P9-DMR-010

THE MIDDLE AGES
David / Simpson

THE SIXTEENTH CENTURY
Logan / Greenblatt

THE EARLY SEVENTEENTH CENTURY
Lewalski / Maus

THE RESTORATION AND THE EIGHTEENTH CENTURY
Lipking / Noggle

THE ROMANTIC PERIOD
Stillinger / Lynch

THE VICTORIAN AGE
Christ / Robson

THE TWENTIETH CENTURY AND AFTER
Stallworthy / Ramazani

The Norton Anthology of English Literature

EIGHTH EDITION
THE MAJOR AUTHORS

VOLUME B

THE ROMANTIC PERIOD THROUGH
THE TWENTIETH CENTURY AND AFTER

Carol T. Christ
PROFESSOR EMERITUS OF ENGLISH, UNIVERSITY OF CALIFORNIA, BERKELEY
PRESIDENT, SMITH COLLEGE

Alfred David
PROFESSOR OF ENGLISH EMERITUS, INDIANA UNIVERSITY

Barbara K. Lewalski
WILLIAM R. KENAN PROFESSOR OF ENGLISH AND OF HISTORY AND LITERATURE,
HARVARD UNIVERSITY

Lawrence Lipking
PROFESSOR OF ENGLISH AND CHESTER D. TRIPP PROFESSOR OF HUMANITIES,
NORTHWESTERN UNIVERSITY

George M. Logan
JAMES CAPPON PROFESSOR OF ENGLISH, QUEEN'S UNIVERSITY

Deidre Shauna Lynch
ASSOCIATE PROFESSOR OF ENGLISH, INDIANA UNIVERSITY

Katharine Eisaman Maus
JAMES BRANCH CABELL PROFESSOR OF ENGLISH, UNIVERSITY OF VIRGINIA

James Noggle
ASSOCIATE PROFESSOR OF ENGLISH AND
WHITEHEAD ASSOCIATE PROFESSOR OF CRITICAL THOUGHT,
WELLESLEY COLLEGE

Jahan Ramazani
EDGAR F. SHANNON PROFESSOR OF ENGLISH, UNIVERSITY OF VIRGINIA

Catherine Robson
ASSOCIATE PROFESSOR OF ENGLISH AND CHANCELLOR'S FELLOW,
UNIVERSITY OF CALIFORNIA, DAVIS

James Simpson
PROFESSOR OF ENGLISH AND AMERICAN LITERATURE, HARVARD UNIVERSITY

Jon Stallworthy
PROFESSOR OF ENGLISH LITERATURE, OXFORD UNIVERSITY

Jack Stillinger
CENTER FOR ADVANCED STUDY PROFESSOR OF ENGLISH,
UNIVERSITY OF ILLINOIS

Editors Emeriti

E. Talbot Donaldson, LATE OF INDIANA UNIVERSITY • Hallett Smith, LATE OF THE
HUNTINGTON LIBRARY • Robert M. Adams, LATE OF THE UNIVERSITY OF CALIFOR-
NIA, LOS ANGELES • Samuel Holt Monk, LATE OF THE UNIVERSITY OF MINNESOTA
• George H. Ford, LATE OF THE UNIVERSITY OF ROCHESTER • David Daiches, LATE
OF THE INSTITUTE OF ADVANCED STUDIES, UNIVERSITY OF EDINBURGH

The Norton Anthology of English Literature

EIGHTH EDITION

THE MAJOR AUTHORS

VOLUME B

THE ROMANTIC PERIOD THROUGH THE TWENTIETH CENTURY AND AFTER

Stephen Greenblatt, *General Editor*

COGAN UNIVERSITY PROFESSOR OF THE HUMANITIES,
HARVARD UNIVERSITY

M. H. Abrams, *Founding Editor Emeritus*

CLASS OF 1916 PROFESSOR OF ENGLISH EMERITUS,
CORNELL UNIVERSITY

W • W • NORTON & COMPANY • *New York* • *London*

W. W. Norton & Company has been independent since its founding in 1923, when William Warder Norton and Mary D. Herter Norton first published lectures delivered at the People's Institute, the adult education division of New York City's Cooper Union. The Nortons soon expanded their program beyond the Institute, publishing books by celebrated academics from America and abroad. By mid-century, the two major pillars of Norton's publishing program— trade books and college texts—were firmly established. In the 1950s, the Norton family transferred control of the company to its employees, and today—with a staff of four hundred and a comparable number of trade, college, and professional titles published each year— W. W. Norton & Company stands as the largest and oldest publishing house owned wholly by its employees.

Editor: Julia Reidhead
Managing Editor, College: Marian Johnson
Developmental Editor: Kurt Wildermuth
Electronic Media Editor: Eileen Connell
Production Manager: Diane O'Connor
Associate Editor: Erin Granville
Copy Editors: Alice Falk, Katharine Ings, Candace Levy, Alan Shaw, Ann Tappert
Permissions Managers: Nancy Rodwan and Katrina Washington
Editorial Assistant: Catherine Spencer
Text Design: Antonina Krass
Art Research: Neil Ryder Hoos

Composition by Binghamton Valley Composition
Manufacturing by RR Donnelley

Copyright © 2006, 2001, 1996, 1987, 1975, 1968, 1962
by W. W. Norton & Company, Inc.
Copyright renewed 1990 by W. W. Norton & Company, Inc.

All rights reserved
Printed in the United States of America

Since this page cannot legibly accommodate all the copyright notices,
Permissions Acknowledgments constitutes an extension of the copyright page.

ISBN 0-393-92831-4 (pbk.)

W. W. Norton & Company, Inc., 500 Fifth Avenue, New York, N.Y. 10110
www.wwnorton.com

W. W. Norton & Company Ltd., Castle House, 75/76 Wells Street, London W1T 3QT

3 4 5 6 7 8 9 0

Contents

The Victorian Age (1830–1901)   1885

The Twentieth Century and After   2293

Preface to
the Eighth Edition

The outpouring of English literature overflows all boundaries, including the capacious boundaries of the Major Authors edition of *The Norton Anthology of English Literature*. But these pages manage to contain many of the most remarkable works written in English during centuries of restless creative effort. We have included epic poems and short lyrics; love songs and satires; tragedies and comedies written for performance on the commercial stage, and private meditations meant to be perused in silence; prayers, popular ballads, prophecies, ecstatic visions, erotic fantasies, sermons, short stories, letters in verse and prose, critical essays, polemical tracts, several entire novels, and a great deal more. Such works generally form the core of courses that are designed to introduce students to English literature, with its history not only of gradual development, continuity, and dense internal echoes, but also of sudden change and startling innovation.

One of the joys of literature in English is its spectacular abundance. Even within the geographical confines of England, Scotland, Wales, and Ireland, where the majority of texts brought together in this collection originated, one can find more than enough distinguished and exciting works to fill the pages of this anthology many times over. The abundance is all the greater if one takes, as the editors of this anthology do, a broad understanding of the term *literature*. The meaning of the term has in the course of several centuries shifted from the whole body of writing produced in a particular language to a subset of that writing consisting of works that claim special attention because of their unusual formal beauty or expressive power. Certain literary works, arousing enduring admiration, have achieved sufficient prominence to serve as widespread models for other writers and thus to constitute something approximating a canon. But just as there have never been in English-speaking countries academies empowered to regulate the use of language, so too there have never been firmly settled guidelines for canonizing particular texts. Any individual text's claim to attention is subject to constant debate and revision; established texts are jostled both by new arrivals and by previously neglected claimants; and the boundaries between the literary and whatever is thought to be "nonliterary" are constantly challenged and redrawn. The heart of this collection consists of poems, plays, and prose fiction, but, like the language in which they are written, these categories are themselves products of ongoing historical transformations, and we have included many texts that call into question any conception of literature as denoting only a limited set of particular kinds of writing. English literature as a field arouses not a sense of order but what Yeats calls "the emotion of multitude."

This anthology aims to enable its readers to gauge the achievement of the principal authors it represents by providing generous samplings of their most characteristic and brilliant work. We have tried, whenever possible, not to give a brief glimpse but rather to facilitate a satisfying, sustained engagement with each writer. But we have also included some individual works whose compelling interest merits their representation in these pages, even though the scope of this book does not permit a wider survey of the author's writings.

By the designation "major authors," the editors call attention to an unusual power to excite and reward close attention. Our grasp of this power—our notion of where to look for it, how to identify it, and what to do when we find it—does not stand still. The questions that we ask and the pleasures that we seek change over time, and with these changes the literary landscape is transformed. Hence there are twelve new writers in this Eighth Edition, six of whom are women. To cite a few examples: Margery Kempe, a medieval woman who had the temerity to insist loudly upon the importance of her own spiritual life and left behind a remarkable autobiographical memoir; John Wilmot, the Second Earl of Rochester, and Eliza Haywood, who scandalized their contemporaries, though for very different reasons, and produced fascinating, transgressive works of art; and John Clare, a poor agricultural laborer who became one of the great nature poets of the early nineteenth century. Several of the authors and works newly included—Robert Louis Stevenson's *The Strange Case of Dr. Jekyll and Mr. Hyde* and Rudyard Kipling's *The Man Who Would Be King*—have long thrilled readers (and inspired popular films), but their inclusion in this edition highlights the narrative cunning and imaginative intensity through which they achieve their effects. Other new offerings represent the flowering of major contemporary talents, such as two brilliant Canadian writers, Alice Munro and Anne Carson.

Where do we draw the boundaries? Following the lead of most college courses, we have separated off, on pragmatic grounds, English literature from American literature, but, in keeping with the multinational, multicultural, and hugely expansive character of the language, we have incorporated, particularly for the modern period, a substantial number of texts by authors from other countries. This border-crossing is not just a phenomenon of modernity. It is fitting that among the first works here is *Beowulf*, a powerful epic written in the Germanic language known as Old English about a singularly restless Scandinavian hero. *Beowulf*'s remarkable translator in *The Norton Anthology of English Literature*, Seamus Heaney, is one of the great contemporary masters of English literature—he was awarded the Nobel Prize for Literature in 1995—but it would be potentially misleading to call him an "English poet" for he was born in Northern Ireland and is not in fact English. It would be still more misleading to call him a "British poet," as if the British Empire were the most salient fact about the language he speaks and writes or the culture by which he was shaped. What does matter is that the language in which Heaney writes is English, and this fact links him powerfully with the authors in these volumes, a linguistic community that stubbornly refuses to fit comfortably within any firm geographical or ethnic or national boundaries. So too, to glance at other authors and writings in the anthology, in the sixteenth century William Tyndale, in exile in the Low Countries and inspired by German religious reformers, translated the New Testament from Greek and thereby changed the course of the English language; in the seventeenth century Aphra Behn deeply touched her readers with a story that moves from Africa, where its hero is born, to South America, where Behn herself may have witnessed some of the tragic events she describes; and early in the twentieth century Joseph Conrad, born in Ukraine of Polish parents, wrote in eloquent English a celebrated novella whose deeply ambivalent endorsement of European empire was trenchantly challenged at the century's end by such writers as Brian Friel (born in County Tyrone, Northern Ireland), J. M. Coetzee (born in Cape Town, South Africa), and Salman Rushdie (born in Bombay, India).

A vital literary culture is always on the move. This principle was the watchword of M. H. Abrams, the distinguished literary critic who first conceived *The Norton Anthology of English Literature*, brought together the original team of editors, and, with characteristic insight, diplomacy, and humor, oversaw seven editions and graciously offered counsel on this eighth edition. Abrams wisely understood that the dense continuities that underlie literary performance are perpetually challenged and revitalized by innovation. He understood too that scholarly discoveries and the shifting interests of readers constantly alter the landscape of literary history. Hence from the start he envisaged that, if the anthology were to be successful, it would have to undergo a process of periodic revision and reselection, an ambitious enterprise that would draw upon the energy and ideas of new editors brought in to work with the seasoned team.

The Eighth Edition of the Major Authors *Norton Anthology* represents the most thorough-going instance in its long publishing history of this generational renewal. Across the whole chronological breadth of the volumes, new editors joined forces with the existing editors in a spirit of close collaboration. The revitalized team has considered afresh each of the selections and rethought all the other myriad aspects of the anthology. In doing so, we have, as in past years, profited from a remarkable flow of voluntary corrections and suggestions proposed by students, as well as teachers, who view the anthology with a loyal but critical eye. Moreover, we have again solicited and received detailed information on the works actually assigned, proposals for deletions and additions, and suggestions for improving the editorial matter, from over two hundred reviewers from around the world, almost all of them teachers who use the book in a course. The active participation of an engaged and dedicated community of readers has been crucial as the editors of the *Norton Anthology* grapple with the task of strengthening the selection of more traditional texts even while adding many texts that reflect the transformation and expansion of the field of English studies. The great challenge (and therefore the interest) of the task is linked to the space constraints that even this hefty volume must observe. The virtually limitless resources of the Web site make at least some of the difficult choices less vexing, but the editorial team kept clearly in view the central importance in the classroom of the printed pages. The final decisions on what to include were made by the editors, but we were immeasurably assisted by our ongoing collaboration with teachers and students.

We have in this edition continued to expand the selection of writing by women in all of the historical periods. The sustained work of scholars in recent years has recovered dozens of significant authors who had been marginalized or neglected by a male-dominated literary tradition and has deepened our understanding of those women writers who had managed, against considerable odds, to claim a place in that tradition. The First Edition of the Major Authors *Norton Anthology* included no women writers; this Eighth Edition includes twenty-six, of whom six are newly added. Poets and dramatists whose names were scarcely mentioned even in the specialized literary histories of earlier generations—Aemilia Lanyer, Lady Mary Wroth, Margaret Cavendish, Anna Letitia Barbauld, Charlotte Smith, Letitia Elizabeth Landon, and many others—now appear in the company of their male contemporaries. There are in addition three complete long prose works by women—Aphra Behn's *Oroonoko*, Eliza Haywood's *Fantomina*, and Virginia Woolf's *A Room of One's Own*—along with new selections from such celebrated fiction writers as Jean Rhys and Alice Munro.

The novel is, of course, a stumbling block for an anthology. The length of many great novels defies their incorporation in any volume that hopes to include a broad spectrum of literature. At the same time it is difficult to excerpt representative passages from narratives whose power often depends upon amplitude or upon the slow development of character or upon the on-rushing urgency of the story. Therefore, better to represent the achievements of novelists, the publisher is making available the full list of 180 Norton Critical Editions, any one of which may be packaged for free with the Major Authors edition (one-volume paperbound, one-volume clothbound, or two-splits package).

Now, as in the past, cultures define themselves by the songs they sing and the stories they tell. But the central importance of visual media in contemporary culture has heightened our awareness of the ways in which songs and stories have always been closely linked to the images that societies have fashioned. The Major Authors edition of *The Norton Anthology of English Literature* features fifty-eight pages of color plates. In addition, black-and-white engravings and illustrations by Hogarth, Blake, and Dante Gabriel Rossetti provide compelling examples of the hybrid art of the "visual narrative." In selecting visual material—from the Sutton Hoo treasure of the seventh century to Anish Kapoor's immense *Marsyas* in the twenty-first century—the editors had several aims: to provide images that conjure up, whether directly or indirectly, the individual writers in each section; to provide images that relate specifically to works in the anthology; and to provide images that shape and illuminate the culture of a particular literary period. We have tried to choose visually striking images that will capture students' attention and provoke discussion, and our captions draw attention to important details and cross-reference related literary texts.

Period-by-Period Revisions

The scope of the extensive revisions we have undertaken can be conveyed more fully by a list of some of the principal texts and features that have been added to the present edition.

The Middle Ages. The period, edited by Alfred David and James Simpson, is divided into three sections: Anglo-Saxon Literature, Anglo-Norman Literature, and Middle English Literature of the Fourteenth and Fifteenth Centuries. The heart of the Anglo-Saxon section is the great epic *Beowulf*, in a translation, specially commissioned for *The Norton Anthology of English Literature*, by Seamus Heaney. Another acclaimed translation, Marie Borroff's modern rendering of *Sir Gawain and the Green Knight* is featured in the Middle English section. New selections from Langland's *Piers Plowman*, the female mystic Julian of Norwich, and the religious visionary Margery Kempe together form an important new topical cluster, "Christ's Humanity." Also in the cluster, and strengthening our representation of medieval drama, is the powerful *York Play of the Crucifixion.*

The Sixteenth Century. Two celebrated plays are at the core of this section: Marlowe's *Doctor Faustus* and Shakespeare's *Twelfth Night*, the latter included for the first time in the Major Authors edition. The editors, George Logan and Stephen Greenblatt, have strengthened the selection of poems with six additional sonnets by Shakespeare and a revealing verse exchange between Queen Elizabeth and her glittering courtier, Sir Walter Ralegh.

The Early Seventeenth Century. New to this section, edited by Barbara Lewalski and Katharine Eisaman Maus, are two powerful poems—John Donne's "Good Friday, 1613. Riding Westward" and Andrew Marvell's "An Horatian Ode"—along with the most famous chapter from Hobbes's *Leviathan.* A substantial selection from Milton's *Paradise Lost* remains the section's centerpiece. Complete longer works include John Donne's soul-searching *Satire 3*, Aemilia Lanyer's country-house poem "The Description of Cookham," and Milton's "Lycidas."

The Restoration and the Eighteenth Century. The editors, Lawrence Lipking and James Noggle, include for the first time a selection of poems by the scandalous libertine John Wilmot, second earl of Rochester, along with a wry yet touching poem of "imperfect enjoyment" by Aphra Behn. We introduce as well *Fantomina*, a novella of sexual role-playing by an author new to the *Norton Anthology*, Eliza Haywood. Other longer texts presented in complete form in this section include Dryden's satires "Absalom and Achitophel" and "MacFlecknoe," Aphra Behn's novel *Oroonoko,* Pope's *The Rape of the Lock* and "Epistle to Dr. Abuthnot," Hogarth's graphic satire "Marriage A-la-Mode," Johnson's *Vanity of Human Wishes* and *Rasselas,* and Gray's "Elegy Written in a Country Churchyard."

The Romantic Period. In addition to a new poem by Anna Letitia Barbauld, the period editors, Jack Stillinger and Deidre Shauna Lynch, introduce two new figures to the galaxy of Romantic poets. The first, Charlotte Smith, is represented by a number of her *Elegiac Sonnets,* poems that she published when she was in debtor's prison with her husband and children, and by a substantial selection from *The Emigrants,* her long poem about migrants who have fled revolutionary persecution. The second, John Clare, was a poor farm laborer who became one of the most celebrated naturalists and poets of the age.

The Victorian Age. Among the significant additions to this section, edited by Carol Christ and Catherine Robson, are Robert Louis Stevenson's *The Strange Case of Dr. Jekyll and Mr. Hyde* and three works by Rudyard Kipling, including his novella *The Man Who Would Be King.* Both Stevenson and Kipling are new to the Major Authors edition. Also included for the first time are Elizabeth Barrett Browning's long poem "The Runaway Slave at Pilgrim's Point" and Alfred, Lord Tennyson's "Mariana." Complete longer works include Tennyson's *The Passing of Arthur*; Robert Browning's "Fra Lippo Lippi," " 'Childe Roland,' " "Andrea del Sarto," and "Caliban upon Setebos"; Matthew Arnold's "The Scholar Gypsy"; Christina Rossetti's *Goblin Market*; and Oscar Wilde's comedy *The Importance of Being Earnest.*

The Twentieth Century and After. Several new and reselected writers mark this major revision by the editors, Jon Stallworthy and Jahan Ramazani. The section features a brilliant play, Brian Friel's *Translations*, which has vital connections to literary and cultural issues that extend throughout the volume. Canadian writers—the poet Anne Carson and the prose writer Alice Munro—appear for the first time. There is a new story by Jean Rhys, a new selection from J. M. Coetzee's *Waiting for the Barbarians*, and new poems from Yeats, Auden, and Walcott. There is, as before, a remarkable array of complete longer texts, including Conrad's *Heart of Darkness*, Woolf's *A Room of One's Own*, Eliot's *The Waste Land*, Mansfield's "The Garden Party," and Beckett's *Endgame*. Seamus Heaney's works, to which two new poems have been added, provide the occasion to look back again to the beginning of this volume with Heaney's translation of *Beowulf*. This translation is a reminder that the most recent works can double back upon the distant past, and that words set down by men and women who have crumbled into dust can speak to us with astonishing directness.

Editorial Procedures

The Major Authors edition adheres to the core principles that have always characterized *The Norton Anthology of English Literature*. Period introductions, headnotes, and annotations are designed to give readers the information they need to understand each text, without imposing interpretations. The aim of these editorial materials is to make the anthology self-sufficient, so that it can be read anywhere—in a coffee bar, on a bus, or under a tree. Above all, we have tried to keep in mind the actual classroom situation. Teachability is central to every aspect of these volumes.

Our fidelity to a trusted and well-tried format may make it difficult for long-time users to take in, at first glance, how thorough-going the revisions of the Eighth Edition actually are. The editorial team undertook to rethink and update virtually everything in these pages, from the endpaper maps, scrutinized for accuracy by Catherine Robson and redrawn by cartographer Adrian Kitzinger, to the appendix on English money, which, thanks to James Noggle's clever chart, now provides answers to the perennial question, But what was money actually worth? Similarly, the appendix on "Religions in England," completely rewritten by Katharine Maus, and the one on "Geographic Nomenclature," revised by Jahan Ramazani, quickly illuminate what students have often found obscure. The anthology also includes a section, "Poems in Process," revised and expanded by Deidre Lynch, with the help of Alfred David and James Simpson. This section reproduces from manuscripts and printed texts the genesis and evolution of a number of poems whose final form is printed in the volume. And, thanks to James Simpson, we now have a freshly conceived and thoroughly rewritten appendix on "Literary Terminology," recast as a quick-reference alphabetical glossary, with examples from works in *The Norton Anthology of English Literature*.

Drawing upon the latest scholarship and upon their classroom experience, the editors have substantially rewritten the period introductions and headnotes. We have updated as well the Selected Bibliographies and have carefully revised the Texts/Contexts timelines. And, for the first time, we have provided in-text cross-references to the extensive *Norton Literature Online* Web site. With all aspects of the anthology's apparatus our intention is to facilitate direct and informed access to the extraordinary works of literature assembled here.

The Norton Anthology of English Literature prides itself on the scholarly accuracy and readability of its texts. To ease students' access, we have normalized spelling and capitalization in texts up to and including the Romantic period to follow the conventions of modern English; we leave unaltered, however, texts in which modernizing would change semantic or metrical qualities. From the Victorian period onward, we have restored the original spelling and punctuation to selections retained from the previous edition in the belief that the authors' choices, when they pose no difficulties for student readers, should be respected.

We continue other editorial procedures that have proved useful in the past. After each work, we cite (when known) the date of composition on the left and the date of first publication on the right; in some instances, the latter is followed by the date of a revised edition for which the author was responsible. We have used square brackets to indicate titles supplied by the editors for the convenience of readers. When a portion of a text has been omitted, we have indicated that omission with three asterisks. If the omitted portion is important for following the plot or argument, we have provided a brief summary within the text or in a footnote. Finally, we have reconsidered annotations throughout and increased the number of marginal glosses for archaic, dialect, or unfamiliar words.

Additional Resources

With the Eighth Edition of *The Norton Anthology of English Literature*, the publisher is proud to launch an extensive new online resource—Norton Literature Online (wwnorton.com/literature)—the gateway to all of the outstanding literature resources available from Norton. Students who activate the registration code included in each new copy of the *Norton Anthology* will find at Norton Literature Online a deep and broad array of general resources, among them a glossary of literary terms, advice on writing about literature and using MLA documentation style, study aids and quizzes, an author portrait gallery featuring 380 authors, more than 100 maps, and over 90 minutes of recorded readings and musical selections. To encourage students to explore Norton Literature Online, cross-references in the anthology draw attention to relevant materials, notably to the 27 topical clusters in the much-praised Norton Topics Online site. Prepared by the anthology editors, the topics include the editors' introductions, a gathering of annotated texts and images, and study questions and research links relevant to each topic. For use with the Eighth Edition, three entirely new Twentieth Century topics—"Imagining Ireland," "Modernist Experiment," and "Representing the Great War"—and a recast Romantic topic, "The Satanic and Byronic Hero," have been added, among other updates and improvements. Norton Literature Online is also the portal to the Online Archive (wwnorton.com/nael/noa), which offers more than 150 downloadable texts from the Middle Ages through the early Victorian period, as well as some 80 audio files. An ongoing project, the Online Archive is being expanded with all public-domain texts trimmed from *The Norton Anthology of English Literature* over seven editions. A new feature of the Archive, a Publication Chronology, lists over 1,000 texts and the edition in which each was introduced, dropped, and sometimes reintroduced. As such, the table and the archive of texts now being assembled (a massive project of a few years' duration) are a unique window on changing interests in the teaching of English literature over four decades.

Teaching with The Norton Anthology of English Literature: *A Guide for*

Instructors has been reconceived for ease of use and substantially rewritten by Sondra Archimedes, University of California, Santa Cruz; Elizabeth Fowler, University of Virginia; Laura Runge, University of South Florida; and Philip Schwyzer, University of Exeter. The Guide offers extensive help, from planning a course and developing a syllabus and course objectives to preparing exams. For authors and works, the Guide entries provide a "hook" to start a lively class discussion; a Quick Read section to refresh instructors on essential information about a text or author; Teaching Suggestions that call out interesting textual or contextual features; Teaching Clusters of suggested groups or pairs of texts; and Discussions Questions. Built into the *Guide for Instructors* is a Media Guide, by Philip Schwyzer, which offers specific suggestions for integrating the anthology's rich multimedia resources with the text and for incorporating them into traditional or distance-learning courses. Finally, the Norton Resource Library (www.wwnorton.com/nrl), by Philip Schwyzer, offers instructors brief period introductions and "class sessions" to facilitate close reading, art galleries and literary links, enhanced period timelines, essay assignments, sample syllabi, and instructions for customizing the material. These materials are compatible with WebCT and other course-management systems.

The editors are deeply grateful to the hundreds of teachers worldwide who have helped us to improve the Major Authors edition of *The Norton Anthology of English Literature*. A list of the advisors who prepared in-depth reviews and the instructors who replied to a detailed questionnaire follows on a separate page, under Acknowledgments. The editors would like to express appreciation for their assistance to Elizabeth Anker (University of Virginia), Sandie Byrne (Oxford University), Timothy Campbell (Indiana University), Sarita Cargas (Oxford University), Jason Coats (University of Virginia), Joseph W. Childers (University of California, Riverside), Daniel Cook (University of California, Davis), Linda David, William Flesch (Brandeis University), Robert Folkenflik (University of California, Irvine), Robert D. Fulk (Indiana University), Omaar Hena (University of Virginia), Tom Keirstead (Indiana University), Shayna Kessel (University of Southern California), Joanna Lipking (Northwestern University), Ian Little (Liverpool University), Tricia Lootens (University of Georgia), Erin Minear (Harvard University), Elaine Musgrave (University of California, Davis), J. Morgan Myers (University of Virginia), Kate Nash (University of Virginia), Ruth Perry (M.I.T.), Emily Peterson (Harvard University), Kate Pilson (Harvard University), Jane Potter (Oxford Brookes University), Leah Price (Harvard University), Angelique Richardson (Exeter University), Philip Schwyzer (Exeter University), and Ramie Targoff (Brandeis University). We especially thank John W. Sider (Westmont College) for his meticulous review of standing annotations and myriad suggestions for improvements. We also thank the many people at Norton who contributed to the Eighth Edition: Julia Reidhead, who served not only as the inhouse supervisor but also as an unfailingly wise and effective collaborator in every aspect of planning and accomplishing this Eighth Edition; Marian Johnson, Managing Editor, College, who kept the project moving forward with a remarkable blend of focused energy, intelligence, and common sense; Kurt Wildermuth, developmental and project editor; Alice Falk, Katharine Ings, Candace Levy, Alan Shaw, and Ann Tappert, manuscript editors; Eileen Connell, electronic media editor; Diane O'Connor, production manager; Nancy Rodwan and

Katrina Washington, permissions managers; Toni Krass, designer; Neil Ryder Hoos, art researcher; Erin Granville, associate editor; and Catherine Spencer, editorial assistant. All these friends provided the editors with indispensable help in meeting the challenge of representing the unparalleled range and variety of English literature.

We dedicate this Eighth Edition of *The Norton Anthology of English Literature* to our friend, mentor, and inspiring guide, M. H. Abrams. His shaping power over these volumes and the profession it serves will long endure.

Acknowledgments

Among our many critics, advisors, and friends, the following were of especial help toward the preparation of the Major Authors, Eighth Edition by providing either advice or critiques of particular periods of the anthology: Jesse Airaudi (Baylor University), Daniel Adams (St. John's University), Kenneth Alrutz (Miami University), David L. Anderson (Butler County Community College), Robert Anderson (Oakland University), Peter Auksi (University of Western Ontario), James E. Barcus (Baylor University), David Barnard (University of Regina), Ian Baucom (Duke University), Dr. Richard Beadle (St John's College, Cambridge University), Lance Bertelsen (University of Texas at Austin), Scott Boltwood (Emory and Henry College), James S. Brown (Charleston Southern University), James Bryant-Trerise (Clackamas Community College), Natalie B. Cole (Oakland University), David Collins (Westminster College), Sherry Covington (East Texas Baptist University), Valentine Cunningham (Oxford University), Richard Dolan, Jr. (Georgia State University), Deborah Dooley (Nazareth College), Timothy Drake (Queen's University), Ian Duncan (University of California, Berkeley), Robert Einarsson (Grant MacEwan College), Marilyn M. Ewing (Eastern Oregon University), Mary Elizabeth Ellzey (Shepherd College), Robert Forman (St. John's University), Patsy Fowler (Gonzaga University), Bill Franklin (North Central Texas College), Rosanne Gasse, (Brandon University), Teriann Gaston (University of Texas at Arlington), Vincent Gillespie (Oxford University), Cynthia Griffith (Danville Community College), John Gordon (Connecticut College), Robert Haight (Kalamazoo Valley Community College), Keith Hale (South Texas Community College), Kelly Hall (Florida State University), Shari Hammond (Southwest Virginia Community College), Elizabeth Hanson, (Queen's University), Alan F. Hickman (University of Arkansas at Pine Bluff), Karen R. Jacobs (Louisiana Tech University), Emrys Jones (Oxford University), Suzanne Keen (Washington and Lee University), Flo Keyes (Castleton State College), Kathleen Kincade (Indiana State University), Bruce King, Melisa Klimaszewski (Oakland University), Jonathan Kramnick (Rutgers University), David Kuijt (University of Maryland), Janice Lasseter (Samford University), Shawn Liang (Mohawk Valley Community College), Jane Lilienfeld (Lincoln University), Peter Lindenbaum (Indiana University), Oliver Lovesey (Okanagan University College), Scott Lucas (The Citadel), Jeanette Lynes (St. Francis Xavier University), Krista Lysack (University of Western Ontario), Father Germain Marc'hadour (Angers, France), Leah S. Marcus (Vanderbilt University), Wayne Martindale (Wheaton College), Brian May (Northern Illinois University), Laurence W. Mazzeno (Alvernia College), Michael L. McInturff (Birmingham-Southern College), James McWard (Johnson County Community College), Heather L. Meakin (Case Western Reserve University), Steve Michael (Wayland Baptist University), Clarence H. Miller (St. Louis University), Sandra Moore (Mississippi Delta Community College), Michael Moses (Duke University), Joanne

S. Norman (Bishop's University), Pat Panzarelth (St. Bonaventure University), David Phillips (Charleston Southern University), Adela Pinch (University of Michigan), Tison Pugh (University of Central Florida), James A. W. Rembert (The Citadel), Rick Simmons (Louisiana Tech University), Phillip Rogers (Queen's University), Mary Beth Rose (University of Illinois at Chicago), Heidi Sjostrom (Marquette University), Billy B. Smith (Ranger College), Malinda Snow (Georgia State University), Janet Sorensen (Indiana University), Michele Stanco (Università degli Studi di Napoli "Federico II"), Jackina Stark (Ozark Christian College), Ralph S. Stevens (Coppin State College), Marta Straznicky (Queen's University), Kennetha Stringer (Drury University), Barbara Sudol (St. John's University), James Sullivan (California State University at LA), Greg Underwood (Pearl River Community College), John Wall (North Carolina State University), Phillip Wedgeworth (Jones County Junior College), Laura White (University of Nebraska, Lincoln), John Wilson (College of the Ozarks), Johnny Wink (Ouachita Baptist University), and David Wyatt (University of Maryland).

The Norton Anthology
of English Literature

EIGHTH EDITION

MAJOR AUTHORS

VOLUME B

THE ROMANTIC PERIOD THROUGH
THE TWENTIETH CENTURY AND AFTER

The Romantic Period
1785–1830

1789–1815:	Revolutionary and Napoleonic period in France.—1789: The Revolution begins with the assembly of the States-General in May and the storming of the Bastille on July 14.—1793: King Louis XVI executed; England joins the alliance against France.—1793–94: The Reign of Terror under Robespierre. 1804: Napoleon crowned emperor.—1815: Napoleon defeated at Waterloo
1807:	British slave trade outlawed (slavery abolished throughout the empire, including the West Indies, twenty-six years later)
1811–20:	The Regency—George, Prince of Wales, acts as regent for George III, who has been declared incurably insane
1819:	Peterloo Massacre
1820:	Accession of George IV

The Romantic period, though by far the shortest, is at least as complex and diverse as any other period in British literary history. For much of the twentieth century, scholars singled out five poets—Wordsworth, Coleridge, Byron, Percy Shelley, and Keats, adding Blake belatedly to make a sixth—and constructed notions of a unified Romanticism on the basis of their works. But there were problems all along: even the two closest collaborators of the 1790s, Wordsworth and Coleridge, would fit no single definition; Byron despised both Coleridge's philosophical speculations and Wordsworth's poetry; Shelley and Keats were at opposite poles from each other stylistically and philosophically; Blake was not at all like any of the other five.

Nowadays, although the six poets remain, by most measures of canonicity, the principal canonical figures, we recognize a greater range of accomplishments. In 1798, the year of Wordsworth and Coleridge's first *Lyrical Ballads*, neither of the authors had much of a reputation; Wordsworth was not even included among the 1,112 entries in David Rivers's *Literary Memoirs of Living Authors of Great Britain* of that year, and *Lyrical Ballads* was published anonymously because, as Coleridge told the publisher, "Wordsworth's name is nothing—to a large number of people mine *stinks*." Some of the best-regarded poets of the time were women—Anna Barbauld, Charlotte Smith, Mary Robinson—and Wordsworth and Coleridge (junior colleagues of Robinson when she was poetry editor of the *Morning Post* in the late 1790s) looked up to them and learned their craft from them. The rest of the then-established figures were the later eighteenth-century poets who are printed at the end of volume 1 of this anthology—Gray, Collins, Crabbe, and Cowper in particular. Only Byron, among the now-canonical poets, was instantly famous; and Felicia

Hemans and Letitia Landon ran him a close race as best-sellers. The Romantic period had a great many more participants than the six principal male poets and was shaped by a multitude of political, social, and economic changes.

REVOLUTION AND REACTION

Following a widespread practice of historians of English literature, we use "Romantic period" to refer to the span between the year 1785, the midpoint of the decade in which Samuel Johnson died and Blake, Burns, and Smith published their first poems, and 1830, by which time the major writers of the preceding century were either dead or no longer productive. This was a turbulent period, during which England experienced the ordeal of change from a primarily agricultural society, where wealth and power had been concentrated in the landholding aristocracy, to a modern industrial nation. And this change occurred in a context of revolution—first the American and then the more radical French—and of war, of economic cycles of inflation and depression, and of the constant threat to the social structure from imported revolutionary ideologies to which the ruling classes responded by the repression of traditional liberties.

The early period of the French Revolution, marked by the Declaration of the Rights of Man and the storming of the Bastille, evoked enthusiastic support from English liberals and radicals alike. Three important books epitomize the radical social thinking stimulated by the Revolution. Mary Wollstonecraft's *A Vindication of the Rights of Men* (1790) justified the French Revolution against Edmund Burke's attack in his *Reflections on the Revolution in France* (1790). Tom Paine's *Rights of Man* (1791–92) also advocated for England a democratic republic that was to be achieved, if lesser pressures failed, by popular revolution. More important as an influence on Wordsworth and Percy Shelley was William Godwin's *Enquiry Concerning Political Justice* (1793), which foretold an inevitable but peaceful evolution of society to a final stage in which property would be equally distributed and government would wither away. But English sympathizers dropped off as the Revolution followed its increasingly grim course: the accession to power by Jacobin extremists, intent on purifying their new republic by purging it of its enemies; the "September Massacres" of the imprisoned nobility in 1792, followed by the execution of the king and queen; the new French Republic's invasion of the Rhineland and the Netherlands, which brought England into the war against France; the guillotining of thousands in the Reign of Terror under Robespierre; and, after the execution in their turn of the men who had directed the Terror, the emergence of Napoleon, first as dictator then as emperor of France. As Wordsworth wrote in *The Prelude*,

> become Oppressors in their turn,
> Frenchmen had changed a war of self-defence
> For one of Conquest, losing sight of all
> Which they had struggled for. . . . (11.206–09)

Napoleon, the brilliant tactician whose rise through the ranks of the army had seemed to epitomize the egalitarian principles of the Revolution, had become an arch-aggressor, a despot, and would-be founder of a new imperial dynasty. By 1800 liberals found they had no side they could wholeheartedly espouse. Napoleon's defeat at Waterloo in 1815 proved to be the triumph, not of progress and reform, but of reactionary despotisms throughout continental Europe.

In England this was a period of harsh, repressive measures. Public meetings were prohibited, the right of habeas corpus (the legal principle protecting individuals from arbitrary imprisonment) was suspended for the first time in over a hundred years, and advocates of even moderate political change were charged with treason. Efforts during these war years to repeal the laws that barred Protestants who did not conform to the Anglican Church from the universities and government came to nothing: in the new climate of counter-revolutionary alarm, it was easy to portray even a slight abridgement of the privileges of the established Church as a measure that, validating the Jacobins' campaigns to de-Christianize France, would aid the enemy cause. Another early casualty of this counterrevolution was the movement to abolish the slave trade, a cause supported initially by a wide cross-section of English society. In the 1780s and 1790s numerous writers, both white (Barbauld, Robinson, Coleridge, and Wordsworth) and black (Ottobah Cugoano and Olaudah Equiano), attacked the greed of the owners of the West Indian sugar plantations and detailed the horrors of the traffic in African flesh that provided them with their labor power. But the bloodshed that accompanied political change in France strengthened the hand of apologists for slavery, by making any manner of reform seem the prelude to violent insurrection. Parliament rejected a bill abolishing the trade in 1791, and sixteen years—marked by slave rebellions and by the planters' brutal reprisals—elapsed before it passed a new version of the bill.

The frustration of the abolitionist cause is an emblematic chapter in the larger story of how a reactionary government sacrificed hopes of reform while it mobilized the nation's resources for war. Yet this was the very time when economic and social changes were creating a desperate need for corresponding changes in political arrangements. For one thing, new classes inside England—manufacturing rather than agricultural—were beginning to demand a voice in government proportionate to their wealth. The "Industrial Revolution"—the shift in manufacturing that resulted from the invention of power-driven machinery to replace hand labor—had begun in the mid-eighteenth century with improvements in machines for processing textiles, and was given immense impetus when James Watt perfected the steam engine in 1765. In the succeeding decades steam replaced wind and water as the primary source of power for all sorts of manufacturing processes, beginning that dynamic of ever-accelerating economic expansion and technological development that we still identify as the hallmark of the modern age. A new laboring population massed in sprawling mill towns such as Manchester, whose population increased by a factor of five in fifty years. In agricultural communities the destruction of home industry was accompanied by the acceleration of the process of enclosing open fields and wastelands (usually, in fact, "commons" that had provided the means of subsistence for entire communities) and incorporating them into larger, privately owned holdings. Enclosure was by and large necessary for the more efficient methods of agriculture required to feed the nation's growing population (although some of the land that the wealthy acquired through parliamentary acts of enclosure they in fact incorporated into their private estates). But enclosure was socially destructive, breaking up villages, creating a landless class who either migrated to the industrial towns or remained as farm laborers, subsisting on starvation wages and the little they could obtain from parish charity. The landscape of England began to take on its modern appearance—the hitherto open rural areas subdivided into a checkerboard of fields enclosed by hedges and stone walls, with the factories of the cities casting a pall of smoke over vast areas of cheaply built houses and slum tenements. Meanwhile, the population was increasingly polarized into what Disraeli later called the "Two Nations"—the two classes of capital and labor, the rich and the poor.

No attempt was made to regulate this shift from the old economic world to the new, since even liberal reformers were committed to the philosophy of laissez-faire. This theory of "let alone," set out in Adam Smith's *The Wealth of Nations* in 1776, holds that the general welfare can be ensured only by the free operation of economic laws; the government should maintain a policy of strict noninterference and leave people to pursue, unfettered, their private interests. On the one hand, laissez-faire thinking might have helped pave the way for the long-postponed emancipation of the slave population of the West Indies; by 1833, when Parliament finally ended slavery, the anomaly that their unfree labor represented for the new economic and social orthodoxies evidently had become intolerable. But for the great majority of the laboring class at home, the results of laissez-faire and the "freedom" of contract it secured were inadequate wages and long hours of work under harsh discipline and in sordid conditions. Investigators' reports on the coal mines, where male and female children of ten or even five years of age were harnessed to heavy coal-sledges that they dragged by crawling on their hands and knees, read like scenes from Dante's *Inferno*. With the end of the war in 1815, the nation's workforce was enlarged by demobilized troops at the very moment when demand for manufactured goods, until now augmented by the needs of the military, fell dramatically. The result was an unemployment crisis that persisted through the 1820s. Since the workers had no vote and were prevented by law from unionizing, their only recourses were petitions, protest meetings, and riots, to which the ruling class responded with even more repressive measures. The introduction of new machinery into the mills resulted in further loss of jobs, provoking sporadic attempts by the displaced workers to destroy the machines. After one such outbreak of "Luddite" machine-breaking, the House of Lords—despite Byron's eloquent protest—passed a bill (1812) making death the penalty for destroying the frames used for weaving in the stocking industry. In 1819 hundreds of thousands of workers organized meetings to demand parliamentary reform. In August of that year, a huge but orderly assembly at St. Peter's Fields, Manchester, was charged by saber-wielding troops, who killed nine and severely injured hundreds more; this was the notorious "Peterloo Massacre," so named with sardonic reference to the Battle of Waterloo, and condemned by Shelley in his poem for the working class "England in 1819."

Suffering was largely confined to the poor, however, while the landed classes and industrialists prospered. So did many merchants, who profited from the new markets opened up as the British Empire expanded aggressively, compensating with victories against the French for the traumatic loss of America in 1783. England's merchants profited, too, thanks to the marketing successes that, over time, converted once-exotic imports from these colonies into everyday fare for the English. In the eighteenth century tea and sugar had been transformed in this way, and in the nineteenth century other commodities followed suit: the Indian muslin, for instance, that was the fabric of choice for gentlemen's cravats and fashionable ladies' gowns, and the laudanum (Indian opium dissolved in alcohol) that so many ailing writers of the period appear to have found irresistible. The West End of London and new seaside resorts like Brighton became in the early nineteenth century consumers' paradises, sites where West Indian planters and nabobs (a Hindi word that entered English as a name for those who owed their fortunes to Indian gain) could be glimpsed displaying their purchasing power in a manner that made them moralists' favorite examples of nouveau riche vulgarity. The word *shopping* came into English usage in this era. Luxury villas sprang up in London, and the prince regent, who in 1820 became George IV, built himself palaces and pleasure domes, retreats from his not very onerous public responsibilities.

But even, or especially, in private life at home, the prosperous could not escape being touched by the great events of this period. French revolutionary principles were feared by English conservatives almost as much for their challenge to the "proper" ordering of the relations between men and women as for their challenge to traditional political arrangements. Yet the account of what it meant to be English that developed in reaction to this challenge—an account emphasizing the special virtues of the English sense of home and family—was in its way equally revolutionary. The war that the English waged almost without intermission between 1793 and 1815 was one that in an unprecedented manner had a "home front": the menaced sanctuary of the domestic fireside became the symbol of what the nation's military might was safeguarding. What popularity the monarchy held on to during this turbulent period was thus a function not of the two King Georges' traditional exercise of a monarch's sovereign powers but instead of the publicity, tailored to suit this nationalist rhetoric, that emphasized each one's domestic bliss within a "royal family." Conceptions of proper femininity altered as well under the influence of this new idealization and nationalization of the home, this project (as Burke put it) of "binding up the constitution of our country with our dearest domestic ties."

And that alteration both put new pressures on women and granted them new opportunities. As in earlier English history, women in the Romantic period were provided only limited schooling, were subjected to a rigid code of sexual behavior, and (especially after marriage) were bereft of legal rights. In this period women began, as well, to be deluged by books, sermons, and magazine articles that insisted vehemently on the physical and mental differences between the sexes and instructed women that, because of these differences, they should accept that their roles in life involved child rearing, housekeeping, and nothing more. (Of course, in tendering this advice promoters of female domesticity conveniently ignored the definitions of duty that industrialists imposed on the poor women who worked in their mills.) Yet a paradoxical byproduct of the connections that the new nationalist rhetoric forged between the well-being of the state and domestic life was that the identity of the patriot became one a woman might attempt, with some legitimacy, to claim. Within the framework created by the new accounts of English national identity, a woman's private virtues now had a public relevance. They had to be seen as crucial to the nation's welfare. Those virtues might well be manifested in the work of raising patriotic sons, but, as the thousands of women in this period who made their ostensibly natural feminine feelings of pity their alibi for participation in abolitionism demonstrated, they could be turned to nontraditional uses as well.

The new idea that, as the historian Linda Colley has put it, a woman's place was not simply in the home but also in the nation could also justify or at least extenuate the affront to proper feminine modesty represented by publication— by a woman's entry into the public sphere of authorship. "Bluestockings"— educated women—remained targets of masculine scorn. This became, nonetheless, the first era in literary history in which women writers began to compete with men in their numbers, sales, and literary reputations: just in the category of poetry, some nine hundred women are listed in J. R. de J. Jackson's comprehensive bibliography, *Romantic Poetry by Women*. These female authors had to tread carefully, to be sure, to avoid suggesting that (as one male critic fulminated) they wished the nation's "affectionate wives, kind mothers, and lovely daughters" to be metamorphosed into "studious philosophers" and "busy politicians." And figures like Wollstonecraft, who in the *Vindication of the Rights of Woman* grafted a radical proposal about gender equality onto a more orthodox argument about the education women needed to be proper mothers, remained exceptional. Later women writers tended cautiously to either ignore her example or define themselves against it.

Only in the Victorian period would Wollstonecraft's cause of women's rights rally enough support for substantial legal reform to begin, and that process would not be completed until the twentieth century. In the early nineteenth century the pressures for political reform focused on the rights of men, as distinct from women. Middle-class and working-class men, entering into strategic and short-lived alliances, made the restructuring of the British electoral system their common cause. Finally, at a time of acute economic distress, and after unprecedented disorders that threatened to break out into revolution, the first Reform Bill was passed in 1832. It did away with the rotten boroughs (depopulated areas whose seats in the House of Commons were at the disposal of a few noblemen), redistributed parliamentary representation to include the industrial cities, and extended the franchise. Although about half the middle class, almost all the working class, and all women remained without a vote, the principle of the peaceful adjustment of conflicting interests by parliamentary majority had been firmly established. Reform was to go on, by stages, until Britain acquired universal adult suffrage in 1928.

"THE SPIRIT OF THE AGE"

Writers working in the period 1785–1830 did not think of themselves as "Romantic"; the word was not applied until half a century later, by English historians. Contemporary reviewers treated them as independent individuals, or else grouped them (often maliciously, but with some basis in fact) into a number of separate schools: the "Lake School" of Wordsworth, Coleridge, and Robert Southey; the "Cockney School," a derogatory term for the Londoners Leigh Hunt, William Hazlitt, and associated writers, including Keats; and the "Satanic School" of Percy Shelley, Byron, and their followers.

Many writers, however, felt that there was something distinctive about their time—not a shared doctrine or literary quality, but a pervasive intellectual and imaginative climate, which some of them called "the spirit of the age." They had the sense that (as Keats wrote) "Great spirits now on earth are sojourning," and that there was evidence of the experimental boldness that marks a literary renaissance. In his "Defence of Poetry" Shelley claimed that the literature of the age "has arisen as it were from a new birth," and that "an electric life burns" within the words of its best writers, "less their spirit than the spirit of the age." He explained this spirit as an accompaniment of revolution, and others agreed. Francis Jeffrey, the foremost conservative reviewer of the day, connected "the revolution in our literature" with "the agitations of the French Revolution, and the discussions as well as the hopes and terrors to which it gave occasion." Hazlitt, who devoted a series of essays entitled *The Spirit of the Age* to assessing his contemporaries, maintained that the new poetry of the school of Wordsworth "had its origin in the French Revolution."

The imagination of many Romantic-period writers was preoccupied with revolution, and from that fact and idea they derived the framework that enabled them to think of themselves as inhabiting a distinctive period in history. The deep familiarity that many late-eighteenth-century Englishmen and -women had with the prophetic writings of the Bible contributed from the start to their readiness to attribute a tremendous significance to the political transformations set in motion in 1789. Religious belief predisposed many to view these convulsions as something more than local historical events and to cast them instead as harbingers of a new age in the history of *all* human beings. Seeing the hand of God in the events in France and understanding those events as the fulfillment of prophecies of the coming millennium came easily to figures such as Barbauld, Coleridge, Wollstonecraft, and, above all, Blake: all were affiliated with the traditions of radical Protestant Dissent, in which accounts of the imminence of the Apocalypse and the coming of the Kingdom of God had long been central. A quarter-century later, their millenarian interpretation of the Revolution would be recapitulated by radical writers such as Percy Shelley and Hazlitt, who, though they tended to place their faith in notions of progress and the diffusion of knowledge and tended to identify a rational citizenry and not God as the moving force of history, were just as convinced as their predecessors were that the Revolution had marked humanity's chance to start history over again (a chance that had been lost but was perhaps recoverable).

Another method that writers of this period took when they sought to salvage the millennial hopes that had, for many, been dashed by the bloodshed of the Terror involved granting a crucial role to the creative imagination. Some writers rethought apocalyptic transformation so that it no longer depended on the political action of collective humanity but depended instead (in a shift from the external to the internal) on the individual consciousness. The new heaven and earth promised in the prophecies could, in this account, be gained by the individual who had achieved a new, spiritualized, and visionary way of seeing. An apocalypse of the imagination could liberate the individual from time, from what Blake called the "mind-forg'd manacles" of imprisoning orthodoxies and from what Percy Shelley called "the curse which binds us to be subjected to the accident of surrounding impressions."

Wordsworth, whose formulations of this notion of a revolution in imagination would prove immensely influential, wrote in *The Prelude* the classic description of the spirit of the early 1790s. "Europe at that time was thrilled with joy, / France standing on top of the golden hours, / And human nature seeming born again" (6.340–42). "Not favored spots alone, but the whole earth, / The beauty wore of promise" (6.117–18). Something of this sense of possibility and anticipation of spiritual regeneration (captured in that phrase "born again") survived the disenchantment with politics that Wordsworth experienced later in the decade. His sense of the emancipatory opportunities brought in by the new historical moment carried over to the year 1797, when, working in tandem, he and Coleridge revolutionized the theory and practice of poetry. The product of their exuberant daily discussions was the *Lyrical Ballads* of 1798.

POETIC THEORY AND POETIC PRACTICE

Wordsworth undertook to justify those poems by means of a critical manifesto, or statement of poetic principles, which appeared first as a short Advertisement in the original *Lyrical Ballads* and then as an extended Preface to the second edition in 1800, which he enlarged still further in the third edition of 1802. In it he set himself in opposition to the literary ancien régime, those writers of the eighteenth century who, in his view, had imposed on poetry artificial conventions that distorted its free and natural expression. Many of Wordsworth's later critical writings were attempts to clarify, buttress, or qualify points made in this first declaration. Coleridge said that the Preface was "half a child of my own brain"; and although he developed doubts about some of Wordsworth's unguarded statements, he did not question the rightness of Wordsworth's attempt to overthrow the reigning tradition. Of course, many writers in eighteenth-century England had anticipated Wordsworth's attempt, as well as the definitions of the "authentic" language of poetry it assumed. Far from unprecedented, efforts to displace the authority of a poet such as Pope can be dated back to only a few years after Pope's death in 1744; by 1800 readers were accustomed to hear, for instance, that Pope's propensities for satire had derailed true poetry by elevating wit over feeling. Moreover, the last half of the eighteenth century, a time when philosophers and moralists highlighted in new ways the role that emotional sensitivity ("sensibility") plays in mental and social life, had seen the emergence of many of the critical concepts, as well as a number of the poetic subjects and forms, that later would be exploited by Wordsworth and his contemporaries.

Wordsworth's Preface nevertheless deserves its reputation as a turning point in literary history, for Wordsworth gathered up isolated ideas, organized them into a coherent theory, and made them the rationale for his own achievements. We can safely use concepts in the Preface as points of departure for a survey of some of the distinctive elements in the poetry of the Romantic period—especially if we bear in mind that during this era of revolution definitions of good poetry, like definitions of the good society, were sure to create as much contention as consensus.

The Concept of the Poet and the Poem

Seeking a stable foundation on which social institutions might be constructed, eighteenth-century British philosophers had devoted much energy to demonstrating that human nature must be everywhere the same, because it everywhere derived from individuals' shared sensory experience of an external world that could be objectively represented. As the century went on, however, philosophers began emphasizing—and poets began developing a new language for—individual variations in perception and the capacity the receptive consciousness has to filter and to re-create reality. This was the shift Wordsworth registered when in the Preface he located the source of a poem not in outer nature but in the psychology of the individual poet, and specified that the essential materials of a poem were not the external people and events it represented but the inner feelings of the author, or external objects only after these have been transformed by the author's feelings. Wordsworth in 1802 described all good poetry as, at the moment of composition, "the spontaneous overflow of powerful feelings." Other Romantic theories concurred by referring to the mind, emotions, and imagination of the poet for the origin, content, and defining attributes of a poem. Using a metaphor that parallels Wordsworth's "overflow," and that Wordsworth would revive in a late poem, Mary Robinson and Coleridge identified some of their key poems of the 1790s as "effusions"—ardent outpourings of feeling. Coleridge subsequently drew on German precedents and introduced into English criticism an account of the organic form of literary works; in this account the work is conceptualized as a self-originating and self-organizing process, parallel to the growth of a plant, that begins with a seedlike idea in the poet's imagination, grows by assimilating both the poet's feelings and the materials of sensory experience, and evolves into an organic whole in which the parts are integrally related to each other and to the whole.

In keeping with the view that poetry expresses the poet's feelings, the lyric poem written in the first person, which for much of literary history was regarded as a minor kind, became a major Romantic form and was often described as the most essentially poetic of all the genres. And in most Romantic lyrics the "I" is no longer a conventionally typical lyric speaker, such as the Petrarchan lover or Cavalier gallant of Elizabethan and seventeenth-century love poems, but one who shares recognizable traits with the poet. The experiences and states of mind expressed by the lyric speaker often accord closely with the known facts of the poet's life and the personal confessions in the poet's letters and journals. This reinvention of the lyric complicated established understandings of the gender of authorship. It may not be an accident, some critics suggest, that Wordsworth in the Preface defines poetry as "the real language of men" and the Poet as a "man speaking to men": Wordsworth, who began to publish when women such as Robinson and Charlotte Smith occupied the vanguard of the new personal poetry, might have decided that to establish the distinctiveness of his project he needed to counterbalance his emphasis on his feelings with an emphasis on those feelings' "manly" dignity. This is not to say that women writers' relationship to the new ideas about poetry was straightforward either. In one of her prefaces Smith says that she anticipates being criticized for "bringing forward 'with querulous egotism,' the mention of myself." For many female poets the other challenge those ideas about poetry posed might have consisted in their potential to reinforce the old, prejudicial idea that their sex—traditionally seen as creatures of feeling rather than intellect—wrote about their own experiences because they were capable of nothing else. For male poets the risks of poetic self-revelation were different—and in some measure they were actively seized by those who, like Coleridge and Shelley, intimated darkly that the introspective tendency and emotional sensitivity that made someone a poet could also lead him to melancholy and madness.

It was not only the lyric that registered these new accounts of the poet. Byron confounded his contemporaries' expectations about which poetic genre was best suited to self-revelation by inviting his audience to equate the heroes of *Childe Harold*, *Manfred*, and *Don Juan* with their author, and to see these fictional protagonists' experiences as disclosing the deep truths of his secret self. Wordsworth's *Prelude* represents an extreme instance of this tendency to self-reference. Though the poem is of epic length and seriousness, its subject is not, as is customary in an epic, history on a world-changing scale but the growth of the poet's mind.

The Prelude exemplifies two other important tendencies. Like Blake, Coleridge in early poems, and later on Shelley, Wordsworth presents himself as, in his words, "a chosen son" or "Bard." That is, he assumes the persona of a poet-prophet, a composite figure modeled on Milton, the biblical prophets, and figures of a national music, the harp-playing patriots, Celtic or Anglo-Saxon, whom eighteenth-century poets and antiquarians had located in a legendary Dark Ages Britain. Adopting this bardic guise, Wordsworth puts himself forward as a spokesman for civilization at a time of crisis—a time, as Wordsworth said in The Prelude, of the "melancholy waste of hopes o'erthrown." (Spokesman is appropriate here: almost always, the bardic poet-prophet was a distinctively male persona.) The Prelude is also an instance of a central literary form of English, as of European, Romanticism—a long work about the crisis and renewal of the self, recounted as the story of an interior journey taken in quest of one's true identity and destined spiritual home and vocation. Blake's Milton, Keats's Endymion and Fall of Hyperion, and, in Victorian poetry, Elizabeth Barrett Browning's Aurora Leigh also exemplify this form. Late in the period there are equivalent developments in prose: spiritual autobiographies (Coleridge's Biographia Literaria, Thomas De Quincey's Confessions of an English Opium Eater) undergo a revival, at the same time that Lamb and Hazlitt rediscover the essay as a medium of self-revelation.

Spontaneity and the Impulses of Feeling

Wordsworth defined good poetry not merely as the overflow but as the "spontaneous overflow" of feelings. In traditional poetics, poetry had been regarded as supremely an art—an art that in modern times is practiced by poets who have assimilated classical precedents, are aware of the "rules" governing the kind of poem they are writing, and (except for the happy touches that, as Pope said, are "beyond the reach of art") deliberately employ tested means to achieve premeditated effects on an audience. But to Wordsworth, although the composition of a poem originates from "emotion recollected in tranquillity" and may be preceded and followed by reflection, the immediate act of composition must be spontaneous—arising from impulse and free from rules. Keats listed as an "axiom" a similar proposition—that "if poetry comes not as naturally as the leaves to a tree it had better not come at all."

Other Romantics voiced similar declarations of artistic independence from inherited precepts, sometimes in a manner involving, paradoxically, a turn from the here-and-now toward a remote, preliterate, and primitive past. If the ancient bard was a charismatic figure for many Romantics, this was in part because imagining the songs he might have sung made it easier to think about an alternative to the mundane language of modernity—about a natural, oral poetry, blissfully unconscious of modern decorums. (Though they chafed against this expectation, writers from the rural working class—Burns and later John Clare—could be expected, by virtue of their perceived distance from the restraint and refinement of civilized discourse, to play a comparable role inside modern culture, that of peasant poet or natural genius.) When, after Waterloo, writers like Byron, Hunt, and the Shelleys traveled to Italy, taking these bardic ideals with them, they became enthralled with the arts of the improvisatore and improvisatrice, men and women whose electrifying oral performances of poetry involved no texts but those of immediate inspiration. One of the writers who praised and emulated that rhapsodic spontaneity, Percy Shelley, thought it "an error to assert that the finest passages of poetry are produced by labor and study." He suggested instead that these were the products of an unconscious creativity: "A great statue or picture grows under the power of the artist as a child in the mother's womb."

The emphasis in this period on the spontaneous activity of the imagination is linked to a belief (which links the Romantics' literary productions to the poetry and fiction of sensibility written earlier in the eighteenth century) in the essential role of passion, whether in the province of art, philosophy, or morality. The intuitive feelings of "the heart" had to supplement the judgments of the purely logical faculty, "the head." "Deep thinking," Coleridge wrote, "is attainable only by a man of deep feeling"; hence, "a metaphysical solution that does not tell you something in the heart is grievously to be suspected as apocryphal."

Romantic "Nature Poetry"

Wordsworth identified *Lyrical Ballads* as his effort to counteract the degradation in taste that had resulted from "the increasing accumulation of men in cities": the revolution in style he proposed in the Preface was meant in part to undo the harmful effects of urbanization. Because he and many fellow writers kept their distance from city life, and because natural scenes so often provide the occasions for their writing, Romantic poetry for present-day readers has become almost synonymous with "nature poetry." In the Essay that supplements his Preface, Wordsworth portrays himself as remedying the failings of predecessors who, he argues, were unable truthfully to depict natural phenomena such as a moonlit sky: from Dryden to Pope, he asserts, there are almost no images of external nature "from which it can be inferred that the eye of the Poet had been steadily fixed upon his object." Neither Romantic theory nor practice, however, justifies the opinion that Romantic poets valued description for its own sake, though many poems of the period are almost unmatched in their ability to capture the sensuous nuances of the natural scene, and the writers participated enthusiastically in the touring of picturesque scenery that was a new leisure activity of their age. But in the Essay Supplementary to the Preface, Wordsworth's complaint against eighteenth-century poetic imagery continues: take an image from an early-eighteenth-century poem, and it will show no signs either, he says, that the Poet's "feelings had urged him to work upon it in the spirit of genuine imagination." For Wordsworth the ability to observe objects accurately is a necessary but not sufficient condition for poetry, "as its exercise supposes all the higher qualities of the mind to be passive, and in a state of subjection to external objects." And while many of the great Romantic lyrics—Wordsworth's "Tintern Abbey," Coleridge's "Frost at Midnight," Keats's "Nightingale," Smith's *Beachy Head*—remark on an aspect or a change of aspect in the natural scene, this serves only as stimulus to the most characteristic human activity, that of thinking. The longer Romantic "nature poems" are in fact usually meditative, using the presented scene to suggest a personal crisis; the organizing principle of the poem involves that crisis's development and resolution.

In addition, Romantic poems habitually endow the landscape with human life, passion, and expressiveness. Many poets respond to the outer universe as a vital entity that participates in the feelings of the observer (an idea of sympathetic exchange between nature and humanity that Mary Shelley, however, would probe fiercely in her novel *The Last Man*). James Thomson and other descriptive poets of the eighteenth century had depicted the created universe as giving direct access to the deity. In "Tintern Abbey" and other poems, Wordsworth not only exhibits toward the landscape attitudes and sentiments that human beings had earlier felt for God; he also loves it in the way human beings love a father, a mother, or a beloved. Still, there was a competing sense, evident especially in the poetry of Blake and Percy Shelley, that natural objects were meaningful primarily for the correspondences linking them to an inner or spiritual world. In their poems a rose, a sunflower, a cloud, or a mountain is presented not as something to be observed and imaged but as an object imbued with a significance beyond itself. "I always seek in what I see," Shelley said, "the likeness of something beyond the present and tangible object." And by Blake, mere nature, as perceived by the physical eye, was spurned "as the dust upon my feet, no part of me." Annotating a copy of Wordsworth's 1815 *Poems,* Blake deplored what *he* perceived as Wordsworth's commitment to unspiritualized observation: "Natural objects always did, and now do, weaken, deaden, and obliterate imagination in men."

The Glorification of the Ordinary

Also discussing Wordsworth, Hazlitt declared his school of poetry the literary equivalent of the French Revolution, which translated political change into poetical experiment. "Kings and queens were dethroned from their rank and station in legitimate tragedy or epic poetry, as they were decapitated elsewhere. . . . The paradox [these poets] set out with was that all things are by nature, equally fit subjects for poetry; or that if there is any preference to give, those that are the meanest [i.e., most humble] and most unpromising are the best." Hazlitt had in mind Wordsworth's statement that the aim of *Lyrical Ballads* was "to choose incidents and situations from common life" and to use a "language really spoken by men": for Wordsworth's polemical purposes, it is in "humble and rustic life" that this language is found. Later eighteenth-century writers had already experimented with the simple treatment of simple subjects. Burns—like the young Wordsworth, a sympathizer with the Revolution—had with great success represented "the rural scenes and rural pleasures of [his] natal Soil," and in a language aiming to be true to the rhythms of his regional Scots dialect. Women poets especially—Barbauld, Robinson, Baillie—assimilated to their poems the subject matter of everyday life. But Wordsworth underwrote his poetic practice with a theory that inverted the traditional hierarchy of poetic genres, subjects, and styles: it elevated humble life and the plain style, which in earlier theory were appropriate only for the pastoral, the genre at the bottom of the traditional hierarchy, into the principal subject and medium for poetry in general. And in his practice, as Hazlitt also noted, Wordsworth went further and turned for the subjects of serious poems not only to humble country folk but to the disgraced, outcast, and delinquent—"convicts, female vagrants, gypsies . . . idiot boys and mad mothers." Hence the scorn of Lord Byron, who facetiously summoned ghosts from the eighteenth century to help him demonstrate that Wordsworth's innovations had been taking literature in the wrong direction:

> "Peddlers," and "Boats," and "Wagons"! Oh! ye shades
> Of Pope and Dryden, are we come to this?

Yet Wordsworth's project was not simply to represent the world as it is but, as he announced in his Preface, to throw over "situations from common life . . . a certain coloring of imagination, whereby ordinary things should be presented to the mind in an unusual aspect." No one can read his poems without noticing the reverence with which he invests words that for earlier writers had been derogatory—words such as "common," "ordinary," "everyday," "humble." Wordsworth's aim was to shatter the lethargy of custom so as to refresh our sense of wonder in the everyday, the trivial, and the lowly. In the eighteenth century Samuel Johnson had said that "wonder is a pause of reason"—"the effect of novelty upon ignorance." But for many Romantics, to arouse in the sophisticated mind that sense of wonder presumed to be felt by the ignorant and the innocent—to renew the universe, Percy Shelley wrote, "after it has been blunted by reiteration"—was a major function of poetry. Commenting on the special imaginative quality of Wordsworth's early verse, Coleridge remarked: "To combine the child's sense of wonder and novelty with the appearances, which every day for perhaps forty years had rendered familiar . . . this is the character and privilege of genius." Contributing to this poetry of the child's-eye view, Baillie and Barbauld wrote poems centered on an observer's effort to imagine the unknowable perspective of beings for whom thought and sensation are new or not begun—in Baillie's case, a "waking infant," in Barbauld's, a "little invisible being who is expected soon to become visible" but is still in its mother's womb.

The Supernatural, the Romance, and Psychological Extremes

In most of his poems, Coleridge, like Wordsworth, dealt with everyday things, and in "Frost at Midnight" he showed how well he too could achieve the effect of wonder in the familiar. But Coleridge tells us in *Biographia Literaria* that, according to the division of labor that organized their collaboration on *Lyrical Ballads*, his assignment was to achieve wonder by a frank violation of natural laws and of the ordinary course of events: in his poems "the incidents and agents were to be, in part at least, supernatural." And in *The Rime of the Ancient Mariner, Christabel,* and "Kubla Khan," Coleridge opened up to modern poetry a realm of mystery and magic. Stories of bewitchings, hauntings, and possession—shaped by antiquated treatises on demonology, folklore, and Gothic novels—supplied him with the means of impressing upon readers a sense of occult powers and unknown modes of being.

Materials like these were often grouped together under the rubric "romance," a term that would some time after the fact give the "Romantic" period its name. On the one hand romances were writings that turned, in their quest for settings conducive to supernatural happenings, to "strange fits of passion" and strange adventures, to distant pasts, faraway places, or both— Keats's "perilous seas, in faery lands forlorn" or the China of "Kubla Khan." On the other hand romance also named a homegrown, native tradition of literature, made unfamiliar and alien by the passage of time. For many authors, starting with Horace Walpole, whose *Castle of Otranto* (1764) began the tradition of Gothic fiction, writing under the banner of romance meant reclaiming their national birthright: a literature of untrammeled imagination— associated, above all, with Spenser and the Shakespeare of fairy magic and witchcraft—that had been forced underground by the Enlightenment's emphasis on reason and refinement. Byron negotiated between romance's two sets of associations in *Childe Harold,* having his hero travel in far-off Albania and become entranced by the inhabitants' savage songs, but also giving the poem the subtitle "A Romaunt" (an archaic spelling of romance) and writing it in Spenserian stanzas. This was the same stanzaic form, neglected for much of the eighteenth century, that Keats drew on for *The Eve of St. Agnes,* the poem in which he proved himself a master of that Romantic mode that establishes a medieval setting for events that violate our sense of realism and the natural order. The Romantic period's "medieval revival" was also promoted by women: Robinson, for instance (author of "Old English," "Monkish," and "Gothic" Tales), as well as Letitia Landon, Felicia Hemans, Joanna Baillie, and others, women who often matched the arch-medievalist Sir Walter Scott in the historical learning they brought to their compositions.

The "addition of strangeness to beauty" that Walter Pater near the end of the nineteenth century would identify as a key Romantic tendency is seen not only in this concern with the exotic and archaic landscapes of romance, but also in the Romantic interest in the mysteries of mental life and determination to investigate psychological extremes. Wordsworth explored visionary states of consciousness that are common among children but violate the categories of adult judgment. Coleridge and De Quincey shared an interest in dreams and nightmares and in the altered consciousness they experienced under their addiction to opium. In his odes as in the quasi-medieval "ballad" "La Belle Dame sans Merci" Keats recorded strange mixtures of pleasure and pain with extraordinary sensitivity, pondering the destructive aspects of sexuality and the erotic quality of the longing for death. And Byron made repeated use of the fascination of the forbidden and the appeal of the terrifying yet seductive Satanic hero.

There were, of course, writers who resisted these poetic engagements with fantasized landscapes and strange passions. Significant dissent came from women, who, given accounts of their sex as especially susceptible to the delusions of romantic love, had particular reason to continue the Enlightenment program and promote the rational regulation of emotion. Barbauld wrote a poem gently advising the young Coleridge not to prolong his stay in the "fairy bower" of romance but to engage actively with the world as it is. Often satirical when she assesses characters who imagine themselves the pitiable victims of their own powerful feelings, Jane Austen had her heroine in *Persuasion,* while conversing with a melancholy, Byron-reading young man, caution him against overindulgence in Byron's "impassioned descriptions of hopeless agony" and "prescribe" to him a "larger allowance of prose in his daily study." And yet this heroine, having "been forced into prudence in her youth," has "learned romance as she grew older." The reversal of the sequence that usually orders the story line of female socialization suggests a receptivity to romance's allure that links even Austen to the spirit of the age.

Individualism and Alienation

Another feature of Byron's poetry that attracted notice and, in some quarters, censure was its insistence on his or his hero's self-sufficiency. Hazlitt, for instance, borrowed lines from Shakespeare's *Coriolanus* to object to Byron's habit of spurning human connection "[a]s if a man were author of himself, / And owned no other kin." The audacious individualism that Hazlitt questions here (a questioning that he carries on in part by enacting his own reliance on others and supplementing his words with Shakespeare's) was, however, central to the celebrations of creativity occupying many Romantic-period writers:

indeed, in the Preface to *Lyrical Ballads*, Wordsworth (as if anticipating and preemptively defying Hazlitt) had already characterized his poetic experimentation as an exercise in artistic self-sufficiency. The Preface has been read as a document in which Wordsworth, proving himself a self-made man, arranges for his disinheritance—arranges to cut himself off, he says, "from a large portion of the phrases and figures of speech which from father to son have long been regarded as the common inheritance of Poets." The German philosophers who generated many of the characteristic ideas of European Romanticism had likewise developed an account of how individuals might author and create themselves. In the work of Kant and others, the human mind was described as creating the universe it perceived and so creating its own experience. Mind is "not passive," Kant's admirer Coleridge wrote, but "made in God's image, and that too in the sublimest sense—the Image of the *Creator*." And Wordsworth declared in *The Prelude* that the individual mind "Doth, like an Agent of the one great Mind, / Create, creator and receiver both." The Romantic period, the epoch of free enterprise, imperial expansion, and boundless revolutionary hope, was also an epoch of individualism in which philosophers and poets alike put an extraordinarily high estimate on human potentialities and powers.

In representing this expanded scope for individual initiative, much poetry of the period redefined heroism and made a ceaseless striving for the unattainable its crucial element. Viewed by moralists of previous ages as sin or lamentable error, longings that can never be satisfied—in Percy Shelley's phrase, "the desire of the moth for a star"—came to be revalued as the glory of human nature. "Less than everything," Blake announced, "cannot satisfy man." Discussions of the nature of art developed similarly. The German philosopher Friedrich Schlegel's proposal that poetry "should forever be becoming and never be perfected" supplied a way to understand the unfinished, "fragment" poems of the period (Coleridge's "Kubla Khan" most famously) not as failures but instead as confirmations that the most poetic poetry was defined as much by what was absent as by what was present: the poem, in this understanding, was a fragmentary trace of an original conception that was too grand ever to be fully realized. This defiant attitude toward limits also made many writers impatient with the conceptions of literary genre they inherited from the past. The result was that, creating new genres from old, they produced an astonishing variety of hybrid forms constructed on fresh principles of organization and style: "elegiac sonnets," "lyrical ballads," the poetic autobiography of *The Prelude*, Percy Shelley's "lyric drama" of cosmic reach, *Prometheus Unbound*, and (in the field of prose) the "historical novels" of Scott and the complex interweaving of letters, reported oral confessions, and interpolated tales that is Mary Shelley's *Frankenstein*. Blake went furthest: the composite art of word and image and "illuminated printing" he created for his poems daringly reinvented the concept of the book.

In this context many writers' choice to portray poetry as a product of solitude and poets as loners might be understood as a means of reinforcing the individuality of their vision. (The sociability of the extroverted narrator of *Don Juan*, who is forever buttonholing "the gentle reader," is exceptional—Byron's way of harkening back to the satire of the eighteenth century.) And the pervasiveness of nature poetry in the period can be attributed to a determination to idealize the natural scene as a site where the individual could find freedom from social laws, an idealization that was easier to sustain when nature was, as often in the era, represented not as cultivated fields but as uninhabitable wild wastes, unploughed uplands, caves, and chasms. Rural *community*, threatened by the enclosures that were breaking up village life, was a tenuous presence in poetry as well.

Wordsworth's imagination is typically released, for instance, by the sudden apparition of a single figure, stark and solitary against a natural background; the words "solitary," "by one self," "alone" sound through his poems. In the poetry of Coleridge, Shelley, and Byron (before *Don Juan* launched Byron's own satire on Byronism), the desolate landscapes are often the haunts of disillusioned visionaries and accursed outlaws, figures whose thwarted ambitions and torments connect them, variously, to Cain, the Wandering Jew, Satan, and even Napoleon. A variant of this figure is Prometheus, the hero of classical mythology, who is Satan-like in setting himself in opposition to God, but who, unlike Satan, is the champion rather than the enemy of the human race. Mary Shelley subjected this hero, central to her husband's mythmaking, to ironic rewriting in *Frankenstein*: Victor Frankenstein, a "Modern Prometheus," is far from championing humankind. For other women writers of the period, and for Shelley in novels following *Frankenstein,* the equivalent to these half-charismatic, half-condemnable figures of alienation is the woman of "genius." In a world in which—as Wollstonecraft complained in the *Rights of Woman*— "all women are to be levelled by meekness and docility, into one character of . . . gentle compliance," the woman who in "unfeminine" fashion claimed a distinctive individuality did not gain authority but risked ostracism. As for the woman of genius, in writings by Robinson, Hemans, and Landon particularly, her story was often told as a modern variation on ancient legends of the Greek Sappho, the ill-fated female poet who had triumphed in poetry but died of love. Pressured by the emergent Victorianism of the 1820s and playing it safe, Hemans and Landon especially were careful to associate genius with self-inflicted sorrow and happiness with a woman's embrace of her domestic calling.

WRITING IN THE MARKETPLACE AND THE COURTS

Even Romantics who wished to associate literature with isolated poets holding mute converse with their souls had to acknowledge that in real life the writer did not dwell in solitude but confronted, and was accountable to, a crowd. For many commentators the most revolutionary aspect of the age was the spread of literacy and the dramatic expansion of the potential audience for literature. This revolution, like the Revolution in France, occasioned a conservative reaction: the worry, frequently expressed as books ceased to be written exclusively for an elite, that this bigger audience (by 1830, about half England's population of fourteen million) would be less qualified to judge or understand what it read. Beginning in 1780, more members of the working classes had learned to read as a result of lessons provided in Sunday schools (informal sites for the education of the poor that long antedated state-supported schools). At the same time reading matter became more plentiful and cheaper, thanks to innovations in retailing—the cut-rate sales of remaindered books and the spread of circulating libraries where volumes could be "rented"—and thanks to technological developments. By the end of the period, printing presses were driven by steam engines, and the manufacture of paper had been mechanized; publishers had mastered publicity, the art (as it was called) of "the puff." Surveying the consequences of these changes, Coleridge muttered darkly about that "misgrowth," "a Reading Public," making it sound like something freakish. Books had become a big business, one enrolling increasing numbers of individuals who found it possible to do without the assistance of wealthy patrons and who, accordingly, looked to this public for their hopes of survival. A few writers became celebrities, invested with a glamor that formerly had been reserved for royalty and that we nowadays save for movie stars. This was the case for the best-selling Byron, particularly, whose enthusiastic public could by the 1830s purchase dinner services imprinted with illustrations from his life and works.

How such popular acclaim was to be understood and how the new reading public that bestowed it (and took it away) could possibly be reformed or monitored when, as Coleridge's term "misgrowth" suggests, its limits and composition seemed unknowable: these were pressing questions for the age. Opponents of the French Revolution and political reform at home pondered a frightening possibility: if "events . . . [had] made us a world of readers" (as Coleridge put it, thinking of how newspapers had proliferated in response to the political upheavals), it might also be true that readers could *make* events in turn, that the new members of the audience for print would demand a part in the drama of national politics. Conservatives were well aware of arguments conjecturing that the Revolution had been the result of the invention of the printing press three centuries before. They certainly could not forget that Paine's *Rights of Man*—not the reading matter for the poor the Sunday-school movement had envisioned—had sold an astonishing two hundred thousand copies in a year. Distributed by clubs of workers who pooled money for this purpose, read aloud in alehouses or as listeners worked in the fields, those copies reached a total audience that was much more numerous still.

However, the British state had lacked legal provisions for the prepublication censorship of books since 1695, which was when the last Licensing Act had lapsed. Throughout the Romantic period therefore the Crown tried out other methods for policing reading and criminalizing certain practices of authoring and publishing. Paine was in absentia found guilty of sedition, for instance, and in 1817 the radical publisher William Hone narrowly escaped conviction for blasphemy. Another government strategy was to use taxes to inflate the prices of printed matter and so keep political information out of the hands of the poor without exactly violating the freedom of the press. In the meantime worries about how the nation would fare now that "the people" read were matched by worries about how to regulate the reading done by women. In 1807 the bowdlerized edition was born, as the Reverend Thomas Bowdler and his sister Henrietta produced *The Family Shakespeare,* concocting a Bard who, his indelicacies expurgated, could be sanctioned family fare.

Commentators who condemned the publishing industry as a scene of criminality also cited the frequency with which, during this chaotic time, bestselling books ended up republished in unauthorized, "pirated" editions. Novels were the pirates' favorite targets. But the radical underground of London's printing industry also appropriated one of the most politically daring works of Percy Shelley, *Queen Mab,* and by keeping it in print, and accessible in cheap editions, thwarted attempts to posthumously sanitize the poet's reputation. And in 1817 Robert Southey, the Poet Laureate, was embarrassed to find his insurrectionary drama of 1794, *Wat Tyler,* republished without his permission. There was no chance, Southey learned, that the thieves who had filched his intellectual property and put this souvenir of his youthful radicalism back into circulation would be punished: the judiciary ruled that copyright law was for the law-abiding and did not apply to "sedition."

OTHER LITERARY FORMS

Prose

Although we now know the Romantic period as an age of poetry, centered on works of imagination, nonfiction prose forms—essays, reviews, political pamphlets—flourished during the epoch, as writers seized the opportunity to speak to and for the era's new audiences. In eighteenth-century England, prose, particularly in the urbane, accessible style that writers such as Addison and Hume cultivated in their essays, had been valued as the medium of sociable exchange that could integrate different points of view and unify the public space known as the "republic of letters." That ideal of civil discussion came under pressure in the Romantic period, however, since by then many intellectuals were uncertain whether a republic of letters could survive the arrival of those new readers, "the people," and whether in this age of class awareness such a thing as a unified public culture was even possible. Those uncertainties are never far from the surface in the masterpieces of Romantic prose—a category that ranges from the pamphleteering that drew Burke, Wollstonecraft, and Paine into the Revolution controversy of the 1790s, to the periodical essays, with suggestive titles like *The Watchman* and *The Friend*, in which Coleridge turned controversialist, to the magazine writing of Hazlitt, Lamb, and De Quincey in the 1820s.

The issue of how the writer should relate to audience—as watchman or friend?—was especially tricky, because this period, when so many more people defined themselves as readers, saw the emergence of a new species of specialist reader. This was the critic, who, perhaps problematically, was empowered to tell all the others what to read. Following the establishment in 1802 of the *Edinburgh Review* and in 1809 of the *Quarterly Review,* a new professionalized breed of book reviewer claimed a degree of cultural authority to which eighteenth-century critics had never aspired. Whereas later-eighteenth-century periodicals such as the *Monthly Review* and *Critical Review* had aimed to notice almost everything in print, the *Edinburgh* and *Quarterly* limited themselves to about fifteen books per issue. The selectivity enabled them to make decisive statements about what would count as culture and what would fall beyond the pale. They also conceptualized criticism as a space of discipline, in which the reputations of the writers under review were as likely to be marred as they were to be made. The stern Latin motto of the *Edinburgh* (founded by lawyers) translates as "the judge is condemned when the guilty go free." The continuing tension in the relations between criticism and literature and doubt about whether critical prose can be literature—whether it can have artistic value as well as social utility—are legacies from the Romantic era. Hazlitt wondered self-consciously in an essay on criticism whether his was not in fact a critical rather than a poetical age and whether "no great works of genius appear, because so much is said and written about them."

Hazlitt participated importantly in another development. In 1820 the founding editor of the *London Magazine* gathered a group of writers, Hazlitt, Lamb, and De Quincey, who in the *London*'s pages collectively developed the Romantic form known as the familiar essay: intimate-feeling commentaries, often presented as if prompted by incidents in the authors' private lives, on an eclectic range of topics, from pork to prize-fighting. In some of his essays, Hazlitt modeled an account of the individual's response to works of art as most important not for how, for instance, it prepares that person for public citizenship, but for what it helps him discover about his personality. For their essays Lamb and De Quincey developed a style that harkened back to writers who flourished before the republic of letters and who had more idiosyncratic eccentricities than eighteenth-century decorum would have allowed. Though these essayists were very differently circumstanced from the Romantic poets who were their friends—paid by the page and writing to a deadline, for a start—their works thus parallel the poets' in also turning toward the personal and subjective. One consequence of the essayists' cultivation of intimacy and preference for the impressionistic over the systematic is that, when we track the history of prose to the 1820s, we see it end up in a place very different from the one it occupies at the start of the Romantic period. Participants in the Revolution controversy of the 1790s had claimed to speak for all England. By the close of the period the achievement of the familiar essay was to have brought the medium of prose within the category of "the literary"—but by distancing it from public life.

Drama

Whether the plays composed during the Romantic period can qualify as literature has been, by contrast, more of a puzzle. England throughout this period had a vibrant theatrical culture. Theater criticism, practiced with flair by Hazlitt and Lamb, emerged as a new prose genre; actors like Sarah Siddons and Edmund Kean numbered the poets among their admirers and found their way into Romantic poetry; Mary Robinson was known as an actor before she was known as an author. But there were many restrictions limiting what could be staged in England and many calls for reform. As places where crowds gathered, theaters were always closely watched by suspicious government officials. The English had habitually extolled their theater as a site of social mixing—a mirror to the political order in that it supplied all the classes in the nation (those who, depending on how their tickets were priced, frequented the box, the pit, or the gallery) with another sort of representative assembly. But during this era *dis*order seemed the rule: riots broke out at Covent Garden in 1792 and 1809. The link between drama and disorder was one reason that new dramas had to meet the approval of a censor before they could be performed, a rule in place since 1737. Another restriction was that only the theaters royal (in London, Drury Lane and Covent Garden) had the legal right to produce "legitimate" (spoken word) drama, leaving the other stages limited to entertainments—pantomimes and melodramas mainly—in which dialogue was by regulation always combined with music. An evening's entertainment focused on legitimate drama would not have been so different. The stages and auditoriums of the two theaters royal were huge spaces, which encouraged their managers to favor grandiose spectacles or, more precisely, multimedia experiences, involving musicians, dancers, and artists who designed scenery, besides players and playwrights.

This theatrical culture's demotion of *words* might explain why the poets of the era, however stagestruck, found drama uncongenial. Nonetheless, almost all tried their hands at the form, tempted by the knowledge that the plays of certain of their (now less esteemed) contemporaries—Hannah Cowley and Charles Maturin, for example—had met with immense acclaim. Some of the poets' plays were composed to be read rather than performed: "closet dramas," such as Byron's *Manfred,* Shelley's *Prometheus Unbound,* and most of Baillie's *Plays on the Passions,* permitted experimentation with topic and form. Others were written expressly for the stage, but their authors were hampered by their inexperience and tendency, exacerbated by the censorship that encouraged them to seek safe subject matter in the past, to imitate the style of Elizabethan and Jacobean drama. There were exceptions to this discouraging record. Coleridge's tragedy *Remorse,* for instance, was a minor hit and ran for twenty nights in 1813. The most capable dramatist among the poets was, surprisingly, Percy Shelley. His powerful tragedy *The Cenci* (1820), the story of a monstrous father who rapes his daughter and is murdered by her in turn, was deemed unstageable on political rather than artistic or technical grounds. It had no chance of getting by the Examiner of Plays; indeed, by thematizing the unspeakable topic of incest, Shelley predicted his own censoring.

The Novel

Novels at the start of the Romantic period were immensely popular but—as far as critics and some of the form's half-ashamed practitioners were concerned—not quite respectable. Loose in structure, they seemed to require fewer skills than other literary genres. This genre lacked the classic pedigree claimed by poetry and drama. It attracted (or so detractors declared) an undue proportion of readers who were women, and who, by consuming its escapist stories of romantic love, risked developing false ideas of life. It likewise attracted (so some of these same critics complained) too many *writers* who were women. (By the 1780s women were publishing as many novels as men.) Because of its popularity, the form also focused commentators' anxieties about the expansion of the book market and commercialization of literature: hence late-eighteenth-century reviewers of new novels often sarcastically described them as mass-produced commodities, not authored exactly, but instead stamped out automatically in "novel-mills." Matters changed decisively, however, starting around 1814. Reviews of Scott's *Waverley* series of historical novels and then a review that Scott wrote of Jane Austen's *Emma* declared a renaissance—"a new style of novel." By this time, too, the genre had its historians, who delineated the novel's origins and rise and in this manner established its particularity against the more reputable literary forms. It was having a canon created for it too; figures like Barbauld and Scott compiled and introduced collections of the best novels. So equipped, the novel began to endanger poetry's long-held monopoly on literary prestige.

There had in fact been earlier signs of these new ambitions for the genre, although reviewers did not then know what to make of them. The last decade of the eighteenth century saw bold experiments with novels' form and subject matter—in particular, new ways of linking fiction with philosophy and history. Rather than, as one reviewer put it, contentedly remaining in a "region of their own," some novels showed signs of having designs on the real world. The writers now known as the Jacobin novelists used the form to test political theories and represent the political upheavals of the age. Thus in *Caleb Williams, or, Things as They Are,* the philosopher William Godwin (husband of Mary Wollstonecraft and father of Mary Shelley) set out, he said, to "write a tale, that shall constitute an epoch in the mind of the reader, that no one, after he had read it, shall ever be exactly the same": the result was a chilling novel of surveillance and entrapment in which a servant recounts the persecutions he suffers at the hands of the master whose secret past he has detected. (The disturbing cat-and-mouse game between the two gets rewritten two decades later as the conclusion to *Frankenstein,* a novel that, among many other things, represents Shelley's tribute to the philosophical fictions of her parents.) Loyalists attacked the Jacobins with their own weapons and, in making novels their ammunition, contributed in turn to enhancing the genre's cultural presence.

Another innovation in novel-writing took shape, strangely enough, as a recovery of what was old. Writers whom we now describe as the Gothic novelists revisited the romance, the genre identified as the primitive forerunner of the modern novel, looking to a medieval (i.e., "Gothic") Europe that they pictured as a place of gloomy castles, devious Catholic monks, and stealthy ghosts. These authors—first Walpole, followed by Clara Reeve, Sophia Lee, Matthew Lewis, and the hugely popular Ann Radcliffe—developed for the novel a repertory of settings and story lines meant to purvey to readers the pleasurable terror of regression to a premodern, prerational state. This Gothic turn was another instance of the period's "romance revival," another variation on the effort to renew the literature of the present by reworking the past. Gothic fiction was thus promoted in terms running parallel to those in accounts of the powers of poetry: when novels break with humdrum reality, Anna Barbauld explained, "our imagination, darting forth, explores with rapture the new world which is laid open to its view, and rejoices in the expansion of its powers."

Possibly this "new world" was meant to supply Romantic-period readers with an escape route from the present and from what Godwin called "things as they are." Certainly, the pasts that Gothic novelists conjure up are conceived of in fanciful, freewheeling ways; it is comical just how often a Radcliffe heroine who is supposed to inhabit sixteenth-century France can act like a proper English girl on the marriage market in the 1790s. But even that example of anachronism might suggest that some Gothic novelists were inviting readers to assess their stories as engaging the questions of the day. Gothic horrors gave many writers a language in which to examine the nature of power—the elements of sadism and masochism in the relations between men and women, for instance. And frequently the Gothic novelists probe the very ideas of historical accuracy and legitimacy that critics use against them, and meditate on who is authorized to tell the story of the past and who is not.

The ascendancy of the novel in the early nineteenth century is in many ways a function of fiction writers' new self-consciousness about their relation to works of history. By 1814 the novelist and historian encroached on each other's territory more than ever. This was not exactly because nineteenth-century novelists were renewing their commitment to probability and realism (although, defining themselves against the critically reviled Gothic novelists, many were), but rather because the nature of things historical was also being reinvented. In light of the Revolution, history's traditional emphasis on public affairs and great men had begun to give way to an emphasis on beliefs, customs, everyday habits—the approach we now identify with social history. Novelists pursued similar interests: in works like *Castle Rackrent,* Maria Edgeworth, for instance, provides an almost anthropological account of the way of life of a bygone Ireland. The only novelist before Scott whom the influential *Edinburgh Review* took seriously, Edgeworth builds into her "national tales" details about local practices that demonstrate how people's ways of seeing are rooted in the particularities of their native places. Scott learned from her, incorporating her regionalism into his new style of historical novels, in which, with deeply moving results, he also portrayed the past as a place of adventure, pageantry, and grandeur.

Scott and Edgeworth establish the master theme of the early-nineteenth-century novel: the question of how the individual consciousness intermeshes with larger social structures, of how far character is the product of history and how far it is not. Jane Austen's brilliance as a satirist of the English leisure class often prompts literary historians to compare her works to witty Restoration and eighteenth-century comedies. But she too helped bring this theme to the forefront of novel-writing, devising new ways of articulating the relationship between the psychological history of the individual and the history of society, and, with unsurpassed psychological insight, creating unforgettable heroines who live in time and change. As with other Romantics, Austen's topic is revolution—revolutions of the mind. The momentous event in her fictions, which resemble Wordsworth's poetry in finding out the extraordinary in the everyday, is the change of mind that creates the possibility of love. Contrasting his own "big bow-wow strain" with Austen's nuance, Scott wrote that Austen "had a talent for describing the involvements and feelings and characters of ordinary life, which is to me the most wonderful I ever met with." Nineteenth-century reviewers of his triumphant *Waverley* series were certain that Scott's example foretold the future of novel-writing. He, however, recognized the extent to which Austen had also changed the genre in which she worked, by developing a new novelistic language for the workings of the mind in flux.

Additional information about the Romantic Period, including primary texts and images, is available at Norton Literature Online (www.wwnorton.com/literature). Online topics are

- *Tintern Abbey,* Tourism, and Romantic Landscape
- The Satanic and Byronic Hero
- The French Revolution
- Romantic Orientalism

THE ROMANTIC PERIOD

TEXTS	CONTEXTS
1773 Anna Letitia Aikin (later Barbauld), *Poems*	
1774 J. W. von Goethe, *The Sorrows of Young Werther*	
	1775 American War of Independence (1775–83)
1776 Adam Smith, *The Wealth of Nations*	
1778 Frances Burney, *Evelina*	
1779 Samuel Johnson, *Lives of the English Poets* (1779–81)	
	1780 Gordon Riots in London
1781 Immanuel Kant, *Critique of Pure Reason.* Jean-Jacques Rousseau, *Confessions.* J. C. Friedrich Schiller, *The Robbers*	
	1783 William Pitt becomes prime minister (serving until 1801 and again in 1804–06)
1784 Charlotte Smith, *Elegiac Sonnets*	**1784** Death of Samuel Johnson
1785 William Cowper, *The Task*	
1786 William Beckford, *Vathek.* Robert Burns, *Poems, Chiefly in the Scottish Dialect*	
	1787 W. A. Mozart, *Don Giovanni.* Society for the Abolition of the Slave Trade founded
1789 Jeremy Bentham, *Principles of Morals and Legislation.* William Blake, *Songs of Innocence*	**1789** Fall of the Bastille (beginning of the French Revolution)
1790 Joanna Baillie, *Poems.* Blake, *The Marriage of Heaven and Hell.* Edmund Burke, *Reflections on the Revolution in France*	**1790** J. M. W. Turner first exhibits at the Royal Academy
1791 William Gilpin, *Observations on the River Wye.* Thomas Paine, *Rights of Man.* Ann Radcliffe, *The Romance of the Forest*	**1791** Revolution in Santo Domingo (modern Haiti)
1792 Mary Wollstonecraft, *A Vindication of the Rights of Woman*	**1792** September Massacres in Paris. First gas lights in Britain
1793 William Godwin, *Political Justice*	**1793** Execution of Louis XVI and Marie Antoinette. France declares war against Britain (and then Britain against France). The Reign of Terror
1794 Blake, *Songs of Experience.* Godwin, *Caleb Williams.* Radcliffe, *The Mysteries of Udolpho*	**1794** The fall of Robespierre. Trials for high treason of members of the London Corresponding Society
	1795 Pitt's Gagging Acts suppress freedom of speech and assembly in Britain

TEXTS	CONTEXTS
1796 Matthew Gregory Lewis, *The Monk*	
	1797 Death of complications resulting from childbirth of Mary Wollstonecraft
1798 Joanna Baillie, *Plays on the Passions,* volume 1. Bentham, *Political Economy.* Thomas Malthus, *An Essay on the Principle of Population.* William Wordsworth and Samuel Taylor Coleridge, *Lyrical Ballads*	**1798** Rebellion in Ireland
1800 Maria Edgeworth, *Castle Rackrent.* Mary Robinson, *Lyrical Tales*	
	1801 Parliamentary Union of Ireland and Great Britain
	1802 Treaty of Amiens. *Edinburgh Review* founded. John Constable first exhibits at the Royal Academy
	1804 Napoleon crowned emperor. Founding of the republic of Haiti
1805 Walter Scott, *The Lay of the Last Minstrel*	**1805** The French fleet defeated by the British at Trafalgar
1807 Wordsworth, *Poems in Two Volumes*	**1807** Abolition of the slave trade in Britain
1808 Goethe, *Faust,* part 1	**1808** Ludwig van Beethoven, *Symphonies* 5 and 6
	1809 *Quarterly Review* founded
	1811 The Prince of Wales becomes regent for George III, who is declared incurably insane
1812 Lord Byron, *Childe Harold's Pilgrimage,* cantos 1 and 2. Felicia Hemans, *The Domestic Affections*	**1812** War between Britain and the United States (1812–15)
1813 Jane Austen, *Pride and Prejudice*	
1814 Walter Scott, *Waverley.* Wordsworth, *The Excursion*	
	1815 Napoleon defeated at Waterloo. Corn Laws passed, protecting economic interests of the landed aristocracy
1816 Byron, *Childe Harold,* cantos 3 and 4. Coleridge, *Christabel,* "Kubla Khan." Percy Shelley, *Alastor*	
1817 Byron, *Manfred.* Coleridge, *Biographia Literaria* and *Sibylline Leaves.* John Keats, *Poems*	**1817** *Blackwood's Edinburgh Magazine* founded. Death of Princess Charlotte. Death of Jane Austen
1818 Austen, *Northanger Abbey.* Keats, *Endymion.* Thomas Love Peacock, *Nightmare Abbey.* Mary Shelley, *Frankenstein*	

TEXTS	CONTEXTS
1819 Byron, *Don Juan,* cantos 1 and 2	**1819** "Peterloo Massacre" in Manchester
1820 John Clare, *Poems Descriptive of Rural Life.* Keats, *Lamia, Isabella, The Eve of St. Agnes, and Other Poems.* Percy Shelley, *Prometheus Unbound*	**1820** Death of George III; accession of George IV. *London Magazine* founded
1821 Thomas De Quincey, *Confessions of an English Opium-Eater.* Percy Shelley, *Adonais*	**1821** Deaths of Keats in Rome and Napoleon at St. Helena
	1822 Franz Schubert, *Unfinished Symphony.* Death of Percy Shelley in the Bay of Spezia, near Lerici, Italy
1824 Letitia Landon, *The Improvisatrice*	**1824** Death of Byron in Missolonghi
1827 Clare, *The Shepherd's Calendar*	
1828 Hemans, *Records of Woman*	**1828** Parliamentary repeal of the Test and Corporation Acts excluding Dissenters from state offices
	1829 Catholic Emancipation
1830 Charles Lyell, *Principles of Geology* (1830–33). Alfred Tennyson, *Poems, Chiefly Lyrical*	**1830** Death of George IV; accession of William IV. Revolution in France
	1832 First Reform Bill

ANNA LETITIA BARBAULD
1743–1825

Anna Barbauld, born Anna Letitia Aikin, received an unusual education from her father, a minister and a teacher, after 1758, at the Warrington Academy in Lancashire, the great educational center for the Nonconformist community, whose religion barred them from admission to the universities of Oxford and Cambridge. Over the course of the eighteenth century, Dissenting academies such as Warrington had developed a modern curriculum in the natural sciences, as well as in modern languages and English literature. This progressive educational program deviated significantly from the classics-based curriculum, scarcely altered since the sixteenth century, that was supplied by the old universities. Barbauld benefited from the curriculum the Dissenters had designed with their sons in mind and mastered French and Italian, and then Latin and Greek, while still a girl.

She made her literary debut with *Poems,* which went through five editions between 1773 and 1777 and immediately established her as a leading poet. In 1774 she married Rochemont Barbauld, a Dissenting minister, and with him comanaged a school at Palgrave, in Suffolk. Thereafter, becoming increasingly famous and respected in literary circles as (according to the custom of the day) "Mrs. Barbauld," she divided her time between the teaching of younger pupils at Palgrave and a series of writings focused on education, politics, and literature. She published *Devotional Pieces* (1775), three volumes of *Lessons for Children* (1778–79), and *Hymns in Prose for Children* (1781), all of which were reprinted many times. William Hazlitt records a common experience in recalling that he read her works "before those of any other author, male or female, when I was learning to spell words of one syllable in her storybooks for children."

She wrote political pamphlets in the 1790s, opposing Britain's declaration of war against France, defending democratic government and popular education, and campaigning for the repeal of the Test Acts that had long excluded Nonconformist Protestants (those who would not subscribe, as a "test" of their loyalty, to the thirty-nine Articles of the Established Church) from the public life of the nation. Her 1791 "Epistle to William Wilberforce" attacked Britain's involvement in the slave trade. She accompanied her poetry and political writing with editing, producing an edition of William Collins's poems (1797), six volumes of the correspondence of the mid-eighteenth-century novelist Samuel Richardson (1804), fifty volumes of *The British Novelists* (beginning in 1810), and a popular anthology of poetry and prose for young women called *The Female Speaker* (1811). *The British Novelists* was the first attempt to establish a national canon in fiction paralleling the multivolume collections of British poets (such as the one associated with Samuel Johnson's prefaces) that had been appearing since the 1770s. Her introductory essay, "On the Origin and Progress of Novel-Writing," is a pioneering statement concerning the educational value of novels.

Barbauld's last major work in poetry was *Eighteen Hundred and Eleven* (1812), a bitter diagnosis of contemporary British life and politics, which lamented the war with France (then in its seventeenth year), the poverty of leadership, the fallen economy, colonialism, and the failure of genius (at the conclusion, the Spirit of Genius emigrates to South America). Critics, even the more liberal ones, were antagonized by a woman writer's use of the scourge of Juvenalian satire, and their response was anguished and unanimously negative; and Barbauld seems not to have attempted another long work after this (she was, by this time, in her late sixties). After Barbauld's death, her niece Lucy Aikin brought out her aunt's *Works* (two volumes), including several previously unpublished pieces.

The Mouse's Petition[1]

Found in the trap where he had been confined all night by Dr. Priestley,
for the sake of making experiments with different kinds of air

"Parcere subjectis, et debellare superbos."
—Virgil

Oh hear a pensive prisoner's prayer,
For liberty that sighs;
And never let thine heart be shut
Against the wretch's cries.

5   For here forlorn and sad I sit,
Within the wiry gate;
And tremble at th' approaching morn,
Which brings impending fate.

If e'er thy breast with freedom glow'd,
10   And spurn'd a tyrant's chain,
Let not thy strong oppressive force
A free-born mouse detain.

Oh do not stain with guiltless blood
Thy hospitable hearth;
15   Nor triumph that thy wiles betray'd
A prize so little worth.

The scatter'd gleanings of a feast
My frugal meals supply;
But if thine unrelenting heart
20   That slender boon deny,

The cheerful light, the vital air,
Are blessings widely given;
Let nature's commoners enjoy
The common gifts of heaven.

25   The well-taught philosophic mind
To all compassion gives;
Casts round the world an equal eye,
And feels for all that lives.

If mind, as ancient sages taught,[2]
30   A never dying flame,

---

1. Addressed to the clergyman, political theorist, and scientist Joseph Priestley (1733–1804), who at this time was the most distinguished teacher at the Nonconformist Protestant Warrington Academy, where Barbauld's father was also a member of the faculty. The imagined speaker (the petitioning mouse) is destined to participate in just the sort of experiment that led Priestley, a few years later, to the discovery of "phlogiston"—what we now call oxygen. Tradition has it that when Barbauld showed him the lines, Priestley set the mouse free. According to Barbauld's modern editors, the poem was many times reprinted and was a favorite to assign students for memorizing. The Latin epigraph is from *The Aeneid* 6.853, "To spare the humbled, and to tame in war the proud."
2. Lines 29–36 play on the idea of transmigration of souls, a doctrine that Priestley believed until the early 1770s.

Still shifts through matter's varying forms,
In every form the same,

Beware, lest in the worm you crush
A brother's soul you find;
35 And tremble lest thy luckless hand
Dislodge a kindred mind.

Or, if this transient gleam of day
Be *all* of life we share,
Let pity plead within thy breast
40 That little *all* to spare.

So may thy hospitable board
With health and peace be crown'd;
And every charm of heartfelt ease
Beneath thy roof be found.

45 So, when destruction lurks unseen,
Which men, like mice, may share,
May some kind angel clear thy path,
And break the hidden snare.

ca. 1771   1773

A Summer Evening's Meditation[1]

'Tis past! The sultry tyrant of the south
Has spent his short-lived rage; more grateful° hours   *pleasing*
Move silent on; the skies no more repel
The dazzled sight, but with mild maiden beams
5 Of tempered lustre court the cherished eye
To wander o'er their sphere; where, hung aloft,
Dian's bright crescent, like a silver bow
New strung in heaven, lifts high its beamy horns
Impatient for the night, and seems to push
10 Her brother° down the sky. Fair Venus shines   *Apollo*
Even in the eye of day; with sweetest beam
Propitious shines, and shakes a trembling flood
Of softened radiance from her dewy locks.
The shadows spread apace; while meekened[2] Eve,
15 Her cheek yet warm with blushes, slow retires
Through the Hesperian gardens of the west,
And shuts the gates of day. 'Tis now the hour
When Contemplation from her sunless haunts,

1. This poem looks backward to poems such as William Collins's "Ode to Evening" (1747), Anne Finch's "A Nocturnal Reverie" (1713), and even to Milton's description in book 2 of *Paradise Lost* of Satan's daring navigation of the realm of Chaos. At the same time Barbauld's excursion-and-return structure anticipates the high flights (and returns) of later lyrics by Coleridge, Percy Shelley, and Keats. But her account of the journey, with its references to Diana's crescent (line 7) and Venus's sweetest beams (10 and 11) is *differently* gendered: this soul that launches "into the trackless deeps" (82) is clearly female.
2. Softened, made meek.

The cool damp grotto, or the lonely depth
20 Of unpierced woods, where wrapt in solid shade
She mused away the gaudy hours of noon,
And fed on thoughts unripened by the sun,
Moves forward; and with radiant finger points
To yon blue concave swelled by breath divine,
25 Where, one by one, the living eyes of heaven
Awake, quick kindling o'er the face of ether
One boundless blaze; ten thousand trembling fires,
And dancing lustres, where the unsteady eye,
Restless and dazzled, wanders unconfined
30 O'er all this field of glories; spacious field,
And worthy of the Master: he, whose hand
With hieroglyphics elder than the Nile
Inscribed the mystic tablet, hung on high
To public gaze, and said, "Adore, O man!
35 The finger of thy God." From what pure wells
Of milky light, what soft o'erflowing urn,
Are all these lamps so fill'd? these friendly lamps,
For ever streaming o'er the azure deep
To point our path, and light us to our home.
40 How soft they slide along their lucid spheres!
And silent as the foot of Time, fulfill
Their destined courses: Nature's self is hushed,
And, but° a scattered leaf, which rustles through   *except for*
The thick-wove foliage, not a sound is heard
45 To break the midnight air; though the raised ear,
Intensely listening, drinks in every breath.
How deep the silence, yet how loud the praise!
But are they silent all? or is there not
A tongue in every star, that talks with man,
50 And woos him to be wise? nor woos in vain:
This dead of midnight is the noon of thought,
And Wisdom mounts her zenith with the stars.
At this still hour the self-collected soul
Turns inward, and beholds a stranger there
55 Of high descent, and more than mortal rank;
An embryo God; a spark of fire divine,
Which must burn on for ages, when the sun,—
Fair transitory creature of a day!—
Has closed his golden eye, and wrapt in shades
60 Forgets his wonted journey through the east.

Ye citadels of light, and seats of Gods!
Perhaps my future home, from whence the soul,
Revolving° periods past, may oft look back   *Meditating on*
With recollected tenderness on all
65 The various busy scenes she left below,
Its deep-laid projects and its strange events,
As on some fond and doting tale that soothed
Her infant hours—O be it lawful now
To tread the hallowed circle of your courts,
70 And with mute wonder and delighted awe

Approach your burning confines. Seized in thought,
On Fancy's wild and roving wing I sail,
From the green borders of the peopled Earth,
And the pale Moon, her duteous fair attendant;
75   From solitary Mars; from the vast orb
Of Jupiter, whose huge gigantic bulk
Dances in ether like the lightest leaf;
To the dim verge, the suburbs of the system,
Where cheerless Saturn 'midst his watery moons[3]
80   Girt with a lucid zone,° in gloomy pomp,   belt
Sits like an exiled monarch: fearless thence
I launch into the trackless deeps of space,
Where, burning round, ten thousand suns appear,
Of elder beam, which ask no leave to shine
85   Of our terrestrial star, nor borrow light
From the proud regent of our scanty day;
Sons of the morning, first-born of creation,
And only less than Him who marks their track,
And guides their fiery wheels. Here must I stop,
90   Or is there aught beyond? What hand unseen
Impels me onward through the glowing orbs
Of habitable nature, far remote,
To the dread confines of eternal night,
To solitudes of vast unpeopled space,
95   The deserts of creation, wide and wild;
Where embryo systems and unkindled suns
Sleep in the womb of chaos? fancy droops,
And thought astonished stops her bold career.
But O thou mighty mind! whose powerful word
100 Said, thus let all things be, and thus they were,[4]
Where shall I seek thy presence? how unblamed
Invoke thy dread perfection?
Have the broad eyelids of the morn beheld thee?
Or does the beamy shoulder of Orion
105 Support thy throne? O look with pity down
On erring, guilty man! not in thy names
Of terror clad; not with those thunders armed
That conscious Sinai felt, when fear appalled
The scattered tribes;[5]—thou hast a gentler voice,
110 That whispers comfort to the swelling heart,
Abashed, yet longing to behold her Maker.

But now my soul, unused to stretch her powers
In flight so daring, drops her weary wing,
And seeks again the known accustomed spot,
115 Drest up with sun, and shade, and lawns, and streams,
A mansion fair, and spacious for its guest,
And full replete with wonders. Let me here,
Content and grateful, wait the appointed time,
And ripen for the skies: the hour will come

3. Saturn marked the outmost bounds of the solar system until the discovery of Uranus in 1781.
4. An echo of Genesis 1.3.
5. When God came down to deliver the Ten Com-

mandments "there were thunders and lightnings . . . so that all the people . . . trembled" (Exodus 19.16).

120   When all these splendours bursting on my sight
      Shall stand unveiled, and to my ravished sense
      Unlock the glories of the world unknown.

1773

The Rights of Woman[1]

    Yes, injured Woman! rise, assert thy right!
    Woman! too long degraded, scorned, opprest;
    O born to rule in partial° Law's despite,   *biased*
    Resume thy native empire o'er the breast!

5   Go forth arrayed in panoply° divine;   *suit of armor*
    That angel pureness which admits no stain;
    Go, bid proud Man his boasted rule resign,
    And kiss the golden sceptre of thy reign.

    Go, gird thyself with grace; collect thy store
10 Of bright artillery glancing from afar;
    Soft melting tones thy thundering cannon's roar,
    Blushes and fears thy magazine° of war.   *storehouse of arms*

    Thy rights are empire: urge no meaner claim,—
    Felt, not defined, and if debated, lost;
15 Like sacred mysteries, which withheld from fame,
    Shunning discussion, are revered the most.

    Try all that wit and art suggest to bend
    Of thy imperial foe the stubborn knee;
    Make treacherous Man thy subject, not thy friend;
20 Thou mayst command, but never canst be free.

    Awe the licentious, and restrain the rude;
    Soften the sullen, clear the cloudy brow:
    Be, more than princes' gifts, thy favours sued;—
    She hazards all, who will the least allow.

25 But hope not, courted idol of mankind,
    On this proud eminence secure to stay;
    Subduing and subdued, thou soon shalt find
    Thy coldness soften, and thy pride give way.

    Then, then, abandon each ambitious thought,
30 Conquest or rule thy heart shall feebly move,
    In Nature's school, by her soft maxims taught,
    That separate rights are lost in mutual love.

ca. 1792–95   1825

1. A response—seemingly favorable until the last two stanzas—to Mary Wollstonecraft's *A Vindication of the Rights of Woman* (1792). In chapter 4 of *Vindication*, Wollstonecraft had singled out Barbauld's poem "To a Lady with Some Painted Flowers" as evidence that even women of sense were capable of adopting the masculine-centered gender code that identified the feminine with the ornamental and the frivolous.

To a Little Invisible Being
Who Is Expected Soon to Become Visible

Germ of new life, whose powers expanding slow
For many a moon their full perfection wait,—
Haste, precious pledge of happy love, to go
Auspicious borne through life's mysterious gate.

5   What powers lie folded in thy curious frame,—
Senses from objects locked, and mind from thought!
How little canst thou guess thy lofty claim
To grasp at all the worlds the Almighty wrought!

And see, the genial season's warmth to share,
10   Fresh younglings° shoot, and opening roses glow!   *young plants*
Swarms of new life exulting fill the air,—
Haste, infant bud of being, haste to blow!°   *bloom*

For thee the nurse prepares her lulling songs,
The eager matrons count the lingering day;
15   But far the most thy anxious parent longs
On thy soft cheek a mother's kiss to lay.

She only asks to lay her burden down,
That her glad arms that burden may resume;
And nature's sharpest pangs her wishes crown,
20   That free thee living from thy living tomb.

She longs to fold to her maternal breast
Part of herself, yet to herself unknown;
To see and to salute the stranger guest,
Fed with her life through many a tedious moon.

25   Come, reap thy rich inheritance of love!
Bask in the fondness of a Mother's eye!
Nor wit nor eloquence her heart shall move
Like the first accents of thy feeble cry.

Haste, little captive, burst thy prison doors!
30   Launch on the living world, and spring to light!
Nature for thee displays her various stores,
Opens her thousand inlets of delight.

If charmed verse or muttered prayers had power,
With favouring spells to speed thee on thy way,
35   Anxious I'd bid my beads° each passing hour,   *offer a prayer*
Till thy wished smile thy mother's pangs o'erpay.°   *more than compensate*

ca. 1795?   1825

Washing-Day

> *. . . and their voice,*
> *Turning again towards childish treble, pipes*
> *And whistles in its sound.*[1]

The Muses are turned gossips; they have lost
The buskined° step, and clear high-sounding phrase,   *tragic, elevated*
Language of gods. Come then, domestic Muse,
In slipshod measure loosely prattling on
5 Of farm or orchard, pleasant curds and cream,
Or drowning flies, or shoe lost in the mire
By little whimpering boy, with rueful face;
Come, Muse; and sing the dreaded Washing-Day.
Ye who beneath the yoke of wedlock bend,
10 With bowed soul, full well ye ken° the day   *know*
Which week, smooth sliding after week, brings on
Too soon;—for to that day nor peace belongs
Nor comfort;—ere the first gray streak of dawn,
The red-armed washers come and chase repose.
15 Nor pleasant smile, nor quaint device of mirth,
E'er visited that day: the very cat,
From the wet kitchen scared, and reeking hearth,
Visits the parlour,—an unwonted° guest.   *unaccustomed*
The silent breakfast-meal is soon dispatched;
20 Uninterrupted, save by anxious looks
Cast at the lowering sky, if sky should lower.
From that last evil, O preserve us, heavens!
For should the skies pour down, adieu to all
Remains of quiet: then expect to hear
25 Of sad disasters,—dirt and gravel stains
Hard to efface, and loaded lines at once
Snapped short,—and linen-horse° by dog thrown down,   *drying rack*
And all the petty miseries of life.
Saints have been calm while stretched upon the rack,
30 And Guatimozin[2] smiled on burning coals;
But never yet did housewife notable
Greet with a smile a rainy washing-day.
—But grant the welkin° fair, require not thou   *sky*
Who call'st thyself perchance the master there,
35 Or study swept or nicely dusted coat,
Or usual 'tendance;—ask not, indiscreet,
Thy stockings mended, though the yawning rents
Gape wide as Erebus;° nor hope to find   *the underworld*
Some snug recess impervious: shouldst thou try
40 The 'customed garden walks, thine eye shall rue
The budding fragrance of thy tender shrubs,
Myrtle or rose, all crushed beneath the weight
Of coarse checked apron,—with impatient hand

1. Loosely quoted from Shakespeare's *As You Like It* 2.7.160–62.
2. The last Aztec emperor (Cuanhtémoc, d. 1525), who was tortured and executed by the Spanish conquistadors.

Twitched off when showers impend: or crossing lines
45 Shall mar thy musings, as the wet cold sheet
Flaps in thy face abrupt. Woe to the friend
Whose evil stars have urged him forth to claim
On such a day the hospitable rites!
Looks, blank at best, and stinted courtesy,
50 Shall he receive. Vainly he feeds his hopes
With dinner of roast chicken, savoury pie,
Or tart or pudding:—pudding he nor tart
That day shall eat; nor, though the husband try,
Mending what can't be helped, to kindle mirth
55 From cheer deficient, shall his consort's brow
Clear up propitious:—the unlucky guest
In silence dines, and early slinks away.
I well remember, when a child, the awe
This day struck into me; for then the maids,
60 I scarce knew why, looked cross, and drove me from them;
Nor soft caress could I obtain, nor hope
Usual indulgencies; jelly or creams,
Relic of costly suppers, and set by
For me, their petted one; or buttered toast,
65 When butter was forbid; or thrilling tale
Of ghost or witch, or murder—so I went
And sheltered me beside the parlour fire:
There my dear grandmother, eldest of forms,
Tended the little ones, and watched from harm,
70 Anxiously fond, though oft her spectacles
With elfin cunning hid, and oft the pins
Drawn from her ravelled stocking, might have soured
One less indulgent.—
At intervals my mother's voice was heard,
75 Urging dispatch: briskly the work went on,
All hands employed to wash, to rinse, to wring,
To fold, and starch, and clap,° and iron, and plait.   *flatten*
Then would I sit me down, and ponder much
Why washings were. Sometimes through hollow bowl
80 Of pipe amused we blew, and sent aloft
The floating bubbles; little dreaming then
To see, Mongolfier,[3] thy silken ball
Ride buoyant through the clouds—so near approach
The sports of children and the toils of men.
85 Earth, air, and sky, and ocean, hath its bubbles,[4]
And verse is one of them—this most of all.

1797

3. Brothers Joseph-Michel and Jacques-Étienne Mongolfier successfully launched the first hot-air balloon, at Annonay, France, in 1783.

4. Cf. Shakespeare's *Macbeth* 1.3.77: "The earth hath bubbles, as the water has."

CHARLOTTE SMITH
1749–1806

The melancholy of Charlotte Smith's poems was no mere literary posture. After her father married for the second time, she herself was married off, at the age of fifteen, and bore a dozen children (three of whom died in infancy or childhood), before permanently separating from her husband, Benjamin Smith, because of his abusive temper, infidelities, and financial irresponsibility. She began writing to make money when her husband was imprisoned for debt in 1783. Her first book, *Elegiac Sonnets, and Other Essays by Charlotte Smith of Bignor Park, in Sussex,* came out in 1785 and went through nine expanding editions in the following sixteen years.

Beginning with the 1788 publication of *Emmeline,* Smith also enjoyed considerable success as a novelist, rapidly producing nine more novels within the decade, including *Desmond* (1792), *The Old Manor House* (1793), *The Banished Man* (1794), and *The Young Philosopher* (1798). The liberal political views espoused in these fictions made the books key contributions to the Revolution Controversy in Britain. This was also the case with her eight-hundred-line blank verse poem *The Emigrants* (1793), which both evokes the suffering endured by political refugees from France and links their plight to that of the poet herself, who as a woman has discovered the emptiness of her native land's "boast / Of equal law." Such views earned Smith a place of dishonor, alongside Mary Wollstonecraft and Anna Letitia Barbauld, in Richard Polwhele's conservative satire *The Unsex'd Females* (1797), which scolds her for having suffered "her mind to be infected with the Gallic mania." We are more likely now to follow Stuart Curran, Smith's modern editor, and hail *The Emigrants* as "the finest piece of extended blank verse in English between Cowper's *The Task* (1785) and Wordsworth's unpublished initial version of *The Prelude* (1799)."

The sonnet as a form, after its great flourishing in the Renaissance in the hands of Sidney, Spenser, Shakespeare, Donne, and Milton, dropped out of fashion in the eighteenth century. It was, Samuel Johnson declared in his *Dictionary* (1755), "not very suitable to the English language." Its revival toward the end of that century—by Coleridge in the 1790s; Wordsworth (who wrote some five hundred sonnets beginning in 1802); and in the next generation, Shelley and Keats—was largely the result of Smith's influential refashioning of the sonnet as a medium of mournful feeling. Coleridge noted in the introduction to his privately printed "sheet of sonnets" in 1796 that "Charlotte Smith and [William Lisle] Bowles are they who first made the Sonnet popular among the present English"; but Bowles's *Fourteen Sonnets* of 1789, imitating those that Smith first published five years earlier (which by 1789 had reached a fifth edition), rode on a wave of popularity of the form that she had already established.

Coleridge in his 1796 introductory essay on the sonnet, using Smith as a principal example, remarked that "those Sonnets appear to me the most exquisite, in which moral Sentiments, Affections, or Feelings, are deduced from, and associated with, the scenery of Nature." Subsequently, of course, the connecting of feelings and nature became a central theme and strategy in Romantic poetry, especially in the genre that has come to be known as "the greater Romantic lyric." But Smith's engagement with nature differs from Coleridge's and Wordsworth's in its quasi-scientific insistence on the faithful rendering of detail: it is not surprising to learn that she addressed a sonnet to the "goddess of botany." That close-up view of nature is rendered exquisitely in her last long poem, the posthumously published *Beachy Head* (1807).

FROM ELEGIAC SONNETS

Written at the Close of Spring

The garlands fade that Spring so lately wove,
  Each simple flower, which she had nursed in dew,
Anemonies,[1] that spangled every grove,
  The primrose wan, and hare-bell mildly blue.
5 No more shall violets linger in the dell,
  Or purple orchis variegate the plain,
Till Spring again shall call forth every bell,
  And dress with humid hands her wreaths again.—
Ah! poor humanity! so frail, so fair,
10 Are the fond visions of thy early day,
Till tyrant passion, and corrosive care,
  Bid all thy fairy colors fade away!
Another May new buds and flowers shall bring;
Ah! why has happiness—no second Spring?

1784

To Sleep

Come, balmy Sleep! tired nature's soft resort!
  On these sad temples all thy poppies shed;
And bid gay dreams, from Morpheus'° airy court,   *Greek god of sleep*
  Float in light vision round my aching head!
5 Secure of all thy blessings, partial° Power!   *friendly*
  On his hard bed the peasant throws him down;
And the poor sea boy, in the rudest hour,
  Enjoys thee more than he who wears a crown.[1]
Clasp'd in her faithful shepherd's guardian arms,
10 Well may the village girl sweet slumbers prove
And they, O gentle Sleep! still taste thy charms,
  Who wake to labor, liberty, and love.
But still thy opiate aid dost thou deny
To calm the anxious breast; to close the streaming eye.

1784

To Night

I love thee, mournful, sober-suited Night!
  When the faint moon, yet lingering in her wane,
And veil'd in clouds, with pale uncertain light
  Hangs o'er the waters of the restless main.

---

1. Anemonies. *Anemony Nemeroso.* The wood
Anemony [Smith's note].
1. "Wilt thou upon the high and giddy mast / seal
up the ship boy's eyes, and rock his brains / In

cradle of the rude impetuous surge?" Shakespeare's *Henry IV* [Smith's note; "imperious surge"
in the original].

5   In deep depression sunk, the enfeebled mind
      Will to the deaf cold elements complain,
      And tell the embosom'd grief, however vain,
    To sullen surges and the viewless wind.
    Though no repose on thy dark breast I find,
10   I still enjoy thee—cheerless as thou art;
      For in thy quiet gloom the exhausted heart
    Is calm, though wretched; hopeless, yet resign'd.
    While to the winds and waves its sorrows given,
    May reach—though lost on earth—the ear of Heaven!

1788

Written in the Church-Yard at Middleton in Sussex[1]

    Press'd by the Moon, mute arbitress of tides,
      While the loud equinox its power combines,
      The sea no more its swelling surge confines,
    But o'er the shrinking land sublimely rides.
5   The wild blast, rising from the Western cave,
      Drives the huge billows from their heaving bed;
      Tears from their grassy tombs the village dead,
    And breaks the silent sabbath of the grave!
    With shells and sea-weed mingled, on the shore
10   Lo! their bones whiten in the frequent wave;
      But vain to them the winds and waters rave;
    They hear the warring elements no more:
    While I am doom'd—by life's long storm opprest,
    To gaze with envy on their gloomy rest.

1789

On Being Cautioned against Walking on an Headland Overlooking the Sea, Because It Was Frequented by a Lunatic

    Is there a solitary wretch who hies
      To the tall cliff, with starting pace or slow,
      And, measuring, views with wild and hollow eyes
      Its distance from the waves that chide below;
5   Who, as the sea-born gale with frequent sighs
      Chills his cold bed upon the mountain turf,
      With hoarse, half-utter'd lamentation, lies

1. Middleton is a village on the margin of the sea, in Sussex, containing only two or three houses. There were formerly several acres of ground between its small church and the sea, which now, by its continual encroachments, approaches within a few feet of this half ruined and humble edifice. The wall, which once surrounded the churchyard, is entirely swept away, many of the graves broken up, and the remains of bodies interred washed into the sea: whence human bones are found among the sand and shingles on the shore [Smith's note].

Murmuring responses to the dashing surf?
In moody sadness, on the giddy brink,
10   I see him more with envy than with fear;
He has no *nice felicities* that shrink[1]
    From giant horrors; wildly wandering here,
He seems (uncursed with reason) not to know
The depth or the duration of his woe.

1797

The Sea View[1]

The upland shepherd, as reclined he lies
    On the soft turf that clothes the mountain brow,
Marks the bright sea-line mingling with the skies;
    Or from his course celestial, sinking slow,
5   The summer-sun in purple radiance low,
Blaze on the western waters; the wide scene
    Magnificent, and tranquil, seems to spread
Even o'er the rustic's breast a joy serene,
    When, like dark plague-spots by the Demons shed,
10   Charged deep with death, upon the waves, far seen,
    Move the war-freighted ships; and fierce and red,
    Flash their destructive fire.—The mangled dead
And dying victims then pollute the flood.
Ah! thus man spoils Heaven's glorious works with blood!

1797

The Emigrants[1]

From *Book 1*

SCENE, *on the Cliffs to the Eastward of the Town of
Brighthelmstone in Sussex.*

TIME, *a Morning in November, 1792.*

Slow in the Wintry Morn, the struggling light
Throws a faint gleam upon the troubled waves;

1. " 'Tis delicate felicity that shrinks / when rocking winds are loud." Walpole [Smith's note; the passage from Walpole has not been identified].
1. Suggested by the recollection of having seen, some years since, on a beautiful evening of Summer, an engagement between two armed ships, from the high down called the Beacon Hill, near Brighthelmstone [Smith's note, referring to a location near Brighton].
1. As the Revolution unfolded in France, growing numbers of aristocrats, aghast at their loss of power and increasingly in fear for their lives, abandoned their estates and riches and sought refuge in England. Following the new Republic's abolition of state religion and confiscation of Church lands, these nobles were joined in their exile by Catholic clerics. Book 1 of *The Emigrants* traces how these people cope, and fail to cope, with the disintegra-

tion of the system that had sanctioned their social privilege. It is set, as Smith indicates, in November 1792, just after the downfall of the French monarchy and the declaration of a Republic. Its "scene" is atop the cliffs at Brighthelmstone (Brighton), across the Channel from France. Book 2, set five months later, at a time following the execution of Louis XVI and the outbreak of war between Britain and France, narrates how the emigrants, forming a counterrevolutionary army, invade France to wage war on their own countrymen. Here Smith emphasizes the situation of the women this foolhardy army leaves behind, abandoned to an unwanted independence in a strange land.
    Smith dedicated *The Emigrants* to William Cowper, whose easy, informal blank verse in *The Task* (1785) was an immediate influence on her own.

Their foaming tops, as they approach the shore
And the broad surf that never ceasing breaks
On the innumerous pebbles, catch the beams
Of the pale Sun, that with reluctance gives
To this cold northern Isle, its shorten'd day.
Alas! how few the morning wakes to joy!
How many murmur at oblivious night
For leaving them so soon; for bearing thus
Their fancied bliss (the only bliss they taste!),
On her black wings away!—Changing° the dreams   *exchanging*
That sooth'd their sorrows, for calamities
(And every day brings its own sad proportion)
For doubts, diseases, abject dread of Death,
And faithless friends, and fame and fortune lost;
Fancied or real wants; and wounded pride,
That views the day star,° but to curse his beams.   *the sun*
    Yet He, whose Spirit into being call'd
This wond'rous World of Waters; He who bids
The wild wind lift them till they dash the clouds,
And speaks to them in thunder; or whose breath,
Low murmuring o'er the gently heaving tides,
When the fair Moon, in summer night serene,
Irradiates with long trembling lines of light
Their undulating surface; that great Power,
Who, governing the Planets, also knows
If but a Sea-Mew falls, whose nest is hid
In these incumbent° cliffs; He surely means   *overhanging*
To us, his reasoning Creatures, whom He bids
Acknowledge and revere his awful° hand,   *awe-inspiring*
Nothing but good: Yet Man, misguided Man,
Mars the fair work that he was bid enjoy,
And makes himself the evil he deplores.
How often, when my weary soul recoils
From proud oppression, and from legal crimes
(For such are in this Land, where the vain boast
Of equal Law is mockery, while the cost
Of seeking for redress is sure to plunge
Th' already injur'd to more certain ruin
And the wretch starves, before his Counsel pleads)
How often do I half abjure Society,
And sigh for some lone Cottage, deep embower'd
In the green woods, that these steep chalky Hills
Guard from the strong South West; where round their base
The Beach² wide flourishes, and the light Ash
With slender leaf half hides the thymy° turf!—   *abounding in thyme*
There do I wish to hide me; well content
If on the short grass, strewn with fairy flowers,
I might repose thus shelter'd; or when Eve
In Orient crimson° lingers in the west,   *the setting sun*
Gain the high mound, and mark these waves remote
(Lucid tho' distant), blushing with the rays
Of the far-flaming Orb, that sinks beneath them;

2. Possibly a variant spelling of *beech* (the tree).

55 For I have thought, that I should then behold
The beauteous works of God, unspoil'd by Man
And less affected then, by human woes
I witness'd not; might better learn to bear
Those that injustice, and duplicity
60 And faithlessness and folly, fix on me:
For never yet could I derive relief,
When my swol'n heart was bursting with its sorrows,
From the sad thought, that others like myself
Live but to swell affliction's countless tribes!
65 —Tranquil seclusion I have vainly sought;
Peace, who delights in solitary shade,
No more will spread for me her downy wings,
But, like the fabled Danaïds—or the wretch,
Who ceaseless, up the steep acclivity,
70 Was doom'd to heave the still rebounding rock,³
Onward I labour; as the baffled wave,
Which yon rough beach repulses, that returns
With the next breath of wind, to fail again.—
Ah! Mourner—cease these wailings: cease and learn,
75 That not the Cot sequester'd, where the briar
And wood-bine wild, embrace the mossy thatch,
(Scarce seen amid the forest gloom obscure!)
Or more substantial farm, well fenced and warm,
Where the full barn, and cattle fodder'd round
80 Speak rustic plenty; nor the statelier dome
By dark firs shaded, or the aspiring pine,
Close by the village Church (with care conceal'd
By verdant foliage, lest the poor man's grave
Should mar the smiling prospect of his Lord),
85 Where offices° well rang'd, or dove-cote stock'd,   outbuildings
Declare manorial residence; not these
Or any of the buildings, new and trim
With windows circling towards the restless Sea,
Which ranged in rows, now terminate my walk,
90 Can shut out for an hour the spectre Care,
That from the dawn of reason, follows still
Unhappy Mortals,'till the friendly grave
(Our sole secure asylum) "ends the chace."⁴
    Behold, in witness of this mournful truth,
95 A group approach me, whose dejected looks,
Sad Heralds of distress! proclaim them Men
Banish'd for ever⁵ and for conscience sake
From their distracted Country, whence the name
Of Freedom misapplied, and much abus'd
100 By lawless Anarchy, has driven them far
To wander; with the prejudice they learn'd

3. In Greek mythology Sisyphus was condemned forever to push a rock uphill, only to have it roll back down just before it reached the top. The Danaides were condemned to pour water into leaky vessels.
4. I have a confused notion, that this expression, with nearly the same application, is to be found in [Edward] Young: but I cannot refer to it [Smith's note; the quotation has never been identified].
5. Catholic clergymen, banished from France by the revolutionists.

From Bigotry (the Tut'ress of the blind),
Thro' the wide World unshelter'd; their sole hope,
That German spoilers, thro' that pleasant land
105 May carry wide the desolating scourge
Of War and Vengeance;[6] yet unhappy Men,
Whate'er your errors, I lament your fate:
And, as disconsolate and sad ye hang
Upon the barrier of the rock, and seem
110 To murmur your despondence, waiting long
Some fortunate reverse that never comes;
Methinks in each expressive face, I see
Discriminated° anguish; there droops one,   *distinct, marked*
Who in a moping cloister long consum'd
115 This life inactive, to obtain a better,
And thought that meagre abstinence, to wake
From his hard pallet with the midnight bell,
To live on eleemosynary bread,°   *alms*
And to renounce God's works, would please that God.
120 And now the poor pale wretch receives, amaz'd,
The pity, strangers give to his distress,
Because these strangers are, by his dark creed,
Condemn'd as Heretics—and with sick heart
Regrets° his pious prison, and his beads.[7]—   *recalls with regret*
125 Another, of more haughty port, declines
The aid he needs not; while in mute despair
His high indignant thoughts go back to France,
Dwelling on all he lost—the Gothic dome,
That vied with splendid palaces;[8] the beds
130 Of silk and down, the silver chalices,
Vestments with gold enwrought for blazing altars;
Where, amid clouds of incense, he held forth
To kneeling crowds the imaginary bones
Of Saints suppos'd, in pearl and gold enchas'd,°   *decoratively set*
135 And still with more than living Monarchs' pomp
Surrounded; was believ'd by mumbling bigots
To hold the keys of Heaven, and to admit
Whom he thought good to share it.—Now alas!
He, to whose daring soul and high ambition
140 The World seem'd circumscrib'd; who, wont to dream
Of Fleuri, Richelieu, Alberoni,[9] men
Who trod on Empire, and whose politics
Were not beyond the grasp of his vast mind,
Is, in a Land once hostile, still prophan'd

6. An Austro-Prussian army invaded France in August 1792 but was driven back.
7. Lest the same attempts at misrepresentation should now be made, as have been made on former occasions, it is necessary to repeat, that nothing is farther from my thoughts, than to reflect invidiously on the Emigrant clergy, whose steadiness of principle excites veneration, as much as their sufferings compassion. Adversity has now taught them the charity and humility they perhaps wanted, when they made it a part of their faith, that salvation could be obtained in no other religion than their own [Smith's note].
8. Let it not be considered as an insult to men in fallen fortune, if these luxuries (undoubtedly inconsistent with their profession) be here enumerated.—France is not the only country, where the splendour and indulgences of the higher, and the poverty and depression of the inferior Clergy, have alike proved injurious to the cause of Religion [Smith's note].
9. Three cardinals who held important political offices.

145   By disbelief, and rites un-orthodox,
     The object of compassion.—At his side,
     Lighter of heart than these, but heavier far
     Than he was wont, another victim comes,
     An Abbé—who with less contracted brow
150   Still smiles and flatters, and still talks of Hope;
     Which, sanguine as he is, he does not feel,
     And so he cheats the sad and weighty pressure
     Of evils present;—Still, as Men misled
     By early prejudice (so hard to break),
155   I mourn your sorrows; for I too have known
     Involuntary exile; and while yet
     England had charms for me, have felt how sad
     It is to look across the dim cold sea,
     That melancholy rolls its refluent° tides   *ebbing*
160   Between us and the dear regretted land
     We call our own—as now ye pensive wait
     On this bleak morning, gazing on the waves
     That seem to leave your shore; from whence the wind
     Is loaded to your ears, with the deep groans
165   Of martyr'd Saints and suffering Royalty,
     While to your eyes the avenging power of Heaven
     Appears in aweful anger to prepare
     The storm of vengeance, fraught with plagues and death.
     Even he of milder heart, who was indeed
170   The simple shepherd in a rustic scene,
     And,'mid the vine-clad hills of Languedoc,
     Taught to the bare-foot peasant, whose hard hands
     Produc'd[1] the nectar he could seldom taste,
     Submission to the Lord for whom he toil'd;
175   He, or his brethren, who to Neustria's sons°   *the men of Normandy*
     Enforc'd religious patience, when, at times,
     On their indignant hearts Power's iron hand
     Too strongly struck; eliciting some sparks
     Of the bold spirit of their native North;
180   Even these Parochial Priests, these humbled men,
     Whose lowly undistinguish'd cottages
     Witness'd a life of purest piety,
     While the meek tenants were, perhaps, unknown
     Each to the haughty Lord of his domain,
185   Who mark'd them not; the Noble scorning still
     The poor and pious Priest, as with slow pace
     He glided thro' the dim arch'd avenue
     Which to the Castle led; hoping to cheer
     The last sad hour of some laborious life
190   That hasten'd to its close—even such a Man
     Becomes an exile; staying not to try
     By temperate zeal to check his madd'ning flock,

---

1. See the finely descriptive Verses written at Montauban in France in 1750, by Dr. Joseph Warton. Printed in Dodsley's *Miscellanies*, Vol. IV, page 203 [Smith's note; the lines begin, "Tarn, how delightful wind thy willow'd waves, / But ah! they fructify a land of slaves! / In vain thy barefoot, sun-burnt peasants hide / With luscious grapes yon hill's romantic side; / No cups nectareous shall their toils repay . . ."]. Languedoc is in southern France, just above the Pyrenees.

Who, at the novel sound of Liberty
(Ah! most intoxicating sound to slaves!),
195   Start into licence.—Lo! dejected now,
The wandering Pastor mourns, with bleeding heart,
His erring people, weeps and prays for them,
And trembles for the account that he must give
To Heaven for souls entrusted to his care.—
200   Where the cliff, hollow'd by the wintry storm,
Affords a seat with matted sea-weed strewn,
A softer form reclines; around her run,
On the rough shingles,° or the chalky bourn,   *pebbles*
Her gay unconscious children, soon amus'd;
205   Who pick the fretted stone, or glossy shell,
Or crimson plant marine: or they contrive
The fairy vessel, with its ribband sail
And gilded paper pennant: in the pool,
Left by the salt wave on the yielding sands,
210   They launch the mimic navy.—Happy age!
Unmindful of the miseries of Man!—
Alas! too long a victim to distress,
Their Mother, lost in melancholy thought,
Lull'd for a moment by the murmurs low
215   Of sullen billows, wearied by the task
Of having here, with swol'n and aching eyes
Fix'd on the grey horizon, since the dawn
Solicitously watch'd the weekly sail
From her dear native land, now yields awhile
220   To kind forgetfulness, while Fancy brings,
In waking dreams, that native land again!
Versailles² appears—its painted galleries,
And rooms of regal splendour; rich with gold,
Where, by long mirrors multiply'd, the crowd
225   Paid willing homage—and, united there,
Beauty gave charms to empire.—Ah! too soon
From the gay visionary pageant rous'd,
See the sad mourner start!—and, drooping, look
With tearful eyes and heaving bosom round
230   On drear reality—where dark'ning waves,
Urg'd by the rising wind, unheeded foam
Near her cold rugged seat. * * *

1793

2. Louis XIV's opulent palace, south of Paris.

WILLIAM BLAKE
1757–1827

What William Blake called his "Spiritual Life" was as varied, free, and dramatic as his "Corporeal Life" was simple, limited, and unadventurous. His father was a London tradesman. His only formal education was in art: at the age of ten he entered a drawing school, and later he studied for a time at the school of the Royal Academy of Arts. At fourteen he entered an apprenticeship for seven years to a well-known engraver, James Basire, and began reading widely in his free time and trying his hand at poetry. At twenty-four he married Catherine Boucher, daughter of a market gardener. She was then illiterate, but Blake taught her to read and to help him in his engraving and printing. In the early and somewhat sentimentalized biographies, Catherine is represented as an ideal wife for an unorthodox and impecunious genius. Blake, however, must have been a trying domestic partner, and his vehement attacks on the torment caused by a possessive, jealous female will, which reached their height in 1793 and remained prominent in his writings for another decade, probably reflect a troubled period at home. The couple was childless.

The Blakes for a time enjoyed a moderate prosperity while Blake gave drawing lessons, illustrated books, and engraved designs made by other artists. When the demand for his work slackened, Blake in 1800 moved to a cottage at Felpham, on the Sussex seacoast, to take advantage of the patronage of the wealthy amateur of the arts and biographer William Hayley (also a supporter of Charlotte Smith), who with the best of narrow intentions tried to transform Blake into a conventional artist and breadwinner. But the caged eagle soon rebelled. Hayley, Blake wrote, "is the Enemy of my Spiritual Life while he pretends to be the Friend of my Corporeal."

At Felpham in 1803 occurred an event that left a permanent mark on Blake's mind and art—an altercation with one John Schofield, a private in the Royal Dragoons. Blake ordered the soldier out of his garden and, when Schofield replied with threats and curses against Blake and his wife, pushed him the fifty yards to the inn where he was quartered. Schofield brought charges that Blake had uttered seditious statements about king and country. Since England was at war with France, sedition was a hanging offense. Blake was acquitted—an event, according to a newspaper account, "which so gratified the auditory that the court was . . . thrown into an uproar by their noisy exultations." Nevertheless Schofield, his fellow soldier Cock, and other participants in the trial haunted Blake's imagination and were enlarged to demonic characters who play a sinister role in *Jerusalem*. The event exacerbated Blake's sense that ominous forces were at work in the contemporary world and led him to complicate the symbolic and allusive style by which he veiled the radical religious, moral, and political opinions that he expressed in his poems.

The dominant literary and artistic fashion of Blake's youth involved the notion that the future of British culture would involve the recovery, through archaeology as well as literary history, of an all but lost past. As an apprentice engraver who learned to draw by sketching the medieval monuments of London churches, Blake began his artistic career in the thick of that antiquarianism. It also informs his early lyric poetry. *Poetical Sketches*, published when he was twenty-six, suggests Blake's affinities with a group of later-eighteenth-century writers that includes Thomas Warton, poet and student of Middle English romance and Elizabethan verse; Thomas Gray, translator from Old Icelandic and Welsh and author, in 1757, of "The Bard," a poem about the English conquest of Wales; Thomas Percy, the editor of the ballad collection *Reliques of Ancient English Poetry* (1765); and James Macpherson, who came before the public in the 1760s claiming to be the translator of the epic verse of a third-century Gaelic bard named Ossian. Like these figures, Blake located the sources of poetic inspiration in an archaic native tradition that, according to the prevailing view of national history, had ended up eclipsed after the seventeenth century, when French court culture, manners, and morals began their cultural ascendancy. Even in their orientation to a visionary culture, the bards of Blake's later Prophetic Books retain an association with this imagined version of a primitive past.

Poetical Sketches was the only book of Blake's to be set in type according to customary methods. In 1788 he began to experiment with relief etching, a method that he called "illuminated printing" (a term associating his works with the illuminated manuscripts of the Middle Ages) and used to produce most of his books of poems. Working directly on a copper plate with pens, brushes, and an acid-resistant medium, he wrote the text in reverse (so that it would print in the normal order) and also drew the illustration; he then etched the plate in acid to eat away the untreated copper and leave the design standing in relief. The pages printed from such plates were colored by hand in water colors, often by Catherine Blake, and stitched together to make up a volume. This process was laborious and time-consuming, and Blake printed very few copies of his books; for example, of *Songs of Innocence and of Experience* only twenty-eight copies (some of them incomplete) are known to exist; of *The Book of Thel*, sixteen; of *The Marriage of Heaven and Hell*, nine; and of *Jerusalem*, five.

To read a Blake poem without the pictures is to miss something important: Blake places words and images in a relationship that is sometimes mutually enlightening and sometimes turbulent, and that relationship is an aspect of the poem's argument. In this mode of relief etching, he published *Songs of Innocence* (1789), then added supplementary poems and printed *Songs of Innocence and of Experience* (1794). The two groups of poems represent the world as it is envisioned by what he calls "two contrary states of the human soul."

Gradually Blake's thinking about human history and his experience of life and suffering articulated themselves in the "Giant Forms" and their actions, which came to constitute a complete mythology. As Blake's mythical character Los said, speaking for all imaginative artists, "I must Create a System or be enslaved by another Man's." This coherent but constantly altering and enlarging system composed the subject matter first of Blake's "minor prophecies," completed by 1795, and then of the major prophetic books on which he continued working until about 1820: *The Four Zoas, Milton,* and *Jerusalem.*

In his sixties Blake gave up poetry to devote himself to pictorial art. In the course of his life, he produced hundreds of paintings and engravings, many of them illustrations for the work of other poets, including a representation of Chaucer's Canterbury pilgrims, a superb set of designs for the Book of Job, and a series of illustrations of Dante, on which he was still hard at work when he died. At the time of his death, Blake was little known as an artist and almost entirely unknown as a poet. In the mid-nineteenth century he acquired a group of admirers among the Pre-Raphaelites, who regarded him as a precursor. Since the mid-1920s Blake has finally come into his own, both in poetry and in painting, as one of the most dedicated, intellectually challenging, and astonishingly original artists. His marked influence ranges from William Butler Yeats, who edited Blake's writings and modeled his own system of mythology on Blake's, to Allen Ginsberg and other Beat writers, Philip Pullman's *His Dark Materials* trilogy, and the graphic novels of the present day.

The explication of Blake's cryptic prophetic books has been the preoccupation of many scholars. Blake wrote them in the persona, or "voice," of "the Bard! / Who Present, Past, & Future sees"—that is, as a British poet who follows Spenser, and especially Milton, in a lineage going back to the prophets of the Bible. "The Nature of my Work," he said, "is Visionary or Imaginative." What Blake meant by the key terms *vision* and *imagination,* however, is often misinterpreted by taking literally what he, speaking the traditional language of his great predecessors, intended in a figurative sense. "That which can be made Explicit to the Idiot," he declared, "is not worth my care." Blake was a born ironist who enjoyed mystifying his well-meaning but literal-minded friends and who took a defiant pleasure in shocking the dull and complacent "angels" of his day by being deliberately outrageous in representing his work and opinions.

Blake declared that "all he knew was in the Bible" and that "The Old & New Testaments are the Great Code of Art." This is an exaggeration of the truth that all his prophetic writings deal, in various formulations, with some aspects of the overall biblical plot of the creation and the Fall, the history of the generations of humanity in the fallen world, redemption, and the promise of a recovery of Eden and of a New Jerusalem. These events, however, Blake interprets in what he calls "the spiritual sense." For such a procedure he had considerable precedent, not in the neoplatonic and occult thinkers with whom some modern commentators align him, but in the "spiritual" interpreters of the Bible among the radical Protestant sects in seventeenth- and eighteenth-century England. In *The French Revolution, America: A Prophecy, Europe: A Prophecy,* and the trenchant prophetic satire *The Marriage of Heaven and Hell*—all of which Blake wrote in the early 1790s while he was an ardent supporter of the French Revolution—he, like Wordsworth, Coleridge, Southey, and a number of radical English theologians, represented the contemporary Revolution as the purifying violence that, according to biblical prophecy, portended the imminent redemption of humanity and the world. (For discussion of these apocalyptic expectations, see "The French Revolution" at Norton Literature Online.) In Blake's later poems Orc, the fiery spirit of violent revolution, gives way as a central personage to Los, the type of the visionary imagination in the fallen world.

BLAKE'S MYTHMAKING

Blake's first attempt to articulate his full myth of humanity's present, past, and future was *The Four Zoas,* begun in 1796 or 1797. A passage from the opening statement of its theme exemplifies the long verse line (what Blake called "the march of long resounding strong heroic verse") in which he wrote his Prophetic Books and will serve also to outline the Books' vision:

> Four Mighty Ones are in every Man; a Perfect Unity
> Cannot Exist, but from the Universal Brotherhood of Eden,
> The Universal Man. To Whom be Glory Evermore, Amen. . . .
> Los was the fourth immortal starry one, & in the Earth
> Of a bright Universe Empery attended day & night
> Days & nights of revolving joy, Urthona was his name
> In Eden; in the Auricular Nerves of Human life
> Which is the Earth of Eden, he his Emanations propagated. . . .
>   Daughter of Beulah, Sing
> His fall into Division & his Resurrection to Unity.

Blake's mythical premise, or starting point, is not a transcendent God but the "Universal Man" who is God and who incorporates the cosmos as well. (Blake elsewhere describes this founding image as "the Human Form Divine" and names him "Albion.") The Fall, in this myth, is not the fall of humanity away from God but a falling apart of primal people, a "fall into Division." In this event the original sin is what Blake calls "Selfhood," the attempt of an isolated part to be self-sufficient. The breakup of the all-inclusive Universal Man in Eden into exiled parts, it is evident, serves to identify the Fall with the creation—the creation not only of man and of nature as we ordinarily know them but also of a separate sky god who is alien from humanity. Universal Man divides first into the "Four Mighty Ones" who are the Zoas, or chief powers and component aspects of humanity, and these in turn divide sexually into male Spectres and female Emanations. (Thus in the quoted passage the Zoa known in the unfallen state of Eden as Urthona, the imaginative power, separates into the form of Los in the fallen world.) In addition to Eden there are three successively lower "states" of being in the fallen world, which Blake calls Beulah (a pastoral condition of easy and relaxed innocence, without clash of "contraries"), Generation (the realm of common human experience, suffering, and conflicting contraries), and Ulro (Blake's hell, the lowest state, or limit, of bleak rationality, tyranny, static negation, and isolated Selfhood). The fallen world moves through the cycles of its history, successively approaching and falling away from redemption, until, by the agency of the Redeemer (who is equated with the human imagination and is most potently operative in the prophetic poet), it will culminate in an apocalypse. In terms of his controlling image of the Universal Man, Blake describes this apocalypse as a return to the original, undivided condition, "his Resurrection to Unity."

What is confusing to many readers is that Blake alternates this representation of the Fall (as a fragmentation of the one Primal Man into separate parts) with a different kind of representation, in terms of two sharply opposed ways of seeing the universe. In this latter mode the Fall is a catastrophic change from imaginative insight (which sees the cosmos as unified and humanized) to sight by the physical eye (which sees the cosmos as a multitude of isolated individuals in an inhuman and alien nature). In terms of this distinction, the apocalypse toward which Blake as imaginative artist strives unceasingly will enable men and women once again to envision all beings as participant in the individual life that he calls "the Universal Brotherhood of Eden"— that is, a humanized world in which all individuals, in familial union, can feel at home.

The text for Blake's writings is that of *The Complete Poetry and Prose of William Blake,* edited by David V. Erdman and Harold Bloom (rev. ed., Berkeley, 1982). Blake's erratic spelling and punctuation have been altered when the original form might mislead the reader. The editors are grateful for the expert advice of Joseph Viscomi and Robert Essick in editing the selections from Blake.

There Is No Natural Religion[1]

[a]

The Argument. Man has no notion of moral fitness but from Education. Naturally he is only a natural organ subject to Sense.

I. Man cannot naturally Percieve but through his natural or bodily organs.

II. Man by his reasoning power can only compare & judge of what he has already perciev'd.

III. From a perception of only 3 senses or 3 elements none could deduce a fourth or fifth.

IV. None could have other than natural or organic thoughts if he had none but organic perceptions.

V. Man's desires are limited by his perceptions; none can desire what he has not perciev'd.

VI. The desires & perceptions of man, untaught by any thing but organs of sense, must be limited to objects of sense.

Conclusion. If it were not for the Poetic or Prophetic character the Philosophic & Experimental would soon be at the ratio of all things, & stand still unable to do other than repeat the same dull round over again.

1788

1. In this selection Blake presents his version of English empiricism, which derives all mental content (including the evidences from which, in "nat- ural religion," reason is held to prove the existence of God) from perceptions by the physical senses.

There Is No Natural Religion[1]

[b]

I. Man's perceptions are not bounded by organs of perception; he percieves more than sense (tho' ever so acute) can discover.

II. Reason, or the ratio[2] of all we have already known, is not the same that it shall be when we know more.

[III lacking]

IV. The bounded is loathed by its possessor. The same dull round even of a universe would soon become a mill with complicated wheels.

V. If the many become the same as the few when possess'd, More! More! is the cry of a mistaken soul. Less than All cannot satisfy Man.

VI. If any could desire what he is incapable of possessing, despair must be his eternal lot.

VII. The desire of Man being Infinite, the possession is Infinite & himself Infinite.

Application. He who sees the Infinite in all things sees God. He who sees the Ratio only sees himself only.

Therefore God becomes as we are, that we may be as he is.

1788

FROM SONGS OF INNOCENCE AND OF EXPERIENCE[1]

SHEWING THE TWO CONTRARY STATES OF THE HUMAN SOUL

FROM SONGS OF INNOCENCE

Introduction

Piping down the valleys wild
Piping songs of pleasant glee
On a cloud I saw a child,
And he laughing said to me,

1. In this third document Blake presents his assertions (in opposition to those in the preceding tract) that knowledge is not limited to the physical senses, but is as unbounded as the infinite desires of humankind and its godlike capacity for infinite vision.
2. In Latin ratio signifies both "reason" and "calculation." Blake applies the term derogatorily to the 18th-century concept of reason as a calculating faculty whose operations are limited to sense perceptions.
1. Songs of Innocence was etched in 1789, and in 1794 was combined with additional poems under the title Songs of Innocence and of Experience; this collection was reprinted at various later times with varying arrangements of the poems. In his songs of innocence Blake assumes the stance that he is writing "happy songs / Every child may joy to hear," but they do not all depict an innocent and happy world; many of them incorporate injustice, evil, and suffering. These aspects of the fallen world,

however, are represented as they appear to a "state" of the human soul that Blake calls "innocence" and that he expresses in a simple pastoral language, in the tradition both of Isaac Watts's widely read Divine Songs for Children (1715) and of the picture-books for child readers pioneered by mid-eighteenth-century booksellers such as John Newbery. The vision of the same world, as it appears to the "contrary" state of the soul that Blake calls "experience," is an ugly and terrifying one of poverty, disease, prostitution, war, and social, institutional, and sexual repression, epitomized in the ghastly representation of modern London. Though each stands as an independent poem, a number of the songs of innocence have a matched counterpart, or "contrary," in the songs of experience. Thus "Infant Joy" is paired with "Infant Sorrow," and the meek "Lamb" reveals its other aspect of divinity in the flaming, wrathful "Tyger."

Title page for *Songs of Innocence* (1789)

```
 5   "Pipe a song about a Lamb";
     So I piped with merry chear;
     "Piper pipe that song again"—
     So I piped, he wept to hear.

     "Drop thy pipe thy happy pipe
10   Sing thy songs of happy chear";
     So I sung the same again
     While he wept with joy to hear.

     "Piper sit thee down and write
     In a book that all may read"—
15   So he vanish'd from my sight.
     And I pluck'd a hollow reed,

     And I made a rural pen,
     And I stain'd the water clear,
     And I wrote my happy songs
20   Every child may joy to hear.
```

1789

The Ecchoing Green

The Sun does arise,
And make happy the skies.
The merry bells ring
To welcome the Spring.
5   The sky-lark and thrush,
The birds of the bush,
Sing louder around,
To the bells' chearful sound.
While our sports shall be seen
10   On the Ecchoing Green.

Old John with white hair
Does laugh away care,
Sitting under the oak,
Among the old folk.
15   They laugh at our play,
And soon they all say:
"Such, such were the joys.
When we all, girls & boys,
In our youth-time were seen,
20   On the Ecchoing Green."

Till the little ones weary
No more can be merry
The sun does descend,
And our sports have an end:
25   Round the laps of their mothers,
Many sisters and brothers,
Like birds in their nest,
Are ready for rest;
And sport no more seen,
30   On the darkening Green.

1789

The Lamb[1]

Little Lamb, who made thee?
  Dost thou know who made thee?
Gave thee life & bid thee feed,
By the stream & o'er the mead;
5   Gave thee clothing of delight,
Softest clothing wooly bright;
Gave thee such a tender voice,
Making all the vales rejoice!
  Little Lamb who made thee?
10   Dost thou know who made thee?

1. The opening of this poem mimes the form of the catechistic questions and answers customarily used for children's religious instruction.

Little Lamb I'll tell thee,
Little Lamb I'll tell thee!
He is callèd by thy name,
For he calls himself a Lamb;
15   He is meek & he is mild,
He became a little child;
I a child & thou a lamb,
We are callèd by his name.
    Little Lamb God bless thee.
20   Little Lamb God bless thee.

1789

The Little Black Boy

My mother bore me in the southern wild,
And I am black, but O! my soul is white;
White as an angel is the English child,
But I am black as if bereav'd of light.

5 My mother taught me underneath a tree,
And sitting down before the heat of day,
She took me on her lap and kissèd me,
And pointing to the east, began to say:

"Look on the rising sun: there God does live
10 And gives his light, and gives his heat away;
And flowers and trees and beasts and men receive
Comfort in morning, joy in the noon day.

"And we are put on earth a little space,
That we may learn to bear the beams of love,
15 And these black bodies and this sun-burnt face
Is but a cloud, and like a shady grove.

"For when our souls have learn'd the heat to bear,
The cloud will vanish; we shall hear his voice,
Saying: 'Come out from the grove, my love & care,
20 And round my golden tent like lambs rejoice.' "

Thus did my mother say, and kissèd me;
And thus I say to little English boy:
When I from black and he from white cloud free,
And round the tent of God like lambs we joy,

25 I'll shade him from the heat till he can bear
To lean in joy upon our father's knee.
And then I'll stand and stroke his silver hair,
And be like him, and he will then love me.

1789

The Chimney Sweeper

When my mother died I was very young,
And my father sold me while yet my tongue
Could scarcely cry " 'weep! 'weep! 'weep! 'weep!"[1]
So your chimneys I sweep & in soot I sleep.

5 There's little Tom Dacre, who cried when his head
That curl'd like a lamb's back, was shav'd, so I said,
"Hush, Tom! never mind it, for when your head's bare,
You know that the soot cannot spoil your white hair."

And so he was quiet, & that very night,
10 As Tom was a-sleeping he had such a sight!
That thousands of sweepers, Dick, Joe, Ned, & Jack,
Were all of them lock'd up in coffins of black;

And by came an Angel who had a bright key,
And he open'd the coffins & set them all free;
15 Then down a green plain, leaping, laughing they run,
And wash in a river and shine in the Sun.

Then naked & white, all their bags left behind,
They rise upon clouds, and sport in the wind.
And the Angel told Tom, if he'd be a good boy,
20 He'd have God for his father & never want joy.

And so Tom awoke; and we rose in the dark
And got with our bags & our brushes to work.
Tho' the morning was cold, Tom was happy & warm;
So if all do their duty, they need not fear harm.

1789

The Divine Image

To Mercy, Pity, Peace, and Love,
All pray in their distress,
And to these virtues of delight
Return their thankfulness.

5 For Mercy, Pity, Peace, and Love,
Is God, our father dear:
And Mercy, Pity, Peace, and Love,
Is Man, his child and care.

For Mercy has a human heart,
10 Pity, a human face,
And Love, the human form divine,
And Peace, the human dress.

1. The child's lisping attempt at the chimney sweeper's street cry, "Sweep! Sweep!"

Then every man of every clime,
That prays in his distress,
15 Prays to the human form divine,
Love, Mercy, Pity, Peace.

And all must love the human form,
In heathen, Turk, or Jew.
Where Mercy, Love, & Pity dwell,
20 There God is dwelling too.

1789

Holy Thursday[1]

'Twas on a Holy Thursday, their innocent faces clean,
The children walking two & two, in red & blue & green;
Grey headed beadles[2] walkd before with wands as white as snow,
Till into the high dome of Paul's they like Thames' waters flow.

5 O what a multitude they seemd, these flowers of London town!
Seated in companies they sit with radiance all their own.
The hum of multitudes was there, but multitudes of lambs,
Thousands of little boys & girls raising their innocent hands.

Now like a mighty wind they raise to heaven the voice of song,
10 Or like harmonious thunderings the seats of heaven among.
Beneath them sit the agèd men, wise guardians of the poor;
Then cherish pity, lest you drive an angel from your door.[3]

ca. 1784   1789

Nurse's Song

When the voices of children are heard on the green
And laughing is heard on the hill,
My heart is at rest within my breast
And everything else is still.

5 "Then come home my children, the sun is gone down
And the dews of night arise;
Come, come, leave off play, and let us away
Till the morning appears in the skies."

"No, no, let us play, for it is yet day
10 And we cannot go to sleep;

---

1. In the Anglican Church the Thursday celebrating the ascension of Jesus (thirty-nine days after Easter). It was the custom on this day to march the poor (frequently orphaned) children from the charity schools of London to a service at St. Paul's Cathedral.

2. Lower church officers, one of whose duties is to keep order.
3. Cf. Hebrews 13.2: "Be not forgetful to entertain strangers: for thereby some have entertained angels unawares."

Besides, in the sky, the little birds fly
And the hills are all coverd with sheep."

"Well, well, go & play till the light fades away
And then go home to bed."
15 The little ones leaped & shouted & laugh'd
And all the hills ecchoèd.

ca. 1784   1789

Infant Joy

"I have no name,
I am but two days old."
What shall I call thee?
"I happy am,
5 Joy is my name."
Sweet joy befall thee!

Pretty joy!
Sweet joy but two days old,
Sweet joy I call thee;
10 Thou dost smile,
I sing the while—
Sweet joy befall thee.

1789

FROM SONGS OF EXPERIENCE

Introduction

Hear the voice of the Bard!
Who Present, Past, & Future sees;
Whose ears have heard
The Holy Word
5 That walk'd among the ancient trees;[1]

Calling the lapsèd Soul[2]
And weeping in the evening dew,
That might controll[3]
The starry pole,
10 And fallen, fallen light renew!

---

1. Genesis 3.8: "And [Adam and Eve] heard the voice of the Lord God walking in the garden in the cool of the day." The Bard, or poet-prophet, whose imagination is not bound by time, has heard the voice of the Lord in Eden.
2. The syntax leaves it ambiguous whether it is "the Bard" or "the Holy Word" who calls to the fallen ("lapsèd") soul and to the fallen earth to stop the natural cycle of light and darkness.
3. The likely syntax is that "Soul" is the subject of "might controll."

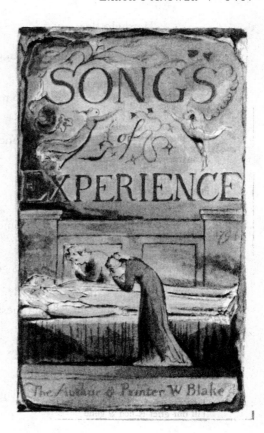

Separate title page for *Songs of Experience* (1794)

      "O Earth, O Earth, return!
      Arise from out the dewy grass;
      Night is worn,
      And the morn
15   Rises from the slumberous mass.

      "Turn away no more;
      Why wilt thou turn away?
      The starry floor
      The watry shore[4]
20   Is giv'n thee till the break of day."

                             1794

Earth's Answer[1]

Earth rais'd up her head,
From the darkness dread & drear.

---

4. In Blake's recurrent symbolism the starry sky ("floor") signifies rigid rational order, and the sea signifies chaos.

1. The Earth explains why she, the natural world, cannot by her unaided endeavors renew the fallen light.

Her light fled:
Stony dread!
5 And her locks cover'd with grey despair.

"Prison'd on watry shore
Starry Jealousy does keep my den,
Cold and hoar
Weeping o'er
10 I hear the Father of the ancient men.[2]

"Selfish father of men,
Cruel, jealous, selfish fear!
Can delight
Chain'd in night
15 The virgins of youth and morning bear?

"Does spring hide its joy
When buds and blossoms grow?
Does the sower
Sow by night,
20 Or the plowman in darkness plow?

"Break this heavy chain
That does freeze my bones around;
Selfish! vain!
Eternal bane!
25 That free Love with bondage bound."

1794

The Clod & the Pebble

"Love seeketh not Itself to please,
Nor for itself hath any care;
But for another gives its ease,
And builds a Heaven in Hell's despair."

5 So sang a little Clod of Clay,
Trodden with the cattle's feet;
But a Pebble of the brook,
Warbled out these metres meet:

"Love seeketh only Self to please,
10 To bind another to its delight;
Joys in another's loss of ease,
And builds a Hell in Heaven's despite."

1794

2. This is the character that Blake later named "Urizen" in his prophetic works. He is the tyrant who binds the mind to the natural world and also imposes a moral bondage on sexual desire and other modes of human energy.

Holy Thursday

Is this a holy thing to see,
In a rich and fruitful land,
Babes reduced to misery,
Fed with cold and usurous hand?

5 Is that trembling cry a song?
Can it be a song of joy?
And so many children poor?
It is a land of poverty!

And their sun does never shine,
10 And their fields are bleak & bare,
And their ways are fill'd with thorns;
It is eternal winter there.

For where-e'er the sun does shine,
And where-e'er the rain does fall,
15 Babe can never hunger there,
Nor poverty the mind appall.

1794

The Chimney Sweeper

A little black thing among the snow
Crying " 'weep, 'weep," in notes of woe!
"Where are thy father & mother? say?"
"They are both gone up to the church to pray.

5 "Because I was happy upon the heath,
And smil'd among the winter's snow;
They clothed me in the clothes of death,
And taught me to sing the notes of woe.

"And because I am happy, & dance & sing,
10 They think they have done me no injury,
And are gone to praise God & his Priest & King,
Who make up a heaven of our misery."

1790–92   1794

Nurse's Song

When the voices of children are heard on the green
And whisperings are in the dale,
The days of my youth rise fresh in my mind,
My face turns green and pale.

5 Then come home my children, the sun is gone down
   And the dews of night arise;
   Your spring & your day are wasted in play,
   And your winter and night in disguise.

                                                              1794

The Sick Rose

O Rose, thou art sick.
The invisible worm
That flies in the night
In the howling storm

5 Has found out thy bed
   Of crimson joy,
   And his dark secret love
   Does thy life destroy.

                                                              1794

The Tyger[1]

Tyger! Tyger! burning bright
In the forests of the night,
What immortal hand or eye
Could frame thy fearful symmetry?

5 In what distant deeps or skies
   Burnt the fire of thine eyes?
   On what wings dare he aspire?
   What the hand dare seize the fire?

   And what shoulder, & what art,
10 Could twist the sinews of thy heart?
   And when thy heart began to beat,
   What dread hand? & what dread feet?

   What the hammer? what the chain?
   In what furnace was thy brain?
15 What the anvil? what dread grasp
   Dare its deadly terrors clasp?

   When the stars threw down their spears[2]
   And water'd heaven with their tears,
   Did he smile his work to see?
20 Did he who made the Lamb make thee?

1. For the author's revisions while composing "The Tyger," see "Poems in Process," in the appendices to this volume.

2. "Threw down" is ambiguous and may signify that the stars either "surrendered" or "hurled down" their spears.

"The Tyger"

Tyger! Tyger! burning bright
In the forests of the night,
What immortal hand or eye
Dare frame thy fearful symmetry?

1790–92   1794

My Pretty Rose Tree

A flower was offerd to me;
Such a flower as May never bore,
But I said, "I've a Pretty Rose-tree,"
And I passed the sweet flower o'er.

5 Then I went to my Pretty Rose-tree,
To tend her by day and by night.
But my Rose turnd away with jealousy,
And her thorns were my only delight.

1794

Ah Sun-flower

Ah Sun-flower! weary of time,
Who countest the steps of the Sun,
Seeking after that sweet golden clime
Where the traveller's journey is done;

5 Where the Youth pined away with desire,
And the pale Virgin shrouded in snow,
Arise from their graves and aspire,
Where my Sun-flower wishes to go.

1794

The Garden of Love

I went to the Garden of Love,
And saw what I never had seen:
A Chapel was built in the midst,
Where I used to play on the green.

5 And the gates of this Chapel were shut,
And "Thou shalt not" writ over the door;
So I turn'd to the Garden of Love,
That so many sweet flowers bore,

And I saw it was filled with graves,
10 And tomb-stones where flowers should be;
And Priests in black gowns were walking their rounds,
And binding with briars my joys & desires.

1794

London

I wander thro' each charter'd[1] street,
Near where the charter'd Thames does flow,
And mark in every face I meet
Marks of weakness, marks of woe.

5 In every cry of every Man,
In every Infant's cry of fear,
In every voice, in every ban,[2]
The mind-forg'd manacles I hear:

1. "Given liberty," but also, ironically, "preempted as private property, and rented out."
2. The various meanings of *ban* are relevant (political and legal prohibition, curse, public condemnation) as well as "banns" (marriage proclamation).

How the Chimney-sweeper's cry
10   Every blackning Church appalls,
And the hapless Soldier's sigh
Runs in blood down Palace walls.

But most thro' midnight streets I hear
How the youthful Harlot's curse
15   Blasts the new-born Infant's tear,[3]
And blights with plagues the Marriage hearse.[4]

1794

The Human Abstract[1]

Pity would be no more,
If we did not make somebody Poor;
And Mercy no more could be,
If all were as happy as we;

5   And mutual fear brings peace,
Till the selfish loves increase;
Then Cruelty knits a snare,
And spreads his baits with care.

He sits down with holy fears,
10   And waters the ground with tears;
Then Humility takes its root
Underneath his foot.

Soon spreads the dismal shade
Of Mystery over his head;
15   And the Catterpiller and Fly
Feed on the Mystery.

And it bears the fruit of Deceit,
Ruddy and sweet to eat;
And the Raven his nest has made
20   In its thickest shade.

The Gods of the earth and sea,
Sought thro' Nature to find this Tree,
But their search was all in vain:
There grows one in the Human Brain.

1790–92   1794

3. Most critics read this line as implying prenatal blindness, resulting from a parent's venereal disease (the "plagues" of line 16) by earlier infection from the harlot.
4. In the older sense: "converts the marriage bed into a bier." Or possibly, because the current sense of the word had also come into use in Blake's day, "converts the marriage coach into a funeral hearse."
1. The matched contrary to "The Divine Image" in *Songs of Innocence.* The virtues of the earlier poem, "Mercy, Pity, Peace, and Love," are now represented as possible marks for exploitation, cruelty, conflict, and hypocritical humility.

Infant Sorrow

My mother groand! my father wept.
Into the dangerous world I leapt,
Helpless, naked, piping loud;
Like a fiend hid in a cloud.

5 Struggling in my father's hands,
Striving against my swadling bands;
Bound and weary I thought best
To sulk upon my mother's breast.

1794

A Poison Tree

I was angry with my friend:
I told my wrath, my wrath did end.
I was angry with my foe:
I told it not, my wrath did grow.

5 And I waterd it in fears,
Night & morning with my tears;
And I sunnèd it with smiles,
And with soft deceitful wiles.

And it grew both day and night,
10 Till it bore an apple bright.
And my foe beheld it shine,
And he knew that it was mine,

And into my garden stole,
When the night had veild the pole;
15 In the morning glad I see
My foe outstretchd beneath the tree.

1794

To Tirzah[1]

Whate'er is Born of Mortal Birth
Must be consumèd with the Earth
To rise from Generation free;
Then what have I to do with thee?[2]

1. Tirzah was the capital of the northern kingdom of Israel and is conceived by Blake in opposition to Jerusalem, capital of the southern kingdom of Judah, whose tribes had been redeemed from captivity. In this poem, which was added to late versions of Songs of Experience, Tirzah is represented as the mother—in the realm of material nature and "Generation"—of the mortal body, with its restrictive senses.
2. Echoing the words of Christ to his mother at the marriage in Cana, John 2.4: "Woman, what have I to do with thee? mine hour is not yet come."

5   The Sexes sprung from Shame & Pride,
     Blow'd° in the morn, in evening died;   *blossomed*
     But Mercy changd Death into Sleep;
     The Sexes rose to work & weep.

     Thou, Mother of my Mortal part,
10   With cruelty didst mould my Heart,
     And with false self-deceiving tears
     Didst bind my Nostrils, Eyes, & Ears.

     Didst close my Tongue in senseless clay
     And me to Mortal Life betray.
15   The Death of Jesus set me free;
     Then what have I to do with thee?

                                                      ca. 1805

A Divine Image[1]

     Cruelty has a Human Heart
     And Jealousy a Human Face,
     Terror, the Human Form Divine,
     And Secrecy, the Human Dress.

5   The Human Dress is forgèd Iron,
     The Human Form, a fiery Forge,
     The Human Face, a Furnace seal'd,
     The Human Heart, its hungry Gorge.°   *maw, stomach*

1790–91

The Book of Thel

Although Blake dated the etched poem 1789, its composition probably extended to 1791, so that he was working on it at the time he was writing the *Songs of Innocence* and some of the *Songs of Experience*. The Book of Thel treats the same two "states"; now, however, Blake employs the narrative instead of the lyrical mode and embodies aspects of the developing myth that was fully enacted in his later prophetic books. And like the major prophecies, this poem is written in the fourteener, a long line of seven stresses.

The name *Thel* possibly derives from the Greek word for "wish" or "will" and may be intended to suggest the failure of desire, because of timidity, to fulfill itself. Thel is represented as a virgin dwelling in the Vales of Har, which seems equivalent to the sheltered state of pastoral peace and innocence in Blake's *Songs of Innocence*. Here, however, Thel feels useless and unfulfilled, and appeals for comfort, unavailingly, to various beings who are contented with their roles in Har. Finally, the Clay invites Thel to try the experiment of assuming embodied life. Part 4 (plate 6) expresses the brutal shock of the revelation to Thel of the experience of sexual desire—a revelation

1. Blake omitted this poem from all but one copy of *Songs of Experience*, probably because "The Human Abstract" served as a more comprehensive and subtle contrary to "The Divine Image" in *Songs of Innocence*.

from which she flees in terror back to her sheltered, if unsatisfying, existence in Har.

Some commentators propose that Thel is an unborn soul who rejects the ordeal of an embodied life in the material world. Others propose that Thel is a human virgin who shrinks from experiencing a life of adult sexuality. It is possible, however, to read Blake's little myth as comprehending both these areas of significance. The reader does not need to know Blake's mythology inside and out to recognize the broad symbolic reach of this poem in ordinary human experience—the elemental failure of nerve to meet the challenge of life as it is, the timid incapacity to risk the conflict, physicality, pain, and loss without which there is no possibility either of growth or of creativity.

The Book of Thel

PLATE i[1]

Thel's Motto

Does the Eagle know what is in the pit?
Or wilt thou go ask the Mole?
Can Wisdom be put in a silver rod?
Or Love in a golden bowl?[2]

PLATE 1

1

The daughters of Mne[3] Seraphim led round their sunny flocks,
All but the youngest; she in paleness sought the secret air,
To fade away like morning beauty from her mortal day;
Down by the river of Adona her soft voice is heard,
5 And thus her gentle lamentation falls like morning dew:

"O life of this our spring! why fades the lotus of the water?
Why fade these children of the spring? born but to smile & fall.
Ah! Thel is like a watry bow, and like a parting cloud,
Like a reflection in a glass, like shadows in the water,
10 Like dreams of infants, like a smile upon an infant's face,
Like the dove's voice, like transient day, like music in the air.
Ah! gentle may I lay me down, and gentle rest my head,
And gentle sleep the sleep of death, and gentle hear the voice
Of him that walketh in the garden in the evening time."[4]

15 The Lilly of the valley breathing in the humble grass
Answer'd the lovely maid and said: "I am a watry weed,
And I am very small, and love to dwell in lowly vales;

1. The plate numbers identify the page, each with its own pictorial design, as originally printed by Blake. These numbers are reproduced here because they are frequently used in references to Blake's writings.
2. Ecclesiastes 12.5–6 describes a time when "fears shall be in the way . . . and desire shall fail: because man goeth to his long home, and the mourners go about the streets: Or ever the silver cord be loosed, or the golden bowl be broken." Per-

haps Blake changed the silver cord to a rod to make it, with the golden bowl, a sexual symbol.
3. There has been much speculation about this curious term. It may be an abbreviation for the name "Mnetha," the goddess of the Vales of Har in Blake's earlier poem Tiriel.
4. Genesis 3.8: "And they heard the voice of the Lord God walking in the garden in the cool of the day."

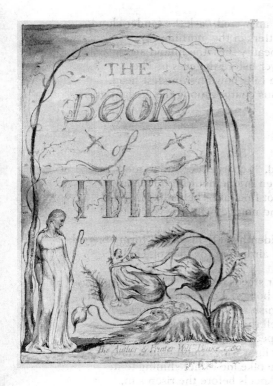

Title page of *The Book of Thel*
(1789), plate ii. Copy N, ca. 1815

So weak, the gilded butterfly scarce perches on my head;
Yet I am visited from heaven, and he that smiles on all
20 Walks in the valley and each morn over me spreads his hand,
Saying: 'Rejoice, thou humble grass, thou new-born lilly flower,
Thou gentle maid of silent valleys and of modest brooks;
For thou shalt be clothed in light, and fed with morning manna,
Till summer's heat melts thee beside the fountains and the springs
25 To flourish in eternal vales.' Then why should Thel complain?

PLATE 2

Why should the mistress of the vales of Har utter a sigh?"

She ceasd & smild in tears, then sat down in her silver shrine.

Thel answer'd: "O thou little virgin of the peaceful valley,
Giving to those that cannot crave, the voiceless, the o'ertired;
5 Thy breath doth nourish the innocent lamb, he smells thy milky garments,
He crops thy flowers, while thou sittest smiling in his face,
Wiping his mild and meekin° mouth from all contagious taints.   *humble*
Thy wine doth purify the golden honey; thy perfume,
Which thou dost scatter on every little blade of grass that springs,
10 Revives the milkèd cow, & tames the fire-breathing steed.
But Thel is like a faint cloud kindled at the rising sun:
I vanish from my pearly throne, and who shall find my place?"

"Queen of the vales," the Lilly answered, "ask the tender cloud,
And it shall tell thee why it glitters in the morning sky,
15 And why it scatters its bright beauty thro' the humid air.
Descend, O little cloud, & hover before the eyes of Thel."
The Cloud descended, and the Lilly bowd her modest head,
And went to mind her numerous charge among the verdant grass.

PLATE 3

2

"O little Cloud," the virgin said, "I charge thee tell to me,
Why thou complainest not when in one hour thou fade away:
Then we shall seek thee but not find; ah, Thel is like to Thee.
I pass away, yet I complain, and no one hears my voice."

5 The Cloud then shew'd his golden head & his bright form emerg'd,
Hovering and glittering on the air before the face of Thel.

"O virgin, know'st thou not our steeds drink of the golden springs
Where Luvah[5] doth renew his horses? Look'st thou on my youth,
And fearest thou because I vanish and am seen no more,
10 Nothing remains? O maid, I tell thee, when I pass away,
It is to tenfold life, to love, to peace, and raptures holy:
Unseen descending, weigh my light wings upon balmy flowers,
And court the fair eyed dew, to take me to her shining tent;
The weeping virgin trembling kneels before the risen sun,
15 Till we arise link'd in a golden band, and never part,
But walk united, bearing food to all our tender flowers."

"Dost thou O little Cloud? I fear that I am not like thee;
For I walk through the vales of Har and smell the sweetest flowers,
But I feed not the little flowers; I hear the warbling birds,
20 But I feed not the warbling birds; they fly and seek their food;
But Thel delights in these no more, because I fade away,
And all shall say, 'Without a use this shining woman liv'd,
Or did she only live to be at death the food of worms?' "

The Cloud reclind upon his airy throne and answer'd thus:

25 "Then if thou art the food of worms, O virgin of the skies,
How great thy use, how great thy blessing! Every thing that lives
Lives not alone, nor for itself; fear not, and I will call
The weak worm from its lowly bed, and thou shalt hear its voice.
Come forth, worm of the silent valley, to thy pensive queen."

30 The helpless worm arose, and sat upon the Lilly's leaf,
And the bright Cloud saild on, to find his partner in the vale.

---

5. The earliest mention in Blake's work of one of his "Giant Forms," the Zoas. Luvah is the mythical embodiment of the passional and sexual aspect of humankind. He is represented here, like the Greek Phoebus Apollo, as the driver of the chariot of the sun; he repairs to the Vales of Har simply to rest and water his horses. The cloud in this passage describes the cycle of water, from cloud to rain and (by the vaporizing action of the sun on water) back to the cloud.

PLATE 4

3

Then Thel astonish'd view'd the Worm upon its dewy bed.

"Art thou a Worm? Image of weakness, art thou but a Worm?
I see thee like an infant wrapped in the Lilly's leaf;
Ah, weep not, little voice, thou can'st not speak, but thou can'st weep.
5   Is this a Worm? I see thee lay helpless & naked, weeping,
And none to answer, none to cherish thee with mother's smiles."

The Clod of Clay heard the Worm's voice, & raisd her pitying head;
She bow'd over the weeping infant, and her life exhal'd
In milky fondness; then on Thel she fix'd her humble eyes.

10   "O beauty of the vales of Har! we live not for ourselves;
Thou seest me the meanest thing, and so I am indeed;
My bosom of itself is cold, and of itself is dark,

PLATE 5

But he that loves the lowly, pours his oil upon my head,
And kisses me, and binds his nuptial bands around my breast,
And says: 'Thou mother of my children, I have lovèd thee,
And I have given thee a crown that none can take away.'
5   But how this is, sweet maid, I know not, and I cannot know;
I ponder, and I cannot ponder; yet I live and love."

The daughter of beauty wip'd her pitying tears with her white veil,
And said: "Alas! I knew not this, and therefore did I weep.
That God would love a Worm, I knew, and punish the evil foot
10   That, wilful, bruis'd its helpless form; but that he cherish'd it
With milk and oil I never knew; and therefore did I weep,
And I complaind in the mild air, because I fade away,
And lay me down in thy cold bed, and leave my shining lot."

"Queen of the vales," the matron Clay answered, "I heard thy sighs,
15   And all thy moans flew o'er my roof, but I have call'd them down.
Wilt thou, O Queen, enter my house? 'tis given thee to enter
And to return; fear nothing, enter with thy virgin feet."

PLATE 6

4

The eternal gates' terrific porter lifted the northern bar:[6]
Thel enter'd in & saw the secrets of the land unknown.
She saw the couches of the dead, & where the fibrous roots
Of every heart on earth infixes deep its restless twists:
5   A land of sorrows & of tears where never smile was seen.

6. Homer, in *Odyssey* 13, described the Cave of the Naiades, of which the northern gate is for mortals and the southern gate for gods. The neopla-tonist Porphyry had allegorized it as an account of the descent of the soul into matter and then its return.

She wanderd in the land of clouds thro' valleys dark, listning
Dolours & lamentations; waiting oft beside a dewy grave,
She stood in silence, listning to the voices of the ground,
Till to her own grave plot she came, & there she sat down,
10   And heard this voice of sorrow breathed from the hollow pit:

"Why cannot the Ear be closed to its own destruction?
Or the glistning Eye to the poison of a smile?
Why are Eyelids stord with arrows ready drawn,
Where a thousand fighting men in ambush lie?
15   Or an Eye of gifts & graces, show'ring fruits & coinèd gold?
Why a Tongue impress'd with honey from every wind?
Why an Ear, a whirlpool fierce to draw creations in?
Why a Nostril wide inhaling terror, trembling, & affright?
Why a tender curb upon the youthful burning boy?
20   Why a little curtain of flesh on the bed of our desire?"

The Virgin started from her seat, & with a shriek
Fled back unhinderd till she came into the vales of Har.

1789–91

The Marriage of Heaven and Hell

This, the most immediately accessible of Blake's longer works, is a vigorous, deliberately outrageous, and at times comic onslaught against timidly conventional and self-righteous members of society as well as against stock opinions of orthodox Christian piety and morality. The seeming simplicity of Blake's satiric attitude, however, is deceptive.

Initially, Blake accepts the terminology of standard Christian morality ("what the religious call Good & Evil") but reverses its values. In this conventional use Evil, which is manifested by the class of beings called Devils and which consigns wrongdoers to the orthodox Hell, is everything associated with the body and its desires and consists essentially of energy, abundance, actions, and freedom. Conventional Good, which is manifested by Angels and guarantees its adherents a place in the orthodox Heaven, is associated with the Soul (regarded as entirely separate from the body) and consists of the contrary qualities of reason, restraint, passivity, and prohibition. Blandly adopting these conventional oppositions, Blake elects to assume the diabolic persona—what he calls "the voice of the Devil"—and to utter "Proverbs of Hell."

But this stance is only a first stage in Blake's complex irony, designed to startle the reader into recognizing the inadequacy of conventional moral categories. As he also says in the opening summary, "Without Contraries is no progression," and "Reason and Energy" are both "necessary to Human existence." It turns out that Blake subordinates his reversal of conventional values under a more inclusive point of view, according to which the real Good, as distinguished from the merely ironic Good, is not abandonment of all restraints but a "marriage," or union of the contraries, of desire and restraint, energy and reason, the promptings of Hell and the denials of Heaven—or as Blake calls these contraries in plate 16, "the Prolific" and "the Devouring." These two classes, he adds, "should be enemies," and "whoever tries to reconcile them seeks to destroy existence." Implicit in Blake's satire is the view that the good and abundant life consists in the sustained tension, without victory or suppression, of co-present oppositions.

When Blake composed this unique work in the early 1790s, his city of London was teeming with religious mystics, astrologers, and sometimes bawdy freethinkers who were determined to challenge the Established Church's monopoly on spirituality and who were reviving the link, created in the seventeenth century, between enthusiasm in religion and political revolution. The work is also a response to the writings of the visionary Swedish theologian Emanuel Swedenborg, whom Blake had at first admired but then had come to recognize as a conventional Angel in the disguise of a radical Devil. In plate 3 the writings of Swedenborg are described as the winding clothes Blake discards as he is resurrected from the tomb of his past self, as a poet-prophet who heralds the apocalyptic promise of his age. Blake shared the expectations of a number of radical English writers, including the young poets Wordsworth, Coleridge, and Southey, that the French Revolution was the violent stage that, as the biblical prophets foresaw, immediately preceded the millennium. The double role of *The Marriage* as both satire and revolutionary prophecy is made explicit in *A Song of Liberty*, which Blake etched in 1792 and added as a coda.

The Marriage of Heaven and Hell

PLATE 2

The Argument

Rintrah[1] roars & shakes his fires in the burdend air;
Hungry clouds swag on the deep.
Once meek, and in a perilous path,
The just man kept his course along
5   The vale of death.
Roses are planted where thorns grow,
And on the barren heath
Sing the honey bees.

Then the perilous path was planted,
10   And a river, and a spring,
On every cliff and tomb;
And on the bleached bones
Red clay[2] brought forth;

Till the villain left the paths of ease,
15   To walk in perilous paths, and drive
The just man into barren climes.

Now the sneaking serpent walks
In mild humility,
And the just man rages in the wilds
20   Where lions roam.

---

1. Rintrah plays the role of the angry Old Testament prophet Elijah as well as of John the Baptist, the voice "crying in the wilderness" (Matthew 3), preparing the way for Christ the Messiah. It has been plausibly suggested that stanzas 2–5 summarize the course of biblical history to the present time. "Once" (line 3) refers to Old Testament history after the Fall; "Then" (line 9) is the time of the birth of Christ. "Till" (line 14) identifies the era when Christianity was perverted into an insti-

tutional religion. "Now" (line 17) is the time of the wrathful portent of the French Revolution. In this final era the hypocritical serpent represents the priest of the "angels" in the poem, while "the just man" is embodied in Blake, a raging poet and prophet in the guise of a devil. "Swag" (line 2): sag, hang down.

2. In Hebrew the literal meaning of "Adam," or created man. The probable reference is to the birth of the Redeemer, the new Adam.

Rintrah roars & shakes his fires in the burdend air;
Hungry clouds swag on the deep.

PLATE 3

As a new heaven is begun, and it is now thirty-three years since its advent,
the Eternal Hell revives. And lo! Swedenborg[3] is the Angel sitting at the tomb;
his writings are the linen clothes folded up. Now is the dominion of Edom, &
the return of Adam into Paradise; see Isaiah xxxiv & XXXV Chap.[4]

Without Contraries is no progression. Attraction and Repulsion, Reason and
Energy, Love and Hate, are necessary to Human existence.

From these contraries spring what the religious call Good & Evil. Good is
the passive that obeys Reason. Evil is the active springing from Energy.

Good is Heaven. Evil is Hell.

PLATE 4

The Voice of the Devil

All Bibles or sacred codes have been the causes of the following Errors:

1. That Man has two real existing principles; Viz: a Body & a Soul.

2. That Energy, calld Evil, is alone from the Body, & that Reason, calld
Good, is alone from the Soul.

3. That God will torment Man in Eternity for following his Energies.

But the following Contraries to these are True:

1. Man has no Body distinct from his Soul; for that calld Body is a portion
of Soul discernd by the five Senses, the chief inlets of Soul in this age.

2. Energy is the only life, and is from the Body; and Reason is the bound
or outward circumference of Energy.

3. Energy is Eternal Delight.

PLATE 5

Those who restrain desire, do so because theirs is weak enough to be
restraind; and the restrainer or reason usurps its place & governs the
unwilling.

And being restraind, it by degrees becomes passive, till it is only the shadow
of desire.

The history of this is written in *Paradise Lost*,[5] & the Governor or Reason is
call'd Messiah.

3. Emanuel Swedenborg (1688–1772), Swedish scientist and religious philosopher, had predicted, on the basis of his visions, that the Last Judgment and the coming of the Kingdom of Heaven would occur in 1757. This was precisely the year of Blake's birth. Now, in 1790, Blake is thirty-three, the age at which Christ had been resurrected from the tomb; correspondingly, Blake rises from the tomb of his past life in his new role as imaginative artist who will redeem his age. But, Blake ironically comments, the works he will engrave in his resurrection will constitute the Eternal Hell, the contrary brought into simultaneous being by Swedenborg's limited New Heaven.
4. Isaiah 34 prophesies "the day of the Lord's vengeance," a time of violent destruction and bloodshed; Isaiah 35 prophesies the redemption to follow, in which "the desert shall . . . blossom as

the rose," "in the wilderness shall waters break out, and streams in the desert," and "no lion shall be there," but "an highway shall be there . . . and it shall be called The way of holiness" (cf. "The Argument," lines 3–11, 20). Blake combines with these chapters Isaiah 63, in which "Edom" is the place from which comes the man whose garments are red with the blood he has spilled; for as he says, "the day of vengeance is in mine heart, and the year of my redeemed is come." Blake interprets this last phrase as predicting the time when Adam would regain his lost Paradise. Also relevant is Genesis 36.1, where the Edomites are identified as the descendants of the disinherited Esau, cheated out of his father's blessing by Jacob.
5. What follows, to the end of this section, is Blake's "diabolical" reading of Milton's *Paradise Lost*. For other Romantic comments on the mag-

And the original Archangel, or possessor of the command of the heavenly host, is calld the Devil or Satan, and his children are call'd Sin & Death.[6]

But in the Book of Job, Milton's Messiah is call'd Satan.[7]

For this history has been adopted by both parties.

It indeed appear'd to Reason as if Desire was cast out; but the Devil's account is, that the Messi[PLATE 6]ah fell, & formed a heaven of what he stole from the Abyss.

This is shewn in the Gospel, where he prays to the Father to send the comforter or Desire that Reason may have Ideas to build on;[8] the Jehovah of the Bible being no other than he who dwells in flaming fire. Know that after Christ's death, he became Jehovah.

But in Milton, the Father is Destiny, the Son, a Ratio[9] of the five senses, & the Holy-ghost, Vacuum!

Note. The reason Milton wrote in fetters when he wrote of Angels & God, and at liberty when of Devils & Hell, is because he was a true Poet and of the Devil's party without knowing it.

A Memorable Fancy[1]

As I was walking among the fires of hell, delighted with the enjoyments of Genius, which to Angels look like torment and insanity, I collected some of their Proverbs; thinking that as the sayings used in a nation mark its character, so the Proverbs of Hell shew the nature of Infernal wisdom better than any description of buildings or garments.

When I came home, on the abyss of the five senses, where a flat sided steep frowns over the present world, I saw a mighty Devil folded in black clouds, hovering on the sides of the rock; with cor[PLATE 7]roding fires he wrote the following sentence[2] now perceived by the minds of men, & read by them on earth:

> How do you know but ev'ry Bird that cuts the airy way,
> Is an immense world of delight, clos'd by your senses five?

Proverbs of Hell[3]

In seed time learn, in harvest teach, in winter enjoy.
Drive your cart and your plow over the bones of the dead.
The road of excess leads to the palace of wisdom.
Prudence is a rich ugly old maid courted by Incapacity.
5 He who desires but acts not, breeds pestilence.

nificence of Milton's Satan see "The Satanic and Byronic Hero" at Norton Literature Online.
6. Satan's giving birth to Sin and then incestuously begetting Death upon her is described in *Paradise Lost* 2.745ff.; the war in heaven, referred to three lines below, in which the Messiah defeated Satan and drove him out of heaven, is described in 6.824ff.
7. In the Book of Job, Satan plays the role of Job's moral accuser and physical tormentor.
8. Possibly John 14.16–17, where Christ says he "will pray the Father, and he shall give you another Comforter . . . Even the Spirit of truth."
9. The Latin *ratio* means both "reason" and "sum." Blake applies the term to the 18th-century view, following the empiricist philosophy of John Locke,

that the content of the mind, on which the faculty of reason operates, is limited to the sum of the experience acquired by the five senses.
1. A parody of what Swedenborg called "memorable relations" of his literal-minded visions of the eternal world.
2. The "mighty Devil" is Blake, as he sees himself reflected in the shiny plate on which he is etching this very passage with "corroding fires," i.e., the acid used in the etching process. See also the third from last sentence in plate 14.
3. A "diabolic" version of the Book of Proverbs in the Old Testament, which also incorporates sly allusions to 18th-century books of piety such as Isaac Watts's *Divine Songs*.

The cut worm forgives the plow.
Dip him in the river who loves water.
A fool sees not the same tree that a wise man sees.
He whose face gives no light, shall never become a star.
10 Eternity is in love with the productions of time.
The busy bee has no time for sorrow.
The hours of folly are measur'd by the clock; but of wisdom, no clock can
   measure.
All wholsom food is caught without a net or a trap.
Bring out number, weight, & measure in a year of dearth.
15 No bird soars too high, if he soars with his own wings.
A dead body revenges not injuries.
The most sublime act is to set another before you.
If the fool would persist in his folly he would become wise.
Folly is the cloke of knavery.
20 Shame is Pride's cloke.

PLATE 8

Prisons are built with stones of Law, Brothels with bricks of Religion.
The pride of the peacock is the glory of God.
The lust of the goat is the bounty of God.
The wrath of the lion is the wisdom of God.
5 The nakedness of woman is the work of God.
Excess of sorrow laughs. Excess of joy weeps.
The roaring of lions, the howling of wolves, the raging of the stormy sea,
   and the destructive sword, are portions of eternity too great for the eye
   of man.
The fox condemns the trap, not himself.
Joys impregnate. Sorrows bring forth.
10 Let man wear the fell of the lion, woman the fleece of the sheep.
The bird a nest, the spider a web, man friendship.
The selfish smiling fool & the sullen frowning fool shall be both thought
   wise, that they may be a rod.
What is now proved was once only imagin'd.
The rat, the mouse, the fox, the rabbit watch the roots; the lion, the tyger,
   the horse, the elephant, watch the fruits.
15 The cistern contains; the fountain overflows.
One thought fills immensity.
Always be ready to speak your mind, and a base man will avoid you.
Every thing possible to be believ'd is an image of truth.
The eagle never lost so much time as when he submitted to learn of the
   crow.

PLATE 9

The fox provides for himself, but God provides for the lion.
Think in the morning, Act in the noon, Eat in the evening, Sleep in the
   night.
He who has sufferd you to impose on him knows you.
As the plow follows words, so God rewards prayers.

5 The tygers of wrath are wiser than the horses of instruction.
Expect poison from the standing water.
You never know what is enough unless you know what is more than
    enough.
Listen to the fool's reproach! it is a kingly title!
The eyes of fire, the nostrils of air, the mouth of water, the beard of earth.
10 The weak in courage is strong in cunning.
The apple tree never asks the beech how he shall grow, nor the lion the
    horse, how he shall take his prey.
The thankful reciever bears a plentiful harvest.
If others had not been foolish, we should be so.
The soul of sweet delight can never be defil'd.
15 When thou seest an Eagle, thou seest a portion of Genius; lift up thy head!
As the catterpiller chooses the fairest leaves to lay her eggs on, so the priest
    lays his curse on the fairest joys.
To create a little flower is the labour of ages.
Damn braces; Bless relaxes.
The best wine is the oldest, the best water the newest.
20 Prayers plow not! Praises reap not!
Joys laugh not! Sorrows weep not!

PLATE 10

The head Sublime, the heart Pathos, the genitals Beauty, the hands & feet
    Proportion.
As the air to a bird or the sea to a fish, so is contempt to the contemptible.
The crow wish'd every thing was black, the owl that every thing was white.
Exuberance is Beauty.
5 If the lion was advised by the fox, he would be cunning.
Improvement makes strait roads, but the crooked roads without
    Improvement are roads of Genius.
Sooner murder an infant in its cradle than nurse unacted desires.
Where man is not, nature is barren.
Truth can never be told so as to be understood, and not be believ'd.
10   Enough! or Too much.

———————

PLATE 11

    The ancient Poets animated all sensible objects with Gods or Geniuses,
calling them by the names and adorning them with the properties of woods,
rivers, mountains, lakes, cities, nations, and whatever their enlarged & numerous senses could perceive.

    And particularly they studied the genius of each city & country, placing it
under its mental deity.

    Till a system was formed, which some took advantage of & enslav'd the
vulgar by attempting to realize or abstract the mental deities from their objects;
thus began Priesthood,

    Choosing forms of worship from poetic tales.

    And at length they pronounced that the Gods had ordered such things.

    Thus men forgot that All deities reside in the human breast.

PLATE 12

A Memorable Fancy[4]

The Prophets Isaiah and Ezekiel dined with me, and I asked them how they dared so roundly to assert that God spake to them; and whether they did not think at the time that they would be misunderstood, & so be the cause of imposition.

Isaiah answer'd: "I saw no God, nor heard any, in a finite organical perception; but my senses discover'd the infinite in every thing, and as I was then perswaded, & remain confirm'd, that the voice of honest indignation is the voice of God, I cared not for consequences, but wrote."

Then I asked: "Does a firm perswasion that a thing is so, make it so?"

He replied: "All poets believe that it does, & in ages of imagination this firm perswasion removed mountains; but many are not capable of a firm perswasion of any thing."

Then Ezekiel said: "The philosophy of the East taught the first principles of human perception. Some nations held one principle for the origin & some another; we of Israel taught that the Poetic Genius (as you now call it) was the first principle and all the others merely derivative, which was the cause of our despising the Priests & Philosophers of other countries, and prophecying that all Gods [PL 13] would at last be proved to originate in ours & to be the tributaries of the Poetic Genius; it was this that our great poet, King David, desired so fervently & invokes so pathetically, saying by this he conquers enemies & governs kingdoms; and we so loved our God, that we cursed in his name all the deities of surrounding nations, and asserted that they had rebelled; from these opinions the vulgar came to think that all nations would at last be subject to the Jews."

"This," said he, "like all firm perswasions, is come to pass, for all nations believe the Jews' code and worship the Jews' god, and what greater subjection can be?"

I heard this with some wonder, & must confess my own conviction. After dinner I ask'd Isaiah to favour the world with his lost works; he said none of equal value was lost. Ezekiel said the same of his.

I also asked Isaiah what made him go naked and barefoot three years? He answered, "the same that made our friend Diogenes,[5] the Grecian."

I then asked Ezekiel why he eat dung, & lay so long on his right & left side?[6] He answered, "the desire of raising other men into a perception of the infinite; this the North American tribes practise, & is he honest who resists his genius or conscience only for the sake of present ease or gratification?"

———————

PLATE 14

The ancient tradition that the world will be consumed in fire at the end of six thousand years is true, as I have heard from Hell.

For the cherub with his flaming sword is hereby commanded to leave his guard at the tree of life;[7] and when he does, the whole creation will be con-

---

4. Blake parodies Swedenborg's accounts, in his *Memorable Relations,* of his conversations with the inhabitants during his spiritual trips to heaven.
5. Greek Cynic (4th century), whose extreme repudiation of civilized customs gave rise to anecdotes that he had renounced clothing. In Isaiah

20.2–3 the prophet, at the Lord's command, walked "naked and barefoot" for three years.
6. The Lord gave these instructions to the prophet Ezekiel (4.4–6).
7. In Genesis 3.24, when the Lord drove Adam and Eve from the Garden of Eden, he had placed

sumed, and appear infinite and holy, whereas it now appears finite & corrupt.

This will come to pass by an improvement of sensual enjoyment.

But first the notion that man has a body distinct from his soul is to be expunged; this I shall do, by printing in the infernal method, by corrosives, which in Hell are salutary and medicinal, melting apparent surfaces away, and displaying the infinite which was hid.[8]

If the doors of perception were cleansed every thing would appear to man as it is, infinite.

For man has closed himself up, till he sees all things thro' narrow chinks of his cavern.

PLATE 15

A Memorable Fancy

I was in a Printing house[9] in Hell & saw the method in which knowledge is transmitted from generation to generation.

In the first chamber was a Dragon-Man, clearing away the rubbish from a cave's mouth; within, a number of Dragons were hollowing the cave.

In the second chamber was a Viper folding round the rock & the cave, and others adorning it with gold, silver, and precious stones.

In the third chamber was an Eagle with wings and feathers of air; he caused the inside of the cave to be infinite; around were numbers of Eagle-like men, who built palaces in the immense cliffs.

In the fourth chamber were Lions of flaming fire, raging around & melting the metals into living fluids.

In the fifth chamber were Unnam'd forms, which cast the metals into the expanse.

There they were receiv'd by Men who occupied the sixth chamber, and took the forms of books & were arranged in libraries.[1]

PLATE 16

The Giants[2] who formed this world into its sensual existence, and now seem to live in it in chains, are in truth the causes of its life & the sources of all activity; but the chains are the cunning of weak and tame minds which have power to resist energy; according to the proverb, the weak in courage is strong in cunning.

Thus one portion of being is the Prolific, the other, the Devouring; to the Devourer it seems as if the producer was in his chains, but it is not so; he only takes portions of existence and fancies that the whole.

But the Prolific would cease to be Prolific unless the Devourer as a sea received the excess of his delights.

Some will say, "Is not God alone the Prolific?" I answer, "God only Acts & Is, in existing beings or Men."

These two classes of men are always upon earth, & they should be enemies;

Cherubim and a flaming sword at the eastern end "to keep the way of the tree of life."

8. See n. 2, p. 1433.

9. A covert pun runs through this section: workers, ink-blackened, who did the dirty work in the printing houses of the period were humorously known as "printer's devils."

1. In this "Memorable Fancy" Blake allegorizes his procedure in designing, etching, printing, and binding his works of imaginative genius.

2. In this section human creative energies, called "the Prolific," in their relation to their indispensable contrary, "the Devourer."

1438 / WILLIAM BLAKE

whoever tries [PLATE 17] to reconcile them seeks to destroy existence.

Religion is an endeavour to reconcile the two.

Note. Jesus Christ did not wish to unite but to separate them, as in the Parable of sheep and goats! & he says, "I came not to send Peace but a Sword."[3]

Messiah or Satan or Tempter was formerly thought to be one of the Antediluvians[4] who are our Energies.

A Memorable Fancy

An Angel came to me and said: "O pitiable foolish young man! O horrible! O dreadful state! consider the hot burning dungeon thou art preparing for thyself to all eternity, to which thou art going in such career."

I said: "Perhaps you will be willing to shew me my eternal lot, & we will contemplate together upon it and see whether your lot or mine is most desirable."

So he took me thro' a stable & thro' a church & down into the church vault at the end of which was a mill; thro' the mill we went, and came to a cave; down the winding cavern we groped our tedious way till a void boundless as a nether sky appeared beneath us, & we held by the roots of trees and hung over this immensity, but I said: "If you please, we will commit ourselves to this void, and see whether Providence is here also, if you will not I will." But he answered: "Do not presume, O young man, but as we here remain, behold thy lot which will soon appear when the darkness passes away."[5]

So I remaind with him sitting in the twisted [PLATE 18] root of an oak; he was suspended in a fungus which hung with the head downward into the deep.

By degrees we beheld the infinite Abyss, fiery as the smoke of a burning city; beneath us at an immense distance was the sun, black but shining; round it were fiery tracks on which revolv'd vast spiders, crawling after their prey, which flew, or rather swum in the infinite deep, in the most terrific shapes of animals sprung from corruption; & the air was full of them, & seemed composed of them; these are Devils, and are called Powers of the air. I now asked my companion which was my eternal lot? He said, "Between the black & white spiders."

But now, from between the black & white spiders a cloud and fire burst and rolled thro the deep, blackning all beneath, so that the nether deep grew black as a sea & rolled with a terrible noise. Beneath us was nothing now to be seen but a black tempest, till looking east between the clouds & the waves, we saw a cataract of blood mixed with fire, and not many stones' throw from us appeared and sunk again the scaly fold of a monstrous serpent. At last to the east, distant about three degrees, appeared a fiery crest above the waves. Slowly it reared like a ridge of golden rocks till we discovered two globes of crimson fire, from which the sea fled away in clouds of smoke. And now we saw it was the head of Leviathan;[6] his forehead was divided into streaks of green & purple like those on a tyger's forehead; soon we saw his mouth & red

---

3. Matthew 10.34. The parable of the sheep and the goats is in Matthew 25.32–33.
4. Those who lived before Noah's Flood.
5. The "stable" is that where Jesus was born, which, allegorically, leads to the "church" founded in his name and to the "vault" where this institution effectually buried him. The "mill" in Blake is a symbol of mechanical and analytic philosophy; through this the pilgrims pass into the twisting cave of rationalistic theology and descend to an

underworld that is an empty abyss. The point of this Blakean equivalent of a carnival funhouse is that only after you have thoroughly confused yourself by this tortuous approach, and only if you then (as in the next two paragraphs) stare at this topsyturvy emptiness long enough, will the void gradually assume the semblance of the comic horrors of the fantasized Hell of religious orthodoxy.
6. The biblical sea monster.

gills hang just above the raging foam, tinging the black deep with beams of blood, advancing toward [PLATE 19] us with all the fury of a spiritual existence.

My friend the Angel climb'd up from his station into the mill. I remain'd alone, & then this appearance was no more, but I found myself sitting on a pleasant bank beside a river by moon light, hearing a harper who sung to the harp, & his theme was: "The man who never alters his opinion is like standing water, & breeds reptiles of the mind."

But I arose, and sought for the mill, & there I found my Angel, who surprised asked me how I escaped?

I answered: "All that we saw was owing to your metaphysics: for when you ran away, I found myself on a bank by moonlight hearing a harper. But now we have seen my eternal lot, shall I shew you yours? He laughd at my proposal; but I by force suddenly caught him in my arms, & flew westerly thro' the night, til we were elevated above the earth's shadow; then I flung myself with him directly into the body of the sun. Here I clothed myself in white, & taking in my hand Swedenborg's volumes, sunk from the glorious clime, and passed all the planets till we came to Saturn. Here I staid to rest & then leap'd into the void between Saturn & the fixed stars.[7]

"Here," said I, "is your lot, in this space, if space it may be calld." Soon we saw the stable and the church, & I took him to the altar and open'd the Bible, and lo! it was a deep pit, into which I descended, driving the Angel before me. Soon we saw seven houses of brick;[8] one we enterd; in it were a [PLATE 20] number of monkeys, baboons, & all of that species, chaind by the middle, grinning and snatching at one another, but withheld by the shortness of their chains. However, I saw that they sometimes grew numerous, and then the weak were caught by the strong, and with a grinning aspect, first coupled with & then devourd, by plucking off first one limb and then another till the body was left a helpless trunk. This, after grinning & kissing it with seeming fondness, they devourd too; and here & there I saw one savourily picking the flesh off of his own tail. As the stench terribly annoyd us both, we went into the mill, & I in my hand brought the skeleton of a body, which in the mill was Aristotle's Analytics.[9]

So the Angel said: "Thy phantasy has imposed upon me, & thou oughtest to be ashamed."

I answered: "We impose on one another, & it is but lost time to converse with you whose works are only Analytics."

Opposition is true Friendship.

PLATE 21

I have always found that Angels have the vanity to speak of themselves as the only wise; this they do with a confident insolence sprouting from systematic reasoning.

Thus Swedenborg boasts that what he writes is new; tho' it is only the Contents or Index of already publish'd books.

A man carried a monkey about for a shew, & because he was a little wiser

---

7. In the Ptolemaic world picture, Saturn was in the outermost planetary sphere; beyond it was the sphere of the fixed stars.
8. The "seven churches which are in Asia," to which John addresses the Book of Revelation 1.4.

Blake now forces on the angel his own diabolic view of angelic biblical exegesis, theological speculation and disputation, and Hell.
9. Aristotle's treatises on logic.

than the monkey, grew vain, and conceiv'd himself as much wiser than seven men. It is so with Swedenborg; he shews the folly of churches & exposes hypocrites, till he imagines that all are religious, & himself the single [PLATE 22] one on earth that ever broke a net.

Now hear a plain fact: Swedenborg has not written one new truth. Now hear another: he has written all the old falshoods.

And now hear the reason: He conversed with Angels who are all religious, & conversed not with Devils, who all hate religion, for he was incapable thro' his conceited notions.

Thus Swedenborg's writings are a recapitulation of all superficial opinions, and an analysis of the more sublime, but no further.

Have now another plain fact: Any man of mechanical talents may from the writings of Paracelsus or Jacob Behmen[1] produce ten thousand volumes of equal value with Swedenborg's, and from those of Dante or Shakespear, an infinite number.

But when he has done this, let him not say that he knows better than his master, for he only holds a candle in sunshine.

A Memorable Fancy

Once I saw a Devil in a flame of fire, who arose before an Angel that sat on a cloud, and the Devil utterd these words:

"The worship of God is, Honouring his gifts in other men, each according to his genius, and loving the [PLATE 23] greatest men best. Those who envy or calumniate great men hate God, for there is no other God."

The Angel hearing this became almost blue; but mastering himself, he grew yellow, & at last white, pink, & smiling, and then replied:

"Thou Idolater, is not God One? & is not he visible in Jesus Christ? and has not Jesus Christ given his sanction to the law of ten commandments, and are not all other men fools, sinners, & nothings?"

The Devil answer'd; "Bray a fool in a mortar with wheat, yet shall not his folly be beaten out of him.[2] If Jesus Christ is the greatest man, you ought to love him in the greatest degree. Now hear how he has given his sanction to the law of ten commandments: did he not mock at the sabbath, and so mock the sabbath's God?[3] murder those who were murderd because of him? turn away the law from the woman taken in adultery?[4] steal the labor of others to support him? bear false witness when he omitted making a defence before Pilate?[5] covet when he pray'd for his disciples, and when he bid them shake off the dust of their feet against such as refused to lodge them?[6] I tell you, no virtue can exist without breaking these ten commandments. Jesus was all virtue, and acted from im[PLATE 24]pulse, not from rules."

When he had so spoken, I beheld the Angel, who stretched out his arms embracing the flame of fire, & he was consumed and arose as Elijah.[7]

1. Jakob Boehme (1575–1624), a German shoemaker who developed a theosophical system that has had persisting influence on both theological and metaphysical speculation. Paracelsus (1493–1541), a Swiss physician and a pioneer in empirical medicine, was also a prominent theorist of the occult.
2. Proverbs 27.22: "Though thou shouldst bray a fool in a mortar among wheat with a pestle, yet will not his foolishness depart from him." "Bray": pound into small pieces.
3. Mark 2.27: "The sabbath was made for man."
4. Cf. John 8.2–11.
5. Cf. Matthew 27.13–14.
6. Matthew 10.14: "Whosoever shall not receive you . . . when ye depart . . . shake off the dust of your feet."
7. In 2 Kings 2.11 the prophet Elijah "went up by a whirlwind into heaven," borne by "a chariot of fire."

Note. This Angel, who is now become a Devil, is my particular friend; we often read the Bible together in its infernal or diabolical sense, which the world shall have if they behave well.

I have also The Bible of Hell,[8] which the world shall have whether they will or no.

One Law for the Lion & Ox is Oppression.

1790–93   1790–93

PLATE 25

8. I.e., the poems and designs that Blake is working on.

ROBERT BURNS
1759–1796

When Robert Burns published his first volume of *Poems* in 1786, he was immediately hailed by the Edinburgh establishment as an instance of the natural genius, a "Heaven-taught ploughman" whose poems owed nothing to literary study, but instead represented the spontaneous overflow of his native feelings. Burns took care to call attention to those qualities in his verse—the undisciplined energy and rustic simplicity—that suited the temper of an age worried that modern refinement and propriety had undermined the vigor of poetry. But even though he cast himself (in the half-modest, half-defiant words of his Preface to *Poems*) as someone "unacquainted with the necessary requisites for commencing Poet by rule," Burns was in fact a widely read (although largely self-educated) man and a careful craftsman who turned to two earlier traditions for his poetic models. One of these was an oral tradition of folklore and folk song. The other was the highly developed literary tradition of poetry written in the Scots dialect of English.

His father—William Burnes, as he spelled his name—was a God-fearing and hard-working farmer of Ayrshire, a county in southwestern Scotland, who, unable to make a go of it in a period of hard times and high rents, died in 1784 broken in body and spirit. Robert, with his brother Gilbert, was forced to do the heavy work of a man while still a boy and began to show signs of the heart trouble of which he was to die when only thirty-seven. Although his father had the Scottish esteem for education and saw to it that his sons attended school whenever they could, Burns's education in literature, theology, politics, and philosophy came mainly from his own reading. At the age of fifteen, he fell in love and was inspired by that event to write his first song. "Thus," he said, "with me began Love and Poesy." After he reached maturity, he practiced at both. He began a series of love affairs, fathering in 1785 the first of a number of illegitimate children. He also extended greatly the range and quantity of his attempts at poetry. So rapid was his development that by the time he published the Kilmarnock edition, at the age of twenty-seven, he had written all but a few of his greatest long poems.

The Kilmarnock volume (so named from the town in which it was published) is one of the most remarkable first volumes by any British poet, and it had a great and immediate success. Burns was acclaimed "Caledonia's Bard" and championed by intellectuals and gentlefolk when he visited the city of Edinburgh soon after his book came out. The peasant-poet demonstrated that he could more than hold his own as an urbane conversationalist and debater. But he was also wise enough to realize that once the novelty wore off, his eminence in this society would not endure. He had a fierce pride that was quick to resent any hint of contempt or condescension toward himself as a man of low degree. His sympathies were democratic, and even in 1793 and 1794, when partisans of parliamentary reform were being prosecuted for sedition in Edinburgh and Glasgow, he remained (like William Blake in London) an outspoken admirer of the republican revolutions in America and France. In religion, too, he was a radical. Against the strict Calvinism of the Presbyterian kirk (church) in which he had been raised, Burns was known to profess "the Religion of Sentiment and Reason." A letter of December 1789, in which he seizes the chance to play a free-thinking Son "of Satan," merrily proclaims his intention to take up a theme that will, he says, be "pregnant with all the stores of Learning, from Moses & Confucius to [Benjamin] Franklin & [Joseph] Priestl[e]y—in short . . . I intend to write Baudy." Burns's satires on the kirk and taste for bawdy vulgarity could offend. Furthermore, his promiscuity gained him considerable notoriety, less because womanizing was out of the common order for the time than because he flaunted it. Many of the friendships that he made in high society fell apart, and Burns's later visits to Edinburgh were less successful than the first.

In 1788 Burns was given a commission as excise officer, or tax inspector, and he settled down with Jean Armour, a former lover, now his wife, at Ellisland, near Dumfries, combining his official duties with farming. This was the fourth farm on which Burns had worked; and when it, like the others, failed, he moved his family to the lively country town of Dumfries. Here he was fairly happy, despite recurrent illness and a chronic shortage of money. He performed his official duties efficiently and was respected by his fellow townspeople and esteemed by his superiors; he was a devoted family man and father; and he accumulated a circle of intimates to whom he could repair for conversation and conviviality. In 1787 James Johnson, an engraver, had enlisted Burns's aid in collecting Scottish folk songs for an anthology called *The Scots Musical Museum*. Burns soon became the real editor for several volumes of this work, devoting all of his free time to collecting, editing, restoring, and imitating traditional songs, and to writing verses of his own to traditional dance tunes. Almost all of his creative work during the last twelve years of his life went into the writing of songs for the *Musical Museum* and for George Thomson's *Select Collection of Original Scottish Airs*. This was for Burns a devoted labor of love and patriotism, done anonymously, for which he refused to accept any pay, although badly in need of money; and he continued the work when he was literally on his deathbed.

Because of its use of Scots dialect, the language spoken by most eighteenth-century Scottish people (lower and upper class alike), and because, in addition, of its lyricism and engagement with folk culture, Burns's verse is often said to anticipate William Wordsworth's idea of a poetry founded on "a selection of language really used by men." This account is based primarily on his songs. By far the major portion of the poems that he published under his own name are concerned with men and manners and are written in the literary forms that had been favored by earlier eighteenth-century poets. They include brilliant satire in a variety of modes, a number of fine verse epistles to friends and fellow poets, and one masterpiece of mock-heroic (or at any rate seriocomic) narrative, "Tam o' Shanter." It can be argued that, next to Pope, Burns is the greatest eighteenth-century master of these literary types. (Byron would later claim those forms for his own generation.) Yet Burns's writings in satire, epistle, and mock-heroic are remote from Pope's in their heartiness and verve, no less than in their dialect and intricate stanza forms. The reason for the difference is that Burns turned for his models not to Horace and the English neoclassic tradition but to the native tradition that had been established in the golden age of Scottish poetry by Robert Henryson, William Dunbar, Gavin Douglas, and other Scottish Chaucerians of the fifteenth and sixteenth centuries. He knew this literature through his eighteenth-century Scottish predecessors, especially Allan Ramsay and Robert Fergusson, who had collected some of the old poems and written new ones based on the old models. Burns improved greatly on these predecessors, but he derived from them much that is characteristic in his literary forms, subjects, diction, and stanzas.

Burns's songs, which number more than three hundred, have, however, in themselves been enough to sustain his poetic reputation. They made him, for a start, a central figure for his contemporaries' discussions of how music, valued by them for awakening sympathies that reason could not rouse, might serve as the foundation of a national identity. (William Wordsworth would explore this new notion of "national music"—of ethnically marked melody—in his 1805 poem "The Solitary Reaper.") But beyond being the bard of Scots nationalism, Burns is a songwriter for all English-speaking people. Evidence of that standing is supplied each New Year's Eve, when, moved once again to acknowledge their common bondage to time, men and women join hands and sing "Auld Lang Syne," to an old tune that Burns refitted with his new words.

The texts printed here are based on *The Poems and Songs of Robert Burns*, ed. James Kinsley, 3 vols. (Oxford, 1968).

Holy Willie's Prayer[1]

And send the Godly in a pet to pray—
POPE

Argument

Holy Willie was a rather oldish batchelor Elder in the parish of Mauchline, and much and justly famed for that polemical chattering which ends in tippling Orthodoxy, and for that Spiritualized Bawdry which refines to Liquorish Devotion.—In a Sessional process with a gentleman in Mauchline, a Mr. Gavin Hamilton, Holy Willie, and his priest, Father Auld, after full hearing in the Presbytry of Ayr, came off but second best; owing partly to the oratorical powers of Mr. Robt. Aiken, Mr. Hamilton's Counsel; but chiefly to Mr. Hamilton's being one of the most irreproachable and truly respectable characters in the country.—On losing his Process, the Muse overheard him at his devotions as follows—

O thou that in the heavens does dwell!
Wha, as it pleases best thysel,
Sends ane to heaven and ten to h-ll,
    A' for thy glory!
5 And no for ony gude or ill
    They've done before thee.[2]

1. This satire, in the form of a dramatic monologue, was inspired by William Fisher, a self-righteous elder in the same Ayrshire parish that in 1785 had forced Burns and Betty Paton to do public penance in church for "fornication," and is directed against a basic Calvinist tenet of the old Scottish kirk. Holy Willie assumes that he is one of a small minority, God's "elect"—in other words that he has been predestined for grace, no matter what deeds he does in this world. The sessional processes were court proceedings carried on under the auspices of the Kirk. The epigraph is from *The Rape of the Lock.*
2. Here as elsewhere Burns use the virtuosic

stanza form known as the "standard Habbie" (named for "The Life and Death of Habbie Simpson" a ballad in this form by Robert Sempill, a 17th-century poet who, also hailing from the west of Scotland, was a countryman of Burns's). In each sestet three lines of iambic tetrameter that rhyme *aaa* are followed by a dimeter rhyming *b*, another line of tetrameter rhyming *a,* and a final dimeter rhyming *b*. Associated at its origins with the troubadour poetry of Europe, the form came to Scotland during the Renaissance and had been revived in the 18th century by Ramsay and Fergusson as a distinctively national Scots measure.

I bless and praise thy matchless might,
When thousands thou has left in night,
That I am here before thy sight,
    For gifts and grace,
A burning and a shining light
        To a' this place.

What was I, or my generation,
That I should get such exaltation?
I, wha deserv'd most just damnation,
    For broken laws
Sax° thousand years ere my creation,   six
        Thro' Adam's cause!

When from my mother's womb I fell,
Thou might hae plunged me deep in hell,
To gnash my gooms, and weep, and wail,[3]
    In burning lakes,
Where damned devils roar and yell
        Chain'd to their stakes.

Yet I am here, a chosen sample,
To shew thy grace is great and ample:
I'm here, a pillar o' thy temple
        Strong as a rock,
A guide, a ruler and example
        To a' thy flock.

O Lord thou kens what zeal I bear,
When drinkers drink, and swearers swear,
And singin' there, and dancin' here,
        Wi' great an' sma';
For I am keepet by thy fear,
        Free frae them a'.

But yet—O Lord—confess I must—
At times I'm fash'd° wi' fleshly lust;   troubled
And sometimes too, in warldly trust
        Vile Self gets in;
But thou remembers we are dust,
        Defil'd wi' sin.

O Lord—yestreen°—thou kens°—wi' Meg—   yesterday / knowest
Thy pardon I sincerely beg!
O may't ne'er be a living plague,
        To my dishonor!
And I'll ne'er lift a lawless leg
        Again upon her.

---

3. An echo of Matthew 8.12, "the children of the kingdom shall be cast out into outer darkness: there shall be weeping and gnashing of teeth."

Besides, I farther maun° avow,   *must*
50 Wi' Leezie's lass, three times—I trow°—   *believe*
But Lord, that Friday I was fou°   *drunk*
      When I cam near her;
Or else, thou kens, thy servant true
      Wad never steer° her.   *molest*

55 Maybe thou lets this fleshly thorn
Buffet thy servant e'en and morn,[4]
Lest he o'er proud and high should turn,
      That he's sae gifted;
If sae, thy hand maun e'en be borne
60   Untill thou lift it.

Lord bless thy Chosen in this place,
For here thou has a chosen race:
But God, confound their stubborn face,
      And blast their name,
65 Wha bring thy rulers to disgrace
      And open shame.

Lord mind Gaun Hamilton's[5] deserts!
He drinks, and swears, and plays at cartes,°   *cards*
Yet has sae mony taking arts
70   Wi' Great and Sma',
Frae God's ain priest the people's hearts
      He steals awa.

And when we chasten'd him therefore,
Thou kens how he bred sic a splore,°   *disturbance*
75 And set the warld in a roar
      O' laughin at us:
Curse thou his basket and his store,
      Kail° and potatoes.   *broth*

Lord hear my earnest cry and prayer
80 Against that Presbytry of Ayr!
Thy strong right hand, Lord, make it bare
      Upon their heads!
Lord visit them, and dinna spare,
      For their misdeeds!

85 O Lord my God, that glib-tongu'd Aiken!
My very heart and flesh are quaking
To think how I sat, sweating, shaking,
      And piss'd wi' dread,
While Auld wi' hingin° lip gaed sneaking   *hanging*
90   And hid his head!

4. An echo of 2 Corinthians 12.7, "there was given to me a thorn in the flesh, the messenger of Satan to buffet me, lest I should be exalted above measure."
5. Burns's friend Gavin Hamilton, whom Holy Willie had brought up on moral charges before the Kirk Session of the Presbytery of Ayr. As Burns explains in the Argument, Hamilton was successfully defended by his counsel, Robert Aiken (referred to in line 85).

Lord, in thy day o'vengeance try him!
Lord visit him that did employ him!
And pass not in thy mercy by them,
    Nor hear their prayer;
95 But for thy people's sake destroy them,
    And dinna spare!

But Lord, remember me and mine
Wi' mercies temporal and divine!
That I for grace and gear° may shine,   *wealth*
100   Excell'd by nane!
And a' the glory shall be thine!
Amen! Amen!

1789   1789

To a Mouse

On Turning Her up in Her Nest with the Plough, November, 1785[1]

Wee, sleeket,° cowran, tim'rous beastie,   *sleek*
O, what a panic's in thy breastie!
Thou need na start awa sae hasty,
    Wi' bickering brattle![2]
5 I wad be laith° to rin an' chase thee   *loath*
    Wi' murd'ring pattle!°   *plowstaff*

I'm truly sorry Man's dominion
Has broken Nature's social union,
An' justifies that ill opinion,
10   Which makes thee startle,
At me, thy poor, earth-born companion,
    An' fellow mortal!

I doubt na, whyles,° but thou may thieve;   *sometimes*
What then? poor beastie, thou maun° live!   *must*
15 A daimen-icker in a thrave[3]
    'S a sma' request:
I'll get a blessin wi' the lave,°   *remainder*
    An' never miss 't!

Thy wee-bit housie, too, in ruin!
20 It's silly wa's° the win's are strewin!   *frail walls*
An' naething, now, to big° a new ane,   *build*
    O' foggage° green!   *coarse grass*
An' bleak December's winds ensuin,
    Baith snell° an' keen!   *bitter*

1. Burns's brother claimed that this poem was composed while the poet was actually holding the plow.
2. With headlong scamper.
3. An occasional ear in twenty-four sheaves.

25   Thou saw the fields laid bare an' waste,
An' weary Winter comin fast,
An' cozie here, beneath the blast,
      Thou thought to dwell,
Till crash! the cruel coulter° past   *cutter blade*
30   Out thro' thy cell.

That wee-bit heap o' leaves an' stibble°   *stubble*
Has cost thee monie a weary nibble!
Now thou 's turn'd out, for a' thy trouble,
      But° house or hald,[4]   *without*
35   To thole° the Winter's sleety dribble,   *endure*
      An' cranreuch° cauld!   *hoarfrost*

But Mousie, thou art no thy-lane,°   *not alone*
In proving foresight may be vain:
The best laid schemes o' Mice an' Men
40   Gang aft agley,[5]
An' lea'e us nought but grief an' pain,
      For promis'd joy!

Still, thou art blest, compar'd wi' me!
The present only toucheth thee:
45   But Och! I backward cast my e'e,
      On prospects drear!
An' forward tho' I canna see,
      I guess an' fear!

1785   1786

To a Louse

On Seeing One on a Lady's Bonnet at Church

Ha! whare ye gaun, ye crowlan° ferlie!°   *crawling / wonder*
Your impudence protects you sairly:°   *sorely*
I canna say but ye strunt° rarely,   *strut*
      Owre gawze and lace;
5   Tho' faith, I fear ye dine but sparely,
      On sic a place.

Ye ugly, creepan, blastet wonner,°   *wonder*
Detested, shunn'd, by saunt an' sinner,
How daur ye set your fit° upon her,   *foot*
10   Sae fine a Lady!
Gae somewhere else and seek your dinner,
      On some poor body.

---

4. Hold, holding (i.e., land).   5. Go oft awry.

Swith,° in some beggar's haffet° squattle;°   *swift / locks / sprawl*
There ye may creep, and sprawl, and sprattle,°   *struggle*
15 Wi' ither kindred, jumping cattle,
    In shoals and nations;
Whare horn nor bane[1] ne'er daur unsettle,
    Your thick plantations.

Now haud you there, ye're out o' sight,
20 Below the fatt'rels,° snug and tight,   *ribbon ends*
Na faith ye yet![2] ye'll no be right,
    Till ye've got on it,
The vera tapmost, towrin height
    O' Miss's bonnet.

25 My sooth! right bauld ye set your nose out,
As plump an' gray as onie grozet:°   *gooseberry*
O for some rank, mercurial rozet,°   *rosin*
    Or fell,° red smeddum,°   *sharp / powder*
I'd gie you sic a hearty dose o't,
30   Wad dress your droddum!°   *buttocks*

I wad na been surpriz'd to spy
You on an auld wife's flainen toy,°   *flannel cap*
Or aiblins° some bit duddie° boy,   *perhaps / ragged*
    On 's wylecoat;°   *undershirt*
35 But Miss's fine Lunardi,[3] fye!
    How daur ye do 't?

O Jenny dinna toss your head,
An' set your beauties a' abread!°   *abroad*
Ye little ken what cursed speed
40   The blastie's° makin!   *creature's*
Thae° winks and finger-ends, I dread,   *those*
    Are notice takin!

O wad some Pow'r the giftie gie us
To see oursels as others see us!
45 It wad frae monie a blunder free us
    An' foolish notion:
What airs in dress an' gait wad lea'e us,
    And ev'n Devotion![4]

1785   1786

1. I.e., fine-tooth comb made of horn or bone ("bane").
2. Confound you!
3. A balloon-shaped bonnet, named after Vincenzo Lunardi, who made a number of balloon flights in the mid-1780s.
4. I.e., even pretended piety.

Tam o' Shanter: A Tale[1]

Of Brownyis and of Bogillis full is this buke.
GAWIN DOUGLAS.

When chapman billies[2] leave the street,
And drouthy° neebors neebors meet,   *thirsty*
As market-days are wearing late,
An' folk begin to tak the gate;°   *road*
5   While we sit bousing at the nappy,°   *strong ale*
And getting fou° and unco° happy,   *drunk / very*
We think na on the lang Scots miles,
The mosses, waters, slaps,° and styles,   *gaps (in walls)*
That lie between us and our hame,
10 Whare sits our sulky sullen dame,
Gathering her brows like gathering storm,
Nursing her wrath to keep it warm.

     This truth fand° honest Tam o' Shanter,   *found*
As he frae Ayr ae night did canter,
15 (Auld Ayr, wham ne'er a town surpasses,
For honest men and bonny lasses).

     O Tam! hadst thou but been sae wise,
As ta'en thy ain wife Kate's advice!
She tauld thee weel thou was a skellum,°   *good-for-nothing*
20 A blethering,° blustering, drunken blellum;°   *chattering / babbler*
That frae November till October,
Ae market-day thou was nae sober;
That ilka° melder,[3] wi' the miller,   *every*
Thou sat as lang as thou had siller;°   *silver, money*
25 That every naig° was ca'd° a shoe on,   *nag / driven*
The smith and thee gat roaring fou on;
That at the Lord's house, even on Sunday,
Thou drank wi' Kirkton Jean till Monday.
She prophesied that late or soon,
30 Thou would be found deep drown'd in Doon;

---

1. This poem, written to order for a book on Scottish antiquities, is based on a witch story told about Alloway Kirk, an old ruin near Burns's house in Ayr. As a mock-heroic rendering of folk material, "Tam o' Shanter" is comparable to *The Nun's Priest's Tale* of Chaucer. Burns recognized that the poem was his most sustained and finished artistic performance; it discovers "a spice of roguish waggery" but also shows "a force of genius and a finishing polish that I despair of ever excelling." The verve and seriocomic sympathy with which Burns manages this misadventure of a confirmed tippler won Wordsworth, a water drinker, to passionate advocacy against the moralists who objected to Burns's ribaldry: "Who, but some impenetrable dunce or narrow-minded puritan in works of art, ever read without delight the picture which he has drawn of the convivial exaltation of the rustic adventurer, Tam o' Shanter?" ("Letter to a Friend of Burns," 1816). The epigraph is from the prologue to book 6 of Gavin Douglas's 16th-century Scots translation of Virgil's *Aeneid*. In this book the epic hero Aeneas, soon to be the founder of Rome, descends into the world of the dead.

Scots can be easier to understand when heard than when read. For tips on pronunciation listen to the reading of "Tam o' Shanter" at Norton Literature Online.
2. Peddler fellows.
3. The amount of corn processed at a single grinding.

Or catch'd wi' warlocks in the mirk,°   *night*
By Alloway's auld haunted kirk.

    Ah, gentle dames! it gars° me greet°   *makes / weep*
To think how mony counsels sweet,
35 How mony lengthen'd sage advices,
The husband frae the wife despises!

    But to our tale: Ae market-night,
Tam had got planted unco right;
Fast by an ingle,° bleezing° finely,   *fireplace / blazing*
40 Wi' reaming swats,° that drank divinely;   *foaming new ale*
And at his elbow, Souter° Johnny,   *shoemaker*
His ancient, trusty, drouthy crony;
Tam lo'ed him like a vera brither;
They had been fou for weeks thegither.
45 The night drave on wi' sangs and clatter;
And ay the ale was growing better:
The landlady and Tam grew gracious,
Wi' favours secret, sweet, and precious:
The Souter tauld his queerest stories;
50 The landlord's laugh was ready chorus:
The storm without might rair° and rustle,   *roar*
Tam did na mind the storm a whistle.

    Care, mad to see a man sae happy,
E'en drown'd himsel amang the nappy:
55 As bees flee hame wi' lades o' treasure,
The minutes wing'd their way wi' pleasure:
Kings may be blest, but Tam was glorious,
O'er a' the ills o' life victorious!

    But pleasures are like poppies spread,
60 You seize the flower, its bloom is shed;
Or like the snow falls in the river,
A moment white—then melts for ever;
Or like the borealis race,
That flit ere you can point their place;
65 Or like the rainbow's lovely form
Evanishing amid the storm.—
Nae man can tether time or tide;
The hour approaches Tam maun° ride;   *must*
That hour, o' night's black arch the key-stane,
70 That dreary hour, he mounts his beast in;
And sic a night he taks the road in,
As ne'er poor sinner was abroad in.

    The wind blew as 'twad blawn its last;
The rattling showers rose on the blast;
75 The speedy gleams the darkness swallow'd;
Loud, deep, and lang, the thunder bellow'd:
That night, a child might understand,
The Deil had business on his hand.

Weel mounted on his gray mare, Meg,
80 A better never lifted leg,[4]
Tam skelpit° on thro' dub° and mire,   *slapped / puddle*
Despising wind, and rain, and fire;
Whiles holding fast his gude blue bonnet;
Whiles crooning o'er some auld Scots sonnet;
85 Whiles glowring° round wi' prudent cares,   *staring*
Lest bogles° catch him unawares.   *hobgoblins*
Kirk-Alloway was drawing nigh,
Whare ghaists° and houlets° nightly cry.—   *ghosts / owls*

By this time he was cross the ford,
90 Whare in the snaw, the chapman smoor'd;[5]
And past the birks° and meikle stane,°   *birches / big stone*
Whare drunken Charlie brak's neck-bane;
And thro' the whins, and by the cairn,[6]
Whare hunters fand the murder'd bairn;
95 And near the thorn, aboon the well,
Where Mungo's mither hang'd hersel.—
Before him Doon pours all his floods;
The doubling storm roars thro' the woods;
The lightnings flash from pole to pole;
100 Near and more near the thunders roll:
When, glimmering thro' the groaning trees,
Kirk-Alloway seemed in a bleeze;°   *blaze*
Thro' ilka bore° the beams were glancing;   *hole*
And loud resounded mirth and dancing.—

105 Inspiring bold John Barleycorn!
What dangers thou canst make us scorn!
Wi' tippeny,[7] we fear nae evil;
Wi' usquabae,° we'll face the devil!—   *whisky*
The swats sae ream'd in Tammie's noddle,
110 Fair play, he car'd na deils a boddle.[8]
But Maggie stood right sair astonish'd,
Till, by the heel and hand admonish'd,
She ventured forward on the light;
And, vow! Tam saw an unco° sight!   *strange*
115 Warlocks and witches in a dance;
Nae cotillion brent° new frae France,   *brand*
But hornpipes, jigs, strathspeys,[9] and reels,
Put life and mettle in their heels.
A winnock-bunker° in the east,   *window seat*
120 There sat auld Nick, in shape o' beast;
A touzie tyke,° black, grim, and large,   *shaggy dog*
To gie them music was his charge:
He screw'd the pipes and gart° them skirl,°   *made / screech*

4. Compare this "lifted leg" to Willie's use of the
term about himself in line 47 of "Holy Willie's
Prayer." Tam's horse, Meg (also called Maggie),
occasions the poem's bawdiest wordplay.
5. The peddler smothered.
6. Stones heaped up as a memorial. "Whins":

furze (an evergreen shrub).
7. Twopenny (usually of weak beer).
8. I.e., he didn't care a farthing about devils (a
"boddle" is a very small copper coin).
9. Slow Highland dance.

Till roof and rafters a' did dirl.°—   *rattle*
125 Coffins stood round, like open presses,
That shaw'd the dead in their last dresses;
And by some devilish cantraip° slight   *charm, trick*
Each in its cauld hand held a light.—
By which heroic Tam was able
130 To note upon the haly° table,   *holy*
A murderer's banes in gibbet airns;°   *irons*
Twa span-lang,[1] wee, unchristened bairns;
A thief, new-cutted frae a rape,°   *rope*
Wi' his last gasp his gab° did gape;   *mouth*
135 Five tomahawks, wi' blude red-rusted;
Five scymitars, wi' murder crusted;
A garter, which a babe had strangled;
A knife, a father's throat had mangled,
Whom his ain son o' life bereft,
140 The grey hairs yet stack° to the heft;   *stuck*
Wi' mair o' horrible and awefu',
Which even to name wad be unlawfu'.

As Tammie glowr'd, amaz'd, and curious,
The mirth and fun grew fast and furious:
145 The piper loud and louder blew;
The dancers quick and quicker flew;
They reel'd, they set, they cross'd, they cleekit,° *joined hands*
Till ilka carlin° swat and reekit,   *old woman*
And coost her duddies to the wark,[2]
150 And linket° at it in her sark![3]   *tripped lightly*

Now, Tam, O Tam! had thae been queans,° *girls*
A' plump and strapping in their teens,
Their sarks, instead o' creeshie flannen,° *greasy flannel*
Been snaw-white seventeen hunder linnen![4]
155 Thir° breeks o' mine, my only pair,   *these*
That ance were plush, o' gude blue hair,
I wad hae gi'en them off my hurdies,° *buttocks*
For ae blink o' the bonie burdies!° *bonny (pretty) girls*

But wither'd beldams,° auld and droll, *hags*
160 Rigwoodie° hags wad spean° a foal, *bony / wean*
Lowping° and flinging on a crummock,° *leaping / staff*
I wonder didna turn thy stomach.

But Tam kend what was what fu' brawlie,° *finely*
There was ae winsome wench and wawlie° *strapping*
165 That night enlisted in the core,°   *corps*
(Lang after kend on Carrick shore;
For mony a beast to dead she shot,
And perish'd mony a bony boat,

1. Two spans long (a span is the distance from outstretched thumb to little finger).
2. Cast off her clothes for the work.
3. Shirt (underclothes).
4. Very fine linen, woven on a loom with seventeen hundred strips.

And shook baith meikle corn and bear,°	*barley*
170 And kept the country-side in fear:)	
Her cutty° sark, o' Paisley harn,°	*short / yarn*
That while a lassie she had worn,	
In longitude tho' sorely scanty,	
It was her best, and she was vauntie.°—	*proud*
175 Ah! little kend thy reverend grannie,	
That sark she coft° for her wee Nannie,	*bought*
Wi' twa pund Scots ('twas a' her riches),	
Wad ever grac'd a dance of witches!	
But here my Muse her wing maun cour;°	*lower*
180 Sic flights are far beyond her pow'r;	
To sing how Nannie lap and flang,	
(A souple jade° she was, and strang),	*disreputable woman*
And how Tam stood, like ane bewitch'd,	
And thought his very een° enrich'd;	*eyes*
185 Even Satan glowr'd, and fidg'd fu' fain,[5]	
And hotch'd° and blew wi' might and main:	*jerked*
Till first ae caper, syne° anither,	*then*
Tam tint° his reason a' thegither,	*lost*
And roars out, 'Weel done, Cutty-sark!'	
190 And in an instant all was dark:	
And scarcely had he Maggie rallied,	
When out the hellish legion sallied.	
As bees bizz out wi' angry fyke,°	*fuss*
When plundering herds° assail their byke;°	*herdsmen / hive*
195 As open° pussie's mortal foes,	*begin to bark*
When, pop! she starts before their nose;	
As eager runs the market-crowd,	
When 'Catch the thief!' resounds aloud;	
So Maggie runs the witches follow,	
200 Wi' mony an eldritch° skreech and hollow.	*unearthly*
Ah, Tam! Ah, Tam! thou'll get thy fairin'!°	*deserts*
In hell they'll roast thee like a herrin!	
In vain thy Kate awaits thy comin!	
Kate soon will be a woefu' woman!	
205 Now, do thy speedy utmost, Meg,	
And win the key-stane of the brig;[6]	
There at them thou thy tail may toss,	
A running stream they dare na cross.	
But ere the key-stane she could make,	
210 The fient a tail she had to shake!	
For Nannie, far before the rest,	
Hard upon noble Maggie prest,	
And flew at Tam wi' furious ettle;°	*intent*

5. Fidgeted with pleasure.
6. It is a well known fact that witches, or any evil spirits, have no power to follow a poor wight any farther than the middle of the next running stream.—It may be proper likewise to mention to the benighted traveler, that when he falls in with *bogles*, whatever danger may be in his going forward, there is much more hazard in turning back [Burns's note]. "Brig": bridge.

But little wist she Maggie's mettle—
215 Ae spring brought off her master hale,°   whole
But left behind her ain gray tail:
The carlin claught° her by the rump,   clutched
And left poor Maggie scarce a stump.[7]

Now, wha this tale o' truth shall read,
220 Ilk man and mother's son, take heed:
Whene'er to drink you are inclin'd,
Or cutty-sarks run in your mind,
Think, ye may buy the joys o'er dear,
Remember Tam o' Shanter's mare.

1790   1791

A Red, Red Rose[1]

O my Luve's like a red, red rose,
     That's newly sprung in June;
O my Luve's like the melodie
     That's sweetly played in tune.

5   As fair art thou, my bonie lass,
        So deep in luve am I;
    And I will love thee still, my Dear,
        Till a' the seas gang dry.

    Till a' the seas gang dry, my Dear,
10   And the rocks melt wi' the sun:
    O I will love thee still, my Dear,
        While the sands o' life shall run.

    And fare thee weel, my only Luve!
        And fare thee weel, a while!
15 And I will come again, my Luve,
        Tho' it were ten thousand mile!

1794   1796

Song: For a' that and a' that[1]

Is there, for honest Poverty
     That hangs his head, and a' that;
The coward-slave, we pass him by,
     We dare be poor for a' that!
5   For a' that, and a' that,

---

7. I.e., she had no tail left at all.
1. Like many of Burns's lyrics, this one incorporates elements from several current folk songs.

1. This song was set to a dance tune, known as
Lady Macintosh's Reel, that Burns had drawn on
for previous songs.

Our toils obscure, and a' that,
The rank is but the guinea's stamp,°   *inscription on a coin*
The Man's the gowd° for a' that.   *gold*

What though on hamely fare we dine,
10   Wear hodden grey,[2] and a' that.
Gie fools their silks, and knaves their wine,
A Man's a Man for a' that.
For a' that, and a' that,
Their tinsel show, and a' that;
15   The honest man, though e'er sae poor,
Is king o' men for a' that.

Ye see yon birkie° ca'd a lord,   *fellow*
Wha struts, and stares, and a' that,
Though hundreds worship at his word,
20   He's but a coof° for a' that.   *dolt*
For a' that, and a' that,
His ribband, star and a' that,
The man of independant mind,
He looks and laughs at a' that.

25   A prince can mak a belted knight,
A marquis, duke, and a' that;
But an honest man's aboon° his might,   *above*
Guid faith he mauna fa' that![3]
For a' that, and a' that,
30   Their dignities, and a' that,
The pith o' Sense, and pride o' Worth,
Are higher rank than a' that.

Then let us pray that come it may,
As come it will for a' that,
35   That Sense and Worth, o'er a' the earth
Shall bear the gree,° and a' that.   *win the prize*
For a' that, and a' that,
It's coming yet for a' that,
That Man to Man the warld o'er,
40   Shall brothers be for a' that.

1795   1795

2. A coarse cloth of undyed wool.   3. Must not claim that.

MARY WOLLSTONECRAFT
1759–1797

Mary Wollstonecraft's father inherited a substantial fortune and set himself up as a gentleman farmer. He was, however, both extravagant and incompetent, and as one farm after another failed, he became moody and violent and sought solace in heavy bouts of drinking and in tyrannizing his submissive wife. Mary was the second of five children and the oldest daughter. She later told her husband, William Godwin, that she used to throw herself in front of her mother to protect her from her husband's blows, and that she sometimes slept outside the door of her parents' bedroom to intervene if her father should break out in a drunken rage. The solace of Mary's early life was her fervent attachment to Fanny Blood, an accomplished girl two years her senior; their friendship, which began when Mary was sixteen, endured and deepened until Fanny's death.

At the age of nineteen, Mary Wollstonecraft left home to take a position as companion to a well-to-do widow living in Bath, where for the first time she had the opportunity to observe—and scorn—the social life of the upper classes at the most fashionable of English resort cities. Having left her job in 1780 to nurse her dying mother through a long and harrowing illness, Wollstonecraft next went to live with the Bloods, where her work helped sustain the struggling family. Her sister Eliza meanwhile had married and, in 1784, after the birth of a daughter, suffered a nervous breakdown. Convinced that her sister's collapse was the result of her husband's cruelty and abuse, Wollstonecraft persuaded her to abandon husband and child and flee to London. Because a divorce at that time was not commonly available, and a fugitive wife could be forced to return to her husband, the two women hid in secret quarters while awaiting the grant of a legal separation. The infant, automatically given into the father's custody, died before she was a year old.

The penniless women, together with Fanny Blood and Wollstonecraft's other sister, Everina, established a girls' school at Newington Green, near London. The project flourished at first, and at Newington, Wollstonecraft was befriended by the Reverend Richard Price, the radical author who was soon to play a leading role in the British debates about the Revolution in France, and whose kindly guidance helped shape her social and political opinions. Blood, although already ill with tuberculosis, went to Lisbon to marry her longtime suitor, Hugh Skeys, and quickly became pregnant. Wollstonecraft rushed to Lisbon to attend her friend's childbirth, only to have Fanny die in her arms; the infant died soon afterward. The loss threw Wollstonecraft (already subject to bouts of depression) into black despair, which was heightened when she found that the school at Newington was in bad financial straits and had to be closed. Tormented by creditors, she rallied her energies to write her first book, *Thoughts on the Education of Daughters* (1786), a conventional and pious series of essays, and took up a position as governess for several daughters in the Anglo-Irish family of Viscount Kingsborough, a man of great wealth whose seat was in County Cork, Ireland.

The Kingsboroughs were well intentioned and did their best to introduce Wollstonecraft into the busy trivialities of their social life. But the ambiguity of her position as governess, halfway between a servant and a member of the family, was galling. An antagonism developed between Wollstonecraft and Lady Kingsborough, in part because the children feared their mother and adored their governess. Wollstonecraft was dismissed. She returned to London, where Joseph Johnson in 1788 published *Mary, a Fiction*, a novel, as Wollstonecraft described it, about "the mind of a woman who has thinking powers." Johnson also published her book for children, *Original Stories from Real Life*, a considerable success that was translated into German and quickly achieved a second English edition illustrated with engravings by William Blake. Wollstonecraft was befriended and subsidized by Johnson, the major publisher in England of radical and reformist books, and she took a prominent place among the writers (including notables such as Barbauld and Coleridge) whom he regularly entertained at his rooms in St. Paul's Churchyard. She published translations from French and German (she had taught herself both languages) and began reviewing books for Johnson's newly founded journal, the *Analytical Review*. Though still in straitened circumstances, she helped support her two sisters and her improvident and importunate father, and was also generous with funds—and with advice—to one of her brothers and to the indigent family of Fanny Blood.

In 1790 Edmund Burke's *Reflections on the Revolution in France*—an eloquent and powerful attack on the French Revolution and its English sympathizers—quickly evoked Wollstonecraft's response, *A Vindication of the Rights of Men*. This was a formidable piece of argumentation; its most potent passages represent the disabilities and sufferings of the English lower classes and impugn the motives and sentiments of Burke. This work, the first book-length reply to Burke, scored an immediate success, although it was soon submerged in the flood of other replies, most notably Tom Paine's classic *Rights of Man* (1791–92). In 1792 Wollstonecraft focused her defense of the underprivileged on her own sex and wrote, in six weeks of intense effort, *A Vindication of the Rights of Woman*.

Earlier writers in both France and England had proposed that, given equivalent educations, women would equal men in achievement. Wollstonecraft was particularly indebted to the historian Catharine Macaulay, whose *Letters on Education* (1790) she had reviewed enthusiastically. At the same time Wollstonecraft was contributing to a long-running discussion of human rights that in Britain dated back to John Locke's publication of the *Second Treatise of Civil Government* (1690). Prefaced with a letter addressed to the French politician Bishop Talleyrand, the *Vindication* was in part her rejoinder to the inconsistent actions of France's National Assembly, which in 1791 had formally denied to all Frenchwomen the rights of citizens, even as, ironically enough, it set about celebrating the "universal rights of man."

Her book was also unprecedented in its firsthand observations of the disabilities and indignities suffered by women and in the articulateness and passion with which it exposed and decried this injustice. Wollstonecraft's views were conspicuously radical at a time when women had no political rights; were limited to a few lowly vocations as servants, nurses, governesses, and petty shopkeepers; and were legally nonpersons who lost their property to their husbands at marriage and were incapable of instituting an action in the courts of law. An impressive feature of her book, for all its vehemence, is the clear-sightedness and balance of her analysis of the social conditions of the time, as they affect men as well as women. She perceives that women constitute an oppressed class that cuts across the standard hierarchy of social classes; she shows that women, because they are denied their rights as human beings, have been forced to seek their ends by means of coquetry and cunning, the weapons of the weak; and, having demonstrated that it is contrary to reason to expect virtue from those who are not free, she also recognizes that men, no less than women, inherit their roles, and that the wielding of irresponsible power corrupts the oppressor no less than it distorts the oppressed. Hence her surprising and telling comparisons between women on the one hand and men of the nobility and military on the other as classes whose values and behavior have been distorted because their social roles prevent them from becoming fully human. In writing this pioneering work, Wollstonecraft found the cause that she was to pursue the rest of her life.

In December 1792 Wollstonecraft went to Paris to observe the Revolution at firsthand. During the years that she lived in France, 1793–94, the early period of moderation was succeeded by extremism and violence. In Paris she joined a group of English, American, and European expatriates sympathetic to the Revolution and fell in love with Gilbert Imlay, a personable American who had briefly been an officer in the American Revolutionary Army and was the author of a widely read book on the Kentucky backwoods, where he had been an explorer. He played the role in Paris of an American frontiersman and child of nature, but was in fact an adventurer who had left America to avoid prosecution for debt and for freewheeling speculations in Kentucky land. He was also unscrupulous in his relations with women. The two became lovers, and Wollstonecraft bore a daughter, Fanny Imlay, in May 1794. Imlay, who was often absent on mysterious business deals, left mother and daughter for a visit to London that he kept protracting. After the publication of her book *An Historical and Moral View of the Origin and Progress of the French Revolution* (1794), Wollstonecraft followed Imlay to London, where, convinced that he no longer loved her, she tried to commit suicide. The attempt, however, was discovered and prevented by Imlay. To get her out of the way, he persuaded her to take a trip as his business envoy to the Scandinavian countries. Although this was then a region of poor or impassible roads and primitive accommodations, the intrepid Wollstonecraft traveled there for four months, sometimes in the wilds, accompanied by the year-old Fanny and a French nursemaid.

Back in London, Wollstonecraft discovered that Imlay was living with a new mistress, an actress. Finally convinced he was lost to her, she hurled herself from a bridge into the Thames but was rescued by a passerby. Imlay departed with his actress to Paris. Wollstonecraft, resourceful as always, used the letters she had written to Imlay to compose a book, *Letters Written during a Short Residence in Sweden, Norway, and Denmark* (1796), full of sharp observations of politics, the lives of Scandinavian women, and the austere northern landscape.

In the same year Wollstonecraft renewed an earlier acquaintance with the philosopher William Godwin. His *Inquiry Concerning Political Justice* (1793), the most drastic proposal for restructuring the political and social order yet published in England, together with his novel of terror, *Caleb Williams* (1794), which embodies his social views, had made him the most famed radical writer of his time. The austerely rationalistic philosopher, then forty years of age, had an unexpected capacity for deep feeling, and what began as a flirtation soon ripened into affection and (as their letters show) passionate physical love. She wrote Godwin, with what was for the time remarkable outspokenness on the part of a woman: "Now by these presents [i.e., this document] let me assure you that you are not only in my heart, but my veins, this morning. I turn from you half abashed—yet you haunt me, and some look, word or touch thrills through my whole frame. . . . When the heart and reason accord there is no flying from voluptuous sensations, do what a woman can." Wollstonecraft was soon pregnant once more, and Godwin (who had in his *Inquiry* attacked the institution of marriage as a base form of property rights in human beings) braved the ridicule of his radical friends and conservative enemies by marrying her.

They set up a household together, but Godwin also kept separate quarters in which to do his writing, and they further salvaged their principles by agreeing to live separate social lives. Wollstonecraft was able to enjoy this arrangement for only six months. She began writing *The Wrongs of Woman*, a novel about marriage and motherhood that uses its Gothic setting inside a dilapidated madhouse to explore how women are confined both by unjust marriage laws and by their own romantic illusions. On August 30, 1797, she gave birth to a daughter, Mary Wollstonecraft Godwin, later the author of *Frankenstein* and wife of Percy Shelley. The delivery was not difficult, but resulted in massive blood poisoning. After ten days of agony, she lapsed into a coma and died. Her last whispered words were about her husband: "He is the kindest, best man in the world." Godwin wrote to a friend, announcing her death: "I firmly believe that there does not exist her equal in the world. I know from experience we were formed to make each other happy."

To distract himself in his grief, Godwin published in 1798 *Memoirs of the Author of "A Vindication of the Rights of Woman,"* in which he told, with the total candor on which he prided himself, of her affairs with Imlay and himself, her attempts at suicide, and her free thinking in matters of religion and sexual relationships. In four companion volumes of her *Posthumous Works*, he indiscreetly included her love letters to

Imlay along with the unfinished *Wrongs of Woman*. The reaction to these revelations was immediate and ugly. The conservative satirist the Reverend Richard Polwhele, for instance, remarked gloatingly on how it appeared to him providential that as a proponent of sexual equality Wollstonecraft should have died in childbirth—"a death that strongly marked the distinction of the sexes, by pointing out the destiny of women, and the diseases to which they are liable." The unintended consequence of Godwin's candor was that Wollstonecraft came to be saddled with a scandalous reputation so enduring that through the Victorian era advocates of the equality of women circumspectly avoided explicit reference to her *Vindication*. Even John Stuart Mill, in his *Subjection of Women* (1869), neglected to mention the work. It was only in the twentieth century, and especially in the later decades, that Wollstonecraft's *Vindication* gained recognition as a classic in the literature not only of women's rights but of social analysis as well.

From A Vindication of the Rights of Woman[1]

Introduction

After considering the historic page, and viewing the living world with anxious solicitude, the most melancholy emotions of sorrowful indignation have depressed my spirits, and I have sighed when obliged to confess, that either nature has made a great difference between man and man, or that the civilization which has hitherto taken place in the world has been very partial. I have turned over various books written on the subject of education, and patiently observed the conduct of parents and the management of schools; but what has been the result?—a profound conviction that the neglected education of my fellow-creatures is the grand source of the misery I deplore; and that women, in particular, are rendered weak and wretched by a variety of concurring causes, originating from one hasty conclusion. The conduct and manners of women, in fact, evidently prove that their minds are not in a healthy state; for, like the flowers which are planted in too rich a soil, strength and usefulness are sacrificed to beauty; and the flaunting leaves, after having pleased a fastidious eye, fade, disregarded on the stalk, long before the season when they ought to have arrived at maturity.—One cause of this barren blooming I attribute to a false system of education, gathered from the books written on this subject by men who, considering females rather as women than human creatures, have been more anxious to make them alluring mistresses than affectionate wives and rational mothers; and the understanding of the sex has been so bubbled[2] by this specious homage, that the civilized women of the present century, with a few exceptions, are only anxious to inspire love, when they ought to cherish a nobler ambition, and by their abilities and virtues exact respect.

In a treatise, therefore, on female rights and manners, the works which have been particularly written for their improvement must not be overlooked; especially when it is asserted, in direct terms, that the minds of women are enfeebled by false refinement; that the books of instruction, written by men of genius, have had the same tendency as more frivolous productions; and that, in the true style of Mahometanism, they are treated as a kind of subordinate

1. The text is from the second revised edition of 1792, as edited by Carol H. Poston for the Norton Critical Edition of *A Vindication* (1975). The editors gratefully acknowledge Poston's permission to use the information in her annotations.
2. In an archaic sense: deluded, cheated.

beings, and not as a part of the human species,[3] when improvable reason is allowed to be the dignified distinction which raises men above the brute creation, and puts a natural sceptre in a feeble hand.

Yet, because I am a woman, I would not lead my readers to suppose that I mean violently to agitate the contested question respecting the equality or inferiority of the sex; but as the subject lies in my way, and I cannot pass it over without subjecting the main tendency of my reasoning to misconstruction, I shall stop a moment to deliver, in a few words, my opinion.—In the government of the physical world it is observable that the female in point of strength is, in general, inferior to the male. This is the law of nature; and it does not appear to be suspended or abrogated in favor of woman. A degree of physical superiority cannot, therefore, be denied—and it is a noble prerogative! But not content with this natural pre-eminence, men endeavor to sink us still lower, merely to render us alluring objects for a moment; and women, intoxicated by the adoration which men, under the influence of their senses, pay them, do not seek to obtain a durable interest in their hearts, or to become the friends of the fellow creatures who find amusement in their society.

I am aware of an obvious inference:—from every quarter have I heard exclamations against masculine women; but where are they to be found? If by this appellation men mean to inveigh against their ardor in hunting, shooting, and gaming, I shall most cordially join in the cry; but if it be against the imitation of manly virtues, or, more properly speaking, the attainment of those talents and virtues, the exercise of which ennobles the human character, and which raise females in the scale of animal being, when they are comprehensively termed mankind;—all those who view them with a philosophic eye must, I should think, wish with me, that they may every day grow more and more masculine.

This discussion naturally divides the subject. I shall first consider women in the grand light of human creatures, who, in common with men, are placed on this earth to unfold their faculties; and afterwards I shall more particularly point out their peculiar designation.

I wish also to steer clear of an error which many respectable writers have fallen into; for the instruction which has hitherto been addressed to women, has rather been applicable to *ladies*, if the little indirect advice, that is scattered through Sandford and Merton,[4] be excepted; but, addressing my sex in a firmer tone, I pay particular attention to those in the middle class, because they appear to be in the most natural state.[5] Perhaps the seeds of false refinement, immorality, and vanity, have ever been shed by the great. Weak, artificial beings, raised above the common wants and affections of their race, in a premature unnatural manner, undermine the very foundation of virtue, and spread corruption through the whole mass of society! As a class of mankind they have the strongest claim to pity; the education of the rich tends to render them vain and helpless, and the unfolding mind is not strengthened by the practice of those duties which dignify the human character.—They only live to amuse themselves, and by the same law which in nature invariably produces certain effects, they soon only afford barren amusement.

3. It was a common but mistaken opinion among Europeans that the Koran, the sacred text of Islam, teaches that women have no souls.
4. *The History of Sandford and Merton*, by Thomas Day, was a very popular story for children, published in three volumes (1786–89). In it a tutor, the Reverend Mr. Barlow, frequently cites the superiority in moral principles of Harry Sandford, the son of a poor farmer, over Tommy Merton, the spoiled son of a rich family.
5. The middle class is viewed as more "natural" than the upper classes because it is uncorrupted by the artificialities of leisure-class life.

But as I purpose taking a separate view of the different ranks of society, and of the moral character of women, in each, this hint is, for the present, sufficient, and I have only alluded to the subject, because it appears to me to be the very essence of an introduction to give a cursory account of the contents of the work it introduces.

My own sex, I hope, will excuse me, if I treat them like rational creatures, instead of flattering their *fascinating* graces, and viewing them as if they were in a state of perpetual childhood, unable to stand alone. I earnestly wish to point out in what true dignity and human happiness consists—I wish to persuade women to endeavor to acquire strength, both of mind and body, and to convince them that the soft phrases, susceptibility of heart, delicacy of sentiment, and refinement of taste, are almost synonymous with epithets of weakness, and that those beings who are only the objects of pity and that kind of love, which has been termed its sister, will soon become objects of contempt.

Dismissing then those pretty feminine phrases, which the men condescendingly use to soften our slavish dependence, and despising that weak elegancy of mind, exquisite sensibility, and sweet docility of manners, supposed to be the sexual characteristics of the weaker vessel, I wish to shew that elegance is inferior to virtue, that the first object of laudable ambition is to obtain a character as a human being, regardless of the distinction of sex; and that secondary views should be brought to this simple touchstone.

This is a rough sketch of my plan; and should I express my conviction with the energetic emotions that I feel whenever I think of the subject, the dictates of experience and reflection will be felt by some of my readers. Animated by this important object, I shall disdain to cull[6] my phrases or polish my style;—I aim at being useful, and sincerity will render me unaffected; for, wishing rather to persuade by the force of my arguments, than dazzle by the elegance of my language, I shall not waste my time in rounding periods,[7] or in fabricating the turgid bombast of artificial feelings, which, coming from the head, never reach the heart. I shall be employed about things, not words!—and, anxious to render my sex more respectable members of society, I shall try to avoid that flowery diction which has slided from essays into novels, and from novels into familiar letters and conversation.

These pretty superlatives, dropping glibly from the tongue, vitiate the taste, and create a kind of sickly delicacy that turns away from simple unadorned truth; and a deluge of false sentiments and over-stretched feelings, stifling the natural emotions of the heart, render the domestic pleasures insipid, that ought to sweeten the exercise of those severe duties, which educate a rational and immortal being for a nobler field of action.

The education of women has, of late, been more attended to than formerly; yet they are still reckoned a frivolous sex, and ridiculed or pitied by the writers who endeavour by satire or instruction to improve them. It is acknowledged that they spend many of the first years of their lives in acquiring a smattering of accomplishments;[8] meanwhile strength of body and mind are sacrificed to libertine notions of beauty, to the desire of establishing themselves,—the only way women can rise in the world,—by marriage. And this desire making mere

---

6. Be selective in.
7. I.e., in rounding out elaborate sentences. "Period": a formal sentence composed of balanced clauses.
8. The lessons in music, dancing, sketching, and needlework that were central elements in the education provided for genteel young ladies and that were supposed to enhance their value on the marriage market.

animals of them, when they marry they act as such children may be expected
to act:—they dress; they paint, and nickname God's creatures.[9]—Surely these
weak beings are only fit for a seraglio![1]—Can they be expected to govern a
family with judgment, or take care of the poor babes whom they bring into
the world?

If then it can be fairly deduced from the present conduct of the sex, from
the prevalent fondness for pleasure which takes place of ambition and those
nobler passions that open and enlarge the soul; that the instruction which
women have hitherto received has only tended, with the constitution of civil
society, to render them insignificant objects of desire—mere propagators of
fools!—if it can be proved that in aiming to accomplish them, without cultivating their understandings, they are taken out of their sphere of duties, and
made ridiculous and useless when the short-lived bloom of beauty is over,[2] I
presume that *rational* men will excuse me for endeavoring to persuade them
to become more masculine and respectable.

Indeed the word masculine is only a bugbear: there is little reason to fear
that women will acquire too much courage or fortitude; for their apparent
inferiority with respect to bodily strength, must render them, in some degree,
dependent on men in the various relations of life; but why should it be
increased by prejudices that give a sex to virtue, and confound simple truths
with sensual reveries?

Women are, in fact, so much degraded by mistaken notions of female excellence, that I do not mean to add a paradox when I assert, that this artificial
weakness produces a propensity to tyrannize, and gives birth to cunning, the
natural opponent of strength, which leads them to play off those contemptible
infantine airs that undermine esteem even whilst they excite desire. Let men
become more chaste and modest, and if women do not grow wiser in the same
ratio it will be clear that they have weaker understandings. It seems scarcely
necessary to say, that I now speak of the sex in general. Many individuals have
more sense than their male relatives; and, as nothing preponderates where
there is a constant struggle for an equilibrium, without[3] it has naturally more
gravity, some women govern their husbands without degrading themselves,
because intellect will always govern.

Chap. 2. The Prevailing Opinion of a Sexual Character Discussed

To account for, and excuse the tyranny of man, many ingenious arguments
have been brought forward to prove, that the two sexes, in the acquirement
of virtue, ought to aim at attaining a very different character: or, to speak
explicitly, women are not allowed to have sufficient strength of mind to acquire
what really deserves the name of virtue. Yet it should seem, allowing them to
have souls, that there is but one way appointed by Providence to lead *mankind*
to either virtue or happiness.

If then women are not a swarm of ephemeron[4] triflers, why should they be

---

9. Hamlet, charging Ophelia with the faults characteristic of women, says: "You jig, you amble, and
you lisp, and / nickname God's creatures, and make
your wantonness your ignorance" (Shakespeare,
Hamlet 3.1.143–45).
1. Harem, the women's quarters in a Muslim
household.
2. A lively writer, I cannot recollect his name, asks
what business women turned of forty have to do in

the world? [Wollstonecraft's note]. Poston, in her
edition of the *Vindication*, suggests that Wollstonecraft is recalling a passage in Frances Burney's novel *Evelina* (1778), where the licentious
Lord Merton exclaims: "I don't know what the devil
a woman lives for after thirty; she is only in other
folks' way."
3. Unless.
4. A flying insect that lives only one day.

kept in ignorance under the specious name of innocence? Men complain, and with reason, of the follies and caprices of our sex, when they do not keenly satirize our headstrong passions and groveling vices.—Behold, I should answer, the natural effect of ignorance! The mind will ever be unstable that has only prejudices to rest on, and the current will run with destructive fury when there are no barriers to break its force. Women are told from their infancy, and taught by the example of their mothers, that a little knowledge of human weakness, justly termed cunning, softness of temper, *outward* obedience, and a scrupulous attention to a puerile kind of propriety, will obtain for them the protection of man; and should they be beautiful, every thing else is needless, for, at least, twenty years of their lives.

Thus Milton describes our first frail mother; though when he tells us that women are formed for softness and sweet attractive grace,[5] I cannot comprehend his meaning, unless, in the true Mahometan strain, he meant to deprive us of souls, and insinuate that we were beings only designed by sweet attractive grace, and docile blind obedience, to gratify the senses of man when he can no longer soar on the wing of contemplation.

How grossly do they insult us who thus advise us only to render ourselves gentle, domestic brutes! For instance, the winning softness so warmly, and frequently, recommended, that governs by obeying. What childish expressions, and how insignificant is the being—can it be an immortal one? who will condescend to govern by such sinister methods! "Certainly," says Lord Bacon, "man is of kin to the beasts by his body; and if he be not of kin to God by his spirit, he is a base and ignoble creature!"[6] Men, indeed, appear to me to act in a very unphilosophical manner when they try to secure the good conduct of women by attempting to keep them always in a state of childhood. Rousseau[7] was more consistent when he wished to stop the progress of reason in both sexes, for if men eat of the tree of knowledge, women will come in for a taste; but, from the imperfect cultivation which their understandings now receive, they only attain a knowledge of evil.

Children, I grant, should be innocent; but when the epithet is applied to men, or women, it is but a civil term for weakness. For if it be allowed that women were destined by Providence to acquire human virtues, and by the exercise of their understandings, that stability of character which is the firmest ground to rest our future hopes upon, they must be permitted to turn to the fountain of light, and not forced to shape their course by the twinkling of a mere satellite. Milton, I grant, was of a very different opinion; for he only bends to the indefeasible right of beauty, though it would be difficult to render two passages which I now mean to contrast, consistent. But into similar inconsistencies are great men often led by their senses.

To whom thus Eve with *perfect beauty* adorn'd.
My Author and Disposer, what thou bidst
Unargued I obey; So God ordains;

---

5. Milton asserts the authority of man over woman, on the grounds that "for contemplation he and valor formed, / For softness she and sweet attractive grace; / He for God only, she for God in him" (*Paradise Lost* 4.298ff.).
6. Francis Bacon's "Of Atheism" (1597).
7. Throughout his writings Jean-Jacques Rousseau (1712–1778) argued against the notion that civilization and rationality brought moral perfec-

tion, proposing that virtuous societies were instead the primitive ones that remained closest to nature. Rousseau's opinions about women, also alluded to in this chapter, are outlined in *Émile* (1762), a blend of educational treatise and novel. In book 5 Rousseau describes the education of the perfect woman, Sophie, brought up to provide Émile with a perfect wife.

> God is *thy law, thou mine*: to know no more
> Is Woman's *happiest* knowledge and her *praise*.[8]

These are exactly the arguments that I have used to children; but I have added, your reason is now gaining strength, and, till it arrives at some degree of maturity, you must look up to me for advice—then you ought to *think*, and only rely on God.

Yet in the following lines Milton seems to coincide with me; when he makes Adam thus expostulate with his Maker.

> Hast thou not made me here thy substitute,
> And these inferior far beneath me set?
> Among *unequals* what society
> Can sort, what harmony or true delight?
> Which must be mutual, in proportion due
> Giv'n and receiv'd; but in *disparity*
> The one intense, the other still remiss
> Cannot well suit with either, but soon prove
> Tedious alike: of *fellowship* I speak
> Such as I seek, fit to participate
> All rational delight[9]—

In treating, therefore, of the manners of women, let us, disregarding sensual arguments, trace what we should endeavor to make them in order to co-operate, if the expression be not too bold, with the supreme Being.

By individual education, I mean, for the sense of the word is not precisely defined, such an attention to a child as will slowly sharpen the senses, form the temper,[1] regulate the passions as they begin to ferment, and set the understanding to work before the body arrives at maturity; so that the man may only have to proceed, not to begin, the important task of learning to think and reason.

To prevent any misconstruction, I must add, that I do not believe that a private education[2] can work the wonders which some sanguine writers have attributed to it. Men and women must be educated, in a great degree, by the opinions and manners of the society they live in. In every age there has been a stream of popular opinion that has carried all before it, and given a family character, as it were, to the century. It may then fairly be inferred, that, till society be differently constituted, much cannot be expected from education. It is, however, sufficient for my present purpose to assert, that, whatever effect circumstances have on the abilities, every being may become virtuous by the exercise of its own reason; for if but one being was created with vicious inclinations, that is positively bad, what can save us from atheism? or if we worship a God, is not that God a devil?

Consequently, the most perfect education, in my opinion, is such an exercise of the understanding as is best calculated to strengthen the body and form the heart. Or, in other words, to enable the individual to attain such habits of virtue as will render it independent. In fact, it is a farce to call any being virtuous whose virtues do not result from the exercise of its own reason. This was Rousseau's opinion respecting men: I extend it to women, and confidently

8. *Paradise Lost* 4.634–38 (Wollstonecraft's italics).
9. *Paradise Lost* 8.381–91 (Wollstonecraft's italics).
1. Temperament, character.
2. Education at home.

assert that they have been drawn out of their sphere by false refinement, and not by an endeavour to acquire masculine qualities. Still the regal homage which they receive is so intoxicating, that till the manners of the times are changed, and formed on more reasonable principles, it may be impossible to convince them that the illegitimate power, which they obtain, by degrading themselves, is a curse, and that they must return to nature and equality, if they wish to secure the placid satisfaction that unsophisticated affections impart. But for this epoch we must wait—wait, perhaps, till kings and nobles, enlightened by reason, and, preferring the real dignity of man to childish state,[3] throw off their gaudy hereditary trappings: and if then women do not resign the arbitrary power of beauty—they will prove that they have *less* mind than man.

I may be accused of arrogance; still I must declare what I firmly believe, that all the writers who have written on the subject of female education and manners from Rousseau to Dr. Gregory,[4] have contributed to render women more artificial, weak characters, than they would otherwise have been; and, consequently, more useless members of society. I might have expressed this conviction in a lower key; but I am afraid it would have been the whine of affectation, and not the faithful expression of my feelings, of the clear result, which experience and reflection have led me to draw. When I come to that division of the subject, I shall advert to the passages that I more particularly disapprove of, in the works of the authors I have just alluded to; but it is first necessary to observe, that my objection extends to the whole purport of those books, which tend, in my opinion, to degrade one half of the human species, and render women pleasing at the expense of every solid virtue.

Though, to reason on Rousseau's ground, if man did attain a degree of perfection of mind when his body arrived at maturity, it might be proper, in order to make a man and his wife *one*, that she should rely entirely on his understanding; and the graceful ivy, clasping the oak that supported it, would form a whole in which strength and beauty would be equally conspicuous. But, alas! husbands, as well as their helpmates, are often only overgrown children; nay, thanks to early debauchery, scarcely men in their outward form— and if the blind lead the blind, one need not come from heaven to tell us the consequence.

Many are the causes that, in the present corrupt state of society, contribute to enslave women by cramping their understandings and sharpening their senses. One, perhaps, that silently does more mischief than all the rest, is their disregard of order.

To do every thing in an orderly manner, is a most important precept, which women, who, generally speaking, receive only a disorderly kind of education, seldom attend to with that degree of exactness that men, who from their infancy are broken into method, observe. This negligent kind of guess-work, for what other epithet can be used to point out the random exertions of a sort of instinctive common sense, never brought to the test of reason? prevents their generalizing matters of fact—so they do to-day, what they did yesterday, merely because they did it yesterday.

This contempt of the understanding in early life has more baneful consequences than is commonly supposed; for the little knowledge which women

3. Pomp, costly display.
4. John Gregory, Scottish author of a widely read book on the education of women, *A Father's Legacy to His Daughters* (1774).

of strong minds attain, is, from various circumstances, of a more desultory kind than the knowledge of men, and it is acquired more by sheer observations on real life, than from comparing what has been individually observed with the results of experience generalized by speculation. Led by their dependent situation and domestic employments more into society, what they learn is rather by snatches; and as learning is with them, in general, only a secondary thing, they do not pursue any one branch with that persevering ardour necessary to give vigor to the faculties, and clearness to the judgment. In the present state of society, a little learning is required to support the character of a gentleman; and boys are obliged to submit to a few years of discipline. But in the education of women, the cultivation of the understanding is always subordinate to the acquirement of some corporeal accomplishment; even while enervated by confinement and false notions of modesty, the body is prevented from attaining that grace and beauty which relaxed half-formed limbs never exhibit. Besides, in youth their faculties are not brought forward by emulation; and having no serious scientific study, if they have natural sagacity it is turned too soon on life and manners. They dwell on effects, and modifications, without tracing them back to causes; and complicated rules to adjust behaviour are a weak substitute for simple principles.

As a proof that education gives this appearance of weakness to females, we may instance the example of military men, who are, like them, sent into the world before their minds have been stored with knowledge or fortified by principles. The consequences are similar; soldiers acquire a little superficial knowledge, snatched from the muddy current of conversation, and, from continually mixing with society, they gain, what is termed a knowledge of the world; and this acquaintance with manners and customs has frequently been confounded with a knowledge of the human heart. But can the crude fruit of casual observation, never brought to the test of judgment, formed by comparing speculation and experience, deserve such a distinction? Soldiers, as well as women, practice the minor virtues with punctilious politeness. Where is then the sexual difference, when the education has been the same? All the difference that I can discern, arises from the superior advantage of liberty, which enables the former to see more of life.

It is wandering from my present subject, perhaps, to make a political remark; but, as it was produced naturally by the train of my reflections, I shall not pass it silently over.

Standing armies can never consist of resolute, robust men; they may be well disciplined machines, but they will seldom contain men under the influence of strong passions, or with very vigorous faculties. And as for any depth of understanding, I will venture to affirm, that it is as rarely to be found in the army as amongst women; and the cause, I maintain, is the same. It may be further observed, that officers are also particularly attentive to their persons, fond of dancing, crowded rooms, adventures, and ridicule.[5] Like the *fair* sex, the business of their lives is gallantry.—They were taught to please, and they only live to please. Yet they do not lose their rank in the distinction of sexes, for they are still reckoned superior to women, though in what their superiority consists, beyond what I have just mentioned, it is difficult to discover.

5. Why should women be censured with petulant acrimony, because they seem to have a passion for a scarlet coat? Has not education placed them more on a level with soldiers than any other class of men? [Wollstonecraft's note].

The great misfortune is this, that they both acquire manners before morals, and a knowledge of life before they have, from reflection, any acquaintance with the grand ideal outline of human nature. The consequence is natural; satisfied with common nature, they become a prey to prejudices, and taking all their opinions on credit, they blindly submit to authority. So that, if they have any sense, it is a kind of instinctive glance, that catches proportions, and decides with respect to manners; but fails when arguments are to be pursued below the surface, or opinions analyzed.

May not the same remark be applied to women? Nay, the argument may be carried still further, for they are both thrown out of a useful station by the unnatural distinctions established in civilized life. Riches and hereditary honours have made cyphers of women to give consequence to the numerical figure;[6] and idleness has produced a mixture of gallantry and despotism into society, which leads the very men who are the slaves of their mistresses to tyrannize over their sisters, wives, and daughters. This is only keeping them in rank and file, it is true. Strengthen the female mind by enlarging it, and there will be an end to blind obedience; but, as blind obedience is ever sought for by power, tyrants and sensualists are in the right when they endeavour to keep women in the dark, because the former only want slaves, and the latter a play-thing. The sensualist, indeed, has been the most dangerous of tyrants, and women have been duped by their lovers, as princes by their ministers, whilst dreaming that they reigned over them.

I now principally allude to Rousseau, for his character of Sophia is, undoubtedly, a captivating one, though it appears to me grossly unnatural; however it is not the superstructure, but the foundation of her character, the principles on which her education was built, that I mean to attack; nay, warmly as I admire the genius of that able writer, whose opinions I shall often have occasion to cite, indignation always takes place of admiration, and the rigid frown of insulted virtue effaces the smile of complacency, which his eloquent periods are wont to raise, when I read his voluptuous reveries. Is this the man, who, in his ardor for virtue, would banish all the soft arts of peace, and almost carry us back to Spartan discipline? Is this the man who delights to paint the useful struggles of passion, the triumphs of good dispositions, and the heroic flights which carry the glowing soul out of itself?—How are these mighty sentiments lowered when he describes the pretty foot and enticing airs of his little favorite! But, for the present, I waive the subject, and, instead of severely reprehending the transient effusions of overweening sensibility, I shall only observe, that whoever has cast a benevolent eye on society, must often have been gratified by the sight of a humble mutual love, not dignified by sentiment, or strengthened by a union in intellectual pursuits. The domestic trifles of the day have afforded matters for cheerful converse, and innocent caresses have softened toils which did not require great exercise of mind or stretch of thought: yet, has not the sight of this moderate felicity excited more tenderness than respect? An emotion similar to what we feel when children are playing, or animals sporting,[7] whilst the contemplation of the noble struggles of suf-

6. Much as a zero added to a number multiplies its value by a factor of ten, in a hierarchical society women magnify the status of the men with whom they are allied.

7. Similar feelings has Milton's pleasing picture of paradisiacal happiness ever raised in my mind; yet, instead of envying the lovely pair, I have, with con-

scious dignity, or Satanic pride, turned to hell for sublimer objects. In the same style, when viewing some noble monument of human art, I have traced the emanation of the Deity in the order I admired, till, descending from that giddy height, I have caught myself contemplating the grandest of all human sights;—for fancy quickly placed, in some fering merit has raised admiration, and carried our thoughts to that world where sensation will give place to reason.

Women are, therefore, to be considered either as moral beings, or so weak that they must be entirely subjected to the superior faculties of men.

Let us examine this question. Rousseau declares that a woman should never, for a moment, feel herself independent, that she should be governed by fear to exercise her natural cunning, and made a coquetish slave in order to render her a more alluring object of desire, a *sweeter* companion to man, whenever he chooses to relax himself. He carries the arguments, which he pretends to draw from the indications of nature, still further, and insinuates that truth and fortitude, the corner stones of all human virtue, should be cultivated with certain restrictions, because, with respect to the female character, obedience is the grand lesson which ought to be impressed with unrelenting rigor.[8]

What nonsense! when will a great man arise with sufficient strength of mind to puff away the fumes which pride and sensuality have thus spread over the subject! If women are by nature inferior to men, their virtues must be the same in quality, if not in degree, or virtue is a relative idea; consequently, their conduct should be founded on the same principles, and have the same aim.

Connected with man as daughters, wives, and mothers, their moral character may be estimated by their manner of fulfilling those simple duties; but the end, the grand end of their exertions should be to unfold their own faculties and acquire the dignity of conscious virtue. They may try to render their road pleasant; but ought never to forget, in common with man, that life yields not the felicity which can satisfy an immortal soul. I do not mean to insinuate, that either sex should be so lost in abstract reflections or distant views, as to forget the affections and duties that lie before them, and are, in truth, the means appointed to produce the fruit of life; on the contrary, I would warmly recommend them, even while I assert, that they afford most satisfaction when they are considered in their true, sober light.

Probably the prevailing opinion, that woman was created for man, may have taken its rise from Moses's poetical story;[9] yet, as very few, it is presumed, who have bestowed any serious thought on the subject, ever supposed that Eve was, literally speaking, one of Adam's ribs, the deduction must be allowed to fall to the ground; or, only be so far admitted as it proves that man, from the remotest antiquity, found it convenient to exert his strength to subjugate his companion, and his invention to shew that she ought to have her neck bent under the yoke, because the whole creation was only created for his convenience or pleasure.

Let it not be concluded that I wish to invert the order of things; I have already granted, that, from the constitution of their bodies, men seem to be designed by Providence to attain a greater degree of virtue.[1] I speak collectively of the whole sex; but I see not the shadow of a reason to conclude that their virtues should differ in respect to their nature. In fact, how can they, if virtue

---

solitary recess, an outcast of fortune, rising superior to passion and discontent [Wollstonecraft's note].

8. Rousseau had written in *Émile*: "What is most wanted in a woman is gentleness; formed to obey a creature so imperfect as man, a creature often vicious and always faulty, she should early learn to submit to injustice and to suffer the wrongs inflicted on her by her husband without com-

plaint."

9. The story of the creation of Eve from the rib of Adam (Genesis 2.21–22). Traditionally, the first five books of the Old Testament were attributed to the authorship of Moses.

1. In the third paragraph of her Introduction (p. 1460 above), Wollstonecraft had said that men are, in general, physically stronger than women.

has only one eternal standard? I must therefore, if I reason consequentially, as strenuously maintain that they have the same simple direction, as that there is a God.

It follows then that cunning should not be opposed to wisdom, little cares to great exertions, or insipid softness, varnished over with the name of gentleness, to that fortitude which grand views alone can inspire.

I shall be told that woman would then lose many of her peculiar graces, and the opinion of a well known poet might be quoted to refute my unqualified assertion. For Pope has said, in the name of the whole male sex,

> Yet ne'er so sure our passion to create,
> As when she touch'd the brink of all we hate.[2]

In what light this sally places men and women, I shall leave to the judicious to determine; meanwhile I shall content myself with observing, that I cannot discover why, unless they are mortal, females should always be degraded by being made subservient to love or lust.

To speak disrespectfully of love is, I know, high treason against sentiment and fine feelings; but I wish to speak the simple language of truth, and rather to address the head than the heart. To endeavor to reason love out of the world, would be to out-Quixote Cervantes,[3] and equally offend against common sense; but an endeavor to restrain this tumultuous passion, and prove that it should not be allowed to dethrone superior powers, or to usurp the sceptre which the understanding should ever coolly wield, appears less wild.

Youth is the season for love in both sexes; but in those days of thoughtless enjoyment provision should be made for the more important years of life, when reflection takes place of sensation. But Rousseau, and most of the male writers who have followed his steps, have warmly inculcated that the whole tendency of female education ought to be directed to one point:—to render them pleasing.

Let me reason with the supporters of this opinion who have any knowledge of human nature, do they imagine that marriage can eradicate the habitude of life? The woman who has only been taught to please will soon find that her charms are oblique sunbeams, and that they cannot have much effect on her husband's heart when they are seen every day, when the summer is passed and gone. Will she then have sufficient native energy to look into herself for comfort, and cultivate her dormant faculties? or, is it not more rational to expect that she will try to please other men; and, in the emotions raised by the expectation of new conquests, endeavor to forget the mortification her love or pride has received? When the husband ceases to be a lover—and the time will inevitably come, her desire of pleasing will then grow languid, or become a spring of bitterness; and love, perhaps, the most evanescent of all passions, gives place to jealousy or vanity.

I now speak of women who are restrained by principle or prejudice; such women, though they would shrink from an intrigue with real abhorrence, yet, nevertheless, wish to be convinced by the homage of gallantry that they are cruelly neglected by their husbands; or, days and weeks are spent in dreaming of the happiness enjoyed by congenial souls till their health is undermined and their spirits broken by discontent. How then can the great art of pleasing

---

2. Alexander Pope's *Moral Essays* 2, "Of the Characters of Women," lines 51–52.

3. I.e., to outdo the hero of Cervantes's *Don Quixote* (1605) in trying to accomplish the impossible.

be such a necessary study? it is only useful to a mistress; the chaste wife, and serious mother, should only consider her power to please as the polish of her virtues, and the affection of her husband as one of the comforts that render her task less difficult and her life happier.—But, whether she be loved or neglected, her first wish should be to make herself respectable,[4] and not to rely for all her happiness on a being subject to like infirmities with herself.

The worthy Dr. Gregory fell into a similar error. I respect his heart; but entirely disapprove of his celebrated Legacy to his Daughters.

He advises them to cultivate a fondness for dress, because a fondness for dress, he asserts, is natural to them. I am unable to comprehend what either he or Rousseau mean, when they frequently use this indefinite term.[5] If they told us that in a pre-existent state the soul was fond of dress, and brought this inclination with it into a new body, I should listen to them with a half smile, as I often do when I hear a rant about innate elegance.—But if he only meant to say that the exercise of the faculties will produce this fondness—I deny it.— It is not natural; but arises, like false ambition in men, from a love of power.

Dr. Gregory goes much further; he actually recommends dissimulation, and advises an innocent girl to give the lie to her feelings, and not dance with spirit, when gaiety of heart would make her feel eloquent without making her gestures immodest. In the name of truth and common sense, why should not one woman acknowledge that she can take more exercise than another? or, in other words, that she has a sound constitution; and why, to damp innocent vivacity, is she darkly to be told that men will draw conclusions which she little thinks of?[6]—Let the libertine draw what inference he pleases; but, I hope, that no sensible mother will restrain the natural frankness of youth by instilling such indecent cautions. Out of the abundance of the heart the mouth speaketh;[7] and a wiser than Solomon hath said, that the heart should be made clean,[8] and not trivial ceremonies observed, which is not very difficult to fulfill with scrupulous exactness when vice reigns in the heart.

Women ought to endeavor to purify their heart; but can they do so when their uncultivated understandings make them entirely dependent on their senses for employment and amusement, when no noble pursuit sets them above the little vanities of the day, or enables them to curb the wild emotions that agitate a reed over which every passing breeze has power? To gain the affections of a virtuous man is affectation necessary? Nature has given woman a weaker frame than man; but, to ensure her husband's affections, must a wife, who by the exercise of her mind and body whilst she was discharging the duties of a daughter, wife, and mother, has allowed her constitution to retain its natural strength, and her nerves a healthy tone, is she, I say, to condescend to use art and feign a sickly delicacy in order to secure her husband's affection? Weakness may excite tenderness, and gratify the arrogant pride of man; but the lordly caresses of a protector will not gratify a noble mind that pants for, and deserves to be respected. Fondness is a poor substitute for friendship!

In a seraglio, I grant, that all these arts are necessary; the epicure must have his palate tickled, or he will sink into apathy; but have women so little ambition

---

4. I.e., morally worthy of respect.
5. I.e., "natural."
6. In *A Father's Legacy to His Daughters*, Gregory had advised a girl, when she dances, not "to forget the delicacy of [her] sex," lest she be "thought to discover a spirit she little dreams of"—i.e., lest she

betray her capacity for physical pleasure.
7. Matthew 12.34.
8. Psalm 51 (attributed to David, the "wiser than Solomon"), 10: "Create in me a clean heart, O God; and renew a right spirit within me."

as to be satisfied with such a condition? Can they supinely dream life away in the lap of pleasure, or the languor of weariness, rather than assert their claim to pursue reasonable pleasures and render themselves conspicuous by practising the virtues which dignify mankind? Surely she has not an immortal soul who can loiter life away merely employed to adorn her person, that she may amuse the languid hours, and soften the cares of a fellow-creature who is willing to be enlivened by her smiles and tricks, when the serious business of life is over.

Besides, the woman who strengthens her body and exercises her mind will, by managing her family and practising various virtues, become the friend, and not the humble dependent of her husband; and if she, by possessing such substantial qualities, merit his regard, she will not find it necessary to conceal her affection, nor to pretend to an unnatural coldness of constitution to excite her husband's passions. In fact, if we revert to history, we shall find that the women who have distinguished themselves have neither been the most beautiful nor the most gentle of their sex.

Nature, or, to speak with strict propriety, God, has made all things right; but man has sought him out many inventions to mar the work. I now allude to that part of Dr. Gregory's treatise, where he advises a wife never to let her husband know the extent of her sensibility or affection. Voluptuous precaution, and as ineffectual as absurd.—Love, from its very nature, must be transitory. To seek for a secret that would render it constant, would be as wild a search as for the philosopher's stone, or the grand panacea:[9] and the discovery would be equally useless, or rather pernicious to mankind. The most holy band of society is friendship. It has been well said, by a shrewd satirist, "that rare as true love is, true friendship is still rarer."[1]

This is an obvious truth, and the cause not lying deep, will not elude a slight glance of inquiry.

Love, the common passion, in which chance and sensation take place of choice and reason, is, in some degree, felt by the mass of mankind; for it is not necessary to speak, at present, of the emotions that rise above or sink below love. This passion, naturally increased by suspense and difficulties, draws the mind out of its accustomed state, and exalts the affections; but the security of marriage, allowing the fever of love to subside, a healthy temperature is thought insipid, only by those who have not sufficient intellect to substitute the calm tenderness of friendship, the confidence of respect, instead of blind admiration, and the sensual emotions of fondness.

This is, must be, the course of nature.—Friendship or indifference inevitably succeeds love.—And this constitution seems perfectly to harmonize with the system of government which prevails in the moral world. Passions are spurs to action, and open the mind; but they sink into mere appetites, become a personal and momentary gratification, when the object is gained, and the satisfied mind rests in enjoyment. The man who had some virtue whilst he was struggling for a crown, often becomes a voluptuous tyrant when it graces his brow; and, when the lover is not lost in the husband, the dotard, a prey to childish caprices, and fond jealousies, neglects the serious duties of life, and

9. A medicine reputed to cure all diseases. "The philosopher's stone," in alchemy, had the power of transmuting base metals into gold.

1. Maxim 473 of La Rochefoucauld (1613–1680), the great French writer of epigrams.

the caresses which should excite confidence in his children are lavished on the overgrown child, his wife.

In order to fulfil the duties of life, and to be able to pursue with vigour the various employments which form the moral character, a master and mistress of a family ought not to continue to love each other with passion. I mean to say, that they ought not to indulge those emotions which disturb the order of society, and engross the thoughts that should be otherwise employed. The mind that has never been engrossed by one object wants vigor—if it can long be so, it is weak.

A mistaken education, a narrow, uncultivated mind, and many sexual prejudices, tend to make women more constant than men; but, for the present, I shall not touch on this branch of the subject. I will go still further, and advance, without dreaming of a paradox, that an unhappy marriage is often very advantageous to a family, and that the neglected wife is, in general, the best mother.[2] And this would almost always be the consequence if the female mind were more enlarged: for, it seems to be the common dispensation of Providence, that what we gain in present enjoyment should be deducted from the treasure of life, experience; and that when we are gathering the flowers of the day and revelling in pleasure, the solid fruit of toil and wisdom should not be caught at the same time. The way lies before us, we must turn to the right or left; and he who will pass life away in bounding from one pleasure to another, must not complain if he acquire neither wisdom nor respectability of character.

Supposing, for a moment, that the soul is not immortal, and that man was only created for the present scene,—I think we should have reason to complain that love, infantine fondness, ever grew insipid and palled upon the sense. Let us eat, drink, and love for to-morrow we die, would be, in fact, the language of reason, the morality of life; and who but a fool would part with a reality for a fleeting shadow? But, if awed by observing the improbable[3] powers of the mind, we disdain to confine our wishes or thoughts to such a comparatively mean field of action; that only appears grand and important, as it is connected with a boundless prospect and sublime hopes, what necessity is there for falsehood in conduct, and why must the sacred majesty of truth be violated to detain a deceitful good that saps the very foundation of virtue? Why must the female mind be tainted by coquetish arts to gratify the sensualist, and prevent love from subsiding into friendship, or compassionate tenderness, when there are not qualities on which friendship can be built? Let the honest heart shew itself, and *reason* teach passion to submit to necessity; or, let the dignified pursuit of virtue and knowledge raise the mind above those emotions which rather imbitter than sweeten the cup of life, when they are not restrained within due bounds.

I do not mean to allude to the romantic passion, which is the concomitant of genius.—Who can clip its wing? But that grand passion not proportioned to the puny enjoyments of life, is only true to the sentiment, and feeds on itself. The passions which have been celebrated for their durability have always been unfortunate. They have acquired strength by absence and constitutional melancholy.—The fancy has hovered around a form of beauty dimly seen—

2. Wollstonecraft's point is that a woman who is not preoccupied with her husband (and his attentions to her) has more time and attention for her children.

3. Poston points out that this may be a misprint in the second edition for "improvable," which occurs in the first edition.

but familiarity might have turned admiration into disgust; or, at least, into indifference, and allowed the imagination leisure to start fresh game. With perfect propriety, according to his view of things, does Rousseau make the mistress of his soul, Eloisa, love St. Preux, when life was fading before her;[4] but this is no proof of the immortality of the passion.

Of the same complexion is Dr. Gregory's advice respecting delicacy of sentiment,[5] which he advises a woman not to acquire, if she have determined to marry. This determination, however, perfectly consistent with his former advice, he calls *indelicate*, and earnestly persuades his daughters to conceal it, though it may govern their conduct;—as if it were indelicate to have the common appetites of human nature.

Noble morality! and consistent with the cautious prudence of a little soul that cannot extend its views beyond the present minute division of existence. If all the faculties of woman's mind are only to be cultivated as they respect her dependence on man; if, when a husband be obtained, she have arrived at her goal, and meanly proud rests satisfied with such a paltry crown, let her grovel contentedly, scarcely raised by her employments above the animal kingdom; but, if, struggling for the prize of her high calling,[6] she look beyond the present scene, let her cultivate her understanding without stopping to consider what character the husband may have whom she is destined to marry. Let her only determine, without being too anxious about present happiness, to acquire the qualities that ennoble a rational being, and a rough inelegant husband may shock her taste without destroying her peace of mind. She will not model her soul to suit the frailties of her companion, but to bear with them: his character may be a trial, but not an impediment to virtue.

If Dr. Gregory confined his remark to romantic expectations of constant love and congenial feelings, he should have recollected that experience will banish what advice can never make us cease to wish for, when the imagination is kept alive at the expence of reason.

I own it frequently happens that women who have fostered a romantic unnatural delicacy of feeling, waste their[7] lives in *imagining* how happy they should have been with a husband who could love them with a fervid increasing affection every day, and all day. But they might as well pine married as single— and would not be a jot more unhappy with a bad husband than longing for a good one. That a proper education; or, to speak with more precision, a well stored mind, would enable a woman to support a single life with dignity, I grant; but that she should avoid cultivating her taste, lest her husband should occasionally shock it, is quitting a substance for a shadow. To say the truth, I do not know of what use is an improved taste, if the individual be not rendered more independent of the casualties of life; if new sources of enjoyment, only dependent on the solitary operations of the mind, are not opened. People of taste, married or single, without distinction, will ever be disgusted by various things that touch not less observing minds. On this conclusion the argument

4. In Rousseau's *Julie, ou la Nouvelle Héloise* (1761), Julie, after a life of fidelity to her husband, reveals on her deathbed that she has never lost her passion for St. Preux, her lover when she was young. Wollstonecraft accepts the common opinion that Julie represents Madame d'Houdetot, with whom Rousseau was in love when he wrote the novel.
5. I.e., too elevated and refined a notion of what to expect in a man.
6. An echo of Philippians 3.14, where St. Paul writes, "I press toward the mark for the prize of the high calling of God in Christ Jesus."
7. For example, the herd of Novelists [Wollstonecraft's note]. The author's reference is to women who have formed their expectations of love as it is misrepresented in the sentimental novels of their time.

must not be allowed to hinge; but in the whole sum of enjoyment is taste to be denominated a blessing?

The question is, whether it procures most pain or pleasure? The answer will decide the propriety of Dr. Gregory's advice, and shew how absurd and tyrannic it is thus to lay down a system of slavery; or to attempt to educate moral beings by any other rules than those deduced from pure reason, which apply to the whole species.

Gentleness of manners, forbearance, and long-suffering, are such amiable Godlike qualities, that in sublime poetic strains the Deity has been invested with them; and, perhaps, no representation of his goodness so strongly fastens on the human affections as those that represent him abundant in mercy and willing to pardon. Gentleness, considered in this point of view, bears on its front all the characteristics of grandeur, combined with the winning graces of condescension; but what a different aspect it assumes when it is the submissive demeanour of dependence, the support of weakness that loves, because it wants protection; and is forbearing, because it must silently endure injuries; smiling under the lash at which it dare not snarl. Abject as this picture appears, it is the portrait of an accomplished woman, according to the received opinion of female excellence, separated by specious reasoners from human excellence. Or, they[8] kindly restore the rib, and make one moral being of a man and woman; not forgetting to give her all the "submissive charms."[9] How women are to exist in that state where there is to be neither marrying nor giving in marriage,[1] we are not told. For though moralists have agreed that the tenor of life seems to prove that *man* is prepared by various circumstances for a future state, they constantly concur in advising *woman* only to provide for the present. Gentleness, docility, and a spaniel-like affection are, on this ground, consistently recommended as the cardinal virtues of the sex; and, disregarding the arbitrary economy of nature, one writer has declared that it is masculine for a woman to be melancholy. She was created to be the toy of man, his rattle, and it must jingle in his ears whenever, dismissing reason, he chooses to be amused.

To recommend gentleness, indeed, on a broad basis is strictly philosophical. A frail being should labor to be gentle. But when forbearance confounds right and wrong, it ceases to be a virtue; and, however convenient it may be found in a companion—that companion will ever be considered as an inferior, and only inspire a vapid tenderness, which easily degenerates into contempt. Still, if advice could really make a being gentle, whose natural disposition admitted not of such a fine polish, something towards the advancement of order would be attained; but if, as might quickly be demonstrated, only affectation be produced by this indiscriminate counsel, which throws a stumbling-block in the way of gradual improvement, and true melioration of temper, the sex is not much benefited by sacrificing solid virtues to the attainment of superficial graces, though for a few years they may procure the individuals regal sway.

As a philosopher, I read with indignation the plausible epithets which men use to soften their insults; and, as a moralist, I ask what is meant by such

<hr/>

8. *Vide* [see] Rousseau and Swedenborg [Wollstonecraft's note]. Rousseau's view was that a wife constituted an integral moral being only in concert with her husband. Emanuel Swedenborg (1688–1772), the Swedish theosophist, held that in the married state in heaven male and female are embodied in a single angelic form.

9. Milton says of Adam and Eve in *Paradise Lost* 4.497–99 that "he in delight / Both of her beauty and submissive charms / Smiled with superior love."

1. "For in the resurrection they neither marry, nor are given in marriage, but are as the angels of God in heaven" (Matthew 22.30).

heterogeneous associations, as fair defects, amiable weaknesses, &c.?[2] If there be but one criterion of morals, but one archetype of man, women appear to be suspended by destiny, according to the vulgar tale of Mahomet's coffin;[3] they have neither the unerring instinct of brutes, nor are allowed to fix the eye of reason on a perfect model. They were made to be loved, and must not aim at respect, lest they should be hunted out of society as masculine.

But to view the subject in another point of view. Do passive indolent women make the best wives? Confining our discussion to the present moment of existence, let us see how such weak creatures perform their part. Do the women who, by the attainment of a few superficial accomplishments, have strengthened the prevailing prejudice, merely contribute to the happiness of their husbands? Do they display their charms merely to amuse them? And have women, who have early imbibed notions of passive obedience, sufficient character to manage a family or educate children? So far from it, that, after surveying the history of woman, I cannot help, agreeing with the severest satirist, considering the sex as the weakest as well as the most oppressed half of the species. What does history disclose but marks of inferiority, and how few women have emancipated themselves from the galling yoke of sovereign man?—So few, that the exceptions remind me of an ingenious conjecture respecting Newton: that he was probably a being of a superior order, accidentally caged in a human body.[4] Following the same train of thinking, I have been led to imagine that the few extraordinary women who have rushed in eccentrical directions out of the orbit prescribed to their sex, were *male* spirits, confined by mistake in female frames. But if it be not philosophical to think of sex when the soul is mentioned, the inferiority must depend on the organs; or the heavenly fire, which is to ferment the clay, is not given in equal portions.

But avoiding, as I have hitherto done, any direct comparison of the two sexes collectively, or frankly acknowledging the inferiority of woman, according to the present appearance of things, I shall only insist that men have increased that inferiority till women are almost sunk below the standard of rational creatures. Let their faculties have room to unfold, and their virtues to gain strength, and then determine where the whole sex must stand in the intellectual scale. Yet let it be remembered, that for a small number of distinguished women I do not ask a place.

It is difficult for us purblind mortals to say to what height human discoveries and improvements may arrive when the gloom of despotism subsides, which makes us stumble at every step; but, when morality shall be settled on a more solid basis, then, without being gifted with a prophetic spirit, I will venture to predict that woman will be either the friend or slave of man. We shall not, as at present, doubt whether she is a moral agent, or the link which unites man with brutes.[5] But, should it then appear, that like the brutes they were prin-

2. In *Paradise Lost* 10.891–92 the fallen Adam refers to Eve as "this fair defect / Of Nature"; and in *Moral Essays* 2.43 Pope describes women as "Fine by defect, and delicately weak."
3. A legend has it that Muhammad's coffin hovers suspended in his tomb.
4. A possible reminiscence of Pope's *An Essay on Man* 2.31–34: "Superior beings [i.e., angels] . . . / Admired such wisdom in an earthly shape, / And showed a Newton as we show an ape."
5. Rousseau doubted that a woman, of herself, was a moral agent. There had been a long dispute

about the question of woman being part of humankind. In the *Summa Theologica* (Question XVII, Art. 1) St. Thomas Aquinas concedes, with Aristotle, that the "production of woman comes from a defect in the active power, or from some material indisposition, or even from some external influence, such as that of a south wind, which is moist" (English Dominican translation of St. Thomas, edited by Anton C. Pegis, *The Basic Writings of Saint Thomas Aquinas* [New York, 1945], I, 880) [Poston's note].

cipally created for the use of man, he will let them patiently bite the bridle, and not mock them with empty praise; or, should their rationality be proved, he will not impede their improvement merely to gratify his sensual appetites. He will not, with all the graces of rhetoric, advise them to submit implicitly their understanding to the guidance of man. He will not, when he treats of the education of women, assert that they ought never to have the free use of reason, nor would he recommend cunning and dissimulation to beings who are acquiring, in like manner as himself, the virtues of humanity.

Surely there can be but one rule of right, if morality has an eternal foundation, and whoever sacrifices virtue, strictly so called, to present convenience, or whose *duty* it is to act in such a manner, lives only for the passing day, and cannot be an accountable creature.

The poet then should have dropped his sneer when he says,

> If weak women go astray,
> The stars are more in fault than they.[6]

For that they are bound by the adamantine chain of destiny is most certain, if it be proved that they are never to exercise their own reason, never to be independent, never to rise above opinion, or to feel the dignity of a rational will that only bows to God, and often forgets that the universe contains any being but itself and the model of perfection to which its ardent gaze is turned, to adore attributes that, softened into virtues, may be imitated in kind, though the degree overwhelms the enraptured mind.

If, I say, for I would not impress by declamation when Reason offers her sober light, if they be really capable of acting like rational creatures, let them not be treated like slaves; or, like the brutes who are dependent on the reason of man, when they associate with him; but cultivate their minds, give them the salutary, sublime curb of principle, and let them attain conscious dignity by feeling themselves only dependent on God. Teach them, in common with man, to submit to necessity, instead of giving, to render them more pleasing, a sex to morals.

Further, should experience prove that they cannot attain the same degree of strength of mind, perseverance, and fortitude, let their virtues be the same in kind, though they may vainly struggle for the same degree; and the superiority of man will be equally clear, if not clearer; and truth, as it is a simple principle, which admits of no modification, would be common to both. Nay, the order of society as it is at present regulated would not be inverted, for woman would then only have the rank that reason assigned her, and arts could not be practised to bring the balance even, much less to turn it.

These may be termed Utopian dreams.—Thanks to that Being who impressed them on my soul, and gave me sufficient strength of mind to dare to exert my own reason, till, becoming dependent only on him for the support of my virtue, I view, with indignation, the mistaken notions that enslave my sex.

I love man as my fellow; but his scepter, real or usurped, extends not to me, unless the reason of an individual demands my homage; and even then the submission is to reason, and not to man. In fact, the conduct of an accountable being must be regulated by the operations of its own reason; or on what foundation rests the throne of God?

---

6. Matthew Prior, "Hans Carvel," lines 11–12, alluding to Shakespeare's *Julius Caesar* 1.2.141–42: "The fault, dear Brutus, is not in our stars, / But in ourselves."

It appears to me necessary to dwell on these obvious truths, because females have been insulated, as it were; and, while they have been stripped of the virtues that should clothe humanity, they have been decked with artificial graces that enable them to exercise a short-lived tyranny. Love, in their bosoms, taking place of every nobler passion, their sole ambition is to be fair, to raise emotion instead of inspiring respect; and this ignoble desire, like the servility in absolute monarchies, destroys all strength of character. Liberty is the mother of virtue, and if women be, by their very constitution, slaves, and not allowed to breathe the sharp invigorating air of freedom, they must ever languish like exotics,[7] and be reckoned beautiful flaws in nature.

As to the argument respecting the subjection in which the sex has ever been held, it retorts on man. The many have always been enthralled by the few; and monsters, who scarcely have shewn any discernment of human excellence, have tyrannized over thousands of their fellow-creatures. Why have men of superiour endowments submitted to such degradation? For, is it not universally acknowledged that kings, viewed collectively, have ever been inferior, in abilities and virtue, to the same number of men taken from the common mass of mankind—yet, have they not, and are they not still treated with a degree of reverence that is an insult to reason? China is not the only country where a living man has been made a God.[8] *Men* have submitted to superior strength to enjoy with impunity the pleasure of the moment—*women* have only done the same, and therefore till it is proved that the courtier, who servilely resigns the birthright of a man, is not a moral agent, it cannot be demonstrated that woman is essentially inferior to man because she has always been subjugated.

Brutal force has hitherto governed the world, and that the science of politics is in its infancy, is evident from philosophers scrupling to give the knowledge most useful to man that determinate distinction.

I shall not pursue this argument any further than to establish an obvious inference, that as sound politics diffuse liberty, mankind, including woman, will become more wise and virtuous.

From *Chap. 4. Observations on the State of Degradation to Which Woman Is Reduced by Various Causes*

* * *

In the middle rank of life, to continue the comparison,[9] men, in their youth, are prepared for professions, and marriage is not considered as the grand feature in their lives; whilst women, on the contrary, have no other scheme to sharpen their faculties. It is not business, extensive plans, or any of the excursive flights of ambition, that engross their attention; no, their thoughts are not employed in rearing such noble structures. To rise in the world, and have the liberty of running from pleasure to pleasure, they must marry advantageously, and to this object their time is sacrificed, and their persons often legally prostituted. A man when he enters any profession has his eye steadily fixed on some future advantage (and the mind gains great strength by having all its efforts directed to one point), and, full of his business, pleasure is considered

---

7. Hot-house plants, which do not thrive in the English climate. There is also an echo here of the language of the Mansfield Judgment of 1772, the legal decision that effectually prohibited slavery within England by declaring "the air of England . . . too pure for slaves to breathe in."

8. The emperors of China were regarded as deities.

9. I.e., her comparison between the social expectations that shape men and those that shape women and lead them to "degradation."

as mere relaxation; whilst women seek for pleasure as the main purpose of existence. In fact, from the education, which they receive from society, the love of pleasure may be said to govern them all; but does this prove that there is a sex in souls? It would be just as rational to declare that the courtiers in France, when a destructive system of despotism had formed their character, were not men, because liberty, virtue, and humanity, were sacrificed to pleasure and vanity.—Fatal passions, which have ever domineered over the *whole* race!

The same love of pleasure, fostered by the whole tendency of their education, gives a trifling turn to the conduct of women in most circumstances: for instance, they are ever anxious about secondary things; and on the watch for adventures, instead of being occupied by duties.

A man, when he undertakes a journey, has, in general, the end in view; a woman thinks more of the incidental occurrences, the strange things that may possibly occur on the road; the impression that she may make on her fellow-travellers; and, above all, she is anxiously intent on the care of the finery that she carries with her, which is more than ever a part of herself, when going to figure on a new scene; when, to use an apt French turn of expression, she is going to produce a sensation.—Can dignity of mind exist with such trivial cares?

In short, women, in general, as well as the rich of both sexes, have acquired all the follies and vices of civilization, and missed the useful fruit. It is not necessary for me always to premise, that I speak of the condition of the whole sex, leaving exceptions out of the question. Their senses are inflamed, and their understandings neglected, consequently they become the prey of their senses, delicately termed sensibility, and are blown about by every momentary gust of feeling. Civilized women are, therefore, so weakened by false refinement, that, respecting morals, their condition is much below what it would be were they left in a state nearer to nature. Ever restless and anxious, their over exercised sensibility not only renders them uncomfortable themselves, but troublesome, to use a soft phrase, to others. All their thoughts turn on things calculated to excite emotion; and feeling, when they should reason, their conduct is unstable, and their opinions are wavering—not the wavering produced by deliberation or progressive views, but by contradictory emotions. By fits and starts they are warm in many pursuits; yet this warmth, never concentrated into perseverance, soon exhausts itself; exhaled by its own heat, or meeting with some other fleeting passion, to which reason has never given any specific gravity, neutrality ensues. Miserable, indeed, must be that being whose cultivation of mind has only tended to inflame its passions! A distinction should be made between inflaming and strengthening them. The passions thus pampered, whilst the judgment is left unformed, what can be expected to ensue?—Undoubtedly, a mixture of madness and folly!

This observation should not be confined to the *fair* sex; however, at present, I only mean to apply it to them.

Novels, music, poetry, and gallantry, all tend to make women the creatures of sensation, and their character is thus formed in the mold of folly during the time they are acquiring accomplishments, the only improvement they are excited, by their station in society, to acquire. This overstretched sensibility naturally relaxes the other powers of the mind, and prevents intellect from attaining that sovereignty which it ought to attain to render a rational creature useful to others, and content with its own station: for the exercise of the understanding, as life advances, is the only method pointed out by nature to calm the passions.

Satiety has a very different effect, and I have often been forcibly struck by an emphatical description of damnation:—when the spirit is represented as continually hovering with abortive eagerness round the defiled body, unable to enjoy any thing without the organs of sense. Yet, to their senses, are women made slaves, because it is by their sensibility that they obtain present power.

And will moralists pretend to assert, that this is the condition in which one half of the human race should be encouraged to remain with listless inactivity and stupid acquiescence? Kind instructors! what were we created for? To remain, it may be said, innocent; they mean in a state of childhood.—We might as well never have been born, unless it were necessary that we should be created to enable man to acquire the noble privilege of reason, the power of discerning good from evil, whilst we lie down in the dust from whence we were taken, never to rise again.—

It would be an endless task to trace the variety of meannesses, cares, and sorrows, into which women are plunged by the prevailing opinion, that they were created rather to feel than reason, and that all the power they obtain, must be obtained by their charms and weakness:

Fine by defect, and amiably weak![1]

And, made by this amiable weakness entirely dependent, excepting what they gain by illicit sway, on man, not only for protection, but advice, is it surprising that, neglecting the duties that reason alone points out, and shrinking from trials calculated to strengthen their minds, they only exert themselves to give their defects a graceful covering, which may serve to heighten their charms in the eye of the voluptuary, though it sink them below the scale of moral excellence?

Fragile in every sense of the word, they are obliged to look up to man for every comfort. In the most trifling dangers they cling to their support, with parasitical tenacity, piteously demanding succour; and their *natural* protector extends his arm, or lifts up his voice, to guard the lovely trembler—from what? Perhaps the frown of an old cow, or the jump of a mouse; a rat, would be a serious danger. In the name of reason, and even common sense, what can save such beings from contempt; even though they be soft and fair?

These fears, when not affected, may produce some pretty attitudes; but they shew a degree of imbecility which degrades a rational creature in a way women are not aware of—for love and esteem are very distinct things.

I am fully persuaded that we should hear of none of these infantine airs, if girls were allowed to take sufficient exercise, and not confined in close rooms till their muscles are relaxed, and their powers of digestion destroyed. To carry the remark still further, if fear in girls, instead of being cherished, perhaps, created, were treated in the same manner as cowardice in boys, we should quickly see women with more dignified aspects. It is true, they could not then with equal propriety be termed the sweet flowers that smile in the walk of man; but they would be more respectable members of society, and discharge the important duties of life by the light of their own reason. "Educate women like men," says Rousseau, "and the more they resemble our sex the less power

---

1. Pope's actual words were "Fine by defect, and delicately weak" (*Moral Essays* 2.43).

will they have over us."[2] This is the very point I aim at. I do not wish them to have power over men; but over themselves.

In the same strain have I heard men argue against instructing the poor; for many are the forms that aristocracy assumes. "Teach them to read, and write," say they, "and you take them out of the station assigned them by nature." An eloquent Frenchman has answered them, I will borrow his sentiments. But they know not, when they make man a brute, that they may expect every instant to see him transformed into a ferocious beast.[3] Without knowledge there can be no morality!

Ignorance is a frail base for virtue! Yet, that it is the condition for which woman was organized, has been insisted upon by the writers who have most vehemently argued in favor of the superiority of man; a superiority not in degree, but essence; though, to soften the argument, they have labored to prove, with chivalrous generosity, that the sexes ought not to be compared; man was made to reason, woman to feel: and that together, flesh and spirit, they make the most perfect whole, by blending happily reason and sensibility into one character.

And what is sensibility? "Quickness of sensation; quickness of perception; delicacy." Thus is it defined by Dr. Johnson;[4] and the definition gives me no other idea than of the most exquisitely polished instinct. I discern not a trace of the image of God in either sensation or matter. Refined seventy times seven,[5] they are still material; intellect dwells not there; nor will fire ever make lead gold!

I come round to my old argument; if woman be allowed to have an immortal soul, she must have, as the employment of life, an understanding to improve. And when, to render the present state more complete, though every thing proves it to be but a fraction of a mighty sum, she is incited by present gratification to forget her grand destination, nature is counteracted, or she was born only to procreate and rot. Or, granting brutes, of every description, a soul, though not a reasonable one, the exercise of instinct and sensibility may be the step, which they are to take, in this life, towards the attainment of reason in the next; so that through all eternity they will lag behind man, who, why we cannot tell, had the power given him of attaining reason in his first mode of existence.

When I treat of the peculiar duties of women, as I should treat of the peculiar duties of a citizen or father, it will be found that I do not mean to insinuate that they should be taken out of their families, speaking of the majority. "He that hath wife and children," says Lord Bacon, "hath given hostages to fortune; for they are impediments to great enterprises, either of virtue or mischief. Certainly the best works, and of greatest merit for the public, have proceeded from the unmarried or childless men."[6] I say the same of women. But, the welfare of society is not built on extraordinary exertions; and were it more reasonably organized, there would be still less need of great abilities, or heroic virtues.

2. In *Émile* Rousseau means this as a warning to women that if they are brought up to be like men, they will lose their sexual power over men.
3. Poston suggests that Wollstonecraft has in mind the comment by Mirabeau, the Revolutionary statesman, to the Abbé Sieyès, who had been rudely treated in the French Constituent Assembly in 1790: "My dear abbé, you have loosed the bull: do you expect he is not to make use of his horns?"

4. In his *Dictionary of the English Language* (1755).
5. Jesus replies, when asked whether a brother's repeated sin should be forgiven "till seven times": "I say not unto thee, Until seven times: but, Until seventy times seven" (Matthew 18.22).
6. From Francis Bacon's essay "Of Marriage and the Single Life."

In the regulation of a family, in the education of children, understanding, in an unsophisticated sense, is particularly required: strength both of body and mind; yet the men who, by their writings, have most earnestly labored to domesticate women, have endeavored, by arguments dictated by a gross appetite, which satiety had rendered fastidious, to weaken their bodies and cramp their minds. But, if even by these sinister methods they really *persuaded* women, by working on their feelings, to stay at home, and fulfil the duties of a mother and mistress of a family, I should cautiously oppose opinions that led women to right conduct, by prevailing on them to make the discharge of such important duties the main business of life, though reason were insulted. Yet, and I appeal to experience, if by neglecting the understanding they be as much, nay, more detached from these domestic employments, than they could be by the most serious intellectual pursuit, though it may be observed, that the mass of mankind will never vigorously pursue an intellectual object,[7] I may be allowed to infer that reason is absolutely necessary to enable a woman to perform any duty properly, and I must again repeat, that sensibility is not reason.

The comparison with the rich still occurs to me; for, when men neglect the duties of humanity, women will follow their example; a common stream hurries them both along with thoughtless celerity. Riches and honors prevent a man from enlarging his understanding, and enervate all his powers by reversing the order of nature, which has ever made true pleasure the reward of labor. Pleasure—enervating pleasure is, likewise, within women's reach without earning it. But, till hereditary possessions are spread abroad, how can we expect men to be proud of virtue? And, till they are, women will govern them by the most direct means, neglecting their dull domestic duties to catch the pleasure that sits lightly on the wing of time.

"The power of the woman," says some author, "is her sensibility";[8] and men, not aware of the consequence, do all they can to make this power swallow up every other. Those who constantly employ their sensibility will have most: for example; poets, painters, and composers.[9] Yet, when the sensibility is thus increased at the expence of reason, and even the imagination, why do philosophical men complain of their fickleness? The sexual attention of man particularly acts on female sensibility, and this sympathy has been exercised from their youth up. A husband cannot long pay those attentions with the passion necessary to excite lively emotions, and the heart, accustomed to lively emotions, turns to a new lover, or pines in secret, the prey of virtue or prudence. I mean when the heart has really been rendered susceptible, and the taste formed; for I am apt to conclude, from what I have seen in fashionable life, that vanity is oftener fostered than sensibility by the mode of education, and the intercourse between the sexes, which I have reprobated; and that coquetry more frequently proceeds from vanity than from that inconstancy, which overstrained sensibility naturally produces.

Another argument that has had great weight with me, must, I think, have

---

7. The mass of mankind are rather the slaves of their appetites than of their passions [Wollstonecraft's note].
8. The sentiment is a commonplace, but Wollstonecraft may be referring to Edmund Burke's phrase: "The beauty of women is considerably owing to their weakness, or delicacy . . ." (Edmund Burke, *A Philosophical Enquiry into the Origin of Our Ideas of the Sublime and Beautiful* [London,

1759 (repr. The Scolar Press, 1970)], p. 219) [Poston's note].
9. Men of these descriptions pour it into their compositions, to amalgamate the gross materials; and, molding them with passion, give to the inert body a soul; but, in woman's imagination, love alone concentrates these ethereal beams [Wollstonecraft's note].

some force with every considerate benevolent heart. Girls who have been thus weakly educated, are often cruelly left by their parents without any provision; and, of course, are dependent on, not only the reason, but the bounty of their brothers. These brothers are, to view the fairest side of the question, good sort of men, and give as a favor, what children of the same parents had an equal right to. In this equivocal humiliating situation, a docile female may remain some time, with a tolerable degree of comfort. But, when the brother marries, a probable circumstance, from being considered as the mistress of the family, she is viewed with averted looks as an intruder, an unnecessary burden on the benevolence of the master of the house, and his new partner.

Who can recount the misery, which many unfortunate beings, whose minds and bodies are equally weak, suffer in such situations—unable to work, and ashamed to beg? The wife, a cold-hearted, narrow-minded, woman, and this is not an unfair supposition; for the present mode of education does not tend to enlarge the heart any more than the understanding, is jealous of the little kindness which her husband shews to his relations; and her sensibility not rising to humanity, she is displeased at seeing the property of *her* children lavished on an helpless sister.

These are matters of fact, which have come under my eye again and again. The consequence is obvious, the wife has recourse to cunning to undermine the habitual affection, which she is afraid openly to oppose; and neither tears nor caresses are spared till the spy is worked out of her home, and thrown on the world, unprepared for its difficulties; or sent, as a great effort of generosity, or from some regard to propriety, with a small stipend, and an uncultivated mind, into joyless solitude.

These two women may be much upon a par, with respect to reason and humanity; and changing situations, might have acted just the same selfish part; but had they been differently educated, the case would also have been very different. The wife would not have had that sensibility, of which self is the centre, and reason might have taught her not to expect, and not even to be flattered by, the affection of her husband, if it led him to violate prior duties. She would wish not to love him merely because he loved her, but on account of his virtues; and the sister might have been able to struggle for herself instead of eating the bitter bread of dependence.

I am, indeed, persuaded that the heart, as well as the understanding, is opened by cultivation; and by, which may not appear so clear, strengthening the organs; I am not now talking of momentary flashes of sensibility, but of affections. And, perhaps, in the education of both sexes, the most difficult task is so to adjust instruction as not to narrow the understanding, whilst the heart is warmed by the generous juices of spring, just raised by the electric fermentation of the season; nor to dry up the feelings by employing the mind in investigations remote from life.

With respect to women, when they receive a careful education, they are either made fine ladies, brimful of sensibility, and teeming with capricious fancies; or mere notable women.[1] The latter are often friendly, honest creatures, and have a shrewd kind of good sense joined with worldly prudence, that often render them more useful members of society than the fine sentimental lady, though they possess neither greatness of mind nor taste. The intellectual world is shut against them; take them out of their family or neigh-

1. I.e., energetic in running a household.

borhood, and they stand still; the mind finding no employment, for literature affords a fund of amusement which they have never sought to relish, but frequently to despise. The sentiments and taste of more cultivated minds appear ridiculous, even in those whom chance and family connections have led them to love; but in mere acquaintance they think it all affectation.

A man of sense can only love such a woman on account of her sex, and respect her, because she is a trusty servant. He lets her, to preserve his own peace, scold the servants, and go to church in clothes made of the very best materials. A man of her own size of understanding would, probably, not agree so well with her; for he might wish to encroach on her prerogative, and manage some domestic concerns himself. Yet women, whose minds are not enlarged by cultivation, or the natural selfishness of sensibility expanded by reflection, are very unfit to manage a family; for, by an undue stretch of power, they are always tyrannizing to support a superiority that only rests on the arbitrary distinction of fortune. The evil is sometimes more serious, and domestics are deprived of innocent indulgences, and made to work beyond their strength, in order to enable the notable woman to keep a better table, and outshine her neighbours in finery and parade. If she attend to her children, it is, in general, to dress them in a costly manner—and, whether this attention arise from vanity or fondness, it is equally pernicious.

Besides, how many women of this description pass their days; or, at least, their evenings, discontentedly. Their husbands acknowledge that they are good managers, and chaste wives; but leave home to seek for more agreeable, may I be allowed to use a significant French word, *piquant*[2] society; and the patient drudge, who fulfils her task, like a blind horse in a mill, is defrauded of her just reward; for the wages due to her are the caresses of her husband; and women who have so few resources in themselves, do not very patiently bear this privation of a natural right.

A fine lady, on the contrary, has been taught to look down with contempt on the vulgar employments of life; though she has only been incited to acquire accomplishments that rise a degree above sense; for even corporeal accomplishments cannot be acquired with any degree of precision unless the understanding has been strengthened by exercise. Without a foundation of principles taste is superficial, grace must arise from something deeper than imitation. The imagination, however, is heated, and the feelings rendered fastidious, if not sophisticated; or, a counterpoise of judgment is not acquired, when the heart still remains artless, though it becomes too tender.

These women are often amiable; and their hearts are really more sensible to general benevolence, more alive to the sentiments that civilize life, than the square-elbowed family drudge; but, wanting a due proportion of reflection and self-government, they only inspire love; and are the mistresses of their husbands, whilst they have any hold on their affections; and the platonic friends of his male acquaintance. These are the fair defects in nature; the women who appear to be created not to enjoy the fellowship of man, but to save him from sinking into absolute brutality, by rubbing off the rough angles of his character; and by playful dalliance to give some dignity to the appetite that draws him to them.—Gracious Creator of the whole human race! hast thou created such a being as woman, who can trace thy wisdom in thy works, and feel that thou alone art by thy nature exalted above her,—for no better purpose?—Can she

2. Stimulating.

believe that she was only made to submit to man, her equal, a being, who, like her, was sent into the world to acquire virtue?—Can she consent to be occupied merely to please him; merely to adorn the earth, when her soul is capable of rising to thee?—And can she rest supinely dependent on man for reason, when she ought to mount with him the arduous steeps of knowledge?—

Yet, if love be the supreme good, let women be only educated to inspire it, and let every charm be polished to intoxicate the senses; but, if they be moral beings, let them have a chance to become intelligent; and let love to man be only a part of that glowing flame of universal love, which, after encircling humanity, mounts in grateful incense to God.

* * *

1792

WILLIAM WORDSWORTH
1770–1850

William Wordsworth was born in Cockermouth in West Cumberland, just on the northern fringe of the English Lake District. When his mother died, the eight-year-old boy was sent to school at Hawkshead, near Esthwaite Lake, in the heart of that sparsely populated region that he and Coleridge were to transform into one of the poetic centers of England. William and his three brothers boarded in the cottage of Ann Tyson, who gave the boys simple comfort, ample affection, and freedom to roam the countryside at will. A vigorous, unruly, and sometimes moody boy, William spent his free days and occasionally "half the night" in the sports and rambles described in the first two books of *The Prelude*, "drinking in" (to use one of his favorite metaphors) the natural sights and sounds, and getting to know the cottagers, shepherds, and solitary wanderers who moved through his imagination into his later poetry. He also found time to read voraciously in the books owned by his young headmaster, William Taylor, who encouraged him in his inclination to poetry.

John Wordsworth, the poet's father, died suddenly when William was thirteen, leaving to his five children mainly the substantial sum owed him by Lord Lonsdale, whom he had served as attorney and as steward of the huge Lonsdale estate. This harsh nobleman had yet to pay the debt when he died in 1802. Wordsworth was nevertheless able in 1787 to enter St. John's College, Cambridge University, where four years later he took his degree without distinction.

During the summer vacation of his third year at Cambridge (1790), Wordsworth and his closest college friend, the Welshman Robert Jones, journeyed on foot through France and the Alps (described in *The Prelude* 6) at the time when the French were joyously celebrating the first anniversary of the fall of the Bastille. Upon completing his course at Cambridge, Wordsworth spent four months in London, set off on another walking tour with Robert Jones through Wales (the time of the memorable ascent of Mount Snowdon in *The Prelude* 14), and then went back alone to France to master the language and qualify as a traveling tutor.

During his year in France (November 1791 to December 1792), Wordsworth became a fervent supporter of the French Revolution—which seemed to him and many others to promise a "glorious renovation" of society—and he fell in love with Annette Vallon, the daughter of a French surgeon at Blois. The two planned to marry, despite their differences in religion and political inclinations (Annette belonged to an old Catholic family whose sympathies were Royalist). But almost immediately after their daughter, Caroline, was born, lack of money forced Wordsworth to return to England. The outbreak of war made it impossible for him to rejoin Annette and Caroline. Wordsworth's guilt over this abandonment, his divided loyalties between England and France, and his gradual disillusion with the course of the Revolution brought him—according to his account in *The Prelude* 10 and 11—to the verge of an emotional breakdown, when "sick, wearied out with contrarieties," he "yielded up moral questions in despair." His suffering, his near-collapse, and the successful effort, after his break with his past, to reestablish "a saving intercourse with my true self," are the experiences that underlie many of his greatest poems.

At this critical point, a friend died and left Wordsworth a sum of money just sufficient to enable him to live by his poetry. In 1795 he settled in a rent-free house at Racedown, Dorsetshire, with his beloved sister, Dorothy, who now began her long career as confidante, inspirer, and secretary. At that same time Wordsworth met Samuel Taylor Coleridge. Two years later he moved to Alfoxden House, Somersetshire, to be near Coleridge, who lived four miles away at Nether Stowey. Here he entered at the age of twenty-seven on the delayed springtime of his poetic career.

Even while he had been an undergraduate at Cambridge, Coleridge claimed that he had detected signs of genius in Wordsworth's rather conventional poem about his tour in the Alps, *Descriptive Sketches,* published in 1793. Now he hailed Wordsworth unreservedly as "the best poet of the age." The two men met almost daily, talked for hours about poetry, and wrote prolifically. So close was their association that we find the same phrases occurring in poems by Wordsworth and Coleridge, as well as in the remarkable journals that Dorothy kept at the time; the two poets collaborated in some writings and freely traded thoughts and passages for others; and Coleridge even undertook to complete a few poems that Wordsworth had left unfinished. This close partnership, along with the hospitality the two households offered to another young radical writer, John Thelwall, aroused the paranoia of people in the neighborhood. Already fearful of a military invasion by France, they became convinced that Wordsworth and Coleridge were political plotters, not poets. The government sent spies to investigate, and the Wordsworths lost their lease.

Although brought to this abrupt end, that short period of collaboration resulted in one of the most important books of the era, *Lyrical Ballads, with a Few Other Poems,* published anonymously in 1798. This short volume opened with Coleridge's *Ancient Mariner* and included three other poems by Coleridge, some lyrics in which Wordsworth celebrated the experience of nature, and a number of verse anecdotes drawn from the lives of the rural poor. (The verse forms and the subject matter of this last set of poems—which includes "Simon Lee," "We Are Seven," and "The Thorn"— make evident the debt, announced in the very title of *Lyrical Ballads,* that Wordsworth's and Coleridge's book owed to the folk ballads that were being transcribed and anthologized in the later eighteenth century by collectors such as Thomas Percy and Robert Burns.) The book closed with Wordsworth's great descriptive and meditative poem in blank verse, "Tintern Abbey." This poem inaugurated what modern critics call Wordsworth's "myth of nature": his presentation of the "growth" of his mind to maturity, a process unfolding through the interaction between the inner world of the mind and the shaping force of external Nature.

William Hazlitt said that when he heard Coleridge read some of the newly written poems of *Lyrical Ballads* aloud, "the sense of a new style and a new spirit in poetry came over me," with something of the effect "that arises from the turning up of the fresh soil, or of the first welcome breath of spring." The reviewers were less enthusiastic, warning that, because of their simple language and subject matter, poems such as "Simon Lee" risked "vulgarity" or silliness. Nevertheless *Lyrical Ballads* sold out in two years, and Wordsworth published under his own name a new edition, dated 1800, to which he added a second volume of poems. In his famous Preface to this edition, planned in close consultation with Coleridge, Wordsworth outlined a critical program that provided a retroactive rationale for the "experiments" the poems represented.

Late in 1799 William and Dorothy moved back permanently to their native lakes, settling at Grasmere in the little house later named Dove Cottage. Coleridge, following them, rented at Keswick, thirteen miles away. In 1802 Wordsworth finally came into his father's inheritance and, after an amicable settlement with Annette Vallon, married Mary Hutchinson, whom he had known since childhood. His life after that time had many sorrows: the drowning in 1805 of his favorite brother, John, a sea captain; the death in 1812 of two of his and Mary's five children; a growing rift with Coleridge, culminating in a bitter quarrel (1810) from which they were not completely reconciled for almost two decades; and, from the 1830s on, Dorothy's physical and mental illness. Over these years Wordsworth became, nonetheless, increasingly prosperous and famous. He also displayed a political and religious conservatism that disappointed readers who, like Hazlitt, had interpreted his early work as the expression of a "levelling Muse" that promoted democratic change. In 1813 a government sinecure, the position of stamp distributor (that is, revenue collector) for Westmorland, was bestowed on him—concrete evidence of his recognition as a national poet and of the alteration in the government's perception of his politics. Gradually, Wordsworth's residences, as he moved into more and more comfortable quarters, became standard stops for sightseers touring the Lakes. By 1843 he was poet laureate of Great Britain. He died in 1850 at the age of eighty. Only then did his executors publish his masterpiece, *The Prelude,* the autobiographical poem that he had written in two parts in 1799, expanded to its full length in 1805, and then continued to revise almost to the last decade of his long life.

Most of Wordsworth's greatest poetry had been written by 1807, when he published *Poems, in Two Volumes;* and after *The Excursion* (1814) and the first collected edition of his poems (1815), although he continued to write prolifically, his powers appeared to decline. The causes of that decline have been much debated. One seems to be inherent in the very nature of his writing. Wordsworth is above all the poet of the remembrance of things past or, as he put it, of "emotion recollected in tranquillity." Some object or event in the present triggers a sudden renewal of feelings he had experienced in youth; the result is a poem exhibiting the discrepancy between what Wordsworth called "two consciousnesses": himself as he is now and himself as he once was. But the memory of one's early emotional experience is not an inexhaustible resource for poetry, as Wordsworth recognized. He said in *The Prelude* 12, while describing the recurrence of "spots of time" from his memories of childhood:

> The days gone by
> Return upon me almost from the dawn
> Of life: the hiding places of Man's power
> Open; I would approach them, but they close.
> I see by glimpses now; when age comes on,
> May scarcely see at all.

The past that Wordsworth recollected was one of moments of intense experience, and of emotional turmoil that is ordered, in the calmer present, into a hard-won equilibrium. As time went on, however, he gained what, in the "Ode to Duty" (composed in 1804), he longed for, "a repose which ever is the same"—but at the expense of the agony and excitation that, under the calm surface, empower his best and most characteristic poems.

Occasionally in his middle and later life a jolting experience would revive the intensity of Wordsworth's remembered emotion, and also his earlier poetic strength. The moving sonnet "Surprised by Joy," for example, was written in his forties at the abrupt realization that time was beginning to diminish his grief at the death some years earlier of his little daughter Catherine. And when Wordsworth was sixty-five years old, the sudden report of the death of James Hogg called up the memory of other poets whom

Wordsworth had loved and outlived; the result was his "Extempore Effusion," in which he returns to the simple quatrains of the early *Lyrical Ballads* and recovers the elegiac voice that had mourned Lucy, thirty-five years before.

FROM LYRICAL BALLADS

We Are Seven[1]

————A simple Child,
That lightly draws its breath,
And feels its life in every limb,
What should it know of death?

5   I met a little cottage Girl:
She was eight years old, she said;
Her hair was thick with many a curl
That clustered round her head.

She had a rustic, woodland air,
10 And she was wildly clad:
Her eyes were fair, and very fair;
—Her beauty made me glad.

"Sisters and brothers, little Maid,
How many may you be?"
15 "How many? Seven in all," she said,
And wondering looked at me.

"And where are they? I pray you tell."
She answered, "Seven are we;
And two of us at Conway[2] dwell,
20 And two are gone to sea.

"Two of us in the church-yard lie,
My sister and my brother;
And, in the church-yard cottage, I
Dwell near them with my mother."

25 "You say that two at Conway dwell,
And two are gone to sea,
Yet ye are seven! I pray you tell,
Sweet Maid, how this may be."

Then did the little Maid reply,
30 "Seven boys and girls are we;

---

1. Written at Alfoxden in the spring of 1798. . . . The little girl who is the heroine I met within the area of Goodrich Castle [in the Wye Valley north of Tintern Abbey] in the year 1793 [Wordsworth's note, 1843]. Wordsworth also tells us that, "while walking to and fro," he composed the last stanza first, beginning with the last line, and that Coleridge contributed the first stanza.
2. A seaport town in north Wales.

Two of us in the church-yard lie,
Beneath the church-yard tree."

"You run about, my little Maid,
Your limbs they are alive;
35   If two are in the church-yard laid,
Then ye are only five."

"Their graves are green, they may be seen,"
The little Maid replied,
"Twelve steps or more from my mother's door,
40   And they are side by side.

"My stockings there I often knit,
My kerchief there I hem;
And there upon the ground I sit,
And sing a song to them.

45   "And often after sun-set, Sir,
When it is light and fair,
I take my little porringer,[3]
And eat my supper there.

"The first that died was sister Jane;
50   In bed she moaning lay,
Till God released her of her pain;
And then she went away.

"So in the church-yard she was laid;
And, when the grass was dry,
55   Together round her grave we played,
My brother John and I.

"And when the ground was white with snow,
And I could run and slide,
My brother John was forced to go,
60   And he lies by her side."

"How many are you, then," said I,
"If they two are in heaven?"
Quick was the little Maid's reply,
"O Master! we are seven."

65   "But they are dead; those two are dead!
Their spirits are in heaven!"
'Twas throwing words away; for still
The little Maid would have her will,
And said, "Nay, we are seven!"

1798   1798

3. Bowl for porridge.

Lines Written in Early Spring

I heard a thousand blended notes,
While in a grove I sate reclined,
In that sweet mood when pleasant thoughts
Bring sad thoughts to the mind.

5   To her fair works did Nature link
The human soul that through me ran;
And much it grieved my heart to think
What man has made of man.

Through primrose tufts, in that green bower,
10   The periwinkle[1] trailed its wreaths,
And 'tis my faith that every flower
Enjoys the air it breathes.

The birds around me hopped and played,
Their thoughts I cannot measure:—
15   But the least motion which they made,
It seemed a thrill of pleasure.

The budding twigs spread out their fan,
To catch the breezy air;
And I must think, do all I can,
20   That there was pleasure there.

If this belief from heaven be sent,
If such be Nature's holy plan,[2]
Have I not reason to lament
What man has made of man?

1798   1798

Expostulation and Reply[1]

"Why, William, on that old grey stone,
Thus for the length of half a day,
Why, William, sit you thus alone,
And dream your time away?

1. A trailing evergreen plant with small blue flowers (U.S. myrtle).
2. The version of these two lines in the *Lyrical Ballads* of 1798 reads: "If I these thoughts may not prevent, / If such be of my creed the plan."
1. This and the following companion poem have often been attacked—and defended—as Wordsworth's own statement about the comparative merits of nature and of books. But they are a dialogue between two friends who rally one another by the usual device of overstating parts of a whole truth. In the 1798 Advertisement to *Lyrical Ballads*, Wordsworth said that the pieces originated in a conversation "with a friend who was somewhat unreasonably attached to modern books of moral philosophy." In 1843 he noted that the idea of learning when the mind is in a state of "wise passiveness" made this poem a favorite of the Quakers, who rejected religious ritual for informal and spontaneous worship.

5 "Where are your books?—that light bequeathed
To Beings else forlorn and blind!
Up! up! and drink the spirit breathed
From dead men to their kind.

"You look round on your Mother Earth,
10 As if she for no purpose bore you;
As if you were her first-born birth,
And none had lived before you!"

One morning thus, by Esthwaite lake,
When life was sweet, I knew not why,
15 To me my good friend Matthew spake,
And thus I made reply.

"The eye—it cannot choose but see;
We cannot bid the ear be still;
Our bodies feel, where'er they be,
20 Against or with our will.

"Nor less I deem that there are Powers
Which of themselves our minds impress;
That we can feed this mind of ours
In a wise passiveness.

25 "Think you, 'mid all this mighty sum
Of things for ever speaking,
That nothing of itself will come,
But we must still be seeking?

"—Then ask not wherefore, here, alone,
30 Conversing² as I may,
I sit upon this old grey stone,
And dream my time away."

Spring 1798   1798

The Tables Turned

An Evening Scene on the Same Subject

Up! up! my Friend, and quit your books;
Or surely you'll grow double:°   double over
Up! up! my Friend, and clear your looks;
Why all this toil and trouble?

5 The sun, above the mountain's head,
A freshening lustre mellow
Through all the long green fields has spread,
His first sweet evening yellow.

---

2. In the old sense of "communing" (with the "things for ever speaking").

Books! 'tis a dull and endless strife:
10 Come, hear the woodland linnet,°   *small finch*
How sweet his music! on my life,
There's more of wisdom in it.

And hark! how blithe the throstle° sings!   *song thrush*
He, too, is no mean preacher:
15 Come forth into the light of things,
Let Nature be your Teacher.

She has a world of ready wealth,
Our minds and hearts to bless—
Spontaneous wisdom breathed by health,
20 Truth breathed by cheerfulness.

One impulse from a vernal wood
May teach you more of man,
Of moral evil and of good,
Than all the sages can.

25 Sweet is the lore which Nature brings;
Our meddling intellect
Mis-shapes the beauteous forms of things:—
We murder to dissect.

Enough of Science and of Art;
30 Close up those barren leaves;°   *pages*
Come forth, and bring with you a heart
That watches and receives.

1798   1798

Lines[1]

Composed a Few Miles above Tintern Abbey, on Revisiting the Banks of the Wye during a Tour, July 13, 1798

Five years have past; five summers, with the length
Of five long winters! and again I hear
These waters, rolling from their mountain-springs
With a soft inland murmur.[2]—Once again
5 Do I behold these steep and lofty cliffs,

1. No poem of mine was composed under circumstances more pleasant for me to remember than this. I began it upon leaving Tintern, after crossing the Wye, and concluded it just as I was entering Bristol in the evening, after a ramble of 4 or 5 days, with my sister. Not a line of it was altered, and not any part of it written down till I reached Bristol [Wordsworth's note, 1843]. The poem was printed as the last item in *Lyrical Ballads*.
   Wordsworth had first visited the Wye valley and the ruins of Tintern Abbey, in Monmouthshire, while on a solitary walking tour in August 1793, when he was twenty-three years old. (See "Tintern Abbey, Tourism, and Romantic Landscape" at Norton Literature Online.) The puzzling difference between the present landscape and the remembered "picture of the mind" (line 61) gives rise to an intricately organized meditation, in which the poet reviews his past, evaluates the present, and (through his sister as intermediary) anticipates the future; he ends by rounding back quietly on the scene that had been his point of departure.
2. The river is not affected by the tides a few miles above Tintern [Wordsworth's note, 1798 ff.]. Until 1845 the text had "sweet" for "soft," meaning fresh, not salty.

That on a wild secluded scene impress
Thoughts of more deep seclusion; and connect
The landscape with the quiet of the sky.
The day is come when I again repose
10   Here, under this dark sycamore, and view
These plots of cottage-ground, these orchard-tufts,
Which at this season, with their unripe fruits,
Are clad in one green hue, and lose themselves
'Mid groves and copses. Once again I see
15   These hedge-rows, hardly hedge-rows, little lines
Of sportive wood run wild: these pastoral farms,
Green to the very door; and wreaths of smoke
Sent up, in silence, from among the trees!
With some uncertain notice, as might seem
20   Of vagrant dwellers in the houseless woods,
Or of some Hermit's cave, where by his fire
The Hermit sits alone.

                              These beauteous forms,
Through a long absence, have not been to me
As is a landscape to a blind man's eye:
25   But oft, in lonely rooms, and 'mid the din
Of towns and cities, I have owed to them
In hours of weariness, sensations sweet,
Felt in the blood, and felt along the heart;
And passing even into my purer mind,
30   With tranquil restoration:—feelings too
Of unremembered pleasure: such, perhaps,
As have no slight or trivial influence
On that best portion of a good man's life,
His little, nameless, unremembered, acts
35   Of kindness and of love. Nor less, I trust,
To them I may have owed another gift,
Of aspect more sublime; that blessed mood,
In which the burthen° of the mystery,   *burden*
In which the heavy and the weary weight
40   Of all this unintelligible world,
Is lightened:—that serene and blessed mood,
In which the affections gently lead us on,—
Until, the breath of this corporeal frame
And even the motion of our human blood
45   Almost suspended, we are laid asleep
In body, and become a living soul:
While with an eye made quiet by the power
Of harmony, and the deep power of joy,
We see into the life of things.

                              If this
50   Be but a vain belief, yet, oh! how oft—
In darkness and amid the many shapes
Of joyless daylight; when the fretful stir
Unprofitable, and the fever of the world,
Have hung upon the beatings of my heart—

55 How oft, in spirit, have I turned to thee,
    O sylvan Wye! thou wanderer thro' the woods,
    How often has my spirit turned to thee!

        And now, with gleams of half-extinguished thought,
        With many recognitions dim and faint,
60   And somewhat of a sad perplexity,
        The picture of the mind revives again:
        While here I stand, not only with the sense
        Of present pleasure, but with pleasing thoughts
        That in this moment there is life and food
65   For future years. And so I dare to hope,
        Though changed, no doubt, from what I was when first
        I came among these hills; when like a roe°   deer
        I bounded o'er the mountains, by the sides
        Of the deep rivers, and the lonely streams,
70   Wherever nature led: more like a man
        Flying from something that he dreads, than one
        Who sought the thing he loved. For nature then
        (The coarser pleasures of my boyish days,
        And their glad animal movements all gone by)
75   To me was all in all.—I cannot paint
        What then I was. The sounding cataract
        Haunted me like a passion: the tall rock,
        The mountain, and the deep and gloomy wood,
        Their colours and their forms, were then to me
80   An appetite; a feeling and a love,
        That had no need of a remoter charm,
        By thought supplied, nor any interest
        Unborrowed from the eye.—That time is past,
        And all its aching joys are now no more,
85   And all its dizzy raptures.[3] Not for this
        Faint° I, nor mourn nor murmur; other gifts   lose heart
        Have followed; for such loss, I would believe,
        Abundant recompense. For I have learned
        To look on nature, not as in the hour
90   Of thoughtless youth; but hearing oftentimes
        The still, sad music of humanity,
        Nor harsh nor grating, though of ample power
        To chasten and subdue. And I have felt
        A presence that disturbs me with the joy
95   Of elevated thoughts; a sense sublime
        Of something far more deeply interfused,
        Whose dwelling is the light of setting suns,
        And the round ocean and the living air,
        And the blue sky, and in the mind of man:
100   A motion and a spirit, that impels
        All thinking things, all objects of all thought,

3. Lines 66ff. contain Wordsworth's famed description of the three stages of his growing up, defined in terms of his evolving relations to the natural scene: the young boy's purely physical responsiveness (lines 73–74); the postadolescent's aching, dizzy, and equivocal passions—a love that is more like dread (lines 67–72, 75–85: this was his state of mind on the occasion of his first visit); his present state (lines 85ff.), in which for the first time he adds thought to sense.

And rolls through all things. Therefore am I still
A lover of the meadows and the woods,
And mountains; and of all that we behold
105 From this green earth; of all the mighty world
Of eye, and ear,—both what they half create,[4]
And what perceive; well pleased to recognise
In nature and the language of the sense,
The anchor of my purest thoughts, the nurse,
110 The guide, the guardian of my heart, and soul
Of all my moral being.

                      Nor perchance,
If I were not thus taught, should I the more
Suffer my genial spirits[5] to decay:
For thou art with me here upon the banks
115 Of this fair river; thou my dearest Friend,[6]
My dear, dear Friend; and in thy voice I catch
The language of my former heart, and read
My former pleasures in the shooting lights
Of thy wild eyes. Oh! yet a little while
120 May I behold in thee what I was once,
My dear, dear Sister! and this prayer I make,
Knowing that Nature never did betray
The heart that loved her; 'tis her privilege,
Through all the years of this our life, to lead
125 From joy to joy: for she can so inform
The mind that is within us, so impress
With quietness and beauty, and so feed
With lofty thoughts, that neither evil tongues,[7]
Rash judgments, nor the sneers of selfish men,
130 Nor greetings where no kindness is, nor all
The dreary intercourse of daily life,
Shall e'er prevail against us, or disturb
Our cheerful faith, that all which we behold
Is full of blessings. Therefore let the moon
135 Shine on thee in thy solitary walk;
And let the misty mountain-winds be free
To blow against thee: and, in after years,
When these wild ecstasies shall be matured
Into a sober pleasure; when thy mind
140 Shall be a mansion for all lovely forms,
Thy memory be as a dwelling-place
For all sweet sounds and harmonies; oh! then,
If solitude, or fear, or pain, or grief,
Should be thy portion,° with what healing thoughts   inheritance, dowry
145 Of tender joy wilt thou remember me,
And these my exhortations! Nor, perchance—

---

4. This line has a close resemblance to an admirable line of Young, the exact expression of which I cannot recollect [Wordsworth's note, 1798 ff.]. Edward Young in *Night Thoughts* (1744) says that the human senses "half create the wondrous world they see."
5. Creative powers. ("Genial" is here the adjectival form of the noun *genius*.)
6. His sister, Dorothy.
7. In the opening of *Paradise Lost* 7, Milton describes himself as fallen on "evil days" and "evil tongues" and with "dangers compassed round" (lines 26–27).

If I should be where I no more can hear
Thy voice, nor catch from thy wild eyes these gleams
Of past existence[8]—wilt thou then forget
150 That on the banks of this delightful stream
We stood together; and that I, so long
A worshipper of Nature, hither came
Unwearied in that service; rather say
With warmer love—oh! with far deeper zeal
155 Of holier love. Nor wilt thou then forget,
That after many wanderings, many years
Of absence, these steep woods and lofty cliffs,
And this green pastoral landscape, were to me
More dear, both for themselves and for thy sake!

July 1798   1798

Preface to *Lyrical Ballads*   (1802) To the first edition of *Lyrical Ballads*,
published jointly with Coleridge in 1798, Wordsworth prefixed an "Advertisement"
asserting that the majority of the poems were "to be considered as experiments" to
determine "how far the language of conversation in the middle and lower classes of
society is adapted to the purposes of poetic pleasure." In the second, two-volume
edition of 1800, Wordsworth, aided by frequent conversations with Coleridge,
expanded the Advertisement into a preface that justified the poems not as experiments, but as exemplifying the principles of all good poetry. The Preface was enlarged
for the third edition of *Lyrical Ballads*, published two years later. This last version of
1802 is reprinted here.

Although some of its ideas had antecedents in the later eighteenth century, the
Preface as a whole deserves its reputation as a revolutionary manifesto about the
nature of poetry. Like many radical statements, however, it claims to go back to
the implicit principles that governed the great poetry of the past but have been perverted in recent practice. Most discussions of the Preface, following the lead of Coleridge in chapters 14 and 17 of his *Biographia Literaria*, have focused on Wordsworth's
assertions about the valid language of poetry, on which he bases his attack on the
"poetic diction" of eighteenth-century poets. As Coleridge pointed out, Wordsworth's
argument about this issue is far from clear. However, Wordsworth's questioning of
the underlying premises of neoclassical poetry went even further. His Preface implicitly denies the traditional assumption that the poetic genres constitute a hierarchy,
from epic and tragedy at the top down through comedy, satire, pastoral, to the short
lyric at the lowest reaches of the poetic scale; he also rejects the traditional principle
of "decorum," which required the poet to arrange matters so that the poem's subject
(especially the social class of its protagonists) and its level of diction conformed to
the status of the literary kind on the poetic scale.

When Wordsworth asserted in the Preface that he deliberately chose to represent
"incidents and situations from common life," he translated his democratic sympathies
into critical terms, justifying his use of peasants, children, outcasts, criminals, and
madwomen as serious subjects of poetic and even tragic concern. He also undertook
to write in "a selection of language really used by men," on the grounds that there
can be no "essential difference between the language of prose and metrical composition." In making this claim Wordsworth attacked the neoclassical principle that
required the language, in many kinds of poems, to be elevated over everyday speech

---

8. I.e., reminders of his own "past existence" five years earlier (see lines 116–19).

by a special, more refined and dignified diction and by artful figures of speech. Wordsworth's views about the valid language of poetry are based on the new premise that
"all good poetry is the spontaneous overflow of powerful feelings"—spontaneous, that
is, at the moment of composition, even though the process is influenced by prior
thought and acquired poetic skill.

Wordsworth's assertions about the materials and diction of poetry have been greatly
influential in expanding the range of serious literature to include the common people
and ordinary things and events, as well as in justifying a poetry of sincerity rather
than of artifice, expressed in the ordinary language of its time. But in the long view
other aspects of his Preface have been no less significant in establishing its importance, not only as a turning point in English criticism but also as a central document
in modern culture, Wordsworth feared that a new urban, industrial society's mass
media and mass culture (glimpsed in the Preface when he refers derisively to contemporary Gothic novels and German melodramas) were threatening to blunt the human
mind's "discriminatory powers" and to "reduce it to a state of almost savage torpor."
He attributed to imaginative literature the primary role in keeping the human beings
who live in such societies emotionally alive and morally sensitive. Literature, that is,
could keep humans essentially human.

From Preface to *Lyrical Ballads, with Pastoral and Other Poems* (1802)

[THE SUBJECT AND LANGUAGE OF POETRY]

The first volume of these poems has already been submitted to general
perusal. It was published, as an experiment, which, I hoped, might be of some
use to ascertain, how far, by fitting to metrical arrangement a selection of the
real language of men in a state of vivid sensation, that sort of pleasure and
that quantity of pleasure may be imparted, which a poet may rationally endeavour to impart.

I had formed no very inaccurate estimate of the probable effect of those
poems: I flattered myself that they who should be pleased with them would read
them with more than common pleasure: and, on the other hand, I was well
aware, that by those who should dislike them they would be read with more than
common dislike. The result has differed from my expectation in this only, that I
have pleased a greater number than I ventured to hope I should please.

For the sake of variety, and from a consciousness of my own weakness, I
was induced to request the assistance of a friend, who furnished me with the
poems of the *Ancient Mariner*, the *Foster-Mother's Tale*, the *Nightingale*, and
the poem entitled *Love*. I should not, however, have requested this assistance,
had I not believed that the poems of my friend[1] would in a great measure have
the same tendency as my own, and that, though there would be found a difference, there would be found no discordance in the colours of our style; as
our opinions on the subject of poetry do almost entirely coincide.

Several of my friends are anxious for the success of these poems from a
belief, that, if the views with which they were composed were indeed realized,
a class of poetry would be produced, well adapted to interest mankind permanently, and not unimportant in the multiplicity, and in the quality of its
moral relations: and on this account they have advised me to prefix a systematic

1. The "friend" of course is Coleridge.

defence of the theory upon which the poems were written. But I was unwilling to undertake the task, because I knew that on this occasion the reader would look coldly upon my arguments, since I might be suspected of having been principally influenced by the selfish and foolish hope of *reasoning* him into an approbation of these particular poems: and I was still more unwilling to undertake the task, because, adequately to display my opinions, and fully to enforce my arguments, would require a space wholly disproportionate to the nature of a preface. For to treat the subject with the clearness and coherence of which I believe it susceptible, it would be necessary to give a full account of the present state of the public taste in this country, and to determine how far this taste is healthy or depraved; which, again, could not be determined, without pointing out, in what manner language and the human mind act and re-act on each other, and without retracing the revolutions, not of literature alone, but likewise of society itself. I have therefore altogether declined to enter regularly upon this defence; yet I am sensible, that there would be some impropriety in abruptly obtruding upon the public, without a few words of introduction, poems so materially different from those upon which general approbation is at present bestowed.

It is supposed, that by the act of writing in verse an author makes a formal engagement that he will gratify certain known habits of association; that he not only thus apprizes the reader that certain classes of ideas and expressions will be found in his book, but that others will be carefully excluded. This exponent or symbol held forth by metrical language must in different eras of literature have excited very different expectations: for example, in the age of Catullus, Terence, and Lucretius and that of Statius or Claudian,[2] and in our own country, in the age of Shakespeare and Beaumont and Fletcher, and that of Donne and Cowley, or Dryden, or Pope. I will not take upon me to determine the exact import of the promise which by the act of writing in verse an author, in the present day, makes to his reader; but I am certain, it will appear to many persons that I have not fulfilled the terms of an engagement thus voluntarily contracted. They who have been accustomed to the gaudiness and inane phraseology of many modern writers, if they persist in reading this book to its conclusion, will, no doubt, frequently have to struggle with feelings of strangeness and awkwardness: they will look round for poetry, and will be induced to inquire by what species of courtesy these attempts can be permitted to assume that title. I hope therefore the reader will not censure me, if I attempt to state what I have proposed to myself to perform; and also (as far as the limits of a preface will permit) to explain some of the chief reasons which have determined me in the choice of my purpose: that at least he may be spared any unpleasant feeling of disappointment, and that I myself may be protected from the most dishonorable accusation which can be brought against an author, namely, that of an indolence which prevents him from endeavouring to ascertain what is his duty, or, when this duty is ascertained, prevents him from performing it.

The principal object, then, which I proposed to myself in these poems was to choose incidents and situations from common life, and to relate or describe them, throughout, as far as was possible, in a selection of language really used by men; and, at the same time, to throw over them a certain colouring of

2. Wordsworth's implied contrast is between the naturalness and simplicity of the first three Roman poets (who wrote in the last two centuries B.C.E.) and the elaborate artifice of the last two Roman poets (Statius wrote in the 1st and Claudian in the 4th century C.E.).

imagination, whereby ordinary things should be presented to the mind in an unusual way; and, further, and above all, to make these incidents and situations interesting by tracing in them, truly though not ostentatiously, the primary laws of our nature: chiefly, as far as regards the manner in which we associate ideas in a state of excitement. Low and rustic life was generally chosen, because in that condition, the essential passions of the heart find a better soil in which they can attain their maturity, are less under restraint, and speak a plainer and more emphatic language; because in that condition of life our elementary feelings co-exist in a state of greater simplicity, and, consequently, may be more accurately contemplated, and more forcibly communicated; because the manners of rural life germinate from those elementary feelings; and, from the necessary character of rural occupations, are more easily comprehended; and are more durable; and lastly, because in that condition the passions of men are incorporated with the beautiful and permanent forms of nature. The language, too, of these men is adopted (purified indeed from what appear to be its real defects, from all lasting and rational causes of dislike or disgust) because such men hourly communicate with the best objects from which the best part of language is originally derived; and because, from their rank in society and the sameness and narrow circle of their intercourse, being less under the influence of social vanity they convey their feelings and notions in simple and unelaborated expressions. Accordingly, such a language, arising out of repeated experience and regular feelings, is a more permanent, and a far more philosophical language, than that which is frequently substituted for it by poets, who think that they are conferring honour upon themselves and their art, in proportion as they separate themselves from the sympathies of men, and indulge in arbitrary and capricious habits of expression, in order to furnish food for fickle tastes, and fickle appetites, of their own creation.[3]

I cannot, however, be insensible of the present outcry against the triviality and meanness both of thought and language, which some of my contemporaries have occasionally introduced into their metrical compositions; and I acknowledge, that this defect, where it exists, is more dishonorable to the writer's own character than false refinement or arbitrary innovation, though I should contend at the same time that it is far less pernicious in the sum of its consequences. From such verses the poems in these volumes will be found distinguished at least by one mark of difference, that each of them has a worthy *purpose*. Not that I mean to say, that I always began to write with a distinct purpose formally conceived; but I believe that my habits of meditation have so formed my feelings, as that my descriptions of such objects as strongly excite those feelings, will be found to carry along with them a *purpose*. If in this opinion I am mistaken, I can have little right to the name of a poet. For all good poetry is the spontaneous overflow of powerful feelings: but though this be true, poems to which any value can be attached, were never produced on any variety of subjects but by a man who, being possessed of more than usual organic sensibility, had also thought long and deeply. For our continued influxes of feeling are modified and directed by our thoughts, which are indeed the representatives of all our past feelings; and, as by contemplating the relation of these general representatives to each other we discover what is really

---

3. It is worth while here to observe that the affecting parts of Chaucer are almost always expressed in language pure and universally intelligible even to this day [Wordsworth's note].

important to men, so, by the repetition and continuance of this act, our feelings will be connected with important subjects, till at length, if we be originally possessed of much sensibility, such habits of mind will be produced, that, by obeying blindly and mechanically the impulses of those habits, we shall describe objects, and utter sentiments, of such a nature and in such connection with each other, that the understanding of the being to whom we address ourselves, if he be in a healthful state of association, must necessarily be in some degree enlightened, and his affections ameliorated.

I have said that each of these poems has a purpose. I have also informed my reader what this purpose will be found principally to be: namely, to illustrate the manner in which our feelings and ideas are associated in a state of excitement. But, speaking in language somewhat more appropriate, it is to follow the fluxes and refluxes of the mind when agitated by the great and simple affections of our nature. This object I have endeavored in these short essays to attain by various means; by tracing the maternal passion through many of its more subtile[4] windings, as in the poems of the *Idiot Boy* and the *Mad Mother*; by accompanying the last struggles of a human being, at the approach of death, cleaving in solitude to life and society, as in the poem of the *Forsaken Indian*; by shewing, as in the stanzas entitled *We Are Seven*, the perplexity and obscurity which in childhood attend our notion of death, or rather our utter inability to admit that notion; or by displaying the strength of fraternal, or to speak more philosophically, of moral attachment when early associated with the great and beautiful objects of nature, as in *The Brothers*; or, as in the Incident of *Simon Lee*, by placing my reader in the way of receiving from ordinary moral sensations another and more salutary impression than we are accustomed to receive from them. It has also been part of my general purpose to attempt to sketch characters under the influence of less impassioned feelings, as in the *Two April Mornings, The Fountain, The Old Man Travelling, The Two Thieves*, &c., characters of which the elements are simple, belonging rather to nature than to manners,[5] such as exist now, and will probably always exist, and which from their constitution may be distinctly and profitably contemplated. I will not abuse the indulgence of my reader by dwelling longer upon this subject; but it is proper that I should mention one other circumstance which distinguishes these poems from the popular poetry of the day; it is this, that the feeling therein developed gives importance to the action and situation, and not the action and situation to the feeling. My meaning will be rendered perfectly intelligible by referring my reader to the poems entitled *Poor Susan* and the *Childless Father*, particularly to the last stanza of the latter poem.

I will not suffer a sense of false modesty to prevent me from asserting, that I point my reader's attention to this mark of distinction, far less for the sake of these particular poems than from the general importance of the subject. The subject is indeed important! For the human mind is capable of being excited without the application of gross[6] and violent stimulants; and he must have a very faint perception of its beauty and dignity who does not know this, and who does not further know, that one being is elevated above another, in proportion as he possesses this capability. It has therefore appeared to me, that to endeavour to produce or enlarge this capability is one of the best serv-

4. Subtle.
5. Social custom.

6. Coarse.

ices in which, at any period, a writer can be engaged; but this service, excellent at all times, is especially so at the present day. For a multitude of causes, unknown to former times, are now acting with a combined force to blunt the discriminating powers of the mind, and, unfitting it for all voluntary exertion, to reduce it to a state of almost savage torpor. The most effective of these causes are the great national events which are daily taking place, and the increasing accumulation of men in cities, where the uniformity of their occupations produces a craving for extraordinary incident, which the rapid communication of intelligence hourly gratifies.[7] To this tendency of life and manners the literature and theatrical exhibitions of the country have conformed themselves. The invaluable works of our elder writers, I had almost said the works of Shakespeare and Milton, are driven into neglect by frantic novels, sickly and stupid German tragedies,[8] and deluges of idle and extravagant stories in verse.—When I think upon this degrading thirst after outrageous stimulation, I am almost ashamed to have spoken of the feeble effort with which I have endeavoured to counteract it; and, reflecting upon the magnitude of the general evil, I should be oppressed with no dishonorable melancholy, had I not a deep impression of certain inherent and indestructible qualities of the human mind, and likewise of certain powers in the great and permanent objects that act upon it which are equally inherent and indestructible; and did I not further add to this impression a belief, that the time is approaching when the evil will be systematically opposed, by men of greater powers, and with far more distinguished success.

Having dwelt thus long on the subjects and aim of these poems, I shall request the reader's permission to apprize him of a few circumstances relating to their *style*, in order, among other reasons, that I may not be censured for not having performed what I never attempted. The reader will find that personifications of abstract ideas[9] rarely occur in these volumes; and, I hope, are utterly rejected as an ordinary device to elevate the style, and raise it above prose. I have proposed to myself to imitate, and, as far as is possible, to adopt the very language of men; and assuredly such personifications do not make any natural or regular part of that language. They are, indeed, a figure of speech occasionally prompted by passion, and I have made use of them as such; but I have endeavoured utterly to reject them as a mechanical device of style, or as a family language which writers in metre seem to lay claim to by prescription. I have wished to keep my reader in the company of flesh and blood, persuaded that by so doing I shall interest him. I am, however, well aware that others who pursue a different track may interest him likewise; I do not interfere with their claim, I only wish to prefer a different claim of my own. There will also be found in these volumes little of what is usually called poetic diction;[1] I have taken as much pains to avoid it as others ordinarily take to produce it; this I have done for the reason already alleged, to bring my language near to the language of men, and further, because the pleasure which I have proposed to myself to impart is of a kind very different from that which

7. This was the period of the wars against France, of industrial urbanization, and of the rapid proliferation in England of daily newspapers.
8. Wordsworth had in mind the "Gothic" terror novels by writers such as Ann Radcliffe and Matthew Gregory Lewis and the sentimental melodrama, then immensely popular in England, of August von Kotzebue and his German contemporaries.
9. This practice was common in 18th-century poetry. Samuel Johnson, for instance, in *The Vanity of Human Wishes* (1749), has "Observation . . . survey[ing] mankind" and "Vengeance listen[ing] to the fool's request" (lines 1–2, 14).
1. In the sense of words, phrases, and figures of speech not commonly used in conversation or prose that are regarded as especially appropriate to poetry.

is supposed by many persons to be the proper object of poetry. I do not know how, without being culpably particular, I can give my reader a more exact notion of the style in which I wished these poems to be written than by informing him that I have at all times endeavoured to look steadily at my subject, consequently, I hope that there is in these poems little falsehood of description, and that my ideas are expressed in language fitted to their respective importance. Something I must have gained by this practice, as it is friendly to one property of all good poetry, namely, good sense; but it has necessarily cut me off from a large portion of phrases and figures of speech which from father to son have long been regarded as the common inheritance of poets. I have also thought it expedient to restrict myself still further, having abstained from the use of many expressions, in themselves proper and beautiful, but which have been foolishly repeated by bad poets, till such feelings of disgust are connected with them as it is scarcely possible by any art of association to overpower.

If in a poem there should be found a series of lines, or even a single line, in which the language, though naturally arranged and according to the strict laws of metre, does not differ from that of prose, there is a numerous class of critics, who, when they stumble upon these prosaisms as they call them, imagine that they have made a notable discovery, and exult over the poet as over a man ignorant of his own profession. Now these men would establish a canon of criticism which the reader will conclude he must utterly reject, if he wishes to be pleased with these volumes. And it would be a most easy task to prove to him, that not only the language of a large portion of everygood poem, even of the most elevated character, must necessarily, except with reference to the metre, in no respect differ from that of good prose, but likewise that some of the most interesting parts of the best poems will be found to be strictly the language of prose, when prose is well written. The truth of this assertion might be demonstrated by innumerable passages from almost all the poetical writings, even of Milton himself. I have not space for much quotation; but, to illustrate the subject in a general manner, I will here adduce a short composition of Gray, who was at the head of those who by their reasonings have attempted to widen the space of separation betwixt prose and metrical composition, and was more than any other man curiously elaborate in the structure of his own poetic diction.[2]

> In vain to me the smiling mornings shine,
> And reddening Phoebus lifts his golden fire:
> The birds in vain their amorous descant join,
> Or cheerful fields resume their green attire:
> These ears, alas! for other notes repine;
> *A different object do these eyes require;*
> *My lonely anguish melts no heart but mine;*
> *And in my breast the imperfect joys expire;*
> Yet Morning smiles the busy race to cheer,
> And new-born pleasure brings to happier men;
> The fields to all their wonted tribute bear;
> To warm their little loves the birds complain.

2. Thomas Gray (author in 1751 of the "Elegy Written in a Country Churchyard") had written, in a letter to Richard West, that "the language of the age is never the language of poetry." The poem that follows is Gray's "Sonnet on the Death of Richard West."

I fruitless mourn to him that cannot hear
And weep the more because I weep in vain.

It will easily be perceived that the only part of this sonnet which is of any value is the lines printed in italics: it is equally obvious, that, except in the rhyme, and in the use of the single word "fruitless" for fruitlessly, which is so far a defect, the language of these lines does in no respect differ from that of prose.

By the foregoing quotation I have shewn that the language of prose may yet be well adapted to poetry; and I have previously asserted that a large portion of the language of every good poem can in no respect differ from that of good prose. I will go further. I do not doubt that it may be safely affirmed, that there neither is, nor can be, any essential difference between the language of prose and metrical composition. We are fond of tracing the resemblance between poetry and painting, and, accordingly, we call them sisters: but where shall we find bonds of connection sufficiently strict to typify the affinity betwixt metrical and prose composition? They both speak by and to the same organs; the bodies in which both of them are clothed may be said to be of the same substance, their affections are kindred and almost identical, not necessarily differing even in degree; poetry[3] sheds no tears "such as Angels weep,"[4] but natural and human tears; she can boast of no celestial ichor[5] that distinguishes her vital juices from those of prose; the same human blood circulates through the veins of them both.

* * *

["WHAT IS A POET?"]

Taking up the subject, then, upon general grounds, I ask what is meant by the word "poet"? What is a poet? To whom does he address himself? And what language is to be expected from him? He is a man speaking to men: a man, it is true, endued with more lively sensibility, more enthusiasm and tenderness, who has a greater knowledge of human nature, and a more comprehensive soul, than are supposed to be common among mankind; a man pleased with his own passions and volitions, and who rejoices more than other men in the spirit of life that is in him; delighting to contemplate similar volitions and passions as manifested in the goings-on of the universe, and habitually impelled to create them where he does not find them. To these qualities he has added a disposition to be affected more than other men by absent things as if they were present; an ability of conjuring up in himself passions, which are indeed far from being the same as those produced by real events, yet (especially in those parts of the general sympathy which are pleasing and delightful) do more nearly resemble the passions produced by real events, than any thing which, from the motions of their own minds merely, other men are accustomed to feel in themselves; whence, and from practice, he has acquired a greater readiness and power in expressing what he thinks and feels, and especially those thoughts and feelings which, by his own choice, or from

3. I here use the word "poetry" (though against my own judgment) as opposed to the word "prose," and synonymous with metrical composition. But much confusion has been introduced into criticism by this contradistinction of poetry and prose, instead of the more philosophical one of poetry and matter of fact, or science. The only strict antithesis to prose is metre; nor is this, in truth, a *strict* antithesis; because lines and passages of metre so naturally occur in writing prose, that it would be scarcely possible to avoid them, even were it desirable [Wordsworth's note].
4. Milton's *Paradise Lost* 1.620.
5. In Greek mythology the fluid in the veins of the gods.

the structure of his own mind, arise in him without immediate external excitement.

But, whatever portion of this faculty we may suppose even the greatest poet to possess, there cannot be a doubt but that the language which it will suggest to him, must, in liveliness and truth, fall far short of that which is uttered by men in real life, under the actual pressure of those passions, certain shadows of which the poet thus produces, or feels to be produced, in himself. However exalted a notion we would wish to cherish of the character of a poet, it is obvious, that, while he describes and imitates passions, his situation is alto-gether slavish and mechanical, compared with the freedom and power of real and substantial action and suffering. So that it will be the wish of the poet to bring his feelings near to those of the persons whose feelings he describes, nay, for short spaces of time perhaps, to let himself slip into an entire delusion, and even confound and identify his own feelings with theirs; modifying only the language which is thus suggested to him, by a consideration that he describes for a particular purpose, that of giving pleasure. Here, then, he will apply the principle on which I have so much insisted, namely, that of selection; on this he will depend for removing what would otherwise be painful or dis-gusting in the passion; he will feel that there is no necessity to trick out[6] or to elevate nature: and, the more industriously he applies this principle, the deeper will be his faith that no words, which his fancy or imagination can suggest, will be to be compared with those which are the emanations of reality and truth.

But it may be said by those who do not object to the general spirit of these remarks, that, as it is impossible for the poet to produce upon all occasions language as exquisitely fitted for the passion as that which the real passion itself suggests, it is proper that he should consider himself as in the situation of a translator, who deems himself justified when he substitutes excellences of another kind for those which are unattainable by him; and endeavours occasionally to surpass his original, in order to make some amends for the general inferiority to which he feels that he must submit. But this would be to encourage idleness and unmanly despair. Further, it is the language of men who speak of what they do not understand; who talk of poetry as a matter of amusement and idle pleasure; who will converse with us as gravely about a *taste* for poetry, as they express it, as if it were a thing as indifferent as a taste for rope-dancing, or Frontiniac[7] or sherry. Aristotle, I have been told, hath said, that poetry is the most philosophic of all writing;[8] it is so: its object is truth, not individual and local, but general, and operative; not standing upon external testimony, but carried alive into the heart by passion; truth which is its own testimony, which gives strength and divinity to the tribunal to which it appeals, and receives them from the same tribunal. Poetry is the image of man and nature. The obstacles which stand in the way of the fidelity of the biographer and historian, and of their consequent utility, are incalculably greater than those which are to be encountered by the poet who has an ade-quate notion of the dignity of his art. The poet writes under one restriction only, namely, that of the necessity of giving immediate pleasure to a human being possessed of that information which may be expected from him, not as a lawyer, a physician, a mariner, an astronomer or a natural philosopher, but as a man. Except this one restriction, there is no object standing between the

6. Dress up.
7. A sweet wine made from muscat grapes.
8. Aristotle in fact said that "poetry is more phil-osophic than history, since its statements are of the nature of universals, whereas those of history are singulars" (*Poetics* 1451b).

poet and the image of things; between this, and the biographer and historian there are a thousand.

Nor let this necessity of producing immediate pleasure be considered as a degradation of the poet's art. It is far otherwise. It is an acknowledgment of the beauty of the universe, an acknowledgment the more sincere because it is not formal, but indirect; it is a task light and easy to him who looks at the world in the spirit of love: further, it is a homage paid to the native and naked dignity of man, to the grand elementary principle of pleasure, by which he knows, and feels, and lives, and moves.[9] We have no sympathy but what is propagated by pleasure: I would not be misunderstood; but wherever we sympathize with pain it will be found that the sympathy is produced and carried on by subtle combinations with pleasure. We have no knowledge, that is, no general principles drawn from the contemplation of particular facts, but what has been built up by pleasure, and exists in us by pleasure alone. The man of science, the chemist and mathematician, whatever difficulties and disgusts they may have had to struggle with, know and feel this. However painful may be the objects with which the anatomist's knowledge is connected, he feels that his knowledge is pleasure; and where he has no pleasure he has no knowledge. What then does the poet? He considers man and the objects that surround him as acting and re-acting upon each other, so as to produce an infinite complexity of pain and pleasure; he considers man in his own nature and in his ordinary life as contemplating this with a certain quantity of immediate knowledge, with certain convictions, intuitions, and deductions which by habit become of the nature of intuitions; he considers him as looking upon this complex scene of ideas and sensations, and finding every where objects that immediately excite in him sympathies which, from the necessities of his nature, are accompanied by an overbalance of enjoyment.

To this knowledge which all men carry about with them, and to these sympathies in which without any other discipline than that of our daily life we are fitted to take delight, the poet principally directs his attention. He considers man and nature as essentially adapted to each other, and the mind of man as naturally the mirror of the fairest and most interesting qualities of nature. And thus the poet, prompted by this feeling of pleasure which accompanies him through the whole course of his studies, converses with general nature with affections akin to those, which, through labour and length of time, the man of science has raised up in himself, by conversing with those particular parts of nature which are the objects of his studies. The knowledge both of the poet and the man of science is pleasure; but the knowledge of the one cleaves to us as a necessary part of our existence, our natural and unalienable inheritance; the other is a personal and individual acquisition, slow to come to us, and by no habitual and direct sympathy connecting us with our fellow-beings. The man of science seeks truth as a remote and unknown benefactor; he cherishes and loves it in his solitude: the poet, singing a song in which all human beings join with him, rejoices in the presence of truth as our visible friend and hourly companion. Poetry is the breath and finer spirit of all knowledge; it is the impassioned expression which is in the countenance of all science. Emphatically may it be said of the poet, as Shakespeare hath said of man, "that he looks before and after."[1] He is the rock of defence of human nature; an upholder and preserver, carrying everywhere with him relationship

9. A bold echo of the words of St. Paul, that in God "we live, and move, and have our being" (Acts 17.28).
1. Cf. Shakespeare's *Hamlet* 4.4.9.27.

and love. In spite of difference of soil and climate, of language and manners, of laws and customs, in spite of things silently gone out of mind and things violently destroyed, the poet binds together by passion and knowledge the vast empire of human society, as it is spread over the whole earth, and over all time. The objects of the poet's thoughts are every where; though the eyes and senses of man are, it is true, his favorite guides, yet he will follow wheresoever he can find an atmosphere of sensation in which to move his wings. Poetry is the first and last of all knowledge—it is as immortal as the heart of man. If the labours of men of science should ever create any material revolution, direct or indirect, in our condition, and in the impressions which we habitually receive, the poet will sleep then no more than at present, but he will be ready to follow the steps of the man of science, not only in those general indirect effects, but he will be at his side, carrying sensation into the midst of the objects of the science itself. The remotest discoveries of the chemist, the botanist, or mineralogist, will be as proper objects of the poet's art as any upon which it can be employed, if the time should ever come when these things shall be familiar to us, and the relations under which they are contemplated by the followers of these respective sciences shall be manifestly and palpably material to us as enjoying and suffering beings.[2] If the time should ever come when what is now called science, thus familiarized to men, shall be ready to put on, as it were, a form of flesh and blood, the poet will lend his divine spirit to aid the transfiguration, and will welcome the being thus produced, as a dear and genuine inmate of the household of man.—It is not, then, to be supposed that any one, who holds that sublime notion of poetry which I have attempted to convey, will break in upon the sanctity and truth of his pictures by transitory and accidental ornaments, and endeavour to excite admiration of himself by arts, the necessity of which must manifestly depend upon the assumed meanness of his subject.

What I have thus far said applies to poetry in general; but especially to those parts of composition where the poet speaks through the mouth of his characters; and upon this point it appears to have such weight that I will conclude, there are few persons, of good sense, who would not allow that the dramatic parts of composition are defective, in proportion as they deviate from the real language of nature, and are coloured by a diction of the poet's own, either peculiar to him as an individual poet, or belonging simply to poets in general, to a body of men who, from the circumstance of their compositions being in metre, it is expected will employ a particular language.

It is not, then, in the dramatic parts of composition that we look for this distinction of language; but still it may be proper and necessary where the poet speaks to us in his own person and character. To this I answer by referring my reader to the description which I have before given of a poet. Among the qualities which I have enumerated as principally conducing to form a poet, is implied nothing differing in kind from other men, but only in degree. The sum of what I have there said is, that the poet is chiefly distinguished from other men by a greater promptness to think and feel without immediate external excitement, and a greater power in expressing such thoughts and feelings as are produced in him in that manner. But these passions and thoughts and feelings are the general passions and thoughts and feelings of men. And with what are they connected? Undoubtedly with our moral sentiments and animal

2. Wordsworth is at least right in anticipating the poetry of the machine. His sonnet "Steamboats, Viaducts, and Railways" is an early instance, as is Joanna Baillie's "Address to a Steamvessel."

sensations, and with the causes which excite these; with the operations of the elements and the appearances of the visible universe; with storm and sunshine, with the revolutions[3] of the seasons, with cold and heat, with loss of friends and kindred, with injuries and resentments, gratitude and hope, with fear and sorrow. These, and the like, are the sensations and objects which the poet describes, as they are the sensations of other men, and the objects which interest them. The poet thinks and feels in the spirit of the passions of men. How, then, can his language differ in any material degree from that of all other men who feel vividly and see clearly? It might be *proved* that it is impossible. But supposing that this were not the case, the poet might then be allowed to use a peculiar language, when expressing his feelings for his own gratification, or that of men like himself. But poets do not write for poets alone, but for men. Unless therefore we are advocates for that admiration which depends upon ignorance, and that pleasure which arises from hearing what we do not understand, the poet must descend from this supposed height, and, in order to excite rational sympathy, he must express himself as other men express themselves. * * *

["EMOTION RECOLLECTED IN TRANQUILLITY"]

I have said that poetry is the spontaneous overflow of powerful feelings: it takes its origin from emotion recollected in tranquillity: the emotion is contemplated till by a species of reaction the tranquillity gradually disappears, and an emotion, kindred to that which was before the subject of contemplation, is gradually produced, and does itself actually exist in the mind. In this mood successful composition generally begins, and in a mood similar to this it is carried on; but the emotion, of whatever kind and in whatever degree, from various causes is qualified by various pleasures, so that in describing any passions whatsoever, which are voluntarily described, the mind will upon the whole be in a state of enjoyment. Now, if nature be thus cautious in preserving in a state of enjoyment a being thus employed, the poet ought to profit by the lesson thus held forth to him, and ought especially to take care, that whatever passions he communicates to his reader, those passions, if his reader's mind be sound and vigorous, should always be accompanied with an overbalance of pleasure. Now the music of harmonious metrical language, the sense of difficulty overcome, and the blind association of pleasure which has been previously received from works of rhyme or metre of the same or similar construction, an indistinct perception perpetually renewed of language closely resembling that of real life, and yet, in the circumstance of metre, differing from it so widely, all these imperceptibly make up a complex feeling of delight, which is of the most important use in tempering the painful feeling which will always be found intermingled with powerful descriptions of the deeper passions. This effect is always produced in pathetic and impassioned poetry; while, in lighter compositions, the ease and gracefulness with which the poet manages his numbers are themselves confessedly a principal source of the gratification of the reader. I might perhaps include all which it is *necessary* to say upon this subject by affirming, what few persons will deny, that, of two descriptions, either of passions, manners, or characters, each of them equally well executed, the one in prose and the other in verse, the verse will be read a hundred times where the prose is read once. * * *

3. Recurrence.

I know that nothing would have so effectually contributed to further the end which I have in view, as to have shewn of what kind the pleasure is, and how the pleasure is produced, which is confessedly produced by metrical composition essentially different from that which I have here endeavoured to recommend: for the reader will say that he has been pleased by such composition; and what can I do more for him? The power of any art is limited; and he will suspect, that, if I propose to furnish him with new friends, it is only upon condition of his abandoning his old friends. Besides, as I have said, the reader is himself conscious of the pleasure which he has received from such composition, composition to which he has peculiarly attached the endearing name of poetry; and all men feel an habitual gratitude, and something of an honorable bigotry for the objects which have long continued to please them: we not only wish to be pleased, but to be pleased in that particular way in which we have been accustomed to be pleased. There is a host of arguments in these feelings; and I should be the less able to combat them successfully, as I am willing to allow, that, in order entirely to enjoy the poetry which I am recommending, it would be necessary to give up much of what is ordinarily enjoyed. But, would my limits have permitted me to point out how this pleasure is produced, I might have removed many obstacles, and assisted my reader in perceiving that the powers of language are not so limited as he may suppose; and that it is possible that poetry may give other enjoyments, of a purer, more lasting, and more exquisite nature. This part of my subject I have not altogether neglected; but it has been less my present aim to prove, that the interest excited by some other kinds of poetry is less vivid, and less worthy of the nobler powers of the mind, than to offer reasons for presuming, that, if the object which I have proposed to myself were adequately attained, a species of poetry would be produced, which is genuine poetry; in its nature well adapted to interest mankind permanently, and likewise important in the multiplicity and quality of its moral relations.

From what has been said, and from a perusal of the poems, the reader will be able clearly to perceive the object which I have proposed to myself: he will determine how far I have attained this object; and, what is a much more important question, whether it be worth attaining; and upon the decision of these two questions will rest my claim to the approbation of the public.

1800, 1802

Strange fits of passion have I known[1]

Strange fits of passion have I known:
And I will dare to tell,
But in the Lover's ear alone,
What once to me befel.

5   When she I loved looked every day
Fresh as a rose in June,

---

1. This and the four following pieces are often grouped by editors as the "Lucy poems," even though "A slumber did my spirit seal" does not identify the "she" who is the subject of that poem. All but the last were written in 1799, while Words- worth and his sister were in Germany and homesick. There has been diligent speculation about the identity of Lucy, but it remains speculation. The one certainty is that she is not the girl of Wordsworth's "Lucy Gray."

I to her cottage bent my way,
Beneath an evening moon.

10 Upon the moon I fixed my eye,
All over the wide lea;
With quickening pace my horse drew nigh
Those paths so dear to me.

And now we reached the orchard-plot;
And, as we climbed the hill,
15 The sinking moon to Lucy's cot
Came near, and nearer still.

In one of those sweet dreams I slept,
Kind Nature's gentlest boon!
And all the while my eyes I kept
20 On the descending moon.

My horse moved on; hoof after hoof
He raised, and never stopped:
When down behind the cottage roof,
At once, the bright moon dropped.

25 What fond and wayward thoughts will slide
Into a Lover's head!
"O mercy!" to myself I cried,
"If Lucy should be dead!"[2]

1799   1800

She dwelt among the untrodden ways[1]

She dwelt among the untrodden ways
    Beside the springs of Dove,[2]
A Maid whom there were none to praise
    And very few to love:

5 A violet by a mossy stone
    Half hidden from the eye!
—Fair as a star, when only one
    Is shining in the sky.

She lived unknown, and few could know
10   When Lucy ceased to be;

2. An additional stanza in an earlier manuscript version demonstrates how a poem can be improved by omission of a passage that is, in itself, excellent poetry: "I told her this: her laughter light / Is ringing in my ears; / And when I think upon that night / My eyes are dim with tears."

1. For the author's revisions while composing this poem, see "Poems in Process," in the appendices to this volume.
2. There are several rivers by this name in England, including one in the Lake District.

But she is in her grave, and, oh,
The difference to me!

1799   1800

Three years she grew

Three years she grew in sun and shower,
Then Nature said, "A lovelier flower
On earth was never sown;
This Child I to myself will take;
5   She shall be mine, and I will make
A Lady of my own.[1]

"Myself will to my darling be
Both law and impulse: and with me
The Girl, in rock and plain,
10   In earth and heaven, in glade and bower,
Shall feel an overseeing power
To kindle or restrain.

"She shall be sportive as the fawn
That wild with glee across the lawn
15   Or up the mountain springs;
And hers shall be the breathing balm,
And hers the silence and the calm
Of mute insensate things.

"The floating clouds their state shall lend
20   To her; for her the willow bend;
Nor shall she fail to see
Even in the motions of the Storm
Grace that shall mould the Maiden's form
By silent sympathy.

25   "The stars of midnight shall be dear
To her; and she shall lean her ear
In many a secret place
Where rivulets dance their wayward round,
And beauty born of murmuring sound
30   Shall pass into her face.

"And vital feelings of delight
Shall rear her form to stately height,
Her virgin bosom swell;
Such thoughts to Lucy I will give
35   While she and I together live
Here in this happy dell."

---

1. I.e., Lucy was three years old when Nature made this promise; line 37 makes clear that Lucy had reached
the maturity foretold in the sixth stanza when she died.

Thus Nature spake—the work was done—
How soon my Lucy's race was run!
She died, and left to me
40 This heath, this calm, and quiet scene;
The memory of what has been,
And never more will be.

1799   1800

A slumber did my spirit seal

A slumber did my spirit seal;
    I had no human fears:
She seemed a thing that could not feel
    The touch of earthly years.

5   No motion has she now, no force;
    She neither hears nor sees;
Rolled round in earth's diurnal° course,   *daily*
    With rocks, and stones, and trees.

1799   1800

I travelled among unknown men

I travelled among unknown men,
    In lands beyond the sea;
Nor, England! did I know till then
    What love I bore to thee.

5   'Tis past, that melancholy dream!
    Nor will I quit thy shore
A second time; for still I seem
    To love thee more and more.

Among thy mountains did I feel
10   The joy of my desire;
And she I cherished turned her wheel
    Beside an English fire.

Thy mornings showed, thy nights concealed
    The bowers where Lucy played;
15 And thine too is the last green field
    That Lucy's eyes surveyed.

ca. 1801   1807

Nutting[1]

——————— It seems a day
(I speak of one from many singled out)
One of those heavenly days that cannot die;
When, in the eagerness of boyish hope,
5   I left our cottage-threshold, sallying forth
With a huge wallet° o'er my shoulder slung,   *bag, knapsack*
A nutting-crook in hand; and turned my steps
Tow'rd some far-distant wood, a Figure quaint,
Tricked out in proud disguise of cast-off weeds°   *clothes*
10 Which for that service had been husbanded,
By exhortation of my frugal Dame[2]—
Motley accoutrement, of power to smile
At thorns, and brakes, and brambles,—and, in truth,
More ragged than need was! O'er pathless rocks,
15 Through beds of matted fern, and tangled thickets,
Forcing my way, I came to one dear nook
Unvisited, where not a broken bough
Drooped with its withered leaves, ungracious sign
Of devastation; but the hazels rose
20 Tall and erect, with tempting clusters hung,
A virgin scene!—A little while I stood,
Breathing with such suppression of the heart
As joy delights in; and, with wise restraint
Voluptuous, fearless of a rival, eyed
25 The banquet;—or beneath the trees I sate
Among the flowers, and with the flowers I played;
A temper known to those, who, after long
And weary expectation, have been blest
With sudden happiness beyond all hope.
30 Perhaps it was a bower beneath whose leaves
The violets of five seasons re-appear
And fade, unseen by any human eye;
Where fairy water-breaks[3] do murmur on
For ever; and I saw the sparkling foam,
35 And—with my cheek on one of those green stones
That, fleeced with moss, under the shady trees,
Lay round me, scattered like a flock of sheep—
I heard the murmur and the murmuring sound,
In that sweet mood when pleasure loves to pay
40 Tribute to ease; and, of its joy secure,
The heart luxuriates with indifferent things,
Wasting its kindliness on stocks[4] and stones,
And on the vacant air. Then up I rose,

---

1. Wordsworth said in 1843 that these lines, written in Germany in 1798, were "intended as part of
a poem on my own life [*The Prelude*], but struck
out as not being wanted there." He published them
in the second edition of *Lyrical Ballads*, 1800.
2. Ann Tyson, with whom Wordsworth lodged

while at Hawkshead grammar school.
3. Places where the flow of a stream is broken by
rocks.
4. Tree stumps. ("Stocks and stones" is a conventional expression for "inanimate things.")

And dragged to earth both branch and bough, with crash
45   And merciless ravage: and the shady nook
Of hazels, and the green and mossy bower,
Deformed and sullied, patiently gave up
Their quiet being: and, unless I now
Confound my present feelings with the past,
50   Ere from the mutilated bower I turned
Exulting, rich beyond the wealth of kings,
I felt a sense of pain when I beheld
The silent trees, and saw the intruding sky.—
Then, dearest Maiden,[5] move along these shades
55   In gentleness of heart; with gentle hand
Touch—for there is a spirit in the woods.

1798   1800

The Ruined Cottage[1]

First Part

'Twas summer and the sun was mounted high.
Along the south the uplands feebly glared
Through a pale steam, and all the northern downs
In clearer air ascending shewed far off
5   Their surfaces with shadows dappled o'er
Of deep embattled clouds: far as the sight
Could reach those many shadows lay in spots
Determined and unmoved, with steady beams
Of clear and pleasant sunshine interposed;
10   Pleasant to him who on the soft cool moss
Extends his careless limbs beside the root
Of some huge oak whose aged branches make
A twilight of their own, a dewy shade
Where the wren warbles while the dreaming man,
15   Half-conscious of that soothing melody,
With side-long eye looks out upon the scene,
By those impending branches made more soft,
More soft and distant. Other lot was mine.
Across a bare wide Common I had toiled
20   With languid feet which by the slipp'ry ground
Were baffled still, and when I stretched myself
On the brown earth my limbs from very heat

5. In a manuscript passage originally intended to lead up to "Nutting," the maiden is called Lucy.
1. Wordsworth wrote *The Ruined Cottage* in 1797–98, then revised it several times before he finally published an expanded version of the story as book 1 of *The Excursion*, in 1814. *The Ruined Cottage* was not published as an independent poem until 1949, when it appeared in the fifth volume of *The Poetical Works of William Wordsworth*, edited by Ernest de Selincourt and Helen Darbishire, who printed a version known as "MS. B." The text reprinted here is from "MS. D," dated 1799, as transcribed by James Butler in the Cornell Wordsworth volume, *"The Ruined Cottage" and "The Pedlar"* (1979).

Concerning the principal narrator, introduced in line 33, Wordsworth said in 1843, "had I been born in a class which would have deprived me of what is called a liberal education, it is not unlikely that being strong in body; I should have taken to a way of life such as that in which my Pedlar passed the greater part of his days. . . . [T]he character I have represented in his person is chiefly an idea of what I fancied my own character might have become in his circumstances."

Could find no rest nor my weak arm disperse
The insect host which gathered round my face
25 And joined their murmurs to the tedious noise
Of seeds of bursting gorse that crackled round.
I rose and turned towards a group of trees
Which midway in that level stood alone,
And thither come at length, beneath a shade
30 Of clustering elms that sprang from the same root
I found a ruined house, four naked walls
That stared upon each other. I looked round
And near the door I saw an aged Man,
Alone, and stretched upon the cottage bench;
35 An iron-pointed staff lay at his side.
With instantaneous joy I recognized
That pride of nature and of lowly life,
The venerable Armytage, a friend
As dear to me as is the setting sun.
40   Two days before
We had been fellow-travellers. I knew
That he was in this neighbourhood and now
Delighted found him here in the cool shade.
He lay, his pack of rustic merchandize
45 Pillowing his head—I guess he had no thought
Of his way-wandering life. His eyes were shut;
The shadows of the breezy elms above
Dappled his face. With thirsty heat oppress'd
At length I hailed him, glad to see his hat
50 Bedewed with water-drops, as if the brim
Had newly scoop'd a running stream. He rose
And pointing to a sun-flower bade me climb
The [   ]² wall where that same gaudy flower
Looked out upon the road. It was a plot
55 Of garden-ground, now wild, its matted weeds
Marked with the steps of those whom as they pass'd,
The goose-berry trees that shot in long lank slips,
Or currants hanging from their leafless stems
In scanty strings, had tempted to o'erleap
60 The broken wall. Within that cheerless spot,
Where two tall hedgerows of thick willow boughs
Joined in a damp cold nook, I found a well
Half-choked [with willow flowers and weeds.]³
I slaked my thirst and to the shady bench
65 Returned, and while I stood unbonneted
To catch the motion of the cooler air
The old Man said, "I see around me here
Things which you cannot see: we die, my Friend,
Nor we alone, but that which each man loved
70 And prized in his peculiar nook of earth
Dies with him or is changed, and very soon
Even of the good is no memorial left.

2. The brackets here and in later lines mark blank spaces left unfilled in the manuscript.

3. Wordsworth penciled the bracketed phrase into a gap left in the manuscript.

The Poets in their elegies and songs
Lamenting the departed call the groves,
75   They call upon the hills and streams to mourn,
And senseless[4] rocks, nor idly; for they speak
In these their invocations with a voice
Obedient to the strong creative power
Of human passion. Sympathies there are
80   More tranquil, yet perhaps of kindred birth,
That steal upon the meditative mind
And grow with thought. Beside yon spring I stood
And eyed its waters till we seemed to feel
One sadness, they and I. For them a bond
85   Of brotherhood is broken: time has been
When every day the touch of human hand
Disturbed their stillness, and they ministered
To human comfort. When I stooped to drink,
A spider's web hung to the water's edge,
90   And on the wet and slimy foot-stone lay
The useless fragment of a wooden bowl;
It moved my very heart. The day has been
When I could never pass this road but she
Who lived within these walls, when I appeared,
95   A daughter's welcome gave me, and I loved her
As my own child. O Sir! the good die first,
And they whose hearts are dry as summer dust
Burn to the socket. Many a passenger°   *passerby, traveler*
Has blessed poor Margaret for her gentle looks
100   When she upheld the cool refreshment drawn
From that forsaken spring, and no one came
But he was welcome, no one went away
But that it seemed she loved him. She is dead,
The worm is on her cheek, and this poor hut,
105   Stripp'd of its outward garb of household flowers,
Of rose and sweet-briar, offers to the wind
A cold bare wall whose earthy top is tricked
With weeds and the rank spear-grass. She is dead,
And nettles rot and adders sun themselves
110   Where we have sate together while she nurs'd
Her infant at her breast. The unshod Colt,
The wandring heifer and the Potter's ass,
Find shelter now within the chimney-wall
Where I have seen her evening hearth-stone blaze
115   And through the window spread upon the road
Its chearful light.—You will forgive me, Sir,
But often on this cottage do I muse
As on a picture, till my wiser mind
Sinks, yielding to the foolishness of grief.
120   She had a husband, an industrious man,
Sober and steady; I have heard her say
That he was up and busy at his loom
In summer ere the mower's scythe had swept

---

4. Incapable of sensation or perception.

The dewy grass, and in the early spring
125 Ere the last star had vanished. They who pass'd
At evening, from behind the garden-fence
Might hear his busy spade, which he would ply
After his daily work till the day-light
Was gone and every leaf and flower were lost
130 In the dark hedges. So they pass'd their days
In peace and comfort, and two pretty babes
Were their best hope next to the God in Heaven.
—You may remember, now some ten years gone,
Two blighting seasons when the fields were left
135 With half a harvest.[5] It pleased heaven to add
A worse affliction in the plague of war:
A happy land was stricken to the heart;
'Twas a sad time of sorrow and distress:
A wanderer among the cottages,
140 I with my pack of winter raiment saw
The hardships of that season: many rich
Sunk down as in a dream among the poor,
And of the poor did many cease to be,
And their place knew them not. Meanwhile, abridg'd°   *deprived*
145 Of daily comforts, gladly reconciled
To numerous self-denials, Margaret
Went struggling on through those calamitous years
With chearful hope: but ere the second autumn
A fever seized her husband. In disease
150 He lingered long, and when his strength returned
He found the little he had stored to meet
The hour of accident or crippling age
Was all consumed. As I have said, 'twas now
A time of trouble; shoals of artisans
155 Were from their daily labour turned away
To hang for bread on parish charity,[6]
They and their wives and children—happier far
Could they have lived as do the little birds
That peck along the hedges or the kite
160 That makes her dwelling in the mountain rocks.
Ill fared it now with Robert, he who dwelt
In this poor cottage; at his door he stood
And whistled many a snatch of merry tunes
That had no mirth in them, or with his knife
165 Carved uncouth figures on the heads of sticks,
Then idly sought about through every nook
Of house or garden any casual task
Of use or ornament, and with a strange,
Amusing but uneasy novelty
170 He blended where he might the various tasks

5. As James Butler points out in his introduction, Wordsworth is purposely distancing his story in time. The "two blighting seasons" in fact occurred in 1794–95, only a few years before Wordsworth wrote *The Ruined Cottage*, when a bad harvest was followed by one of the worst winters on record. Much of the seed grain was destroyed in the ground, and the price of wheat nearly doubled.
6. The so-called able-bodied poor were entitled to receive from the parish in which they were settled the food, the clothing, and sometimes the cash that would help them over a crisis.

Of summer, autumn, winter, and of spring.
But this endured not; his good-humour soon
Became a weight in which no pleasure was,
And poverty brought on a petted° mood   *ill-tempered*
175   And a sore temper: day by day he drooped,
And he would leave his home, and to the town
Without an errand would he turn his steps
Or wander here and there among the fields.
One while he would speak lightly of his babes
180   And with a cruel tongue: at other times
He played with them wild freaks of merriment:
And 'twas a piteous thing to see the looks
Of the poor innocent children. 'Every smile,'
Said Margaret to me here beneath these trees,
185   'Made my heart bleed,' " At this the old Man paus'd
And looking up to those enormous elms
He said, " 'Tis now the hour of deepest noon,
At this still season of repose and peace,
This hour when all things which are not at rest
190   Are chearful, while this multitude of flies
Fills all the air with happy melody,
Why should a tear be in an old man's eye?
Why should we thus with an untoward mind
And in the weakness of humanity
195   From natural wisdom turn our hearts away,
To natural comfort shut our eyes and ears,
And feeding on disquiet thus disturb
The calm of Nature with our restless thoughts?"

END OF THE FIRST PART

Second Part

He spake with somewhat of a solemn tone:
200   But when he ended there was in his face
Such easy chearfulness, a look so mild
That for a little time it stole away
All recollection, and that simple tale
Passed from my mind like a forgotten sound.
205   A while on trivial things we held discourse,
To me soon tasteless. In my own despite
I thought of that poor woman as of one
Whom I had known and loved. He had rehearsed
Her homely tale with such familiar power,
210   With such a[n active]⁷ countenance, an eye
So busy, that the things of which he spake
Seemed present, and, attention now relaxed,
There was a heartfelt chillness in my veins.
I rose, and turning from that breezy shade
215   Went out into the open air and stood
To drink the comfort of the warmer sun.
Long time I had not stayed ere, looking round
Upon that tranquil ruin, I returned

7. Wordsworth penciled the bracketed phrase into a gap left in the manuscript.

And begged of the old man that for my sake
220 He would resume his story. He replied,
"It were a wantonness° and would demand   *reckless ill-doing*
Severe reproof, if we were men whose hearts
Could hold vain dalliance with the misery
Even of the dead, contented thence to draw
225 A momentary pleasure never marked
By reason, barren of all future good.
But we have known that there is often found
In mournful thoughts, and always might be found,
A power to virtue friendly; were't not so,
230 I am a dreamer among men, indeed
An idle dreamer. 'Tis a common tale,
By moving accidents[8] uncharactered,
A tale of silent suffering, hardly clothed
In bodily form, and to the grosser sense
235 But ill adapted, scarcely palpable
To him who does not think. But at your bidding
I will proceed.
                     While thus it fared with them
To whom this cottage till that hapless year
Had been a blessed home, it was my chance
240 To travel in a country far remote,
And glad I was when, halting by yon gate
That leads from the green lane, again I saw
These lofty elm-trees. Long I did not rest:
With many pleasant thoughts I cheer'd my way
245 O'er the flat common. At the door arrived,
I knocked, and when I entered with the hope
Of usual greeting, Margaret looked at me
A little while, then turned her head away
Speechless, and sitting down upon a chair
250 Wept bitterly. I wist not what to do
Or how to speak to her. Poor wretch! at last
She rose from off her seat—and then, oh Sir!
I cannot tell how she pronounced my name:
With fervent love, and with a face of grief
255 Unutterably helpless, and a look
That seem'd to cling upon me, she enquir'd
If I had seen her husband. As she spake
A strange surprize and fear came to my heart,
Nor had I power to answer ere she told
260 That he had disappeared—just two months gone.
He left his house; two wretched days had passed,
And on the third by the first break of light,
Within her casement full in view she saw
A purse of gold.[9] 'I trembled at the sight,'
265 Said Margaret, 'for I knew it was his hand

---

8. Othello speaks "of most disastrous chances, / Of moving accidents by flood and field, / Of hairbreadth 'scapes" (Shakespeare, *Othello* 1.3.133–35).
9. The "bounty" that her husband had been paid for enlisting in the militia. The shortage of volunteers and England's sharply rising military needs had in some counties forced the bounty up from about £1 in 1757 to more than £16 in 1796 (J. R. Western, *English Militia in the Eighteenth Century*, 1965).

That placed it there, and on that very day
By one, a stranger, from my husband sent,
The tidings came that he had joined a troop
Of soldiers going to a distant land.
270 He left me thus—Poor Man! he had not heart
To take a farewell of me, and he feared
That I should follow with my babes, and sink
Beneath the misery of a soldier's life.'
This tale did Margaret tell with many tears:
275 And when she ended I had little power
To give her comfort, and was glad to take
Such words of hope from her own mouth as serv'd
To cheer us both: but long we had not talked
Ere we built up a pile of better thoughts,
280 And with a brighter eye she looked around
As if she had been shedding tears of joy.
We parted. It was then the early spring;
I left her busy with her garden tools;
And well remember, o'er that fence she looked,
285 And while I paced along the foot-way path
Called out, and sent a blessing after me
With tender chearfulness and with a voice
That seemed the very sound of happy thoughts.
    I roved o'er many a hill and many a dale
290 With this my weary load, in heat and cold,
Through many a wood, and many an open ground,
In sunshine or in shade, in wet or fair,
Now blithe, now drooping, as it might befal,
My best companions now the driving winds
295 And now the 'trotting brooks'[1] and whispering trees
And now the music of my own sad steps,
With many a short-lived thought that pass'd between
And disappeared. I came this way again
Towards the wane of summer, when the wheat
300 Was yellow, and the soft and bladed grass
Sprang up afresh and o'er the hay-field spread
Its tender green. When I had reached the door
I found that she was absent. In the shade
Where now we sit I waited her return.
305 Her cottage in its outward look appeared
As chearful as before; in any shew
Of neatness little changed, but that I thought
The honeysuckle crowded round the door
And from the wall hung down in heavier wreathes,
310 And knots of worthless stone-crop[2] started out
Along the window's edge, and grew like weeds
Against the lower panes. I turned aside
And stroll'd into her garden.—It was chang'd:
The unprofitable bindweed spread his bells
315 From side to side and with unwieldy wreaths

---

1. From Robert Burns ("To William Simpson," line 87).

2. A plant with yellow flowers that grows on walls and rocks.

Had dragg'd the rose from its sustaining wall
And bent it down to earth; the border-tufts—
Daisy and thrift and lowly camomile
And thyme—had straggled out into the paths
320 Which they were used° to deck. Ere this an hour   *accustomed*
Was wasted. Back I turned my restless steps,
And as I walked before the door it chanced
A stranger passed, and guessing whom I sought
He said that she was used to ramble far.
325 The sun was sinking in the west, and now
I sate with sad impatience. From within
Her solitary infant cried aloud.
The spot though fair seemed very desolate,
The longer I remained more desolate.
330 And, looking round, I saw the corner-stones,
Till then unmark'd, on either side the door
With dull red stains discoloured and stuck o'er
With tufts and hairs of wool, as if the sheep
That feed upon the commons³ thither came
335 Familiarly and found a couching-place
Even at her threshold.—The house-clock struck eight;
I turned and saw her distant a few steps.
Her face was pale and thin, her figure too
Was chang'd. As she unlocked the door she said,
340 'It grieves me you have waited here so long,
But in good truth I've wandered much of late
And sometimes, to my shame I speak, have need
Of my best prayers to bring me back again.'
While on the board she spread our evening meal
345 She told me she had lost her elder child,
That he for months had been a serving-boy
Apprenticed by the parish. 'I perceive
You look at me, and you have cause. Today
I have been travelling far, and many days
350 About the fields I wander, knowing this
Only, that what I seek I cannot find.
And so I waste my time: for I am changed;
And to myself,' said she, 'have done much wrong,
And to this helpless infant. I have slept
355 Weeping, and weeping I have waked; my tears
Have flow'd as if my body were not such
As others are, and I could never die.
But I am now in mind and in my heart
More easy, and I hope,' said she, 'that heaven
360 Will give me patience to endure the things
Which I behold at home.' It would have grieved
Your very heart to see her. Sir, I feel
The story linger in my heart. I fear
'Tis long and tedious, but my spirit clings
365 To that poor woman: so familiarly
Do I perceive her manner, and her look

---

3. Land belonging to the local community as a whole.

And presence, and so deeply do I feel
Her goodness, that not seldom in my walks
A momentary trance comes over me;
370 And to myself I seem to muse on one
By sorrow laid asleep or borne away,
A human being destined to awake
To human life, or something very near
To human life, when he shall come again
375 For whom she suffered. Sir, it would have griev'd
Your very soul to see her: evermore
Her eye-lids droop'd, her eyes were downward cast;
And when she at her table gave me food
She did not look at me. Her voice was low,
380 Her body was subdued. In every act
Pertaining to her house-affairs appeared
The careless stillness which a thinking mind
Gives to an idle matter—still she sighed,
But yet no motion of the breast was seen,
385 No heaving of the heart. While by the fire
We sate together, sighs came on my ear;
I knew not how, and hardly whence they came.
I took my staff, and when I kissed her babe
The tears stood in her eyes. I left her then
390 With the best hope and comfort I could give;
She thanked me for my will, but for my hope
It seemed she did not thank me.
                                        I returned
And took my rounds along this road again
Ere on its sunny bank the primrose flower
395 Had chronicled the earliest day of spring.
I found her sad and drooping; she had learn'd
No tidings of her husband: if he lived
She knew not that he lived; if he were dead
She knew not he was dead. She seemed the same
400 In person [or]⁴ appearance, but her house
Bespoke a sleepy hand of negligence;
The floor was neither dry nor neat, the hearth
Was comfortless [   ],
The windows too were dim, and her few books,
405 Which, one upon the other, heretofore
Had been piled up against the corner-panes
In seemly order, now with straggling leaves
Lay scattered here and there, open or shut
As they had chanced to fall. Her infant babe
410 Had from its mother caught the trick of grief
And sighed among its playthings. Once again
I turned towards the garden-gate and saw
More plainly still that poverty and grief
Were now come nearer to her: the earth was hard,
415 With weeds defaced and knots of withered grass;
No ridges there appeared of clear black mould,

4. The word *or* was erased here; later manuscripts read "and."

No winter greenness; of her herbs and flowers
It seemed the better part were gnawed away
Or trampled on the earth; a chain of straw
420 Which had been twisted round the tender stem
Of a young apple-tree lay at its root;
The bark was nibbled round by truant sheep.
Margaret stood near, her infant in her arms,
And seeing that my eye was on the tree
425 She said, 'I fear it will be dead and gone
Ere Robert come again.' Towards the house
Together we returned, and she inquired
If I had any hope. But for her Babe
And for her little friendless Boy, she said,
430 She had no wish to live, that she must die
Of sorrow. Yet I saw the idle loom
Still in its place. His Sunday garments hung
Upon the self-same nail, his very staff
Stood undisturbed behind the door. And when
435 I passed this way beaten by Autumn winds
She told me that her little babe was dead
And she was left alone. That very time,
I yet remember, through the miry lane
She walked with me a mile, when the bare trees
440 Trickled with foggy damps, and in such sort
That any heart had ached to hear her begg'd
That wheresoe'er I went I still would ask
For him whom she had lost. We parted then,
Our final parting, for from that time forth
445 Did many seasons pass ere I returned
Into this tract again.
                          Five tedious years
She lingered in unquiet widowhood,
A wife and widow. Needs must it have been
A sore heart-wasting. I have heard, my friend,
450 That in that broken arbour she would sit
The idle length of half a sabbath day—
There, where you see the toadstool's lazy head—
And when a dog passed by she still would quit
The shade and look abroad. On this old Bench
455 For hours she sate, and evermore her eye
Was busy in the distance, shaping things
Which made her heart beat quick. Seest thou that path?
(The green-sward now has broken its grey line)
There to and fro she paced through many a day
460 Of the warm summer, from a belt of flax
That girt her waist spinning the long-drawn thread
With backward steps.—Yet ever as there passed
A man whose garments shewed the Soldier's red,
Or crippled Mendicant in Sailor's garb,
465 The little child who sate to turn the wheel
Ceased from his toil, and she with faltering voice,
Expecting still to learn her husband's fate,
Made many a fond inquiry; and when they

Whose presence gave no comfort were gone by,
470 Her heart was still more sad. And by yon gate
Which bars the traveller's road she often stood
And when a stranger horseman came, the latch
Would lift, and in his face look wistfully,
Most happy if from aught discovered there
475 Of tender feeling she might dare repeat
The same sad question. Meanwhile her poor hut
Sunk to decay, for he was gone whose hand
At the first nippings of October frost
Closed up each chink and with fresh bands of straw
480 Chequered the green-grown thatch. And so she lived
Through the long winter, reckless and alone,
Till this reft house by frost, and thaw, and rain
Was sapped; and when she slept the nightly damps
Did chill her breast, and in the stormy day
485 Her tattered clothes were ruffled by the wind
Even at the side of her own fire. Yet still
She loved this wretched spot, nor would for worlds
Have parted hence; and still that length of road
And this rude bench one torturing hope endeared,
490 Fast rooted at her heart, and here, my friend,
In sickness she remained, and here she died,
Last human tenant of these ruined walls."
      The old Man ceased: he saw that I was mov'd;
From that low Bench, rising instinctively,
495 I turned aside in weakness, nor had power
To thank him for the tale which he had told.
I stood, and leaning o'er the garden-gate
Reviewed that Woman's suff'rings, and it seemed
To comfort me while with a brother's love
500 I blessed her in the impotence of grief.
At length [towards] the [Cottage I returned]⁵
Fondly, and traced with milder interest
That secret spirit of humanity
Which, 'mid the calm oblivious tendencies
505 Of nature, 'mid her plants, her weeds, and flowers,
And silent overgrowings, still survived.
The old man, seeing this, resumed and said,
"My Friend, enough to sorrow have you given,
The purposes of wisdom ask no more;
510 Be wise and chearful, and no longer read
The forms of things with an unworthy eye.
She sleeps in the calm earth, and peace is here.
I well remember that those very plumes,
Those weeds, and the high spear-grass on that wall,
515 By mist and silent rain-drops silver'd o'er,
As once I passed did to my heart convey
So still an image of tranquillity,
So calm and still, and looked so beautiful
Amid the uneasy thoughts which filled my mind,

5. The words inside the brackets were added in MS. E.

520   That what we feel of sorrow and despair
        From ruin and from change, and all the grief
        The passing shews of being leave behind,
        Appeared an idle dream that could not live
        Where meditation was. I turned away
525   And walked along my road in happiness."
            He ceased. By this the sun declining shot
        A slant and mellow radiance which began
        To fall upon us where beneath the trees
        We sate on that low bench, and now we felt,
530   Admonished thus, the sweet hour coming on.
        A linnet warbled from those lofty elms,
        A thrush sang loud, and other melodies,
        At distance heard, peopled the milder air.
        The old man rose and hoisted up his load.
535   Together casting then a farewell look
        Upon those silent walls, we left the shade
        And ere the stars were visible attained
        A rustic inn, our evening resting-place.

THE END

1797–ca.1799   1949

Michael[1]

A Pastoral Poem

    If from the public way you turn your steps
    Up the tumultuous brook of Green-head Ghyll,[2]
    You will suppose that with an upright path
    Your feet must struggle; in such bold ascent
5   The pastoral mountains front you, face to face.
    But, courage! for around that boisterous brook
    The mountains have all opened out themselves,
    And made a hidden valley of their own.
    No habitation can be seen; but they
10   Who journey thither find themselves alone
    With a few sheep, with rocks and stones, and kites°   *hawks*
    That overhead are sailing in the sky.
    It is in truth an utter solitude;

1. This poem is founded on the actual misfortunes of a family at Grasmere. For the account of the sheepfold, see Dorothy Wordsworth's *Grasmere Journals,* October 11, 1800 (p. 1597). Wordsworth wrote to Thomas Poole, on April 9, 1801, that he had attempted to picture a man "agitated by two of the most powerful affections of the human heart; the parental affection, and the love of property, *landed* property, including the feelings of inheritance, home, and personal and family independence." In another letter, sent, along with a copy of the 1800 *Lyrical Ballads,* January 14, 1801, to Charles James Fox, the leader of the opposition in Parliament, Wordsworth commented in a similar vein on how a "little tract of land" could serve, for the class of men whom he had represented in "Michael," as "a kind of permanent rallying point for their domestic feelings"; he also remarked, with regret, that this class, "small independent *proprietors* of land," was "rapidly disappearing." The subtitle shows Wordsworth's shift of the term "pastoral" from aristocratic make-believe to the tragic suffering of people in what he called "humble and rustic life."
2. A ravine forming the bed of a stream. Greenhead Ghyll is not far from Wordsworth's cottage at Grasmere. The other places named in the poem are also in that vicinity.

Nor should I have made mention of this Dell
15 But for one object which you might pass by,
Might see and notice not. Beside the brook
Appears a straggling heap of unhewn stones!
And to that simple object appertains
A story—unenriched with strange events,
20 Yet not unfit, I deem, for the fireside,
Or for the summer shade. It was the first
Of those domestic tales that spake to me
Of Shepherds, dwellers in the valleys, men
Whom I already loved;—not verily
25 For their own sakes, but for the fields and hills
Where was their occupation and abode.
And hence this Tale, while I was yet a Boy
Careless of books, yet having felt the power
Of Nature, by the gentle agency
30 Of natural objects, led me on to feel
For passions that were not my own, and think
(At random and imperfectly indeed)
On man, the heart of man, and human life.
Therefore, although it be a history
35 Homely and rude, I will relate the same
For the delight of a few natural hearts;
And, with yet fonder feeling, for the sake
Of youthful Poets, who among these hills
Will be my second self when I am gone.

40   Upon the forest-side in Grasmere Vale
There dwelt a Shepherd, Michael was his name;
An old man, stout of heart, and strong of limb.
His bodily frame had been from youth to age
Of an unusual strength: his mind was keen,
45 Intense, and frugal, apt for all affairs,
And in his shepherd's calling he was prompt
And watchful more than ordinary men.
Hence had he learned the meaning of all winds,
Of blasts of every tone; and, oftentimes,
50 When others heeded not, he heard the South°   south wind
Make subterraneous music, like the noise
Of bagpipers on distant Highland hills.
The Shepherd, at such warning, of his flock
Bethought him, and he to himself would say,
55 "The winds are now devising work for me!"
And, truly, at all times, the storm, that drives
The traveller to a shelter, summoned him
Up to the mountains: he had been alone
Amid the heart of many thousand mists,
60 That came to him, and left him, on the heights.
So lived he till his eightieth year was past.
And grossly that man errs, who should suppose
That the green valleys, and the streams and rocks,
Were things indifferent to the Shepherd's thoughts.
65 Fields, where with cheerful spirits he had breathed

The common air; hills, which with vigorous step
He had so often climbed; which had impressed
So many incidents upon his mind
Of hardship, skill or courage, joy or fear;
70 Which, like a book, preserved the memory
Of the dumb animals, whom he had saved,
Had fed or sheltered, linking to such acts
The certainty of honourable gain;
Those fields, those hills—what could they less? had laid
75 Strong hold on his affections, were to him
A pleasurable feeling of blind love,
The pleasure which there is in life itself.

    His days had not been passed in singleness.
His Helpmate was a comely matron, old—
80 Though younger than himself full twenty years.
She was a woman of a stirring life,
Whose heart was in her house: two wheels she had
Of antique form; this large, for spinning wool;
That small, for flax; and if one wheel had rest,
85 It was because the other was at work.
The Pair had but one inmate in their house,
An only Child, who had been born to them
When Michael, telling° o'er his years, began   counting
To deem that he was old,—in shepherd's phrase,
90 With one foot in the grave. This only Son,
With two brave sheep-dogs tried° in many a storm,   tested
The one of an inestimable worth,
Made all their household. I may truly say,
That they were as a proverb in the vale
95 For endless industry. When day was gone,
And from their occupations out of doors
The Son and Father were come home, even then,
Their labour did not cease; unless when all
Turned to the cleanly supper-board, and there,
100 Each with a mess of pottage and skimmed milk,
Sat round the basket piled with oaten cakes,
And their plain home-made cheese. Yet when the meal
Was ended, Luke (for so the Son was named)
And his old Father both betook themselves
105 To such convenient work as might employ
Their hands by the fire-side; perhaps to card
Wool for the Housewife's spindle, or repair
Some injury done to sickle, flail, or scythe,
Or other implement of house or field.

110   Down from the ceiling, by the chimney's edge,
That in our ancient uncouth country style
With huge and black projection overbrowed
Large space beneath, as duly as the light
Of day grew dim the Housewife hung a lamp;
115 An aged utensil, which had performed
Service beyond all others of its kind.

Early at evening did it burn—and late,
Surviving comrade of uncounted hours,
Which, going by from year to year, had found,
120 And left the couple neither gay perhaps
Nor cheerful, yet with objects and with hopes,
Living a life of eager industry.
And now, when Luke had reached his eighteenth year,
There by the light of his old lamp they sate,
125 Father and Son, while far into the night
The Housewife plied her own peculiar work,
Making the cottage through the silent hours
Murmur as with the sound of summer flies.
This light was famous in its neighbourhood,
130 And was a public symbol of the life
That thrifty Pair had lived. For, as it chanced,
Their cottage on a plot of rising ground
Stood single, with large prospect, north and south,
High into Easedale, up to Dunmail-Raise,
135 And westward to the village near the lake;
And from this constant light, so regular
And so far seen, the House itself, by all
Who dwelt within the limits of the vale,
Both old and young, was named THE EVENING STAR.

140   Thus living on through such a length of years,
The Shepherd, if he loved himself, must needs
Have loved his Helpmate; but to Michael's heart
This son of his old age was yet more dear—
Less from instinctive tenderness, the same
145 Fond spirit that blindly works in the blood of all—
Than that a child, more than all other gifts
That earth can offer to declining man,
Brings hope with it, and forward-looking thoughts,
And stirrings of inquietude, when they
150 By tendency of nature needs must fail.
Exceeding was the love he bare to him,
His heart and his heart's joy! For oftentimes
Old Michael, while he was a babe in arms,
Had done him female service, not alone
155 For pastime and delight, as is the use
Of fathers, but with patient mind enforced
To acts of tenderness; and he had rocked
His cradle, as with a woman's gentle hand.

     And, in a later time, ere yet the Boy
160 Had put on boy's attire, did Michael love,
Albeit of a stern unbending mind,
To have the Young-one in his sight, when he
Wrought in the field, or on his shepherd's stool
Sate with a fettered sheep before him stretched
165 Under the large old oak, that near his door
Stood single, and, from matchless depth of shade,
Chosen for the Shearer's covert from the sun,

Thence in our rustic dialect was called
The CLIPPING TREE, a name which yet it bears.
170 There, while they two were sitting in the shade,
With others round them, earnest all and blithe,
Would Michael exercise his heart with looks
Of fond correction and reproof bestowed
Upon the Child, if he disturbed the sheep
175 By catching at their legs, or with his shouts
Scared them, while they lay still beneath the shears.

And when by Heaven's good grace the boy grew up
A healthy Lad, and carried in his cheek
Two steady roses that were five years old;
180 Then Michael from a winter coppice³ cut
With his own hand a sapling, which he hooped
With iron, making it throughout in all
Due requisites a perfect shepherd's staff,
And gave it to the Boy; wherewith equipt
185 He as a watchman oftentimes was placed
At gate or gap, to stem or turn the flock;
And, to his office prematurely called,
There stood the urchin, as you will divine,
Something between a hindrance and a help;
190 And for this cause not always, I believe,
Receiving from his Father hire° of praise;   *wages*
Though nought was left undone which staff, or voice,
Or looks, or threatening gestures, could perform.

But soon as Luke, full ten years old, could stand
195 Against the mountain blasts; and to the heights,
Not fearing toil, nor length of weary ways,
He with his Father daily went, and they
Were as companions, why should I relate
That objects which the Shepherd loved before
200 Were dearer now? that from the Boy there came
Feelings and emanations—things which were
Light to the sun and music to the wind;
And that the old Man's heart seemed born again?

Thus in his Father's sight the Boy grew up:
205 And now, when he had reached his eighteenth year,
He was his comfort and his daily hope.

While in this sort the simple household lived
From day to day, to Michael's ear there came
Distressful tidings. Long before the time
210 Of which I speak, the Shepherd had been bound
In surety for his brother's son, a man
Of an industrious life, and ample means;
But unforeseen misfortunes suddenly
Had prest upon him; and old Michael now

3. Grove of small trees.

215   Was summoned to discharge the forfeiture,
      A grievous penalty, but little less
      Than half his substance.[4] This unlooked-for claim,
      At the first hearing, for a moment took
      More hope out of his life than he supposed
220   That any old man ever could have lost.
      As soon as he had armed himself with strength
      To look his trouble in the face, it seemed
      The Shepherd's sole resource to sell at once
      A portion of his patrimonial fields.
225   Such was his first resolve; he thought again,
      And his heart failed him. "Isabel," said he,
      Two evenings after he had heard the news,
      "I have been toiling more than seventy years,
      And in the open sunshine of God's love
230   Have we all lived; yet if these fields of ours
      Should pass into a stranger's hand, I think
      That I could not lie quiet in my grave.
      Our lot is a hard lot; the sun himself
      Has scarcely been more diligent than I;
235   And I have lived to be a fool at last
      To my own family. An evil man
      That was, and made an evil choice, if he
      Were false to us; and if he were not false,
      There are ten thousand to whom loss like this
240   Had been no sorrow. I forgive him;—but
      'Twere better to be dumb than to talk thus.

      "When I began, my purpose was to speak
      Of remedies and of a cheerful hope.
      Our Luke shall leave us, Isabel; the land
245   Shall not go from us, and it shall be free;°   *unmortgaged*
      He shall possess it, free as is the wind
      That passes over it. We have, thou know'st,
      Another kinsman—he will be our friend
      In this distress. He is a prosperous man,
250   Thriving in trade—and Luke to him shall go,
      And with his kinsman's help and his own thrift
      He quickly will repair this loss, and then
      He may return to us. If here he stay,
      What can be done? Where every one is poor,
      What can be gained?"
255   At this the old Man paused,
      And Isabel sat silent, for her mind
      Was busy, looking back into past times.
      There's Richard Bateman,[5] thought she to herself,
      He was a parish-boy[6]—at the church-door
260   They made a gathering for him, shillings, pence

---

4. Michael has guaranteed a loan for his nephew and now has lost the collateral, which amounts to half his financial worth.
5. The story alluded to here is well known in the country. The chapel is called Ings Chapel and is on the road leading from Kendal to Ambleside [Wordsworth's note, 1802–05].
6. A poor boy supported financially by the poor rates (taxes) paid out by the wealthier members of his parish.

And halfpennies, wherewith the neighbours bought
A basket, which they filled with pedlar's wares;
And, with this basket on his arm, the lad
Went up to London, found a master there,
265 Who, out of many, chose the trusty boy
To go and overlook his merchandise
Beyond the seas; where he grew wondrous rich,
And left estates and monies to the poor,
And, at his birth-place, built a chapel floored
270 With marble, which he sent from foreign lands.
These thoughts, and many others of like sort,
Passed quickly through the mind of Isabel,
And her face brightened. The old Man was glad,
And thus resumed:—"Well, Isabel! this scheme
275 These two days, has been meat and drink to me.
Far more than we have lost is left us yet.
—We have enough—I wish indeed that I
Were younger;—but this hope is a good hope.
Make ready Luke's best garments, of the best
280 Buy for him more, and let us send him forth
To-morrow, or the next day, or to-night:
—If he *could* go, the Boy should go to-night."

Here Michael ceased, and to the fields went forth
With a light heart. The Housewife for five days
285 Was restless morn and night, and all day long
Wrought on with her best fingers to prepare
Things needful for the journey of her son.
But Isabel was glad when Sunday came
To stop her in her work: for, when she lay
290 By Michael's side, she through the last two nights
Heard him, how he was troubled in his sleep:
And when they rose at morning she could see
That all his hopes were gone. That day at noon
She said to Luke, while they two by themselves
295 Were sitting at the door, "Thou must not go:
We have no other Child but thee to lose,
None to remember—do not go away,
For if thou leave thy Father he will die."
The Youth made answer with a jocund voice;
300 And Isabel, when she had told her fears,
Recovered heart. That evening her best fare
Did she bring forth, and all together sat
Like happy people round a Christmas fire.

With daylight Isabel resumed her work;
305 And all the ensuing week the house appeared
As cheerful as a grove in Spring: at length
The expected letter from their kinsman came,
With kind assurances that he would do
His utmost for the welfare of the Boy;
310 To which, requests were added, that forthwith
He might be sent to him. Ten times or more

The letter was read over; Isabel
Went forth to show it to the neighbours round;
Nor was there at that time on English land
315 A prouder heart than Luke's. When Isabel
Had to her house returned, the old Man said,
"He shall depart to-morrow." To this word
The Housewife answered, talking much of things
Which, if at such short notice he should go,
320 Would surely be forgotten. But at length
She gave consent, and Michael was at ease.

Near the tumultuous brook of Green-head Ghyll,
In that deep valley, Michael had designed
To build a Sheep-fold;[7] and, before he heard
325 The tidings of his melancholy loss,
For this same purpose he had gathered up
A heap of stones, which by the streamlet's edge
Lay thrown together, ready for the work.
With Luke that evening thitherward he walked:
330 And soon as they had reached the place he stopped,
And thus the old Man spake to him:—"My Son,
To-morrow thou wilt leave me: with full heart
I look upon thee, for thou art the same
That wert a promise to me ere thy birth,
335 And all thy life hast been my daily joy.
I will relate to thee some little part
Of our two histories; 'twill do thee good
When thou art from me, even if I should touch
On things thou canst not know of.——After thou
340 First cam'st into the world—as oft befals
To new-born infants—thou didst sleep away
Two days, and blessings from thy Father's tongue
Then fell upon thee. Day by day passed on,
And still I loved thee with increasing love.
345 Never to living ear came sweeter sounds
Than when I heard thee by our own fire-side
First uttering, without words, a natural tune;
While thou, a feeding babe, didst in thy joy
Sing at thy Mother's breast. Month followed month,
350 And in the open fields my life was passed
And on the mountains; else I think that thou
Hadst been brought up upon thy Father's knees.
But we were playmates, Luke: among these hills,
As well thou knowest, in us the old and young
355 Have played together, nor with me didst thou
Lack any pleasure which a boy can know."
Luke had a manly heart; but at these words
He sobbed aloud. The old Man grasped his hand,
And said, "Nay, do not take it so—I see
360 That these are things of which I need not speak.

7. A sheepfold [pen for sheep] in these mountains is an unroofed building of stone walls, with different
divisions [Wordsworth's note, 1802–05].

　　　　—Even to the utmost I have been to thee
　　　　A kind and a good Father: and herein
　　　　I but repay a gift which I myself
　　　　Received at others' hands; for, though now old
365　　Beyond the common life of man, I still
　　　　Remember them who loved me in my youth.
　　　　Both of them sleep together: here they lived,
　　　　As all their Forefathers had done; and when
　　　　At length their time was come, they were not loth
370　　To give their bodies to the family mould.°　　　　　　grave plot
　　　　I wished that thou should'st live the life they lived:
　　　　But, 'tis a long time to look back, my Son,
　　　　And see so little gain from threescore years.
　　　　These fields were burthened° when they came to me;　　mortgaged
375　　Till I was forty years of age, not more
　　　　Than half of my inheritance was mine.
　　　　I toiled and toiled; God blessed me in my work,
　　　　And till these three weeks past the land was free.
　　　　—It looks as if it never could endure
380　　Another Master. Heaven forgive me, Luke,
　　　　If I judge ill for thee, but it seems good
　　　　That thou should'st go."
　　　　　　　　　　　　At this the old Man paused;
　　　　Then, pointing to the stones near which they stood,
　　　　Thus, after a short silence, he resumed:
385　　"This was a work for us; and now, my Son,
　　　　It is a work for me. But, lay one stone—
　　　　Here, lay it for me, Luke, with thine own hands.
　　　　Nay, Boy, be of good hope;—we both may live
　　　　To see a better day. At eighty-four
390　　I still am strong and hale;—do thou thy part;
　　　　I will do mine.—I will begin again
　　　　With many tasks that were resigned to thee:
　　　　Up to the heights, and in among the storms,
　　　　Will I without thee go again, and do
395　　All works which I was wont to do alone,
　　　　Before I knew thy face.—Heaven bless thee, Boy!
　　　　Thy heart these two weeks has been beating fast
　　　　With many hopes; it should be so—yes—yes—
　　　　I knew that thou could'st never have a wish
400　　To leave me, Luke: thou hast been bound to me
　　　　Only by links of love: when thou art gone,
　　　　What will be left to us!—But, I forget
　　　　My purposes. Lay now the corner-stone,
　　　　As I requested; and hereafter, Luke,
405　　When thou art gone away, should evil men
　　　　Be thy companions, think of me, my Son,
　　　　And of this moment; hither turn thy thoughts,
　　　　And God will strengthen thee: amid all fear
　　　　And all temptation, Luke, I pray that thou
410　　May'st bear in mind the life thy Fathers lived,
　　　　Who, being innocent, did for that cause
　　　　Bestir them in good deeds. Now, fare thee well—

When thou return'st, thou in this place wilt see
A work which is not here: a covenant
415 'Twill be between us; but, whatever fate
Befal thee, I shall love thee to the last,
And bear thy memory with me to the grave."

The Shepherd ended here; and Luke stooped down,
And, as his Father had requested, laid
420 The first stone of the Sheep-fold. At the sight
The old Man's grief broke from him; to his heart
He pressed his Son, he kissèd him and wept;
And to the house together they returned.
—Hushed was that House in peace, or seeming peace,
425 Ere the night fell:—with morrow's dawn the Boy
Began his journey, and when he had reached
The public way, he put on a bold face;
And all the neighbours, as he passed their doors,
Came forth with wishes and with farewell prayers,
430 That followed him till he was out of sight.

A good report did from their Kinsman come,
Of Luke and his well-doing: and the Boy
Wrote loving letters, full of wondrous news,
Which, as the Housewife phrased it, were throughout
435 "The prettiest letters that were ever seen."
Both parents read them with rejoicing hearts.
So, many months passed on: and once again
The Shepherd went about his daily work
With confident and cheerful thoughts; and now
440 Sometimes when he could find a leisure hour
He to that valley took his way, and there
Wrought at the Sheep-fold. Meantime Luke began
To slacken in his duty; and, at length,
He in the dissolute city gave himself
445 To evil courses: ignominy and shame
Fell on him, so that he was driven at last
To seek a hiding-place beyond the seas.

There is a comfort in the strength of love;
'Twill make a thing endurable, which else
450 Would overset the brain, or break the heart:
I have conversed with more than one who well
Remember the old Man, and what he was
Years after he had heard this heavy news.
His bodily frame had been from youth to age
455 Of an unusual strength. Among the rocks
He went, and still looked up to sun and cloud,
And listened to the wind; and, as before
Performed all kinds of labour for his sheep,
And for the land, his small inheritance.
460 And to that hollow dell from time to time
Did he repair, to build the Fold of which
His flock had need. 'Tis not forgotten yet

The pity which was then in every heart
For the old Man—and 'tis believed by all
465 That many and many a day he thither went,
And never lifted up a single stone.

    There, by the Sheep-fold, sometimes was he seen
Sitting alone, or with his faithful Dog,
Then old, beside him, lying at his feet.
470 The length of full seven years, from time to time,
He at the building of this Sheep-fold wrought,
And left the work unfinished when he died.
Three years, or little more, did Isabel
Survive her Husband: at her death the estate
475 Was sold, and went into a stranger's hand.
The Cottage which was named the EVENING STAR
Is gone—the ploughshare has been through the ground
On which it stood;[8] great changes have been wrought
In all the neighbourhood:—yet the oak is left
480 That grew beside their door; and the remains
Of the unfinished Sheep-fold may be seen
Beside the boisterous brook of Green-head Ghyll.

Oct. 11–Dec. 9, 1800   1800

Resolution and Independence[1]

1

There was a roaring in the wind all night;
The rain came heavily and fell in floods;
But now the sun is rising calm and bright;
The birds are singing in the distant woods;
5 Over his own sweet voice the Stock-dove broods;
The Jay makes answer as the Magpie chatters;
And all the air is filled with pleasant noise of waters.

2

All things that love the sun are out of doors;
The sky rejoices in the morning's birth;
10 The grass is bright with rain-drops;—on the moors
The hare is running races in her mirth;
And with her feet she from the plashy earth
Raises a mist; that, glittering in the sun,
Runs with her all the way, wherever she doth run.

8. The land on which Michael's sheep had grazed
has been turned over to cultivation.
1. For the meeting with the old leech gatherer, see
Dorothy Wordsworth's *Grasmere Journals*, October
3, 1800 (p. 1596). Wordsworth himself tells us, in
a note of 1843, that "I was in the state of feeling
described in the beginning of the poem, while
crossing over Barton Fell from Mr. Clarkson's, at
the foot of Ullswater, towards Askam. The image
of the hare I then observed on the ridge of the
Fell." He wrote the poem eighteen months after
this event (see *Grasmere Journals*, May 4 and 7,
1802; pp. 1602 and 1603).

3

¹⁵ I was a Traveller then upon the moor;
I saw the hare that raced about with joy;
I heard the woods and distant waters roar;
Or heard them not, as happy as a boy:
The pleasant season did my heart employ:
²⁰ My old remembrances went from me wholly;
And all the ways of men, so vain and melancholy.

4

But, as it sometimes chanceth, from the might
Of joy in minds that can no further go,
As high as we have mounted in delight
²⁵ In our dejection do we sink as low;
To me that morning did it happen so;
And fears and fancies thick upon me came;
Dim sadness—and blind thoughts, I knew not, nor could name.

5

I heard the sky-lark warbling in the sky;
³⁰ And I bethought me of the playful hare:
Even such a happy Child of earth am I;
Even as these blissful creatures do I fare;
Far from the world I walk, and from all care;
But there may come another day to me—
³⁵ Solitude, pain of heart, distress, and poverty.

6

My whole life I have lived in pleasant thought,
As if life's business were a summer mood;
As if all needful things would come unsought
To genial° faith, still rich in genial good;   *creative*
⁴⁰ But how can He expect that others should
Build for him, sow for him, and at his call
Love him, who for himself will take no heed at all?

7

I thought of Chatterton,[2] the marvellous Boy,
The sleepless Soul that perished in his pride;
⁴⁵ Of Him[3] who walked in glory and in joy
Following his plough, along the mountain-side:
By our own spirits are we deified:
We Poets in our youth begin in gladness;
But thereof come in the end despondency and madness.

---

2. After his early death through drug overdose, a death believed by many to have been a suicide, the poet Thomas Chatterton (1752–1770) became a prime symbol of neglected boy genius for the Romantics. He came to public attention in his hometown of Bristol in the West of England as the discoverer of the long-lost manuscripts of a local 15th-century monk named "Thomas Rowley." Rowley's works—in fact Chatterton's own inventions—included many poems. His pseudo-Chaucerian "An Excelente Balade of Charitie"

used the rhyme royal stanza form that Wordsworth employs here. Reports of the frustrations that Chatterton experienced in his attempts to interest the London literary establishment in such "discoveries" provided the seed for that Romantic myth-making in which Wordsworth, Coleridge, and Keats participated.
3. Robert Burns, here considered, as Chatterton is, a natural poet who died young and poor, without adequate recognition, and who seemed to have hastened his death through dissipation.

8

50 Now, whether it were by peculiar grace,
  A leading from above, a something given,
  Yet it befel, that, in this lonely place,
  When I with these untoward thoughts had striven,
  Beside a pool bare to the eye of heaven
55 I saw a Man before me unawares:
  The oldest man he seemed that ever wore grey hairs.

9

  As a huge stone is sometimes seen to lie
  Couched on the bald top of an eminence;
  Wonder to all who do the same espy,
60 By what means it could thither come, and whence;
  So that it seems a thing endued with sense:
  Like a sea-beast crawled forth, that on a shelf
  Of rock or sand reposeth, there to sun itself;

10

  Such seemed this Man,[4] not all alive nor dead,
65 Nor all asleep—in his extreme old age:
  His body was bent double, feet and head
  Coming together in life's pilgrimage;
  As if some dire constraint of pain, or rage
  Of sickness felt by him in times long past,
70 A more than human weight upon his frame had cast.

11

  Himself he propped, limbs, body, and pale face,
  Upon a long grey staff of shaven wood:
  And, still as I drew near with gentle pace,
  Upon the margin of that moorish flood
75 Motionless as a cloud the old Man stood,
  That heareth not the loud winds when they call;
  And moveth all together, if it move at all.

12

  At length, himself unsettling, he the pond
  Stirred with his staff, and fixedly did look
80 Upon the muddy water, which he conned,°   *studied*
  As if he had been reading in a book:
  And now a stranger's privilege I took;
  And, drawing to his side, to him did say,
  "This morning gives us promise of a glorious day."

13

85 A gentle answer did the old Man make,
  In courteous speech which forth he slowly drew:
  And him with further words I thus bespake,

---

4. In Wordsworth's analysis of this passage he says that the stone is endowed with something of life, the sea beast is stripped of some of its life to assimilate it to the stone, and the old man divested of enough life and motion to make "the two objects unite and coalesce in just comparison." He used the passage to demonstrate his theory of how the "conferring, the abstracting, and the modifying powers of the Imagination . . . are all brought into conjunction" (Preface to the *Poems* of 1815). Cf. Coleridge's brief definitions of the imagination in *Biographia Literaria*, chap. 13 (p. 1663).

"What occupation do you there pursue?
This is a lonesome place for one like you."
90 Ere he replied, a flash of mild surprise
Broke from the sable orbs of his yet-vivid eyes.

14

His words came feebly, from a feeble chest,
But each in solemn order followed each,
With something of a lofty utterance drest—
95 Choice word and measured phrase, above the reach
Of ordinary men; a stately speech;
Such as grave Livers[5] do in Scotland use,
Religious men, who give to God and man their dues.

15

He told, that to these waters he had come
100 To gather leeches,[6] being old and poor:
Employment hazardous and wearisome!
And he had many hardships to endure:
From pond to pond he roamed, from moor to moor;
Housing, with God's good help, by choice or chance;
105 And in this way he gained an honest maintenance.

16

The old Man still stood talking by my side;
But now his voice to me was like a stream
Scarce heard; nor word from word could I divide;
And the whole body of the Man did seem
110 Like one whom I had met with in a dream;
Or like a man from some far region sent,
To give me human strength, by apt admonishment.

17

My former thoughts returned: the fear that kills;
And hope that is unwilling to be fed;
115 Cold, pain, and labour, and all fleshly ills;
And mighty Poets in their misery dead.
—Perplexed, and longing to be comforted,
My question eagerly did I renew,
"How is it that you live, and what is it you do?"

18

120 He with a smile did then his words repeat;
And said, that, gathering leeches, far and wide
He travelled; stirring thus about his feet
The waters of the pools where they abide.
"Once I could meet with them on every side;
125 But they have dwindled long by slow decay;
Yet still I persevere, and find them where I may."

---

5. Those who live gravely (as opposed to "loose livers," those who live for a life of pleasure).
6. Used by medical attendants to draw their patients' blood for curative purposes. A leech gath-erer, bare legged in shallow water, stirred the water to attract them and, when they fastened them-selves to his legs, picked them off.

19

While he was talking thus, the lonely place,
The old Man's shape, and speech—all troubled me:
In my mind's eye I seemed to see him pace
130   About the weary moors continually,
Wandering about alone and silently.
While I these thoughts within myself pursued,
He, having made a pause, the same discourse renewed.

20

And soon with this he other matter blended,
135   Cheerfully uttered, with demeanour kind,
But stately in the main; and when he ended,
I could have laughed myself to scorn to find
In that decrepit Man so firm a mind.
"God," said I, "be my help and stay⁷ secure;
140   I'll think of the Leech-gatherer on the lonely moor!"

May 3–July 4, 1802   1807

I wandered lonely as a cloud¹

I wandered lonely as a cloud
That floats on high o'er vales and hills,
When all at once I saw a crowd,
A host, of golden daffodils;
5   Beside the lake, beneath the trees,
Fluttering and dancing in the breeze.

Continuous as the stars that shine
And twinkle on the milky way,
They stretched in never-ending line
10   Along the margin of a bay:
Ten thousand saw I at a glance,
Tossing their heads in sprightly dance.

The waves beside them danced; but they
Out-did the sparkling waves in glee:
15   A poet could not but be gay,
In such a jocund company:
I gazed—and gazed—but little thought
What wealth the show to me had brought:

For oft, when on my couch I lie
20   In vacant or in pensive mood,
They flash upon that inward eye
Which is the bliss of solitude;

---

7. Support (a noun).
1. For the original experience, two years earlier,

see Dorothy Wordsworth's *Grasmere Journals*,
April 15, 1802 (p. 1600).

And then my heart with pleasure fills,
And dances with the daffodils.

1804   1807

My heart leaps up

My heart leaps up when I behold
    A rainbow in the sky:
So was it when my life began;
So is it now I am a man;
5 So be it when I shall grow old,
    Or let me die!
The Child is father of the Man;
And I could wish my days to be
Bound each to each by natural piety.[1]

Mar. 26, 1802   1807

Ode: Intimations of Immortality   In 1843 Wordsworth said about this
Ode to Isabella Fenwick:

This was composed during my residence at Town End, Grasmere; two years at
least passed between the writing of the four first stanzas and the remaining part.
To the attentive and competent reader the whole sufficiently explains itself; but
there may be no harm in adverting here to particular feelings or *experiences* of
my own mind on which the structure of the poem partly rests. Nothing was more
difficult for me in childhood than to admit the notion of death as a state applicable to my own being. I have said elsewhere [in the opening stanza of "We Are
Seven"]:

    —A simple child,
    That lightly draws its breath,
    And feels its life in every limb,
    What should it know of death!—

But it was not so much from [feelings] of animal vivacity that *my* difficulty came
as from a sense of the indomitableness of the spirit within me. I used to brood
over the stories of Enoch and Elijah [Genesis 5.22–24; 2 Kings 2.11], and almost
to persuade myself that, whatever might become of others, I should be translated,
in something of the same way, to heaven. With a feeling congenial to this, I was
often unable to think of external things as having external existence, and I communed with all that I saw as something not apart from, but inherent in, my own
immaterial nature. Many times while going to school have I grasped at a wall or
tree to recall myself from this abyss of idealism to the reality. At that time I was
afraid of such processes. In later periods of life I have deplored, as we have all
reason to do, a subjugation of an opposite character, and have rejoiced over the
remembrances, as is expressed in the lines—

---

1. Perhaps as distinguished from piety based on the Bible, in which the rainbow is the token of God's
promise to Noah and his descendants never again to send a flood to destroy the earth.

> Obstinate questionings
> Of sense and outward things,
> Fallings from us, vanishings; etc.

To that dreamlike vividness and splendor which invest objects of sight in child-hood, everyone, I believe, if he would look back, could bear testimony, and I need not dwell upon it here: but having in the Poem regarded it as presumptive evidence of a prior state of existence, I think it right to protest against a conclu-sion, which has given pain to some good and pious persons, that I meant to inculcate such a belief. It is far too shadowy a notion to be recommended to faith, as more than an element in our instincts of immortality. * * * [W]hen I was impelled to write this Poem on the 'Immortality of the Soul,' I took hold of the notion of pre-existence as having sufficient foundation in humanity for authorizing me to make for my purpose the best use of it I could as a Poet.

When he dictated this long note to Isabella Fenwick, at the age of seventy-two or seventy-three, Wordsworth was troubled by objections that his apparent claim for the preexistence of the soul violated the Christian belief that the soul, although it survives after death, does not exist before the birth of an individual. His claim in the note is that he refers to the preexistence of the soul not in order to set out a religious doctrine but only so as to deal "as a Poet" with a common human experience: that the passing of youth involves the loss of a freshness and radiance investing everything one sees. Coleridge's "Dejection: An Ode," which he wrote (in its earliest version) after he had heard the first four stanzas of Wordsworth's poem, employs a similar figurative tech-nique for a comparable, though more devastating, experience of loss.

The original published text of this poem (in 1807) had as its title only "Ode," and then as epigraph *"Paulo maiora canamus"* (Latin for "Let us sing of somewhat higher things") from Virgil's *Eclogue 4*.

Ode

Intimations of Immortality from Recollections of Early Childhood

> The Child is Father of the Man;
> And I could wish my days to be
> Bound each to each by natural piety.[1]

1

There was a time when meadow, grove, and stream,
The earth, and every common sight,
  To me did seem
  Apparelled in celestial light,
5 The glory and the freshness of a dream.
It is not now as it hath been of yore;—
  Turn wheresoe'er I may,
  By night or day,
The things which I have seen I now can see no more.

2

10   The Rainbow comes and goes,
   And lovely is the Rose,
   The Moon doth with delight
Look round her when the heavens are bare,

---

1. The concluding lines of Wordsworth's "My heart leaps up" (p. 1538).

15   Waters on a starry night
        Are beautiful and fair;
        The sunshine is a glorious birth;
        But yet I know, where'er I go,
        That there hath past away a glory from the earth.

                            3
        Now, while the birds thus sing a joyous song,
20   And while the young lambs bound
            As to the tabor's² sound,
        To me alone there came a thought of grief:
        A timely utterance³ gave that thought relief,
        And I again am strong:
25   The cataracts blow their trumpets from the steep;
        No more shall grief of mine the season wrong;
        I hear the Echoes through the mountains throng,
        The Winds come to me from the fields of sleep,⁴
            And all the earth is gay;
30   Land and sea
            Give themselves up to jollity,
            And with the heart of May
        Doth every Beast keep holiday;—
            Thou Child of Joy,
35   Shout round me, let me hear thy shouts, thou happy
        Shepherd-boy!

                            4
        Ye blessed Creatures, I have heard the call
            Ye to each other make; I see
        The heavens laugh with you in your jubilee;
            My heart is at your festival,
40   My head hath its coronal,⁵
        The fulness of your bliss, I feel—I feel it all.
            Oh evil day! if I were sullen
            While Earth herself is adorning,
            This sweet May-morning,
45   And the Children are culling
                On every side,
            In a thousand valleys far and wide,
            Fresh flowers; while the sun shines warm,
        And the Babe leaps up on his Mother's arm:—
50   I hear, I hear, with joy I hear!
        —But there's a Tree, of many, one,
        A single Field which I have looked upon,
        Both of them speak of something that is gone:
            The Pansy at my feet
55   Doth the same tale repeat:

2. A small drum often used to beat time for dancing.
3. Perhaps "My heart leaps up," perhaps "Resolution and Independence," perhaps not a poem at
all.
4. Of the many suggested interpretations, the sim-

plest is "from the fields where they were sleeping."
Wordsworth often associated a rising wind with the
revival of spirit and of poetic inspiration (see, e.g.,
the opening passage of The Prelude, p. 1553).
5. Circlet of wildflowers, with which the shepherd
boys trimmed their hats in May.

Whither is fled the visionary gleam?
Where is it now, the glory and the dream?

5

Our birth is but a sleep and a forgetting:
The Soul that rises with us, our life's Star,[6]
60   Hath had elsewhere its setting,
        And cometh from afar:
     Not in entire forgetfulness,
     And not in utter nakedness,
But trailing clouds of glory do we come
65   From God, who is our home:
Heaven lies about us in our infancy!
Shades of the prison-house begin to close
     Upon the growing Boy,
But He beholds the light, and whence it flows,
70   He sees it in his joy;
The Youth, who daily farther from the east
     Must travel, still is Nature's Priest,
     And by the vision splendid
     Is on his way attended;
75 At length the Man perceives it die away,
And fade into the light of common day.

6

Earth fills her lap with pleasures of her own;
Yearnings she hath in her own natural kind,
And, even with something of a Mother's mind,
80   And no unworthy aim,
     The homely[7] Nurse doth all she can
To make her Foster-child, her Inmate Man,
     Forget the glories he hath known,
And that imperial palace whence he came.

7

85 Behold the Child among his new-born blisses,
A six years' Darling of a pigmy size!
See, where 'mid work of his own hand he lies,
Fretted[8] by sallies of his mother's kisses,
With light upon him from his father's eyes!
90 See, at his feet, some little plan or chart,
Some fragment from his dream of human life,
Shaped by himself with newly-learnèd art;
     A wedding or a festival,
     A mourning or a funeral;
95   And this hath now his heart,
     And unto this he frames his song:
     Then will he fit his tongue
To dialogues of business, love, or strife;
     But it will not be long
100   Ere this be thrown aside,

6. The sun, as metaphor for the soul.
7. In the old sense: simple and friendly.

8. Irritated; or possibly in the old sense: checkered over.

And with new joy and pride
The little Actor cons° another part;   studies
Filling from time to time his "humorous stage"[9]
With all the Persons, down to palsied Age,
105   That Life brings with her in her equipage;
        As if his whole vocation
        Were endless imitation.

                            8

Thou, whose exterior semblance doth belie
        Thy Soul's immensity;
110   Thou best Philosopher, who yet dost keep
Thy heritage, thou Eye among the blind,
That, deaf and silent, read'st the eternal deep,
Haunted for ever by the eternal mind,—
        Mighty Prophet! Seer blest!
115   On whom those truths do rest,
Which we are toiling all our lives to find,
In darkness lost, the darkness of the grave;
Thou, over whom thy Immortality
Broods like the Day, a Master o'er a Slave,
120   A Presence which is not to be put by;
Thou little Child, yet glorious in the might
Of heaven-born freedom on thy being's height,
Why with such earnest pains dost thou provoke
The years to bring the inevitable yoke,
125   Thus blindly with thy blessedness at strife?
Full soon thy Soul shall have her earthly freight,
And custom lie upon thee with a weight,
Heavy as frost, and deep almost as life!

                            9

        O joy! that in our embers
130   Is something that doth live,
        That nature yet remembers
        What was so fugitive!°   fleeting
The thought of our past years in me doth breed
Perpetual benediction: not indeed
135   For that which is most worthy to be blest;
Delight and liberty, the simple creed
Of Childhood, whether busy or at rest,
With new-fledged hope still fluttering in his breast:—
        Not for these I raise
140   The song of thanks and praise;
        But for those obstinate questionings
        Of sense and outward things,
        Fallings from us, vanishings;
        Blank misgivings of a Creature

---

9. From a sonnet by the Elizabethan poet Samuel Daniel. In Daniel's era *humorous* meant "capricious" and also referred to the various characters and temperaments ("humors") represented in drama.

145 Moving about in worlds not realised,[1]
High instincts before which our mortal Nature
Did tremble like a guilty Thing surprised:
But for those first affections,
Those shadowy recollections,
150 Which, be they what they may,
Are yet the fountain light of all our day,
Are yet a master light of all our seeing;
Uphold us, cherish, and have power to make
Our noisy years seem moments in the being
155 Of the eternal Silence: truths that wake,
To perish never;
Which neither listlessness, nor mad endeavour,
Nor Man nor Boy,
Nor all that is at enmity with joy,
160 Can utterly abolish or destroy!
Hence in a season of calm weather
Though inland far we be,
Our Souls have sight of that immortal sea
Which brought us hither,
165 Can in a moment travel thither,
And see the Children sport upon the shore,
And hear the mighty waters rolling evermore.

10

Then sing, ye Birds, sing, sing a joyous song!
And let the young Lambs bound
170 As to the tabor's sound!
We in thought will join your throng,
Ye that pipe and ye that play,
Ye that through your hearts to-day
Feel the gladness of the May!
175 What though the radiance which was once so bright
Be now for ever taken from my sight,
Though nothing can bring back the hour
Of splendour in the grass, of glory in the flower;
We will grieve not, rather find
180 Strength in what remains behind;
In the primal sympathy
Which having been must ever be;
In the soothing thoughts that spring
Out of human suffering;
185 In the faith that looks through death,
In years that bring the philosophic mind.

11

And O, ye Fountains, Meadows, Hills, and Groves,
Forebode° not any severing of our loves!   predict, portend
Yet in my heart of hearts I feel your might;
190 I only have relinquished one delight
To live beneath your more habitual sway.

---

1. Not seeming real (see Wordsworth's comment about "this abyss of idealism" in the headnote on p. 1538).

I love the Brooks which down their channels fret,
Even more than when I tripped lightly as they;
The innocent brightness of a new-born Day
195   Is lovely yet;
The Clouds that gather round the setting sun
Do take a sober colouring from an eye
That hath kept watch o'er man's mortality;
Another race hath been, and other palms are won.[2]
200   Thanks to the human heart by which we live,
Thanks to its tenderness, its joys, and fears,
To me the meanest flower that blows can give
Thoughts that do often lie too deep for tears.

1802–04   1807

Ode to Duty[1]

Jam non consilio bonus, sed more eo perductus, ut non tantum recte facere possim, sed nisi recte facere non possim.[2]

Stern Daughter of the Voice of God![3]
O Duty! if that name thou love
Who art a light to guide, a rod
To check the erring, and reprove;
5 Thou, who art victory and law
When empty terrors overawe;
From vain temptations dost set free;
And calm'st the weary strife of frail humanity!

There are who ask not if thine eye
10 Be on them; who, in love and truth,
Where no misgiving is, rely
Upon the genial sense[4] of youth:
Glad Hearts! without reproach or blot;
Who do thy work, and know it not:
15 Oh! if through confidence misplaced
They fail, thy saving arms, dread Power! around them cast.

---

2. In Greece foot races were often run for the prize of a branch or wreath of palm. Wordsworth's line echoes Paul, 1 Corinthians 9.24, who uses such races as a metaphor for life: "Know ye not that they which run in a race run all, but one receiveth the prize?"

1. This Ode . . . is on the model of Gray's "Ode to Adversity" which is copied from Horace's "Ode to Fortune." Many and many a time have I been twitted by my wife and sister for having forgotten this dedication of myself to the stern lawgiver [Wordsworth's note, 1843].

In this poem, a striking departure from his earlier forms and ideas, Wordsworth abandons the descriptive-meditative pattern of his "Tintern Abbey" and "Ode: Intimations of Immortality." Where in the Preface to *Lyrical Ballads* of 1802 he had both disparaged the 18th-century poet Thomas Gray and rejected the personifications that were customary in 18th-century poetry, Wordsworth here reverts to a standard 18th-century form, an ode addressed to a personified abstraction.

2. Now I am not good by conscious intent, but have been so trained by habit that I not only can act rightly but am unable to act other than rightly (Latin). Added in 1837, this epigraph is an adaptation from *Moral Epistles* 120.10 by Seneca (4 B.C.E.–65 C.E.), Stoic philosopher and writer of tragedies.

3. Cf. Milton's *Paradise Lost* 9.652–54. Eve for a moment resists the serpent's recommendation of the forbidden fruit by stating, "God so commanded, and left that Command / Sole Daughter of his voice; the rest, we live / Law to ourselves, our Reason is our Law."

4. Innate vitality.

Serene will be our days and bright,
And happy will our nature be,
When love is an unerring light,
20 And joy its own security.
And they a blissful course may hold
Even now, who, not unwisely bold,
Live in the spirit of this creed;
Yet seek thy firm support, according to their need.

25 I, loving freedom, and untried;
No sport of every random gust,
Yet being to myself a guide,
Too blindly have reposed my trust:
And oft, when in my heart was heard
30 Thy timely mandate, I deferred
The task, in smoother walks to stray;
But thee I now would serve more strictly, if I may.

Through no disturbance of my soul,
Or strong compunction⁵ in me wrought,
35 I supplicate for thy control;
But in the quietness of thought:
Me this unchartered freedom tires;
I feel the weight of chance-desires:
My hopes no more must change their name,
40 I long for a repose that ever is the same.

Stern Lawgiver! yet thou dost wear
The Godhead's most benignant grace;
Nor know we any thing so fair
As is the smile upon thy face:
45 Flowers laugh before thee on their beds
And fragrance in thy footing treads;
Thou dost preserve the stars from wrong;
And the most ancient heavens, through Thee, are fresh and strong.

To humbler functions, awful Power!
50 I call thee: I myself commend
Unto thy guidance from this hour;
Oh, let my weakness have an end!
Give unto me, made lowly wise,⁶
The spirit of self-sacrifice;
55 The confidence of reason give;
And in the light of truth thy Bondman⁷ let me live!

1804   1807

5. In the older sense: sting of conscience, or remorse.
6. Another echo from Milton. The angel Raphael had advised Adam (*Paradise Lost* 8.173–74), "Be

lowly wise: / Think only what concerns thee and thy being."
7. Man in bondage, serf or slave.

The Solitary Reaper[1]

Behold her, single in the field,
Yon solitary Highland Lass!
Reaping and singing by herself;
Stop here, or gently pass!
5 Alone she cuts and binds the grain,
And sings a melancholy strain;
O listen! for the Vale profound
Is overflowing with the sound.

No Nightingale did ever chaunt
10 More welcome notes to weary bands
Of travellers in some shady haunt,
Among Arabian sands:
A voice so thrilling ne'er was heard
In spring-time from the Cuckoo-bird,
15 Breaking the silence of the seas
Among the farthest Hebrides.[2]

Will no one tell me what she sings?[3]
Perhaps the plaintive numbers° flow   *verses*
For old, unhappy, far-off things,
20 And battles long ago:
Or is it some more humble lay,
Familiar matter of to-day?
Some natural sorrow, loss, or pain,
That has been, and may be again?

25 Whate'er the theme, the Maiden sang
As if her song could have no ending;
I saw her singing at her work,
And o'er the sickle bending;—
I listened, motionless and still;
30 And, as I mounted up the hill,
The music in my heart I bore,
Long after it was heard no more.

Nov. 5, 1805   1807

---

1. One of the rare poems not based on Wordsworth's own experience. In a note published with the poem in 1807, Wordsworth says that it was suggested by a passage in Thomas Wilkinson's *Tours to the British Mountains* (1824), which he had seen in manuscript: "Passed a female who was reaping alone: she sung in Erse [the Gaelic language of Scotland] as she bended over her sickle; the sweetest human voice I ever heard: her strains were tenderly melancholy, and felt delicious, long after they were heard no more." In 1803 William and Mary Wordsworth, Dorothy Wordsworth, and Coleridge toured Scotland, making a pilgrimage to Robert Burns's grave and visiting places mentioned in Walter Scott's historical notes to his *Minstrelsy of the Scottish Border.*
2. Islands off the west coast of Scotland.
3. The poet does not understand Erse, the language in which she sings.

Elegiac Stanzas

Suggested by a Picture of Peele Castle, in a Storm, Painted by Sir George Beaumont[1]

I was thy neighbour once, thou rugged Pile!°   *building*
Four summer weeks I dwelt in sight of thee:
I saw thee every day; and all the while
Thy Form was sleeping on a glassy sea.

5   So pure the sky, so quiet was the air!
So like, so very like, was day to day!
Whene'er I looked, thy Image still was there;
It trembled, but it never passed away.

How perfect was the calm! it seemed no sleep;
10 No mood, which season takes away, or brings:
I could have fancied that the mighty Deep
Was even the gentlest of all gentle Things.

Ah! THEN, if mine had been the Painter's hand,
To express what then I saw; and add the gleam,
15 The light that never was, on sea or land,
The consecration, and the Poet's dream;

I would have planted thee, thou hoary Pile
Amid a world how different from this!
Beside a sea that could not cease to smile;
20 On tranquil land, beneath a sky of bliss.

Thou shouldst have seemed a treasure-house divine
Of peaceful years; a chronicle of heaven;
—Of all the sunbeams that did ever shine
The very sweetest had to thee been given.

25 A Picture had it been of lasting ease,
Elysian[2] quiet, without toil or strife;
No motion but the moving tide, a breeze,
Or merely silent Nature's breathing life.

Such, in the fond illusion of my heart,
30 Such Picture would I at that time have made:
And seen the soul of truth in every part,
A stedfast peace that might not be betrayed.

So once it would have been,—'tis so no more;
I have submitted to a new control:

---

1. A wealthy landscape painter who was Wordsworth's patron and close friend. Peele Castle is on
an island opposite Rampside, Lancashire, where
Wordsworth had spent a month in 1794, twelve
years before he saw Beaumont's painting.
2. Referring to Elysium, in classical mythology the
peaceful place where those favored by the gods
dwelled after death.

35 A power is gone, which nothing can restore;
    A deep distress hath humanised my Soul.[3]

    Not for a moment could I now behold
    A smiling sea, and be what I have been:
    The feeling of my loss will ne'er be old;
40 This, which I know, I speak with mind serene.

    Then, Beaumont, Friend! who would have been the Friend,
    If he had lived, of Him whom I deplore,°   mourn
    This work of thine I blame not, but commend;
    This sea in anger, and that dismal shore.

45 O 'tis a passionate Work!—yet wise and well,
    Well chosen is the spirit that is here;
    That Hulk° which labours in the deadly swell,   ship
    This rueful sky, this pageantry of fear!

    And this huge Castle, standing here sublime,
50 I love to see the look with which it braves,
    Cased in the unfeeling armour of old time,
    The lightning, the fierce wind, and trampling waves.

    Farewell, farewell the heart that lives alone,
    Housed in a dream, at distance from the Kind!°   humankind
55 Such happiness, wherever it be known,
    Is to be pitied; for 'tis surely blind.

    But welcome fortitude, and patient cheer,
    And frequent sights of what is to be borne!
    Such sights, or worse, as are before me here.—
60 Not without hope we suffer and we mourn.

Summer 1806   1807

SONNETS

Composed upon Westminster Bridge,
September 3, 1802[1]

    Earth has not any thing to show more fair:
    Dull would he be of soul who could pass by
    A sight so touching in its majesty:

3. Captain John Wordsworth, William's brother, had been drowned in a shipwreck on February 5, 1805. He is referred to in lines 41–42.
1. The date of this experience was not September 3, but July 31, 1802. Its occasion was a trip to France, made possible by a brief truce in the war (see Dorothy Wordsworth's *Grasmere Journals*, July 1802, p. 1603). Wordsworth's conflicted feelings about this return to France, where he had once supported the Revolution and loved Annette Vallon, inform a number of personal and political sonnets that he wrote in 1802, among them the four that follow.

This City now doth, like a garment, wear
5   The beauty of the morning; silent, bare,
Ships, towers, domes, theatres, and temples lie
Open unto the fields, and to the sky;
All bright and glittering in the smokeless air.
Never did sun more beautifully steep
10   In his first splendour, valley, rock, or hill;
Ne'er saw I, never felt, a calm so deep!
The river glideth at his own sweet will:
Dear God! the very houses seem asleep;
And all that mighty heart is lying still!

1802   1807

It is a beauteous evening

It is a beauteous evening, calm and free,
The holy time is quiet as a Nun
Breathless with adoration; the broad sun
Is sinking down in its tranquillity;
5   The gentleness of heaven broods o'er the Sea:
Listen! the mighty Being is awake,
And doth with his eternal motion make
A sound like thunder—everlastingly.
Dear Child! dear Girl! that walkest with me here,[2]
10   If thou appear untouched by solemn thought,
Thy nature is not therefore less divine:
Thou liest in Abraham's bosom[3] all the year;
And worshipp'st at the Temple's inner shrine,
God being with thee when we know it not.

Aug. 1802   1807

London, 1802[4]

Milton! thou should'st be living at this hour:
England hath need of thee: she is a fen
Of stagnant waters: altar, sword, and pen,
Fireside, the heroic wealth of hall and bower,
5   Have forfeited their ancient English dower°   endowment, gift
Of inward happiness. We are selfish men;

2. The girl walking with Wordsworth is Caroline, his daughter by Annette Vallon. For the event described see Dorothy Wordsworth's *Grasmere Journals,* July 1802 (p. 1603).
3. Where the souls destined for heaven rest after death. Luke 16.22: "And it came to pass, that the beggar died, and was carried by the angels into Abraham's bosom."
4. One of a series "written immediately after my return from France to London, when I could not but be struck, as here described, with the vanity and parade of our own country . . . as contrasted with the quiet, and I may say the desolation, that the revolution had produced in France. This must be borne in mind, or else the reader may think that in this and the succeeding sonnets I have exaggerated the mischief engendered and fostered among us by undisturbed wealth" [Wordsworth's note, 1843].

Oh! raise us up, return to us again;
And give us manners, virtue, freedom, power.
Thy soul was like a Star, and dwelt apart:
10   Thou hadst a voice whose sound was like the sea:
Pure as the naked heavens, majestic, free,
So didst thou travel on life's common way,
In cheerful godliness; and yet thy heart
The lowliest duties on herself did lay.

Sept. 1802   1807

The world is too much with us

The world is too much with us; late and soon,
Getting and spending, we lay waste our powers:
Little we see in Nature that is ours;
We have given our hearts away, a sordid boon!⁵
5   This Sea that bares her bosom to the moon;
The winds that will be howling at all hours,
And are up-gathered now like sleeping flowers;
For this, for every thing, we are out of tune;
It moves us not.—Great God! I'd rather be
10   A Pagan suckled in a creed outworn;
So might I, standing on this pleasant lea,
Have glimpses that would make me less forlorn;
Have sight of Proteus rising from the sea;
Or hear old Triton⁶ blow his wreathèd horn.

1802–04   1807

Surprised by joy⁷

Surprised by joy—impatient as the Wind
I turned to share the transport—Oh! with whom
But Thee, deep buried in the silent tomb,
That spot which no vicissitude can find?
5   Love, faithful love, recalled thee to my mind—
But how could I forget thee? Through what power,
Even for the least division of an hour,
Have I been so beguiled as to be blind
To my most grievous loss!—That thought's return
10   Was the worst pang that sorrow ever bore,

5. Gift. It is the act of giving the heart away that is sordid.
6. A sea deity, usually represented as blowing on a conch shell. Proteus was an old man of the sea who (in the *Odyssey*) could assume a variety of shapes. The description of Proteus echoes *Paradise Lost* 3.603–04, and that of Triton echoes Edmund

Spenser's *Colin Clouts Come Home Againe*, lines 244–45.
7. This was in fact suggested by my daughter Catherine, long after her death [Wordsworth's note]. Catherine Wordsworth died June 4, 1812, at the age of four.

Save one, one only, when I stood forlorn,
Knowing my heart's best treasure was no more;
That neither present time, nor years unborn
Could to my sight that heavenly face restore.

1813–14   1815

Mutability[8]

From low to high doth dissolution climb,
And sink from high to low, along a scale
Of awful° notes, whose concord shall not fail;   awe-inspiring
A musical but melancholy chime,
5   Which they can hear who meddle not with crime,
Nor avarice, nor over-anxious care.
Truth fails not; but her outward forms that bear
The longest date do melt like frosty rime,
That in the morning whitened hill and plain
10   And is no more; drop like the tower sublime
Of yesterday, which royally did wear
His crown of weeds, but could not even sustain
Some casual shout that broke the silent air,
Or the unimaginable touch of Time.

1821   1822

Steamboats, Viaducts, and Railways[9]

Motions and Means, on land and sea at war
With old poetic feeling, not for this,
Shall ye, by Poets even, be judged amiss!
Nor shall your presence, howsoe'er it mar
5   The loveliness of Nature, prove a bar
To the Mind's gaining that prophetic sense
Of future change, that point of vision, whence
May be discovered what in soul ye are.
In spite of all that beauty may disown
10   In your harsh features, Nature doth embrace
Her lawful offspring in Man's art; and Time,
Pleased with your triumphs o'er his brother Space,
Accepts from your bold hands the proffered crown
Of hope, and smiles on you with cheer sublime.

1833   1835

---

8. This late sonnet was included in an otherwise
rather uninspired sequence, *Ecclesiastical Sonnets*,
dealing with the history and ceremonies of the
Church of England.
9. In late middle age Wordsworth demonstrates,

as he had predicted in the Preface to *Lyrical Ballads*, that the poet will assimilate to his subject
matter the "material revolution" produced by science.

The Prelude   *The Prelude*, now regarded as Wordsworth's crowning achievement, was unknown to the public at the time of his death in April 1850. When, three months later, it was published from manuscript by Wordsworth's literary executors, its title was given to it by the poet's wife, Mary. Wordsworth had referred to it variously as "the poem to Coleridge," "the poem on the growth of my own mind," and "the poem on my own poetical education."

For some seventy-five years this posthumous publication of 1850 was the only known text. Then in 1926 Ernest de Selincourt, working from manuscripts, printed an earlier version of the poem that Wordsworth had completed in 1805. Since that time other scholars have established the existence of a still earlier and much shorter version of *The Prelude,* in two parts, that Wordsworth had composed in 1798–99. The following seems to have been the process of composition that produced the three principal versions of the poem:

1. The *Two-Part Prelude* of 1799. Wordsworth originally planned, early in 1798, to include an account of his own development as a poet in his projected but never-completed philosophical poem *The Recluse.* While living in Germany during the autumn and winter of 1798–99, he composed a number of passages about his early experiences with nature. What had been intended to be part of *The Recluse,* however, quickly evolved into an independent autobiographical poem, and by late 1799, when Wordsworth settled with his sister, Dorothy, at Grasmere, he had written a two-part, 978-line poem which describes his life from infancy, through his years at Hawkshead School, to the age of seventeen. This poem corresponds, by and large, to the contents of books 1 and 2 of the later versions of *The Prelude.*

2. The 1805 *Prelude.* Late in 1801 Wordsworth began to expand the poem on his poetic life, and in 1804 he set to work intensively on the project. His initial plan was to write it in five books, but he soon decided to enlarge it to incorporate an account of his experiences in France and of his mental crisis after the failure of his hopes in the French Revolution, and to end the poem with his settlement at Grasmere and his taking up the great task of *The Recluse.* He completed the poem, in thirteen books, in May 1805. This is the version that Wordsworth read to Coleridge after the latter's return from Malta (see Coleridge's "To William Wordsworth," p. 1656).

3. The 1850 *Prelude.* For the next thirty-five years, Wordsworth tinkered with the text. He polished the style and softened some of the challenges to religious orthodoxy that he had set out in his earlier statements about the godlike powers of the human mind in its communion with nature; he did not, however, in any essential way alter its subject matter or overall design. *The Prelude* that was published in July 1850 is in fourteen books, it incorporated Wordsworth's latest revisions, which had been made in 1839, as well as some alterations introduced by his literary executors. The selections printed here—from W. J. B. Owen's Cornell Wordsworth volume, *The Fourteen-Book Prelude* (1985)—are from the manuscript of this final version. Our reasons for choosing this version are set forth in Jack Stillinger's "Textual Primitivism and the Editing of Wordsworth," *Studies in Romanticism* 28 (1989): 3–28.

When Wordsworth enlarged the two-part *Prelude* of 1799, he not only made it a poem of epic length but also heightened the style and introduced various thematic parallels with earlier epics, especially *Paradise Lost.* The expanded poem, however, is a personal history that turns on a mental crisis and recovery, and for such a narrative design the chief prototype is not the classical or Christian epic but the spiritual autobiography of crisis. St. Augustine's *Confessions* established this central Christian form late in the fourth century. Jean-Jacques Rousseau's *Confessions,* published between 1780 and 1789, and quickly translated into English from French, renewed this autobiographical form for writers of Wordsworth's generation.

As in many versions of spiritual autobiography, Wordsworth's persistent metaphor is that of life as a circular journey whose end (as T. S. Eliot put it in *Four Quartets,* his adaptation of the traditional form) is "to arrive where we started / And know the

place for the first time" (*Little Gidding*, lines 241–42). Wordsworth's *Prelude* opens
with a literal journey whose chosen goal (1.72, 106–07) is "a known Vale whither my
feet should turn"—that is, the Vale of Grasmere. *The Prelude* narrates a number of
later journeys, most notably the crossing of the Alps in book 6 and, at the beginning
of the final book, the climactic ascent of Mount Snowdon. In the course of the poem,
such literal journeys become the metaphoric vehicle for a spiritual journey—the
quest, within the poet's memory, and in the very process of composing his poem, for
his lost early self and his proper spiritual home. At its end the poem, rounding back
on its beginning, leaves the poet at home in the Vale of Grasmere, ready finally to
begin his great project *The Recluse* (14.302–11, 374–85). It is in this sense that the
poem is a "prelude"—preparation for the "honorable toil" (1.626) for which, having
discovered his vocation, the mature writer is ready at last.

Although the episodes of *The Prelude* are recognizable events from Wordsworth's
life, they are interpreted in retrospect, reordered in sequence, and retold as dramas
involving the interaction between the mind and nature and between the creative
imagination and the force of history. And although the narrator is recognizably William Wordsworth, addressing the entire poem as a communication to his friend Coleridge, he adopts the prophetic persona, modeled on the poet-prophets of the Bible,
which John Milton had adopted in narrating *Paradise Lost* (13.300–11). In this way
Wordsworth, like his great English predecessor, assumes the authority to speak as a
national poet whose function is to reconstitute the grounds of hope in a dark time of
postrevolutionary reaction and despair. As Wordsworth describes it (2.433–42), he
speaks out

> in these times of fear,
> This melancholy waste of hopes overthrown,
> . . . 'mid indifference and apathy
> And wicked exultation, when good men,
> On every side, fall off, we know not how,
> To selfishness, disguised in gentle names
> Of peace and quiet and domestic love
>   . . . this time
> Of dereliction and dismay. . . .

FROM THE PRELUDE
OR
GROWTH OF A POET'S MIND

AN AUTOBIOGRAPHICAL POEM

Book First
Introduction, Childhood, and School-time

> O there is blessing in this gentle breeze,
> A visitant that, while he fans my cheek,
> Doth seem half-conscious of the joy he brings
> From the green fields, and from yon azure sky.
> 5 Whate'er his mission, the soft breeze can come
> To none more grateful than to me; escaped
> From the vast City,° where I long have pined   *London*
> A discontented Sojourner—Now free,

Free as a bird to settle where I will.
10   What dwelling shall receive me? in what vale
Shall be my harbour? underneath what grove
Shall I take up my home? and what clear stream
Shall with its murmur lull me into rest?
The earth is all before me:[1] with a heart
15   Joyous, nor scared at its own liberty,
I look about; and should the chosen guide
Be nothing better than a wandering cloud,
I cannot miss my way. I breathe again;
Trances of thought and mountings of the heart
20   Come fast upon me: it is shaken off,
That burthen of my own unnatural self,
The heavy weight of many a weary day
Not mine, and such as were not made for me.
Long months of peace (if such bold word accord
25   With any promises of human life),
Long months of ease and undisturbed delight
Are mine in prospect;° whither shall I turn,   *anticipation*
By road or pathway, or through trackless field,
Up hill or down, or shall some floating thing
30   Upon the River point me out my course?
Dear Liberty! Yet what would it avail,
But for a gift that consecrates the joy?
For I, methought, while the sweet breath of heaven
Was blowing on my body, felt, within,
35   A correspondent breeze, that gently moved
With quickening virtue,[2] but is now become
A tempest, a redundant° energy,   *abundant*
Vexing its own creation. Thanks to both,
And their congenial° powers that, while they join   *kindred*
40   In breaking up a long continued frost,
Bring with them vernal° promises, the hope   *springtime*
Of active days urged on by flying hours;
Days of sweet leisure taxed with patient thought
Abstruse, nor wanting punctual service high,
45   Matins and vespers, of harmonious verse![3]
    Thus far, O Friend![4] did I, not used to make
A present joy the matter of a Song,[5]
Pour forth, that day, my soul in measured strains,

1. One of many echoes from *Paradise Lost*, where the line is applied to Adam and Eve as, at the conclusion of the poem, they begin their new life after being expelled from Eden: "The world was all before them" (12.646).
2. Revivifying power. ("To quicken" is to give or restore life.)
3. I.e., verses equivalent to morning prayers (matins) and evening prayers (vespers). The opening passage (lines 1–45), which Wordsworth calls in book 7, line 4, a "glad preamble," replaces the traditional epic device, such as Milton had adopted in *Paradise Lost*, of an opening prayer to the Muse for inspiration. To be "inspired," in the literal sense, is to be breathed or blown into by a divinity (in Latin *spirare* means both "to breathe" and "to blow"). Wordsworth begins his poem with a "blessing" from an outer "breeze," which (lines 34–45)

is called the "breath of heaven" and evokes in him, in response, an inner, "correspondent" breeze, a burst of inspiration. The power of this revivifying breeze and breath, at once material and spiritual, is represented in other Romantic poems, such as Coleridge's "The Eolian Harp" and Percy Shelley's "Ode to the West Wind" as well as in the opening letter of Mary Shelley's *Frankenstein*.
4. Samuel Taylor Coleridge, to whom Wordsworth addresses the whole of the *Prelude*. For Coleridge's response, after the poem was read to him, see "To William Wordsworth" (p. 1656).
5. In the Preface to *Lyrical Ballads*, Wordsworth says that his poetry usually originates in "emotion recollected in tranquillity"; hence not, as in the preceding preamble, during the experience that it records.

That would not be forgotten, and are here
50   Recorded:—to the open fields I told
A prophecy:—poetic numbers° came   *verse*
Spontaneously, to clothe in priestly robe
A renovated° Spirit singled out,   *renewed*
Such hope was mine, for holy services:
55   My own voice cheered me, and, far more, the mind's
Internal echo of the imperfect sound;
To both I listened, drawing from them both
A chearful confidence in things to come.
      Content, and not unwilling now to give
60   A respite to this passion,[6] I paced on
With brisk and eager steps; and came at length
To a green shady place where down I sate
Beneath a tree, slackening my thoughts by choice,
And settling into gentler happiness.
65   'Twas Autumn, and a clear and placid day,
With warmth, as much as needed, from a sun
Two hours declined towards the west, a day
With silver clouds, and sunshine on the grass,
And, in the sheltered and the sheltering grove,
70   A perfect stillness. Many were the thoughts
Encouraged and dismissed, till choice was made
Of a known Vale[7] whither my feet should turn,
Nor rest till they had reached the very door
Of the one Cottage which methought I saw.
75   No picture of mere memory ever looked
So fair; and while upon the fancied scene
I gazed with growing love, a higher power
Than Fancy gave assurance of some work
Of glory, there forthwith to be begun,
80   Perhaps too there performed.[8] Thus long I mused,
Nor e'er lost sight of what I mused upon,
Save where, amid the stately grove of Oaks,
Now here—now there—an acorn, from its cup
Dislodged, through sere leaves rustled, or at once
85   To the bare earth dropped with a startling sound.
      From that soft couch I rose not, till the sun
Had almost touched the horizon; casting then
A backward glance upon the curling cloud
Of city smoke, by distance ruralized,
90   Keen as a Truant or a Fugitive,
But as a Pilgrim resolute, I took,
Even with the chance equipment of that hour,
The road that pointed tow'rd the chosen Vale.
      It was a splendid evening: and my Soul
95   Once more made trial of her strength, nor lacked
Eolian visitations;[9] but the harp
Was soon defrauded, and the banded host

---

6. I.e., "and willing to prolong the passion."
7. Grasmere, where Wordsworth settled with his sister, Dorothy, in December 1799.
8. I.e., *The Recluse,* which Wordsworth planned to be his major poetic work.

9. Influences to which his soul responded as an Eolian harp, placed in an open window, responds with music to gusts of a breeze. For a description of this instrument, see Coleridge's *The Eolian Harp,* n. 1, p. 1612.

Of harmony dispersed in straggling sounds;
And lastly utter silence! "Be it so;
100 Why think of any thing but present good?"
So, like a Home-bound Labourer, I pursued
My way, beneath the mellowing sun, that shed
Mild influence;¹ nor left in me one wish
Again to bend the sabbath of that time²
105 To a servile yoke. What need of many words?
A pleasant loitering journey, through three days
Continued, brought me to my hermitage.
I spare to tell of what ensued, the life
In common things,—the endless store of things
110 Rare, or at least so seeming, every day
Found all about me in one neighbourhood;
The self-congratulation,° and from morn   *self-rejoicing*
To night unbroken cheerfulness serene.
But speedily an earnest longing rose
115 To brace myself to some determined aim,
Reading or thinking; either to lay up
New stores, or rescue from decay the old
By timely interference: and therewith
Came hopes still higher, that with outward life
120 I might endue° some airy phantasies   *invest*
That had been floating loose about for years;
And to such Beings temperately deal forth
The many feelings that oppressed my heart.
That hope hath been discouraged; welcome light
125 Dawns from the East, but dawns—to disappear
And mock me with a sky that ripens not
Into a steady morning: if my mind,
Remembering the bold promise of the past,
Would gladly grapple with some noble theme,
130 Vain is her wish: where'er she turns, she finds
Impediments from day to day renewed.
       And now it would content me to yield up
Those lofty hopes awhile for present gifts
Of humbler industry. But, O dear Friend!
135 The Poet, gentle Creature as he is,
Hath, like the Lover, his unruly times,
His fits when he is neither sick nor well,
Though no distress be near him but his own
Unmanageable thoughts: his mind, best pleas'd
140 While she, as duteous as the Mother Dove,
Sits brooding,³ lives not always to that end,
But, like the innocent Bird, hath goadings on
That drive her, as in trouble, through the groves:
With me is now such passion, to be blamed
145 No otherwise than as it lasts too long.
       When as becomes a Man who would prepare

1. An astrological term for the effect of stars on human life.
2. That time of rest.
3. An echo of Milton's reference in *Paradise Lost* to the original act of creation in his invocation to the Holy Spirit: Thou "Dovelike satst brooding on the vast Abyss / And mad'st it pregnant" (1.21–22).

For such an arduous Work, I through myself
Make rigorous inquisition, the report
Is often chearing; for I neither seem
150 To lack that first great gift, the vital Soul,
Nor general Truths, which are themselves a sort
Of Elements and Agents, Under-powers,
Subordinate helpers of the living Mind:
Nor am I naked of external things,
155 Forms, images, nor numerous other aids
Of less regard, though won perhaps with toil,
And needful to build up a Poet's praise.
Time, place, and manners do I seek, and these
Are found in plenteous store, but no where such
160 As may be singled out with steady choice:
No little band of yet remembered names
Whom I in perfect confidence might hope
To summon back from lonesome banishment,
And make them dwellers in the hearts of men
165 Now living, or to live in future years.
Sometimes the ambitious Power of choice, mistaking
Proud spring-tide swellings for a regular sea,
Will settle on some British theme, some old
Romantic Tale by Milton left unsung:[4]
170 More often turning to some gentle place
Within the groves of Chivalry, I pipe
To Shepherd Swains, or seated, harp in hand,
Amid reposing knights by a River side
Or fountain, listen to the grave reports
175 Of dire enchantments faced, and overcome
By the strong mind, and Tales of warlike feats
Where spear encountered spear, and sword with sword
Fought, as if conscious of the blazonry
That the shield bore, so glorious was the strife;
180 Whence inspiration for a song that winds
Through ever changing scenes of votive quest,[5]
Wrongs to redress, harmonious tribute paid
To patient courage and unblemished truth,
To firm devotion, zeal unquenchable,
185 And Christian meekness hallowing faithful loves.[6]
Sometimes, more sternly moved, I would relate
How vanquished Mithridates northward passed,
And, hidden in the cloud of years, became
Odin, the Father of a Race by whom
190 Perished the Roman Empire;[7] how the friends
And followers of Sertorius, out of Spain

4. In *Paradise Lost* 9.24–41 Milton relates that, in seeking a subject for his epic poem, he rejected "fabled Knights" and medieval romance.
5. A quest undertaken to fulfill a vow.
6. An echo of the prefatory statement to Spenser's *Faerie Queene*, line 9: "Fierce warres and faithfull loves shall moralize my song."
7. Mithridates VI, king of Pontus, was defeated by the Roman Pompey in 66 B.C.E. In his *Decline and* *Fall of the Roman Empire* (published between 1776 and 1788), the historian Edward Gibbon had discussed Mithridates as a historical prototype for the legendary Norse god Odin. Mithridates' determination to found a family line that would take revenge on the conquering Romans links him to other figures whom Wordsworth here considers as potential subjects for his poem, all of them battlers against tyranny.

Flying, found shelter in the Fortunate Isles;
And left their usages, their arts, and laws
To disappear by a slow gradual death;
195   To dwindle and to perish, one by one,
Starved in those narrow bounds: but not the soul
Of Liberty, which fifteen hundred years
Survived, and, when the European came
With skill and power that might not be withstood,
200   Did, like a pestilence, maintain its hold,
And wasted down by glorious death that Race
Of natural Heroes;[8]—or I would record
How, in tyrannic times, some high-souled Man,
Unnamed among the chronicles of Kings,
205   Suffered in silence for truth's sake: or tell
How that one Frenchman, through continued force
Of meditation on the inhuman deeds
Of those who conquered first the Indian isles,
Went, single in his ministry, across
210   The Ocean;—not to comfort the Oppressed,
But, like a thirsty wind, to roam about,
Withering the Oppressor:[9]—how Gustavus sought
Help at his need in Dalecarlia's mines:[1]
How Wallace[2] fought for Scotland, left the name
215   Of Wallace to be found, like a wild flower,
All over his dear Country, left the deeds
Of Wallace, like a family of Ghosts,
To people the steep rocks and river banks,
Her natural sanctuaries, with a local soul
220   Of independence and stern liberty.
Sometimes it suits me better to invent
A Tale from my own heart, more near akin
To my own passions, and habitual thoughts,
Some variegated Story, in the main
225   Lofty, but the unsubstantial Structure melts
Before the very sun that brightens it,
Mist into air dissolving! Then, a wish,
My last and favourite aspiration, mounts,
With yearning, tow'rds some philosophic Song
230   Of Truth[3] that cherishes our daily life;
With meditations passionate, from deep
Recesses in man's heart, immortal verse
Thoughtfully fitted to the Orphean lyre;[4]
But from this awful burthen I full soon

---

8. Sertorius, a Roman general allied with Mithridates, fought off the armies of Pompey and others until he was assassinated in 72 B.C.E. There is a legend that after his death his followers, to escape Roman tyranny, fled from Spain to the Canary Islands (known in ancient times as "the Fortunate Isles," line 192), where their descendants flourished until subjugated and decimated by invading Spaniards late in the 15th century.
9. Dominique de Gourges, a French gentleman who went in 1568 to Florida to avenge the massacre of the French by the Spaniards there [foot-

note in *The Prelude* of 1850].
1. Gustavus I of Sweden (1496–1530) worked to advance Sweden's liberation from Danish rule while toiling in disguise as a miner in his country's Dalecarlia mines.
2. William Wallace, Scottish patriot, fought against the English until captured and executed in 1305.
3. I.e., *The Recluse.*
4. The lyre of Orpheus. In Greek myth Orpheus was able to enchant not only human listeners but also the natural world by his singing and playing.

235 Take refuge, and beguile myself with trust
     That mellower years will bring a riper mind
     And clearer insight. Thus my days are passed
     In contradiction; with no skill to part
     Vague longing, haply bred by want of power,
240 From paramount impulse—not to be withstood;
     A timorous capacity from prudence;
     From circumspection, infinite delay.[5]
     Humility and modest awe themselves
     Betray me, serving often for a cloke
245 To a more subtile selfishness; that now
     Locks every function up in blank° reserve,°   absolute / inaction
     Now dupes me, trusting to an anxious eye
     That with intrusive restlessness beats off
     Simplicity, and self-presented truth.
250   Ah! better far than this, to stray about
     Voluptuously,° through fields and rural walks,   luxuriously
     And ask no record of the hours, resigned
     To vacant musing, unreproved neglect
     Of all things, and deliberate holiday:
255 Far better never to have heard the name
     Of zeal and just ambition, than to live
     Baffled and plagued by a mind that every hour
     Turns recreant° to her task, takes heart again,   unfaithful
     Then feels immediately some hollow thought
260 Hang like an interdict° upon her hopes.   prohibition
     This is my lot; for either still I find
     Some imperfection in the chosen theme;
     Or see of absolute accomplishment
     Much wanting, so much wanting, in myself
265 That I recoil and droop, and seek repose
     In listlessness from vain perplexity;
     Unprofitably travelling toward the grave,
     Like a false Steward who hath much received,
     And renders nothing back.[6]
                              Was it for this[7]
270 That one, the fairest of all rivers, loved
     To blend his murmurs with my Nurse's song;
     And, from his alder shades and rocky falls,
     And from his fords and shallows, sent a voice
     That flowed along my dreams? For this didst Thou,
275 O Derwent! winding among grassy holms[8]
     Where I was looking on, a Babe in arms,
     Make ceaseless music, that composed my thoughts
     To more than infant softness, giving me,
     Amid the fretful dwellings of mankind,
280 A foretaste, a dim earnest, of the calm

5. The syntax is complex and inverted; in outline the sense of lines 238–42 seems to be: "With no ability ('skill') to distinguish between vague desire (perhaps, 'haply,' resulting from lack of power) and ruling impulse; between endless procrastination and carefulness ('circumspection')."
6. The reference is to Christ's parable of the stew- ard who fails to use his talents (literally, the coins his master has entrusted to him and, figuratively, his God-given abilities) in Matthew 25.14–30.
7. The two-part *Prelude* that Wordsworth wrote in 1798–99 begins at this point.
8. Flat ground next to a river.

That Nature breathes among the hills and groves?
    When he had left the mountains, and received
On his smooth breast the shadow of those Towers
That yet survive, a shattered Monument
285   Of feudal sway, the bright blue River passed
Along the margin of our Terrace Walk;[9]
A tempting Playmate whom we dearly loved.
O many a time have I, a five years' Child,
In a small mill-race[1] severed from his stream,
290   Made one long bathing of a summer's day;
Basked in the sun, and plunged, and basked again,
Alternate all a summer's day, or scoured[2]
The sandy fields, leaping through flow'ry groves
Of yellow ragwort; or when rock and hill,
295   The woods and distant Skiddaw's[3] lofty height,
Were bronzed with deepest radiance, stood alone
Beneath the sky, as if I had been born
On Indian plains, and from my Mother's hut
Had run abroad in wantonness,° to sport,   *frolic*
300   A naked Savage, in the thunder shower.
    Fair seed-time had my soul, and I grew up
Fostered alike by beauty and by fear;
Much favoured in my birth-place, and no less
In that beloved Vale[4] to which erelong
305   We were transplanted—there were we let loose
For sports of wider range. Ere I had told
Ten birth-days, when among the mountain slopes
Frost, and the breath of frosty wind, had snapped
The last autumnal Crocus, 'twas my joy,
310   With store of Springes° o'er my Shoulder slung,   *bird snares*
To range the open heights where woodcocks ran
Along the smooth green turf. Through half the night,
Scudding away from snare to snare, I plied
That anxious visitation;—moon and stars
315   Were shining o'er my head; I was alone,
And seemed to be a trouble to the peace
That dwelt among them. Sometimes it befel,
In these night-wanderings, that a strong desire
O'erpowered my better reason, and the Bird
320   Which was the Captive of another's toil[5]
Became my prey; and when the deed was done
I heard, among the solitary hills,
Low breathings coming after me, and sounds
Of undistinguishable motion, steps
325   Almost as silent as the turf they trod.
    Nor less, when Spring had warmed the cultured° Vale,   *cultivated*
Roved we as plunderers where the Mother-bird

9. The Derwent River flows by Cockermouth Castle and then past the garden terrace behind Wordsworth's father's house in Cockermouth, Cumberland.
1. The current that drives a mill wheel.
2. Run swiftly over.
3. A mountain nine miles east of Cockermouth.
4. The valley of Esthwaite, the location of Hawkshead, where Wordsworth attended school.
5. Snare or labor.

Had in high places built her lodge; though mean°   *of little value*
Our object, and inglorious, yet the end°   *outcome*
330 Was not ignoble. Oh! when I have hung
Above the Raven's nest, by knots of grass
And half-inch fissures in the slippery rock
But ill-sustained; and almost (so it seemed)
Suspended by the blast that blew amain,
335 Shouldering the naked crag; Oh, at that time,
While on the perilous ridge I hung alone,
With what strange utterance did the loud dry wind
Blow through my ears! the sky seemed not a sky
Of earth, and with what motion moved the clouds!
340   Dust as we are, the immortal Spirit grows
Like harmony in music; there is a dark
Inscrutable workmanship that reconciles
Discordant elements, makes them cling together
In one society. How strange that all
345 The terrors, pains, and early miseries,
Regrets, vexations, lassitudes, interfused
Within my mind, should e'er have borne a part,
And that a needful part, in making up
The calm existence that is mine when I
350 Am worthy of myself! Praise to the end!
Thanks to the means which Nature deigned to employ!
Whether her fearless visitings or those
That came with soft alarm like hurtless lightning
Opening the peaceful clouds, or she would use
355 Severer interventions, ministry
More palpable, as best might suit her aim.
    One summer evening (led by her) I found
A little Boat tied to a Willow-tree
Within a rocky cave, its usual home.
360 Straight I unloosed her chain, and, stepping in,
Pushed from the shore. It was an act of stealth
And troubled pleasure, nor without the voice
Of mountain-echoes did my Boat move on,
Leaving behind her still, on either side,
365 Small circles glittering idly in the moon,
Until they melted all into one track
Of sparkling light. But now, like one who rows
(Proud of his skill) to reach a chosen point
With an unswerving line, I fixed my view
370 Upon the summit of a craggy ridge,
The horizon's utmost boundary; for above
Was nothing but the stars and the grey sky.
She was an elfin Pinnace;° lustily   *small boat*
I dipped my oars into the silent lake;
375 And, as I rose upon the stroke, my boat
Went heaving through the Water like a swan:
When, from behind that craggy Steep, till then
The horizon's bound, a huge peak, black and huge,
As if with voluntary power instinct,°   *endowed*

380   Upreared its head.[6]—I struck, and struck again,
        And, growing still in stature, the grim Shape
        Towered up between me and the stars, and still,
        For so it seemed, with purpose of its own
        And measured motion, like a living Thing

385   Strode after me. With trembling oars I turned,
        And through the silent water stole my way
        Back to the Covert° of the Willow-tree;   *shelter*
        There, in her mooring-place, I left my Bark,—
        And through the meadows homeward went, in grave

390   And serious mood; but after I had seen
        That spectacle, for many days, my brain
        Worked with a dim and undetermined sense
        Of unknown modes of being; o'er my thoughts
        There hung a darkness, call it solitude

395   Or blank desertion. No familiar Shapes
        Remained, no pleasant images of trees,
        Of sea or Sky, no colours of green fields,
        But huge and mighty Forms, that do not live
        Like living men, moved slowly through the mind

400   By day, and were a trouble to my dreams.
           Wisdom and Spirit of the Universe!
        Thou Soul that art the eternity of thought,
        That giv'st to forms and images a breath
        And everlasting Motion! not in vain,

405   By day or star-light, thus from my first dawn
        Of Childhood didst thou intertwine for me
        The passions that build up our human Soul,
        Not with the mean° and vulgar° works of man,   *inferior / commonplace*
        But with high objects, with enduring things,

410   With life and nature, purifying thus
        The elements of feeling and of thought,
        And sanctifying, by such discipline,
        Both pain and fear; until we recognize
        A grandeur in the beatings of the heart.

415   Nor was this fellowship vouchsafed to me
        With stinted kindness. In November days
        When vapours, rolling down the valley, made
        A lonely scene more lonesome; among woods
        At noon, and 'mid the calm of summer nights,

420   When, by the margin of the trembling Lake,
        Beneath the gloomy hills homeward I went
        In solitude, such intercourse was mine:
        Mine was it, in the fields both day and night,
        And by the waters, all the summer long.

425   —And in the frosty season, when the sun
        Was set, and visible for many a mile,
        The cottage windows blazed through twilight gloom,
        I heeded not their summons,—happy time

---

6. To direct his boat in a straight line, the rower (sitting facing the stern of the boat) has fixed his eye on a point on the ridge above the nearby shore, which blocks out the landscape behind. As he moves farther out, the black peak rises into his altering angle of vision and seems to stride closer with each stroke of the oars.

It was indeed for all of us; for me
430 It was a time of rapture!—Clear and loud
The village Clock toll'd six—I wheeled about,
Proud and exulting like an untired horse
That cares not for his home.—All shod with steel,°   *i.e., on skates*
We hissed along the polished ice, in games
435 Confederate, imitative of the chase
And woodland pleasures,—the resounding horn,
The Pack loud-chiming and the hunted hare.
So through the darkness and the cold we flew,
And not a voice was idle: with the din
440 Smitten, the precipices rang aloud;
The leafless trees and every icy crag
Tinkled like iron; while far distant hills
Into the tumult sent an alien sound
Of melancholy, not unnoticed while the stars,
445 Eastward, were sparkling clear, and in the west
The orange sky of evening died away.
Not seldom from the uproar I retired
Into a silent bay,—or sportively
Glanced sideway,[7] leaving the tumultous throng
450 To cut across the reflex° of a star   *reflection*
That fled, and, flying still before me, gleamed
Upon the glassy plain: and oftentimes,
When we had given our bodies to the wind,
And all the shadowy banks on either side
455 Came sweeping through the darkness, spinning still
The rapid line of motion, then at once
Have I, reclining back upon my heels,
Stopped short; yet still the solitary cliffs
Wheeled by me—even as if the earth had rolled
460 With visible motion her diurnal° round!   *daily*
Behind me did they stretch in solemn train,°   *succession*
Feebler and feebler, and I stood and watched
Till all was tranquil as a dreamless sleep.
     Ye presences of Nature, in the sky,
465 And on the earth! Ye visions of the hills!
And Souls[8] of lonely places! can I think
A vulgar hope was yours when ye employed
Such ministry, when ye, through many a year,
Haunting me thus among my boyish sports,
470 On caves and trees, upon the woods and hills,
Impressed upon all forms the characters°   *signs*
Of danger or desire; and thus did make
The surface of the universal earth
With triumph and delight, with hope and fear,
Work° like a sea?   *seethe*
475   Not uselessly employed,
Might I pursue this theme through every change
Of exercise and play, to which the year

---

7. Moved off obliquely.
8. Wordsworth refers both to a single "Spirit" or "Soul" of the universe as a whole (e.g., lines 401–

02) and to plural "Presences" and "Souls" animating the various parts of the universe.

Did summon us in his delightful round.
　　　—We were a noisy crew; the sun in heaven
480　Beheld not vales more beautiful than ours,
Nor saw a Band in happiness and joy
Richer, or worthier of the ground they trod.
I could record with no reluctant voice
The woods of Autumn, and their hazel bowers
485　With milk-white clusters hung; the rod and line,
True symbol of hope's foolishness, whose strong
And unreproved enchantment led us on,
By rocks and pools shut out from every star
All the green summer, to forlorn cascades
490　Among the windings hid of mountain brooks.
　　　—Unfading recollections! at this hour
The heart is almost mine with which I felt,
From some hill-top on sunny afternoons,
The paper-Kite, high among fleecy clouds,
495　Pull at her rein, like an impatient Courser;°　　　　　　　　*swift horse*
Or, from the meadows sent on gusty days,
Beheld her breast the wind, then suddenly
Dashed headlong, and rejected by the storm.
　　　Ye lowly Cottages in which we dwelt,
500　A ministration of your own was yours!
Can I forget you, being as ye were
So beautiful among the pleasant fields
In which ye stood? or can I here forget
The plain and seemly countenance with which
505　Ye dealt out your plain Comforts? Yet had ye
Delights and exultations of your own.
Eager and never weary, we pursued
Our home-amusements by the warm peat-fire
At evening, when with pencil, and smooth slate
510　In square divisions parcelled out, and all
With crosses and with cyphers scribbled o'er,
We schemed and puzzled, head opposed to head,
In strife too humble to be named in verse;⁹
Or round the naked table, snow-white deal,°　　　　　　　　*pine or fir*
515　Cherry, or maple, sate in close array,
And to the Combat, Lu or Whist, led on
A thick-ribbed Army, not as in the world
Neglected and ungratefully thrown by
Even for the very service they had wrought,
520　But husbanded through many a long campaign.
Uncouth assemblage was it, where no few
Had changed their functions; some, plebeian cards
Which Fate, beyond the promise of their birth,
Had dignified, and called to represent
525　The Persons of departed Potentates.¹
Oh, with what echoes on the board they fell!

9. I.e., ticktacktoe. With his phrasing in this passage, Wordsworth pokes fun at 18th-century poetic diction, which avoided everyday terms by using elaborate paraphrases.

1. The cards have changed their functions in ways that remind us that the first version of *The Prelude* was begun soon after the downfall of the French monarchy during the Revolution. The "Potentate"

Ironic diamonds; Clubs, Hearts, Diamonds, Spades,
A congregation piteously akin!
Cheap matter offered they to boyish wit,
530 Those sooty Knaves, precipitated down
With scoffs and taunts like Vulcan[2] out of heaven;
The paramount Ace, a moon in her eclipse,
Queens gleaming through their Splendor's last decay,
And Monarchs surly at the wrongs sustained
535 By royal visages.[3] Meanwhile abroad
Incessant rain was falling, or the frost
Raged bitterly, with keen and silent tooth;
And, interrupting oft that eager game,
From under Esthwaite's splitting fields of ice
540 The pent-up air, struggling to free itself,
Gave out to meadow-grounds and hills, a loud
Protracted yelling, like the noise of wolves
Howling in Troops along the Bothnic Main.[4]
    Nor, sedulous° as I have been to trace   *diligent*
545 How Nature by extrinsic passion first
Peopled the mind with forms sublime or fair
And made me love them, may I here omit
How other pleasures have been mine, and joys
Of subtler origin; how I have felt,
550 Not seldom even in that tempestuous time,
Those hallowed and pure motions of the sense
Which seem, in their simplicity, to own
An intellectual[5] charm;—that calm delight
Which, if I err not, surely must belong
555 To those first-born° affinities that fit   *innate*
Our new existence to existing things,
And, in our dawn of being, constitute
The bond of union between life and joy.
    Yes, I remember when the changeful earth
560 And twice five summers on my mind had stamped
The faces of the moving year, even then
I held unconscious intercourse with beauty
Old as creation, drinking in a pure
Organic pleasure from the silver wreaths
565 Of curling mist, or from the level plain
Of waters, colored by impending° clouds.   *overhanging*
    The sands of Westmorland, the creeks and bays
Of Cumbria's° rocky limits, they can tell   *Cumberland's*
How, when the Sea threw off his evening shade,
570 And to the Shepherd's hut on distant hills
Sent welcome notice of the rising moon,
How I have stood, to fancies such as these
A Stranger, linking with the Spectacle

---

cards—the kings, queens, and jacks—have over time been lost from the pack and so selected "plebeian," or commoner, cards have come to be used in their place.
2. Roman god of fire and forge. His mother, Juno, when he was born lame, threw him down from Olympus, the home of the gods.

3. Wordsworth implicitly parallels the boys' card games to the mock-epic description of the aristocratic game of ombre in Pope's *The Rape of the Lock* 3.37–98.
4. A northern gulf of the Baltic Sea.
5. Spiritual, as opposed to sense perceptions.

No conscious memory of a kindred sight,
575 And bringing with me no peculiar sense
Of quietness or peace, yet have I stood,
Even while mine eye hath moved o'er many a league[6]
Of shining water, gathering, as it seemed,
Through every hair-breadth in that field of light,
580 New pleasure, like a bee among the flowers.
　　Thus oft amid those fits of vulgar[7] joy
Which, through all seasons, on a Child's pursuits
Are prompt Attendants; 'mid that giddy bliss
Which like a tempest works along the blood
585 And is forgotten: even then I felt
Gleams like the flashing of a shield,—the earth
And common face of Nature spake to me
Rememberable things; sometimes, 'tis true,
By chance collisions and quaint accidents
590 (Like those ill-sorted unions, work supposed
Of evil-minded fairies), yet not vain
Nor profitless, if haply they impressed
Collateral° objects and appearances, _secondary_
Albeit lifeless then, and doomed to sleep
595 Until maturer seasons called them forth
To impregnate and to elevate the mind.
—And, if the vulgar joy by its own weight
Wearied itself out of the memory,
The scenes which were a witness of that joy
600 Remained, in their substantial lineaments
Depicted on the brain, and to the eye
Were visible, a daily sight: and thus
By the impressive discipline of fear,
By pleasure and repeated happiness,
605 So frequently repeated, and by force
Of obscure feelings representative
Of things forgotten; these same scenes so bright,
So beautiful, so majestic in themselves,
Though yet the day was distant, did become
610 Habitually dear; and all their forms
And changeful colours by invisible links
Were fastened to the affections.° _feelings_
　　　　　　　　　　　I began
My Story early, not misled, I trust,
By an infirmity of love for days
615 Disowned by memory,[8] fancying flowers where none,
Not even the sweetest, do or can survive
For him at least whose dawning day they cheered;
Nor will it seem to Thee, O Friend! so prompt
In sympathy, that I have lengthened out,
620 With fond and feeble tongue, a tedious tale.
　　Meanwhile, my hope has been, that I might fetch

6. A distance equal to approximately three miles.
7. Ordinary, commonplace.
8. I.e., he hopes that he has not mistakenly attributed his later thoughts and feelings to a time of life
he can no longer remember.

Invigorating thoughts from former years;
Might fix the wavering balance of my mind,
And haply meet reproaches too, whose power
625 May spur me on, in manhood now mature,
To honorable toil. Yet should these hopes
Prove vain, and thus should neither I be taught
To understand myself, nor thou to know
With better knowledge how the heart was framed
630 Of him thou lovest, need I dread from thee
Harsh judgments, if the Song be loth to quit
Those recollected hours that have the charm
Of visionary things, those lovely forms
And sweet sensations that throw back our life,
635 And almost make remotest infancy
A visible scene, on which the sun is shining?
    One end at least hath been attained—my mind
Hath been revived; and, if this genial[9] mood
Desert me not, forthwith shall be brought down
640 Through later years the story of my life:
The road lies plain before me,—'tis a theme
Single, and of determined bounds; and hence
I chuse it rather, at this time, than work
Of ampler or more varied argument,
645 Where I might be discomfited and lost;
And certain hopes are with me that to thee
This labour will be welcome, honoured Friend!

Book Second
School-time continued

Thus far, O Friend! have we, though leaving much
Unvisited, endeavoured to retrace
The simple ways in which my childhood walked,
Those chiefly, that first led me to the love
5 Of rivers, woods, and fields. The passion yet
Was in its birth, sustained, as might befal,
By nourishment that came unsought; for still,
From week to week, from month to month, we lived
A round of tumult. Duly° were our games   *appropriately*
10 Prolonged in summer till the day-light failed;
No chair remained before the doors, the bench
And threshold steps were empty; fast asleep
The Labourer, and the old Man who had sate,
A later Lingerer, yet the revelry
15 Continued, and the loud uproar; at last,
When all the ground was dark, and twinkling stars
Edged the black clouds, home and to bed we went,
Feverish, with weary joints and beating minds.
Ah! is there One who ever has been young

---

9. Productive, creative.

20   Nor needs a warning voice to tame the pride
        Of intellect, and virtue's self-esteem?
        One is there,[1] though the wisest and the best
        Of all mankind, who covets not at times
        Union that cannot be; who would not give,
25   If so he might, to duty and to truth
        The eagerness of infantine desire?
        A tranquillizing spirit presses now
        On my corporeal frame, so wide appears
        The vacancy between me and those days,
30   Which yet have such self-presence° in my mind,   actuality
        That, musing on them, often do I seem
        Two consciousnesses, conscious of myself
        And of some other Being. A rude mass
        Of native rock, left midway in the Square
35   Of our small market Village, was the goal
        Or centre of these sports; and, when, returned
        After long absence, thither I repaired,
        Gone was the old grey stone, and in its place
        A smart Assembly-room usurped the ground
40   That had been ours.[2] There let the fiddle scream,
        And be ye happy! Yet, my Friends,[3] I know
        That more than one of you will think with me
        Of those soft starry nights, and that old Dame
        From whom the Stone was named, who there had sate
45   And watched her table with its huckster's wares°   peddler's goods
        Assiduous, through the length of sixty years.
        —We ran a boisterous course, the year span round
        With giddy motion. But the time approached
        That brought with it a regular desire
50   For calmer pleasures, when the winning forms
        Of Nature were collaterally attached[4]
        To every scheme of holiday delight,
        And every boyish sport, less grateful° else   pleasing
        And languidly pursued.
                                 When summer came,
55   Our pastime was, on bright half-holidays,
        To sweep along the plain of Windermere
        With rival oars; and the selected bourne°   destination
        Was now an Island musical with birds
        That sang and ceased not; now a sister isle,
60   Beneath the oaks' umbrageous° covert, sown   shaded
        With lilies of the valley like a field;
        And now a third small island,[5] where survived,
        In solitude, the ruins of a shrine
        Once to our Lady dedicate, and served
65   Daily with chaunted rites. In such a race,
        So ended, disappointment could be none,
        Uneasiness, or pain, or jealousy;

---

1. I.e., "Is there anyone . . . ?"
2. The Hawkshead Town Hall, built in 1790.
3. Coleridge and John Wordsworth (William's brother), who had visited Hawkshead together

with William in November 1799.
4. Associated as an accompaniment.
5. The island of Lady Holm, former site of a chapel dedicated to the Virgin Mary.

We rested in the Shade, all pleased alike,
Conquered and Conqueror. Thus the pride of strength,
70   And the vain-glory of superior skill,
Were tempered, thus was gradually produced
A quiet independence of the heart:
And, to my Friend who knows me, I may add,
Fearless of blame, that hence, for future days,
75   Ensued a diffidence and modesty;
And I was taught to feel, perhaps too much,
The self-sufficing power of solitude.
         Our daily meals were frugal, Sabine fare![6]
More than we wished we knew the blessing then
80   Of vigorous hunger—hence corporeal strength
Unsapped by delicate viands;° for, exclude   food
A little weekly stipend,[7] and we lived
Through three divisions of the quartered year
In pennyless poverty. But now, to school
85   From the half-yearly holidays returned,
We came with weightier purses, that sufficed
To furnish treats more costly than the Dame
Of the old grey stone, from her scanty board, supplied.
Hence rustic dinners on the cool green ground,
90   Or in the woods, or by a river side,
Or shady fountains,° while among the leaves   springs, streams
Soft airs were stirring, and the mid-day sun
Unfelt shone brightly round us in our joy.
         Nor is my aim neglected if I tell
95   How sometimes, in the length of those half years,
We from our funds drew largely—proud to curb,
And eager to spur on, the gallopping Steed:
And with the cautious Inn-keeper, whose Stud
Supplied our want, we haply might employ
100   Sly subterfuges, if the Adventure's bound
Were distant, some famed Temple[8] where of yore°   long ago
The Druids worshipped, or the antique Walls
Of that large Abbey which within the Vale
Of Nightshade, to St Mary's honour built,
105   Stands yet, a mouldering Pile,° with fractured arch,   building in ruin
Belfry, and Images, and living Trees;
A holy Scene![9]—Along the smooth green Turf
Our Horses grazed:—to more than inland peace
Left by the west wind sweeping overhead
110   From a tumultuous ocean, trees and towers
In that sequestered Valley may be seen
Both silent and both motionless alike;
Such the deep shelter that is there, and such
The safeguard for repose and quietness.

6. Like the meals of the Roman poet Horace on his Sabine farm.
7. In his last year at school, Wordsworth had an allowance of sixpence a week; his younger brother Christopher, threepence. After the Midsummer and Christmas holidays (line 85), the boys received a larger sum, ranging up to a guinea.
8. The stone circle at Swinside, on the lower Duddon River, mistakenly believed at the time to have been a Druid temple.
9. Furness Abbey, some twenty miles south of Hawkshead.

115   Our Steeds remounted, and the summons given,
    With whip and spur we through the Chauntry[1] flew
    In uncouth race, and left the cross-legged Knight
    And the Stone-abbot, and that single Wren
    Which one day sang so sweetly in the Nave
120   Of the old Church, that, though from recent Showers
    The earth was comfortless, and, touched by faint
    Internal breezes, sobbings of the place
    And respirations, from the roofless walls
    The shuddering ivy dripped large drops, yet still
125   So sweetly 'mid the gloom the invisible Bird
    Sang to herself, that there I could have made
    My dwelling-place, and lived for ever there
    To hear such music. Through the Walls we flew,
    And down the Valley, and, a circuit made
130   In wantonness° of heart, through rough and smooth   *playfulness*
    We scampered homewards. Oh, ye rocks and streams,
    And that still Spirit shed from evening air!
    Even in this joyous time I sometimes felt
    Your presence, when with slackened step we breathed[2]
135   Along the sides of the steep hills, or when,
    Lighted by gleams of moonlight from the sea,
    We beat with thundering hoofs the level sand.
       Midway on long Winander's Eastern shore,
    Within the crescent of a pleasant Bay,
140   A Tavern[3] stood, no homely-featured House,
    Primeval like its neighbouring Cottages;
    But 'twas a splendid place, the door beset
    With Chaises, Grooms, and Liveries,—and within
    Decanters, Glasses, and the blood-red Wine.
145   In ancient times, or ere the Hall was built
    On the large Island,[4] had this Dwelling been
    More worthy of a Poet's love, a Hut
    Proud of its one bright fire and sycamore shade.
    But, though the rhymes were gone that once inscribed
150   The threshold, and large golden characters°   *letters*
    Spread o'er the spangled sign-board had dislodged
    The old Lion, and usurped his place in slight
    And mockery of the rustic Painter's hand,
    Yet to this hour the spot to me is dear
155   With all its foolish pomp. The garden lay
    Upon a slope surmounted by the plain
    Of a small Bowling-green: beneath us stood
    A grove, with gleams of water through the trees
    And over the tree-tops; nor did we want
160   Refreshment, strawberries, and mellow cream.
    There, while through half an afternoon we played
    On the smooth platform, whether skill prevailed
    Or happy blunder triumphed, bursts of glee
    Made all the mountains ring. But ere night-fall,

1. A chapel endowed for masses to be sung for the donor.
2. Slowed to let the horses catch their breath.
3. The White Lion at Bowness.
4. The Hall on Belle Isle in Lake Windermere had been built in the early 1780s.

165 When in our pinnace° we returned, at leisure   *small boat*
    Over the shadowy Lake, and to the beach
    Of some small Island steered our course with one,
    The Minstrel of our Troop, and left him there,
    And rowed off gently, while he blew his flute
170 Alone upon the rock,—Oh then the calm
    And dead still water lay upon my mind
    Even with a weight of pleasure, and the sky,
    Never before so beautiful, sank down
    Into my heart, and held me like a dream!
175   Thus were my sympathies enlarged, and thus
    Daily the common range of visible things
    Grew dear to me: already I began
    To love the sun; a boy I loved the sun,
    Not as I since have loved him, as a pledge
180 And surety of our earthly life, a light
    Which we behold, and feel we are alive;
    Nor for his bounty to so many worlds,
    But for this cause, that I had seen him lay
    His beauty on the morning hills, had seen
185 The western mountain touch his setting orb,
    In many a thoughtless hour, when, from excess
    Of happiness, my blood appear'd to flow
    For its own pleasure, and I breathed with joy;
    And from like feelings, humble though intense,
190 To patriotic and domestic love
    Analogous, the moon to me was dear;
    For I would dream away my purposes,
    Standing to gaze upon her while she hung
    Midway between the hills, as if she knew
195 No other region; but belonged to thee,
    Yea, appertained by a peculiar right
    To thee, and thy grey huts,[5] thou one dear Vale!
       Those incidental charms which first attached
    My heart to rural objects, day by day
200 Grew weaker, and I hasten on to tell
    How Nature, intervenient[6] till this time
    And secondary, now at length was sought
    For her own sake. But who shall[7] parcel out
    His intellect, by geometric rules,
205 Split like a province into round and square?
    Who knows the individual hour in which
    His habits were first sown, even as a seed?
    Who that shall point, as with a wand, and say,
    "This portion of the river of my mind
210 Came from yon fountain"? Thou, my friend! art one
    More deeply read in thy own thoughts; to thee
    Science[8] appears but what in truth she is,
    Not as our glory and our absolute boast,
    But as a succedaneum,[9] and a prop

5. Cottages built of gray stones.
6. I.e., entering incidentally into his other concerns.
7. Is able to.

8. In the old sense: learning.
9. In medicine a drug substituted for a different drug. Wordsworth, however, uses the term to signify a remedy, or palliative.

215   To our infirmity. No officious° slave   *intrusive*
Art thou of that false secondary power[1]
By which we multiply distinctions, then
Deem that our puny boundaries are things
That we perceive, and not that we have made.
220   To thee, unblinded by these formal arts,
The unity of all hath been revealed;
And thou wilt doubt with me, less aptly skilled
Than many are to range the faculties
In scale and order, class the cabinet[2]
225   Of their sensations, and in voluble phrase[3]
Run through the history and birth of each
As of a single independent thing.
Hard task, vain hope, to analyse the mind,
If each most obvious and particular thought,
230   Not in a mystical and idle sense,
But in the words of reason deeply weighed,
Hath no beginning.
                Blest the infant Babe,
(For with my best conjecture I would trace
Our Being's earthly progress) blest the Babe,
235   Nursed in his Mother's arms, who sinks to sleep
Rocked on his Mother's breast; who, when his soul
Claims manifest kindred with a human soul,
Drinks in the feelings of his Mother's eye![4]
For him, in one dear Presence, there exists
240   A virtue which irradiates and exalts
Objects through widest intercourse of sense.
No outcast he, bewildered and depressed;
Along his infant veins are interfused
The gravitation and the filial bond
245   Of nature that connect him with the world.
Is there a flower to which he points with hand
Too weak to gather it, already love
Drawn from love's purest earthly fount for him
Hath beautified that flower; already shades
250   Of pity cast from inward tenderness
Do fall around him upon aught that bears
Unsightly marks of violence or harm.
Emphatically such a Being lives,
Frail Creature as he is, helpless as frail,
255   An inmate of° this active universe.   *a dweller in*
For feeling has to him imparted power
That through the growing faculties of sense
Doth, like an Agent of the one great Mind,
Create, creator and receiver both,
260   Working but in alliance with the works

1. The analytic faculty of the mind, as contrasted with the power to apprehend "the unity of all" (line 221).
2. To classify, as if arranged in a display case.
3. In fluent words.
4. Like the modern psychologist, Wordsworth recognized the importance of earliest infancy in the development of the individual mind, although he had then to invent the terms with which to analyze the process.

Which it beholds.[5]—Such, verily, is the first
Poetic spirit of our human life,
By uniform control of after years
In most abated or suppressed, in some,
265 Through every change of growth and of decay,
Preeminent till death.
                From early days,
Beginning not long after that first time
In which, a Babe, by intercourse of touch,
I held mute dialogues with my Mother's heart,[6]
270 I have endeavoured to display the means
Whereby this infant sensibility,
Great birth-right of our being, was in me
Augmented and sustained. Yet is a path
More difficult before me, and I fear
275 That, in its broken windings, we shall need
The chamois'[7] sinews, and the eagle's wing:
For now a trouble came into my mind
From unknown causes. I was left alone,
Seeking the visible world, nor knowing why.
280 The props of my affections were removed,[8]
And yet the building stood, as if sustained
By its own spirit! All that I beheld
Was dear, and hence to finer influxes°   *influences*
The mind lay open, to a more exact
285 And close communion. Many are our joys
In youth, but Oh! what happiness to live
When every hour brings palpable access
Of knowledge, when all knowledge is delight,
And sorrow is not there! The seasons came,
290 And every season, wheresoe'er I moved,
Unfolded° transitory qualities   *revealed*
Which, but for this most watchful power of love,
Had been neglected, left a register
Of permanent relations, else unknown.[9]
295 Hence life, and change, and beauty; solitude
More active even than "best society,"[1]
Society made sweet as solitude
By inward concords, silent, inobtrusive;
And gentle agitations of the mind
300 From manifold distinctions, difference
Perceived in things where, to the unwatchful eye,
No difference is, and hence, from the same source,
Sublimer joy: for I would walk alone

5. The infant, in the sense of security and love shed by his mother's presence on outer things, perceives what would otherwise be an alien world as a place to which he has a relationship like that of a son to a mother (lines 239–45). On such grounds Wordsworth asserts that the mind partially creates, by altering, the world it seems simply to perceive.
6. I.e., both infant and mother feel the pulse of the other's heart.
7. An agile species of antelope inhabiting mountainous regions of Europe.

8. Wordsworth's mother had died the month before his eighth birthday.
9. I.e., had it not been for the watchful power of love (line 292), the "transitory qualities" (291) would have been neglected, and the "permanent relations" now recorded in his memory would have been unknown.
1. A partial quotation of a line spoken by Adam to Eve in *Paradise Lost* 9.249: "For solitude sometimes is best society."

Under the quiet stars, and at that time
305　Have felt whate'er there is of power in sound
To breathe an elevated mood, by form
Or Image unprofaned: and I would stand,
If the night blackened with a coming storm,
Beneath some rock, listening to notes that are
310　The ghostly° language of the ancient earth,　　　　　　*disembodied*
Or make their dim abode in distant winds.
Thence did I drink the visionary power;
And deem not profitless those fleeting moods
Of shadowy exultation: not for this,
315　That they are kindred to our purer mind
And intellectual life;[2] but that the soul,
Remembering how she felt, but what she felt
Remembering not, retains an obscure sense
Of possible sublimity, whereto
320　With growing faculties she doth aspire,
With faculties still growing, feeling still
That, whatsoever point they gain, they yet
Have something to pursue.
　　　　　　　　　　　And not alone
'Mid gloom and tumult, but no less 'mid fair
325　And tranquil scenes, that universal power
And fitness in the latent qualities
And essences of things, by which the mind
Is moved with feelings of delight, to me
Came strengthened with a superadded soul,
330　A virtue not its own.—My morning walks
Were early;—oft before the hours of School
I travelled round our little Lake, five miles
Of pleasant wandering; happy time! more dear
For this, that One was by my side, a Friend[3]
335　Then passionately loved; with heart how full
Would he peruse these lines! for many years
Have since flowed in between us, and, our minds
Both silent to each other, at this time
We live as if those hours had never been.
340　Nor seldom did I lift our Cottage latch
Far earlier, and ere one smoke-wreath had risen
From human dwelling, or the thrush, high perched,
Piped to the woods his shrill *reveillé*,[4] sate
Alone upon some jutting eminence
345　At the first gleam of dawn-light, when the Vale,
Yet slumbering, lay in utter solitude.
How shall I seek the origin, where find
Faith in the marvellous things which then I felt?
Oft in those moments such a holy calm
350　Would overspread my soul, that bodily eyes[5]
Were utterly forgotten, and what I saw

2. I.e., not because they are related to the non-
sensuous ("intellectual") aspect of our life.
3. Identified as John Fleming in a note to the 1850
edition.
4. The signal given to awaken soldiers.
5. As opposed to the mind's eye, inner vision.

Appeared like something in myself, a dream,
A prospect° in the mind.   *scene*
                    'Twere long to tell
What spring and autumn, what the winter snows,
355 And what the summer shade, what day and night,
Evening and morning, sleep and waking thought,
From sources inexhaustible, poured forth
To feed the spirit of religious love,
In which I walked with Nature. But let this
360 Be not forgotten, that I still retained
My first creative sensibility,
That by the regular action of the world
My soul was unsubdued. A plastic° power   *shaping*
Abode with me, a forming hand, at times
365 Rebellious, acting in a devious mood,
A local Spirit of his own, at war
With general tendency, but, for the most,
Subservient strictly to external things
With which it communed. An auxiliar light
370 Came from my mind which on the setting sun
Bestowed new splendor; the melodious birds,
The fluttering breezes, fountains that ran on
Murmuring so sweetly in themselves, obeyed
A like dominion; and the midnight storm
375 Grew darker in the presence of my eye;
Hence my obeisance, my devotion hence,
And hence my transport.°   *exaltation*
                    Nor should this, perchance,
Pass unrecorded, that I still° had loved   *always*
The exercise and produce of a toil
380 Than analytic industry to me
More pleasing, and whose character I deem
Is more poetic, as resembling more
Creative agency. The Song would speak
Of that interminable building reared
385 By observation of affinities
In objects where no brotherhood exists
To passive minds. My seventeenth year was come;
And, whether from this habit rooted now
So deeply in my mind, or from excess
390 Of the great social principle of life
Coercing all things into sympathy,
To unorganic Natures were transferred
My own enjoyments; or the Power of truth,
Coming in revelation, did converse
395 With things that really are;[6] I, at this time,
Saw blessings spread around me like a sea.
Thus while the days flew by and years passed on,
From Nature overflowing on my soul

---

6. Wordsworth is careful to indicate that there are alternative explanations for his sense that life pervades the inorganic as well as the organic world: it may be the result either of a way of perceiving that has been habitual since infancy or of a projection of his own inner life, or else it may be the perception of an objective truth.

I had received so much, that every thought
400 Was steeped in feeling; I was only then
Contented when with bliss ineffable
I felt the sentiment of Being spread
O'er all that moves, and all that seemeth still;
O'er all that, lost beyond the reach of thought
405 And human knowledge, to the human eye
Invisible, yet liveth to the heart;
O'er all that leaps, and runs, and shouts, and sings,
Or beats the gladsome air; o'er all that glides
Beneath the wave, yea, in the wave itself,
410 And mighty depth of waters. Wonder not
If high the transport, great the joy I felt,
Communing in this sort through earth and Heaven
With every form of Creature, as it looked
Towards the Uncreated° with a countenance   God
415 Of adoration, with an eye of love.[7]
One song they sang, and it was audible,
Most audible, then, when the fleshly ear,
O'ercome by humblest prelude of that strain,
Forgot her functions and slept undisturbed.
420   If this be error, and another faith
Find easier access to the pious mind,[8]
Yet were I grossly destitute of all
Those human sentiments that make this earth
So dear, if I should fail with grateful voice
425 To speak of you, Ye Mountains, and Ye Lakes,
And sounding Cataracts, Ye Mists and Winds
That dwell among the Hills where I was born.
If in my Youth I have been pure in heart,
If, mingling with the world, I am content
430 With my own modest pleasures, and have lived,
With God and Nature communing, removed
From little enmities and low desires,
The gift is yours: if in these times of fear,
This melancholy waste° of hopes o'erthrown,   wasteland
435 If, 'mid indifference and apathy
And wicked exultation, when good men,
On every side, fall off, we know not how,
To selfishness, disguised in gentle names
Of peace and quiet and domestic love,
440 Yet mingled, not unwillingly, with sneers
On visionary minds; if, in this time
Of dereliction and dismay,[9] I yet
Despair not of our Nature, but retain
A more than Roman confidence, a faith
445 That fails not, in all sorrow my support,

7. Wordsworth did not add lines 412–14, which frame his experience of the "one life" in Christian terms, until the last revision of *The Prelude*, in 1839.
8. Compare "Tintern Abbey" lines 43–50, ending with "If this / Be but a vain belief . . ." (p. 1492).

9. The era, some ten years after the start of the French Revolution, was one of violent reaction. Many earlier sympathizers were abandoning their radical beliefs, and the British government was clamping down on all forms of political expression that resembled, even faintly, French ideas.

The blessing of my life, the gift is yours,
Ye Winds and sounding Cataracts, 'tis yours,
Ye Mountains! thine, O Nature! Thou hast fed
My lofty speculations; and in thee,
450 For this uneasy heart of ours, I find
A never-failing principle of joy
And purest passion.
              Thou, my Friend! wert reared
In the great City, 'mid far other scenes;[1]
But we, by different roads, at length have gained
455 The self-same bourne.° And for this cause to Thee   *destination*
I speak, unapprehensive of contempt,
The insinuated scoff of coward tongues,
And all that silent language which so oft,
In conversation between Man and Man,
460 Blots from the human countenance all trace
Of beauty and of love. For Thou hast sought
The truth in solitude, and, since the days
That gave thee liberty, full long desired,
To serve in Nature's Temple, thou hast been
465 The most assiduous of her Ministers,[2]
In many things my Brother, chiefly here
In this our deep devotion.
                    Fare Thee well!
Health, and the quiet of a healthful mind,
Attend Thee! seeking oft the haunts of Men,
470 And yet more often living with thyself
And for thyself, so haply shall thy days
Be many, and a blessing to mankind.

From Book Fifth
Books

[THE BOY OF WINANDER]

    There was a Boy;[1]—ye knew him well, Ye Cliffs
And Islands of Winander!—many a time
At evening, when the earliest stars began
To move along the edges of the hills,
370 Rising or setting, would he stand alone,
Beneath the trees, or by the glimmering lake;
And there, with fingers interwoven, both hands
Pressed closely palm to palm and to his mouth
Uplifted, he, as through an instrument,
375 Blew mimic hootings to the silent owls

1. A reminiscence of Coleridge's "Frost at Midnight," lines 51–52: "For I was reared / In the great
city, pent 'mid cloisters dim."
2. Wordsworth may be recalling the conclusion of
Coleridge's "France: An Ode" (1798), where, disillusioned about the promise of liberty by the
French Revolution, he writes that, while standing

on a "sea-cliff's verge," "O Liberty! my spirit felt
thee there." Wordsworth added lines 461–64 some
years after Coleridge's death in 1834.
1. In an early manuscript version of this passage,
Wordsworth uses the first-person pronoun. The
experience he describes was thus apparently his
own.

That they might answer him.—And they would shout
Across the watery Vale, and shout again,
Responsive to his call,—with quivering peals,
And long halloos, and screams, and echoes loud
380 Redoubled and redoubled; concourse wild
Of jocund din! and when a lengthened pause
Of silence came, and baffled his best skill,
Then, sometimes, in that silence, while he hung
Listening, a gentle shock of mild surprize
385 Has carried far into his heart[2] the voice
Of mountain torrents; or the visible scene
Would enter unawares into his mind
With all its solemn imagery, its rocks,
Its woods, and that uncertain heaven, received
390 Into the bosom of the steady lake.
    This Boy was taken from his Mates, and died
In childhood, ere he was full twelve years old.
Fair is the Spot, most beautiful the Vale
Where he was born: the grassy Church-yard hangs
395 Upon a slope above the Village School;
And through that Church-yard when my way has led
On summer evenings, I believe that there
A long half-hour together I have stood
Mute—looking at the grave in which he lies!
400   Even now appears before the mind's clear eye
That self-same Village Church; I see her sit
(The thronèd Lady whom erewhile we hailed)
On her green hill, forgetful of this Boy
Who slumbers at her feet, forgetful, too,
405 Of all her silent neighbourhood of graves,
And listening only to the gladsome sounds
That, from the rural School ascending, play
Beneath her, and about her. May she long
Behold a race of Young Ones like to those
410 With whom I herded! (easily, indeed,
We might have fed upon a fatter soil
Of Arts and Letters, but be that forgiven)
A race of *real* children; not too wise,
Too learnèd, or too good: but wanton,° fresh,   *playful*
415 And bandied up and down by love and hate;
Not unresentful where self-justified;
Fierce, moody, patient, venturous, modest, shy;
Mad at their sports like withered leaves in winds:
Though doing wrong and suffering, and full oft
420 Bending beneath our life's mysterious weight
Of pain, and doubt, and fear; yet yielding not
In happiness to the happiest upon earth.
Simplicity in habit, truth in speech,
Be these the daily strengtheners of their minds!

2. Thomas De Quincey responded to this line in *Recollections of the Lakes and the Lake Poets*: "This very expression, 'far,' by which space and its infinities are attributed to the human heart, and to its capacities of re-echoing the sublimities of nature, has always struck me as with a flash of sublime revelation."

425 May books and nature be their early joy!
And knowledge, rightly honored with that name,
Knowledge not purchased by the loss of power!

From Book Sixth
Cambridge, and the Alps

["HUMAN NATURE SEEMING BORN AGAIN"]

When the third summer freed us from restraint,[1]
A youthful Friend, he too a Mountaineer,
325 Not slow to share my wishes, took his staff,
And, sallying forth, we journeyed, side by side,
Bound to the distant Alps. A hardy slight
Did this unprecedented course imply
Of College studies and their set rewards;[2]
330 Nor had, in truth, the scheme been formed by me
Without uneasy forethought of the pain,
The censures, and ill-omening of those
To whom my worldly interests were dear.
But Nature then was Sovereign in my mind,
335 And mighty Forms, seizing a youthful fancy,
Had given a charter[3] to irregular hopes.
In any age of uneventful calm
Among the Nations, surely would my heart
Have been possessed by similar desire;
340 But Europe at that time was thrilled with joy,
France standing on the top of golden hours,
And human nature seeming born again.

[CROSSING SIMPLON PASS]

* * * That very day,
525 From a bare ridge we also first beheld
Unveiled the summit of Mont Blanc, and grieved
To have a soulless image on the eye
Which had usurped upon a living thought
That never more could be.[4] The wondrous Vale
530 Of Chamouny[5] stretched far below, and soon
With its dumb° cataracts, and streams of ice,   silent
A motionless array of mighty waves,
Five rivers broad and vast, made rich amends,
And reconciled us to realities.

1. After reviewing briefly his second and third years at Cambridge, Wordsworth here describes his trip through France and Switzerland with a college friend, Robert Jones, during the succeeding summer vacation, in 1790. France was then in the "golden hours" of the early period of the Revolution; the fall of the Bastille had occurred on July 14 of the preceding year.
2. Universities in Britain allow longer vacations than those in North America, on the assumption that they will be used for study. In the upcoming term Wordsworth faces his final examinations. His ranking in those will determine his career prospects.
3. Privileged freedom.
4. The "image" is the actual sight of Mont Blanc, as against what the poet has imagined the famous Swiss mountain to be.
5. Chamonix, a valley in eastern France, north of Mont Blanc.

535 There small birds warble from the leafy trees,
The eagle soars high in the element;
There doth the Reaper bind the yellow sheaf,
The Maiden spread the hay-cock in the sun,
While Winter like a well-tamed lion walks,
540 Descending from the Mountain to make sport
Among the Cottages by beds of flowers.
　　Whate'er in this wide circuit we beheld,
Or heard, was fitted to our unripe state
Of intellect and heart. With such a book
545 Before our eyes we could not chuse but read
Lessons of genuine brotherhood, the plain
And universal reason of mankind,
The truths of Young and Old. Nor, side by side
Pacing, two social Pilgrims, or alone
550 Each with his humour,[6] could we fail to abound
In dreams and fictions pensively composed,
Dejection taken up for pleasure's sake,
And gilded sympathies; the willow wreath,[7]
And sober posies[8] of funereal flowers
555 Gathered, among those solitudes sublime,
From formal gardens of the Lady Sorrow,
Did sweeten many a meditative hour.
　　Yet still in me with those soft luxuries
Mixed something of stern mood, an under thirst
560 Of vigor seldom utterly allayed.
And from that source how different a sadness
Would issue, let one incident make known.
When from the Vallais we had turned, and clomb°　　*climbed*
Along the Simplon's steep and rugged road,[9]
565 Following a band of Muleteers, we reached
A halting-place where all together took
Their noon-tide meal. Hastily rose our Guide,
Leaving *us* at the Board;° awhile we lingered,　　*i.e., eating the meal*
Then paced the beaten downward way that led
570 Right to a rough stream's edge and there broke off.
The only track now visible was one
That from the torrent's further brink held forth
Conspicuous invitation to ascend
A lofty mountain. After brief delay
575 Crossing the unbridged stream, that road we took
And clomb with eagerness, till anxious fears
Intruded, for we failed to overtake
Our Comrades gone before. By fortunate chance,
While every moment added doubt to doubt,
580 A Peasant met us, from whose mouth we learned
That to the Spot which had perplexed us first
We must descend, and there should find the road,
Which in the stony channel of the Stream

6. Temperament, or state of mind.
7. Clichéd symbol of sorrow. "Gilded": laid on like gilt; i.e., superficial.
8. Small bunches of flowers.
9. The Simplon Pass through the Alps.

Lay a few steps, and then along its banks,
585 And that our future course, all plain to sight,
Was downwards, with the current of that Stream.
Loth to believe what we so grieved to hear,
For still we had hopes that pointed to the clouds,
We questioned him again, and yet again;
590 But every word that from the Peasant's lips
Came in reply, translated by our feelings,
Ended in this, *that we had crossed the Alps.*[1]
    Imagination—here the Power so called
Through sad incompetence of human speech—
595 That awful° Power rose from the Mind's abyss   awe-inspiring
Like an unfathered vapour[2] that enwraps
At once some lonely Traveller. I was lost,
Halted without an effort to break through;
But to my conscious soul I now can say,
600 "I recognize thy glory"; in such strength
Of usurpation, when the light of sense
Goes out, but with a flash that has revealed
The invisible world, doth Greatness make abode,
There harbours, whether we be young or old;
605 Our destiny, our being's heart and home,
Is with infinitude, and only there;
With hope it is, hope that can never die,
Effort, and expectation, and desire,
And something evermore about to be.
610 Under such banners militant the Soul
Seeks for no trophies, struggles for no spoils,
That may attest her prowess, blest in thoughts
That are their own perfection and reward,
Strong in herself, and in beatitude[3]
615 That hides her like the mighty flood of Nile
Poured from his fount of Abyssinian clouds
To fertilize the whole Egyptian plain.
    The melancholy slackening that ensued
Upon those tidings by the Peasant given
620 Was soon dislodged; downwards we hurried fast
And, with the half-shaped road, which we had missed,
Entered a narrow chasm. The brook and road
Were fellow-Travellers in this gloomy Strait,
And with them did we journey several hours
625 At a slow pace. The immeasurable height
Of woods decaying, never to be decayed,
The stationary blasts of waterfalls,
And in the narrow rent at every turn
Winds thwarting winds, bewildered and forlorn,
630 The torrents shooting from the clear blue sky,
The rocks that muttered close upon our ears,

---

1. As Dorothy Wordsworth baldly put it later on, "The ambition of youth was disappointed at these tidings." The visionary experience that follows (lines 593–617) occurred not in the Alps but at the time of writing the passage, as the 1805 text explic-itly says: "Imagination! lifting up itself / Before the eye and progress of my Song."
2. Sudden vapor from no apparent source.
3. The ultimate blessedness or happiness.

Black drizzling crags that spake by the way-side
As if a voice were in them, the sick sight
And giddy prospect of the raving stream,
635 The unfettered clouds, and region of the Heavens,
Tumult and peace, the darkness and the light—
Were all like workings of one mind, the features
Of the same face, blossoms upon one tree,
Characters of the great Apocalypse,
640 The types and symbols of Eternity,[4]
Of first and last, and midst, and without end.[5]

From Book Tenth
France continued[1]

[THE REVOLUTION: PARIS AND ENGLAND]

Cheared with this hope,[2] to Paris I returned;
And ranged, with ardor heretofore unfelt,
50 The spacious City, and in progress passed
The Prison[3] where the unhappy Monarch lay,
Associate with his Children and his Wife,
In Bondage; and the Palace[4] lately stormed,
With roar of Cannon, by a furious Host.
55 I crossed the Square (an empty Area then!)
Of the Carousel, where so late had lain
The Dead, upon the Dying heaped; and gazed
On this and other Spots, as doth a Man
Upon a Volume whose contents he knows
60 Are memorable, but from him locked up,
Being written in a tongue he cannot read;
So that he questions the mute leaves° with pain,   *pages*
And half-upbraids their silence. But, that night,
I felt most deeply in what world I was,
65 What ground I trod on, and what air I breathed.
High was my Room and lonely, near the roof
Of a large Mansion or Hotel,° a Lodge   *town house*
That would have pleased me in more quiet times,
Nor was it wholly without pleasure, then.
70 With unextinguished taper I kept watch,
Reading at intervals; the fear gone by
Pressed on me almost like a fear to come.

4. The objects in this natural scene are like the written words ("characters") of the Apocalypse—i.e., of the Book of Revelation, the last book of the New Testament. "Types": signs foreshadowing the future.
5. Cf. Revelation 1.8: "I am Alpha and Omega, the beginning and the ending, saith the Lord." The phrase is repeated in Revelation 21.6, after the fulfillment of the last things. In *Paradise Lost* 5.153–65 Milton says that the things created declare their Creator, and calls on all to extol "him first, him last, him midst, and without end."
1. Book 10 deals with the period between October 1792 and August 1794.

2. I.e., hope that, with the Declaration of the Republic and the French army's recent defeat of an Austrian and Prussian invasion, there would be no more need for violence.
3. I.e., the "Temple" (it had once housed the religious Order of Templars), where starting in September 1792 the deposed king was held prisoner awaiting trial for his crimes against the people.
4. The Tuileries. On August 10, 1792, the palace was marched upon by a crowd intent on seizing Louis XVI, whose Swiss guards opened fire on the insurgents. The bodies of the thousands who died in the conflict were cremated in the great square of the "Carousel" (line 56), in front of the palace.

I thought of those September massacres,
Divided from me by one little month,
75 Saw them and touched;[5] the rest was conjured up
From tragic fictions, or true history,
Remembrances and dim admonishments.
The Horse is taught his manage,[6] and no Star
Of wildest course but treads back his own steps;
80 For the spent hurricane the air provides
As fierce a Successor; the tide retreats
But to return out of its hiding place
In the great Deep; all things have second birth;
The earthquake is not satisfied at once;
85 And in this way I wrought upon myself
Until I seemed to hear a voice that cried
To the whole City, "Sleep no more."[7] The Trance
Fled with the Voice to which it had given birth,
But vainly comments of a calmer mind
90 Promised soft peace and sweet forgetfulness.
The place, all hushed and silent as it was,
Appeared unfit for the repose of Night,
Defenceless as a wood where Tygers roam.

       * * * In this frame of mind,
Dragged by a chain of harsh necessity,
So seemed it,—now I thankfully acknowledge,
Forced by the gracious providence of Heaven—
225 To England I returned,[8] else (though assured
That I both was, and must be, of small weight,
No better than a Landsman on the deck
Of a ship struggling with a hideous storm)
Doubtless I should have then made common cause
230 With some who perished, haply° perished too,[9]   *perhaps*
A poor mistaken and bewildered offering,
Should to the breast of Nature have gone back
With all my resolutions, all my hopes,
A Poet only to myself, to Men
235 Useless, and even, belovèd Friend, a Soul
To thee unknown![1]

            * * *

What then were my emotions, when in Arms
Britain put forth her free-born strength in league,
265 O pity and shame! with those confederate Powers?[2]
Not in my single self alone I found,
But in the minds of all ingenuous Youth,

5. I.e., his imagination of the September massacres was so vivid as to be palpable.
6. The French *manège*, the prescribed action and paces of a trained horse.
7. Macbeth's hallucination after his murder of the king. "Methought I heard a voice cry, 'Sleep no more, / Macbeth does murder sleep' " (Shakespeare, *Macbeth* 2.2.33–34). Louis XVI was guillotined on January 21, 1793.
8. Forced by the "harsh necessity" of a lack of money, Wordsworth returned to England late in 1792.
9. Wordsworth sympathized with the moderate party of the Girondins, almost all of whom were guillotined or committed suicide following Robespierre's rise to power in the National Convention.
1. Wordsworth did not meet Coleridge, the "beloved Friend," until 1795.
2. England joined Austria and Prussia in the war against France in February 1793.

Change and subversion from that hour. No shock
Given to my moral nature had I known
270 Down to that very moment; neither lapse
Nor turn of sentiment that might be named
A revolution, save at this one time;
All else was progress on the self-same path
On which, with a diversity of pace,
275 I had been travelling: this a stride at once
Into another region.—As a light
And pliant hare-bell° swinging in the breeze   *bluebell*
On some gray rock, its birth-place, so had I
Wantoned, fast rooted on the ancient tower
280 Of my beloved Country, wishing not
A happier fortune than to wither there.
Now was I from that pleasant station torn
And tossed about in whirlwind. I rejoiced,
Yea, afterwards, truth most painful to record!
285 Exulted, in the triumph of my Soul,
When Englishmen by thousands were o'erthrown,
Left without glory on the field, or driven,
Brave hearts, to shameful flight.[3] It was a grief,—
Grief call it not, 'twas any thing but that,—
290 A conflict of sensations without name,
Of which *he* only who may love the sight
Of a Village Steeple as I do can judge,
When, in the Congregation bending all
To their great Father, prayers were offered up,
295 Or praises, for our Country's victories,
And, 'mid the simple Worshippers, perchance
I only, like an uninvited Guest,
Whom no one owned, sate silent, shall I add,
Fed on the day of vengeance yet to come?

* * *

[THE REIGN OF TERROR. NIGHTMARES]

—Domestic carnage now filled the whole year
With Feast-days;[4] old Men from the Chimney-nook,
The Maiden from the bosom of her Love,
The Mother from the Cradle of her Babe,
360 The Warrior from the Field, all perished, all,
Friends, enemies, of all parties, ages, ranks,
Head after head, and never heads enough
For those that bade them fall. They found their joy,
They made it, proudly eager as a Child
365 (If like desires of innocent little ones
May with such heinous appetites be compared),
Pleased in some open field to exercise

3. The French defeated the English in the battle of Hondschoote, September 6, 1793.
4. I.e., festivals celebrated by human slaughter ("carnage"). Wordsworth alludes ironically to the patriotic festivals created to replace Catholic feast days within the new Republic's calendar. Lines 356–63 describe the Reign of Terror organized by Robespierre's Committee of Public Safety. In 1794 a total of 1,376 people were guillotined in Paris in forty-nine days.

A toy that mimics with revolving wings
The motion of a windmill, though the air
370   Do of itself blow fresh and make the Vanes
Spin in his eyesight, *that* contents him not,
But, with the play-thing at arm's length, he sets
His front against the blast, and runs amain
That it may whirl the faster.

                       *   *   *

Most melancholy at that time, O Friend!
Were my day-thoughts, my nights were miserable;
Through months, through years, long after the last beat
400   Of those atrocities, the hour of sleep
To me came rarely charged with natural gifts,
Such ghastly Visions had I of despair
And tyranny, and implements of death,
And innocent victims sinking under fear,
405   And momentary hope, and worn-out prayer,
Each in his separate cell, or penned in crowds
For sacrifice, and struggling with forced mirth
And levity in dungeons where the dust
Was laid with tears. Then suddenly the scene
410   Changed, and the unbroken dream entangled me
In long orations which I strove to plead
Before unjust tribunals—with a voice
Labouring, a brain confounded, and a sense
Death-like of treacherous desertion, felt
415   In the last place of refuge, my own soul.

Book Twelfth
Imagination and Taste, how impaired and restored

[SPOTS OF TIME]

    * * * I shook the habit off[1]
205   Entirely and for ever, and again
In Nature's presence stood, as now I stand,
A sensitive Being, a *creative* Soul.
    There are in our existence spots of time,[2]
That with distinct pre-eminence retain
210   A renovating virtue,° whence, depressed   *power of renewal*
By false opinion and contentious thought,
Or aught of heavier or more deadly weight,
In trivial occupations, and the round
Of ordinary intercourse, our minds

1. The acquired habit of logical analysis, which had marred his earlier feelings for the natural world.
2. Wordsworth's account in the lines that follow of two memories from childhood was originally drafted for book 1 of the two-part *Prelude* of 1799. By transferring these early memories to the end of his completed autobiography, rather than presenting them in its opening books, he enacts his own theory about how remembrance of things past nourishes the mind. He shows that it does so, as he says, "down to this *very* time" (line 327): the poetic imagination he brings to the composition of this book has been revived by recollections.

215 Are nourished and invisibly repaired;
    A virtue by which pleasure is inhanced,
    That penetrates, enables us to mount,
    When high, more high, and lifts us up when fallen.
    This efficacious Spirit chiefly lurks
220 Among those passages of life that give
    Profoundest knowledge how and to what point
    The mind is lord and master—outward sense³
    The obedient Servant of her will. Such moments
    Are scattered every where, taking their date
225 From our first Childhood. I remember well
    That once, while yet my inexperienced hand
    Could scarcely hold a bridle, with proud hopes
    I mounted, and we journied towards the hills:
    An ancient Servant of my Father's house
230 Was with me, my encourager and Guide.
    We had not travelled long ere some mischance
    Disjoined me from my Comrade, and, through fear
    Dismounting, down the rough and stony Moor
    I led my horse, and, stumbling on, at length
235 Came to a bottom,° where in former times   valley
    A Murderer had been hung in iron chains.
    The Gibbet mast⁴ had mouldered down, the bones
    And iron case were gone, but on the turf
    Hard by, soon after that fell deed was wrought,
240 Some unknown hand had carved the Murderer's name.
    The monumental Letters were inscribed
    In times long past, but still from year to year,
    By superstition of the neighbourhood,
    The grass is cleared away, and to that hour
245 The characters° were fresh and visible.   letters
    A casual glance had shewn them, and I fled,
    Faultering and faint and ignorant of the road:
    Then, reascending the bare common,° saw   field
    A naked Pool that lay beneath the hills,
250 The Beacon⁵ on its summit, and, more near,
    A Girl who bore a Pitcher on her head,
    And seemed with difficult steps to force her way
    Against the blowing wind. It was in truth
    An ordinary sight; but I should need
255 Colors and words that are unknown to man
    To paint the visionary dreariness
    Which, while I looked all round for my lost Guide,
    Invested Moorland waste and naked Pool,
    The Beacon crowning the lone eminence,
260 The Female and her garments vexed and tossed
    By the strong wind.—When, in the blessed hours
    Of early love, the loved One⁶ at my side,
    I roamed, in daily presence of this scene,

3. Perception of the external world.
4. The post with a projecting arm used for hanging criminals.
5. A signal beacon on a hill above Penrith.
6. Mary Hutchinson.

Upon the naked Pool and dreary Crags,
265 And on the melancholy Beacon, fell
A spirit of pleasure, and Youth's golden gleam;
And think ye not with radiance more sublime
For these remembrances, and for the power
They had left behind? So feeling comes in aid
270 Of feeling, and diversity of strength
Attends us, if but once we have been strong.
Oh! mystery of Man, from what a depth
Proceed thy honors! I am lost, but see
In simple child-hood something of the base
275 On which thy greatness stands; but this I feel,
That from thyself it comes, that thou must give,
Else never canst receive. The days gone by
Return upon me almost from the dawn
Of life: the hiding-places of Man's power
280 Open; I would approach them, but they close.
I see by glimpses now; when age comes on
May scarcely see at all, and I would give,
While yet we may, as far as words can give,
Substance and life to what I feel, enshrining,
285 Such is my hope, the spirit of the past
For future restoration.—Yet another
Of these memorials.
              One Christmas-time,[7]
On the glad Eve of its dear holidays,
Feverish, and tired, and restless, I went forth
290 Into the fields, impatient for the sight
Of those led Palfreys[8] that should bear us home,
My Brothers and myself. There rose a Crag
That, from the meeting point of two highways
Ascending, overlooked them both, far stretched;
295 Thither, uncertain on which road to fix
My expectation, thither I repaired,
Scout-like, and gained the summit; 'twas a day
Tempestuous, dark, and wild, and on the grass
I sate, half-sheltered by a naked wall;
300 Upon my right hand couched a single sheep,
Upon my left a blasted hawthorn stood:
With those Companions at my side, I sate,
Straining my eyes intensely, as the mist
Gave intermitting prospect of the copse
305 And plain beneath. Ere we to School returned
That dreary time, ere we had been ten days
Sojourners in my Father's House, he died,[9]
And I and my three Brothers, Orphans then,
Followed his Body to the Grave. The Event,
310 With all the sorrow that it brought, appeared
A chastisement; and when I called to mind

7. In 1783. Wordsworth, aged thirteen, was at Hawkshead School with two of his brothers.
8. Small saddle horses.

9. John Wordsworth died on December 30, 1783. William's mother had died five years earlier.

That day so lately passed, when from the Crag
I looked in such anxiety of hope,
With trite reflections of morality,
315   Yet in the deepest passion, I bowed low
To God, who thus corrected my desires;
And afterwards, the wind and sleety rain
And all the business[1] of the Elements,
The single Sheep, and the one blasted tree,
320   And the bleak music of that old stone wall,
The noise of wood and water, and the mist
That on the line of each of those two Roads
Advanced in such indisputable shapes;[2]
All these were kindred spectacles and sounds
325   To which I oft repaired, and thence would drink
As at a fountain; and on winter nights,
Down to this *very* time, when storm and rain
Beat on my roof, or haply° at noon-day,   *perhaps*
While in a grove I walk whose lofty trees,
330   Laden with summer's thickest foliage, rock
In a strong wind, some working of the spirit,
Some inward agitations, thence are brought,[3]
Whate'er their office, whether to beguile
Thoughts over-busy in the course they took,
335   Or animate an hour of vacant ease.

From Book Fourteenth
Conclusion

[THE VISION ON MOUNT SNOWDON.]

In one of those Excursions (may they ne'er
Fade from remembrance!), through the Northern tracts
Of Cambria ranging with a youthful Friend,
I left Bethgellert's huts at couching-time,
5   And westward took my way, to see the sun
Rise from the top of Snowdon.[1] To the door
Of a rude Cottage at the Mountain's base
We came, and rouzed the Shepherd who attends
The adventurous Stranger's steps, a trusty Guide;
10   Then, cheered by short refreshment, sallied forth.
—It was a close, warm, breezeless summer night,

1. Busy-ness; motions.
2. I.e., shapes one did not dare question. Cf. Hamlet's declaration to the ghost of his father: "Thou com'st in such questionable shape / That I will speak to thee" (Shakespeare, *Hamlet* 1.4.24–25).
3. Another instance of Wordsworth's inner response to an outer breeze (cf. 1.33–38, p. 1554).
1. Wordsworth climbed Mount Snowdon—the highest peak in Wales ("Cambria"), and some ten miles from the sea—with Robert Jones, the friend with whom he had also tramped through the Alps (book 6). The climb started from the village of Bethgelert at "couching-time" (line 4), the time of night when the sheep lie down to sleep. This event had taken place in 1791 (or possibly 1793); Wordsworth presents it out of its chronological order to introduce at this point a great natural "type" or "emblem" (lines 66, 70) for the mind, and especially for the activity of the imagination, whose "restoration" he has described in the two preceding books.

Wan, dull, and glaring,[2] with a dripping fog
Low-hung and thick, that covered all the sky.
But, undiscouraged, we began to climb
15 The mountain-side. The mist soon girt us round,
And, after ordinary Travellers' talk
With our Conductor, pensively we sank
Each into commerce with his private thoughts:
Thus did we breast the ascent, and by myself
20 Was nothing either seen or heard that checked
Those musings or diverted, save that once
The Shepherd's Lurcher,° who, among the crags,   *hunting dog*
Had to his joy unearthed a Hedgehog, teased
His coiled-up Prey with barkings turbulent.
25 This small adventure, for even such it seemed
In that wild place, and at the dead of night,
Being over and forgotten, on we wound
In silence as before. With forehead bent
Earthward, as if in opposition set
30 Against an enemy, I panted up
With eager pace, and no less eager thoughts.
Thus might we wear a midnight hour away,
Ascending at loose distance each from each,
And I, as chanced, the foremost of the Band:
35 When at my feet the ground appeared to brighten,
And with a step or two seemed brighter still;
Nor was time given to ask, or learn, the cause;
For instantly a light upon the turf
Fell like a flash; and lo! as I looked up,
40 The Moon hung naked in a firmament
Of azure without cloud, and at my feet
Rested a silent sea of hoary mist.
A hundred hills their dusky backs upheaved
All over this still Ocean;[3] and beyond,
45 Far, far beyond, the solid vapours stretched,
In Headlands, tongues, and promontory shapes,
Into the main Atlantic, that appeared
To dwindle, and give up his majesty,
Usurped upon far as the sight could reach.
50 Not so the ethereal Vault; encroachment none
Was there, nor loss;[4] only the inferior stars
Had disappeared, or shed a fainter light
In the clear presence of the full-orbed Moon;
Who, from her sovereign elevation, gazed
55 Upon the billowy ocean, as it lay
All meek and silent, save that through a rift
Not distant from the shore whereon we stood,
A fixed, abysmal, gloomy breathing-place,

---

2. In north of England dialect, *glairie*, applied to
the weather, means dull, rainy.
3. In Milton's description of God's creation of the
land from the waters, "the mountains huge appear
/ Emergent, and their broad bare backs upheave /

Into the clouds" (*Paradise Lost* 7.285–87).
4. The mist projected in various shapes over the
Irish Sea, but did not "encroach" on the heavens
overhead.

Mounted the roar of waters—torrents—streams
60 Innumerable, roaring with one voice!
Heard over earth and sea, and in that hour,
For so it seemed, felt by the starry heavens.
    When into air had partially dissolved
That Vision, given to Spirits of the night,
65 And three chance human Wanderers, in calm thought
Reflected, it appeared to me the type
Of a majestic Intellect, its acts
And its possessions, what it has and craves,
What in itself it is, and would become.
70 There I beheld the emblem of a Mind
That feeds upon infinity, that broods
Over the dark abyss, intent to hear
Its voices issuing forth to silent light
In one continuous stream; a mind sustained
75 By recognitions of transcendent power
In sense, conducting to ideal form;
In soul, of more than mortal privilege.[5]
One function, above all, of such a mind
Had Nature shadowed there, by putting forth,
80 'Mid circumstances awful° and sublime,   *awe-inspiring*
That mutual domination which she loves
To exert upon the face of outward things,
So moulded, joined, abstracted; so endowed
With interchangeable supremacy,
85 That Men least sensitive see, hear, perceive,
And cannot chuse but feel. The power which all
Acknowledge when thus moved, which Nature thus
To bodily sense exhibits, is the express
Resemblance of that glorious faculty
90 That higher minds bear with them as their own.[6]
This is the very spirit in which they deal
With the whole compass of the universe:
They, from their native selves, can send abroad
Kindred mutations; for themselves create
95 A like existence; and whene'er it dawns
Created for them, catch it;—or are caught
By its inevitable mastery,
Like angels stopped upon the wing by sound
Of harmony from heaven's remotest spheres.
100 Them the enduring and the transient both
Serve to exalt; they build up greatest things
From least suggestions; ever on the watch,
Willing to work and to be wrought upon,
They need not extraordinary calls
105 To rouse them, in a world of life they live;
By sensible° impressions not enthralled,   *sensory*

5. The sense of lines 74–77 seems to be that the mind of someone who is gifted beyond the ordinary lot of mortals recognizes its power to transcend the senses by converting sensory objects into ideal forms.

6. The "glorious faculty" is the imagination, which transfigures and re-creates what is given to it by the senses, much as, in Wordsworth's account of this night on Snowdon, the moonlit mist transfigures the familiar landscape.

But, by their quickening impulse, made more prompt
To hold fit converse with the spiritual world,
And with the generations of mankind
110   Spread over time, past, present, and to come,
Age after age, till Time shall be no more.
Such minds are truly from the Deity,
For they are powers; and hence the highest bliss
That flesh can know is theirs,—the consciousness
115   Of whom they are, habitually infused
Through every image, and through every thought,
And all affections° by communion raised   *emotions*
From earth to heaven, from human to divine.
Hence endless occupation for the Soul,
120   Whether discursive or intuitive;[7]
Hence chearfulness for acts of daily life,
Emotions which best foresight need not fear,
Most worthy then of trust when most intense:
Hence, amid ills that vex, and wrongs that crush
125   Our hearts, if here the words of holy Writ
May with fit reverence be applied, that peace
Which passeth understanding,[8]—that repose
In moral judgements which from this pure source
Must come, or will by Man be sought in vain.

*   *   *

[CONCLUSION: "THE MIND OF MAN"]

And now, O Friend![9] this History is brought
To its appointed close: the discipline
And consummation° of a Poet's mind   *completion*
305   In every thing that stood most prominent
Have faithfully been pictured; we have reached
The time (our guiding object from the first)
When we may, not presumptuously, I hope,
Suppose my powers so far confirmed, and such
310   My knowledge, as to make me capable
Of building up a Work that shall endure.

* * * Having now
Told what best merits mention, further pains
Our present purpose seems not to require,
And I have other tasks. Recall to mind
375   The mood in which this labour was begun.
O Friend! the termination of my course
Is nearer now, much nearer; yet even then,
In that distraction, and intense desire,
I said unto the life which I had lived,

---

7. An echo of Archangel Raphael's account to Adam of the soul's powers of reason (*Paradise Lost* 5.488–89). Discursive reason, mainly a human quality according to Raphael, undertakes to reach truths through a logical sequence of premises, observations, and conclusions; "intuitive" reason, mainly angelic, comprehends truths immediately. 8. Philippians 4.7: "The peace of God, which passeth all understanding." This passage of Christian piety was added by Wordsworth in a late revision. 9. Coleridge.

380 Where art thou? Hear I not a voice from thee
Which 'tis reproach to hear?[1] Anon I rose
As if on wings, and saw beneath me stretched
Vast prospect of the world which I had been
And was; and hence this Song, which like a Lark
385 I have protracted, in the unwearied heavens
Singing, and often with more plaintive voice
To earth attempered° and her deep-drawn sighs,　　　　　　　*adapted*
Yet centering all in love, and in the end
All gratulant,° if rightly understood.[2]　　　　　　　　　　*joyful*

*　　*　　*

Oh! yet a few short years of useful life,
And all will be complete, thy[3] race be run,
Thy monument of glory will be raised;
435 Then, though, too weak to tread the ways of truth,
This Age fall back to old idolatry,
Though Men return to servitude as fast
As the tide ebbs, to ignominy and shame
By Nations sink together,[4] we shall still
440 Find solace—knowing what we have learnt to know,
Rich in true happiness if allowed to be
Faithful alike in forwarding a day
Of firmer trust, joint laborers in the Work
(Should Providence such grace to us vouchsafe°)　　　　　　*grant*
445 Of their deliverance, surely yet to come.
Prophets of Nature, we to them will speak
A lasting inspiration, sanctified
By reason, blest by faith: what we have loved
Others will love, and we will teach them how,
450 Instruct them how the mind of Man becomes
A thousand times more beautiful than the earth
On which he dwells, above this Frame of things
(Which 'mid all revolutions in the hopes
And fears of Men doth still remain unchanged)
455 In beauty exalted, as it is itself
Of quality and fabric more divine.

1798–1839　　　　　　　　　　　　　　　　　　　　　　　　1850

---

1. As he approaches the end, Wordsworth recalls the beginning of *The Prelude.* The reproachful voice is that which asked the question, "Was it for this?" in 1.269ff.
2. The poet finds that suffering and frustration are justified when seen as part of the overall design of the life he has just reviewed. The passage echoes the conclusion of Pope's *An Essay on Man* 1.291–92: "All discord, harmony not understood; / All partial evil, universal good."
3. Coleridge's.
4. I.e., though men—whole nations of them together—sink to ignominy (disgrace) and shame.

DOROTHY WORDSWORTH
1771–1855

Dorothy Wordsworth has an enduring place in English literature even though she wrote almost no word for publication. Not until long after her death did scholars gradually retrieve and print her letters, a few poems, and a series of journals that she kept sporadically between 1798 and 1828 because, she wrote, "I shall give William Pleasure by it." It has always been known, from tributes to her by her brother and Coleridge, that she exerted an important influence on the lives and writings of both these men. It is now apparent that she also possessed a power surpassing that of the two poets for precise observation of people and the natural world, together with a genius for terse, luminous, and delicately nuanced description in prose.

Dorothy was born on Christmas Day 1771, twenty-one months after William; she was the only girl of five Wordsworth children. From her seventh year, when her mother died, she lived with various relatives—some of them tolerant and affectionate, others rigid and tyrannical—and saw William and her other brothers only occasionally, during the boys' summer vacations from school. In 1795, when she was twenty-four, an inheritance that William received enabled her to carry out a long-held plan to join her brother in a house at Racedown, and the two spent the rest of their long lives together, first in Dorsetshire and Somersetshire, in the southwest of England, then in their beloved Lake District. She uncomplainingly subordinated her own talents to looking after her brother and his household. She also became William's secretary, tirelessly copying and recopying the manuscripts of his poems to ready them for publication. Despite the scolding of a great-aunt, who deemed "rambling about . . . on foot" unladylike, she accompanied her brother, too, in vigorous cross-country walks in which they sometimes covered as much as thirty-three miles in a day.

All her adult life she was overworked; after a severe illness in 1835, she suffered a physical and mental collapse. She spent the rest of her existence as an invalid. Hardest for her family to endure was the drastic change in her temperament: from a high-spirited and compassionate woman she became (save for brief intervals of lucidity) querulous, demanding, and at times violent. In this half-life she lingered for twenty years, attended devotedly by William until his death five years before her own in 1855.

Our principal selections are from the journal Dorothy kept in 1798 at Alfoxden, Somersetshire, where the Wordsworths had moved from Racedown to be near Coleridge at Nether Stowey, as well as from her journals while at Grasmere (1800–03), with Coleridge residing some thirteen miles away at Greta Hall, Keswick. Her records cover the period when both men emerged as major poets, and in their achievements Dorothy played an indispensable role. In book 11 of *The Prelude*, William says that in the time of his spiritual crisis, Dorothy "maintained for me a saving intercourse / With my true self" and "preserved me still / A Poet"; in a letter of 1797, Coleridge stressed the delicacy and tact in the responses of William's "exquisite sister" to the world of sense: "Her manners are simple, ardent, impressive. . . . Her information various—her eye watchful in minutest observation of nature—and her taste a perfect electrometer—it bends, protrudes, and draws in, at subtlest beauties & most recondite faults."

The verbal sketches of natural scenes given in the journal passages that we reprint are often echoed in Wordsworth's and Coleridge's poems. Of at least equal importance for Wordsworth was her chronicling of the busy wayfaring life of rural England. These were exceedingly hard times for country people, when the suffering caused by the displacement of small farms and of household crafts by large-scale farms and industries was aggravated by the economic distress caused by protracted Continental wars (see Wordsworth's comment in *The Ruined Cottage*, lines 133ff., p. 1515). Peddlers, maimed war veterans, leech gatherers, adult and infant beggars, ousted farm families, fugitives, and women abandoned by husbands or lovers streamed along the rural roads and into William's brooding poetic imagination—often by way of Dorothy's prose records.

The journals also show the intensity of Dorothy's love for her brother. Inevitably in our era, the mutual devotion of the orphaned brother and sister has evoked psychoanalytic speculation. It is important to note that Mary Hutchinson, a gentle and openhearted young woman, had been Dorothy's closest friend since childhood, and that Dorothy encouraged William's courtship and marriage, even though she realized that it entailed her own displacement as a focus of her brother's life. All the evidence indicates that their lives in a single household never strained the affectionate relationship between the two women; indeed Dorothy, until she became an invalid, added to her former functions as William's chief support, housekeeper, and scribe a loving ministration to her brother's children.

Because the manuscript of the Alfoxden journal has disappeared, the text printed here is from the transcript published by William Knight in 1897. The selections from the Grasmere journals reproduce Pamela Woof's exact transcription of the manuscripts in the Wordsworth Library at Dove Cottage (Oxford University Press, 1991). Dorothy Wordsworth's poems, written mainly for children in her brother's household and surviving as manuscripts in one or another family commonplace book, were not collected until 1987, when Susan M. Levin edited thirty of them in an appendix ("The Collected Poems of Dorothy Wordsworth") to her *Dorothy Wordsworth and Romanticism*. The two poems included here are reprinted from this source.

From The Alfoxden Journal

Jan. 31, 1798. Set forward to Stowey[1] at half-past five. A violent storm in the wood; sheltered under the hollies. When we left home the moon immensely large, the sky scattered over with clouds. These soon closed in, contracting the dimensions of the moon without concealing her.[2] The sound of the pattering shower, and the gusts of wind, very grand. Left the wood when nothing remained of the storm but the driving wind, and a few scattering drops of rain. Presently all clear, Venus first showing herself between the struggling clouds; afterwards Jupiter appeared. The hawthorn hedges, black and pointed, glittering with millions of diamond drops; the hollies shining with broader patches of light. The road to the village of Holford glittered like another stream. On our return, the wind high—a violent storm of hail and rain at the Castle of Comfort.[3] All the Heavens seemed in one perpetual motion when the rain ceased; the moon appearing, now half veiled, and now retired behind heavy clouds, the stars still moving, the roads very dirty.

* * *

Feb. 3. A mild morning, the windows open at breakfast, the redbreasts singing in the garden. Walked with Coleridge over the hills. The sea at first obscured by vapour; that vapour afterwards slid in one mighty mass along the sea-shore; the islands and one point of land clear beyond it. The distant country (which was purple in the clear dull air), overhung by straggling clouds that sailed over it, appeared like the darker clouds, which are often seen at a great distance apparently motionless, while the nearer ones pass quickly over them, driven by the lower winds. I never saw such a union of earth, sky, and sea.

1. I.e., to Coleridge's cottage at Nether Stowey, three miles from Alfoxden.
2. Cf. Coleridge's *Christabel*, lines 16–19
(p. 1636).
3. A tavern halfway between Holford and Nether Stowey.

The clouds beneath our feet spread themselves to the water, and the clouds of the sky almost joined them. Gathered sticks in the wood; a perfect stillness. The redbreasts sang upon the leafless boughs. Of a great number of sheep in the field, only one standing. Returned to dinner at five o'clock. The moonlight still and warm as a summer's night at nine o'clock.

Feb. 4. Walked a great part of the way to Stowey with Coleridge. The morning warm and sunny. The young lasses seen on the hill-tops, in the villages and roads, in their summer holiday clothes—pink petticoats and blue. Mothers with their children in arms, and the little ones that could just walk, tottering by their side. Midges or small flies spinning in the sunshine; the songs of the lark and redbreast; daisies upon the turf; the hazels in blossom; honeysuckles budding. I saw one solitary strawberry flower under a hedge. The furze gay with blossom. The moss rubbed from the pailings by the sheep, that leave locks of wool, and the red marks with which they are spotted, upon the wood.[4]

*   *   *

Feb. 8. Went up the Park, and over the tops of the hills, till we came to a new and very delicious pathway, which conducted us to the Coombe.[5] Sat a considerable time upon the heath. Its surface restless and glittering with the motion of the scattered piles of withered grass, and the waving of the spiders' threads.[6] On our return the mist still hanging over the sea, but the opposite coast clear, and the rocky cliffs distinguishable. In the deep Coombe, as we stood upon the sunless hill, we saw miles of grass, light and glittering, and the insects passing.

Feb. 9. William gathered sticks.

Feb. 10. Walked to Woodlands, and to the waterfall. The adder's-tongue and the ferns green in the low damp dell. These plants now in perpetual motion from the current of the air; in summer only moved by the drippings of the rocks.[7] A cloudy day.

*   *   *

Mar. 7. William and I drank tea at Coleridge's. A cloudy sky. Observed nothing particularly interesting—the distant prospect obscured. One only leaf upon the top of a tree—the sole remaining leaf—danced round and round like a rag blown by the wind.[8]

Mar. 8. Walked in the Park in the morning. I sate under the fir trees. Coleridge came after dinner, so we did not walk again. A foggy morning, but a clear sunny day.

Mar. 9. A clear sunny morning, went to meet Mr and Mrs Coleridge. The day very warm.

Mar. 10. Coleridge, Wm, and I walked in the evening to the top of the hill. We all passed the morning in sauntering about the park and gardens, the children playing about, the old man at the top of the hill gathering furze; interesting groups of human creatures, the young frisking and dancing in the sun, the elder quietly drinking in the life and soul of the sun and air.

Mar. 11. A cold day. The children went down towards the sea. William and

---

4. Cf. Wordsworth's *The Ruined Cottage*, lines 330–36 (p. 1519).
5. Hodder's Coombe in the Quantock Hills, near Alfoxden. A combe is a deep valley on the flank of a hill.
6. Cf. Coleridge's *The Rime of the Ancient Mari-*

ner, line 184 (p. 1621).
7. Cf. the description of the dell in Coleridge's "This Lime-Tree Bower My Prison," lines 13–20 (p. 1614).
8. Cf. *Christabel,* lines 49ff. (p. 1636).

I walked to the top of the hills above Holford. Met the blacksmith. Pleasant to see the labourer on Sunday jump with the friskiness of a cow upon a sunny day.

* * *

1798   1897

From The Grasmere Journals

1800

May 14 1800 [*Wednesday*]. Wm & John set off into Yorkshire[1] after dinner at ½ past 2 o'clock—cold pork in their pockets. I left them at the turning of the Low-wood bay under the trees. My heart was so full that I could hardly speak to W when I gave him a farewell kiss. I sate a long time upon a stone at the margin of the lake, & after a flood of tears my heart was easier. The lake looked to me I knew not why dull and melancholy, and the weltering on the shores seemed a heavy sound. I walked as long as I could amongst the stones of the shore. The wood rich in flowers. A beautiful yellow, palish yellow flower, that looked thick round & double, & smelt very sweet—I supposed it was a ranunculus—Crowfoot, the grassy-leaved Rabbit-toothed white flower, strawberries, geranium—scentless violet, anemones two kinds, orchises, prim-roses. The heckberry very beautiful, the crab coming out as a low shrub. Met a blind man, driving a very large beautiful Bull & a cow—he walked with two sticks. Came home by Clappersgate. The valley very green, many sweet views up to Rydale head when I could juggle away the fine houses, but they disturbed me even more than when I have been happier—one beautiful view of the Bridge, without Sir Michael's.[2] Sate down very often, tho' it was cold. I resolved to write a journal of the time till W & J return, & I set about keeping my resolve because I will not quarrel with myself, & because I shall give Wm Pleasure by it when he comes home again. At Rydale a woman of the village, stout & well-dressed, begged a halfpenny—she had never she said done it before—but these hard times!—Arrived at home with a bad head-ache, set some slips of privett. The evening cold, had a fire—my face now flame-coloured. It is nine o'clock. I shall soon go to bed. A young woman begged at the door—she had come from Manchester on Sunday morn with two shillings & a slip of paper which she supposed a Bank note—it was a cheat. She had buried her husband & three children within a year & a half—all in one grave—burying very dear—paupers all put in one place—20 shillings paid for as much ground as will bury a man—a stone to be put over it or the right will be lost—11/6[3] each time the ground is opened. Oh! that I had a letter from William!

* * *

Friday 3rd October. Very rainy all the morning—little Sally learning to mark. Wm walked to Ambleside after dinner. I went with him part of the way—he talked much about the object of his Essay for the 2nd volume of LB.[4] I returned

---

1. William and his younger brother John, on the way to visit Mary Hutchinson, whom William was to marry two and a half years later.
2. Sir Michael le Fleming's estate, Rydal Hall.

"Without": outside or beyond.
3. Eleven shillings, six pence.
4. The Preface to the second edition of *Lyrical Ballads*, 1800.

expecting the Simpsons—they did not come. I should have met Wm but my teeth ached & it was showery & late—he returned after 10. Amos Cottle's[5] death in the Morning Post. Wrote to S. Lowthian.[6]

N.B. When Wm & I returned from accompanying Jones we met an old man almost double,[7] he had on a coat thrown over his shoulders above his waistcoat & coat. Under this he carried a bundle & had an apron on & a night cap. His face was interesting. He had dark eyes & a long nose—John who afterwards met him at Wythburn took him for a Jew. He was of Scotch parents but had been born in the army. He had had a wife "& a good woman & it pleased God to bless us with ten children"—all these were dead but one of whom he had not heard for many years, a sailor—his trade was to gather leeches, but now leeches are scarce & he had not strength for it—he lived by begging & was making his way to Carlisle where he should buy a few godly books to sell. He said leeches were very scarce partly owing to this dry season, but many years they have been scarce—he supposed it owing to their being much sought after, that they did not breed fast, & were of slow growth. Leeches were formerly 2/ 6 [per] 100; they are now 30/. He had been hurt in driving a cart his leg broke his body driven over his skull fractured—he felt no pain till he recovered from his first insensibility. It was then late in the evening—when the light was just going away.

* * *

Saturday [Oct.] 11th. A fine October morning—sat in the house working all the morning. Wm composing—Sally Ashburner learning to mark. After Dinner we walked up Greenhead Gill in search of a sheepfold.[8] We went by Mr Oliff's & through his woods. It was a delightful day & the views looked excessively chearful & beautiful chiefly that from Mr Oliff's field where our house is to be built. The colours of the mountains soft & rich, with orange fern—The Cattle pasturing upon the hill-tops Kites sailing as in the sky above our heads— Sheep bleating & in lines & chains & patterns scattered over the mountains. They come down & feed on the little green islands in the beds of the torrents & so may be swept away. The Sheepfold is falling away it is built nearly in the form of a heart unequally divided. Look down the brook & see the drops rise upwards & sparkle in the air, at the little falls, the higher sparkles the tallest. We walked along the turf of the mountain till we came to a Cattle track— made by the cattle which come upon the hills. We drank tea at Mr Simpson's returned at about nine—a fine mild night.

Sunday 12th October. Beautiful day. Sate in the house writing in the morning while Wm went into the Wood to compose. Wrote to John in the morning— copied poems for the LB, in the evening wrote to Mrs Rawson. Mary Jameson & Sally Ashburner dined. We pulled apples after dinner, a large basket full. We walked before tea by Bainriggs to observe the many coloured foliage the oaks dark green with yellow leaves—The birches generally still green, some near the water yellowish. The Sycamore crimson & crimson-tufted—the mountain ash a deep orange—the common ash Lemon colour but many ashes still fresh in

5. The brother of Joseph Cottle, Bristol publisher of the first edition of *Lyrical Ballads*.
6. Sally Lowthian, who had been a servant in the house of the Wordsworths' father.
7. William's "Resolution and Independence," composed one and a half years later, incorporated various details of Dorothy's description of the leech gatherer. See May 4 and 7, 1802 (pp. 1602 and 1603), for William working on the poem he originally called "The Leech Gatherer."
8. The sheepfold (pen for sheep) in William's "Michael"; lines 1–17 of the poem describe the walk up Greenhead Ghyll.

their summer green. Those that were discoloured chiefly near the water. William composing in the Evening. Went to bed at 12 o'clock.

* * *

1801

Tuesday [*Nov.*] *24th.* A rainy morning. We all were well except that my head ached a little & I took my Breakfast in bed. I read a little of Chaucer, prepared the goose for dinner, & then we all walked out—I was obliged to return for my fur tippet & Spenser[9] it was so cold. We had intended going to Easedale but we shaped our course to Mr Gell's cottage. It was very windy & we heard the wind everywhere about us as we went along the Lane but the walls sheltered us—John Green's house looked pretty under Silver How—as we were going along we were stopped at once, at the distance perhaps of 50 yards from our favorite Birch tree it was yielding to the gusty wind with all its tender twigs, the sun shone upon it & it glanced in the wind like a flying sunshiny shower—it was a tree in shape with stem & branches but it was like a Spirit of water—The sun went in & it resumed its purplish appearance the twigs still yielding to the wind but not so visibly to us. The other Birch trees that were near it looked bright & chearful—but it was a Creature by its own self among them. We could not get into Mr Gell's grounds—the old tree fallen from its undue exaltation above the Gate. A shower came on when we were at Benson's. We went through the wood—it became fair, there was a rainbow which spanned the lake from the Island house to the foot of Bainriggs. The village looked populous & beautiful. Catkins are coming out palm trees budding— the alder with its plumb coloured buds. We came home over the stepping stones the Lake was foamy with white waves. I saw a solitary butter flower in the wood. *I* found it not easy to get over the stepping stones—reached home at dinner time. Sent Peggy Ashburner some goose. She sent me some honey— with a thousand thanks—"alas the gratitude of men has & c"[1] I went in to set her right about this & sate a while with her. She talked about Thomas's having sold his land—"Ay" says she I said many a time "He's not come fra London to buy our Land however" then she told me with what pains & industry they had made up their taxes interest &c &c—how they all got up at 5 o'clock in the morning to spin & Thomas carded, & that they had paid off a hundred pound of the interest. She said she used to take such pleasure in the cattle & sheep— "O how pleased I used to be when they fetched them down, & when I had been a bit poorly I would gang out upon a hill & look over t' fields & see them & it used to do me so much good you cannot think"—Molly said to me when I came in "poor Body! she's very ill but one does not know how long she may last. Many a fair face may gang before her." We sate by the fire without work for some time then Mary read a poem of Daniell upon Learning.[2] After tea Wm read Spenser now & then a little aloud to us. We were making his waistcoat. We had a note from Mrs C., with bad news from poor C very ill. William walked to John's grove—I went to meet him—moonlight but it rained. I met him before I had got as far as John Baty's he had been surprized & terrified by a sudden rushing

9. A close-fitting jacket worn by women and children. A tippet is a stole or scarf.
1. A quotation from William's "Simon Lee": "Alas! the gratitude of men / Has oft'ner left me

mourning."
2. Samuel Daniel's long poem *Musophilus: Containing a General Defense of Learning* (1599).

of winds which seemed to bring earth sky & lake together, as if the whole were going to enclose him in—he was glad he was in a high Road.

In speaking of our walk on Sunday Evening the 22nd November I forgot to notice one most impressive sight—it was the moon & the moonlight seen through hurrying driving clouds immediately behind the Stone man upon the top of the hill on the Forest side. Every tooth & every edge of Rock was visible, & the Man stood like a Giant watching from the Roof of a lofty castle. The hill seemed perpendicular from the darkness below it. It was a sight that I could call to mind at any time it was so distinct.

* * *

1802

Thursday [*Mar.* 4]. Before we had quite finished Breakfast Calvert's man brought the horses for Wm.[3] We had a deal to do to shave—pens to make—poems to put in order for writing, to settle the dress pack up &c &. The man came before the pens were made & he was obliged to leave me with only two—Since he has left me (at ½ past 11) it is now 2 I have been putting the Drawers into order, laid by his clothes which we had thrown here & there & everywhere, filed two months' newspapers & got my dinner 2 boiled eggs & 2 apple tarts. I have set Molly on to clear the garden a little, & I myself have helped. I transplanted some snowdrops—The Bees are busy—Wm has a nice bright day. It was hard frost in the night—The Robins are singing sweetly—Now for my walk. I *will* be busy, I *will* look well & be well when he comes back to me. O the Darling! Here is one of his bitten apples! I can hardly find in my heart to throw it into the fire. I must wash myself, then off—I walked round the two Lakes crossed the stepping stones at Rydale Foot. Sate down where we always sit. I was full of thoughts about my darling. Blessings on him. I came home at the foot of our own hill under Loughrigg. They are making sad ravages in the woods—Benson's Wood is going & the wood above the River. The wind has blown down a small fir tree on the Rock that terminates John's path—I suppose the wind of Wednesday night. I read German after my return till tea time. After tea I worked & read the LB, enchanted with the Idiot Boy. Wrote to Wm then went to Bed. It snowed when I went to Bed.

* * *

Monday [*Mar.* 22]. A rainy day—William very poorly. Mr Luff came in after dinner & brought us 2 letters from Sara H. & one from poor Annette. I read Sara's letters while he was here. I finished my letters to M. & S. & wrote to my Br Richard. We talked a good deal about C. & other interesting things. We resolved to see Annette, & that Wm should go to Mary.[4] We wrote to Coleridge not to expect us till Thursday or Friday.

Tuesday [*Mar.* 23]. A mild morning William worked at the Cuckow poem.[5] I sewed beside him. After dinner he slept I read German, & at the closing in of day went to sit in the Orchard—he came to me, & walked backwards & forwards. We talked about C—Wm repeated the poem to me—I left him there

---

3. For a journey to Keswick, to visit Coleridge.
4. It had been arranged several months earlier that William was to marry Mary Hutchinson ("Sara H" is Mary's sister, with whom Coleridge had fallen in love). Now the Wordsworths resolve to go to

France to settle affairs with Annette Vallon, mother of William's daughter, Caroline. William did not conceal the facts of his early love affair from his family, or from Mary Hutchinson.
5. "To the Cuckoo."

& in 20 minutes he came in, rather tired with attempting to write—he is now reading Ben Jonson I am going to read German it is about 10 o'clock, a quiet night. The fire flutters & the watch ticks I hear nothing else save the Breathing of my Beloved & he now & then pushes his book forward & turns over a leaf. Fletcher is not come home. No letter from C.

* * *

Thursday [Apr.] 15th. It was a threatening misty morning—but mild. We set off after dinner from Eusemere—Mrs Clarkson went a short way with us but turned back. The wind was furious & we thought we must have returned. We first rested in the large Boat-house, then under a furze Bush opposite Mr Clarksons, saw the plough going in the field. The wind seized our breath the Lake was rough. There was a Boat by itself floating in the middle of the Bay below Water Millock—We rested again in the Water Millock Lane. The haw-thorns are black & green, the birches here & there greenish but there is yet more of purple to be seen on the Twigs. We got over into a field to avoid some cows—people working, a few primroses by the roadside, wood-sorrel flower, the anemone, scentless violets, strawberries, & that starry yellow flower which Mrs C calls pile wort. When we were in the woods beyond Gowbarrow park we saw a few daffodils close to the water side.[6] We fancied that the lake had floated the seeds ashore & that the little colony had so sprung up—But as we went along there were more & yet more & at last under the boughs of the trees, we saw that there was a long belt of them along the shore, about the breadth of a country turnpike road. I never saw daffodils so beautiful they grew among the mossy stones about & about them, some rested their heads upon these stones as on a pillow for weariness & the rest tossed & reeled & danced & seemed as if they verily laughed with the wind that blew upon them over the lake, they looked so gay ever glancing ever changing. This wind blew directly over the lake to them. There was here & there a little knot & a few stragglers a few yards higher up but they were so few as not to disturb the simplicity & unity & life of that one busy highway—We rested again & again. The Bays were stormy & we heard the waves at different distances & in the middle of the water like the sea—Rain came on, we were wet when we reached Luffs but we called in. Luckily all was chearless & gloomy so we faced the storm—we *must* have been wet if we had waited—put on dry clothes at Dobson's. I was very kindly treated by a young woman, the Landlady looked sour but it is her way. She gave us a goodish supper. Excellent ham & potatoes. We paid 7/ when we came away. William was sitting by a bright fire when I came downstairs. He soon made his way to the Library piled up in a corner of the window. He brought out a volume of Enfield's Speaker,[7] another miscel-lany, & an odd volume of Congreve's plays. We had a glass of warm rum & water—We enjoyed ourselves & wished for Mary. It rained & blew when we went to bed. NB Deer in Gowbarrow park like skeletons.

Friday 16th April (Good Friday). When I undrew my curtains in the morn-ing, I was much affected by the beauty of the prospect & the change. The sun shone, the wind has passed away, the hills looked chearful, the river was very bright as it flowed into the lake. The Church rises up behind a little knot of Rocks, the steeple not so high as an ordinary 3 story house. Bees, in a row in

6. William did not compose his poem on the daf-fodils, "I wandered lonely as a cloud," until two years later. Comparison with the poem will show how extensive was his use of Dorothy's prose description (see p. 1537).
7. William Enfield's *The Speaker* (1774), a volume of selections suitable for elocution.

the garden under the wall. After Wm had shaved we set forward. The valley is at first broken by little rocky woody knolls that make retiring places, fairy valleys in the vale, the river winds along under these hills travelling not in a bustle but not slowly to the lake. We saw a fisherman in the flat meadow on the other side of the water. He came towards us & threw his line over the two arched Bridge. It is a Bridge of a heavy construction, almost bending inwards in the middle, but it is grey & there is a look of ancientry in the architecture of it that pleased me. As we go on the vale opens out more into one vale with somewhat of a cradle Bed. Cottages with groups of trees on the side of the hills. We passed a pair of twin Children 2 years old—& Sate on the next bridge which we crossed a single arch. We rested again upon the Turf & looked at the same Bridge. We observed arches in the water occasioned by the large stones sending it down in two streams—a Sheep came plunging through the river, stumbled up the Bank & passed close to us, it had been frightened by an insignificant little Dog on the other side, its fleece dropped a glittering shower under its belly—Primroses by the roadside, pile wort that shone like stars of gold in the Sun, violets, strawberries, retired & half buried among the grass. When we came to the foot of Brothers water I left William sitting on the Bridge & went along the path on the right side of the Lake through the wood—I was delighted with what I saw. The water under the boughs of the bare old trees, the simplicity of the mountains & the exquisite beauty of the path. There was one grey cottage. I repeated the Glowworm[8] as I walked along—I hung over the gate, & thought I could have stayed for ever. When I returned I found William writing a poem descriptive of the sights & sounds we saw & heard. There was the gentle flowing of the stream, the glittering lively lake, green fields without a living creature to be seen on them, behind us, a flat pasture with 42 cattle feeding to our left the road leading to the hamlet, no smoke there, the sun shone on the bare roofs. The people were at work ploughing, harrowing & sowing—Lasses spreading dung, a dog's barking now & then, cocks crowing, birds twittering, the snow in patches at the top of the highest hills, yellow palms, purple & green twigs on the Birches, ashes with their glittering spikes quite bare. The hawthorn a bright green with black stems under the oak. The moss of the oak glossy. We then went on, passed two sisters at work, *they first passed us*, one with two pitch forks in her hand. The other had a spade. We had some talk with them. They laughed aloud after we were gone perhaps half in wantonness, half boldness. William finished his poem before we got to the foot of Kirkstone.[9] * * *

* * *

Thursday [*Apr.*] 29. A beautiful morning. The sun shone & all was pleasant. We sent off our parcel to Coleridge by the waggon. Mr Simpson heard the Cuckow today. Before we went out after I had written down the Tinker (which William finished this morning)[1] Luff called. He was very lame, limped into the kitchen—he came on a little Pony. We then went to John's Grove, sate a while at first. Afterwards William lay, & I lay in the trench under the fence—he with his eyes shut & listening to the waterfalls & the Birds. There was no one waterfall above another[2]—it was a sound of waters in the air—the voice of the air. William heard me breathing & rustling now & then but we both lay still,

8. William's poem beginning "Among all lovely things my Love had been," composed four days earlier; "my Love" in this line is Dorothy.
9. The short lyric "Written in March."

1. William never published his comic poem "The Tinker." It was first printed in 1897.
2. I.e., no waterfall could be heard individually.

& unseen by one another—he thought that it would be as sweet thus to lie so in the grave, to hear the *peaceful* sounds of the earth & just to know that our dear friends were near. The Lake was still. There was a Boat out. Silver How reflected with delicate purple & yellowish hues as I have seen Spar—Lambs on the island & running races together by the half dozen in the round field near us. The copses green*ish*, hawthorn green.—Came home to dinner then went to Mr Simpson. We rested a long time under a wall. Sheep & lambs were in the field—cottages smoking. As I lay down on the grass, I observed the glittering silver line on the ridges of the Backs of the sheep, owing to their situation respecting the Sun—which made them look beautiful but with something of strangeness, like animals of another kind—as if belonging to a more splendid world. Met old Mr S at the door—Mrs S poorly—I got mullens & pansies—I was sick & ill & obliged to come home soon. We went to bed immediately—I slept up stairs. The air coldish where it was felt somewhat frosty.

* * *

Tuesday May 4th. William had slept pretty well & though he went to bed nervous & jaded in the extreme he rose refreshed. I wrote the Leech Gatherer[3] for him which he had begun the night before & of which he wrote several stanzas in bed this Monday morning. It was very hot, we called at Mr Simpson's door as we passed but did not go in. We rested several times by the way, read & repeated the Leech Gatherer. We were almost melted before we were at the top of the hill. We saw Coleridge on the Wytheburn side of the water. He crossed the Beck to us. Mr Simpson was fishing there. William & I ate a Luncheon, then went on towards the waterfall. It is a glorious wild solitude under that lofty purple crag. It stood upright by itself. Its own self & its shadow below, one mass—all else was sunshine. We went on further. A Bird at the top of the crags was flying round & round & looked in thinness & transparency, shape & motion like a moth. We climbed the hill but looked in vain for a shade except at the foot of the great waterfall, & there we did not like to stay on account of the loose stones above our heads. We came down & rested upon a moss covered Rock, rising out of the bed of the River. There we lay ate our dinner & stayed there till about 4 o'clock or later—Wm & C repeated & read verses. I drank a little Brandy & water & was in Heaven. The Stags horn is very beautiful & fresh springing upon the fells. Mountain ashes, green. We drank tea at a farm house. The woman had not a pleasant countenance, but was civil enough. She had a pretty Boy a year old whom she suckled. We parted from Coleridge at Sara's Crag after having looked at the Letters which C carved in the morning. I kissed them all. Wm deepened the T with C's penknife.[4] We sate afterwards on the wall, seeing the sun go down & the reflections in the still water. C looked well & parted from us chearfully, hopping up upon the side stones. On the Rays we met a woman with 2 little girls one in her arms the other about 4 years old walking by her side, a pretty little thing, but half starved. She had on a pair of slippers that had belonged to some gentleman's child, down at the heels—it was not easy to keep them on—but, poor thing! young as she was, she walked carefully with them. Alas too young

3. The poem that was published as "Resolution and Independence." For its origin see the entry for October 3, 1800 (p. 1596).
4. The rock, which has since been blasted away to make room for a new road, contained the carved letters W. W., M. H., D. W., S.T.C., J. W., S. H. (M. H. and S. H. are Mary and Sara Hutchinson; J. W. is John Wordsworth.)

for such cares & such travels—The Mother when we accosted her told us that her husband had left her & gone off with another woman & how she *"pursued"* them. Then her fury kindled & her eyes rolled about. She changed again to tears. She was a Cockermouth woman—30 years of age a child at Cockermouth when I was—I was moved & gave her a shilling, I believe 6^d more than I ought to have given. We had the crescent moon with the "auld moon in her arms."[5]—We rested often:—always upon the Bridges. Reached home at about 10 o'clock. The Lloyds had been here in our absence. We went soon to bed. I repeated verses to William while he was in bed—he was soothed & I left him. "This is the Spot"[6] over & over again.

* * *

6th May Thursday 1802. A sweet morning we have put the finishing stroke to our Bower & here we are sitting in the orchard. It is one o'clock. We are sitting upon a seat under the wall which I found my Brother building up when I came to him with his apple—he had intended that it should have been done before I came. It is a nice cool shady spot. The small Birds are singing—Lambs bleating, Cuckow calling—The Thrush sings by Fits. Thomas Ashburner's axe is going quietly (without passion) in the orchard—Hens are cackling, Flies humming, the women talking together at their doors—Plumb & pear trees are in Blossom—apple trees greenish—the opposite woods green, the crows are cawing. We have heard Ravens. The ash trees are in blossom, Birds flying all about us. The stitchwort is coming out, there is one budding Lychnis, the primroses are passing their prime. Celandine violets & wood sorrel for ever more little—geraniums & pansies on the wall. We walked in the evening to Tail End to enquire about hurdles for the orchard shed & about Mr Luff's flower—The flower dead—no hurdles. I went to look at the falling wood— Wm also when he had been at Benson's went with me. They have left a good many small oak trees but we dare not hope that they are all to remain. The Ladies are come to Mr Gell's cottage. We saw them as we went & their light when we returned. When we came in we found a Magazine & Review & a letter from Coleridge with verses to Hartley & Sara H. We read the Review,[7] &c. The moon was a perfect Boat a silver Boat when we were out in the evening. The Birch Tree is all over green in *small* leaf more light & elegant than when it is full out. It bent to the breezes as if for the love of its own delightful motions. Sloe thorns & Hawthorns in the hedges.

Friday 7th May. William had slept uncommonly well so, feeling himself strong, he fell to work at the Leech gatherer—He wrote hard at it till dinner time, then he gave over tired to death—he had finished the poem.[8] * * *

* * *

[July.] On Thursday morning, 29th, we arrived in London.[9] Wm left me at the Inn—I went to bed &c &c &c—After various troubles and disasters we left London on Saturday morning at ½ past 5 or 6, the 31st of July (I have forgot which). We mounted the Dover Coach at Charing Cross. It was a beautiful morning. The City, St. Paul's, with the River & a multitude of little Boats,

5. From the "Ballad of Sir Patrick Spens." Coleridge quoted the stanza, of which this phrase is part, as epigraph to "Dejection: An Ode" (p. 1652).
6. William never completed this poem.
7. The *Monthly Review* for March 1802.

8. Later entries show, however, that William kept working on the manuscript until July 4.
9. On the way to France to visit Annette Vallon and Caroline (see the entry for March 22, 1802; p. 1599).

made a most beautiful sight as we crossed Westminster Bridge. The houses
were not overhung by their cloud of smoke & they were spread out endlessly,
yet the sun shone so brightly with such a pure light that there was even something like the purity of one of nature's own grand spectacles.[1] We rode on
chearfully now with the Paris Diligence before us, now behind—we walked
up the steep hills, beautiful prospects everywhere, till we even reached Dover.
* * * We arrived at Calais at 4 o'clock on Sunday morning the 31st of July.[2]
We stayed in the vessel till ½ past 7, then Wm went for Letters, at about ½
past 8 or 9. We found out Annette & C chez Madame Avril dans la Rue de la
Tête d'or. We lodged opposite two Ladies in tolerably decent-sized rooms but
badly furnished, & with large store of bad smells & dirt in the yard, & all about.
The weather was very hot. We walked by the sea-shore almost every evening
with Annette & Caroline or Wm & I alone. I had a bad cold & could not bathe
at first but William did. It was a pretty sight to see as we walked upon the
Sands when the tide was low perhaps a hundred people bathing about ¼ of a
mile distant from us, and we had delightful walks after the heat of the day was
passed away—seeing far off in the west the Coast of England like a cloud
crested with Dover Castle, which was but like the summit of the cloud—the
Evening star & the glory of the sky. The Reflections in the water were more
beautiful than the sky itself, purple waves brighter than precious stones for
ever melting away upon the sands. * * *

* * *

[*Sept. 24 and following.*] Mary first met us in the avenue. She looked so fat
and well that we were made very happy by the sight of her—then came Sara,
& last of all Joanna.[3] Tom was forking corn standing upon the corn cart. We
dressed ourselves immediately & got tea—the garden looked gay with asters
& sweet peas—I looked at everything with tranquillity & happiness but I was
ill both on Saturday & Sunday & continued to be poorly most of the time of
our stay. Jack & George came on Friday Evening 1st October. On Saturday
2nd we rode to Hackness, William Jack George & Sara single, I behind Tom.
On Sunday 3rd Mary & Sara were busy packing. On Monday 4th October
1802, my Brother William was married to Mary Hutchinson. I slept a good
deal of the night & rose fresh & well in the morning—at a little after 8 o'clock
I saw them go down the avenue towards the Church. William had parted from
me up stairs. I gave him the wedding ring—with how deep a blessing! I took
it from my forefinger where I had worn it the whole of the night before—he
slipped it again onto my finger and blessed me fervently. When they were
absent my dear little Sara prepared the breakfast. I kept myself as quiet as I
could, but when I saw the two men running up the walk, coming to tell us it
was over, I could stand it no longer & threw myself on the bed where I lay in
stillness, neither hearing or seeing any thing, till Sara came upstairs to me &
said "They are coming." This forced me from the bed where I lay & I moved
I knew not how straight forward, faster than my strength could carry me till I
met my beloved William & fell upon his bosom. He & John Hutchinson led

1. Cf. William's sonnet "Composed upon Westminster Bridge" (p. 1548).
2. The actual date was August 1. One of the walks
by the sea that Dorothy goes on to describe was
the occasion for William's sonnet "It is a beauteous
evening."
3. The Wordsworths have come to Gallow Hill,

Yorkshire, for the marriage of William and Mary.
The people mentioned are Mary's sisters and
brothers (Sara, Joanna, Tom, Jack, and George
Hutchinson). Out of consideration for Dorothy's
overwrought feelings, only Joanna, Jack, and Tom
attended the ceremony at Brampton Church.

me to the house & there I stayed to welcome my dear Mary. As soon as we had breakfasted we departed.[4] It rained when we set off. Poor Mary was much agitated when she parted from her Brothers & Sisters & her home. Nothing particular occurred till we reached Kirby. We had sunshine & showers, pleasant talk, love & chearfulness. * * * It rained very hard when we reached Windermere. We sate in the rain at Wilcock's to change horses, & arrived at Grasmere at about 6 o'clock on Wednesday Evening, the 6th of October 1802. Molly was overjoyed to see us,—for my part I cannot describe what I felt, & our dear Mary's feelings would I dare say not be easy to speak of. We went by candle light into the garden & were astonished at the growth of the Brooms, Portugal Laurels, &c &c &—The next day, Thursday, we unpacked the Boxes. On Friday 8th we baked Bread, & Mary & I walked, first upon the Hill side, & then in John's Grove, then in view of Rydale, the first walk that I had taken with my Sister.

* * *

24th December 1802, Christmas Eve. William is now sitting by me at ½ past 10 o'clock. I have been beside him ever since tea running the heel of a stocking, repeating some of his sonnets to him, listening to his own repeating, reading some of Milton's & the Allegro & Penseroso. It is a quiet keen frost. Mary is in the parlour below attending to the baking of cakes & Jenny Fletcher's pies. Sara is in bed in the tooth ache, & so we are—beloved William is turning over the leaves of Charlotte Smith's sonnets, but he keeps his hand to his poor chest pushing aside his breastplate.[5] Mary is well & I am well, & Molly is as blithe as last year at this time. Coleridge came this morning with Wedgwood.[6] We all turned out of Wm's bedroom one by one to meet him— he looked well. We had to tell him of the Birth of his little Girl, born yesterday morning at 6 o'clock.[7] W went with them to Wytheburn in the Chaise, & M & I met Wm on the Rays. It was not an unpleasant morning to the feelings—far from it—the sun shone now & then, & there was no wind, but all things looked chearless & distinct, no meltings of sky into mountains—the mountains like stone-work wrought up with huge hammers.—Last Sunday was as mild a day as I ever remember—We all set off together to walk. I went to Rydale & Wm returned with me. M & S[8] went round the Lakes. There were flowers of various kinds the topmost bell of a fox-glove, geraniums, daisies—a buttercup in the water (but this I saw two or three days before) small yellow flowers (I do not know their name) in the turf a large bunch of strawberry blossoms. Wm sate a while with me, then went to meet M. & S.—Last Saturday I dined at Mr Simpson's also a beautiful mild day. Monday was a frosty day, & it has been frost ever since. On Saturday I dined with Mrs Simpson. It is today Christmas-day Saturday 25th December 1802. I am 31 years of age.—It is a dull frosty day.

* * *

1800–02   1897

4. Dorothy accompanied William and Mary on the three-day journey back to their cottage at Grasmere.
5. Probably an undergarment covering the chest.
6. Tom Wedgwood, whose father had founded the

famous pottery works, was a friend and generous patron of Coleridge.
7. Coleridge's daughter, Sara (1802–1852).
8. Mary and her sister Sara Hutchinson.

Grasmere—A Fragment

Peaceful our valley, fair and green,
And beautiful her cottages,
Each in its nook, its sheltered hold,
Or underneath its tuft of trees.

5 Many and beautiful they are;
But there is *one* that I love best,
A lowly shed, in truth, it is,
A brother of the rest.

Yet when I sit on rock or hill,
10 Down looking on the valley fair,
That Cottage with its clustering trees
Summons my heart; it settles there.

Others there are whose small domain
Of fertile fields and hedgerows green
15 Might more seduce a wanderer's mind
To wish that *there* his home had been.

Such wish be his! I blame him not,
My fancies they perchance are wild
—I love that house because it is
20 The very Mountains' child.

Fields hath it of its own, green fields,
But they are rocky steep and bare;
Their fence is of the mountain stone,
And moss and lichen flourish there.

25 And when the storm comes from the North
It lingers near that pastoral spot,
And, piping through the mossy walls,
It seems delighted with its lot.

And let it take its own delight;
30 And let it range the pastures bare;
Until it reach that group of trees,
—It may not enter there!

A green unfading grove it is,
Skirted with many a lesser tree,
35 Hazel and holly, beech and oak,
A bright and flourishing company.

Precious the shelter of those trees;
They screen the cottage that I love;
The sunshine pierces to the roof,
40 And the tall pine-trees tower above.

When first I saw that dear abode,
It was a lovely winter's day:
After a night of perilous storm
The west wind ruled with gentle sway;

45 A day so mild, it might have been
The first day of the gladsome spring;
The robins warbled, and I heard
One solitary throstle sing.

A Stranger, Grasmere, in thy Vale,
50 All faces then to me unknown,
I left my sole companion-friend
To wander out alone.

Lured by a little winding path,
I quitted soon the public road,
55 A smooth and tempting path it was,
By sheep and shepherds trod.

Eastward, toward the lofty hills,
This pathway led me on
Until I reached a stately Rock,
60 With velvet moss o'ergrown.

With russet oak and tufts of fern
Its top was richly garlanded;
Its sides adorned with eglantine
Bedropp'd with hips of glossy red.

65 There, too, in many a sheltered chink
The foxglove's broad leaves flourished fair,
And silver birch whose purple twigs
Bend to the softest breathing air.

Beneath that Rock my course I stayed,
70 And, looking to its summit high,
"Thou wear'st," said I, "a splendid garb,
Here winter keeps his revelry.

"Full long a dweller on the Plains,
I griev'd when summer days were gone;
75 No more I'll grieve; for Winter here
Hath pleasure gardens of his own.

"What need of flowers? The splendid moss
Is gayer than an April mead;
More rich its hues of various green,
80 Orange, and gold, & glittering red."

—Beside that gay and lovely Rock
There came with merry voice

A foaming streamlet glancing by;
It seemed to say "Rejoice!"

85 My youthful wishes all fulfill'd,
Wishes matured by thoughtful choice,
I stood an Inmate of this vale
How *could* I but rejoice?

ca. 1802–05   1892

Thoughts on My Sick-Bed[1]

And has the remnant of my life
Been pilfered of this sunny Spring?
And have its own prelusive sounds
Touched in my heart no echoing string?

5 Ah! say not so—the hidden life
Couchant° within this feeble frame   *lying*
Hath been enriched by kindred gifts,
That, undesired, unsought-for, came

With joyful heart in youthful days
10 When fresh each season in its Round
I welcomed the earliest Celandine
Glittering upon the mossy ground;

With busy eyes I pierced the lane
In quest of known and *un*known things,
15 —The primrose a lamp on its fortress rock,
The silent butterfly spreading its wings,

The violet betrayed by its noiseless breath,
The daffodil dancing in the breeze,
The carolling thrush, on his naked perch,
20 Towering above the budding trees.

Our cottage-hearth no longer our home,
Companions of Nature were we,
The Stirring, the Still, the Loquacious, the Mute—
To all we gave our sympathy.

25 Yet never in those careless days
When spring-time in rock, field, or bower
Was but a fountain of earthly hope
A promise of fruits & the *splendid* flower.

---

1. In a letter of May 25, 1832, William Wordsworth's daughter Dora mentions this as "an affecting poem which she [her aunt Dorothy] has written
on the pleasure she received from the first spring
flowers that were carried up to her when confined
to her sick room." The lines refer to half a dozen
or more poems by William, including "I wandered
lonely as a cloud" (in line 18) and "Tintern Abbey"
(lines 45–52).

No! then I never felt a bliss
30 That might with *that* compare
Which, piercing to my couch of rest,
Came on the vernal air.

When loving Friends an offering brought,
The first flowers of the year,
35 Culled from the precincts of our home,
From nooks to Memory dear.

With some sad thoughts the work was done,
Unprompted and unbidden,
But joy it brought to my *hidden* life,
40 To consciousness no longer hidden.

I felt a Power unfelt before,
Controlling weakness, languor, pain;
It bore me to the Terrace walk
I trod the Hills again;—

45 No prisoner in this lonely room,
I *saw* the green Banks of the Wye,
Recalling thy prophetic words,
Bard, Brother, Friend from infancy!

No need of motion, or of strength,
50 Or even the breathing air:
—I thought of Nature's loveliest scenes;
And with Memory I was there.

May 1832   1978

SAMUEL TAYLOR COLERIDGE
1772–1834

In *The Prelude* Wordsworth, recording his gratitude to the mountains, lakes, and winds "that dwell among the hills where I was born," commiserates with Coleridge because "thou, my Friend! wert reared / In the great City, 'mid far other scenes." Samuel Taylor Coleridge had in fact been born in the small town of Ottery St. Mary, in rural Devonshire, but on the death of his father he had been sent to school at Christ's Hospital in London. He was a dreamy, enthusiastic, and extraordinarily precocious schoolboy. Charles Lamb, his schoolmate and lifelong friend, in his essay on Christ's Hospital has given us a vivid sketch of Coleridge's loneliness, his learning, and his eloquence. When in 1791 Coleridge entered Jesus College, Cambridge, he was an accomplished scholar; but he found little intellectual stimulation at the university, fell into idleness, dissoluteness, and debt, then in despair fled to London and enlisted in the Light Dragoons under the alias of Silas Tomkyn Comberbache—one of the most inept cavalrymen in the long history of the British army. Although rescued by his brothers and sent back to Cambridge, he left in 1794 without a degree.

In June 1794 Coleridge met Robert Southey, then a student at Oxford who, like himself, had poetic aspirations, was a radical in religion and politics, and sympathized with the republican experiment in France. Together the two young men planned to establish an ideal democratic community in America for which Coleridge coined the name "Pantisocracy," signifying an equal rule by all. A plausible American real-estate agent persuaded them that the ideal location would be on the banks of the Susquehanna in Pennsylvania. Twelve men undertook to go; and because perpetuation of the scheme required offspring, hence wives, Coleridge dutifully became engaged to Sara Fricker, conveniently at hand as the sister of Southey's fiancée. The Pantisocracy scheme collapsed, but at Southey's insistence Coleridge went through with the marriage, "resolved," as he said, "but wretched." Later Coleridge's radicalism waned, and he became a conservative in politics—a highly philosophical one—and a staunch Anglican in religion.

In 1795 Coleridge met Wordsworth and at once judged him to be "the best poet of the age." When in 1797 Wordsworth brought his sister, Dorothy, to settle at Alfoxden, only three miles from the Coleridges at Nether Stowey, the period of intimate communication and poetic collaboration began that was the golden time of Coleridge's life. An annual allowance of £150, granted to Coleridge by Thomas and Josiah Wedgwood, sons of the founder of the famous pottery firm, came just in time to deflect him from assuming a post as a Unitarian minister. After their joint publication of *Lyrical Ballads* in 1798, Coleridge and the Wordsworths spent a winter in Germany, where Coleridge attended the University of Göttingen and began the lifelong study of German philosophers and critics—Kant, Schiller, Schelling, and Fichte—that helped alter profoundly his thinking about philosophy, religion, and aesthetics.

Back in England, Coleridge in 1800 followed the Wordsworths to the Lake District, settling at Greta Hall, Keswick. He had become gradually disaffected from his wife, and now he fell helplessly and hopelessly in love with Sara Hutchinson, whose sister, Mary, Wordsworth married in 1802. In accord with the medical prescription of that time, Coleridge had been taking laudanum (opium dissolved in alcohol) to ease the painful physical ailments from which he had suffered from an early age. In 1800–01 heavy dosages during attacks of rheumatism made opium a necessity to him, and Coleridge soon recognized that the drug was a greater evil than the diseases it did not cure. "Dejection: An Ode," published in 1802, was Coleridge's despairing farewell to health, happiness, and poetic creativity. A two-year sojourn on the Mediterranean island of Malta, intended to restore his health, instead completed his decline. When he returned to England in the late summer of 1806, he was a broken man, a drug addict, estranged from his wife, suffering from agonies of remorse, and subject to terrifying nightmares of guilt and despair from which his own shrieks awakened him. By 1810, when he and Wordsworth quarreled bitterly, it must have seemed that he could not fall any lower.

Under these conditions Coleridge's literary efforts, however sporadic and fragmentary, were little short of heroic. In 1808 he debuted as a speaker at one of the new lecturing institutions that sprang up in British cities in the early nineteenth century. His lectures on poetry, like his later series on Shakespeare, became part of the social calendar for fashionable Londoners—women, excluded still from universities, particularly. He wrote for newspapers and single-handedly undertook to write, publish, and distribute a periodical, *The Friend*, which lasted for some ten months beginning in June 1809. A tragedy, *Remorse*, had in 1813 a successful run of twenty performances at the Drury Lane theater. In 1816 he took up residence at Highgate, a northern suburb of London, under the supervision of the excellent and endlessly forbearing physician James Gillman, who managed to control, although not to eliminate, Coleridge's consumption of opium. The next three years were Coleridge's most sustained period of literary activity. While continuing to lecture and to write for the newspapers on a variety of subjects, he published *Biographia Literaria*, *Zapolya* (a drama), a book consisting of the essays in *The Friend* (revised and greatly enlarged), two collections of poems, and several important treatises on philosophical and religious subjects. In these treatises and those that followed over the next fifteen years, he emerged as the heir to the conservatism of Edmund Burke, an opponent to secularism and a defender of the Anglican Church, and an unapologetic intellectual elitist with an ambitious account of the role elites might play in modern states, outlined in his discussions of national culture and of the "clerisy" who would take responsibility for preserving it.

The remaining years of his life, which he spent with Dr. and Mrs. Gillman, were quieter and happier than any he had known since the turn of the century. He came to a peaceful understanding with his wife and was reconciled with Wordsworth, with whom he toured the Rhineland in 1828. His rooms at Highgate became a center for friends, for the London literati, and for a steady stream of pilgrims from England and America. They came to hear one of the wonders of the age, the Sage of Highgate's conversation—or monologue—for even in his decline, Coleridge's talk never lost the almost hypnotic power that Hazlitt has immortalized in "My First Acquaintance with Poets." Mary Shelley appears to have been haunted by the memory of the evening when, a small child, she hid behind a sofa to listen to Coleridge, one of her father's visitors, recite *The Rime of the Ancient Mariner*, and a stanza from that poem of dark mystery found its way into *Frankenstein*, just as her recollections of that visitor's voice contributed to her depictions of the irresistible hold her novel's storytellers have over their auditors. When he died, Coleridge left his friends with the sense that an incomparable intellect had vanished from the world.

Coleridge's friends, however, abetted by his own merciless self-judgments, set current the opinion, still common, that he was great in promise but not in performance. Even in his buoyant youth he described his own character as "indolence capable of energies"; and it is true that while his mind was incessantly active and fertile, he lacked application and staying power. He also manifested early in life a profound sense of guilt and a need for public expiation. After drug addiction sapped his strength and will, he often adapted (or simply adopted) passages from other writers, with little or no acknowledgment, and sometimes in a context that seems designed to reveal that he relies on sources that he does not credit. Whatever the tangled motives for his procedure, Coleridge has repeatedly been charged with gross plagiarism, from his day to ours. After *The Ancient Mariner*, most of the poems he completed were written, like the first version of "Dejection: An Ode," in a spasm of intense effort. Writings that required sustained planning and application were either left unfinished or, like *Biographia Literaria*, made up of brilliant sections padded out with filler, sometimes lifted from other writers, in a desperate effort to meet a deadline. Many of his speculations Coleridge merely confided to his notebooks and the ears of his friends, incorporated in letters, and poured out in the margins of his own and other people's books.

Even so, it is only when measured against his own potentialities that Coleridge's achievements appear limited. In an 1838 essay the philosopher John Stuart Mill hailed the recently deceased Coleridge as one of "the two great seminal minds of England": according to Mill, Coleridge's conservatism had, along with the very different utilitarian philosophy of Jeremy Bentham (the other seminal mind identified in Mill's essay), revolutionized the political thought of the day. Coleridge was also one of the important and influential literary theorists of the nineteenth century. One of his major legacies is the notion that culture, the nation's artistic and spiritual heritage, represents a force with the power to combat the fragmentation of a modern, market-driven society and to restore a common, collective life. This was an idea that he worked out largely in opposition to Bentham's utilitarianism, the newly prestigious discipline of political economy, and the impoverished, soulless account of human nature that these systems of thought offered. And in *Biographia Literaria* and elsewhere, Coleridge raised the stakes for literary criticism, making it into a kind of writing that could address the most difficult and abstract questions—questions about, for instance, the relations between literary language and ordinary language, or between poetry and philosophy, or between perception and imagination. Above all, Coleridge's writings in verse—whether we consider the poetry of Gothic demonism in *Christabel* or the meditative conversation poems like "Frost at Midnight" or "This Lime-Tree Bower My Prison"—are the achievements of a remarkably innovative poet.

The Eolian Harp[1]

Composed at Clevedon, Somersetshire

My pensive Sara! thy soft cheek reclined
Thus on mine arm, most soothing sweet it is
To sit beside our cot, our cot o'ergrown
With white-flowered jasmin, and the broad-leaved myrtle,
5   (Meet emblems they of Innocence and Love!)
And watch the clouds, that late were rich with light,
Slow saddening round, and mark the star of eve
Serenely brilliant (such should wisdom be)
Shine opposite! How exquisite the scents
10   Snatched from yon bean-field! and the world so hushed!
The stilly murmur of the distant sea
Tells us of silence.

And that simplest lute,
Placed length-ways in the clasping casement, hark!
How by the desultory breeze caressed,
15   Like some coy maid half yielding to her lover,
It pours such sweet upbraiding,° as must needs   scolding
Tempt to repeat the wrong! And now, its strings
Boldlier swept, the long sequacious° notes   regularly following
Over delicious surges sink and rise,
20   Such a soft floating witchery of sound
As twilight Elfins make, when they at eve
Voyage on gentle gales from Fairy-Land,
Where Melodies round honey-dropping flowers,
Footless and wild, like birds of Paradise,[2]
25   Nor pause, nor perch, hovering on untamed wing!
O the one life within us and abroad,
Which meets all motion and becomes its soul,
A light in sound, a sound-like power in light,
Rhythm in all thought, and joyance[3] every where—
30   Methinks, it should have been impossible
Not to love all things in a world so filled;
Where the breeze warbles, and the mute still air
Is Music slumbering on her instrument.

---

1. Named for Aeolus, god of the winds, the harp has strings stretched over a rectangular sounding box. When placed in an opened window, the harp (also called "Eolian lute," "Eolian lyre," "wind harp") responds to the altering wind by sequences of musical chords. This instrument, which seems to voice nature's own music, was a favorite household furnishing in the period and was repeatedly alluded to in Romantic poetry. It served also as one of the recurrent Romantic images for the mind—either the mind in poetic inspiration, as in the last stanza of Shelley's "Ode to the West Wind" (p. 1743), or else the mind in perception, responding to an intellectual breeze by trembling into consciousness, as in this poem, lines 44–48.
   Coleridge wrote this poem to Sara Fricker, whom he married on October 4, 1795, and took to a cottage (the "cot" of lines 3 and 64) at Clevedon, overlooking the Bristol Channel. He later several times expanded and altered the original version;

the famous lines 26–29, for example, were not added until 1817. Originally it was titled "Effusion XXXV" and was one of thirty-six such effusions that Coleridge included in a 1796 volume of verse; revised and retitled, it became what he called a "conversation poem"—the designation used since his day for a sustained blank-verse lyric of description and meditation, in the mode of conversation addressed to a silent auditor. This was the form that Coleridge perfected in "Frost at Midnight" and that Wordsworth adopted in "Tintern Abbey."
2. Brilliantly colored birds found in New Guinea and adjacent islands. The native practice of removing the legs when preparing the skin led Europeans to believe that the birds were footless and spent their lives hovering in the air and feeding on nectar.
3. An archaic term for enjoyment, coined in the 16th century by Spenser and reintroduced by Coleridge.

And thus, my love! as on the midway slope
35 Of yonder hill I stretch my limbs at noon,
Whilst through my half-closed eye-lids I behold
The sunbeams dance, like diamonds, on the main,°   *ocean*
And tranquil muse upon tranquillity;
Full many a thought uncalled and undetained,
40 And many idle flitting phantasies,
Traverse my indolent and passive brain,
As wild and various as the random gales
That swell and flutter on this subject lute!

And what if all of animated nature
45 Be but organic harps diversely framed,
That tremble into thought, as o'er them sweeps
Plastic and vast, one intellectual breeze,
At once the Soul of each, and God of All?

But thy more serious eye a mild reproof
50 Darts, O beloved woman! nor such thoughts
Dim and unhallowed dost thou not reject,
And biddest me walk humbly with my God.
Meek daughter in the family of Christ!
Well hast thou said and holily dispraised
55 These shapings of the unregenerate[4] mind;
Bubbles that glitter as they rise and break
On vain Philosophy's aye-babbling° spring.   *ever babbling*
For never guiltless may I speak of him,
The Incomprehensible! save when with awe
60 I praise him, and with Faith that inly feels;
Who with his saving mercies healed me,
A sinful and most miserable man,
Wildered and dark, and gave me to possess
Peace, and this cot, and thee, heart-honored Maid!

1795   1796

This Lime-Tree Bower My Prison

In the June of 1797, some long-expected Friends paid a visit to the
author's cottage; and on the morning of their arrival, he met with
an accident, which disabled him from walking during the whole
time of their stay. One evening, when they had left him for a few
hours, he composed the following lines in the garden-bower.[1]

Well, they are gone, and here must I remain,
This lime-tree bower my prison! I have lost

4. Spiritually unredeemed; not born again.
1. The time was in fact July 1797; the visiting
friends were William and Dorothy Wordsworth
and Charles Lamb; the accident was the fault of
Mrs. Coleridge—"dear Sara," Coleridge wrote,
"accidentally emptied a skillet of boiling milk on
my foot"; and the bower consisted of lime (i.e., lin-

den) trees in the garden of Thomas Poole, next
door to Coleridge's cottage at Nether Stowey.
Coleridge related these facts in a letter to Robert
Southey, July 17, 1797, in which he transcribed
the first version of this poem. In the earliest printed
text, the title is followed by "Addressed to Charles
Lamb, of the India-House, London."

Beauties and feelings, such as would have been
Most sweet to my remembrance even when age
5 Had dimmed mine eyes to blindness! They, meanwhile,
Friends, whom I never more may meet again,
On springy[2] heath, along the hill-top edge,
Wander in gladness, and wind down, perchance,
To that still roaring dell, of which I told;
10 The roaring dell, o'erwooded, narrow, deep,
And only speckled by the mid-day sun;
Where its slim trunk the ash from rock to rock
Flings arching like a bridge;—that branchless ash,
Unsunned and damp, whose few poor yellow leaves
15 Ne'er tremble in the gale, yet tremble still,
Fanned by the water-fall! and there my friends
Behold the dark green file of long lank weeds,
That all at once (a most fantastic sight!)
Still nod and drip beneath the dripping edge
Of the blue clay-stone.[3]

20   Now, my friends emerge
Beneath the wide wide Heaven—and view again
The many-steepled tract magnificent
Of hilly fields and meadows, and the sea,
With some fair bark,° perhaps, whose sails light up   *boat*
25 The slip of smooth clear blue betwixt two Isles
Of purple shadow! Yes! they wander on
In gladness all; but thou, methinks, most glad,
My gentle-hearted Charles! for thou hast pined
And hungered after Nature, many a year,
30 In the great City pent,[4] winning thy way
With sad yet patient soul, through evil and pain
And strange calamity![5] Ah! slowly sink
Behind the western ridge, thou glorious sun!
Shine in the slant beams of the sinking orb,
35 Ye purple heath-flowers! richlier burn, ye clouds!
Live in the yellow light, ye distant groves!
And kindle, thou blue ocean! So my Friend
Struck with deep joy may stand, as I have stood,
Silent with swimming sense; yea, gazing round
40 On the wide landscape, gaze till all doth seem
Less gross than bodily; and of such hues
As veil the Almighty Spirit, when yet he makes
Spirits perceive his presence.

                    A delight
Comes sudden on my heart, and I am glad
45 As I myself were there! Nor in this bower,
This little lime-tree bower, have I not marked

---

2. *Elastic*, I mean [Coleridge's note].
3. Cf. Dorothy Wordsworth's description of the "low damp dell" in her *Alfoxden Journal*, February 10, 1798 (p. 1595).
4. Despite Coleridge's claim, Charles Lamb eminently preferred London over what he called "dead Nature." For Lamb's love of city life, see his letter to Wordsworth at Norton Literature Online.
5. Some ten months earlier Charles Lamb's sister, Mary, had stabbed their mother to death in a fit of insanity.

Much that has soothed me. Pale beneath the blaze
Hung the transparent foliage; and I watched
Some broad and sunny leaf, and loved to see
50 The shadow of the leaf and stem above
Dappling its sunshine! And that walnut-tree
Was richly tinged, and a deep radiance lay
Full on the ancient ivy, which usurps
Those fronting elms, and now, with blackest mass
55 Makes their dark branches gleam a lighter hue
Through the late twilight: and though now the bat
Wheels silent by, and not a swallow twitters,
Yet still the solitary humble bee
Sings in the bean-flower! Henceforth I shall know
60 That Nature ne'er deserts the wise and pure;
No plot so narrow, be but Nature there,
No waste so vacant, but may well employ
Each faculty of sense, and keep the heart
Awake to Love and Beauty! and sometimes
65 'Tis well to be bereft of promised good,
That we may lift the Soul, and contemplate
With lively joy the joys we cannot share.
My gentle-hearted Charles! when the last rook
Beat its straight path along the dusky air
70 Homewards, I blessed it! deeming its black wing
(Now a dim speck, now vanishing in light)
Had crossed the mighty orb's dilated glory,
While thou stood'st gazing; or when all was still,
Flew creeking o'er thy head, and had a charm
75 For thee, my gentle-hearted Charles, to whom
No sound is dissonant which tells of Life.

1797   1800

The Rime of the Ancient Mariner[1]

IN SEVEN PARTS

*Facile credo, plures esse Naturas invisibiles quam visibiles in rerum
universitate. Sed horum* [sic] *omnium familiam quis nobis enarrabit,
et gradus et cognationes et discrimina et singulorum munera? Quid
agunt? quae loca habitant? Harum rerum notitiam semper ambivit
ingenium humanum, nunquam attigit. Juvat, interea, non diffiteor,
quandoque in animo, tanquam in tabulâ, majoris et melioris mundi
imaginem contemplari: ne mens assuefacta hodiernae vitae minutiis*

1. Coleridge describes the origin of this poem in
the opening section of chap. 14 of *Biographia Literaria*. In a comment made to the Reverend Alexander Dyce in 1835 and in a note on "We Are
Seven" dictated in 1843, Wordsworth added some
details. The poem, based on a dream of Coleridge's
friend Cruikshank, was originally planned as a collaboration between Coleridge and Wordsworth, to
pay the expense of a walking tour they took with
Dorothy Wordsworth in November 1797. Before
he dropped out of the enterprise, Wordsworth suggested the shooting of the albatross and the navi-

gation of the ship by the dead men; he also
contributed lines 13–16 and 226–27.
  When printed in *Lyrical Ballads* (1798), this
poem was titled "The Rime of the Ancyent Mari-
nere" and contained many archaic words and spellings, which, Wordsworth believed, hurt the sales
of their volume. In later editions Coleridge revised
the poem, in part by pruning those archaisms. He
also added the Latin epigraph and the marginal
glosses written in the old-fashioned style of 17th-
century learning.

se contrahat nimis, et tota subsidat in pusillas cogitationes. Sed
veritati interea invigilandum est, modusque servandus, ut certa ab
incertis, diem a nocte, distinguamus.

T. Burnet, *Archaeol. Phil.* p. 68.[2]

Part 1

An ancient Mariner meeteth three gallants bidden to a wedding-feast, and detaineth one.	It is an ancient Mariner And he stoppeth one of three. "By thy long grey beard and glittering eye, Now wherefore stopp'st thou me?

The Bridegroom's doors are opened wide,⠀⠀⠀⠀⠀⠀5
And I am next of kin;
The guests are met, the feast is set:
May'st hear the merry din."

He holds him with his skinny hand,
"There was a ship," quoth he.⠀⠀⠀⠀⠀⠀10
"Hold off! unhand me, grey-beard loon!"
Eftsoons[3] his hand dropt he.

The wedding guest is spellbound by the eye of the old sea-faring man, and constrained to hear his tale.

He holds him with his glittering eye—
The wedding-guest stood still,
And listens like a three years' child:⠀⠀⠀⠀⠀⠀15
The Mariner hath his will.[4]

The wedding-guest sat on a stone:
He cannot choose but hear;
And thus spake on that ancient man,
The bright-eyed Mariner.⠀⠀⠀⠀⠀⠀20

"The ship was cheered, the harbor cleared,
Merrily did we drop
Below the kirk,[5] below the hill,
Below the light house top.

The Mariner tells how the ship sailed southward with a good wind and fair weather, till it reached the line.

The sun came up upon the left,⠀⠀⠀⠀⠀⠀25
Out of the sea came he!
And he shone bright, and on the right
Went down into the sea.

2. "I readily believe that there are more invisible than visible Natures in the universe. But who will explain for us the family of all these beings, and the ranks and relations and distinguishing features and functions of each? What do they do? What places do they inhabit? The human mind has always sought the knowledge of these things, but never attained it. Meanwhile I do not deny that it is helpful sometimes to contemplate in the mind, as on a tablet, the image of a greater and better world, lest the intellect, habituated to the petty things of daily life, narrow itself and sink wholly into trivial thoughts. But at the same time we must be watchful for the truth and keep a sense of proportion, so that we may distinguish the certain from the uncertain, day from night." Adapted by Coleridge from Thomas Burnet, *Archaeologiae Philosophicae* (1692).
3. At once.
4. I.e., the Mariner has gained control of the will of the wedding guest by hypnosis—or, as it was called in Coleridge's time, by "mesmerism."
5. Church.

Higher and higher every day,
Till over the mast at noon[6]—"
The wedding-guest here beat his breast, 30
For he heard the loud bassoon.

The Wedding Guest heareth the bridal music; but the mariner continueth his tale.

The bride hath paced into the hall,
Red as a rose is she;
Nodding their heads before her goes 35
The merry minstrelsy.

The wedding-guest he beat his breast,
Yet he cannot choose but hear;
And thus spake on that ancient man,
The bright-eyed Mariner. 40

The ship driven by a storm toward the south pole.

"And now the storm-blast came, and he
Was tyrannous and strong:
He struck with his o'ertaking wings,
And chased us south along.

With sloping masts and dipping prow, 45
As who pursued with yell and blow
Still treads the shadow of his foe,
And forward bends his head,
The ship drove fast, loud roared the blast,
And southward aye[7] we fled. 50

And now there came both mist and snow,
And it grew wondrous cold:
And ice, mast-high, came floating by,
As green as emerald.

The land of ice, and of fearful sounds where no living thing was to be seen.

And through the drifts the snowy clifts 55
Did send a dismal sheen:
Nor shapes of men nor beasts we ken[8]—
The ice was all between.

The ice was here, the ice was there,
The ice was all around: 60
It cracked and growled, and roared and howled,
Like noises in a swound![9]

Till a great sea-bird, called the Albatross, came through the snow-fog, and was received with great joy and hospitality.

At length did cross an Albatross,
Thorough the fog it came;
As if it had been a Christian soul, 65
We hailed it in God's name.

It ate the food it ne'er had eat,
And round and round it flew.

6. The ship had reached the equator.
7. Always.
8. Knew.
9. Swoon.

The ice did split with a thunder-fit;
The helmsman steered us through!   70

And lo! the Albatross proveth a bird of good omen, and followeth the ship as it returned northward through fog and floating ice.

And a good south wind sprung up behind;
The Albatross did follow,
And every day, for food or play,
Came to the mariners' hollo!

In mist or cloud, on mast or shroud,[1]   75
It perched for vespers nine;
Whiles all the night, through fog-smoke white,
Glimmered the white moon-shine."

The ancient Mariner inhospitably killeth the pious bird of good omen.

"God save thee, ancient Mariner!
From the fiends, that plague thee thus!—   80
Why look'st thou so?"—With my cross-bow
I shot the Albatross.

Part 2

The Sun now rose upon the right:[2]
Out of the sea came he,
Still hid in mist, and on the left   85
Went down into the sea.

And the good south wind still blew behind,
But no sweet bird did follow,
Nor any day for food or play
Came to the mariners' hollo!   90

His shipmates cry out against the ancient Mariner, for killing the bird of good luck.

And I had done a hellish thing,
And it would work 'em woe:
For all averred, I had killed the bird
That made the breeze to blow.
Ah wretch! said they, the bird to slay,   95
That made the breeze to blow!

But when the fog cleared off, they justify the same, and thus make themselves accomplices in the crime.

Nor dim nor red, like God's own head,
The glorious Sun uprist:
Then all averred, I had killed the bird
That brought the fog and mist.   100
'Twas right, said they, such birds to slay,
That bring the fog and mist.

The fair breeze continues; the ship enters the Pacific Ocean, and sails northward, even till it reaches the Line.[3]

The fair breeze blew, the white foam flew,
The furrow followed free;
We were the first that ever burst   105
Into that silent sea.

---

1. Rope supporting the mast.
2. Having rounded Cape Horn, the ship heads north into the Pacific.
3. I.e., the equator. Unless it is simply an error

(Coleridge misreading his own poem), this gloss anticipates the ship's later arrival at the equator, on its trip north from the region of the South Pole, as described in lines 381–84.

The ship hath been
suddenly becalmed.

Down dropt the breeze, the sails dropt down,
'Twas sad as sad could be;
And we did speak only to break
The silence of the sea! 110

All in a hot and copper sky,
The bloody Sun, at noon,
Right up above the mast did stand,
No bigger than the Moon.

Day after day, day after day, 115
We stuck, nor breath nor motion;
As idle as a painted ship
Upon a painted ocean.

And the Albatross
begins to be avenged.

Water, water, every where,
And all the boards did shrink; 120
Water, water, every where,
Nor any drop to drink.

The very deep did rot: O Christ!
That ever this should be!
Yea, slimy things did crawl with legs 125
Upon the slimy sea.

About, about, in reel and rout
The death-fires⁴ danced at night;
The water, like a witch's oils,
Burnt green, and blue and white. 130

A spirit had followed
them; one of the
invisible inhabitants
of this planet, neither
departed souls nor
angels; concerning
whom the learned

And some in dreams assured were
Of the spirit that plagued us so;
Nine fathom deep he had followed us
From the land of mist and snow.

Jew, Josephus, and the Platonic Constantinopolitan, Michael Psellus, may be consulted. They are very
numerous, and there is no climate or element without one or more.

And every tongue, through utter drought, 135
Was withered at the root;
We could not speak, no more than if
We had been choked with soot.

The shipmates, in
their sore distress,
would fain throw the
whole guilt on the
ancient Mariner: in
sign whereof they
hang the dead sea
bird round his neck.

Ah! well-a-day! what evil looks
Had I from old and young! 140
Instead of the cross, the Albatross
About my neck was hung.

4. Usually glossed as St. Elmo's fire—an atmospheric electricity on a ship's mast or rigging—believed by superstitious sailors to portend disaster. Possibly the reference is instead to phosphorescence resulting from the decomposition of organic matter in the sea (see line 123).

Part 3

There passed a weary time. Each throat
Was parched, and glazed each eye.
A weary time! a weary time!   145
How glazed each weary eye,
The ancient Mariner When looking westward, I beheld
beholdeth a sign in A something in the sky.
the element afar off.

At first it seemed a little speck,
And then it seemed a mist;   150
It moved and moved, and took at last
A certain shape, I wist.[5]

A speck, a mist, a shape, I wist!
And still it neared and neared:
As if it dodged a water-sprite,[6]   155
It plunged and tacked and veered.

At its nearer   With throats unslaked, with black lips baked,
approach, it seemeth   We could nor laugh nor wail;
him to be a ship; and Through utter drought all dumb we stood!
at a dear ransom he
freeth his speech   I bit my arm, I sucked the blood,   160
from the bonds of   And cried, A sail! a sail!
thirst.

With throats unslaked, with black lips baked,
Agape they heard me call:
A flash of joy;   Gramercy![7] they for joy did grin,
And all at once their breath drew in,   165
As they were drinking all.

And horror follows.   See! see! (I cried) she tacks no more!
For can it be a ship   Hither to work us weal;[8]
that comes onward   Without a breeze, without a tide,
without wind or tide? She steadies with upright keel!   170

The western wave was all a-flame.
The day was well nigh done!
Almost upon the western wave
Rested the broad bright Sun;
When that strange shape drove suddenly   175
Betwixt us and the Sun.

It seemeth him but   And straight the Sun was flecked with bars,
the skeleton of a   (Heaven's Mother send us grace!)
ship.   As if through a dungeon-grate he peered
With broad and burning face.   180

---

5. Knew.
6. A supernatural being that supervises the natural elements (but Coleridge may in fact have been

using the term to mean water-*spout*).
7. Great thanks; from the French *grand-merci*.
8. Benefit.

Alas! (thought I, and my heart beat loud)
How fast she nears and nears!
Are those her sails that glance in the Sun,
Like restless gossameres?[9]

And its ribs are seen as bars on the face of the setting Sun. The specter-woman and her death-mate, and no other on board the skeleton-ship.

Are those her ribs through which the Sun   185
Did peer, as through a grate?
And is that Woman all her crew?
Is that a Death? and are there two?
Is Death that woman's mate?

Like vessel, like crew!

Her lips were red, her looks were free,   190
Her locks were yellow as gold:
Her skin was as white as leprosy,
The Night-mare Life-in-Death was she,
Who thicks man's blood with cold.

Death and Life-in-death have diced for the ship's crew, and she (the latter) winneth the ancient Mariner.

The naked hulk[1] alongside came,   195
And the twain were casting dice;
"The game is done! I've won! I've won!"
Quoth she, and whistles thrice.

No twilight within the courts of the sun.

The Sun's rim dips; the stars rush out:
At one stride comes the dark;   200
With far-heard whisper, o'er the sea,
Off shot the spectre-bark.[2]

At the rising of the Moon,

We listened and looked sideways up!
Fear at my heart, as at a cup,
My life-blood seemed to sip!   205
The stars were dim, and thick the night,
The steersman's face by his lamp gleamed white;
From the sails the dew did drip—
Till clomb above the eastern bar
The horned Moon, with one bright star   210
Within the nether tip.[3]

One after another,

One after one, by the star-dogged Moon,
Too quick for groan or sigh,
Each turned his face with a ghastly pang,
And cursed me with his eye.   215

His shipmates drop down dead.

Four times fifty living men,
(And I heard nor sigh nor groan)
With heavy thump, a lifeless lump,
They dropped down one by one.

But Life-in-Death begins her work on the ancient Mariner.

The souls did from their bodies fly,—   220
They fled to bliss or woe!
And every soul, it passed me by,
Like the whizz of my cross-bow!

9. Filmy cobwebs floating in the air.
1. Large ship.
2. Ghost ship.
3. An omen of impending evil.

Part 4

*The wedding guest
feareth that a spirit is
talking to him.*

"I fear thee, ancient Mariner!
I fear thy skinny hand!   225
And thou art long, and lank, and brown,
As is the ribbed sea-sand.

I fear thee and thy glittering eye,
And thy skinny hand, so brown."—

*But the ancient Mar-
iner assureth him of
his bodily life, and
proceedeth to relate
his horrible penance.*

Fear not, fear not, thou wedding-guest!   230
This body dropt not down.

Alone, alone, all, all alone,
Alone on a wide wide sea!
And never a saint took pity on
My soul in agony.   235

*He despiseth the
creatures of the
calm,*

The many men, so beautiful!
And they all dead did lie:
And a thousand thousand slimy things
Lived on; and so did I.

*And envieth that
they should live, and
so many lie dead.*

I looked upon the rotting sea,   240
And drew my eyes away;
I looked upon the rotting deck,
And there the dead men lay.

I looked to heaven, and tried to pray;
But or ever a prayer had gusht,   245
A wicked whisper came, and made
My heart as dry as dust.

I closed my lids, and kept them close,
And the balls like pulses beat;
For the sky and the sea, and the sea and the sky   250
Lay like a load on my weary eye,
And the dead were at my feet.

*But the curse liveth
for him in the eye of
the dead men.*

The cold sweat melted from their limbs,
Nor rot nor reek did they:
The look with which they looked on me   255
Had never passed away.

An orphan's curse would drag to hell
A spirit from on high;
But oh! more horrible than that
Is the curse in a dead man's eye!   260
Seven days, seven nights, I saw that curse,
And yet I could not die.

*In his loneliness and
fixedness he yearneth
towards the journey-
ing Moon, and the
stars that still
sojourn, yet still
move onward; and
everywhere the blue sky belongs to them, and is their appointed rest, and their native country and their
own natural homes, which they enter unannounced, as lords that are certainly expected and yet there
is a silent joy at their arrival.*

The moving Moon went up the sky,
And no where did abide:
Softly she was going up,   265
And a star or two beside—

Her beams bemocked the sultry main,
Like April hoar-frost spread;
But where the ship's huge shadow lay,
The charmed water burnt alway   270
A still and awful red.

*By the light of the
Moon he beholdeth
God's creatures of
the great calm.*

Beyond the shadow of the ship,
I watched the water-snakes:
They moved in tracks of shining white,
And when they reared, the elfish light   275
Fell off in hoary flakes.

Within the shadow of the ship
I watched their rich attire:
Blue, glossy green, and velvet black,
They coiled and swam; and every track   280
Was a flash of golden fire.

*Their beauty and
their happiness.*

O happy living things! no tongue
Their beauty might declare:
A spring of love gushed from my heart,

*He blesseth them in
his heart.*

And I blessed them unaware: 285
Sure my kind saint took pity on me,
And I blessed them unaware.

*The spell begins to
break.*

The selfsame moment I could pray;
And from my neck so free
The Albatross fell off, and sank   290
Like lead into the sea.

Part 5

Oh sleep! it is a gentle thing,
Beloved from pole to pole!
To Mary Queen the praise be given!
She sent the gentle sleep from Heaven,   295
That slid into my soul.

*By grace of the holy
Mother, the ancient
Mariner is refreshed
with rain.*

The silly[4] buckets on the deck,
That had so long remained,
I dreamt that they were filled with dew;
And when I awoke, it rained.   300

4. Simple, homely.

My lips were wet, my throat was cold,
My garments all were dank;
Sure I had drunken in my dreams,
And still my body drank.

I moved, and could not feel my limbs: 305
I was so light—almost
I thought that I had died in sleep,
And was a blessed ghost.

He heareth sounds
and seeth strange
sights and commo-
tions in the sky and
the element.

And soon I heard a roaring wind:
It did not come anear; 310
But with its sound it shook the sails,
That were so thin and sere.

The upper air burst into life!
And a hundred fire-flags sheen,[5]
To and fro they were hurried about! 315
And to and fro, and in and out,
The wan stars danced between.

And the coming wind did roar more loud,
And the sails did sigh like sedge;[6]
And the rain poured down from one black cloud; 320
The Moon was at its edge.

The thick black cloud was cleft, and still
The Moon was at its side:
Like waters shot from some high crag,
The lightning fell with never a jag, 325
A river steep and wide.

The bodies of the
ship's crew are
inspired, and the
ship moves on;

The loud wind never reached the ship,
Yet now the ship moved on!
Beneath the lightning and the moon
The dead men gave a groan. 330

They groaned, they stirred, they all uprose,
Nor spake, nor moved their eyes;
It had been strange, even in a dream,
To have seen those dead men rise.

The helmsman steered, the ship moved on; 335
Yet never a breeze up blew;
The mariners all 'gan work the ropes,
Where they were wont to do;
They raised their limbs like lifeless tools—
We were a ghastly crew. 340

5. Shone. These fire-flags are probably St. Elmo's fire (see n. 4, p. 1619), but Coleridge may be describing the Aurora Australis, or Southern Lights, and possibly also lightning.
6. A rushlike plant growing in wet soil.

The body of my brother's son
Stood by me, knee to knee:
The body and I pulled at one rope,
But he said nought to me.

But not by the souls
of the men, nor by
dæmons[7] of earth or
middle air, but by a
blessed troop of
angelic spirits, sent
down by the invoca-
tion of the guardian
saint.

"I fear thee, ancient Mariner!"   345
Be calm, thou Wedding-Guest!
'Twas not those souls that fled in pain,
Which to their corses[8] came again,
But a troop of spirits blest:

For when it dawned—they dropped their arms,   350
And clustered round the mast;
Sweet sounds rose slowly through their mouths,
And from their bodies passed.

Around, around, flew each sweet sound,
Then darted to the Sun;   355
Slowly the sounds came back again,
Now mixed, now one by one.

Sometimes a-dropping from the sky
I heard the sky-lark sing;
Sometimes all little birds that are,   360
How they seemed to fill the sea and air
With their sweet jargoning![9]

And now 'twas like all instruments,
Now like a lonely flute;
And now it is an angel's song,   365
That makes the heavens be mute.

It ceased; yet still the sails made on
A pleasant noise till noon,
A noise like of a hidden brook
In the leafy month of June,   370
That to the sleeping woods all night
Singeth a quiet tune.

Till noon we quietly sailed on,
Yet never a breeze did breathe:
Slowly and smoothly went the ship,   375
Moved onward from beneath.

7. Supernatural beings halfway between mortals   8. Corpses.
and gods (the type of spirit that Coleridge describes   9. Warbling (Middle English).
in the gloss beside lines 131–34).

The lonesome spirit from the south-pole carries on the ship as far as the line, in obedience to the angelic troop, but still requireth vengeance.

Under the keel nine fathom deep,
From the land of mist and snow,
The spirit slid: and it was he
That made the ship to go. 380
The sails at noon left off their tune,
And the ship stood still also.

The Sun, right up above the mast,
Had fixed her to the ocean:
But in a minute she 'gan stir, 385
With a short uneasy motion—
Backwards and forwards half her length
With a short uneasy motion.

Then like a pawing horse let go,
She made a sudden bound: 390
It flung the blood into my head,
And I fell down in a swound.

The Polar Spirit's fellow dæmons, the invisible inhabitants of the element, take part in his wrong; and two of them relate, one to the other, that penance long and heavy for the ancient Mariner hath been accorded to the Polar Spirit, who returneth southward.

How long in that same fit I lay,
I have not[1] to declare;
But ere my living life returned, 395
I heard and in my soul discerned
Two voices in the air.

"Is it he?" quoth one, "Is this the man?
By him who died on cross,
With his cruel bow he laid full low 400
The harmless Albatross.

The spirit who bideth by himself
In the land of mist and snow,
He loved the bird that loved the man
Who shot him with his bow." 405

The other was a softer voice,
As soft as honey-dew:
Quoth he, "The man hath penance done,
And penance more will do."

Part 6

FIRST VOICE

"But tell me, tell me! speak again, 410
Thy soft response renewing—
What makes that ship drive on so fast?
What is the ocean doing?"

SECOND VOICE

"Still as a slave before his lord,
The ocean hath no blast; 415

___
1. I.e., have not the knowledge.

His great bright eye most silently
Up to the Moon is cast—

If he may know which way to go;
For she guides him smooth or grim.
See, brother, see! how graciously   420
She looketh down on him."

FIRST VOICE

The Mariner hath been cast into a trance; for the angelic power causeth the vessel to drive northward faster than human life could endure.

"But why drives on that ship so fast,
Without or wave or wind?"

SECOND VOICE

"The air is cut away before,
And closes from behind.   425

Fly, brother, fly! more high, more high!
Or we shall be belated:
For slow and slow that ship will go,
When the Mariner's trance is abated."

The supernatural motion is retarded; the Mariner awakes, and his penance begins anew.

I woke, and we were sailing on   430
As in a gentle weather:
'Twas night, calm night, the moon was high;
The dead men stood together.

All stood together on the deck,
For a charnel-dungeon fitter: 435
All fixed on me their stony eyes,
That in the Moon did glitter.

The pang, the curse, with which they died,
Had never passed away:
I could not draw my eyes from theirs,   440
Nor turn them up to pray.

The curse is finally expiated.

And now this spell was snapt: once more
I viewed the ocean green,
And looked far forth, yet little saw
Of what had else been seen—   445

Like one, that on a lonesome road
Doth walk in fear and dread,
And having once turned round walks on,
And turns no more his head;
Because he knows, a frightful fiend   450
Doth close behind him tread.

But soon there breathed a wind on me,
Nor sound nor motion made:
Its path was not upon the sea,
In ripple or in shade.   455

It raised my hair, it fanned my cheek
Like a meadow-gale of spring—
It mingled strangely with my fears,
Yet it felt like a welcoming.

Swiftly, swiftly flew the ship,   460
Yet she sailed softly too:
Sweetly, sweetly blew the breeze—
On me alone it blew.

*And the ancient
Mariner beholdeth
his native country.*

Oh! dream of joy! is this indeed
The light-house top I see?   465
Is this the hill? is this the kirk?
Is this mine own countree?

We drifted o'er the harbour-bar,
And I with sobs did pray—
O let me be awake, my God!   470
Or let me sleep alway.

The harbour-bay was clear as glass,
So smoothly it was strewn!
And on the bay the moonlight lay,
And the shadow of the moon.   475

The rock shone bright, the kirk no less,
That stands above the rock:
The moonlight steeped in silentness
The steady weathercock.

And the bay was white with silent light,   480
Till rising from the same,

*The angelic spirits
leave the dead
bodies,*

Full many shapes, that shadows were,
In crimson colours came.

*And appear in their
own forms of light.*

A little distance from the prow
Those crimson shadows were: 485
I turned my eyes upon the deck—
Oh, Christ! what saw I there!

Each corse lay flat, lifeless and flat,
And, by the holy rood!
A man all light, a seraph-man,[2]   490
On every corse there stood.

This seraph-band, each waved his hand:
It was a heavenly sight!
They stood as signals to the land,
Each one a lovely light;   495

---

2. A shining celestial being, highest in the ranks of the angels. "Rood": cross.

This seraph-band, each waved his hand,
No voice did they impart—
No voice; but oh! the silence sank
Like music on my heart.

But soon I heard the dash of oars,   500
I heard the Pilot's cheer;
My head was turned perforce away,
And I saw a boat appear.

The Pilot and the Pilot's boy,
I heard them coming fast: 505
Dear Lord in Heaven! it was a joy
The dead men could not blast.

I saw a third—I heard his voice:
It is the Hermit good!
He singeth loud his godly hymns   510
That he makes in the wood.
He'll shrieve[3] my soul, he'll wash away
The Albatross's blood.

Part 7

The Hermit of the wood,

This Hermit good lives in that wood
Which slopes down to the sea.   515
How loudly his sweet voice he rears!
He loves to talk with marineres
That come from a far countree.

He kneels at morn, and noon, and eve—
He hath a cushion plump: 520
It is the moss that wholly hides
The rotted old oak-stump.

The skiff-boat neared: I heard them talk,
"Why, this is strange, I trow!
Where are those lights so many and fair,   525
That signal made but now?"

Approacheth the ship with wonder.

"Strange, by my faith!" the Hermit said—
"And they answered not our cheer!
The planks looked warped! and see those sails,
How thin they are and sere!   530
I never saw aught like to them,
Unless perchance it were

Brown skeletons of leaves that lag
My forest-brook along;
When the ivy-tod[4] is heavy with snow,   535

---

3. Absolve.   4. Clump of ivy.

And the owlet whoops to the wolf below,
That eats the she-wolf's young."

"Dear Lord! it hath a fiendish look"—
(The Pilot made reply)
"I am a-feared"—"Push on, push on!"   540
Said the Hermit cheerily.

The boat came closer to the ship,
But I nor spake nor stirred;
The boat came close beneath the ship,
And straight a sound was heard.   545

The ship suddenly sinketh.

Under the water it rumbled on,
Still louder and more dread:
It reached the ship, it split the bay;
The ship went down like lead.

The ancient Mariner is saved in the Pilot's boat.

Stunned by that loud and dreadful sound,   550
Which sky and ocean smote,
Like one that hath been seven days drowned
My body lay afloat;
But swift as dreams, myself I found
Within the Pilot's boat.   555

Upon the whirl, where sank the ship,
The boat spun round and round;
And all was still, save that the hill
Was telling of the sound.

I moved my lips—the Pilot shrieked   560
And fell down in a fit;
The holy Hermit raised his eyes,
And prayed where he did sit.

I took the oars: the Pilot's boy,
Who now doth crazy go,   565
Laughed loud and long, and all the while
His eyes went to and fro.
"Ha! ha!" quoth he, "full plain I see,
The Devil knows how to row."

And now, all in my own countree,   570
I stood on the firm land!
The Hermit stepped forth from the boat,
And scarcely he could stand.

The ancient Mariner earnestly entreateth the Hermit to shrieve him; and the penance of life falls on him.

"O shrieve me, shrieve me, holy man!"
The Hermit crossed his brow.[5]   575
"Say quick," quoth he, "I bid thee say—
What manner of man art thou?"

5. Made the sign of the cross on his forehead. "Shrieve me": hear my confession and grant me absolution.

Forthwith this frame of mine was wrenched
With a woful agony,
Which forced me to begin my tale;   580
And then it left me free.

And ever and anon throughout his future life an agony constraineth him to travel from land to land.

Since then, at an uncertain hour,
That agony returns:
And till my ghastly tale is told,
This heart within me burns.   585

I pass, like night, from land to land;
I have strange power of speech;
That moment that his face I see,
I know the man that must hear me:
To him my tale I teach.   590

What loud uproar bursts from that door!
The wedding-guests are there:
But in the garden-bower the bride
And bride-maids singing are:
And hark the little vesper bell,   595
Which biddeth me to prayer!

O Wedding-Guest! this soul hath been
Alone on a wide wide sea:
So lonely 'twas, that God himself
Scarce seemed there to be.   600

O sweeter than the marriage-feast,
'Tis sweeter far to me,
To walk together to the kirk
With a goodly company!—

To walk together to the kirk,   605
And all together pray,
While each to his great Father bends,
Old men, and babes, and loving friends,
And youths and maidens gay!

And to teach, by his own example, love and reverence to all things that God made and loveth.

Farewell, farewell! but this I tell   610
To thee, thou Wedding-Guest!
He prayeth well, who loveth well
Both man and bird and beast.

He prayeth best, who loveth best
All things both great and small;   615
For the dear God who loveth us,
He made and loveth all.[6]

6. Coleridge said in 1830, answering the objection of the poet Anna Barbauld that the poem "lacked a moral": "I told her that in my own judgment the poem had too much; and that the only, or chief fault, if I might say so, was the obtrusion of the moral sentiment so openly on the reader as a principle or cause of action in a work of pure imagination. It ought to have had no more moral than the *Arabian Nights'* tale of the merchant's sitting down to eat dates by the side of a well and throwing

The Mariner, whose eye is bright,
Whose beard with age is hoar,
Is gone: and now the Wedding-Guest   620
Turned from the bridegroom's door.

He went like one that hath been stunned,
And is of sense forlorn:[7]
A sadder and a wiser man,
He rose the morrow morn.   625

1797   1798

Kubla Khan

Or, A Vision in a Dream. A Fragment

In[1] the summer of the year 1797, the Author, then in ill health, had retired to
a lonely farm house between Porlock and Linton, on the Exmoor confines of
Somerset and Devonshire. In consequence of a slight indisposition, an anodyne had been prescribed, from the effect of which he fell asleep in his chair
at the moment that he was reading the following sentence, or words of the
same substance, in *Purchas's Pilgrimage*: "Here the Khan Kubla commanded
a palace to be built, and a stately garden thereunto: and thus ten miles of
fertile ground were inclosed with a wall."[2] The author continued for about
three hours in a profound sleep, at least of the external senses,[3] during which
time he has the most vivid confidence, that he could not have composed less
than from two to three hundred lines; if that indeed can be called composition
in which all the images rose up before him as things, with a parallel production
of the correspondent expressions, without any sensation or consciousness of
effort. On awaking he appeared to himself to have a distinct recollection of
the whole, and taking his pen, ink, and paper, instantly and eagerly wrote down
the lines that are here preserved. At this moment he was unfortunately called
out by a person on business from Porlock, and detained by him above an hour,
and on his return to his room, found, to his no small surprise and mortification,
that though he still retained some vague and dim recollection of the general
purport of the vision, yet, with the exception of some eight or ten scattered
lines and images, all the rest had passed away like the images on the surface
of a stream into which a stone had been cast, but, alas! without the after
restoration of the latter:

---

the shells aside, and lo! a genie starts up and says
he *must* kill the aforesaid merchant *because* one of
the date shells had, it seems, put out the eye of the
genie's son."
7. Bereft.
1. In the texts of 1816–29, this note began with
an additional short paragraph: "The following fragment is here published at the request of a poet of
great and deserved celebrity, and, as far as the
Author's own opinions are concerned, rather as a
psychological curiosity, than on the ground of any
supposed *poetic* merits." The "poet of . . . celebrity" was Lord Byron.
2. "In Xamdu did Cublai Can build a stately Palace, encompassing sixteene miles of plaine ground
with a wall, wherein are fertile Meddowes, pleasant Springs, delightfull Streames, and all sorts of

beasts of chase and game, and in the middest
thereof a sumptuous house of pleasure, which may
be removed from place to place." From Samuel
Purchas's book of travelers' tales, *Purchas his Pilgrimage* (1613). The historical Kublai Khan
founded the Mongol dynasty in China in the 13th
century.
3. In a note on a manuscript copy of "Kubla
Khan," Coleridge gave a more precise account of
the nature of this "sleep": "This fragment with a
good deal more, not recoverable, composed, in a
sort of reverie brought on by two grains of opium,
taken to check a dysentery, at a farmhouse
between Porlock and Linton, a quarter of a mile
from Culbone Church, in the fall of the year,
1797."

Then all the charm
Is broken—all that phantom-world so fair
Vanishes, and a thousand circlets spread,
And each mis-shape[s] the other. Stay awhile,
Poor youth! who scarcely dar'st lift up thine eyes—
The stream will soon renew its smoothness, soon
The visions will return! And lo! he stays,
And soon the fragments dim of lovely forms
Come trembling back, unite, and now once more
The pool becomes a mirror.

[From Coleridge's *The Picture; or, the Lover's Resolution*,
lines 91–100]

Yet from the still surviving recollections in his mind, the Author has frequently purposed to finish for himself what had been originally, as it were, given to him. Αὔριον ἄδιον ἄσω:[4] but the to-morrow is yet to come.

As a contrast to this vision, I have annexed a fragment of a very different character, describing with equal fidelity the dream of pain and disease.[5]—1816.

In Xanadu did Kubla Khan
A stately pleasure-dome decree:
Where Alph,[6] the sacred river, ran
Through caverns measureless to man
5   Down to a sunless sea.
So twice five miles of fertile ground
With walls and towers were girdled round:
And there were gardens bright with sinuous rills
Where blossomed many an incense-bearing tree;
10   And here were forests ancient as the hills,
Enfolding sunny spots of greenery.

But oh! that deep romantic chasm which slanted
Down the green hill athwart a cedarn cover!
A savage place! as holy and enchanted
15   As e'er beneath a waning moon was haunted
By woman wailing for her demon-lover!
And from this chasm, with ceaseless turmoil seething,
As if this earth in fast thick pants were breathing,
A mighty fountain momently was forced:
20   Amid whose swift half-intermitted burst
Huge fragments vaulted like rebounding hail,
Or chaffy grain beneath the thresher's flail:
And 'mid these dancing rocks at once and ever
It flung up momently the sacred river.
25   Five miles meandering with a mazy motion
Through wood and dale the sacred river ran,
Then reached the caverns measureless to man,

4. I shall sing a sweeter song tomorrow (Greek; recalled from Theocritus's *Idyls* 1.145).
   A number of Coleridge's assertions in this preface have been debated by critics: whether the poem was written in 1797 or later, whether it was actually composed in a "dream" or opium reverie, even whether it is a fragment or in fact is complete. All critics agree, however, that this visionary poem of demonic inspiration is much more than a mere "psychological curiosity."
5. Coleridge refers to "The Pains of Sleep."
6. Derived probably from the Greek river Alpheus, which flows into the Ionian Sea. Its waters were fabled to rise again in Sicily as the fountain of Arethusa.

And sank in tumult to a lifeless ocean:
And 'mid this tumult Kubla heard from far
30 Ancestral voices prophesying war!

The shadow of the dome of pleasure
Floated midway on the waves;
Where was heard the mingled measure
From the fountain and the caves.
35 It was a miracle of rare device,
A sunny pleasure-dome with caves of ice!

A damsel with a dulcimer
In a vision once I saw:
It was an Abyssinian maid,
40 And on her dulcimer she played,
Singing of Mount Abora.[7]
Could I revive within me
Her symphony and song,
To such a deep delight 'twould win me,
45 That with music loud and long,
I would build that dome in air,
That sunny dome! those caves of ice!
And all who heard should see them there,
And all should cry, Beware! Beware!
50 His flashing eyes, his floating hair!
Weave a circle round him thrice,[8]
And close your eyes with holy dread,
For he on honey-dew hath fed,
And drunk the milk of Paradise.[9]

ca. 1797–98   1816

Christabel[1]

Preface

The first part of the following poem was written in the year 1797, at Stowey,
in the county of Somerset. The second part, after my return from Germany,
in the year 1800, at Keswick, Cumberland. It is probable, that if the poem
had been finished at either of the former periods, or if even the first and second
part had been published in the year 1800, the impression of its originality
would have been much greater than I dare at present expect. But for this, I

---

7. Apparently a reminiscence of Milton's *Paradise Lost* 4.280–82: "where Abassin Kings their issue guard / Mount Amara (though this by some supposed / True Paradise) under the Ethiop line."
8. A magic ritual, to protect the inspired poet from intrusion.
9. Lines 50ff. echo in part the description, in Plato's *Ion* 533–34, of inspired poets, who are "like Bacchic maidens who draw milk and honey from the rivers when they are under the influence of Dionysus but not when they are in their right mind."

1. Coleridge had planned to publish *Christabel* in the 2nd edition of *Lyrical Ballads* (1800) but had not been able to complete the poem. When *Christabel* was finally published in 1816 in its present fragmentary state, he still hoped to finish it, for the Preface contained this sentence (deleted in the edition of 1834): "But as, in my very first conception of the tale, I had the whole present to my mind, with the wholeness, no less than with the liveliness of a vision; I trust that I shall be able to embody in verse the three parts yet to come, in the course of the present year."

have only my own indolence to blame. The dates are mentioned for the exclusive purpose of precluding charges of plagiarism or servile imitation from myself. For there is amongst us a set of critics, who seem to hold, that every possible thought and image is traditional; who have no notion that there are such things as fountains in the world, small as well as great; and who would therefore charitably derive every rill they behold flowing, from a perforation made in some other man's tank. I am confident, however, that as far as the present poem is concerned, the celebrated poets[2] whose writings I might be suspected of having imitated, either in particular passages, or in the tone and the spirit of the whole, would be among the first to vindicate me from the charge, and who, on any striking coincidence, would permit me to address them in this doggerel version of two monkish Latin hexameters.

> Tis mine and it is likewise yours;
> But an if this will not do;
> Let it be mine, good friend! for I
> Am the poorer of the two.

I have only to add, that the metre of the Christabel is not, properly speaking, irregular, though it may seem so from its being founded on a new principle: namely, that of counting in each line the accents, not the syllables.[3] Though the latter may vary from seven to twelve, yet in each line the accents will be found to be only four. Nevertheless this occasional variation in number of syllables is not introduced wantonly, or for the mere ends of convenience, but in correspondence with some transition, in the nature of the imagery or passion.

Part 1

'Tis the middle of night by the castle clock,
And the owls have awakened the crowing cock;
Tu—whit!——Tu—whoo!
And hark, again! the crowing cock,
5   How drowsily it crew.

Sir Leoline, the Baron rich,
Hath a toothless mastiff bitch;
From her kennel beneath the rock
She maketh answer to the clock,
10   Four for the quarters, and twelve for the hour;
Ever and aye,° by shine and shower,   always
Sixteen short howls, not over loud;
Some say, she sees my lady's shroud.

Is the night chilly and dark?
15   The night is chilly, but not dark.

2. Sir Walter Scott and Lord Byron, who had read and admired *Christabel* while it circulated in manuscript. Coleridge has in mind Scott's *Lay of the Last Minstrel* (1805) and Byron's *Siege of Corinth* (1816), which showed the influence of *Christabel*, especially in their meter.
3. Much of the older English versification, following the example of Anglo-Saxon poetry, had been based on stress, or "accent," and some of it shows as much freedom in varying the number of syllables as does *Christabel*. The poem, however, is a radical departure from the theory and practice of versification in the 18th century, which had been based on a recurrent number of syllables in each line.

The thin gray cloud is spread on high,
It covers but not hides the sky.
The moon is behind, and at the full;
And yet she looks both small and dull.
20 The night is chill, the cloud is gray:
'Tis a month before the month of May,
And the Spring comes slowly up this way.

The lovely lady, Christabel,
Whom her father loves so well,
25 What makes her in the wood so late,
A furlong from the castle gate?
She had dreams all yesternight
Of her own betrothed knight;
And she in the midnight wood will pray
30 For the weal° of her lover that's far away.   well-being

She stole along, she nothing spoke,
The sighs she heaved were soft and low,
And naught was green upon the oak,
But moss and rarest mistletoe:⁴
35 She kneels beneath the huge oak tree,
And in silence prayeth she.

The lady sprang up suddenly,
The lovely lady, Christabel!
It moaned as near, as near can be,
40 But what it is, she cannot tell.—
On the other side it seems to be,
Of the huge, broad-breasted, old oak tree.

The night is chill; the forest bare;
Is it the wind that moaneth bleak?
45 There is not wind enough in the air
To move away the ringlet curl
From the lovely lady's cheek—
There is not wind enough to twirl
The one red leaf, the last of its clan,
50 That dances as often as dance it can,
Hanging so light, and hanging so high,
On the topmost twig that looks up at the sky.

Hush, beating heart of Christabel!
Jesu, Maria, shield her well!
55 She folded her arms beneath her cloak,
And stole to the other side of the oak.
    What sees she there?

There she sees a damsel bright,
Drest in a silken robe of white,

---

4. In Celtic Britain the mistletoe (a parasitic plant) had been held in veneration when it was found growing—as it rarely does—on an oak tree. (Its usual host is the apple tree.)

60   That shadowy in the moonlight shone:
       The neck that made that white robe wan,
       Her stately neck, and arms were bare;
       Her blue-veined feet unsandal'd were,
       And wildly glittered here and there
65   The gems entangled in her hair.
       I guess, 'twas frightful there to see
       A lady so richly clad as she—
       Beautiful exceedingly!

       "Mary mother, save me now!"
70   (Said Christabel,) "And who art thou?"

       The lady strange made answer meet,°   *appropriate*
       And her voice was faint and sweet:—
       "Have pity on my sore distress,
       I scarce can speak for weariness:
75   Stretch forth thy hand, and have no fear!"
       Said Christabel, "How camest thou here?"
       And the lady, whose voice was faint and sweet,
       Did thus pursue her answer meet:—

       "My sire is of a noble line,
80   And my name is Geraldine:
       Five warriors seized me yestermorn,
       Me, even me, a maid forlorn:
       They choked my cries with force and fright,
       And tied me on a palfrey white.
85   The palfrey was as fleet as wind,
       And they rode furiously behind.
       They spurred amain,° their steeds were white: *at top speed*
       And once we crossed the shade of night.
       As sure as Heaven shall rescue me,
90   I have no thought what men they be;
       Nor do I know how long it is
       (For I have lain entranced I wis⁵)
       Since one, the tallest of the five,
       Took me from the palfrey's back,
95   A weary woman, scarce alive.
       Some muttered words his comrades spoke:
       He placed me underneath this oak;
       He swore they would return with haste;
       Whither they went I cannot tell—
100   I thought I heard, some minutes past,
       Sounds as of a castle bell.
       Stretch forth thy hand" (thus ended she),
       "And help a wretched maid to flee."

       Then Christabel stretched forth her hand
105   And comforted fair Geraldine:
       "O well, bright dame! may you command

5. I believe (Coleridge's misinterpretation of the Middle English adverb *ywis*, meaning "certainly").

The service of Sir Leoline;
And gladly our stout chivalry
Will he send forth and friends withal
110   To guide and guard you safe and free
Home to your noble father's hall."

She rose: and forth with steps they passed
That strove to be, and were not, fast.
Her gracious stars the lady blest,
115   And thus spake on sweet Christabel:
"All our household are at rest,
The hall as silent as the cell;°   *a monastery*
Sir Leoline is weak in health,
And may not well awakened be,
120   But we will move as if in stealth,
And I beseech your courtesy,
This night, to share your couch with me."

They crossed the moat, and Christabel
Took the key that fitted well;
125   A little door she opened straight,
All in the middle of the gate;
The gate that was ironed within and without,
Where an army in battle array had marched out.
The lady sank, belike through pain,
130   And Christabel with might and main
Lifted her up, a weary weight,
Over the threshold of the gate:[6]
Then the lady rose again,
And moved, as she were not in pain.

135   So free from danger, free from fear,
They crossed the court: right glad they were.
And Christabel devoutly cried
To the Lady by her side;
"Praise we the Virgin all divine
140   Who hath rescued thee from thy distress!"
"Alas, alas!" said Geraldine,
"I cannot speak for weariness."
So free from danger, free from fear,
They crossed the court: right glad they were.

145   Outside her kennel the mastiff old
Lay fast asleep, in moonshine cold.
The mastiff old did not awake,
Yet she an angry moan did make!
And what can ail the mastiff bitch?
150   Never till now she uttered yell
Beneath the eye of Christabel.
Perhaps it is the owlet's scritch:
For what can ail the mastiff bitch?

---

6. According to legend, a witch cannot cross the threshold by her own power because it has been blessed against evil spirits.

They passed the hall, that echoes still,
155 Pass as lightly as you will!
The brands were flat, the brands were dying,
Amid their own white ashes lying;
But when the lady passed, there came
A tongue of light, a fit of flame;
160 And Christabel saw the lady's eye,
And nothing else saw she thereby,
Save the boss of the shield of Sir Leoline tall,
Which hung in a murky old niche in the wall.
"O softly tread," said Christabel,
165 "My father seldom sleepeth well."

Sweet Christabel her feet doth bare,
And, jealous of the listening air,
They steal their way from stair to stair,
Now in glimmer, and now in gloom,
170 And now they pass the Baron's room,
As still as death with stifled breath!
And now have reached her chamber door;
And now doth Geraldine press down
The rushes⁷ of the chamber floor.

175 The moon shines dim in the open air,
And not a moonbeam enters here.
But they without its light can see
The chamber carved so curiously,
Carved with figures strange and sweet,
180 All made out of the carver's brain,
For a lady's chamber meet:
The lamp with twofold silver chain
Is fastened to an angel's feet.
The silver lamp burns dead and dim;
185 But Christabel the lamp will trim.
She trimmed the lamp, and made it bright,
And left it swinging to and fro,
While Geraldine, in wretched plight,
Sank down upon the floor below.

190 "O weary lady, Geraldine,
I pray you, drink this cordial wine!
It is a wine of virtuous powers;
My mother made it of wild flowers."

"And will your mother pity me,
195 Who am a maiden most forlorn?"
Christabel answered—"Woe is me!
She died the hour that I was born.
I have heard the grey-haired friar tell,
How on her death-bed she did say,
200 That she should hear the castle-bell
Strike twelve upon my wedding day.

---

7. Often used as a floor covering in the Middle Ages.

O mother dear! that thou wert here!"
"I would," said Geraldine, "she were!"

But soon with altered voice, said she—
205 "Off, wandering mother![8] Peak and pine!
I have power to bid thee flee."
Alas! what ails poor Geraldine?
Why stares she with unsettled eye?
Can she the bodiless dead espy?
210 And why with hollow voice cries she,
"Off, woman, off! this hour is mine—
Though thou her guardian spirit be,
Off, woman, off! 'tis given to me."

Then Christabel knelt by the lady's side,
215 And raised to heaven her eyes so blue—
"Alas!" said she, "this ghastly ride—
Dear lady! it hath wildered you!"
The lady wiped her moist cold brow,
And faintly said, " 'tis over now!"

220 Again the wild-flower wine she drank:
Her fair large eyes 'gan glitter bright,
And from the floor whereon she sank,
The lofty lady stood upright;
She was most beautiful to see,
225 Like a lady of a far countrée.

And thus the lofty lady spake—
"All they who live in the upper sky,
Do love you, holy Christabel!
And you love them, and for their sake
230 And for the good which me befell,
Even I in my degree will try,
Fair maiden, to requite you well.
But now unrobe yourself; for I
Must pray, ere yet in bed I lie."

235 Quoth Christabel, "So let it be!"
And as the lady bade, did she.
Her gentle limbs did she undress,
And lay down in her loveliness.

But through her brain of weal and woe
240 So many thoughts moved to and fro,
That vain it were her lids to close;
So half-way from the bed she rose,
And on her elbow did recline
To look at the lady Geraldine.

8. A term that could designate a fit of hysteria. "Peak and pine": Shakespeare's *Macbeth* 1.3.22.

245 Beneath the lamp the lady bowed,
 And slowly rolled her eyes around;
 Then drawing in her breath aloud,
 Like one that shuddered, she unbound
 The cincture° from beneath her breast: *belt*
250 Her silken robe, and inner vest,
 Dropt to her feet, and full in view,
 Behold! her bosom and half her side——
 A sight to dream of, not to tell!
 O shield her! shield sweet Christabel!⁹

255 Yet Geraldine nor speaks nor stirs;
 Ah! what a stricken look was hers!
 Deep from within she seems half-way
 To lift some weight with sick assay,°   *attempt*
 And eyes the maid and seeks delay;
260 Then suddenly as one defied
 Collects herself in scorn and pride,
 And lay down by the maiden's side!—
 And in her arms the maid she took,
    Ah well-a-day!
265 And with low voice and doleful look
 These words did say:
 "In the touch of this bosom there worketh a spell,
 Which is lord of thy utterance, Christabel!
 Thou knowest to-night, and wilt know to-morrow
270 This mark of my shame, this seal of my sorrow;
   But vainly thou warrest,
    For this is alone in
    Thy power to declare,
    That in the dim forest
275   Thou heard'st a low moaning,
 And found'st a bright lady, surpassingly fair:
 And didst bring her home with thee in love and in charity,
 To shield her and shelter her from the damp air."

The Conclusion to Part 1

 It was a lovely sight to see
280 The lady Christabel, when she
 Was praying at the old oak tree.
   Amid the jagged shadows
   Of mossy leafless boughs,
   Kneeling in the moonlight,
285   To make her gentle vows;
 Her slender palms together prest,
 Heaving sometimes on her breast;
 Her face resigned to bliss or bale°—   *evil, sorrow*
 Her face, oh call it fair not pale,
290 And both blue eyes more bright than clear,
 Each about to have a tear.

9. In several manuscripts and the first printing, this line reads "And she is to sleep by [*or* with] Christabel."

With open eyes (ah woe is me!)
Asleep, and dreaming fearfully,
Fearfully dreaming, yet I wis,
295 Dreaming that alone, which is—
O sorrow and shame! Can this be she,
The lady, who knelt at the old oak tree?
And lo! the worker of these harms,
That holds the maiden in her arms,
300 Seems to slumber still and mild,
As a mother with her child.

A star hath set, a star hath risen,
O Geraldine! since arms of thine
Have been the lovely lady's prison.
305 O Geraldine! one hour was thine—
Thou'st had thy will! By tairn[1] and rill,
The night-birds all that hour were still.
But now they are jubilant anew,
From cliff and tower, tu—whoo! tu—whoo!
310 Tu—whoo! tu—whoo! from wood and fell![2]

And see! the lady Christabel
Gathers herself from out her trance;
Her limbs relax, her countenance
Grows sad and soft; the smooth thin lids
315 Close o'er her eyes; and tears she sheds—
Large tears that leave the lashes bright!
And oft the while she seems to smile
As infants at a sudden light!
Yea, she doth smile, and she doth weep,
320 Like a youthful hermitess,
Beauteous in a wilderness,
Who, praying always, prays in sleep.
And, if she move unquietly,
Perchance, 'tis but the blood so free,
325 Comes back and tingles in her feet.
No doubt, she hath a vision sweet.
What if her guardian spirit 'twere?
What if she knew her mother near?
But this she knows, in joys and woes,
330 That saints will aid if men will call:
For the blue sky bends over all!

Part 2

"Each matin bell," the Baron saith,
"Knells us back to a world of death."
These words Sir Leoline first said,
335 When he rose and found his lady dead:
These words Sir Leoline will say,
Many a morn to his dying day!

---

1. Tarn, a mountain pool.   2. Elevated moor, or hill.

And hence the custom and law began,
That still at dawn the sacristan,[3]
340 Who duly pulls the heavy bell,
Five and forty beads must tell[4]
Between each stroke—a warning knell,
Which not a soul can choose but hear
From Bratha Head to Wyndermere.[5]

345 Saith Bracy the bard, "So let it knell!
And let the drowsy sacristan
Still count as slowly as he can!
There is no lack of such, I ween,°   *believe*
As well fill up the space between.
350 In Langdale Pike° and Witch's Lair,   *Peak*
And Dungeon-ghyll[6] so foully rent,
With ropes of rock and bells of air
Three sinful sextons' ghosts are pent,
Who all give back, one after t'other,
355 The death-note to their living brother;
And oft too, by the knell offended,
Just as their one! two! three! is ended,
The devil mocks the doleful tale
With a merry peal from Borodale."

360 The air is still! through mist and cloud
That merry peal comes ringing loud;
And Geraldine shakes off her dread,
And rises lightly from the bed;
Puts on her silken vestments white,
365 And tricks her hair in lovely plight,°   *plait*
And nothing doubting of her spell
Awakens the lady Christabel.
"Sleep you, sweet lady Christabel?
I trust that you have rested well."

370 And Christabel awoke and spied
The same who lay down by her side—
O rather say, the same whom she
Raised up beneath the old oak tree!
Nay, fairer yet! and yet more fair!
375 For she belike hath drunken deep
Of all the blessedness of sleep!
And while she spake, her looks, her air
Such gentle thankfulness declare,
That (so it seemed) her girded vests
380 Grew tight beneath her heaving breasts.
"Sure I have sinned!" said Christabel,
"Now heaven be praised if all be well!"
And in low faltering tones, yet sweet,

3. Church officer who digs the graves and rings the bells.
4. Pray while "telling" (keeping count on) the beads of a rosary.
5. These and the following names are of localities in the English Lake District.
6. Ravine forming the bed of a stream.

Did she the lofty lady greet
385 With such perplexity of mind
As dreams too lively leave behind.

So quickly she rose, and quickly arrayed
Her maiden limbs, and having prayed
That He, who on the cross did groan,
390 Might wash away her sins unknown,
She forthwith led fair Geraldine
To meet her sire, Sir Leoline.

The lovely maid and the lady tall
Are pacing both into the hall,
395 And pacing on through page and groom,
Enter the Baron's presence room.

The Baron rose, and while he prest
His gentle daughter to his breast,
With cheerful wonder in his eyes
400 The lady Geraldine espies,
And gave such welcome to the same,
As might beseem so bright a dame!

But when he heard the lady's tale,
And when she told her father's name,
405 Why waxed Sir Leoline so pale,
Murmuring o'er the name again,
Lord Roland de Vaux of Tryermaine?

Alas! they had been friends in youth;
But whispering tongues can poison truth;
410 And constancy lives in realms above;
And life is thorny; and youth is vain;
And to be wroth with one we love,
Doth work like madness in the brain.
And thus it chanced, as I divine,
415 With Roland and Sir Leoline.
Each spake words of high disdain
And insult to his heart's best brother:
They parted—ne'er to meet again!
But never either found another
420 To free the hollow heart from paining—
They stood aloof, the scars remaining,
Like cliffs which had been rent asunder;
A dreary sea now flows between;—
But neither heat, nor frost, nor thunder,
425 Shall wholly do away, I ween,
The marks of that which once hath been.

Sir Leoline, a moment's space,
Stood gazing on the damsel's face:
And the youthful Lord of Tryermaine
430 Came back upon his heart again.

O then the Baron forgot his age,
His noble heart swelled high with rage;
He swore by the wounds in Jesu's side,
He would proclaim it far and wide
435   With trump and solemn heraldry,
That they who thus had wronged the dame,
Were base as spotted infamy!
"And if they dare deny the same,
My herald shall appoint a week,
440   And let the recreant traitors seek
My tourney court[7]—that there and then
I may dislodge their reptile souls
From the bodies and forms of men!"
He spake: his eye in lightning rolls!
445   For the lady was ruthlessly seized; and he kenned
In the beautiful lady the child of his friend!

And now the tears were on his face,
And fondly in his arms he took
Fair Geraldine, who met the embrace,
450   Prolonging it with joyous look.
Which when she viewed, a vision fell
Upon the soul of Christabel,
The vision of fear, the touch and pain!
She shrunk and shuddered, and saw again—
455   (Ah, woe is me! Was it for thee,
Thou gentle maid! such sights to see?)
Again she saw that bosom old,
Again she felt that bosom cold,
And drew in her breath with a hissing sound:
460   Whereat the Knight turned wildly round,
And nothing saw, but his own sweet maid
With eyes upraised, as one that prayed.

The touch, the sight, had passed away,
And in its stead that vision blest,
465   Which comforted her after-rest,
While in the lady's arms she lay,
Had put a rapture in her breast,
And on her lips and o'er her eyes
Spread smiles like light!
                              With new surprise,
470   "What ails then my beloved child?"
The Baron said—His daughter mild
Made answer, "All will yet be well!"
I ween, she had no power to tell
Aught else: so mighty was the spell.

475   Yet he, who saw this Geraldine,
Had deemed her sure a thing divine.
Such sorrow with such grace she blended,

7. Arena for tournaments.

As if she feared, she had offended
Sweet Christabel, that gentle maid!
480 And with such lowly tones she prayed,
She might be sent without delay
Home to her father's mansion.
                           "Nay!
Nay, by my soul!" said Leoline.
"Ho! Bracy, the bard, the charge be thine!
485 Go thou, with music sweet and loud,
And take two steeds with trappings proud,
And take the youth whom thou lov'st best
To bear thy harp, and learn thy song,
And clothe you both in solemn vest,
490 And over the mountains haste along,
Lest wandering folk, that are abroad,
Detain you on the valley road.
And when he has crossed the Irthing flood,
My merry bard! he hastes, he hastes
495 Up Knorren Moor, through Halegarth Wood,
And reaches soon that castle good
Which stands and threatens Scotland's wastes.

"Bard Bracy! bard Bracy! your horses are fleet,
Ye must ride up the hall, your music so sweet,
500 More loud than your horses' echoing feet!
And loud and loud to Lord Roland call,
Thy daughter is safe in Langdale hall!
Thy beautiful daughter is safe and free—
Sir Leoline greets thee thus through me.
505 He bids thee come without delay
With all thy numerous array;
And take thy lovely daughter home:
And he will meet thee on the way
With all his numerous array
510 White with their panting palfreys' foam:
And by mine honour! I will say,
That I repent me of the day
When I spake words of fierce disdain
To Roland de Vaux of Tryermaine!—
515 —For since that evil hour hath flown,
Many a summer's sun hath shone;
Yet ne'er found I a friend again
Like Roland de Vaux of Tryermaine."

The lady fell, and clasped his knees,
520 Her face upraised, her eyes o'erflowing;
And Bracy replied, with faltering voice,
His gracious hail on all bestowing!—
"Thy words, thou sire of Christabel,
Are sweeter than my harp can tell;
525 Yet might I gain a boon of thee,
This day my journey should not be,
So strange a dream hath come to me;

That I had vowed with music loud
To clear yon wood from thing unblest,
530 Warned by a vision in my rest!
For in my sleep I saw that dove,
That gentle bird, whom thou dost love,
And call'st by thy own daughter's name—
Sir Leoline! I saw the same
535 Fluttering, and uttering fearful moan,
Among the green herbs in the forest alone.
Which when I saw and when I heard,
I wonder'd what might ail the bird;
For nothing near it could I see,
540 Save the grass and green herbs underneath the old tree.

"And in my dream methought I went
To search out what might there be found;
And what the sweet bird's trouble meant,
That thus lay fluttering on the ground.
545 I went and peered, and could descry
No cause for her distressful cry;
But yet for her dear lady's sake
I stooped, methought, the dove to take,
When lo! I saw a bright green snake
550 Coiled around its wings and neck,
Green as the herbs on which it couched,
Close by the dove's its head it crouched;
And with the dove it heaves and stirs,
Swelling its neck as she swelled hers!
555 I woke; it was the midnight hour,
The clock was echoing in the tower;
But though my slumber was gone by,
This dream it would not pass away—
It seems to live upon my eye!
560 And thence I vowed this self-same day,
With music strong and saintly song
To wander through the forest bare,
Lest aught unholy loiter there."

Thus Bracy said: the Baron, the while,
565 Half-listening heard him with a smile;
Then turned to Lady Geraldine,
His eyes made up of wonder and love;
And said in courtly accents fine,
"Sweet maid, Lord Roland's beauteous dove,
570 With arms more strong than harp or song,
Thy sire and I will crush the snake!"
He kissed her forehead as he spake,
And Geraldine, in maiden wise,°   *manner*
Casting down her large bright eyes,
575 With blushing cheek and courtesy fine
She turned her from Sir Leoline;
Softly gathering up her train,
That o'er her right arm fell again;

And folded her arms across her chest,
580   And couched her head upon her breast,
And looked askance at Christabel——
Jesu Maria, shield her well!

A snake's small eye blinks dull and shy,
And the lady's eyes they shrunk in her head,
585   Each shrunk up to a serpent's eye,
And with somewhat of malice, and more of dread,
At Christabel she looked askance!—
One moment—and the sight was fled!
But Christabel in dizzy trance
590   Stumbling on the unsteady ground
Shuddered aloud, with a hissing sound;
And Geraldine again turned round,
And like a thing, that sought relief,
Full of wonder and full of grief,
595   She rolled her large bright eyes divine
Wildly on Sir Leoline.

The maid, alas! her thoughts are gone,
She nothing sees—no sight but one!
The maid, devoid of guile and sin,
600   I know not how, in fearful wise
So deeply had she drunken in
That look, those shrunken serpent eyes,
That all her features were resigned
To this sole image in her mind;
605   And passively did imitate
That look of dull and treacherous hate!
And thus she stood, in dizzy trance,
Still picturing that look askance
With forced unconscious sympathy
610   Full before her father's view——
As far as such a look could be,
In eyes so innocent and blue!
And when the trance was o'er, the maid
Paused awhile, and inly prayed:
615   Then falling at the Baron's feet,
"By my mother's soul do I entreat
That thou this woman send away!"
She said: and more she could not say:
For what she knew she could not tell,
620   O'er-mastered by the mighty spell.

Why is thy cheek so wan and wild,
Sir Leoline? Thy only child
Lies at thy feet, thy joy, thy pride,
So fair, so innocent, so mild;
625   The same, for whom thy lady died!
O by the pangs of her dear mother
Think thou no evil of thy child!
For her, and thee, and for no other,
She prayed the moment ere she died:

630   Prayed that the babe for whom she died,
      Might prove her dear lord's joy and pride!
          That prayer her deadly pangs beguiled,
              Sir Leoline!
          And wouldst thou wrong thy only child,
635   Her child and thine?

      Within the Baron's heart and brain
      If thoughts, like these, had any share,
      They only swelled his rage and pain,
      And did but work confusion there.
640   His heart was cleft with pain and rage,
      His cheeks they quivered, his eyes were wild,
      Dishonoured thus in his old age;
      Dishonoured by his only child,
      And all his hospitality
645   To the wrong'd daughter of his friend
      By more than woman's jealousy
      Brought thus to a disgraceful end—
      He rolled his eye with stern regard
      Upon the gentle minstrel bard,
650   And said in tones abrupt, austere—
      "Why, Bracy! dost thou loiter here?
      I bade thee hence!" The bard obeyed;
      And turning from his own sweet maid,
      The aged knight, Sir Leoline,
655   Led forth the lady Geraldine!

                  The Conclusion to Part 2

      A little child, a limber elf,
      Singing, dancing to itself,
      A fairy thing with red round cheeks,
      That always finds, and never seeks,
660   Makes such a vision to the sight
      As fills a father's eyes with light;
      And pleasures flow in so thick and fast
      Upon his heart, that he at last
      Must needs express his love's excess
665   With words of unmeant bitterness.
      Perhaps 'tis pretty to force together
      Thoughts so all unlike each other;
      To mutter and mock a broken charm,
      To dally with wrong that does no harm.
670   Perhaps 'tis tender too and pretty
      At each wild word to feel within
      A sweet recoil of love and pity.
      And what, if in a world of sin
      (O sorrow and shame should this be true!)
675   Such giddiness of heart and brain
      Comes seldom save from rage and pain,
      So talks as it's most used to do.

1798–1800   1816

Frost at Midnight[1]

The frost performs its secret ministry,
Unhelped by any wind. The owlet's cry
Came loud—and hark, again! loud as before.
The inmates of my cottage, all at rest,
5   Have left me to that solitude, which suits
Abstruser musings: save that at my side
My cradled infant slumbers peacefully.
'Tis calm indeed! so calm, that it disturbs
And vexes meditation with its strange
10   And extreme silentness. Sea, hill, and wood,
This populous village! Sea, and hill, and wood,
With all the numberless goings on of life,
Inaudible as dreams! the thin blue flame
Lies on my low burnt fire, and quivers not;
15   Only that film,[2] which fluttered on the grate,
Still flutters there, the sole unquiet thing.
Methinks, its motion in this hush of nature
Gives it dim sympathies with me who live,
Making it a companionable form,
20   Whose puny flaps and freaks the idling Spirit
By its own moods interprets, every where
Echo or mirror seeking of itself,
And makes a toy of Thought.

                  But O! how oft,
How oft, at school, with most believing mind,
25   Presageful, have I gazed upon the bars,
To watch that fluttering stranger! and as oft
With unclosed lids, already had I dreamt
Of my sweet birth-place,[3] and the old church-tower,
Whose bells, the poor man's only music, rang
30   From morn to evening, all the hot Fair-day,
So sweetly, that they stirred and haunted me
With a wild pleasure, falling on mine ear
Most like articulate sounds of things to come!
So gazed I, till the soothing things I dreamt
35   Lulled me to sleep, and sleep prolonged my dreams!
And so I brooded all the following morn,
Awed by the stern preceptor's[4] face, mine eye

---

1. The scene is Coleridge's cottage at Nether Stowey; the infant in line 7 is his son Hartley, then aged seventeen months.
2. In all parts of the kingdom these films are called *strangers* and supposed to portend the arrival of some absent friend [Coleridge's note]. The "film" is a piece of soot fluttering on the bar of the grate. Cf. Cowper's *The Task* 4.292–95, in which the poet describes how, dreaming before the parlor fire, he watches "The sooty films that play upon the bars, / Pendulous and foreboding, in the view / Of superstition prophesying still, / Though still deceived, some stranger's near approach." Several editions of Cowper's poems were advertised on the verso of the last page of Coleridge's text in the 1798 volume in which "Frost at Midnight" was first published.
3. Coleridge was born at Ottery St. Mary, Devonshire, but went to school in London, beginning at the age of nine.
4. The Reverend James Boyer at Coleridge's school, Christ's Hospital.

Fixed with mock study on my swimming book:
Save if the door half opened, and I snatched
40 A hasty glance, and still my heart leaped up,
For still I hoped to see the stranger's face,
Townsman, or aunt, or sister more beloved,
My play-mate when we both were clothed alike!⁵

    Dear Babe, that sleepest cradled by my side,
45 Whose gentle breathings, heard in this deep calm,
Fill up the interspersed vacancies
And momentary pauses of the thought!
My babe so beautiful! it thrills my heart
With tender gladness, thus to look at thee,
50 And think that thou shalt learn far other lore
And in far other scenes! For I was reared
In the great city, pent 'mid cloisters dim,
And saw nought lovely but the sky and stars.
But thou, my babe! shalt wander like a breeze
55 By lakes and sandy shores, beneath the crags
Of ancient mountain, and beneath the clouds,
Which image in their bulk both lakes and shores
And mountain crags: so shalt thou see and hear
The lovely shapes and sounds intelligible
60 Of that eternal language, which thy God
Utters, who from eternity doth teach
Himself in all, and all things in himself.
Great universal Teacher! he shall mould
Thy spirit, and by giving make it ask.

65   Therefore all seasons shall be sweet to thee,
Whether the summer clothe the general earth
With greenness, or the redbreast sit and sing
Betwixt the tufts of snow on the bare branch
Of mossy apple-tree, while the nigh thatch
70 Smokes in the sun-thaw; whether the eave-drops fall
Heard only in the trances of the blast,
Or if the secret ministry of frost
Shall hang them up in silent icicles,
Quietly shining to the quiet Moon.

Feb. 1798   1798

---

5. I.e., when both Coleridge and his sister Ann still wore infant clothes, before he was deemed old enough to be breeched.

Dejection: An Ode[1]

> Late, late yestreen I saw the new Moon,
> With the old Moon in her arms;
> And I fear, I fear, my Master dear!
> We shall have a deadly storm.
> *Ballad of Sir Patrick Spence*

I

Well! If the Bard was weather-wise, who made
The grand old ballad of Sir Patrick Spence,
This night, so tranquil now, will not go hence
Unroused by winds, that ply a busier trade
5 Than those which mould yon cloud in lazy flakes,
Or the dull sobbing draft, that moans and rakes
    Upon the strings of this Eolian lute,[2]
    Which better far were mute.
  For lo! the New-moon winter-bright!
10 And overspread with phantom light,
  (With swimming phantom light o'erspread
  But rimmed and circled by a silver thread)
I see the old Moon in her lap, foretelling
The coming on of rain and squally blast.
15 And oh! that even now the gust were swelling,
  And the slant night-shower driving loud and fast!
Those sounds which oft have raised me, whilst they awed,
    And sent my soul abroad,
Might now perhaps their wonted° impulse give,   *customary*
20 Might startle this dull pain, and make it move and live!

2

A grief without a pang, void, dark, and drear,
  A stifled, drowsy, unimpassioned grief,
  Which finds no natural outlet, no relief,
    In word, or sigh, or tear—
25 O Lady![3] in this wan and heartless mood,
To other thoughts by yonder throstle woo'd,
  All this long eve, so balmy and serene,
Have I been gazing on the western sky,
  And its peculiar tint of yellow green:
30 And still I gaze—and with how blank an eye!

1. This poem originated in a verse letter of 340 lines, called "A Letter to ———," that Coleridge wrote on the night of April 4, 1802, after hearing the opening stanzas of "Ode: Intimations of Immortality," which Wordsworth had just composed. The "Letter" was addressed to Sara Hutchinson (whom Coleridge sometimes called "Asra"), the sister of Wordsworth's fiancée, Mary. It picked up the theme of a loss in the quality of perceptual experience that Wordsworth had presented at the beginning of his "Ode." In his original poem Coleridge lamented at length his unhappy marriage and the hopelessness of his love for Sara Hutchinson. In the next six months Coleridge deleted more than half the original lines, revised and reordered the remaining passages, and so transformed a long verse confession into the compact and dignified "Dejection: An Ode." He published the "Ode," in substantially its present form, on October 4, 1802, Wordsworth's wedding day—and also the seventh anniversary of Coleridge's own disastrous marriage to Sara Fricker.
2. A stringed instrument played upon by the wind (see "The Eolian Harp," n. 1, p. 1612).
3. In the original version "Sara"—i.e., Sara Hutchinson. After intervening versions, in which the poem was addressed first to "William" (Wordsworth) and then to "Edmund," Coleridge introduced the noncommittal "Lady" in 1817.

And those thin clouds above, in flakes and bars,
That give away their motion to the stars;
Those stars, that glide behind them or between,
Now sparkling, now bedimmed, but always seen:
35 Yon crescent Moon as fixed as if it grew
In its own cloudless, starless lake of blue;
I see them all so excellently fair,
I see, not feel, how beautiful they are!

3

My genial° spirits fail;   creative
40   And what can these avail
To lift the smothering weight from off my breast?
        It were a vain endeavour,
        Though I should gaze for ever
On that green light that lingers in the west:
45 I may not hope from outward forms to win
The passion and the life, whose fountains are within.

4

O Lady! we receive but what we give,
And in our life alone does nature live:
Ours is her wedding-garment, ours her shroud!⁴
50   And would we aught° behold, of higher worth,   anything
Than that inanimate cold world allowed
To the poor loveless ever-anxious crowd,
        Ah! from the soul itself must issue forth,
A light, a glory,⁵ a fair luminous cloud
55   Enveloping the Earth—
And from the soul itself must there be sent
        A sweet and potent voice, of its own birth,
Of all sweet sounds the life and element!

5

O pure of heart! thou need'st not ask of me
60 What this strong music in the soul may be!
What, and wherein it doth exist,
This light, this glory, this fair luminous mist,
This beautiful and beauty-making power.
        Joy, virtuous Lady! Joy that ne'er was given,
65 Save to the pure, and in their purest hour,
Life, and Life's effluence, cloud at once and shower,
Joy, Lady! is the spirit and the power,
Which wedding Nature to us gives in dower,
        A new Earth and new Heaven,⁶
70 Undreamt of by the sensual and the proud—
Joy is the sweet voice, Joy the luminous cloud—

---

4. I.e., nature's wedding garment and shroud are ours to give to her.
5. A "glory" is a halo. Coleridge often uses the term to identify in particular the phenomenon that occurs in the mountains when a walker sees his or her own figure projected by the sun in the mist, enlarged and with light encircling its head. Cf. Wordsworth's *Prelude* 8.268–70.

6. The sense becomes clearer if line 68 is punctuated in the way that Coleridge punctuated it when quoting the passage in one of his essays: "Which, wedding Nature to us, gives in dower." I.e., Joy marries us to Nature and gives us, for our dowry, "a new Earth and a new Heaven," a phrase echoing Revelation 21.1.

We in ourselves rejoice!
And thence flows all that charms or ear or sight,
All melodies the echoes of that voice,
75   All colours a suffusion from that light.

6

There was a time when, though my path was rough,
  This joy within me dallied with distress,
And all misfortunes were but as the stuff
  Whence Fancy made me dreams of happiness:
80 For hope grew round me, like the twining vine,
And fruits, and foliage, not my own, seemed mine.
But now afflictions bow me down to earth:
Nor care I that they rob me of my mirth,
  But oh! each visitation°   *i.e., of affliction*
85 Suspends what nature gave me at my birth,
  My shaping spirit of Imagination.
For not to think of what I needs must feel,
  But to be still and patient, all I can;
And haply by abstruse research to steal
90   From my own nature all the natural man—
This was my sole resource, my only plan:
Till that which suits a part infects the whole,
And now is almost grown the habit of my soul.

7

Hence, viper thoughts, that coil around my mind,
95   Reality's dark dream!
I turn from you, and listen to the wind,
  Which long has raved unnoticed. What a scream
Of agony by torture lengthened out
That lute sent forth! Thou Wind, that ravest without,
100   Bare crag, or mountain-tairn,[7] or blasted tree,
Or pine-grove whither woodman never clomb,°   *climbed*
Or lonely house, long held the witches' home,
  Methinks were fitter instruments for thee,
Mad Lutanist! who in this month of showers,
105 Of dark brown gardens, and of peeping flowers,
Mak'st Devils' yule,[8] with worse than wintry song,
The blossoms, buds, and timorous leaves among.
  Thou Actor, perfect in all tragic sounds!
Thou mighty Poet, e'en to frenzy bold!
110   What tell'st thou now about?
  'Tis of the rushing of a host in rout,
With groans of trampled men, with smarting wounds—
At once they groan with pain, and shudder with the cold!
But hush! there is a pause of deepest silence!
115   And all that noise, as of a rushing crowd,
With groans, and tremulous shudderings—all is over—
  It tells another tale, with sounds less deep and loud!
  A tale of less affright,
  And tempered with delight,

7. Tarn, or mountain pool.
8. Christmas as, in a perverted form, it is celebrated by devils.

120   As Otway's⁹ self had framed the tender lay,
            'Tis of a little child
            Upon a lonesome wild,
        Not far from home, but she hath lost her way:
        And now moans low in bitter grief and fear,
125   And now screams loud, and hopes to make her mother hear.

                                8

        'Tis midnight, but small thoughts have I of sleep:
        Full seldom may my friend such vigils keep!
        Visit her, gentle Sleep! with wings of healing,
            And may this storm be but a mountain-birth,¹
130   May all the stars hang bright above her dwelling,
            Silent as though they watched the sleeping Earth!
                With light heart may she rise,
                Gay fancy, cheerful eyes,
            Joy lift her spirit, joy attune her voice;
135   To her may all things live, from pole to pole,
            Their life the eddying of her living soul!
                O simple spirit, guided from above,
            Dear Lady! friend devoutest of my choice,
            Thus mayest thou ever, evermore rejoice.

Apr. 4, 1802   1802

                        The Pains of Sleep¹

            Ere on my bed my limbs I lay,
            It hath not been my use to pray
            With moving lips or bended knees;
            But silently, by slow degrees,
5   My spirit I to Love compose,
            In humble trust mine eye-lids close,
            With reverential resignation,
            No wish conceived, no thought exprest,
            Only a sense of supplication;
10   A sense o'er all my soul imprest
            That I am weak, yet not unblest,
            Since in me, round me, every where
            Eternal strength and wisdom are.

            But yester-night I prayed aloud
15   In anguish and in agony,

<hr>

9. Thomas Otway (1652–1685), a dramatist noted for the pathos of his tragic passages. The poet originally named was "William," and the allusion was probably to Wordsworth's "Lucy Gray."
1. Probably, "May this be a typical mountain storm, short though violent," although Coleridge might have intended an allusion to Horace's phrase "the mountain labored and brought forth a mouse."
1. Coleridge included a draft of this poem in a letter to Robert Southey, September 11, 1803, in which he wrote that "my spirits are dreadful, owing entirely to the Horrors of every night—I truly dread to sleep. It is no shadow with me, but substantial Misery foot-thick, that makes me sit by my bedside of a morning, & cry—. I have abandoned all opiates except Ether be one; & that only in *fits*. . . . " The last sentence indicates what Coleridge did not know—that his guilty nightmares were probably withdrawal symptoms from opium. The dreams he describes are very similar to those that De Quincey represents as "The Pains of Opium" in his *Confessions of an English Opium-Eater.*

Up-starting from the fiendish crowd
Of shapes and thoughts that tortured me:
A lurid light, a trampling throng,
Sense of intolerable wrong,
20   And whom I scorned, those only strong!
Thirst of revenge, the powerless will
Still baffled, and yet burning still!
Desire with loathing strangely mixed
On wild or hateful objects fixed.
25   Fantastic passions! maddening brawl!
And shame and terror over all!
Deeds to be hid which were not hid,
Which all confused I could not know,
Whether I suffered, or I did:
30   For all seemed guilt, remorse or woe,
My own or others still the same
Life-stifling fear, soul-stifling shame.

So two nights passed: the night's dismay
Saddened and stunned the coming day.
35   Sleep, the wide blessing, seemed to me
Distemper's worst calamity.
The third night, when my own loud scream
Had waked me from the fiendish dream,
O'ercome with sufferings strange and wild,
40   I wept as I had been a child;
And having thus by tears subdued
My anguish to a milder mood,
Such punishments, I said, were due
To natures deepliest stained with sin,—
45   For aye entempesting anew
The unfathomable hell within,
The horror of their deeds to view,
To know and loathe, yet wish and do!
Such griefs with such men well agree,
50   But wherefore, wherefore fall on me?
To be beloved is all I need,
And whom I love, I love indeed.

1803   1816

To William Wordsworth

Composed on the Night after His Recitation of a Poem on the Growth of an Individual Mind[1]

Friend of the wise! and teacher of the good!
Into my heart have I received that lay°   *song*

1. This was the poem (later called *The Prelude*), addressed to Coleridge, that Wordsworth had completed in 1805. After Coleridge returned from Malta, very low in health and spirits, Wordsworth read the poem aloud to him during the evenings of almost two weeks. Coleridge wrote most of the present response immediately after the reading was completed, on January 7, 1807.

More than historic, that prophetic lay
Wherein (high theme by thee first sung aright)
5 Of the foundations and the building up
Of a Human Spirit thou hast dared to tell
What may be told, to the understanding mind
Revealable; and what within the mind
By vital breathings secret as the soul
10 Of vernal° growth, oft quickens in the heart   springtime
Thoughts all too deep for words!²—

                              Theme hard as high!
Of smiles spontaneous, and mysterious fears
(The first-born they of Reason and twin birth),
Of tides obedient to external force,
15 And currents self-determined, as might seem,
Or by some inner power; of moments awful,°   awe-inspiring
Now in thy inner life, and now abroad,
When power streamed from thee, and thy soul received
The light reflected, as a light bestowed—
20 Of fancies fair, and milder hours of youth,
Hyblean³ murmurs of poetic thought
Industrious in its joy, in vales and glens
Native or outland, lakes and famous hills!
Or on the lonely high-road, when the stars
25 Were rising; or by secret mountain-streams,
The guides and the companions of thy way!

    Of more than Fancy, of the Social Sense
Distending wide, and man beloved as man,
Where France in all her towns lay vibrating
30 Like some becalmed bark beneath the burst
Of Heaven's immediate thunder, when no cloud
Is visible, or shadow on the main.
For thou wert there, thine own brows garlanded,
Amid the tremor of a realm aglow,
35 Amid a mighty nation jubilant,
When from the general heart of human kind
Hope sprang forth like a full-born Deity!
——Of that dear Hope afflicted and struck down,
So summoned homeward, thenceforth calm and sure
40 From the dread watch-tower of man's absolute self,
With light unwaning on her eyes, to look
Far on—herself a glory to behold,
The Angel of the vision! Then (last strain)
Of Duty, chosen laws controlling choice,
45 Action and joy!—An Orphic song⁴ indeed,
A song divine of high and passionate thoughts
To their own music chanted!

---

2. Wordsworth had described the effect on his
mind of the animating breeze ("vital breathings")
in *The Prelude* 1.1–44. "Thoughts . . . words" echoes the last line of Wordsworth's "Intimations"
ode. Coleridge goes on to summarize the major

themes and events of *The Prelude*.
3. Sweet. Hybla, in ancient Sicily, was famous for
its honey.
4. As enchanting and oracular as the song of the
legendary Orpheus. There may also be an allusion

O great Bard!
Ere yet that last strain dying awed the air,
With steadfast eye I viewed thee in the choir
50 Of ever-enduring men. The truly great
Have all one age, and from one visible space
Shed influence! They, both in power and act,
Are permanent, and Time is not with them,
Save as it worketh for them, they in it.
55 Nor less a sacred roll, than those of old,
And to be placed, as they, with gradual fame
Among the archives of mankind, thy work
Makes audible a linked lay of Truth,
Of Truth profound a sweet continuous lay,
60 Not learnt, but native, her own natural notes!
Ah! as I listened with a heart forlorn,
The pulses of my being beat anew:
And even as life returns upon the drowned,
Life's joy rekindling roused a throng of pains—
65 Keen pangs of Love, awakening as a babe
Turbulent, with an outcry in the heart;
And fears self-willed, that shunned the eye of hope;
And hope that scarce would know itself from fear;
Sense of past youth, and manhood come in vain,
70 And genius given, and knowledge won in vain;
And all which I had culled in wood-walks wild,
And all which patient toil had reared, and all,
Commune with thee had opened out—but flowers
Strewed on my corse, and borne upon my bier,
75 In the same coffin, for the self-same grave!

That way no more! and ill beseems it me,
Who came a welcomer in herald's guise,
Singing of glory, and futurity,
To wander back on such unhealthful road,
80 Plucking the poisons of self-harm! And ill
Such intertwine beseems triumphal wreaths
Strewed before thy advancing!

Nor do thou,
Sage Bard! impair the memory of that hour
Of thy communion with my nobler mind[5]
85 By pity or grief, already felt too long!
Nor let my words import more blame than needs.
The tumult rose and ceased: for peace is nigh
Where wisdom's voice has found a listening heart.
Amid the howl of more than wintry storms,
90 The halcyon[6] hears the voice of vernal hours
Already on the wing.

---

to the Orphic mysteries, involving spiritual death
and rebirth (see lines 61–66). "The Angel of the
vision" (line 43) probably alludes to "the great
vision of the guarded mount" in Milton's "Lycidas,"
line 161.

5. I.e., during the early association between the
two poets (1797–98).
6. A fabled bird, able to calm the sea where it
nested in winter.

Eve following eve,[7]
Dear tranquil time, when the sweet sense of Home
Is sweetest! moments for their own sake hailed
And more desired, more precious for thy song,
95   In silence listening, like a devout child,
My soul lay passive, by thy various strain
Driven as in surges now beneath the stars,
With momentary stars of my own birth,
Fair constellated foam, still darting off
100   Into the darkness; now a tranquil sea,
Outspread and bright, yet swelling to the moon.

And when—O Friend! my comforter and guide!
Strong in thyself, and powerful to give strength!—
Thy long sustained Song finally closed,
105   And thy deep voice had ceased—yet thou thyself
Wert still before my eyes, and round us both
That happy vision of beloved faces—
Scarce conscious, and yet conscious of its close
I sate, my being blended in one thought
110   (Thought was it? or aspiration? or resolve?)
Absorbed, yet hanging still upon the sound—
And when I rose, I found myself in prayer.

1807   1817

Epitaph[1]

Stop, Christian Passer-by!—Stop, child of God,
And read with gentle breast. Beneath this sod
A poet lies, or that which once seem'd he.—
O, lift one thought in prayer for S. T. C.;
5   That he who many a year with toil of breath
Found death in life, may here find life in death!
Mercy for praise—to be forgiven for[2] fame
He ask'd, and hoped, through Christ. Do thou the same!

1833   1834

Biographia Literaria   In March 1815 Coleridge was preparing a collected edition of his poems and planned to include "a general preface . . . on the principles of philosophic and genial criticism." As was typical for Coleridge, the materials developed as he worked on them until, on July 29, he declared that the preface had expanded to become a book in its own right, an "Autobiographia Literaria." In a characteristic Romantic reinvention of autobiography, the work merged personal experience with philosophical speculation, as well as with what Coleridge identified

---

7. The evenings during which Wordsworth read his poem aloud.
1. Written by Coleridge the year before he died. One version that he sent in a letter had as a title: "Epitaph on a Poet little known, yet better known

by the Initials of his name than by the Name Itself."
2. "For" in the sense of "instead of" [Coleridge's note].

as "digression and anecdotes." It was to consist of two main parts, "my literary life and opinions, as far as poetry and *poetical* criticism [are] concerned" and a critique of Wordsworth's theory of poetic diction. This work was ready by September 17, 1815, but the *Biographia Literaria,* in two volumes, was not published until July 1817. The delay was caused by a series of miscalculations by his printer, which forced Coleridge to add 150 pages of miscellaneous materials to pad out the length of the second volume.

Coleridge had been planning a detailed critique of Wordsworth's theory of poetic diction ever since 1802, when he had detected "a radical difference in our theoretical opinions respecting poetry." In the selection from chapter 17, Coleridge agrees with Wordsworth's general aim of reforming the artifices of current poetic diction, but he sharply denies Wordsworth's claim that there is no essential difference between the language of poetry and the language spoken by people in real life. The other selections printed here are devoted mainly to the central principle of Coleridge's own critical theory, the distinction between the mechanical "fancy" and the organic imagination, which is tersely summarized in the conclusion to chapter 13. The definition of poetry at the end of chapter 14, develops at greater length the nature of the "synthetic and magical power . . . of imagination," which, for Coleridge, has the capacity to dissolve the divisions (between, for instance, the perceiving human subject and his or her objects of perception) that characterize human beings' fallen state.

From Biographia Literaria

From *Chapter 4*

[MR. WORDSWORTH'S EARLIER POEMS]

* * * During the last year of my residence at Cambridge, I became acquainted with Mr. Wordsworth's first publication, entitled *Descriptive Sketches;*[1] and seldom, if ever, was the emergence of an original poetic genius above the literary horizon more evidently announced. In the form, style, and manner of the whole poem, and in the structure of the particular lines and periods, there is a harshness and acerbity connected and combined with words and images all a-glow which might recall those products of the vegetable world, where gorgeous blossoms rise out of the hard and thorny rind and shell within which the rich fruit was elaborating. The language was not only peculiar and strong, but at times knotty and contorted, as by its own impatient strength; while the novelty and struggling crowd of images, acting in conjunction with the difficulties of the style, demanded always a greater closeness of attention than poetry (at all events than descriptive poetry) has a right to claim. It not seldom therefore justified the complaint of obscurity. In the following extract I have sometimes fancied that I saw an emblem of the poem itself and of the author's genius as it was then displayed:

> 'Tis storm; and hid in mist from hour to hour,
> All day the floods a deepening murmur pour;
> The sky is veiled, and every cheerful sight:
> Dark is the region as with coming night;
> And yet what frequent bursts of overpowering light!
> Triumphant on the bosom of the storm,

---

1. Published 1793, the year before Coleridge left Cambridge; a long descriptive-meditative poem in closed couplets, recounting Wordsworth's walking tour in the Alps in 1790. Wordsworth describes the same tour in *The Prelude,* book 6.

Glances the fire-clad eagle's wheeling form;
Eastward, in long perspective glittering, shine
The wood-crowned cliffs that o'er the lake recline;
Wide o'er the Alps a hundred streams unfold,
At once to pillars turned that flame with gold;
Behind his sail the peasant strives to shun
The West, that burns like one dilated sun,
Where in a mighty crucible expire
The mountains, glowing hot, like coals of fire.[2]

The poetic Psyche, in its process to full development, undergoes as many changes as its Greek namesake, the butterfly.[3] And it is remarkable how soon genius clears and purifies itself from the faults and errors of its earliest products; faults which, in its earliest compositions, are the more obtrusive and confluent because, as heterogeneous elements which had only a temporary use, they constitute the very-*ferment* by which themselves are carried off. Or we may compare them to some diseases, which must work on the humors and be thrown out on the surface in order to secure the patient from their future recurrence. I was in my twenty-fourth year when I had the happiness of knowing Mr. Wordsworth personally;[4] and, while memory lasts, I shall hardly forget the sudden effect produced on my mind by his recitation of a manuscript poem which still remains unpublished, but of which the stanza and tone of style were the same as those of *The Female Vagrant* as originally printed in the first volume of the *Lyrical Ballads*.[5] There was here no mark of strained thought or forced diction, no crowd or turbulence of imagery, and, as the poet hath himself well described in his lines on revisiting the Wye,[6] manly reflection and human associations had given both variety and an additional interest to natural objects which in the passion and appetite of the first love they had seemed to him neither to need or permit. The occasional obscurities, which had risen from an imperfect control over the resources of his native language, had almost wholly disappeared, together with that worse defect of arbitrary and illogical phrases, at once hackneyed and fantastic, which hold so distinguished a place in the *technique* of ordinary poetry and will, more or less, alloy the earlier poems of the truest genius, unless the attention has been specifically directed to their worthlessness and incongruity. I did not perceive anything particular in the mere style of the poem alluded to during its recitation, except indeed such difference as was not separable from the thought and manner; and the Spenserian stanza which always, more or less, recalls to the reader's mind Spenser's own style, would doubtless have authorized in my then opinion a more frequent descent to the phrases of ordinary life than could, without an ill effect, have been hazarded in the heroic couplet. It was not however the freedom from false taste, whether as to common defects or to those more properly his own, which made so unusual an impression on my feelings immediately, and subsequently on my judgment. It was the union of deep feeling with profound thought; the fine balance of truth in observing with the imaginative faculty in modifying the objects observed; and above all the original

2. *Descriptive Sketches* (1815 version), lines 332ff.
3. In Greek, Psyche is the common name for the soul and the butterfly [Coleridge's note].
4. The meeting occurred in September 1795.
5. *Salisbury Plain* (1793–94), which was left in

manuscript until Wordsworth published a revised version in 1842 under the title "Guilt and Sorrow." An excerpt from *Salisbury Plain* was printed as "The Female Vagrant," in *Lyrical Ballads* (1798).
6. Wordsworth's "Tintern Abbey," lines 76ff.

gift of spreading the tone, the *atmosphere,* and with it the depth and height of the ideal world, around forms, incidents, and situations of which, for the common view, custom had bedimmed all the luster, had dried up the sparkle and the dewdrops. "To find no contradiction in the union of old and new, to contemplate the Ancient of Days and all his works with feelings as fresh as if all had then sprang forth at the first creative fiat,[7] characterizes the mind that feels the riddle of the world and may help to unravel it. To carry on the feelings of childhood into the powers of manhood; to combine the child's sense of wonder and novelty with the appearances which every day for perhaps forty years had rendered familiar;

> With sun and moon and stars throughout the year,
> And man and woman;[8]

this is the character and privilege of genius, and one of the marks which distinguish genius from talents. And therefore it is the prime merit of genius, and its most unequivocal mode of manifestation, so to represent familiar objects as to awaken in the minds of others a kindred feeling concerning them, and that freshness of sensation which is the constant accompaniment of mental no less than of bodily convalescence. Who has not a thousand times seen snow fall on water? Who has not watched it with a new feeling from the time that he has read Burns' comparison of sensual pleasure

> To snow that falls upon a river
> A moment white—then gone forever![9]

In poems, equally as in philosophic disquisitions, genius produces the strongest impressions of novelty while it rescues the most admitted truths from the impotence caused by the very circumstance of their universal admission. Truths of all others the most awful and mysterious, yet being at the same time of universal interest, are too often considered as *so* true, that they lose all the life and efficiency of truth and lie bedridden in the dormitory of the soul side by side with the most despised and exploded errors." *The Friend,* p. 76, no. 5.[1]

[ON FANCY AND IMAGINATION—THE INVESTIGATION OF THE DISTINCTION IMPORTANT TO THE FINE ARTS]

This excellence, which in all Mr. Wordsworth's writings is more or less predominant and which constitutes the character of his mind, I no sooner felt than I sought to understand. Repeated meditations led me first to suspect (and a more intimate analysis of the human faculties, their appropriate marks, functions, and effects, matured my conjecture into full conviction) that fancy and imagination were two distinct and widely different faculties, instead of being, according to the general belief, either two names with one meaning, or at furthest the lower and higher degree of one and the same power. It is not, I own, easy to conceive a more apposite translation of the Greek *phantasia* than the Latin *imaginatio;* but it is equally true that in all societies there exists an instinct of growth, a certain collective unconscious good sense working progressively to desynonymize those words originally of the same meaning which

---

7. The first divine command: "Let there be light."
8. Altered from Milton's sonnet "To Mr. Cyriack Skinner upon His Blindness."

9. Altered from Burns's "Tam o' Shanter," lines 61–62.
1. A periodical published by Coleridge (1809–10).

the conflux of dialects had supplied to the more homogeneous languages, as the Greek and German: and which the same cause, joined with accidents of translation from original works of different countries, occasion in mixed languages like our own. The first and most important point to be proved is, that two conceptions perfectly distinct are confused under one and the same word, and (this done) to appropriate that word exclusively to one meaning, and the synonym (should there be one) to the other. But if (as will be often the case in the arts and sciences) no synonym exists, we must either invent or borrow a word. In the present instance the appropriation had already begun and been legitimated in the derivative adjective: Milton had a highly *imaginative*, Cowley a very *fanciful*, mind. If therefore I should succeed in establishing the actual existence of two faculties generally different, the nomenclature would be at once determined. To the faculty by which I had characterized Milton we should confine the term *imagination*; while the other would be contra-distinguished as *fancy*. Now were it once fully ascertained that this division is no less grounded in nature than that of delirium from mania, or Otway's

> Lutes, lobsters, seas of milk, and ships of amber,[2]

from Shakespeare's

> What! have his daughters brought him to this pass?[3]

or from the preceding apostrophe to the elements, the theory of the fine arts and of poetry in particular could not, I thought, but derive some additional and important light. It would in its immediate effects furnish a torch of guidance to the philosophical critic, and ultimately to the poet himself. In energetic minds truth soon changes by domestication into power; and from directing in the discrimination and appraisal of the product becomes influencive in the production. To admire on principle is the only way to imitate without loss of originality. * * *

From *Chapter 13*

[ON THE IMAGINATION, OR ESEMPLASTIC[4] POWER]

* * * The IMAGINATION, then, I consider either as primary, or secondary. The primary IMAGINATION I hold to be the living power and prime agent of all human perception, and as a repetition in the finite mind of the eternal act of creation in the infinite I AM. The secondary I consider as an echo of the former, coexisting with the conscious will, yet still as identical with the primary in the *kind* of its agency, and differing only in *degree*, and in the *mode* of its operation. It dissolves, diffuses, dissipates, in order to recreate; or where this process is rendered impossible, yet still, at all events, it struggles to idealize and to unify. It is essentially *vital*, even as all objects (*as* objects) are essentially fixed and dead.

FANCY, on the contrary, has no other counters to play with but fixities and definites. The fancy is indeed no other than a mode of memory emancipated from the order of time and space; and blended with, and modified by that

2. Thomas Otway, in *Venice Preserved* (1682), wrote "laurels" in place of "lobsters" (5.2.151).
3. *King Lear* 3.4.59.

4. Coleridge coined this word and used it to mean "molding into unity."

empirical phenomenon of the will which we express by the word CHOICE. But equally with the ordinary memory it must receive all its materials ready made from the law of association.[5] * * *

Chapter 14

OCCASION OF THE *LYRICAL BALLADS*, AND THE OBJECTS ORIGINALLY
PROPOSED—PREFACE TO THE SECOND EDITION—THE ENSUING
CONTROVERSY, ITS CAUSES AND ACRIMONY—PHILOSOPHIC DEFINITIONS
OF A POEM AND POETRY WITH SCHOLIA.[6]

During the first year that Mr. Wordsworth and I were neighbours,[7] our conversations turned frequently on the two cardinal points of poetry, the power of exciting the sympathy of the reader by a faithful adherence to the truth of nature, and the power of giving the interest of novelty by the modifying colors of imagination.[8] The sudden charm which accidents of light and shade, which moonlight or sunset diffused over a known and familiar landscape, appeared to represent the practicability of combining both. These are the poetry of nature. The thought suggested itself (to which of us I do not recollect) that a series of poems might be composed of two sorts. In the one, the incidents and agents were to be, in part at least, supernatural; and the excellence aimed at was to consist in the interesting of the affections by the dramatic truth of such emotions as would naturally accompany such situations, supposing them real. And real in *this* sense they have been to every human being who, from whatever source of delusion, has at any time believed himself under supernatural agency. For the second class, subjects were to be chosen from ordinary life; the characters and incidents were to be such as will be found in every village and its vicinity where there is a meditative and feeling mind to seek after them, or to notice them when they present themselves.

In this idea originated the plan of the *Lyrical Ballads;* in which it was agreed that my endeavours should be directed to persons and characters supernatural, or at least romantic; yet so as to transfer from our inward nature a human interest and a semblance of truth sufficient to procure for these shadows of imagination that willing suspension of disbelief for the moment, which constitutes poetic faith. Mr. Wordsworth, on the other hand, was to propose to himself as his object to give the charm of novelty to things of every day, and to excite a feeling analogous to the supernatural, by awakening the mind's attention from the lethargy of custom and directing it to the loveliness and the wonders of the world before us; an inexhaustible treasure, but for which, in consequence of the film of familiarity and selfish solicitude, we have eyes yet see not, ears that hear not, and hearts that neither feel nor understand.[9]

With this view I wrote *The Ancient Mariner,* and was preparing, among other poems, *The Dark Ladie,* and the *Christabel,* in which I should have more nearly

---

5. Coleridge conceives God's creation to be a continuing process, which has an analogy in the creative perception ("primary imagination") of all human minds. The creative process is repeated, or "echoed," on still a third level, by the "secondary imagination" of the poet, which dissolves the products of primary perception to shape them into a new and unified creation—the imaginative passage or poem. The "fancy," on the other hand, can only manipulate "fixities and definites" that, linked by

association, come to it ready-made from perception.
6. Additional remarks, after a philosophic demonstration.
7. At Nether Stowey and Alfoxden, Somerset, in 1797.
8. Cf. Wordsworth's account in his Preface to *Lyrical Ballads* (p. 1495).
9. Cf. Isaiah 6.9–10.

realized my ideal than I had done in my first attempt. But Mr. Wordsworth's industry had proved so much more successful and the number of his poems so much greater, that my compositions, instead of forming a balance, appeared rather an interpolation of heterogeneous matter.[1] Mr. Wordsworth added two or three poems written in his own character, in the impassioned, lofty, and sustained diction which is characteristic of his genius. In this form the *Lyrical Ballads* were published; and were presented by him, as an *experiment*,[2] whether subjects which from their nature rejected the usual ornaments and extra-colloquial style of poems in general might not be so managed in the language of ordinary life as to produce the pleasurable interest which it is the peculiar business of poetry to impart. To the second edition[3] he added a preface of considerable length; in which, notwithstanding some passages of apparently a contrary import, he was understood to contend for the extension of this style to poetry of all kinds, and to reject as vicious and indefensible all phrases and forms of style that were not included in what he (unfortunately, I think, adopting an equivocal expression) called the language of *real* life. From this preface, prefixed to poems in which it was impossible to deny the presence of original genius, however mistaken its direction might be deemed, arose the whole long-continued controversy.[4] For from the conjunction of perceived power with supposed heresy I explain the inveteracy[5] and in some instances, I grieve to say, the acrimonious passions with which the controversy has been conducted by the assailants.

Had Mr. Wordsworth's poems been the silly, the childish things which they were for a long time described as being; had they been really distinguished from the compositions of other poets merely by meanness[6] of language and inanity of thought; had they indeed contained nothing more than what is found in the parodies and pretended imitations of them; they must have sunk at once, a dead weight, into the slough of oblivion, and have dragged the preface along with them. But year after year increased the number of Mr. Wordsworth's admirers. They were found too not in the lower classes of the reading public, but chiefly among young men of strong sensibility and meditative minds; and their admiration (inflamed perhaps in some degree by opposition) was distinguished by its intensity, I might almost say, by its *religious* fervor. These facts, and the intellectual energy of the author, which was more or less consciously felt where it was outwardly and even boisterously denied, meeting with sentiments of aversion to his opinions and of alarm at their consequences, produced an eddy of criticism which would of itself have borne up the poems by the violence with which it whirled them round and round. With many parts of this preface, in the sense attributed to them and which the words undoubtedly seem to authorize, I never concurred; but, on the contrary objected to them as erroneous in principle, and as contradictory (in appearance at least) both to other parts of the same preface and to the author's own practice in the greater number of the poems themselves. Mr. Wordsworth in his recent collection[7] has, I find, degraded this prefatory disquisition to the end of his second volume, to be read or not at the reader's choice. But he has not, as far as I can discover, announced any change in his poetic creed. At all events,

1. The first edition of *Lyrical Ballads*, published anonymously in 1798, contained nineteen poems by Wordsworth, four by Coleridge.
2. *Experiments* was the word used by Wordsworth in his *Advertisement* to the first edition.
3. Published in 1800.

4. The controversy over Wordsworth's theory and poetical practice in the literary journals of the day.
5. Deep-rooted prejudice.
6. Vulgarity.
7. *Poems*, 2 vols., 1815.

considering it as the source of a controversy in which I have been honored more than I deserve by the frequent conjunction of my name with his, I think it expedient to declare once for all in what points I coincide with his opinions, and in what points I altogether differ. But in order to render myself intelligible I must previously, in as few words as possible, explain my ideas, first, of a POEM; and secondly, of POETRY itself, in *kind* and in *essence*.

The office of philosophical *disquisition* consists in just *distinction*; while it is the privilege of the philosopher to preserve himself constantly aware that distinction is not division. In order to obtain adequate notions of any truth, we must intellectually separate its distinguishable parts; and this is the technical of philosophy. But having so done, we must then restore them in our conceptions to the unity in which they actually coexist; and this is the *result* of philosophy. A poem contains the same elements as a prose composition; the difference therefore must consist in a different combination of them, in consequence of a different object proposed. According to the difference of the object will be the difference of the combination. It is possible that the object may be merely to facilitate the recollection of any given facts or observations by artificial arrangement; and the composition will be a poem, merely because it is distinguished from prose by meter, or by rhyme, or by both conjointly. In this, the lowest sense, a man might attribute the name of a poem to the well-known enumeration of the days in the several months:

> Thirty days hath September,
> April, June, and November, etc.

and others of the same class and purpose. And as a particular pleasure is found in anticipating the recurrence of sounds and quantities, all compositions that have this charm superadded, whatever be their contents, *may* be entitled poems.

So much for the superficial *form*. A difference of object and contents supplies an additional ground of distinction. The immediate purpose may be the communication of truths; either of truth absolute and demonstrable, as in works of science; or of facts experienced and recorded, as in history. Pleasure, and that of the highest and most permanent kind, may *result* from the *attainment* of the end; but it is not itself the immediate end. In other works the communication of pleasure may be the immediate purpose; and though truth, either moral or intellectual, ought to be the *ultimate* end, yet this will distinguish the character of the author, not the class to which the work belongs. Blessed indeed is that state of society in which the immediate purpose would be baffled by the perversion of the proper ultimate end; in which no charm of diction or imagery could exempt the Bathyllus even of an Anacreon, or the Alexis of Virgil,[8] from disgust and aversion!

But the communication of pleasure may be the immediate object of a work not metrically composed; and that object may have been in a high degree attained, as in novels and romances. Would then the mere superaddition of meter, with or without rhyme, entitle *these* to the name of poems? The answer is that nothing can permanently please which does not contain in itself the reason why it is so, and not otherwise. If meter be superadded, all other parts must be made consonant with it. They must be such as to justify the perpetual and distinct attention to each part which an exact correspondent recurrence

---

8. The reference is to poems of homosexual love. Bathyllus was a beautiful boy praised by Anacreon, a Greek lyric poet (ca. 560–475 B.C.E.); Alexis was a young man loved by the shepherd Corydon in Virgil's *Eclogue* 2.

of accent and sound are calculated to excite. The final definition then, so deduced, may be thus worded. A poem is that species of composition which is opposed to works of science by proposing for its *immediate* object pleasure, not truth; and from all other species (having *this* object in common with it) it is discriminated by proposing to itself such delight from the *whole* as is compatible with a distinct gratification from each component *part*.

Controversy is not seldom excited in consequence of the disputants attaching each a different meaning to the same word; and in few instances has this been more striking than in disputes concerning the present subject. If a man chooses to call every composition a poem which is rhyme, or measure, or both, I must leave his opinion uncontroverted. The distinction is at least competent to characterize the writer's intention. If it were subjoined that the whole is likewise entertaining or affecting as a tale or as a series of interesting reflections, I of course admit this as another fit ingredient of a poem and an additional merit. But if the definition sought for be that of a *legitimate* poem, I answer it must be one the parts of which mutually support and explain each other; all in their proportion harmonizing with, and supporting the purpose and known influences of metrical arrangement. The philosophic critics of all ages coincide with the ultimate judgment of all countries in equally denying the praises of a just poem on the one hand to a series of striking lines or distichs,[9] each of which absorbing the whole attention of the reader to itself disjoins it from its context and makes it a separate whole, instead of a harmonizing part; and on the other hand, to an unsustained composition, from which the reader collects rapidly the general result unattracted by the component parts. The reader should be carried forward, not merely or chiefly by the mechanical impulse of curiosity, or by a restless desire to arrive at the final solution; but by the pleasurable activity of mind excited by the attractions of the journey itself. Like the motion of a serpent, which the Egyptians made the emblem of intellectual power; or like the path of sound through the air; at every step he pauses and half recedes, and from the retrogressive movement collects the force which again carries him onward. *"Praecipitandus est liber spiritus,"*[1] says Petronius Arbiter most happily. The epithet *liber* here balances the preceding verb; and it is not easy to conceive more meaning condensed in fewer words.

But if this should be admitted as a satisfactory character of a poem, we have still to seek for a definition of poetry. The writings of Plato, and Bishop Taylor, and the *Theoria Sacra* of Burnet,[2] furnish undeniable proofs that poetry of the highest kind may exist without meter, and even without the contradistinguishing objects of a poem. The first chapter of Isaiah (indeed a very large proportion of the whole book) is poetry in the most emphatic sense; yet it would be not less irrational than strange to assert that pleasure, and not truth, was the immediate object of the prophet. In short, whatever *specific* import we attach to the word poetry, there will be found involved in it, as a necessary consequence, that a poem of any length neither can be, nor ought to be, all poetry. Yet if a harmonious whole is to be produced, the remaining parts must be preserved in *keeping*[3] with the poetry; and this can be no otherwise effected

9. Pairs of lines.
1. "The *free* spirit [of the poet] must be hurled onward." From the *Satyricon,* by the Roman satirist Petronius Arbiter (1st century c.e.).
2. Thomas Burnet (1635?–1715), author of *The Sacred Theory of the Earth.* Bishop Jeremy Taylor (1613–1667), author of *Holy Living* and *Holy*

Dying. Coleridge greatly admired the elaborate and sonorous prose of both these writers. He took from a work by Burnet the Latin motto for *The Rime of the Ancient Mariner.*
3. A term from the theory of painting for the maintenance of the harmony of a composition.

than by such a studied selection and artificial arrangement as will partake of *one,* though not a *peculiar,* property of poetry. And this again can be no other than the property of exciting a more continuous and equal attention than the language of prose aims at, whether colloquial or written.

My own conclusions on the nature of poetry, in the strictest use of the word, have been in part anticipated in the preceding disquisition on the fancy and imagination. What is poetry? is so nearly the same question with, what is a poet? that the answer to the one is involved in the solution of the other. For it is a distinction resulting from the poetic genius itself, which sustains and modifies the images, thoughts, and emotions of the poet's own mind.

The poet, described in *ideal* perfection, brings the whole soul of man into activity, with the subordination of its faculties to each other, according to their relative worth and dignity. He diffuses a tone and spirit of unity that blends and (as it were) *fuses,* each into each, by that synthetic and magical power to which we have exclusively appropriated the name of imagination. This power, first put in action by the will and understanding and retained under their irremissive,[4] though gentle and unnoticed, control (*laxis effertur habenis*)[5] reveals itself in the balance or reconciliation of opposite or discordant qualities:[6] of sameness, with difference; of the general, with the concrete; the idea, with the image; the individual, with the representative; the sense of novelty and freshness, with old and familiar objects; a more than usual state of emotion, with more than usual order; judgment ever awake and steady self-possession, with enthusiasm and feeling profound or vehement; and while it blends and harmonizes the natural and the artificial, still subordinates art to nature; the manner to the matter; and our admiration of the poet to our sympathy with the poetry. "Doubtless," as Sir John Davies observes of the soul (and his words may with slight alteration be applied, and even more appropriately, to the poetic IMAGINATION):

> Doubtless this could not be, but that she turns
>   Bodies to spirit by sublimation strange,
> As fire converts to fire the things it burns,
>   As we our food into our nature change.
>
> From their gross matter she abstracts their forms,
>   And draws a kind of quintessence from things;
> Which to her proper nature she transforms,
>   To bear them light on her celestial wings.
>
> Thus does she, when from individual states
>   She doth abstract the universal kinds;
> Which then reclothed in divers names and fates
>   Steal access through our senses to our minds.[7]

Finally, GOOD SENSE is the BODY of poetic genius, FANCY its DRAPERY,[8] MOTION its LIFE, and IMAGINATION the SOUL that is everywhere, and in each; and forms all into one graceful and intelligent whole.

---

4. Continuous.
5. Driven with loosened reins (Latin).
6. Here Coleridge introduces the concept, which became central to the American New Critics of the mid-20th century, that the best poetry incorpo-

rates and reconciles opposite or discordant elements.
7. Adapted from John Davies's *Nosce Teipsum* ("Know Thyself"), a philosophical poem (1599).
8. Clothing.

From *Chapter 17*

[EXAMINATION OF THE TENETS PECULIAR TO MR. WORDSWORTH]

As far then as Mr. Wordsworth in his preface contended, and most ably contended, for a reformation in our poetic diction, as far as he has evinced the truth of passion, and the *dramatic* propriety of those figures and metaphors in the original poets which, stripped of their justifying reasons and converted into mere artifices of connection or ornament, constitute the characteristic falsity in the poetic style of the moderns; and as far as he has, with equal acuteness and clearness, pointed out the process by which this change was effected and the resemblances between that state into which the reader's mind is thrown by the pleasurable confusion of thought from an unaccustomed train of words and images and that state which is induced by the natural language of impassioned feeling, he undertook a useful task and deserves all praise, both for the attempt and for the execution. The provocations to this remonstrance in behalf of truth and nature were still of perpetual recurrence before and after the publication of this preface. * * *

My own differences from certain supposed parts of Mr. Wordsworth's theory ground themselves on the assumption that his words had been rightly interpreted, as purporting that the proper diction for poetry in general consists altogether in a language taken, with due exceptions, from the mouths of men in real life, a language which actually constitutes the natural conversation of men under the influence of natural feelings.[9] My objection is, first, that in *any* sense this rule is applicable only to *certain* classes of poetry; secondly, that even to these classes it is not applicable, except in such a sense as hath never by anyone (as far as I know or have read) been denied or doubted; and, lastly, that as far as, and in that degree in which it is *practicable*, yet as a *rule* it is useless, if not injurious, and therefore either need not or ought not to be practiced. * * *

[RUSTIC LIFE (ABOVE ALL, *LOW* AND RUSTIC LIFE) ESPECIALLY UNFAVORABLE TO THE FORMATION OF A HUMAN DICTION—THE BEST PARTS OF LANGUAGE THE PRODUCTS OF PHILOSOPHERS, NOT CLOWNS[1] OR SHEPHERDS]

As little can I agree with the assertion that from the objects with which the rustic hourly communicates the best part of language is formed. For first, if to communicate with an object implies such an acquaintance with it, as renders it capable of being discriminately reflected on; the distinct knowledge of an uneducated rustic would furnish a very scanty vocabulary. The few things, and modes of action, requisite for his bodily conveniences, would alone be individualized; while all the rest of nature would be expressed by a small number of confused general terms. Secondly, I deny that the words and combinations of words derived from the objects, with which the rustic is familiar, whether with distinct or confused knowledge, can be justly said to form the *best* part of language. It is more than probable that many classes of the brute creation possess discriminating sounds, by which they can convey to each other notices of such objects as concern their food, shelter, or safety. Yet we hesitate to call the aggregate of such sounds a language, otherwise than meta-

---

9. Wordsworth's Preface to *Lyrical Ballads* (1800): "A selection of the real language of men in a state of vivid sensation. . . . Low and rustic life
was generally chosen. . . . The language, too, of these men is adopted."
1. Rustic people.

phorically. The best part of human language, properly so called, is derived from reflection on the acts of the mind itself. It is formed by a voluntary appropriation of fixed symbols to internal acts, to processes and results of imagination, the greater part of which have no place in the consciousness of uneducated man; though in civilized society, by imitation and passive remembrance of what they hear from their religious instructors and other superiors, the most uneducated share in the harvest which they neither sowed or reaped. * * *

[THE LANGUAGE OF MILTON AS MUCH THE LANGUAGE OF *REAL* LIFE, YEA, INCOMPARABLY MORE SO THAN THAT OF THE COTTAGER]

Here let me be permitted to remind the reader that the positions which I controvert are contained in the sentences—"a selection of the REAL language of men"; "the language of these men (i.e., men in low and rustic life) I propose to myself to imitate, and as far as possible to adopt the very language of men." "Between the language of prose and that of metrical composition there neither is, nor can be any essential difference." It is against these exclusively that my opposition is directed.

I object, in the very first instance, to an equivocation in the use of the word "real." Every man's language varies according to the extent of his knowledge, the activity of his faculties, and the depth or quickness of his feelings. Every man's language has, first, its *individualities;* secondly, the common properties of the *class* to which he belongs; and thirdly, words and phrases of *universal* use. The language of Hooker, Bacon, Bishop Taylor, and Burke[2] differs from the common language of the learned class only by the superior number and novelty of the thoughts and relations which they had to convey. The language of Algernon Sidney[3] differs not at all from that which every well-educated gentleman would wish to write, and (with due allowances for the undeliberateness and less connected train of thinking natural and proper to conversation) such as he would wish to talk. Neither one nor the other differ half as much from the general language of cultivated society as the language of Mr. Wordsworth's homeliest composition differs from that of a common peasant. For "real" therefore we must substitute *ordinary*, or *lingua communis.*[4] And this, we have proved, is no more to be found in the phraseology of low and rustic life than in that of any other class. Omit the peculiarities of each, and the result of course must be common to all. And assuredly the omissions and changes to be made in the language of rustics before it could be transferred to any species of poem, except the drama or other professed imitation, are at least as numerous and weighty as would be required in adapting to the same purpose the ordinary language of tradesmen and manufacturers. Not to mention that the language so highly extolled by Mr. Wordsworth varies in every county, nay, in every village, according to the accidental character of the clergyman, the existence or nonexistence of schools; or even, perhaps, as the exciseman, publican, or barber happen to be, or not to be, zealous politicians and readers of the weekly newspaper *pro bono publico.*[5] Anterior to cultivation the

2. Richard Hooker (1554–1600), author of *The Laws of Ecclesiastical Polity;* Francis Bacon (1561–1626), essayist and philosopher, and Jeremy Taylor were all, together with the late-18th-century politician and opponent of the French Revolution Edmund Burke (1729–1797), lauded for their prose styles.

3. Republican soldier and statesman (1622–1683), author of *Discourses Concerning Government,* executed for his part in the Rye House Plot to assassinate Charles II.
4. The common language (Latin).
5. For the public welfare (Latin).

lingua communis of every country, as Dante has well observed, exists every where in parts and no where as a whole.[6]

Neither is the case rendered at all more tenable by the addition of the words "in a state of excitement."[7] For the nature of a man's words, when he is strongly affected by joy, grief, or anger, must necessarily depend on the number and quality of the general truths, conceptions, and images, and of the words expressing them, with which his mind had been previously stored. For the property of passion is not to *create*, but to set in increased activity. At least, whatever new connections of thoughts or images, or (which is equally, if not more than equally, the appropriate effect of strong excitement) whatever generalizations of truth or experience the heat of passion may produce, yet the terms of their conveyance must have pre-existed in his former conversations, and are only collected and crowded together by the unusual stimulation. It is indeed very possible to adopt in a poem the unmeaning repetitions, habitual phrases, and other blank counters which an unfurnished or confused understanding interposes at short intervals in order to keep hold of his subject which is still slipping from him, and to give him time for recollection; or in mere aid of vacancy, as in the scanty companies of a country stage the same player pops backwards and forwards, in order to prevent the appearance of empty spaces, in the procession of *Macbeth* or *Henry VIIIth*. But what assistance to the poet or ornament to the poem these can supply, I am at a loss to conjecture. Nothing assuredly can differ either in origin or in mode more widely from the apparent tautologies of intense and turbulent feeling in which the passion is greater and of longer endurance than to be exhausted or satisfied by a single representation of the image or incident exciting it. Such repetitions I admit to be a beauty of the highest kind; as illustrated by Mr. Wordsworth himself from the song of Deborah. "At her feet he bowed, he fell, he lay down; at her feet he bowed, he fell; where he bowed, there he fell down dead."[8]

1815   1817

6. In *De Vulgari Eloquentia* ("On the Speech of the people") Dante discusses—and affirms—the fitness for poetry of the unlocalized Italian vernacular.
7. Wordsworth: "the manner in which we associate ideas in a state of excitement."
8. Judges 5.27. Cited by Wordsworth in a note to *The Thorn* as an example of the natural repetitiousness of "impassioned feelings."

GEORGE GORDON, LORD BYRON
1788–1824

In his *History of English Literature*, written in the late 1850s, the French critic Hippolyte Taine gave only a few condescending pages to Wordsworth, Coleridge, Percy Shelley, and Keats and then devoted a long chapter to Lord Byron, "the greatest and most English of these artists; he is so great and so English that from him alone we shall learn more truths of his country and of his age than from all the rest together." This comment reflects the fact that Byron had achieved an immense European reputation during his own lifetime, while admirers of his English contemporaries were much more limited in number. Through much of the nineteenth century he continued to be rated as one of the greatest of English poets and the very prototype of literary Romanticism. His influence was manifested everywhere, among the major poets and novelists (Balzac and Stendhal in France, Pushkin and Dostoyevsky in

Russia, and Melville in America), painters (especially Delacroix), and composers (including Beethoven and Berlioz).

Yet even as poets, painters, and composers across Europe and the Americas struck Byronic attitudes, Byron's place within the canon of English Romantic poetry was becoming insecure. The same Victorian critics who first described the Romantic period *as* a literary period warned readers against the immorality of Byron's poetry, finding in his voluptuous imagination and aristocratic disdain for the commonplace an affront to their own middle-class values: "Close thy Byron; open thy Goethe," Thomas Carlyle urged in *Sartor Resartus* (1834), meaning to redirect the nation toward healthier reading matter. After getting a glimpse of the scandalous stuff recorded in Byron's journals, Felicia Hemans ceased to wear the brooch in which she had preserved a lock of the poet's hair: she could venerate him no longer. Indeed, Byron would have had qualms about being considered a representative figure of a period that also included Wordsworth (memorialized in Byron's *Don Juan* as "Wordy") or Keats (a shabby Cockney brat, Byron claimed) or scribbling women such as Hemans. These reservations were reciprocated. Of Byron's best-known male contemporaries, only Shelley thought highly of either the man or his work (although there are signs that, among the naysayers, the negative reactions were tinged with some resentment at Byron's success in developing a style that spoke to a popular audience). Byron in fact insisted that, measured against the poetic practice of Alexander Pope, he and his contemporaries were "all in the wrong, one as much as another. . . . We are upon a wrong revolutionary poetical system, or systems, not worth a damn in itself." Pope's Horatian satires, along with Laurence Sterne's novel *Tristram Shandy*, exerted a significant influence on the style that Byron developed for his epic survey of modern folly, *Don Juan*.

Still, even as he had recourse to old-fashioned eighteenth-century models, Byron cultivated a skepticism about established systems of belief that, in its restlessness and defiance, expressed the intellectual and social ferment of his era. And through much of his best poetry, he shared his contemporaries' fascination with the internal dramas of the individual mind (although Byron explored personality in an improvisatory and mercurial manner that could not have been more different from Wordsworth's autobiographical accounts of his psychological development). Readers marveled over the intensity of the feelings his verse communicated—"its force, fire, and thought," said the novelist Lady Sydney Morgan—and the vividness of the sense of self they found in it. Byron's chief claim to be considered an arch-Romantic is that he provided the age with what Taine called its "ruling personage; that is, the model that contemporaries invest with their admiration and sympathy." This personage is the "Byronic hero." He is first sketched in the opening canto of *Childe Harold,* then recurs in various guises in the verse romances and dramas that followed. In his developed form, as we find it in *Manfred,* he is an alien, mysterious, and gloomy spirit, superior in his passions and powers to the common run of humanity, whom he regards with disdain. He harbors the torturing memory of an enormous, nameless guilt that drives him toward an inevitable doom. And he exerts an attraction on other characters that is the more compelling because it involves their terror at his obliviousness to ordinary human concerns and values. This figure, infusing the archrebel in a nonpolitical form with a strong erotic interest, was imitated in life as well as in art and helped shape the intellectual and the cultural history of the later nineteenth century. The literary descendants of the Byronic hero include Heathcliff in *Wuthering Heights,* Captain Ahab in *Moby-Dick,* and the hero of Pushkin's great poem *Eugene Onegin.* Byron also lived on in the guise of the Undead, thanks to the success of a novella by his former friend and traveling companion John Polidori, whose "The Vampyre" (1819) mischievously made Byron its model for the title character. Earlier Byron had in his writings helped introduce the English to the Eastern Mediterranean's legends of bloodsucking evil spirits; it was left to Polidori, however, to portray the vampire as a habitué of England's most fashionable social circles. The fact that, for all their menace, vampires—from Bela Lugosi's Count Dracula to Anne Rice's L'Estat—remain models of well-dressed, aristocratic elegance represents yet another tribute to the staying power of Byron's image.

Byron's contemporaries insisted on identifying the author with his fictional characters, reading his writing as veiled autobiography even when it dealt with supernatural themes. (They also read other people's writing this way: to Polidori's chagrin, authorship of "The Vampyre" was attributed to Byron.) Byron's letters and the testimony of his friends show, however, that, except for recurrent moods of deep depression, his own temperament was in many respects opposite to that of his heroes. While he was passionate and willful, he was also a witty conversationalist capable of taking an ironic attitude toward his own activities as well as those of others. But although Byronism was largely a fiction, produced by a collaboration between Byron's imagination and that of his public, the fiction was historically more important than the actual person.

Byron was descended from two aristocratic families, both of them colorful, violent, and dissolute. His grandfather was an admiral nicknamed "Foulweather Jack"; his great-uncle was the fifth Baron Byron, known to his rural neighbors as the "Wicked Lord," who was tried by his peers for killing his kinsman William Chaworth in a drunken duel; his father, Captain John Byron, was a rake and fortune hunter who rapidly spent his way through the fortunes of two wealthy wives. Byron's mother was a Scotswoman, Catherine Gordon of Gight, the last descendant of a line of lawless Scottish lairds. After her husband died (Byron was then three), she brought up her son in near poverty in Aberdeen, where he was indoctrinated with the Calvinistic morality of Scottish Presbyterianism. Catherine Byron was an ill-educated and extremely irascible woman who nevertheless had an abiding love for her son; they fought violently when together, but corresponded affectionately enough when apart, until her death in 1811.

When Byron was ten the death of his great-uncle, preceded by that of more immediate heirs to the title, made him the sixth Lord Byron. In a fashion suitable to his new status, he was sent to Harrow School, then to Trinity College, Cambridge. He had a deformed foot, made worse by inept surgical treatment, about which he felt acute embarrassment. His lameness made him avid for athletic prowess; he played cricket and made himself an expert boxer, fencer, and horseman and a powerful swimmer. Both at Cambridge and at his ancestral estate of Newstead, he engaged with more than ordinary zeal in the expensive pursuits and fashionable dissipations of a young Regency lord. As a result, despite a sizable and increasing income, he got into financial difficulties from which he did not entirely extricate himself until late in his life. In the course of his schooling, he formed many close and devoted friendships, the most important with John Cam Hobhouse, a sturdy political liberal and commonsense moralist who exerted a steadying influence throughout Byron's turbulent life.

Despite his distractions at the university, Byron found time to try his hand at lyric verse, some of which was published in 1807 in a slim and conventional volume titled *Hours of Idleness*. This was treated so harshly by the *Edinburgh Review* that Byron was provoked to write in reply his first important poem, *English Bards and Scotch Reviewers*, a vigorous satire in which he incorporated brilliant ridicule (whose tactlessness he later came to regret) of important contemporaries, including Scott, Wordsworth, and Coleridge.

After attaining his M.A. degree and his legal independence from his guardians, Byron set out with Hobhouse in 1809 on a tour through Portugal and Spain to Malta, and then to little-known Albania, Greece, and Asia Minor. There, in the classic locale for Greek love, he encountered a culture that accepted sexual relations between older aristocratic men and beautiful boys, and he accumulated materials that, sometimes rather slyly, he incorporated into many of his important poems, including his last work, *Don Juan*. The first literary product was *Childe Harold*; he wrote the opening two cantos while on the tour that the poem describes; published them in 1812 soon after his return to England; and, in his own oft-quoted phrase, "awoke one morning and found myself famous." He became the celebrity of fashionable London, and increased his literary success with a series of highly readable Eastern tales; in these the Byronic hero, represented against various exotic backdrops as a "Giaour" (an "infidel" within Muslim society), or a "Corsair" (a pirate), or in other forms, flaunts his misanthropy and undergoes violent and romantic adventures that current gossip attributed to the author. In his chronic shortage of money, Byron could well have used the huge income from these publications, but instead maintained his status as an aristocratic amateur by giving the royalties away. Occupying his inherited seat in the House of Lords, he also became briefly active on the liberal side of the Whig party and spoke courageously in defense of the Nottingham weavers who had resorted to smashing the newly invented textile machines that had thrown them out of work. He also supported other liberal measures, including that of Catholic Emancipation.

Byron was extraordinarily handsome—"so beautiful a countenance," Coleridge wrote, "I scarcely ever saw . . . his eyes the open portals of the sun—things of light, and for light." Because of a constitutional tendency to obesity, however, he was able to maintain his looks only by resorting again and again to a starvation diet of biscuits, soda water, and strong purgatives. Often as a result of female initiative rather than his own, Byron entered into a sequence of liaisons with ladies of fashion. One of these, the flamboyant and eccentric young Lady Caroline Lamb, caused him so much distress by her pursuit that Byron turned for relief to marriage with Annabella Milbanke, who was in every way Lady Caroline's opposite, for she was unworldly and intellectual (with a special passion for mathematics) and naively believed that she could reform her husband. This ill-starred marriage produced a daughter (Augusta Ada) and many scenes in which Byron, goaded by financial difficulties, behaved so frantically that his wife suspected his sanity; after only one year the union ended in a legal separation. The final blow came when Lady Byron discovered her husband's incestuous relations with his half-sister, Augusta Leigh. The two had been raised apart, so that they were almost strangers when they met as adults. Byron's affection for his sister, however guilty, was genuine and endured all through his life. This affair, enhanced by rumors about Byron's earlier liaisons with men, proved a delicious morsel even to the jaded palate of a public that was used to eating up stories of aristocratic vice. Byron was ostracized by all but a few friends and was finally forced to leave England forever on April 25, 1816.

Byron now resumed the travels incorporated in the third and fourth cantos of *Childe Harold*. At Geneva he lived for several months in close and intellectually fruitful relation to Percy and Mary Shelley, who were accompanied by Mary's stepsister, Claire Clairmont—a misguided seventeen-year-old who had forced herself on Byron while he was still in England and who in January 1817 bore him a daughter, Allegra. In the fall of 1817, Byron established himself in Venice, where he began a year and a half of debauchery that, he estimated, involved liaisons with more than two hundred women. This period, however, was also one of great literary creativity. Often working through the night, he finished his tragedy *Manfred*; wrote the fourth canto of *Childe Harold*; and then, feeling more and more trapped by the poetic modes that had won him his popularity, tested out an entirely new mode in *Beppo: A Venetian Story*, a comic verse tale about a deceived husband in which he previewed the playful narrative manner and the ottava rima stanzas of *Don Juan*. In December 1818 he began the composition of *Don Juan*.

Exhausted and bored by promiscuity, Byron in 1819 settled into a placid and relatively faithful relationship with Teresa Guiccioli, the young wife of the elderly Count Alessandro Guiccioli; according to the Italian upper-class mores of the times, having contracted a marriage of convenience, she could now with some propriety take Byron as her lover. Through the countess's nationalistic family, the Gambas, Byron became involved with a group of political conspirators seeking to end the Austrian Empire's control over northern Italy. When the Gambas were forced by the authorities to move to Pisa, Byron followed them there and, for the second time, joined the Shelleys. There grew up about them the "Pisan Circle," which in addition to the Gambas included their friends Thomas Medwin and Edward and Jane Williams, as well as the Greek nationalist leader Prince Mavrocordatos, the picturesque Irish Count Taaffe, and the adventurer Edward Trelawny, a great teller of tall tales who seems to have stepped out of one of Byron's romances. Leigh Hunt, the journalist and essayist, joined them, drawing Byron and Percy Shelley into his plan to make Italy the base for a radical political journal, *The Liberal*. This circle was gradually broken up, however, first by the Shelleys' anger over Byron's treatment of his daughter Allegra (Byron had sent the child to be brought up as a Catholic in an Italian convent, where she died of a fever in 1822); then by the expulsion of the Gambas, whom Byron followed to Genoa; and finally by the drowning of Percy Shelley and Edward Williams in July 1822.

Byron meanwhile had been steadily at work on a series of closet tragedies (including *Cain, Sardanapalus,* and *Marino Faliero*) and on his devastating satire on the life and death of George III, *The Vision of Judgment*. But increasingly he devoted himself to the continuation of *Don Juan*. He had always been diffident in his self-judgments and easily swayed by literary advice. But now, confident that he had at last found his métier, he kept on, in spite of persistent objections against the supposed immorality of the poem by the English public, by his publisher John Murray, by his friends and well-wishers, and by his extremely decorous lover, the Countess Guiccioli—by almost everyone, in fact, except the idealist Shelley, who thought *Juan* incomparably better than anything he himself could write and insisted "that every word of it is pregnant with immortality."

Byron finally broke off literature for action when he organized an expedition to assist in the Greek war for independence from the Ottoman Empire. He knew too well the conditions in Greece, and had too skeptical an estimate of human nature, to entertain hope of success; but, in part because his own writings had helped kindle European enthusiasm for the Greek cause, he now felt honor-bound to try what could be done. In the dismal, marshy town of Missolonghi, he lived a Spartan existence, training troops whom he had subsidized and exhibiting practical grasp and a power of leadership amid a chaos of factionalism, intrigue, and military ineptitude. Worn out, he succumbed to a series of feverish attacks and died just after he had reached his thirty-sixth birthday. To this day Byron is revered by the Greek people as a national hero.

Students of Byron still feel, as his friends had felt, the magnetism of his volatile temperament. As Mary Shelley wrote six years after his death, when she read Thomas Moore's edition of his *Letters and Journals*: "The Lord Byron I find there is our Lord Byron—the fascinating—faulty—childish—philosophical being—daring the world—docile to a private circle—impetuous and indolent—gloomy and yet more gay than any other." Of his contradictions Byron was well aware; he told his friend Lady Blessington: "I am so changeable, being everything by turns and nothing long— I am such a strange *mélange* of good and evil, that it would be difficult to describe me." Yet he remained faithful to his code: a determination to tell the truth as he saw it about the world and about himself (his refusal to suppress or conceal any of his moods is in part what made him seem so contradictory) and a dedication to the freedom of nations and individuals. As he went on to say to Lady Blessington: "There are but two sentiments to which I am constant—a strong love of liberty, and a detestation of cant."

The poetry texts printed here are taken from Jerome J. McGann's edition, *Lord Byron: The Complete Poetical Works* (Oxford, 1980–93).

Written after Swimming from Sestos to Abydos[1]

May 9, 1810

1

If in the month of dark December
Leander, who was nightly wont
(What maid will not the tale remember?)
To cross thy stream, broad Hellespont!

2

5   If when the wintry tempest roared
He sped to Hero, nothing loth,
And thus of old thy current pour'd,
Fair Venus! how I pity both!

3

For *me*, degenerate modern wretch,
10   Though in the genial month of May,
My dripping limbs I faintly stretch,
And think I've done a feat to-day.

4

But since he cross'd the rapid tide,
According to the doubtful story,
15   To woo,—and—Lord knows what beside,
And swam for Love, as I for Glory;

5

'Twere hard to say who fared the best:
Sad mortals! thus the Gods still plague you!
He lost his labour, I my jest:
20   For he was drown'd, and I've the ague.

1810   1812

She walks in beauty[1]

1

She walks in beauty, like the night
Of cloudless climes and starry skies;
And all that's best of dark and bright

---

1. The Hellespont (now called the Dardanelles) is the narrow strait between Europe and Asia. In the ancient story, retold in Christopher Marlowe's *Hero and Leander,* young Leander of Abydos, on the Asian side, swam nightly to visit Hero, a priestess of the goddess Venus at Sestos, until he was drowned when he made the attempt in a storm. Byron and a young Lieutenant Ekenhead swam the Hellespont in the reverse direction on May 3, 1810. Byron alternated between complacency and humor in his many references to the event. In a note to the poem, he mentions that the distance was "upwards of four English miles, though the actual breadth is barely one. The rapidity of the current is such that no boat can row directly across. . . . The water was extremely cold, from the melting of the mountain snows."

1. From *Hebrew Melodies* (1815), a collection of lyrics on Old Testament themes that Byron composed to accompany the musician Isaac Nathan's settings of traditional synagogue chants. Byron wrote these lines about his beautiful cousin by marriage, Anne Wilmot, who at the ball where they first met wore a black mourning gown brightened with spangles. In their context as the opening poem of *Hebrew Melodies,* the lines praise any one of a number of Old Testament heroines. To hear the poem sung to Nathan's music, consult Norton Literature Online.

Meet in her aspect and her eyes:
5 Thus mellow'd to that tender light
   Which heaven to gaudy day denies.

2

One shade the more, one ray the less,
   Had half impair'd the nameless grace
Which waves in every raven tress,
10   Or softly lightens o'er her face;
Where thoughts serenely sweet express
   How pure, how dear their dwelling place.

3

And on that cheek, and o'er that brow,
   So soft, so calm, yet eloquent,
15 The smiles that win, the tints that glow,
   But tell of days in goodness spent,
A mind at peace with all below,
   A heart whose love is innocent!

June 1814   1815

They say that Hope is happiness

Felix qui potuit rerum cognoscere causas.[1]
                                        VIRGIL

1

They say that Hope is happiness—
   But genuine Love must prize the past;
And Mem'ry wakes the thoughts that bless:
   They rose the first—they set the last.

2

5 And all that mem'ry loves the most
   Was once our only hope to be:
And all that hope adored and lost
   Hath melted into memory.

3

Alas! it is delusion all—
10   The future cheats us from afar:
Nor can we be what we recall,
   Nor dare we think on what we are.

1814   1829

1. Happy is he who has been able to learn the causes of things (Latin; *Georgics* 2.490).

When we two parted

1

When we two parted
  In silence and tears,
Half broken-hearted
  To sever for years,
5 Pale grew thy cheek and cold,
    Colder thy kiss;
Truly that hour foretold
  Sorrow to this.

2

The dew of the morning
10 Sunk chill on my brow—
It felt like the warning
  Of what I feel now.
Thy vows are all broken,
  And light is thy fame;
15 I hear thy name spoken,
  And share in its shame.

3

They name thee before me,
  A knell to mine ear;
A shudder comes o'er me—
20 Why wert thou so dear?
They know not I knew thee,
  Who knew thee too well:—
Long, long shall I rue thee,
  Too deeply to tell.

4

25 In secret we met—
  In silence I grieve,
That thy heart could forget,
  Thy spirit deceive.
If I should meet thee
30 After long years,
How should I greet thee!—
  With silence and tears.

1815   1815

Darkness[1]

I had a dream, which was not all a dream.
The bright sun was extinguish'd, and the stars

1. A powerful blank-verse description of the end of life on Earth. New geological sciences and an accompanying interest in what the fossil record indicated about the extinction of species made such speculations hardly less common in Byron's time than in ours. Mary Shelley would later take up the theme in her novel *The Last Man* (1826).

Did wander darkling° in the eternal space,   °*in the dark*
Rayless, and pathless, and the icy earth
5   Swung blind and blackening in the moonless air;
Morn came, and went—and came, and brought no day,
And men forgot their passions in the dread
Of this their desolation; and all hearts
Were chill'd into a selfish prayer for light:
10 And they did live by watchfires—and the thrones,
The palaces of crowned kings—the huts,
The habitations of all things which dwell,
Were burnt for beacons; cities were consumed,
And men were gathered round their blazing homes
15 To look once more into each other's face;
Happy were those who dwelt within the eye
Of the volcanos, and their mountain-torch:
A fearful hope was all the world contain'd;
Forests were set on fire—but hour by hour
20 They fell and faded—and the crackling trunks
Extinguish'd with a crash—and all was black.
The brows of men by the despairing light
Wore an unearthly aspect, as by fits
The flashes fell upon them; some lay down
25 And hid their eyes and wept; and some did rest
Their chins upon their clenched hands, and smiled;
And others hurried to and fro, and fed
Their funeral piles with fuel, and looked up
With mad disquietude on the dull sky,
30 The pall of a past world; and then again
With curses cast them down upon the dust,
And gnash'd their teeth and howl'd: the wild birds shriek'd,
And, terrified, did flutter on the ground,
And flap their useless wings; the wildest brutes
35 Came tame and tremulous; and vipers crawl'd
And twined themselves among the multitude,
Hissing, but stingless—they were slain for food:
And War, which for a moment was no more,
Did glut himself again;—a meal was bought
40 With blood, and each sate sullenly apart
Gorging himself in gloom: no love was left;
All earth was but one thought—and that was death,
Immediate and inglorious; and the pang
Of famine fed upon all entrails—men
45 Died, and their bones were tombless as their flesh;
The meagre by the meagre were devoured,
Even dogs assail'd their masters, all save one,
And he was faithful to a corse, and kept
The birds and beasts and famish'd men at bay,
50 Till hunger clung° them, or the dropping dead   °*withered*
Lured their lank jaws; himself sought out no food,
But with a piteous and perpetual moan,
And a quick desolate cry, licking the hand
Which answered not with a caress—he died.
55 The crowd was famish'd by degrees; but two

Of an enormous city did survive,
And they were enemies; they met beside
The dying embers of an altar-place,
Where had been heap'd a mass of holy things
60 For an unholy usage; they raked up,
And shivering scraped with their cold skeleton hands
The feeble ashes, and their feeble breath
Blew for a little life, and made a flame
Which was a mockery; then they lifted up
65 Their eyes as it grew lighter, and beheld
Each other's aspects—saw, and shriek'd, and died—
Even of their mutual hideousness they died,
Unknowing who he was upon whose brow
Famine had written Fiend. The world was void,
70 The populous and the powerful—was a lump,
Seasonless, herbless,° treeless, manless, lifeless—   *without vegetation*
A lump of death—a chaos of hard clay.
The rivers, lakes, and ocean all stood still,
And nothing stirred within their silent depths;
75 Ships sailorless lay rotting on the sea,
And their masts fell down piecemeal; as they dropp'd
They slept on the abyss without a surge—
The waves were dead; the tides were in their grave,
The moon their mistress had expired before;
80 The winds were withered in the stagnant air,
And the clouds perish'd; Darkness had no need
Of aid from them—She was the universe.

1816   1816

So, we'll go no more a roving[1]

1

So, we'll go no more a roving
    So late into the night,
Though the heart be still as loving,
    And the moon be still as bright.

2

5 For the sword outwears its sheath,
    And the soul wears out the breast,
And the heart must pause to breathe,
    And love itself have rest.

1. Composed in the Lenten aftermath of a period of late-night carousing during the Carnival season in Venice, and included in a letter to Thomas Moore, February 28, 1817. Byron wrote, "I find 'the sword wearing out the scabbard,' though I have but just turned the corner of twenty-nine." The poem is based on the refrain of a bawdy Scottish song, "The Jolly Beggar": "And we'll gang nae mair a roving / Sae late into the nicht."

3
Though the night was made for loving,
10   And the day returns too soon,
Yet we'll go no more a roving
By the light of the moon.

1817   1830

Childe Harold's Pilgrimage

Childe Harold is a travelogue narrated by a melancholy, passionate, well-read, and very eloquent tourist. Byron wrote most of the first two cantos while on the tour through Spain, Portugal, Albania, and Greece that these cantos describe. When he published them, in 1812, they made him at one stroke the best-known and most talked about poet in England. Byron took up *Childe Harold* again in 1816, during the European tour he made after the breakup of his marriage. Canto 3, published in 1816, moves through Belgium, up the Rhine, then to Switzerland and the Alps. Canto 4, published in 1818, describes Italy's great cities, in particular their ruins and museums and the stories these tell of the bygone glories of the Roman Empire.

Byron chose for his poem the Spenserian stanza, and like James Thomson (in *The Castle of Indolence*) and other eighteenth-century predecessors, he attempted in the first canto to imitate, in a seriocomic fashion, the archaic language of his Elizabethan model. (*Childe* is the ancient term for a young noble awaiting knighthood.) But he soon dropped the archaisms, and in the last two cantos he confidently adapts Spenser's mellifluous stanza to his own autobiographical and polemical purposes. The virtuoso range of moods and subjects in *Childe Harold* was a quality on which contemporaries commented admiringly. Equally fascinating is the tension between the body of the poem and the long notes (for the most part omitted here) that Byron appended to its sometimes dashing and sometimes sorrowing chronicle of his pilgrimage in the countries of chivalry and romance—notes that feature cosmopolitan reflections on the contrasts among cultures as well as sardonic, hard-hitting critiques of the evolving political order of Europe.

In the preface to his first two cantos, Byron had insisted that the narrator, Childe Harold, was "a fictitious character," merely "the child of imagination." In the manuscript version of these cantos, however, he had called his hero "Childe Burun," the early form of his own family name. The world insisted on identifying the character as well as the travels of the protagonist with those of the author, and in the fourth canto Byron, abandoning the third-person *dramatis persona,* spoke out frankly in the first person. In the preface to that canto, he declares that there will be "less of the pilgrim" here than in any of the preceding cantos, "and that little slightly, if at all, separated from the author speaking in his own person. The fact is, that I had become weary of drawing a line which every one seemed determined not to perceive."

FROM CHILDE HAROLD'S PILGRIMAGE

A ROMAUNT[1]

From Canto 1

["SIN'S LONG LABYRINTH"]

1

Oh, thou! in Hellas° deem'd of heav'nly birth,   *Greece*
 Muse! form'd or fabled at the minstrel's will!
 Since sham'd full oft by later lyres on earth,
 Mine dares not call thee from thy sacred hill:
5 Yet there I've wander'd by thy vaunted rill;
 Yes! sigh'd o'er Delphi's long-deserted shrine,
 Where, save that feeble fountain, all is still;
 Nor mote° my shell awake the weary Nine[2]   *may*
 To grace so plain a tale—this lowly lay° of mine. *song*

2

10 Whilome[3] in Albion's° isle there dwelt a youth, *England's*
 Who ne in virtue's ways did take delight;
 But spent his days in riot most uncouth,
 And vex'd with mirth the drowsy ear of Night.
 Ah, me! in sooth he was a shameless wight,° *creature*
15 Sore given to revel and ungodly glee;
 Few earthly things found favour in his sight
 Save concubines and carnal companie,
 And flaunting wassailers[4] of high and low degree.

3

 Childe Harold was he hight:°—but whence his name *called*
20 And lineage long, it suits me not to say;
 Suffice it, that perchance they were of fame,
 And had been glorious in another day:
 But one sad losel[5] soils a name for aye,
 However mighty in the olden time;
25 Nor all that heralds rake from coffin'd clay,
 Nor florid prose, nor honied lies of rhyme
 Can blazon evil deeds, or consecrate a crime.

4

 Childe Harold bask'd him in the noon-tide sun,
 Disporting there like any other fly;
30 Nor deem'd before his little day was done
 One blast might chill him into misery.
 But long ere scarce a third of his pass'd by,
 Worse than adversity the Childe befell;

1. A romance or narrative of adventure.
2. The Muses, whose "vaunted rill" (line 5) was the Castalian spring. "Shell": lyre. Hermes is fabled to have invented the lyre by stretching strings over the hollow of a tortoise shell.
3. Once upon a time; one of the many archaisms that Byron borrowed from Spenser.
4. Noisy, insolent drinkers (Byron is thought to refer to his own youthful carousing with friends at Newstead Abbey).
5. Rascal. Byron's great-uncle, the fifth Lord Byron, had killed a kinsman in a drunken duel.

He felt the fulness of satiety:
35   Then loath'd he in his native land to dwell,
Which seem'd to him more lone than Eremite's⁶ sad cell.

5

For he through Sin's long labyrinth had run,
Nor made atonement when he did amiss,
Had sigh'd to many though he lov'd but one,
40   And that lov'd one, alas! could ne'er be his.
Ah, happy she! to 'scape from him whose kiss
Had been pollution unto aught so chaste;
Who soon had left her charms for vulgar bliss,
And spoil'd her goodly lands to gild his waste,
45 Nor calm domestic peace had ever deign'd to taste.

6

And now Childe Harold was sore sick at heart,
And from his fellow bacchanals would flee;
'Tis said, at times the sullen tear would start,
But Pride congeal'd the drop within his ee:°   eye
50   Apart he stalk'd in joyless reverie,
And from his native land resolv'd to go,
And visit scorching climes beyond the sea;
With pleasure drugg'd he almost long'd for woe,
And e'en for change of scene would seek the shades below.

From Canto 3

["ONCE MORE UPON THE WATERS"]

1

Is thy face like thy mother's, my fair child!
Ada!¹ sole daughter of my house and heart?
When last I saw thy young blue eyes they smiled,
And then we parted,—not as now we part,
But with a hope.—
5   Awaking with a start,
The waters heave around me; and on high
The winds lift up their voices: I depart,
Whither I know not; but the hour's gone by,
When Albion's lessening shores could grieve or glad mine eye.

2

10   Once more upon the waters! yet once more!
And the waves bound beneath me as a steed
That knows his rider. Welcome, to their roar!
Swift be their guidance, wheresoe'er it lead!
Though the strain'd mast should quiver as a reed,
15   And the rent canvas fluttering strew the gale,

6. A religious hermit.
1. Byron's daughter Augusta Ada, born in December 1815, a month before her parents separated.

Byron's "hope" (line 5) had been for a reconciliation, but he was never to see Ada again.

Still must I on; for I am as a weed,
Flung from the rock, on Ocean's foam, to sail
Where'er the surge may sweep, the tempest's breath prevail.

3

In my youth's summer[2] I did sing of One,
20 The wandering outlaw of his own dark mind;
Again I seize the theme then but begun,
And bear it with me, as the rushing wind
Bears the cloud onwards: in that Tale I find
The furrows of long thought, and dried-up tears,
25 Which, ebbing, leave a sterile track behind,
O'er which all heavily the journeying years
Plod the last sands of life,—where not a flower appears.

4

Since my young days of passion—joy, or pain,
Perchance my heart and harp have lost a string,
30 And both may jar:[3] it may be, that in vain
I would essay as I have sung to sing.
Yet, though a dreary strain, to this I cling;
So that it wean me from the weary dream
Of selfish grief or gladness—so it fling
35 Forgetfulness around me—it shall seem
To me, though to none else, a not ungrateful theme.

5

He, who grown aged in this world of woe,
In deeds, not years, piercing the depths of life,
So that no wonder waits him; nor below
40 Can love, or sorrow, fame, ambition, strife,
Cut to his heart again with the keen knife
Of silent, sharp endurance: he can tell
Why thought seeks refuge in lone caves, yet rife
With airy images, and shapes which dwell
45 Still unimpair'd, though old, in the soul's haunted cell.

6

'Tis to create, and in creating live
A being more intense, that we endow
With form our fancy, gaining as we give
The life we image, even as I do now.
50 What am I? Nothing; but not so art thou,
Soul of my thought![4] with whom I traverse earth,
Invisible but gazing, as I glow
Mix'd with thy spirit, blended with thy birth,
And feeling still with thee in my crush'd feelings' dearth.

7

55 Yet must I think less wildly:—I *have* thought
Too long and darkly, till my brain became,
In its own eddy boiling and o'erwrought,
A whirling gulf of phantasy and flame:

2. Byron wrote canto 1 at age twenty-one; he is now twenty-eight.
3. Sound discordant.
4. I.e., Childe Harold, his literary creation.

And thus, untaught in youth my heart to tame,
60   My springs of life were poison'd. 'Tis too late!
Yet am I chang'd; though still enough the same
In strength to bear what time can not abate,
And feed on bitter fruits without accusing Fate.

8

Something too much of this:—but now 'tis past,
65   And the spell closes with its silent seal.⁵
Long absent HAROLD re-appears at last;
He of the breast which fain no more would feel,
Wrung with the wounds which kill not, but ne'er heal;
Yet Time, who changes all, had alter'd him
70   In soul and aspect as in age: years steal
Fire from the mind as vigour from the limb;
And life's enchanted cup but sparkles near the brim.

9

His had been quaff'd too quickly, and he found
The dregs were wormwood; but he fill'd again,
75   And from a purer fount, on holier ground,
And deem'd its spring perpetual; but in vain!
Still round him clung invisibly a chain
Which gall'd for ever, fettering though unseen,
And heavy though it clank'd not; worn with pain,
80   Which pined although it spoke not, and grew keen,
Entering with every step, he took, through many a scene.

10

Secure in guarded coldness, he had mix'd
Again in fancied safety with his kind,
And deem'd his spirit now so firmly fix'd
85   And sheath'd with an invulnerable mind,
That, if no joy, no sorrow lurk'd behind;
And he, as one, might midst the many stand
Unheeded, searching through the crowd to find
Fit speculation! such as in strange land
90   He found in wonder-works of God and Nature's hand.

11

But who can view the ripened rose, nor seek
To wear it? who can curiously behold
The smoothness and the sheen of beauty's cheek,
Nor feel the heart can never all grow old?
95   Who can contemplate Fame through clouds unfold
The star which rises o'er her steep, nor climb?
Harold, once more within the vortex, roll'd
On with the giddy circle, chasing Time,
Yet with a nobler aim than in his youth's fond° prime.   foolish

12

100   But soon he knew himself the most unfit
Of men to herd with Man; with whom he held

5. I.e., he sets the seal of silence on his personal tale ("spell").

Little in common; untaught to submit
His thoughts to others, though his soul was quell'd
In youth by his own thoughts; still uncompell'd,
105 He would not yield dominion of his mind
To spirits against whom his own rebell'd;
Proud though in desolation; which could find
A life within itself, to breathe without mankind.

13

Where rose the mountains, there to him were friends;
110 Where roll'd the ocean, thereon was his home;
Where a blue sky, and glowing clime, extends,
He had the passion and the power to roam;
The desert, forest, cavern, breaker's foam,
Were unto him companionship; they spake
115 A mutual language, clearer than the tome°   book
Of his land's tongue, which he would oft forsake
For Nature's pages glass'd° by sunbeams on the lake.   made glassy

14

Like the Chaldean,[6] he could watch the stars,
Till he had peopled them with beings bright
120 As their own beams; and earth, and earth-born jars,
And human frailties, were forgotten quite:
Could he have kept his spirit to that flight
He had been happy; but this clay will sink
Its spark immortal, envying it the light
125 To which it mounts, as if to break the link
That keeps us from yon heaven which woos us to its brink.

15

But in Man's dwellings he became a thing
Restless and worn, and stern and wearisome,
Droop'd as a wild-born falcon with clipt wing,
130 To whom the boundless air alone were home:
Then came his fit again, which to o'ercome,
As eagerly the barr'd-up bird will beat
His breast and beak against his wiry dome
Till the blood tinge his plumage, so the heat
135 Of his impeded soul would through his bosom eat.

16

Self-exiled Harold wanders forth again,
With nought of hope left, but with less of gloom;
The very knowledge that he lived in vain,
That all was over on this side the tomb,
140 Had made Despair a smilingness assume,
Which, though 'twere wild,—as on the plundered wreck
When mariners would madly meet their doom
With draughts intemperate on the sinking deck,—
Did yet inspire a cheer, which he forbore to check.

6. A people of ancient Babylonia, expert in astronomy.

[WATERLOO]

17

145 Stop!—for thy tread is on an Empire's dust!
An Earthquake's spoil is sepulchered below!
Is the spot mark'd with no colossal bust?
Nor column trophied for triumphal show?[7]
None; but the moral's truth tells simpler so,
150 As the ground was before, thus let it be;—
How that red rain hath made the harvest grow!
And is this all the world has gained by thee,
Thou first and last of fields! king-making Victory?

18

And Harold stands upon this place of skulls,
155 The grave of France, the deadly Waterloo![8]
How in an hour the power which gave annuls
Its gifts, transferring fame as fleeting too!
In "pride of place" here last the eagle flew,[9]
Then tore with bloody talon the rent plain,
160 Pierced by the shaft of banded nations[1] through;
Ambition's life and labours all were vain;
He wears the shattered links of the world's broken chain.[2]

19

Fit retribution! Gaul[3] may champ the bit
And foam in fetters;—but is Earth more free?
165 Did nations combat to make One submit;
Or league to teach all kings true sovereignty?
What! shall reviving Thraldom again be
The patched-up idol of enlightened days?
Shall we, who struck the Lion down, shall we
170 Pay the Wolf homage? proffering lowly gaze
And servile knees to thrones? No; prove[4] before ye praise!

20

If not, o'er one fallen despot boast no more!
In vain fair cheeks were furrowed with hot tears
For Europe's flowers long rooted up before
175 The trampler of her vineyards; in vain years
Of death, depopulation, bondage, fears,
Have all been borne, and broken by the accord
Of roused-up millions: all that most endears

7. Referring to the triumphal arches erected in ancient Rome to honor conquering generals, a custom Napoleon had revived.
8. Napoleon's defeat at Waterloo, near Brussels, had occurred only the year before, on June 18, 1815. The battlefield, where almost fifty thousand English, Prussian, and French soldiers were killed in a single day, quickly became a gruesome tourist attraction.
9. "Pride of place," is a term of falconry, and means the highest pitch of flight [Byron's note, which continues by referring to the use of the term in Shakespeare's *Macbeth* 2.4]. The eagle was the symbol of Napoleon.
1. The Grand Alliance formed in opposition to Napoleon.
2. Napoleon was then a prisoner at St. Helena.
3. France. Byron, like other liberals, saw the defeat of the Napoleonic tyranny as a victory for tyrannical kings and the forces of reaction throughout Europe.
4. Await the test (proof) of experience.

Glory, is when the myrtle wreathes a sword
180   Such as Harmodius drew on Athens' tyrant lord.[5]

21

There was a sound of revelry by night,[6]
And Belgium's capital had gathered then
Her Beauty and her Chivalry, and bright
The lamps shone o'er fair women and brave men;
185   A thousand hearts beat happily; and when
Music arose with its voluptuous swell,
Soft eyes look'd love to eyes which spake again,
And all went merry as a marriage-bell;
But hush! hark! a deep sound strikes like a rising knell!

22

190   Did ye not hear it?—No; 'twas but the wind,
Or the car rattling o'er the stony street;
On with the dance! let joy be unconfined;
No sleep till morn, when Youth and Pleasure meet
To chase the glowing Hours with flying feet—
195   But, hark!—that heavy sound breaks in once more,
As if the clouds its echo would repeat;
And nearer, clearer, deadlier than before!
Arm! Arm! and out—it is—the cannon's opening roar!

23

Within a windowed niche of that high hall
200   Sate Brunswick's fated chieftain;[7] he did hear
That sound the first amidst the festival,
And caught its tone with Death's prophetic ear;
And when they smiled because he deem'd it near,
His heart more truly knew that peal too well
205   Which stretch'd his father on a bloody bier,
And roused the vengeance blood alone could quell:
He rush'd into the field, and, foremost fighting, fell.

24

Ah! then and there was hurrying to and fro,
And gathering tears, and tremblings of distress,
210   And cheeks all pale, which but an hour ago
Blush'd at the praise of their own loveliness;
And there were sudden partings, such as press
The life from out young hearts, and choking sighs
Which ne'er might be repeated; who could guess
215   If ever more should meet those mutual eyes,
Since upon nights so sweet such awful morn could rise?

5. In 514 B.C.E. Harmodius and Aristogeiton, hiding their daggers in myrtle (symbol of love), killed Hipparchus, tyrant of Athens.
6. A famous ball, given by the duchess of Richmond on the eve of the battle of Quatre Bras, which opened the conflict at Waterloo.

7. The duke of Brunswick, nephew of George III of England, was killed in the battle of Quatre Bras. His father, commanding the Prussian army against Napoleon, had been killed at Auerstedt in 1806 (line 205).

25

And there was mounting in hot haste: the steed,
The mustering squadron, and the clattering car,
Went pouring forward in impetuous speed,
220   And swiftly forming in the ranks of war;
And the deep thunder peal on peal afar;
And near, the beat of the alarming drum
Roused up the soldier ere the morning star;
While throng'd the citizens with terror dumb,
225   Or whispering, with white lips—"The foe! They come! they come!"

26

And wild and high the "Cameron's gathering" rose!
The war-note of Lochiel,[8] which Albyn's° hills   *Scotland's*
Have heard, and heard, too, have her Saxon foes:—
How in the noon of night that pibroch[9] thrills,
230   Savage and shrill! But with the breath which fills
Their mountain-pipe, so fill the mountaineers
With the fierce native daring which instils
The stirring memory of a thousand years,
And Evan's, Donald's[1] fame rings in each clansman's ears!

27

235   And Ardennes[2] waves above them her green leaves,
Dewy with nature's tear-drops, as they pass,
Grieving, if aught inanimate e'er grieves,
Over the unreturning brave,—alas!
Ere evening to be trodden like the grass
240   Which now beneath them, but above shall grow
In its next verdure, when this fiery mass
Of living valour, rolling on the foe
And burning with high hope, shall moulder cold and low.

28

Last noon beheld them full of lusty life,
245   Last eve in Beauty's circle proudly gay,
The midnight brought the signal-sound of strife,
The morn the marshalling in arms,—the day
Battle's magnificently-stern array!
The thunder-clouds close o'er it, which when rent
250   The earth is covered thick with other clay,
Which her own clay shall cover, heaped and pent,
Rider and horse,—friend, foe,—in one red burial blent!

*   *   *

---

8. "Cameron's gathering" is the clan song of the Camerons, whose chief was called "Lochiel," after his estate.
9. Bagpipe music, usually warlike in character.
1. Sir Evan and Donald Cameron, famous warriors in the Stuart cause in the Jacobite risings of 1689 and 1745.
2. The wood of Soignes is supposed to be a remnant of the "forest of Ardennes" famous in Boiardo's *Orlando*, and immortal in Shakespeare's *As You Like It*. It is also celebrated in Tacitus as being the spot of successful defence by the Germans against the Roman encroachments—I have ventured to adopt the name connected with nobler associations than those of mere slaughter [Byron's note]. *Orlando Innamorato* is a 15th-century Italian epic of love and adventure.

Don Juan   Byron began his masterpiece (pronounced in the English fashion, *Don Joó-un*) in July 1818, published it in installments beginning with cantos 1 and 2 in 1819, and continued working on it almost until his death. Initially he improvised the poem from episode to episode. "I *have* no plan," he said, "I *had* no plan; but I had or have materials." The work was composed with remarkable speed (the 888 lines of canto 13, for example, were dashed off within a week), and it aims at the effect of improvisation rather than of artful compression; it asks to be read rapidly, at a conversational pace.

The poem breaks off with the sixteenth canto, but even in its unfinished state *Don Juan* is the longest satirical poem, and indeed one of the longest poems of any kind, in English. Its hero, the Spanish libertine, had in the original legend been superhuman in his sexual energy and wickedness. Throughout Byron's version the unspoken but persistent joke is that this archetypal lady-killer of European legend is in fact more acted upon than active. Unfailingly amiable and well intentioned, he is guilty largely of youth, charm, and a courteous and compliant spirit. The women do all the rest.

The chief models for the poem were the Italian seriocomic versions of medieval chivalric romances; the genre had been introduced by Pulci in the fifteenth century and was adopted by Ariosto in his *Orlando Furioso* (1532). From these writers Byron caught the mixed moods and violent oscillations between the sublime and the ridiculous as well as the colloquial management of the complex ottava rima—an eight-line stanza in which the initial interlaced rhymes (*ababab*) build up to the comic turn in the final couplet (*cc*). Byron was influenced in the English use of this Italian form by a mildly amusing poem published in 1817, under the pseudonym of "Whistlecraft," by his friend John Hookham Frere. Other recognizable antecedents of *Don Juan* are Jonathan Swift's *Gulliver's Travels* and Samuel Johnson's *Rasselas,* both of which had employed the naive traveler as a satiric device, and Laurence Sterne's novel *Tristram Shandy,* with its comic exploitation of a narrative medium blatantly subject to the whimsy of the author. But even the most original literary works play variations on inherited conventions. Shelley at once recognized his friend's poem as "something wholly new and relative to the age."

Byron's literary advisers thought the poem unacceptably immoral, and John Murray took the precaution of printing the first two installments (cantos 1–2, then 3–5) without identifying Byron as the author or himself as the publisher. The eleven completed cantos that followed were, because of Murray's continuing jitters, brought out in 1823–24 by the radical publisher John Hunt. In those cantos Byron's purpose deepened. He set out to create a comic yet devastatingly critical history of the Europe of his own age, sending the impressionable Juan from West to East and back again, from his native Spain to a Russian court (by way of a primitive Greek island and the 1790 siege of the Turkish town of Ismail) and then into the English gentry's country manors. These journeys, which facilitated Byron's satire on almost all existing forms of political organization, would, according to the scheme that he projected for the poem as a whole, ultimately have taken Juan to a death by guillotining in Revolutionary France.

Yet the controlling element of *Don Juan* is not the narrative but the narrator. His running commentary on Juan's misadventures, his reminiscences, and his opinionated remarks on the epoch of political reaction in which he is actually telling Juan's story together add another level to the poem's engagement with history. The narrator's reflections also at the same time lend unity to *Don Juan's* effervescent variety. Tellingly, the poem opens with the first-person pronoun and immediately lets us into the storyteller's predicament: "I want a hero. . . ." The voice then goes on, for almost two thousand stanzas, with effortless volubility and shifts of mood. The poet who in his brilliant successful youth created the gloomy Byronic hero, in his later and sadder life created a character (not the hero, but the narrator of *Don Juan*) who is one of the great comic inventions in English literature.

FROM DON JUAN

Fragment[1]

I would to Heaven that I were so much Clay—
    As I am blood—bone—marrow, passion—feeling—
Because at least the past were past away—
    And for the future—(but I write this reeling
5 Having got drunk exceedingly to day
    So that I seem to stand upon the ceiling)
I say—the future is a serious matter—
And so—for Godsake—Hock[2] and Soda water.

From Canto 1

[JUAN AND DONNA JULIA]

1

I want a hero: an uncommon want,
    When every year and month sends forth a new one,
Till, after cloying the gazettes with cant,
    The age discovers he is not the true one;
5 Of such as these I should not care to vaunt,
    I'll therefore take our ancient friend Don Juan,
We all have seen him in the pantomime[1]
Sent to the devil, somewhat ere his time.

*   *   *

5

Brave men were living before Agamemnon[2]
    And since, exceeding valorous and sage,
35 A good deal like him too, though quite the same none;
    But then they shone not on the poet's page,
And so have been forgotten—I condemn none,
    But can't find any in the present age
Fit for my poem (that is, for my new one);
40 So, as I said, I'll take my friend Don Juan.

6

Most epic poets plunge in *"medias res,"*[3]
    (Horace makes this the heroic turnpike road)[4]

---

1. This stanza was written on the back of a page of the manuscript of canto 1. For the author's revisions while composing two stanzas of *Don Juan,* see "Poems in Process," in the appendices to this volume.
2. A white Rhine wine, from the German *Hochheimer.*
1. The Juan legend was a popular subject in English pantomime.
2. In Homer's *Iliad* the king commanding the Greeks in the siege of Troy. This line is translated from a Latin ode by Horace.
3. Into the middle of things (Latin; Horace's *Art of Poetry* 148).
4. I.e., the smoothest road for heroic poetry.

And then your hero tells, whene'er you please,
    What went before—by way of episode,
45 While seated after dinner at his ease,
    Beside his mistress in some soft abode,
Palace, or garden, paradise, or cavern,
Which serves the happy couple for a tavern.

7

That is the usual method, but not mine—
50   My way is to begin with the beginning;
The regularity of my design
    Forbids all wandering as the worst of sinning,
And therefore I shall open with a line
    (Although it cost me half an hour in spinning)
55 Narrating somewhat of Don Juan's father,
And also of his mother, if you'd rather.

8

In Seville was he born, a pleasant city,
    Famous for oranges and women—he
Who has not seen it will be much to pity,
60   So says the proverb—and I quite agree;
Of all the Spanish towns is none more pretty,
    Cadiz perhaps—but that you soon may see:—
Don Juan's parents lived beside the river,
A noble stream, and call'd the Guadalquivir.

9

65 His father's name was Jóse[5]—*Don*, of course,
    A true Hidalgo,° free from every stain   *noble man*
Of Moor or Hebrew blood, he traced his source
    Through the most Gothic gentlemen of Spain;
A better cavalier ne'er mounted horse,
70   Or, being mounted, e'er got down again,
Than Jóse, who begot our hero, who
Begot—but that's to come——Well, to renew:

10

His mother was a learned lady, famed
    For every branch of every science known—
75 In every christian language ever named,
    With virtues equall'd by her wit alone,
She made the cleverest people quite ashamed,
    And even the good with inward envy groan,
Finding themselves so very much exceeded
80 In their own way by all the things that she did.

11

Her memory was a mine: she knew by heart
    All Calderon and greater part of Lopé,[6]
So that if any actor miss'd his part
    She could have served him for the prompter's copy;

5. Normally "José"; Byron transferred the accent to keep his meter.

6. Calderón de la Barca and Lope de Vega, the great Spanish dramatists of the early 17th century.

85 For her Feinagle's[7] were an useless art,
    And he himself obliged to shut up shop—he
Could never make a memory so fine as
That which adorn'd the brain of Donna Inez.

12

Her favourite science was the mathematical,
90   Her noblest virtue was her magnanimity,
Her wit (she sometimes tried at wit) was Attic[8] all,
    Her serious sayings darken'd to sublimity;
In short, in all things she was fairly what I call
    A prodigy—her morning dress was dimity,°   *cotton*
95 Her evening silk, or, in the summer, muslin,
And other stuffs, with which I won't stay puzzling.

13

She knew the Latin—that is, "the Lord's prayer,"
    And Greek—the alphabet—I'm nearly sure;
She read some French romances here and there,
100   Although her mode of speaking was not pure;
For native Spanish she had no great care,
    At least her conversation was obscure;
Her thoughts were theorems, her words a problem,
As if she deem'd that mystery would ennoble 'em.

           *   *   *

22

'Tis pity learned virgins ever wed
170   With persons of no sort of education,
Or gentlemen, who, though well-born and bred,
    Grow tired of scientific conversation:
I don't choose to say much upon this head,
    I'm a plain man, and in a single station,
175 But—Oh! ye lords of ladies intellectual,
Inform us truly, have they not hen-peck'd you all?

23

Don Jóse and his lady quarrell'd—*why,*
    Not any of the many could divine,
Though several thousand people chose to try,
180   'Twas surely no concern of theirs nor mine;
I loathe that low vice curiosity,
    But if there's any thing in which I shine
'Tis in arranging all my friends' affairs.
Not having, of my own, domestic cares.

24

185 And so I interfered, and with the best
    Intentions, but their treatment was not kind;
I think the foolish people were possess'd,

---

7. Gregor von Feinagle, a German expert on the art of memory, who had lectured in England in 1811.

8. Athenian. *Attic salt* is a term for the famed wit of the Athenians.

For neither of them could I ever find,
Although their porter afterwards confess'd—
190   But that's no matter, and the worst's behind,
For little Juan o'er me threw, down stairs,
A pail of housemaid's water unawares.

25

A little curly-headed, good-for-nothing,
    And mischief-making monkey from his birth;
195   His parents ne'er agreed except in doting
        Upon the most unquiet imp on earth;
Instead of quarrelling, had they been but both in
    Their senses, they'd have sent young master forth
To school, or had him soundly whipp'd at home,
200   To teach him manners for the time to come.

26

Don José and the Donna Inez led
    For some time an unhappy sort of life,
Wishing each other, not divorced, but dead;
    They lived respectably as man and wife,
205   Their conduct was exceedingly well-bred,
        And gave no outward signs of inward strife,
Until at length the smother'd fire broke out,
And put the business past all kind of doubt.

27

For Inez call'd some druggists and physicians,
210   And tried to prove her loving lord was *mad*,[9]
But as he had some lucid intermissions,
    She next decided he was only *bad*;
Yet when they ask'd her for her depositions,
    No sort of explanation could be had,
215   Save that her duty both to man and God
Required this conduct—which seem'd very odd.

28

She kept a journal, where his faults were noted,
    And open'd certain trunks of books and letters,
All which might, if occasion served, be quoted;
220   And then she had all Seville for abettors,
Besides her good old grandmother (who doted);
    The hearers of her case became repeaters,
Then advocates, inquisitors, and judges,
Some for amusement, others for old grudges.

29

225   And then this best and meekest woman bore
        With such serenity her husband's woes,
Just as the Spartan ladies did of yore,
    Who saw their spouses kill'd, and nobly chose

---

9. Lady Byron had thought her husband might be insane and sought medical advice on the matter. This and other passages obviously allude to his wife, although Byron insisted that Donna Inez was not intended to be a caricature of Lady Byron. In her determination to preserve her son's innocence, Donna Inez also shares traits with Byron's mother.

Never to say a word about them more—
230   Calmly she heard each calumny that rose,
And saw *his* agonies with such sublimity,
That all the world exclaim'd "What magnanimity!"

* * *

32
Their friends had tried at reconciliation,
250   Then their relations, who made matters worse;
('Twere hard to say upon a like occasion
    To whom it may be best to have recourse—
I can't say much for friend or yet relation):
    The lawyers did their utmost for divorce,
255   But scarce a fee was paid on either side
Before, unluckily, Don Jóse died.

33
He died: and most unluckily, because,
    According to all hints I could collect
From counsel learned in those kinds of laws,
260   (Although their talk's obscure and circumspect)
His death contrived to spoil a charming cause;°   law case
    A thousand pities also with respect
To public feeling, which on this occasion
Was manifested in a great sensation.

* * *

37
Dying intestate,° Juan was sole heir   without a will
290   To a chancery suit, and messuages,[1] and lands,
Which, with a long minority and care,
    Promised to turn out well in proper hands:
Inez became sole guardian, which was fair,
    And answer'd but to nature's just demands;
295   An only son left with an only mother
Is brought up much more wisely than another.

38
Sagest of women, even of widows, she
    Resolved that Juan should be quite a paragon,
And worthy of the noblest pedigree:
300   (His sire was of Castile, his dam from Arragon).
Then for accomplishments of chivalry,
    In case our lord the king should go to war again,
He learn'd the arts of riding, fencing, gunnery,
And how to scale a fortress—or a nunnery.

39
305   But that which Donna Inez most desired,
    And saw into herself each day before all

---

1. Houses and the adjoining lands. "Chancery suit": a case in what was then the highest English court, notorious for its delays.

The learned tutors whom for him she hired,
Was, that his breeding should be strictly moral;
Much into all his studies she inquired,
310   And so they were submitted first to her, all,
Arts, sciences, no branch was made a mystery
To Juan's eyes, excepting natural history.[2]

40

The languages, especially the dead,
The sciences, and most of all the abstruse,
315   The arts, at least all such as could be said
To be the most remote from common use,
In all these he was much and deeply read;
But not a page of anything that's loose,
Or hints continuation of the species,
320   Was ever suffer'd, lest he should grow vicious.

41

His classic studies made a little puzzle,
Because of filthy loves of gods and goddesses,
Who in the earlier ages made a bustle,
But never put on pantaloons or boddices;
325   His reverend tutors had at times a tussle,
And for their Aeneids, Iliads, and Odysseys,
Were forced to make an odd sort of apology,
For Donna Inez dreaded the mythology.

42

Ovid's a rake, as half his verses show him,
330   Anacreon's morals are a still worse sample,
Catullus scarcely has a decent poem,
I don't think Sappho's Ode a good example,
Although Longinus[3] tells us there is no hymn
Where the sublime soars forth on wings more ample;
335   But Virgil's songs are pure, except that horrid one
Beginning with "*Formosum Pastor Corydon.*"[4]

43

Lucretius' irreligion[5] is too strong
For early stomachs, to prove wholesome food;
I can't help thinking Juvenal[6] was wrong,
340   Although no doubt his real intent was good,
For speaking out so plainly in his song,
So much indeed as to be downright rude;
And then what proper person can be partial
To all those nauseous epigrams of Martial?

2. Includes biology, physiology, and particularly botany, popular in the era in part because study of plants' stamens and pistils offered a form of surreptitious sex education.
3. In *On the Sublime* 10, the Greek rhetorician Longinus praises a passage of erotic longing from one of Sappho's odes.
4. Virgil's *Eclogue* 2 begins: "The shepherd, Corydon, burned with love for the handsome Alexis."
5. In *De Rerum Natura* (*On the Nature of Things*), Lucretius argues that the universe can be explained in entirely materialist terms without reference to any god.
6. The Latin satires of Juvenal attacked the corruption of Roman society in the 1st century C.E. and displayed its vices.

44

345 Juan was taught from out the best edition,
　　Expurgated by learned men, who place,
Judiciously, from out the schoolboy's vision,
　　The grosser parts; but fearful to deface
Too much their modest bard by this omission,
350　　And pitying sore his mutilated case,
They only add them all in an appendix,[7]
Which saves, in fact, the trouble of an index.

* * *

52

For my part I say nothing—nothing—but
410　　*This* I will say—my reasons are my own—
That if I had an only son to put
　　To school (as God be praised that I have none)
'Tis not with Donna Inez I would shut
　　Him up to learn his catechism alone,
415 No—No—I'd send him out betimes to college,
For there it was I pick'd up my own knowledge.

53

For there one learns—'tis not for me to boast,
　　Though I acquired—but I pass over *that,*
As well as all the Greek I since have lost:
420　　I say that there's the place—but *"Verbum sat,"*[8]
I think I pick'd up too, as well as most,
　　Knowledge of matters—but no matter *what—*
I never married—but, I think, I know
That sons should not be educated so.

54

425 Young Juan now was sixteen years of age,
　　Tall, handsome, slender, but well knit; he seem'd
Active, though not so sprightly, as a page;
　　And every body but his mother deem'd
Him almost man; but she flew in a rage,
430　　And bit her lips (for else she might have scream'd),
If any said so, for to be precocious
Was in her eyes a thing the most atrocious.

55

Amongst her numerous acquaintance, all
　　Selected for discretion and devotion,
435 There was the Donna Julia, whom to call
　　Pretty were but to give a feeble notion
Of many charms in her as natural
　　As sweetness to the flower, or salt to ocean,
Her zone to Venus,[9] or his bow to Cupid,
440 (But this last simile is trite and stupid).

---

7. Fact! There is, or was, such an edition, with all
the obnoxious epigrams of Martial placed by themselves at the end [Byron's note]. Martial, another
Latin poet, was a contemporary of Juvenal.

8. A word [to the wise] is sufficient (Latin).
9. The belt ("zone") of Venus made its wearer sexually irresistible.

1698 / George Gordon, Lord Byron

56

The darkness of her Oriental eye
    Accorded with her Moorish origin;
(Her blood was not all Spanish, by the by;
    In Spain, you know, this is a sort of sin).
445 When proud Grenada fell, and, forced to fly,
    Boabdil wept,[1] of Donna Julia's kin
Some went to Africa, some staid in Spain,
Her great great grandmamma chose to remain.

57

She married (I forget the pedigree)
450   With an Hidalgo, who transmitted down
His blood less noble than such blood should be;
    At such alliances his sires would frown,
In that point so precise in each degree
    That they bred *in and in*, as might be shown,
455 Marrying their cousins—nay, their aunts and nieces,
Which always spoils the breed, if it increases.

58

This heathenish cross restored the breed again,
    Ruin'd its blood, but much improved its flesh;
For, from a root the ugliest in Old Spain
460   Sprung up a branch as beautiful as fresh;
The sons no more were short, the daughters plain:
    But there's a rumour which I fain would hush,
'Tis said that Donna Julia's grandmamma
Produced her Don more heirs at love than law.

59

465 However this might be, the race° went on   *family line*
    Improving still through every generation,
Until it center'd in an only son,
    Who left an only daughter; my narration
May have suggested that this single one
470   Could be but Julia (whom on this occasion
I shall have much to speak about), and she
Was married, charming, chaste,[2] and twenty-three.

60

Her eye (I'm very fond of handsome eyes)
    Was large and dark, suppressing half its fire
475 Until she spoke, then through its soft disguise
    Flash'd an expression more of pride than ire,
And love than either; and there would arise
    A something in them which was not desire,
But would have been, perhaps, but for the soul
480 Which struggled through and chasten'd down the whole.

---

1. The Moorish king of Granada (the last Islamic enclave in Spain) wept when his capital fell and he and his people were forced to emigrate to Africa (1492).
2. I.e., faithful to her husband.

61

Her glossy hair was cluster'd o'er a brow
   Bright with intelligence, and fair and smooth;
Her eyebrow's shape was like the aerial bow,
   Her cheek all purple with the beam of youth,
485 Mounting, at times, to a transparent glow,
   As if her veins ran lightning; she, in sooth,
Possess'd an air and grace by no means common:
Her stature tall—I hate a dumpy woman.

62

Wedded she was some years, and to a man
490   Of fifty, and such husbands are in plenty;
And yet, I think, instead of such a ONE
   'Twere better to have TWO of five and twenty,
Especially in countries near the sun:
   And now I think on't, "mi vien in mente,"[3]
495 Ladies even of the most uneasy virtue
Prefer a spouse whose age is short of thirty.

63

'Tis a sad thing, I cannot choose but say,
   And all the fault of that indecent sun,
Who cannot leave alone our helpless clay,
500   But will keep baking, broiling, burning on,
That howsoever people fast and pray
   The flesh is frail, and so the soul undone:
What men call gallantry, and gods adultery,
Is much more common where the climate's sultry.

64

505 Happy the nations of the moral north!
   Where all is virtue, and the winter season
Sends sin, without a rag on, shivering forth;
   ('Twas snow that brought St. Francis back to reason);
Where juries cast up what a wife is worth
510   By laying whate'er sum, in mulct,[4] they please on
The lover, who must pay a handsome price,
Because it is a marketable vice.

65

Alfonso was the name of Julia's lord,
   A man well looking for his years, and who
515 Was neither much beloved, nor yet abhorr'd;
   They lived together as most people do,
Suffering each other's foibles by accord,
   And not exactly either *one* or *two*;
Yet he was jealous, though he did not show it,
520 For jealousy dislikes the world to know it.

* * *

3. It comes to my mind (Italian).   4. By way of a fine or legal penalty.

69

545 Juan she saw, and, as a pretty child,
  Caress'd him often, such a thing might be
Quite innocently done, and harmless styled,
  When she had twenty years, and thirteen he;
But I am not so sure I should have smiled
550   When he was sixteen, Julia twenty-three,
These few short years make wondrous alterations,
Particularly amongst sun-burnt nations.

70

Whate'er the cause might be, they had become
  Changed; for the dame grew distant, the youth shy,
555 Their looks cast down, their greetings almost dumb,
  And much embarrassment in either eye;
There surely will be little doubt with some
  That Donna Julia knew the reason why,
But as for Juan, he had no more notion
560 Than he who never saw the sea of ocean.

71

Yet Julia's very coldness still was kind,
  And tremulously gentle her small hand
Withdrew itself from his, but left behind
  A little pressure, thrilling, and so bland
565 And slight, so very slight, that to the mind
  'Twas but a doubt; but ne'er magician's wand
Wrought change with all Armida's[5] fairy art
Like what this light touch left on Juan's heart.

72

And if she met him, though she smiled no more,
570   She look'd a sadness sweeter than her smile,
As if her heart had deeper thoughts in store
  She must not own, but cherish'd more the while,
For that compression in its burning core;
  Even innocence itself has many a wile,
575 And will not dare to trust itself with truth,
And love is taught hypocrisy from youth.

     * * *

75

Poor Julia's heart was in an awkward state;
  She felt it going, and resolved to make
595 The noblest efforts for herself and mate,
  For honour's, pride's, religion's, virtue's sake;
Her resolutions were most truly great,
  And almost might have made a Tarquin[6] quake;
She pray'd the Virgin Mary for her grace,
600 As being the best judge of a lady's case.

5. The sorceress in Torquato Tasso's *Jerusalem Delivered* (1581) who seduces Rinaldo into forgetting his vows as a crusader.
6. A member of a legendary family of Roman kings noted for tyranny and cruelty; perhaps a reference specifically to Lucius Tarquinus, the villain of Shakespeare's *The Rape of Lucrece*.

76

She vow'd she never would see Juan more,
　　And next day paid a visit to his mother,
And look'd extremely at the opening door,
　　Which, by the Virgin's grace, let in another;
605　Grateful she was, and yet a little sore—
　　Again it opens, it can be no other,
'Tis surely Juan now—No! I'm afraid
That night the Virgin was no further pray'd.

77

She now determined that a virtuous woman
610　　Should rather face and overcome temptation,
That flight was base and dastardly, and no man
　　Should ever give her heart the least sensation;
That is to say, a thought beyond the common
　　Preference, that we must feel upon occasion,
615　For people who are pleasanter than others,
But then they only seem so many brothers.

78

And even if by chance—and who can tell?
　　The devil's so very sly—she should discover
That all within was not so very well,
620　　And, if still free, that such or such a lover
Might please perhaps, a virtuous wife can quell
　　Such thoughts, and be the better when they're over;
And if the man should ask, 'tis but denial:
I recommend young ladies to make trial.

79

625　And then there are such things as love divine,
　　Bright and immaculate, unmix'd and pure,
Such as the angels think so very fine,
　　And matrons, who would be no less secure,
Platonic, perfect, "just such love as mine":
630　　Thus Julia said—and thought so, to be sure,
And so I'd have her think, were I the man
On whom her reveries celestial ran.

*　　*　　*

86

So much for Julia. Now we'll turn to Juan,
　　Poor little fellow! he had no idea
Of his own case, and never hit the true one;
　　In feelings quick as Ovid's Miss Medea,[7]
685　He puzzled over what he found a new one,
　　But not as yet imagined it could be a
Thing quite in course, and not at all alarming,
Which, with a little patience, might grow charming.

---

7. In *Metamorphoses* 7 Ovid tells the story of Medea's mad infatuation for Jason.

* * *

90

Young Juan wander'd by the glassy brooks
  Thinking unutterable things; he threw
715 Himself at length within the leafy nooks
  Where the wild branch of the cork forest grew;
There poets find materials for their books,
  And every now and then we read them through,
So that their plan and prosody are eligible,
720 Unless, like Wordsworth, they prove unintelligible.

91

He, Juan (and not Wordsworth), so pursued
  His self-communion with his own high soul,
Until his mighty heart, in its great mood,
  Had mitigated part, though not the whole
725 Of its disease; he did the best he could
  With things not very subject to control,
And turn'd, without perceiving his condition,
Like Coleridge, into a metaphysician.

92

He thought about himself, and the whole earth,
730 Of man the wonderful, and of the stars,
And how the deuce they ever could have birth;
  And then he thought of earthquakes, and of wars,
How many miles the moon might have in girth,
  Of air-balloons, and of the many bars
735 To perfect knowledge of the boundless skies;
And then he thought of Donna Julia's eyes.

93

In thoughts like these true wisdom may discern
  Longings sublime, and aspirations high,
Which some are born with, but the most part learn
740 To plague themselves withal, they know not why:
'Twas strange that one so young should thus concern
  His brain about the action of the sky;
If *you* think 'twas philosophy that this did,
I can't help thinking puberty assisted.

94

745 He pored upon the leaves, and on the flowers,
  And heard a voice in all the winds; and then
He thought of wood nymphs and immortal bowers,
  And how the goddesses came down to men:
He miss'd the pathway, he forgot the hours,
750 And when he look'd upon his watch again,
He found how much old Time had been a winner—
He also found that he had lost his dinner.

* * *

103

'Twas on a summer's day—the sixth of June:—
    I like to be particular in dates,
Not only of the age, and year, but moon;
820   They are a sort of post-house, where the Fates
Change horses, making history change its tune,
    Then spur away o'er empires and o'er states,
Leaving at last not much besides chronology,
Excepting the post-obits[8] of theology.

104

825 'Twas on the sixth of June, about the hour
    Of half-past six—perhaps still nearer seven,
When Julia sate within as pretty a bower
    As e'er held houri in that heathenish heaven
Described by Mahomet, and Anacreon Moore,[9]
830   To whom the lyre and laurels have been given,
With all the trophies of triumphant song—
He won them well, and may he wear them long!

105

She sate, but not alone; I know not well
    How this same interview had taken place,
835 And even if I knew, I should not tell—
    People should hold their tongues in any case;
No matter how or why the thing befell,
    But there were she and Juan, face to face—
When two such faces are so,'twould be wise,
840   But very difficult, to shut their eyes.

106

How beautiful she look'd! her conscious[1] heart
    Glow'd in her cheek, and yet she felt no wrong.
Oh Love! how perfect is thy mystic art,
    Strengthening the weak, and trampling on the strong,
845 How self-deceitful is the sagest part
    Of mortals whom thy lure hath led along—
The precipice she stood on was immense,
So was her creed° in her own innocence.   *belief*

107

She thought of her own strength, and Juan's youth,
850   And of the folly of all prudish fears,
Victorious virtue, and domestic truth,
    And then of Don Alfonso's fifty years:
I wish these last had not occurr'd, in sooth,

---

8. I.e., postobit bonds (*post obitum,* "after death" [Latin]): loans to an heir that fall due after the death of the person whose estate he or she is to inherit. Byron's meaning is probably that only theology purports to tell us what rewards are due in heaven.
9. Byron's friend the poet Thomas Moore, who in

1800 had translated the *Odes* of the ancient Greek Anacreon and whose popular Orientalist poem *Lalla Rookh* (1817) had portrayed the "heathenish heaven" of Islam as populated by "houris," beautiful maidens who in the afterlife will give heroes their reward.
1. Secretly aware (of her feelings).

Because that number rarely much endears,
855   And through all climes, the snowy and the sunny,
Sounds ill in love, whate'er it may in money.

               *   *   *

113

The sun set, and up rose the yellow moon:
   The devil's in the moon for mischief; they
Who call'd her CHASTE, methinks, began too soon
900   Their nomenclature; there is not a day,
The longest, not the twenty-first of June,
   Sees half the business in a wicked way
On which three single hours of moonshine smile—
And then she looks so modest all the while.

114

905 There is a dangerous silence in that hour,
   A stillness, which leaves room for the full soul
To open all itself, without the power
   Of calling wholly back its self-control;
The silver light which, hallowing tree and tower,
910   Sheds beauty and deep softness o'er the whole,
Breathes also to the heart, and o'er it throws
A loving languor, which is not repose.

115

And Julia sate with Juan, half embraced
   And half retiring from the glowing arm,
915 Which trembled like the bosom where 'twas placed;
   Yet still she must have thought there was no harm,
Or else 'twere easy to withdraw her waist;
   But then the situation had its charm,
And then—God knows what next—I can't go on;
920 I'm almost sorry that I e'er begun.

116

Oh Plato! Plato! you have paved the way,
   With your confounded fantasies, to more
Immoral conduct by the fancied sway
   Your system feigns o'er the controlless core
925 Of human hearts, than all the long array
   Of poets and romancers:—You're a bore,
A charlatan, a coxcomb—and have been,
At best, no better than a go-between.

117

And Julia's voice was lost, except in sighs,
930   Until too late for useful conversation;
The tears were gushing from her gentle eyes,
   I wish, indeed, they had not had occasion,
But who, alas! can love, and then be wise?
   Not that remorse did not oppose temptation,

935 A little still she strove, and much repented,
And whispering "I will ne'er consent"—consented.

* * *

126

'Tis sweet to win, no matter how, one's laurels
By blood or ink; 'tis sweet to put an end
To strife; 'tis sometimes sweet to have our quarrels,
Particularly with a tiresome friend;
1005 Sweet is old wine in bottles, ale in barrels;
Dear is the helpless creature we defend
Against the world; and dear the schoolboy spot
We ne'er forget, though there we are forgot.

127

But sweeter still than this, than these, than all,
1010 Is first and passionate love—it stands alone,
Like Adam's recollection of his fall;
The tree of knowledge has been pluck'd—all's known—
And life yields nothing further to recall
Worthy of this ambrosial sin, so shown,
1015 No doubt in fable, as the unforgiven
Fire which Prometheus² filch'd for us from heaven.

* * *

133

Man's a phenomenon, one knows not what,
And wonderful beyond all wondrous measure;
'Tis pity though, in this sublime world, that
1060 Pleasure's a sin, and sometimes sin's a pleasure;
Few mortals know what end they would be at,
But whether glory, power, or love, or treasure,
The path is through perplexing ways, and when
The goal is gain'd, we die, you know—and then—

134

1065 What then?—I do not know, no more do you—
And so good night.—Return we to our story:
'Twas in November, when fine days are few,
And the far mountains wax a little hoary,
And clap a white cape on their mantles blue;
1070 And the sea dashes round the promontory,
And the loud breaker boils against the rock,
And sober suns must set at five o'clock.

135

'Twas, as the watchmen say, a cloudy night;
No moon, no stars, the wind was low or loud
1075 By gusts, and many a sparkling hearth was bright
With the piled wood, round which the family crowd;

2. The Titan Prometheus incurred the wrath of Zeus by stealing fire from heaven for humans.

There's something cheerful in that sort of light,
    Even as a summer sky's without a cloud:
I'm fond of fire, and crickets, and all that,
1080 A lobster-salad, and champagne, and chat.

136

'Twas midnight—Donna Julia was in bed,
    Sleeping, most probably—when at her door
Arose a clatter might awake the dead,
    If they had never been awoke before,
1085 And that they have been so we all have read,
    And are to be so, at the least, once more—
The door was fasten'd, but with voice and fist
First knocks were heard, then "Madam—Madam—hist!

137

"For God's sake, Madam—Madam—here's my master,
1090   With more than half the city at his back—
Was ever heard of such a curst disaster!
    'Tis not my fault—I kept good watch—Alack!
Do, pray undo the bolt a little faster—
    They're on the stair just now, and in a crack°   *moment*
1095 Will all be here; perhaps he yet may fly—
    Surely the window's not so *very* high!"

138

By this time Don Alfonso was arrived,
    With torches, friends, and servants in great number;
The major part of them had long been wived,
1100   And therefore paused not to disturb the slumber
Of any wicked woman, who contrived
    By stealth her husband's temples to encumber:[3]
Examples of this kind are so contagious,
Were one not punish'd, all would be outrageous.

139

1105 I can't tell how, or why, or what suspicion
    Could enter into Don Alfonso's head;
But for a cavalier of his condition°   *rank*
    It surely was exceedingly ill-bred
Without a word of previous admonition,
1110   To hold a levee[4] round his lady's bed,
And summon lackeys, arm'd with fire and sword,
To prove himself the thing he most abhorr'd.

140

Poor Donna Julia! starting as from sleep,
    (Mind—that I do not say—she had not slept)
1115 Began at once to scream, and yawn, and weep;
    Her maid Antonia, who was an adept,
Contrived to fling the bed-clothes in a heap,
    As if she had just now from out them crept:

---

3. I.e., with horns that, growing on the forehead, were the traditional emblem of the cuckolded husband.
4. Morning reception.

I can't tell why she should take all this trouble
1120 To prove her mistress had been sleeping double.

141

But Julia mistress, and Antonia maid,
   Appear'd like two poor harmless women, who
Of goblins, but still more of men afraid,
   Had thought one man might be deterr'd by two,
1125 And therefore side by side were gently laid,
   Until the hours of absence should run through,
And truant husband should return, and say,
"My dear, I was the first who came away."

142

Now Julia found at length a voice, and cried,
1130   "In heaven's name, Don Alfonso, what d'ye mean?
Has madness seized you? would that I had died
   Ere such a monster's victim I had been!
What may this midnight violence betide,
   A sudden fit of drunkenness or spleen?
1135 Dare you suspect me, whom the thought would kill?
Search, then, the room!"—Alfonso said, "I will."

143

He search'd, *they* search'd, and rummaged every where,
   Closet and clothes'-press, chest and window-seat,
And found much linen, lace, and seven pair
1140   Of stockings, slippers, brushes, combs, complete,
With other articles of ladies fair,
   To keep them beautiful, or leave them neat:
Arras[5] they prick'd and curtains with their swords,
And wounded several shutters, and some boards.

144

1145 Under the bed they search'd, and there they found—[6]
   No matter what—it was not that they sought;
They open'd windows, gazing if the ground
   Had signs or footmarks, but the earth said nought;
And then they stared each others' faces round:
1150   'Tis odd, not one of all these seekers thought,
And seems to me almost a sort of blunder,
Of looking *in* the bed as well as under.

145

During this inquisition Julia's tongue
   Was not asleep—"Yes, search and search," she cried,
1155 "Insult on insult heap, and wrong on wrong!
   It was for this that I became a bride!
For this in silence I have suffer'd long
   A husband like Alfonso at my side;
But now I'll bear no more, nor here remain,
1160 If there be law, or lawyers, in all Spain.

5. A tapestry hanging on a wall.   6. Perhaps a chamber pot.

1708 / GEORGE GORDON, LORD BYRON

146

"Yes, Don Alfonso! husband now no more,
　　If ever you indeed deserved the name,
Is't worthy of your years?—you have threescore,
　　Fifty, or sixty—it is all the same—
1165　Is't wise or fitting causeless to explore
　　For facts against a virtuous woman's fame?
Ungrateful, perjured, barbarous Don Alfonso,
How dare you think your lady would go on so?"

* * *

159

1265　The Senhor Don Alfonso stood confused;
　　Antonia bustled round the ransack'd room,
And, turning up her nose, with looks abused
　　Her master, and his myrmidons,[7] of whom
Not one, except the attorney, was amused;
1270　He, like Achates,[8] faithful to the tomb,
So there were quarrels, cared not for the cause,
Knowing they must be settled by the laws.

160

With prying snub-nose, and small eyes, he stood,
　　Following Antonia's motions here and there,
1275　With much suspicion in his attitude;
　　For reputations he had little care;
So that a suit or action were made good,
　　Small pity had he for the young and fair,
And ne'er believed in negatives, till these
1280　Were proved by competent false witnesses.

161

But Don Alfonso stood with downcast looks,
　　And, truth to say, he made a foolish figure;
When, after searching in five hundred nooks,
　　And treating a young wife with so much rigour,
1285　He gain'd no point, except some self-rebukes,
　　Added to those his lady with such vigour
Had pour'd upon him for the last half-hour,
Quick, thick, and heavy—as a thunder-shower.

162

At first he tried to hammer an excuse,
1290　　To which the sole reply was tears, and sobs,
And indications of hysterics, whose
　　Prologue is always certain throes, and throbs,
Gasps, and whatever else the owners choose:—
　　Alfonso saw his wife, and thought of Job's;[9]

---

7. Servants, so named for the followers Achilles led to the Trojan War.
8. The *fidus Achates* ("faithful Achates") of Virgil's *Aeneid*, whose loyalty to Aeneas has become proverbial.

9. Job's wife advised her afflicted husband to "curse God, and die." He replied, "Thou speakest as one of the foolish women speaketh" (Job 2.9–10).

1295 He saw too, in perspective, her relations,
    And then he tried to muster all his patience.

163

He stood in act to speak, or rather stammer,
    But sage Antonia cut him short before
The anvil of his speech received the hammer,
1300   With "Pray sir, leave the room, and say no more,
Or madam dies."—Alfonso mutter'd "D—n her,"
    But nothing else, the time of words was o'er;
He cast a rueful look or two, and did,
He knew not wherefore, that which he was bid.

164

1305 With him retired his *"posse comitatus,"*[1]
    The attorney last, who linger'd near the door,
Reluctantly, still tarrying there as late as
    Antonia let him—not a little sore
At this most strange and unexplain'd *"hiatus"*
1310   In Don Alfonso's facts, which just now wore
An awkward look; as he resolved the case
The door was fasten'd in his legal face.

165

No sooner was it bolted, than—Oh shame!
    Oh sin! Oh sorrow! and Oh womankind!
1315 How can you do such things and keep your fame,
    Unless this world, and t'other too, be blind?
Nothing so dear as an unfilch'd good name!
    But to proceed—for there is more behind:
With much heart-felt reluctance be it said,
1320 Young Juan slipp'd, half-smother'd, from the bed.

166

He had been hid—I don't pretend to say
    How, nor can I indeed describe the where—
Young, slender, and pack'd easily, he lay,
    No doubt, in little compass, round or square;
1325 But pity him I neither must nor may
    His suffocation by that pretty pair;
'Twere better, sure, to die so, than be shut
With maudlin Clarence in his Malmsey butt.[2]

* * *

169

1345 What's to be done? Alfonso will be back
    The moment he has sent his fools away.
Antonia's skill was put upon the rack,
    But no device could be brought into play—

1. The complete form of the modern word *posse* (*posse comitatus* means literally "power of the county" [Latin], i.e., the body of citizens summoned by a sheriff to preserve order in the county).

2. Clarence, brother of Edward IV and of the future Richard III, was reputed to have been assassinated by being drowned in a cask ("butt") of malmsey, a sweet and aromatic wine.

And how to parry the renew'd attack?
1350   Besides, it wanted but few hours of day:
Antonia puzzled; Julia did not speak,
But press'd her bloodless lip to Juan's cheek.

170

He turn'd his lip to hers, and with his hand
    Call'd back the tangles of her wandering hair;
1355 Even then their love they could not all command,
    And half forgot their danger and despair:
Antonia's patience now was at a stand—
    "Come, come, 'tis no time now for fooling there,"
She whisper'd, in great wrath—"I must deposit
1360 This pretty gentleman within the closet."

* * *

173

Now, Don Alfonso entering, but alone,
    Closed the oration of the trusty maid:
She loiter'd, and he told her to be gone,
1380   An order somewhat sullenly obey'd;
However, present remedy was none,
    And no great good seem'd answer'd if she staid:
Regarding both with slow and sidelong view,
She snuff'd the candle, curtsied, and withdrew.

174

1385 Alfonso paused a minute—then begun
    Some strange excuses for his late proceeding;
He would not justify what he had done,
    To say the best, it was extreme ill-breeding;
But there were ample reasons for it, none
1390   Of which he specified in this his pleading:
His speech was a fine sample, on the whole,
Of rhetoric, which the learn'd call "rigmarole."

* * *

180

Alfonso closed his speech, and begg'd her pardon,
    Which Julia half withheld, and then half granted,
1435 And laid conditions, he thought, very hard on,
    Denying several little things he wanted:
He stood like Adam lingering near his garden,
    With useless penitence perplex'd and haunted,
Beseeching she no further would refuse,
1440 When lo! he stumbled o'er a pair of shoes.

181

A pair of shoes!—what then? not much, if they
    Are such as fit with lady's feet, but these
(No one can tell how much I grieve to say)
    Were masculine; to see them, and to seize,
1445 Was but a moment's act.—Ah! Well-a-day!

My teeth begin to chatter, my veins freeze—
Alfonso first examined well their fashion,
And then flew out into another passion.

182

He left the room for his relinquish'd sword,
1450   And Julia instant to the closet flew,
"Fly, Juan, fly! for heaven's sake—not a word—
    The door is open—you may yet slip through
The passage you so often have explored—
    Here is the garden-key—Fly—fly—Adieu!
1455 Haste—haste!—I hear Alfonso's hurrying feet—
    Day has not broke—there's no one in the street."

183

None can say that this was not good advice,
    The only mischief was, it came too late;
Of all experience 'tis the usual price,
1460   A sort of income-tax laid on by fate:
Juan had reach'd the room-door in a trice,
    And might have done so by the garden-gate,
But met Alfonso in his dressing-gown,
Who threaten'd death—so Juan knock'd him down.

184

1465 Dire was the scuffle, and out went the light,
    Antonia cried out "Rape!" and Julia "Fire!"
But not a servant stirr'd to aid the fight.
    Alfonso, pommell'd to his heart's desire,
Swore lustily he'd be revenged this night;
1470   And Juan, too, blasphemed an octave higher,
His blood was up; though young, he was a Tartar,[3]
And not at all disposed to prove a martyr.

185

Alfonso's sword had dropp'd ere he could draw it,
    And they continued battling hand to hand,
1475 For Juan very luckily ne'er saw it;
    His temper not being under great command,
If at that moment he had chanced to claw it,
    Alfonso's days had not been in the land
Much longer.—Think of husbands', lovers' lives!
1480 And how ye may be doubly widows—wives!

186

Alfonso grappled to detain the foe,
    And Juan throttled him to get away,
And blood ('twas from the nose) began to flow;
    At last, as they more faintly wrestling lay,
1485 Juan contrived to give an awkward blow,
    And then his only garment quite gave way;
He fled, like Joseph,[4] leaving it; but there,
I doubt, all likeness ends between the pair.

---

3. A formidable opponent.
4. In Genesis 39.7ff. the chaste Joseph flees from the advances of Potiphar's wife, leaving "his garment in her hand."

187

Lights came at length, and men, and maids, who found
1490   An awkward spectacle their eyes before;
Antonia in hysterics, Julia swoon'd,
  Alfonso leaning, breathless, by the door;
Some half-torn drapery scatter'd on the ground,
  Some blood, and several footsteps, but no more:
1495 Juan the gate gain'd, turn'd the key about,
And liking not the inside, lock'd the out.

188

Here ends this canto.—Need I sing, or say,
  How Juan, naked, favour'd by the night,
Who favours what she should not, found his way,
1500   And reach'd his home in an unseemly plight?
The pleasant scandal which arose next day,
  The nine days' wonder which was brought to light,
And how Alfonso sued for a divorce,
Were in the English newspapers, of course.

189

1505 If you would like to see the whole proceedings,
  The depositions, and the cause at full,
The names of all the witnesses, the pleadings
  Of counsel to nonsuit,[5] or to annul,
There's more than one edition, and the readings
1510   Are various, but they none of them are dull,
The best is that in shorthand ta'en by Gurney,[6]
Who to Madrid on purpose made a journey.

190

But Donna Inez, to divert the train
  Of one of the most circulating scandals
1515 That had for centuries been known in Spain,
  Since Roderic's Goths, or older Genseric's Vandals,[7]
First vow'd (and never had she vow'd in vain)
  To Virgin Mary several pounds of candles;
And then, by the advice of some old ladies,
1520 She sent her son to be embark'd at Cadiz.

191

She had resolved that he should travel through
  All European climes, by land or sea,
To mend his former morals, or get new,
  Especially in France and Italy,
1525 (At least this is the thing most people do).
  Julia was sent into a nunnery,
And there, perhaps, her feelings may be better
Shown in the following copy of her letter:

5. Judgment against the plaintiff for failure to establish his case.
6. William B. Gurney (1777–1855), official shorthand writer for the houses of Parliament and a famous court reporter.
7. The Germanic tribes that overran Spain and other parts of southern Europe in the 5th through 8th centuries, notorious for rape and violence.

192

"They tell me 'tis decided; you depart:
1530   'Tis wise—'tis well, but not the less a pain;
I have no further claim on your young heart,
        Mine was the victim, and would be again;
To love too much has been the only art
        I used;—I write in haste, and if a stain
1535 Be on this sheet,'tis not what it appears,
My eyeballs burn and throb, but have no tears.

193

"I loved, I love you, for that love have lost
        State, station, heaven, mankind's, my own esteem,
And yet can not regret what it hath cost,
1540   So dear is still the memory of that dream;
Yet, if I name my guilt,'tis not to boast,
        None can deem harshlier of me than I deem:
I trace this scrawl because I cannot rest—
I've nothing to reproach, nor to request.

194

1545 "Man's love is of his life a thing apart,
        'Tis woman's whole existence; man may range
The court, camp, church, the vessel, and the mart,
        Sword, gown, gain, glory, offer in exchange
Pride, fame, ambition, to fill up his heart,
1550   And few there are whom these can not estrange;
Man has all these resources, we but one,
To love again, and be again undone.

195

"My breast has been all weakness, is so yet;
        I struggle, but cannot collect my mind;
1555 My blood still rushes where my spirit's set,
        As roll the waves before the settled wind;
My brain is feminine, nor can forget—
        To all, except your image, madly blind;
As turns the needle[8] trembling to the pole
1560 It ne'er can reach, so turns to you, my soul.

196

"You will proceed in beauty, and in pride,
        Beloved and loving many; all is o'er
For me on earth, except some years to hide
        My shame and sorrow deep in my heart's core;
1565 These I could bear, but cannot cast aside
        The passion which still rends it as before,
And so farewell—forgive me, love me—No,
That word is idle now—but let it go.

197

"I have no more to say, but linger still,
1570   And dare not set my seal upon this sheet,

8. Of a compass.

And yet I may as well the task fulfil,
    My misery can scarce be more complete:
I had not lived till now, could sorrow kill;
    Death flies the wretch who fain the blow would meet,
1575 And I must even survive this last adieu,
    And bear with life, to love and pray for you!"

198

This note was written upon gilt-edged paper
    With a neat crow-quill, rather hard, but new;
Her small white fingers scarce could reach the taper,[9]
1580   But trembled as magnetic needles do,
And yet she did not let one tear escape her;
    The seal a sunflower; "*Elle vous suit partout,*"[1]
The motto, cut upon a white cornelian;
The wax was superfine, its hue vermilion.

199

1585 This was Don Juan's earliest scrape; but whether
    I shall proceed with his adventures is
Dependent on the public altogether;
    We'll see, however, what they say to this,
Their favour in an author's cap's a feather,
1590   And no great mischief's done by their caprice;
And if their approbation we experience,
    Perhaps they'll have some more about a year hence.

200

My poem's epic, and is meant to be
    Divided in twelve books; each book containing,
1595 With love, and war, a heavy gale at sea,
    A list of ships, and captains, and kings reigning,
New characters; the episodes are three:
    A panorama view of hell's in training,
After the style of Virgil and of Homer,
1600 So that my name of Epic's no misnomer.

201

All these things will be specified in time,
    With strict regard to Aristotle's rules,
The *vade mecum*[2] of the true sublime,
    Which makes so many poets, and some fools;
1605 Prose poets like blank-verse, I'm fond of rhyme,
    Good workmen never quarrel with their tools;
I've got new mythological machinery,[3]
And very handsome supernatural scenery.

9. The candle (to melt wax to seal the letter).
1. She follows you everywhere (French). This motto was inscribed on one of Byron's seals and on a jewel he gave to John Edleston, the boy with whom he had a romantic friendship while at Cambridge. Their friendship was memorialized in Byron's 1807 poem "The Cornelian."

2. Go with me (Latin, literal trans.); handbook. Byron is deriding the neoclassical view that Aristotle's *Poetics* proposes "rules" for writing epic and tragedy.
3. The assemblage of supernatural personages and incidents introduced into a literary work.

202

There's only one slight difference between
1610   Me and my epic brethren gone before,
And here the advantage is my own, I ween;
    (Not that I have not several merits more,
But this will more peculiarly be seen)
    They so embellish, that 'tis quite a bore
1615 Their labyrinth of fables to thread through,
Whereas this story's actually true.

203

If any person doubt it, I appeal
    To history, tradition, and to facts,
To newspapers, whose truth all know and feel,
1620   To plays in five, and operas in three acts;
All these confirm my statement a good deal,
    But that which more completely faith exacts
Is, that myself, and several now in Seville,
Saw Juan's last elopement with the devil.[4]

204

1625 If ever I should condescend to prose,
    I'll write poetical commandments, which
Shall supersede beyond all doubt all those
    That went before; in these I shall enrich
My text with many things that no one knows,
1630   And carry precept to the highest pitch:
I'll call the work "Longinus o'er a Bottle,
Or, Every Poet his own Aristotle."

205

Thou shalt believe in Milton, Dryden, Pope;[5]
    Thou shalt not set up Wordsworth, Coleridge, Southey;
1635 Because the first is crazed beyond all hope,
    The second drunk, the third so quaint and mouthey:
With Crabbe it may be difficult to cope,
    And Campbell's Hippocrene[6] is somewhat drouthy:
Thou shalt not steal from Samuel Rogers, nor—
1640 Commit—flirtation with the muse of Moore.

206

Thou shalt not covet Mr. Sotheby's Muse,
    His Pegasus,[7] nor any thing that's his;
Thou shalt not bear false witness like "the Blues,"[8]

4. The usual plays on the Juan legend ended with Juan in hell; an early-20th-century version is Bernard Shaw's *Man and Superman*.
5. This is one of many passages, in prose and verse, in which Byron vigorously defends Dryden and Pope against his Romantic contemporaries.
6. Fountain on Mount Helicon whose waters supposedly gave inspiration. George Crabbe, whom Byron admired, was the author of *The Village* and other realistic poems of rural life. Thomas Campbell, Samuel Rogers, and Thomas Moore were lesser poets of the Romantic period; the last two were close friends of Byron and members of London's liberal Whig circles.
7. The winged horse symbolizing poetic inspiration. The wealthy William Sotheby, minor poet and translator, is satirized, as Botherby, in Byron's *Beppo*.
8. I.e., bluestockings, a contemporary term for female intellectuals, among whom Byron numbered his wife (line 1644).

(There's one, at least, is very fond of this);
1645 Thou shalt not write, in short, but what I choose:
This is true criticism, and you may kiss—
Exactly as you please, or not, the rod,
But if you don't, I'll lay it on, by G—d!⁹

207

If any person should presume to assert
1650 This story is not moral, first I pray
That they will not cry out before they're hurt,
Then that they'll read it o'er again, and say,
(But, doubtless, nobody will be so pert)
That this is not a moral tale, though gay;
1655 Besides, in canto twelfth, I mean to show
The very place where wicked people go.

* * *

213

But now at thirty years my hair is gray—
(I wonder what it will be like at forty?
I thought of a peruke° the other day)   wig
1700 My heart is not much greener; and, in short, I
Have squander'd my whole summer while 'twas May,
And feel no more the spirit to retort; I
Have spent my life, both interest and principal,
And deem not, what I deem'd, my soul invincible.

214

1705 No more—no more—Oh! never more on me
The freshness of the heart can fall like dew,
Which out of all the lovely things we see
Extracts emotions beautiful and new,
Hived in our bosoms like the bag o' the bee:
1710 Think'st thou the honey with those objects grew?
Alas! 'twas not in them, but in thy power
To double even the sweetness of a flower.

215

No more—no more—Oh! never more, my heart,
Canst thou be my sole world, my universe!
1715 Once all in all, but now a thing apart,
Thou canst not be my blessing or my curse:
The illusion's gone for ever, and thou art
Insensible, I trust, but none the worse,
And in thy stead I've got a deal of judgment,
1720 Though heaven knows how it ever found a lodgement.

---

9. Byron's parody of the Ten Commandments seemed blasphemous to some commentators. Radical publishers like William Hone, who in 1817 had been put on trial for the ostensible blasphemy of political satires that used the form of the Anglican Church's creed and catechism bitterly noted a double standard: books brought out by the ultra-respectable John Murray were not subject to the same reprisals as Hone's books.

216

My days of love are over, me no more
    The charms of maid, wife, and still less of widow,
Can make the fool of which they made before,
    In short, I must not lead the life I did do;
1725 The credulous hope of mutual minds is o'er,
    The copious use of claret is forbid too,
So for a good old gentlemanly vice,
I think I must take up with avarice.

217

Ambition was my idol, which was broken
1730   Before the shrines of Sorrow and of Pleasure;
And the two last have left me many a token
    O'er which reflection may be made at leisure:
Now, like Friar Bacon's brazen head, I've spoken,
    "Time is, Time was, Time's past,"[1] a chymic treasure[2]
1735 Is glittering youth, which I have spent betimes—
My heart in passion, and my head on rhymes.

218

What is the end of fame? 'tis but to fill
    A certain portion of uncertain paper:
Some liken it to climbing up a hill,
1740   Whose summit, like all hills', is lost in vapour;
For this men write, speak, preach, and heroes kill,
    And bards burn what they call their "midnight taper,"
To have, when the original is dust,
A name, a wretched picture, and worse bust.[3]

219

1745 What are the hopes of man? old Egypt's King
    Cheops erected the first pyramid
And largest, thinking it was just the thing
    To keep his memory whole, and mummy hid;
But somebody or other rummaging,
1750   Burglariously broke his coffin's lid:
Let not a monument give you or me hopes,
Since not a pinch of dust remains of Cheops.

220

But I, being fond of true philosophy,
    Say very often to myself, "Alas!
1755 All things that have been born were born to die,
    And flesh (which Death mows down to hay) is grass;[4]
You've pass'd your youth not so unpleasantly,
    And if you had it o'er again—'twould pass—

1. Spoken by a bronze bust in Robert Greene's *Friar Bacon and Friar Bungay* (1594). This comedy was based on legends about the magical power of Roger Bacon, the 13th-century Franciscan monk who was said to have built with diabolical assistance a brazen head capable of speech.
2. "Chymic": alchemic; i.e., the "treasure" is counterfeit gold.
3. Byron was unhappy with the portrait bust of him recently made by the Danish sculptor Thorwaldsen.
4. An echo of Isaiah 40.6 and 1 Peter 1.24: "All flesh is grass."

So thank your stars that matters are no worse,
1760   And read your Bible, sir, and mind your purse."

221

But for the present, gentle reader! and
      Still gentler purchaser! the bard—that's I—
Must, with permission, shake you by the hand,
      And so your humble servant, and good bye!
1765   We meet again, if we should understand
      Each other; and if not, I shall not try
Your patience further than by this short sample—
'Twere well if others follow'd my example.

222

"Go, little book, from this my solitude!
1770   I cast thee on the waters, go thy ways!
And if, as I believe, thy vein be good,
      The world will find thee after many days."
When Southey's read, and Wordsworth understood,
      I can't help putting in my claim to praise—
1775   The four first rhymes are Southey's every line:[5]
For God's sake, reader! take them not for mine.

From Canto 2

[JUAN AND HAIDEE]

III

How long in his damp trance young Juan lay
      He knew not, for the earth was gone for him,
And Time had nothing more of night nor day
      For his congealing blood, and senses dim;
885   And how this heavy faintness pass'd away
      He knew not, till each painful pulse and limb,
And tingling vein seem'd throbbing back to life,
For Death, though vanquish'd, still retired with strife.

112

His eyes he open'd, shut, again unclosed,
890   For all was doubt and dizziness; methought
He still was in the boat, and had but dozed,
      And felt again with his despair o'erwrought,
And wish'd it death in which he had reposed,
      And then once more his feelings back were brought,
895   And slowly by his swimming eyes was seen
A lovely female face of seventeen.

113

'Twas bending close o'er his, and the small mouth
      Seem'd almost prying into his for breath;
And chafing him, the soft warm hand of youth

5. The lines are part of the last stanza of Southey's "Epilogue to the Lay of the Laureate."

900   Recall'd his answering spirits back from death;
    And, bathing his chill temples, tried to soothe
       Each pulse to animation, till beneath
    Its gentle touch and trembling care, a sigh
    To these kind efforts made a low reply.

114

905   Then was the cordial pour'd, and mantle flung
       Around his scarce-clad limbs; and the fair arm
    Raised higher the faint head which o'er it hung;
       And her transparent cheek, all pure and warm,
    Pillow'd his death-like forehead; then she wrung
910   His dewy curls, long drench'd by every storm;
    And watch'd with eagerness each throb that drew
    A sigh from his heaved bosom—and hers, too.

115

    And lifting him with care into the cave,
       The gentle girl, and her attendant,—one
915   Young, yet her elder, and of brow less grave,
       And more robust of figure,—then begun
    To kindle fire, and as the new flames gave
       Light to the rocks that roof'd them, which the sun
    Had never seen, the maid, or whatsoe'er
920   She was, appear'd distinct, and tall, and fair.

116

    Her brow was overhung with coins of gold,
       That sparkled o'er the auburn of her hair,
    Her clustering hair, whose longer locks were roll'd
       In braids behind, and though her stature were
925   Even of the highest for a female mould,
       They nearly reach'd her heel; and in her air
    There was a something which bespoke command,
    As one who was a lady in the land.

117

    Her hair, I said, was auburn; but her eyes
930   Were black as death, their lashes the same hue,
    Of downcast length, in whose silk shadow lies
       Deepest attraction, for when to the view
    Forth from its raven fringe the full glance flies,
       Ne'er with such force the swiftest arrow flew;
935   'Tis as the snake late coil'd, who pours his length,
    And hurls at once his venom and his strength.

*   *   *

123

    And these two tended him, and cheer'd him both
       With food and raiment, and those soft attentions,
    Which are (as I must own) of female growth,
980   And have ten thousand delicate inventions:
    They made a most superior mess of broth,

A thing which poesy but seldom mentions,
But the best dish that e'er was cook'd since Homer's
Achilles order'd dinner for new comers.[1]

124

985   I'll tell you who they were, this female pair,
     Lest they should seem princesses in disguise;
Besides, I hate all mystery, and that air
     Of clap-trap, which your recent poets prize;
And so, in short, the girls they really were
990   They shall appear before your curious eyes,
Mistress and maid; the first was only daughter
Of an old man, who lived upon the water.

125

A fisherman he had been in his youth,
     And still a sort of fisherman was he;
995   But other speculations were, in sooth,
     Added to his connection with the sea,
Perhaps not so respectable, in truth:
     A little smuggling, and some piracy,
Left him, at last, the sole of many masters
1000   Of an ill-gotten million of piastres.[2]

126

A fisher, therefore, was he—though of men,
     Like Peter the Apostle,[3]—and he fish'd
For wandering merchant vessels, now and then,
     And sometimes caught as many as he wish'd;
1005   The cargoes he confiscated, and gain
     He sought in the slave-market too, and dish'd
Full many a morsel for that Turkish trade,
By which, no doubt, a good deal may be made.

127

He was a Greek, and on his isle had built
1010   (One of the wild and smaller Cyclades)[4]
A very handsome house from out his guilt,
     And there he lived exceedingly at ease;
Heaven knows what cash he got, or blood he spilt,
     A sad[5] old fellow was he, if you please,
1015   But this I know, it was a spacious building,
Full of barbaric carving, paint, and gilding.

128

He had an only daughter, call'd Haidee,
     The greatest heiress of the Eastern Isles;
Besides, so very beautiful was she,
1020   Her dowry was as nothing to her smiles:

---

1. A reference to the lavish feast with which Achilles entertained Ajax, Phoenix, and Ulysses (*Iliad* 9.193ff.).
2. Near-Eastern coins.
3. Christ's words to Peter and Andrew, both fishermen: "Follow me, and I will make you fishers of men" (Matthew 4.19).
4. A group of islands in the Aegean Sea.
5. In the playful sense: wicked.

Still in her teens, and like a lovely tree
   She grew to womanhood, and between whiles
Rejected several suitors, just to learn
How to accept a better in his turn.

129

1025 And walking out upon the beach, below
   The cliff, towards sunset, on that day she found,
Insensible,°—not dead, but nearly so,—   *unconscious*
   Don Juan, almost famish'd, and half drown'd;
But being naked, she was shock'd, you know,
1030   Yet deem'd herself in common pity bound,
As far as in her lay, "to take him in,
A stranger"[6] dying, with so white a skin.

130

But taking him into her father's house
   Was not exactly the best way to save,
1035 But like conveying to the cat the mouse,
   Or people in a trance into their grave;
Because the good old man had so much *"νους,"*[7]
   Unlike the honest Arab thieves so brave,
He would have hospitably cured the stranger,
1040 And sold him instantly when out of danger.

131

And therefore, with her maid, she thought it best
   (A virgin always on her maid relies)
To place him in the cave for present rest:
   And when, at last, he open'd his black eyes,
1045 Their charity increased about their guest;
   And their compassion grew to such a size,
It open'd half the turnpike-gates to heaven—
(St. Paul says 'tis the toll which must be given).[8]

*   *   *

141

And Haidee met the morning face to face;
   Her own was freshest, though a feverish flush
Had dyed it with the headlong blood, whose race
   From heart to cheek is curb'd into a blush,
1125 Like to a torrent which a mountain's base,
   That overpowers some Alpine river's rush,
Checks to a lake, whose waves in circles spread;
Or the Red Sea—but the sea is not red.

142

And down the cliff the island virgin came,
1130   And near the cave her quick light footsteps drew,

---

6. Cf. Matthew 25.35: "I was a stranger, and ye took me in."
7. *Nous*, intelligence (Greek); in England pronounced so as to rhyme with *mouse*.
8. 1 Corinthians 13.13: "And now abideth faith, hope, charity, these three; but the greatest of these is charity."

While the sun smiled on her with his first flame,
  And young Aurora° kiss'd her lips with dew,   *dawn*
Taking her for a sister; just the same
  Mistake you would have made on seeing the two,
1135 Although the mortal, quite as fresh and fair,
  Had all the advantage too of not being air.

143

And when into the cavern Haidee stepp'd
  All timidly, yet rapidly, she saw
That like an infant Juan sweetly slept;
1140   And then she stopp'd, and stood as if in awe,
(For sleep is awful)° and on tiptoe crept   *awe-inspiring*
  And wrapt him closer, lest the air, too raw,
Should reach his blood, then o'er him still as death
Bent, with hush'd lips, that drank his scarce-drawn breath.

*   *   *

148

And she bent o'er him, and he lay beneath,
  Hush'd as the babe upon its mother's breast,
Droop'd as the willow when no winds can breathe,
1180   Lull'd like the depth of ocean when at rest,
Fair as the crowning rose of the whole wreath,
  Soft as the callow° cygnet° in its nest;   *young / swan*
In short, he was a very pretty fellow,
Although his woes had turn'd him rather yellow.

149

1185 He woke and gazed, and would have slept again,
  But the fair face which met his eyes forbade
Those eyes to close, though weariness and pain
  Had further sleep a further pleasure made;
For woman's face was never form'd in vain
1190   For Juan, so that even when he pray'd
He turn'd from grisly saints, and martyrs hairy,
To the sweet portraits of the Virgin Mary.

150

And thus upon his elbow he arose,
  And look'd upon the lady, in whose cheek
1195 The pale contended with the purple rose,
  As with an effort she began to speak;
Her eyes were eloquent, her words would pose,
  Although she told him, in good modern Greek,
With an Ionian accent, low and sweet,
1200 That he was faint, and must not talk, but eat.

*   *   *

168

And every day by day-break—rather early
  For Juan, who was somewhat fond of rest—
She came into the cave, but it was merely

1340   To see her bird reposing in his nest;
    And she would softly stir his locks so curly,
       Without disturbing her yet slumbering guest,
    Breathing all gently o'er his cheek and mouth,
    As o'er a bed of roses the sweet south.[9]

169

1345   And every morn his colour freshlier came,
       And every day help'd on his convalescence;
    'Twas well, because health in the human frame
       Is pleasant, besides being true love's essence,
    For health and idleness to passion's flame
1350   Are oil and gunpowder; and some good lessons
    Are also learnt from Ceres[1] and from Bacchus,
    Without whom Venus will not long attack us.

170

    While Venus fills the heart (without heart really
       Love, though good always, is not quite so good)
1355   Ceres presents a plate of vermicelli,—
       For love must be sustain'd like flesh and blood,—
    While Bacchus pours out wine, or hands a jelly:
       Eggs, oysters too, are amatory food;
    But who is their purveyor from above
1360   Heaven knows,—it may be Neptune, Pan, or Jove.

171

    When Juan woke he found some good things ready,
       A bath, a breakfast, and the finest eyes
    That ever made a youthful heart less steady,
       Besides her maid's, as pretty for their size;
1365   But I have spoken of all this already—
       And repetition's tiresome and unwise,—
    Well—Juan, after bathing in the sea,
    Came always back to coffee and Haidée.

172

    Both were so young, and one so innocent,
1370   That bathing pass'd for nothing; Juan seem'd
    To her, as 'twere, the kind of being sent,
       Of whom these two years she had nightly dream'd,
    A something to be loved, a creature meant
       To be her happiness, and whom she deem'd
1375   To render happy; all who joy would win
    Must share it,—Happiness was born a twin.

173

    It was such pleasure to behold him, such
       Enlargement of existence to partake
    Nature with him, to thrill beneath his touch,
1380   To watch him slumbering, and to see him wake:
    To live with him for ever were too much;
       But then the thought of parting made her quake:

9. The south wind.
1. Ceres, goddess of the grain; Bacchus, god of wine and revelry.

He was her own, her ocean-treasure, cast
Like a rich wreck—her first love, and her last.

174

1385   And thus a moon° roll'd on, and fair Haidee   *month*
     Paid daily visits to her boy, and took
Such plentiful precautions, that still he
     Remain'd unknown within his craggy nook;
At last her father's prows put out to sea,
1390   For certain merchantmen upon the look,
Not as of yore to carry off an Io,[2]
But three Ragusan vessels, bound for Scio.[3]

175

Then came her freedom, for she had no mother,
     So that, her father being at sea, she was
1395 Free as a married woman, or such other
     Female, as where she likes may freely pass,
Without even the encumbrance of a brother,
     The freest she that ever gazed on glass:°   *in a mirror*
I speak of christian lands in this comparison,
1400 Where wives, at least, are seldom kept in garrison.

176

Now she prolong'd her visits and her talk
     (For they must talk), and he had learnt to say
So much as to propose to take a walk,—
     For little had he wander'd since the day
1405 On which, like a young flower snapp'd from the stalk,
     Drooping and dewy on the beach he lay,—
And thus they walk'd out in the afternoon,
And saw the sun set opposite the moon.

177

It was a wild and breaker-beaten coast,
1410   With cliffs above, and a broad sandy shore,
Guarded by shoals and rocks as by an host,
     With here and there a creek, whose aspect wore
A better welcome to the tempest-tost;
     And rarely ceas'd the haughty billow's roar,
1415 Save on the dead long summer days, which make
The outstretch'd ocean glitter like a lake.

178

And the small ripple spilt upon the beach
     Scarcely o'erpass'd the cream of your champagne,
When o'er the brim the sparkling bumpers reach,
1420   That spring-dew of the spirit! the heart's rain!
Few things surpass old wine; and they may preach
     Who please,—the more because they preach in vain,—
Let us have wine and woman, mirth and laughter,
Sermons and soda water the day after.

---

2. A mistress of Zeus who was persecuted by his jealous wife, Hera, and kidnapped by Phoenician merchants.

3. The Italian name for Chios, an island near Turkey. "Ragusan": Ragusa (or Dubrovnik) is an Adriatic port located in what is now Croatia.

179

1425   Man, being reasonable, must get drunk;
      The best of life is but intoxication:
  Glory, the grape, love, gold, in these are sunk
      The hopes of all men, and of every nation;
  Without their sap, how branchless were the trunk
1430   Of life's strange tree, so fruitful on occasion:
  But to return,—Get very drunk; and when
  You wake with head-ache, you shall see what then.

180

  Ring for your valet—bid him quickly bring
     Some hock and soda-water, then you'll know
1435   A pleasure worthy Xerxes[4] the great king;
     For not the blest sherbet, sublimed with snow,
  Nor the first sparkle of the desert-spring,
     Nor Burgundy in all its sunset glow,
  After long travel, ennui, love, or slaughter,
1440   Vie with that draught of hock and soda-water.

181

  The coast—I think it was the coast that I
     Was just describing—Yes, it *was* the coast—
  Lay at this period quiet as the sky,
     The sands untumbled, the blue waves untost,
1445   And all was stillness, save the sea-bird's cry,
     And dolphin's leap, and little billow crost
  By some low rock or shelve, that made it fret
  Against the boundary it scarcely wet.

182

  And forth they wandered, her sire being gone,
1450   As I have said, upon an expedition;
  And mother, brother, guardian, she had none,
     Save Zoe, who, although with due precision
  She waited on her lady with the sun,
     Thought daily service was her only mission,
1455   Bringing warm water, wreathing her long tresses,
  And asking now and then for cast-off dresses.

183

  It was the cooling hour, just when the rounded
     Red sun sinks down behind the azure hill,
  Which then seems as if the whole earth it bounded,
1460   Circling all nature, hush'd, and dim, and still,
  With the far mountain-crescent half surrounded
     On one side, and the deep sea calm and chill
  Upon the other, and the rosy sky,
  With one star sparkling through it like an eye.

---

4. The 5th-century Persian king was said to have offered a reward to anyone who could discover a new kind of pleasure.

184

1465 And thus they wander'd forth, and hand in hand,
   Over the shining pebbles and the shells,
Glided along the smooth and harden'd sand,
   And in the worn and wild receptacles
Work'd by the storms, yet work'd as it were plann'd,
1470   In hollow halls, with sparry roofs and cells,
They turn'd to rest; and, each clasp'd by an arm,
Yielded to the deep twilight's purple charm.

185

They look'd up to the sky, whose floating glow
   Spread like a rosy ocean, vast and bright;
1475 They gazed upon the glittering sea below,
   Whence the broad moon rose circling into sight;
They heard the wave's splash, and the wind so low,
   And saw each other's dark eyes darting light
Into each other—and, beholding this,
1480 Their lips drew near, and clung into a kiss;

186

A long, long kiss, a kiss of youth and love,
   And beauty, all concentrating like rays
Into one focus, kindled from above;
   Such kisses as belong to early days,
1485 Where heart, and soul, and sense, in concert move,
   And the blood's lava, and the pulse a blaze,
Each kiss a heart-quake,—for a kiss's strength,
I think, it must be reckon'd by its length.

187

By length I mean duration; theirs endured
1490   Heaven knows how long—no doubt they never reckon'd;
And if they had, they could not have secured
   The sum of their sensations to a second:
They had not spoken; but they felt allured,
   As if their souls and lips each other beckon'd,
1495 Which, being join'd, like swarming bees they clung—
Their hearts the flowers from whence the honey sprung.

188

They were alone, but not alone as they
   Who shut in chambers think it loneliness;
The silent ocean, and the starlight bay,
1500   The twilight glow, which momently grew less,
The voiceless sands, and dropping caves, that lay
   Around them, made them to each other press,
As if there were no life beneath the sky
Save theirs, and that their life could never die.

189

1505 They fear'd no eyes nor ears on that lone beach,
   They felt no terrors from the night, they were
All in all to each other: though their speech

Was broken words, they *thought* a language there,—
And all the burning tongues the passions teach
1510 Found in one sigh the best interpreter
Of nature's oracle—first love,—that all
Which Eve has left her daughters since her fall.

190

Haidee[5] spoke not of scruples, ask'd no vows,
Nor offer'd any; she had never heard
1515 Of plight and promises to be a spouse,
Or perils by a loving maid incurr'd;
She was all which pure ignorance allows,
And flew to her young mate like a young bird;
And, never having dreamt of falsehood, she
1520 Had not one word to say of constancy.

191

She loved, and was beloved—she adored,
And she was worshipp'd; after nature's fashion,
Their intense souls, into each other pour'd,
If souls could die, had perish'd in that passion,—
1525 But by degrees their senses were restored,
Again to be o'ercome, again to dash on;
And, beating 'gainst *his* bosom, Haidee's heart
Felt as if never more to beat apart.

192

Alas! they were so young, so beautiful,
1530 So lonely, loving, helpless, and the hour
Was that in which the heart is always full,
And, having o'er itself no further power,
Prompts deeds eternity can not annul,
But pays off moments in an endless shower
1535 Of hell-fire—all prepared for people giving
Pleasure or pain to one another living.

193

Alas! for Juan and Haidee! they were
So loving and so lovely—till then never,
Excepting our first parents, such a pair
1540 Had run the risk of being damn'd for ever;
And Haidee, being devout as well as fair,
Had, doubtless, heard about the Stygian river,[6]
And hell and purgatory—but forgot
Just in the very crisis she should not.

194

1545 They look upon each other, and their eyes
Gleam in the moonlight; and her white arm clasps
Round Juan's head, and his around hers lies
Half buried in the tresses which it grasps;

---

5. Byron said, with reference to Haidee: "I was, and am, penetrated with the conviction that women only know evil from men, whereas men have no criterion to judge of purity or goodness but woman."
6. The Styx, which flows through Hades.

She sits upon his knee, and drinks his sighs,
1550   He hers, until they end in broken gasps;
And thus they form a group that's quite antique,
Half naked, loving, natural, and Greek.

195

And when those deep and burning moments pass'd,
    And Juan sunk to sleep within her arms,
1555 She slept not, but all tenderly, though fast,
    Sustain'd his head upon her bosom's charms;
And now and then her eye to heaven is cast,
    And then on the pale cheek her breast now warms,
Pillow'd on her o'erflowing heart, which pants
1560 With all it granted, and with all it grants.

196

An infant when it gazes on a light,
    A child the moment when it drains the breast,
A devotee when soars the Host[7] in sight,
    An Arab with a stranger for a guest,
1565 A sailor when the prize has struck[8] in fight,
    A miser filling his most hoarded chest,
Feel rapture; but not such true joy are reaping
As they who watch o'er what they love while sleeping.

197

For there it lies so tranquil, so beloved,
1570   All that it hath of life with us is living;
So gentle, stirless, helpless, and unmoved,
    And all unconscious of the joy 'tis giving;
All it hath felt, inflicted, pass'd, and proved,
    Hush'd into depths beyond the watcher's diving;
1575 There lies the thing we love with all its errors
And all its charms, like death without its terrors.

198

The lady watch'd her lover—and that hour
    Of Love's, and Night's, and Ocean's solitude,
O'erflow'd her soul with their united power;
1580   Amidst the barren sand and rocks so rude
She and her wave-worn love had made their bower,
    Where nought upon their passion could intrude,
And all the stars that crowded the blue space
Saw nothing happier than her glowing face.

199

1585 Alas! the love of women! it is known
    To be a lovely and a fearful thing;
For all of theirs upon that die is thrown,
    And if 'tis lost, life hath no more to bring
To them but mockeries of the past alone,
1590   And their revenge is as the tiger's spring,

---

7. The bread or wafer that a priest consecrates to celebrate Mass.

8. When a captured vessel (a "prize") lowers its flag in token of surrender.

Deadly, and quick, and crushing; yet, as real
Torture is theirs, what they inflict they feel.

200

    They are right; for man, to man so oft unjust,
      Is always so to women; one sole bond
1595 Awaits them, treachery is all their trust;
      Taught to conceal, their bursting hearts despond
Over their idol, till some wealthier lust
      Buys them in marriage—and what rests beyond?
A thankless husband, next a faithless lover,
1600 Then dressing, nursing, praying, and all's over.

201

Some take a lover, some take drams° or prayers,   *drink*
    Some mind their household, others dissipation,
Some run away, and but exchange their cares,
    Losing the advantage of a virtuous station;
1605 Few changes e'er can better their affairs,
    Theirs being an unnatural situation,
From the dull palace to the dirty hovel:
Some play the devil, and then write a novel.[9]

202

Haidee was Nature's bride, and knew not this;
1610   Haidee was Passion's child, born where the sun
Showers triple light, and scorches even the kiss
    Of his gazelle-eyed daughters; she was one
Made but to love, to feel that she was his
    Who was her chosen: what was said or done
1615 Elsewhere was nothing—She had nought to fear,
Hope, care, nor love beyond, her heart beat *here*.

203

And oh! that quickening of the heart, that beat!
    How much it costs us! yet each rising throb
Is in its cause as its effect so sweet,
1620   That Wisdom, ever on the watch to rob
Joy of its alchymy, and to repeat
    Fine truths, even Conscience, too, has a tough job
To make us understand each good old maxim,
So good—I wonder Castlereagh[1] don't tax 'em.

204

1625 And now 'twas done—on the lone shore were plighted
    Their hearts; the stars, their nuptial torches, shed
Beauty upon the beautiful they lighted:
    Ocean their witness, and the cave their bed,

9. The impetuous Lady Caroline Lamb, having thrown herself at Byron and been after a time rejected, incorporated incidents from the affair in her novel *Glenarvon* (1816).
1. Robert Stewart, Viscount Castlereagh, detested by Byron for the ruthlessness he had shown in 1798 as the government's chief secretary for Ireland and for the foreign policy he later pursued as foreign secretary (1812–22). His belligerence with political opponents contributed to his unpopularity. Byron refers to a famously testy speech in which Castlereagh complained of "an ignorant impatience of taxation."

By their own feelings hallow'd and united,
1630   Their priest was Solitude, and they were wed:
And they were happy, for to their young eyes
Each was an angel, and earth paradise.[2]

       *   *   *

208

But Juan! had he quite forgotten Julia?
       And should he have forgotten her so soon?
I can't but say it seems to me most truly a
1660   Perplexing question; but, no doubt, the moon
Does these things for us, and whenever newly a
       Strong palpitation rises,'tis her boon,
Else how the devil is it that fresh features
Have such a charm for us poor human creatures?

209

1665 I hate inconstancy—I loathe, detest,
       Abhor, condemn, abjure the mortal made
Of such quicksilver clay that in his breast
       No permanent foundation can be laid;
Love, constant love, has been my constant guest,
1670   And yet last night, being at a masquerade,
I saw the prettiest creature, fresh from Milan,
Which gave me some sensations like a villain.

210

But soon Philosophy came to my aid,
       And whisper'd "think of every sacred tie!"
1675 "I will, my dear Philosophy!" I said,
       "But then her teeth, and then, Oh heaven! her eye!
I'll just inquire if she be wife or maid,
       Or neither—out of curiosity."
"Stop!" cried Philosophy, with air so Grecian,
1680 (Though she was masqued then as a fair Venetian).

211

"Stop!" so I stopp'd.—But to return: that which
       Men call inconstancy is nothing more
Than admiration due where nature's rich
       Profusion with young beauty covers o'er
1685 Some favour'd object; and as in the niche
       A lovely statue we almost adore,
This sort of adoration of the real
Is but a heightening of the "beau ideal."[3]

212

'Tis the perception of the beautiful,
1690   A fine extension of the faculties,

---

2. This episode rewrites *Aeneid* 4 in which, influenced by the malicious goddess Juno's love spells, the hero Aeneas and Dido, queen of Carthage, consummate their union in the cave in which they have taken refuge from a storm.

3. Ideal beauty (French), a common phrase in discussions of aesthetics.

Platonic, universal, wonderful,
    Drawn from the stars, and filter'd through the skies,
Without which life would be extremely dull;
    In short, it is the use of our own eyes,
1695 With one or two small senses added, just
    To hint that flesh is form'd of fiery dust.

213

Yet 'tis a painful feeling, and unwilling,
    For surely if we always could perceive
In the same object graces quite as killing
1700   As when she rose upon us like an Eve,
'Twould save us many a heart-ache, many a shilling,
    (For we must get them anyhow, or grieve),
Whereas, if one sole lady pleased for ever,
How pleasant for the heart, as well as liver!

* * *

216

In the mean time, without proceeding more
    In this anatomy, I've finish'd now
Two hundred and odd stanzas as before,
    That being about the number I'll allow
1725 Each canto of the twelve, or twenty-four;
    And, laying down my pen, I make my bow,
Leaving Don Juan and Haidee to plead
For them and theirs with all who deign to read.

1818–23   1819–24

PERCY BYSSHE SHELLEY
1792–1822

Percy Bysshe Shelley, radical in every aspect of his life and thought, emerged from a solidly conservative background. His ancestors had been Sussex aristocrats since early in the seventeenth century; his grandfather, Sir Bysshe Shelley, made himself the richest man in Horsham, Sussex; his father, Timothy Shelley, was a hardheaded and conventional member of Parliament. Percy Shelley was in line for a baronetcy and, as befitted his station, was sent to be educated at Eton and Oxford. As a youth he was slight of build, eccentric in manner, and unskilled in sports or fighting and, as a consequence, was mercilessly bullied by older and stronger boys. He later said that he saw the petty tyranny of schoolmasters and schoolmates as representative of man's general inhumanity to man, and dedicated his life to a war against injustice and oppression. As he described the experience in the Dedication to Laon and Cythna:

So without shame, I spake:—"I will be wise,
    And just, and free, and mild, if in me lies
Such power, for I grow weary to behold
    The selfish and the strong still tyrannise
Without reproach or check." I then controuled
My tears, my heart grew calm, and I was meek and bold.

At Oxford in the autumn of 1810, Shelley's closest friend was Thomas Jefferson Hogg, a self-centered, self-confident young man who shared Shelley's love of philosophy and scorn of orthodoxy. The two collaborated on a pamphlet, *The Necessity of Atheism*, which claimed that God's existence cannot be proved on empirical grounds, and, provocatively, they mailed it to the bishops and heads of the colleges at Oxford. Shelley refused to repudiate the document and, to his shock and grief, was peremptorily expelled, terminating a university career that had lasted only six months. This event opened a breach between Shelley and his father that widened over the years.

Shelley went to London, where he took up the cause of Harriet Westbrook, the pretty and warmhearted daughter of a well-to-do tavern keeper, whose father, Shelley wrote to Hogg, "has persecuted her in a most horrible way by endeavoring to compel her to go to school." Harriet threw herself on Shelley's protection, and "gratitude and admiration," he wrote, "all demand that I shall love her *forever*." He eloped with Harriet to Edinburgh and married her, against his conviction that marriage was a tyrannical and degrading social institution. He was then eighteen years of age; his bride, sixteen. The couple moved restlessly from place to place, living on a small allowance granted reluctantly by their families. In February 1812, accompanied by Harriet's sister Eliza, they traveled to Dublin to distribute Shelley's *Address to the Irish People* and otherwise take part in the movement for Catholic emancipation and for the amelioration of that oppressed and poverty-stricken people.

Back in London, Shelley became a disciple of the radical social philosopher William Godwin, author of the *Inquiry Concerning Political Justice*. In 1813 he printed privately his first important work, *Queen Mab*, a long poem set in the fantastic frame of the journey of a disembodied soul through space, to whom the fairy Mab reveals in visions the woeful past, the dreadful present, and a utopian future. Announcing that "there is no God!" Mab decries institutional religion and codified morality as the roots of social evil, prophesying that all institutions will wither away and humanity will return to its natural condition of goodness and felicity.

In the following spring Shelley, who had drifted apart from Harriet, fell in love with the beautiful Mary Wollstonecraft Godwin, daughter of Mary Wollstonecraft and William Godwin. Convinced that cohabitation without love is immoral, he abandoned Harriet, fled to France with Mary (taking along her stepsister, Claire Clairmont), and—in accordance with his belief in nonexclusive love—invited Harriet to come live with them in the relationship of a sister. Shelley's elopement with Mary outraged her father, despite the facts that his own views of marriage had been no less radical than Shelley's and that Shelley, himself in financial difficulties, had earlier taken over Godwin's very substantial debts. When he returned to London, Shelley found that the general public, his family, and most of his friends regarded him as not only an atheist and a revolutionary but also a gross immoralist. When two years later Harriet, pregnant by an unknown lover, drowned herself in a fit of despair, the courts denied Shelley the custody of their two children. (His first child with Mary Godwin, a girl born prematurely, had died earlier, only twelve days after her birth in February 1815.) Percy and Mary married in December 1816, and in spring 1818 they moved to Italy. Thereafter he envisioned himself as an alien and outcast, rejected by the human race to whose welfare he had dedicated his powers and his life.

In Italy he resumed his restless way of life, evading the people to whom he owed money by moving from town to town and house to house. His health was usually bad. Although the death of his grandfather in 1815 had provided a substantial income, he dissipated so much of it by his warmhearted but imprudent support of William Godwin, Leigh Hunt, and other needy acquaintances that he was constantly short of funds. Within nine months, in 1818–19, both Clara and William, the children Mary had borne in 1815 and 1817, died. Grief over these deaths destroyed the earlier harmony of the Shelleys' marriage; the birth in November 1819 of another son, Percy Florence (their only child to survive to adulthood), was not enough to mend the rift.

In these circumstances, close to despair and knowing that he almost entirely lacked an audience, Shelley wrote his greatest works. In 1819 he completed *Prometheus Unbound* and a tragedy, *The Cenci*. He wrote also numerous lyric poems; a visionary call for a proletarian revolution, "The Mask of Anarchy"; a witty satire on Wordsworth, *Peter Bell the Third*; and a penetrating political essay, "A Philosophical View of Reform." His works of the next two years include "A Defence of Poetry"; *Epipsychidion*, a rhapsodic vision of love as a spiritual union beyond earthly limits; *Adonais*, his elegy on the death of Keats; and *Hellas*, a lyrical drama evoked by the Greek war for liberation from the Turks. These writings, unlike the early *Queen Mab*, are the products of a mind chastened by tragic experience, deepened by philosophical speculation, and stored with the harvest of his reading—which Shelley carried on, as his friend Hogg said, "in season and out of season, at table, in bed, and especially during a walk," until he became one of the most erudite of poets. His delight in scientific discoveries and speculations continued, but his earlier zest for Gothic terrors and the social theories of the radical eighteenth-century optimists gave way to an absorption in Greek tragedy, Milton's *Paradise Lost*, and the Bible. Although he did not give up his hopes for a millennial future (he wore a ring with the motto *Il buon tempo verrà*— "the good time will come"), he now attributed the evils of society to humanity's own moral failures and grounded the possibility of radical social reform on a reform of the moral and imaginative faculties through the redeeming power of love. Though often represented as a simpleminded doctrinaire, Shelley in fact possessed a complex and energetically inquisitive intelligence that never halted at a fixed mental position; his writings reflect stages in a ceaseless exploration.

The poems of Shelley's maturity also show the influence of his study of Plato and the Neoplatonists. Shelley found congenial the Platonic division of the cosmos into two worlds—the ordinary world of change, mortality, evil, and suffering and an ideal world of perfect and eternal Forms, of which the world of sense experience is only a distant and illusory reflection. The earlier interpretations of Shelley as a downright Platonic idealist, however, have been drastically modified by modern investigations of his reading and writings. He was a close student of British empiricist philosophy, which limits knowledge to valid reasoning on what is given in sense experience, and within this tradition he felt a special affinity to the radical skepticism of David Hume. A number of Shelley's works, such as "Mont Blanc," express his view of the narrow limits of what human beings can know with certainty and exemplify his refusal to let his hopes harden into a philosophical or religious creed. To what has been called the "skeptical idealism" of the mature Shelley, hope in a redemption from present social ills is not an intellectual certainty but a moral obligation. Despair is self-fulfilling; we must continue to hope because, by keeping open the possibility of a better future, hope releases the imaginative and creative powers that are the only means of achieving that end.

When in 1820 the Shelleys settled finally at Pisa, he came closer to finding contentment than at any other time in his adult life. A group of friends, Shelley's "Pisan Circle," gathered around them, including for a while Lord Byron and the swashbuckling young Cornishman Edward Trelawny. Chief in Shelley's affections were Edward Williams, a retired lieutenant of a cavalry regiment serving in India, and his charming common-law wife, Jane, with whom Shelley became infatuated and to whom he addressed some of his best lyrics and verse letters. The end came suddenly, and in a way prefigured uncannily in the last stanza of *Adonais*, in which he had described his spirit as a ship driven by a violent storm out into the dark unknown. On July 8, 1822, Shelley and Edward Williams were sailing their open boat, the *Don Juan*, on the Gulf of Spezia. A violent squall swamped the boat. When several days later the bodies were washed ashore, they were cremated, and Shelley's ashes were buried in the Protestant Cemetery at Rome, near the graves of John Keats and William Shelley, the poet's young son.

Both Shelley's character and his poetry have been the subject of violently contradictory, and often partisan, estimates. His actions according to his deep convictions often led to disastrous consequences for himself and those near to him; and even recent scholars, while repudiating the vicious attacks by Shelley's contemporaries, attribute some of those actions to a self-assured egotism that masked itself as idealism. Yet Byron, who knew Shelley intimately and did not pay moral compliments lightly, wrote to his publisher John Murray, in response to attacks on Shelley at the time of his death: "You are all brutally mistaken about Shelley, who was, without exception, the *best* and least selfish man I ever knew." Shelley's politics, vilified during his lifetime, made him a literary hero to later political radicals: the Chartists in the middle of the nineteenth century, Marx and Engels at the end, and for much of the twentieth century, many of the guiding lights of the British Labour Party. As a poet Shelley was greatly admired by Robert Browning, Swinburne, and other Victorians; but in the mid-twentieth century he was repeatedly charged with intellectual and emotional immaturity, shoddy workmanship, and incoherent imagery by influential writers such as F. R. Leavis and his followers in Britain and the New Critics in America. More recently, however, many sympathetic studies have revealed the coherent intellectual understructure of his poems and have confirmed Wordsworth's early recognition that "Shelley is one of the best *artists* of us all: I mean in workmanship of style." Shelley, it has become clear, greatly expanded the metrical and stanzaic resources of English versification. His poems exhibit a broad range of voices, from the high but ordered passion of "Ode to the West Wind," through the heroic dignity of the utterances of Prometheus, to the approximation of what is inexpressible in the description of Asia's transfiguration and in the visionary conclusion of *Adonais*. Most surprising, for a poet who almost entirely lacked an audience, is the urbanity, the assured command of the tone and language of a cultivated man of the world, exemplified in passages that Shelley wrote all through his mature career and especially in the lyrics and verse letters that he composed during the last year of his life.

The texts printed here are those prepared by Donald H. Reiman and Neil Fraistat for *Shelley's Poetry and Prose*, a Norton Critical Edition, 2nd ed. (2001); Reiman has also edited for this anthology a few poems not included in that edition.

Mutability

We are as clouds that veil the midnight moon;
　　How restlessly they speed, and gleam, and quiver,
Streaking the darkness radiantly!—yet soon
　　Night closes round, and they are lost for ever:

5　Or like forgotten lyres,° whose dissonant strings　　　*wind harps*
　　Give various response to each varying blast,
To whose frail frame no second motion brings
　　One mood or modulation like the last.

We rest.—A dream has power to poison sleep;
10　We rise.—One wandering thought pollutes the day;
We feel, conceive or reason, laugh or weep;
　　Embrace fond woe, or cast our cares away:

It is the same!—For, be it joy or sorrow,
　　The path of its departure still is free:
15　Man's yesterday may ne'er be like his morrow;
　　Nought may endure but Mutability.

ca. 1814–15　　　　　　　　　　　　　　　　　　　　1816

To Wordsworth[1]

Poet of Nature, thou hast wept to know
That things depart which never may return:
Childhood and youth, friendship and love's first glow,
Have fled like sweet dreams, leaving thee to mourn.
5   These common woes I feel. One loss is mine
Which thou too feel'st, yet I alone deplore.
Thou wert as a lone star, whose light did shine
On some frail bark° in winter's midnight roar: small ship
Thou hast like to a rock-built refuge stood
10   Above the blind and battling multitude:
In honoured poverty thy voice did weave
Songs consecrate to truth and liberty,[2]—
Deserting these, thou leavest me to grieve,
Thus having been, that thou shouldst cease to be.

ca. 1814–15   1816

Mont Blanc[1]

Lines Written in the Vale of Chamouni

I

The everlasting universe of things
Flows through the mind, and rolls its rapid waves,
Now dark—now glittering—now reflecting gloom—
Now lending splendour, where from secret springs
5   The source of human thought its tribute brings
Of waters,—with a sound but half its own.
Such as a feeble brook will oft assume
In the wild woods, among the mountains lone,
Where waterfalls around it leap forever,

1. Shelley's grieved comment on the poet of nature and of social radicalism after his views had become conservative.
2. Perhaps an allusion to "Sonnets Dedicated to Liberty," the title that Wordsworth gave to the section of sonnets such as "London, 1802" when he republished them in his *Poems* of 1807.
1. "Mont Blanc," in which Shelley both echoes and argues with the poetry of natural description written by Wordsworth and Coleridge, was first published as the conclusion to the *History of a Six Weeks' Tour*. This was a book that Percy and Mary Shelley wrote together detailing the excursion that they and Claire Clairmont took in July 1816 to the valley of Chamonix, in what is now southeastern France. That valley lies at the foot of Mont Blanc, the highest mountain in the Alps and in all Europe.
   In the *History* Percy Shelley commented on his poem: "It was composed under the immediate impression of the deep and powerful feelings excited by the objects it attempts to describe; and, as an indisciplined overflowing of the soul rests its claim to approbation on an attempt to imitate the untamable wildness and inaccessible solemnity from which those feelings sprang." He was inspired

to write the poem while standing on a bridge spanning the river Arve, which flows through the valley of Chamonix and is fed from above by the meltoff of the glacier, the Mer de Glace.
   In a letter to Thomas Love Peacock drafted in the same week as "Mont Blanc," Shelley had recalled that the count de Buffon, a French pioneer of the science we now know as geology, had proposed a "sublime but gloomy theory—that this globe which we inhabit will at some future period be changed to a mass of frost." This sense, which Shelley takes from Buffon, of a Nature that is utterly alien and indifferent to human beings (and whose history takes shape on a timescale of incomprehensible immensity) is counterposed throughout "Mont Blanc" with Shelley's interest, fueled by his reading of 18th-century skeptics such as David Hume, in questions about the human mind, its powers, and the limits of knowledge. "All things exist as they are perceived: at least in relation to the percipient," Shelley would later write in "A Defence of Poetry" (p. 1785). In "Mont Blanc" the priority that this statement gives to the mind over the external world is challenged by the sheer destructive power of the mountain.

10 Where woods and winds contend, and a vast river
Over its rocks ceaselessly bursts and raves.

2

Thus thou, Ravine of Arve—dark, deep Ravine—
Thou many-coloured, many-voiced vale,
Over whose pines, and crags, and caverns sail
15 Fast cloud shadows and sunbeams: awful° scene,   *awe-inspiring*
Where Power in likeness of the Arve comes down
From the ice gulphs that gird his secret throne,
Bursting through these dark mountains like the flame
Of lightning through the tempest;—thou dost lie,
20 Thy giant brood of pines around thee clinging,
Children of elder° time, in whose devotion   *earlier, ancient*
The chainless winds still come and ever came
To drink their odours, and their mighty swinging
To hear—an old and solemn harmony;
25 Thine earthly rainbows stretched across the sweep
Of the etherial waterfall, whose veil
Robes some unsculptured² image; the strange sleep
Which when the voices of the desart fail
Wraps all in its own deep eternity;—
30 Thy caverns echoing to the Arve's commotion,
A loud, lone sound no other sound can tame;
Thou art pervaded with that ceaseless motion,
Thou art the path of that unresting sound—
Dizzy Ravine! and when I gaze on thee
35 I seem as in a trance sublime and strange
To muse on my own separate phantasy,
My own, my human mind, which passively
Now renders and receives fast influencings,
Holding an unremitting interchange
40 With the clear universe of things around;³
One legion of wild thoughts, whose wandering wings
Now float above thy darkness, and now rest
Where that or thou art no unbidden guest,
In the still cave of the witch Poesy,⁴
45 Seeking among the shadows that pass by
Ghosts of all things that are, some shade of thee,
Some phantom, some faint image; till the breast
From which they fled recalls them, thou art there!⁵

3

Some say that gleams of a remoter world
50 Visit the soul in sleep,—that death is slumber,
And that its shapes the busy thoughts outnumber
Of those who wake and live.—I look on high;

---

2. I.e., not formed by humans.
3. This passage is remarkably parallel to a passage Shelley could not have read in *The Prelude*, first published in 1850, in which Wordsworth discovers, in the landscape viewed from Mount Snowdon, the "type" or "emblem" of the human mind in its interchange with nature (see *The Prelude*

14.63ff., p. 1590).
4. I.e., in the part of the mind that creates poetry.
5. I.e., the thoughts (line 41) seek, in the poet's creative faculty, some shade, phantom, or image of the Ravine of the Arve; and when the breast, which has forgotten these images, recalls them again—there, suddenly, the Arve exists.

Has some unknown omnipotence unfurled
The veil of life and death? or do I lie
55 In dream, and does the mightier world of sleep
Spread far around and inaccessibly
Its circles? For the very spirit fails,
Driven like a homeless cloud from steep to steep
That vanishes among the viewless° gales!   *invisible*
60 Far, far above, piercing the infinite sky,
Mont Blanc appears,—still, snowy, and serene—
Its subject mountains their unearthly forms
Pile around it, ice and rock; broad vales between
Of frozen floods, unfathomable deeps,
65 Blue as the overhanging heaven, that spread
And wind among the accumulated steeps;
A desart peopled by the storms alone,
Save° when the eagle brings some hunter's bone,   *except*
And the wolf tracts° her there—how hideously   *tracks*
70 Its shapes are heaped around! rude, bare, and high,
Ghastly, and scarred, and riven.°—Is this the scene   *split*
Where the old Earthquake-dæmon[6] taught her young
Ruin? Were these their toys? or did a sea
Of fire, envelope once this silent snow?
75 None can reply—all seems eternal now.
The wilderness has a mysterious tongue
Which teaches awful doubt, or faith so mild,
So solemn, so serene, that man may be
But for such faith[7] with nature reconciled;
80 Thou hast a voice, great Mountain, to repeal
Large codes of fraud and woe; not understood
By all, but which[8] the wise, and great, and good
Interpret, or make felt, or deeply feel.

4

The fields, the lakes, the forests, and the streams,
85 Ocean, and all the living things that dwell
Within the dædal[9] earth; lightning, and rain,
Earthquake, and fiery flood, and hurricane,
The torpor of the year when feeble dreams
Visit the hidden buds, or dreamless sleep
90 Holds every future leaf and flower;—the bound
With which from that detested trance they leap;
The works and ways of man, their death and birth,
And that of him and all that his may be;
All things that move and breathe with toil and sound
95 Are born and die; revolve, subside and swell.

6. A supernatural being, halfway between mortals and the gods. Here it represents the force that makes earthquakes. Shelley views this landscape as the product of violent geological upheavals in the past.
7. I.e., "simply by holding such faith." In Shelley's balance of possibilities, the landscape is equally capable either of instilling such a Wordsworthian faith (in the possibility of reconciling humans and nature, lines 78–79) or of producing the "awful" (i.e., "awesome") doubt (that nature is totally alien to human needs and values). For Wordsworth's faith in the correspondence of Nature and human thoughts and his conviction that "Nature never did betray / The heart that loved her," see "Tintern Abbey," lines 122–23.
8. The reference is to "voice," line 80.
9. Intricately formed; derived from Daedalus, builder of the labyrinth in Crete.

Power dwells apart in its tranquillity
Remote, serene, and inaccessible:
And *this*, the naked countenance of earth,
On which I gaze, even these primæval mountains
100 Teach the adverting° mind. The glaciers creep   *observant*
Like snakes that watch their prey, from their far fountains,
Slow rolling on; there, many a precipice,
Frost and the Sun in scorn of mortal power
Have piled: dome, pyramid, and pinnacle,
105 A city of death, distinct with many a tower
And wall impregnable of beaming ice.
Yet not a city, but a flood of ruin
Is there, that from the boundaries of the sky
Rolls its perpetual stream; vast pines are strewing
110 Its destined path, or in the mangled soil
Branchless and shattered stand: the rocks, drawn down
From yon remotest waste, have overthrown
The limits of the dead and living world,
Never to be reclaimed. The dwelling-place
115 Of insects, beasts, and birds, becomes its spoil;
Their food and their retreat for ever gone,
So much of life and joy is lost. The race
Of man, flies far in dread; his work and dwelling
Vanish, like smoke before the tempest's stream,
120 And their place is not known. Below, vast caves
Shine in the rushing torrents' restless gleam,
Which from those secret chasms in tumult welling[1]
Meet in the vale, and one majestic River,[2]
The breath and blood of distant lands, for ever
125 Rolls its loud waters to the ocean waves,
Breathes its swift vapours to the circling air.

5

Mont Blanc yet gleams on high:—the power is there,
The still and solemn power of many sights,
And many sounds, and much of life and death.
130 In the calm darkness of the moonless nights,
In the lone glare of day, the snows descend
Upon that Mountain; none beholds them there,
Nor when the flakes burn in the sinking sun,
Or the star-beams dart through them:—Winds contend
135 Silently there, and heap the snow with breath
Rapid and strong, but silently! Its home
The voiceless lightning in these solitudes
Keeps innocently, and like vapour broods
Over the snow. The secret strength of things
140 Which governs thought, and to the infinite dome
Of heaven is as a law, inhabits thee!
And what were thou,° and earth, and stars, and sea,   *Mont Blanc*

---

1. This description (as well as that in lines 9–11) seems to be an echo of Coleridge's description of the chasm and sacred river in the recently published "Kubla Khan," lines 12–24.

2. The Arve, which flows into Lake Geneva. Nearby the river Rhone flows out of Lake Geneva to begin its course through France and into the Mediterranean.

If to the human mind's imaginings
Silence and solitude were vacancy?

1816   1817

Hymn to Intellectual Beauty[1]

1

The awful shadow of some unseen Power
  Floats though unseen amongst us,—visiting
  This various world with as inconstant wing
As summer winds that creep from flower to flower.—
5 Like moonbeams that behind some piny mountain shower,[2]
    It visits with inconstant glance
    Each human heart and countenance;
Like hues and harmonies of evening,—
    Like clouds in starlight widely spread,—
10   Like memory of music fled,—
    Like aught that for its grace may be
Dear, and yet dearer for its mystery.

2

Spirit of BEAUTY, that dost consecrate
  With thine own hues all thou dost shine upon
15   Of human thought or form,—where art thou gone?
Why dost thou pass away and leave our state,
This dim vast vale of tears, vacant and desolate?
    Ask why the sunlight not forever
    Weaves rainbows o'er yon mountain river,
20 Why aught° should fail and fade that once is shewn,   *anything*
    Why fear and dream and death and birth
    Cast on the daylight of this earth
    Such gloom,—why man has such a scope
For love and hate, despondency and hope?

3

25 No voice from some sublimer world hath ever
  To sage or poet these responses given—
  Therefore the name of God and ghosts and Heaven,
Remain the records of their vain endeavour,[3]
Frail spells—whose uttered charm might not avail to sever,
30   From all we hear and all we see,
    Doubt, chance, and mutability.
Thy light alone—like mist o'er mountains driven,
    Or music by the night wind sent
    Through strings of some still instrument,°   *wind harp*

---

1. "Intellectual" means nonmaterial, that which is beyond access to the human senses. In this poem intellectual beauty is something postulated to account for occasional states of awareness that lend splendor, grace, and truth both to the natural world and to people's moral consciousness.

2. Used as a verb.
3. The names (line 27) represent nothing better than the feeble guesses that philosophers and poets have made in attempting to answer the questions posed in stanza 2, but these guesses also delude us as though they were magic spells.

35   Or moonlight on a midnight stream,
      Gives grace and truth to life's unquiet dream.

4

      Love, Hope, and Self-esteem, like clouds depart
         And come, for some uncertain moments lent.
         Man were immortal, and omnipotent,
40   Didst thou, unknown and awful as thou art,
      Keep with thy glorious train firm state within his heart.[4]
            Thou messenger of sympathies,
            That wax and wane in lovers' eyes—
      Thou—that to human thought art nourishment,
45   Like darkness to a dying flame![5]
            Depart not as thy shadow came,
            Depart not—lest the grave should be,
      Like life and fear, a dark reality.

5

      While yet a boy I sought for ghosts, and sped
50   Through many a listening chamber, cave and ruin,
         And starlight wood, with fearful steps pursuing
      Hopes of high talk with the departed dead.
      I called on poisonous names with which our youth is fed;[6]
            I was not heard—I saw them not—
55   When musing deeply on the lot
      Of life, at that sweet time when winds are wooing
            All vital things that wake to bring
            News of buds and blossoming,—
            Sudden, thy shadow fell on me;
60   I shrieked, and clasped my hands in extacy!

6

      I vowed that I would dedicate my powers
         To thee and thine—have I not kept the vow?
         With beating heart and streaming eyes, even now
      I call the phantoms of a thousand hours
65   Each from his voiceless grave: they have in visioned bowers
            Of studious zeal or love's delight
            Outwatched with me the envious night[7]—
      They know that never joy illumed my brow
            Unlinked with hope that thou wouldst free
70   This world from its dark slavery,
            That thou—O awful Loveliness,
      Wouldst give whate'er these words cannot express.

7

      The day becomes more solemn and serene
         When noon is past—there is a harmony

4. I.e., "man would be immortal . . . if thou didst keep."
5. Darkness may be said to nourish the dying flame by providing the contrast that offsets its light.
6. Lines 49–52 refer to Shelley's youthful experi-
ments with magic. The "poisonous names" may be the religious terms ("God and ghosts and Heaven") of line 27.
7. I.e., stayed up until the night, envious of their delight, had reluctantly departed.

75   In autumn, and a lustre in its sky,
       Which through the summer is not heard or seen,
       As if it could not be, as if it had not been!
          Thus let thy power, which like the truth
          Of nature on my passive youth
80   Descended, to my onward life supply
          Its calm—to one who worships thee,
          And every form containing thee,
       Whom, Spirit fair, thy spells did bind
       To fear[8] himself, and love all human kind.

1816   1817

Ozymandias[1]

    I met a traveller from an antique land,
    Who said—"Two vast and trunkless° legs of stone   *without a torso*
    Stand in the desert. . . . Near them, on the sand,
    Half sunk a shattered visage lies, whose frown,
5   And wrinkled lip, and sneer of cold command,
    Tell that its sculptor well those passions read
    Which yet survive,° stamped on these lifeless things,   *outlive*
    The hand that mocked them, and the heart that fed;[2]
    And on the pedestal, these words appear:
10   My name is Ozymandias, King of Kings,
    Look on my Works, ye Mighty, and despair!
    Nothing beside remains. Round the decay
    Of that colossal Wreck, boundless and bare
    The lone and level sands stretch far away."

1817   1818

A Song: "Men of England"[1]

    Men of England, wherefore plough
    For the lords who lay ye low?
    Wherefore weave with toil and care
    The rich robes your tyrants wear?

5   Wherefore feed and clothe and save
    From the cradle to the grave

8. Probably in the old sense: "to stand in awe of."
1. According to Diodorus Siculus, Greek historian of the 1st century B.C.E., the largest statue in Egypt had the inscription "I am Ozymandias, king of kings; if anyone wishes to know what I am and where I lie, let him surpass me in some of my exploits." Ozymandias was the Greek name for Ramses II of Egypt, 13th century B.C.E.
2. "The hand" is the sculptor's, who had "mocked" (both imitated and satirized) the sculptured pas-

sions; "the heart" is the king's, which has "fed" his passions.
1. This and the two following poems were written at a time of turbulent unrest, after the return of troops from the Napoleonic Wars had precipitated a great economic depression. The "Song," expressing Shelley's hope for a proletarian revolution, was originally planned as one of a series for workers. It has become, as the poet wished, a hymn of the British labor movement.

Those ungrateful drones who would
Drain your sweat—nay, drink your blood?

Wherefore, Bees of England, forge
10   Many a weapon, chain, and scourge,
That these stingless drones may spoil
The forced produce of your toil?

Have ye leisure, comfort, calm,
Shelter, food, love's gentle balm?
15   Or what is it ye buy so dear
With your pain and with your fear?

The seed ye sow, another reaps;
The wealth ye find, another keeps;
The robes ye weave, another wears;
20   The arms ye forge, another bears.

Sow seed—but let no tyrant reap:
Find wealth—let no impostor heap:
Weave robes—let not the idle wear:
Forge arms—in your defence to bear.

25   Shrink to your cellars, holes, and cells—
In halls ye deck another dwells.
Why shake the chains ye wrought? Ye see
The steel ye tempered glance on ye.

With plough and spade and hoe and loom
30   Trace your grave and build your tomb
And weave your winding-sheet—till fair
England be your Sepulchre.

1819   1839

England in 1819

An old, mad, blind, despised, and dying King;[1]
Princes, the dregs of their dull race, who flow
Through public scorn,—mud from a muddy spring;
Rulers who neither see nor feel nor know,
5   But leechlike to their fainting country cling
Till they drop, blind in blood, without a blow.
A people starved and stabbed in th' untilled field;[2]
An army, whom liberticide[3] and prey
Makes as a two-edged sword to all who wield;

1. George III, who had been declared insane in
1811. He died in 1820.
2. Alluding to the Peterloo Massacre on August
16, 1819. In St. Peter's field, near Manchester, a
troop of cavalry had charged into a crowd attending
a peaceful rally in support of parliamentary reform.
"Peterloo" is an ironic combination of "St. Peter's"
and "Waterloo."
3. The killing of liberty.

10   Golden and sanguine laws[4] which tempt and slay;
     Religion Christless, Godless—a book sealed;
     A senate, Time's worst statute, unrepealed—
     Are graves from which a glorious Phantom[5] may
     Burst, to illumine our tempestuous day.

1819   1839

Ode to the West Wind[1]

O wild West Wind, thou breath of Autumn's being,
Thou, from whose unseen presence the leaves dead
Are driven, like ghosts from an enchanter fleeing,

Yellow, and black, and pale, and hectic[2] red,
5   Pestilence-stricken multitudes: O Thou,
Who chariotest to their dark wintry bed

The winged seeds, where they lie cold and low,
Each like a corpse within its grave, until
Thine azure sister of the Spring[3] shall blow

10   Her clarion[4] o'er the dreaming earth, and fill
(Driving sweet buds like flocks to feed in air)
With living hues and odours plain and hill:

Wild Spirit, which art moving everywhere;
Destroyer and Preserver;[5] hear, O hear!

2

15   Thou on whose stream, 'mid the steep sky's commotion,
Loose clouds like Earth's decaying leaves are shed,
Shook from the tangled boughs of Heaven and Ocean,

Angels[6] of rain and lightning: there are spread
On the blue surface of thine aery surge,
20   Like the bright hair uplifted from the head

4. Laws bought with gold and leading to bloodshed.
5. I.e., a revolution.
1. This poem was conceived and chiefly written in a wood that skirts the Arno, near Florence, and on a day when that tempestuous wind, whose temperature is at once mild and animating, was collecting the vapours which pour down the autumnal rains [Shelley's note]. As in other major Romantic poems—for example, the opening of Wordsworth's *Prelude*, Coleridge's "Dejection: An Ode," and the conclusion to Shelley's *Adonais*—the rising wind, linked with the cycle of the seasons, is presented as the correspondent in the external world to an inner change, a burst of creative power that is paralleled to the inspiration of prophets. In many languages the words for *wind, breath, soul,* and *inspiration* are identical or related. Thus Shelley's west wind is a "spirit" (the Latin *spiritus:* wind, breath, soul, and the root word for *inspiration*), the

"breath of Autumn's being," which on earth, sky, and sea destroys in autumn to revive in the spring. In some philosophical histories of the period, the spirit of liberty was said to have deserted Europe for the Americas. In blowing from the west, the wind may carry liberty back again.

Shelley's sonnet-length stanza, developed from the interlaced three-line units of the Italian *terza rima* (*aba bcb cdc,* etc.), consists of a set of four such tercets, closed by a couplet rhyming with the middle line of the preceding tercet: *aba bcb cdc ded ee.*
2. Referring to the kind of fever that occurs in tuberculosis.
3. The west wind that will blow in the spring.
4. A high, shrill trumpet.
5. Refers to the Hindu gods Siva the Destroyer and Vishnu the Preserver.
6. In the old sense of messengers.

Of some fierce Mænad,[7] even from the dim verge
Of the horizon to the zenith's height,
The locks of the approaching storm. Thou Dirge

Of the dying year, to which this closing night
25 Will be the dome of a vast sepulchre,
Vaulted with all thy congregated might

Of vapours,° from whose solid atmosphere   clouds
Black rain and fire and hail will burst: O hear!

3

Thou who didst waken from his summer dreams
30 The blue Mediterranean, where he lay,
Lulled by the coil of his chrystalline streams,[8]

Beside a pumice isle in Baiæ's bay,[9]
And saw in sleep old palaces and towers
Quivering within the wave's intenser day,

35 All overgrown with azure moss and flowers
So sweet, the sense faints picturing them! Thou
For whose path the Atlantic's level powers

Cleave themselves into chasms, while far below
The sea-blooms and the oozy woods which wear
40 The sapless foliage of the ocean, know

Thy voice, and suddenly grow grey with fear,
And tremble and despoil themselves:[1] O hear!

4

If I were a dead leaf thou mightest bear;
If I were a swift cloud to fly with thee;
45 A wave to pant beneath thy power, and share

The impulse of thy strength, only less free
Than thou, O Uncontrollable! If even
I were as in my boyhood, and could be

The comrade of thy wanderings over Heaven,
50 As then, when to outstrip thy skiey speed
Scarce seemed a vision; I would ne'er have striven

As thus with thee in prayer in my sore need.
Oh! lift me as a wave, a leaf, a cloud!
I fall upon the thorns of life! I bleed!

7. A female worshipper who danced frenziedly in
the worship of Dionysus (Bacchus), the Greek god
of wine and vegetation. As vegetation god he was
fabled to die in the fall and to be resurrected in the
spring.
8. The currents that flow in the Mediterranean
Sea, sometimes with a visible difference in color.

9. West of Naples, the locale of imposing villas
built in the glory days of imperial Rome. Their
ruins are reflected in the waters of the bay.
1. The vegetation at the bottom of the sea . . .
sympathizes with that of the land in the change of
seasons, and is consequently influenced by the
winds which announce it [Shelley's note].

55 A heavy weight of hours has chained and bowed
One too like thee: tameless, and swift, and proud.

5

Make me thy lyre,[2] even as the forest is:
What if my leaves are falling like its own!
The tumult of thy mighty harmonies

60 Will take from both a deep, autumnal tone,
Sweet though in sadness. Be thou, Spirit fierce,
My spirit! Be thou me, impetuous one!

Drive my dead thoughts over the universe
Like withered leaves to quicken a new birth![3]
65 And, by the incantation of this verse,

Scatter, as from an unextinguished hearth
Ashes and sparks, my words among mankind!
Be through my lips to unawakened Earth

The trumpet of a prophecy! O Wind,
70 If Winter comes, can Spring be far behind?

1819   1820

Prometheus Unbound

Prometheus Unbound   Shelley composed this work in Italy between the
autumn of 1818 and the close of 1819 and published it the following summer. Upon
its completion he wrote in a letter, "It is a drama, with characters and mechanism of
a kind yet unattempted; and I think the execution is better than any of my former
attempts." It is based on the *Prometheus Bound* of Aeschylus, which dramatizes the
sufferings of Prometheus, unrepentant champion of humanity, who, because he had
stolen fire from heaven, was condemned by Zeus to be chained to Mount Caucasus
and to be tortured by a vulture feeding on his liver; in a lost sequel Aeschylus reconciled Prometheus with his oppressor. Shelley continued Aeschylus's story but transformed it into a symbolic drama about the origin of evil and the possibility of
overcoming it. In such early writings as *Queen Mab*, Shelley had expressed his belief
that injustice and suffering could be eliminated by an external revolution that would
wipe out or radically reform the causes of evil, attributed to existing social, political,
and religious institutions. Implicit in *Prometheus Unbound*, on the other hand, is the
view that both evil and the possibility of reform are the moral responsibility of men
and women. Social chaos and wars are a gigantic projection of human moral disorder
and inner division and conflict; tyrants are the outer representatives of the tyranny
of our baser over our better elements; hatred for others is a product of self-contempt;
and external political reform is impossible unless we have first reformed our own
nature at its roots, by substituting selfless love for divisive hatred. Shelley thus incorporates into his secular myth—of universal regeneration by a triumph of humanity's
moral imagination—the ethical teaching of Christ on the Mount, together with the
classical morality represented in the *Prometheus* of Aeschylus.

2. The Eolian lyre, which responds to the wind
with rising and falling musical chords.

3. This line may play on the secondary sense of
"leaves" as pages in a book.

FROM PROMETHEUS UNBOUND

A Lyrical Drama in Four Acts

Audisne hæc Amphiarae, sub terram abdite?[1]

Preface

The Greek tragic writers, in selecting as their subject any portion of their national history or mythology, employed in their treatment of it a certain arbitrary discretion. They by no means conceived themselves bound to adhere to the common interpretation or to imitate in story as in title their rivals and predecessors. Such a system would have amounted to a resignation of those claims to preference over their competitors which incited the composition. The Agamemnonian story was exhibited on the Athenian theatre with as many variations as dramas.

I have presumed to employ a similar licence.—The *Prometheus Unbound* of Æschylus, supposed the reconciliation of Jupiter with his victim as the price of the disclosure of the danger threatened to his empire by the consummation of his marriage with Thetis. Thetis, according to this view of the subject, was given in marriage to Peleus, and Prometheus by the permission of Jupiter delivered from his captivity by Hercules.[2]—Had I framed my story on this model I should have done no more than have attempted to restore the lost drama of Æschylus; an ambition, which, if my preference to this mode of treating the subject had incited me to cherish, the recollection of the high comparison such an attempt would challenge, might well abate. But in truth I was averse from a catastrophe so feeble as that of reconciling the Champion with the Oppressor of mankind. The moral interest of the fable which is so powerfully sustained by the sufferings and endurance of Prometheus, would be annihilated if we could conceive of him as unsaying his high language, and quailing before his successful and perfidious adversary. The only imaginary being resembling in any degree Prometheus, is Satan; and Prometheus is, in my judgement, a more poetical character than Satan because, in addition to courage and majesty and firm and patient opposition to omnipotent force, he is susceptible of being described as exempt from the taints of ambition, envy, revenge, and a desire for personal aggrandisement, which in the Hero of *Paradise Lost,* interfere with the interest. The character of Satan engenders in the mind a pernicious casuistry[3] which leads us to weigh his faults with his wrongs and to excuse the former because the latter exceed all measure. In the minds of those who consider that magnificent fiction with a religious feeling, it engenders something worse. But Prometheus is, as it were, the type of the

---

1. Cicero, *Tusculan Disputations* 2.60: "Do you hear this, O Amphiaraus, concealed under the earth?" In Greek myth Amphiaraus was a seer. Fleeing from an unsuccessful assault on Thebes, he was saved from his pursuers by Zeus, who by a thunderbolt opened a cleft in the earth that swallowed him up.

In his *Disputations* Cicero is arguing for the Stoic doctrine of the need to master pain and suffering. He quotes this line (a Latin translation from Aeschylus's lost drama *Epigoni*) in the course of an anecdote about Dionysius of Heraclea, who, tormented by kidney stones, abjures the doctrine of his Stoic teacher Zeno that pain is not an evil. By way of reproof his fellow-Stoic Cleanthes strikes his foot on the ground and utters this line. Cicero interprets it as an appeal to Zeno the Stoic master (under the name of Amphiaraus).

2. Shelley's description of the subject of Aeschylus's lost drama, *Prometheus Unbound,* is a speculation based on surviving fragments.

3. Slippery reasoning.

highest perfection of moral and intellectual nature, impelled by the purest and the truest motives to the best and noblest ends.

This Poem was chiefly written upon the mountainous ruins of the Baths of Caracalla, among the flowery glades, and thickets of odoriferous blossoming trees which are extended in ever winding labyrinths upon its immense platforms and dizzy arches suspended in the air. The bright blue sky of Rome, and the effect of the vigorous awakening of spring in that divinest climate, and the new life with which it drenches the spirits even to intoxication, were the inspiration of this drama.

The imagery which I have employed will be found in many instances to have been drawn from the operations of the human mind, or from those external actions by which they are expressed. This is unusual in modern Poetry; although Dante and Shakespeare are full of instances of the same kind: Dante indeed more than any other poet and with greater success. But the Greek poets, as writers to whom no resource of awakening the sympathy of their contemporaries was unknown, were in the habitual use of this power, and it is the study of their works (since a higher merit would probably be denied me) to which I am willing that my readers should impute this singularity.

One word is due in candour to the degree in which the study of contemporary writings may have tinged my composition, for such has been a topic of censure with regard to poems far more popular, and indeed more deservedly popular than mine. It is impossible that any one who inhabits the same age with such writers as those who stand in the foremost ranks of our own, can conscientiously assure himself, that his language and tone of thought may not have been modified by the study of the productions of those extraordinary intellects. It is true, that, not the spirit of their genius, but the forms in which it has manifested itself, are due, less to the peculiarities of their own minds, than to the peculiarity of the moral and intellectual condition of the minds among which they have been produced. Thus a number of writers possess the form, whilst they want the spirit of those whom, it is alleged, they imitate; because the former is the endowment of the age in which they live, and the latter must be the uncommunicated lightning of their own mind.

The peculiar style of intense and comprehensive imagery which distinguishes the modern literature of England, has not been, as a general power, the product of the imitation of any particular writer. The mass of capabilities remains at every period materially the same; the circumstances which awaken it to action perpetually change. If England were divided into forty republics, each equal in population and extent to Athens, there is no reason to suppose but that, under institutions not more perfect than those of Athens, each would produce philosophers and poets equal to those who (if we except Shakespeare) have never been surpassed. We owe the great writers of the golden age of our literature to that fervid awakening of the public mind which shook to dust the oldest and most oppressive form of the Christian Religion. We owe Milton to the progress and developement of the same spirit; the sacred Milton was, let it ever be remembered, a Republican,[4] and a bold enquirer into morals and religion. The great writers of our own age are, we have reason to suppose, the companions and forerunners of some unimagined change in our social con-

---

4. I.e., Milton hoped that the overthrow of the monarchy during the Civil War would lead to England's rebirth as a republic.

dition or the opinions which cement it. The cloud of mind is discharging its collected lightning, and the equilibrium between institutions and opinions is now restoring, or is about to be restored.[5]

As to imitation; Poetry is a mimetic art. It creates, but it creates by combination and representation. Poetical abstractions are beautiful and new, not because the portions of which they are composed had no previous existence in the mind of man or in nature, but because the whole produced by their combination has some intelligible and beautiful analogy with those sources of emotion and thought, and with the contemporary condition of them: one great poet is a masterpiece of nature, which another not only ought to study but must study. He might as wisely and as easily determine that his mind should no longer be the mirror of all that is lovely in the visible universe, as exclude from his contemplation the beautiful which exists in the writings of a great contemporary. The pretence of doing it would be a presumption in any but the greatest; the effect, even in him, would be strained, unnatural and ineffectual. A Poet, is the combined product of such internal powers as modify the nature of others, and of such external influences as excite and sustain these powers; he is not one, but both. Every man's mind is in this respect modified by all the objects of nature and art, by every word and every suggestion which he ever admitted to act upon his consciousness; it is the mirror upon which all forms are reflected, and in which they compose one form. Poets, not otherwise than philosophers, painters, sculptors and musicians, are in one sense the creators and in another the creations of their age. From this subjection the loftiest do not escape. There is a similarity between Homer and Hesiod, between Æschylus and Euripides, between Virgil and Horace, between Dante and Petrarch, between Shakespeare and Fletcher, between Dryden and Pope; each has a generic resemblance under which their specific distinctions are arranged. If this similarity be the result of imitation, I am willing to confess that I have imitated.

Let this opportunity be conceded to me of acknowledging that I have, what a Scotch philosopher characteristically terms, "a passion for reforming the world:"[6] what passion incited him to write and publish his book, he omits to explain. For my part I had rather be damned with Plato and Lord Bacon, than go to Heaven with Paley and Malthus.[7] But it is a mistake to suppose that I dedicate my poetical compositions solely to the direct enforcement of reform, or that I consider them in any degree as containing a reasoned system on the theory of human life. Didactic poetry is my abhorrence; nothing can be equally well expressed in prose that is not tedious and supererogatory in verse. My purpose has hitherto been simply to familiarise the highly refined imagination of the more select classes of poetical readers with beautiful idealisms of moral excellence; aware that until the mind can love, and admire, and trust, and hope, and endure, reasoned principles of moral conduct are seeds cast upon the highway of life which the unconscious passenger tramples into dust,

5. See Shelley's similar tribute to his great contemporaries in the concluding paragraph of his "Defence of Poetry" (p. 1797).
6. This is the title of chap. 16 in *The Principles of Moral Science* (1805), by the Scottish writer Robert Forsyth.
7. Thomas Malthus's *An Essay on the Principle of Population* (1798) argued that the rate of increase in population will soon exceed the rate of increase in the food supply necessary to sustain it. William Paley wrote *Evidences of Christianity* (1794), which undertakes to prove that the design apparent in natural phenomena, and especially in the human body, entails the existence of God as the great Designer. Shelley ironically expresses his contempt for the doctrines of both these thinkers, which he conceives as arguments for accepting uncomplainingly the present state of the world.

although they would bear the harvest of his happiness. Should I live to accomplish what I purpose, that is, produce a systematical history of what appear to me to be the genuine elements of human society,[8] let not the advocates of injustice and superstition flatter themselves that I should take Æschylus rather than Plato as my model.

The having spoken of myself with unaffected freedom will need little apology with the candid; and let the uncandid consider that they injure me less than their own hearts and minds by misrepresentation. Whatever talents a person may possess to amuse and instruct others, be they ever so inconsiderable, he is yet bound to exert them: if his attempt be ineffectual, let the punishment of an unaccomplished purpose have been sufficient; let none trouble themselves to heap the dust of oblivion upon his efforts; the pile they raise will betray his grave which might otherwise have been unknown.

Prometheus Unbound

From *Act 1*

SCENE: *A Ravine of Icy Rocks in the Indian Caucasus.* PROMETHEUS *is discovered bound to the Precipice.* PANTHEA *and* IONE[1] *are seated at his feet. Time, Night. During the Scene, Morning slowly breaks.*

PROMETHEUS   Monarch of Gods and Dæmons, and all Spirits
  But One,[2] who throng those bright and rolling Worlds
  Which Thou and I alone of living things
  Behold with sleepless eyes! regard this Earth
5 Made multitudinous with thy slaves, whom thou
  Requitest for knee-worship, prayer and praise,
  And toil, and hecatombs[3] of broken hearts,
  With fear and self contempt and barren hope;
  Whilst me, who am thy foe, eyeless° in hate,   blinded
10 Hast thou made reign and triumph, to thy scorn,
  O'er mine own misery and thy vain revenge.—
  Three thousand years of sleep-unsheltered hours
  And moments—aye° divided by keen pangs   always
  Till they seemed years, torture and solitude,
15 Scorn and despair,—these are mine empire:—
  More glorious far than that which thou surveyest
  From thine unenvied throne, O Mighty God!
  Almighty, had I deigned[4] to share the shame
  Of thine ill tyranny, and hung not here
20 Nailed to this wall of eagle-baffling mountain,
  Black, wintry, dead, unmeasured; without herb,°   vegetation
  Insect, or beast, or shape or sound of life.
  Ah me, alas, pain, pain ever, forever!

---

8. Shelley did not live to write this history.
1. Ione, Panthea, and Asia (introduced in the following scene) are sisters and Oceanids—i.e., daughters of Oceanus.
2. Demogorgon (see 2.4). "Daemons": super-

natural beings, intermediary between gods and mortals. Prometheus is addressing Jupiter.
3. Large sacrificial offerings.
4. I.e., you would have been all-powerful, if I had deigned.

No change, no pause, no hope!—Yet I endure.
25 I ask the Earth, have not the mountains felt?
I ask yon Heaven—the all-beholding Sun,
Has it not seen? The Sea, in storm or calm,
Heaven's ever-changing Shadow, spread below—
Have its deaf waves not heard my agony?
30 Ah me, alas, pain, pain ever, forever!

The crawling glaciers pierce me with the spears
Of their moon-freezing chrystals; the bright chains
Eat with their burning cold into my bones.
Heaven's winged hound, polluting from thy lips
35 His beak in poison not his own, tears up
My heart;[5] and shapeless sights come wandering by,
The ghastly people of the realm of dream,
Mocking me: and the Earthquake-fiends are charged
To wrench the rivets from my quivering wounds
40 When the rocks split and close again behind;
While from their loud abysses howling throng
The genii of the storm, urging the rage
Of whirlwind, and afflict me with keen hail.
And yet to me welcome is Day and Night,
45 Whether one breaks the hoar frost of the morn,
Or starry, dim, and slow, the other climbs
The leaden-coloured East; for then they lead
Their wingless, crawling Hours,[6] one among whom
—As some dark Priest hales° the reluctant victim— *drags*
50 Shall drag thee, cruel King, to kiss the blood
From these pale feet,[7] which then might trample thee
If they disdained not such a prostrate slave.
Disdain? Ah no! I pity thee.[8]—What Ruin
Will hunt thee undefended through wide Heaven!
55 How will thy soul, cloven to its depth with terror,
Gape like a Hell within! I speak in grief,
Not exultation, for I hate no more,
As then, ere misery made me wise.—The Curse
Once breathed on thee I would recall.[9] Ye Mountains,
60 Whose many-voiced Echoes, through the mist
Of cataracts, flung the thunder of that spell!
Ye icy Springs, stagnant with wrinkling frost,
Which vibrated to hear me, and then crept
Shuddering through India! Thou serenest Air,
65 Through which the Sun walks burning without beams!
And ye swift Whirlwinds, who on poised wings
Hung mute and moveless o'er yon hushed abyss,

5. The vulture, tearing daily at Prometheus's heart, was kissed by Jupiter by way of reward.
6. The Hours were represented in Greek myth and art by human figures with wings.
7. One of a number of implied parallels between the agony of Prometheus and the passion of Christ.

8. At this early point occurs the crisis of the action: the beginning of Prometheus's change of heart from hate to compassion, consummated in lines 303–05.
9. I.e., remember. But the word's alternative sense, "revoke," will later become crucial.

As thunder louder than your own made rock
The orbed world! If then my words had power
—Though I am changed so that aught evil wish
Is dead within, although no memory be
Of what is hate—let them not lose it now![1]
What was that curse? for ye all heard me speak.[2]

* * *

PHANTASM

Fiend, I defy thee! with a calm, fixed mind,
    All that thou canst inflict I bid thee do;
Foul Tyrant both of Gods and Humankind,
    One only being shalt thou not subdue.
        Rain then thy plagues upon me here,
        Ghastly disease and frenzying fear;
        And let alternate frost and fire
        Eat into me, and be thine ire
Lightning and cutting hail and legioned forms
Of furies, driving by upon the wounding storms.

Aye, do thy worst. Thou art Omnipotent.
    O'er all things but thyself I gave thee power,
And my own will. Be thy swift mischiefs sent
    To blast mankind, from yon etherial tower.
        Let thy malignant spirit move
        Its darkness over those I love:
        On me and mine I imprecate°   call down
        The utmost torture of thy hate
And thus devote to sleepless agony
This undeclining head while thou must reign on high.

But thou who art the God and Lord—O thou
    Who fillest with thy soul this world of woe,
To whom all things of Earth and Heaven do bow
    In fear and worship—all-prevailing foe!
        I curse thee! let a sufferer's curse
        Clasp thee, his torturer, like remorse,
        Till thine Infinity shall be
        A robe of envenomed agony;[3]
And thine Omnipotence a crown of pain
To cling like burning gold round thy dissolving brain.

Heap on thy soul by virtue of this Curse
    Ill deeds, then be thou damned, beholding good,
    Both infinite as is the Universe,

1. Let my words not lose their power now.
2. In the passage here omitted, none dares, for
fear of the god's vengeance, to repeat the curse
Prometheus had proclaimed against Jupiter. Prometheus is finally forced to call up the Phantasm
of Jupiter himself, who, in the next excerpt, repeats

the words of Prometheus's curse.
3. Like the poisoned shirt of the centaur Nessus,
which consumed Hercules' flesh when he put it
on. The next two lines allude to the mock crowning
of Christ with a crown of thorns.

295   And thou, and thy self-torturing solitude.
        An awful Image of calm power
        Though now thou sittest, let the hour
        Come, when thou must appear to be
        That which thou art internally.
300   And after many a false and fruitless crime
     Scorn track thy lagging fall through boundless space and time.

                                [*The Phantasm vanishes.*]

PROMETHEUS   Were these my words, O Parent?
THE EARTH   They were thine.
PROMETHEUS   It doth repent me: words are quick and vain;
     Grief for awhile is blind, and so was mine.
305   I wish no living thing to suffer pain.

THE EARTH

    Misery, O misery to me,
    That Jove at length should vanquish thee.
    Wail, howl aloud, Land and Sea,
    The Earth's rent heart shall answer ye.
310 Howl, Spirits of the living and the dead,
Your refuge, your defence lies fallen and vanquished.

FIRST ECHO
Lies fallen and vanquished?

SECOND ECHO
Fallen and vanquished!

IONE[4]
    Fear not—'tis but some passing spasm,
315   The Titan is unvanquished still.[5]

             *   *   *

FURY   Behold, an emblem—those who do endure
595   Deep wrongs for man, and scorn and chains, but heap
    Thousand-fold torment on themselves and him.
PROMETHEUS   Remit the anguish of that lighted stare—
    Close those wan lips—let that thorn-wounded brow
    Stream not with blood—it mingles with thy tears
600 Fix, fix those tortured orbs in peace and death
So thy sick throes shake not that crucifix,
So those pale fingers play not with thy gore.—
O horrible! Thy name I will not speak,
It hath become a curse.[6] I see, I see

4. Ione, Panthea, and Asia (in the following scene) are sisters and Oceanids—i.e., daughters of Oceanus.
5. In the omitted passage the herald Mercury, at Jupiter's command, brings a group of Furies (in Greek myth, avengers of crimes against the gods) who tempt Prometheus to despair by revealing the loathsome potentialities for evil in humankind's conscious and unconscious mind. In the climactic temptation a Fury tears aside a veil to reveal a representation ("emblem," line 594) of the suffering Christ on the cross.
6. I.e., the name "Christ" has become, literally, a curse word and metaphorically, a curse to humankind, in that His religion of love is used to justify religious wars and bloody oppression.

The wise, the mild, the lofty and the just,
Whom thy slaves hate for being like to thee,
Some hunted by foul lies from their heart's home,
An early-chosen, late-lamented home,
As hooded ounces[7] cling to the driven hind,°   doe
Some linked to corpses in unwholesome cells:
Some—hear I not the multitude laugh loud?—
Impaled in lingering fire: and mighty realms
Float by my feet like sea-uprooted isles
Whose sons are kneaded down in common blood
By the red light of their own burning homes.
FURY   Blood thou canst see, and fire; and canst hear groans;
Worse things, unheard, unseen, remain behind.
PROMETHEUS   Worse?
FURY   In each human heart terror survives
The ravin it has gorged:[8] the loftiest fear
All that they would disdain to think were true:
Hypocrisy and custom make their minds
The fanes° of many a worship, now outworn.   temples
They dare not devise good for man's estate
And yet they know not that they do not dare.
The good want power, but to weep barren tears.[9]
The powerful goodness want: worse need for them.
The wise want love, and those who love want wisdom;
And all best things are thus confused to ill.
Many are strong and rich,—and would be just,—
But live among their suffering fellow men
As if none felt: they know not what they do.[1]
PROMETHEUS   Thy words are like a cloud of winged snakes
And yet, I pity those they torture not.
FURY   Thou pitiest them? I speak no more!   [Vanishes.]
PROMETHEUS   Ah woe!
Ah woe! Alas! pain, pain ever, forever!
I close my tearless eyes, but see more clear
Thy works within my woe-illumed mind,
Thou subtle Tyrant![2] . . . Peace is in the grave—
The grave hides all things beautiful and good—
I am a God and cannot find it there,
Nor would I seek it: for, though dread revenge,
This is defeat, fierce King, not victory.
The sights with which thou torturest gird my soul
With new endurance, till the hour arrives
When they shall be no types of things which are.
PANTHEA   Alas! what sawest thou?
PROMETHEUS   There are two woes:

7. Cheetahs, or leopards, used in hunting (hoods were sometimes placed over their eyes to make them easier to control).
8. The prey that it has greedily devoured.
9. I.e., the good lack ("want") power except to weep "barren tears."

1. The Fury ironically echoes Christ's plea for forgiveness of his crucifiers: "Father, forgive them: for they know not what they do" (Luke 23.34).
2. Jupiter (also addressed as "fierce King," line 642).

To speak and to behold; thou spare me one.[3]
Names are there, Nature's sacred watchwords—they
Were borne aloft in bright emblazonry.[4]
650 The nations thronged around, and cried aloud
As with one voice, "Truth, liberty and love!"
Suddenly fierce confusion fell from Heaven
Among them—there was strife, deceit and fear;
Tyrants rushed in, and did divide the spoil.
655 This was the shadow of the truth I saw.
THE EARTH   I felt thy torture, Son, with such mixed joy
As pain and Virtue give.—To cheer thy state
I bid ascend those subtle and fair spirits
Whose homes are the dim caves of human thought
660 And who inhabit, as birds wing the wind,
Its world-surrounding ether;[5] they behold
Beyond that twilight realm, as in a glass,°   mirror
The future—may they speak comfort to thee!

* * *

From Act 2

SCENE 4—*The Cave of* DEMOGORGON. ASIA *and* PANTHEA.[6]

PANTHEA   What veiled form sits on that ebon throne?
ASIA   The veil has fallen! . . .
PANTHEA   I see a mighty Darkness
Filling the seat of power; and rays of gloom
Dart round, as light from the meridian Sun,
5 Ungazed upon and shapeless—neither limb
Nor form—nor outline;[7] yet we feel it is
A living Spirit.
DEMOGORGON   Ask what thou wouldst know.
ASIA   What canst thou tell?
DEMOGORGON   All things thou dar'st demand.
ASIA   Who made the living world?
DEMOGORGON   God.
ASIA   Who made all
10 That it contains—thought, passion, reason, will,
Imagination?

---

3. I.e., spare me the woe of speaking (about what I have beheld).
4. As in a brilliant display of banners.
5. A medium, weightless and infinitely elastic, once supposed to permeate the universe.
6. Act 2 has opened with Asia—the feminine principle and embodiment of love, who was separated from Prometheus at the moment of his fall into divisive hate—in a lovely Indian valley at the first hour of the dawn of the spring season of redemption. Asia and her sister Panthea have been led, by a sweet and irresistible compulsion, first to the portal and then down into the depths of the cave of

Demogorgon—the central enigma of Shelley's poem.
   As the father of all that exists, Demogorgon may represent the ultimate reason for the way things are. As such, Shelley appears to argue, Demogorgon must be a mystery inaccessible to knowledge and must be ignorant of the principle controlling him. In this scene Demogorgon can give only riddling answers to Asia's questions about the "why" of creation, good, and evil.
7. Echoing Milton's description of Death, *Paradise Lost* 2.666–73.

DEMOGORGON   God, Almighty God.

ASIA   Who made that sense[8] which, when the winds of Spring
    In rarest visitation, or the voice
    Of one beloved heard in youth alone,
5   Fills the faint eyes with falling tears, which dim
    The radiant looks of unbewailing flowers,
    And leaves this peopled earth a solitude
    When it returns no more?

DEMOGORGON   Merciful God.

ASIA   And who made terror, madness, crime, remorse,
10   Which from the links of the great chain of things
    To every thought within the mind of man
    Sway and drag heavily—and each one reels
    Under the load towards the pit of death;
    Abandoned hope, and love that turns to hate;
15   And self-contempt, bitterer to drink than blood;
    Pain whose unheeded and familiar speech
    Is howling and keen shrieks, day after day;
    And Hell, or the sharp fear of Hell?[9]

DEMOGORGON   He reigns.

ASIA   Utter his name—a world pining in pain
20   Asks but his name; curses shall drag him down.

DEMOGORGON   He reigns.

ASIA   I feel, I know it—who?

DEMOGORGON   He reigns.

ASIA   Who reigns? There was the Heaven and Earth at first
    And Light and Love;—then Saturn,[1] from whose throne
    Time fell, an envious shadow; such the state
35   Of the earth's primal spirits beneath his sway
    As the calm joy of flowers and living leaves
    Before the wind or sun has withered them
    And semivital worms; but he refused
    The birthright of their being, knowledge, power,
40   The skill which wields the elements, the thought
    Which pierces this dim Universe like light,
    Self-empire and the majesty of love,
    For thirst of which they fainted. Then Prometheus
    Gave wisdom, which is strength, to Jupiter
45   And with this law alone: "Let man be free,"
    Clothed him with the dominion of wide Heaven.
    To know nor faith nor love nor law, to be
    Omnipotent but friendless, is to reign;
    And Jove now reigned; for on the race of man
50   First famine, and then toil, and then disease,

8. Presumably the sense by which one is aware of
the "unseen Power" that Shelley calls "Intellectual
Beauty" (see "Hymn to Intellectual Beauty," stanza
2, p. 1739).
9. The nouns "hope," "love," etc. (lines 24–28) are
all objects of the verb "made" (line 19).

1. In Greek myth Saturn's reign was the golden
age. In Shelley's version Saturn refused to grant
mortals knowledge and science, so that it was an
age of ignorant innocence in which the deepest
human needs remained unfulfilled.

Strife, wounds, and ghastly death unseen before,
Fell; and the unseasonable seasons drove,
With alternating shafts of frost and fire,
Their shelterless, pale tribes to mountain caves;
55 And in their desart° hearts fierce wants he sent   *empty*
And mad disquietudes, and shadows idle
Of unreal good, which levied mutual war,
So ruining the lair wherein they raged.
Prometheus saw, and waked the legioned hopes
60 Which sleep within folded Elysian flowers,
Nepenthe, Moly, Amaranth,² fadeless blooms;
That they might hide with thin and rainbow wings
The shape of Death; and Love he sent to bind
The disunited tendrils of that vine
65 Which bears the wine of life, the human heart;
And he tamed fire which, like some beast of prey,
Most terrible, but lovely, played beneath
The frown of man, and tortured to his will
Iron and gold, the slaves and signs of power,
70 And gems and poisons, and all subtlest forms,
Hidden beneath the mountains and the waves.
He gave man speech, and speech created thought,
Which is the measure of the Universe;
And Science struck the thrones of Earth and Heaven
75 Which shook, but fell not; and the harmonious mind
Poured itself forth in all-prophetic song,
And music lifted up the listening spirit
Until it walked, exempt from mortal care,
Godlike, o'er the clear billows of sweet sound;
80 And human hands first mimicked and then mocked³
With moulded limbs more lovely than its own
The human form, till marble grew divine,
And mothers, gazing, drank the love men see
Reflected in their race, behold, and perish.⁴—
85 He told the hidden power of herbs and springs,
And Disease drank and slept—Death grew like sleep.—
He taught the implicated° orbits woven   *intertwined*
Of the wide-wandering stars, and how the Sun
Changes his lair, and by what secret spell
90 The pale moon is transformed, when her broad eye
Gazes not on the interlunar⁵ sea;
He taught to rule, as life directs the limbs,
The tempest-winged chariots of the Ocean,

2. These are medicinal drugs and flowers in Greek myth. Asia is describing (lines 59–97) the various sciences and arts given to humans by Prometheus, the culture bringer.
3. I.e., sculptors first merely reproduced but later improved on and heightened the beauty of the human form, so that the original was inferior to, and hence "mocked" by, the copy.
4. Expectant mothers looked at the beautiful statues so that their children might, by prenatal influence, be born with the beauty that makes beholders die of love.
5. The phase between old and new moons, when the moon is invisible.

And the Celt knew the Indian.[6] Cities then
Were built, and through their snow-like columns flowed
The warm winds, and the azure æther shone,
And the blue sea and shadowy hills were seen . . .
Such the alleviations of his state
Prometheus gave to man—for which he hangs
Withering in destined pain—but who rains down
Evil, the immedicable plague, which while
Man looks on his creation like a God
And sees that it is glorious, drives him on,
The wreck of his own will, the scorn of Earth,
The outcast, the abandoned, the alone?—
Not Jove: while yet his frown shook Heaven, aye when
His adversary from adamantine° chains   *unbreakable*
Cursed him, he trembled like a slave. Declare
Who is his master? Is he too a slave?
DEMOGORGON   All spirits are enslaved which serve things evil:
  Thou knowest if Jupiter be such or no.
ASIA   Whom calledst thou God?
DEMOGORGON   I spoke but as ye speak—
  For Jove is the supreme of living things.
ASIA   Who is the master of the slave?
DEMOGORGON   —If the Abysm
  Could vomit forth its secrets:—but a voice
  Is wanting, the deep truth is imageless;
  For what would it avail to bid thee gaze
  On the revolving world? what to bid speak
  Fate, Time, Occasion, Chance and Change? To these
  All things are subject but eternal Love.
ASIA   So much I asked before, and my heart gave
  The response thou hast given; and of such truths
  Each to itself must be the oracle.—
  One more demand . . . and do thou answer me
  As my own soul would answer, did it know
  That which I ask.—Prometheus shall arise
  Henceforth the Sun of this rejoicing world:
  When shall the destined hour arrive?
DEMOGORGON   Behold![7]
ASIA   The rocks are cloven, and through the purple night
  I see Cars drawn by rainbow-winged steeds
  Which trample the dim winds—in each there stands
  A wild-eyed charioteer, urging their flight.
  Some look behind, as fiends pursued them there
  And yet I see no shapes but the keen stars:
  Others with burning eyes lean forth, and drink
  With eager lips the wind of their own speed,
  As if the thing they loved fled on before,

6. The reference is to the ships in which the Celtic (here, non-Greco-Roman) races of Europe were able to sail to India.

7. Demogorgon's answer is a gesture: he points to the approaching chariots ("Cars").

And now—even now they clasped it; their bright locks
Stream like a comet's flashing hair: they all
Sweep onward.—

140 DEMOGORGON   These are the immortal Hours
Of whom thou didst demand.—One waits for thee.

ASIA A Spirit with a dreadful countenance
Checks its dark chariot by the craggy gulph.
Unlike thy brethren, ghastly charioteer,

145 What art thou? whither wouldst thou bear me? Speak!

SPIRIT I am the shadow of a destiny
More dread than is my aspect—ere yon planet
Has set, the Darkness which ascends with me
Shall wrap in lasting night Heaven's kingless throne.

ASIA What meanest thou?

150 PANTHEA   That terrible shadow[8] floats
Up from its throne, as may the lurid° smoke   red-glaring
Of earthquake-ruined cities o'er the sea.—
Lo! it ascends the Car . . . the coursers fly
Terrified; watch its path among the stars
Blackening the night!

155 ASIA   Thus I am answered—strange!

PANTHEA See, near the verge° another chariot stays;   horizon
An ivory shell inlaid with crimson fire
Which comes and goes within its sculptured rim
Of delicate strange tracery—the young Spirit

160 That guides it, has the dovelike eyes of hope.
How its soft smiles attract the soul!—as light
Lures winged insects[9] through the lampless air.

SPIRIT

My coursers are fed with the lightning,
They drink of the whirlwind's stream

165 And when the red morning is brightning
They bathe in the fresh sunbeam;
They have strength for their swiftness, I deem:
Then ascend with me, daughter of Ocean.

I desire—and their speed makes night kindle;

170 I fear—they outstrip the Typhoon;
Ere the cloud piled on Atlas[1] can dwindle
We encircle the earth and the moon:
We shall rest from long labours at noon:
Then ascend with me, daughter of Ocean.

SCENE 5—*The Car pauses within a Cloud on the Top of a snowy Mountain.* ASIA,
PANTHEA, *and the* SPIRIT OF THE HOUR.

8. Demogorgon (the "Darkness" of line 148), who
is ascending (lines 150–55) to dethrone Jupiter.
9. The ancient image of the soul, or *psyche*, was a
moth. The chariot described here will carry Asia to
a reunion with Prometheus.
1. A mountain in North Africa that the Greeks
regarded as so high that it supported the heavens.

SPIRIT

On the brink of the night and the morning
  My coursers are wont to respire,²
But the Earth has just whispered a warning
  That their flight must be swifter than fire:
5   They shall drink the hot speed of desire!

ASIA Thou breathest on their nostrils—but my breath
  Would give them swifter speed.
SPIRIT   Alas, it could not.
PANTHEA O Spirit! pause and tell whence is the light
  Which fills the cloud? the sun is yet unrisen.
10 SPIRIT   The sun will rise not until noon.³—Apollo
  Is held in Heaven by wonder—and the light
  Which fills this vapour, as the aerial hue
  Of fountain-gazing roses fills the water,
  Flows from thy mighty sister.
PANTHEA   Yes, I feel . . .
15 ASIA What is it with thee, sister? Thou art pale.
PANTHEA How thou art changed! I dare not look on thee;
  I feel, but see thee not. I scarce endure
  The radiance of thy beauty.⁴ Some good change
  Is working in the elements which suffer
20 Thy presence thus unveiled.—The Nereids tell
  That on the day when the clear hyaline°   glassy sea
  Was cloven at thy uprise, and thou didst stand
  Within a veined shell,⁵ which floated on
  Over the calm floor of the chrystal sea,
25 Among the Ægean isles, and by the shores
  Which bear thy name, love, like the atmosphere
  Of the sun's fire filling the living world,
  Burst from thee, and illumined Earth and Heaven
  And the deep ocean and the sunless caves,
30 And all that dwells within them; till grief cast
  Eclipse upon the soul from which it came:
  Such art thou now, nor is it I alone,
  Thy sister, thy companion, thine own chosen one,
  But the whole world which seeks thy sympathy.
35 Hearest thou not sounds i' the air which speak the love
  Of all articulate beings? Feelest thou not
  The inanimate winds enamoured of thee?—List!   [Music.]
ASIA Thy words are sweeter than aught else but his
  Whose echoes they are—yet all love is sweet,
40 Given or returned; common as light is love

---

2. Catch their breath.
3. The time of the reunion of Prometheus and Asia.
4. In an earlier scene Panthea had envisioned in a dream the radiant and eternal inner form of Prometheus emerging through his "wound-worn limbs." The corresponding transfiguration of Asia,

prepared for by her descent to the underworld to question Demogorgon, now takes place.
5. The story told by the Nereids (sea nymphs) serves to associate Asia with Aphrodite, goddess of love, emerging (as in Botticelli's painting) from the Mediterranean on a seashell.

And its familiar voice wearies not ever.
Like the wide Heaven, the all-sustaining air,
It makes the reptile equal to the God . . .
They who inspire it most are fortunate
45 As I am now; but those who feel it most
Are happier still, after long sufferings
As I shall soon become.

PANTHEA   List! Spirits speak.

VOICE (*in the air, singing*)[6]
      Life of Life! thy lips enkindle
            With their love the breath between them
50   And thy smiles before they dwindle
            Make the cold air fire; then screen them
      In those looks where whoso gazes
      Faints, entangled in their mazes.

      Child of Light! thy limbs are burning
55   Through the vest which seems to hide them
      As the radiant lines of morning
            Through the clouds ere they divide them,
      And this atmosphere divinest
      Shrouds thee wheresoe'er thou shinest.

60   Fair are others;—none beholds thee
            But thy voice sounds low and tender
      Like the fairest, for it folds thee
            From the sight, that liquid splendour,
      And all feel, yet see thee never
65   As I feel now, lost forever!

      Lamp of Earth! where'er thou movest
            Its dim shapes are clad with brightness
      And the souls of whom thou lovest
            Walk upon the winds with lightness
70   Till they fail, as I am failing,
      Dizzy, lost . . . yet unbewailing!

                              ASIA
      My soul is an enchanted Boat
      Which, like a sleeping swan, doth float
      Upon the silver waves of thy sweet singing,
75   And thine doth like an Angel sit
            Beside the helm conducting it
      Whilst all the winds with melody are ringing.
            It seems to float ever—forever—
            Upon that many winding River

6. The voice attempts to describe, in a dizzying whirl of optical paradoxes, what it feels like to look on the naked essence of love and beauty.

80 Between mountains, woods, abysses,
       A Paradise of wildernesses,
    Till like one in slumber bound
    Borne to the Ocean, I float down, around,
    Into a Sea profound, of ever-spreading sound.

85   Meanwhile thy spirit lifts its pinions°   *wings*
       In Music's most serene dominions,
    Catching the winds that fan that happy Heaven.
       And we sail on, away, afar,
       Without a course—without a star—
90 But by the instinct of sweet Music driven
       Till, through Elysian garden islets
       By thee, most beautiful of pilots,
       Where never mortal pinnace° glided,   *small boat*
       The boat of my desire is guided—
95 Realms where the air we breathe is Love
    Which in the winds and on the waves doth move,
    Harmonizing this Earth with what we feel above.

       We have past Age's icy caves,
       And Manhood's dark and tossing waves
00 And Youth's smooth ocean, smiling to betray;
       Beyond the glassy gulphs we flee
       Of shadow-peopled Infancy,
    Through Death and Birth to a diviner day,[7]
       A Paradise of vaulted bowers
05   Lit by downward-gazing flowers
       And watery paths that wind between
       Wildernesses calm and green,
    Peopled by shapes too bright to see,
    And rest, having beheld—somewhat like thee,
10 Which walk upon the sea, and chaunt melodiously!

From *Act 3*

SCENE 1—*Heaven.* JUPITER *on his Throne;* THETIS *and the other Deities assembled.*

JUPITER   Ye congregated Powers of Heaven who share
    The glory and the strength of him ye serve,
    Rejoice! henceforth I am omnipotent.
    All else had been subdued to me—alone
5   The soul of man, like unextinguished fire,
    Yet burns towards Heaven with fierce reproach and doubt
    And lamentation and reluctant prayer,
    Hurling up insurrection, which might make

---

7. Asia is describing what it feels like to be transfigured—in the image of moving backward in the stream of time, through youth and infancy and birth, in order to die to this life and be born again to a "diviner" existence.

Our antique empire insecure, though built
10   On eldest faith, and Hell's coeval,[8] fear.
And though my curses through the pendulous° air   overhanging
Like snow on herbless peaks, fall flake by flake
And cling to it[9]—though under my wrath's night
It climb the crags of life, step after step,
15   Which wound it, as ice wounds unsandalled feet,
It yet remains supreme o'er misery,
Aspiring . . . unrepressed; yet soon to fall:
Even now have I begotten a strange wonder,
That fatal Child,[1] the terror of the Earth,
20   Who waits but till the destined Hour arrive,
Bearing from Demogorgon's vacant throne
The dreadful might of ever living limbs
Which clothed that awful spirit unbeheld—
To redescend, and trample out the spark[2] . . .

25   Pour forth Heaven's wine, Idæan Ganymede,
And let it fill the dædal[3] cups like fire
And from the flower-inwoven soil divine
Ye all triumphant harmonies arise
As dew from Earth under the twilight stars;
30   Drink! be the nectar circling through your veins
The soul of joy, ye everliving Gods,
Till exultation burst in one wide voice
Like music from Elysian winds.—
                                        And thou
Ascend beside me, veiled in the light
35   Of the desire which makes thee one with me,
Thetis, bright Image of Eternity!—
When thou didst cry, "Insufferable might![4]
God! spare me! I sustain not the quick flames,
The penetrating presence; all my being,
40   Like him whom the Numidian seps[5] did thaw
Into a dew with poison, is dissolved,
Sinking through its foundations"—even then
Two mighty spirits, mingling, made a third
Mightier than either—which unbodied now
45   Between us, floats, felt although unbeheld,
Waiting the incarnation, which ascends—
Hear ye the thunder of the fiery wheels
Griding[6] the winds?—from Demogorgon's throne.—
Victory! victory! Feel'st thou not, O World,

8. Of the same age.
9. "It" (as also in lines 14 and 16) is "the soul of man" (line 5).
1. The son of Jupiter and Thetis. Jupiter believes that he has begotten a child who will assume the bodily form of the conquered Demogorgon and then return to announce his victory and the defeat of the resistance of Prometheus.
2. Of Prometheus's defiance.
3. Skillfully wrought (from the name of the Greek craftsman Daedalus). Ganymede (line 25) had been seized on Mount Ida by an eagle and carried to heaven to be Jupiter's cupbearer.
4. This description of Jupiter's rape of Thetis is a grotesque parody of the reunion of Prometheus and Asia.
5. A serpent of Numidia (North Africa) whose bite was thought to cause putrefaction.
6. Cutting with a rasping sound.

The Earthquake of his chariot thundering up
Olympus?
        [*The Car of the* HOUR *arrives.* DEMOGORGON *descends and moves towards the Throne of* JUPITER.]
        Awful Shape, what art thou? Speak!
DEMOGORGON   Eternity—demand no direr name.
Descend, and follow me down the abyss;
I am thy child,[7] as thou wert Saturn's child,
Mightier than thee; and we must dwell together
Henceforth in darkness.—Lift thy lightnings not.
The tyranny of Heaven none may retain,
Or reassume, or hold succeeding thee . . .
Yet if thou wilt—as 'tis the destiny
Of trodden worms to writhe till they are dead—
Put forth thy might.
JUPITER   Detested prodigy!
Even thus beneath the deep Titanian prisons[8]
I trample thee! . . . thou lingerest?
                 Mercy! mercy!
No pity—no release, no respite! . . . Oh,
That thou wouldst make mine enemy my judge.
Even where he hangs, seared by my long revenge
On Caucasus—he would not doom me thus.—
Gentle and just and dreadless, is he not
The monarch of the world? what then art thou? . . .
No refuge! no appeal— . . .
               Sink with me then—
We two will sink in the wide waves of ruin
Even as a vulture and a snake outspent
Drop, twisted in inextricable fight,[9]
Into a shoreless sea.—Let Hell unlock
Its mounded Oceans of tempestuous fire,
And whelm on them° into the bottomless void   *wash them*
The desolated world and thee and me,
The conqueror and the conquered, and the wreck
Of that for which they combated.
                Ai! Ai![1]
The elements obey me not . . . I sink . . .
Dizzily down—ever, forever, down—
And, like a cloud, mine enemy above
Darkens my fall with victory!—Ai! Ai!

From SCENE 4—*A Forest. In the Background a Cave.* PROMETHEUS, ASIA, PAN-
THEA, IONE, *and the* SPIRIT OF THE EARTH.[2]

---

7. Ironically, and in a figurative sense: Demogorgon's function follows from Jupiter's actions.
8. After they overthrew the Titans, Jupiter and the
Olympian gods imprisoned them in Tartarus, deep
beneath the earth.
9. The eagle (or vulture) and the snake locked in
equal combat—a favorite Shelleyan image.
1. Traditional Greek cry of sorrow.

2. After Jupiter's annihilation (described in scene
2), Hercules unbinds Prometheus, who is reunited
with Asia and retires to a cave "where we will
sit and talk of time and change / . . . ourselves
unchanged." In the speech that concludes the act
(reprinted here) the Spirit of the Hour describes
what happened in the human world when he
sounded the apocalyptic trumpet.

* * *

[*The* SPIRIT OF THE HOUR *enters.*]

PROMETHEUS   We feel what thou hast heard and seen—yet speak.
SPIRIT OF THE HOUR   Soon as the sound had ceased whose thunder filled
        The abysses of the sky, and the wide earth,
100   There was a change . . . the impalpable thin air
        And the all-circling sunlight were transformed
        As if the sense of love dissolved in them
        Had folded itself round the sphered world.
        My vision then grew clear and I could see
105   Into the mysteries of the Universe.[3]
        Dizzy as with delight I floated down,
        Winnowing the lightsome air with languid plumes,
        My coursers sought their birthplace in the sun
        Where they henceforth will live exempt from toil,
110   Pasturing flowers of vegetable fire—
        And where my moonlike car will stand within
        A temple, gazed upon by Phidian forms,[4]
        Of thee, and Asia and the Earth, and me
        And you fair nymphs, looking the love we feel,
115   In memory of the tidings it has borne,
        Beneath a dome fretted with graven flowers,
        Poised on twelve columns of resplendent stone
        And open to the bright and liquid sky.
        Yoked to it by an amphisbænic snake[5]
120   The likeness of those winged steeds will mock[6]
        The flight from which they find repose.—Alas,
        Whither has wandered now my partial[7] tongue
        When all remains untold which ye would hear!—
        As I have said, I floated to the Earth:
125   It was, as it is still, the pain of bliss
        To move, to breathe, to be; I wandering went
        Among the haunts and dwellings of mankind
        And first was disappointed not to see
        Such mighty change as I had felt within
130   Expressed in outward things; but soon I looked,
        And behold! thrones were kingless, and men walked
        One with the other even as spirits do,
        None fawned, none trampled; hate, disdain or fear,
        Self-love or self-contempt on human brows
135   No more inscribed, as o'er the gate of hell,
        "All hope abandon, ye who enter here";[8]
        None frowned, none trembled, none with eager fear
        Gazed on another's eye of cold command
        Until the subject of a tyrant's will

---

3. I.e., the earth's atmosphere clarifies, no longer refracting the sunlight, and so allows the Spirit of the Hour to see what is happening on earth.
4. The crescent-shaped ("moonlike") chariot, its apocalyptic mission accomplished, will be frozen to stone and will be surrounded by the sculptured forms of other agents in the drama. Phidias (5th century B.C.E.) was the noblest of Greek sculptors.

5. A mythical snake with a head at each end; it serves here as a symbolic warning that a reversal of the process is always possible.
6. "Imitate" and also, in their immobility, "mock at" the flight they represent.
7. Biased or, possibly, telling only part of the story.
8. The inscription over the gate of hell in Dante's *Inferno* 3.9.

Became, worse fate, the abject of his own[9]
Which spurred him, like an outspent° horse, to death.   *exhausted*
None wrought his lips in truth-entangling lines
Which smiled the lie his tongue disdained to speak;
None with firm sneer trod out in his own heart
The sparks of love and hope, till there remained
Those bitter ashes, a soul self-consumed,
And the wretch crept, a vampire among men,
Infecting all with his own hideous ill.
None talked that common, false, cold, hollow talk
Which makes the heart deny the *yes* it breathes
Yet question that unmeant hypocrisy
With such a self-mistrust as has no name.
And women too, frank, beautiful and kind
As the free Heaven which rains fresh light and dew
On the wide earth, past: gentle, radiant forms,
From custom's evil taint exempt and pure;
Speaking the wisdom once they could not think,
Looking emotions once they feared to feel
And changed to all which once they dared not be,
Yet being now, made Earth like Heaven—nor pride
Nor jealousy nor envy nor ill shame,
The bitterest of those drops of treasured gall,
Spoilt the sweet taste of the nepenthe,[1] love.

Thrones, altars, judgement-seats and prisons; wherein
And beside which, by wretched men were borne
Sceptres, tiaras, swords and chains, and tomes
Of reasoned wrong glozed on[2] by ignorance,
Were like those monstrous and barbaric shapes,
The ghosts of a no more remembered fame,
Which from their unworn obelisks[3] look forth
In triumph o'er the palaces and tombs
Of those who were their conquerors, mouldering round.
Those imaged to the pride of Kings and Priests
A dark yet mighty faith, a power as wide
As is the world it wasted, and are now
But an astonishment; even so the tools
And emblems of its last captivity
Amid the dwellings of the peopled Earth,
Stand, not o'erthrown, but unregarded now.
And those foul shapes, abhorred by God and man—
Which under many a name and many a form
Strange, savage, ghastly, dark and execrable
Were Jupiter,[4] the tyrant of the world;
And which the nations panic-stricken served

9. I.e., he was so abjectly enslaved that his own will accorded with the tyrant's will.
1. A drug (probably opium) that brings forgetfulness of pain and sorrow.
2. Annotated, explained.
3. The Egyptian obelisks (tapering shafts of stone), brought to Rome by its conquering armies,

included hieroglyphs that—because they were still undeciphered in Shelley's time—seemed "monstrous and barbaric shapes" (line 168).
4. The "foul shapes" (line 180) were statues of the gods who, whatever their names, were all really manifestations of Jupiter.

185　With blood, and hearts broken by long hope, and love
　　　Dragged to his altars soiled and garlandless
　　　And slain amid men's unreclaiming tears,
　　　Flattering the thing they feared, which fear was hate—
　　　Frown, mouldering fast, o'er their abandoned shrines.
190　The painted veil, by those who were, called life,[5]
　　　Which mimicked, as with colours idly spread,
　　　All men believed and hoped, is torn aside—
　　　The loathsome mask has fallen, the man remains
　　　Sceptreless, free, uncircumscribed—but man:
195　Equal, unclassed, tribeless, and nationless,
　　　Exempt from awe, worship, degree,—the King
　　　Over himself; just, gentle, wise—but man:
　　　Passionless? no—yet free from guilt or pain
　　　Which were, for his will made, or suffered them,
200　Nor yet exempt, though ruling them like slaves,
　　　From chance and death and mutability,
　　　The clogs of that which else might oversoar
　　　The loftiest star of unascended Heaven
　　　Pinnacled dim in the intense inane.[6]

From Act 4[7]

SCENE—*A Part of the Forest near the Cave of* PROMETHEUS.

*　　*　　*

DEMOGORGON

　　　This is the Day which down the void Abysm
555　At the Earth-born's spell[8] yawns for Heaven's Despotism,
　　　　And Conquest is dragged Captive through the Deep;[9]
　　　Love from its awful° throne of patient power　　　　　　　　　　　awesome
　　　In the wise heart, from the last giddy hour
　　　　Of dread endurance, from the slippery, steep,
560　And narrow verge of crag-like Agony, springs
　　　And folds over the world its healing wings.

5. I.e., which was thought to be life by humans as they were before their regeneration.
6. I.e., a dim point in the extreme of empty space. The sense of lines 198–204 is if regenerate man were to be released from all earthly and biological impediments ("clogs"), he would become what even the stars are not—a pure ideal.
7. The original drama, completed in the spring of 1819, consisted of three acts. Later that year Shelley added a jubilant fourth act. In Revelation 21 the apocalyptic replacement of the old world by "a new heaven and new earth" had been symbolized by the marriage of the Lamb with the New Jerusalem. Shelley's fourth act, somewhat like the conclusion of Blake's *Jerusalem*, expands this figure into a cosmic epithalamion, representing a union of divided elements that enacts everywhere the reunion of Prometheus and Asia taking place offstage.
Shelley's model is the Renaissance masque, which combines song and dance with spectacular

displays. Panthea and Ione serve as commentators on the action, which is divided into three episodes. In the first episode the purified "Spirits of the human mind" unite in a ritual dance with the Hours of the glad new day. In the second episode (lines 194–318), there appear emblematic representations of the moon and the earth, each bearing an infant whose hour has come round at last. Shelley based this description in part on Ezekiel 1, the vision of the chariot of divine glory, which had traditionally been interpreted as a portent of apocalypse. The third episode (lines 319–502) is the bacchanalian dance of the love-intoxicated Moon around her brother and paramour, the rejuvenescent Earth.
8. Prometheus's spell—the magically effective words of pity, rather than vengefulness, that he spoke in act 1.
9. Ephesians 4.8: "When [Christ] ascended up on high, he led captivity captive."

Gentleness, Virtue, Wisdom and Endurance,—
These are the seals of that most firm assurance
    Which bars the pit over Destruction's strength;
And if, with infirm hand, Eternity,
Mother of many acts and hours, should free
    The serpent that would clasp her with his length[1]—
These are the spells by which to reassume
An empire o'er the disentangled Doom.[2]

To suffer woes which Hope thinks infinite;
To forgive wrongs darker than Death or Night;
    To defy Power which seems Omnipotent;
To love, and bear; to hope, till Hope creates
From its own wreck the thing it contemplates;
    Neither to change nor falter nor repent:
This, like thy glory, Titan! is to be
Good, great and joyous, beautiful and free;
This is alone Life, Joy, Empire and Victory.

1818–19   1820

The Cloud

I bring fresh showers for the thirsting flowers,
    From the seas and streams;
I bear light shade for the leaves when laid
    In their noon-day dreams.
5 From my wings are shaken the dews that waken
    The sweet buds every one,
When rocked to rest on their mother's° breast,   *earth's*
    As she dances about the Sun.
I wield the flail[1] of the lashing hail,
10   And whiten the green plains under,
And then again I dissolve it in rain,
    And laugh as I pass in thunder.

I sift the snow on the mountains below,
    And their great pines groan aghast;
15 And all the night 'tis my pillow white,
    While I sleep in the arms of the blast.
Sublime on the towers of my skiey bowers,
    Lightning my pilot sits;
In a cavern under is fettered the thunder,
20   It struggles and howls at fits;°   *fitfully*
Over Earth and Ocean, with gentle motion,
    This pilot is guiding me,

1. A final reminder that the serpent incessantly
struggles to break loose and start the cycle of
humanity's fall all over again.
2. Shelley's four cardinal virtues (line 562), which
seal the serpent in the pit, also constitute the

magic formulas ("spells") by which to remaster
him, should he again break loose.
1. Either a weapon fashioned as a ball and chain
or a tool for threshing grain.

Lured by the love of the genii that move
    In the depths of the purple sea;[2]
25 Over the rills, and the crags, and the hills,
    Over the lakes and the plains,
Wherever he dream, under mountain or stream,
    The Spirit he loves remains;
And I all the while bask in Heaven's blue smile,[3]
30   Whilst he is dissolving in rains.

The sanguine Sunrise, with his meteor eyes,
    And his burning plumes outspread,[4]
Leaps on the back of my sailing rack,[5]
    When the morning star shines dead;
35 As on the jag of a mountain crag,
    Which an earthquake rocks and swings,
An eagle alit one moment may sit
    In the light of its golden wings.
And when Sunset may breathe, from the lit Sea beneath,
40   Its ardours of rest and of love,
And the crimson pall° of eve may fall   *rich coverlet*
    From the depth of Heaven above,
With wings folded I rest, on mine aëry nest,
    As still as a brooding dove.[6]
45 That orbed maiden with white fire laden
    Whom mortals call the Moon,
Glides glimmering o'er my fleece-like floor,
    By the midnight breezes strewn;
And wherever the beat of her unseen feet,
50   Which only the angels hear,
May have broken the woof,° of my tent's thin roof,   *texture*
    The stars peep behind her, and peer;
And I laugh to see them whirl and flee,
    Like a swarm of golden bees,
55 When I widen the rent in my wind-built tent,
    Till the calm rivers, lakes, and seas,
Like strips of the sky fallen through me on high,
    Are each paved with the moon and these.[7]

I bind the Sun's throne with a burning zone°   *belt, sash*
60   And the Moon's with a girdle of pearl;
The volcanos are dim and the stars reel and swim
    When the whirlwinds my banner unfurl.
From cape to cape, with a bridge-like shape,
    Over a torrent sea,
65 Sunbeam-proof, I hang like a roof—
    The mountains its columns be!
The triumphal arch, through which I march

2. I.e., atmospheric electricity, guiding the cloud (line 18), discharges as lightning when "lured" by the attraction of an opposite charge.
3. The upper part of the cloud remains exposed to the sun.
4. The sun's corona. "Meteor eyes": as bright as a burning meteor.

5. High, broken clouds, driven by the wind.
6. An echo of Milton's description of his Muse, identified with the Holy Spirit, who "with mighty wings outspread / Dove-like sat'st brooding on the vast abyss" (*Paradise Lost* 1.20–21).
7. The stars reflected in the water.

With hurricane, fire, and snow,
  When the Powers of the Air, are chained to my chair,°   *chariot*
70 Is the million-coloured Bow;
The sphere-fire° above its soft colours wove   *sunlight*
  While the moist Earth was laughing below.

I am the daughter of Earth and Water,
  And the nursling of the Sky;
75 I pass through the pores, of the ocean and shores;
  I change, but I cannot die—
For after the rain, when with never a stain
  The pavilion of Heaven is bare,
And the winds and sunbeams, with their convex gleams,
80   Build up the blue dome of Air⁸—
I silently laugh at my own cenotaph,⁹
  And out of the caverns of rain,
Like a child from the womb, like a ghost from the tomb,
  I arise, and unbuild it again.—

1820   1820

To a Sky-Lark¹

Hail to thee, blithe Spirit!
  Bird thou never wert—
That from Heaven, or near it,
  Pourest thy full heart
5 In profuse strains of unpremeditated art.

Higher still and higher
  From the earth thou springest
Like a cloud of fire;
  The blue deep thou wingest,
10 And singing still dost soar, and soaring ever singest.

In the golden lightning
  Of the sunken Sun—
O'er which clouds are brightning,
  Thou dost float and run;
15 Like an unbodied joy whose race is just begun.

The pale purple even°   *evening*
  Melts around thy flight,
Like a star of Heaven
  In the broad day-light
20 Thou art unseen,—but yet I hear thy shrill delight,

8. The blue color of the sky. The phenomenon, as Shelley indicates, results from the way "sunbeams" are filtered by the earth's atmosphere.
9. The memorial monument of the dead cloud is the cloudless blue dome of the sky. (The point is that a cenotaph is a monument that does not contain a corpse.)
1. The European skylark is a small bird that sings only in flight, often when it is too high to be visible.

Keen as are the arrows
  Of that silver sphere,[2]
Whose intense lamp narrows
  In the white dawn clear
25   Until we hardly see—we feel that it is there.

All the earth and air
  With thy voice is loud,
As when Night is bare
  From one lonely cloud
30   The moon rains out her beams—and Heaven is overflowed.

What thou art we know not;
  What is most like thee?
From rainbow clouds there flow not
  Drops so bright to see
35   As from thy presence showers a rain of melody.

Like a Poet hidden
  In the light of thought,
Singing hymns unbidden,
  Till the world is wrought
40   To sympathy with hopes and fears it heeded not:

Like a high-born maiden
  In a palace-tower,
Soothing her love-laden
  Soul in secret hour,
45   With music sweet as love—which overflows her bower:

Like a glow-worm golden
  In a dell of dew,
Scattering unbeholden
  Its aerial hue
50   Among the flowers and grass which screen it from the view:

Like a rose embowered
  In its own green leaves—
By warm winds deflowered—
  Till the scent it gives
55   Makes faint with too much sweet those heavy-winged thieves:[3]

Sound of vernal° showers   springtime
  On the twinkling grass,
Rain-awakened flowers,
  All that ever was
60   Joyous, and clear and fresh, thy music doth surpass.

Teach us, Sprite° or Bird,   spirit
  What sweet thoughts are thine;
I have never heard

---

2. The morning star, Venus.   3. The "warm winds," line 53.

Praise of love or wine
65 That panted forth a flood of rapture so divine:

Chorus Hymeneal[4]
Or triumphal chaunt
Matched with thine would be all
But an empty vaunt,
70 A thing wherein we feel there is some hidden want.

What objects are the fountains
Of thy happy strain?
What fields or waves or mountains?
What shapes of sky or plain?
75 What love of thine own kind? what ignorance of pain?

With thy clear keen joyance
Languor cannot be—
Shadow of annoyance
Never came near thee;
80 Thou lovest—but ne'er knew love's sad satiety.

Waking or asleep,
Thou of death must deem
Things more true and deep
Than we mortals dream,
85 Or how could thy notes flow in such a chrystal stream?

We look before and after,
And pine for what is not—
Our sincerest laughter
With some pain is fraught—
90 Our sweetest songs are those that tell of saddest thought.

Yet if we could scorn
Hate and pride and fear;
If we were things born
Not to shed a tear,
95 I know not how thy joy we ever should come near.

Better than all measures
Of delightful sound—
Better than all treasures
That in books are found—
100 Thy skill to poet were, thou Scorner of the ground!

Teach me half the gladness
That thy brain must know,
Such harmonious madness
From my lips would flow
105 The world should listen then—as I am listening now.

1820   1820

4. Marital (from Hymen, Greek god of marriage).

Adonais   John Keats died in Rome on February 23, 1821, and was buried there in the Protestant Cemetery. Shelley had met Keats, had invited him to be his guest at Pisa, and had gradually come to realize that he was "among the writers of the highest genius who have adorned our age" (Preface to *Adonais*). The name "Adonais" is derived from Adonis, the handsome youth who had been loved by the goddess Venus and slain by a wild boar. He was restored to life on the condition that he spend only part of every year with Venus in heaven and the other part with Proserpine in the underworld. This cycle of rebirth and death, symbolic of the alternate return of summer and winter, suggests why Adonis was central to ancient fertility myths. Shelley in his poem gives the role of the boar to the anonymous author of a vituperative review of Keats's *Endymion* in the *Quarterly Review*, April 1818 (now known to be John Wilson Croker), whom Shelley mistakenly believed to be responsible for Keats's illness and death.

Shelley in a letter described *Adonais*, which he wrote in April–June 1821 and had printed in Pisa in July, as a "highly wrought piece of art." Its artistry consists in part in the care with which it follows the conventions of the pastoral elegy, established more than two thousand years earlier by the Greek Sicilian poets Theocritus, Bion, and Moschus—Shelley had translated into English Bion's *Lament for Adonis* and Moschus's *Lament for Bion*. We recognize the centuries-old poetic ritual in many verbal echoes and in devices such as the mournful and accusing invocation to a muse (stanzas 2–4), the sympathetic participation of nature in the grieving (stanzas 14–17), the procession of appropriate mourners (stanzas 30–35), the denunciation of unworthy practitioners of the pastoral or literary art (stanzas 17, 27–29, 36–37), and above all, in the turn from despair at the finality of human death (lines 1, 64, 190: "*He* will awake no more, oh, never more!") to consolation in the sudden and contradictory discovery that the grave is a gate to a higher existence (line 343: "Peace, peace! he is not dead, he doth not sleep").

Published first in Pisa, Italy, in 1821, *Adonais* was not issued in England until 1829, in an edition sponsored by the so-called Cambridge Apostles (the minor poet R. M. Milnes and the more famous poets Alfred Tennyson and A. H. Hallam). The appearance of this edition marked the beginning of Keats's posthumous emergence from obscurity.

Adonais

An Elegy on the Death of John Keats, Author of Endymion, Hyperion, etc.

[Thou wert the morning star among the living,
　　Ere thy fair light had fled—
Now, having died, thou art as Hesperus, giving
　　New splendour to the dead.][1]

I

I weep for Adonais—he is dead!
O, weep for Adonais! though our tears
Thaw not the frost which binds so dear a head!
And thou, sad Hour,[2] selected from all years
5　To mourn our loss, rouse thy obscure compeers,°　　　*companions*

---

1. Shelley prefixed to *Adonais* a Greek epigram attributed to Plato; this is Shelley's translation of the Greek. The planet Venus appears both as the morning star, Lucifer, and as the evening star, Hesperus or Vesper. Shelley makes of this phenomenon a key symbol for Adonais's triumph over death, in stanzas 44–46.

2. Shelley follows the classical mode of personifying the hours, which mark the passage of time and turn of the seasons.

And teach them thine own sorrow, say: with me
Died Adonais; till the Future dares
Forget the Past, his fate and fame shall be
An echo and a light unto eternity!

2

Where wert thou mighty Mother,[3] when he lay,
When thy Son lay, pierced by the shaft which flies
In darkness?[4] where was lorn° Urania   *forlorn*
When Adonais died? With veiled eyes,
'Mid listening Echoes, in her Paradise
She sate, while one,[5] with soft enamoured breath,
Rekindled all the fading melodies,
With which, like flowers that mock the corse° beneath, *corpse*
He had adorned and hid the coming bulk of death.

3

O, weep for Adonais—he is dead!
Wake, melancholy Mother, wake and weep!
Yet wherefore? Quench within their burning bed
Thy fiery tears, and let thy loud heart keep
Like his, a mute and uncomplaining sleep;
For he is gone, where all things wise and fair
Descend;—oh, dream not that the amorous Deep° *abyss*
Will yet restore him to the vital air;
Death feeds on his mute voice, and laughs at our despair.

4

Most musical of mourners, weep again!
Lament anew, Urania!—He[6] died,
Who was the Sire of an immortal strain,
Blind, old, and lonely, when his country's pride,
The priest, the slave, and the liberticide,
Trampled and mocked with many a loathed rite
Of lust and blood; he went, unterrified,
Into the gulph of death; but his clear Sprite° *spirit*
Yet reigns o'er earth; the third among the sons of light.[7]

5

Most musical of mourners, weep anew!
Not all to that bright station dared to climb;
And happier they their happiness who knew,
Whose tapers° yet burn through that night of time *candles*
In which suns perished; others more sublime,
Struck by the envious wrath of man or God,
Have sunk, extinct in their refulgent° prime; *radiant*

3. Urania. She had originally been the Muse of astronomy, but the name was also an epithet for Venus. Shelley converts Venus Urania, who in Greek myth had been the lover of Adonis, into the mother of Adonais.
4. Alludes to the anonymity of the review of *Endymion*.
5. I.e., the echo of Keats's voice in his poems.
6. Milton, regarded as precursor of the great

poetic tradition in which Keats wrote. He had adopted Urania as the muse of *Paradise Lost*. Lines 31–35 describe Milton's life during the restoration of the Stuart monarchy.
7. In "A Defence of Poetry," Shelley says that Milton was the third great epic poet, along with Homer and Dante. The stanza following describes the lot of other poets, up to Shelley's own time.

And some yet live, treading the thorny road,
45   Which leads, through toil and hate, to Fame's serene abode.

6

But now, thy youngest, dearest one, has perished—
The nursling of thy widowhood, who grew,
Like a pale flower by some sad maiden cherished,
And fed with true love tears, instead of dew;[8]
50   Most musical of mourners, weep anew!
Thy extreme[9] hope, the loveliest and the last,
The bloom, whose petals nipt before they blew°   bloomed
Died on the promise of the fruit, is waste;
The broken lily lies—the storm is overpast.

7

55   To that high Capital,° where kingly Death   Rome
Keeps his pale court in beauty and decay,
He came; and bought, with price of purest breath,
A grave among the eternal.—Come away!
Haste, while the vault of blue Italian day
60   Is yet his fitting charnel-roof! while still
He lies, as if in dewy sleep he lay;
Awake him not! surely he takes his fill
Of deep and liquid rest, forgetful of all ill.

8

He will awake no more, oh, never more!—
65   Within the twilight chamber spreads apace,
The shadow of white Death, and at the door
Invisible Corruption waits to trace
His extreme way to her dim dwelling-place;
The eternal Hunger sits, but pity and awe
70   Soothe her pale rage, nor dares she to deface
So fair a prey, till darkness, and the law
Of change, shall 'oer his sleep the mortal curtain draw.

9

O, weep for Adonais!—The quick° Dreams,   living
The passion-winged Ministers of thought,
75   Who were his flocks,[1] whom near the living streams
Of his young spirit he fed, and whom he taught
The love which was its music, wander not,—
Wander no more, from kindling brain to brain,
But droop there, whence they sprung; and mourn their lot
80   Round the cold heart, where, after their sweet pain,
They ne'er will gather strength, or find a home again.

10

And one[2] with trembling hands clasps his cold head,
And fans him with her moonlight wings, and cries;
"Our love, our hope, our sorrow, is not dead;
85   See, on the silken fringe of his faint eyes,

8. An allusion to an incident in Keats's *Isabella*.
9. Last, as well as highest.
1. The products of Keats's imagination, figura-

tively represented (according to the conventions of the pastoral elegy) as his sheep.
2. One of the Dreams (line 73).

Like dew upon a sleeping flower, there lies
A tear some Dream has loosened from his brain."
Lost Angel of a ruined Paradise!
She knew not 'twas her own; as with no stain
90 She faded, like a cloud which had outwept its rain.

11

One from a lucid° urn of starry dew   luminous
Washed his light limbs as if embalming them;
Another clipt her profuse locks, and threw
The wreath upon him, like an anadem,°   rich garland
95 Which frozen tears instead of pearls begem;
Another in her wilful grief would break
Her bow and winged reeds, as if to stem
A greater loss with one which was more weak;
And dull the barbed fire against his frozen cheek.

12

100 Another Splendour on his mouth alit,
That mouth, whence it was wont° to draw the breath   accustomed
Which gave it strength to pierce the guarded wit,[3]
And pass into the panting heart beneath
With lightning and with music: the damp death
105 Quenched its caress upon his icy lips;
And, as a dying meteor stains a wreath
Of moonlight vapour, which the cold night clips,
It flushed through his pale limbs, and past to its eclipse.

13

And others came . . . Desires and Adorations,
110 Winged Persuasions and veiled Destinies,
Splendours, and Glooms, and glimmering Incarnations
Of hopes and fears, and twilight Phantasies;
And Sorrow, with her family of Sighs,
And Pleasure, blind with tears, led by the gleam
115 Of her own dying smile instead of eyes,
Came in slow pomp;—the moving pomp might seem
Like pageantry of mist on an autumnal stream.

14

All he had loved, and moulded into thought,
From shape, and hue, and odour, and sweet sound,
120 Lamented Adonais. Morning sought
Her eastern watchtower, and her hair unbound,
Wet with the tears which should adorn the ground,
Dimmed the aerial eyes that kindle day;
Afar the melancholy thunder moaned,
125 Pale Ocean in unquiet slumber lay,
And the wild winds flew round, sobbing in their dismay.

15

Lost Echo sits amid the voiceless mountains,
And feeds her grief with his remembered lay,°   song

3. The cautious intellect (of the listener).

And will no more reply to winds or fountains,
130   Or amorous birds perched on the young green spray,
Or herdsman's horn, or bell at closing day;
Since she can mimic not his lips, more dear
Than those for whose disdain she pined away
Into a shadow of all sounds:[4]—a drear
135 Murmur, between their songs, is all the woodmen hear.

16

Grief made the young Spring wild, and she threw down
Her kindling buds, as if she Autumn were,
Or they dead leaves; since her delight is flown
For whom should she have waked the sullen year?
140   To Phoebus was not Hyacinth so dear[5]
Nor to himself Narcissus, as to both
Thou Adonais: wan they stand and sere[6]
Amid the faint companions of their youth,
With dew all turned to tears; odour, to sighing ruth.°   pity

17

145 Thy spirit's sister, the lorn nightingale[7]
Mourns not her mate with such melodious pain;
Not so the eagle, who like thee could scale
Heaven, and could nourish in the sun's domain
Her mighty youth with morning,[8] doth complain,°   lament
150   Soaring and screaming round her empty nest,
As Albion° wails for thee: the curse of Cain   England
Light on his head[9] who pierced thy innocent breast,
And scared the angel soul that was its earthly guest!

18

Ah woe is me! Winter is come and gone,
155   But grief returns with the revolving year;
The airs and streams renew their joyous tone;
The ants, the bees, the swallows reappear;
Fresh leaves and flowers deck the dead Seasons' bier;
The amorous birds now pair in every brake,°   thicket
160   And build their mossy homes in field and brere;°   briar
And the green lizard, and the golden snake,
Like unimprisoned flames, out of their trance awake.

19

Through wood and stream and field and hill and Ocean
A quickening life from the Earth's heart has burst
165   As it has ever done, with change and motion,
From the great morning of the world when first
God dawned on Chaos; in its stream immersed

4. Because of her unrequited love for Narcissus, who was enamored of his own reflection (line 141), the nymph Echo pined away until she was only a reflected sound.
5. Young Hyacinthus was loved by Phoebus Apollo, who accidentally killed him in a game of quoits. Apollo made the hyacinth flower spring from his blood.
6. Dried, withered.
7. To whom Keats had written "Ode to a Nightingale."
8. In the legend the aged eagle, to renew his youth, flies toward the sun until his old plumage is burned off and the film cleared from his eyes.
9. The reviewer of Endymion.

The lamps of Heaven flash with a softer light;
All baser things pant with life's sacred thirst;
170   Diffuse themselves; and spend in love's delight,
The beauty and the joy of their renewed might.

20

The leprous corpse touched by this spirit tender
Exhales itself in flowers of gentle breath;
Like incarnations of the stars, when splendour
175   Is changed to fragrance, they illumine death
And mock the merry worm that wakes beneath;
Nought we know, dies. Shall that alone which knows
Be as a sword consumed before the sheath[1]
By sightless° lightning?—th' intense atom glows   *invisible*
180 A moment, then is quenched in a most cold repose.

21

Alas! that all we loved of him should be,
But for our grief, as if it had not been,
And grief itself be mortal! Woe is me!
Whence are we, and why are we? of what scene
185   The actors or spectators? Great and mean°   *low*
Meet massed in death, who lends what life must borrow.
As long as skies are blue, and fields are green,
Evening must usher night, night urge the morrow,
Month follow month with woe, and year wake year to sorrow.

22

190 *He* will awake no more, oh, never more!
"Wake thou," cried Misery, "childless Mother, rise
Out of thy sleep, and slake,° in thy heart's core,   *assuage*
A wound more fierce than his with tears and sighs."
And all the Dreams that watched Urania's eyes,
195   And all the Echoes whom their sister's song[2]
Had held in holy silence, cried: "Arise!"
Swift as a Thought by the snake Memory stung,
From her ambrosial rest the fading Splendour° sprung.   *Urania*

23

She rose like an autumnal Night, that springs
200   Out of the East, and follows wild and drear
The golden Day, which, on eternal wings,
Even as a ghost abandoning a bier,
Had left the Earth a corpse. Sorrow and fear
So struck, so roused, so rapt Urania;
205   So saddened round her like an atmosphere
Of stormy mist; so swept her on her way
Even to the mournful place where Adonais lay.

24

Out of her secret Paradise she sped,
Through camps and cities rough with stone, and steel,

1. The "sword" is the mind that knows; the   2. I.e., the Echo in line 127.
"sheath" is its vehicle, the material body.

210   And human hearts, which to her aery tread
      Yielding not, wounded the invisible
      Palms of her tender feet where'er they fell:
      And barbed tongues, and thoughts more sharp than they
      Rent° the soft Form they never could repel,   tore
215   Whose sacred blood, like the young tears of May,
    Paved with eternal flowers that undeserving way.

                        25

      In the death chamber for a moment Death
      Shamed by the presence of that living Might
      Blushed to annihilation, and the breath
220   Revisited those lips, and life's pale light
      Flashed through those limbs, so late her dear delight.
      "Leave me not wild and drear and comfortless,
      As silent lightning leaves the starless night!
      Leave me not!" cried Urania: her distress
225   Roused Death: Death rose and smiled, and met her vain caress.

                        26

      "Stay yet awhile! speak to me once again;
      Kiss me, so long but as a kiss may live;
      And in my heartless³ breast and burning brain
      That word, that kiss shall all thoughts else survive
230   With food of saddest memory kept alive,
      Now thou art dead, as if it were a part
      Of thee, my Adonais! I would give
      All that I am to be as thou now art!
    But I am chained to Time, and cannot thence depart!

                        27

235   "Oh gentle child, beautiful as thou wert,
      Why didst thou leave the trodden paths of men
      Too soon, and with weak hands though mighty heart
      Dare° the unpastured dragon in his den?⁴   challenge
      Defenceless as thou wert, oh where was then
240   Wisdom the mirrored shield, or scorn the spear?⁵
      Or hadst thou waited the full cycle, when
      Thy spirit should have filled its crescent sphere,⁶
    The monsters of life's waste had fled from thee like deer.

                        28

      "The herded wolves, bold only to pursue;
245   The obscene ravens, clamorous o'er the dead;
      The vultures to the conqueror's banner true
      Who feed where Desolation first has fed,
      And whose wings rain contagion;—how they fled,
      When like Apollo, from his golden bow,

3. Because her heart had been given to Adonais.
4. I.e., the hostile reviewers.
5. The allusion is to Perseus, who had cut off
Medusa's head while avoiding the direct sight of
her (which would have turned him to stone) by
looking only at her reflection in his shield.
6. I.e., when thy spirit, like the full moon, should
have reached its maturity.

250   The Pythian of the age[7] one arrow sped
       And smiled!—The spoilers tempt no second blow,
    They fawn on the proud feet that spurn them lying low.

                        29

       "The sun comes forth, and many reptiles spawn;
       He sets, and each ephemeral insect[8] then
255   Is gathered into death without a dawn,
       And the immortal stars awake again;
       So is it in the world of living men:
       A godlike mind soars forth, in its delight
       Making earth bare and veiling heaven,[9] and when
260   It sinks, the swarms that dimmed or shared its light
    Leave to its kindred lamps[1] the spirit's awful night."

                        30

       Thus ceased she: and the mountain shepherds came,
       Their garlands sere, their magic mantles° rent;   cloaks
       The Pilgrim of Eternity,[2] whose fame
265   Over his living head like Heaven is bent,
       An early but enduring monument,
       Came, veiling all the lightnings of his song
       In sorrow; from her wilds Ierne sent
       The sweetest lyrist[3] of her saddest wrong,
270   And love taught grief to fall like music from his tongue.

                        31

       Midst others of less note, came one frail Form,[4]
       A phantom among men; companionless
       As the last cloud of an expiring storm
       Whose thunder is its knell;° he, as I guess,   funeral bell
275   Had gazed on Nature's naked loveliness,
       Actæon-like, and now he fled astray
       With feeble steps o'er the world's wilderness,
       And his own thoughts, along that rugged way,
    Pursued, like raging hounds, their father and their prey.[5]

                        32

280   A pardlike° Spirit beautiful and swift—   leopardlike
       A Love in desolation masked;—a Power
       Girt round with weakness;—it can scarce uplift
       The weight of the superincumbent hour;[6]
       It is a dying lamp, a falling shower,
285   A breaking billow;—even whilst we speak
       Is it not broken? On the withering flower

7. Byron, who had directed against critics of the age his satiric poem *English Bards and Scotch Reviewers* (1809). The allusion is to Apollo, called "the Pythian" because he had slain the dragon Python.
8. Insect that lives and dies in a single day.
9. As the sun reveals the earth but veils the other stars.
1. The other stars (i.e., creative minds), of lesser brilliance than the sun.
2. Byron, who had referred to his Childe Harold as one of the "wanderers o'er Eternity" (3.669).
3. Thomas Moore (1779–1852), from Ireland ("Ierne"), who had written poems about the oppression of his native land.
4. Shelley, represented in one of his aspects—such as the Poet in *Alastor*, rather than the author of *Prometheus Unbound*.
5. Actaeon, while hunting, came upon the naked Diana bathing and, as a punishment, was turned into a stag and torn to pieces by his own hounds.
6. The heavy, overhanging hour of Keats's death.

The killing sun smiles brightly: on a cheek
The life can burn in blood, even while the heart may break.

33

His head was bound with pansies overblown,
290   And faded violets, white, and pied, and blue;
And a light spear topped with a cypress cone,
Round whose rude shaft dark ivy tresses grew[7]
Yet dripping with the forest's noonday dew,
Vibrated, as the ever-beating heart
295   Shook the weak hand that grasped it; of that crew
He came the last, neglected and apart;
A herd-abandoned deer struck by the hunter's dart.

34

All stood aloof, and at his partial moan
Smiled through their tears; well knew that gentle band
300   Who in another's fate now wept his own;
As in the accents of an unknown land,
He sung new sorrow; sad Urania scanned
The Stranger's mien, and murmured: "who art thou?"
He answered not, but with a sudden hand
305   Made bare his branded and ensanguined° brow,   *bloodied*
Which was like Cain's or Christ's[8]—Oh! that it should be so!

35

What softer voice is hushed over the dead?
Athwart what brow is that dark mantle thrown?
What form leans sadly o'er the white death-bed,
310   In mockery of monumental stone,[9]
The heavy heart heaving without a moan?
If it be He,[1] who, gentlest of the wise,
Taught, soothed, loved, honoured the departed one;
Let me not vex, with inharmonious sighs
315   The silence of that heart's accepted sacrifice.

36

Our Adonais has drunk poison—oh!
What deaf and viperous murderer could crown
Life's early cup with such a draught of woe?
The nameless worm[2] would now itself disown:
320   It felt, yet could escape the magic tone
Whose prelude held all envy, hate, and wrong,
But what was howling in one breast alone,
Silent with expectation of the song,[3]
Whose master's hand is cold, whose silver lyre unstrung.

---

7. Like the thyrsus, the leaf-entwined and cone-topped staff carried by Dionysus, to whom leopards (see line 280) are sacred. The pansies, which are "overblown," i.e., past their bloom, are emblems of sorrowful thought. The cypress is an emblem of mourning.
8. His bloody ("ensanguined") brow bore a mark like that with which God had branded Cain for murdering Abel—or like that left by Christ's crown of thorns.
9. In imitation of a memorial statue.
1. Leigh Hunt, close friend of both Keats and Shelley.
2. Snake—the anonymous reviewer.
3. The promise of later greatness in Keats's early poems "held . . . silent" the expression of "all envy, hate, and wrong" except the reviewer's.

37

325 Live thou, whose infamy is not thy fame!
Live! fear no heavier chastisement from me,
Thou noteless blot on a remembered name!
But be thyself, and know thyself to be!
And ever at thy season be thou free
330 To spill the venom when thy fangs o'erflow:
Remorse and Self-contempt shall cling to thee;
Hot Shame shall burn upon thy secret brow,
And like a beaten hound tremble thou shalt—as now.

38

Nor let us weep that our delight is fled
335 Far from these carrion kites⁴ that scream below;
He wakes or sleeps with the enduring dead;
Thou canst not soar where he is sitting now.—
Dust to the dust! but the pure spirit shall flow
Back to the burning fountain whence it came,
340 A portion of the Eternal,⁵ which must glow
Through time and change, unquenchably the same,
Whilst thy cold embers choke the sordid hearth of shame.

39

Peace, peace! he is not dead, he doth not sleep—
He hath awakened from the dream of life—
345 'Tis we, who lost in stormy visions, keep
With phantoms an unprofitable strife,
And in mad trance, strike with our spirit's knife
Invulnerable nothings.—*We* decay
Like corpses in a charnel; fear and grief
350 Convulse us and consume us day by day,
And cold hopes swarm like worms within our living clay.

40

He has outsoared the shadow of our night;⁶
Envy and calumny° and hate and pain,   *slander*
And that unrest which men miscall delight,
355 Can touch him not and torture not again;
From the contagion of the world's slow stain
He is secure, and now can never mourn
A heart grown cold, a head grown grey in vain;
Nor, when the spirit's self has ceased to burn,
360 With sparkless ashes load an unlamented urn.

41

He lives, he wakes—'tis Death is dead, not he;
Mourn not for Adonais.—Thou young Dawn
Turn all thy dew to splendour, for from thee
The spirit thou lamentest is not gone;

4. A species of hawk that feeds on dead flesh.
5. Shelley adopts for this poem the Neoplatonic view that all life and all forms emanate from the Absolute, the eternal One. The Absolute is imaged as both a radiant light source and an overflowing fountain, which circulates continuously through the dross of matter (stanza 43) and back to its source.
6. He has soared beyond the shadow cast by the earth as it intercepts the sun's light.

365 Ye caverns and ye forests, cease to moan!
Cease ye faint flowers and fountains, and thou Air
Which like a mourning veil thy scarf hadst thrown
O'er the abandoned Earth, now leave it bare
Even to the joyous stars which smile on its despair![7]

42

370 He is made one with Nature: there is heard
His voice in all her music, from the moan
Of thunder, to the song of night's sweet bird;[8]
He is a presence to be felt and known
In darkness and in light, from herb and stone,
375 Spreading itself where'er that Power may move
Which has withdrawn his being to its own;
Which wields the world with never wearied love,
Sustains it from beneath, and kindles it above.

43

He is a portion of the loveliness
380 Which once he made more lovely: he doth bear
His part, while the one Spirit's plastic[9] stress
Sweeps through the dull dense world, compelling there,
All new successions to the forms they wear;
Torturing th' unwilling dross that checks its flight
385 To its own likeness, as each mass may bear;[1]
And bursting in its beauty and its might
From trees and beasts and men into the Heaven's light.

44

The splendours of the firmament of time
May be eclipsed, but are extinguished not;
390 Like stars to their appointed height they climb
And death is a low mist which cannot blot
The brightness it may veil.[2] When lofty thought
Lifts a young heart above its mortal lair,
And love and life contend in it, for what°   *whatever*
395 Shall be its earthly doom,° the dead live there[3]   *destiny*
And move like winds of light on dark and stormy air.

45

The inheritors of unfulfilled renown[4]
Rose from their thrones, built beyond mortal thought,
Far in the Unapparent. Chatterton
400 Rose pale, his solemn agony had not

---

7. Shelley's science is, as usual, accurate: it is the envelope of air around the earth that, by diffusing and reflecting sunlight, veils the stars so that they are invisible during the day.
8. The nightingale, in allusion to Keats's "Ode to a Nightingale."
9. Formative, shaping.
1. I.e., to the degree that a particular substance will permit.
2. The radiance of stars (i.e., of poets) persists, even when they are temporarily "eclipsed" by another heavenly body, or obscured by the veil of

the earth's atmosphere.
3. I.e., in the thought of the "young heart."
4. Poets who (like Keats) died young, before achieving their full measure of fame: the seventeen-year-old Thomas Chatterton (1752–1770) was believed to have committed suicide out of despair over his poverty and lack of recognition, Sir Philip Sidney (1554–1586) died in battle at thirty-two, and the Roman poet Lucan (39–65 C.E.) killed himself at twenty-six to escape a sentence of death for having plotted against the tyrant Nero.

Yet faded from him; Sidney, as he fought
And as he fell and as he lived and loved
Sublimely mild, a Spirit without spot,
Arose; and Lucan, by his death approved:° *justified*
405 Oblivion as they rose shrank like a thing reproved.

46

And many more, whose names on Earth are dark
But whose transmitted effluence cannot die
So long as fire outlives the parent spark,
Rose, robed in dazzling immortality.
410 "Thou art become as one of us," they cry,
"It was for thee yon kingless sphere has long
Swung blind in unascended majesty,
Silent alone amid an Heaven of song.
Assume thy winged throne, thou Vesper of our throng!"[5]

47

415 Who mourns for Adonais? oh come forth
Fond° wretch! and know thyself and him aright. *foolish*
Clasp with thy panting soul the pendulous[6] Earth;
As from a centre, dart thy spirit's light
Beyond all worlds, until its spacious might° *power*
420 Satiate the void circumference: then shrink
Even to a point within our day and night;[7]
And keep thy heart light lest it make thee sink
When hope has kindled hope, and lured thee to the brink.

48

Or go to Rome, which is the sepulchre
425 O, not of him, but of our joy: 'tis nought
That ages, empires, and religions there
Lie buried in the ravage they have wrought;
For such as he can lend,—they[8] borrow not
Glory from those who made the world their prey;
430 And he is gathered to the kings of thought
Who waged contention with their time's decay,
And of the past are all that cannot pass away.

49

Go thou to Rome,—at once the Paradise,
The grave, the city, and the wilderness;
435 And where its wrecks° like shattered mountains rise, *ruins*
And flowering weeds, and fragrant copses[9] dress
The bones of Desolation's nakedness
Pass, till the Spirit of the spot shall lead
Thy footsteps to a slope of green access[1]

5. Adonais assumes his place in the sphere of Vesper, the evening star, hitherto unoccupied ("kingless"), hence also "silent" amid the music of the other spheres.
6. Suspended, floating in space.
7. The poet bids the mourner to stretch his imagination so as to reach the poet's own cosmic viewpoint and then allow it to contract ("shrink") back to its ordinary vantage point on Earth—where, unlike Adonais in his heavenly place, we have an alternation of day and night.
8. Poets such as Keats.
9. Undergrowth. In Shelley's time the ruins of ancient Rome were overgrown with weeds and shrubs, almost as if the ground were returning to its natural state.
1. The Protestant Cemetery, Keats's burial place. The next line is a glancing allusion to Shelley's three-year-old son, William, also buried there.

440   Where, like an infant's smile, over the dead,
       A light of laughing flowers along the grass is spread.

                              50
       And grey walls moulder round,[2] on which dull Time
       Feeds, like slow fire upon a hoary brand;[3]
       And one keen pyramid with wedge sublime,[4]
445   Pavilioning the dust of him who planned
       This refuge for his memory, doth stand
       Like flame transformed to marble; and beneath,
       A field is spread, on which a newer band
       Have pitched in Heaven's smile their camp of death[5]
450 Welcoming him we lose with scarce extinguished breath.

                              51
       Here pause: these graves are all too young as yet
       To have outgrown the sorrow which consigned
       Its charge to each; and if the seal is set,
       Here, on one fountain of a mourning mind,[6]
455   Break it not thou! too surely shalt thou find
       Thine own well full, if thou returnest home,
       Of tears and gall. From the world's bitter wind
       Seek shelter in the shadow of the tomb.
     What Adonais is, why fear we to become?

                              52
460   The One remains, the many change and pass;
       Heaven's light forever shines, Earth's shadows fly;
       Life, like a dome of many-coloured glass,
       Stains the white radiance of Eternity,
       Until Death tramples it to fragments.[7]—Die,
465   If thou wouldst be with that which thou dost seek!
       Follow where all is fled!—Rome's azure sky,
       Flowers, ruins, statues, music, words, are weak
     The glory they transfuse with fitting truth to speak.

                              53
       Why linger, why turn back, why shrink, my Heart?
470   Thy hopes are gone before; from all things here
       They have departed; thou shouldst now depart!
       A light is past° from the revolving year,   passed
       And man, and woman; and what still is dear
       Attracts to crush, repels to make thee wither.
475   The soft sky smiles,—the low wind whispers near:
       'Tis Adonais calls! oh, hasten thither,
     No more let Life divide what Death can join together.

2. The wall of ancient Rome formed one boundary
of the cemetery.
3. A burning log, white with ash.
4. The tomb of Caius Cestius, a Roman tribune,
just outside the cemetery.
5. A common name for a cemetery in Italy is *cam-
posanto*, "holy camp or ground." Shelley is punning
seriously on the Italian word.

6. Shelley's mourning for his son.
7. Earthly life colors ("stains") the pure white light
of the One, which is the source of all light (see
lines 339–40, n. 5). The azure sky, flowers, etc., of
lines 466–68 exemplify earthly colors that, however beautiful, fall far short of the "glory" of the
pure Light that they transmit but also refract
("transfuse").

54

That Light whose smile kindles the Universe,
That Beauty in which all things work and move,
480   That Benediction which the eclipsing Curse
Of birth can quench not, that sustaining Love
Which through the web of being blindly wove
By man and beast and earth and air and sea,
Burns bright or dim, as each are mirrors of[8]
485   The fire for which all thirst;[9] now beams on me,
Consuming the last clouds of cold mortality.

55

The breath whose might I have invoked in song[1]
Descends on me; my spirit's bark is driven,
Far from the shore, far from the trembling throng
490   Whose sails were never to the tempest given;
The massy earth and sphered skies are riven![2]
I am borne darkly, fearfully, afar;
Whilst burning through the inmost veil of Heaven,
The soul of Adonais, like a star,
495   Beacons from the abode where the Eternal are.

1821   1821

A Defence of Poetry

In 1820 Shelley's good friend Thomas Love Peacock published an ironic essay, "The Four Ages of Poetry," implicitly directed against the towering claims for poetry and the poetic imagination made by his Romantic contemporaries. In this essay, which is available at Norton Literature Online, Peacock adopted the premise of Wordsworth and some other Romantic critics—that poetry in its origin was a primitive use of language and mind—but from this premise he proceeded to draw the conclusion that poetry had become a useless anachronism in his own Age of Bronze, a time defined by new sciences (including economics and political theory) and technologies that had the potential to improve the world. Peacock was a poet as well as an excellent prose satirist, and Shelley saw the joke; but he also recognized that the view that Peacock, as a satirist, had assumed was very close to that actually held in his day by Utilitarian philosophers and the material-minded public, which either attacked or contemptuously ignored the imaginative faculty and its achievements. He therefore undertook, as he good-humoredly wrote to Peacock, "to break a lance with you . . . in honor of my mistress Urania" (giving the cause for which he battled the name that Milton had used for the muse inspiring *Paradise Lost*), even though he was only "the knight of the shield of shadow and the lance of gossamere." The result was "A Defence of Poetry," planned to consist of three parts. The last two parts were never written, and even the existing section, written in 1821, remained unpublished until 1840, eighteen years after Shelley's death.

Shelley's emphasis in this essay is not on the particularity of individual poems but on the universal and permanent qualities and values that, he believes, all great poems,

---

8. I.e., according to the degree that each reflects.
9. The "thirst" of the human spirit is to return to the fountain and fire (the "burning fountain," line 339) that are its source.
1. Two years earlier Shelley had "invoked" (prayed

to, and also asked for) "the breath of Autumn's being" in his "Ode to the West Wind" (p. 1743).
2. In her 1839 edition of her husband's works, Mary Shelley asked: "who but will regard as a prophecy the last stanza of the 'Adonais'?"

as products of imagination, have in common. Shelley in addition extends the term *poet* to include all creative minds that break out of the conditions of their historical time and place in order to envision such values. This category includes not only writers in prose as well as verse but also artists, legislators, prophets, and the founders of new social and religious institutions.

The "Defence" is an eloquent and enduring claim for the indispensability of the visionary and creative imagination in all the great human concerns. Few later social critics have equaled the cogency of Shelley's attack on our acquisitive society and its narrowly material concepts of utility and progress. Such a bias has opened the way to enormous advances in the physical sciences and our material well-being, but without a proportionate development of our "poetic faculty," the moral imagination. The result, Shelley says, is that "man, having enslaved the elements, remains himself a slave."

From A Defence of Poetry

or Remarks Suggested by an Essay Entitled "The Four Ages of Poetry"

According to one mode of regarding those two classes of mental action, which are called reason and imagination, the former may be considered as mind contemplating the relations borne by one thought to another, however produced; and the latter, as mind acting upon those thoughts so as to colour them with its own light, and composing from them, as from elements, other thoughts, each containing within itself the principle of its own integrity. The one[1] is the *to poiein*,[2] or the principle of synthesis, and has for its objects those forms which are common to universal nature and existence itself; the other is the *to logizein*,[3] or principle of analysis, and its action regards the relations of things, simply as relations; considering thoughts, not in their integral unity, but as the algebraical representations which conduct to certain general results. Reason is the enumeration of quantities already known; imagination is the perception of the value of those quantities, both separately and as a whole. Reason respects the differences, and imagination the similitudes of things. Reason is to Imagination as the instrument to the agent, as the body to the spirit, as the shadow to the substance.

Poetry, in a general sense, may be defined to be "the expression of the Imagination": and poetry is connate with the origin of man. Man is an instrument over which a series of external and internal impressions are driven, like the alternations of an ever-changing wind over an Æolian lyre,[4] which move it by their motion to ever-changing melody. But there is a principle within the human being, and perhaps within all sentient beings, which acts otherwise than in the lyre, and produces not melody, alone, but harmony, by an internal adjustment of the sounds or motions thus excited to the impressions which excite them. It is as if the lyre could accommodate its chords to the motions of that which strikes them, in a determined proportion of sound; even as the musician can accommodate his voice to the sound of the lyre. A child at play by itself will express its delight by its voice and motions; and every inflexion of tone and every gesture will bear exact relation to a corresponding antitype

---

1. The imagination. "The other" (later in the sentence) is the reason.
2. Making. The Greek word from which the English term *poet* derives means "maker," and "maker" was often used as equivalent to "poet" by Renaissance critics such as Sir Philip Sidney in his

Defence of Poesy, which Shelley had carefully studied.
3. Calculating, reasoning.
4. A wind harp (see Coleridge, "The Eolian Harp," p. 1612).

in the pleasurable impressions which awakened it; it will be the reflected image of that impression; and as the lyre trembles and sounds after the wind has died away, so the child seeks, by prolonging in its voice and motions the duration of the effect, to prolong also a consciousness of the cause. In relation to the objects which delight a child, these expressions are, what poetry is to higher objects. The savage (for the savage is to ages what the child is to years) expresses the emotions produced in him by surrounding objects in a similar manner; and language and gesture, together with plastic[5] or pictorial imitation, become the image of the combined effect of those objects, and of his apprehension of them. Man in society, with all his passions and his pleasures, next becomes the object of the passions and pleasures of man; an additional class of emotions produces an augmented treasure of expressions; and language, gesture, and the imitative arts, become at once the representation and the medium, the pencil and the picture, the chisel and the statue, the chord and the harmony. The social sympathies, or those laws from which as from its elements society results, begin to develope themselves from the moment that two human beings coexist; the future is contained within the present as the plant within the seed; and equality, diversity, unity, contrast, mutual dependence, become the principles alone capable of affording the motives according to which the will of a social being is determined to action, inasmuch as he is social; and constitute pleasure in sensation, virtue in sentiment, beauty in art, truth in reasoning, and love in the intercourse of kind. Hence men, even in the infancy of society, observe a certain order in their words and actions, distinct from that of the objects and the impressions represented by them, all expression being subject to the laws of that from which it proceeds. But let us dismiss those more general considerations which might involve an enquiry into the principles of society itself, and restrict our view to the manner in which the imagination is expressed upon its forms.

In the youth of the world, men dance and sing and imitate natural objects, observing[6] in these actions, as in all others, a certain rhythm or order. And, although all men observe a similar, they observe not the same order, in the motions of the dance, in the melody of the song, in the combinations of language, in the series of their imitations of natural objects. For there is a certain order or rhythm belonging to each of these classes of mimetic representation, from which the hearer and the spectator receive an intenser and purer pleasure than from any other: the sense of an approximation to this order has been called taste, by modern writers. Every man in the infancy of art, observes an order which approximates more or less closely to that from which this highest delight results: but the diversity is not sufficiently marked, as that its gradations should be sensible,[7] except in those instances where the predominance of this faculty of approximation to the beautiful (for so we may be permitted to name the relation between this highest pleasure and its cause) is very great. Those in whom it exists in excess are poets, in the most universal sense of the word; and the pleasure resulting from the manner in which they express the influence of society or nature upon their own minds, communicates itself to others, and gathers a sort of reduplication from that community. Their language is vitally metaphorical; that is, it marks the before unapprehended relations of things, and perpetuates their apprehension, until the words which represent them, become through time signs for portions or classes of thoughts[8]

5. Sculptural.
6. Following, obeying.

7. Discernible.
8. I.e., abstract concepts.

instead of pictures of integral thoughts; and then if no new poets should arise to create afresh the associations which have been thus disorganized, language will be dead to all the nobler purposes of human intercourse. These similitudes or relations are finely said by Lord Bacon to be "the same footsteps of nature impressed upon the various subjects of the world"[9]—and he considers the faculty which perceives them as the storehouse of axioms common to all knowledge. In the infancy of society every author is necessarily a poet, because language itself is poetry; and to be a poet is to apprehend the true and the beautiful, in a word the good which exists in the relation, subsisting, first between existence and perception, and secondly between perception and expression. Every original language near to its source is in itself the chaos of a cyclic poem:[1] the copiousness of lexicography and the distinctions of grammar are the works of a later age, and are merely the catalogue and the form of the creations of Poetry.

But Poets, or those who imagine and express this indestructible order, are not only the authors of language and of music, of the dance and architecture and statuary and painting: they are the institutors of laws, and the founders of civil society and the inventors of the arts of life and the teachers, who draw into a certain propinquity with the beautiful and the true that partial apprehension of the agencies of the invisible world which is called religion.[2] Hence all original religions are allegorical, or susceptible of allegory, and like Janus[3] have a double face of false and true. Poets, according to the circumstances of the age and nation in which they appeared, were called in the earlier epochs of the world legislators or prophets:[4] a poet essentially comprises and unites both these characters. For he not only beholds intensely the present as it is, and discovers those laws according to which present things ought to be ordered, but he beholds the future in the present, and his thoughts are the germs of the flower and the fruit of latest time. Not that I assert poets to be prophets in the gross sense of the word, or that they can foretell the form as surely as they foreknow the spirit of events: such is the pretence of superstition which would make poetry an attribute of prophecy, rather than prophecy an attribute of poetry. A Poet participates in the eternal, the infinite, and the one; as far as relates to his conceptions, time and place and number are not. The grammatical forms which express the moods of time, and the difference of persons and the distinction of place are convertible with respect to the highest poetry without injuring it as poetry, and the choruses of Æschylus, and the book of Job, and Dante's Paradise would afford, more than any other writings, examples of this fact, if the limits of this essay did not forbid citation. The creations of sculpture, painting, and music, are illustrations still more decisive.

Language, colour, form, and religious and civil habits of action are all the instruments and materials of poetry; they may be called poetry by that figure of speech which considers the effect as a synonime of the cause. But poetry in a more restricted sense[5] expresses those arrangements of language, and especially metrical language, which are created by that imperial faculty, whose

9. Francis Bacon's *The Advancement of Learning* 3.1.
1. A group of poems (e.g., "the Arthurian cycle") that deal with the same subject.
2. Here Shelley enlarges the scope of the term *poetry* to denote all the creative achievements, or imaginative breakthroughs, of humankind, including noninstitutional religious insights.
3. Roman god of beginnings and endings, often represented by two heads facing opposite directions.
4. Sir Philip Sidney had pointed out, in his *Defence of Poesy*, that *vates,* the Roman term for "poet," signifies "a diviner, fore-seer, or Prophet."
5. I.e., restricted to specifically verbal poetry, as against the inclusive sense in which Shelley has been applying the term.

throne is curtained within the invisible nature of man. And this springs from the nature itself of language, which is a more direct representation of the actions and passions of our internal being, and is susceptible of more various and delicate combinations, than colour, form, or motion, and is more plastic and obedient to the controul of that faculty of which it is the creation. For language is arbitrarily produced by the Imagination and has relation to thoughts alone; but all other materials, instruments and conditions of art, have relations among each other, which limit and interpose between conception and expression. The former[6] is as a mirror which reflects, the latter as a cloud which enfeebles, the light of which both are mediums of communication. Hence the fame of sculptors, painters and musicians, although the intrinsic powers of the great masters of these arts, may yield in no degree to that of those who have employed language as the hieroglyphic of their thoughts, has never equalled that of poets in the restricted sense of the term; as two performers of equal skill will produce unequal effects from a guitar and a harp. The fame of legislators and founders of religions, so long as their institutions last, alone seems to exceed that of poets in the restricted sense; but it can scarcely be a question whether, if we deduct the celebrity which their flattery of the gross opinions of the vulgar usually conciliates, together with that which belonged to them in their higher character of poets, any excess will remain.

We have thus circumscribed the meaning of the word Poetry within the limits of that art which is the most familiar and the most perfect expression of the faculty itself. It is necessary however to make the circle still narrower, and to determine the distinction between measured and unmeasured language;[7] for the popular division into prose and verse is inadmissible in accurate philosophy.

Sounds as well as thoughts have relation both between each other and towards that which they represent, and a perception of the order of those relations has always been found connected with a perception of the order of the relations of thoughts. Hence the language of poets has ever affected a certain uniform and harmonious recurrence of sound, without which it were not poetry, and which is scarcely less indispensable to the communication of its influence, than the words themselves, without reference to that peculiar order. Hence the vanity of translation; it were as wise to cast a violet into a crucible that you might discover the formal principle of its colour and odour, as seek to transfuse from one language into another the creations of a poet. The plant must spring again from its seed or it will bear no flower—and this is the burthen of the curse of Babel.[8]

An observation of the regular mode of the recurrence of this harmony in the language of poetical minds, together with its relation to music, produced metre, or a certain system of traditional forms of harmony of language. Yet it is by no means essential that a poet should accommodate his language to this traditional form, so that the harmony which is its spirit, be observed. The practise is indeed convenient and popular, and to be preferred, especially in such composition as includes much form and action: but every great poet must inevitably innovate upon the example of his predecessors in the exact structure

6. I.e., language, as opposed to the media of sculpture, painting, and music.
7. I.e., in meter versus in prose.
8. When the descendants of Noah, who spoke a single language, undertook to build the Tower of Babel, which would reach heaven, God cut short the attempt by multiplying languages so that the builders could no longer communicate (see Genesis 11.1–9).

of his peculiar versification. The distinction between poets and prose writers is a vulgar error. The distinction between philosophers and poets has been anticipated.[9] Plato was essentially a poet—the truth and splendour of his imagery and the melody of his language is the most intense that it is possible to conceive. He rejected the measure of the epic, dramatic, and lyrical forms, because he sought to kindle a harmony in thoughts divested of shape and action, and he forbore to invent any regular plan of rhythm which would include, under determinate forms, the varied pauses of his style. Cicero[1] sought to imitate the cadence of his periods but with little success. Lord Bacon was a poet.[2] His language has a sweet and majestic rhythm, which satisfies the sense, no less than the almost superhuman wisdom of his philosophy satisfies the intellect; it is a strain which distends, and then bursts the circumference of the hearer's mind, and pours itself forth together with it into the universal element with which it has perpetual sympathy. All the authors of revolutions in opinion are not only necessarily poets as they are inventors, nor even as their words unveil the permanent analogy of things by images which participate in the life of truth; but as their periods are harmonious and rhythmical and contain in themselves the elements of verse; being the echo of the eternal music. Nor are those supreme poets, who have employed traditional forms of rhythm on account of the form and action of their subjects, less capable of perceiving and teaching the truth of things, than those who have omitted that form. Shakespeare, Dante and Milton (to confine ourselves to modern writers) are philosophers of the very loftiest power.

A poem is the very image of life expressed in its eternal truth. There is this difference between a story and a poem, that a story is a catalogue of detached facts, which have no other bond of connexion than time, place, circumstance, cause and effect; the other is the creation of actions according to the unchangeable forms of human nature, as existing in the mind of the creator, which is itself the image of all other minds. The one is partial, and applies only to a definite period of time, and a certain combination of events which can never again recur; the other is universal, and contains within itself the germ of a relation to whatever motives or actions have place in the possible varieties of human nature. Time, which destroys the beauty and the use of the story of particular facts, stript of the poetry which should invest them, augments that of Poetry, and for ever develops new and wonderful applications of the eternal truth which it contains. Hence epitomes[3] have been called the moths of just history;[4] they eat out the poetry of it. The story of particular facts is as a mirror which obscures and distorts that which should be beautiful: Poetry is a mirror which makes beautiful that which is distorted.

The parts of a composition may be poetical, without the composition as a whole being a poem. A single sentence may be considered as a whole though it be found in a series of unassimilated portions; a single word even may be a spark of inextinguishable thought. And thus all the great historians, Herodotus, Plutarch, Livy,[5] were poets; and although the plan of these writers, especially that of Livy, restrained them from developing this faculty in its highest

---

9. I.e., in what Shelley has already said.
1. Marcus Tullius Cicero, the great Roman orator of the 1st century B.C.E.
2. See the *Filium Labyrinthi* and the *Essay on Death* particularly [Shelley's note].
3. Abstracts, summaries.
4. By Bacon in *The Advancement of Learning*

2.2.4.
5. Titus Livius (59 B.C.E.–17 C.E.) wrote an immense history of Rome. Herodotus (ca. 480–ca. 425 B.C.E.) wrote the first systematic history of Greece. Plutarch (ca. 46–ca. 120 C.E.) wrote *Parallel Lives* (of eminent Greeks and Romans).

degree, they make copious and ample amends for their subjection, by filling all the interstices of their subjects with living images.

Having determined what is poetry, and who are poets, let us proceed to estimate its effects upon society.

Poetry is ever accompanied with pleasure: all spirits on which it falls, open themselves to receive the wisdom which is mingled with its delight. In the infancy of the world, neither poets themselves nor their auditors are fully aware of the excellence of poetry: for it acts in a divine and unapprehended manner, beyond and above consciousness; and it is reserved for future generations to contemplate and measure the mighty cause and effect in all the strength and splendour of their union. Even in modern times, no living poet ever arrived at the fulness of his fame; the jury which sits in judgement upon a poet, belonging as he does to all time, must be composed of his peers: it must be impanelled by Time from the selectest of the wise of many generations. A Poet is a nightingale, who sits in darkness and sings to cheer its own solitude with sweet sounds; his auditors are as men entranced by the melody of an unseen musician, who feel that they are moved and softened, yet know not whence or why. The poems of Homer and his contemporaries were the delight of infant Greece; they were the elements of that social system which is the column upon which all succeeding civilization has reposed. Homer embodied the ideal perfection of his age in human character; nor can we doubt that those who read his verses were awakened to an ambition of becoming like to Achilles, Hector and Ulysses: the truth and beauty of friendship, patriotism and persevering devotion to an object, were unveiled to the depths in these immortal creations: the sentiments of the auditors must have been refined and enlarged by a sympathy with such great and lovely impersonations, until from admiring they imitated, and from imitation they identified themselves with the objects of their admiration. Nor let it be objected, that these characters are remote from moral perfection, and that they can by no means be considered as edifying patterns for general imitation. Every epoch under names more or less specious has deified its peculiar errors; Revenge is the naked Idol of the worship of a semi-barbarous age; and Self-deceit is the veiled Image of unknown evil before which luxury and satiety lie prostrate. But a poet considers the vices of his contemporaries as the temporary dress in which his creations must be arrayed, and which cover without concealing the eternal proportions of their beauty. An epic or dramatic personage is understood to wear them around his soul, as he may the antient armour or the modern uniform around his body; whilst it is easy to conceive a dress more graceful than either. The beauty of the internal nature cannot be so far concealed by its accidental vesture, but that the spirit of its form shall communicate itself to the very disguise, and indicate the shape it hides from the manner in which it is worn. A majestic form and graceful motions will express themselves through the most barbarous and tasteless costume. Few poets of the highest class have chosen to exhibit the beauty of their conceptions in its naked truth and splendour; and it is doubtful whether the alloy of costume, habit, etc., be not necessary to temper this planetary music[6] for mortal ears.

The whole objection, however, of the immorality of poetry[7] rests upon a misconception of the manner in which poetry acts to produce the moral

6. The music made by the revolving crystalline spheres of the planets, inaudible to human ears.
7. In the preceding paragraph Shelley has been implicitly dealing with the charge, voiced by Plato in his *Republic*, that poetry is immoral because it represents evil characters acting evilly.

improvement of man. Ethical science[8] arranges the elements which poetry has created, and propounds schemes and proposes examples of civil and domestic life: nor is it for want of admirable doctrines that men hate, and despise, and censure, and deceive, and subjugate one another. But Poetry acts in another and diviner manner. It awakens and enlarges the mind itself by rendering it the receptacle of a thousand unapprehended combinations of thought. Poetry lifts the veil from the hidden beauty of the world, and makes familiar objects be as if they were not familiar; it reproduces[9] all that it represents, and the impersonations clothed in its Elysian light stand thenceforward in the minds of those who have once contemplated them, as memorials of that gentle and exalted content[1] which extends itself over all thoughts and actions with which it coexists. The great secret of morals is Love; or a going out of our own nature, and an identification of ourselves with the beautiful which exists in thought, action, or person, not our own. A man, to be greatly good, must imagine intensely and comprehensively; he must put himself in the place of another and of many others; the pains and pleasures of his species must become his own. The great instrument of moral good is the imagination;[2] and poetry administers to the effect by acting upon the cause. Poetry enlarges the circumference of the imagination by replenishing it with thoughts of ever new delight, which have the power of attracting and assimilating to their own nature all other thoughts, and which form new intervals and interstices whose void for ever craves fresh food. Poetry strengthens that faculty which is the organ of the moral nature of man, in the same manner as exercise strengthens a limb. A Poet therefore would do ill to embody his own conceptions of right and wrong, which are usually those of his place and time, in his poetical creations, which participate in neither. By this assumption of the inferior office of interpreting the effect, in which perhaps after all he might acquit himself but imperfectly, he would resign the glory in a participation in the cause.[3] There was little danger that Homer, or any of the eternal Poets, should have so far misunderstood themselves as to have abdicated this throne of their widest dominion. Those in whom the poetical faculty, though great, is less intense, as Euripides, Lucan, Tasso,[4] Spenser, have frequently affected[5] a moral aim, and the effect of their poetry is diminished in exact proportion to the degree in which they compel us to advert to this purpose.[6]

* * *

It is difficult to define pleasure in its highest sense; the definition involving a number of apparent paradoxes. For, from an inexplicable defect of harmony in the constitution of human nature, the pain of the inferior is frequently connected with the pleasures of the superior portions of our being. Sorrow,

8. Moral philosophy.
9. Produces anew, re-creates.
1. Contentment.
2. Central to Shelley's theory is the concept (developed by 18th-century philosophers) of the sympathetic imagination—the faculty by which an individual is enabled to identify with the thoughts and feelings of others. Shelley insists that the faculty in poetry that enables us to share the joys and sufferings of invented characters is also the basis of all morality, for it compels us to feel for others as we feel for ourselves.
3. The "effect," or the explicit moral standards into which imaginative insights are translated at a particular time or place, is contrasted to the

"cause" of all morality, the imagination itself.
4. Tasso Torquato (1544–1595), Italian poet, author of *Jerusalem Delivered*, an epic poem about a crusade. Euripides (ca. 484–406 B.C.E.), Greek writer of tragedies. Lucan (39–65 C.E.), Roman poet, author of the *Pharsalia*.
5. Assumed, adopted.
6. In the following, omitted passage, Shelley reviews the history of drama and poetry in relation to civilization and morality and proceeds to refute the charge that poets are less useful than "reasoners and merchants." He begins by defining *utility* in terms of pleasure and then distinguishes between the lower (physical and material) and the higher (imaginative) pleasures.

terror, anguish, despair itself are often the chosen expressions of an approximation to the highest good. Our sympathy in tragic fiction depends on this principle; tragedy delights by affording a shadow of the pleasure which exists in pain. This is the source also of the melancholy which is inseparable from the sweetest melody. The pleasure that is in sorrow is sweeter than the pleasure of pleasure itself. And hence the saying, "It is better to go to the house of mourning, than to the house of mirth."[7] Not that this highest species of pleasure is necessarily linked with pain. The delight of love and friendship, the ecstasy of the admiration of nature, the joy of the perception and still more of the creation of poetry is often wholly unalloyed.

The production and assurance of pleasure in this highest sense is true utility. Those who produce and preserve this pleasure are Poets or poetical philosophers.

The exertions of Locke, Hume, Gibbon, Voltaire, Rousseau,[8] and their disciples, in favour of oppressed and deluded humanity, are entitled to the gratitude of mankind. Yet it is easy to calculate the degree of moral and intellectual improvement which the world would have exhibited, had they never lived. A little more nonsense would have been talked for a century or two; and perhaps a few more men, women, and children, burnt as heretics. We might not at this moment have been congratulating each other on the abolition of the Inquisition in Spain.[9] But it exceeds all imagination to conceive what would have been the moral condition of the world if neither Dante, Petrarch, Boccaccio, Chaucer, Shakespeare, Calderon, Lord Bacon, nor Milton, had ever existed; if Raphael and Michael Angelo had never been born; if the Hebrew poetry had never been translated; if a revival of the study of Greek literature had never taken place; if no monuments of antient sculpture had been handed down to us; and if the poetry of the religion of the antient world had been extinguished together with its belief. The human mind could never, except by the intervention of these excitements, have been awakened to the invention of the grosser sciences, and that application of analytical reasoning to the aberrations of society, which it is now attempted to exalt over the direct expression of the inventive and creative faculty itself.

We have more moral, political and historical wisdom, than we know how to reduce into practice; we have more scientific and economical knowledge than can be accommodated to the just distribution of the produce which it multiplies. The poetry in these systems of thought, is concealed by the accumulation of facts and calculating processes. There is no want of knowledge respecting what is wisest and best in morals, government, and political economy, or at least, what is wiser and better than what men now practise and endure. But we let "I dare not wait upon I would, like the poor cat i' the adage."[1] We want[2] the creative faculty to imagine that which we know; we want the generous impulse to act that which we imagine; we want the poetry of life: our calculations have outrun conception; we have eaten more than we can digest. The cultivation of those sciences which have enlarged the limits of the empire of man over the external world, has, for want of the poetical faculty, proportion-

7. Ecclesiastes 7.2.
8. I follow the classification adopted by the author of Four Ages of Poetry. But Rousseau was essentially a poet. The others, even Voltaire, were mere reasoners [Shelley's note].
9. The Inquisition had been suspended following the Spanish Revolution of 1820, the year before

Shelley wrote this essay; it was not abolished permanently until 1834.
1. The words with which Lady Macbeth encourages her husband's ambition (Shakespeare, *Macbeth* 1.7.44–45).
2. Lack.

ally circumscribed those of the internal world; and man, having enslaved the elements, remains himself a slave. To what but a cultivation of the mechanical arts in a degree disproportioned to the presence of the creative faculty, which is the basis of all knowledge, is to be attributed the abuse of all invention for abridging and combining labour, to the exasperation of the inequality of mankind? From what other cause has it arisen that these inventions which should have lightened, have added a weight to the curse imposed on Adam?[3] Poetry, and the principle of Self, of which money is the visible incarnation, are the God and Mammon of the world.[4]

The functions of the poetical faculty are two-fold; by one it creates new materials of knowledge, and power and pleasure; by the other it engenders in the mind a desire to reproduce and arrange them according to a certain rhythm and order which may be called the beautiful and the good. The cultivation of poetry is never more to be desired than at periods when, from an excess of the selfish and calculating principle, the accumulation of the materials of external life exceed the quantity of the power of assimilating them to the internal laws of human nature. The body has then become too unwieldy for that which animates it.

Poetry is indeed something divine. It is at once the centre and circumference of knowledge; it is that which comprehends all science, and that to which all science must be referred. It is at the same time the root and blossom of all other systems of thought; it is that from which all spring, and that which adorns all; and that which, if blighted, denies the fruit and the seed, and witholds from the barren world the nourishment and the succession of the scions of the tree of life. It is the perfect and consummate surface and bloom of things; it is as the odour and the colour of the rose to the texture of the elements which compose it, as the form and the splendour of unfaded beauty to the secrets of anatomy and corruption. What were Virtue, Love, Patriotism, Friendship etc.—what were the scenery of this beautiful Universe which we inhabit—what were our consolations on this side of the grave—and what were our aspirations beyond it—if Poetry did not ascend to bring light and fire from those eternal regions where the owl-winged faculty of calculation dare not ever soar? Poetry is not like reasoning, a power to be exerted according to the determination of the will. A man cannot say, "I will compose poetry." The greatest poet even cannot say it: for the mind in creation is as a fading coal which some invisible influence, like an inconstant wind, awakens to transitory brightness: this power arises from within, like the colour of a flower which fades and changes as it is developed, and the conscious portions of our natures are unprophetic either of its approach or its departure. Could this influence be durable in its original purity and force, it is impossible to predict the greatness of the results; but when composition begins, inspiration is already on the decline, and the most glorious poetry that has ever been communicated to the world is probably a feeble shadow of the original conception of the poet. I appeal to the greatest Poets of the present day, whether it be not an error to assert that the finest passages of poetry are produced by labour and study. The toil and the delay recommended by critics can be justly interpreted to mean no more than a careful observation of the inspired moments, and an artificial connexion of the spaces between their suggestions by the intertexture of con-

3. God says to Adam: "cursed is the ground for thy sake. . . . Thorns also and thistles shall it bring forth. . . . In the sweat of thy face shalt thou eat bread, till thou return unto the ground" (Genesis 3.17–19).
4. Matthew 6.24: "Ye cannot serve God and Mammon."

ventional expressions; a necessity only imposed by the limitedness of the poetical faculty itself. For Milton conceived the Paradise Lost as a whole before he executed it in portions. We have his own authority also for the Muse having "dictated" to him the "unpremeditated song,"[5] and let this be an answer to those who would allege the fifty-six various readings of the first line of the Orlando Furioso.[6] Compositions so produced are to poetry what mosaic is to painting. This instinct and intuition of the poetical faculty is still more observable in the plastic and pictorial arts: a great statue or picture grows under the power of the artist as a child in the mother's womb; and the very mind which directs the hands in formation is incapable of accounting to itself for the origin, the gradations, or the media of the process.

Poetry is the record of the best and happiest[7] moments of the happiest and best minds. We are aware of evanescent visitations of thought and feeling sometimes associated with place or person, sometimes regarding our own mind alone, and always arising unforeseen and departing unbidden, but elevating and delightful beyond all expression: so that even in the desire and the regret they leave, there cannot but be pleasure, participating as it does in the nature of its object. It is as it were the interpenetration of a diviner nature through our own; but its footsteps are like those of a wind over a sea, where the coming calm erases, and whose traces remain only as on the wrinkled sand which paves it. These and corresponding conditions of being are experienced principally by those of the most delicate sensibility[8] and the most enlarged imagination; and the state of mind produced by them is at war with every base desire. The enthusiasm of virtue, love, patriotism, and friendship is essentially linked with these emotions; and whilst they last, self appears as what it is, an atom to a Universe. Poets are not only subject to these experiences as spirits of the most refined organization, but they can colour all that they combine with the evanescent hues of this etherial world; a word, or a trait in the representation of a scene or a passion, will touch the enchanted chord, and reanimate, in those who have ever experienced these emotions, the sleeping, the cold, the buried image of the past. Poetry thus makes immortal all that is best and most beautiful in the world; it arrests the vanishing apparitions which haunt the interlunations[9] of life, and veiling them or in language or in form sends them forth among mankind, bearing sweet news of kindred joy to those with whom their sisters abide—abide, because there is no portal of expression from the caverns of the spirit which they inhabit into the universe of things. Poetry redeems from decay the visitations of the divinity in man.

Poetry turns all things to loveliness; it exalts the beauty of that which is most beautiful, and it adds beauty to that which is most deformed; it marries exultation and horror, grief and pleasure, eternity and change; it subdues to union under its light yoke all irreconcilable things. It transmutes all that it touches, and every form moving within the radiance of its presence is changed by wondrous sympathy to an incarnation of the spirit which it breathes; its secret alchemy turns to potable gold[1] the poisonous waters which flow from death through life; it strips the veil of familiarity from the world, and lays bare the naked and sleeping beauty which is the spirit of its forms.

All things exist as they are perceived: at least in relation to the percipient.

5. *Paradise Lost* 9.21–24.
6. The epic poem by the 16th-century Italian poet Ariosto, noted for his care in composition.
7. In the double sense of "most joyous" and "most apt or felicitous in invention."
8. Sensitivity, capacity for sympathetic feeling.

9. The dark intervals between the old and new moons.
1. Alchemists aimed to produce a drinkable ("potable") form of gold that would be an elixir of life, curing all diseases.

"The mind is its own place, and of itself can make a heaven of hell, a hell of heaven."[2] But poetry defeats the curse which binds us to be subjected to the accident of surrounding impressions. And whether it spreads its own figured curtain or withdraws life's dark veil from before the scene of things, it equally creates for us a being within our being. It makes us the inhabitants of a world to which the familiar world is a chaos. It reproduces the common universe of which we are portions and percipients, and it purges from our inward sight the film of familiarity which obscures from us the wonder of our being. It compels us to feel that which we perceive, and to imagine that which we know. It creates anew the universe after it has been annihilated in our minds by the recurrence of impressions blunted by reiteration.[3] It justifies that bold and true word of Tasso: *Non merita nome di creatore, se non Iddio ed il Poeta.*[4]

A Poet, as he is the author to others of the highest wisdom, pleasure, virtue and glory, so he ought personally to be the happiest, the best, the wisest, and the most illustrious of men. As to his glory, let Time be challenged to declare whether the fame of any other institutor of human life be comparable to that of a poet. That he is the wisest, the happiest, and the best, inasmuch as he is a poet, is equally incontrovertible: the greatest poets have been men of the most spotless virtue, of the most consummate prudence, and, if we could look into the interior of their lives, the most fortunate of men: and the exceptions, as they regard those who possessed the poetic faculty in a high yet inferior degree, will be found on consideration to confirm rather than destroy the rule. Let us for a moment stoop to the arbitration of popular breath, and usurping and uniting in our own persons the incompatible characters of accuser, witness, judge and executioner, let us decide without trial, testimony, or form that certain motives of those who are "there sitting where we dare not soar"[5] are reprehensible. Let us assume that Homer was a drunkard, that Virgil was a flatterer, that Horace was a coward, that Tasso was a madman, that Lord Bacon was a peculator, that Raphael was a libertine, that Spenser was a poet laureate.[6] It is inconsistent with this division of our subject to cite living poets, but Posterity has done ample justice to the great names now referred to. Their errors have been weighed and found to have been dust in the balance; if their sins "were as scarlet, they are now white as snow";[7] they have been washed in the blood of the mediator and the redeemer Time. Observe in what a ludicrous chaos the imputations of real or fictitious crime have been confused in the contemporary calumnies against poetry and poets;[8] consider how little is, as it appears—or appears, as it is; look to your own motives, and judge not, lest ye be judged.[9]

Poetry, as has been said, in this respect differs from logic, that it is not

---

2. Satan's speech, *Paradise Lost* 1.254–55.
3. Shelley's version of a widespread Romantic doctrine that the poetic imagination transforms the familiar into the miraculous and re-creates the old world into a new world. See, e.g., Coleridge's *Biographia Literaria*, chap. 4: "To carry on the feelings of childhood into the powers of manhood; to combine the child's sense of wonder and novelty with the appearances which every day for perhaps forty years has rendered familiar; . . . this is the character and privilege of genius" (p. 1660).
4. "No one merits the name of Creator except God and the Poet." Quoted by Pierantonio Serassi in his *Life of Torquato Tasso* (1785).
5. Satan's scornful words to the angels who dis-

cover him after he has surreptitiously entered Eden: "Ye knew me once no mate / For you, sitting where ye durst not soar" (*Paradise Lost* 4.828–29).
6. Charges that had in fact been made against these men. The use of "poet laureate" as a derogatory term was a dig at Robert Southey, who held that honor at the time Shelley was writing. "Peculator": an embezzler of public money. Raphael is the 16th-century Italian painter.
7. Isaiah 1.18.
8. Shelley alludes especially to the charges of immorality by contemporary reviewers against Lord Byron and himself.
9. Christ's warning in Matthew 7.1.

subject to the controul of the active powers of the mind, and that its birth and recurrence has no necessary connexion with consciousness or will. It is presumptuous to determine that these[1] are the necessary conditions of all mental causation, when mental effects are experienced insusceptible of being referred to them. The frequent recurrence of the poetical power, it is obvious to suppose, may produce in the mind an habit of order and harmony correlative with its own nature and with its effects upon other minds. But in the intervals of inspiration, and they may be frequent without being durable, a poet becomes a man, and is abandoned to the sudden reflux of the influences under which others habitually live. But as he is more delicately organized than other men, and sensible[2] to pain and pleasure, both his own and that of others, in a degree unknown to them, he will avoid the one and pursue the other with an ardour proportioned to this difference. And he renders himself obnoxious to calumny,[3] when he neglects to observe the circumstances under which these objects of universal pursuit and flight have disguised themselves in one another's garments.

But there is nothing necessarily evil in this error, and thus cruelty, envy, revenge, avarice, and the passions purely evil, have never formed any portion of the popular imputations on the lives of poets.

I have thought it most favourable to the cause of truth to set down these remarks according to the order in which they were suggested to my mind, by a consideration of the subject itself, instead of following that of the treatise that excited me to make them public.[4] Thus although devoid of the formality of a polemical reply; if the view they contain be just, they will be found to involve a refutation of the doctrines of the Four Ages of Poetry, so far at least as regards the first division of the subject. I can readily conjecture what should have moved the gall of the learned and intelligent author of that paper; I confess myself, like him, unwilling to be stunned by the Theseids of the hoarse Codri of the day. Bavius and Maevius[5] undoubtedly are, as they ever were, insufferable persons. But it belongs to a philosophical critic to distinguish rather than confound.

The first part of these remarks has related to Poetry in its elements and principles; and it has been shewn, as well as the narrow limits assigned them would permit, that what is called poetry, in a restricted sense, has a common source with all other forms of order and of beauty according to which the materials of human life are susceptible of being arranged, and which is poetry in an universal sense.

The second part[6] will have for its object an application of these principles to the present state of the cultivation of Poetry, and a defence of the attempt to idealize the modern forms of manners and opinions, and compel them into a subordination to the imaginative and creative faculty. For the literature of

---

1. I.e., consciousness or will. Shelley again proposes that some mental processes are unconscious—outside our control or awareness.
2. I.e., sensitive to, conscious of. Cf. Wordsworth's Preface to *Lyrical Ballads* (p. 1495): "What is a poet? . . . He is a man speaking to men: a man, it is true, endued with more lively sensibility, more enthusiasm, and tenderness, who has a greater knowledge of human nature, and a more comprehensive soul, than are supposed to be common among mankind."
3. Exposed to slander.

4. Peacock's "Four Ages of Poetry."
5. Would-be poets satirized by Virgil and Horace. "Theseids": epic poems about Theseus. Codrus (plural "Codri") was the Roman author of a long, dull *Theseid* attacked by Juvenal and others. In 1794 and 1795 the conservative critic William Gifford had borrowed from Virgil and Horace and published the *Baviad* and the *Maeviad*, hard-hitting and highly influential satires on popular poetry and drama.
6. Shelley, however, completed only the first part.

England, an energetic developement of which has ever preceded or accompanied a great and free developement of the national will, has arisen as it were from a new birth. In spite of the low-thoughted envy which would undervalue contemporary merit, our own will be a memorable age in intellectual achievements, and we live among such philosophers and poets as surpass beyond comparison any who have appeared since the last national struggle for civil and religious liberty.[7] The most unfailing herald, companion, and follower of the awakening of a great people to work a beneficial change in opinion or institution, is Poetry. At such periods there is an accumulation of the power of communicating and receiving intense and impassioned conceptions respecting man and nature. The persons in whom this power resides, may often, as far as regards many portions of their nature, have little apparent correspondence with that spirit of good of which they are the ministers. But even whilst they deny and abjure, they are yet compelled to serve, the Power which is seated upon the throne of their own soul. It is impossible to read the compositions of the most celebrated writers of the present day without being startled with the electric life which burns within their words. They measure the circumference and sound the depths of human nature with a comprehensive and all-penetrating spirit, and they are themselves perhaps the most sincerely astonished at its manifestations, for it is less their spirit than the spirit of the age. Poets are the hierophants[8] of an unapprehended inspiration, the mirrors of the gigantic shadows which futurity casts upon the present, the words which express what they understand not; the trumpets which sing to battle, and feel not what they inspire: the influence which is moved not, but moves.[9] Poets are the unacknowledged legislators of the World.

1821   1840

---

7. In the age of Milton and the English Civil Wars.
8. Priests who are expositors of sacred mysteries.

9. Aristotle had said that God is the "Unmoved Mover" of the universe.

JOHN CLARE
1793–1864

Since the mid-eighteenth century, when critics had begun to worry that the authentic vigor of poetry was being undermined in their age of modern learning and refinement, they had looked for untaught primitive geniuses among the nation's peasantry. In the early-nineteenth-century literary scene, John Clare was the nearest thing to a "natural poet" there was. An earlier and greater peasant poet, Robert Burns, had managed to acquire a solid liberal education. Clare, however, was born at Helpston, a Northamptonshire village, the son of a field laborer and a mother who was entirely illiterate, and he obtained only enough schooling to enable him to read and write. Although he was a sickly and fearful child, he had to work hard in the field, where he found himself composing verse "for downright pleasure in giving vent to my feelings." The fragments of an autobiography that he wrote later in life describe movingly, and with humor, the stratagems that as a young man he devised in order to find the time and the materials for writing. A blank notebook could cost him a week's wages. In 1820 publication of his *Poems Descriptive of Rural Life and Scenery* attracted critical attention, and on a trip to London, he was made much of by leading writers of the day.

But his celebrity soon dimmed, and his three later books of verse were financial failures. Under these and other disappointments his mind gave way in 1837, and he spent almost all the rest of his life in an asylum. The place was for him a refuge as well as a confinement, for he was treated kindly, allowed to wander about the countryside, and encouraged to go on writing his verses. Some of his best achievements are the poems composed during his madness.

Clare did not, of course, write independently of literary influences, for he had studied the poetry of James Thomson, William Cowper, Burns, Milton, Wordsworth, and Coleridge. But he stayed true to his own experience of everyday country sights and customs. His nightingale poem, written in a long-established literary tradition, has many more particulars of nature than any of those by his predecessors, and his homely mouse, in the third poem printed below, is a bit of pure rustic impressionism in a way that even Burns's moralized mouse is not (see "To a Mouse," p. 1446). Some of Clare's introspective asylum poems achieve so haunting a poignancy and are spoken in so quietly distinctive a voice that they have made the great mass of manuscripts he left at his death an exciting place of discovery for recent scholars.

Those same manuscripts are a site of contention among current textual theorists. Words are everywhere misspelled in them, standard syntax is regularly ignored, and there is almost no punctuation in the lines. In his own day Clare was respelled, punctuated, and otherwise made presentable by his publisher, John Taylor (who did the same for John Keats, another of his poets who took a casual view of such matters). Modern scholars, eager to recover exactly what Clare wrote—in effect, to free him from the impositions and constraints of well-intentioned nineteenth-century editors— are restoring the idiosyncrasies but, in the process, are constructing a poet who is so full of what we would normally call mistakes as to be, for all practical purposes, inaccessible to the general reader. (For example, the manuscripts have "were" for "where," "your" for "you're," "anker" for "hanker," "hugh" for "huge.") The texts printed below, which are presented as "reading" versions of Clare's own words, are the product of a principled modernization by the editors of this anthology. They are based, where the materials are available, on authoritative manuscript versions recovered and now made standard by Eric Robinson and his associates in a succession of editions published by Oxford University Press.

The Nightingale's Nest

Up this green woodland ride° let's softly rove,   *riding path*
And list° the nightingale—she dwelleth here.   *listen to*
Hush! let the wood gate softly clap, for fear
The noise may drive her from her home of love;
5 For here I've heard her many a merry year—
At morn and eve, nay, all the livelong day,
As though she lived on song. This very spot,
Just where that old man's beard[1] all wildly trails
Rude arbours o'er the road and stops the way—
10 And where that child its blue-bell flowers hath got,
Laughing and creeping through the mossy rails°—   *fence rails*
There have I hunted like a very boy,
Creeping on hands and knees through matted thorns
To find her nest and see her feed her young.
15 And vainly did I many hours employ:

---

1. *Clematis vitalba,* a vine.

All seemed as hidden as a thought unborn.
And where these crimping° fern leaves ramp° among   *curling / shoot up*
The hazel's under-boughs, I've nestled down
And watched her while she sung; and her renown
20 Hath made me marvel that so famed a bird[2]
Should have no better dress than russet brown.
Her wings would tremble in her ecstasy,
And feathers stand on end, as 'twere with joy,
And mouth wide open to release her heart
25 Of its out-sobbing songs. The happiest part
Of summer's fame she shared, for so to me
Did happy fancies shapen her employ;[3]
But if I touched a bush or scarcely stirred,
All in a moment stopt. I watched in vain:
30 The timid bird had left the hazel bush,
And at a distance hid to sing again.
Lost in a wilderness of listening leaves,
Rich ecstasy would pour its luscious strain,
Till envy spurred the emulating thrush
35 To start less wild and scarce inferior songs;
For cares with him for half the year remain,
To damp the ardour of his speckled breast,
While nightingales to summer's life belongs,
And naked trees and winter's nipping wrongs
40 Are strangers to her music and her rest.
Her joys are evergreen, her world is wide—
Hark! there she is as usual—let's be hush—
For in this black-thorn clump, if rightly guessed,
Her curious house is hidden. Part aside
45 These hazel branches in a gentle way,
And stoop right cautious 'neath the rustling boughs,
For we will have another search to-day,
And hunt this fern-strewn thorn clump round and round;
And where this seeded wood grass idly bows,
50 We'll wade right through, it is a likely nook:
In such like spots, and often on the ground,
They'll build where rude boys never think to look—
Aye, as I live! her secret nest is here,
Upon this whitethorn stulp!° I've searched about   *stump*
55 For hours in vain. There! put that bramble by—
Nay, trample on its branches and get near.
How subtle is the bird! she started out
And raised a plaintive note of danger nigh,
Ere we were past the brambles; and now, near
60 Her nest, she sudden stops—as choking fear
That might betray her home. So even now
We'll leave it as we found it: safety's guard
Of pathless solitude shall keep it still.
See, there she's sitting on the old oak bough,

2. The nightingale had been celebrated by, among others, Chaucer, Spenser, Shakespeare, Milton, and, closer to Clare's time, William Cowper, Charlotte Smith, Mary Robinson, Coleridge, Wordsworth, and Keats. In lines 22, 24–25, and 33, Clare echoes lines 57–58 of Keats's "Ode to a Nightingale."
3. Give shape to her (the nightingale's) regular activities.

65 Mute in her fears; our presence doth retard
Her joys, and doubt turns all her rapture chill.

Sing on, sweet bird! may no worse hap° befall   *fate*
Thy visions, than the fear that now deceives.
We will not plunder music of its dower,°   *dowry, gift*
70 Nor turn this spot of happiness to thrall;°   *misery*
For melody seems hid in every flower,
That blossoms near thy home. These harebells all
Seems bowing with the beautiful in song;
And gaping cuckoo° with its spotted leaves   *a spring flower*
75 Seems blushing of the singing it has heard.
How curious is the nest; no other bird
Uses such loose materials, or weaves
Their dwellings in such spots: dead oaken leaves
Are placed without, and velvet moss within,
80 And little scraps of grass, and, scant and spare,
Of what seems scarce materials, down and hair;
For from man's haunts she seemeth nought to win.
Yet nature is the builder and contrives
Homes for her children's comfort even here;
85 Where solitude's disciples spend their lives
Unseen save when a wanderer passes near
That loves such pleasant places. Deep adown,
The nest is made an hermit's mossy cell.
Snug lie her curious eggs, in number five,
90 Of deadened green, or rather olive brown;
And the old prickly thorn-bush guards them well.
And here we'll leave them, still unknown to wrong,
As the old woodland's legacy of song.

1825–30   1835

Pastoral Poesy

True poesy is not in words,
But images that thoughts express,
By which the simplest hearts are stirred
To elevated happiness.

5 Mere books would be but useless things
Where none had taste or mind to read,
Like unknown lands where beauty springs
And none are there to heed.

But poesy is a language meet,°   *suitable, proper*
10 And fields are every one's employ;°   *concern*
The wild flower 'neath the shepherd's feet
Looks up and gives him joy;

A language that is ever green,
That feelings unto all impart,

15 As hawthorn blossoms, soon as seen,
    Give May to every heart.

    The pictures that our summer minds
    In summer's dwellings meet;
    The fancies that the shepherd finds
20 To make his leisure sweet;

    The dust mills that the cowboy delves
    In banks for dust to run,[1]
    Creates a summer in ourselves—
    He does as we have done.

25 An image to the mind is brought,
    Where happiness enjoys
    An easy thoughtlessness of thought
    And meets excess of joys.

    The world is in that little spot
30 With him—and all beside
    Is nothing, all a life forgot,
    In feelings satisfied.

    And such is poesy; its power
    May varied lights employ,
35 Yet to all minds it gives the dower
    Of self-creating joy.

    And whether it be hill or moor,
    I feel where'er I go
    A silence that discourses more
40 That any tongue can do.

    Unruffled quietness hath made
    A peace in every place,
    And woods are resting in their shade
    Of social loneliness.

45 The storm, from which the shepherd turns
    To pull his beaver° down,   beaver hat
    While he upon the heath sojourns,
    Which autumn pleaches° brown,   bleaches

    Is music, aye, and more indeed
50 To those of musing mind
    Who through the yellow woods proceed
    And listen to the wind.

    The poet in his fitful glee
    And fancy's many moods
55 Meets it as some strange melody,
    And poem of the woods.

1. The boy tending the cows has (as an amusement) dug miniature millstreams in the dirt.

It sings and whistles in his mind,
And then it talks aloud,
While by some leaning tree reclined
60 He shuns a coming cloud,

That sails its bulk against the sun,
A mountain in the light—
He heeds not for the storm begun
But dallies with delight.

65 And now a harp that flings around
The music of the wind,
The poet often hears the sound
When beauty fills the mind.

The morn with saffron° strips and gray,   *orange-yellow*
70 Or blushing to the view,
Like summer fields when run away
In weeds of crimson hue,

Will simple shepherds' hearts imbue
With nature's poesy,
75 Who inly fancy while they view
How grand must heaven be.

With every musing mind she steals
Attendance[2] on their way;
The simplest thing her heart reveals
80 Is seldom thrown away.

The old man, full of leisure hours,
Sits cutting at his door
Rude fancy sticks to tie his flowers
—They're sticks and nothing more

85 With many passing by his door—
But pleasure has its bent;°   *inclination*
With him 'tis happiness and more,
Heart satisfied content.

Those box-edged borders that impart
90 Their fragrance near his door
Hath been the comfort of his heart
For sixty years and more.

That mossy thatch above his head
In winter's drifting showers
95 To him and his old partner made
A music many hours.

2. She (nature) demands attention (to her beauties).

It patted to their hearts a joy[3]
That humble comfort made—
A little fire to keep them dry
100 And shelter over head.

And such no matter what they call
Each all are nothing less
Than poesy's power that gives to all
A cheerful blessedness.

105 So would I my own mind employ,
And my own heart impress,
That poesy's self's a dwelling joy
Of humble quietness.

So would I for the biding° joy   *abiding, lasting*
110 That to such thoughts belong,
That I life's errand may employ
As harmless as a song.

1824–32   1935

[Mouse's Nest]

I found a ball of grass among the hay
And progged° it as I passed and went away;   *prodded*
And when I looked I fancied something stirred,
And turned again and hoped to catch the bird—
5 When out an old mouse bolted in the wheat
With all her young ones hanging at her teats;
She looked so odd and so grotesque to me,
I ran and wondered what the thing could be,
And pushed the knapweed[1] bunches where I stood,
10 When the mouse hurried from the crawling brood.
The young ones squeaked, and when I went away
She found her nest again among the hay.
The water o'er the pebbles scarce could run
And broad old cesspools[2] glittered in the sun.

1835–37   1935

A Vision

I

I lost the love of heaven above;
I spurn'd the lust of earth below;
I felt the sweets of fancied love,—
And hell itself my only foe.

3. The patter of the rain on the thatch (lines 93–94) enhanced the comfort of the fire and shelter indoors.

1. A plant with knobs of purple flowers.
2. Low spots where water has collected.

2

5 I lost earth's joys but felt the glow
Of heaven's flame abound in me:
Till loveliness and I did grow
The bard of immortality.

3

I loved, but woman fell away;
10 I hid me from her faded fame:
I snatch'd the sun's eternal ray,—
And wrote till earth was but a name.

4

In every language upon earth,
On every shore, o'er every sea,
15 I gave my name immortal birth,
And kept my spirit with the free.

Aug. 2, 1844   1924

I Am

1

I am—yet what I am, none cares or knows;
  My friends forsake me like a memory lost:—
I am the self-consumer of my woes;—
  They rise and vanish in oblivion's host,
5 Like shadows in love's frenzied stifled throes:—
And yet I am, and live—like vapours tossed

2

Into the nothingness of scorn and noise,—
  Into the living sea of waking dreams,
Where there is neither sense of life or joys,
10   But the vast shipwreck of my life's esteems;
Even the dearest that I love the best
Are strange—nay, rather, stranger than the rest.

3

I long for scenes where man hath never trod,
  A place where woman never smiled or wept,
15 There to abide with my Creator, God,
  And sleep as I in childhood sweetly slept,
Untroubling and untroubled where I lie,
The grass below—above, the vaulted sky.

1842–46   1848

An Invite to Eternity

1

Wilt thou go with me, sweet maid,
Say maiden, wilt thou go with me
Through the valley depths of shade,
Of night and dark obscurity,
5   Where the path hath lost its way,
Where the sun forgets the day,
Where there's nor life nor light to see,
Sweet maiden, wilt thou go with me?

2

Where stones will turn to flooding streams,
10   Where plains will rise like ocean waves,
Where life will fade like visioned dreams
And mountains darken into caves,
Say maiden, wilt thou go with me
Through this sad non-identity,
15   Where parents live and are forgot
And sisters live and know us not?

3

Say maiden, wilt thou go with me
In this strange death of life to be,
To live in death and be the same
20   Without this life, or home, or name,
At once to be and not to be,
That was and is not—yet to see
Things pass like shadows—and the sky
Above, below, around us lie?

4

25   The land of shadows wilt thou trace
And look—nor know each other's face,
The present mixed with reasons gone
And past and present all as one?
Say maiden, can thy life be led
30   To join the living with the dead?
Then trace thy footsteps on with me—
We're wed to one eternity.

1847   1848

Clock a Clay[1]

1

In the cowslip's peeps I lie,[2]
Hidden from the buzzing fly,
While green grass beneath me lies,
Pearled wi' dew like fishes' eyes;
5   Here I lie, a Clock a Clay,
Waiting for the time o' day.

2

While grassy forests quake surprise,
And the wild wind sobs and sighs,
My gold home rocks as like to fall
10   On its pillars green and tall;
When the pattering rain drives by
Clock a Clay keeps warm and dry.

3

Day by day and night by night,
All the week I hide from sight;
15   In the cowslip's peeps I lie,
In rain and dew still warm and dry;
Day and night and night and day,
Red black-spotted Clock a Clay.

4

My home it shakes in wind and showers,
20   Pale green pillar topped wi' flowers,
Bending at the wild wind's breath,
Till I touch the grass beneath;
Here still I live, lone Clock a Clay,
Watching for the time of day.

ca. 1848   1873

The Peasant Poet

He loved the brook's soft sound,
The swallow swimming by;
He loved the daisy-covered ground,
The cloud-bedappled sky.
5   To him the dismal storm appeared
The very voice of God,
And where the evening rack° was reared   *mass of clouds*
Stood Moses with his rod.

1. The ladybird, or ladybug. The sixth and last lines allude to the children's game of telling the hour by the number of taps it takes to make the ladybird fly away home.
2. Cf. the opening lines of Ariel's song in act 5 of Shakespeare's *The Tempest*: "Where the bee sucks, there suck I: / In a cowslip's bell I lie." "Peeps": i.e., pips—single blossoms of flowers growing in a cluster. "Cowslip": a yellow primrose.

And everything his eyes surveyed,
10 The insects i' the brake,
Were creatures God Almighty made—
He loved them for His sake:
A silent man in life's affairs,
A thinker from a boy,
15 A peasant in his daily cares—
The poet in his joy.

1842–64   1920

Song

I hid my love when young while I
Couldn't bear the buzzing of a fly;
I hid my love to my despite
Till I could not bear to look at light.
5 I dare not gaze upon her face
But left her memory in each place;
Where'er I saw a wild flower lie
I kissed and bade my love goodbye.

I met her in the greenest dells,
10 Where dewdrops pearl the wood bluebells;
The lost breeze kissed her bright blue eye,
The bee kissed and went singing by.
A sunbeam found a passage there,
A gold chain round her neck so fair;
15 As secret as the wild bee's song
She lay there all the summer long.

I hid my love in field and town
Till e'en the breeze would knock me down.
The bees seemed singing ballads o'er
20 The fly's buzz turned a lion's roar;
And even silence found a tongue
To haunt me all the summer long:
The riddle nature could not prove
Was nothing else but secret love.

1842–64   1920

Song

I peeled bits o' straws and I got switches too
From the grey peeling willow as idlers do,
And I switched at the flies as I sat all alone
Till my flesh, blood, and marrow wasted to dry bone.
5 My illness was love, though I knew not the smart,
But the beauty o' love was the blood o' my heart.

Crowded places, I shunned them as noises too rude
And flew to the silence of sweet solitude,
Where the flower in green darkness buds, blossoms, and fades,
10   Unseen of a' shepherds and flower-loving maids.
The hermit bees find them but once and away;
There I'll bury alive and in silence decay.

I looked on the eyes o' fair woman too long,
Till silence and shame stole the use o' my tongue;
15   When I tried to speak to her I'd nothing to say,
So I turned myself round, and she wandered away.
When she got too far off—why, I'd something to tell,
So I sent sighs behind her and talked to mysel'.

Willow switches I broke, and I peeled bits o' straws,
20   Ever lonely in crowds, in nature's own laws—
My ballroom the pasture, my music the bees,
My drink was the fountain, my church the tall trees.
Who ever would love or be tied to a wife
When it makes a man mad a' the days o' his life?

1842–64   1920

FELICIA DOROTHEA HEMANS
1793–1835

Born in Liverpool and brought up in Wales, Felicia Hemans published her first two volumes—*Poems* and *England and Spain, or Valour and Patriotism*—when she was fifteen. She followed these four years later with *The Domestic Affections and Other Poems* (1812) and from 1816 on into the 1830s produced new books of poetry almost annually: short sentimental lyrics, tales and "historic scenes," translations, songs for music, sketches of women, hymns for children. She also published literary criticism in magazines and wrote three plays. Her work was widely read, anthologized, memorized, and set to music throughout the nineteenth century and was especially popular and influential in the United States, where the first of many collected editions of her poems appeared in 1825. When she died she was eulogized by many poets, including William Wordsworth, Letitia Landon, and Elizabeth Barrett—a sign of the high regard in which she was held by her contemporaries.

A tablet erected by her brothers in the cathedral of St. Asaph, in north Wales, reads in part, "In memory of Felicia Hemans, whose character is best pourtrayed in her writings." But there are several characters in her poems, and some of them seem not entirely compatible with some of the others. She is frequently thought of as the poet (in the nineteenth century as "the poetess") of domestic affections, at the center of a cult of domesticity in which the home is conceptualized as a haven apart from the stresses of the public world, to which only men are suited. Her poems have been viewed as celebrations of a feminine ethic founded on women's—especially mothers'—capacities for forbearance, piety, and long suffering. Among her most popular pieces in this vein, "Evening Prayer, at a Girls' School" depicts the happy ignorance of schoolgirls whose enjoyment of life will end when they reach womanhood, and "Indian Woman's Death-Song" is the lament of a Native American woman whose husband has abandoned her, sung as she plunges in her canoe over a cataract to suicide with an infant in her arms.

Many of Hemans's longer narratives, by contrast, recount the exploits of women warriors who, to avenge personal, family, or national injustice or insult, destroy enemies in a manner not conventionally associated with female behavior. In *The Widow of Crescentius,* Stephania stalks and poisons the German emperor Otho, the murderer of her husband; in "The Wife of Asdrubal," a mother publicly kills her own children and herself to show contempt for her husband, a betrayer of the Carthaginians whom he governed; the heroine of "The Bride of the Greek Isle," boarding the ship of the pirates who have killed her husband, annihilates them (and herself) in a conflagration rivaling the monumental explosion described in "Casabianca." Among the numerous themes of her work, patriotism and military action recur frequently; there may be a biographical basis for these motifs, given that her two oldest brothers distinguished themselves in the Peninsular War and her military husband (who deserted her and their five sons in 1818) had also served in Spain. But some of her most famous patriotic and military poems are now being viewed as critiques of the virtues and ideologies they had been thought by earlier readers to inculcate. "The Homes of England," for example, has been read as both asserting and undermining the idea that all homes are equal, ancestral estates and cottages alike; and in "Casabianca," the boy's automatic steadfastness has been interpreted as empty obedience rather than admirable loyalty.

Hemans was the highest paid writer in *Blackwood's Magazine* during her day. Her books sold more copies than those of any other contemporary poet except Byron and Walter Scott. She was a shrewd calculator of the literary marketplace and a genius in her negotiations with publishers (which she carried on entirely through the mails). Her self-abasing women of the domestic affections and her scimitar-wielding superwomen of the revenge narratives exist side by side throughout her works. These and other seeming dissonances clearly enhanced the strong appeal of her poems to a wide range of readers, men as well as women.

England's Dead

Son of the ocean isle!
Where sleep your mighty dead?
Show me what high and stately pile
Is rear'd o'er Glory's bed.

5   Go, stranger! track the deep,
Free, free the white sail spread!
Wave may not foam, nor wild wind sweep,
Where rest not England's dead.

On Egypt's burning plains,
10   By the pyramid o'ersway'd,
With fearful power the noonday reigns,
And the palm trees yield no shade.[1]

But let the angry sun
From heaven look fiercely red,

---

1. English forces defeated the French at Alexandria in the spring of 1801. The rest of the references—to 18th- and early-19th-century battles in India (lines 17–24), America (lines 25–32), Spain (lines 33–40), and on the sea (lines 41–48)—are more general.

15   Unfelt by those whose task is done!—
        There slumber England's dead.

        The hurricane hath might
        Along the Indian shore,
    And far by Ganges' banks at night,
20   Is heard the tiger's roar.

        But let the sound roll on!
        It hath no tone of dread,
    For those that from their toils are gone;—
        There slumber England's dead.

25   Loud rush the torrent floods
        The western wilds among,
    And free, in green Columbia's woods,
        The hunter's bow is strung.

        But let the floods rush on!
30   Let the arrow's flight be sped!
    Why should *they* reck whose task is done?—
        There slumber England's dead!

        The mountain storms rise high
        In the snowy Pyrenees,
35   And toss the pine boughs through the sky,
        Like rose leaves on the breeze.

        But let the storm rage on!
        Let the fresh wreaths be shed!
    For the Roncesvalles' field[2] is won,—
40   *There* slumber England's dead.

        On the frozen deep's repose
        'Tis a dark and dreadful hour,
    When round the ship the ice-fields close,
        And the northern night clouds lower.

45   But let the ice drift on!
        Let the cold-blue desert spread!
    Their course with mast and flag is done,—
        Even there sleep England's dead.

        The warlike of the isles,
50   The men of field and wave!
    Are not the rocks their funeral piles,
        The seas and shores their grave?

        Go, stranger! track the deep,
        Free, free the white sail spread!

---

2. Roncesvalles, the mountain pass in the Pyrenees between France and Spain, was a scene of action during the Peninsular War (1808–14).

55   Wave may not foam, nor wild wind sweep,
       Where rest not England's dead.

1822

Casabianca[1]

The boy stood on the burning deck
   Whence all but he had fled;
The flame that lit the battle's wreck
   Shone round him o'er the dead.

5   Yet beautiful and bright he stood,
   As born to rule the storm;
A creature of heroic blood,
   A proud, though childlike form.

The flames roll'd on—he would not go
10   Without his Father's word;
That Father, faint in death below,
   His voice no longer heard.

He call'd aloud:—"Say, Father, say
   If yet my task is done?"
15   He knew not that the chieftain lay
   Unconscious of his son.

"Speak, Father!" once again he cried,
   "If I may yet be gone!
And"—but the booming shots replied,
20   And fast the flames roll'd on.

Upon his brow he felt their breath,
   And in his waving hair,
And look'd from that lone post of death
   In still, yet brave despair.

25   And shouted but once more aloud,
   "My Father! must I stay?"
While o'er him fast, through sail and shroud,
   The wreathing fires made way.

They wrapt the ship in splendour wild,
30   They caught the flag on high,
And stream'd above the gallant child,
   Like banners in the sky.

1. Young Casabianca, a boy about thirteen years old, son to the Admiral of the *Orient*, remained at his post (in the Battle of the Nile) after the ship had taken fire, and all the guns had been abandoned; and perished in the explosion of the vessel, when the flames had reached the powder [Hemans's note]. The Battle of the Nile, in which Nelson captured and destroyed the French fleet in Aboukir Bay, took place on August 1, 1798. Admiral Casabianca and his son (who was in fact only ten) were among those killed by the British forces.

There came a burst of thunder sound—
    The boy—oh! where was he?
35 Ask of the winds that far around
    With fragments strew'd the sea!—

With mast, and helm, and pennon fair,
    That well had borne their part,
But the noblest thing which perish'd there
40   Was that young faithful heart!

1826

The Homes of England

Where's the coward that would not dare
To fight for such a land?
        —*Marmion*[1]

The stately Homes of England,
    How beautiful they stand!
Amidst their tall ancestral trees,
    O'er all the pleasant land.
5 The deer across their greensward bound
    Through shade and sunny gleam,
And the swan glides past them with the sound
    Of some rejoicing stream.

The merry Homes of England!
10   Around their hearths by night,
What gladsome looks of household love
    Meet in the ruddy light!
There woman's voice flows forth in song,
    Or childhood's tale is told,
15 Or lips move tunefully along
    Some glorious page of old.

The blessed Homes of England!
    How softly on their bowers
Is laid the holy quietness
20   That breathes from Sabbath-hours!
Solemn, yet sweet, the church-bell's chime
    Floats through their woods at morn;
All other sounds, in that still time,
    Of breeze and leaf are born.

25 The Cottage Homes of England!
    By thousands on her plains,
They are smiling o'er the silvery brooks,

1. From Sir Walter Scott's long poem *Marmion* (1808), 4.633–34, a tale of betrayal and bloody conflict between the English and the Scots. When she first published the poem, in *Blackwood's*, April 1827, Hemans used as epigraph a passage from the work of another Scottish author, Joanna Baillie's *Ethwald: A Tragedy*, part 2 (1802), 1.2.76–82.

And round the hamlet-fanes.°   *village churches*
Through glowing orchards forth they peep,
30   Each from its nook of leaves,
And fearless there the lowly sleep,
    As the bird beneath their eaves.

The free, fair Homes of England!
    Long, long, in hut and hall,
35   May hearts of native proof be rear'd
    To guard each hallow'd wall!
And green for ever be the groves,
    And bright the flowery sod,
Where first the child's glad spirit loves
40   Its country and its God!

1827

A Spirit's Return

"This is to be a mortal,
And seek the things beyond mortality!"
—MANFRED[1]

Thy voice prevails—dear friend, my gentle friend!
This long-shut heart for thee shall be unsealed,
And though thy soft eye mournfully will bend
Over the troubled stream, yet once revealed
5   Shall its freed waters flow; then rocks must close
For evermore, above their dark repose.

Come while the gorgeous mysteries of the sky
Fused in the crimson sea of sunset lie;
Come to the woods, where all strange wandering sound
10   Is mingled into harmony profound;
Where the leaves thrill with spirit, while the wind
Fills with a viewless° being, unconfined,   *invisible*
The trembling reeds and fountains—our own dell,
With its green dimness and Aeolian° breath,   *wind-blown*
15   Shall suit th' unveiling of dark records well—
Hear me in tenderness and silent faith!

Thou knew'st me not in life's fresh vernal morn—
I would thou hadst!—for then my heart on thine
Had poured a worthier love; now, all o'erworn
20   By its deep thirst for something too divine,
It hath but fitful music to bestow,
Echoes of harp-strings broken long ago.

1. A spirit's verdict on Manfred's quest, spoken just after Manfred is convulsed by the disappearance of the Phantom of his beloved Astarte (*Manfred* 2.4.158–59). Hemans's poem can be read as commentary on Byron's play, Percy Shelley's *Alas-* *tor,* and Keats's *Endymion* (see the note to lines 216–17 below), all of which depict a protagonist's problems in communicating with an otherworldly lover.

Yet even in youth companionless I stood,
As a lone forest-bird 'midst ocean's foam;
25 For me the silver cords of brotherhood
Were early loosed; the voices from my home
Passed one by one, and melody and mirth
Left me a dreamer by a silent hearth.

But, with the fulness of a heart that burned
30 For the deep sympathies of mind, I turned
From that unanswering spot, and fondly sought
In all wild scenes with thrilling murmurs fraught,
In every still small voice and sound of power,
And flute-note of the wind through cave and bower,
35 A perilous delight!—for then first woke
My life's lone passion, the mysterious quest
Of secret knowledge; and each tone that broke
From the wood-arches or the fountain's breast,
Making my quick soul vibrate as a lyre,
40 But ministered to that strange inborn fire.
'Midst the bright silence of the mountain dells,
In noon-tide hours or golden summer-eves,
My thoughts have burst forth as a gale that swells
Into a rushing blast, and from the leaves
45 Shakes out response. O thou rich world unseen!
Thou curtained realm of spirits!—thus my cry
Hath troubled air and silence—dost thou lie
Spread all around, yet by some filmy screen
Shut from us ever? The resounding woods,
50 Do their depths teem with marvels?—and the floods,
And the pure fountains, leading secret veins
Of quenchless melody through rock and hill,
Have they bright dwellers?—are their lone domains
Peopled with beauty, which may never still
55 *Our* weary thirst of soul?—Cold, weak and cold,
Is earth's vain language, piercing not one fold
Of our deep being! Oh, for gifts more high!
For a seer's glance to rend mortality!
For a charmed rod, to call from each dark shrine
60 The oracles divine!

I woke from those high fantasies, to know
My kindred with the earth—I woke to love:
O gentle friend! to love in doubt and woe,
Shutting the heart the worshipped name above,
65 Is to love deeply—and *my* spirit's dower
Was a sad gift, a melancholy power
Of so adoring—with a buried care,
And with the o'erflowing of a voiceless prayer,
And with a deepening dream, that day by day,
70 In the still shadow of its lonely sway,
Folded me closer, till the world held nought
Save the *one* being to my centred thought.

There was no music but his voice to hear,
No joy but such as with *his* step drew near;
75 Light was but where he looked—life where he moved;
Silently, fervently, thus, thus I loved.
Oh! but such love is fearful!—and I knew
Its gathering doom:—the soul's prophetic sight
Even then unfolded in my breast, and threw
80 O'er all things round a full, strong, vivid light,
Too sorrowfully clear!—an undertone
Was given to Nature's harp, for me alone
Whispering of grief.—Of grief?—be strong, awake,
Hath not thy love been victory, O, my soul?
85 Hath not its conflict won a voice to shake
Death's fastnesses?—a magic to control
Worlds far removed?—from o'er the grave to thee
Love hath made answer; and *thy* tale should be
Sung like a lay of triumph!—Now return,
90 And take thy treasure from its bosomed urn,[2]
And lift it once to light!

               In fear, in pain,
I said I loved—but yet a heavenly strain
Of sweetness floated down the tearful stream,
A joy flashed through the trouble of my dream!
95 I knew myself beloved!—we breathed no vow,
No mingling visions might our fate allow,
As unto happy hearts; but still and deep,
Like a rich jewel gleaming in a grave,
Like golden sand in some dark river's wave,
100 So did my soul that costly knowledge keep
So jealously!°—a thing o'er which to shed,   *watchfully*
When stars alone beheld the drooping head,
Lone tears! yet ofttimes burdened with the excess
Of our strange nature's quivering happiness.

105 But, oh! sweet friend! we dream not of love's might
Till death has robed with soft and solemn light
The image we enshrine!—Before *that* hour,
We have but glimpses of the o'ermastering power
Within us laid!—*then* doth the spirit-flame
110 With sword-like lightning rend its mortal frame;
The wings of that which pants to follow fast
Shake their clay-bars, as with a prisoned blast—
The sea is in our souls!

               He died—*he* died
On whom my lone devotedness was cast!
115 I might not keep one vigil by his side,
I, whose wrung heart watched with him to the last!
I might not once his fainting head sustain,
Nor bathe his parched lips in the hour of pain,

2. Suggests an urn in which funerary ashes are kept.

Nor say to him, "Farewell!"—He passed away—
120   Oh! had *my* love been there, its conquering sway
Had won him back from death! but thus removed,
Borne o'er the abyss no sounding-line hath proved,
Joined with the unknown, the viewless—he became
Unto my thoughts another, yet the same—
125   Changed—hallowed—glorified!—and his low grave
Seemed a bright mournful altar—mine, all mine:—
Brother and friend soon left me *that* sole shrine,
The birthright of the faithful!—*their* world's wave
Soon swept them from its brink.—Oh! deem thou not
130   That on the sad and consecrated spot
My soul grew weak!—I tell thee that a power
There kindled heart and lip—a fiery shower
My words were made—a might was given to prayer,
And a strong grasp to passionate despair,
135   And a dead triumph!—Know'st thou what I sought?
For what high boon my struggling spirit wrought?—
Communion with the dead!—I sent a cry,
Through the veiled empires of eternity,
A voice to cleave them! By the mournful truth,
140   By the lost promise of my blighted youth,
By the strong chain a mighty love can bind
On the beloved, the spell of mind o'er mind;
By words, which in themselves are magic high,
Armed and inspired, and winged with agony;
145   By tears, which comfort not, but burn, and seem
To bear the heart's blood in their passion stream;
I summoned, I adjured!°—with quickened sense,   *entreated*
With the keen vigil of a life intense,
I watched, an answer from the winds to wring,
150   I listened, if perchance the stream might bring
Token from worlds afar: I taught *one* sound
Unto a thousand echoes—one profound
Imploring accent to the tomb, the sky—
One prayer to night—"Awake, appear, reply!"
155   Hast thou been told that from the viewless bourne,°   *invisible region*
The dark way never hath allowed return?
That all, which tears can move, with life is fled—
That earthly love is powerless on the dead?
Believe it not!—there is a large lone star
160   Now burning o'er yon western hill afar,
And under its clear light there lies a spot
Which well might utter forth—Believe it not!

I sat beneath that planet—I had wept
My woe to stillness, every night-wind slept;
165   A hush was on the hills; the very streams
Went by like clouds, or noiseless founts in dreams,
And the dark tree o'ershadowing me that hour,
Stood motionless, even as the gray church-tower
Whereon I gazed unconsciously:—there came
170   A low sound, like the tremor of a flame,

Or like the light quick shiver of a wing,
Flitting through twilight woods, across the air;
And I looked up!—Oh! for strong words to bring
Conviction o'er thy thought!—Before me there,
175   He, the departed, stood!—Ay, face to face,
So near, and yet how far!—his form, his mien,
Gave to remembrance back each burning trace
Within:—Yet something awfully serene,
Pure, sculpture-like, on the pale brow, that wore
180   Of the once-beating heart no token more;
And stillness on the lip—and o'er the hair
A gleam, that trembled through the breathless air;
And an unfathomed calm, that seemed to lie
In the grave sweetness of the illumined eye;
185   Told of the gulfs between our beings set,
And, as that unsheathed spirit-glance I met,
Made my soul faint:—with *fear?* Oh! *not* with fear!
With the sick feeling that in *his* far sphere
My love could be as nothing! But he spoke—
190   How shall I tell thee of the startling thrill
In that low voice, whose breezy tones could fill
My bosom's infinite? O, friend! I woke
Then first to heavenly life!—Soft, solemn, clear
Breathed the mysterious accents on mine ear,
195   Yet strangely seemed as if the while they rose
From depths of distance, o'er the wide repose
Of slumbering waters wafted, or the dells
Of mountains, hollow with sweet-echo cells;
But, as they murmured on, the mortal chill
200   Passed from me, like a mist before the morn,
And, to that glorious intercourse upborne
By slow degrees, a calm, divinely still,
Possessed my frame: I sought that lighted eye—
From its intense and searching purity
205   I drank in *soul!*—I questioned of the dead—
Of the hushed, starry shores their footsteps tread,
And I was answered:—if remembrance there,
With dreamy whispers fill the immortal air;
If thought, here piled from many a jewel-heap,
210   Be treasure in that pensive land to keep;
If love, o'ersweeping change, and blight, and blast
Find *there* the music of his home at last;
I asked, and I was answered:—Full and high
Was that communion with eternity,
215   Too rich for aught so fleeting!—Like a knell
Swept o'er my sense its closing words, "Farewell,
On earth we meet no more!"[3]—and all was gone—
The pale bright settled brow—the thrilling tone,

3. This is the answer to Manfred's question to the Phantom of Astarte (2.4.154): "Say, shall we meet again?" Astarte vanishes, and Nemesis says, "She's gone, and will not be recall'd." Hemans's lines also echo Endymion's renunciation of his dream goddess at a crucial moment in Keats's *Endymion* (4.657–59): "The hour may come / When we shall meet in pure elysium. / On earth I may not love thee."

The still and shining eye! and never more
220 May twilight gloom or midnight hush restore
That radiant guest! One full-fraught hour of heaven,
To earthly passion's wild implorings given,
Was made my own—the ethereal fire hath shivered
The fragile censer[4] in whose mould it quivered
225 Brightly, consumingly! What now is left?
A faded world, of glory's hues bereft—
A void, a chain!—I dwell 'midst throngs, apart,
In the cold silence of the stranger's heart;
A fixed, immortal shadow stands between
230 My spirit and life's fast receding scene;
A gift hath severed me from human ties,
A power is gone from all earth's melodies,
Which never may return: their chords are broken,
The music of another land hath spoken—
235 No after-sound is sweet!—this weary thirst!
And I have heard celestial fountains burst!—
What *here* shall quench it?
                          Dost thou not rejoice,
When the spring sends forth an awakening voice
Through the young woods?—Thou dost!—And in the birth
240 Of early leaves, and flowers, and songs of mirth,
Thousands, like thee, find gladness!—Couldst thou know
How every breeze then summons *me* to go!
How all the light of love and beauty shed
By those rich hours, but woos me to the dead!
245 The *only* beautiful that change no more—
The only loved!—the dwellers on the shore
Of spring fulfilled!—The dead!—*whom* call we so?
They that breathe purer air, that feel, that know
Things wrapt from us!—Away!—within me pent,
250 That which is barred from its own element
Still droops or struggles!—But the day *will* come—
Over the deep the free bird finds its home,
And the stream lingers 'midst the rocks, yet greets
The sea at last; and the winged flower-seed meets
255 A soil to rest in:—shall not *I*, too, be,
My spirit-love! upborne to dwell with thee?
Yes! by the power whose conquering anguish stirred
The tomb, whose cry beyond the stars was heard,
Whose agony of triumph won thee back
260 Through the dim pass no mortal step may track,
Yet shall we meet!—that glimpse of joy divine
Proved thee for ever and for ever mine!

1830

---

4. Container in which incense is burned.

JOHN KEATS
1795–1821

John Keats's father was head stableman at a London livery stable; he married his employer's daughter and inherited the business. The poet's mother, by all reports, was an affectionate but negligent parent to her children; remarrying almost immediately after a fall from a horse killed her first husband, she left the eight-year-old John (her firstborn), his brothers, and a sister with their grandmother and did not reenter their lives for four years. The year before his father's death, Keats had been sent to the Reverend John Clarke's private school at Enfield, famous for its progressive curriculum, where he was a noisy, high-spirited boy; despite his small stature (when full-grown, he was barely over five feet in height), he distinguished himself in sports and fistfights. Here he had the good fortune to have as a mentor Charles Cowden Clarke, son of the headmaster, who later became a writer and an editor; he encouraged Keats's passion for reading and, both at school and in the course of their later friendship, introduced him to Spenser and other poets, to music, and to the theater.

When Keats's mother returned to her children, she was already ill, and in 1810 she died of tuberculosis. Although the livery stable had prospered, and £8,000 had been left in trust to the children by Keats's grandmother, the estate remained tied up in the law courts for all of Keats's lifetime. The children's guardian, Richard Abbey, an unimaginative and practical-minded businessman, took Keats out of school at the age of fifteen and bound him apprentice to Thomas Hammond, a surgeon and apothecary at Edmonton. In 1815 Keats carried on his medical studies at Guy's Hospital, London, and the next year qualified to practice as an apothecary-surgeon—but almost immediately, over his guardian's protests, he abandoned medicine for poetry.

This decision was influenced by Keats's friendship with Leigh Hunt, then editor of the *Examiner* and a leading political radical, poet, and prolific writer of criticism and periodical essays. Hunt, the first successful author of Keats's acquaintance, added his enthusiastic encouragement of Keats's poetic efforts to that of Clarke. More important, he introduced him to writers greater than Hunt himself—William Hazlitt, Charles Lamb, and Percy Shelley—as well as to Benjamin Robert Haydon, painter of grandiose historical and religious canvases. Through Hunt, Keats also met John Hamilton Reynolds and then Charles Wentworth Dilke and Charles Brown, who became his intimate friends and provided him with an essential circumstance for a fledgling poet: a sympathetic and appreciative audience.

The rapidity and sureness of Keats's development has no match. Although he did not begin writing poetry until his eighteenth year, by 1816 in the bold sonnet "On First Looking into Chapman's Homer" he had found his voice. Later that same year he wrote "Sleep and Poetry," in which he laid out for himself a program deliberately modeled on the careers of the greatest poets, asking only

> for ten years, that I may overwhelm
> Myself in poesy; so I may do the deed
> That my own soul has to itself decreed.

For even while his health was good, Keats felt a foreboding of early death and applied himself to his art with a desperate urgency. In 1817 he went on to compose *Endymion,* an ambitious undertaking of more than four thousand lines. It is a rich allegory of a mortal's quest for an ideal feminine counterpart and a flawless happiness beyond earthly possibility; in a number of passages, it already exhibits the sure movement and phrasing of his mature poetic style. But Keats's critical judgment and aspiration exceeded his achievement: long before he completed it, he declared impatiently that he carried on with the "slipshod" *Endymion* only as a "trial of invention" and began to block out *Hyperion,* conceived on the model of Milton's *Paradise Lost* in that most demanding of forms, the epic poem. His success in achieving the Miltonic manner is one of the reasons why Keats abandoned *Hyperion* before it was finished, for he recognized that he was uncommonly susceptible to poetic influences and regarded this as a threat to his individuality. "I will write independently," he insisted. "The Genius of Poetry must work out its own salvation in a man." He had refused the chance of intimacy with Shelley "that I might have my own unfettered scope"; he had broken away from Leigh Hunt's influence lest he get "the reputation of Hunt's *élève* [pupil]"; now he shied away from domination by Milton's powerfully infectious style.

In sentimental, later-nineteenth-century accounts of "poor Keats," 1818 was cast as the year in which this rising genius, already frail and sensitive, was mortally crushed by vicious reviews. Percy Shelley helped initiate this myth in *Adonais*, which describes Keats as "a pale flower." Byron, who did not like Keats's verse, put it unsentimentally: Keats, he wrote, was "snuffed out by an article." It is true that the critics were brutal to Keats, those associated with the Tory journals especially; for them his poetry proved an irresistible target precisely because it had been promoted by the radical Hunt. *Endymion* was mauled in the *Quarterly Review,* and one of the articles on "the Cockney School of Poetry" that appeared in *Blackwood's Magazine* condemned Keats as hopelessly vulgar, a writer who wanted to be a poet of nature but thought, as a social-climbing, undereducated Londoner would, that nature was "flowers seen in window-pots." "It is a better and wiser thing to be a starved apothecary than a starved poet," the reviewer scolded: "so back to the shop Mr John." Keats had for his own part the good sense to recognize that the attacks were motivated by political prejudice and class snobbery, and he had already passed his own severe judgment on *Endymion*: "My own domestic criticism," he said, "has given me pain without comparison beyond what *Blackwood* or the *Quarterly* could possibly inflict." More important was the financial distress of his brother George and his young bride, who emigrated to Kentucky and lost their money in an ill-advised investment. Keats, short of funds and needing to supplement the family income, had now to find ways to make money from his writing: he turned to journalism and began planning plays. His brother Tom contracted tuberculosis, and the poet, in devoted attendance, helplessly watched him waste away until his death that December. In the summer of that year, Keats had taken a strenuous walking tour in the English Lake District, Scotland, and Ireland. It was a glorious adventure but a totally exhausting one in wet, cold weather, and he returned in August with a chronically ulcerated throat made increasingly ominous by the shadow of the tuberculosis that had killed his mother and brother. And in the late fall of that same year, Keats fell unwillingly but deeply in love with Fanny Brawne, the eighteen-year-old girl next door. They became engaged, knowing, though, that Keats's poverty and worsening health might well make their marriage impossible.

In this period of turmoil, Keats achieved the culmination of his brief poetic career. Between January and September of 1819, masterpiece followed masterpiece in astonishing succession: *The Eve of St. Agnes,* "La Belle Dame sans Merci," all of the "great odes," *Lamia,* and a sufficient number of fine sonnets to make him, with Wordsworth, the major Romantic craftsman in that form. All of these poems possess the distinctive qualities of the work of Keats's maturity: a slow-paced, gracious movement; a concreteness of description in which all the senses—tactile, gustatory, kinetic, visceral, as well as visual and auditory—combine to give the total apprehension of an experience; a delight at the sheer existence of things outside himself, the poet seeming to lose his own identity in a total identification with the object he contemplates; and a concentrated felicity of phrasing that reminded his friends, as it has many critics since, of the language of Shakespeare. Under the richly sensuous surface, we find Keats's characteristic presentation of all experience as a tangle of inseparable but irreconcilable opposites. He finds melancholy in delight and pleasure in pain; he feels the highest intensity of love as an approximation to death; he inclines equally toward a life of indolence and "sensation" and toward a life of thought; he is aware both of the attraction of an imaginative dream world without "disagreeables" and the remorseless pressure of the actual; he aspires at the same time to aesthetic detachment and to social responsibility.

His letters, hardly less remarkable than his poetry, show that Keats felt on his pulses the conflicts he dramatized in his major poems. Above all, they reveal him wrestling with the problem of evil and suffering—what to make of our lives in the discovery that "the world is full of misery and heartbreak, pain, sickness and oppression." To the end of his life, he refused to seek solace for the complexity and contradictions of experience either in the abstractions of inherited philosophical doctrines or in the absolutes of a religious creed. At the close of his poetic career, in the latter part of 1819, Keats began to rework the epic *Hyperion* into the form of a dream vision that he called *The Fall of Hyperion*. In the introductory section of this fragment the poet is told by the prophetess Moneta that he has hitherto been merely a dreamer; he must know that

> The poet and the dreamer are distinct,
> Diverse, sheer opposite, antipodes,

and that the height of poetry can be reached only by

> those to whom the miseries of the world
> Are misery, and will not let them rest.

He was seemingly planning to undertake a new direction and subject matter, when illness and death intervened.

On the night of February 3, 1820, he coughed up blood. As a physician he refused to evade the truth: "I cannot be deceived in that colour; that drop of blood is my death warrant. I must die." That spring and summer a series of hemorrhages rapidly weakened him. In the autumn he allowed himself to be persuaded to seek the milder climate of Italy in the company of Joseph Severn, a young painter, but these last months were only what he called "a posthumous existence." He died in Rome on February 23, 1821, and was buried in the Protestant Cemetery, where Mary and Percy Shelley had already interred their little son William, and where Percy's ashes, too, would be deposited in 1822. At times the agony of his disease, the seeming frustration of his hopes for great poetic achievement, and the despair of his passion for Fanny Brawne compelled even Keats's brave spirit to bitterness and jealousy, but he always recovered his gallantry. His last letter, written to Charles Brown, concludes: "I can scarcely bid you good bye even in a letter. I always made an awkward bow. God bless you! John Keats."

No one can read Keats's poems and letters without an undersense of the tragic waste of an extraordinary intellect and genius cut off so early. What he might have done is beyond conjecture; what we do know is that his poetry, when he stopped writing at the age of twenty-four, exceeds the accomplishment at the same age of Chaucer, Shakespeare, and Milton.

The texts here are taken from Jack Stillinger's edition, *The Poems of John Keats* (Cambridge, Mass., 1978).

On First Looking into Chapman's Homer[1]

> Much have I travell'd in the realms of gold,
> And many goodly states and kingdoms seen;

---

1. Keats's mentor Charles Cowden Clarke introduced him to Homer in the robust translation by the Elizabethan poet and dramatist George Chapman. They read through the night, and Keats walked home at dawn. This sonnet reached Clarke by the ten o'clock mail that same morning. It was the gold-hunter Balboa, not Cortez, the Spanish conqueror of Mexico, who caught his first sight of the Pacific from the heights of Darien, in Panama, but none of Keats's contemporaries noticed the error.

Round many western islands have I been
Which bards in fealty to Apollo hold.
5   Oft of one wide expanse had I been told
That deep-brow'd Homer ruled as his demesne;[2]
Yet did I never breathe its pure serene[3]
Till I heard Chapman speak out loud and bold:
Then felt I like some watcher of the skies
10   When a new planet swims into his ken;°   view
Or like stout Cortez when with eagle eyes
He star'd at the Pacific—and all his men
Look'd at each other with a wild surmise—
Silent, upon a peak in Darien.

Oct. 1816   1816

From Sleep and Poetry[1]

[O FOR TEN YEARS]

O for ten years, that I may overwhelm
Myself in poesy; so I may do the deed
That my own soul has to itself decreed.
Then will I pass the countries that I see
100   In long perspective, and continually
Taste their pure fountains. First the realm I'll pass
Of Flora, and old Pan:[2] sleep in the grass,
Feed upon apples red, and strawberries,
And choose each pleasure that my fancy sees;
105   Catch the white-handed nymphs in shady places,
To woo sweet kisses from averted faces,—
Play with their fingers, touch their shoulders white
Into a pretty shrinking with a bite
As hard as lips can make it: till agreed,
110   A lovely tale of human life we'll read.
And one will teach a tame dove how it best
May fan the cool air gently o'er my rest;
Another, bending o'er her nimble tread,
Will set a green robe floating round her head,
115   And still will dance with ever varied ease,
Smiling upon the flowers and the trees:
Another will entice me on, and on
Through almond blossoms and rich cinnamon;
Till in the bosom of a leafy world

---

2. Realm, feudal possession.
3. Clear expanse of air.
1. At the age of twenty-one, Keats set himself a regimen of poetic training modeled on the course followed by the greatest poets. Virgil had established the pattern of beginning with pastoral writing and proceeding gradually to the point at which he was ready to undertake the epic, and this pattern had been deliberately followed by Spenser and Milton. Keats's version of this program, as he describes it here, is to begin with the realm "of

Flora, and old Pan" (line 102) and, within ten years, to climb up to the level of poetry dealing with "the agonies, the strife / Of human hearts" (lines 124–25). The program Keats set himself is illuminated by his analysis of Wordsworth's progress in his letter to J. H. Reynolds of May 3, 1818 (p. 1874).
2. I.e., the carefree pastoral world. Flora was the Roman goddess of flowers. Pan was the Greek god of pastures, woods, and animal life.

120 We rest in silence, like two gems upcurl'd
In the recesses of a pearly shell.

And can I ever bid these joys farewell?
Yes, I must pass them for a nobler life,
Where I may find the agonies, the strife
125 Of human hearts: for lo! I see afar,
O'er sailing the blue cragginess, a car³
And steeds with streamy manes—the charioteer
Looks out upon the winds with glorious fear:
And now the numerous tramplings quiver lightly
130 Along a huge cloud's ridge; and now with sprightly
Wheel downward come they into fresher skies,
Tipt round with silver from the sun's bright eyes.
Still downward with capacious whirl they glide;
And now I see them on a green-hill's side
135 In breezy rest among the nodding stalks.
The charioteer with wond'rous gesture talks
To the trees and mountains; and there soon appear
Shapes of delight, of mystery, and fear,
Passing along before a dusky space
140 Made by some mighty oaks: as they would chase
Some ever-fleeting music on they sweep.
Lo! how they murmur, laugh, and smile, and weep:
Some with upholden hand and mouth severe;
Some with their faces muffled to the ear
145 Between their arms; some, clear in youthful bloom,
Go glad and smilingly athwart° the gloom;   *against*
Some looking back, and some with upward gaze;
Yes, thousands in a thousand different ways
Flit onward—now a lovely wreath of girls
150 Dancing their sleek hair into tangled curls;
And now broad wings. Most awfully intent,
The driver of those steeds is forward bent,
And seems to listen: O that I might know
All that he writes with such a hurrying glow.

155 The visions all are fled—the car is fled
Into the light of heaven, and in their stead
A sense of real things comes doubly strong,
And, like a muddy stream, would bear along
My soul to nothingness: but I will strive
160 Against all doubtings, and will keep alive
The thought of that same chariot, and the strange
Journey it went.

* * *

Oct.–Dec. 1816   1817

3. Chariot. The description that follows recalls the traditional portrayal of Apollo, god of the sun and poetry, and represents the higher poetic imagina- tion, which bodies forth the matters "of delight, of mystery, and fear" (line 138) that characterize the grander poetic genres.

On Seeing the Elgin Marbles[1]

My spirit is too weak—mortality
  Weighs heavily on me like unwilling sleep,
  And each imagined pinnacle and steep
Of godlike hardship tells me I must die
5 Like a sick eagle looking at the sky.
  Yet 'tis a gentle luxury to weep
  That I have not the cloudy winds to keep
Fresh for the opening of the morning's eye.
Such dim-conceived glories of the brain
10 Bring round the heart an undescribable feud;
So do these wonders a most dizzy pain,
  That mingles Grecian grandeur with the rude
Wasting of old time—with a billowy main°—   *ocean*
A sun—a shadow of a magnitude.

Mar. 1 or 2, 1817   1817

From Endymion: A Poetic Romance[1]

"The stretched metre of an antique song"

INSCRIBED TO THE MEMORY OF THOMAS CHATTERTON

Preface

   Knowing within myself the manner in which this Poem has been produced, it is not without a feeling of regret that I make it public.

   What manner I mean, will be quite clear to the reader, who must soon perceive great inexperience, immaturity, and every error denoting a feverish attempt, rather than a deed accomplished. The two first books, and indeed the two last, I feel sensible are not of such completion as to warrant their passing the press; nor should they if I thought a year's castigation would do them any good;—it will not: the foundations are too sandy. It is just that this youngster

1. Lord Elgin had brought to England in 1806 many of the marble statues and friezes that adorned the Parthenon at Athens. In 1817 Keats, along with his artist friend Haydon, viewed the marbles at the British Museum, which had just purchased them, an acqusition that was and remains controversial. Keats's sonnet first appeared on the same day in both Leigh Hunt's *Examiner* and, through Keats's friend Reynolds, *The Champion*, and then was reprinted in Haydon's magazine *Annals of the Fine Arts*.
1. This poem of more than four thousand lines (based on the classical myth of a mortal beloved by the goddess of the moon) tells of Endymion's long and agonized search for an immortal goddess whom he had seen in several visions. In the course of his wanderings, he comes upon an Indian maid who had been abandoned by the followers of Bacchus, god of wine and revelry. To his utter despair,

he succumbs to a sensual passion for her, in apparent betrayal of his love for his heavenly ideal. The conclusion to Keats's "romance" offers a way of resolving this opposition, which runs throughout the poem, between the inevitably mortal pleasures of this world and the possibility of delights that would be eternal: the Indian maid reveals that she is herself Cynthia (Diana), goddess of the moon, the celestial subject of his earlier visions.
   The verse epigraph is adapted from Shakespeare's Sonnet 17, line 12: "And stretchèd metre of an antique song." Thomas Chatterton (1752–1770), to whom *Endymion* is dedicated, and who is the "marvellous Boy" of Wordsworth's "Resolution and Independence," wrote a number of brilliant pseudoarchaic poems that he attributed to an imaginary 15th-century poet, Thomas Rowley. Keats described him as "the most English of poets except Shakespeare."

should die away: a sad thought for me, if I had not some hope that while it is dwindling I may be plotting, and fitting myself for verses fit to live.

This may be speaking too presumptuously, and may deserve a punishment: but no feeling man will be forward to inflict it: he will leave me alone, with the conviction that there is not a fiercer hell than the failure in a great object. This is not written with the least atom of purpose to forestall criticisms of course, but from the desire I have to conciliate men who are competent to look, and who do look with a zealous eye, to the honour of English literature.

The imagination of a boy is healthy, and the mature imagination of a man is healthy; but there is a space of life between, in which the soul is in a ferment, the character undecided, the way of life uncertain, the ambition thick-sighted: thence proceeds mawkishness, and all the thousand bitters which those men I speak of must necessarily taste in going over the following pages.

I hope I have not in too late a day touched the beautiful mythology of Greece,[2] and dulled its brightness: for I wish to try once more,[3] before I bid it farewell.

Teignmouth, April 10, 1818

From *Book 1*

[A THING OF BEAUTY]

A thing of beauty is a joy for ever:
Its loveliness increases; it will never
Pass into nothingness; but still will keep
A bower quiet for us, and a sleep
5 Full of sweet dreams, and health, and quiet breathing.
Therefore, on every morrow, are we wreathing
A flowery band to bind us to the earth,
Spite° of despondence, of the inhuman dearth   *despite*
Of noble natures, of the gloomy days,
10 Of all the unhealthy and o'er-darkened ways
Made for our searching: yes, in spite of all,
Some shape of beauty moves away the pall
From our dark spirits. Such the sun, the moon,
Trees old, and young sprouting a shady boon
15 For simple sheep; and such are daffodils
With the green world they live in; and clear rills°   *small streams*
That for themselves a cooling covert make
'Gainst the hot season; the mid forest brake,°   *thicket*
Rich with a sprinkling of fair musk-rose blooms:
20 And such too is the grandeur of the dooms°   *judgments*
We have imagined for the mighty dead;
All lovely tales that we have heard or read:

2. In 1820 an anonymous reviewer of Keats's final volume of poems cited this phrase and, in a complaint that suggests the political charge that the poetic use of classical mythology could carry at this time, wrote disparagingly of "the nonsense that Mr. Keats . . . and Mr. Percy Bysshe Shelley, and some of the poets about town, have been talking of 'the beautiful mythology of Greece' "; "To some persons . . . that mythology comes recommended chiefly by its grossness—its alliance to the sensitive pleasures which belong to the animal."

3. In *Hyperion*, which Keats was already planning.

An endless fountain of immortal drink,
Pouring unto us from the heaven's brink.

25   Nor do we merely feel these essences
For one short hour; no, even as the trees
That whisper round a temple become soon
Dear as the temple's self, so does the moon,
The passion poesy, glories infinite,
30   Haunt us till they become a cheering light
Unto our souls, and bound to us so fast,
That, whether there be shine, or gloom o'ercast,
They alway must be with us, or we die.

        Therefore, 'tis with full happiness that I
35   Will trace the story of Endymion.
The very music of the name has gone
Into my being, and each pleasant scene
Is growing fresh before me as the green
Of our own vallies. * * *

[THE "PLEASURE THERMOMETER"]

        "Peona!⁴ ever have I long'd to slake
770   My thirst for the world's praises: nothing base,
No merely slumberous phantasm, could unlace
The stubborn canvas for my voyage prepar'd—
Though now 'tis tatter'd; leaving my bark bar'd
And sullenly drifting: yet my higher hope
775   Is of too wide, too rainbow-large a scope,
To fret at myriads of earthly wrecks.
Wherein lies happiness? In that which becks°   beckons
Our ready minds to fellowship divine,
A fellowship with essence; till we shine,
780   Full alchemiz'd,⁵ and free of space. Behold
The clear religion of heaven! Fold
A rose leaf round thy finger's taperness,
And soothe thy lips: hist,° when the airy stress   listen
Of music's kiss impregnates the free winds,
785   And with a sympathetic touch unbinds
Eolian⁶ magic from their lucid wombs:
Then old songs waken from enclouded tombs;
Old ditties sigh above their father's grave;

4. The sister to whom Endymion confides his troubles. Of lines 769–857 Keats said to his publisher, John Taylor: "When I wrote it, it was the regular stepping of the Imagination towards a Truth. My having written that Argument will perhaps be of the greatest Service to me of anything I ever did—It set before me at once the gradations of Happiness even like a kind of Pleasure Thermometer, and is my first step towards the chief attempt in the Drama—the playing of different Natures with Joy and Sorrow." The gradations on this "Pleasure Thermometer" mark the stages on the way to what Keats calls "happiness" (line 777)—his secular version of the religious concept of "felicity" that, in the orthodox view, is to be achieved by a surrender of oneself to God. For Keats the way to happiness lies through a fusion of ourselves, first sensuously, with the lovely objects of nature and art (lines 781–97), then on a higher level, with other human beings through "love and friendship" (line 801) and, ultimately, sexual love.
5. Transformed by alchemy from a base to a precious metal.
6. From Aeolus, god of winds.

Ghosts of melodious prophecyings rave

790 Round every spot where trod Apollo's foot;
Bronze clarions awake, and faintly bruit,[7]
Where long ago a giant battle was;
And, from the turf, a lullaby doth pass
In every place where infant Orpheus[8] slept.
795 Feel we these things?—that moment have we stept
Into a sort of oneness, and our state
Is like a floating spirit's. But there are
Richer entanglements, enthralments far
More self-destroying, leading, by degrees,
800 To the chief intensity: the crown of these
Is made of love and friendship, and sits high
Upon the forehead of humanity.
All its more ponderous and bulky worth
Is friendship, whence there ever issues forth
805 A steady splendour; but at the tip-top
There hangs by unseen film, an orbed drop
Of light, and that is love: its influence,
Thrown in our eyes, genders a novel sense,
At which we start and fret; till in the end,
810 Melting into its radiance, we blend,
Mingle, and so become a part of it,—
Nor with aught else can our souls interknit
So wingedly: when we combine therewith,
Life's self is nourish'd by its proper pith,[9]
815 And we are nurtured like a pelican brood.[1]
Aye, so delicious is the unsating food,[2]
That men, who might have tower'd in the van°   *forefront*
Of all the congregated world, to fan
And winnow from the coming step of time
820 All chaff of custom, wipe away all slime
Left by men-slugs and human serpentry,
Have been content to let occasion die,
Whilst they did sleep in love's elysium.°   *heaven*
And, truly, I would rather be struck dumb,
825 Than speak against this ardent listlessness:
For I have ever thought that it might bless
The world with benefits unknowingly;
As does the nightingale, upperched high,
And cloister'd among cool and bunched leaves—
830 She sings but to her love, nor e'er conceives
How tiptoe Night holds back her dark-grey hood.[3]
Just so may love, although 'tis understood
The mere commingling of passionate breath,
Produce more than our searching witnesseth:
835 What I know not: but who, of men, can tell

---

7. Make a sound.
8. The musician of Greek legend, whose beautiful music could move even inanimate things.
9. Its own elemental substance.
1. Young pelicans were once thought to feed on their mother's flesh. In a parallel way our life is nourished by another's life, with which it fuses in love.
2. Food that never satiates, that never ceases to satisfy.
3. I.e., in order to hear better.

That flowers would bloom, or that green fruit would swell
To melting pulp, that fish would have bright mail,
The earth its dower of river, wood, and vale,
The meadows runnels, runnels pebble-stones,
840   The seed its harvest, or the lute its tones,
Tones ravishment, or ravishment its sweet,
If human souls did never kiss and greet?

    "Now, if this earthly love has power to make
Men's being mortal, immortal; to shake
845   Ambition from their memories, and brim
Their measure of content; what merest whim,
Seems all this poor endeavour after fame,
To one, who keeps within his stedfast aim
A love immortal, an immortal too.
850   Look not so wilder'd; for these things are true,
And never can be born of atomies°   *mites*
That buzz about our slumbers, like brain-flies,
Leaving us fancy-sick. No, no, I'm sure,
My restless spirit never could endure
855   To brood so long upon one luxury,
Unless it did, though fearfully, espy
A hope beyond the shadow of a dream."

Apr.–Nov. 1817   1818

On Sitting Down to Read *King Lear* Once Again[1]

O golden-tongued Romance, with serene lute!
    Fair plumed syren,[2] queen of far-away!
    Leave melodizing on this wintry day,
Shut up thine olden pages, and be mute.
5   Adieu! for, once again, the fierce dispute
    Betwixt damnation and impassion'd clay
    Must I burn through; once more humbly assay°   *test*
The bitter-sweet of this Shakespearean fruit.
Chief Poet! and ye clouds of Albion,[3]
10   Begetters of our deep eternal theme!
When through the old oak forest I am gone,
    Let me not wander in a barren dream:
But, when I am consumed in the fire,
    Give me new phoenix[4] wings to fly at my desire.

Jan. 22, 1818   1838

1. Keats pauses, while revising *Endymion: A Poetic Romance,* to read again Shakespeare's great tragedy. The word "syren" (line 2) indicates Keats's feeling that "Romance" was enticing him from the poet's prime duty, to deal with "the agonies, the strife / Of human hearts" (*Sleep and Poetry,* lines 124–25).

2. Syrens (sirens) were sea nymphs whose singing lured listeners to their deaths.
3. Old name for England. *King Lear* is set in Celtic Britain.
4. The fabulous bird that periodically burns itself to death to rise anew from the ashes.

When I have fears that I may cease to be[1]

When I have fears that I may cease to be
  Before my pen has glean'd my teeming brain,
Before high piled books, in charactry,[2]
  Hold like rich garners the full ripen'd grain;
5 When I behold, upon the night's starr'd face,
  Huge cloudy symbols of a high romance,
And think that I may never live to trace
  Their shadows, with the magic hand of chance;
And when I feel, fair creature of an hour,
10   That I shall never look upon thee more,
Never have relish in the fairy power
  Of unreflecting love;—then on the shore
Of the wide world I stand alone, and think
Till love and fame to nothingness do sink.

Jan. 1818   1848

To Homer

Standing aloof in giant ignorance,
  Of thee I hear and of the Cyclades,[1]
As one who sits ashore and longs perchance
  To visit dolphin-coral in deep seas.
5 So wast thou blind;—but then the veil was rent,
  For Jove uncurtain'd heaven to let thee live,
And Neptune made for thee a spumy tent,
  And Pan made sing for thee his forest-hive;
Aye on the shores of darkness there is light,
10   And precipices show untrodden green,
There is a budding morrow in midnight,
  There is a triple sight in blindness keen;
Such seeing hadst thou, as it once befel
To Dian, Queen of Earth, and Heaven, and Hell.[2]

1818   1848

The Eve of St. Agnes[1]

I

St. Agnes' Eve—Ah, bitter chill it was!
The owl, for all his feathers, was a-cold;

1. The first, and one of the most successful, of Keats's attempts at the sonnet in the Shakespearean rhyme scheme.
2. Characters; printed letters of the alphabet.
1. A group of islands in the Aegean Sea, off Greece. Keats's allusion is to his ignorance of the Greek language. Schooling in Greek was a badge of gentlemanly identity in the period.
2. In late pagan cults Diana was worshiped as a three-figured goddess, the deity of nature and of the moon as well as the queen of hell. The "triple sight" that blind Homer paradoxically commands is of these three regions and also of heaven, sea, and earth (the realms of Jove, Neptune, and Pan, lines 6–8).
1. St. Agnes, martyred ca. 303 at the age of thirteen, is the patron saint of virgins. Legend has it that if a chaste young woman performs the proper

    The hare limp'd trembling through the frozen grass,
    And silent was the flock in woolly fold:
5   Numb were the Beadsman's[2] fingers, while he told
    His rosary, and while his frosted breath,
    Like pious incense from a censer old,
    Seem'd taking flight for heaven, without a death,
Past the sweet Virgin's picture, while his prayer he saith.

2

10   His prayer he saith, this patient, holy man;
    Then takes his lamp, and riseth from his knees,
    And back returneth, meagre,° barefoot, wan,   *lean*
    Along the chapel aisle by slow degrees:
15   The sculptur'd dead, on each side, seem to freeze,
    Emprison'd in black, purgatorial rails:
    Knights, ladies, praying in dumb° orat'ries,°   *silent / chapels*
    He passeth by; and his weak spirit fails
To think[3] how they may ache in icy hoods and mails.

3

    Northward he turneth through a little door,
20   And scarce three steps, ere Music's golden tongue
    Flatter'd° to tears this aged man and poor;   *beguiled*
    But no—already had his deathbell rung;
    The joys of all his life were said and sung:
    His was harsh penance on St. Agnes' Eve:
25   Another way he went, and soon among
    Rough ashes sat he for his soul's reprieve,°   *salvation*
And all night kept awake, for sinners' sake to grieve.

4

    That ancient Beadsman heard the prelude soft;
    And so it chanc'd, for many a door was wide,
30   From hurry to and fro. Soon, up aloft,
    The silver, snarling trumpets 'gan to chide:
    The level chambers, ready with their pride,°   *ostentation*
    Were glowing to receive a thousand guests:
    The carved angels, ever eager-eyed,
35   Star'd, where upon their heads the cornice rests,
With hair blown back, and wings put cross-wise on their breasts.

5

    At length burst in the argent revelry,[4]
    With plume, tiara, and all rich array,
    Numerous as shadows haunting fairily
40   The brain, new stuff'd, in youth, with triumphs gay
    Of old romance.° These let us wish away,   *stories*
    And turn, sole-thoughted, to one Lady there,

---

ritual, she will dream of her future husband on the evening before St. Agnes's Day, January 21. Keats combines this superstition with the Romeo and Juliet theme of young love thwarted by feuding families and tells the story in a sequence of evolving Spenserian stanzas. The poem is Keats's first complete success in sustained narrative romance. For the author's revisions while composing stanzas

26 and 30 of *The Eve of St. Agnes,* see "Poems in Process," in the appendices to this volume.
2. One who is paid to pray for his benefactor. He "tells" (counts) the beads of his rosary to keep track of his prayers.
3. I.e., when he thinks.
4. Silver-adorned revelers.

Whose heart had brooded, all that wintry day,
On love, and wing'd St. Agnes' saintly care,
45   As she had heard old dames full many times declare.

6

They told her how, upon St. Agnes' Eve,
Young virgins might have visions of delight,
And soft adorings from their loves receive
Upon the honey'd middle of the night,
50   If ceremonies due they did aright;
As, supperless to bed they must retire,
And couch supine their beauties, lily white;
Nor look behind, nor sideways, but require
Of heaven with upward eyes for all that they desire.

7

55   Full of this whim was thoughtful Madeline:
The music, yearning like a god in pain,
She scarcely heard: her maiden eyes divine,
Fix'd on the floor, saw many a sweeping train[5]
Pass by—she heeded not at all: in vain
60   Came many a tiptoe, amorous cavalier,
And back retir'd, not cool'd by high disdain;
But she saw not: her heart was otherwhere:
She sigh'd for Agnes' dreams, the sweetest of the year.

8

She danc'd along with vague, regardless eyes,
65   Anxious her lips, her breathing quick and short:
The hallow'd hour was near at hand: she sighs
Amid the timbrels,° and the throng'd resort   *tambourines*
Of whisperers in anger, or in sport;
'Mid looks of love, defiance, hate, and scorn,
70   Hoodwink'd with faery fancy; all amort,[6]
Save to St. Agnes[6] and her lambs unshorn,[7]
And all the bliss to be before to-morrow morn.

9

So, purposing each moment to retire,
She linger'd still. Meantime, across the moors,
75   Had come young Porphyro, with heart on fire
For Madeline. Beside the portal doors,
Buttress'd from moonlight,[8] stands he, and implores
All saints to give him sight of Madeline,
But for one moment in the tedious hours,
80   That he might gaze and worship all unseen;
Perchance speak, kneel, touch, kiss—in sooth such things have been.

10

He ventures in: let no buzz'd whisper tell:
All eyes be muffled, or a hundred swords

5. Skirts sweeping along the ground.
6. Entirely oblivious or dead ("amort") to everything except St. Agnes. "Hoodwinked": covered by a hood or blindfolded.
7. On St. Agnes's Day it was the custom to offer lambs' wool at the altar, to be made into cloth by nuns.
8. Sheltered from the moonlight by the buttresses (the supports projecting from the wall).

Will storm his heart, Love's fev'rous citadel:
For him, those chambers held barbarian hordes,
Hyena foemen, and hot-blooded lords,
Whose very dogs would execrations howl
Against his lineage: not one breast affords
Him any mercy, in that mansion foul,
Save one old beldame,[9] weak in body and in soul.

II

Ah, happy chance! the aged creature came,
Shuffling along with ivory-headed wand,°   *staff*
To where he stood, hid from the torch's flame,
Behind a broad hall-pillar, far beyond
The sound of merriment and chorus bland:°   *soft*
He startled her; but soon she knew his face,
And grasp'd his fingers in her palsied hand,
Saying, "Mercy, Porphyro! hie thee from this place;
They are all here to-night, the whole blood-thirsty race!

12

"Get hence! get hence! there's dwarfish Hildebrand;
He had a fever late, and in the fit
He cursed thee and thine, both house and land:
Then there's that old Lord Maurice, not a whit
More tame for his gray hairs—Alas me! flit!
Flit like a ghost away."—"Ah, Gossip[1] dear,
We're safe enough; here in this arm-chair sit,
And tell me how"—"Good Saints! not here, not here;
Follow me, child, or else these stones will be thy bier."°   *tomb*

13

He follow'd through a lowly arched way,
Brushing the cobwebs with his lofty plume,
And as she mutter'd "Well-a—well-a-day!"
He found him in a little moonlight room,
Pale, lattic'd, chill, and silent as a tomb.
"Now tell me where is Madeline," said he,
"O tell me, Angela, by the holy loom
Which none but secret sisterhood may see,
When they St. Agnes' wool are weaving piously."

14

"St. Agnes! Ah! it is St. Agnes' Eve—
Yet men will murder upon holy days:
Thou must hold water in a witch's sieve,[2]
And be liege-lord of all the Elves and Fays,
To venture so: it fills me with amaze
To see thee, Porphyro!—St. Agnes' Eve!
God's help! my lady fair the conjuror plays[3]
This very night: good angels her deceive!
But let me laugh awhile, I've mickle° time to grieve."   *much*

9. Old (and, usually, homely) woman; an ironic
development in English from the French meaning,
"lovely lady."
1. In the old sense: godmother or old friend.

2. A sieve made to hold water by witchcraft.
3. I.e., uses magic in her attempt to evoke the
vision of her lover.

15

Feebly she laugheth in the languid moon,
While Porphyro upon her face doth look,
Like puzzled urchin on an aged crone
130 Who keepeth clos'd a wond'rous riddle-book,
As spectacled she sits in chimney nook.
But soon his eyes grew brilliant, when she told
His lady's purpose; and he scarce could brook°   *restrain*
Tears, at the thought of those enchantments cold,
135 And Madeline asleep in lap of legends old.

16

Sudden a thought came like a full-blown rose,
Flushing his brow, and in his pained heart
Made purple riot: then doth he propose
A stratagem, that makes the beldame start:
140 "A cruel man and impious thou art:
Sweet lady, let her pray, and sleep, and dream
Alone with her good angels, far apart
From wicked men like thee. Go, go!—I deem
Thou canst not surely be the same that thou didst seem."

17

145 "I will not harm her, by all saints I swear,"
Quoth Porphyro: "O may I ne'er find grace
When my weak voice shall whisper its last prayer,
If one of her soft ringlets I displace,
Or look with ruffian passion in her face:
150 Good Angela, believe me by these tears;
Or I will, even in a moment's space,
Awake, with horrid shout, my foemen's ears,
And beard° them, though they be more fang'd than wolves and *confront*
  bears."

18

"Ah! why wilt thou affright a feeble soul?
155 A poor, weak, palsy-stricken, churchyard thing,
Whose passing-bell° may ere the midnight toll;   *death knell*
Whose prayers for thee, each morn and evening,
Were never miss'd."—Thus plaining,° doth she bring *complaining*
A gentler speech from burning Porphyro;
160 So woful, and of such deep sorrowing,
That Angela gives promise she will do
Whatever he shall wish, betide her weal or woe.[4]

19

Which was, to lead him, in close secrecy,
Even to Madeline's chamber, and there hide
165 Him in a closet, of such privacy
That he might see her beauty unespied,
And win perhaps that night a peerless bride,
While legion'd fairies pac'd the coverlet,

---

4. I.e., whether good or ill befalls her.

And pale enchantment held her sleepy-eyed.
70 Never on such a night have lovers met,
Since Merlin paid his Demon all the monstrous debt.[5]

20

"It shall be as thou wishest," said the Dame:
"All cates° and dainties shall be stored there   delicacies
Quickly on this feast-night: by the tambour frame[6]
75 Her own lute thou wilt see: no time to spare,
For I am slow and feeble, and scarce dare
On such a catering trust my dizzy head.
Wait here, my child, with patience; kneel in prayer
The while: Ah! thou must needs the lady wed,
80 Or may I never leave my grave among the dead."

21

So saying, she hobbled off with busy fear.
The lover's endless minutes slowly pass'd;
The dame return'd, and whisper'd in his ear
To follow her; with aged eyes aghast
85 From fright of dim espial. Safe at last,
Through many a dusky gallery, they gain
The maiden's chamber, silken, hush'd, and chaste;
Where Porphyro took covert, pleas'd amain.°   mightily
His poor guide hurried back with agues° in her brain.   shivering

22

90 Her falt'ring hand upon the balustrade,
Old Angela was feeling for the stair,
When Madeline, St. Agnes' charmed maid,
Rose, like a mission'd spirit,[7] unaware:
With silver taper's light, and pious care,
95 She turn'd, and down the aged gossip led
To a safe level matting. Now prepare,
Young Porphyro, for gazing on that bed;
She comes, she comes again, like ring-dove fray'd° and fled.   frightened

23

Out went the taper as she hurried in;
100 Its little smoke, in pallid moonshine, died:
She clos'd the door, she panted, all akin
To spirits of the air, and visions wide:
No uttered syllable, or, woe betide!
But to her heart, her heart was voluble,
105 Paining with eloquence her balmy side;
As though a tongueless nightingale[8] should swell
Her throat in vain, and die, heart-stifled, in her dell.

5. Probably the episode in the Arthurian legends in which Merlin, the magician, lost his life when the wily Vivien turned one of his own spells against him.
6. A drum-shaped embroidery frame.
7. I.e., like an angel sent on a mission.
8. An allusion to Ovid's story, in the *Metamorphoses*, of Philomel, who was raped by Tereus, her sister's husband. He cut out Philomel's tongue to prevent her from speaking of his crime, but she managed to weave her story and make herself understood to her sister, Procne. Just as Tereus was about to kill both women, Philomel and Procne were metamorphosed into a nightingale and a swallow.

24

A casement° high and triple-arch'd there was,   *window*
All garlanded with carven imag'ries
210   Of fruits, and flowers, and bunches of knot-grass,
And diamonded with panes of quaint device,
Innumerable of stains and splendid dyes,
As are the tiger-moth's deep-damask'd wings;
And in the midst, 'mong thousand heraldries,
215   And twilight saints, and dim emblazonings,
A shielded scutcheon blush'd with blood of queens and kings.⁹

25

Full on this casement shone the wintry moon,
And threw warm gules¹ on Madeline's fair breast,
As down she knelt for heaven's grace and boon;°   *gift, blessing*
220   Rose-bloom fell on her hands, together prest,
And on her silver cross soft amethyst,
And on her hair a glory,° like a saint: *halo*
She seem'd a splendid angel, newly drest,
Save wings, for heaven:—Porphyro grew faint:
225   She knelt, so pure a thing, so free from mortal taint.

26

Anon his heart revives: her vespers done,
Of all its wreathed pearls her hair she frees;²
Unclasps her warmed jewels one by one;
Loosens her fragrant boddice; by degrees
230   Her rich attire creeps rustling to her knees:
Half-hidden, like a mermaid in sea-weed,
Pensive awhile she dreams awake, and sees,
In fancy, fair St. Agnes in her bed,
But dares not look behind, or all the charm is fled.

27

235   Soon, trembling in her soft and chilly nest,
In sort of wakeful swoon, perplex'd³ she lay,
Until the poppied warmth of sleep oppress'd
Her soothed limbs, and soul fatigued away;
Flown, like a thought, until the morrow-day;
240   Blissfully haven'd both from joy and pain;
Clasp'd like a missal where swart Paynims pray;⁴
Blinded alike from sunshine and from rain,
As though a rose should shut, and be a bud again.

28

Stol'n to this paradise, and so entranced,
245   Porphyro gazed upon her empty dress,

---

9. I.e., among the genealogical emblems ("herald-ries") and other devices ("emblazonings"), a heraldic shield signified by its colors that the family was of royal blood.
1. Red (heraldry).
2. The Pre-Raphaelite-inspired painter Daniel Maclise represented this moment in Keats's romance in his painting of 1868, *Madeline after Prayer*. For a reproduction of the painting, see the color insert.
3. In a confused state between waking and sleeping.
4. Variously interpreted; perhaps: held tightly, cherished (or else kept shut, fastened with a clasp), like a Christian prayer book ("missal") in a land where the religion is that of dark-skinned pagans ("swart Paynims").

And listen'd to her breathing, if it chanced
To wake into a slumberous tenderness;
Which when he heard, that minute did he bless,
And breath'd himself: then from the closet crept,
Noiseless as fear in a wide wilderness,
And over the hush'd carpet, silent, stept,
And 'tween the curtains peep'd, where, lo!—how fast she slept.

29

Then by the bed-side, where the faded moon
Made a dim, silver twilight, soft he set
A table, and, half anguish'd, threw thereon
A cloth of woven crimson, gold, and jet:—
O for some drowsy Morphean amulet![5]
The boisterous, midnight, festive clarion,[6]
The kettle-drum, and far-heard clarionet,
Affray° his ears, though but in dying tone:—   *frighten*
The hall door shuts again, and all the noise is gone.

30

And still she slept an azure-lidded sleep,
In blanched linen, smooth, and lavender'd,
While he from forth the closet brought a heap
Of candied apple, quince, and plum, and gourd;°   *melon*
With jellies soother than the creamy curd,
And lucent syrops, tinct with cinnamon;
Manna and dates, in argosy transferr'd
From Fez,[7] and spiced dainties, every one,
From silken Samarcand to cedar'd Lebanon.

31

These delicates he heap'd with glowing hand
On golden dishes and in baskets bright
Of wreathed silver: sumptuous they stand
In the retired quiet of the night,
Filling the chilly room with perfume light.—
"And now, my love, my seraph[8] fair, awake!
Thou art my heaven, and I thine eremite:[9]
Open thine eyes, for meek St. Agnes' sake,
Or I shall drowse beside thee, so my soul doth ache."

32

Thus whispering, his warm, unnerved° arm   *unmanned, weak*
Sank in her pillow. Shaded was her dream
By the dusk curtains:—'twas a midnight charm
Impossible to melt as iced stream:
The lustrous salvers° in the moonlight gleam;   *trays*
Broad golden fringe upon the carpet lies:
It seem'd he never, never could redeem
From such a stedfast spell his lady's eyes;
So mus'd awhile, entoil'd in woofed phantasies.[1]

5. Sleep-producing charm.
6. High-pitched trumpet.
7. I.e., jellies softer ("soother") than the curds of cream, clear ("lucent") syrups tinged with cinnamon, and sweet gums ("manna") and dates trans- ported in a great merchant ship ("argosy") from Fez, in Morocco.
8. One of the highest orders of angels.
9. Hermit, religious solitary.
1. Entangled in a weave of fantasies.

33

Awakening up, he took her hollow lute,—
290 Tumultuous,—and, in chords that tenderest be,
He play'd an ancient ditty, long since mute,
In Provence call'd, "La belle dame sans mercy":[2]
Close to her ear touching the melody;—
Wherewith disturb'd, she utter'd a soft moan:
295 He ceased—she panted quick—and suddenly
Her blue affrayed eyes wide open shone:
Upon his knees he sank, pale as smooth-sculptured stone.

34

Her eyes were open, but she still beheld,
Now wide awake, the vision of her sleep:
300 There was a painful change, that nigh° expell'd   *nearly*
The blisses of her dream so pure and deep:
At which fair Madeline began to weep,
And moan forth witless words with many a sigh;
While still her gaze on Porphyro would keep;
305 Who knelt, with joined hands and piteous eye,
Fearing to move or speak, she look'd so dreamingly.

35

"Ah, Porphyro!" said she, "but even now
Thy voice was at sweet tremble in mine ear,
Made tuneable with every sweetest vow;
310 And those sad eyes were spiritual and clear:
How chang'd thou art! how pallid, chill, and drear!
Give me that voice again, my Porphyro,
Those looks immortal, those complainings dear!
Oh leave me not in this eternal woe,
315 For if thou diest, my love, I know not where to go."

36

Beyond a mortal man impassion'd far
At these voluptuous accents, he arose,
Ethereal, flush'd, and like a throbbing star
Seen mid the sapphire heaven's deep repose;
320 Into her dream he melted, as the rose
Blendeth its odour with the violet,—
Solution° sweet: meantime the frost-wind blows   *fusion*
Like Love's alarum pattering the sharp sleet
Against the window-panes; St. Agnes' moon hath set.

37

325 'Tis dark: quick pattereth the flaw-blown° sleet: *gust-blown*
"This is no dream, my bride, my Madeline!"
'Tis dark: the iced gusts still rave and beat:
"No dream, alas! alas! and woe is mine!
Porphyro will leave me here to fade and pine.—
330 Cruel! what traitor could thee hither bring?

2. "The Lovely Lady without Pity," title of a work by the medieval poet Alain Chartier. Keats later adopted the title for his own ballad.

I curse not, for my heart is lost in thine,
Though thou forsakest a deceived thing;—
A dove forlorn and lost with sick unpruned wing."

38

"My Madeline! sweet dreamer! lovely bride!
335   Say, may I be for aye thy vassal blest?
Thy beauty's shield, heart-shap'd and vermeil° dyed?   *vermilion*
Ah, silver shrine, here will I take my rest
After so many hours of toil and quest,
A famish'd pilgrim,—saved by miracle.
340   Though I have found, I will not rob thy nest
Saving of thy sweet self; if thou think'st well
To trust, fair Madeline, to no rude infidel.

39

"Hark! 'tis an elfin-storm from faery land,
Of haggard[3] seeming, but a boon indeed:
345   Arise—arise! the morning is at hand;—
The bloated wassaillers[4] will never heed:—
Let us away, my love, with happy speed;
There are no ears to hear, or eyes to see,—
Drown'd all in Rhenish and the sleepy mead:[5]
350   Awake! arise! my love, and fearless be,
For o'er the southern moors I have a home for thee."

40

She hurried at his words, beset with fears,
For there were sleeping dragons all around,
At glaring watch, perhaps, with ready spears—
355   Down the wide stairs a darkling[6] way they found.—
In all the house was heard no human sound.
A chain-droop'd lamp was flickering by each door;
The arras,° rich with horseman, hawk, and hound,   *tapestry*
Flutter'd in the besieging wind's uproar;
360   And the long carpets rose along the gusty floor.

41

They glide, like phantoms, into the wide hall;
Like phantoms, to the iron porch, they glide;
Where lay the Porter, in uneasy sprawl,
With a huge empty flaggon by his side:
365   The wakeful bloodhound rose, and shook his hide,
But his sagacious eye an inmate owns:[7]
By one, and one, the bolts full easy slide:—
The chains lie silent on the footworn stones;—
The key turns, and the door upon its hinges groans.

42

370   And they are gone: ay, ages long ago
These lovers fled away into the storm.

3. Wild, untamed (originally, a wild hawk).
4. Drunken carousers.
5. Rhine wine and the sleep-producing mead (a
heavy fermented drink made with honey).
6. In the dark.
7. Acknowledges a member of the household.

That night the Baron dreamt of many a woe,
And all his warrior-guests, with shade and form
Of witch, and demon, and large coffin-worm,
375 Were long be-nightmar'd. Angela the old
Died palsy-twitch'd, with meagre face deform;
The Beadsman, after thousand aves[8] told,
For aye° unsought for slept among his ashes cold.   *ever*

Jan.–Feb. 1819   1820

Bright star, would I were stedfast as thou art[1]

Bright star, would I were stedfast as thou art—
    Not in lone splendor hung aloft the night,
And watching, with eternal lids apart,
    Like nature's patient, sleepless eremite,[2]
5 The moving waters at their priestlike task
    Of pure ablution[3] round earth's human shores,
Or gazing on the new soft-fallen mask
    Of snow upon the mountains and the moors;
No—yet still stedfast, still unchangeable,
10   Pillow'd upon my fair love's ripening breast,
To feel for ever its soft swell and fall,
    Awake for ever in a sweet unrest,
Still, still to hear her tender-taken breath,
And so live ever—or else swoon to death.[4]

1819   1838

La Belle Dame sans Merci: A Ballad[1]

I

O what can ail thee, knight at arms,
    Alone and palely loitering?
The sedge° has wither'd from the lake,   *rushes*
    And no birds sing.

8. The prayers beginning *Ave Maria* ("Hail Mary").
1. While on a tour of the Lake District in 1818, Keats had said that the austere scenes "refine one's sensual vision into a sort of north star which can never cease to be open lidded and steadfast over the wonders of the great Power." The thought developed into this sonnet, which Keats drafted in 1819, then copied into his volume of Shakespeare's poems at the end of September or the beginning of October 1820, while on his way to Italy, where he died.
2. Hermit, religious solitary.
3. Washing, as part of a religious rite.
4. In the earlier version: "Half passionless, and so

swoon on to death."
1. The title, though not the subject, was taken from a medieval poem by Alain Chartier and means "The Lovely Lady without Pity." The story of a mortal destroyed by his love for a supernatural femme fatale has been told repeatedly in myth, fairy tale, and ballad. The text printed here is Keats's earlier version of the poem, as transcribed by Charles Brown. The version published in 1820 begins, "Ah, what can ail thee, wretched wight."
Keats imitates a frequent procedure of folk ballads by casting the poem into the dialogue form. The first three stanzas are addressed to the knight, and the rest of the poem is his reply.

2

5 O what can ail thee, knight at arms,
    So haggard and so woe-begone?
The squirrel's granary is full,
    And the harvest's done.

3

I see a lily on thy brow
10   With anguish moist and fever dew,
And on thy cheeks a fading rose
    Fast withereth too.

4

I met a lady in the meads,
    Full beautiful, a fairy's child;
15 Her hair was long, her foot was light,
    And her eyes were wild.

5

I made a garland for her head,
    And bracelets too, and fragrant zone;[2]
She look'd at me as she did love,
20   And made sweet moan.

6

I set her on my pacing steed,
    And nothing else saw all day long,
For sidelong would she bend, and sing
    A fairy's song.

7

25 She found me roots of relish° sweet,   *flavor*
    And honey wild, and manna dew,
And sure in language strange she said—
    I love thee true.

8

She took me to her elfin grot°   *cave*
30   And there she wept, and sigh'd full sore,
And there I shut her wild wild eyes
    With kisses four.[3]

9

And there she lulled me asleep,
    And there I dream'd—Ah! woe betide!
35 The latest° dream I ever dream'd   *last*
    On the cold hill's side.

---

2. Belt (of flowers).
3. Keats commented in a letter to his brother and sister-in-law, "Why four kisses—you will say—why four because I wish to restrain the headlong impetuosity of my Muse—she would have fain said 'score' without hurting the rhyme—but we must temper the Imagination as the Critics say with Judgment. I was obliged to choose an even number that both eyes might have fair play."

10

I saw pale kings, and princes too,
   Pale warriors, death pale were they all;
They cried—"La belle dame sans merci
40   Hath thee in thrall!"

11

I saw their starv'd lips in the gloom°   *twilight*
   With horrid warning gaped wide,
And I awoke and found me here
   On the cold hill's side.

12

45 And this is why I sojourn here,
   Alone and palely loitering,
Though the sedge is wither'd from the lake,
   And no birds sing.

Apr. 1819   1820

Sonnet to Sleep

O soft embalmer of the still midnight,
   Shutting with careful fingers and benign
Our gloom-pleas'd eyes, embower'd from the light,
   Enshaded in forgetfulness divine:
5 O soothest° Sleep! if so it please thee, close,   *softest*
   In midst of this thine hymn, my willing eyes,
Or wait the Amen ere thy poppy[1] throws
   Around my bed its lulling charities.
Then save me or the passed day will shine
10   Upon my pillow, breeding many woes:
Save me from curious° conscience, that still hoards   *scrupulous*
   Its strength for darkness, burrowing like the mole;
Turn the key deftly in the oiled wards,[2]
   And seal the hushed casket of my soul.

Apr. 1819   1838

---

1. Opium is made from the dried juice of the opium poppy.

2. The ridges in a lock that correspond to the notches of the key.

Ode to Psyche[1]

O Goddess! hear these tuneless numbers,° wrung   *verses*
  By sweet enforcement and remembrance dear,
And pardon that thy secrets should be sung
  Even into thine own soft-conchèd[2] ear:
5 Surely I dreamt to-day, or did I see
  The winged Psyche with awaken'd eyes?
I wander'd in a forest thoughtlessly,
  And, on the sudden, fainting with surprise,
Saw two fair creatures, couched side by side
10   In deepest grass, beneath the whisp'ring roof
    Of leaves and trembled blossoms, where there ran
      A brooklet, scarce espied:
'Mid hush'd, cool-rooted flowers, fragrant-eyed,
    Blue, silver-white, and budded Tyrian,[3]
15 They lay calm-breathing on the bedded grass;
    Their arms embraced, and their pinions° too;   *wings*
    Their lips touch'd not, but had not bade adieu,
As if disjoinèd by soft-handed slumber,
And ready still past kisses to outnumber
20   At tender eye-dawn of aurorean love:[4]
      The winged boy I knew;
But who wast thou, O happy, happy dove?
      His Psyche true!

O latest born and loveliest vision far
25   Of all Olympus' faded hierarchy![5]
Fairer than Phoebe's sapphire-region'd star,[6]
  Or Vesper,° amorous glow-worm of the sky;   *evening star*
Fairer than these, though temple thou hast none,
    Nor altar heap'd with flowers;
30 Nor virgin-choir to make delicious moan
    Upon the midnight hours;

---

1. This poem initiated the sequence of great odes that Keats wrote in the spring of 1819. It is copied into the same journal-letter that included the "Sonnet to Sleep" and several other sonnets as well as a comment about "endeavoring to discover a better sonnet stanza than we have." It is therefore likely that Keats's experiments with sonnet schemes led to the development of the intricate and varied stanzas of his odes and also that he abandoned the sonnet on discovering the richer possibilities of the more spacious form.

Psyche, which gives us our modern term *psychology,* means mind or soul (and also butterfly) in Greek. In the story told by the Roman author Apuleius in the 2nd century, Psyche was a lovely mortal beloved by Cupid, the "winged boy" (line 21), son of Venus. To keep their love a secret from his mother, who envied Psyche's beauty, he visited his lover only in the dark of night, and had her promise never to try to discover his identity. After Psyche broke the promise, she endured various tribulations as a penance and then was finally wedded to Cupid and translated to heaven as an immortal. To

this goddess, added to the pantheon of pagan gods too late to have been the center of a cult, Keats in the last two stanzas promises to establish a place of worship within his own mind, with himself as poet-priest and prophet.
2. Soft and shaped like a seashell.
3. The purple dye once made in ancient Tyre.
4. Aurora was the goddess of the dawn.
5. The ranks of the gods who lived on Mount Olympus, according to the classical mythology now eclipsed (made "faded") by Christianity. "You must recollect that Psyche was not embodied as a goddess before the time of Apuleius the Platonist who lived after the Augustan age, and consequently the Goddess was never worshiped or sacrificed to with any of the ancient fervour—and perhaps never thought of in the old religion—I am more orthodox tha[n] to let a hethen Goddess be so neglected" (Keats, in a long letter written over several months to George and Georgiana Keats in America, April 30, 1819).
6. The moon, supervised by the goddess Phoebe (Diana).

No voice, no lute, no pipe, no incense sweet
　　From chain-swung censer teeming;
No shrine, no grove, no oracle, no heat
35　　Of pale-mouth'd prophet dreaming.

O brightest! though too late for antique vows,[7]
　Too, too late for the fond believing lyre,
When holy were the haunted° forest boughs,　　　　　　*spirit-filled*
　Holy the air, the water, and the fire;
40 Yet even in these days so far retir'd
　　From happy pieties, thy lucent fans,°　　　　　　*shining wings*
　Fluttering among the faint Olympians,
I see, and sing, by my own eyes inspired.
So let me be thy choir, and make a moan
45　　Upon the midnight hours;
Thy voice, thy lute, thy pipe, thy incense sweet
　　From swinged censer teeming;
Thy shrine, thy grove, thy oracle, thy heat
　　Of pale-mouth'd prophet dreaming.

50 Yes, I will be thy priest, and build a fane°　　　　　*temple*
　　In some untrodden region of my mind,
Where branched thoughts, new grown with pleasant pain,
　　Instead of pines shall murmur in the wind:
Far, far around shall those dark-cluster'd trees
55　　Fledge the wild-ridged mountains steep by steep;[8]
And there by zephyrs, streams,° and birds, and bees,　　*breezes*
　　The moss-lain Dryads° shall be lull'd to sleep;　　*wood nymphs*
And in the midst of this wide quietness
A rosy sanctuary will I dress
60 With the wreath'd trellis of a working brain,
　　With buds, and bells, and stars without a name,
With all the gardener Fancy e'er could feign,
　　Who breeding flowers, will never breed the same:
And there shall be for thee all soft delight
65　　That shadowy thought can win,
A bright torch, and a casement ope at night,
　　To let the warm Love[9] in!

Apr. 1819　　　　　　　　　　　　　　　　　　　　1820

7. I.e., of worshipers.
8. I.e., the trees shall stand, rank against rank, like
layers of feathers.
9. I.e., Cupid, god of love.

Ode to a Nightingale[1]

I

My heart aches, and a drowsy numbness pains
   My sense, as though of hemlock[2] I had drunk,
Or emptied some dull opiate to the drains
   One minute past, and Lethe[3]-wards had sunk:
5 'Tis not through envy of thy happy lot,
   But being too happy in thine happiness,—
      That thou, light-winged Dryad of the trees,
        In some melodious plot
   Of beechen green, and shadows numberless,
10   Singest of summer in full-throated ease.

2

O, for a draught of vintage!° that hath been   *wine*
   Cool'd a long age in the deep-delved earth,
Tasting of Flora[4] and the country green,
   Dance, and Provençal song,[5] and sunburnt mirth!
15 O for a beaker full of the warm South,
   Full of the true, the blushful Hippocrene,[6]
      With beaded bubbles winking at the brim,
        And purple-stained mouth;
That I might drink, and leave the world unseen,
20   And with thee fade away into the forest dim:

3

Fade far away, dissolve, and quite forget
   What thou among the leaves hast never known,
The weariness, the fever, and the fret
   Here, where men sit and hear each other groan;
25 Where palsy shakes a few, sad, last gray hairs,
   Where youth grows pale, and spectre-thin, and dies;[7]
      Where but to think is to be full of sorrow
        And leaden-eyed despairs,
   Where Beauty cannot keep her lustrous eyes,
30   Or new Love pine at them beyond to-morrow.

4

Away! away! for I will fly to thee,
   Not charioted by Bacchus and his pards,

---

1. Charles Brown, with whom Keats was then living in Hampstead, wrote: "In the spring of 1819 a nightingale had built her nest near my house. Keats felt a tranquil and continual joy in her song; and one morning he took his chair from the breakfast table to the grass plot under a plum tree, where he sat for two or three hours. When he came into the house, I perceived he had some scraps of paper in his hand, and these he was quietly thrusting behind the books. On inquiry, I found those scraps, four or five in number, contained his poetic feeling on the song of our nightingale."
2. A poisonous herb, not the North American evergreen tree; a sedative if taken in small doses.
3. River in Hades whose waters cause forgetfulness.
4. The Roman goddess of flowers or the flowers themselves.
5. Provence, in southern France, was in the late Middle Ages renowned for its troubadours—writers and singers of love songs.
6. Fountain of the Muses on Mount Helicon, hence the waters of inspiration, here applied metaphorically to a beaker of wine.
7. Keats's brother Tom, wasted by tuberculosis, had died the preceding winter.

But on the viewless wings of Poesy,[8]
  Though the dull brain perplexes and retards:
35 Already with thee! tender is the night,
    And haply the Queen-Moon is on her throne,
      Cluster'd around by all her starry Fays;°   *fairies*
        But here there is no light,
  Save what from heaven is with the breezes blown
40   Through verdurous° glooms and winding mossy ways.   *green-foliaged*

5

I cannot see what flowers are at my feet,
  Nor what soft incense hangs upon the boughs,
But, in embalmed° darkness, guess each sweet   *perfumed*
  Wherewith the seasonable month endows
45 The grass, the thicket, and the fruit-tree wild;
    White hawthorn, and the pastoral eglantine;[9]
      Fast fading violets cover'd up in leaves;
        And mid-May's eldest child,
  The coming musk-rose, full of dewy wine,
50   The murmurous haunt of flies on summer eves.

6

Darkling° I listen; and, for many a time   *in darkness*
  I have been half in love with easeful Death,
Call'd him soft names in many a mused° rhyme,   *meditated*
  To take into the air my quiet breath;
55 Now more than ever seems it rich to die,
  To cease upon the midnight with no pain,
    While thou art pouring forth thy soul abroad
      In such an ecstasy!
  Still wouldst thou sing, and I have ears in vain—
60   To thy high requiem° become a sod.   *mass for the dead*

7

Thou wast not born for death, immortal Bird!
  No hungry generations tread thee down;
The voice I hear this passing night was heard
  In ancient days by emperor and clown:°   *peasant*
65 Perhaps the self-same song that found a path
  Through the sad heart of Ruth,[1] when, sick for home,
    She stood in tears amid the alien corn;°   *wheat*
      The same that oft-times hath
  Charm'd magic casements,° opening on the foam   *windows*
70   Of perilous seas, in faery lands forlorn.

8

Forlorn! the very word is like a bell
  To toll me back from thee to my sole self!
Adieu! the fancy[2] cannot cheat so well

---

8. I.e., by getting drunk not on wine (the "vintage" of stanza 2) but on the invisible ("viewless") wings of the poetic imagination. (Bacchus, god of wine, was sometimes represented in a chariot drawn by "pards"—leopards.)

9. Sweetbrier or honeysuckle.
1. The young widow in the biblical Book of Ruth.
2. I.e., imagination, "the viewless wings of Poesy" of line 33.

As she is fam'd to do, deceiving elf.
75 Adieu! adieu! thy plaintive anthem° fades   *hymn*
   Past the near meadows, over the still stream,
      Up the hill-side; and now 'tis buried deep
      In the next valley-glades:
   Was it a vision, or a waking dream?
80   Fled is that music:—Do I wake or sleep?

May 1819   1819

Ode on a Grecian Urn[1]

1

Thou still unravish'd bride of quietness,
   Thou foster-child of silence and slow time,
Sylvan[2] historian, who canst thus express
   A flowery tale more sweetly than our rhyme:
5 What leaf-fring'd legend haunts about thy shape
   Of deities or mortals, or of both,
      In Tempe or the dales of Arcady?[3]
   What men or gods are these? What maidens loth?
What mad pursuit? What struggle to escape?
10   What pipes and timbrels? What wild ecstasy?

2

Heard melodies are sweet, but those unheard
   Are sweeter; therefore, ye soft pipes, play on;
Not to the sensual ear,[4] but, more endear'd,
   Pipe to the spirit ditties of no tone:
15 Fair youth, beneath the trees, thou canst not leave
   Thy song, nor ever can those trees be bare;
      Bold lover, never, never canst thou kiss,
   Though winning near the goal—yet, do not grieve;
      She cannot fade, though thou hast not thy bliss,
20   For ever wilt thou love, and she be fair!

3

Ah, happy, happy boughs! that cannot shed
   Your leaves, nor ever bid the spring adieu;
   And, happy melodist, unwearied,

1. Another poem that Keats published in Haydon's *Annals of the Fine Arts*. This urn, with its sculptured reliefs of revelry and panting young lovers in chase and in flight, of a pastoral piper under spring foliage, and of the quiet procession of priest and townspeople, resembles parts of various vases, sculptures, and paintings, but it existed in all its particulars only in Keats's imagination. In the urn—which captures moments of intense experience in attitudes of grace and immobilizes them in marble—Keats found the perfect correlative for his concern with the longing for permanence in a world of change. The interpretation of the details with which he develops this concept, however, is hotly disputed. The disputes begin with the opening phrase: is "still" an adverb ("as yet"), or is it an adjective ("motionless"), as the punctuation of the *Annals* version, which adds a comma after "still," suggests? And the two concluding lines have accumulated as much critical discussion as the "two-handed engine" in Milton's "Lycidas" or the most difficult cruxes in Shakespeare's plays.
2. Rustic, representing a woodland scene.
3. The valleys of Arcadia, a state in ancient Greece often used as a symbol of the pastoral ideal. "Tempe": a beautiful valley in Greece that has come to represent rural beauty.
4. The ear of sense (as opposed to that of the "spirit," or imagination).

For ever piping songs for ever new;
25   More happy love! more happy, happy love!
For ever warm and still to be enjoy'd,
For ever panting, and for ever young;
All breathing human passion far above,
That leaves a heart high-sorrowful and cloy'd,
30   A burning forehead, and a parching tongue.

4

Who are these coming to the sacrifice?
To what green altar, O mysterious priest,
Lead'st thou that heifer lowing at the skies,
And all her silken flanks with garlands drest?
35   What little town by river or sea shore,
Or mountain-built with peaceful citadel,
Is emptied of this folk, this pious morn?
And, little town, thy streets for evermore
Will silent be; and not a soul to tell
40   Why thou art desolate, can e'er return.

5

O Attic[5] shape! Fair attitude![6] with brede
Of marble men and maidens overwrought,[7]
With forest branches and the trodden weed;
Thou, silent form, dost tease us out of thought
45   As doth eternity: Cold Pastoral!
When old age shall this generation waste,
Thou shalt remain, in midst of other woe
Than ours, a friend to man, to whom thou say'st,
"Beauty is truth, truth beauty,"[8]—that is all
50   Ye know on earth, and all ye need to know.

1819   1820

Ode on Melancholy   This is Keats's best-known statement of his recurrent theme of the mingled contrarieties of life. The remarkable last stanza, in which Melancholy becomes a veiled goddess worshiped in secret religious rites, implies that it is the tragic human destiny that beauty, joy, and life itself owe not only their quality but their value to the fact that they are transitory and turn into their opposites. Melancholy—a synonym for depression, involving a paralyzing self-consciousness engendered by an excess of thought—is a highly literary and even bookish ailment, as Keats knew. Shakespeare's Hamlet and Milton's speaker in "Il Penseroso" are the

5. Greek. Attica was the region of Greece in which Athens was located.
6. Probably used in its early, technical sense: the pose struck by a figure in statuary or painting.
7. Ornamented all over ("overwrought") with an interwoven pattern ("brede"). The adjective "overwrought" might also modify "maidens" and even "men" and so hint at the emotional anguish of the figures portrayed on the urn.
8. The quotation marks around this phrase are found in the volume of poems Keats published in 1820, but there are no quotation marks in the version printed in *Annals of the Fine Arts* that same year or in the transcripts of the poem made by

Keats's friends. This discrepancy has multiplied the diversity of critical interpretations of the last two lines. Critics disagree whether the whole of these lines is said by the urn, or "Beauty is truth, truth beauty" by the urn and the rest by the lyric speaker; whether the "ye" in the last line is addressed to the lyric speaker, to the readers, to the urn, or to the figures on the urn; whether "all ye know" is that beauty is truth, or this plus the statement in lines 46–48; and whether "beauty is truth" is a profound metaphysical proposition, an overstatement representing the limited point of view of the urn, or simply nonsensical.

disorder's most famous sufferers. Keats was also an admirer of Robert Burton's encyclopedic *Anatomy of Melancholy* (1621).

The poem once had the following initial stanza, which Keats canceled in manuscript:

> Though you should build a bark of dead men's bones,
>   And rear a phantom gibbet for a mast,
> Stitch creeds together for a sail, with groans
>   To fill it out, bloodstained and aghast;
> Although your rudder be a Dragon's tail,
>   Long sever'd, yet still hard with agony,
>   Your cordage large uprootings from the skull
> Of bald Medusa: certes you would fail
>   To find the Melancholy, whether she
>   Dreameth in any isle of Lethe dull.

Ode on Melancholy

1

No, no, go not to Lethe,[1] neither twist
  Wolf's-bane, tight-rooted, for its poisonous wine;
Nor suffer thy pale forehead to be kiss'd
  By nightshade, ruby grape of Proserpine;[2]
5 Make not your rosary of yew-berries,[3]
    Nor let the beetle, nor the death-moth be
    Your mournful Psyche,[4] nor the downy owl
  A partner in your sorrow's mysteries;[5]
    For shade to shade will come too drowsily,
10   And drown the wakeful anguish of the soul.[6]

2

But when the melancholy fit shall fall
  Sudden from heaven like a weeping cloud,
That fosters the droop-headed flowers all,
  And hides the green hill in an April shroud;
15 Then glut thy sorrow on a morning rose,
    Or on the rainbow of the salt sand-wave,
      Or on the wealth of globed peonies;
  Or if thy mistress some rich anger shows,
    Emprison her soft hand, and let her rave,
20   And feed deep, deep upon her peerless eyes.

3

She[7] dwells with Beauty—Beauty that must die;
  And Joy, whose hand is ever at his lips
Bidding adieu; and aching Pleasure nigh,

---

1. The waters of forgetfulness in Hades.
2. The wife of Pluto and queen of the underworld. "Nightshade" and "wolf's-bane" (line 2) are poisonous plants.
3. A symbol of death.
4. In ancient times Psyche (the soul) was sometimes represented as a butterfly or moth, fluttering out of the mouth of a dying man. The allusion may also be to the death's-head moth, which has skull-like markings on its back. The "beetle" of line 6 refers to replicas of the large black beetle, the scarab, which were often placed by Egyptians in their tombs as a symbol of resurrection.
5. Secret rituals.
6. I.e., sorrow needs contrast to sustain its intensity.
7. Usually taken to refer to Melancholy rather than to "thy mistress" in line 18.

Turning to poison while the bee-mouth sips:
25   Ay, in the very temple of Delight
Veil'd Melancholy has her sovran shrine,
    Though seen of none save him whose strenuous tongue
Can burst Joy's grape against his palate fine;[8]
His soul shall taste the sadness of her might,
30   And be among her cloudy trophies hung.[9]

1819   1820

Ode on Indolence[1]

"They toil not, neither do they spin."[2]

I

One morn before me were three figures seen,
    With bowed necks, and joined hands, side-faced;
And one behind the other stepp'd serene,
    In placid sandals, and in white robes graced:
5   They pass'd, like figures on a marble urn,
        When shifted round to see the other side;
            They came again: as when the urn once more
Is shifted round, the first seen shades return;
    And they were strange to me, as may betide
10   With vases, to one deep in Phidian[3] lore.

2

How is it, shadows, that I knew ye not?
    How came ye muffled in so hush a masque?
Was it a silent deep-disguised plot
    To steal away, and leave without a task
15   My idle days? Ripe was the drowsy hour;
        The blissful cloud of summer-indolence
            Benumb'd my eyes; my pulse grew less and less;
Pain had no sting, and pleasure's wreath no flower.
    O, why did ye not melt, and leave my sense
20   Unhaunted quite of all but—nothingness?

3

A third time pass'd they by, and, passing, turn'd
    Each one the face a moment whiles to me;
Then faded, and to follow them I burn'd
    And ached for wings, because I knew the three:
25   The first was a fair maid, and Love her name;

8. Sensitive, refined.
9. A reference to the Greek and Roman practice of hanging trophies in the temples of the gods.
1. On March 19, 1819, Keats wrote to George and Georgiana Keats: "This morning I am in a sort of temper indolent and supremely careless. . . . Neither Poetry, nor Ambition, nor Love have any alertness of countenance as they pass by me: they seem rather like three figures on a greek vase—a Man and two women—whom no one but myself could distinguish in their disguisement. This is the only

happiness; and is a rare instance of advantage in the body overpowering the Mind." The ode was probably written soon after this time, but was not published until 1848, long after the poet's death.
2. Matthew 6.28. Christ's comment on the lilies of the field—a parable justifying those who trust to God rather than worry about how they will feed or clothe themselves.
3. Phidias was the great Athenian sculptor of the 5th century B.C.E. who designed the marble sculptures for the Parthenon.

The second was Ambition, pale of cheek,
   And ever watchful with fatigued eye;
The last, whom I love more, the more of blame
   Is heap'd upon her, maiden most unmeek,—
30   I knew to be my demon[4] Poesy.

4

They faded, and, forsooth! I wanted wings:
   O folly! What is Love? and where is it?
And for that poor Ambition—it springs
   From a man's little heart's short fever-fit;
35 For Poesy!—no,—she has not a joy,—
   At least for me,—so sweet as drowsy noons,
     And evenings steep'd in honied indolence;
O, for an age so shelter'd from annoy,
   That I may never know how change the moons,
40   Or hear the voice of busy common-sense!

5

A third time came they by;—alas! wherefore?
   My sleep had been embroider'd with dim dreams;
My soul had been a lawn besprinkled o'er
   With flowers, and stirring shades, and baffled beams:
45 The morn was clouded, but no shower fell,
   Though in her lids hung the sweet tears of May;
     The open casement press'd a new-leaved vine,
   Let in the budding warmth and throstle's lay;°   *thrush's song*
O shadows! 'twas a time to bid farewell!
50   Upon your skirts had fallen no tears of mine.

6

So, ye three ghosts, adieu! Ye cannot raise
   My head cool-bedded in the flowery grass;
For I would not be dieted with praise,
   A pet-lamb in a sentimental farce![5]
55 Fade softly from my eyes, and be once more
   In masque-like figures on the dreamy urn;
     Farewell! I yet have visions for the night,
And for the day faint visions there is store;
     Vanish, ye phantoms, from my idle spright,°   *spirit*
60 Into the clouds, and never more return!

Spring 1819   1848

Lamia   In a note printed at the end of the poem, Keats cited as his source the
following story in Robert Burton's *Anatomy of Melancholy* (1621):

---

4. Meaning both devil and, as in Greek myth, the
spirit that attends constantly on the human
individual.
5. In a letter of June 9, 1819, Keats wrote: "I have
been very idle lately, very averse to writing; both
from the overpowering idea of our dead poets and

from abatement of my love of fame. I hope I am a
little more of a Philosopher than I was, consequently a little less of a versifying Pet-lamb....
You will judge of my 1819 temper when I tell you
that the thing I have most enjoyed this year has
been writing an ode to Indolence."

One Menippus Lycius, a young man twenty-five years of age, that going betwixt Cenchreas and Corinth, met such a phantasm in the habit of a fair gentlewoman, which, taking him by the hand, carried him home to her house, in the suburbs of Corinth. . . . The young man, a philosopher, otherwise staid and discreet, able to moderate his passions, though not this of love, tarried with her a while to his great content, and at last married her, to whose wedding, amongst other guests, came Apollonius; who, by some probable conjectures, found her out to be a serpent, a lamia; and that all her furniture was, like Tantalus's gold, described by Homer, no substance but mere illusions. When she saw herself descried, she wept, and desired Apollonius to be silent, but he would not be moved, and thereupon she, plate, house, and all that was in it, vanished in an instant: many thousands took notice of this fact, for it was done in the midst of Greece.

In ancient demonology a "lamia" was a monster in woman's form who preyed on human beings. There are various clues that Keats invested the ancient legend with allegorical significance (see especially 2.229–38). Its interpretation, however, and even the inclination of Keats's sympathies in the contest between Lamia and Apollonius, have been disputed. Perhaps Keats simply failed to make up his mind or wavered in the course of composition. In any case the poem presents an inevitably fatal situation, in which no one is entirely blameless or blameworthy and no character monopolizes either our sympathy or our antipathy.

The poem, written between late June and early September 1819, is a return, after the Spenserian stanzas of *The Eve of St. Agnes,* to the pentameter couplets Keats had used in *Endymion* and other early poems. But Keats had in the meantime been studying John Dryden's closed and strong-paced couplets. The initial lines of Dryden's version of Boccaccio's story *Cymon and Iphigenia* demonstrate the kind of narrative model that helped Keats make the technical transition from the fluent but sprawling gracefulness of the opening of *Endymion* to the vigor and economy of the opening of *Lamia:*

> In that sweet isle where Venus keeps her court,
> And every grace, and all the loves, resort;
> Where either sex is formed of softer earth,
> And takes the bent of pleasure from their birth;
> There lived a Cyprian lord, above the rest
> Wise, wealthy, with a numerous issue blessed. . . .

Lamia

Part 1

Upon a time, before the faery broods
Drove Nymph and Satyr[1] from the prosperous woods,
Before King Oberon's bright diadem,
Sceptre, and mantle, clasp'd with dewy gem,
5   Frighted away the Dryads and the Fauns
From rushes green, and brakes,° and cowslip'd lawns,   thickets
The ever-smitten Hermes[2] empty left
His golden throne, bent warm on amorous theft:
From high Olympus had he stolen light,

---

1. Nymphs and satyrs—like the dryads and fauns in line 5—were minor classical deities of the woods and fields, said here to have been driven off by Oberon, king of the fairies, who were supernatural beings of the postclassical era.

2. Or Mercury; wing-footed messenger at the summons of Jove (line 11), Hermes was notoriously amorous.

10 On this side of Jove's clouds, to escape the sight
   Of his great summoner, and made retreat
   Into a forest on the shores of Crete.
   For somewhere in that sacred island dwelt
   A nymph, to whom all hoofed Satyrs knelt;
15 At whose white feet the languid Tritons³ poured
   Pearls, while on land they wither'd and adored.
   Fast by the springs where she to bathe was wont,
   And in those meads where sometime she might haunt,
   Were strewn rich gifts, unknown to any Muse,
20 Though Fancy's casket were unlock'd to choose.
   Ah, what a world of love was at her feet!
   So Hermes thought, and a celestial heat
   Burnt from his winged heels to either ear,
   That from a whiteness, as the lily clear,
25 Blush'd into roses 'mid his golden hair,
   Fallen in jealous curls about his shoulders bare.⁴

   From vale to vale, from wood to wood, he flew,
   Breathing upon the flowers his passion new,
   And wound with many a river to its head,
30 To find where this sweet nymph prepar'd her secret bed:
   In vain; the sweet nymph might nowhere be found,
   And so he rested, on the lonely ground,
   Pensive, and full of painful jealousies
   Of the Wood-Gods, and even the very trees.
35 There as he stood, he heard a mournful voice,
   Such as once heard, in gentle heart, destroys
   All pain but pity: thus the lone voice spake:
   "When from this wreathed tomb shall I awake!
   When move in a sweet body fit for life,
40 And love, and pleasure, and the ruddy strife
   Of hearts and lips! Ah, miserable me!"
   The God, dove-footed,⁵ glided silently
   Round bush and tree, soft-brushing, in his speed,
   The taller grasses and full-flowering weed,
45 Until he found a palpitating snake,
   Bright, and cirque-couchant⁶ in a dusky brake.

   She was a gordian⁷ shape of dazzling hue,
   Vermilion-spotted, golden, green, and blue;
   Striped like a zebra, freckled like a pard,°   *leopard*
50 Eyed like a peacock,⁸ and all crimson barr'd;
   And full of silver moons, that, as she breathed,
   Dissolv'd, or brighter shone, or interwreathed
   Their lustres with the gloomier tapestries—
   So rainbow-sided, touch'd with miseries,

3. Minor sea gods.
4. I.e., the curls clung jealously to his bare shoulders. This line is the first of a number of Alexandrines, a six-foot line, used to vary the metrical movement—a device that Keats learned from Dryden. Another such device is the triplet, occurring first in lines 61–63.

5. I.e., quietly as a dove.
6. Lying in a circular coil. Keats borrows the language of heraldry.
7. Intricately twisted, like the knot tied by King Gordius, which no one could undo.
8. Having multicolored spots, like the "eyes" in a peacock's tail.

55   She seem'd, at once, some penanced lady elf,
       Some demon's mistress, or the demon's self.
       Upon her crest she wore a wannish[9] fire
       Sprinkled with stars, like Ariadne's tiar:[1]
       Her head was serpent, but ah, bitter-sweet!
60   She had a woman's mouth with all its pearls[2] complete:
       And for her eyes: what could such eyes do there
       But weep, and weep, that they were born so fair?
       As Proserpine still weeps for her Sicilian air.[3]
       Her throat was serpent, but the words she spake
65   Came, as through bubbling honey, for Love's sake,
       And thus; while Hermes on his pinions° lay,   *wings*
       Like a stoop'd falcon[4] ere he takes his prey.

       "Fair Hermes, crown'd with feathers, fluttering light,
       I had a splendid dream of thee last night:
70   I saw thee sitting, on a throne of gold,
       Among the Gods, upon Olympus old,
       The only sad one; for thou didst not hear
       The soft, lute-finger'd Muses chaunting clear,
       Nor even Apollo when he sang alone,
75   Deaf to his throbbing throat's long, long melodious moan.
       I dreamt I saw thee, robed in purple flakes,
       Break amorous through the clouds, as morning breaks,
       And, swiftly as a bright Phœbean dart,[5]
       Strike for the Cretan isle; and here thou art!
80   Too gentle Hermes, hast thou found the maid?"
       Whereat the star of Lethe[6] not delay'd
       His rosy eloquence, and thus inquired:
       "Thou smooth-lipp'd serpent, surely high inspired!
       Thou beauteous wreath, with melancholy eyes,
85   Possess whatever bliss thou canst devise,
       Telling me only where my nymph is fled,—
       Where she doth breathe!" "Bright planet, thou hast said,"
       Return'd the snake, "but seal with oaths, fair God!"
       "I swear," said Hermes, "by my serpent rod,
90   And by thine eyes, and by thy starry crown!"
       Light flew his earnest words, among the blossoms blown.
       Then thus again the brilliance feminine:
       "Too frail of heart! for this lost nymph of thine,
       Free as the air, invisibly, she strays
95   About these thornless wilds; her pleasant days
       She tastes unseen; unseen her nimble feet
       Leave traces in the grass and flowers sweet;

9. Rather dark.
1. Ariadne's jeweled wedding crown, or tiara ("tiar"), was given to her by the god Bacchus, who took her as his wife after she was abandoned by her faithless mortal lover Theseus. The crown, transformed into a constellation of stars in the sky, is represented in Titian's *Bacchus and Ariadne*, which Keats had seen when the painting was exhibited in London in 1816. Keats's memories of this painting may also inform his reference to Bacchus's chariot and leopards in "Ode to a Nightingale," line 32.

2. "Pearls" had become almost a synonym for teeth in Elizabethan love poems.
3. Proserpine had been carried off to Hades by Pluto from the field of Enna, in Sicily.
4. *Stoop* is the term for the plunge of a falcon on his prey.
5. A ray of Phoebus Apollo, god of the sun.
6. Hermes, when he appeared like a star on the banks of Lethe, in the darkness of Hades. (One of Hermes' offices was to guide the souls of the dead to the lower regions.)

From weary tendrils, and bow'd branches green,
She plucks the fruit unseen, she bathes unseen:
100 And by my power is her beauty veil'd
To keep it unaffronted, unassail'd
By the love-glances of unlovely eyes,
Of Satyrs, Fauns, and blear'd Silenus'[7] sighs.
Pale grew her immortality, for woe
105 Of all these lovers, and she grieved so
I took compassion on her, bade her steep
Her hair in weïrd° syrops, that would keep   magical
Her loveliness invisible, yet free
To wander as she loves, in liberty.
110 Thou shalt behold her, Hermes, thou alone,
If thou wilt, as thou swearest, grant my boon!"
Then, once again, the charmed God began
An oath, and through the serpent's ears it ran
Warm, tremulous, devout, psalterian.[8]
115 Ravish'd, she lifted her Circean head,
Blush'd a live damask,[9] and swift-lisping said,
"I was a woman, let me have once more
A woman's shape, and charming as before.
I love a youth of Corinth—O the bliss!
120 Give me my woman's form, and place me where he is.
Stoop, Hermes, let me breathe upon thy brow,
And thou shalt see thy sweet nymph even now."
The God on half-shut feathers sank serene,
She breath'd upon his eyes, and swift was seen
125 Of both the guarded nymph near-smiling on the green.
It was no dream; or say a dream it was,
Real are the dreams of Gods, and smoothly pass
Their pleasures in a long immortal dream.
One warm, flush'd moment, hovering, it might seem
130 Dash'd by the wood-nymph's beauty, so he burn'd;
Then, lighting on the printless verdure, turn'd
To the swoon'd serpent, and with languid arm,
Delicate, put to proof the lythe Caducean charm.[1]
So done, upon the nymph his eyes he bent
135 Full of adoring tears and blandishment,
And towards her stept: she, like a moon in wane,
Faded before him, cower'd, nor could restrain
Her fearful sobs, self-folding like a flower
That faints into itself at evening hour:
140 But the God fostering her chilled hand,
She felt the warmth, her eyelids open'd bland,°   softly
And, like new flowers at morning song of bees,
Bloom'd, and gave up her honey to the lees.°   dregs
Into the green-recessed woods they flew;
145 Nor grew they pale, as mortal lovers do.

7. Satyr, a tutor of Bacchus, usually represented as a fat, jolly drunkard.
8. Either "like a psalm" or "like the sound of the psaltery" (an ancient stringed instrument).
9. The color of a damask rose (large and fragrant pink rose). "Circean": like that of Circe, the enchantress in the *Odyssey*.
1. I.e., put to the test the magic of the flexible Caduceus (the name given to Hermes' wand).

Left to herself, the serpent now began
To change; her elfin blood in madness ran,
Her mouth foam'd, and the grass, therewith besprent,°   sprinkled
Wither'd at dew so sweet and virulent;
150 Her eyes in torture fix'd, and anguish drear,
Hot, glaz'd, and wide, with lid-lashes all sear,
Flash'd phosphor and sharp sparks, without one cooling tear.
The colours all inflam'd throughout her train,
She writh'd about, convuls'd with scarlet pain:
155 A deep volcanian yellow took the place
Of all her milder-mooned body's grace;[2]
And, as the lava ravishes the mead,
Spoilt all her silver mail, and golden brede;[3]
Made gloom of all her frecklings, streaks and bars,
160 Eclips'd her crescents, and lick'd up her stars:
So that, in moments few, she was undrest
Of all her sapphires, greens, and amethyst,
And rubious-argent:° of all these bereft,   silvery red
Nothing but pain and ugliness were left.
165 Still shone her crown; that vanish'd, also she
Melted and disappear'd as suddenly;
And in the air, her new voice luting soft,
Cried, "Lycius! gentle Lycius!"—Borne aloft
With the bright mists about the mountains hoar°   white
170 These words dissolv'd: Crete's forests heard no more.

Whither fled Lamia, now a lady bright,
A full-born beauty new and exquisite?
She fled into that valley they pass o'er
Who go to Corinth from Cenchreas' shore;[4]
175 And rested at the foot of those wild hills,
The rugged founts of the Peæran rills,
And of that other ridge whose barren back
Stretches, with all its mist and cloudy rack,
South-westward to Cleone. There she stood
180 About a young bird's flutter from a wood,
Fair, on a sloping green of mossy tread,
By a clear pool, wherein she passioned[5]
To see herself escap'd from so sore ills,
While her robes flaunted with the daffodils.

185 Ah, happy Lycius!—for she was a maid
More beautiful than ever twisted braid,
Or sigh'd, or blush'd, or on spring-flowered lea°   meadow
Spread a green kirtle° to the minstrelsy: gown
A virgin purest lipp'd, yet in the lore
190 Of love deep learned to the red heart's core:
Not one hour old, yet of sciential brain
To unperplex bliss from its neighbour pain;

2. I.e., the yellow of sulfur (thrown up by a volcano) replaced her former silvery moon color.
3. Embroidery, interwoven pattern. "Mail": interlinked rings, as in a coat of armor.
4. Cenchrea (Keats's "Cenchreas") was a harbor of Corinth, in southern Greece.
5. Felt intense excitement.

Define their pettish limits, and estrange
Their points of contact, and swift counterchange;[6]
195 Intrigue with the specious chaos,[7] and dispart
Its most ambiguous atoms with sure art;
As though in Cupid's college she had spent
Sweet days a lovely graduate, still unshent,°   unspoiled
And kept his rosy terms[8] in idle languishment.

200   Why this fair creature chose so fairily
By the wayside to linger, we shall see;
But first 'tis fit to tell how she could muse
And dream, when in the serpent prison-house,
Of all she list,° strange or magnificent: wished
205 How, ever, where she will'd, her spirit went;
Whether to faint Elysium,[9] or where
Down through tress-lifting waves the Nereids[1] fair
Wind into Thetis' bower by many a pearly stair;
Or where God Bacchus drains his cups divine,
210 Stretch'd out, at ease, beneath a glutinous pine;
Or where in Pluto's gardens palatine°   palatial
Mulciber's columns gleam in far piazzian line.[2]
And sometimes into cities she would send
Her dream, with feast and rioting to blend;
215 And once, while among mortals dreaming thus,
She saw the young Corinthian Lycius
Charioting foremost in the envious race,
Like a young Jove with calm uneager face,
And fell into a swooning love of him.
220 Now on the moth-time of that evening dim
He would return that way, as well she knew,
To Corinth from the shore; for freshly blew
The eastern soft wind, and his galley now
Grated the quaystones with her brazen prow
225 In port Cenchreas, from Egina isle
Fresh anchor'd; whither he had been awhile
To sacrifice to Jove, whose temple there
Waits with high marble doors for blood and incense rare.
Jove heard his vows, and better'd his desire;
230 For by some freakful chance he made retire
From his companions, and set forth to walk,
Perhaps grown wearied of their Corinth talk:
Over the solitary hills he fared,
Thoughtless at first, but ere eve's star appeared
235 His phantasy was lost, where reason fades,
In the calm'd twilight of Platonic shades.[3]

---

6. I.e., of knowledgeable ("sciential") brain to dis-entangle ("unperplex") bliss from its closely related pain, to define their quarreled-over ("pettish") lim-its, and to separate out ("estrange") their points of contact and the swift changes of each condition into its opposite. Cf. Keats's "Ode on Melancholy," lines 21–26 (p. 1849).
7. I.e., turn to her own artful purpose the seeming ("specious") chaos.
8. The terms spent studying in "Cupid's college."
9. Region inhabited by the virtuous after death.
1. Sea nymphs, of whom Thetis (line 208, the mother of Achilles) was one.
2. I.e., columns made by Mulciber (Vulcan, god of fire and metalworking) gleam in long lines around open courts (piazzas).
3. I.e., he was absorbed in musing about the obscurities of Plato's philosophy.

Lamia beheld him coming, near, more near—
Close to her passing, in indifference drear,
His silent sandals swept the mossy green;
240 So neighbour'd to him, and yet so unseen
She stood: he pass'd, shut up in mysteries,
His mind wrapp'd like his mantle, while her eyes
Follow'd his steps, and her neck regal white
Turn'd—syllabling thus, "Ah, Lycius bright,
245 And will you leave me on the hills alone?
Lycius, look back! and be some pity shown."
He did; not with cold wonder fearingly,
But Orpheus-like at an Eurydice;[4]
For so delicious were the words she sung,
250 It seem'd he had lov'd them a whole summer long:
And soon his eyes had drunk her beauty up,
Leaving no drop in the bewildering cup,
And still the cup was full,—while he, afraid
Lest she should vanish ere his lip had paid
255 Due adoration, thus began to adore;
Her soft look growing coy, she saw his chain so sure:
"Leave thee alone! Look back! Ah, Goddess, see
Whether my eyes can ever turn from thee!
For pity do not this sad heart belie[5]—
260 Even as thou vanishest so I shall die.
Stay! though a Naiad of the rivers, stay!
To thy far wishes will thy streams obey:
Stay! though the greenest woods be thy domain,
Alone they can drink up the morning rain:
265 Though a descended Pleiad,[6] will not one
Of thine harmonious sisters keep in tune
Thy spheres, and as thy silver proxy shine?
So sweetly to these ravish'd ears of mine
Came thy sweet greeting, that if thou shouldst fade
270 Thy memory will waste me to a shade:—
For pity do not melt!"—"If I should stay,"
Said Lamia, "here, upon this floor of clay,
And pain my steps upon these flowers too rough,
What canst thou say or do of charm enough
275 To dull the nice[7] remembrance of my home?
Thou canst not ask me with thee here to roam
Over these hills and vales, where no joy is,—
Empty of immortality and bliss!
Thou art a scholar, Lycius, and must know
280 That finer spirits cannot breathe below
In human climes, and live: Alas! poor youth,
What taste of purer air hast thou to soothe
My essence? What serener palaces,
Where I may all my many senses please,

4. As Orpheus looked at Eurydice in Hades. Orpheus was allowed by Pluto to lead Eurydice back to Earth on condition that he not look back at her, but he could not resist doing so and hence lost her once more.
5. Be false to.
6. One of the seven sisters composing the constellation Pleiades. The lines that follow allude to the ancient belief that the planets traveled inside crystalline spheres whose movements produced heavenly music.
7. Detailed, minutely accurate.

285 And by mysterious sleights a hundred thirsts appease?
It cannot be—Adieu!" So said, she rose
Tiptoe with white arms spread. He, sick to lose
The amorous promise of her lone complain,
Swoon'd, murmuring of love, and pale with pain.
290 The cruel lady, without any show
Of sorrow for her tender favourite's woe,
But rather, if her eyes could brighter be,
With brighter eyes and slow amenity,°   *pleasure*
Put her new lips to his, and gave afresh
295 The life she had so tangled in her mesh:
And as he from one trance was wakening
Into another, she began to sing,
Happy in beauty, life, and love, and every thing,
A song of love, too sweet for earthly lyres,
300 While, like held breath, the stars drew in their panting fires.
And then she whisper'd in such trembling tone,
As those who, safe together met alone
For the first time through many anguish'd days,
Use other speech than looks; bidding him raise
305 His drooping head, and clear his soul of doubt,
For that she was a woman, and without
Any more subtle fluid in her veins
Than throbbing blood, and that the self-same pains
Inhabited her frail-strung heart as his.
310 And next she wonder'd how his eyes could miss
Her face so long in Corinth, where, she said,
She dwelt but half retir'd, and there had led
Days happy as the gold coin could invent
Without the aid of love; yet in content
315 Till she saw him, as once she pass'd him by,
Where 'gainst a column he leant thoughtfully
At Venus' temple porch, 'mid baskets heap'd
Of amorous herbs and flowers, newly reap'd
Late on that eve, as 'twas the night before
320 The Adonian feast;[8] whereof she saw no more,
But wept alone those days, for why should she adore?
Lycius from death awoke into amaze,
To see her still, and singing so sweet lays;
Then from amaze into delight he fell
325 To hear her whisper woman's lore so well;
And every word she spake entic'd him on
To unperplex'd delight[9] and pleasure known.
Let the mad poets say whate'er they please
Of the sweets of Fairies, Peris,[1] Goddesses,
330 There is not such a treat among them all,
Haunters of cavern, lake, and waterfall,
As a real woman, lineal indeed
From Pyrrha's pebbles[2] or old Adam's seed.
Thus gentle Lamia judg'd, and judg'd aright,

8. The feast of Adonis, beloved by Venus.
9. I.e., delight not mixed with its neighbor, pain (see line 192).
1. Fairylike creatures in Persian mythology.

2. Descended from the pebbles with which, in Greek myth, Pyrrha and Deucalion repeopled the earth after the flood.

335 That Lycius could not love in half a fright,
     So threw the goddess off, and won his heart
     More pleasantly by playing woman's part,
     With no more awe than what her beauty gave,
     That, while it smote, still guaranteed to save.
340 Lycius to all made eloquent reply,
     Marrying to every word a twinborn sigh;
     And last, pointing to Corinth, ask'd her sweet,
     If 'twas too far that night for her soft feet.
     The way was short, for Lamia's eagerness
345 Made, by a spell, the triple league decrease
     To a few paces; not at all surmised
     By blinded Lycius, so in her comprized.[3]
     They pass'd the city gates, he knew not how,
     So noiseless, and he never thought to know.

350   As men talk in a dream, so Corinth all,
     Throughout her palaces imperial,
     And all her populous streets and temples lewd,[4]
     Mutter'd, like tempest in the distance brew'd,
     To the wide-spreaded night above her towers.
355 Men, women, rich and poor, in the cool hours,
     Shuffled their sandals o'er the pavement white,
     Companion'd or alone; while many a light
     Flared, here and there, from wealthy festivals,
     And threw their moving shadows on the walls,
360 Or found them cluster'd in the corniced shade
     Of some arch'd temple door, or dusky colonnade.

         Muffling his face, of greeting friends in fear,
     Her fingers he press'd hard, as one came near
     With curl'd gray beard, sharp eyes, and smooth bald crown,
365 Slow-stepp'd, and robed in philosophic gown:
     Lycius shrank closer, as they met and past,
     Into his mantle, adding wings to haste,
     While hurried Lamia trembled: "Ah," said he,
     "Why do you shudder, love, so ruefully?
370 Why does your tender palm dissolve in dew?"—
     "I'm wearied," said fair Lamia: "tell me who
     Is that old man? I cannot bring to mind
     His features:—Lycius! wherefore did you blind
     Yourself from his quick eyes?" Lycius replied,
375 " 'Tis Apollonius sage, my trusty guide
     And good instructor; but to-night he seems
     The ghost of folly haunting my sweet dreams."

         While yet he spake they had arrived before
     A pillar'd porch, with lofty portal door,
380 Where hung a silver lamp, whose phosphor glow

---

3. Bound up, absorbed.
4. Temples of Venus, whose worship sometimes involved ritual prostitution. The city of Corinth was notorious in antiquity as a site of commerce and prostitution.

Reflected in the slabbed steps below,
Mild as a star in water; for so new,
And so unsullied was the marble hue,
So through the crystal polish, liquid fine,
385   Ran the dark veins, that none but feet divine
Could e'er have touch'd there. Sounds Æolian[5]
Breath'd from the hinges, as the ample span
Of the wide doors disclos'd a place unknown
Some time to any, but those two alone,
390   And a few Persian mutes, who that same year
Were seen about the markets: none knew where
They could inhabit; the most curious
Were foil'd, who watch'd to trace them to their house:
And but the flitter-winged verse must tell,
395   For truth's sake, what woe afterwards befel,
'Twould humour many a heart to leave them thus,
Shut from the busy world of more incredulous.

Part 2

Love in a hut, with water and a crust,
Is—Love, forgive us!—cinders, ashes, dust;
Love in a palace is perhaps at last
More grievous torment than a hermit's fast:—
5   That is a doubtful tale from faery land,
Hard for the non-elect to understand.
Had Lycius liv'd to hand his story down,
He might have given the moral a fresh frown,
Or clench'd it quite: but too short was their bliss
10   To breed distrust and hate, that make the soft voice hiss.
Besides, there, nightly, with terrific glare,
Love, jealous grown of so complete a pair,
Hover'd and buzz'd his wings, with fearful roar,
Above the lintel of their chamber door,
15   And down the passage cast a glow upon the floor.

    For all this came a ruin: side by side
They were enthroned, in the even tide,
Upon a couch, near to a curtaining
Whose airy texture, from a golden string,
20   Floated into the room, and let appear
Unveil'd the summer heaven, blue and clear,
Betwixt two marble shafts:—there they reposed,
Where use had made it sweet, with eyelids closed,
Saving a tythe which love still open kept,
25   That they might see each other while they almost slept;
When from the slope side of a suburb hill,
Deafening the swallow's twitter, came a thrill
Of trumpets—Lycius started—the sounds fled,
But left a thought, a buzzing in his head.
30   For the first time, since first he harbour'd in

5. Like sounds from the wind harp (Aeolus is god of winds), which responds musically to a current of air.

That purple-lined palace of sweet sin,
His spirit pass'd beyond its golden bourn°   *boundary*
Into the noisy world almost forsworn.
The lady, ever watchful, penetrant,
35 Saw this with pain, so arguing a want
Of something more, more than her empery°   *empire*
Of joys; and she began to moan and sigh
Because he mused beyond her, knowing well
That but a moment's thought is passion's passing bell.°   *death knell*
40 "Why do you sigh, fair creature?" whisper'd he:
"Why do you think?" return'd she tenderly:
"You have deserted me;—where am I now?
Not in your heart while care weighs on your brow:
No, no, you have dismiss'd me; and I go
45 From your breast houseless: ay, it must be so."
He answer'd, bending to her open eyes,
Where he was mirror'd small in paradise,
"My silver planet, both of eve and morn!⁶
Why will you plead yourself so sad forlorn,
50 While I am striving how to fill my heart
With deeper crimson, and a double smart?
How to entangle, trammel up and snare
Your soul in mine, and labyrinth you there
Like the hid scent in an unbudded rose?
55 Ay, a sweet kiss—you see your mighty woes.⁷
My thoughts! shall I unveil them? Listen then!
What mortal hath a prize, that other men
May be confounded and abash'd withal,
But lets it sometimes pace abroad majestical,
60 And triumph, as in thee I should rejoice
Amid the hoarse alarm of Corinth's voice.
Let my foes choke, and my friends shout afar,
While through the thronged streets your bridal car°   *chariot*
Wheels round its dazzling spokes."—The lady's cheek
65 Trembled; she nothing said, but, pale and meek,
Arose and knelt before him, wept a rain
Of sorrows at his words; at last with pain
Beseeching him, the while his hand she wrung,
To change his purpose. He thereat was stung,
70 Perverse, with stronger fancy to reclaim
Her wild and timid nature to his aim:
Besides, for all his love, in self despite,
Against his better self, he took delight
Luxurious in her sorrows, soft and new.
75 His passion, cruel grown, took on a hue
Fierce and sanguineous as 'twas possible
In one whose brow had no dark veins to swell.
Fine was the mitigated fury, like
Apollo's presence when in act to strike
80 The serpent—Ha, the serpent! certes, she

6. The planet Venus, which is both the morning
and the evening star.

7. Playfully: "You see how great your troubles
were!"

Was none. She burnt, she lov'd the tyranny,
And, all subdued, consented to the hour
When to the bridal he should lead his paramour.
Whispering in midnight silence, said the youth,

85   "Sure some sweet name thou hast, though, by my truth,
I have not ask'd it, ever thinking thee
Not mortal, but of heavenly progeny,
As still I do. Hast any mortal name,
Fit appellation for this dazzling frame?

90   Or friends or kinsfolk on the citied earth,
To share our marriage feast and nuptial mirth?"
"I have no friends," said Lamia, "no, not one;
My presence in wide Corinth hardly known:
My parents' bones are in their dusty urns

95   Sepulchred, where no kindled incense burns,
Seeing all their luckless race are dead, save me,
And I neglect the holy rite for thee.
Even as you list invite your many guests;
But if, as now it seems, your vision rests

100 With any pleasure on me, do not bid
Old Apollonius—from him keep me hid."
Lycius, perplex'd at words so blind and blank,
Made close inquiry; from whose touch she shrank,
Feigning a sleep; and he to the dull shade

105 Of deep sleep in a moment was betray'd.

    It was the custom then to bring away,
The bride from home at blushing shut of day,
Veil'd, in a chariot, heralded along
By strewn flowers, torches, and a marriage song,

110 With other pageants: but this fair unknown
Had not a friend. So being left alone,
(Lycius was gone to summon all his kin)
And knowing surely she could never win
His foolish heart from its mad pompousness,

115 She set herself, high-thoughted, how to dress
The misery in fit magnificence.
She did so, but 'tis doubtful how and whence
Came, and who were her subtle servitors.
About the halls, and to and from the doors,

120 There was a noise of wings, till in short space
The glowing banquet-room shone with wide-arched grace.
A haunting music, sole perhaps and lone
Supportress of the faery-roof, made moan
Throughout, as fearful the whole charm might fade.

125 Fresh carved cedar, mimicking a glade
Of palm and plantain, met from either side,
High in the midst, in honour of the bride:
Two palms and then two plantains, and so on,
From either side their stems branch'd one to one

130 All down the aisled place; and beneath all
There ran a stream of lamps straight on from wall to wall.
So canopied, lay an untasted feast

Teeming with odours. Lamia, regal drest,
Silently paced about, and as she went,
135 In pale contented sort of discontent,
Mission'd her viewless° servants to enrich   *invisible*
The fretted[8] splendour of each nook and niche.
Between the tree-stems, marbled plain at first,
Came jasper pannels; then, anon, there burst
140 Forth creeping imagery of slighter trees,
And with the larger wove in small intricacies.
Approving all, she faded at self-will,
And shut the chamber up, close, hush'd and still,
Complete and ready for the revels rude,
145 When dreadful° guests would come to spoil her solitude.   *terrifying*

The day appear'd, and all the gossip rout.
O senseless Lycius! Madman! wherefore flout
The silent-blessing fate, warm cloister'd hours,
And show to common eyes these secret bowers?
150 The herd approach'd; each guest, with busy brain,
Arriving at the portal, gaz'd amain,°   *intently*
And enter'd marveling: for they knew the street,
Remember'd it from childhood all complete
Without a gap, yet ne'er before had seen
155 That royal porch, that high-built fair demesne;°   *estate*
So in they hurried all, maz'd, curious and keen:
Save one, who look'd thereon with eye severe,
And with calm-planted steps walk'd in austere;
'Twas Apollonius: something too he laugh'd,
160 As though some knotty problem, that had daft°   *baffled*
His patient thought, had now begun to thaw,
And solve and melt:—'twas just as he foresaw.

He met within the murmurous vestibule
His young disciple. " 'Tis no common rule,
165 Lycius," said he, "for uninvited guest
To force himself upon you, and infest
With an unbidden presence the bright throng
Of younger friends; yet must I do this wrong,
And you forgive me." Lycius blush'd, and led
170 The old man through the inner doors broad-spread;
With reconciling words and courteous mien°   *appearance*
Turning into sweet milk the sophist's° spleen.   *scholar's*

Of wealthy lustre was the banquet-room,
Fill'd with pervading brilliance and perfume:
175 Before each lucid pannel fuming stood
A censer fed with myrrh and spiced wood,
Each by a sacred tripod held aloft,
Whose slender feet wide-swerv'd upon the soft
Wool-woofed° carpets: fifty wreaths of smoke   *woven*
180 From fifty censers their light voyage took
To the high roof, still mimick'd as they rose

---

8. Adorned with fretwork (interlaced patterns).

Along the mirror'd walls by twin-clouds odorous.
Twelve sphered tables, by silk seats insphered,
High as the level of a man's breast rear'd
185 On libbard's° paws, upheld the heavy gold   *leopard's*
Of cups and goblets, and the store thrice told
Of Ceres' horn,[9] and, in huge vessels, wine
Come from the gloomy tun with merry shine.
Thus loaded with a feast the tables stood,
190 Each shrining in the midst the image of a God.

    When in an antichamber every guest
Had felt the cold full sponge to pleasure press'd,
By minist'ring slaves, upon his hands and feet,
And fragrant oils with ceremony meet°   *suitable*
195 Pour'd on his hair, they all mov'd to the feast
In white robes, and themselves in order placed
Around the silken couches, wondering
Whence all this mighty cost and blaze of wealth could spring.

    Soft went the music the soft air along,
200 While fluent Greek a vowel'd undersong
Kept up among the guests, discoursing low
At first, for scarcely was the wine at flow;
But when the happy vintage touch'd their brains,
Louder they talk, and louder come the strains
205 Of powerful instruments:—the gorgeous dyes,
The space, the splendour of the draperies,
The roof of awful richness, nectarous cheer,
Beautiful slaves, and Lamia's self, appear,
Now, when the wine has done its rosy deed,
210 And every soul from human trammels freed,
No more so strange; for merry wine, sweet wine,
Will make Elysian shades not too fair, too divine.

    Soon was God Bacchus at meridian height;
Flush'd were their cheeks, and bright eyes double bright:
215 Garlands of every green, and every scent
From vales deflower'd, or forest-trees branch-rent,
In baskets of bright osier'd[1] gold were brought
High as the handles heap'd, to suit the thought
Of every guest; that each, as he did please,
220 Might fancy-fit his brows, silk-pillow'd at his ease.

    What wreath for Lamia? What for Lycius?
What for the sage, old Apollonius?
Upon her aching forehead be there hung
The leaves of willow and of adder's tongue;[2]
225 And for the youth, quick, let us strip for him
The thyrsus,[3] that his watching eyes may swim
Into forgetfulness; and, for the sage,

9. The horn of plenty, overflowing with the products of Ceres, goddess of grain.
1. Plaited. An "osier" is a strip of willow used in weaving baskets.

2. A fern whose spikes resemble a serpent's tongue.
3. The vine-covered staff of Bacchus, used to signify drunkenness.

Let spear-grass and the spiteful thistle wage
War on his temples. Do not all charms fly
230 At the mere touch of cold philosophy?⁴
There was an awful° rainbow once in heaven: *awe-inspiring*
We know her woof, her texture; she is given
In the dull catalogue of common things.
Philosophy will clip an Angel's wings,
235 Conquer all mysteries by rule and line,
Empty the haunted air, and gnomed mine⁵—
Unweave a rainbow, as it erewhile made
The tender-person'd Lamia melt into a shade.

By her glad Lycius sitting, in chief place,
240 Scarce saw in all the room another face,
Till, checking his love trance, a cup he took
Full brimm'd, and opposite sent forth a look
'Cross the broad table, to beseech a glance
From his old teacher's wrinkled countenance,
245 And pledge⁶ him. The bald-head philosopher
Had fix'd his eye, without a twinkle or stir
Full on the alarmed beauty of the bride,
Brow-beating her fair form, and troubling her sweet pride.
Lycius then press'd her hand, with devout touch,
250 As pale it lay upon the rosy couch:
'Twas icy, and the cold ran through his veins;
Then sudden it grew hot, and all the pains
Of an unnatural heat shot to his heart.
"Lamia, what means this? Wherefore dost thou start?
255 Know'st thou that man?" Poor Lamia answer'd not.
He gaz'd into her eyes, and not a jot
Own'd° they the lovelorn piteous appeal: *acknowledged*
More, more he gaz'd: his human senses reel:
Some hungry spell that loveliness absorbs;
260 There was no recognition in those orbs.
"Lamia!" he cried—and no soft-toned reply.
The many heard, and the loud revelry
Grew hush; the stately music no more breathes;
The myrtle⁷ sicken'd in a thousand wreaths.
265 By faint degrees, voice, lute, and pleasure ceased;
A deadly silence step by step increased,
Until it seem'd a horrid presence there,
And not a man but felt the terror in his hair.
"Lamia!" he shriek'd; and nothing but the shriek
270 With its sad echo did the silence break.
"Begone, foul dream!" he cried, gazing again
In the bride's face, where now no azure vein
Wander'd on fair-spaced temples; no soft bloom
Misted the cheek; no passion to illume

---

4. In the sense of "natural philosophy," or science. Benjamin Haydon tells in his *Autobiography* how, at a hard-drinking and high-spirited dinner party, Keats had agreed with Charles Lamb (to what extent jokingly, it is not clear) that Newton's *Optics* "had destroyed all the poetry of the rainbow by reducing it to the prismatic colors."
5. Gnomes were guardians of mines.
6. Drink a toast to.
7. Sacred to Venus, hence an emblem of love.

275 The deep-recessed vision:—all was blight;
Lamia, no longer fair, there sat a deadly white.
"Shut, shut those juggling[8] eyes, thou ruthless man!
Turn them aside, wretch! or the righteous ban
Of all the Gods, whose dreadful images
280 Here represent their shadowy presences,
May pierce them on the sudden with the thorn
Of painful blindness; leaving thee forlorn,
In trembling dotage to the feeblest fright
Of conscience, for their long offended might,
285 For all thine impious proud-heart sophistries,
Unlawful magic, and enticing lies.
Corinthians! look upon that gray-beard wretch!
Mark how, possess'd, his lashless eyelids stretch
Around his demon eyes! Corinthians, see!
290 My sweet bride withers at their potency."
"Fool!" said the sophist, in an under-tone
Gruff with contempt; which a death-nighing moan
From Lycius answer'd, as heart-struck and lost,
He sank supine beside the aching ghost.
295 "Fool! Fool!" repeated he, while his eyes still
Relented not, nor mov'd; "from every ill
Of life have I preserv'd thee to this day,
And shall I see thee made a serpent's prey?"
Then Lamia breath'd death breath; the sophist's eye,
300 Like a sharp spear, went through her utterly,
Keen, cruel, perceant,° stinging: she, as well   *piercing*
As her weak hand could any meaning tell,
Motion'd him to be silent; vainly so,
He look'd and look'd again a level—No!
305 "A Serpent!" echoed he; no sooner said,
Than with a frightful scream she vanished:
And Lycius' arms were empty of delight,
As were his limbs of life, from that same night.
On the high couch he lay!—his friends came round—
310 Supported him—no pulse, or breath they found,
And, in its marriage robe, the heavy body wound.

July–Aug. 1819   1820

To Autumn[1]

I

Season of mists and mellow fruitfulness,
    Close bosom-friend of the maturing sun;
    Conspiring with him how to load and bless

8. Deceiving, full of trickery.
1. Two days after this ode was composed, Keats wrote to J. H. Reynolds: "I never liked stubble fields so much as now—Aye, better than the chilly green of the spring. Somehow a stubble plain looks warm—in the same way that some pictures look warm—this struck me so much in my Sunday's walk that I composed upon it." For the author's revisions while composing "To Autumn," see "Poems in Process," in the appendices to this volume.

With fruit the vines that round the thatch-eves run;
5 To bend with apples the moss'd cottage-trees,
    And fill all fruit with ripeness to the core;
        To swell the gourd, and plump the hazel shells
    With a sweet kernel; to set budding more,
    And still more, later flowers for the bees,
10 Until they think warm days will never cease,
        For summer has o'er-brimm'd their clammy cells.

2

Who hath not seen thee oft amid thy store?
    Sometimes whoever seeks abroad may find
Thee sitting careless on a granary floor,
15   Thy hair soft-lifted by the winnowing² wind;
Or on a half-reap'd furrow sound asleep,
    Drows'd with the fume of poppies, while thy hook°   scythe
        Spares the next swath and all its twined flowers:
And sometimes like a gleaner thou dost keep
20   Steady thy laden head across a brook;
    Or by a cyder-press, with patient look,
        Thou watchest the last oozings hours by hours.

3

Where are the songs of spring? Ay, where are they?
    Think not of them, thou hast thy music too,—
25 While barred clouds bloom the soft-dying day,
    And touch the stubble-plains with rosy hue;
Then in a wailful choir the small gnats mourn
    Among the river sallows,° borne aloft   willows
        Or sinking as the light wind lives or dies;
30 And full-grown lambs loud bleat from hilly bourn;°   region
    Hedge-crickets sing; and now with treble soft
    The red-breast whistles from a garden-croft;³
        And gathering swallows twitter in the skies.

Sept. 19, 1819   1820

Letters

Letters   Keats's letters serve as a running commentary on his life, reading, thinking, and writing. They are, in his career, the equivalent of the essays, prefaces, and
defenses of poetry produced by his contemporaries. His early reputation as a poet of
pure luxury, sensation, and art for art's sake has undergone a radical change since,
in the twentieth century, critics began to pay close attention to the letters. For Keats
thought hard and persistently about life and art, and any seed of an ethical or critical
idea that he picked up from his contemporaries (in particular, Hazlitt, Coleridge,
Wordsworth) instantly germinated and flourished in the rich soil of his imagination.
What T. S. Eliot said about the Metaphysical poets applies to Keats in his letters: his
"mode of feeling was directly and freshly altered by [his] reading and thought." And
like Donne, he looked not only into the heart but, literally, "into the cerebral cortex,
the nervous system, and the digestive tract." A number of Keats's casual comments
on the poet and on poetry included here—especially those dealing with "negative

2. To "winnow" is to fan the chaff from the grain.   3. An enclosed plot of farmland.

capability" and the kind of imaginative identification with someone or something outside ourselves that we now call empathy—have become standard points of reference in aesthetic theory. But Keats regarded nothing that he said as final; each statement constituted only a stage in his continuing exploration into what he called "the mystery."

The text printed here is that of the edition of the *Letters* by Hyder E. Rollins (1958), which reproduces the original manuscripts precisely.

LETTERS

To Benjamin Bailey[1]

[THE AUTHENTICITY OF THE IMAGINATION]

[November 22, 1817]

My dear Bailey,

* * * O I wish I was as certain of the end of all your troubles as that of your momentary start about the authenticity of the Imagination. I am certain of nothing but of the holiness of the Heart's affections and the truth of Imagination—What the imagination seizes as Beauty must be truth[2]—whether it existed before or not—for I have the same Idea of all our Passions as of Love they are all in their sublime, creative of essential Beauty—In a Word, you may know my favorite Speculation by my first Book and the little song[3] I sent in my last—which is a representation from the fancy of the probable mode of operating in these Matters—The Imagination may be compared to Adam's dream[4]—he awoke and found it truth. I am the more zealous in this affair, because I have never yet been able to perceive how any thing can be known for truth by consequitive reasoning[5]—and yet it must be—Can it be that even the greatest Philosopher ever when arrived at his goal without putting aside numerous objections—However it may be, O for a Life of Sensations[6] rather than of Thoughts! It is "a Vision in the form of Youth" a Shadow of reality to come—and this consideration has further conv[i]nced me for it has come as auxiliary to another favorite Speculation of mine, that we shall enjoy ourselves here after by having what we called happiness on Earth repeated in a finer tone and so repeated[7]—And yet such a fate can only befall those who delight in sensation rather than hunger as you do after Truth—Adam's dream will do here and seems to be a conviction that Imagination and its empyreal[8] reflection is the same as human Life and its spiritual repetition. But as I was saying— the simple imaginative Mind may have its rewards in the repeti[ti]on of its

---

1. One of Keats's closest friends. Keats had stayed with him the month before at Oxford, where Bailey was an undergraduate.
2. At the close of "Ode on a Grecian Urn," Keats also grapples with these categories. Where Keats uses "truth" we might substitute the words *real* or *reality*.
3. The song was "O Sorrow," from book 4 of *Endymion*.
4. In Milton's *Paradise Lost* 8.452–90 Adam dreams that Eve has been created and awakes to

find her real. Adam also describes an earlier prefigurative dream in the same work, 8.283–311.
5. Consecutive reasoning—reasoning that moves by logical steps.
6. Probably not only sense experiences but also the intuitive perceptions of truths, as opposed to truth achieved by consecutive reasoning.
7. Cf. the "Pleasure Thermometer" in *Endymion* 1.777ff. (p. 1827).
8. Heavenly.

own silent Working coming continually on the spirit with a fine suddenness—
to compare great things with small—have you never by being surprised with
an old Melody—in a delicious place—by a delicious voice, fe[l]t over again
your very speculations and surmises at the time it first operated on your soul—
do you not remember forming to yourself the singer's face more beautiful
[than] it was possible and yet with the elevation of the Moment you did not
think so—even then you were mounted on the Wings of Imagination so high—
that the Prototype must be here after—that delicious face you will see—What
a time! I am continually running away from the subject—sure this cannot be
exactly the case with a complex Mind—one that is imaginative and at the same
time careful of its fruits—who would exist partly on sensation partly on
thought—to whom it is necessary that years should bring the philosophic
Mind[9]—such an one I consider your's and therefore it is necessary to your
eternal Happiness that you not only drink this old Wine of Heaven which I
shall call the redigestion of our most ethereal Musings on Earth; but also
increase in knowledge and know all things. I am glad to hear you are in a fair
Way for Easter—you will soon get through your unpleasant reading and
then!—but the world is full of troubles and I have not much reason to think
myself pesterd with many—I think Jane or Marianne has a better opinion of
me than I deserve—for really and truly I do not think my Brothers illness
connected with mine—you know more of the real Cause than they do—nor
have I any chance of being rack'd as you have been[1]—you perhaps at one time
thought there was such a thing as Worldly Happiness to be arrived at, at
certain periods of time marked out—you have of necessity from your disposition been thus led away—I scarcely remember counting upon any Happiness—I look not for it if it be not in the present hour—nothing startles me
beyond the Moment. The setting sun will always set me to rights—or if a
Sparrow come before my Window I take part in its existence and pick about
the Gravel. The first thing that strikes me on hea[r]ing a Misfortune having
befalled another is this. "Well it cannot be helped.—he will have the pleasure
of trying the resourses of his spirit, and I beg now my dear Bailey that hereafter should you observe any thing cold in me not to [put] it to the account
of heartlessness but abstraction—for I assure you I sometimes feel not the
influence of a Passion or Affection during a whole week—and so long this
sometimes continues I begin to suspect myself and the genuiness of my
feelings at other times—thinking them a few barren Tragedy-tears. * * *

Your affectionate friend
John Keats—

9. An echo of Wordsworth, "Ode: Intimations of
Immortality," line 187.
1. Keats's friends Jane and Mariane Reynolds
feared that his ill health at this time threatened
tuberculosis, from which his brother Tom was suffering. Bailey had recently experienced pain (been
"racked") because of an unsuccessful love affair.

To George and Thomas Keats

[NEGATIVE CAPABILITY]

[December 21, 27 (?), 1817]

My dear Brothers

I must crave your pardon for not having written ere this. * * * I spent Friday evening with Wells[1] & went the next morning to see *Death on the Pale horse*. It is a wonderful picture, when West's[2] age is considered; But there is nothing to be intense upon; no women one feels mad to kiss; no face swelling into reality. the excellence of every Art is its intensity, capable of making all disagreeables evaporate, from their being in close relationship with Beauty & Truth[3]—Examine King Lear & you will find this examplified throughout; but in this picture we have unpleasantness without any momentous depth of speculation excited, in which to bury its repulsiveness—The picture is larger than Christ rejected—I dined with Haydon[4] the sunday after you left, & had a very pleasant day, I dined too (for I have been out too much lately) with Horace Smith & met his two Brothers with Hill & Kingston & one Du Bois,[5] they only served to convince me, how superior humour is to wit in respect to enjoyment—These men say things which make one start, without making one feel, they are all alike; their manners are alike; they all know fashionables; they have a mannerism in their very eating & drinking, in their mere handling a Decanter—They talked of Kean[6] & his low company—Would I were with that company instead of yours said I to myself! I know such like acquaintance will never do for me & yet I am going to Reynolds, on wednesday—Brown & Dilke[7] walked with me & back from the Christmas pantomime.[8] I had not a dispute but a disquisition with Dilke, on various subjects; several things dovetailed in my mind, & at once it struck me, what quality went to form a Man of Achievement especially in Literature & which Shakespeare possessed so enormously— I mean *Negative Capability*,[9] that is when man is capable of being in uncertainties, Mysteries, doubts, without any irritable reaching after fact & reason— Coleridge, for instance, would let go by a fine isolated verisimilitude caught from the Penetralium[1] of mystery, from being incapable of remaining content

---

1. Charles Wells, a former schoolmate of Tom Keats.
2. Benjamin West (1738–1820), painter of historical pictures, was an American who moved to England and became president of the Royal Academy. The *Christ Rejected* mentioned a few sentences farther on is also by West.
3. Keats's solution to a problem at least as old as Aristotle's *Poetics*: why do we take pleasure in the aesthetic representation of a subject that in life would be ugly or painful?
4. Keats's close friend Benjamin Haydon, painter of large-scale historical and religious pictures.
5. Smith was one of the best-known literary wits of the day; the others mentioned were men of letters or of literary interests.
6. Edmund Kean, noted Shakespearean actor. His popularity in the early 19th century was contentious because he made no secret of his humble class origins. Keats had written an article on Kean for the *Champion*.
7. Charles Armitage Brown, John Hamilton Reyn-

olds, and Charles Wentworth Dilke were all writers and friends of Keats. Keats interrupted the writing of this letter after the dash; beginning with "Brown & Dilke" he is writing several days after the preceding sentences.
8. Christmas pantomimes were performed each year at Drury Lane and Covent Garden theaters.
9. This famous and elusive phrase has been much discussed. Keats coins it so as to distinguish between, on the one hand, a poetry that is evidently shaped by the writer's personal interests and beliefs and, on the other hand, a poetry of impersonality that records the writer's receptivity to the "uncertainties" of experience. This second kind of poetry, in which a sense of beauty overcomes considerations of truth versus falsehood, is that produced by the poet of "negative capability." Cf. Keats's dislike, in his letter to John Hamilton Reynolds, February 3, 1818, of "poetry that has a palpable design upon us" (p. 1872).
1. The Latin *penetralia* signified the innermost and most secret parts of a temple.

with half knowledge. This pursued through Volumes would perhaps take us no further than this, that with a great poet the sense of Beauty overcomes every other consideration, or rather obliterates all consideration.

Shelley's poem[2] is out & there are words about its being objected too, as much as Queen Mab was. Poor Shelley I think he has his Quota of good qualities, in sooth la!! Write soon to your most sincere friend & affectionate Brother

John

To John Hamilton Reynolds[1]

[WORDSWORTH'S POETRY]

[February 3, 1818]

My dear Reynolds,

* * * It may be said that we ought to read our Contemporaries. that Wordsworth &c should have their due from us. but for the sake of a few fine imaginative or domestic passages, are we to be bullied into a certain Philosophy engendered in the whims of an Egotist—Every man has his speculations, but every man does not brood and peacock over them till he makes a false coinage and deceives himself—Many a man can travel to the very bourne[2] of Heaven, and yet want confidence to put down his halfseeing. Sancho[3] will invent a Journey heavenward as well as any body. We hate poetry that has a palpable design upon us—and if we do not agree, seems to put its hand in its breeches pocket.[4] Poetry should be great & unobtrusive, a thing which enters into one's soul, and does not startle it or amaze it with itself but with its subject.—How beautiful are the retired flowers! how would they lose their beauty were they to throng into the highway crying out, "admire me I am a violet! dote upon me I am a primrose! Modern poets differ from the Elizabethans in this. Each of the moderns like an Elector of Hanover governs his petty state, & knows how many straws are swept daily from the Causeways in all his dominions & has a continual itching that all the Housewives should have their coppers well scoured: the antients were ~~Emperors of large~~ Emperors of vast Provinces, they had only heard of the remote ones and scarcely cared to visit them.—I will cut all this—I will have no more of Wordsworth or Hunt[5] in particular—Why should we be of the tribe of Manasseh, when we can wander with Esau?[6] why should we kick against the Pricks, when we can walk on Roses? Why should we be owls, when we can be Eagles? Why be teased with "nice Eyed wagtails," when we have in sight "the Cherub Contemplation"?[7]—Why with Wordsworths "Matthew with

---

2. *Laon and Cythna* (1817), whose treatment of incest created scandal and which had to be withdrawn by the author. Shelley revised and republished it as *The Revolt of Islam* (1818). In *Queen Mab* (1813) Shelley had presented a radical program for the achievement of a millennial earthly state through the elimination of "kings, priests, and statesmen."
1. A close friend who was at this time an insurance clerk and also an able poet and man of letters.
2. Boundary.
3. Sancho Panza, the earthy squire in Cervantes's

Don Quixote.
4. I.e., sulks and refuses to interact with.
5. Leigh Hunt, a poet who earlier had strongly influenced Keats's style.
6. I.e., why should we carry on a conventional way of life (as did the tribe of Manasseh in Old Testament history) when we can become adventurers (like Esau, who sold his birthright in Genesis 25.29–34 and became an outlaw).
7. Milton, "Il Penseroso," line 54. "Nice Eyed wagtails": from Hunt's *Nymphs.*

a bough of wilding in his hand" when we can have Jacques "under an oak &c"[8]—The secret of the Bough of Wilding will run through your head faster than I can write it—Old Matthew spoke to him some years ago on some nothing, & because he happens in an Evening Walk to imagine the figure of the old man—he must stamp it down in black & white, and it is henceforth sacred—I don't mean to deny Wordsworth's grandeur & Hunt's merit, but I mean to say we need not be teazed with grandeur & merit—when we can have them uncontaminated & unobtrusive. Let us have the old Poets, & robin Hood[9] Your letter and its sonnets gave me more pleasure than will the 4th Book of Childe Harold[1] & the whole of any body's life & opinions. * * *

Y[r] sincere friend and Coscribbler

John Keats.

To John Taylor[1]

[KEATS'S AXIOMS IN POETRY]

[February 27, 1818]

My dear Taylor,

Your alteration strikes me as being a great improvement—the page looks much better. * * * It is a sorry thing for me that any one should have to overcome Prejudices in reading my Verses—that affects me more than any hypercriticism on any particular Passage. In *Endymion* I have most likely but moved into the Go-cart from the leading strings.[2] In Poetry I have a few Axioms, and you will see how far I am from their Centre. 1st I think Poetry should surprise by a fine excess and not by Singularity—it should strike the Reader as a wording of his own highest thoughts, and appear almost a Remembrance—2nd Its touches of Beauty should never be half way therby making the reader breathless instead of content: the rise, the progress, the setting of imagery should like the Sun come natural natural too him—shine over him and set soberly although in magnificence leaving him in the Luxury of twilight—but it is easier to think what Poetry should be than to write it—and this leads me on to another axiom. That if Poetry comes not as naturally as the Leaves to a tree it had better not come at all. However it may be with me I cannot help looking into new countries with "O for a Muse of fire to ascend!"[3]—If Endymion serves me as a Pioneer perhaps I ought to be content. I have great reason to be content, for thank God I can read and perhaps understand Shakspeare to his depths, and I have I am sure many friends, who, if I fail, will attribute any change in my Life and Temper to Humbleness rather than to Pride—to a cowering under the Wings of great Poets rather than to a

8. Shakespeare's *As You Like It* 2.1.31. The Wordsworth phrase is from his poem "The Two April Mornings." A "wilding" is a wild apple tree.
9. A reference to two sonnets on Robin Hood, written by Reynolds, which he had sent to Keats.
1. Canto 4 of Byron's *Childe Harold's Pilgrimage* was being eagerly awaited by English readers.
1. Partner in the publishing firm of Taylor and Hessey, to whom Keats wrote this letter while *Endymion* was being put through the press.

2. Go-carts were the wheeled walkers in which 19th-century toddlers learned to walk. Leading-strings were the harnesses with which they were guided and supported while they learned. Keats's point appears to be that as a poet he has not advanced and may even have regressed in *Endymion*.
3. Altered from Shakespeare's *Henry V*, Prologue, line 1.

Bitterness that I am not appreciated. I am anxious to get Endymion printed that I may forget it and proceed. * * *

Your sincere and oblig⁴ friend

John Keats—

P.S. You shall have a sho[r]t *Preface* in good time—

To John Hamilton Reynolds

[MILTON, WORDSWORTH, AND THE CHAMBERS OF HUMAN LIFE]

[May 3, 1818]

My dear Reynolds.

* * * Were I to study physic or rather Medicine again,—I feel it would not make the least difference in my Poetry; when the Mind is in its infancy a Bias is in reality a Bias, but when we have acquired more strength, a Bias becomes no Bias. Every department of knowledge we see excellent and calculated towards a great whole. I am so convinced of this, that I am glad at not having given away my medical Books, which I shall again look over to keep alive the little I know thitherwards; and moreover intend through you and Rice to become a sort of Pip-civilian.[1] An extensive knowledge is needful to thinking people—it takes away the heat and fever; and helps, by widening speculation, to ease the Burden of the Mystery:[2] a thing I begin to understand a little, and which weighed upon you in the most gloomy and true sentence in your Letter. The difference of high Sensations with and without knowledge appears to me this—in the latter case we are falling continually ten thousand fathoms deep and being blown up again without wings[3] and with all [the] horror of a ~~Case~~ bare shoulderd Creature—in the former case, our shoulders are fledged[4] and we go thro' the same ~~Fir~~ air and space without fear. * * *

You say "I fear there is little chance of any thing else in this life." You seem by that to have been going through with a more painful and acute ~~test~~ zest the same labyrinth that I have—I have come to the same conclusion thus far. My Branchings out therefrom have been numerous: one of them is the consideration of Wordsworth's genius and as a help, in the manner of gold being the meridian Line of worldly wealth,—how he differs from Milton.[5]—And here I have nothing but surmises, from an uncertainty whether Miltons apparently less anxiety for Humanity proceeds from his seeing further or no than Wordsworth: And whether Wordsworth has in truth epic passions, and martyrs himself to the human heart, the main region of his song[6]—In regard to his genius alone—we find what he says true as far as we have experienced and we can judge no further but by larger experience—for axioms in philosophy are not axioms until they are proved upon our pulses: We read fine——things but

---

1. Apparently "a small-scale layman." James Rice, a lawyer, was one of Keats's favorite friends.
2. Wordsworth, "Tintern Abbey," line 38.
3. Recalls the description of Satan's flight through Chaos (Milton, *Paradise Lost* 2.933–34).
4. Grow wings.
5. I.e., as gold is the standard of material wealth (in the way that the meridian line of Greenwich

Observatory, England, is the reference for measuring degrees of longitude), so Milton is the standard of poetic value, by which we may measure Wordsworth.
6. In the Prospectus to *The Recluse*, Wordsworth, laying out his poetic program, had identified "the Mind of Man" as "My haunt, and the main region of my song" (lines 40–41).

never feel them to [the] full until we have gone the same steps as the Author.—
I know this is not plain; you will know exactly my meaning when I say, that
now I shall relish Hamlet more than I ever have done—Or, better—You are
sensible no man can set down Venery[7] as a bestial or joyless thing until he is
sick of it and therefore all philosophizing on it would be mere wording. Until
we are sick, we understand not;—in fine, as Byron says, "Knowledge is Sorrow";[8] and I go on to say that "Sorrow is Wisdom"—and further for aught we
can know for certainty! "Wisdom is folly." * * *

I will return to Wordsworth—whether or no he has an extended vision or a
circumscribed grandeur—whether he is an eagle in his nest, or on the wing—
And to be more explicit and to show you how tall I stand by the giant, I will
put down a simile of human life as far as I now perceive it; that is, to the point
to which I say we both have arrived at—Well—I compare human life to a large
Mansion of Many Apartments, two of which I can only describe, the doors of
the rest being as yet shut upon me—The first we step into we call the infant
or thoughtless Chamber, in which we remain as long as we do not think—We
remain there a long while, and notwithstanding the doors of the second Chamber remain wide open, showing a bright appearance, we care not to hasten to
it; but are at length imperceptibly impelled by the awakening of the thinking
principle—within us—we no sooner get into the second Chamber, which I
shall call the Chamber of Maiden-Thought,[9] than we become intoxicated with
the light and the atmosphere, we see nothing but pleasant wonders, and think
of delaying there for ever in delight: However among the effects this breathing
is father of is that tremendous one of sharpening one's vision into the ~~head~~
heart and nature of Man—of convincing ones nerves that the World is full of
Misery and Heartbreak, Pain, Sickness and oppression—whereby This Chamber of Maiden Thought becomes gradually darken'd and at the same time on
all sides of it many doors are set open—but all dark—all leading to dark passages—We see not the ballance of good and evil. We are in a Mist—We are
now in that state—We feel the "burden of the Mystery," To this point was
Wordsworth come, as far as I can conceive when he wrote "Tintern Abbey"
and it seems to me that his Genius is explorative of those dark Passages. Now
if we live, and go on thinking, we too shall explore them. he is a Genius and
superior [to] us, in so far as he can, more than we, make discoveries, and shed
a light in them—Here I must think Wordsworth is deeper than Milton—
though I think it has depended more upon the general and gregarious advance
of intellect, than individual greatness of Mind—From the Paradise Lost and
the other Works of Milton, I hope it is not too presuming, even between
ourselves to say, his Philosophy, human and divine, may be tolerably understood by one not much advanced in years, In his time englishmen were just
emancipated from a great superstition—and Men had got hold of certain
points and resting places in reasoning which were too newly born to be
doubted, and too much ~~oppressed~~ opposed by the Mass of Europe not to be
thought etherial and authentically divine—who could gainsay his ideas on
virtue, vice, and Chastity in Comus, just at the time of the dismissal of Cod-
pieces[1] and a hundred other disgraces? who would not rest satisfied with his

7. Sexual indulgence.
8. *Manfred* 1.1.10: "Sorrow is knowledge."
9. I.e., innocent thought, with the implication (as
in "maiden voyage") of a first undertaking.

1. In the 15th and 16th centuries, the codpiece
was a flap, often ornamental, that covered an opening in the front of men's breeches. In Milton's
masque the chastity of a young lady is put to the

hintings at good and evil in the Paradise Lost, when just free from the inquisition and burrning in Smithfield?[2] The Reformation produced such immediate and great benefits, that Protestantism was considered under the immediate eye of heaven, and its own remaining Dogmas and superstitions, then, as it were, regenerated, constituted those resting places and seeming sure points of Reasoning—from that I have mentioned, Milton, whatever he may have thought in the sequel,[3] appears to have been content with these by his writings—He did not think into the human heart, as Wordsworth has done—Yet Milton as a Philosop[h]er, had sure as great powers as Wordsworth—What is then to be inferr'd? O many things—It proves there is really a grand march of intellect—, It proves that a mighty providence subdues the mightiest Minds to the service of the time being, whether it be in human Knowledge or Religion— * * * Tom[4] has spit a leetle blood this afternoon, and that is rather a damper—but I know—the truth is there is something real in the World Your third Chamber of Life shall be a lucky and a gentle one—stored with the wine of love—and the Bread of Friendship— * * *

Your affectionate friend
John Keats.

To Richard Woodhouse[1]

[October 27, 1818]

My dear Woodhouse,

Your Letter gave me a great satisfaction; more on account of its friendliness, than any relish of that matter in it which is accounted so acceptable in the "genus irritabile"[2] The best answer I can give you is in a clerklike manner to make some observations on two principle points, which seem to point like indices into the midst of the whole pro and con, about genius, and views and atchievements and ambition and cœtera. 1st As to the poetical Character itself, (I mean that sort of which, if I am any thing, I am a Member; that sort distinguished from the wordsworthian or egotistical sublime; which is a thing per se and stands alone) it is not itself—it has no self—it is every thing and nothing—It has no character—it enjoys light and shade; it lives in gusto,[3] be it foul or fair, high or low, rich or poor, mean or elevated—It has as much delight in conceiving an Iago as an Imogen.[4] What shocks the virtuous philosop[h]er, delights the camelion[5] Poet. It does no harm from its relish of the dark side of things any more than from its taste for the bright one; because they both end in speculation.[6] A Poet is the most unpoetical of any thing in

---

proof by the evil enchanter Comus.
2. An open place northwest of the walls of the City of London where, in the 16th century, heretics were burned.
3. Later on.
4. Keats's younger brother, then eighteen, who was dying of tuberculosis.
1. A young lawyer with literary interests who early recognized Keats's talents and prepared, or preserved, manuscript copies of many of his poems and letters.
2. "The irritable race," a phrase Horace had applied to poets (*Epistles* 2.2.102).

3. Hazlitt had defined gusto in his 1816 essay as "power or passion."
4. Iago is the villain in Shakespeare's *Othello* and Imogen the virtuous heroine in his *Cymbeline*.
5. The chameleon is a lizard that camouflages itself by changing its color to match its surroundings.
6. I.e., without affecting our practical judgment or actions. Cf. Keats's discussion of the poet of "negative capability" in his letter to George and Thomas Keats begun on December 21, 1817 (p. 1871).

existence; because he has no Identity—he is continually in for[7]—and filling some other Body—The Sun, the Moon, the Sea and Men and Women who are creatures of impulse are poetical and have about them an unchangeable attribute—the poet has none; no identity—he is certainly the most unpoetical of all God's Creatures. If then he has no self, and if I am a Poet, where is the Wonder that I should say I would write no more? Might I not at that very instant [have] been cogitating on the Characters of saturn and Ops?[8] It is a wretched thing to confess; but is a very fact that not one word I ever utter can be taken for granted as an opinion growing out of my identical nature—how can it, when I have no nature? When I am in a room with People if I ever am free from speculating on creations of my own brain, then not myself goes home to myself: but the identity of every one in the room begins to to press upon me[9] that, I am in a very little time an[ni]hilated—not only among Men; it would be the same in a Nursery of children: I know not whether I make myself wholly understood: I hope enough so to let you see that no dependence is to be placed on what I said that day.

In the second place I will speak of my views, and of the life I purpose to myself—I am ambitious of doing the world some good: if I should be spared that may be the work of maturer years—in the interval I will assay to reach to as high a summit in Poetry as the nerve bestowed upon me will suffer. The faint conceptions I have of Poems to come brings the blood frequently into my forehead—All I hope is that I may not lose all interest in human affairs— that the solitary indifference I feel for applause even from the finest Spirits, will not blunt any acuteness of vision I may have. I do not think it will—I feel assured I should write from the mere yearning and fondness I have for the Beautiful even if my night's labours should be burnt every morning and no eye ever shine upon them. But even now I am perhaps not speaking from myself; but from some character in whose soul I now live. I am sure however that this next sentence is from myself. I feel your anxiety, good opinion and friendliness in the highest degree, and am

Your's most sincerely

John Keats

To George and Georgiana Keats[1]

[THE VALE OF SOUL-MAKING]

[February 14–May 3, 1819]

My dear Brother & Sister—

* * * I have this moment received a note from Haslam[2] in which he expects the death of his Father who has been for some time in a state of insensibility— his mother bears up he says very well—I shall go to [town] tommorrow to see

---

7. Instead of "in for," Keats may have intended to write "informing."

8. Characters in Keats's *Hyperion.* Woodhouse had recently written Keats to express concern at a remark by the poet that, because former writers had preempted the best poetic materials and styles, there was nothing new left for the modern poet.

9. Perhaps "*so* to press upon me."

1. Keats's brother and his wife, who had emigrated to Louisville, Kentucky, in 1818. This is part of a long letter that Keats wrote over a period of several months, and into which he transcribed several of his poems, including "Ode to Psyche." The date of this first extract is March 19.

2. William Haslam, a young businessman and close friend.

him. This is the world—thus we cannot expect to give way many hours to pleasure—Circumstances are like Clouds continually gathering and bursting—While we are laughing the seed of some trouble is put into he the wide arable land of events—while we are laughing it sprouts [it] grows and suddenly bears a poison fruit which we must pluck—Even so we have leisure to reason on the misfortunes of our friends; our own touch us too nearly for words. Very few men have ever arrived at a complete disinterestedness[3] of Mind: very few have been influenced by a pure desire of the benefit of others—in the greater part of the Benefactors of & to Humanity some meretricious motive has sullied their greatness—some melodramatic scenery has facinated them—From the manner in which I feel Haslam's misfortune I perceive how far I am from any humble standard of disinterestedness—Yet this feeling ought to be carried to its highest pitch, as there is no fear of its ever injuring society—which it would do I fear pushed to an extremity—For in wild nature the Hawk would loose his Breakfast of Robins and the Robin his of Worms The Lion must starve as well as the swallow—The greater part of Men make their way with the same instinctiveness, the same unwandering eye from their purposes, the same animal eagerness as the Hawk—The Hawk wants a Mate, so does the Man—look at them both they set about it and procure on[e] in the same manner—They want both a nest and they both set about one in the same manner—they get their food in the same manner—The noble animal Man for his amusement smokes his pipe—the Hawk balances about the Clouds—that is the only difference of their leisures. This it is that makes the Amusement of Life—to a speculative Mind. I go among the Feilds and catch a glimpse of a stoat[4] or a fieldmouse peeping out of the withered grass—the creature hath a purpose and its eyes are bright with it—I go amongst the buildings of a city and I see a Man hurrying along—to what? The Creature has a purpose and his eyes are bright with it. But then as Wordsworth says, "we have all one human heart"[5]—there is an ellectric fire in human nature tending to purify—so that among these human creature[s] there is continually some birth of new heroism—The pity is that we must wonder at it: as we should at finding a pearl in rubbish—I have no doubt that thousands of people never heard of have had hearts comp[l]etely disinterested: I can remember but two—Socrates and Jesus—their Histories evince it—What I heard a little time ago, Taylor observe with respect to Socrates, may be said of Jesus—That he was so great as man that though he transmitted no writing of his own to posterity, we have his Mind and his sayings and his greatness handed to us by others. It is to be lamented that the history of the latter was written and revised by Men interested in the pious frauds of Religion. Yet through all this I see his splendour. Even here though I myself am pursueing the same instinctive course as the veriest human animal you can think of—I am however young writing at random—straining at particles of light in the midst of a great darkness—without knowing the bearing of any one assertion of any one opinion. Yet may I not in this be free from sin? May there not be superior beings amused with any graceful, though instinctive attitude my mind [may] fall into, as I am entertained with the alertness of a Stoat or the anxiety of a Deer? Though a quarrel in the streets is a thing to be hated, the energies displayed in it are fine; the commonest Man shows a grace in his quarrel—By a superior being our reasoning[s] may take

---

3. Transcendence of self-interest, of one's selfish instincts.

4. A weasel.
5. "The Old Cumberland Beggar," line 153.

the same tone—though erroneous they may be fine—This is the very thing in which consists poetry; and if so it is not so fine a thing as philosophy—For the same reason that an eagle is not so fine a thing as a truth—Give me this credit—Do you not think I strive—to know myself? Give me this credit—and you will not think that on my own accou[n]t I repeat Milton's lines

> "How charming is divine Philosophy
> Not harsh and crabbed as dull fools suppose
> But musical as is Apollo's lute"—[6]

No—no for myself—feeling grateful as I do to have got into a state of mind to relish them properly—Nothing ever becomes real till it is experienced—Even a Proverb is no proverb to you till your Life has illustrated it— * * *

* * * I have been reading lately two very different books Robertson's America and Voltaire's Siecle De Louis xiv[7] It is like walking arm and arm between Pizarro and the great-little Monarch.[8] In How lementabl[e] a case do we see the great body of the people in both instances: in the first, where Men might seem to inherit quiet of Mind from unsophisticated senses; from uncontamination of civilisation; and especially from their being as it were estranged from the mutual helps of Society and its mutual injuries—and thereby more immediately under the Protection of Providence—even there they had mortal pains to bear as bad; or even worse than Baliffs,[9] Debts and Poverties of civilised Life—The whole appears to resolve into this—that Man is originally "a poor forked creature"[1] subject to the same mischances as the beasts of the forest, destined to hardships and disquietude of some kind or other. If he improves by degrees his bodily accommodations and comforts—at each stage, at each accent there are waiting for him a fresh set of annoyances—he is mortal and there is still a heaven with its Stars abov[e] his head. The most interesting question that can come before us is, How far by the persevering endeavours of a seldom appearing Socrates Mankind may be made happy—I can imagine such happiness carried to an extreme—but what must it end in?—Death—and who could in such a case bear with death—the whole troubles of life which are now frittered away in a series of years, would the[n] be accumulated for the last days of a being who instead of hailing its approach, would leave this world as Eve left Paradise—But in truth I do not at all believe in this sort of perfectibility—the nature of the world will not admit of it—the inhabitants of the world will correspond to itself—Let the fish philosophise the ice away from the Rivers in winter time and they shall be at continual play in the tepid delight of summer. Look at the Poles and at the sands of Africa, Whirlpools and volcanoes—Let men exterminate them and I will say that they may arrive at earthly Happiness—The point at which Man may arrive is as far as the paralel state in inanimate nature and no further—For instance suppose a rose to have sensation, it blooms on a beautiful morning it enjoys itself—but there comes a cold wind, a hot sun—it can not escape it, it cannot destroy its annoyances—they are as native to the world as itself: no more can man be happy in spite, the world[l]y elements will prey upon his nature—The common cog-

6. *Comus*, lines 475–77.
7. Two books of history, Voltaire's *Le Siècle de Louis XIV* (1751) and William Robertson's *The History of America* (1777). In this second extract from the journal-letter, Keats is writing toward the end of April (on the 21st or 28th).
8. Francisco Pizarro, the Spanish explorer whose exploits are described in Robertson's *America*. The "Monarch" is Louis XIV of France.
9. Bailiffs: officers of the law whose duties included making arrests for bad debts.
1. Shakespeare's *King Lear* 3.4.95–97. Lear says of "Poor Tom," "Unaccommodated man is no more but such a poor, bare, forked animal as thou art."

nomen of this world among the misguided and superstitious is "a vale of tears" from which we are to be redeemed by a certain arbitrary interposition of God and taken to Heaven—What a little circumscribe[d] straightened notion! Call the world if you Please "The vale of Soul-making" Then you will find out the use of the world (I am speaking now in the highest terms for human nature admitting it to be immortal which I will here take for granted for the purpose of showing a thought which has struck me concerning it) I say "*Soul making*" Soul as distinguished from an Intelligence—There may be intelligences or sparks of the divinity in millions—but they are not Souls ~~the~~ till they acquire identities, till each one is personally itself. I[n]telligences are atoms of perception—they know and they see and they are pure, in short they are God—how then are Souls to be made? How then are these sparks which are God to have identity given them—so as ever to possess a bliss peculiar to each ones individual existence? How, but by the medium of a world like this? This point I sincerely wish to consider because I think it a grander system of salvation than the chrystean religion—or rather it is a system of Spirit-creation[2]—This is effected by three grand materials acting the one upon the other for a series of years—These three Materials are the *Intelligence*—the *human heart* (as distinguished from intelligence or Mind) and the *World* or *Elemental space* suited for the proper action of *Mind and Heart* on each other for the purpose of forming the *Soul* or *Intelligence destined to possess the sense of Identity*. I can scarcely express what I but dimly perceive—and yet I think I perceive it—that you may judge the more clearly I will put it in the most homely form possible—I will call the *world* a School instituted for the purpose of teaching little children to read—I will call the *human heart* the *horn Book*[3] used in that School—and I will call the *Child able to read, the Soul* made from that *school* and its *hornbook*. Do you not see how necessary a World of Pains and troubles is to school an Intelligence and make it a soul? A Place where the heart must feel and suffer in a thousand diverse ways! Not merely is the Heart a Hornbook, It is the Minds Bible, it is the Minds experience, it is the teat from which the Mind or intelligence sucks its identity—As various as the Lives of Men are—so various become their souls, and thus does God make individual beings, Souls, Identical Souls of the sparks of his own essence—This appears to me a faint sketch of a system of Salvation which does not affront our reason and humanity—I am convinced that many difficulties which christians labour under would vanish before it—There is one wh[i]ch even now Strikes me—the Salvation of Children—In them the Spark or intelligence returns to God without any identity—it having had no time to learn of, and be altered by, the heart—or seat of the human Passions—It is pretty generally suspected that the chr[i]stian scheme has been coppied from the ancient persian and greek Philosophers. Why may they not have made this simple thing even more simple for common apprehension by introducing Mediators and Personages in the same manner as in the hethen mythology abstractions are personified—Seriously I think it probable that this System of Soul-making—may have been the

2. Keats is struggling for an analogy that will embody his solution to the ancient riddle of evil, as an alternative to what he understands to be the Christian view: that evil exists as a test of the individual's worthiness of salvation in heaven, and this world is only a proving ground for a later and better life. Keats proposes that the function of the human experience of sorrow and pain is to feed and discipline the formless and unstocked "intelligence" that we possess at birth and thus to shape it into a rich and coherent "identity," or "soul." This result provides a justification ("salvation") for our suffering in terms of our earthly life: i.e., experience is its own reward.

3. A child's primer, which used to consist of a sheet of paper mounted on thin wood, protected by a sheet of transparent horn.

Parent of all the more palpable and personal Schemes of Redemption, among the Zoroastrians the Christians and the Hindoos. For as one part of the human species must have their carved Jupiter; so another part must have the palpable and named Mediatior and saviour, their Christ their Oromanes and their Vishnu[4]—If what I have said should not be plain enough, as I fear it may not be, I will [put] you in the place where I began in this series of thoughts—I mean, I began by seeing how man was formed by circumstances—and what are circumstances?—but touchstones of his heart—? and what are touch stones?—but proovings of his hearrt?[5]—and what are proovings of his heart but fortifiers or alterers of his nature? and what is his altered nature but his soul?—and what was his soul before it came into the world and had These provings and alterations and perfectionings?—An intelligences—without Identity—and how is this Identity to be made? Through the medium of the Heart? And how is the heart to become this Medium but in a world of Circumstances?—There now I think what with Poetry and Theology you may thank your Stars that my pen is not very long winded— * * *

This is the 3d of May & every thing is in delightful forwardness; the violets are not withered, before the peeping of the first rose; You must let me know every thing, how parcels go & come, what papers you have, & what Newspapers you want, & other things—God bless you my dear Brother & Sister

Your ever Affectionate Brother
John Keats—

To Fanny Brawne

[FANNY BRAWNE AS KEATS'S "FAIR STAR"]

[July 25, 1819]

My sweet Girl,

I hope you did not blame me much for not obeying your request of a Letter on Saturday: we have had four in our small room playing at cards night and morning leaving me no undisturb'd opportunity to write. Now Rice and Martin are gone I am at liberty. Brown to my sorrow confirms the account you give of your ill health. You cannot conceive how I ache to be with you: how I would die for one hour——for what is in the world? I say you cannot conceive; it is impossible you should look with such eyes upon me as I have upon you: it cannot be. Forgive me if I wander a little this evening, for I have been all day employ'd in a very abstr[a]ct Poem[1] and I am in deep love with you—two things which must excuse me. I have, believe me, not been an age in letting you take possession of me; the very first week I knew you I wrote myself your vassal; but burnt the Letter as the very next time I saw you I thought you manifested some dislike to me. If you should ever feel for Man at the first sight what I did for you, I am lost. Yet I should not quarrel with you, but hate myself if such a thing were to happen—only I should burst if the thing were not as fine as a Man as you are as a Woman. Perhaps I am too vehement, then fancy me

---

4. The deity who creates and preserves the world, in Hindu belief. Oromanes (Ahriman) was the principle of evil, locked in a persisting struggle with Ormazd, the principle of good, in the Zoroastrian religion of ancient Persia.
5. I.e., experiences by which the human heart is put to the test.
1. Probably *The Fall of Hyperion*.

on my knees, especially when I mention a part of you Letter which hurt me; you say speaking of Mr. Severn[2] "but you must be satisfied in knowing that I admired you much more than your friend." My dear love, I cannot believe there ever was or ever could be any thing to admire in me especially as far as sight goes—I cannot be admired, I am not a thing to be admired. You are, I love you; all I can bring you is a swooning admiration of your Beauty. I hold that place among Men which snub-nos'd brunettes with meeting eyebrows do among women—they are trash to me—unless I should find one among them with a fire in her heart like the one that burns in mine. You absorb me in spite of myself—you alone: for I look not forward with any pleasure to what is call'd being settled in the world; I tremble at domestic cares—yet for you I would meet them, though if it would leave you the happier I would rather die than do so. I have two luxuries to brood over in my walks, your Loveliness and the hour of my death. O that I could have possession of them both in the same minute. I hate the world: it batters too much the wings of my self-will, and would I could take a sweet poison from your lips to send me out of it. From no others would I take it. I am indeed astonish'd to find myself so careless of all cha[r]ms but yours—remembring as I do the time when even a bit of ribband was a matter of interest with me. What softer words can I find for you after this—what it is I will not read. Nor will I say more here, but in a Postscript answer any thing else you may have mentioned in your Letter in so many words—for I am distracted with a thousand thoughts. I will imagine you Venus tonight and pray, pray, pray to your star like a Hethen.[3]

Your's ever, fair Star,

John Keats.

To Percy Bysshe Shelley[1]

[LOAD EVERY RIFT WITH ORE]

[August 16, 1820]

My dear Shelley,

I am very much gratified that you, in a foreign country, and with a mind almost over occupied, should write to me in the strain of the Letter beside me. If I do not take advantage of your invitation it will be prevented by a circumstance I have very much at heart to prophesy[2]—There is no doubt that an english winter would put an end to me, and do so in a lingering hateful manner, therefore I must either voyage or journey to Italy as a soldier marches up to a battery. My nerves at present are the worst part of me, yet they feel soothed when I think that come what extreme may, I shall not be destined to remain in one spot long enough to take a hatred of any four particular bed-posts. I am glad you take any pleasure in my poor Poem;[3]—which I would willingly take the trouble to unwrite, if possible, did I care so much as I have done about Reputation. I received a copy of the Cenci,[4] as from yourself from

---

2. Joseph Severn, who later looked after Keats in Rome during his final illness.
3. See Keats's sonnet "Bright star" (p. 1840) for parallels to this and other remarks in the present letter.
1. Written in reply to a letter urging Keats (who was ill) to spend the winter with the Shelleys in Pisa.

2. His own death.
3. Keats's *Endymion*, Shelley had written, contains treasures, "though treasures poured forth with indistinct profusion." Keats here responds with advice in kind.
4. Shelley's blank-verse tragedy, *The Cenci*, had been published in the spring of 1820.

Hunt. There is only one part of it I am judge of; the Poetry, and dramatic effect, which by many spirits now a days is considered the mammon. A modern work it is said must have a purpose,[5] which may be the God—*an artist* must serve Mammon—he must have "self concentration" selfishness perhaps. You I am sure will forgive me for sincerely remarking that you might curb your magnanimity and be more of an artist, and "load every rift"[6] of your subject with ore. The thought of such discipline must fall like cold chains upon you, who perhaps never sat with your wings furl'd for six Months together. And is not this extraordina[r]y talk for the writer of Endymion? whose mind was like a pack of scattered cards—I am pick'd up and sorted to a pip.[7] My Imagination is a Monastry and I am its Monk—you must explain my metap[cs][8] to yourself. I am in expectation of Prometheus[9] every day. Could I have my own wish for its interest effected you would have it still in manuscript—or be but now putting an end to the second act. I remember you advising me not to publish my first-blights, on Hampstead heath—I am returning advice upon your hands. Most of the Poems in the volume I send you[1] have been written above two years, and would never have been publish'd but from a hope of gain; so you see I am inclined enough to take your advice now. I must exp[r]ess once more my deep sense of your kindness, adding my sincere thanks and respects for M[rs] Shelley. In the hope of soon seeing you I remain

most sincerely yours,
John Keats—

To Charles Brown[1]

[KEATS'S LAST LETTER]

Rome. 30 November 1820.

My dear Brown,

'Tis the most difficult thing in the world to me to write a letter. My stomach continues so bad, that I feel it worse on opening any book,—yet I am much better than I was in Quarantine.[2] Then I am afraid to encounter the proing and conning of any thing interesting to me in England. I have an habitual feeling of my real life having past, and that I am leading a posthumous existence. God knows how it would have been—but it appears to me—however, I will not speak of that subject. I must have been at Bedhampton nearly at the time you were writing to me from Chichester[3]—how unfortunate—and to pass on the river too! There was my star predominant![4] I cannot answer any thing in your letter, which followed me from Naples to Rome, because I am afraid

---

5. Wordsworth had said this in his Preface to *Lyrical Ballads*. For "Mammon" see Matthew 6.24 and Luke 16.13: "Ye cannot serve God and mammon."
6. From Spenser's description of the Cave of Mammon in *The Faerie Queene* 2.7.28: "With rich metall loaded every rifte."
7. Perfectly ordered; all the suits in the deck matched up ("pips" are the conventional spots on playing cards).
8. Metaphysics.
9. *Prometheus Unbound*, of which Shelley had promised Keats a copy.
1. Keats's volume of 1820, including *Lamia, The Eve of St. Agnes*, and the odes. When Shelley

drowned he had this small book open in his pocket.
1. Written to Keats's friend Charles Armitage Brown from the house on the Spanish Steps, in the Piazza di Spagna, where Keats was being tended in his mortal illness by the devoted Joseph Severn.
2. When it landed at Naples, Keats's ship had been quarantined for ten miserably hot days.
3. Bedhampton and Chichester are both near the harbor town of Portsmouth, where Keats had embarked for Naples two months before.
4. I.e., that was my usual luck. Cf. Shakespeare's *The Winter's Tale* 1.2.202–03: "It is a bawdy planet, that will strike / Where 'tis predominant."

to look it over again. I am so weak (in mind) that I cannot bear the sight of any hand writing of a friend I love so much as I do you. Yet I ride the little horse,—and, at my worst, even in Quarantine, summoned up more puns, in a sort of desperation, in one week than in any year of my life. There is one thought enough to kill me—I have been well, healthy, alert &c, walking with her[5]—and now—the knowledge of contrast, feeling for light and shade, all that information (primitive sense) necessary for a poem are great enemies to the recovery of the stomach. There, you rogue, I put you to the torture,—but you must bring your philosophy to bear—as I do mine, really—or how should I be able to live? Dr Clarke is very attentive to me; he says, there is very little the matter with my lungs, but my stomach, he says, is very bad. I am well disappointed in hearing good news from George,—for it runs in my head we shall all die young. I have not written to x x x x x yet,[6] which he must think very neglectful; being anxious to send him a good account of my health, I have delayed it from week to week. If I recover, I will do all in my power to correct the mistakes made during sickness; and if I should not, all my faults will be forgiven. I shall write to x x x to-morrow, or next day. I will write to x x x x x in the middle of next week. Severn is very well, though he leads so dull a life with me. Remember me to all friends, and tell x x x x I should not have left London without taking leave of him, but from being so low in body and mind. Write to George as soon as you receive this, and tell him how I am, as far as you can guess;—and also a note to my sister—who walks about my imagination like a ghost—she is so like Tom.[7] I can scarcely bid you good bye even in a letter. I always made an awkward bow.

God bless you!
John Keats.

5. Fanny Brawne.
6. Charles Brown, whose manuscript transcription is the only text for this letter, substituted crosses for the names of Keats's friends to conceal their identities.

7. Keats's youngest brother, whom Fanny, his only sister, closely resembled, had died of tuberculosis on December 1, 1818. George was John Keats's younger brother.

The Victorian Age
1830–1901

1832: The First Reform Bill
1837: Victoria becomes queen
1846: The Corn Laws repealed
1850: Tennyson succeeds Wordsworth as poet laureate
1851: The Great Exhibition in London
1859: Charles Darwin's *Origin of Species* published
1870–71: Franco-Prussian War
1901: Death of Victoria

In 1897 Mark Twain was visiting London during the Diamond Jubilee celebrations honoring the sixtieth anniversary of Queen Victoria's coming to the throne. "British history is two thousand years old," Twain observed, "and yet in a good many ways the world has moved farther ahead since the Queen was born than it moved in all the rest of the two thousand put together." And if the whole world had "moved" during that long lifetime and reign of Victoria's, it was in her own country itself that the change was most marked and dramatic, a change that brought England to its highest point of development as a world power.

In the eighteenth century the pivotal city of Western civilization had been Paris; by the second half of the nineteenth century this center of influence had shifted to London, a city that expanded from about two million inhabitants when Victoria came to the throne to six and a half million at the time of her death. The rapid growth of London is one of the many indications of the most important development of the age: the shift from a way of life based on the ownership of land to a modern urban economy based on trade and manufacturing. "We have been living, as it were, the life of three hundred years in thirty" was the impression formed by Dr. Thomas Arnold during the early stages of England's industrialization. By the end of the century—after the resources of steam power had been more fully exploited for fast railways and iron ships, looms, printing presses, and farmers' combines, and after the introduction of the telegraph, intercontinental cable, photography, anesthetics, and universal compulsory education—a late Victorian could look back with astonishment on these developments during his or her lifetime. Walter Besant, one of these late Victorians, observed that so completely transformed were "the mind and habits of the ordinary Englishman" by 1897, "that he would not, could he see him, recognize his own grandfather."

Because England was the first country to become industrialized, its transformation was an especially painful one: it experienced a host of social and economic problems consequent to rapid and unregulated industrialization. England also experienced an enormous increase in wealth. An early start enabled England to capture markets all over the globe. Cotton and other manufactured products were exported in English ships, a merchant fleet whose size was without parallel in other countries. The profits gained from trade led also to extensive capital investments in all continents. After England had become the world's workshop, London became, from 1870 on, the world's banker. England gained particular profit from the development of its own colonies, which, by 1890, comprised more than a quarter of all the territory on the surface of the earth; one in four people was a subject of Queen Victoria. By the end of the century England was the world's foremost imperial power.

The reactions of Victorian writers to the fast-paced expansion of England were various. Thomas Babington Macaulay (1800–1859) relished the spectacle with strenuous enthusiasm. During the prosperous 1850s Macaulay's essays and histories, with their recitations of the statistics of industrial growth, constituted a Hymn to Progress as well as a celebration of the superior qualities of the English people—"the greatest and most highly civilized people that ever the world saw." Other writers felt that leadership in commerce and industry was being paid for at a terrible price in human happiness, that a so-called progress had been gained only by abandoning traditional rhythms of life and traditional patterns of human relationships. The melancholy poetry of Matthew Arnold often strikes this note:

> For what wears out the life of mortal men?
> 'Tis that from change to change their being rolls;
> 'Tis that repeated shocks, again, again,
> Exhaust the energy of strongest souls.

Although many Victorians shared a sense of satisfaction in the industrial and political preeminence of England during the period, they also suffered from an anxious sense of something lost, a sense too of being displaced persons in a world made alien by technological changes that had been exploited too quickly for the adaptive powers of the human psyche.

QUEEN VICTORIA AND THE VICTORIAN TEMPER

Queen Victoria's long reign, from 1837 to 1901, defines the historical period that bears her name. The question naturally arises whether the distinctive character of those years justifies the adjective *Victorian*. In part Victoria herself encouraged her own identification with the qualities we associate with the adjective—earnestness, moral responsibility, domestic propriety. As a young wife, as the mother of nine children, and as the black-garbed Widow of Windsor in the forty years after her husband's death in 1861, Victoria represented the domestic fidelities her citizens embraced. After her death Henry James wrote, "I mourn the safe and motherly old middle-class queen, who held the nation warm under the fold of her big, hideous Scotch-plaid shawl." Changes in the reproduction of visual images aided in making her the icon she became. She is the first British monarch of whom we have photographs. These pictures, and the ease and cheapness with which they were reproduced, facilitated her representing her country's sense of itself during her reign.

Victoria came to the throne in a decade that does seem to mark a different historical consciousness among Britain's writers. In 1831 John Stuart Mill asserts, "we are living in an age of transition." In the same year Thomas Carlyle writes, "The Old has passed away, but alas, the New appears not in its stead; the Time is still in pangs of travail with the New." Although the historical changes that created the England of the 1830s had been in progress for many decades, writers of the thirties shared a sharp new sense of modernity, of a break with the past, of historical self-consciousness. They responded to their sense of the historical moment with a strenuous call to action that they self-consciously distinguished from the attitude of the previous generation.

In 1834 Carlyle urged his contemporaries, "Close thy *Byron*; open thy *Goethe*." He was saying, in effect, to abandon the introspection of the Romantics and to turn to the higher moral purpose that he found in Goethe. The popular novelist Edward Bulwer-Lytton in his *England and the English* (1833) made a similar judgment. "When Byron passed away," he wrote, ". . . we turned to the actual and practical career of life: we awoke from the morbid, the dreaming, 'the moonlight and dimness of the mind,' and by a natural reaction addressed ourselves to the active and daily objects which lay before us." This sense of historical self-consciousness, of strenuous social enterprise, and of growing national achievement led writers as early as the 1850s and 1860s to define their age as Victorian. The very fact that Victoria reigned for so long sustained the concept of a distinctive historical period that writers defined even as they lived it.

When Queen Victoria died, a reaction developed against many of the achievements of the previous century; this reinforced the sense that the Victorian age was a distinct period. In the earlier decades of the twentieth century, writers took pains to separate themselves from the Victorians. It was then the fashion for most literary critics to treat their Victorian predecessors as somewhat absurd creatures, stuffily complacent prigs with whose way of life they had little in common. Writers of the Georgian period (1911–36) took great delight in puncturing overinflated Victorian balloons, as Lytton Strachey, a member of Virginia Woolf's circle, did in *Eminent Victorians* (1918). A subtler example occurs in Woolf's *Orlando* (1928), a fictionalized survey of English literature from Elizabethan times to 1928, in which the Victorians are presented in terms of dampness, rain, and proliferating vegetation:

> Ivy grew in unparalleled profusion. Houses that had been of bare stone were smothered in greenery. . . . And just as the ivy and the evergreen rioted in the damp earth outside, so did the same fertility show itself within. The life of the average woman was a succession of childbirths. . . . Giant cauliflowers towered deck above deck till they rivaled . . . the elm trees themselves. Hens laid incessantly eggs of no special tint. . . . The whole sky itself as it spread wide above the British Isles was nothing but a vast feather bed.

This witty description not only identifies a distinguishing quality of Victorian life and literature—a superabundant energy—but reveals the author's distaste for its smothering profusion. Woolf was the daughter of Sir Leslie Stephen (1832–1904), an eminent Victorian. In her later life, when assessing her father's powerful personality, Woolf recorded in her diary that she could never have become a writer if he had not died when he did. Growing up under such towering shadows, she and her generation mocked their predecessors to make them less intimidating. In his reminiscences *Portraits from Life* (1937), the novelist Ford Madox Ford recalled his feelings of terror when he confronted the works of Carlyle and Ruskin, which he likened to an overpowering range of high mountains. The mid-Victorians, he wrote, were "a childish nightmare to me."

The Georgian reaction against the Victorians is now only a matter of the history of taste, but its aftereffects still sometimes crop up when the term *Victorian* is employed in an exclusively pejorative sense, as prudish or old-fashioned. Contemporary historians and critics find the Victorian period a richly complex example of a society struggling with the issues and problems we identify with modernism. But to give the period the single designation *Victorian* reduces its complexity. Since it is a period of almost seventy years, we can hardly expect generalizations to be uniformly applicable. It is, therefore, helpful to subdivide the age into three phases: early Victorian (1830–48), mid-Victorian (1848–70), and late Victorian (1870–1901). It is also helpful to consider the final decade, the nineties, as a bridge between two centuries.

THE EARLY PERIOD (1830–48): A TIME OF TROUBLES

In the early 1830s two historical events occurred of momentous consequence for England. In 1830 the Liverpool and Manchester Railway opened, becoming the first steam-powered, public railway line in the world. A burst of railway construction followed. By 1850 6,621 miles of railway line connected all of England's major cities. By 1900 England had 15,195 lines of track and an underground railway system beneath London. The train transformed England's landscape, supported the growth of its commerce, and shrank the distances between its cities. The opening of England's first railway coincided with the opening of the country's Reform Parliament. The railway had increased the pressure for parliamentary reform. "Parliamentary reform must follow soon after the opening of this road," a Manchester man observed in 1830. "A million of persons will pass over it in the course of this year, and see that hitherto unseen village of Newton; and they must be convinced of the absurdity of its sending two members to Parliament while Manchester sends none." Despite the growth of manufacturing cities consequent to the Industrial Revolution, England was still governed by an archaic electoral system whereby some of the new industrial cities were unrepresented in Parliament while "rotten boroughs" (communities that had become depopulated) elected the nominees of the local squire to Parliament.

By 1830 a time of economic distress had brought England close to revolution. Manufacturing interests, who refused to tolerate their exclusion from the political process any longer, led working men in agitating for reform. Fearing the kind of revolution it had seen in Europe, Parliament passed a Reform Bill in 1832 that transformed England's class structure. The Reform Bill of 1832 extended the right to vote to all males owning property worth £10 or more in annual rent. In effect the voting public thereafter included the lower middle classes but not the working classes, who did not obtain the vote until 1867, when a second Reform Bill was passed. Even more important than the extension of the franchise was the virtual abolition of the rotten boroughs and the redistribution of parliamentary representation. Because it broke up the monopoly of power that the conservative landowners had so long enjoyed (the Tory party had been in office almost continuously from 1783 to 1830), the Reform Bill represents the beginning of a new age, in which middle-class economic interests gained increasing power.

Yet even the newly constituted Parliament was unable to find legislative solutions to the problems facing the nation. The economic and social diffi-culties attendant on industrialization were so severe that the 1830s and 1840s became known as the Time of Troubles. After a period of prosperity from 1832 to 1836, a crash in 1837, followed by a series of bad harvests, produced a period of unemployment, desperate poverty, and rioting. Conditions in the new industrial and coal-mining areas were terrible. Workers and their families in the slums of such cities as Manchester lived in horribly crowded, unsanitary housing; and the conditions under which men, women, and children toiled in mines and factories were unimaginably brutal. Elizabeth Barrett's poem "The Cry of the Children" (1843) expresses her horrified response to an official report on child labor that described five-year-olds sitting alone in darkness to open and close ventilation doors, and twelve-year-olds dragging heavy tubs of coal through low-ceilinged mine passages for sixteen hours a day.

The owners of mines and factories regarded themselves as innocent of blame for such conditions, for they were wedded to an economic theory of laissez-faire, which assumed that unregulated working conditions would ultimately benefit everyone. A sense of the seemingly hopeless complexity of the situation during the Hungry Forties is provided by an entry for 1842 in the diary of the statesman Charles Greville, an entry written at the same time that Carlyle was making his contribution to the "Condition of England Question," *Past and Present*. Conditions in the north of England, Greville reports, were "appalling."

> There is an immense and continually increasing population, no adequate demand for labor, . . . no confidence, but a universal alarm, disquietude, and discontent. Nobody can sell anything. . . . Certainly I have never seen . . . so serious a state of things as that which now stares us in the face; and this after thirty years of uninterrupted peace, and the most ample scope afforded for the development of all our resources. . . . One remark-able feature in the present condition of affairs is that nobody can account for it, and nobody pretends to be able to point out any remedy.

In reality many remedies were proposed. One of the most striking was put forward by the Chartists, a large organization of workers. In 1838 the orga-nization drew up a "People's Charter" advocating the extension of the right to vote, the use of secret balloting, and other legislative reforms. For ten years the Chartist leaders engaged in agitation to have their program adopted by Parliament. Their fiery speeches, delivered at conventions designed to collect signatures for petitions to Parliament, created fears of revolution. In "Locksley Hall" (1842), Alfred, Lord Tennyson seems to have had the Chartist demon-strations in mind when he wrote: "Slowly comes a hungry people, as a lion, creeping nigher, / Glares at one that nods and winks behind a slowly-dying fire." Although the Chartist movement had fallen apart by 1848, it succeeded in creating an atmosphere open to reform. One of the most important reforms was the abolition of the high tariffs on imported grains, tariffs known as the Corn Laws (the word *corn* in England refers to wheat and other grains). These high tariffs had been established to protect English farm products from having to compete with low-priced products imported from abroad. Landowners and farmers fought to keep these tariffs in force so that high prices for their wheat would be ensured; but the rest of the population suffered severely from the exorbitant price of bread or, in years of bad crops, from scarcity of food. In 1845 serious crop failures in England and the outbreak of potato blight in Ireland convinced Sir Robert Peel, the Tory prime minister, that traditional protectionism must be abandoned. In 1846 the Corn Laws were repealed by Parliament, and the way was paved for the introduction of a system of free trade whereby goods could be imported with the payment of only minimal tariff duties. Although free trade did not eradicate the slums of Manchester, it worked well for many years and helped relieve the major crisis of the Victorian economy. In 1848, when revolutions were breaking out all over Europe, England was relatively unaffected. A large Chartist demonstration in London seemed to threaten violence, but it came to nothing. The next two decades were relatively calm and prosperous.

This Time of Troubles left its mark on some early Victorian literature. "Insurrection is a most sad necessity," Carlyle writes in his *Past and Present*, "and governors who wait for that to instruct them are surely getting into the fatalest courses." A similar refrain runs through Carlyle's history *The French Revolution* (1837). Memories of the French Reign of Terror lasted longer than memories of British victories over Napoleon at Trafalgar and Waterloo, memories freshened by later outbreaks of civil strife, "the red fool-fury of the Seine" as Tennyson described one of the violent overturnings of government in France. The most marked response to the industrial and political scene, however, comes in the "Condition of England" novels of the 1840s and early 1850s. Vivid records of these times are to be found in the fiction of Charles Kingsley (1819–1875); Elizabeth Gaskell (1810–1865); and Benjamin Disraeli (1804–1881), a novelist who became prime minister. For his novel *Sybil* (1845), Disraeli chose an appropriate subtitle, *The Two Nations*—a phrase that pointed out the line dividing the England of the rich from the other nation, the England of the poor.

THE MID-VICTORIAN PERIOD (1848–70): ECONOMIC PROSPERITY, THE GROWTH OF EMPIRE, AND RELIGIOUS CONTROVERSY

In the decades following the Time of Troubles some Victorian writers, such as Charles Dickens, continued to make critical attacks on the shortcomings of the Victorian social scene. Even more critical and indignant than Dickens was John Ruskin, who turned from a purely moral and aesthetic criticism of art during this period to denounce the evils of Victorian industry, as in his *The Stones of Venice* (1851–53), which combines a history of architecture with stern prophecies about the doom of technological culture, or in his attacks on laissez-faire economics in *Unto This Last* (1862). Generally speaking, however, the realistic novels of Anthony Trollope (1815–1882), with their comfortable tolerance and equanimity, are a more characteristic reflection of the mid-Victorian attitude toward the social and political scene than are Ruskin's lamentations. Overall, this second phase of the Victorian period had many harassing problems, but it was a time of prosperity. On the whole its institutions worked well. Even the badly bungled war against Russia in the Crimea (1854–56) did not seriously affect the growing sense of satisfaction that the challenging difficulties of the 1840s had been solved or would be solved by English wisdom and energy. The monarchy was proving its worth in a modern setting. The queen and her husband, Prince Albert, were models of middle-class domesticity and devotion to duty. The aristocracy was discovering that free trade was enriching rather than impoverishing their estates; agriculture flourished together with trade and industry. And through a succession of Factory Acts in Parliament, which restricted child labor and limited hours of employment, the condition of the working classes was also being gradually improved. When we speak of Victorian complacency or stability or optimism, we are usually referring to this mid-Victorian phase—"The Age of Improvement," as the historian Asa Briggs has called it. "Of all the decades in our history," writes G. M. Young, "a wise man would choose the eighteen-fifties to be young in."

In 1851 Prince Albert opened the Great Exhibition in Hyde Park, where a gigantic glass greenhouse, the Crystal Palace, had been erected to display the exhibits of modern industry and science. The Crystal Palace was one of the first buildings constructed according to modern architectural principles in which materials such as glass and iron are employed for purely functional ends (much late Victorian furniture, on the other hand, with its fantastic and irrelevant ornamentation, was constructed according to the opposite principle). The building, as well as the exhibits, symbolized the triumphant feats of Victorian technology. As Benjamin Disraeli wrote to a friend in 1862: "It is a privilege to live in this age of rapid and brilliant events. What an error to consider it a utilitarian age. It is one of infinite romance."

England's technological progress, together with its prosperity, led to an enormous expansion of its influence around the globe. Its annual export of goods nearly trebled in value between 1850 and 1870. Not only the export of goods but that of people and capital increased. Between 1853 and 1880 2,466,000 emigrants left Britain, many bound for British colonies. By 1870 British capitalists had invested £800 million abroad; in 1850 the total had been only £300 million. This investment, of people, money, and technology, created the British Empire. Important building blocks of the empire were put in place in the mid-Victorian period. In the 1850s and 1860s there was large-scale immigration to Australia; in 1867 Parliament unified the Canadian provinces into the Dominion of Canada. In 1857 Parliament took over the government of India from the private East India Company, which had controlled the country, and started to put in place its civil service government. In 1876 Queen Victoria was named empress of India. Although the competitive scramble for African colonies did not take place until the final decades of the century, the model of empire was created earlier, made possible by technological revolution in communication and transportation. Much as Rome had built roads through Europe in the years of the Roman Empire, Britain built railways and strung telegraph wires. It also put in place a framework for education and government that preserves British influence in former colonies even today. Britain's motives, in creating its empire, were many. It sought wealth, markets for manufactured goods, sources for raw materials, and world power and influence. Many English people also saw the expansion of empire as a moral responsibility—what Rudyard Kipling, in another context, termed "the White Man's burden." Queen Victoria stated that the imperial mission was "to protect the poor natives and advance civilization." Missionary societies flourished, spreading Christianity in India, Asia, and Africa.

At the same time that the British missionary enterprise was expanding, there was increasing debate about religious belief. By the mid-Victorian period the Church of England had evolved into three major divisions: Evangelical, or Low Church; Broad Church; and High Church. The Evangelicals emphasized spiritual transformation of the individual by conversion and a strictly moral Christian life. Zealously dedicated to good causes (they were responsible for the emancipation of all slaves in the British Empire as early as 1833), advocates of a strict Puritan code of morality, and righteously censorious of worldliness in others, the Evangelicals became a powerful and active minority in the early part of the nineteenth century. Much of the power of the Evangelicals depended on the fact that their view of life and religion was virtually identical with that of a much larger group external to the Church of England: the Nonconformists, or Dissenters—that is, Baptists, Methodists, Congregationalists, and other Protestant denominations. The High Church was also associated with a group external to the Church of England; it was the "Catholic" side of the Church, emphasizing the importance of tradition, ritual, and authority. In the 1830s a High Church movement took shape, known both as "the Oxford movement," because it originated at Oxford University, and as "Tractarianism," because its leaders developed their arguments in a series of pamphlets or tracts. Led by John Henry Newman, who later converted to Roman Catholicism, Tractarians argued that the Church could maintain its power and authority only by resisting liberal tendencies and holding to its original traditions. The Broad Church resisted the doctrinal and ecclesiastical controversies that separated the High Church and Evangelical divisions. Open to modern advances in thought, its adherents emphasized the broadly inclusive nature of the Church.

Some rationalist challenges to religious belief that developed before the Victorian period maintained their influence. The most significant was Utilitarianism, also known as Benthamism or Philosophical Radicalism. Utilitarianism derived from the thought of Jeremy Bentham (1748–1832) and his disciple James Mill (1773–1836), the father of John Stuart Mill. Bentham believed that all human beings seek to maximize pleasure and minimize pain. The criterion by which we should judge a morally correct action, therefore, is the extent to which it provides the greatest pleasure to the greatest number. Measuring religion by this moral arithmetic, Benthamites concluded that it was an outmoded superstition; it did not meet the rationalist test of value. Utilitarianism was widely influential in providing a philosophical basis for political and social reforms, but it aroused considerable opposition on the part of those who felt it failed to recognize people's spiritual needs. Raised according to strict utilitarian principles by his father, John Stuart Mill came to be critical of them. In the mental and spiritual crisis portrayed in his *Autobiography* (1873), Mill describes his realization that his utilitarian upbringing had left him no power to feel. In *Sartor Resartus* (1833–34) Carlyle describes a similar spiritual crisis in which he struggles to rediscover the springs of religious feeling in the face of his despair at the specter of a universe governed only by utilitarian principles. Later both Dickens, in his portrayal of Thomas Gradgrind in *Hard Times* (1854), "a man of facts and calculations" who is "ready to weigh and measure any parcel of human nature," and Ruskin, in his *Unto This Last*, attack utilitarianism.

In mid-Victorian England, however, the challenge to religious belief gradually shifted from the Utilitarians to some of the leaders of science, in particular to Thomas Henry Huxley, who popularized the theories of Charles Darwin. Although many English scientists were themselves individuals of strong religious convictions, the impact of their scientific discoveries seemed consistently damaging to established faiths. Complaining in 1851 about the "flimsiness" of his own religious faith, Ruskin exclaimed: "If only the Geologists would let me alone, I could do very well, but those dreadful hammers! I hear the clink of them at the end of every cadence of the Bible verses."

The damage lamented by Ruskin was effected in two ways. First the scientific attitude of mind was applied toward a study of the Bible. This kind of investigation, developed especially in Germany, was known as the "Higher Criticism." Instead of treating the Bible as a sacredly infallible document, scientifically minded scholars examined it as a mere text of history and presented evidence about its composition that believers, especially in Protestant countries, found disconcerting, to say the least. A noteworthy example of such Higher Criticism studies was David Friedrich Strauss's *Das Leben Jesu*, which was translated by George Eliot in 1846 as *The Life of Jesus*. The second kind of damage was effected by the view of humanity implicit in the discoveries of geology and astronomy, the new and "Terrible Muses" of literature, as Tennyson called them in a late poem. Geology, by extending the history of the earth backward millions of years, reduced the stature of the human species in time. John Tyndall, an eminent physicist, said in an address at Belfast in 1874 that in the eighteenth century people had an "unwavering trust" in the "chronology of the Old Testament" but in Victorian times they had to become accustomed to

> the idea that not for six thousand, nor for sixty thousand, nor for six thousand thousand, but for aeons embracing untold millions of years, this earth has been the theater of life and death. The riddle of the rocks has been read by the geologist and paleontologist, from sub-Cambrian depths to the deposits thickening over the sea bottoms of today. And upon the leaves of that stone book are . . . stamped the characters, plainer and surer than those formed by the ink of history, which carry the mind back into abysses of past time.

The discoveries of astronomers, by extending a knowledge of stellar distances to dizzying expanses, were likewise disconcerting. Carlyle's friend John Sterling remarked in a letter of 1837 how geology "gives one the same sort of bewildering view of the abysmal extent of Time that Astronomy does of Space." To Tennyson's speaker in *Maud* (1855) the stars are "innumerable" tyrants of "iron skies." They are "Cold fires, yet with power to burn and brand / His nothingness into man."

In the mid-Victorian period biology reduced humankind even further into "nothingness." Darwin's great treatise *The Origin of Species* (1859) was interpreted by the nonscientific public in a variety of ways. Some chose to assume that evolution was synonymous with progress, but most readers recognized that Darwin's theory of natural selection conflicted not only with the concept of creation derived from the Bible but also with long-established assumptions of the values attached to humanity's special role in the world. Darwin's later treatise *The Descent of Man* (1871) raised more explicitly the haunting question of our identification with the animal kingdom. If the principle of survival of the fittest was accepted as the key to conduct, there remained the inquiry: fittest for what? As John Fowles writes in his 1968 novel about Victorian England, *The French Lieutenant's Woman*, Darwin's theories made the Victorians feel "infinitely isolated." "By the 1860s the great iron structures of their philosophies, religions, and social stratifications were already beginning to look dangerously corroded to the more perspicacious."

Disputes about evolutionary science, like the disputes about religion, are a reminder that beneath the placidly prosperous surface of the mid-Victorian age there were serious conflicts and anxieties. In the same year as the Great Exhibition, with its celebration of the triumphs of trade and industry, Charles Kingsley wrote, "The young men and women of our day are fast parting from their parents and each other; the more thoughtful are wandering either towards Rome, towards sheer materialism, or towards an unchristian and unphilosophic spiritualism."

THE LATE PERIOD (1870–1901): DECAY OF VICTORIAN VALUES

The third phase of the Victorian age is more difficult to categorize. At first glance its point of view seems merely an extension of mid-Victorianism, whose golden glow lingered on through the Jubilee years of 1887 and 1897 (years celebrating the fiftieth and sixtieth anniversaries of the queen's accession) down to 1914. For many affluent Victorians, this final phase of the century was a time of serenity and security, the age of house parties and long weekends in the country. In the amber of Henry James's prose is immortalized a sense of the comfortable pace of these pleasant, food-filled gatherings. Life in London, too, was for many an exhilarating heyday. In *My Life and Loves* the Irish-American Frank Harris (1854–1931), often a severe critic of the English scene, records his recollections of the gaiety of London in the 1880s: "London: who would give even an idea of its varied delights: London, the center of civilization, the queen city of the world without a peer in the multitude of its attractions, as superior to Paris as Paris is to New York." The exhilarating sense of London's delights reflects in part the proliferation of things: commodities, inventions, products that were changing the texture of modern life. England had become committed not only to continuing technological change but also to a culture of consumerism, generating new products for sale.

The wealth of England's empire provided the foundation on which its economy was built. The final decades of the century saw the apex of British imperialism, yet the cost of the empire became increasingly apparent in rebellions, massacres, and bungled wars, such as the Indian Mutiny in 1857; the Jamaica Rebellion in 1865; the massacre of General Gordon and his troops at Khartoum, in the Sudan, in 1885, where he had been sent to evacuate the British in the face of a religiously inspired revolt; and the Anglo-Boer War, at the end of the century, in which England engaged in a long, bloody, and unpopular struggle to annex two independent republics in the south of Africa controlled by Dutch settlers called Boers. In addition the "Irish Question," as it was called, became especially divisive in the 1880s, when home rule for Ireland became a topic of heated debate—a proposed reform that was unsuccessfully advocated by Prime Minister Gladstone and other leaders. And outside the British Empire, other developments challenged Victorian stability and security. The sudden emergence of Bismarck's Germany after the defeat of France in 1871 was progressively to confront England with powerful threats to its naval and military position and also to its preeminence in trade and industry. The recovery of the United States after the Civil War likewise provided new and serious competition not only in industry but also in agriculture. As the westward expansion of railroads in the United States and Canada opened up the vast, grain-rich prairies, the typical English farmer had to confront lower grain prices and a dramatically different scale of productivity, which England could not match. In 1873 and 1874 such severe economic depressions occurred that the rate of emigration rose to an alarming degree. Another change in the mid-Victorian balance of power was the growth of labor as a political and economic force. In 1867, under Disraeli's guidance, a second Reform Bill had been passed that extended the right to vote to sections of the working classes; and this, together with the subsequent development of trade unions, made labor a powerful political force that included a wide variety of kinds of socialism. Some labor leaders were disciples of the Tory-socialism of John Ruskin and shared his idealistic conviction that the middle-class economic and political system, with its distrust of state interference, was irresponsible and immoral. Other labor leaders had been influenced instead by the revolutionary theories of Karl Marx and Friedrich Engels as expounded in their *Communist Manifesto* of 1847 and in Marx's *Das Kapital* (1867, 1885, 1895). The first English author of note to embrace Marxism was the poet and painter William Morris, who shared with Marx a conviction that utopia could be achieved only after the working classes had, by revolution, taken control of government and industry.

In much of the literature of this final phase of Victorianism we can sense an overall change of attitudes. Some of the late Victorian writers expressed the change openly by simply attacking the major mid-Victorian idols. Samuel Butler, for example, set about demolishing Darwin, Tennyson, and Prime Minister Gladstone, figures whose aura of authority reminded him of his own father. For the more worldly and casual-mannered Prime Minister Disraeli, on the other hand, Butler could express considerable admiration: "Earnestness was his greatest danger, but if he did not quite overcome it (as who indeed can? it is the last enemy that shall be subdued), he managed to veil it with a fair amount of success." In his novel *The Way of All Flesh* (1903), much of which was written in the 1870s, Butler satirized family life, in particular the tyrannical self-righteousness of a Victorian father, his own father (a clergyman) serving as his model. In a different vein Walter Pater and his followers concluded that the striving of their predecessors was ultimately pointless, that the answers to our problems are not to be found, and that our role is to enjoy the fleeting moments of beauty in "this short day of frost and sun." It is symptomatic of this shift in point of view that Edward FitzGerald's beautiful translation (1859) of *The Rubáiyát of Omar Khayyám*, with its melancholy theme that life's problems are insoluble, went virtually unnoticed in the 1860s but became a popular favorite in subsequent decades.

THE NINETIES

The changes in attitude that had begun cropping up in the 1870s became much more conspicuous in the final decade of the century and give the nineties a special aura of notoriety. Of course the changes were not in evidence everywhere. At the empire's outposts in India and Africa, the English were building railways and administering governments with the same strenuous energy as in the mid-Victorian period. The stories of Kipling and Joseph Conrad variously record the struggles of such people. Also embodying the task of sustaining an empire were the soldiers and sailors who fought in various colonial wars, most notably in the war against the Boers in South Africa (1899–1902). But back in England, Victorian standards were breaking down on several fronts. One colorful embodiment of changing values was Victoria's son and heir, Edward, Prince of Wales, who was entering his fiftieth year as the nineties began. A pleasure-seeking easygoing person, Edward was the antithesis of his father, Prince Albert, an earnest-minded intellectual who had devoted his life to hard work and to administrative responsibilities. Edward's carryings-on were a favorite topic for newspaper articles, one of which noted how this father of five children "openly maintained scandalous relations with ballet dancers and chorus singers."

Much of the writing of the decade illustrates a breakdown of a different sort. Melancholy, not gaiety, is characteristic of its spirit. Artists of the nineties, representing the aesthetic movement, were very much aware of living at the end of a great century and often cultivated a deliberately fin de siècle ("end-of-century") pose. A studied languor, a weary sophistication, a search for new ways of titillating jaded palates can be found in both the poetry and the prose of the period. *The Yellow Book,* a periodical that ran from 1894 to 1897, is generally taken to represent the aestheticism of the nineties. The startling black-and-white drawings and designs of its art editor, Aubrey Beardsley, the prose of George Moore and Max Beerbohm, and the poetry of Ernest Dowson illustrate different aspects of the movement. In 1893 the Austrian critic Max Nordau summed up what seemed to him to be happening, in a book that was as sensational as its title: *Degeneration.*

From our perspective, however, it is easy to see in the nineties the beginning of the modernist movement in literature; a number of the great writers of the twentieth century—Yeats, Hardy, Conrad, Shaw—were already publishing.

In Dickens's *David Copperfield* (1850) the hero affirms: "I have always been thoroughly in earnest." Forty-five years later Oscar Wilde's comedy *The Importance of Being Earnest* (1895) turns the typical mid-Victorian word *earnest* into a pun, a key joke in this comic spectacle of earlier Victorian values being turned upside down. As Richard Le Gallienne (a novelist of the nineties) remarked in *The Romantic Nineties* (1926): "Wilde made dying Victorianism laugh at itself, and it may be said to have died of the laughter."

THE ROLE OF WOMEN

Political and legal reforms in the course of the Victorian period had given citizens many rights. In 1844 Friedrich Engels observed: "England is unquestionably the freest—that is the least unfree—country in the world, North America not excepted." England had indeed done much to extend its citizens' liberties, but women did not share in these freedoms. They could not vote or hold political office. (Although petitions to Parliament advocating women's suffrage were introduced as early as the 1840s, women did not get the vote until 1918.) Until the passage of the Married Women's Property Acts (1870–1908), married women could not own or handle their own property. While men could divorce their wives for adultery, wives could divorce their husbands only if adultery were combined with cruelty, bigamy, incest, or bestiality. Educational and employment opportunities for women were limited. These inequities stimulated a spirited debate about women's roles known as the "Woman Question." Some of the social changes that such discussion helped foster eventually affected the lives of all, or many, of the country's female population; nevertheless, it is important to recognize that this Victorian debate, despite the inclusive claims of its title was, with a few exceptions, conducted by the middle classes about middle-class women.

Arguments for women's rights were based on the same libertarian principles that had formed the basis of extended rights for men. In Hardy's last novel, *Jude the Obscure* (1895), his heroine justifies leaving her husband by quoting a passage from Mill's *On Liberty* (1859). She might have quoted another work by Mill, *The Subjection of Women* (1869), which, like Mary Wollstonecraft's *A Vindication of the Rights of Woman* (1792), challenges long-established assumptions about women's role in society. Legislative measures over the course of the nineteenth century gradually brought about changes in a number of areas.

The Custody Act of 1839 gave a mother the right to petition the court for access to her minor children and custody of children under seven (raised to sixteen in 1878). The Divorce and Matrimonial Causes Act of 1857 established a civil divorce court (divorce previously could be granted only by an ecclesiastical court) and provided a deserted wife the right to apply for a protection order that would allow her rights to her property. Although divorce remained so expensive as to be available only to the very rich, these changes in marriage and divorce laws, together with the Married Women's Property Acts, began to establish a basis for the rights of women in marriage.

In addition to pressuring Parliament for legal reform, feminists worked to enlarge female educational opportunities. In 1837 none of England's three universities was open to women. Tennyson's long poem *The Princess* (1847), with its fantasy of a women's college from whose precincts all males are excluded, was inspired by contemporary discussions of the need for women to obtain an education more advanced than that provided by the popular finishing schools such as Miss Pinkerton's Academy in William Makepeace Thackeray's *Vanity Fair* (1847–48). Although by the end of the poem Princess Ida has repented of her Amazonian scheme, she and the prince look forward to a future in which man will be "more of woman, she of man." The poem reflects a climate of opinion that led in 1848 to the establishment of the first women's college in London, an example later recommended by Thomas Henry Huxley, a strong advocate of advanced education for women. By the end of Victoria's reign, women could take degrees at twelve universities or university colleges and could study, although not earn a degree, at Oxford and Cambridge.

There was also agitation for improved employment opportunities for women. Writers as diverse as Charlotte Brontë, Elizabeth Barrett Browning, and Florence Nightingale complained that middle-class women were taught trivial accomplishments to fill up days in which there was nothing important to do. Had they been aware of such complaints, women from the majority lower-class population might have found it hard to show sympathy: the working lives of poor English women had always been strenuous, inside and outside the house, but industrial society brought unprecedented pressures. Although the largest proportion of working women labored as servants in the homes of the more affluent, the explosive growth of mechanized industries, especially in the textile trade, created new and grueling forms of paid employment. Hundreds of thousands of lower-class women worked at factory jobs under appalling conditions, while the need for coal to fuel England's industrial development brought women into the mines for the first time. A series of Factory Acts (1802–78) gradually regulated the conditions of labor in mines and factories, eventually reducing the sixteen-hour day and banning women from mine work altogether; but even with such changes, the lot of the country's poorest women, whether factory operatives or housemaids, seamstresses or field laborers, was undoubtedly hard. Bad working conditions and underemployment drove thousands of women into prostitution, which in the nineteenth century became increasingly professionalized—and the subject of an almost obsessive public concern, whose manifestations included frequent literary and artistic representation.

For the most part, prostitution was a trade for working-class women, but there was considerable anxiety about the possible fates of what contemporary journalists called the "surplus" or "redundant" women of the middle classes— that is, women who remained unmarried because of the imbalance in numbers between the sexes. Such women (of whom there were approximately half a million in mid-Victorian England) had few employment opportunities, none of them attractive or profitable. Emigration was frequently proposed as a solution to the problem, but the number of single female emigrants was never high enough to significantly affect the population imbalance. The only occupation at which an unmarried middle-class woman could earn a living and maintain some claim to gentility was that of a governess, but a governess could expect no security of employment, only minimal wages, and an ambiguous status, somewhere between servant and family member, that isolated her within the household. Perhaps because the governess so clearly indicated the precariousness of the unmarried middle-class woman's status in Victorian England, the governess novel, of which the most famous examples are *Jane Eyre* (1847) and *Vanity Fair*, became a popular genre through which to explore women's roles in society.

As such novels indicate, Victorian society was preoccupied not only with legal and economic limitations on women's lives but with the very nature of woman. In *The Subjection of Women*, John Stuart Mill argues that "what is now called the nature of women is eminently an artificial thing—the result of forced repression in some directions, unnatural stimulation in others." In Tennyson's *The Princess* the king voices a more traditional view of male and female roles, a view that has come to be known as the doctrine of "separate spheres":

> Man for the field and woman for the hearth:
> Man for the sword and for the needle she:
> Man with the head and woman with the heart:
> Man to command and woman to obey.

The king's relegation of women to the hearth and heart reflects an ideology that claimed that woman had a special nature peculiarly fit for her domestic role. Most aptly epitomized by the title of Coventry Patmore's immensely popular poem *The Angel in the House* (1854–62), this concept of womanhood stressed woman's purity and selflessness. Protected and enshrined within the home, her role was to create a place of peace where man could take refuge from the difficulties of modern life. In "Of Queens' Gardens" (1865), John Ruskin writes:

> This is the true nature of home—it is the place of Peace; the shelter, not only from all injury, but from all terror, doubt, and division. In so far as it is not this, it is not home; so far as the anxieties of the outer life penetrate into it, and the inconsistently-minded, unknown, unloved, or hostile society of the outer world is allowed either by husband or wife to cross the threshold, it ceases to be home; it is then only a part of that outer world which you have roofed over, and lighted fire in. But so far as it is a sacred place, a vestal temple, a temple of the hearth watched over by

Household Gods, . . . so far it vindicates the name, and fulfills the praise, of home.

Such an exalted conception of home placed great pressure on the woman who ran it to be, in Ruskin's words, "enduringly, incorruptibly good; instinctively, infallibly wise—wise, not for self-development, but for self-renunciation." It is easy to recognize the oppressive aspects of this domestic ideology. Paradoxically, however, it was used not only by antifeminists, eager to keep woman in her place, but by some feminists as well, in justifying the special contribution that woman could make to public life.

In his preface to *The Portrait of a Lady* (1881) Henry James writes: "Millions of presumptuous girls, intelligent or not intelligent, daily affront their destiny, and what is it open to their destiny to *be*, at the most, that we should make an ado about it?" Every major Victorian novelist makes the "ado" that James describes in addressing the question of woman's vocation; by the 1890s the "New Woman," an emerging form of emancipated womanhood, was endlessly debated in a wave of fiction and magazine articles. Ultimately, as Victorian texts illustrate, the basic problem was not only political, economic, and educational. It was how women were regarded, and regarded themselves, as members of a society.

LITERACY, PUBLICATION, AND READING

Literacy increased significantly during the Victorian period, although precise figures are difficult to calculate. In 1837 about half of the adult male population could read and write to some extent; by the end of the century, basic literacy was almost universal, the product in part of compulsory national education, required by 1880 to the age of ten. There was also an explosion of things to read. Because of technological changes in printing—presses powered by steam, paper made from wood pulp rather than rags, and, toward the end of the century, typesetting machines—publishers could bring out more printed material more cheaply than ever before. The number of newspapers, periodicals, and books increased exponentially during the Victorian period. Books remained fairly expensive, and most readers borrowed them from commercial lending libraries. (There were few public libraries until the final decades of the century.) After the repeal of the stamp tax and duties on advertisements just after midcentury, an extensive popular press developed.

The most significant development in publishing from the point of view of literary culture was the growth of the periodical. In the first thirty years of the Victorian period, 170 new periodicals were started in London alone. There were magazines for every taste: cheap and popular magazines that published sensational tales; religious monthlies; weekly newspapers; satiric periodicals noted for their political cartoons (the most famous of these was *Punch*); women's magazines; monthly miscellanies publishing fiction, poetry, and articles on current affairs; and reviews and quarterlies, ostensibly reviewing new books but using the reviews, which were always unsigned, as occasions for essays on the subjects in question. The chief reviews and monthly magazines had a great deal of power and influence; they defined issues in public affairs, and they made and broke literary reputations. They also published the major writers of the period: the fiction of Dickens, Thackeray, Eliot, Trollope, and Gaskell; the essays of Carlyle, Mill, Arnold, and Ruskin; and the poetry of Tennyson and the Brownings all appeared in monthly magazines.

The circumstances of periodical publication exerted a shaping force on literature. Novels and long works of nonfiction prose were published in serial form. Although serial publication of works began in the late eighteenth century, it was the publication of Dickens's *Pickwick Papers* (1836–37) in individual numbers that established its popularity. All of Dickens's novels and many of those of his contemporaries were published in serial form. Readers therefore read these works in relatively short, discrete installments over a period that could extend more than a year, with time for reflection and interpretation in between. Serial publication encouraged a certain kind of plotting and pacing and allowed writers to take account of their readers' reactions as they constructed subsequent installments. Writers created a continuing world, punctuated by the ends of installments, which served to stimulate the curiosity that would keep readers buying subsequent issues. Serial publication also created a distinctive sense of a community of readers, a sense encouraged by the practice of reading aloud in family gatherings.

As the family reading of novels suggests, the middle-class reading public enjoyed a common reading culture. Poets such as Tennyson and Elizabeth Barrett Browning and anthologies such as Palgrave's *Golden Treasury* (1861) appealed to a large body of readers; prose writers such as Carlyle, Arnold, and Ruskin achieved a status as sages; and the major Victorian novelists were popular writers. Readers shared the expectation that literature would not only delight but instruct, that it would be continuous with the lived world, and that it would illuminate social problems. "Tennyson," one of his college friends warned him, "we cannot live in Art." These expectations weighed more heavily on some writers than others. Tennyson wore his public mantle with considerable ambivalence; Arnold abandoned the private mode of lyric poetry in order to speak about public issues in lectures and essays.

By the 1870s the sense of a broad readership, with a shared set of social concerns, had begun to dissolve. Writers had begun to define themselves in opposition to a general public; poets like the Pre-Raphaelites pursued art for art's sake, doing exactly what Tennyson's friend had warned against; mass publication included less and less serious literature. By the end of Victoria's reign, writers could no longer assume a unified reading public.

THE NOVEL

The novel was the dominant form in Victorian literature. Initially published, for the most part, in serial form, novels subsequently appeared in three-volume editions, or "three-deckers." "Large loose baggy monsters," Henry James called them, reflecting his dissatisfaction with their sprawling panoramic expanse. As their size suggests, Victorian novels seek to represent a large and comprehensive social world, with the variety of classes and social settings that constitute a community. They contain a multitude of characters and a number of plots, setting in motion the kinds of patterns that reveal the author's vision of the deep structures of the social world—how, in George Eliot's words, "the mysterious mixture behaves under the varying experiments of Time." They presents themselves as realistic, that is, as representing a social world that shares the features of the one we inhabit. The French novelist Stendhal (1783–1842) called the novel "a mirror wandering down a road," but the metaphor of the mirror is somewhat deceptive, since it implies that writers exert no shaping force on their material. It would be more accurate to speak not of realism but of realisms, since each novelist presents a specific vision of reality whose representational force he or she seeks to persuade us to acknowledge through a variety of techniques and conventions. The worlds of Dickens, of Trollope, of Eliot, of the Brontës hardly seem continuous with each other, but their authors share the attempt to convince us that the characters and events they imagine resemble those we experience in actual life.

The experience that Victorian novelists most frequently depict is the set of social relationships in the middle-class society developing around them. It is a society where the material conditions of life indicate social position, where money defines opportunity, where social class enforces a powerful sense of stratification, yet where chances for class mobility exist. Pip can aspire to the great expectations that provide the title for Dickens's novel; Jane Eyre can marry her employer, a landed gentleman. Most Victorian novels focus on a protagonist whose effort to define his or her place in society is the main concern of the plot. The novel thus constructs a tension between surrounding social conditions and the aspiration of the hero or heroine, whether it be for love, social position, or a life adequate to his or her imagination. This tension makes the novel the natural form to use in portraying woman's struggle for self-realization in the context of the constraints imposed upon her. For both men and women writers, the heroine is often, therefore, the representative protagonist whose search for fulfillment emblematizes the human condition. The great heroines of Victorian fiction—Jane Eyre, Maggie Tulliver, Dorothea Brooke, Isabel Archer, Tess of the d'Urbervilles, even Becky Sharp—all seem in some way to illustrate George Eliot's judgment, voiced in the Prelude to *Middlemarch* (1871–72), of "a certain spiritual grandeur ill-matched with meanness of opportunity."

From the beginning of the nineteenth century, the novel was more than a fertile medium for the portrayal of women; women writers were, for the first time, not figures on the margins but major authors. Jane Austen, the Brontës, Elizabeth Gaskell, George Eliot—all helped define the genre. When Charlotte Brontë screwed up her courage to write to the poet laureate, Robert Southey, to ask his advice about a career as a writer, he warned her, "Literature cannot be the business of a woman's life, and it ought not to be." Charlotte Brontë put this letter, with one other from Southey, in an envelope, with the inscription "Southey's advice to be kept forever. My twenty-first birthday." Brontë's ability ultimately to depart from Southey's advice derived in part from how amenable the novel was to women writers. It concerned the domestic life that women knew well—courtship, family relationships, marriage. It was a popular form whose market women could enter easily. It did not carry the burden of an august tradition as poetry did, nor did it build on the learning of a university education. In his essay "The Lady Novelists" (1852) George Henry Lewes declared, "The advent of female literature promises woman's view of life, woman's experience." His common-law wife, George Eliot, together with many of her sister novelists, fulfilled his prophecy.

Whether written by women or men, the Victorian novel was extraordinarily various. It encompassed a wealth of styles and genres from the extravagant comedy of Dickens to the Gothic romances of the Brontë sisters, from the satire of Thackeray to the probing psychological fiction of Eliot, from the social and political realism of Trollope to the sensation novels of Wilkie Collins. Later in the century a number of popular genres developed—crime, mystery, and horror novels, as well as science fiction and detective stories. For the Victorians the novel was both a principal form of entertainment and a spur to social sympathy. There was not a social topic that the novel did not address. Dickens, Gaskell, and many lesser novelists tried to stimulate efforts for social reform through their depiction of social problems. Writing at the beginning of the twentieth century, Joseph Conrad defined the novel in a way that could speak for the Victorians: "What is a novel if not a conviction of our fellow-men's existence strong enough to take upon itself a form of imagined life clearer than reality and whose accumulated verisimilitude of selected episodes puts to shame the pride of documentary history?"

POETRY

Victorian poetry developed in the context of the novel. As the novel emerged as the dominant form of literature, poets sought new ways of telling stories in verse; examples include Tennyson's *Maud*, Elizabeth Barrett Browning's *Aurora Leigh* (1857), Robert Browning's *The Ring and the Book* (1868–69), and Arthur Hugh Clough's *Amours de Voyage* (1857–58). Poets and critics debated what the appropriate subjects of such long narrative poems should be. Some, like Matthew Arnold, held that poets should use the heroic materials of the past; others, like Elizabeth Barrett Browning, felt that poets should represent "their age, not Charlemagne's." Poets also experimented with character and perspective. *Amours de Voyage* is a long epistolary poem that tells the story of a failed romance through letters written by its various characters; *The Ring and the Book* presents its plot—an old Italian murder story—through ten different perspectives.

Victorian poetry also developed in the shadow of Romanticism. By 1837, when Victoria ascended the throne, all the major Romantic poets, save William Wordsworth, were dead, but they had died young, and many readers consequently still regarded them as their contemporaries. Not even twenty years separated the birth dates of Tennyson and Browning from that of John Keats, but they lived more than three times as long as he did. All the Victorian poets show the strong influence of the Romantics, but they cannot sustain the confidence that the Romantics felt in the power of the imagination. The Victorians often rewrite Romantic poems with a sense of belatedness and distance. When, in his poem "Resignation," Arnold addresses his sister upon revisiting a landscape, much as Wordsworth had addressed his sister in "Tintern Abbey," he tells her the rocks and sky "seem to bear rather than rejoice." Tennyson frequently represents his muse as an embowered woman, cut off from the world and doomed to death. The speakers of Browning's poems who embrace the visions that their imaginations present are madmen. When Hardy writes "The Darkling Thrush," in December 1900, Keats's nightingale has become "an aged thrush, frail, gaunt, and small."

Victorian poets build upon this sense of belated Romanticism in a number of different ways. Some poets writing in the second half of the century, like Dante Gabriel Rossetti and Algernon Charles Swinburne, embrace an attenuated Romanticism, art pursued for its own sake. Reacting against what he sees as the insufficiency of an allegory of the state of one's own mind as the basis of poetry, Arnold seeks an objective basis for poetic emotion and finally gives up writing poems altogether when he decides that the present age lacks the culture necessary to support great poetry. The more fruitful reaction to the subjectivity of Romantic poetry, however, was not Arnold's but Browning's. Turning from the mode of his early poetry, modeled on Percy Bysshe Shelley, Browning began writing dramatic monologues—poems, he said, that are "Lyric in expression" but "Dramatic in principle, and so many utterances of so many imaginary persons, not mine." Tennyson simultaneously developed a more lyric form of the dramatic monologue. The idea of creating a lyric poem in the voice of a speaker ironically distinct from the poet is the great achievement of Victorian poetry, one developed extensively in the twentieth century. In *Poetry and the Age* (1953), the modernist poet and critic Randall Jarrell acknowledges this fact: "The dramatic monologue, which once had depended for its effect upon being a departure from the norm of poetry, now became in one form or other the norm."

The formal experimentation of Victorian poetry, both in long narrative and in the dramatic monologue, may make it seem eclectic, but Victorian poetry shares a number of characteristics. It tends to be pictorial, using detail to construct visual images that represent the emotion or situation the poem concerns. In his review of Tennyson's first volume of poetry, Arthur Henry Hallam defines this kind of poetry as "picturesque," as combining visual impressions in such a way that they create a picture that carries the dominant emotion of the poem. This aesthetic brings poets and painters close together. Contemporary artists frequently illustrated Victorian poems, and poems themselves often present paintings. Victorian poetry also uses sound in a distinctive way. Whether it be the mellifluousness of Tennyson or Swinburne, with its emphasis on beautiful cadences, alliteration, and vowel sounds, or the roughness of Browning or Gerard Manley Hopkins, a roughness adopted in part in reaction against Tennyson, the sound of Victorian poetry reflects an attempt to use poetry as a medium with a presence almost independent of sense. The resulting style can become so syntactically elaborate that it is easy to parody, as in Hopkins's description of Browning as a man "bouncing up from table with his mouth full of bread and cheese" or T. S. Eliot's criticism of Swinburne's poetry, where "meaning is merely the hallucination of meaning." Yet it is important to recognize that these poets use sound to convey meaning, to quote Hallam's review of Tennyson once more, "where words would not." "The tone becomes the sign of the feeling." In all of these developments—the experimentation with narrative and perspective, the dramatic monologue, the use of visual detail and sound—Victorian poets seek to represent psychology in a different way. Their most distinctive achievement is a poetry of mood and character. They therefore sat in uneasy relationship to the public expectation that poets be sages with something to teach. Tennyson, Browning, and Arnold showed varying discomfort with this public role; poets beginning to write in the second half of the century distanced themselves from their public by embracing an identity as bohemian rebels. Women poets encountered a different set of difficulties in developing their poetic voice. When, in Barrett Browning's epic about the growth of a woman poet, Aurora Leigh's cousin Romney discourages her poetic ambitions by telling her that women are "weak for art" but "strong for life and duty," he articulates the prejudice of an age. Women poets view their vocation in the context of the constraints and expectations upon their sex. Perhaps because of this, their poems are less complicated by the experiments in perspective than those of their male contemporaries.

PROSE

Although Victorian poets felt ambivalent about the didactic mission the public expected of the man of letters, writers of nonfictional prose aimed specifically to instruct. Although the term *nonfictional prose* is clumsy and not quite exact (the Victorians themselves referred instead to history, biography, theology, criticism), it has its uses not only to distinguish these prose writers from the novelists but also to indicate the centrality of argument and persuasion to Victorian intellectual life. The growth of the periodical press, described earlier, provided the vehicle and marketplace for nonfictional prose. It reflects a vigorous sense of shared intellectual life and the public urgency of social and moral issues. On a wide range of controversial topics—religious, political, and aesthetic—writers seek to convince their readers to share their convictions and values. Such writers seem at times almost secular priests. Indeed, in the fifth lecture of *On Heroes, Hero-Worship, and the Heroic in History* (1841), Carlyle defines the writer precisely in these terms: "Men of Letters are a perpetual Priesthood, from age to age, teaching all Men that God is still present in their life. . . . In the true Literary Man, there is thus ever, acknowledged or not by the world, a sacredness." The modern man of letters, Carlyle argues, differs from his earlier counterpart in that he writes for money. "Never, till about a hundred years ago, was there seen any figure of a Great Soul living apart in that anomalous manner; endeavouring to speak forth the inspiration that was in him by Printed Books, and find place and subsistence by what the world would please him for doing that." This combination, of a new market position for nonfictional writing and an exalted sense of the didactic function of the writer, produces a quintessential Victorian form.

On behalf of nonfictional prose, Walter Pater argued in his essay "Style" (1889) that it was "the special and opportune art of the modern world." He believed not that it was superior to verse but that it more readily conveys the "chaotic variety and complexity" of modern life, the "incalculable" intellectual diversity of the "master currents of the present time." Pater's characterization of prose helps us understand what its writers were attempting to do. Despite the diversity of styles and subjects, Victorian prose writers were engaged in shaping belief in a bewilderingly complex and changing world. Their modes of persuasion differ. Mill and Huxley rely on clear reasoning, logical argument, and the kind of lucid style favored by essayists of the eighteenth century. Carlyle and Ruskin write a prose that is more Romantic in character, that seeks to move readers as well as convince them. Whatever the differences in their rhetorical techniques, however, they share an urgency of exposition. Not only by what they said but by how they said it, Victorian prose writers were claiming a place for literature in a scientific and materialistic culture. Arnold and Pater share this as an explicit aim. Each in his own way argues that culture—the intensely serious appreciation of great works of literature—provides the kind of immanence and meaning that people once found in religion. For Arnold this is an intensely moral experience; for Pater it is aesthetic. Together they develop the basis for the claims of modern literary criticism.

DRAMA AND THEATER

Though the Victorian age can lay claim to greatness for its poetry, its prose, and its novels, it would be difficult to make such a high claim for its plays, at least until the final decade of the century. Here we must distinguish between playwriting on the one hand and theatrical activity on the other. For the theater, throughout the period, was a flourishing and popular institution, in which were performed not merely conventional dramas but a rich variety of theatrical entertainments, many with lavish spectacular effects—burlesques, extravaganzas, highly scenic and altered versions of Shakespeare's plays, melodramas, pantomimes, and musicals. Robert Corrigan gives figures that suggest the extent of the popularity of such entertainment: "In the decade between 1850 and 1860 the number of theaters built throughout the country was doubled, and in the middle of the sixties, in London alone, 150,000 would be attending the theater on any given day. Only when we realize that the theatre was to Victorian England what television is to us today will we be able to comprehend both its wide appeal and its limited artistic achievement." The popularity of theatrical entertainment made theater a powerful influence on other genres. Dickens was devoted to the theater and composed many of the scenes of his novels with theatrical techniques. Thackeray represents himself as the puppet master of his characters in *Vanity Fair* and employs the stock gestures and expressions of melodramatic acting in his illustrations for the novel. Tennyson, Browning, and Henry James tried their hands at writing plays, though with no commercial success. Successful plays on stage were written by the lesser lights of literature such as Dion Boucicault (1820–1890), the period's most prolific and popular dramatist. The comic operas of W. S. Gilbert and Arthur Sullivan prove the exception to this judgment. Their satire of Victorian values and institutions, what Gilbert called their "topsyturvydom," and their grave and quasi-respectful treatment of the ridiculous not only make them delightful in themselves but anticipate the techniques of Shaw and Wilde. Around 1890, when the socially controversial plays of the Norwegian dramatist Henrik Ibsen (1828–1906) became known in England, Arthur Pinero (1855–1934) and Bernard Shaw began writing "problem plays," which addressed difficult social issues. In the 1890s Shaw and Oscar Wilde transformed British theater with their comic masterpieces. Although they did not like each other's work, they both created a kind of comedy that took aim at Victorian pretense and hypocrisy.

Additional information about the Victorian Age, including primary texts and images, is available at Norton Literature Online (www.wwnorton.com/literature). Online topics are

- Industrialism—Progress or Decline?
- The Woman Question
- The Painterly Image in Poetry
- Victorian Imperialism

TEXTS	CONTEXTS
1830 Alfred Lord Tennyson, *Poems, Chiefly Lyrical*	1830 Opening of Liverpool and Manchester Railway
1832 Sir Charles Lyell, *Principles of Geology*	1832 First Reform Bill
1833 Thomas Carlyle, *Sartor Resartus*	1833 Factory Act. Abolition of Slavery Act. Beginning of Oxford Movement
1836 Charles Dickens, *Pickwick Papers*	1836 First train in London
1837 Carlyle, *The French Revolution*	1837 Victoria becomes queen
	1838 "People's Charter" issued by Chartist Movement
	1840 Queen marries Prince Albert
1842 Tennyson, *Poems*. Robert Browning, *Dramatic Lyrics*	1842 Chartist Riots. Copyright Act. Mudie's Circulating Library
1843 John Ruskin, *Modern Painters* (vol. 1)	
	1845–46 Potato famine in Ireland. Mass emigration to North America
1846 George Eliot, *The Life of Jesus* (translation)	1846 Repeal of Corn Laws. Robert Browning marries Elizabeth Barrett
1847 Charlotte Brontë, *Jane Eyre*. Emily Brontë, *Wuthering Heights*	1847 Ten Hours Factory Act
1848 Elizabeth Gaskell, *Mary Barton*. William Makepeace Thackeray, *Vanity Fair*	1848 Revolution on the Continent. Second Republic established in France. Founding of Pre-Raphaelite Brotherhood
1850 Tennyson, *In Memoriam*. William Wordsworth, *The Prelude* (posthumous publication)	1850 Tennyson succeeds Wordsworth as Poet Laureate
1851 Ruskin, *Stones of Venice*	1851 Great Exhibition of science and industry at the Crystal Palace
1853 Matthew Arnold, *Poems*	
1854 Dickens, *Hard Times*	1854 Crimean War. Florence Nightingale organizes nurses to care for sick and wounded
1855 Robert Browning, *Men and Women*	
1857 Elizabeth Barrett Browning, *Aurora Leigh*	1857 Indian Mutiny. Matrimonial Causes Act
1859 Charles Darwin, *The Origin of Species*. John Stuart Mill, *On Liberty*. Tennyson, *Idylls of the King* (books 1–4)	
1860 Dickens, *Great Expectations*. Eliot, *The Mill on the Floss*	1860 Italian unification
	1861 Death of Prince Albert
	1861–65 American Civil War
1862 Christina Rossetti, *Goblin Market*	
1864 R. Browning, *Dramatis Personae*	

TEXTS	CONTEXTS
1865 Lewis Carroll, *Alice's Adventures in Wonderland*	1865 Jamaica Rebellion
1866 Algernon Charles Swinburne, *Poems and Ballads*	
1867 Karl Marx, *Das Kapital*	1867 Second Reform Bill
	1868 Opening of Suez Canal
1869 Arnold, *Culture and Anarchy*. Mill, *The Subjection of Women*	
	1870 Married Women's Property Act. Victory in Franco-Prussian War makes Germany a world power. Elementary Education Act
1871 Darwin, *Descent of Man*	1871 Newnham College (first women's Oxbridge college) founded at Cambridge
1872 Eliot, *Middlemarch*	
1873 Walter Pater, *Studies in the History of the Renaissance*	
	1877 Queen Victoria made empress of India. Gerard Manley Hopkins joins Jesuit order
	1878 Electric street lighting in London
	1882 Married Women's Property Act
1885 W. S. Gilbert and Arthur Sullivan, *The Mikado*	1885 Massacre of General Gordon and his forces and fall of Khartoum
1886 Robert Louis Stevenson, *Doctor Jekyll and Mr. Hyde*	
1888 Rudyard Kipling, *Plain Tales from the Hills*	
1889 William Butler Yeats, *Crossways*	
	1890 First subway line in London
1891 Thomas Hardy, *Tess of the D'Urbervilles*. Bernard Shaw, *The Quintessence of Ibsenism*. Oscar Wilde, *The Picture of Dorian Grey*. Arthur Conan Doyle, *Adventures of Sherlock Holmes*	1891 Free elementary education
1893 Shaw, *Mrs. Warren's Profession*	1893 Independent Labour Party
1895 Wilde, *The Importance of Being Earnest*. Hardy, *Jude the Obscure*	1895 Oscar Wilde arrested and imprisoned for homosexuality
1896 A. E. Housman, *A Shropshire Lad*	
1898 Hardy, *Wessex Poems*	1898 Discovery of radium
	1899 Irish Literary Theater founded in Dublin
	1899–1902 Anglo-Boer War
1900 Joseph Conrad, *Lord Jim*	
	1901 Death of Queen Victoria; succession of Edward VII

THOMAS CARLYLE
1795–1881

W. B. Yeats once asked William Morris which writers had inspired the socialist movement of the 1880s, and Morris replied: "Oh, Ruskin and Carlyle, but somebody should have been beside Carlyle and punched his head every five minutes." Morris's mixed feelings of admiration and exasperation are typical of the response Thomas Carlyle evokes in many readers. Anyone approaching his prose for the first time should expect to be sometimes bewildered. Like Bernard Shaw, Carlyle discovered, early in life, that exaggeration can be a highly effective way of gaining the attention of an audience. But it can also be a way of distracting an audience unfamiliar with the idiosyncrasies of his rhetoric and unprepared for the distinctive enjoyments his writings can provide.

One of the idiosyncrasies of his prose is that it is meant to be read aloud. "His paragraphs," as Ralph Waldo Emerson observes, "are all a sort of splendid conversation." As a talker Carlyle was as famous in his day as Samuel Johnson in his. Charles Darwin testified that he was "the best worth listening to of any man I know." No Boswell has adequately recorded this talk, but no Boswell was needed, for Carlyle's prose adopts the rhythm, idiosyncrasy, and spontaneity of the spoken voice. It is a noisy and emphatic voice, startling on a first reading.

Carlyle was forty-one years old when Victoria became queen of England. He had been born in the same year as John Keats, yet he is rarely grouped with his contemporaries among the Romantic writers. Instead his name is linked with younger men such as Charles Dickens, Robert Browning, and John Ruskin, the early generation of Victorian writers, for whom he became (according to Elizabeth Barrett Browning) "the great teacher of the age." The classification is fitting, for it was Carlyle's role to foresee the problems that were to preoccupy the Victorians and early to report on his experiences in confronting these problems. After 1837 his loud voice began to attract an audience; and he soon became one of the most influential figures of the age, affecting the attitudes of scientists, statesmen, and especially of writers. His wife once complained that Emerson had no ideas (except mad ones) that he had not derived from Carlyle. " 'But pray, Mrs. Carlyle,' replied a friend, 'who has?' "

Carlyle was born in Ecclefechan, a village in Scotland, the eldest child of a large family. His mother, at the time of her marriage, was illiterate. His father, James Carlyle, a stonemason and later a farmer, was proudly characterized by his son as a peasant. The key to the character of James Carlyle was the Scottish Calvinism that he instilled into the members of his household. Frugality, hard work, a tender but undemonstrative family loyalty, and a peculiar blend of self-denial and self-righteousness were characteristic features of Carlyle's childhood home.

With his father's aid the young Carlyle was educated at Annan Academy and at Edinburgh University, the subject of his special interest being mathematics; he left without taking a degree. It was his parents' hope that their son would become a clergyman, but in this respect Thomas made a severe break with his ancestry. He was a prodigious reader; and his exposure to such skeptical writers as David Hume, Voltaire, and Edward Gibbon had undermined his faith. Gibbon's *Decline and Fall of the Roman Empire* (1776–88), he told Emerson, was "the splendid bridge from the old world to the new." By the time he was twenty-three Carlyle had crossed the bridge and had abandoned his Christian faith and his proposed career as a clergyman. During the period in which he was thinking through his religious position, he supported himself by teaching school in Scotland and, later, by tutoring private pupils; but from 1824 to the end of his life he relied exclusively on his writings for his livelihood. His early writings consisted of translations, biographies, and critical studies of Johann Wolfgang von Goethe and other German authors, to whose view of life he was deeply attracted. The German Romantics (loosely grouped by Carlyle under the label "Mystics") were the second most important influence on his life and character, exceeded only by his early family experiences. Aided by the writings of these German poets and philosophers, he arrived finally at a faith in life that served as a substitute for the Christian faith he had lost.

His most significant early essay, "Characteristics," appeared in *The Edinburgh Review* in 1831. A year earlier he had begun writing *Sartor Resartus*, an account of the life and opinions of an imaginary philosopher, Professor Diogenes Teufelsdröckh, a work that he had great difficulty in persuading anyone to publish. In book form *Sartor* first appeared in America in 1836, where Carlyle's follower Emerson had prepared an enthusiastic audience for this unusual work. His American following (which was later to become a vast one) did little at first, however, to relieve the poverty in which he still found himself after fifteen years of writing. In 1837 the tide at last turned when he published *The French Revolution*. "O it has been a great success, dear," his wife assured him; but her husband, embittered by the long struggle, was incredulous that the sought-for recognition had at last come to him.

It was in character for his wife, Jane Welsh Carlyle, to be less surprised by his success than he was. That Thomas Carlyle was a genius had been an article of faith to her from her first meeting with him in 1821. A witty, intelligent, and intellectually ambitious young woman, the daughter of a doctor of good family, Jane Welsh had many suitors. When in 1826 she finally accepted Carlyle, her family and friends were shocked. This peasant's son, of no fixed employment, seemed a preposterous choice. Subsequent events seemed to confirm her family's verdict. Not long after marriage Carlyle insisted on their retiring to a remote farm at Craigenputtock, where for six years (1828–34) this sociable woman was obliged to live in isolation and loneliness. After they moved to London in 1834 and settled in a house on Cheyne Walk in Chelsea, Jane Carlyle was considerably happier and enjoyed her role at the center of the intellectual and artistic circle that surrounded her husband. Her husband, however, remained a difficult man to live with. His stomach ailments, irascible nerves, and preoccupation with his writings, as well as the lionizing to which he was subjected, left him with little inclination for domestic amenities or for encouraging his wife's considerable intellectual talents. As a young girl she had wanted to be a writer; her letters, some of the most remarkable of the century, show that she had considerable literary talent.

This marriage of the Carlyles has aroused almost as much interest as that of the Brownings. Their friend the Reverend W. H. Brookfield (whose marriage was an unhappy one) once said cynically that marrying is "dipping into a pitcher of snakes for the chance of an eel," and some biographers have argued that Jane Welsh Carlyle drew a snake instead of an eel. Yet if we study her letters, it is evident that she wanted to marry a man of genius who would change the world. Despite the years she endured of comparative poverty, poor health, and loneliness, she had the satisfaction of recognizing her husband's triumph when the peasant's son she had chosen returned to Scotland to deliver his inaugural address as lord rector of Edinburgh University. While he was away, to Carlyle's great grief, she died.

During the first thirty years of his residence in London Carlyle wrote extensive historical works and many pamphlets concerning contemporary issues. After *The French Revolution* he edited, in 1845, the *Letters and Speeches of Oliver Cromwell*, a Puritan leader of heroic dimensions in Carlyle's eyes, and later wrote a full-length biography, *The History of Friedrich II of Prussia, Called Frederick the Great* (1858–65). Carlyle's pamphleteering is seen at its best in *Past and Present* (1843) and in its most violent phase in his *Latter-Day Pamphlets* (1850). Following the death of his wife, he wrote very little. For the remaining fifteen years of his life, he confined himself to reading or to talking to the stream of visitors who called at Cheyne Walk to listen to the "Sage of Chelsea," as he came to be called. In 1874 he accepted the Prussian Order of Merit from Bismarck but declined an English baronetcy offered by Disraeli. In 1881 he died and was buried near his family in Ecclefechan churchyard.

To understand Carlyle's role as historian, biographer, and social critic, it is essential to understand his attitude toward religion. Like many Victorians, Carlyle underwent a crisis of religious belief. By the time he was twenty-three, he had been shorn of his faith in Christianity. At this stage, as Carlyle observed with dismay, many people seemed content simply to stop or, worse, to adopt antispiritual ideas. A Utilitarian such as James Mill or some of his commonsensical professors at the University of Edinburgh regarded society and the universe as machines. To such thinkers the machines might sometimes seem complex, but they were not mysterious, for machines are subject to humankind's control and understanding through reason and observation. To Carlyle, and to many others, life without a sense of the divine was a meaningless nightmare. In the first part of "The Everlasting No," a chapter of *Sartor Resartus,* he memorably depicts the horrors of such a soulless world that drove him in 1822 to thoughts of suicide. The eighteenth-century Enlightenment had left him not in light but in darkness.

In developing his views of religion, Carlyle used the metaphor of the "Clothes Philosophy." The naked individual seeks clothing for protection. One solution, represented by Coleridge and his followers, was to repudiate the skepticism of Voltaire and Hume and to return to the protective beliefs and rituals of the Christian Church. To Carlyle such a return was pointless. The traditional Christian coverings were worn out—"Hebrew Old Clothes," he called them. His own solution, described in "The Everlasting Yea," was to tailor a new suit of beliefs from German philosophy, shreds of Scottish Calvinism, and his own observations. The following summarizes his basic religious attitude: "Gods die with the men who have conceived them. But the god-stuff roars eternally, like the sea. . . . Even the gods must be born again. We must be born again." Although this passage is from *The Plumed Serpent* (1926) by D. H. Lawrence (a writer who resembles Carlyle at many points), it might have come from any one of Carlyle's own books—most especially from *Sartor Resartus,* in which he describes his being born again—his "Fire-baptism"—into a new secular faith. Carlyle was thus in many ways the quintessential nineteenth-century mystic; yet at the same time, many contemporary critics note, his writings also gesture toward postmodernism. Certainly his self-aware, genre-defying, and often contradictory prose exposes the inherent difficulty of assuming that literature or philosophy can ever achieve a unified, foundational truth.

Nevertheless, Carlyle often talked like a *vitalist;* that is, as though the presence of energy in the world was, in itself, a sign of the godhead. Carlyle therefore judges everything in terms of the presence or absence of some vital spark. The minds of people, books, societies, Churches, or even landscapes are rated as alive or dead, dynamic or merely mechanical. The government of Louis XVI, for example, was obviously moribund, doomed to be swept away by the dynamic forces of the French Revolution. The government of Victorian England seemed likewise to be doomed unless infused with vital energies of leadership and an awareness of the real needs of humankind. When an editor complained that his essay "Characteristics" was "inscrutable," Carlyle remarked: "My own fear was that it might be too *scrutable;* for it indicates decisively enough that Society (in my view) is utterly condemned to destruction, and even now beginning its long travail-throes of Newbirth."

In his inquiry into the principles of government and social order, Carlyle, like many of his contemporaries, is seeking to understand a world of great social unrest and historical change. This preoccupation with revolution and the destruction of the old orders suggests that Carlyle's politics were radical, but his position is bewilderingly difficult to classify. During the Hungry Forties he was one of the most outspoken critics of middle-class bunglings and of the economic theory of laissez-faire that, in his opinion, was ultimately responsible for those bunglings. On behalf of the millions of people suffering from the miseries attendant on a major breakdown of industry and agriculture he worked strenuously. At other times, because of his insistence on strong and heroic leadership, Carlyle appears to be a violent conservative or, as some have argued, virtually a fascist. He had no confidence that democratic institutions could work efficiently. A few individuals in every age are, in his view, leaders; the rest are followers and are happy only as followers. Society should be organized so that these gifted leaders can have scope to govern effectively. Such leaders are, for Carlyle, heroes. Bernard Shaw, who learned much from Carlyle, would call them "supermen." Liberals and democrats, however, might call them dictators. Although Carlyle was aware that the Western world was committed to a faith in a system of balloting and of legislative debate, he was confident that the system would eventually break down. The democratic assumption that all voters are equally capable of choice and the assumption that people value liberty more than they value order seemed to him non-sense. Carlyle's authoritarianism intensified as he grew older. When the governor of Jamaica violently repressed a rebellion of black plantation workers, Carlyle served as chair of his defense fund, arguing that England owed the governor honor and thanks for his defense of civilization.

Carlyle's prose style reflects the intensity of his views. At the time he began to write, the essayists of the eighteenth century, Samuel Johnson in particular, were the models of good prose. Carlyle recognized that their style, however admirable an instrument for reasoning, analysis, and generalized exposition, did not suit his purposes. Like a poet, he wanted to convey the sense of experience itself. Like a preacher or prophet, he wanted to exhort or inspire his readers rather than to develop a chain of logical argument. Like a psychoanalyst, he wanted to explore the unconscious and irrational levels of human life, the hidden nine-tenths of the iceberg rather than the conscious and rational fraction above the surface. To this end he developed his highly individual manner of writing, with its vivid imagery of fire and barnyard and zoo, its mixture of biblical rhythms and explosive talk, and its inverted and unorthodox syntax. Classicists may complain, as Walter Savage Landor did, that the result is not English. Carlyle would reply that it is not eighteenth-century English, but that his style was appropriate for a Victorian who reports of revolutions in society and in thought. In reply to a friend who had protested about his stylistic experiments, Carlyle exclaimed: "Do you reckon this really a time for Purism of Style? I do not: with whole ragged battalions of Scott's Novel Scotch, with Irish, German, French, and even Newspaper Cockney . . . storming in on us, and the whole structure of our Johnsonian English breaking up from its foundations—revolution *there* as visible as anywhere else?" George Eliot wrote (in an essay of 1855) that Carlyle was "more of an artist than a philosopher." As she said: "No novelist has made his creations live for us more thoroughly." Carlyle is best regarded, that is, as a man of letters, the inventor of a distinctive and extremely effective prose medium, and one who strove tirelessly to create a new spiritual and political philosophy adequate to the age.

From Past and Present[1]

From *Democracy*

If the Serene Highnesses and Majesties do not take note of that,[2] then, as I perceive, *that* will take note of itself! The time for levity, insincerity, and idle babble and play-acting, in all kinds, is gone by; it is a serious, grave time. Old long-vexed questions, not yet solved in logical words or parliamentary laws, are fast solving themselves in facts, somewhat unblessed to behold! This largest of questions, this question of Work and Wages, which ought, had we heeded Heaven's voice, to have begun two generations ago or more, cannot be delayed longer without hearing Earth's voice. "Labour" will verily need to be somewhat "organized," as they say,—God knows with what difficulty. Man will actually need to have his debts and earnings a little better paid by man; which, let Parliaments speak of them, or be silent of them, are eternally his due from man, and cannot, without penalty and at length not without death-penalty,[3] be withheld. How much ought to cease among us straightway; how much ought to begin straightway, while the hours yet are!

Truly they are strange results to which this of leaving all to "Cash"; of quietly shutting up the God's Temple, and gradually opening wide-open the Mammon's Temple, with "Laissez-faire, and Every man for himself,"[4]—have led us in these days! We have Upper, speaking Classes, who indeed do "speak" as never man spake before;[5] the withered flimsiness, godless baseness and barrenness of whose Speech might of itself indicate what kind of Doing and practical Governing went on under it! For Speech is the gaseous element out of which most kinds of Practice and Performance, especially all kinds of moral Performance, condense themselves, and take shape; as the one is, so will the other be. Descending, accordingly, into the Dumb Class in its Stockport Cellars and Poor-Law Bastilles,[6] have we not to announce that they are hitherto unexampled in the History of Adam's Posterity?

Life was never a May-game for men: in all times the lot of the dumb millions born to toil was defaced with manifold sufferings, injustices, heavy burdens, avoidable and unavoidable; not play at all, but hard work that made the sinews sore and the heart sore. As bond-slaves, *villani, bordarii, sochemanni,* nay indeed as dukes, earls and kings, men were oftentimes made weary of their

1. In 1843 there were reputedly one and a half million unemployed in England (out of a population of eighteen million). The closing of factories and the reduction of wages led to severe rioting in the manufacturing districts. Bread-hungry mobs (as well as the Chartist mobs who demanded political reforms) caused many observers to dread that a large-scale revolution was imminent. Carlyle was so appalled by the plight of the industrial workers that he postponed his research into the life and times of Cromwell to air his views on the contemporary crisis. *Past and Present*, a book written in seven weeks, was a call for heroic leadership. Cromwell and other historic leaders are cited, but the principal example from the past is Abbot Samson, a medieval monk who established order in the monasteries under his charge. Carlyle hoped that the "Captains of Industry" might provide a comparable leadership in 1843. He was aware that the spread of democracy was inevitable, but he had little confidence in it as a method of producing leaders. Nor did he have any confidence, at this time, in the landed aristocracy, who seemed to him preoccupied with foxhunting, preserving their game, and upholding the tariffs on grain (Corn Laws). In place of a "Do nothing Aristocracy" there was need for a "Working Aristocracy." This first selection is from book 3, chap. 13.

2. The previous chapter, "Reward," had urged that English manufacturers needed the help of everyone and that Parliament should remove the tariffs (Corn Laws) restricting the growth of trade and industry.

3. I.e., by the outbreak of a revolution, as in France.

4. The pursuit of wealth (Mammon is the devil of covetousness) according to a noninterventionist economic policy. *Laissez-faire* literally means "let it be" (French).

5. John 7.46.

6. I.e., workhouses for the unemployed. "Stockport Cellars": in a cellar in the slum district of Stockport, an industrial town near Manchester, three children were poisoned by their starving parents, who wanted to collect insurance benefits from a burial society.

life; and had to say, in the sweat of their brow[7] and of their soul, Behold, it is not sport, it is grim earnest, and our back can bear no more! Who knows not what massacrings and harryings there have been; grinding, long-continuing, unbearable injustices,—till the heart had to rise in madness, and some *"Eu Sachsen, nimith euer sachses,* You Saxons, out with your gully-knives, then!" You Saxons, some "arrestment," partial "arrestment of the Knaves and Dastards" has become indispensable!—The page of Dryasdust[8] is heavy with such details.

And yet I well venture to believe that in no time, since the beginnings of Society, was the lot of those same dumb millions of toilers so entirely unbearable as it is even in the days now passing over us. It is not to die, or even to die of hunger, that makes a man wretched; many men have died; all men must die,—the last exit of us all is in a Fire-Chariot of Pain.[9] But it is to live miserable we know not why; to work sore and yet gain nothing; to be heartworn, weary, yet isolated, unrelated, girt-in with a cold universal Laissez-faire: it is to die slowly all our life long, imprisoned in a deaf, dead, Infinite Injustice, as in the accursed iron belly of a Phalaris' Bull![1] This is and remains for ever intolerable to all men whom God has made. Do we wonder at French Revolutions, Chartisms, Revolts of Three Days?[2] The times, if we will consider them, are really unexampled.

Never before did I hear of an Irish Widow reduced to "prove her sisterhood by dying of typhus-fever and infecting seventeen persons,"—saying in such undeniable way, "You *see,* I was your sister!"[3] Sisterhood, brotherhood, was often forgotten; but not till the rise of these ultimate Mammon and Shotbelt Gospels[4] did I ever see it so expressly denied. If no pious Lord or *Law-ward* would remember it, always some pious Lady (*"Hlaf-dig,"* Benefactress, *"Loaf-giveress,"* they say she is,—blessings on her beautiful heart!) was there, with mild mother-voice and hand, to remember it; some pious thoughtful *Elder,* what we now call "Prester," *Presbyter* or "Priest," was there to put all men in mind of it, in the name of the God who had made all.

Not even in Black Dahomey[5] was it ever, I think, forgotten to the typhus-fever length. Mungo Park,[6] resourceless, had sunk down to die under the Negro Village-Tree, a horrible White object in the eyes of all. But in the poor Black Woman, and her daughter who stood aghast at him, whose earthly wealth and funded capital consisted of one small calabash of rice, there lived a heart richer than *"Laissez-faire":* they, with a royal munificence, boiled their rice for him; they sang all night to him, spinning assiduous on their cotton distaffs, as he lay to sleep: "Let us pity the poor white man; no mother has he to fetch him milk, no sister to grind him corn!" Thou poor black Noble One,— thou *Lady* too: did not a God make thee too; was there not in thee too something of a God!—

Gurth,[7] born thrall of Cedric the Saxon, has been greatly pitied by Dryasdust and others. Gurth, with the brass collar round his neck, tending Cedric's pigs

7. Genesis 3.19.
8. An imaginary author of dull histories.
9. 2 Kings 2.11.
1. Phalaris was a Sicilian tyrant (6th century B.C.E.) whose victims were roasted alive by being confined inside the brass figure of a bull under which a fire was lit.
2. The 1830 revolution in France (July 27–29).
3. An incident referred to several times in *Past and Present.* Dickens in *Bleak House* (1851) also showed how indifference to the lack of sanitation

in London slums led to the spread of disease to other parts of the city.
4. The attitudes of land-owning aristocracy who were committed to preserving their exclusive right to shoot game birds and animals.
5. A state in west Africa where human sacrifice and cannibalism persisted.
6. Explorer and author (1771–1806); he was killed by Africans.
7. A swineherd described in Scott's *Ivanhoe* (1819).

in the glades of the wood, is not what I call an exemplar of human felicity: but Gurth, with the sky above him, with the free air and tinted boscage and umbrage round him, and in him at least the certainty of supper and social lodging when he came home; Gurth to me seems happy, in comparison with many a Lancashire and Buckinghamshire man, of these days, not born thrall of anybody! Gurth's brass collar did not gall him: Cedric *deserved* to be his Master. The pigs were Cedric's, but Gurth too would get his parings of them. Gurth had the inexpressible satisfaction of feeling himself related indissolubly, though in a rude brass-collar way, to his fellow-mortals in this Earth. He had superiors, inferiors, equals.—Gurth is now "emancipated" long since; has what we call "Liberty." Liberty, I am told, is a Divine thing. Liberty when it becomes the "Liberty to die by starvation" is not so divine!

Liberty? The true liberty of a man, you would say, consisted in his finding out, or being forced to find out, the right path, and to walk thereon. To learn, or to be taught, what work he actually was able for; and then by permission, persuasion, and even compulsion, to set about doing of the same! That is his true blessedness, honour, "liberty" and maximum of wellbeing: if liberty be not that, I for one have small care about liberty. You do not allow a palpable madman to leap over precipices; you violate his liberty, you that are wise; and keep him, were it in strait-waistcoats, away from the precipices! Every stupid, every cowardly and foolish man is but a less palpable madman: his true liberty were that a wiser man, that any and every wiser man, could, by brass collars, or in whatever milder or sharper way, lay hold of him when he was going wrong, and order and compel him to go a little righter. O, if thou really art my *Senior,* Seigneur, my *Elder,* Presbyter or Priest,—if thou art in very deed my *Wiser,* may a beneficent instinct lead and impel thee to "conquer" me, to command me! If thou do know better than I what is good and right, I conjure[8] thee in the name of God, force me to do it; were it by never such brass collars, whips and handcuffs, leave me not to walk over precipices! That I have been called, by all the Newspapers, a "free man" will avail me little, if my pilgrimage have ended in death and wreck. O that the Newspapers had called me slave, coward, fool, or what it pleased their sweet voices to name me, and I had attained not death, but life!—Liberty requires new definitions.

A conscious abhorrence and intolerance of Folly, of Baseness, Stupidity, Poltroonery and all that brood of things, dwells deep in some men: still deeper in others an *un*conscious abhorrence and intolerance, clothed moreover by the beneficent Supreme Powers in what stout appetites, energies, egoisms so-called, are suitable to it;—these latter are your Conquerors, Romans, Normans, Russians, Indo-English; Founders of what we call Aristocracies. Which indeed have they not the most "divine right" to found;—being themselves very truly *Aristoi,* BRAVEST, BEST; and conquering generally a confused rabble of WORST, or at lowest, clearly enough, of WORSE? I think their divine right, tried, with affirmatory verdict, in the greatest Law-Court known to me, was good! A class of men who are dreadfully exclaimed against by Dryasdust; of whom nevertheless beneficent Nature has oftentimes had need; and may, alas, again have need.

When, across the hundredfold poor scepticisms, trivialisms, and constitutional cobwebberies of Dryasdust, you catch any glimpse of a William the Conqueror, a Tancred of Hauteville[9] or such like,—do you not discern veritably some rude outline of a true God-made King; whom not the Champion of England[1] cased in tin, but all Nature and the Universe were calling to the throne? It is absolutely necessary that he get thither. Nature does not mean her poor Saxon children to perish, of obesity, stupor or other malady, as yet: a stern Ruler and Line of Rulers therefore is called in,—a stern but most beneficent *perpetual House-Surgeon* is by Nature herself called in, and even the appropriate *fees* are provided for him! Dryasdust talks lamentably about Hereward and the Fen Counties; fate of earl Waltheof;[2] Yorkshire and the North reduced to ashes; all of which is undoubtedly lamentable. But even Dryasdust apprises me of one fact: "A child, in this William's reign, might have carried a purse of gold from end to end of England." My erudite friend, it is a fact which outweighs a thousand! Sweep away thy constitutional, sentimental, and other cobwebberies; look eye to eye, if thou still have any eye, in the face of this big burly William Bastard: thou wilt see a fellow of most flashing discernment, of most strong lion-heart;—in whom, as it were, within a frame of oak and iron, the gods have planted the soul of "a man of genius"! Dost thou call that nothing? I call it an immense thing!—Rage enough was in this Willelmus Conquaestor, rage enough for his occasions;—and yet the essential element of him, as of all such men, is not scorching *fire*, but shining illuminative *light*. Fire and light are strangely interchangeable; nay, at bottom, I have found them different forms of the same most godlike "elementary substance" in our world: a thing worth stating in these days. The essential element of this Conquaestor is, first of all, the most sun-eyed perception of what *is* really what on this God's-Earth;—which, thou wilt find, does mean at bottom "Justice," and "Virtues" not a few: *Conformity* to what the Maker has seen good to make; that, I suppose, will mean Justice and a Virtue or two?—

Dost thou think Willelmus Conquaestor would have tolerated ten years' jargon, one hour's jargon, on the propriety of killing Cotton-manufactures by partridge Corn-Laws?[3] I fancy, this was not the man to knock out of his night's-rest with nothing but a noisy bedlamism in your mouth![4] "Assist us still better to bush the partridges; strangle Plugson who spins the shirts?"—*"Par la Splendeur de Dieu!"*[5]—Dost thou think Willelmus Conquaestor, in this new time, with Steam-engine Captains of Industry on one hand of him, and Joe-Manton Captains of Idleness[6] on the other, would have doubted which *was* really the BEST; which did deserve strangling, and which not?

I have a certain indestructible regard for Willelmus Conquaestor. A resident House-Surgeon, provided by Nature for her beloved English People, and even

King William I of England (ca. 1028–1087; reigned 1066–87), surnamed *the Conqueror* after the Battle of Hastings in 1066. Being an illegitimate son, he also bore the surname of William the Bastard. Although some historians condemn William as a ruthless ruler, he is ranked by Carlyle as a hero because of his strong and efficient government. William fulfilled the requirements of the kingly hero described by Carlyle in his lectures *On Heroes*: a man fittest "to *command* over us . . . to tell us what we are to *do*."

1. An official who goes through a formality, at coronation ceremonies, of demanding whether anyone challenges the right of the monarch to ascend the throne. He wears full armor ("cased in tin") and is a symbol of outworn feudal customs.

2. His execution in 1075, on a supposedly trumped-up charge, is cited as a blot on William's record as king. Hereward the Wake was an outlaw whose exploits against William the Conqueror made him seem a romantic figure like Robin Hood.

3. See nn. 1, 2, p. 1912.

4. I.e., not the man to disturb with your mad ravings. Bedlam, the hospital of St. Mary in Bethlehem, was London's most famous lunatic asylum.

5. By the splendor of God! (French): one of William's oaths. Plugson of Undershot was Carlyle's fictive representative of the new class of industrial leaders.

6. The idle aristocracy who wasted time shooting partridges with guns made by Joseph Manton, a London gunsmith. This speech sums up the pleas of the High Tariff lobby in Parliament. "Keep the Corn Laws intact so that the aristocratic landlords may continue to enjoy shooting partridges on their estates; subdue the manufacturing leaders by preventing trade."

furnished with the requisite fees, as I said; for he by no means felt himself doing Nature's work, this Willelmus, but his own work exclusively! And his own work withal it was; informed *"par la Splendeur de Dieu."*—I say, it is necessary to get the work out of such a man, however harsh that be! When a world, not yet doomed for death, is rushing down to ever-deeper Baseness and Confusion, it is a dire necessity of Nature's to bring in her ARISTOCRACIES, her BEST, even by forcible methods. When their descendants or representatives cease entirely to *be* the Best, Nature's poor world will very soon rush down again to Baseness; and it becomes a dire necessity of Nature's to cast them out. Hence French Revolutions, Five-point Charters,[7] Democracies, and a mournful list of *Etceteras,* in these our afflicted times.

* * *

Democracy, the chase of Liberty in that direction, shall go its full course; unrestrained by him of Pferdefuss-Quacksalber,[8] or any of *his* household. The Toiling Millions of Mankind, in most vital need and passionate instinctive desire of Guidance, shall cast away False-Guidance; and hope, for an hour, that No-Guidance will suffice them: but it can be for an hour only. The smallest item of human Slavery is the oppression of man by his Mock-Superiors; the palpablest, but I say at bottom the smallest. Let him shake off such oppression, trample it indignantly under his feet; I blame him not, I pity and commend him. But oppression by your Mock-Superiors well shaken off, the grand problem yet remains to solve: That of finding government by your Real-Superiors! Alas, how shall we ever learn the solution of that, benighted, bewildered, sniffing, sneering, godforgetting unfortunates as we are? It is a work for centuries; to be taught us by tribulations, confusions, insurrections, obstructions; who knows if not by conflagration and despair! It is a lesson inclusive of all other lessons; the hardest of all lessons to learn.

Captains of Industry[9]

If I believed that Mammonism with its adjuncts was to continue henceforth the one serious principle of our existence, I should reckon it idle to solicit remedial measures from any Government, the disease being insusceptible of remedy. Government can do much, but it can in no wise do all. Government, as the most conspicuous object in Society, is called upon to give signal of what shall be done; and, in many ways, to preside over further, and command the doing of it. But the Government cannot do, by all its signalling and commanding, what the Society is radically indisposed to do. In the long-run every Government is the exact symbol of its People, with their wisdom and unwisdom; we have to say, Like People like Government.—The main substance of this immense Problem of Organizing Labour, and first of all of Managing the Working Classes, will, it is very clear, have to be solved by those who stand practically in the middle of it; by those who themselves work and preside over work. Of all that can be enacted by any Parliament in regard to it, the germs must already lie potentially extant in those two Classes, who are to obey such enactment. A Human Chaos *in* which there is no light, you vainly attempt to irradiate by light shed *on* it: order never can arise there.

---

7. The Chartist movement for political reform called first for six, then for five major changes to the existing system of parliamentary democracy.

8. Horse foot quack doctor (a fake German name invented by Carlyle).

9. From book 4, chap. 4.

But it is my firm conviction that the "Hell of England" will *cease* to be that of "not making money"; that we shall get a nobler Hell and a nobler Heaven! I anticipate light *in* the Human Chaos, glimmering, shining more and more; under manifold true signals from without That light shall shine. Our deity no longer being Mammon,—O Heavens, each man will then say to himself: "Why such deadly haste to make money? I shall not go to Hell, even if I do not make money! There is another Hell, I am told!" Competition, at railway-speed, in all branches of commerce and work will then abate:—good felt-hats for the head, in every sense, instead of seven-feet lath-and-plaster hats on wheels,[1] will then be discoverable! Bubble-periods,[2] with their panics and commercial crises, will again become infrequent; steady modest industry will take the place of gambling speculation. To be a noble Master, among noble Workers, will again be the first ambition with some few; to be a rich Master only the second. How the Inventive Genius of England, with the whirr of its bobbins and billy-rollers[3] shoved somewhat into the backgrounds of the brain, will contrive and devise, not cheaper produce exclusively, but fairer distribution of the produce at its present cheapness! By degrees, we shall again have a Society with something of Heroism in it, something of Heaven's Blessing on it; we shall again have, as my German friend[4] asserts, "instead of Mammon-Feudalism with unsold cotton-shirts and Preservation of the Game, noble just Industrialism and Government by the Wisest!"

It is with the hope of awakening here and there a British man to know himself for a man and divine soul, that a few words of parting admonition, to all persons to whom the Heavenly Powers have lent power of any kind in this land, may now be addressed. And first to those same Master-Workers, Leaders of Industry; who stand nearest, and in fact powerfullest, though not most prominent, being as yet in too many senses a Virtuality rather than an Actuality.

The Leaders of Industry, if Industry is ever to be led, are virtually the Captains of the World; if there be no nobleness in them, there will never be an Aristocracy more. But let the Captains of Industry consider: once again, are they born of other clay than the old Captains of Slaughter; doomed for ever to be not Chivalry, but a mere gold-plated *Doggery*,—what the French well name *Canaille*, "Doggery" with more or less gold carrion at its disposal? Captains of Industry are the true Fighters, henceforth recognizable as the only true ones: Fighters against Chaos, Necessity and the Devils and Jötuns;[5] and lead on Mankind in that great, and alone true, and universal warfare; the stars in their courses fighting for them, and all Heaven and all Earth saying audibly, Well done! Let the Captains of Industry retire into their own hearts, and ask solemnly, If there is nothing but vulturous hunger for fine wines, valet reputation and gilt carriages, discoverable there? Of hearts made by the Almighty God I will not believe such a thing. Deep-hidden under wretchedest god-forgetting Cants, Epicurisms, Dead-Sea Apisms;[6] forgotten as under foullest fat Lethe[7] mud and weeds, there is yet, in all hearts born into this God's-

---

1. A London hatter's mode of advertising.
2. Periods of violent fluctuation in the stock market caused by unsound speculating.
3. Machines used to prepare cotton or wool for spinning.
4. Teufelsdröckh, the hero of *Sartor Resartus* (1833–34).

5. Giants of Scandinavian mythology.
6. A reference to a Muslim story in which members of a tribe living near the Dead Sea were transformed into apes because they had ignored the prophecies of Moses.
7. The river of forgetfulness in the classical underworld.

World, a spark of the Godlike slumbering. Awake, O nightmare sleepers; awake, arise, or be for ever fallen![8] This is not playhouse poetry; it is sober fact. Our England, our world cannot live as it is. It will connect itself with a God again, or go down with nameless throes and fire-consummation to the Devils. Thou who feelest aught of such a Godlike stirring in thee, any faintest intimation of it as through heavy-laden dreams, follow *it*, I conjure thee. Arise, save thyself, be one of those that save thy country.

Bucaniers,[9] Chactaw Indians, whose supreme aim in fighting is that they may get the scalps, the money, that they may amass scalps and money; out of such came no Chivalry, and never will! Out of such came only gore and wreck, infernal rage and misery; desperation quenched in annihilation. Behold it, I bid thee, behold there, and consider! What is it that thou have a hundred thousand-pound bills laid up in thy strong-room, a hundred scalps hung up in thy wigwam? I value not them or thee. Thy scalps and thy thousand-pound bills are as yet nothing, if no nobleness from within irradiate them; if no Chivalry, in action, or in embryo ever struggling towards birth and action, be there.

Love of men cannot be bought by cash-payment; and without love, men cannot endure to be together. You cannot lead a Fighting World without having it regimented, chivalried: the thing, in a day, becomes impossible; all men in it, the highest at first, the very lowest at last, discern consciously, or by a noble instinct, this necessity. And can you any more continue to lead a Working World unregimented, anarchic? I answer, and the Heavens and Earth are now answering, No! The thing becomes not "in a day" impossible; but in some two generations it does. Yes, when fathers and mothers, in Stockport hunger-cellars, begin to eat their children, and Irish widows have to prove their relationship by dying of typhus-fever; and amid Governing "Corporations of the Best and Bravest," busy to preserve their game by "bushing," dark millions of God's human creatures start up in mad Chartisms, impracticable Sacred-Months, and Manchester Insurrections;[1]—and there is a virtual Industrial Aristocracy as yet only half-alive, spell-bound amid money-bags and ledgers; and an actual Idle Aristocracy seemingly near dead in somnolent delusions, in trespasses and double-barrels,[2] "sliding," as on inclined-planes, which every new year they *soap* with new Hansard's-jargon under God's sky, and so are "sliding" ever faster, towards a "scale"[3] and balance-scale whereon is written *Thou art found Wanting;*[4]—in such days, after a generation or two, I say, it does become, even to the low and simple, very palpably impossible! No Working World, any more than a Fighting World, can be led on without a noble Chivalry of Work, and laws and fixed rules which follow out of that,— far nobler than any Chivalry of Fighting was. As an anarchic multitude on mere Supply-and-demand, it is becoming inevitable that we dwindle in horrid suicidal convulsion, and self-abrasion, frightful to the imagination, into *Chactaw* Workers. With wigwams and scalps,—with palaces and thousand-pound

---

8. Satan's appeal to the devils in Milton's *Paradise Lost* 1.330.
9. Buccaneers.
1. In 1819 a large open-air labor meeting in Manchester was broken up by charging cavalry. Thirteen men and women were massacred, and many others were wounded. "Bushing": protecting game from poachers who use nets, by positioning bushes or branches on the grounds.
2. I.e., the only concern of the landed aristocrats

is to keep trespassers off their game preserves and reserve shooting rights to themselves.
3. The "sliding scale" refers to the system of variable tariffs within the Corn Laws that benefited the aristocratic landlords. "Hansard's-jargon": parliamentary oratory, as in Hansard's printed record of debates in the Houses of Parliament.
4. The message of the miraculous writing on the wall in Daniel 5.

bills; with savagery, depopulation, chaotic desolation! Good Heavens, will not one French Revolution and Reign of Terror suffice us, but must there be two? There will be two if needed; there will be twenty if needed; there will be precisely as many as needed. The Laws of Nature will have themselves fulfilled. That is a thing certain to me.

Your gallant battle-hosts and work-hosts, as the others did, will need to be made loyally yours; they must and will be regulated, methodically secured in their just share of conquest under you;—joined with you in veritable brotherhood, sonhood, by quite other and deeper ties than those of temporary day's wages! How would mere redcoated regiments, to say nothing of chivalries, fight for you, if you could discharge them on the evening of the battle, on payment of the stipulated shillings,—and they discharge you on the morning of it! Chelsea Hospitals,[5] pensions, promotions, rigorous lasting covenant on the one side and on the other, are indispensable even for a hired fighter. The Feudal Baron, much more,—how could he subsist with mere temporary mercenaries round him, at sixpence a day; ready to go over to the other side, if sevenpence were offered? He could not have subsisted;—and his noble instinct saved him from the necessity of even trying! The Feudal Baron had a Man's Soul in him; to which anarchy, mutiny, and the other fruits of temporary mercenaries, were intolerable: he had never been a Baron otherwise, but had continued a Chactaw and Bucanier. He felt it precious, and at last it became habitual, and his fruitful enlarged existence included it as a necessity, to have men round him who in heart loved him; whose life he watched over with rigour yet with love; who were prepared to give their life for him, if need came. It was beautiful; it was human! Man lives not otherwise, nor can live contented, anywhere or anywhen. Isolation is the sum-total of wretchedness to man. To be cut off, to be left solitary: to have a world alien, not your world; all a hostile camp for you; not a home at all, of hearts and faces who are yours, whose you are! It is the frightfullest enchantment; too truly a work of the Evil One. To have neither superior, nor inferior, nor equal, united manlike to you. Without father, without child, without brother. Man knows no sadder destiny. "How is each of us," exclaims Jean Paul,[6] "so lonely in the wide bosom of the All!" Encased each as in his transparent "ice-palace"; our brother visible in his, making signals and gesticulations to us;—visible, but for ever unattainable: on his bosom we shall never rest, nor he on ours. It was not a God that did this; no!

Awake, ye noble Workers, warriors in the one true war: all this must be remedied. It is you who are already half-alive, whom I will welcome into life; whom I will conjure in God's name to shake off your enchanted sleep, and live wholly! Cease to count scalps, goldpurses; not in these lies your or our salvation. Even these, if you count only these, will not be left. Let bucaniering be put far from you; alter, speedily abrogate all laws of the bucaniers, if you would gain any victory that shall endure. Let God's justice, let pity, nobleness and manly valour, with more gold-purses or with fewer, testify themselves in this your brief Life-transit to all the Eternities, the Gods and Silences. It is to you I call; for ye are not dead, ye are already half-alive: there is in you a sleepless dauntless energy, the prime-matter of all nobleness in man. Honour to you in your kind. It is to you I call: ye know at least this, That the mandate

5. Homes for disabled veterans.
6. Jean Paul Richter (1763–1825), German humorist.

of God to His creature man is: Work! The future Epic of the World rests not with those that are near dead, but with those that are alive, and those that are coming into life.

Look around you. Your world-hosts are all in mutiny, in confusion, destitution; on the eve of fiery wreck and madness! They will not march farther for you, on the sixpence a day and supply-and-demand principle; they will not; nor ought they, nor can they. Ye shall reduce them to order, begin reducing them. To order, to just subordination; noble loyalty in return for noble guidance. Their souls are driven nigh mad; let yours be sane and ever saner. Not as a bewildered bewildering mob; but as a firm regimented mass, with real captains over them, will these men march any more. All human interests, combined human endeavours, and social growths in this world, have, at a certain stage of their development, required organizing: and Work, the grandest of human interests, does now require it.

God knows, the task will be hard: but no noble task was ever easy. This task will wear away your lives, and the lives of your sons and grandsons: but for what purpose, if not for tasks like this, were lives given to men? Ye shall cease to count your thousand-pound scalps, the noble of you shall cease! Nay, the very scalps, as I say, will not long be left if you count on these. Ye shall cease wholly to be barbarous vulturous Chactaws, and become noble European Nineteenth-Century Men. Ye shall know that Mammon, in never such gigs[7] and flunkey "respectabilities," is not the alone God; that of himself he is but a Devil, and even a Brute-god.

Difficult? Yes, it will be difficult. The short-fibre cotton; that too was difficult. The waste cotton-shrub, long useless, disobedient, as the thistle by the wayside,—have ye not conquered it; made it into beautiful bandana webs; white woven shirts for men; bright-tinted air-garments wherein flit goddesses? Ye have shivered mountains asunder, made the hard iron pliant to you as soft putty: the Forest-giants, Marsh-jötuns bear sheaves of golden grain; Aegir the Seademon[8] himself stretches his back for a sleek highway to you, and on Firehorses and Windhorses ye career. Ye are most strong. Thor red-bearded, with his blue sun-eyes, with his cheery heart and strong thunder-hammer, he and you have prevailed. Ye are most strong, ye Sons of the icy North, of the far East,—far marching from your rugged Eastern Wildernesses, hitherward from the grey Dawn of Time! Ye are Sons of the *Jötun-land*; the land of Difficulties Conquered. Difficult? You must try this thing. Once try it with the understanding that it will and shall have to be done. Try it as ye try the paltrier thing, making of money! I will bet on you once more, against all Jötuns, Tailor-gods,[9] Double-barrelled Law-wards, and Denizens of Chaos whatsoever.

1843   1843

---

7. Light carriages; to own one was a sign of respectability.

8. From Scandinavian mythology.
9. False gods.

ELIZABETH BARRETT BROWNING
1806–1861

During her lifetime Elizabeth Barrett Browning was one of England's most famous poets. Passionately admired by contemporaries as diverse as John Ruskin, Algernon Charles Swinburne, and Emily Dickinson for her moral and emotional ardor and her energetic engagement with the issues of her day, she was better known than her husband, Robert Browning, at the time of her death. Her work fell into disrepute with the modernist reaction against what was seen as the inappropriate didacticism and rhetorical excess of Victorian poetry; but recently scholars interested in her exploration of what it means to be a woman poet and in her response to social and political events have restored her status as a major writer.

Barrett Browning received an unusual education for a woman of her time. Availing herself of her brother's tutor, she studied Latin and Greek. She read voraciously in history, philosophy, and literature and began to write poetry from an early age—her first volume of poetry was published when she was thirteen. But as her intellectual and literary powers matured, her personal life became increasingly circumscribed both by ill health and by a tyrannically protective father, who had forbidden any of his eleven children to marry. By the age of thirty-nine, Elizabeth Barrett was a prominent woman of letters who lived in semiseclusion as an invalid in her father's house, where she occasionally received visitors in her room. One of these visitors was Robert Browning, who, moved by his admiration of her poetry, wrote to tell her "I do as I say, love these books with all my heart—and I love you too." He thereby initiated a courtship that culminated in 1846 in their secret marriage and elopement to Italy, for which her father never forgave her. In Italy Barrett Browning regained much health and strength, bearing and raising a son, Pen, to whom she was ardently devoted, and becoming deeply involved in Italian nationalist politics. She and her husband made their home in Florence, at the house called Casa Guidi, where she died in 1861.

Barrett Browning's poetry is characterized by a fervent moral sensibility. In her early work she tended to use the visionary modes of Romantic narrative poetry, but she turned increasingly to contemporary topics, particularly to liberal causes of her day. For example, in 1843, when government investigations exposed the exploitation of children employed in coal mines and factories, she wrote "The Cry of the Children," a powerful indictment of the appalling use of child labor. Like Harriet Beecher Stowe in *Uncle Tom's Cabin* (1851–52), Barrett Browning uses literature as a tool of social protest and reform, lending her voice, for example, to the cause of American abolitionism in "The Runaway Slave at Pilgrim's Point." In later poems she took up the cause of the *risorgimento*, the movement to unify Italy as a nation-state, in which Italy's struggle for freedom and identity found resonance with her own.

For many years Elizabeth Barrett Browning was best-known for her *Sonnets from the Portuguese* (1850), a sequence of forty-four sonnets presented under the guise of a translation from the Portuguese language, in which she recorded the stages of her love for Robert Browning. But increasingly, her verse novel *Aurora Leigh* (1857) has attracted critical attention. The poem depicts the growth of a woman poet and is thus, as Cora Kaplan observes, the first work in English by a woman writer in which the heroine herself is an author. When Barrett Browning first envisioned the poem, she wrote, "My chief *intention* just now is the writing of a sort of novel-poem . . . running into the midst of our conventions, and rushing into drawing-rooms and the like 'where angels fear to tread'; and so, meeting face to face and without mask the Humanity of the age, and speaking the truth as I conceive of it out plainly." The poem is a portrait of the artist as a young woman committed to a socially inclusive realist art. It is a daring work both in its presentation of social issues concerning women and in its claims for Aurora's poetic vocation; on her twentieth birthday, to pursue her career as a poet, Aurora refuses a proposal of marriage from her cousin Romney, who wants her to be his helpmate in the liberal causes he has embraced. Later in the poem, she rescues a fallen woman and takes her to Italy, where they settle together and confront a chastened Romney.

Immensely popular in its own day, *Aurora Leigh* had extravagant admirers (like Ruskin, who asserted that it was the greatest poem written in English) and critics who found fault with both its poetry and its morality. With its crowded canvas and melodramatic plot, it seems closer to the novel than to poetry, but it is important to view the poem in the context of the debate about appropriate poetic subject matter that engaged other Victorian poets. Unlike Matthew Arnold, who believed that the present age had not produced actions heroic enough to be the subject of great poetry, and unlike Alfred, Lord Tennyson, who used Arthurian legend to represent contemporary concerns, Barrett Browning felt that the present age contained the materials for an epic poetry. Virginia Woolf writes that "Elizabeth Barrett was inspired by a flash of true genius when she rushed into the drawing-room and said that here, where we live and work, is the true place for the poet." *Aurora Leigh* succeeds in giving us what Woolf describes as "a sense of life in general, of people who are unmistakably Victorian, wrestling with the problems of their own time, all brightened, intensified, and compacted by the fire of poetry. . . . Aurora Leigh, with her passionate interest in social questions, her conflict as artist and woman, her longing for knowledge and freedom, is the true daughter of her age."

The Cry of the Children[1]

"Φεῦ, φεῦ, τί προσδέρκεσθέ μ' ὄμμασιν, τέκνα;"
—*Medea*[2]

Do ye hear the children weeping, O my brothers,
        Ere the sorrow comes with years?
They are leaning their young heads against their mothers,
        And *that* cannot stop their tears.
5 The young lambs are bleating in the meadows,
        The young birds are chirping in the nest,
The young fawns are playing with the shadows,
        The young flowers are blowing toward the west—
But the young, young children, O my brothers,
10   They are weeping bitterly!
They are weeping in the playtime of the others,
        In the country of the free.

Do you question the young children in the sorrow
        Why their tears are falling so?
15 The old man may weep for his to-morrow
        Which is lost in Long Ago;
The old tree is leafless in the forest,
        The old year is ending in the frost,
The old wound, if stricken, is the sorest,

1. Barrett Browning wrote "The Cry of the Children" in response to the report of a parliamentary commission, to which her friend R. H. Horne contributed, on the labor of children in mines and factories. Many of the details of Barrett Browning's poem derive from the report.

2. Alas, my children, why do you look at me? (Greek), from Euripides' tragedy *Medea*. Medea speaks these lines before killing her children in vengeance against her husband, who has taken a new wife. (The poem's title is spoken by the chorus.)

20   The old hope is hardest to be lost:
But the young, young children, O my brothers,
    Do you ask them why they stand
Weeping sore° before the bosoms of their mothers,   *bitterly*
    In our happy Fatherland?

25   They look up with their pale and sunken faces,
    And their looks are sad to see,
For the man's hoary anguish draws and presses
    Down the cheeks of infancy;
"Your old earth," they say, "is very dreary,"
30   "Our young feet," they say, "are very weak;
Few paces have we taken, yet are weary—
    Our grave-rest is very far to seek:
Ask the aged why they weep, and not the children,
    For the outside earth is cold,
35   And we young ones stand without, in our bewildering,
    And the graves are for the old."

"True," say the children, "it may happen
    That we die before our time:
Little Alice died last year, her grave is shapen
40   Like a snowball, in the rime.°   *frost*
We looked into the pit prepared to take her:
    Was no room for any work in the close clay!
From the sleep wherein she lieth none will wake her,
    Crying, 'Get up, little Alice! it is day.'
45   If you listen by that grave, in sun and shower,
    With your ear down, little Alice never cries;
Could we see her face, be sure we should not know her,
    For the smile has time for growing in her eyes:
And merry go her moments, lulled and stilled in
50   The shroud by the kirk° chime.   *church*
It is good when it happens," say the children,
    "That we die before our time."

Alas, alas, the children! they are seeking
    Death in life, as best to have:
55   They are binding up their hearts away from breaking,
    With a ceremen° from the grave.   *shroud*
Go out, children, from the mine and from the city,
    Sing out, children, as the little thrushes do;
Pluck your handfuls of the meadow-cowslips pretty,
60   Laugh aloud, to feel your fingers let them through!
But they answer, "Are your cowslips of the meadows
    Like our weeds anear the mine?[3]
Leave us quiet in the dark of the coal-shadows,
    From your pleasures fair and fine!

---

3. A commissioner mentions the fact of weeds being thus confounded with the idea of flowers [Barrett Browning's note].

65   "For oh," say the children, "we are weary,
        And we cannot run or leap;
    If we cared for any meadows, it were merely
        To drop down in them and sleep.
    Our knees tremble sorely in the stooping,
70   We fall upon our faces, trying to go;
    And, underneath our heavy eyelids drooping,
        The reddest flower would look as pale as snow.
    For, all day, we drag our burden tiring
        Through the coal-dark, underground;
75   Or, all day, we drive the wheels of iron
        In the factories, round and round.

    "For, all day, the wheels are droning, turning;
        Their wind comes in our faces,
    Till our hearts turn, our heads with pulses burning,
80   And the walls turn in their places:
    Turns the sky in the high window blank and reeling,
        Turns the long light that drops adown the wall,
    Turn the black flies that crawl along the ceiling,
        All are turning, all the day, and we with all.
85   And all day, the iron wheels are droning,
        And sometimes we could pray,
    'O ye wheels,' (breaking out in a mad moaning)
        'Stop! be silent for to-day!' "

    Ay, be silent! Let them hear each other breathing
90   For a moment, mouth to mouth!
    Let them touch each other's hands, in a fresh wreathing
        Of their tender human youth!
    Let them feel that this cold metallic motion
        Is not all the life God fashions or reveals:
95   Let them prove their living souls against the notion
        That they live in you, or under you, O wheels!
    Still, all day, the iron wheels go onward,
        Grinding life down from its mark;
    And the children's souls, which God is calling sunward,
100   Spin on blindly in the dark.

    Now tell the poor young children; O my brothers,
        To look up to Him and pray;
    So the blessed One who blesseth all the others,
        Will bless them another day.
105   They answer, "Who is God that He should hear us,
        While the rushing of the iron wheels is stirred?
    When we sob aloud, the human creatures near us
        Pass by, hearing not, or answer not a word.
    And *we* hear not (for the wheels in their resounding)
110   Strangers speaking at the door:
    Is it likely God, with angels singing round Him,
        Hears our weeping any more?

    Two words, indeed, of praying we remember,
        And at midnight's hour of harm,

115 'Our Father,' looking upward in the chamber,
        We say softly for a charm.
    We know no other words except 'Our Father.'
        And we think that, in some pause of angels' song,
    God may pluck them with the silence sweet to gather,
120   And hold both within His right hand which is strong.
    'Our Father!' If He heard us, He would surely
        (For they call Him good and mild)
    Answer, smiling down the steep world very purely,
        'Come and rest with me, my child.'

125 "But, no!" say the children, weeping faster,
        "He is speechless as a stone:
    And they tell us, of His image is the master
        Who commands us to work on.
    Go to!" say the children,—"up in Heaven,
130   Dark, wheel-like, turning clouds are all we find.
    Do not mock us; grief has made us unbelieving:
    We look up for God, but tears have made us blind."
    Do you hear the children weeping and disproving,
        O my brothers, what ye preach?
135 For God's possible is taught by His world's loving,[4]
        And the children doubt of each.

    And well may the children weep before you!
        They are weary ere they run;
    They have never seen the sunshine, nor the glory
140   Which is brighter than the sun.
    They know the grief of man, without its wisdom;
        They sink in man's despair, without its calm;
    Are slaves, without the liberty in Christdom,
        Are martyrs, by the pang without the palm:[5]
145 Are worn as if with age, yet unretrievingly
        The harvest of its memories cannot reap,—
    Are orphans of the earthly love and heavenly.
        Let them weep! let them weep!

    They look up with their pale and sunken faces,
150   And their look is dread to see,
    For they mind you of their angels in high places,
        With eyes turned on Deity.
    "How long," they say, "how long, O cruel nation,
        Will you stand, to move the world, on a child's heart,—
155 Stifle down with a mailed heel its palpitation,
        And tread onward to your throne amid the mart?
    Our blood splashes upward, O gold-heaper,
        And your purple[6] shows your path!
    But the child's sob in the silence curses deeper
160   Than the strong man in his wrath."

                                                        1843

4. I.e., we gain our sense of the possibilities of God's love from our experience of love in the world.
5. Palm branch, symbol of victory.
6. Color associated with royalty and (in poetry) with blood.

From Sonnets from the Portuguese

21

Say over again, and yet once over again,
That thou dost love me. Though the word repeated
Should seem "a cuckoo song,"¹ as thou dost treat it,
Remember, never to the hill or plain,
5   Valley and wood, without her cuckoo strain
Comes the fresh Spring in all her green completed.
Belovèd, I, amid the darkness greeted
By a doubtful spirit voice, in that doubt's pain
Cry, "Speak once more—thou lovest!" Who can fear
10   Too many stars, though each in heaven shall roll,
Too many flowers, though each shall crown the year?
Say thou dost love me, love me, love me—toll
The silver iterance!°—only minding, Dear,   repetition
To love me also in silence with thy soul.

22

When our two souls stand up erect and strong,
Face to face, silent, drawing nigh and nigher,
Until the lengthening wings break into fire
At either curvèd point—what bitter wrong
5   Can the earth do to us, that we should not long
Be here contented? Think. In mounting higher,
The angels would press on us and aspire
To drop some golden orb of perfect song
Into our deep, dear silence. Let us stay
10   Rather on earth, Belovèd,—where the unfit
Contrarious moods of men recoil away
And isolate pure spirits, and permit
A place to stand and love in for a day,
With darkness and the death-hour rounding it.

32

The first time that the sun rose on thine oath
To love me, I looked forward to the moon
To slacken all those bonds which seemed too soon
And quickly tied to make a lasting troth.
5   Quick-loving hearts, I thought, may quickly loathe;
And, looking on myself, I seemed not one
For such man's love!—more like an out-of-tune
Worn viol, a good singer would be wroth
To spoil his song with, and which, snatched in haste,
10   Is laid down at the first ill-sounding note.
I did not wrong myself so, but I placed
A wrong on *thee*. For perfect strains may float

1. The cuckoo has a repeating call.

'Neath master-hands, from instruments defaced—
And great souls, at one stroke, may do and dote.

43

How do I love thee? Let me count the ways.
I love thee to the depth and breadth and height
My soul can reach, when feeling out of sight
For the ends of Being and ideal Grace.
5   I love thee to the level of everyday's
Most quiet need, by sun and candlelight.
I love thee freely, as men strive for Right;
I love thee purely, as they turn from Praise.
I love thee with the passion put to use
10   In my old griefs, and with my childhood's faith.
I love thee with a love I seemed to lose
With my lost saints—I love thee with the breath,
Smiles, tears, of all my life!—and, if God choose,
I shall but love thee better after death.

1845–47   1850

The Runaway Slave at Pilgrim's Point[1]

I

I stand on the mark beside the shore
   Of the first white pilgrim's bended knee,
Where exile turned to ancestor,
   And God was thanked for liberty.
5   I have run through the night, my skin is as dark,
I bend my knee down on this mark:
   I look on the sky and the sea.

II

O pilgrim-souls, I speak to you!
   I see you come proud and slow
10   From the land of the spirits pale as dew
   And round me and round me ye go.
O pilgrims, I have gasped and run
All night long from the whips of one
   Who in your names works sin and woe!

III

15   And thus I thought that I would come
   And kneel here where ye knelt before,
And feel your souls around me hum
   In undertone to the ocean's roar;

1. Plymouth Rock, Massachusetts, where the Pilgrims landed in November 1620.

And lift my black face, my black hand,
20 Here, in your names, to curse this land
    Ye blessed in freedom's, evermore.

IV

I am black, I am black,
    And yet God made me, they say:
But if He did so, smiling back
25   He must have cast his work away
Under the feet of his white creatures,
With a look of scorn, that the dusky features
    Might be trodden again to clay.

V

And yet He has made dark things
30   To be glad and merry as light:
There's a little dark bird sits and sings,
    There's a dark stream ripples out of sight,
And the dark frogs chant in the safe morass,°   *marsh*
And the sweetest stars are made to pass
35   O'er the face of the darkest night.

VI

But *we* who are dark, we are dark!
    Ah God, we have no stars!
About our souls in care and cark°   *anxiety*
    Our blackness shuts like prison-bars:
40 The poor souls crouch so far behind
That never a comfort can they find
    By reaching through the prison-bars.

VII

Indeed we live beneath the sky,
    That great smooth Hand of God stretched out
45 On all His children fatherly,
    To save them from the dread and doubt
Which would be if, from this low place,
All opened straight up to His face
    Into the grand eternity.

VIII

50 And still God's sunshine and His frost,
    They make us hot, they make us cold,
As if we were not black and lost;
    And the beasts and birds, in wood and fold,
Do fear and take us for very men:
55 Could the whip-poor-will or the cat of the glen°   *bobcat*
    Look into my eyes and be bold?

IX

I am black, I am black!
   But, once, I laughed in girlish glee,
For one of my colour stood in the track
60   Where the drivers drove, and looked at me,
And tender and full was the look he gave—
Could a slave look *so* at another slave?—
   I look at the sky and the sea.

X

And from that hour our spirits grew
65   As free as if unsold, unbought:
Oh, strong enough, since we were two,
   To conquer the world, we thought.
The drivers drove us day by day;
We did not mind, we went one way,
70   And no better a freedom sought.

XI

In the sunny ground between the canes,°   *sugar canes*
   He said "I love you" as he passed;
When the shingle-roof rang sharp with the rains,
   I heard how he vowed it fast:
75 While others shook he smiled in the hut,
As he carved me a bowl of the cocoa-nut
   Through the roar of the hurricanes.

XII

I sang his name instead of a song,
   Over and over I sang his name,
80 Upward and downward I drew it along
   My various notes,—the same, the same!
I sang it low, that the slave-girls near
Might never guess, from aught they could hear,
   It was only a name—a name.

XIII

85 I look on the sky and the sea.
   We were two to love, and two to pray:
Yes, two, O God, who cried to Thee,
   Though nothing didst Thou say!
Coldly Thou sat'st behind the sun:
90 And now I cry who am but one,
   Thou wilt not speak to-day.

XIV

We were black, we were black,
   We had no claim to love and bliss,

What marvel if each went to wrack?°   ruin
95   They wrung my cold hands out of his,
They dragged him—where? I crawled to touch
His blood's mark in the dust . . . not much,
    Ye pilgrim-souls, though plain as *this*!

XV

Wrong, followed by a deeper wrong!
100   Mere grief's too good for such as I:
So the white men brought the shame ere long
    To strangle the sob of my agony.
They would not leave me for my dull
Wet eyes!—it was too merciful
105   To let me weep pure tears and die.

XVI

I am black, I am black!
    I wore a child upon my breast,
An amulet that hung too slack,
    And, in my unrest, could not rest:
110   Thus we went moaning, child and mother,
One to another, one to another,
    Until all ended for the best.

XVII

For hark! I will tell you low, low,
    I am black, you see,—
115   And the babe who lay on my bosom so,
    Was far too white, too white for me;
As white as the ladies who scorned to pray
Beside me at church but yesterday,
    Though my tears had washed a place for my knee.

XVIII

120   My own, own child! I could not bear
    To look in his face, it was so white;
I covered him up with a kerchief there,
    I covered his face in close and tight:
And he moaned and struggled, as well might be,
125   For the white child wanted his liberty—
    Ha, ha! he wanted the master-right.

XIX

He moaned and beat with his head and feet,
    His little feet that never grew;
He struck them out, as it was meet,
130   Against my heart to break it through:
I might have sung and made him mild,
But I dared not sing to the white-faced child
    The only song I knew.

XX

I pulled the kerchief very close:
135   He could not see the sun, I swear,
More, then, alive, than now he does
    From between the roots of the mango . . . where?
I know where.   Close!   A child and mother
Do wrong to look at one another
140   When one is black and one is fair.

XXI

Why, in that single glance I had
    Of my child's face, . . . I tell you all,
I saw a look that made me mad!
    The *master's* look, that used to fall
145 On my soul like his lash . . . or worse!
And so, to save it from my curse,
    I twisted it round in my shawl.

XXII

And he moaned and trembled from foot to head,
    He shivered from head to foot;
150 Till after a time, he lay instead
    Too suddenly still and mute.
I felt, beside, a stiffening cold:
I dared to lift up just a fold,
    As in lifting a leaf of the mango-fruit.

XXIII

155 But *my* fruit . . . ha, ha!—there, had been
    (I laugh to think on 't at this hour!)
Your fine white angels (who have seen
    Nearest the secret of God's power)
And plucked my fruit to make them wine,
160 And sucked the soul of that child of mine
    As the humming-bird sucks the soul of the flower.

XXIV

Ha, ha, the trick of the angels white!
    They freed the white child's spirit so.
I said not a word, but day and night
165   I carried the body to and fro,
And it lay on my heart like a stone, as chill.
—The sun may shine out as much as he will:
    I am cold, though it happened a month ago.

XXV

From the white man's house, and the black man's hut,
170   I carried the little body on;

The forest's arms did round us shut,
    And silence through the trees did run:
They asked no question as I went,
They stood too high for astonishment,
175   They could see God sit on His throne.

XXVI

My little body, kerchiefed fast,
    I bore it on through the forest, on;
And when I felt it was tired at last,
    I scooped a hole beneath the moon:
180   Through the forest-tops the angels far,
With a white sharp finger from every star,
    Did point and mock at what was done.

XXVII

Yet when it was all done aright,—
    Earth, 'twixt me and my baby, strewed,—
185   All, changed to black earth,—nothing white,—
    A dark child in the dark!—ensued
Some comfort, and my heart grew young;
I sate down smiling there and sung
    The song I learnt in my maidenhood.

XXVIII

190   And thus we two were reconciled,
    The white child and black mother, thus;
For as I sang it soft and wild,
    The same song, more melodious,
Rose from the grave whereon I sate:
195   It was the dead child singing that,
    To join the souls of both of us.

XXIX

I look on the sea and the sky.
    Where the pilgrims' ships first anchored lay
The free sun rideth gloriously,
200   But the pilgrim-ghosts have slid away
Through the earliest streaks of the morn:
My face is black, but it glares with a scorn
    Which they dare not meet by day.

XXX

Ha!—in their stead, their hunter sons!
205   Ha, ha! they are on me—they hunt in a ring!
Keep off! I brave you all at once,
    I throw off your eyes like snakes that sting!
You have killed the black eagle at nest, I think:
Did you ever stand still in your triumph, and shrink
210   From the stroke of her wounded wing?

XXXI

(Man, drop that stone you dared to lift!—)
   I wish you who stand there five abreast,
Each, for his own wife's joy and gift,
   A little corpse as safely at rest
215 As mine in the mangoes! Yes, but *she*
May keep live babies on her knee,
   And sing the song she likes the best.

XXXII

I am not mad: I am black.
   I see you staring in my face—
220 I know you staring, shrinking back,
   Ye are born of the Washington-race,[2]
And this land is the free America,
And this mark on my wrist—(I prove° what I say)   *demonstrate*
   Ropes tied me up here to the flogging-place.

XXXIII

225 You think I shrieked then? Not a sound!
   I hung, as a gourd hangs in the sun;
I only cursed them all around
   As softly as I might have done
My very own child: from these sands
230 Up to the mountains, lift your hands,
   O slaves, and end what I begun!

XXXIV

Whips, curses; these must answer those!
   For in this UNION you have set
Two kinds of men in adverse rows,
235   Each loathing each; and all forget
The seven wounds in Christ's body fair,
While HE sees gaping everywhere
   Our countless wounds that pay no debt.

XXXV

Our wounds are different. Your white men
240   Are, after all, not gods indeed,
Nor able to make Christs again
   Do good with bleeding. *We* who bleed
(Stand off!) we help not in our loss!
We are too heavy for our cross,
245   And fall and crush you and your seed.

XXXVI

I fall, I swoon! I look at the sky.
   The clouds are breaking on my brain;

2. I.e., the white race (the race of George Washington, the first president of the United States).

I am floated along, as if I should die
        Of liberty's exquisite pain.
250 In the name of the white child waiting for me
    In the death-dark where we may kiss and agree,
    White men, I leave you all curse-free
        In my broken heart's disdain!

1846   1848, 1850

From Aurora Leigh

From *Book 1*

[THE EDUCATION OF AURORA LEIGH][1]

Then, land!—then, England! oh, the frosty cliffs[2]
Looked cold upon me. Could I find a home
Among those mean red houses through the fog?
And when I heard my father's language first
255 From alien lips which had no kiss for mine
I wept aloud, then laughed, then wept, then wept,
And some one near me said the child was mad
Through much sea-sickness. The train swept us on:
Was this my father's England? the great isle?
260 The ground seemed cut up from the fellowship
Of verdure, field from field,[3] as man from man;
The skies themselves looked low and positive,
As almost you could touch them with a hand,
And dared to do it they were so far off
265 From God's celestial crystals;[4] all things blurred
And dull and vague. Did Shakespeare and his mates
Absorb the light here?—not a hill or stone
With heart to strike a radiant colour up
Or active outline on the indifferent air.

270 I think I see my father's sister stand
Upon the hall-step of her country-house
To give me welcome. She stood straight and calm,
Her somewhat narrow forehead braided tight
As if for taming accidental thoughts
275 From possible pulses;[5] brown hair pricked with gray
By frigid use of life (she was not old,
Although my father's elder by a year),
A nose drawn sharply, yet in delicate lines;
A close mild mouth, a little soured about
280 The ends, through speaking unrequited loves

---

1. Aurora Leigh, the only child of an Italian
mother and an English father, is raised in Italy by
her father after her mother's death when Aurora is
four years old. When she is thirteen her father also
dies, and the orphaned girl is sent to live in
England with her father's sister, who is to be
responsible for the girl's education.

2. The white chalk cliffs at Dover.
3. English fields were separated from each other
by hedgerows.
4. Perhaps a reference to the ancient notion that
the sky was composed of several crystalline spheres
orbiting the earth.
5. I.e., pulsation in her temples from excitement.

Or peradventure niggardly° half-truths;   *miserly*
Eyes of no colour,—once they might have smiled,
But never, never have forgot themselves
In smiling; cheeks, in which was yet a rose
285 Of perished summers, like a rose in a book,
Kept more for ruth° than pleasure,—if past bloom,   *remorse*
Past fading also.
                    She had lived, we'll say,
A harmless life, she called a virtuous life,
A quiet life, which was not life at all
290 (But that, she had not lived enough to know),
Between the vicar and the county squires,
The lord-lieutenant[6] looking down sometimes
From the empyrean° to assure their souls   *highest heaven*
Against chance vulgarisms, and, in the abyss,
295 The apothecary,[7] looked on once a year
To prove their soundness of humility.
The poor-club[8] exercised her Christian gifts
Of knitting stockings, stitching petticoats,
Because we are of one flesh, after all,
300 And need one flannel[9] (with a proper sense
Of difference in the quality)—and still
The book-club, guarded from your modern trick
Of shaking dangerous questions from the crease,[1]
Preserved her intellectual.° She had lived   *intellectual gifts*
305 A sort of cage-bird life, born in a cage,
Accounting that to leap from perch to perch
Was act and joy enough for any bird.
Dear heaven, how silly are the things that live
In thickets, and eat berries!
                              I, alas,
310 A wild bird scarcely fledged, was brought to her cage,
And she was there to meet me. Very kind.
Bring the clean water, give out the fresh seed.

She stood upon the steps to welcome me,
Calm, in black garb. I clung about her neck,—
315 Young babes, who catch at every shred of wool
To draw the new light closer, catch and cling
Less blindly. In my ears my father's word
Hummed ignorantly, as the sea in shells,
"Love, love, my child." She, black there with my grief,
320 Might feel my love—she was his sister once—
I clung to her. A moment she seemed moved,
Kissed me with cold lips, suffered me to cling,
And drew me feebly through the hall into
The room she sat in.
                    There, with some strange spasm

6. Governor of the county.
7. Pharmacist, who in England at the time could prescribe as well as sell medicine.
8. Club devoted to making things for the poor.
9. I.e., flannel petticoat.

1. The fold between two pages of a book, which had to be cut to open the pages. Presumably, modern books were more apt to reveal dangerous material when the crease was cut.

325 Of pain and passion, she wrung loose my hands
    Imperiously, and held me at arm's length,
    And with two grey-steel naked-bladed eyes
    Searched through my face,—ay, stabbed it through and through,
    Through brows and cheeks and chin, as if to find
330 A wicked murderer in my innocent face,
    If not here, there perhaps. Then, drawing breath,
    She struggled for her ordinary calm—
    And missed it rather,—told me not to shrink,
    As if she had told me not to lie or swear,—
335 "She loved my father and would love me too
    As long as I deserved it." Very kind.

    I understood her meaning afterward;
    She thought to find my mother in my face,
    And questioned it for that. For she, my aunt,
340 Had loved my father truly, as she could,
    And hated, with the gall of gentle souls,
    My Tuscan² mother who had fooled away
    A wise man from wise courses, a good man
    From obvious duties, and, depriving her,
345 His sister, of the household precedence,
    Had wronged his tenants, robbed his native land,
    And made him mad, alike by life and death,
    In love and sorrow. She had pored° for years   pored over
    What sort of woman could be suitable
350 To her sort of hate, to entertain it with,
    And so, her very curiosity
    Became hate too, and all the idealism
    She ever used in life was used for hate,
    Till hate, so nourished, did exceed at last
355 The love from which it grew, in strength and heat,
    And wrinkled her smooth conscience with a sense
    Of disputable virtue (say not, sin)
    When Christian doctrine was enforced at church.

    And thus my father's sister was to me
360 My mother's hater. From that day she did
    Her duty to me (I appreciate it
    In her own word as spoken to herself),
    Her duty, in large measure, well pressed out
    But measured always. She was generous, bland,
365 More courteous than was tender, gave me still
    The first place,—as if fearful that God's saints
    Would look down suddenly and say "Herein
    You missed a point, I think, through lack of love."
    Alas, a mother never is afraid
370 Of speaking angrily to any child,
    Since love, she knows, is justified of love.
    And I, I was a good child on the whole,
    A meek and manageable child. Why not?
    I did not live, to have the faults of life:

2. From Tuscany, a region in central Italy.

375 There seemed more true life in my father's grave
     Than in all England. Since *that* threw me off
     Who fain would cleave (his latest will, they say,
     Consigned me to his land), I only thought
     Of lying quiet there where I was thrown
380 Like sea-weed on the rocks, and suffering her
     To prick me to a pattern with her pin,[3]
     Fibre from fibre, delicate leaf from leaf,
     And dry out from my drowned anatomy
     The last sea-salt left in me.
                                        So it was.
385 I broke the copious curls upon my head
     In braids, because she liked smooth-ordered hair.
     I left off saying my sweet Tuscan words
     Which still at any stirring of the heart
     Came up to float across the English phrase
390 As lilies (*Bene* or *Che che*[4]), because
     She liked my father's child to speak his tongue.
     I learnt the collects[5] and the catechism,
     The creeds, from Athanasius back to Nice,[6]
     The Articles, the Tracts *against* the times[7]
395 (By no means Buonaventure's "Prick of Love"[8]),
     And various popular synopses of
     Inhuman doctrines never taught by John,[9]
     Because she liked instructed piety.
     I learnt my complement of classic French
400 (Kept pure of Balzac and neologism[1])
     And German also, since she liked a range
     Of liberal education,—tongues,° not books.   languages
     I learnt a little algebra, a little
     Of the mathematics,—brushed with extreme flounce[2]
405 The circle of the sciences, because
     She misliked women who are frivolous.
     I learnt the royal genealogies
     Of Oviedo,[3] the internal laws
     Of the Burmese empire,—by how many feet
410 Mount Chimborazo outsoars Teneriffe,
     What navigable river joins itself
     To Lara,[4] and what census of the year five
     Was taken at Klagenfurt,[5]—because she liked
     A general insight into useful facts.

3. As in embroidery.
4. No, no, indeed (Italian). *"Bene"*: it is well (Italian).
5. Seasonal opening prayers in the Anglican Church service.
6. Articles of Christian faith such as those proclaimed by Athanasius, an Egyptian theologian of the 4th century C.E., and at the early Church council held at Nicaea in the same era.
7. In the 1830s leaders of the conservative High Church party, such as John Henry Newman, had published *Tracts for the Times,* which expounded arguments against efforts by liberals to modernize the Anglican Church. Aurora's version of the title is hence ironic. "Articles": the thirty-nine articles are the principles of faith of the Church of England.

8. St. Bonaventure's doctrine that the power of the heart to love leads to higher illumination than the power of the mind to reason.
9. I.e., the author of the Gospel.
1. A new word or expression. Honoré de Balzac (1799–1850), a French novelist whose realism made him improper reading for a young English lady of the 19th century.
2. An ornamental edge to a skirt. "Extreme": outermost.
3. Spanish historian (16th century), who wrote a book on the genealogies of Spanish noblemen.
4. A town in Spain on the river Arlanza. Mount Chimborazo is one of the highest peaks of the Andes. Teneriffe is a mountain in the Canary Islands.
5. A town in Austria.

415 I learnt much music,—such as would have been
     As quite impossible in Johnson's day[6]
     As still it might be wished—fine sleights of hand
     And unimagined fingering, shuffling off
     The hearer's soul through hurricanes of notes
420 To a noisy Tophet;° and I drew . . . costumes   hell
     From French engravings, nereids° neatly draped   sea nymphs
     (With smirks of simmering godship): I washed in[7]
     Landscapes from nature (rather say, washed out).
     I danced the polka and Cellarius,[8]
425 Spun glass, stuffed birds, and modeled flowers in wax,
     Because she liked accomplishments in girls.
     I read a score of books on womanhood
     To prove, if women do not think at all,
     They may teach thinking (to a maiden aunt
430 Or else the author),—books that boldly assert
     Their right of comprehending husband's talk
     When not too deep, and even of answering
     With pretty "may it please you," or "so it is,"—
     Their rapid insight and fine aptitude,
435 Particular worth and general missionariness,
     As long as they keep quiet by the fire
     And never say "no" when the world says "ay,"
     For that is fatal,—their angelic reach
     Of virtue, chiefly used to sit and darn,
440 And fatten household sinners,—their, in brief,
     Potential faculty in everything
     Of abdicating power in it: she owned
     She liked a woman to be womanly,
     And English women, she thanked God and sighed
445 (Some people always sigh in thanking God),
     Were models to the universe. And last
     I learnt cross-stitch,[9] because she did not like
     To see me wear the night with empty hands
     A-doing nothing. So, my shepherdess
450 Was something after all (the pastoral saints
     Be praised for't), leaning lovelorn with pink eyes
     To match her shoes, when I mistook the silks;
     Her head uncrushed by that round weight of hat
     So strangely similar to the tortoise shell
     Which slew the tragic poet.[1]
455   By the way,
     The works of women are symbolical.
     We sew, sew, prick our fingers, dull our sight,
     Producing what? A pair of slippers, sir,
     To put on when you're weary—or a stool
460 To stumble over and vex you . . . "curse that stool!"

6. Allusion to the story about Samuel Johnson (1709–1784), who, when informed of the difficulty of a piece of music a young lady was playing, replied, "I would it had been impossible."
7. As in painting with watercolors.
8. A kind of waltz.

9. I.e., embroidery.
1. According to tradition, the Greek playwright Aeschylus was killed by an eagle who, mistaking his bald head for a stone, dropped a tortoise on it to break the shell.

Or else at best, a cushion, where you lean
And sleep, and dream of something we are not
But would be for your sake. Alas, alas!
This hurts most, this—that, after all, we are paid
The worth of our work, perhaps.
465   In looking down
Those years of education (to return)
I wonder if Brinvilliers suffered more
In the water-torture[2] . . . flood succeeding flood
To drench the incapable throat and split the veins . . .
470 Than I did. Certain of your feebler souls
Go out° in such a process; many pine   die
To a sick, inodorous light; my own endured:
I had relations in the Unseen, and drew
The elemental nutriment and heat
475 From nature, as earth feels the sun at nights,
Or as a babe sucks surely in the dark.
I kept the life thrust on me, on the outside
Of the inner life with all its ample room
For heart and lungs, for will and intellect,
480 Inviolable by conventions. God,
I thank thee for that grace of thine!
                                   At first
I felt no life which was not patience,—did
The thing she bade me, without heed to a thing
Beyond it, sat in just the chair she placed,
485 With back against the window, to exclude
The sight of the great lime-tree on the lawn,[3]
Which seemed to have come on purpose from the woods
To bring the house a message,—ay, and walked
Demurely in her carpeted low rooms,
490 As if I should not, harkening my own steps,
Misdoubt° I was alive. I read her books,   doubt
Was civil to her cousin, Romney Leigh,
Gave ear to her vicar, tea to her visitors,
And heard them whisper, when I changed a cup
495 (I blushed for joy at that),—"The Italian child,
For all her blue eyes and her quiet ways,
Thrives ill in England: she is paler yet
Than when we came the last time; she will die."

From *Book 2*

[AURORA'S ASPIRATIONS][4]

Times followed one another. Came a morn
I stood upon the brink of twenty years,
And looked before and after, as I stood

2. Marie Marguerite, Marquise de Brinvilliers, a celebrated criminal who was beheaded in 1676, was tortured by having water forced down her throat.
3. Cf. Coleridge's "This Lime-Tree Bower My Prison" (1800), in which the lime tree becomes the

vehicle of a realization that Nature never deserts the wise and pure even when they seem to be cut off from her most beautiful vistas.
4. Stifled by her aunt's oppressive conventionality, Aurora has found three sources of comfort and

Woman and artist,—either incomplete,
5   Both credulous of completion. There I held
The whole creation in my little cup,
And smiled with thirsty lips before I drank
"Good health to you and me, sweet neighbour mine,
And all these peoples."
                              I was glad, that day;
10 The June was in me, with its multitudes
Of nightingales all singing in the dark,
And rosebuds reddening where the calyx[5] split.
I felt so young, so strong, so sure of God!
So glad, I could not choose be very wise!
15 And, old at twenty, was inclined to pull
My childhood backward in a childish jest
To see the face of't once more, and farewell!
In which fantastic mood I bounded forth
At early morning,—would not wait so long
20 As even to snatch my bonnet by the strings,
But, brushing a green trail across the lawn
With my gown in the dew, took will and away
Among the acacias of the shrubberies,
To fly my fancies in the open air
25 And keep° my birthday, till my aunt awoke   observe
To stop good dreams. Meanwhile I murmured on
As honeyed bees keep humming to themselves,
"The worthiest poets have remained uncrowned
Till death has bleached their foreheads to the bone;
30 And so with me it must be unless I prove
Unworthy of the grand adversity,
And certainly I would not fail so much.
What, therefore, if I crown myself to-day
In sport, not pride, to learn the feel of it,
35 Before my brows be numbed as Dante's own
To all the tender pricking of such leaves?
Such leaves! what leaves?"
                              I pulled the branches down
To choose from.
                    "Not the bay![6] I choose no bay
(The fates deny us if we are overbold),
40 Nor myrtle—which means chiefly love; and love
Is something awful which one dares not touch
So early o' mornings. This verbena strains
The point of passionate fragrance; and hard by,
This guelder-rose,° at far too slight a beck   cranberry bush
45 Of the wind, will toss about her flower-apples.
Ah—there's my choice,—that ivy on the wall,
That headlong ivy! not a leaf will grow

---

inspiration: poetic aspirations, fostered by the discovery of her father's library; the beauty of the natural world; and the intellectual companionship of her cousin Romney Leigh, an idealistic young man troubled by the misery of the poor and inspired by contemporary notions of social reform.

5. The protective outer leaves covering a flower or bud.
6. Laurel, associated with poetry and prophecy by the ancient Greeks, who also crowned the athletic victors in the Pythian games with a laurel wreath.

But thinking of a wreath. Large leaves, smooth leaves,
Serrated like my vines, and half as green.
50 I like such ivy, bold to leap a height
'Twas strong to climb; as good to grow on graves
As twist about a thyrsus;[7] pretty too
(And that's not ill) when twisted round a comb."
Thus speaking to myself, half singing it,
55 Because some thoughts are fashioned like a bell
To ring with once being touched, I drew a wreath
Drenched, blinding me with dew, across my brow,
And fastening it behind so, turning faced
. . . My public!—cousin Romney—with a mouth
Twice graver than his eyes.
60   I stood there fixed,—
My arms up, like the caryatid,[8] sole
Of some abolished temple, helplessly
Persistent in a gesture which derides
A former purpose. Yet my blush was flame,
As if from flax, not stone.
65   "Aurora Leigh,
The earliest of Auroras!"[9]
                                        Hand stretched out
I clasped, as shipwrecked men will clasp a hand,
Indifferent to the sort of palm. The tide
Had caught me at my pastime, writing down
70 My foolish name too near upon the sea
Which drowned me with a blush as foolish. "You,
My cousin!"
                    The smile died out in his eyes
And dropped upon his lips, a cold dead weight,
For just a moment, "Here's a book I found!
75 No name writ on it—poems, by the form;
Some Greek upon the margin,—lady's Greek
Without the accents.[1] Read it? Not a word.
I saw at once the thing had witchcraft in't,
Whereof the reading calls up dangerous spirits:
I rather bring it to the witch."
80   "My book.
You found it" . . .
                    "In the hollow by the stream
That beech leans down into—of which you said
The Oread in it has a Naiad's[2] heart
And pines for waters."
                                        "Thank you."
                                                            "Thanks to *you*
85 My cousin! that I have seen you not too much
Witch, scholar, poet, dreamer, and the rest,

---

7. Staff twined with ivy that was carried, according to Greek myth, by Dionysus, god of wine and fertility.
8. Classical column in the form of a draped female figure.
9. Dawns; from Aurora, Roman goddess of the dawn.
1. Romney is gently mocking Aurora for her apparent ignorance of the complex rules of classical Greek accentuation.
2. Water nymph's. "Oread": tree nymph.

      To be a woman also."
                     With a glance
      The smile rose in his eyes again and touched
      The ivy on my forehead, light as air.
90   I answered gravely "Poets needs must be
      Or° men or women—more's the pity."   *either*
                                  "Ah,
      But men, and still less women, happily,
      Scarce need be poets. Keep to the green wreath,
      Since even dreaming of the stone and bronze
95   Brings headaches, pretty cousin, and defiles
      The clean white morning dresses."
                              "So you judge!
      Because I love the beautiful I must
      Love pleasure chiefly, and be overcharged
      For ease and whiteness! well, you know the world,
100   And only miss your cousin,'tis not much.
      But learn this; I would rather take my part
      With God's Dead, who afford to walk in white
      Yet spread His glory, than keep quiet here
      And gather up my feet from even a step
105   For fear to soil my gown in so much dust.
      I choose to walk at all risks.—Here, if heads
      That hold a rhythmic thought, must ache perforce,
      For my part I choose headaches,—and to-day's
      My birthday,"
                   "Dear Aurora, choose instead
      To cure them. You have balsams."°   *soothing cures*
110   "I perceive.
      The headache is too noble for my sex.
      You think the heartache would sound decenter,
      Since that's the woman's special, proper ache,
      And altogether tolerable, except
115   To a woman."

[AURORA'S REJECTION OF ROMNEY][3]

                   There he glowed on me
      With all his face and eyes. "No other help?"
      Said he—"no more than so?"
345   "What help?" I asked.
      "You'd scorn my help,—as Nature's self, you say,
      Has scorned to put her music in my mouth
      Because a woman's. Do you now turn round
      And ask for what a woman cannot give?"

350   "For what she only can, I turn and ask,"
      He answered, catching up my hands in his,

3. Romney and Aurora have been arguing about whether art, particularly a young woman's poetry, is useful in a world that, according to Romney, is full of human suffering. Romney claims that women have no ability to generalize from their personal experiences and are, therefore, doomed to be trivial poets and ineffectual social reformers. Aurora is quick to agree that to be merely an inferior poet would be intolerable to her, but while she admires Romney's lofty concern for humanity, she remains untempted to join forces with him.

And dropping on me from his high-eaved brow
The full weight of his soul,—"I ask for love,
And that, she can; for life in fellowship
355 Through bitter duties—that, I know she can;
For wifehood—will she?"
                              "Now," I said, "may God
Be witness 'twixt us two!" and with the word,
Meseemed[4] I floated into a sudden light
Above his stature,—"am I proved too weak
360 To stand alone, yet strong enough to bear
Such leaners on my shoulder? poor to think,
Yet rich enough to sympathise with thought?
Incompetent to sing, as blackbirds can,
Yet competent to love, like HIM?"
                              I paused;
365 Perhaps I darkened, as the lighthouse will
That turns upon the sea. "It's always so.
Anything does for a wife."
                              "Aurora, dear,
And dearly honoured,"—he pressed in at once
With eager utterance,—"you translate me ill.
370 I do not contradict my thought of you
Which is most reverent, with another thought
Found less so. If your sex is weak for art
(And I, who said so, did but honour you
By using truth in courtship), it is strong
375 For life and duty. Place your fecund heart
In mine, and let us blossom for the world
That wants love's colour in the grey of time.
My talk, meanwhile, is arid to you, ay,
Since all my talk can only set you where
380 You look down coldly on the arena-heaps
Of headless bodies, shapeless, indistinct!
The Judgment-Angel scarce would find his way
Through such a heap of generalised distress
To the individual man with lips and eyes,
385 Much less Aurora. Ah, my sweet, come down,
And hand in hand we'll go where yours shall touch
These victims, one by one! till, one by one,
The formless, nameless trunk of every man
Shall seem to wear a head with hair you know,
390 And every woman catch your mother's face
To melt you into passion."
                              "I am a girl,"
I answered slowly; "you do well to name
My mother's face. Though far too early, alas,
God's hand did interpose 'twixt it and me,
395 I know so much of love as used to shine
In that face and another. Just so much;
No more indeed at all. I have not seen
So much love since, I pray you pardon me,

4. It seemed to me.

As answers even to make a marriage with
400 In this cold land of England. What you love
Is not a woman, Romney, but a cause:
You want a helpmate, not a mistress, sir,
A wife to help your ends,—in her no end.
Your cause is noble, your ends excellent,
405 But I, being most unworthy of these and that,
Do otherwise conceive of love. Farewell."

"Farewell, Aurora? you reject me thus?"
He said.
          "Sir, you were married long ago.
You have a wife already whom you love,
410 Your social theory. Bless you both, I say.
For my part, I am scarcely meek enough
To be the handmaid of a lawful spouse.
Do I look a Hagar,[5] think you?"
                              "So you jest."

"Nay, so, I speak in earnest," I replied.
415 "You treat of° marriage too much like, at least,   talk about
A chief apostle: you would bear with you
A wife . . . a sister . . . shall we speak it out?
A sister of charity."
                    "Then, must it be
Indeed farewell? And was I so far wrong
420 In hope and in illusion, when I took
The woman to be nobler than the man,
Yourself the noblest woman, in the use
And comprehension of what love is,—love,
That generates the likeness of itself
425 Through all heroic duties? so far wrong,
In saying bluntly, venturing truth on love,
'Come, human creature, love and work with me,'—
Instead of 'Lady, thou art wondrous fair,
'And, where the Graces[6] walk before, the Muse
430 'Will follow at the lightning of their eyes,
'And where the Muse walks, lovers need to creep:
'Turn round and love me, or I die of love.' "

With quiet indignation I broke in.
"You misconceive the question like a man,
435 Who sees a woman as the complement
Of his sex merely. You forget too much
That every creature, female as the male,
Stands single in responsible act and thought
As also in birth and death. Whoever says
440 To a loyal woman, 'Love and work with me,'
Will get fair answers if the work and love,
Being good themselves, are good for her—the best
She was born for. Women of a softer mood,

5. In Genesis 16 Sarah's maidservant, who bore a
child, Ishmael, by Sarah's husband, Abraham.

6. In classical mythology goddesses who personified beauty and charm.

Surprised by men when scarcely awake to life,
445 Will sometimes only hear the first word, love,
And catch up with it any kind of work,
Indifferent, so that dear love go with it.
I do not blame such women, though, for love,
They pick much oakum;[7] earth's fanatics make
450 Too frequently heaven's saints. But *me* your work
Is not the best for,—nor your love the best,
Nor able to commend the kind of work
For love's sake merely. Ah, you force me, sir,
To be overbold in speaking of myself:
455 I too have my vocation,—work to do,
The heavens and earth have set me since I changed
My father's face for theirs, and, though your world
Were twice as wretched as you represent,
Most serious work, most necessary work
460 As any of the economists'. Reform,
Make trade a Christian possibility,
And individual right no general wrong;
Wipe out earth's furrows of the Thine and Mine,
And leave one green for men to play at bowls,[8]
465 With innings for them all! . . . What then, indeed,
If mortals are not greater by the head
Than any of their prosperities? what then,
Unless the artist keep up open roads
Betwixt the seen and unseen,—bursting through
470 The best of your conventions with his best,
The speakable, imaginable best
God bids him speak, to prove what lies beyond
Both speech and imagination? A starved man
Exceeds a fat beast: we'll not barter, sir,
475 The beautiful for barley.—And, even so,
I hold you will not compass your poor ends
Of barley-feeding and material ease,
Without a poet's individualism
To work your universal. It takes a soul,
480 To move a body: it takes a high-souled man,
To move the masses, even to a cleaner stye:
It takes the ideal, to blow a hair's-breadth off
The dust of the actual.—Ah, your Fouriers[9] failed,
Because not poets enough to understand
485 That life develops from within.——For me,
Perhaps I am not worthy, as you say,
Of work like this: perhaps a woman's soul
Aspires, and not creates: yet we aspire,
And yet I'll try out your perhapses, sir,
490 And if I fail . . . why, burn me up my straw[1]
Like other false works—I'll not ask for grace;
Your scorn is better, cousin Romney. I

---

7. Fiber derived by untwisting (picking) old rope, a task frequently assigned to workhouse inmates.
8. A game of skill played on a smooth lawn with weighted wooden balls.
9. I.e., utopian thinkers; François-Marie-Charles Fourier (1772–1837), a French political theorist who advocated communal property as a basis for social harmony.
1. I.e., destroy my poetry. See 1 Corinthians 3.12–15.

Who love my art, would never wish it lower
To suit my stature. I may love my art.
495   You'll grant that even a woman may love art,
Seeing that to waste true love on anything
Is womanly, past question."

From *Book 5*

[POETS AND THE PRESENT AGE]

The critics say that epics have died out
140   With Agamemnon and the goat-nursed gods;[2]
I'll not believe it. I could never deem,
As Payne Knight[3] did (the mythic mountaineer
Who travelled higher than he was born to live,
And showed sometimes the goitre[4] in his throat
145   Discoursing of an image seen through fog),
That Homer's heroes measured twelve feet high.
They were but men:—his Helen's hair turned grey
Like any plain Miss Smith's who wears a front;[5]
And Hector's infant whimpered at a plume[6]
150   As yours last Friday at a turkey-cock.
All actual heroes are essential men,
And all men possible heroes: every age,
Heroic in proportions, double-faced,
Looks backward and before, expects a morn
And claims an epos.°   *epic poem*
155   Ay, but every age
Appears to souls who live in't (ask Carlyle)[7]
Most unheroic. Ours, for instance, ours:
The thinkers scout it,° and the poets abound   *dismiss it scornfully*
Who scorn to touch it with a finger-tip:
160   A pewter age,[8]—mixed metal, silver-washed;
An age of scum, spooned off the richer past,
An age of patches for old gaberdines,°   *coats*
An age of mere transition,[9] meaning nought
Except that what succeeds° must shame it quite   *follows*
165   If God please. That's wrong thinking, to my mind,
And wrong thoughts make poor poems.
                                     Every age,
Through being beheld too close, is ill-discerned
By those who have not lived past it. We'll suppose
Mount Athos carved, as Alexander schemed,

2. Zeus, the ruler of the ancient Greek gods, was nursed by a goat. Agamemnon: the commander of the Greeks in the Trojan War.
3. Richard Payne Knight (1750–1824), a classical philologist who claimed that Lord Elgin had wasted his labor taking the marble friezes from the Parthenon in Greece to England because the marbles were not all Greek.
4. A disease often contracted in high mountain areas because of the low iodine content of the water.
5. A piece of false hair worn over the forehead by women.
6. In the *Iliad*, book 6, the Trojan hero Hector reaches for his infant son, but the child clings to his nurse, frightened of his father's helmet and crest.
7. In *Heroes, Hero-Worship, and the Heroic in History* (1841), Carlyle argues that the present age needs a renewed perception of the heroic.
8. Allusion to the convention, which originates in Hesiod (Greek poet, ca. 8th century B.C.E), of describing civilization's decline through a succession of ages named for increasingly less precious materials: i.e., the Golden Age, the Silver Age, the Bronze Age.
9. In *The Spirit of the Age* (1831), John Stuart Mill calls the present age "an age of transition."

170   To some colossal statue of a man.[1]
      The peasants, gathering brushwood in his ear,
      Had guessed as little as the browsing goats
      Of form or feature of humanity
      Up there,—in fact, had travelled five miles off
175   Or ere the giant image broke on them,
      Full human profile, nose and chin distinct,
      Mouth, muttering rhythms of silence up the sky
      And fed at evening with the blood of suns;
      Grand torso,—hand, that flung perpetually
180   The largesse of a silver river down
      To all the country pastures. 'Tis even thus
      With times we live in,—evermore too great
      To be apprehended near.
                     But poets should
      Exert a double vision; should have eyes
185   To see near things as comprehensively
      As if afar they took their point of sight,
      And distant things as intimately deep
      As if they touched them. Let us strive for this.
      I do distrust the poet who discerns
190   No character or glory in his times,
      And trundles back his soul five hundred years,
      Past moat and drawbridge, into a castle-court,
      To sing—oh, not of lizard or of toad
      Alive i' the ditch there,—'twere excusable,
195   But of some black chief, half knight, half sheep-lifter,°   *sheep stealer*
      Some beauteous dame, half chattel and half queen,
      As dead as must be, for the greater part,
      The poems made on their chivalric bones;
      And that's no wonder: death inherits death.

200   Nay, if there's room for poets in this world
      A little overgrown (I think there is),
      Their sole work is to represent the age,
      Their age, not Charlemagne's,[2]—this live, throbbing age,
      That brawls, cheats, maddens, calculates, aspires,
205   And spends more passion, more heroic heat,
      Betwixt the mirrors of its drawing-rooms,
      Than Roland[3] with his knights at Roncesvalles.
      To flinch from modern varnish, coat or flounce,
      Cry out for togas and the picturesque,
210   Is fatal,—foolish too. King Arthur's self
      Was commonplace to Lady Guenever;
      And Camelot to minstrels seemed as flat
      As Fleet Street[4] to our poets.
                      Never flinch,

1. Deinocrates, a Macedonian architect (4th century B.C.E.), is said to have suggested to Alexander the Great that Mount Athos be carved into the statue of a conqueror with a city in his left hand and a basin in his right, where all the waters of the region could be collected and used to water the pasture lands below.
2. Frankish conqueror (742–814), who created a European empire.
3. Legendary medieval hero, whose adventures are told in the epic poem *Chanson de Roland* (11th century); his last battle is fought at Roncesvalles, a Spanish village.
4. A center for book shops and newspaper and publishing offices in London.

But still, unscrupulously epic, catch
215 Upon the burning lava of a song
The full-veined, heaving, double-breasted Age:
That, when the next shall come, the men of that
May touch the impress° with reverent hand, and say   *impression*
"Behold,—behold the paps° we all have sucked!   *breasts*
220 This bosom seems to beat still, or at least
It sets ours beating: this is living art,
Which thus presents and thus records true life."

1853–56   1857

ALFRED, LORD TENNYSON
1809–1892

In his own lifetime Tennyson was the most popular of poets; his works, from 1850 onward, occupied a significant space on the bookshelves of almost every family of readers in England and the United States. Such popularity inevitably provoked a reaction in the decades following his death. In the course of repudiating their Victorian predecessors, the Edwardians and Georgians established the fashion of making fun of Tennyson's achievements. Samuel Butler (1835–1902), who anticipated early-twentieth-century tastes, has a characteristic entry in his *Notebooks*: "Talking it over, we agreed that Blake was no good because he learnt Italian at sixty in order to study Dante, and we knew Dante was no good because he was so fond of Virgil, and Virgil was no good because Tennyson ran [followed] him, and as for Tennyson—well, Tennyson goes without saying." Butler's flippant dismissal expresses an attitude that is no longer fashionable: Tennyson's stature as one of the major poets of the English language seems uncontroversial today.

Like his poetry, Tennyson's life and character have been reassessed in recent times. To many of his contemporaries he seemed a remote wizard secure in his laureate's robes, a man whose life had been sheltered, marred only by the loss of his best friend in youth. During much of his career Tennyson may have been isolated, but his was not a sheltered life in the real sense of the word. His childhood home, a parsonage, was a household dominated by frictions and loyalties and broodings over ancestral inheritances, in which the children showed marked strains of instability and eccentricity.

Alfred Tennyson was the fourth son in a family of twelve children. One of his brothers had to be confined to an insane asylum for life; another was long addicted to opium; another had violent quarrels with his father, the Reverend Dr. George Tennyson. This father, a man of considerable learning, had been born the eldest son of a wealthy landowner and had, therefore, expected to be heir to his family's estates. Instead he was disinherited in favor of his younger brother and had to make his own livelihood by joining the clergy, a profession that he disliked. After George Tennyson had settled in a small rectory in Somersby, his brooding sense of dissatisfaction led to increasingly violent bouts of drunkenness; he was nevertheless able to act as his sons' tutor in classical and modern languages to prepare them for entering the university.

Before leaving this strange household for Cambridge, Tennyson had already demonstrated a flair for writing verse—precocious exercises in the manner of John Milton or Byron or the Elizabethan dramatists. He had even published a volume in 1827, in collaboration with his brother Charles, *Poems by Two Brothers*. This feat drew him to the attention of a group of gifted undergraduates at Cambridge, "the Apostles," who encouraged him to devote his life to poetry. Up until that time the young man had known scarcely anyone outside the circle of his own family. Despite his massive frame and powerful physique, he was painfully shy, and the friendships he found at Cambridge as well as the intellectual and political discussions in which he participated gave him confidence and widened his horizons as a poet. The most important of these friendships was with Arthur Hallam, a leader of the Apostles, who later became engaged to Tennyson's sister Emily. Hallam's sudden death, in 1833, seemed an overwhelming calamity to his friend. Not only the long elegy *In Memoriam* (1850) but many of Tennyson's other poems are tributes to this early friendship.

Tennyson's career at Cambridge was interrupted and finally broken off in 1831 by family dissensions and financial need, and he returned home to study and practice the craft of poetry. His early volumes (1830 and 1832) were attacked as "obscure" or "affected" by some of the reviewers. Tennyson suffered acutely under hostile criticism, but he also profited from it. His 1842 volume demonstrated a remarkable leap forward, and in 1850 he at last attained fame and full critical recognition with *In Memoriam*. In the same year he became poet laureate in succession to William Wordsworth. The struggle during the previous twenty years had been made especially painful by the long postponement of his marriage to Emily Sellwood, whom he had loved since 1836 but could not marry, because of poverty, until 1850.

His life thereafter was a comfortable one. He was as popular as Byron had been, and the earnings from his poetry (sometimes exceeding £10,000 a year) enabled him to purchase a house in the country and to enjoy the kind of seclusion he liked. His notoriety was enhanced, like that of Bernard Shaw and Walt Whitman, by his colorful appearance. Huge and shaggy in cloak and broad-brimmed hat, gruff in manner, he impressed everyone as what is called a "character." The pioneering photographer Julia Cameron, who took magnificent portraits of him, called him "the most beautiful old man on earth." Like Dylan Thomas in the twentieth century, Tennyson had a booming voice that electrified listeners when he read his poetry, "mouthing out his hollow o's and a's, / Deep-chested music," as he would covertly describe himself in an early version of his Arthurian epic. Moreover, for many Victorian readers, he seemed not only a great poetical phrase maker and a striking individual but also a wise man whose occasional pronouncements on politics or world affairs represented the national voice itself. In 1884 he accepted a peerage. In 1892 he died and was buried in Westminster Abbey.

It is often said that success was bad for Tennyson and that after *In Memoriam* his poetic power seriously declined. That in his last forty-two years certain of his mannerisms became accentuated is true. One of the difficulties of his dignified blank verse was, as he said himself, that it is hard to describe commonplace objects and "at the same time to retain poetical elevation." This difficulty is evident, for example, in *Enoch Arden* (1864), a long blank verse narrative of everyday life in a fishing village, in which a basketful of fish is ornately described as "Enoch's ocean spoil / In ocean-smelling osier." In his later poems dealing with national affairs, there is also an increased shrillness of tone—a mannerism accentuated by Tennyson's realizing that he, like Charles Dickens, had a vast public behind him to back up his pronouncements.

It would be unwise, however, to ignore all of Tennyson's later productions. In 1855 he published his experimental monologue *Maud*, in which he presents an alienated hero who feels great bitterness toward society. In 1859 appeared four books of his *Idylls of the King*, a large-scale epic that occupied most of his energies in the second half of his career. The *Idylls* uses the body of Arthurian legend to construct a vision of civilization's rise and fall. In this civilization women both inspire men's highest efforts and sow the seeds of those efforts' destruction. The *Idylls* provides Tennyson's most extensive social vision, one that typifies much social thought of the age in its concern with medieval ideals of social community, heroism, and courtly love and in its despairing sense of the cycles of historical change.

W. H. Auden stated that Tennyson had "the finest ear, perhaps, of any English poet." The interesting point is that Tennyson did not "have" such an ear: he developed it. Studies of the original versions of his poems in the 1830 and 1832 volumes demonstrate how hard he worked at his craftsmanship. Like Geoffrey Chaucer or Alexander Pope or John Keats, Tennyson studied his predecessors assiduously to perfect his technique. Anyone wanting to learn the traditional craft of English verse can study profitably the various stages of revision that poems such as "The Lotos-Eaters" were subjected to by this painstaking and artful poet. Some lines written in 1988 by the American poet Karl Shapiro effectively characterize Tennyson's accomplishments in these areas:

> Long-lived, the very image of English Poet,
> Whose songs still break out tears in the generations,
> Whose poetry for practitioners still astounds,
> Who crafted his life and letters like a watch.

Tennyson's early poetry shows other skills as well. One of these was a capacity for linking scenery to states of mind. As early as 1835 J. S. Mill identified the special kind of scene painting to be found in poems such as "Mariana" (1830): "not the power of producing that rather vapid species of composition usually termed descriptive poetry . . . but the power of *creating* scenery, in keeping with some state of human feeling so fitted to it as to be the embodied symbol of it, and to summon up the state of feeling itself, with a force not to be surpassed by anything but reality."

The state of feeling to which Tennyson was most intensely drawn was a melancholy isolation, often portrayed through the consciousness of an abandoned woman, as in "Mariana." Tennyson's absorption with such emotions in his early poetry evoked considerable criticism. His friend R. C. Trench warned him, "Tennyson, we cannot live in Art," and Mill urged him to "cultivate, and with no half devotion, philosophy as well as poetry." Advice of this kind Tennyson was already predisposed to heed. The death of Hallam and the religious uncertainties that he had himself experienced, together with his own extensive study of writings by geologists, astronomers, and biologists, led him to confront many of the religious issues that bewildered his and later generations. The result was *In Memoriam*, a long elegy written over a period of seventeen years, embodying the poet's reflections on the relation of human beings to God and to nature.

Tennyson's exploration of these vast subjects prompted some readers, such as T. H. Huxley, to consider him an intellectual giant, a thinker who had mastered the scientific thought of his century and fully confronted the issues it raised. Others dismissed Tennyson, in this phase, as a lightweight. Auden went so far as to call him the "stupidest" of English poets. He added, "There was little about melancholia that he didn't know; there was little else that he did." Perhaps T. S. Eliot's evaluation of *In Memoriam* is the more thought-provoking: the poem, he wrote, is remarkable not "because of the quality of its faith but because of the quality of its doubt." Tennyson's mind was slow, ponderous, brooding; for the composition of *In Memoriam* such qualities of mind were assets, not liabilities. Very different are the poems Tennyson writes of events of the moment over which his thoughts and feelings have had no time to brood. Several of these are what he himself called "newspaper verse." They are letters to the editor in effect, with the heat we expect of such productions. "The Charge of the Light Brigade" (1854), inspired by a report in the London *Times* of a cavalry charge at Balaclava during the Crimean War, is one of the most fascinating of his productions in this category.

Tennyson's poems of contemporary events were inevitably popular in his own day. So too were those poems in which, as in "Locksley Hall" (1842), he dipped into the future. The technological changes wrought by Victorian inventors and engineers fascinated him, sometimes giving him an exultant assurance of human progress. At other times the horrors of industrialism's by-products in the slums, the persistence of barbarity and bloodshed, and the greed of the newly rich destroyed his hopes that humanity was evolving upward. In the final book of *Idylls of the King* (1869), Arthur laments that his "realm / Reels back into the beast": Tennyson was similarly haunted by the possibility of retrogression.

For despite Tennyson's fascination with technological developments, he was essentially a poet of the countryside, a man whose whole being was conditioned by the recurring rhythms of rural rather than urban life. He had the country dweller's awareness of traditional roots and sense of the past. It is appropriate that so many of his poems are about the past, not about the present or future. Tennyson said that "the words 'far, far away' had always a strange charm" for him, even in his childhood; he was haunted by what he called "the passion of the past." The past became his great theme, whether it be his own past (such as the times he shared with Hallam), his country's past (as in *Idylls of the King*), or the past of the world itself, as expressed in these lines from *In Memoriam*:

> There rolls the deep where grew the tree.
> O earth, what changes hast thou seen!
> There where the long street roars hath been
> The stillness of the central sea.

Though Tennyson more often is inspired by the recorded past of humankind, he is the first major writer to express this awareness of the vast extent of geological time that has haunted human consciousness since Victorian scientists exposed the history of the earth's crust.

Mariana[1]

"Mariana in the moated grange."
Measure for Measure

With blackest moss the flower-plots
    Were thickly crusted, one and all;
The rusted nails fell from the knots
    That held the pear to the gable wall.
5   The broken sheds looked sad and strange:
    Unlifted was the clinking latch;
    Weeded° and worn the ancient thatch   *full of weeds*
Upon the lonely moated grange.
    She only said, "My life is dreary,
10   He cometh not," she said;
    She said, "I am aweary, aweary,
    I would that I were dead!"

Her tears fell with the dews at even;
    Her tears fell ere the dews were dried;
15 She could not look on the sweet heaven,
    Either at morn or eventide.
After the flitting of the bats,
    When thickest dark did trance° the sky,   *cross*

1. Mariana, in Shakespeare's *Measure for Measure* 3.1.255, waits in a grange (an outlying farmhouse) for her lover, who has deserted her.

She drew her casement curtain by,
20 And glanced athwart° the glooming flats.   *across*
    She only said, "The night is dreary,
        He cometh not," she said;
    She said, "I am aweary, aweary,
        I would that I were dead!"

25 Upon the middle of the night,
        Waking she heard the nightfowl crow;
    The cock sung out an hour ere light;
        From the dark fen° the oxen's low   *marshland*
    Came to her; without hope of change,
30   In sleep she seemed to walk forlorn,
        Till cold winds woke the gray-eyed morn
    About the lonely moated grange.
        She only said, "The day is dreary,
            He cometh not," she said;
35   She said, "I am aweary, aweary,
            I would that I were dead!"

    About a stonecast° from the wall   *stone's throw*
        A sluice with blackened waters slept,
    And o'er it many, round and small,
40   The clustered marish-mosses² crept.
    Hard° by a poplar shook alway,   *close*
        All silver-green with gnarlèd bark:
    For leagues no other tree did mark
    The level waste, the rounding gray.
45   She only said, "My life is dreary,
            He cometh not," she said;
        She said, "I am aweary, aweary,
            I would that I were dead!"

    And ever when the moon was low,
50   And the shrill winds were up and away,
    In the white curtain, to and fro,
        She saw the gusty shadow sway.
    But when the moon was very low,
        And wild winds bound within their cell,³
55   The shadow of the poplar fell
    Upon her bed, across her brow.
        She only said, "The night is dreary,
            He cometh not," she said;
        She said, "I am aweary, aweary,
60   I would that I were dead!"

    All day within the dreamy house,
        The doors upon their hinges creaked;
    The blue fly sung in the pane; the mouse

2. The little marsh-moss lumps that float on the surface of water [Tennyson's note].

3. According to Virgil, Aeolus, god of winds, kept the winds imprisoned in a cave (*Aeneid* 1.50–59).

Behind the moldering wainscot° shrieked,   *wooden paneling*
65   Or from the crevice peered about.
      Old faces glimmered through the doors,
      Old footsteps trod the upper floors,
      Old voices called her from without.
            She only said, "My life is dreary,
70   He cometh not," she said;
            She said, "I am aweary, aweary,
               I would that I were dead!"

      The sparrow's chirrup on the roof,
      The slow clock ticking, and the sound
75   Which to the wooing wind aloof
      The poplar made, did all confound
      Her sense; but most she loathed the hour
      When the thick-moted sunbeam lay
      Athwart the chambers, and the day
80   Was sloping toward his western bower.
            Then, said she, "I am very dreary,
               He will not come," she said;
            She wept, "I am aweary, aweary,
               Oh God, that I were dead!"

                                                    1830

The Lady of Shalott[1]

Part 1

      On either side the river lie
      Long fields of barley and of rye,
      That clothe the wold° and meet the sky;   *rolling plain*
      And through the field the road runs by
5   To many-towered Camelot;
      And up and down the people go,
      Gazing where the lilies blow°   *bloom*
      Round an island there below,
            The island of Shalott.

10   Willows whiten, aspens quiver,
      Little breezes dusk and shiver
      Through the wave that runs forever
      By the island in the river
            Flowing down to Camelot.
15   Four gray walls, and four gray towers,

1. The story of the Lady of Shalott is a version of the tale of "Elaine the fair maid of Astolat," which appears in book 18 of Sir Thomas Malory's *Morte Darthur* (1470). Tennyson, however, claimed he did not know Malory's version when he wrote his draft in 1832, identifying his source as a 14th-century tale about "la Damigella di Scalot": "I met the story first in some Italian *novelle:* but the web, mirror, island, etc., were my own. Indeed, I doubt whether I should ever have put it in that shape if I had been aware of the Maid of Astolat in *Morte Arthur.*" Tennyson subjected this poem to numerous revisions over the years.

        Overlook a space of flowers,
        And the silent isle imbowers
            The Lady of Shalott.

        By the margin, willow-veiled,
20   Slide the heavy barges trailed
        By slow horses; and unhailed
        The shallop° flitteth silken-sailed   *light open boat*
            Skimming down to Camelot:
        But who hath seen her wave her hand?
25   Or at the casement seen her stand?
        Or is she known in all the land,
            The Lady of Shalott?

        Only reapers, reaping early
        In among the bearded barley,
30   Hear a song that echoes cheerly
        From the river winding clearly,
            Down to towered Camelot;
        And by the moon the reaper weary,
        Piling sheaves in uplands airy,
35   Listening, whispers " 'Tis the fairy
            Lady of Shalott."

Part 2

        There she weaves by night and day
        A magic web with colors gay.
        She has heard a whisper say,
40   A curse is on her if she stay°   *pause*
            To look down to Camelot.
        She knows not what the curse may be,
        And so she weaveth steadily,
        And little other care hath she,
45   The Lady of Shalott.

        And moving through a mirror clear²
        That hangs before her all the year,
        Shadows of the world appear.
        There she sees the highway near
50   Winding down to Camelot;
        There the river eddy whirls,
        And there the surly village churls,°   *peasants*
        And the red cloaks of market girls,
            Pass onward from Shalott.

55   Sometimes a troop of damsels glad,
        An abbot on an ambling pad,°   *easy-paced horse*
        Sometimes a curly shepherd lad,
        Or long-haired page in crimson clad,
            Goes by to towered Camelot;

---

2. Weavers used mirrors, placed facing their looms, to see the progress of their work.

60 And sometimes through the mirror blue
    The knights come riding two and two:
    She hath no loyal knight and true,
            The Lady of Shalott.

    But in her web she still delights
65 To weave the mirror's magic sights,
    For often through the silent nights
    A funeral, with plumes and lights
            And music, went to Camelot;
    Or when the moon was overhead,
70 Came two young lovers lately wed:
    "I am half sick of shadows," said
            The Lady of Shalott.

Part 3

    A bowshot from her bower eaves,
    He rode between the barley sheaves,
75 The sun came dazzling through the leaves,
    And flamed upon the brazen greaves[3]
            Of bold Sir Lancelot.
    A red-cross knight forever kneeled
    To a lady in his shield,
80 That sparkled on the yellow field,
            Beside remote Shalott.

    The gemmy bridle glittered free,
    Like to some branch of stars we see
    Hung in the golden Galaxy.
85 The bridle bells rang merrily
            As he rode down to Camelot;
    And from his blazoned baldric[4] slung
    A mighty silver bugle hung,
    And as he rode his armor rung,
90   Beside remote Shalott.

    All in the blue unclouded weather
    Thick-jeweled shone the saddle leather,
    The helmet and the helmet-feather
    Burned like one burning flame together,
95   As he rode down to Camelot;
    As often through the purple night,
    Below the starry clusters bright,
    Some bearded meteor, trailing light,
            Moves over still Shalott.

100 His broad clear brow in sunlight glowed;
    On burnished hooves his war horse trode;
    From underneath his helmet flowed

3. Armor protecting the leg below the knee.
4. A belt worn diagonally from one shoulder to the
opposite hip, supporting a sword or bugle. "Blazoned": painted with a heraldic device.

His coal-black curls as on he rode,
    As he rode down to Camelot.
105 From the bank and from the river
He flashed into the crystal mirror,
"Tirra lirra,"[5] by the river
    Sang Sir Lancelot.

She left the web, she left the loom,
110 She made three paces through the room,
She saw the water lily bloom,
She saw the helmet and the plume,
    She looked down to Camelot.
Out flew the web and floated wide;
115 The mirror cracked from side to side;
"The curse is come upon me," cried
    The Lady of Shalott.

Part 4

In the stormy east wind straining,
The pale yellow woods were waning,
120 The broad stream in his banks complaining,
Heavily the low sky raining
    Over towered Camelot;
Down she came and found a boat
Beneath a willow left afloat,
125 And round about the prow she wrote
    The Lady of Shalott.

And down the river's dim expanse
Like some bold seër in a trance,
Seeing all his own mischance—
130 With a glassy countenance
    Did she look to Camelot.
And at the closing of the day
She loosed the chain, and down she lay;
The broad stream bore her far away,
135   The Lady of Shalott.

Lying, robed in snowy white
That loosely flew to left and right—
The leaves upon her falling light—
Through the noises of the night
140   She floated down to Camelot;
And as the boat-head wound along
The willowy hills and fields among,
They heard her singing her last song,
    The Lady of Shalott.

145 Heard a carol, mournful, holy,
Chanted loudly, chanted lowly,

---

5. Cf. Autolycus's song in Shakespeare's *The Winter's Tale* 4.3.9.

This 1857 engraving, created by Dante Gabriel Rossetti for publisher Edward Moxon's illustrated collection of Tennyson's poetry, shows Lancelot musing "a little space" on the Lady of Shalott in her boat.

> Till her blood was frozen slowly,
> And her eyes were darkened wholly,[6]
>   Turned to towered Camelot.
> 150 For ere she reached upon the tide
> The first house by the waterside,
> Singing in her song she died,
>   The Lady of Shalott.
>
> Under tower and balcony,
> 155 By garden wall and gallery,
> A gleaming shape she floated by,
> Dead-pale between the houses high,
>   Silent into Camelot.
> Out upon the wharfs they came,
> 160 Knight and burgher, lord and dame,
> And round the prow they read her name,
>   *The Lady of Shalott.*

6. In the 1832 version this line read: "And her smooth face sharpened slowly." George Eliot informed Tennyson that she preferred the earlier version.

Who is this? and what is here?
And in the lighted palace near
165 Died the sound of royal cheer;
And they crossed themselves for fear,
　　All the knights at Camelot:
But Lancelot mused a little space;
He said, "She has a lovely face;
170 God in his mercy lend her grace,
　　The Lady of Shalott."

1831–32　　　　　　　　　　　　　　　　　　　　1832, 1842

The Lotos-Eaters[1]

"Courage!" he[2] said, and pointed toward the land,
"This mounting wave will roll us shoreward soon."
In the afternoon they came unto a land[3]
In which it seemèd always afternoon.
5　All round the coast the languid air did swoon,
Breathing like one that hath a weary dream.
Full-faced above the valley stood the moon;
And, like a downward smoke, the slender stream
Along the cliff to fall and pause and fall did seem.

10　A land of streams! some, like a downward smoke,
Slow-dropping veils of thinnest lawn,° did go;　　　　*fine thin linen*
And some through wavering lights and shadows broke,
Rolling a slumbrous sheet of foam below.
They saw the gleaming river seaward flow
15　From the inner land; far off, three mountaintops
Three silent pinnacles of aged snow,
Stood sunset-flushed; and, dewed with showery drops,
Up-clomb° the shadowy pine above the woven copse.　　*climbed up*

The charmèd sunset lingered low adown
20　In the red West; through mountain clefts the dale
Was seen far inland, and the yellow down[4]
Bordered with palm, and many a winding vale
And meadow, set with slender galingale;[5]

---

1. Based on a short episode from the *Odyssey* (9.82–97) in which the weary Greek veterans of the Trojan War are tempted by a desire to abandon their long voyage homeward. As Odysseus later reported: "On the tenth day we set foot on the land of the lotos-eaters who eat a flowering food. . . . I sent forth certain of my company [who] . . . mixed with the men of the lotos-eaters who gave . . . them of the lotos to taste. Now whosoever of them did eat the honey-sweet fruit of the lotos had no more wish to bring tidings nor to come back, but there he chose to abide . . . forgetful of his homeward way."
　Tennyson expands Homer's brief account into an elaborate picture of weariness and the desire for rest and death. The descriptions in the first stanzas are similar to Spenser's *The Faerie Queene* (1590) 2.6 and employ the same stanza form. The final section derives, in part, from Lucretius's conception of the gods in *De Rerum Natura* (ca. 55 B.C.E.).
2. Odysseus (or Ulysses).
3. The repetition of "land" from line 1 was deliberate; Tennyson said that this "no rhyme" was "lazier" in its effect. This technique of repeating words, phrases, and sounds continues; cf. "afternoon" (lines 3–4) and the rhyming of "adown" and "down" (lines 19 and 21).
4. An open plain on high ground.
5. A plant resembling tall coarse grass.

A land where all things always seemed the same!
25 And round about the keel with faces pale,
Dark faces pale against that rosy flame,
The mild-eyed melancholy Lotos-eaters came.

Branches they bore of that enchanted stem,
Laden with flower and fruit, whereof they gave
30 To each, but whoso did receive of them
And taste, to him the gushing of the wave
Far far away did seem to mourn and rave
On alien shores; and if his fellow spake,
His voice was thin, as voices from the grave;
35 And deep-asleep he seemed, yet all awake,
And music in his ears his beating heart did make.

They sat them down upon the yellow sand,
Between the sun and moon upon the shore;
And sweet it was to dream of Fatherland,
40 Of child, and wife, and slave; but evermore
Most weary seemed the sea, weary the oar,
Weary the wandering fields of barren foam,
Then some one said, "We will return no more";
And all at once they sang, "Our island home°   Ithaca
45 Is far beyond the wave; we will no longer roam."

Choric Song[6]

1

There is sweet music here that softer falls
Than petals from blown roses on the grass,
Or night-dews on still waters between walls
Of shadowy granite, in a gleaming pass;
50 Music that gentlier on the spirit lies,
Than tired[7] eyelids upon tired eyes;
Music that brings sweet sleep down from the blissful skies.
Here are cool mosses deep,
And through the moss the ivies creep,
55 And in the stream the long-leaved flowers weep,
And from the craggy ledge the poppy hangs in sleep.

2

Why are we weighed upon with heaviness,
And utterly consumed with sharp distress,
While all things else have rest from weariness?
60 All things have rest: why should we toil alone,
We only toil, who are the first of things,
And make perpetual moan,
Still from one sorrow to another thrown;
Nor ever fold our wings,

6. Sung by the mariners.
7. Tennyson wanted the word to be pronounced as *tie-yerd* rather than *tier'd* or *tire-èd*, thus "mak-ing the word neither monosyllable or disyllabic, but a dreamy child of the two."

65 And cease from wanderings,
    Nor steep our brows in slumber's holy balm;
    Nor harken what the inner spirit sings,
    "There is no joy but calm!"—
    Why should we only toil, the roof and crown of things?[8]

3

70 Lo! in the middle of the wood,
    The folded leaf is wooed from out the bud
    With winds upon the branch, and there
    Grows green and broad, and takes no care,
    Sun-steeped at noon, and in the moon
75 Nightly dew-fed; and turning yellow
    Falls, and floats adown the air.
    Lo! sweetened with summer light,
    The full-juiced apple, waxing over-mellow,
    Drops in a silent autumn night.
80 All its allotted length of days
    The flower ripens in its place,
    Ripens and fades, and falls, and hath no toil,
    Fast-rooted in the fruitful soil.

4

    Hateful is the dark blue sky,
85 Vaulted o'er the dark blue sea.
    Death is the end of life; ah, why
    Should life all labor be?
    Let us alone. Time driveth onward fast,
    And in a little while our lips are dumb.
90 Let us alone. What is it that will last?
    All things are taken from us, and become
    Portions and parcels of the dreadful past.
    Let us alone. What pleasure can we have
    To war with evil? Is there any peace
95 In ever climbing up the climbing wave?
    All things have rest, and ripen toward the grave
    In silence—ripen, fall, and cease:
    Give us long rest or death, dark death, or dreamful ease.[9]

5

    How sweet it were, hearing the downward stream,
100 With half-shut eyes ever to seem
    Falling asleep in a half-dream!
    To dream and dream, like yonder amber light,
    Which will not leave the myrrh-bush[1] on the height;
    To hear each other's whispered speech;
105 Eating the Lotos day by day,
    To watch the crisping° ripples on the beach,   *curling*
    And tender curving lines of creamy spray;

8. Cf. *The Faerie Queene* 2.6.17: "Why then dost thou, O man, that of them all / Art Lord, and eke of nature Sovereaine, / Wilfully . . . wast thy joyous houres in needlesse paine?"
9. Cf. *The Faerie Queen* 1.9.40: "Sleepe after toyle, port after stormie seas, / Ease after warre, death after life does greatly please."
1. Myrrh, a resin used in perfume and incense, is associated with sweetness and comfort.

To lend our hearts and spirits wholly
To the influence of mild-minded melancholy;
10 To muse and brood and live again in memory,
With those old faces of our infancy
Heaped over with a mound of grass,
Two handfuls of white dust, shut in an urn of brass!

6

Dear is the memory of our wedded lives,
15 And dear the last embraces of our wives
And their warm tears; but all hath suffered change;
For surely now our household hearths are cold,
Our sons inherit us,° our looks are strange,   succeed us as our heirs
And we should come like ghosts to trouble joy.
20 Or else the island princes[2] overbold
Have eat our substance, and the minstrel sings
Before them of the ten years' war in Troy,
And our great deeds, as half-forgotten things.
Is there confusion in the little isle?
25 Let what is broken so remain.
The Gods are hard to reconcile;
'Tis hard to settle order once again.
There *is* confusion worse than death,
Trouble on trouble, pain on pain,
30 Long labor unto aged breath,
Sore tasks to hearts worn out by many wars
And eyes grown dim with gazing on the pilot-stars.

7

But, propped on beds of amaranth and moly,[3]
How sweet—while warm airs lull us, blowing lowly—
135 With half-dropped eyelid still,
Beneath a heaven dark and holy,
To watch the long bright river drawing slowly
His waters from the purple hill—
To hear the dewy echoes calling
140 From cave to cave through the thick-twined vine—
To watch the emerald-colored water falling
Through many a woven acanthus[4] wreath divine!
Only to hear and see the far-off sparkling brine,
Only to hear were sweet, stretched out beneath the pine.

8

145 The Lotos blooms below the barren peak,
The Lotos blows by every winding creek;
All day the wind breathes low with mellower tone;
Through every hollow cave and alley lone
Round and round the spicy downs the yellow Lotos dust is blown.
150 We have had enough of action, and of motion we,
Rolled to starboard, rolled to larboard, when the surge was seething free,

2. The suitors of Penelope, Odysseus's wife; during his long absence they have settled themselves
as guests in his hall as they pressure her to remarry.
3. A flower with magical properties mentioned by

Homer. "Amaranth": a legendary unfading flower.
4. A plant resembling a thistle. Its leaves were the
model for ornaments on Corinthian columns.

Where the wallowing monster spouted his foam-fountains in the sea.
Let us swear an oath, and keep it with an equal mind,
In the hollow Lotos land to live and lie reclined
155 On the hills like Gods together, careless of mankind.
For they lie beside their nectar, and the bolts° are hurled   thunderbolts
Far below them in the valleys, and the clouds are lightly curled
Round their golden houses, girdled with the gleaming world;
Where they smile in secret, looking over wasted lands,
160 Blight and famine, plague and earthquake, roaring deeps and fiery sands,
Clanging fights, and flaming towns, and sinking ships, and praying hands.
But they smile, they find a music centred in a doleful song
Steaming up, a lamentation and an ancient tale of wrong,
Like a tale of little meaning though the words are strong;
165 Chanted from an ill-used race of men that cleave the soil,
Sow the seed, and reap the harvest with enduring toil,
Storing yearly little dues of wheat, and wine and oil;
Till they perish and they suffer—some, 'tis whispered—down in hell
Suffer endless anguish, others in Elysian valleys dwell,
170 Resting weary limbs at last on beds of asphodel.[5]
Surely, surely, slumber is more sweet than toil, the shore
Than labor in the deep mid-ocean, wind and wave and oar;
O, rest ye, brother mariners, we will not wander more.

1832, 1842

Ulysses[1]

It little profits that an idle king,
By this still hearth, among these barren crags,
Matched with an aged wife, I mete and dole
Unequal laws[2] unto a savage race,
5 That hoard, and sleep, and feed,[3] and know not me.
I cannot rest from travel; I will drink
Life to the lees. All times I have enjoyed
Greatly, have suffered greatly, both with those
That loved me, and alone; on shore, and when
10 Through scudding drifts the rainy Hyades[4]
Vexed the dim sea. I am become a name;
For always roaming with a hungry heart

5. A yellow lilylike flower supposed to grow in Elysium—in classical mythology a paradise for heroes favored by the gods.
1. According to Dante, after the fall of Troy, Ulysses never returned to his island home of Ithaca. Instead he persuaded some of his followers to seek new experiences by a voyage of exploration westward out beyond the Strait of Gibraltar. In his inspiring speech to his aging crew he said: "Consider your origin: you were not made to live as brutes, but to pursue virtue and knowledge" (Inferno 26). Tennyson modified Dante's 14th-century version by combining it with Homer's account (Odyssey 19–24). Thus Tennyson has Ulysses make his speech in Ithaca some time after he has returned home; reunited with his wife,

Penelope, and his son, Telemachus; and, presumably, resumed his administrative responsibilities involved in governing his kingdom.
Tennyson stated that this poem expressed his own "need of going forward and braving the struggle of life" after the death of Arthur Hallam.
2. Measure out rewards and punishments.
3. Cf. Shakespeare's Hamlet 4.4.9.23–25: "What is a man / If his chief good . . . Be but to sleep and feed?—a beast, no more."
4. A group of stars (literally, "rainy ones") in the constellation Taurus; their heliacal rising and setting generally coincided with the season of heavy rains. "Scudding drifts": driving showers of spray and rain.

Much have I seen and known—cities of men
And manners, climates, councils, governments,
15 Myself not least, but honored of them all—
And drunk delight of battle with my peers,
Far on the ringing plains of windy Troy,
I am a part of all that I have met;
Yet all experience is an arch wherethrough
20 Gleams that untraveled world whose margin fades
Forever and forever when I move.
How dull it is to pause, to make an end,
To rust unburnished, not to shine in use![5]
As though to breathe were life! Life piled on life
25 Were all too little, and of one to me
Little remains; but every hour is saved
From that eternal silence, something more,
A bringer of new things; and vile it were
For some three suns to store and hoard myself,
30 And this gray spirit yearning in desire
To follow knowledge like a sinking star,
Beyond the utmost bound of human thought.

   This is my son, mine own Telemachus,
To whom I leave the scepter and the isle—
35 Well-loved of me, discerning to fulfill
This labor, by slow prudence to make mild
A rugged people, and through soft degrees
Subdue them to the useful and the good.
Most blameless is he, centered in the sphere
40 Of common duties, decent not to fail
In offices of tenderness, and pay
Meet° adoration to my household gods,   *suitable, fitting*
When I am gone. He works his work, I mine.

   There lies the port; the vessel puffs her sail;
45 There gloom the dark, broad seas. My mariners,
Souls that have toiled, and wrought, and thought with me—
That ever with a frolic welcome took
The thunder and the sunshine,[6] and opposed
Free hearts, free foreheads[7]—you and I are old;
50 Old age hath yet his honor and his toil.
Death closes all; but something ere the end,
Some work of noble note, may yet be done,
Not unbecoming men that strove with Gods.
The lights begin to twinkle from the rocks;
55 The long day wanes; the slow moon climbs; the deep
Moans round with many voices. Come, my friends,
'Tis not too late to seek a newer world.
Push off, and sitting well in order smite
The sounding furrows; for my purpose holds

5. Cf. Ulysses' speech in Shakespeare's *Troilus and Cressida* 3.3.144–47: "Perseverance, dear my lord, / Keeps honour bright. To have done is to hang / Quite out of fashion, like a rusty mail / In monumental mock'ry."
6. I.e., varying fortunes.
7. Confidence.

60 To sail beyond the sunset, and the baths[8]
    Of all the western stars, until I die.
    It may be that the gulfs will wash us down;
    It may be we shall touch the Happy Isles,[9]
    And see the great Achilles,[1] whom we knew.
65 Though much is taken, much abides; and though
    We are not now that strength which in old days
    Moved earth and heaven, that which we are, we are—
    One equal temper of heroic hearts,
    Made weak by time and fate, but strong in will
70 To strive, to seek, to find, and not to yield.

1833   1842

Tithonus[1]

    The woods decay, the woods decay and fall,
    The vapors weep their burthen to the ground,
    Man comes and tills the field and lies beneath,
    And after many a summer dies the swan.[2]
5   Me only cruel immortality
    Consumes; I wither slowly in thine arms,[3]
    Here at the quiet limit of the world,
    A white-haired shadow roaming like a dream
    The ever-silent spaces of the East,
10 Far-folded mists, and gleaming halls of morn.
        Alas! for this gray shadow, once a man—
    So glorious in his beauty and thy choice,
    Who madest him thy chosen, that he seemed
    To his great heart none other than a God!
15 I asked thee, "Give me immortality."
    Then didst thou grant mine asking with a smile,
    Like wealthy men who care not how they give.
    But thy strong Hours indignant worked their wills,
    And beat me down and marred and wasted me,
20 And though they could not end me, left me maimed
    To dwell in presence of immortal youth,
    Immortal age beside immortal youth,
    And all I was in ashes. Can thy love,
    Thy beauty, make amends, though even now,
25 Close over us, the silver star,[4] thy guide,
    Shines in those tremulous eyes that fill with tears
    To hear me? Let me go; take back thy gift.
    Why should a man desire in any way

8. The outer ocean or river that the Greeks believed surrounded the flat circle of the earth; the stars descended into it.
9. In Greek myth the Islands of the Blessed, a paradise of perpetual summer, located in the far-western ocean, where the virtuous and heroes dwell forever after death (often identified with Elysium).
1. The greatest of the Greek warriors at Troy, where he was killed.
1. A Trojan prince loved by the goddess of the dawn, Eos or Aurora, who obtained for him the gift of living forever but neglected to ask for the gift of everlasting youth.
2. Some species of swans live for at least fifty years.
3. Aurora's arms.
4. The morning star that precedes the dawn.

To vary from the kindly race of men,
30   Or pass beyond the goal of ordinance[5]
Where all should pause, as is most meet for all?
    A soft air fans the cloud apart; there comes
A glimpse of that dark world where I was born.
Once more the old mysterious glimmer steals
35   From thy pure brows, and from thy shoulders pure,
And bosom beating with a heart renewed.
Thy cheek begins to redden through the gloom,
Thy sweet eyes brighten slowly close to mine,
Ere yet they blind the stars, and the wild team[6]
40   Which love thee, yearning for thy yoke, arise,
And shake the darkness from their loosened manes,
And beat the twilight into flakes of fire.
    Lo! ever thus thou growest beautiful
In silence, then before thine answer given
45   Departest, and thy tears are on my cheek.
    Why wilt thou ever scare me with thy tears,
And make me tremble lest a saying learnt,
In days far-off, on that dark earth, be true?
"The Gods themselves cannot recall their gifts."
50   Ay me! ay me! with what another heart
In days far-off, and with what other eyes
I used to watch—if I be he that watched—
The lucid outline forming round thee; saw
The dim curls kindle into sunny rings;
55   Changed with thy mystic change, and felt my blood
Glow with the glow that slowly crimsoned all
Thy presence and thy portals, while I lay,
Mouth, forehead, eyelids, growing dewy-warm
With kisses balmier than half-opening buds
60   Of April, and could hear the lips that kissed
Whispering I knew not what of wild and sweet,
Like that strange song I heard Apollo sing,
While Ilion like a mist rose into towers.[7]
    Yet hold me not forever in thine East;
65   How can my nature longer mix with thine?
Coldly thy rosy shadows bathe me, cold
Are all thy lights, and cold my wrinkled feet
Upon thy glimmering thresholds, when the steam
Floats up from those dim fields about the homes
70   Of happy men that have the power to die,
And grassy barrows° of the happier dead.   *burial mounds*
Release me, and restore me to the ground.
Thou seest all things, thou wilt see my grave;
Thou wilt renew thy beauty morn by morn,
75   I earth in earth forget these empty courts,
And thee returning on thy silver wheels.

1833, 1859   1860

5. What is decreed or ordained as human destiny.
6. The horses that draw Aurora's chariot into the sky at daybreak.

7. The walls of Troy ("Ilion") were supposed to have been built to the strains of the god Apollo's music.

Break, Break, Break

Break, break, break,
  On thy cold gray stones, O Sea!
And I would that my tongue could utter
  The thoughts that arise in me.

5 O, well for the fisherman's boy,
  That he shouts with his sister at play!
O, well for the sailor lad,
  That he sings in his boat on the bay!

And the stately ships go on
10   To their haven under the hill;
But O for the touch of a vanished hand,
  And the sound of a voice that is still!

Break, break, break,
  At the foot of thy crags, O Sea!
15 But the tender grace of a day that is dead
  Will never come back to me.

1834   1842

Locksley Hall[1]

Comrades, leave me here a little, while as yet 'tis early morn;
Leave me here, and when you want me, sound upon the bugle horn.

'Tis the place, and all around it, as of old, the curlews call,
Dreary gleams[2] about the moorland flying over Locksley Hall;

5 Locksley Hall, that in the distance overlooks the sandy tracts,
And the hollow ocean-ridges roaring into cataracts.

Many a night from yonder ivied casement, ere I went to rest,
Did I look on great Orion sloping slowly to the west.

Many a night I saw the Pleiads,[3] rising through the mellow shade,
10 Glitter like a swarm of fireflies tangled in a silver braid.

---

1. The situation in this poem—of a young man's being jilted by a woman who chose to marry a wealthy landowner—may have been suggested to Tennyson by the experience of his brother Frederick, a hot-tempered man who had fallen in love with his cousin Julia Tennyson and who was similarly unsuccessful. It may also have been inspired by Tennyson's own frustrated courtship of Rosa Baring, who rejected the young poet in favor of a wealthy suitor. Concerning the ranting tone of the speaker (a tone accentuated by the heavily marked trochaic meter), Tennyson said: "The whole poem represents young life, its good side, its deficiencies, and its yearnings."
2. Tennyson stated that the noun "gleams" refers not to "curlews" flying but to streaks of light.
3. Or the Pleiades, seven stars in the constellation Taurus.

Here about the beach I wandered, nourishing a youth sublime
With the fairy tales of science, and the long result of time;

When the centuries behind me like a fruitful land reposed;
When I clung to all the present for the promise that it closed°   enclosed

5   When I dipped into the future far as human eye could see,
Saw the vision of the world and all the wonder that would be.—

In the spring a fuller crimson comes upon the robin's breast;
In the spring the wanton lapwing gets himself another crest;

In the spring a livelier iris changes on the burnished dove;[4]
10   In the spring a young man's fancy lightly turns to thoughts of love.

Then her cheek was pale and thinner than should be for one so young,
And her eyes on all my motions with a mute observance hung.

And I said, "My cousin Amy, speak, and speak the truth to me,
Trust me, cousin, all the current of my being sets to thee."

15   On her pallid cheek and forehead came a color and a light,
As I have seen the rosy red flushing in the northern night.

And she turned—her bosom shaken with a sudden storm of sighs—
All the spirit deeply dawning in the dark of hazel eyes—

Saying, "I have hid my feelings, fearing they should do me wrong";
20   Saying, "Dost thou love me, cousin?" weeping, "I have loved thee long."

Love took up the glass of Time, and turned it in his glowing hands;
Every moment, lightly shaken, ran itself in golden sands.

Love took up the harp of Life, and smote on all the chords with might;
Smote the chord of Self, that, trembling, passed in music out of sight.

35   Many a morning on the moorland did we hear the copses ring,
And her whisper thronged my pulses with the fullness of the spring.

Many an evening by the waters did we watch the stately ships,
And our spirits rushed together at the touching of the lips.

O my cousin, shallow-hearted! O my Amy, mine no more!
40   O the dreary, dreary moorland! O the barren, barren shore!

Falser than all fancy fathoms, falser than all songs have sung,
Puppet to a father's threat, and servile to a shrewish tongue!

Is it well to wish thee happy?—having known me—to decline
On a range of lower feelings and a narrower heart than mine!

4. The rainbowlike colors of a dove's throat plumage are intensified in the mating season.

45   Yet it shall be; thou shalt lower to his level day by day,
     What is fine within thee growing coarse to sympathize with clay.

     As the husband is, the wife is; thou art mated with a clown,°   boor
     And the grossness of his nature will have weight to drag thee down.

     He will hold thee, when his passion shall have spent its novel force,
50   Something better than his dog, a little dearer than his horse.

     What is this? his eyes are heavy; think not they are glazed with wine.
     Go to him, it is thy duty; kiss him, take his hand in thine.

     It may be my lord is weary, that his brain is overwrought;
     Soothe him with thy finer fancies, touch him with thy lighter thought.

55   He will answer to the purpose, easy things to understand—
     Better thou wert dead before me, though I slew thee with my hand!

     Better thou and I were lying, hidden from the heart's disgrace,
     Rolled in one another's arms, and silent in a last embrace.

     Cursed be the social wants that sin against the strength of youth!
60   Cursed be the social lies that warp us from the living truth!

     Cursed be the sickly forms that err from honest Nature's rule!
     Cursed be the gold that gilds the straitened° forehead of the fool!   narrowed

     Well—'tis well that I should bluster!—Hadst thou less unworthy proved—
     Would to God—for I had loved thee more than ever wife was loved.

65   Am I mad, that I should cherish that which bears but bitter fruit?
     I will pluck it from my bosom, though my heart be at the root.

     Never, though my mortal summers to such length of years should come
     As the many-wintered crow⁵ that leads the clanging rookery home.

     Where is comfort? in division of the records of the mind?
70   Can I part her from herself, and love her, as I knew her, kind?

     I remember one that perished; sweetly did she speak and move;
     Such a one do I remember, whom to look at was to love.

     Can I think of her as dead, and love her for the love she bore?
     No—she never loved me truly; love is love for evermore.

75   Comfort? comfort scorned of devils! this is truth the poet⁶ sings,
     That a sorrow's crown of sorrow is remembering happier things.

     Drug thy memories, lest thou learn it, lest thy heart be put to proof,
     In the dead unhappy night, and when the rain is on the roof.

---

5. A rook, a long-lived bird.   6. Dante; see *Inferno* 5.121–23.

Like a dog, he hunts in dreams, and thou art staring at the wall,
Where the dying night-lamp flickers, and the shadows rise and fall.

Then a hand shall pass before thee, pointing to his drunken sleep,
To thy widowed[7] marriage-pillows, to the tears that thou wilt weep.

Thou shalt hear the "Never, never," whispered by the phantom years.
And a song from out the distance in the ringing of thine ears;

And an eye shall vex thee, looking ancient kindness on thy pain.
Turn thee, turn thee on thy pillow; get thee to thy rest again.

Nay, but Nature brings thee solace; for a tender voice will cry.
'Tis a purer life than thine, a lip to drain thy trouble dry.

Baby lips will laugh me down; my latest rival brings thee rest.
Baby fingers, waxen touches, press me from the mother's breast.

O, the child too clothes the father with a dearness not his due.
Half is thine and half is his; it will be worthy of the two.

O, I see thee old and formal, fitted to thy petty part,
With a little hoard of maxims preaching down a daughter's heart.

"They were dangerous guides the feelings—she herself was not exempt—
Truly, she herself had suffered"—Perish in thy self-contempt!

Overlive it—lower yet—be happy! wherefore should I care?
I myself must mix with action, lest I wither by despair.

What is that which I should turn to, lighting upon days like these?
Every door is barred with gold, and opens but to golden keys.

Every gate is thronged with suitors, all the markets overflow.
I have but an angry fancy; what is that which I should do?

I had been content to perish, falling on the foeman's ground,
When the ranks are rolled in vapor, and the winds are laid with sound.[8]

But the jingling of the guinea helps the hurt that Honor feels,
And the nations do but murmur, snarling at each other's heels.

Can I but relive in sadness? I will turn that earlier page.
Hide me from my deep emotion, O thou wondrous Mother-Age![9]

Make me feel the wild pulsation that I felt before the strife,
When I heard my days before me, and the tumult of my life;

---

7. Presumably figurative. Her marriage having become a mockery, she is widowed.
8. It was once believed that the firing of artillery stilled the winds.

9. A happier past at life's beginning, which generated a more confident anticipation of the future (see also line 185).

Yearning for the large excitement that the coming years would yield,
Eager-hearted as a boy when first he leaves his father's field,

And at night along the dusky highway near and nearer drawn,
Sees in heaven the light of London flaring like a dreary dawn;

115 And his spirit leaps within him to be gone before him then,
Underneath the light he looks at, in among the throngs of men;

Men, my brothers, men the workers, ever reaping something new;
That which they have done but earnest° of the things that they   *pledge*
    shall do.

For I dipped into the future, far as human eye could see,
120 Saw the Vision of the world, and all the wonder that would be;

Saw the heavens fill with commerce, argosies of magic sails,[1]
Pilots of the purple twilight, dropping down with costly bales;

Heard the heavens fill with shouting, and there rained a ghastly dew
From the nations' airy navies grappling in the central blue;

125 Far along the world-wide whisper of the south wind rushing warm,
With the standards of the peoples plunging through the thunderstorm;

Till the war drum throbbed no longer, and the battle flags were furled
In the Parliament of man, the Federation of the world.

There the common sense of most shall hold a fretful realm in awe,
130 And the kindly earth shall slumber, lapped in° universal law.   *encompassed by*

So I triumphed ere my passion sweeping through me left me dry,
Left me with the palsied heart, and left me with the jaundiced eye;

Eye, to which all order festers, all things here are out of joint.
Science moves, but slowly, slowly, creeping on from point to point;

135 Slowly comes a hungry people, as a lion, creeping nigher,
Glares at one that nods and winks behind a slowly-dying fire.

Yet I doubt not through the ages one increasing purpose runs,
And the thoughts of men are widened with the process of the suns.

What is that to him that reaps not harvest of his youthful joys,
140 Though the deep heart of existence beat forever like a boy's?

Knowledge comes, but wisdom lingers, and I linger on the shore,
And the individual withers, and the world is more and more.

Knowledge comes, but wisdom lingers, and he bears a laden breast,
Full of sad experience, moving toward the stillness of his rest.

1. Probably airships, such as balloons. "Argosies": merchant vessels.

Hark, my merry comrades call me, sounding on the bugle horn,
They to whom my foolish passion were a target for their scorn.

Shall it not be scorn to me to harp on such a moldered string?
I am shamed through all my nature to have loved so slight a thing.

Weakness to be wroth with weakness! woman's pleasure, woman's pain—
Nature made them blinder motions bounded in a shallower brain.

Woman is the lesser man, and all thy passions, matched with mine,
Are as moonlight unto sunlight, and as water unto wine—

Here at least, where nature sickens, nothing. Ah, for some retreat
Deep in yonder shining Orient, where my life began to beat.

Where in wild Mahratta-battle[2] fell my father evil-starred—
I was left a trampled orphan, and a selfish uncle's ward.

Or to burst all links of habit—there to wander far away,
On from island unto island at the gateways of the day.

Larger constellations burning, mellow moons and happy skies,
Breadths of tropic shade and palms in cluster, knots of Paradise.

Never comes the trader, never floats an European flag,
Slides the bird o'er lustrous woodland, swings the trailer° from the *vine*
  crag;

Droops the heavy-blossomed bower, hangs the heavy-fruited tree—
Summer isles of Eden lying in dark purple spheres of sea.

There methinks would be enjoyment more than in this march of mind,
In the steamship, in the railway, in the thoughts that shake mankind.

There the passions cramped no longer shall have scope and breathing space;
I will take some savage woman, she shall rear my dusky race.

Iron-jointed, supple-sinewed, they shall dive, and they shall run,
Catch the wild goat by the hair, and hurl their lances in the sun;

Whistle back the parrot's call, and leap the rainbows of the brooks,
Not with blinded eyesight poring over miserable books—

Fool, again the dream, the fancy! but I *know* my words are wild,
But I count the gray barbarian lower than the Christian child.

I, to herd with narrow foreheads, vacant of our glorious gains,
Like a beast with lower pleasures, like a beast with lower pains!

Mated with a squalid savage—what to me were sun or clime?
I the heir of all the ages, in the foremost files of time—

---

2. Reference to wars waged by a Hindu people against the British forces in India (1803 and 1817).

I that rather held it better men should perish one by one,
180 Than that earth should stand at gaze like Joshua's moon in Ajalon![3]

Not in vain the distance beacons. Forward, forward let us range,
Let the great world spin forever down the ringing grooves[4] of change.

Through the shadow of the globe we sweep into the younger day;
Better fifty years of Europe than a cycle of Cathay.[5]

185 Mother-Age—for mine I knew not—help me as when life begun;
Rift the hills, and roll the waters, flash the lightnings, weigh the sun.

O, I see the crescent promise of my spirit hath not set.
Ancient founts of inspiration well through all my fancy yet.

Howsoever these things be, a long farewell to Locksley Hall!
190 Now for me the woods may wither, now for me the roof-tree fall.

Comes a vapor from the margin,° blackening over heath and   *riverbank*
    holt,°   *wood*
Cramming all the blast before it, in its breast a thunderbolt.

Let it fall on Locksley Hall, with rain or hail, or fire or snow;
For the mighty wind arises, roaring seaward, and I go.

1837–38   1842

In Memoriam A. H. H.

When Arthur Hallam died suddenly at the age of twenty-two, probably of a stroke, Tennyson felt that his life had been shattered. Hallam was not only Tennyson's closest friend, and his sister's fiancé, but a critic and champion of his poetry. Widely regarded as the most promising young man of his generation, Hallam had written a review of Tennyson's first book of poetry that is still one of the best assessments of it. When Tennyson lost Hallam's love and support, he was overwhelmed with doubts about his own life and vocation and about the meaning of the universe and humankind's place in it, doubts reinforced by his study of geology and other sciences. To express the variety of his feelings and reflections, he began to compose a series of lyrics. Tennyson later arranged these "short swallow-flights of song," as he called them, written at intervals over a period of seventeen years, into one long elegy. Although the resulting poem has many affinities with traditional elegies like Milton's "Lycidas" (1638) and Shelley's *Adonais* (1821), its structure is strikingly different. It is made up of individual lyric units that are seemingly self-contained but take their full meaning from their place in the whole. As T. S. Eliot has written, "It is unique: it is a long poem made by putting together lyrics, which have only the unity and continuity of a diary, the concentrated diary of a man confessing himself." Though intensely personal, the elegy expressed the religious doubts of his age. It is also a love poem. Like Shakespeare's sonnets, to which the poem alludes, *In Memoriam* vests its most intense emotion in male relationships.

3. At Joshua's command the sun and moon stood still while the Israelites completed the slaughter of their enemies in the valley of Ajalon (Joshua 10.12–13).

4. Railroad tracks. Tennyson at one time had the impression that train wheels ran in grooved rails.
5. China, regarded in the 19th century as a static, unprogressive country.

The sections of the poem record a progressive development from despair to some sort of hope. Some of the early sections of the poem resemble traditional pastoral elegies, including those portraying the voyage during which Hallam's body was brought to England for burial (sections 9 to 15 and 19). Other early sections portraying the speaker's loneliness, in which even Christmas festivities seem joyless (sections 28 to 30), are more distinctive. The poem's internal chronology covers a span of around three years, and with the passage of time, indicated by anniversaries and by recurring changes of the seasons, the speaker comes to accept the loss and to assert his belief in life and in an afterlife. In particular the recurring Christmases (sections 28, 78, 104) indicate the stages of his development, yet the pattern of progress in the poem is not a simple unimpeded movement upward. Dramatic conflicts recur throughout. Thus the most intense expression of doubt occurs not at the beginning of *In Memoriam* but as late as sections 54, 55, and 56.

The quatrain form in which the whole poem is written is usually called the "*In Memoriam* stanza," although it had been occasionally used by earlier poets. So rigid a form taxed Tennyson's ingenuity in achieving variety, but it is one of several means by which the diverse parts of the poem are knitted together.

The introductory section, consisting of eleven stanzas, is commonly referred to as the "Prologue," although Tennyson did not assign a title to it. It was written in 1849 after the rest of the poem was complete.

FROM IN MEMORIAM A. H. H.

OBIIT MDCCCXXXIII[1]

Strong Son of God, immortal Love,
    Whom we, that have not seen thy face,
    By faith, and faith alone, embrace,
Believing where we cannot prove;[2]

5 Thine are these orbs[3] of light and shade;
    Thou madest Life in man and brute;
    Thou madest Death; and lo, thy foot
Is on the skull which thou hast made.

Thou wilt not leave us in the dust:
10   Thou madest man, he knows not why,
    He thinks he was not made to die;
And thou hast made him: thou art just.

Thou seemest human and divine,
    The highest, holiest manhood, thou.
15   Our wills are ours, we know not how;
Our wills are ours, to make them thine.

Our little systems[4] have their day;
    They have their day and cease to be;

1. He died 1833 (Latin).
2. Cf. John 20.24–29, in which Jesus rebukes Thomas for his doubts concerning the Resurrection: "Blessed are they that have not seen, and yet have believed."
3. The sun and moon (according to Tennyson's note).
4. Of religion and philosophy.

> They are but broken lights of thee,
> 20 And thou, O Lord, art more than they.
>
> We have but faith: we cannot know,
> For knowledge is of things we see;
> And yet we trust it comes from thee,
> A beam in darkness: let it grow.
>
> 25 Let knowledge grow from more to more,
> But more of reverence in us dwell;
> That mind and soul, according well,
> May make one music as before,[5]
>
> But vaster. We are fools and slight;
> 30 We mock thee when we do not fear:
> But help thy foolish ones to bear;
> Help thy vain worlds to bear thy light.
>
> Forgive what seemed my sin in me,
> What seemed my worth since I began;
> 35 For merit lives from man to man,
> And not from man, O Lord, to thee.
>
> Forgive my grief for one removed,
> Thy creature, whom I found so fair.
> I trust he lives in thee, and there
> 40 I find him worthier to be loved.
>
> Forgive these wild and wandering cries,
> Confusions of a wasted° youth;   desolated
> Forgive them where they fail in truth,
> And in thy wisdom make me wise.

1849

1

> I held it truth, with him who sings
> To one clear harp in divers tones,[6]
> That men may rise on stepping stones
> Of their dead selves to higher things.
>
> 5 But who shall so forecast the years
> And find in loss a gain to match?
> Or reach a hand through time to catch
> The far-off interest of tears?
>
> Let Love clasp Grief lest both be drowned,
> 10 Let darkness keep her raven gloss.

---

5. As in the days of fixed religious faith.
6. Identified by Tennyson as the German poet Johann Wolfgang von Goethe (1749–1832).

Ah, sweeter to be drunk with loss,
To dance with Death, to beat the ground,

Than that the victor Hours should scorn
The long result of love, and boast,
15   "Behold the man that loved and lost,
But all he was is overworn."

2

Old yew, which graspest at the stones
    That name the underlying dead,
    Thy fibres net the dreamless head,
Thy roots are wrapped about the bones.

5 The seasons bring the flower again,
    And bring the firstling to the flock;
    And in the dusk of thee the clock
Beats out the little lives of men.

O, not for thee the glow, the bloom,
10   Who changest not in any gale,
    Nor branding summer suns avail
To touch thy thousand years of gloom[7]

And gazing on thee, sullen tree,
    Sick for° thy stubborn hardihood,   *envying*
15   I seem to fail from out my blood
And grow incorporate into thee.

3

O Sorrow, cruel fellowship,
    O Priestess in the vaults of Death,
    O sweet and bitter in a breath,
What whispers from thy lying lip?

5 "The stars," she whispers, "blindly run;
    A web is woven across the sky;
    From out waste places comes a cry,
And murmurs from the dying sun;

"And all the phantom, Nature, stands—
10   With all the music in her tone,
    A hollow echo of my own—
A hollow form with empty hands."

7. The ancient yew tree, growing in the grounds near the clock tower and church where Hallam was to be buried, seems neither to blossom in spring nor to change from its dark mournful color in summer. "Thousand years": cf. Book of Common Prayer, Psalm 90: "For a thousand years in Thy sight are but as yesterday when it is past, and as a watch in the night."

> And shall I take a thing so blind,
>   Embrace her° as my natural good;   *Sorrow*
> 15   Or crush her, like a vice of blood,
> Upon the threshold of the mind?

4

> To Sleep I give my powers away;
>   My will is bondsman to the dark;
>   I sit within a helmless bark,
> And with my heart I muse and say:
>
> 5 O heart, how fares it with thee now,
>   That thou should fail from thy desire,
>   Who scarcely darest to inquire,
> "What is it makes me beat so low?"
>
> Something it is which thou hast lost,
> 10   Some pleasure from thine early years.
>   Break thou deep vase of chilling tears,
> That grief hath shaken into frost![8]
>
> Such clouds of nameless trouble cross
>   All night below the darkened eyes;
> 15   With morning wakes the will, and cries,
> "Thou shalt not be the fool of loss."

5

> I sometimes hold it half a sin
>   To put in words the grief I feel;
>   For words, like Nature, half reveal
> And half conceal the Soul within.
>
> 5 But, for the unquiet heart and brain,
>   A use in measured language lies;
>   The sad mechanic exercise,
> Like dull narcotics, numbing pain.
>
> In words, like weeds,° I'll wrap me o'er,   *mourning garments*
> 10   Like coarsest clothes against the cold;
>   But that large grief which these enfold
> Is given in outline and no more.

6

> One writes, that "Other friends remain,"
>   That "Loss is common to the race"—

---

8. Water can be brought below freezing-point and not turn into ice—if it be kept still; but if it be moved suddenly it turns into ice and may break a vase [Tennyson's note].

And common is the commonplace,
And vacant chaff° well meant for grain.   *husks*

5   That loss is common would not make
    My own less bitter, rather more:
    Too common! Never morning wore
To evening, but some heart did break.

O father, wheresoe'er thou be,
10   Who pledgest° now thy gallant son;   *toasts*
    A shot, ere half thy draft be done,
Hath stilled the life that beat from thee.

O mother, praying God will save
    Thy sailor—while thy head is bowed,
15   His heavy-shotted hammock-shroud
Drops in his vast and wandering grave.[9]

Ye know no more than I who wrought
    At that last hour to please him well;[1]
    Who mused on all I had to tell,
20   And something written, something thought;

Expecting still his advent home;
    And ever met him on his way
    With wishes, thinking, "here today,"
Or "here tomorrow will he come."

25   O somewhere, meek, the unconscious dove,
    That sittest ranging° golden hair;   *arranging*
    And glad to find thyself so fair,
Poor child, that waitest for thy love!

For now her father's chimney glows
30   In expectation of a guest;
    And thinking "this will please him best,"
She takes a riband or a rose;

For he will see them on tonight;
    And with the thought her color burns;
35   And, having left the glass, she turns
Once more to set a ringlet right;

And, even when she turned, the curse
    Had fallen, and her future Lord
    Was drowned in passing through the ford,
40   Or killed in falling from his horse.

O what to her shall be the end?
    And what to me remains of good?

---

9. Sailors buried at sea were often wrapped in their own hammocks. "Heavy-shotted": heavily weighted.

1. According to his son, Tennyson discovered that he had been writing a letter to Hallam during the very hour in which his friend died.

To her, perpetual maidenhood,
And unto me no second friend.

7

Dark house,[2] by which once more I stand
  Here in the long unlovely street,
  Doors, where my heart was used to beat
So quickly, waiting for a hand,

5 A hand that can be clasped no more—
  Behold me, for I cannot sleep,
  And like a guilty thing I creep
At earliest morning to the door.

He is not here; but far away
10 The noise of life begins again,
  And ghastly through the drizzling rain
On the bald street breaks the blank day.

8

A happy lover who has come
  To look on her that loves him well,
  Who 'lights° and rings the gateway bell,   *alights*
And learns her gone and far from home;

5 He saddens, all the magic light
  Dies off at once from bower and hall,
  And all the place is dark, and all
The chambers emptied of delight:

So find I every pleasant spot
10 In which we two were wont to meet,
  The field, the chamber, and the street,
For all is dark where thou art not.

Yet as that other, wandering there
  In those deserted walks, may find
15 A flower beat with rain and wind,
Which once she fostered up with care;

So seems it in my deep regret,
  O my forsaken heart, with thee
  And this poor flower of poesy
20 Which little cared for fades not yet.

But since it pleased a vanished eye,[3]
  I go to plant it on his tomb,

2. The house on Wimpole Street, in London, where Hallam had lived.

3. Hallam expressed enthusiasm for Tennyson's early poetry in a review written in 1831.

That if it can it there may bloom,
Or dying, there at least may die.

9

Fair ship, that from the Italian shore⁴
    Sailest the placid ocean-plains
    With my lost Arthur's loved remains,
Spread thy full wings, and waft him o'er.

5   So draw him home to those that mourn
    In vain; a favorable speed
    Ruffle thy mirrored mast, and lead
Through prosperous floods his holy urn.

All night no ruder air perplex
10   Thy sliding keel, till Phosphor,° bright   *morning star*
    As our pure love, through early light
Shall glimmer on the dewy decks.

Sphere all your lights around, above;
    Sleep, gentle heavens, before the prow;
15   Sleep, gentle winds, as he sleeps now,
My friend, the brother of my love;

My Arthur, whom I shall not see
    Till all my widowed race be run;
    Dear as the mother to the son,
20 More than my brothers are to me.

10

I hear the noise about thy keel;
    I hear the bell struck in the night;
    I see the cabin window bright;
I see the sailor at the wheel.

5   Thou bring'st the sailor to his wife,
    And traveled men from foreign lands;
    And letters unto trembling hands;
And, thy dark freight, a vanished life.

So bring him; we have idle dreams;
10   This look of quiet flatters thus
    Our home-bred fancies. O, to us,
The fools of habit, sweeter seems

To rest beneath the clover sod,
    That takes the sunshine and the rains,

4. Hallam's body was conveyed back to England by ship from Trieste, Italy.

15   Or where the kneeling hamlet drains
  The chalice of the grapes of God;[5]

  Than if with thee the roaring wells
   Should gulf him fathom-deep in brine,
   And hands so often clasped in mine,
20   Should toss with tangle° and with shells.   *seaweed*

11

  Calm is the morn without a sound,
   Calm as to suit a calmer grief,
   And only through the faded leaf
  The chestnut pattering to the ground;

5   Calm and deep peace on this high wold,°   *open countryside*
   And on these dews that drench the furze,
   And all the silvery gossamers
  That twinkle into green and gold;

  Calm and still light on yon great plain
10   That sweeps with all its autumn bowers,
   And crowded farms and lessening towers,
  To mingle with the bounding main;

  Calm and deep peace in this wide air,
   These leaves that redden to the fall,
15   And in my heart, if calm at all,
  If any calm, a calm despair;

  Calm on the seas, and silver sleep,
   And waves that sway themselves in rest,
   And dead calm in that noble breast
20   Which heaves but with the heaving deep.

12

  Lo, as a dove when up she springs
   To bear through Heaven a tale of woe,
   Some dolorous message knit below
  The wild pulsation of her wings;

5   Like her I go; I cannot stay;
   I leave this mortal ark behind,
   A weight of nerves without a mind,
  And leave the cliffs, and haste away

---

5. Reference to a burial inside a church building rather than in the churchyard.

O'er ocean-mirrors rounded large,
10   And reach the glow of southern skies,
    And see the sails at distance rise,
And linger weeping on the marge,°   *shore*

And saying; "Comes he thus, my friend?
    Is this the end of all my care?"
15   And circle moaning in the air:
"Is this the end? Is this the end?"

And forward dart again, and play
    About the prow, and back return
    To where the body sits, and learn
20 That I have been an hour away.

13

Tears of the widower, when he sees
    A late-lost form that sleep reveals,
    And moves his doubtful arms, and feels
Her place is empty, fall like these;

5 Which weep a loss forever new,
    A void where heart on heart reposed;
    And, where warm hands have pressed and closed,
Silence, till I be silent too;

Which weep the comrade of my choice,
10   An awful thought, a life removed,
    The human-hearted man I loved,
A Spirit, not a breathing voice.

Come, Time, and teach me, many years,
    I do not suffer in a dream;
15   For now so strange do these things seem,
Mine eyes have leisure for their tears,

My fancies time to rise on wing,
    And glance about the approaching sails,
    As though they brought but merchants' bales,
20 And not the burthen that they bring.

14

If one should bring me this report,
    That thou° hadst touched the land today,   *the ship*
    And I went down unto the quay;⁶
And found thee lying in the port;

6. By 1850 the accepted pronunciation of "quay" would rhyme with *key*, but Tennyson reverts to an earlier pronunciation, *kay*.

5   And standing, muffled round with woe,
      Should see thy passengers in rank
      Come stepping lightly down the plank
    And beckoning unto those they know;

    And if along with these should come
10   The man I held as half divine,
      Should strike a sudden hand in mine,
    And ask a thousand things of home;

    And I should tell him all my pain,
      And how my life had drooped of late,
15   And he should sorrow o'er my state
    And marvel what possessed my brain;

    And I perceived no touch of change,
      No hint of death in all his frame,
      But found him all in all the same,
20   I should not feel it to be strange.

15

    Tonight the winds begin to rise
      And roar from yonder dropping day;
      The last red leaf is whirled away,
    The rooks are blown about the skies;

5   The forest cracked, the waters curled,
      The cattle huddled on the lea;
      And wildly dashed on tower and tree
    The sunbeam strikes along the world:

    And but for fancies, which aver
10   That all thy motions gently pass
      Athwart a plane of molten glass,[7]
    I scarce could brook the strain and stir

    That makes the barren branches loud;
      And but for fear it is not so,
15   The wild unrest that lives in woe
    Would dote and pore on yonder cloud

    That rises upward always higher,
      And onward drags a laboring breast,
      And topples round the dreary west,
20   A looming bastion fringed with fire.

* * *

---

7. I.e., a calm sea.

19

The Danube to the Severn[8] gave
    The darkened heart that beat no more;
    They laid him by the pleasant shore,
And in the hearing of the wave.

5   There twice a day the Severn fills;
    The salt sea water passes by,
    And hushes half the babbling Wye,[9]
And makes a silence in the hills.

The Wye is hushed nor moved along,
10   And hushed my deepest grief of all,
    When filled with tears that cannot fall,
I brim with sorrow drowning song.

The tide flows down, the wave again
    Is vocal in its wooded walls;[1]
15   My deeper anguish also falls,
And I can speak a little then.

*   *   *

21

I sing to him that rests below
    And, since the grasses round me wave,
    I take the grasses of the grave,[2]
And make them pipes whereon to blow.

5   The traveler hears me now and then,
    And sometimes harshly will he speak:
    "This fellow would make weakness weak,
And melt the waxen hearts of men."

Another answers: "Let him be,
10   He loves to make parade of pain,
    That with his piping he may gain
The praise that comes to constancy."

A third is wroth: "Is this an hour
    For private sorrow's barren song,

8. Hallam died at Vienna on the river Danube. His burial place is on the banks of the Severn, a tidal river in the southwest of England.
9. A tributary of the Severn.
1. The water of the Wye River is dammed up as the tide flows in, and its sound is silenced until, with the turn of the tide, its "wave" once more becomes "vocal"; these stanzas were written at Tintern Abbey in the Wye valley.
2. The poet assumes that the burial was in the churchyard; in fact, on January 3, 1834, at St. Andrews in Clevedon, Somersetshire, Hallam's body was interred in a vault inside the church.

15   When more and more the people throng
            The chairs and thrones of civil power?

        "A time to sicken and to swoon,
            When Science reaches forth her arms[3]
            To feel from world to world, and charms
20   Her secret from the latest moon?"[4]

        Behold, ye speak an idle thing;
            Ye never knew the sacred dust.
            I do but sing because I must,
        And pipe but as the linnets sing:

25   And one is glad; her note is gay,
            For now her little ones have ranged;
            And one is sad; her note is changed,
        Because her brood is stolen away.

                        22

        The path by which we twain did go,
            Which led by tracts that pleased us well,
            Through four sweet years arose and fell,
        From flower to flower, from snow to snow;

5   And we with singing cheered the way,
            And, crowned with all the season lent,
            From April on to April went,
        And glad at heart from May to May.

        But where the path we walked began
10   To slant the fifth autumnal slope,[5]
            As we descended following Hope,
        There sat the Shadow feared of man;

        Who broke our fair companionship,
            And spread his mantle dark and cold,
15   And wrapped thee formless in the fold,
        And dulled the murmur on thy lip,

        And bore thee where I could not see
            Nor follow, though I walk in haste,
            And think that somewhere in the waste
20   The Shadow sits and waits for me.

3. Astronomical instruments, such as telescopes.
4. Probably alluding to the discovery in 1846 of
the planet Neptune and one of its moons.

5. Hallam died just before the beginning of
autumn (September 15, 1833) in the fifth year of
the friendship.

23

Now, sometimes in my sorrow shut,
  Or breaking into song by fits,
  Alone, alone, to where he sits,
The Shadow cloaked from head to foot,

5 Who keeps the keys of all the creeds,
  I wander, often falling lame,
  And looking back to whence I came,
Or on to where the pathway leads;

And crying, How changed from where it ran
10 Through lands where not a leaf was dumb,
  But all the lavish hills would hum
The murmur of a happy Pan;[6]

When each by turns was guide to each,
  And Fancy light from Fancy caught,
15 And Thought leapt out to wed with Thought
Ere Thought could wed itself with Speech;

And all we met was fair and good,
  And all was good that Time could bring,
  And all the secret of the Spring
20 Moved in the chambers of the blood;

And many an old philosophy
  On Argive[7] heights divinely sang,
  And round us all the thicket rang
To many a flute of Arcady.[8]

24

And was the day of my delight
  As pure and perfect as I say?
  The very source and fount of day
Is dashed with wandering isles of night.[9]

5 If all was good and fair we met,
  This earth had been the Paradise
  It never looked to human eyes
Since our first sun arose and set.

And is it that the haze of grief
10 Makes former gladness loom so great?

6. In Greek mythology the god of woods and pastures.
7. Of Argos, an ancient city-state in the northeastern Peloponnesus; more generally, Greek.

8. A sheep-raising region in Greece associated with pastoral poetry.
9. Moving spots on the sun.

The lowness of the present state,
That sets the past in this relief?

Or that the past will always win
    A glory from its being far,
15   And orb into the perfect star
We saw not when we moved therein?[1]

25

I know that this was Life—the track
    Whereon with equal feet we fared;
    And then, as now, the day prepared
The daily burden for the back.

5   But this it was that made me move
    As light as carrier birds in air;
    I loved the weight I had to bear,
Because it needed help of Love;

Nor could I weary, heart or limb,
10   When mighty Love would cleave in twain
    The lading° of a single pain,   *burden*
And part it, giving half to him.

26

Still onward winds the dreary way;
    I with it, for I long to prove
    No lapse of moons can canker Love,
Whatever fickle tongues may say.

5   And if that eye which watches guilt
    And goodness, and hath power to see
    Within the green the mouldered tree,
And towers fallen as soon as built—

O, if indeed that eye foresee
10   Or see—in Him is no before—
    In more of life true life no more
And Love the indifference to be,

Then might I find, ere yet the morn
    Breaks hither over Indian seas,
15   That Shadow waiting with the keys,
To shroud me from my proper scorn.[2]

1. The poet wonders whether Earth would have the deceptive appearance of being a perfect orb if viewed from afar, on another planet.
2. The Deity, being outside time, sees (rather than foresees) whether or not the rest of life ("more of life," line 11) will be pointless. If pointless, then the way for the speaker to deal with his self-scorn ("proper scorn") might be to seek death.

27

I envy not in any moods
    The captive void of noble rage,
    The linnet born within the cage,
That never knew the summer woods;

5   I envy not the beast that takes
    His license in the field of time,
    Unfettered by the sense of crime,
To whom a conscience never wakes;

Nor, what may count itself as blest,
10   The heart that never plighted troth
    But stagnates in the weeds of sloth;
Nor any want-begotten rest.[3]

I hold it true, whate'er befall;
    I feel it, when I sorrow most;
15   'Tis better to have loved and lost
Than never to have loved at all.

28

The time draws near the birth of Christ.[4]
    The moon is hid, the night is still;
    The Christmas bells from hill to hill
Answer each other in the mist.

5   Four voices of four hamlets round,
    From far and near, on mead and moor,
    Swell out and fail, as if a door
Were shut between me and the sound;

Each voice four changes[5] on the wind,
10   That now dilate, and now decrease,
    Peace and goodwill, goodwill and peace,
Peace and goodwill, to all mankind.

This year I slept and woke with pain,
    I almost wished no more to wake,
15   And that my hold on life would break
Before I heard those bells again;

But they my troubled spirit rule,
    For they controlled me when a boy;

3. Complacency resulting from some deficiency ("want").
4. The first Christmas after Hallam's death (1833); the setting is Tennyson's family home in Lincolnshire.
5. Different sequences in which church bells are pealed.

They bring me sorrow touched with joy,
20   The merry, merry bells of Yule.

29

With such compelling cause to grieve
    As daily vexes household peace,
    And chains regret to his decease,
How dare we keep our Christmas eve;

5   Which brings no more a welcome guest
    To enrich the threshold of the night
    With showered largess of delight
In dance and song and game and jest?

Yet go, and while the holly boughs
10   Entwine the cold baptismal font,
    Make one wreath more for Use and Wont,[6]
That guard the portals of the house;

Old sisters of a day gone by,
    Gray nurses, loving nothing new;
15   Why should they miss their yearly due
Before their time? They too will die.

30

With trembling fingers did we weave
    The holly round the Christmas hearth;
    A rainy cloud possessed the earth,
And sadly fell our Christmas eve.

5   At our old pastimes in the hall
    We gamboled, making vain pretense
    Of gladness, with an awful sense
Of one mute Shadow watching all.

We paused: the winds were in the beech;
10   We heard them sweep the winter land;
    And in a circle hand-in-hand
Sat silent, looking each at each.

Then echo-like our voices rang;
    We sung, though every eye was dim,
15   A merry song we sang with him
Last year; impetuously we sang.

We ceased; a gentler feeling crept
    Upon us: surely rest is meet.°   *proper, appropriate*

6. Personifying the spirits who expect customary observances of the Christmas season to be followed.

"They rest," we said, "their sleep is sweet,"
20   And silence followed, and we wept.

Our voices took a higher range;
    Once more we sang: "They do not die
    Nor lose their mortal sympathy,
Nor change to us, although they change;

25   "Rapt from[7] the fickle and the frail
    With gathered power, yet the same,
    Pierces the keen seraphic flame
From orb to orb, from veil[8] to veil."

Rise, happy morn, rise, holy morn,
30   Draw forth the cheerful day from night:
    O Father, touch the east, and light
The light that shone when Hope was born.

*   *   *

34

My own dim life should teach me this,
    That life shall live forevermore,
    Else earth is darkness at the core,
And dust and ashes all that is;

5   This round of green, this orb of flame,
    Fantastic beauty; such as lurks
    In some wild poet, when he works
Without a conscience or an aim.

What then were God to such as I?
10   'Twere hardly worth my while to choose
    Of things all mortal, or to use
A little patience ere I die;

'Twere best at once to sink to peace,
    Like birds the charming serpent[9] draws,
15   To drop head-foremost in the jaws
Of vacant darkness and to cease.

35

Yet if some voice that man could trust
    Should murmur from the narrow house,

---

7. Carried away from.
8. An image representing the boundary between different worlds, especially that between Earth and heaven (cf. section 56, line 28). "From orb to orb": the angelic spirit ("flame") of the dead moves from star to star.
9. Some snakes are reputed to capture their prey by hypnotizing it.

"The cheeks drop in, the body bows;
Man dies, nor is there hope in dust";

5   Might I not say? "Yet even here,
But for one hour, O Love, I strive
To keep so sweet a thing alive."
But I should turn mine ears and hear

The moanings of the homeless sea,
10   The sound of streams that swift or slow
Draw down Aeonian[1] hills, and sow
The dust of continents to be;

And Love would answer with a sigh,
"The sound of that forgetful shore[2]
15   Will change my sweetness more and more,
Half-dead to know that I shall die."

O me, what profits it to put
An idle case? If Death were seen
At first as Death, Love had not been,
20   Or been in narrowest working shut,

Mere fellowship of sluggish moods,
Or in his coarsest Satyr-shape[3]
Had bruised the herb and crushed the grape,
And basked and battened° in the woods.[4]   *grown fat*

*   *   *

39

Old warder of these buried bones,
And answering now my random stroke
With fruitful cloud and living smoke,
Dark yew, that graspest at the stones

5   And dippest toward the dreamless head,
To thee too comes the golden hour
When flower is feeling after flower;[5]
But Sorrow—fixed upon the dead,

And darkening the dark graves of men—
10   What whispered from her lying lips?

1. Eons old, seemingly everlasting.
2. I.e., of Lethe, the river in the classical underworld whose water caused forgetfulness.
3. In Greek mythology satyrs were half-man, half-beast (goat or horse) in appearance, desires, and behavior.
4. Lines 18–24 may be paraphrased: if we knew death to be final and that no afterlife were possible,
love could not exist except on a primitive or bestial level.
5. The ancient yew tree in the graveyard was described in section 2 as never changing. Now the poet discovers that in the flowering season, if the tree is struck ("my random stroke"), it gives off a cloud of golden pollen.

Thy gloom is kindled at the tips,[6]
And passes into gloom again.

*   *   *

47

That each, who seems a separate whole,
   Should move his rounds,[7] and fusing all
   The skirts[8] of self again, should fall
Remerging in the general Soul,

5   Is faith as vague as all unsweet.
   Eternal form shall still divide
   The eternal soul from all beside;
And I shall know him when we meet;

And we shall sit at endless feast,
10   Enjoying each the other's good.
   What vaster dream can hit the mood
Of Love on earth? He seeks at least

Upon the last and sharpest height,
   Before the spirits fade away,
15   Some landing place, to clasp and say,
"Farewell! We lose ourselves in light."[9]

48

If these brief lays, of Sorrow born,
   Were taken to be such as closed
   Grave doubts and answers here proposed,
Then these were such as men might scorn.

5   Her° care is not to part and prove;   *Sorrow's*
   She takes, when harsher moods remit,
   What slender shade of doubt may flit,
And makes it vassal unto love;

And hence, indeed, she sports with words,
10   But better serves a wholesome law,
   And holds it sin and shame to draw
The deepest measure from the chords;

6. Only the tips of the yew branches are in flower.
7. I.e., go through the customary circuit of life.
8. Outer edges or fringes.
9. These lines express the hope that, as Tennyson wrote, "individuality lasts after death, and we are not utterly absorbed into the Godhead. If we are to be finally merged into the Universal Soul, Love asks to have at least one more parting before we lose ourselves."

Nor dare she trust a larger lay,°   *song*
    But rather loosens from the lip
15   Short swallow-flights of song, that dip
Their wings in tears, and skim away.

*   *   *

50

Be near me when my light is low,
    When the blood creeps, and the nerves prick
    And tingle; and the heart is sick,
And all the wheels of being slow.

5   Be near me when the sensuous frame
    Is racked with pangs that conquer trust;
    And Time, a maniac scattering dust,
And Life, a Fury slinging flame.

Be near me when my faith is dry,
10   And men the flies of latter spring,
    That lay their eggs, and sting and sing
And weave their petty cells and die.

Be near me when I fade away,
    To point the term of human strife,
15   And on the low dark verge of life
The twilight of eternal day.

*   *   *

54

O, yet we trust that somehow good
    Will be the final goal of ill,
    To pangs of nature, sins of will,
Defects of doubt, and taints of blood;

5   That nothing walks with aimless feet;
    That not one life shall be destroyed,
    Or cast as rubbish to the void,
When God hath made the pile complete;

That not a worm is cloven in vain;
10   That not a moth with vain desire
    Is shriveled in a fruitless fire,
Or but° subserves another's gain.   *only*

Behold, we know not anything;
    I can but trust that good shall fall

15   At last—far off—at last, to all,
        And every winter change to spring.

        So runs my dream; but what am I?
            An infant crying in the night;
            An infant crying for the light,
20   And with no language but a cry.

55

        The wish, that of the living whole
            No life may fail beyond the grave,
            Derives it not from what we have
        The likest God within the soul?[1]

5   Are God and Nature then at strife,
            That Nature lends such evil dreams?
            So careful of the type she seems,
        So careless of the single life,

        That I, considering everywhere
10   Her secret meaning in her deeds,
            And finding that of fifty seeds
        She often brings but one to bear,

        I falter where I firmly trod,
            And falling with my weight of cares
15   Upon the great world's altar-stairs
        That slope through darkness up to God,

        I stretch lame hands of faith, and grope,
            And gather dust and chaff, and call
            To what I feel is Lord of all,
20   And faintly trust the larger hope.[2]

56

        "So careful of the type?" but no.
            From scarpèd[3] cliff and quarried stone
            She° cries, "A thousand types are gone;   *Nature*
        I care for nothing, all shall go.

5   "Thou makest thine appeal to me:
            I bring to life, I bring to death;
            The spirit does but mean the breath:
        I know no more." And he, shall he,

---

1. According to Tennyson, the "inner conscience—
the divine in man."

2. As expressed in lines 1 and 2.
3. Cut away so that the strata are exposed.

Man, her last work, who seemed so fair,
10   Such splendid purpose in his eyes,
        Who rolled the psalm to wintry skies,
        Who built him fanes° of fruitless prayer,   *temples*

        Who trusted God was love indeed
            And love Creation's final law—
15   Though Nature, red in tooth and claw
        With ravine, shrieked against his creed—

        Who loved, who suffered countless ills,
            Who battled for the True, the Just,
            Be blown about the desert dust,
20   Or sealed within the iron hills?⁴

        No more? A monster then, a dream,
            A discord. Dragons of the prime,°   *primeval age*
            That tare° each other in their slime,   *tore (archaic)*
        Were mellow music matched with° him.   *compared to*

25   O life as futile, then, as frail!
            O for thy voice to soothe and bless!
            What hope of answer, or redress?
        Behind the veil, behind the veil.

57

        Peace; come away: the song of woe
            Is after all an earthly song.
            Peace; come away: we do him wrong
        To sing so wildly: let us go.

5   Come; let us go: your cheeks are pale;
            Methinks my friend is richly shrined;
            But half my life I leave behind.
        But I shall pass, my work will fail.

        Yet in these ears, till hearing dies,
10   One set slow bell will seem to toll
            The passing of the sweetest soul
        That ever looked with human eyes.

        I hear it now, and o'er and o'er,
            Eternal greetings to the dead;
15   And "Ave,° Ave, Ave," said,   *Hail (Latin)*
        "Adieu, adieu," forevermore.

4. Preserved like fossils in rock.

58

In those sad words I took farewell.
   Like echoes in sepulchral halls,
   As drop by drop the water falls
In vaults and catacombs, they fell;

5 And, falling, idly broke the peace
   Of hearts that beat from day to day,
   Half-conscious of their dying clay,
And those cold crypts where they shall cease.

The high Muse answered: "Wherefore grieve
10   Thy brethren with a fruitless tear?
   Abide a little longer here,
And thou shalt take a nobler leave."

59

O Sorrow, wilt thou live with me
   No casual mistress, but a wife,
   My bosom friend and half of life;
As I confess it needs must be?

5 O Sorrow, wilt thou rule my blood,
   Be sometimes lovely like a bride,
   And put thy harsher moods aside,
If thou wilt have me wise and good?

My centered passion cannot move,
10   Nor will it lessen from today;
   But I'll have leave at times to play
As with the creature of my love;

And set thee forth, for thou art mine,
   With so much hope for years to come,
15   That, howsoe'er I know thee, some
Could hardly tell what name were thine.

       *   *   *

64

Dost thou look back on what hath been,
   As some divinely gifted man,
   Whose life in low estate began
And on a simple village green;

5   Who breaks his birth's invidious bar,
      And grasps the skirts of happy chance,
      And breasts the blows of circumstance,
    And grapples with his evil star;

    Who makes by force his merit known
10   And lives to clutch the golden keys,[5]
      To mold a mighty state's decrees,
    And shape the whisper of the throne;

    And moving up from high to higher,
      Becomes on Fortune's crowning slope
15   The pillar of a people's hope,
    The centre of a world's desire;

    Yet feels, as in a pensive dream,
      When all his active powers are still,
      A distant dearness in the hill,
20   A secret sweetness in the stream,

    The limit of his narrower fate,
      While yet beside its vocal springs
      He played at counselors and kings,
    With one that was his earliest mate;

25   Who plows with pain his native lea
      And reaps the labour of his hands,
      Or in the furrow musing stands:
    "Does my old friend remember me?"

* * *

67

    When on my bed the moonlight falls,
      I know that in thy place of rest
      By that broad water[6] of the west
    There comes a glory on the walls:

5   Thy marble bright in dark appears,
      As slowly steals a silver flame
      Along the letters of thy name,
    And o'er the number of thy years.

    The mystic glory swims away,
10   From off my bed the moonlight dies;
      And closing eaves of wearied eyes
    I sleep till dusk is dipped in gray;

    And then I know the mist is drawn
      A lucid veil from coast to coast,

---

5. Badges of high public office.   6. The Severn River.

15   And in the dark church like a ghost
        Thy tablet glimmers to the dawn.

                    *   *   *

70

        I cannot see the features right,
            When on the gloom I strive to paint
            The face I know; the hues are faint
        And mix with hollow masks of night;

5   Cloud-towers by ghostly masons wrought,
            A gulf that ever shuts and gapes,
            A hand that points, and pallèd shapes
        In shadowy thoroughfares of thought;

        And crowds that stream from yawning doors,
10   And shoals of puckered faces drive;
            Dark bulks that tumble half alive,
        And lazy lengths on boundless shores;

        Till all at once beyond the will
            I hear a wizard music roll,
15   And through a lattice on the soul
        Looks thy fair face and makes it still.

71

        Sleep, kinsman thou to death and trance
            And madness, thou has forged at last
            A night-long present of the past
        In which we went through summer France.[7]

5   Hadst thou such credit with the soul?
            Then bring an opiate trebly strong,
            Drug down the blindfold sense of wrong,
        That so my pleasure may be whole;

        While now we talk as once we talked
10   Of men and minds, the dust of change,
            The days that grow to something strange,
        In walking as of old we walked

        Beside the river's wooded reach,
            The fortress, and the mountain ridge,
15   The cataract flashing from the bridge,
        The breaker breaking on the beach.

7. In the summer of 1830 Hallam and Tennyson went through southern France en route to Spain.

72

Risest thou thus, dim dawn, again,[8]
   And howlest, issuing out of night,
   With blasts that blow the poplar white,
And lash with storm the streaming pane?

5   Day, when my crowned estate[9] begun
   To pine in that reverse of doom,[1]
   Which sickened every living bloom,
And blurred the splendor of the sun;

Who usherest in the dolorous hour
10   With thy quick tears that make the rose
   Pull sideways, and the daisy close
Her crimson fringes to the shower;

Who mightst have heaved a windless flame
   Up the deep East, or, whispering, played
15   A checker-work of beam and shade
Along the hills, yet looked the same,

As wan, as chill, as wild as now;
   Day, marked as with some hideous crime,
   When the dark hand struck down through time,
20   And canceled nature's best: but thou,

Lift as thou mayst thy burthened brows
   Through clouds that drench the morning star,
   And whirl the ungarnered sheaf afar,
And sow the sky with flying boughs,

25   And up thy vault with roaring sound
   Climb thy thick noon, disastrous day;
   Touch thy dull goal of joyless gray,
And hide thy shame beneath the ground.

* * *

75

I leave thy praises unexpressed
   In verse that brings myself relief,
   And by the measure of my grief
I leave thy greatness to be guessed.

---

8. September 15, 1834, the first anniversary of
Hallam's death.
9. State of happiness.

1. The reversal or disaster that doom brought
upon him when Hallam died.

5   What practice howsoe'er expert
      In fitting aptest words to things,
      Or voice the richest-toned that sings,
    Hath power to give thee as thou wert?

    I care not in these fading days
10   To raise a cry that lasts not long,
      And round thee with the breeze of song
    To stir a little dust of praise.

    Thy leaf has perished in the green,
      And, while we breathe beneath the sun,
15   The world which credits what is done
    Is cold to all that might have been.

    So here shall silence guard thy fame;
      But somewhere, out of human view,
      Whate'er thy hands are set to do
20   Is wrought with tumult of acclaim.

*   *   *

78

    Again at Christmas[2] did we weave
      The holly round the Christmas hearth;
      The silent snow possessed the earth,
    And calmly fell our Christmas eve.

5   The yule clog° sparkled keen with frost,   *log*
      No wing of wind the region swept,
      But over all things brooding slept
    The quiet sense of something lost.

    As in the winters left behind,
10   Again our ancient games had place,
      The mimic picture's[3] breathing grace,
    And dance and song and hoodman-blind.[4]

    Who showed a token of distress?
      No single tear, no mark of pain—
15   O sorrow, then can sorrow wane?
    O grief, can grief be changed to less?

    O last regret, regret can die!
      No—mixed with all this mystic frame,

---

2. The second Christmas (1834) after Hallam's death.
3. A game in which the participants pose in the manner of some famous statue or painting and the spectators try to guess what work of art is being portrayed.
4. The player in the game of blindman's buff who wears a blindfold or hood.

Her deep relations are the same,
20   But with long use her tears are dry.

*   *   *

82

I wage not any feud with Death
    For changes wrought on form and face;
    No lower life that earth's embrace
May breed with him can fright my faith.

5   Eternal process moving on,
    From state to state the spirit walks;
    And these are but the shattered stalks,
Or ruined chrysalis of one.

Nor blame I Death, because he bare
10   The use of virtue out of earth;
    I know transplanted human worth
Will bloom to profit, otherwhere.

For this alone on Death I wreak
    The wrath that garners in my heart:
15   He put our lives so far apart
We cannot hear each other speak.

83

Dip down upon the northern shore,
    O sweet new-year° delaying long;   spring 1835
    Thou doest expectant Nature wrong;
Delaying long, delay no more.

5   What stays thee from the clouded noons,
    Thy sweetness from its proper place?
    Can trouble live with April days,
Or sadness in the summer moons?

Bring orchis, bring the foxglove spire,
10   The little speedwell's° darling blue,   spring flower
    Deep tulips dashed with fiery dew,
Laburnums, dropping-wells of fire.

O thou, new-year, delaying long,
    Delayest the sorrow in my blood,
15   That longs to burst a frozen bud
And flood a fresher throat with song.

84

When I contemplate all alone
    The life that had been thine below,
    And fix my thoughts on all the glow
To which thy crescent would have grown,

5   I see thee sitting crowned with good,
    A central warmth diffusing bliss
    In glance and smile, and clasp and kiss,
On all the branches of thy blood;

Thy blood, my friend, and partly mine;
10   For now the day was drawing on,
    When thou shouldst link thy life with one
Of mine own house, and boys of thine

Had babbled "Uncle" on my knee;
    But that remorseless iron hour
15   Made cypress of her orange flower,[5]
Despair of hope, and earth of thee.

I seem to meet their least desire,
    To clap their cheeks, to call them mine.
    I see their unborn faces shine
20   Beside the never-lighted fire.

I see myself an honored guest,
    Thy partner in the flowery walk
    Of letters, genial table talk,
Or deep dispute, and graceful jest;

25   While now thy prosperous labor fills
    The lips of men with honest praise,
    And sun by sun the happy days
Descend below the golden hills

With promise of a morn as fair;
30   And all the train of bounteous hours
    Conduct, by paths of growing powers,
To reverence and the silver hair;

Till slowly worn her earthly robe,
    Her lavish mission richly wrought,
35   Leaving great legacies of thought,
Thy spirit should fail from off the globe;

What time mine own might also flee,
    As linked with thine in love and fate,

---

5. Orange blossoms are associated with brides—here the poet's sister Emily Tennyson, to whom Hallam
had been engaged. Cypress branches are associated with funerals.

And, hovering o'er the dolorous strait
40   To the other shore, involved in thee,

Arrive at last the blessed goal,
And He that died in Holy Land
Would reach us out the shining hand,
And take us as a single soul.

45   What reed was that on which I leant?
Ah, backward fancy, wherefore wake
The old bitterness again, and break
The low beginnings of content?

*   *   *

86

Sweet after showers, ambrosial air,
That rollest from the gorgeous gloom
Of evening over brake° and bloom   *thicket*
And meadow, slowly breathing bare

5   The round of space,[6] and rapt below
Through all the dewy-tasseled wood,
And shadowing down the hornèd flood[7]
In ripples, fan my brows and blow

The fever from my cheek, and sigh
10   The full new life that feeds thy breath
Throughout my frame, till Doubt and Death,
Ill brethren, let the fancy fly

From belt to belt of crimson seas
On leagues of odor streaming far,
15   To where in yonder orient star
A hundred spirits whisper "Peace."

87

I passed beside the reverend walls[8]
In which of old I wore the gown;
I roved at random through the town,
And saw the tumult of the halls;

5   And heard once more in college fanes°   *chapels*
The storm their high-built organs make,
And thunder-music, rolling, shake
The prophet blazoned on the panes;

6. The "ambrosial air" is slowly clearing the clouds   7. Between two promontories [Tennyson's note].
from the sky.   8. Of Trinity College, Cambridge University.

And caught once more the distant shout,
10   The measured pulse of racing oars
    Among the willows; paced the shores
And many a bridge, and all about

The same gray flats again, and felt
    The same, but not the same; and last
15   Up that long walk of limes I passed
To see the rooms in which he dwelt.

Another name was on the door.
    I lingered; all within was noise
    Of songs, and clapping hands, and boys
20 That crashed the glass and beat the floor;

Where once we held debate, a band
    Of youthful friends,[9] on mind and art,
    And labor, and the changing mart,
And all the framework of the land;

25 When one would aim an arrow fair,
    But send it slackly from the string;
    And one would pierce an outer ring,
And one an inner, here and there;

And last the master bowman, he,
30   Would cleave the mark. A willing ear
    We lent him. Who but hung to hear
The rapt oration flowing free

From point to point, with power and grace
    And music in the bounds of law,
35   To those conclusions when we saw
The God within him light his face,

And seem to lift the form, and glow
    In azure orbits heavenly-wise;
    And over those ethereal eyes
40 The bar of Michael Angelo?[1]

88

Wild bird,[2] whose warble, liquid sweet,
    Rings Eden through the budded quicks,[3]
    O tell me where the senses mix,
O tell me where the passions meet,

9. The Apostles, an undergraduate club to which
Tennyson and Hallam had belonged.
1. Hallam, like the Italian artist Michelangelo
(1475–1564), had a prominent ridge of bone above
his eyes.
2. Probably a nightingale.
3. Hawthorn hedges.

5   Whence radiate: fierce extremes employ
       Thy spirits in the darkening leaf,
       And in the midmost heart of grief
    Thy passion clasps a secret joy;

    And I—my harp would prelude woe—
10   I cannot all command the strings;
       The glory of the sum of things
    Will flash along the chords and go.

89

Witch elms that counterchange the floor
    Of this flat lawn with dusk and bright;[4]
    And thou, with all thy breadth and height
Of foliage, towering sycamore;

5   How often, hither wandering down,
    My Arthur found your shadows fair,
    And shook to all the liberal air
The dust and din and steam of town!

He brought an eye for all he saw;
10   He mixed in all our simple sports;
    They pleased him, fresh from brawling courts
And dusty purlieus° of the law.[5]   *regions*

O joy to him in this retreat,
    Immantled in ambrosial dark,
15   To drink the cooler air, and mark
The landscape winking through the heat!

O sound to rout the brood of cares,
    The sweep of scythe in morning dew,
    The gust that round the garden flew,
20   And tumbled half the mellowing pears!

O bliss, when all in circle drawn
    About him, heart and ear were fed
    To hear him, as he lay and read
The Tuscan poets[6] on the lawn!

25   Or in the all-golden afternoon
    A guest, or happy sister, sung,
    Or here she brought the harp and flung
A ballad to the brightening moon.

4. Shadows of the elm tree checker the lawn at Somersby, the Tennysons' country home.
5. Hallam became a law student in London after leaving Cambridge.
6. A group of 13th- and 14th-century poets in central Italy (Tuscany); the best-known of them are Dante and Petrarch.

Nor less it pleased in livelier moods,
30   Beyond the bounding hill to stray,
      And break the livelong summer day
With banquet in the distant woods;

Whereat we glanced from theme to theme,
      Discussed the books to love or hate,
35   Or touched the changes of the state,
Or threaded some Socratic dream;[7]

But if I praised the busy town,
      He loved to rail against it still,
      For "ground in yonder social mill
40 We rub each other's angles down,

"And merge," he said, "in form and gloss
      The picturesque of man and man."
      We talked: the stream beneath us ran,
The wine-flask lying couched in moss,

45 Or cooled within the glooming wave;
      And last, returning from afar,
      Before the crimson-circled star[8]
Had fallen into her father's[9] grave,

And brushing ankle-deep in flowers,
50   We heard behind the woodbine veil
      The milk that bubbled in° the pail,   *into*
And buzzings of the honeyed hours.

                    *   *   *

91

When rosy plumelets tuft the larch,
      And rarely° pipes the mounted thrush,   *exquisitely*
      Or underneath the barren bush
Flits by the sea-blue bird° of March;   *kingfisher*

5   Come, wear the form by which I know
      Thy spirit in time among thy peers;
      The hope of unaccomplished years
Be large and lucid round thy brow.

When summer's hourly-mellowing change
10   May breathe, with many roses sweet,

---

7. I.e., worked our way through some discourse of Socrates (as recorded by Plato).
8. Venus, which will sink into the west as the Sun has done.

9. According to the nebular hypothesis, planets condensed out of the sun's atmosphere; in this sense the Sun is the "father" of planets.

Upon the thousand waves of wheat
That ripple round the lowly grange,°   *outlying farmhouse*

Come; not in watches of the night,
But where the sunbeam broodeth warm,
15   Come, beauteous in thine after form,
And like a finer light in light.

* * *

93

I shall not see thee. Dare I say
No spirit ever brake the band
That stays him from the native land
Where first he walked when clasped in clay?[1]

5   No visual shade of someone lost,
But he, the Spirit himself, may come
Where all the nerve of sense is numb,
Spirit to Spirit, Ghost to Ghost.

Oh, therefore from thy sightless° range   *invisible*
10   With gods in unconjectured bliss,
Oh, from the distance of the abyss
Of tenfold-complicated change,

Descend, and touch, and enter; hear
The wish too strong for words to name,
15   That in this blindness of the frame°   *human body*
My Ghost may feel that thine is near.

94

How pure at heart and sound in head,
With what divine affections bold
Should be the man whose thought would hold
An hour's communion with the dead.

5   In vain shalt thou, or any, call
The spirits from their golden day,
Except, like them, thou too canst say,
My spirit is at peace with all.

They haunt the silence of the breast,
10   Imaginations calm and fair,
The memory like a cloudless air,
The conscience as a sea at rest;

1. I.e., when he was alive and in fleshly form.

But when the heart is full of din,
   And doubt beside the portal waits,
15   They can but listen at the gates,
And hear the household jar° within.   *noise*

95

By night we lingered on the lawn,
   For underfoot the herb was dry;
   And genial warmth; and o'er the sky
The silvery haze of summer drawn;

5   And calm that let the tapers burn
   Unwavering: not a cricket chirred;
   The brook alone far off was heard,
And on the board the fluttering urn.[2]

And bats went round in fragrant skies,
10   And wheeled or lit the filmy shapes[3]
   That haunt the dusk, with ermine capes
And woolly breasts and beaded eyes;

While now we sang old songs that pealed
   From knoll to knoll, where, couched at ease,
15   The white kine° glimmered, and the trees   *cows*
Laid their dark arms[4] about the field.

But when those others, one by one,
   Withdrew themselves from me and night,
   And in the house light after light
20 Went out, and I was all alone,

A hunger seized my heart; I read
   Of that glad year which once had been,
   In those fallen leaves which kept their green,
The noble letters of the dead.

25   And strangely on the silence broke
   The silent-speaking words, and strange
   Was love's dumb cry defying change
To test his worth; and strangely spoke

The faith, the vigor, bold to dwell
30   On doubts that drive the coward back,
   And keen through wordy snares to track
Suggestion to her inmost cell.

So word by word, and line by line,
   The dead man touched me from the past,

2. Vessel for boiling water for tea or coffee, heated by a fluttering flame.
3. The white-winged night moths called ermine moths.
4. Cast the shadows of their branches.

35   And all at once it seemed at last
The[5] living soul was flashed on mine.

And mine in this was wound, and whirled
    About empyreal° heights of thought,   *heavenly*
    And came on that which is, and caught
40 The deep pulsations of the world,

Aeonian music[6] measuring out
    The steps of Time—the shocks of Chance—
    The blows of Death. At length my trance
Was canceled, stricken through with doubt.[7]

45 Vague words! but ah, how hard to frame
    In matter-molded forms of speech,
    Or even for intellect to reach
Through memory that which I became.

Till now the doubtful dusk revealed
50   The knolls once more where, couched at ease,
    The white kine glimmered, and the trees
Laid their dark arms about the field;

And sucked from out the distant gloom
    A breeze began to tremble o'er
55   The large leaves of the sycamore,
And fluctuate all the still perfume,

And gathering freshlier overhead,
    Rocked the full-foliaged elms, and swung
    The heavy-folded rose, and flung
60 The lilies to and fro, and said,

"The dawn, the dawn," and died away;
    And East and West, without a breath,
    Mixed their dim lights, like life and death,
To broaden into boundless day.

5. "His" in the 1st edition. Also in the 1st edition, line 37 read: "And mine in his was wound."
6. Music of the universe, which has pulsated for eons.
7. In a letter of 1874, replying to an inquiry about his experience of mystical trances, Tennyson wrote: "A kind of waking trance I have frequently had, quite up from boyhood, when I have been all alone. This has generally come upon me through repeating my own name two or three times to myself silently, till all at once, as it were out of the intensity of the consciousness of individuality, the individuality itself seemed to dissolve and fade away into boundless being, and this not a confused state, but the clearest of the clearest, the surest of the surest, the weirdest of the weirdest, utterly beyond words, where death was an almost laughable impossibility, the loss of personality (if so it were) seeming no extinction but the only true life. . . . This might . . . be the state which St. Paul describes, 'Whether in the body I cannot tell, or whether out of the body I cannot tell.' . . . I am ashamed of my feeble description. Have I not said the state is utterly beyond words? But in a moment, when I come back to my normal state of 'sanity,' I am ready to fight for *mein liebes Ich* [my dear self], and hold that it will last for aeons of aeons" (*Alfred Lord Tennyson, A Memoir*, 1897, vol. 1, 320).

96

You say, but with no touch of scorn,
   Sweet-hearted, you,[8] whose light blue eyes
   Are tender over drowning flies,
You tell me, doubt is Devil-born.

5   I know not: one indeed I knew
   In many a subtle question versed,
   Who touched a jarring lyre at first,
But ever strove to make it true;

Perplexed in faith, but pure in deeds,
10   At last he beat his music out.
   There lives more faith in honest doubt,
Believe me, than in half the creeds.

He fought his doubts and gathered strength,
   He would not make his judgment blind,
15   He faced the specters of the mind
And laid them; thus he came at length

To find a stronger faith his own,
   And Power was with him in the night,
   Which makes the darkness and the light,
20   And dwells not in the light alone,

But in the darkness and the cloud,
   As over Sinaï's peaks of old,
   While Israel made their gods of gold,
Although the trumpet blew so loud.[9]

*   *   *

99

Risest thou thus, dim dawn, again,[1]
   So loud with voices of the birds,
   So thick with lowings of the herds,
Day, when I lost the flower of men;

5   Who tremblest through thy darkling red
   On yon swollen brook that bubbles fast[2]
   By meadows breathing of the past,
And woodlands holy to the dead;

8. A woman of simple faith.
9. After veiling Mount Sinai in a "thick cloud" and signifying the divine presence by "the voice of the trumpet" (Exodus 19.16), God addresses Moses from the "thick darkness" (20.21). Meanwhile Aaron made, and the Israelites worshipped, a golden calf (32.1–6).
1. September 15, 1835, the second anniversary of Hallam's death.
2. I.e., reflections of the clouded red light of dawn quiver on the surface of the fast-moving water.

Who murmurest in the foliage eaves
10   A song that slights the coming care,[3]
     And Autumn laying here and there
A fiery finger on the leaves;

Who wakenest with thy balmy breath
     To myriads on the genial° earth,   *generative*
15   Memories of bridal, or of birth,[4]
And unto myriads more, of death.

Oh, wheresoever those[5] may be,
     Betwixt the slumber of the poles,
     Today they count as kindred souls;
20 They know me not, but mourn with me.

*   *   *

103

On that last night before we went
     From out the doors where I was bred,[6]
     I dreamed a vision of the dead,
Which left my after-morn content.

5   Methought I dwelt within a hall,
     And maidens with me; distant hills
     From hidden summits fed with rills
A river sliding by the wall.

The hall with harp and carol rang.
10   They sang of what is wise and good
     And graceful. In the center stood
A statue veiled, to which they sang;

And which, though veiled, was known to me,
     The shape of him I loved, and love
15   Forever. Then flew in a dove
And brought a summons from the sea;

And when they learnt that I must go,
     They wept and wailed, but led the way
     To where the little shallop° lay   *light open boat*
20 At anchor in the flood below;

And on by many a level mead,°   *meadow*
     And shadowing bluff that made the banks,
     We glided winding under ranks
Of iris and the golden reed;

3. I.e., that disregards future events such as death or the coming of autumn.
4. Cf. "Epilogue," lines 117–28 (p. 2022).
5. I.e., the many who remember death.
6. In 1837 Tennyson and his family moved away from their home in Lincolnshire, which had been closely associated with his friendship with Hallam. In section 104 the move seems to occur in 1835, the year of the third Christmas after Hallam's death.

25   And still as vaster grew the shore
          And rolled the floods in grander space,
          The maidens gathered strength and grace
      And presence, lordlier than before;

      And I myself, who sat apart
30   And watched them, waxed° in every limb;   *grown*
          I felt the thews of Anakim,[7]
      The pulses of a Titan's[8] heart;

      As one would sing the death of war,
          And one would chant the history
35   Of that great race which is to be,[9]
      And one the shaping of a star;

      Until the forward-creeping tides
          Began to foam, and we to draw
          From deep to deep, to where we saw
40   A great ship lift her shining sides.[1]

      The man we loved was there on deck,
          But thrice as large as man he bent
          To greet us. Up the side I went,
      And fell in silence on his neck;

45   Whereat those maidens with one mind
          Bewailed their lot; I did them wrong:
          "We served thee here," they said, "so long,
      And wilt thou leave us now behind?"

      So rapt° I was, they could not win   *entranced*
50   An answer from my lips, but he
          Replying, "Enter likewise ye
      And go with us:" they entered in.

      And while the wind began to sweep
          A music out of sheet and shroud,
55   We steered her toward a crimson cloud
      That landlike slept along the deep.

104

      The time draws near the birth of Christ;[2]
          The moon is hid, the night is still;

7. Plural of *Anak*; a reference to the giant sons of Anak (see Numbers 13.33).
8. Giant of Greek mythology.
9. See the account of the "crowning race" in "Epilogue," lines 128–44.
1. Cf. *The Passing of Arthur*, lines 361–469, in which Bedivere is left behind as Arthur's barge, the ship of death, sails away. In the present dream vision the speaker is taken aboard, as are his companions, who represent the creative arts of this world—"all the human powers and talents that do not pass with life but go along with it," as Tennyson said of this passage.
2. The third Christmas (1835) after Hallam's death.

A single church below the hill
Is pealing, folded in the mist.

5   A single peal of bells below,
        That wakens at this hour of rest
        A single murmur in the breast,
    That these are not the bells I know.

    Like strangers' voices here they sound,
10   In lands where not a memory strays,
        Nor landmark breathes of other days,
    But all is new unhallowed ground.

105

Tonight ungathered let us leave
    This laurel, let this holly stand:[3]
    We live within the stranger's land,
And strangely falls our Christmas eve.

5   Our father's dust is left alone
        And silent under other snows:
        There in due time the woodbine blows,°   blooms
    The violet comes, but we are gone.

    No more shall wayward grief abuse
10   The genial hour with mask and mime;
        For change of place, like growth of time,
    Has broke the bond of dying use.

    Let cares that petty shadows cast,
        By which our lives are chiefly proved,
15   A little spare the night I loved,
    And hold it solemn to the past.

    But let no footstep beat the floor,
        Nor bowl of wassail mantle warm;[4]
        For who would keep an ancient form
20   Through which the spirit breathes no more?

    Be neither song, nor game, nor feast;
        Nor harp be touched, nor flute be blown;
        No dance, no motion, save alone
    What lightens in the lucid east

25   Of rising worlds[5] by yonder wood.
        Long sleeps the summer in the seed;

---

3. Cf. section 29, in which the family in their former home still continued to gather holly. In the new home the customary observances lapse.
4. I.e., let no bowl of hot punch warm the mantelpiece.
5. The scintillating motion of the stars that rise [Tennyson's note].

Run out your measured arcs, and lead
The closing cycle rich in good.

106

Ring out, wild bells, to the wild sky,
  The flying cloud, the frosty light:
  The year is dying in the night;
Ring out, wild bells, and let him die.

5 Ring out the old, ring in the new,
  Ring, happy bells, across the snow:
  The year is going, let him go;
Ring out the false, ring in the true.

Ring out the grief that saps the mind,
10   For those that here we see no more;
  Ring out the feud of rich and poor,
Ring in redress to all mankind.

Ring out a slowly dying cause,
  And ancient forms of party strife;
15   Ring in the nobler modes of life,
With sweeter manners, purer laws.

Ring out the want, the care, the sin,
  The faithless coldness of the times:
  Ring out, ring out my mournful rhymes,
20 But ring the fuller minstrel in.

Ring out false pride in place and blood,
  The civic slander and the spite;
  Ring in the love of truth and right,
Ring in the common love of good.

25 Ring out old shapes of foul disease;
  Ring out the narrowing lust of gold;
  Ring out the thousand wars of old,
Ring in the thousand years of peace.

Ring in the valiant man and free,
30   The larger heart, the kindlier hand;
  Ring out the darkness of the land,
Ring in the Christ that is to be.[6]

6. These allusions to the second coming of Christ and to the millennium are derived from Revelation 20, but Tennyson has interpreted the biblical account in his own way. He once told his son of his conviction that "the forms of Christian religion would alter; but that the spirit of Christ would still grow from more to more."

107

It is the day when he was born.°   *February 1*
   A bitter day that early sank
   Behind a purple-frosty bank
Of vapor, leaving night forlorn.

5   The time admits not flowers or leaves
   To deck the banquet. Fiercely flies
   The blast of North and East, and ice
Makes daggers at the sharpened eaves,

And bristles all the brakes° and thorns   *thickets*
10   To yon hard crescent, as she hangs
   Above the wood which grides[7] and clangs
Its leafless ribs and iron horns

Together, in the drifts[8] that pass
   To darken on the rolling brine
15   That breaks the coast. But fetch the wine,
Arrange the board and brim the glass;

Bring in great logs and let them lie,
   To make a solid core of heat;
   Be cheerful-minded, talk and treat
20   Of all things even as he were by;

We keep the day. With festal cheer,
   With books and music, surely we
   Will drink to him, whate'er he be,
And sing the songs he loved to hear.

108

I will not shut me from my kind,
   And, lest I stiffen into stone,
   I will not eat my heart alone,
Nor feed with sighs a passing wind:

5   What profit lies in barren faith,
   And vacant yearning, though with might
   To scale the heaven's highest height,
Or dive below the wells of Death?

What find I in the highest place,
10   But mine own phantom chanting hymns?
   And on the depths of death there swims
The reflex of a human face.°   *his own face*

---

7. Clashes with a strident noise.   8. Either cloud drifts or clouds of snow.

I'll rather take what fruit may be
　　Of sorrow under human skies:
15　　'Tis held that sorrow makes us wise,
　　Whatever wisdom sleep with thee.°　　　　　　　　　*Hallam*

109

Heart-affluence in discursive talk
　　From household fountains never dry;
　　The critic clearness of an eye
That saw through all the Muses' walk;[9]

5　Seraphic intellect and force
　　To seize and throw the doubts of man;
　　Impassioned logic, which outran
The hearer in its fiery course;

High nature amorous of the good,
10　　But touched with no ascetic gloom;
　　And passion pure in snowy bloom
Through all the years of April blood;

A love of freedom rarely felt,
　　Of freedom in her regal seat
15　　Of England; not the schoolboy heat,
The blind hysterics of the Celt;[1]

And manhood fused with female grace
　　In such a sort, the child would twine
　　A trustful hand, unasked, in thine,
20　And find his comfort in thy face;

All these have been, and thee mine eyes
　　Have looked on: if they looked in vain,
　　My shame is greater who remain,
Nor let thy wisdom make me wise.

*　*　*

115

Now fades the last long streak of snow,
　　Now burgeons every maze of quick°　　　　　　*hawthorn hedge*
　　About the flowering squares,° and thick　　　　　　*fields*
By ashen roots the violets blow.

9. The realm of art and literature.
1. A member or descendant of one of the groups of peoples populating ancient Britain.

⁵ Now rings the woodland loud and long,
    The distance takes a lovelier hue,
    And drowned in yonder living blue
    The lark becomes a sightless song.

    Now dance the lights on lawn and lea,
¹⁰   The flocks are whiter down the vale,
    And milkier every milky sail
    On winding stream or distant sea;

    Where now the seamew° pipes, or dives   *a seabird*
    In yonder greening gleam, and fly
¹⁵   The happy birds, that change their sky
    To build and brood, that live their lives

    From land to land; and in my breast
    Spring wakens too, and my regret
    Becomes an April violet,
²⁰ And buds and blossoms like the rest.

*   *   *

118

Contèmplate all this work of Time,
    The giant laboring in his youth;
    Nor dream of human love and truth,
As dying Nature's earth and lime;[2]

⁵ But trust that those we call the dead
    Are breathers of an ampler day
    For ever nobler ends. They° say,   *Scientists*
The solid earth whereon we tread

In tracts of fluent heat began,
¹⁰   And grew to seeming-random forms,
    The seeming prey of cyclic storms,
Till at the last arose the man;

Who throve and branched from clime to clime,
    The herald of a higher race,
¹⁵   And of himself in higher place
If so he type[3] this work of time

Within himself, from more to more;
    Or, crowned with attributes of woe
    Like glories, move his course, and show
²⁰ That life is not as idle ore,

---

2. Two of the perishable organic ingredients of the human body.   3. Emulate, prefigure as a type.

But iron dug from central gloom,
  And heated hot with burning fears,
  And dipped in baths of hissing tears,
And battered with the shocks of doom

25 To shape and use. Arise and fly
  The reeling Faun,[4] the sensual feast;
  Move upward, working out the beast,
And let the ape and tiger die.

119

Doors,[5] where my heart was used to beat
  So quickly, not as one that weeps
  I come once more; the city sleeps;
I smell the meadow in the street;

5 I hear a chirp of birds; I see
  Betwixt the black fronts long-withdrawn
  A light blue lane of early dawn,
And think of early days and thee,

And bless thee, for thy lips are bland,°   *gentle*
10 And bright the friendship of thine eye;
  And in my thoughts with scarce a sigh
I take the pressure of thine hand.

120

I trust I have not wasted breath:
  I think we are not wholly brain,
  Magnetic mockeries;[6] not in vain,
Like Paul[7] with beasts, I fought with Death;

5 Not only cunning° casts in clay: *skillful*
  Let Science prove we are, and then
  What matters Science unto men,
At least to me? I would not stay.

Let him, the wiser man who springs
10 Hereafter, up from childhood shape
  His action like the greater ape,
But I was *born* to other things.

4. In Roman mythology a half-human, half-beast deity of the woods and mountains.
5. The doors of Hallam's house on London's Wimpole Street. Cf. section 7.
6. Mechanisms operated by responses to electrical forces.
7. 1 Corinthians 15.32.

121

Sad Hesper° o'er the buried sun   *evening star*
   And ready, thou, to die with him,
   Thou watchest all things ever dim
And dimmer, and a glory done.

5   The team is loosened from the wain,°   *hay wagon*
   The boat is drawn upon the shore;
   Thou listenest to the closing door,
And life is darkened in the brain.

Bright Phosphor,° fresher for the night,   *morning star*
10   By thee the world's great work is heard
   Beginning, and the wakeful bird;
Behind thee comes the greater light.[8]

The market boat is on the stream,
   And voices hail it from the brink;
15   Thou hear'st the village hammer clink,
And see'st the moving of the team.

Sweet Hesper-Phosphor, double name[9]
   For what is one, the first, the last,
   Thou, like my present and my past,
20   Thy place is changed; thou art the same.

*   *   *

123

There rolls the deep where grew the tree.
   O earth, what changes hast thou seen!
   There where the long street roars hath been
The stillness of the central sea.[1]

5   The hills are shadows, and they flow
   From form to form, and nothing stands;
   They melt like mist, the solid lands,
Like clouds they shape themselves and go.

But in my spirit will I dwell,
10   And dream my dream, and hold it true;

8. Cf. Genesis 1.16: "the greater light to rule the day."
9. The planet Venus, named for the Roman goddess of love, is both the evening star and the morning star (visible at different times in different seasons).
1. In a passage from *The Principles of Geology* (1832), a book well known to Tennyson, Sir Charles Lyell discusses the "interchange of sea and land" that has occurred "on the surface of our globe": "In the Mediterranean alone, many flourishing inland towns and a still greater number of ports now stand where the sea rolled its waves since the era when civilized nations first grew in Europe."

For though my lips may breathe adieu,
I cannot think the thing farewell.

124

That which we dare invoke to bless;
   Our dearest faith; our ghastliest doubt;
   He, They, One, All; within, without;
The Power in darkness whom we guess—

5 I found Him not in world or sun,
   Or eagle's wing, or insect's eye,[2]
   Nor through the questions men may try,
The petty cobwebs we have spun.

If e'er when faith had fallen asleep,
10 I heard a voice, "believe no more,"
   And heard an ever-breaking shore
That tumbled in the Godless deep,

A warmth within the breast would melt
   The freezing reason's colder part,
15 And like a man in wrath the heart
Stood up and answered, "I have felt."

No, like a child in doubt and fear:
   But that blind clamor made me wise;
   Then was I as a child that cries,
20 But, crying, knows his father near;

And what I am beheld again
   What is, and no man understands;
   And out of darkness came the hands
That reach through nature, molding men.

         *   *   *

126

Love is and was my lord and king,
   And in his presence I attend
   To hear the tidings of my friend,
Which every hour his couriers bring.

5 Love is and was my king and lord,
   And will be, though as yet I keep

---

2. He does not discover satisfactory proof of God's existence in the 18th-century argument that because objects in nature are designed there must exist a designer.

Within the court on earth, and sleep
Encompassed by his faithful guard,

And hear at times a sentinel
10   Who moves about from place to place,
And whispers to the worlds of space,
In the deep night, that all is well.

127

And all is well, though faith and form[3]
Be sundered in the night of fear;
Well roars the storm to those that hear
A deeper voice across the storm,

5   Proclaiming social truth shall spread,
And justice, even though thrice again
The red fool-fury of the Seine
Should pile her barricades with dead.[4]

But ill for him that wears a crown,
10   And him, the lazar,[5] in his rags!
They tremble, the sustaining crags;
The spires of ice are toppled down,

And molten up, and roar in flood;
The fortress crashes from on high,
15   The brute earth lightens[6] to the sky,
And the great Aeon[7] sinks in blood,

And compassed by the fires of hell,
While thou, dear spirit, happy star,
O'erlook'st the tumult from afar,
20 And smilest, knowing all is well.

*   *   *

129

Dear friend, far off, my lost desire,
So far, so near in woe and weal,°   *happiness*
O loved the most, when most I feel
There is a lower and a higher;

---

3. Traditional institutions through which faith was formerly expressed, such as the Church.
4. Reference to revolutionary uprisings in France, in each of which a king lost his throne (line 9): in 1789 against Louis XVI, in 1830 against Charles X, and in 1848 against Louis-Philippe. If, as Tennyson recollected, section 127 was finished at a date earlier than 1848, the reference to three revolutions (line 6) was prophetic. Seine: the river that runs through Paris.
5. Pauper suffering from disease.
6. Is lit up by fire.
7. A vast tract of time, here perhaps modern Western civilization.

5   Known and unknown, human, divine;
     Sweet human hand and lips and eye;
     Dear heavenly friend that canst not die,
  Mine, mine, forever, ever mine;

  Strange friend, past, present, and to be;
10   Loved deeplier, darklier understood;
     Behold, I dream a dream of good,
  And mingle all the world with thee.

130

  Thy voice is on the rolling air
     I hear thee where the waters run;
     Thou standest in the rising sun,
  And in the setting thou art fair.

5   What art thou then? I cannot guess;
     But though I seem in star and flower
     To feel thee some diffusive power,
  I do not therefore love thee less.

  My love involves the love before;
10   My love is vaster passion now;
     Tho' mix'd with God and Nature thou,
  I seem to love thee more and more.

  Far off thou art, but ever nigh;
     I have thee still, and I rejoice;
15   I prosper, circled with thy voice;
  I shall not lose thee tho' I die.

131

  O living will[8] that shalt endure
     When all that seems shall suffer shock,
     Rise in the spiritual rock,[9]
  Flow through our deeds and make them pure,

5   That we may lift from out of dust
     A voice as unto him that hears,
     A cry above the conquered years
  To one that with us works, and trust,

  With faith that comes of self-control,
10   The truths that never can be proved
     Until we close with all we loved,
  And all we flow from, soul in soul.

8. Tennyson later commented that he meant here the moral will of humankind.
9. Christ. Cf. 1 Corinthians 10.4: "And did all drink the same spiritual drink; for they drank of that spiritual Rock that followed them: and that Rock was Christ."

From Epilogue[1]

* * *

And rise, O moon, from yonder down,
110   Till over down and over dale
   All night the shining vapor sail
And pass the silent-lighted town,

The white-faced halls, the glancing rills,
   And catch at every mountain head,
115   And o'er the friths° that branch and spread   *inlets of the sea*
Their sleeping silver through the hills;

And touch with shade the bridal doors,
   With tender gloom the roof, the wall;
   And breaking let the splendor fall
120 To spangle all the happy shores

By which they rest, and ocean sounds,
   And, star and system rolling past,
   A soul shall draw from out the vast
And strike his being into bounds,

125 And, moved through life of lower phase,
   Result in man,[2] be born and think,
   And act and love, a closer link
Betwixt us and the crowning race

Of those that, eye to eye, shall look
130   On knowledge; under whose command
   Is Earth and Earth's, and in their hand
Is Nature like an open book;

No longer half-akin to brute,
   For all we thought and loved and did,
135   And hoped, and suffered, is but seed
Of what in them is flower and fruit;

Whereof the man that with me trod
   This planet was a noble type°   *model, example*
   Appearing ere the times were ripe,
140 That friend of mine who lives in God,

That God, which ever lives and loves,
   One God, one law, one element,
   And one far-off divine event,
To which the whole creation moves.

1833–50   1850

1. The "Epilogue" describes the wedding day of Tennyson's sister Cecilia to Edmund Lushington. At the conclusion (printed here) the speaker reflects on the moonlit wedding night and the kind of offspring that will result from their union.

2. A child will be conceived and will develop in embryo through various stages. This development is similar to human evolution from the animal to the human level and perhaps to a future higher stage of development.

The Charge of the Light Brigade[1]

1

Half a league,[2] half a league,
Half a league onward,
All in the valley of Death
   Rode the six hundred.
5 "Forward the Light Brigade!
Charge for the guns!" he said.
Into the valley of Death
   Rode the six hundred.[3]

2

"Forward, the Light Brigade!"
10 Was there a man dismayed?
Not though the soldier knew
   Someone had blundered.
Theirs not to make reply,
Theirs not to reason why,
15 Theirs but to do and die.
Into the valley of Death
   Rode the six hundred.

3

Cannon to right of them,
Cannon to left of them,
20 Cannon in front of them
   Volleyed and thundered;
Stormed at with shot and shell,
Boldly they rode and well,
Into the jaws of Death,
25 Into the mouth of hell
   Rode the six hundred.

4

Flashed all their sabers bare,
Flashed as they turned in air
Sab'ring the gunners there,
30 Charging an army, while
   All the world wondered.
Plunged in the battery smoke
Right through the line they broke;
Cossack and Russian
35 Reeled from the saber stroke
   Shattered and sundered.

---

1. During the Crimean War (1854–56), owing to confusion of orders, a brigade of British cavalry charged some entrenched batteries of Russian artillery. This blunder cost the lives of three-quarters of the six hundred horsemen engaged (see Cecil Woodham-Smith, *The Reason Why*, 1954). Tennyson rapidly composed his "ballad" (as he called the poem) after reading an account of the battle in a newspaper.
2. About a mile and a half.
3. In the recording Tennyson made of this poem, "hundred" sounds like "hunderd"—a Lincolnshire pronunciation that reinforces the rhyme with "thundered," etc. "Valley of Death": see Psalms 23.4 ("Yea, though I walk through the valley of the shadow of death").

> Then they rode back, but not,
>   Not the six hundred.

5

>   Cannon to right of them,
> 40 Cannon to left of them,
>   Cannon behind them
>   Volleyed and thundered;
>   Stormed at with shot and shell,
>   While horse and hero fell.
> 45 They that had fought so well
>   Came through the jaws of Death,
>   Back from the mouth of hell,
>   All that was left of them,
>   Left of six hundred.

6

> 50 When can their glory fade?
>   O the wild charge they made!
>   All the world wondered.
>   Honor the charge they made!
>   Honor the Light Brigade,
> 55   Noble six hundred!

1854   1854

Idylls of the King

When John Milton was considering subjects suitable for an epic poem, one of those he entertained was the story of the British king Arthur, a semilegendary leader of about 500 C.E. who fought off the Saxon invaders who had swarmed into Britain after the withdrawal of the Roman legions. Tennyson likewise saw that the Arthurian story had epic potential and selected it for his lifework as "the greatest of all poetical subjects." At intervals, during a period of fifty years, he labored over the twelve books that make up his *Idylls of the King,* completing the work in 1888.

The principal source of Tennyson's stories of Arthur and his knights was Sir Thomas Malory's *Morte Darthur,* a version that Malory translated into English prose from French sources in 1470. As Talbot Donaldson suggested, one basis of the appeal of the Arthurian stories, like the legends of Robin Hood and stories of the American West, is that they represent the struggle of individuals to restore order when chaos and anarchy are ascendant, a task performed in the face of seemingly overwhelming odds. The individual stories in Tennyson's *Idylls* have the same basic appeal, but the overall design of the whole poem is more ambitious and impressive. The epic represents the rise and fall of a civilization, and its underlying theme is that after two thousand years of Christianity, Western civilization may be going through a cycle in which it must confront the possibilities of a renewal in the future or an apocalyptic extinction. The first book, *The Coming of Arthur,* introduces the basic myth of a springtime hero transforming a wasteland and inspiring faith and hope in the highest values of civilized life among his devoted followers, the knights of his Round Table. Succeeding books move through summer and autumn and culminate in the bleak wintry scene of Arthur's last battle in which his order perishes in a civil war; the leader of the enemy forces is his own nephew, Sir Modred.

Throughout the later books of the *Idylls* the forces of opposition grow in strength, and discontent and resentment infect leading figures of the Round Table itself. The most glaring example is the adulterous relationship between Guinevere, Arthur's "sumptuous" queen (as Tennyson once described her), and the king's chief lieutenant and friend, Sir Lancelot. Many other fallings away subsequently come to light, such as the deceitful betrayal by Sir Gawain in the ninth book, *Pelleas and Ettarre*, and the cynical conduct of Sir Tristram, whose story is told in the bitter tenth book, *The Last Tournament*. Even Merlin, Arthur's trusted magician and counselor, becomes corrupted and can perform no further offices for the king (*Merlin and Vivien*). *The Passing of Arthur* depicts the apocalyptic end of this long process of disintegration and decay.

FROM IDYLLS OF THE KING

The Passing of Arthur[1]

That story which the bold Sir Bedivere,[2]
First made and latest left of all the knights,
Told, when the man was no more than a voice
In the white winter of his age, to those
5   With whom he dwelt, new faces, other minds.

For on their march to westward, Bedivere,
Who slowly paced among the slumbering host,
Heard in his tent the moanings of the King:

"I found Him in the shining of the stars,
10   I marked Him in the flowering of His fields,
But in His ways with men I find Him not.
I waged His wars, and now I pass and die.
O me! for why is all around us here
As if some lesser god had made the world,
15   But had not force to shape it as he would,
Till the High God behold it from beyond,
And enter it, and make it beautiful?
Or else as if the world were wholly fair,
But that these eyes of men are dense and dim,
20   And have not power to see it as it is:
Perchance, because we see not to the close;—
For I, being simple, thought to work His will,
And have but stricken with the sword in vain;
And all whereon I leaned in wife and friend
25   Is traitor to my peace, and all my realm
Reels back into the beast, and is no more.
My God, thou hast forgotten me in my death:[3]
Nay—God my Christ—I pass but shall not die."

---

1. The principal source for *The Passing of Arthur* is Malory's *Morte Darthur* 21.4–5. Preceding the action of this idyll, Arthur has been in France with his nephew Gawain, fighting against the forces of Lancelot. Learning at that time of the gathering of an army against him in England, under the leadership of his nephew, Modred, Arthur returns there to engage in his last battle. Upon landing at Dover, Gawain is slain.
2. A knight who has long been close to the king, described in *The Coming of Arthur*, lines 173–74: "Bedivere, the first of all his knights / Knighted by Arthur at his crowning."
3. Cf. Jesus' cry in Matthew 27.46: "My God, my God, why hast thou forsaken me?"

Then, ere that last weird battle in the west,
30   There came on Arthur sleeping, Gawain killed
In Lancelot's war, the ghost of Gawain blown
Along a wandering wind, and past his ear
Went shrilling. "Hollow, hollow all delight!
Hail, King! tomorrow thou shalt pass away.
35   Farewell! there is an isle of rest for thee.
And I am blown along a wandering wind,
And hollow, hollow, hollow all delight."
And fainter onward, like wild birds that change
Their season in the night and wail their way
40   From cloud to cloud, down the long wind the dream
Shrilled; but in going mingled with dim cries
Far in the moonlit haze among the hills,
As of some lonely city sacked by night,
When all is lost, and wife and child with wail
45   Pass to new lords; and Arthur woke and called,
"Who spake? A dream. O light upon the wind,
Thine, Gawain, was the voice—are these dim cries
Thine? or doth all that haunts the waste and wild
Mourn, knowing it will go along with me?"

50   This heard the bold Sir Bedivere and spake:
"O me, my King, let pass whatever will,
Elves, and the harmless glamour of the field;[4]
But in their stead thy name and glory cling
To all high places like a golden cloud
55   Forever: but as yet thou shalt not pass.
Light was Gawain in life, and light in death
Is Gawain, for the ghost is as the man;
And care not thou for dreams from him, but rise—
I hear the steps of Modred in the west,
60   And with him many of thy people, and knights
Once thine, whom thou hast loved, but grosser grown
Than heathen, spitting at their vows and thee.
Right well in heart they know thee for the King.
Arise, go forth and conquer as of old."

65   Then spake King Arthur to Sir Bedivere:
"Far other is this battle in the west
Whereto we move, than when we strove in youth,
And brake the petty kings, and fought with Rome,
Or thrust the heathen from the Roman wall,[5]
70   And shook him through the north. Ill doom° is mine   *destiny*
To war against my people and my knights.
The king who fights his people fights himself.
And they my knights, who loved me once, the stroke
That strikes them dead is as my death to me.
75   Yet let us hence, and find or feel a way

---

4. Tennyson said the reference is to "the legends which cluster round the King's name." One legend told of the elves' bestowing gifts on Arthur as a child.

5. Hadrian's Wall, built in northern Britain, by the 2nd-century Roman emperor Hadrian as a defense against invaders from the north.

Through this blind haze, which ever since I saw
One lying in the dust at Almesbury,[6]
Hath folded in the passes of the world."

Then rose the King and moved his host by night,
80 And ever pushed Sir Modred, league by league,
Back to the sunset bound of Lyonnesse[7]—
A land of old upheaven from the abyss
By fire, to sink into the abyss again;
Where fragments of forgotten peoples dwelled,
85 And the long mountains ended in a coast
Of ever-shifting sand, and far away
The phantom circle of a moaning sea.
There the pursuer could pursue no more,
And he that fled no further fly the King;
90 And there, that day when the great light of heaven
Burned at his lowest in the rolling year,
On the waste sand by the waste sea they closed.
Nor ever yet had Arthur fought a fight
Like this last, dim, weird battle of the west.
95 A deathwhite mist slept over sand and sea:
Whereof the chill, to him who breathed it, drew
Down with his blood, till all his heart was cold
With formless fear; and even on Arthur fell
Confusion, since he saw not whom he fought.
100 For friend and foe were shadows in the mist,
And friend slew friend not knowing whom he slew;[8]
And some had visions out of golden youth,
And some beheld the faces of old ghosts
Look in upon the battle; and in the mist
105 Was many a noble deed, many a base,
And chance and craft and strength in single fights,
And ever and anon with host to host
Shocks, and the splintering spear, the hard mail hewn,
Shield-breakings, and the clash of brands,° the crash   *swords*
110 Of battleaxes on shattered helms, and shrieks
After the Christ, of those who falling down
Looked up for heaven, and only saw the mist;
And shouts of heathen and the traitor knights,
Oaths, insult, filth, and monstrous blasphemies,
115 Sweat, writhings, anguish, laboring of the lungs
In that close mist, and cryings for the light,
Moans of the dying, and voices of the dead.

Last, as by some one deathbed after wail
Of suffering, silence follows, or through death
120 Or deathlike swoon, thus over all that shore,

6. The convent to which Guinevere withdraws in
the eleventh idyll; during the king's farewell visit
to her there, she lies in the dust at his feet.
7. Legendary land, extending west from Cornwall,
that sank into the sea.
8. Cf. the description of a battle by the Greek

writer Thucydides (ca. 455–ca. 400 B.C.E.) in his
History of the Peloponnesian War (7.44), in which
the invaders become confused by darkness and
slaughter many of their own men, and Matthew
Arnold's 1851 reworking of this scene in "Dover
Beach," lines 35–37 (p. 2106).

Save for some whisper of the seething seas,
A dead hush fell; but when the dolorous day
Grew drearier toward twilight falling, came
A bitter wind, clear from the North, and blew
125 The mist aside, and with that wind the tide
Rose, and the pale King glanced across the field
Of battle: but no man was moving there;
Nor any cry of Christian heard thereon,
Nor yet of heathen; only the wan wave
130 Brake in among dead faces, to and fro
Swaying the helpless hands, and up and down
Tumbling the hollow helmets of the fallen,
And shivered brands that once had fought with Rome,
And rolling far along the gloomy shores
135 The voice of days of old and days to be.

Then spake King Arthur to Sir Bedivere,
And whiter than the mist that all day long
Had held the field of battle was the King:

"Hearest thou this great voice that shakes the world,
140 And wastes the narrow realm whereon we move,
And beats upon the faces of the dead,
My dead, as though they had not died for me?—
O Bedivere, for on my heart hath fallen
Confusion, till I know not what I am,
145 Nor whence I am, nor whether I be King.
Behold, I seem but King among the dead."

Then spake the bold Sir Bedivere: "My King,
King everywhere! and so the dead have kings,
There also will I worship thee as King.
150 Yet still thy life is whole, and still I live
Who love thee; but who hates thee, he that brought
The heathen back among us, yonder stands,
Modred, unharmed, the traitor of thine house."

Then spake the King: "My house hath been my doom.
155 But call not thou this traitor of my house
Who hath but dwelled beneath one roof with me.
My house are rather they who sware my vows,
Yea, even while they brake them, owned° me King.   acknowledged
And well for thee, saying in my dark hour,
160 When all the purport of my throne hath failed,
That quick or dead thou holdest me for King.
King am I, whatsoever be their cry;
And one last act of kinghood shalt thou see
Yet, ere I pass." And uttering this the King
165 Made at the man: then Modred smote his liege
Hard on that helm which many a heathen sword
Had beaten thin; while Arthur at one blow,
Striking the last stroke with Excalibur,
Slew him, and all but slain himself, he fell.

170   So all day long the noise of battle rolled
       Among the mountains by the winter sea;
       Until King Arthur's Table, man by man,
       Had fallen in Lyonnesse about their lord,
       King Arthur. Then, because his wound was deep,
175   The bold Sir Bedivere uplifted him,
       And bore him to a chapel nigh the field,
       A broken chancel with a broken cross,
       That stood on a dark strait of barren land:
       On one side lay the Ocean, and on one
180   Lay a great water, and the moon was full.

       Then spake King Arthur to Sir Bedivere:
       "The sequel of today unsolders all
       The goodliest fellowship of famous knights
       Whereof this world holds record. Such a sleep
185   They sleep—the men I loved. I think that we
       Shall never more, at any future time,
       Delight our souls with talk of knightly deeds,
       Walking about the gardens and the halls
       Of Camelot, as in the days that were.
190   I perish by this people which I made,—
       Though Merlin sware that I should come again
       To rule once more;[9] but, let what will be, be,
       I am so deeply smitten through the helm
       That without help I cannot last til morn.
195   Thou therefore take my brand Excalibur,
       Which was my pride: for thou rememberest how
       In those old days, one summer noon, an arm
       Rose up from out the bosom of the lake,
       Clothed in white samite,[1] mystic, wonderful,
200   Holding the sword—and how I rowed across
       And took it, and have worn it, like a king;
       And, wheresoever I am sung or told
       In aftertime, this also shall be known:
       But now delay not: take Excalibur,
205   And fling him far into the middle mere:°   *middle of the lake*
       Watch what thou seëst, and lightly° bring me word."   *quickly*

       To him replied the bold Sir Bedivere:
       "It is not meet,° Sir King, to leave thee thus,   *fitting*
       Aidless, alone, and smitten through the helm—
210   A little thing may harm a wounded man;
       Yet I thy hest° will all perform at full,   *command*
       Watch what I see, and lightly bring thee word."

       So saying, from the ruined shrine he stepped,
       And in the moon athwart° the place of tombs,   *across*
215   Where lay the mighty bones of ancient men,

9. Cf. Malory, *Morte Darthur* 21.7: "Some men yet say in many parts of England that King Arthur is not dead, but by the will of our Lord in another place. And men say that he will come again."
1. A rich silk fabric.

Old knights, and over them the sea-wind sang
Shrill, chill, with flakes of foam. He, stepping down
By zigzag paths, and juts of pointed rock,
Came on the shining levels of the lake.

220   There drew he forth the brand Excalibur,
And o'er him, drawing it, the winter moon,
Brightening the skirts of a long cloud, ran forth
And sparkled keen with frost against the hilt:
For all the haft° twinkled with diamond sparks,   hilt
225   Myriads of topaz-lights, and jacinth°-work   red gem
Of subtlest jewelry. He gazed so long
That both his eyes were dazzled as he stood,
This way and that dividing the swift mind,
In act to throw: but at the last it seemed
230   Better to leave Excalibur concealed
There in the many-knotted waterflags,
That whistled stiff and dry about the marge.°   shore
So strode he back slow to the wounded King.

      Then spake King Arthur to Sir Bedivere:
235   "Hast thou performed my mission which I gave?
What is it thou hast seen? or what hast heard?"
      And answer made the bold Sir Bedivere:
"I heard the ripple washing in the reeds,
And the wild water lapping on the crag."

240   To whom replied King Arthur, faint and pale:
"Thou hast betrayed thy nature and thy name,
Not rendering true answer, as beseemed
Thy fëalty, nor like a noble knight:
For surer sign had followed, either hand,
245   Or voice, or else a motion of the mere.
This is a shameful thing for men to lie.
Yet now, I charge thee, quickly go again,
As thou art lief° and dear, and do the thing   beloved
I bade thee, watch, and lightly bring me word."

250   Then went Sir Bedivere the second time
Across the ridge, and paced beside the mere,
Counting the dewy pebbles, fixed in thought;
But when he saw the wonder of the hilt,
How curiously and strangely chased,[2] he smote
255   His palms together, and he cried aloud:

      "And if indeed I cast the brand away,
Surely a precious thing, one worthy note,
Should thus be lost forever from the earth,
Which might have pleased the eyes of many men.
260   What good should follow this, if this were done?
What harm, undone? Deep harm to disobey,
Seeing obedience is the bond of rule.

2. Decorated. "Curiously": skillfully.

Were it well to obey then, if a king demand
An act unprofitable, against himself?
265 The King is sick, and knows not what he does.
What record, or what relic of my lord
Should be to aftertime, but empty breath
And rumors of a doubt? But were this kept,
Stored in some treasure-house of mighty kings,
270 Some one might show it at a joust of arms,
Saying, 'King Arthur's sword, Excalibur,
Wrought by the lonely maiden of the Lake.
Nine years she wrought it, sitting in the deeps
Upon the hidden bases of the hills.'
275 So might some old man speak in the aftertime
To all the people, winning reverence.
But now much honor and much fame were lost."

So spake he, clouded with his own conceit,[3]
And hid Excalibur the second time,
280 And so strode back slow to the wounded king.

Then spoke King Arthur, breathing heavily:
"What is it thou hast seen? or what hast heard?"

And answer made the bold Sir Bedivere:
"I heard the water lapping on the crag,
285 And the long ripple washing in the reeds."

To whom replied King Arthur, much in wrath:
"Ah, miserable and unkind, untrue,
Unknightly, traitor-hearted! Woe is me!
Authority forgets a dying king,
290 Laid widowed of the power in his eye
That bowed the will. I see thee what thou art,
For thou, the latest-left of all my knights,
In whom should meet the offices of all,
Thou wouldst betray me for the precious hilt;
295 Either from lust of gold, or like a girl
Valuing the giddy pleasure of the eyes.
Yet, for a man may fail in duty twice,
And the third time may prosper, get thee hence:
But, if thou spare to fling Excalibur,
300 I will arise and slay thee with my hands."

Then quickly rose Sir Bedivere, and ran,
And, leaping down the ridges lightly, plunged
Among the bullrush beds, and clutched the sword,
And strongly wheeled and threw it. The great brand
305 Made lightnings in the splendor of the moon,
And flashing round and round and whirled in an arch,
Shot like a streamer of the northern morn,[4]
Seen where the moving isles of winter shock[5]

3. Vain and foolish fancies.
4. The northern lights.

5. Where the icebergs collide.

By night, with noises of the Northern Sea.
310 So flashed and fell the brand Excalibur:
But ere he dipped the surface, rose an arm
Clothed in white samite, mystic, wonderful,
And caught him by the hilt, and brandished him
Three times, and drew him under in the mere.
315 And lightly went the other to the King.

Then spoke King Arthur, drawing thicker breath:
"Now see I by thine eyes that this is done.
Speak out: what is it thou hast heard, or seen?"

And answer made the bold Sir Bedivere:
320 "Sir King, I closed mine eyelids, lest the gems
Should blind my purpose, for I never saw,
Nor shall see, here or elsewhere, till I die,
Not though I live three lives of mortal men,
So great a miracle as yonder hilt,
325 Then with both hands I flung him, wheeling him;
But when I looked again, behold an arm,
Clothed in white samite, mystic, wonderful,
That caught him by the hilt, and brandished him
Three times, and drew him under in the mere."

330 And answer made King Arthur, breathing hard:
"My end draws nigh; 'tis time that I were gone.
Make broad thy shoulders to receive my weight,
And bear me to the margin; yet I fear
My wound hath taken cold, and I shall die."

335 So saying, from the pavement he half rose,
Slowly, with pain, reclining on his arm,
And looking wistfully with wide blue eyes
As in a picture. Him Sir Bedivere
Remorsefully regarded through his tears,
340 And would have spoken, but he found not words;
Then took with care, and kneeling on one knee,
O'er both his shoulders drew the languid hands,
And rising bore him through the place of tombs.

But, as he walked, King Arthur panted hard,
345 Like one that feels a nightmare on his bed
When all the house is mute. So sighed the King,
Muttering and murmuring at his ear, "Quick, quick!
I fear it is too late, and I shall die."
But the other swiftly strode from ridge to ridge,
350 Clothed with his breath, and looking, as he walked,
Larger than human on the frozen hills.
He heard the deep behind him, and a cry
Before. His own thought drove him like a goad.
Dry clashed his harness in the icy caves
355 And barren chasms, and all to left and right
The bare black cliff clanged round him, as he based

His feet on juts of slippery crag that rang
Sharp-smitten with the dint of armèd heels—
And on a sudden, lo! the level lake,
360   And the long glories of the winter moon.

Then saw they how there hove a dusky barge,
Dark as a funeral scarf from stem to stern,
Beneath them; and descending they were ware°   *aware*
That all the decks were dense with stately forms,
365   Black-stoled, black-hooded, like a dream—by these
Three Queens with crowns of gold: and from them rose
A cry that shivered to the tingling stars,
And, as it were one voice, an agony
Of lamentation, like a wind that shrills
370   All night in a waste land, where no one comes,
Or hath come, since the making of the world.

Then murmured Arthur, "Place me in the barge."
So to the barge they came. There those three Queens
Put forth their hands, and took the King, and wept.
375   But she, that rose the tallest of them all
And fairest, laid his head upon her lap,
And loosed the shattered casque,° and chafed his hands,   *helmet*
And called him by his name, complaining loud,
And dropping bitter tears against a brow
380   Striped with dark blood: for all his face was white
And colorless, and like the withered moon
Smote by the fresh beam of the springing east;
And all his greaves and cuisses[6] dashed with drops
Of onset;[7] and the light and lustrous curls—
385   That made his forehead like a rising sun
High from the daïs-throne—were parched with dust;
Or, clotted into points and hanging loose,
Mixed with the knightly growth that fringed his lips.
So like a shattered column lay the King;
390   Not like that Arthur who, with lance in rest,
From spur to plume a star of tournament,
Shot through the lists at Camelot, and charged
Before the eyes of ladies and of kings.

Then loudly cried the bold Sir Bedivere:
395   "Ah! my Lord Arthur, whither shall I go?
Where shall I hide my forehead and my eyes?
For now I see the true old times are dead,
When every morning brought a noble chance,
And every chance brought out a noble knight.
400   Such times have been not since the light[8] that led
The holy Elders with the gift of myrrh.
But now the whole Round Table is dissolved

6. Armor to protect the front of the thighs.
"Greaves": armor to protect the leg below the knee.
7. Blood from battle.

8. I.e., the star that guided the three kings
("Elders") to the infant Jesus at Bethlehem. See
Matthew 2.1–12.

Which was an image of the mighty world,
And I, the last, go forth companionless,
405   And the days darken round me, and the years,
Among new men, strange faces, other minds."

      And slowly answered Arthur from the barge:
"The old order changeth, yielding place to new,
And God fulfills himself in many ways,
410   Lest one good custom should corrupt the world.
Comfort thyself: what comfort is in me?
I have lived my life, and that which I have done
May He within himself make pure! but thou,
If thou shouldst never see my face again,
415   Pray for my soul. More things are wrought by prayer
Than this world dreams of. Wherefore, let thy voice
Rise like a fountain for me night and day.
For what are men better than sheep or goats
That nourish a blind life within the brain,
420   If, knowing God, they lift not hands of prayer
Both for themselves and those who call them friend?
For so the whole round earth is every way
Bound by gold chains about the feet of God.
But now farewell. I am going a long way
425   With these thou seëst—if indeed I go
(For all my mind is clouded with a doubt)—
To the island-valley of Avilion;⁹
Where falls not hail, or rain, or any snow,
Nor ever wind blows loudly: but it lies
430   Deep-meadowed, happy, fair with orchard lawns
And bowery hollows crowned with summer sea,
Where I will heal me of my grievous wound."

      So said he, and the barge with oar and sail
Moved from the brink, like some full-breasted swan
435   That, fluting a wild carol ere her death,
Ruffles her pure cold plume, and takes the flood
With swarthy webs.° Long stood Sir Bedivere   *webbed feet*
Revolving many memories, till the hull
Looked one black dot against the verge of dawn,
440   And on the mere the wailing died away.

      But when that moan had passed for evermore,
The stillness of the dead world's winter dawn
Amazed him, and he groaned, "The King is gone."
And therewithal came on him the weird rhyme,¹
445   "From the great deep to the great deep he goes."

      Whereat he slowly turned and slowly clomb
The last hard footstep of that iron crag;
Thence marked the black hull moving yet, and cried,

---

9. Or Avalon; in Celtic mythology and medieval
romance, the Vale of the Blessed where heroes
enjoyed life after death.

1. In *The Coming of Arthur*, lines 402–10, Merlin
speaks a mysterious prophecy, in verse, concerning
Arthur's birth.

"He passes to be King among the dead,
450 And after healing of his grievous wound
He comes again; but—if he come no more—
O me, be yon dark Queens in yon black boat,
Who shrieked and wailed, the three whereat we gazed
On that high day, when, clothed with living light,
455 They stood before his throne in silence, friends
Of Arthur, who should help him at his need?"[2]

Then from the dawn it seemed there came, but faint
As from beyond the limit of the world,
Like the last echo born of a great cry,
460 Sounds, as if some fair city were one voice
Around a king returning from his wars.

Thereat once more he moved about, and clomb
Even to the highest he could climb, and saw,
Straining his eyes beneath an arch of hand,
465 Or thought he saw, the speck that bare the King,
Down that long water opening on the deep
Somewhere far off, pass on and on, and go
From less to less and vanish into light.
And the new sun rose bringing the new year.

1833–69   1869

Crossing the Bar[1]

Sunset and evening star,
    And one clear call for me!
And may there be no moaning of the bar,[2]
    When I put out to sea,

5   But such a tide as moving seems asleep,
    Too full for sound and foam,
When that which drew from out the boundless deep
    Turns again home.

Twilight and evening bell,
10   And after that the dark!
And may there be no sadness of farewell,
    When I embark;

For though from out our bourne° of Time and Place   *boundary*
    The flood may bear me far,
15 I hope to see my Pilot face to face
    When I have crossed the bar.

1889   1889

---

2. In *The Coming of Arthur*, lines 275–78, Arthur's half-sister Bellicent describes his coronation.
1. Although not the last poem written by Tenny-son, "Crossing the Bar" appears, at his request, as the final poem in all collections of his work.
2. Mournful sound of the ocean beating on a sand bar at the mouth of a harbor.

ELIZABETH GASKELL
1810–1865

It is ironic that the writer whom contemporaries and future generations knew as "Mrs. Gaskell" once instructed her sister-in-law that it was "a silly piece of bride-like affectation not to sign yourself by your proper name." Despite the wifely identity that the name Mrs. Gaskell connotes, Elizabeth Gaskell, as she always signed herself, wrote fiction on contemporary social topics that stimulated considerable controversy. Her first novel, *Mary Barton* (1848), presents a sympathetic picture of the hardships and the grievances of the working class. Another early novel, *Ruth* (1853), portrays the seduction and rehabilitation of an unmarried mother.

Elizabeth Cleghorn Gaskell was born in 1810 in Chelsea, on the outskirts of London, to a family that followed Unitarianism, a Christian movement that rejected the doctrine of the Trinity and advocated religious tolerance. Her mother died when Gaskell was one, and the girl was sent to rural Knutsford, in Cheshire, to be raised by her aunt. At the age of twenty-one, she met and married William Gaskell, a Unitarian minister whose chapel was in the industrial city of Manchester. For the first ten years of her marriage, she led the life of a minister's wife, bearing five children, keeping a house, and helping her husband serve his congregation. When her fourth child and only son, William, died at the age of one year, Gaskell became depressed. Her husband encouraged her to write as a way of allaying her grief, and so she produced *Mary Barton*, subtitled *A Tale of Manchester Life*. In the preface to the novel, she wrote that she was inspired by thinking "how deep might be the romance in the lives of some of those who elbowed me daily in the busy streets of the town in which I resided. I had always felt a deep sympathy with the careworn men, who looked as if doomed to struggle through their lives in strange alternations between work and want." Observing the mutual distrust of the rich and the poor, and their accompanying resentments, Gaskell hoped that her novel would help create within her middle-class readership understanding and sympathy for the working classes.

Anonymously published, the novel was widely reviewed and discussed. Gaskell was soon identified as the author; she subsequently developed a wide acquaintance in literary circles. She wrote five more novels and about thirty short stories, many of which were published in Charles Dickens's journal *Household Words* and its successor, *All the Year Round*. The contrasting experiences Gaskell's life had given her of two ways of life, of rural Knutsford and industrial Manchester, defined the poles of her fiction. Her second novel, *Cranford* (1853), presents a delicate picture of the small events of country village life, a subject to which she returns with greater range and psychological depth in her last novel, *Wives and Daughters* (1866). In *North and South* (1855), Gaskell brings together the two worlds of her fiction in the story of Margaret Hale, a young woman from a village in the south of England who moves to a factory town in the north.

One of the writers Gaskell's literary fame led her to know was Charlotte Brontë, with whom she became friends. When Brontë died in 1855, Gaskell was approached by Patrick Brontë to write the story of his daughter's life. Gaskell's *Life of Charlotte Brontë* (1857) is a masterpiece of English biography and one of her finest portrayals of character. Her focus in the *Life* on the relationship between Brontë's identity as a writer and her role as daughter, sister, and wife reflects the balance Gaskell herself sought between the stories she wove and the people she cared for. Referred to by Dickens as "my dear Scheherazade," Gaskell wrote not just to entertain but also to critique society and to promote social reform.

The Old Nurse's Story[1]

You know, my dears, that your mother was an orphan, and an only child; and I dare say you have heard that your grandfather was a clergyman up in Westmoreland, where I come from. I was just a girl in the village school, when, one day, your grandmother came in to ask the mistress if there was any scholar there who would do for a nurse-maid; and mighty proud I was, I can tell ye, when the mistress called me up, and spoke to my being a good girl at my needle, and a steady honest girl, and one whose parents were very respectable, though they might be poor. I thought I should like nothing better than to serve the pretty young lady, who was blushing as deep as I was, as she spoke of the coming baby, and what I should have to do with it. However, I see you don't care so much for this part of my story, as for what you think is to come, so I'll tell you at once I was engaged,[2] and settled at the parsonage before Miss Rosamond (that was the baby, who is now your mother) was born. To be sure, I had little enough to do with her when she came, for she was never out of her mother's arms, and slept by her all night long; and proud enough was I sometimes when missis trusted her to me. There never was such a baby before or since, though you've all of you been fine enough in your turns; but for sweet winning ways, you've none of you come up to your mother. She took after her mother, who was a real lady born; a Miss Furnivall, a granddaughter of Lord Furnivall's in Northumberland. I believe she had neither brother nor sister, and had been brought up in my lord's family till she had married your grandfather, who was just a curate, son to a shopkeeper in Carlisle—but a clever fine gentleman as ever was—and one who was a right-down hard worker in his parish, which was very wide, and scattered all abroad over the Westmoreland Fells. When your mother, little Miss Rosamond, was about four or five years old, both her parents died in a fortnight—one after the other. Ah! that was a sad time. My pretty young mistress and me was looking for another baby, when my master came home from one of his long rides, wet and tired, and took the fever he died of; and then she never held up her head again, but just lived to see her dead baby, and have it laid on her breast before she sighed away her life. My mistress had asked me, on her death-bed, never to leave Miss Rosamond; but if she had never spoken a word, I would have gone with the little child to the end of the world.

The next thing, and before we had well stilled our sobs, the executors and guardians came to settle the affairs. They were my poor young mistress's own cousin, Lord Furnivall, and Mr. Esthwaite, my master's brother, a shopkeeper in Manchester; not so well to do then, as he was afterwards, and with a large family rising about him. Well! I don't know if it were their settling, or because of a letter my mistress wrote on her death-bed to her cousin, my lord; but somehow it was settled that Miss Rosamond and me were to go to Furnivall Manor House, in Northumberland, and my lord spoke as if it had been her mother's wish that she should live with his family, and as if he had no objections, for that one or two more or less could make no difference in so grand a household. So, though that was not the way in which I should have wished

1. Originally published anonymously in the 1852 Christmas number of Dickens's journal *Household Words*; it was later republished in Gaskell's *Lizzie*

Leigh, and Other Tales (1855).
2. Hired.

the coming of my bright and pretty pet to have been looked at—who was like a sunbeam in any family, be it never so grand—I was well pleased that all the folks in the Dale should stare and admire, when they heard I was going to be young lady's maid at my Lord Furnivall's at Furnivall Manor.

But I made a mistake in thinking we were to go and live where my lord did. It turned out that the family had left Furnivall Manor House fifty years or more. I could not hear that my poor young mistress had ever been there, though she had been brought up in the family; and I was sorry for that, for I should have liked Miss Rosamond's youth to have passed where her mother's had been.

My lord's gentleman, from whom I asked as many questions as I durst, said that the Manor House was at the foot of the Cumberland Fells, and a very grand place; that an old Miss Furnivall, a great-aunt of my lord's, lived there, with only a few servants; but that it was a very healthy place, and my lord had thought that it would suit Miss Rosamond very well for a few years, and that her being there might perhaps amuse his old aunt.

I was bidden by my lord to have Miss Rosamond's things ready by a certain day. He was a stern, proud man, as they say all the Lord Furnivalls were; and he never spoke a word more than was necessary. Folk did say he had loved my young mistress; but that, because she knew that his father would object, she would never listen to him, and married Mr. Esthwaite; but I don't know. He never married at any rate. But he never took much notice of Miss Rosamond; which I thought he might have done if he had cared for her dead mother. He sent his gentleman with us to the Manor House, telling him to join him at Newcastle that same evening; so there was no great length of time for him to make us known to all the strangers before he, too, shook us off; and we were left, two lonely young things (I was not eighteen), in the great old Manor House. It seems like yesterday that we drove there. We had left our own dear parsonage very early, and we had both cried as if our hearts would break, though we were travelling in my lord's carriage, which I had thought so much of once. And now it was long past noon on a September day, and we stopped to change horses for the last time at a little smoky town, all full of colliers and miners. Miss Rosamond had fallen asleep, but Mr. Henry told me to waken her, that she might see the park and the Manor House as we drove up. I thought it rather a pity; but I did what he bade me, for fear he should complain of me to my lord. We had left all signs of a town or even a village, and were then inside the gates of a large wild park—not like the parks here in the south, but with rocks, and the noise of running water, and gnarled thorn-trees, and old oaks, all white and peeled with age.

The road went up about two miles, and then we saw a great and stately house, with many trees close around it, so close that in some places their branches dragged against the walls when the wind blew; and some hung broken down; for no one seemed to take much charge of the place;—to lop the wood, or to keep the moss-covered carriage-way in order. Only in front of the house all was clear. The great oval drive was without a weed; and neither tree nor creeper was allowed to grow over the long, many-windowed front; at both sides of which a wing projected, which were each the ends of other side fronts; for the house, although it was so desolate, was even grander than I expected. Behind it rose the Fells, which seemed unenclosed and bare enough; and on the left hand of the house as you stood facing it, was a little old-fashioned flower-garden, as I found out afterwards. A door opened out upon it from the west front; it had been scooped out of the thick dark wood for some old Lady Furnivall; but the branches of the great forest trees had grown and over-shadowed it again, and there were very few flowers that would live there at that time.

When we drove up to the great front entrance, and went into the hall I thought we should be lost—it was so large, and vast, and grand. There was a chandelier all of bronze, hung down from the middle of the ceiling; and I had never seen one before, and looked at it all in amaze. Then, at one end of the hall, was a great fire-place, as large as the sides of the houses in my country, with massy andirons and dogs[3] to hold the wood; and by it were heavy old-fashioned sofas. At the opposite end of the hall, to the left as you went in—on the western side—was an organ built into the wall, and so large that it filled up the best part of that end. Beyond it, on the same side, was a door; and opposite, on each side of the fire-place, were also doors leading to the east front; but those I never went through as long as I stayed in the house, so I can't tell you what lay beyond.

The afternoon was closing in, and the hall, which had no fire lighted in it, looked dark and gloomy; but we did not stay there a moment. The old servant who had opened the door for us bowed to Mr. Henry, and took us in through the door at the further side of the great organ, and led us through several smaller halls and passages into the west drawing-room, where he said that Miss Furnivall was sitting. Poor little Miss Rosamond held very tight to me, as if she were scared and lost in that great place, and, as for myself, I was not much better. The west drawing-room was very cheerful-looking, with a warm fire in it, and plenty of good comfortable furniture about. Miss Furnivall was an old lady not far from eighty, I should think, but I do not know. She was thin and tall, and had a face as full of fine wrinkles as if they had been drawn all over it with a needle's point. Her eyes were very watchful, to make up, I suppose, for her being so deaf as to be obliged to use a trumpet.[4] Sitting with her, working at the same great piece of tapestry, was Mrs. Stark, her maid and companion, and almost as old as she was. She had lived with Miss Furnivall ever since they both were young, and now she seemed more like a friend than a servant; she looked so cold and grey, and stony, as if she had never loved or cared for any one; and I don't suppose she did care for any one, except her mistress; and, owing to the great deafness of the latter, Mrs. Stark treated her very much as if she were a child. Mr. Henry gave some message from my lord, and then he bowed good-bye to us all,—taking no notice of my sweet little Miss Rosamond's out-stretched hand—and left us standing there, being looked at by the two old ladies through their spectacles.

I was right glad when they rung for the old footman who had shown us in at first, and told him to take us to our rooms. So we went out of that great drawing-room, and into another sitting-room, and out of that, and then up a great flight of stairs, and along a broad gallery—which was something like a library, having books all down one side, and windows and writing-tables all down the other—till we came to our rooms, which I was not sorry to hear were just over the kitchens; for I began to think I should be lost in that wil-derness of a house. There was an old nursery, that had been used for all the little lords and ladies long ago, with a pleasant fire burning in the grate, and

3. Large decorative fireplace supports.
4. A horn-shaped device used by the hard of hearing to amplify sound.

the kettle boiling on the hob, and tea things spread out on the table; and out of that room was the night-nursery, with a little crib for Miss Rosamond close to my bed. And old James called up Dorothy, his wife, to bid us welcome; and both he and she were so hospitable and kind, that by-and-by Miss Rosamond and me felt quite at home; and by the time tea was over, she was sitting on Dorothy's knee, and chattering away as fast as her little tongue could go. I soon found out that Dorothy was from Westmoreland, and that bound her and me together, as it were; and I would never wish to meet with kinder people than were old James and his wife. James had lived pretty nearly all his life in my lord's family, and thought there was no one so grand as they. He even looked down a little on his wife; because, till he had married her, she had never lived in any but a farmer's household. But he was very fond of her, as well he might be. They had one servant under them, to do all the rough work. Agnes they called her; and she and me, and James and Dorothy, with Miss Furnivall and Mrs. Stark, made up the family; always remembering my sweet little Miss Rosamond! I used to wonder what they had done before she came, they thought so much of her now. Kitchen and drawing-room, it was all the same. The hard, sad Miss Furnivall, and the cold Mrs. Stark, looked pleased when she came fluttering in like a bird, playing and pranking hither and thither, with a continual murmur, and pretty prattle of gladness. I am sure, they were sorry many a time when she flitted away into the kitchen, though they were too proud to ask her to stay with them, and were a little surprised at her taste; though, to be sure, as Mrs. Stark said, it was not to be wondered at, remembering what stock her father had come of. The great, old rambling house, was a famous[5] place for little Miss Rosamond. She made expeditions all over it, with me at her heels; all, except the east wing, which was never opened, and whither we never thought of going. But in the western and north-ern part was many a pleasant room; full of things that were curiosities to us, though they might not have been to people who had seen more. The windows were darkened by the sweeping boughs of the trees, and the ivy which had overgrown them: but, in the green gloom, we could manage to see old China jars and carved ivory boxes, and great heavy books, and, above all, the old pictures!

Once, I remember, my darling would have Dorothy go with us to tell us who they all were; for they were all portraits of some of my lord's family, though Dorothy could not tell us the names of every one. We had gone through most of the rooms, when we came to the old state drawing-room over the hall, and there was a picture of Miss Furnivall; or, as she was called in those days, Miss Grace, for she was the younger sister. Such a beauty she must have been! but with such a set, proud look, and such scorn looking out of her handsome eyes, with her eyebrows just a little raised, as if she wondered how any one could have the impertinence to look at her; and her lip curled at us, as we stood there gazing. She had a dress on, the like of which I had never seen before, but it was all the fashion when she was young; a hat of some soft white stuff like beaver, pulled a little over her brows, and a beautiful plume of feathers sweeping round it on one side; and her gown of blue satin was open in front to a quilted white stomacher.[6]

---

5. Exciting, wonderful.
6. Ornamental covering for the front of the body.

"Beaver": felted wool.

"Well, to be sure!" said I, when I had gazed my fill. "Flesh is grass,[7] they do say; but who would have thought that Miss Furnivall had been such an out-and-out beauty, to see her now?"

"Yes," said Dorothy. "Folks change sadly. But if what my master's father used to say was true, Miss Furnivall, the elder sister, was handsomer than Miss Grace. Her picture is here somewhere; but, if I show it you, you must never let on, even to James, that you have seen it. Can the little lady hold her tongue, think you?" asked she.

I was not so sure, for she was such a little sweet, bold, open-spoken child, so I set her to hide herself; and then I helped Dorothy to turn a great picture, that leaned with its face towards the wall, and was not hung up as the others were. To be sure, it beat Miss Grace for beauty; and, I think, for scornful pride, too, though in that matter it might be hard to choose. I could have looked at it an hour, but Dorothy seemed half frightened of having shown it to me, and hurried it back again, and bade me run and find Miss Rosamond, for that there were some ugly places about the house, where she should like ill for the child to go. I was a brave, high-spirited girl, and thought little of what the old woman said, for I liked hide-and-seek as well as any child in the parish; so off I ran to find my little one.

As winter drew on, and the days grew shorter, I was sometimes almost certain that I heard a noise as if some one was playing on the great organ in the hall. I did not hear it every evening; but, certainly, I did very often; usually when I was sitting with Miss Rosamond, after I had put her to bed, and keeping quite still and silent in the bedroom. Then I used to hear it booming and swelling away in the distance. The first night, when I went down to my supper, I asked Dorothy who had been playing music, and James said very shortly that I was a gowk to take the wind soughing[8] among the trees for music; but I saw Dorothy look at him very fearfully, and Bessy, the kitchen-maid, said something beneath her breath, and went quite white. I saw they did not like my question, so I held my peace till I was with Dorothy alone, when I knew I could get a good deal out of her. So, the next day, I watched my time, and I coaxed and asked her who it was that played the organ; for I knew that it was the organ and not the wind well enough, for all I had kept silence before James. But Dorothy had had her lesson, I'll warrant, and never a word could I get from her. So then I tried Bessy, though I had always held my head rather above her, as I was evened[9] to James and Dorothy, and she was little better than their servant. So she said I must never, never tell; and, if I ever told, I was never to say *she* had told me; but it was a very strange noise, and she had heard it many a time, but most of all on winter nights, and before storms; and folks did say, it was the old lord playing on the great organ in the hall, just as he used to do when he was alive; but who the old lord was, or why he played, and why he played on stormy winter evenings in particular, she either could not or would not tell me. Well! I told you I had a brave heart; and I thought it was rather pleasant to have that grand music rolling about the house, let who would be the player; for now it rose above the great gusts of wind, and wailed and triumphed just like a living creature, and then it fell to a softness most complete; only it was always music and tunes, so it was nonsense to call

7. Cf. 1 Peter 1.24 ("For all flesh is as grass, and all the glory of men as the flower of grass. The grass withereth, and the flower thereof falleth away").

8. Moaning. "Shortly": curtly. "Gowk": fool.
9. Of equal status.

it the wind. I thought, at first, it might be Miss Furnivall who played, unknown to Bessy; but, one day when I was in the hall by myself, I opened the organ and peeped all about it, and around it, as I had done to the organ in Crosthwaite Church once before, and I saw it was all broken and destroyed inside, though it looked so brave[1] and fine; and then, though it was noon-day, my flesh began to creep a little, and I shut it up, and ran away pretty quickly to my own bright nursery; and I did not like hearing the music for some time after that, any more than James and Dorothy did. All this time Miss Rosamond was making herself more and more beloved. The old ladies liked her to dine with them at their early dinner; James stood behind Miss Furnivall's chair, and I behind Miss Rosamond's, all in state; and, after dinner, she would play about in a corner of the great drawing-room, as still as any mouse, while Miss Furnivall slept, and I had my dinner in the kitchen. But she was glad enough to come to me in the nursery afterwards; for, as she said, Miss Furnivall was so sad, and Mrs. Stark so dull; but she and I were merry enough; and, by-and-by, I got not to care for that weird rolling music, which did one no harm, if we did not know where it came from.

That winter was very cold. In the middle of October the frosts began, and lasted many, many weeks. I remember, one day at dinner, Miss Furnivall lifted up her sad, heavy eyes, and said to Mrs. Stark, "I am afraid we shall have a terrible winter," in a strange kind of meaning way. But Mrs. Stark pretended not to hear, and talked very loud of something else. My little lady and I did not care for the frost;—not we! As long as it was dry we climbed up the steep brows, behind the house, and went up on the Fells, which were bleak and bare enough, and there we ran races in the fresh, sharp air; and once we came down by a new path that took us past the two old gnarled holly-trees, which grew about half-way down by the east side of the house. But the days grew shorter and shorter; and the old lord, if it was he, played away more and more stormily and sadly on the great organ. One Sunday afternoon,—it must have been towards the end of November—I asked Dorothy to take charge of little Missey when she came out of the drawing-room, after Miss Furnivall had had her nap; for it was too cold to take her with me to church, and yet I wanted to go. And Dorothy was glad enough to promise, and was so fond of the child that all seemed well; and Bessy and I set off very briskly, though the sky hung heavy and black over the white earth, as if the night had never fully gone away; and the air, though still, was very biting and keen.

"We shall have a fall of snow," said Bessy to me. And sure enough, even while we were in church, it came down thick, in great large flakes, so thick it almost darkened the windows. It had stopped snowing before we came out, but it lay soft, thick and deep beneath our feet, as we tramped home. Before we got to the hall the moon rose, and I think it was lighter then,—what with the moon, and what with the white dazzling snow—than it had been when we went to church, between two and three o'clock. I have not told you that Miss Furnivall and Mrs. Stark never went to church: they used to read the prayers together, in their quiet gloomy way; they seemed to feel the Sunday very long without their tapestry-work to be busy at. So when I went to Dorothy in the kitchen, to fetch Miss Rosamond and take her up-stairs with me, I did not much wonder when the old woman told me that the ladies had kept the child with them, and that she had never come to the kitchen, as I had bidden her,

1. Excellent.

when she was tired of behaving pretty in the drawing-room. So I took off my things and went to find her, and bring her to her supper in the nursery. But when I went into the best drawing-room, there sat the two old ladies, very still and quiet, dropping out a word now and then, but looking as if nothing so bright and merry as Miss Rosamond had ever been near them. Still I thought she might be hiding from me; it was one of her pretty ways; and that she had persuaded them to look as if they knew nothing about her; so I went softly peeping under this sofa, and behind that chair, making believe I was sadly frightened at not finding her.

"What's the matter, Hester?" said Mrs. Stark sharply. I don't know if Miss Furnivall had seen me, for, as I told you, she was very deaf, and she sat quite still, idly staring into the fire, with her hopeless face. "I'm only looking for my little Rosy-Posy," replied I, still thinking that the child was there, and near me, though I could not see her.

"Miss Rosamond is not here," said Mrs. Stark. "She went away more than an hour ago to find Dorothy." And she too turned and went on looking into the fire.

My heart sank at this, and I began to wish I had never left my darling. I went back to Dorothy and told her. James was gone out for the day, but she and me and Bessy took lights, and went up into the nursery first and then we roamed over the great large house, calling and entreating Miss Rosamond to come out of her hiding place, and not frighten us to death in that way. But there was no answer; no sound.

"Oh!" said I at last, "Can she have got into the east wing and hidden there?"

But Dorothy said it was not possible, for that she herself had never been in there; that the doors were always locked, and my lord's steward had the keys, she believed; at any rate, neither she nor James had ever seen them: so, I said I would go back and see if, after all, she was not hidden in the drawing-room, unknown to the old ladies; and if I found her there, I said, I would whip her well for the fright she had given me; but I never meant to do it. Well, I went back to the west drawing-room, and I told Mrs. Stark we could not find her anywhere, and asked for leave to look all about the furniture there, for I thought now, that she might have fallen asleep in some warm hidden corner; but no! we looked, Miss Furnivall got up and looked, trembling all over, and she was no where there; then we set off again, every one in the house, and looked in all the places we had searched before, but we could not find her. Miss Furnivall shivered and shook so much, that Mrs. Stark took her back into the warm drawing-room; but not before they had made me promise to bring her to them when she was found. Well-a-day! I began to think she never would be found, when I bethought me to look out into the great front court, all covered with snow. I was up-stairs when I looked out; but, it was such clear moonlight, I could see quite plain two little footprints, which might be traced from the hall door, and round the corner of the east wing. I don't know how I got down, but I tugged open the great, stiff hall door; and, throwing the skirt of my gown over my head for a cloak, I ran out. I turned the east corner, and there a black shadow fell on the snow; but when I came again into the moonlight, there were the little footmarks going up—up to the Fells. It was bitter cold; so cold that the air almost took the skin off my face as I ran, but I ran on, crying to think how my poor little darling must be perished[2] and frightened.

2. Extremely cold.

I was within sight of the holly-trees, when I saw a shepherd coming down the hill, bearing something in his arms wrapped in his maud.[3] He shouted to me, and asked me if I had lost a bairn;[4] and, when I could not speak for crying, he bore towards me, and I saw my wee bairnie lying still, and white, and stiff, in his arms, as if she had been dead. He told me he had been up the Fells to gather in his sheep, before the deep cold of night came on, and that under the holly-trees (black marks on the hill-side, where no other bush was for miles around) he had found my little lady—my lamb—my queen—my darling—stiff and cold, in the terrible sleep which is frost-begotten. Oh! the joy, and the tears of having her in my arms once again! for I would not let him carry her; but took her, maud and all, into my own arms, and held her near my own warm neck and heart, and felt the life stealing slowly back again into her little gentle limbs. But she was still insensible when we reached the hall, and I had no breath for speech. We went in by the kitchen door.

"Bring the warming-pan," said I; and I carried her up-stairs and began undressing her by the nursery fire, which Bessy had kept up. I called my little lammie all the sweet and playful names I could think of,—even while my eyes were blinded by my tears; and at last, oh! at length she opened her large blue eyes. Then I put her into her warm bed, and sent Dorothy down to tell Miss Furnivall that all was well; and I made up my mind to sit by my darling's bedside the live-long night. She fell away into a soft sleep as soon as her pretty head had touched the pillow, and I watched by her till morning light; when she wakened up bright and clear—or so I thought at first—and, my dears, so I think now.

She said, that she had fancied that she should like to go to Dorothy, for that both the old ladies were asleep, and it was very dull in the drawing-room; and that, as she was going through the west lobby, she saw the snow through the high window falling—falling—soft and steady; but she wanted to see it lying pretty and white on the ground; so she made her way into the great hall; and then, going to the window, she saw it bright and soft upon the drive; but while she stood there, she saw a little girl, not so old as she was, "but so pretty," said my darling, "and this little girl beckoned to me to come out; and oh, she was so pretty and so sweet, I could not choose but go." And then this other little girl had taken her by the hand, and side by side the two had gone round the east corner.

"Now you are a naughty little girl, and telling stories," said I. "What would your good mamma, that is in heaven, and never told a story in her life, say to her little Rosamond, if she heard her—and I dare say she does—telling stories!"

"Indeed, Hester," sobbed out my child; "I'm telling you true. Indeed I am."

"Don't tell me!" said I, very stern. "I tracked you by your foot-marks through the snow; there were only yours to be seen: and if you had had a little girl to go hand-in-hand with you up the hill, don't you think the foot-prints would have gone along with yours?"

"I can't help it, dear, dear Hester," said she, crying, "if they did not; I never looked at her feet, but she held my hand fast and tight in her little one, and it was very, very cold. She took me up the Fell-path, up to the holly trees; and there I saw a lady weeping and crying; but when she saw me, she hushed her

3. Shawl of gray plaid used by shepherds in the region.   4. Child.

weeping, and smiled very proud and grand, and took me on her knees, and began to lull me to sleep; and that's all, Hester—but that is true; and my dear mamma knows it is," said she, crying. So I thought the child was in a fever, and pretended to believe her, as she went over her story—over and over again, and always the same. At last Dorothy knocked at the door with Miss Rosamond's breakfast; and she told me the old ladies were down in the eating-parlour, and that they wanted to speak to me. They had both been into the night-nursery the evening before, but it was after Miss Rosamond was asleep; so they had only looked at her—not asked me any questions.

"I shall catch it," thought I to myself, as I went along the north gallery. "And yet," I thought, taking courage, "it was in their charge I left her; and it's they that's to blame for letting her steal away unknown and unwatched." So I went in boldly, and told my story. I told it all to Miss Furnivall, shouting it close to her ear; but when I came to the mention of the other little girl out in the snow, coaxing and tempting her out, and willing her up to the grand and beautiful lady by the Holly-tree, she threw her arms up—her old and withered arms—and cried aloud, "Oh! Heaven, forgive! Have mercy!"

Mrs. Stark took hold of her; roughly enough, I thought; but she was past Mrs. Stark's management, and spoke to me, in a kind of wild warning and authority.

"Hester! keep her from that child! It will lure her to her death! That evil child! Tell her it is a wicked, naughty child." Then, Mrs. Stark hurried me out of the room; where, indeed, I was glad enough to go; but Miss Furnivall kept shrieking out, "Oh! have mercy! Wilt Thou never forgive! It is many a long year ago——"

I was very uneasy in my mind after that. I durst never leave Miss Rosamond, night or day, for fear lest she might slip off again, after some fancy or other; and all the more, because I thought I could make out that Miss Furnivall was crazy, from their odd ways about her; and I was afraid lest something of the same kind (which might be in the family, you know) hung over my darling. And the great frost never ceased all this time; and, whenever it was a more stormy night than usual, between the gusts, and through the wind, we heard the old lord playing on the great organ. But, old lord, or not, wherever Miss Rosamond went, there I followed; for my love for her, pretty helpless orphan, was stronger than my fear for the grand and terrible sound. Besides, it rested with me to keep her cheerful and merry, as beseemed her age. So we played together, and wandered together, here and there, and everywhere; for I never dared to lose sight of her again in that large and rambling house. And so it happened, that one afternoon, not long before Christmas day, we were playing together on the billiard-table in the great hall (not that we knew the right way of playing, but she liked to roll the smooth ivory balls with her pretty hands, and I liked to do whatever she did); and, by-and-bye, without our noticing it, it grew dusk indoors, though it was still light in the open air, and I was thinking of taking her back into the nursery, when, all of a sudden, she cried out:

"Look, Hester! look! there is my poor little girl out in the snow!"

I turned towards the long narrow windows, and there, sure enough, I saw a little girl, less than my Miss Rosamond—dressed all unfit to be out-of-doors such a bitter night—crying, and beating against the window-panes, as if, she wanted to be let in. She seemed to sob and wail, till Miss Rosamond could bear it no longer, and was flying to the door to open it, when, all of a sudden, and close upon us, the great organ pealed out so loud and thundering, it fairly made me tremble; and all the more, when I remembered me that, even in the stillness of that dead-cold weather, I had heard no sound of little battering hands upon the window-glass, although the Phantom Child had seemed to put forth all its force; and, although I had seen it wail and cry, no faintest touch of sound had fallen upon my ears. Whether I remembered all this at the very moment, I do not know; the great organ sound had so stunned me into terror; but this I know, I caught up Miss Rosamond before she got the hall-door opened, and clutched her, and carried her away, kicking and scream-ing, into the large bright kitchen, where Dorothy and Agnes were busy with their mince-pies.

"What is the matter with my sweet one?" cried Dorothy, as I bore in Miss Rosamond, who was sobbing as if her heart would break.

"She won't let me open the door for my little girl to come in; and she'll die if she is out on the Fells all night. Cruel, naughty Hester," she said, slapping me; but she might have struck harder, for I had seen a look of ghastly terror on Dorothy's face, which made my very blood run cold.

"Shut the back kitchen door fast, and bolt it well," said she to Agnes. She said no more; she gave me raisins and almonds to quiet Miss Rosamond: but she sobbed about the little girl in the snow, and would not touch any of the good things. I was thankful when she cried herself to sleep in bed. Then I stole down to the kitchen, and told Dorothy I had made up my mind. I would carry my darling back to my father's house in Applethwaite; where, if we lived humbly, we lived at peace. I said I had been frightened enough with the old lord's organ-playing; but now, that I had seen for myself this little moaning child, all decked out as no child in the neighborhood could be, beating and battering to get in, yet always without any sound or noise—with the dark wound on its right shoulder; and that Miss Rosamond had known it again for the phantom that had nearly lured her to her death (which Dorothy knew was true); I would stand it no longer.

I saw Dorothy change color once or twice. When I had done, she told me she did not think I could take Miss Rosamond with me, for that she was my lord's ward, and I had no right over her; and she asked me, would I leave the child that I was so fond of, just for sounds and sights that could do me no harm; and that they had all had to get used to in their turns? I was all in a hot, trembling passion; and I said it was very well for her to talk, that knew what these sights and noises betokened, and that had, perhaps, had something to do with the Spectre-child while it was alive. And I taunted her so, that she told me all she knew, at last; and then I wished I had never been told, for it only made me more afraid than ever.

She said she had heard the tale from old neighbors, that were alive when she was first married; when folks used to come to the hall sometimes, before it had got such a bad name on the country side: it might not be true, or it might, what she had been told.

The old lord was Miss Furnivall's father—Miss Grace, as Dorothy called her, for Miss Maude was the elder, and Miss Furnivall by rights. The old lord was eaten up with pride. Such a proud man was never seen or heard of; and his daughters were like him. No one was good enough to wed them, although they had choice enough; for they were the great beauties of their day, as I had seen by their portraits, where they hung in the state drawing-room. But, as the old saying is, "Pride will have a fall;" and these two haughty beauties fell in love with the same man, and he no better than a foreign musician, whom their father had down from London to play music with him at the Manor House. For, above all things, next to his pride, the old lord loved music. He could play on nearly every instrument that ever was heard of; and it was a strange thing it did not soften him; but he was a fierce dour old man, and had broken his poor wife's heart with his cruelty, they said. He was mad after music, and would pay any money for it. So he got this foreigner to come; who made such beautiful music, that they said the very birds on the trees stopped their singing to listen. And, by degrees, this foreign gentleman got such a hold over the old lord, that nothing would serve him but that he must come every year; and it was he that had the great organ brought from Holland and built up in the hall, where it stood now. He taught the old lord to play on it; but many and many a time, when Lord Furnivall was thinking of nothing but his fine organ, and his finer music, the dark foreigner was walking abroad in the woods with one of the young ladies; now Miss Maude, and then Miss Grace.

Miss Maude won the day and carried off the prize, such as it was; and he and she were married, all unknown to any one; and before he made his next yearly visit, she had been confined of[5] a little girl at a farm-house on the Moors, while her father and Miss Grace thought she was away at Doncaster Races. But though she was a wife and a mother, she was not a bit softened, but as haughty and as passionate as ever; and perhaps more so, for she was jealous of Miss Grace, to whom her foreign husband paid a deal of court—by way of blinding her—as he told his wife. But Miss Grace triumphed over Miss Maude, and Miss Maude grew fiercer and fiercer, both with her husband and with her sister; and the former—who could easily shake off what was disagreeable, and hide himself in foreign countries—went away a month before his usual time that summer, and half threatened that he would never come back again. Meanwhile, the little girl was left at the farm-house, and her mother used to have her horse saddled and gallop wildly over the hills to see her once every week, at the very least—for where she loved, she loved; and where she hated, she hated. And the old lord went on playing—playing on his organ; and the servants thought the sweet music he made had soothed down his awful temper, of which (Dorothy said) some terrible tales could be told. He grew infirm too, and had to walk with a crutch; and his son—that was the present Lord Furnivall's father—was with the army in America, and the other son at sea; so Miss Maude had it pretty much her own way, and she and Miss Grace grew colder and bitterer to each other every day; till at last they hardly ever spoke, except when the old lord was by. The foreign musician came again the next summer, but it was for the last time; for they led him such a life with their jealousy and their passions, that he grew weary, and went away, and never was heard of again. And Miss Maude, who had always meant to have her marriage acknowledged when her father should be dead, was left now a deserted wife— whom nobody knew to have been married—with a child that she dared not own, although she loved it to distraction; living with a father whom she feared, and a sister whom she hated. When the next summer passed over and the dark foreigner never came, both Miss Maude and Miss Grace grew gloomy and sad; they had a haggard look about them, though they looked handsome as ever. But by and by Miss Maude brightened; for her father grew more and more infirm, and more than ever carried away by his music; and she and Miss Grace lived almost entirely apart, having separate rooms, the one on the west side—

5. Given birth to.

Miss Maude on the east—those very rooms which were now shut up. So she thought she might have her little girl with her, and no one need ever know except those who dared not speak about it, and were bound to believe that it was, as she said, a cottager's child she had taken a fancy to. All this, Dorothy said, was pretty well known; but what came afterwards no one knew, except Miss Grace, and Mrs. Stark, who was even then her maid, and much more of a friend to her than ever her sister had been. But the servants supposed, from words that were dropped, that Miss Maude had triumphed over Miss Grace, and told her that all the time the dark foreigner had been mocking her with pretended love—he was her own husband; the colour left Miss Grace's cheek and lips that very day for ever, and she was heard to say many a time that sooner or later she would have her revenge; and Mrs. Stark was for ever spying about the east rooms.

One fearful night, just after the New Year had come in, when the snow was lying thick and deep, and the flakes were still falling—fast enough to blind any one who might be out and abroad—there was a great and violent noise heard, and the old lord's voice above all, cursing and swearing awfully,—and the cries of a little child,—and the proud defiance of a fierce woman,—and the sound of a blow,—and a dead stillness,—and moans and wailings dying away on the hill-side! Then the old lord summoned all his servants, and told them, with terrible oaths, and words more terrible, that his daughter had disgraced herself, and that he had turned her out of doors,—her, and her child,—and that if ever they gave her help,—or food—or shelter,—he prayed that they might never enter Heaven. And, all the while, Miss Grace stood by him, white and still as any stone; and when he had ended she heaved a great sigh, as much as to say her work was done, and her end was accomplished. But the old lord never touched his organ again, and died within the year; and no wonder! for, on the morrow of that wild and fearful night, the shepherds, coming down the Fell side, found Miss Maude sitting, all crazy and smiling, under the holly-trees, nursing a dead child,—with a terrible mark on its right shoulder. "But that was not what killed it," said Dorothy; "it was the frost and the cold—every wild creature was in its hole, and every beast in its fold,—while the child and its mother were turned out to wander on the Fells! And now you know all! and I wonder if you are less frightened now?"

I was more frightened than ever; but I said I was not. I wished Miss Rosamond and myself well out of that dreadful house for ever; but I would not leave her, and I dared not take her away. But oh! how I watched her, and guarded her! We bolted the doors, and shut the window-shutters fast, an hour or more before dark, rather than leave them open five minutes too late. But my little lady still heard the weird child crying and mourning; and not all we could do or say, could keep her from wanting to go to her, and let her in from the cruel wind and the snow. All this time, I kept away from Miss Furnivall and Mrs. Stark, as much as ever I could; for I feared them—I knew no good could be about them, with their grey hard faces, and their dreamy eyes, looking back into the ghastly years that were gone. But, even in my fear, I had a kind of pity—for Miss Furnivall, at least. Those gone down to the pit[6] can hardly have a more hopeless look than that which was ever on her face. At last I even got so sorry for her—who never said a word but what was quite forced from her—that I prayed for her; and I taught Miss Rosamond to pray for one who

6. Hell.

had done a deadly sin; but often when she came to those words, she would listen, and start up from her knees, and say, "I hear my little girl plaining[7] and crying very sad—Oh! let her in, or she will die!"

One night—just after New Year's Day had come at last, and the long winter had taken a turn as I hoped—I heard the west drawing-room bell ring three times, which was the signal for me. I would not leave Miss Rosamond alone, for all she was asleep—for the old lord had been playing wilder than ever— and I feared lest my darling should waken to hear the spectre child; see her I knew she could not, I had fastened the windows too well for that. So, I took her out of her bed and wrapped her up in such outer clothes as were most handy, and carried her down to the drawing-room, where the old ladies sat at their tapestry work as usual. They looked up when I came in, and Mrs. Stark asked, quite astounded, "Why did I bring Miss Rosamond there, out of her warm bed?" I had begun to whisper, "Because I was afraid of her being tempted out while I was away, by the wild child in the snow," when she stopped me short (with a glance at Miss Furnivall) and said Miss Furnivall wanted me to undo some work she had done wrong, and which neither of them could see to unpick. So, I laid my pretty dear on the sofa, and sat down on a stool by them, and hardened my heart against them as I heard the wind rising and howling.

Miss Rosamond slept on sound, for all the wind blew so; and Miss Furnivall said never a word, nor looked round when the gusts shook the windows. All at once she started up to her full height, and put up one hand as if to bid us listen.

"I hear voices!" said she. "I hear terrible screams—I hear my father's voice!"

Just at that moment, my darling wakened with a sudden start: "My little girl is crying, oh, how she is crying!" and she tried to get up and go to her, but she got her feet entangled in the blanket, and I caught her up; for my flesh had begun to creep at these noises, which they heard while we could catch no sound. In a minute or two the noises came, and gathered fast, and filled our ears; we, too, heard voices and screams, and no longer heard the winter's wind that raged abroad. Mrs. Stark looked at me, and I at her, but we dared not speak. Suddenly Miss Furnivall went towards the door, out into the ante-room, through the west lobby, and opened the door into the great hall. Mrs. Stark followed, and I durst not be left, though my heart almost stopped beating for fear. I wrapped my darling tight in my arms, and went out with them. In the hall the screams were louder than ever; they sounded to come from the east wing—nearer and nearer—close on the other side of the locked-up doors— close behind them. Then I noticed that the great bronze chandelier seemed all alight, though the hall was dim, and that a fire was blazing in the vast hearth-place, though it gave no heat; and I shuddered up with terror, and folded my darling closer to me. But as I did so, the east door shook, and she, suddenly struggling to get free from me, cried, "Hester! I must go! My little girl is there; I hear her; she is coming! Hester, I must go!"

I held her tight with all my strength; with a set will, I held her. If I had died, my hands would have grasped her still; I was so resolved in my mind. Miss Furnivall stood listening, and paid no regard to my darling, who had got down to the ground, and whom I, upon my knees now, was holding with both my arms clasped round her neck; she still striving and crying to get free.

7. Lamenting.

All at once, the east door gave way with a thundering crash, as if torn open in a violent passion, and there came into that broad and mysterious light, the figure of a tall old man, with grey hair and gleaming eyes. He drove before him, with many a relentless gesture of abhorrence, a stern and beautiful woman, with a little child clinging to her dress.

"Oh Hester! Hester!" cried Miss Rosamond. "It's the lady! the lady below the holly-trees; and my little girl is with her. Hester! Hester! let me go to her; they are drawing me to them. I feel them—I feel them. I must go!"

Again she was almost convulsed by her efforts to get away; but I held her tighter and tighter; till I feared I should do her a hurt; but rather that than let her go towards those terrible phantoms. They passed along towards the great hall-door, where the winds howled and ravened for their prey; but before they reached that, the lady turned; and I could see that she defied the old man with a fierce and proud defiance; but then she quailed—and then she threw up her arms wildly and piteously to save her child—her little child—from a blow from his uplifted crutch.

And Miss Rosamond was torn as by a power stronger than mine, and writhed in my arms, and sobbed (for by this time the poor darling was growing faint).

"They want me to go with them on to the Fells—they are drawing me to them. Oh, my little girl! I would come, but cruel, wicked Hester holds me very tight." But when she saw the uplifted crutch she swooned away, and I thanked God for it. Just at this moment—when the tall old man, his hair streaming as in the blast of a furnace, was going to strike the little shrinking child—Miss Furnivall, the old woman by my side, cried out, "Oh, father! father! spare the little innocent child!" But just then I saw—we all saw—another phantom shape itself, and grow clear out of the blue and misty light that filled the hall; we had not seen her till now, for it was another lady who stood by the old man, with a look of relentless hate and triumphant scorn. That figure was very beautiful to look upon, with a soft white hat drawn down over the proud brows, and a red and curling lip. It was dressed in an open robe of blue satin. I had seen that figure before. It was the likeness of Miss Furnivall in her youth; and the terrible phantoms moved on, regardless of old Miss Furnivall's wild entreaty,—and the uplifted crutch fell on the right shoulder of the little child, and the younger sister looked on, stony and deadly serene. But at that moment, the dim lights, and the fire that gave no heat, went out of themselves, and Miss Furnivall lay at our feet stricken down by the palsy—death-stricken.

Yes! she was carried to her bed that night never to rise again. She lay with her face to the wall, muttering low but muttering alway: "Alas! alas! what is done in youth can never be undone in age! What is done in youth can never be undone in age!"

1852

ROBERT BROWNING
1812–1889

During the years of his marriage, Robert Browning was sometimes referred to as "Mrs. Browning's husband." Elizabeth Barrett was at that time a famous poet, whereas her husband was a relatively unknown experimenter whose poems were greeted with misunderstanding or indifference. Not until the 1860s did he at last gain a public and become recognized as the rival or equal of Alfred, Lord Tennyson. In the twentieth century his reputation persisted but in an unusual way: his poetry was admired by two groups of readers widely different in tastes. To one group, among whom were the Browning societies that flourished in England and America, Browning was a wise philosopher and religious teacher who resolved the doubts that troubled Matthew Arnold and Tennyson.

The second group of readers enjoyed Browning less for his attempt to solve problems of religious doubt than for his attempt to solve the problems of how poetry should be written. Poets such as Ezra Pound and Robert Lowell recognized that more than any other nineteenth-century poet, it was Browning who energetically hacked through a trail that subsequently became the main road of twentieth-century poetry. In *Poetry and the Age* (1953) Randall Jarrell remarked that "the dramatic monologue, which once had depended for its effect upon being a departure from the norm of poetry, now became in one form or another the norm."

The dramatic monologue, as Browning uses it, separates the speaker from the poet in such a way that the reader must work through the words of the speaker to discover the meaning of the poet. For example, in the well-known early monologue "My Last Duchess" (1842), we listen to the duke as he speaks of his dead wife. From his one-sided conversation we piece together the situation, both past and present, and we infer what sort of woman the duchess really was and what sort of man the duke is. Ultimately, we may also infer what the poet himself thinks of the speaker he has created. In this poem it is fairly easy to reach such a judgment, although the pleasure of the poem results from our reconstruction of a story quite different from the one the duke thinks he is telling. Many of Browning's poems are far less stable, and it is difficult to discern the relationship of the poet to his speaker. In reading "A Grammarian's Funeral" (1855), for example, can we be sure that the central character is a hero? Or is he merely a fool? In " 'Childe Roland to the Dark Tower Came' " (1855) is the speaker describing a phantasmagoric landscape of his own paranoid imagining, or is the poem a fable of courage and defiance in a modern wasteland?

In addition to his experiments with the dramatic monologue, Browning also experimented with language and syntax. The grotesque rhymes and jaw-breaking diction that he often employs have been repugnant to some critics; George Santayana, for instance, dismissed him as a clumsy barbarian. But to those who appreciate Browning, the incongruities of language are a humorous and appropriate counterpart to an imperfect world. Ezra Pound's tribute to "Old Hippety-Hop o' the accents," as he addresses Browning, is both affectionate and memorable:

> Heart that was big as the bowels of Vesuvius
> Words that were winged as her sparks in eruption,
> Eagled and thundered as Jupiter Pluvius
> Sound in your wind past all signs o' corruption.

Robert Browning was born in Camberwell, a London suburb. His father, a bank clerk, was a learned man with an extensive library. His mother was a kindly, religious-minded woman, interested in music, whose love for her brilliant son was warmly reciprocated. Until the time of his marriage, at the age of thirty-four, Browning was rarely absent from his parents' home. He attended a boarding school near Camberwell, traveled a little (to Russia and Italy), and was a student at the University of

London for a short period, but he preferred to pursue his education at home, where he was tutored in foreign languages, music, boxing, and horsemanship and where he read omnivorously. From this unusual education he acquired a store of knowledge on which to draw for the background of his poems.

The "obscurity" of which his contemporaries complained in his earlier poetry may be partly accounted for by the circumstances of Browning's education, but it also reflects his anxious desire to avoid exposing himself too explicitly before his readers. His first poem, *Pauline* (1833), published when he was twenty-one, had been modeled on the example of Percy Bysshe Shelley, the most personal of poets. When an otherwise admiring review by John Stuart Mill noted that the young author was afflicted with an "intense and morbid self-consciousness," Browning was overwhelmed with embarrassment. He resolved to avoid confessional writings thereafter.

One way of reducing the personal element in his poetry was to write plays instead of soul-searching narratives or lyrics. In 1836, encouraged by the actor W. C. Macready, Browning began work on his first play, *Strafford*, a historical tragedy that lasted only four nights when it was produced in London in 1837. For ten years the young writer struggled to write for the theater, but all his stage productions remained failures. Nevertheless, writing dialogue for actors led him to explore another form more congenial to his genius—the dramatic monologue, a form that enabled him through imaginary speakers to avoid explicit autobiography. His first collection of such monologues, *Dramatic Lyrics*, appeared in 1842; but it received no more critical enthusiasm than did his plays.

Browning's resolution to avoid the subjective manner of Shelley did not preclude his being influenced by the earlier poet in other ways. At fourteen, when he first discovered Shelley's works, he became an atheist and liberal. Although he grew away from the atheism, after a struggle, and also the extreme phases of his liberalism, he retained from Shelley's influence something permanent and more difficult to define: an ardent dedication to ideals (often undefined ideals) and an energetic striving toward goals (often undefined goals).

Browning's ardent romanticism also found expression in his love affair with Elizabeth Barrett, which had the dramatic ingredients of Browning's own favorite story of St. George rescuing the maiden from the dragon. Few would have forecast the outcome when Browning met Elizabeth Barrett in 1845. She was six years older than he was, a semi-invalid, jealously guarded by her possessively tyrannical father. But love, as the poet was to say later, is best; and love swept aside all obstacles. After their elopement to Italy, the former semi-invalid was soon enjoying far better health and a full life. The husband likewise seemed to thrive during the years of this remarkable marriage. His most memorable volume of poems, *Men and Women* (1855), reflects his enjoyment of Italy: its picturesque landscapes and lively street scenes as well as its monuments from the past—its Renaissance past in particular.

The happy fifteen-year sojourn in Italy ended in 1861 with Elizabeth's death. The widower returned to London with his son. During the twenty-eight years remaining to him, the quantity of verse he produced did not diminish. *Dramatis Personae* (1864) is a volume containing some of his most intriguing monologues, such as "Caliban upon Setebos." And in 1868 he published his longest and most significant single poem, *The Ring and the Book*, which was inspired by his discovery of an old book of legal records concerning a murder trial in seventeenth-century Rome. His poem tells the story of a brutally sadistic husband, Count Guido Franceschini. The middle-aged Guido grows dissatisfied with his young wife, Pompilia, and accuses her of having adulterous relations with a handsome priest who, like St. George, had tried to rescue her from the appalling situation in which her husband confined her. Eventually Guido stabs his wife to death and is himself executed. In a series of twelve books, Browning retells this tale of violence, presenting it from the contrasting points of view of participants and spectators. Because of its vast scale, *The Ring and the Book* is like a Victorian novel, but in its experiments with multiple points of view it anticipates later works such as Joseph Conrad's novel *Lord Jim* (1900) and Akira Kurosawa's film *Rashōmon* (1950).

After *The Ring and the Book* several more volumes appeared. In general, Browning's writings during the last two decades of his life exhibit a certain mechanical repetition of mannerism and an excess of argumentation—tendencies into which he may have been led by the unqualified enthusiasm of his admirers, for it was during this period that he gained his great following. When he died, in 1889, he was buried in Westminster Abbey.

During the London years Browning became extremely fond of social life. He dined at the homes of friends and at clubs, where he enjoyed port wine and conversation. He would talk loudly and emphatically about many topics—except his own poetry, about which he was usually reticent. Despite his bursts of outspokenness, Browning's character seemed, in Thomas Hardy's words, "*the* literary puzzle of the nineteenth century." Like William Butler Yeats, he was a poet preoccupied with masks. On the occasion of his burial, his friend Henry James reflected that many oddities and many great writers have been buried in Westminster Abbey, "but none of the odd ones have been so great and none of the great ones been so odd."

Just as Browning's character is hard to identify so also are his poems difficult to relate to the age in which they were written. Bishops and painters of the Renaissance, physicians of the Roman Empire, musicians of eighteenth-century Germany—as we explore this gallery of talking portraits we seem to be in a world of time long past, remote from the world of steam engines and disputes about human beings' descent from the ape. Yet our first impression is misleading. Many of these portraits explore problems that confronted Browning's contemporaries, especially problems of faith and doubt, of good and evil, and of the function of the artist in modern life. "Caliban upon Setebos," for example, is a highly topical critique of Darwinism and of natural (as opposed to supernatural) religions. Browning's own attitude toward these topics is partially concealed because of his use of speakers and of settings from earlier ages, yet we do encounter certain recurrent religious assumptions that we can safely assign to the poet himself. The most recurrent is that God has created an imperfect world as a kind of testing ground, a "vale of soul-making," as John Keats had said. It followed, for Browning's purposes, that the human soul must be immortal and that heaven itself be perfect. As Abt Vogler affirms: "On the earth the broken arcs; in the heaven, a perfect round." Armed with such a faith, Browning sometimes gives the impression that he was himself untroubled by the doubts that gnawed at the hearts of Tennyson, Arnold, and other figures in the mid-Victorian period. Yet Browning's apparent optimism is consistently being tested by his bringing to light the evils of human nature. His gallery of villains—murderers, sadistic husbands, mean and petty manipulators— is an extraordinary one. Few writers, in fact, seem to have been more aware of the existence of evil.

A second aspect of Browning's poetry that separates it from the Victorian age is its style. The most representative Victorian poets such as Tennyson and Dante Gabriel Rossetti write in the manner of Keats, John Milton, and Edmund Spenser, and of classical poets such as Virgil. Theirs is the central stylistic tradition in English poetry, one that favors smoothly polished texture, elevated diction and subjects, and pleasing liquidity of sound. Browning draws from a different tradition, more colloquial and discordant, a tradition that includes the poetry of John Donne, the soliloquies of William Shakespeare, and certain features of the narrative style of Geoffrey Chaucer. Of most significance are Browning's affinities with Donne. Both poets sacrifice, on occasion, the pleasures of harmony and of a consistent elevation of tone by using a harshly discordant style and unexpected juxtapositions that startle us into an awareness of a world of everyday realities and trivialities. Readers who dislike this kind of poetry in Browning or in Donne argue that it suffers from prosiness. Oscar Wilde once described the novelist George Meredith as "a prose Browning." And so, he added, was Browning. Wilde's joke may help us to relate Browning to his contemporaries. For if Browning seems out of step with other Victorian poets, he is by no means out of step with his contemporaries in prose. The grotesque, which plays such a prominent role in the style and subject matter of Carlyle and Dickens and in the aesthetic theories of John Ruskin, is equally prominent in Browning's verse:

> Fee, faw, fum! bubble and squeak!
> Blessedest Thursday's the fat of the week.
> Rumble and tumble, sleek and rough,
> Stinking and savory, smug and gruff.

Like Thomas Carlyle's *Sartor Resartus* (1833–34), these lines from "Holy-Cross Day" (1855) present a situation of grave seriousness with noisy jocularity. It was fitting that Browning and Carlyle remained good friends, even though the elder writer kept urging Browning to give up verse in favor of prose.

The link between Browning and the Victorian prose writers is not limited to style. With the later generation of Victorian novelists, George Eliot, George Meredith, and Henry James, Browning shares a central preoccupation. Like Eliot in particular, he was interested in exposing the devious ways in which our minds work and the complexity of our motives. "My stress lay on incidents in the development of a human soul," he wrote; "little else is worth study." His psychological insights can be illustrated in poems such as "The Bishop Orders His Tomb" (1845) and "Andrea del Sarto" (1855). Although these are spoken monologues, not inner monologues in the manner of James Joyce, the insight into the workings of the mind is similarly acute. As in reading Joyce, we must be on our guard to follow the rapid shifts of the speaker's mental processes as jumps are made from one cluster of associations to another. A further challenge for the reader of Browning is to identify what has been left out. As was remarked in a letter by the 1890s poet Ernest Dowson, Browning's "masterpieces in verse" demonstrate both "subtlety" and "the tact of omission." "My Last Duchess," he added, "is pure Henry James."

But Browning's role as a forerunner of twentieth-century literature should not blind us to his essential Victorianism. Energy is the most characteristic aspect of his writing and of the man (Ivan Turgenev compared Browning's handshake to an electric shock). Gerard Manley Hopkins described Browning as "a man bouncing up from table with his mouth full of bread and cheese and saying that he meant to stand no blasted nonsense." This buoyancy imparts a creative vitality to all of Browning's writings.

Porphyria's Lover[1]

> The rain set early in tonight,
>   The sullen wind was soon awake,
> It tore the elm-tops down for spite,
>   And did its worst to vex the lake:
> 5   I listened with heart fit to break.
> When glided in Porphyria; straight
>   She shut the cold out and the storm,
> And kneeled and made the cheerless grate
>   Blaze up, and all the cottage warm;
> 10   Which done, she rose, and from her form
> Withdrew the dripping cloak and shawl,
>   And laid her soiled gloves by, untied
> Her hat and let the damp hair fall,

---

1. One of a pair of monologues originally published as "Madhouse Cells," a title that emphasized the speaker's abnormal state of mind.

And, last, she sat down by my side
15   And called me. When no voice replied,
She put my arm about her waist,
    And made her smooth white shoulder bare,
And all her yellow hair displaced,
    And, stooping, made my cheek lie there,
20   And spread, o'er all, her yellow hair,
Murmuring how she loved me—she
    Too weak, for all her heart's endeavor,
To set its struggling passion free
    From pride, and vainer ties dissever,
25   And give herself to me forever.
But passion sometimes would prevail,
    Nor could tonight's gay feast restrain
A sudden thought of one so pale
    For love of her, and all in vain:
30   So, she was come through wind and rain.
Be sure I looked up at her eyes
    Happy and proud; at last I knew
Porphyria worshiped me: surprise
    Made my heart swell, and still it grew
35   While I debated what to do.
That moment she was mine, mine, fair,
    Perfectly pure and good: I found
A thing to do, and all her hair
    In one long yellow string I wound
40   Three times her little throat around,
And strangled her. No pain felt she;
    I am quite sure she felt no pain.
As a shut bud that holds a bee,
    I warily oped her lids: again
45   Laughed the blue eyes without a stain.
And I untightened next the tress
    About her neck; her cheek once more
Blushed bright beneath my burning kiss:
    I propped her head up as before,
50   Only, this time my shoulder bore
Her head, which droops upon it still:
    The smiling rosy little head,
So glad it has its utmost will,
    That all it scorned at once is fled,
55   And I, its love, am gained instead!
Porphyria's love: she guessed not how
    Her darling one wish would be heard.
And thus we sit together now,
    And all night long we have not stirred,
60   And yet God has not said a word!

1834   1836, 1842

Soliloquy of the Spanish Cloister

1

Gr-r-r—there go, my heart's abhorrence!
Water your damned flowerpots, do!
If hate killed men, Brother Lawrence,
God's blood,[1] would not mine kill you!
5 What? your myrtle bush wants trimming?
Oh, that rose has prior claims—
Needs its leaden vase filled brimming?
Hell dry you up with its flames!

2

At the meal we sit together:
10 *Salve tibi!*[2] I must hear
Wise talk of the kind of weather,
Sort of season, time of year:
*Not a plenteous cork crop: scarcely
Dare we hope oak-galls,*[3] I doubt:
15 *What's the Latin name for "parsley"?*
What's the Greek name for Swine's Snout?[4]

3

Whew! We'll have our platter burnished,
Laid with care on our own shelf!
With a fire-new spoon we're furnished,
20 And a goblet for ourself,
Rinsed like something sacrificial
Ere 'tis fit to touch our chaps°   jaws
Marked with L. for our initial!
(He-he! There his lily snaps!)

4

25 *Saint,* forsooth! While brown Dolores
Squats outside the Convent bank
With Sanchicha, telling stories,
Steeping tresses in the tank,
Blue-black, lustrous, thick like horsehairs,
30 —Can't I see his dead eye glow,
Bright as 'twere a Barbary corsair's?[5]
(That is, if he'd let it show!)

5

When he finishes refection,°   dinner
Knife and fork he never lays
35 Cross-wise, to my recollection,
As do I, in Jesu's praise.
I the Trinity illustrate,

1. An oath (archaic).
2. Hail to thee! (Latin); i.e., "your health!" This and other speeches in italics in this stanza are the words of Brother Lawrence.
3. Abnormal outgrowths on oak trees, used for tanning.
4. Dandelion (19th-century use).
5. Pirate of the Barbary Coast of northern Africa, renowned for fierceness and lechery.

Drinking watered orange pulp—
In three sips the Arian[6] frustrate;
40   While he drains his at one gulp.

6

Oh, those melons? If he's able
      We're to have a feast! so nice!
One goes to the Abbot's table,
      All of us get each a slice.
45   How go on your flowers? None double?
      Not one fruit-sort can you spy?
Strange!—And I, too, at such trouble,
      Keep them close-nipped on the sly!

7

There's a great text in Galatians,[7]
50   Once you trip on it, entails
Twenty-nine distinct damnations,
      One sure, if another fails:
If I trip him just a-dying,
      Sure of heaven as sure can be,
55   Spin him round and send him flying
      Off to hell, a Manichee?[8]

8

Or, my scrofulous French novel
      On gray paper with blunt type!
Simply glance at it, you grovel
60   Hand and foot in Belial's° gripe: *the devil's*
If I double down its pages
      At the woeful sixteenth print,
When he gathers his greengages,
      Ope a sieve and slip it in't?

9

65   Or, there's Satan!—one might venture
      Pledge one's soul to him, yet leave
Such a flaw in the indenture
      As he'd miss till, past retrieve,
Blasted lay that rose-acacia[9]
70   We're so proud of! *Hy, Zy, Hine*[1]
'St, there's Vespers![2] *Plena gratiâ
      Ave, Virgo!*[3] Gr-r-r—you swine!

ca. 1839   1842

---

6. Heretical follower of Arius (256–336), who denied the doctrine of the Trinity.
7. The speaker hopes to obtain Lawrence's damnation by luring him into a heresy when he may prove unable to interpret "Galatians" in an unswervingly orthodox way. In Galatians 5.15–23 St. Paul specifies an assortment of "works of the flesh" that lead to damnation, which could make up a total of "twenty-nine" (line 51).
8. A heretic, a follower of Mani (3rd century), Persian religious leader.
9. The speaker would pledge his own soul to Satan

in return for blasting Lawrence and his "rose-acacia," but the pledge would be so cleverly worded that the speaker would not have to pay his debt to Satan. There would be an escape clause ("flaw in the indenture") for himself.
1. Perhaps the opening of a mysterious curse against Lawrence.
2. Evening prayers.
3. Full of grace, Hail, Virgin! (Latin). The speaker's twisted state of mind may be reflected in his mixed-up version of the prayer to Mary: "Ave, Maria, gratia plena."

My Last Duchess[1]

Ferrara

That's my last Duchess painted on the wall,
Looking as if she were alive. I call
That piece a wonder, now: Frà Pandolf's[2] hands
Worked busily a day, and there she stands.
5   Will 't please you sit and look at her? I said
"Frà Pandolf" by design, for never read
Strangers like you that pictured countenance,
The depth and passion of its earnest glance,
But to myself they turned (since none puts by
10   The curtain I have drawn for you, but I)
And seemed as they would ask me, if they durst,
How such a glance came there; so, not the first
Are you to turn and ask thus. Sir, 'twas not
Her husband's presence only, called that spot
15   Of joy into the Duchess' cheek: perhaps
Frà Pandolf chanced to say "Her mantle laps
Over my lady's wrist too much," or "Paint
Must never hope to reproduce the faint
Half-flush that dies along her throat": such stuff
20   Was courtesy, she thought, and cause enough
For calling up that spot of joy. She had
A heart—how shall I say?—too soon made glad,
Too easily impressed; she liked whate'er
She looked on, and her looks went everywhere.
25   Sir, 'twas all one! My favor at her breast,
The dropping of the daylight in the West,
The bough of cherries some officious fool
Broke in the orchard for her, the white mule
She rode with round the terrace—all and each
30   Would draw from her alike the approving speech,
Or blush, at least. She thanked men—good! but thanked
Somehow—I know not how—as if she ranked
My gift of a nine-hundred-years-old name
With anybody's gift. Who'd stoop to blame
35   This sort of trifling? Even had you skill
In speech—(which I have not)—to make your will
Quite clear to such an one, and say, "Just this
Or that in you disgusts me; here you miss,
Or there exceed the mark"—and if she let
40   Herself be lessoned so, nor plainly set
Her wits to yours, forsooth, and made excuse
—E'en then would be some stooping; and I choose
Never to stoop. Oh sir, she smiled, no doubt,
Whene'er I passed her; but who passed without
45   Much the same smile? This grew; I gave commands;

---

1. The poem is based on incidents in the life of
Alfonso II, Duke of Ferrara in Italy, whose first
wife, Lucrezia, a young woman, died in 1561 after
three years of marriage. Following her death, the
duke negotiated through an agent to marry a niece
of the Count of Tyrol. Browning represents the
duke as addressing this agent.
2. Friar Pandolf, an imaginary painter.

Then all smiles stopped together. There she stands
As if alive. Will 't please you rise? We'll meet
The company below, then. I repeat,
The Count your master's known munificence
50   Is ample warrant that no just pretense
Of mine for dowry will be disallowed;
Though his fair daughter's self, as I avowed
At starting, is my object. Nay, we'll go
Together down, sir. Notice Neptune, though,
55   Taming a sea horse, thought a rarity,
Which Claus of Innsbruck[3] cast in bronze for me!

1842   1842

The Bishop Orders His Tomb at Saint Praxed's Church[1]

Rome, 15—

Vanity, saith the preacher, vanity![2]
Draw round my bed: is Anselm keeping back?
Nephews—sons mine . . . ah God, I know not! Well—
She, men would have to be your mother once,
5   Old Gandolf envied me, so fair she was!
What's done is done, and she is dead beside,
Dead long ago, and I am Bishop since,
And as she died so must we die ourselves,
And thence ye may perceive the world's a dream.
10   Life, how and what is it? As here I lie
In this state chamber, dying by degrees,
Hours and long hours in the dead night, I ask
"Do I live, am I dead?" Peace, peace seems all.
Saint Praxed's ever was the church for peace;
15   And so, about this tomb of mine. I fought
With tooth and nail to save my niche, ye know:
—Old Gandolf cozened° me, despite my care;   *cheated*
Shrewd was that snatch from out the corner south
He graced his carrion with,[3] God curse the same!

3. An unidentified or imaginary sculptor. The Count of Tyrol had his capital at Innsbruck.
1. In "Fra Lippo Lippi" Browning represents the dawn of the Renaissance in Italy, with its fresh zest for human experiences in this world. In this monologue he portrays a later stage of the Renaissance when such worldliness, full-blown, had infected some of the leading clergy of Italy. Browning's portrait of the dying bishop is, however, not primarily a satire against corruption in the church. It is a brilliant exposition of the workings of a mind, a mind that has been conditioned by special historical circumstances. The Victorian historian of art John Ruskin said of this poem:

  I know of no other piece of modern English, prose or poetry, in which there is so much told, as in these lines, of the Renaissance spirit—its

worldliness, inconsistency, pride, hypocrisy, ignorance of itself, love of art, of luxury, and of good Latin. It is nearly all that I have said of the central Renaissance in thirty pages of the *Stones of Venice*, put into as many lines, Browning's also being the antecedent work.

  St. Praxed's Church was named in honor of St. Praxedes, a Roman virgin of the 2nd century who gave her riches to poor Christians. Both the bishop and his predecessor, Gandolf, are imaginary persons.
2. Cf. Ecclesiastes 1.2.
3. Bishop Gandolf shrewdly chose a prize spot in the southern corner of the church for his burial place. The tomb that the speaker is ordering will also be inside the church, as was common for important people in this era.

20 Yet still my niche is not so cramped but thence
    One sees the pulpit o' the epistle side,[4]
    And somewhat of the choir, those silent seats,
    And up into the aery dome where live
    The angels, and a sunbeam's sure to lurk:
25 And I shall fill my slab of basalt[5] there,
    And 'neath my tabernacle[6] take my rest,
    With those nine columns round me, two and two,
    The odd one at my feet where Anselm stands:
    Peach-blossom marble all, the rare, the ripe
30 As fresh-poured red wine of a mighty pulse.[7]
    —Old Gandolf with his paltry onion-stone,[8]
    Put me where I may look at him! True peach,
    Rosy and flawless: how I earned the prize!
    Draw close: that conflagration of my church
35 —What then? So much was saved if aught were missed!
    My sons, ye would not be my death? Go dig
    The white-grape vineyard where the oil-press stood,
    Drop water gently till the surface sink,
    And if ye find . . . Ah God, I know not, I! . . .
40 Bedded in store of rotten fig leaves soft,
    And corded up in a tight olive-frail,[9]
    Some lump, ah God, of *lapis lazuli*,[1]
    Big as a jew's head cut off at the nape,[2]
    Blue as a vein o'er the Madonna's breast . . .
45 Sons, all have I bequeathed you, villas, all,
    That brave Frascati[3] villa with its bath,
    So, let the blue lump poise between my knees,
    Like God the Father's globe on both his hands
    Ye worship in the Jesu Church[4] so gay,
50 For Gandolf shall not choose but see and burst!
    Swift as a weaver's shuttle fleet our years:[5]
    Man goeth to the grave, and where is he?
    Did I say basalt for my slab, sons? Black[6]—
    'Twas ever antique-black I meant! How else
55 Shall ye contrast my frieze[7] to come beneath?
    The bas-relief[8] in bronze ye promised me,
    Those Pans and Nymphs ye wot° of, and perchance   *know*
    Some tripod, thyrsus, with a vase or so,
    The Saviour at his sermon on the mount,
60 Saint Praxed in a glory, and one Pan
    Ready to twitch the Nymph's last garment off,
    And Moses with the tables[9] . . . but I know

4. The Epistles of the New Testament are read from the right-hand side of the altar (as one faces it).
5. Dark-colored igneous rock.
6. Stone canopy or tentlike roof, presumably supported by the "nine columns" under which the sculptured effigy of the bishop would lie on the "slab of basalt."
7. A pulpy mash of fermented grapes from which a strong wine might be poured off.
8. An inferior marble that peels in layers.
9. Basket for holding olives.
1. Valuable bright blue stone.
2. Perhaps a reference to the head of John the

Baptist, cut off at Salomé's request (Matthew 14.6–11).
3. Suburb of Rome, used as a resort by wealthy Italians.
4. Il Gesù, a Jesuit church in Rome. In a chapel in this church the figure of an angel (rather than God) holds a huge lump of lapis lazuli in his hands.
5. Cf. Job 7.6.
6. I.e., black marble.
7. Continuous band of sculpture.
8. Sculpture in which the figures do not project far from the background surface.
9. The sculpture would consist of a mixture of pagan and Christian iconography. "Tripod": seat

Ye mark° me not! What do they whisper thee,   *heed*
Child of my bowels, Anselm? Ah, ye hope
65 To revel down my villas while I gasp
Bricked o'er with beggar's moldy travertine°   *Italian limestone*
Which Gandolf from his tomb-top chuckles at!
Nay, boys, ye love me—all of jasper, then!
'Tis jasper ye stand pledged to, lest I grieve
70 My bath must needs be left behind, alas!
One block, pure green as a pistachio nut,
There's plenty jasper somewhere in the world—
And have I not Saint Praxed's ear to pray
Horses for ye, and brown Greek manuscripts,
75 And mistresses with great smooth marbly limbs?
—That's if ye carve my epitaph aright,
Choice Latin, picked phrase, Tully's¹ every word,
No gaudy ware like Gandolf's second line—
Tully, my masters? Ulpian² serves his need!
80 And then how I shall lie through centuries,
And hear the blessed mutter of the mass,
And see God made and eaten all day long,³
And feel the steady candle flame, and taste
Good strong thick stupefying incense-smoke!
85 For as I lie here, hours of the dead night,
Dying in state and by such slow degrees,
I fold my arms as if they clasped a crook,°   *bishop's staff*
And stretch my feet forth straight as stone can point,
And let the bedclothes, for a mortcloth,⁴ drop
90 Into great laps and folds of sculptor's-work:
And as yon tapers dwindle, and strange thoughts
Grow, with a certain humming in my ears,
About the life before I lived this life,
And this life too, popes, cardinals, and priests,
95 Saint Praxed at his sermon on the mount,⁵
Your tall pale mother with her talking eyes,
And new-found agate urns as fresh as day,
And marble's language, Latin pure, discreet
—Aha, ELUCESCEBAT⁶ quoth our friend?
100 No Tully, said I, Ulpian at the best!
Evil and brief hath been my pilgrimage.⁷
All *lapis*, all, sons! Else I give the Pope
My villas! Will ye ever eat my heart?
Ever your eyes were as a lizard's quick,
105 They glitter like your mother's for my soul,

on which the Oracle of Delphi made prophecies. "Thyrsus": a staff twined with ivy that was carried, according to Greek mythology, by Dionysus, god of wine and fertility. "Glory": halo. "Tables": the stone tablets on which the Ten Commandments were written. Such intermingling of pagan and Christian traditions, characteristic of the Renaissance, had been attacked in 1841 in *Contrasts*, a book on architecture by A. W. Pugin, a Roman Catholic.
1. I.e., Marcus Tullius Cicero (106–43 B.C.E.), orator and statesman who was one of the great stylists of classical Latin prose.
2. Late Latin author of legal commentaries (d.

228 C.E.); not a model of good style.
3. Reference to the doctrine of transubstantiation.
4. Rich cloth spread over a dead body or coffin.
5. The bishop is confusing St. Praxed (a woman) with Jesus—an indication that his mind is wandering.
6. He was illustrious (Latin); word from Gandolf's epitaph. The bishop considers the form of the verb to be in "gaudy" bad taste (line 78). If the epitaph had been copied from Cicero instead of from Ulpian, the word would have been *elucebat*.
7. Cf. Genesis 47.9.

Or ye would heighten my impoverished frieze,
Piece out its starved design, and fill my vase
With grapes, and add a vizor and a Term,[8]
And to the tripod ye would tie a lynx[9]
110   That in his struggle throws the thyrsus down,
To comfort me on my entablature[1]
Whereon I am to lie till I must ask
"Do I live, am I dead?" There, leave me, there!
For ye have stabbed me with ingratitude
115   To death—ye wish it—God, ye wish it! Stone—
Gritstone,[2] a-crumble! Clammy squares which sweat
As if the corpse they keep were oozing through—
And no more *lapis* to delight the world!
Well go! I bless ye. Fewer tapers there,
120   But in a row: and, going, turn your backs
—Aye, like departing altar-ministrants,
And leave me in my church, the church for peace,
That I may watch at leisure if he leers—
Old Gandolf, at me, from his onion-stone,
125   As still he envied me, so fair she was!

1844   1845

Love among the Ruins

1

Where the quiet-colored end of evening smiles,
        Miles and miles
On the solitary pastures where our sheep
        Half-asleep
5   Tinkle homeward through the twilight, stray or stop
        As they crop—
Was the site once of a city great and gay
        (So they say),
Of our country's very capital, its prince
10   Ages since
Held his court in, gathered councils, wielding far
        Peace or war.

2

Now—the country does not even boast a tree,
        As you see,
15   To distinguish slopes of verdure, certain rills
        From the hills
Intersect and give a name to (else they run
        Into one),
Where the domed and daring palace shot its spires

---

8. Statue of Terminus, the Roman god of boundaries, usually represented without arms. "Vizor": part of a helmet, often represented in sculpture.
9. An animal that traditionally accompanied Bacchus.
1. Horizontal platform supporting a statue or effigy.
2. Coarse sandstone.

20   Up like fires
        O'er the hundred-gated circuit of a wall
                Bounding all,
        Made of marble, men might march on nor be pressed,
                Twelve abreast.

3

25   And such plenty and perfection, see, of grass
                Never was!
        Such a carpet as, this summertime, o'erspreads
                And embeds
        Every vestige of the city, guessed alone,
30   Stock or stone—
        Where a multitude of men breathed joy and woe
                Long ago;
        Lust of glory pricked their hearts up, dread of shame
                Struck them tame;
35   And that glory and that shame alike, the gold
                Bought and sold.

4

        Now—the single little turret that remains
                On the plains,
        By the caper overrooted, by the gourd
40   Overscored,
        While the patching houseleek's[1] head of blossom winks
                Through the chinks—
        Marks the basement whence a tower in ancient time
                Sprang sublime,
45   And a burning ring, all round, the chariots traced
                As they raced,
        And the monarch and his minions and his dames
                Viewed the games.

5

        And I know, while thus the quiet-colored eve
50   Smiles to leave
        To their folding, all our many-tinkling fleece
                In such peace,
        And the slopes and rills in undistinguished gray
                Melt away—
55   That a girl with eager eyes and yellow hair
                Waits me there
        In the turret whence the charioteers caught soul
                For the goal,
        When the king looked, where she looks now, breathless, dumb
60   Till I come.

6

        But he looked upon the city, every side,
                Far and wide,
        All the mountains topped with temples, all the glades'

---

1. Common European plant with petals clustered in the shape of rosettes.

Colonnades,
65 All the causeys,² bridges, aqueducts—and then,
All the men!
When I do come, she will speak not, she will stand,
Either hand
On my shoulder, give her eyes the first embrace
70   Of my face,
Ere we rush, ere we extinguish sight and speech
Each on each.

7

In one year they sent a million fighters forth
South and north,
75 And they built their gods a brazen° pillar high   *brass*
As the sky,
Yet reserved a thousand chariots in full force—
Gold, of course.
Oh heart! oh blood that freezes, blood that burns!
80   Earth's returns
For whole centuries of folly, noise, and sin!
Shut them in,
With their triumphs and their glories and the rest!
Love is best.

1853   1855

"Childe Roland to the Dark Tower Came"¹

(See Edgar's Song in "Lear")

1

My first thought was, he lied in every word,
That hoary cripple, with malicious eye
Askance° to watch the working of his lie   *squinting sidewise*
On mine, and mouth scarce able to afford
5 Suppression of the glee, that pursed and scored
Its edge, at one more victim gained thereby.

2

What else should he be set for, with his staff?
What, save to waylay with his lies, ensnare

---

2. Causeways or roads raised above low ground.
1. Browning stated that this poem "came upon me as a kind of dream," and that it was written in one day. Although the poem was among those of his own writings that pleased him most, he was reluctant to explain what the dream (or nightmare) signified. He once agreed with a friend's suggestion that the meaning might be expressed in the statement: "He that endureth to the end shall be saved" (cf. Matthew 24.13). Most readers have responded to the poem in this way, finding in the story of Roland's quest an inspiring expression of defiance and courage. Other readers find that the poem expresses despair more than enduring hope, and it

is at least true that the landscape is as grim and nightmarelike as in 20th-century writings such as T. S. Eliot's "The Hollow Men" (1925) or Franz Kafka's "In the Penal Colony" (1919).
The lines from Shakespeare's *King Lear* 3.4 (lines 158–60), from which the title is taken, are spoken when Lear is about to enter a hovel on the heath, and Edgar, feigning madness, chants the fragment of a song reminiscent of quests and challenges in fairy tales: "Child Roland to the dark tower come, / His word was still, 'Fie, fo, and fum; / I smell the blood of a British man." "Childe": a youth of gentle birth, usually a candidate for knighthood.

All travelers who might find him posted there,
10 And ask the road? I guessed what skull-like laugh
Would break, what crutch 'gin° write my epitaph   *would begin to*
For pastime in the dusty thoroughfare,

3

If at his counsel I should turn aside
    Into that ominous tract which, all agree,
15   Hides the Dark Tower. Yet acquiescingly
I did turn as he pointed: neither pride
Nor hope rekindling at the end descried,
        So much as gladness that some end might be.

4

For, what with my whole world-wide wandering,
20   What with my search drawn out through years, my hope
        Dwindled into a ghost not fit to cope
With that obstreperous joy success would bring,
I hardly tried now to rebuke the spring
        My heart made, finding failure in its scope.

5

25 As when a sick man very near to death
    Seems dead indeed, and feels begin and end
        The tears and takes the farewell of each friend,
And hears one bid the other go, draw breath
Freelier outside ("since all is o'er," he saith,
30   "And the blow fallen no grieving can amend"),

6

While some discuss if near the other graves
    Be room enough for this, and when a day
        Suits best for carrying the corpse away,
With care about the banners, scarves and staves:[2]
35 And still the man hears all, and only craves
        He may not shame such tender love and stay.

7

Thus, I had so long suffered in this quest,
    Heard failure prophesied so oft, been writ
        So many times among "The Band"—to wit,
40 The knights who to the Dark Tower's search addressed
    Their steps—that just to fail as they, seemed best,
        And all the doubt was now—should I be fit?

8

So, quiet as despair, I turned from him,
    That hateful cripple, out of his highway
45   Into the path he pointed. All the day
Had been a dreary one at best, and dim
Was settling to its close, yet shot one grim
        Red leer to see the plain catch its estray.[3]

2. The trappings of an imagined funeral.
3. Literally, a domestic animal that has strayed away from its home.

9

For mark! no sooner was I fairly found
50   Pledged to the plain, after a pace or two,
         Than, pausing to throw backward a last view
O'er the safe road, 'twas gone; gray plain all round:
Nothing but plain to the horizon's bound.
         I might go on; naught else remained to do.

10

55   So, on I went. I think I never saw
         Such starved ignoble nature; nothing throve:
         For flowers—as well expect a cedar grove!
But, cockle, spurge,[4] according to their law
Might propagate their kind, with none to awe,
60   You'd think; a burr had been a treasure trove.

11

No! penury, inertness and grimace,
         In some strange sort, were the land's portion. "See
         Or shut your eyes," said Nature peevishly,
"It nothing skills:[5] I cannot help my case;
65   'Tis the Last Judgment's fire must cure this place,
         Calcine[6] its clods and set my prisoners free."

12

If there pushed any ragged thistle stalk
         Above its mates, the head was chopped; the bents[7]
         Were jealous else. What made those holes and rents
70   In the dock's° harsh swarth leaves, bruised as to balk   coarse plant
All hope of greenness? 'tis a brute must walk
         Pashing° their life out, with a brute's intents.   smashing

13

As for the grass, it grew as scant as hair
         In leprosy; thin dry blades pricked the mud
75   Which underneath looked kneaded up with blood.
One stiff blind horse, his every bone a-stare,
Stood stupefied, however he came there:
         Thrust out past service from the devil's stud!

14

Alive? he might be dead for aught I know,
80   With that red gaunt and colloped° neck a-strain,   ridged
         And shut eyes underneath the rusty mane;
Seldom went such grotesqueness with such woe;
I never saw a brute I hated so;
         He must be wicked to deserve such pain.

15

85   I shut my eyes and turned them on my heart.
         As a man calls for wine before he fights,

4. A bitter-juiced weed. "Cockle": a weed that
bears burrs.
5. I.e., it is no use.

6. Turn to powder by heat.
7. Coarse stiff grasses.

I asked one draught of earlier, happier sights,
Ere fitly I could hope to play my part.
Think first, fight afterwards—the soldier's art:
90   One taste of the old time sets all to rights.

16

Not it! I fancied Cuthbert's reddening face
      Beneath its garniture of curly gold,
      Dear fellow, till I almost felt him fold
An arm in mine to fix me to the place,
95   That way he used. Alas, one night's disgrace!
      Out went my heart's new fire and left it cold.

17

Giles then, the soul of honor—there he stands
      Frank as ten years ago when knighted first.
      What honest man should dare (he said) he durst.
100 Good—but the scene shifts—faugh! what hangman hands
Pin to his breast a parchment? His own bands
      Read it. Poor traitor, spit upon and cursed!

18

Better this present than a past like that;
      Back therefore to my darkening path again!
105   No sound, no sight as far as eye could strain.
Will the night send a howlet° or a bat?   owl
I asked: when something on the dismal flat
      Came to arrest my thoughts and change their train.

19

A sudden little river crossed my path
110   As unexpected as a serpent comes.
      No sluggish tide congenial to the glooms;
This, as it frothed by, might have been a bath
For the fiend's glowing hoof—to see the wrath
      Of its black eddy bespate° with flakes and spumes.   bespattered

20

115 So petty yet so spiteful! All along,
      Low scrubby alders kneeled down over it;
      Drenched willows flung them headlong in a fit
Of mute despair, a suicidal throng:
The river which had done them all the wrong,
120   Whate'er that was, rolled by, deterred no whit.

21

Which, while I forded—good saints, how I feared
      To set my foot upon a dead man's cheek,
      Each step, or feel the spear I thrust to seek
For hollows, tangled in his hair or beard!
125 —It may have been a water rat I speared,
      But, ugh! it sounded like a baby's shriek.

22

Glad was I when I reached the other bank.
      Now for a better country. Vain presage!

Who were the strugglers, what war did they wage,
130   Whose savage trample thus could pad the dank
Soil to a plash?° Toads in a poisoned tank,   *puddle*
Or wild cats in a red-hot iron cage—

23

The fight must so have seemed in that fell cirque.°   *dreadful arena*
What penned them there, with all the plain to choose?
135   No footprint leading to that horrid mews,[8]
None out of it. Mad brewage set to work
Their brains, no doubt, like galley slaves the Turk
Pits for his pastime, Christians against Jews.

24

And more than that—a furlong on—why, there!
140   What bad use was that engine for, that wheel,
Or brake,[9] not wheel—that harrow fit to reel
Men's bodies out like silk? with all the air
Of Tophet's° tool, on earth left unaware,   *hell's*
Or brought to sharpen its rusty teeth of steel.

25

145   Then came a bit of stubbed ground, once a wood,
Next a marsh, it would seem, and now mere earth
Desperate and done with; (so a fool finds mirth,
Makes a thing and then mars it, till his mood
Changes and off he goes!) within a rood[1]
150   Bog, clay and rubble, sand and stark black dearth.

26

Now blotches rankling, colored gay and grim,
Now patches where some leanness of the soil's
Broke into moss or substances like boils;
Then came some palsied oak, a cleft in him
155   Like a distorted mouth that splits its rim
Gaping at death, and dies while it recoils.

27

And just as far as ever from the end!
Naught in the distance but the evening, naught
To point my footstep further! At the thought,
160   A great black bird, Apollyon's[2] bosom friend,
Sailed past, nor beat his wide wing dragon-penned[3]
That brushed my cap—perchance the guide I sought.

28

For, looking up, aware I somehow grew,
'Spite of the dusk, the plain had given place
165   All round to mountains—with such name to grace

---

8. Enclosed stable yard.
9. A toothed machine used for separating the fibers of flax or hemp; here an instrument of torture.
1. I.e., a short distance (6–8 yards).

2. In Revelation 9.11 Apollyon is "the angel of the bottomless pit." In Bunyan's *Pilgrim's Progress* (1678) he is a hideous "monster"; "he had wings like a dragon."
3. With wings or pinions like those of a dragon.

Mere ugly heights and heaps now stolen in view.
How thus they had surprised me—solve it, you!
How to get from them was no clearer case.

29

Yet half I seemed to recognize some trick
170   Of mischief happened to me, God knows when—
    In a bad dream perhaps. Here ended, then,
Progress this way. When, in the very nick
Of giving up, one time more, came a click
    As when a trap shuts—you're inside the den!

30

175 Burningly it came on me all at once,
    This was the place! those two hills on the right,
    Crouched like two bulls locked horn in horn in fight;
While to the left, a tall scalped mountain . . . Dunce,
Dotard, a-dozing at the very nonce,°   *moment*
180   After a life spent training for the sight!

31

What in the midst lay but the Tower itself?
    The round squat turret, blind as the fool's heart,[4]
    Built of brown stone, without a counterpart
In the whole world. The tempest's mocking elf
185 Points to the shipman thus the unseen shelf
    He strikes on, only when the timbers start.°   *separate; come loose*

32

Not see? because of night perhaps?—why, day
    Came back again for that! before it left,
    The dying sunset kindled through a cleft:
190 The hills, like giants at a hunting, lay,
Chin upon hand, to see the game at bay—
    "Now stab and end the creature—to the heft!"[5]

33

Not hear? when noise was everywhere! it tolled
    Increasing like a bell. Names in my ears
195   Of all the lost adventurers my peers—
How such a one was strong, and such was bold,
And such was fortunate, yet each of old
    Lost, lost! one moment knelled the woe of years.

34

There they stood, ranged along the hillsides, met
200   To view the last of me, a living frame
    For one more picture! in a sheet of flame
I saw them and I knew them all. And yet

---

4. Cf. Psalm 14.1: "The fool hath said in his heart,   5. Handle of dagger or sword.
There is no God."

Dauntless the slug-horn[6] to my lips I set,
And blew. *"Childe Roland to the Dark Tower came."*

1852   1855

Fra Lippo Lippi[1]

I am poor brother Lippo, by your leave!
You need not clap your torches to my face.
Zooks,[2] what's to blame? you think you see a monk!
What, 'tis past midnight, and you go the rounds,
5   And here you catch me at an alley's end
Where sportive ladies leave their doors ajar?
The Carmine's[3] my cloister: hunt it up,
Do—harry out, if you must show your zeal,
Whatever rat, there, haps on his wrong hole,
10   And nip each softling of a wee white mouse,
Weke, weke, that's crept to keep him company!
Aha, you know your betters! Then, you'll take
Your hand away that's fiddling on my throat,
And please to know me likewise. Who am I?
15   Why, one, sir, who is lodging with a friend
Three streets off—he's a certain . . . how d'ye call?
Master—a . . . Cosimo of the Medici,[4]
I' the house that caps the corner. Boh! you were best!
Remember and tell me, the day you're hanged,
20   How you affected such a gullet's gripe![5]
But you,[6] sir, it concerns you that your knaves
Pick up a manner nor discredit you:
Zooks, are we pilchards,° that they sweep the streets   small fish
And count fair prize what comes into this net?
25   He's Judas to a tittle, that man is![7]
Just such a face! Why, sir, you make amends.
Lord, I'm not angry! Bid your hangdogs go
Drink out this quarter-florin[8] to the health
Of the munificent House that harbors me
30   (And many more beside, lads! more beside!)
And all's come square again. I'd like his face—

6. The war cry or slogan of a clan about to engage in battle (Scottish). In 1770, however, the poet Thomas Chatterton was misled into using it to mean a kind of trumpet or horn. Browning followed Chatterton's example, although the original meaning would also be relevant here.
1. This monologue portrays the dawn of the Renaissance in Italy at a point when the medieval attitude toward life and art was about to be displaced by a fresh appreciation of earthly pleasures. It was from Giorgio Vasari's *Lives of the Painters* (1550) that Browning derived most of his information about the life of the Florentine painter and friar Lippo Lippi (1406–1469), but the theory of art propounded by Lippi in the poem was developed by the poet.
2. A shortened version of *Gadzooks,* a mild oath

now obscure in meaning but perhaps resembling a phrase still in use: "God's truth."
3. Santa Maria del Carmine, a church and cloister of the Carmelite order of friars to which Lippi belonged.
4. Lippi's patron, a banker and virtual ruler of Florence (1389–1464).
5. I.e., how you had the arrogance to choke the gullet of someone with my connections.
6. The officer in charge of the patrol of policemen or watchmen.
7. I.e., one of the watchmen has a face that would serve as a model for a painting of Judas. "To a tittle": to a tee; absolutely.
8. I.e., buy a drink worth a quarter of a florin (the florin was a gold coin first minted in Florence).

His, elbowing on his comrade in the door
With the pike and lantern—for the slave that holds
John Baptist's head a-dangle by the hair
35 With one hand ("Look you, now," as who should say)
And his weapon in the other, yet unwiped!
It's not your chance to have a bit of chalk,
A wood-coal° or the like? or you should see!   °piece of charcoal
Yes, I'm the painter, since you style me so.
40 What, brother Lippo's doings, up and down,
You know them and they take you? like enough!
I saw the proper twinkle in your eye—
'Tell you, I liked your looks at very first.
Let's sit and set things straight now, hip to haunch.
45 Here's spring come, and the nights one makes up bands
To roam the town and sing out carnival,[9]
And I've been three weeks shut within my mew,°   °private den
A-painting for the great man, saints and saints
And saints again. I could not paint all night—
50 Ouf! I leaned out of window for fresh air.
There came a hurry of feet and little feet,
A sweep of lute-strings, laughs, and whiffs of song—
Flower o' the broom,
Take away love, and our earth is a tomb!
55 *Flower o' the quince,*
I let Lisa go, and what good in life since?[1]
Flower o' the thyme—and so on. Round they went.
Scarce had they turned the corner when a titter
Like the skipping of rabbits by moonlight—three slim shapes,
60 And a face that looked up . . . zooks, sir, flesh and blood,
That's all I'm made of! Into shreds it went,
Curtain and counterpane and coverlet,
All the bed-furniture—a dozen knots,
There was a ladder! Down I let myself,
65 Hands and feet, scrambling somehow, and so dropped,
And after them. I came up with the fun
Hard by Saint Laurence,[2] hail fellow, well met—
Flower o' the rose,
If I've been merry, what matter who knows!
70 And so as I was stealing back again
To get to bed and have a bit of sleep
Ere I rise up tomorrow and go work
On Jerome knocking at his poor old breast
With his great round stone to subdue the flesh,[3]
75 You snap me of the sudden. Ah, I see!
Though your eye twinkles still, you shake your head—
Mine's shaved—a monk, you say—the sting's in that!
If Master Cosimo announced himself,
Mum's the word naturally; but a monk!

9. Season of revelry before the commencement of
Lent.
1. This and other interspersed flower songs are
called *stornelli* in Italy.
2. San Lorenzo, a church in Florence. "Hard by":
next to.
3. A picture of Saint Jerome (ca. 340–420), whose
ascetic observances were hardly a congenial subject for a painter such as Lippi.

80 Come, what am I a beast for? tell us, now!
  I was a baby when my mother died
  And father died and left me in the street.
  I starved there, God knows how, a year or two
  On fig skins, melon parings, rinds and shucks,
85 Refuse and rubbish. One fine frosty day,
  My stomach being empty as your hat,
  The wind doubled me up and down I went.
  Old Aunt Lapaccia trussed me with one hand
  (Its fellow° was a stinger as I knew),   *i.e., her other hand*
90 And so along the wall, over the bridge,
  By the straight cut to the convent. Six words there,
  While I stood munching my first bread that month:
  "So, boy, you're minded," quoth the good fat father
  Wiping his own mouth, 'twas refection time°—   *mealtime*
95 "To quit this very miserable world?
  Will you renounce" . . . "the mouthful of bread?" thought I;
  By no means! Brief, they made a monk of me;
  I did renounce the world, its pride and greed,
  Palace, farm, villa, shop, and banking house,
100 Trash, such as these poor devils of Medici
   Have given their hearts to—all at eight years old.
   Well, sir, I found in time, you may be sure,
   'Twas not for nothing—the good bellyful,
   The warm serge and the rope that goes all round,⁴
105 And day-long blessed idleness beside!
   "Let's see what the urchin's fit for"—that came next.
   Not overmuch their way, I must confess.
   Such a to-do! They tried me with their books:
   Lord, they'd have taught me Latin in pure waste!
110 *Flower o' the clove,*
   All the Latin I construe is "amo," I love!
   But, mind you, when a boy starves in the streets
   Eight years together, as my fortune was,
   Watching folk's faces to know who will fling
115 The bit of half-stripped grape bunch he desires,
   And who will curse or kick him for his pains—
   Which gentleman processional and fine,
   Holding a candle to the Sacrament,
   Will wink and let him lift a plate and catch
120 The droppings of the wax to sell again,
   Or holla for the Eight° and have him whipped—   *Florentine magistrates*
   How say I?—nay, which dog bites, which lets drop
   His bone from the heap of offal in the street—
   Why, soul and sense of him grow sharp alike,
125 He learns the look of things, and none the less
   For admonition from the hunger-pinch.
   I had a store of such remarks, be sure,
   Which, after I found leisure, turned to use.
   I drew men's faces on my copybooks,

---

4. The material ("serge") and belt ("rope") of a monk's clothing.

The Romantic Period
(1785–1830)

La Prise de la Bastille, le 14 Juillet 1789, Claude Cholat, 1789

This amateur painting (in gouache on cardboard) was made "on the spot" by one of the participants in the five-hour siege, a local wine merchant, and presented to the French National Assembly two years later. The storming of the Bastille—the fortress and state prison in Paris, a hated symbol of absolutism—marked the entry of the lower classes ("the people") into the Revolution. The anniversary of the event, July 14, is the principal French national holiday. RÉUNION DES MUSÉES NATIONAUX/ART RESOURCE, NY.

Plate 1 of *The Marriage of Heaven and Hell*, William Blake, 1790–93

This title page of a work composed in the early years of the French Revolution (see p. 1430) juxtaposes lighthearted activities (birds and humans soaring, strolling, playing music, dancing, embracing) with bleak and ominous surroundings (the leaflessness of the trees, the intensity of the flames). The larger reclining figures at the bottom of the page, sexy but genderless, are usually read as a devil and an angel whose embrace symbolizes the union ("marriage") of contraries running throughout the work. LIBRARY OF CONGRESS, WASHINGTON DC, USA/BRIDGEMAN ART LIBRARY.

The Sick Rose, William Blake, 1794

Blake's "illumination" (the poem is plate 39 of *Songs of Innocence and of Experience*; see p. 1420) further complicates an already highly ambiguous poetic text. In the picture are two worms—one eating a leaf in the upper left corner, the other coming out of the fallen blossom at the bottom—and three female figures, two of which, situated on the thorny stems above the engraved text, appear to be in postures of despair. The third female figure, emerging from the blossom, has arms flung forward in an expression of either ecstasy or terror. LIBRARY OF CONGRESS, WASHINGTON DC, USA/BRIDGEMAN ART LIBRARY.

Glad Day, or *The Dance of Albion*, William Blake, ca. 1793

Blake kept returning to this image of liberation. He first designed it in 1780, shortly after finishing his apprenticeship as an engraver, when the vision of a rising sun and a radiant human body may have expressed his own youthful sense of freedom. But later, in an age of revolution, he identified the figure as Albion—"Albion rose from where he labourd at the Mill with Slaves." For Blake the giant Albion represents the ancient form of Britain, a universal man who has fallen on evil, repressive times but is destined to awake and to unite all people in a dance of liberty, both political and spiritual. Eventually, in *Jerusalem* (ca. 1820), Blake's last great prophetic work, the figure of Albion merged with Jesus, risen from the tomb as an embodiment of "the human form divine"—immortal and perpetually creative. BRITISH MUSEUM, LONDON, UK/BRIDGEMAN ART LIBRARY.

First draft of *The Eve of St. Agnes*, John Keats, 1819

The extant holograph of *The Eve of St. Agnes*—here a part of the page containing stanza 30 (see p. 1837)—is possibly the messiest and most fragile manuscript in all of English poetry. The poem's Spenserian stanzas require an elaborate calculation of rhymes ahead of time to line up the quadruple b-rhymes and triple c-rhymes needed for each stanza. In page after page of this first draft, Keats's final wording varies in only a phrase or two (if that much) from the version that was published in 1820, still the standard text. THE HARVARD KEATS COLLECTION, HOUGHTON LIBRARY, HARVARD UNIVERSITY, CAMBRIDGE.

Interior of Tintern Abbey, J. M. W. Turner, 1794

Turner painted this watercolor at the age of nineteen, a year after Wordsworth made his first visit to the abbey (1793) and four years before the poet returned for a second visit (1798), as recorded in the famous "Lines . . ." pondering the changes that have taken place in both the speaker and the scene in the interim (see p. 1491). In Turner's version—as, in a different way, in Wordsworth's—the ruined symbol of religion, towering above two tiny human figures, presumably tourists, in the lower left, is in the process of being taken over (allegorically superseded) by the more powerful force of nature. VICTORIA & ALBERT MUSEUM, LONDON/ART RESOURCE, NY.

Lord Byron, by Thomas Phillips, 1835 (after an original of 1813)

Garbed theatrically in an Albanian soldier's dress that he had purchased while on his travels, Byron appears in this portrait as one of his own exotic heroes. The profits from his "Eastern" tales *Lara* and *The Corsair* in fact helped pay the painter's fees for the portrait, which Byron commissioned in 1813, choosing to be pictured not as a member of the British Establishment but as an outsider. The archives of London's National Portrait Gallery record more than forty portraits of Byron done during his lifetime, as well as a waxwork model from life made by Madame Tussaud in 1816: a statistic that suggests the poet's keen awareness of the magnetism and marketability of his image. NATIONAL PORTRAIT GALLERY, LONDON, UK/BRIDGEMAN ART LIBRARY.

Grasmere Lake from the northwest shore

Wordsworth saw the vale and lake of Grasmere for the first time when he was a teenager, in the 1780s, hiking over from Hawkshead, a few miles to the south, where he was in school, and coming through the cleft in the top center of the picture. He returned in 1799 and lived and wrote his poems there—in a succession of houses called Dove Cottage, Allan Bank, the Rectory, and Rydal Mount—for the next fifty years. Patrick Ward/Corbis.

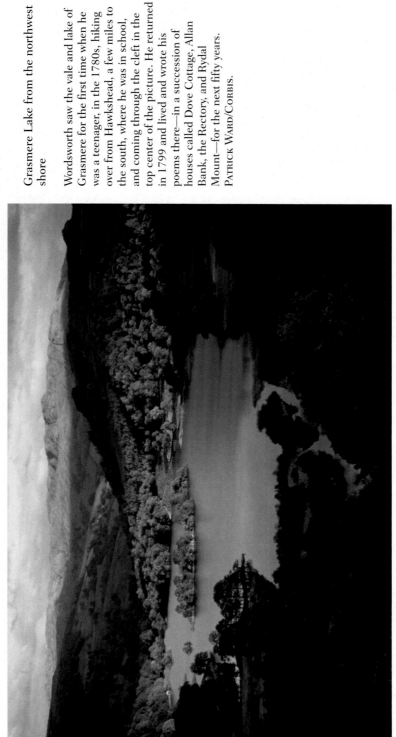

Manfred on the Jungfrau, John Martin, 1837

Manfred, about to throw himself off the cliff, is seized and held back by a passing chamois hunter. Martin's watercolor (based on his oil painting of 1826, no longer extant) emphasizes the sublimity and dramatic intensity of the Alpine setting and presents another version of the "deep romantic chasm" central to the imagery of Coleridge's "Kubla Khan" (see p. 1632). BIRMINGHAM MUSEUMS AND ART GALLERY, UK/BRIDGEMAN ART LIBRARY.

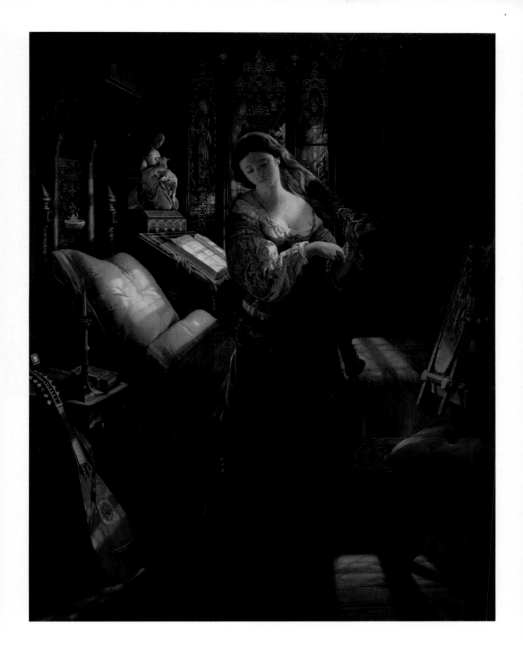

Madeline after Prayer, Daniel Maclise, 1868

Maclise's painting illustrates the particulars of Madeline's freeing her hair "of all its wreathed pearls" (*The Eve of St. Agnes,* line 227; see p. 1836) and more generally the stanzas describing the "casement high and triple-arch'd" and other furnishings of her bedroom. The pre-Raphaelite-influenced picture captures the rich colors and textures of the situation, but Keats's *words* actually provide many more details than the painting, including the hidden observer of this scene, Madeline's lover, Porphyro, who grows faint on seeing Madeline's appearance as a "splendid angel." THE BOARD OF TRUSTEES OF THE NATIONAL MUSEUMS AND GALLERIES ON MERSEYSIDE, WALKER ART GALLERY, LIVERPOOL, UK.

The Nightmare, by Henry Fuseli, ca. 1783–1791

The first version of this painting created a sensation when the Swiss-born artist Fuseli exhibited it at London's Royal Academy in 1781. Even Horace Walpole, who had used his own nightmare of "a gigantic hand in armour" when composing his Gothic novel, *The Castle of Otranto,* found Fuseli's trademark blend of violence, eroticism, and the irrational excessively disturbing: "shockingly mad, madder than ever; quite mad" was Walpole's verdict on the witchcraft scene that Fuseli exhibited four years later. It is no surprise to learn that during the 1920s Sigmund Freud kept an engraving of *The Nightmare* on display. SNARK/ART RESOURCE, NY.

Illustration of *The Rime of the Ancient Mariner,* Gustave Doré, 1876

Coleridge's poems—especially *The Ancient Mariner* and "Kubla Khan," with their abundance of color, texture, and mysterious detail—have been illustrated many times. Doré's elaborate engravings, originally published in an edition of the poem in 1876, are perhaps the best known of all, "darkly brooding, richly detailed, almost symphonic in their comprehensiveness and complexity," as one critic has described them. This plate illustrates lines 59–60, "The ice was here, the ice was there, / The ice was all around" (see p. 1617). FROM *THE RIME OF THE ANCIENT MARINER,* DOVER PUBLICATIONS, INC.

The Victorian Age
(1830–1901)

Slave Ship (Slavers Throwing Overboard the Dead and Dying—Typhoon Coming On),
J. M. W. Turner, 1840

The subject of Turner's painting—slaves thrown overboard, still in chains, as a storm
approaches—is the occasion for apocalyptic use of light and color. For several years John
Ruskin owned this painting, a gift from his father; but he later sold it, finding the subject
"too painful to live with." While many contemporaries criticized the painting for what they
saw as its extravagance, Ruskin praised it as Turner's noblest work, in a passage from *Modern
Painters* that is one of Ruskin's own finest passages of prose painting. Burstein Collec-
tion/Corbis.

Ophelia, John Everett Millais, 1851–52

Millais's painting illustrates the lines from *Hamlet* (4.7.137–54) in which Gertrude describes Ophelia's drowning herself. Many of the individual plants and flowers—the pansies on her dress, the violets around her neck—derive from the queen's speech and Ophelia's mad scene (4.5.163–94). Like much Pre-Raphaelite art, the painting sets an erotic subject in the midst of photographically precise, symbolic detail. The model for the painting was Elizabeth Siddal (later to become Dante Gabriel Rossetti's wife), who posed for the picture in a warm bath. ERICH LESSING/ART RESOURCE, NY.

Work, Ford Madox Brown, 1852, 1856–63

Brown's painting constructs a comprehensive picture of Victorian society through the relationships of various classes of the population to work. The excavators at the center represent work in its essential, physical form; the leisured gentry on horseback at the top of the painting have no need to work; the ragged girl in the foreground cares for her orphaned brothers and sisters. Under the trees are vagrants and distressed haymakers. Thomas Carlyle and F. D. Maurice, "brain workers" whose social ideas influenced the painting, stand on the right. MANCHESTER CITY ART GALLERY, MANCHESTER, UK.

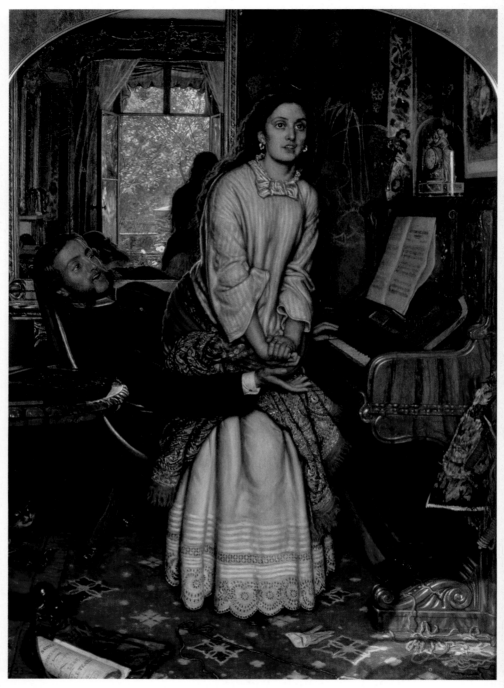

The Awakening Conscience, William Holman Hunt, 1853–54

Every detail of Hunt's painting of a fallen woman, hearing the voice of conscience while in the arms of her lover, has symbolic resonance—the soiled glove on the carpet, the bird that has escaped the cat, the songs on the piano ("Oft in the Stilly Night") and on the floor ("Tears, Idle Tears"), the window through which the woman gazes, reflected in the mirror behind the couple. Like Millais's *Ophelia,* the painting surrounds and interprets its subject with a crowded canvas of discrete, photographically rendered objects. TATE GALLERY, LONDON/ART RESOURCE, NY.

ul's Beauty, Dante Gabriel ...ssetti, 1864–70

...o titled *Sibylla Palmifera* ...e palm-bearing sibyl), *...ul's Beauty* represents the ...attainable ideal that ...pires the artist. Painted as ...ompanion to the sonnet of ...same name, the picture ...ves to represent and evoke ...e erotic and aesthetic ab-...ption the poem allegorizes. ...ssetti devoted the last fif-...n years of his painting ca-...r to these looming frontal ...traits with richly decorated ...ckgrounds, the details of ...ich carry symbolic signifi-...nce (in this painting, the ...h of life, the cupid, the ...pies, the skull, the butter-...s). THE BOARD OF ...USTEES OF THE NATIONAL ...SEUMS AND GALLERIES ON ...RSEYSIDE, LADY LEVER ART ...LLERY, LIVERPOOL, ENGLAND.

Body's Beauty, Dante Gabriel Rossetti, 1864–73

Also titled *Lady Lilith* (after Adam's first wife, who ran away to become a witch), *Body's Beauty* represents sensual absorption. Paired with the sonnet of the same name, the painting associates the sexual allure of the woman at the center with the golden hair that represents her value, and her narcissistic contemplation of herself with the art that she embodies. Like the Lady of Shalott, Lady Lilith is a weaver, but a deadly one—the poppies and roses surrounding her link death and sexuality. DELAWARE ART MUSEUM, WILMINGTON, USA/SAMUEL AND MARY R. BANCROFT MEMORIAL/ BRIDGEMAN ART LIBRARY.

The Beguiling of Merlin, Edward Burne-Jones, 1870–74

Burne-Jones draws on a medieval version of the Arthurian legend for this painting, in which Merlin's pupil, Nimuë (also called Nimiane, Vivian, or Vivien), uses one of Merlin's own spells to imprison him in a hawthorn tree. The winding branches of the tree, echoed in the Medusa-like snakes of Nimuë's hair, create a flat decorative surface. Although the Nimuë of the story is a femme fatale enchanting the helpless Merlin, her posture and expression and the similarity of the two faces make the painting ambiguous. The Board of Trustees of the National Museums and Galleries on Merseyside, Lady Lever Art Gallery, Liverpool, England.

The Passing of Arthur, Julia Margaret Cameron, 1875

Using photography in the way that earlier artists had used engravings to illustrate literary texts, Cameron produced a set of tableaux vivants to illustrate Tennyson's *Idylls of the King,* posing family and friends in costume in a combination of reality and fantasy that recalls the Pre-Raphaelites. This photograph illustrates lines 361–93 of *The Passing of Arthur* (see p. 2033), where the three queens attend the dying king in the barge that takes him to Avalon. Hulton-Deutsch Collection/Corbis.

Nocturne in Black and Gold, the Falling Rocket, James A. M. Whistler, 1875

Whistler's impressionist painting of fireworks approaches the abstraction suggested in his title. He emphatically rejected the precise depiction of objects in earlier Victorian painting. When the critic John Ruskin saw the painting in Grosvenor Gallery, he wrote in *Fors Clavigera* that he "never expected to hear a coxcomb ask two hundred guineas for flinging a pot of paint in the public's face." Whistler sued Ruskin for libel and won; but he was awarded damages of only one farthing, and the trial left him financially ruined. THE DETROIT INSTITUTE OF ARTS, USA/BRIDGEMAN ART LIBRARY. GIFT OF DEXTER M. FERRY, JR.

Climax, Aubrey Beardsley, 1893

After seeing a drawing in *Studio* magazine of Salome holding the head of John the Baptist, Oscar Wilde asked the artist, Aubrey Beardsley, to illustrate the English translation of his play *Salome*. The engraving makes the sexuality of the two figures ambiguous, and links them through the likeness of their faces and their Medusa-like hair. The decorative surface of the drawing absorbs its morbid, erotic subject in aesthetic pattern. FROM *BEST WORKS OF AUBREY BEARDSLEY*, DOVER PUBLICATIONS, INC.

The Twentieth Century and After

Les Demoiselles d'Avignon, Pablo Picasso, 1907

This masterpiece by Spanish expatriate painter Pablo Picasso helped unleash the experimental energies of modern art. The painting breaks with formal traditions of one-point perspective and human modeling, violently fracturing space in jagged planes. At the same time it defies conventions of sexual decorum in the visual arts, confronting the viewer with five naked prostitutes in a brothel. The masklike faces, particularly of the women to the right, echo African art; they suggest the crucial role non-Western art will play in the development of modernism. The abstract faces, angular forms, and formally fragmented bodies intimate the revolutionary techniques of analytic cubism that Picasso and his French collaborator Georges Braque would develop in Paris from 1907 to 1914. THE MUSEUM OF MODERN ART/LICENSED BY SCALA/ART RESOURCE, NY.

The Merry-Go-Round, Mark Gertler, 1916

Painted in the midst of World War I, *The Merry-Go-Round* explores the insufferable condition of life on the home front and on the battlefields. Its circularity describes the frustration of the deadlock on the Western Front, while its mingling of automatized soldiers and women conveys the sense of psychological menace pervading civilian society. The grinning puppet-like figures and the fun-fair setting convey an atmosphere of ghastly levity, in which war becomes a game. Glaring artificial colors contribute to the impression of a violent and confined world, where even nature is mechanical. TATE GALLERY, LONDON/ART RESOURCE, NY.

Over the Top, 1st Artists' Rifles at Marcoing, 30th December 1917,
John Northcote Nash, 1918

John Nash enlisted in the Artists' Rifles in 1916 and survived several attempts at going "over
the top" before his appointment as a War Artist two years later. In this painting he powerfully
recollects the futile danger of an attack near Cambrai in 1917. A line of soldiers clambers out
of a crude, wound-red trench to trudge through snow toward an unseen enemy. Several men
are killed immediately, then fall prostrate or fall back into the ready-made grave of their
recent refuge. Years later Nash recalled that the advance had from the outset been doomed,
"was in fact pure murder," designed to divert attention from a bombing raid elsewhere. Of the
eighty men who set out, only twelve, including Nash, returned. IMPERIAL WAR MUSEUM,
LONDON, UK/BRIDGEMAN ART LIBRARY.

Tube Shelter Perspective (1941) and *Family Group* (1947), Henry Moore

In their disparate treatments of space and community, these works powerfully demonstrate the antithetic atmospheres of war and peace. Moore took up sketching during World War I because of a scarcity of sculpting material. His impression of crowds sheltering in the London Underground during an air raid, ranged in parallel lines down a seemingly endless tunnel, evokes the involuntary intimacy of strangers—forced into proximity, yet still isolated and anonymous. *Family Group*, by contrast, expresses a postwar moment of relative security, when the birth of Moore's only daughter coincided with the government's promotion of traditional family values, and Moore's return to sculpture found a ready market for large-scale public art. Two parents, infants on their knees, sit in a cozy circle, their bodies merging in a physical expression of unity. The holes within the sculpture recall the wartime tunnel, transforming it from a void that swallows masses of people to a harmonious space controlled by the bodies. *FAMILY GROUP*: CHRISTIE'S IMAGES/CORBIS; *TUBE SHELTER PERSPECTIVE*: HENRY MOORE FOUNDATION; TATE GALLERY, LONDON/ART RESOURCE, NY.

Painting, Francis Bacon, 1946

Bacon's nightmarish association of the slaughterhouse with the emblems of political and religious power conjures both the suffering and the hypocrisy of the twentieth century. The bust of a man, his face overshadowed by an open umbrella, surrounded by microphones, the whole superimposed upon a butcher's display, evokes the discrepancy between rhetoric and means of power. While the umbrella offers a ludicrous symbol of respectability, the visual parallels between man and meat draw attention to the brutal foundations of political influence. The man's broad shoulders resemble the squared outline of the carcass behind him. The red and white of his face, and his exposed teeth, suggest the flesh and bone of the beef. Incongruous religious references, in the cruciform spread of the carcass and the churchlike decorations on the walls, augment the painting's insinuations of corruption. THE ESTATE OF FRANCIS BACON/ARS, NY/DACS, LONDON; DIGITAL IMAGE; THE MUSEUM OF MODERN ART/LICENSED BY SCALA/ART RESOURCE, NY.

Model with Unfinished Self-Portrait, David Hockney, 1977

In *Model with Unfinished Self-Portrait* layers of illusion, realism undermined by artifice, and pictures within pictures draw our attention to the deceptive nature of painting. At first we seem to see in mirror image a model (Gregory Evans, Hockney's lover) sleeping while the artist paints; but as the title implies, the figure in fact lies in front of *Self-Portrait with Blue Guitar,* a painting developed concurrently with *Model,* depicting Hockney as Picasso, drawing a guitar. Hockney used the relationship between the canvases to reinforce his persona: *Model* invokes Picasso's technique of combining naturalistic with stylized or unfinished elements; while *Self-Portrait,* which eventually incorporated a bust of Dora Maar, Picasso's mistress, encourages an analogy between Picasso, Hockney, and their respective muses. PRIVATE COLLECTION/BRIDGEMAN ART LIBRARY.

Naked Man, Back View, Lucian Freud, 1993

Freud's nudes study the details of the human body with an unflinching fascination that is modern in its refusal to censor or sentimentalize. Bowery, Freud's model, was a two-hundred-pound nightclub performer, famous for the gorgeous and outrageous costumes he used to reinvent himself in public. Yet Freud, recalling their first encounter, remembered the shape of his lower limbs rather than his outfit, observing that "his calves went right down to his feet, almost avoiding the whole business of ankles altogether." His depiction of Bowery in the nude strongly evokes the magnificence and the vulnerability of a body better known for its sartorial transformations. Courtesy of Acquavella Galleries, Inc. © 1993 The Metropolitan Museum of Art, Purchase Lila Acheson Wallace Gift (1993.71).

Marsyas, Anish Kapoor, October 9, 2002–April 6, 2003

Designed as a temporary installation to fill the vast central Turbine Hall at London's Tate Modern, *Marsyas* consists of a dark-red plastic membrane joining together three steel rings, two positioned vertically at either end and the third hung horizontally between. Its title refers to Marsyas, the satyr whom, in Greek mythology, Apollo flayed alive, and the membrane's color and contortions evoke flesh, even mutilated flesh. Yet the whole structure also has an ethereal quality, opening around each ring like the throat of an enormous flower. Suspended in the air, its intense, monochromatic surface resisting spatial recession, it seeks, as Kapoor has commented, "to make body into sky." COPYRIGHT 2002 ANISH KAPOOR; TATE GALLERY, LONDON/ART RESOURCE, NY.

130 Scrawled them within the antiphonary's marge,⁵
Joined legs and arms to the long music-notes,
Found eyes and nose and chin for A's and B's,
And made a string of pictures of the world
Betwixt the ins and outs of verb and noun,
135 On the wall, the bench, the door. The monks looked black.
"Nay," quoth the Prior,⁶ "turn him out, d' ye say?
In no wise. Lose a crow and catch a lark.
What if at last we get our man of parts,°   skill, genius
We Carmelites, like those Camaldolese
140 And Preaching Friars,⁷ to do our church up fine
And put the front on it that ought to be!"
And hereupon he bade me daub away.
Thank you! my head being crammed, the walls a blank,
Never was such prompt disemburdening.
145 First, every sort of monk, the black and white,
I drew them, fat and lean: then, folk at church,
From good old gossips waiting to confess
Their cribs° of barrel droppings, candle ends—   petty thefts
To the breathless fellow at the altar-foot,
150 Fresh from his murder, safe⁸ and sitting there
With the little children round him in a row
Of admiration, half for his beard and half
For that white anger of his victim's son
Shaking a fist at him with one fierce arm,
155 Signing himself with the other because of Christ
(Whose sad face on the cross sees only this
After the passion° of a thousand years)   sufferings
Till some poor girl, her apron o'er her head
(Which the intense eyes looked through), came at eve
160 On tiptoe, said a word, dropped in a loaf,
Her pair of earrings and a bunch of flowers
(The brute took growling), prayed, and so was gone.
I painted all, then cried " 'Tis ask and have;
Choose, for more's ready!"—laid the ladder flat,
165 And showed my covered bit of cloister wall.
The monks closed in a circle and praised loud
Till checked, taught what to see and not to see,
Being simple bodies—"That's the very man!
Look at the boy who stoops to pat the dog!
170 That woman's like the Prior's niece who comes
To care about his asthma: it's the life!"
But there my triumph's straw-fire flared and funked;⁹
Their betters took their turn to see and say:
The Prior and the learned pulled a face
175 And stopped all that in no time. "How? what's here?
Quite from the mark of painting, bless us all!
Faces, arms, legs and bodies like the true

5. Margin of a music book used for choral singing.
6. Head of a Carmelite convent.
7. Benedictine and Dominican religious orders, respectively.
8. Having claimed sanctuary in the church.
9. Went up in smoke.

As much as pea and pea! it's devil's game!
Your business is not to catch men with show,
180 With homage to the perishable clay,
But lift them over it, ignore it all,
Make them forget there's such a thing as flesh.
Your business is to paint the souls of men—
Man's soul, and it's a fire, smoke . . . no, it's not . . .
185 It's vapor done up like a newborn babe—
(In that shape when you die it leaves your mouth)
It's . . . well, what matters talking, it's the soul!
Give us no more of body than shows soul!
Here's Giotto,[1] with his Saint a-praising God,
190 That sets us praising—why not stop with him?
Why put all thoughts of praise out of our head
With wonder at lines, colors, and what not?
Paint the soul, never mind the legs and arms!
Rub all out, try at it a second time.
195 Oh, that white smallish female with the breasts,
She's just° my niece . . . Herodias,[2] I would say—   exactly like
Who went and danced and got men's heads cut off!
Have it all out!" Now, is this sense, I ask?
A fine way to paint soul, by painting body
200 So ill, the eye can't stop there, must go further
And can't fare worse! Thus, yellow does for white
When what you put for yellow's simply black,
And any sort of meaning looks intense
When all beside itself means and looks naught.
205 Why can't a painter lift each foot in turn,
Left foot and right foot, go a double step,
Make his flesh liker and his soul more like,
Both in their order? Take the prettiest face,
The Prior's niece . . . patron-saint—is it so pretty
210 You can't discover if it means hope, fear,
Sorrow or joy? won't beauty go with these?
Suppose I've made her eyes all right and blue,
Can't I take breath and try to add life's flash,
And then add soul and heighten them threefold?
215 Or say there's beauty with no soul at all—
(I never saw it—put the case the same—)
If you get simple beauty and naught else,
You get about the best thing God invents:
That's somewhat: and you'll find the soul you have missed,
220 Within yourself, when you return him thanks.
"Rub all out!" Well, well, there's my life, in short,
And so the thing has gone on ever since.
I'm grown a man no doubt, I've broken bounds:
You should not take a fellow eight years old
225 And make him swear to never kiss the girls.
I'm my own master, paint now as I please—

---

1. Great Florentine painter (1276–1337), whose stylized pictures of religious subjects were admired as models of pre-Renaissance art.
2. I.e., Salomé (her mother was Herodias, the sister-in-law of King Herod). Because John the Baptist had aroused her mother's displeasure, Salomé asked for his head on a platter after she danced (Matthew 14.6–11).

Having a friend, you see, in the Corner-house![3]
Lord, it's fast holding by the rings in front—
Those great rings serve more purposes than just
230   To plant a flag in, or tie up a horse!
And yet the old schooling sticks, the old grave eyes
Are peeping o'er my shoulder as I work,
The heads shake still—"It's art's decline, my son!
You're not of the true painters, great and old;
235   Brother Angelico's the man, you'll find;
Brother Lorenzo[4] stands his single peer:
Fag on° at flesh, you'll never make the third!"   *work hard*
Flower o' the pine,
You keep your mistr . . . manners, and I'll stick to mine!
240   I'm not the third, then: bless us, they must know!
Don't you think they're the likeliest to know,
They with their Latin? So, I swallow my rage,
Clench my teeth, suck my lips in tight, and paint
To please them—sometimes do and sometimes don't;
245   For, doing most, there's pretty sure to come
A turn, some warm eve finds me at my saints—
A laugh, a cry, the business of the world—
(*Flower o' the peach,*
Death for us all, and his own life for each!)
250   And my whole soul revolves, the cup runs over,
The world and life's too big to pass for a dream,
And I do these wild things in sheer despite,
And play the fooleries you catch me at,
In pure rage! The old mill-horse, out at grass
255   After hard years, throws up his stiff heels so,
Although the miller does not preach to him
The only good of grass is to make chaff.°   *straw*
What would men have? Do they like grass or no[5]—
May they or mayn't they? all I want's the thing
260   Settled forever one way. As it is,
You tell too many lies and hurt yourself:
You don't like what you only like too much,
You do like what, if given you at your word,
You find abundantly detestable.
265   For me, I think I speak as I was taught;
I always see the garden[6] and God there
A-making man's wife: and, my lesson learned,
The value and significance of flesh,
I can't unlearn ten minutes afterwards.

270   You understand me: I'm a beast, I know.
But see, now—why, I see as certainly
As that the morning star's about to shine,

3. The Medici palace.
4. Fra Angelico (1387–1455) and Lorenzo Monaco (1370–1425), whose paintings were in the approved traditional manner.
5. I.e., while horses are allowed to enjoy playing in the grass, human beings are taught by the

Church that physical experience is valuable only in its relation to their future condition in the afterlife. The biblical text "all flesh is as grass" (1 Peter 1.24) lurks within Lippi's question.
6. I.e., Eden.

2076 / ROBERT BROWNING

What will hap some day. We've a youngster here
Comes to our convent, studies what I do,
275 Slouches and stares and lets no atom drop:
His name is Guidi[7]—he'll not mind the monks—
They call him Hulking Tom, he lets them talk—
He picks my practice up—he'll paint apace,
I hope so—though I never live so long,
280 I know what's sure to follow. You be judge!
You speak no Latin more than I, belike;
However, you're my man, you've seen the world
—The beauty and the wonder and the power,
The shapes of things, their colors, lights and shades,
285 Changes, surprises—and God made it all!
—For what? Do you feel thankful, aye or no,
For this fair town's face, yonder river's line,
The mountain round it and the sky above,
Much more the figures of man, woman, child,
290 These are the frame to? What's it all about?
To be passed over, despised? or dwelt upon,
Wondered at? oh, this last of course!—you say.
But why not do as well as say—paint these
Just as they are, careless what comes of it?
295 God's works—paint any one, and count it crime
To let a truth slip. Don't object, "His works
Are here already; nature is complete:
Suppose you reproduce her—(which you can't)
There's no advantage! You must beat her, then."
300 For, don't you mark?° we're made so that we love   observe
First when we see them painted, things we have passed
Perhaps a hundred times nor cared to see;
And so they are better, painted—better to us,
Which is the same thing. Art was given for that;
305 God uses us to help each other so,
Lending our minds out. Have you noticed, now,
Your cullion's° hanging face? A bit of chalk,   rascal's
And trust me but you should, though! How much more,
If I drew higher things with the same truth!
310 That were to take the Prior's pulpit-place,
Interpret God to all of you! Oh, oh,
It makes me mad to see what men shall do
And we in our graves! This world's no blot for us,
Nor blank; it means intensely, and means good:
315 To find its meaning is my meat and drink.
"Aye, but you don't so instigate to prayer!"
Strikes in the Prior: "when your meaning's plain
It does not say to folk—remember matins,
Or, mind you fast next Friday!" Why, for this
320 What need of art at all? A skull and bones,
Two bits of stick nailed crosswise, or, what's best,

7. Guidi or Masaccio (1401–1428), a painter who may have been Lippi's master rather than his pupil, although Browning, in a letter to the press in 1870, argued that Lippi had been born earlier. Like Lippi, Masaccio was in revolt against the medieval theory of art. His frescoes in the chapel of Santa Maria del Carmine are considered his masterpiece.

A bell to chime the hour with, does as well.
I painted a Saint Laurence[8] six months since
At Prato, splashed the fresco[9] in fine style:
325 "How looks my painting, now the scaffold's down?"
I ask a brother: "Hugely," he returns—
"Already not one phiz° of your three slaves   *face*
Who turn the Deacon off his toasted side,
But it's scratched and prodded to our heart's content,
330 The pious people have so eased their own
With coming to say prayers there in a rage:
We get on fast to see the bricks beneath.
Expect another job this time next year,
For pity and religion grow i' the crowd—
335 Your painting serves its purpose!" Hang the fools!

      —That is—you'll not mistake an idle word
Spoke in a huff by a poor monk, God wot,°   *knows*
Tasting the air this spicy night which turns
The unaccustomed head like Chianti wine!
340 Oh, the church knows! don't misreport me, now!
It's natural a poor monk out of bounds
Should have his apt word to excuse himself:
And hearken how I plot to make amends.
I have bethought me: I shall paint a piece
345 . . . There's for you! Give me six months, then go, see
Something in Sant' Ambrogio's![1] Bless the nuns!
They want a cast o' my office.[2] I shall paint
God in the midst, Madonna and her babe,
Ringed by a bowery flowery angel brood,
350 Lilies and vestments and white faces, sweet
As puff on puff of grated orris-root[3]
When ladies crowd to Church at midsummer.
And then i' the front, of course a saint or two—
Saint John, because he saves the Florentines,
355 Saint Ambrose, who puts down in black and white
The convent's friends and gives them a long day,
And Job,[4] I must have him there past mistake,
The man of Uz (and Us without the z,
Painters who need his patience). Well, all these
360 Secured at their devotion, up shall come
Out of a corner when you least expect,
As one by a dark stair into a great light,
Music and talking, who but Lippo! I!—
Mazed,° motionless and moonstruck—I'm the man!   *confused*
365 Back I shrink—what is this I see and hear?
I, caught up with my monk's things by mistake,
My old serge gown and rope that goes all round,

8. A scene representing the fiery martyrdom of
Saint Laurence.
9. Painted on a freshly plastered surface. It must
be painted quickly before the plaster dries. Prato
is a town near Florence.
1. A convent church in Florence.
2. Sample of my work. The completed painting,

which Browning saw in Florence, is Lippi's *Coronation of the Virgin* (1441).
3. A powder (like talcum) made from sweet-
smelling roots of a flower.
4. The prosperous man who endured immense
suffering without once questioning God's will (see
the book of Job).

I, in this presence, this pure company!
Where's a hole, where's a corner for escape?
370 Then steps a sweet angelic slip of a thing
Forward, puts out a soft palm—"Not so fast!"
—Addresses the celestial presence, "nay—
He made you and devised you, after all,
Though he's none of you! Could Saint John there draw—
375 His camel-hair[5] make up a painting-brush?
We come to brother Lippo for all that,
Iste perfecit opus!"[6] So, all smile—
I shuffle sideways with my blushing face
Under the cover of a hundred wings
380 Thrown like a spread of kirtles° when you're gay   *skirts*
And play hot cockles,[7] all the doors being shut,
Till, wholly unexpected, in there pops
The hothead husband! Thus I scuttle off
To some safe bench behind, not letting go
385 The palm of her, the little lily thing
That spoke the good word for me in the nick,
Like the Prior's niece . . . Saint Lucy, I would say.
And so all's saved for me, and for the church
A pretty picture gained. Go, six months hence!
390 Your hand, sir, and good-by: no lights, no lights!
The street's hushed, and I know my own way back,
Don't fear me! There's the gray beginning. Zooks!

ca. 1853   1855

Andrea del Sarto[1]

(called "The Faultless Painter")

But do not let us quarrel any more,
No, my Lucrezia; bear with me for once:
Sit down and all shall happen as you wish.
You turn your face, but does it bring your heart?
5 I'll work then for your friend's friend, never fear,
Treat his own subject after his own way,
Fix his own time, accept too his own price,
And shut the money into this small hand

---

5. Cf. Mark 1.6: "And John was clothed with camel's hair."
6. This man made the work! (Latin). In this painting, as later completed, these words appear beside a figure that Browning took to be Lippi's self-portrait.
7. A game in which a player wears a blindfold.
1. This portrait of Andrea del Sarto (1486–1531) was derived from a biography written by his pupil Giorgio Vasari, author of *The Lives of the Painters* (1550). Vasari's account seeks to explain why his Florentine master, one of the most skillful painters of the Renaissance, never altogether fulfilled the promise he had shown early in his career and why he had never arrived (in Vasari's opinion) at the

level of such artists as Raphael. Vasari noted that Andrea suffered from "a certain timidity of mind . . . which rendered it impossible that those evidences of ardor and animation, which are proper to the more exalted character, should ever appear in him."
 Browning also follows Vasari's account of Andrea's marriage to a beautiful widow, Lucrezia, "an artful woman who made him do as she pleased in all things." Vasari reports that Andrea's "immoderate love for her soon caused him to neglect the studies demanded by his art" and that this infatuation had "more influence over him than the glory and honor towards which he had begun to make such hopeful advances."

When next it takes mine. Will it? tenderly?
10 Oh, I'll content him—but tomorrow, Love!
I often am much wearier than you think,
This evening more than usual, and it seems
As if—forgive now—should you let me sit
Here by the window with your hand in mine
15 And look a half-hour forth on Fiesole,[2]
Both of one mind, as married people use,°   usually are
Quietly, quietly the evening through,
I might get up tomorrow to my work
Cheerful and fresh as ever. Let us try.
20 Tomorrow, how you shall be glad for this!
Your soft hand is a woman of itself,
And mine the man's bared breast she curls inside.
Don't count the time lost, neither; you must serve
For each of the five pictures we require:
25 It saves° a model. So! keep looking so—   saves the expense of
My serpentining beauty, rounds on rounds![3]
—How could you ever prick those perfect ears,
Even to put the pearl there! oh, so sweet—
My face, my moon, my everybody's moon,
30 Which everybody looks on and calls his,
And, I suppose, is looked on by in turn,
While she looks—no one's: very dear, no less.[4]
You smile? why, there's my picture ready made,
There's what we painters call our harmony!
35 A common grayness silvers everything[5]—
All in a twilight, you and I alike
—You, at the point of your first pride in me
(That's gone you know)—but I, at every point;
My youth, my hope, my art, being all toned down
40 To yonder sober pleasant Fiesole.
There's the bell clinking from the chapel top;
That length of convent wall across the way
Holds the trees safer, huddled more inside;
The last monk leaves the garden; days decrease,
45 And autumn grows, autumn in everything.
Eh? the whole seems to fall into a shape
As if I saw alike my work and self
And all that I was born to be and do,
A twilight-piece. Love, we are in God's hand.
50 How strange now, looks the life he makes us lead;
So free we seem, so fettered fast we are!
I feel he laid the fetter: let it lie!
This chamber for example—turn your head—
All that's behind us! You don't understand
55 Nor care to understand about my art,
But you can hear at least when people speak:
And that cartoon,° the second from the door   drawing

2. A suburb on the hills overlooking Florence.   dear to him.
3. Coils of hair like the coils of a serpent.   5. The predominant color in many of Andrea's
4. Her affections are centered on no one person,   paintings is silver gray.
not even on her husband, yet she is nevertheless

2080 / ROBERT BROWNING

—It is the thing, Love! so such things should be—
Behold Madonna!—I am bold to say.
60 I can do with my pencil what I know,
What I see, what at bottom of my heart
I wish for, if I ever wish so deep—
Do easily, too—when I say, perfectly,
I do not boast, perhaps: yourself are judge,
65 Who listened to the Legate's[6] talk last week,
And just as much they used to say in France.
At any rate 'tis easy, all of it!
No sketches first, no studies, that's long past:
I do what many dream of, all their lives,
70 —Dream? strive to do, and agonize to do,
And fail in doing. I could count twenty such
On twice your fingers, and not leave this town,
Who strive—you don't know how the others strive
To paint a little thing like that you smeared
75 Carelessly passing with your robes afloat—
Yet do much less, so much less, Someone[7] says
(I know his name, no matter)—so much less!
Well, less is more, Lucrezia: I am judged.
There burns a truer light of God in them,
80 In their vexed beating stuffed and stopped-up brain,
Heart, or whate'er else, than goes on to prompt
This low-pulsed forthright craftsman's hand of mine.
Their works drop groundward, but themselves, I know,
Reach many a time a heaven that's shut to me,
85 Enter and take their place there sure enough,
Though they come back and cannot tell the world.
My works are nearer heaven, but I sit here.
The sudden blood of these men! at a word—
Praise them, it boils, or blame them, it boils too.
90 I, painting from myself and to myself,
Know what I do, am unmoved by men's blame
Or their praise either. Somebody remarks
Morello's[8] outline there is wrongly traced,
His hue mistaken; what of that? or else,
95 Rightly traced and well ordered; what of that?
Speak as they please, what does the mountain care?
Ah, but a man's reach should exceed his grasp,
Or what's a heaven for? All is silver-gray
Placid and perfect with my art: the worse!
100 I know both what I want and what might gain,
And yet how profitless to know, to sigh
"Had I been two, another and myself,
Our head would have o'erlooked the world!" No doubt.
Yonder's a work now, of that famous youth
105 The Urbinate[9] who died five years ago.
('Tis copied,[1] George Vasari sent it me.)

6. A deputy of the pope.
7. Probably the artist Michelangelo (1475–1564).
8. A mountain peak outside Florence.
9. Raphael (1483–1520), or Raffaello Sanzio,
born at Urbino.
1. In saying that the painting is a copy, Andrea
may perhaps be concerned to prevent Lucrezia
from selling it.

Well, I can fancy how he did it all,
Pouring his soul, with kings and popes to see,
Reaching, that heaven might so replenish him,
Above and through his art—for it gives way;
That arm is wrongly put—and there again—
A fault to pardon in the drawing's lines,
Its body, so to speak: its soul is right,
He means right—that, a child may understand.
Still, what an arm! and I could alter it:
But all the play, the insight and the stretch—
Out of me, out of me! And wherefore out?
Had you enjoined them on me, given me soul,
We might have risen to Rafael, I and you!
Nay, Love, you did give all I asked, I think—
More than I merit, yes, by many times.
But had you—oh, with the same perfect brow,
And perfect eyes, and more than perfect mouth,
And the low voice my soul hears, as a bird
The fowler's pipe,[2] and follows to the snare—
Had you, with these the same, but brought a mind!
Some women do so. Had the mouth there urged
"God and the glory! never care for gain.
The present by the future, what is that?
Live for fame, side by side with Agnolo!°   Michelangelo
Rafael is waiting: up to God, all three!"
I might have done it for you. So it seems:
Perhaps not. All is as God overrules.
Beside, incentives come from the soul's self;
The rest avail not. Why do I need you?
What wife had Rafael, or has Agnolo?
In this world, who can do a thing, will not;
And who would do it, cannot, I perceive:
Yet the will's somewhat°—somewhat, too, the power—   of some importance
And thus we half-men struggle. At the end,
God, I conclude, compensates, punishes.
'Tis safer for me, if the award be strict,
That I am something underrated here.
Poor this long while, despised, to speak the truth.
I dared not, do you know, leave home all day,
For fear of chancing on the Paris lords.
The best is when they pass and look aside;
But they speak sometimes; I must bear it all.
Well may they speak! That Francis,[3] that first time,
And that long festal year at Fontainebleau!
I surely then could sometimes leave the ground,
Put on the glory, Rafael's daily wear,
In that humane great monarch's golden look—
One finger in his beard or twisted curl

2. Whistle or call used by hunters to lure wild fowl
into range.
3. King Francis I of France (1494–1547; reigned
1515–47) had invited Andrea to his court at Fontainebleau and warmly encouraged him in his

painting. On returning to Florence, however,
Andrea is reputed to have stolen some funds
entrusted to him by Francis; and to please Lucrezia
he built a house with the money. Now he is afraid
of being insulted by "Paris lords" on the streets.

155   Over his mouth's good mark that made the smile,
      One arm about my shoulder, round my neck,
      The jingle of his gold chain in my ear,
      I painting proudly with his breath on me,
      All his court round him, seeing with his eyes,
160   Such frank French eyes, and such a fire of souls
      Profuse, my hand kept plying by those hearts—
      And, best of all, this, this, this face beyond,
      This in the background, waiting on my work,
      To crown the issue with a last reward!
165   A good time, was it not, my kingly days?
      And had you not grown restless . . . but I know—
      'Tis done and past; 'twas right, my instinct said;
      Too live the life grew, golden and not gray,
      And I'm the weak-eyed bat no sun should tempt
170   Out of the grange° whose four walls make his world.   *farmhouse*
      How could it end in any other way?
      You called me, and I came home to your heart.
      The triumph was—to reach and stay there; since
      I reached it ere the triumph, what is lost?
175   Let my hands frame your face in your hair's gold,
      You beautiful Lucrezia that are mine!
      "Rafael did this, Andrea painted that;
      The Roman's is the better when you pray,
      But still the other's Virgin was his wife—"
180   Men will excuse me. I am glad to judge
      Both pictures in your presence; clearer grows
      My better fortune, I resolve to think.
      For, do you know, Lucrezia, as God lives,
      Said one day Agnolo, his very self,
185   To Rafael . . . I have known it all these years . . .
      (When the young man was flaming out his thoughts
      Upon a palace wall for Rome to see,
      Too lifted up in heart because of it)
      "Friend, there's a certain sorry little scrub
190   Goes up and down our Florence, none cares how,
      Who, were he set to plan and execute
      As you are, pricked on by your popes and kings,
      Would bring the sweat into that brow of yours!"
      To Rafael's—And indeed the arm is wrong.
195   I hardly dare . . . yet, only you to see,
      Give the chalk here—quick, thus the line should go!
      Aye, but the soul! he's Rafael! rub it out!
      Still, all I care for, if he spoke the truth,
      (What he? why, who but Michel Agnolo?
200   Do you forget already words like those?)
      If really there was such a chance, so lost—
      Is, whether you're—not grateful—but more pleased.
      Well, let me think so. And you smile indeed!
      This hour has been an hour! Another smile?
205   If you would sit thus by me every night
      I should work better, do you comprehend?
      I mean that I should earn more, give you more.

See, it is settled dusk now; there's a star;
Morello's gone, the watch-lights show the wall,
10 The cue-owls[4] speak the name we call them by.
Come from the window, love—come in, at last,
Inside the melancholy little house
We built to be so gay with. God is just.
King Francis may forgive me: oft at nights
15 When I look up from painting, eyes tired out,
The walls become illumined, brick from brick
Distinct, instead of mortar, fierce bright gold,
That gold of his I did cement them with!
Let us but love each other. Must you go?
20 That Cousin here again? he waits outside?
Must see you—you, and not with me? Those loans?
More gaming debts to pay?[5] you smiled for that?
Well, let smiles buy me! have you more to spend?
While hand and eye and something of a heart
25 Are left me, work's my ware, and what's it worth?
I'll pay my fancy. Only let me sit
The gray remainder of the evening out,
Idle, you call it, and muse perfectly
How I could paint, were I but back in France,
30 One picture, just one more—the Virgin's face,
Not yours this time! I want you at my side
To hear them—that is, Michel Agnolo—
Judge all I do and tell you of its worth.
Will you? Tomorrow, satisfy your friend.
35 I take the subjects for his corridor,
Finish the portrait out of hand—there, there,
And throw him in another thing or two
If he demurs; the whole should prove enough
To pay for this same Cousin's freak.° Beside,   whim
40 What's better and what's all I care about,
Get you the thirteen scudi° for the ruff!   Italian coins
Love, does that please you? Ah, but what does he,
The Cousin! What does he to please you more?

I am grown peaceful as old age tonight.
45 I regret little, I would change still less.
Since there my past life lies, why alter it?
The very wrong to Francis!—it is true
I took his coin, was tempted and complied,
And built this house and sinned, and all is said.
50 My father and my mother died of want.[6]
Well, had I riches of my own? you see
How one gets rich! Let each one bear his lot.
They were born poor, lived poor, and poor they died:

---

4. Scops owls; the term is Browning's coinage from the Italian *chiù* or *ciù*, a name that imitates their cry.
5. Lucrezia's "Cousin" (or lover or friend) owes gambling debts to a creditor. Andrea has already contracted (lines 5–10) to pay off these debts by painting some pictures according to the creditor's specifications. Now he agrees to pay off further debts.
6. According to Vasari, Andrea's infatuation for Lucrezia prompted him to stop supporting his poverty-stricken parents.

And I have labored somewhat in my time
255 And not been paid profusely. Some good son
Paint my two hundred pictures—let him try!
No doubt, there's something strikes a balance. Yes,
You loved me quite enough, it seems tonight.
This must suffice me here. What would one have?
260 In heaven, perhaps, new chances, one more chance—
Four great walls in the New Jerusalem,[7]
Meted on each side by the angel's reed,°   measuring rod
For Leonard,[8] Rafael, Agnolo and me
To cover—the three first without a wife,
265 While I have mine! So—still they overcome
Because there's still Lucrezia—as I choose.

Again the Cousin's whistle! Go, my Love.

ca. 1853   1855

Caliban upon Setebos

Shakespeare's *Tempest* provided Browning with the idea for his speaker (Caliban is Prospero's brutish slave, half-man, half-beast) and the subject of his musings (Setebos is briefly referred to in the play as the god of Caliban's mother, the witch Sycorax). From these beginnings Browning writes a poem that reflects on two closely related controversies of the Victorian period. The first concerned the nature of God and God's responsibility for the existence of pain in the world. The second debate, stimulated by the publication of Darwin's *Origin of Species* (1859), focused on humanity's origins and our relation to other beings.

As the poem's epigraph reveals, Browning is interested in the idea that the human conception of the divine is conditioned by our own limitations, or by our understanding of ourselves. Caliban, a lower being, draws his notion of the god who he believes dictates his fortunes from three main sources: his observations of life on the island, his own character, and his experiences with Prospero, his master. The first of these, his knowledge of the behavior and sufferings of animal life, gives rise to his "natural theology": that is, his tendency to understand the character of his god from evidences provided by nature rather than from the evidence of supernatural revelation. From his perceptions of his own motivations and the conduct of his earthly ruler comes Caliban's conception of Setebos's willful power. Caliban admires power and thinks of his god as a being who selects at random some creatures who are to be saved and others who are condemned to suffer. His musings thus connect in complex ways with key and pressing issues for the religious and scientific communities of the Victorian era: through the lens of this most unlikely philosopher, Browning raises the topics both of eternal salvation and of natural selection. Significantly, Caliban feels the need to posit a higher divine being, or presence, that exists "over Setebos": puzzling about this other deity, "the Quiet," Browning's speaker delves into fundamental questions of origin and the construction of myth.

An obstacle for the reader is Caliban's use of the third-person pronoun to refer to himself. Thus " 'Will sprawl" means "Caliban will sprawl" (an apostrophe before the verb usually indicates that Caliban is the implied subject). Setebos is also referred to in the third person but with an initial capital letter ("He").

7. Cf. Revelation 21.10–21.   8. Leonardo da Vinci (1452–1519).

Caliban upon Setebos

Or Natural Theology in the Island

"Thou thoughtest that I was altogether such a one as thyself."[1]

['Will sprawl, now that the heat of day is best,
Flat on his belly in the pit's much mire,
With elbows wide, fists clenched to prop his chin.
And, while he kicks both feet in the cool slush,
5   And feels about his spine small eft-things° course,   *water lizards*
Run in and out each arm, and make him laugh:
And while above his head a pompion° plant,   *pumpkin*
Coating the cave-top as a brow its eye,
Creeps down to touch and tickle hair and beard,
10 And now a flower drops with a bee inside,
And now a fruit to snap at, catch and crunch—
He looks out o'er yon sea which sunbeams cross
And recross till they weave a spider web
(Meshes of fire, some great fish breaks at times)
15 And talks to his own self, howe'er he please,
Touching that other, whom his dam° called God.   *mother*
Because to talk about Him, vexes—ha,
Could He but know! and time to vex is now,
When talk is safer than in wintertime.
20 Moreover Prosper and Miranda[2] sleep
In confidence he drudges at their task,
And it is good to cheat the pair, and gibe,°   *insult them*
Letting the rank tongue blossom into speech.]

Setebos, Setebos, and Setebos!
25 'Thinketh, He dwelleth i' the cold o' the moon.

'Thinketh He made it, with the sun to match,
But not the stars; the stars came otherwise;
Only made clouds, winds, meteors, such as that:
Also this isle, what lives and grows thereon,
30 And snaky sea which rounds and ends the same.

'Thinketh, it came of being ill at ease:
He hated that He cannot change His cold,
Nor cure its ache. 'Hath spied an icy fish
That longed to 'scape the rock-stream where she lived,
35 And thaw herself within the lukewarm brine
O' the lazy sea her stream thrusts far amid,
A crystal spike 'twixt two warm walls of wave;[3]
Only, she ever sickened, found repulse
At the other kind of water, not her life,
40 (Green-dense and dim-delicious, bred o' the sun)

---

1. Psalm 50.21. The speaker is God.
2. Prospero's daughter.
3. I.e., the thin stream of cold water that is driven into the warm ocean like a spike between walls.

Flounced back from bliss she was not born to breathe,
And in her old bounds buried her despair,
Hating and loving warmth alike: so He.

'Thinketh, He made thereat the sun, this isle,
45   Trees and the fowls here, beast and creeping thing.
Yon otter, sleek-wet, black, lithe as a leech;
Yon auk,° one fire-eye in a ball of foam,   *seabird*
That floats and feeds; a certain badger brown
He hath watched hunt with that slant white-wedge eye
50   By moonlight; and the pie° with the long tongue   *magpie*
That pricks deep into oakwarts for a worm,
And says a plain word when she finds her prize,
But will not eat the ants; the ants themselves
That build a wall of seeds and settled stalks
55   About their hole—He made all these and more,
Made all we see, and us, in spite: how else?
He could not, Himself, make a second self
To be His mate; as well have made Himself:
He would not make what he mislikes or slights,
60   An eyesore to Him, or not worth His pains:
But did, in envy, listlessness, or sport,
Make what Himself would fain,° in a manner, be—   *gladly*
Weaker in most points, stronger in a few,
Worthy, and yet mere playthings all the while,
65   Things He admires and mocks too—that is it.
Because, so brave, so better though they be,
It nothing skills if He begin to plague.⁴
Look now, I melt a gourd-fruit into mash,
Add honeycomb and pods, I have perceived,
70   Which bite like finches when they bill and kiss—
Then, when froth rises bladdery,° drink up all,   *bubbly*
Quick, quick, till maggots scamper through my brain;
Last, throw me on my back i' the seeded thyme,
And wanton, wishing I were born a bird.
75   Put case, unable to be what I wish,
I yet could make a live bird out of clay:
Would not I take clay, pinch my Caliban
Able to fly?—for, there, see, he hath wings,
And great comb like the hoopoe's⁵ to admire,
80   And there, a sting to do his foes offense,
There, and I will that he begin to live,
Fly to yon rock-top, nip me off the horns
Of griggs° high up that make the merry din,   *grasshoppers*
Saucy through their veined wings, and mind me not.
85   In which feat, if his leg snapped, brittle clay,
And he lay stupid-like—why, I should laugh;
And if he, spying me, should fall to weep,
Beseech me to be good, repair his wrong,

4. I.e., the superior virtues of Setebos's creatures   5. Bird with bright plumage.
are no help to them if he decides to torture them.

Bid his poor leg smart less or grow again—
90　Well, as the chance were, this might take or else
　　Not take my fancy: I might hear his cry,
　　And give the mankin° three sound legs for one,　　　　*little man*
　　Or pluck the other off, leave him like an egg,
　　And lessoned° he was mine and merely clay.　　　　*thus taught*
95　Were this no pleasure, lying in the thyme,
　　Drinking the mash, with brain become alive,
　　Making and marring clay at will? So He.
　　'Thinketh, such shows nor right nor wrong in Him,
　　Nor kind, nor cruel: He is strong and Lord.
100　'Am strong myself compared to yonder crabs
　　That march now from the mountain to the sea;
　　'Let twenty pass, and stone the twenty-first,
　　Loving not, hating not, just choosing so.
　　'Say, the first straggler that boasts purple spots
105　Shall join the file, one pincer twisted off;
　　'Say, this bruised fellow shall receive a worm,
　　And two worms he whose nippers end in red;
　　As it likes me each time, I do: so He.

　　Well then, 'supposeth He is good i' the main,
110　Placable if His mind and ways were guessed,
　　But rougher than His handiwork, be sure!
　　Oh, He hath made things worthier than Himself,
　　And envieth that, so helped, such things do more
　　Than He who made them! What consoles but this?
115　That they, unless through Him, do naught at all,
　　And must submit: what other use in things?
　　'Hath cut a pipe of pithless elder-joint
　　That, blown through, gives exact the scream o' the jay
　　When from her wing you twitch the feathers blue:
120　Sound this, and little birds that hate the jay
　　Flock within stone's throw, glad their foe is hurt:
　　Put case such pipe could prattle and boast forsooth,
　　"I catch the birds, I am the crafty thing,
　　I make the cry my maker cannot make
125　With his great round mouth; he must blow through mine!"
　　Would not I smash it with my foot? So He.

　　But wherefore rough, why cold and ill at ease?
　　Aha, that is a question! Ask, for that,
　　What knows—the something over Setebos
130　That made Him, or He, may be, found and fought,
　　Worsted, drove off and did to nothing,° perchance.　　*completely overcame*
　　There may be something quiet o'er His head,
　　Out of His reach, that feels nor° joy nor grief,　　　　*neither*
　　Since both derive from weakness in some way.
135　I joy because the quails come; would not joy
　　Could I bring quails here when I have a mind:
　　This Quiet, all it hath a mind to, doth.
　　'Esteemeth° stars the outposts of its couch,　　　　*he believes*

But never spends much thought nor care that way.
140 It may look up, work up—the worse for those
It works on! 'Careth but for Setebos[6]
The many-handed as a cuttlefish,
Who, making Himself feared through what He does,
Looks up, first, and perceives he cannot soar
145 To what is quiet and hath happy life;
Next looks down here, and out of very spite
Makes this a bauble-world to ape yon real,
These good things to match those as hips[7] do grapes.
'Tis solace making baubles, aye, and sport.
150 Himself peeped late, eyed Prosper at his books
Careless and lofty, lord now of the isle:
Vexed, 'stitched a book of broad leaves, arrow-shaped,
Wrote thereon, he knows what, prodigious words;
Has peeled a wand and called it by a name;
155 Weareth at whiles for an enchanter's robe
The eyed skin of a supple oncelot;[8]
And hath an ounce[9] sleeker than youngling mole,
A four-legged serpent he makes cower and couch,
Now snarl, now hold its breath and mind his eye,
160 And saith she is Miranda and my wife:
'Keeps for his Ariel[1] a tall pouch-bill crane
He bids go wade for fish and straight° disgorge;   *immediately*
Also a sea beast, lumpish, which he snared,
Blinded the eyes of, and brought somewhat tame,
165 And split its toe-webs, and now pens the drudge
In a hole o' the rock and calls him Caliban;
A bitter heart that bides its time and bites.
'Plays thus at being Prosper in a way,
Taketh his mirth with make-believes: so He.
170 His dam held that the Quiet made all things
Which Setebos vexed only: 'holds not so.
Who made them weak, meant weakness He might vex.
Had He meant other, while His hand was in,
Why not make horny eyes no thorn could prick,
175 Or plate my scalp with bone against the snow,
Or overscale my flesh 'neath joint and joint,
Like an orc's° armor? Aye—so spoil His sport!   *sea monster's*
He is the One now: only He doth all.

'Saith, He may like, perchance, what profits Him.
180 Aye, himself loves what does him good; but why?
'Gets good no otherwise. This blinded beast
Loves whoso places flesh-meat on his nose,
But, had he eyes, would want no help, but hate
Or love, just as it liked him: He hath eyes.
185 Also it pleaseth Setebos to work,

---

6. Caliban's concern is to appease only Setebos, not the other deity—the Quiet.
7. Hard fruits produced by wild roses.
8. Browning may have invented this term from the Spanish *oncela* or from the French *ocelot* (i.e., a leopard or spotted wildcat).
9. A lynx or other wild feline of moderate size or a snow leopard.
1. In *The Tempest* a spirit who serves Prospero.

Use all His hands, and exercise much craft,
By no means for the love of what is worked.
'Tasteth, himself, no finer good i' the world
When all goes right, in this safe summertime,
190 And he wants little, hungers, aches not much,
Than trying what to do with wit and strength.
'Falls to make something: 'piled yon pile of turfs,
And squared and stuck there squares of soft white chalk,
And, with a fish-tooth, scratched a moon on each,
195 And set up endwise certain spikes of tree,
And crowned the whole with a sloth's skull a-top,
Found dead i' the woods, too hard for one to kill.
No use at all i' the work, for work's sole sake;
'Shall some day knock it down again: so He.

200 'Saith He is terrible: watch His feats in proof!
One hurricane will spoil six good months' hope.
He hath a spite against me, that I know,
Just as He favors Prosper, who knows why?
So it is, all the same, as well I find.
205 'Wove wattles half the winter, fenced them firm
With stone and stake to stop she-tortoises
Crawling to lay their eggs here: well, one wave,
Feeling the foot of Him upon its neck,
Gaped as a snake does, lolled out its large tongue,
210 And licked the whole labor flat; so much for spite.
'Saw a ball° flame down late (yonder it lies)   *meteorite*
Where, half an hour before, I slept i' the shade:
Often they scatter sparkles: there is force!
'Dug up a newt He may have envied once
215 And turned to stone, shut up inside a stone.
Please Him and hinder this?—What Prosper does?[2]
Aha, if He would tell me how! Not He!
There is the sport: discover how or die!
All need not die, for of the things o' the isle
220 Some flee afar, some dive, some run up trees;
Those at His mercy—why, they please Him most
When . . . when . . . well, never try the same way twice!
Repeat what act has pleased, He may grow wroth.
You must not know His ways, and play Him off,
225 Sure of the issue.° 'Doth the like himself: *outcome*
'Spareth a squirrel that it nothing fears
But steals[3] the nut from underneath my thumb,
And when I threat, bites stoutly in defense:
'Spareth an urchin° that contrariwise   *hedgehog*
230 Curls up into a ball, pretending death
For fright at my approach: the two ways please.
But what would move my choler more than this,
That either creature counted on its life
Tomorrow and next day and all days to come,

2. I.e., shall I please Setebos, as Prospero does,   was punished?
and thus prevent my being punished as the newt   3. I.e., that is fearless enough to steal.

235 Saying, forsooth, in the inmost of its heart,
"Because he did so yesterday with me,
And otherwise with such another brute,
So must he do henceforth and always."—Aye?
Would teach the reasoning couple what "must" means!
240 'Doth as he likes, or wherefore Lord? So He.

'Conceiveth all things will continue thus,
And we shall have to live in fear of Him
So long as He lives, keeps His strength: no change,
If He have done His best, make no new world
245 To please Him more, so leave off watching this—
If He surprise not even the Quiet's self
Some strange day—or, suppose, grow into it
As grubs grow butterflies: else, here are we,
And there is He, and nowhere help at all.
250 'Believeth with the life, the pain shall stop.
His dam held different, that after death
He both plagued enemies and feasted friends:
Idly![4] He doth His worst in this our life,
Giving just respite lest we die through pain,
255 Saving last pain for worst—with which, an end.
Meanwhile, the best way to escape His ire
Is, not to seem too happy. 'Sees, himself,
Yonder two flies, with purple films and pink,
Bask on the pompion-bell above: kills both.
260 'Sees two black painful beetles roll their ball
On head and tail as if to save their lives:
Moves them the stick away they strive to clear.

Even so, 'would have Him misconceive, suppose
This Caliban strives hard and ails no less,
265 And always, above all else, envies Him;
Wherefore he mainly dances on dark nights,
Moans in the sun, gets under holes to laugh,
And never speaks his mind save housed as now:
Outside, 'groans, curses. If He caught me here,
270 O'erheard this speech, and asked "What chucklest at?"
'Would, to appease Him, cut a finger off,
Or of my three kid yearlings burn the best,
Or let the toothsome apples rot on tree,
Or push my tame beast for the orc to taste:
275 While myself lit a fire, and made a song
And sung it, *"What I hate, be consecrate*
To celebrate Thee and Thy state, no mate
For Thee; what see for envy in poor me?"
Hoping the while, since evils sometimes mend,
280 Warts rub away and sores are cured with slime,
That some strange day, will either the Quiet catch
And conquer Setebos, or likelier He
Decrepit may doze, doze, as good as die.

---

4. I.e., Caliban thinks his mother's opinion was wrong or idle. Setebos's sport with his creatures is confined to this world: there is no afterlife.

[What, what? A curtain o'er the world at once!
285　Crickets stop hissing; not a bird—or, yes,
There scuds His raven[5] that has told Him all!
It was fool's play this prattling! Ha! The wind
Shoulders the pillared dust, death's house o' the move,[6]
And fast invading fires begin! White blaze—
290　A tree's head snaps—and there, there, there, there, there,
His thunder follows! Fool to gibe at Him!
Lo! 'Lieth flat and loveth Setebos!
'Maketh his teeth meet through his upper lip,
Will let those quails fly, will not eat this month
295　One little mess of whelks,° so he may 'scape!]　　　　*shellfish*

ca. 1860　　　　　　　　　　　　　　　　　　　　　　　　　1864

---

5. In Norse mythology ravens brought the daily news to Odin, the most powerful god.

6. The whirlwind stirs up a column of dust that Caliban associates with a house of death.

MATTHEW ARNOLD
1822–1888

How is a full and enjoyable life to be lived in a modern industrial society? This was the recurrent topic in the poetry and prose of Matthew Arnold. In his poetry the question itself is raised; in his prose some answers are attempted. "The misapprehensiveness [wrongheadedness] of his age is exactly what a poet is sent to remedy," wrote Robert Browning, and yet it is to Arnold's work, not Browning's, that the statement seems more applicable. In response to rapid and potentially dislocating social changes, Arnold strove to help his contemporaries achieve a richer intellectual and emotional existence.

Matthew Arnold was born in Laleham, a village in the valley of the Thames. It seems appropriate that his childhood was spent near a river, for clear-flowing streams were later to appear in his poems as symbols of serenity. At the age of six, Arnold was moved to Rugby School, where his father, Dr. Thomas Arnold, had become headmaster. As a clergyman Dr. Arnold was a leader of the liberal or Broad Church and hence one of the principal opponents of John Henry Newman. As a headmaster he became famous as an educational reformer, a teacher who instilled in his pupils an earnest preoccupation with moral and social issues and also an awareness of the connection between liberal studies and modern life. At Rugby his eldest son, Matthew, was directly exposed to the powerful force of the father's mind and character. The son's attitude toward this force was a mixture of attraction and repulsion. That he was permanently influenced by his father is evident in his poems and in his writings on religion, education, and politics; but like many sons of clergymen, he made a determined effort in his youth to be different. As a student at Oxford he behaved like a dandy. Elegantly and colorfully dressed, alternately languid or merry in manner, he refused to be serious and irritated more solemn undergraduate friends and acquaintances with his irreverent jokes. "His manner displeases, from its seeming foppery," wrote Charlotte Brontë after talking with the young man in later years. "The shade of Dr. Arnold," she added, "seemed to me to frown on his young representative." The son of Dr. Arnold thus appeared to have no connection with Rugby School's standards of earnestness. Even his studies did not seem to occupy him seriously. By a session of cramming, he managed to earn second-class honors in his final examinations, a near disaster that was redeemed by his election to a fellowship at Oriel College.

Arnold's biographers usually dismiss his youthful frivolity of spirit as only a temporary pose or mask, but it permanently colored his prose style, brightening his most serious criticism with geniality and wit. For most readers the jauntiness of his prose is a virtue, though others find it offensive. Anyone suspicious of urbanity and irony would applaud Walt Whitman's sour comment that Arnold is "one of the dudes [dandies, or city slickers] of literature." A more appropriate estimate of his manner is provided by Arnold's own description of the French writer Charles-Augustin Sainte-Beuve: "a critic of measure, not exuberant; of the centre, not provincial . . . with gay and amiable temper, his manner as good as his matter—the *'critique souriant'* [smiling critic]."

Unlike authors such as Alfred, Lord Tennyson and Thomas Carlyle who committed themselves solely to their literary pursuits, Arnold confined his writing and reading to his spare time. In 1847 he took the post of private secretary to Lord Lansdowne; and in 1851, the year of his marriage, he became an inspector of schools, a demanding and time-consuming position that he held for thirty-five years. Although his work as an inspector may have reduced his output as a writer, it had several advantages. His extensive traveling in England took him to the homes of the more ardently Protestant middle classes, and when he criticized the dullness of middle-class life (as he often did), his scorn was based on intimate knowledge. His position also led to travel on the Continent to study the schools of Europe. As a critic of English education, he was thus able to make helpful comparisons and to draw on a stock of fresh ideas in the same way as in his literary criticism he used his familiarity with French, German, Italian, and classical literatures to talk knowledgeably about the distinctive qualities of English writers. Despite the monotony of much of his work as an inspector, Arnold became convinced of its importance. It contributed to what he regarded as his century's most important need: the development of a satisfactory national system of education.

In 1849 Arnold published *The Strayed Reveler*, his first volume of poetry. Eight years later, as a tribute to his poetic achievement, he was elected to the professorship of poetry at Oxford, a part-time position that he held for ten years. Later, like Charles Dickens and William Makepeace Thackeray before him, Arnold toured America to make money by lecturing. His lectures could leave audiences indifferent, but sometimes they were highly acclaimed: thus the *Washington Post* reported that, following a two-hour address in the U.S. capital, the African American leader Frederick Douglass "moved that a tremendous vote of thanks be tendered to the speaker." A further inducement for his two visits (in 1883 and 1886) was the opportunity of seeing his daughter Lucy, who had married an American. In 1888 Arnold died of a sudden heart attack.

Arnold's career as a writer can be roughly divided into four periods. In the 1850s most of his poems appeared; in the 1860s, literary criticism and social criticism; in the 1870s, his religious and educational writings; and in the 1880s, his second set of essays in literary criticism.

Today Arnold is perhaps better known as a writer of prose than as a poet, although individual poems such as "Dover Beach" (1867) continue to be widely popular. In his own era his decision to spend hardly any time composing poetry after 1860 was considered wrongheaded by some: "Tell Mat not to write any more of those prose things like *Literature and Dogma*," Tennyson wrote in a letter, wishing that Arnold would instead "give us something like his 'Thyrsis,' 'Scholar Gypsy,' or 'Forsaken Merman.' " Others have felt that he made the right move: Arnold's poetry has been criticized, in both the nineteenth and the twentieth centuries, on numerous grounds. Some have disliked its excessive reliance on italics instead of on meter to emphasize the meaning of a line, while others object to the prosy flatness of certain passages or, conversely, to overelaborated similes in others. Yet despite these cavils, many readers find much to cherish and admire. Given Arnold's sophistication as a writer, it is perhaps surprising that his evocations of nature function so memorably in his poetry: rather than simply providing a picturesque backdrop, the setting—seashore or river or mountaintop—draws the poem's meaning together. In this respect, as in many others, Arnold displays a debt to William Wordsworth, whose poetry he greatly admired; but he also draws on his own bond with particular landscapes, especially those associated with his youth and early adulthood. The stanzas of "The Scholar Gypsy" (1853), for instance—suffused in a deep familiarity with the changing patterns of the rural scene, from the "frail-leafed, white anemone" and "dark bluebells drenched with dews" of May to the "scarlet poppies" and "pale pink convolvulus" of August—record with sensuous care the distinct seasons of the English countryside and Arnold's nostalgic memories of the rambles of his Oxford days.

Arnold's own verdict on the qualities of his poetry is interesting. In an 1869 letter to his mother, he writes:

> My poems represent, on the whole, the main movement of mind of the last quarter of a century, and thus they will probably have their day as people become conscious to themselves of what that movement of mind is, and interested in the literary productions which reflect it. It might be fairly urged that I have less poetical sentiment than Tennyson, and less intellectual vigor and abundance than Browning; yet, because I have perhaps more of a fusion of the two than either of them, and have more regularly applied that fusion to the main line of modern development, I am likely enough to have my turn, as they have had theirs.

The emphasis in the letter on "movement of mind" suggests that Arnold's poetry and prose should be studied together. Such an approach can be fruitful provided that it does not obscure the important difference between Arnold the poet and Arnold the critic. T. S. Eliot once said of his own writings that "in one's prose reflections one may be legitimately occupied with ideals, whereas in the writing of verse, one can deal only with actuality." Arnold's writings offer a nice verification of Eliot's seeming paradox. As a poet he usually records his own experiences, his own feelings of loneliness and isolation as a lover, his longing for a serenity that he cannot find, his melancholy sense of the passing of youth (more than for many men, Arnold's thirtieth birthday was an awe-inspiring landmark after which he felt, he said, "three parts iced over"). Above all he records his despair in a universe in which humanity's role seemed an incongruous as it was later to seem to Thomas Hardy. In a memorable passage of his "Stanzas from the Grande Chartreuse" (1855), he describes himself as "Wandering between two worlds, one dead, / The other powerless to be born." And addressing the representatives of a faith that seems to him dead, he cries: "Take me, cowled forms, and fence me round, / Till I possess my soul again." As a poet, then, like T. S. Eliot and W. H. Auden, Arnold provides a record of a troubled individual in a troubled society. This was "actuality" as he experienced it—an actuality, like Eliot's and Auden's, representative of his era. As a prose writer, a formulator of "ideals," he seeks a different role—to be what Auden calls the "healer" of a diseased society, or as he himself called Goethe, the "Physician of the iron age." And in this difference we have a clue to answering the question of why Arnold virtually abandoned the writing of poetry to move into criticism. One reason was his dissatisfaction with the kind of poetry he was writing.

In one of his fascinating letters to his friend Arthur Hugh Clough in the 1850s (letters that provide the best insight we have into Arnold's mind and tastes), this note of dissatisfaction is struck: "I am glad you like the *Gypsy Scholar*—but what does it *do* for you? Homer *animates*—Shakespeare *animates*—in its poor way I think *Sohrab and Rustum animates*—the *Gypsy Scholar* at best awakens a pleasing melancholy. But this is not what we want." It is evident that early in his career Arnold had evolved a theory of what poetry should do for its readers, a theory based, in part, on his impression of what classical poetry had achieved. To help make life bearable, poetry, in

2094 / Matthew Arnold

Arnold's view, must bring joy. As he says in the 1853 preface to his *Poems*, it must "inspirit and rejoice the reader"; it must "convey a charm, and infuse delight." Such a demand does not exclude tragic poetry but does exclude works "in which suffering finds no vent in action; in which a continual state of mental distress is prolonged." Of Charlotte Brontë's novel *Villette* (1853) he says witheringly: "The writer's mind contains nothing but hunger, rebellion, and rage . . . No fine writing can hide this thoroughly, and it will be fatal to her in the long run." Judged by such a standard, most nineteenth-century poems, including his own long poem *Empedocles on Etna* (1852), were unsatisfactory. And when Arnold tried to write poems that would meet his own requirements—*Sohrab and Rustum* (1853) or *Balder Dead* (1855)—he felt that something was lacking. By the late 1850s he thus found himself at a dead end. Turning aside to literary criticism enabled him partially to escape the dilemma. In his prose his melancholy and "morbid" personality was subordinated to the resolutely cheerful and purposeful character he had created for himself by an effort of will.

Arnold's two volumes of *Essays in Criticism* (1865, 1888) repeatedly show how authors as different as Marcus Aurelius, Leo Tolstoy, Homer, and Wordsworth provide the virtues he sought in his reading. Among these virtues was plainness of style. Although he could on occasion recommend the richness of language of such poets as John Keats or Tennyson—their "natural magic," as he called it—Arnold usually preferred literature that was unadorned. And beyond stylistic excellences, the principal virtue he admired as a critic was the quality of "high seriousness." In a world in which the role of formal religion appeared to be shrinking, Arnold increasingly emphasized that the poet must be a serious thinker who could offer guidance to his readers. This belief perhaps caused him to undervalue other qualities in literature: in "The Study of Poetry" (1880), for instance, he displays little appreciation for Chaucer's humor and chooses instead to castigate him for his lack of high seriousness.

In "The Function of Criticism at the Present Time" (1864), Arnold makes clear that he regarded good literary criticism, like literature itself, as a potent force in producing what he conceived as a civilized society. From a close study of this essay one could forecast the third stage of his career: his excursion into the criticism of society that was to culminate in *Culture and Anarchy* (1869) and *Friendship's Garland* (1871).

Arnold's starting point as a critic of society is different from that of Carlyle and John Ruskin. The older prophets attacked the Victorian middle classes on the grounds of their materialism, their selfish indifference to the sufferings of the poor—their immorality, in effect. Arnold argued instead that the "Philistines," as he called them, were not so much wicked as ignorant, narrow-minded, and suffering from the dullness of their private lives. This novel analysis was reinforced by Arnold's conviction that the world of the future, both in England and in America, would be a middle-class world and therefore would be dominated by a class inadequately equipped either to lead or to enjoy civilized living.

To establish this point Arnold employed cajolery, satire, and even quotations from current newspapers with considerable effect. He also used memorable catch phrases (such as "sweetness and light") that sometimes pose an obstacle to understanding the complexities of his position. His view of civilization, for example, was pared down to a four-point formula of the four "powers": conduct, intellect and knowledge, beauty, and social life and manners. Applying this simple formula to a range of civilizations, Arnold had a scale by which to judge the virtues as well as the inadequacies of different countries. When he turned this instrument on his own country, he usually awarded the Victorian middle classes an A in the first category (i.e., conduct) but a failing grade in the other three categories. Unsurprisingly, he also had pronounced opinions on what he viewed as the distinct national characters of different peoples: this strain in Arnold's writing appears in, for example, his lectures *On the Study of Celtic Literature* (1867).

Arnold's relentless exposure of middle-class narrow-mindedness in his own country eventually led him into the arena of religious controversy. As a critic of religious institutions he was arguing, in effect, that just as the middle classes did not know how to lead full lives, neither did they know how to read the Bible intelligently or attend church intelligently. Of the Christian religion he remarked that there are two things "that surely must be clear to anybody with eyes in his head. One is, that men cannot do without it; the other that they cannot do with it as it is." His three full-length studies of the Bible, including *Literature and Dogma* (1873), are thus best considered a postscript to his social criticism. The Bible, to Arnold, was a great work of literature like the *Odyssey*, and the Church of England was a great national institution like Parliament. Both Bible and Church must be preserved not because historical Christianity was credible but because both, when properly understood, were agents of what he called "culture"—they contributed to making humanity more civilized.

Culture is perhaps Arnold's most familiar catchwood, although what he meant by it has sometimes been misunderstood. He used the term to capture the qualities of an open-minded intelligence (as described in "The Function of Criticism")—a refusal to take things on authority. In this respect Arnold appears close to T. H. Huxley and J. S. Mill. But the word also connotes a full awareness of humanity's past and a capacity to enjoy the best works of art, literature, history, and philosophy that have come down to us from that past. As a way of viewing life in all its aspects, including the social, political, and religious, culture represents for Arnold the most effective cure for the ills of a sick society. It is his principal prescription.

The attempt to define culture brings us to a final aspect of Arnold's career as a critic: his writings on education, in which he sought to make cultural values, as he said, "prevail." Most obviously these writings comprise his reply to Huxley (his admirably reasoned essay "Literature and Science," 1882) and his volumes of official reports written as an inspector of schools. Less obviously, they comprise all his prose. At their core is his belief that good education is *the* crucial need. Arnold was essentially a great teacher. He has the faults of a teacher—a tendency to repeat himself, to lean too hard on formulaic phrases—and he displays something of the lectern manner at times. He also has the great teacher's virtues, in particular the ability to skillfully convey to us the conviction on which all his arguments are based. This conviction is that the humanist tradition of which he is the expositor can enable the individual man or woman to live life more fully and to change the course of society. He believes that a democratic society can thrive only if its citizens become educated in what he saw as the great Western tradition, "the best that is known and thought." These values, which some readers find elitist, make Arnold both timely and controversial. Arnold fought for these values with the gloves on—kid gloves, his opponents used to say—and he provided a lively exhibition of footwork that is a pleasure to observe. Yet the gracefulness of the display should not obscure the fact that he lands hard blows squarely on his opponents.

Although his lifelong attacks against the inadequacies of Puritanism make Arnold one of the most anti-Victorian figures of his age, behind his attacks is a characteristically Victorian assumption: that the Puritan middle classes *can* be changed, that they are, as we would more clumsily say, educable. In 1852, writing to Clough on the subject of equality (a political objective in which he believed by conviction if not by instinct), Arnold observed: "I am more and more convinced that the world tends to become more comfortable for the mass, and more uncomfortable for those of any natural gift or distinction—and it is as well perhaps that it should be so—for hitherto the gifted have astonished and delighted the world, but not trained or inspired or in any real way changed it." Arnold's gifts as a poet and critic enabled him to do both: to delight the world and to change it.

To Marguerite—Continued

Yes! in the sea of life enisled,°   *encircled*
With echoing straits between us thrown,
Dotting the shoreless watery wild,
We mortal millions live *alone*.
5   The islands feel the enclasping flow,
And then their endless bounds they know.

But when the moon their hollows lights,
And they are swept by balms of spring,
And in their glens, on starry nights,
10   The nightingales divinely sing;
And lovely notes, from shore to shore,
Across the sounds and channels pour—

Oh! then a longing like despair
Is to their farthest caverns sent;
15   For surely once, they feel, we were
Parts of a single continent!
Now round us spreads the watery plain—
Oh might our marges meet again!

Who ordered that their longing's fire
20   Should be, as soon as kindled, cooled?
Who renders vain their deep desire?—
A God, a God their severance ruled!
And bade betwixt their shores to be
The unplumbed, salt, estranging sea.

1849   1852

The Buried Life

Light flows our war of mocking words, and yet,
Behold, with tears mine eyes are wet!
I feel a nameless sadness o'er me roll.
Yes, yes, we know that we can jest,
5   We know, we know that we can smile!
But there's a something in this breast,
To which thy light words bring no rest,
And thy gay smiles no anodyne.
Give me thy hand, and hush awhile,
10   And turn those limpid eyes on mine,
And let me read there, love! thy inmost soul.

Alas! is even love too weak
To unlock the heart, and let it speak?
Are even lovers powerless to reveal
15   To one another what indeed they feel?

I knew the mass of men concealed
Their thoughts, for fear that if revealed
They would by other men be met
With blank indifference, or with blame reproved;
20 I knew they lived and moved
Tricked° in disguises, alien to the rest   *dressed up*
Of men, and alien to themselves—and yet
The same heart beats in every human breast!

But we, my love!—doth a like spell benumb
25 Our hearts, our voices?—must we too be dumb?
Ah! well for us, if even we,
Even for a moment, can get free
Our heart, and have our lips unchained;
For that which seals them hath been deep-ordained!

30 Fate, which foresaw
How frivolous a baby man would be—
By what distractions he would be possessed,
How he would pour himself in every strife,
And well-nigh change his own identity—
35 That it might keep from his capricious play
His genuine self, and force him to obey
Even in his own despite his being's law,
Bade through the deep recesses of our breast
The unregarded river of our life
40 Pursue with indiscernible flow its way;
And that we should not see
The buried stream, and seem to be
Eddying at large in blind uncertainty,
Though driving on with it eternally.

45 But often, in the world's most crowded streets,¹
But often, in the din of strife,
There rises an unspeakable desire
After the knowledge of our buried life;
A thirst to spend our fire and restless force
50 In tracking out our true, original course;
A longing to inquire
Into the mystery of this heart which beats
So wild, so deep in us—to know
Whence our lives come and where they go.
55 And many a man in his own breast then delves,
But deep enough, alas! none ever mines.
And we have been on many thousand lines,
And we have shown, on each, spirit and power;
But hardly have we, for one little hour,
60 Been on our own line, have we been ourselves—

---

1. This passage, like many others in Arnold's poetry, illustrates William Wordsworth's effect on his writings. In this instance cf. Wordsworth's "Tintern Abbey (1798), lines 25–27: "But oft, in lonely rooms, and 'mid the din / Of towns and cities, I have owed to them, / In hours of weariness, sensations sweet." Cf. also *The Prelude* (1850) 7.626: "How oft amid those overflowing streets . . ."

Hardly had skill to utter one of all
The nameless feelings that course through our breast,
But they course on forever unexpressed.
And long we try in vain to speak and act
65 Our hidden self, and what we say and do
Is eloquent, is well—but 'tis not true!
And then we will no more be racked
With inward striving, and demand
Of all the thousand nothings of the hour
70 Their stupefying power;
Ah yes, and they benumb us at our call!
Yet still, from time to time, vague and forlorn,
From the soul's subterranean depth upborne
As from an infinitely distant land,
75 Come airs, and floating echoes, and convey
A melancholy into all our day.[2]

Only—but this is rare—
When a beloved hand is laid in ours,
When, jaded with the rush and glare
80 Of the interminable hours,
Our eyes can in another's eyes read clear,
When our world-deafened ear
Is by the tones of a loved voice caressed—
A bolt is shot back somewhere in our breast,
85 And a lost pulse of feeling stirs again.
The eye sinks inward, and the heart lies plain,
And what we mean, we say, and what we would, we know.
A man becomes aware of his life's flow,
And hears its winding murmur; and he sees
90 The meadows where it glides, the sun, the breeze.

And there arrives a lull in the hot race
Wherein he doth forever chase
That flying and elusive shadow, rest.
An air of coolness plays upon his face,
95 And an unwonted calm pervades his breast.
And then he thinks he knows
The hills where his life rose,
And the sea where it goes.   1852

The Scholar Gypsy

The story of a seventeenth-century student who left Oxford and joined a band of gypsies had made a strong impression on Arnold. In the poem he wistfully imagines that the spirit of this scholar is still to be encountered in the Cumner countryside near Oxford, having achieved immortality by a serene pursuit of the secret of human existence. Like Keats's nightingale, the scholar has escaped "the weariness, the fever, and the fret" of modern life.

At the outset the poet addresses a shepherd who has been helping him in his search for traces of the scholar. The shepherd is addressed as *you*. After line 61, with the

2. Cf. Wordsworth's "Ode: Intimations of Immortality" (1807), lines 149–51: "Those shadowy recollections, / Which, be they what they may, / Are yet the fountain light of all our day."

shift to *thou* and *thy,* the person addressed is the scholar, and the poet thereafter sometimes uses the pronoun *we* to indicate he is speaking for all humanity of later generations.

About the setting Arnold wrote to his brother Tom on May 15, 1857: "You alone of my brothers are associated with that life at Oxford, the *freest* and most delightful part, perhaps, of my life, when with you and Clough and Walrond I shook off all the bonds and formalities of the place, and enjoyed the spring of life and that unforgotten Oxfordshire and Berkshire country. Do you remember a poem of mine called 'The Scholar Gipsy'? It was meant to fix the remembrance of those delightful wanderings of ours in the Cumner Hills."

The passage from Joseph Glanvill's *Vanity of Dogmatizing* (1661) that inspired the poem was included by Arnold as a note:

> There was very lately a lad in the University of Oxford, who was by his poverty forced to leave his studies there; and at last to join himself to a company of vagabond gypsies. Among these extravagant people, by the insinuating subtilty of his carriage, he quickly got so much of their love and esteem as that they discovered to him their mystery. After he had been a pretty while exercised in the trade, there chanced to ride by a couple of scholars, who had formerly been of his acquaintance. They quickly spied out their old friend among the gypsies; and he gave them an account of the necessity which drove him to that kind of life, and told them that the people he went with were not such imposters as they were taken for, but that they had a traditional kind of learning among them, and could do wonders by the power of imagination, their fancy binding that of others: that himself had learned much of their art, and when he had compassed the whole secret, he intended, he said, to leave their company, and give the world an account of what he had learned.

The Scholar Gypsy

Go, for they call you, shepherd, from the hill;
  Go, shepherd, and untie the wattled cotes![1]
    No longer leave thy wistful flock unfed,
    Nor let thy bawling fellows rack their throats,
5   Nor the cropped herbage shoot another head.
      But when the fields are still,
  And the tired men and dogs all gone to rest,
    And only the white sheep are sometimes seen
    Cross and recross the strips of moon-blanched green,
10 Come, shepherd, and again begin the quest!

Here, where the reaper was at work of late—
  In this high field's dark corner, where he leaves
    His coat, his basket, and his earthen cruse,[2]
    And in the sun all morning binds the sheaves,
15   Then here, at noon, comes back his stores to use—
      Here will I sit and wait,
  While to my ear from uplands far away
    The bleating of the folded° flocks is borne,   *penned up*
    With distant cries of reapers in the corn[3]—
20 All the live murmur of a summer's day.

1. Sheepfolds woven from sticks.   3. Grain or wheat.
2. Pot or jug for carrying his drink.

Screened is this nook o'er the high, half-reaped field,
 And here till sundown, shepherd! will I be.
  Through the thick corn the scarlet poppies peep,
 And round green roots and yellowing stalks I see
25   Pale pink convolvulus in tendrils creep;
   And air-swept lindens yield
 Their scent, and rustle down their perfumed showers
  Of bloom on the bent grass where I am laid,
  And bower me from the August sun with shade;
30 And the eye travels down to Oxford's towers.

 And near me on the grass lies Glanvill's book—
  Come, let me read the oft-read tale again!
   The story of the Oxford scholar poor,
  Of pregnant parts[4] and quick inventive brain,
35   Who, tired of knocking at preferment's door,
    One summer morn forsook
  His friends, and went to learn the gypsy lore,
   And roamed the world with that wild brotherhood,
   And came, as most men deemed, to little good,
40 But came to Oxford and his friends no more.

 But once, years after, in the country lanes,
  Two scholars, whom at college erst° he knew,   *long ago*
   Met him, and of his way of life inquired;
  Whereat he answered, that the gypsy crew,
45   His mates, had arts to rule as they desired
    The workings of men's brains,
  And they can bind them to what thoughts they will.
   "And I," he said, "the secret of their art,
   When fully learned, will to the world impart;
50 But it needs heaven-sent moments for this skill."

 This said, he left them, and returned no more.—
  But rumors hung about the countryside,
   That the lost Scholar long was seen to stray,
  Seen by rare glimpses, pensive and tongue-tied,
55   In hat of antique shape, and cloak of grey,
    The same the gypsies wore.
  Shepherds had met him on the Hurst[5] in spring;
   At some lone alehouse in the Berkshire moors,
   On the warm ingle-bench, the smock-frocked boors[6]
60 Had found him seated at their entering,

 But, 'mid their drink and clatter, he would fly.
  And I myself seem half to know thy looks,
   And put the shepherds, wanderer! on thy trace;
  And boys who in lone wheatfields scare the rooks[7]
65   I ask if thou hast passed their quiet place;

---

4. Of rich conception, many ideas.
5. A hill near Oxford. All the place-names in the
poem (except those in the final two stanzas) refer
to the countryside near Oxford.
6. Rustics. "Ingle-bench": fireside bench.
7. Crows.

Or in my boat I lie
Moored to the cool bank in the summer heats,
'Mid wide grass meadows which the sunshine fills,
And watch the warm, green-muffled Cumner hills,
70   And wonder if thou haunt'st their shy retreats.

For most, I know, thou lov'st retired ground!
Thee at the ferry Oxford riders blithe,
Returning home on summer nights, have met
Crossing the stripling Thames at Bab-lock-hithe,[8]
75   Trailing in the cool stream thy fingers wet,
As the punt's rope chops round;[9]
And leaning backward in a pensive dream,
And fostering in thy lap a heap of flowers
Plucked in shy fields and distant Wychwood bowers,
80   And thine eyes resting on the moonlit stream.

And then they land, and thou art seen no more!—
Maidens, who from the distant hamlets come
To dance around the Fyfield elm in May,
Oft through the darkening fields have seen thee roam,
85   Or cross a stile into the public way.
Oft thou hast given them store
Of flowers—the frail-leafed, white anemone,
Dark bluebells drenched with dews of summer eves,
And purple orchises with spotted leaves—
90   But none hath words she can report of thee.

And, above Godstow Bridge, when hay time's here
In June, and many a scythe in sunshine flames,
Men who through those wide fields of breezy grass
Where black-winged swallows haunt the glittering Thames,
95   To bathe in the abandoned lasher[1] pass,
Have often passed thee near
Sitting upon the river bank o'ergrown;
Marked thine outlandish garb, thy figure spare,
Thy dark vague eyes, and soft abstracted air—
100   But, when they came from bathing, thou wast gone!

At some lone homestead in the Cumner hills,
Where at her open door the housewife darns,
Thou hast been seen, or hanging on a gate
To watch the threshers in the mossy barns.
105   Children, who early range these slopes and late
For cresses from the rills,
Have known thee eying, all an April day,
The springing pastures and the feeding kine;°   *cattle*

---

8. Or Bablock Hythe (a *hithe* or *hythe* is a landing place on a river). "The stripling Thames": the narrow upper reaches of the river before it broadens out to its full width.
9. The scholar's flat-bottomed boat ("punt") is tied up by a rope at the riverbank near the ferry crossing like the speaker's boat (in the previous stanza), which was "moored to the cool bank." The motion of the boat as it is stirred by the current of the river causes the chopping sound of the rope in the water.
1. Water that spills over a dam or weir.

And marked thee, when the stars come out and shine,
110   Through the long dewy grass move slow away.

In autumn, on the skirts of Bagley Wood—
    Where most the gypsies by the turf-edged way
        Pitch their smoked tents, and every bush you see
    With scarlet patches tagged and shreds of grey,
115   Above the forest ground called Thessaly—
            The blackbird, picking food,
    Sees thee, nor stops his meal, nor fears at all;
        So often has he known thee past him stray,
        Rapt, twirling in thy hand a withered spray,
120   And waiting for the spark from heaven to fall.

And once, in winter, on the causeway chill
    Where home through flooded fields foot-travelers go,
        Have I not passed thee on the wooden bridge,
    Wrapped in thy cloak and battling with the snow,
125   Thy face tow'rd Hinksey and its wintry ridge?
            And thou hast climbed the hill,
    And gained the white brow of the Cumner range;
        Turned once to watch, while thick the snowflakes fall,
        The line of festal light in Christ Church hall[2]—
130   Then sought thy straw in some sequestered grange.°   *farmhouse*

But what—I dream! Two hundred years are flown
    Since first thy story ran through Oxford halls,
        And the grave Glanvill did the tale inscribe
    That thou wert wandered from the studious walls
135   To learn strange arts, and join a gypsy tribe;
            And thou from earth art gone
    Long since, and in some quiet churchyard laid—
        Some country nook, where o'er thy unknown grave
        Tall grasses and white flowering nettles wave,
140   Under a dark, red-fruited yew tree's shade.

—No, no, thou hast not felt the lapse of hours!
    For what wears out the life of mortal men?
        'Tis that from change to change their being rolls;
    'Tis that repeated shocks, again, again,
145   Exhaust the energy of strongest souls
            And numb the elastic powers.
    Till having used our nerves with bliss and teen,°   *vexation*
        And tired upon a thousand schemes our wit,
        To the just-pausing Genius[3] we remit
150   Our worn-out life, and are—what we have been.

Thou hast not lived, why should'st thou perish, so?
    Thou hadst *one* aim, *one* business, *one* desire;

2. The dining hall of this Oxford college.
3. Perhaps the spirit of the universe, which pauses
briefly to receive back the life given to us. (In

Roman mythology a *genius* was an attendant
spirit.)

Else wert thou long since numbered with the dead!
Else hadst thou spent, like other men, thy fire!
155   The generations of thy peers are fled,
      And we ourselves shall go;
But thou possessest an immortal lot,
    And we imagine thee exempt from age
    And living as thou liv'st on Glanvill's page,
160 Because thou hadst—what we, alas! have not.

For early didst thou leave the world, with powers
    Fresh, undiverted to the world without,
      Firm to their mark, not spent on other things;
    Free from the sick fatigue, the languid doubt,
165   Which much to have tried, in much been baffled, brings.
      O life unlike to ours!
Who fluctuate idly without term or scope,
    Of whom each strives, nor knows for what he strives,
    And each half[4] lives a hundred different lives;
170 Who wait like thee, but not, like thee, in hope.

Thou waitest for the spark from heaven! and we,
    Light half-believers of our casual creeds,
      Who never deeply felt, nor clearly willed,
Whose insight never has borne fruit in deeds,
175   Whose vague resolves never have been fulfilled;
      For whom each year we see
Breeds new beginnings, disappointments new;
    Who hesitate and falter life away,
    And lose tomorrow the ground won today—
180 Ah! do not we, wanderer! await it too?

Yes, we await it!—but it still delays,
    And then we suffer! and amongst us one,[5]
      Who most has suffered, takes dejectedly
His seat upon the intellectual throne;
185   And all his store of sad experience he
      Lays bare of wretched days;
Tells us his misery's birth and growth and signs,
    And how the dying spark of hope was fed,
    And how the breast was soothed, and how the head,
190 And all his hourly varied anodynes.

This for our wisest! and we others pine,
    And wish the long unhappy dream would end,
      And waive all claim to bliss, and try to bear;
With close-lipped patience for our only friend,
195   Sad patience, too near neighbor to despair—
      But none has hope like thine!
Thou through the fields and through the woods dost stray,
    Roaming the countryside, a truant boy,

4. An adverb modifying "lives."
5. Probably Goethe, although possibly referring to

Tennyson, whose *In Memoriam* had appeared in 1850.

Nursing thy project in unclouded joy,
200   And every doubt long blown by time away.

O born in days when wits were fresh and clear,
    And life ran gaily as the sparkling Thames;
        Before this strange disease of modern life,
    With its sick hurry, its divided aims,
205   Its heads o'ertaxed, its palsied hearts, was rife—
            Fly hence, our contact fear!
        Still fly, plunge deeper in the bowering wood!
            Averse, as Dido did with gesture stern
            From her false friend's approach in Hades turn,[6]
210   Wave us away, and keep thy solitude!

Still nursing the unconquerable hope,
    Still clutching the inviolable shade,
        With a free, onward impulse brushing through,
    By night, the silvered branches of the glade—
215   Far on the forest skirts, where none pursue.
            On some mild pastoral slope
        Emerge, and resting on the moonlit pales
        Freshen thy flowers as in former years
        With dew, or listen with enchanted ears,
220   From the dark dingles,° to the nightingales!   *small deep valleys*

But fly our paths, our feverish contact fly!
    For strong the infection of our mental strife,
        Which, though it gives no bliss, yet spoils for rest;
    And we should win thee from thy own fair life,
225   Like us distracted, and like us unblest.
            Soon, soon thy cheer would die,
        Thy hopes grow timorous, and unfixed thy powers,
            And thy clear aims be cross and shifting made;
            And then thy glad perennial youth would fade,
230   Fade, and grow old at last, and die like ours.

Then fly our greetings, fly our speech and smiles!
    —As some grave Tyrian trader, from the sea,
        Descried at sunrise an emerging prow
    Lifting the cool-haired creepers stealthily,
235   The fringes of a southward-facing brow
            Among the Aegean isles;
        And saw the merry Grecian coaster come,
            Freighted with amber grapes, and Chian wine,
            Green, bursting figs, and tunnies° steeped in brine—   *tuna fish*
240   And knew the intruders on his ancient home,

The young lighthearted masters of the waves—
    And snatched his rudder, and shook out more sail;

---

6. Dido committed suicide after her lover, Aeneas, deserted her. When he later encountered her in Hades, she silently turned away from him (see Virgil's *Aeneid*, book 6).

And day and night held on indignantly
O'er the blue Midland waters with the gale,
245   Betwixt the Syrtes[7] and soft Sicily,
               To where the Atlantic raves
Outside the western straits; and unbent sails
          There, where down cloudy cliffs, through sheets of foam,
Shy traffickers, the dark Iberians[8] come;
250   And on the beach undid his corded bales.[9]

1853

Dover Beach

The sea is calm tonight.
The tide is full, the moon lies fair
Upon the straits—on the French coast the light
Gleams and is gone; the cliffs of England stand,
5   Glimmering and vast, out in the tranquil bay.
Come to the window, sweet is the night air!
Only, from the long line of spray
Where the sea meets the moon-blanched land,
Listen! you hear the grating roar
10   Of pebbles which the waves draw back, and fling,
At their return, up the high strand,
Begin, and cease, and then again begin,
With tremulous cadence slow, and bring
The eternal note of sadness in.

15   Sophocles long ago
Heard it on the Aegean, and it brought
Into his mind the turbid ebb and flow
Of human misery;[1] we
Find also in the sound a thought,
20   Hearing it by this distant northern sea.

---

7. Shoals off the coast of North Africa.

8. Dark inhabitants of Spain and Portugal—perhaps associated with gypsies.

9. The elaborate simile of the final two stanzas has been variously interpreted. The trader from Tyre (a Phoenician city, on the coast of what is now Lebanon) is disconcerted to see a new business rival, "the merry Grecian coaster," emerging from one of his habitual trading ports in the Greek islands. Like the Scholar Gypsy, when similarly intruded on by hearty extroverts, he resolves to flee and seek a less competitive sphere of life.

The reference (line 249) to the Iberians as "shy traffickers" (traders) is explained by Kenneth Allott as having been derived from Herodotus's History (4.196). Herodotus describes a distinctive method of selling goods established by merchants from Carthage who used to sail through the Strait of Gibraltar to trade with the inhabitants of the coast of West Africa. The Carthaginians would leave bales of their merchandise on display along the beaches and, without having seen their prospective customers, would return to their ships. The shy natives would then come down from their inland hiding places and set gold beside the bales they wished to buy. When the natives withdrew in their turn, the Carthaginians would return to the beach and decide whether payments were adequate, a process repeated until agreement was reached. On the Atlantic coasts this method of bargaining persisted into the 19th century. As William Beloe, a translator of the ancient Greek historian, noted in 1844: "In this manner they transact their exchange without seeing one another, or without the least instance of dishonesty . . . on either side." For the solitary Tyrian trader such a procedure, with its avoidance of "contact" (line 221), would have been especially appropriate.

1. A reference to a chorus in *Antigone* that compares human sorrow to the sound of the waves moving the sand beneath them (lines 585–91).

The Sea of Faith
Was once, too, at the full, and round earth's shore
Lay like the folds of a bright girdle furled.[2]
But now I only hear
25   Its melancholy, long, withdrawing roar,
Retreating, to the breath
Of the night wind, down the vast edges drear
And naked shingles[3] of the world.

Ah, love, let us be true
30   To one another! for the world, which seems
To lie before us like a land of dreams,
So various, so beautiful, so new,
Hath really neither joy, nor love, nor light,
Nor certitude, nor peace, nor help for pain;
35   And we are here as on a darkling plain
Swept with confused alarms of struggle and flight,
Where ignorant armies[4] clash by night.

ca. 1851   1867

Stanzas from the Grande Chartreuse[1]

Through Alpine meadows soft-suffused
With rain, where thick the crocus blows,
Past the dark forges long disused,
The mule track from Saint Laurent goes.
5   The bridge is crossed, and slow we ride,
Through forest, up the mountainside.

The autumnal evening darkens round,
The wind is up, and drives the rain;
While, hark! far down, with strangled sound
10   Doth the Dead Guier's[2] stream complain,
Where that wet smoke, among the woods,
Over his boiling cauldron broods.

2. This difficult line means, in general, that at high tide the sea envelops the land closely. Its forces are "gathered" up (to use William Wordsworth's term) like the "folds" of bright clothing ("girdle") that have been compressed ("furled"). At ebb tide, as the sea retreats, it is unfurled and spread out. It still surrounds the shoreline but not as an "enclasping flow" (as in "To Marguerite—Continued").
3. Beaches covered with pebbles.
4. Perhaps alluding to conflicts in Arnold's own time such as occurred during the revolutions of 1848 in Europe, or at the Siege of Rome by the French in 1849 (the poem's date of composition is unknown, although generally assumed to be 1851). But the passage also refers back to another battle, one that occurred more than two thousand years earlier when an Athenian army was attempting an invasion of Sicily at nighttime. As this "night battle" was described by the ancient Greek histo-

rian Thucydides in his History of the Peloponnesian War (7.44), the invaders became confused by darkness and slaughtered many of their own men. Hence "ignorant armies."
1. A monastery situated high in the French Alps. It was established in 1084 by Saint Bruno, founder of the Carthusians (line 30), whose austere regimen of solitary contemplation, fasting, and religious exercises (lines 37–44) had remained virtually unchanged for centuries. Arnold visited the site on September 7, 1851, accompanied by his bride. His account may be compared with that by William Wordsworth (Prelude [1850] 6.414–88), who had made a similar visit in 1790.
2. The Guiers Mort River flows down from the monastery and joins the Guiers Vif in the valley below; in French, Mort and Vif mean "dead" and "alive," respectively. Wordsworth speaks of the two rivers as "the sister streams of Life and Death."

Swift rush the spectral vapors white
Past limestone scars° with ragged pines,   *cliffs*
15   Showing—then blotting from our sight!—
Halt—through the cloud-drift something shines!
High in the valley, wet and drear,
The huts of Courrerie appear.

Strike leftward! cries our guide; and higher
20   Mounts up the stony forest way.
At last the encircling trees retire;
Look! through the showery twilight grey
What pointed roofs are these advance?—
A palace of the Kings of France?

25   Approach, for what we seek is here!
Alight, and sparely sup, and wait
For rest in this outbuilding near;
Then cross the sward and reach that gate.
Knock; pass the wicket!° Thou art come   *gate*
30   To the Carthusians' world-famed home.

The silent courts, where night and day
Into their stone-carved basins cold
The splashing icy fountains play—
The humid corridors behold!
35   Where, ghostlike in the deepening night,
Cowled forms brush by in gleaming white.

The chapel, where no organ's peal
Invests the stern and naked prayer—
With penitential cries they kneel
40   And wrestle; rising then, with bare
And white uplifted faces stand,
Passing the Host from hand to hand;[3]

Each takes, and then his visage wan
Is buried in his cowl once more.
45   The cells!—the suffering Son of Man
Upon the wall—the knee-worn floor—
And where they sleep, that wooden bed,
Which shall their coffin be, when dead![4]

The library, where tract and tome
50   Not to feed priestly pride are there,
To hymn the conquering march of Rome,
Nor yet to amuse, as ours are!
They paint of souls the inner strife,
Their drops of blood, their death in life.

3. Arnold, during his short visit, may not actually
have witnessed Mass in the monastery. During the
service the consecrated wafer ("the Host") is not
passed from the hand of the officiating priest to
the hands of the communicant (as is the practice

in Arnold's own Anglican Church) but is placed
directly on the tongue of the communicant (who
kneels rather than stands).
4. A Carthusian is buried on a wooden plank but
does not sleep in a coffin.

55 The garden, overgrown—yet mild,
    See, fragrant herbs[5] are flowering there!
    Strong children of the Alpine wild
    Whose culture is the brethren's care;
    Of human tasks their only one,
60 And cheerful works beneath the sun.

    Those halls, too, destined to contain
    Each its own pilgrim-host of old,
    From England, Germany, or Spain—
    All are before me! I behold
65 The House, the Brotherhood austere!
    —And what am I, that I am here?

    For rigorous teachers seized my youth,
    And purged its faith, and trimmed its fire,
    Showed me the high, white star of Truth,
70 There bade me gaze, and there aspire.
    Even now their whispers pierce the gloom:
    What dost thou in this living tomb?

    Forgive me, masters of the mind![6]
    At whose behest I long ago
75 So much unlearnt, so much resigned—
    I come not here to be your foe!
    I seek these anchorites, not in ruth,[7]
    To curse and to deny your truth;

    Not as their friend, or child, I speak!
80 But as, on some far northern strand,
    Thinking of his own Gods, a Greek
    In pity and mournful awe might stand
    Before some fallen Runic stone[8]—
    For both were faiths, and both are gone.

85 Wandering between two worlds, one dead,
    The other powerless to be born,
    With nowhere yet to rest my head,
    Like these, on earth I wait forlorn.
    Their faith, my tears, the world deride—
90 I come to shed them at their side.

    Oh, hide me in your gloom profound,
    Ye solemn seats of holy pain!
    Take me, cowled forms, and fence me round,
    Till I possess my soul again;

5. From which the liqueur Chartreuse is manufactured. Sales of this liqueur provide the principal revenues for the monastery's upkeep.
6. Writers whose insistence on testing religious beliefs in the light of fact and reason persuaded Arnold that faith in Christianity (especially in the Roman Catholic or Anglo-Catholic forms) was no longer tenable in the modern world.

7. Remorse for having adopted the rationalist view of Christianity.
8. A monument inscribed in Teutonic letters (runes), emblematic of a Nordic religion that has become extinct. The relic reminds the Greek that his own religion is likewise dying and will soon be extinct.

95 Till free my thoughts before me roll,
  Not chafed by hourly false control!

  For the world cries your faith is now
  But a dead time's exploded dream;
  My melancholy, sciolists[9] say,
100 Is a passed mode, an outworn theme—
  As if the world had ever had
  A faith, or sciolists been sad!

  Ah, if it *be* passed, take away,
  At least, the restlessness, the pain;
105 Be man henceforth no more a prey
  To these out-dated stings again!
  The nobleness of grief is gone—
  Ah, leave us not the fret alone!

  But—if you[1] cannot give us ease—
110 Last of the race of them who grieve
  Here leave us to die out with these
  Last of the people who believe!
  Silent, while years engrave the brow;
  Silent—the best are silent now.

115 Achilles[2] ponders in his tent,
  The kings of modern thought[3] are dumb;
  Silent they are, though not content,
  And wait to see the future come.
  They have the grief men had of yore,
120 But they contend and cry no more.

  Our fathers[4] watered with their tears
  This sea of time whereon we sail,
  Their voices were in all men's ears
  Who passed within their puissant hail.
125 Still the same ocean round us raves,
  But we stand mute, and watch the waves.

  For what availed it, all the noise
  And outcry of the former men?—
  Say, have their sons achieved more joys,
130 Say, is life lighter now than then?
  The sufferers died, they left their pain—
  The pangs which tortured them remain.

---

9. Superficial-minded persons who pretend to know the answers to all questions.

1. It is not clear whether the speaker has resumed addressing his "rigorous teachers" (line 67) or (as would seem more likely) a combination of the sciolists, who scorn the speaker's melancholy, and the worldly, who scorn the faith of the monks. See his address to the "sons of the world" (lines 161–68).

2. Until the death of Patroclus, he refused to participate in the Trojan War; hence he is similar to modern intellectual leaders who refuse to speak out about their frustrated sense of alienation.

3. Variously but never satisfactorily identified as John Henry Newman or Thomas Carlyle (the latter was said to have preached the gospel of silence in forty volumes). Another advocate of stoical silence was the French poet Alfred de Vigny (1797–1863).

4. Predecessors among the Romantic writers such as Byron.

What helps it now, that Byron bore,
With haughty scorn which mocked the smart,
135   Through Europe to the Aetolian shore[5]
The pageant of his bleeding heart?
That thousands counted every groan,
And Europe made his woe her own?

What boots° it, Shelley! that the breeze   *avails*
140   Carried thy lovely wail away,
Musical through Italian trees
Which fringe thy soft blue Spezzian bay?[6]
Inheritors of thy distress
Have restless hearts one throb the less?

145   Or are we easier, to have read,
O Obermann![7] the sad, stern page,
Which tells us how thou hidd'st thy head
From the fierce tempest of thine age
In the lone brakes° of Fontainebleau,   *thickets*
150   Or chalets near the Alpine snow?

Ye slumber in your silent grave!
The world, which for an idle day
Grace to your mood of sadness gave,
Long since hath flung her weeds° away.   *mourning clothes*
155   The eternal trifler[8] breaks your spell;
But we—we learnt your lore too well!

Years hence, perhaps, may dawn an age,
More fortunate, alas! than we,
Which without hardness will be sage,
160   And gay without frivolity.
Sons of the world, oh, speed those years;
But, while we wait, allow our tears!

Allow them! We admire with awe
The exulting thunder of your race;
165   You give the universe your law,
You triumph over time and space!
Your pride of life, your tireless powers,
We laud them, but they are not ours.

We are like children reared in shade
170   Beneath some old-world abbey wall,
Forgotten in a forest glade,
And secret from the eyes of all.
Deep, deep the greenwood round them waves,
Their abbey, and its close° of graves!   *enclosure*

5. Region in Greece where Byron died.
6. The Gulf of Spezia in Italy, where Percy Bysshe
Shelley was drowned.

7. Melancholy hero of *Obermann* (1804), a novel
by the French writer Étienne Sénancour.
8. The sciolist, as in line 99.

175 But, where the road runs near the stream,
     Oft through the trees they catch a glance
     Of passing troops in the sun's beam—
     Pennon, and plume, and flashing lance!
     Forth to the world those soldiers fare,
180 To life, to cities, and to war!

     And through the wood, another way,
     Faint bugle notes from far are borne,
     Where hunters gather, staghounds bay,
     Round some fair forest-lodge at morn.
185 Gay dames are there, in sylvan green;
     Laughter and cries—those notes between!

     The banners flashing through the trees
     Make their blood dance and chain their eyes;
     That bugle music on the breeze
190 Arrests them with a charmed surprise.
     Banner by turns and bugle woo:
     Ye shy recluses, follow too!

     O children, what do ye reply?—
     "Action and pleasure, will ye roam
195 Through these secluded dells to cry
     And call us?—but too late ye come!
     Too late for us your call ye blow,
     Whose bent° was taken long ago.   *natural inclination*

     "Long since we pace this shadowed nave;
200 We watch those yellow tapers shine,
     Emblems of hope over the grave,
     In the high altar's depth divine;
     The organ carries to our ear
     Its accents of another sphere.[9]

205 "Fenced early in this cloistral round
     Of reverie, of shade, of prayer,
     How should we grow in other ground?
     How can we flower in foreign air?
     —Pass, banners, pass, and bugles, cease;
210 And leave our desert to its peace!"

1852(?)   1855

---

9. The organ music is from the abbey in the greenwood (line 174), as contrasted with the monastery on the mountaintop in which there is no organ (line 37).

From The Function of Criticism at the Present Time[1]

Many objections have been made to a proposition which, in some remarks of mine on translating Homer,[2] I ventured to put forth; a proposition about criticism, and its importance at the present day. I said: "Of the literature of France and Germany, as of the intellect of Europe in general, the main effort, for now many years, has been a critical effort; the endeavor, in all branches of knowledge, theology, philosophy, history, art, science, to see the object as in itself it really is." I added, that owing to the operation in English literature of certain causes, "almost the last thing for which one would come to English literature is just that very thing which now Europe most desires—criticism"; and that the power and value of English literature was thereby impaired. More than one rejoinder declared that the importance I here assigned to criticism was excessive, and asserted the inherent superiority of the creative effort of the human spirit over its critical effort. And the other day, having been led by a Mr. Shairp's excellent notice of Wordsworth[3] to turn again to his biography, I found, in the words of this great man, whom I, for one, must always listen to with the profoundest respect, a sentence passed on the critic's business, which seems to justify every possible disparagement of it. Wordsworth says in one of his letters:

> The writers in these publications (the Reviews), while they prosecute their inglorious employment, cannot be supposed to be in a state of mind very favorable for being affected by the finer influences of a thing so pure as genuine poetry.

And a trustworthy reporter[4] of his conversation quotes a more elaborate judgment to the same effect:

> Wordsworth holds the critical power very low, infinitely lower than the inventive; and he said today that if the quantity of time consumed in writing critiques on the works of others were given to original composition, of whatever kind it might be, it would be much better employed; it would make a man find out sooner his own level, and it would do infinitely less mischief. A false or malicious criticism may do much injury to the minds of others; a stupid invention, either in prose or verse, is quite harmless.

It is almost too much to expect of poor human nature, that a man capable of producing some effect in one line of literature, should, for the greater good of society, voluntarily doom himself to impotence and obscurity in another. Still less is this to be expected from men addicted to the composition of the

1. This essay served as an introduction to *Essays in Criticism* (1865).
2. *On Translating Homer* (1861).
3. J. C. Shairp's essay "Wordsworth: The Man and the Poet" was published in 1864. Arnold comments in a footnote:

I cannot help thinking that a practice, common in England during the last century, and still followed in France, of printing a notice of this kind—a notice by a competent critic—to serve as an introduction to an eminent author's works, might be revived among us with advantage. To

introduce all succeeding editions of Wordsworth, Mr. Shairp's notice might, it seems to me, excellently serve; it is written from the point of view of an admirer, nay, of a disciple, and that is right; but then the disciple must be also, as in this case he is, a critic, a man of letters, not, as too often happens, some relation or friend with no qualification for his task except affection for his author.

4. Christopher Wordsworth, *Memoirs of William Wordsworth* (1851).

"false or malicious criticism" of which Wordsworth speaks. However, everybody would admit that a false or malicious criticism had better never have been written. Everybody, too, would be willing to admit, as a general proposition, that the critical faculty is lower than the inventive. But is it true that criticism is really, in itself, a baneful and injurious employment; is it true that all time given to writing critiques on the works of others would be much better employed if it were given to original composition, of whatever kind this may be? Is it true that Johnson had better have gone on producing more *Irenes*[5] instead of writing his *Lives of the Poets*; nay, is it certain that Wordsworth himself was better employed in making his Ecclesiastical Sonnets than when he made his celebrated Preface[6] so full of criticism, and criticism of the works of others? Wordsworth was himself a great critic, and it is to be sincerely regretted that he has not left us more criticism; Goethe was one of the greatest of critics, and we may sincerely congratulate ourselves that he has left us so much criticism. Without wasting time over the exaggeration which Wordsworth's judgment on criticism clearly contains, or over an attempt to trace the causes—not difficult, I think, to be traced—which may have led Wordsworth to this exaggeration, a critic may with advantage seize an occasion for trying his own conscience, and for asking himself of what real service, at any given moment, the practice of criticism either is or may be made to his own mind and spirit, and to the minds and spirits of others.

The critical power is of lower rank than the creative. True; but in assenting to this proposition, one or two things are to be kept in mind. It is undeniable that the exercise of a creative power, that a free creative activity, is the highest function of man; it is proved to be so by man's finding in it his true happiness. But it is undeniable, also, that men may have the sense of exercising this free creative activity in other ways than in producing great works of literature or art; if it were not so, all but a very few men would be shut out from the true happiness of all men. They may have it in well-doing, they may have it in learning, they may have it even in criticizing. This is one thing to be kept in mind. Another is, that the exercise of the creative power in the production of great works of literature or art, however high this exercise of it may rank, is not at all epochs and under all conditions possible; and that therefore labor may be vainly spent in attempting it, which might with more fruit be used in preparing for it, in rendering it possible. This creative power works with elements, with materials; what if it has not those materials, those elements, ready for its use? In that case it must surely wait till they are ready. Now, in literature—I will limit myself to literature, for it is about literature that the question arises—the elements with which the creative power works are ideas; the best ideas on every matter which literature touches, current at the time. At any rate we may lay it down as certain that in modern literature no manifestation of the creative power not working with these can be very important or fruitful. And I say *current* at the time, not merely accessible at the time; for creative literary genius does not principally show itself in discovering new ideas, that is rather the business of the philosopher. The grand work of literary genius is a work of synthesis and exposition, not of analysis and discovery; its gift lies in the faculty of being happily inspired by a certain intellectual and spiritual

5. *Irene* (1749) is a clumsy play by Samuel Johnson (1709–1784), whose *Lives of the Poets* (1779–81) is a major work of criticism.

6. To *Lyrical Ballads* (1800). "Ecclesiastical Sonnets": a sonnet sequence (1821–22) by Wordsworth, usually regarded as minor verse.

atmosphere, by a certain order of ideas, when it finds itself in them; of dealing divinely with these ideas, presenting them in the most effective and attractive combinations—making beautiful works with them, in short. But it must have the atmosphere, it must find itself amidst the order of ideas, in order to work freely; and these it is not so easy to command. This is why great creative epochs in literature are so rare, this is why there is so much that is unsatisfactory in the productions of many men of real genius; because, for the creation of a masterwork of literature two powers must concur, the power of the man and the power of the moment, and the man is not enough without the moment; the creative power has, for its happy exercise, appointed elements, and those elements are not in its own control.

Nay, they are more within the control of the critical power. It is the business of the critical power, as I said in the words already quoted, "in all branches of knowledge, theology, philosophy, history, art, science, to see the object as in itself it really is." Thus it tends, at last, to make an intellectual situation of which the creative power can profitably avail itself. It tends to establish an order of ideas, if not absolutely true, yet true by comparison with that which it displaces; to make the best ideas prevail. Presently these new ideas reach society, the touch of truth is the touch of life, and there is a stir and growth everywhere; out of this stir and growth come the creative epochs of literature.

Or, to narrow our range, and quit these considerations of the general march of genius and of society—considerations which are apt to become too abstract and impalpable—everyone can see that a poet, for instance, ought to know life and the world before dealing with them in poetry; and life and the world being in modern times very complex things, the creation of a modern poet, to be worth much, implies a great critical effort behind it; else it must be a comparatively poor, barren, and short-lived affair. This is why Byron's poetry had so little endurance in it, and Goethe's so much; both Byron and Goethe had a great productive power, but Goethe's was nourished by a great critical effort providing the true materials for it, and Byron's was not; Goethe knew life and the world, the poet's necessary subjects, much more comprehensively and thoroughly than Byron. He knew a great deal more of them, and he knew them much more as they really are.

It has long seemed to me that the burst of creative activity in our literature, through the first quarter of this century, had about it in fact something premature; and that from this cause its productions are doomed, most of them, in spite of the sanguine hopes which accompanied and do still accompany them, to prove hardly more lasting than the productions of far less splendid epochs. And this prematureness comes from its having proceeded without having its proper data, without sufficient materials to work with. In other words, the English poetry of the first quarter of this century, with plenty of energy, plenty of creative force, did not know enough. This makes Byron so empty of matter, Shelley so incoherent, Wordsworth even, profound as he is, yet so wanting in completeness and variety. Wordsworth cared little for books, and disparaged Goethe. I admire Wordsworth, as he is, so much that I cannot wish him different; and it is vain, no doubt, to imagine such a man different from what he is, to suppose that he *could* have been different. But surely the one thing wanting to make Wordsworth an even greater poet than he is—his thought richer, and his influence of wider application—was that he should have read more books, among them, no doubt, those of that Goethe whom he disparaged without reading him.

But to speak of books and reading may easily lead to a misunderstanding here. It was not really books and reading that lacked to our poetry at this epoch: Shelley had plenty of reading, Coleridge had immense reading. Pindar and Sophocles[7]—as we all say so glibly, and often with so little discernment of the real import of what we are saying—had not many books; Shakespeare was no deep reader. True; but in the Greece of Pindar and Sophocles, in the England of Shakespeare, the poet lived in a current of ideas in the highest degree animating and nourishing to the creative power; society was, in the fullest measure, permeated by fresh thought, intelligent and alive. And this state of things is the true basis for the creative power's exercise, in this it finds its data, its materials, truly ready for its hand; all the books and reading in the world are only valuable as they are helps to this. Even when this does not actually exist, books and reading may enable a man to construct a kind of semblance of it in his own mind, a world of knowledge and intelligence in which he may live and work. This is by no means an equivalent to the artist for the nationally diffused life and thought of the epochs of Sophocles or Shakespeare; but, besides that it may be a means of preparation for such epochs, it does really constitute, if many share in it, a quickening and sustaining atmosphere of great value. Such an atmosphere the many-sided learning and the long and widely combined critical effort of Germany formed for Goethe, when he lived and worked. There was no national glow of life and thought there as in the Athens of Pericles or the England of Elizabeth.[8] That was the poet's weakness. But there was a sort of equivalent for it in the complete culture and unfettered thinking of a large body of Germans. That was his strength. In the England of the first quarter of this century there was neither a national glow of life and thought, such as we had in the age of Elizabeth, nor yet a culture and a force of learning and criticism such as were to be found in Germany. Therefore the creative power of poetry wanted, for success in the highest sense, materials and a basis; a thorough interpretation of the world was necessarily denied to it.

At first sight it seems strange that out of the immense stir of the French Revolution and its age should not have come a crop of works of genius equal to that which came out of the stir of the great productive time of Greece, or out of that of the Renascence, with its powerful episode the Reformation. But the truth is that the stir of the French Revolution took a character which essentially distinguished it from such movements as these. These were, in the main, disinterestedly intellectual and spiritual movements; movements in which the human spirit looked for its satisfaction in itself and in the increased play of its own activity. The French Revolution took a political, practical character. The movement, which went on in France under the old *régime,* from 1700 to 1789, was far more really akin than that of the Revolution itself to the movement of the Renascence; the France of Voltaire and Rousseau[9] told far more powerfully upon the mind of Europe than the France of the Revolution. Goethe reproached this last expressly with having "thrown quiet culture back."[1] Nay, and the true key to how much in our Byron, even in our Words-

7. Greek tragedian (ca. 496–406 B.C.E.). Pindar (518–438 B.C.E.), Greek lyric poet.
8. Elizabeth I (1533–1603; reigned 1558–1603). Pericles (ca. 495–429 B.C.E.), the leading statesman of Athens during the period of the city's most outstanding achievements in art, literature, and politics.

9. Jean-Jacques Rousseau (1712–1778), Swissborn French philosopher and political theorist. Voltaire (1694–1778), pen name of the French writer François Marie Arouet.
1. See "Vier Jahreszeiten Herbst" (1796) in his *Werke* (1887) 1.354.

worth, is this!—that they had their source in a great movement of feeling, not in a great movement of mind. The French Revolution, however—that object of so much blind love and so much blind hatred—found undoubtedly its motive power in the intelligence of men, and not in their practical sense; this is what distinguishes it from the English Revolution of Charles the First's time.[2] This is what makes it a more spiritual event than our Revolution, an event of much more powerful and worldwide interest, though practically less successful; it appeals to an order of ideas which are universal, certain, permanent. 1789 asked of a thing, Is it rational? 1642 asked of a thing, Is it legal? or, when it went furthest, Is it according to conscience? This is the English fashion, a fashion to be treated, within its own sphere, with the highest respect; for its success, within its own sphere, has been prodigious. But what is law in one place is not law in another; what is law here today is not law even here tomorrow; and as for conscience, what is binding on one man's conscience is not binding on another's. The old woman who threw her stool at the head of the surpliced minister in St. Giles's Church at Edinburgh[3] obeyed an impulse to which millions of the human race may be permitted to remain strangers. But the prescriptions of reason are absolute, unchanging, of universal validity; *to count by tens is the easiest way of counting*—that is a proposition of which everyone, from here to the Antipodes, feels the force; at least I should say so if we did not live in a country where it is not impossible that any morning we may find a letter in the *Times* declaring that a decimal coinage is an absurdity.[4] That a whole nation should have been penetrated with an enthusiasm for pure reason, and with an ardent zeal for making its prescriptions triumph, is a very remarkable thing, when we consider how little of mind, or anything so worthy and quickening as mind, comes into the motives which alone, in general, impel great masses of men. In spite of the extravagant direction given to this enthusiasm, in spite of the crimes and follies in which it lost itself, the French Revolution derives from the force, truth, and universality of the ideas which it took for its law, and from the passion with which it could inspire a multitude for these ideas, a unique and still living power; it is—it will probably long remain—the greatest, the most animating event in history. And as no sincere passion for the things of the mind, even though it turn out in many respects an unfortunate passion, is ever quite thrown away and quite barren of good, France has reaped from hers one fruit—the natural and legitimate fruit though not precisely the grand fruit she expected: she is the country in Europe where *the people* is most alive.

But the mania for giving an immediate political and practical application to all these fine ideas of the reason was fatal. Here an Englishman is in his element: on this theme we can all go on for hours. And all we are in the habit of saying on it has undoubtedly a great deal of truth. Ideas cannot be too much prized in and for themselves, cannot be too much lived with; but to transport them abruptly into the world of politics and practice, violently to revolutionize this world to their bidding—that is quite another thing. There is the world of

2. Disputes between Charles I (1600–1649; reigned 1625–49) and Parliament led in 1642 to civil war and ultimately to the king's beheading. (Eleven years later his son, Charles II, was recalled from exile and proclaimed king.)
3. In 1637 rioting broke out in Scotland against a new kind of church service prescribed by Charles I. The riot was started by an old woman hurling a stool at a clergyman, whom she accused of saying Mass.
4. In 1863 a proposal in Parliament to introduce the French decimal system for weights and measures had provoked articles in the London *Times* defending the English system (of ounces and pounds or inches and feet) as more practical. Decimal coinage was finally instituted in 1971.

ideas and there is the world of practice; the French are often for suppressing the one and the English the other; but neither is to be suppressed. A member of the House of Commons said to me the other day: "That a thing is an anomaly, I consider to be no objection to it whatever." I venture to think he was wrong; that a thing is an anomaly *is* an objection to it, but absolutely and in the sphere of ideas: it is not necessarily, under such and such circumstances, or at such and such a moment, an objection to it in the sphere of politics and practice. Joubert[5] has said beautifully: *"C'est la force et le droit qui règlent toutes choses dans le monde; la force en attendant le droit."*—"Force and right are the governors of this world; force till right is ready." *Force till right is ready;* and till right is ready, force, the existing order of things, is justified, is the legitimate ruler. But right is something moral, and implies inward recognition, free assent of the will; we are not ready for right—*right,* so far as we are concerned, is *not ready*—until we have attained this sense of seeing it and willing it. The way in which for us it may change and transform force, the existing order of things, and become, in its turn, the legitimate ruler of the world, should depend on the way in which, when our time comes, we see it and will it. Therefore for other people enamored of their own newly discerned right, to attempt to impose it upon us as ours, and violently to substitute their right for our force, is an act of tyranny, and to be resisted. It sets at nought the second great half of our maxim, *force till right is ready.* This was the grand error of the French Revolution; and its movement of ideas, by quitting the intellectual sphere and rushing furiously into the political sphere, ran, indeed a prodigious and memorable course, but produced no such intellectual fruit as the movement of ideas of the Renascence, and created, in opposition to itself, what I may call an *epoch of concentration.* The great force of that epoch of concentration was England; and the great voice of that epoch of concentration was Burke.[6] It is the fashion to treat Burke's writings on the French Revolution as superannuated and conquered by the event; as the eloquent but unphilosophical tirades of bigotry and prejudice. I will not deny that they are often disfigured by the violence and passion of the moment, and that in some directions Burke's view was bounded, and his observation therefore at fault. But on the whole, and for those who can make the needful corrections, what distinguishes these writings is their profound, permanent, fruitful, philosophical truth, They contain the true philosophy of an epoch of concentration, dissipate the heavy atmosphere which its own nature is apt to engender round it, and make its resistance rational instead of mechanical.

But Burke is so great because, almost alone in England, he brings thought to bear upon politics, he saturates politics with thought. It is his accident[7] that his ideas were at the service of an epoch of concentration, not of an epoch of expansion; it is his characteristic that he so lived by ideas, and had such a source of them welling up within him, that he could float even an epoch of concentration and English Tory politics with them. It does not hurt him that Dr. Price[8] and the Liberals were enraged with him; it does not even hurt him that George the Third and the Tories were enchanted with him. His greatness is that he lived in a world which neither English Liberalism nor English Tory-

5. Joseph Joubert (1754–1824), French moralist about whom Arnold wrote in his *Essays in Criticism.*
6. Edmund Burke (1729–1797), prominent statesman and author of *Reflections on the French*

Revolution (1790), which expressed the conservative opposition to revolutionary theories.
7. Fortune.
8. Richard Price (1723–1791), a prorevolutionary clergyman who was an opponent of Burke's.

ism is apt to enter—the world of ideas, not the world of catchwords and party habits. So far is it from being really true of him that he "to party gave up what was meant for mankind,"[9] that at the very end of his fierce struggle with the French Revolution, after all his invectives against its false pretensions, hollowness, and madness, with his sincere convictions of its mischievousness, he can close a memorandum on the best means of combating it, some of the last pages he ever wrote[1]—the *Thoughts on French Affairs*, in December 1791— with these striking words:

> The evil is stated, in my opinion, as it exists. The remedy must be where power, wisdom, and information, I hope, are more united with good intentions than they can be with me. I have done with this subject, I believe, forever. It has given me many anxious moments for the last two years. *If a great change is to be made in human affairs, the minds of men will be fitted to it; the general opinions and feelings will draw that way. Every fear, every hope will forward it; and then they who persist in opposing this mighty current in human affairs, will appear rather to resist the decrees of Providence itself, than the mere designs of men. They will not be resolute and firm, but perverse and obstinate.*

That return of Burke upon himself has always seemed to me one of the finest things in English literature, or indeed in any literature. That is what I call living by ideas: when one side of a question has long had your earnest support, when all your feelings are engaged, when you hear all round you no language but one, when your party talks this language like a steam engine and can imagine no other—still to be able to think, still to be irresistibly carried, if so it be, by the current of thought to the opposite side of the question, and, like Balaam, to be unable to speak anything *but what the Lord has put in your mouth.*[2] I know nothing more striking, and I must add that I know nothing more un-English.

For the Englishman in general is like my friend the Member of Parliament, and believes, point-blank, that for a thing to be an anomaly is absolutely no objection to it whatever. He is like the Lord Auckland[3] of Burke's day, who, in a memorandum on the French Revolution, talks of certain "miscreants, assuming the name of philosophers, who have presumed themselves capable of establishing a new system of society." The Englishman has been called a political animal, and he values what is political and practical so much that ideas easily become objects of dislike in his eyes, and thinkers, "miscreants," because ideas and thinkers have rashly meddled with politics and practice. This would be all very well if the dislike and neglect confined themselves to ideas transported out of their own sphere, and meddling rashly with practice; but they are inevitably extended to ideas as such, and to the whole life of intelligence; practice is everything, a free play of the mind is nothing. The notion of the free play of the mind upon all subjects being a pleasure in itself, being an object of desire, being an essential provider of elements without which a nation's spirit, whatever compensations it may have for them, must,

---

9. From Oliver Goldsmith's poem "Retaliation" (1774).
1. Arnold was mistaken; Burke continued to write for another six years after 1791. According to Arnold's editor, R. H. Super, the mistake was caused by misunderstanding a passage in one of

Burke's letters.
2. Balaam, a false and worldly prophet, pronounced a blessing on the Israelites instead of the curse he had intended (Numbers 22.38).
3. William Eden, first Baron Auckland (1744–1814), statesman and diplomat.

in the long run, die of inanition, hardly enters into an Englishman's thoughts. It is noticeable that the word *curiosity,* which in other languages is used in a good sense, to mean, as a high and fine quality of man's nature, just this disinterested love of a free play of the mind on all subjects, for its own sake—it is noticeable, I say, that this word has in our language no sense of the kind, no sense but a rather bad and disparaging one. But criticism, real criticism, is essentially the exercise of this very quality. It obeys an instinct prompting it to try to know the best that is known and thought in the world, irrespectively of practice, politics, and everything of the kind; and to value knowledge and thought as they approach this best, without the intrusion of any other considerations whatever. This is an instinct for which there is, I think, little original sympathy in the practical English nature, and what there was of it has undergone a long benumbing period of blight and suppression in the epoch of concentration which followed the French Revolution.

But epochs of concentration cannot well endure forever; epochs of expansion, in the due course of things, follow them. Such an epoch of expansion seems to be opening in this country. In the first place all danger of a hostile forcible pressure of foreign ideas upon our practice has long disappeared; like the traveler in the fable, therefore, we begin to wear our cloak a little more loosely.[4] Then, with a long peace, the ideas of Europe steal gradually and amicably in, and mingle, though in infinitesimally small quantities at a time, with our own notions. Then, too, in spite of all that is said about the absorbing and brutalizing influence of our passionate material progress, it seems to me indisputable that this progress is likely, though not certain, to lead in the end to an apparition of intellectual life; and that man, after he has made himself perfectly comfortable and has now to determine what to do with himself next, may begin to remember that he has a mind, and that the mind may be made the source of great pleasure. I grant it is mainly the privilege of faith, at present, to discern this end to our railways, our business, and our fortune-making; but we shall see if, here as elsewhere, faith is not in the end the true prophet. Our ease, our traveling, and our unbounded liberty to hold just as hard and securely as we please to the practice to which our notions have given birth, all tend to beget an inclination to deal a little more freely with these notions themselves, to canvass them a little, to penetrate a little into their real nature. Flutterings of curiosity, in the foreign sense of the word, appear amongst us, and it is in these that criticism must look to find its account. Criticism first; a time of true creative activity, perhaps—which, as I have said, must inevitably be preceded amongst us by a time of criticism—hereafter, when criticism has done its work.

It is of the last importance that English criticism should clearly discern what rule for its course, in order to avail itself of the field now opening to it, and to produce fruit for the future, it ought to take. The rule may be summed up in one word—*disinterestedness.*[5] And how is criticism to show disinterestedness? By keeping aloof from what is called "the practical view of things"; by resolutely following the law of its own nature, which is to be a free play of the mind on all subjects which it touches. By steadily refusing to lend itself to any of those

4. In Aesop's fable of the wind and the sun, the two compete to see who is more powerful. The sun wins by causing the traveler to take off his coat (the goal of both), whereas the wind can only make him hold it closely.

5. This key word in Arnold's argument connotes independence and objectivity of mind. It means not having an interest, in the sense of an ax to grind. It does not mean lack of interest.

ulterior, political, practical considerations about ideas, which plenty of people will be sure to attach to them, which perhaps ought often to be attached to them, which in this country at any rate are certain to be attached to them quite sufficiently, but which criticism has really nothing to do with. Its business is, as I have said, simply to know the best that is known and thought in the world, and by in its turn making this known, to create a current of true and fresh ideas. Its business is to do this with inflexible honesty, with due ability; but its business is to do no more, and to leave alone all questions of practical consequences and applications, questions which will never fail to have due prominence given to them. Else criticism, besides being really false to its own nature, merely continues in the old rut which it has hitherto followed in this country, and will certainly miss the chance now given to it. For what is at present the bane of criticism in this country? It is that practical considerations cling to it and stifle it. It subserves interests not its own. Our organs of criticism are organs of men and parties having practical ends to serve, and with them those practical ends are the first thing and the play of mind the second; so much play of mind as is compatible with the prosecution of those practical ends is all that is wanted. An organ like the *Revue des Deux Mondes*,[6] having for its main function to understand and utter the best that is known and thought in the world, existing, it may be said, as just an organ for a free play of the mind, we have not. But we have the *Edinburgh Review,* existing as an organ of the old Whigs, and for as much play of mind as may suit its being that; we have the *Quarterly Review,* existing as an organ of the Tories, and for as much play of mind as may suit its being that; we have the *British Quarterly Review,* existing as an organ of the political Dissenters, and for as much play of mind as may suit its being that; we have the *Times,* existing as an organ of the common, satisfied, well-to-do Englishman, and for as much play of mind as may suit its being that. And so on through all the various fractions, political and religious, of our society; every fraction has, as such, its organ of criticism, but the notion of combining all fractions in the common pleasure of a free disinterested play of mind meets with no favor. Directly this play of mind wants to have more scope, and to forget the pressure of practical considerations a little, it is checked, it is made to feel the chain. We saw this the other day in the extinction, so much to be regretted, of the *Home and Foreign Review.*[7] Perhaps in no organ of criticism in this country was there so much knowledge, so much play of mind; but these could not save it. The *Dublin Review* subordinates play of mind to the practical business of English and Irish Catholicism, and lives. It must needs be that men should act in sects and parties, that each of these sects and parties should have its organ, and should make this organ subserve the interests of its action; but it would be well, too, that there should be a criticism, not the minister of these interests, not their enemy, but absolutely and entirely independent of them. No other criticism will ever attain any real authority or make any real way towards its end—the creating a current of true and fresh ideas.

It is because criticism has so little kept in the pure intellectual sphere, has so little detached itself from practice, has been so directly polemical and controversial, that it has so ill accomplished, in this country, its best spiritual work, which is to keep man from a self-satisfaction which is retarding and

---

6. An international magazine of exceptionally high quality, founded in Paris in 1829.

7. A liberal Catholic periodical, founded in 1862, which ceased publication in 1864.

vulgarizing, to lead him towards perfection, by making his mind dwell upon what is excellent in itself, and the absolute beauty and fitness of things. A polemical practical criticism makes men blind even to the ideal imperfection of their practice, makes them willingly assert its ideal perfection, in order the better to secure it against attack; and clearly this is narrowing and baneful for them. If they were reassured on the practical side, speculative considerations of ideal perfection they might be brought to entertain, and their spiritual horizon would thus gradually widen. Sir Charles Adderley[8] says to the Warwickshire farmers:

> Talk of the improvement of breed! Why, the race we ourselves represent, the men and women, the old Anglo-Saxon race, are the best breed in the whole world. . . . The absence of a too enervating climate, too unclouded skies, and a too luxurious nature, has produced so vigorous a race of people, and has rendered us so superior to all the world.

Mr. Roebuck says to the Sheffield cutlers:[9]

> I look around me and ask what is the state of England? Is not property safe? Is not every man able to say what he likes? Can you not walk from one end of England to the other in perfect security? I ask you whether, the world over or in past history, there is anything like it? Nothing. I pray that our unrivaled happiness may last.

Now obviously there is a peril for poor human nature in words and thoughts of such exuberant self-satisfaction, until we find ourselves safe in the streets of the Celestial City.

> *Das wenige verschwindet leicht dem Blicke*
> *Der vorwärts sieht, wie viel noch übrig bleibt*—[1]

says Goethe; "the little that is done seems nothing when we look forward and see how much we have yet to do." Clearly this is a better line of reflection for weak humanity, so long as it remains on this earthly field of labor and trial.

But neither Sir Charles Adderley nor Mr. Roebuck is by nature inaccessible to considerations of this sort. They only lose sight of them owing to the controversial life we all lead, and the practical form which all speculation takes with us. They have in view opponents whose aim is not ideal, but practical; and in their zeal to uphold their own practice against these innovators, they go so far as even to attribute to this practice an ideal perfection. Somebody has been wanting to introduce a six-pound franchise, or to abolish church-rates,[2] or to collect agricultural statistics by force, or to diminish local self-government. How natural, in reply to such proposals, very likely improper or ill-timed, to go a little beyond the mark and to say stoutly, "Such a race of people as we stand, so superior to all the world! The old Anglo-Saxon race, the best breed in the whole world! I pray that our unrivaled happiness may last! I ask you whether, the world over or in past history, there is anything like it?" And so long as criticism answers this dithyramb by insisting that the old Anglo-Saxon race would be still more superior to all others if it had no church-

8. Conservative politician and wealthy landowner (1814–1905).
9. Makers of knives and forks. John Arthur Roebuck (1801–1879), radical politician and representative in Parliament for the industrial city of Sheffield, famous for its metalworking trades.

1. Goethe's *Iphigenie auf Tauris* (1787) 1.2.91–92.
2. Taxes supporting the Church of England. "Six-pound franchise": a radical proposal to extend the right to vote to anyone owning land worth £6 annual rent.

rates, or that our unrivaled happiness would last yet longer with a six-pound franchise, so long will the strain, "The best breed in the whole world!" swell louder and louder, everything ideal and refining will be lost out of sight, and both the assailed and their critics will remain in a sphere, to say the truth, perfectly unvital, a sphere in which spiritual progression is impossible. But let criticism leave church-rates and the franchise alone, and in the most candid spirit, without a single lurking thought of practical innovation, confront with our dithyramb this paragraph on which I stumbled in a newspaper immediately after reading Mr. Roebuck:

> A shocking child murder has just been committed at Nottingham.[3] A girl named Wragg left the workhouse there on Saturday morning with her young illegitimate child. The child was soon afterwards found dead on Mapperly Hills, having been strangled. Wragg is in custody.

Nothing but that; but, in juxtaposition with the absolute eulogies of Sir Charles Adderley and Mr. Roebuck, how eloquent, how suggestive are those few lines! "Our old Anglo-Saxon breed, the best in the whole world!"—how much that is harsh and ill-favored there is in this best! *Wragg!* If we are to talk of ideal perfection, of "the best in the whole world," has anyone reflected what a touch of grossness in our race, what an original shortcoming in the more delicate spiritual perceptions, is shown by the natural growth amongst us of such hideous names—Higginbottom, Stiggins, Bugg! In Ionia and Attica[4] they were luckier in this respect than "the best race in the world"; by the Ilissus[5] there was no Wragg, poor thing! And "our unrivaled happiness"—what an element of grimness, bareness, and hideousness mixes with it and blurs it; the workhouse, the dismal Mapperly Hills[6]—how dismal those who have seen them will remember—the gloom, the smoke, the cold, the strangled illegitimate child! "I ask you whether, the world over or in past history, there is anything like it?" Perhaps not, one is inclined to answer; but at any rate, in that case, the world is very much to be pitied. And the final touch—short, bleak and inhuman: *Wragg is in custody.* The sex lost in the confusion of our unrivaled happiness; or (shall I say?) the superfluous Christian name lopped off by the straightforward vigor of our old Anglo-Saxon breed! There is profit for the spirit in such contrasts as this; criticism serves the cause of perfection by establishing them. By eluding sterile conflict, by refusing to remain in the sphere where alone narrow and relative conceptions have any worth and validity, criticism may diminish its momentary importance, but only in this way has it a chance of gaining admittance for those wider and more perfect conceptions to which all its duty is really owed. Mr. Roebuck will have a poor opinion of an adversary who replies to his defiant songs of triumph only by murmuring under his breath, *Wragg is in custody;* but in no other way will these songs of triumph be induced gradually to moderate themselves, to get rid of what in them is excessive and offensive, and to fall into a softer and truer key.

It will be said that it is a very subtle and indirect action which I am thus prescribing for criticism, and that, by embracing in this manner the Indian[7] virtue of detachment and abandoning the sphere of practical life, it condemns

---

3. It occurred on September 10, 1864.
4. The district in Greece that includes Athens. Ionia: area of the west coast of Asia Minor where Homer was believed to have lived.
5. A stream south of Athens.

6. Adjacent to the coal-mining and industrial area of Nottingham (later associated with the writings of D. H. Lawrence).
7. I.e., Hindu.

itself to a slow and obscure work. Slow and obscure it may be, but it is the only proper work of criticism. The mass of mankind will never have any ardent zeal for seeing things as they are; very inadequate ideas will always satisfy them. On these inadequate ideas reposes, and must repose, the general practice of the world. That is as much as saying that whoever sets himself to see things as they are will find himself one of a very small circle; but it is only by this small circle resolutely doing its own work that adequate ideas will ever get current at all. The rush and roar of practical life will always have a dizzying and attracting effect upon the most collected spectator, and tend to draw him into its vortex; most of all will this be the case where that life is so powerful as it is in England. But it is only by remaining collected, and refusing to lend himself to the point of view of the practical man, that the critic can do the practical man any service, and it is only by the greatest sincerity in pursuing his own course, and by at last convincing even the practical man of his sincerity, that he can escape misunderstandings which perpetually threaten him.

For the practical man is not apt for fine distinctions, and yet in these distinctions truth and the highest culture greatly find their account. But it is not easy to lead a practical man—unless you reassure him as to your practical intentions, you have no chance of leading him—to see that a thing which he has always been used to look at from one side only, which he greatly values, and which, looked at from that side, quite deserves, perhaps, all the prizing and admiring which he bestows upon it—that this thing, looked at from another side, may appear much less beneficent and beautiful, and yet retain all its claims to our practical allegiance. Where shall we find language innocent enough, how shall we make the spotless purity of our intentions evident enough, to enable us to say to the political Englishman that the British Constitution itself, which, seen from the practical side, looks such a magnificent organ of progress and virtue, seen from the speculative side—with its compromises, its love of facts, its horror of theory, its studied avoidance of clear thoughts—that, seen from this side, our august Constitution sometimes looks—forgive me, shade of Lord Somers!—a colossal machine for the manufacture of Philistines?[8] How is Cobbett[9] to say this and not be misunderstood, blackened as he is with the smoke of a lifelong conflict in the field of political practice? how is Mr. Carlyle to say it and not be misunderstood, after his furious raid into this field with his *Latter-day Pamphlets*? how is Mr. Ruskin, after his pugnacious political economy?[1] I say, the critic must keep out of the region of immediate practice in the political, social, humanitarian sphere if he wants to make a beginning for that more free speculative treatment of things, which may perhaps one day make its benefits felt even in this sphere, but in a natural and thence irresistible manner.

*   *   *

If I have insisted so much on the course which criticism must take where politics and religion are concerned, it is because, where these burning matters

8. The unenlightened middle classes, whose opposition to the defenders of culture is akin to that of the biblical tribe that fought against the people of Israel, "the children of light." Arnold's repeated use of this parallel has established the term in our language. John Somers (1651–1716), statesman responsible for formulating the Declaration of Rights.

9. William Cobbett (1762–1835), vehement reformer and champion of the poor and oppressed.
1. Reference to *Unto This Last* (1862), in which John Ruskin shifted from art criticism to an attack on traditional theories of economics. In *Latter-Day Pamphlets* (1850), Thomas Carlyle expressed bitter antidemocratic views.

are in question, it is most likely to go astray. I have wished, above all, to insist on the attitude which criticism should adopt towards things in general; on its right tone and temper of mind. But then comes another question as to the subject matter which literary criticism should most seek. Here, in general, its course is determined for it by the idea which is the law of its being; the idea of a disinterested endeavour to learn and propagate the best that is known and thought in the world, and thus to establish a current of fresh and true ideas. By the very nature of things, as England is not all the world, much of the best that is known and thought in the world cannot be of English growth, must be foreign; by the nature of things, again, it is just this that we are least likely to know, while English thought is streaming in upon us from all sides, and takes excellent care that we shall not be ignorant of its existence. The English critic of literature, therefore, must dwell much on foreign thought, and with particular heed on any part of it, which, while significant and fruitful in itself, is for any reason specially likely to escape him. Again, judging is often spoken of as the critic's one business, and so in some sense it is; but the judgment which almost insensibly forms itself in a fair and clear mind, along with fresh knowledge, is the valuable one; and thus knowledge, and ever fresh knowledge, must be the critic's great concern for himself. And it is by communicating fresh knowledge, and letting his own judgment pass along with it—but insensibly, and in the second place, not the first, as a sort of companion and clue, not as an abstract lawgiver—that the critic will generally do most good to his readers. Sometimes, no doubt, for the sake of establishing an author's place in literature, and his relation to a central standard (and if this is not done, how are we to get at our *best in the world*?) criticism may have to deal with a subject matter so familiar that fresh knowledge is out of the question, and then it must be all judgment; an enunciation and detailed application of principles. Here the great safeguard is never to let oneself become abstract, always to retain an intimate and lively consciousness of the truth of what one is saying, and, the moment this fails us, to be sure that something is wrong. Still under all circumstances, this mere judgment and application of principles is, in itself, not the most satisfactory work to the critic; like mathematics, it is tautological, and cannot well give us, like fresh learning, the sense of creative activity.

But stop, some one will say; all this talk is of no practical use to us whatever; this criticism of yours is not what we have in our minds when we speak of criticism; when we speak of critics and criticism, we mean critics and criticism of the current English literature of the day; when you offer to tell criticism its function, it is to this criticism that we expect you to address yourself. I am sorry for it, for I am afraid I must disappoint these expectations. I am bound by my own definition of criticism: *a disinterested endeavour to learn and propagate the best that is known and thought in the world.* How much of current English literature comes into this "best that is known and thought in the world"? Not very much I fear; certainly less, at this moment, than of the current literature of France or Germany. Well, then, am I to alter my definition of criticism, in order to meet the requirements of a number of practicing English critics, who, after all, are free in their choice of a business? That would be making criticism lend itself just to one of those alien practical considerations, which, I have said, are so fatal to it. One may say, indeed, to those who have to deal with the mass—so much better disregarded—of current English literature, that they may at all events endeavour, in dealing with this, to try it, so far as they can, by the standard of the best that is known and thought in the world; one may say, that to get anywhere near this standard, every critic should try and possess one great literature, at least, besides his own; and the more unlike his own, the better. But, after all, the criticism I am really concerned with—the criticism which alone can much help us for the future, the criticism which, throughout Europe, is at the present day meant, when so much stress is laid on the importance of criticism and the critical spirit—is a criticism which regards Europe as being, for intellectual and spiritual purposes, one great confederation, bound to a joint action and working to a common result, and whose members have, for their proper outfit, a knowledge of Greek, Roman, and Eastern antiquity, and of one another. Special, local, and temporary advantages being put out of account, that modern nation will in the intellectual and spiritual sphere make most progress, which most thoroughly carries out this program. And what is that but saying that we too, all of us, as individuals, the more thoroughly we carry it out, shall make the more progress?

There is so much inviting us!—what are we to take? what will nourish us in growth towards perfection? That is the question which, with the immense field of life and of literature lying before him, the critic has to answer; for himself first, and afterwards for others. In this idea of the critic's business the essays brought together in the following pages have had their origin; in this idea, widely different as are their subjects, they have, perhaps, their unity.

I conclude with what I said at the beginning: to have the sense of creative activity is the great happiness and the great proof of being alive, and it is not denied to criticism to have it; but then criticism must be sincere, simple, flexible, ardent, ever widening its knowledge. Then it may have, in no contemptible measure, a joyful sense of creative activity; a sense which a man of insight and conscience will prefer to what he might derive from a poor, starved, fragmentary, inadequate creation. And at some epochs no other creation is possible.

Still, in full measure, the sense of creative activity belongs only to genuine creation; in literature we must never forget that. But what true man of letters ever can forget it? It is no such common matter for a gifted nature to come into possession of a current of true and living ideas, and to produce amidst the inspiration of them, that we are likely to underrate it. The epochs of Aeschylus[2] and Shakespeare make us feel their pre-eminence. In an epoch like those is, no doubt, the true life of literature; there is the promised land, towards which criticism can only beckon. That promised land it will not be ours to enter, and we shall die in the wilderness:[3] but to have desired to enter it, to have saluted it from afar, is already, perhaps, the best distinction among contemporaries; it will certainly be the best title to esteem with posterity.

1864, 1865

2. Greek tragedian (525–456 B.C.E.).
3. An allusion to the fate of rebellious Israelites (Numbers 14.26–35).

2126 / MATTHEW ARNOLD

From Culture and Anarchy[1]

From Chapter 1. Sweetness and Light

The impulse of the English race towards moral development and self-conquest has nowhere so powerfully manifested itself as in Puritanism. Nowhere has Puritanism found so adequate an expression as in the religious organization of the Independents.[2] The modern Independents have a newspaper, the *Nonconformist*, written with great sincerity and ability. The motto, the standard, the profession of faith which this organ of theirs carries aloft, is: "The Dissidence of Dissent and the Protestantism of the Protestant religion." There is sweetness and light, and an ideal of complete harmonious human perfection! One need not go to culture and poetry to find language to judge it. Religion, with its instinct for perfection, supplies language to judge it, language, too, which is in our mouths every day. "Finally, be of one mind, united in feeling," says St. Peter.[3] There is an ideal which judges the Puritan ideal: "The Dissidence of Dissent and the Protestantism of the Protestant religion!" And religious organizations like this are what people believe in, rest in, would give their lives for! Such, I say, is the wonderful virtue of even the beginnings of perfection, of having conquered even the plain faults of our animality, that the religious organization which has helped us to do it can seem to us something precious, salutary, and to be propagated, even when it wears such a brand of imperfection on its forehead as this. And men have got such a habit of giving to the language of religion a special application, of making it a mere jargon, that for the condemnation which religion itself passes on the shortcomings of their religious organizations they have no ear; they are sure to cheat themselves and to explain this condemnation away. They can only be reached by the criticism which culture, like poetry, speaking of language not to be sophisticated, and resolutely testing these organizations by the ideal of a human perfection complete on all sides, applies to them.

But men of culture and poetry, it will be said, are again and again failing, and failing conspicuously, in the necessary first stage to a harmonious perfection, in the subduing of the great obvious faults of our animality, which it is the glory of these religious organizations to have helped us to subdue. True, they do often so fail. They have often been without the virtues as well as the faults of the Puritan; it has been one of their dangers that they so felt the Puritan's faults that they too much neglected the practice of his virtues. I will not, however, exculpate them at the Puritan's expense. They have often failed

1. Arnold began *Culture and Anarchy* in the context of the turbulent political debate that preceded the passage of the second Reform Bill in 1867. The political climate seemed to some to threaten anarchy, to which Arnold opposed culture. A characteristic quality of the cultured state of mind is summed up, for his purposes, in his formula "sweetness and light," a phrase suggesting reasonableness of temper and intellectual insight. Arnold derived the phrase from a fable contrasting the spider with the bee in Jonathan Swift's *The Battle of the Books* (1704). The spider (representing a narrow, self-centered, and uncultured mind) spins out of itself "nothing at all but flybane and cobweb." The bee (representing a cultured mind that has drawn nourishment from the humanist tradition) ranges far and wide and makes in its hive honey and also wax out of which candles may be made.

Therefore, the bee, Swift says, furnishes humankind "with the two noblest of things, which are sweetness and light."

The selections printed here illustrate aspects of Arnold's indictment of the middle classes for their lack of sweetness and light. The first and third expose the narrowness and dullness of middle-class Puritan religious institutions in both the 17th and 19th centuries. The second, "Doing As One Likes," shows the limitations of the middle-class political bias and the irresponsibility of laissez-faire economics. Here Arnold is most close to Thomas Carlyle and John Ruskin.

2. A 17th-century Puritan group (of which Oliver Cromwell was an adherent), allied with the Congregationalists.

3. Cf. 1 Peter 3.8.

in morality, and morality is indispensable. And they have been punished for their failure, as the Puritan has been rewarded for his performance. They have been punished wherein they erred; but their ideal of beauty, of sweetness and light, and a human nature complete on all its sides, remains the true ideal of perfection still; just as the Puritan's ideal of perfection remains narrow and inadequate, although for what he did well he has been richly rewarded. Notwithstanding the mighty results of the Pilgrim Fathers' voyage, they and their standard of perfection are rightly judged when we figure to ourselves Shakespeare or Virgil[4]—souls in whom sweetness and light, and all that in human nature is most humane, were eminent—accompanying them on their voyage, and think what intolerable company Shakespeare and Virgil would have found them! In the same way let us judge the religious organizations which we see all around us. Do not let us deny the good and the happiness which they have accomplished; but do not let us fail to see clearly that their idea of human perfection is narrow and inadequate, and that the Dissidence of Dissent and the Protestantism of the Protestant religion will never bring humanity to its true goal. As I said with regard to wealth: Let us look at the life of those who live in and for it—so I say with regard to the religious organizations. Look at the life imaged in such a newspaper as the *Nonconformist*—a life of jealousy of the Establishment,[5] disputes, tea-meetings, openings of chapels, sermons; and then think of it as an ideal of a human life completing itself on all sides, and aspiring with all its organs after sweetness, light, and perfection!

From The Study of Poetry[1]

"The future of poetry is immense, because in poetry, where it is worthy of its high destinies, our race, as time goes on, will find an ever surer and surer stay. There is not a creed which is not shaken, not an accredited dogma which is not shown to be questionable, not a received tradition which does not threaten to dissolve. Our religion has materialized itself in the fact, in the supposed fact; it has attached its emotion to the fact, and now the fact is failing it. But for poetry the idea is everything; the rest is a world of illusion, of divine illusion. Poetry attaches its emotion to the idea; the idea *is* the fact. The strongest part of our religion today is its unconscious poetry."

Let me be permitted to quote these words of my own, as uttering the thought which should, in my opinion, go with us and govern us in all our study of poetry. In the present work[2] it is the course of one great contributory stream to the world-river of poetry that we are invited to follow. We are here invited

---

4. Roman poet (70–19 B.C.E.).
5. The Church of England or the Established Church.
1. Aside from its vindication of the importance of literature, this essay is an interesting example of the variety of Arnold's reading. To know literature in only one language seemed to him not to know literature. His personal *Notebooks* show that throughout his active life he continued to read books in French, German, Italian, Latin, and Greek. His favorite authors in these languages are used by him as a means of testing English poetry. The testing is sometimes a severe one. Readers may also protest that despite Arnold's wit, his essay

is limited by an incomplete recognition of the values of comic literature, a shortcoming abundantly evident in the discussion of Chaucer. Nevertheless, whether we agree or disagree with some of Arnold's verdicts, we can be attracted by the combination of traditionalism and impressionism on which these verdicts are based, and we can enjoy the memorable phrasemaking in which the verdicts are expressed. "The Study of Poetry" has been extraordinarily potent in shaping literary tastes in England and in America.
2. An anthology of English poetry for which this essay served as the introduction.

to trace the stream of English poetry. But whether we set ourselves, as here, to follow only one of the several streams that make the mighty river of poetry, or whether we seek to know them all, our governing thought should be the same. We should conceive of poetry worthily, and more highly than it has been the custom to conceive of it. We should conceive of it as capable of higher uses, and called to higher destinies, than those which in general men have assigned to it hitherto. More and more mankind will discover that we have to turn to poetry to interpret life for us, to console us, to sustain us. Without poetry, our science will appear incomplete; and most of what now passes with us for religion and philosophy will be replaced by poetry. Science, I say, will appear incomplete without it. For finely and truly does Wordsworth call poetry "the impassioned expression which is in the countenance of all science";[3] and what is a countenance without its expression? Again, Wordsworth finely and truly calls poetry "the breath and finer spirit of all knowledge": our religion, parading evidences such as those on which the popular mind relies now; our philosophy, pluming itself on its reasonings about causation and finite and infinite being; what are they but the shadows and dreams and false shows of knowledge? The day will come when we shall wonder at ourselves for having trusted to them, for having taken them seriously; and the more we perceive their hollowness, the more we shall prize "the breath and finer spirit of knowledge" offered to us by poetry.

But if we conceive thus highly of the destinies of poetry, we must also set our standard for poetry high, since poetry, to be capable of fulfilling such high destinies, must be poetry of a high order of excellence. We must accustom ourselves to a high standard and to a strict judgment. * * *

The best poetry is what we want; the best poetry will be found to have a power of forming, sustaining, and delighting us, as nothing else can. A clearer, deeper sense of the best in poetry, and of the strength and joy to be drawn from it, is the most precious benefit which we can gather from a poetical collection such as the present. And yet in the very nature and conduct of such a collection there is inevitably something which tends to obscure in us the consciousness of what our benefit should be, and to distract us from the pursuit of it. We should therefore steadily set it before our minds at the outset, and should compel ourselves to revert constantly to the thought of it as we proceed.

Yes; constantly in reading poetry, a sense for the best, the really excellent, and of the strength and joy to be drawn from it, should be present in our minds and should govern our estimate of what we read. But this real estimate, the only true one, is liable to be superseded, if we are not watchful, by two other kinds of estimate, the historic estimate and the personal estimate, both of which are fallacious. A poet or a poem may count to us historically, they may count to us on grounds personal to ourselves, and they may count to us really. They may count to us historically. The course of development of a nation's language, thought, and poetry, is profoundly interesting; and by regarding a poet's work as a stage in this course of development we may easily bring ourselves to make it of more importance as poetry than in itself it really is, we may come to use a language of quite exaggerated praise in criticizing it; in short, to overrate it. So arises in our poetic judgments the fallacy caused by the estimate which we may call historic. Then, again, a poet or a poem may

3. Preface to *Lyrical Ballads* (1800).

count to us on grounds personal to ourselves. Our personal affinities, likings, and circumstances, have great power to sway our estimate of this or that poet's work, and to make us attach more importance to it as poetry than in itself it really possesses, because to us it is, or has been, of high importance. Here also we overrate the object of our interest, and apply to it a language of praise which is quite exaggerated. And thus we get the source of a second fallacy in our poetic judgments—the fallacy caused by an estimate which we may call personal.

* * *

* * * The historic estimate is likely in especial to affect our judgment and our language when we are dealing with ancient poets; the personal estimate when we are dealing with poets our contemporaries, or at any rate modern. The exaggerations due to the historic estimate are not in themselves, perhaps, of very much gravity. Their report hardly enters the general ear; probably they do not always impose even on the literary men who adopt them. But they lead to a dangerous abuse of language. So we hear Caedmon,[4] amongst our own poets, compared to Milton. I have already noticed the enthusiasm of one accomplished French critic for "historic origins."[5] Another eminent French critic, M. Vitet, comments upon that famous document of the early poetry of his nation, the *Chanson de Roland*.[6] It is indeed a most interesting document. The *joculator* or *jongleur*[7] Taillefer, who was with William the Conqueror's army at Hastings,[8] marched before the Norman troops, so said the tradition, singing "of Charlemagne and of Roland and of Oliver, and of the vassals who died at Roncevaux"; and it is suggested that in the *Chanson de Roland* by one Turoldus or *Thefoulde*, a poem preserved in a manuscript of the twelfth century in the Bodleian Library at Oxford, we have certainly the matter, perhaps even some of the words, of the chant which Taillefer sang. The poem has vigor and freshness; it is not without pathos. But M. Vitet is not satisfied with seeing in it a document of some poetic value, and of very high historic and linguistic value; he sees in it a grand and beautiful work, a monument of epic genius. In its general design he finds the grandiose conception, in its details he finds the constant union of simplicity with greatness, which are the marks, he truly says, of the genuine epic, and distinguish it from the artificial epic of literary ages. One thinks of Homer; this is the sort of praise which is given to Homer, and justly given. Higher praise there cannot well be, and it is the praise due to epic poetry of the highest order only, and to no other. Let us try, then, the *Chanson de Roland* at its best. Roland, mortally wounded, lays himself down under a pine tree, with his face turned towards Spain and the enemy—

> De plusurs choses à remembrer li prist,
> De tantes teres cume li bers cunquist,
> De dulce France, des humes de sun lign,
> De Carlemagne sun seignor ki l'nurrit.[9]

4. A 7th-century Old English poet.
5. Charles d'Héricault (1823–1899), a French critic cited earlier in a passage omitted here. Arnold had mildly reprimanded him for his "historical" bias in praising a 15th-century poet, Clément Marot, at the expense of classical 17th-century poets such as Racine.
6. An 11th-century epic poem in Old French that tells of the 8th-century wars of Charlemagne against the Moors in Spain and of the bravery of

the French leaders Roland and Oliver. Ludovic Vitet (1802–1873) wrote on it in his *Essais Historiques et Littéraires* (1862).
7. Jester or minstrel (French).
8. The battle in 1066 in which Harold II was killed and the English army defeated.
9. "Then began he to call many things to remembrance—all the lands which his valor conquered and pleasant France, and the men of his lineage, and Charlemagne his liege lord who nourished

That is primitive work, I repeat, with an undeniable poetic quality of its own. It deserves such praise, and such praise is sufficient for it. But now turn to Homer—

    Ὣς φάτο τοὺς δ' ἤδη κάτεχεν φυσίζοος αἶα
    ἐν Λακεδαίμονι αὖθι, φίλῃ ἐν πατρίδι γαίῃ.[1]

We are here in another world, another order of poetry altogether; here is rightly due such supreme praise as that which M. Vitet gives to the *Chanson de Roland*. If our words are to have any meaning, if our judgments are to have any solidity, we must not heap that supreme praise upon poetry of an order immeasurably inferior.

Indeed there can be no more useful help for discovering what poetry belongs to the class of the truly excellent, and can therefore do us most good, than to have always in one's mind lines and expressions of the great masters, and to apply them as a touchstone to other poetry. Of course we are not to require this other poetry to resemble them; it may be very dissimilar. But if we have any tact we shall find them, when we have lodged them well in our minds, an infallible touchstone for detecting the presence or absence of high poetic quality, and also the degree of this quality, in all other poetry which we may place beside them. Short passages, even single lines, will serve our turn quite sufficiently. Take the two lines which I have just quoted from Homer, the poet's comment on Helen's mention of her brothers—or take his

    Ἆ δειλώ, τί σφῶϊ δόμεν Πηλῆϊ ἄνακτι
    θνητῷ; ὑμεῖς δ' ἐστὸν ἀγήρω τ' ἀθανάτω τε.
    ἦ ἵνα δυστήνοισι μετ' ἀνδράσιν ἄλγε' ἔχητον;[2]

the address of Zeus to the horses of Peleus—or take finally his

    Καὶ σέ, γέρον, τὸ πρὶν μὲν ἀκούομεν ὄλβιον εἶναι.[3]

the words of Achilles to Priam, a suppliant before him. Take that incomparable line and a half of Dante, Ugolino's tremendous words—

    Io no piangeva; sì dentro impietrai.
    Piangevan elli . . .[4]

take the lovely words of Beatrice to Virgil—

    Io son fatta da Dio, sua mercè, tale,
    Che la vostra miseria non mi tange,
    Nè fiamma d'esto incendio non m'assale . . .[5]

take the simple, but perfect, single line—

    In la sua volontade è nostra pace.[6]

---

him." *Chanson de Roland* 3.939–42 [Arnold's note].

1. "So said she; they long since in Earth's soft arms were reposing, / There, in their own dear land, their fatherland, Lacedaemon." *Iliad* 3.243–44 (translated by Dr. Hawtrey) [Arnold's note].

2. "Ah, unhappy pair, why gave we you to King Peleus, to a mortal? but ye are without old age, and immortal. Was it that with men born to misery ye might have sorrow?" *Iliad* 17.443–45 [Arnold's note].

3. "Nay, and thou too, old man, in former days wast, as we hear, happy." *Iliad* 24.543 [Arnold's

note]. Priam, king of Troy, has begged Achilles to return the body of his son Hector, whom the Greek warrior had killed.

4. "I wailed not, so of stone I grew within; *they* wailed." *Inferno* 33.49–50 [Arnold's note].

5. "Of such sort hath God, thanked be His mercy, made me, that your misery toucheth me not, neither doth the flame of this fire strike me." *Inferno* 2.91–93 [Arnold's note]. The Roman poet Virgil is Dante's guide.

6. "In His will is our peace." *Paradiso* 3.85 [Arnold's note].

Take of Shakespeare a line or two of Henry the Fourth's expostulation with
sleep—

> Wilt thou upon the high and giddy mast
> Seal up the shipboy's eyes, and rock his brains
> In cradle of the rude imperious surge . . . [7]

and take, as well, Hamlet's dying request to Horatio—

> If thou didst ever hold me in thy heart,
> Absent thee from felicity awhile,
> And in this harsh world draw thy breath in pain,
> To tell my story . . . [8]

Take of Milton that Miltonic passage—

> Darkened so, yet shone
> Above them all the archangel; but his face
> Deep scars of thunder had intrenched, and care
> Sat on his faded cheek . . . [9]

add two such lines as—

> And courage never to submit or yield
> And what is else not to be overcome . . . [1]

and finish with the exquisite close to the loss of Proserpine, the loss

> . . . which cost Ceres all that pain
> To seek her through the world.[2]

These few lines, if we have tact and can use them, are enough even of themselves to keep clear and sound our judgments about poetry, to save us from
fallacious estimates of it, to conduct us to a real estimate.

The specimens I have quoted differ widely from one another, but they have
in common this: the possession of the very highest poetical quality. If we are
thoroughly penetrated by their power, we shall find that we have acquired a
sense enabling us, whatever poetry may be laid before us, to feel the degree
in which a high poetical quality is present or wanting there. Critics give themselves great labour to draw out what in the abstract constitutes the characters
of a high quality of poetry. It is much better simply to have recourse to concrete
examples—to take specimens of poetry of the high, the very highest quality,
and to say: The characters of a high quality of poetry are what is expressed
there. They are far better recognized by being felt in the verse of the master,
than by being perused in the prose of the critic. Nevertheless if we are urgently
pressed to give some critical account of them, we may safely, perhaps, venture
on laying down, not indeed how and why the characters arise, but where and
in what they arise. They are in the matter and substance of the poetry, and
they are in its manner and style. Both of these, the substance and matter on
the one hand, the style and manner on the other, have a mark, an accent, of
high beauty, worth, and power. But if we are asked to define this mark and
accent in the abstract, our answer must be: No, for we should thereby be

---

7. *2 Henry IV* 3.1.18–20.
8. *Hamlet* 5.2.288–91.
9. *Paradise Lost* 1.599–602.
1. *Paradise Lost* 1.108–9.

2. *Paradise Lost* 4.271–72. Ceres, the Roman goddess of grain, searched for her daughter Proserpina, not knowing that she had been abducted by
Pluto, the god of the underworld.

darkening the question, not clearing it. The mark and accent are as given by the substance and matter of that poetry, by the style and manner of that poetry, and of all other poetry which is akin to it in quality.

Only one thing we may add as to the substance and matter of poetry, guiding ourselves by Aristotle's profound observation that the superiority of poetry over history consists in its possessing a higher truth and a higher seriousness (φιλοσοφώτερον καὶ σπουδαιότερον).[3] Let us add, therefore, to what we have said, this: that the substance and matter of the best poetry acquire their special character from possessing, in an eminent degree, truth and seriousness. We may add yet further, what is in itself evident, that to the style and manner of the best poetry their special character, their accent, is given by their diction, and, even yet more, by their movement. And though we distinguish between the two characters, the two accents, of superiority, yet they are nevertheless vitally connected one with the other. The superior character of truth and seriousness, in the matter and substance of the best poetry, is inseparable from the superiority of diction and movement marking its style and manner. The two superiorities are closely related, and are in steadfast proportion one to the other. So far as high poetic truth and seriousness are wanting to a poet's matter and substance, so far also, we may be sure, will a high poetic stamp of diction and movement be wanting to his style and manner. In proportion as this high stamp of diction and movement, again, is absent from a poet's style and manner, we shall find, also, that high poetic truth and seriousness are absent from his substance and matter.

So stated, these are but dry generalities; their whole force lies in their application. And I could wish every student of poetry to make the application of them for himself. Made by himself, the application would impress itself upon his mind far more deeply than made by me. Neither will my limits allow me to make any full application of the generalities above propounded; but in the hope of bringing out, at any rate, some significance in them, and of establishing an important principle more firmly by their means, I will, in the space which remains to me, follow rapidly from the commencement the course of our English poetry with them in my view.

*　*　*

Chaucer's * * * poetical importance does not need the assistance of the historic estimate; it is real. He is a genuine source of joy and strength, which is flowing still for us and will flow always. He will be read, as time goes on, far more generally than he is read now. His language is a cause of difficulty for us; but so also, and I think in quite as great a degree, is the language of Burns.[4] In Chaucer's case, as in that of Burns, it is a difficulty to be unhesitatingly accepted and overcome.

If we ask ourselves wherein consists the immense superiority of Chaucer's poetry over the romance poetry—why it is that in passing from this to Chaucer we suddenly feel ourselves to be in another world, we shall find that his superiority is both in the substance of his poetry and in the style of his poetry. His superiority in substance is given by his large, free, simple, clear yet kindly view of human life—so unlike the total want, in the romance poets, of all intelligent command of it. Chaucer has not their helplessness; he has gained the power to survey the world from a central, a truly human point of view. We have only

---

3. Aristotle's *Poetics* 9.
4. Robert Burns (1759–1796), whose language is difficult because he frequently uses Scottish dialect.

to call to mind the Prologue to *The Canterbury Tales*. The right comment upon it is Dryden's: "It is sufficient to say, according to the proverb, that *here is God's plenty*." And again: "He is a perpetual fountain of good sense."[5] It is by a large, free, sound representation of things, that poetry, this high criticism of life, has truth of substance; and Chaucer's poetry has truth of substance.

Of his style and manner, if we think first of the romance poetry and then of Chaucer's divine liquidness of diction, his divine fluidity of movement, it is difficult to speak temperately. They are irresistible, and justify all the rapture with which his successors speak of his "gold dewdrops of speech."[6] Johnson misses the point entirely when he finds fault with Dryden for ascribing to Chaucer the first refinement of our numbers, and says that Gower[7] also can show smooth numbers and easy rhymes. The refinement of our numbers means something far more than this. A nation may have versifiers with smooth numbers and easy rhymes, and yet may have no real poetry at all. Chaucer is the father of our splendid English poetry; he is our "well of English undefiled,"[8] because by the lovely charm of his diction, the lovely charm of his movement, he makes an epoch and founds a tradition. In Spenser, Shakespeare, Milton, Keats, we can follow the tradition of the liquid diction, the fluid movement, of Chaucer; at one time it is his liquid diction of which in these poets we feel the virtue, and at another time it is his fluid movement. And the virtue is irresistible.

Bounded as is my space, I must yet find room for an example of Chaucer's virtue, as I have given examples to show the virtue of the great classics. I feel disposed to say that a single line is enough to show the charm of Chaucer's verse; that merely one line like this—

O martyr souded[9] in virginitee!

has a virtue of manner and movement such as we shall not find in all the verse of romance poetry—but this is saying nothing. The virtue is such as we shall not find, perhaps, in all English poetry, outside the poets whom I have named as the special inheritors of Chaucer's tradition. A single line, however, is too little if we have not the strain of Chaucer's verse well in our memory; let us take a stanza. It is from *The Prioress's Tale*, the story of the Christian child murdered in a Jewry—[1]

> My throte is cut unto my nekke-bone
> Saidè this child, and as by way of kinde
> I should have deyd, yea, longè time agone;
> But Jesu Christ, as ye in bookès finde,
> Will that his glory last and be in minde,
> And for the worship of his mother dere
> Yet may I sing O *Alma* loud and clere.

Wordsworth has modernized this Tale, and to feel how delicate and evanescent is the charm of verse, we have only to read Wordsworth's first three lines of this stanza after Chaucer's—

5. Both quotations are from John Dryden's preface to his *Fables Ancient and Modern* (1700).
6. "The Life of Our Lady," a poem by John Lydgate (ca. 1370–ca.1451).
7. John Gower (ca. 1325–1408), friend of Chaucer and author of the *Confessio Amantis*, a long poem in octosyllabic couplets. Samuel Johnson (1709–1784), critic, essayist, and poet.
8. Said of Chaucer by Edmund Spenser in *The Faerie Queene* (1590) 4.2.32.
9. The French *soudé*: soldered, fixed fast [Arnold's note]. From *The Canterbury Tales*, *The Prioress's Tale* (line 127); Chaucer wrote "souded to" rather than "souded in."
1. Jewish ghetto.

> My throat is cut unto the bone, I trow,
> Said this young child, and by the law of kind
> I should have died, yea, many hours ago.

The charm is departed. It is often said that the power of liquidness and fluidity in Chaucer's verse was dependent upon a free, a licentious dealing with language, such as is now impossible; upon a liberty, such as Burns too enjoyed, of making words like *neck, bird,* into a dissyllable by adding to them, and words like *cause, rhyme,* into a dissyllable by sounding the *e* mute. It is true that Chaucer's fluidity is conjoined with this liberty, and is admirably served by it; but we ought not to say that it was dependent upon it. It was dependent upon his talent. Other poets with a like liberty do not attain to the fluidity of Chaucer; Burns himself does not attain to it. Poets, again, who have a talent akin to Chaucer's, such as Shakespeare or Keats, have known how to attain to his fluidity without the like liberty.

And yet Chaucer is not one of the great classics. His poetry transcends and effaces, easily and without effort, all the romance poetry of Catholic Christendom; it transcends and effaces all the English poetry contemporary with it, it transcends and effaces all the English poetry subsequent to it down to the age of Elizabeth. Of such avail is poetic truth of substance, in its natural and necessary union with poetic truth of style. And yet, I say, Chaucer is not one of the great classics. He has not their accent. What is wanting to him is suggested by the mere mention of the name of the first great classic of Christendom, the immortal poet who died eighty years before Chaucer—Dante. The accent of such verse as

> *In la sua volontade è nostra pace . . .*

is altogether beyond Chaucer's reach; we praise him, but we feel that this accent is out of the question for him. It may be said that it was necessarily out of the reach of any poet in the England of that stage of growth. Possibly; but we are to adopt a real, not a historic, estimate of poetry. However we may account for its absence, something is wanting, then, to the poetry of Chaucer, which poetry must have before it can be placed in the glorious class of the best. And there is no doubt what that something is. It is the σπουδαιότης, the high and excellent seriousness, which Aristotle assigns as one of the grand virtues of poetry. The substance of Chaucer's poetry, his view of things and his criticism of life, has largeness, freedom, shrewdness, benignity; but it has not this high seriousness. Homer's criticism of life has it, Dante's has it, Shakespeare's has it. It is this chiefly which gives to our spirits what they can rest upon; and with the increasing demands of our modern ages upon poetry, this virtue of giving us what we can rest upon will be more and more highly esteemed. A voice from the slums of Paris, fifty or sixty years after Chaucer, the voice of poor Villon out of his life of riot and crime, has at its happy moments (as, for instance, in the last stanza of *La Belle Heaulmière*)[2] more of this important poetic virtue of seriousness than all the productions of Chaucer. But its apparition[3] in Villon, and in men like Villon, is fitful; the greatness of

---

2. The name *Heaulmière* is said to be derived from a headdress (helm) worn as a mask by courtesans. In Villon's ballad a poor old creature of this class laments her days of youth and beauty. The last stanza of the ballad runs thus—"*Ainsi le bon temps regretons / Entrenous, pauvres vieilles sottes, / Assises bas, à croppetons, / Tout en ung tas comme pelottes; / A petit feu de chenevottes / Tost allumeés, tost estaincles, / Et jadis fusmes si mignottes! / Ainsi*

en prend à maintz et maintes." [It may be translated:] "Thus amongst ourselves we regret the good time, poor silly old things, low-seated on our heels, all in a heap like so many balls; by a little fire of hemp stalks, soon lighted, soon spent. And once we were such darlings! So fares it with many and many a one" [Arnold's note]. François Villon (1431–1484), French poet and vagabond.
3. Appearance.

the great poets, the power of their criticism of life, is that their virtue is sustained.

To our praise, therefore, of Chaucer as a poet there must be this limitation: he lacks the high seriousness of the great classics, and therewith an important part of their virtue. Still, the main fact for us to bear in mind about Chaucer is his sterling value according to that real estimate which we firmly adopt for all poets. He has poetic truth of substance, though he has not high poetic seriousness, and corresponding to his truth of substance he has an exquisite virtue of style and manner. With him is born our real poetry.

For my present purpose I need not dwell on our Elizabethan poetry, or on the continuation and close of this poetry in Milton. We all of us profess to be agreed in the estimate of this poetry; we all of us recognize it as great poetry, our greatest, and Shakespeare and Milton as our poetical classics. The real estimate, here, has universal currency. With the next age of our poetry divergency and difficulty begin. An historic estimate of that poetry has established itself; and the question is, whether it will be found to coincide with the real estimate.

The age of Dryden, together with our whole eighteenth century which followed it, sincerely believed itself to have produced poetical classics of its own, and even to have made advance, in poetry, beyond all its predecessors. Dryden regards as not seriously disputable the opinion "that the sweetness of English verse was never understood or practiced by our fathers."[4] Cowley[5] could see nothing at all in Chaucer's poetry. Dryden heartily admired it, and, as we have seen, praised its matter admirably; but of its exquisite manner and movement all he can find to say is that "there is the rude sweetness of a Scotch tune in it, which is natural and pleasing, though not perfect."[6] Addison,[7] wishing to praise Chaucer's numbers, compares them with Dryden's own. And all through the eighteenth century, and down even into our own times, the stereotyped phrase of approbation for good verse found in our early poetry has been, that it even approached the verse of Dryden, Addison, Pope, and Johnson.

Are Dryden and Pope poetical classics? Is the historic estimate, which represents them as such, and which has been so long established that it cannot easily give way, the real estimate? Wordsworth and Coleridge, as is well known, denied it; but the authority of Wordsworth and Coleridge does not weigh much with the young generation, and there are many signs to show that the eighteenth century and its judgments are coming into favor again. Are the favorite poets of the eighteenth century classics?

It is impossible within my present limits to discuss the question fully. And what man of letters would not shrink from seeming to dispose dictatorially of the claims of two men who are, at any rate, such masters in letters as Dryden and Pope; two men of such admirable talent, both of them, and one of them, Dryden, a man, on all sides, of such energetic and genial power? And yet, if we are to gain the full benefit from poetry, we must have the real estimate of it. I cast about for some mode of arriving, in the present case, at such an estimate without offense. And perhaps the best way is to begin, as it is easy to begin, with cordial praise.

When we find Chapman,[8] the Elizabethan translator of Homer, expressing himself in his preface thus: "Though truth in her very nakedness sits in so

---

4. *Essay on Dramatic Poesy* (1668).
5. Abraham Cowley (1618–1667), English poet.
6. Preface to his *Fables*.
7. Joseph Addison (1672–1719), essayist and

poet.
8. George Chapman (ca. 1559–1634), poet and dramatist; the quotation is from his translation (1598–1611) of the *Iliad*.

deep a pit, that from Gades to Aurora and Ganges few eyes can sound her, I hope yet those few here will so discover and confirm that, the date being out of her darkness in this morning of our poet, he shall now gird his temples with the sun," we pronounce that such a prose is intolerable. When we find Milton writing: "And long it was not after, when I was confirmed in this opinion, that he, who would not be frustrate of his hope to write well hereafter in laudable things, ought himself to be a true poem"[9]—we pronounce that such a prose has its own grandeur, but that it is obsolete and inconvenient. But when we find Dryden telling us: "What Virgil wrote in the vigor of his age, in plenty and at ease, I have undertaken to translate in my declining years; struggling with wants, oppressed with sickness, curbed in my genius, liable to be misconstrued in all I write"[1]—then we exclaim that here at last we have the true English prose, a prose such as we would all gladly use if we only knew how. Yet Dryden was Milton's contemporary.

But after the Restoration the time had come when our nation felt the imperious need of a fit prose. So, too, the time had likewise come when our nation felt the imperious need of freeing itself from the absorbing preoccupation which religion in the Puritan age had exercised. It was impossible that this freedom should be brought about without some negative excess, without some neglect and impairment of the religious life of the soul; and the spiritual history of the eighteenth century shows us that the freedom was not achieved without them. Still, the freedom was achieved; the preoccupation, an undoubtedly baneful and retarding one if it had continued, was got rid of. And as with religion amongst us at that period, so it was also with letters. A fit prose was a necessity; but it was impossible that a fit prose should establish itself amongst us without some touch of frost to the imaginative life of the soul. The needful qualities for a fit prose are regularity, uniformity, precision, balance. The men of letters, whose destiny it may be to bring their nation to the attainment of a fit prose, must of necessity, whether they work in prose or in verse, give a predominating, an almost exclusive attention to the qualities of regularity, uniformity, precision, balance. But an almost exclusive attention to these qualities involves some repression and silencing of poetry.

We are to regard Dryden as the puissant and glorious founder, Pope as the splendid high priest, of our age of prose and reason, of our excellent and indispensable eighteenth century. For the purposes of their mission and destiny their poetry, like their prose, is admirable. Do you ask me whether Dryden's verse, take it almost where you will, is not good?

> A milk-white Hind, immortal and unchanged,
> Fed on the lawns and in the forest ranged.[2]

I answer: Admirable for the purposes of the inaugurator of an age of prose and reason. Do you ask me whether Pope's verse, take it almost where you will, is not good?

> To Hounslow Heath I point, and Banstead Down;
> Thence comes your mutton, and these chicks my own.[3]

I answer: Admirable for the purposes of the high priest of an age of prose and reason. But do you ask me whether such verse proceeds from men with an

9. "Apology for Smectymnuus" (1642).
1. "Postscript to the Reader" (1698) in his translation of Virgil.

2. The Hind and the Panther (1687) 1.1–2.
3. Imitations of Horace (1737), Satire 2.2.143–44.

adequate poetic criticism of life, from men whose criticism of life has a high seriousness, or even, without that high seriousness, has poetic largeness, freedom, insight, benignity? Do you ask me whether the application of ideas to life in the verse of these men, often a powerful application, no doubt, is a powerful *poetic* application? Do you ask me whether the poetry of these men has either the matter or the inseparable manner of such an adequate poetic criticism; whether it has the accent of

> Absent thee from felicity awhile . . .

or of

> And what is else not to be overcome . . .

or of

> O martyr souded in virginitee!

I answer: It has not and cannot have them; it is the poetry of the builders of an age of prose and reason. Though they may write in verse, though they may in a certain sense be masters of the art of versification, Dryden and Pope are not classics of our poetry, they are classics of our prose.

Gray[4] is our poetical classic of that literature and age; the position of Gray is singular, and demands a word of notice here. He has not the volume or the power of poets who, coming in times more favorable, have attained to an independent criticism of life. But he lived with the great poets, he lived, above all, with the Greeks, through perpetually studying and enjoying them; and he caught their poetic point of view for regarding life, caught their poetic manner. The point of view and the manner are not self-sprung in him, he caught them of others; and he had not the free and abundant use of them. But whereas Addison and Pope never had the use of them, Gray had the use of them at times. He is the scantiest and frailest of classics in our poetry, but he is a classic.[5]

* * *

At any rate the end to which the method and the estimate are designed to lead, and from leading to which, if they do lead to it, they get their whole value—the benefit of being able clearly to feel and deeply to enjoy the best, the truly classic, in poetry—is an end, let me say it once more at parting, of supreme importance. We are often told that an era is opening in which we are to see multitudes of a common sort of readers, and masses of a common sort of literature; that such readers do not want and could not relish anything better than such literature, and that to provide it is becoming a vast and profitable industry. Even if good literature entirely lost currency with the world, it would still be abundantly worth while to continue to enjoy it by oneself. But it never will lose currency with the world, in spite of momentary appearances; it never will lose supremacy. Currency and supremacy are insured to it, not indeed by the world's deliberate and conscious choice, but by something far deeper—by the instinct of self-preservation in humanity.

1880

4. Thomas Gray (1716–1771), British poet.
5. After Gray, the only other poet discussed by Arnold is Burns (not printed here). Arnold con-

cludes that "Burns, like Chaucer, comes short of the high seriousness of the great classics."

CHRISTINA ROSSETTI
1830–1894

Referring to the title of George Gissing's 1893 novel about women who choose not to marry, the critic Jerome McGann calls Christina Rossetti "one of nineteenth-century England's greatest 'Odd Women.' " Her life had little apparent incident. She was the youngest child in the Rossetti family. Her father was an exiled Italian patriot who wrote poetry and commentaries on Dante that tried to find evidence in his poems of mysterious ancient conspiracies; her mother was an Anglo-Italian who had worked as a governess. Their household was a lively gathering place for Italian exiles, full of conversation of politics and culture; and Christina, like her brothers Dante Gabriel and William Michael, was encouraged to develop an early love for art and literature and to draw and write poetry from a very early age. When she was an adolescent, her life changed dramatically: her father became a permanent invalid, the family's economic situation worsened, and her own health deteriorated. Subsequently she, her mother, and her sister became intensely involved with the Anglo-Catholic movement within the Church of England. For the rest of her life, Rossetti governed herself by strict religious principles, giving up theater, opera, and chess; on two occasions she canceled plans for marriage because of religious scruples, breaking her first engagement when her fiancé reverted to Roman Catholicism and ultimately refusing to marry a second suitor because he seemed insufficiently concerned with religion. She lived a quiet life, occupying herself with charitable work—including ten years of volunteer service at a penitentiary for fallen women—with caring for her family, and with writing poetry.

Rossetti's first volume of poetry, *Goblin Market and Other Poems* (1862), contains all the different poetic modes that mark her achievement—pure lyric, narrative fable, ballad, and the devotional verse to which she increasingly turned in her later years. The most remarkable poem in the book is the title piece, which early established its popularity as a seemingly simple moral fable for children. Later readers have likened it to S. T. Coleridge's *The Rime of the Ancient Mariner* (1798) and have detected in it a complex representation of the religious themes of temptation and sin, and of redemption by vicarious suffering; the fruit that tempts Laura, however, clearly is not from the tree of knowledge but from the orchard of sensual delights. In its deceptively simple style *Goblin Market,* like many of Rossetti's poems, demonstrates her affinity with the early aims of the Pre-Raphaelite group, though her work as a whole resists this classification. A consciousness of gender often leads her to criticize the conventional representation of women in Pre-Raphaelite art, as in her sonnet "In an Artist's Studio" (1896), and a stern religious vision controls the sensuous impulses typical of Pre-Raphaelite poetry and painting. Virginia Woolf has described the distinctive combination of sensuousness and religious severity in Rossetti's work:

> Your poems are full of gold dust and "sweet geraniums' varied brightness"; your eye noted incessantly how rushes are "velvet headed," and lizards have a "strange metallic mail"—your eye, indeed, observed with a sensual pre-Raphaelite intensity that must have surprised Christina the Anglo-Catholic. But to her you owed perhaps the fixity and sadness of your muse. . . . No sooner have you feasted on beauty with your eyes than your mind tells you that beauty is vain and beauty passes. Death, oblivion, and rest lap round your songs with their dark wave.

William Michael Rossetti wrote of his sister, "She was replete with the spirit of self-postponement." Christina Rossetti was a poet who created, in Sandra M. Gilbert and Susan Gubar's phrase, "an aesthetics of renunciation." She writes a poetry of deferral, of deflection, of negation, whose very denials and constraints give her a powerful way to articulate a poetic self in critical relationship to the little that the world offers. Like Emily Dickinson, she often, as in "Winter: My Secret" (1862) uses a coy playfulness and sardonic wit to reduce the self but at the same time to preserve for it a secret inner space. And like Dickinson, she wrote many poems of an extraordinarily pure lyric beauty that made Virginia Woolf compare Rossetti's work to that of classical composers: "Your instinct was so sure, so direct, so intense that it produced poems that sing like music in one's ears—like a melody by Mozart or an air by Gluck."

Song

She sat and sang alway
　　By the green margin of a stream,
Watching the fishes leap and play
　　Beneath the glad sunbeam.

5　　I sat and wept alway
　　Beneath the moon's most shadowy beam,
Watching the blossoms of the May
　　Weep leaves into the stream.

I wept for memory;
10　　She sang for hope that is so fair:
My tears were swallowed by the sea;
　　Her songs died on the air.

1848   1862

Song

When I am dead, my dearest,
　　Sing no sad songs for me;
Plant thou no roses at my head,
　　Nor shady cypress tree:[1]
5　　Be the green grass above me
　　With showers and dewdrops wet;
And if thou wilt, remember,
　　And if thou wilt, forget.

I shall not see the shadows,
10　　I shall not feel the rain;
I shall not hear the nightingale
　　Sing on, as if in pain:
And dreaming through the twilight
　　That doth not rise nor set,
15　　Haply° I may remember,　　　　　　　　　　*perhaps*
　　And haply may forget.

1848   1862

1. The cypress tree is associated with mourning.

After Death

The curtains were half drawn, the floor was swept
  And strewn with rushes, rosemary and may[1]
  Lay thick upon the bed on which I lay,
Where thro' the lattice ivy-shadows crept.
5 He leaned above me, thinking that I slept
  And could not hear him; but I heard him say:
  "Poor child, poor child": and as he turned away
Came a deep silence, and I knew he wept.
He did not touch the shroud, or raise the fold
10   That hid my face, or take my hand in his,
    Or ruffle the smooth pillows for my head:
    He did not love me living; but once dead
  He pitied me; and very sweet it is
To know he still is warm tho' I am cold.

1849   1862

Dead before Death

Ah! changed and cold, how changed and very cold!
  With stiffened smiling lips and cold calm eyes:
  Changed, yet the same; much knowing, little wise;
This was the promise of the days of old!
5 Grown hard and stubborn in the ancient mould,
  Grown rigid in the sham of lifelong lies:
  We hoped for better things as years would rise,
But it is over as a tale once told.
All fallen the blossom that no fruitage bore,
10   All lost the present and the future time,
All lost, all lost, the lapse that went before:
So lost till death shut-to the opened door,
  So lost from chime to everlasting chime,
So cold and lost for ever evermore.

1854   1862

Cobwebs

It is a land with neither night nor day,
  Nor heat nor cold, nor any wind, nor rain,
  Nor hills nor valleys; but one even plain
Stretches thro' long unbroken miles away:
5 While thro' the sluggish air a twilight grey
  Broodeth; no moons or seasons wax and wane,
  No ebb and flow are there along the main,°   *ocean*

1. Flowers associated with death.

No bud-time no leaf-falling, there for aye:°—   *forever*
No ripple on the sea, no shifting sand,
10   No beat of wings to stir the stagnant space,
No pulse of life thro' all the loveless land:
And loveless sea; no trace of days before,
      No guarded home, no toil-won resting place,
No future hope no fear for evermore.

1855   1896

A Triad

Three sang of love together: one with lips
      Crimson, with cheeks and bosom in a glow,
Flushed to the yellow hair and finger tips;
      And one there sang who soft and smooth as snow
5   Bloomed like a tinted hyacinth at a show;
And one was blue with famine after love,
      Who like a harpstring snapped rang harsh and low
The burden of what those were singing of.
One shamed herself in love; one temperately
10   Grew gross in soulless love, a sluggish wife;
One famished died for love. Thus two of three
      Took death for love and won him after strife;
One droned in sweetness like a fattened bee:
      All on the threshold, yet all short of life.

1856   1862

In an Artist's Studio[1]

One face looks out from all his canvases,
      One selfsame figure sits or walks or leans;
      We found her hidden just behind those screens,
That mirror gave back all her loveliness.
5   A queen in opal or in ruby dress,
      A nameless girl in freshest summer-greens,
      A saint, an angel;—every canvas means
The same one meaning, neither more nor less.
He feeds upon her face by day and night,
10   And she with true kind eyes looks back on him
Fair as the moon and joyful as the light:
      Not wan with waiting, not with sorrow dim;
Not as she is, but was when hope shone bright;
      Not as she is, but as she fills his dream.

1856   1896

1. According to Christina's brother William Michael, this poem focuses on the work of their older brother, Dante Gabriel: "The reference is apparently to our brother's studio, and to his constantly repeated heads of the lady whom he afterwards married, Miss Siddal."

A Birthday

My heart is like a singing bird
    Whose nest is in a watered shoot;°   *slim branch*
My heart is like an apple tree
    Whose boughs are bent with thickset fruit;
5 My heart is like a rainbow shell
    That paddles in a halcyon° sea;   *tranquil*
My heart is gladder than all these
    Because my love is come to me.

Raise me a dais of silk and down;
10   Hang it with vair° and purple dyes;   *squirrel fur*
Carve it in doves and pomegranates,
    And peacocks with a hundred eyes;
Work it in gold and silver grapes,
    In leaves and silver fleurs-de-lys;
15 Because the birthday of my life
    Is come, my love is come to me.

1857   1862

An Apple-Gathering

I plucked pink blossoms from mine apple tree
    And wore them all that evening in my hair:
Then in due season when I went to see
    I found no apples there.

5 With dangling basket all along the grass
    As I had come I went the selfsame track:
My neighbours mocked me while they saw me pass
    So empty-handed back.

Lilian and Lilias smiled in trudging by,
10   Their heaped-up basket teazed me like a jeer;
Sweet-voiced they sang beneath the sunset sky,
    Their mother's home was near.

Plump Gertrude passed me with her basket full,
    A stronger hand than hers helped it along;
15 A voice talked with her thro' the shadows cool
    More sweet to me than song.

Ah Willie, Willie, was my love less worth
    Than apples with their green leaves piled above?
I counted rosiest apples on the earth
20   Of far less worth than love.

So once it was with me you stooped to talk
    Laughing and listening in this very lane:

> To think that by this way we used to walk
>> We shall not walk again!
>
> 25   I let my neighbours pass me, ones and twos
>> And groups; the latest said the night grew chill,
> And hastened: but I loitered, while the dews
>> Fell fast I loitered still.

1857   1862

Up-Hill

> Does the road wind up-hill all the way?
>> Yes, to the very end.
> Will the day's journey take the whole long day?
>> From morn to night, my friend.
>
> 5   But is there for the night a resting-place?
>> A roof for when the slow dark hours begin.
> May not the darkness hide it from my face?
>> You cannot miss that inn.
>
> Shall I meet other wayfarers at night?
> 10   Those who have gone before.
> Then must I knock, or call when just in sight?
>> They will not keep you standing at that door.
>
> Shall I find comfort, travel-sore and weak?
>> Of labour you shall find the sum.
> 15   Will there be beds for me and all who seek?
>> Yea, beds for all who come.

1858   1862

Goblin Market

> Morning and evening
> Maids heard the goblins cry:
> "Come buy our orchard fruits,
> Come buy, come buy:
> 5   Apples and quinces,
> Lemons and oranges,
> Plump unpecked cherries,
> Melons and raspberries,
> Bloom-down-cheeked peaches,
> 10   Swart-headed mulberries,
> Wild free-born cranberries,
> Crab-apples, dewberries,
> Pine-apples, blackberries,
> Apricots, strawberries;—

15   All ripe together
      In summer weather,—
      Morns that pass by,
      Fair eves that fly;
      Come buy, come buy:
20   Our grapes fresh from the vine,
      Pomegranates full and fine,
      Dates and sharp bullaces,
      Rare pears and greengages,
      Damsons[1] and bilberries,
25   Taste them and try:
      Currants and gooseberries,
      Bright-fire-like barberries,
      Figs to fill your mouth,
      Citrons from the South,
30   Sweet to tongue and sound to eye;
      Come buy, come buy."

      Evening by evening
      Among the brookside rushes,
      Laura bowed her head to hear,
35   Lizzie veiled her blushes:
      Crouching close together
      In the cooling weather,
      With clasping arms and cautioning lips,
      With tingling cheeks and finger tips.
40   "Lie close," Laura said,
      Pricking up her golden head:
      "We must not look at goblin men,
      We must not buy their fruits:
      Who knows upon what soil they fed
45   Their hungry thirsty roots?"
      "Come buy," call the goblins
      Hobbling down the glen.
      "Oh," cried Lizzie, "Laura, Laura,
      You should not peep at goblin men."
50   Lizzie covered up her eyes,
      Covered close lest they should look;
      Laura reared her glossy head,
      And whispered like the restless brook:
      "Look, Lizzie, look, Lizzie,
55   Down the glen tramp little men.
      One hauls a basket,
      One bears a plate,
      One lugs a golden dish
      Of many pounds weight.
60   How fair the vine must grow
      Whose grapes are so luscious;
      How warm the wind must blow
      Thro' those fruit bushes."
      "No," said Lizzie: "No, no, no;

1. Bullaces, greengages, and damsons are varieties of plums.

65 Their offers should not charm us,
    Their evil gifts would harm us."
    She thrust a dimpled finger
    In each ear, shut eyes and ran:
    Curious Laura chose to linger
70 Wondering at each merchant man.
    One had a cat's face,
    One whisked a tail,
    One tramped at a rat's pace,
    One crawled like a snail,
75 One like a wombat prowled obtuse and furry,
    One like a ratel² tumbled hurry skurry.
    She heard a voice like voice of doves
    Cooing all together:
    They sounded kind and full of loves
80 In the pleasant weather.

    Laura stretched her gleaming neck
    Like a rush-imbedded swan,
    Like a lily from the beck,°   *small brook*
    Like a moonlit poplar branch,
85 Like a vessel at the launch
    When its last restraint is gone.

    Backwards up the mossy glen
    Turned and trooped the goblin men,
    With their shrill repeated cry,
90 "Come buy, come buy."
    When they reached where Laura was
    They stood stock still upon the moss,
    Leering at each other,
    Brother with queer brother;
95 Signalling each other,
    Brother with sly brother.
    One set his basket down,
    One reared° his plate;   *raised*
    One began to weave a crown
100 Of tendrils, leaves and rough nuts brown
    (Men sell not such in any town);
    One heaved the golden weight
    Of dish and fruit to offer her:
    "Come buy, come buy," was still their cry.
105 Laura stared but did not stir,
    Longed but had no money:
    The whisk-tailed merchant bade her taste
    In tones as smooth as honey,
    The cat-faced purr'd,
110 The rat-paced spoke a word
    Of welcome, and the snail-paced even was heard;
    One parrot-voiced and jolly

2. South African mammal resembling a badger (pronounced *ray-tell*).

Cried "Pretty Goblin" still° for "Pretty Polly;"—   *always*
One whistled like a bird.

115 But sweet-tooth Laura spoke in haste:
"Good folk, I have no coin;
To take were to purloin:
I have no copper in my purse,
I have no silver either,
120 And all my gold is on the furze
That shakes in windy weather
Above the rusty heather."
"You have much gold upon your head,"
They answered all together:
125 "Buy from us with a golden curl."
She clipped a precious golden lock,
She dropped a tear more rare than pearl,
Then sucked their fruit globes fair or red:
Sweeter than honey from the rock.
130 Stronger than man-rejoicing wine,[3]
Clearer than water flowed that juice;
She never tasted such before,
How should it cloy with length of use?
She sucked and sucked and sucked the more
135 Fruits which that unknown orchard bore;
She sucked until her lips were sore;
Then flung the emptied rinds away
But gathered up one kernel-stone,
And knew not was it night or day
140 As she turned home alone.

Lizzie met her at the gate
Full of wise upbraidings:
"Dear, you should not stay so late,
Twilight is not good for maidens;
145 Should not loiter in the glen
In the haunts of goblin men.
Do you not remember Jeanie,
How she met them in the moonlight,
Took their gifts both choice and many,
150 Ate their fruits and wore their flowers
Plucked from bowers
Where summer ripens at all hours?
But ever in the noonlight
She pined and pined away;
155 Sought them by night and day,
Found them no more but dwindled and grew grey;
Then fell with the first snow,
While to this day no grass will grow
Where she lies low:
160 I planted daisies there a year ago
That never blow.°   *bloom*

3. Psalm 104.15. "Sweeter . . . rock," Psalm 81.16.

You should not loiter so."
"Nay, hush," said Laura:
"Nay, hush, my sister:
165 I ate and ate my fill,
Yet my mouth waters still;
Tomorrow night I will
Buy more:" and kissed her:
"Have done with sorrow;
170 I'll bring you plums tomorrow
Fresh on their mother twigs,
Cherries worth getting;
You cannot think what figs
My teeth have met in,
175 What melons icy-cold
Piled on a dish of gold
Too huge for me to hold,
What peaches with a velvet nap,
Pellucid grapes without one seed:
180 Odorous indeed must be the mead
Whereon they grow, and pure the wave they drink
With lilies at the brink,
And sugar-sweet their sap."

Golden head by golden head,
185 Like two pigeons in one nest
Folded in each other's wings,
They lay down in their curtained bed:
Like two blossoms on one stem,
Like two flakes of new-fall'n snow,
190 Like two wands of ivory
Tipped with gold for awful° kings.   *awe-inspiring*
Moon and stars gazed in at them,
Wind sang to them lullaby,
Lumbering owls forbore to fly,
195 Not a bat flapped to and fro
Round their rest:
Cheek to cheek and breast to breast
Locked together in one nest.

Early in the morning
200 When the first cock crowed his warning,
Neat like bees, as sweet and busy,
Laura rose with Lizzie:
Fetched in honey, milked the cows,
Aired and set to rights the house,
205 Kneaded cakes of whitest wheat,
Cakes for dainty mouths to eat,
Next churned butter, whipped up cream,
Fed their poultry, sat and sewed;
Talked as modest maidens should:
210 Lizzie with an open heart,
Laura in an absent dream,
One content, one sick in part;

GOBLIN MARKET
and other poems
by Chriſtina Roſſetti

"Golden head by golden head"

London and Cambridge
Macmillan and Co. 1862

This frontispiece is one of the two illustrations that Dante Gabriel Rossetti provided for his sister's first volume of poetry in 1862.

> One warbling for the mere bright day's delight,
> One longing for the night.
>
> At length slow evening came:
> They went with pitchers to the reedy brook;
> Lizzie most placid in her look,
> Laura most like a leaping flame.
> They drew the gurgling water from its deep;
> Lizzie plucked purple and rich golden flags,°   *irises*
> Then turning homewards said: "The sunset flushes
> Those furthest loftiest crags;
> Come, Laura, not another maiden lags,
> No wilful squirrel wags,
> The beasts and birds are fast asleep."
> But Laura loitered still among the rushes
> And said the bank was steep.
>
> And said the hour was early still,
> The dew not fall'n, the wind not chill:
> Listening ever, but not catching
> The customary cry,
> "Come buy, come buy,"
> With its iterated jingle

Line numbers: 215, 220, 225, 230

Of sugar-baited words:
235 Not for all her watching
Once discerning even one goblin
Racing, whisking, tumbling, hobbling;
Let alone the herds
That used to tramp along the glen,
240 In groups or single,
Of brisk fruit-merchant men.

Till Lizzie urged, "O Laura, come;
I hear the fruit-call but I dare not look:
You should not loiter longer at this brook:
245 Come with me home.
The stars rise, the moon bends her arc,
Each glowworm winks her spark,
Let us get home before the night grows dark:
For clouds may gather
250 Tho' this is summer weather,
Put out the lights and drench us thro';
Then if we lost our way what should we do?"

Laura turned cold as stone
To find her sister heard that cry alone,
255 That goblin cry,
"Come buy our fruits, come buy."
Must she then buy no more such dainty fruit?
Must she no more such succous° pasture find,   *juicy, succulent*
Gone deaf and blind?
260 Her tree of life drooped from the root:
She said not one word in her heart's sore ache;
But peering thro' the dimness, nought discerning,
Trudged home, her pitcher dripping all the way;
So crept to bed, and lay
265 Silent till Lizzie slept;
Then sat up in a passionate yearning,
And gnashed her teeth for baulked desire, and wept
As if her heart would break.

Day after day, night after night,
270 Laura kept watch in vain
In sullen silence of exceeding pain.
She never caught again the goblin cry:
"Come buy, come buy;"—
She never spied the goblin men
275 Hawking their fruits along the glen:
But when the noon waxed bright
Her hair grew thin and gray;
She dwindled, as the fair full moon doth turn
To swift decay and burn
280 Her fire away.

One day remembering her kernel-stone
She set it by a wall that faced the south;

Dewed it with tears, hoped for a root,
Watched for a waxing shoot,
285 But there came none;
It never saw the sun,
It never felt the trickling moisture run:
While with sunk eyes and faded mouth
She dreamed of melons, as a traveller sees
290 False waves in desert drouth
With shade of leaf-crowned trees,
And burns the thirstier in the sandful breeze.

She no more swept the house,
Tended the fowls or cows,
295 Fetched honey, kneaded cakes of wheat,
Brought water from the brook:
But sat down listless in the chimney-nook
And would not eat.

Tender Lizzie could not bear
300 To watch her sister's cankerous care
Yet not to share.
She night and morning
Caught the goblins' cry:
"Come buy our orchard fruits,
305 Come buy, come buy:"—
Beside the brook, along the glen,
She heard the tramp of goblin men,
The voice and stir
Poor Laura could not hear;
310 Longed to buy fruit to comfort her,
But feared to pay too dear.
She thought of Jeanie in her grave,
Who should have been a bride;
But who for joys brides hope to have
315 Fell sick and died
In her gay prime,
In earliest Winter time,
With the first glazing rime,
With the first snow-fall of crisp Winter time.

320 Till Laura dwindling
Seemed knocking at Death's door:
Then Lizzie weighed° no more   *evaluated, considered*
Better and worse;
But put a silver penny in her purse,
325 Kissed Laura, crossed the heath with clumps of furze
At twilight, halted by the brook:
And for the first time in her life
Began to listen and look.

Laughed every goblin
330 When they spied her peeping:
Came towards her hobbling,

Flying, running, leaping,
Puffing and blowing,
Chuckling, clapping, crowing,
335   Clucking and gobbling,
Mopping and mowing,[4]
Full of airs and graces,
Pulling wry faces,

Demure grimaces,
340   Cat-like and rat-like,
Ratel-and wombat-like,
Snail-paced in a hurry,
Parrot-voiced and whistler,
Helter skelter, hurry skurry,
345   Chattering like magpies,
Fluttering like pigeons,
Gliding like fishes,—
Hugged her and kissed her,
Squeezed and caressed her:
350   Stretched up their dishes,
Panniers, and plates:
"Look at our apples
Russet and dun,
Bob at our cherries,
355   Bite at our peaches,
Citrons and dates,
Grapes for the asking,
Pears red with basking
Out in the sun,
360   Plums on their twigs;
Pluck them and suck them,
Pomegranates, figs."—

"Good folk," said Lizzie,
Mindful of Jeanie:
365   "Give me much and many:"—
Held out her apron,
Tossed them her penny.
"Nay, take a seat with us,
Honour and eat with us,"
370   They answered grinning:
"Our feast is but beginning.
Night yet is early,
Warm and dew-pearly,
Wakeful and starry:
375   Such fruits as these
No man can carry;
Half their bloom would fly,
Half their dew would dry,
Half their flavour would pass by.
380   Sit down and feast with us,

4. Grimacing, making faces.

Be welcome guest with us,
Cheer you and rest with us."—
"Thank you," said Lizzie: "But one waits
At home alone for me:
385   So without further parleying,
If you will not sell me any
Of your fruits tho' much and many,
Give me back my silver penny
I tossed you for a fee."—

390   They began to scratch their pates,
No longer wagging, purring,
But visibly demurring,
Grunting and snarling.
One called her proud,
395   Cross-grained, uncivil;
Their tones waxed loud,
Their looks were evil.
Lashing their tails
They trod and hustled her,
400   Elbowed and jostled her,
Clawed with their nails,
Barking, mewing, hissing, mocking,
Tore her gown and soiled her stocking,
Twitched her hair out by the roots,
405   Stamped upon her tender feet,
Held her hands and squeezed their fruits
Against her mouth to make her eat.

White and golden Lizzie stood,
Like a lily in a flood,—
410   Like a rock of blue-veined stone
Lashed by tides obstreperously,—
Like a beacon left alone
In a hoary roaring sea,
Sending up a golden fire,—
415   Like a fruit-crowned orange-tree
White with blossoms honey-sweet
Sore beset by wasp and bee,—
Like a royal virgin town
Topped with gilded dome and spire
420   Close beleaguered by a fleet
Mad to tug her standard down.

One may lead a horse to water,
Twenty cannot make him drink.
Tho' the goblins cuffed and caught her,
425   Coaxed and fought her,
Bullied and besought her,
Scratched her, pinched her black as ink,
Kicked and knocked her,
Mauled and mocked her,
430   Lizzie uttered not a word;

Would not open lip from lip
Lest they should cram a mouthful in:
But laughed in heart to feel the drip
Of juice that syruped all her face,
435 And lodged in dimples of her chin,
And streaked her neck which quaked like curd.
At last the evil people
Worn out by her resistance
Flung back her penny, kicked their fruit
440 Along whichever road they took,
Not leaving root or stone or shoot;
Some writhed into the ground,
Some dived into the brook
With ring and ripple,
445 Some scudded on the gale without a sound,
Some vanished in the distance.

In a smart, ache, tingle,
Lizzie went her way;
Knew not was it night or day;
450 Sprang up the bank, tore thro' the furze,
Threaded copse and dingle,
And heard her penny jingle
Bouncing in her purse,
Its bounce was music to her ear.
455 She ran and ran
As if she feared some goblin man
Dogged her with gibe or curse
Or something worse:
But not one goblin skurried after,
460 Nor was she pricked by fear;
The kind heart made her windy-paced
That urged her home quite out of breath with haste
And inward laughter.

She cried "Laura," up the garden,
465 "Did you miss me?
Come and kiss me.
Never mind my bruises,
Hug me, kiss me, suck my juices
Squeezed from goblin fruits for you,
470 Goblin pulp and goblin dew.
Eat me, drink me, love me;
Laura, make much of me:
For your sake I have braved the glen
And had to do with goblin merchant men."

475 Laura started from her chair,
Flung her arms up in the air,
Clutched her hair:
"Lizzie, Lizzie, have you tasted
For my sake the fruit forbidden?
480 Must your light like mine be hidden,

Your young life like mine be wasted,
Undone in mine undoing
And ruined in my ruin,
Thirsty, cankered, goblin-ridden?"—
485   She clung about her sister,
Kissed and kissed and kissed her:
Tears once again
Refreshed her shrunken eyes,
Dropping like rain
490   After long sultry drouth;
Shaking with aguish° fear, and pain,   *feverish*
She kissed and kissed her with a hungry mouth.

Her lips began to scorch,
That juice was wormwood to her tongue,
495   She loathed the feast:
Writhing as one possessed she leaped and sung,
Rent all her robe, and wrung
Her hands in lamentable haste,
And beat her breast.
500   Her locks streamed like the torch
Borne by a racer at full speed,
Or like the mane of horses in their flight,
Or like an eagle when she stems⁵ the light
Straight toward the sun,
505   Or like a caged thing freed,
Or like a flying flag when armies run.

Swift fire spread thro' her veins, knocked at her heart,
Met the fire smouldering there
And overbore its lesser flame;
510   She gorged on bitterness without a name:
Ah! fool, to choose such part
Of soul-consuming care!
Sense failed in the mortal strife:
Like the watch-tower of a town
515   Which an earthquake shatters down,
Like a lightning-stricken mast,
Like a wind-uprooted tree
Spun about,
Like a foam-topped waterspout
520   Cast down headlong in the sea,
She fell at last;
Pleasure past and anguish past,
Is it death or is it life?

Life out of death.
525   That night long Lizzie watched by her,
Counted her pulse's flagging stir,
Felt for her breath,
Held water to her lips, and cooled her face

5. Makes headway against.

With tears and fanning leaves:
530 But when the first birds chirped about their eaves,
And early reapers plodded to the place
Of golden sheaves,
And dew-wet grass
Bowed in the morning winds so brisk to pass,
535 And new buds with new day
Opened of cup-like lilies on the stream,
Laura awoke as from a dream,
Laughed in the innocent old way,
Hugged Lizzie but not° twice or thrice;   *not only*
540 Her gleaming locks showed not one thread of grey,
Her breath was sweet as May
And light danced in her eyes.

Days, weeks, months, years
Afterwards, when both were wives
545 With children of their own;
Their mother-hearts beset with fears,
Their lives bound up in tender lives;
Laura would call the little ones
And tell them of her early prime,
550 Those pleasant days long gone
Of not-returning time:
Would talk about the haunted glen,
The wicked, quaint° fruit-merchant men,   *strange*
Their fruits like honey to the throat
555 But poison in the blood;
(Men sell not such in any town:)
Would tell them how her sister stood
In deadly peril to do her good,
And win the fiery antidote:
560 Then joining hands to little hands
Would bid them cling together,
"For there is no friend like a sister
In calm or stormy weather;
To cheer one on the tedious way,
565 To fetch one if one goes astray,
To lift one if one totters down,
To strengthen whilst one stands."

1859   1862

"No, Thank You, John"

I never said I loved you, John:
    Why will you teaze me day by day,
And wax a weariness to think upon
    With always "do" and "pray"?

5 You know I never loved you, John;
    No fault of mine made me your toast:

Why will you haunt me with a face as wan
    As shows an hour-old ghost?

I dare say Meg or Moll would take
10   Pity upon you, if you'd ask:
And pray don't remain single for my sake
    Who can't perform that task.

I have no heart?—Perhaps I have not;
    But then you're mad to take offence
15 That I don't give you what I have not got:
    Use your own common sense.

Let bygones be bygones:
    Don't call me false, who owed not to be true:
I'd rather answer "No" to fifty Johns
20   Than answer "Yes" to you.

Let's mar our pleasant days no more,
    Song-birds of passage, days of youth:
Catch at today, forget the days before:
    I'll wink° at your untruth.   *close (both) eyes*

25 Let us strike hands as hearty friends;
    No more, no less; and friendship's good:
Only don't keep in view ulterior ends,
    And points not understood

In open treaty. Rise above
30   Quibbles and shuffling off and on:
Here's friendship for you if you like; but love,—
    No, thank you, John.

1860   1862

Promises Like Pie-Crust

Promise me no promises,
    So will I not promise you:
Keep we both our liberties,
    Never false and never true:
5 Let us hold the die uncast,
    Free to come as free to go:
For I cannot know your past,
    And of mine what can you know?

You, so warm, may once have been
10   Warmer towards another one:
I, so cold, may once have seen
    Sunlight, once have felt the sun:
Who shall show us if it was

Thus indeed in time of old?
15   Fades the image from the glass,
And the fortune is not told.

If you promised, you might grieve
For lost liberty again:
If I promised, I believe
20   I should fret to break the chain.
Let us be the friends we were,
Nothing more but nothing less:
Many thrive on frugal fare
Who would perish of excess.

1861   1896

Cardinal Newman[1]

In the grave, whither thou goest[2]

O weary Champion of the Cross, lie still:
Sleep thou at length the all-embracing sleep:
Long was thy sowing-day, rest now and reap:
Thy fast was long, feast now thy spirit's fill.
5   Yea, take thy fill of love, because thy will
Chose love not in the shallows but the deep:
Thy tides were springtides, set against the neap[3]
Of calmer souls: thy flood rebuked their rill.°   *small stream*
Now night has come to thee—please God, of rest:
10   So some time must it come to every man;
To first and last, where many last are first.[4]
Now fixed and finished thine eternal plan,
Thy best has done its best, thy worst its worst:
Thy best its best, Please God, thy best its best.

1890

Sleeping at Last

Sleeping at last, the trouble & tumult over,
Sleeping at last, the struggle & horror past,
Cold & white out of sight of friend & of lover
Sleeping at last.

5   No more a tired heart downcast or overcast,
No more pangs that wring or shifting fears that hover,
Sleeping at last in a dreamless sleep locked fast.

---

1. Written on the occasion of the death of John
Henry Newman (1801–1890).
2. Ecclesiastes 9.10.
3. Tides that do not rise to the high-water mark of

the spring tides.
4. Rossetti alludes to the parable of the vineyard,
in which "the last shall be first." See Matthew
20.16, Luke 13.30.

> Fast asleep. Singing birds in their leafy cover
> Cannot wake her, nor shake her the gusty blast.
> 10   Under the purple thyme and the purple clover
> Sleeping at last.

1896

GERARD MANLEY HOPKINS
1844–1889

It has been said that the most important date in Gerard Manley Hopkins's career was 1918, twenty-nine years after his death, for it was then that the first publication of his poems made them accessible to the world of readers. During his lifetime these remarkable poems, most of them celebrating the wonders of God's creation, had been known only to a small circle of friends, including his literary executor, the poet Robert Bridges, who waited until 1918 before releasing them to a publisher. Partly because his work was first made public in a twentieth-century volume, but especially because of his striking experiments in meter and diction, Hopkins was widely hailed as a pioneering figure of "modern" literature, miraculously unconnected with his fellow Victorian poets (who during the 1920s and 1930s were largely out of fashion among critical readers). And this way of classifying and evaluating his writings has long persisted. In 1936 a substantial selection of his poems led off *The Faber Book of Modern Verse*, one of the most influential anthologies of the century, featuring poets such as W. H. Auden, Dylan Thomas, and T. S. Eliot (the only one whose selections occupy more pages than those allotted to Hopkins). And the first four editions of *The Norton Anthology of English Literature* (1962–79) grouped Hopkins with these twentieth-century poets. To reclassify him is not to repudiate his earlier reputation as a "modern" but rather to suggest that his work can be better understood and appreciated if it is restored to the Victorian world out of which it developed.

Hopkins was born near London into a large and cultivated family in comfortable circumstances. After a brilliant career at Highgate School, he entered Oxford in 1863, where he was exposed to a variety of Victorian ways of thinking, both secular and religious. Among the influential leaders at Oxford was Matthew Arnold, professor of poetry; but more important for Hopkins was his tutor, Walter Pater, an aesthetician whose emphasis on the intense apprehension of sensuous beauty struck a responsive chord in Hopkins. At Oxford he was also exposed to the Broad Church theology of one of the tutors at his college (Balliol), Benjamin Jowett. But Hopkins became increasingly attracted first to the High Church movement represented at Oxford by Edward Pusey, and then to Roman Catholicism. Profoundly influenced by John Henry Newman's conversion to Rome and by subsequent conversations with Newman, Hopkins entered the Roman Catholic Church in 1866. The estrangement from his family that resulted from his conversion was very painful for him; his parents' letters to him were so "terrible" (he reported to Newman) that he could not bear to "read them twice." And this alienation was heightened by his decision not only to become a Roman Catholic but to become a priest and, in particular, a Jesuit priest, for many Victorian Protestants regarded the Jesuit order with a special distrust. For the rest of his life, Hopkins served as a priest and teacher in various places, among them Oxford, Liverpool, and Lancashire. In 1884 he was appointed professor of classics at University College in Dublin.

At school and at Oxford in the early 1860s, Hopkins had written poems in the vein of John Keats. He burned most of these early writings after his conversion (although drafts survive), for he believed that his vocation must require renouncing such personal satisfactions as the writing of poems. Only after his superiors in the church encouraged him to do so did he resume writing poetry. Yet during the seven years of silence, as his letters show, he had been thinking about experimenting with what he called a "new rhythm." The result, in 1876, was his rhapsodic lyric-narrative, "The Wreck of the Deutschland," a long ode about the wreck of a ship in which five Franciscan nuns were drowned. The style of the poem was so distinctive that the editor of the Jesuit magazine to which he had submitted it "dared not print it," as Hopkins reported. During the remaining fourteen years of his life, Hopkins wrote poems but seldom submitted them for publication, partly because he was convinced that poetic fame was incompatible with his religious vocation but also because of a fear that readers would be discouraged by the eccentricity of his work.

Hopkins's sense of his own uniqueness is in accord with the larger philosophy that informs his poetry. Drawing on the theology of Duns Scotus, a medieval philosopher, he felt that everything in the universe was characterized by what he called *inscape,* the distinctive design that constitutes individual identity. This identity is not static but dynamic. Each being in the universe "selves," that is, enacts its identity. And the human being, the most highly selved, the most individually distinctive being in the universe, recognizes the inscape of other beings in an act that Hopkins calls *instress,* the apprehension of an object in an intense thrust of energy toward it that enables one to realize its specific distinctiveness. Ultimately, the instress of inscape leads one to Christ, for the individual identity of any object is the stamp of divine creation on it. In the act of instress, therefore, the human being becomes a celebrant of the divine, at once recognizing God's creation and enacting his or her own God-given identity within it.

Poetry for Hopkins enacts this celebration. It is instress, and it realizes the inscape of its subject in its own distinctive design. Hopkins wrote, "But as air, melody, is what strikes me most of all in music and design in painting, so design, pattern or what I am in the habit of calling 'inscape' is what I above all aim at in poetry." To create inscape, Hopkins seeks to give each poem a unique design that captures the initial inspiration when he is "caught" by his subject. Many of the characteristics of Hopkins's style—his disruption of conventional syntax, his coining and compounding of words, his use of ellipsis and repetition—can be understood as ways of representing the stress and action of the brain in moments of inspiration. He creates compounds to represent the unique interlocking of the characteristics of an object—"piecebright," "dapple-dawn-drawn," "blue-bleak." He omits syntactical connections to fuse qualities more intensely—"the dearest freshness deep down things." He creates puns to suggest how God's creation rhymes and chimes in a divine patterning. He violates conventional syntactic order to represent the shape of mental experience. In the act of imaginative apprehension, a language particular to the moment generates itself.

Hopkins also uses a new rhythm to give each poem its distinctive design. In the new metric system he created, which he called *sprung rhythm,* lines have a given number of stresses, but the number and placement of unstressed syllables is highly variable. Hopkins rarely marks all the intended stresses, only those that readers might not anticipate. To indicate stressed syllables, Hopkins often uses both the stress (') and the "great stress" ("). A curved line marks an "outride"—one or more syllables added to a foot but not counted in the scansion of the line; they indicate a stronger stress on the preceding syllable and a short pause after the outride. Here, for example, is the scansion for the first three lines of "The Windhover":

> I caúght this mórning mórning's mínion, kíng-
> dom of dáylight's daúphin, dapple-dawn-drawn Fálcon, in his ríding
> Of the rólling level underneáth him steady aír, and stríding

Hopkins argued that sprung rhythm was the natural rhythm of common speech and written prose, as well as of music. He found a model for it in Old English poetry and in nursery rhymes, but he claimed that it had not been used in English poetry since the Elizabethan age.

The density and difficulty that result from Hopkins's unconventional rhythm and syntax make his poetry seem modern, but his concern with the imagination's shaping of the natural world puts him very much in the Romantic tradition; and his creation of a rough and difficult style, designed to capture the mind's own motion, resembles the style of Robert Browning. "A horrible thing has happened to me," Hopkins wrote in 1864, "I have begun to *doubt* Tennyson." He criticizes Tennyson for using the grand style as a smooth and habitual poetic speech. Like Algernon Charles Swinburne, Walter Pater, and Henry James as well as Browning, Hopkins displays a new mannerism, characteristic of the latter part of the nineteenth century, which paradoxically combines an elaborate aestheticism with a more complex representation of consciousness.

In Hopkins's early poetry his singular apprehension of the beauty of individual objects always brings him to an ecstatic illumination of the presence of God. But in his late poems, the so-called terrible sonnets, his distinctive individuality comes to isolate him from the God who made him thus. Hopkins wrote, "To me there is no resemblance: searching nature, I taste *self* but at one tankard, that of my own being." In the terrible sonnets Hopkins confronts the solipsism to which his own stress on individuality seems to lead him. Like the mad speakers of so many Victorian dramatic monologues, he cannot escape a world solely of his own imagining. Yet even these poems of despair, which simultaneously echo the bleaker side of the Romantic tradition and anticipate more modern attitudes, reflect a traditional religious vision: the dark night of the soul as described by the Spanish mystic Saint John of the Cross.

In his introduction to *The Oxford Book of Modern Verse*, Yeats calls Hopkins's poetry "a last development of poetical diction." Yeats's remark indicates the anomaly that Hopkins's work poses. Perhaps it is only appropriate for a writer who stressed the uniqueness of inscape to strike us with the individuality of his achievement.

God's Grandeur

The world is charged with the grandeur of God.
   It will flame out, like shining from shook foil;[1]
   It gathers to a greatness, like the ooze of oil
Crushed.[2] Why do men then now not reck his rod?
5 Generations have trod, have trod, have trod;
   And all is seared with trade; bleared, smeared with toil;
   And wears man's smudge and shares man's smell: the soil
Is bare now, nor can foot feel, being shod.

And for° all this, nature is never spent;   *despite*
10   There lives the dearest freshness deep down things;
And though the last lights off the black West went
   Oh, morning, at the brown brink eastward, springs—
Because the Holy Ghost over the bent
   World broods with warm breast and with ah! bright wings.

1877   1918

1. Hopkins explained this image in a letter: "I mean foil in its sense of leaf or tinsel. . . . Shaken goldfoil gives off broad glares like sheet lightning and also, and this is true of nothing else, owing to its zigzag dints and creasings and network of small many cornered facets, a sort of fork lightning too."
2. I.e., from the crushing of olives.

The Starlight Night

Look at the stars! look, look up at the skies!
  O look at all the fire-folk sitting in the air!
  The bright boroughs, the circle-citadels there!
Down in dim woods the diamond delves!° the elves'-eyes!   *quarries*
5 The grey lawns cold where gold, where quickgold;[1] lies!
  Wind-beat whitebeam! airy abeles° set on a flare!   *white poplars*
  Flake-doves sent floating forth at a farmyard scare!—
Ah well! it is all a purchase, all is a prize.

Buy then! bid then!—What?—Prayer, patience, alms, vows.
10 Look, look: a May-mess,[2] like on orchard boughs!
  Look! March-bloom, like on mealed-with-yellow sallows![3]
These are indeed the barn; withindoors house
The shocks. This piece-bright paling[4] shuts the spouse
  Christ home, Christ and his mother and all his hallows.°   *saints*

1877   1918

As Kingfishers Catch Fire

As kingfishers catch fire, dragonflies draw flame;
  As tumbled over rim in roundy wells
  Stones ring; like each tucked° string tells, each hung bell's *plucked*
Bow swung finds tongue to fling out broad its name;
5 Each mortal thing does one thing and the same:
  Deals out that being indoors° each one dwells;   *within*
  Selves[1]—goes itself; *myself* it speaks and spells,
Crying *What I do is me: for that I came.*

I say more: the just man justices;[2]
10 Keeps gráce: thát keeps all his goings graces;
Acts in God's eye what in God's eye he is—
  Chríst. For Christ plays in ten thousand places,
Lovely in limbs, and lovely in eyes not his
  To the Father through the features of men's faces.

1877   1918

Spring

Nothing is so beautiful as Spring—
  When weeds, in wheels, shoot long and lovely and lush;

---

1. Coined by analogy with quicksilver. The starlight night resembles the lawns below it, where the dew, reflecting the starlight, looks like gold.
2. A profusion of growing things such as May blossoms.

3. Willows, here with yellow spots like meal.
4. Picket fence. "Shocks": sheaves of grain.
1. Fulfills its individuality.
2. Acts in a just manner.

Thrush's eggs look little low heavens, and thrush
Through the echoing timber does so rinse and wring
5   The ear, it strikes like lightnings to hear him sing;
    The glassy peartree leaves and blooms, they brush
    The descending blue; that blue is all in a rush
With richness; the racing lambs too have fair their fling.

What is all this juice and all this joy?
10   A strain of the earth's sweet being in the beginning
In Eden garden.—Have, get, before it cloy,
    Before it cloud, Christ, lord, and sour with sinning,
Innocent mind and Mayday in girl and boy,
    Most, O maid's child,[1] thy choice and worthy the winning.

1877   1918

The Windhover[1]

To Christ our Lord

I caught this morning morning's minion,° king-   darling
    dom of daylight's dauphin,[2] dapple-dawn-drawn Falcon, in his riding
    Of the rolling level underneath him steady air, and striding
High there, how he rung upon the rein of a wimpling[3] wing
5 In his ecstasy! then off, off forth on swing,
    As a skate's heel sweeps smooth on a bow-bend: the hurl and gliding
    Rebuffed the big wind. My heart in hiding
Stirred for a bird,—the achieve of, the mastery of the thing!

Brute beauty and valour and act, oh, air, pride, plume, here
10   Buckle![4] AND the fire that breaks from thee then, a billion
Times told lovelier, more dangerous, O my chevalier!°   knight

No wonder of it: shéer plód makes plough down sillion[5]
Shine, and blue-bleak embers, ah my dear,
    Fall, gall[6] themselves, and gash gold-vermilion.

1877   1918

Pied[1] Beauty

Glory be to God for dappled things—
    For skies of couple-colour as a brinded[2] cow;
        For rose-moles all in stipple upon trout that swim;
    Fresh-firecoal chestnut-falls,[3] finches' wings;

1. Jesus, son of the Virgin Mary.
1. Kestrel, a small falcon noted for hovering in the air.
2. A prince who is heir to the French throne.
3. Rippling. "Rung upon the rein": circled at the end of a rein.
4. The verb can be read as imperative or indicative. All three meanings are relevant: to prepare for

action, to fasten together, to collapse.
5. The ridge between two furrows of a plowed field.
6. Break the surface of.
1. Of two or more colors in blotches, variegated.
2. Brownish orange in color with streaks of gray.
3. I.e., freshly fallen chestnuts, bright as coals.

5   Landscape plotted and pieced—fold, fallow, and plough;[4]
     And áll trádes, their gear and tackle and trim.°   equipment

     All things counter, original, spare,[5] strange;
       Whatever is fickle, freckled (who knows how?)
         With swift, slow; sweet, sour; adazzle, dim;
10   He fathers-forth whose beauty is past change:
                                    Praise him.

1877   1918

Hurrahing in Harvest

     Summer ends now; now, barbarous in beauty, the stooks[1] rise
     Around; up above, what wind-walks! what lovely behaviour
     Of silk-sack clouds! has wilder, wilful-wavier
     Meal-drift moulded ever and melted across skies?

5   I walk, I lift up, I lift up heart, eyes,
     Down all that glory in the heavens to glean our Saviour;
     And, éyes, heárt, what looks, what lips yet gave you a
     Rapturous love's greeting of realer, of rounder replies?

     And the azurous hung hills are his world-wielding shoulder
10   Majestic—as a stallion stalwart, very-violet-sweet!—
     These things, these things were here and but the beholder
     Wanting; which two when they once meet,
     The heart rears wings bold and bolder
     And hurls for him, O half hurls earth for him off under his feet.

1877   1918

Binsey Poplars

felled 1879

     My aspens dear, whose airy cages quelled,
       Quelled or quenched in leaves the leaping sun,
         All felled, felled, are all felled;
           Of a fresh and following folded rank
5   Not spared, not one
                 That dandled a sandalled
               Shadow that swam or sank
       On meadow and river and wind-wandering
                 weed-winding bank.

10   O if we but knew what we do
           When we delve° or hew—   dig

---

4. Divided into fields used as pastures ("fold"),   5. Rare. "Counter": contrary.
lying fallow, or plowed for cultivation. The land-   1. Sheaves of grain.
scape thus appears like patches of different colors.

2164 / GERARD MANLEY HOPKINS

Hack and rack° the growing green!   *torture*
 Since country is so tender
 To touch, her being só slender,
15 That, like this sleek and seeing ball°   *the eye*
 But a prick will make no eye at all,

Where we, even where we mean
 To mend her we end her,
 When we hew or delve:
20 After-comers cannot guess the beauty been.
 Ten or twelve, only ten or twelve
 Strokes of havoc únselve°   *rob of self*
 The sweet especial scene,
 Rural scene, a rural scene,
25 Sweet especial rural scene.

1879   1918

Duns Scotus's Oxford[1]

Towery city and branchy between towers;
Cuckoo-echoing, bell-swarmèd, lark-charmèd, rook-racked, river-rounded;
The dapple-eared lily below thee; that country and town did
Once encounter in, here coped and poisèd powers;

5 Thou hast a base and brickish skirt there, sours
That neighbour-nature thy grey beauty is grounded
Best in;[2] graceless growth, thou hast confounded
Rural rural keeping—folk, flocks, and flowers.

Yet ah! this air I gather and I release
10 He lived on; these weeds and waters, these walls are what
He haunted who of all men most sways my spirits to peace;

Of realty° the rarest-veinèd unraveller; a not   *reality*
Rivalled insight, be rival Italy or Greece;
Who fired France for Mary without spot.[3]

1879   1918

1. Duns Scotus, the medieval theologian, lectured at Oxford about 1301. His idea that individuality is the final perfection of any creature influenced Hopkins's conception of inscape. When Hopkins came on two of Scotus's commentaries in 1872, he wrote that he was immediately "flush with a new stroke of enthusiasm . . . when I took in any inscape of the sky or sea I thought of Scotus."
2. Hopkins contrasts the "here" of the "grey beauty" of the medieval city of Oxford, where country and town are both protected ("coped," as within a priest's cloak) and in equilibrium ("poisèd powers"), with the "there" of its new surburban "brickish skirt": housing developments and industrial complexes that were built around the perimeter of the city in the 19th century.
3. In Paris, Scotus was influential in defending the doctrine of the Immaculate Conception—i.e., that Mary was born without original sin.

Felix Randal

Felix Randal the farrier,° O is he dead then? my duty   *blacksmith*
all ended,
Who have watched his mould of man, big-boned and hardy-handsome
Pining, pining, till time when reason rambled in it and some
Fatal four disorders, fleshed there, all contended?

5   Sickness broke him. Impatient, he cursed at first, but mended
Being anointed[1] and all; though a heavenlier heart began some
Months earlier, since I had our sweet reprieve and ransom[2]
Tendered to him. Ah well, God rest him all road ever[3] he offended!

This seeing the sick endears them to us, us too it endears.
10   My tongue had taught thee comfort, touch had quenched thy tears,
Thy tears that touched my heart, child, Felix, poor Felix Randal;
How far from then forethought of, all thy more boisterous years,
When thou at the random[4] grim forge, powerful amidst peers,
Didst fettle° for the great grey drayhorse his bright and battering   *prepare*
sandal!

1880   1918

Spring and Fall:[1]

to a young child

Márgarét, áre you gríeving
Over Goldengrove unleaving?
Leáves, líke the things of man, you
With your fresh thoughts care for, can you?
5   Áh! ás the heart grows older
It will come to such sights colder
By and by, nor spare a sigh
Though worlds of wanwood leafmeal[2] lie;
And yet you *will* weep and know why.
10   Now no matter, child, the name:
Sórrow's spríngs áre the same.
Nor mouth had, no nor mind, expressed
What heart heard of, ghost° guessed: *spirit*
It ís the blight man was born for,
15   It is Margaret you mourn for.

1880   1918

---

1. In Extreme Unction (the sacrament for the dying.)
2. Holy Communion preceded by confession and absolution.
3. In whatever way.
4. Built with stones of irregular size and shape.
1. This deceptively simple poem is deeply informed by Christian theology: according to Cath-olic doctrine, the fall of Adam and Eve brought into the world both mortality and the legacy of Original Sin for all human beings ("the blight man was born for").
2. Coined by analogy with piecemeal. "Wan-wood": pale or dim; the forest may be pale because of light-colored autumn leaves or dim because light is filtered through the leaves.

[Carrion Comfort][1]

Not, I'll not, carrion comfort, Despair, not feast on thee,[2]
Not untwist—slack they may be—these last strands of man
In me ór, most weary, cry *I can no more.* I can;
Can something, hope, wish day come, not choose not to be.

5 But ah, but O thou terrible, why wouldst thou rude on me
    Thy wring-world right foot rock?[3] lay a lionlimb against me?
        scan
With darksome devouring eyes my bruisèd bones? and fan,
    O in turns of tempest, me heaped there; me frantic to avoid
        thee and flee?

Why? That my chaff might fly; my grain lie,[4] sheer and clear.
10 Nay in all that toil, that coil,° since (seems) I kissed the rod,   *tumult*
Hand rather,[5] my heart lo! lapped strength, stole joy, would
    laugh, chéer.
Cheer whom though? The Hero whose heaven-handling
    flung me, fóot tród
Me? or me that fought him? O which one? is it each one?
    That night, that year
Of now done darkness I wretch lay wrestling with (my God!)
    my God.

1885   1918

No worst, there is none

No worst, there is none. Pitched past pitch of grief,
More pangs will, schooled at forepangs, wilder wring.
Comforter, where, where is your comforting?
Mary, mother of us, where is your relief?

5 My cries heave, herds-long;[1] huddle in a main, a chief-
woe, world-sorrow; on an age-old anvil wince and sing—
Then lull, then leave off. Fury had shrieked "No lingering! Let me be fell: force[2] I must be brief."
    O the mind, mind has mountains; cliffs of fall
10 Frightful, sheer, no-man-fathomed. Hold them cheap
May who ne'er hung there. Nor does long our small
Durance° deal with that steep or deep. Here! creep,   *endurance*

1. This title was supplied by Bridges. The poem is one of the "terrible sonnets," as are the three following poems.
2. The satisfaction of giving in to despair as a kind of "comfort" is implicitly likened to a vulture's satisfaction in feasting on dead flesh.
3. I.e., why would you roughly rock me with your world-wringing right foot?
4. Metaphors of winnowing, or removing the

empty husks ("chaff") that are blown away from the valuable grain that remains, appear frequently in the Bible to represent the separation of virtue from wickedness. See, e.g., Psalm 1.4, Luke 3.16–17.
5. I.e., the hand that wields the rod.
1. Like the succession of cries made by cattle that have been following one another in a long line.
2. Necessarily, inevitably. "Fell": fierce.

Wretch, under a comfort serves in a whirlwind: all
Life death does end and each day dies with sleep.

1885   1918

I wake and feel the fell of dark, not day

I wake and feel the fell° of dark, not day.   bitterness
What hours, O what black hoürs we have spent
This night! what sights you, heart, saw; ways you went!
And more must, in yet longer light's delay.

5   With witness I speak this. But where I say
Hours I mean years, mean life. And my lament
Is cries countless, cries like dead letters[1] sent
To dearest him that lives alas! away.

I am gall, I am heartburn. God's most deep decree
10 Bitter would have me taste: my taste was me;
Bones built in me, flesh filled, blood brimmed the curse.

Selfyeast of spirit a dull dough sours. I see
The lost are like this, and their scourge to be
As I am mine, their sweating selves; but worse.

1885   1918

Thou art indeed just, Lord

Justus quidem tu es, Domine, si disputem tecum; verumtamen justa
loquar ad te: Quare via impiorum prosperatur? &c.[1]

Thou art indeed just, Lord, if I contend
With thee; but, sir, so what I plead is just.
Why do sinners' ways prosper? and why must
Disappointment all I endeavour end?

5   Wert thou my enemy, O thou my friend,
How wouldst thou worse, I wonder, than thou dost
Defeat, thwart me? Oh, the sots and thralls of lust
Do in spare hours more thrive than I that spend,

Sir, life upon thy cause. See, banks and brakes°   thickets
10 Now, leavèd how thick! lacèd they are again
With fretty chervil,[2] look, and fresh wind shakes

---

1. Letters undelivered or returned to the sender
by the post office.
1. "Righteous art thou, O Lord, when I plead with
thee: yet let me talk with thee of thy judgments:

Wherefore doth the way of the wicked prosper?"
(Jeremiah 12.1). The Latin was Hopkins's title.
2. A kind of herb, related to parsley.

Them; birds build—but not I build; no, but strain,
Time's eunuch, and not breed one work that wakes.
Mine, O thou lord of life, send my roots rain.

1889   1918

ROBERT LOUIS STEVENSON
1850–1894

Robert Louis (originally Lewis) Balfour Stevenson was born in Edinburgh on November 13, 1850, the only child of Margaret Balfour and Thomas Stevenson, a well-known marine engineer and designer of lighthouses. His family was part of the respectable Scottish middle classes, a membership that would both benefit Stevenson—although there were difficult stretches in his relationship with his father, he generally did not have to worry about money—and leave him with a restlessness for adventure and excitement. Driven at the same time by a quest for a climate that would ease his chronically diseased lungs, Stevenson traveled more broadly than any other prominent Victorian writer. And yet it could be argued that although he was constantly on the move in far-flung lands, Stevenson returned again and again in his creative fiction, explicitly or implicitly, to the tensions of his own personal and national heritage—to the pronounced conflicts of his upbringing and of Scotland's somber, religiously oppressive society.

An awkward sensitive boy, Stevenson was subjected to the disciplinary strictures of his stern Presbyterian father and to the more affectionate, although also deeply devout, care of his mother and his nurse. Plagued by night terrors and bouts of sickness, the young Stevenson seemed "in body . . . assuredly badly set up," as a schoolmate said in later years; "his limbs were long, lean, and spidery, and his chest flat, so as almost to suggest some malnutrition." This constitutional weakness was to afflict Stevenson throughout his life, and he enjoyed only short periods of reasonable health. As a student at Edinburgh University, Stevenson soon began to avoid the engineering classes that would have enabled him to follow in his father's footsteps, and embarked instead on a course of reading—"an extensive and highly rational system of truancy," as he called it—to learn how to become a writer. In time, as a compromise to placate his father, he switched to the study of law; although he never practiced as a lawyer, he did pass the Scottish bar examination in 1875. But his interests clearly lay elsewhere: in this period Stevenson began dressing like a bohemian, reading scandalous French poetry, and hanging around brothels, where the prostitutes nicknamed him "Velvet Jack." By all accounts he was a witty and attentive conversationalist; his friend the folklorist and writer Andrew Lang later described him in verse as a "Buffoon and lover, poet and sensualist: / A deal of Ariel, just a streak of Puck, / Much Antony, of Hamlet most of all."

At the age of twenty-two, Stevenson further distanced himself from his father by confessing that he had turned both socialist and agnostic; he subsequently began to spend increasingly longer periods in France, partly because of respiratory troubles but also to be in the company of painters and writers. Back in Britain he developed important and useful friendships with artistic and literary figures, including Sidney Colvin, a professor of art, and the poet and editor W. E. Henley; with their support Stevenson started to publish essays and books of travel writing. As if to complete his breach with bourgeois Scottish respectability, Stevenson then fell in love with Fanny Osbourne, an American woman ten years his senior, who was estranged from her husband but not yet divorced.

In 1879 Stevenson's global wanderings began in earnest, starting with a trip to California to marry the newly divorced Fanny. Despite constant travel and recurrent illness, Stevenson found the time and energy to write. *Treasure Island,* begun as an amusement for his stepson, was his first popular success: serialized in 1881 and published in book form in 1883, the story of the cabin boy Jim Hawkins's adventures includes a covert portrait of Stevenson's one-legged friend Henley in the figure of the pirate Long John Silver. Soon thereafter he published another children's classic: *A Child's Garden of Verses* (1885), a collection of poems dedicated to his former nurse. In the years to come, Stevenson worked in numerous genres, including short fiction, swashbuckling romances, historical adventures (*Kidnapped,* 1886, a story set in Scotland just after the Jacobite rebellion of 1745, and its sequel, *Catriona,* 1893), and more gothic undertakings, such as the bleak and brooding novel *The Master of Ballantrae* (1889).

The work that first established Stevenson's critical reputation, however, was a horror story that prefigured *The Master of Ballantrae*'s fascination with the darker side of human nature and reflected his long-standing interest in the idea of a double life: *The Strange Case of Dr. Jekyll and Mr. Hyde,* written in 1885 and published the following year. The novella rapidly became a best seller in both Britain and America, and like Mary Shelley's *Frankenstein* of 1818 (to which *Jekyll and Hyde* pays homage at various moments) and Bram Stoker's *Dracula* (1897), the story has enjoyed a continuous and lively presence in popular culture up to the present day. Yet our familiarity with the outline of the tale may not prepare us for the psychological and ethical complexity of the original. Certainly the novelist's friends found *Jekyll and Hyde* genuinely unnerving: the writer and historian J. A. Symonds wrote to Stevenson that the story "has left such a deeply painful impression on my heart that I do not know how I am ever to turn to it again," while Lang commented that "we would welcome a spectre, a ghoul, or even a vampire, rather than meet Mr. Edward Hyde." For some, many aspects of the novella have seemed markedly Scottish in flavor: the novelist G. K. Chesterton insisted that its London is really Edinburgh, its Englishmen actually Scotsmen—"No modern English lawyer," he protested of the character Mr. Utterson, "ever read a book of dry divinity in the evening, merely because it was Sunday." Nevertheless, the distinctive tone and theme of *Jekyll and Hyde* have led many critics to characterize it—often together with another work that shares its preoccupation with the divided self, Oscar Wilde's *Picture of Dorian Gray* (1891)—as an expression of quintessentially fin de siècle anxieties.

From 1888 onward the Stevensons embarked on a series of journeys in the South Seas, once again in the hope that the climate would benefit Robert's health. They eventually settled in Samoa, where Stevenson became a favorite with the locals (who called him Tusitala, or "teller of tales") before he died of a cerebral hemorrhage in 1894. At the time of his death, Stevenson was only forty-four years old and still furiously at work, this time on a historical novel titled *Weir of Hermiston.*

The Strange Case of Dr. Jekyll and Mr. Hyde

Story of the Door

Mr. Utterson the lawyer was a man of a rugged countenance, that was never lighted by a smile; cold, scanty and embarrassed in discourse; backward in sentiment; lean, long, dusty, dreary and yet somehow lovable. At friendly meetings, and when the wine was to his taste, something eminently human beaconed from his eye; something indeed which never found its way into his talk, but which spoke not only in these silent symbols of the after-dinner face, but more often and loudly in the acts of his life. He was austere with himself;

2170 / Robert Louis Stevenson

drank gin when he was alone, to mortify a taste for vintages; and though he enjoyed the theatre, had not crossed the doors of one for twenty years. But he had an approved[1] tolerance for others; sometimes wondering, almost with envy, at the high pressure of spirits involved in their misdeeds; and in any extremity inclined to help rather than to reprove. "I incline to Cain's heresy,"[2] he used to say quaintly: "I let my brother go to the devil in his own way." In this character, it was frequently his fortune to be the last reputable acquaintance and the last good influence in the lives of down-going men. And to such as these, so long as they came about his chambers, he never marked a shade of change in his demeanour.

No doubt the feat was easy to Mr. Utterson; for he was undemonstrative at the best, and even his friendship seemed to be founded in a similar catholicity[3] of good-nature. It is the mark of a modest man to accept his friendly circle ready-made from the hands of opportunity; and that was the lawyer's way. His friends were those of his own blood or those whom he had known the longest; his affections, like ivy, were the growth of time, they implied no aptness in the object. Hence, no doubt, the bond that united him to Mr. Richard Enfield, his distant kinsman, the well-known man about town. It was a nut to crack for many, what these two could see in each other, or what subject they could find in common. It was reported by those who encountered them in their Sunday walks, that they said nothing, looked singularly dull, and would hail with obvious relief the appearance of a friend. For all that, the two men put the greatest store by these excursions, counted them the chief jewel of each week, and not only set aside occasions of pleasure, but even resisted the calls of business, that they might enjoy them uninterrupted.

It chanced on one of these rambles that their way led them down a by-street in a busy quarter of London. The street was small and what is called quiet, but it drove a thriving trade on the week-days. The inhabitants were all doing well, it seemed, and all emulously hoping to do better still, and laying out the surplus of their gains in coquetry;[4] so that the shop fronts stood along that thoroughfare with an air of invitation, like rows of smiling saleswomen. Even on Sunday, when it veiled its more florid charms and lay comparatively empty of passage, the street shone out in contrast to its dingy neighbourhood, like a fire in a forest; and with its freshly painted shutters, well-polished brasses, and general cleanliness and gaiety of note, instantly caught and pleased the eye of the passenger.[5]

Two doors from one corner, on the left hand going east, the line was broken by the entry of a court; and just at that point, a certain sinister block of building thrust forward its gable on the street. It was two storeys high; showed no window, nothing but a door on the lower storey and a blind forehead of discoloured wall on the upper; and bore in every feature, the marks of prolonged and sordid negligence. The door, which was equipped with neither bell nor knocker, was blistered and distained.[6] Tramps slouched into the recess and struck matches on the panels; children kept shop upon the steps; the schoolboy had tried his knife on the mouldings; and for close on a generation, no one had appeared to drive away these random visitors or to repair their ravages.

1. Proved.
2. Refusal of responsibility for one's fellow man. After Cain kills his brother, Abel, and God asks where Abel is, Cain responds, "Am I my brother's keeper?" (Genesis 4.9).
3. Universality.
4. Attractive display.
5. Passerby.
6. Discolored.

Mr. Enfield and the lawyer were on the other side of the by-street; but when they came abreast of the entry, the former lifted up his cane and pointed.

"Did you ever remark that door?" he asked; and when his companion had replied in the affirmative, "It is connected in my mind," added he, "with a very odd story."

"Indeed?" said Mr. Utterson, with a slight change of voice, "and what was that?"

"Well, it was this way," returned Mr. Enfield: "I was coming home from some place at the end of the world, about three o'clock of a black winter morning, and my way lay through a part of town where there was literally nothing to be seen but lamps. Street after street, and all the folks asleep— street after street, all lighted up as if for a procession and all as empty as a church—till at last I got into that state of mind when a man listens and listens and begins to long for the sight of a policeman. All at once, I saw two figures: one a little man who was stumping along eastward at a good walk, and the other a girl of maybe eight or ten who was running as hard as she was able down a cross street. Well, sir, the two ran into one another naturally enough at the corner; and then came the horrible part of the thing; for the man trampled calmly over the child's body and left her screaming on the ground. It sounds nothing to hear, but it was hellish to see. It wasn't like a man; it was like some damned Juggernaut.[7] I gave a view halloa,[8] took to my heels, collared my gentleman, and brought him back to where there was already quite a group about the screaming child. He was perfectly cool and made no resistance, but gave me one look, so ugly that it brought out the sweat on me like running. The people who had turned out were the girl's own family; and pretty soon, the doctor, for whom she had been sent, put in his appearance. Well, the child was not much the worse, more frightened, according to the Sawbones;[9] and there you might have supposed would be an end to it. But there was one curious circumstance. I had taken a loathing to my gentleman at first sight. So had the child's family, which was only natural. But the doctor's case was what struck me. He was the usual cut and dry apothecary, of no particular age and colour, with a strong Edinburgh accent, and about as emotional as a bagpipe. Well, sir, he was like the rest of us; every time he looked at my prisoner, I saw that Sawbones turn sick and white with the desire to kill him. I knew what was in his mind, just as he knew what was in mine; and killing being out of the question, we did the next best. We told the man we could and would make such a scandal out of this, as should make his name stink from one end of London to the other. If he had any friends or any credit,[1] we undertook that he should lose them. And all the time, as we were pitching it in red hot, we were keeping the women off him as best we could, for they were as wild as harpies.[2] I never saw a circle of such hateful faces; and there was the man in the middle, with a kind of black, sneering coolness—frightened too, I could see that—but carrying it off, sir, really like Satan. 'If you choose to make capital out of this accident,' said he, 'I am naturally helpless. No gentleman but wishes to avoid a scene,' says he. 'Name your figure.' Well, we

---

7. A relentless force that crushes individuals in its path. Originally a title of Krishna (an avatar of the Hindu god Vishnu); at an annual festival his statue was drawn on an enormous cart, under whose wheels many worshippers threw themselves to be crushed.

8. Shout.
9. Doctor (slang).
1. Good name.
2. In classical mythology monsters with women's faces and bodies and birds' wings and claws.

2172 / Robert Louis Stevenson

screwed him up to a hundred pounds for the child's family; he would have clearly liked to stick out; but there was something about the lot of us that meant mischief, and at last he struck.[3] The next thing was to get the money; and where do you think he carried us but to that place with the door?— whipped out a key, went in, and presently came back with the matter of ten pounds in gold and a cheque for the balance on Coutts's,[4] drawn payable to bearer and signed with a name that I can't mention, though it's one of the points of my story, but it was a name at least very well known and often printed. The figure was stiff; but the signature was good for more than that, if it was only genuine. I took the liberty of pointing out to my gentleman that the whole business looked apocryphal, and that a man does not, in real life, walk into a cellar door at four in the morning and come out of it with another man's cheque for close upon a hundred pounds. But he was quite easy and sneering. 'Set your mind at rest,' says he, 'I will stay with you till the banks open and cash the cheque myself.' So we all set off, the doctor, and the child's father, and our friend and myself, and passed the rest of the night in my chambers; and next day, when we had breakfasted, went in a body to the bank. I gave in the check myself, and said I had every reason to believe it was a forgery. Not a bit of it. The cheque was genuine."

"Tut-tut," said Mr. Utterson.

"I see you feel as I do," said Mr. Enfield. "Yes, it's a bad story. For my man was a fellow that nobody could have to do with, a really damnable man; and the person that drew the cheque is the very pink of the proprieties, celebrated too, and (what makes it worse) one of your fellows who do what they call good. Black mail, I suppose; an honest man paying through the nose for some of the capers of his youth. Black Mail House is what I call that place with the door, in consequence. Though even that, you know, is far from explaining all," he added, and with the words fell into a vein of musing.

From this he was recalled by Mr. Utterson asking rather suddenly: "And you don't know if the drawer of the cheque lives there?"

"A likely place, isn't it?" returned Mr. Enfield. "But I happen to have noticed his address; he lives in some square or other."

"And you never asked about the—place with the door?" said Mr. Utterson.

"No, sir: I had a delicacy," was the reply. "I feel very strongly about putting questions; it partakes too much of the style of the day of judgment. You start a question, and it's like starting a stone. You sit quietly on the top of a hill; and away the stone goes, starting others; and presently some bland old bird (the last you would have thought of) is knocked on the head in his own back garden and the family have to change their name. No, sir, I make it a rule of mine: the more it looks like Queer Street,[5] the less I ask."

"A very good rule, too," said the lawyer.

"But I have studied the place for myself," continued Mr. Enfield. "It seems scarcely a house. There is no other door, and nobody goes in or out of that one but, once in a great while, the gentleman of my adventure. There are three windows looking on the court on the first floor;[6] none below; the windows are always shut but they're clean. And then there is a chimney which is generally smoking; so somebody must live there. And yet it's not so sure; for the buildings

---

3. Gave in.
4. A prestigious London bank.
5. I.e., looks like someone is in trouble or a bad fix (slang).
6. I.e., the first floor above the ground floor (what Americans call the second floor).

are so packed together about that court, that it's hard to say where one ends and another begins."

The pair walked on again for a while in silence; and then "Enfield," said Mr. Utterson, "that's a good rule of yours."

"Yes, I think it is," returned Enfield.

"But for all that," continued the lawyer, "there's one point I want to ask: I want to ask the name of that man who walked over the child."

"Well," said Mr. Enfield, "I can't see what harm it would do. It was a man of the name of Hyde."

"H'm," said Mr. Utterson. "What sort of a man is he to see?"

"He is not easy to describe. There is something wrong with his appearance; something displeasing, something downright detestable. I never saw a man I so disliked, and yet I scarce know why. He must be deformed somewhere; he gives a strong feeling of deformity, although I couldn't specify the point. He's an extraordinary looking man, and yet I really can name nothing out of the way. No, sir; I can make no hand of it; I can't describe him. And it's not want of memory; for I declare I can see him this moment."

Mr. Utterson again walked some way in silence and obviously under a weight of consideration. "You are sure he used a key?" he inquired at last.

"My dear sir . . ." began Enfield, surprised out of himself.

"Yes, I know," said Utterson; "I know it must seem strange. The fact is, if I do not ask you the name of the other party, it is because I know it already. You see, Richard, your tale has gone home. If you have been inexact in any point, you had better correct it."

"I think you might have warned me," returned the other with a touch of sullenness. "But I have been pedantically exact, as you call it. The fellow had a key; and what's more, he has it still. I saw him use it, not a week ago."

Mr. Utterson sighed deeply but said never a word; and the young man presently resumed. "Here is another lesson to say nothing," said he. "I am ashamed of my long tongue. Let us make a bargain never to refer to this again."

"With all my heart," said the lawyer. "I shake hands on that, Richard."

Search for Mr. Hyde

That evening Mr. Utterson came home to his bachelor house in sombre spirits and sat down to dinner without relish. It was his custom of a Sunday, when this meal was over, to sit close by the fire, a volume of some dry divinity[7] on his reading desk, until the clock of the neighbouring church rang out the hour of twelve, when he would go soberly and gratefully to bed. On this night, however, as soon as the cloth was taken away, he took up a candle and went into his business room. There he opened his safe, took from the most private part of it a document endorsed on the envelope as Dr. Jekyll's Will, and sat down with a clouded brow to study its contents. The will was holograph,[8] for Mr. Utterson, though he took charge of it now that it was made, had refused to lend the least assistance in the making of it; it provided not only that, in case of the decease of Henry Jekyll, M.D., D.C.L., LL.D., F.R.S.,[9] etc., all his possessions were to pass into the hands of his "friend and benefactor Edward

7. Theology.
8. In the author's handwriting.

9. Doctor of Medicine, Doctor of Civil Law, Doctor of Laws, and Fellow of the Royal Society.

Hyde," but that in case of Dr. Jekyll's "disappearance or unexplained absence for any period exceeding three calendar months," the said Edward Hyde should step into the said Henry Jekyll's shoes without further delay and free from any burthen or obligation, beyond the payment of a few small sums to the members of the doctor's household. This document had long been the lawyer's eyesore. It offended him both as a lawyer and as a lover of the sane and customary sides of life, to whom the fanciful was the immodest. And hitherto it was his ignorance of Mr. Hyde that had swelled his indignation; now, by a sudden turn, it was his knowledge. It was already bad enough when the name was but a name of which he could learn no more. It was worse when it began to be clothed upon with detestable attributes; and out of the shifting, insubstantial mists that had so long baffled his eye, there leaped up the sudden, definite presentment[1] of a fiend.

"I thought it was madness," he said, as he replaced the obnoxious paper in the safe, "and now I begin to fear it is disgrace."

With that he blew out his candle, put on a greatcoat, and set forth in the direction of Cavendish Square, that citadel of medicine,[2] where his friend, the great Dr. Lanyon, had his house and received his crowding patients. "If anyone knows, it will be Lanyon," he had thought.

The solemn butler knew and welcomed him; he was subjected to no stage of delay, but ushered direct from the door to the dining-room where Dr. Lanyon sat alone over his wine. This was a hearty, healthy, dapper, red-faced gentleman, with a shock of hair prematurely white, and a boisterous and decided manner. At sight of Mr. Utterson, he sprang up from his chair and welcomed him with both hands. The geniality, as was the way of the man, was somewhat theatrical to the eye; but it reposed on genuine feeling. For these two were old friends, old mates both at school and college, both thorough respecters of themselves and of each other, and, what does not always follow, men who thoroughly enjoyed each other's company.

After a little rambling talk, the lawyer led up to the subject which so disagreeably preoccupied his mind.

"I suppose, Lanyon," said he, "you and I must be the two oldest friends that Henry Jekyll has?"

"I wish the friends were younger," chuckled Dr. Lanyon. "But I suppose we are. And what of that? I see little of him now."

"Indeed?" said Utterson. "I thought you had a bond of common interest."

"We had," was the reply. "But it is more than ten years since Henry Jekyll became too fanciful for me. He began to go wrong, wrong in mind; and though of course I continue to take an interest in him for old sake's sake, as they say, I see and I have seen devilish little of the man. Such unscientific balderdash," added the doctor, flushing suddenly purple, "would have estranged Damon and Pythias."[3]

This little spirit of temper was somewhat of a relief to Mr. Utterson. "They have only differed on some point of science," he thought; and being a man of no scientific passions (except in the matter of conveyancing,[4]) he even added: "It is nothing worse than that!" He gave his friend a few seconds to recover his composure, and then approached the question he had come to put. "Did

---

1. Image.
2. A once-aristocratic neighborhood where fashionable doctors had their offices.
3. Two inseparable youths in Greek legend whose

willingness to die for each other symbolizes true friendship.
4. Legal transfer of property by writing deeds.

you ever come across a protégé of his—one Hyde?" he asked.

"Hyde?" repeated Lanyon. "No. Never heard of him. Since my time."

That was the amount of information that the lawyer carried back with him to the great, dark bed on which he tossed to and fro, until the small hours of the morning began to grow large. It was a night of little ease to his toiling mind, toiling in mere⁵ darkness and besieged by questions.

Six o'clock struck on the bells of the church that was so conveniently near to Mr. Utterson's dwelling, and still he was digging at the problem. Hitherto it had touched him on the intellectual side alone; but now his imagination also was engaged, or rather enslaved; and as he lay and tossed in the gross darkness of the night and the curtained room, Mr. Enfield's tale went by before his mind in a scroll of lighted pictures. He would be aware of the great field of lamps of a nocturnal city; then of the figure of a man walking swiftly; then of a child running from the doctor's; and then these met, and that human Juggernaut trod the child down and passed on regardless of her screams. Or else he would see a room in a rich house, where his friend lay asleep, dreaming and smiling at his dreams; and then the door of that room would be opened, the curtains of the bed plucked apart, and the sleeper recalled,⁶ and lo! there would stand by his side a figure to whom power was given, and even at that dead hour, he must rise and do its bidding. The figure in these two phases haunted the lawyer all night; and if at any time he dozed over, it was but to see it glide more stealthily through sleeping houses, or move the more swiftly and still the more swiftly, even to dizziness, through wider labyrinths of lamp-lighted city, and at every street corner crush a child and leave her screaming. And still the figure had no face by which he might know it; even in his dreams, it had no face, or one that baffled him and melted before his eyes; and thus it was that there sprang up and grew apace in the lawyer's mind a singularly strong, almost an inordinate, curiosity to behold the features of the real Mr. Hyde. If he could but once set eyes on him, he thought the mystery would lighten and perhaps roll altogether away, as was the habit of mysterious things when well examined. He might see a reason for his friend's strange preference or bondage (call it which you please) and even for the startling clause of the will. At least it would be a face worth seeing: the face of a man who was without bowels of mercy:⁷ a face which had but to show itself to raise up, in the mind of the unimpressionable Enfield, a spirit of enduring hatred.

From that time forward, Mr. Utterson began to haunt the door in the by-street of shops. In the morning before office hours, at noon when business was plenty, and time scarce, at night under the face of the fogged city moon, by all lights and at all hours of solitude or concourse, the lawyer was to be found on his chosen post.

"If he be Mr. Hyde," he had thought, "I shall be Mr. Seek."

And at last his patience was rewarded. It was a fine dry night; frost in the air; the streets as clean as a ballroom floor; the lamps, unshaken by any wind, drawing a regular pattern of light and shadow. By ten o'clock, when the shops were closed, the by-street was very solitary and, in spite of the low growl of London from all round, very silent. Small sounds carried far; domestic sounds out of the houses were clearly audible on either side of the roadway; and the rumour⁸ of the approach of any passenger preceded him by a long time. Mr.

5. Pure.
6. Revived, awakened.
7. Compassion.
8. Noise.

Utterson had been some minutes at his post, when he was aware of an odd, light footstep drawing near. In the course of his nightly patrols, he had long grown accustomed to the quaint effect with which the footfalls of a single person, while he is still a great way off, suddenly spring out distinct from the vast hum and clatter of the city. Yet his attention had never before been so sharply and decisively arrested; and it was with a strong, superstitious prevision of success that he withdrew into the entry of the court.

The steps drew swiftly nearer, and swelled out suddenly louder as they turned the end of the street. The lawyer, looking forth from the entry, could soon see what manner of man he had to deal with. He was small and very plainly dressed, and the look of him, even at that distance, went somehow strongly against the watcher's inclination. But he made straight for the door, crossing the roadway to save time; and as he came, he drew a key from his pocket like one approaching home.

Mr. Utterson stepped out and touched him on the shoulder as he passed. "Mr. Hyde, I think?"

Mr. Hyde shrank back with a hissing intake of the breath. But his fear was only momentary; and though he did not look the lawyer in the face, he answered coolly enough: "That is my name. What do you want?"

"I see you are going in," returned the lawyer. "I am an old friend of Dr. Jekyll's—Mr. Utterson of Gaunt Street—you must have heard my name; and meeting you so conveniently, I thought you might admit me."

"You will not find Dr. Jekyll; he is from home," replied Mr. Hyde, blowing in the key. And then suddenly, but still without looking up, "How did you know me?" he asked.

"On your side," said Mr. Utterson, "will you do me a favour?"

"With pleasure," replied the other. "What shall it be?"

"Will you let me see your face?" asked the lawyer.

Mr. Hyde appeared to hesitate, and then, as if upon some sudden reflection, fronted about with an air of defiance; and the pair stared at each other pretty fixedly for a few seconds. "Now I shall know you again," said Mr. Utterson. "It may be useful."

"Yes," returned Mr. Hyde, "it is as well we have met; and à propos, you should have my address." And he gave a number of a street in Soho.[9]

"Good God!" thought Mr. Utterson, "can he, too, have been thinking of the will?" But he kept his feelings to himself and only grunted in acknowledgment of the address.

"And now," said the other, "how did you know me?"

"By description," was the reply.

"Whose description?"

"We have common friends," said Mr. Utterson.

"Common friends?" echoed Mr. Hyde, a little hoarsely. "Who are they?"

"Jekyll, for instance," said the lawyer.

"He never told you," cried Mr. Hyde, with a flush of anger. "I did not think you would have lied."

"Come," said Mr. Utterson, "that is not fitting language."

The other snarled aloud into a savage laugh; and the next moment, with extraordinary quickness, he had unlocked the door and disappeared into the house.

9. Seedy district in central London. "À propos": by the way (French).

The lawyer stood awhile when Mr. Hyde had left him, the picture of disquietude. Then he began slowly to mount the street, pausing every step or two and putting his hand to his brow like a man in mental perplexity. The problem he was thus debating as he walked, was one of a class that is rarely solved. Mr. Hyde was pale and dwarfish, he gave an impression of deformity without any nameable malformation, he had a displeasing smile, he had borne himself to the lawyer with a sort of murderous mixture of timidity and boldness, and he spoke with a husky, whispering and somewhat broken voice; all these were points against him, but not all of these together could explain the hitherto unknown disgust, loathing and fear with which Mr. Utterson regarded him. "There must be something else," said the perplexed gentleman. "There *is* something more, if I could find a name for it. God bless me, the man seems hardly human! Something troglodytic, shall we say? or can it be the old story of Dr. Fell? or is it the mere radiance of a foul soul that thus transpires through, and transfigures, its clay continent?[1] The last, I think; for, O my poor old Harry Jekyll, if ever I read Satan's signature upon a face, it is on that of your new friend."

Round the corner from the by-street, there was a square of ancient, handsome houses, now for the most part decayed from their high estate and let in flats and chambers to all sorts and conditions of men: map-engravers, architects, shady lawyers and the agents of obscure enterprises. One house, however, second from the corner, was still occupied entire; and at the door of this, which wore a great air of wealth and comfort, though it was now plunged in darkness except for the fanlight, Mr. Utterson stopped and knocked. A well-dressed, elderly servant opened the door.

"Is Dr. Jekyll at home, Poole?" asked the lawyer.

"I will see, Mr. Utterson," said Poole, admitting the visitor, as he spoke, into a large, low-roofed, comfortable hall, paved with flags,[2] warmed (after the fashion of a country house) by a bright, open fire, and furnished with costly cabinets of oak. "Will you wait here by the fire, sir? or shall I give you a light in the dining-room?"

"Here, thank you," said the lawyer, and he drew near and leaned on the tall fender.[3] This hall, in which he was now left alone, was a pet fancy of his friend the doctor's; and Utterson himself was wont to speak of it as the pleasantest room in London. But to-night there was a shudder in his blood; the face of Hyde sat heavy on his memory; he felt (what was rare with him) a nausea and distaste of life; and in the gloom of his spirits, he seemed to read a menace in the flickering of the firelight on the polished cabinets and the uneasy starting of the shadow on the roof. He was ashamed of his relief, when Poole presently returned to announce that Dr. Jekyll was gone out.

"I saw Mr. Hyde go in by the old dissecting-room door, Poole," he said. "Is that right, when Dr. Jekyll is from home?"

"Quite right, Mr. Utterson, sir," replied the servant. "Mr. Hyde has a key."

"Your master seems to repose a great deal of trust in that young man, Poole," resumed the other musingly.

"Yes, sir, he do indeed," said Poole. "We have all orders to obey him."

"I do not think I ever met Mr. Hyde?" asked Utterson.

1. Container. "Troglodytic": like a prehistoric cave dweller or apelike. Dr. Fell: figure from the nursery rhyme "I do not like thee Dr. Fell; / The reason why I cannot tell."
2. Flagstones.
3. Metal frame in front of a fireplace.

"O, dear no, sir. He never *dines* here," replied the butler. "Indeed we see very little of him on this side of the house; he mostly comes and goes by the laboratory."

"Well, good-night, Poole."

"Good-night, Mr. Utterson."

And the lawyer set out homeward with a very heavy heart. "Poor Harry Jekyll," he thought, "my mind misgives me he is in deep waters! He was wild when he was young; a long while ago to be sure; but in the law of God, there is no statute of limitations. Ay, it must be that; the ghost of some old sin, the cancer of some concealed disgrace: punishment coming, *pede claudo*,[4] years after memory has forgotten and self-love condoned the fault." And the lawyer, scared by the thought, brooded awhile on his own past, groping in all the corners of memory, lest by chance some Jack-in-the-Box of an old iniquity should leap to light there. His past was fairly blameless; few men could read the rolls of their life with less apprehension; yet he was humbled to the dust by the many ill things he had done, and raised up again into a sober and fearful gratitude by the many that he had come so near to doing, yet avoided. And then by a return on his former subject, he conceived a spark of hope. "This Master Hyde, if he were studied," thought he, "must have secrets of his own; black secrets, by the look of him; secrets compared to which poor Jekyll's worst would be like sunshine. Things cannot continue as they are. It turns me cold to think of this creature stealing like a thief to Harry's bedside; poor Harry, what a wakening! And the danger of it; for if this Hyde suspects the existence of the will, he may grow impatient to inherit. Ay, I must put my shoulder to the wheel—if Jekyll will but let me," he added, "if Jekyll will only let me." For once more he saw before his mind's eye, as clear as a transparency, the strange clauses of the will.

Dr. Jekyll Was Quite at Ease

A fortnight later, by excellent good fortune, the doctor gave one of his pleasant dinners to some five or six old cronies, all intelligent, reputable men and all judges of good wine; and Mr. Utterson so contrived that he remained behind after the others had departed. This was no new arrangement, but a thing that had befallen many scores of times. Where Utterson was liked, he was liked well. Hosts loved to detain the dry lawyer, when the light-hearted and the loose-tongued had already their foot on the threshold; they liked to sit awhile in his unobtrusive company, practising for solitude, sobering their minds in the man's rich silence after the expense and strain of gaiety. To this rule, Dr. Jekyll was no exception; and as he now sat on the opposite side of the fire—a large, well-made, smooth-faced man of fifty, with something of a slyish cast perhaps, but every mark of capacity and kindness—you could see by his looks that he cherished for Mr. Utterson a sincere and warm affection.

"I have been wanting to speak to you, Jekyll," began the latter. "You know that will of yours?"

A close observer might have gathered that the topic was distasteful; but the doctor carried it off gaily. "My poor Utterson," said he, "you are unfortunate in such a client. I never saw a man so distressed as you were by my will; unless

4. With lame foot (Latin). From the Roman poet Horace's *Odes* 3.2.32: "Rarely has Vengeance with her lame foot abandoned the wicked man with a head start on her."

it were that hide-bound pedant, Lanyon, at what he called my scientific heresies. O, I know he's a good fellow—you needn't frown—an excellent fellow, and I always mean to see more of him; but a hide-bound pedant for all that; an ignorant, blatant pedant. I was never more disappointed in any man than Lanyon."

"You know I never approved of it," pursued Utterson, ruthlessly disregarding the fresh topic.

"My will? Yes, certainly, I know that," said the doctor, a trifle sharply. "You have told me so."

"Well, I tell you so again," continued the lawyer. "I have been learning something of young Hyde."

The large handsome face of Dr. Jekyll grew pale to the very lips, and there came a blackness about his eyes. "I do not care to hear more," said he. "This is a matter I thought we had agreed to drop."

"What I heard was abominable," said Utterson.

"It can make no change. You do not understand my position," returned the doctor, with a certain incoherency of manner. "I am painfully situated, Utterson; my position is a very strange—a very strange one. It is one of those affairs that cannot be mended by talking."

"Jekyll," said Utterson, "you know me: I am a man to be trusted. Make a clean breast of this in confidence; and I make no doubt I can get you out of it."

"My good Utterson," said the doctor, "this is very good of you, this is downright good of you, and I cannot find words to thank you in. I believe you fully; I would trust you before any man alive, ay, before myself, if I could make the choice; but indeed it isn't what you fancy; it is not so bad as that; and just to put your good heart at rest, I will tell you one thing: the moment I choose, I can be rid of Mr. Hyde. I give you my hand upon that; and I thank you again and again; and I will just add one little word, Utterson, that I'm sure you'll take in good part: this is a private matter, and I beg of you to let it sleep."

Utterson reflected a little, looking in the fire.

"I have no doubt you are perfectly right," he said at last, getting to his feet.

"Well, but since we have touched upon this business, and for the last time I hope," continued the doctor, "there is one point I should like you to understand. I have really a very great interest in poor Hyde. I know you have seen him; he told me so; and I fear he was rude. But I do sincerely take a great, a very great interest in that young man; and if I am taken away, Utterson, I wish you to promise me that you will bear with him and get his rights for him. I think you would, if you knew all; and it would be a weight off my mind if you would promise."

"I can't pretend that I shall ever like him," said the lawyer.

"I don't ask that," pleaded Jekyll, laying his hand upon the other's arm; "I only ask for justice; I only ask you to help him for my sake, when I am no longer here."

Utterson heaved an irrepressible sigh. "Well," said he, "I promise."

The Carew Murder Case

Nearly a year later, in the month of October, 18—, London was startled by a crime of singular ferocity and rendered all the more notable by the high position of the victim. The details were few and startling. A maid servant living alone in a house not far from the river, had gone upstairs to bed about eleven. Although a fog rolled over the city in the small hours, the early part of the night was cloudless, and the lane, which the maid's window overlooked, was brilliantly lit by the full moon. It seems she was romantically given, for she sat down upon her box, which stood immediately under the window, and fell into a dream of musing. Never (she used to say, with streaming tears, when she narrated that experience), never had she felt more at peace with all men or thought more kindly of the world. And as she so sat she became aware of an aged and beautiful gentleman with white hair, drawing near along the lane; and advancing to meet him, another and very small gentleman, to whom at first she paid less attention. When they had come within speech (which was just under the maid's eyes) the older man bowed and accosted the other with a very pretty manner of politeness. It did not seem as if the subject of his address were of great importance; indeed, from his pointing, it sometimes appeared as if he were only inquiring his way; but the moon shone on his face as he spoke, and the girl was pleased to watch it, it seemed to breathe such an innocent and old-world kindness of disposition, yet with something high too, as of a well-founded self-content. Presently her eye wandered to the other, and she was surprised to recognise in him a certain Mr. Hyde, who had once visited her master and for whom she had conceived a dislike. He had in his hand a heavy cane, with which he was trifling; but he answered never a word, and seemed to listen with an ill-contained impatience. And then all of a sudden he broke out in a great flame of anger, stamping with his foot, brandishing the cane, and carrying on (as the maid described it) like a madman. The old gentleman took a step back, with the air of one very much surprised and a trifle hurt; and at that Mr. Hyde broke out of all bounds and clubbed him to the earth. And next moment, with ape-like fury, he was trampling his victim under foot and hailing down a storm of blows, under which the bones were audibly shattered and the body jumped upon the roadway. At the horror of these sights and sounds, the maid fainted.

It was two o'clock when she came to herself and called for the police. The murderer was gone long ago; but there lay his victim in the middle of the lane, incredibly mangled. The stick with which the deed had been done, although it was of some rare and very tough and heavy wood, had broken in the middle under the stress of this insensate cruelty; and one splintered half had rolled in the neighbouring gutter—the other, without doubt, had been carried away by the murderer. A purse and a gold watch were found upon the victim; but no cards or papers, except a sealed and stamped envelope, which he had been probably carrying to the post,[5] and which bore the name and address of Mr. Utterson.

This was brought to the lawyer the next morning, before he was out of bed; and he had no sooner seen it and been told the circumstances, than he shot out a solemn lip. "I shall say nothing till I have seen the body," said he; "this may be very serious. Have the kindness to wait while I dress." And with the same grave countenance he hurried through his breakfast and drove to the police station, whither the body had been carried. As soon as he came into the cell, he nodded.

"Yes," said he, "I recognise him. I am sorry to say that this is Sir Danvers Carew."

5. I.e., postal letter box.

"Good God, sir," exclaimed the officer, "is it possible?" And the next moment his eye lighted up with professional ambition. "This will make a deal of noise," he said. "And perhaps you can help us to the man." And he briefly narrated what the maid had seen, and showed the broken stick.

Mr. Utterson had already quailed at the name of Hyde; but when the stick was laid before him, he could doubt no longer; broken and battered as it was, he recognised it for one that he had himself presented many years before to Henry Jekyll.

"Is this Mr. Hyde a person of small stature?" he inquired.

"Particularly small and particularly wicked-looking, is what the maid calls him," said the officer.

Mr. Utterson reflected; and then, raising his head, "If you will come with me in my cab," he said, "I think I can take you to his house."

It was by this time about nine in the morning, and the first fog of the season. A great chocolate-coloured pall lowered[6] over heaven, but the wind was continually charging and routing these embattled vapours; so that as the cab crawled from street to street, Mr. Utterson beheld a marvellous number of degrees and hues of twilight; for here it would be dark like the back-end of evening; and there would be a glow of a rich, lurid brown, like the light of some strange conflagration; and here, for a moment, the fog would be quite broken up, and a haggard shaft of daylight would glance in between the swirling wreaths. The dismal quarter of Soho seen under these changing glimpses, with its muddy ways, and slatternly passengers, and its lamps, which had never been extinguished or had been kindled afresh to combat this mournful reinvasion of darkness, seemed, in the lawyer's eyes, like a district of some city in a nightmare. The thoughts of his mind, besides, were of the gloomiest dye; and when he glanced at the companion of his drive, he was conscious of some touch of that terror of the law and the law's officers, which may at times assail the most honest.

As the cab drew up before the address indicated, the fog lifted a little and showed him a dingy street, a gin palace, a low French eating house, a shop for the retail of penny numbers[7] and twopenny salads, many ragged children huddled in the doorways, and many women of many different nationalities passing out, key in hand, to have a morning glass; and the next moment the fog settled down again upon that part, as brown as umber, and cut him off from his blackguardly surroundings. This was the home of Henry Jekyll's favourite; of a man who was heir to quarter of a million sterling.[8]

An ivory-faced and silvery-haired old woman opened the door. She had an evil face, smoothed by hypocrisy; but her manners were excellent. Yes, she said, this was Mr. Hyde's, but he was not at home; he had been in that night very late, but had gone away again in less than an hour; there was nothing strange in that; his habits were very irregular, and he was often absent; for instance, it was nearly two months since she had seen him till yesterday.

"Very well, then, we wish to see his rooms," said the lawyer; and when the woman began to declare it was impossible, "I had better tell you who this person is," he added. "This is Inspector Newcomen of Scotland Yard."

A flash of odious joy appeared upon the woman's face. "Ah!" said she, "he is in trouble! What has he done?"

---

6. Was gloomy and threatening.
7. Cheap serial installments of popular fiction.

"Gin palace:" cheap bar.
8. I.e., pounds sterling.

Mr. Utterson and the inspector exchanged glances. "He don't seem a very popular character," observed the latter. "And now, my good woman, just let me and this gentleman have a look about us."

In the whole extent of the house, which but for the old woman remained otherwise empty, Mr. Hyde had only used a couple of rooms; but these were furnished with luxury and good taste. A closet was filled with wine; the plate was of silver, the napery[9] elegant; a good picture hung upon the walls, a gift (as Utterson supposed) from Henry Jekyll, who was much of a connoisseur; and the carpets were of many piles and agreeable in colour. At this moment, however, the rooms bore every mark of having been recently and hurriedly ransacked; clothes lay about the floor, with their pockets inside out; lock-fast drawers stood open; and on the hearth there lay a pile of gray ashes, as though many papers had been burned. From these embers the inspector disinterred the butt end of a green cheque book, which had resisted the action of the fire; the other half of the stick was found behind the door; and as this clinched his suspicions, the officer declared himself delighted. A visit to the bank, where several thousand pounds were found to be lying to the murderer's credit, completed his gratification.

"You may depend upon it, sir," he told Mr. Utterson: "I have him in my hand. He must have lost his head, or he never would have left the stick or, above all, burned the cheque book. Why, money's life to the man. We have nothing to do but wait for him at the bank, and get out the handbills."

This last, however, was not so easy of accomplishment; for Mr. Hyde had numbered few familiars—even the master of the servant maid had only seen him twice; his family could nowhere be traced; he had never been photographed; and the few who could describe him differed widely, as common observers will. Only on one point, were they agreed; and that was the haunting sense of unexpressed deformity with which the fugitive impressed his beholders.

Incident of the Letter

It was late in the afternoon, when Mr. Utterson found his way to Dr. Jekyll's door, where he was at once admitted by Poole, and carried down by the kitchen offices and across a yard which had once been a garden, to the building which was indifferently[1] known as the laboratory or the dissecting rooms. The doctor had bought the house from the heirs of a celebrated surgeon; and his own tastes being rather chemical than anatomical, had changed the destination[2] of the block at the bottom of the garden. It was the first time that the lawyer had been received in that part of his friend's quarters; and he eyed the dingy, windowless structure with curiosity, and gazed round with a distasteful sense of strangeness as he crossed the theatre,[3] once crowded with eager students and now lying gaunt and silent, the tables laden with chemical apparatus, the floor strewn with crates and littered with packing straw, and the light falling dimly through the foggy cupola. At the further end, a flight of stairs mounted to a door covered with red baize; and through this, Mr. Utterson was at last received into the doctor's cabinet.[4] It was a large room, fitted round with glass

---

9. Table linen.
1. Without distinction.
2. Purpose.
3. Room with tiers of rising seats surrounding a

central platform, used for lectures and medical demonstrations.
4. Small private room. "Baize": coarse woolen material.

presses, furnished, among other things, with a cheval-glass[5] and a business table, and looking out upon the court by three dusty windows barred with iron. A fire burned in the grate; a lamp was set lighted on the chimney shelf, for even in the houses the fog began to lie thickly; and there, close up to the warmth, sat Dr. Jekyll, looking deadly sick. He did not rise to meet his visitor, but held out a cold hand and bade him welcome in a changed voice.

"And now," said Mr. Utterson, as soon as Poole had left them, "you have heard the news?"

The doctor shuddered. "They were crying it in the square," he said. "I heard them in my dining-room."

"One word," said the lawyer. "Carew was my client, but so are you, and I want to know what I am doing. You have not been mad enough to hide this fellow?"

"Utterson, I swear to God," cried the doctor, "I swear to God I will never set eyes on him again. I bind my honour to you that I am done with him in this world. It is all at an end. And indeed he does not want my help; you do not know him as I do; he is safe, he is quite safe; mark my words, he will never more be heard of."

The lawyer listened gloomily; he did not like his friend's feverish manner. "You seem pretty sure of him," said he; "and for your sake, I hope you may be right. If it came to a trial, your name might appear."

"I am quite sure of him," replied Jekyll; "I have grounds for certainty that I cannot share with anyone. But there is one thing on which you may advise me. I have—I have received a letter; and I am at a loss whether I should show it to the police. I should like to leave it in your hands, Utterson; you would judge wisely, I am sure; I have so great a trust in you."

"You fear, I suppose, that it might lead to his detection?" asked the lawyer.

"No," said the other. "I cannot say that I care what becomes of Hyde; I am quite done with him. I was thinking of my own character, which this hateful business has rather exposed."

Utterson ruminated awhile; he was surprised at his friend's selfishness, and yet relieved by it. "Well," said he, at last, "let me see the letter."

The letter was written in an odd, upright hand and signed "Edward Hyde": and it signified, briefly enough, that the writer's benefactor, Dr. Jekyll, whom he had long so unworthily repaid for a thousand generosities, need labour under no alarm for his safety, as he had means of escape on which he placed a sure dependence. The lawyer liked this letter well enough; it put a better colour on the intimacy than he had looked for; and he blamed himself for some of his past suspicions.

"Have you the envelope?" he asked.

"I burned it," replied Jekyll, "before I thought what I was about. But it bore no postmark. The note was handed in."

"Shall I keep this and sleep upon it?" asked Utterson.

"I wish you to judge for me entirely," was the reply. "I have lost confidence in myself."

"Well, I shall consider," returned the lawyer. "And now one word more: it was Hyde who dictated the terms in your will about that disappearance?"

The doctor seemed seized with a qualm of faintness; he shut his mouth tight and nodded.

---

5. Large freestanding mirror, hinged on a frame. "Presses": cupboards with glass doors.

"I knew it," said Utterson. "He meant to murder you. You have had a fine escape."

"I have had what is far more to the purpose," returned the doctor solemnly: "I have had a lesson—O God, Utterson, what a lesson I have had!" And he covered his face for a moment with his hands.

On his way out, the lawyer stopped and had a word or two with Poole. "By the bye," said he, "there was a letter handed in to-day: what was the messenger like?" But Poole was positive nothing had come except by post; "and only circulars by that," he added.

This news sent off the visitor with his fears renewed. Plainly the letter had come by the laboratory door; possibly, indeed, it had been written in the cabinet; and if that were so, it must be differently judged, and handled with the more caution. The newsboys, as he went, were crying themselves hoarse along the footways: "Special edition. Shocking murder of an M.P."[6] That was the funeral oration of one friend and client; and he could not help a certain apprehension lest the good name of another should be sucked down in the eddy of the scandal. It was, at least, a ticklish decision that he had to make; and self-reliant as he was by habit, he began to cherish a longing for advice. It was not to be had directly; but perhaps, he thought, it might be fished for.

Presently after, he sat on one side of his own hearth, with Mr. Guest, his head clerk, upon the other, and midway between, at a nicely calculated distance from the fire, a bottle of a particular old wine that had long dwelt unsunned in the foundations of his house. The fog still slept on the wing above the drowned city, where the lamps glimmered like carbuncles;[7] and through the muffle and smother of these fallen clouds, the procession of the town's life was still rolling in through the great arteries with a sound as of a mighty wind. But the room was gay with firelight. In the bottle the acids were long ago resolved; the imperial dye[8] had softened with time, as the colour grows richer in stained windows; and the glow of hot autumn afternoons on hillside vineyards, was ready to be set free and to disperse the fogs of London. Insensibly the lawyer melted. There was no man from whom he kept fewer secrets than Mr. Guest; and he was not always sure that he kept as many as he meant. Guest had often been on business to the doctor's; he knew Poole; he could scarce have failed to hear of Mr. Hyde's familiarity about the house; he might draw conclusions: was it not as well, then, that he should see a letter which put that mystery to rights? and above all since Guest, being a great student and critic of handwriting, would consider the step natural and obliging? The clerk, besides, was a man of counsel; he would scarce read so strange a document without dropping a remark; and by that remark Mr. Utterson might shape his future course.

"This is a sad business about Sir Danvers," he said.

"Yes, sir, indeed. It has elicited a great deal of public feeling," returned Guest. "The man, of course, was mad."

"I should like to hear your views on that," replied Utterson. "I have a document here in his handwriting; it is between ourselves, for I scarce know what to do about it; it is an ugly business at the best. But there it is; quite in your way: a murderer's autograph."

Guest's eyes brightened, and he sat down at once and studied it with passion. "No, sir," he said: "not mad; but it is an odd hand."

6. Member of Parliament.   8. Purple.
7. Precious fiery-red stones.

"And by all accounts a very odd writer," added the lawyer.

Just then the servant entered with a note.

"Is that from Dr. Jekyll, sir?" inquired the clerk. "I thought I knew the writing. Anything private, Mr. Utterson?"

"Only an invitation to dinner. Why? Do you want to see it?"

"One moment. I thank you, sir;" and the clerk laid the two sheets of paper alongside and sedulously compared their contents. "Thank you, sir," he said at last, returning both; "it's a very interesting autograph."

There was a pause, during which Mr. Utterson struggled with himself. "Why did you compare them, Guest?" he inquired suddenly.

"Well, sir," returned the clerk, "there's a rather singular resemblance; the two hands are in many points identical: only differently sloped."

"Rather quaint,"[9] said Utterson.

"It is, as you say, rather quaint," returned Guest.

"I wouldn't speak of this note, you know," said the master.

"No, sir," said the clerk. "I understand."

But no sooner was Mr. Utterson alone that night than he locked the note into his safe, where it reposed from that time forward. "What!" he thought. "Henry Jekyll forge for a murderer!" And his blood ran cold in his veins.

Remarkable Incident of Dr. Lanyon

Time ran on; thousands of pounds were offered in reward, for the death of Sir Danvers was resented as a public injury; but Mr. Hyde had disappeared out of the ken of the police as though he had never existed. Much of his past was unearthed, indeed, and all disreputable: tales came out of the man's cruelty, at once so callous and violent; of his vile life, of his strange associates, of the hatred that seemed to have surrounded his career; but of his present whereabouts, not a whisper. From the time he had left the house in Soho on the morning of the murder, he was simply blotted out; and gradually, as time drew on, Mr. Utterson began to recover from the hotness of his alarm, and to grow more at quiet with himself. The death of Sir Danvers was, to his way of thinking, more than paid for by the disappearance of Mr. Hyde. Now that that evil influence had been withdrawn, a new life began for Dr. Jekyll. He came out of his seclusion, renewed relations with his friends, became once more their familiar guest and entertainer; and whilst he had always been known for charities, he was now no less distinguished for religion. He was busy, he was much in the open air, he did good; his face seemed to open and brighten, as if with an inward consciousness of service; and for more than two months, the doctor was at peace.

On the 8th of January Utterson had dined at the doctor's with a small party; Lanyon had been there; and the face of the host had looked from one to the other as in the old days when the trio were inseparable friends. On the 12th, and again on the 14th, the door was shut against the lawyer. "The doctor was confined to the house," Poole said, "and saw no one." On the 15th, he tried again, and was again refused; and having now been used for the last two months to see his friend almost daily, he found this return of solitude to weigh upon his spirits. The fifth night he had in Guest to dine with him; and the sixth he betook himself to Dr. Lanyon's.

There at least he was not denied admittance; but when he came in, he was

9. Odd, unusual.

shocked at the change which had taken place in the doctor's appearance. He had his death-warrant written legibly upon his face. The rosy man had grown pale; his flesh had fallen away; he was visibly balder and older; and yet it was not so much these tokens of a swift physical decay that arrested the lawyer's notice, as a look in the eye and quality of manner that seemed to testify to some deep-seated terror of the mind. It was unlikely that the doctor should fear death; and yet that was what Utterson was tempted to suspect. "Yes," he thought; "he is a doctor, he must know his own state and that his days are counted; and the knowledge is more than he can bear." And yet when Utterson remarked on his ill-looks, it was with an air of great firmness that Lanyon declared himself a doomed man.

"I have had a shock," he said, "and I shall never recover. It is a question of weeks. Well, life has been pleasant; I liked it; yes, sir, I used to like it. I sometimes think if we knew all, we should be more glad to get away."

"Jekyll is ill, too," observed Utterson. "Have you seen him?"

But Lanyon's face changed, and he held up a trembling hand. "I wish to see or hear no more of Dr. Jekyll," he said in a loud, unsteady voice. "I am quite done with that person; and I beg that you will spare me any allusion to one whom I regard as dead."

"Tut-tut," said Mr. Utterson; and then after a considerable pause, "Can't I do anything?" he inquired. "We are three very old friends, Lanyon; we shall not live to make others."

"Nothing can be done," returned Lanyon; "ask himself."

"He will not see me," said the lawyer.

"I am not surprised at that," was the reply. "Some day, Utterson, after I am dead, you may perhaps come to learn the right and wrong of this. I cannot tell you. And in the meantime, if you can sit and talk with me of other things, for God's sake, stay and do so; but if you cannot keep clear of this accursed topic, then, in God's name, go, for I cannot bear it."

As soon as he got home, Utterson sat down and wrote to Jekyll, complaining of his exclusion from the house, and asking the cause of this unhappy break with Lanyon; and the next day brought him a long answer, often very pathetically worded, and sometimes darkly mysterious in drift. The quarrel with Lanyon was incurable. "I do not blame our old friend," Jekyll wrote, "but I share his view that we must never meet. I mean from henceforth to lead a life of extreme seclusion; you must not be surprised, nor must you doubt my friendship, if my door is often shut even to you. You must suffer me to go my own dark way. I have brought on myself a punishment and a danger that I cannot name. If I am the chief of sinners, I am the chief of sufferers also. I could not think that this earth contained a place for sufferings and terrors so unmanning; and you can do but one thing, Utterson, to lighten this destiny, and that is to respect my silence." Utterson was amazed; the dark influence of Hyde had been withdrawn, the doctor had returned to his old tasks and amities; a week ago, the prospect had smiled with every promise of a cheerful and an honoured age; and now in a moment, friendship, and peace of mind, and the whole tenor of his life were wrecked. So great and unprepared a change pointed to madness; but in view of Lanyon's manner and words, there must lie for it some deeper ground.

A week afterwards Dr. Lanyon took to his bed, and in something less than a fortnight he was dead. The night after the funeral, at which he had been sadly affected, Utterson locked the door of his business room, and sitting there by the light of a melancholy candle, drew out and set before him an envelope addressed by the hand and sealed with the seal of his dead friend. "PRIVATE: for the hands of G. J. Utterson ALONE, and in case of his predecease *to be destroyed unread*," so it was emphatically superscribed; and the lawyer dreaded to behold the contents. "I have buried one friend today," he thought: "what if this should cost me another?" And then he condemned the fear as a disloyalty, and broke the seal. Within there was another enclosure, likewise sealed, and marked upon the cover as "not to be opened till the death or disappearance of Dr. Henry Jekyll." Utterson could not trust his eyes. Yes, it was disappearance; here again, as in the mad will which he had long ago restored to its author, here again were the idea of a disappearance and the name of Henry Jekyll bracketted. But in the will, that idea had sprung from the sinister suggestion of the man Hyde; it was set there with a purpose all too plain and horrible. Written by the hand of Lanyon, what should it mean? A great curiosity came on the trustee, to disregard the prohibition and dive at once to the bottom of these mysteries; but professional honour and faith to his dead friend were stringent obligations; and the packet slept in the inmost corner of his private safe.

It is one thing to mortify curiosity, another to conquer it; and it may be doubted if, from that day forth, Utterson desired the society of his surviving friend with the same eagerness. He thought of him kindly; but his thoughts were disquieted and fearful. He went to call indeed; but he was perhaps relieved to be denied admittance; perhaps, in his heart, he preferred to speak with Poole upon the doorstep and surrounded by the air and sounds of the open city, rather than to be admitted into that house of voluntary bondage, and to sit and speak with its inscrutable recluse. Poole had, indeed, no very pleasant news to communicate. The doctor, it appeared, now more than ever confined himself to the cabinet over the laboratory, where he would sometimes even sleep; he was out of spirits, he had grown very silent, he did not read; it seemed as if he had something on his mind. Utterson became so used to the unvarying character of these reports, that he fell off little by little in the frequency of his visits.

Incident at the Window

It chanced on Sunday, when Mr. Utterson was on his usual walk with Mr. Enfield, that their way lay once again through the by-street; and that when they came in front of the door, both stopped to gaze on it.

"Well," said Enfield, "that story's at an end at least. We shall never see more of Mr. Hyde."

"I hope not," said Utterson. "Did I ever tell you that I once saw him, and shared your feeling of repulsion?"

"It was impossible to do the one without the other," returned Enfield. "And by the way, what an ass you must have thought me, not to know that this was a back way to Dr. Jekyll's! It was partly your own fault that I found it out, even when I did."

"So you found it out, did you?" said Utterson. "But if that be so, we may step into the court and take a look at the windows. To tell you the truth, I am uneasy about poor Jekyll; and even outside, I feel as if the presence of a friend might do him good."

The court was very cool and a little damp, and full of premature twilight, although the sky, high up overhead, was still bright with sunset. The middle one of the three windows was half way open; and sitting close beside it, taking the air with an infinite sadness of mien, like some disconsolate prisoner, Utterson saw Dr. Jekyll.

"What! Jekyll!" he cried. "I trust you are better."

"I am very low, Utterson," replied the doctor, drearily, "very low. It will not last long, thank God."

"You stay too much indoors," said the lawyer. "You should be out, whipping up the circulation like Mr. Enfield and me. (This is my cousin—Mr. Enfield—Dr. Jekyll.) Come now; get your hat and take a quick turn with us."

"You are very good," sighed the other. "I should like to very much; but no, no, no, it is quite impossible; I dare not. But indeed, Utterson, I am very glad to see you; this is really a great pleasure; I would ask you and Mr. Enfield up, but the place is really not fit."

"Why then," said the lawyer, good-naturedly, "the best thing we can do is to stay down here and speak with you from where we are."

"That is just what I was about to venture to propose," returned the doctor with a smile. But the words were hardly uttered, before the smile was struck out of his face and succeeded by an expression of such abject terror and despair, as froze the very blood of the two gentlemen below. They saw it but for a glimpse, for the window was instantly thrust down; but that glimpse had been sufficient, and they turned and left the court without a word. In silence, too, they traversed the by-street; and it was not until they had come into a neighbouring thoroughfare, where even upon a Sunday there were still some stirrings of life, that Mr. Utterson at last turned and looked at his companion. They were both pale; and there was an answering horror in their eyes.

"God forgive us, God forgive us," said Mr. Utterson.

But Mr. Enfield only nodded his head very seriously, and walked on once more in silence.

The Last Night

Mr. Utterson was sitting by his fireside one evening after dinner, when he was surprised to receive a visit from Poole.

"Bless me, Poole, what brings you here?" he cried; and then taking a second look at him, "What ails you?" he added; "is the doctor ill?"

"Mr. Utterson," said the man, "there is something wrong."

"Take a seat, and here is a glass of wine for you," said the lawyer. "Now, take your time, and tell me plainly what you want."

"You know the doctor's ways, sir," replied Poole, "and how he shuts himself up. Well, he's shut up again in the cabinet; and I don't like it, sir—I wish I may die if I like it. Mr. Utterson, sir, I'm afraid."

"Now, my good man," said the lawyer, "be explicit. What are you afraid of?"

"I've been afraid for about a week," returned Poole, doggedly disregarding the question, "and I can bear it no more."

The man's appearance amply bore out his words; his manner was altered for the worse; and except for the moment when he had first announced his terror, he had not once looked the lawyer in the face. Even now, he sat with the glass of wine untasted on his knee, and his eyes directed to a corner of the floor. "I can bear it no more," he repeated.

"Come," said the lawyer, "I see you have some good reason, Poole; I see there is something seriously amiss. Try to tell me what it is."

"I think there's been foul play," said Poole, hoarsely.

"Foul play!" cried the lawyer, a good deal frightened and rather inclined to be irritated in consequence. "What foul play? What does the man mean?"

"I daren't say, sir," was the answer; "but will you come along with me and see for yourself?"

Mr. Utterson's only answer was to rise and get his hat and great coat; but he observed with wonder the greatness of the relief that appeared upon the butler's face, and perhaps with no less, that the wine was still untasted when he set it down to follow.

It was a wild, cold, seasonable night of March, with a pale moon, lying on her back as though the wind had tilted her, and a flying wrack of the most diaphanous and lawny[1] texture. The wind made talking difficult, and flecked the blood into the face. It seemed to have swept the streets unusually bare of passengers, besides; for Mr. Utterson thought he had never seen that part of London so deserted. He could have wished it otherwise; never in his life had he been conscious of so sharp a wish to see and touch his fellow-creatures; for struggle as he might, there was born in upon his mind a crushing anticipation of calamity. The square, when they got there, was all full of wind and dust, and the thin trees in the garden were lashing themselves along the railing. Poole, who had kept all the way a pace or two ahead, now pulled up in the middle of the pavement, and in spite of the biting weather, took off his hat and mopped his brow with a red pocket-handkerchief. But for all the hurry of his coming, these were not the dews of exertion that he wiped away, but the moisture of some strangling anguish; for his face was white and his voice, when he spoke, harsh and broken.

"Well, sir," he said, "here we are, and God grant there be nothing wrong."

"Amen, Poole," said the lawyer.

Thereupon the servant knocked in a very guarded manner; the door was opened on the chain; and a voice asked from within, "Is that you, Poole?"

"It's all right," said Poole. "Open the door."

The hall, when they entered it, was brightly lighted up; the fire was built high; and about the hearth the whole of the servants, men and women, stood huddled together like a flock of sheep. At the sight of Mr. Utterson, the housemaid broke into hysterical whimpering; and the cook, crying out "Bless God! it's Mr. Utterson," ran forward as if to take him in her arms.

"What, what? Are you all here?" said the lawyer peevishly. "Very irregular, very unseemly; your master would be far from pleased."

"They're all afraid," said Poole.

Blank silence followed, no one protesting; only the maid lifted up her voice and now wept loudly.

"Hold your tongue!" Poole said to her, with a ferocity of accent that testified to his own jangled nerves; and indeed, when the girl had so suddenly raised the note of her lamentation, they had all started and turned towards the inner door with faces of dreadful expectation. "And now," continued the butler, addressing the knife-boy, "reach me a candle, and we'll get this through hands[2] at once." And then he begged Mr. Utterson to follow him, and led the way to the back garden.

---

1. Of fine linen. "Wrack": i.e., rack, a mass of high clouds driven by the wind.

2. We'll deal with this.

"Now, sir," said he, "you come as gently as you can. I want you to hear, and I don't want you to be heard. And see here, sir, if by any chance he was to ask you in, don't go."

Mr. Utterson's nerves, at this unlooked-for termination, gave a jerk that nearly threw him from his balance; but he recollected his courage and followed the butler into the laboratory building and through the surgical theatre, with its lumber[3] of crates and bottles, to the foot of the stair. Here Poole motioned him to stand on one side and listen; while he himself, setting down the candle and making a great and obvious call on his resolution, mounted the steps and knocked with a somewhat uncertain hand on the red baize of the cabinet door.

"Mr. Utterson, sir, asking to see you," he called; and even as he did so, once more violently signed to the lawyer to give ear.

A voice answered from within: "Tell him I cannot see anyone," it said complainingly.

"Thank you, sir," said Poole, with a note of something like triumph in his voice; and taking up his candle, he led Mr. Utterson back across the yard and into the great kitchen, where the fire was out and the beetles were leaping on the floor.

"Sir," he said, looking Mr. Utterson in the eyes, "was that my master's voice?"

"It seems much changed," replied the lawyer, very pale, but giving look for look.

"Changed? Well, yes, I think so," said the butler. "Have I been twenty years in this man's house, to be deceived about his voice? No, sir; master's made away with; he was made away with, eight days ago, when we heard him cry out upon the name of God; and *who's* in there instead of him, and *why* it stays there, is a thing that cries to Heaven, Mr. Utterson!"

"This is a very strange tale, Poole; this is rather a wild tale, my man," said Mr. Utterson, biting his finger. "Suppose it were as you suppose, supposing Dr. Jekyll to have been—well, murdered, what could induce the murderer to stay? That won't hold water; it doesn't commend itself to reason."

"Well, Mr. Utterson, you are a hard man to satisfy, but I'll do it yet," said Poole. "All this last week (you must know) him, or it, or whatever it is that lives in that cabinet, has been crying night and day for some sort of medicine and cannot get it to his mind. It was sometimes his way—the master's, that is—to write his orders on a sheet of paper and throw it on the stair. We've had nothing else this week back; nothing but papers, and a closed door, and the very meals left there to be smuggled in when nobody was looking. Well, sir, every day, ay, and twice and thrice in the same day, there have been orders and complaints, and I have been sent flying to all the wholesale chemists in town. Every time I brought the stuff back, there would be another paper telling me to return it, because it was not pure, and another order to a different firm. This drug is wanted bitter bad, sir, whatever for."

"Have you any of these papers?" asked Mr. Utterson.

Poole felt in his pocket and handed out a crumpled note, which the lawyer, bending nearer to the candle, carefully examined. Its contents ran thus: "Dr. Jekyll presents his compliments to Messrs. Maw. He assures them that their last sample is impure and quite useless for his present purpose. In the year

---

3. Stored accumulation.

18—, Dr. J. purchased a somewhat large quantity from Messrs. M. He now begs them to search with the most sedulous care, and should any of the same quality be left, to forward it to him at once. Expense is no consideration. The importance of this to Dr. J. can hardly be exaggerated." So far the letter had run composedly enough, but here with a sudden splutter of the pen, the writer's emotion had broken loose. "For God's sake," he had added, "find me some of the old."

"This is a strange note," said Mr. Utterson; and then sharply, "How do you come to have it open?"

"The man at Maw's was main angry, sir, and he threw it back to me like so much dirt," returned Poole.

"This is unquestionably the doctor's hand, do you know?" resumed the lawyer.

"I thought it looked like it," said the servant rather sulkily; and then, with another voice, "But what matters hand of write?" he said. "I've seen him!"

"Seen him?" repeated Mr. Utterson. "Well?"

"That's it!" said Poole. "It was this way. I came suddenly into the theatre from the garden. It seems he had slipped out to look for this drug or whatever it is; for the cabinet door was open, and there he was at the far end of the room digging among the crates. He looked up when I came in, gave a kind of cry, and whipped upstairs into the cabinet. It was but for one minute that I saw him, but the hair stood upon my head like quills. Sir, if that was my master, why had he a mask upon his face? If it was my master, why did he cry out like a rat, and run from me? I have served him long enough. And then . . ." The man paused and passed his hand over his face.

"These are all very strange circumstances," said Mr. Utterson, "but I think I begin to see daylight. Your master, Poole, is plainly seized with one of those maladies that both torture and deform the sufferer; hence, for aught I know, the alteration of his voice; hence the mask and the avoidance of his friends; hence his eagerness to find this drug, by means of which the poor soul retains some hope of ultimate recovery—God grant that he be not deceived! There is my explanation; it is sad enough, Poole, ay, and appalling to consider; but it is plain and natural, hangs well together, and delivers us from all exorbitant alarms."

"Sir," said the butler, turning to a sort of mottled pallor, "that thing was not my master, and there's the truth. My master"—here he looked round him and began to whisper—"is a tall, fine build of a man, and this was more of a dwarf." Utterson attempted to protest. "O, sir," cried Poole, "do you think I do not know my master after twenty years? Do you think I do not know where his head comes to in the cabinet door, where I saw him every morning of my life? No, sir, that thing in the mask was never Dr. Jekyll—God knows what it was, but it was never Dr. Jekyll; and it is the belief of my heart that there was murder done."

"Poole," replied the lawyer, "if you say that, it will become my duty to make certain. Much as I desire to spare your master's feelings, much as I am puzzled by this note which seems to prove him to be still alive, I shall consider it my duty to break in that door."

"Ah, Mr. Utterson, that's talking!" cried the butler.

"And now comes the second question," resumed Utterson: "Who is going to do it?"

"Why, you and me," was the undaunted reply.

"That's very well said," returned the lawyer; "and whatever comes of it, I shall make it my business to see you are no loser."

"There is an axe in the theatre," continued Poole; "and you might take the kitchen poker for yourself."

The lawyer took that rude but weighty instrument into his hand, and balanced it. "Do you know, Poole," he said, looking up, "that you and I are about to place ourselves in a position of some peril?"

"You may say so, sir, indeed," returned the butler.

"It is well, then, that we should be frank," said the other. "We both think more than we have said; let us make a clean breast. This masked figure that you saw, did you recognise it?"

"Well, sir, it went so quick, and the creature was so doubled up, that I could hardly swear to that," was the answer. "But if you mean, was it Mr. Hyde?— why, yes, I think it was! You see, it was much of the same bigness; and it had the same quick, light way with it; and then who else could have got in by the laboratory door? You have not forgot, sir, that at the time of the murder he had still the key with him? But that's not all. I don't know, Mr. Utterson, if ever you met this Mr. Hyde?"

"Yes," said the lawyer, "I once spoke with him."

"Then you must know as well as the rest of us that there was something queer about that gentleman—something that gave a man a turn—I don't know rightly how to say it, sir, beyond this: that you felt it in your marrow kind of cold and thin."

"I own I felt something of what you describe," said Mr. Utterson.

"Quite so, sir," returned Poole. "Well, when that masked thing like a monkey jumped from among the chemicals and whipped into the cabinet, it went down my spine like ice. O, I know it's not evidence, Mr. Utterson; I'm book-learned enough for that; but a man has his feelings, and I give you my bible-word it was Mr. Hyde!"

"Ay, ay," said the lawyer. "My fears incline to the same point. Evil, I fear, founded—evil was sure to come—of that connection. Ay, truly, I believe you; I believe poor Harry is killed; and I believe his murderer (for what purpose, God alone can tell) is still lurking in his victim's room. Well, let our name be vengeance. Call Bradshaw."

The footman came at the summons, very white and nervous.

"Pull yourself together, Bradshaw," said the lawyer. "This suspense, I know, is telling upon all of you; but it is now our intention to make an end of it. Poole, here, and I are going to force our way into the cabinet. If all is well, my shoulders are broad enough to bear the blame. Meanwhile, lest anything should really be amiss, or any malefactor seek to escape by the back, you and the boy must go round the corner with a pair of good sticks and take your post at the laboratory door. We give you ten minutes, to get to your stations."

As Bradshaw left, the lawyer looked at his watch. "And now, Poole, let us get to ours," he said; and taking the poker under his arm, led the way into the yard. The scud[4] had banked over the moon, and it was now quite dark. The wind, which only broke in puffs and draughts into that deep well of building, tossed the light of the candle to and fro about their steps, until they came into the shelter of the theatre, where they sat down silently to wait. London hummed solemnly all around; but nearer at hand, the stillness was only broken

4. Loose clouds driven rapidly before the wind.

by the sounds of a footfall moving to and fro along the cabinet floor.

"So it will walk all day, sir," whispered Poole; "ay, and the better part of the night. Only when a new sample comes from the chemist, there's a bit of a break. Ah, it's an ill-conscience that's such an enemy to rest! Ah, sir, there's blood foully shed in every step of it! But hark again, a little closer—put your heart in your ears, Mr. Utterson, and tell me, is that the doctor's foot?"

The steps fell lightly and oddly, with a certain swing, for all they went so slowly; it was different indeed from the heavy creaking tread of Henry Jekyll. Utterson sighed. "Is there never anything else?" he asked.

Poole nodded. "Once," he said. "Once I heard it weeping!"

"Weeping? how that?" said the lawyer, conscious of a sudden chill of horror.

"Weeping like a woman or a lost soul," said the butler. "I came away with that upon my heart, that I could have wept too."

But now the ten minutes drew to an end. Poole disinterred the axe from under a stack of packing straw; the candle was set upon the nearest table to light them to the attack; and they drew near with bated breath to where that patient foot was still going up and down, up and down, in the quiet of the night.

"Jekyll," cried Utterson, with a loud voice, "I demand to see you." He paused a moment, but there came no reply. "I give you fair warning, our suspicions are aroused, and I must and shall see you," he resumed; "if not by fair means, then by foul—if not of your consent, then by brute force!"

"Utterson," said the voice, "for God's sake, have mercy!"

"Ah, that's not Jekyll's voice—it's Hyde's!" cried Utterson. "Down with the door, Poole!"

Poole swung the axe over his shoulder; the blow shook the building, and the red baize door leaped against the lock and hinges. A dismal screech, as of mere animal terror, rang from the cabinet. Up went the axe again, and again the panels crashed and the frame bounded; four times the blow fell; but the wood was tough and the fittings were of excellent workmanship; and it was not until the fifth, that the lock burst in sunder and the wreck of the door fell inwards on the carpet.

The besiegers, appalled by their own riot and the stillness that had succeeded, stood back a little and peered in. There lay the cabinet before their eyes in the quiet lamplight, a good fire glowing and chattering on the hearth, the kettle singing its thin strain, a drawer or two open, papers neatly set forth on the business table, and nearer the fire, the things laid out for tea: the quietest room, you would have said, and, but for the glazed presses full of chemicals, the most commonplace that night in London.

Right in the midst there lay the body of a man sorely contorted and still twitching. They drew near on tip-toe, turned it on its back and beheld the face of Edward Hyde. He was dressed in clothes far too large for him, clothes of the doctor's bigness; the cords of his face still moved with a semblance of life, but life was quite gone: and by the crushed phial in the hand and the strong smell of kernels[5] that hung upon the air, Utterson knew that he was looking on the body of a self-destroyer.

"We have come too late," he said sternly, "whether to save or punish. Hyde is gone to his account; and it only remains for us to find the body of your master."

5. I.e., pits: cyanide smells of bitter almond or of peach pits.

The far greater proportion of the building was occupied by the theatre, which filled almost the whole ground story and was lighted from above, and by the cabinet, which formed an upper story at one end and looked upon the court. A corridor joined the theatre to the door on the by-street; and with this the cabinet communicated separately by a second flight of stairs. There were besides a few dark closets and a spacious cellar. All these they now thoroughly examined. Each closet needed but a glance, for all were empty, and all, by the dust that fell from their doors, had stood long unopened. The cellar, indeed, was filled with crazy lumber, mostly dating from the times of the surgeon who was Jekyll's predecessor; but even as they opened the door they were advertised of the uselessness of further search, by the fall of a perfect mat of cobweb which had for years sealed up the entrance. Nowhere was there any trace of Henry Jekyll, dead or alive.

Poole stamped on the flags of the corridor. "He must be buried here," he said, hearkening to the sound.

"Or he may have fled," said Utterson, and he turned to examine the door in the by-street. It was locked; and lying near by on the flags, they found the key, already stained with rust.

"This does not look like use," observed the lawyer.

"Use!" echoed Poole. "Do you not see, sir, it is broken? much as if a man had stamped on it."

"Ay," continued Utterson, "and the fractures, too, are rusty." The two men looked at each other with a scare. "This is beyond me, Poole," said the lawyer. "Let us go back to the cabinet."

They mounted the stair in silence, and still with an occasional awestruck glance at the dead body, proceeded more thoroughly to examine the contents of the cabinet. At one table, there were traces of chemical work, various measured heaps of some white salt being laid on glass saucers, as though for an experiment in which the unhappy man had been prevented.

"That is the same drug that I was always bringing him," said Poole; and even as he spoke, the kettle with a startling noise boiled over.

This brought them to the fireside, where the easy-chair was drawn cosily up, and the tea things stood ready to the sitter's elbow, the very sugar in the cup. There were several books on a shelf; one lay beside the tea things open, and Utterson was amazed to find it a copy of a pious work, for which Jekyll had several times expressed a great esteem, annotated, in his own hand, with startling blasphemies.

Next, in the course of their review of the chamber, the searchers came to the cheval glass, into whose depths they looked with an involuntary horror. But it was so turned as to show them nothing but the rosy glow playing on the roof, the fire sparkling in a hundred repetitions along the glazed front of the presses, and their own pale and fearful countenances stooping to look in.

"This glass have seen some strange things, sir," whispered Poole.

"And surely none stranger than itself," echoed the lawyer in the same tones. "For what did Jekyll"—he caught himself up at the word with a start, and then conquering the weakness—"what could Jekyll want with it?" he said.

"You may say that!" said Poole.

Next they turned to the business table. On the desk, among the neat array of papers, a large envelope was uppermost, and bore, in the doctor's hand, the name of Mr. Utterson. The lawyer unsealed it, and several enclosures fell to the floor. The first was a will, drawn in the same eccentric terms as the one which he had returned six months before, to serve as a testament in case of death and as a deed of gift in case of disappearance; but in place of the name of Edward Hyde, the lawyer, with indescribable amazement, read the name of Gabriel John Utterson. He looked at Poole, and then back at the paper, and last of all at the dead malefactor stretched upon the carpet.

"My head goes round," he said. "He has been all these days in possession; he had no cause to like me; he must have raged to see himself displaced; and he has not destroyed this document."

He caught up the next paper; it was a brief note in the doctor's hand and dated at the top. "O Poole!" the lawyer cried, "he was alive and here this day. He cannot have been disposed of in so short a space; he must be still alive, he must have fled! And then, why fled? and how? and in that case, can we venture to declare this suicide? O, we must be careful. I foresee that we may yet involve your master in some dire catastrophe."

"Why don't you read it, sir?" asked Poole.

"Because I fear," replied the lawyer solemnly. "God grant I have no cause for it!" And with that he brought the paper to his eyes and read as follows:

"MY DEAR UTTERSON,—When this shall fall into your hands, I shall have disappeared, under what circumstances I have not the penetration to foresee, but my instinct and all the circumstances of my nameless situation tell me that the end is sure and must be early. Go then, and first read the narrative which Lanyon warned me he was to place in your hands; and if you care to hear more, turn to the confession of

"Your unworthy and unhappy friend,
"HENRY JEKYLL."

"There was a third enclosure?" asked Utterson.

"Here, sir," said Poole, and gave into his hands a considerable packet sealed in several places.

The lawyer put it in his pocket. "I would say nothing of this paper. If your master has fled or is dead, we may at least save his credit. It is now ten; I must go home and read these documents in quiet; but I shall be back before midnight, when we shall send for the police."

They went out, locking the door of the theatre behind them; and Utterson, once more leaving the servants gathered about the fire in the hall, trudged back to his office to read the two narratives in which this mystery was now to be explained.

Dr. Lanyon's Narrative

On the ninth of January, now four days ago, I received by the evening delivery a registered envelope, addressed in the hand of my colleague and old school-companion, Henry Jekyll. I was a good deal surprised by this; for we were by no means in the habit of correspondence; I had seen the man, dined with him, indeed, the night before; and I could imagine nothing in our intercourse that should justify formality of registration. The contents increased my wonder; for this is how the letter ran:

"10th December, 18—

"Dear Lanyon,—You are one of my oldest friends; and although we may have differed at times on scientific questions, I cannot remember, at least on my side, any break in our affection. There was never a day when, if you had said to me, 'Jekyll, my life, my honour, my reason, depend upon you,' I would not have sacrificed my left hand to help you. Lanyon, my life, my honour, my reason, are all at your mercy; if you fail me to-night I am lost. You might suppose, after this preface, that I am going to ask you for something dishonourable to grant. Judge for yourself.

"I want you to postpone all other engagements for to-night—ay, even if you were summoned to the bedside of an emperor; to take a cab, unless your carriage should be actually at the door; and with this letter in your hand for consultation, to drive straight to my house. Poole, my butler, has his orders; you will find him waiting your arrival with a locksmith. The door of my cabinet is then to be forced: and you are to go in alone; to open the glazed press (letter E) on the left hand, breaking the lock if it be shut; and to draw out, *with all its contents as they stand*, the fourth drawer from the top or (which is the same thing) the third from the bottom. In my extreme distress of mind, I have a morbid fear of misdirecting you; but even if I am in error, you may know the right drawer by its contents: some powders, a phial and a paper book. This drawer I beg of you to carry back with you to Cavendish Square exactly as it stands.

"That is the first part of the service: now for the second. You should be back, if you set out at once on the receipt of this, long before midnight; but I will leave you that amount of margin, not only in the fear of one of those obstacles that can neither be prevented nor foreseen, but because an hour when your servants are in bed is to be preferred for what will then remain to do. At midnight, then, I have to ask you to be alone in your consulting room, to admit with your own hand into the house a man who will present himself in my name, and to place in his hands the drawer that you will have brought with you from my cabinet. Then you will have played your part and earned my gratitude completely. Five minutes afterwards, if you insist upon an explanation, you will have understood that these arrangements are of capital importance; and that by the neglect of one of them, fantastic as they must appear, you might have charged your conscience with my death or the shipwreck of my reason.

"Confident as I am that you will not trifle with this appeal, my heart sinks and my hand trembles at the bare thought of such a possibility. Think of me at this hour, in a strange place, labouring under a blackness of distress that no fancy can exaggerate, and yet well aware that, if you will but punctually serve me, my troubles will roll away like a story that is told. Serve me, my dear Lanyon, and save

"Your friend,
H. J."

"P. S.—I had already sealed this up when a fresh terror struck upon my soul. It is possible that the post-office may fail me, and this letter not come into your hands until to-morrow morning. In that case, dear Lanyon, do my errand when it shall be most convenient for you in the course of the day; and once more expect my messenger at midnight. It may then already be too late; and if that night passes without event, you will know that you have seen the last of Henry Jekyll."

Upon the reading of this letter, I made sure my colleague was insane; but till that was proved beyond the possibility of doubt, I felt bound to do as he requested. The less I understood of this farrago,[6] the less I was in a position to judge of its importance; and an appeal so worded could not be set aside without a grave responsibility. I rose accordingly from table, got into a hansom, and drove straight to Jekyll's house. The butler was awaiting my arrival; he had received by the same post as mine a registered letter of instruction, and had sent at once for a locksmith and a carpenter. The tradesmen came while we were yet speaking; and we moved in a body to old Dr. Denman's surgical theatre, from which (as you are doubtless aware) Jekyll's private cabinet is most conveniently entered. The door was very strong, the lock excellent; the carpenter avowed he would have great trouble and have to do much damage, if force were to be used; and the locksmith was near despair. But this last was a handy fellow, and after two hours' work, the door stood open. The press marked E was unlocked; and I took out the drawer, had it filled up with straw and tied in a sheet, and returned with it to Cavendish Square.

Here I proceeded to examine its contents. The powders were neatly enough made up, but not with the nicety of the dispensing chemist; so that it was plain they were of Jekyll's private manufacture: and when I opened one of the wrappers I found what seemed to me a simple crystalline salt of a white colour. The phial, to which I next turned my attention, might have been about half full of a blood-red liquor, which was highly pungent to the sense of smell and seemed to me to contain phosphorus and some volatile ether. At the other ingredients I could make no guess. The book was an ordinary version book[7] and contained little but a series of dates. These covered a period of many years, but I observed that the entries ceased nearly a year ago and quite abruptly. Here and there a brief remark was appended to a date, usually no more than a single word: "double" occurring perhaps six times in a total of several hundred entries; and once very early in the list and followed by several marks of exclamation, "total failure!!!" All this, though it whetted my curiosity, told me little that was definite. Here were a phial of some tincture, a paper of some salt, and the record of a series of experiments that had led (like too many of Jekyll's investigations) to no end of practical usefulness. How could the presence of these articles in my house affect either the honour, the sanity, or the life of my flighty colleague? If his messenger could go to one place, why could he not go to another? And even granting some impediment, why was this gentleman to be received by me in secret? The more I reflected the more convinced I grew that I was dealing with a case of cerebral disease; and though I dismissed my servants to bed, I loaded an old revolver, that I might be found in some posture of self-defence.

Twelve o'clock had scarce rung out over London, ere the knocker sounded very gently on the door. I went myself at the summons, and found a small man crouching against the pillars of the portico.

"Are you come from Dr. Jekyll?" I asked.

He told me "yes" by a constrained gesture; and when I had bidden him

6. Mixture.

7. School notebook used to record translations.

enter, he did not obey me without a searching backward glance into the dark-ness of the square. There was a policeman not far off, advancing with his bull's eye[8] open; and at the sight, I thought my visitor started and made greater haste.

These particulars struck me, I confess, disagreeably; and as I followed him into the bright light of the consulting room, I kept my hand ready on my weapon. Here, at last, I had a chance of clearly seeing him. I had never set eyes on him before, so much was certain. He was small, as I have said; I was struck besides with the shocking expression of his face, with his remarkable combination of great muscular activity and great apparent debility of consti-tution, and—last but not least—with the odd, subjective disturbance caused by his neighbourhood. This bore some resemblance to incipient rigour,[9] and was accompanied by a marked sinking of the pulse. At the time, I set it down to some idiosyncratic, personal distaste, and merely wondered at the acuteness of the symptoms; but I have since had reason to believe the cause to lie much deeper in the nature of man, and to turn on some nobler hinge than the principle of hatred.

This person (who had thus, from the first moment of his entrance, struck in me what I can only describe as a disgustful curiosity) was dressed in a fashion that would have made an ordinary person laughable; his clothes, that is to say, although they were of rich and sober fabric, were enormously too large for him in every measurement—the trousers hanging on his legs and rolled up to keep them from the ground, the waist of the coat below his haunches, and the collar sprawling wide upon his shoulders. Strange to relate, this ludicrous accoutrement was far from moving me to laughter. Rather, as there was something abnormal and misbegotten in the very essence of the creature that now faced me—something seizing,[1] surprising and revolting— this fresh disparity seemed but to fit in with and to reinforce it; so that to my interest in the man's nature and character, there was added a curiosity as to his origin, his life, his fortune and status in the world.

These observations, though they have taken so great a space to be set down in, were yet the work of a few seconds. My visitor was, indeed, on fire with sombre excitement.

"Have you got it?" he cried. "Have you got it?" And so lively was his impa-tience that he even laid his hand upon my arm and sought to shake me.

I put him back, conscious at his touch of a certain icy pang along my blood. "Come, sir," said I. "You forget that I have not yet the pleasure of your acquain-tance. Be seated, if you please." And I showed him an example, and sat down myself in my customary seat and with as fair an imitation of my ordinary manner to a patient, as the lateness of the hour, the nature of my preoccu-pations, and the horror I had of my visitor, would suffer me to muster.

"I beg your pardon, Dr. Lanyon," he replied civilly enough. "What you say is very well founded; and my impatience has shown its heels to my politeness. I come here at the instance[2] of your colleague, Dr. Henry Jekyll, on a piece of business of some moment; and I understood . . ." He paused and put his hand to his throat, and I could see, in spite of his collected manner, that he was wrestling against the approaches of the hysteria—"I understood, a drawer . . ."

But here I took pity on my visitor's suspense, and some perhaps on my own growing curiosity.

8. Sliding door of his lantern.
9. Sudden chill.

1. Powerfully impressive.
2. Request.

"There it is, sir," said I, pointing to the drawer, where it lay on the floor behind a table and still covered with the sheet.

He sprang to it, and then paused, and laid his hand upon his heart: I could hear his teeth grate with the convulsive action of his jaws; and his face was so ghastly to see that I grew alarmed both for his life and reason.

"Compose yourself," said I.

He turned a dreadful smile to me, and as if with the decision of despair, plucked away the sheet. At sight of the contents, he uttered one loud sob of such immense relief that I sat petrified. And the next moment, in a voice that was already fairly well under control, "Have you a graduated[3] glass?" he asked.

I rose from my place with something of an effort and gave him what he asked.

He thanked me with a smiling nod, measured out a few minims[4] of the red tincture and added one of the powders. The mixture, which was at first of a reddish hue, began, in proportion as the crystals melted, to brighten in colour, to effervesce audibly, and to throw off small fumes of vapour. Suddenly and at the same moment, the ebullition[5] ceased and the compound changed to a dark purple, which faded again more slowly to a watery green. My visitor, who had watched these metamorphoses with a keen eye, smiled, set down the glass upon the table, and then turned and looked upon me with an air of scrutiny.

"And now," said he, "to settle what remains. Will you be wise? will you be guided? will you suffer me to take this glass in my hand and to go forth from your house without further parley? or has the greed of curiosity too much command of you? Think before you answer, for it shall be done as you decide. As you decide, you shall be left as you were before, and neither richer nor wiser, unless the sense of service rendered to a man in mortal distress may be counted as a kind of riches of the soul. Or, if you shall so prefer to choose, a new province of knowledge and new avenues to fame and power shall be laid open to you, here, in this room, upon the instant; and your sight shall be blasted by a prodigy to stagger the unbelief of Satan."

"Sir," said I, affecting a coolness that I was far from truly possessing, "you speak enigmas, and you will perhaps not wonder that I hear you with no very strong impression of belief. But I have gone too far in the way of inexplicable services to pause before I see the end."

"It is well," replied my visitor. "Lanyon, you remember your vows: what follows is under the seal of our profession. And now, you who have so long been bound to the most narrow and material views, you who have denied the virtue of transcendental medicine, you who have derided your superiors—behold!"

He put the glass to his lips and drank at one gulp. A cry followed; he reeled, staggered, clutched at the table and held on, staring with injected[6] eyes, gasping with open mouth; and as I looked there came, I thought, a change—he seemed to swell—his face became suddenly black and the features seemed to melt and alter—and the next moment, I had sprung to my feet and leaped back against the wall, my arm raised to shield me from that prodigy, my mind submerged in terror.

"O God!" I screamed, and "O God!" again and again; for there before my

3. Marked with lines to indicate quantities.
4. Drops (a minim is a liquid measure equal to ¹⁄₄₈₀th of an ounce).
5. Bubbling.
6. Swollen.

eyes—pale and shaken, and half fainting, and groping before him with his hands, like a man restored from death—there stood Henry Jekyll!

What he told me in the next hour, I cannot bring my mind to set on paper. I saw what I saw, I heard what I heard, and my soul sickened at it; and yet now when that sight has faded from my eyes, I ask myself if I believe it, and I cannot answer. My life is shaken to its roots; sleep has left me; the deadliest terror sits by me at all hours of the day and night; I feel that my days are numbered, and that I must die; and yet I shall die incredulous. As for the moral turpitude that man unveiled to me, even with tears of penitence, I cannot, even in memory, dwell on it without a start of horror. I will say but one thing, Utterson, and that (if you can bring your mind to credit it) will be more than enough. The creature who crept into my house that night was, on Jekyll's own confession, known by the name of Hyde and hunted for in every corner of the land as the murderer of Carew.

HASTIE LANYON.

Henry Jekyll's Full Statement of the Case

I was born in the year 18— to a large fortune, endowed besides with excellent parts,[7] inclined by nature to industry, fond of the respect of the wise and good among my fellow-men, and thus, as might have been supposed, with every guarantee of an honourable and distinguished future. And indeed the worst of my faults was a certain impatient gaiety of disposition, such as has made the happiness of many, but such as I found it hard to reconcile with my imperious desire to carry my head high, and wear a more than commonly grave countenance before the public. Hence it came about that I concealed my pleasures; and that when I reached years of reflection, and began to look round me and take stock of my progress and position in the world, I stood already committed to a profound duplicity of life. Many a man would have even blazoned such irregularities as I was guilty of; but from the high views that I had set before me, I regarded and hid them with an almost morbid sense of shame. It was thus rather the exacting nature of my aspirations than any particular degradation in my faults, that made me what I was, and, with even a deeper trench than in the majority of men, severed in me those provinces of good and ill which divide and compound man's dual nature. In this case, I was driven to reflect deeply and inveterately on that hard law of life, which lies at the root of religion and is one of the most plentiful springs of distress. Though so profound a double-dealer, I was in no sense a hypocrite; both sides of me were in dead earnest; I was no more myself when I laid aside restraint and plunged in shame, than when I laboured, in the eye of day, at the furtherance of knowledge or the relief of sorrow and suffering. And it chanced that the direction of my scientific studies, which led wholly towards the mystic and the transcendental, reacted and shed a strong light on this consciousness of the perennial war among my members. With every day, and from both sides of my intelligence, the moral and the intellectual, I thus drew steadily nearer to that truth, by whose partial discovery I have been doomed to such a dreadful shipwreck: that man is not truly one, but truly two. I say two, because the state of my own knowledge does not pass beyond that point. Others will follow, others

7. Abilities.

will outstrip me on the same lines; and I hazard the guess that man will be ultimately known for a mere polity of multifarious, incongruous and independent denizens. I for my part, from the nature of my life, advanced infallibly in one direction and in one direction only. It was on the moral side, and in my own person, that I learned to recognise the thorough and primitive duality of man; I saw that, of the two natures that contended in the field of my consciousness, even if I could rightly be said to be either, it was only because I was radically both; and from an early date, even before the course of my scientific discoveries had begun to suggest the most naked possibility of such a miracle, I had learned to dwell with pleasure, as a beloved day-dream, on the thought of the separation of these elements. If each, I told myself, could but be housed in separate identities, life would be relieved of all that was unbearable; the unjust might go his way, delivered from the aspirations and remorse of his more upright twin; and the just could walk steadfastly and securely on his upward path, doing the good things in which he found his pleasure, and no longer exposed to disgrace and penitence by the hands of this extraneous evil. It was the curse of mankind that these incongruous faggots[8] were thus bound together—that in the agonised womb of consciousness, these polar twins should be continuously struggling. How, then, were they dissociated?

I was so far in my reflections when, as I have said, a side light began to shine upon the subject from the laboratory table. I began to perceive more deeply than it has ever yet been stated, the trembling immateriality, the mist-like transience, of this seemingly so solid body in which we walk attired. Certain agents I found to have the power to shake and to pluck back that fleshly vestment, even as a wind might toss the curtains of a pavilion. For two good reasons, I will not enter deeply into this scientific branch of my confession. First, because I have been made to learn that the doom and burthen of our life is bound forever on man's shoulders, and when the attempt is made to cast it off, it but returns upon us with more unfamiliar and more awful pressure. Second, because, as my narrative will make, alas! too evident, my discoveries were incomplete. Enough, then, that I not only recognised my natural body for the mere aura and effulgence of certain of the powers that made up my spirit, but managed to compound a drug by which these powers should be dethroned from their supremacy, and a second form and countenance substituted, none the less natural to me because they were the expression, and bore the stamp, of lower elements in my soul.

I hesitated long before I put this theory to the test of practice. I knew well that I risked death; for any drug that so potently controlled and shook the very fortress of identity, might by the least scruple[9] of an overdose or at the least inopportunity in the moment of exhibition, utterly blot out that immaterial tabernacle which I looked to it to change. But the temptation of a discovery so singular and profound, at last overcame the suggestions of alarm. I had long since prepared my tincture; I purchased at once, from a firm of wholesale chemists, a large quantity of a particular salt which I knew, from my experiments, to be the last ingredient required; and late one accursed night, I compounded the elements, watched them boil and smoke together in the glass, and when the ebullition had subsided, with a strong glow of courage, drank off the potion.

8. Bundles of sticks used for fuel.
9. A minute amount (literally, an apothecaries' weight equal to about 1.3 grams).

The most racking pangs succeeded: a grinding in the bones, deadly nausea, and a horror of the spirit that cannot be exceeded at the hour of birth or death. Then these agonies began swiftly to subside, and I came to myself as if out of a great sickness. There was something strange in my sensations, something indescribably new and, from its very novelty, incredibly sweet. I felt younger, lighter, happier in body; within I was conscious of a heady recklessness, a current of disordered sensual images running like a mill race[1] in my fancy, a solution of the bonds of obligation, an unknown but not an innocent freedom of the soul. I knew myself, at the first breath of this new life, to be more wicked, tenfold more wicked, sold a slave to my original evil; and the thought, in that moment, braced and delighted me like wine. I stretched out my hands, exulting in the freshness of these sensations; and in the act, I was suddenly aware that I had lost in stature.

There was no mirror, at that date, in my room; that which stands beside me as I write, was brought there later on and for the very purpose of these trans-formations. The night, however, was far gone into the morning—the morning, black as it was, was nearly ripe for the conception of the day—the inmates of my house were locked in the most rigorous hours of slumber; and I deter-mined, flushed as I was with hope and triumph, to venture in my new shape as far as to my bedroom. I crossed the yard, wherein the constellations looked down upon me, I could have thought, with wonder, the first creature of that sort that their unsleeping vigilance had yet disclosed to them; I stole through the corridors, a stranger in my own house; and coming to my room, I saw for the first time the appearance of Edward Hyde.

I must here speak by theory alone, saying not that which I know, but that which I suppose to be most probable. The evil side of my nature, to which I had now transferred the stamping efficacy, was less robust and less developed than the good which I had just deposed. Again, in the course of my life, which had been, after all, nine-tenths a life of effort, virtue and control, it had been much less exercised and much less exhausted. And hence, as I think, it came about that Edward Hyde was so much smaller, slighter and younger than Henry Jekyll. Even as good shone upon the countenance of the one, evil was written broadly and plainly on the face of the other. Evil besides (which I must still believe to be the lethal side of man) had left on that body an imprint of deformity and decay. And yet when I looked upon that ugly idol in the glass, I was conscious of no repugnance, rather of a leap of welcome. This, too, was myself. It seemed natural and human. In my eyes it bore a livelier image of the spirit, it seemed more express and single, than the imperfect and divided countenance I had been hitherto accustomed to call mine. And in so far I was doubtless right. I have observed that when I wore the semblance of Edward Hyde, none could come near to me at first without a visible misgiving of the flesh. This, as I take it, was because all human beings, as we meet them, are commingled out of good and evil: and Edward Hyde, alone in the ranks of mankind, was pure evil.

I lingered but a moment at the mirror: the second and conclusive experiment had yet to be attempted; it yet remained to be seen if I had lost my identity beyond redemption and must flee before daylight from a house that was no longer mine; and hurrying back to my cabinet, I once more prepared and drank

1. Water current that drives a mill wheel.

the cup, once more suffered the pangs of dissolution, and came to myself once more with the character, the stature and the face of Henry Jekyll.

That night I had come to the fatal cross roads. Had I approached my discovery in a more noble spirit, had I risked the experiment while under the empire of generous or pious aspirations, all must have been otherwise, and from these agonies of death and birth, I had come forth an angel instead of a fiend. The drug had no discriminating action; it was neither diabolical nor divine; it but shook the doors of the prison-house of my disposition; and like the captives of Philippi, that which stood within ran forth.[2] At that time my virtue slumbered; my evil, kept awake by ambition, was alert and swift to seize the occasion; and the thing that was projected was Edward Hyde. Hence, although I had now two characters as well as two appearances, one was wholly evil, and the other was still the old Henry Jekyll, that incongruous compound of whose reformation and improvement I had already learned to despair. The movement was thus wholly towards the worse.

Even at that time, I had not yet conquered my aversion to the dryness of a life of study. I would still be merrily disposed at times; and as my pleasures were (to say the least) undignified, and I was not only well known and highly considered, but growing towards the elderly man, this incoherency of my life was daily growing more unwelcome. It was on this side that my new power tempted me until I fell in slavery. I had but to drink the cup, to doff at once the body of the noted professor, and to assume, like a thick cloak, that of Edward Hyde. I smiled at the notion; it seemed to me at the time to be humorous; and I made my preparations with the most studious care. I took and furnished that house in Soho, to which Hyde was tracked by the police; and engaged as housekeeper a creature whom I well knew to be silent and unscrupulous. On the other side, I announced to my servants that a Mr. Hyde (whom I described) was to have full liberty and power about my house in the square; and to parry mishaps, I even called and made myself a familiar object, in my second character. I next drew up that will to which you so much objected; so that if anything befell me in the person of Dr. Jekyll, I could enter on that of Edward Hyde without pecuniary loss. And thus fortified, as I supposed, on every side, I began to profit by the strange immunities of my position.

Men have before hired bravos[3] to transact their crimes, while their own person and reputation sat under shelter. I was the first that ever did so for his pleasures. I was the first that could thus plod in the public eye with a load of genial respectability, and in a moment, like a schoolboy, strip off these lendings[4] and spring headlong into the sea of liberty. But for me, in my impenetrable mantle, the safety was complete. Think of it—I did not even exist! Let me but escape into my laboratory door, give me but a second or two to mix and swallow the draught that I had always standing ready; and whatever he had done, Edward Hyde would pass away like the stain of breath upon a mirror; and there in his stead, quietly at home, trimming the midnight lamp in his study, a man who could afford to laugh at suspicion, would be Henry Jekyll.

2. Cf. Acts 16.26: when the apostle Paul and his friend Silas were imprisoned at Philippi, a city in eastern Macedonia, an earthquake freed all the prisoners (none of whom fled).

3. Thugs.
4. Borrowed clothing; a reference to King Lear's cry on the heath "Off, off you lendings!" (Shakespeare, King Lear 3.4.97).

The pleasures which I made haste to seek in my disguise were, as I have said, undignified; I would scarce use a harder term. But in the hands of Edward Hyde, they soon began to turn towards the monstrous. When I would come back from these excursions, I was often plunged into a kind of wonder at my vicarious depravity. This familiar[5] that I called out of my own soul, and sent forth alone to do his good pleasure, was a being inherently malign and villainous; his every act and thought centered on self; drinking pleasure with bestial avidity from any degree of torture to another; relentless like a man of stone. Henry Jekyll stood at times aghast before the acts of Edward Hyde; but the situation was apart from ordinary laws, and insidiously relaxed the grasp of conscience. It was Hyde, after all, and Hyde alone, that was guilty. Jekyll was no worse; he woke again to his good qualities seemingly unimpaired; he would even make haste, where it was possible, to undo the evil done by Hyde. And thus his conscience slumbered.

Into the details of the infamy at which I thus connived (for even now I can scarce grant that I committed it) I have no design of entering; I mean but to point out the warnings and the successive steps with which my chastisement approached. I met with one accident which, as it brought on no consequence, I shall no more than mention. An act of cruelty to a child aroused against me the anger of a passer-by, whom I recognised the other day in the person of your kinsman; the doctor and the child's family joined him; there were moments when I feared for my life; and at last, in order to pacify their too just resentment, Edward Hyde had to bring them to the door, and pay them in a cheque drawn in the name of Henry Jekyll. But this danger was easily eliminated from the future, by opening an account at another bank in the name of Edward Hyde himself; and when, by sloping my own hand backward, I had supplied my double with a signature, I thought I sat beyond the reach of fate.

Some two months before the murder of Sir Danvers, I had been out for one of my adventures, had returned at a late hour, and woke the next day in bed with somewhat odd sensations. It was in vain I looked about me; in vain I saw the decent furniture and tall proportions of my room in the square; in vain that I recognised the pattern of the bed curtains and the design of the mahogany frame; something still kept insisting that I was not where I was, that I had not wakened where I seemed to be, but in the little room in Soho where I was accustomed to sleep in the body of Edward Hyde. I smiled to myself, and, in my psychological way began lazily to inquire into the elements of this illusion, occasionally, even as I did so, dropping back into a comfortable morning doze. I was still so engaged when, in one of my more wakeful moments, my eyes fell upon my hand. Now the hand of Henry Jekyll (as you have often remarked) was professional in shape and size: it was large, firm, white and comely. But the hand which I now saw, clearly enough, in the yellow light of a mid-London morning, lying half shut on the bed clothes, was lean, corded, knuckly, of a dusky pallor and thickly shaded with a swart[6] growth of hair. It was the hand of Edward Hyde.

I must have stared upon it for near half a minute, sunk as I was in the mere stupidity of wonder, before terror woke up in my breast as sudden and startling as the crash of cymbals; and bounding from my bed, I rushed to the mirror. At the sight that met my eyes, my blood was changed into something exquisitely thin and icy. Yes, I had gone to bed Henry Jekyll, I had awakened Edward

---

5. Spirit or demon.   6. Dark.

Hyde. How was this to be explained? I asked myself; and then, with another bound of terror—how was it to be remedied? It was well on in the morning; the servants were up; all my drugs were in the cabinet—a long journey down two pair of stairs, through the back passage, across the open court and through the anatomical theatre, from where I was then standing horror-struck. It might indeed be possible to cover my face; but of what use was that, when I was unable to conceal the alteration in my stature? And then with an overpowering sweetness of relief, it came back upon my mind that the servants were already used to the coming and going of my second self. I had soon dressed, as well as I was able, in clothes of my own size: had soon passed through the house, where Bradshaw stared and drew back at seeing Mr. Hyde at such an hour and in such a strange array; and ten minutes later, Dr. Jekyll had returned to his own shape and was sitting down, with a darkened brow, to make a feint of breakfasting.

Small indeed was my appetite. This inexplicable incident, this reversal of my previous experience, seemed, like the Babylonian finger on the wall,[7] to be spelling out the letters of my judgment; and I began to reflect more seriously than ever before on the issues and possibilities of my double existence. That part of me which I had the power of projecting, had lately been much exercised and nourished; it had seemed to me of late as though the body of Edward Hyde had grown in stature, as though (when I wore that form) I were conscious of a more generous tide of blood; and I began to spy a danger that, if this were much prolonged, the balance of my nature might be permanently overthrown, the power of voluntary change be forfeited, and the character of Edward Hyde become irrevocably mine. The power of the drug had not been always equally displayed. Once, very early in my career, it had totally failed me; since then I had been obliged on more than one occasion to double, and once, with infinite risk of death, to treble the amount; and these rare uncertainties had cast hitherto the sole shadow on my contentment. Now, however, and in the light of that morning's accident, I was led to remark that whereas, in the beginning, the difficulty had been to throw off the body of Jekyll, it had of late gradually but decidedly transferred itself to the other side. All things therefore seemed to point to this: that I was slowly losing hold of my original and better self, and becoming slowly incorporated with my second and worse.

Between these two, I now felt I had to choose. My two natures had memory in common, but all other faculties were most unequally shared between them. Jekyll (who was composite) now with the most sensitive apprehensions, now with a greedy gusto, projected and shared in the pleasures and adventures of Hyde; but Hyde was indifferent to Jekyll, or but remembered him as the mountain bandit remembers the cavern in which he conceals himself from pursuit. Jekyll had more than a father's interest; Hyde had more than a son's indifference. To cast in my lot with Jekyll, was to die to those appetites which I had long secretly indulged and had of late begun to pamper. To cast it in with Hyde, was to die to a thousand interests and aspirations, and to become, at a blow and forever, despised and friendless. The bargain might appear unequal; but there was still another consideration in the scales; for while Jekyll would suffer smartingly in the fires of abstinence, Hyde would be not even conscious of all that he had lost. Strange as my circumstances were, the terms of this

7. In Daniel 5.5–31; the writing foretold the overthrow of Belshazzar, the Babylonian king, because of his transgressions against the Lord.

2206 / <small>Robert Louis Stevenson</small>

debate are as old and commonplace as man; much the same inducements and alarms cast the die for any tempted and trembling sinner; and it fell out with me, as it falls with so vast a majority of my fellows, that I chose the better part and was found wanting in the strength to keep to it.

Yes, I preferred the elderly and discontented doctor, surrounded by friends and cherishing honest hopes; and bade a resolute farewell to the liberty, the comparative youth, the light step, leaping impulses and secret pleasures, that I had enjoyed in the disguise of Hyde. I made this choice perhaps with some unconscious reservation, for I neither gave up the house in Soho, nor destroyed the clothes of Edward Hyde, which still lay ready in my cabinet. For two months, however, I was true to my determination; for two months I led a life of such severity as I had never before attained to, and enjoyed the compensations of an approving conscience. But time began at last to obliterate the freshness of my alarm; the praises of conscience began to grow into a thing of course; I began to be tortured with throes and longings, as of Hyde struggling after freedom; and at last, in an hour of moral weakness, I once again compounded and swallowed the transforming draught.

I do not suppose that, when a drunkard reasons with himself upon his vice, he is once out of five hundred times affected by the dangers that he runs through his brutish, physical insensibility; neither had I, long as I had considered my position, made enough allowance for the complete moral insensibility and insensate readiness to evil, which were the leading characters of Edward Hyde. Yet it was by these that I was punished. My devil had been long caged, he came out roaring. I was conscious, even when I took the draught, of a more unbridled, a more furious propensity to ill. It must have been this, I suppose, that stirred in my soul that tempest of impatience with which I listened to the civilities of my unhappy victim; I declare, at least, before God, no man morally sane could have been guilty of that crime upon so pitiful a provocation; and that I struck in no more reasonable spirit than that in which a sick child may break a plaything. But I had voluntarily stripped myself of all those balancing instincts by which even the worst of us continues to walk with some degree of steadiness among temptations; and in my case, to be tempted, however slightly, was to fall.

Instantly the spirit of hell awoke in me and raged. With a transport of glee, I mauled the unresisting body, tasting delight from every blow; and it was not till weariness had begun to succeed, that I was suddenly, in the top fit of my delirium, struck through the heart by a cold thrill of terror. A mist dispersed; I saw my life to be forfeit; and fled from the scene of these excesses, at once glorifying and trembling, my lust of evil gratified and stimulated, my love of life screwed to the topmost peg.[8] I ran to the house in Soho, and (to make assurance doubly sure) destroyed my papers; thence I set out through the lamplit streets, in the same divided ecstasy of mind, gloating on my crime, light-headedly devising others in the future, and yet still hastening and still hearkening in my wake for the steps of the avenger. Hyde had a song upon his lips as he compounded the draught, and as he drank it, pledged[9] the dead man. The pangs of transformation had not done tearing him, before Henry Jekyll, with streaming tears of gratitude and remorse, had fallen upon his knees

---

8. Strained to the highest point.   9. Drank a toast to.

and lifted his clasped hands to God. The veil of self-indulgence was rent from head to foot.[1] I saw my life as a whole: I followed it up from the days of childhood, when I had walked with my father's hand, and through the self-denying toils of my professional life, to arrive again and again, with the same sense of unreality, at the damned horrors of the evening. I could have screamed aloud; I sought with tears and prayers to smother down the crowd of hideous images and sounds with which my memory swarmed against me; and still, between the petitions, the ugly face of my iniquity stared into my soul. As the acuteness of this remorse began to die away, it was succeeded by a sense of joy. The problem of my conduct was solved. Hyde was thenceforth impossible; whether I would or not, I was now confined to the better part of my existence; and O, how I rejoiced to think it! with what willing humility, I embraced anew the restrictions of natural life! with what sincere renunciation, I locked the door by which I had so often gone and come, and ground the key under my heel!

The next day, came the news that the murder had been overlooked,[2] that the guilt of Hyde was patent to the world, and that the victim was a man high in public estimation. It was not only a crime, it had been a tragic folly. I think I was glad to know it; I think I was glad to have my better impulses thus buttressed and guarded by the terrors of the scaffold. Jekyll was now my city of refuge; let but Hyde peep out an instant, and the hands of all men would be raised to take and slay him.

I resolved in my future conduct to redeem the past; and I can say with honesty that my resolve was fruitful of some good. You know yourself how earnestly in the last months of last year, I laboured to relieve suffering; you know that much was done for others, and that the days passed quietly, almost happily for myself. Nor can I truly say that I wearied of this beneficent and innocent life; I think instead that I daily enjoyed it more completely; but I was still cursed with my duality of purpose; and as the first edge of my penitence wore off, the lower side of me, so long indulged, so recently chained down, began to growl for license. Not that I dreamed of resuscitating Hyde; the bare idea of that would startle me to frenzy: no, it was in my own person, that I was once more tempted to trifle with my conscience; and it was as an ordinary secret sinner, that I at last fell before the assaults of temptation.

There comes an end to all things; the most capacious measure is filled at last; and this brief condescension to my evil finally destroyed the balance of my soul. And yet I was not alarmed; the fall seemed natural, like a return to the old days before I had made my discovery. It was a fine, clear, January day, wet under foot where the frost had melted, but cloudless overhead; and the Regent's Park[3] was full of winter chirrupings and sweet with spring odours. I sat in the sun on a bench; the animal within me licking the chops of memory; the spiritual side a little drowsed, promising subsequent penitence, but not yet moved to begin. After all, I reflected, I was like my neighbours; and then I smiled, comparing myself with other men, comparing my active goodwill with the lazy cruelty of their neglect. And at the very moment of that vain-glorious thought, a qualm came over me, a horrid nausea and the most deadly shud-

---

1. See Matthew 27.51: "the veil of the temple was rent in twain, from the top to the bottom."

2. Seen from above.
3. A large park in northwest London.

dering. These passed away, and left me faint; and then as in its turn the faintness subsided, I began to be aware of a change in the temper of my thoughts, a greater boldness, a contempt of danger, a solution of the bonds of obligation. I looked down; my clothes hung formlessly on my shrunken limbs; the hand that lay on my knee was corded and hairy. I was once more Edward Hyde. A moment before I had been safe of all men's respect, wealthy, beloved—the cloth laying for me in the dining-room at home; and now I was the common quarry of mankind, hunted, houseless, a known murderer, thrall to the gallows.

My reason wavered, but it did not fail me utterly. I have more than once observed that, in my second character, my faculties seemed sharpened to a point and my spirits more tensely elastic; thus it came about that, where Jekyll perhaps might have succumbed, Hyde rose to the importance of the moment. My drugs were in one of the presses of my cabinet; how was I to reach them? That was the problem that (crushing my temples in my hands) I set myself to solve. The laboratory door I had closed. If I sought to enter by the house, my own servants would consign me to the gallows. I saw I must employ another hand, and thought of Lanyon. How was he to be reached? how persuaded? Supposing that I escaped capture in the streets, how was I to make my way into his presence? and how should I, an unknown and displeasing visitor, prevail on the famous physician to rifle the study of his colleague, Dr. Jekyll? Then I remembered that of my original character, one part remained to me: I could write my own hand; and once I had conceived that kindling spark, the way that I must follow became lighted up from end to end.

Thereupon, I arranged my clothes as best I could, and summoning a passing hansom, drove to an hotel in Portland Street, the name of which I chanced to remember. At my appearance (which was indeed comical enough, however tragic a fate these garments covered) the driver could not conceal his mirth. I gnashed my teeth upon him with a gust of devilish fury; and the smile withered from his face—happily for him—yet more happily for myself, for in another instant I had certainly dragged him from his perch. At the inn, as I entered, I looked about me with so black a countenance as made the attendants tremble; not a look did they exchange in my presence; but obsequiously took my orders, led me to a private room, and brought me wherewithal to write. Hyde in danger of his life was a creature new to me; shaken with inordinate anger, strung to the pitch of murder, lusting to inflict pain. Yet the creature was astute; mastered his fury with a great effort of the will; composed his two important letters, one to Lanyon and one to Poole; and that he might receive actual evidence of their being posted, sent them out with directions that they should be registered.

Thenceforward, he sat all day over the fire in the private room, gnawing his nails; there he dined, sitting alone with his fears, the waiter visibly quailing before his eye; and thence, when the night was fully come, he set forth in the corner of a closed cab, and was driven to and fro about the streets of the city. He, I say—I cannot say, I. That child of Hell had nothing human; nothing lived in him but fear and hatred. And when at last, thinking the driver had begun to grow suspicious, he discharged the cab and ventured on foot, attired in his misfitting clothes, an object marked out for observation, into the midst of the nocturnal passengers, these two base passions raged within him like a tempest. He walked fast, hunted by his fears, chattering to himself, skulking through the less frequented thoroughfares, counting the minutes that still divided him from midnight. Once a woman spoke to him, offering, I think, a box of lights.[4] He smote her in the face, and she fled.

When I came to myself at Lanyon's, the horror of my old friend perhaps affected me somewhat: I do not know; it was at least but a drop in the sea to the abhorrence with which I looked back upon these hours. A change had come over me. It was no longer the fear of the gallows, it was the horror of being Hyde that racked me. I received Lanyon's condemnation partly in a dream; it was partly in a dream that I came home to my own house and got into bed. I slept after the prostration of the day, with a stringent and profound slumber which not even the nightmares that wrung me could avail to break. I awoke in the morning shaken, weakened, but refreshed. I still hated and feared the thought of the brute that slept within me, and I had not of course forgotten the appalling dangers of the day before; but I was once more at home, in my own house and close to my drugs; and gratitude for my escape shone so strong in my soul that it almost rivalled the brightness of hope.

I was stepping leisurely across the court after breakfast, drinking the chill of the air with pleasure, when I was seized again with those indescribable sensations that heralded the change; and I had but the time to gain the shelter of my cabinet, before I was once again raging and freezing with the passions of Hyde. It took on this occasion a double dose to recall me to myself; and alas! six hours after, as I sat looking sadly in the fire, the pangs returned, and the drug had to be re-administered. In short, from that day forth it seemed only by a great effort as of gymnastics, and only under the immediate stimulation of the drug, that I was able to wear the countenance of Jekyll. At all hours of the day and night, I would be taken with the premonitory shudder; above all, if I slept, or even dozed for a moment in my chair, it was always as Hyde that I awakened. Under the strain of this continually impending doom and by the sleeplessness to which I now condemned myself, ay, even beyond what I had thought possible to man, I became, in my own person, a creature eaten up and emptied by fever, languidly weak both in body and mind, and solely occupied by one thought: the horror of my other self. But when I slept, or when the virtue of the medicine wore off, I would leap almost without transition (for the pangs of transformation grew daily less marked) into the possession of a fancy brimming with images of terror, a soul boiling with causeless hatreds, and a body that seemed not strong enough to contain the raging energies of life. The powers of Hyde seemed to have grown with the sickliness of Jekyll. And certainly the hate that now divided them was equal on each side. With Jekyll, it was a thing of vital instinct. He had now seen the full deformity of that creature that shared with him some of the phenomena of consciousness, and was co-heir with him to death: and beyond these links of community, which in themselves made the most poignant part of his distress, he thought of Hyde, for all his energy of life, as of something not only hellish but inorganic. This was the shocking thing; that the slime of the pit seemed to utter cries and voices; that the amorphous dust gesticulated and sinned; that what was dead, and had no shape, should usurp the offices of life. And this again, that that insurgent horror was knit to him closer than a wife, closer than an eye; lay caged in his flesh, where he heard it mutter and felt it struggle to be born; and at every hour of weakness, and in the confidence of slumber, prevailed against him, and deposed him out of life. The hatred of

4. Matches.

Hyde for Jekyll, was of a different order. His terror of the gallows drove him continually to commit temporary suicide, and return to his subordinate station of a part instead of a person; but he loathed the necessity, he loathed the despondency into which Jekyll was now fallen, and he resented the dislike with which he was himself regarded. Hence the apelike tricks that he would play me, scrawling in my own hand blasphemies on the pages of my books, burning the letters and destroying the portrait of my father; and indeed, had it not been for his fear of death, he would long ago have ruined himself in order to involve me in the ruin. But his love of life is wonderful; I go further: I, who sicken and freeze at the mere thought of him, when I recall the abjection and passion of this attachment, and when I know how he fears my power to cut him off by suicide, I find it in my heart to pity him.

It is useless, and the time awfully fails me, to prolong this description; no one has ever suffered such torments, let that suffice; and yet even to these, habit brought—no, not alleviation—but a certain callousness of soul, a certain acquiescence of despair; and my punishment might have gone on for years, but for the last calamity which has now fallen, and which has finally severed me from my own face and nature. My provision of the salt, which had never been renewed since the date of the first experiment, began to run low. I sent out for a fresh supply, and mixed the draught; the ebullition followed, and the first change of colour, not the second; I drank it and it was without efficiency. You will learn from Poole how I have had London ransacked; it was in vain; and I am now persuaded that my first supply was impure, and that it was that unknown impurity which lent efficacy to the draught.

About a week has passed, and I am now finishing this statement under the influence of the last of the old powders. This, then, is the last time, short of a miracle, that Henry Jekyll can think his own thoughts or see his own face (now how sadly altered!) in the glass. Nor must I delay too long to bring my writing to an end; for if my narrative has hitherto escaped destruction, it has been by a combination of great prudence and great good luck. Should the throes of change take me in the act of writing it, Hyde will tear it in pieces; but if some time shall have elapsed after I have laid it by, his wonderful self-ishness and circumscription to the moment will probably save it once again from the action of his apelike spite. And indeed the doom that is closing on us both, has already changed and crushed him. Half an hour from now, when I shall again and forever reindue[5] that hated personality, I know how I shall sit shuddering and weeping in my chair, or continue, with the most strained and fearstruck ecstasy of listening, to pace up and down this room (my last earthly refuge) and give ear to every sound of menace. Will Hyde die upon the scaffold? or will he find courage to release himself at the last moment? God knows; I am careless;[6] this is my true hour of death, and what is to follow concerns another than myself. Here then, as I lay down the pen and proceed to seal up my confession, I bring the life of that unhappy Henry Jekyll to an end.

1885   1886

---

5. Put on again.   6. Indifferent.

OSCAR WILDE
1854–1900

In Oscar Wilde's comedy *The Importance of Being Earnest* (1895) there is an account of a rakish character, Ernest Worthing, whose death in a Paris hotel is reported by the manager. Five years later Wilde died in Paris (where he was living in exile) attended by a hotel manager. The coincidence seems a curious paradigm of Wilde's career, for the connections between his life and his art were unusually close. Indeed, in his last years he told André Gide that he seemed to have put his genius into his life and only his talent into his writings.

His father, Sir William, was a distinguished surgeon in Dublin, where Wilde was born and grew up. After studying classics at Trinity College, Dublin, he won a scholarship to Oxford and there established a brilliant academic record. At Oxford he came under the influence of the aesthetic theories of John Ruskin (who was at the time professor of fine arts) and, more important, of Walter Pater. With characteristic hyperbole Wilde affirmed of Pater's *Studies in the History of the Renaissance* (1873): "It is my golden book; I never travel anywhere without it. But it is the very flower of decadence; the last trumpet should have sounded the moment it was written."

After graduating in 1878, Wilde moved to London, where his fellow Irishmen Bernard Shaw and William Butler Yeats were also to settle. Here Wilde quickly established himself both as a writer and as a spokesperson for the school of "art for art's sake." In Wilde's view this school included not only French poets and critics but also a line of English poets going back through Dante Gabriel Rossetti and the Pre-Raphaelites to John Keats. In 1882 he visited America for a long (and successful) lecture tour, during which he startled audiences by airing the gospel of the "aesthetic movement." In one of these lectures, he asserted that "to disagree with three fourths of all England on all points of view is one of the first elements of sanity."

For his role as a spokesperson for aestheticism, Wilde had many gifts. From all accounts he was a dazzling conversationalist. Yeats reported, after first listening to him: "I never before heard a man talking with perfect sentences, as if he had written them all overnight with labour and yet all spontaneous." Wilde delighted his listeners not only by his polished wordplay but also by uttering opinions that were both outrageous and incongruous—for example, his solemn affirmation that Queen Victoria was one of the three women he most admired and whom he would have married "with pleasure" (the other two were the actress Sarah Bernhardt and Lillie Langtry, reputedly a mistress of Victoria's son Edward, Prince of Wales).

In addition to his mastery of witty conversation, Wilde had the gifts of an actor who delights in gaining attention. Pater had been a very shy and reticent man, but there was nothing reticent about his disciple, who had early discovered that a flamboyant style of dress was one of the most effective means of gaining attention. Like the dandies of the earlier decades of the nineteenth century (including Benjamin Disraeli and Charles Dickens), Wilde favored colorful costumes in marked contrast to the sober black suits of the late-Victorian middle classes. A green carnation in his buttonhole and velvet knee breeches became for Wilde badges of his youthful iconoclasm; and even when he approached middle age, he continued to emphasize the gap between generations. In a letter written when he was forty-two years old, he remarks: "The opinions of the old on matters of Art are, of course, of no value whatever."

Wilde's campaign quickly gained an amused response from middle-class quarters. In 1881 W. S. Gilbert and Sir Arthur Sullivan staged their comic opera *Patience*, which mocked the affectations of the aesthetes in the character of Bunthorne, especially in his song "If You're Anxious for to Shine in the High Aesthetic Line."

Wilde's successes for seventeen years in England and America were, of course, not limited to his self-advertising stunts as a dandy. In his writings he excelled in a variety

2212 / Oscar Wilde

of genres: as a critic of literature and of society (*The Decay of Lying*, 1889, and *The Soul of Man under Socialism*, 1891) and also as a novelist, poet, and dramatist. Much of his prose, including *The Critic as Artist* (1890), develops Pater's aestheticism, particularly its sense of the superiority of art to life and its lack of obligation to any standards of mimesis. His novel *The Picture of Dorian Gray*, which created a sensation when it was published in 1891, takes a somewhat different perspective. The novel is a strikingly ingenious story of a handsome young man and his selfish pursuit of sensual pleasures. Until the end of the book he remains fresh and healthy in appearance while his portrait mysteriously changes into a horrible image of his corrupted soul. Although the preface to the novel (reprinted here) emphasizes that art and morality are totally separate, in the novel, at least in its later chapters, Wilde seems to be portraying the evils of self-regarding hedonism.

As a poet Wilde felt overshadowed by the Victorian predecessors whom he admired—Robert Browning, D. G. Rossetti, and Algernon Charles Swinburne—and had trouble finding his own voice. Many of the poems in his first volume (1881) are highly derivative, but pieces such as "Impression du Matin" (1885) and "The Harlot's House" (1881) offer a distinctive perspective on city streets that seems to anticipate early poems by T. S. Eliot. His most outstanding success, however, was as a writer of comedies; staged in London and New York from 1892 through 1895, these included *Lady Windermere's Fan, A Woman of No Importance, An Ideal Husband,* and *The Importance of Being Earnest.*

In the spring of 1895 this triumphant success suddenly crumbled when Wilde was arrested and sentenced to prison, with hard labor, for two years. Although Wilde was married and the father of two children, he did not hide his relationships with men, and in fact ended up shaping, to his personal cost, a long-standing public image of "the homosexual." When he began a romance (in 1891) with the handsome young poet Lord Alfred Douglas, he set in motion the events that brought about his ruin. In 1895 Lord Alfred's father, the marquess of Queensberry, accused Wilde of homosexuality; Wilde recklessly sued for libel, lost the case, and was thereupon arrested and convicted for what had only recently come onto the statute books as a serious offense. (A late addition to the Criminal Law Amendment Act of 1885, known as the Labouchère Amendment after the member of Parliament who had proposed it, effectively criminalized all forms of sexual relations between men.) The revulsion of feeling against him in Britain and America was violent, and the aesthetic movement suffered a severe setback not only with the public but among writers as well.

His two years in jail led Wilde to write two sober and emotionally high-pitched works, his poem *The Ballad of Reading Gaol* (1898) and his prose confession *De Profundis* (1905). After leaving prison, Wilde, a ruined man, emigrated to France, where he lived out the last three years of his life under an assumed name. Before his departure from England he had been divorced and declared a bankrupt, and in France he had to rely on friends for financial support. Wilde is buried in Paris in the Père Lachaise cemetery.

From The Critic as Artist[1]

[CRITICISM ITSELF AN ART]

ERNEST   Gilbert, you sound too harsh a note. Let us go back to the more gracious fields of literature. What was it you said? That it was more difficult to talk about a thing than to do it?

---

1. In "the library of a house in Piccadilly," Gilbert and Ernest, two sophisticated young men, are talking about the use and function of criticism. Earlier in the dialogue Ernest had complained that criticism is officious and useless: "Why should the artist be troubled by the shrill clamour of criticism?"

GILBERT [*After a pause.*]   Yes: I believe I ventured upon that simple truth. Surely you see now that I am right? When man acts he is a puppet. When he describes he is a poet. The whole secret lies in that. It was easy enough on the sandy plains by windy Ilion[2] to send the notched arrow from the painted bow, or to hurl against the shield of hide and flamelike brass the long ash-handled spear. It was easy for the adulterous queen to spread the Tyrian carpets for her lord,[3] and then, as he lay couched in the marble bath, to throw over his head the purple net, and call to her smooth-faced lover to stab through the meshes at the heart that should have broken at Aulis.[4] For Antigone[5] even, with Death waiting for her as her bridegroom, it was easy to pass through the tainted air at noon, and climb the hill, and strew with kindly earth the wretched naked corse that had no tomb. But what of those who wrote about these things? What of those who gave them reality, and made them live forever? Are they not greater than the men and women they sing of? "Hector that sweet knight is dead."[6] And Lucian[7] tells us how in the dim underworld Menippus saw the bleaching skull of Helen, and marveled that it was for so grim a favour that all those horned ships were launched, those beautiful mailed men laid low, those towered cities brought to dust. Yet, every day the swanlike daughter of Leda comes out on the battlements, and looks down at the tide of war. The greybeards wonder at her loveliness, and she stands by the side of the king.[8] In his chamber of stained ivory lies her leman.[9] He is polishing his dainty armour, and combing the scarlet plume. With squire and page, her husband passes from tent to tent. She can see his bright hair, and hears, or fancies that she hears, that clear cold voice. In the courtyard below, the son of Priam is buckling on his brazen cuirass. The white arms of Andromache[1] are around his neck. He sets his helmet on the ground, lest their babe should be frightened. Behind the embroidered curtains of his pavilion sits Achilles,[2] in perfumed raiment, while in harness of gilt and silver the friend of his soul[3] arrays himself to go forth to fight. From a curiously carven chest that his mother Thetis had brought to his shipside, the Lord of the Myrmidons[4] takes out that mystic chalice that the lip of man had never touched, and cleanses it with brimstone, and with fresh water cools it, and, having washed his hands, fills with

Why should those who cannot create take upon themselves to estimate the value of creative work?" Gilbert, in his reply, argues that criticism is creative in its own right. He digresses to compare the life of action unfavorably with the life of art: actions are dangerous and their results unpredictable; "if we lived long enough to see the results of our actions it may be that those who call themselves good would be sickened by a dull remorse, and those whom the world calls evil stirred by a noble joy." The excerpt printed here begins immediately following this digression.

2. Troy. Gilbert is referring to Homer's *Iliad*.
3. Agamemnon, king of Mycenae. Aeschylus's tragedy of that name tells how his wife, Clytemnestra ("the adulterous queen"), and his cousin Aegisthus ("her smooth-faced lover") conspired to murder him. He hubristically walked on carpets dyed purple, a color derived from shellfish off Tyre (a city located in what is today Lebanon).
4. Where Agamemnon sacrificed his daughter Iphigenia (so that the Greek fleet could sail for Troy), thus incurring Clytemnestra's wrath.
5. Antigone defied Creon, king of Thebes, by

sprinkling earth on the body of her brother whose burial Creon had forbidden, and was punished by death; see Sophocles' play *Antigone* (ca. 441 B.C.E.).
6. Cf. Shakespeare's *Love's Labour's Lost* 5.2.647: "The sweet war-man [Hector] is dead and rotten."
7. Greek satirist (b. ca. 120 C.E.), one of whose main influences was Menippus (early 3rd century B.C.E.), a Greek philosopher who was the first to express his views in a seriocomic style. The reference is to Lucian's *Dialogues of the Dead*.
8. Priam. Homer in *Iliad* 3.156–58 describes the old men of Troy admiring the beauty of Helen, daughter of Leda and of Zeus (who came to Leda in the form of a swan).
9. Lover (i.e., Paris).
1. Wife of Hector, one of the sons of Priam and the finest Trojan warrior.
2. Son of Peleus and of the sea nymph Thetis; Achilles was the greatest Greek warrior fighting in the Trojan War. The scene set here is a tissue of recollections from the *Iliad*.
3. I.e., Patroclus.
4. Warriors who accompanied Achilles to Troy.

black wine its burnished hollow, and spills the thick grape-blood upon the ground in honor of Him whom at Dodona[5] barefooted prophets worshipped, and prays to Him, and knows not that he prays in vain, and that by the hands of two knights from Troy, Panthous' son, Euphorbus, whose love-locks were looped with gold, and the Priamid,[6] the lion-hearted, Patroclus, the comrade of comrades, must meet his doom. Phantoms, are they? Heroes of mist and mountain? Shadows in a song? No: they are real. Action! What is action? It dies at the moment of its energy. It is a base concession to fact. The world is made by the singer for the dreamer.

ERNEST   While you talk it seems to me to be so.

GILBERT   It is so in truth. On the mouldering citadel of Troy lies the lizard like a thing of green bronze. The owl has built her nest in the palace of Priam. Over the empty plain wander shepherd and goatherd with their flocks, and where, on the wine-surfaced, oily sea, οἶνοψ πόντος,[7] as Homer calls it, copper-prowed and streaked with vermilion, the great galleys of the Danaoi[8] came in their gleaming crescent, the lonely tunny-fisher[9] sits in his little boat and watches the bobbing corks of his net. Yet, every morning the doors of the city are thrown open, and on foot, or in horse-drawn chariot, the warriors go forth to battle, and mock their enemies from behind their iron masks. All day long the fight rages, and when night comes the torches gleam by the tents, and the cresset[1] burns in the hall. Those who live in marble or on painted panel know of life but a single exquisite instant, eternal indeed in its beauty, but limited to one note of passion or one mood of calm. Those whom the poet makes live have their myriad emotions of joy and terror, of courage and despair, of pleasure and of suffering. The seasons come and go in glad or saddening pageant, and with winged or leaden feet the years pass by before them. They have their youth and their manhood, they are children, and they grow old. It is always dawn for St. Helena, as Veronese saw her at the window.[2] Through the still morning air the angels bring her the symbol of God's pain.[3] The cool breezes of the morning lift the gilt threads from her brow. On that little hill by the city of Florence, where the lovers of Giorgione[4] are lying, it is always the solstice of noon, made so languorous by summer suns that hardly can the slim naked girl dip into the marble tank the round bubble of clear glass, and the long fingers of the lute player rest idly upon the chords. It is twilight always for the dancing nymphs whom Corot[5] set free among the silver poplars of France. In eternal twilight they move, those frail diaphanous figures, whose tremulous white feet seem not to touch the dew-drenched grass they tread on. But those who walk in epos,[6] drama, or romance, see through the labouring months the young moons wax and wane, and watch the night from evening unto morning star, and from sunrise unto sunsetting can note the shifting day with all its gold and shadow. For them, as for us, the flowers bloom and wither, and the Earth, that Green-tressed Goddess as Coleridge calls

---

5. Seat of a very ancient oracle of Zeus.
6. The son of Priam, i.e., Hector. With Euphorbus's help he killed Patroclus, and in turn he was slain by Achilles.
7. Wine-dark sea (Greek).
8. Greeks.
9. Tuna-fishers.
1. Metal basket holding fuel burned for illumination, often hung from the ceiling.
2. One of the best-known works of the Italian

painter Paolo Veronese (Paolo Caliari, 1528–1588) is *Helena's Vision*.
3. I.e., the cross.
4. Italian painter (ca. 1477–1511), the most brilliant colorist of his time. The painting is *The Concert*.
5. Jean-Baptiste-Camille Corot (1796–1875), French painter best-known for his shimmering trees.
6. Epic poetry.

her,[7] alters her raiment for their pleasure. The statue is concentrated to one moment of perfection. The image stained upon the canvas possesses no spiritual element of growth or change. If they know nothing of death, it is because they know little of life, for the secrets of life and death belong to those, and those only, whom the sequence of time affects, and who possess not merely the present but the future, and can rise or fall from a past of glory or of shame. Movement, that problem of the visible arts, can be truly realized by Literature alone. It is Literature that shows us the body in its swiftness and the soul in its unrest.

ERNEST Yes; I see now what you mean. But, surely, the higher you place the creative artist, the lower must the critic rank.

GILBERT Why so?

ERNEST Because the best that he can give us will be but an echo of rich music, a dim shadow of clear-outlined form. It may, indeed, be that life is chaos, as you tell me that it is; that its martyrdoms are mean and its heroisms ignoble; and that it is the function of Literature to create, from the rough material of actual existence, a new world that will be more marvellous, more enduring, and more true than the world that common eyes look upon, and through which common natures seek to realize their perfection. But surely, if this new world has been made by the spirit and touch of a great artist, it will be a thing so complete and perfect that there will be nothing left for the critic to do. I quite understand now, and indeed admit most readily, that it is far more difficult to talk about a thing than to do it. But it seems to me that this sound and sensible maxim, which is really extremely soothing to one's feelings, and should be adopted as its motto by every Academy of Literature all over the world, applies only to the relations that exist between Art and Life, and not to any relations that there may be between Art and Criticism.

GILBERT But, surely, Criticism is itself an art. And just as artistic creation implies the working of the critical faculty, and, indeed, without it cannot be said to exist at all, so Criticism is really creative in the highest sense of the word. Criticism is, in fact, both creative and independent.

ERNEST Independent?

GILBERT Yes; independent. Criticism is no more to be judged by any low standard of imitation or resemblance than is the work of poet or sculptor. The critic occupies the same relation to the work of art that he criticizes as the artist does to the visible world of form and colour, or the unseen world of passion and of thought. He does not even require for the perfection of his art the finest materials. Anything will serve his purpose. And just as out of the sordid and sentimental amours of the silly wife of a small country doctor in the squalid village of Yonville-l'Abbaye, near Rouen, Gustave Flaubert[8] was able to create a classic, and make a masterpiece of style, so, from subjects of little or of no importance, such as the pictures in this year's Royal Academy,[9] or in any year's Royal Academy for that matter, Mr. Lewis Morris's poems, M. Ohnet's novels, or the plays of Mr. Henry Arthur Jones,[1]

---

7. Cf. S. T. Coleridge's "Hymn to the Earth" (1834), line 10, where Earth is called "Green-haired Goddess."
8. French novelist (1821–1880); the reference is to his novel *Madame Bovary* (1857).
9. The Royal Academy of Arts, founded in 1768, holds an annual summer exhibition of new work.

1. Wilde is mischievously suggesting his low opinion of the contemporary writers just named. Morris (1833–1907) was a popular Welsh poet and essayist often ridiculed by the critics; Georges Ohnet (1848–1918) was a French novelist and dramatist; and Jones (1851–1929) was one of the leading English playwrights of his time.

the true critic can, if it be his pleasure so to direct or waste his faculty of contemplation, produce work that will be flawless in beauty and instinct with intellectual subtlety. Why not? Dullness is always an irresistible temptation for brilliancy, and stupidity is the permanent *Bestia Trionfans*[2] that calls wisdom from its cave. To an artist so creative as the critic, what does subject matter signify? No more and no less than it does to the novelist and the painter. Like them, he can find his motives everywhere. Treatment is the test. There is nothing that has not in it suggestion or challenge.

ERNEST   But is Criticism really a creative art?

GILBERT   Why should it not be? It works with materials, and puts them into a form that is at once new and delightful. What more can one say of poetry? Indeed, I would call criticism a creation within a creation. For just as the great artists, from Homer and Aeschylus, down to Shakespeare and Keats, did not go directly to life for their subject matter, but sought for it in myth, and legend, and ancient tale, so the critic deals with materials that others have, as it were, purified for him, and to which imaginative form and colour have been already added. Nay, more, I would say that the highest Criticism, being the purest form of personal impression, is in its way more creative than creation, as it has least reference to any standard external to itself, and is, in fact, its own reason for existing, and, as the Greeks would put it, in itself, and to itself, an end. Certainly, it is never trammeled by any shackles of verisimilitude. No ignoble considerations of probability, that cowardly concession to the tedious repetitions of domestic or public life, affect it ever. One may appeal from fiction unto fact. But from the soul there is no appeal.

ERNEST   From the soul?

GILBERT   Yes, from the soul. That is what the highest criticism really is, the record of one's own soul. It is more fascinating than history, as it is concerned simply with oneself. It is more delightful than philosophy, as its subject is concrete and not abstract, real and not vague. It is the only civilized form of autobiography, as it deals not with the events, but with the thoughts of one's life, not with life's physical accidents of deed or circumstance, but with the spiritual moods and imaginative passions of the mind. I am always amused by the silly vanity of those writers and artists of our day who seem to imagine that the primary function of the critic is to chatter about their second-rate work. The best that one can say of most modern creative art is that it is just a little less vulgar than reality, and so the critic, with his fine sense of distinction and sure instinct of delicate refinement, will prefer to look into the silver mirror or through the woven veil, and will turn his eyes away from the chaos and clamour of actual existence, though the mirror be tarnished and the veil be torn. His sole aim is to chronicle his own impressions. It is for him that pictures are painted, books written, and marble hewn into form.

ERNEST   I seem to have heard another theory of Criticism.

GILBERT   Yes: it has been said by one whose gracious memory we all revere,[3]

<hr/>

2. Triumphant beast (Wilde's mixture of Italian and Latin); a reference to *Spaccio della Bestia Trionfante* (*Expulsion of the Triumphant Beast*, 1584), a philosophical allegory by the Italian philosopher Giordano Bruno.
3. I.e., Matthew Arnold, whose poem "Thyrsis" (1866; lines 91–100) evokes the legend of Proserpina, a goddess associated with the pastoral landscapes of Sicily. Arnold believed that it would be "in vain" to summon Proserpina to visit the Cumnor hills landscape (near Oxford), but Wilde's speaker here flatters Arnold that the summons was so beautiful that it was "not in vain." For the prose passage about the "aim of Criticism," see Arnold's "The Function of Criticism at the Present Time" (1864; p. 2112).

and the music of whose pipe once lured Proserpina from her Sicilian fields, and made those white feet stir, and not in vain, the Cumnor cowslips, that the proper aim of Criticism is to see the object as in itself it really is. But this is a very serious error, and takes no cognizance of Criticism's most perfect form, which is in its essence purely subjective, and seeks to reveal its own secret and not the secret of another. For the highest Criticism deals with art not as expressive but as impressive purely.

ERNEST   But is that really so?

GILBERT   Of course it is. Who cares whether Mr. Ruskin's views on Turner[4] are sound or not? What does it matter? That mighty and majestic prose of his, so fervid and so fiery-colored in its noble eloquence, so rich in its elaborate symphonic music, so sure and certain, at its best, in subtle choice of word and epithet, is at least as great a work of art as any of those wonderful sunsets that bleach or rot on their corrupted canvases in England's Gallery; greater indeed, one is apt to think at times, not merely because its equal beauty is more enduring, but on account of the fuller variety of its appeal, soul speaking to soul in those long-cadenced lines, not through form and colour alone, though through these, indeed, completely and without loss, but with intellectual and emotional utterance, with lofty passion and with loftier thought, with imaginative insight, and with poetic aim; greater, I always think, even as Literature is the greater art. Who, again, cares whether Mr. Pater has put into the portrait of Mona Lisa[5] something that Leonardo never dreamed of? The painter may have been merely the slave of an archaic smile, as some have fancied, but whenever I pass into the cool galleries of the Palace of the Louvre, and stand before that strange figure "set in its marble chair in that cirque of fantastic rocks, as in some faint light under sea," I murmur to myself, "She is older than the rocks among which she sits; like the vampire, she has been dead many times, and learned the secrets of the grave; and has been a diver in deep seas, and keeps their fallen day about her: and trafficked for strange webs with Eastern merchants; and, as Leda, was the mother of Helen of Troy, and, as St. Anne, the mother of Mary; and all this has been to her but as the sound of lyres and flutes, and lives only in the delicacy with which it has moulded the changing lineaments, and tinged the eyelids and the hands." And I say to my friend, "The presence that thus so strangely rose beside the waters is expressive of what in the ways of a thousand years man had come to desire"; and he answers me, "Hers is the head upon which all 'the ends of the world are come,' and the eyelids are a little weary."

And so the picture becomes more wonderful to us than it really is, and reveals to us a secret of which, in truth, it knows nothing, and the music of the mystical prose is as sweet in our ears as was that flute-player's music that lent to the lips of La Gioconda[6] those subtle and poisonous curves. Do you ask me what Leonardo would have said had any one told him of this picture that "all the thoughts and experience of the world had etched and moulded therein that which they had of power to refine and make expressive the outward form, the animalism of Greece, the lust of Rome, the reverie

---

4. For John Ruskin's defense of the paintings of J. M. W. Turner, see *Modern Painters* (1843), especially his praise of Turner's *The Slave Ship*.
5. All remaining references in this paragraph and the first in the next are to Walter Pater's *Studies in*

the *History of the Renaissance*.
6. I.e., the *Mona Lisa* (the portrait was of the wife of Francesco del Gioconda—hence "La Gioconda").

of the Middle Age with its spiritual ambition and imaginative loves, the return of the Pagan world, the sins of the Borgias?" He would probably have answered that he had contemplated none of these things, but had concerned himself simply with certain arrangements of lines and masses, and with new and curious colour-harmonies of blue and green. And it is for this very reason that the criticism which I have quoted is criticism of the highest kind. It treats the work of art simply as a starting point for a new creation. It does not confine itself—let us at least suppose so for the moment—to discovering the real intention of the artist and accepting that as final. And in this it is right, for the meaning of any beautiful created thing is, at least, as much in the soul of him who looks at it, as it was in his soul who wrought it. Nay, it is rather the beholder who lends to the beautiful thing its myriad meanings, and makes it marvelous for us, and sets it in some new relation to the age, so that it becomes a vital portion of our lives, and symbol of what we pray for, or perhaps of what, having prayed for, we fear that we may receive. The longer I study, Ernest, the more clearly I see that the beauty of the visible arts is, as the beauty of music, impressive[7] primarily, and that it may be marred, and indeed often is so, by any excess of intellectual intention on the part of the artist. For when the work is finished it has, as it were, an independent life of its own, and may deliver a message far other than that which was put into its lips to say. Sometimes, when I listen to the overture to *Tannhäuser*,[8] I seem indeed to see that comely knight treading delicately on the flower-strewn grass, and to hear the voice of Venus calling to him from the caverned hill. But at other times it speaks to me of a thousand different things, of myself, it may be, and my own life, or of the lives of others whom one has loved and grown weary of loving, or of the passions that man has known, or of the passions that man has not known, and so has sought for. Tonight it may fill one with that ΕΡΩΣ ΤΩΝ ΑΔΥΝΑΤΩΝ, that *amour de l'impossible*,[9] which falls like a madness on many who think they live securely and out of reach of harm, so that they sicken suddenly with the poison of unlimited desire, and, in the infinite pursuit of what they may not obtain, grow faint and swoon or stumble. Tomorrow, like the music of which Aristotle and Plato tell us, the noble Dorian music of the Greek,[1] it may perform the office of a physician, and give us an anodyne against pain, and heal the spirit that is wounded, and "bring the soul into harmony with all right things." And what is true about music is true about all the arts. Beauty has as many meanings as man has moods. Beauty is the symbol of symbols. Beauty reveals everything, because it expresses nothing. When it shows us itself, it shows us the whole fiery-coloured world.

ERNEST   But is such work as you have talked about really criticism?

GILBERT   It is the highest Criticism, for it criticizes not merely the individual work of art, but Beauty itself, and fills with wonder a form which the artist may have left void, or not understood, or understood incompletely.

ERNEST   The highest Criticism, then, is more creative than creation, and the

---

7. I.e., designed to create an impression of the senses.

8. The 1845 opera by Richard Wagner, based on the legend of a 14th-century German poet who fell under the spell of Venus and lived with her in a mountain, Hörselberg.

9. Love of the impossible, in Greek (in capital letters, perhaps to give the effect of an inscription)

and in French.

1. Both Plato (*Republic* 3) and Aristotle (*Politics* 8) praise the educational appropriateness of the Dorian mode (Aristotle calls it especially steady and manly), as opposed to eastern music; the Dorians were a people of ancient Greece, the last of the northern invaders (ca. 1100–950 B.C.E.).

primary aim of the critic is to see the object as in itself it really is not; that is your theory, I believe?

GILBERT   Yes, that is my theory. To the critic the work of art is simply a suggestion for a new work of his own, that need not necessarily bear any obvious resemblance to the thing it criticizes. The one characteristic of a beautiful form is that one can put into it whatever one wishes, and see in it whatever one chooses to see; and the Beauty, that gives to creation its universal and aesthetic element, makes the critic a creator in his turn, and whispers of a thousand different things which were not present in the mind of him who carved the statue or painted the panel or graved the gem.

It is sometimes said by those who understand neither the nature of the highest Criticism nor the charm of the highest Art, that the pictures that the critic loves most to write about are those that belong to the anecdotage of painting, and that deal with scenes taken out of literature or history. But this is not so. Indeed, pictures of this kind are far too intelligible. As a class, they rank with illustrations, and even considered from this point of view are failures, as they do not stir the imagination, but set definite bounds to it. For the domain of the painter is, as I suggested before, widely different from that of the poet. To the latter belongs life in its full and absolute entirety; not merely the beauty that men look at, but the beauty that men listen to also; not merely the momentary grace of form or the transient gladness of colour, but the whole sphere of feeling, the perfect cycle of thought. The painter is so far limited that it is only through the mask of the body that he can show us the mystery of the soul; only through conventional images that he can handle ideas; only through its physical equivalents that he can deal with psychology. And how inadequately does he do it then, asking us to accept the torn turban of the Moor for the noble rage of Othello, or a dotard in a storm for the wild madness of Lear! Yet it seems as if nothing could stop him. Most of our elderly English painters spend their wicked and wasted lives in poaching upon the domain of the poets, marring their motives by clumsy treatment, and striving to render, by visible form or colour, the marvel of what is invisible, the splendour of what is not seen. Their pictures are, as a natural consequence, insufferably tedious. They have degraded the invisible arts into the obvious arts, and the one thing not worth looking at is the obvious. I do not say that poet and painter may not treat of the same subject. They have always done so, and will always do so. But while the poet can be pictorial or not, as he chooses, the painter must be pictorial always. For a painter is limited, not to what he sees in nature, but to what upon canvas may be seen.

And so, my dear Ernest, pictures of this kind will not really fascinate the critic. He will turn from them to such works as make him brood and dream and fancy, to works that possess the subtle quality of suggestion, and seem to tell one that even from them there is an escape into a wider world. It is sometimes said that the tragedy of an artist's life is that he cannot realize his ideal. But the true tragedy that dogs the steps of most artists is that they realize their ideal too absolutely. For, when the ideal is realized, it is robbed of its wonder and its mystery, and becomes simply a new starting point for an ideal that is other than itself. This is the reason why music is the perfect type of art. Music can never reveal its ultimate secret. This, also, is the explanation of the value of limitations in art. The sculptor gladly surrenders imitative colour, and the painter the actual dimensions of form, because by such renunciations they are able to avoid too definite a presentation of the Real, which would be mere imitation, and too definite a realization of the Ideal, which would be too purely intellectual. It is through its very incompleteness that Art becomes complete in beauty, and so addresses itself, not to the faculty of recognition nor to the faculty of reason, but to the aesthetic sense alone, which, while accepting both reason and recognition as stages of apprehension, subordinates them both to a pure synthetic impression of the work of art as a whole, and, taking whatever alien emotional elements the work may possess, uses their very complexity as a means by which a richer unity may be added to the ultimate impression itself. You see, then, how it is that the aesthetic critic rejects these obvious modes of art that have but one message to deliver, and having delivered it become dumb and sterile, and seeks rather for such modes as suggest reverie and mood, and by their imaginative beauty make all interpretations true, and no interpretation final. Some resemblance, no doubt, the creative work of the critic will have to the work that has stirred him to creation, but it will be such resemblance as exists, not between Nature and the mirror that the painter of landscape or figure may be supposed to hold up to her, but between Nature and the work of the decorative artist. Just as on the flowerless carpets of Persia, tulip and rose blossom indeed and are lovely to look on, though they are not reproduced in visible shape or line; just as the pearl and purple of the sea shell is echoed in the church of St. Mark at Venice; just as the vaulted ceiling of the wondrous chapel at Ravenna is made gorgeous by the gold and green and sapphire of the peacock's tail, though the birds of Juno[2] fly not across it; so the critic reproduces the work that he criticizes in a mode that is never imitative, and part of whose charm may really consist in the rejection of resemblance, and shows us in this way not merely the meaning but also the mystery of Beauty, and, by transforming each art into literature, solves once for all the problem of Art's unity.

But I see it is time for supper. After we have discussed some Chambertin and a few ortolans,[3] we will pass on to the question of the critic considered in the light of the interpreter.

ERNEST   Ah! you admit, then, that the critic may occasionally be allowed to see the object as in itself it really is.

GILBERT   I am not quite sure. Perhaps I may admit it after supper. There is a subtle influence in supper.

1890, 1891

Preface to *The Picture of Dorian Gray*

The artist is the creator of beautiful things.
To reveal art and conceal the artist is art's aim.
The critic is he who can translate into another manner or a new
material his impression of beautiful things.

---

2. Peacocks, associated in classical mythology with the goddess Juno (in Greek, Hera) because she is said to have set in the bird's tail the eyes of hundred-eyed Argus, who died in her service.

3. Small birds esteemed by epicures for their delicate flavor. "Chambertin": one of the finest wines of Burgundy.

The highest, as the lowest, form of criticism is a mode of auto-
biography.
Those who find ugly meanings in beautiful things are corrupt without being
charming. This is a fault.
Those who find beautiful meanings in beautiful things are the
cultivated. For these there is hope.
They are the elect to whom beautiful things mean only Beauty.
There is no such thing as a moral or an immoral book.
Books are well written, or badly written. That is all.
The nineteenth-century dislike of Realism is the rage of Caliban[1] seeing his
own face in a glass.
The nineteenth-century dislike of Romanticism is the rage of
Caliban not seeing his own face in a glass.
The moral life of man forms part of the subject matter of the artist, but
the morality of art consists in the perfect use of an imperfect medium.
No artist desires to prove anything. Even things that are true can be
proved.
No artist has ethical sympathies. An ethical sympathy in an artist is
an unpardonable mannerism of style.
No artist is ever morbid. The artist can express everything.
Thought and language are to the artist instruments of an art.
Vice and Virtue are to the artist materials for an art.
From the point of view of form, the type of all the arts is the art of the musician.
From the point of view of feeling, the actor's craft is the type.
All art is at once surface and symbol.
Those who go beneath the surface do so at their peril.
Those who read the symbol do so at their peril.
It is the spectator, and not life, that art really mirrors.
Diversity of opinion about a work of art shows that the work is new,
complex, and vital.
When critics disagree the artist is in accord with himself. We
can forgive a man for making a useful thing as long as he does not admire it.
The only excuse for making a useless thing is that one admires it intensely.
All art is quite useless.

1891

The Importance of Being Earnest

Of the four stage comedies by Wilde,
his last, *The Importance of Being Earnest*, is generally regarded as his masterpiece. It
was first staged in February 1895 and was an immediate hit. Only one critic failed to
find it delightful; curiously, this was Wilde's fellow playwright from Ireland, Bernard
Shaw, who, though amused, found Wilde's wit "hateful" and "sinister," and thought
the play exhibited "real degeneracy." Despite Shaw's complaints, the first London
production ran for eighty-six performances; but when Wilde was sentenced to prison,
production ceased for several years. Shortly before his death it was revived in London
and New York, and it has subsequently become a classic.

In its original version the play was in four acts. At the request of the stage producer,
Wilde reduced it to three acts—the version almost always used in performances and

1. The character in Shakespeare's *The Tempest* who is half-human, half-monster.

therefore the version reprinted here. A few of the notes in the text cite passages from the four-act version.

The play was first published in 1899. Earlier, in an interview, Wilde had described his overall aim in writing it: "It has as its philosophy . . . that we should treat all the trivial things of life seriously, and all the serious things of life with sincere and studied triviality." Just before his death he remarked that although he was pleased with the "bright and happy" tone and temper of his play, he wished it might have had a "higher seriousness of intent." Later critics have found this seriousness of intent in the play's deconstruction of Victorian moral and social values. Like another Victorian master-piece of the absurd, *Alice's Adventures in Wonderland* (1865), *The Importance of Being Earnest* empties manners and morals of their underlying sense to create a nominalist world where earnest is not a quality of character but a name, where words, to paraphrase Humpty Dumpty in *Through the Looking-Glass* (1871), mean what you choose them to mean, neither more nor less.

The literary ancestry of Wilde's play has been variously identified. In its witty word-play and worldly attitudes it has been likened to comedies of the Restoration period such as William Congreve's *Love for Love* (1695). In its genial and lighthearted tone, it has some affinities with the festive comedies of Shakespeare, such as *Twelfth Night* (ca. 1601), and with Oliver Goldsmith's *She Stoops to Conquer* (1773). A more imme-diate predecessor was *Engaged* (1877), a comic play by W. S. Gilbert that anticipated some of the burlesque effects exploited by Wilde, such as the inviolable imperturb-ability of the speakers and the interrupting of sentimental scenes by the consumption of food. Gilbert's advice to the actors who were putting on his *Engaged* is worth citing as a clue to how *The Importance of Being Earnest* may be most effectively imagined as a stage representation:

> It is absolutely essential to the success of this piece that it should be played with the most perfect earnestness and gravity throughout. . . . Directly the actors show that they are conscious of the absurdity of their utterances the piece begins to drag.

The Importance of Being Earnest

First Act

SCENE—*Morning room in* ALGERNON's *flat in Half-Moon Street.*[1]

The room is luxuriously and artistically furnished. The sound of a piano is heard in the adjoining room.

[LANE *is arranging afternoon tea on the table, and after the music has ceased,* ALGERNON *enters.*]

ALGERNON Did you hear what I was playing, Lane?

LANE I didn't think it polite to listen, sir.

ALGERNON I'm sorry for that, for your sake. I don't play accurately—anyone can play accurately—but I play with wonderful expression. As far as the piano is concerned, sentiment is my forte. I keep science for Life.

LANE Yes, sir.

ALGERNON And, speaking of the science of Life, have you got the cucumber sandwiches cut for Lady Bracknell?[2]

---

1. A highly fashionable location (at the time of the play) in the West End of London.
2. Bracknell is the name of a place in Berkshire where the mother of Lord Alfred Douglas had her summer home, which Wilde had visited.

LANE Yes, sir. [*Hands them on a salver.*]

ALGERNON [*Inspects them, takes two, and sits down on the sofa.*] Oh! . . . by the way, Lane, I see from your book[3] that on Thursday night, when Lord Shoreham and Mr. Worthing were dining with me, eight bottles of champagne are entered as having been consumed.

LANE Yes, sir; eight bottles and a pint.

ALGERNON Why is it that at a bachelor's establishment the servants invariably drink the champagne? I ask merely for information.

LANE I attribute it to the superior quality of the wine, sir. I have often observed that in married households the champagne is rarely of a first-rate brand.

ALGERNON Good Heavens! Is marriage so demoralizing as that?

LANE I believe it *is* a very pleasant state, sir. I have had very little experience of it myself up to the present. I have only been married once. That was in consequence of a misunderstanding between myself and a young person.

ALGERNON [*Languidly.*] I don't know that I am much interested in your family life, Lane.

LANE No, sir; it is not a very interesting subject. I never think of it myself.

ALGERNON Very natural, I am sure. That will do, Lane, thank you.

LANE Thank you, sir.   [LANE *goes out.*]

ALGERNON Lane's views on marriage seem somewhat lax. Really, if the lower orders don't set us a good example, what on earth is the use of them? They seem, as a class, to have absolutely no sense of moral responsibility.

[*Enter* LANE.]

LANE Mr. Ernest Worthing.

[*Enter* JACK.]   [LANE *goes out.*]

ALGERNON How are you, my dear Ernest? What brings you up to town?

JACK Oh, pleasure, pleasure! What else should bring one anywhere? Eating as usual, I see, Algy!

ALGERNON [*Stiffly.*] I believe it is customary in good society to take some slight refreshment at five o'clock. Where have you been since last Thursday?

JACK [*Sitting down on the sofa.*] In the country.

ALGERNON What on earth do you do there?

JACK [*Pulling off his gloves.*] When one is in town one amuses oneself. When one is in the country one amuses other people. It is excessively boring.

ALGERNON And who are the people you amuse?

JACK [*Airily.*] Oh, neighbours, neighbours.

ALGERNON Got nice neighbours in your part of Shropshire?

JACK Perfectly horrid! Never speak to one of them.

ALGERNON How immensely you must amuse them! [*Goes over and takes sandwich.*] By the way, Shropshire is your county, is it not?

JACK Eh? Shropshire?[4] Yes, of course. Hallo! Why all these cups? Why cucumber sandwiches? Why such reckless extravagance in one so young? Who is coming to tea?

ALGERNON Oh! merely Aunt Augusta and Gwendolen.

---

3. Cellar book, in which records were kept of wines.

4. As we learn later, the estate is in Hertfordshire, a long distance from Shropshire. In the four-act version of the play, when this discrepancy is pointed out by Algernon, Jack replies: "My dear fellow! Surely you don't expect me to be accurate about geography? No gentleman is accurate about geography. Why, I got a prize for geography when I was at school. I can't be expected to know anything about it now."

JACK   How perfectly delightful!

ALGERNON   Yes, that is all very well; but I am afraid Aunt Augusta won't quite approve of your being here.

JACK   May I ask why?

ALGERNON   My dear fellow, the way you flirt with Gwendolen is perfectly disgraceful. It is almost as bad as the way Gwendolen flirts with you.

JACK   I am in love with Gwendolen. I have come up to town expressly to propose to her.

ALGERNON   I thought you had come up for pleasure? . . . I call that business.

JACK   How utterly unromantic you are!

ALGERNON   I really don't see anything romantic in proposing. It is very romantic to be in love. But there is nothing romantic about a definite proposal. Why, one may be accepted. One usually is, I believe. Then the excitement is all over. The very essence of romance is uncertainty. If ever I get married, I'll certainly try to forget the fact.

JACK   I have no doubt about that, dear Algy. The Divorce Court was specially invented for people whose memories are so curiously constituted.

ALGERNON   Oh! there is no use speculating on that subject. Divorces are made in Heaven—[JACK *puts out his hand to take a sandwich.* ALGERNON *at once interferes.*] Please don't touch the cucumber sandwiches. They are ordered specially for Aunt Augusta. [*Takes one and eats it.*]

JACK   Well, you have been eating them all the time.

ALGERNON   That is quite a different matter. She is my aunt. [*Takes plate from below.*] Have some bread and butter. The bread and butter is for Gwendolen. Gwendolen is devoted to bread and butter.

JACK [*Advancing to table and helping himself.*]   And very good bread and butter it is too.

ALGERNON   Well, my dear fellow, you need not eat as if you were going to eat it all. You behave as if you were married to her already. You are not married to her already, and I don't think you ever will be.

JACK   Why on earth do you say that?

ALGERNON   Well, in the first place, girls never marry the men they flirt with. Girls don't think it right.

JACK   Oh, that is nonsense!

ALGERNON   It isn't. It is a great truth. It accounts for the extraordinary number of bachelors that one sees all over the place. In the second place, I don't give my consent.

JACK   Your consent!

ALGERNON   My dear fellow, Gwendolen is my first cousin. And before I allow you to marry her, you will have to clear up the whole question of Cecily. [*Rings bell.*]

JACK   Cecily! What on earth do you mean? What do you mean, Algy, by Cecily? I don't know anyone of the name of Cecily.

   [*Enter* LANE.]

ALGERNON   Bring me that cigarette case Mr. Worthing left in the smoking-room the last time he dined here.

LANE   Yes, sir.   [LANE *goes out.*]

JACK   Do you mean to say you have had my cigarette case all this time? I wish to goodness you had let me know. I have been writing frantic letters to Scotland Yard[5] about it. I was very nearly offering a large reward.

---

5. Police headquarters in London.

ALGERNON   Well, I wish you would offer one. I happen to be more than usually hard up.[6]

JACK   There is no good offering a large reward now that the thing is found. [*Enter* LANE *with the cigarette case on a salver.* ALGERNON *takes it at once.* LANE *goes out.*]

ALGERNON   I think that is rather mean of you, Ernest, I must say. [*Opens case and examines it.*] However, it makes no matter, for, now that I look at the inscription inside, I find that the thing isn't yours after all.

JACK   Of course it's mine. [*Moving to him.*] You have seen me with it a hundred times, and you have no right whatsoever to read what is written inside. It is a very ungentlemanly thing to read a private cigarette case.

ALGERNON   Oh! it is absurd to have a hard-and-fast rule about what one should read and what one shouldn't. More than half of modern culture depends on what one shouldn't read.

JACK   I am quite aware of the fact, and I don't propose to discuss modern culture. It isn't the sort of thing one should talk of in private. I simply want my cigarette case back.

ALGERNON   Yes; but this isn't your cigarette case. This cigarette case is a present from someone of the name of Cecily, and you said you didn't know anyone of that name.

JACK   Well, if you want to know, Cecily happens to be my aunt.

ALGERNON   Your aunt!

JACK   Yes. Charming old lady she is, too. Lives at Tunbridge Wells.[7] Just give it back to me, Algy.

ALGERNON   [*retreating to back of sofa.*]   But why does she call herself little Cecily if she is your aunt and lives at Tunbridge Wells? [*Reading.*] "From little Cecily with her fondest love."

JACK   [*Moving to sofa and kneeling upon it.*]   My dear fellow, what on earth is there in that? Some aunts are tall, some aunts are not tall. That is a matter that surely an aunt may be allowed to decide for herself. You seem to think that every aunt should be exactly like your aunt! That is absurd! For Heaven's sake give me back my cigarette case. [*Follows Algy round the room.*]

ALGERNON   Yes. But why does your aunt call you her uncle? "From little Cecily, with her fondest love to her dear Uncle Jack." There is no objection, I admit, to an aunt being a small aunt, but why an aunt, no matter what her size may be, should call her own nephew her uncle, I can't quite make out. Besides, your name isn't Jack at all; it is Ernest.

JACK   It isn't Ernest; it's Jack.

ALGERNON   You have always told me it was Ernest. I have introduced you to everyone as Ernest. You answer to the name of Ernest. You look as if your name was Ernest. You are the most earnest looking person I ever saw in my life. It is perfectly absurd your saying that your name isn't Ernest. It's on your cards. Here is one of them. [*Taking it from case.*] "Mr. Ernest Worthing, B. 4, The Albany."[8] I'll keep this as a proof that your name is Ernest if ever you attempt to deny it to me, or to Gwendolen, or to anyone else. [*Puts the card in his pocket.*]

JACK   Well, my name is Ernest in town and Jack in the country, and the cigarette case was given to me in the country.

6. Short of money.
7. A fashionable resort town south of London.
8. A former residence of the duke of Albany (brother of George IV) near Piccadilly that had been converted into elegant apartments.

ALGERNON   Yes, but that does not account for the fact that your small Aunt
   Cecily, who lives at Tunbridge Wells, calls you her dear uncle. Come, old
   boy, you had much better have the thing out at once.

JACK   My dear Algy, you talk exactly as if you were a dentist. It is very vulgar
   to talk like a dentist when one isn't a dentist. It produces a false impression.

ALGERNON   Well, that is exactly what dentists always do. Now, go on! Tell me
   the whole thing. I may mention that I have always suspected you of being
   a confirmed and secret Bunburyist; and I am quite sure of it now.

JACK   Bunburyist? What on earth do you mean by a Bunburyist?

ALGERNON   I'll reveal to you the meaning of that incomparable expression as
   soon as you are kind enough to inform me why you are Ernest in town and
   Jack in the country.

JACK   Well, produce my cigarette case first.

ALGERNON   Here it is. [Hands cigarette case.] Now produce your explanation,
   and pray make it improbable. [Sits on sofa.]

JACK   My dear fellow, there is nothing improbable about my explanation
   at all. In fact it's perfectly ordinary. Old Mr. Thomas Cardew, who adopted
   me when I was a little boy, made me in his will guardian to his granddaughter, Miss Cecily Cardew. Cecily, who addresses me as her uncle
   from motives of respect that you could not possibly appreciate, lives at my
   place in the country under the charge of her admirable governess, Miss
   Prism.

ALGERNON   Where is that place in the country, by the way?

JACK   That is nothing to you, dear boy. You are not going to be invited. . . . I
   may tell you candidly that the place is not in Shropshire.

ALGERNON   I suspected that, my dear fellow! I have Bunburyed all over Shropshire on two separate occasions. Now, go on. Why are you Ernest in town
   and Jack in the country?

JACK   My dear Algy, I don't know whether you will be able to understand my
   real motives. You are hardly serious enough. When one is placed in the
   position of guardian, one has to adopt a very high moral tone on all subjects.
   It's one's duty to do so. And as a high moral tone can hardly be said to
   conduce very much to either one's health or one's happiness, in order to get
   up to town I have always pretended to have a younger brother of the name
   of Ernest, who lives in the Albany, and gets into the most dreadful scrapes.
   That, my dear Algy, is the whole truth pure and simple.

ALGERNON   The truth is rarely pure and never simple. Modern life would be
   very tedious if it were either, and modern literature a complete impossibility!

JACK   That wouldn't be at all a bad thing.

ALGERNON   Literary criticism is not your forte, my dear fellow. Don't try it.
   You should leave that to people who haven't been at a University. They do
   it so well in the daily papers. What you really are is a Bunburyist. I was
   quite right in saying you were a Bunburyist. You are one of the most
   advanced Bunburyists I know.

JACK   What on earth do you mean?

ALGERNON   You have invented a very useful young brother called Ernest, in
   order that you may be able to come up to town as often as you like. I have
   invented an invaluable permanent invalid called Bunbury, in order that I
   may be able to go down into the country whenever I choose. Bunbury is
   perfectly invaluable. If it wasn't for Bunbury's extraordinary bad health, for
   instance, I wouldn't be able to dine with you at Willis's tonight, for I have

been really engaged[9] to Aunt Augusta for more than a week.

JACK I haven't asked you to dine with me anywhere tonight.

ALGERNON I know. You are absurdly careless about sending out invitations. It is very foolish of you. Nothing annoys people so much as not receiving invitations.

JACK You had much better dine with your Aunt Augusta.

ALGERNON I haven't the smallest intention of doing anything of the kind. To begin with, I dined there on Monday, and once a week is quite enough to dine with one's own relations. In the second place, whenever I do dine there I am always treated as a member of the family, and sent down with[1] either no woman at all, or two. In the third place, I know perfectly well whom she will place me next to, tonight. She will place me next Mary Farquhar, who always flirts with her own husband across the dinner table. That is not very pleasant. Indeed, it is not even decent . . . and that sort of thing is enormously on the increase. The amount of women in London who flirt with their own husbands is perfectly scandalous. It looks so bad. It is simply washing one's clean linen in public. Besides, now that I know you to be a confirmed Bunburyist, I naturally want to talk to you about Bunburying. I want to tell you the rules.

JACK I'm not a Bunburyist at all. If Gwendolen accepts me, I am going to kill my brother, indeed I think I'll kill him in any case. Cecily is a little too much interested in him. It is rather a bore. So I am going to get rid of Ernest. And I strongly advise you to do the same with Mr. . . . with your invalid friend who has the absurd name.

ALGERNON Nothing will induce me to part with Bunbury, and if you ever get married, which seems to me extremely problematic, you will be very glad to know Bunbury. A man who marries without knowing Bunbury has a very tedious time of it.

JACK That is nonsense. If I marry a charming girl like Gwendolen, and she is the only girl I ever saw in my life that I would marry, I certainly won't want to know Bunbury.

ALGERNON Then your wife will. You don't seem to realize, that in married life three is company and two is none.

JACK [*Sententiously.*] That, my dear young friend, is the theory that the corrupt French Drama has been propounding for the last fifty years.[2]

ALGERNON Yes; and that the happy English home has proved in half the time.

JACK For heaven's sake, don't try to be cynical. It's perfectly easy to be cynical.

ALGERNON My dear fellow, it isn't easy to be anything nowadays. There's such a lot of beastly competition about. [*The sound of an electric bell is heard.*] Ah! that must be Aunt Augusta. Only relatives, or creditors, ever ring in that Wagnerian manner.[3] Now, if I get her out of the way for ten minutes, so that you can have an opportunity for proposing to Gwendolen, may I dine with you tonight at Willis's?

JACK I suppose so, if you want to.

---

9. I.e., committed to attend her dinner party. "Willis's": a first-class restaurant in the vicinity of St. James's Street, in the center of London.
1. I.e., required to escort, as a dinner partner.
2. Almost all the plays by the leading French playwrights of the second half of the 19th century (Alexandre Dumas *fils*, Émile Augier, and Victorien

Sardou) focus on marital infidelity. As Brander Matthews, an American critic, noted in 1882, "the trio—husband, wife, and lover" had become "almost universal" in the French theater.
3. Insistently loud, like some of the music in the large-scale operas of Richard Wagner (1813–1883).

ALGERNON   Yes, but you must be serious about it. I hate people who are not
serious about meals. It is so shallow of them.
  [*Enter* LANE.]
LANE   Lady Bracknell and Miss Fairfax.
  [ALGERNON *goes forward to meet them. Enter* LADY BRACKNELL *and*
  GWENDOLEN.]
LADY BRACKNELL   Good afternoon, dear Algernon, I hope you are behaving
  very well.
ALGERNON   I'm feeling very well, Aunt Augusta.
LADY BRACKNELL   That's not quite the same thing. In fact the two things rarely
  go together. [*Sees* JACK *and bows to him with icy coldness.*]
ALGERNON [*To* GWENDOLEN.]   Dear me, you are smart!⁴
GWENDOLEN   I am always smart! Aren't I, Mr. Worthing?
JACK   You're quite perfect, Miss Fairfax.
GWENDOLEN   Oh! I hope I am not that. It would leave no room for develop-
  ments, and I intend to develop in many directions. [GWENDOLEN *and* JACK
  sit down together in the corner.]
LADY BRACKNELL   I'm sorry if we are a little late, Algernon, but I was obliged
  to call on dear Lady Harbury. I hadn't been there since her poor husband's
  death. I never saw a woman so altered; she looks quite twenty years younger.
  And now I'll have a cup of tea, and one of those nice cucumber sandwiches
  you promised me.
ALGERNON   Certainly, Aunt Augusta. [*Goes over to tea-table.*]
LADY BRACKNELL   Won't you come and sit here, Gwendolen?
GWENDOLEN   Thanks, mamma,⁵ I'm quite comfortable where I am.
ALGERNON [*Picking up empty plate in horror.*]   Good heavens! Lane! Why
  are there no cucumber sandwiches? I ordered them specially.
LANE [*Gravely.*]   There were no cucumbers in the market this morning, sir. I
  went down twice.
ALGERNON   No cucumbers!
LANE   No, sir. Not even for ready money.⁶
ALGERNON   That will do, Lane, thank you.
LANE   Thank you, sir.
ALGERNON   I am greatly distressed, Aunt Augusta, about there being no
  cucumbers, not even for ready money.
LADY BRACKNELL   It really makes no matter, Algernon. I had some crumpets⁷
  with Lady Harbury, who seems to me to be living entirely for pleasure now.
ALGERNON   I hear her hair has turned quite gold from grief.
LADY BRACKNELL   It certainly has changed its colour. From what cause I, of
  course, cannot say. [ALGERNON *crosses and hands tea.*] Thank you. I've quite
  a treat for you tonight, Algernon. I am going to send you down with Mary
  Farquhar. She is such a nice woman, and so attentive to her husband. It's
  delightful to watch them.
ALGERNON   I am afraid, Aunt Augusta, I shall have to give up the pleasure of
  dining with you tonight after all.
LADY BRACKNELL [*Frowning.*]   I hope not, Algernon. It would put my table
  completely out. Your uncle would have to dine upstairs.⁸ Fortunately he is
  accustomed to that.

---

4. Elegantly fashionable.
5. Pronounced with the accent on the second syllable.
6. Immediate payment in cash (rather than on

credit).
7. Round griddle breads, served toasted.
8. Because otherwise she would have more
women than men at the table.

ALGERNON   It is a great bore, and, I need hardly say, a terrible disappointment to me, but the fact is I have just had a telegram to say that my poor friend Bunbury is very ill again. [*Exchanges glances with* JACK.] They seem to think I should be with him.

LADY BRACKNELL   It is very strange. This Mr. Bunbury seems to suffer from curiously bad health.

ALGERNON   Yes; poor Bunbury is a dreadful invalid.

LADY BRACKNELL   Well, I must say, Algernon, that I think it is high time that Mr. Bunbury made up his mind whether he was going to live or to die. This shilly-shallying with the question is absurd. Nor do I in any way approve of the modern sympathy with invalids. I consider it morbid. Illness of any kind is hardly a thing to be encouraged in others. Health is the primary duty of life. I am always telling that to your poor uncle, but he never seems to take much notice . . . as far as any improvement in his ailments goes. I should be obliged if you would ask Mr. Bunbury, from me, to be kind enough not to have a relapse on Saturday, for I rely on you to arrange my music for me. It is my last reception, and one wants something that will encourage conversation, particularly at the end of the season[9] when everyone has practically said whatever they had to say, which, in most cases, was probably not much.

ALGERNON   I'll speak to Bunbury, Aunt Augusta, if he is still conscious, and I think I can promise you he'll be all right by Saturday. Of course the music is a great difficulty. You see, if one plays good music, people don't listen, and if one plays bad music, people don't talk. But I'll run over the program I've drawn out, if you will kindly come into the next room for a moment.

LADY BRACKNELL   Thank you, Algernon. It is very thoughtful of you. [*Rising, and following* ALGERNON.] I'm sure the program will be delightful, after a few expurgations. French songs I cannot possibly allow. People always seem to think that they are improper, and either look shocked, which is vulgar, or laugh, which is worse. But German sounds a thoroughly respectable language, and indeed, I believe is so. Gwendolen, you will accompany me.

GWENDOLEN   Certainly, mamma.

> [LADY BRACKNELL *and* ALGERNON *go into the music room,* GWENDOLEN *remains behind.*]

JACK   Charming day it has been, Miss Fairfax.

GWENDOLEN   Pray don't talk to me about the weather, Mr. Worthing. Whenever people talk to me about the weather, I always feel quite certain that they mean something else. And that makes me so nervous.

JACK   I do mean something else.

GWENDOLEN   I thought so. In fact, I am never wrong.

JACK   And I would like to be allowed to take advantage of Lady Bracknell's temporary absence . . .

GWENDOLEN   I would certainly advise you to do so. Mamma has a way of coming back suddenly into a room that I have often had to speak to her about.

JACK [*Nervously.*]   Miss Fairfax, ever since I met you I have admired you more than any girl . . . I have ever met since . . . I met you.

GWENDOLEN   Yes, I am quite aware of the fact. And I often wish that in public, at any rate, you had been more demonstrative. For me you have always had

---

9. The social season, extending from May through July, when people of fashion came into London from their country estates for entertainments and parties.

an irresistible fascination. Even before I met you I was far from indifferent to you. [JACK *looks at her in amazement.*] We live, as I hope you know, Mr. Worthing, in an age of ideals. The fact is constantly mentioned in the more expensive monthly magazines, and has reached the provincial pulpits, I am told: and my ideal has always been to love someone of the name of Ernest. There is something in that name that inspires absolute confidence. The moment Algernon first mentioned to me that he had a friend called Ernest, I knew I was destined to love you.

JACK   You really love me, Gwendolen?

GWENDOLEN   Passionately!

JACK   Darling! You don't know how happy you've made me.

GWENDOLEN   My own Ernest!

JACK   But you don't really mean to say that you couldn't love me if my name wasn't Ernest?

GWENDOLEN   But your name is Ernest.

JACK   Yes, I know it is. But supposing it was something else? Do you mean to say you couldn't love me then?

GWENDOLEN   [*Glibly.*]   Ah! that is clearly a metaphysical speculation, and like most metaphysical speculations has very little reference at all to the actual facts of real life, as we know them.

JACK   Personally, darling, to speak quite candidly, I don't much care about the name of Ernest . . . I don't think the name suits me at all.

GWENDOLEN   It suits you perfectly. It is a divine name. It has a music of its own. It produces vibrations.

JACK   Well, really, Gwendolen, I must say that I think there are lots of other much nicer names. I think Jack, for instance, a charming name.

GWENDOLEN   Jack? . . . No, there is very little music in the name Jack, if any at all, indeed. It does not thrill. It produces absolutely no vibrations. . . . I have known several Jacks, and they all, without exception, were more than usually plain. Besides, Jack is a notorious domesticity for John! And I pity any woman who is married to a man called John. She would probably never be allowed to know the entrancing pleasure of a single moment's solitude. The only really safe name is Ernest.

JACK   Gwendolen, I must get christened at once—I mean we must get married at once. There is no time to be lost.

GWENDOLEN   Married, Mr. Worthing?

JACK [*Astounded.*]   Well . . . surely. You know that I love you, and you led me to believe, Miss Fairfax, that you were not absolutely indifferent to me.

GWENDOLEN   I adore you. But you haven't proposed to me yet. Nothing has been said at all about marriage. The subject has not even been touched on.

JACK   Well . . . may I propose to you now?

GWENDOLEN   I think it would be an admirable opportunity. And to spare you any possible disappointment, Mr. Worthing, I think it only fair to tell you quite frankly beforehand that I am fully determined to accept you.

JACK   Gwendolen!

GWENDOLEN   Yes, Mr. Worthing, what have you got to say to me?

JACK   You know what I have got to say to you.

GWENDOLEN   Yes, but you don't say it.

JACK   Gwendolen, will you marry me? [*Goes on his knees.*]

GWENDOLEN   Of course I will, darling. How long you have been about it! I am afraid you have had very little experience in how to propose.

JACK   My own one, I have never loved anyone in the world but you.

GWENDOLEN   Yes, but men often propose for practice. I know my brother Gerald does. All my girlfriends tell me so. What wonderfully blue eyes you have, Ernest! They are quite, quite blue. I hope you will always look at me just like that, especially when there are other people present.

[*Enter* LADY BRACKNELL.]

LADY BRACKNELL   Mr. Worthing! Rise, sir, from this semi-recumbent posture. It is most indecorous.

GWENDOLEN   Mamma! [*He tries to rise; she restrains him.*] I must beg you to retire. This is no place for you. Besides, Mr. Worthing has not quite finished yet.

LADY BRACKNELL   Finished what, may I ask?

GWENDOLEN   I am engaged to Mr. Worthing, mamma.

[*They rise together.*]

LADY BRACKNELL   Pardon me, you are not engaged to anyone. When you do become engaged to someone, I, or your father, should his health permit him, will inform you of the fact. An engagement should come on a young girl as a surprise, pleasant or unpleasant, as the case may be. It is hardly a matter that she could be allowed to arrange for herself. . . . And now I have a few questions to put to you, Mr. Worthing. While I am making these inquiries, you, Gwendolen, will wait for me below in the carriage.

GWENDOLEN [*Reproachfully.*]   Mamma!

LADY BRACKNELL   In the carriage, Gwendolen! [GWENDOLEN *goes to the door. She and* JACK *blow kisses to each other behind* LADY BRACKNELL'*s back.* LADY BRACKNELL *looks vaguely about as if she could not understand what the noise was. Finally turns round.*] Gwendolen, the carriage!

GWENDOLEN   Yes, mamma. [*Goes out, looking back at* JACK.]

LADY BRACKNELL [*Sitting down.*]   You can take a seat, Mr. Worthing.
    [*Looks in her pocket for notebook and pencil.*]

JACK   Thank you, Lady Bracknell, I prefer standing.

LADY BRACKNELL [*Pencil and notebook in hand.*]   I feel bound to tell you that you are not down on my list of eligible young men, although I have the same list as the dear Duchess of Bolton has. We work together, in fact. However, I am quite ready to enter your name, should your answers be what a really affectionate mother requires. Do you smoke?

JACK   Well, yes, I must admit I smoke.

LADY BRACKNELL   I am glad to hear it. A man should always have an occupation of some kind. There are far too many idle men in London as it is. How old are you?

JACK   Twenty-nine.

LADY BRACKNELL   A very good age to be married at. I have always been of opinion that a man who desires to get married should know either everything or nothing. Which do you know?

JACK [*After some hesitation.*]   I know nothing, Lady Bracknell.

LADY BRACKNELL   I am pleased to hear it. I do not approve of anything that tampers with natural ignorance. Ignorance is like a delicate exotic fruit; touch it and the bloom is gone. The whole theory of modern education is radically unsound. Fortunately in England, at any rate, education produces no effect whatsoever. If it did, it would prove a serious danger to the upper classes, and probably lead to acts of violence in Grosvenor Square.[1] What is your income?

---

1. A fashionable residential area in the West End of London.

JACK Between seven and eight thousand a year.

LADY BRACKNELL [*Makes a note in her book.*] In land, or in investments?

JACK In investments, chiefly.

LADY BRACKNELL That is satisfactory. What between the duties expected of one during one's lifetime, and the duties exacted from one after one's death,[2] land has ceased to be either a profit or a pleasure. It gives one position, and prevents one from keeping it up. That's all that can be said about land.

JACK I have a country house with some land, of course, attached to it, about fifteen hundred acres, I believe; but I don't depend on that for my real income. In fact, as far as I can make out, the poachers are the only people who make anything out of it.

LADY BRACKNELL A country house! How many bedrooms? Well, that point can be cleared up afterwards. You have a town house, I hope? A girl with a simple, unspoiled nature, like Gwendolen, could hardly be expected to reside in the country.

JACK Well, I own a house in Belgrave Square,[3] but it is let by the year to Lady Bloxham. Of course, I can get it back whenever I like, at six months' notice.

LADY BRACKNELL Lady Bloxham? I don't know her.

JACK Oh, she goes about very little. She is a lady considerably advanced in years.

LADY BRACKNELL Ah, nowadays that is no guarantee of respectability of character. What number in Belgrave Square?

JACK 149.

LADY BRACKNELL [*Shaking her head.*] The unfashionable side. I thought there was something. However, that could easily be altered.

JACK Do you mean the fashion, or the side?

LADY BRACKNELL [*Sternly.*] Both, if necessary, I presume. What are your politics?

JACK Well, I am afraid I really have none. I am a Liberal Unionist.[4]

LADY BRACKNELL Oh, they count as Tories. They dine with us. Or come in the evening, at any rate. Now to minor matters. Are your parents living?

JACK I have lost both my parents.

LADY BRACKNELL Both? To lose one parent may be regarded as a misfortune— to lose *both* seems like carelessness. Who was your father? He was evidently a man of some wealth. Was he born in what the Radical papers call the purple of commerce, or did he rise from the ranks of aristocracy?

JACK I am afraid I really don't know. The fact is, Lady Bracknell, I said I had lost my parents. It would be nearer the truth to say that my parents seem to have lost me. . . . I don't actually know who I am by birth. I was . . . well, I was found.

LADY BRACKNELL Found!

JACK The late Mr. Thomas Cardew, an old gentleman of a very charitable and kindly disposition, found me, and gave me the name of Worthing, because he happened to have a first-class ticket for Worthing in his pocket at the time. Worthing is a place in Sussex. It is a seaside resort.

LADY BRACKNELL Where did the charitable gentleman who had a first-class ticket for this seaside resort find you?

2. The wordplay is on "death duties"—i.e., inheritance taxes.
3. Another fashionable residential area in the West End.

4. A splinter group of members of the Liberal Party who in 1886, led by Joseph Chamberlain, joined forces with the Conservative Party (the "Tories") in opposing home rule for Ireland.

JACK [*Gravely.*]   In a handbag.

LADY BRACKNELL   A handbag?

JACK [*Very seriously.*]   Yes, Lady Bracknell. I was in a handbag—a somewhat large, black leather handbag, with handles to it—an ordinary handbag, in fact.

LADY BRACKNELL   In what locality did this Mr. James, or Thomas, Cardew come across this ordinary handbag?

JACK   In the cloak room at Victoria Station. It was given to him in mistake for his own.[5]

LADY BRACKNELL   The cloak room at Victoria Station?

JACK   Yes. The Brighton line.

LADY BRACKNELL   The line is immaterial. Mr. Worthing, I confess I feel somewhat bewildered by what you have just told me. To be born, or at any rate, bred in a handbag, whether it had handles or not, seems to me to display a contempt for the ordinary decencies of family life that reminds one of the worst excesses of the French Revolution. And I presume you know what that unfortunate movement led to? As for the particular locality in which the handbag was found, a cloak room at a railway station might serve to conceal a social indiscretion—has probably, indeed, been used for that purpose before now—but it could hardly be regarded as an assured basis for a recognized position in good society.

JACK   May I ask you then what you would advise me to do? I need hardly say I would do anything in the world to ensure Gwendolen's happiness.

LADY BRACKNELL   I would strongly advise you, Mr. Worthing, to try and acquire some relations as soon as possible, and to make a definite effort to produce at any rate one parent, of either sex, before the season is quite over.[6]

JACK   Well, I don't see how I could possibly manage to do that. I can produce the handbag at any moment, it is in my dressing room at home. I really think that should satisfy you, Lady Bracknell.

LADY BRACKNELL   Me, sir! What has it to do with me? You can hardly imagine that I and Lord Bracknell would dream of allowing our only daughter—a girl brought up with the utmost care—to marry into a cloak room, and form an alliance with a parcel? Good morning, Mr. Worthing!

[LADY BRACKNELL *sweeps out in majestic indignation.*]

JACK   Good morning! [ALGERNON, *from the other room, strikes up the Wedding March.* JACK *looks perfectly furious, and goes to the door.*] For goodness' sake don't play that ghastly tune, Algy! How idiotic you are!

[*The music stops, and* ALGERNON *enters cheerily.*]

ALGERNON   Didn't it go off all right, old boy? You don't mean to say Gwendolen refused you? I know it is a way she has. She is always refusing people. I think it is most ill-natured of her.

---

5. In the four-act version of the play, Jack explains further what happened to Mr. Cardew: "He did not discover the error till he arrived at his own house. All subsequent efforts to ascertain who I was were unavailing."

6. In the four-act version of the play, Jack later comments to Algernon about Lady Bracknell's demands about locating parents: "After all what does it matter whether a man has ever had a father and mother or not? Mothers, of course, are all right. They pay a chap's bills and don't bother him. But fathers bother a chap and never pay his bills. I don't know a single chap at the club who speaks to his father." And Algernon remarks: "Yes. Fathers are certainly not popular just at present. . . . They are like these chaps, the minor poets. They are never quoted."

2234 / OSCAR WILDE

JACK   Oh, Gwendolen is as right as a trivet.[7] As far as she is concerned, we
   are engaged. Her mother is perfectly unbearable. Never met such a Gorgon[8]
   . . . I don't really know what a Gorgon is like, but I am quite sure that Lady
   Bracknell is one. In any case, she is a monster, without being a myth, which
   is rather unfair . . . I beg your pardon, Algy, I suppose I shouldn't talk about
   your own aunt in that way before you.

ALGERNON   My dear boy, I love hearing my relations abused. It is the only
   thing that makes me put up with them at all. Relations are simply a tedious
   pack of people who haven't got the remotest knowledge of how to live, nor
   the smallest instinct about when to die.

JACK   Oh, that is nonsense!

ALGERNON   It isn't!

JACK   Well, I won't argue about the matter. You always want to argue about
   things.

ALGERNON   That is exactly what things were originally made for.

JACK   Upon my word, if I thought that, I'd shoot myself . . . [A pause.] You
   don't think there is any chance of Gwendolen becoming like her mother in
   about a hundred and fifty years, do you, Algy?

ALGERNON   All women become like their mothers. That is their tragedy. No
   man does. That's his.

JACK   Is that clever?

ALGERNON   It is perfectly phrased! and quite as true as any observation in
   civilized life should be.

JACK   I am sick to death of cleverness. Everybody is clever nowadays. You
   can't go anywhere without meeting clever people. The thing has become an
   absolute public nuisance. I wish to goodness we had a few fools left.

ALGERNON   We have.

JACK   I should extremely like to meet them. What do they talk about?

ALGERNON   The fools? Oh! about the clever people, of course.

JACK   What fools!

ALGERNON   By the way, did you tell Gwendolen the truth about your being
   Ernest in town, and Jack in the country?

JACK   [In a very patronizing manner.]   My dear fellow, the truth isn't quite the
   sort of thing one tells to a nice sweet refined girl. What extraordinary ideas
   you have about the way to behave to a woman!

ALGERNON   The only way to behave to a woman is to make love to[9] her, if she
   is pretty, and to someone else if she is plain.

JACK   Oh, that is nonsense.

ALGERNON   What about your brother? What about the profligate Ernest?

JACK   Oh, before the end of the week I shall have got rid of him. I'll say he
   died in Paris of apoplexy. Lots of people die of apoplexy, quite suddenly,
   don't they?

ALGERNON   Yes, but it's hereditary, my dear fellow. It's a sort of thing that
   runs in families. You had much better say a severe chill.

JACK   You are sure a severe chill isn't hereditary, or anything of that kind?

ALGERNON   Of course it isn't!

---

7. Proverbial expression meaning reliably steady,
like a tripod ("trivet") used to support pots over a
fire.
8. In classical mythology a snake-haired female

monster; at the sight of her, other creatures turned
to stone.
9. Woo, court.

JACK   Very well, then. My poor brother Ernest is carried off suddenly in Paris, by a severe chill. That gets rid of him.[1]

ALGERNON   But I thought you said that . . . Miss Cardew was a little too much interested in your poor brother Ernest? Won't she feel his loss a good deal?

JACK   Oh, that is all right. Cecily is not a silly romantic girl, I am glad to say. She has got a capital appetite, goes on long walks, and pays no attention at all to her lessons.

ALGERNON   I would rather like to see Cecily.

JACK   I will take very good care you never do. She is excessively pretty, and she is only just eighteen.

ALGERNON   Have you told Gwendolen yet that you have an excessively pretty ward who is only just eighteen?

JACK   Oh! one doesn't blurt these things out to people. Cecily and Gwendolen are perfectly certain to be extremely great friends. I'll bet you anything you like that half an hour after they have met, they will be calling each other sister.

ALGERNON   Women only do that when they have called each other a lot of other things first. Now, my dear boy, if we want to get a good table at Willis's, we really must go and dress. Do you know it is nearly seven?

JACK   [Irritably.] Oh! it always is nearly seven.

ALGERNON   Well, I'm hungry.

JACK   I never knew you when you weren't. . . .

ALGERNON   What shall we do after dinner? Go to the theatre?

JACK   Oh no! I loathe listening.

ALGERNON   Well, let us go to the club?

JACK   Oh, no! I hate talking.

ALGERNON   Well, we might trot around to the Empire[2] at ten?

JACK   Oh no! I can't bear looking at things. It is so silly.

ALGERNON   Well, what shall we do?

JACK   Nothing!

ALGERNON   It is awfully hard work doing nothing. However, I don't mind hard work where there is no definite object of any kind.

[Enter LANE.]

LANE   Miss Fairfax.

[Enter GWENDOLEN. LANE goes out.]

ALGERNON   Gwendolen, upon my word!

GWENDOLEN   Algy, kindly turn your back. I have something very particular to say to Mr. Worthing.

ALGERNON   Really, Gwendolen, I don't think I can allow this at all.

GWENDOLEN   Algy, you always adopt a strictly immoral attitude towards life. You are not quite old enough to do that. [ALGERNON retires to the fireplace.]

JACK   My own darling!

GWENDOLEN   Ernest, we may never be married. From the expression on mamma's face I fear we never shall. Few parents nowadays pay any regard to what their children say to them. The old-fashioned respect for the young

1. In the four-act version of the play, Jack explains further: "I'll wear mourning for him, of course; that would be only decent. I don't at all mind wearing mourning. I think that all black, with a good pearl pin, rather smart. Then I'll go down home and break the news to my household."
2. A music hall in Leicester Square that featured light entertainment.

is fast dying out. Whatever influence I ever had over mamma, I lost at the age of three. But although she may prevent us from becoming man and wife, and I may marry someone else, and marry often, nothing that she can possibly do can alter my eternal devotion to you.

JACK   Dear Gwendolen!

GWENDOLEN   The story of your romantic origin, as related to me by mamma, with unpleasing comments, has naturally stirred the deeper fibres of my nature. Your Christian name has an irresistible fascination. The simplicity of your character makes you exquisitely incomprehensible to me. Your town address at the Albany I have. What is your address in the country?

JACK   The Manor House, Woolton, Hertfordshire.

[ALGERNON, *who has been carefully listening, smiles to himself, and writes the address on his shirt-cuff.*[3] *Then picks up the Railway Guide.*]

GWENDOLEN   There is a good postal service, I suppose? It may be necessary to do something desperate. That of course will require serious consideration. I will communicate with you daily.

JACK   My own one!

GWENDOLEN   How long do you remain in town?

JACK   Till Monday.

GWENDOLEN   Good! Algy, you may turn round now.

ALGERNON   Thanks, I've turned round already.

GWENDOLEN   You may also ring the bell.

JACK   You will let me see you to your carriage, my own darling?

GWENDOLEN   Certainly.

JACK [*To* LANE, *who now enters.*]   I will see Miss Fairfax out.

LANE   Yes, sir. [JACK *and* GWENDOLEN *go off.*]

[LANE *presents several letters on a salver to* ALGERNON. *It is to be surmised that they are bills, as* ALGERNON *after looking at the envelopes, tears them up.*]

ALGERNON   A glass of sherry, Lane.

LANE   Yes, sir.

ALGERNON   Tomorrow, Lane, I'm going Bunburying.

LANE   Yes, sir.

ALGERNON   I shall probably not be back till Monday. You can put up my dress clothes, my smoking jacket,[4] and all the Bunbury suits . . .

LANE   Yes, sir. [*Handing sherry.*]

ALGERNON   I hope tomorrow will be a fine day, Lane.

LANE   It never is, sir.

ALGERNON   Lane, you're a perfect pessimist.

LANE   I do my best to give satisfaction, sir.

[*Enter* JACK. LANE *goes off.*]

JACK   There's a sensible, intellectual girl! the only girl I ever cared for in my life. [ALGERNON *is laughing immoderately.*] What on earth are you so amused at?

ALGERNON   Oh, I'm a little anxious about poor Bunbury, that is all.

JACK   If you don't take care, your friend Bunbury will get you into a serious scrape some day.

3. Because shirt cuffs were heavily starched they provided a good surface on which to make notes.
4. Coat worn when gentlemen assembled in a room designated for smoking. The object was to avoid contaminating their regular clothing with the smell of cigars or pipes, which was considered offensive to ladies. "Put up": pack up.

ALGERNON   I love scrapes. They are the only things that are never serious.

JACK   Oh, that's nonsense, Algy. You never talk anything but nonsense.

ALGERNON   Nobody ever does.

[JACK *looks indignantly at him, and leaves the room.* ALGERNON *lights a cigarette, reads his shirt-cuff, and smiles.*]

ACT-DROP[5]

Second Act

SCENE—*Garden at the Manor House. A flight of grey stone steps leads up to the house. The garden, an old-fashioned one, full of roses. Time of year, July. Basket chairs, and a table covered with books, are set under a large yew tree.*

[MISS PRISM[6] *discovered seated at the table.* CECILY *is at the back watering flowers.*]

MISS PRISM [*Calling.*]   Cecily, Cecily! Surely such a utilitarian occupation as the watering of flowers is rather Moulton's duty than yours? Especially at a moment when intellectual pleasures await you. Your German grammar is on the table. Pray open it at page fifteen. We will repeat yesterday's lesson.

CECILY [*Coming over very slowly.*]   But I don't like German. It isn't at all a becoming language. I know perfectly well that I look quite plain after my German lesson.

MISS PRISM   Child, you know how anxious your guardian is that you should improve yourself in every way. He laid particular stress on your German, as he was leaving for town yesterday. Indeed, he always lays stress on your German when he is leaving for town.

CECILY   Dear Uncle Jack is so very serious! Sometime he is so serious that I think he cannot be quite well.

MISS PRISM [*Drawing herself up.*]   Your guardian enjoys the best of health, and his gravity of demeanour is especially to be commended in one so comparatively young as he is. I know no one who has a higher sense of duty and responsibility.

CECILY   I suppose that is why he often looks a little bored when we three are together.

MISS PRISM   Cecily! I am surprised at you. Mr. Worthing has many troubles in his life. Idle merriment and triviality would be out of place in his conversation. You must remember his constant anxiety about that unfortunate young man his brother.

CECILY   I wish Uncle Jack would allow that unfortunate young man, his brother, to come down here sometimes. We might have a good influence over him, Miss Prism. I am sure you certainly would. You know German, and geology, and things of that kind influence a man very much. [CECILY *begins to write in her diary.*]

MISS PRISM [*Shaking her head.*]   I do not think that even I could produce any effect on a character that according to his own brother's admission is irretrievably weak and vacillating. Indeed I am not sure that I would desire to

5. A special curtain lowered during theatrical performances to denote intervals between acts or scenes.

6. The name recalls Charles Dickens's *Little Dor-* *rit* (1855–57), in which Mrs. General, a prim and proper teacher of manners for young ladies, trains them to repeat "prunes and prism" aloud because this exercise "gives a pretty form to the lips."

reclaim him. I am not in favor of this modern mania for turning bad people into good people at a moment's notice. As a man sows so let him reap.[7] You must put away your diary, Cecily. I really don't see why you should keep a diary at all.

CECILY   I keep a diary in order to enter the wonderful secrets of my life. If I didn't write them down I should probably forget all about them.

MISS PRISM   Memory, my dear Cecily, is the diary that we all carry about with us.

CECILY   Yes, but it usually chronicles the things that have never happened, and couldn't possibly have happened. I believe that Memory is responsible for nearly all the three-volume novels that Mudie[8] sends us.

MISS PRISM   Do not speak slightingly of the three-volume novel, Cecily. I wrote one myself in earlier days.

CECILY   Did you really, Miss Prism? How wonderfully clever you are! I hope it did not end happily? I don't like novels that end happily. They depress me so much.

MISS PRISM   The good ended happily, and the bad unhappily. That is what Fiction means.

CECILY   I suppose so. But it seems very unfair. And was your novel ever published?

MISS PRISM   Alas! no. The manuscript unfortunately was abandoned. I use the word in the sense of lost or mislaid. To your work, child, these speculations are profitless.

CECILY [Smiling.]   But I see dear Dr. Chasuble[9] coming up through the garden.

MISS PRISM [Rising and advancing.]   Dr. Chasuble! This is indeed a pleasure.
        [Enter CANON CHASUBLE.]

CHASUBLE   And how are we this morning? Miss Prism, you are, I trust, well?

CECILY   Miss Prism has just been complaining of a slight headache. I think it would do her so much good to have a short stroll with you in the Park, Dr. Chasuble.

MISS PRISM   Cecily, I have not mentioned anything about a headache.

CECILY   No, dear Miss Prism, I know that, but I felt instinctively that you had a headache. Indeed I was thinking about that, and not about my German lesson, when the Rector came in.

CHASUBLE   I hope, Cecily, you are not inattentive.

CECILY   Oh, I am afraid I am.

CHASUBLE   That is strange. Were I fortunate enough to be Miss Prism's pupil, I would hang upon her lips. [MISS PRISM glares.] I spoke metaphorically.— My metaphor was drawn from bees. Ahem! Mr. Worthing, I suppose, has not returned from town yet?

MISS PRISM   We do not expect him till Monday afternoon.

CHASUBLE   Ah yes, he usually likes to spend his Sunday in London. He is not one of those whose sole aim is enjoyment, as, by all accounts, that unfortunate young man his brother seems to be. But I must not disturb Egeria[1] and her pupil any longer.

---

7. Cf. Galatians 6.7.
8. Mudie's Circulating Library, which lent copies of new three-volume novels (usually sentimental tales) to subscribers for a moderate fee. Mudie's power in controlling the book market, especially for novels, was on the wane by 1895.

9. A chasuble is an ornate garment worn by a priest.
1. In Roman legend a nymph who gave counsel to the second king of Rome. Her name was therefore also used as an epithet for a woman who provides guidance.

MISS PRISM   Egeria? My name is Laetitia, Doctor.

CHASUBLE [*Bowing.*]   A classical allusion merely, drawn from the Pagan authors. I shall see you both no doubt at Evensong?[2]

MISS PRISM   I think, dear Doctor, I will have a stroll with you. I find I have a headache after all, and a walk might do it good.

CHASUBLE   With pleasure, Miss Prism, with pleasure. We might go as far as the schools and back.

MISS PRISM   That would be delightful. Cecily, you will read your Political Economy[3] in my absence. The chapter on the Fall of the Rupee[4] you may omit. It is somewhat too sensational. Even these metallic problems have their melodramatic side. [*Goes down the garden with* DR. CHASUBLE.]

CECILY [*Picks up books and throws them back on table.*]   Horrid Political Economy! Horrid Geography! Horrid, horrid German!

[*Enter* MERRIMAN *with a card on a salver.*]

MERRIMAN   Mr. Ernest Worthing has just driven over from the station. He has brought his luggage with him.

CECILY [*Takes the card and reads it.*]   "Mr. Ernest Worthing, B. 4, The Albany, W." Uncle Jack's brother! Did you tell him Mr. Worthing was in town?

MERRIMAN   Yes, Miss. He seemed very much disappointed. I mentioned that you and Miss Prism were in the garden. He said he was anxious to speak to you privately for a moment.

CECILY   Ask Mr. Ernest Worthing to come here. I suppose you had better talk to the housekeeper about a room for him.

MERRIMAN   Yes, Miss.   [MERRIMAN *goes off.*]

CECILY   I have never met any really wicked person before. I feel rather frightened. I am so afraid he will look just like everyone else. [*Enter* ALGERNON, *very gay and debonair.*] He does!

ALGERNON [*Raising his hat.*]   You are my little cousin Cecily, I'm sure.

CECILY   You are under some strange mistake. I am not little. In fact, I believe I am more than usually tall for my age. [ALGERNON *is rather taken aback.*] But I am your cousin Cecily. You, I see from your card, are Uncle Jack's brother, my cousin Ernest, my wicked cousin Ernest.

ALGERNON   Oh! I am not really wicked at all, cousin Cecily. You mustn't think that I am wicked.

CECILY   If you are not, then you have certainly been deceiving us all in a very inexcusable manner. I hope you have not been leading a double life, pretending to be wicked and being really good all the time. That would be hypocrisy.

ALGERNON [*Looks at her in amazement.*]   Oh! Of course I have been rather reckless.

CECILY   I am glad to hear it.

ALGERNON   In fact, now you mention the subject, I have been very bad in my own small way.

CECILY   I don't think you should be so proud of that, though I am sure it must have been very pleasant.

ALGERNON   It is much pleasanter being here with you.

CECILY   I can't understand how you are here at all. Uncle Jack won't be back till Monday afternoon.

---

2. Evening church services.
3. I.e., book about economics.
4. The basic unit of currency in India. British civil

servants who worked in India were paid in rupees and would suffer from its fall in value.

ALGERNON   That is a great disappointment. I am obliged to go up by the first train on Monday morning. I have a business appointment that I am anxious . . . to miss.

CECILY   Couldn't you miss it anywhere but in London?

ALGERNON   No: the appointment is in London.

CECILY   Well, I know, of course, how important it is not to keep a business engagement, if one wants to retain any sense of the beauty of life, but still I think you had better wait till Uncle Jack arrives. I know he wants to speak to you about your emigrating.

ALGERNON   About my what?

CECILY   Your emigrating. He has gone up to buy your outfit.

ALGERNON   I certainly wouldn't let Jack buy my outfit. He has no taste in neckties at all.

CECILY   I don't think you will require neckties. Uncle Jack is sending you to Australia.[5]

ALGERNON   Australia? I'd sooner die.

CECILY   Well, he said at dinner on Wednesday night, that you would have to choose between this world, the next world, and Australia.

ALGERNON   Oh, well! The accounts I have received of Australia and the next world are not particularly encouraging. This world is good enough for me, cousin Cecily.

CECILY   Yes, but are you good enough for it?

ALGERNON   I'm afraid I'm not that. That is why I want you to reform me. You might make that your mission, if you don't mind, cousin Cecily.

CECILY   I'm afraid I've no time, this afternoon.

ALGERNON   Well, would you mind my reforming myself this afternoon?

CECILY   It is rather Quixotic of you. But I think you should try.

ALGERNON   I will. I feel better already.

CECILY   You are looking a little worse.

ALGERNON   That is because I am hungry.

CECILY   How thoughtless of me. I should have remembered that when one is going to lead an entirely new life, one requires regular and wholesome meals. Won't you come in?

ALGERNON   Thank you. Might I have a buttonhole[6] first? I never have any appetite unless I have a buttonhole first.

CECILY   A Maréchal Niel?[7] [Picks up scissors.]

ALGERNON   No, I'd sooner have a pink rose.

CECILY   Why? [Cuts a flower.]

ALGERNON   Because you are like a pink rose, cousin Cecily.

CECILY   I don't think it can be right for you to talk to me like that. Miss Prism never says such things to me.

ALGERNON   Then Miss Prism is a shortsighted old lady. [CECILY puts the rose in his buttonhole.] You are the prettiest girl I ever saw.

CECILY   Miss Prism says that all good looks are a snare.

ALGERNON   They are a snare that every sensible man would like to be caught in.

5. The British had originally viewed Australia as a place to which they banished their criminals. By this time, however, it was perceived in some quarters as a place, like Canada, to which families might send harmless but useless members, who would be paid an allowance to remain abroad.

6. I.e., a flower to wear in the buttonhole of his coat lapel.

7. A chrome-yellow variety of rose named after Adolphe Niel (1802–1869), one of the generals of Napoleon III.

CECILY Oh! I don't think I would care to catch a sensible man. I shouldn't know what to talk to him about.

[*They pass into the house.* MISS PRISM *and* DR. CHASUBLE *return.*]

MISS PRISM You are too much alone, dear Dr. Chasuble. You should get married. A misanthrope I can understand—a womanthrope, never!

CHASUBLE [*With a scholar's shudder.*][8] Believe me, I do not deserve so neologistic a phrase. The precept as well as the practice of the Primitive Church[9] was distinctly against matrimony.

MISS PRISM [*Sententiously.*] That is obviously the reason why the Primitive Church has not lasted up to the present day. And you do not seem to realize, dear Doctor, that by persistently remaining single, a man converts himself into a permanent public temptation. Men should be more careful; this very celibacy leads weaker vessels astray.

CHASUBLE But is a man not equally attractive when married?

MISS PRISM No married man is ever attractive except to his wife.

CHASUBLE And often, I've been told, not even to her.

MISS PRISM That depends on the intellectual sympathies of the woman. Maturity can always be depended on. Ripeness can be trusted. Young women are green. [DR. CHASUBLE *starts.*] I spoke horticulturally. My metaphor was drawn from fruits. But where is Cecily?

CHASUBLE Perhaps she followed us to the schools.

[*Enter* JACK *slowly from the back of the garden. He is dressed in the deepest mourning, with crape hat-band and black gloves.*]

MISS PRISM Mr. Worthing!

CHASUBLE Mr. Worthing?

MISS PRISM This is indeed a surprise. We did not look for you till Monday afternoon.

JACK [*Shakes* MISS PRISM's *hand in a tragic manner.*] I have returned sooner than I expected. Dr. Chasuble, I hope you are well?

CHASUBLE Dear Mr. Worthing, I trust this garb of woe does not betoken some terrible calamity?

JACK My brother.

MISS PRISM More shameful debts and extravagance?

CHASUBLE Still leading his life of pleasure?

JACK [*Shaking his head.*] Dead!

CHASUBLE Your brother Ernest dead?

JACK Quite dead.

MISS PRISM What a lesson for him! I trust he will profit by it.

CHASUBLE Mr. Worthing, I offer you my sincere condolence. You have at least the consolation of knowing that you were always the most generous and forgiving of brothers.

JACK Poor Ernest! He had many faults, but it is a sad, sad blow.

CHASUBLE Very sad indeed. Were you with him at the end?

JACK No. He died abroad; in Paris, in fact. I had a telegram last night from the manager of the Grand Hotel.

CHASUBLE Was the cause of death mentioned?

JACK A severe chill, it seems.

MISS PRISM As a man sows, so shall he reap.

---

8. He shudders because instead of using the correct word for woman hater, *misogynist*, she has coined her own term, one that is etymologically nonsensical.

9. The early Christian Church, of the 1st to 4th centuries.

CHASUBLE [*Raising his hand.*]   Charity, dear Miss Prism, charity! None of us are perfect. I myself am peculiarly susceptible to drafts. Will the interment take place here?

JACK   No. He seemed to have expressed a desire to be buried in Paris.

CHASUBLE   In Paris! [*Shakes his head.*] I fear that hardly points to any very serious state of mind at the last. You would no doubt wish me to make some slight allusion to this tragic domestic affliction next Sunday. [JACK *presses his hand convulsively.*] My sermon on the meaning of the manna in the wilderness can be adapted to almost any occasion, joyful, or, as in the present case, distressing. [*All sigh.*] I have preached it at harvest celebrations, christenings, confirmations, on days of humiliation and festal days. The last time I delivered it was in the Cathedral, as a charity sermon on behalf of the Society for the Prevention of Discontent among the Upper Orders. The Bishop, who was present, was much struck by some of the analogies I drew.

JACK   Ah! That reminds me, you mentioned christenings, I think, Dr. Chasuble? I suppose you know how to christen all right? [DR. CHASUBLE *looks astounded.*] I mean, of course, you are continually christening, aren't you?

MISS PRISM   It is, I regret to say, one of the Rector's most constant duties in this parish. I have often spoken to the poorer classes on the subject. But they don't seem to know what thrift is.

CHASUBLE   But is there any particular infant in whom you are interested, Mr. Worthing? Your brother was, I believe, unmarried, was he not?

JACK   Oh yes.

MISS PRISM [*Bitterly.*]   People who live entirely for pleasure usually are.

JACK   But it is not for any child, dear Doctor. I am very fond of children. No! the fact is, I would like to be christened myself, this afternoon, if you have nothing better to do.

CHASUBLE   But surely, Mr. Worthing, you have been christened already?

JACK   I don't remember anything about it.

CHASUBLE   But have you any grave doubts on the subject?

JACK   I certainly intend to have. Of course I don't know if the thing would bother you in any way, or if you think I am a little too old now.

CHASUBLE   Not at all. The sprinkling, and, indeed, the immersion of adults is a perfectly canonical practice.

JACK   Immersion!

CHASUBLE   You need have no apprehensions. Sprinkling is all that is necessary, or indeed I think advisable. Our weather is so changeable. At what hour would you wish the ceremony performed?

JACK   Oh, I might trot round about five if that would suit you.

CHASUBLE   Perfectly, perfectly! In fact I have two similar ceremonies to perform at that time. A case of twins that occurred recently in one of the outlying cottages on your own estate. Poor Jenkins the carter, a most hard-working man.

JACK   Oh! I don't see much fun in being christened along with other babies. It would be childish. Would half-past five do?

CHASUBLE   Admirably! Admirably! [*Takes out watch.*] And now, dear Mr. Worthing, I will not intrude any longer into a house of sorrow. I would merely beg you not to be too much bowed down by grief. What seem to us bitter trials are often blessings in disguise.

MISS PRISM This seems to me a blessing of an extremely obvious kind.
  [*Enter* CECILY *from the house.*]
CECILY Uncle Jack! Oh, I am pleased to see you back. But what horrid clothes
  you have got on! Do go and change them.
MISS PRISM Cecily!
CHASUBLE My child! my child! [CECILY *goes towards* JACK; *he kisses her brow
  in a melancholy manner.*]
CECILY What is the matter, Uncle Jack? Do look happy! You look as if you
  had toothache, and I have got such a surprise for you. Who do you think is
  in the dining room? Your brother!
JACK Who?
CECILY Your brother Ernest. He arrived about half an hour ago.
JACK What nonsense! I haven't got a brother!
CECILY Oh, don't say that. However badly he may have behaved to you in the
  past he is still your brother. You couldn't be so heartless as to disown him.
  I'll tell him to come out. And you will shake hands with him, won't you,
  Uncle Jack? [*Runs back into the house.*]
CHASUBLE These are very joyful tidings.
MISS PRISM After we had all been resigned to his loss, his sudden return
  seems to me peculiarly distressing.
JACK My brother is in the dining room? I don't know what it all means. I
  think it is perfectly absurd.
    [*Enter* ALGERNON *and* CECILY *hand in hand. They come slowly up to*
    JACK.]
JACK Good heavens! [*Motions* ALGERNON *away.*]
ALGERNON Brother John, I have come down from town to tell you that I am
  very sorry for all the trouble I have given you, and that I intend to lead a
  better life in the future. [JACK *glares at him and does not take his hand.*]
CECILY Uncle Jack, you are not going to refuse your own brother's hand?
JACK Nothing will induce me to take his hand. I think his coming down here
  disgraceful. He knows perfectly well why.
CECILY Uncle Jack, do be nice. There is some good in everyone. Ernest has
  just been telling me about his poor invalid friend Mr. Bunbury whom he
  goes to visit so often. And surely there must be much good in one who is
  kind to an invalid, and leaves the pleasures of London to sit by a bed of
  pain.
JACK Oh! he has been talking about Bunbury, has he?
CECILY Yes, he has told me all about poor Mr. Bunbury, and his terrible state
  of health.
JACK Bunbury! Well, I won't have him talk to you about Bunbury or about
  anything else. It is enough to drive one perfectly frantic.
ALGERNON Of course I admit that the faults were all on my side. But I must
  say that I think that Brother John's coldness to me is peculiarly painful. I
  expected a more enthusiastic welcome, especially considering it is the first
  time I have come here.
CECILY Uncle Jack, if you don't shake hands with Ernest, I will never forgive
  you.
JACK Never forgive me?
CECILY Never, never, never!
JACK Well, this is the last time I shall ever do it. [*Shakes hands with* ALGERNON
  and glares.]

2244 / Oscar Wilde

CHASUBLE It's pleasant, is it not, to see so perfect a reconciliation? I think we might leave the two brothers together.

MISS PRISM Cecily, you will come with us.

CECILY Certainly, Miss Prism. My little task of reconciliation is over.

CHASUBLE You have done a beautiful action today, dear child.

MISS PRISM We must not be premature in our judgments.

CECILY I feel very happy. [*They all go off.*]

JACK You young scoundrel, Algy, you must get out of this place as soon as possible. I don't allow any Bunburying here.

[*Enter* MERRIMAN.]

MERRIMAN I have put Mr. Ernest's things in the room next to yours, sir. I suppose that is all right?

JACK What?

MERRIMAN Mr. Ernest's luggage, sir. I have unpacked it and put it in the room next to your own.

JACK His luggage?

MERRIMAN Yes, sir. Three portmanteaus, a dressing case, two hat-boxes, and a large luncheon basket.[1]

ALGERNON I am afraid I can't stay more than a week this time.

JACK Merriman, order the dogcart[2] at once. Mr. Ernest has been suddenly called back to town.

MERRIMAN Yes, sir.   [*Goes back into the house.*]

ALGERNON What a fearful liar you are, Jack. I have not been called back to town at all.

JACK Yes, you have.

ALGERNON I haven't heard anyone call me.

JACK Your duty as a gentleman calls you back.

ALGERNON My duty as a gentleman has never interfered with my pleasures in the smallest degree.

JACK I can quite understand that.

ALGERNON Well, Cecily is a darling.

JACK You are not to talk of Miss Cardew like that. I don't like it.

ALGERNON Well, I don't like your clothes. You look perfectly ridiculous in them. Why on earth don't you go up and change? It is perfectly childish to be in deep mourning for a man who is actually staying for a whole week with you in your house as a guest. I call it grotesque.

JACK You are certainly not staying with me for a whole week as a guest or anything else. You have got to leave . . . by the four-five train.

ALGERNON I certainly won't leave you so long as you are in mourning. It would be most unfriendly. If I were in mourning you would stay with me, I suppose. I should think it very unkind if you didn't.

JACK Well, will you go if I change my clothes?

ALGERNON Yes, if you are not too long. I never saw anybody take so long to dress, and with such little result.

---

1. According to *Cassell's Domestic Dictionary* (1877–79), "a convenient little receptacle in which gentlemen who are going out shooting for the day, or artists who wish to sketch, can carry their luncheon with them." "Portmanteaus": large leather suitcases. A "dressing case" (also according to *Cassell's*) was "ordinarily made of rosewood, mahogany or coromandel wood." It was supposed to include "scent bottles, jars for pomade and tooth-powders, hair brushes and combs, shaving, nail and tooth brushes, razors and strop, nail scissors, button-hook, tweezer, nail file and penknife" [noted by Russell Jackson].
2. A horse-drawn cart with seats, originally designed to carry hunters and their hunting dogs.

JACK Well, at any rate, that is better than being always overdressed as you are.

ALGERNON If I am occasionally a little overdressed, I make up for it by being always immensely overeducated.

JACK Your vanity is ridiculous, your conduct an outrage, and your presence in my garden utterly absurd. However, you have got to catch the four-five, and I hope you will have a pleasant journey back to town. This Bunburying, as you call it, has not been a great success for you. [*Goes into the house.*]

ALGERNON I think it has been a great success. I'm in love with Cecily, and that is everything.

> [*Enter* CECILY *at the back of the garden. She picks up the can and begins to water the flowers.*]

But I must see her before I go, and make arrangements for another Bunbury. Ah, there she is.

CECILY Oh, I merely came back to water the roses. I thought you were with Uncle Jack.

ALGERNON He's gone to order the dogcart for me.

CECILY Oh, is he going to take you for a nice drive?

ALGERNON He's going to send me away.

CECILY Then have we got to part?

ALGERNON I am afraid so. It's very painful parting.

CECILY It is always painful to part from people whom one has known for a very brief space of time. The absence of old friends one can endure with equanimity. But even a momentary separation from anyone to whom one has just been introduced is almost unbearable.

ALGERNON Thank you.

> [*Enter* MERRIMAN.]

MERRIMAN The dogcart is at the door, sir. [ALGERNON *looks appealingly at* CECILY.]

CECILY It can wait, Merriman . . . for . . . five minutes.

MERRIMAN Yes, Miss. [*Exit* MERRIMAN.]

ALGERNON I hope, Cecily, I shall not offend you if I state quite frankly and openly that you seem to me to be in every way the visible personification of absolute perfection.

CECILY I think your frankness does you great credit, Ernest. If you will allow me I will copy your remarks into my diary. [*Goes over to table and begins writing in diary.*]

ALGERNON Do you really keep a diary? I'd give anything to look at it. May I?

CECILY Oh no. [*Puts her hand over it.*] You see, it is simply a very young girl's record of her own thoughts and impressions, and consequently meant for publication. When it appears in volume form I hope you will order a copy. But pray, Ernest, don't stop. I delight in taking down from dictation. I have reached "absolute perfection." You can go on. I am quite ready for more.

ALGERNON [*Somewhat taken aback.*] Ahem! Ahem!

CECILY Oh, don't cough, Ernest. When one is dictating one should speak fluently and not cough. Besides, I don't know how to spell a cough. [*Writes as* ALGERNON *speaks.*]

ALGERNON [*Speaking very rapidly.*] Cecily, ever since I first looked upon your wonderful and incomparable beauty, I have dared to love you wildly, passionately, devotedly, hopelessly.

CECILY I don't think that you should tell me that you love me wildly, passionately, devotedly, hopelessly. Hopelessly doesn't seem to make much sense, does it?

ALGERNON   Cecily!

[*Enter* MERRIMAN.]

MERRIMAN   The dogcart is waiting, sir.

ALGERNON   Tell it to come round next week, at the same hour.

MERRIMAN [*Looks at* CECILY, *who makes no sign.*]   Yes, sir.

[MERRIMAN *retires.*]

CECILY   Uncle Jack would be very much annoyed if he knew you were staying on till next week, at the same hour.

ALGERNON   Oh, I don't care about Jack. I don't care for anybody in the whole world but you. I love you, Cecily. You will marry me, won't you?

CECILY   You silly boy! Of course. Why, we have been engaged for the last three months.

ALGERNON   For the last three months?

CECILY   Yes, it will be exactly three months on Thursday.

ALGERNON   But how did we become engaged?

CECILY   Well, ever since dear Uncle Jack first confessed to us that he had a younger brother who was very wicked and bad, you of course have formed the chief topic of conversation between myself and Miss Prism. And of course a man who is much talked about is always very attractive. One feels there must be something in him after all. I daresay it was foolish of me, but I fell in love with you, Ernest.

ALGERNON   Darling! And when was the engagement actually settled?

CECILY   On the 14th of February last. Worn out by your entire ignorance of my existence, I determined to end the matter one way or the other, and after a long struggle with myself I accepted you under this dear old tree here. The next day I bought this little ring in your name, and this is the little bangle with the true lovers' knot I promised you always to wear.

ALGERNON   Did I give you this? It's very pretty, isn't it?

CECILY   Yes, you've wonderfully good taste, Ernest. It's the excuse I've always given for your leading such a bad life. And this is the box in which I keep all your dear letters. [*Kneels at table, opens box, and produces letters tied up with blue ribbon.*]

ALGERNON   My letters! But my own sweet Cecily, I have never written you any letters.

CECILY   You need hardly remind me of that, Ernest. I remember only too well that I was forced to write your letters for you. I always wrote three times a week, and sometimes oftener.

ALGERNON   Oh, do let me read them, Cecily?

CECILY   Oh, I couldn't possibly. They would make you far too conceited. [*Replaces box.*] The three you wrote me after I had broken off the engagement are so beautiful, and so badly spelled, that even now I can hardly read them without crying a little.

ALGERNON   But was our engagement ever broken off?

CECILY   Of course it was. On the 22nd of last March. You can see the entry if you like. [*Shows diary.*] "Today I broke off my engagement with Ernest. I feel it is better to do so. The weather still continues charming."

ALGERNON   But why on earth did you break it off? What had I done? I had done nothing at all. Cecily, I am very much hurt indeed to hear you broke it off. Particularly when the weather was so charming.

CECILY It would hardly have been a really serious engagement if it hadn't been broken off at least once. But I forgave you before the week was out.

ALGERNON [Crossing to her, and kneeling.] What a perfect angel you are, Cecily.

CECILY You dear romantic boy. [He kisses her, she puts her fingers through his hair.] I hope your hair curls naturally, does it?

ALGERNON Yes, darling, with a little help from others.

CECILY I am so glad.

ALGERNON You'll never break off our engagement again, Cecily?

CECILY I don't think I could break it off now that I have actually met you. Besides, of course, there is the question of your name.

ALGERNON Yes, of course. [Nervously.]

CECILY You must not laugh at me, darling, but it had always been a girlish dream of mine to love someone whose name was Ernest. [ALGERNON rises, CECILY also.] There is something in that name that seems to inspire absolute confidence. I pity any poor married woman whose husband is not called Ernest.

ALGERNON But, my dear child, do you mean to say you could not love me if I had some other name?

CECILY But what name?

ALGERNON Oh, any name you like—Algernon—for instance . . .

CECILY But I don't like the name of Algernon.

ALGERNON Well, my own dear, sweet, loving little darling, I really can't see why you should object to the name of Algernon. It is not at all a bad name. In fact, it is rather an aristocratic name. Half of the chaps who get into the Bankruptcy Court are called Algernon. But seriously, Cecily . . . [Moving to her.] . . . if my name was Algy, couldn't you love me?

CECILY [Rising.] I might respect you, Ernest, I might admire your character, but I fear that I should not be able to give you my undivided attention.

ALGERNON Ahem! Cecily! [Picking up hat.] Your Rector here is, I suppose, thoroughly experienced in the practice of all the rites and ceremonials of the Church?

CECILY Oh, yes. Dr. Chasuble is a most learned man. He has never written a single book, so you can imagine how much he knows.

ALGERNON I must see him at once on a most important christening—I mean on most important business.

CECILY Oh!

ALGERNON I shan't be away more than half an hour.

CECILY Considering that we have been engaged since February the 14th, and that I only met you today for the first time, I think it is rather hard that you should leave me for so long a period as half an hour. Couldn't you make it twenty minutes?

ALGERNON I'll be back in no time. [Kisses her and rushes down the garden.]

CECILY What an impetuous boy he is! I like his hair so much. I must enter his proposal in my diary.

    [Enter MERRIMAN.]

MERRIMAN A Miss Fairfax has just called to see Mr. Worthing. On very important business, Miss Fairfax states.

CECILY Isn't Mr. Worthing in his library?

MERRIMAN Mr. Worthing went over in the direction of the Rectory some time ago.

CECILY   Pray ask the lady to come out here; Mr. Worthing is sure to be back soon. And you can bring tea.

MERRIMAN   Yes, Miss.   [Goes out.]

CECILY   Miss Fairfax! I suppose one of the many good elderly women who are associated with Uncle Jack in some of his philanthropic work in London. I don't quite like women who are interested in philanthropic work. I think it is so forward of them.

[Enter MERRIMAN.]

MERRIMAN   Miss Fairfax.

[Enter GWENDOLEN.]   [Exit MERRIMAN.]

CECILY [Advancing to meet her.]   Pray let me introduce myself to you. My name is Cecily Cardew.

GWENDOLEN   Cecily Cardew? [Moving to her and shaking hands.] What a very sweet name! Something tells me that we are going to be great friends. I like you already more than I can say. My first impressions of people are never wrong.

CECILY   How nice of you to like me so much after we have known each other such a comparatively short time. Pray sit down.

GWENDOLEN [Still standing up.]   I may call you Cecily, may I not?

CECILY   With pleasure!

GWENDOLEN   And you will always call me Gwendolen, won't you?

CECILY   If you wish.

GWENDOLEN   Then that is all quite settled, is it not?

CECILY   I hope so. [A pause. They both sit down together.]

GWENDOLEN   Perhaps this might be a favorable opportunity for my mentioning who I am. My father is Lord Bracknell. You have never heard of papa, I suppose?

CECILY   I don't think so.

GWENDOLEN   Outside the family circle, papa, I am glad to say, is entirely unknown. I think that is quite as it should be. The home seems to me to be the proper sphere for the man. And certainly once a man begins to neglect his domestic duties he becomes painfully effeminate, does he not? And I don't like that. It makes men so very attractive. Cecily, mamma, whose views on education are remarkably strict, has brought me up to be extremely short-sighted; it is part of her system; so do you mind my looking at you through my glasses?

CECILY   Oh! not at all, Gwendolen. I am very fond of being looked at.

GWENDOLEN [After examining CECILY carefully through a lorgnette.]   You are here on a short visit, I suppose.

CECILY   Oh no! I live here.

GWENDOLEN [Severely.]   Really? Your mother, no doubt, or some female relative of advanced years, resides here also?

CECILY   Oh no! I have no mother, nor, in fact, any relations.

GWENDOLEN   Indeed?

CECILY   My dear guardian, with the assistance of Miss Prism, has the arduous task of looking after me.

GWENDOLEN   Your guardian?

CECILY   Yes, I am Mr. Worthing's ward.

GWENDOLEN   Oh! It is strange he never mentioned to me that he had a ward. How secretive of him! He grows more interesting hourly. I am not sure, however, that the news inspires me with feelings of unmixed delight. [Rising *and going to her.*] I am very fond of you, Cecily; I have liked you ever since I met you! But I am bound to state that now that I know that you are Mr. Worthing's ward, I cannot help expressing a wish you were—well just a little older than you seem to be—and not quite so very alluring in appearance. In fact, if I may speak candidly——

CECILY   Pray do! I think that whenever one has anything unpleasant to say, one should always be quite candid.

GWENDOLEN   Well, to speak with perfect candour, Cecily, I wish that you were fully forty-two, and more than usually plain for your age. Ernest has a strong upright nature. He is the very soul of truth and honour. Disloyalty would be as impossible to him as deception. But even men of the noblest possible moral character are extremely susceptible to the influence of the physical charms of others. Modern, no less than Ancient History, supplies us with many most painful examples of what I refer to. If it were not so, indeed, History would be quite unreadable.

CECILY   I beg your pardon, Gwendolen, did you say Ernest?

GWENDOLEN   Yes.

CECILY   Oh, but it is not Mr. Ernest Worthing who is my guardian. It is his brother—his elder brother.

GWENDOLEN [*Sitting down again.*]   Ernest never mentioned to me that he had a brother.

CECILY   I am sorry to say they have not been on good terms for a long time.

GWENDOLEN   Ah! that accounts for it. And now that I think of it I have never heard any man mention his brother. The subject seems distasteful to most men. Cecily, you have lifted a load from my mind. I was growing almost anxious. It would have been terrible if any cloud had come across a friendship like ours, would it not? Of course you are quite, quite sure that it is not Mr. Ernest Worthing who is your guardian?

CECILY   Quite sure. [*A pause.*] In fact, I am going to be his.

GWENDOLEN [*Inquiringly.*]   I beg your pardon?

CECILY [*Rather shy and confidingly.*]   Dearest Gwendolen, there is no reason why I should make a secret of it to you. Our little county newspaper is sure to chronicle the fact next week. Mr. Ernest Worthing and I are engaged to be married.

GWENDOLEN [*Quite politely, rising.*]   My darling Cecily, I think there must be some slight error. Mr. Ernest Worthing is engaged to me. The announcement will appear in the *Morning Post*[3] on Saturday at the latest.

CECILY [*Very politely, rising.*]   I am afraid you must be under some misconception. Ernest proposed to me exactly ten minutes ago. [*Shows diary.*]

GWENDOLEN [*Examines diary through her lorgnette carefully.*]   It is certainly very curious, for he asked me to be his wife yesterday afternoon at 5:30. If you would care to verify the incident, pray do so. [*Produces diary of her own.*] I never travel without my diary. One should always have something sensational to read in the train. I am so sorry, dear Cecily, if it is any disappointment to you, but I am afraid *I* have the prior claim.

CECILY   It would distress me more than I can tell you, dear Gwendolen, if it caused you any mental or physical anguish, but I feel bound to point out that since Ernest proposed to you he clearly has changed his mind.

GWENDOLEN [*Meditatively.*]   If the poor fellow has been entrapped into any

---

3. A popular journal featuring society gossip and also announcements of engagements and marriages.

foolish promise I shall consider it my duty to rescue him at once, and with a firm hand.

CECILY [*Thoughtfully and sadly.*] Whatever unfortunate entanglement my dear boy may have got into, I will never reproach him with it after we are married.

GWENDOLEN Do you allude to me, Miss Cardew, as an entanglement? You are presumptuous. On an occasion of this kind it becomes more than a moral duty to speak one's mind. It becomes a pleasure.

CECILY Do you suggest, Miss Fairfax, that I entrapped Ernest into an engagement? How dare you? This is no time for wearing the shallow mask of manners. When I see a spade I call it a spade.

GWENDOLEN [*Satirically.*] I am glad to say that I have never seen a spade. It is obvious that our social spheres have been widely different.

> [*Enter* MERRIMAN, *followed by the footman. He carries a salver, table-cloth, and plate stand.* CECILY *is about to retort. The presence of the servants exercises a restraining influence, under which both girls chafe.*]

MERRIMAN Shall I lay tea here as usual, Miss?

CECILY [*Sternly, in a calm voice.*] Yes, as usual.

> [MERRIMAN *begins to clear table and lay cloth. A long pause.* CECILY *and* GWENDOLEN *glare at each other.*]

GWENDOLEN Are there many interesting walks in the vicinity, Miss Cardew?

CECILY Oh! yes! a great many. From the top of one of the hills quite close one can see five counties.

GWENDOLEN Five counties! I don't think I should like that. I hate crowds.

CECILY [*Sweetly.*] I suppose that is why you live in town?

> [GWENDOLEN *bites her lip, and beats her foot nervously with her parasol.*]

GWENDOLEN [*Looking round.*] Quite a well-kept garden this is, Miss Cardew.

CECILY So glad you like it, Miss Fairfax.

GWENDOLEN I had no idea there were any flowers in the country.

CECILY Oh, flowers are as common here, Miss Fairfax, as people are in London.

GWENDOLEN Personally I cannot understand how anybody manages to exist in the country, if anybody who is anybody does. The country always bores me to death.

CECILY Ah! This is what the newspapers call agricultural depression, is it not? I believe the aristocracy are suffering very much from it just at present.[4] It is almost an epidemic amongst them, I have been told. May I offer you some tea, Miss Fairfax?

GWENDOLEN [*With elaborate politeness.*] Thank you. [*Aside.*] Detestable girl! But I require tea!

CECILY [*Sweetly.*] Sugar?

GWENDOLEN [*Superciliously.*] No, thank you. Sugar is not fashionable any more. [CECILY *looks angrily at her, takes up the tongs and puts four lumps of sugar into the cup.*]

CECILY [*Severely.*] Cake or bread and butter?

GWENDOLEN [*In a bored manner.*] Bread and butter, please. Cake is rarely seen at the best houses nowadays.

---

4. From the 1870s on, landowners (including aristocrats) had been suffering severe losses because of adverse economic conditions.

THE IMPORTANCE OF BEING EARNEST, ACT 2 / 2251

CECILY [*Cuts a very large slice of cake, and puts it on the tray.*]   Hand that to
   Miss Fairfax.
        [MERRIMAN *does so, and goes out with footman.* GWENDOLEN *drinks
        the tea and makes a grimace. Puts down cup at once, reaches out her
        hand to the bread and butter, looks at it, and finds it is cake. Rises in
        indignation.*]
GWENDOLEN   You have filled my tea with lumps of sugar, and though I asked
   most distinctly for bread and butter, you have given me cake. I am known
   for the gentleness of my disposition, and the extraordinary sweetness of my
   nature, but I warn you, Miss Cardew, you may go too far.
CECILY [*Rising.*]   To save my poor, innocent, trusting boy from the machi-
   nations of any other girl there are no lengths to which I would not go.
GWENDOLEN   From the moment I saw you I distrusted you. I felt that you
   were false and deceitful. I am never deceived in such matters. My first
   impressions of people are invariably right.
CECILY   It seems to me, Miss Fairfax, that I am trespassing on your valuable
   time. No doubt you have many other calls of a similar character to make in
   the neighborhood.
        [*Enter* JACK.]
GWENDOLEN [*Catching sight of him.*]   Ernest! My own Ernest!
JACK   Gwendolen! Darling! [*Offers to kiss her.*]
GWENDOLEN [*Drawing back.*]   A moment! May I ask if you are engaged to be
   married to this young lady? [*Points to* CECILY.]
JACK [*Laughing.*]   To dear little Cecily! Of course not! What could have put
   such an idea into your pretty little head?
GWENDOLEN   Thank you. You may! [*Offers her cheek.*]
CECILY [*Very sweetly.*]   I knew there must be some misunderstanding, Miss
   Fairfax. The gentleman whose arm is at present round your waist is my dear
   guardian, Mr. John Worthing.
GWENDOLEN   I beg your pardon?
CECILY   This is Uncle Jack.
GWENDOLEN [*Receding.*]   Jack! Oh!
        [*Enter* ALGERNON.]
CECILY   Here is Ernest.
ALGERNON [*Goes straight over to* CECILY *without noticing anyone else.*]   My own
   love! [*Offers to kiss her.*]
CECILY [*Drawing back.*]   A moment, Ernest! May I ask you—are you engaged
   to be married to this young lady?
ALGERNON [*Looking round.*]   To what young lady? Good heavens! Gwendolen!
CECILY   Yes! to good heavens, Gwendolen, I mean to Gwendolen.
ALGERNON [*Laughing.*]   Of course not! What could have put such an idea into
   your pretty little head?
CECILY   Thank you. [*Presenting her cheek to be kissed.*] You may. [ALGERNON
   kisses her.]
GWENDOLEN   I felt there was some slight error, Miss Cardew. The gentleman
   who is now embracing you is my cousin, Mr. Algernon Moncrieff.
CECILY. [*Breaking away from* ALGERNON.]   Algernon Moncrieff! Oh! [*The two
   girls move towards each other and put their arms round each other's waists as
   if for protection.*]
CECILY   Are you called Algernon?
ALGERNON   I cannot deny it.

CECILY Oh!

GWENDOLEN Is your name really John?

JACK [*Standing rather proudly.*] I could deny it if I liked, I could deny anything if I liked. But my name certainly is John. It has been John for years.

CECILY [*To* GWENDOLEN.] A gross deception has been practiced on both of us.

GWENDOLEN My poor wounded Cecily!

CECILY My sweet wronged Gwendolen!

GWENDOLEN [*Slowly and seriously.*] You will call me sister, will you not? [*They embrace.* JACK *and* ALGERNON *groan and walk up and down.*]

CECILY [*Rather brightly.*] There is just one question I would like to be allowed to ask my guardian.

GWENDOLEN An admirable idea! Mr. Worthing, there is just one question I would like to be permitted to put to you. Where is your brother Ernest? We are both engaged to be married to your brother Ernest, so it is a matter of some importance to us to know where your brother Ernest is at present.

JACK [*Slowly and hesitatingly.*] Gwendolen—Cecily—it is very painful for me to be forced to speak the truth. It is the first time in my life that I have ever been reduced to such a painful position, and I am really quite inexperienced in doing anything of the kind. However I will tell you quite frankly that I have no brother Ernest. I have no brother at all. I never had a brother in my life, and I certainly have not the smallest intention of ever having one in the future.

CECILY [*Surprised.*] No brother at all?

JACK [*Cheerily.*] None!

GWENDOLEN [*Severely.*] Had you never a brother of any kind?

JACK [*Pleasantly.*] Never. Not even of any kind.

GWENDOLEN I am afraid it is quite clear, Cecily, that neither of us is engaged to be married to anyone.

CECILY It is not a very pleasant position for a young girl suddenly to find herself in. Is it?

GWENDOLEN Let us go into the house. They will hardly venture to come after us there.

CECILY No, men are so cowardly, aren't they?

[*They retire into the house with scornful looks.*]

JACK This ghastly state of things is what you call Bunburying, I suppose?

ALGERNON Yes, and a perfectly wonderful Bunbury it is. The most wonderful Bunbury I have ever had in my life.

JACK Well, you've no right whatsoever to Bunbury here.

ALGERNON That is absurd. One has a right to Bunbury anywhere one chooses. Every serious Bunburyist knows that.

JACK Serious Bunburyist! Good heavens!

ALGERNON Well, one must be serious about something, if one wants to have any amusement in life. I happen to be serious about Bunburying. What on earth you are serious about I haven't got the remotest idea. About everything, I should fancy. You have such an absolutely trivial nature.

JACK Well, the only small satisfaction I have in the whole of this wretched business is that your friend Bunbury is quite exploded. You won't be able to run down to the country quite so often as you used to do, dear Algy. And a very good thing too.

ALGERNON Your brother is a little off-colour, isn't he, dear Jack? You won't

be able to disappear to London quite so frequently as your wicked custom
was. And not a bad thing either.

JACK As for your conduct towards Miss Cardew, I must say that your taking
in a sweet, simple, innocent girl like that is quite inexcusable. To say nothing
of the fact that she is my ward.

ALGERNON I can see no possible defence at all for your deceiving a brilliant,
clever, thoroughly experienced young lady like Miss Fairfax. To say nothing
of the fact that she is my cousin.

JACK I wanted to be engaged to Gwendolen, that is all. I love her.

ALGERNON Well, I simply wanted to be engaged to Cecily. I adore her.

JACK There is certainly no chance of your marrying Miss Cardew.

ALGERNON I don't think there is much likelihood, Jack, of you and Miss Fairfax being united.

JACK Well, that is no business of yours.

ALGERNON If it was my business, I wouldn't talk about it. [*Begins to eat muffins.*] It is very vulgar to talk about one's business. Only people like stock-
brokers do that, and then merely at dinner parties.

JACK How can you sit there, calmly eating muffins when we are in this horrible trouble, I can't make out. You seem to me to be perfectly heartless.

ALGERNON Well, I can't eat muffins in an agitated manner. The butter would
probably get on my cuffs. One should always eat muffins quite calmly. It is
the only way to eat them.

JACK I say it's perfectly heartless your eating muffins at all, under the
circumstances.

ALGERNON When I am in trouble, eating is the only thing that consoles me.
Indeed, when I am in really great trouble, as anyone who knows me intimately will tell you, I refuse everything except food and drink. At the present
moment I am eating muffins because I am unhappy. Besides, I am particularly fond of muffins. [*Rising.*]

JACK [*Rising.*] Well, that is no reason why you should eat them all in that
greedy way. [*Takes muffins from* ALGERNON.]

ALGERNON [*Offering tea cake.*] I wish you would have tea cake instead. I don't
like tea cake.

JACK Good heavens! I suppose a man may eat his own muffins in his own
garden.

ALGERNON But you have just said it was perfectly heartless to eat muffins.

JACK I said it was perfectly heartless of you, under the circumstances. That
is a very different thing.

ALGERNON That may be. But the muffins are the same. [*He seizes the muffin
dish from* JACK.]

JACK Algy, I wish to goodness you would go.

ALGERNON You can't possibly ask me to go without having some dinner. It's
absurd. I never go without my dinner. No one ever does, except vegetarians
and people like that. Besides I have just made arrangements with Dr. Chasuble to be christened at a quarter to six under the name of Ernest.

JACK My dear fellow, the sooner you give up that nonsense the better. I made
arrangements this morning with Dr. Chasuble to be christened myself at 5:
30, and I naturally will take the name of Ernest. Gwendolen would wish it.
We can't both be christened Ernest. It's absurd. Besides, I have a perfect
right to be christened if I like. There is no evidence at all that I ever have
been christened by anybody. I should think it extremely probable I never

was, and so does Dr. Chasuble. It is entirely different in your case. You have been christened already.

ALGERNON   Yes, but I have not been christened for years.

JACK   Yes, but you have been christened. That is the important thing.

ALGERNON   Quite so. So I know my constitution can stand it. If you are not quite sure about your ever having been christened, I must say I think it rather dangerous your venturing on it now. It might make you very unwell. You can hardly have forgotten that someone very closely connected with you was very nearly carried off this week in Paris by a severe chill.

JACK   Yes, but you said yourself that a severe chill was not hereditary.

ALGERNON   It usen't to be, I know—but I daresay it is now. Science is always making wonderful improvements in things.

JACK [*Picking up the muffin dish.*]   Oh, that is nonsense; you are always talking nonsense.

ALGERNON   Jack, you are at the muffins again! I wish you wouldn't. There are only two left. [*Takes them.*] I told you I was particularly fond of muffins.

JACK   But I hate tea cake.

ALGERNON   Why on earth then do you allow tea cake to be served up for your guests? What ideas you have of hospitality!

JACK   Algernon! I have already told you to go. I don't want you here. Why don't you go!

ALGERNON   I haven't quite finished my tea yet! and there is still one muffin left. [*Jack groans, and sinks into a chair.* ALGERNON *still continues eating.*]

ACT-DROP

Third Act

SCENE—*Morning room*[5] *at the Manor House.*

[GWENDOLEN *and* CECILY *are at the window, looking out into the garden.*]

GWENDOLEN   The fact that they did not follow us at once into the house, as anyone else would have done, seems to me to show that they have some sense of shame left.

CECILY   They have been eating muffins. That looks like repentance.

GWENDOLEN [*After a pause.*]   They don't seem to notice us at all. Couldn't you cough?

CECILY   But I haven't got a cough.

GWENDOLEN   They're looking at us. What effrontery!

CECILY   They're approaching. That's very forward of them.

GWENDOLEN   Let us preserve a dignified silence.

CECILY   Certainly. It's the only thing to do now.

[*Enter* JACK *followed by* ALGERNON. *They whistle some dreadful popular air from a British Opera.*[6]]

GWENDOLEN   This dignified silence seems to produce an unpleasant effect.

CECILY   A most distasteful one.

GWENDOLEN   But we will not be the first to speak.

---

5. A relatively informally furnished room for receiving visitors making morning calls (usually close friends of the host or hostess). Afternoon visitors, on the other hand, would be received in the drawing room, a much more formal and elegant setting.
6. Probably a reference to one of the operas of W. S. Gilbert and Sir Arthur Sullivan.

CECILY Certainly not.

GWENDOLEN Mr. Worthing, I have something very particular to ask you. Much depends on your reply.

CECILY Gwendolen, your common sense is invaluable. Mr. Moncrieff, kindly answer me the following question. Why did you pretend to be my guardian's brother?

ALGERNON In order that I might have an opportunity of meeting you.

CECILY [To GWENDOLEN.] That certainly seems a satisfactory explanation, does it not?

GWENDOLEN Yes, dear, if you can believe him.

CECILY I don't. But that does not affect the wonderful beauty of his answer.

GWENDOLEN True. In matters of grave importance, style, not sincerity is the vital thing. Mr. Worthing, what explanation can you offer to me for pretending to have a brother? Was it in order that you might have an opportunity of coming up to town to see me as often as possible?

JACK Can you doubt it, Miss Fairfax?

GWENDOLEN I have the gravest doubts upon the subject. But I intend to crush them. This is not the moment for German scepticism.[7] [Moving to CECILY.] Their explanations appear to be quite satisfactory, especially Mr. Worthing's. That seems to me to have the stamp of truth upon it.

CECILY I am more than content with what Mr. Moncrieff said. His voice alone inspires one with absolute credulity.

GWENDOLEN Then you think we should forgive them?

CECILY Yes. I mean no.

GWENDOLEN True! I had forgotten. There are principles at stake that one cannot surrender. Which of us should tell them? The task is not a pleasant one.

CECILY Could we not both speak at the same time?

GWENDOLEN An excellent idea! I nearly always speak at the same time as other people. Will you take the time from me?

CECILY Certainly. [GWENDOLEN beats time with uplifted finger.]

GWENDOLEN AND CECILY [Speaking together.] Your Christian names are still an insuperable barrier. That is all!

JACK AND ALGERNON [Speaking together.] Our Christian names! Is that all? But we are going to be christened this afternoon.

GWENDOLEN [To JACK.] For my sake you are prepared to do this terrible thing?

JACK I am.

CECILY [To ALGERNON.] To please me you are ready to face this fearful ordeal?

ALGERNON I am!

GWENDOLEN How absurd to talk of the equality of the sexes! Where questions of self-sacrifice are concerned, men are infinitely beyond us.

JACK We are. [Clasps hands with ALGERNON.]

CECILY They have moments of physical courage of which we women know absolutely nothing.

GWENDOLEN [To JACK.] Darling!

ALGERNON [To CECILY.] Darling. [They fall into each other's arms.]
[Enter MERRIMAN. When he enters he coughs loudly, seeing the situation.]

7. Many 19th-century German scholars (e.g., D. F. Strauss) were notorious among the British for being skeptical in their analyses of religious texts.

MERRIMAN   Ahem! Ahem! Lady Bracknell!

JACK   Good heavens!

[*Enter* LADY BRACKNELL. *The couples separate in alarm. Exit* MERRI-MAN.]

LADY BRACKNELL   Gwendolen! What does this mean?

GWENDOLEN   Merely that I am engaged to be married to Mr. Worthing, mamma.

LADY BRACKNELL   Come here. Sit down. Sit down immediately. Hesitation of any kind is a sign of mental decay in the young, of physical weakness in the old. [*Turns to* JACK.] Apprised, sir, of my daughter's sudden flight by her trusty maid, whose confidence I purchased by means of a small coin, I followed her at once by a luggage train.[8] Her unhappy father is, I am glad to say, under the impression that she is attending a more than usually lengthy lecture by the University Extension Scheme on the Influence of a Permanent Income on Thought. I do not propose to undeceive him. Indeed I have never undeceived him on any question. I would consider it wrong. But of course, you will clearly understand that all communication between yourself and my daughter must cease immediately from this moment. On this point, as indeed on all points, I am firm.

JACK   I am engaged to be married to Gwendolen, Lady Bracknell!

LADY BRACKNELL   You are nothing of the kind, sir. And now, as regards Algernon! . . . Algernon!

ALGERNON   Yes, Aunt Augusta.

LADY BRACKNELL   May I ask if it is in this house that your invalid friend Mr. Bunbury resides?

ALGERNON [*Stammering.*]   Oh! No! Bunbury doesn't live here. Bunbury is somewhere else at present. In fact, Bunbury is dead.

LADY BRACKNELL   Dead! When did Mr. Bunbury die? His death must have been extremely sudden.

ALGERNON [*Airily.*]   Oh! I killed Bunbury this afternoon. I mean poor Bunbury died this afternoon.

LADY BRACKNELL   What did he die of?

ALGERNON   Bunbury? Oh, he was quite exploded.

LADY BRACKNELL   Exploded! Was he the victim of a revolutionary outrage? I was not aware that Mr. Bunbury was interested in social legislation. If so, he is well punished for his morbidity.

ALGERNON   My dear Aunt Augusta, I mean he was found out! The doctors found out that Bunbury could not live, that is what I mean—so Bunbury died.

LADY BRACKNELL   He seems to have had great confidence in the opinion of his physicians. I am glad, however, that he made up his mind at the last to some definite course of action, and acted under proper medical advice. And now that we have finally got rid of this Mr. Bunbury, may I ask, Mr. Worthing, who is that young person whose hand my nephew Algernon is now holding in what seems to me a peculiarly unnecessary manner?

JACK   That lady is Miss Cecily Cardew, my ward.

[LADY BRACKNELL *bows coldly to* CECILY.]

ALGERNON   I am engaged to be married to Cecily, Aunt Augusta.

LADY BRACKNELL   I beg your pardon?

CECILY   Mr. Moncrieff and I are engaged to be married, Lady Bracknell.

---

8. Freight train.

LADY BRACKNELL [*With a shiver, crossing to the sofa and sitting down.*] I do not know whether there is anything peculiarly exciting in the air of this particular part of Hertfordshire, but the number of engagements that go on seems to me considerably above the proper average that statistics have laid down for our guidance. I think some preliminary inquiry on my part would not be out of place. Mr. Worthing, is Miss Cardew at all connected with any of the larger railway stations in London? I merely desire information. Until yesterday I had no idea that there were any families or persons whose origin was a Terminus.[9] [JACK *looks perfectly furious, but restrains himself.*]

JACK [*In a clear, cold voice.*] Miss Cardew is the granddaughter of the late Mr. Thomas Cardew of 149, Belgrave Square, S.W.; Gervase Park, Dorking, Surrey; and the Sporran, Fifeshire, N.B.[1]

LADY BRACKNELL That sounds not unsatisfactory. Three addresses always inspire confidence, even in tradesmen. But what proof have I of their authenticity?

JACK I have carefully preserved the Court Guides[2] of the period. They are open to your inspection, Lady Bracknell.

LADY BRACKNELL [*Grimly.*] I have known strange errors in that publication.

JACK Miss Cardew's family solicitors are Messrs. Markby, Markby, and Markby.

LADY BRACKNELL Markby, Markby, and Markby? A firm of the very highest position in their profession. Indeed I am told that one of the Mr. Markbys is occasionally to be seen at dinner parties. So far I am satisfied.

JACK [*Very irritably.*] How extremely kind of you, Lady Bracknell! I have also in my possession, you will be pleased to hear, certificates of Miss Cardew's birth, baptism, whooping cough, registration, vaccination, confirmation, and the measles; both the German and the English variety.

LADY BRACKNELL Ah! A life crowded with incident, I see; though perhaps somewhat too exciting for a young girl. I am not myself in favor of premature experiences. [*Rises, looks at her watch.*] Gwendolen! the time approaches for our departure. We have not a moment to lose. As a matter of form, Mr. Worthing, I had better ask you if Miss Cardew has any little fortune?

JACK Oh! about a hundred and thirty thousand pounds in the Funds.[3] That is all. Good-bye, Lady Bracknell. So pleased to have seen you.

LADY BRACKNELL [*Sitting down again.*] A moment, Mr. Worthing. A hundred and thirty thousand pounds! And in the Funds! Miss Cardew seems to me a most attractive young lady, now that I look at her. Few girls of the present day have any really solid qualities, any of the qualities that last, and improve with time. We live, I regret to say, in an age of surfaces. [*To* CECILY.] Come over here, dear. [CECILY *goes across.*] Pretty child! your dress is sadly simple, and your hair seems almost as Nature might have left it. But we can soon alter all that. A thoroughly experienced French maid produces a really marvellous result in a very brief space of time. I remember recommending one to young Lady Lancing, and after three months her own husband did not know her.

JACK [*Aside.*] And after six months nobody knew her.[4]

LADY BRACKNELL [*Glares at* JACK *for a few moments. Then bends, with a practiced smile, to* CECILY.] Kindly turn round, sweet child. [CECILY *turns completely*

9. Station at the end of a railway line.
1. Presumably North Britain, i.e., Scotland.
2. Directories commonly used in this era.

3. Interest-bearing government bonds.
4. I.e., she became socially unacceptable because of her scandalous behavior.

round.] No, the side view is what I want. [CECILY *presents her profile.*] Yes, quite as I expected. There are distinct social possibilities in your profile. The two weak points in our age are its want of principle and its want of profile. The chin a little higher, dear. Style largely depends on the way the chin is worn. They are worn very high, just at present. Algernon!

ALGERNON   Yes, Aunt Augusta!

LADY BRACKNELL   There are distinct social possibilities in Miss Cardew's profile.

ALGERNON   Cecily is the sweetest, dearest, prettiest girl in the whole world. And I don't care twopence about social possibilities.

LADY BRACKNELL   Never speak disrespectfully of Society, Algernon. Only people who can't get into it do that. [*To* CECILY.] Dear child, of course you know that Algernon has nothing but his debts to depend upon. But I do not approve of mercenary marriages. When I married Lord Bracknell I had no fortune of any kind. But I never dreamed for a moment of allowing that to stand in my way. Well, I suppose I must give my consent.

ALGERNON   Thank you, Aunt Augusta.

LADY BRACKNELL   Cecily, you may kiss me!

CECILY [*Kisses her.*]   Thank you, Lady Bracknell.

LADY BRACKNELL   You may also address me as Aunt Augusta for the future.

CECILY   Thank you, Aunt Augusta.

LADY BRACKNELL   The marriage, I think, had better take place quite soon.

ALGERNON   Thank you, Aunt Augusta.

CECILY   Thank you, Aunt Augusta.

LADY BRACKNELL   To speak frankly, I am not in favour of long engagements. They give people the opportunity of finding out each other's character before marriage, which I think is never advisable.

JACK   I beg your pardon for interrupting you, Lady Bracknell, but this engagement is quite out of the question. I am Miss Cardew's guardian, and she cannot marry without my consent until she comes of age. That consent I absolutely decline to give.

LADY BRACKNELL   Upon what grounds may I ask? Algernon is an extremely, I may almost say an ostentatiously, eligible young man. He has nothing, but he looks everything. What more can one desire?

JACK   It pains me very much to have to speak frankly to you, Lady Bracknell, about your nephew, but the fact is that I do not approve at all of his moral character. I suspect him of being untruthful. [ALGERNON *and* CECILY *look at him in indignant amazement.*]

LADY BRACKNELL   Untruthful! My nephew Algernon? Impossible! He is an Oxonian.[5]

JACK   I fear there can be no possible doubt about the matter. This afternoon, during my temporary absence in London on an important question of romance, he obtained admission to my house by means of the false pretence of being my brother. Under an assumed name he drank, I've just been informed by my butler, an entire pint bottle of my Perrier-Jouet, Brut, '89;[6] a wine I was specially reserving for myself. Continuing his disgraceful deception, he succeeded in the course of the afternoon in alienating the affections of my only ward. He subsequently stayed to tea, and devoured every single

---

5. I.e., he had been a student at Oxford (in medieval Latin, *Oxonia*).

6. An outstanding brand and year of dry champagne.

muffin. And what makes his conduct all the more heartless is, that he was perfectly well aware from the first that I have no brother, that I never had a brother, and that I don't intend to have a brother, not even of any kind. I distinctly told him so myself yesterday afternoon.

LADY BRACKNELL   Ahem! Mr. Worthing, after careful consideration I have decided entirely to overlook my nephew's conduct to you.

JACK   That is very generous of you, Lady Bracknell. My own decision, however, is unalterable. I decline to give my consent.

LADY BRACKNELL   [To CECILY.]   Come here, sweet child. [CECILY goes over.] How old are you, dear?

CECILY   Well, I am really only eighteen, but I always admit to twenty when I go to evening parties.

LADY BRACKNELL   You are perfectly right in making some slight alteration. Indeed, no woman should ever be quite accurate about her age. It looks so calculating. . . . [In a meditative manner.] Eighteen, but admitting to twenty at evening parties. Well, it will not be very long before you are of age and free from the restraints of tutelage. So I don't think your guardian's consent is, after all, a matter of any importance.

JACK   Pray excuse me, Lady Bracknell, for interrupting you again, but it is only fair to tell you that according to the terms of her grandfather's will Miss Cardew does not come legally of age till she is thirty-five.

LADY BRACKNELL   That does not seem to me to be a grave objection. Thirty-five is a very attractive age. London society is full of women of the very highest birth who have, of their own free choice, remained thirty-five for years. Lady Dumbleton is an instance in point. To my own knowledge she has been thirty-five ever since she arrived at the age of forty, which was many years ago now. I see no reason why our dear Cecily should not be even still more attractive at the age you mention than she is at present. There will be a large accumulation of property.

CECILY   Algy, could you wait for me till I was thirty-five?

ALGERNON   Of course I could, Cecily. You know I could.

CECILY   Yes, I felt it instinctively, but I couldn't wait all that time. I hate waiting even five minutes for anybody. It always makes me rather cross. I am not punctual myself, I know, but I do like punctuality in others, and waiting, even to be married, is quite out of the question.

ALGERNON   Then what is to be done, Cecily?

CECILY   I don't know, Mr. Moncrieff.

LADY BRACKNELL   My dear Mr. Worthing, as Miss Cardew states positively that she cannot wait till she is thirty-five—a remark which I am bound to say seems to me to show a somewhat impatient nature—I would beg of you to reconsider your decision.

JACK   But my dear Lady Bracknell, the matter is entirely in your own hands. The moment you consent to my marriage with Gwendolen, I will most gladly allow your nephew to form an alliance with my ward.

LADY BRACKNELL   [Rising and drawing herself up.]   You must be quite aware that what you propose is out of the question.

JACK   Then a passionate celibacy is all that any of us can look forward to.

LADY BRACKNELL   This is not the destiny I propose for Gwendolen. Algernon, of course, can choose for himself. [Pulls out her watch.] Come, dear; [GWEN-DOLEN rises.] we have already missed five, if not six, trains. To miss any more might expose us to comment on the platform.

2260 / Oscar Wilde

[*Enter* DR. CHASUBLE.]

CHASUBLE Everything is quite ready for the christenings.

LADY BRACKNELL The christenings, sir! Is not that somewhat premature!

CHASUBLE [*Looking rather puzzled, and pointing to* JACK *and* ALGERNON.] Both these gentlemen have expressed a desire for immediate baptism.

LADY BRACKNELL At their age? The idea is grotesque and irreligious! Algernon, I forbid you to be baptized. I will not hear of such excesses. Lord Bracknell would be highly displeased if he learned that that was the way in which you wasted your time and money.

CHASUBLE Am I to understand then that there are to be no christenings at all this afternoon?

JACK I don't think that, as things are now, it would be of much practical value to either of us, Dr. Chasuble.

CHASUBLE I am grieved to hear such sentiments from you, Mr. Worthing. They savour of the heretical views of the Anabaptists,[7] views that I have completely refuted in four of my unpublished sermons. However, as your present mood seems to be one peculiarly secular, I will return to the church at once. Indeed, I have just been informed by the pew-opener[8] that for the last hour and a half Miss Prism has been waiting for me in the vestry.

LADY BRACKNELL [*Starting.*] Miss Prism! Did I hear you mention a Miss Prism?

CHASUBLE Yes, Lady Bracknell. I am on my way to join her.

LADY BRACKNELL Pray allow me to detain you for a moment. This matter may prove to be one of vital importance to Lord Bracknell and myself. Is this Miss Prism a female of repellent aspect, remotely connected with education?

CHASUBLE [*Somewhat indignantly.*] She is the most cultivated of ladies, and the very picture of respectability.

LADY BRACKNELL It is obviously the same person. May I ask what position she holds in your household?

CHASUBLE [*Severely.*] I am a celibate, madam.

JACK [*Interposing.*] Miss Prism, Lady Bracknell, has been for the last three years Miss Cardew's esteemed governess and valued companion.

LADY BRACKNELL In spite of what I hear of her, I must see her at once. Let her be sent for.

CHASUBLE [*Looking off.*] She approaches; she is nigh.

[*Enter* MISS PRISM *hurriedly.*]

MISS PRISM I was told you expected me in the vestry, dear Canon. I have been waiting for you there for an hour and three quarters. [*Catches sight of* LADY BRACKNELL *who has fixed her with a stony glare.* MISS PRISM *grows pale and quails. She looks anxiously round as if desirous to escape.*]

LADY BRACKNELL [*In a severe, judicial voice.*] Prism! [MISS PRISM *bows her head in shame.*] Come here, Prism! [MISS PRISM *approaches in a humble manner.*] Prism! Where is that baby? [*General consternation.* THE CANON *starts back in horror.* ALGERNON *and* JACK *pretend to be anxious to shield* CECILY *and* GWENDOLEN *from hearing the details of a terrible public scandal.*] Twenty-eight years ago, Prism, you left Lord Bracknell's house, Number

---

7. A radical Protestant sect of the 17th century, whose repudiation of infant baptism was regarded as heretical by Anglicans.

8. A person employed at church services to usher worshippers to their pews and open the doors for them.

104, Upper Grosvenor Street, in charge of a perambulator that contained a baby, of the male sex. You never returned. A few weeks later, through the elaborate investigations of the Metropolitan police, the perambulator was discovered at midnight, standing by itself in a remote corner of Bayswater.[9] It contained the manuscript of a three-volume novel of more than usually revolting sentimentality. [MISS PRISM *starts in involuntary indignation.*] But the baby was not there! [*Everyone looks at* MISS PRISM.] Prism! Where is that baby? [*A pause.*]

MISS PRISM   Lady Bracknell, I admit with shame that I do not know. I only wish I did. The plain facts of the case are these. On the morning of the day you mention, a day that is forever branded on my memory, I prepared as usual to take the baby out in its perambulator. I had also with me a somewhat old, but capacious handbag, in which I had intended to place the manuscript of a work of fiction that I had written during my few unoccupied hours. In a moment of mental abstraction, for which I never can forgive myself, I deposited the manuscript in the bassinette, and placed the baby in the handbag.

JACK   [*Who has been listening attentively.*]   But where did you deposit the handbag?

MISS PRISM   Do not ask me, Mr. Worthing.

JACK   Miss Prism, this is a matter of no small importance to me. I insist on knowing where you deposited the handbag that contained that infant.

MISS PRISM   I left it in the cloak room of one of the larger railway stations in London.

JACK   What railway station?

MISS PRISM   [*Quite crushed.*]   Victoria. The Brighton line. [*Sinks into a chair.*]

JACK   I must retire to my room for a moment. Gwendolen, wait here for me.

GWENDOLEN   If you are not too long, I will wait here for you all my life.

[*Exit* JACK *in great excitement.*]

CHASUBLE   What do you think this means, Lady Bracknell?

LADY BRACKNELL   I dare not even suspect, Dr. Chasuble. I need hardly tell you that in families of high position strange coincidences are not supposed to occur. They are hardly considered the thing.

[*Noises heard overhead as if someone was throwing trunks about. Everyone looks up.*]

CECILY   Uncle Jack seems strangely agitated.

CHASUBLE   Your guardian has a very emotional nature.

LADY BRACKNELL   This noise is extremely unpleasant. It sounds as if he was having an argument. I dislike arguments of any kind. They are always vulgar, and often convincing.

CHASUBLE   [*Looking up.*]   It has stopped now. [*The noise is redoubled.*]

LADY BRACKNELL   I wish he would arrive at some conclusion.

GWENDOLEN   This suspense is terrible. I hope it will last.

[*Enter* JACK *with a handbag of black leather in his hand.*]

JACK   [*Rushing over to* MISS PRISM.]   Is this the handbag, Miss Prism? Examine it carefully before you speak. The happiness of more than one life depends on your answer.

MISS PRISM   [*Calmly.*]   It seems to be mine. Yes, here is the injury it received through the upsetting of a Gower Street omnibus in younger and happier

---

9. A once fashionable locality in the West End near Kensington Gardens.

days. Here is the stain on the lining caused by the explosion of a temperance beverage, an incident that occurred at Leamington. And here, on the lock, are my initials. I had forgotten that in an extravagant mood I had had them placed there. The bag is undoubtedly mine. I am delighted to have it so unexpectedly restored to me. It has been a great inconvenience being without it all these years.

JACK [*In a pathetic voice.*] Miss Prism, more is restored to you than this handbag. I was the baby you placed in it.

MISS PRISM [*Amazed.*] You!

JACK [*Embracing her.*] Yes . . . mother!

MISS PRISM [*Recoiling in indignant astonishment.*] Mr. Worthing! I am unmarried!

JACK Unmarried! I do not deny that is a serious blow. But after all, who has the right to cast a stone[1] against one who has suffered? Cannot repentance wipe out an act of folly? Why should there be one law for men, and another for women? Mother, I forgive you. [*Tries to embrace her again.*]

MISS PRISM [*Still more indignant.*] Mr. Worthing, there is some error. [*Pointing to LADY BRACKNELL.*] There is the lady who can tell you who you really are.

JACK [*After a pause.*] Lady Bracknell, I hate to seem inquisitive, but would you kindly inform me who I am?

LADY BRACKNELL I am afraid that the news I have to give you will not altogether please you. You are the son of my poor sister, Mrs. Moncrieff, and consequently Algernon's elder brother.

JACK Algy's elder brother! Then I have a brother after all. I knew I had a brother! I always said I had a brother! Cecily—how could you have ever doubted that I had a brother? [*Seizes hold of ALGERNON.*] Dr. Chasuble, my unfortunate brother. Miss Prism, my unfortunate brother. Gwendolen, my unfortunate brother. Algy, you young scoundrel, you will have to treat me with more respect in the future. You have never behaved to me like a brother in all your life.

ALGERNON Well, not till today, old boy, I admit. I did my best, however, though I was out of practice. [*Shakes hands.*]

GWENDOLEN [*To JACK.*] My own! But what own are you? What is your Christian name, now that you have become someone else?

JACK Good heavens! . . . I had quite forgotten that point. Your decision on the subject of my name is irrevocable, I suppose?

GWENDOLEN I never change, except in my affections.

CECILY What a noble nature you have, Gwendolen!

JACK Then the question had better be cleared up at once. Aunt Augusta, a moment. At the time when Miss Prism left me in the handbag, had I been christened already?

LADY BRACKNELL Every luxury that money could buy, including christening, had been lavished on you by your fond and doting parents.

JACK Then I was christened! That is settled. Now, what name was I given? Let me know the worst.

MISS PRISM [*Embarrassed.*] It was sure to be a sure. Yes, here is the initial. I received —

---

1. When the scribes and Pharisees brought to Jesus an adulterous woman with the reminder that the law of Moses required her to be stoned, he answered: "He that is without sin among you, let him first cast a stone at her" (John 8.7).

LADY BRACKNELL   Being the eldest son you were naturally christened after your father.

JACK [*Irritably.*]   Yes, but what was my father's Christian name?

LADY BRACKNELL [*Meditatively.*]   I cannot at the present moment recall what the General's Christian name was. But I have no doubt he had one. He was eccentric, I admit. But only in later years. And that was the result of the Indian climate, and marriage, and indigestion, and other things of that kind.

JACK   Algy! Can't you recollect what our father's Christian name was?

ALGERNON   My dear boy, we were never even on speaking terms. He died before I was a year old.

JACK   His name would appear in the Army Lists of the period, I suppose, Aunt Augusta?

LADY BRACKNELL   The General was essentially a man of peace, except in his domestic life. But I have no doubt his name would appear in any military directory.

JACK   The Army Lists of the last forty years are here. These delightful records should have been my constant study. [*Rushes to bookcase and tears the books out.*] M. Generals . . . Mallam, Maxbohm,[2] Magley, what ghastly names they have—Markby, Migsby, Mobbs, Moncrieff! Lieutenant 1840, Captain, Lieutenant Colonel, Colonel, General 1869, Christian names, Ernest John. [*Puts book very quietly down and speaks quite calmly.*] I always told you, Gwendolen, my name was Ernest, didn't I? Well it is Ernest after all. I mean it naturally is Ernest.

LADY BRACKNELL   Yes, I remember now that the General was called Ernest. I knew I had some particular reason for disliking the name.

GWENDOLEN   Ernest! My own Ernest! I felt from the first that you could have no other name!

JACK   Gwendolen, it is a terrible thing for a man to find out suddenly that all his life he has been speaking nothing but the truth. Can you forgive me?

GWENDOLEN   I can. For I feel that you are sure to change.

JACK   My own one!

CHASUBLE [*To* MISS PRISM.]   Laetitia! [*Embraces her.*]

MISS PRISM [*Enthusiastically.*]   Frederick! At last!

ALGERNON   Cecily! [*Embraces her.*] At last!

JACK   Gwendolen! [*Embraces her.*] At last!

LADY BRACKNELL   My nephew, you seem to be displaying signs of triviality.

JACK   On the contrary, Aunt Augusta, I've now realized for the first time in my life the vital Importance of Being Earnest.

CURTAIN

performed 1895   1899

---

2. A play on the name of Max Beerbohm (1872–1956), English essayist, caricaturist, and parodist.

RUDYARD KIPLING
1865–1936

Like many children born to upper- or middle-class Britons living in India in the Victorian era, Rudyard Kipling was sent to Great Britain at the age of six to begin his education. For the next six years in England, he was desperately unhappy; his parents had chosen to board him in a rigidly Calvinistic foster home, and he was treated with considerable cruelty. His parents finally removed him when he was twelve and sent him to a private school, where his experience was far better. His views in later life were deeply affected by the English schoolboy code of honor and duty, especially when it involved loyalty to a group or team. At seventeen he rejoined his parents in India, where his father taught sculpture at the Bombay School of Art. By the time he returned to England seven years later, the poems and stories he had written while working as a newspaper reporter in India had brought him early fame. In 1892 he married an American woman; they lived in Brattleboro, Vermont, until a fierce quarrel with his brother-in-law drove him back to England in 1896. Kipling settled on a country estate and purchased, at the turn of the century, an expensive early-model automobile. He seems to have been the first English author to own an automobile—an appropriate distinction, because he was intrigued by all kinds of machinery and feats of engineering. In this keen interest, as in many tastes, he differed markedly from his contemporaries in the nineties, the aesthetes. Kipling was also the first English author to receive the Nobel Prize for Literature (1907).

In the final decades of the nineteenth century, India was the most important colony of Britain's empire—the "Jewel in the Crown," as Prime Minister Benjamin Disraeli had dubbed it. The English were consequently curious about the world of India, a world that Kipling's stories and poems helped them envision. Indeed, Leonard Woolf, Virginia Woolf's husband, wrote of his own experience in India in the early years of the twentieth century: "I could never make up my mind whether Kipling had moulded his characters accurately in the image of Anglo-Indian society or whether we were moulding our characters accurately in the image of a Kipling story." During his seven years in India in the 1880s, Kipling gained a rich experience of colonial life, which he presented in his stories and poems. His first volume of stories, *Plain Tales from the Hills* (1888), explores some of the psychological and moral problems of the Anglo-Indians and their relationship with the people they had colonized. In his two volumes of the *Jungle Book* (1894, 1895) he draws on the Indian scene to create a world of jungle animals. Capable, on occasion, of constructing offensive stereotypes, Kipling at other times demonstrates a remarkably detailed and intelligent interest in Indian culture, as in his complex novel *Kim* (1901): amid a welter of representations of different modes of existence, the contemplative and religious way of life of the Indian *lama*, or monk, is treated with no less respect and sympathy than the active and worldly way of life of the Victorian English governing classes.

In his poems Kipling also draws on the Indian scene, most commonly as it is viewed through the eyes of the men sent out from England to garrison the country and fight off invaders on the northwest frontiers. Kipling is usually thought of as the poet of British imperialism, as indeed he often was; but these poems about ordinary British soldiers in India contain little by way of flag-waving celebrations of the triumph of empire. The soldier who speaks in "The Widow at Windsor" (1892) is simply bewildered by the events in which he has taken part. As one of the soldiers of the queen (one of "Missis Victorier's sons"), he has done his duty, but he does not see the empire as a divine design to which he has contributed. Kipling develops a new subject in the working-class imperial soldier (a subject, we should note, who frequently gives voice to deeply racist attitudes), and thus a new way to portray modern social experience.

The common man's perspective, expressed in the accent of the London cockney, was one of the qualities that gained Kipling an immediate audience for his *Barrack-*

Room Ballads (1890, 1892). For many years Kipling was extremely popular. What attracted his vast audience was not just the novelty of his subjects but also his mastery of swinging verse rhythms. To some degree Kipling's literary ancestry helps explain his success. In part he learned his craft as a poet from traditional sources. His own family had connections with the Pre-Raphaelites, and he was considerably influenced by such immediate literary predecessors as Robert Browning and Algernon Charles Swinburne. But two of the forces strongly influencing his style and rhythms were not traditional. One of these was the Protestant hymn. Both his parents were children of Methodist clergymen, and chapel singing, as well as preaching, affected him profoundly. "Three generations of Wesleyan ministers . . . lie behind me," he noted; the family tradition can be heard in such secular sermons as "If" (1910) and the elegiac hymn "Recessional" (1897). The second influence came from what seems an antithetical secular quarter: the songs of the music hall. As a teenager in London, Kipling had enjoyed music hall entertainments, which were to reach their peak of popularity in the 1890s. Like Tennyson, Kipling knew how to make poems that call to be set to music, verses such as "Mandalay" (1890) or "Gentlemen-Rankers" (1892), with its memorable refrain: "We're poor little lambs who've lost our way, / Baa! Baa! Baa!" Much of Kipling's poetry is best appreciated with the melodies and ambience of the music hall in mind.

In recent years Kipling's stories have received more attention than his poems. By portraying the British community in India and its relationship with the people it ruled, Kipling created a rich and various fictional world that reflects on England's imperialism as lived by the officers of the empire in all their peculiar social relationships. "The Man Who Would Be King" (1888) presents an intriguing approach to the topic. The narrator, a newspaper editor, tells us of his dealings with a couple of "Loafers." Peachey Carnehan and Daniel Dravot have no official positions in India but are quick to exploit any opportunities their European status may afford them; this pair of rogues heads out to the mountainous region of Kafiristan, intent on establishing their own dynasty. An action-packed tale of adventure in faraway places with strange-sounding names, the story also invites us to think critically about the general project of empire—about the assumptions it holds, the methods it employs, and the human cost of its endeavors.

After leaving India, Kipling gradually turned to English subjects in his fiction, but the cataclysm of World War I did much to diminish his output. As chair of the Imperial War Graves Commission, he played a difficult and important public role, responsible for (among other things) choosing the words to be inscribed on countless monuments and memorials across the globe. Kipling's task was all the more poignant because the body of his only son, who had died in the battle of Loos (1915), was never found. A deeply melancholy autobiography, *Something of Myself,* was published in 1937, the year after Kipling's death.

The Man Who Would Be King[1]

"Brother to a Prince and fellow to a beggar if he be found worthy."[2]

The law, as quoted, lays down a fair conduct of life, and one not easy to follow. I have been fellow to a beggar again and again under circumstances

---

1. Kipling based his story on the true-life exploits of an American adventurer, Josiah Harlan, who awarded himself the title of prince after occupying a region in the Hindu Kush in the late 1830s.
2. Meant to suggest the principles of Freemasonry, a secret fraternal society that developed from the masons' guild in medieval Britain. By Victorian times it had grown to a prominent national organization, whose members were bound to help each other in times of distress. Kipling was a member.

which prevented either of us finding out whether the other was worthy. I have still to be brother to a Prince, though I once came near to kinship with what might have been a veritable King and was promised the reversion of[3] a Kingdom—army, law-courts, revenue and policy all complete. But, to-day, I greatly fear that my King is dead, and if I want a crown I must go and hunt it for myself.

The beginning of everything was in a railway train upon the road to Mhow from Ajmir.[4] There had been a Deficit in the Budget, which necessitated traveling, not Second-class, which is only half as dear as First-class, but by Intermediate, which is very awful indeed. There are no cushions in the Intermediate class, and the population are either Intermediate, which is Eurasian, or native, which for a long night journey is nasty, or Loafer,[5] which is amusing though intoxicated. Intermediates do not patronize refreshment-rooms. They carry their food in bundles and pots, and buy sweets from the native sweetmeat-sellers, and drink the roadside water. That is why in the hot weather Intermediates are taken out of the carriages dead, and in all weathers are most properly looked down upon.

My particular Intermediate happened to be empty till I reached Nasirabad, when a huge gentleman in shirt-sleeves entered, and, following the custom of Intermediates, passed the time of day. He was a wanderer and a vagabond like myself, but with an educated taste for whiskey. He told tales of things he had seen and done, of out-of-the-way corners of the Empire into which he had penetrated, and of adventures in which he risked his life for a few days' food. "If India was filled with men like you and me, not knowing more than the crows where they'd get their next day's rations, it isn't seventy millions of revenue the land would be paying—it's seven hundred millions," said he; and as I looked at his mouth and chin I was disposed to agree with him. We talked politics—the politics of Loaferdom that sees things from the underside where the lath and plaster is not smoothed off[6]—and we talked postal arrangements because my friend wanted to send a telegram back from the next station to Ajmir, which is the turning-off place from the Bombay to the Mhow line as you travel westward. My friend had no money beyond eight annas which he wanted[7] for dinner, and I had no money at all, owing to the hitch in the Budget before mentioned. Further, I was going into a wilderness where, though I should resume touch with the Treasury, there were no telegraph offices. I was, therefore, unable to help him in any way.

"We might threaten a Station-master, and make him send a wire on tick,"[8] said my friend, "but that'd mean inquiries for you and for me, and I've got my hands full these days. Did you say you are traveling back along this line within any days?"

"Within ten," I said.

"Can't you make it eight?" said he. "Mine is rather urgent business."

"I can send your telegram within ten days if that will serve you," I said.

"I couldn't trust the wire to fetch him now I think of it. It's this way. He leaves Delhi on the 23d for Bombay. That means he'll be running through Ajmir about the night of the 23d."

---

3. Right to inherit.
4. These, and the other places mentioned at the beginning of the story, are in northern India.
5. A European in India with no official attachment or position.

6. I.e., the unfinished side of a wall.
7. Needed. "Annas": there are sixteen annas in a rupee, the basic monetary unit of India.
8. On credit.

"But I'm going into the Indian Desert," I explained.

"Well *and* good," said he. "You'll be changing at Marwar Junction to get into Jodhpore territory—you must do that—and he'll be coming through Marwar Junction in the early morning of the 24th by the Bombay Mail. Can you be at Marwar Junction on that time? 'Twon't be inconveniencing you because I know that there's precious few pickings to be got out of these Central India States—even though you pretend to be correspondent of the *Backwoodsman*."[9]

"Have you ever tried that trick?" I asked.

"Again and again, but the Residents[1] find you out, and then you get escorted to the Border before you've time to get your knife into them. But about my friend here. I *must* give him a word o' mouth to tell him what's come to me or else he won't know where to go. I would take it more than kind of you if you was to come out of Central India in time to catch him at Marwar Junction, and say to him:—'He has gone South for the week.' He'll know what that means. He's a big man with a red beard, and a great swell[2] he is. You'll find him sleeping like a gentleman with all his luggage round him in a Second-class compartment. But don't you be afraid. Slip down the window, and say:—'He has gone South for the week,' and he'll tumble.[3] It's only cutting your time of stay in those parts by two days. I ask you as a stranger—going to the West,"[4] he said, with emphasis.

"Where have *you* come from?" said I.

"From the East," said he, "and I am hoping that you will give him the message on the Square[5]—for the sake of my Mother as well as your own."

Englishmen are not usually softened by appeals to the memory of their mothers, but for certain reasons, which will be fully apparent, I saw fit to agree.

"It's more than a little matter," said he, "and that's why I ask you to do it—and now I know that I can depend on you doing it. A Second-class carriage at Marwar Junction, and a red-haired man asleep in it. You'll be sure to remember. I get out at the next station, and I must hold on there till he comes or sends me what I want."

"I'll give the message if I catch him," I said, "and for the sake of your Mother as well as mine I'll give you a word of advice. Don't try to run the Central India States just now as the correspondent of the *Backwoodsman*. There's a real one knocking about here, and it might lead to trouble."

"Thank you," said he, simply, "and when will the swine be gone? I can't starve because he's ruining my work. I wanted to get hold of the Degumber Rajah down here about his father's widow, and give him a jump."

"What did he do to his father's widow, then?"

"Filled her up with red pepper and slippered her to death as she hung from a beam. I found that out myself, and I'm the only man that would dare going into the State to get hush-money for it. They'll try to poison me, same as they did in Chortumna when I went on the loot there. But you'll give the man at Marwar Junction my message?"

He got out at a little roadside station, and I reflected. I had heard, more

9. This fictitious newspaper appears to be based on the Allahabad *Pioneer*, for which Kipling worked as a roving correspondent. "Central India States": quasi-independent "Native States," as they were also known, presided over by Indian royalty.
1. British political officers appointed to oversee affairs at the courts of Indian rulers.
2. Fashionable fellow.
3. Catch on, understand.
4. This phrase and the following one are from the code of the Freemasons.
5. Honestly.

than once, of men personating correspondents of newspapers and bleeding small Native States with threats of exposure, but I had never met any of the caste before. They lead a hard life, and generally die with great suddenness. The Native States have a wholesome horror of English newspapers, which may throw light on their peculiar methods of government, and do their best to choke correspondents with champagne, or drive them out of their mind with four-in-hand barouches.[6] They do not understand that nobody cares a straw for the internal administration of Native States so long as oppression and crime are kept within decent limits, and the ruler is not drugged, drunk, or diseased from one end of the year to the other. Native States were created by Providence in order to supply picturesque scenery, tigers, and tall-writing.[7] They are the dark places of the earth, full of unimaginable cruelty, touching the Railway and the Telegraph on one side, and, on the other, the days of Harun-al-Raschid.[8] When I left the train I did business with divers Kings, and in eight days passed through many changes of life. Sometimes I wore dress-clothes and consorted with Princes and Politicals,[9] drinking from crystal and eating from silver. Sometimes I lay out upon the ground and devoured what I could get, from a plate made of a flapjack, and drank the running water, and slept under the same rug as my servant. It was all in the day's work.

Then I headed for the Great Indian Desert upon the proper date, as I had promised, and the night Mail set me down at Marwar Junction, where a funny little, happy-go-lucky, native-managed railway runs to Jodhpore. The Bombay Mail from Delhi makes a short halt at Marwar. She arrived as I got in, and I had just time to hurry to her platform and go down the carriages. There was only one Second-class on the train. I slipped the window, and looked down upon a flaming red beard, half covered by a railway rug. That was my man, fast asleep, and I dug him gently in the ribs. He woke with a grunt, and I saw his face in the light of the lamps. It was a great and shining face.

"Tickets again?" said he.

"No," said I. "I am to tell you that he is gone South for the week. He is gone South for the week!"

The train had begun to move out. The red man rubbed his eyes. "He has gone South for the week," he repeated. "Now that's just like his impidence. Did he say that I was to give you anything?—'Cause I won't."

"He didn't," I said, and dropped away, and watched the red lights die out in the dark. It was horribly cold, because the wind was blowing off the sands. I climbed into my own train—not an Intermediate Carriage this time—and went to sleep.

If the man with the beard had given me a rupee I should have kept it as a memento of a rather curious affair. But the consciousness of having done my duty was my only reward.

Later on I reflected that two gentlemen like my friends could not do any good if they foregathered and personated correspondents of newspapers, and might, if they "stuck up"[1] one of the little rat-trap states of Central India or Southern Rajputana, get themselves into serious difficulties. I therefore took some trouble to describe them as accurately as I could remember to people who would be interested in deporting them; and succeeded, so I was later

---

6. Fashionable four-wheeled carriages.
7. Tall tales.
8. The caliph of Baghdad (763–809), who figures in many tales of the *Arabian Nights*.

9. I.e., Residents.
1. Fraudulently extorted money from. "Foregathered": met.

informed, in having them headed back from Degumber borders.

Then I became respectable, and returned to an Office where there were no Kings and no incidents except the daily manufacture of a newspaper. A newspaper office seems to attract every conceivable sort of person, to the prejudice of discipline. Zenana-mission ladies[2] arrive, and beg that the Editor will instantly abandon all his duties to describe a Christian prize-giving in a back-slum of a perfectly inaccessible village; Colonels who have been overpassed for commands sit down and sketch the outline of a series of ten, twelve, or twenty-four leading articles on Seniority *versus* Selection; missionaries wish to know why they have not been permitted to escape from their regular vehicles of abuse and swear at a brother missionary under special patronage of the editorial We; stranded theatrical companies troop up to explain that they cannot pay for their advertisements, but on their return from New Zealand or Tahiti will do so with interest; inventors of patent punkah[3]-pulling machines, carriage couplings and unbreakable swords and axle-trees call with specifications in their pockets and hours at their disposal; tea-companies enter and elaborate their prospectuses with the office pens; secretaries of ball-committees clamour to have the glories of their last dance more fully expounded; strange ladies rustle in and say:—"I want a hundred lady's cards printed *at once*, please," which is manifestly part of an Editor's duty; and every dissolute ruffian that ever tramped the Grand Trunk Road[4] makes it his business to ask for employment as a proof-reader. And, all the time, the telephone-bell is ringing madly, and Kings are being killed on the Continent, and Empires are saying—"You're another," and Mister Gladstone is calling down brimstone upon the British Dominions,[5] and the little black copy-boys are whining, "*kaa-pi chay-ha-yeh*" (copy wanted) like tired bees, and most of the paper is as blank as Modred's shield.[6]

But that is the amusing part of the year. There are other six months wherein none ever come to call, and the thermometer walks inch by inch up to the top of the glass, and the office is darkened to just above reading-light, and the press machines are red-hot of touch, and nobody writes anything but accounts of amusements in the Hill-stations[7] or obituary notices. Then the telephone becomes a tinkling terror, because it tells you of the sudden deaths of men and women that you knew intimately, and the prickly-heat covers you as with a garment, and you sit down and write:—"A slight increase of sickness is reported from the Khuda Janta Khan[8] District. The outbreak is purely sporadic in its nature, and, thanks to the energetic efforts of the District authorities, is now almost at an end. It is, however, with deep regret we record the death, etc."

Then the sickness really breaks out, and the less recording and reporting the better for the peace of the subscribers. But the Empires and the Kings continue to divert themselves as selfishly as before, and the Foreman thinks that a daily paper really ought to come out once in twenty-four hours, and all

2. Female missionaries doing work among Indian women, who were customarily confined to a part of the house called the *Zenana*.
3. Large swinging fan, usually worked by hand.
4. Major road connecting Calcutta and Delhi.
5. Places under British control. William Ewart Gladstone (1809–1898), leader of the Liberal Party from 1868 to 1875 and 1880 to 1894, and four times prime minister; he strongly opposed overseas expansion. "Brimstone": i.e., fire and brimstone, the supposed torments of hell.
6. In British legend the shield of King Arthur's traitorous nephew was blank because he had done no deeds of valor.
7. Official outposts in the northern hills, to which many British people in India would retire during the hottest months.
8. "God Knows Town"; i.e., Nowheresville.

2270 / Rudyard Kipling

the people at the Hill-stations in the middle of their amusements say:—"Good gracious! Why can't the paper be sparkling? I'm sure there's plenty going on up here."

That is the dark half of the moon, and, as the advertisements say, "must be experienced to be appreciated."

It was in that season, and a remarkably evil season, that the paper began running the last issue of the week on Saturday night, which is to say, Sunday morning, after the custom of a London paper. This was a great convenience, for immediately after the paper was put to bed,[9] the dawn would lower the thermometer from 96° to almost 84° for half an hour, and in that chill—you have no idea how cold is 84° on the grass until you begin to pray for it—a very tired man could set off to sleep ere the heat roused him.

One Saturday night it was my pleasant duty to put the paper to bed alone. A King or courtier or a courtesan or a community was going to die or get a new Constitution, or do something that was important on the other side of the world, and the paper was to be held open till the latest possible minute in order to catch the telegram. It was a pitchy black night, as stifling as a June night can be, and the *loo*, the red-hot wind from the westward, was booming among the tinder-dry trees and pretending that the rain was on its heels. Now and again a spot of almost boiling water would fall on the dust with the flop of a frog, but all our weary world knew that was only pretence. It was a shade cooler in the press-room than the office, so I sat there, while the type clicked and clicked and the night-jars hooted at the windows, and the all but naked compositors wiped the sweat from their foreheads and called for water. The thing that was keeping us back, whatever it was, would not come off, though the *loo* dropped and the last type was set, and the whole round earth stood still in the choking heat, with its finger on its lip, to wait the event. I drowsed, and wondered whether the telegraph was a blessing, and whether this dying man, or struggling people, was aware of the inconvenience the delay was causing. There was no special reason beyond the heat and worry to make tension, but, as the clock hands crept up to three o'clock and the machines spun their fly-wheels two and three times to see that all was in order, before I said the word that would set them off, I could have shrieked aloud.

Then the roar and rattle of the wheels shivered the quiet into little bits. I rose to go away, but two men in white clothes stood in front of me. The first one said:—"It's him!" The second said:—"So it is!" And they both laughed almost as loudly as the machinery roared, and mopped their foreheads. "We see there was a light burning across the road and we were sleeping in that ditch there for coolness, and I said to my friend here, 'The office is open. Let's come along and speak to him as turned us back from the Degumber State,'" said the smaller of the two. He was the man I had met in the Mhow train, and his fellow was the red-bearded man of Marwar Junction. There was no mistaking the eyebrows of the one or the beard of the other.

I was not pleased, because I wished to go to sleep, not to squabble with loafers. "What do you want?" I asked.

"Half an hour's talk with you cool and comfortable, in the office," said the red-bearded man. "We'd *like* some drink—the Contrack doesn't begin yet, Peachey, so you needn't look—but what we really want is advice. We don't want money. We ask you as a favour, because you did us a bad turn about Degumber."

---

9. The final preparations were made for printing the newspaper.

I led from the press-room to the stifling office with the maps on the walls, and the red-haired man rubbed his hands. "That's something like," said he. "This was the proper shop to come to. Now, Sir, let me introduce to you Brother[1] Peachey Carnehan, that's him, and Brother Daniel Dravot, that is *me*, and the less said about our professions the better, for we have been most things in our time. Soldier, sailor, compositor, photographer, proof-reader, street-preacher, and correspondents of the *Backwoodsman* when we thought the paper wanted one. Carnehan is sober, and so am I. Look at us first and see that's sure. It will save you cutting into my talk. We'll take one of your cigars apiece, and you shall see us light."

I watched the test. The men were absolutely sober, so I gave them each a tepid peg.[2]

"Well *and* good," said Carnehan of the eyebrows, wiping the froth from his moustache. "Let me talk now, Dan. We have been all over India, mostly on foot. We have been boiler-fitters, engine-drivers, petty contractors, and all that, and we have decided that India isn't big enough for such as us."

They certainly were too big for the office. Dravot's beard seemed to fill half the room and Carnehan's shoulders the other half, as they sat on the big table. Carnehan continued: "The country isn't half worked out because they that governs it won't let you touch it. They spend all their blessed time in governing it, and you can't lift a spade, nor chip a rock, nor look for oil, nor anything like that without all the Government saying—'Leave it alone and let us govern.' Therefore, such as it is, we will let it alone, and go away to some other place where a man isn't crowded and can come to his own. We are not little men, and there is nothing that we are afraid of except Drink, and we have signed a Contrack on that. *Therefore*, we are going away to be Kings."

"Kings in our own right," muttered Dravot.

"Yes, of course," I said. "You've been tramping in the sun, and it's a very warm night, and hadn't you better sleep over the notion? Come to-morrow."

"Neither drunk nor sunstruck," said Dravot. "We have slept over the notion half a year, and require to see Books and Atlases, and we have decided that there is only one place now in the world that two strong men can Sar-a-*whack*.[3] They call it Kafiristan.[4] By my reckoning it's the top right-hand corner of Afghanistan, not more than three hundred miles from Pesha-wur. They have two and thirty heathen idols there, and we'll be the thirty-third. It's a mountainous country, and the women of those parts are very beautiful."

"But that is provided against in the Contrack," said Carnehan. "Neither Women nor Liquor, Daniel."

"And that's all we know, except that no one has gone there, and they fight, and in any place where they fight, a man who knows how to drill men can always be a King. We shall go to those parts and say to any King we find— 'D'you want to vanquish your foes?' and we will show him how to drill men; for that we know better than anything else. Then we will subvert that King and seize his Throne and establish a Dy-nasty."

"You'll be cut to pieces before you're fifty miles across the Border," I said. "You have to travel through Afghanistan to get to that country. It's one mass of mountains and peaks and glaciers, and no Englishman has been through

---

1. A title meant to recall the Freemason connection.
2. A drink.
3. A reference to Sir James Brooke (1803–1868), "the White Rajah of Sarawak," who, in return for helping the rajah of Sarawak, in Borneo, put down a rebellion, succeeded him after his death and established a dynasty.
4. A real place, in the Hindu Kush.

it. The people are utter brutes, and even if you reached them you couldn't do anything."

"That's more like," said Carnehan: "If you could think us a little more mad we would be more pleased. We have come to you to know about this country, to read a book about it, and to be shown maps. We want you to tell us that we are fools and to show us your books." He turned to the bookcases.

"Are you at all in earnest?" I said.

"A little," said Dravot, sweetly. "As big a map as you have got, even if it's all blank where Kafiristan is, and any books you've got. We can read, though we aren't very educated."

I uncased the big thirty-two-miles-to-the-inch map of India, and two smaller Frontier maps, hauled down volume INF-KAN of the *Encyclopaedia Britannica*, and the men consulted them.

"See here!" said Dravot, his thumb on the map. "Up to Jagdallak, Peachey and me know the road. We was there with Roberts's Army.[5] We'll have to turn off to the right at Jagdallak through Laghmann territory. Then we get among the hills—fourteen thousand feet—fifteen thousand—it will be cold work there, but it don't look very far on the map."

I handed him Wood on the *Sources of the Oxus*.[6] Carnehan was deep in the *Encyclopaedia*.

"They're a mixed lot," said Dravot, reflectively; "and it won't help us to know the names of their tribes. The more tribes the more they'll fight, and the better for us. From Jagdallak to Ashang. H'mm!"

"But all the information about the country is as sketchy and inaccurate as can be," I protested. "No one knows anything about it really. Here's the file of the *United Services' Institute*. Read what Bellew says."

"Blow Bellew!" said Carnehan. "Dan, they're an all-fired lot of heathens, but this book here says they think they're related to us English."

I smoked while the men pored over Raverty, Wood, the maps, and the *Encyclopaedia*.

"There is no use your waiting," said Dravot, politely. "It's about four o'clock now. We'll go before six o'clock if you want to sleep, and we won't steal any of the papers. Don't you sit up. We're two harmless lunatics and if you come, to-morrow evening, down to the Serai[7] we'll say good-bye to you."

"You *are* two fools," I answered. "You'll be turned back at the Frontier or cut up the minute you set foot in Afghanistan. Do you want any money or a recommendation downcountry? I can help you to the chance of work next week."

"Next week we shall be hard at work ourselves, thank you," said Dravot. "It isn't so easy being a King as it looks. When we've got our Kingdom in going order we'll let you know, and you can come up and help us to govern it."

"Would two lunatics make a Contrack like that?" said Carnehan, with subdued pride, showing me a greasy half-sheet of note-paper on which was written the following. I copied it, then and there, as a curiosity:

This Contract between me and you persuing witnesseth in the name of God— Amen and so forth.

---

5. In the Second Afghan War (1878–80), a force under the command of General Frederick Roberts made a three-hundred-mile forced march through the area.

6. The Oxus is a river whose sources are in the area.

7. Place or building for the accommodation of travelers and their pack animals.

(One)	That me and you will settle this matter together: i. e., to be Kings of Kafiristan.
(Two)	That you and me will not, while this matter is being settled, look at any Liquor, nor any Woman, black, white or brown, so as to get mixed up with one or the other harmful.
(Three)	That we conduct ourselves with dignity and discretion and if one of us gets into trouble the other will stay by him.

Signed by you and me this day.
Peachey Taliaferro Carnehan.
Daniel Dravot.
Both Gentlemen at Large.

"There was no need for the last article," said Carnehan, blushing modestly; "but it looks regular. Now you know the sort of men that loafers are—we *are* loafers, Dan, until we get out of India—and *do* you think that we would sign a Contrack like that unless we was in earnest? We have kept away from the two things that make life worth having."

"You won't enjoy your lives much longer if you are going to try this idiotic adventure. Don't set the office on fire," I said, "and go away before nine o'clock."

I left them still poring over the maps and making notes on the back of the "Contrack." "Be sure to come down to the Serai to-morrow," were their parting words.

The Kumharsen Serai is the great foursquare sink of humanity where the strings of camels and horses from the North load and unload. All the nationalities of Central Asia may be found there, and most of the folk of India proper. Balkh and Bokhara there meet Bengal and Bombay, and try to draw eye-teeth. You can buy ponies, turquoises, Persian pussy-cats, saddle-bags, fat-tailed sheep and musk in the Kumharsen Serai, and get many strange things for nothing. In the afternoon I went down there to see whether my friends intended to keep their word or were lying about drunk.

A priest attired in fragments of ribbons and rags stalked up to me, gravely twisting a child's paper whirligig.[8] Behind was his servant bending under the load of a crate of mud toys. The two were loading up two camels, and the inhabitants of the Serai watched them with shrieks of laughter.

"The priest is mad," said a horse-dealer to me. "He is going up to Kabul to sell toys to the Amir.[9] He will either be raised to honor or have his head cut off. He came in here this morning and has been behaving madly ever since."

"The witless are under the protection of God," stammered a flat-cheeked Usbeg[1] in broken Hindi. "They foretell future events."

"Would they could have foretold that my caravan would have been cut up by the Shinwaris almost within shadow of the Pass!"[2] grunted the Eusufzai agent of a Rajputana trading-house whose goods had been feloniously diverted into the hands of other robbers just across the Border, and whose misfortunes were the laughing-stock of the bazar. "Ohé, priest, whence come you and whither do you go?"

"From Roum[3] have I come," shouted the priest, waving his whirligig; "from

---

8. Pinwheel.
9. The ruler of Afghanistan, based in the city of Kabul.
1. Person from Uzbekistan.
2. The Khyber or Khaiber Pass, running thirty-

three miles through the mountains. Then on the northwest frontier of British India, it now links Afghanistan and Pakistan.
3. Turkey.

Roum, blown by the breath of a hundred devils across the sea! O thieves, robbers, liars, the blessing of Pir Khan on pigs, dogs, and perjurers! Who will take the Protected of God to the North to sell charms that are never still to the Amir? The camels shall not gall,[4] the sons shall not fall sick, and the wives shall remain faithful while they are away, of the men who give me place in their caravan. Who will assist me to slipper the King of the Roos[5] with a golden slipper with a silver heel? The protection of Pir Khan be upon his labors!" He spread out the skirts of his gaberdine and pirouetted between the lines of tethered horses.

"There starts a caravan from Peshawur to Kabul in twenty days, *Huzrut,*"[6] said the Eusufzai trader. "My camels go therewith. Do thou also go and bring us good-luck."

"I will go even now!" shouted the priest. "I will depart upon my winged camels, and be at Peshawur in a day! Ho! Hazar[7] Mir Khan," he yelled to his servant, "drive out the camels, but let me first mount my own."

He leaped on the back of his beast as it knelt, and, turning round to me, cried:—"Come thou also, Sahib, a little along the road, and I will sell thee a charm—an amulet that shall make thee King of Kafiristan."

Then the light broke upon me, and I followed the two camels out of the Serai till we reached open road and the priest halted.

"What d' you think o' that?" said he in English. "Carnehan can't talk their patter, so I've made him my servant. He makes a handsome servant. 'Tisn't for nothing that I've been knocking about the country for fourteen years. Didn't I do that talk neat? We'll hitch on to a caravan at Peshawur till we get to Jagdallak, and then we'll see if we can get donkeys for our camels, and strike into Kafiristan. Whirligigs for the Amir, O Lor! Put your hand under the camel-bags and tell me what you feel."

I felt the butt of a Martini,[8] and another and another.

"Twenty of 'em," said Dravot, placidly. "Twenty of 'em, and ammunition to correspond, under the whirligigs and the mud dolls."

"Heaven help you if you are caught with those things!" I said. "A Martini is worth her weight in silver among the Pathans."[9]

"Fifteen hundred rupees of capital—every rupee we could beg, borrow, or steal—are invested on these two camels," said Dravot. "We won't get caught. We're going through the Khaiber with a regular caravan. Who'd touch a poor mad priest?"

"Have you got everything you want?" I asked, overcome with astonishment.

"Not yet, but we shall soon. Give us a memento of your kindness, *Brother.* You did me a service yesterday, and that time in Marwar. Half my Kingdom shall you have, as the saying is." I slipped a small charm compass from my watch-chain and handed it up to the priest.

"Good-bye," said Dravot, giving me hand cautiously. "It's the last time we'll shake hands with an Englishman these many days. Shake hands with him, Carnehan," he cried, as the second camel passed me.

Carnehan leaned down and shook hands. Then the camels passed away along the dusty road, and I was left alone to wonder. My eye could detect no failure in the disguises. The scene in Serai attested that they were complete to the native mind. There was just the chance, therefore, that Carnehan and

---

4. Become sore.
5. Czar of Russia.
6. Presence (an honorary form of address).
7. Get ready.
8. Rifle issued to British infantry.
9. The principal tribe in Afghanistan.

Dravot would be able to wander through Afghanistan without detection. But, beyond, they would find death, certain and awful death.

Ten days later a native friend of mine, giving me the news of the day from Peshawur, wound up his letter with:—"There has been much laughter here on account of a certain mad priest who is going in his estimation to sell petty gauds and insignificant trinkets which he ascribes as great charms to H. H.[1] the Amir of Bokhara. He passed through Peshawur and associated himself to the Second Summer caravan that goes to Kabul. The merchants are pleased, because through superstition they imagine that such mad fellows bring good-fortune."

The two, then, were beyond the Border. I would have prayed for them, but, that night, a real King died in Europe, and demanded an obituary notice.

The wheel of the world swings through the same phases again and again. Summer passed and winter thereafter, and came and passed again. The daily paper continued and I with it, and upon the third summer there fell a hot night, a night-issue, and a strained waiting for something to be telegraphed from the other side of the world, exactly as had happened before. A few great men had died in the past two years, the machines worked with more clatter, and some of the trees in the Office garden were a few feet taller. But that was all the difference.

I passed over to the press-room, and went through just such a scene as I have already described. The nervous tension was stronger than it had been two years before, and I felt the heat more acutely. At three o'clock I cried, "Print off," and turned to go, when there crept to my chair what was left of a man. He was bent into a circle, his head was sunk between his shoulders, and he moved his feet one over the other like a bear. I could hardly see whether he walked or crawled—this rag-wrapped, whining cripple who addressed me by name, crying that he was come back. "Can you give me a drink?" he whimpered. "For the Lord's sake, give me a drink!"

I went back to the office, the man following with groans of pain, and I turned up the lamp.

"Don't you know me?" he gasped, dropping into a chair, and he turned his drawn face, surmounted by a shock of grey hair, to the light.

I looked at him intently. Once before had I seen eyebrows that met over the nose in an inch-broad black band, but for the life of me I could not tell where.

"I don't know you," I said, handing him the whiskey. "What can I do for you?"

He took a gulp of the spirit raw, and shivered in spite of the suffocating heat.

"I've come back," he repeated; "and I was the King of Kafiristan—me and Dravot—crowned Kings we was! In this office we settled it—you setting there and giving us the books. I am Peachey—Peachey Taliaferro Carnehan, and you've been setting here ever since—O Lord!"

I was more than a little astonished, and expressed my feelings accordingly.

"It's true," said Carnehan, with a dry cackle, nursing his feet, which were wrapped in rags. "True as gospel. Kings we were, with crowns upon our heads—me and Dravot—poor Dan—oh, poor, poor Dan, that would never take advice, not though I begged of him!"

"Take the whiskey," I said, "and take your own time. Tell me all you can

1. His Highness.

recollect of everything from beginning to end. You got across the border on your camels, Dravot dressed as a mad priest and you his servant. Do you remember that?"

"I ain't mad—yet, but I shall be that way soon. Of course I remember. Keep looking at me, or maybe my words will go all to pieces. Keep looking at me in my eyes and don't say anything."

I leaned forward and looked into his face as steadily as I could. He dropped one hand upon the table and I grasped it by the wrist. It was twisted like a bird's claw, and upon the back was a ragged, red, diamond-shaped scar.

"No, don't look there. Look at *me*," said Carnehan.

"That comes afterward, but for the Lord's sake don't distrack me. We left with that caravan, me and Dravot playing all sorts of antics to amuse the people we were with. Dravot used to make us laugh in the evenings when all the people was cooking their dinners—cooking their dinners, and . . . what did they do then? They lit little fires with sparks that went into Dravot's beard, and we all laughed—fit to die. Little red fires they was, going into Dravot's big red beard—so funny." His eyes left mine and he smiled foolishly.

"You went as far as Jagdallak with that caravan," I said, at a venture, "after you had lit those fires. To Jagdallak, where you turned off to try to get into Kafiristan."

"No, we didn't neither. What are you talking about? We turned off before Jagdallak, because we heard the roads was good. But they wasn't good enough for our two camels—mine and Dravot's. When we left the caravan, Dravot took off all his clothes and mine too, and said we would be heathen, because the Kafirs[2] didn't allow Mohammedans to talk to them. So we dressed betwixt and between, and such a sight as Daniel Dravot I never saw yet nor expect to see again. He burned half his beard, and slung a sheep-skin over his shoulder, and shaved his head into patterns. He shaved mine, too, and made me wear outrageous things to look like a heathen. That was in a most mountaineous country, and our camels couldn't go along any more because of the mountains. They were tall and black, and coming home I saw them fight like wild goats—there are lots of goats in Kafiristan. And these mountains, they never keep still, no more than goats. Always fighting they are, and don't let you sleep at night."

"Take some more whiskey," I said, very slowly. "What did you and Daniel Dravot do when the camels could go no further because of the rough roads that led into Kafiristan?"

"What did which do? There was a party called Peachey Taliaferro Carnehan that was with Dravot. Shall I tell you about him? He died out there in the cold. Slap from the bridge fell old Peachey, turning and twisting in the air like a penny whirligig that you can sell to the Amir—No; they was two for three ha'pence, those whirligigs, or I am much mistaken and woful sore. And then these camels were no use, and Peachey said to Dravot—'For the Lord's sake, let's get out of this before our heads are chopped off,' and with that they killed the camels all among the mountains, not having anything in particular to eat, but first they took off the boxes with the guns and the ammunition, till two men came along driving four mules. Dravot up and dances in front of them, singing,—'Sell me four mules.' Says the first man,—'If you are rich enough to buy, you are rich enough to rob;' but before ever he could put his hand to his

2. Non-Muslims.

knife, Dravot breaks his neck over his knee, and the other party runs away. So Carnehan loaded the mules with the rifles that was taken off the camels, and together we starts forward into those bitter cold mountaineous parts, and never a road broader than the back of your hand."

He paused for a moment, while I asked him if he could remember the nature of the country through which he had journeyed.

"I am telling you as straight as I can, but my head isn't as good as it might be. They drove nails through it to make me hear better how Dravot died. The country was mountaineous and the mules were most contrary, and the inhabitants was dispersed and solitary. They went up and up, and down and down, and that other party, Carnehan, was imploring of Dravot not to sing and whistle so loud, for fear of bringing down the tremenjus avalanches. But Dravot says that if a King couldn't sing it wasn't worth being King, and whacked the mules over the rump, and never took no heed for ten cold days. We came to a big level valley all among the mountains, and the mules were near dead, so we killed them, not having anything in special for them or us to eat. We sat upon the boxes, and played odd and even[3] with the cartridges that was jolted out.

"Then ten men with bows and arrows ran down that valley, chasing twenty men with bows and arrows, and the row was tremenjus. They was fair men—fairer than you or me—with yellow hair and remarkable well built.[4] Says Dravot, unpacking the guns—'This is the beginning of the business. We'll fight for the ten men,' and with that he fires two rifles at the twenty men, and drops one of them at two hundred yards from the rock where we was sitting. The other men began to run, but Carnehan and Dravot sits on the boxes picking them off at all ranges, up and down the valley. Then we goes up to the ten men that had run across the snow too, and they fires a footy[5] little arrow at us. Dravot he shoots above their heads and they all falls down flat. Then he walks over and kicks them, and then he lifts them up and shakes hands all round to make them friendly like. He calls them and gives them the boxes to carry, and waves his hand for all the world as though he was King already. They takes the boxes and him across the valley and up the hill into a pine wood on the top, where there was half a dozen big stone idols. Dravot he goes to the biggest—a fellow they call Imbra—and lays a rifle and a cartridge at his feet, rubbing his nose respectful with his own nose, patting him on the head, and saluting in front of it. He turns round to the men and nods his head, and says,—'That's all right. I'm in the know too, and all these old jim-jams[6] are my friends.' Then he opens his mouth and points down it, and when the first man brings him food, he says—'No;' and when the second man brings him food, he says—'No;' but when one of the old priests and the boss of the village brings him food, he says—'Yes;' very haughty, and eats it slow. That was how we came to our first village, without any trouble, just as though we had tumbled from the skies. But we tumbled from one of those damned rope-bridges, you see, and you couldn't expect a man to laugh much after that."

"Take some more whiskey and go on," I said. "That was the first village you came into. How did you get to be King?"

"I wasn't King," said Carnehan. "Dravot he was the King, and a handsome

3. A game in which a player guesses the number of objects that another player is holding.
4. There was a legend that Alexander the Great had left a Greek colony in the area in the 4th cen-

tury B.C.E.
5. Paltry, insignificant.
6. Knickknacks.

man he looked with the gold crown on his head and all. Him and the other party stayed in that village, and every morning Dravot sat by the side of old Imbra, and the people came and worshipped. That was Dravot's order. Then a lot of men came into the valley, and Carnehan and Dravot picks them off with the rifles before they knew where they was, and runs down into the valley and up again the other side, and finds another village, same as the first one, and the people all falls down flat on their faces, and Dravot says,—'Now what is the trouble between you two villages?' and the people points to a woman, as fair as you or me, that was carried off, and Dravot takes her back to the first village and counts up the dead—eight there was. For each dead man Dravot pours a little milk on the ground and waves his arms like a whirligig and 'That's all right,' says he. Then he and Carnehan takes the big boss of each village by the arm and walks them down into the valley, and shows them how to scratch a line with a spear right down the valley, and gives each a sod of turf from both sides o' the line. Then all the people comes down and shouts like the devil and all, and Dravot says,—'Go and dig the land, and be fruitful and multiply,'[7] which they did, though they didn't understand. Then we asks the names of things in their lingo—bread and water and fire and idols and such, and Dravot leads the priest of each village up to the idol, and says he must sit there and judge the people, and if anything goes wrong he is to be shot.

"Next week they was all turning up the land in the valley as quiet as bees and much prettier, and the priests heard all the complaints and told Dravot in dumb show what it was about. 'That's just the beginning,' says Dravot. 'They think we're Gods.' He and Carnehan picks out twenty good men and shows them how to click off a rifle, and form fours, and advance in line, and they was very pleased to do so, and clever to see the hang of it. Then he takes out his pipe and his baccy-pouch and leaves one at one village and one at the other, and off we two goes to see what was to be done in the next valley. That was all rock, and there was a little village there, and Carnehan says,—'Send 'em to the old valley to plant,' and takes 'em there and gives 'em some land that wasn't took before. They were a poor lot, and we blooded 'em with a kid[8] before letting 'em into the new Kingdom. That was to impress the people, and then they settled down quiet, and Carnehan went back to Dravot, who had got into another valley, all snow and ice and most mountaineous. There was no people there, and the Army got afraid, so Dravot shoots one of them, and goes on till he finds some people in a village, and the Army explains that unless the people wants to be killed they had better not shoot their little matchlocks;[9] for they had matchlocks. We makes friends with the priest and I stays there alone with two of the Army, teaching the men how to drill, and a thundering big Chief comes across the snow with kettle-drums and horns twanging, because he heard there was a new God kicking about. Carnehan sights for the brown[1] of the men half a mile across the snow and wings one of them. Then he sends a message to the Chief that, unless he wished to be killed, he must come and shake hands with me and leave his arms behind. The Chief comes alone first, and Carnehan shakes hands with him and whirls his arms about, same as Dravot used, and very much surprised that Chief was, and strokes my

---

7. God's command to Adam and Eve (Genesis 1.28).
8. I.e., a kid goat, a fake religious ritual.
9. Primitive muskets.

1. A hunting term, meaning to fire into the middle of a group of game birds rather than aiming at a particular one.

eyebrows. Then Carnehan goes alone to the Chief, and asks him in dumb show if he had an enemy he hated. 'I have,' says the Chief. So Carnehan weeds out the pick of his men, and sets the two of the Army to show them drill, and at the end of two weeks the men can manoeuvre about as well as Volunteers. So he marches with the Chief to a great big plain on the top of a mountain, and the Chief's men rushes into a village and takes it; we three Martinis firing into the brown of the enemy. So we took that village too, and I gives the Chief a rag from my coat and says, 'Occupy till I come;'[2] which was scriptural. By way of a reminder, when me and the Army was eighteen hundred yards away, I drops a bullet near him standing on the snow, and all the people falls flat on their faces. Then I sends a letter to Dravot, wherever he be by land or by sea."

At the risk of throwing the creature out of train I interrupted,—"How could you write a letter up yonder?"

"The letter?—Oh!—The letter! Keep looking at me between the eyes, please. It was a string-talk letter, that we'd learned the way of it from a blind beggar in the Punjab."

I remember that there had once come to the office a blind man with a knotted twig and a piece of string which he wound round the twig according to some cipher of his own. He could, after the lapse of days or hours, repeat the sentence which he had reeled up. He had reduced the alphabet to eleven primitive sounds; and tried to teach me his method, but failed.

"I sent that letter to Dravot," said Carnehan; "and told him to come back because this Kingdom was growing too big for me to handle, and then I struck for the first valley, to see how the priests were working. They called the village we took along with the Chief, Bashkai, and the first village we took, Er-Heb. The priests at Er-Heb was doing all right, but they had a lot of pending cases about land to show me, and some men from another village had been firing arrows at night. I went out and looked for that village and fired four rounds at it from a thousand yards. That used all the cartridges I cared to spend, and I waited for Dravot, who had been away two or three months, and I kept my people quiet.

"One morning I heard the devil's own noise of drums and horns, and Dan Dravot marches down the hill with his Army and a tail of hundreds of men, and, which was the most amazing—a great gold crown on his head. 'My Gord, Carnehan,' says Daniel, 'this is a tremenjus business, and we've got the whole country as far as it's worth having. I am the son of Alexander by Queen Semi-ramis,[3] and you're my younger brother and a God too! It's the biggest thing we've ever seen. I've been marching and fighting for six weeks with the Army, and every footy[4] little village for fifty miles has come in rejoiceful; and more than that, I've got the key of the whole show, as you'll see, and I've got a crown for you! I told 'em to make two of 'em at a place called Shu, where the gold lies in the rock like suet in mutton. Gold I've seen, and turquoise I've kicked out of the cliffs, and there's garnets in the sands of the river, and here's a chunk of amber that a man brought me. Call up all the priests and, here, take your crown.'

"One of the men opens a black hair bag and I slips the crown on. It was too small and too heavy, but I wore it for the glory. Hammered gold it was—five pound weight, like a hoop of a barrel.

2. In Jesus' parable of the talents, a nobleman gives each of his servants a coin to invest with those instructions (Luke 19.13).

3. Legendary Assyrian queen.
4. Worthless.

" 'Peachey,' says Dravot, 'we don't want to fight no more. The Craft's[5] the trick, so help me!' and he brings forward that same Chief that I left at Bash-kai—Billy Fish we called him afterward, because he was so like Billy Fish that drove the big tank-engine at Mach on the Bolan[6] in the old days. 'Shake hands with him,' says Dravot, and I shook hands and nearly dropped, for Billy Fish gave me the Grip.[7] I said nothing, but tried him with the Fellow Craft Grip. He answers, all right, and I tried the Master's Grip, but that was a slip. 'A Fellow Craft he is!' I says to Dan. 'Does he know the word?' 'He does,' says Dan, 'and all the priests know. It's a miracle! The Chiefs and the priests can work a Fellow Craft Lodge in a way that's very like ours, and they've cut the marks on the rocks, but they don't know the Third Degree, and they've come to find out. It's Gord's Truth. I've known these long years that the Afghans knew up to the Fellow Craft Degree, but this is a miracle. A God and a Grand-Master of the Craft am I, and a Lodge in the Third Degree I will open, and we'll raise the head priests and the Chiefs of the villages.'

" 'It's against all the law,' I says, 'holding a Lodge without warrant from any one; and we never held office in any Lodge.'

" 'It's a master-stroke of policy,' says Dravot. 'It means running the country as easy as a four-wheeled bogy[8] on a down grade. We can't stop to inquire now, or they'll turn against us. I've forty Chiefs at my heel, and passed and raised according to their merit they shall be. Billet these men on the villages and see that we run up a Lodge of some kind. The temple of Imbra will do for the Lodge-room. The women must make aprons as you show them. I'll hold a levee[9] of Chiefs to-night and Lodge to-morrow.'

"I was fair run off my legs, but I wasn't such a fool as not to see what a pull this Craft business gave us. I showed the priests' families how to make aprons of the degrees, but for Dravot's apron the blue border and marks was made of turquoise lumps on white hide, not cloth. We took a great square stone in the temple for the Master's chair, and little stones for the officers' chairs, and painted the black pavement with white squares, and did what we could to make things regular.

"At the levee which was held that night on the hillside with big bonfires, Dravot gives out that him and me were Gods and sons of Alexander, and Past Grand-Masters in the Craft, and was come to make Kafiristan a country where every man should eat in peace and drink in quiet, and specially obey us. Then the Chiefs come round to shake hands, and they was so hairy and white and fair it was just shaking hands with old friends. We gave them names according as they was like men we had known in India—Billy Fish, Holly Wilworth, Pikky Kergan that was Bazar-master when I was at Mhow, and so on and so on.

"The most amazing miracle was at Lodge next night. One of the old priests was watching us continuous, and I felt uneasy, for I knew we'd have to fudge the Ritual, and I didn't know what the men knew. The old priest was a stranger come in from beyond the village of Bashkai. The minute Dravot puts on the Master's apron that the girls had made for him, the priest fetches a whoop and a howl, and tries to overturn the stone that Dravot was sitting on. 'It's all up now,' I says. 'That comes of meddling with the Craft without warrant!' Dravot never winked an eye, not when ten priests took and tilted over the

5. Freemasonry.
6. The Bolan Pass, which was brought under British control in 1879 during the Second Afghan War.
7. Freemason handshake.
8. Railway truck.
9. Gathering.

Grand-Master's chair—which was to say the stone of Imbra. The priest begins rubbing the bottom end of it to clear away the black dirt, and presently he shows all the other priests the Master's Mark, same as was on Dravot's apron, cut into the stone. Not even the priests of the temple of Imbra knew it was there. The old chap falls flat on his face at Dravot's feet and kisses 'em. 'Luck again,' says Dravot, across the Lodge to me, 'they say it's the missing Mark that no one could understand the why of. We're more than safe now.' Then he bangs the butt of his gun for a gavel and says:—'By virtue of the authority vested in me by my own right hand and the help of Peachey, I declare myself Grand-Master of all Freemasonry in Kafiristan in this the Mother Lodge o' the country, and King of Kafiristan equally with Peachey!' At that he puts on his crown and I puts on mine—I was doing Senior Warden—and we opens the Lodge in most ample form. It was a amazing miracle! The priests moved in Lodge through the first two degrees almost without telling, as if the memory was coming back to them. After that, Peachey and Dravot raised such as was worthy—high priests and Chiefs of far-off villages. Billy Fish was the first, and I can tell you we scared the soul out of him. It was not in any way according to Ritual, but it served our turn. We didn't raise more than ten of the biggest men, because we didn't want to make the Degree common. And they was clamoring to be raised.

" 'In another six months,' says Dravot, 'we'll hold another Communication[1] and see how you are working.' Then he asks them about their villages, and learns that they was fighting one against the other and were fair sick and tired of it. And when they wasn't doing that they was fighting with the Mohammedans. 'You can fight those when they come into our country,' says Dravot. 'Tell off[2] every tenth man of your tribes for a Frontier guard, and send two hundred at a time to this valley to be drilled. Nobody is going to be shot or speared any more so long as he does well, and I know that you won't cheat me because you're white people—sons of Alexander—and not like common, black Mohammedans. You are *my* people and by God,' says he, running off into English at the end—'I'll make a damned fine Nation of you, or I'll die in the making!'

"I can't tell all we did for the next six months because Dravot did a lot I couldn't see the hang off, and he learned their lingo in a way I never could. My work was to help the people plough, and now and again go out with some of the Army and see what the other villages were doing, and make 'em throw rope-bridges across the ravines which cut up the country horrid. Dravot was very kind to me, but when he walked up and down in the pine wood pulling that bloody red beard of his with both fists I knew he was thinking plans I could not advise him about, and I just waited for orders.

"But Dravot never showed me disrespect before the people. They were afraid of me and the Army, but they loved Dan. He was the best of friends with the priests and the Chiefs; but any one could come across the hills with a complaint and Dravot would hear him out fair, and call four priests together and say what was to be done. He used to call in Billy Fish from Bashkai, and Pikky Kergan from Shu, and an old Chief we called Kafuzelum—it was like enough to his real name—and hold councils with 'em when there was any fighting to be done in small villages. That was his Council of War, and the four priests of Bashkai, Shu, Khawak, and Madora was his Privy Council. Between the lot

1. In Freemasonry an official Lodge meeting, in which all members have a part.

2. Count off.

of 'em they sent me, with forty men and twenty rifles, and sixty men carrying turquoises, into the Ghorband country to buy those hand-made Martini rifles, that come out of the Amir's workshops at Kabul, from one of the Amir's Herati regiments that would have sold the very teeth out of their mouths for turquoises.

"I stayed in Ghorband a month, and gave the Governor there the pick of my baskets for hush-money, and bribed the Colonel of the regiment some more, and, between the two and the tribes-people, we got more than a hundred hand-made Martinis, a hundred good Kohat Jezails[3] that'll throw to six hundred yards, and forty man-loads of very bad ammunition for the rifles. I came back with what I had, and distributed 'em among the men that the Chiefs sent to me to drill. Dravot was too busy to attend to those things, but the old Army that we first made helped me, and we turned out five hundred men that could drill, and two hundred that knew how to hold arms pretty straight. Even those cork-screwed, hand-made guns was a miracle to them. Dravot talked big about powder-shops and factories, walking up and down in the pine wood when the winter was coming on.

" 'I won't make a Nation,' says he. 'I'll make an Empire! These men aren't niggers; they're English! Look at their eyes—look at their mouths. Look at the way they stand up. They sit, on chairs in their own houses. They're the Lost Tribes,[4] or something like it, and they've grown to be English. I'll take a census in the spring if the priests don't get frightened. There must be a fair two million of 'em in these hills. The villages are full o' little children. Two million people—two hundred and fifty thousand fighting men—and all English! They only want the rifles and a little drilling. Two hundred and fifty thousand men, ready to cut in on Russia's right flank when she tries for India! Peachey, man,' he says, chewing his beard in great hunks, 'we shall be Emperors—Emperors of the Earth! Rajah Brooke will be a suckling to us. I'll treat with the Viceroy[5] on equal terms. I'll ask him to send me twelve picked English—twelve that I know of—to help us govern a bit. There's Mackray, Sergeant-pensioner at Segowli—many's the good dinner he's given me, and his wife a pair of trousers. There's Donkin, the Warder of Tounghoo Jail; there's hundreds that I could lay my hand on if I was in India. The Viceroy shall do it for me. I'll send a man through in the spring for those men, and I'll write for a dispensation from the Grand-Lodge for what I've done as Grand-Master. That—and all the Sniders[6] that'll be thrown out when the native troops in India take up the Martini. They'll be worn smooth, but they'll do for fighting in these hills. Twelve English, a hundred thousand Sniders run through the Amir's country in driblets—I'd be content with twenty thousand in one year—and we'd be an Empire. When everything was shipshape, I'd hand over the crown—this crown I'm wearing now—to Queen Victoria on my knees, and she'd say: "Rise up, Sir Daniel Dravot." Oh, it's big! It's big, I tell you! But there's so much to be done in every place—Bashkai, Khawak, Shu, and everywhere else.'

" 'What is it?' I says. 'There are no more men coming in to be drilled this autumn. Look at those fat, black clouds. They're bringing the snow.'

" 'It isn't that,' says Daniel, putting his hand very hard on my shoulder; 'and I don't wish to say anything that's against you, for no other living man would have followed me and made me what I am as you have done. You're a first-

---

3. Afghan muskets.
4. Of the twelve original Hebrew tribes mentioned in the Bible, ten were lost by assimilating with neighboring peoples.

5. Head of the British administration in India. Rajah Brooke: see n. 3, p. 2271. "Suckling": infant.
6. Older rifles being replaced by Martinis.

class Commander-in-Chief, and the people know you; but—it's a big country, and somehow you can't help me, Peachey, in the way I want to be helped.'

" 'Go to your blasted priests, then!' I said, and I was sorry when I made that remark, but it did hurt me sore to find Daniel talking so superior when I'd drilled all the men, and done all he told me.

" 'Don't let's quarrel, Peachey,' says Daniel, without cursing. 'You're a King, too, and the half of this Kingdom is yours; but can't you see, Peachey, we want cleverer men than us now—three or four of 'em, that we can scatter about for our Deputies. It's a hugeous great State, and I can't always tell the right thing to do, and I haven't time for all I want to do, and here's the winter coming on and all.' He put half his beard into his mouth, and it was as red as the gold of his crown.

" 'I'm sorry, Daniel,' says I. 'I've done all I could. I've drilled the men and shown the people how to stack their oats better; and I've brought in those tinware rifles from Ghorband—but I know what you're driving at. I take it Kings always feel oppressed that way.'

" 'There's another thing too,' says Dravot, walking up and down. 'The winter's coming and these people won't be giving much trouble and if they do we can't move about. I want a wife.'

" 'For Gord's sake leave the women alone!' I says. 'We've both got all the work we can, though I *am* a fool. Remember the Contrack, and keep clear o' women.'

" 'The Contrack only lasted till such time as we was Kings; and Kings we have been these months past,' says Dravot, weighing his crown in his hand. 'You go get a wife too, Peachey—a nice, strappin', plump girl that'll keep you warm in the winter. They're prettier than English girls, and we can take the pick of 'em. Boil 'em once or twice in hot water, and they'll come as fair as chicken and ham.'

" 'Don't tempt me!' I says. 'I will not have any dealings with a woman not till we are a dam' side more settled than we are now. I've been doing the work o' two men, and you've been doing the work o' three. Let's lie off a bit, and see if we can get some better tobacco from Afghan country and run in some good liquor; but no women.'

" 'Who's talking o' *women?*' says Dravot. 'I said *wife*—a Queen to breed a King's son for the King. A Queen out of the strongest tribe, that'll make them your blood-brothers, and that'll lie by your side and tell you all the people thinks about you and their own affairs. That's what I want.'

" 'Do you remember that Bengali woman I kept at Mogul Serai when I was a plate-layer?'[7] says I. 'A fat lot o' good she was to me. She taught me the lingo and one or two other things; but what happened? She ran away with the Station-master's servant and half my month's pay. Then she turned up at Dadur Junction in tow of a half-caste, and had the impidence to say I was her husband—all among the drivers in the running-shed!'

" 'We've done with that,' says Dravot. 'These women are whiter than you or me, and a Queen I will have for the winter months.'

" 'For the last time o' asking, Dan, do *not*,' I says. 'It'll only bring us harm. The Bible says that Kings ain't to waste their strength on women,[8] 'specially when they've got a new raw Kingdom to work over.'

" 'For the last time of answering, I will,' said Dravot, and he went away

---

7. Layer of railway track.
8. "Give not thy strength unto women, nor thy ways to that which destroyeth kings" (Proverbs 31.3).

2284 / Rudyard Kipling

through the pine-trees looking like a big red devil. The low sun hit his crown and beard on one side and the two blazed like hot coals.

"But getting a wife was not as easy as Dan thought. He put it before the Council, and there was no answer till Billy Fish said that he'd better ask the girls. Dravot damned them all round. 'What's wrong with me?' he shouts, standing by the idol Imbra. 'Am I a dog or am I not enough of a man for your wenches? Haven't I put the shadow of my hand over this country? Who stopped the last Afghan raid?' It was me really, but Dravot was too angry to remember. 'Who brought your guns? Who repaired the bridges? Who's the Grand-Master of the sign cut in the stone?' and he thumped his hand on the block that he used to sit on in Lodge, and at Council, which opened like Lodge always. Billy Fish said nothing, and no more did the others. 'Keep your hair on, Dan,' said I; 'and ask the girls. That's how it's done at Home, and these people are quite English.'

" 'The marriage of the King is a matter of State,' says Dan, in a white-hot rage, for he could feel, I hope, that he was going against his better mind. He walked out of the Council-room, and the others sat still, looking at the ground.

" 'Billy Fish,' says I to the Chief of Bashkai, 'what's the difficulty here? A straight answer to a true friend,' 'You know,' says Billy Fish. 'How should a man tell you who know everything? How can daughters of men marry Gods or Devils? It's not proper.'

"I remembered something like that in the Bible;[9] but if, after seeing us as long as they had, they still believed we were Gods, it wasn't for me to undeceive them.

" 'A God can do anything,' says I. 'If the King is fond of a girl he'll not let her die.' 'She'll have to,' said Billy Fish. 'There are all sorts of Gods and Devils in these mountains, and now and again a girl marries one of them and isn't seen any more. Besides, you two know the Mark cut in the stone. Only the Gods know that. We thought you were men till you showed the sign of the Master.'

"I wished then that we had explained about the loss of the genuine secrets of a Master-Mason at the first go-off; but I said nothing. All that night there was a blowing of horns in a little dark temple half-way down the hill, and I heard a girl crying fit to die. One of the priests told us that she was being prepared to marry the King.

" 'I'll have no nonsense of that kind,' says Dan. 'I don't want to interfere with your customs, but I'll take my own wife.' 'The girl's a little bit afraid,' says the priest. 'She thinks she's going to die, and they are a-heartening of her up down in the temple.'

" 'Hearten her very tender, then,' says Dravot, 'or I'll hearten you with the butt of a gun so that you'll never want to be heartened again.' He licked his lips, did Dan, and stayed up walking about more than half the night, thinking of the wife that he was going to get in the morning. I wasn't any means comfortable, for I knew that dealings with a woman in foreign parts, though you was a crowned King twenty times over, could not but be risky. I got up very early in the morning while Dravot was asleep, and I saw the priests talking together in whispers, and the Chiefs talking together too, and they looked at me out of the corners of their eyes.

9. "That the sons of God saw the daughters of men that they were fair; and they took them wives of all which they chose" (Genesis 6.2).

" 'What is up, Fish?' I says to the Bashkai man, who was wrapped up in his furs and looking splendid to behold.

" 'I can't rightly say,' says he; 'but if you can induce the King to drop all this nonsense about marriage, you'll be doing him and me and yourself a great service.'

" 'That I do believe,' says I. 'But sure, you know, Billy, as well as me, having fought against and for us, that the King and me are nothing more than two of the finest men that God Almighty ever made. Nothing more, I do assure you.'

" 'That may be,' says Billy Fish, 'and yet I should be sorry if it was.' He sinks his head upon his great fur cloak for a minute and thinks. 'King,' says he, 'be you man or God or Devil, I'll stick by you to-day. I have twenty of my men with me, and they will follow me. We'll go to Bashkai until the storm blows over.'

"A little snow had fallen in the night, and everything was white except the greasy fat clouds that blew down and down from the north. Dravot came out with his crown on his head, swinging his arms and stamping his feet, and looking more pleased than Punch.[1]

" 'For the last time, drop it, Dan,' says I, in a whisper. 'Billy Fish here says that there will be a row.'

" 'A row among my people!' says Dravot. 'Not much. Peachey, you're a fool not to get a wife too. Where's the girl?' says he, with a voice as loud as the braying of a jackass. 'Call up all the Chiefs and priests, and let the Emperor see if his wife suits him.'

"There was no need to call any one. They were all there leaning on their guns and spears round the clearing in the centre of the pine wood. A deputation of priests went down to the little temple to bring up the girl, and the horns blew up fit to wake the dead. Billy Fish saunters round and gets as close to Daniel as he could, and behind him stood his twenty men with matchlocks. Not a man of them under six feet. I was next to Dravot, and behind me was twenty men of the regular Army. Up comes the girl, and a strapping wench she was, covered with silver and turquoises, but white as death, and looking back every minute at the priests.

" 'She'll do,' said Dan, looking her over. 'What's to be afraid of, lass? Come and kiss me.' He puts his arm round her. She shuts her eyes, gives a bit of a squeak, and down goes her face in the side of Dan's flaming red beard.

" 'The slut's bitten me!' says he, clapping his hand to his neck, and, sure enough, his hand was red with blood. Billy Fish and two of his matchlockmen catches hold of Dan by the shoulders and drags him into the Bashkai lot, while the priests howl in their lingo,—'Neither God nor Devil, but a man!' I was all taken aback, for a priest cut at me in front, and the Army behind began firing into the Bashkai men.

" 'God A-mighty!' says Dan. 'What is the meaning o' this?'

" 'Come back! Come away!' says Billy Fish. 'Ruin and Mutiny is the matter. We'll break for Bashkai if we can.'

"I tried to give some sort of orders to my men—the men o' the regular Army—but it was no use, so I fired into the brown of 'em with an English Martini and drilled three beggars in a line. The valley was full of shouting, howling creatures, and every soul was shrieking, 'Not a God nor a Devil, but

---

1. Common expression: the character in the Punch-and-Judy puppet show has a fixed grin and is delighted with his evil deeds.

only a man!' The Bashkai troops stuck to Billy Fish all they were worth, but their matchlocks wasn't half as good as the Kabul breech-loaders, and four of them dropped. Dan was bellowing like a bull, for he was very wrathy; and Billy Fish had a hard job to prevent him running out at the crowd.

" 'We can't stand,' says Billy Fish. 'Make a run for it down the valley! The whole place is against us.' The matchlock-men ran, and we went down the valley in spite of Dravot's protestations. He was swearing horribly and crying out that he was a King. The priests rolled great stones on us, and the regular Army fired hard, and there wasn't more than six men, not counting Dan, Billy Fish, and Me, that came down to the bottom of the valley alive.

"Then they stopped firing and the horns in the temple blew again. 'Come away—for Gord's sake come away!' says Billy Fish. 'They'll send runners out to all the villages before ever we get to Bashkai. I can protect you there, but I can't do anything now.'

"My own notion is that Dan began to go mad in his head from that hour. He stared up and down like a stuck pig. Then he was all for walking back alone and killing the priests with his bare hands; which he could have done. 'An Emperor am I,' says Daniel, 'and next year I shall be a Knight of the Queen.'

" 'All right, Dan,' says I; 'but come along now while there's time.'

" 'It's your fault,' says he, 'for not looking after your Army better. There was mutiny in the midst and you didn't know—you damned engine-driving, plate-laying, missionary's-pass-hunting hound!' He sat upon a rock and called me every foul name he could lay tongue to. I was too heart-sick to care, though it was all his foolishness that brought the smash.

" 'I'm sorry, Dan,' says I, 'but there's no accounting for natives. This business is our Fifty-Seven.[2] Maybe we'll make something out of it yet, when we've got to Bashkai.'

" 'Let's get to Bashkai, then,' says Dan, 'and, by God, when I come back here again I'll sweep the valley so there isn't a bug in a blanket left!'

"We walked all that day, and all that night Dan was stumping up and down on the snow, chewing his beard and muttering to himself.

" 'There's no hope o' getting clear,' said Billy Fish. 'The priests will have sent runners to the villages to say that you are only men. Why didn't you stick on as Gods till things was more settled? I'm a dead man,' says Billy Fish, and he throws himself down on the snow and begins to pray to his Gods.

"Next morning we was in a cruel bad country—all up and down, no level ground at all, and no food either. The six Bashkai men looked at Billy Fish hungry-wise as if they wanted to ask something, but they said never a word. At noon we came to the top of a flat mountain all covered with snow, and when we climbed up into it, behold, there was an Army in position waiting in the middle!

" 'The runners have been very quick,' says Billy Fish, with a little bit of a laugh. 'They are waiting for us.'

"Three or four men began to fire from the enemy's side, and a chance shot took Daniel in the calf of the leg. That brought him to his senses. He looks across the snow at the Army, and sees the rifles that we had brought into the country.

" 'We're done for,' says he. 'They are Englishmen, these people,—and it's

2. Mutiny of 1857, when regiments of the Bengal army rebelled against their British officers.

my blasted nonsense that has brought you to this. Get back, Billy Fish, and take your men away; you've done what you could, and now cut for it. Carnehan,' says he, 'shake hands with me and go along with Billy. Maybe they won't kill you. I'll go and meet 'em alone. It's me that did it. Me, the King!'

" 'Go!' says I. 'Go to Hell, Dan. I'm with you here. Billy Fish, you clear out, and we two will meet those folk.'

" 'I'm a Chief,' says Billy Fish, quite quiet. 'I stay with you. My men can go.'

"The Bashkai fellows didn't wait for a second word, but ran off, and Dan and me and Billy Fish walked across to where the drums were drumming and the horns were horning. It was cold—awful cold. I've got that cold in the back of my head now. There's a lump of it there."

The punkah-coolies[3] had gone to sleep. Two kerosene lamps were blazing in the office, and the perspiration poured down my face and splashed on the blotter as I leaned forward. Carnehan was shivering, and I feared that his mind might go. I wiped my face, took a fresh grip of the piteously mangled hands, and said: "What happened after that?"

The momentary shift of my eyes had broken the clear current.

"What was you pleased to say?" whined Carnehan. "They took them without any sound. Not a little whisper all along the snow, not though the King knocked down the first man that set hand on him—not though old Peachey fired his last cartridge into the brown of 'em. Not a single solitary sound did those swines make. They just closed up tight, and I tell you their furs stunk. There was a man called Billy Fish, a good friend of us all, and they cut his throat, Sir, then and there, like a pig; and the King kicks up the bloody snow and says:—'We've had a dashed fine run for our money. What's coming next?' But Peachey, Peachey Taliaferro, I tell you, Sir, in confidence as betwixt two friends, he lost his head, Sir. No, he didn't neither. The King lost his head, so he did, all along o' one of those cunning rope-bridges. Kindly let me have the paper-cutter, Sir. It tilted this way. They marched him a mile across that snow to a rope-bridge over a ravine with a river at the bottom. You may have seen such. They prodded him behind like an ox. 'Damn your eyes!' says the King. 'D'you suppose I can't die like a gentleman?' He turns to Peachey—Peachey that was crying like a child. 'I've brought you to this, Peachey,' says he. 'Brought you out of your happy life to be killed in Kafiristan, where you was late Commander-in-Chief of the Emperor's forces. Say you forgive me, Peachey.' 'I do,' says Peachey. 'Fully and freely do I forgive you, Dan.' 'Shake hands, Peachey,' says he. 'I'm going now. Out he goes, looking neither right nor left, and when he was plumb in the middle of those dizzy dancing ropes, 'Cut, you beggars,' he shouts; and they cut, and old Dan fell, turning round and round and round twenty thousand miles, for he took half an hour to fall till he struck the water, and I could see his body caught on a rock with the gold crown close beside.

"But do you know what they did to Peachey between two pine trees? They crucified him, Sir, as Peachey's hand will show. They used wooden pegs for his hands and his feet; and he didn't die. He hung there and screamed, and they took him down next day, and said it was a miracle that he wasn't dead. They took him down—poor old Peachey that hadn't done them any harm— that hadn't done them any . . ."

He rocked to and fro and wept bitterly, wiping his eyes with the back of his

---

3. Servants who operate punkahs, or fans.

scarred hands and moaning like a child for some ten minutes.

"They was cruel enough to feed him up in the temple, because they said he was more of a God than old Daniel that was a man. Then they turned him out on the snow, and told him to go home, and Peachey came home in about a year, begging along the roads quite safe; for Daniel Dravot he walked before and said:—'Come along, Peachey. It's a big thing we're doing.' The mountains they danced at night, and the mountains they tried to fall on Peachey's head, but Dan he held up his hand, and Peachey came along bent double. He never let go of Dan's hand, and he never let go of Dan's head. They gave it to him as a present in the temple, to remind him not to come again, and though the crown was pure gold, and Peachey was starving, never would Peachey sell the same. You knew Dravot, Sir! You knew Right Worshipful Brother Dravot! Look at him now!"

He fumbled in the mass of rags round his bent waist; brought out a black horsehair bag embroidered with silver thread; and shook therefrom on to my table—the dried, withered head of Daniel Dravot! The morning sun that had long been paling the lamps struck the red beard and blind, sunken eyes; struck, too, a heavy circlet of gold studded with raw turquoises, that Carnehan placed tenderly on the battered temples.

"You behold now," said Carnehan, "the Emperor in his habit as he lived[4]— the King of Kafiristan with his crown upon his head. Poor old Daniel that was a monarch once!"

I shuddered, for, in spite of defacements manifold, I recognized the head of the man of Marwar Junction. Carnehan rose to go. I attempted to stop him. He was not fit to walk abroad. "Let me take away the whiskey, and give me a little money," he gasped. "I was a King once. I'll go to the Deputy Commissioner and ask to set in the Poorhouse till I get my health. No, thank you, I can't wait till you get a carriage for me. I've urgent private affairs—in the south—at Marwar."

He shambled out of the office and departed in the direction of the Deputy Commissioner's house. That day at noon I had occasion to go down the blinding hot Mall, and I saw a crooked man crawling along the white dust of the roadside, his hat in his hand, quavering dolorously after the fashion of street-singers at Home. There was not a soul in sight, and he was out of all possible earshot of the houses. And he sang through his nose, turning his head from right to left:

> "The Son of Man goes forth to war,
>   A golden crown to gain;
> His blood-red banner streams afar—
>   Who follows in his train?"[5]

I waited to hear no more, but put the poor wretch into my carriage and drove him off to the nearest missionary for eventual transfer to the Asylum. He repeated the hymn twice while he was with me, whom he did not in the least recognize, and I left him singing it to the missionary.

Two days later I inquired after his welfare of the Superintendent of the Asylum.

---

4. Allusion to Hamlet's description of his father's ghost: "My father, in his habit as he lived" (Shakespeare, *Hamlet* 3.4.126).
5. A well-known hymn, by Reginald Heber (1783–

1826), corrected in later editions to the actual words of the first line: "The Son of God goes forth to war."

"He was admitted suffering from sunstroke. He died early yesterday morning," said the Superintendent. "Is it true that he was half an hour bareheaded in the sun at midday?"

"Yes," said I, "but do you happen to know if he had anything upon him by any chance when he died?"

"Not to my knowledge," said the Superintendent.

And there the matter rests.

1888

The White Man's Burden[1]

Take up the White Man's burden—
    Send forth the best ye breed—
Go bind your sons to exile
    To serve your captives' need;
5   To wait in heavy harness,
    On fluttered folk and wild—
Your new-caught, sullen peoples,
    Half-devil and half-child.

Take up the White Man's burden—
10   In patience to abide,
To veil the threat of terror
    And check the show of pride;
By open speech and simple,
    An hundred times made plain,
15 To seek another's profit,
    And work another's gain.

Take up the White Man's burden—
    The savage wars of peace—
Fill full the mouth of Famine
20   And bid the sickness cease;
And when your goal is nearest
    The end for others sought,
Watch Sloth and heathen Folly
    Bring all your hope to nought.

25 Take up the White Man's burden—
    No tawdry rule of kings,
But toil of serf and sweeper[2]—
    The tale of common things.
The ports ye shall not enter,
30   The roads ye shall not tread,

1. This poem was conceived for Queen Victoria's Jubilee in 1897, but Kipling abandoned it in favor of "Recessional." He returned to the poem when disagreements between Spain and the United States over Spanish colonial rule in Cuba and elsewhere sparked the Spanish-American War in 1898. In its revised form the poem reacts to resistance in the Philippines to the United States' assumption of colonial power.
2. Street sweeper, who in India would belong to the lowest caste.

Go make them with your living,
    And mark them with your dead.

Take up the White Man's burden—
    And reap his old reward:
35 The blame of those ye better,
        The hate of those ye guard—
    The cry of hosts ye humour
        (Ah, slowly!) toward the light:—
    'Why brought ye us from bondage,
40   Our loved Egyptian night?'³

Take up the White Man's burden—
    Ye dare not stoop to less—
    Nor call too loud on Freedom
        To cloak your weariness;
45 By all ye cry or whisper,
        By all ye leave or do,
    The silent, sullen peoples
        Shall weigh your Gods and you.

Take up the White Man's burden—
50   Have done with childish days—
    The lightly proffered laurel,⁴
        The easy, ungrudged praise.
    Comes now, to search your manhood
        Through all the thankless years,
55 Cold, edged with dear-bought wisdom,
        The judgment of your peers!

1899

If—

If you can keep your head when all about you
    Are losing theirs and blaming it on you;
If you can trust yourself when all men doubt you,
    But make allowance for their doubting too;
5 If you can wait and not be tired by waiting,
    Or being lied about, don't deal in lies,
Or being hated don't give way to hating,
    And yet don't look too good, nor talk too wise:

If you can dream—and not make dreams your master;
10   If you can think—and not make thoughts your aim,
If you can meet with Triumph and Disaster

---

3. Cf. Exodus 16.2–3. When the Israelites were suffering from hunger in the wilderness, they criticized Moses and Aaron for taking them from what they saw as the relative comfort of Egyptian slavery.

4. A symbol of military distinction in the triumphs celebrated by victorious Roman generals (later, Roman emperors wore a laurel crown as part of their official regalia).

And treat those two impostors just the same;
If you can bear to hear the truth you've spoken
Twisted by knaves to make a trap for fools,
15   Or watch the things you gave your life to, broken,
And stoop and build 'em up with worn-out tools:

If you can make one heap of all your winnings
And risk it on one turn of pitch-and-toss,[1]
And lose, and start again at your beginnings
20   And never breathe a word about your loss;
If you can force your heart and nerve and sinew
To serve your turn long after they are gone,
And so hold on when there is nothing in you
Except the Will which says to them: 'Hold on!'

25   If you can talk with crowds and keep your virtue,
Or walk with Kings—nor° lose the common touch,   *and not*
If neither foes nor loving friends can hurt you,
If all men count with you, but none too much;
If you can fill the unforgiving minute
30   With sixty seconds' worth of distance run,
Yours is the Earth and everything that's in it,
And—which is more—you'll be a Man, my son!

1910

---

1. A game, played with coins, that combines skill (tossing a coin as close as possible to a fixed mark) and luck (flipping coins and keeping those that come up heads).

The Twentieth Century
and After

HISTORICAL BACKGROUND

The roots of modern literature are in the late nineteenth century. The aesthetic movement, with its insistence on "art for art's sake," assaulted middle-class assumptions about the nature and function of art. Rejecting Victorian notions of the artist's moral and educational duties, aestheticism helped widen the breach between writers and the general public, resulting in the "alienation" of the modern artist from society. This alienation is evident in the lives and work of the French symbolists and other late-nineteenth-century bohemians who repudiated conventional notions of respectability, and it underlies key works of modern literature, such as James Joyce's *Portrait of the Artist as a Young Man* and T. S. Eliot's *Waste Land*.

The growth of public education in England as a result of the Education Act of 1870, which finally made elementary schooling compulsory and universal, led to the rapid emergence of a mass literate population, at whom a new mass-produced popular literature and new cheap journalism (the "yellow press") were directed. The audience for literature split up into "highbrows," "middle-brows," and "lowbrows," and the segmentation of the reading public, developing with unprecedented speed and to an unprecedented degree, helped widen the gap between popular art and art esteemed only by the sophisticated and the expert. This breach yawned ever wider with the twentieth-century emergence of modernist iconoclasm and avant-garde experiment in literature, music, and the visual arts.

Queen Victoria's contemporaries felt her Jubilee in 1887 and, even more, her Diamond Jubilee in 1897 marked the end of an era. The reaction against middle-class Victorian attitudes that is central to modernism was already under way in the two decades before the queen's death in 1901. Samuel Butler savagely attacked the Victorian conceptions of the family, education, and religion in his novel *The Way of All Flesh* (completed in 1884, posthumously published in 1903), the bitterest indictment in English literature of the Victorian way of life. And the high tide of anti-Victorianism was marked by the publication in 1918 of a classic of ironic debunking, Lytton Strachey's collection of biographical essays *Eminent Victorians*.

A pivotal figure between Victorianism and modernism, Thomas Hardy marked the end of the Victorian period and the dawn of the new age in "The Darkling Thrush," a poem originally titled "By the Century's Deathbed" and postdated December 31, 1900, the last day of the nineteenth century. The poem marks the demise of a century of relative conviction and optimism, and it intimates the beginnings of a new era in its skeptical irresolution, its bleak sense of the modern world as "hard and dry"—favorite adjectives of later writers such as Ezra Pound and T. E. Hulme:

> The land's sharp features seemed to be
> The Century's corpse outleant,
> His crypt the cloudy canopy,
> The wind his death-lament.
> The ancient pulse of germ and birth
> Was shrunken hard and dry,
> And every spirit upon earth
> Seemed fervourless as I.

This poem and other works by Hardy, A. E. Housman, and Joseph Conrad exemplify the pessimism of imaginative writing in the last decade of the nineteenth century and the first decade of the twentieth. Stoicism—a stiff-upper-lip determination to endure whatever fate may bring—also characterizes the literature written in the transitional period between the Victorian era and modernism, including the work of minor authors such as Robert Louis Stevenson and Rudyard Kipling.

By the dawn of the twentieth century, traditional stabilities of society, religion, and culture seemed to have weakened, the pace of change to be accelerating. The unsettling force of modernity profoundly challenged traditional ways of structuring and making sense of human experience. Because of the rapid pace of social and technological change, because of the mass dislocation of populations by war, empire, and economic migration, because of the mixing in close quarters of cultures and classes in rapidly expanding cities, modernity disrupted the old order, upended ethical and social codes, cast into doubt previously stable assumptions about self, community, the world, and the divine.

Early-twentieth-century writers were keenly aware that powerful concepts and vocabularies were emerging in anthropology, psychology, philosophy, and the visual arts that reimagined human identity in radically new ways. Sigmund Freud's seminal *Interpretation of Dreams* was published in 1900, and soon psychoanalysis was changing how people saw and described rationality, the self, and personal development. In his prose and poetry D. H. Lawrence adapted the Oedipus complex to interpret and present his relationships with his parents, though rejecting Freud's negative definition of the unconscious. By the time of his death in 1939, Freud had become, as W. H. Auden wrote in an elegy for him, "a whole climate of opinion // under whom we conduct our different lives." Also in the early twentieth century, Sir James Frazer's

Golden Bough (1890–1915) and other works of anthropology were altering basic conceptions of culture, religion, and myth. Eliot observed that Frazer's work "influenced our generation profoundly," and the critic Lionel Trilling suggested that "perhaps no book has had so decisive an effect upon modern literature as Frazer's." For both anthropologists and modern writers, Western religion was now decentered by being placed in a comparative context as one of numerous related mythologies, with Jesus Christ linked to "primitive" fertility gods thought to die and revive in concert with the seasons. Furthering this challenge to religious doctrine were the writings of Friedrich Nietzsche, the nineteenth-century German philosopher who declared the death of God, repudiated Christianity, and offered instead a harshly tragic conception of life: people look "deeply into the true nature of things" and realize "that no action of theirs can work any change," but they nevertheless laugh and stoically affirm their fate. W. B. Yeats, who remarks in a 1902 letter that his eyes are exhausted from reading "that strong enchanter," greets death and destruction in a Nietzschean spirit of tragic exultation.

These profound changes in modern intellectual history coincided with changes of a more mundane sort, for everyday life was also undergoing rapid transformation during the first years of the twentieth century. Electricity was spreading, cinema and radio were proliferating, and new pharmaceuticals such as aspirin were being developed. As labor was increasingly managed and rationalized, as more and more people crowded into cities, as communications and transportation globalized space and accelerated time, literature could not stand still, and modern writers sought to create new forms that could register these profound alterations in human experience. This was a period of scientific revolution, as exemplified in German physics by Max Planck's quantum theory (1900) and Albert Einstein's theory of relativity (1905), and T. S. Eliot reflects the increasing dominance of science when he argues that the poet surrenders to tradition and thus extinguishes rather than expresses personality: "It is in this depersonalization that art may be said to approach the condition of science," he claims, adding that "the mind of the poet is the shred of platinum" that catalyzes change but itself remains "inert, neutral, and unchanged" ("Tradition and the Individual Talent").

The early twentieth century also brought countless advances in technology: the first wireless communication across the Atlantic occurred in 1901, the Wright Brothers flew the first airplane in 1903, and Henry Ford introduced the first mass-produced car, the Model T or "Tin Lizzie," in 1913. Not that modern writers univocally embraced such changes. Although some were more sanguine, many modern writers were paradoxically repulsed by aspects of modernization. Mass-produced appliances and products, such as the "gramophone" and canned goods ("tins"), are objects of revulsion in Eliot's *Waste Land*, for example. Because scientific materialism and positivism, according to which empirical explanations could be found for everything, were weakening the influence of organized religion, many writers looked to literature as an alternative. His "simple-minded" Protestantism spoiled by science, Yeats says in his autobiography, he "made a new religion, almost an infallible church of poetic tradition." Whether or not they welcomed the demise of tradition, habit, and certitude in favor of the new, modern writers articulated the effects of modernity's relentless change, loss, and destabilization. "Things fall apart," Yeats wrote, "the centre cannot hold." Eliot describes in *Four Quartets* his quest for the "still point of the turning world." The modernist drive to "make it new"—in

Ezra Pound's famous slogan—thus arises in part out of an often ambivalent consciousness of the relentless mutations brought by modernization.

The position of women, too, was rapidly changing during this period. The Married Woman's Property Act of 1882 allowed married women to own property in their own right, and women were admitted to universities at different times during the latter part of the century. Since the days of Mary Wollstonecraft, women in Great Britain had been arguing and lobbying for the right to vote, but in the first decades of the twentieth century, Emmeline Pankhurst and her daughter Christabel encouraged suffragettes, as they were known, to take a more militant approach, which included boycotts, bombings, and hunger strikes. The long fight for women's suffrage was finally won in 1918 for women thirty and over, and in 1928 for women twenty-one and over. These shifts in attitudes toward women, in the roles women played in the national life, and in the relations between the sexes are reflected in a variety of ways in the literature of the period.

Britain's modern political history begins with the Anglo-Boer War (1899–1902), fought by the British to establish political and economic control over the Boer republics (self-governing states) of South Africa. It was an imperial war against which many British intellectuals protested and one that the British in the end were slightly ashamed of having won. The war spanned the reign of Queen Victoria, who died in 1901, and Edward VII, who held the throne from 1901 to 1910. This latter decade is known as the Edwardian period, and the king stamped his extrovert and self-indulgent character upon it. The wealthy made it a vulgar age of conspicuous enjoyment, but most writers and artists kept well away from involvement in high society: in general this period had no equivalent to Queen Victoria's friendship with Tennyson. The alienation of artists and intellectuals from political rulers and middle-class society was proceeding apace. From 1910 (when George V came to the throne) until World War I broke out in August 1914, Britain achieved a temporary equilibrium between Victorian earnestness and Edwardian flashiness; in retrospect the Georgian period seems peculiarly golden, the last phase of assurance and stability before the old order throughout Europe broke up in violence. Yet even then, under the surface, there was restlessness and experimentation. The age of Rupert Brooke's idyllic sonnets on the English countryside was also the age of T. S. Eliot's first experiments in a radically new kind of poetry, James Joyce's and Virginia Woolf's in radically new forms of fiction.

Edwardian as a term applied to English cultural history suggests a period in which the social and economic stabilities of the Victorian age—country houses with numerous servants, a flourishing and confident middle class, a strict hierarchy of social classes—remained unimpaired, though on the level of ideas a sense of change and liberation existed. *Georgian* refers largely to the lull before the storm of World War I. That war, as the bitterly skeptical and antiheroic work of Wilfred Owen, Siegfried Sassoon, Isaac Rosenberg, and other war poets makes clear, produced major shifts in attitude toward Western myths of progress and civilization. The postwar disillusion of the 1920s resulted, in part, from the sense of utter social and political collapse during a war in which unprecedented millions were killed.

By the beginning of World War I, nearly a quarter of the earth's surface and more than a quarter of the world's population were under British dominion, including the vast African territories acquired in the preceding hundred years. Some of the colonies in the empire were settler nations with large European populations, such as Canada, Australia, and New Zealand, and in 1907 the empire granted them the new status of dominions, recognizing their relative control over internal affairs. Over time these largely independent nations came to be known as the British Commonwealth, an association of self-governing countries. The twentieth century witnessed the emergence of internationally acclaimed literary voices from these dominions, from the early-century New Zealander Katherine Mansfield to the late-century Australian Les Murray and Canadians Alice Munro and Anne Carson. The rest of the colonies in the British Empire consisted primarily of indigenous populations that had little or no political power, but nationalist movements were gaining strength in the early years of the century—as when, in 1906, the Congress movement in India first demanded *swaraj* ("self-rule") soon to become the mantra of Indian nationalism. In Britain imperialist and anti-imperialist sentiments often met head on in Parliament and the press, the debate involving writers as far apart as Rudyard Kipling and E. M. Forster.

A steadily rising Irish nationalism resulted in increasingly violent protests against the cultural, economic, and political subordination of Ireland to the British Crown and government. During the Easter Rising of 1916, Irish rebels in Dublin staged a revolt against British rule, and by executing fifteen Irish leaders, the British inadvertently intensified the drive for independence, finally achieved in 1921–22 when the southern counties were declared the Irish Free State. (The six counties of Northern Ireland remained, however, part of Great Britain.) No one can fully understand Yeats or Joyce without some awareness of the Irish struggle for independence, and the way in which the Irish literary revival of the late nineteenth and early twentieth centuries (with Yeats at the forefront) reflected a determination to achieve a vigorous national life cultur-ally even if the road seemed blocked politically.

Depression and unemployment in the early 1930s, followed by the rise of Hitler and the shadow of Fascism and Nazism over Europe, with its threat of another war, deeply affected the emerging poets and novelists of the time. While Eliot, Lawrence, Wyndham Lewis, Yeats, Pound, and others of the older generation turned to the political right, the impotence of capitalist govern-ments in the face of Fascism combined with economic dislocation to turn the majority of young intellectuals (and not only intellectuals) in the 1930s to the political left. The 1930s were the so-called red decade, because only the left seemed to offer any solution in various forms of socialism, communism, and left liberalism. The early poetry of W. H. Auden and his contemporaries cried out for "the death of the old gang" (in Auden's phrase) and a clean sweep politically and economically, while the right-wing army's rebellion against the left-wing republican government in Spain, which started in the summer of 1936 and soon led to full-scale civil war, was regarded as a rehearsal for an inevitable second world war and thus further emphasized the inadequacy of politicians. Yet though the younger writers of the period expressed the up-to-date, radical political views of the left, they were less technically inventive than the first-generation modernists, such as Eliot, Joyce, and Woolf. The outbreak of World War II in September 1939—following shortly on Hitler's pact with the Soviet Union, which so shocked and disillusioned many of the young left-wing writers that they subsequently moved politically to the cen-ter—marked the sudden end of the red decade. What was from the beginning expected to be a long and costly war brought inevitable exhaustion. The dim-inution of British political power, its secondary status in relation to the United

States as a player in the Cold War, brought about a painful reappraisal of Britain's place in the world, even as countries that had lost the war—West Germany and Japan—were, in economic terms, winning the peace that followed.

In winning a war, Great Britain lost an empire. The largest, most powerful, best organized of the modern European empires, it had expropriated enormous quantities of land, raw materials, and labor from its widely scattered overseas territories. India, long the jewel in the imperial Crown, won its independence in 1947, along with the newly formed Muslim state of Pakistan. The postwar wave of decolonization that began in South Asia spread to Africa and the Caribbean: in 1957 Ghana was the first nation in sub-Saharan Africa to become independent, unleashing an unstoppable wave of liberation from British rule that freed Nigeria in 1960, Sierra Leone in 1961, Uganda in 1962, Kenya in 1963; in the Caribbean, Jamaica and Trinidad and Tobago in 1962, Barbados and Guyana in 1966, and Saint Lucia in 1979. India and Pakistan elected to remain within a newly expanded and reconceived British Commonwealth, but other former colonies did not. The Irish Republic withdrew from the Commonwealth in 1949; the Republic of South Africa, in 1961. Postwar decolonization coincided with and encouraged the efflorescence of postcolonial writing that would bring about the most dramatic geographic shift in literature in English since its inception. Writers from Britain's former colonies published influential and innovative novels, plays, and poems, hybridizing their local traditions and varieties of English with those of the empire. The names of the Nobel Prize winners Wole Soyinka, Nadine Gordimer, Derek Walcott, V. S. Naipaul, and J. M. Coetzee were added to the annals of literature in English.

While Britain was decolonizing its empire, the former empire was colonizing Britain, as Louise Bennett wryly suggests in her poem "Colonization in Reverse." Encouraged by the postwar labor shortage in England and the scarcity of work at home, waves of Caribbean migrants journeyed to and settled in "the motherland," the first group on the *Empire Windrush* that sailed from Jamaica to Tilbury Docks in 1948. Migrants followed from India, Pakistan, Bangladesh, Africa, and other regions of the "New Commonwealth." Even as immigration laws became more restrictive in the 1960s, relatives of earlier migrants and refugees from these and other nations continued to arrive, transforming Britain into an increasingly multiracial society and infusing energy into British arts and literature. But people of Caribbean, African, and South Asian origin, who brought distinctive vernaculars and cultural traditions with them, painfully discovered that their official status as British subjects often did not translate into their being welcomed as full-fledged members of British society. The friction between color-blind and ethnically specific notions of Englishness prompted a large-scale and ongoing rethinking of national identity in Britain. Among the arrivals in England were many who journeyed there to study in the late 1940s and 1950s and eventually became prominent writers, such as Bennett, Soyinka, Kamau (then Edward) Brathwaite, and Chinua Achebe. In the 1970s and 1980s a younger generation of black and Asian British writers emerged—some born in the U.K., some in the ex-empire— including Salman Rushdie, Hanif Kureishi, John Agard, and Caryl Phillips, and in the 1990s and the first decade of the new millennium, still younger writers including Jackie Kay and Zadie Smith.

London, as the capital of the empire, had long dominated the culture as well as the politics and the economy of the British Isles. London spoke for Britain in the impeccable southern English intonations of the radio announcers of the state-owned British Broadcasting Corporation (known as the BBC), but from the end of World War II this changed. Regional dialects and multicultural accents were admitted to the airwaves. Regional radio and television stations sprang up. In the 1940s and 1950s the BBC produced a weekly program called "Caribbean Voices," which proved an important stimulus to anglophone writing in the West Indies. The Arts Council, which had subsidized the nation's drama, literature, music, painting, and plastic arts from London, delegated much of its grant-giving responsibility to regional arts councils. This gave a new confidence to writers and artists outside London—the Beatles were launched from Liverpool—and has since contributed to a notable renaissance of regional literature.

From the 1960s London ceased to be essentially the sole cultural stage of the United Kingdom, and though its Parliament remained the sole political stage until 1999, successive governments came under increasing pressure from the regions and the wider world. After decades of predominantly Labour governments, Margaret Thatcher led the Conservatives to power in the general election of 1979, becoming thereby the country's first woman to hold the office of prime minister, an office she was to hold for an unprecedented twelve years. Pursuing a vision of a "new," more productive Britain, she curbed the power of the unions and began to dismantle the "welfare state," privatizing nationalized industries and utilities in the interests of an aggressive free-market economy. Initially her policies seemed to have a bracing effect on a nation still sunk in postwar, postimperial torpor, but writers such as Ian McEwan and Caryl Churchill and filmmakers such as Derek Jarman protested that Conservative reforms widened the gap between rich and poor, black and white, north and south, and between the constituent parts of the United Kingdom.

Thatcher was deposed by her own party in 1990, and the Conservatives were routed in the election of 1997. The electorate's message was clear, and Tony Blair, the new Labour prime minister, moved to restore the rundown Health Service and system of state education. Honoring other of his campaign pledges, he offered Scotland its own parliament and Wales its own assembly, each with tax-raising powers and a substantial budget for the operation of its social services, and each holding its first elections in 1999. Though a commanding figure in British politics, Blair faced increasing skepticism over his justification for joining forces with the U.S.-led invasion and occupation of Iraq in 2003.

Meanwhile the Labour government made significant progress toward solving the bitter and bloody problems of Northern Ireland, where, since the late 1960s, the Irish Republican Army (IRA) had waged a violent campaign for a united Ireland and against British rule, met by violent suppression by the British Army and reprisals by Protestant Unionists, who sought to keep Northern Ireland a part of the United Kingdom. In the 1990s politics finally took precedence over armed struggle in the Republican movement. In 1998 the Good Friday Agreement, also known as the Belfast Agreement, led to elections to a Northern Ireland Assembly, which met for the first time in 1999, and the leaders of the main Roman Catholic and Protestant parties were jointly awarded the Nobel Peace Prize. Although hope persisted that peaceful coexistence and substantial self-governance in Ulster could continue, disagreements between the parties over IRA weapons and alleged spying led to the suspension of the Northern Ireland Assembly and Executive Committee in 2002.

POETRY

The years leading up to World War I saw the start of a poetic revolution. The imagist movement, influenced by the philosopher poet T. E. Hulme's insistence on hard, clear, precise images, arose in reaction to what it saw as Romantic fuzziness and facile emotionalism in poetry. (Like other modernists, the imagists somewhat oversimplified the nineteenth-century aesthetic against which they defined their own artistic ideal, while scanting underlying continuities.) The movement developed initially in London, where the modernist American poet Ezra Pound was living, and quickly migrated across the Atlantic, and its early members included Hulme, Pound, H. D. (Hilda Doolittle), Amy Lowell, Richard Aldington, John Gould Fletcher, and F. S. Flint. As Flint explained in an article in March 1913, partly dictated by Pound, imagists insisted on "direct treatment of the 'thing,' whether subjective or objective," on the avoidance of all words "that did not contribute to the presentation," and on a freer metrical movement than a strict adherence to the "sequence of a metronome" could allow. Inveighing in manifestos against Victorian discursiveness, the imagists wrote short, sharply etched, descriptive lyrics, but they lacked a technique for the production of longer and more complex poems.

Other new ideas about poetry helped provide this technique, many of them associated with another American in London, T. S. Eliot. Sir Herbert Grierson's 1912 edition of John Donne's poems both reflected and encouraged a new enthusiasm for seventeenth-century Metaphysical poetry. The revived interest in Metaphysical "wit" brought with it a desire on the part of pioneering poets to introduce into their work a much higher degree of intellectual complexity than had been found among the Victorians or the Georgians. The full subtlety of French symbolist poetry also now came to be appreciated; it had been admired in the 1890s, but more for its dreamy suggestiveness than for its imagistic precision and complexity. At the same time modernist writers wanted to bring poetic language and rhythms closer to those of conversation, or at least to spice the formalities of poetic utterance with echoes of the colloquial and even the slangy. Irony, which made possible several levels of discourse simultaneously, and wit, with the use of puns (banished from serious poetry for more than two hundred years), helped achieve that union of thought and passion that Eliot, in his review of Grierson's anthology of Metaphysical poetry (1921), saw as characteristic of the Metaphysicals and wished to bring back into poetry. A new critical movement and a new creative movement in poetry went hand in hand, with Eliot the high priest of both. He extended the scope of imagism by bringing the English Metaphysicals and the French symbolists (as well as the English Jacobean dramatists) to the rescue, thus adding new criteria of complexity and allusiveness to the criteria of concreteness and precision stressed by the imagists. Eliot also introduced into modern English and American poetry the kind of irony achieved by shifting suddenly from the formal to the colloquial, or by oblique allusions to objects or ideas that contrasted sharply with the surface meaning of the poem. Nor were Eliot and the imagists alone in their efforts to reinvent poetry. From 1912 D. H. Lawrence began writing poems freer in form and emotion, wanting to unshackle verse from the constraints of the "gem-like" lyric and approach even the "insurgent naked throb of the instant moment." Thus between, say, 1911 (the first year covered by Edward Marsh's anthologies of Georgian poetry) and 1922 (the year of the publication of *The Waste Land*), a major revolution occurred in English—and for that matter American—poetic theory and practice, one that determined the way in which many poets now think about their art.

This modernist revolution was by no means an isolated literary phenomenon. Writers on both sides of the English Channel were influenced by the French impressionist, postimpressionist, and cubist painters' radical reexamination of the nature of reality. The influence of Italian futurism was likewise strong on the painter and writer Wyndham Lewis, whose short-lived journal *Blast* was meant to be as shocking in its visual design as in its violent rhetoric. The poet Mina Loy shared the futurist fascination with modernity and speed, while repudiating its misogyny and jingoism, as evidenced by her "Feminist Manifesto." Pound wrote books about the French sculptor Henri Gaudier-Brzeska and the American composer George Antheil, and indeed the jagged rhythms and wrenching dissonances of modern music influenced a range of writers. Wilfred Owen wrote in 1918: "I suppose I am doing in poetry what the advanced composers are doing in music"; and Eliot, while writing *The Waste Land* three years later, was so impressed by a performance of the composer Igor Stravinsky's *Le Sacre du Printemps* (*The Rite of Spring*) that he stood up at the end and cheered.

The posthumous 1918 publication by Robert Bridges of Gerard Manley Hopkins's poetry encouraged experimentation in language and rhythms, as evidenced by the verse's influence on Eliot, Auden, and the Welshman Dylan Thomas. Hopkins combined precision of the individual image with a complex ordering of images and a new kind of metrical patterning he named "sprung rhythm," in which the stresses of a line could be more freely distributed.

Meanwhile Yeats's remarkable oeuvre, stretching across the whole modern period, reflected varying developments of the age yet maintained an unmistakably individual accent. Beginning with the ideas of the aesthetes, turning to a tougher and sparer ironic language without losing its characteristic verbal magic, working out its author's idiosyncratic notions of symbolism, developing in its full maturity into a rich symbolic and Metaphysical poetry with its own curiously haunting cadences and with imagery both shockingly realistic and movingly suggestive, Yeats's work encapsulates a history of English poetry between 1890 and 1939.

In his poem "Remembering the 'Thirties," Donald Davie declared: "A neutral tone is nowadays preferred." That tone—Auden's coolly clinical tone—dominated the poetry of the decade. The young poets of the early 1930s—Auden, Stephen Spender, C. Day Lewis, Louis MacNeice—were the first generation to grow up in the shadow of the first-generation modern poets. Hopkins's attention to sonorities, Hardy's experiments in stanzaic patterns, Yeats's ambivalent meditations on public themes, Eliot's satiric treatment of a mechanized and urbanized world, and Owen's pararhymed enactments of pity influenced Auden and the other poets in his circle. But these younger poets also had to distinguish themselves from the still-living eminences in poetry, and they did so by writing poems more low-pitched and ironic than Yeats's, for example, or more individually responsive to and active in the social world than Eliot's.

As World War II began, the neutral tone gave way to, as in Auden's work, an increasingly direct and humane voice and to the vehemence of what came to be known as the New Apocalypse. The poets of this movement, most notably Dylan Thomas, owed something of their imagistic audacity and rhetorical violence to the French surrealists, whose poetry was introduced to English readers in translations and in *A Short Survey of Surrealism* (1936) by David Gascoyne, one of the New Apocalypse poets. Many of the surrealists, such as Salvador Dalí and André Breton, were both poets and painters, and in their verbal as well as their visual art they sought to express, often by free association, the operation of the unconscious mind.

With the coming of the 1950s, however, the pendulum swung back. A new generation of poets, including Donald Davie, Thom Gunn, and Philip Larkin, reacted against what seemed to them the verbal excesses and extravagances of Dylan Thomas and Edith Sitwell, as well as the arcane myths and knotty allusiveness of Yeats, Eliot, and Pound. "The Movement," as this new group came to be called, aimed once again for a neutral tone, a purity of diction, in which to render an unpretentious fidelity to mundane experience. Larkin, its most notable exponent, rejected the intimidating gestures of an imported modernism in favor of a more civil and accessible "native" tradition that went back to Hardy, Housman, and the Georgian pastoralists of the 1910s.

Not everyone in England followed the lead of Larkin and the Movement, some rejecting the Movement's notion of a limited, rationalist, polished poetics. In the late 1950s and the 1960s Ted Hughes began to write poems in which predators and victims in the natural world suggest the violence and irrationality of modern history, including the carnage of World War I, in which his father had fought. Geoffrey Hill also saw a rationalist humanism as inadequate to the ethical and religious challenges of twentieth-century war, genocide, and atrocity, which he evoked in a strenuous language built on the traditions of high modernism and Metaphysical poetry.

Since the 1980s the spectrum of Britain's poets has become more diverse in class, ethnicity, gender, and region than ever before, bringing new voices into the English literary tradition. Born in the northern industrial city of Leeds, Tony Harrison brings the local vernacular, the oral energy and resonance of Yorkshire idiom and rhythms, into contact with traditional English and classical verse. Born in Scotland to an Irish mother in a left-wing, working-class Catholic family, Carol Ann Duffy grew up amid Irish, Scottish, and Standard varieties of English, and this youthful experience helped equip her to speak in different voices in her feminist monologues.

Post–World War II Ireland—both North and South—was among the most productive spaces for poetry in the second half of the twentieth century. Born just two and a half weeks after Yeats died, Seamus Heaney, his most celebrated successor, responds to the horrors of sectarian bloodshed in Northern Ireland with subtlety and acute ethical sensitivity in poems that draw on both Irish genres and sonorities and the English literary tradition of Wordsworth, Hopkins, and Ted Hughes. Paul Muldoon, one of Heaney's former students in Belfast, also writes about the Troubles in Northern Ireland but through eerily distorted fixed forms and multiple screens of irony, combining experimental zaniness with formal reserve. Born in the Irish Republic, Eavan Boland has made a space within the largely male tradition of Irish verse—with its standard, mythical emblems of femininity—for Irish women's historical experiences of suffering and survival.

The massive postwar change in the geographical contours of poetry written in English involved, in part, the emergence of new voices and styles from the "Old Commonwealth," or dominions, such as Canada and Australia. Self-conscious about being at the margins of the former empire, Les Murray fashions a brash, playful, overbrimming poetry that mines the British and classical traditions while remaking them in what he styles his "redneck" Australian manner. Anne Carson continues Canadian poetry's dialogue with its British literary origins, imaginatively transporting, for example, the Victorian writers Charlotte and Emily Brontë into a Canadian landscape, but she also illustrates a heightened interest in U.S. poetry and popular culture, bringing into the literary mix influences that range from ancient Greek poetry to Ezra Pound and Sylvia Plath, television and video.

From the former colonies of the British Empire in the so-called Third World came some of the most important innovations in the language and thematic reach of poetry in English. Born under British rule, students of colonial educations that repressed or denigrated native languages and traditions, these postcolonial poets grew up with an acute awareness of the riches of their own cultural inheritances, as well as a deep knowledge of the British literary canon. They expanded the range of possibilities in English-language poetry by hybridizing traditions of the British Isles with their indigenous images and speech rhythms, creoles and genres. Some of these writers, such as the Nobel laureate Derek Walcott, the most eminent West Indian poet, have drawn largely on British, American, and classical European models, though Walcott creolizes the rhythms, diction, and sensibility of English-language poetry. "I have Dutch, nigger, and English in me," declares the mulatto hero of "The Schooner *Flight*, "and either I'm nobody, or I'm a nation." Other poets have emphasized even more strongly Afro-Caribbean inheritances in speech and culture. When colonial prejudices still branded West Indian English, or Creole, a backward language, a "corruption" of English, the Afro-Jamaican poets Claude McKay and Louise Bennett claimed its wit, vibrancy, and proverbial richness for poetry. In the late 1960s the Barbadian Kamau (then Edward) Brathwaite revalued the linguistic, musical, and mythic survivals of Africa in the Caribbean—resources long repressed because of colonial attitudes. In poetry as well as fiction, Nigeria was the most prolific anglophone African nation around the time of independence, said to be the "golden age" of letters in sub-Saharan Africa. Wole Soyinka, later the first black African to win the Nobel Prize, stretched English syntax and figurative language in poems dense with Yoruba-inspired wordplay and myth. At the same time poets from India were bringing its great variety of indigenous cultures into English-language poetry. A. K. Ramanujan's sharply etched poems interfuse Anglo-modernist principles with the south Indian legacies of Tamil and Kannada poetry. All of these poets respond with emotional ambivalence and linguistic versatility to the experience of living after colonialism, between non-Western traditions and modernity, in a period of explosive change in the relation between Western and "native" cultures.

A century that began with a springtime of poetic innovation drew to its close with the full flowering of older poets such as Walcott, Hill, and Heaney, and the twenty-first century opened with welcome signs of fresh growth in English-language poetry, including new books by Paul Muldoon, Anne Carson, and Carol Ann Duffy.

FICTION

Novels—"loose baggy monsters," in Henry James's phrase—can be, can do, can include anything at all. The form defies prescriptions and limits. Yet its variety converges on persistent issues such as the construction of the self within society, the reproduction of the real world, and the temporality of human experience and of narrative. The novel's flexibility and porousness, its omnivorousness and multivoicedness have enabled writers to take advantage of modernity's global dislocation and mixture of peoples, while meeting the challenges to the imagination of mass death and world war, of the relentless and rapid mutations in modern cultures and societies, in evolving knowledge and belief.

The twentieth century's novels may be divided roughly into three main subperiods: high modernism through the 1920s, celebrating personal and textual inwardness, complexity, and difficulty; the reaction against modernism, involving a return to social realism, moralism, and assorted documentary endeavors, in the 1930s, 1940s, and 1950s; and the period after the collapse of the British Empire (especially from the time of the countercultural revolution of the 1960s), in which the fictional claims of various realisms—urban, proletarian, provincial English (e.g., northern), regional (e.g., Scottish and Irish), immigrant, postcolonial, feminist, gay—are asserted alongside, but also through, a continuing self-consciousness about language and form and meaning that is, in effect, the enduring legacy of modernism. By the end of the century, modernism had given way to the striking pluralism of postmodernism and postcolonialism. Yet the roots of the late-century panoramic mix of voices and styles lay in the early part of the century, when writers on the margins of "Englishness"—a Pole, Joseph Conrad; an Irishman, James Joyce; an American, Henry James; an Englishwoman, Virginia Woolf; and a working-class Englishman, D. H. Lawrence—were the most instrumental inventors of the modernist "English" novel.

The high modernists wrote in the wake of the shattering of confidence in the old certainties about the deity and the Christian faith, about the person, knowledge, materialism, history, the old grand narratives, which had, more or less, sustained the Western novel through the nineteenth century. They boldly ventured into this general shaking of belief in the novel's founding assumptions—that the world, things, and selves were knowable, that language was a reliably revelatory instrument, that the author's story gave history meaning and moral shape, that narratives should fall into ethically instructive beginnings, middles, and endings. Trying to be true to the new skepticisms and hesitations, the modernists also attempted to construct credible new alternatives to the old belief systems.

The once-prevailing nineteenth-century notions of ordinary reality came under serious attack. In her famous 1919 essay "Modern Fiction," Virginia Woolf explicitly assaulted the "materialism" of the realistic Edwardian heirs of Victorian naturalist confidence, Arnold Bennett, H. G. Wells, and John Galsworthy. For Woolf, as for other modernists, what was knowable, and thus representable, was not out there as some given, fixed, transcribable essence. Reality existed, rather, only as it was perceived. Hence the introduction of the impressionistic, flawed, even utterly unreliable narrator—a substitute for the classic nineteenth-century authoritative narrating voice, usually the voice of the author or some close substitute. Even a relatively reliable narrator, such as Conrad's Marlow, the main narrating voice of *Heart of Darkness*, as of *Lord Jim*, dramatized the struggle to know, penetrate, and interpret reality, with his large rhetoric of the invisible, inaudible, impossible, unintelligible, and so unsayable. The real was offered, thus, as refracted and reflected in the novel's representative consciousness. "Look within," Woolf urged the novelist. Reality and its truth had gone inward.

Woolf's subject would be "an ordinary mind on an ordinary day." The life that mattered most would now be mental life. And so the modernist novel turned resolutely inward, its concern being now with consciousness—a flow of reflections, momentary impressions, disjunctive bits of recall and half-memory, simultaneously revealing both the past and the way the past is repressed. Psychoanalysis partly enabled this concentration: to narrate the reality of persons as the life of the mind in all its complexity and inner tumult—consciousness, unconsciousness, id, libido, and so on. And the apparent truths of this inward life were, of course, utterly tricky, scattered, fragmentary, spotty, now illuminated, now twilit, now quite occluded. For Woolf, Joyce's *Ulysses* was a prime expression of this desired impressionistic agenda: "he is concerned at all costs to reveal the flickerings of that innermost flame which flashes its messages through the brain."

The characters of Joyce and Woolf are caught, then, as they are immersed in the so-called stream of consciousness; and some version of an interior flow of thought becomes the main modernist access to "character." The reader overhears the characters speaking, so to say, from within their particular consciousnesses, but not always directly. The modernists felt free also to enter their characters' minds, to speak as it were on their behalf, in the technique known as "free indirect style" (*style indirect libre* in French).

A marked feature of the new fictional selfhood was a fraught condition of existential loneliness. Conrad's Lord Jim, Joyce's Leopold Bloom and Stephen Dedalus, Lawrence's Paul Morel and Birkin, and Woolf's Mrs. Dalloway were people on their own, individuals bereft of the old props, Church, Bible, ideological consensus, and so doomed to make their own puzzled way through life's labyrinths without much confidence in belief, in the knowable solidity of the world, above all in language as a tool of knowledge about self and other. Jacob of Woolf's *Jacob's Room* remains stubbornly unknowable to his closest friends and loved ones, above all to his novelist. The walls and cupboards of Rhoda's room in *The Waves*, also by Woolf, bend disconcertingly around her bed; she tries in vain to restore her sense of the solidity of things by touching the bottom bed rail with her toes; her mind "pours" out of her; the very boundaries of her self soften, slip, dissolve. The old conclusive plots—everything resolved on the novel's last page, on the model of the detective story—gave place to irresolute open endings: the unending vista of the last paragraph in Lawrence's *Sons and Lovers*; the circularity by which the last sentence of Joyce's *Finnegans Wake* hooks back to be completed in the novel's first word, so that reading simply starts over.

Novelists built modern myths on the dry bones of the old Christian ones. In his review of *Ulysses* ("*Ulysses*, Order, and Myth," 1923), T. S. Eliot famously praised the novel for replacing the old "narrative method" by a new "mythical method": Joyce's Irish Jew, Bloom, is mythicized as a modern Ulysses, his day's odyssey often ironically reviving episodes in Homer's *Odyssey*. This manipulation of "a continuous parallel between contemporaneity and antiquity," was, Eliot thought, "a step toward making the modern world possible for art," much in keeping with the new anthropology and psychology as well as with what Yeats was doing in verse. Such private myth-making could, of course, take worrying turns. The "religion of the blood" that D. H. Lawrence celebrated led directly to the fascist sympathies of his *Aaron's Rod* and the revived Aztec blood cult of *The Plumed Serpent*.

Language and textuality, reading and writing, were now central to these highly metafictional novels, which are often about writers and artists, and surrogates for artists, such as Woolf's Mrs. Ramsay with her dinners and Mrs. Dalloway with her party, producers of what Woolf called the "unpublished works of women." But this self-reflexivity was not necessarily consoling—Mrs. Flanders's vision blurs and an inkblot spreads across the postcard we find her writing in the opening page of *Jacob's Room*. Perhaps the greatest modernist example of language gone rampant, *Finnegans Wake* taxes even its most dedicated readers and verges on unreadability for others.

The skeptical modernist linguistic turn, the rejection of materialist externality and of the Victorians' realist project, left ineradicable traces on later fiction, but modernism's revolutions were not absolute or permanent. *Ulysses* and *Finnegans Wake* were influential but unrepeatable. And even within the greatest modernist fictions the worldly and the material, political and moral questions never dried up. Woolf and Joyce, for example, celebrate the perplexities of urban life in London and Dublin, and, indeed, modernist fiction is largely an art of the great city. Lawrence was preoccupied with the condition of England, industrialism, provincial life. Satire was one of modernism's recurrent notes. So it was not odd for the right-wing novelists who came through in the 1920s, such as Wyndham Lewis and Evelyn Waugh, to resort to the social subject and the satiric stance, nor for their left-leaning contemporaries—who came to be seen as even more characteristic of the red decade of the 1930s—such as Graham Greene and George Orwell, to engage with the human condition in ways that Dickens or Balzac, let alone Bennett-Wells-Galsworthy, would have recognized as not all that distant from their own spirit.

Despite the turn to documentary realism in the 1930s, the modernist emphasis on linguistic self-consciousness did not disappear. Instead the new writers politicized the modern novel's linguistic self-consciousness: they deployed the discourse of the unemployed or of the West Midlands' proletariat, for example, for political ends. The comically chaotic meeting of English and German languages in Christopher Isherwood's Berlin stories is central to the fiction's dire warning about Anglo-German politics; Newspeak in George Orwell's *Nineteen-Eighty-Four* is the culmination of the author's nearly two decades of politically motivated engagement with the ways of English speakers at home and abroad. In this politicized aftermath of the modernist experiment, novelists such as Aldous Huxley in *Brave New World* satirically engage the socio-politico-moral matter of the 1930s in part through reflections on the corruptions of language.

Where World War I was a great engine of modernism, endorsing the chaos of shattered belief, the fragility of language and of the human subject, the Spanish Civil War and then World War II confirmed the English novel in its return to registering the social scene and the historical event. World War II provoked whole series of more or less realist fictions, including Evelyn Waugh's *Sword of Honour* trilogy, as well as powerful singletons such as Graham Greene's *Ministry of Fear* and Waugh's *Brideshead Revisited*. The new fictions of the post–World War II period speak with the satirical energies of the young demobilized officer class (Kingsley Amis's *Lucky Jim* set the disgruntled tone), and of the ordinary provincial citizen finding a fictional voice yet again in the new Welfare State atmosphere of the 1950s, as in Alan Sillitoe's proletarian Nottingham novel *Saturday Night and Sunday Morning*.

Questing for new moral bases for the post-Holocaust nuclear age, William Golding published the first of many intense post-Christian moral fables with *The Lord of the Flies*, and Iris Murdoch the first of many novels of moral philosophy with *Under the Net*, both in 1954. Murdoch espoused the "sovereignty of good" and the importance of the novel's loving devotion to "the otherness of the other person." Murdoch and Golding were consciously retrospective (as were the contemporary Roman Catholic novelists Greene, Waugh, and Muriel Spark) in their investment in moral form. But even such firmly grounded determinations could not calm the anxieties of belatedness. As the century drew on, British fiction struggled with a disconcertingly pervasive sense of posteriority—postwar flatness, postimperial diminutions of power and influence, and the sense of the grand narratives now losing their force as never before.

Some younger novelists, such as Ian McEwan and Martin Amis (son of Kingsley), became obsessed with Germany (the now accusingly prosperous old foe), and with the still haunting ghosts of the *Hitlerzeit*—and not least after 1989, when the Berlin Wall came down and wartime European horrors stirred into vivid focus. The dereliction of the once-grand imperial center, London, became a main topic for McEwan and for Amis, as well as for the later Kingsley Amis and the ex-Rhodesian Doris Lessing. Whereas Conrad, E. M. Forster (*A Passage to India*), and Jean Rhys (*Wide Sargasso Sea*) had been harshly accusatory about Britain's overseas behavior, now nostalgia for old imperial days shrouded the pages of Lawrence Durrell's *Alexandria Quartet* and Paul Scott's *Raj Quartet* and *Staying On*. Observers of English fiction worried that the only tasks left for it were to ruminate over past history and rehash old stories. The modernist Joycean strategy of resurrecting ancient narratives to revitalize present consciousness had given way to a fear that the postmodern novelist was condemned to a disabled career of parroting old stuff. *On est parlé*, "one is spoken," rather than speaking for oneself, thinks the main character of Julian Barnes's *Flaubert's Parrot*, reflecting in some dismay on this dilemma. Ventriloquial reproduction of old voices became Peter Ackroyd's trademark. Worries about being merely possessed by the past came to seem central to late-twentieth-century English fiction, as in A. S. Byatt's *Possession*, which is about the magnetism of past (Victorian) writers and writings.

Yet this was also a time for the spectacular emergence of many robust new voices, particularly from assorted margins—writers for whom the enervation at the English center represented an opportunity for telling their untold stories. After a sensational trial in 1960, the ban on D. H. Lawrence's erotically explicit *Lady Chatterley's Lover* was finally lifted, ensuring greater freedom in the narrative exploration of sexuality. Relaxing views on gender roles, the influx of women into the workplace, and the collapse of the grand patriarchal narratives also gave impetus to feminist revisionary narratives of history, and the remaking of narrative technique as more fluid and free. In the 1980s and 1990s prominent and inventive women's voices included those of Jeanette Winterson, celebrator of women's arts and bodiliness, and Angela Carter, feminist neomythographer, reviser of fairy tales, rewriter of the Marquis de Sade, espouser of raucous and rebellious heroines. Among the chorus of voices seeking to express with new intimacy and vividness experiences once held taboo were those of uncloseted gay writers, such as Alan Hollinghurst, pioneer of the openly male-homosexual literary novel of the post–World War II period, and Adam Mars-Jones, short-story chronicler of the HIV/AIDS crisis. The literary counterpart for political decolonization and devolution within the British Isles was the emergence of a multitude of regional and national voices outside the south of England, many deploying a vigorously local idiom, such as the Scottish novelist Irvine Welsh and the Irish writer Roddy Doyle, who reached mass international audiences through 1990s film versions of their novels *Trainspotting* (Welsh) and *The Commitments* (Doyle).

While postimperial anxieties and exhaustion seemed to beset many postwar English writers, postcolonial novelists were energetically claiming for literature in English untold histories, hybrid identities, and vibrantly creolized vocabularies. A major phase in the huge geographic shift in the center of gravity of English-language fiction occurred during the postwar decolonization of much of South Asia, Africa, and the Caribbean, when Chinua Achebe's *Things Fall Apart* (1958) was published, just two years before Nigerian independence. Retelling the story of colonial incursion from an indigenous viewpoint, Achebe's influential novel intricately represents an African community before and after the arrival of whites, in a language made up of English and Igbo words, encompassed by a narrative that enmeshes African proverbs and oral tales with English realism and modernist reflexivity. A few years later and on the eve of his natal island's independence, the Trinidad-born writer V. S. Naipaul published his first major novel, *A House for Mr. Biswas* (1961), one of many works that brilliantly develop the potential of a translucent realist fiction to explore issues such as migrant identities, cross-cultural mimicry, and the spaces of colonialism. The Indian-born Salman Rushdie, more restive than Naipaul in relation to Englishness and English literary traditions, has exuberantly championed hybrid narrative forms made out of the fresh convergence of modern European fiction and "Third World" orality, magical realism, and polyglossia, his novels, such as *Midnight's Children* (1981) and *The Satanic Verses* (1988), wryly offering a "chutnification of history" in South Asia and in an Asianized England. The colonies where English literature had once been used to impose imperial models of "civilization" now gave rise to novelists who, ironically, outstripped in imaginative freshness, cultural energy, and narrative inventiveness their counterparts from the seat of the empire.

White fiction writers from the colonies and dominions, many of them women, and many of them resident in England, such as Katherine Mansfield, Doris Lessing, and Jean Rhys, had long brought fresh perspectives to the novel from the outposts of empire, each of these eminent writers sharply etching a feminist critique of women's lives diminished by subordination to the colonial order. South Africa, not least because of its fraught racial and political history, can count among its progeny some of the most celebrated fiction writers of the late twentieth century. Nadine Gordimer has extended the potential of an ethical narrative realism to probe the fierce moral challenges of apartheid and its aftermath, whereas J. M. Coetzee has used self-reflexively postmodern and allegorical forms to inquire into the tangled complexities and vexed complicities of white South African experience.

Late-twentieth-century and early-twenty-first-century "English" fiction would have looked startlingly thin and poverty-stricken were it not for the large presence in Britain of writers of non-European origin. Like the first modern novelists, many of the novelists who have most enriched English-language fiction in recent decades are migrants, émigrés, and expatriates, such as Naipaul and Rushdie, and such as the delicately ironic realist Kazuo Ishiguro, from Japan, and the postsurreal fabulist Wilson Harris, from Guyana. Still others are the sons and daughters of non-European immigrants to Britain, such as two of the most visible exemplars of the often comically cross-cultural fiction of a new multiracial England, Hanif Kureishi and Zadie Smith, both born on the peripheries of London, Kureishi to a Pakistani father and English mother, Smith to a Jamaican mother and English father. These and other "British" novelists of color, giving voice to new and emergent experiences of immigration, hybridization, and cross-racial encounter, take advantage of the novel's fecund polymorphousness with little anxiety about belatedness, no fright over parroting, and no neomodernist worries about attempting realistic encounters with the world.

DRAMA

Late Victorians from one perspective, Oscar Wilde and Bernard Shaw can also be seen as early moderns, forerunners of the twentieth century's renovators of dramatic form. The wit of Wilde's drawing-room comedies is combative and generative of paradoxes, but beneath the glitter of his verbal play are serious—if heavily coded—reflections on social, political, and feminist issues. Shaw brought still another kind of wit into drama—not Wilde's lighthearted sparkle but the provocative paradox that was meant to tease and disturb, to challenge the complacency of the audience. Over time the desire to unsettle, to shock, even to alienate the audience became one hallmark of modern drama.

Wilde and Shaw were both born in Ireland, and it was in Dublin that the century's first major theatrical movement originated. To nourish Irish poetic drama and foster the Irish literary renaissance, Yeats and Lady Augusta Gregory founded the Irish Literary Theatre in 1899, with Yeats's early nationalist play *The Countess Cathleen* as its first production. In 1902 the Irish Literary Theatre was able to maintain a permanent all-Irish company and changed its name to the Irish National Theatre, which moved in 1904 to the Abbey Theatre, by which name it has been known ever since. J. M. Synge brought the speech and imagination of Irish country people into theater, but the Abbey's 1907 staging of his play *The Playboy of the Western World* so offended orthodox religious and nationalist sentiment that the audience rioted. While defending Synge and other pioneers of Irish drama, Yeats also continued to write his own plays, which drew themes from old Irish legend and which, after 1913, stylized and ritualized theatrical performance on the model of Japanese Noh drama. In the 1920s Sean O'Casey brought new vitality to the Abbey Theatre, using the Easter Rising and Irish civil war as a background for controversial plays (one of which again sparked riots) that combined tragic melodrama, humor of character, and irony of circumstance. In England T. S. Eliot attempted with considerable success to revive a ritual poetic drama with his *Murder in the Cathedral* (1935), though his later attempts to combine religious symbolism with the chatter of entertaining society comedy, as in *The Cocktail Party* (1950), were uneven.

Despite the achievements of Yeats, Synge, O'Casey, and Eliot, it cannot be said of Irish and British drama, as it can of poetry and fiction in the first half of the century, that a technical revolution changed the whole course of literary history. The major innovations in the first half of the twentieth century were on the Continent. German expressionist drama developed out of the dark, psychological focus of the later plays of the Swedish dramatist August Strindberg (1849–1912). Another worldwide influence was the "epic" drama of the leftist German dramatist Bertolt Brecht (1898–1956): to foster ideological awareness, he rejected the idea that the audience should identify with a play's characters and become engrossed in its plot; the playwright should break the illusion of reality through the alienation effect (*Verfremdungseffekt*) and foreground the play's theatrical constructedness and historical specificity. The French dramatist Antonin Artaud (1896–1948) also defied realism and rationalism, but unlike Brecht, his theory of the theater of cruelty sought a transformative, mystical communion with the audience through incantations and sounds, physical gestures and strange scenery. Another French dramatist, the Romanian-born Eugène Ionesco (1909–1994), helped inaugurate the theater of the absurd just after World War II, in plays that enact people's hopeless efforts to communicate and that comically intimate a tragic vision of life devoid of meaning or purpose. In such Continental drama the influences of symbolism (on the later Strindberg), Marxism (on Brecht), and surrealism (on Artaud and Ionesco) contributed to the shattering of naturalistic convention in drama, making the theater a space where linear plot gave way to fractured scenes and circular action, transparent conversation was displaced by misunderstanding and verbal opacity, a predictable and knowable universe was unsettled by eruptions of the irrational and the absurd.

In Britain the impact of these Continental innovations was delayed by a conservative theater establishment until the late 1950s and 1960s, when they converged with the countercultural revolution to transform the nature of English-language theater. Meanwhile the person who played the most significant role in the anglophone absorption of modernist experiment was the Irishman Samuel Beckett. He changed the history of drama with his first produced play, written in French in 1948 and translated by the author as *Waiting for Godot* (premiered in Paris in 1953, in London in 1955). The play astonishingly did away with plot ("Nothing happens—twice," as one critic put it), as did *Endgame* (1958) and Beckett's later plays, such as *Not I* (1973) and *That Time* (1976). In the shadow of the mass death of World War II, the plotlessness, the minimal characterization and setting, the absurdist intimation of an existential darkness without redemption, the tragicomic melding of anxiety, circular wordplay, and slapstick action in Beckett's plays gave impetus to a seismic shift in British writing for the theater.

The epicenter of the new developments in British drama was the Royal Court Theatre, symbolically located a little away from London's West End "theater land" (the rough equivalent of Broadway in New York). From 1956 the Royal Court was the home of the English Stage Company. Together they provided a venue and a vision that provoked and enabled a new wave of writers. John Osborne's *Look Back in Anger* (1956), the hit of the ESC's first season (significantly helped by the play's television broadcast), offered the audience "lessons in feeling" through a searing depiction of class-based indignation, emotional cruelty, and directionless angst, all in a surprisingly nonmetropolitan setting. At the Royal Court the working-class naturalism of the so-called "kitchen sink" dramatists and other "angry young men" of the 1950s, such as Arnold Wesker, author of the trilogy *Chicken Soup with Barley* (1958), also broke with the genteel proprieties and narrowly upper-class set designs that, in one unadventurous drawing-room comedy after another, had dominated the British stage for decades. The political consciousness of the new theater was still more evident in John Arden's plays produced for the Royal Court, such as *Sergeant Musgrave's Dance* (1959), which explores colonial oppression, communal guilt for wartime atrocities, and pacifism in the stylized setting of an isolated mining town. By the later 1960s the influence of the counter-culture on British theater was unavoidable. Joe Orton challenged bourgeois sentiment in a series of classically precise, blackly comic, and sexually ambiguous parodies, such as his farce *What the Butler Saw* (1969).

While plays of social and political critique were one response to the postwar period, Beckett and the theater of the absurd inspired another group of Royal Court writers to refocus theater on language, symbolism, and existential realities. Informed by kitchen-sink naturalism and absurdism, Harold Pinter's "comedies of menace" map out a social trajectory from his early study of working-class stress and inarticulate anxiety, *The Room* (1957), through the film-noirish black farce of *The Dumb Waiter* (1960) and the emotional power plays of *The Caretaker* (1960), to the savagely comic study of middle-class escape from working-class mores in *The Homecoming* (1965). Later plays reflect on patrician suspicion and betrayal, though in the 1980s his work acquired a more overtly political voice. Though less bleak than Pinter, Tom Stoppard is no less indebted to Beckett's wordplay, skewed conversations, and theatrical technique, as evidenced by *Rosencrantz and Guildenstern Are Dead* (1967) and other plays, many of which embed within themselves earlier literary works (such as *Godot* and *Hamlet*) and thus offer virtuoso postmodernist reflections on art, language, and performance. This enjoyment and exploitation of self-conscious theatricality arises partly out of the desire to show theater as different from film and television and is also apparent in the 1970s productions of another playwright: the liturgical stylization of Peter Shaffer's *Equus* (1973) and the bleak mental landscape of his Antonio Salieri in *Amadeus* (1979) emphasize the stage as battleground and site of struggle (an effect lost in their naturalistic film versions). Stoppard's time shifts and memory lapses in *Travesties* (1974) allow a nonnaturalistic study of the role of memory and imagination in the creative process, a theme he returns to in *Arcadia* (1993), a stunning double-exposure account of a Romantic poet and his modern critical commentators occupying the same physical space but never reaching intellectual common ground.

Legal reform intensified the postwar ferment in British theater. Since the Theatres Act of 1843, writers for the public stage had been required to submit their playscripts to the Lord Chamberlain's office for state censorship, but in 1968 a new Theatres Act abolished that office. With this new freedom from conservative mores and taste, Howard Brenton, Howard Barker, Edward Bond, and David Hare were able to write challenging studies of violence, social deprivation, and political and sexual aggression, often using mythical settings and epic stories to construct austere tableaux of power and oppression. Bond's *Lear* (1971) typifies his ambitious combination of soaring lyrical language and alienatingly realistic violence. Directors such as Peter Brook took advantage of the new freedom in plays that emphasized, as had Artaud's theater of cruelty, physical gesture, bodily movement, and ritualized spectacle. The post-1968 liberalization also encouraged the emergence of new theater groups addressing specific political agendas, many of them inspired by Brecht's "epic" theater's distancing, discontinuous, and socially critical style. Companies such as Monstrous Regiment, Gay Sweatshop, Joint Stock, and John McGrath's 7: 84 worked collaboratively with dramatists who were invited to help devise and develop shows. Increasingly in the 1970s published plays were either transcriptions of the first production or "blueprints for the alchemy of live performance" (Micheline Wandor). In Ireland the founding of the Field Day Theatre Company in 1980 by the well-established playwright Brian Friel and actor Stephen Rea had similar motives of collaborative cultural catalysis. Their first production, Friel's *Translations* (1980), exploring linguistic colonialism and the fragility of cultural identity in nineteenth-century Ireland, achieved huge international success.

This ethos of collaboration and group development helped foster the first major cohort of women dramatists to break through onto mainstream stages. Working with Joint Stock and Monstrous Regiment in the late 1970s on plays such as the gender-bending anticolonial *Cloud Nine* (1979), Caryl Churchill developed plays out of workshops exploring gender, class, and colonialism. She carefully transcribes and overlaps the speech of her characters to create a seamlessly interlocking web of discourse, a streamlined version of the ebb and flow of normal speech. In *Top Girls* (1982) and *Serious Money* (1987), plays that anatomize the market-driven ethos of the 1980s, she explores modern society with the wit and detachment of Restoration comedy. Pam Gems studies the social and sexual politics of misogyny and feminism in her campy theatrical explorations of strong women—*Queen Cristina* (1977), *Piaf* (1978), *Camille* (1984)—while Sarah Daniels reinterprets the naturalism of kitchen-sink drama by adding to it the linguistic stylization of Churchill.

Massive strides in the diversification of English-language theater occurred during the era of decolonization, when two eminent poets, Derek Walcott and Wole Soyinka, helped breathe new life into anglophone drama. As early as the 1950s Derek Walcott was writing and directing plays about Caribbean history and experience, re-creating in his drama a West Indian "oral culture, of chants, jokes, folk-songs, and fables," at a time when theater in the Caribbean tended to imitate European themes and styles. After moving to Trinidad in 1958, he founded what came to be known as the Trinidad Theatre Workshop, and for much of the next twenty years devoted himself to directing and writing plays that included *Dream on Monkey Mountain*, first produced in 1967, in which Eurocentric and Afrocentric visions of Caribbean identity collide. Since then, a notable breakthrough in Caribbean theater has been the collaborative work of the Sistren Theatre Collective in Jamaica, which, following the lead of Louise Bennett and other West Indian poets, draws on women's personal histories in dramatic performances that make vivid use of Jamaican speech, expression, and rhythm. Meanwhile in Africa, Wole Soyinka, who had been involved with the Royal Court Theatre in the late 1950s when Brecht's influence was first being absorbed, returned to Nigeria in the year of its independence to write and direct plays that fused Euromodernist dramatic techniques with conventions from Yoruba popular and traditional drama. His play *Death and the King's Horseman*, premiered in Nigeria in 1976, represents a tragic confrontation between colonial officials and the guardians of Yoruba rituals and beliefs. While Soyinka has been a towering presence in sub-Saharan Africa, other playwrights, such as the fellow Nigerian Femi Osofisan and the South African Athol Fugard, have used the stage to probe issues of class, race, and the often violent legacy of colonialism. In England playwrights of Caribbean, African, and Asian origin or descent, such as Mustapha Matura, Caryl

Phillips, and Hanif Kureishi, the latter of whom is best-known internationally for his screenplays for *My Beautiful Laundrette* (1985), *Sammy and Rosie Get Laid* (1988), *My Son the Fanatic* (1998), and *The Mother* (2004), have revitalized British drama with a host of new vocabularies, new techniques, new visions of identity in an increasingly cross-ethnic and transnational world. The century that began with its first great dramatic movement in Ireland was followed by a century that began with English-language drama more diverse in its accents and styles, more international in its bearings and vision than ever before.

Additional information about the Twentieth Century and After, including primary texts and images, is available at Norton Literature Online (www .wwnorton.literature). Online topics are

- Representing the Great War
- Modernist Experiment
- Imagining Ireland

THE TWENTIETH CENTURY AND AFTER

TEXTS	CONTEXTS
1899, 1902 Joseph Conrad, *Heart of Darkness*	
	1900 Max Planck, quantum theory
	1901 First wireless communication across the Atlantic
	1901–10 Reign of Edward VII
	1902 End of the Anglo-Boer War
	1903 Henry Ford introduces the first mass-produced car. Wright Brothers make the first successful airplane flight
	1905 Albert Einstein, theory of special relativity. Impressionist exhibition, London
1910 Bernard Shaw, *Pygmalion*	**1910** Postimpressionist exhibition, London
	1910–36 Reign of George V
1913 Ezra Pound, "A Few Don'ts by an Imagiste"	
1914 James Joyce, *Dubliners*. Thomas Hardy, *Satires of Circumstance*	**1914–18** World War I
1914–15 *Blast*	
1916 Joyce, *A Portrait of the Artist as a Young Man*	**1916** Easter Rising in Dublin
1917 T. S. Eliot, "The Love Song of J. Alfred Prufrock"	
1918 Gerard Manley Hopkins, *Poems*	**1918** Armistice. Franchise Act grants vote to women thirty and over
1920 D. H. Lawrence, *Women in Love*. Wilfred Owen, *Poems*	**1920** Treaty of Versailles. League of Nations formed
1921 William Butler Yeats, *Michael Robartes and the Dancer*	**1921–22** Formation of Irish Free State with Northern Ireland (Ulster) remaining part of Great Britain
1922 Katherine Mansfield, *The Garden Party and Other Stories*. Joyce, *Ulysses*. Eliot, *The Waste Land*.	
1924 Forster, *A Passage to India*	
1927 Virginia Woolf, *To the Lighthouse*	
1928 Yeats, *The Tower*	**1928** Women twenty-one and over granted voting rights
1929 Woolf, *A Room of One's Own*. Robert Graves, *Goodbye to All That*	**1929** Stock market crash; Great Depression begins
	1933 Hitler comes to power in Germany
1935 Eliot, *Murder in the Cathedral*	

TEXTS	CONTEXTS
	1936–39 Spanish Civil War
	1936 Edward VIII succeeds George V, but abdicates in favor of his brother, crowned as George VI
1937 David Jones, *In Parenthesis*	
1939 Joyce, *Finnegans Wake*. Yeats, *Last Poems and Two Plays*	1939–45 World War II
1940 W. H. Auden, *Another Time*	1940 Fall of France. Battle of Britain
	1941–45 The Holocaust
1943 Eliot, *Four Quartets*	
1945 Auden, *Collected Poems*. George Orwell, *Animal Farm*	1945 First atomic bombs dropped, on Japan
1946 Dylan Thomas, *Deaths and Entrances*	
	1947 India and Pakistan become independent nations
	1948 *Empire Windrush* brings West Indians to U.K.
1949 Orwell, *Nineteen-Eighty-Four*	
	1950 Apartheid laws passed in South Africa
1953 Premiere of Samuel Beckett's *Waiting for Godot*	
	1956 Suez Crisis
	1957 Ghana becomes independent
1958 Chinua Achebe, *Things Fall Apart*	
	1960 Nigeria becomes independent
	1961 Berlin Wall erected
1962 Doris Lessing, *The Golden Notebook*	1962 Cuban missile crisis. Uganda, Jamaica, Trinidad and Tobago become independent
1964 Philip Larkin, *The Whitsun Weddings*	
	1965 U.S. troops land in South Vietnam
1966 Nadine Gordimer, *The Late Bourgeois World*. Tom Stoppard, *Rosencrantz and Guildenstern Are Dead*. Jean Rhys, *Wide Sargasso Sea*	1966 Barbados and Guyana become independent
	1969 Apollo moon landing
1971 V. S. Naipaul, *In a Free State*	1971 Indo-Pakistan War, leading to creation of Bangladesh
	1972 Britain enters European Common Market
	1973 U.S. troops leave Vietnam
1975 Seamus Heaney, *North*	

TEXTS	CONTEXTS
1979 Caryl Churchill, *Cloud 9*	1979 Islamic Revolution in Iran; the Shah flees. Soviets invade Afghanistan
	1979–90 Margaret Thatcher is British prime minister
1980 J. M. Coetzee, *Waiting for the Barbarians*	1980–88 Iran-Iraq War
1981 Salman Rushdie, *Midnight's Children*. Brian Friel, *Translations*	
	1982 Falklands War
1985 Production of Hanif Kureishi's *My Beautiful Laundrette*	
1988 Rushdie, *The Satanic Verses*	
1989 Kazuo Ishiguro, *The Remains of the Day*	1989 Fall of the Berlin Wall. Tiananmen Square, Beijing, demonstration and massacre
1990 Derek Walcott, *Omeros*	
	1991 Collapse of the Soviet Union
1992 Thom Gunn, *The Man with Night Sweats*	
1993 Tom Stoppard, *Arcadia*	
	1994 Democracy comes to South Africa
1997 Arundhati Roy, *The God of Small Things*	1997 Labour Party victory in the U.K. ends eighteen years of Conservative government
	1998 British handover of Hong Kong to China. Northern Ireland Assembly established
1999 Carol Ann Duffy, *The World's Wife*	
2000 Zadie Smith, *White Teeth*	
	2001 September 11 attacks destroy World Trade Center
2002 Paul Muldoon, *Moy Sand and Gravel*	2002 Euro becomes sole currency in most of European Union
	2003 Invasion of Iraq led by U.S. and U.K.

THOMAS HARDY
1840–1928

Thomas Hardy was born near Dorchester, in that area of southwest England that he was to make the "Wessex" of his novels. He attended local schools until the age of fifteen, when he was apprenticed to a Dorchester architect with whom he worked for six years. In 1861 he went to London to continue his studies and to practice as an architect. Meanwhile he was completing his general education informally through his own erratic reading and was becoming more and more interested in both fiction and poetry. After some early attempts at writing both short stories and poems, he decided to concentrate on fiction. His first novel was rejected by the publishers in 1868 on the recommendation of George Meredith, who nevertheless advised Hardy to write another. The result was *Desperate Remedies,* published anonymously in 1871, followed the next year by his first real success (also published anonymously), *Under the Greenwood Tree.* His career as a novelist was now well launched; Hardy gave up his architectural work and produced a series of novels that ended with *Jude the Obscure* in 1895. The hostile reception of this novel—lambasted as *Jude the Obscene*—sent him back to poetry. Straddling the Victorian and modern periods, he published all his novels in the nineteenth century, all but the first of his poetry collections, *Wessex and Other Verses* (1898), in the twentieth. His remarkable epic-drama of the Napoleonic Wars, *The Dynasts,* came out in three parts between 1903 and 1908; after this he wrote mostly lyric poetry.

Hardy's novels, set in a predominantly rural "Wessex," show the forces of nature outside and inside individuals combining to shape human destiny. Against a background of immemorial agricultural labor, with ancient monuments such as Stonehenge or an old Roman amphitheater reminding us of the human past, he presents characters at the mercy of their own passions or finding temporary salvation in the age-old rhythms of rural work or rural recreation. Men and women in Hardy's fiction are not masters of their fates; they are at the mercy of the indifferent forces that manipulate their behavior and their relations with others, but they can achieve dignity through endurance, heroism, or simple strength of character. The characteristic Victorian novelist—e.g., Dickens or Thackeray—was concerned with the behavior and problems of people in a given social milieu, which were described in detail; Hardy preferred to go directly for the elemental in human behavior with a minimum of contemporary social detail. Most of his novels are tragic, exploring the bitter ironies of life with an almost malevolent staging of coincidence to emphasize the disparity between human desire and ambition on the one hand and what fate has in store for the characters on the other. But fate is not a wholly external force. Men and women are driven by the demands of their own nature as much as by anything outside them. Perhaps the darkest of Hardy's novels, *Tess of the D'Urbervilles* (1891) is the story of an intelligent and sensitive young woman, daughter of a poor family, driven to murder and so to death by hanging, by a painfully ironic concatenation of events and circumstances. Published in the same year as *Tess,* the story anthologized here, "On the Western Circuit," similarly has at its center a young country woman seduced by a sophisticated city man; her "ruin" (see also Hardy's poem "The Ruined Maid") leads—contrary to the good intentions of the three protagonists, and again as the result of bitter irony—to *his* ruin and a lifetime of misery for all concerned.

Hardy denied that he was a pessimist, calling himself a "meliorist"—that is, one who believes that the world can be made better by human effort. But there is little sign of meliorism in either his most important novels or his lyric poetry. A number of his poems, such as the one he wrote about the *Titanic* disaster, "The Convergence of the Twain," illustrate the perversity of fate, the disastrous or ironic coincidence. Other poems go beyond this mood to present with quiet gravity and a carefully controlled elegiac feeling some aspect of human sorrow or loss or frustration or regret, always grounded in a particular, fully realized situation. "Hap" shows Hardy in the characteristic mood of complaining about the irony of human destiny in a universe ruled by chance, but a poem such as "The Walk" (one of a group of poems written after the death of his first wife in 1912) gives, with remarkable power, concrete embodiment to a sense of loss.

Hardy's poetry, like his prose, often has a self-taught air about it; both can seem, on first reading, roughly hewn. He said he wanted to avoid "the jewelled line," and like many modern and contemporary poets, he sought instead what he called "dissonances, and other irregularities" in his art, because these convey more authenticity and spontaneity. "Art is a disproportioning . . . of realities," he declared. Though he adheres to the metered line, Hardy roughens prosody and contorts syntax, and he creates irregular and complex stanza forms. His diction includes archaisms and deliberately awkward coinages (e.g., "Powerfuller" and "unblooms" in "Hap"). He distorts many conventions of traditional genres such as the sonnet, the love poem, the war poem, and the elegy. Though rooted in the Victorian period, Hardy thus looks ahead to the dislocations of poetic form carried out by subsequent poets of the twentieth century.

The sadness in Hardy—his inability to believe in the government of the world by a benevolent God, his sense of the waste and frustration involved in human life, his insistent irony when faced with moral or metaphysical questions—is part of the late-Victorian mood, found also, say, in A. E. Housman's poetry and, earlier, in Edward FitzGerald's *Rubáiyát of Omar Khayyám,* published when Hardy was nineteen. What has been termed "the disappearance of God" affected him more deeply than it did many of his contemporaries, because until he was twenty-five he seriously considered becoming an Anglican priest. Yet his characteristic themes and attitudes cannot be related simply to the reaction to new scientific and philosophical ideas (Darwin's theory of evolution, for example) that we see in many forms in late-nineteenth-century literature. The favorite poetic mood of both Tennyson and Arnold was also an elegiac one (e.g., in Tennyson's "Break, Break, Break" and Arnold's "Dover Beach"), but the mood of Hardy's poetry differs from Victorian sorrow; it is sterner, more skeptical, as though braced by a long look at the worst. It is this sternness, this ruggedness of his poetry, together with its verbal and emotional integrity, its formal variety and tonal complexity, its quietly searching individual accent, that helped bring about the steady rise in Hardy's reputation as a poet. Ezra Pound remarked in a 1934 letter: "Nobody has taught me anything about writing since Thomas Hardy died." W. H. Auden begins an essay with this testament to the effect of Hardy's verse: "I cannot write objectively about Thomas Hardy because I was once in love with him." And Hardy appears as the major figure—with more poems than either Yeats or Eliot—in Philip Larkin's influential *Oxford Book of Twentieth-Century English Verse* (1973).

Hap[1]

   If but some vengeful god would call to me
   From up the sky, and laugh: 'Thou suffering thing,
   Know that thy sorrow is my ecstasy,
   That thy love's loss is my hate's profiting!'

5 Then would I bear it, clench myself, and die,
   Steeled by the sense of ire° unmerited;   *anger*
   Half-eased in that a Powerfuller than I
   Had willed and meted° me the tears I shed.   *allotted, given*

1. I.e., chance (as also "Casualty," line 11).

But not so. How arrives it joy lies slain,
10 And why unblooms the best hope ever sown?
—Crass Casualty obstructs the sun and rain,
And dicing Time for gladness casts a moan. . . .
These purblind Doomsters[2] had as readily strown
Blisses about my pilgrimage as pain.

1866   1898

Neutral Tones

We stood by a pond that winter day,
And the sun was white, as though chidden of° God,   rebuked by
And a few leaves lay on the starving sod;°   turf
    —They had fallen from an ash, and were gray.

5   Your eyes on me were as eyes that rove
Over tedious riddles of years ago;
And some words played between us to and fro
    On which lost the more by our love.

The smile on your mouth was the deadest thing
10 Alive enough to have strength to die;
And a grin of bitterness swept thereby
    Like an ominous bird a-wing . . .

Since then, keen lessons that love deceives,
And wrings with wrong, have shaped to me
15 Your face, and the God-curst sun, and a tree,
    And a pond edged with grayish leaves.

1867   1898

Drummer Hodge

1

They throw in Drummer Hodge, to rest
    Uncoffined—just as found:
His landmark is a kopje-crest
    That breaks the veldt[1] around;
5   And foreign constellations[2] west°   set
    Each night above his mound.

2

Young Hodge the Drummer never knew—
    Fresh from his Wessex home—
The meaning of the broad Karoo,[3]

2. Half-blind judges.
1. South African Dutch (Afrikaans) word for a plain or prairie. "Kopje-crest": Afrikaans for a small hill. The poem is a lament for an English soldier killed in the Anglo-Boer War (1899–1902).
2. Those visible only in the Southern Hemisphere.
3. A dry tableland region in South Africa (usually spelled "Karroo").

10   The Bush,⁴ the dusty loam,
   And why uprose to nightly view
        Strange stars amid the gloam.

3

   Yet portion of that unknown plain
        Will Hodge for ever be;
15   His homely Northern breast and brain
        Grow to some Southern tree,
   And strange-eyed constellations reign
        His stars eternally.

1899, 1901

The Darkling¹ Thrush

   I leant upon a coppice gate²
        When Frost was spectre-gray,
   And Winter's dregs made desolate
        The weakening eye of day.
5   The tangled bine-stems³ scored the sky
        Like strings of broken lyres,
   And all mankind that haunted nigh°   *near*
        Had sought their household fires.

   The land's sharp features seemed to be
10   The Century's corpse outleant,⁴
   His crypt the cloudy canopy,
        The wind his death-lament.
   The ancient pulse of germ and birth
        Was shrunken hard and dry,
15   And every spirit upon earth
        Seemed fervourless as I.

   At once a voice arose among
        The bleak twigs overhead
   In a full-hearted evensong
20   Of joy illimited;
   An aged thrush, frail, gaunt, and small,
        In blast-beruffled plume,
   Had chosen thus to fling his soul
        Upon the growing gloom.

25   So little cause for carolings
        Of such ecstatic sound
   Was written on terrestrial things
        Afar or nigh around,
   That I could think there trembled through

4. British colonial word for an uncleared area of land.
1. In the dark.
2. Gate leading to a small wood or thicket.

3. Twining stems of shrubs.
4. Leaning out (of its coffin); i.e., the 19th century was dead. This poem was dated December 31, 1900.

30   His happy good-night air
        Some blessed Hope, whereof he knew
        And I was unaware.

1900, 1901

The Ruined Maid

'O 'Melia,[1] my dear, this does everything crown!
Who could have supposed I should meet you in Town?
And whence such fair garments, such prosperi-ty?'—
'O didn't you know I'd been ruined?' said she.

5   —'You left us in tatters, without shoes or socks,
Tired of digging potatoes, and spudding up docks;[2]
And now you've gay bracelets and bright feathers three!'—
'Yes: that's how we dress when we're ruined,' said she.

—'At home in the barton° you said "thee" and "thou",   *farmyard*
10 And "thik oon", and "theäs oon", and "t'other"; but now
Your talking quite fits 'ee for high compa-ny!'—
'Some polish is gained with one's ruin,' said she.

—'Your hands were like paws then, your face blue and bleak
But now I'm bewitched by your delicate cheek,
15 And your little gloves fit as on any la-dy!'—
'We never do work when we're ruined,' said she.

—'You used to call home-life a hag-ridden dream,
And you'd sigh, and you'd sock;° but at present you seem   *sigh*
To know not of megrims° or melancho-ly!'—   *low spirits*
20 'True. One's pretty lively when ruined,' said she.

—'I wish I had feathers, a fine sweeping gown,
And a delicate face, and could strut about Town!'—
'My dear—a raw country girl, such as you be,
Cannot quite expect that. You ain't ruined,' said she.

1866   1901

Channel Firing[1]

That night your great guns, unawares,
Shook all our coffins as we lay,
And broke the chancel[2] window-squares,
We thought it was the Judgement-day

---

1. Diminutive form of Amelia.
2. Digging up a species of thick-rooted weed.
1. Written in April 1914, when Anglo-German
naval rivalry was growing steadily more acute; the

title refers to gunnery practice in the English
Channel. Four months later (August 4), World
War I broke out.
2. Part of church nearest to the altar.

5 And sat upright. While drearisome
 Arose the howl of wakened hounds:
 The mouse let fall the altar-crumb,
 The worms drew back into the mounds,

 The glebe cow[3] drooled. Till God called, 'No;
10 It's gunnery practise out at sea
 Just as before you went below;
 The world is as it used to be:

 'All nations striving strong to make
 Red war yet redder. Mad as hatters[4]
15 They do no more for Christès[5] sake
 Than you who are helpless in such matters.

 'That this is not the judgement-hour
 For some of them's a blessed thing,
 For if it were they'd have to scour
20 Hell's floor for so much threatening. . . .

 'Ha, ha. It will be warmer when
 I blow the trumpet (if indeed
 I ever do; for you are men,
 And rest eternal sorely need).'

25 So down we lay again. 'I wonder,
 Will the world ever saner be,'
 Said one, 'than when He sent us under
 In our indifferent century!'

 And many a skeleton shook his head.
30 'Instead of preaching forty year,'
 My neighbour Parson Thirdly said,
 'I wish I had stuck to pipes and beer.'

 Again the guns disturbed the hour,
 Roaring their readiness to avenge,
35 As far inland as Stourton Tower,
 And Camelot, and starlit Stonehenge.[6]

1914   1914

3. I.e., cow on a small plot of land belonging to a church (a "glebe" is a small field).
4. Cf. the Mad Hatter in Lewis Carroll's *Alice's Adventures in Wonderland* (1865).
5. The archaic spelling and pronunciation suggest a ballad note of doom.
6. The sound of guns preparing for war across the

Channel reaches Alfred's ("Stourton") Tower (near Stourton in Dorset), commemorating King Alfred's defeat of a Danish invasion in 878; also the site of King Arthur's court at Camelot (supposedly near Glastonbury) and the famous prehistoric stone circle of Stonehenge on Salisbury Plain.

The Convergence of the Twain

(*Lines on the loss of the* Titanic)[1]

I

In a solitude of the sea
Deep from human vanity,
And the Pride of Life that planned her, stilly couches she.

2

Steel chambers, late the pyres
Of her salamandrine[2] fires,
Cold currents thrid,[3] and turn to rhythmic tidal lyres.

3

Over the mirrors meant
To glass the opulent
The sea-worm crawls—grotesque, slimed, dumb, indifferent.

4

Jewels in joy designed
To ravish the sensuous mind
Lie lightless, all their sparkles bleared and black and blind.

5

Dim moon-eyed fishes near
Gaze at the gilded gear
And query: 'What does this vaingloriousness down here?' . . .

6

Well: while was fashioning
This creature of cleaving wing,
The Immanent Will[4] that stirs and urges everything

7

Prepared a sinister mate
For her—so gaily great—
A Shape of Ice, for the time far and dissociate.

8

And as the smart ship grew
In stature, grace, and hue,
In shadowy silent distance grew the Iceberg too.

9

Alien they seemed to be:
No mortal eye could see
The intimate welding of their later history,

5

10

15

20

25

1. The *Titanic* was the largest and most luxurious ocean liner of the day. Considered unsinkable, it sank with great loss of life on April 15, 1912, on the ship's maiden voyage, from Southampton to the United States, after colliding with an iceberg. "Twain": two.

2. I.e., destructive. The salamander was supposed to be able to survive fire.
3. A variant form of the verb *thread*.
4. The force (blind, but slowly gaining consciousness throughout history) that drives the world, according to Hardy's philosophy.

10

Or sign that they were bent
By paths coincident
30 On being anon° twin halves of one august° event,   soon / important

11

Till the Spinner of the Years
Said 'Now!' And each one hears,
And consummation comes, and jars two hemispheres.

1912   1912, 1914

Ah, Are You Digging on My Grave?

'Ah, are you digging on my grave
        My loved one?—planting rue?'[1]
—'No: yesterday he went to wed
One of the brightest wealth has bred.
5   'It cannot hurt her now,' he said,
        "That I should not be true." '

'Then who is digging on my grave?
        My nearest dearest kin?'
—'Ah, no; they sit and think, "What use!
10 What good will planting flowers produce?
No tendance of her mound can loose
        Her spirit from Death's gin." '°   trap

'But some one digs upon my grave?
        My enemy?—prodding sly?'
15 —'Nay: when she heard you had passed the Gate
That shuts on all flesh soon or late,
She thought you no more worth her hate,
        And cares not where you lie.'

'Then, who is digging on my grave?
20   Say—since I have not guessed!'
—'O it is I, my mistress dear,
Your little dog, who still lives near,
And much I hope my movements here
        Have not disturbed your rest?'

25 'Ah, yes! You dig upon my grave . . .
        Why flashed it not on me
That one true heart was left behind!
What feeling do we ever find
To equal among human kind
30   A dog's fidelity!'

---

1. A yellow-flowered herb, traditionally an emblem of sorrow (*rue* is also an archaic word for "sorrow").

'Mistress, I dug upon your grave
        To bury a bone, in case
I should be hungry near this spot
        When passing on my daily trot.
35 I am sorry, but I quite forgot
        It was your resting-place.'

1914

In Time of 'The Breaking of Nations'[1]

1

Only a man harrowing clods
        In a slow silent walk
With an old horse that stumbles and nods
        Half asleep as they stalk.

2

5   Only thin smoke without flame
        From the heaps of couch-grass;
Yet this will go onward the same
        Though Dynasties pass.

3

Yonder a maid and her wight°   man
10   Come whispering by:
War's annals will cloud into night
        Ere their story die.

1915   1916, 1917

He Never Expected Much

[or]

A CONSIDERATION
(A reflection) On my Eighty-Sixth Birthday

Well, World, you have kept faith with me,
        Kept faith with me;
Upon the whole you have proved to be
        Much as you said you were.
5   Since as a child I used to lie
Upon the leaze° and watch the sky,   pasture
Never, I own, expected I
        That life would all be fair.

'Twas then you said, and since have said,
10   Times since have said,

---

1. Cf. "Thou art my battle axe and weapon of war: for with thee will I break in pieces the nations" (Jeremiah 51.20). The poem was written during World War I.

In that mysterious voice you shed
From clouds and hills around:
'Many have loved me desperately,
Many with smooth serenity,
15   While some have shown contempt of me
Till they dropped underground.

'I do not promise overmuch,
Child; overmuch;
Just neutral-tinted haps° and such,'   *happenings*
20   You said to minds like mine.
Wise warning for your credit's sake!
Which I for one failed not to take,
And hence could stem such strain and ache
As each year might assign.

1926   1928

JOSEPH CONRAD
1857–1924

Joseph Conrad was born Józef Teodor Konrad Korzeniowski in Poland (then under Russian rule), son of a Polish patriot who suffered exile in Russia for his Polish nationalist activities and died in 1869, leaving Conrad to be brought up by a maternal uncle. At the age of fifteen he amazed his family and friends by announcing his passionate desire to go to sea; he was eventually allowed to go to Marseilles, France, in 1874, and from there he made a number of voyages on French merchant ships to Martinique and other islands in the Caribbean. In 1878 he signed on an English ship that brought him to the east coast English port of Lowestoft, where (still as an ordinary seaman) he joined the crew of a small coasting vessel plying between Lowestoft and Newcastle. In six voyages between these two ports he learned English. Thus launched on a career in the British merchant service, Conrad sailed on a variety of British ships to East Asia, Australia, India, South America, and Africa, eventually gaining his master's certificate in 1886, the year he became a naturalized British subject. He received his first command in 1888, and in 1890 took a steamboat up the Congo River in nightmarish circumstances (described in *Heart of Darkness*, 1899) that permanently afflicted his health and his imagination.

In the early 1890s he was already thinking of turning some of his Malayan experiences into English fiction, and in 1892–93, when serving as first mate on the *Torrens* sailing from London to Adelaide, he revealed to a sympathetic passenger that he had begun a novel (*Almayer's Folly*), while on the return journey he impressed the young novelist John Galsworthy, who was on board, with his conversation. Conrad found it difficult to obtain a command, and this difficulty, together with the interest aroused by *Almayer's Folly* when it was published in 1895, helped turn him away from the sea to a career as a writer. He settled in London and in 1896 married an Englishwoman. This son of a Polish patriot turned merchant seaman turned writer was henceforth—after twenty years at sea—an English novelist.

In his travels through Asian, African, and Caribbean landscapes that eventually made their way into his fiction, Conrad witnessed at close range the workings of

European empires, including the British, French, Belgian, Dutch, and German, that at the time controlled most of the earth's surface and were extracting from it vast quantities of raw materials and profiting from forced or cheap labor. In the essay "Geography and Some Explorers," Conrad describes the imperial exploitation he observed in Africa as "the vilest scramble for loot that ever disfigured the history of human conscience and geographical exploration." What he saw of the uses and abuses of imperial power helped make him deeply skeptical. Marlow, the intermediate narrator of *Heart of Darkness*, reflects: "The conquest of the earth, which mostly means the taking it away from those who have a different complexion or slightly flatter noses than ourselves, is not a pretty thing when you look into it too much. What redeems it is the idea only. An idea at the back of it. . . ." And yet in this novella, the ideas at the back of colonialism's ruthless greed and violence are hardly shown to redeem anything at all.

Conrad's questioning of the ethics of empire, perhaps harkening back to his childhood experience as a Pole under Russian occupation, is part of his many-faceted exploration of the ethical ambiguities in human experience. In his great novel *Lord Jim* (1900), which like *Heart of Darkness* uses the device of an intermediate narrator, he probes the meaning of a gross failure of duty on the part of a romantic and idealistic young sailor, and by presenting the hero's history from a series of different points of view sustains the ethical questioning to the end. By deploying intermediate narrators and multiple points of view in his fiction, he suggests the complexity of experience and the difficulty of judging human actions.

Although Conrad's plots and exotic settings recall imperial romance and Victorian tales of adventure, he helped develop modern narrative strategies—frame narration, fragmented perspective, flashbacks and flash-forwards, psychologically laden symbolism—that disrupt chronology, render meaning indeterminate, reveal unconscious drives, blur boundaries between civilization and barbarism, and radically cast in doubt epistemological and ethical certainties. Another indication of Conrad's modernist proclivities is the alienation of his characters. Many of his works expose the difficulty of true communion, while also paradoxically exposing how communion is sometimes unexpectedly forced on us, often with someone who may be on the surface our moral opposite, so that we are compelled into a mysterious recognition of our opposite as our true self. Other stories and novels—and Conrad wrote prolifically despite his late start—explore the ways in which the codes we live by are tested in moments of crisis, revealing either their inadequacy or our own. Imagination can corrupt (as with Lord Jim) or save (as in *The Shadow-Line*, 1917), and a total lack of it can either see a person through (Captain MacWhirr in *Typhoon*, 1902) or render a person comically ridiculous (Captain Mitchell in *Nostromo*, 1904). Set in an imaginary Latin American republic, *Nostromo* subtly studies the corrupting effects of politics and "material interests" on personal relationships. Conrad wrote two other political novels—*The Secret Agent* (1906) and *Under Western Eyes* (1911). The latter is a story of Dostoyevskian power about a Russian student who becomes involuntarily associated with antigovernment violence in czarist Russia and is maneuvered by circumstances into a position where, although a government spy, he has to pretend to be a revolutionary among revolutionaries. Having to pretend consistently to be the opposite of what he is, this character, like others in Conrad's fiction, is alienated, trapped, unable to communicate. Conrad was as much a pessimist as Hardy, but Conrad aesthetically embodied his pessimism in subtler ways.

He was also a great master of English prose, an astonishing fact given that English was his third language after Polish and French, that he was twenty-one before he learned English, and that to the end of his life he spoke English with a strong foreign accent. He approached English's linguistic and literary conventions aslant, but the seeming handicap of his foreignness helped him bring to the English novel a fresh geopolitical understanding, a formal seriousness, and a psychological depth, all of which opened up new possibilities for imaginative literature in English, as indicated by his profound, if vexed, influence on later writers as different from himself as the Nigerian Chinua Achebe and the Anglo-Trinidadian V. S. Naipaul.

Heart of Darkness

Heart of Darkness   This story is derived from Conrad's experience in the Congo in 1890. Like Marlow, the narrator of the story, Conrad had as a child determined one day to visit the heart of Africa. "It was in 1868, when nine years old or thereabouts, that while looking at a map of Africa at the time and putting my finger on the blank space then representing the unsolved mystery of that continent, I said to myself with absolute assurance and an amazing audacity which are no longer in my character now: 'When I grow up I shall go *there*' " (*A Personal Record*, 1912).

Conrad was promised a job as a Congo River pilot through the influence of his distant cousin Marguerite Poradowska, who lived in Brussels and knew important officials of the Belgian company that exploited the Congo. At this time the Congo, although nominally an independent state, the Congo Free State (État Indépendent du Congo), was virtually the personal property of Leopold II, king of Belgium, who made a fortune out of it. Later, the appalling abuses involved in the naked colonial exploitation that went on in the Congo were exposed to public view, and international criticism compelled the setting up of a committee of inquiry in 1904. From 1885 to 1908 masses of Congolese men were worked to death, women were raped, hands were cut off, villages were looted and burned. What Conrad saw in 1890 shocked him profoundly and shook his view of the moral basis of colonialism, of exploration and trade in newly discovered countries, indeed of civilization in general. "*Heart of Darkness* is experience, too," Conrad wrote in his 1917 "Author's Note," "but it is experience pushed a little (and only very little) beyond the actual facts of the case for the perfectly legitimate, I believe, purpose of bringing it home to the minds and bosoms of the readers." And later he told Edward Garnett: "Before the Congo I was just a mere animal."

Conrad arrived in Africa in May 1890 and made his way up the Congo River very much as described in *Heart of Darkness*. At Kinshasa (which Conrad spells Kinchassa) on Stanley Pool, which he reached after an exhausting two-hundred-mile trek from Matadi, near the mouth of the river, Conrad was taken aback to learn that the steamer of which he was to be captain had been damaged and was undergoing repairs. He was sent as supernumerary on another steamer to learn the river. This steamer was sent to Stanley Falls to collect and bring back to Kinshasa one Georges Antoine Klein, an agent of the company who had fallen so gravely ill that he died on board. Conrad then fell seriously ill and eventually returned to London in January 1891 without ever having served as a Congo River pilot. The Congo experience permanently impaired his health; it also permanently haunted his imagination. The nightmare atmosphere of *Heart of Darkness* is an accurate reflection of Conrad's response to his traumatic experience.

The theme of the story is partly the "choice of nightmares" facing whites in the Congo—either to become like the commercially minded manager, who sees Africa, its people, and its resources solely as instruments of financial gain, or to become like Kurtz, the self-tortured and corrupted idealist (inspired by Klein). The manager is a "hollow man" (T. S. Eliot used a quotation from this story as one epigraph for his poem "The Hollow Men"); his only objections to Kurtz are commercial, not moral: Kurtz's methods are "unsound" and would therefore lose the company money. At the last Kurtz seems to recognize the moral horror of his having succumbed to the dark temptations that African life posed for the European. "He had summed up—he had judged." But the story also has other levels of meaning, and the counterpointing of Western civilization in Europe with what that civilization has done in Africa (see the concluding interview between Marlow and Kurtz's "intended"—based on an interview between Conrad and the dead Klein's fiancée) throws out several of these. The story first appeared in *Blackwood's Magazine* in 1899 and was revised for book publication in 1902 as part of *Youth: A Narrative, and Two Other Stories.*

Heart of Darkness

1

The *Nellie*, a cruising yawl,[1] swung to her anchor without a flutter of the sails, and was at rest. The flood had made, the wind was nearly calm, and being bound down the river, the only thing for it was to come to and wait for the turn of the tide.

The sea-reach of the Thames stretched before us like the beginning of an interminable waterway. In the offing the sea and the sky were welded together without a joint, and in the luminous space the tanned sails of the barges drifting up with the tide seemed to stand still in red clusters of canvas sharply peaked, with gleams of varnished sprits. A haze rested on the low shores that ran out to sea in vanishing flatness. The air was dark above Gravesend,[2] and farther back still seemed condensed into a mournful gloom, brooding motionless over the biggest, and the greatest, town on earth.

The Director of Companies was our captain and our host. We four affectionately watched his back as he stood in the bows looking to seaward. On the whole river there was nothing that looked half so nautical. He resembled a pilot, which to a seaman is trustworthiness personified. It was difficult to realise his work was not out there in the luminous estuary, but behind him, within the brooding gloom.

Between us there was, as I have already said somewhere, the bond of the sea. Besides holding our hearts together through long periods of separation, it had the effect of making us tolerant of each other's yarns—and even convictions. The Lawyer—the best of old fellows—had, because of his many years and many virtues, the only cushion on deck, and was lying on the only rug. The Accountant had brought out already a box of dominoes, and was toying architecturally with the bones. Marlow sat cross-legged right aft, leaning against the mizzenmast. He had sunken cheeks, a yellow complexion, a straight back, an ascetic aspect, and, with his arms dropped, the palms of hands outwards, resembled an idol. The Director, satisfied the anchor had good hold, made his way aft and sat down amongst us. We exchanged a few words lazily. Afterwards there was silence on board the yacht. For some reason or other we did not begin that game of dominoes. We felt meditative, and fit for nothing but placid staring. The day was ending in a serenity of still and exquisite brilliance. The water shone pacifically; the sky, without a speck, was a benign immensity of unstained light; the very mist on the Essex marshes was like a gauzy and radiant fabric, hung from the wooded rises inland, and draping the low shores in diaphanous folds. Only the gloom to the west, brooding over the upper reaches, became more sombre every minute, as if angered by the approach of the sun.

And at last, in its curved and imperceptible fall, the sun sank low, and from glowing white changed to a dull red without rays and without heat, as if about

1. Two-masted boat.
2. River port on the south bank of the Thames twenty-four miles east (downriver) of London.

to go out suddenly, stricken to death by the touch of that gloom brooding over a crowd of men.

Forthwith a change came over the waters, and the serenity became less brilliant but more profound. The old river in its broad reach rested unruffled at the decline of day, after ages of good service done to the race that peopled its banks, spread out in the tranquil dignity of a waterway leading to the uttermost ends of the earth. We looked at the venerable stream not in the vivid flush of a short day that comes and departs for ever, but in the august light of abiding memories. And indeed nothing is easier for a man who has, as the phrase goes, "followed the sea" with reverence and affection, than to evoke the great spirit of the past upon the lower reaches of the Thames. The tidal current runs to and fro in its unceasing service, crowded with memories of men and ships it has borne to the rest of home or to the battles of the sea. It had known and served all the men of whom the nation is proud, from Sir Francis Drake to Sir John Franklin,[3] knights all, titled and untitled—the great knights-errant of the sea. It had borne all the ships whose names are like jewels flashing in the night of time, from the *Golden Hind* returning with her round flanks full of treasure, to be visited by the Queen's Highness and thus pass out of the gigantic tale, to the *Erebus* and *Terror*, bound on other conquests—and that never returned. It had known the ships and the men. They had sailed from Deptford, from Greenwich, from Erith—the adventurers and the settlers; kings' ships and the ships of men on 'Change; captains, admirals, the dark "interlopers"[4] of the Eastern trade, and the commissioned "generals" of East India fleets. Hunters for gold or pursuers of fame, they all had gone out on that stream, bearing the sword, and often the torch, messengers of the might within the land, bearers of a spark from the sacred fire. What greatness had not floated on the ebb of that river into the mystery of an unknown earth! . . . The dreams of men, the seed of commonwealths, the germs of empires.

The sun set; the dusk fell on the stream, and lights began to appear along the shore. The Chapman lighthouse, a three-legged thing erect on a mud-flat, shone strongly. Lights of ships moved in the fairway[5]—a great stir of lights going up and going down. And farther west on the upper reaches the place of the monstrous town was still marked ominously on the sky, a brooding gloom in sunshine, a lurid glare under the stars.

"And this also," said Marlow suddenly, "has been one of the dark places of the earth."

He was the only man of us who still "followed the sea." The worst that could be said of him was that he did not represent his class. He was a seaman, but he was a wanderer too, while most seamen lead, if one may so express it, a sedentary life. Their minds are of the stay-at-home order, and their home is always with them—the ship; and so is their country—the sea. One ship is very much like another, and the sea is always the same. In the immutability of their

---

3. Sir John Franklin (1786–1847), Arctic explorer who in 1845 commanded an expedition consisting of the ships *Erebus* and *Terror* in search of the Northwest Passage. The ships never returned. Sir Francis Drake (ca. 1540–1596), Elizabethan naval hero and explorer, sailed around the world on his ship *The Golden Hind*. Queen Elizabeth knighted Drake aboard his ship, loaded with captured Spanish treasure, on his return.
4. Private ships muscling in on the monopoly of the East India Company, which was founded in 1600, lost its trading monopoly in 1813, and transferred its governmental functions to the Crown in 1858. Deptford, on the south bank of the Thames, on the eastern edge of London, was once an important dockyard. Greenwich is on the south bank of the Thames immediately east of Deptford. Erith is eight miles farther east. " 'Change": the Stock Exchange.
5. Navigable part of a river, through which ships enter and depart.

surroundings the foreign shores, the foreign faces, the changing immensity of life, glide past, veiled not by a sense of mystery but by a slightly disdainful ignorance; for there is nothing mysterious to a seaman unless it be the sea itself, which is the mistress of his existence and as inscrutable as Destiny. For the rest, after his hours of work, a casual stroll or a casual spree on shore suffices to unfold for him the secret of a whole continent, and generally he finds the secret not worth knowing. The yarns of seamen have a direct simplicity, the whole meaning of which lies within the shell of a cracked nut. But Marlow was not typical (if his propensity to spin yarns be excepted), and to him the meaning of an episode was not inside like a kernel but outside, enveloping the tale which brought it out only as a glow brings out a haze, in the likeness of one of these misty halos that sometimes are made visible by the spectral illumination of moonshine.

His remark did not seem at all surprising. It was just like Marlow. It was accepted in silence. No one took the trouble to grunt even; and presently he said, very slow:

"I was thinking of very old times, when the Romans first came here, nineteen hundred years ago—the other day. . . . Light came out of this river since—you say Knights? Yes; but it is like a running blaze on a plain, like a flash of lightning in the clouds. We live in the flicker—may it last as long as the old earth keeps rolling! But darkness was here yesterday. Imagine the feelings of a commander of a fine—what d'ye call 'em?—trireme[6] in the Mediterranean, ordered suddenly to the north; run overland across the Gauls in a hurry; put in charge of one of these craft the legionaries—a wonderful lot of handy men they must have been too—used to build, apparently by the hundred, in a month or two, if we may believe what we read. Imagine him here—the very end of the world, a sea the colour of lead, a sky the colour of smoke, a kind of ship about as rigid as a concertina—and going up this river with stores, or orders, or what you like. Sandbanks, marshes, forests, savages—precious little to eat fit for a civilised man, nothing but Thames water to drink. No Falernian wine[7] here, no going ashore. Here and there a military camp lost in a wilderness, like a needle in a bundle of hay—cold, fog, tempests, disease, exile, and death—death skulking in the air, in the water, in the bush. They must have been dying like flies here. Oh yes—he did it. Did it very well, too, no doubt, and without thinking much about it either, except afterwards to brag of what he had gone through in his time, perhaps. They were men enough to face the darkness. And perhaps he was cheered by keeping his eye on a chance of promotion to the fleet at Ravenna[8] by and by, if he had good friends in Rome and survived the awful climate. Or think of a decent young citizen in a toga—perhaps too much dice, you know—coming out here in the train of some prefect, or tax-gatherer, or trader, even, to mend his fortunes. Land in a swamp, march through the woods, and in some inland post feel the savagery, the utter savagery, had closed round him—all that mysterious life of the wilderness that stirs in the forest, in the jungles, in the hearts of wild men. There's no initiation either into such mysteries. He has to live in the midst of the incomprehensible, which is also detestable. And it has a fascination, too, that goes to work upon him. The fascination of the abomination—you know. Imag-

6. Ancient Greek and Roman galley with three ranks of oars.
7. Wine from a famed wine-making district in Campania (Italy).

8. A city in northern Italy once directly on the Adriatic Sea and an important naval station in Roman times. It is now about six miles from the sea, connected with it by a canal.

ine the growing regrets, the longing to escape, the powerless disgust, the surrender, the hate."

He paused.

"Mind," he began again, lifting one arm from the elbow, the palm of the hand outwards, so that, with his legs folded before him, he had the pose of a Buddha preaching in European clothes and without a lotus-flower—"Mind, none of us would feel exactly like this. What saves us is efficiency—the devotion to efficiency. But these chaps were not much account, really. They were no colonists; their administration was merely a squeeze, and nothing more, I suspect. They were conquerors, and for that you want only brute force—nothing to boast of, when you have it, since your strength is just an accident arising from the weakness of others. They grabbed what they could get for the sake of what was to be got. It was just robbery with violence, aggravated murder on a great scale, and men going at it blind—as is very proper for those who tackle a darkness. The conquest of the earth, which mostly means the taking it away from those who have a different complexion or slightly flatter noses than ourselves, is not a pretty thing when you look into it too much. What redeems it is the idea only. An idea at the back of it; not a sentimental pretence but an idea; and an unselfish belief in the idea—something you can set up, and bow down before, and offer a sacrifice to. . . ."

He broke off. Flames glided in the river, small green flames, red flames, white flames, pursuing, overtaking, joining, crossing each other—then separating slowly or hastily. The traffic of the great city went on in the deepening night upon the sleepless river. We looked on, waiting patiently—there was nothing else to do till the end of the flood; but it was only after a long silence, when he said, in a hesitating voice, "I suppose you fellows remember I did once turn fresh-water sailor for a bit," that we knew we were fated, before the ebb began to run, to hear about one of Marlow's inconclusive experiences.

"I don't want to bother you much with what happened to me personally," he began, showing in this remark the weakness of many tellers of tales who seem so often unaware of what their audience would best like to hear; "yet to understand the effect of it on me you ought to know how I got out there, what I saw, how I went up that river to the place where I first met the poor chap. It was the farthest point of navigation and the culminating point of my experience. It seemed somehow to throw a kind of light on everything about me—and into my thoughts. It was sombre enough too—and pitiful—not extraordinary in any way—not very clear either. No, not very clear. And yet it seemed to throw a kind of light.

"I had then, as you remember, just returned to London after a lot of Indian Ocean, Pacific, China Seas—a regular dose of the East—six years or so, and I was loafing about, hindering you fellows in your work and invading your homes, just as though I had got a heavenly mission to civilise you. It was very fine for a time, but after a bit I did get tired of resting. Then I began to look for a ship—I should think the hardest work on earth. But the ships wouldn't even look at me. And I got tired of that game too.

"Now when I was a little chap I had a passion for maps. I would look for hours at South America, or Africa, or Australia, and lose myself in all the glories of exploration. At that time there were many blank spaces on the earth, and when I saw one that looked particularly inviting on a map (but they all look that) I would put my finger on it and say, When I grow up I will go there. The North Pole was one of these places, I remember. Well, I haven't been there yet, and shall not try now. The glamour's off. Other places were scattered about the Equator, and in every sort of latitude all over the two hemispheres. I have been in some of them, and . . . well, we won't talk about that. But there was one yet—the biggest, the most blank, so to speak—that I had a hankering after.

"True, by this time it was not a blank space any more. It had got filled since my boyhood with rivers and lakes and names. It had ceased to be a blank space of delightful mystery—a white patch for a boy to dream gloriously over. It had become a place of darkness. But there was in it one river especially, a mighty big river, that you could see on the map, resembling an immense snake uncoiled, with its head in the sea, its body at rest curving afar over a vast country, and its tail lost in the depths of the land. And as I looked at the map of it in a shop-window, it fascinated me as a snake would a bird—a silly little bird. Then I remembered there was a big concern, a Company for trade on that river. Dash it all! I thought to myself, they can't trade without using some kind of craft on that lot of fresh water—steamboats! Why shouldn't I try to get charge of one? I went on along Fleet Street,[9] but could not shake off the idea. The snake had charmed me.

"You understand it was a Continental concern, that Trading Society; but I have a lot of relations living on the Continent, because it's cheap and not so nasty as it looks, they say.

"I am sorry to own I began to worry them. This was already a fresh departure for me. I was not used to get things that way, you know. I always went my own road and on my own legs where I had a mind to go. I wouldn't have believed it of myself; but, then—you see—I felt somehow I must get there by hook or by crook. So I worried them. The men said, 'My dear fellow,' and did nothing. Then—would you believe it?—I tried the women. I, Charlie Marlow, set the women to work—to get a job. Heavens! Well, you see, the notion drove me. I had an aunt, a dear enthusiastic soul. She wrote: 'It will be delightful. I am ready to do anything, anything for you. It is a glorious idea. I know the wife of a very high personage in the Administration, and also a man who has lots of influence with,' etc. etc. She was determined to make no end of fuss to get me appointed skipper of a river steamboat, if such was my fancy.

"I got my appointment—of course; and I got it very quick. It appears the Company had received news that one of their captains had been killed in a scuffle with the natives. This was my chance, and it made me the more anxious to go. It was only months and months afterwards, when I made the attempt to recover what was left of the body, that I heard the original quarrel arose from a misunderstanding about some hens. Yes, two black hens. Fresleven—that was the fellow's name, a Dane—thought himself wronged somehow in the bargain, so he went ashore and started to hammer the chief of the village with a stick. Oh, it didn't surprise me in the least to hear this, and at the same time to be told that Fresleven was the gentlest, quietest creature that ever walked on two legs. No doubt he was; but he had been a couple of years already out there engaged in the noble cause, you know, and he probably felt the need at last of asserting his self-respect in some way. Therefore he whacked the old nigger mercilessly, while a big crowd of his people watched him, thunder-struck, till some man—I was told the chief's son—in desperation at hearing the old chap yell, made a tentative jab with a spear at the white man—and of

9. Street in central London.

course it went quite easy between the shoulder-blades. Then the whole population cleared into the forest, expecting all kinds of calamities to happen,
while, on the other hand, the steamer Fresleven commanded left also in a bad
panic, in charge of the engineer, I believe. Afterwards nobody seemed to trouble much about Fresleven's remains, till I got out and stepped into his shoes.
I couldn't let it rest, though; but when an opportunity offered at last to meet
my predecessor, the grass growing through his ribs was tall enough to hide his
bones. They were all there. The supernatural being had not been touched after
he fell. And the village was deserted, the huts gaped black, rotting, all askew
within the fallen enclosures. A calamity had come to it, sure enough. The
people had vanished. Mad terror had scattered them, men, women, and children, through the bush, and they had never returned. What became of the
hens I don't know either. I should think the cause of progress got them, anyhow. However, through this glorious affair I got my appointment, before I had
fairly begun to hope for it.

"I flew around like mad to get ready, and before forty-eight hours I was
crossing the Channel to show myself to my employers, and sign the contract.
In a very few hours I arrived in a city that always makes me think of a whited
sepulchre. Prejudice no doubt. I had no difficulty in finding the Company's
offices. It was the biggest thing in the town, and everybody I met was full of
it. They were going to run an over-sea empire, and make no end of coin by
trade.

"A narrow and deserted street in deep shadow, high houses, innumerable
windows with venetian blinds, a dead silence, grass sprouting between the
stones, imposing carriage archways right and left, immense double doors
standing ponderously ajar. I slipped through one of these cracks, went up a
swept and ungarnished staircase, as arid as a desert, and opened the first door
I came to. Two women, one fat and the other slim, sat on straw-bottomed
chairs, knitting black wool. The slim one got up and walked straight at me—
still knitting with downcast eyes—and only just as I began to think of getting
out of her way, as you would for a somnambulist, stood still, and looked up.
Her dress was as plain as an umbrella-cover, and she turned round without a
word and preceded me into a waiting-room. I gave my name, and looked about.
Deal table in the middle, plain chairs all round the walls, on one end a large
shining map, marked with all the colours of a rainbow. There was a vast
amount of red—good to see at any time, because one knows that some real
work is done in there, a deuce of a lot of blue, a little green, smears of orange,
and, on the East Coast, a purple patch, to show where the jolly pioneers of
progress drink the jolly lager-beer. However, I wasn't going into any of these.
I was going into the yellow. Dead in the centre. And the river was there—
fascinating—deadly—like a snake. Ough! A door opened, a white-haired secretarial head, but wearing a compassionate expression, appeared, and a skinny
forefinger beckoned me into the sanctuary. Its light was dim, and a heavy
writing desk squatted in the middle. From behind that structure came out an
impression of pale plumpness in a frockcoat. The great man himself. He was
five feet six, I should judge, and had his grip on the handle-end of ever so
many millions. He shook hands, I fancy, murmured vaguely, was satisfied with
my French. *Bon voyage.*

"In about forty-five seconds I found myself again in the waiting-room with
the compassionate secretary, who, full of desolation and sympathy, made me

sign some document. I believe I undertook amongst other things not to disclose any trade secrets. Well, I am not going to.

"I began to feel slightly uneasy. You know I am not used to such ceremonies, and there was something ominous in the atmosphere. It was just as though I had been let into some conspiracy—I don't know—something not quite right; and I was glad to get out. In the outer room the two women knitted black wool feverishly. People were arriving, and the younger one was walking back and forth introducing them. The old one sat on her chair. Her flat cloth slippers were propped up on a foot-warmer, and a cat reposed on her lap. She wore a starched white affair on her head, had a wart on one cheek, and silver-rimmed spectacles hung on the tip of her nose. She glanced at me above the glasses. The swift and indifferent placidity of that look troubled me. Two youths with foolish and cheery countenances were being piloted over, and she threw at them the same quick glance of unconcerned wisdom. She seemed to know all about them and about me too. An eerie feeling came over me. She seemed uncanny and fateful. Often far away there I thought of these two, guarding the door of Darkness, knitting black wool as for a warm pall, one introducing, introducing continuously to the unknown, the other scrutinising the cheery and foolish faces with unconcerned old eyes. *Ave!* Old knitter of black wool. *Morituri te salutant.*[1] Not many of those she looked at ever saw her again—not half, by a long way.

"There was yet a visit to the doctor. 'A simple formality,' assured me the secretary, with an air of taking an immense part in all my sorrows. Accordingly a young chap wearing his hat over the left eyebrow, some clerk I suppose—there must have been clerks in the business, though the house was as still as a house in a city of the dead—came from somewhere upstairs, and led me forth. He was shabby and careless, with ink-stains on the sleeves of his jacket, and his cravat was large and billowy, under a chin shaped like the toe of an old boot. It was a little too early for the doctor, so I proposed a drink, and thereupon he developed a vein of joviality. As we sat over our vermuths he glorified the Company's business, and by and by I expressed casually my surprise at him not going out there. He became very cool and collected all at once. 'I am not such a fool as I look, quoth Plato to his disciples,' he said sententiously, emptied his glass with great resolution, and we rose.

"The old doctor felt my pulse, evidently thinking of something else the while. 'Good, good for there,' he mumbled, and then with a certain eagerness asked me whether I would let him measure my head. Rather surprised, I said Yes, when he produced a thing like callipers and got the dimensions back and front and every way, taking notes carefully. He was an unshaven little man in a threadbare coat like a gaberdine, with his feet in slippers, and I thought him a harmless fool. 'I always ask leave, in the interests of science, to measure the crania of those going out there,' he said. 'And when they come back too?' I asked. 'Oh, I never see them,' he remarked; 'and, moreover, the changes take place inside, you know.' He smiled, as if at some quiet joke. 'So you are going out there. Famous. Interesting too.' He gave me a searching glance, and made another note. 'Ever any madness in your family?' he asked, in a matter-of-fact tone. I felt very annoyed. 'Is that question in the interests of science too?' 'It

---

1. "Hail! . . . Those who are about to die salute you" (Latin). The Roman gladiators' salute to the emperor on entering the arena.

would be,' he said, without taking notice of my irritation, 'interesting for science to watch the mental changes of individuals, on the spot, but . . . ' 'Are you an alienist?'[2] I interrupted. 'Every doctor should be—a little,' answered that original[3] imperturbably. 'I have a little theory which you Messieurs who go out there must help me to prove. This is my share in the advantages my country shall reap from the possession of such a magnificent dependency. The mere wealth I leave to others. Pardon my questions, but you are the first Englishman coming under my observation . . . ' I hastened to assure him I was not in the least typical. 'If I were,' said I, 'I wouldn't be talking like this with you.' 'What you say is rather profound, and probably erroneous,' he said, with a laugh. 'Avoid irritation more than exposure to the sun. Adieu. How do you English say, eh? Good-bye. Ah! Good-bye. Adieu. In the tropics one must before everything keep calm.' . . . He lifted a warning forefinger. . . . 'Du calme, du calme. Adieu.'

"One thing more remained to do—say good-bye to my excellent aunt. I found her triumphant. I had a cup of tea—the last decent cup of tea for many days—and in a room that most soothingly looked just as you would expect a lady's drawing-room to look, we had a long quiet chat by the fireside. In the course of these confidences it became quite plain to me I had been represented to the wife of the high dignitary, and goodness knows to how many more people besides, as an exceptional and gifted creature—a piece of good fortune for the Company—a man you don't get hold of every day. Good heavens! and I was going to take charge of a two-penny-halfpenny river-steamboat with a penny whistle attached! It appeared, however, I was also one of the Workers, with a capital—you know. Something like an emissary of light, something like a lower sort of apostle. There had been a lot of such rot let loose in print and talk just about that time, and the excellent woman, living right in the rush of all that humbug, got carried off her feet. She talked about 'weaning those ignorant millions from their horrid ways,' till, upon my word, she made me quite uncomfortable. I ventured to hint that the Company was run for profit.

" 'You forget, dear Charlie, that the labourer is worthy of his hire,' she said brightly. It's queer how out of touch with truth women are. They live in a world of their own, and there had never been anything like it, and never can be. It is too beautiful altogether, and if they were to set it up it would go to pieces before the first sunset. Some confounded fact we men have been living contentedly with ever since the day of creation would start up and knock the whole thing over.

"After this I got embraced, told to wear flannel, be sure to write often, and so on—and I left. In the street—I don't know why—a queer feeling came to me that I was an impostor. Odd thing that I, who used to clear out for any part of the world at twenty-four hours' notice, with less thought than most men give to the crossing of a street, had a moment—I won't say of hesitation, but of startled pause, before this commonplace affair. The best way I can explain it to you is by saying that, for a second or two, I felt as though, instead of going to the centre of a continent, I were about to set off for the centre of the earth.

"I left in a French steamer, and she called in every blamed port they have out there, for, as far as I could see, the sole purpose of landing soldiers and

2. Doctor who treats mental diseases. (The term has now been replaced by psychiatrist.)

3. Eccentric person.

custom-house officers. I watched the coast. Watching a coast as it slips by the ship is like thinking about an enigma. There it is before you—smiling, frowning, inviting, grand, mean, insipid, or savage, and always mute with an air of whispering, Come and find out. This one was almost featureless, as if still in the making, with an aspect of monotonous grimness. The edge of a colossal jungle, so dark green as to be almost black, fringed with white surf, ran straight, like a ruled line, far, far away along a blue sea whose glitter was blurred by a creeping mist. The sun was fierce, the land seemed to glisten and drip with steam. Here and there greyish-whitish specks showed up clustered inside the white surf, with a flag flying above them perhaps—settlements some centuries old, and still no bigger than pin-heads on the untouched expanse of their background. We pounded along, stopped, landed soldiers; went on, landed custom-house clerks to levy toll in what looked like a God-forsaken wilderness, with a tin shed and a flag-pole lost in it; landed more soldiers—to take care of the custom-house clerks presumably. Some, I heard, got drowned in the surf; but whether they did or not, nobody seemed particularly to care. They were just flung out there, and on we went. Every day the coast looked the same, as though we had not moved; but we passed various places—trading places—with names like Gran' Bassam, Little Popo; names that seemed to belong to some sordid farce acted in front of a sinister back-cloth. The idleness of a passenger, my isolation amongst all these men with whom I had no point of contact, the oily and languid sea, the uniform sombreness of the coast, seemed to keep me away from the truth of things, within the toil of a mournful and senseless delusion. The voice of the surf heard now and then was a positive pleasure, like the speech of a brother. It was something natural, that had its reason, that had a meaning. Now and then a boat from the shore gave one a momentary contact with reality. It was paddled by black fellows. You could see from afar the white of their eyeballs glistening. They shouted, sang; their bodies streamed with perspiration; they had faces like grotesque masks—these chaps; but they had bone, muscle, a wild vitality, an intense energy of movement, that was as natural and true as the surf along their coast. They wanted no excuse for being there. They were a great comfort to look at. For a time I would feel I belonged still to a world of straightforward facts; but the feeling would not last long. Something would turn up to scare it away. Once, I remember, we came upon a man-of-war anchored off the coast. There wasn't even a shed there, and she was shelling the bush. It appears the French had one of their wars going on thereabouts. Her ensign dropped limp like a rag; the muzzles of the long six-inch guns stuck out all over the low hull; the greasy, slimy swell swung her up lazily and let her down, swaying her thin masts. In the empty immensity of earth, sky, and water, there she was, incomprehensible, firing into a continent. Pop, would go one of the six-inch guns; a small flame would dart and vanish, a little white smoke would disappear, a tiny projectile would give a feeble screech—and nothing happened. Nothing could happen. There was a touch of insanity in the proceeding, a sense of lugubrious drollery in the sight; and it was not dissipated by somebody on board assuring me earnestly there was a camp of natives—he called them enemies!—hidden out of sight somewhere.

"We gave her her letters (I heard the men in that lonely ship were dying of fever at the rate of three a day) and went on. We called at some more places with farcical names, where the merry dance of death and trade goes on in a still and earthy atmosphere as of an overheated catacomb; all along the formless coast bordered by dangerous surf, as if Nature herself had tried to ward off intruders; in and out of rivers, streams of death in life, whose banks were rotting into mud, whose waters, thickened into slime, invaded the contorted mangroves,[4] that seemed to writhe at us in the extremity of an impotent despair. Nowhere did we stop long enough to get a particularised impression, but the general sense of vague and oppressive wonder grew upon me. It was like a weary pilgrimage amongst hints for nightmares.

"It was upward of thirty days before I saw the mouth of the big river. We anchored off the seat of the government. But my work would not begin till some two hundred miles farther on. So as soon as I could I made a start for a place thirty miles higher up.

"I had my passage on a little sea-going steamer. Her captain was a Swede, and knowing me for a seaman, invited me on the bridge. He was a young man, lean, fair, and morose, with lanky hair and a shuffling gait. As we left the miserable little wharf, he tossed his head contemptuously at the shore. 'Been living there?' he asked. I said, 'Yes.' 'Fine lot these government chaps—are they not?' he went on, speaking English with great precision and considerable bitterness. 'It is funny what some people will do for a few francs a month. I wonder what becomes of that kind when it goes up country?' I said to him I expected to see that soon. 'So-o-o!' he exclaimed. He shuffled athwart, keeping one eye ahead vigilantly. 'Don't be too sure,' he continued. 'The other day I took up a man who hanged himself on the road. He was a Swede, too.' 'Hanged himself! Why, in God's name?' I cried. He kept on looking out watchfully. 'Who knows? The sun too much for him, or the country perhaps.'

"At last we opened a reach. A rocky cliff appeared, mounds of turned-up earth by the shore, houses on a hill, others with iron roofs, amongst a waste of excavations, or hanging to the declivity. A continuous noise of the rapids above hovered over this scene of inhabited devastation. A lot of people, mostly black and naked, moved about like ants. A jetty[5] projected into the river. A blinding sunlight drowned all this at times in a sudden recrudescence of glare. 'There's your Company's station,' said the Swede, pointing to three wooden barrack-like structures on the rocky slope. 'I will send your things up. Four boxes did you say? So. Farewell.'

"I came upon a boiler wallowing in the grass, then found a path leading up the hill. It turned aside for the boulders, and also for an undersized railway truck lying there on its back with its wheels in the air. One was off. The thing looked as dead as the carcass of some animal. I came upon more pieces of decaying machinery, a stack of rusty nails. To the left a clump of trees made a shady spot, where dark things seemed to stir feebly. I blinked, the path was steep. A horn tooted to the right, and I saw the black people run. A heavy and dull detonation shook the ground, a puff of smoke came out of the cliff, and that was all. No change appeared on the face of the rock. They were building a railway. The cliff was not in the way or anything; but this objectless blasting was all the work going on.

"A slight clinking behind me made me turn my head. Six black men advanced in a file, toiling up the path. They walked erect and slow, balancing small baskets full of earth on their heads, and the clink kept time with their footsteps. Black rags were wound round their loins, and the short ends behind waggled to and fro like tails. I could see every rib, the joints of their limbs were

4. Tropical evergreen trees or shrubs with roots and stems forming dense thickets. 5. Wharf or pier.

like knots in a rope; each had an iron collar on his neck, and all were connected together with a chain whose bights swung between them, rhythmically clinking. Another report from the cliff made me think suddenly of that ship of war I had seen firing into a continent. It was the same kind of ominous voice; but these men could by no stretch of imagination be called enemies. They were called criminals, and the outraged law, like the bursting shells, had come to them, an insoluble mystery from the sea. All their meagre breasts panted together, the violently dilated nostrils quivered, the eyes stared stonily uphill. They passed me within six inches, without a glance, with that complete, death-like indifference of unhappy savages. Behind this raw matter one of the reclaimed, the product of the new forces at work, strolled despondently, carrying a rifle by its middle. He had a uniform jacket with one button off, and seeing a white man on the path, hoisted his weapon to his shoulder with alacrity. This was simple prudence, white men being so much alike at a distance that he could not tell who I might be. He was speedily reassured, and with a large, white, rascally grin, and a glance at his charge, seemed to take me into partnership in his exalted trust. After all, I also was a part of the great cause of these high and just proceedings.

"Instead of going up, I turned and descended to the left. My idea was to let that chain-gang get out of sight before I climbed the hill. You know I am not particularly tender; I've had to strike and to fend off. I've had to resist and to attack sometimes—that's only one way of resisting—without counting the exact cost, according to the demands of such sort of life as I had blundered into. I've seen the devil of violence, and the devil of greed, and the devil of hot desire; but, by all the stars! these were strong, lusty, red-eyed devils, that swayed and drove men—men, I tell you. But as I stood on this hillside, I foresaw that in the blinding sunshine of that land I would become acquainted with a flabby, pretending, weak-eyed devil of a rapacious and pitiless folly. How insidious he could be, too, I was only to find out several months later and a thousand miles farther. For a moment I stood appalled, as though by a warning. Finally I descended the hill, obliquely, towards the trees I had seen.

"I avoided a vast artificial hole somebody had been digging on the slope, the purpose of which I found it impossible to divine. It wasn't a quarry or a sandpit, anyhow. It was just a hole. It might have been connected with the philanthropic desire of giving the criminals something to do. I don't know. Then I nearly fell into a very narrow ravine, almost no more than a scar in the hillside. I discovered that a lot of imported drainage-pipes for the settlement had been tumbled in there. There wasn't one that was not broken. It was a wanton smash-up. At last I got under the trees. My purpose was to stroll into the shade for a moment; but no sooner within than it seemed to me I had stepped into the gloomy circle of some Inferno. The rapids were near, and an uninterrupted, uniform, headlong, rushing noise filled the mournful stillness of the grove, where not a breath stirred, not a leaf moved, with a mysterious sound—as though the tearing pace of the launched earth had suddenly become audible.

"Black shapes crouched, lay, sat between the trees, leaning against the trunks, clinging to the earth, half coming out, half effaced within the dim light, in all the attitudes of pain, abandonment, and despair. Another mine on the cliff went off, followed by a slight shudder of the soil under my feet. The work was going on. The work! And this was the place where some of the helpers had withdrawn to die.

"They were dying slowly—it was very clear. They were not enemies, they were not criminals, they were nothing earthly now—nothing but black shadows of disease and starvation, lying confusedly in the greenish gloom. Brought from all the recesses of the coast in all the legality of time contracts, lost in uncongenial surroundings, fed on unfamiliar food, they sickened, became inefficient, and were then allowed to crawl away and rest. These moribund shapes were free as air—and nearly as thin. I began to distinguish the gleam of eyes under the trees. Then, glancing down, I saw a face near my hand. The black bones reclined at full length with one shoulder against the tree, and slowly the eyelids rose and the sunken eyes looked up at me, enormous and vacant, a kind of blind, white flicker in the depths of the orbs, which died out slowly. The man seemed young—almost a boy—but you know with them it's hard to tell. I found nothing else to do but to offer him one of my good Swede's ship's biscuits I had in my pocket. The fingers closed slowly on it and held—there was no other movement and no other glance. He had tied a bit of white worsted[6] round his neck—Why? Where did he get it? Was it a badge—an ornament—a charm—a propitiatory act? Was there any idea at all connected with it? It looked startling round his black neck, this bit of white thread from beyond the seas.

"Near the same tree two more bundles of acute angles sat with their legs drawn up. One, with his chin propped on his knees, stared at nothing, in an intolerable and appalling manner: his brother phantom rested its forehead, as if overcome with a great weariness; and all about others were scattered in every pose of contorted collapse, as in some picture of a massacre or a pestilence. While I stood horror-struck, one of these creatures rose to his hands and knees, and went off on all-fours towards the river to drink. He lapped out of his hand, then sat up in the sunlight, crossing his shins in front of him, and after a time let his woolly head fall on his breastbone.

"I didn't want any more loitering in the shade, and I made haste towards the station. When near the buildings I met a white man, in such an unexpected elegance of get-up that in the first moment I took him for a sort of vision. I saw a high starched collar, white cuffs, a light alpaca[7] jacket, snowy trousers, a clear necktie, and varnished boots. No hat. Hair parted, brushed, oiled, under a green-lined parasol held in a big white hand. He was amazing, and had a penholder behind his ear.

"I shook hands with this miracle, and I learned he was the Company's chief accountant, and that all the book-keeping was done at this station. He had come out for a moment, he said, 'to get a breath of fresh air.' The expression sounded wonderfully odd, with its suggestion of sedentary desk-life. I wouldn't have mentioned the fellow to you at all, only it was from his lips that I first heard the name of the man who is so indissolubly connected with the memories of that time. Moreover, I respected the fellow. Yes; I respected his collars, his vast cuffs, his brushed hair. His appearance was certainly that of a hairdresser's dummy; but in the great demoralisation of the land he kept up his appearance. That's backbone. His starched collars and got-up shirt-fronts were achievements of character. He had been out nearly three years; and, later, I could not help asking him how he managed to sport such linen. He had just the faintest blush, and said modestly, 'I've been teaching one of the native women about the station. It was difficult. She had a distaste for the work.'

---

6. Fine wool fabric.
7. Made from the wool of a South American animal by that name.

Thus this man had verily accomplished something. And he was devoted to his books, which were in apple-pie order.

"Everything else in the station was in a muddle,—heads, things, buildings. Strings of dusty niggers with splay feet arrived and departed; a stream of manufactured goods, rubbishy cottons, beads, and brass-wire sent into the depths of darkness, and in return came a precious trickle of ivory.

"I had to wait in the station for ten days—an eternity. I lived in a hut in the yard, but to be out of the chaos I would sometimes get into the accountant's office. It was built of horizontal planks, and so badly put together that, as he bent over his high desk, he was barred from neck to heels with narrow strips of sunlight. There was no need to open the big shutter to see. It was hot there too; big flies buzzed fiendishly, and did not sting, but stabbed. I sat generally on the floor, while, of faultless appearance (and even slightly scented), perching on a high stool, he wrote, he wrote. Sometimes he stood up for exercise. When a truckle-bed with a sick man (some invalided agent from up country) was put in there, he exhibited a gentle annoyance. 'The groans of this sick person' he said, 'distract my attention. And without that it is extremely difficult to guard against clerical errors in this climate.'

"One day he remarked, without lifting his head, 'In the interior you will no doubt meet Mr Kurtz.' On my asking who Mr Kurtz was, he said he was a first-class agent; and seeing my disappointment at this information, he added slowly, laying down his pen, 'He is a very remarkable person.' Further questions elicited from him that Mr Kurtz was at present in charge of a trading-post, a very important one, in the true ivory-country, at 'the very bottom of there. Sends in as much ivory as all the others put together . . . ' He began to write again. The sick man was too ill to groan. The flies buzzed in a great peace.

"Suddenly there was a growing murmur of voices and a great tramping of feet. A caravan had come in. A violent babble of uncouth sounds burst out on the other side of the planks. All the carriers were speaking together, and in the midst of the uproar the lamentable voice of the chief agent was heard 'giving it up' tearfully for the twentieth time that day. . . . He rose slowly. 'What a frightful row,' he said. He crossed the room gently to look at the sick man, and returning, said to me, 'He does not hear.' 'What! Dead?' I asked, startled. 'No, not yet,' he answered, with great composure. Then, alluding with a toss of the head to the tumult in the station-yard, 'When one has got to make correct entries, one comes to hate those savages—hate them to the death.' He remained thoughtful for a moment. 'When you see Mr Kurtz,' he went on, 'tell him from me that everything here'—he glanced at the desk—'is very satisfactory. I don't like to write to him—with those messengers of ours you never know who may get hold of your letter—at that Central Station.' He stared at me for a moment with his mild, bulging eyes. 'Oh, he will go far, very far,' he began again. 'He will be a somebody in the Administration before long. They, above—the Council in Europe, you know—mean him to be.'

"He turned to his work. The noise outside had ceased, and presently in going out I stopped at the door. In the steady buzz of flies the homeward-bound agent was lying flushed and insensible; the other, bent over his books, was making correct entries of perfectly correct transactions; and fifty feet below the doorstep I could see the still tree-tops of the grove of death.

"Next day I left that station at last, with a caravan of sixty men, for a two-hundred-mile tramp.

"No use telling you much about that. Paths, paths, everywhere; a stamped-in network of paths spreading over the empty land, through long grass, through burnt grass, through thickets, down and up chilly ravines, up and down stony hills ablaze with heat; and a solitude, a solitude, nobody, not a hut. The population had cleared out a long time ago. Well, if a lot of mysterious niggers armed with all kinds of fearful weapons suddenly took to travelling on the road between Deal and Gravesend, catching the yokels right and left to carry heavy loads for them, I fancy every farm and cottage thereabouts would get empty very soon. Only here the dwellings were gone too. Still, I passed through several abandoned villages. There's something pathetically childish in the ruins of grass walls. Day after day, with the stamp and shuffle of sixty pair of bare feet behind me, each pair under a 60-lb. load. Camp, cook, sleep, strike camp, march. Now and then a carrier dead in harness, at rest in the long grass near the path, with an empty water-gourd and his long staff lying by his side. A great silence around and above. Perhaps on some quiet night the tremor of far-off drums, sinking, swelling, a tremor vast, faint; a sound weird, appealing, suggestive, and wild—and perhaps with as profound a meaning as the sound of bells in a Christian country. Once a white man in an unbuttoned uniform, camping on the path with an armed escort of lank Zanzibaris,[8] very hospitable and festive—not to say drunk. Was looking after the upkeep of the road, he declared. Can't say I saw any road or any upkeep, unless the body of a middle-aged negro, with a bullet-hole in the forehead, upon which I absolutely stumbled three miles farther on, may be considered as a permanent improvement. I had a white companion too, not a bad chap, but rather too fleshy and with the exasperating habit of fainting on the hot hillsides, miles away from the least bit of shade and water. Annoying, you know, to hold your own coat like a parasol over a man's head while he is coming-to. I couldn't help asking him once what he meant by coming there at all. 'To make money, of course. What do you think?' he said scornfully. Then he got fever, and had to be carried in a hammock slung under a pole. As he weighed sixteen stone[9] I had no end of rows with the carriers. They jibbed, ran away, sneaked off with their loads in the night—quite a mutiny. So, one evening, I made a speech in English with gestures, not one of which was lost to the sixty pairs of eyes before me, and the next morning I started the hammock off in front all right. An hour afterwards I came upon the whole concern wrecked in a bush—man, hammock, groans, blankets, horrors. The heavy pole had skinned his poor nose. He was very anxious for me to kill somebody, but there wasn't the shadow of a carrier near. I remembered the old doctor—'It would be interesting for science to watch the mental changes of individuals, on the spot.' I felt I was becoming scientifically interesting. However, all that is to no purpose. On the fifteenth day I came in sight of the big river again, and hobbled into the Central Station. It was on a back water surrounded by scrub and forest, with a pretty border of smelly mud on one side, and on the three others enclosed by a crazy fence of rushes. A neglected gap was all the gate it had, and the first glance at the place was enough to let you see the flabby devil was running that show. White men with long staves in their hands appeared languidly from amongst the buildings, strolling up to take a look at me, and then retired out of sight some-

---

8. Natives of Zanzibar, an island off the east coast of Africa, once part of the sultanate of Zanzibar and a British protectorate, now part of the independent state of Tanzania. Zanzibaris were used as mercenaries throughout Africa.
9. One stone equals 14 pounds. The man weighed 224 pounds.

where. One of them, a stout, excitable chap with black moustaches, informed me with great volubility and many digressions, as soon as I told him who I was, that my steamer was at the bottom of the river. I was thunderstruck. What, how, why? Oh, it was 'all right.' The 'manager himself' was there. All quite correct. 'Everybody had behaved splendidly! splendidly!'—'You must,' he said in agitation, 'go and see the general manager at once. He is waiting!'

"I did not see the real significance of that wreck at once. I fancy I see it now, but I am not sure—not at all. Certainly the affair was too stupid—when I think of it—to be altogether natural. Still . . . But at the moment it presented itself simply as a confounded nuisance. The steamer was sunk. They had started two days before in a sudden hurry up the river with the manager on board, in charge of some volunteer skipper, and before they had been out three hours they tore the bottom out of her on stones, and she sank near the south bank. I asked myself what I was to do there, now my boat was lost. As a matter of fact, I had plenty to do in fishing my command out of the river. I had to set about it the very next day. That, and the repairs when I brought the pieces to the station, took some months.

"My first interview with the manager was curious. He did not ask me to sit down after my twenty-mile walk that morning. He was commonplace in complexion, in feature, in manners, and in voice. He was of middle size and of ordinary build. His eyes, of the usual blue, were perhaps remarkably cold, and he certainly could make his glance fall on one as trenchant and heavy as an axe. But even at these times the rest of his person seemed to disclaim the intention. Otherwise there was only an indefinable, faint expression of his lips, something stealthy—a smile—not a smile—I remember it, but I can't explain. It was unconscious, this smile was, though just after he had said something it got intensified for an instant. It came at the end of his speeches like a seal applied on the words to make the meaning of the commonest phrase appear absolutely inscrutable. He was a common trader, from his youth up employed in these parts—nothing more. He was obeyed, yet he inspired neither love nor fear, nor even respect. He inspired uneasiness. That was it! Uneasiness. Not a definite mistrust—just uneasiness—nothing more. You have no idea how effective such a . . . a . . . faculty can be. He had no genius for organising, for initiative, or for order even. That was evident in such things as the deplorable state of the station. He had no learning, and no intelligence. His position had come to him—why? Perhaps because he was never ill . . . He had served three terms of three years out there . . . Because triumphant health in the general rout of constitutions is a kind of power in itself. When he went home on leave he rioted on a large scale—pompously. Jack ashore—with a difference—in externals only. This one could gather from his casual talk. He originated nothing, he could keep the routine going—that's all. But he was great. He was great by this little thing that it was impossible to tell what could control such a man. He never gave that secret away. Perhaps there was nothing within him. Such a suspicion made one pause—for out there there were no external checks. Once when various tropical diseases had laid low almost every 'agent' in the station, he was heard to say, 'Men who come out here should have no entrails.' He sealed the utterance with that smile of his, as though it had been a door opening into a darkness he had in his keeping. You fancied you had seen things—but the seal was on. When annoyed at meal-times by the constant quarrels of the white men about precedence, he ordered an immense round table to be made, for which a special house had to be built. This was the station's mess-room. Where he sat was the first place—the rest were nowhere. One felt this to be his unalterable conviction. He was neither civil nor uncivil. He was quiet. He allowed his 'boy'—an overfed young negro from the coast—to treat the white men, under his very eyes, with provoking insolence.

"He began to speak as soon as he saw me. I had been very long on the road. He could not wait. Had to start without me. The up-river stations had to be relieved. There had been so many delays already that he did not know who was dead and who was alive, and how they got on—and so on, and so on. He paid no attention to my explanations, and, playing with a stick of sealing-wax, repeated several times that the situation was 'very grave, very grave.' There were rumours that a very important station was in jeopardy, and its chief, Mr Kurtz, was ill. Hoped it was not true. Mr Kurtz was . . . I felt weary and irritable. Hang Kurtz, I thought. I interrupted him by saying I had heard of Mr Kurtz on the coast. 'Ah! So they talk of him down there,' he murmured to himself. Then he began again, assuring me Mr Kurtz was the best agent he had, an exceptional man, of the greatest importance to the Company; therefore I could understand his anxiety. He was, he said, 'very, very uneasy.' Certainly he fidgeted on his chair a good deal, exclaimed, 'Ah, Mr Kurtz!' broke the stick of sealing-wax and seemed dumbfounded by the accident. Next thing he wanted to know 'how long it would take to' . . . I interrupted him again. Being hungry, you know, and kept on my feet too, I was getting savage. 'How can I tell?' I said, 'I haven't even seen the wreck yet—some months, no doubt.' All this talk seemed to me so futile. 'Some months,' he said. 'Well, let us say three months before we can make a start. Yes. That ought to do the affair.' I flung out of his hut (he lived all alone in a clay hut with a sort of verandah) muttering to myself my opinion of him. He was a chattering idiot. Afterwards I took it back when it was borne in upon me startlingly with what extreme nicety he had estimated the time requisite for the 'affair.'

"I went to work the next day, turning, so to speak, my back on that station. In that way only it seemed to me I could keep my hold on the redeeming facts of life. Still, one must look about sometimes; and then I saw this station, these men strolling aimlessly about in the sunshine of the yard. I asked myself sometimes what it all meant. They wandered here and there with their absurd long staves in their hands, like a lot of faithless pilgrims bewitched inside a rotten fence. The word 'ivory' rang in the air, was whispered, was sighed. You would think they were praying to it. A taint of imbecile rapacity blew through it all, like a whiff from some corpse. By Jove! I've never seen anything so unreal in my life. And outside, the silent wilderness surrounding this cleared speck on the earth struck me as something great and invincible, like evil or truth, waiting patiently for the passing away of this fantastic invasion.

"Oh, these months! Well, never mind. Various things happened. One evening a grass shed full of calico, cotton prints, beads, and I don't know what else, burst into a blaze so suddenly that you would have thought the earth had opened to let an avenging fire consume all that trash. I was smoking my pipe quietly by my dismantled steamer, and saw them all cutting capers in the light, with their arms lifted high, when the stout man with moustaches came tearing down to the river, a tin pail in his hand, assured me that everybody was 'behaving splendidly, splendidly,' dipped about a quart of water and tore back again. I noticed there was a hole in the bottom of his pail.

"I strolled up. There was no hurry. You see the thing had gone off like a box of matches. It had been hopeless from the very first. The flame had leaped high, driven everybody back, lighted up everything—and collapsed. The shed was already a heap of embers glowing fiercely. A nigger was being beaten near by. They said he had caused the fire in some way; be that as it may, he was screeching most horribly. I saw him, later, for several days, sitting in a bit of shade looking very sick and trying to recover himself: afterwards he arose and went out—and the wilderness without a sound took him into its bosom again. As I approached the glow from the dark I found myself at the back of two men, talking. I heard the name of Kurtz pronounced, then the words, 'take advantage of this unfortunate accident.' One of the men was the manager. I wished him a good evening. 'Did you ever see anything like it—eh? it is incredible,' he said, and walked off. The other man remained. He was a first-class agent, young, gentlemanly, a bit reserved, with a forked little beard and a hooked nose. He was standoffish with the other agents, and they on their side said he was the manager's spy upon them. As to me, I had hardly ever spoken to him before. We got into talk, and by and by we strolled away from the hissing ruins. Then he asked me to his room, which was in the main building of the station. He struck a match, and I perceived that this young aristocrat had not only a silver-mounted dressing-case but also a whole candle all to himself. Just at that time the manager was the only man supposed to have any right to candles. Native mats covered the clay walls; a collection of spears, assegais,[1] shields, knives, was hung up in trophies. The business entrusted to this fellow was the making of bricks—so I had been informed; but there wasn't a fragment of a brick anywhere in the station, and he had been there more than a year—waiting. It seems he could not make bricks without something, I don't know what—straw maybe. Anyway, it could not be found there, and as it was not likely to be sent from Europe, it did not appear clear to me what he was waiting for. An act of special creation perhaps. However, they were all waiting—all the sixteen or twenty pilgrims of them—for something; and upon my word it did not seem an uncongenial occupation, from the way they took it, though the only thing that ever came to them was disease—as far as I could see. They beguiled the time by backbiting and intriguing against each other in a foolish kind of way. There was an air of plotting about that station, but nothing came of it, of course. It was as unreal as everything else—as the philanthropic pretence of the whole concern, as their talk, as their government, as their show of work. The only real feeling was a desire to get appointed to a trading-post where ivory was to be had, so that they could earn percentages. They intrigued and slandered and hated each other only on that account—but as to effectually lifting a little finger—oh no. By heavens! there is something after all in the world allowing one man to steal a horse while another must not look at a halter. Steal a horse straight out. Very well. He has done it. Perhaps he can ride. But there is a way of looking at a halter that would provoke the most charitable of saints into a kick.

"I had no idea why he wanted to be sociable, but as we chatted in there it suddenly occurred to me the fellow was trying to get at something—in fact, pumping me. He alluded constantly to Europe, to the people I was supposed to know there—putting leading questions as to my acquaintances in the sepulchral city, and so on. His little eyes glittered like mica[2] discs—with curiosity—though he tried to keep up a bit of superciliousness. At first I was astonished,

---

1. Slender iron-tipped spears.   2. Glassy mineral.

but very soon I became awfully curious to see what he would find out from me. I couldn't possibly imagine what I had in me to make it worth his while. It was very pretty to see how he baffled himself, for in truth my body was full only of chills, and my head had nothing in it but that wretched steamboat business. It was evident he took me for a perfectly shameless prevaricator. At last he got angry, and, to conceal a movement of furious annoyance, he yawned. I rose. Then I noticed a small sketch in oils, on a panel, representing a woman, draped and blindfolded, carrying a lighted torch. The background was sombre—almost black. The movement of the woman was stately, and the effect of the torchlight on the face was sinister.

"It arrested me, and he stood by civilly, holding an empty half-pint champagne bottle (medical comforts) with the candle stuck in it. To my question he said Mr Kurtz had painted this—in this very station more than a year ago—while waiting for means to go to his trading-post. 'Tell me, pray,' said I, 'who is this Mr Kurtz?'

" 'The chief of the Inner Station,' he answered in a short tone, looking away. 'Much obliged,' I said, laughing. 'And you are the brickmaker of the Central Station. Every one knows that.' He was silent for a while. 'He is a prodigy,' he said at last. 'He is an emissary of pity, and science, and progress, and devil knows what else. We want,' he began to declaim suddenly, 'for the guidance of the cause entrusted to us by Europe, so to speak, higher intelligence, wide sympathies, a singleness of purpose.' 'Who says that?' I asked. 'Lots of them,' he replied. 'Some even write that; and so *he* comes here, a special being, as you ought to know.' 'Why ought I to know?' I interrupted, really surprised. He paid no attention. 'Yes. To-day he is chief of the best station, next year he will be assistant-manager, two years more and . . . but I daresay you know what he will be in two years' time. You are of the new gang—the gang of virtue. The same people who sent him specially also recommended you. Oh, don't say no. I've my own eyes to trust.' Light dawned upon me. My dear aunt's influential acquaintances were producing an unexpected effect upon that young man. I nearly burst into a laugh. 'Do you read the Company's confidential correspondence?' I asked. He hadn't a word to say. It was great fun. 'When Mr Kurtz,' I continued severely, 'is General Manager, you won't have the opportunity.'

"He blew the candle out suddenly, and we went outside. The moon had risen. Black figures strolled about listlessly, pouring water on the glow, whence proceeded a sound of hissing; steam ascended in the moonlight; the beaten nigger groaned somewhere. 'What a row the brute makes!' said the indefatigable man with the moustaches, appearing near us. 'Serve him right. Transgression—punishment—bang! Pitiless, pitiless. That's the only way. This will prevent all conflagrations for the future. I was just telling the manager . . .' He noticed my companion, and became crestfallen all at once. 'Not in bed yet,' he said, with a kind of servile heartiness; 'it's so natural. Ha! Danger—agitation.' He vanished. I went on to the river-side, and the other followed me. I heard a scathing murmur at my ear, 'Heap of muffs—go to.' The pilgrims could be seen in knots gesticulating, discussing. Several had still their staves in their hands. I verily believe they took these sticks to bed with them. Beyond the fence the forest stood up spectrally in the moonlight, and through the dim stir, through the faint sounds of that lamentable courtyard, the silence of the land went home to one's very heart—its mystery, its greatness, the amazing reality of its concealed life. The hurt nigger moaned feebly somewhere near by, and then fetched a deep sigh that made me mend my pace away from there. I felt a hand introducing itself under my arm. 'My dear sir,' said the fellow, 'I don't want to be misunderstood, and especially by you, who will see Mr Kurtz long before I can have that pleasure. I wouldn't like him to get a false idea of my disposition. . . . '

"I let him run on, this papier-mâché Mephistopheles, and it seemed to me that if I tried I could poke my forefinger through him, and would find nothing inside but a little loose dirt, maybe. He, don't you see, had been planning to be assistant-manager by and by under the present man, and I could see that the coming of that Kurtz had upset them both not a little. He talked precipitately, and I did not try to stop him. I had my shoulders against the wreck of my steamer, hauled up on the slope like a carcass of some big river animal. The smell of mud, of primeval mud, by Jove! was in my nostrils, the high stillness of primeval forest was before my eyes; there were shiny patches on the black creek. The moon had spread over everything a thin layer of silver—over the rank grass, over the mud, upon the wall of matted vegetation standing higher than the wall of a temple, over the great river I could see through a sombre gap glittering, glittering, as it flowed broadly by without a murmur. All this was great, expectant, mute, while the man jabbered about himself. I wondered whether the stillness on the face of the immensity looking at us two were meant as an appeal or as a menace. What were we who had strayed in here? Could we handle that dumb thing, or would it handle us? I felt how big, how confoundedly big, was that thing that couldn't talk and perhaps was deaf as well. What was in there? I could see a little ivory coming out from there, and I had heard Mr Kurtz was in there. I had heard enough about it too—God knows! Yet somehow it didn't bring any image with it—no more than if I had been told an angel or a fiend was in there. I believed it in the same way one of you might believe there are inhabitants in the planet Mars. I knew once a Scotch sailmaker who was certain, dead sure, there were people in Mars. If you asked him for some idea how they looked and behaved, he would get shy and mutter something about 'walking on all-fours.' If you as much as smiled, he would—though a man of sixty—offer to fight you. I would not have gone so far as to fight for Kurtz, but I went for him near enough to a lie. You know I hate, detest, and can't bear a lie, not because I am straighter than the rest of us, but simply because it appals me. There is a taint of death, a flavour of mortality in lies—which is exactly what I hate and detest in the world—what I want to forget. It makes me miserable and sick, like biting something rotten would do. Temperament, I suppose. Well, I went near enough to it by letting the young fool there believe anything he liked to imagine as to my influence in Europe. I became in an instant as much of a pretence as the rest of the bewitched pilgrims. This simply because I had a notion it somehow would be of help to that Kurtz whom at the time I did not see—you understand. He was just a word for me. I did not see the man in the name any more than you do. Do you see him? Do you see the story? Do you see anything? It seems to me I am trying to tell you a dream—making a vain attempt, because no relation of a dream can convey the dream-sensation, that commingling of absurdity, surprise, and bewilderment in a tremor of struggling revolt, that notion of being captured by the incredible which is of the very essence of dreams. . . . "

He was silent for a while.

". . . No, it is impossible; it is impossible to convey the life-sensation of any given epoch of one's existence—that which makes its truth, its meaning—its subtle and penetrating essence. It is impossible. We live, as we dream—alone. . . ."

He paused again as if reflecting, then added:

"Of course in this you fellows see more than I could then. You see me, whom you know. . . ."

It had become so pitch dark that we listeners could hardly see one another. For a long time already he, sitting apart, had been no more to us than a voice. There was not a word from anybody. The others might have been asleep, but I was awake. I listened, I listened on the watch for the sentence, for the word, that would give me the clue to the faint uneasiness inspired by this narrative that seemed to shape itself without human lips in the heavy night-air of the river.

". . . Yes—I let him run on," Marlow began again, "and think what he pleased about the powers that were behind me. I did! And there was nothing behind me! There was nothing but that wretched, old, mangled steamboat I was leaning against, while he talked fluently about 'the necessity for every man to get on.' 'And when one comes out here, you conceive, it is not to gaze at the moon.' Mr Kurtz was a 'universal genius,' but even a genius would find it easier to work with 'adequate tools—intelligent men.' He did not make bricks—why, there was a physical impossibility in the way—as I was well aware; and if he did secretarial work for the manager, it was because 'no sensible man rejects wantonly the confidence of his superiors.' Did I see it? I saw it. What more did I want? What I really wanted was rivets, by heaven! Rivets. To get on with the work—to stop the hole. Rivets I wanted. There were cases of them down at the coast—cases—piled up—burst—split! You kicked a loose rivet at every second step in that station yard on the hillside. Rivets had rolled into the grove of death. You could fill your pockets with rivets for the trouble of stooping down—and there wasn't one rivet to be found where it was wanted. We had plates that would do, but nothing to fasten them with. And every week the messenger, a lone negro, letter-bag on shoulder and staff in hand, left our station for the coast. And several times a week a coast caravan came in with trade goods—ghastly glazed calico that made you shudder only to look at it, glass beads value about a penny a quart, confounded spotted cotton handkerchiefs. And no rivets. Three carriers could have brought all that was wanted to set that steamboat afloat.

"He was becoming confidential now, but I fancy my unresponsive attitude must have exasperated him at last, for he judged it necessary to inform me he feared neither God nor devil, let alone any mere man. I said I could see that very well, but what I wanted was a certain quantity of rivets—and rivets were what really Mr Kurtz wanted, if he had only known it. Now letters went to the coast every week. . . . 'My dear sir,' he cried, 'I write from dictation.' I demanded rivets. There was a way—for an intelligent man. He changed his manner; became very cold, and suddenly began to talk about a hippopotamus; wondered whether sleeping on board the steamer (I stuck to my salvage night and day) I wasn't disturbed. There was an old hippo that had the bad habit of getting out on the bank and roaming at night over the station grounds. The pilgrims used to turn out in a body and empty every rifle they could lay hands on at him. Some even had sat up o' nights for him. All this energy was wasted, though. 'That animal has a charmed life,' he said; 'but you can say this only of brutes in this country. No man—you apprehend me?—no man here bears a charmed life.' He stood there for a moment in the moonlight with his delicate hooked nose set a little askew, and his mica eyes glittering without a wink, then, with a curt Good-night, he strode off. I could see he was disturbed and considerably puzzled, which made me feel more hopeful than I had been for days. It was a great comfort to turn from that chap to my influential friend, the battered, twisted, ruined, tinpot steamboat. I clambered on board. She rang under my feet like an empty Huntley & Palmer biscuit-tin kicked along a gutter; she was nothing so solid in make, and rather less pretty in shape, but I had expended enough hard work on her to make me love her. No influential friend would have served me better. She had given me a chance to come out a bit—to find out what I could do. No, I don't like work. I had rather laze about and think of all the fine things that can be done. I don't like work—no man does—but I like what is in the work—the chance to find yourself. Your own reality—for yourself, not for others—what no other man can ever know. They can only see the mere show, and never can tell what it really means.

"I was not surprised to see somebody sitting aft, on the deck, with his legs dangling over the mud. You see I rather chummed with the few mechanics there were in that station, whom the other pilgrims naturally despised—on account of their imperfect manners, I suppose. This was the foreman—a boiler-maker by trade—a good worker. He was a lank, bony, yellow-faced man, with big intense eyes. His aspect was worried, and his head was as bald as the palm of my hand; but his hair in falling seemed to have stuck to his chin, and had prospered in the new locality, for his beard hung down to his waist. He was a widower with six young children (he had left them in charge of a sister of his to come out there), and the passion of his life was pigeon-flying. He was an enthusiast and a connoisseur. He would rave about pigeons. After work hours he used sometimes to come over from his hut for a talk about his children and his pigeons; at work, when he had to crawl in the mud under the bottom of the steamboat, he would tie up that beard of his in a kind of white serviette[3] he brought for the purpose. It had loops to go over his ears. In the evening he could be seen squatted on the bank rinsing that wrapper in the creek with great care, then spreading it solemnly on a bush to dry.

"I slapped him on the back and shouted 'We shall have rivets!' He scrambled to his feet exclaiming 'No! Rivets!' as though he couldn't believe his ears. Then in a low voice, 'You . . . eh?' I don't know why we behaved like lunatics. I put my finger to the side of my nose and nodded mysteriously. 'Good for you!' he cried, snapped his fingers above his head, lifting one foot. I tried a jig. We capered on the iron deck. A frightful clatter came out of that hulk, and the virgin forest on the other bank of the creek sent it back in a thundering roll upon the sleeping station. It must have made some of the pilgrims sit up in their hovels. A dark figure obscured the lighted doorway of the manager's hut, vanished, then, a second or so after, the doorway itself vanished too. We stopped, and the silence driven away by the stamping of our feet flowed back again from the recesses of the land. The great wall of vegetation, an exuberant and entangled mass of trunks, branches, leaves, boughs, festoons, motionless in the moonlight, was like a rioting invasion of soundless life, a rolling wave of plants, piled up, crested, ready to topple over the creek, to sweep every little man of us out of his little existence. And it moved not. A deadened burst of mighty splashes and snorts reached us from afar, as though an ichthyosaurus[4] had been taking a bath of glitter in the great river. 'After all,' said the boiler-maker in a reasonable tone, 'why shouldn't we get the rivets?' Why not, indeed! I did not know of any reason why we shouldn't. 'They'll come in three weeks,' I said confidently.

---

3. Table napkin.

4. Large prehistoric marine creature.

2350 / JOSEPH CONRAD

"But they didn't. Instead of rivets there came an invasion, an infliction, a visitation. It came in sections during the next three weeks, each section headed by a donkey carrying a white man in new clothes and tan shoes, bowing from that elevation right and left to the impressed pilgrims. A quarrelsome band of footsore sulky niggers trod on the heels of the donkey; a lot of tents, camp-stools, tin boxes, white cases, brown bales would be shot down in the court-yard, and the air of mystery would deepen a little over the muddle of the station. Five such instalments came, with their absurd air of disorderly flight with the loot of innumerable outfit shops and provision stores, that, one would think, they were lugging, after a raid, into the wilderness for equitable division. It was an inextricable mess of things decent in themselves but that human folly made look like the spoils of thieving.

"This devoted band called itself the Eldorado[5] Exploring Expedition, and I believe they were sworn to secrecy. Their talk, however, was the talk of sordid buccaneers: it was reckless without hardihood, greedy without audacity, and cruel without courage; there was not an atom of foresight or of serious inten-tion in the whole batch of them, and they did not seem aware these things are wanted for the work of the world. To tear treasure out of the bowels of the land was their desire, with no more moral purpose at the back of it than there is in burglars breaking into a safe. Who paid the expenses of the noble enter-prise I don't know; but the uncle of our manager was leader of that lot.

"In exterior he resembled a butcher in a poor neighbourhood, and his eyes had a look of sleepy cunning. He carried his fat paunch with ostentation on his short legs, and during the time his gang infested the station spoke to no one but his nephew. You could see these two roaming about all day long with their heads close together in an everlasting confab.[6]

"I had given up worrying myself about the rivets. One's capacity for that kind of folly is more limited than you would suppose. I said Hang!—and let things slide. I had plenty of time for meditation, and now and then I would give some thought to Kurtz. I wasn't very interested in him. No. Still, I was curious to see whether this man, who had come out equipped with moral ideas of some sort, would climb to the top after all, and how he would set about his work when there."

2

"One evening as I was lying flat on the deck of my steamboat, I heard voices approaching—and there were the nephew and the uncle strolling along the bank. I laid my head on my arm again, and had nearly lost myself in a doze, when somebody said in my ear, as it were: 'I am as harmless as a little child, but I don't like to be dictated to. Am I the manager—or am I not? I was ordered to send him there. It's incredible.' . . . I became aware that the two were stand-ing on the shore alongside the forepart of the steamboat, just below my head. I did not move; it did not occur to me to move: I was sleepy. 'It *is* unpleasant,' grunted the uncle. 'He has asked the Administration to be sent there,' said the other, 'with the idea of showing what he could do; and I was instructed accord-ingly. Look at the influence that man must have. Is it not frightful?' They both agreed it was frightful, then made several bizarre remarks: 'Make rain and fine

5. Fabled land of gold (*el dorado,* Spanish for "the gilded") imagined by the Spanish conquistadors to exist in South America.
6. Confabulation, talk.

weather—one man—the Council—by the nose'—bits of absurd sentences that got the better of my drowsiness, so that I had pretty near the whole of my wits about me when the uncle said, 'The climate may do away with this difficulty for you. Is he alone there?' 'Yes,' answered the manager; 'he sent his assistant down the river with a note to me in these terms: "Clear this poor devil out of the country, and don't bother sending more of that sort. I had rather be alone than have the kind of men you can dispose of with me." It was more than a year ago. Can you imagine such impudence?' 'Anything since then?' asked the other hoarsely. 'Ivory,' jerked the nephew; 'lots of it—prime sort—lots—most annoying, from him.' 'And with that?' questioned the heavy rumble. 'Invoice,' was the reply fired out, so to speak. Then silence. They had been talking about Kurtz.

"I was broad awake by this time, but, lying perfectly at ease, remained still, having no inducement to change my position. 'How did that ivory come all this way?' growled the elder man, who seemed very vexed. The other explained that it had come with a fleet of canoes in charge of an English half-caste clerk Kurtz had with him; that Kurtz had apparently intended to return himself, the station being by that time bare of goods and stores, but after coming three hundred miles, had suddenly decided to go back, which he started to do alone in a small dugout with four paddlers, leaving the half-caste to continue down the river with the ivory. The two fellows there seemed astounded at anybody attempting such a thing. They were at a loss for an adequate motive. As for me, I seemed to see Kurtz for the first time. It was a distinct glimpse: the dugout, four paddling savages, and the lone white man turning his back suddenly on the headquarters, on relief, on thoughts of home—perhaps; setting his face towards the depths of the wilderness, towards his empty and desolate station. I did not know the motive. Perhaps he was just simply a fine fellow who stuck to his work for its own sake. His name, you understand, had not been pronounced once. He was 'that man.' The half-caste, who, as far as I could see, had conducted a difficult trip with great prudence and pluck, was invariably alluded to as 'that scoundrel.' The 'scoundrel' had reported that the 'man' had been very ill—had recovered imperfectly. . . . The two below me moved away then a few paces, and strolled back and forth at some little distance. I heard: 'Military post—doctor—two hundred miles—quite alone now— unavoidable delays—nine months—no news—strange rumours.' They approached again, just as the manager was saying, 'No one, as far as I know, unless a species of wandering trader—a pestilential fellow, snapping ivory from the natives.' Who was it they were talking about now? I gathered in snatches that this was some man supposed to be in Kurtz's district, and of whom the manager did not approve. 'We will not be free from unfair competition till one of these fellows is hanged for an example,' he said. 'Certainly,' grunted the other; 'get him hanged! Why not? Anything—anything can be done in this country. That's what I say; nobody here, you understand, *here*, can endanger your position. And why? You stand the climate—you outlast them all. The danger is in Europe; but there before I left I took care to—' They moved off and whispered, then their voices rose again. 'The extraordinary series of delays is not my fault. I did my possible.'[7] The fat man sighed, 'Very

---

7. Literal rendering of the French *J'ai fait mon possible* (I have done all I could). Conrad sprinkles the conversation of his Belgian characters with Gallicisms to remind us that their words, though reported in English, were spoken in French. Other examples are "a species of wandering trader" (above), "Conceive you" (below), "I would be desolated" (p. 2359).

sad.' 'And the pestiferous absurdity of his talk,' continued the other; 'he bothered me enough when he was here. "Each station should be like a beacon on the road towards better things, a centre for trade of course, but also for humanising, improving, instructing." Conceive you—that ass! And he wants to be manager! No, it's—' Here he got choked by excessive indignation, and I lifted my head the least bit. I was surprised to see how near they were—right under me. I could have spat upon their hats. They were looking on the ground, absorbed in thought. The manager was switching his leg with a slender twig: his sagacious relative lifted his head. 'You have been well since you came out this time?' he asked. The other gave a start. 'Who? I? Oh! Like a charm—like a charm. But the rest—oh, my goodness! All sick. They die so quick, too, that I haven't the time to send them out of the country—it's incredible!' 'H'm. Just so,' grunted the uncle. 'Ah! my boy, trust to this—I say, trust to this.' I saw him extend his short flipper of an arm for a gesture that took in the forest, the creek, the mud, the river—seemed to beckon with a dishonouring flourish before the sunlit face of the land a treacherous appeal to the lurking death, to the hidden evil, to the profound darkness of its heart. It was so startling that I leaped to my feet and looked back at the edge of the forest, as though I had expected an answer of some sort to that black display of confidence. You know the foolish notions that come to one sometimes. The high stillness confronted these two figures with its ominous patience, waiting for the passing away of a fantastic invasion.

"They swore aloud together—out of sheer fright, I believe—then, pretending not to know anything of my existence, turned back to the station. The sun was low; and leaning forward side by side, they seemed to be tugging painfully uphill their two ridiculous shadows of unequal length, that trailed behind them slowly over the tall grass without bending a single blade.

"In a few days the Eldorado Expedition went into the patient wilderness, that closed upon it as the sea closes over a diver. Long afterwards the news came that all the donkeys were dead. I know nothing as to the fate of the less valuable animals. They, no doubt, like the rest of us, found what they deserved. I did not inquire. I was then rather excited at the prospect of meeting Kurtz very soon. When I say very soon I mean it comparatively. It was just two months from the day we left the creek when we came to the bank below Kurtz's station.

"Going up that river was like travelling back to the earliest beginnings of the world, when vegetation rioted on the earth and the big trees were kings. An empty stream, a great silence, an impenetrable forest. The air was warm, thick, heavy, sluggish. There was no joy in the brilliance of sunshine. The long stretches of the waterway ran on, deserted, into the gloom of overshadowed distances. On silvery sandbanks hippos and alligators sunned themselves side by side. The broadening waters flowed through a mob of wooded islands; you lost your way on that river as you would in a desert, and butted all day long against shoals, trying to find the channel, till you thought yourself bewitched and cut off for ever from everything you had known once—somewhere—far away—in another existence perhaps. There were moments when one's past came back to one, as it will sometimes when you have not a moment to spare to yourself; but it came in the shape of an unrestful and noisy dream, remembered with wonder amongst the overwhelming realities of this strange world of plants, and water, and silence. And this stillness of life did not in the least resemble a peace. It was the stillness of an implacable force brooding over an inscrutable intention. It looked at you with a vengeful aspect. I got used to it afterwards; I did not see it any more; I had no time. I had to keep guessing at the channel; I had to discern, mostly by inspiration, the signs of hidden banks; I watched for sunken stones; I was learning to clap my teeth smartly before my heart flew out, when I shaved by a fluke some infernal sly old snag that would have ripped the life out of the tin-pot steamboat and drowned all the pilgrims; I had to keep a look-out for the signs of dead wood we could cut up in the night for next day's steaming. When you have to attend to things of that sort, to the mere incidents of the surface, the reality—the reality, I tell you— fades. The inner truth is hidden—luckily, luckily. But I felt it all the same; I felt often its mysterious stillness watching me at my monkey tricks, just as it watches you fellows performing on your respective tight-ropes for—what is it? half a crown a tumble—"

"Try to be civil, Marlow," growled a voice, and I knew there was at least one listener awake besides myself.

"I beg your pardon. I forgot the heartache which makes up the rest of the price. And indeed what does the price matter, if the trick be well done? You do your tricks very well. And I didn't do badly either, since I managed not to sink that steamboat on my first trip. It's a wonder to me yet. Imagine a blind-folded man set to drive a van over a bad road. I sweated and shivered over that business considerably, I can tell you. After all, for a seaman, to scrape the bottom of the thing that's supposed to float all the time under his care is the unpardonable sin. No one may know of it, but you never forget the thump— eh? A blow on the very heart. You remember it, you dream of it, you wake up at night and think of it—years after—and go hot and cold all over. I don't pretend to say that steamboat floated all the time. More than once she had to wade for a bit, with twenty cannibals splashing around and pushing. We had enlisted some of these chaps on the way for a crew. Fine fellows—cannibals— in their place. They were men one could work with, and I am grateful to them. And, after all, they did not eat each other before my face: they had brought along a provision of hippo-meat which went rotten, and made the mystery of the wilderness stink in my nostrils. Phoo! I can sniff it now. I had the manager on board and three or four pilgrims with their staves—all complete. Sometimes we came upon a station close by the bank, clinging to the skirts of the unknown, and the white men rushing out of a tumble-down hovel, with great gestures of joy and surprise and welcome, seemed very strange—had the appearance of being held there captive by a spell. The word 'ivory' would ring in the air for a while—and on we went again into the silence, along empty reaches, round the still bends, between the high walls of our winding way, reverberating in hollow claps the ponderous beat of the stern-wheel. Trees, trees, millions of trees, massive, immense, running up high; and at their foot, hugging the bank against the stream, crept the little begrimed steamboat, like a sluggish beetle crawling on the floor of a lofty portico. It made you feel very small, very lost, and yet it was not altogether depressing, that feeling. After all, if you were small, the grimy beetle crawled on—which was just what you wanted it to do. Where the pilgrims imagined it crawled to I don't know. To some place where they expected to get something, I bet! For me it crawled towards Kurtz—exclusively; but when the steam-pipes started leaking we crawled very slow. The reaches opened before us and closed behind, as if the forest had stepped leisurely across the water to bar the way for our return. We penetrated deeper and deeper into the heart of darkness. It was very quiet there. At night sometimes the roll of drums behind the curtain of trees would run up the river and remain sustained faintly, as if hovering in the air high over our heads, till the first break of day. Whether it meant war, peace, or prayer we could not tell. The dawns were heralded by the descent of a chill stillness; the woodcutters slept, their fires burned low; the snapping of a twig would make you start. We were wanderers on a prehistoric earth, on an earth that wore the aspect of an unknown planet. We could have fancied ourselves the first of men taking possession of an accursed inheritance, to be subdued at the cost of profound anguish and of excessive toil. But suddenly, as we struggled round a bend, there would be a glimpse of rush walls, of peaked grass-roofs, a burst of yells, a whirl of black limbs, a mass of hands clapping, of feet stamping, of bodies swaying, of eyes rolling, under the droop of heavy and motionless foliage. The steamer toiled along slowly on the edge of a black and incomprehensible frenzy. The prehistoric man was cursing us, praying to us, welcoming us—who could tell? We were cut off from the comprehension of our surroundings; we glided past like phantoms, wondering and secretly appalled, as sane men would be before an enthusiastic outbreak in a madhouse. We could not understand because we were too far and could not remember, because we were travelling in the night of first ages, of those ages that are gone, leaving hardly a sign—and no memories.

"The earth seemed unearthly. We are accustomed to look upon the shackled form of a conquered monster, but there—there you could look at a thing monstrous and free. It was unearthly, and the men were—No, they were not inhuman. Well, you know, that was the worst of it—this suspicion of their not being inhuman. It would come slowly to one. They howled and leaped, and spun, and made horrid faces; but what thrilled you was just the thought of their humanity—like yours—the thought of your remote kinship with this wild and passionate uproar. Ugly. Yes, it was ugly enough; but if you were man enough you would admit to yourself that there was in you just the faintest trace of a response to the terrible frankness of that noise, a dim suspicion of there being a meaning in it which you—you so remote from the night of first ages—could comprehend. And why not? The mind of man is capable of anything—because everything is in it, all the past as well as all the future. What was there after all? Joy, fear, sorrow, devotion, valour, rage—who can tell?—but truth—truth stripped of its cloak of time. Let the fool gape and shudder—the man knows, and can look on without a wink. But he must at least be as much of a man as these on the shore. He must meet that truth with his own true stuff—with his own inborn strength. Principles? Principles won't do. Acquisitions, clothes, pretty rags—rags that would fly off at the first good shake. No; you want a deliberate belief. An appeal to me in this fiendish row—is there? Very well; I hear; I admit, but I have a voice too, and for good or evil mine is the speech that cannot be silenced. Of course, a fool, what with sheer fright and fine sentiments, is always safe. Who's that grunting? You wonder I didn't go ashore for a howl and a dance? Well, no—I didn't. Fine sentiments, you say? Fine sentiments be hanged! I had no time. I had to mess about with white-lead and strips of woollen blanket helping to put bandages on those leaky steam-pipes—I tell you. I had to watch the steering, and circumvent those snags, and get the tin-pot along by hook or by crook. There was surface-truth enough in these things to save a wiser man. And between whiles I had to look after the savage who was fireman. He was an improved specimen; he could fire up a vertical boiler. He was there below me, and, upon my word, to look at him was as edifying as seeing a dog in a parody of breeches and a feather hat, walking on his hind legs. A few months of training had done for that really fine chap. He squinted at the steam-gauge and at the water-gauge with an evident effort of intrepidity—and he had filed teeth too, the poor devil, and the wool of his pate shaved into queer patterns, and three ornamental scars on each of his cheeks. He ought to have been clapping his hands and stamping his feet on the bank, instead of which he was hard at work, a thrall to strange witchcraft, full of improving knowledge. He was useful because he had been instructed; and what he knew was this—that should the water in that transparent thing disappear, the evil spirit inside the boiler would get angry through the greatness of his thirst, and take a terrible vengeance. So he sweated and fired up and watched the glass fearfully (with an impromptu charm, made of rags, tied to his arm, and a piece of polished bone, as big as a watch, stuck flatways through his lower lip), while the wooded banks slipped past us slowly, the short noise was left behind, the interminable miles of silence—and we crept on, towards Kurtz. But the snags were thick, the water was treacherous and shallow, the boiler seemed indeed to have a sulky devil in it, and thus neither that fireman nor I had any time to peer into our creepy thoughts.

"Some fifty miles below the Inner Station we came upon a hut of reeds, an inclined and melancholy pole, with the unrecognisable tatters of what had been a flag of some sort flying from it, and a neatly stacked wood-pile. This was unexpected. We came to the bank, and on the stack of firewood found a flat piece of board with some faded pencil-writing on it. When deciphered it said: 'Wood for you. Hurry up. Approach cautiously.' There was a signature, but it was illegible—not Kurtz—a much longer word. Hurry up. Where? Up the river? 'Approach cautiously.' We had not done so. But the warning could not have been meant for the place where it could be only found after approach. Something was wrong above. But what—and how much? That was the question. We commented adversely upon the imbecility of that telegraphic style. The bush around said nothing, and would not let us look very far, either. A torn curtain of red twill hung in the doorway of the hut, and flapped sadly in our faces. The dwelling was dismantled; but we could see a white man had lived there not very long ago. There remained a rude table—a plank on two posts; a heap of rubbish reposed in a dark corner, and by the door I picked up a book. It had lost its covers, and the pages had been thumbed into a state of extremely dirty softness; but the back had been lovingly stitched afresh with white cotton thread, which looked clean yet. It was an extraordinary find. Its title was, *An Inquiry into some Points of Seamanship*, by a man Towser, Towson—some such name—Master in His Majesty's Navy. The matter looked dreary reading enough, with illustrative diagrams and repulsive tables of figures, and the copy was sixty years old. I handled this amazing antiquity with the greatest possible tenderness, lest it should dissolve in my hands. Within, Towson or Towser was inquiring earnestly into the breaking strain of ships' chains and tackle, and other such matters. Not a very enthralling book; but at the first glance you could see there a singleness of intention, an honest concern for the right way of going to work, which made these humble pages, thought out so many years ago, luminous with another than a professional light. The simple old sailor, with his talk of chains and purchases, made me forget the jungle and the pilgrims in a delicious sensation of having come upon something unmistakably real. Such a book being there was wonderful enough;

but still more astounding were the notes pencilled in the margin, and plainly referring to the text. I couldn't believe my eyes! They were in cipher! Yes, it looked like cipher. Fancy a man lugging with him a book of that description into this nowhere and studying it—and making notes—in cipher at that! It was an extravagant mystery.

"I had been dimly aware for some time of a worrying noise, and when I lifted my eyes I saw the wood-pile was gone, and the manager, aided by all the pilgrims, was shouting at me from the river-side. I slipped the book into my pocket. I assure you to leave off reading was like tearing myself away from the shelter of an old and solid friendship.

"I started the lame engine ahead. 'It must be this miserable trader—this intruder,' exclaimed the manager, looking back malevolently at the place we had left. 'He must be English,' I said. 'It will not save him from getting into trouble if he is not careful,' muttered the manager darkly. I observed with assumed innocence that no man was safe from trouble in this world.

"The current was more rapid now, the steamer seemed at her last gasp, the stern-wheel flopped languidly, and I caught myself listening on tiptoe for the next beat of the float,[8] for in sober truth I expected the wretched thing to give up every moment. It was like watching the last flickers of a life. But still we crawled. Sometimes I would pick out a tree a little way ahead to measure our progress towards Kurtz by, but I lost it invariably before we got abreast. To keep the eyes so long on one thing was too much for human patience. The manager displayed a beautiful resignation. I fretted and fumed and took to arguing with myself whether or no I would talk openly with Kurtz; but before I could come to any conclusion it occurred to me that my speech or my silence, indeed any action of mine, would be a mere futility. What did it matter what any one knew or ignored? What did it matter who was manager? One gets sometimes such a flash of insight. The essentials of this affair lay deep under the surface, beyond my reach, and beyond my power of meddling.

"Towards the evening of the second day we judged ourselves about eight miles from Kurtz's station. I wanted to push on; but the manager looked grave, and told me the navigation up there was so dangerous that it would be advisable, the sun being very low already, to wait where we were till next morning. Moreover, he pointed out that if the warning to approach cautiously were to be followed, we must approach in daylight—not at dusk, or in the dark. This was sensible enough. Eight miles meant nearly three hours' steaming for us, and I could also see suspicious ripples at the upper end of the reach. Nevertheless, I was annoyed beyond expression at the delay, and most unreasonably too, since one night more could not matter much after so many months. As we had plenty of wood, and caution was the word, I brought up in the middle of the stream. The reach was narrow, straight, with high sides like a railway cutting. The dusk came gliding into it long before the sun had set. The current ran smooth and swift, but a dumb immobility sat on the banks. The living trees, lashed together by the creepers and every living bush of the under-growth, might have been changed into stone, even to the slenderest twig, to the lightest leaf. It was not sleep—it seemed unnatural, like a state of trance. Not the faintest sound of any kind could be heard. You looked on amazed, and began to suspect yourself of being deaf—then the night came suddenly, and struck you blind as well. About three in the morning some large fish

8. Automatic water-level regulator opening and closing a water-supply valve.

leaped, and the loud splash made me jump as though a gun had been fired. When the sun rose there was a white fog, very warm and clammy, and more blinding than the night. It did not shift or drive; it was just there, standing all round you like something solid. At eight or nine, perhaps, it lifted as a shutter lifts. We had a glimpse of the towering multitude of trees, of the immense matted jungle, with the blazing little ball of the sun hanging over it—all perfectly still—and then the white shutter came down again, smoothly, as if sliding in greased grooves. I ordered the chain, which we had begun to heave in, to be paid out again. Before it stopped running with a muffled rattle, a cry, a very loud cry, as of infinite desolation, soared slowly in the opaque air. It ceased. A complaining clamour, modulated in savage discords, filled our ears. The sheer unexpectedness of it made my hair stir under my cap. I don't know how it struck the others: to me it seemed as though the mist itself had screamed, so suddenly, and apparently from all sides at once, did this tumultuous and mournful uproar arise. It culminated in a hurried outbreak of almost intolerably excessive shrieking, which stopped short, leaving us stiffened in a variety of silly attitudes, and obstinately listening to the nearly as appalling and excessive silence. 'Good God! What is the meaning—?' stammered at my elbow one of the pilgrims—a little fat man, with sandy hair and red whiskers, who wore side-spring boots, and pink pyjamas tucked into his socks. Two others remained open-mouthed a whole minute, then dashed into the little cabin, to rush out incontinently and stand darting scared glances, with Winchesters at 'ready' in their hands. What we could see was just the steamer we were on, her outlines blurred as though she had been on the point of dissolving, and a misty strip of water, perhaps two feet broad, around her—and that was all. The rest of the world was nowhere, as far as our eyes and ears were concerned. Just nowhere. Gone, disappeared; swept off without leaving a whisper or a shadow behind.

"I went forward, and ordered the chain to be hauled in short, so as to be ready to trip the anchor and move the steamboat at once if necessary. 'Will they attack?' whispered an awed voice. 'We will all be butchered in this fog,' murmured another. The faces twitched with the strain, the hands trembled slightly, the eyes forgot to wink. It was very curious to see the contrast of expressions of the white men and of the black fellows of our crew, who were as much strangers to that part of the river as we, though their homes were only eight hundred miles away. The whites, of course greatly discomposed, had besides a curious look of being painfully shocked by such an outrageous row. The others had an alert, naturally interested expression; but their faces were essentially quiet, even those of the one or two who grinned as they hauled at the chain. Several exchanged short, grunting phrases, which seemed to settle the matter to their satisfaction. Their headman, a young, broad-chested black, severely draped in dark-blue fringed cloths, with fierce nostrils and his hair all done up artfully in oily ringlets, stood near me. 'Aha!' I said, just for good fellowship's sake. 'Catch 'im,' he snapped, with a bloodshot widening of his eyes and a flash of sharp teeth—'catch 'im. Give 'im to us.' 'To you, eh?' I asked; 'what would you do with them?' 'Eat 'im!' he said curtly, and, leaning his elbow on the rail, looked out into the fog in a dignified and profoundly pensive attitude. I would no doubt have been properly horrified, had it not occurred to me that he and his chaps must be very hungry: that they must have been growing increasingly hungry for at least this month past. They had been engaged for six months (I don't think a single one of them had any clear idea of time, as we at the end of countless ages have. They still belonged to the beginnings of time—had no inherited experience to teach them, as it were), and of course, as long as there was a piece of paper written over in accordance with some farcical law or other made down the river, it didn't enter anybody's head to trouble how they would live. Certainly they had brought with them some rotten hippo-meat, which couldn't have lasted very long, anyway, even if the pilgrims hadn't, in the midst of a shocking hullabaloo, thrown a considerable quantity of it overboard. It looked like a high-handed proceeding; but it was really a case of legitimate self-defence. You can't breathe dead hippo waking, sleeping, and eating, and at the same time keep your precarious grip on existence. Besides that, they had given them every week three pieces of brass wire, each about nine inches long; and the theory was they were to buy their provisions with that currency in river-side villages. You can see how *that* worked. There were either no villages, or the people were hostile, or the director, who like the rest of us fed out of tins, with an occasional old he-goat thrown in, didn't want to stop the steamer for some more or less recondite reasons. So, unless they swallowed the wire itself, or made loops of it to snare the fishes with, I don't see what good their extravagant salary could be to them. I must say it was paid with a regularity worthy of a large and honourable trading company. For the rest, the only thing to eat—though it didn't look eatable in the least—I saw in their possession was a few lumps of some stuff like half-cooked dough, of a dirty lavender colour, they kept wrapped in leaves, and now and then swallowed a piece of, but so small that it seemed done more for the look of the thing than for any serious purpose of sustenance. Why in the name of all the gnawing devils of hunger they didn't go for us—they were thirty to five—and have a good tuck-in for once, amazes me now when I think of it. They were big powerful men, with not much capacity to weigh the consequences, with courage, with strength, even yet, though their skins were no longer glossy and their muscles no longer hard. And I saw that something restraining, one of those human secrets that baffle probability, had come into play there. I looked at them with a swift quickening of interest—not because it occurred to me I might be eaten by them before very long, though I own to you that just then I perceived—in a new light, as it were—how unwholesome the pilgrims looked, and I hoped, yes, I positively hoped, that my aspect was not so—what shall I say?—so—unappetising: a touch of fantastic vanity which fitted well with the dream-sensation that pervaded all my days at that time. Perhaps I had a little fever too. One can't live with one's finger everlastingly on one's pulse. I had often 'a little fever,' or a little touch of other things—the playful paw-strokes of the wilderness, the preliminary trifling before the more serious onslaught which came in due course. Yes; I looked at them as you would on any human being, with a curiosity of their impulses, motives, capacities, weaknesses, when brought to the test of an inexorable physical necessity. Restraint! What possible restraint? Was it superstition, disgust, patience, fear—or some kind of primitive honour? No fear can stand up to hunger, no patience can wear it out, disgust simply does not exist where hunger is; and as to superstition, beliefs, and what you may call principles, they are less than chaff in a breeze. Don't you know the devilry of lingering starvation, its exasperating torment, its black thoughts, its sombre and brooding ferocity? Well, I do. It takes a man all his inborn strength to fight hunger properly. It's really easier to face bereavement, dishonour, and the perdition of one's soul—than this kind of prolonged hunger. Sad, but true. And these chaps too had no earthly reason for any kind of scruple. Restraint! I would just as soon have expected restraint from a hyena prowling amongst the corpses of a battlefield. But there was the fact facing me—the fact dazzling, to be seen, like the foam on the depths of the sea, like a ripple on an unfathomable enigma, a mystery greater—when I thought of it—than the curious, inexplicable note of desperate grief in this savage clamour that had swept by us on the river-bank, behind the blind whiteness of the fog.

"Two pilgrims were quarrelling in hurried whispers as to which bank. 'Left.' 'No, no; how can you? Right, right, of course.' 'It is very serious,' said the manager's voice behind me; 'I would be desolated if anything should happen to Mr Kurtz before we came up.' I looked at him, and had not the slightest doubt he was sincere. He was just the kind of man who would wish to preserve appearances. That was his restraint. But when he muttered something about going on at once, I did not even take the trouble to answer him. I knew, and he knew, that it was impossible. Were we to let go our hold of the bottom, we would be absolutely in the air—in space. We wouldn't be able to tell where we were going to—whether up or down stream, or across—till we fetched against one bank or the other—and then we wouldn't know at first which it was. Of course I made no move. I had no mind for a smash-up. You couldn't imagine a more deadly place for a shipwreck. Whether drowned at once or not, we were sure to perish speedily in one way or another. 'I authorise you to take all the risks,' he said, after a short silence. 'I refuse to take any,' I said shortly; which was just the answer he expected, though its tone might have surprised him. 'Well, I must defer to your judgment. You are captain,' he said, with marked civility. I turned my shoulder to him in sign of my appreciation, and looked into the fog. How long would it last? It was the most hopeless lookout. The approach to this Kurtz grubbing for ivory in the wretched bush was beset by as many dangers as though he had been an enchanted princess sleeping in a fabulous castle. 'Will they attack, do you think?' asked the manager, in a confidential tone.

"I did not think they would attack, for several obvious reasons. The thick fog was one. If they left the bank in their canoes they would get lost in it, as we would be if we attempted to move. Still, I had also judged the jungle of both banks quite impenetrable—and yet eyes were in it, eyes that had seen us. The river-side bushes were certainly very thick; but the undergrowth behind was evidently penetrable. However, during the short lift I had seen no canoes anywhere in the reach—certainly not abreast of the steamer. But what made the idea of attack inconceivable to me was the nature of the noise—of the cries we had heard. They had not the fierce character boding of immediate hostile intention. Unexpected, wild, and violent as they had been, they had given me an irresistible impression of sorrow. The glimpse of the steamboat had for some reason filled those savages with unrestrained grief. The danger, if any, I expounded, was from our proximity to a great human passion let loose. Even extreme grief may ultimately vent itself in violence—but more generally takes the form of apathy. . . .

"You should have seen the pilgrims stare! They had no heart to grin, or even to revile me; but I believe they thought me gone mad—with fright, maybe. I delivered a regular lecture. My dear boys, it was no good bothering. Keep a look-out? Well, you may guess I watched the fog for the signs of lifting as a cat watches a mouse; but for anything else our eyes were of no more use to us than if we had been buried miles deep in a heap of cotton-wool. It felt like it too—choking, warm, stifling. Besides, all I said, though it sounded extravagant, was absolutely true to fact. What we afterwards alluded to as an attack was really an attempt at repulse. The action was very far from being aggressive—it was not even defensive, in the usual sense: it was undertaken under the stress of desperation, and in its essence was purely protective.

"It developed itself, I should say, two hours after the fog lifted, and its commencement was at a spot, roughly speaking, about a mile and a half below Kurtz's station. We had just floundered and flopped round a bend, when I saw an islet, a mere grassy hummock of bright green, in the middle of the stream. It was the only thing of the kind; but as we opened the reach more, I perceived it was the head of a long sandbank, or rather of a chain of shallow patches stretching down the middle of the river. They were discoloured, just awash, and the whole lot was seen just under the water, exactly as a man's backbone is seen running down the middle of his back under the skin. Now, as far as I did see, I could go to the right or to the left of this. I didn't know either channel, of course. The banks looked pretty well alike, the depth appeared the same; but as I had been informed the station was on the west side, I naturally headed for the western passage.

"No sooner had we fairly entered it than I became aware it was much narrower than I had supposed. To the left of us there was the long uninterrupted shoal,[9] and to the right a high steep bank heavily overgrown with bushes. Above the bush the trees stood in serried ranks. The twigs overhung the current thickly, and from distance to distance a large limb of some tree projected rigidly over the stream. It was then well on in the afternoon, the face of the forest was gloomy, and a broad strip of shadow had already fallen on the water. In this shadow we steamed up—very slowly, as you may imagine. I sheered her well inshore—the water being deepest near the bank, as the sounding-pole informed me.

"One of my hungry and forbearing friends was sounding in the bows just below me. This steamboat was exactly like a decked scow. On the deck there were two little teak-wood houses, with doors and windows. The boiler was in the fore-end, and the machinery right astern. Over the whole there was a light roof, supported on stanchions. The funnel projected through that roof, and in front of the funnel a small cabin built of light planks served for a pilot-house. It contained a couch, two camp-stools, a loaded Martini-Henry[1] leaning in one corner, a tiny table, and the steering-wheel. It had a wide door in front and a broad shutter at each side. All these were always thrown open, of course. I spent my days perched up there on the extreme fore-end of that roof, before the door. At night I slept, or tried to, on the couch. An athletic black belonging to some coast tribe, and educated by my poor predecessor, was the helmsman. He sported a pair of brass earrings, wore a blue cloth wrapper from the waist to the ankles, and thought all the world of himself. He was the most unstable kind of fool I had ever seen. He steered with no end of a swagger while you were by; but if he lost sight of you, he became instantly the prey of an abject funk, and would let that cripple of a steamboat get the upper hand of him in a minute.

"I was looking down at the sounding-pole, and feeling much annoyed to see

9. Sandbank.
1. Rifle combining the seven-grooved barrel of the Scottish gun maker A. Henry with the block-action breech mechanism introduced by the Swiss inventor F. Martini.

at each try a little more of it stick out of that river, when I saw my poleman give up the business suddenly, and stretch himself flat on the deck, without even taking the trouble to haul his pole in. He kept hold on it though, and it trailed in the water. At the same time the fireman, whom I could also see below me, sat down abruptly before his furnace and ducked his head. I was amazed. Then I had to look at the river mighty quick, because there was a snag in the fairway. Sticks, little sticks, were flying about—thick; they were whizzing before my nose, dropping below me, striking behind me against my pilot-house. All this time the river, the shore, the woods, were very quiet— perfectly quiet. I could only hear the heavy splashing thump of the stern-wheel and the patter of these things. We cleared the snag clumsily. Arrows, by Jove! We were being shot at! I stepped in quickly to close the shutter on the land-side. That fool-helmsman, his hands on the spokes, was lifting his knees high, stamping his feet, champing his mouth, like a reined-in horse. Confound him! And we were staggering within ten feet of the bank. I had to lean right out to swing the heavy shutter, and I saw a face amongst the leaves on the level with my own, looking at me very fierce and steady; and then suddenly, as though a veil had been removed from my eyes, I made out, deep in the tangled gloom, naked breasts, arms, legs, glaring eyes—the bush was swarming with human limbs in movement, glistening, of bronze colour. The twigs shook, swayed, and rustled, the arrows flew out of them, and then the shutter came to. 'Steer her straight,' I said to the helmsman. He held his head rigid, face forward; but his eyes rolled, he kept on lifting and setting down his feet gently, his mouth foamed a little. 'Keep quiet!' I said in a fury. I might just as well have ordered a tree not to sway in the wind. I darted out. Below me there was a great scuffle of feet on the iron deck; confused exclamations; a voice screamed, 'Can you turn back?' I caught sight of a V-shaped ripple on the water ahead. What? Another snag! A fusillade burst out under my feet. The pilgrims had opened with their Winchesters, and were simply squirting lead into that bush. A deuce of a lot of smoke came up and drove slowly forward. I swore at it. Now I couldn't see the ripple or the snag either. I stood in the doorway, peering, and the arrows came in swarms. They might have been poisoned, but they looked as though they wouldn't kill a cat. The bush began to howl. Our wood-cutters raised a warlike whoop; the report of a rifle just at my back deafened me. I glanced over my shoulder, and the pilot-house was yet full of noise and smoke when I made a dash at the wheel. The fool-nigger had dropped everything, to throw the shutter open and let off that Martini-Henry. He stood before the wide opening, glaring, and I yelled at him to come back, while I straightened the sudden twist out of that steamboat. There was no room to turn even if I had wanted to, the snag was somewhere very near ahead in that confounded smoke, there was no time to lose, so I just crowded her into the bank—right into the bank, where I knew the water was deep.

"We tore slowly along the overhanging bushes in a whirl of broken twigs and flying leaves. The fusillade below stopped short, as I had foreseen it would when the squirts got empty. I threw my head back to a glinting whizz that traversed the pilot-house, in at one shutter-hole and out at the other. Looking past that mad helmsman, who was shaking the empty rifle and yelling at the shore, I saw vague forms of men running bent double, leaping, gliding, distinct, incomplete, evanescent. Something big appeared in the air before the shutter, the rifle went overboard, and the man stepped back swiftly, looked at me over his shoulder in an extraordinary, profound, familiar manner, and fell

2362 / JOSEPH CONRAD

upon my feet. The side of his head hit the wheel twice, and the end of what appeared a long cane clattered round and knocked over a little camp-stool. It looked as though after wrenching that thing from somebody ashore he had lost his balance in the effort. The thin smoke had blown away, we were clear of the snag, and looking ahead I could see that in another hundred yards or so I would be free to sheer off, away from the bank; but my feet felt so very warm and wet that I had to look down. The man had rolled on his back and stared straight up at me; both his hands clutched that cane. It was the shaft of a spear that, either thrown or lunged through the opening, had caught him in the side just below the ribs; the blade had gone in out of sight, after making a frightful gash; my shoes were full; a pool of blood lay very still, gleaming dark-red under the wheel; his eyes shone with an amazing lustre. The fusillade burst out again. He looked at me anxiously, gripping the spear like something precious, with an air of being afraid I would try to take it away from him. I had to make an effort to free my eyes from his gaze and attend to the steering. With one hand I felt above my head for the line of the steam whistle, and jerked out screech after screech hurriedly. The tumult of angry and warlike yells was checked instantly, and then from the depths of the woods went out such a tremulous and prolonged wail of mournful fear and utter despair as may be imagined to follow the flight of the last hope from the earth. There was a great commotion in the bush; the shower of arrows stopped, a few dropping shots rang out sharply—then silence, in which the languid beat of the stern-wheel came plainly to my ears. I put the helm hard a-starboard at the moment when the pilgrim in pink pyjamas, very hot and agitated, appeared in the doorway. 'The manager sends me—' he began in an official tone, and stopped short. 'Good God!' he said, glaring at the wounded man.

"We two whites stood over him, and his lustrous and inquiring glance enveloped us both. I declare it looked as though he would presently put to us some question in an understandable language; but he died without uttering a sound, without moving a limb, without twitching a muscle. Only in the very last moment, as though in response to some sign we could not see, to some whisper we could not hear, he frowned heavily, and that frown gave to his black death-mask an inconceivably sombre, brooding, and menacing expression. The lustre of inquiring glance faded swiftly into vacant glassiness. 'Can you steer?' I asked the agent eagerly. He looked very dubious; but I made a grab at his arm, and he understood at once I meant him to steer whether or no. To tell you the truth, I was morbidly anxious to change my shoes and socks. 'He is dead,' murmured the fellow, immensely impressed. 'No doubt about it,' said I, tugging like mad at the shoe-laces. 'And by the way, I suppose Mr Kurtz is dead as well by this time.'

"For the moment that was the dominant thought. There was a sense of extreme disappointment, as though I had found out I had been striving after something altogether without a substance. I couldn't have been more disgusted if I had travelled all this way for the sole purpose of talking with Mr Kurtz. Talking with . . . I flung one shoe overboard, and became aware that that was exactly what I had been looking forward to—a talk with Kurtz. I made the strange discovery that I had never imagined him as doing, you know, but as discoursing. I didn't say to myself, 'Now I will never see him,' or 'Now I will never shake him by the hand,' but, 'Now I will never hear him.' The man presented himself as a voice. Not of course that I did not connect him with some sort of action. Hadn't I been told in all the tones of jealousy and admiration that he had collected, bartered, swindled, or stolen more ivory than all the other agents together? That was not the point. The point was in his being a gifted creature, and that of all his gifts the one that stood out pre-eminently, that carried with it a sense of real presence, was his ability to talk, his words— the gift of expression, the bewildering, the illuminating, the most exalted and the most contemptible, the pulsating stream of light, or the deceitful flow from the heart of an impenetrable darkness.

"The other shoe went flying unto the devil-god of that river. I thought, By Jove! it's all over. We are too late; he has vanished—the gift has vanished, by means of some spear, arrow, or club. I will never hear that chap speak after all—and my sorrow had a startling extravagance of emotion, even such as I had noticed in the howling sorrow of these savages in the bush. I couldn't have felt more of lonely desolation somehow, had I been robbed of a belief or had missed my destiny in life. . . . Why do you sigh in this beastly way, some-body? Absurd? Well, absurd. Good Lord! mustn't a man ever— Here, give me some tobacco." . . .

There was a pause of profound stillness, then a match flared, and Marlow's lean face appeared, worn, hollow, with downward folds and dropped eyelids, with an aspect of concentrated attention; and as he took vigorous draws at his pipe, it seemed to retreat and advance out of the night in the regular flicker of the tiny flame. The match went out.

"Absurd!" he cried. "This is the worst of trying to tell . . . Here you all are, each moored with two good addresses, like a hulk with two anchors, a butcher round one corner, a policeman round another, excellent appetites, and tem-perature normal—you hear—normal from year's end to year's end. And you say, Absurd! Absurd be—exploded! Absurd! My dear boys, what can you expect from a man who out of sheer nervousness had just flung overboard a pair of new shoes? Now I think of it, it is amazing I did not shed tears. I am, upon the whole, proud of my fortitude. I was cut to the quick at the idea of having lost the inestimable privilege of listening to the gifted Kurtz. Of course I was wrong. The privilege was waiting for me. Oh yes, I heard more than enough. And I was right, too. A voice. He was very little more than a voice. And I heard—him—it—this voice—other voices—all of them were so little more than voices—and the memory of that time itself lingers around me, impalpa-ble, like a dying vibration of one immense jabber, silly, atrocious, sordid, sav-age, or simply mean, without any kind of sense. Voices, voices—even the girl herself—now—"

He was silent for a long time.

"I laid the ghost of his gifts at last with a lie," he began suddenly. "Girl! What? Did I mention a girl? Oh, she is out of it—completely. They—the women I mean—are out of it—should be out of it. We must help them to stay in that beautiful world of their own, lest ours gets worse. Oh, she had to be out of it. You should have heard the disinterred body of Mr Kurtz saying, 'My Intended.' You would have perceived directly then how completely she was out of it. And the lofty frontal bone of Mr Kurtz! They say the hair goes on growing sometimes, but this—ah—specimen was impressively bald. The wil-derness had patted him on the head, and, behold, it was like a ball—an ivory ball; it had caressed him, and—lo!—he had withered; it had taken him, loved him, embraced him, got into his veins, consumed his flesh, and sealed his soul to its own by the inconceivable ceremonies of some devilish initiation. He was its spoiled and pampered favourite. Ivory? I should think so. Heaps of it, stacks of it. The old mud shanty was bursting with it. You would think there was not a single tusk left either above or below the ground in the whole country. 'Mostly fossil,' the manager had remarked disparagingly. It was no more fossil than I am; but they call it fossil when it is dug up. It appears these niggers do bury the tusks sometimes—but evidently they couldn't bury this parcel deep enough to save the gifted Mr Kurtz from his fate. We filled the steamboat with it, and had to pile a lot on the deck. Thus he could see and enjoy as long as he could see, because the appreciation of this favour had remained with him to the last. You should have heard him say, 'My ivory.' Oh yes, I heard him. 'My Intended, my ivory, my station, my river, my—' everything belonged to him. It made me hold my breath in expectation of hearing the wilderness burst into a prodigious peal of laughter that would shake the fixed stars in their places. Everything belonged to him—but that was a trifle. The thing was to know what he belonged to, how many powers of darkness claimed him for their own. That was the reflection that made you creepy all over. It was impossible—it was not good for one either—trying to imagine. He had taken a high seat amongst the devils of the land—I mean literally. You can't understand. How could you?—with solid pavement under your feet, surrounded by kind neighbours ready to cheer you or to fall on you, stepping delicately between the butcher and the policeman, in the holy terror of scandal and gallows and lunatic asylums—how can you imagine what particular region of the first ages a man's untrammelled feet may take him into by the way of solitude—utter solitude without a policeman—by the way of silence—utter silence, where no warning voice of a kind neighbour can be heard whispering of public opinion? These little things make all the great difference. When they are gone you must fall back upon your own innate strength, upon your own capacity for faithfulness. Of course you may be too much of a fool to go wrong—too dull even to know you are being assaulted by the powers of darkness. I take it, no fool ever made a bargain for his soul with the devil: the fool is too much of a fool, or the devil too much of a devil—I don't know which. Or you may be such a thunderingly exalted creature as to be altogether deaf and blind to anything but heavenly sights and sounds. Then the earth for you is only a standing place—and whether to be like this is your loss or your gain I won't pretend to say. But most of us are neither one nor the other. The earth for us is a place to live in, where we must put up with sights, with sounds, with smells, too, by Jove!—breathe dead hippo, so to speak, and not be contaminated. And there, don't you see? your strength comes in, the faith in your ability for the digging of unostentatious holes to bury the stuff in—your power of devotion, not to yourself, but to an obscure, back-breaking business. And that's difficult enough. Mind, I am not trying to excuse or even explain—I am trying to account to myself for—for—Mr Kurtz—for the shade of Mr Kurtz. This initiated wraith from the back of Nowhere honoured me with its amazing confidence before it vanished altogether. This was because it could speak English to me. The original Kurtz had been educated partly in England, and—as he was good enough to say himself—his sympathies were in the right place. His mother was half-English, his father was half-French. All Europe contributed to the making of Kurtz; and by and by I learned that, most appropriately, the International Society for the Suppression of Savage Customs had entrusted him with the making of a report, for its future guidance. And he had written it too. I've seen it. I've read it. It was eloquent, vibrating with eloquence, but too high-strung, I think. Seventeen pages of close writing he had found time for! But this must have been before his—let us say—nerves went wrong, and caused him to preside at certain midnight dances ending with unspeakable rites, which—as far as I reluctantly gathered from what I heard at various times—were offered up to him—do you understand?—to Mr Kurtz himself. But it was a beautiful piece of writing. The opening paragraph, however, in the light of later information, strikes me now as ominous. He began with the argument that we whites, from the point of development we had arrived at, 'must necessarily appear to them [savages] in the nature of supernatural beings—we approach them with the might as of a deity,' and so on, and so on. 'By the simple exercise of our will we can exert a power for good practically unbounded,' etc. etc. From that point he soared and took me with him. The peroration was magnificent, though difficult to remember, you know. It gave me the notion of an exotic Immensity ruled by an august Benevolence. It made me tingle with enthusiasm. This was the unbounded power of eloquence—of words—of burning noble words. There were no practical hints to interrupt the magic current of phrases, unless a kind of note at the foot of the last page, scrawled evidently much later, in an unsteady hand, may be regarded as the exposition of a method. It was very simple, and at the end of that moving appeal to every altruistic sentiment it blazed at you, luminous and terrifying, like a flash of lightning in a serene sky: 'Exterminate all the brutes!' The curious part was that he had apparently forgotten all about that valuable post-scriptum, because, later on, when he in a sense came to himself, he repeatedly entreated me to take good care of 'my pamphlet' (he called it), as it was sure to have in the future a good influence upon his career. I had full information about all these things, and, besides, as it turned out, I was to have the care of his memory. I've done enough for it to give me the indisputable right to lay it, if I choose, for an everlasting rest in the dust-bin of progress, amongst all the sweepings and, figuratively speaking, all the dead cats of civilisation. But then, you see, I can't choose. He won't be forgotten. Whatever he was, he was not common. He had the power to charm or frighten rudimentary souls into an aggravated witchdance in his honour; he could also fill the small souls of the pilgrims with bitter misgivings: he had one devoted friend at least, and he had conquered one soul in the world that was neither rudimentary nor tainted with self-seeking. No; I can't forget him, though I am not prepared to affirm the fellow was exactly worth the life we lost in getting to him. I missed my late helmsman awfully—I missed him even while his body was still lying in the pilot-house. Perhaps you will think it passing strange this regret for a savage who was no more account than a grain of sand in a black Sahara. Well, don't you see, he had done something, he had steered; for months I had him at my back—a help—an instrument. It was a kind of partnership. He steered for me—I had to look after him, I worried about his deficiencies, and thus a subtle bond had been created, of which I only became aware when it was suddenly broken. And the intimate profundity of that look he gave me when he received his hurt remains to this day in my memory—like a claim of distant kinship affirmed in a supreme moment.

"Poor fool! If he had only left that shutter alone. He had no restraint, no restraint—just like Kurtz—a tree swayed by the wind. As soon as I had put on a dry pair of slippers, I dragged him out, after first jerking the spear out of his side, which operation I confess I performed with my eyes shut tight. His heels leaped together over the little doorstep; his shoulders were pressed to my breast; I hugged him from behind desperately. Oh! he was heavy, heavy; heavier than any man on earth, I should imagine. Then without more ado I tipped him overboard. The current snatched him as though he had been a wisp of grass, and I saw the body roll over twice before I lost sight of it for ever. All the pilgrims and the manager were then congregated on the awning-deck about the pilot-house, chattering at each other like a flock of excited magpies, and there was a scandalised murmur at my heartless promptitude. What they wanted to keep that body hanging about for I can't guess. Embalm it, maybe. But I had also heard another, and a very ominous, murmur on the deck below. My friends the wood-cutters were likewise scandalised, and with a better show of reason—though I admit that the reason itself was quite inadmissible. Oh, quite! I had made up my mind that if my late helmsman was to be eaten, the fishes alone should have him. He had been a very second-rate helmsman while alive, but now he was dead he might have become a first-class temptation, and possibly cause some startling trouble. Besides, I was anxious to take the wheel, the man in pink pyjamas showing himself a hopeless duffer at the business.

"This I did directly the simple funeral was over. We were going half-speed, keeping right in the middle of the stream, and I listened to the talk about me. They had given up Kurtz, they had given up the station; Kurtz was dead, and the station had been burnt—and so on—and so on. The red-haired pilgrim was beside himself with the thought that at least this poor Kurtz had been properly revenged. 'Say! We must have made a glorious slaughter of them in the bush. Eh? What do you think? Say?' He positively danced, the bloodthirsty little gingery beggar.[2] And he had nearly fainted when he saw the wounded man! I could not help saying, 'You made a glorious lot of smoke, anyhow.' I had seen, from the way the tops of the bushes rustled and flew, that almost all the shots had gone too high. You can't hit anything unless you take aim and fire from the shoulder; but these chaps fired from the hip with their eyes shut. The retreat, I maintained—and I was right—was caused by the screeching of the steam-whistle. Upon this they forgot Kurtz, and began to howl at me with indignant protests.

"The manager stood by the wheel murmuring confidentially about the necessity of getting well away down the river before dark at all events, when I saw in the distance a clearing on the river-side and the outlines of some sort of building. 'What's this?' I asked. He clapped his hands in wonder. 'The station!' he cried. I edged in at once, still going half-speed.

"Through my glasses I saw the slope of a hill interspersed with rare trees and perfectly free from undergrowth. A long decaying building on the summit was half buried in the high grass; the large holes in the peaked roof gaped black from afar; the jungle and the woods made a background. There was no enclosure or fence of any kind; but there had been one apparently, for near the house half a dozen slim posts remained in a row, roughly trimmed, and with their upper ends ornamented with round carved balls. The rails, or whatever there had been between, had disappeared. Of course the forest surrounded all that. The river-bank was clear, and on the water side I saw a white man under a hat like a cart-wheel beckoning persistently with his whole arm. Examining the edge of the forest above and below, I was almost certain I could see movements—human forms gliding here and there. I steamed past prudently, then stopped the engines and let her drift down. The man on the shore began to shout, urging us to land. 'We have been attacked,' screamed the

2. Little redheaded rascal.

manager. 'I know—I know. It's all right,' yelled back the other, as cheerful as you please. 'Come along. It's all right. I am glad.'

"His aspect reminded me of something I had seen—something funny I had seen somewhere. As I manœuvred to get alongside, I was asking myself, 'What does this fellow look like?' Suddenly I got it. He looked like a harlequin.[3] His clothes had been made of some stuff that was brown holland[4] probably, but it was covered with patches all over, with bright patches, blue, red, and yellow— patches on the back, patches on the front, patches on elbows, on knees; coloured binding round his jacket, scarlet edging at the bottom of his trousers; and the sunshine made him look extremely gay and wonderfully neat withal, because you could see how beautifully all this patching had been done. A beardless, boyish face, very fair, no features to speak of, nose peeling, little blue eyes, smiles and frowns chasing each other over that open countenance like sunshine and shadow on a wind-swept plain. 'Look out, captain!' he cried; 'there's a snag lodged in here last night.' What! Another snag? I confess I swore shamefully. I had nearly holed my cripple, to finish off that charming trip. The harlequin on the bank turned his little pug nose up to me. 'You English?' he asked, all smiles. 'Are you?' I shouted from the wheel. The smiles vanished, and he shook his head as if sorry for my disappointment. Then he brightened up. 'Never mind!' he cried encouragingly. 'Are we in time?' I asked. 'He is up there,' he replied, with a toss of the head up the hill, and becoming gloomy all of a sudden. His face was like the autumn sky, overcast one moment and bright the next.

"When the manager, escorted by the pilgrims, all of them armed to the teeth, had gone to the house, this chap came on board. 'I say, I don't like this. These natives are in the bush,' I said. He assured me earnestly it was all right. 'They are simple people,' he added; 'well, I am glad you came. It took me all my time to keep them off.' 'But you said it was all right,' I cried. 'Oh, they meant no harm,' he said; and as I stared he corrected himself, 'Not exactly.' Then vivaciously, 'My faith, your pilot-house wants a clean up!' In the next breath he advised me to keep enough steam on the boiler to blow the whistle in case of any trouble. 'One good screech will do more for you than all your rifles. They are simple people,' he repeated. He rattled away at such a rate he quite overwhelmed me. He seemed to be trying to make up for lots of silence, and actually hinted, laughing, that such was the case. 'Don't you talk with Mr Kurtz?' I said. 'You don't talk with that man—you listen to him,' he exclaimed with severe exaltation. 'But now—' He waved his arm, and in the twinkling of an eye was in the uttermost depths of despondency. In a moment he came up again with a jump, possessed himself of both my hands, shook them continuously, while he gabbled: 'Brother sailor . . . honour . . . pleasure . . . delight . . . introduce myself . . . Russian . . . son of an arch-priest . . . Government of Tambov . . . What? Tobacco! English tobacco; the excellent English tobacco! Now, that's brotherly. Smoke? Where's a sailor that does not smoke?'

"The pipe soothed him, and gradually I made out he had run away from school, had gone to sea in a Russian ship; ran away again; served some time in English ships; was now reconciled with the arch-priest. He made a point of that. 'But when one is young one must see things, gather experience, ideas; enlarge the mind.' 'Here!' I interrupted. 'You can never tell! Here I met Mr

3. Character from Italian comedy traditionally dressed in multicolored clothes.
4. Coarse linen fabric.

Kurtz,' he said, youthfully solemn and reproachful. I held my tongue after that. It appears he had persuaded a Dutch trading-house on the coast to fit him out with stores and goods, and had started for the interior with a light heart, and no more idea of what would happen to him than a baby. He had been wandering about that river for nearly two years alone, cut off from everybody and everything. 'I am not so young as I look. I am twenty-five,' he said. 'At first old Van Shuyten would tell me to go to the devil,' he narrated with keen enjoyment; 'but I stuck to him, and talked and talked, till at last he got afraid I would talk the hind-leg off his favourite dog, so he gave me some cheap things and a few guns, and told me he hoped he would never see my face again. Good old Dutchman, Van Shuyten. I sent him one small lot of ivory a year ago, so that he can't call me a little thief when I get back. I hope he got it. And for the rest I don't care. I had some wood stacked for you. That was my old house. Did you see?'

"I gave him Towson's book. He made as though he would kiss me, but restrained himself. 'The only book I had left, and I thought I had lost it,' he said, looking at it ecstatically. 'So many accidents happen to a man going about alone, you know. Canoes get upset sometimes—and sometimes you've got to clear out so quick when the people get angry.' He thumbed the pages. 'You made notes in Russian?' I asked. He nodded. 'I thought they were written in cipher,' I said. He laughed, then became serious. 'I had lots of trouble to keep these people off,' he said. 'Did they want to kill you?' I asked. 'Oh no!' he cried, and checked himself. 'Why did they attack us?' I pursued. He hesitated, then said shamefacedly, 'They don't want him to go.' 'Don't they?' I said curiously. He nodded a nod full of mystery and wisdom. 'I tell you,' he cried, 'this man has enlarged my mind.' He opened his arms wide, staring at me with his little blue eyes that were perfectly round."

3

"I looked at him, lost in astonishment. There he was before me, in motley, as though he had absconded from a troupe of mimes, enthusiastic, fabulous. His very existence was improbable, inexplicable, and altogether bewildering. He was an insoluble problem. It was inconceivable how he had existed, how he had succeeded in getting so far, how he had managed to remain—why he did not instantly disappear. 'I went a little farther,' he said, 'then still a little farther—till I had gone so far that I don't know how I'll ever get back. Never mind. Plenty time. I can manage. You take Kurtz away quick—quick—I tell you.' The glamour of youth enveloped his particoloured rags, his destitution, his loneliness, the essential desolation of his futile wanderings. For months— for years—his life hadn't been worth a day's purchase; and there he was gallantly, thoughtlessly alive, to all appearance indestructible solely by the virtue of his few years and of his unreflecting audacity. I was seduced into something like admiration—like envy. Glamour urged him on, glamour kept him unscathed. He surely wanted nothing from the wilderness but space to breathe in and to push on through. His need was to exist, and to move onwards at the greatest possible risk, and with a maximum of privation. If the absolutely pure, uncalculating, unpractical spirit of adventure had ever ruled a human being, it ruled this be-patched youth. I almost envied him the possession of this modest and clear flame. It seemed to have consumed all thought of self so completely, that, even while he was talking to you, you forgot that it was he—

the man before your eyes—who had gone through these things. I did not envy him his devotion to Kurtz, though. He had not meditated over it. It came to him, and he accepted it with a sort of eager fatalism. I must say that to me it appeared about the most dangerous thing in every way he had come upon so far.

"They had come together unavoidably, like two ships becalmed near each other, and lay rubbing sides at last. I suppose Kurtz wanted an audience, because on a certain occasion, when encamped in the forest, they had talked all night, or more probably Kurtz had talked. 'We talked of everything,' he said, quite transported at the recollection. 'I forgot there was such a thing as sleep. The night did not seem to last an hour. Everything! Everything! . . . Of love too.' 'Ah, he talked to you of love!' I said, much amused. 'It isn't what you think,' he cried, almost passionately. 'It was in general. He made me see things—things.'

"He threw his arms up. We were on deck at the time, and the head-man of my wood-cutters, lounging near by, turned upon him his heavy and glittering eyes. I looked around, and I don't know why, but I assure you that never, never before, did this land, this river, this jungle, the very arch of this blazing sky, appear to me so hopeless and so dark, so impenetrable to human thought, so pitiless to human weakness. 'And, ever since, you have been with him, of course?' I said.

"On the contrary. It appears their intercourse had been very much broken by various causes. He had, as he informed me proudly, managed to nurse Kurtz through two illnesses (he alluded to it as you would to some risky feat), but as a rule Kurtz wandered alone, far in the depths of the forest. 'Very often coming to this station, I had to wait days and days before he would turn up,' he said. 'Ah, it was worth waiting for!—sometimes.' 'What was he doing? exploring or what?' I asked. 'Oh yes, of course'; he had discovered lots of villages, a lake too—he did not know exactly in what direction; it was danger-ous to inquire too much—but mostly his expeditions had been for ivory. 'But he had no goods to trade with by that time,' I objected. 'There's a good lot of cartridges left even yet,' he answered, looking away. 'To speak plainly, he raided the country,' I said. He nodded. 'Not alone, surely!' He muttered some-thing about the villages round that lake. 'Kurtz got the tribe to follow him, did he?' I suggested. He fidgeted a little. 'They adored him,' he said. The tone of these words was so extraordinary that I looked at him searchingly. It was curi-ous to see his mingled eagerness and reluctance to speak of Kurtz. The man filled his life, occupied his thoughts, swayed his emotions. 'What can you expect?' he burst out; 'he came to them with thunder and lightning, you know—and they had never seen anything like it—and very terrible. He could be very terrible. You can't judge Mr Kurtz as you would an ordinary man. No, no, no! Now—just to give you an idea—I don't mind telling you, he wanted to shoot me too one day—but I don't judge him.' 'Shoot you!' I cried. 'What for?' 'Well, I had a small lot of ivory the chief of that village near my house gave me. You see I used to shoot game for them. Well, he wanted it, and wouldn't hear reason. He declared he would shoot me unless I gave him the ivory and then cleared out of the country, because he could do so, and had a fancy for it, and there was nothing on earth to prevent him killing whom he jolly well pleased. And it was true too. I gave him the ivory. What did I care! But I didn't clear out. No, no. I couldn't leave him. I had to be careful, of course, till we got friendly again for a time. He had his second illness then.

Afterwards I had to keep out of the way; but I didn't mind. He was living for the most part in those villages on the lake. When he came down to the river, sometimes he would take to me, and sometimes it was better for me to be careful. This man suffered too much. He hated all this, and somehow he couldn't get away. When I had a chance I begged him to try and leave while there was time; I offered to go back with him. And he would say yes, and then he would remain; go off on another ivory hunt; disappear for weeks; forget himself amongst these people—forget himself—you know.' 'Why! he's mad,' I said. He protested indignantly. Mr Kurtz couldn't be mad. If I had heard him talk, only two days ago, I wouldn't dare hint at such a thing. . . . I had taken up my binoculars while we talked, and was looking at the shore, sweeping the limit of the forest at each side and at the back of the house. The consciousness of there being people in that bush, so silent, so quiet—as silent and quiet as the ruined house on the hill—made me uneasy. There was no sign on the face of nature of this amazing tale that was not so much told as suggested to me in desolate exclamations, completed by shrugs, in interrupted phrases, in hints ending in deep sighs. The woods were unmoved, like a mask—heavy, like the closed door of a prison—they looked with their air of hidden knowledge, of patient expectation, of unapproachable silence. The Russian was explaining to me that it was only lately that Mr Kurtz had come down to the river, bringing along with him all the fighting men of that lake tribe. He had been absent for several months—getting himself adored, I suppose—and had come down unexpectedly, with the intention to all appearance of making a raid either across the river or down stream. Evidently the appetite for more ivory had got the better of the—what shall I say?—less material aspirations. However, he had got much worse suddenly. 'I heard he was lying helpless, and so I came up—took my chance,' said the Russian. 'Oh, he is bad, very bad.' I directed my glass to the house. There were no signs of life, but there was the ruined roof, the long mud wall peeping above the grass, with three little square window-holes, no two of the same size; all this brought within reach of my hand, as it were. And then I made a brusque movement, and one of the remaining posts of that vanished fence leaped up in the field of my glass. You remember I told you I had been struck at the distance by certain attempts at ornamentation, rather remarkable in the ruinous aspect of the place. Now I had suddenly a nearer view, and its first result was to make me throw my head back as if before a blow. Then I went carefully from post to post with my glass, and I saw my mistake. These round knobs were not ornamental but symbolic; they were expressive and puzzling, striking and disturbing—food for thought and also for the vultures if there had been any looking down from the sky; but at all events for such ants as were industrious enough to ascend the pole. They would have been even more impressive, those heads on the stakes, if their faces had not been turned to the house. Only one, the first I had made out, was facing my way. I was not so shocked as you may think. The start back I had given was really nothing but a movement of surprise. I had expected to see a knob of wood there, you know. I returned deliberately to the first I had seen—and there it was, black, dried, sunken, with closed eyelids—a head that seemed to sleep at the top of that pole, and, with the shrunken dry lips showing a narrow white line of the teeth, was smiling too, smiling continuously at some endless and jocose dream of that eternal slumber.

"I am not disclosing any trade secrets. In fact the manager said afterwards that Mr Kurtz's methods had ruined the district. I have no opinion on that point, but I want you clearly to understand that there was nothing exactly profitable in these heads being there. They only show that Mr Kurtz lacked restraint in the gratification of his various lusts, that there was something wanting in him—some small matter which, when the pressing need arose, could not be found under his magnificent eloquence. Whether he knew of this deficiency himself I can't say. I think the knowledge came to him at last— only at the very last. But the wilderness had found him out early, and had taken on him a terrible vengeance for the fantastic invasion. I think it had whispered to him things about himself which he did not know, things of which he had no conception till he took counsel with this great solitude—and the whisper had proved irresistibly fascinating. It echoed loudly within him because he was hollow at the core. . . . I put down the glass, and the head that had appeared near enough to be spoken to seemed at once to have leaped away from me into inaccessible distance.

"The admirer of Mr Kurtz was a bit crestfallen. In a hurried, indistinct voice he began to assure me he had not dared to take these—say, symbols—down. He was not afraid of the natives; they would not stir till Mr Kurtz gave the word. His ascendancy was extraordinary. The camps of these people sur-rounded the place, and the chiefs came every day to see him. They would crawl . . . 'I don't want to know anything of the ceremonies used when approaching Mr Kurtz,' I shouted. Curious, this feeling that came over me that such details would be more intolerable than those heads drying on the stakes under Mr Kurtz's windows. After all, that was only a savage sight, while I seemed at one bound to have been transported into some lightless region of subtle horrors, where pure, uncomplicated savagery was a positive relief, being something that had a right to exist—obviously—in the sunshine. The young man looked at me with surprise. I suppose it did not occur to him that Mr Kurtz was no idol of mine. He forgot I hadn't heard any of these splendid monologues on, what was it? on love, justice, conduct of life—or what not. If it had come to crawling before Mr Kurtz, he crawled as much as the veriest savage of them all. I had no idea of the conditions, he said: these heads were the heads of rebels. I shocked him excessively by laughing. Rebels! What would be the next definition I was to hear? There had been enemies, criminals, work-ers—and these were rebels. Those rebellious heads looked very subdued to me on their sticks. 'You don't know how such a life tries a man like Kurtz,' cried Kurtz's last disciple. 'Well, and you?' I said. 'I! I! I am a simple man. I have no great thoughts. I want nothing from anybody. How can you compare me to . . . ?' His feelings were too much for speech, and suddenly he broke down. 'I don't understand,' he groaned. 'I've been doing my best to keep him alive, and that's enough. I had no hand in all this. I have no abilities. There hasn't been a drop of medicine or a mouthful of invalid food for months here. He was shamefully abandoned. A man like this, with such ideas. Shamefully! Shamefully! I—I—haven't slept for the last ten nights. . . .'

"His voice lost itself in the calm of the evening. The long shadows of the forest had slipped down hill while we talked, had gone far beyond the ruined hovel, beyond the symbolic row of stakes. All this was in the gloom, while we down there were yet in the sunshine, and the stretch of the river abreast of the clearing glittered in a still and dazzling splendour, with a murky and over-shadowed bend above and below. Not a living soul was seen on the shore. The bushes did not rustle.

"Suddenly round the corner of the house a group of men appeared, as

2372 / JOSEPH CONRAD

though they had come up from the ground. They waded waist-deep in the grass, in a compact body, bearing an improvised stretcher in their midst. Instantly, in the emptiness of the landscape, a cry arose whose shrillness pierced the still air like a sharp arrow flying straight to the very heart of the land; and, as if by enchantment, streams of human beings—of naked human beings—with spears in their hands, with bows, with shields, with wild glances and savage movements, were poured into the clearing by the dark-faced and pensive forest. The bushes shook, the grass swayed for a time, and then everything stood still in attentive immobility.

" 'Now, if he does not say the right thing to them we are all done for,' said the Russian at my elbow. The knot of men with the stretcher had stopped too, half-way to the steamer, as if petrified. I saw the man on the stretcher sit up, lank and with an uplifted arm, above the shoulders of the bearers. 'Let us hope that the man who can talk so well of love in general will find some particular reason to spare us this time,' I said. I resented bitterly the absurd danger of our situation, as if to be at the mercy of that atrocious phantom had been a dishonouring necessity. I could not hear a sound, but through my glasses I saw the thin arm extended commandingly, the lower jaw moving, the eyes of that apparition shining darkly far in its bony head that nodded with grotesque jerks. Kurtz—Kurtz—that means 'short' in German—don't it? Well, the name was as true as everything else in his life—and death. He looked at least seven feet long. His covering had fallen off, and his body emerged from it pitiful and appalling as from a winding-sheet. I could see the cage of his ribs all astir, the bones of his arm waving. It was as though an animated image of death carved out of old ivory had been shaking its hand with menaces at a motionless crowd of men made of dark and glittering bronze. I saw him open his mouth wide—it gave him a weirdly voracious aspect, as though he had wanted to swallow all the air, all the earth, all the men before him. A deep voice reached me faintly. He must have been shouting. He fell back suddenly. The stretcher shook as the bearers staggered forward again, and almost at the same time I noticed that the crowd of savages was vanishing without any perceptible movement of retreat, as if the forest that had ejected these beings so suddenly had drawn them in again as the breath is drawn in a long aspiration.

"Some of the pilgrims behind the stretcher carried his arms—two shot-guns, a heavy rifle, and a light revolver-carbine—the thunderbolts of that pitiful Jupiter. The manager bent over him murmuring as he walked beside his head. They laid him down in one of the little cabins—just a room for a bedplace and a camp-stool or two, you know. We had brought his belated correspondence, and a lot of torn envelopes and open letters littered his bed. His hand roamed feebly amongst these papers. I was struck by the fire of his eyes and the composed languor of his expression. It was not so much the exhaustion of disease. He did not seem in pain. This shadow looked satiated and calm, as though for the moment it had had its fill of all the emotions.

"He rustled one of the letters, and looking straight in my face said, 'I am glad.' Somebody had been writing to him about me. These special recommendations were turning up again. The volume of tone he emitted without effort, almost without the trouble of moving his lips, amazed me. A voice! a voice! It was grave, profound, vibrating, while the man did not seem capable of a whisper. However, he had enough strength in him—factitious no doubt—to very nearly make an end of us, as you shall hear directly.

"The manager appeared silently in the doorway; I stepped out at once and he drew the curtain after me. The Russian, eyed curiously by the pilgrims, was staring at the shore. I followed the direction of his glance.

"Dark human shapes could be made out in the distance, flitting indistinctly against the gloomy border of the forest, and near the river two bronze figures, leaning on tall spears, stood in the sunlight under fantastic head-dresses of spotted skins, warlike and still in statuesque repose. And from right to left along the lighted shore moved a wild and gorgeous apparition of a woman.

"She walked with measured steps, draped in striped and fringed cloths, treading the earth proudly, with a slight jingle and flash of barbarous ornaments. She carried her head high; her hair was done in the shape of a helmet; she had brass leggings to the knee, brass wire gauntlets to the elbow, a crimson spot on her tawny cheek, innumerable necklaces of glass beads on her neck; bizarre things, charms, gifts of witch-men, that hung about her, glittered and trembled at every step. She must have had the value of several elephant tusks upon her. She was savage and superb, wild-eyed and magnificent; there was something ominous and stately in her deliberate progress. And in the hush that had fallen suddenly upon the whole sorrowful land, the immense wilderness, the colossal body of the fecund and mysterious life seemed to look at her, pensive, as though it had been looking at the image of its own tenebrous and passionate soul.

"She came abreast of the steamer, stood still, and faced us. Her long shadow fell to the water's edge. Her face had a tragic and fierce aspect of wild sorrow and of dumb pain mingled with the fear of some struggling, half-shaped resolve. She stood looking at us without a stir, and like the wilderness itself, with an air of brooding over an inscrutable purpose. A whole minute passed, and then she made a step forward. There was a low jingle, a glint of yellow metal, a sway of fringed draperies, and she stopped as if her heart had failed her. The young fellow by my side growled. The pilgrims murmured at my back. She looked at us all as if her life had depended upon the unswerving steadiness of her glance. Suddenly she opened her bared arms and threw them up rigid above her head, as though in an uncontrollable desire to touch the sky, and at the same time the swift shadows darted out on the earth, swept around on the river, gathering the steamer into a shadowy embrace. A formidable silence hung over the scene.

"She turned away slowly, walked on, following the bank, and passed into the bushes to the left. Once only her eyes gleamed back at us in the dusk of the thickets before she disappeared.

" 'If she had offered to come aboard I really think I would have tried to shoot her,' said the man of patches nervously. 'I had been risking my life every day for the last fortnight to keep her out of the house. She got in one day and kicked up a row about those miserable rags I picked up in the storeroom to mend my clothes with. I wasn't decent. At least it must have been that, for she talked like a fury to Kurtz for an hour, pointing at me now and then. I don't understand the dialect of this tribe. Luckily for me, I fancy Kurtz felt too ill that day to care, or there would have been mischief. I don't understand. . . . No—it's too much for me. Ah, well, it's all over now.'

"At this moment I heard Kurtz's deep voice behind the curtain: 'Save me!— save the ivory, you mean. Don't tell me. Save *me*! Why, I've had to save you. You are interrupting my plans now. Sick! Sick! Not so sick as you would like to believe. Never mind. I'll carry my ideas out yet—I will return. I'll show you what can be done. You with your little peddling notions—you are interfering with me. I will return. I . . .'

"The manager came out. He did me the honour to take me under the arm and lead me aside. 'He is very low, very low,' he said. He considered it necessary to sigh, but neglected to be consistently sorrowful. 'We have done all we could for him—haven't we? But there is no disguising the fact, Mr Kurtz has done more harm than good to the Company. He did not see the time was not ripe for vigorous action. Cautiously, cautiously—that's my principle. We must be cautious yet. The district is closed to us for a time. Deplorable! Upon the whole, the trade will suffer. I don't deny there is a remarkable quantity of ivory—mostly fossil. We must save it, at all events—but look how precarious the position is—and why? Because the method is unsound.' 'Do you,' said I, looking at the shore, 'call it "unsound method"?' 'Without doubt,' he exclaimed hotly, 'Don't you?' . . . 'No method at all,' I murmured after a while. 'Exactly,' he exulted. 'I anticipated this. Shows a complete want of judgment. It is my duty to point it out in the proper quarter.' 'Oh,' said I, 'that fellow—what's his name?—the brickmaker, will make a readable report for you.' He appeared confounded for a moment. It seemed to me I had never breathed an atmosphere so vile, and I turned mentally to Kurtz for relief—positively for relief. 'Nevertheless, I think Mr Kurtz is a remarkable man,' I said with emphasis. He started, dropped on me a cold heavy glance, said very quietly, 'He *was*,' and turned his back on me. My hour of favour was over; I found myself lumped along with Kurtz as a partisan of methods for which the time was not ripe: I was unsound! Ah! but it was something to have at least a choice of nightmares.

"I had turned to the wilderness really, not to Mr Kurtz, who, I was ready to admit, was as good as buried. And for a moment it seemed to me as if I also were buried in a vast grave full of unspeakable secrets. I felt an intolerable weight oppressing my breast, the smell of the damp earth, the unseen presence of victorious corruption, the darkness of an impenetrable night. . . . The Russian tapped me on the shoulder. I heard him mumbling and stammering something about 'brother seaman—couldn't conceal—knowledge of matters that would affect Mr Kurtz's reputation.' I waited. For him evidently Mr Kurtz was not in his grave; I suspect that for him Mr Kurtz was one of the immortals. 'Well!' said I at last, 'speak out. As it happens, I am Mr Kurtz's friend—in a way.'

"He stated with a good deal of formality that had we not been 'of the same profession,' he would have kept the matter to himself without regard to consequences. He suspected 'there was an active ill-will towards him on the part of these white men that—' 'You are right,' I said, remembering a certain conversation I had overheard. 'The manager thinks you ought to be hanged.' He showed a concern at this intelligence which amused me at first. 'I had better get out of the way quietly,' he said earnestly. 'I can do no more for Kurtz now, and they would soon find some excuse. What's to stop them? There's a military post three hundred miles from here.' 'Well, upon my word,' said I, 'perhaps you had better go if you have any friends amongst the savages near by.' 'Plenty,' he said. 'They are simple people—and I want nothing, you know.' He stood biting his lip, then: 'I don't want any harm to happen to these whites here, but of course I was thinking of Mr Kurtz's reputation—but you are a brother seaman and—' 'All right,' said I, after a time. 'Mr Kurtz's reputation is safe with me.' I did not know how truly I spoke.

"He informed me, lowering his voice, that it was Kurtz who had ordered the attack to be made on the steamer. 'He hated sometimes the idea of being taken away—and then again . . . . But I don't understand these matters. I am a simple man. He thought it would scare you away—that you would give it up, thinking him dead. I could not stop him. Oh, I had an awful time of it this last month.' 'Very well,' I said. 'He is all right now.' 'Ye-e-es,' he muttered, not very convinced apparently. 'Thanks,' said I; 'I shall keep my eyes open.' 'But quiet—eh?' he urged anxiously. 'It would be awful for his reputation if anybody here—' I promised a complete discretion with great gravity. 'I have a canoe and three black fellows waiting not very far. I am off. Could you give me a few Martini-Henry cartridges?' I could, and did, with proper secrecy. He helped himself, with a wink at me, to a handful of my tobacco. 'Between sailors—you know—good English tobacco.' At the door of the pilot-house he turned round—'I say, haven't you a pair of shoes you could spare?' He raised one leg. 'Look.' The soles were tied with knotted strings sandal-wise under his bare feet. I rooted out an old pair, at which he looked with admiration before tucking it under his left arm. One of his pockets (bright red) was bulging with cartridges, from the other (dark blue) peeped 'Towson's Inquiry,' etc. etc. He seemed to think himself excellently well equipped for a renewed encounter with the wilderness. 'Ah! I'll never, never meet such a man again. You ought to have heard him recite poetry—his own too it was, he told me. Poetry!' He rolled his eyes at the recollection of these delights. 'Oh, he enlarged my mind!' 'Good-bye,' said I. He shook hands and vanished in the night. Sometimes I ask myself whether I had ever really seen him—whether it was possible to meet such a phenomenon! . . .

"When I woke up shortly after midnight his warning came to my mind with its hint of danger that seemed, in the starred darkness, real enough to make me get up for the purpose of having a look round. On the hill a big fire burned, illuminating fitfully a crooked corner of the station-house. One of the agents with a picket of a few of our blacks, armed for the purpose, was keeping guard over the ivory; but deep within the forest, red gleams that wavered, that seemed to sink and rise from the ground amongst confused columnar shapes of intense blackness, showed the exact position of the camp where Mr Kurtz's adorers were keeping their uneasy vigil. The monotonous beating of a big drum filled the air with muffled shocks and a lingering vibration. A steady droning sound of many men chanting each to himself some weird incantation came out from the black, flat wall of the woods as the humming of bees comes out of a hive, and had a strange narcotic effect upon my half-awake senses. I believe I dozed off leaning over the rail, till an abrupt burst of yells, an overwhelming outbreak of a pent-up and mysterious frenzy, woke me up in a bewildered wonder. It was cut short all at once, and the low droning went on with an effect of audible and soothing silence. I glanced casually into the little cabin. A light was burning within, but Mr Kurtz was not there.

"I think I would have raised an outcry if I had believed my eyes. But I didn't believe them at first—the thing seemed so impossible. The fact is I was completely unnerved by a sheer blank fright, pure abstract terror, unconnected with any distinct shape of physical danger. What made this emotion so overpowering was—how shall I define it?—the moral shock I received, as if something altogether monstrous, intolerable to thought and odious to the soul, had been thrust upon me unexpectedly. This lasted of course the merest fraction of a second, and then the usual sense of commonplace, deadly danger, the possibility of a sudden onslaught and massacre, or something of the kind, which I saw impending, was positively welcome and composing. It pacified me, in fact, so much, that I did not raise an alarm.

"There was an agent buttoned up inside an ulster[5] and sleeping on a chair on deck within three feet of me. The yells had not awakened him; he snored very slightly; I left him to his slumbers and leaped ashore. I did not betray Mr Kurtz—it was ordered I should never betray him—it was written I should be loyal to the nightmare of my choice. I was anxious to deal with this shadow by myself alone—and to this day I don't know why I was so jealous of sharing with any one the peculiar blackness of that experience.

"As soon as I got on the bank I saw a trail—a broad trail through the grass. I remember the exultation with which I said to myself, 'He can't walk—he is crawling on all-fours—I've got him.' The grass was wet with dew. I strode rapidly with clenched fists. I fancy I had some vague notion of falling upon him and giving him a drubbing. I don't know. I had some imbecile thoughts. The knitting old woman with the cat obtruded herself upon my memory as a most improper person to be sitting at the other end of such an affair. I saw a row of pilgrims squirting lead in the air out of Winchesters held to the hip. I thought I would never get back to the steamer, and imagined myself living alone and unarmed in the woods to an advanced age. Such silly things—you know. And I remember I confounded the beat of the drum with the beating of my heart, and was pleased at its calm regularity.

"I kept to the track though—then stopped to listen. The night was very clear; a dark blue space, sparkling with dew and starlight, in which black things stood very still. I thought I could see a kind of motion ahead of me. I was strangely cocksure of everything that night. I actually left the track and ran in a wide semicircle (I verily believe chuckling to myself) so as to get in front of that stir, of that motion I had seen—if indeed I had seen anything. I was circumventing Kurtz as though it had been a boyish game.

"I came upon him, and, if he had not heard me coming, I would have fallen over him too, but he got up in time. He rose, unsteady, long, pale, indistinct, like a vapour exhaled by the earth, and swayed slightly, misty and silent before me; while at my back the fires loomed between the trees, and the murmur of many voices issued from the forest. I had cut him off cleverly; but when actually confronting him I seemed to come to my senses, I saw the danger in its right proportion. It was by no means over yet. Suppose he began to shout? Though he could hardly stand, there was still plenty of vigour in his voice. 'Go away—hide yourself,' he said, in that profound tone. It was very awful. I glanced back. We were within thirty yards of the nearest fire. A black figure stood up, strode on long black legs, waving long black arms, across the glow. It had horns—antelope horns, I think—on its head. Some sorcerer, some witch-man no doubt: it looked fiend-like enough. 'Do you know what you are doing?' I whispered. 'Perfectly,' he answered, raising his voice for that single word: it sounded to me far off and yet loud, like a hail through a speaking-trumpet. If he makes a row we are lost, I thought to myself. This clearly was not a case for fisticuffs, even apart from the very natural aversion I had to beat that Shadow—this wandering and tormented thing. 'You will be lost,' I said— 'utterly lost.' One gets sometimes such a flash of inspiration, you know. I did say the right thing, though indeed he could not have been more irretrievably

5. Long overcoat.

lost than he was at this very moment, when the foundations of our intimacy were being laid—to endure—to endure—even to the end—even beyond.

"'I had immense plans,' he muttered irresolutely. 'Yes,' said I; 'but if you try to shout I'll smash your head with—' There was not a stick or a stone near. 'I will throttle you for good,' I corrected myself. 'I was on the threshold of great things,' he pleaded, in a voice of longing, with a wistfulness of tone that made my blood run cold. 'And now for this stupid scoundrel—' 'Your success in Europe is assured in any case,' I affirmed steadily. I did not want to have the throttling of him, you understand—and indeed it would have been very little use for any practical purpose. I tried to break the spell—the heavy, mute spell of the wilderness—that seemed to draw him to its pitiless breast by the awakening of forgotten and brutal instincts, by the memory of gratified and monstrous passions. This alone, I was convinced, had driven him out to the edge of the forest, to the bush, towards the gleam of fires, the throb of drums, the drone of weird incantations; this alone had beguiled his unlawful soul beyond the bounds of permitted aspirations. And, don't you see, the terror of the position was not in being knocked on the head—though I had a very lively sense of that danger too—but in this, that I had to deal with a being to whom I could not appeal in the name of anything high or low. I had, even like the niggers, to invoke him—himself—his own exalted and incredible degradation. There was nothing either above or below him, and I knew it. He had kicked himself loose of the earth. Confound the man! he had kicked the very earth to pieces. He was alone, and I before him did not know whether I stood on the ground or floated in the air. I've been telling you what we said—repeating the phrases we pronounced—but what's the good? They were common everyday words—the familiar, vague sounds exchanged on every waking day of life. But what of that? They had behind them, to my mind, the terrific suggestiveness of words heard in dreams, of phrases spoken in nightmares. Soul! If anybody had ever struggled with a soul, I am the man. And I wasn't arguing with a lunatic either. Believe me or not, his intelligence was perfectly clear—concentrated, it is true, upon himself with horrible intensity, yet clear; and therein was my only chance—barring, of course, the killing him there and then, which wasn't so good, on account of unavoidable noise. But his soul was mad. Being alone in the wilderness, it had looked within itself, and, by heavens! I tell you, it had gone mad. I had—for my sins, I suppose, to go through the ordeal of looking into it myself. No eloquence could have been so withering to one's belief in mankind as his final burst of sincerity. He struggled with himself too. I saw it—I heard it. I saw the inconceivable mystery of a soul that knew no restraint, no faith, and no fear, yet struggling blindly with itself. I kept my head pretty well; but when I had him at last stretched on the couch, I wiped my forehead, while my legs shook under me as though I had carried half a ton on my back down that hill. And yet I had only supported him, his bony arm clasped round my neck—and he was not much heavier than a child.

"When next day we left at noon, the crowd, of whose presence behind the curtain of trees I had been acutely conscious all the time, flowed out of the woods again, filled the clearing, covered the slope with a mass of naked, breathing, quivering, bronze bodies. I steamed up a bit, then swung downstream, and two thousand eyes followed the evolutions of the splashing, thumping, fierce river-demon beating the water with its terrible tail and breathing black smoke into the air. In front of the first rank, along the river, three men, plastered with bright red earth from head to foot, strutted to and fro restlessly. When we came abreast again, they faced the river, stamped their feet, nodded their horned heads, swayed their scarlet bodies; they shook towards the fierce river-demon a bunch of black feathers, a mangy skin with a pendent tail—something that looked like a dried gourd; they shouted periodically together strings of amazing words that resembled no sounds of human language; and the deep murmurs of the crowd, interrupted suddenly, were like the responses of some satanic litany.

"We had carried Kurtz into the pilot-house: there was more air there. Lying on the couch, he stared through the open shutter. There was an eddy in the mass of human bodies, and the woman with helmeted head and tawny cheeks rushed out to the very brink of the stream. She put out her hands, shouted something, and all that wild mob took up the shout in a roaring chorus of articulated, rapid, breathless utterance.

" 'Do you understand this?' I asked.

"He kept on looking out past me with fiery, longing eyes, with a mingled expression of wistfulness and hate. He made no answer, but I saw a smile, a smile of indefinable meaning, appear on his colourless lips that a moment after twitched convulsively. 'Do I not?' he said slowly, gasping, as if the words had been torn out of him by a supernatural power.

"I pulled the string of the whistle, and I did this because I saw the pilgrims on deck getting out their rifles with an air of anticipating a jolly lark. At the sudden screech there was a movement of abject terror through that wedged mass of bodies. 'Don't! don't you frighten them away,' cried some one on deck disconsolately. I pulled the string time after time. They broke and ran, they leaped, they crouched, they swerved, they dodged the flying terror of the sound. The three red chaps had fallen flat, face down on the shore, as though they had been shot dead. Only the barbarous and superb woman did not so much as flinch, and stretched tragically her bare arms after us over the sombre and glittering river.

"And then that imbecile crowd down on the deck started their little fun, and I could see nothing more for smoke.

"The brown current ran swiftly out of the heart of darkness, bearing us down towards the sea with twice the speed of our upward progress; and Kurtz's life was running swiftly too, ebbing, ebbing out of his heart into the sea of inexorable time. The manager was very placid, he had no vital anxieties now, he took us both in with a comprehensive and satisfied glance: the 'affair' had come off as well as could be wished. I saw the time approaching when I would be left alone of the party of 'unsound method.' The pilgrims looked upon me with disfavour. I was, so to speak, numbered with the dead. It is strange how I accepted this unforeseen partnership, this choice of nightmares forced upon me in the tenebrous land invaded by these mean and greedy phantoms.

"Kurtz discoursed. A voice! a voice! It rang deep to the very last. It survived his strength to hide in the magnificent folds of eloquence the barren darkness of his heart. Oh, he struggled! he struggled! The wastes of his weary brain were haunted by shadowy images now—images of wealth and fame revolving obsequiously round his unextinguishable gift of noble and lofty expression. My Intended, my station, my career, my ideas—these were the subjects for the occasional utterances of elevated sentiments. The shade of the original Kurtz frequented the bedside of the hollow sham, whose fate it was to be buried presently in the mould of primeval earth. But both the diabolic love and the unearthly hate of the mysteries it had penetrated fought for the possession of that soul satiated with primitive emotions, avid of lying fame, of sham distinction, of all the appearances of success and power.

"Sometimes he was contemptibly childish. He desired to have kings meet him at railway stations on his return from some ghastly Nowhere, where he intended to accomplish great things. 'You show them you have in you something that is really profitable, and then there will be no limits to the recognition of your ability,' he would say. 'Of course you must take care of the motives— right motives—always.' The long reaches that were like one and the same reach, monotonous bends that were exactly alike, slipped past the steamer with their multitude of secular[6] trees looking patiently after this grimy fragment of another world, the forerunner of change, of conquest, of trade, of massacres, of blessings. I looked ahead—piloting. 'Close the shutter,' said Kurtz suddenly one day; 'I can't bear to look at this.' I did so. There was a silence. 'Oh, but I will wring your heart yet!' he cried at the invisible wilderness.

"We broke down—as I had expected—and had to lie up for repairs at the head of an island. This delay was the first thing that shook Kurtz's confidence. One morning he gave me a packet of papers and a photograph—the lot tied together with a shoe-string. 'Keep this for me,' he said. 'This noxious fool' (meaning the manager) 'is capable of prying into my boxes when I am not looking.' In the afternoon I saw him. He was lying on his back with closed eyes, and I withdrew quietly, but I heard him mutter, 'Live rightly, die, die . . .' I listened. There was nothing more. Was he rehearsing some speech in his sleep, or was it a fragment of a phrase from some newspaper article? He had been writing for the papers and meant to do so again, 'for the furthering of my ideas. It's a duty.'

"His was an impenetrable darkness. I looked at him as you peer down at a man who is lying at the bottom of a precipice where the sun never shines. But I had not much time to give him, because I was helping the engine-driver to take to pieces the leaky cylinders, to straighten a bent connecting-rod, and in other such matters. I lived in an infernal mess of rust, filings, nuts, bolts, spanners, hammers, ratchet-drills—things I abominate, because I don't get on with them. I tended the little forge we fortunately had aboard; I toiled wearily in a wretched scrap-heap—unless I had the shakes too bad to stand.

"One evening coming in with a candle I was startled to hear him say a little tremulously, 'I am lying here in the dark waiting for death.' The light was within a foot of his eyes. I forced myself to murmur, 'Oh, nonsense!' and stood over him as if transfixed.

"Anything approaching the change that came over his features I have never seen before, and hope never to see again. Oh, I wasn't touched. I was fascinated. It was as though a veil had been rent. I saw on that ivory face the expression of sombre pride, of ruthless power, of craven terror—of an intense and hopeless despair. Did he live his life again in every detail of desire, temptation, and surrender during that supreme moment of complete knowledge? He cried in a whisper at some image, at some vision—he cried out twice, a cry that was no more than a breath:

" 'The horror! The horror!'

"I blew the candle out and left the cabin. The pilgrims were dining in the mess-room, and I took my place opposite the manager, who lifted his eyes to give me a questioning glance, which I successfully ignored. He leaned back,

6. Centuries old.

serene, with that peculiar smile of his sealing the unexpressed depths of his meanness. A continuous shower of small flies streamed upon the lamp, upon the cloth, upon our hands and faces. Suddenly the manager's boy put his insolent black head in the doorway, and said in a tone of scathing contempt:

" 'Mistah Kurtz—he dead.'

"All the pilgrims rushed out to see. I remained, and went on with my dinner. I believe I was considered brutally callous. However, I did not eat much. There was a lamp in there—light, don't you know—and outside it was so beastly, beastly dark. I went no more near the remarkable man who had pronounced a judgement upon the adventures of his soul on this earth. The voice was gone. What else had been there? But I am of course aware that next day the pilgrims buried something in a muddy hole.

"And then they very nearly buried me.

"However, as you see, I did not go to join Kurtz there and then. I did not. I remained to dream the nightmare out to the end, and to show my loyalty to Kurtz once more. Destiny. My destiny! Droll thing life is—that mysterious arrangement of merciless logic for a futile purpose. The most you can hope from it is some knowledge of yourself—that comes too late—a crop of unextinguishable regrets. I have wrestled with death. It is the most unexciting contest you can imagine. It takes place in an impalpable greyness, with nothing underfoot, with nothing around, without spectators, without clamour, without glory, without the great desire of victory, without the great fear of defeat, in a sickly atmosphere of tepid scepticism, without much belief in your own right, and still less in that of your adversary. If such is the form of ultimate wisdom, then life is a greater riddle than some of us think it to be. I was within a hair's-breadth of the last opportunity for pronouncement, and I found with humiliation that probably I would have nothing to say. This is the reason why I affirm that Kurtz was a remarkable man. He had something to say. He said it. Since I had peeped over the edge myself, I understand better the meaning of his stare, that could not see the flame of the candle, but was wide enough to embrace the whole universe, piercing enough to penetrate all the hearts that beat in the darkness. He had summed up—he had judged. 'The horror!' He was a remarkable man. After all, this was the expression of some sort of belief; it had candour, it had conviction, it had a vibrating note of revolt in its whisper, it had the appalling face of a glimpsed truth—the strange commingling of desire and hate. And it is not my own extremity I remember best—a vision of greyness without form filled with physical pain, and a careless contempt for the evanescence of all things—even of this pain itself. No! It is his extremity that I seem to have lived through. True, he had made that last stride, he had stepped over the edge, while I had been permitted to draw back my hesitating foot. And perhaps in this is the whole difference; perhaps all the wisdom, and all truth, and all sincerity, are just compressed into that inappreciable moment of time in which we step over the threshold of the invisible. Perhaps! I like to think my summing-up would not have been a word of careless contempt. Better his cry—much better. It was an affirmation, a moral victory paid for by innumerable defeats, by abominable terrors, by abominable satisfactions. But it was a victory! That is why I have remained loyal to Kurtz to the last, and even beyond, when a long time after I heard once more, not his own voice, but the echo of his magnificent eloquence thrown to me from a soul as translucently pure as a cliff of crystal.

"No, they did not bury me, though there is a period of time which I remember mistily, with a shuddering wonder, like a passage through some inconceivable world that had no hope in it and no desire. I found myself back in the sepulchral city resenting the sight of people hurrying through the streets to filch a little money from each other, to devour their infamous cookery, to gulp their unwholesome beer, to dream their insignificant and silly dreams. They trespassed upon my thoughts. They were intruders whose knowledge of life was to me an irritating pretence, because I felt so sure they could not possibly know the things I knew. Their bearing, which was simply the bearing of commonplace individuals going about their business in the assurance of perfect safety, was offensive to me like the outrageous flauntings of folly in the face of a danger it is unable to comprehend. I had no particular desire to enlighten them, but I had some difficulty in restraining myself from laughing in their faces, so full of stupid importance. I daresay I was not very well at that time. I tottered about the streets—there were various affairs to settle—grinning bitterly at perfectly respectable persons. I admit my behaviour was inexcusable, but then my temperature was seldom normal in these days. My dear aunt's endeavours to 'nurse up my strength' seemed altogether beside the mark. It was not my strength that wanted nursing, it was my imagination that wanted soothing. I kept the bundle of papers given me by Kurtz, not knowing exactly what to do with it. His mother had died lately, watched over, as I was told, by his Intended. A clean-shaven man, with an official manner and wearing gold-rimmed spectacles, called on me one day and made inquiries, at first circuitous, afterwards suavely pressing, about what he was pleased to denominate certain 'documents.' I was not surprised, because I had had two rows with the manager on the subject out there. I had refused to give up the smallest scrap out of that package, and I took the same attitude with the spectacled man. He became darkly menacing at last, and with much heat argued that the Company had the right to every bit of information about its 'territories.' And, said he, 'Mr Kurtz's knowledge of unexplored regions must have been necessarily extensive and peculiar—owing to his great abilities and to the deplorable circumstances in which he had been placed: therefore—' I assured him Mr Kurtz's knowledge, however extensive, did not bear upon the problems of commerce or administration. He invoked then the name of science. 'It would be an incalculable loss if,' etc. etc. I offered him the report on the 'Suppression of Savage Customs,' with the postscriptum torn off. He took it up eagerly, but ended by sniffing at it with an air of contempt. 'This is not what we had a right to expect,' he remarked. 'Expect nothing else,' I said. 'There are only private letters.' He withdrew upon some threat of legal proceedings, and I saw him no more; but another fellow, calling himself Kurtz's cousin, appeared two days later, and was anxious to hear all the details about his dear relative's last moments. Incidentally he gave me to understand that Kurtz had been essentially a great musician. 'There was the making of an immense success,' said the man, who was an organist, I believe, with lank grey hair flowing over a greasy coat-collar. I had no reason to doubt his statement; and to this day I am unable to say what was Kurtz's profession, whether he ever had any—which was the greatest of his talents. I had taken him for a painter who wrote for the papers, or else for a journalist who could paint—but even the cousin (who took snuff during the interview) could not tell me what he had been—exactly. He was a universal genius—on that point I agreed with the old chap, who thereupon blew his nose noisily into a large cotton handkerchief and withdrew in senile agitation, bearing off some family letters and memoranda without importance. Ultimately a journalist anxious to know something of the fate of his 'dear colleague' turned up. This visitor informed me Kurtz's proper sphere ought to have been politics 'on the popular side.' He had furry straight eyebrows, bristly hair cropped short, an eyeglass on a broad ribbon, and, becoming expansive, confessed his opinion that Kurtz really couldn't write a bit—'but heavens! how that man could talk! He electrified large meetings. He had faith—don't you see?—he had the faith. He could get himself to believe anything—anything. He would have been a splendid leader of an extreme party.' 'What party?' I asked. 'Any party,' answered the other. 'He was an—an—extremist.' Did I not think so? I assented. Did I know, he asked, with a sudden flash of curiosity, 'what it was that had induced him to go out there?' 'Yes,' said I, and forthwith handed him the famous Report for publication, if he thought fit. He glanced through it hurriedly, mumbling all the time, judged 'it would do,' and took himself off with this plunder.

"Thus I was left at last with a slim packet of letters and the girl's portrait. She struck me as beautiful—I mean she had a beautiful expression. I know that the sunlight can be made to lie too, yet one felt that no manipulation of light and pose could have conveyed the delicate shade of truthfulness upon those features. She seemed ready to listen without mental reservation, without suspicion, without a thought for herself. I concluded I would go and give her back her portrait and those letters myself. Curiosity? Yes; and also some other feeling perhaps. All that had been Kurtz's had passed out of my hands: his soul, his body, his station, his plans, his ivory, his career. There remained only his memory and his Intended—and I wanted to give that up too to the past, in a way—to surrender personally all that remained of him with me to that oblivion which is the last word of our common fate. I don't defend myself. I had no clear perception of what it was I really wanted. Perhaps it was an impulse of unconscious loyalty, or the fulfilment of one of those ironic necessities that lurk in the facts of human existence. I don't know. I can't tell. But I went.

"I thought his memory was like the other memories of the dead that accumulate in every man's life—a vague impress on the brain of shadows that had fallen on it in their swift and final passage; but before the high and ponderous door, between the tall houses of a street as still and decorous as a well-kept alley in a cemetery, I had a vision of him on the stretcher, opening his mouth voraciously, as if to devour all the earth with all its mankind. He lived then before me; he lived as much as he had ever lived—a shadow insatiable of splendid appearances, of frightful realities; a shadow darker than the shadow of the night, and draped nobly in the folds of a gorgeous eloquence. The vision seemed to enter the house with me—the stretcher, the phantom-bearers, the wild crowd of obedient worshippers, the gloom of the forests, the glitter of the reach between the murky bends, the beat of the drum, regular and muffled like the beating of a heart—the heart of a conquering darkness. It was a moment of triumph for the wilderness, an invading and vengeful rush which, it seemed to me, I would have to keep back alone for the salvation of another soul. And the memory of what I had heard him say afar there, with the horned shapes stirring at my back, in the glow of fires, within the patient woods, those broken phrases came back to me, were heard again in their ominous and terrifying simplicity. I remembered his abject pleading, his abject threats, the colossal scale of his vile desires, the meanness, the torment, the tempestuous anguish of his soul. And later on I seemed to see his collected languid manner, when he said one day, 'This lot of ivory now is really mine. The Company did not pay for it. I collected it myself at a very great personal risk. I am afraid they will try to claim it as theirs though. H'm. It is a difficult case. What do you think I ought to do—resist? Eh? I want no more than justice.' . . . He wanted no more than justice—no more than justice. I rang the bell before a mahogany door on the first floor, and while I waited he seemed to stare at me out of the glossy panel—stare with that wide and immense stare embracing, condemning, loathing all the universe. I seemed to hear the whispered cry, 'The horror! The horror!'

"The dusk was falling. I had to wait in a lofty drawing-room with three long windows from floor to ceiling that were like three luminous and bedraped columns. The bent gilt legs and backs of the furniture shone in indistinct curves. The tall marble fireplace had a cold and monumental whiteness. A grand piano stood massively in a corner; with dark gleams on the flat surfaces like a sombre and polished sarcophagus. A high door opened—closed. I rose.

"She came forward, all in black, with a pale head, floating towards me in the dusk. She was in mourning. It was more than a year since his death, more than a year since the news came; she seemed as though she would remember and mourn for ever. She took both my hands in hers and murmured, 'I had heard you were coming.' I noticed she was not very young—I mean not girlish. She had a mature capacity for fidelity, for belief, for suffering. The room seemed to have grown darker, as if all the sad light of the cloudy evening had taken refuge on her forehead. This fair hair, this pale visage, this pure brow, seemed surrounded by an ashy halo from which the dark eyes looked out at me. Their glance was guileless, profound, confident, and trustful. She carried her sorrowful head as though she were proud of that sorrow, as though she would say, I—I alone know how to mourn for him as he deserves. But while we were still shaking hands, such a look of awful desolation came upon her face that I perceived she was one of those creatures that are not the playthings of Time. For her he had died only yesterday. And, by Jove! the impression was so powerful that for me too he seemed to have died only yesterday—nay, this very minute. I saw her and him in the same instant of time—his death and her sorrow—I saw her sorrow in the very moment of his death. Do you understand? I saw them together—I heard them together. She had said, with a deep catch of the breath, 'I have survived'; while my strained ears seemed to hear distinctly, mingled with her tone of despairing regret, the summing-up whisper of his eternal condemnation. I asked myself what I was doing there, with a sensation of panic in my heart as though I had blundered into a place of cruel and absurd mysteries not fit for a human being to behold. She motioned me to a chair. We sat down. I laid the packet gently on the little table, and she put her hand over it. . . . 'You knew him well,' she murmured, after a moment of mourning silence.

" 'Intimacy grows quickly out there,' I said. 'I knew him as well as it is possible for one man to know another.'

" 'And you admired him,' she said. 'It was impossible to know him and not to admire him. Was it?'

" 'He was a remarkable man,' I said unsteadily. Then before the appealing fixity of her gaze, that seemed to watch for more words on my lips, I went on, 'It was impossible not to—'

" 'Love him,' she finished eagerly, silencing me into an appalled dumbness. 'How true! how true! But when you think that no one knew him so well as I! I had all his noble confidence. I knew him best.'

" 'You knew him best,' I repeated. And perhaps she did. But with every word spoken the room was growing darker, and only her forehead, smooth and white, remained illumined by the unextinguishable light of belief and love.

" 'You were his friend,' she went on. 'His friend,' she repeated, a little louder. 'You must have been, if he had given you this, and sent you to me. I feel I can speak to you—and oh! I must speak. I want you—you who have heard his last words—to know I have been worthy of him. . . . It is not pride. . . . Yes! I am proud to know I understood him better than any one on earth—he told me so himself. And since his mother died I have had no one—no one—to—to—'

"I listened. The darkness deepened. I was not even sure whether he had given me the right bundle. I rather suspect he wanted me to take care of another batch of his papers which, after his death, I saw the manager examining under the lamp. And the girl talked, easing her pain in the certitude of my sympathy; she talked as thirsty men drink. I had heard that her engagement with Kurtz had been disapproved by her people. He wasn't rich enough or something. And indeed I don't know whether he had not been a pauper all his life. He had given me some reason to infer that it was his impatience of comparative poverty that drove him out there.

" ' . . . Who was not his friend who had heard him speak once?' she was saying. 'He drew men towards him by what was best in them.' She looked at me with intensity. 'It is the gift of the great,' she went on, and the sound of her low voice seemed to have the accompaniment of all the other sounds, full of mystery, desolation, and sorrow, I had ever heard—the ripple of the river, the soughing of the trees swayed by the wind, the murmurs of the crowds, the faint ring of incomprehensible words cried from afar, the whisper of a voice speaking from beyond the threshold of an eternal darkness. 'But you have heard him! You know!' she cried.

" 'Yes, I know,' I said with something like despair in my heart, but bowing my head before the faith that was in her, before that great and saving illusion that shone with an unearthly glow in the darkness, in the triumphant darkness from which I could not have defended her—from which I could not even defend myself.

" 'What a loss to me—to us!'—she corrected herself with beautiful generosity; then added in a murmur, 'To the world.' By the last gleams of twilight I could see the glitter of her eyes, full of tears—of tears that would not fall.

" 'I have been very happy—very fortunate—very proud,' she went on. 'Too fortunate. Too happy for a little while. And now I am unhappy for—for life.'

"She stood up; her fair hair seemed to catch all the remaining light in a glimmer of gold. I rose too.

" 'And of all this,' she went on mournfully, 'of all his promise, and of all his greatness, of his generous mind, of his noble heart, nothing remains—nothing but a memory. You and I—'

" 'We shall always remember him,' I said hastily.

" 'No!' she cried. 'It is impossible that all this should be lost—that such a life should be sacrificed to leave nothing—but sorrow. You know what vast plans he had. I knew of them too—I could not perhaps understand—but others knew of them. Something must remain. His words, at least, have not died.'

" 'His words will remain,' I said.

" 'And his example,' she whispered to herself. 'Men looked up to him—his goodness shone in every act. His example—'

" 'True,' I said; 'his example too. Yes, his example. I forgot that.'

" 'But I do not. I cannot—I cannot believe—not yet. I cannot believe that I shall never see him again, that nobody will see him again, never, never, never.'

"She put out her arms as if after a retreating figure, stretching them black and with clasped pale hands across the fading and narrow sheen of the window. Never see him! I saw him clearly enough then. I shall see this eloquent phantom as long as I live, and I shall see her too, a tragic and familiar Shade, resembling in this gesture another one, tragic also, and bedecked with powerless charms, stretching bare brown arms over the glitter of the infernal stream, the stream of darkness. She said suddenly very low, 'He died as he lived.'

" 'His end,' said I, with dull anger stirring in me, 'was in every way worthy of his life.'

" 'And I was not with him,' she murmured. My anger subsided before a feeling of infinite pity.

" 'Everything that could be done—' I mumbled.

" 'Ah, but I believed in him more than any one on earth—more than his own mother, more than—himself. He needed me! Me! I would have treasured every sigh, every word, every sign, every glance.'

"I felt like a chill grip on my chest. 'Don't,' I said, in a muffled voice.

" 'Forgive me. I—I—have mourned so long in silence—in silence. . . . You were with him—to the last? I think of his loneliness. Nobody near to understand him as I would have understood. Perhaps no one to hear. . . .'

" 'To the very end,' I said shakily. 'I heard his very last words. . . . ' I stopped in a fright.

" 'Repeat them,' she murmured in a heart-broken tone. 'I want—I want—something—something—to—to live with.'

"I was on the point of crying at her, 'Don't you hear them?' The dusk was repeating them in a persistent whisper all around us, in a whisper that seemed to swell menacingly like the first whisper of a rising wind. 'The horror! The horror!'

" 'His last word—to live with,' she insisted. 'Don't you understand I loved him—I loved him—I loved him!'

"I pulled myself together and spoke slowly.

" 'The last word he pronounced was—your name.'

"I heard a light sigh and then my heart stood still, stopped dead short by an exulting and terrible cry, by the cry of inconceivable triumph and of unspeakable pain. 'I knew it—I was sure!' . . . She knew. She was sure. I heard her weeping; she had hidden her face in her hands. It seemed to me that the house would collapse before I could escape, that the heavens would fall upon my head. But nothing happened. The heavens do not fall for such a trifle. Would they have fallen, I wonder, if I had rendered Kurtz that justice which was his due? Hadn't he said he wanted only justice? But I couldn't. I could not tell her. It would have been too dark—too dark altogether. . . ."[7]

Marlow ceased, and sat apart, indistinct and silent, in the pose of a meditating Buddha. Nobody moved for a time. "We have lost the first of the ebb,"

---

7. Writing to William Blackwood (editor of *Blackwood's Magazine*, where the story first appeared) in May 1902, Conrad referred to "the last pages of Heart of Darkness where the interview of the man and the girl locks in—as it were—the whole 30,000 words of narrative description into one suggestive view of a whole phase of life, and makes of that story something quite on another plane than an anecdote of a man who went mad in the Centre of Africa" (Joseph Conrad, *Letters to William Blackwood and David S. Meldrum*, ed. William Blackburn, 1958).

said the Director suddenly. I raised my head. The offing was barred by a black bank of clouds, and the tranquil waterway leading to the uttermost ends of the earth flowed sombre under an overcast sky—seemed to lead into the heart of an immense darkness.

1898–99   1899, 1902

WILLIAM BUTLER YEATS
1865–1939

William Butler Yeats was born to an Anglo-Irish family in Dublin. His father, J. B. Yeats, had abandoned law to take up painting, at which he made a somewhat precarious living. His mother came from the Pollexfen family that lived near Sligo, in the west of Ireland, where Yeats spent much of his childhood. The Yeatses moved to London in 1874, then returned to Dublin in 1880. Yeats attended first high school and then art school, which he soon left to concentrate on poetry.

Yeats's father was a religious skeptic, but he believed in the "religion of art." Yeats, religious by temperament but unable to believe in Christian orthodoxy, sought all his life to compensate for his lost religion. This search led him to various kinds of mysticism, to folklore, theosophy, spiritualism, and neoplatonism. He said he "made a new religion, almost an infallible church of poetic tradition."

Yeats's childhood and young manhood were spent between Dublin, London, and Sligo, and each of these places contributed something to his poetic development. In London in the 1890s he met the important poets of the day, founded the Irish Literary Society, and acquired late-Romantic, Pre-Raphaelite ideas of poetry: he believed, in this early stage of his career, that a poet's language should be dreamy, evocative, and ethereal. From the countryside around Sligo he gained a knowledge of the life of the peasantry and of their folklore. In Dublin, where he founded the National Literary Society, he was influenced by Irish nationalism and, although often disagreeing with those who wished to use literature for political ends, he nevertheless came to see his poetry as contributing to the rejuvenation of Irish culture.

Yeats's poetry began in the tradition of self-conscious Romanticism, strongly influenced by the English poets Edmund Spenser, Percy Shelley, and, a little later, William Blake, whose works he edited. About the same time he was writing poems (e.g., "The Stolen Child") deriving from his Sligo experience, with quietly precise nature imagery, Irish place-names, and themes from Irish folklore. A little later he drew on the great stories of the heroic age of Irish history and translations of Gaelic poetry into "that dialect which gets from Gaelic its syntax and keeps its still partly Tudor vocabulary." The heroic legends of ancient Ireland and the folk traditions of the modern Irish countryside helped brace his early dreamlike imagery. "The Lake Isle of Innisfree"— "my first lyric with anything in its rhythm of my own music," said Yeats—is both a Romantic evocation of escape into dream, art, and the imagination, and a specifically Irish reverie on freedom and self-reliance.

Yeats vigorously hybridizes Irish and English traditions, and eventually draws into this potent intercultural mix East and South Asian cultural resources, including Japanese Noh theater and Indian meditative practices. Resolutely Irish, he imaginatively reclaims a land colonized by the British; imposes Irish rhythms, images, genres, and syntax on English-language poetry; and revives native myths, place-names, and consciousness. Yet he is also cosmopolitan, insisting on the transnationalism of the collective storehouse of images he calls "Spiritus Mundi" or "Anima Mundi," spending much of his life in England, and cross-pollinating forms, ideas, and images from Ireland and England, Europe and Asia.

Irish nationalism first sent Yeats in search of a consistently simpler and more popular style, to express the elemental facts about Irish life and aspirations. This led him to the concrete image, as did translations from Gaelic folk songs, in which "nothing . . . was abstract, nothing worn-out." But other forces were also working on him. In 1902 a friend gave him the works of the German philosopher Friedrich Nietzsche, to which he responded with great excitement, and it would seem that, in persuading the passive love-poet to get off his knees, Nietzsche's books intensified his search for a more active stance, a more vigorous style. At the start of the twentieth century, Yeats wearied of his early languid aesthetic, declaring his intentions, in a 1901 letter, to make "everything hard and clear" and, in another of 1904, to leave behind "sentiment and sentimental sadness." He wished for poems not of disembodied beauty but that could "carry the normal, passionate, reasoning self, the personality as a whole." In poems of his middle period, such as "Adam's Curse" and "A Coat," Yeats combines the colloquial with the formal, enacting in his more austere diction, casual rhythms, and passionate syntax his will to leave behind the poetic "embroideries" of his youth and walk "naked." The American poet Ezra Pound, who spent winters from 1913 to 1916 with Yeats in a stone cottage in Sussex, strengthened Yeats's resolve to develop a less mannered, more stripped down style.

In 1889 Yeats had met the beautiful actor and Irish nationalist Maud Gonne, with whom he was desperately in love for many years, but who persistently refused to marry him. She became the subject of many of his early love poems, and in later poems, such as "No Second Troy" and "A Prayer for My Daughter," he expresses anger over her self-sacrifice to political activism. He had also met Lady Gregory, Anglo-Irish writer and promoter of Irish literature, in 1896, and Yeats spent many holidays at her aristocratic country house, Coole Park. Disliking the moneygrubbing and prudery of the middle classes, as indicated in "September 1913," he looked for his ideal characters either below them, to peasants and beggars, or above them, to the aristocracy, for each of these had their own traditions and lived according to them. Under Lady Gregory's influence Yeats began to organize the Irish dramatic movement in 1899 and, with her help, founded the Abbey Theater in 1904. His active participation in theatrical production—confronting political censorship, economic problems of paying carpenters and actors, and other aspects of "theatre business, management of men"—also helped toughen his style, as he demonstrates in "The Fascination of What's Difficult." Yeats's long-cherished hope had been to "bring the halves together"—Protestant and Catholic—through a literature infused with Ireland's ancient myths and cultural riches before the divisions between rival Christianities. But in a string of national controversies, he ran afoul of both the Roman Catholic middle class and the Anglo-Irish Protestant ascendancy, and at last, bitterly turning his back on Ireland, moved to England.

Then came the Easter Rising of 1916, led by men and women he had long known, some of whom were executed or imprisoned by the British. Persuaded by Gonne (whose estranged husband was one of the executed leaders) that "tragic dignity had returned to Ireland," Yeats returned. His culturally nationalist work had helped inspire the poet revolutionaries, and so he asked himself, as he put it in the late poem "Man and the Echo," did his work "send out / Certain men the English shot?" Yeats's nationalism and antinationalism, his divided loyalties to Ireland and to England, find powerfully ambivalent expression in "Easter, 1916" and other poems. Throughout his poetry he brilliantly mediates between contending aspects of himself—late-Romantic visionary and astringent modern skeptic, Irish patriot and irreverent antinationalist, shrewd man of action and esoteric dreamer. As he said: "We make out of the quarrel with others, rhetoric, but of the quarrel with ourselves, poetry." Conceiving consciousness as conflict, he fashioned a kind of poetry that could embody the contradictory feelings and ideas of his endless inner debate.

To mark his recommitment to Ireland, Yeats refurbished and renamed Thoor (Castle) Ballylee, the Norman tower on Lady Gregory's land, in which he lived off and on, and which became, along with its inner winding stair, a central symbol in his later poetry. In 1922 he was appointed a senator of the recently established Irish Free State, and he served until 1928, playing an active part not only in promoting the arts but also in general political affairs, in which he supported the views of the minority Protestant landed class. At the same time he was continuing his esoteric studies. He married Georgie (changed by Yeats to George) Hyde Lees in 1917, when he was fifty-two, and she proved so sympathetic to his imaginative needs that the automatic writing she produced for several years (believed by Yeats to have been dictated by spirits) gave him the elements of a symbolic system that he later worked out in his book *A Vision* (1925, 1937). The system was a theory of the movements of history and of the different types of personality, each movement and type being related to a different phase of the moon. At the center of the symbolic system were the interpenetrating cones, or "gyres," that represented the movement through major cycles of history and across antitheses of human personality.

He compressed and embodied his personal mythology in visionary poems of great scope, linguistic force, and incantatory power, such as "The Second Coming" and "Leda and the Swan." In poems of the 1920s and 1930s, winding stairs, spinning tops, "gyres," spirals of all kinds, are important symbols, serving as a means of resolving some of the contraries that had arrested him from the beginning—paradoxes of time and eternity, change and continuity, spirit and the body, life and art. If his earliest poetry was sometimes static, a beautifully stitched tapestry laden with symbols of inner states, his late poetry became more dynamic, its propulsive syntax and muscular rhythms more suited to his themes of lust, rage, and the body. He had once screened these out of his verse as unpoetic, along with war, violence, "the mire of human veins." Now he embraced the mortal world intensely. In "A Dialogue of Self and Soul," the self defies the soul's injunction to leave the world behind: "I am content to live it all again / And yet again, if it be life to pitch / Into the frog-spawn of a blind man's ditch." Yeats no longer sought transcendence of the human, but instead aimed for the active interpenetration of the corporeal and the visionary. In his Nietzsche-inspired poems of "tragic joy," such as "Lapis Lazuli," he affirmed ruin and destruction as necessary to imaginative creation.

One key to Yeats's greatness is that there are many different Yeatses: a hard-nosed skeptic and an esoteric idealist, a nativist and a cosmopolitan, an Irish nationalist and an ironic antinationalist, a Romantic brooding on loss and unrequited desire and a modernist mocking idealism, nostalgia, and contemporary society. Similarly, in his poetic innovations and consolidations, he is both a conservative and a radical. That is, he is a literary traditionalist, working within such inherited genres as love poetry, the elegy, the self-elegy, the sonnet, and the occasional poem on public themes. But he is also a restless innovator who disrupts generic conventions, breaking up the coherence of the sonnet, de-idealizing the dead mourned in elegies, and bringing into public poems an intense personal ambivalence. In matters of form, too, he rhymes but often in off-rhyme, uses standard meters but bunches or scatters their stresses, employs an elegant syntax that nevertheless has the passionate urgency of colloquial speech; his diction, tone, enjambments, and stanzas intermix ceremony with contortion, controlled artifice with wayward unpredictability. A difficulty in reading Yeats—but also one of the great rewards—is comprehending his manysidedness.

Like Pound, T. S. Eliot, and Windham Lewis, Yeats was attracted to right-wing politics, and in the 1930s he was briefly drawn to fascism. His late interest in authoritarian politics arose in part from his desire for a feudal, aristocratic society that, unlike middle-class culture, in his view, might allow the imagination to flourish, and in part from his anticolonialism, since he thought a fascist Spain, for example, would "weaken the British Empire." But eventually he was appalled by all political ideologies, and the grim prophecy of "The Second Coming" seemed to him increasingly apt.

Written in a rugged, colloquial, and concrete language, Yeats's last poems have a controlled yet startling wildness. His return to life, to "the foul rag-and-bone shop of the heart," is one of the most impressive final phases of any poet's career. In one of his last letters he wrote: "When I try to put all into a phrase I say, 'Man can embody truth but he cannot know it.' . . . The abstract is not life and everywhere draws out its contradictions. You can refute Hegel but not the Saint or the Song of Sixpence." He died in southern France just before the beginning of World War II. His grave is, as his poem directed, near Sligo, "under Ben Bulben." He left behind a body of verse that, in variety and power, has been an enduring influence for English-language poets around the globe, from W. H. Auden and Seamus Heaney to Derek Walcott and A. K. Ramanujan.

The Stolen Child[1]

Where dips the rocky highland
Of Sleuth Wood[2] in the lake,
There lies a leafy island
Where flapping herons wake
5   The drowsy water-rats;
There we've hid our faery vats,
Full of berries
And of reddest stolen cherries.
Come away, O human child!
10   *To the waters and the wild*
With a faery, hand in hand,
For the world's more full of weeping than you can understand.

Where the wave of moonlight glosses
The dim grey sands with light,
15   Far off by furthest Rosses
We foot it all the night,
Weaving olden dances,
Mingling hands and mingling glances
Till the moon has taken flight;
20   To and fro we leap
And chase the frothy bubbles,
While the world is full of troubles
And is anxious in its sleep.
Come away, O human child!
25   *To the waters and the wild*
With a faery, hand in hand,
For the world's more full of weeping than you can understand.

Where the wandering water gushes
From the hills above Glen-Car,
30   In pools among the rushes
That scarce could bathe a star,
We seek for slumbering trout
And whispering in their ears
Give them unquiet dreams;
35   Leaning softly out

1. I.e., a child stolen by fairies to be their companion, as in Irish folklore.
2. This and other places mentioned in the poem are in County Sligo, in the west of Ireland, where Yeats spent much of his childhood.

From ferns that drop their tears
Over the young streams.
Come away, O human child!
To the waters and the wild
40 *With a faery, hand in hand,*
For the world's more full of weeping than you can understand.

Away with us he's going,
The solemn-eyed:
He'll hear no more the lowing
45 Of the calves on the warm hillside
Or the kettle on the hob
Sing peace into his breast,
Or see the brown mice bob
Round and round the oatmeal-chest.
50 *For he comes, the human child,*
To the waters and the wild
With a faery, hand in hand,
From a world more full of weeping than he can understand.

1886, 1889

The Rose of the World[1]

Who dreamed that beauty passes like a dream?
For these red lips, with all their mournful pride,
Mournful that no new wonder may betide,
Troy[2] passed away in one high funeral gleam,
5 And Usna's children died.[3]

We and the labouring world are passing by:
Amid men's souls, that waver and give place
Like the pale waters in their wintry race,
Under the passing stars, foam of the sky,
10 Lives on this lonely face.

Bow down, archangels, in your dim abode:
Before you were, or any hearts to beat,
Weary and kind one lingered by His seat;
He made the world to be a grassy road
15 Before her wandering feet.

1892, 1895

1. The Platonic idea of eternal beauty. "I notice upon reading these poems for the first time for several years that the quality symbolized as The Rose differs from the Intellectual Beauty of Shelley and of Spenser in that I have imagined it as suffering with man and not as something pursued and seen from afar" [Yeats, in 1925]. Yeats wrote this poem to Maud Gonne.
2. Ancient city destroyed by the Greeks, according to legend, after the abduction of the beautiful Helen.
3. In Old Irish legend the Ulster warrior Naoise, son of Usna or Usnach (pronounced *Úskna*) carried off the beautiful Deirdre, whom King Conchubar of Ulster had intended to marry, and with his two brothers took her to Scotland. Eventually Conchubar lured the four of them back to Ireland and killed the three brothers.

The Lake Isle of Innisfree[1]

I will arise and go now, and go to Innisfree,
And a small cabin build there, of clay and wattles[2] made:
Nine bean-rows will I have there, a hive for the honey-bee,
And live alone in the bee-loud glade.

5 And I shall have some peace there, for peace comes dropping slow,
Dropping from the veils of the morning to where the cricket sings;
There midnight's all a glimmer, and noon a purple glow,
And evening full of the linnet's wings.

I will arise and go now, for always night and day
10 I hear lake water lapping with low sounds by the shore;
While I stand on the roadway, or on the pavements grey,
I hear it in the deep heart's core.

1890   1890, 1892

The Sorrow of Love[1]

The brawling of a sparrow in the eaves,
The brilliant moon and all the milky sky,
And all that famous harmony of leaves,
Had blotted out man's image and his cry.

5 A girl arose that had red mournful lips
And seemed the greatness of the world in tears,
Doomed like Odysseus and the labouring ships
And proud as Priam murdered with his peers;[2]

Arose, and on the instant clamorous eaves,
10 A climbing moon upon an empty sky,
And all that lamentation of the leaves,
Could but compose man's image and his cry.

1891   1892, 1925

---

1. Inis Fraoigh (Heather Island) is a small island in Lough Gill, near Sligo, in the west of Ireland. In his autobiography Yeats writes: "I had still the ambition, formed in Sligo in my teens, of living in imitation of Thoreau on Innisfree . . . and when walking through Fleet Street [in London] very homesick I heard a little tinkle of water and saw a fountain in a shop-window which balanced a little ball upon its jet, and began to remember lake water. From the sudden remembrance came my poem Innisfree, my first lyric with anything in its rhythm of my own music."
2. Stakes interwoven with twigs or branches.
1. For earlier versions of this poem, see "Poems in Process," in the appendices to this volume.
2. Odysseus (whom the Romans called Ulysses) is the hero of Homer's Odyssey, which describes how, after having fought in the siege of Troy, he wandered for ten years before reaching his home, the Greek island of Ithaca. Priam was king of Troy at the time of the siege and was killed when the Greeks captured the city.

When You Are Old[1]

When you are old and grey and full of sleep,
And nodding by the fire, take down this book,
And slowly read, and dream of the soft look
Your eyes had once, and of their shadows deep;

5 How many loved your moments of glad grace,
And loved your beauty with love false or true,
But one man loved the pilgrim soul in you,
And loved the sorrows of your changing face;

And bending down beside the glowing bars,[2]
10 Murmur, a little sadly, how Love fled
And paced upon the mountains overhead
And hid his face amid a crowd of stars.

1891   1892, 1899

Who Goes with Fergus?[1]

Who will go drive with Fergus now,
And pierce the deep wood's woven shade,
And dance upon the level shore?
Young man, lift up your russet brow,
5 And lift your tender eyelids, maid,
And brood on hopes and fear no more.

And no more turn aside and brood
Upon love's bitter mystery;
For Fergus rules the brazen cars,°   *bronze chariots*
10 And rules the shadows of the wood,
And the white breast of the dim sea
And all dishevelled wandering stars.

1893

The Man Who Dreamed of Faeryland

He stood among a crowd at Drumahair;[1]
His heart hung all upon a silken dress,

1. A poem suggested by a sonnet by the French poet Pierre de Ronsard (1524–1585); it begins: "Quand vous serez bien vieille, au soir, à la chandelle" (When you are quite old, in the evening by candlelight).
2. I.e., of the grate.
1. In a late version of this Irish heroic legend, Fer-

gus, "king of the proud Red Branch Kings," gave up his throne voluntarily to King Conchubar of Ulster to learn by dreaming and meditating the bitter wisdom of the poet and philosopher.
1. This and other place-names in the poem refer to places in County Sligo.

And he had known at last some tenderness,
Before earth took him to her stony care;
5   But when a man poured fish into a pile,
It seemed they raised their little silver heads,
And sang what gold morning or evening sheds
Upon a woven world-forgotten isle
Where people love beside the ravelled[2] seas;
10   That Time can never mar a lover's vows
Under that woven changeless roof of boughs:
The singing shook him out of his new ease.

He wandered by the sands of Lissadell;
His mind ran all on money cares and fears,
15   And he had known at last some prudent years
Before they heaped his grave under the hill;
But while he passed before a plashy place,
A lug-worm with its grey and muddy mouth
Sang that somewhere to north or west or south
20   There dwelt a gay, exulting, gentle race
Under the golden or the silver skies;
That if a dancer stayed his hungry foot
It seemed the sun and moon were in the fruit:
And at that singing he was no more wise.
25   He mused beside the well of Scanavin,
He mused upon his mockers: without fail
His sudden vengeance were a country tale,
When earthy night had drunk his body in;
But one small knot-grass growing by the pool
30   Sang where—unnecessary cruel voice—
Old silence bids its chosen race rejoice,
Whatever ravelled waters rise and fall
Or stormy silver fret the gold of day,
And midnight there enfold them like a fleece
35   And lover there by lover be at peace.
The tale drove his fine angry mood away.

He slept under the hill of Lugnagall;
And might have known at last unhaunted sleep
Under that cold and vapour-turbaned steep,
40   Now that the earth had taken man and all:
Did not the worms that spired about his bones
Proclaim with that unwearied, reedy cry
That God has laid His fingers on the sky,
That from those fingers glittering summer runs
45   Upon the dancer by the dreamless wave.
Why should those lovers that no lovers miss
Dream, until God burn Nature with a kiss?
The man has found no comfort in the grave.

1891, 1930

2. Tangled; here turbulent.

Adam's Curse[1]

We sat together at one summer's end,
That beautiful mild woman, your close friend,
And you and I,[2] and talked of poetry.
I said, "A line will take us hours maybe;
5 Yet if it does not seem a moment's thought,
Our stitching and unstitching has been naught.
Better go down upon your marrow-bones
And scrub a kitchen pavement, or break stones
Like an old pauper, in all kinds of weather;
10 For to articulate sweet sounds together
Is to work harder than all these, and yet
Be thought an idler by the noisy set
Of bankers, schoolmasters, and clergymen
The martyrs call the world."

                   And thereupon
15 That beautiful mild woman for whose sake
There's many a one shall find out all heartache
On finding that her voice is sweet and low
Replied, "To be born woman is to know—
Although they do not talk of it at school—
20 That we must labour to be beautiful."

I said, "It's certain there is no fine thing
Since Adam's fall but needs much labouring.
There have been lovers who thought love should be
So much compounded of high courtesy
25 That they would sigh and quote with learned looks
Precedents out of beautiful old books;
Yet now it seems an idle trade enough."

We sat grown quiet at the name of love;
We saw the last embers of daylight die,
30 And in the trembling blue-green of the sky
A moon, worn as if it had been a shell
Washed by time's waters as they rose and fell
About the stars and broke in days and years.

I had a thought for no one's but your ears:
35 That you were beautiful, and that I strove
To love you in the old high way of love;
That it had all seemed happy, and yet we'd grown
As weary-hearted as that hollow moon.

Nov. 1902   1902, 1922

1. When Adam was evicted from the Garden of Eden, God cursed him with a life of toil and labor (Genesis 3.17–19).

2. The two women in the poem are modeled on Maud Gonne and her sister, Kathleen Pilcher (1868–1919).

No Second Troy

Why should I blame her[1] that she filled my days
With misery, or that she would of late
Have taught to ignorant men most violent ways,
Or hurled the little streets upon the great,
5 Had they but courage equal to desire?
What could have made her peaceful with a mind
That nobleness made simple as a fire,
With beauty like a tightened bow, a kind
That is not natural in an age like this,
10 Being high and solitary and most stern?
Why, what could she have done, being what she is?
Was there another Troy for her to burn?[2]

Dec. 1908   1910

The Fascination of What's Difficult[1]

The fascination of what's difficult
Has dried the sap out of my veins, and rent
Spontaneous joy and natural content
Out of my heart. There's something ails our colt[2]
5 That must, as if it had not holy blood
Nor on Olympus[3] leaped from cloud to cloud,
Shiver under the lash, strain, sweat and jolt
As though it dragged road metal. My curse on plays
That have to be set up in fifty ways,
10 On the day's war with every knave and dolt,
Theatre business, management of men.
I swear before the dawn comes round again
I'll find the stable and pull out the bolt.

Sept. 1909–Mar. 1910   1910

A Coat

I made my song a coat
Covered with embroideries
Out of old mythologies
From heel to throat;

1. Maud Gonne, whose revolutionary activities are at issue in the poem.
2. Helen of Troy was the legendary cause of the Trojan War and thus of Troy's destruction.
1. Written when Yeats was director-manager of the Abbey Theatre. "Subject. To complain of the fascination of what's difficult. It spoils spontaneity and pleasure, and wastes time. Repeat the line ending difficult three times and rhyme on bolt, exalt, colt, jolt" [Yeats's diary for September 1909].
2. Pegasus, in Greek mythology a winged horse associated with poetry.
3. A mountain in Greece; the home of the gods.

5   But the fools caught it,
Wore it in the world's eyes
As though they'd wrought it.
Song, let them take it,
For there's more enterprise
10 In walking naked.

1912   1914

September 1913

What need you,[1] being come to sense,
But fumble in a greasy till°   *cash register*
And add the halfpence to the pence
And prayer to shivering prayer, until
5   You have dried the marrow from the bone;
For men were born to pray and save:
Romantic Ireland's dead and gone,
It's with O'Leary[2] in the grave.

Yet they were of a different kind,
10 The names that stilled your childish play,
They have gone about the world like wind,
But little time had they to pray
For whom the hangman's rope was spun,
And what, God help us, could they save?
15 Romantic Ireland's dead and gone,
It's with O'Leary in the grave.

Was it for this the wild geese[3] spread
The grey wing upon every tide;
For this that all that blood was shed,
20 For this Edward Fitzgerald died,
And Robert Emmet and Wolfe Tone,[4]
All that delirium of the brave?
Romantic Ireland's dead and gone,
It's with O'Leary in the grave.

25 Yet could we turn the years again,
And call those exiles as they were

1. Members of the new, largely Roman Catholic middle class. When the art dealer Hugh Lane (d. 1915) offered to give his collection of French impressionist paintings to the city of Dublin, provided they were permanently housed in a suitable gallery, Yeats became angry over fierce public opposition to funding the project.
2. John O'Leary (1830–1907), Irish nationalist, who, after five years' imprisonment and fifteen years' exile, returned to Dublin in 1885; he rallied the young Yeats to the cause of literary nationalism.
3. Popular name for the Irish who, because of the penal laws against Catholics (1695–1727), were forced to flee to the Continent.
4. Theobald Wolfe Tone (1763–1798), one of the chief founders of the United Irishmen (an Irish nationalist organization) and leader of the 1798 Irish Rising, committed suicide in prison. Lord Edward Fitzgerald (1763–1798), British officer who, after being dismissed from the army for disloyal activities, joined the United Irishmen, helped lead the 1798 Irish Rising, and died in prison. Robert Emmet (1778–1803), a leader of the abortive 1803 Irish Nationalist Revolt, was hanged for treason.

In all their loneliness and pain,
You'd cry, "Some woman's yellow hair
Has maddened every mother's son":
30   They weighed so lightly what they gave.
But let them be, they're dead and gone,
They're with O'Leary in the grave.

Sept. 1913   1913

Easter, 1916[1]

I have met them at close of day
Coming with vivid faces
From counter or desk among grey
Eighteenth-century houses.
5   I have passed with a nod of the head
Or polite meaningless words,
Or have lingered awhile and said
Polite meaningless words,
And thought before I had done
10   Of a mocking tale or a gibe
To please a companion
Around the fire at the club,
Being certain that they and I
But lived where motley[2] is worn:
15   All changed, changed utterly:
A terrible beauty is born.

That woman's days were spent
In ignorant good-will,
Her nights in argument
20   Until her voice grew shrill.
What voice more sweet than hers
When, young and beautiful,
She rode to harriers?[3]
This man had kept a school
25   And rode our wingèd horse;[4]
This other his helper and friend[5]
Was coming into his force;
He might have won fame in the end,

1. During the Easter Rising of 1916, Irish nationalists revolted against the British government and proclaimed an Irish Republic. Nearly sixteen hundred Irish Volunteers and two hundred members of the Citizen Army seized buildings and a park in Dublin. The rebellion began on Easter Monday, April 24, 1916, and was crushed in six days. Over the next two weeks fifteen of the leaders were executed by firing squad. Yeats knew the chief nationalist leaders personally. For more on the Easter Rising, see "Imagining Ireland" at Norton Literature Online.

2. The multicolored clothes of a jester.
3. Constance Gore-Booth (1868–1927), afterward Countess Markievicz, took a prominent role in the uprising. Her death sentence was reduced to imprisonment. The other rebel leaders to whom Yeats refers were executed.
4. Padraic Pearse (1879–1916), founder of a boys' school in Dublin and poet—hence the "winged horse," or Pegasus, the horse of the Muses.
5. Thomas MacDonagh (1878–1916), poet and dramatist.

So sensitive his nature seemed,
30 So daring and sweet his thought.
This other man I had dreamed
A drunken, vainglorious lout.[6]
He had done most bitter wrong
To some who are near my heart,
35 Yet I number him in the song;
He, too, has resigned his part
In the casual comedy;
He, too, has been changed in his turn,
Transformed utterly:
40 A terrible beauty is born.

Hearts with one purpose alone
Through summer and winter seem
Enchanted to a stone
To trouble the living stream.
45 The horse that comes from the road,
The rider, the birds that range
From cloud to tumbling cloud,
Minute by minute they change;
A shadow of cloud on the stream
50 Changes minute by minute;
A horse-hoof slides on the brim,
And a horse plashes within it;
The long-legged moor-hens dive,
And hens to moor-cocks call;
55 Minute by minute they live:
The stone's in the midst of all.

Too long a sacrifice
Can make a stone of the heart.
O when may it suffice?
60 That is Heaven's part, our part
To murmur name upon name,
As a mother names her child
When sleep at last has come
On limbs that had run wild.
65 What is it but nightfall?
No, no, not night but death;
Was it needless death after all?
For England may keep faith
For all that is done and said.[7]
70 We know their dream; enough
To know they dreamed and are dead;
And what if excess of love
Bewildered them till they died?
I write it out in a verse—

6. Major John MacBride (1865–1916), Irish revolutionary and estranged husband of Maud Gonne.
7. In 1914 the English government had passed Home Rule for Ireland into law, but because of World War I had suspended it, promising to implement it later.

75 MacDonagh and MacBride
    And Connolly[8] and Pearse
    Now and in time to be,
    Wherever green is worn,
    Are changed, changed utterly:
80 A terrible beauty is born.

May–Sept. 1916   1916, 1920

The Wild Swans at Coole[1]

    The trees are in their autumn beauty,
    The woodland paths are dry,
    Under the October twilight the water
    Mirrors a still sky;
5   Upon the brimming water among the stones
    Are nine-and-fifty swans.

    The nineteenth autumn has come upon me
    Since I first made my count;[2]
    I saw, before I had well finished,
10 All suddenly mount
    And scatter wheeling in great broken rings
    Upon their clamorous wings.

    I have looked upon those brilliant creatures,
    And now my heart is sore.
15 All's changed since I, hearing at twilight,
    The first time on this shore,
    The bell-beat of their wings above my head,
    Trod with a lighter tread.

    Unwearied still, lover by lover,
20 They paddle in the cold
    Companionable streams or climb the air;
    Their hearts have not grown old;
    Passion or conquest, wander where they will,
    Attend upon them still.

25 But now they drift on the still water,
    Mysterious, beautiful;
    Among what rushes will they build,
    By what lake's edge or pool
    Delight men's eyes when I awake some day
30 To find they have flown away?

Oct. 1916   1917

8. James Connolly (1870–1916), a trade-union
organizer and military commander of the rebellion.
1. Coole Park, in County Galway, was the estate
of the Irish playwright Lady Augusta Gregory

(1852–1932).
2. Yeats made his first long visit to Coole in 1897;
from then on he spent summers there, often staying into the fall.

In Memory of Major Robert Gregory[1]

I

Now that we're almost settled in our house
I'll name the friends that cannot sup with us
Beside a fire of turf° in th' ancient tower,[2]   *peat*
And having talked to some late hour
5   Climb up the narrow winding stair to bed:
Discoverers of forgotten truth
Or mere companions of my youth,
All, all are in my thoughts to-night being dead.

2

Always we'd have the new friend meet the old
10   And we are hurt if either friend seem cold,
And there is salt to lengthen out the smart
In the affections of our heart,
And quarrels are blown up upon that head;
But not a friend that I would bring
15   This night can set us quarrelling,
For all that come into my mind are dead.

3

Lionel Johnson[3] comes the first to mind,
That loved his learning better than mankind,
Though courteous to the worst; much falling he
20   Brooded upon sanctity
Till all his Greek and Latin learning seemed
A long blast upon the horn that brought
A little nearer to his thought
A measureless consummation that he dreamed.

4

25   And that enquiring man John Synge[4] comes next,
That dying chose the living world for text
And never could have rested in the tomb
But that, long travelling, he had come
Towards nightfall upon certain set apart
30   In a most desolate stony place,
Towards nightfall upon a race
Passionate and simple like his heart.

---

1. Robert Gregory (1881–1918) was the only child of Lady Augusta Gregory. The first printing of this elegy included the following note: "(Major Robert Gregory, R.F.C. [Royal Flying Corps], M.C. [Military Cross], Legion of Honour, was killed in action on the Italian Front, January 23, 1918)." For another of Yeats's poems on Gregory's death, see "Representing the Great War" at Norton Literature Online.
2. In 1917 Yeats purchased the Norman tower Thor Ballylee, near Lady Gregory's home in Coole

Park. While that residence was being renovated, Yeats and his wife were living in a house that Lady Gregory had lent them.
3. English poet and scholar (1867–1902); he was "much falling" (line 19) because of his drinking.
4. Irish playwright (1871–1909), associated with the Irish literary renaissance and the Abbey Theatre. When Yeats first met Synge, in 1896, he encouraged him to travel to the Aran Islands ("a most desolate and stony place") and write about its rural residents.

5

And then I think of old George Pollexfen,[5]
In muscular youth well known to Mayo[6] men
35   For horsemanship at meets or at racecourses,
That could have shown how pure-bred horses
And solid men, for all their passion, live
But as the outrageous stars incline
By opposition, square and trine;[7]
40   Having grown sluggish and contemplative.

6

They were my close companions many a year,
A portion of my mind and life, as it were,
And now their breathless faces seem to look
Out of some old picture-book;
45   I am accustomed to their lack of breath,
But not that my dear friend's dear son,
Our Sidney[8] and our perfect man,
Could share in that discourtesy of death.

7

For all things the delighted eye now sees
50   Were loved by him;[9] the old storm-broken trees
That cast their shadows upon road and bridge;
The tower set on the stream's edge;
The ford where drinking cattle make a stir
Nightly, and startled by that sound
55   The water-hen must change her ground;
He might have been your heartiest welcomer.

8

When with the Galway foxhounds he would ride
From Castle Taylor to the Roxborough side[1]
Or Esserkelly plain, few kept his pace;
60   At Mooneen he had leaped a place
So perilous that half the astonished meet
Had shut their eyes; and where was it
He rode a race without a bit?
And yet his mind outran the horses' feet.

9

65   We dreamed that a great painter had been born[2]
To cold Clare[3] rock and Galway rock and thorn,
To that stern colour and that delicate line
That are our secret discipline
Wherein the gazing heart doubles her might.

5. Yeats's maternal uncle (1839–1910), with whom he had spent holidays in Sligo as a young man.
6. County in western Ireland.
7. Terms from astrology, in which both Yeats and his uncle were interested.
8. Sir Philip Sidney (1554–1586), English poet and exemplar of the "Renaissance man"; like Gregory, he was killed in battle.

9. Robert Gregory encouraged Yeats to buy the tower.
1. Big country houses in County Galway. Roxborough was Lady Gregory's childhood home.
2. "Robert Gregory painted the Burren Hills and thereby found what promised to grow into a great style, but he had hardly found it before he was killed" (Yeats, "Ireland and the Arts").
3. County south of Galway.

70   Soldier, scholar, horseman, he,
       And yet he had the intensity
       To have published all to be a world's delight.

                          10

       What other could so well have counselled us
       In all lovely intricacies of a house
75   As he that practised or that understood
       All work in metal or in wood,
       In moulded plaster or in carven stone?
       Soldier, scholar, horseman, he,
       And all he did done perfectly
80   As though he had but that one trade alone.

                          11

       Some burn damp faggots,⁴ others may consume
       The entire combustible world in one small room
       As though dried straw, and if we turn about
       The bare chimney is gone black out
85   Because the work had finished in that flare.
       Soldier, scholar, horseman, he,
       As 'twere all life's epitome,
       What made us dream that he could comb grey hair?

                          12

       I had thought, seeing how bitter is that wind
90   That shakes the shutter, to have brought to mind
       All those that manhood tried, or childhood loved
       Or boyish intellect approved,
       With some appropriate commentary on each;
       Until imagination brought
95   A fitter welcome; but a thought
       Of that late death took all my heart for speech.

June 1918   1918

                  The Second Coming

       Turning and turning in the widening gyre¹
       The falcon cannot hear the falconer;
       Things fall apart; the centre cannot hold;
       Mere anarchy is loosed upon the world,
5   The blood-dimmed tide is loosed, and everywhere
       The ceremony of innocence is drowned;
       The best lack all conviction, while the worst
       Are full of passionate intensity.²

4. Bundles of sticks.
1. Yeats's term (pronounced with a hard g) for a spiraling motion in the shape of a cone. He envisions the two-thousand-year cycle of the Christian age as spiraling toward its end and the next historical cycle as beginning after a violent reversal: "the end of an age, which always receives the revelation of the character of the next age, is represented by the coming of one gyre to its place of greatest expansion and of the other to that of its greatest contraction" [Yeats's note].
2. The poem was written in January 1919, in the aftermath of World War I and the Russian Revolution and on the eve of the Anglo-Irish War.

Surely some revelation is at hand;
10 Surely the Second Coming is at hand.
The Second Coming![3] Hardly are those words out
When a vast image out of *Spiritus Mundi*[4]
Troubles my sight: somewhere in sands of the desert
A shape with lion body and the head of a man,
15 A gaze blank and pitiless as the sun,
Is moving its slow thighs, while all about it
Reel shadows of the indignant desert birds.
The darkness drops again; but now I know
That twenty centuries of stony sleep
20 Were vexed to nightmare by a rocking cradle,
And what rough beast, its hour come round at last,
Slouches towards Bethlehem[5] to be born?

Jan. 1919   1920, 1921

A Prayer for My Daughter

Once more the storm is howling, and half hid
Under this cradle-hood and coverlid
My child sleeps on.[1] There is no obstacle
But Gregory's wood[2] and one bare hill
5 Whereby the haystack- and roof-levelling wind,
Bred on the Atlantic, can be stayed;
And for an hour I have walked and prayed
Because of the great gloom that is in my mind.

I have walked and prayed for this young child an hour
10 And heard the sea-wind scream upon the tower,
And under the arches of the bridge, and scream
In the elms above the flooded stream;
Imagining in excited reverie
That the future years had come,
15 Dancing to a frenzied drum,
Out of the murderous innocence of the sea.

May she be granted beauty and yet not
Beauty to make a stranger's eye distraught,
Or hers before a looking-glass, for such,
20 Being made beautiful overmuch,
Consider beauty a sufficient end,
Lose natural kindness and maybe
The heart-revealing intimacy
That chooses right, and never find a friend.

3. Christ's second coming is heralded by the coming of the Beast of the Apocalypse, or Antichrist (1 John 2.18).
4. The spirit of the universe (Latin); i.e., Yeats said, "a general storehouse of images," a collective unconscious or memory, in which the human race preserves its past memories.

5. Jesus' birthplace.
1. Yeats's daughter and first child, Anne Butler Yeats, was born on February 26, 1919, in Dublin and brought home to Yeats's refitted Norman tower of Thoor Ballylee in Galway.
2. Lady Gregory's wood at Coole, only a few miles from Thoor Ballylee.

25 Helen being chosen found life flat and dull
    And later had much trouble from a fool,[3]
    While that great Queen, that rose out of the spray,[4]
    Being fatherless could have her way
    Yet chose a bandy-leggèd smith for man.
30 It's certain that fine women eat
    A crazy salad with their meat
    Whereby the Horn of Plenty[5] is undone.

    In courtesy I'd have her chiefly learned;
    Hearts are not had as a gift but hearts are earned
35 By those that are not entirely beautiful;
    Yet many, that have played the fool
    For beauty's very self, has charm made wise,
    And many a poor man that has roved,
    Loved and thought himself beloved,
40 From a glad kindness cannot take his eyes.

    May she become a flourishing hidden tree
    That all her thoughts may like the linnet° be,   *small songbird*
    And have no business but dispensing round
    Their magnanimities of sound,
45 Not but in merriment begin a chase,
    Nor but in merriment a quarrel.
    O may she live like some green laurel
    Rooted in one dear perpetual place.

    My mind, because the minds that I have loved,
50 The sort of beauty that I have approved,
    Prosper but little, has dried up of late,
    Yet knows that to be choked with hate
    May well be of all evil chances chief.
    If there's no hatred in a mind
55 Assault and battery of the wind
    Can never tear the linnet from the leaf.

    An intellectual hatred is the worst,
    So let her think opinions are accursed.
    Have I not seen the loveliest woman[6] born
60 Out of the mouth of Plenty's horn,
    Because of her opinionated mind
    Barter that horn and every good
    By quiet natures understood
    For an old bellows full of angry wind?

65 Considering that, all hatred driven hence,
    The soul recovers radical innocence

---

3. Menelaus, Helen's husband. Her abduction by
Paris precipitated the Trojan War.
4. Venus, born from the sea, was the Roman goddess of love; her husband, Vulcan, was the lame
god of fire and metalwork (line 29).

5. In Greek mythology the goat's horn that suckled the god Zeus flowed with nectar and ambrosia;
the cornucopia thus became a symbol of plenty.
6. Maud Gonne.

And learns at last that it is self-delighting,
Self-appeasing, self-affrighting,
And that its own sweet will is Heaven's will;
70 She can, though every face should scowl
And every windy quarter howl
Or every bellows burst, be happy still.

And may her bridegroom bring her to a house
Where all's accustomed, ceremonious;
75 For arrogance and hatred are the wares
Peddled in the thoroughfares.
How but in custom and in ceremony
Are innocence and beauty born?
Ceremony's a name for the rich horn,
80 And custom for the spreading laurel tree.

Feb.–June 1919   1919, 1921

Leda and the Swan[1]

A sudden blow: the great wings beating still
Above the staggering girl, her thighs caressed
By the dark webs, her nape caught in his bill,
He holds her helpless breast upon his breast.

5   How can those terrified vague fingers push
The feathered glory from her loosening thighs?
And how can body, laid in that white rush,
But feel the strange heart beating where it lies?

A shudder in the loins engenders there
10 The broken wall, the burning roof and tower[2]
And Agamemnon dead.
                              Being so caught up,
So mastered by the brute blood of the air,
Did she put on his knowledge with his power
Before the indifferent beak could let her drop?

Sept. 1923   1924, 1928

1. In Greek mythology the god Zeus, in the form of a swan, raped Leda, a mortal. Helen, Clytemnestra, Castor, and Pollux were the children of this union. Yeats saw Leda's rape as the beginning of a new age, analogous with the dove's annunciation to Mary of Jesus' conception: "I imagine the annunciation that founded Greece as made to Leda, remembering that they showed in a Spartan temple, strung up to the roof as a holy relic, an unhatched egg of hers, and that from one of her eggs came love and from the other war" (A Vision). For the author's revisions while composing the poem, see "Poems in Process," in the appendices to this volume.

2. I.e., the destruction of Troy, caused by Helen's abduction by Paris. Agamemnon, the leader of the Greek army that besieged Troy, was murdered by his wife, Clytemnestra, the other daughter of Leda and the swan.

Sailing to Byzantium[1]

1

That is no country for old men. The young
In one another's arms, birds in the trees,
—Those dying generations—at their song,
The salmon-falls, the mackerel-crowded seas,
5   Fish, flesh, or fowl, commend all summer long
Whatever is begotten, born, and dies.
Caught in that sensual music all neglect
Monuments of unageing intellect.

2

An aged man is but a paltry thing,
10   A tattered coat upon a stick, unless
Soul clap its hands and sing,[2] and louder sing
For every tatter in its mortal dress,
Nor is there singing school but studying
Monuments of its own magnificence;
15   And therefore I have sailed the seas and come
To the holy city of Byzantium.

3

O sages standing in God's holy fire
As in the gold mosaic of a wall,[3]
Come from the holy fire, perne in a gyre,[4]
20   And be the singing-masters of my soul.
Consume my heart away; sick with desire
And fastened to a dying animal
It knows not what it is; and gather me
Into the artifice of eternity.

4

25   Once out of nature I shall never take
My bodily form from any natural thing,
But such a form as Grecian goldsmiths make
Of hammered gold and gold enamelling
To keep a drowsy Emperor awake;[5]
30   Or set upon a golden bough to sing
To lords and ladies of Byzantium
Of what is past, or passing, or to come.

Sept. 1926   1927

---

1. Yeats wrote in *A Vision*: "I think that if I could be given a month of Antiquity and leave to spend it where I chose, I would spend it in Byzantium [now Istanbul] a little before Justinian opened St. Sophia and closed the Academy of Plato [in the 6th century C.E.]. . . . I think that in early Byzantium, maybe never before or since in recorded history, religious, aesthetic and practical life were one, that architect and artificers . . . spoke to the multitude and the few alike. The painter, the mosaic worker, the worker in gold and silver, the illuminator of sacred books, were almost impersonal, almost perhaps without the consciousness of individual design, absorbed in their subject-matter and that the vision of a whole people."
2. The poet William Blake (1757–1827) saw the soul of his dead brother rising to heaven, "clapping his hands for joy."
3. The mosaics in San Apollinaire Nuovo, in Ravenna, Italy, depict rows of Christian saints on a gold background; Yeats saw them in 1907.
4. I.e., whirl in a spiral.
5. I have read somewhere that in the Emperor's palace at Byzantium was a tree made of gold and silver, and artificial birds that sang [Yeats's note].

Among School Children

1

I walk through the long schoolroom questioning;
A kind old nun in a white hood replies;
The children learn to cipher° and to sing,   *do arithmetic*
To study reading-books and history,
5 To cut and sew, be neat in everything
In the best modern way—the children's eyes
In momentary wonder stare upon
A sixty-year-old smiling public man.[1]

2

I dream of a Ledaean[2] body, bent
10 Above a sinking fire, a tale that she
Told of a harsh reproof, or trivial event
That changed some childish day to tragedy—
Told, and it seemed that our two natures blent
Into a sphere from youthful sympathy,
15 Or else, to alter Plato's parable,
Into the yolk and white of the one shell.[3]

3

And thinking of that fit of grief or rage
I look upon one child or t'other there
And wonder if she stood so at that age—
20 For even daughters of the swan can share
Something of every paddler's heritage—
And had that colour upon cheek or hair,
And thereupon my heart is driven wild:
She stands before me as a living child.

4

25 Her present image floats into the mind—
Did Quattrocento[4] finger fashion it
Hollow of cheek as though it drank the wind
And took a mess of shadows for its meat?
And I though never of Ledaean kind
30 Had pretty plumage once—enough of that,
Better to smile on all that smile, and show
There is a comfortable kind of old scarecrow.

5

What youthful mother, a shape upon her lap
Honey of generation had betrayed,
35 And that must sleep, shriek, struggle to escape
As recollection or the drug decide,[5]

1. Yeats, as part of his work in the Irish Senate, visited a Montessori school in Waterford in 1926.
2. A body like Leda's. Yeats associated her daughter, Helen of Troy, with Maud Gonne.
3. In the *Symposium*, by the Greek philosopher Plato (ca. 428–ca. 348 B.C.E.), Aristophanes argues that "the primeval man" was both male and female but was divided (like an egg separated into yoke and white; the resulting two beings come together in love to become one again.
4. I.e., the skill of a 15th-century Italian painter.
5. I have taken the "honey of generation" from Porphyry's essay on "The Cave of Nymphs" [Yeats's note]. Porphyry (ca. 234–ca. 305 C.E.) was a Neoplatonic philosopher.

Would think her son, did she but see that shape
With sixty or more winters on its head,
A compensation for the pang of his birth,
40   Or the uncertainty of his setting forth?

6

Plato thought nature but a spume that plays
Upon a ghostly paradigm of things;[6]
Solider Aristotle played the taws
Upon the bottom of a king of kings;[7]
45   World-famous golden-thighed Pythagoras[8]
Fingered upon a fiddle-stick or strings
What a star sang and careless Muses heard:
Old clothes upon old sticks to scare a bird.

7

Both nuns and mothers worship images,
50   But those the candles light are not as those
That animate a mother's reveries,
But keep a marble or a bronze repose.
And yet they too break hearts—O Presences
That passion, piety or affection knows,
55   And that all heavenly glory symbolise—
O self-born mockers of man's enterprise;

8

Labour is blossoming or dancing where
The body is not bruised to pleasure soul,
Nor beauty born out of its own despair,
60   Nor blear-eyed wisdom out of midnight oil.
O chestnut tree, great-rooted blossomer,
Are you the leaf, the blossom or the bole?°   trunk
O body swayed to music, O brightening glance,
How can we know the dancer from the dance?

June 1926   1927

A Dialogue of Self and Soul[1]

1

My Soul. I summon to the winding ancient stair;
        Set all your mind upon the steep ascent,
        Upon the broken, crumbling battlement,
        Upon the breathless starlit air,
5   Upon the star that marks the hidden pole;

6. Plato thought nature merely an image of an ideal world that exists elsewhere.
7. Plato's student Aristotle (384–322 B.C.E.) was "solider" because he regarded this world as the authentic one. He tutored Alexander the Great (356–323 B.C.E.), the "king of kings," and disciplined him with the "taws," or leather strap.
8. Greek philosopher (ca. 580–500 B.C.E), known for his doctrine of the harmony of the spheres and his discovery of the mathematical basis of musical intervals. His disciples, the Pythagoreans, venerated their master as a god with a golden thigh.
1. In a letter of October 2, 1923, Yeats wrote: "I am writing a new tower poem 'Sword and Tower,' which is a choice of rebirth rather than deliverance from birth. I make my Japanese sword and its silk covering my symbol of life." Junzo Sato, a friend, had given him the ceremonial sword in 1920.

Fix every wandering thought upon
That quarter where all thought is done:
Who can distinguish darkness from the soul?

My Self. The consecrated blade upon my knees
10   Is Sato's ancient blade, still as it was,
Still razor-keen, still like a looking-glass
Unspotted by the centuries;
That flowering, silken, old embroidery, torn
From some court-lady's dress and round
15   The wooden scabbard bound and wound,
Can, tattered, still protect, faded adorn.

My Soul. Why should the imagination of a man
Long past his prime remember things that are
Emblematical of love and war?
20   Think of ancestral night that can,
If but imagination scorn the earth
And intellect its wandering
To this and that and t'other thing,
Deliver from the crime of death and birth.

25   *My Self.* Montashigi, third of his family, fashioned it
Five hundred years ago, about it lie
Flowers from I know not what embroidery—
Heart's purple—and all these I set
For emblems of the day against the tower
30   Emblematical of the night,
And claim as by a soldier's right
A charter to commit the crime once more.

My Soul. Such fullness in that quarter overflows
And falls into the basin of the mind
35   That man is stricken deaf and dumb and blind,
For intellect no longer knows
Is from the *Ought,* or *Knower* from the *Known*—
That is to say, ascends to Heaven;
Only the dead can be forgiven;
40   But when I think of that my tongue's a stone.

2

My Self. A living man is blind and drinks his drop.
What matter if the ditches are impure?
What matter if I live it all once more?
Endure that toil of growing up;
45   The ignominy of boyhood; the distress
Of boyhood changing into man;
The unfinished man and his pain
Brought face to face with his own clumsiness;

The finished man among his enemies?—
50   How in the name of Heaven can he escape
That defiling and disfigured shape

The mirror of malicious eyes
Casts upon his eyes until at last
He thinks that shape must be his shape?
55 And what's the good of an escape
If honour find him in the wintry blast?

I am content to live it all again
And yet again, if it be life to pitch
Into the frog-spawn of a blind man's ditch,
60 A blind man battering blind men;
Or into that most fecund ditch of all,
The folly that man does
Or must suffer, if he woos
A proud woman not kindred of his soul.

65 I am content to follow to its source
Every event in action or in thought;
Measure the lot; forgive myself the lot!
When such as I cast out remorse
So great a sweetness flows into the breast
70 We must laugh and we must sing,
We are blest by everything,
Everything we look upon is blest.

July–Dec. 1927   1929

Byzantium[1]

The unpurged images of day recede;
The Emperor's drunken soldiery are abed;
Night resonance recedes, night-walkers' song
After great cathedral gong;
5 A starlit or a moonlit dome[2] disdains
All that man is,
All mere complexities,
The fury and the mire° of human veins.   deep mud

Before me floats an image, man or shade,
10 Shade more than man, more image than a shade;
For Hades' bobbin[3] bound in mummy-cloth
May unwind the winding path;[4]
A mouth that has no moisture and no breath

---

1. On October 4, 1930, Yeats sent his friend Sturge Moore a copy of this poem, saying: "The poem originates from a criticism of yours. You objected to the last verse of 'Sailing to Byzantium' because a bird made by a goldsmith was just as natural as anything else. That showed me that the idea needed exposition." The previous April, Yeats had noted in his diary: "Subject for a poem": "Describe Byzantium as it is in the system towards the end of the first Christian millennium. A walking mummy. Flames at the street corners where the soul is purified, birds of hammered gold singing in the golden trees, in the harbour [dolphins] offering their backs to the wailing dead that they may carry them to Paradise."
2. Of the great church of St. Sophia.
3. Spool. Hades was the Greek god of the underworld, the realm of the dead.
4. I.e., the spool of people's fate, which spins their destiny and which is wound like a mummy, may be unwound and lead to the timeless world of pure spirit.

Breathless mouths may summon;
15 I hail the superhuman;
I call it death-in-life and life-in-death.[5]

Miracle, bird or golden handiwork,
More miracle than bird or handiwork,
Planted on the starlit golden bough,
20 Can like the cocks of Hades crow,
Or, by the moon embittered, scorn aloud
In glory of changeless metal
Common bird or petal
And all complexities of mire or blood.

25 At midnight on the Emperor's pavement flit
Flames that no faggot° feeds, nor steel has lit,   bundle of sticks
Nor storm disturbs, flames begotten of flame,
Where blood-begotten spirits come
And all complexities of fury leave,
30 Dying into a dance,
An agony of trance,
An agony of flame that cannot singe a sleeve.

Astraddle on the dolphin's mire and blood,[6]
Spirit after spirit! The smithies break the flood,
35 The golden smithies of the Emperor!
Marbles of the dancing floor
Break bitter furies of complexity,
Those images that yet
Fresh images beget,
40 That dolphin-torn, that gong-tormented sea.

Sept. 1930   1932

Crazy Jane Talks with the Bishop[1]

I met the Bishop on the road
And much said he and I.
"Those breasts are flat and fallen now
Those veins must soon be dry;
5 Live in a heavenly mansion,
Not in some foul sty."

"Fair and foul are near of kin,
And fair needs foul," I cried.
"My friends are gone, but that's a truth
10 Nor grave nor bed denied,

5. On Roman tombstones the cock is a herald of
rebirth, thus of the continuing cycle of human life.
6. In ancient mythology dolphins were thought to
carry the souls of the dead to the Isles of the

Blessed.
1. One of a series of poems about an old woman
partly modeled on Cracked Mary, an old woman
who lived near Lady Gregory.

Learned in bodily lowliness
And in the heart's pride.

"A woman can be proud and stiff
When on love intent;
15   But Love has pitched his mansion in
The place of excrement;
For nothing can be sole or whole
That has not been rent."

Nov. 1931   1932

Lapis Lazuli

(For Harry Clifton)[1]

I have heard that hysterical women say
They are sick of the palette and fiddle-bow,
Of poets that are always gay,
For everybody knows or else should know
5   That if nothing drastic is done[2]
Aeroplane and Zeppelin[3] will come out,
Pitch like King Billy[4] bomb-balls in
Until the town lie beaten flat.

All perform their tragic play,
10   There struts Hamlet, there is Lear,
That's Ophelia, that Cordelia;
Yet they, should the last scene be there,
The great stage curtain about to drop,
If worthy their prominent part in the play,
15   Do not break up their lines to weep.
They know that Hamlet and Lear are gay;
Gaiety transfiguring all that dread.
All men have aimed at, found and lost;
Black out; Heaven blazing into the head:
20   Tragedy wrought to its uttermost.
Though Hamlet rambles and Lear rages,
And all the drop scenes drop at once
Upon a hundred thousand stages,
It cannot grow by an inch or an ounce.

25   On their own feet they came, or on shipboard,
Camel-back, horse-back, ass-back, mule-back,

1. The English writer Harry Clifton (1908–1978) gave Yeats for his seventieth birthday a piece of lapis lazuli, a deep blue stone, "carved by some Chinese sculptor into the semblance of a mountain with temple, trees, paths, and an ascetic and pupil about to climb the mountain. Ascetic, pupil, hard stone, eternal theme of the sensual east. The heroic cry in the midst of despair. But no, I am wrong, the east has its solutions always and therefore knows nothing of tragedy. It is we, not the east, that must raise the heroic cry" [Yeats to Dorothy Wellesley, July 6, 1935].
2. Because Europe was (in 1936) close to war.
3. German zeppelins, or airships, bombed London during World War I.
4. King William III (William of Orange), who defeated the army of King James II at the Battle of the Boyne, in Ireland, in 1690. In a popular ballad, "King William he threw his bomb-balls in, / And set them on fire."

Old civilisations put to the sword.
Then they and their wisdom went to rack:
No handiwork of Callimachus[5]
30   Who handled marble as if it were bronze,
Made draperies that seemed to rise
When sea-wind swept the corner, stands;
His long lamp chimney shaped like the stem
Of a slender palm, stood but a day;
35   All things fall and are built again
And those that build them again are gay.

Two Chinamen, behind them a third,
Are carved in Lapis Lazuli,
Over them flies a long-legged bird
40   A symbol of longevity;
The third, doubtless a serving-man,
Carries a musical instrument.

Every discolouration of the stone,
Every accidental crack or dent
45   Seems a water-course or an avalanche,
Or lofty slope where it still snows
Though doubtless plum or cherry-branch
Sweetens the little half-way house
Those Chinamen climb towards, and I
50   Delight to imagine them seated there;
There, on the mountain and the sky,
On all the tragic scene they stare.
One asks for mournful melodies;
Accomplished fingers begin to play.
55   Their eyes mid many wrinkles, their eyes,
Their ancient, glittering eyes, are gay.

July 1936   1938

Under Ben Bulben[1]

1

Swear by what the Sages spoke
Round the Mareotic Lake[2]
That the Witch of Atlas knew,
Spoke and set the cocks a-crow.

5. Athenian sculptor (5th century B.C.E.), supposedly the originator of the Corinthian column and
of the use of the running drill to imitate folds in
drapery in statues. Yeats wrote of him: "With Callimachus pure Ionic revives again . . . and upon
the only example of his work known to us, a marble
chair, a Persian is represented, and may one not
discover a Persian symbol in that bronze lamp,
shaped like a palm . . . ? But he was an archaistic
workman, and those who set him to work brought
back public life to an older form" (A Vision).
1. A mountain near Sligo; Yeats's grave is in sight

of it, in Drumcliff churchyard.
2. Lake Mareotis, near Alexandria, Egypt, was an
ancient center of Christian Neoplatonism and of
neo-Pythagorean philosophy. The lake is mentioned in Percy Bysshe Shelley's poem "The Witch
of Atlas." In an essay on Shelley, Yeats interprets
the witch as a symbol of timeless, absolute beauty;
passing in a boat by this and another lake, she "sees
all human life shadowed upon its waters . . . and
because she can see the reality of things she is
described as journeying 'in the calm depths' of 'the
wide lake' we journey over unpiloted."

⁵ Swear by those horsemen, by those women,
Complexion and form prove superhuman,[3]
That pale, long visaged company
That airs an immortality
Completeness of their passions won;
¹⁰ Now they ride the wintry dawn
Where Ben Bulben sets the scene.

Here's the gist of what they mean.

2

Many times man lives and dies
Between his two eternities,
¹⁵ That of race and that of soul,
And ancient Ireland knew it all.
Whether man dies in his bed
Or the rifle knocks him dead,
A brief parting from those dear
²⁰ Is the worst man has to fear.
Though grave-diggers' toil is long,
Sharp their spades, their muscle strong,
They but thrust their buried men
Back in the human mind again.

3

²⁵ You that Mitchel's prayer have heard
"Send war in our time, O Lord!"[4]
Know that when all words are said
And a man is fighting mad,
Something drops from eyes long blind
³⁰ He completes his partial mind,
For an instant stands at ease,
Laughs aloud, his heart at peace,
Even the wisest man grows tense
With some sort of violence
³⁵ Before he can accomplish fate
Know his work or choose his mate.

4

Poet and sculptor do the work
Nor let the modish painter shirk
What his great forefathers did,
⁴⁰ Bring the soul of man to God,
Make him fill the cradles right.

---

3. Superhuman beings or fairies, like the Sidhe, believed to ride through the countryside near Ben Bulben.

4. From *Jail Journal*, by the Irish nationalist John Mitchel (1815–1875).

Measurement began our might:
Forms a stark Egyptian thought,
Forms that gentler Phidias⁵ wrought.

45   Michael Angelo left a proof
On the Sistine Chapel roof,
Where but half-awakened Adam
Can disturb globe-trotting Madam
Till her bowels are in heat,
50   Proof that there's a purpose set
Before the secret working mind:
Profane perfection of mankind.

Quattrocento⁶ put in paint,
On backgrounds for a God or Saint,
55   Gardens where a soul's at ease;
Where everything that meets the eye
Flowers and grass and cloudless sky
Resemble forms that are, or seem
When sleepers wake and yet still dream,
60   And when it's vanished still declare,
With only bed and bedstead there,
That Heavens had opened.

Gyres⁷ run on;
When that greater dream had gone
Calvert and Wilson, Blake and Claude⁸
65   Prepared a rest for the people of God,
Palmer's⁹ phrase, but after that
Confusion fell upon our thought.

5

Irish poets learn your trade
Sing whatever is well made,
70   Scorn the sort now growing up
All out of shape from toe to top,
Their unremembering hearts and heads
Base-born products of base beds.
Sing the peasantry, and then
75   Hard-riding country gentlemen,
The holiness of monks, and after
Porter-drinkers'¹ randy laughter;
Sing the lords and ladies gay
That were beaten into the clay
80   Through seven heroic centuries;²
Cast your mind on other days

5. Greek sculptor (fl. ca. 490–430 B.C.E.).
6. 15th-century Italian art.
7. Yeats's term for conelike spirals or cycles of history.
8. Edward Calvert (1799–1883), English visionary artist and follower of William Blake (1757–1827), English mystical poet and artist. Richard Wilson (1714–1782), English landscape painter

and disciple of Claude Lorraine (1600–1682), French artist.
9. Samuel Palmer (1805–1881), English landscape painter who admired Blake.
1. Drinkers of dark brown bitter beer.
2. Since the Norman conquest of Ireland, in the 12th century.

That we in coming days may be
Still the indomitable Irishry.

6

Under bare Ben Bulben's head
85   In Drumcliff churchyard Yeats is laid,
An ancestor was rector there[3]
Long years ago; a church stands near,
By the road an ancient Cross.
No marble, no conventional phrase,
90   On limestone quarried near the spot
By his command these words are cut:

Cast a cold eye
On life, on death.
Horseman, pass by!

Sept. 1938   1939

The Circus Animals' Desertion

1

I sought a theme and sought for it in vain,
I sought it daily for six weeks or so.
Maybe at last being but a broken man,
I must be satisfied with my heart, although
5   Winter and summer till old age began
My circus animals were all on show,
Those stilted boys, that burnished chariot,
Lion and woman and the Lord knows what.[1]

2

What can I but enumerate old themes,
10   First that sea-rider Oisin[2] led by the nose
Through three enchanted islands, allegorical dreams,
Vain gaiety, vain battle, vain repose,
Themes of the embittered heart, or so it seems,
That might adorn old songs or courtly shows;
15   But what cared I that set him on to ride,
I, starved for the bosom of his fairy bride.

And then a counter-truth filled out its play,
"The Countess Cathleen"[3] was the name I gave it,

3. Yeats's great-grandfather, the Reverend John
Yeats (1774–1846), was rector of Drumcliff
Church, Sligo.
1. Yeats refers to the ancient Irish heroes of his
early work ("Those stilted boys"), the gilded carriage of his play *The Unicorn from the Stars* (1908),
and the lion in several of his poems, including "The
Second Coming."
2. In the long title-poem of Yeats's first successful

book, *The Wanderings of Oisin and Other Poems*
(1889), the legendary poet warrior Oisin (pronounced *Ushēēn*) is enchanted by the beautiful
fairy woman Niamh (pronounced *Neeve*), who
leads him to the Islands of Delight, of Many Fears,
and of Forgetfulness.
3. A play (published in 1892) about an Irish
countess (an idealized version of Maud Gonne)
who sells her soul to the devil to buy food for the

She, pity-crazed, had given her soul away,
20 But masterful Heaven had intervened to save it.
I thought my dear must her own soul destroy
So did fanaticism and hate enslave it,
And this brought forth a dream and soon enough
This dream itself had all my thought and love.

25 And when the Fool and Blind Man stole the bread
Cuchulain fought the ungovernable sea;[4]
Heart mysteries there, and yet when all is said
It was the dream itself enchanted me:
Character isolated by a deed
30 To engross the present and dominate memory.
Players and painted stage took all my love
And not those things that they were emblems of.

3

Those masterful images because complete
Grew in pure mind but out of what began?
35 A mound of refuse or the sweepings of a street,
Old kettles, old bottles, and a broken can,
Old iron, old bones, old rags, that raving slut
Who keeps the till. Now that my ladder's gone
I must lie down where all the ladders start
40 In the foul rag and bone shop of the heart.

1939

From Introduction
[A General Introduction for My Work][1]

I. The First Principle

A poet writes always of his personal life, in his finest work out of its tragedies, whatever it be, remorse, lost love or mere loneliness; he never speaks directly as to someone at the breakfast table, there is always a phantasmagoria. Dante and Milton had mythologies, Shakespeare the characters of English history, of traditional romance; even when the poet seems most himself, when Raleigh and gives potentates the lie,[2] or Shelley 'a nerve o'er which do creep the else unfelt oppressions of mankind',[3] or Byron when 'the heart wears out the breast as the sword wears out the sheath',[4] he is never the bundle of accident and

starving Irish poor but is taken up to heaven (for God "Looks always on the motive, not the deed").
4. In Yeats's play *On Baile's Strand* (1904), the legendary warrior Cuchulain (pronounced *Cu-HOOlin* by Yeats, *KooHULLin* in Irish), crazed by his discovery that he has killed his son, fights with the sea.
1. Written in 1937 and originally printed as "A General Introduction for My Work" in *Essays and Introductions* (1961), the text is excerpted from *Later Essays*, ed. William H. O'Donnell (1994), vol. 5 of *The Collected Works of W. B. Yeats*.

2. From "The Lie," by the English writer and explorer Sir Walter Ralegh (1552–1618): "Tell potentates, they live / Acting by others' action; / Not loved unless they give, / Not strong but by a faction: / If potentates reply, / Give potentates the lie."
3. From "Julian and Maddalo," by the English poet Percy Bysshe Shelley (1792–1822).
4. Cf. "So, we'll go no more a roving," by the English poet George Gordon, Lord Byron (p. 1680, lines 5–6).

incoherence that sits down to breakfast; he has been re-born as an idea, something intended, complete. A novelist might describe his accidence, his incoherence, he must not, he is more type than man, more passion than type. He is Lear, Romeo, Oedipus, Tiresias; he has stepped out of a play and even the woman he loves is Rosalind, Cleopatra, never The Dark Lady.[5] He is part of his own phantasmagoria and we adore him because nature has grown intelligible, and by so doing a part of our creative power. 'When mind is lost in the light of the Self', says the Prashna Upanishad,[6] 'it dreams no more; still in the body it is lost in happiness.' 'A wise man seeks in Self', says the Chāndôgya Upanishad, 'those that are alive and those that are dead and gets what the world cannot give.' The world knows nothing because it has made nothing, we know everything because we have made everything.

II. Subject-Matter

* * *

* * *I am convinced that in two or three generations it will become generally known that the mechanical theory[7] has no reality, that the natural and supernatural are knit together, that to escape a dangerous fanaticism we must study a new science; at that moment Europeans may find something attractive in a Christ posed against a background not of Judaism but of Druidism, not shut off in dead history, but flowing, concrete, phenomenal.

I was born into this faith, have lived in it, and shall die in it; my Christ, a legitimate deduction from the Creed of St Patrick[8] as I think, is that Unity of Being Dante compared to a perfectly proportioned human body, Blake's 'Imagination',[9] what the Upanishads have named 'Self': nor is this unity distant and therefore intellectually understandable, but imminent,[1] differing from man to man and age to age, taking upon itself pain and ugliness, 'eye of newt, and leg of frog'.[2]

Subconscious preoccupation with this theme brought me A Vision,[3] its harsh geometry an incomplete interpretation. The 'Irishry' have preserved their ancient 'deposit' through wars which, during the sixteenth and seventeenth centuries, became wars of extermination; no people, Lecky said at the opening of his Ireland in the Eighteenth Century,[4] have undergone greater persecution, nor did that persecution altogether cease up to our own day. No people hate as we do in whom that past is always alive; there are moments when hatred poisons my life and I accuse myself of effeminacy because I have not given it adequate expression. It is not enough to have put it into the mouth of a rambling peasant poet. Then I remind myself that, though mine is the first English marriage I know of in the direct line, all my family names are English and that

5. The woman to whom many of Shakespeare's de-idealizing sonnets are addressed. The rest of the names refer to characters in Shakespeare's plays and in Sophocles' ancient Greek drama Oedipus the King.
6. One of a series of ancient philosophical dialogues in Sanskrit. From Ten Principal Upanishads (1937), translated by Yeats and the Indian monk Shri Purohit Swami (1882–1941).
7. Theory explaining the universe in strictly naturalistic, Newtonian terms.
8. From the second paragraph of "The Confession of St. Patrick, or His Epistle to the Irish," by the fifth-century saint, the apostle of Ireland.
9. In Jerusalem the English poet William Blake

(1757–1827) describes imagination as the "Divine body of the Lord Jesus." Yeats's ideas about the Unity of Being are drawn from his reading of Dante's Il Convito.
1. In manuscript Yeats wrote "imanent" (a misspelling of "immanent"), but he allowed "imminent" to stand in the typescript.
2. Ingredients of the witches' cauldron in Shakespeare's Macbeth 4.1.
3. Yeats's mystical writings (1925, 1937), in which he sketches out and schematizes many of his theories.
4. A History of Ireland in the Eighteenth Century, by the Irish historian William Edward Hartpole Lecky (1838–1903).

I owe my soul to Shakespeare, to Spenser and to Blake, perhaps to William Morris,[5] and to the English language in which I think, speak and write, that everything I love has come to me through English; my hatred tortures me with love, my love with hate. I am like the Tibetan monk who dreams at his initiation that he is eaten by a wild beast and learns on waking that he himself is eater and eaten. This is Irish hatred and solitude, the hatred of human life that made Swift write *Gulliver*[6] and the epitaph upon his tomb, that can still make us wag between extremes and doubt our sanity.

Again and again I am asked why I do not write in Gaelic; some four or five years ago I was invited to dinner by a London society and found myself among London journalists, Indian students and foreign political refugees. An Indian paper says it was a dinner in my honour, I hope not; I have forgotten though I have a clear memory of my own angry mind. I should have spoken as men are expected to speak at public dinners; I should have paid and been paid conventional compliments; then they would speak of the refugees, from that on all would be lively and topical, foreign tyranny would be arraigned, England seem even to those confused Indians the protector of liberty; I grew angrier and angrier; Wordsworth, that typical Englishman, had published his famous sonnet to François Dominique Toussaint, a Santo Domingo negro:

> There's not a breathing of the common wind
> That will forget thee[7]

in the year when Emmet conspired and died, and he remembered that rebellion as little as the half hanging and the pitch cap that preceded it by half a dozen years.[8] That there might be no topical speeches I denounced the oppression of the people of India; being a man of letters, not a politician, I told how they had been forced to learn everything, even their own Sanscrit, through the vehicle of English till the first discoverers of wisdom had become bywords for vague abstract facility. I begged the Indian writers present to remember that no man can think or write with music and vigour except in his mother tongue. I turned a friendly audience hostile, yet when I think of that scene I am unrepentant and angry.

I could no more have written in Gaelic than can those Indians write in English; Gaelic is my national language, but it is not my mother tongue.

III. *Style and Attitude*

Style is almost unconscious. I know what I have tried to do, little what I have done. Contemporary lyric poems, even those that moved me—'The Stream's Secret', 'Dolores'[9]—seemed too long, but an Irish preference for a swift current might be mere indolence, yet Burns may have felt the same when he read Thomson and Cowper.[1] The English mind is meditative, rich, delib-

---

5. English poet and designer (1834–1896). Edmund Spenser (1552–1599), English poet who, in addition to poetic works such as *The Faerie Queene*, wrote a treatise proposing the extermination of the Irish.
6. *Gulliver's Travels*, by the Irish satirist Jonathan Swift (1667–1745). Yeats's poem "Swift's Epitaph," a loose translation of the Latin on Swift's tomb, claims that "Swift has sailed into his rest; / Savage indignation there / Cannot lacerate his breast."
7. From "To Toussaint L'Ouverture," by the English poet William Wordsworth (1770–1850). L'Ouverture (1743–1803) died in prison after

rebelling against France's rule in Haiti.
8. Paper caps filled with burning pitch were used for torture during the martial law preceding and following the Irish Rising of 1798. Robert Emmet (1778–1803), Irish nationalist executed after the Irish rebellion of 1803.
9. Long poems by Dante Gabriel Rossetti (1828–1882) and Algernon Charles Swinburne (1837–1909), respectively.
1. James Thomson (1700–1748) and William Cowper (1731–1800), poets most famous for their long poems. Robert Burns (1759–1796), Scottish poet of short lyrics.

2420 / WILLIAM BUTLER YEATS

erate; it may remember the Thames[2] valley. I planned to write short lyrics or poetic drama where every speech [would] be short and concentrated, knit by dramatic tension, and I did so with more confidence because young English poets were at that time writing out of emotion at the moment of crisis, though their old slow-moving meditation returned almost at once. Then, and in this English poetry has followed my lead, I tried to make the language of poetry coincide with that of passionate, normal speech. I wanted to write in whatever language comes most naturally when we soliloquise, as I do all day long, upon the events of our own lives or of any life where we can see ourselves for the moment. I sometimes compare myself with the mad old slum women I hear denouncing and remembering; 'how dare you,' I heard one say of some imaginary suitor, 'and you without health or a home'. If I spoke my thoughts aloud they might be as angry and as wild. It was a long time before I had made a language to my liking; I began to make it when I discovered some twenty years ago that I must seek, not as Wordsworth thought words in common use,[3] but a powerful and passionate syntax, and a complete coincidence between period and stanza. Because I need a passionate syntax for passionate subject-matter I compel myself to accept those traditional metres that have developed with the language. Ezra Pound, Turner, Lawrence, wrote admirable free verse, I could not.[4] I would lose myself, become joyless like those mad old women. The translators of the Bible, Sir Thomas Browne,[5] certain translators from the Greek when translators still bothered about rhythm, created a form midway between prose and verse that seems natural to impersonal meditation; but all that is personal soon rots; it must be packed in ice or salt. Once when I was in delirium from pneumonia I dictated a letter to George Moore[6] telling him to eat salt because it was a symbol of eternity; the delirium passed, I had no memory of that letter, but I must have meant what I now mean. If I wrote of personal love or sorrow in free verse, or in any rhythm that left it unchanged, amid all its accident, I would be full of self-contempt because of my egotism and indiscretion, and I foresee the boredom of my reader. I must choose a traditional stanza, even what I alter must seem traditional. I commit my emotion to shepherds, herdsmen, camel-drivers, learned men, Milton's or Shelley's Platonist, that tower Palmer drew.[7] Talk to me of originality and I will turn on you with rage. I am a crowd, I am a lonely man, I am nothing. Ancient salt is best packing. The heroes of Shakespeare convey to us through their looks, or through the metaphorical patterns of their speech, the sudden enlargement of their vision, their ecstasy at the approach of death, 'She should have died hereafter', 'Of many million kisses, the poor last', 'Absent thee from felicity awhile'; they have become God or Mother Goddess, the pelican, 'My baby at my breast',[8] but all must be cold; no actress has ever sobbed when she played Cleopatra, even the shallow brain of a producer has never thought of such a

2. English river that runs through London.
3. In the preface to *Lyrical Ballads* (1800), Wordsworth says that poetry should be written in "language really used by men."
4. In his *Oxford Book of Modern Verse* (1936), Yeats included free verse by the American poet Ezra Pound (1885–1972), the English poet Walter Turner (1889–1946), and the English poet and novelist D. H. Lawrence (1885–1930).
5. English physician and author (1605–1682) with an elaborate prose style.
6. Irish novelist (1852–1933).

7. The English artist Samuel Palmer (1805–1881) drew "The Lonely Tower" (1879) as an illustration of Milton's poem about the pensive man, "Il Penseroso" (1645), in which a scholar in a "high lonely tower" is dedicated to uncovering Plato's insights; in Shelley's "Prince Athanase," the idealistic hero searches for love.
8. From *Macbeth* 5.4, *Anthony and Cleopatra* 4.15, *Hamlet* 5.2, respectively. "Pelican": thought to feed its babies with its blood and thus often a symbol of self-sacrifice.

thing. The supernatural is present, cold winds blow across our hands, upon our faces, the thermometer falls, and because of that cold we are hated by journalists and groundlings. There may be in this or that detail painful tragedy, but in the whole work none. I have heard Lady Gregory say, rejecting some play in the modern manner sent to the Abbey Theatre, 'Tragedy must be a joy to the man who dies.' Nor is it any different with lyrics, songs, narrative poems; neither scholars nor the populace have sung or read anything generation after generation because of its pain. The maid of honour whose tragedy they sing must be lifted out of history with timeless pattern, she is one of the four Maries,[9] the rhythm is old and familiar, imagination must dance, must be carried beyond feeling into the aboriginal ice. Is ice the correct word? I once boasted, copying the phrase from a letter of my father's, that I would write a poem 'cold and passionate as the dawn'.[1]

When I wrote in blank verse I was dissatisfied; my vaguely mediaeval *Countess Cathleen* fitted the measure, but our Heroic Age went better, or so I fancied, in the ballad metre of *The Green Helmet*.[2] There was something in what I felt about Deirdre, about Cuchulain,[3] that rejected the Renaissance and its characteristic metres, and this was a principal reason why I created in dance plays the form that varies blank verse with lyric metres. When I speak blank verse and analyse my feelings I stand at a moment of history when instinct, its traditional songs and dances, its general agreement, is of the past. I have been cast up out of the whale's belly though I still remember the sound and sway that came from beyond its ribs,[4] and, like the Queen in Paul Fort's ballad,[5] I smell of the fish of the sea. The contrapuntal structure of the verse, to employ a term adopted by Robert Bridges,[6] combines the past and present. If I repeat the first line of *Paradise Lost* so as to emphasise its five feet I am among the folk singers, 'Of mán's fírst disobédience ánd the frúit', but speak it as I should I cross it with another emphasis, that of passionate prose, 'Of mán's first disobédience and the frúit', or 'Of mán's fírst disobedience and the frúit', the folk song is still there, but a ghostly voice, an unvariable possibility, an unconscious norm. What moves me and my hearer is a vivid speech that has no laws except that it must not exorcise the ghostly voice. I am awake and asleep, at my moment of revelation, self-possessed in self-surrender; there is no rhyme, no echo of the beaten drum, the dancing foot, that would overset my balance. When I was a boy I wrote a poem upon dancing that had one good line: 'They snatch with their hands at the sleep of the skies.' If I sat down and thought for a year I would discover that but for certain syllabic limitations, a rejection or acceptance of certain elisions, I must wake or sleep.

The Countess Cathleen could speak a blank verse which I had loosened, almost put out of joint, for her need, because I thought of her as mediaeval

9. Mary, Queen of Scots (1542–1587) was served by four women named Mary.
1. From "The Fisherman" (1916): "Before I am old / I shall have written him one / Poem maybe as cold / And passionate as the dawn."
2. *The Countess Cathleen* (1892, later revised) is written in blank verse; *The Green Helmet* (1910), in iambic heptameter, which resembles the meter of a ballad (alternating between four- and three-stress lines).
3. The warrior hero of the Irish mythological Ulster Cycle; he also appears in Yeats's "dance" plays, derived from Japanese Noh drama. "Deir-

dre": in the Ulster Cycle, woman chosen to be queen of Ulster before she elopes with Naoise (pronounced *Neesha*).
4. Cf. Jonah 2.10: "And the Lord spake unto the fish, and it vomited out Jonah upon the dry land."
5. "La Reine à la Mer" ("The Queen of the Sea," 1894–96), by the French poet Paul Fort (1872–1960).
6. English poet (1844–1930), who stressed the poetic tension of the counterpoint between regular meters and the rhythm of poetry as actually spoken.

and thereby connected her with the general European movement. For Deirdre and Cuchulain and all the other figures of Irish legend are still in the whale's belly.

IV. Whither?

The young English poets reject dream and personal emotion; they have thought out opinions that join them to this or that political party; they employ an intricate psychology, action in character, not as in the ballads character in action, and all consider that they have a right to the same close attention that men pay to the mathematician and the metaphysician. One of the more distinguished has just explained that man has hitherto slept but must now awake.[7] They are determined to express the factory, the metropolis, that they may be modern. Young men teaching school in some picturesque cathedral town, or settled for life in Capri or in Sicily, defend their type of metaphor by saying that it comes naturally to a man who travels to his work by Tube.[8] I am indebted to a man of this school who went through my work at my request, crossing out all conventional metaphors,[9] but they seem to me to have rejected also those dream associations which were the whole art of Mallarmé.[1] He had topped a previous wave. As they express not what the Upanishads call 'that ancient Self' but individual intellect, they have the right to choose the man in the Tube because of his objective importance. They attempt to kill the whale, push the Renaissance higher yet, out-think Leonardo;[2] their verse kills the folk ghost and yet would remain verse. I am joined to the 'Irishry' and I expect a counter-Renaissance. No doubt it is part of the game to push that Renaissance; I make no complaint; I am accustomed to the geometrical arrangement of history in A Vision, but I go deeper than 'custom' for my convictions. When I stand upon O'Connell Bridge[3] in the half-light and notice that discordant architecture, all those electric signs, where modern heterogeneity has taken physical form, a vague hatred comes up out of my own dark and I am certain that wherever in Europe there are minds strong enough to lead others the same vague hatred rises; in four or five or in less generations this hatred will have issued in violence and imposed some kind of rule of kindred. I cannot know the nature of that rule, for its opposite fills the light; all I can do to bring it nearer is to intensify my hatred. I am no Nationalist, except in Ireland for passing reasons; State and Nation are the work of intellect, and when you consider what comes before and after them they are, as Victor Hugo said of something or other, not worth the blade of grass God gives for the nest of the linnet.[4]

1937   1961

7. Perhaps W. H. Auden (1907–1973) or C. Day Lewis (1904–1972).
8. London's underground railway. Lewis taught in the spa town of Cheltenham in the early 1930s. D. H. Lawrence lived in Capri and Sicily in the early 1920s.
9. Ezra Pound did this circa 1910.

1. Stéphane Mallarmé (1842–1898), French poet.
2. Leonardo da Vinci (1452–1519), Italian artist and inventor.
3. Over Dublin's river Liffey.
4. Small finch. Victor Hugo (1802–1885), French writer.

VIRGINIA WOOLF
1882–1941

Virginia Woolf was born in London, daughter of Julia Jackson Duckworth, a member of the Duckworth publishing family, and Leslie (later Sir Leslie) Stephen, the Victorian critic, philosopher, biographer, and scholar. She grew up within a large and talented family, educating herself in her father's magnificent library, meeting in childhood many eminent Victorians, and learning Greek from the essayist and critic Walter Pater's sister. Writing and the intellectual life thus came naturally to her. But her youth was shadowed by suffering: her older half-brother sexually abused her; her mother died in 1895, precipitating the first of her mental breakdowns; a beloved half-sister died in childbirth two years later; her father died of cancer in 1904; and a brother died of typhoid in 1906.

After her father's death she settled with her sister and two brothers in Bloomsbury, the district of London that later became associated with the group among whom she moved. The "Bloomsbury Group" was an intellectual coterie frequented at various times by the biographer Lytton Strachey, the economist John Maynard Keynes, the art critic Roger Fry, and the novelist E. M. Forster. When her sister, Vanessa, a notable painter, married Clive Bell, an art critic, in 1907, Woolf and her brother Adrian took another house in Bloomsbury, and there they entertained their literary and artistic friends at evening gatherings, where the conversation sparkled. The Bloomsbury Group thrived at the center of the middle-class and upper-middle-class London intelligentsia. Their intelligence was equaled by their frankness, notably on sexual topics, and the sexual life of Bloomsbury provided ample material for discussion and contributed to Woolf's freedom of thinking about gender relations. The painter Duncan Grant, for example, was at different times the lover of Keynes, Woolf's brother Adrian, and her sister, whose daughter, Angelica, he fathered. Woolf too was bisexual; and thirteen years after her marriage to the journalist and essayist Leonard Woolf, she fell passionately in love with the poet Vita [Victoria] Sackville-West, wife of the bisexual diplomat and author Harold Nicolson. Woolf's relationship with this aristocratic lesbian inspired the most lighthearted and scintillating of her books, *Orlando* (1928), a novel about a transhistorical androgynous protagonist, whose identity shifts from masculine to feminine over centuries.

Underneath Woolf's liveliness and wit—qualities so well known among the Bloomsbury Group—lay psychological tensions created partly by her childhood wounds and partly by her perfectionism, she being her own most exacting critic. The public was unaware until her death that she had been subject to periods of severe depression, particularly after finishing a book. In March 1941 she drowned herself in a river, an act influenced by her dread of World War II (she and Leonard would have been arrested by the Gestapo had the Nazis invaded England) and her fear that she was about to lose her mind and become a burden on her husband, who had supported her emotionally and intellectually. (In 1917 the Woolfs had founded the Hogarth Press, which published some of the most interesting literature of their time, including T. S. Eliot's *Poems* [1919], fiction by Maxim Gorky, Katherine Mansfield, and E. M. Forster, the English translations of Freud, and Virginia's novels.)

As a fiction writer Woolf rebelled against what she called the "materialism" of novelists such as her contemporaries Arnold Bennett and John Galsworthy, who depicted suffering and social injustice through gritty realism, and she sought to render more delicately those aspects of consciousness in which she felt the truth of human experience lay. In her essay "Modern Fiction" she defines the task of the novelist as looking within, as conveying the mind receiving "a myriad impressions," as representing the "luminous halo" or "semi-transparent envelope surrounding us from the beginning of consciousness to the end." In her novels she abandoned linear narratives in favor of interior monologues and stream of consciousness narration, exploring with great subtlety problems of personal identity and personal relationships as well as the significance of time, change, loss, and memory for human personality. After two conventionally realistic novels, *The Voyage Out* (1915) and *Night and Day* (1919), she developed her own style, a carefully modulated flow that brought into prose fiction something of the rhythms and imagery of lyric poetry. While intensely psychological and interior, her novels also found inspiration and material in the physical realities of the body and in the heavily trafficked and populated streets of London. In *Monday or Tuesday* (1921), a series of sketches, she explored the possibilities of moving between action and contemplation, between retrospection and anticipation, between specific external events and delicate tracings of the flow of consciousness. These technical experiments made possible those later novels in which her characteristic method is fully developed—the elegiac *Jacob's Room* (1922); *Mrs. Dalloway* (1925), the first completely successful realization of her style; *To the Lighthouse* (1927), which in part memorializes her parents; *The Waves* (1931), the most experimental and difficult of her novels; and *Between the Acts* (1941), which includes a discontinuous pageant of English history and was published after her death.

Woolf was also a prodigious reviewer and essayist. She began to write criticism in 1905 for the *Times Literary Supplement* and published some five hundred reviews and essays for it and other periodicals, collected in *The Common Reader* (1925) and *The Second Common Reader* (1932); her prose presents itself as suggestive rather than authoritative and has an engaging air of spontaneity. In marked contrast to the formal language of the lecture hall or philosophical treatise, arenas and forms of learning from which women were historically barred, she writes in an informal, personal, playfully polemical tone, which is implicitly linked to her identity as a female writer. In her essays she is equally concerned with her own craft as a writer and with what it was like to be a quite different person living in a different age. At once more informal and more revealing are the six volumes of her *Letters* (1975–80) and five volumes of her *Diary* (1977–84), which she began to write in 1917. These, with their running commentary on her life and work, resemble a painter's sketchbooks and serve as a reminder that her writings, for all their variety, have the coherence found only in the work of the greatest literary artists.

Over the course of her career, Woolf grew increasingly concerned with the position of women, especially professional women, and the constrictions under which they suffered. She wrote several cogent essays on the subject, and women's social subjection also arises in her fiction. Her novel *The Years* (1937) was originally to have reflections on the position of women interspersed amid the action, but she later decided to publish them as a separate book, *Three Guineas* (1938). In *A Room of One's Own* (1929), an essay based on two lectures on "Women and Fiction" delivered to female students at Cambridge, Woolf discusses various male institutions that historically either were denied to or oppressed women. Refused access to education, wealth, and property ownership, women lacked the conditions necessary to write and were unable to develop a literature of their own. Woolf advocated the creation of a literature that would include women's experience and ways of thinking, but instead of encouraging an exclusively female perspective, she proposed literature that would be "androgynous in mind" and resonate equally with men and women.

The Mark on the Wall

Perhaps it was the middle of January in the present year that I first looked up and saw the mark on the wall. In order to fix a date it is necessary to remember what one saw. So now I think of the fire; the steady film of yellow light upon the page of my book; the three chrysanthemums in the round glass bowl on the mantelpiece. Yes, it must have been the winter time, and we had just finished our tea, for I remember that I was smoking a cigarette when I looked up and saw the mark on the wall for the first time. I looked up through the smoke of my cigarette and my eye lodged for a moment upon the burning coals, and that old fancy of the crimson flag flapping from the castle tower came into my mind, and I thought of the cavalcade of red knights riding up the side of the black rock. Rather to my relief the sight of the mark interrupted the fancy, for it is an old fancy, an automatic fancy, made as a child perhaps. The mark was a small round mark, black upon the white wall, about six or seven inches above the mantelpiece.

How readily our thoughts swarm upon a new object, lifting it a little way, as ants carry a blade of straw so feverishly, and then leave it. . . . If that mark was made by a nail, it can't have been for a picture, it must have been for a miniature—the miniature of a lady with white powdered curls, powder-dusted cheeks, and lips like red carnations. A fraud of course, for the people who had this house before us would have chosen pictures in that way—an old picture for an old room. That is the sort of people they were—very interesting people, and I think of them so often, in such queer places, because one will never see them again, never know what happened next. They wanted to leave this house because they wanted to change their style of furniture, so he said, and he was in process of saying that in his opinion art should have ideas behind it when we were torn asunder, as one is torn from the old lady about to pour out tea and the young man about to hit the tennis ball in the back garden of the suburban villa as one rushes past in the train.

But for that mark, I'm not sure about it; I don't believe it was made by a nail after all; it's too big, too round, for that. I might get up, but if I got up and looked at it, ten to one I shouldn't be able to say for certain; because once a thing's done, no one ever knows how it happened. Oh! dear me, the mystery of life; the inaccuracy of thought! The ignorance of humanity! To show how very little control of our possessions we have—what an accidental affair this living is after all our civilisation—let me just count over a few of the things lost in one lifetime, beginning, for that seems always the most mysterious of losses—what cat would gnaw, what rat would nibble—three pale blue canisters of book-binding tools? Then there were the bird cages, the iron hoops, the steel skates, the Queen Anne coal-scuttle, the bagatelle[1] board, the hand organ—all gone, and jewels, too. Opals and emeralds, they lie about the roots of turnips. What a scraping paring affair it is to be sure! The wonder is that I've any clothes on my back, that I sit surrounded by solid furniture at this moment. Why, if one wants to compare life to anything, one must liken it to being blown through the Tube[2] at fifty miles an hour—landing at the other end without a single hairpin in one's hair! Shot out at the feet of God entirely naked! Tumbling head over heels in the asphodel meadows[3] like brown paper parcels pitched down a shoot in the post office! With one's hair flying back like the tail of a race-horse. Yes, that seems to express the rapidity of life, the perpetual waste and repair; all so casual, all so haphazard. . . .

But after life. The slow pulling down of thick green stalks so that the cup of the flower, as it turns over, deluges one with purple and red light. Why, after all, should one not be born there as one is born here, helpless, speechless,

---

1. Game played on oblong table with cue and balls. "Coal-scuttle": metal pail for carrying coal.
2. The London underground railway, or subway.

3. I.e., heaven, the next world (in Greek mythology asphodel flowers grow in the Elysian fields).

unable to focus one's eyesight, groping at the roots of the grass, at the toes of the Giants? As for saying which are trees, and which are men and women, or whether there are such things, that one won't be in a condition to do for fifty years or so. There will be nothing but spaces of light and dark, intersected by thick stalks, and rather higher up perhaps, rose-shaped blots of an indistinct colour—dim pinks and blues—which will, as time goes on, become more definite, become—I don't know what. . . .

And yet that mark on the wall is not a hole at all. It may even be caused by some round black substance, such as a small rose leaf, left over from the summer, and I, not being a very vigilant housekeeper—look at the dust on the mantelpiece, for example, the dust which, so they say, buried Troy[4] three times over, only fragments of pots utterly refusing annihilation, as one can believe.

The tree outside the window taps very gently on the pane. . . . I want to think quietly, calmly, spaciously, never to be interrupted, never to have to rise from my chair, to slip easily from one thing to another, without any sense of hostility, or obstacle. I want to sink deeper and deeper, away from the surface, with its hard separate facts. To steady myself, let me catch hold of the first idea that passes . . . Shakespeare. . . . Well, he will do as well as another. A man who sat himself solidly in an arm-chair, and looked into the fire, so— A shower of ideas fell perpetually from some very high Heaven down through his mind. He leant his forehead on his hand, and people, looking in through the open door—for this scene is supposed to take place on a summer's evening— But how dull this is, this historical fiction! It doesn't interest me at all. I wish I could hit upon a pleasant track of thought, a track indirectly reflecting credit upon myself, for those are the pleasantest thoughts, and very frequent even in the minds of modest mouse-coloured people, who believe genuinely that they dislike to hear their own praises. They are not thoughts directly praising oneself; that is the beauty of them; they are thoughts like this:

"And then I came into the room. They were discussing botany. I said how I'd seen a flower growing on a dust heap on the site of an old house in Kingsway.[5] The seed, I said, must have been sown in the reign of Charles the First. What flowers grew in the reign of Charles the First?" I asked—(but I don't remember the answer). Tall flowers with purple tassels to them perhaps. And so it goes on. All the time I'm dressing up the figure of myself in my own mind, lovingly, stealthily, not openly adoring it, for if I did that, I should catch myself out, and stretch my hand at once for a book in self-protection. Indeed, it is curious how instinctively one protects the image of oneself from idolatry or any other handling that could make it ridiculous, or too unlike the original to be believed in any longer. Or is it not so very curious after all? It is a matter of great importance. Suppose the looking-glass smashes, the image disappears, and the romantic figure with the green of forest depths all about it is there no longer, but only that shell of a person which is seen by other people—what an airless, shallow, bald, prominent world it becomes! A world not to be lived in. As we face each other in omnibuses and underground railways we are looking into the mirror; that accounts for the vagueness, the gleam of glassiness, in our eyes. And the novelists in future will realise more and more the importance of these reflections, for of course there is not one reflection but an almost infinite number; those are the depths they will explore, those the

4. Legendary site of ancient war chronicled in Homer's Greek epic *The Iliad*.

5. Street in London.

phantoms they will pursue, leaving the description of reality more and more out of their stories, taking a knowledge of it for granted, as the Greeks did and Shakespeare perhaps—but these generalisations are very worthless. The military sound of the word is enough. It recalls leading articles, cabinet ministers—a whole class of things indeed which, as a child, one thought the thing itself, the standard thing, the real thing, from which one could not depart save at the risk of nameless damnation. Generalisations bring back somehow Sunday in London, Sunday afternoon walks, Sunday luncheons, and also ways of speaking of the dead, clothes, and habits—like the habit of sitting all together in one room until a certain hour, although nobody liked it. There was a rule for everything. The rule for tablecloths at that particular period was that they should be made of tapestry with little yellow compartments marked upon them, such as you may see in photographs of the carpets in the corridors of the royal palaces. Tablecloths of a different kind were not real tablecloths. How shocking, and yet how wonderful it was to discover that these real things, Sunday luncheons, Sunday walks, country houses, and tablecloths were not entirely real, were indeed half phantoms, and the damnation which visited the disbeliever in them was only a sense of illegitimate freedom. What now takes the place of those things I wonder, those real standard things? Men perhaps, should you be a woman; the masculine point of view which governs our lives, which sets the standard, which establishes Whitaker's Table of Precedency,[6] which has become, I suppose, since the war, half a phantom to many men and women, which soon, one may hope, will be laughed into the dustbin where the phantoms go, the mahogany sideboards and the Landseer[7] prints, Gods and Devils, Hell and so forth, leaving us all with an intoxicating sense of illegitimate freedom—if freedom exists. . . .

In certain lights that mark on the wall seems actually to project from the wall. Nor is it entirely circular. I cannot be sure, but it seems to cast a perceptible shadow, suggesting that if I ran my finger down that strip of the wall it would, at a certain point, mount and descend a small tumulus, a smooth tumulus like those barrows on the South Downs[8] which are, they say, either tombs or camps. Of the two I should prefer them to be tombs, desiring melancholy like most English people, and finding it natural at the end of a walk to think of the bones stretched beneath the turf. . . . There must be some book about it. Some antiquary must have dug up those bones and given them a name. . . . What sort of a man is an antiquary, I wonder? Retired Colonels for the most part, I daresay, leading parties of aged labourers to the top here, examining clods of earth and stone, and getting into correspondence with the neighbouring clergy, which, being opened at breakfast time, gives them a feeling of importance, and the comparison of arrow-heads necessitates cross-country journeys to the country towns, an agreeable necessity both to them and to their elderly wives, who wish to make plum jam or to clean out the study, and have every reason for keeping that great question of the camp or the tomb in perpetual suspension, while the Colonel himself feels agreeably philosophic in accumulating evidence on both sides of the question. It is true

6. *Whitaker's Almanack*, an annual compendium of information, prints a "Table of Precedency," which shows the order in which the various ranks in public life and society proceed on formal occasions.
7. Sir Edwin Henry Landseer (1802–1873),

English painter, reproductions of whose *Stag at Bay*, *Monarch of the Glen*, and similar animal paintings were often found in Victorian homes.
8. A range of low hills in southeastern England. "Barrows": mounds of earth or stones erected by prehistoric peoples, usually as burial places.

that he does finally incline to believe in the camp; and, being opposed, indites a pamphlet which he is about to read at the quarterly meeting of the local society when a stroke lays him low, and his last conscious thoughts are not of wife or child, but of the camp and that arrowhead there, which is now in the case at the local museum, together with the foot of a Chinese murderess, a handful of Elizabethan nails, a great many Tudor clay pipes, a piece of Roman pottery, and the wineglass that Nelson[9] drank out of—proving I really don't know what.

No, no, nothing is proved, nothing is known. And if I were to get up at this very moment and ascertain that the mark on the wall is really—what shall we say?—the head of a gigantic old nail, driven in two hundred years ago, which has now, owing to the patient attrition of many generations of housemaids, revealed its head above the coat of paint, and is taking its first view of modern life in the sight of a white-walled fire-lit room, what should I gain?— Knowledge? Matter for further speculation? I can think sitting still as well as standing up. And what is knowledge? What are our learned men save the descendants of witches and hermits who crouched in caves and in woods brewing herbs, interrogating shrew-mice and writing down the language of the stars? And the less we honour them as our superstitions dwindle and our respect for beauty and health of mind increases. . . . Yes, one could imagine a very pleasant world. A quiet, spacious world, with the flowers so red and blue in the open fields. A world without professors or specialists or house-keepers with the profiles of policemen, a world which one could slice with one's thought as a fish slices the water with his fin, grazing the stems of the water-lilies, hanging suspended over nests of white sea eggs. . . . How peaceful it is down here, rooted in the centre of the world and gazing up through the grey waters, with their sudden gleams of light, and their reflections—if it were not for Whitaker's Almanack—if it were not for the Table of Precedency!

I must jump up and see for myself what that mark on the wall really is—a nail, a rose-leaf, a crack in the wood?

Here is Nature once more at her old game of self-preservation. This train of thought, she perceives, is threatening mere waste of energy, even some collision with reality, for who will ever be able to lift a finger against Whitaker's Table of Precedency? The Archbishop of Canterbury is followed by the Lord High Chancellor; the Lord High Chancellor is followed by the Archbishop of York. Everybody follows somebody, such is the philosophy of Whitaker; and the great thing is to know who follows whom. Whitaker knows, and let that, so Nature counsels, comfort you, instead of enraging you; and if you can't be comforted, if you must shatter this hour of peace, think of the mark on the wall.

I understand Nature's game—her prompting to take action as a way of ending any thought that threatens to excite or to pain. Hence, I suppose, comes our slight contempt for men of action—men, we assume, who don't think. Still, there's no harm in putting a full stop to one's disagreeable thoughts by looking at a mark on the wall.

Indeed, now that I have fixed my eyes upon it, I feel that I have grasped a plank in the sea; I feel a satisfying sense of reality which at once turns the two Archbishops and the Lord High Chancellor to the shadows of shades. Here is something definite, something real. Thus, waking from a midnight dream of

9. Horatio Nelson (1758–1805), British admiral. "Tudor": 15th-century English.

horror, one hastily turns on the light and lies quiescent, worshipping the chest of drawers, worshipping solidity, worshipping reality, worshipping the impersonal world which is a proof of some existence other than ours. That is what one wants to be sure of. . . . Wood is a pleasant thing to think about. It comes from a tree; and trees grow, and we don't know how they grow. For years and years they grow, without paying any attention to us, in meadows, in forests, and by the side of rivers—all things one likes to think about. The cows swish their tails beneath them on hot afternoons; they paint rivers so green that when a moorhen dives one expects to see its feathers all green when it comes up again. I like to think of the fish balanced against the stream like flags blown out; and of water-beetles slowly raising domes of mud upon the bed of the river. I like to think of the tree itself: first of the close dry sensation of being wood; then the grinding of the storm; then the slow, delicious ooze of sap; I like to think of it, too, on winter's nights standing in the empty field with all leaves close-furled, nothing tender exposed to the iron bullets of the moon, a naked mast upon an earth that goes tumbling, tumbling, all night long. The song of birds must sound very loud and strange in June; and how cold the feet of insects must feel upon it, as they make laborious progresses up the creases of the bark, or sun themselves upon the thin green awning of the leaves, and look straight in front of them with diamond-cut red eyes. . . . One by one the fibres snap beneath the immense cold pressure of the earth, then the last storm comes and, falling, the highest branches drive deep into the ground again. Even so, life isn't done with; there are a million patient, watchful lives still for a tree, all over the world, in bedrooms, in ships, on the pavement, living rooms, where men and women sit after tea, smoking cigarettes. It is full of peaceful thoughts, happy thoughts, this tree. I should like to take each one separately— but something is getting in the way. . . . Where was I? What has it all been about? A tree? A river? The Downs?[1] Whitaker's Almanack? The fields of asphodel? I can't remember a thing. Everything's moving, falling, slipping, vanishing. . . . There is a vast upheaval of matter. Someone is standing over me and saying:

"I'm going out to buy a newspaper."

"Yes?"

"Though it's no good buying newspapers. . . . Nothing ever happens. Curse this war; God damn this war! . . . All the same, I don't see why we should have a snail on our wall."

Ah, the mark on the wall! It was a snail.

1921

Modern Fiction

In making any survey, even the freest and loosest, of modern fiction, it is difficult not to take it for granted that the modern practice of the art is somehow an improvement upon the old. With their simple tools and primitive materials, it might be said, Fielding[1] did well and Jane Austen even better, but compare their opportunities with ours! Their masterpieces certainly have a

---

1. Part of the sea off the east coast of Kent.   1. Henry Fielding (1707–1754), English novelist.

strange air of simplicity. And yet the analogy between literature and the process, to choose an example, of making motor cars scarcely holds good beyond the first glance. It is doubtful whether in the course of the centuries, though we have learnt much about making machines, we have learnt anything about making literature. We do not come to write better; all that we can be said to do is to keep moving, now a little in this direction, now in that, but with a circular tendency should the whole course of the track be viewed from a sufficiently lofty pinnacle. It need scarcely be said that we make no claim to stand, even momentarily, upon that vantage-ground. On the flat, in the crowd, half blind with dust, we look back with envy to those happier warriors, whose battle is won and whose achievements wear so serene an air of accomplishment that we can scarcely refrain from whispering that the fight was not so fierce for them as for us. It is for the historian of literature to decide; for him to say if we are now beginning or ending or standing in the middle of a great period of prose fiction, for down in the plain little is visible. We only know that certain gratitudes and hostilities inspire us; that certain paths seem to lead to fertile land, others to the dust and the desert; and of this perhaps it may be worth while to attempt some account.

Our quarrel, then, is not with the classics, and if we speak of quarrelling with Mr Wells, Mr Bennett, and Mr Galsworthy;[2] it is partly that by the mere fact of their existence in the flesh their work has a living, breathing, everyday imperfection which bids us take what liberties with it we choose. But it is also true, that, while we thank them for a thousand gifts, we reserve our unconditional gratitude for Mr Hardy, for Mr Conrad, and in much lesser degree for the Mr Hudson of *The Purple Land, Green Mansions,* and *Far Away and Long Ago.*[3] Mr Wells, Mr Bennett, and Mr Galsworthy have excited so many hopes and disappointed them so persistently that our gratitude largely takes the form of thanking them for having shown us what they might have done but have not done; what we certainly could not do, but as certainly, perhaps, do not wish to do. No single phrase will sum up the charge or grievance which we have to bring against a mass of work so large in its volume and embodying so many qualities, both admirable and the reverse. If we tried to formulate our meaning in one word we should say that these three writers are materialists. It is because they are concerned not with the spirit but with the body that they have disappointed us, and left us with the feeling that the sooner English fiction turns its back upon them, as politely as may be, and marches, if only into the desert, the better for its soul. Naturally, no single word reaches the centre of three separate targets. In the case of Mr Wells it falls notably wide of the mark. And yet even with him it indicates to our thinking the fatal alloy in his genius, the great clod of clay that has got itself mixed up with the purity of his inspiration. But Mr Bennett is perhaps the worst culprit of the three, inasmuch as he is by far the best workman. He can make a book so well constructed and solid in its craftsmanship that it is difficult for the most exacting of critics to see through what chink or crevice decay can creep in. There is not so much as a draught between the frames of the windows, or a crack in the boards. And yet—if life should refuse to live there? That is a risk which the creator of *The Old Wives' Tale,* George Cannon, Edwin Clayhanger,[4] and

2. H. G. Wells (1866–1946), Arnold Bennett (1867–1931), John Galsworthy (1867–1933), English novelists.
3. W. H. Hudson (1841–1922), naturalist and writer, was born in Argentina, although he later lived in London. *The Purple Land* (1885) is about South America; *Green Mansions* (1904), a novel set in South America, was his first real success.
4. Characters in Arnold Bennett's novels; *The Old Wives' Tale* (1908) is the best-known.

hosts of other figures, may well claim to have surmounted. His characters live abundantly, even unexpectedly, but it remains to ask how do they live, and what do they live for? More and more they seem to us, deserting even the well-built villa in the Five Towns,[5] to spend their time in some softly padded first-class railway carriage, pressing bells and buttons innumerable; and the destiny to which they travel so luxuriously becomes more and more unquestionably an eternity of bliss spent in the very best hotel in Brighton.[6] It can scarcely be said of Mr Wells that he is a materialist in the sense that he takes too much delight in the solidity of his fabric. His mind is too generous in its sympathies to allow him to spend much time in making things shipshape and substantial. He is a materialist from sheer goodness of heart, taking upon his shoulders the work that ought to have been discharged by Government officials, and in the plethora of his ideas and facts scarcely having leisure to realize, or forgetting to think important, the crudity and coarseness of his human beings. Yet what more damaging criticism can there be both of his earth and of his Heaven than that they are to be inhabited here and hereafter by his Joans and his Peters?[7] Does not the inferiority of their natures tarnish whatever institutions and ideals may be provided for them by the generosity of their creator? Nor, profoundly though we respect the integrity and humanity of Mr Galsworthy, shall we find what we seek in his pages.

If we fasten, then, one label on all these books, on which is one word, materialists, we mean by it that they write of unimportant things; that they spend immense skill and immense industry making the trivial and the transitory appear the true and the enduring.

We have to admit that we are exacting, and, further, that we find it difficult to justify our discontent by explaining what it is that we exact. We frame our question differently at different times. But it reappears most persistently as we drop the finished novel on the crest of a sigh—Is it worth while? What is the point of it all? Can it be that, owing to one of those little deviations which the human spirit seems to make from time to time, Mr Bennett has come down with his magnificent apparatus for catching life just an inch or two on the wrong side? Life escapes; and perhaps without life nothing else is worth while. It is a confession of vagueness to have to make use of such a figure as this, but we scarcely better the matter by speaking, as critics are prone to do, of reality. Admitting the vagueness which afflicts all criticism of novels, let us hazard the opinion that for us at this moment the form of fiction most in vogue more often misses than secures the thing we seek. Whether we call it life or spirit, truth or reality, this, the essential thing, has moved off, or on, and refuses to be contained any longer in such ill-fitting vestments as we provide. Nevertheless, we go on perseveringly, conscientiously, constructing our two and thirty chapters after a design which more and more ceases to resemble the vision in our minds. So much of the enormous labour of proving the solidity, the likeness to life, of the story is not merely labour thrown away but labour misplaced to the extent of obscuring and blotting out the light of the conception. The writer seems constrained, not by his own free will but by some powerful and unscrupulous tyrant who has him in thrall, to provide a plot, to provide comedy, tragedy, love interest, and an air of probability embalming the whole so impeccable that if all his figures were to come to life they would

5. The pottery towns of Staffordshire in which much of Bennett's fiction was set.
6. Once-fashionable seaside resort on the south-west coast of England.

7. In his novel *Joan and Peter: The Story of an Education* (1918), Wells advocates education to address social problems.

find themselves dressed down to the last button of their coats in the fashion of the hour. The tyrant is obeyed; the novel is done to a turn. But sometimes, more and more often as time goes by, we suspect a momentary doubt, a spasm of rebellion, as the pages fill themselves in the customary way. Is life like this? Must novels be like this?

Look within and life, it seems, is very far from being "like this." Examine for a moment an ordinary mind on an ordinary day. The mind receives a myriad impressions—trivial, fantastic, evanescent, or engraved with the sharpness of steel. From all sides they come, an incessant shower of innumerable atoms; and as they fall, as they shape themselves into the life of Monday or Tuesday,[8] the accent falls differently from of old; the moment of importance came not here but there; so that, if a writer were a free man and not a slave, if he could write what he chose, not what he must, if he could base his work upon his own feeling and not upon convention, there would be no plot, no comedy, no tragedy, no love interest or catastrophe in the accepted style, and perhaps not a single button sewn on as the Bond Street[9] tailors would have it. Life is not a series of gig-lamps[1] symmetrically arranged; life is a luminous halo, a semitransparent envelope surrounding us from the beginning of consciousness to the end. Is it not the task of the novelist to convey this varying, this unknown and uncircumscribed spirit, whatever aberration or complexity it may display, with as little mixture of the alien and external as possible? We are not pleading merely for courage and sincerity; we are suggesting that the proper stuff of fiction is a little other than custom would have us believe it.

It is, at any rate, in some such fashion as this that we seek to define the quality which distinguishes the work of several young writers, among whom Mr James Joyce is the most notable, from that of their predecessors. They attempt to come closer to life, and to preserve more sincerely and exactly what interests and moves them, even if to do so they must discard most of the conventions which are commonly observed by the novelist. Let us record the atoms as they fall upon the mind in the order in which they fall, let us trace the pattern, however disconnected and incoherent in appearance, which each sight or incident scores upon the consciousness. Let us not take it for granted that life exists more fully in what is commonly thought big than in what is commonly thought small. Anyone who has read *The Portrait of the Artist as a Young Man* or, what promises to be a far more interesting work, *Ulysses*,[2] now appearing in the *Little Review*, will have hazarded some theory of this nature as to Mr Joyce's intention. On our part, with such a fragment before us, it is hazarded rather than affirmed; but whatever the intention of the whole, there can be no question but that it is of the utmost sincerity and that the result, difficult or unpleasant as we may judge it, is undeniably important. In contrast with those whom we have called materialists, Mr Joyce is spiritual; he is concerned at all costs to reveal the flickerings of that innermost flame which flashes its messages through the brain, and in order to preserve it he disregards with complete courage whatever seems to him adventitious, whether it be probability, or coherence, or any other of these signposts which for generations have served to support the imagination of a reader when called upon to imagine what he can neither touch nor see. The scene in the cemetery,[3] for

---

8. *Monday or Tuesday* was Woolf's 1921 collection of experimental stories and sketches.
9. Fashionable shopping street in London.
1. Carriage lamps.

2. Written April, 1919 [Woolf's note].
3. The sixth episode ("Hades") of *Ulysses*, where Bloom goes to Paddy Dignam's funeral.

instance, with its brilliancy, its sordidity, its incoherence, its sudden lightning flashes of significance, does undoubtedly come so close to the quick of the mind that, on a first reading at any rate, it is difficult not to acclaim a masterpiece. If we want life itself, here surely we have it. Indeed, we find ourselves fumbling rather awkwardly if we try to say what else we wish, and for what reason a work of such originality yet fails to compare, for we must take high examples, with *Youth* or *The Mayor of Casterbridge*.[4] It fails because of the comparative poverty of the writer's mind, we might say simply and have done with it. But it is possible to press a little further and wonder whether we may not refer our sense of being in a bright yet narrow room, confined and shut in, rather than enlarged and set free, to some limitation imposed by the method as well as by the mind. Is it the method that inhibits the creative power? Is it due to the method that we feel neither jovial nor magnanimous, but centred in a self which, in spite of its tremor of susceptibility, never embraces or creates what is outside itself and beyond? Does the emphasis laid, perhaps didactically, upon indecency contribute to the effect of something angular and isolated? Or is it merely that in any effort of such originality it is much easier, for contemporaries especially, to feel what it lacks than to name what it gives? In any case it is a mistake to stand outside examining "methods". Any method is right, every method is right, that expresses what we wish to express, if we are writers; that brings us closer to the novelist's intention if we are readers. This method has the merit of bringing us closer to what we were prepared to call life itself; did not the reading of *Ulysses* suggest how much of life is excluded or ignored, and did it not come with a shock to open *Tristram Shandy* or even *Pendennis*[5] and be by them convinced that there are not only other aspects of life, but more important ones into the bargain.

However this may be, the problem before the novelist at present, as we suppose it to have been in the past, is to contrive means of being free to set down what he chooses. He has to have the courage to say that what interests him is no longer "this" but "that": out of "that" alone must he construct his work. For the moderns "that", the point of interest, lies very likely in the dark places of psychology. At once, therefore, the accent falls a little differently; the emphasis is upon something hitherto ignored; at once a different outline of form becomes necessary, difficult for us to grasp, incomprehensible to our predecessors. No one but a modern, no one perhaps but a Russian, would have felt the interest of the situation which Tchekov has made into the short story which he calls "Gusev."[6] Some Russian soldiers lie ill on board a ship which is taking them back to Russia. We are given a few scraps of their talk and some of their thoughts; then one of them dies and is carried away; the talk goes on among the others for a time, until Gusev himself dies, and looking "like a carrot or a radish" is thrown overboard. The emphasis is laid upon such unexpected places that at first it seems as if there were no emphasis at all; and then, as the eyes accustom themselves to twilight and discern the shapes of things in a room we see how complete the story is, how profound, and how truly in obedience to his vision Tchekov has chosen this, that, and the other, and placed them together to compose something new. But it is impossible to

4. A story and a novel by, respectively, Joseph Conrad and Thomas Hardy.
5. Novels by, respectively, the English writers Laurence Sterne (1713–1768) and William Make-

peace Thackeray (1811–1863).
6. 1890 story by the Russian writer Anton Pavlovich Chekhov (1860–1904).

say "this is comic," or "that is tragic," nor are we certain, since short stories, we have been taught, should be brief and conclusive, whether this, which is vague and inconclusive, should be called a short story at all.

The most elementary remarks upon modern English fiction can hardly avoid some mention of the Russian influence, and if the Russians are mentioned one runs the risk of feeling that to write of any fiction save theirs is waste of time. If we want understanding of the soul and heart where else shall we find it of comparable profundity? If we are sick of our own materialism the least considerable of their novelists has by right of birth a natural reverence for the human spirit. "Learn to make yourself akin to people. . . . But let this sympathy be not with the mind—for it is easy with the mind—but with the heart, with love towards them." In every great Russian writer we seem to discern the features of a saint, if sympathy for the sufferings of others, love towards them, endeavour to reach some goal worthy of the most exacting demands of the spirit constitute saintliness. It is the saint in them which confounds us with a feeling of our own irreligious triviality, and turns so many of our famous novels to tinsel and trickery. The conclusions of the Russian mind, thus comprehensive and compassionate, are inevitably, perhaps, of the utmost sadness. More accurately indeed we might speak of the inconclusiveness of the Russian mind. It is the sense that there is no answer, that if honestly examined life presents question after question which must be left to sound on and on after the story is over in hopeless interrogation that fills us with a deep, and finally it may be with a resentful, despair. They are right perhaps; unquestionably they see further than we do and without our gross impediments of vision. But perhaps we see something that escapes them, or why should this voice of protest mix itself with our gloom? The voice of protest is the voice of another and an ancient civilisation which seems to have bred in us the instinct to enjoy and fight rather than to suffer and understand. English fiction from Sterne to Meredith[7] bears witness to our natural delight in humour and comedy, in the beauty of earth, in the activities of the intellect, and in the splendour of the body. But any deductions that we may draw from the comparison of two fictions so immeasurably far apart are futile save indeed as they flood us with a view of the infinite possibilities of the art and remind us that there is no limit to the horizon, and that nothing—no "method," no experiment, even of the wildest—is forbidden, but only falsity and pretence. "The proper stuff of fiction" does not exist; everything is the proper stuff of fiction, every feeling, every thought; every quality of brain and spirit is drawn upon; no perception comes amiss. And if we can imagine the art of fiction come alive and standing in our midst, she would undoubtedly bid us break her and bully her, as well as honour and love her, for so her youth is renewed and her sovereignty assured.

1925

---

7. George Meredith (1828–1909), English novelist.

A Room of One's Own[1]

Chapter One

But, you may say, we asked you to speak about women and fiction—what has that got to do with a room of one's own? I will try to explain. When you asked me to speak about women and fiction I sat down on the banks of a river and began to wonder what the words meant. They might mean simply a few remarks about Fanny Burney; a few more about Jane Austen; a tribute to the Brontës and a sketch of Haworth Parsonage under snow; some witticisms if possible about Miss Mitford; a respectful allusion to George Eliot; a reference to Mrs. Gaskell[2] and one would have done. But at second sight the words seemed not so simple. The title women and fiction might mean, and you may have meant it to mean, women and what they are like; or it might mean women and the fiction that they write; or it might mean women and the fiction that is written about them; or it might mean that somehow all three are inextricably mixed together and you want me to consider them in that light. But when I began to consider the subject in this last way, which seemed the most inter-esting, I soon saw that it had one fatal drawback. I should never be able to come to a conclusion. I should never be able to fulfil what is, I understand, the first duty of a lecturer—to hand you after an hour's discourse a nugget of pure truth to wrap up between the pages of your notebooks and keep on the mantelpiece for ever. All I could do was to offer you an opinion upon one minor point—a woman must have money and a room of her own if she is to write fiction; and that, as you will see, leaves the great problem of the true nature of woman and the true nature of fiction unsolved. I have shirked the duty of coming to a conclusion upon these two questions—women and fiction remain, so far as I am concerned, unsolved problems. But in order to make some amends I am going to do what I can to show you how I arrived at this opinion about the room and the money. I am going to develop in your presence as fully and freely as I can the train of thought which led me to think this. Perhaps if I lay bare the ideas, the prejudices, that lie behind this statement you will find that they have some bearing upon women and some upon fiction. At any rate, when a subject is highly controversial—and any question about sex is that—one cannot hope to tell the truth. One can only show how one came to hold whatever opinion one does hold. One can only give one's audi-ence the chance of drawing their own conclusions as they observe the limi-tations, the prejudices, the idiosyncrasies of the speaker. Fiction here is likely to contain more truth than fact. Therefore I propose, making use of all the liberties and licences of a novelist, to tell you the story of the two days that preceded my coming here—how, bowed down by the weight of the subject which you have laid upon my shoulders, I pondered it, and made it work in and out of my daily life. I need not say that what I am about to describe has no existence; Oxbridge[3] is an invention; so is Fernham; "I" is only a convenient

1. This essay is based upon two papers read to the Arts Society at Newnham and the Odtaa at Girton in October 1928. The papers were too long to be read in full, and have since been altered and expanded [Woolf's note]. Newnham and Girton are women's colleges at Cambridge. Odtaa, or "One Damn Thing After Another," was an elite lit-erary society.
2. All English writers: Frances Burney (1752–

1840); Jane Austen (1775–1817); Charlotte (1816–1855), Emily (1818–1848), and Anne (1820–1849) Brontë, who grew up in the parsonage in Haworth (Yorkshire), where their father was curate; Mary Russell Mitford (1787–1855); George Eliot (pseudonym of Marian Evans, 1819–1880); and Elizabeth Gaskell (1810–1865).
3. A common term blending Oxford and Cam-bridge.

2436 / Virginia Woolf

term for somebody who has no real being. Lies will flow from my lips, but there may perhaps be some truth mixed up with them; it is for you to seek out this truth and to decide whether any part of it is worth keeping. If not, you will of course throw the whole of it into the wastepaper basket and forget all about it.

Here then was I (call me Mary Beton, Mary Seton, Mary Carmichael[4] or by any name you please—it is not a matter of any importance) sitting on the banks of a river a week or two ago in fine October weather, lost in thought. That collar I have spoken of, women and fiction, the need of coming to some conclusion on a subject that raises all sorts of prejudices and passions, bowed my head to the ground. To the right and left bushes of some sort, golden and crimson, glowed with the colour, even it seemed burnt with the heat, of fire. On the further bank the willows wept in perpetual lamentation, their hair about their shoulders. The river reflected whatever it chose of sky and bridge and burning tree, and when the undergraduate had oared his boat through the reflections they closed again, completely, as if he had never been. There one might have sat the clock round lost in thought. Thought—to call it by a prouder name than it deserved—had let its line down into the stream. It swayed, minute after minute, hither and thither among the reflections and the weeds, letting the water lift it and sink it, until—you know the little tug—the sudden conglomeration of an idea at the end of one's line: and then the cautious hauling of it in, and the careful laying of it out? Alas, laid on the grass how small, how insignificant this thought of mine looked; the sort of fish that a good fisherman puts back into the water so that it may grow fatter and be one day worth cooking and eating. I will not trouble you with that thought now, though if you look carefully you may find it for yourselves in the course of what I am going to say.

But however small it was, it had, nevertheless, the mysterious property of its kind—put back into the mind, it became at once very exciting, and important; and as it darted and sank, and flashed hither and thither, set up such a wash and tumult of ideas that it was impossible to sit still. It was thus that I found myself walking with extreme rapidity across a grass plot. Instantly a man's figure rose to intercept me. Nor did I at first understand that the gesticulations of a curious-looking object, in a cut-away coat and evening shirt, were aimed at me. His face expressed horror and indignation. Instinct rather than reason came to my help; he was a Beadle;[5] I was a woman. This was the turf; there was the path. Only the Fellows and Scholars are allowed here; the gravel is the place for me. Such thoughts were the work of a moment. As I regained the path the arms of the Beadle sank, his face assumed its usual repose, and though turf is better walking than gravel, no very great harm was done. The only charge I could bring against the Fellows and Scholars of whatever the college might happen to be was that in protection of their turf, which has been rolled for 300 years in succession, they had sent my little fish into hiding.

What idea it had been that had sent me so audaciously trespassing I could not now remember. The spirit of peace descended like a cloud from heaven, for if the spirit of peace dwells anywhere, it is in the courts and quadrangles of Oxbridge on a fine October morning. Strolling through those colleges past those ancient halls the roughness of the present seemed smoothed away; the

4. Reference to the "Scottish Ballad of the Queen's Marys," also called "The Four Marys" (ca. 1563), a ballad about ladies-in-waiting to Mary,
Queen of Scots.
5. Officer in a university who precedes public processions.

body seemed contained in a miraculous glass cabinet through which no sound could penetrate, and the mind, freed from any contact with facts (unless one trespassed on the turf again), was at liberty to settle down upon whatever meditation was in harmony with the moment. As chance would have it, some stray memory of some old essay about revisiting Oxbridge in the long vacation brought Charles Lamb to mind—Saint Charles, said Thackeray,[6] putting a letter of Lamb's to his forehead. Indeed, among all the dead (I give you my thoughts as they came to me), Lamb is one of the most congenial; one to whom one would have liked to say, Tell me then how you wrote your essays? For his essays are superior even to Max Beerbohm's,[7] I thought, with all their perfection, because of that wild flash of imagination, that lightning crack of genius in the middle of them which leaves them flawed and imperfect, but starred with poetry. Lamb then came to Oxbridge perhaps a hundred years ago. Certainly he wrote an essay—the name escapes me[8]—about the manuscript of one of Milton's poems which he saw here. It was *Lycidas* perhaps, and Lamb wrote how it shocked him to think it possible that any word in *Lycidas* could have been different from what it is. To think of Milton changing the words in that poem seemed to him a sort of sacrilege. This led me to remember what I could of *Lycidas* and to amuse myself with guessing which word it could have been that Milton had altered, and why. It then occurred to me that the very manuscript itself which Lamb had looked at was only a few hundred yards away, so that one could follow Lamb's footsteps across the quadrangle to that famous library[9] where the treasure is kept. Moreover, I recollected, as I put this plan into execution, it is in this famous library that the manuscript of Thackeray's *Esmond* is also preserved. The critics often say that *Esmond* is Thackeray's most perfect novel. But the affectation of the style, with its imitation of the eighteenth century, hampers one, so far as I remember; unless indeed the eighteenth-century style was natural to Thackeray—a fact that one might prove by looking at the manuscript and seeing whether the alterations were for the benefit of the style or of the sense. But then one would have to decide what is style and what is meaning, a question which—but here I was actually at the door which leads into the library itself. I must have opened it, for instantly there issued, like a guardian angel barring the way with a flutter of black gown instead of white wings, a deprecating, silvery, kindly gentleman, who regretted in a low voice as he waved me back that ladies are only admitted to the library if accompanied by a Fellow of the College or furnished with a letter of introduction.

That a famous library has been cursed by a woman is a matter of complete indifference to a famous library. Venerable and calm, with all its treasures safe locked within its breast, it sleeps complacently and will, so far as I am concerned, so sleep for ever. Never will I wake those echoes, never will I ask for that hospitality again, I vowed as I descended the steps in anger. Still an hour remained before luncheon, and what was one to do? Stroll on the meadows? sit by the river? Certainly it was a lovely autumn morning; the leaves were fluttering red to the ground; there was no great hardship in doing either. But the sound of music reached my ear. Some service or celebration was going forward. The organ complained magnificently as I passed the chapel door.

---

6. William Makepeace Thackeray (1811–1863), English novelist, wrote *The History of Henry Esmond, Esquire* (1852), mentioned later. Charles Lamb (1775–1834), English critic and essayist.

7. English essayist and parodist (1872–1956).
8. "Oxford in the Vacation" (1823).
9. The library at Trinity College, Cambridge.

Even the sorrow of Christianity sounded in that serene air more like the recollection of sorrow than sorrow itself; even the groanings of the ancient organ
seemed lapped in peace. I had no wish to enter had I the right, and this time
the verger might have stopped me, demanding perhaps my baptismal certificate, or a letter of introduction from the Dean. But the outside of these magnificent buildings is often as beautiful as the inside. Moreover, it was amusing
enough to watch the congregation assembling, coming in and going out again,
busying themselves at the door of the chapel like bees at the mouth of a hive.
Many were in cap and gown; some had tufts of fur on their shoulders; others
were wheeled in bath-chairs; others, though not past middle age, seemed
creased and crushed into shapes so singular that one was reminded of those
giant crabs and crayfish who heave with difficulty across the sand of an aquar-
ium. As I leant against the wall the University indeed seemed a sanctuary in
which are preserved rare types which would soon be obsolete if left to fight
for existence on the pavement of the Strand.[1] Old stories of old deans and old
dons came back to mind, but before I had summoned up courage to whistle—it
used to be said that at the sound of a whistle old Professor ———— instantly
broke into a gallop—the venerable congregation had gone inside. The outside
of the chapel remained. As you know, its high domes and pinnacles can be
seen, like a sailing-ship always voyaging never arriving, lit up at night and
visible for miles, far away across the hills. Once, presumably, this quadrangle
with its smooth lawns, its massive buildings, and the chapel itself was marsh
too, where the grasses waved and the swine rootled. Teams of horses and oxen,
I thought, must have hauled the stone in wagons from far countries, and then
with infinite labour the grey blocks in whose shade I was now standing were
poised in order one on top of another, and then the painters brought their
glass for the windows, and the masons were busy for centuries up on that roof
with putty and cement, spade and trowel.[2] Every Saturday somebody must
have poured gold and silver out of a leathern purse into their ancient fists, for
they had their beer and skittles presumably of an evening. An unending stream
of gold and silver, I thought, must have flowed into this court perpetually to
keep the stones coming and the masons working; to level, to ditch, to dig and
to drain. But it was then the age of faith, and money was poured liberally to
set these stones on a deep foundation, and when the stones were raised, still
more money was poured in from the coffers of kings and queens and great
nobles to ensure that hymns should be sung here and scholars taught. Lands
were granted; tithes were paid. And when the age of faith was over and the
age of reason had come, still the same flow of gold and silver went on; fellowships were founded; lectureships endowed; only the gold and silver flowed
now, not from the coffers of the king, but from the chests of merchants and
manufacturers, from the purses of men who had made, say, a fortune from
industry, and returned, in their wills, a bounteous share of it to endow more
chairs, more lectureships, more fellowships in the university where they had
learnt their craft. Hence the libraries and laboratories; the observatories; the
splendid equipment of costly and delicate instruments which now stands on
glass shelves, where centuries ago the grasses waved and the swine rootled.
Certainly, as I strolled round the court, the foundation of gold and silver
seemed deep enough; the pavement laid solidly over the wild grasses. Men

---

1. A busy thoroughfare in London.
2. King's College Chapel, Cambridge, was built from 1446 to 1547.

with trays on their heads went busily from staircase to staircase. Gaudy blossoms flowered in window-boxes. The strains of the gramophone blared out from the rooms within. It was impossible not to reflect—the reflection whatever it may have been was cut short. The clock struck. It was time to find one's way to luncheon.

It is a curious fact that novelists have a way of making us believe that luncheon parties are invariably memorable for something very witty that was said, or for something very wise that was done. But they seldom spare a word for what was eaten. It is part of the novelist's convention not to mention soup and salmon and ducklings, as if soup and salmon and ducklings were of no importance whatsoever, as if nobody ever smoked a cigar or drank a glass of wine. Here, however, I shall take the liberty to defy that convention and to tell you that the lunch on this occasion began with soles, sunk in a deep dish, over which the college cook had spread a counterpane of the whitest cream, save that it was branded here and there with brown spots like the spots on the flanks of a doe. After that came the partridges, but if this suggests a couple of bald, brown birds on a plate you are mistaken. The partridges, many and various, came with all their retinue of sauces and salads, the sharp and the sweet, each in its order; their potatoes, thin as coins but not so hard; their sprouts, foliated as rosebuds but more succulent. And no sooner had the roast and its retinue been done with than the silent serving-man, the Beadle himself perhaps in a milder manifestation, set before us, wreathed in napkins, a confection which rose all sugar from the waves. To call it pudding and so relate it to rice and tapioca would be an insult. Meanwhile the wineglasses had flushed yellow and flushed crimson; had been emptied; had been filled. And thus by degrees was lit, halfway down the spine, which is the seat of the soul, not that hard little electric light which we call brilliance, as it pops in and out upon our lips, but the more profound, subtle and subterranean glow, which is the rich yellow flame of rational intercourse. No need to hurry. No need to sparkle. No need to be anybody but oneself. We are all going to heaven and Vandyck[3] is of the company—in other words, how good life seemed, how sweet its rewards, how trivial this grudge or that grievance, how admirable friendship and the society of one's kind, as, lighting a good cigarette, one sunk among the cushions in the window-seat.

If by good luck there had been an ash-tray handy, if one had not knocked the ash out of the window in default, if things had been a little different from what they were, one would not have seen, presumably, a cat without a tail. The sight of that abrupt and truncated animal padding softly across the quadrangle changed by some fluke of the subconscious intelligence the emotional light for me. It was as if some one had let fall a shade. Perhaps the excellent hock[4] was relinquishing its hold. Certainly, as I watched the Manx cat pause in the middle of the lawn as if it too questioned the universe, something seemed lacking, something seemed different. But what was lacking, what was different, I asked myself, listening to the talk. And to answer that question I had to think myself out of the room, back into the past, before the war indeed, and to set before my eyes the model of another luncheon party held in rooms not very far distant from these; but different. Everything was different. Mean-

3. Sir Anthony Van Dyck (1599–1641), born in Antwerp but lived for some years in England. He painted many grand portraits of the English royal family and court.
4. Rhine wine.

while the talk went on among the guests, who were many and young, some of this sex, some of that; it went on swimmingly, it went on agreeably, freely, amusingly. And as it went on I set it against the background of that other talk, and as I matched the two together I had no doubt that one was the descendant, the legitimate heir of the other. Nothing was changed; nothing was different save only—here I listened with all my ears not entirely to what was being said, but to the murmur or current behind it. Yes, that was it—the change was there. Before the war at a luncheon party like this people would have said precisely the same things but they would have sounded different, because in those days they were accompanied by a sort of humming noise, not articulate, but musical, exciting, which changed the value of the words themselves. Could one set that humming noise to words? Perhaps with the help of the poets one could. A book lay beside me and, opening it, I turned casually enough to Tennyson. And here I found Tennyson was singing:

> There has fallen a splendid tear
>   From the passion-flower at the gate.
> She is coming, my dove, my dear;
>   She is coming, my life, my fate;
> The red rose cries, "She is near, she is near";
>   And the white rose weeps, "She is late";
> The larkspur listens, "I hear, I hear";
>   And the lily whispers, "I wait."[5]

Was that what men hummed at luncheon parties before the war? And the women?

> My heart is like a singing bird
>   Whose nest is in a water'd shoot;
> My heart is like an apple tree
>   Whose boughs are bent with thick-set fruit;
> My heart is like a rainbow shell
>   That paddles in a halcyon sea;
> My heart is gladder than all these
>   Because my love is come to me.[6]

Was that what women hummed at luncheon parties before the war?

There was something so ludicrous in thinking of people humming such things even under their breath at luncheon parties before the war that I burst out laughing, and had to explain my laughter by pointing at the Manx cat, who did look a little absurd, poor beast, without a tail, in the middle of the lawn. Was he really born so, or had he lost his tail in an accident? The tailless cat, though some are said to exist in the Isle of Man,[7] is rarer than one thinks. It is a queer animal, quaint rather than beautiful. It is strange what a difference a tail makes—you know the sort of things one says as a lunch party breaks up and people are finding their coats and hats.

This one, thanks to the hospitality of the host, had lasted far into the afternoon. The beautiful October day was fading and the leaves were falling from the trees in the avenue as I walked through it. Gate after gate seemed to close with gentle finality behind me. Innumerable beadles were fitting innumerable keys into well-oiled locks; the treasure-house was being made secure for

5. *Maud* 1.22.10.
6. Christina Rossetti's *A Birthday,* first stanza.

7. One of the British Isles in the Irish Sea.

another night. After the avenue one comes out upon a road—I forget its name—which leads you, if you take the right turning, along to Fernham. But there was plenty of time. Dinner was not till half-past seven. One could almost do without dinner after such a luncheon. It is strange how a scrap of poetry works in the mind and makes the legs move in time to it along the road. Those words—

> There has fallen a splendid tear
> From the passion-flower at the gate.
> She is coming, my dove, my dear—

sang in my blood as I stepped quickly along towards Headingley. And then, switching off into the other measure, I sang, where the waters are churned up by the weir:

> My heart is like a singing bird
> Whose nest is in a water'd shoot;
> My heart is like an apple tree . . .

What poets, I cried aloud, as one does in the dusk, what poets they were!

In a sort of jealousy, I suppose, for our own age, silly and absurd though these comparisons are, I went on to wonder if honestly one could name two living poets now as great as Tennyson and Christina Rossetti were then. Obviously it is impossible, I thought, looking into those foaming waters, to compare them. The very reason why the poetry excites one to such abandonment, such rapture, is that it celebrates some feeling that one used to have (at luncheon parties before the war perhaps), so that one responds easily, familiarly, without troubling to check the feeling, or to compare it with any that one has now. But the living poets express a feeling that is actually being made and torn out of us at the moment. One does not recognize it in the first place; often for some reason one fears it; one watches it with keenness and compares it jealously and suspiciously with the old feeling that one knew. Hence the difficulty of modern poetry; and it is because of this difficulty that one cannot remember more than two consecutive lines of any good modern poet. For this reason— that my memory failed me—the argument flagged for want of material. But why, I continued, moving on towards Headingley, have we stopped humming under our breath at luncheon parties? Why has Alfred ceased to sing

> She is coming, my dove, my dear?

Why has Christina ceased to respond

> My heart is gladder than all these
> Because my love is come to me?

Shall we lay the blame on the war? When the guns fired in August 1914, did the faces of men and women show so plain in each other's eyes that romance was killed? Certainly it was a shock (to women in particular with their illusions about education, and so on) to see the faces of our rulers in the light of the shell-fire. So ugly they looked—German, English, French—so stupid. But lay the blame where one will, on whom one will, the illusion which inspired Tennyson and Christina Rossetti to sing so passionately about the coming of their loves is far rarer now than then. One has only to read, to look, to listen, to remember. But why say "blame"? Why, if it was an illusion, not praise the catastrophe, whatever it was, that destroyed illusion and put truth in its place?

For truth . . . those dots mark the spot where, in search of truth, I missed the turning up to Fernham. Yes indeed, which was truth and which was illusion, I asked myself. What was the truth about these houses, for example, dim and festive now with their red windows in the dusk, but raw and red and squalid, with their sweets and their boot-laces, at nine o'clock in the morning? And the willows and the river and the gardens that run down to the river, vague now with the mist stealing over them, but gold and red in the sunlight—which was the truth, which was the illusion about them? I spare you the twists and turns of my cogitations, for no conclusion was found on the road to Heading-ley, and I ask you to suppose that I soon found out my mistake about the turning and retraced my steps to Fernham.

As I have said already that it was an October day, I dare not forfeit your respect and imperil the fair name of fiction by changing the season and describing lilacs hanging over garden walls, crocuses, tulips and other flowers of spring. Fiction must stick to facts, and the truer the facts the better the fiction—so we are told. Therefore it was still autumn and the leaves were still yellow and falling, if anything, a little faster than before, because it was now evening (seven twenty-three to be precise) and a breeze (from the southwest to be exact) had risen. But for all that there was something odd at work:

> *My heart is like a singing bird*
> *Whose nest is in a water'd shoot;*
> *My heart is like an apple tree*
> *Whose boughs are bent with thick-set fruit—*

perhaps the words of Christina Rossetti were partly responsible for the folly of the fancy—it was nothing of course but a fancy—that the lilac was shaking its flowers over the garden walls, and the brimstone butterflies were scudding hither and thither, and the dust of the pollen was in the air. A wind blew, from what quarter I know not, but it lifted the half-grown leaves so that there was a flash of silver grey in the air. It was the time between the lights when colours undergo their intensification and purples and golds burn in window-panes like the beat of an excitable heart; when for some reason the beauty of the world revealed and yet soon to perish (here I pushed into the garden, for, unwisely, the door was left open and no beadles seemed about), the beauty of the world which is so soon to perish, has two edges, one of laughter, one of anguish, cutting the heart asunder. The gardens of Fernham lay before me in the spring twilight, wild and open, and in the long grass, sprinkled and carelessly flung, were daffodils and bluebells, not orderly perhaps at the best of times, and now wind-blown and waving as they tugged at their roots. The windows of the building, curved like ships' windows among generous waves of red brick, changed from lemon to silver under the flight of the quick spring clouds. Somebody was in a hammock, somebody, but in this light they were phantoms only, half guessed, half seen, raced across the grass—would no one stop her?— and then on the terrace, as if popping out to breathe the air, to glance at the garden, came a bent figure, formidable yet humble, with her great forehead and her shabby dress—could it be the famous scholar, could it be J—— H—— herself?[8] All was dim, yet intense too, as if the scarf which the dusk had flung over the garden were torn asunder by star or sword—the flash of some terrible

---

8. Jane Harrison (1850–1928), fellow and lecturer in classical archaeology at Newnham College, Cambridge; author of *Ancient Art and Ritual* (1913) and other influential books.

reality leaping, as its way is, out of the heart of the spring. For youth————

Here was my soup. Dinner was being served in the great dining-hall. Far from being spring it was in fact an evening in October. Everybody was assembled in the big dining-room. Dinner was ready. Here was the soup. It was a plain gravy soup. There was nothing to stir the fancy in that. One could have seen through the transparent liquid any pattern that there might have been on the plate itself. But there was no pattern. The plate was plain. Next came beef with its attendant greens and potatoes—a homely trinity, suggesting the rumps of cattle in a muddy market, and sprouts curled and yellowed at the edge, and bargaining and cheapening, and women with string bags on Monday morning. There was no reason to complain of human nature's daily food, seeing that the supply was sufficient and coal-miners doubtless were sitting down to less. Prunes and custard followed. And if any one complains that prunes, even when mitigated by custard, are an uncharitable vegetable (fruit they are not), stringy as a miser's heart and exuding a fluid such as might run in misers' veins who have denied themselves wine and warmth for eighty years and yet not given to the poor, he should reflect that there are people whose charity embraces even the prune. Biscuits and cheese came next, and here the water-jug was liberally passed round, for it is the nature of biscuits to be dry, and these were biscuits to the core. That was all. The meal was over. Everybody scraped their chairs back; the swing-doors swung violently to and fro; soon the hall was emptied of every sign of food and made ready no doubt for breakfast next morning. Down corridors and up staircases the youth of England went banging and singing. And was it for a guest, a stranger (for I had no more right here in Fernham than in Trinity or Somerville or Girton or Newnham or Christchurch),[9] to say, "The dinner was not good," or to say (we were now, Mary Seton and I, in her sitting-room), "Could we not have dined up here alone?" for if I had said anything of the kind I should have been prying and searching into the secret economies of a house which to the stranger wears so fine a front of gaiety and courage. No, one could say nothing of the sort. Indeed, conversation for a moment flagged. The human frame being what it is, heart, body and brain all mixed together, and not contained in separate compartments as they will be no doubt in another million years, a good dinner is of great importance to good talk. One cannot think well, love well, sleep well, if one has not dined well. The lamp in the spine does not light on beef and prunes. We are all *probably* going to heaven, and Vandyck is, we *hope*, to meet us round the next corner—that is the dubious and qualifying state of mind that beef and prunes at the end of the day's work breed between them. Happily my friend, who taught science, had a cupboard where there was a squat bottle and little glasses—(but there should have been sole and partridge to begin with)—so that we were able to draw up to the fire and repair some of the damages of the day's living. In a minute or so we were slipping freely in and out among all those objects of curiosity and interest which form in the mind in the absence of a particular person, and are naturally to be discussed on coming together again—how somebody has married, another has not; one thinks this, another that; one has improved out of all knowledge, the other most amazingly gone to the bad—with all those speculations upon human nature and the character of the amazing world we live in which spring naturally from such beginnings. While these things were being said, however, I became

9. Oxford college. Somerville is a women's college at Oxford.

shamefacedly aware of a current setting in of its own accord and carrying everything forward to an end of its own. One might be talking of Spain or Portugal, of book or racehorse, but the real interest of whatever was said was none of those things, but a scene of masons on a high roof some five centuries ago. Kings and nobles brought treasure in huge sacks and poured it under the earth. This scene was for ever coming alive in my mind and placing itself by another of lean cows and a muddy market and withered greens and the stringy hearts of old men—these two pictures, disjointed and disconnected and non-sensical as they were, were for ever coming together and combating each other and had me entirely at their mercy. The best course, unless the whole talk was to be distorted, was to expose what was in my mind to the air, when with good luck it would fade and crumble like the head of the dead king when they opened the coffin at Windsor.[1] Briefly, then, I told Miss Seton about the masons who had been all those years on the roof of the chapel, and about the kings and queens and nobles bearing sacks of gold and silver on their shoulders, which they shovelled into the earth; and then how the great financial magnates of our own time came and laid cheques and bonds, I suppose, where the others had laid ingots and rough lumps of gold. All that lies beneath the colleges down there, I said; but this college, where we are now sitting, what lies beneath its gallant red brick and the wild unkempt grasses of the garden? What force is behind the plain china off which we dined, and (here it popped out of my mouth before I could stop it) the beef, the custard and the prunes?

Well, said Mary Seton, about the year 1860—Oh, but you know the story, she said, bored, I suppose, by the recital. And she told me—rooms were hired. Committees met. Envelopes were addressed. Circulars were drawn up. Meetings were held; letters were read out; so-and-so has promised so much; on the contrary, Mr ——— won't give a penny. The *Saturday Review* has been very rude. How can we raise a fund to pay for offices? Shall we hold a bazaar? Can't we find a pretty girl to sit in the front row? Let us look up what John Stuart Mill[2] said on the subject. Can any one persuade the editor of the ——— to print a letter? Can we get Lady ——— to sign it? Lady ——— is out of town. That was the way it was done, presumably, sixty years ago, and it was a prodigious effort, and a great deal of time was spent on it. And it was only after a long struggle and with the utmost difficulty that they got thirty thousand pounds together.[3] So obviously we cannot have wine and partridges and servants carrying tin dishes on their heads, she said. We cannot have sofas and separate rooms. "The amenities," she said, quoting from some book or other, "will have to wait."[4]

At the thought of all those women working year after year and finding it hard to get two thousand pounds together, and as much as they could do to get thirty thousand pounds, we burst out in scorn at the reprehensible poverty of our sex. What had our mothers been doing then that they had no wealth to leave us? Powdering their noses? Looking in at shop windows? Flaunting in the sun at Monte Carlo?[5] There were some photographs on the mantel-piece.

1. Windsor Castle.
2. English philosopher and economist (1806–1873).
3. "We are told that we ought to ask for £30,000 at least. . . . It is not a large sum, considering that there is to be but one college of this sort for Great Britain, Ireland and the Colonies, and considering how easy it is to raise immense sums for boys' schools. But considering how few people really wish women to be educated, it is a good deal."—

Lady Stephen, *Life of Miss Emily Davies* [Woolf's note]. Emily Davies (1830–1921), English educator, who established what was to become Girton College.
4. "Every penny which could be scraped together was set aside for building, and the amenities had to be postponed."—R. Strachey, *The Cause* [Woolf's note].
5. Resort town in Monaco, on the French Riviera.

Mary's mother—if that was her picture—may have been a wastrel in her spare time (she had thirteen children by a minister of the church), but if so her gay and dissipated life had left too few traces of its pleasures on her face. She was a homely body; an old lady in a plaid shawl which was fastened by a large cameo;[6] and she sat in a basket-chair, encouraging a spaniel to look at the camera, with the amused, yet strained expression of one who is sure that the dog will move directly the bulb is pressed. Now if she had gone into business; had become a manufacturer of artificial silk or a magnate on the Stock Exchange; if she had left two or three hundred thousand pounds to Fernham, we could have been sitting at our ease tonight and the subject of our talk might have been archaeology, botany, anthropology, physics, the nature of the atom, mathematics, astronomy, relativity, geography. If only Mrs Seton and her mother and her mother before her had learnt the great art of making money and had left their money, like their fathers and their grandfathers before them, to found fellowships and lectureships and prizes and scholarships appropriated to the use of their own sex, we might have dined very tolerably up here alone off a bird and a bottle of wine; we might have looked forward without undue confidence to a pleasant and honourable lifetime spent in the shelter of one of the liberally endowed professions. We might have been exploring or writing; mooning about the venerable places of the earth; sitting contemplative on the steps of the Parthenon, or going at ten to an office and coming home comfortably at half-past four to write a little poetry. Only, if Mrs Seton and her like had gone into business at the age of fifteen, there would have been—that was the snag in the argument—no Mary. What, I asked, did Mary think of that? There between the curtains was the October night, calm and lovely, with a star or two caught in the yellowing trees. Was she ready to resign her share of it and her memories (for they had been a happy family, though a large one) of games and quarrels up in Scotland, which she is never tired of praising for the fineness of its air and the quality of its cakes, in order that Fernham might have been endowed with fifty thousand pounds or so by a stroke of the pen? For, to endow a college would necessitate the suppression of families altogether. Making a fortune and bearing thirteen children—no human being could stand it. Consider the facts, we said. First there are nine months before the baby is born. Then the baby is born. Then there are three or four months spent in feeding the baby. After the baby is fed there are certainly five years spent in playing with the baby. You cannot, it seems, let children run about the streets. People who have seen them running wild in Russia say that the sight is not a pleasant one. People say, too, that human nature takes its shape in the years between one and five. If Mrs Seton, I said, had been making money, what sort of memories would you have had of games and quarrels? What would you have known of Scotland, and its fine air and cakes and all the rest of it? But it is useless to ask these questions, because you would never have come into existence at all. Moreover, it is equally useless to ask what might have happened if Mrs Seton and her mother and her mother before her had amassed great wealth and laid it under the foundations of college and library, because, in the first place, to earn money was impossible for them, and in the second, had it been possible, the law denied them the right to possess what money they earned. It is only for the last forty-eight years that Mrs Seton has had a penny of her own. For all the centuries before that it would have been her husband's property—a thought which, perhaps, may have

6. Vividly carved stone.

had its share in keeping Mrs Seton and her mothers off the Stock Exchange. Every penny I earn, they may have said, will be taken from me and disposed of according to my husband's wisdom—perhaps to found a scholarship or to endow a fellowship in Balliol or Kings,[7] so that to earn money, even if I could earn money, is not a matter that interests me very greatly. I had better leave it to my husband.

At any rate, whether or not the blame rested on the old lady who was looking at the spaniel, there could be no doubt that for some reason or other our mothers had mismanaged their affairs very gravely. Not a penny could be spared for "amenities"; for partridges and wine, beadles and turf, books and cigars, libraries and leisure. To raise bare walls out of the bare earth was the utmost they could do.

So we talked standing at the window and looking, as so many thousands look every night, down on the domes and towers of the famous city beneath us. It was very beautiful, very mysterious in the autumn moonlight. The old stone looked very white and venerable. One thought of all the books that were assembled down there; of the pictures of old prelates and worthies hanging in the panelled rooms; of the painted windows that would be throwing strange globes and crescents on the pavement; of the tablets and memorials and inscriptions; of the fountains and the grass; of the quiet rooms looking across the quiet quadrangles. And (pardon me the thought) I thought, too, of the admirable smoke and drink and the deep armchairs and the pleasant carpets: of the urbanity, the geniality, the dignity which are the offspring of luxury and privacy and space. Certainly our mothers had not provided us with anything comparable to all this—our mothers who found it difficult to scrape together thirty thousand pounds, our mothers who bore thirteen children to ministers of religion at St Andrews.[8]

So I went back to my inn, and as I walked through the dark streets I pondered this and that, as one does at the end of the day's work. I pondered why it was that Mrs Seton had no money to leave us; and what effect poverty has on the mind; and what effect wealth has on the mind; and I thought of the queer old gentlemen I had seen that morning with tufts of fur upon their shoulders; and I remembered how if one whistled one of them ran; and I thought of the organ booming in the chapel and of the shut doors of the library; and I thought how unpleasant it is to be locked out; and I thought how it is worse perhaps to be locked in; and, thinking of the safety and prosperity of the one sex and of the poverty and insecurity of the other and of the effect of tradition and of the lack of tradition upon the mind of a writer, I thought at last that it was time to roll up the crumpled skin of the day, with its arguments and its impressions and its anger and its laughter, and cast it into the hedge. A thousand stars were flashing across the blue wastes of the sky. One seemed alone with an inscrutable society. All human beings were laid asleep—prone, horizontal, dumb. Nobody seemed stirring in the streets of Oxbridge. Even the door of the hotel sprang open at the touch of an invisible hand—not a boots was sitting up to light me to bed, it was so late.

7. Colleges at Oxford and Cambridge, respectively.
8. Perhaps St. Andrew Holborn, a church in London designed by Sir Christopher Wren (1632–1723).

Chapter Two

The scene, if I may ask you to follow me, was now changed. The leaves were still falling, but in London now, not Oxbridge; and I must ask you to imagine a room, like many thousands, with a window looking across people's hats and vans and motor-cars to other windows, and on the table inside the room a blank sheet of paper on which was written in large letters WOMEN AND FICTION, but no more. The inevitable sequel to lunching and dining at Oxbridge seemed, unfortunately, to be a visit to the British Museum. One must strain off what was personal and accidental in all these impressions and so reach the pure fluid, the essential oil of truth. For that visit to Oxbridge and the luncheon and the dinner had started a swarm of questions. Why did men drink wine and women water? Why was one sex so prosperous and the other so poor? What effect has poverty on fiction? What conditions are necessary for the creation of works of art?—a thousand questions at once suggested themselves. But one needed answers, not questions; and an answer was only to be had by consulting the learned and the unprejudiced, who have removed themselves above the strife of tongue and the confusion of body and issued the result of their reasoning and research in books which are to be found in the British Museum. If truth is not to be found on the shelves of the British Museum, where, I asked myself, picking up a notebook and a pencil, is truth?

Thus provided, thus confident and enquiring, I set out in the pursuit of truth. The day, though not actually wet, was dismal, and the streets in the neighbourhood of the Museum were full of open coal-holes, down which sacks were showering; four-wheeled cabs were drawing up and depositing on the pavement corded boxes containing, presumably, the entire wardrobe of some Swiss or Italian family seeking fortune or refuge or some other desirable commodity which is to be found in the boarding-houses of Bloomsbury in the winter. The usual hoarse-voiced men paraded the streets with plants on barrows. Some shouted; others sang. London was like a workshop. London was like a machine. We were all being shot backwards and forwards on this plain foundation to make some pattern. The British Museum was another department of the factory. The swing-doors swung open; and there one stood under the vast dome, as if one were a thought in the huge bald forehead which is so splendidly encircled by a band of famous names. One went to the counter; one took a slip of paper; one opened a volume of the catalogue, and . . . . . the five dots here indicate five separate minutes of stupefaction, wonder and bewilderment. Have you any notion how many books are written about women in the course of one year? Have you any notion how many are written by men? Are you aware that you are, perhaps, the most discussed animal in the universe? Here had I come with a notebook and a pencil proposing to spend a morning reading, supposing that at the end of the morning I should have transferred the truth to my notebook. But I should need to be a herd of elephants, I thought, and a wilderness of spiders, desperately referring to the animals that are reputed longest lived and most multitudinously eyed, to cope with all this. I should need claws of steel and beak of brass even to penetrate the husk. How shall I ever find the grains of truth embedded in all this mass of paper, I asked myself, and in despair began running my eye up and down the long list of titles. Even the names of the books gave me food for thought. Sex and its nature might well attract doctors and biologists; but what was surprising and difficult of explanation was the fact that sex—woman, that is to say—also attracts agreeable essayists, light-fingered novelists, young men who have taken the M.A. degree; men who have taken no degree; men who have no apparent qualification save that they are not women. Some of these books were, on the face of it, frivolous and facetious; but many, on the other hand, were serious and prophetic, moral and hortatory. Merely to read the titles suggested innumerable schoolmasters, innumerable clergymen mounting their platforms and pulpits and holding forth with a loquacity which far exceeded the hour usually allotted to such discourse on this one subject. It was a most strange phenomenon; and apparently—here I consulted the letter M—one confined to male sex. Women do not write books about men—a fact that I could not help welcoming with relief, for if I had first to read all that men have written about women, then all that women have written about men, the aloe that flowers once in a hundred years would flower twice before I could set pen to paper. So, making a perfectly arbitrary choice of a dozen volumes or so, I sent my slips of paper to lie in the wire tray, and waited in my stall, among the other seekers for the essential oil of truth.

What could be the reason, then, of this curious disparity, I wondered, drawing cart-wheels on the slips of paper provided by the British taxpayer for other purposes. Why are women, judging from this catalogue, so much more interesting to men than men are to women? A very curious fact it seemed, and my mind wandered to picture the lives of men who spend their time in writing books about women; whether they were old or young, married or unmarried, red-nosed or hump-backed—anyhow, it was flattering, vaguely, to feel oneself the object of such attention, provided that it was not entirely bestowed by the crippled and the infirm—so I pondered until all such frivolous thoughts were ended by an avalanche of books sliding down on to the desk in front of me. Now the trouble began. The student who has been trained in research at Oxbridge has no doubt some method of shepherding his question past all distractions till it runs into its answer as a sheep runs into its pen. The student by my side, for instance, who was copying assiduously from a scientific manual was, I felt sure, extracting pure nuggets of the essential ore every ten minutes or so. His little grunts of satisfaction indicated so much. But if, unfortunately, one has had no training in a university, the question far from being shepherded to its pen flies like a frightened flock hither and thither, helter-skelter, pursued by a whole pack of hounds. Professors, schoolmasters, sociologists, clergymen, novelists, essayists, journalists, men who had no qualification save that they were not women, chased my simple and single question—Why are women poor?—until it became fifty questions; until the fifty questions leapt frantically into mid-stream and were carried away. Every page in my notebook was scribbled over with notes. To show the state of mind I was in, I will read you a few of them, explaining that the page was headed quite simply, WOMEN AND POVERTY, in block letters; but what followed was something like this:

> Condition in Middle Ages of,
> Habits in the Fiji Islands of,
> Worshipped as goddesses by,
> Weaker in moral sense than,
> Idealism of,
> Greater conscientiousness of,
> South Sea Islanders, age of puberty among,
> Attractiveness of,
> Offered as sacrifice to,

Small size of brain of,
Profounder sub-consciousness of,
Less hair on the body of,
Mental, moral and physical inferiority of,
Love of children of,
Greater length of life of,
Weaker muscles of,
Strength of affections of,
Vanity of,
Higher education of,
Shakespeare's opinion of,
Lord Birkenhead's opinion of,
Dean Inge's opinion of,
La Bruyère's opinion of,
Dr Johnson's opinion of,
Mr Oscar Browning's[9] opinion of, . . .

Here I drew breath and added, indeed, in the margin, Why does Samuel But-ler[1] say, "Wise men never say what they think of women"? Wise men never say anything else apparently. But, I continued, leaning back in my chair and looking at the vast dome in which I was a single but by now somewhat harassed thought, what is so unfortunate is that wise men never think the same thing about women. Here is Pope:

Most women have no character at all.[2]

And here is La Bruyère:

Les femmes sont extrêmes; elles sont meilleures ou pires que les hommes—[3]

a direct contradiction by keen observers who were contemporary. Are they capable of education or incapable? Napoleon thought them incapable. Dr Johnson thought the opposite.[4] Have they souls or have they not souls? Some savages say they have none. Others, on the contrary, maintain that women are half divine and worship them on that account.[5] Some sages hold that they are shallower in the brain; others that they are deeper in the consciousness. Goethe honoured them; Mussolini[6] despises them. Wherever one looked men thought about women and thought differently. It was impossible to make head or tail of it all, I decided, glancing with envy at the reader next door who was making the neatest abstracts, headed often with an A or a B or a C, while my

9. Famous history lecturer (1837–1923) at King's College, Cambridge. F. E. Smith, earl of Birken-head (1872–1930), was lord chancellor (1919–22) and an opponent of women's suffrage. William Ralph Inge (1860–1954) was dean of St. Paul's Cathedral in London (1911–34). Woolf quotes the opinions of the French moralist Jean de La Bruyère (1645–1696) and of the English writer Samuel Johnson (1609–1784) below.
1. English writer (1835–1902).
2. From "Epistle to a Lady," by the English poet Alexander Pope (1688–1744).
3. Women are extreme: they are better or worse than men (French).
4. " 'Men know that women are an overmatch for them, and therefore they choose the weakest or the most ignorant. If they did not think so, they never could be afraid of women knowing as much as themselves.' . . . In justice to the sex, I think it but candid to acknowledge that, in a subsequent con-versation, he told me that he was serious in what he said."—Boswell, *The Journal of a Tour to the Hebrides* [Woolf's note]. James Boswell (1740–1795), Scottish lawyer, diarist, and writer, renowned for his biography of Samuel Johnson.
5. "The ancient Germans believed that there was something holy in women, and accordingly con-sulted them as oracles."—Frazer, *Golden Bough* [Woolf's note]. Sir James Frazer (1854–1941), Scottish anthropologist.
6. Italian Fascist dictator (1883–1945). Johann Wolfgang von Goethe (1749–1832), German poet, novelist, and playwright.

own notebook rioted with the wildest scribble of contradictory jottings. It was distressing, it was bewildering, it was humiliating. Truth had run through my fingers. Every drop had escaped.

I could not possibly go home, I reflected, and add as a serious contribution to the study of women and fiction that women have less hair on their bodies than men, or that the age of puberty among the South Sea Islanders is nine— or is it ninety?—even the handwriting had become in its distraction indecipherable. It was disgraceful to have nothing more weighty or respectable to show after a whole morning's work. And if I could not grasp the truth about W. (as for brevity's sake I had come to call her) in the past, why bother about W. in the future? It seemed pure waste of time to consult all those gentlemen who specialise in woman and her effect on whatever it may be—politics, children, wages, morality—numerous and learned as they are. One might as well leave their books unopened.

But while I pondered I had unconsciously, in my listlessness, in my desperation, been drawing a picture where I should, like my neighbour, have been writing a conclusion. I had been drawing a face, a figure. It was the face and the figure of Professor von X. engaged in writing his monumental work entitled *The Mental, Moral, and Physical Inferiority of the Female Sex*. He was not in my picture a man attractive to women. He was heavily built; he had a great jowl; to balance that he had very small eyes; he was very red in the face. His expression suggested that he was labouring under some emotion that made him jab his pen on the paper as if he were killing some noxious insect as he wrote, but even when he had killed it that did not satisfy him; he must go on killing it; and even so, some cause for anger and irritation remained. Could it be his wife, I asked, looking at my picture. Was she in love with a cavalry officer? Was the cavalry officer slim and elegant and dressed in astrachan? Had he been laughed at, to adopt the Freudian theory, in his cradle by a pretty girl? For even in his cradle the professor, I thought, could not have been an attractive child. Whatever the reason, the professor was made to look very angry and very ugly in my sketch, as he wrote his great book upon the mental, moral and physical inferiority of women. Drawing pictures was an idle way of finishing an unprofitable morning's work. Yet it is in our idleness, in our dreams, that the submerged truth sometimes comes to the top. A very elementary exercise in psychology, not to be dignified by the name of psychoanalysis, showed me, on looking at my notebook, that the sketch of the angry professor had been made in anger. Anger had snatched my pencil while I dreamt. But what was anger doing there? Interest, confusion, amusement, boredom—all these emotions I could trace and name as they succeeded each other throughout the morning. Had anger, the black snake, been lurking among them? Yes, said the sketch, anger had. It referred me unmistakably to the one book, to the one phrase, which had roused the demon; it was the professor's statement about the mental, moral and physical inferiority of women. My heart had leapt. My cheeks had burnt. I had flushed with anger. There was nothing specially remarkable, however foolish, in that. One does not like to be told that one is naturally the inferior of a little man—I looked at the student next me—who breathes hard, wears a ready-made tie, and has not shaved this fortnight. One has certain foolish vanities. It is only human nature, I reflected, and began drawing cartwheels and circles over the angry professor's face till he looked like a burning bush or a flaming comet—anyhow, an apparition without human semblance or significance. The professor was nothing now but a faggot burning on the top of Hampstead Heath.[7] Soon my own anger was explained and done with; but curiosity remained. How explain the anger of the professors? Why were they angry? For when it came to ana-lysing the impression left by these books there was always an element of heat. This heat took many forms; it showed itself in satire, in sentiment, in curiosity, in reprobation. But there was another element which was often present and could not immediately be identified. Anger, I called it. But it was anger that had gone underground and mixed itself with all kinds of other emotions. To judge from its odd effects, it was anger disguised and complex, not anger simple and open.

Whatever the reason, all these books, I thought, surveying the pile on the desk, are worthless for my purposes. They were worthless scientifically, that is to say, though humanly they were full of instruction, interest, boredom, and very queer facts about the habits of the Fiji Islanders. They had been written in the red light of emotion and not in the white light of truth. Therefore they must be returned to the central desk and restored each to his own cell in the enormous honeycomb. All that I had retrieved from that morning's work had been the one fact of anger. The professors—I lumped them together thus— were angry. But why, I asked myself, having returned the books, why, I repeated, standing under the colonnade among the pigeons and the prehistoric canoes, why are they angry? And, asking myself this question, I strolled off to find a place for luncheon. What is the real nature of what I call for the moment their anger? I asked. Here was a puzzle that would last all the time that it takes to be served with food in a small restaurant somewhere near the British Museum. Some previous luncher had left the lunch edition of the evening paper on a chair, and, waiting to be served, I began idly reading the headlines. A ribbon of very large letters ran across the page. Somebody had made a big score in South Africa. Lesser ribbons announced that Sir Austen Chamberlain was at Geneva.[8] A meat axe with human hair on it had been found in a cellar. Mr Justice ——— commented in the Divorce Courts upon the Shamelessness of Women. Sprinkled about the paper were other pieces of news. A film actress had been lowered from a peak in California and hung suspended in mid-air. The weather was going to be foggy. The most transient visitor to this planet, I thought, who picked up this paper could not fail to be aware, even from this scattered testimony, that England is under the rule of a patriarchy. Nobody in their senses could fail to detect the dominance of the professor. His was the power and the money and the influence. He was the proprietor of the paper and its editor and sub-editor. He was the Foreign Secretary and the Judge. He was the cricketer; he owned the racehorses and the yachts. He was the director of the company that pays two hundred per cent to its shareholders. He left millions to charities and colleges that were ruled by himself. He suspended the film actress in mid-air. He will decide if the hair on the meat axe is human; he it is who will acquit or convict the murderer, and hang him, or let him go free. With the exception of the fog he seemed to control everything. Yet he was angry. I knew that he was angry by this token. When I read what he wrote about women I thought, not of what he was saying, but of himself. When an arguer argues dispassionately he thinks only of the argument; and the reader

---

7. An extensive area of open land on a hill over-looking London. "Faggot": a bundle of sticks.
8. Headquarters of the League of Nations. Cham- berlain (1863–1937) was a British statesman and brother of Neville Chamberlain, British prime min-ister (1937–40).

cannot help thinking of the argument too. If he had written dispassionately about women, had used indisputable proofs to establish his argument and had shown no trace of wishing that the result should be one thing rather than another, one would not have been angry either. One would have accepted the fact, as one accepts the fact that a pea is green or a canary yellow. So be it, I should have said. But I had been angry because he was angry. Yet it seemed absurd, I thought, turning over the evening paper, that a man with all this power should be angry. Or is anger, I wondered, somehow, the familiar, the attendant sprite[9] on power? Rich people, for example, are often angry because they suspect that the poor want to seize their wealth. The professors, or patriarchs, as it might be more accurate to call them, might be angry for that reason partly, but partly for one that lies a little less obviously on the surface. Possibly they were not "angry" at all; often, indeed, they were admiring, devoted, exemplary in the relations of private life. Possibly when the professor insisted a little too emphatically upon the inferiority of women, he was concerned not with their inferiority, but with his own superiority. That was what he was protecting rather hot-headedly and with too much emphasis, because it was a jewel to him of the rarest price. Life for both sexes—and I looked at them, shouldering their way along the pavement—is arduous, difficult, a perpetual struggle. It calls for gigantic courage and strength. More than anything, perhaps, creatures of illusion as we are, it calls for confidence in oneself. Without self-confidence we are as babes in the cradle. And how can we generate this imponderable quality, which is yet so invaluable, most quickly? By thinking that other people are inferior to oneself. By feeling that one has some innate superiority—it may be wealth, or rank, a straight nose, or the portrait of a grandfather by Romney[1]—for there is no end to the pathetic devices of the human imagination—over other people. Hence the enormous importance to a patriarch who has to conquer, who has to rule, of feeling that great numbers of people, half the human race indeed, are by nature inferior to himself. It must indeed be one of the chief sources of his power. But let me turn the light of this observation on to real life, I thought. Does it help to explain some of those psychological puzzles that one notes in the margin of daily life? Does it explain my astonishment the other day when Z, most humane, most modest of men, taking up some book by Rebecca West[2] and reading a passage in it, exclaimed, "The arrant feminist! She says that men are snobs!" The exclamation, to me so surprising—for why was Miss West an arrant feminist for making a possibly true if uncomplimentary statement about the other sex?—was not merely the cry of wounded vanity; it was a protest against some infringement of his power to believe in himself. Women have served all these centuries as looking-glasses possessing the magic and delicious power of reflecting the figure of man at twice its natural size. Without that power probably the earth would still be swamp and jungle. The glories of all our wars would be unknown. We should still be scratching the outlines of deer on the remains of mutton bones and bartering flints for sheepskins or whatever simple ornament took our unsophisticated taste. Supermen and Fingers of Destiny would never have existed. The Czar and the Kaiser[3] would never have worn their crowns or lost them. Whatever may be their use in civilised societies, mirrors are essential to all violent and heroic action. That is why Napoleon and Mussolini[4] both

---

9. Spirit.
1. George Romney (1734–1802), fashionable English portrait painter.
2. Adopted name of Cicily Isabel Fairfield (1892–

1983), English feminist, journalist, and novelist.
3. Rulers of Russia and Germany, respectively.
4. I.e., dictators.

insist so emphatically upon the inferiority of women, for if they were not inferior, they would cease to enlarge. That serves to explain in part the necessity that women so often are to men. And it serves to explain how restless they are under her criticism; how impossible it is for her to say to them this book is bad, this picture is feeble, or whatever it may be, without giving far more pain and rousing far more anger than a man would do who gave the same criticism. For if she begins to tell the truth, the figure in the looking-glass shrinks; his fitness for life is diminished. How is he to go on giving judgement, civilising natives, making laws, writing books, dressing up and speechifying at banquets, unless he can see himself at breakfast and at dinner at least twice the size he really is? So I reflected, crumbling my bread and stirring my coffee and now and again looking at the people in the street. The looking-glass vision is of supreme importance because it charges the vitality; it stimulates the nervous system. Take it away and man may die, like the drug fiend deprived of his cocaine. Under the spell of that illusion, I thought, looking out of the window, half the people on the pavement are striding to work. They put on their hats and coats in the morning under its agreeable rays. They start the day confident, braced, believing themselves desired at Miss Smith's tea party; they say to themselves as they go into the room, I am the superior of half the people here, and it is thus that they speak with that self-confidence, that self-assurance, which have had such profound consequences in public life and lead to such curious notes in the margin of the private mind.

But these contributions to the dangerous and fascinating subject of the psychology of the other sex—it is one, I hope, that you will investigate when you have five hundred a year of your own—were interrupted by the necessity of paying the bill. It came to five shillings and ninepence. I gave the waiter a ten-shilling note and he went to bring me change. There was another ten-shilling note in my purse; I noticed it, because it is a fact that still takes my breath away—the power of my purse to breed ten-shillings notes automatically. I open it and there they are. Society gives me chicken and coffee, bed and lodging, in return for a certain number of pieces of paper which were left me by an aunt, for no other reason than that I share her name.

My aunt, Mary Beton, I must tell you, died by a fall from her horse when she was riding out to take the air in Bombay. The news of my legacy reached me one night about the same time that the act was passed that gave votes to women. A solicitor's letter fell into the post-box and when I opened it I found that she had left me five hundred pounds a year for ever. Of the two—the vote and the money—the money, I own, seemed infinitely the more important. Before that I had made my living by cadging odd jobs from newspapers, by reporting a donkey show here or a wedding there; I had earned a few pounds by addressing envelopes, reading to old ladies, making artificial flowers, teaching the alphabet to small children in a kindergarten. Such were the chief occupations that were open to women before 1918. I need not, I am afraid, describe in any detail the hardness of the work, for you know perhaps women who have done it; nor the difficulty of living on the money when it was earned, for you may have tried. But what still remains with me as a worse infliction than either was the poison of fear and bitterness which those days bred in me. To begin with, always to be doing work that one did not wish to do, and to do it like a slave, flattering and fawning, not always necessarily perhaps, but it seemed necessary and the stakes were too great to run risks; and then the thought of that one gift which it was death to hide—a small one but dear to the possessor—perishing and with it myself, my soul—all this became like a rust eating away the bloom of the spring, destroying the tree at its heart. However, as I say, my aunt died; and whenever I change a ten-shilling note a little of that rust and corrosion is rubbed off; fear and bitterness go. Indeed, I thought, slipping the silver into my purse, it is remarkable, remembering the bitterness of those days, what a change of temper a fixed income will bring about. No force in the world can take from me my five hundred pounds. Food, house and clothing are mine for ever. Therefore not merely do effort and labour cease, but also hatred and bitterness. I need not hate any man; he cannot hurt me. I need not flatter any man; he has nothing to give me. So imperceptibly I found myself adopting a new attitude towards the other half of the human race. It was absurd to blame any class or any sex, as a whole. Great bodies of people are never responsible for what they do. They are driven by instincts which are not within their control. They too, the patriarchs, the professors, had endless difficulties, terrible drawbacks to contend with. Their education had been in some ways as faulty as my own. It had bred in them defects as great. True, they had money and power, but only at the cost of harbouring in their breasts an eagle, a vulture, for ever tearing the liver out and plucking at the lungs—the instinct for possession, the rage for acquisition which drives them to desire other people's fields and goods perpetually; to make frontiers and flags; battleships and poison gas; to offer up their own lives and their children's lives. Walk through the Admiralty Arch[5] (I had reached that monument), or any other avenue given up to trophies and cannon, and reflect upon the kind of glory celebrated there. Or watch in the spring sunshine the stockbroker and the great barrister going indoors to make money and more money and more money when it is a fact that five hundred pounds a year will keep one alive in the sunshine. These are unpleasant instincts to harbour, I reflected. They are bred of the conditions of life; of the lack of civilisation, I thought, looking at the statue of the Duke of Cambridge,[6] and in particular at the feathers in his cocked hat, with a fixity that they have scarcely ever received before. And, as I realised these drawbacks, by degrees fear and bitterness modified themselves into pity and toleration; and then in a year or two, pity and toleration went, and the greatest release of all came, which is freedom to think of things in themselves. That building, for example, do I like it or not? Is that picture beautiful or not? Is that in my opinion a good book or a bad? Indeed my aunt's legacy unveiled the sky to me, and substituted for the large and imposing figure of a gentleman, which Milton recommended for my perpetual adoration, a view of the open sky.

So thinking, so speculating, I found my way back to my house by the river. Lamps were being lit and an indescribable change had come over London since the morning hour. It was as if the great machine after labouring all day had made with our help a few yards of something very exciting and beautiful—a fiery fabric flashing with red eyes, a tawny monster roaring with hot breath. Even the wind seemed flung like a flag as it lashed the houses and rattled the hoardings.

In my little street, however, domesticity prevailed. The house painter was descending his ladder; the nursemaid was wheeling the perambulator carefully in and out back to nursery tea; the coal-heaver was folding his empty sacks on

5. Between the Mall and Trafalgar Square in London, constructed 1906–11 to commemorate Britain's imperial successes.

6. On Whitehall Lane, directly off Trafalgar Square.

top of each other; the woman who keeps the green-grocer's shop was adding up the day's takings with her hands in red mittens. But so engrossed was I with the problem you have laid upon my shoulders that I could not see even these usual sights without referring them to one centre. I thought how much harder it is now than it must have been even a century ago to say which of these employments is the higher, the more necessary. Is it better to be a coal-heaver or a nursemaid; is the charwoman[7] who has brought up eight children of less value to the world than the barrister who has made a hundred thousand pounds? It is useless to ask such questions; for nobody can answer them. Not only do the comparative values of charwomen and lawyers rise and fall from decade to decade, but we have no rods with which to measure them even as they are at the moment. I had been foolish to ask my professor to furnish me with "indisputable proofs" of this or that in his argument about women. Even if one could state the value of any one gift at the moment, those values will change; in a century's time very possibly they will have changed completely. Moreover, in a hundred years, I thought, reaching my own doorstep, women will have ceased to be the protected sex. Logically they will take part in all the activities and exertions that were once denied them. The nursemaid will heave coal. The shop-woman will drive an engine. All assumptions founded on the facts observed when women were the protected sex will have disappeared—as, for example (here a squad of soldiers marched down the street), that women and clergymen and gardeners live longer than other people. Remove that pro-tection, expose them to the same exertions and activities, make them soldiers and sailors and engine-drivers and dock labourers, and will not women die off so much younger, so much quicker, than men that one will say, "I saw a woman today," as one used to say, "I saw an aeroplane." Anything may happen when womanhood has ceased to be a protected occupation, I thought, opening the door. But what bearing has all this upon the subject of my paper, Women and Fiction? I asked, going indoors.

Chapter Three

It was disappointing not to have brought back in the evening some important statement, some authentic fact. Women are poorer than men because—this or that. Perhaps now it would be better to give up seeking for the truth, and receiving on one's head an avalanche of opinion hot as lava, discoloured as dish-water. It would be better to draw the curtains; to shut out distractions; to light the lamp; to narrow the enquiry and to ask the historian, who records not opinions but facts, to describe under what conditions women lived, not throughout the ages, but in England, say in the time of Elizabeth.[8]

For it is a perennial puzzle why no woman wrote a word of that extraordinary literature when every other man, it seemed, was capable of song or sonnet. What were the conditions in which women lived, I asked myself; for fiction, imaginative work that is, is not dropped like a pebble upon the ground, as science may be; fiction is like a spider's web, attached ever so lightly perhaps, but still attached to life at all four corners. Often the attachment is scarcely perceptible; Shakespeare's plays, for instance, seem to hang there complete by themselves. But when the web is pulled askew, hooked up at the edge, torn in the middle, one remembers that these webs are not spun in midair by

---

7. Household worker.   8. She reigned from 1558 to 1603.

incorporeal creatures, but are the work of suffering human beings, and are attached to grossly material things, like health and money and the houses we live in.

I went, therefore, to the shelf where the histories stand and took down one of the latest, Professor Trevelyan's *History of England*.[9] Once more I looked up Women, found "position of," and turned to the pages indicated. "Wife-beating," I read, "was a recognised right of man, and was practised without shame by high as well as low. . . . Similarly," the historian goes on, "the daughter who refused to marry the gentleman of her parents' choice was liable to be locked up, beaten and flung about the room, without any shock being inflicted on public opinion. Marriage was not an affair of personal affection, but of family avarice, particularly in the 'chivalrous' upper classes. . . . Betrothal often took place while one or both of the parties was in the cradle, and marriage when they were scarcely out of the nurses' charge." That was about 1470, soon after Chaucer's time. The next reference to the position of women is some two hundred years later, in the time of the Stuarts.[1] "It was still the exception for women of the upper and middle class to choose their own husbands, and when the husband had been assigned, he was lord and master, so far at least as law and custom could make him. Yet even so," Professor Trevelyan concludes, "neither Shakespeare's women nor those of authentic seventeenth-century memoirs, like the Verneys and the Hutchinsons,[2] seem wanting in personality and character." Certainly, if we consider it, Cleopatra must have had a way with her; Lady Macbeth, one would suppose, had a will of her own; Rosalind,[3] one might conclude, was an attractive girl. Professor Trevelyan is speaking no more than the truth when he remarks that Shakespeare's women do not seem wanting in personality and character. Not being a historian, one might go even further and say that women have burnt like beacons in all the works of all the poets from the beginning of time— Clytemnestra, Antigone, Cleopatra, Lady Macbeth, Phèdre, Cressida, Rosalind, Desdemona, the Duchess of Malfi, among the dramatists; then among the prose writers: Millamant, Clarissa, Becky Sharp, Anna Karenina, Emma Bovary, Madame de Guermantes[4]—the names flock to mind, nor do they recall women "lacking in personality and character." Indeed, if woman had no existence save in the fiction written by men, one would imagine her a person of the utmost importance, very various; heroic and mean; splendid and sordid; infinitely beautiful and hideous in the extreme; as great as a man, some think even greater.[5] But this is woman in fiction. In fact, as Professor Trevelyan

9. G. M. Trevelyan's *History of England* (1926) long held its place as the standard one-volume history of the country.
1. I.e., during the reign of the British house of Stuart (1603–49, 1660–1714).
2. "The ideal family life of the period [1640–50] that ended in such tragic political division has been recorded once for all in the *Memoirs of the Verney Family*" (Trevelyan, *History of England*). Lucy Hutchinson (1620–after 1675) wrote the biography of her husband, Col. John Hutchinson (1615–1664); it was first published in 1806.
3. These three Shakespearean heroines are, respectively, in *Antony and Cleopatra, Macbeth*, and *As You Like It*.
4. Characters in, respectively, Aeschylus's *Agamemnon*; Sophocles' *Antigone*; Shakespeare's *Antony and Cleopatra* and *Macbeth*; Racine's *Phèdre*; Shakespeare's *Troilus and Cressida, As You*

Like It, and *Othello*; Webster's *The Duchess of Malfi*; Congreve's *Way of the World*; Richardson's *Clarissa*; Thackeray's *Vanity Fair*; Tolstoy's *Anna Karenina*; Flaubert's *Madame Bovary*; and Proust's *A la Recherche du Temps Perdu* (*In Search of Lost Time*).
5. "It remains a strange and almost inexplicable fact that in Athena's city, where women were kept in almost Oriental suppression as odalisques or drudges, the stage should yet have produced figures like Clytemnestra and Cassandra, Atossa and Antigone, Phèdre and Medea, and all the other heroines who dominate play after play of the 'misogynist' Euripides. But the paradox of this world where in real life a respectable woman could hardly show her face alone in the street, and yet on the stage woman equals or surpasses man, has never been satisfactorily explained. In modern tragedy the same predominance exists. At all

points out, she was locked up, beaten and flung about the room.

A very queer, composite being thus emerges. Imaginatively she is of the highest importance; practically she is completely insignificant. She pervades poetry from cover to cover; she is all but absent from history. She dominates the lives of kings and conquerors in fiction; in fact she was the slave of any boy whose parents forced a ring upon her finger. Some of the most inspired words, some of the most profound thoughts in literature fall from her lips; in real life she could hardly read, could scarcely spell, and was the property of her husband.

It was certainly an odd monster that one made up by reading the historians first and the poets afterwards—a worm winged like an eagle; the spirit of life and beauty in a kitchen chopping up suet. But these monsters, however amusing to the imagination, have no existence in fact. What one must do to bring her to life was to think poetically and prosaically at one and the same moment, thus keeping in touch with fact—that she is Mrs Martin, aged thirty-six, dressed in blue, wearing a black hat and brown shoes; but not losing sight of fiction either—that she is a vessel in which all sorts of spirits and forces are coursing and flashing perpetually. The moment, however, that one tries this method with the Elizabethan woman, one branch of illumination fails; one is held up by the scarcity of facts. One knows nothing detailed, nothing perfectly true and substantial about her. History scarcely mentions her. And I turned to Professor Trevelyan again to see what history meant to him. I found by looking at his chapter headings that it meant—

"The Manor Court and the Methods of Open-field Agriculture . . . The Cistercians and Sheep-farming . . . The Crusades . . . The University . . . The House of Commons . . . The Hundred Years' War . . . The Wars of the Roses . . . The Renaissance Scholars . . . The Dissolution of the Monasteries . . . Agrarian and Religious Strife . . . The Origin of English Sea-power . . . The Armada . . ." and so on. Occasionally an individual woman is mentioned, an Elizabeth, or a Mary; a queen or a great lady. But by no possible means could middle-class women with nothing but brains and character at their command have taken part in any one of the great movements which, brought together, constitute the historian's view of the past. Nor shall we find her in any collection of anecdotes. Aubrey[6] hardly mentions her. She never writes her own life and scarcely keeps a diary; there are only a handful of her letters in existence. She left no plays or poems by which we can judge her. What one wants, I thought—and why does not some brilliant student at Newnham or Girton supply it?—is a mass of information; at what age did she marry; how many children had she as a rule; what was her house like; had she a room to herself; did she do the cooking; would she be likely to have a servant? All these facts lie somewhere, presumably, in parish registers and account books; the life of the average Elizabethan woman must be scattered about somewhere, could one collect it and make a book of it. It would be ambitious beyond my daring, I thought, looking about the shelves for books that were not there, to suggest to the students of those famous colleges that they should re-write history,

events, a very cursory survey of Shakespeare's work (similarly with Webster, though not with Marlowe or Jonson) suffices to reveal how this dominance, this initiative of women, persists from Rosalind to Lady Macbeth. So too in Racine; six of his tragedies bear their heroines' names; and what male characters of his shall we set against Hermione and

Andromaque, Bérénice and Roxane, Phèdre and Athalie? So again with Ibsen; what men shall we match with Solveig and Nora, Hedda and Hilda Wangel and Rebecca West?"—F. L. Lucas, *Tragedy*, pp. 114–15 [Woolf's note].
6. John Aubrey (1626–1697), English writer, especially of short biographies.

though I own that it often seems a little queer as it is, unreal, lop-sided; but why should they not add a supplement to history? calling it, of course, by some inconspicuous name so that women might figure there without impropriety? For one often catches a glimpse of them in the lives of the great, whisking away into the background, concealing, I sometimes think, a wink, a laugh, perhaps a tear. And, after all, we have lives enough of Jane Austen; it scarcely seems necessary to consider again the influence of the tragedies of Joanna Baillie[7] upon the poetry of Edgar Allan Poe; as for myself, I should not mind if the homes and haunts of Mary Russell Mitford[8] were closed to the public for a century at least. But what I find deplorable, I continued, looking about the bookshelves again, is that nothing is known about women before the eighteenth century. I have no model in my mind to turn about this way and that. Here am I asking why women did not write poetry in the Elizabethan age, and I am not sure how they were educated; whether they were taught to write; whether they had sitting-rooms to themselves; how many women had children before they were twenty-one; what, in short, they did from eight in the morning till eight at night. They had no money evidently; according to Professor Trevelyan they were married whether they liked it or not before they were out of the nursery, at fifteen or sixteen very likely. It would have been extremely odd, even upon this showing, had one of them suddenly written the plays of Shakespeare, I concluded, and I thought of that old gentleman, who is dead now, but was a bishop, I think, who declared that it was impossible for any woman, past, present, or to come, to have the genius of Shakespeare. He wrote to the papers about it. He also told a lady who applied to him for information that cats do not as a matter of fact go to heaven, though they have, he added, souls of a sort. How much thinking those old gentlemen used to save one! How the borders of ignorance shrank back at their approach! Cats do not go to heaven. Women cannot write the plays of Shakespeare.

Be that as it may, I could not help thinking, as I looked at the works of Shakespeare on the shelf, that the bishop was right at least in this; it would have been impossible, completely and entirely, for any woman to have written the plays of Shakespeare in the age of Shakespeare. Let me imagine, since facts are so hard to come by, what would have happened had Shakespeare had a wonderfully gifted sister, called Judith,[9] let us say. Shakespeare himself went, very probably—his mother was an heiress—to the grammar school, where he may have learnt Latin—Ovid, Virgil and Horace—and the elements of grammar and logic. He was, it is well known, a wild boy who poached rabbits, perhaps shot a deer, and had, rather sooner than he should have done, to marry a woman in the neighbourhood, who bore him a child rather quicker than was right. That escapade sent him to seek his fortune in London. He had, it seemed, a taste for the theatre; he began by holding horses at the stage door. Very soon he got work in the theatre, became a successful actor, and lived at the hub of the universe, meeting everybody, knowing everybody, practising his art on the boards, exercising his wits in the streets, and even getting access to the palace of the queen. Meanwhile his extraordinarily gifted sister, let us suppose, remained at home. She was as adventurous, as imaginative, as agog to see the world as he was. But she was not sent to school. She had no chance of learning grammar and logic, let alone of reading Horace and Virgil.

7. English poet and dramatist (1762–1851).
8. Poet and novelist (1787–1855), best-known for sketches of country life.
9. Shakespeare had a daughter named Judith.

She picked up a book now and then, one of her brother's perhaps, and read a few pages. But then her parents came in and told her to mend the stockings or mind the stew and not moon about with books and papers. They would have spoken sharply but kindly, for they were substantial people who knew the conditions of life for a woman and loved their daughter—indeed, more likely than not she was the apple of her father's eye. Perhaps she scribbled some pages up in an apple loft on the sly, but was careful to hide them or set fire to them. Soon, however, before she was out of her teens, she was to be betrothed to the son of a neighbouring wool-stapler.[1] She cried out that marriage was hateful to her, and for that she was severely beaten by her father. Then he ceased to scold her. He begged her instead not to hurt him, not to shame him in this matter of her marriage. He would give her a chain of beads or a fine petticoat, he said; and there were tears in his eyes. How could she disobey him? How could she break his heart? The force of her own gift alone drove her to it. She made up a small parcel of her belongings, let herself down by a rope one summer's night and took the road to London. She was not seventeen. The birds that sang in the hedge were not more musical than she was. She had the quickest fancy, a gift like her brother's, for the tune of words. Like him, she had a taste for the theatre. She stood at the stage door; she wanted to act, she said. Men laughed in her face. The manager—a fat, loose-lipped man—guffawed. He bellowed something about poodles dancing and women acting—no woman, he said, could possibly be an actress. He hinted—you can imagine what. She could get no training in her craft. Could she even seek her dinner in a tavern or roam the streets at midnight? Yet her genius was for fiction and lusted to feed abundantly upon the lives of men and women and the study of their ways. At last—for she was very young, oddly like Shakespeare the poet in her face, with the same grey eyes and rounded brows—at last Nick Greene the actor-manager took pity on her; she found herself with child by that gentleman and so—who shall measure the heat and violence of the poet's heart when caught and tangled in a woman's body?—killed herself one winter's night and lies buried at some cross-roads where the omnibuses now stop outside the Elephant and Castle.[2]

That, more or less, is how the story would run, I think, if a woman in Shakespeare's day had had Shakespeare's genius. But for my part, I agree with the deceased bishop, if such he was—it is unthinkable that any woman in Shakespeare's day should have had Shakespeare's genius. For genius like Shakespeare's is not born among labouring, uneducated, servile people. It was not born in England among the Saxons and the Britons. It is not born today among the working classes. How, then, could it have been born among women whose work began, according to Professor Trevelyan, almost before they were out of the nursery, who were forced to it by their parents and held to it by all the power of law and custom? Yet genius of a sort must have existed among women as it must have existed among the working classes. Now and again an Emily Brontë or a Robert Burns[3] blazes out and proves its presence. But certainly it never got itself on to paper. When, however, one reads of a witch being ducked, of a woman possessed by devils, of a wise woman selling herbs,

---

1. A stapler is a dealer in staple goods (i.e., established goods in trade and marketing); hence a wool-stapler is a dealer in wool (one of the "staple" products of 16th-century England).
2. Suicides were buried at crossroads. The Ele-
phant and Castle was a tavern south of the river Thames, where roads went off to different parts of southern England.
3. Scottish poet (1759–1796).

or even of a very remarkable man who had a mother, then I think we are on the track of a lost novelist, a suppressed poet, of some mute and inglorious[4] Jane Austen, some Emily Brontë who dashed her brains out on the moor or mopped and mowed about the highways crazed with the torture that her gift had put her to. Indeed, I would venture to guess that Anon, who wrote so many poems without signing them, was often a woman. It was a woman Edward Fitzgerald,[5] I think, suggested who made the ballads and the folk-songs, crooning them to her children, beguiling her spinning with them, or the length of the winter's night.

This may be true or it may be false—who can say?—but what is true in it, so it seemed to me, reviewing the story of Shakespeare's sister as I had made it, is that any woman born with a great gift in the sixteenth century would certainly have gone crazed, shot herself, or ended her days in some lonely cottage outside the village, half witch, half wizard, feared and mocked at. For it needs little skill in psychology to be sure that a highly gifted girl who had tried to use her gift for poetry would have been so thwarted and hindered by other people, so tortured and pulled asunder by her own contrary instincts, that she must have lost her health and sanity to a certainty. No girl could have walked to London and stood at a stage door and forced her way into the presence of actor-managers without doing herself a violence and suffering an anguish which may have been irrational—for chastity may be a fetish invented by certain societies for unknown reasons—but were none the less inevitable. Chastity had then, it has even now, a religious importance in a woman's life, and has so wrapped itself round with nerves and instincts that to cut it free and bring it to the light of day demands courage of the rarest. To have lived a free life in London in the sixteenth century would have meant for a woman who was poet and playwright a nervous stress and dilemma which might well have killed her. Had she survived, whatever she had written would have been twisted and deformed, issuing from a strained and morbid imagination. And undoubtedly, I thought, looking at the shelf where there are no plays by women, her work would have gone unsigned. That refuge she would have sought certainly. It was the relic of the sense of chastity that dictated anonymity to women even so late as the nineteenth century. Currer Bell, George Eliot, George Sand,[6] all the victims of inner strife as their writings prove, sought ineffectively to veil themselves by using the name of a man. Thus they did homage to the convention, which if not implanted by the other sex was liberally encouraged by them (the chief glory of a woman is not to be talked of, said Pericles,[7] himself a much-talked-of man), that publicity in women is detestable. Anonymity runs in their blood. The desire to be veiled still possesses them. They are not even now as concerned about the health of their fame as men are, and, speaking generally, will pass a tombstone or a signpost without feeling an irresistible desire to cut their names on it, as Alf, Bert or Chas. must do in obedience to their instinct, which murmurs if it sees a fine woman go by, or even a dog, Ce chien est à moi.[8] And, of course, it may not be a dog, I thought, remembering Parliament Square, the Sieges Allee[9] and other avenues; it may

---

4. An echo of Thomas Gray's "Elegy Written in a Country Churchyard" (1751), line 59: "Some mute inglorious Milton here may rest."
5. Poet and translator (1809–1883).
6. Male pseudonyms, respectively, of Charlotte Brontë, Marian Evans, and Amandine-Aurore-

Lucie Dupin (1804–1876).
7. Athenian statesman (ca. 495–429 B.C.E.).
8. This dog is mine (French).
9. Avenue of Victory, a busy thoroughfare in Berlin. "Parliament Square": London intersection.

be a piece of land or a man with curly black hair. It is one of the great advantages of being a woman that one can pass even a very fine negress without wishing to make an Englishwoman of her.

That woman, then, who was born with a gift of poetry in the sixteenth century, was an unhappy woman, a woman at strife against herself. All the conditions of her life, all her own instincts, were hostile to the state of mind which is needed to set free whatever is in the brain. But what is the state of mind that is most propitious to the act of creation, I asked. Can one come by any notion of the state that furthers and makes possible that strange activity? Here I opened the volume containing the Tragedies of Shakespeare. What was Shakespeare's state of mind, for instance, when he wrote *Lear* and *Antony and Cleopatra*? It was certainly the state of mind most favourable to poetry that there has ever existed. But Shakespeare himself said nothing about it. We only know casually and by chance that he "never blotted a line."[1] Nothing indeed was ever said by the artist himself about his state of mind until the eighteenth century perhaps. Rousseau[2] perhaps began it. At any rate, by the nineteenth century self-consciousness had developed so far that it was the habit for men of letters to describe their minds in confessions and autobiographies. Their lives also were written, and their letters were printed after their deaths. Thus, though we do not know what Shakespeare went through when he wrote *Lear,* we do know what Carlyle went through when he wrote the *French Revolution;* what Flaubert went through when he wrote *Madame Bovary;* what Keats was going through when he tried to write poetry against the coming of death and the indifference of the world.

And one gathers from this enormous modern literature of confession and self-analysis that to write a work of genius is almost always a feat of prodigious difficulty. Everything is against the likelihood that it will come from the writer's mind whole and entire. Generally material circumstances are against it. Dogs will bark; people will interrupt; money must be made; health will break down. Further, accentuating all these difficulties and making them harder to bear is the world's notorious indifference. It does not ask people to write poems and novels and histories; it does not need them. It does not care whether Flaubert finds the right word or whether Carlyle scrupulously verifies this or that fact. Naturally, it will not pay for what it does not want. And so the writer, Keats, Flaubert, Carlyle, suffers, especially in the creative years of youth, every form of distraction and discouragement. A curse, a cry of agony, rises from those books of analysis and confession. "Mighty poets in their misery dead"[3]—that is the burden of their song. If anything comes through in spite of all this, it is a miracle, and probably no book is born entire and uncrippled as it was conceived.

But for women, I thought, looking at the empty shelves, these difficulties were infinitely more formidable. In the first place, to have a room of her own, let alone a quiet room or a sound-proof room, was out of the question, unless her parents were exceptionally rich or very noble, even up to the beginning of the nineteenth century. Since her pin money, which depended on the good will of her father, was only enough to keep her clothed, she was debarred from such alleviations as came even to Keats or Tennyson or Carlyle, all poor men,

---

1. Ben Jonson, *Timber* (1640): "I remember, the players have often mentioned it as an honour to Shakespeare that in his writing (whatsoever he penned) he never blotted out a line."

2. Jean-Jacques Rousseau (1712–1778), early-Romantic French philosopher and memoirist.
3. From Wordsworth's "Resolution and Independence" (1807), line 116.

2462 / Virginia Woolf

from a walking tour, a little journey to France, from the separate lodging which, even if it were miserable enough, sheltered them from the claims and tyrannies of their families. Such material difficulties were formidable; but much worse were the immaterial. The indifference of the world which Keats and Flaubert and other men of genius have found so hard to bear was in her case not indifference but hostility. The world did not say to her as it said to them, Write if you choose; it makes no difference to me. The world said with a guffaw, Write? What's the good of your writing? Here the psychologists of Newnham and Girton might come to our help, I thought, looking again at the blank spaces on the shelves. For surely it is time that the effect of discouragement upon the mind of the artist should be measured, as I have seen a dairy company measure the effect of ordinary milk and Grade A milk upon the body of the rat. They set two rats in cages side by side, and of the two one was furtive, timid and small, and the other was glossy, bold and big. Now what food do we feed women as artists upon? I asked, remembering, I suppose, that dinner of prunes and custard. To answer that question I had only to open the evening paper and to read that Lord Birkenhead is of opinion—but really I am not going to trouble to copy out Lord Birkenhead's opinion upon the writing of women. What Dean Inge says I will leave in peace. The Harley Street specialist[4] may be allowed to rouse the echoes of Harley Street with his vociferations without raising a hair on my head. I will quote, however, Mr Oscar Browning, because Mr Oscar Browning was a great figure in Cambridge at one time, and used to examine the students at Girton and Newnham. Mr Oscar Browning was wont to declare "that the impression left on his mind, after looking over any set of examination papers, was that, irrespective of the marks he might give, the best woman was intellectually the inferior of the worst man." After saying that Mr Browning went back to his rooms—and it is this sequel that endears him and makes him a human figure of some bulk and majesty—he went back to his rooms and found a stable-boy lying on the sofa—"a mere skeleton, his cheeks were cavernous and sallow, his teeth were black, and he did not appear to have the full use of his limbs. . . . 'That's Arthur' [said Mr Browning]. 'He's a dear boy really and most high-minded.' " The two pictures always seem to me to complete each other. And happily in this age of biography the two pictures often do complete each other, so that we are able to interpret the opinions of great men not only by what they say, but by what they do.

But though this is possible now, such opinions coming from the lips of important people must have been formidable enough even fifty years ago. Let us suppose that a father from the highest motives did not wish his daughter to leave home and become writer, painter or scholar. "See what Mr Oscar Browning says," he would say; and there was not only Mr Oscar Browning; there was the *Saturday Review*; there was Mr Greg[5]—the "essentials of a woman's being," said Mr Greg emphatically, "are that *they are supported by, and they minister to, men*"—there was an enormous body of masculine opinion to the effect that nothing could be expected of women intellectually. Even if her father did not read out loud these opinions, any girl could read them for herself; and the reading, even in the nineteenth century, must have lowered her vitality, and told profoundly upon her work. There would always have been that assertion—you cannot do this, you are incapable of doing that—to protest

---

4. On Harley Street in London many medical specialists have their consulting rooms.

5. Sir W. W. Greg (1875–1959), bibliographer and literary scholar.

against, to overcome. Probably for a novelist this germ is no longer of much effect; for there have been women novelists of merit. But for painters it must still have some sting in it; and for musicians, I imagine, is even now active and poisonous in the extreme. The woman composer stands where the actress stood in the time of Shakespeare. Nick Greene, I thought, remembering the story I had made about Shakespeare's sister, said that a woman acting put him in mind of a dog dancing. Johnson repeated the phrase two hundred years later of women preaching. And here, I said, opening a book about music, we have the very words used again in this year of grace, 1928, of women who try to write music. "Of Mlle Germaine Tailleferre one can only repeat Dr John-son's dictum concerning a woman preacher, transposed into terms of music. 'Sir, a woman's composing is like a dog's walking on his hind legs. It is not done well, but you are surprised to find it done at all.' "[6] So accurately does history repeat itself.

Thus, I concluded, shutting Mr Oscar Browning's life and pushing away the rest, it is fairly evident that even in the nineteenth century a woman was not encouraged to be an artist. On the contrary, she was snubbed, slapped, lec-tured and exhorted. Her mind must have been strained and her vitality lowered by the need of opposing this, of disproving that. For here again we come within range of that very interesting and obscure masculine complex which has had so much influence upon the woman's movement; that deepseated desire, not so much that *she* shall be inferior as that *he* shall be superior, which plants him wherever one looks, not only in front of the arts, but barring the way to politics too, even when the risk to himself seems infinitesimal and the suppli-ant humble and devoted. Even Lady Bessborough, I remembered, with all her passion for politics, must humbly bow herself and write to Lord Granville Leveson-Gower:[7] ". . . notwithstanding all my violence in politics and talking so much on that subject, I perfectly agree with you that no woman has any business to meddle with that or any other serious business, farther than giving her opinion (if she is ask'd)." And so she goes on to spend her enthusiasm where it meets with no obstacle whatsoever upon that immensely important subject, Lord Granville's maiden speech in the House of Commons. The spec-tacle is certainly a strange one, I thought. The history of men's opposition to women's emancipation is more interesting perhaps than the story of that emancipation itself. An amusing book might be made of it if some young student at Girton or Newnham would collect examples and deduce a theory— but she would need thick gloves on her hands, and bars to protect her of solid gold.

But what is amusing now, I recollected, shutting Lady Bessborough, had to be taken in desperate earnest once. Opinions that one now pastes in a book labelled cock-a-doodle-dum and keeps for reading to select audiences on sum-mer nights once drew tears, I can assure you. Among your grandmothers and great-grandmothers there were many that wept their eyes out. Florence Night-ingale shrieked loud in her agony.[8] Moreover, it is all very well for you, who have got yourselves to college and enjoy sitting-rooms—or is it only bed-sitting-

---

6. *A Survey of Contemporary Music*, Cecil Gray, p. 246 [Woolf's note].
7. English statesman (1773–1846). Lady Bessbor-ough is Henrietta, countess of Bessborough (1761–1821).
8. See *Cassandra*, by Florence Nightingale,

printed in *The Cause*, by R. Strachey [Woolf's note]. Florence Nightingale (1820–1910), English nurse, who originated and directed a group of field nurses during the Crimean War and is considered the founder of modern nursing.

rooms?—of your own to say that genius should disregard such opinions; that genius should be above caring what is said of it. Unfortunately, it is precisely the men or women of genius who mind most what is said of them. Remember Keats. Remember the words he had cut on his tombstone.[9] Think of Tennyson; think—but I need hardly multiply instances of the undeniable, if very unfortunate, fact that it is the nature of the artist to mind excessively what is said about him. Literature is strewn with the wreckage of men who have minded beyond reason the opinions of others.

And this susceptibility of theirs is doubly unfortunate, I thought, returning again to my original enquiry into what state of mind is most propitious for creative work, because the mind of an artist, in order to achieve the prodigious effort of freeing whole and entire the work that is in him, must be incandescent, like Shakespeare's mind, I conjectured, looking at the book which lay open at *Antony and Cleopatra*. There must be no obstacle in it, no foreign matter unconsumed.

For though we say that we know nothing about Shakespeare's state of mind, even as we say that, we are saying something about Shakespeare's state of mind. The reason perhaps why we know so little of Shakespeare—compared with Donne or Ben Jonson or Milton—is that his grudges and spites and antipathies are hidden from us. We are not held up by some "revelation" which reminds us of the writer. All desire to protest, to preach, to proclaim an injury, to pay off a score, to make the world the witness of some hardship or grievance was fired out of him and consumed. Therefore his poetry flows from him free and unimpeded. If ever a human being got his work expressed completely, it was Shakespeare. If ever a mind was incandescent, unimpeded, I thought, turning again to the bookcase, it was Shakespeare's mind.

Chapter Four

That one would find any woman in that state of mind in the sixteenth century was obviously impossible. One has only to think of the Elizabethan tombstones with all those children kneeling with clasped hands; and their early deaths; and to see their houses with their dark, cramped rooms, to realise that no woman could have written poetry then. What one would expect to find would be that rather later perhaps some great lady would take advantage of her comparative freedom and comfort to publish something with her name to it and risk being thought a monster. Men, of course, are not snobs, I continued, carefully eschewing "the arrant feminism" of Miss Rebecca West; but they appreciate with sympathy for the most part the efforts of a countess to write verse. One would expect to find a lady of title meeting with far greater encouragement than an unknown Miss Austen or a Miss Brontë at that time would have met with. But one would also expect to find that her mind was disturbed by alien emotions like fear and hatred and that her poems showed traces of that disturbance. Here is Lady Winchilsea,[1] for example, I thought, taking down her poems. She was born in the year 1661; she was noble both by birth and by marriage; she was childless; she wrote poetry, and one has only to open her poetry to find her bursting out in indignation against the position of women:

9. "Here lies one whose name was writ in water."
1. Anne Finch, countess of Winchilsea (1661–

1720); the quotations are from her poem "The Introduction."

How are we fallen! fallen by mistaken rules,
And Education's more than Nature's fools;
Debarred from all improvements of the mind,
And to be dull, expected and designed;
And if some one would soar above the rest,
With warmer fancy, and ambition pressed,
So strong the opposing faction still appears,
The hopes to thrive can ne'er outweigh the fears.

Clearly her mind has by no means "consumed all impediments and become incandescent." On the contrary, it is harrassed and distracted with hates and grievances. The human race is split up for her into two parties. Men are the "opposing faction"; men are hated and feared, because they have the power to bar her way to what she wants to do—which is to write.

Alas! a woman that attempts the pen,
Such a presumptuous creature is esteemed,
The fault can by no virtue be redeemed.
They tell us we mistake our sex and way;
Good breeding, fashion, dancing, dressing, play,
Are the accomplishments we should desire;
To write, or read, or think, or to enquire,
Would cloud our beauty, and exhaust our time,
And interrupt the conquests of our prime,
Whilst the dull manage of a servile house
Is held by some our utmost art and use.

Indeed she has to encourage herself to write by supposing that what she writes will never be published; to soothe herself with the sad chant:

To some few friends, and to thy sorrows sing,
For groves of laurel thou wert never meant;
Be dark enough thy shades, and be thou there content.

Yet it is clear that could she have freed her mind from hate and fear and not heaped it with bitterness and resentment, the fire was hot within her. Now and again words issue of pure poetry:

Nor will in fading silks compose,
Faintly the inimitable rose.

—they are rightly praised by Mr Murry,[2] and Pope, it is thought, remembered and appropriated those others:

Now the jonquille o'ercomes the feeble brain;
We faint beneath the aromatic pain.

It was a thousand pities that the woman who could write like that, whose mind was turned to nature and reflection, should have been forced to anger and bitterness. But how could she have helped herself? I asked, imagining the sneers and the laughter, the adulation of the toadies,[3] the scepticism of the professional poet. She must have shut herself up in a room in the country to write, and been torn asunder by bitterness and scruples perhaps, though her

2. John Middleton Murry (1889–1957), English literary critic.

3. Sycophants.

husband was of the kindest, and their married life perfection. She "must have,"
I say, because when one comes to seek out the facts about Lady Winchilsea,
one finds, as usual, that almost nothing is known about her. She suffered
terribly from melancholy, which we can explain at least to some extent when
we find her telling us how in the grip of it she would imagine:

> My lines decried, and my employment thought,
> An useless folly or presumptuous fault:

The employment, which was thus censured, was, as far as one can see, the
harmless one of rambling about the fields and dreaming:

> My hand delights to trace unusual things,
> And deviates from the known and common way,
> Nor will in fading silks compose,
> Faintly the inimitable rose.

Naturally, if that was her habit and that was her delight, she could only expect
to be laughed at; and, accordingly, Pope or Gay[4] is said to have satirised her
"as a blue-stocking with an itch for scribbling." Also it is thought that she
offended Gay by laughing at him. She said that his *Trivia* showed that "he was
more proper to walk before a chair than to ride in one." But this is all "dubious
gossip" and, says Mr Murry, "uninteresting." But there I do not agree with
him, for I should have liked to have had more even of dubious gossip so that
I might have found out or made up some image of this melancholy lady, who
loved wandering in the fields and thinking about unusual things and scorned,
so rashly, so unwisely, "the dull manage of a servile house." But she became
diffuse, Mr Murry says. Her gift is all grown about with weeds and bound with
briars. It had no chance of showing itself for the fine distinguished gift it was.
And so, putting her back on the shelf, I turned to the other great lady, the
Duchess whom Lamb loved, hare-brained, fantastical Margaret of Newcastle,[5]
her elder, but her contemporary. They were very different, but alike in this
that both were noble and both childless, and both were married to the best of
husbands. In both burnt the same passion for poetry and both are disfigured
and deformed by the same causes. Open the Duchess and one finds the same
outburst of rage, "Women live like Bats or Owls, labour like Beasts, and die
like Worms. . . ." Margaret too might have been a poet; in our day all that
activity would have turned a wheel of some sort. As it was, what could bind,
tame or civilise for human use that wild, generous, untutored intelligence? It
poured itself out, higgledy-piggledy, in torrents of rhyme and prose, poetry and
philosophy which stand congealed in quartos and folios that nobody ever
reads. She should have had a microscope put in her hand. She should have
been taught to look at the stars and reason scientifically. Her wits were turned
with solitude and freedom. No one checked her. No one taught her. The
professors fawned on her. At Court they jeered at her. Sir Egerton Brydges[6]
complained of her coarseness—"as flowing from a female of high rank brought
up in the Courts." She shut herself up at Welbeck[7] alone.
  What a vision of loneliness and riot the thought of Margaret Cavendish

4. John Gay (1685–1732), English poet and playwright, author of the poem "Trivia, or The Art of
Walking the Streets of London" (1716), mentioned
below.
5. Margaret Lucas Cavendish, duchess of New-

castle (1623–1673), author of "Female Orations,"
quoted below.
6. English writer (1762–1837).
7. Estate of Margaret's husband, in Nottinghamshire.

brings to mind! as if some giant cucumber had spread itself over all the roses and carnations in the garden and choked them to death. What a waste that the woman who wrote "the best bred women are those whose minds are civilest" should have frittered her time away scribbling nonsense and plunging ever deeper into obscurity and folly till the people crowded round her coach when she issued out. Evidently the crazy Duchess became a bogey to frighten clever girls with. Here, I remembered, putting away the Duchess and opening Dorothy Osborne's[8] letters, is Dorothy writing to Temple about the Duchess's new book. "Sure the poore woman is a little distracted, shee could never bee soe rediculous else as to venture at writeing book's and in verse too, if I should not sleep this fortnight I should not come to that."

And so, since no woman of sense and modesty could write books, Dorothy, who was sensitive and melancholy, the very opposite of the Duchess in temper, wrote nothing. Letters did not count. A woman might write letters while she was sitting by her father's sick-bed. She could write them by the fire whilst the men talked without disturbing them. The strange thing is, I thought, turning over the pages of Dorothy's letters, what a gift that untaught and solitary girl had for the framing of a sentence, for the fashioning of a scene. Listen to her running on:

"After dinner wee sitt and talk till Mr B. com's in question and then I am gon. the heat of the day is spent in reading or working and about sixe or seven a Clock, I walke out into a Common that lyes hard by the house where a great many young wenches keep Sheep and Cow's and sitt in the shades singing of Ballads; I goe to them and compare their voyces and Beauty's to some Ancient Shepherdesses that I have read of and finde a vaste difference there, but trust mee I think these are as innocent as those could bee. I talke to them, and finde they want nothing to make them the happiest People in the world, but the knoledge that they are soe. most commonly when we are in the middest of our discourse one looks aboute her and spyes her Cow's goeing into the Corne and then away they all run, as if they had wing's at theire heels. I that am not soe nimble stay behinde, and when I see them driveing home theire Cattle I think tis time for mee to retyre too. when I have supped I goe into the Garden and soe to the syde of a small River that runs by it where I sitt downe and wish you with mee. . . ."

One could have sworn that she had the makings of a writer in her. But "if I should not sleep this fortnight I should not come to that"—one can measure the opposition that was in the air to a woman writing when one finds that even a woman with a great turn for writing has brought herself to believe that to write a book was to be ridiculous, even to show oneself distracted. And so we come, I continued, replacing the single short volume of Dorothy Osborne's letters upon the shelf, to Mrs Behn.[9]

And with Mrs Behn we turn a very important corner on the road. We leave behind, shut up in their parks among their folios, those solitary great ladies who wrote without audience or criticism, for their own delight alone. We come to town and rub shoulders with ordinary people in the streets. Mrs Behn was a middle-class woman with all the plebeian virtues of humour, vitality and courage; a woman forced by the death of her husband and some unfortunate adventures of her own to make her living by her wits. She had to work on

8. Later, Lady Temple (1627–1695), famous for her letters to her future husband.

9. Aphra Behn (ca. 1640–1689), English poet and playwright, and author of *Oroonoko*.

equal terms with men. She made, by working very hard, enough to live on. The importance of that fact outweighs anything that she actually wrote, even the splendid "A Thousand Martyrs I have made," or "Love in Fantastic Triumph sat," for here begins the freedom of the mind, or rather the possibility that in the course of time the mind will be free to write what it likes. For now that Aphra Behn had done it, girls could go to their parents and say, You need not give me an allowance; I can make money by my pen. Of course the answer for many years to come was, Yes, by living the life of Aphra Behn! Death would be better! and the door was slammed faster than ever. That profoundly interesting subject, the value that men set upon women's chastity and its effect upon their education, here suggests itself for discussion, and might provide an interesting book if any student at Girton or Newnham cared to go into the matter. Lady Dudley, sitting in diamonds among the midges of a Scottish moor, might serve for frontispiece. Lord Dudley, *The Times* said when Lady Dudley died the other day, "a man of cultivated taste and many accomplishments, was benevolent and bountiful, but whimsically despotic. He insisted upon his wife's wearing full dress, even at the remotest shooting-lodge in the Highlands; he loaded her with gorgeous jewels," and so on, "he gave her everything—always excepting any measure of responsibility." Then Lord Dudley had a stroke and she nursed him and ruled his estates with supreme competence for ever after. That whimsical despotism was in the nineteenth century too.

But to return. Aphra Behn proved that money could be made by writing at the sacrifice, perhaps, of certain agreeable qualities; and so by degrees writing became not merely a sign of folly and a distracted mind, but was of practical importance. A husband might die, or some disaster[2] overtake the family. Hundreds of women began as the eighteenth century drew on to add to their pin money, or to come to the rescue of their families by making translations or writing the innumerable bad novels which have ceased to be recorded even in text-books, but are to be picked up in the fourpenny boxes in the Charing Cross Road.[1] The extreme activity of mind which showed itself in the later eighteenth century among women—the talking, and the meeting, the writing of essays on Shakespeare, the translating of the classics—was founded on the solid fact that women could make money by writing. Money dignifies what is frivolous if unpaid for. It might still be well to sneer at "blue stockings with an itch for scribbling," but it could not be denied that they could put money in their purses. Thus, towards the end of the eighteenth century a change came about which, if I were rewriting history, I should describe more fully and think of greater importance than the Crusades or the Wars of the Roses. The middle-class woman began to write. For if *Pride and Prejudice* matters, and *Middlemarch* and *Villette* and *Wuthering Heights*[2] matter, then it matters far more than I can prove in an hour's discourse that women generally, and not merely the lonely aristocrat shut up in her country house among her folios and her flatterers, took to writing. Without those forerunners, Jane Austen and the Brontës and George Eliot could no more have written than Shakespeare could have written without Marlowe, or Marlowe without Chaucer, or Chaucer without those forgotten poets who paved the ways and tamed the natural savagery of the tongue. For masterpieces are not single and solitary

1. A street in London famed for its bookshops.
2. Novels by, respectively, Jane Austen, George

Eliot, Charlotte Brontë, and Emily Brontë. *Emma*, mentioned below, is by Austen.

births; they are the outcome of many years of thinking in common, of thinking by the body of the people, so that the experience of the mass is behind the single voice. Jane Austen should have laid a wreath upon the grave of Fanny Burney, and George Eliot done homage to the robust shade of Eliza Carter[3]— the valiant old woman who tied a bell to her bedstead in order that she might wake early and learn Greek. All women together ought to let flowers fall upon the tomb of Alphra Behn which is, most scandalously but rather appropriately, in Westminster Abbey,[4] for it was she who earned them the right to speak their minds. It is she—shady and amorous as she was—who makes it not quite fantastic for me to say to you tonight: Earn five hundred a year by your wits.

Here, then, one had reached the early nineteenth century. And here, for the first time, I found several shelves given up entirely to the works of women. But why, I could not help asking, as I ran my eyes over them, were they, with very few exceptions, all novels? The original impulse was to poetry. The "supreme head of song" was a poetess. Both in France and in England the women poets precede the women novelists. Moreover, I thought, looking at the four famous names, what had George Eliot in common with Emily Brontë? Did not Charlotte Brontë fail entirely to understand Jane Austen? Save for the possibly relevant fact that not one of them had a child, four more incongruous characters could not have met together in a room—so much so that it is tempting to invent a meeting and a dialogue between them. Yet by some strange force they were all compelled, when they wrote, to write novels. Had it something to do with being born of the middle class, I asked; and with the fact, which Miss Emily Davies[5] a little later was so strikingly to demonstrate, that the middle-class family in the early nineteenth century was possessed only of a single sitting-room between them? If a woman wrote, she would have to write in the common sitting-room. And, as Miss Nightingale was so vehemently to complain,—"women never have an half hour . . . that they can call their own"—she was always interrupted. Still it would be easier to write prose and fiction there than to write poetry or a play. Less concentration is required. Jane Austen wrote like that to the end of her days. "How she was able to effect all this," her nephew writes in his Memoir, "is surprising, for she had no separate study to repair to, and most of the work must have been done in the general sitting-room, subject to all kinds of casual interruptions. She was careful that her occupation should not be suspected by servants or visitors or any persons beyond her own family party."[6] Jane Austen hid her manuscripts or covered them with a piece of blotting-paper. Then, again, all the literary training that a woman had in the early nineteenth century was training in the observation of character, in the analysis of emotion. Her sensibility had been educated for centuries by the influences of the common sitting-room. People's feelings were impressed on her; personal relations were always before her eyes. Therefore, when the middle-class woman took to writing, she naturally wrote novels, even though, as seems evident enough, two of the four famous women here named were not by nature novelists. Emily Brontë should have written poetic plays; the overflow of George Eliot's capacious mind should have spread itself when the creative impulse was spent upon history or biography. They wrote novels, however; one may even go further, I said, taking *Pride and Prej-*

---

3. English poet and translator (1717–1806).
4. Site of Poet's Corner, which contains the tombs of many notable authors.

5. See n. 3, p. 2444.
6. *Memoir of Jane Austen*, by her nephew, James Edward Austen-Leigh [Woolf's note].

udice from the shelf, and say that they wrote good novels. Without boasting or giving pain to the opposite sex, one may say that *Pride and Prejudice* is a good book. At any rate, one would not have been ashamed to have been caught in the act of writing *Pride and Prejudice*. Yet Jane Austen was glad that a hinge creaked, so that she might hide her manuscript before any one came in. To Jane Austen there was something discreditable in writing *Pride and Prejudice*. And, I wondered, would *Pride and Prejudice* have been a better novel if Jane Austen had not thought it necessary to hide her manuscript from visitors? I read a page or two to see; but I could not find any signs that her circumstances had harmed her work in the slightest. That, perhaps, was the chief miracle about it. Here was a woman about the year 1800 writing without hate, without bitterness, without fear, without protest, without preaching. That was how Shakespeare wrote, I thought, looking at *Antony and Cleopatra*; and when people compare Shakespeare and Jane Austen, they may mean that the minds of both had consumed all impediments; and for that reason we do not know Jane Austen and we do not know Shakespeare, and for that reason Jane Austen pervades every word that she wrote, and so does Shakespeare. If Jane Austen suffered in any way from her circumstances it was in the narrowness of life that was imposed upon her. It was impossible for a woman to go about alone. She never travelled; she never drove through London in an omnibus or had luncheon in a shop by herself. But perhaps it was the nature of Jane Austen not to want what she had not. Her gift and her circumstances matched each other completely. But I doubt whether that was true of Charlotte Brontë, I said, opening *Jane Eyre* and laying it beside *Pride and Prejudice*.

I opened it at chapter twelve and my eye was caught by the phrase, "Anybody may blame me who likes." What were they blaming Charlotte Brontë for, I wondered? And I read how Jane Eyre used to go up on to the roof when Mrs. Fairfax was making jellies and looked over the fields at the distant view. And then she longed—and it was for this that they blamed her—that "then I longed for a power of vision which might overpass that limit; which might reach the busy world, towns, regions full of life I had heard of but never seen: that then I desired more of practical experience than I possessed; more of intercourse with my kind, of acquaintance with variety of character than was here within my reach. I valued what was good in Mrs. Fairfax, and what was good in Adèle; but I believed in the existence of other and more vivid kinds of goodness, and what I believed in I wished to behold.

"Who blames me? Many, no doubt, and I shall be called discontented. I could not help it: the restlessness was in my nature; it agitated me to pain sometimes. . . .

"It is vain to say human beings ought to be satisfied with tranquillity: they must have action; and they will make it if they cannot find it. Millions are condemned to a stiller doom than mine, and millions are in silent revolt against their lot. Nobody knows how many rebellions ferment in the masses of life which people earth. Women are supposed to be very calm generally: but women feel just as men feel; they need exercise for their faculties and a field for their efforts as much as their brothers do; they suffer from too rigid a restraint, too absolute a stagnation, precisely as men would suffer; and it is narrow-minded in their more privileged fellow-creatures to say that they ought to confine themselves to making puddings and knitting stockings, to playing on the piano and embroidering bags. It is thoughtless to condemn them, or laugh at them, if they seek to do more or learn more than custom has pronounced necessary for their sex.

"When thus alone I not unfrequently heard Grace Poole's laugh. . . ."

That is an awkward break, I thought. It is upsetting to come upon Grace Poole all of a sudden. The continuity is disturbed. One might say, I continued, laying the book down beside *Pride and Prejudice*, that the woman who wrote those pages had more genius in her than Jane Austen; but if one reads them over and marks that jerk in them, that indignation, one sees that she will never get her genius expressed whole and entire. Her books will be deformed and twisted. She will write in a rage where she should write calmly. She will write foolishly where she should write wisely. She will write of herself where she should write of her characters. She is at war with her lot. How could she help but die young, cramped and thwarted?

One could not but play for a moment with the thought of what might have happened if Charlotte Brontë had possessed say three hundred a year—but the foolish woman sold the copyright of her novels outright for fifteen hundred pounds; had somehow possessed more knowledge of the busy world, and towns and regions full of life; more practical experience, and intercourse with her kind and acquaintance with a variety of character. In those words she puts her finger exactly not only upon her own defects as a novelist but upon those of her sex at that time. She knew, no one better, how enormously her genius would have profited if it had not spent itself in solitary visions over distant fields; if experience and intercourse and travel had been granted her. But they were not granted; they were withheld; and we must accept the fact that all those good novels, *Villette, Emma, Wuthering Heights, Middlemarch*, were written by women without more experience of life than could enter the house of a respectable clergyman; written too in the common sitting-room of that respectable house and by women so poor that they could not afford to buy more than a few quires of paper at a time upon which to write *Wuthering Heights* or *Jane Eyre*. One of them, it is true, George Eliot, escaped after much tribulation, but only to a secluded villa in St John's Wood.[7] And there she settled down in the shadow of the world's disapproval. "I wish it to be understood," she wrote, "that I should never invite any one to come and see me who did not ask for the invitation"; for was she not living in sin with a married man and might not the sight of her damage the chastity of Mrs Smith or whoever it might be that chanced to call? One must submit to the social convention, and be "cut off from what is called the world." At the same time, on the other side of Europe, there was a young man living freely with this gipsy or with that great lady; going to the wars; picking up unhindered and uncensored all that varied experience of human life which served him so splendidly later when he came to write his books. Had Tolstoi[8] lived at the Priory in seclusion with a married lady "cut off from what is called the world," however edifying the moral lesson, he could scarcely, I thought, have written *War and Peace*.

But one could perhaps go a little deeper into the question of novel-writing and the effect of sex upon the novelist. If one shuts one's eyes and thinks of the novel as a whole, it would seem to be a creation owning a certain looking-glass likeness to life, though of course with simplifications and distortions innumerable. At any rate, it is a structure leaving a shape on the mind's eye, built now in squares, now pagoda shaped, now throwing out wings and arcades, now solidly compact and domed like the Cathedral of Saint Sofia at Constantinople. This shape, I thought, thinking back over certain famous nov-

---

7. A suburb in northwest London that developed in the 1840s.

8. Leo Tolstoy (1828–1910), Russian novelist.

els, starts in one the kind of emotion that is appropriate to it. But that emotion at once blends itself with others, for the "shape" is not made by the relation of stone to stone, but by the relation of human being to human being. Thus a novel starts in us all sorts of antagonistic and opposed emotions. Life conflicts with something that is not life. Hence the difficulty of coming to any agreement about novels, and the immense sway that our private prejudices have upon us. On the one hand, we feel You—John the hero—must live, or I shall be in the depths of despair. On the other, we feel, Alas, John, you must die, because the shape of the book requires it. Life conflicts with something that is not life. Then since life it is in part, we judge it as life. James is the sort of man I most detest, one says. Or, This is a farrago of absurdity. I could never feel anything of the sort myself. The whole structure, it is obvious, thinking back on any famous novel, is one of infinite complexity, because it is thus made up of so many different judgments, of so many different kinds of emotion. The wonder is that any book so composed holds together for more than a year or two, or can possibly mean to the English reader what it means for the Russian or the Chinese. But they do hold together occasionally very remarkably. And what holds them together in these rare instances of survival (I was thinking of *War and Peace*) is something that one calls integrity, though it has nothing to do with paying one's bills or behaving honourably in an emergency. What one means by integrity, in the case of the novelist, is the conviction that he gives one that this is the truth. Yes, one feels, I should never have thought that this could be so; I have never known people behaving like that. But you have convinced me that so it is, so it happens. One holds every phrase, every scene to the light as one reads—for Nature seems, very oddly, to have provided us with an inner light by which to judge of the novelist's integrity or disintegrity. Or perhaps it is rather that Nature, in her most irrational mood, has traced in invisible ink on the walls of the mind a premonition which these great artists confirm; a sketch which only needs to be held to the fire of genius to become visible. When one so exposes it and sees it come to life one exclaims in rapture, But this is what I have always felt and known and desired! And one boils over with excitement, and, shutting the book even with a kind of reverence as if it were something very precious, a stand-by to return to as long as one lives, one puts it back on the shelf, I said, taking *War and Peace* and putting it back in its place. If, on the other hand, these poor sentences that one takes and tests rouse first a quick and eager response with their bright colouring and their dashing gestures but there they stop: something seems to check them in their development: or if they bring to light only a faint scribble in that corner and a blot over there, and nothing appears whole and entire, then one heaves a sigh of disappointment and says, Another failure. This novel has come to grief somewhere.

And for the most part, of course, novels do come to grief somewhere. The imagination falters under the enormous strain. The insight is confused; it can no longer distinguish between the true and the false; it has no longer the strength to go on with the vast labour that calls at every moment for the use of so many different faculties. But how would all this be affected by the sex of the novelist, I wondered, looking at *Jane Eyre* and the others. Would the fact of her sex in any way interfere with the integrity of a woman novelist— that integrity which I take to be the backbone of the writer? Now, in the passages I have quoted from *Jane Eyre*, it is clear that anger was tampering with the integrity of Charlotte Brontë the novelist. She left her story, to which her entire devotion was due, to attend to some personal grievance. She remembered that she had been starved of her proper due of experience—she had been made to stagnate in a parsonage mending stockings when she wanted to wander free over the world. Her imagination swerved from indignation and we feel it swerve. But there were many more influences than anger tugging at her imagination and deflecting it from its path. Ignorance, for instance. The portrait of Rochester is drawn in the dark. We feel the influence of fear in it; just as we constantly feel an acidity which is the result of oppression, a buried suffering smouldering beneath her passion, a rancour which contracts those books, splendid as they are, with a spasm of pain.

And since a novel has this correspondence to real life, its values are to some extent those of real life. But it is obvious that the values of women differ very often from the values which have been made by the other sex; naturally, this is so. Yet it is the masculine values that prevail. Speaking crudely, football and sport are "important"; the worship of fashion, the buying of clothes "trivial." And these values are inevitably transferred from life to fiction. This is an important book, the critic assumes, because it deals with war. This is an insignificant book because it deals with the feelings of women in a drawing-room. A scene in a battlefield is more important than a scene in a shop—everywhere and much more subtly the difference of value persists. The whole structure, therefore, of the early nineteenth-century novel was raised, if one was a woman, by a mind which was slightly pulled from the straight, and made to alter its clear vision in deference to external authority. One has only to skim those old forgotten novels and listen to the tone of voice in which they are written to divine that the writer was meeting criticism; she was saying this by way of aggression, or that by way of conciliation. She was admitting that she was "only a woman," or protesting that she was "as good as a man." She met that criticism as her temperament dictated, with docility and diffidence, or with anger and emphasis. It does not matter which it was; she was thinking of something other than the thing itself. Down comes her book upon our heads. There was a flaw in the centre of it. And I thought of all the women's novels that lie scattered, like small pock-marked apples in an orchard, about the secondhand book shops of London. It was the flaw in the centre that had rotted them. She had altered her values in deference to the opinion of others.

But how impossible it must have been for them not to budge either to the right or to the left. What genius, what integrity it must have required in face of all that criticism, in the midst of that purely patriarchal society, to hold fast to the thing as they saw it without shrinking. Only Jane Austen did it and Emily Brontë. It is another feather, perhaps the finest, in their caps. They wrote as women write, not as men write. Of all the thousand women who wrote novels then, they alone entirely ignored the perpetual admonitions of the eternal pedagogue—write this, think that. They alone were deaf to that persistent voice, now grumbling, now patronising, now domineering, now grieved, now shocked, now angry, now avuncular, that voice which cannot let women alone, but must be at them, like some too conscientious governess, adjuring them, like Sir Egerton Brydges, to be refined; dragging even into the criticism of poetry criticism of sex;[9] admonishing them, if they would be good

9. "[She] has a metaphysical purpose, and that is a dangerous obsession, especially with a woman, for women rarely possess men's healthy love of rhetoric. It is a strange lack in the sex which is in other things more primitive and more materialistic."—*New Criterion*, June 1928 [Woolf's note].

and win, as I suppose, some shiny prize, to keep within certain limits which the gentleman in question thinks suitable: ". . . female novelists should only aspire to excellence by courageously acknowledging the limitations of their sex."[1] That puts the matter in a nutshell, and when I tell you, rather to your surprise, that this sentence was written not in August 1828 but in August 1928, you will agree, I think, that however delightful it is to us now, it represents a vast body of opinion—I am not going to stir those old pools, I take only what chance has floated to my feet—that was far more vigorous and far more vocal a century ago. It would have needed a very stalwart young woman in 1828 to disregard all those snubs and chidings and promises of prizes. One must have been something of a firebrand to say to oneself, Oh, but they can't buy literature too. Literature is open to everybody. I refuse to allow you, Beadle though you are, to turn me off the grass. Lock up your libraries if you like; but there is no gate, no lock, no bolt that you can set upon the freedom of my mind.

But whatever effect discouragement and criticism had upon their writing—and I believe that they had a very great effect—that was unimportant compared with the other difficulty which faced them (I was still considering those early nineteenth-century novelists) when they came to set their thoughts on paper—that is that they had no tradition behind them, or one so short and partial that it was of little help. For we think back through our mothers if we are women. It is useless to go to the great men writers for help, however much one may go to them for pleasure. Lamb, Browne, Thackeray, Newman, Sterne, Dickens, De Quincey—whoever it may be—never helped a woman yet, though she may have learnt a few tricks of them and adapted them to her use. The weight, the pace, the stride of a man's mind are too unlike her own for her to lift anything substantial from him successfully. The ape is too distant to be sedulous. Perhaps the first thing she would find, setting pen to paper, was that there was no common sentence ready for her use. All the great novelists like Thackeray and Dickens and Balzac have written a natural prose, swift but not slovenly, expressive but not precious, taking their own tint without ceasing to be common property. They have based it on the sentence that was current at the time. The sentence that was current at the beginning of the nineteenth century ran something like this perhaps: "The grandeur of their works was an argument with them, not to stop short, but to proceed. They could have no higher excitement or satisfaction than in the exercise of their art and endless generations of truth and beauty. Success prompts to exertion; and habit facilitates success." That is a man's sentence; behind it one can see Johnson, Gibbon[2] and the rest. It was a sentence that was unsuited for a woman's use. Charlotte Brontë, with all her splendid gift for prose, stumbled and fell with that clumsy weapon in her hands. George Eliot committed atrocities with it that beggar description. Jane Austen looked at it and laughed at it and devised a perfectly natural, shapely sentence proper for her own use and never departed from it. Thus, with less genius for writing than Charlotte Brontë, she got infinitely more said. Indeed, since freedom and fullness of expression are of the essence of the art, such a lack of tradition, such a scarcity and inade-

1. "If, like the reporter, you believe that female novelists should only aspire to excellence by courageously acknowledging the limitations of their sex (Jane Austen [has] demonstrated how gracefully this gesture can be accomplished). . . ."—*Life and Letters*, August 1928 [Woolf's note].
2. Edward Gibbon (1737–1794), English historian, author of *The History of the Decline and Fall of the Roman Empire*.

quacy of tools, must have told enormously upon the writing of women. More-over, a book is not made of sentences laid end to end, but of sentences built, if an image helps, into arcades or domes. And this shape too has been made by men out of their own needs for their own uses. There is no reason to think that the form of the epic or of the poetic play suits a woman any more than the sentence suits her. But all the older forms of literature were hardened and set by the time she became a writer. The novel alone was young enough to be soft in her hands—another reason, perhaps, why she wrote novels. Yet who shall say that even now "the novel" (I give it inverted commas to mark my sense of the words' inadequacy), who shall say that even this most pliable of all forms is rightly shaped for her use? No doubt we shall find her knocking that into shape for herself when she has the free use of her limbs; and provid-ing some new vehicle, not necessarily in verse, for the poetry in her. For it is the poetry that is still denied outlet. And I went on to ponder how a woman nowadays would write a poetic tragedy in five acts—would she use verse—would she not use prose rather?

But these are difficult questions which lie in the twilight of the future. I must leave them, if only because they stimulate me to wander from my subject into trackless forests where I shall be lost and, very likely, devoured by wild beasts. I do not want, and I am sure that you do not want me, to broach that very dismal subject, the future of fiction, so that I will only pause here one moment to draw your attention to the great part which must be played in that future so far as women are concerned by physical conditions. The book has somehow to be adapted to the body, and at a venture one would say that women's books should be shorter, more concentrated, than those of men, and framed so that they do not need long hours of steady and uninterrupted work. For interruptions there will always be. Again, the nerves that feed the brain would seem to differ in men and women, and if you are going to make them work their best and hardest, you must find out what treatment suits them—whether these hours of lectures, for instance, which the monks devised, pre-sumably, hundreds of years ago, suit them—what alternations of work and rest they need, interpreting rest not as doing nothing but as doing something but something that is different; and what should that difference be? All this should be discussed and discovered; all this is part of the question of women and fiction. And yet, I continued, approaching the bookcase again, where shall I find that elaborate study of the psychology of women by a woman? If through their incapacity to play football women are not going to be allowed to practise medicine——

Happily my thoughts were now given another turn.

Chapter Five

I had come at last, in the course of this rambling, to the shelves which hold books by the living; by women and by men; for there are almost as many books written by women now as by men. Or if that is not yet quite true, if the male is still the voluble sex, it is certainly true that women no longer write novels solely. There are Jane Harrison's books on Greek archaeology; Vernon Lee's books on aesthetics; Gertrude Bell's[3] books on Persia. There are books on all

3. English archaeologist and writer (1868–1926). Harrison (1850–1928), scholar and lecturer at Cam-bridge. Lee (1856–1935), essayist and art critic.

sorts of subjects which a generation ago no woman could have touched. There are poems and plays and criticism; there are histories and biographies, books of travel and books of scholarship and research; there are even a few philosophies and books about science and economics. And though novels predominate, novels themselves may very well have changed from association with books of a different feather. The natural simplicity, the epic age of women's writing, may have gone. Reading and criticism may have given her a wider range, a greater subtlety. The impulse towards autobiography may be spent. She may be beginning to use writing as an art, not as a method of self-expression. Among these new novels one might find an answer to several such questions.

I took down one of them at random. It stood at the very end of the shelf, was called *Life's Adventure,* or some such title, by Mary Carmichael,[4] and was published in this very month of October. It seems to be her first book, I said to myself, but one must read it as if it were the last volume in a fairly long series, continuing all those other books that I have been glancing at—Lady Winchilsea's poems and Aphra Behn's plays and the novels of the four great novelists. For books continue each other, in spite of our habit of judging them separately. And I must also consider her—this unknown woman—as the descendant of all those other women whose circumstances I have been glancing at and see what she inherits of their characteristics and restrictions. So, with a sigh, because novels so often provide an anodyne and not an antidote, glide one into torpid slumbers instead of rousing one with a burning brand, I settled down with a notebook and a pencil to make what I could of Mary Carmichael's first novel, *Life's Adventure.*

To begin with, I ran my eye up and down the page. I am going to get the hang of her sentences first, I said, before I load my memory with blue eyes and brown and the relationship that there may be between Chloe and Roger. There will be time for that when I have decided whether she has a pen in her hand or a pickaxe. So I tried a sentence or two on my tongue. Soon it was obvious that something was not quite in order. The smooth gliding of sentence after sentence was interrupted. Something tore, something scratched; a single word here and there flashed its torch in my eyes. She was "unhanding" herself as they say in the old plays. She is like a person striking a match that will not light, I thought. But why, I asked her as if she were present, are Jane Austen's sentences not of the right shape for you? Must they all be scrapped because Emma and Mr Woodhouse are dead? Alas, I sighed, that it should be so. For while Jane Austen breaks from melody to melody as Mozart from song to song, to read this writing was like being out at sea in an open boat. Up one went, down one sank. This terseness, this shortwindedness, might mean that she was afraid of something; afraid of being called "sentimental" perhaps; or she remembers that women's writing has been called flowery and so provides a superfluity of thorns; but until I have read a scene with some care, I cannot be sure whether she is being herself or some one else. At any rate, she does not lower one's vitality, I thought, reading more carefully. But she is heaping up too many facts. She will not be able to use half of them in a book of this size. (It was about half the length of *Jane Eyre.*) However, by some means or other she succeeded in getting us all—Roger, Chloe, Olivia, Tony and Mr

4. The novel *Love's Creation* was published in London in 1928 under the name Marie Carmichael, the pseudonym for Marie Stopes, a crusader for birth control. The plot and characters resemble those mentioned by Woolf.

Bigham—in a canoe up the river. Wait a moment, I said, leaning back in my chair, I must consider the whole thing more carefully before I go any further.

I am almost sure, I said to myself, that Mary Carmichael is playing a trick on us. For I feel as one feels on a switchback railway when the car, instead of sinking, as one has been led to expect, swerves up again. Mary is tampering with the expected sequence. First she broke the sentence; now she has broken the sequence. Very well, she has every right to do both these things if she does them not for the sake of breaking, but for the sake of creating. Which of the two it is I cannot be sure until she has faced herself with a situation. I will give her every liberty, I said, to choose what that situation shall be; she shall make it of tin cans and old kettles if she likes; but she must convince me that she believes it to be a situation; and then when she has made it she must face it. She must jump. And, determined to do my duty by her as reader if she would do her duty by me as writer, I turned the page and read . . . I am sorry to break off so abruptly. Are there no men present? Do you promise me that behind that red curtain over there the figure of Sir Chartres Biron[5] is not concealed? We are all women, you assure me? Then I may tell you that the very next words I read were these—"Chloe liked Olivia . . ." Do not start. Do not blush. Let us admit in the privacy of our own society that these things sometimes happen. Sometimes women do like women.

"Chloe liked Olivia," I read. And then it struck me how immense a change was there. Chloe liked Olivia perhaps for the first time in literature. Cleopatra did not like Octavia. And how completely *Antony and Cleopatra* would have been altered had she done so! As it is, I thought, letting my mind, I am afraid, wander a little from *Life's Adventure*, the whole thing is simplified, conventionalised, if one dared say it, absurdly. Cleopatra's only feeling about Octavia is one of jealousy. Is she taller than I am? How does she do her hair? The play, perhaps, required no more. But how interesting it would have been if the relationship between the two women had been more complicated. All these relationships between women, I thought, rapidly recalling the splendid gallery of fictitious women, are too simple. So much has been left out, unattempted. And I tried to remember any case in the course of my reading where two women are represented as friends. There is an attempt at it in *Diana of the Crossways*. They are confidantes, of course, in Racine[6] and the Greek tragedies. They are now and then mothers and daughters. But almost without exception they are shown in their relation to men. It was strange to think that all the great women of fiction were, until Jane Austen's day, not only seen by the other sex, but seen only in relation to the other sex. And how small a part of a woman's life is that; and how little can a man know even of that when he observes it through the black or rosy spectacles which sex puts upon his nose. Hence, perhaps, the peculiar nature of woman in fiction; the astonishing extremes of her beauty and horror; her alternations between heavenly goodness and hellish depravity—for so a lover would see her as his love rose or sank, was prosperous or unhappy. This is not so true of the nineteenth-century novelists, of course. Woman becomes much more various and complicated there. Indeed it was the desire to write about women perhaps that led men by degrees to abandon the poetic drama which, with its violence, could make so

5. Chief magistrate of London who in 1928 judged that the novel *The Well of Loneliness*, by the lesbian writer Radclyffe Hall, was an "obscene libel" and ordered all copies destroyed.

6. Jean Racine (1639–1699), French dramatist. "*Diana of the Crossways*": 1885 novel by the English author George Meredith (1828–1909).

little use of them, and to devise the novel as a more fitting receptacle. Even so it remains obvious, even in the writing of Proust,[7] that a man is terribly hampered and partial in his knowledge of women, as a woman in her knowledge of men.

Also, I continued, looking down at the page again, it is becoming evident that women, like men, have other interests besides the perennial interests of domesticity. "Chloe liked Olivia. They shared a laboratory together. . . ." I read on and discovered that these two young women were engaged in mincing liver, which is, it seems, a cure for pernicious anaemia: although one of them was married and had—I think I am right in stating—two small children. Now all that, of course, has had to be left out, and thus the splendid portrait of the fictitious woman is much too simple and much too monotonous. Suppose, for instance, that men were only represented in literature as the lovers of women, and were never the friends of men, soldiers, thinkers, dreamers; how few parts in the plays of Shakespeare could be allotted to them; how literature would suffer! We might perhaps have most of Othello; and a good deal of Antony; but no Caesar, no Brutus, no Hamlet, no Lear, no Jaques—literature would be incredibly impoverished, as indeed literature is impoverished beyond our counting by the doors that have been shut upon women. Married against their will, kept in one room, and to one occupation, how could a dramatist give a full or interesting or truthful account of them? Love was the only possible interpreter. The poet was forced to be passionate or bitter, unless indeed he chose to "hate women," which meant more often than not that he was unattractive to them.

Now if Chloe likes Olivia and they share a laboratory, which of itself will make their friendship more varied and lasting because it will be less personal; if Mary Carmichael knows how to write, and I was beginning to enjoy some quality in her style; if she has a room to herself, of which I am not quite sure; if she has five hundred a year of her own—but that remains to be proved— then I think that something of great importance has happened.

For if Chloe likes Olivia and Mary Carmichael knows how to express it she will light a torch in that vast chamber where nobody has yet been. It is all half lights and profound shadows like those serpentine caves where one goes with a candle peering up and down, not knowing where one is stepping. And I began to read the book again, and read how Chloe watched Olivia put a jar on a shelf and say how it was time to go home to her children. That is a sight that has never been seen since the world began, I exclaimed. And I watched too, very curiously. For I wanted to see how Mary Carmichael set to work to catch those unrecorded gestures, those unsaid or half-said words, which form themselves, no more palpably than the shadows of moths on the ceiling, when women are alone, unlit by the capricious and coloured light of the other sex. She will need to hold her breath, I said, reading on, if she is to do it; for women are so suspicious of any interest that has not some obvious motive behind it, so terribly accustomed to concealment and suppression, that they are off at the flicker of an eye turned observingly in their direction. The only way for you to do it, I thought, addressing Mary Carmichael as if she were there, would be to talk of something else, looking steadily out of the window, and thus note, not with a pencil in a notebook, but in the shortest of shorthand, in words

---

7. Marcel Proust (1871–1922), French novelist and author of the seven-volume *A la Recherche du Temps Perdu* (1913–27).

that are hardly syllabled yet, what happens when Olivia—this organism that has been under the shadow of the rock these million years—feels the light fall on it, and sees coming her way a piece of strange food—knowledge, adventure, art. And she reaches out for it, I thought, again raising my eyes from the page, and has to devise some entirely new combination of her resources, so highly developed for their purposes, so as to absorb the new into the old without disturbing the infinitely intricate and elaborate balance of the whole.

But, alas, I had done what I had determined not to do; I had slipped unthinkingly into praise of my own sex. "Highly developed"—"infinitely intricate"—such are undeniably terms of praise, and to praise one's own sex is always suspect, often silly; moreover, in this case, how could one justify it? One could not go to the map and say Columbus discovered America and Columbus was a woman; or take an apple and remark, Newton discovered the laws of gravitation and Newton was a woman; or look into the sky and say aeroplanes are flying overhead and aeroplanes were invented by women. There is no mark on the wall to measure the precise height of women. There are no yard measures, neatly divided into the fractions of an inch, that one can lay against the qualities of a good mother or the devotion of a daughter, or the fidelity of a sister, or the capacity of a housekeeper. Few women even now have been graded at the universities; the great trials of the professions, army and navy, trade, politics and diplomacy have hardly tested them. They remain even at this moment almost unclassified. But if I want to know all that a human being can tell me about Sir Hawley Butts, for instance, I have only to open Burke or Debrett[8] and I shall find that he took such and such a degree; owns a hall; has an heir; was Secretary to a Board; represented Great Britain in Canada; and has received a certain number of degrees, offices, medals and other distinctions by which his merits are stamped upon him indelibly. Only Providence can know more about Sir Hawley Butts than that.

When, therefore, I say "highly developed," "infinitely intricate," of women, I am unable to verify my words either in Whitaker, Debrett or the University Calendar. In this predicament what can I do? And I looked at the bookcase again. There were the biographies: Johnson and Goethe and Carlyle and Sterne and Cowper and Shelley and Voltaire and Browning and many others. And I began thinking of all those great men who have for one reason or another admired, sought out, lived with, confided in, made love to, written of, trusted in, and shown what can only be described as some need of and dependence upon certain persons of the opposite sex. That all these relationships were absolutely Platonic I would not affirm, and Sir William Joynson Hicks[9] would probably deny. But we should wrong these illustrious men very greatly if we insisted that they got nothing from these alliances but comfort, flattery and the pleasures of the body. What they got, it is obvious, was something that their own sex was unable to supply; and it would not be rash, perhaps, to define it further, without quoting the doubtless rhapsodical words of the poets, as some stimulus, some renewal of creative power which is in the gift only of the opposite sex to bestow. He would open the door of drawing-room or nursery, I thought, and find her among her children perhaps, or with a piece of embroidery on her knee—at any rate, the centre of some different order and

8. Annual reference works of genealogy and the peerage. Sir Hawley Butts, however, seems to be Woolf's invention.

9. English Conservative politician and evangelical religious figure (1865–1932).

system of life, and the contrast between this world and his own, which might be the law courts or the House of Commons, would at once refresh and invigorate; and there would follow, even in the simplest talk, such a natural difference of opinion that the dried ideas in him would be fertilised anew; and the sight of her creating in a different medium from his own would so quicken his creative power that insensibly his sterile mind would begin to plot again, and he would find the phrase or the scene which was lacking when he put on his hat to visit her. Every Johnson has his Thrale,[1] and holds fast to her for some such reasons as these, and when the Thrale marries her Italian music master Johnson goes half mad with rage and disgust, not merely that he will miss his pleasant evenings at Streatham, but that the light of his life will be "as if gone out."

And without being Dr Johnson or Goethe or Carlyle or Voltaire, one may feel, though very differently from these great men, the nature of this intricacy and the power of this highly developed creative faculty among women. One goes into the room—but the resources of the English language would be much put to the stretch, and whole flights of words would need to wing their way illegitimately into existence before a woman could say what happens when she goes into a room. The rooms differ so completely; they are calm or thunderous; open on to the sea, or, on the contrary, give on to a prison yard; are hung with washing; or alive with opals and silks; are hard as horsehair or soft as feathers—one has only to go into any room in any street for the whole of that extremely complex force of femininity to fly in one's face. How should it be otherwise? For women have sat indoors all these millions of years, so that by this time the very walls are permeated by their creative force, which has, indeed, so overcharged the capacity of bricks and mortar that it must needs harness itself to pens and brushes and business and politics. But this creative power differs greatly from the creative power of men. And one must conclude that it would be a thousand pities if it were hindered or wasted, for it was won by centuries of the most drastic discipline, and there is nothing to take its place. It would be a thousand pities if women wrote like men, or lived like men, or looked like men, for if two sexes are quite inadequate, considering the vastness and variety of the world, how should we manage with one only? Ought not education to bring out and fortify the differences rather than the similarities? For we have too much likeness as it is, and if an explorer should come back and bring word of other sexes looking through the branches of other trees at other skies, nothing would be of greater service to humanity; and we should have the immense pleasure into the bargain of watching Professor X rush for his measuring-rods to prove himself "superior."

Mary Carmichael, I thought, still hovering at a little distance above the page, will have her work cut out for her merely as an observer. I am afraid indeed that she will be tempted to become, what I think the less interesting branch of the species—the naturalist-novelist, and not the contemplative. There are so many new facts for her to observe. She will not need to limit herself any longer to the respectable houses of the upper middle classes. She will go without kindness or condescension, but in the spirit of fellowship into those small, scented rooms where sit the courtesan, the harlot and the lady with the pug

---

1. Hester Lynch Thrale (1741–1821), who with her husband, Henry, was for many years friend and hostess to Samuel Johnson at their home in Streatham Place. After Henry's death she married an Italian musician, much to Johnson's distress; his reaction helped end their friendship.

dog. There they still sit in the rough and ready-made clothes that the male writer has had perforce to clap upon their shoulders. But Mary Carmichael will have out her scissors and fit them close to every hollow and angle. It will be a curious sight, when it comes, to see these women as they are, but we must wait a little, for Mary Carmichael will still be encumbered with that self-consciousness in the presence of "sin" which is the legacy of our sexual barbarity. She will still wear the shoddy old fetters of class on her feet.

However, the majority of women are neither harlots nor courtesans; nor do they sit clasping pug dogs to dusty velvet all through the summer afternoon. But what do they do then? and there came to my mind's eye one of those long streets somewhere south of the river whose infinite rows are innumerably populated. With the eye of the imagination I saw a very ancient lady crossing the street on the arm of a middle-aged woman, her daughter, perhaps, both so respectably booted and furred that their dressing in the afternoon must be a ritual, and the clothes themselves put away in cupboards with camphor, year after year, throughout the summer months. They cross the road when the lamps are being lit (for the dusk is their favourite hour), as they must have done year after year. The elder is close on eighty; but if one asked her what her life has meant to her, she would say that she remembered the streets lit for the battle of Balaclava, or had heard the guns fire in Hyde Park for the birth of King Edward the Seventh.[2] And if one asked her, longing to pin down the moment with date and season, but what were you doing on the fifth of April 1868, or the second of November 1875, she would look vague and say that she could remember nothing. For all the dinners are cooked; the plates and cups washed; the children set to school and gone out into the world. Nothing remains of it all. All has vanished. No biography or history has a word to say about it. And the novels, without meaning to, inevitably lie.

All these infinitely obscure lives remain to be recorded, I said, addressing Mary Carmichael as if she were present; and went on in thought through the streets of London feeling in imagination the pressure of dumbness, the accumulation of unrecorded life, whether from the women at the street corners with their arms akimbo, and the rings embedded in their fat swollen fingers, talking with a gesticulation like the swing of Shakespeare's words; or from the violet-sellers and match-sellers and old crones stationed under doorways; or from drifting girls whose faces, like waves in sun and cloud, signal the coming of men and women and the flickering lights of shop windows. All that you will have to explore, I said to Mary Carmichael, holding your torch firm in your hand. Above all, you must illumine your own soul with its profundities and its shallows, and its vanities and its generosities, and say what your beauty means to you or your plainness, and what is your relation to the everchanging and turning world of gloves and shoes and stuffs swaying up and down among the faint scents that come through chemists' bottles down arcades of dress material over a floor of pseudo-marble. For in imagination I had gone into a shop; it was laid with black and white paving; it was hung, astonishingly beautifully, with coloured ribbons. Mary Carmichael might well have a look at that in passing, I thought, for it is a sight that would lend itself to the pen as fittingly as any snowy peak or rocky gorge in the Andes. And there is the girl behind

---

2. In 1841 (since Woolf is writing in 1928, Edward's birth would actually have been before the birth of a woman "close on eighty"). The "battle of Balaclava," famous for the Charge of the Light Brigade, occurred in 1854.

2482 / Virginia Woolf

the counter too—I would as soon have her true history as the hundred and fiftieth life of Napoleon or seventieth study of Keats and his use of Miltonic inversion which old Professor Z and his like are now inditing. And then I went on very warily, on the very tips of my toes (so cowardly am I, so afraid of the lash that was once almost laid on my own shoulders), to murmur that she should also learn to laugh, without bitterness, at the vanities—say rather at the peculiarities, for it is a less offensive word—of the other sex. For there is a spot the size of a shilling at the back of the head which one can never see for oneself. It is one of the good offices that sex can discharge for sex—to describe that spot the size of a shilling at the back of the head. Think how much women have profited by the comments of Juvenal; by the criticism of Strindberg.[3] Think with what humanity and brilliancy men, from the earliest ages, have pointed out to women that dark place at the back of the head! And if Mary were very brave and very honest, she would go behind the other sex and tell us what she found there. A true picture of man as a whole can never be painted until a woman has described that spot the size of a shilling. Mr Woodhouse and Mr Casaubon[4] are spots of that size and nature. Not of course that any one in their senses would counsel her to hold up to scorn and ridicule of set purpose—literature shows the futility of what is written in that spirit. Be truthful, one would say, and the result is bound to be amazingly interesting. Comedy is bound to be enriched. New facts are bound to be discovered.

However, it was high time to lower my eyes to the page again. It would be better, instead of speculating what Mary Carmichael might write and should write, to see what in fact Mary Carmichael did write. So I began to read again. I remembered that I had certain grievances against her. She had broken up Jane Austen's sentence, and thus given me no chance of pluming myself upon my impeccable taste, my fastidious ear. For it was useless to say, "Yes, yes, this is very nice; but Jane Austen wrote much better than you do," when I had to admit that there was no point of likeness between them. Then she had gone further and broken the sequence—the expected order. Perhaps she had done this unconsciously, merely giving things their natural order, as a woman would, if she wrote like a woman. But the effect was somehow baffling; one could not see a wave heaping itself, a crisis coming round the next corner. Therefore I could not plume myself either upon the depths of my feelings and my profound knowledge of the human heart. For whenever I was about to feel the usual things in the usual places, about love, about death, the annoying creature twitched me away, as if the important point were just a little further on. And thus she made it impossible for me to roll out my sonorous phrases about "elemental feelings," the "common stuff of humanity," "depths of the human heart," and all those other phrases which support us in our belief that, however clever we may be on top, we are very serious, very profound and very humane underneath. She made me feel, on the contrary, that instead of being serious and profound and humane, one might be—and the thought was far less seductive—merely lazy minded and conventional into the bargain.

But I read on, and noted certain other facts. She was no "genius"—that was evident. She had nothing like the love of Nature, the fiery imagination, the wild poetry, the brilliant wit, the brooding wisdom of her great predecessors,

3. August Strindberg (1849–1912), Swedish playwright. Juvenal (55 to 60–ca. 127), Roman satirist.
4. The husband of the heroine in George Eliot's *Middlemarch*. Woodhouse is the father of the heroine in Jane Austen's *Emma*.

Lady Winchilsea, Charlotte Brontë, Jane Austen and George Eliot; she could not write with the melody and the dignity of Dorothy Osborne—indeed she was no more than a clever girl whose books will no doubt be pulped by the publishers in ten years' time. But, nevertheless, she had certain advantages which women of far greater gift lacked even half a century ago. Men were no longer to her "the opposing faction"; she need not waste her time railing against them; she need not climb on to the roof and ruin her peace of mind longing for travel, experience and a knowledge of the world and character that were denied her. Fear and hatred were almost gone, or traces of them showed only in a slight exaggeration of the joy of freedom, a tendency to the caustic and satirical, rather than to the romantic, in her treatment of the other sex. Then there could be no doubt that as a novelist she enjoyed some natural advantages of a high order. She had a sensibility that was very wide, eager and free. It responded to an almost imperceptible touch on it. It feasted like a plant newly stood in the air on every sight and sound that came its way. It ranged, too, very subtly and curiously, among almost unknown or unrecorded things; it lighted on small things and showed that perhaps they were not small after all. It brought buried things to light and made one wonder what need there had been to bury them. Awkward though she was and without the unconscious bearing of long descent which makes the least turn of the pen of a Thackeray or a Lamb delightful to the ear, she had—I began to think—mastered the first great lesson; she wrote as a woman, but as a woman who has forgotten that she is a woman, so that her pages were full of that curious sexual quality which comes only when sex is unconscious of itself.

All this was to the good. But no abundance of sensation or fineness of perception would avail unless she could build up out of the fleeting and the personal the lasting edifice which remains unthrown. I had said that I would wait until she faced herself with "a situation." And I meant by that until she proved by summoning, beckoning and getting together that she was not a skimmer of surfaces merely, but had looked beneath into the depths. Now is the time, she would say to herself at a certain moment, when without doing anything violent I can show the meaning of all this. And she would begin— how unmistakable that quickening is!—beckoning and summoning, and there would rise up in memory, half forgotten, perhaps quite trivial things in other chapters dropped by the way. And she would make their presence felt while some one sewed or smoked a pipe as naturally as possible, and one would feel, as she went on writing, as if one had gone to the top of the world and seen it laid out, very majestically, beneath.

At any rate, she was making the attempt. And as I watched her lengthening out for the test, I saw, but hoped that she did not see, the bishops and the deans, the doctors and the professors, the patriarchs and the pedagogues all at her shouting warning and advice. You can't do this and you shan't do that! Fellows and scholars only allowed on the grass! Ladies not admitted without a letter of introduction! Aspiring and graceful female novelists this way! So they kept at her like the crowd at a fence on the race-course, and it was her trial to take her fence without looking to right or left. If you stop to curse you are lost, I said to her; equally, if you stop to laugh. Hesitate or fumble and you are done for. Think only of the jump, I implored her, as if I had put the whole of my money on her back; and she went over it like a bird. But there was a fence beyond that and a fence beyond that. Whether she had the staying power I was doubtful, for the clapping and the crying were fraying to the nerves. But she did her best. Considering that Mary Carmichael was no genius, but an unknown girl writing her first novel in a bed-sitting-room, without enough of those desirable things, time, money and idleness, she did not do so badly, I thought.

Give her another hundred years, I concluded, reading the last chapter—people's noses and bare shoulders showed naked against a starry sky, for some one had twitched the curtain in the drawing-room—give her a room of her own and five hundred a year, let her speak her mind and leave out half that she now puts in, and she will write a better book one of these days. She will be a poet, I said, putting *Life's Adventure,* by Mary Carmichael, at the end of the shelf, in another hundred years' time.

Chapter Six

Next day the light of the October morning was falling in dusty shafts through the uncurtained windows, and the hum of traffic rose from the street. London then was winding itself up again; the factory was astir; the machines were beginning. It was tempting, after all this reading, to look out of the window and see what London was doing on the morning of the twenty-sixth of October 1928. And what was London doing? Nobody, it seemed, was reading *Antony and Cleopatra.* London was wholly indifferent, it appeared, to Shakespeare's plays. Nobody cared a straw—and I do not blame them—for the future of fiction, the death of poetry or the development by the average woman of a prose style completely expressive of her mind. If opinions upon any of these matters had been chalked on the pavement, nobody would have stooped to read them. The nonchalance of the hurrying feet would have rubbed them out in half an hour. Here came an errand-boy; here a woman with a dog on a lead. The fascination of the London street is that no two people are ever alike; each seems bound on some private affair of his own. There were the business-like, with their little bags; there were the drifters rattling sticks upon area railings; there were affable characters to whom the streets serve for clubroom, hailing men in carts and giving information without being asked for it. Also there were funerals to which men, thus suddenly reminded of the passing of their own bodies, lifted their hats. And then a very distinguished gentleman came slowly down a doorstep and paused to avoid collision with a bustling lady who had, by some means or other, acquired a splendid fur coat and a bunch of Parma violets. They all seemed separate, self-absorbed, on business of their own.

At this moment, as so often happens in London, there was a complete lull and suspension of traffic. Nothing came down the street; nobody passed. A single leaf detached itself from the plane tree at the end of the street, and in that pause and suspension fell. Somehow it was like a signal falling, a signal pointing to a force in things which one had overlooked. It seemed to point to a river, which flowed past, invisibly, round the corner, down the street, and took people and eddied them along, as the stream at Oxbridge had taken the undergraduate in his boat and the dead leaves. Now it was bringing from one side of the street to the other diagonally a girl in patent leather boots, and then a young man in a maroon overcoat; it was also bringing a taxi-cab; and it brought all three together at a point directly beneath my window; where the taxi stopped; and the girl and the young man stopped; and they got into the taxi; and then the cab glided off as if it were swept on by the current elsewhere.

The sight was ordinary enough; what was strange was the rhythmical order with which my imagination had invested it; and the fact that the ordinary sight of two people getting into a cab had the power to communicate something of their own seeming satisfaction. The sight of two people coming down the street and meeting at the corner seems to ease the mind of some strain, I thought, watching the taxi turn and make off. Perhaps to think, as I had been thinking these two days, of one sex as distinct from the other is an effort. It interferes with the unity of the mind. Now that effort had ceased and that unity had been restored by seeing two people come together and get into a taxi-cab. The mind is certainly a very mysterious organ, I reflected, drawing my head in from the window, about which nothing whatever is known, though we depend upon it so completely. Why do I feel that there are severances and oppositions in the mind, as there are strains from obvious causes on the body? What does one mean by "the unity of the mind," I pondered, for clearly the mind has so great a power of concentrating at any point at any moment that it seems to have no single state of being. It can separate itself from the people in the street, for example, and think of itself as apart from them, at an upper window looking down on them. Or it can think with other people spontaneously, as, for instance, in a crowd waiting to hear some piece of news read out. It can think back through its fathers or through its mothers, as I have said that a woman writing thinks back through her mothers. Again if one is a woman one is often surprised by a sudden splitting off of consciousness, say in walking down Whitehall,[5] when from being the natural inheritor of that civilisation, she becomes, on the contrary, outside of it, alien and critical. Clearly the mind is always altering its focus, and bringing the world into different perspectives. But some of these states of mind seem, even if adopted spontaneously, to be less comfortable than others. In order to keep oneself continuing in them one is unconsciously holding something back, and gradually the repression becomes an effort. But there may be some state of mind in which one could continue without effort because nothing is required to be held back. And this perhaps, I thought, coming in from the window, is one of them. For certainly when I saw the couple get into the taxi-cab the mind felt as if, after being divided, it had come together again in a natural fusion. The obvious reason would be that it is natural for the sexes to co-operate. One has a profound, if irrational, instinct in favour of the theory that the union of man and woman makes for the greatest satisfaction, the most complete happiness. But the sight of the two people getting into the taxi and the satisfaction it gave me made me also ask whether there are two sexes in the mind corresponding to the two sexes in the body, and whether they also require to be united in order to get complete satisfaction and happiness. And I went on amateurishly to sketch a plan of the soul so that in each of us two powers preside, one male, one female; and in the man's brain, the man predominates over the woman, and in the woman's brain, the woman predominates over the man. The normal and comfortable state of being is that when the two live in harmony together, spiritually cooperating. If one is a man, still the woman part of the brain must have effect; and a woman also must have intercourse with the man in her. Coleridge perhaps meant this when he said that a great mind is androgynous. It is when this fusion takes place that the mind is fully fertilised and uses all its faculties. Perhaps a mind that is purely masculine cannot create, any more than a mind that is purely feminine, I thought. But it would be well to test what one meant

5. London thoroughfare along which are located the chief offices of the British government.

by man-womanly, and conversely by woman-manly, by pausing and looking at a book or two.

Coleridge certainly did not mean, when he said that a great mind is androgynous, that it is a mind that has any special sympathy with women; a mind that takes up their cause or devotes itself to their interpretation. Perhaps the androgynous mind is less apt to make these distinctions than the single-sexed mind. He meant, perhaps, that the androgynous mind is resonant and porous; that it transmits emotion without impediment; that it is naturally creative, incandescent and undivided. In fact one goes back to Shakespeare's mind as the type of the androgynous, of the man-womanly mind, though it would be impossible to say what Shakespeare thought of women. And if it be true that it is one of the tokens of the fully developed mind that it does not think specially or separately of sex, how much harder it is to attain that condition now than ever before. Here I came to the books by living writers, and there paused and wondered if this fact were not at the root of something that had long puzzled me. No age can ever have been as stridently sex-conscious as our own; those innumerable books by men about women in the British Museum are a proof of it. The Suffrage campaign[6] was no doubt to blame. It must have roused in men an extraordinary desire for self-assertion; it must have made them lay an emphasis upon their own sex and its characteristics which they would not have troubled to think about had they not been challenged. And when one is challenged, even by a few women in black bonnets, one retaliates, if one has never been challenged before, rather excessively. That perhaps accounts for some of the characteristics that I remember to have found here, I thought, taking down a new novel by Mr A, who is in the prime of life and very well thought of, apparently, by the reviewers. I opened it. Indeed, it was delightful to read a man's writing again. It was so direct, so straightforward after the writing of women. It indicated such freedom of mind, such liberty of person, such confidence in himself. One had a sense of physical well-being in the presence of this well-nourished, well-educated, free mind, which had never been thwarted or opposed, but had had full liberty from birth to stretch itself in whatever way it liked. All this was admirable. But after reading a chapter or two a shadow seemed to lie across the page. It was a straight dark bar, a shadow shaped something like the letter "I." One began dodging this way and that to catch a glimpse of the landscape behind it. Whether that was indeed a tree or a woman walking I was not quite sure. Back one was always hailed to the letter "I." One began to be tired of "I." Not but what this "I" was a most respectable "I"; honest and logical; as hard as a nut, and polished for centuries by good teaching and good feeding. I respect and admire that "I" from the bottom of my heart. But—here I turned a page or two, looking for something or other—the worst of it is that in the shadow of the letter "I" all is shapeless as mist. Is that a tree? No, it is a woman. But . . . she has not a bone in her body, I thought, watching Phoebe, for that was her name, coming across the beach. Then Alan got up and the shadow of Alan at once obliterated Phoebe. For Alan had views and Phoebe was quenched in the flood of his views. And then Alan, I thought, had passions; and here I turned page after page very fast, feeling that the crisis was approaching, and so it was. It took place on the beach under the sun. It was done very openly. It was done very vigorously. Nothing could have been more indecent. But . . . I had said "but"

6. Movement of the 19th and early-20th centuries seeking the right for women to vote.

too often. One cannot go on saying "but." One must finish the sentence somehow, I rebuked myself. Shall I finish it, "But—I am bored!" But why was I
bored? Partly because of the dominance of the letter "I" and the aridity, which,
like the giant beech tree, it casts within its shade. Nothing will grow there.
And partly for some more obscure reason. There seemed to be some obstacle,
some impediment of Mr A's mind which blocked the fountain of creative
energy and shored it within narrow limits. And remembering the lunch party
at Oxbridge, and the cigarette ash and the Manx cat and Tennyson and Christina Rossetti all in a bunch, it seemed possible that the impediment lay there.
As he no longer hums under his breath, "There has fallen a splendid tear from
the passion-flower at the gate," when Phoebe crosses the beach, and she no
longer replies, "My heart is like a singing bird whose nest is in a water'd shoot,"
when Alan approaches what can he do? Being honest as the day and logical
as the sun, there is only one thing he can do. And that he does, to do him
justice, over and over (I said, turning the pages) and over again. And that, I
added, aware of the awful nature of the confession, seems somehow dull.
Shakespeare's indecency uproots a thousand other things in one's mind, and
is far from being dull. But Shakespeare does it for pleasure; Mr A, as the nurses
say, does it on purpose. He does it in protest. He is protesting against the
equality of the other sex by asserting his own superiority. He is therefore
impeded and inhibited and self-conscious as Shakespeare might have been if
he too had known Miss Clough[7] and Miss Davies. Doubtless Elizabethan literature would have been very different from what it is if the woman's movement had begun in the sixteenth century and not in the nineteenth.

What, then, it amounts to, if this theory of the two sides of the mind holds
good, is that virility has now become self-conscious—men, that is to say, are
now writing only with the male side of their brains. It is a mistake for a woman
to read them, for she will inevitably look for something that she will not find.
It is the power of suggestion that one most misses, I thought, taking Mr B the
critic in my hand and reading, very carefully and very dutifully, his remarks
upon the art of poetry. Very able they were, acute and full of learning; but the
trouble was, that his feelings no longer communicated; his mind seemed separated into different chambers; not a sound carried from one to the other.
Thus, when one takes a sentence of Mr B into the mind it falls plump to the
ground—dead; but when one takes a sentence of Coleridge into the mind, it
explodes and gives birth to all kinds of other ideas, and that is the only sort of
writing of which one can say that it has the secret of perpetual life.

But whatever the reason may be, it is a fact that one must deplore. For it
means—here I had come to rows of books by Mr Galsworthy and Mr Kipling[8]
—that some of the finest works of our greatest living writers fall upon deaf
ears. Do what she will a woman cannot find in them that fountain of perpetual
life which the critics assure her is there. It is not only that they celebrate male
virtues, enforce male values and describe the world of men; it is that the
emotion with which these books are permeated is to a woman incomprehensible. It is coming, it is gathering, it is about to burst on one's head, one begins
saying long before the end. That picture will fall on old Jolyon's head;[9] he will
die of the shock; the old clerk will speak over him two or three obituary words;

7. Anne Jemima Clough (1820–1892), first principal of Newnham College, Cambridge, and advocate for women's suffrage and higher education.
8. John Galsworthy (1867–1933) and Rudyard

Kipling (1865–1936), English novelists.
9. A reference to an event in John Galsworthy's
popular fictional series *The Forsyte Saga* (1922).

and all the swans on the Thames will simultaneously burst out singing. But one will rush away before that happens and hide in the gooseberry bushes, for the emotion which is so deep, so subtle, so symbolical to a man moves a woman to wonder. So with Mr Kipling's officers who turn their backs; and his Sowers who sow the Seed; and his Men who are alone with their Work; and the Flag—one blushes at all these capital letters as if one had been caught eavesdropping at some purely masculine orgy. The fact is that neither Mr Galsworthy nor Mr Kipling has a spark of the woman in him. Thus all their qualities seem to a woman, if one may generalise, crude and immature. They lack suggestive power. And when a book lacks suggestive power, however hard it hits the surface of the mind it cannot penetrate within.

And in that restless mood in which one takes books out and puts them back again without looking at them I began to envisage an age to come of pure, of self-assertive virility, such as the letters of professors (take Sir Walter Raleigh's letters, for instance) seem to forebode, and the rulers of Italy have already brought into being. For one can hardly fail to be impressed in Rome by the sense of unmitigated masculinity; and whatever the value of unmitigated masculinity upon the state, one may question the effect of it upon the art of poetry. At any rate, according to the newspapers, there is a certain anxiety about fiction in Italy. There has been a meeting of academicians whose object it is "to develop the Italian novel." "Men famous by birth, or in finance, industry or the Fascist corporations" came together the other day and discussed the matter, and a telegram was sent to the Duce[1] expressing the hope "that the Fascist era would soon give birth to a poet worthy of it." We may all join in that pious hope, but it is doubtful whether poetry can come out of an incubator. Poetry ought to have a mother as well as a father. The Fascist poem, one may fear, will be a horrid little abortion such as one sees in a glass jar in the museum of some county town. Such monsters never live long, it is said; one has never seen a prodigy of that sort cropping grass in a field. Two heads on one body do not make for length of life.

However, the blame for all this, if one is anxious to lay blame, rests no more upon one sex than upon the other. All seducers and reformers are responsible, Lady Bessborough when she lied to Lord Granville; Miss Davies when she told the truth to Mr Greg. All who have brought about a state of sex-consciousness are to blame, and it is they who drive me, when I want to stretch my faculties on a book, to seek it in that happy age, before Miss Davies and Miss Clough were born, when the writer used both sides of his mind equally. One must turn back to Shakespeare then, for Shakespeare was androgynous; and so was Keats and Sterne and Cowper and Lamb and Coleridge. Shelley perhaps was sexless. Milton and Ben Jonson had a dash too much of the male in them. So had Wordsworth and Tolstoi. In our time Proust was wholly androgynous, if not perhaps a little too much of a woman. But that failing is too rare for one to complain of it, since without some mixture of the kind the intellect seems to predominate and the other faculties of the mind harden and become barren. However, I consoled myself with the reflection that this is perhaps a passing phase; much of what I have said in obedience to my promise to give you the course of my thoughts will seem out of date; much of what flames in my eyes will seem dubious to you who have not yet come of age.

Even so, the very first sentence that I would write here, I said, crossing over

---

1. "The leader," i.e., Mussolini.

to the writing-table and taking up the page headed Women and Fiction, is that it is fatal for any one who writes to think of their sex. It is fatal to be a man or woman pure and simple; one must be woman-manly or man-womanly. It is fatal for a woman to lay the least stress on any grievance; to plead even with justice any cause; in any way to speak consciously as a woman. And fatal is no figure of speech; for anything written with that conscious bias is doomed to death. It ceases to be fertilised. Brilliant and effective, powerful and masterly, as it may appear for a day or two, it must wither at nightfall; it cannot grow in the minds of others. Some collaboration has to take place in the mind between the woman and the man before the act of creation can be accomplished. Some marriage of opposites has to be consummated. The whole of the mind must lie wide open if we are to get the sense that the writer is communicating his experience with perfect fullness. There must be freedom and there must be peace. Not a wheel must grate, not a light glimmer. The curtains must be close drawn. The writer, I thought, once his experience is over, must lie back and let his mind celebrate its nuptials in darkness. He must not look or question what is being done. Rather, he must pluck the petals from a rose or watch the swans float calmly down the river. And I saw again the current which took the boat and the undergraduate and the dead leaves; and the taxi took the man and the woman, I thought, seeing them come together across the street, and the current swept them away, I thought, hearing far off the roar of London's traffic, into that tremendous stream.

Here, then, Mary Beton ceases to speak. She has told you how she reached the conclusion—the prosaic conclusion—that it is necessary to have five hundred a year and a room with a lock on the door if you are to write fiction or poetry. She has tried to lay bare the thoughts and impressions that led her to think this. She has asked you to follow her flying into the arms of a Beadle, lunching here, dining there, drawing pictures in the British Museum, taking books from the shelf, looking out of the window. While she has been doing all these things, you no doubt have been observing her failings and foibles and deciding what effect they have had on her opinions. You have been contradicting her and making whatever additions and deductions seem good to you. That is all as it should be, for in a question like this truth is only to be had by laying together many varieties of error. And I will end now in my own person by anticipating two criticisms, so obvious that you can hardly fail to make them.

No opinion has been expressed, you may say, upon the comparative merits of the sexes even as writers. That was done purposely, because, even if the time had come for such a valuation—and it is far more important at the moment to know how much money women had and how many rooms than to theorise about their capacities—even if the time had come I do not believe that gifts, whether of mind or character, can be weighed like sugar and butter, not even in Cambridge, where they are so adept at putting people into classes and fixing caps on their heads and letters after their names. I do not believe that even the Table of Precedency which you will find in Whitaker's *Almanac* represents a final order of values, or that there is any sound reason to suppose that a Commander of the Bath will ultimately walk in to dinner behind a Master in Lunacy. All this pitting of sex against sex, of quality against quality; all this claiming of superiority and imputing of inferiority, belong to the private-school stage of human existence where there are "sides," and it is necessary for one side to beat another side, and of the utmost importance to walk up to a platform and receive from the hands of the Headmaster himself a highly ornamental pot. As people mature they cease to believe in sides or in Headmasters or in highly ornamental pots. At any rate, where books are concerned, it is notoriously difficult to fix labels of merit in such a way that they do not come off. Are not reviews of current literature a perpetual illustration of the difficulty of judgement? "This great book," "this worthless book," the same book is called by both names. Praise and blame alike mean nothing. No, delightful as the pastime of measuring may be, it is the most futile of all occupations, and to submit to the decrees of the measurers the most servile of attitudes. So long as you write what you wish to write, that is all that matters; and whether it matters for ages or only for hours, nobody can say. But to sacrifice a hair of the head of your vision, a shade of its colour, in deference to some Headmaster with a silver pot in his hand or to some professor with a measuring-rod up his sleeve, is the most abject treachery, and the sacrifice of wealth and chastity which used to be said to be the greatest of human disasters, a mere flea-bite in comparison.

Next I think that you may object that in all this I have made too much of the importance of material things. Even allowing a generous margin for symbolism, that five hundred a year stands for the power to contemplate, that a lock on the door means the power to think for oneself, still you may say that the mind should rise above such things; and that great poets have often been poor men. Let me then quote to you the words of your own Professor of Literature, who knows better than I do what goes to the making of a poet. Sir Arthur Quiller-Couch writes:[2]

"What are the great poetical names of the last hundred years or so? Coleridge, Wordsworth, Byron, Shelley, Landor, Keats, Tennyson, Browning, Arnold, Morris, Rossetti, Swinburne—we may stop there. Of these, all but Keats, Browning, Rossetti were University men; and of these three, Keats, who died young, cut off in his prime, was the only one not fairly well to do. It may seem a brutal thing to say, and it is a sad thing to say: but, as a matter of hard fact, the theory that poetical genius bloweth where it listeth, and equally in poor and rich, holds little truth. As a matter of hard fact, nine out of those twelve were University men: which means that somehow or other they procured the means to get the best education England can give. As a matter of hard fact, of the remaining three you know that Browning was well to do, and I challenge you that, if he had not been well to do, he would no more have attained to write *Saul* or *The Ring and the Book* than Ruskin would have attained to writing *Modern Painters* if his father had not dealt prosperously in business. Rossetti had a small private income; and, moreover, he painted. There remains but Keats; whom Atropos slew young, as she slew John Clare in a mad-house, and James Thomson[3] by the laudanum he took to drug disappointment. These are dreadful facts, but let us face them. It is—however dishonouring to us as a nation—certain that, by some fault in our commonwealth, the poor poet has not in these days, nor has had for two hundred years, a dog's chance. Believe me—and I have spent a great part of ten years in watching some three hundred and twenty elementary schools—we may prate

---

2. *The Art of Writing*, by Sir Arthur Quiller-Couch [Woolf's note].
3. Scottish pre-Romantic poet (1700–1748).

Atropos: in Greek mythology the Fate who cut the thread of life. Clare (1793–1864), English Romantic poet.

A ROOM OF ONE'S OWN / 2491

of democracy, but actually, a poor child in England has little more hope than had the son of an Athenian slave to be emancipated into that intellectual freedom of which great writings are born."

Nobody could put the point more plainly. "The poor poet has not in these days, nor has had for two hundred years, a dog's chance . . . a poor child in England has little more hope than had the son of an Athenian slave to be emancipated into that intellectual freedom of which great writings are born." That is it. Intellectual freedom depends upon material things. Poetry depends upon intellectual freedom. And women have always been poor, not for two hundred years merely, but from the beginning of time. Women have had less intellectual freedom than the sons of Athenian slaves. Women, then, have not had a dog's chance of writing poetry. That is why I have laid so much stress on money and a room of one's own. However, thanks to the toils of those obscure women in the past, of whom I wish we knew more, thanks, curiously enough, to two wars, the Crimean which let Florence Nightingale out of her drawing-room, and the European War which opened the doors to the average woman some sixty years later, these evils are in the way to be bettered. Otherwise you would not be here tonight, and your chance of earning five hundred pounds a year, precarious as I am afraid that it still is, would be minute in the extreme.

Still, you may object, why do you attach so much importance to this writing of books by women when, according to you, it requires so much effort, leads perhaps to the murder of one's aunts, will make one almost certainly late for luncheon, and may bring one into very grave disputes with certain very good fellows? My motives, let me admit, are partly selfish. Like most uneducated Englishwomen, I like reading—I like reading books in the bulk. Lately my diet has become a trifle monotonous; history is too much about wars; biography too much about great men; poetry has shown, I think, a tendency to sterility, and fiction—but I have sufficiently exposed my disabilities as a critic of modern fiction and will say no more about it. Therefore I would ask you to write all kinds of books, hesitating at no subject however trivial or however vast. By hook or by crook, I hope that you will possess yourselves of money enough to travel and to idle, to contemplate the future or the past of the world, to dream over books and loiter at street corners and let the line of thought dip deep into the stream. For I am by no means confining you to fiction. If you would please me—and there are thousands like me—you would write books of travel and adventure, and research and scholarship, and history and biography, and criticism and philosophy and science. By so doing you will certainly profit the art of fiction. For books have a way of influencing each other. Fiction will be much the better for standing cheek by jowl with poetry and philosophy. Moreover, if you consider any great figure of the past, like Sappho, like the Lady Murasaki,[4] like Emily Brontë, you will find that she is an inheritor as well as an originator, and has come into existence because women have come to have the habit of writing naturally; so that even as a prelude to poetry such activity on your part would be invaluable.

But when I look back through these notes and criticise my own train of thought as I made them, I find that my motives were not altogether selfish. There runs through these comments and discursions the conviction—or is it

---

4. Shikibu Murasaki (978?–?1026), Japanese court lady, author of *The Tale of Genji*. Sappho (fl. ca. 610–ca. 580 B.C.E.), Greek lyric poet, who lived on the island of Lesbos.

2492 / VIRGINIA WOOLF

the instinct?—that good books are desirable and that good writers, even if they show every variety of human depravity, are still good human beings. Thus when I ask you to write more books I am urging you to do what will be for your good and for the good of the world at large. How to justify this instinct or belief I do not know, for philosophic words, if one has not been educated at a university, are apt to play one false. What is meant by "reality"? It would seem to be something very erratic, very undependable—now to be found in a dusty road, now in a scrap of newspaper in the street, now in a daffodil in the sun. It lights up a group in a room and stamps some casual saying. It overwhelms one walking home beneath the stars and makes the silent world more real than the world of speech—and then there it is again in an omnibus in the uproar of Piccadilly.[5] Sometimes, too, it seems to dwell in shapes too far away for us to discern what their nature is. But whatever it touches, it fixes and makes permanent. That is what remains over when the skin of the day has been cast into the hedge; that is what is left of past time and of our loves and hates. Now the writer, as I think, has the chance to live more than other people in the presence of this reality. It is his business to find it and collect it and communicate it to the rest of us. So at least I infer from reading *Lear* or *Emma* or *La Recherche du Temps Perdu*. For the reading of these books seems to perform a curious couching operation on the senses; one sees more intensely afterwards; the world seems bared of its covering and given an intenser life. Those are the enviable people who live at enmity with unreality; and those are the pitiable who are knocked on the head by the thing done without knowing or caring. So that when I ask you to earn money and have a room of your own, I am asking you to live in the presence of reality, an invigorating life, it would appear, whether one can impart it or not.

Here I would stop, but the pressure of convention decrees that every speech must end with a peroration. And a peroration addressed to women should have something, you will agree, particularly exalting and ennobling about it. I should implore you to remember your responsibilities, to be higher, more spiritual; I should remind you how much depends upon you, and what an influence you can exert upon the future. But those exhortations can safely, I think, be left to the other sex, who will put them, and indeed have put them, with far greater eloquence than I can compass. When I rummage in my own mind I find no noble sentiments about being companions and equals and influencing the world to higher ends. I find myself saying briefly and prosaically that it is much more important to be oneself than anything else. Do not dream of influencing other people, I would say, if I knew how to make it sound exalted. Think of things in themselves.

And again I am reminded by dipping into newspapers and novels and biographies that when a woman speaks to women she should have something very unpleasant up her sleeve. Women are hard on women. Women dislike women. Women—but are you not sick to death of the word? I can assure you that I am. Let us agree, then, that a paper read by a woman to women should end with something particularly disagreeable.

But how does it go? What can I think of? The truth is, I often like women. I like their unconventionality. I like their subtlety. I like their anonymity. I like—but I must not run on in this way. That cupboard there,—you say it

5. London street that ends in the bustling intersection of Piccadilly Circus.

holds clean table-napkins only; but what if Sir Archibald Bodkin[6] were concealed among them? Let me then adopt a sterner tone. Have I, in the preceding words, conveyed to you sufficiently the warnings and reprobation of mankind? I have told you the very low opinion in which you were held by Mr Oscar Browning. I have indicated what Napoleon once thought of you and what Mussolini thinks now. Then, in case any of you aspire to fiction, I have copied out for your benefit the advice of the critic about courageously acknowledging the limitations of your sex. I have referred to Professor X and given prominence to his statement that women are intellectually, morally and physically inferior to men. I have handed on all that has come my way without going in search of it, and here is a final warning—from Mr John Langdon Davies.[7] Mr John Langdon Davies warns women "that when children cease to be altogether desirable, women cease to be altogether necessary." I hope you will make a note of it.

How can I further encourage you to go about the business of life? Young women, I would say, and please attend, for the peroration is beginning, you are, in my opinion, disgracefully ignorant. You have never made a discovery of any sort of importance. You have never shaken an empire or led an army into battle. The plays of Shakespeare are not by you, and you have never introduced a barbarous race to the blessings of civilisation. What is your excuse? It is all very well for you to say, pointing to the streets and squares and forests of the globe swarming with black and white and coffee-coloured inhabitants, all busily engaged in traffic and enterprise and love-making, we have had other work on our hands. Without our doing, those seas would be unsailed and those fertile lands a desert. We have borne and bred and washed and taught, perhaps to the age of six or seven years, the one thousand six hundred and twenty-three million human beings who are, according to statistics, at present in existence, and that, allowing that some had help, takes time.

There is truth in what you say—I will not deny it. But at the same time may I remind you that there have been at least two colleges for women in existence in England since the year 1866; that after the year 1880 a married woman was allowed by law to possess her own property; and that in 1919—which is a whole nine years ago—she was given a vote? May I also remind you that the most of the professions have been open to you for close on ten years now? When you reflect upon these immense privileges and the length of time during which they have been enjoyed, and the fact that there must be at this moment some two thousand women capable of earning over five hundred a year in one way or another, you will agree that the excuse of lack of opportunity, training, encouragement, leisure and money no longer holds good. Moreover, the economists are telling us that Mrs Seton has had too many children. You must, of course, go on bearing children, but, so they say, in twos and threes, not in tens and twelves.

Thus, with some time on your hands and with some book learning in your brains—you have had enough of the other kind, and are sent to college partly, I suspect, to be uneducated—surely you should embark upon another stage of your very long, very laborious and highly obscure career. A thousand pens are ready to suggest what you should do and what effect you will have. My

---

6. British director of public prosecutions who decided to ban James Joyces's *Ulysses* for obscenity in 1922.

7. *A Short History of Women*, by John Langdon Davies [Woolf's note].

own suggestion is a little fantastic, I admit; I prefer, therefore, to put it in the form of fiction.

I told you in the course of this paper that Shakespeare had a sister; but do not look for her in Sir Sidney Lee's[8] life of the poet. She died young—alas, she never wrote a word. She lies buried where the omnibuses now stop, opposite the Elephant and Castle. Now my belief is that this poet who never wrote a word and was buried at the crossroads still lives. She lives in you and in me, and in many other women who are not here tonight, for they are washing up the dishes and putting the children to bed. But she lives; for great poets do not die; they are continuing presences; they need only the opportunity to walk among us in the flesh. This opportunity, as I think, it is now coming within your power to give her. For my belief is that if we live another century or so—I am talking of the common life which is the real life and not of the little separate lives which we live as individuals—and have five hundred a year each of us and rooms of our own; if we have the habit of freedom and the courage to write exactly what we think; if we escape a little from the common sitting-room and see human beings not always in their relation to each other but in relation to reality; and the sky, too, and the trees or whatever it may be in themselves; if we look past Milton's bogey,[9] for no human being should shut out the view; if we face the fact, for it is a fact, that there is no arm to cling to, but that we go alone and that our relation is to the world of reality and not only to the world of men and women, then the opportunity will come and the dead poet who was Shakespeare's sister will put on the body which she has so often laid down. Drawing her life from the lives of the unknown who were her forerunners, as her brother did before her, she will be born. As for her coming without that preparation, without that effort on our part, without that determination that when she is born again she shall find it possible to live and write her poetry, that we cannot expect, for that would be impossible. But I maintain that she would come if we worked for her, and that so to work, even in poverty and obscurity, is worth while.

1929

Professions for Women[1]

When your secretary invited me to come here, she told me that your Society is concerned with the employment of women and she suggested that I might tell you something about my own professional experiences. It is true I am a woman; it is true I am employed; but what professional experiences have I had? It is difficult to say. My profession is literature; and in that profession there are fewer experiences for women than in any other, with the exception of the stage—fewer, I mean, that are peculiar to women. For the road was cut many years ago—by Fanny Burney, by Aphra Behn, by Harriet Martineau,[2] by

---

8. Biographer and Shakespeare scholar (1859–1926), author of *Life of William Shakespeare* (1898).
9. Milton, with his unhappy first marriage, his campaign for freedom of divorce, and his deliberate subordination of Eve to Adam in *Paradise Lost*, was and often still is held to be (not altogether accurately) what the present age calls a male chauvinist.

1. A paper read to the Women's Service League [Woolf's note]. Woolf here echoes her points in *A Room of One's Own* about a woman's needing money (specifically, five hundred British pounds) and a room in which to write.
2. Economist, moralist, journalist, and novelist (1802–1876). Burney (1752–1840), author of *Evelina* and other novels. Behn (1640–1689), writer of romances and plays.

Jane Austen, by George Eliot—many famous women, and many more unknown and forgotten, have been before me, making the path smooth, and regulating my steps. Thus, when I came to write, there were very few material obstacles in my way. Writing was a reputable and harmless occupation. The family peace was not broken by the scratching of a pen. No demand was made upon the family purse. For ten and sixpence one can buy paper enough to write all the plays of Shakespeare—if one has a mind that way. Pianos and models, Paris, Vienna, and Berlin, masters and mistresses, are not needed by a writer. The cheapness of writing paper is, of course, the reason why women have succeeded as writers before they have succeeded in the other professions.

But to tell you my story—it is a simple one. You have only got to figure to yourselves a girl in a bedroom with a pen in her hand. She had only to move that pen from left to right—from ten o'clock to one. Then it occurred to her to do what is simple and cheap enough after all—to slip a few of those pages into an envelope, fix a penny stamp in the corner, and drop the envelope into the red box at the corner. It was thus that I became a journalist; and my effort was rewarded on the first day of the following month—a very glorious day it was for me—by a letter from an editor containing a cheque for one pound ten shillings and sixpence. But to show you how little I deserve to be called a professional woman, how little I know of the struggles and difficulties of such lives, I have to admit that instead of spending that sum upon bread and butter, rent, shoes and stockings, or butcher's bills, I went out and bought a cat—a beautiful cat, a Persian cat, which very soon involved me in bitter disputes with my neighbours.

What could be easier than to write articles and to buy Persian cats with the profits? But wait a moment. Articles have to be about something. Mine, I seem to remember, was about a novel by a famous man. And while I was writing this review, I discovered that if I were going to review books I should need to do battle with a certain phantom. And the phantom was a woman, and when I came to know her better I called her after the heroine of a famous poem, The Angel in the House.[3] It was she who used to come between me and my paper when I was writing reviews. It was she who bothered and wasted my time and so tormented me that at last I killed her. You who come of a younger and happier generation may not have heard of her—you may not know what I mean by The Angel in the House. I will describe her as shortly as I can. She was intensely sympathetic. She was immensely charming. She was utterly unselfish. She excelled in the difficult arts of family life. She sacrificed herself daily. If there was chicken, she took the leg; if there was a draught she sat in it—in short she was so constituted that she never had a mind or a wish of her own, but preferred to sympathise always with the minds and wishes of others. Above all—I need not say it—she was pure. Her purity was supposed to be her chief beauty—her blushes, her great grace. In those days—the last of Queen Victoria—every house had its Angel. And when I came to write I encountered her with the very first words. The shadow of her wings fell on my page; I heard the rustling of her skirts in the room. Directly, that is to say, I took my pen in my hand to review that novel by a famous man, she slipped behind me and whispered: 'My dear, you are a young woman. You are writing about a book that has been written by a man. Be sympathetic; be tender; flatter; deceive; use all the arts and wiles of our sex. Never let anybody guess that you have a mind of your own. Above all, be pure.' And she made as

3. By Coventry Patmore (1823–1896), published 1854–62.

if to guide my pen. I now record the one act for which I take some credit to myself, though the credit rightly belongs to some excellent ancestors of mine who left me a certain sum of money—shall we say five hundred pounds a year?—so that it was not necessary for me to depend solely on charm for my living. I turned upon her and caught her by the throat. I did my best to kill her. My excuse, if I were to be had up in a court of law, would be that I acted in self-defence. Had I not killed her she would have killed me. She would have plucked the heart out of my writing. For, as I found, directly I put pen to paper, you cannot review even a novel without having a mind of your own, without expressing what you think to be the truth about human relations, morality, sex. And all these questions, according to the Angel of the House, cannot be dealt with freely and openly by women; they must charm, they must conciliate, they must—to put it bluntly—tell lies if they are to succeed. Thus, whenever I felt the shadow of her wing or the radiance of her halo upon my page, I took up the inkpot and flung it at her. She died hard. Her fictitious nature was of great assistance to her. It is far harder to kill a phantom than a reality. She was always creeping back when I thought I had despatched her. Though I flatter myself that I killed her in the end, the struggle was severe; it took much time that had better have been spent upon learning Greek grammar; or in roaming the world in search of adventures. But it was a real experience; it was an experience that was bound to befall all women writers at that time. Killing the Angel in the House was part of the occupation of a woman writer.

But to continue my story. The Angel was dead; what then remained? You may say that what remained was a simple and common object—a young woman in a bedroom with an inkpot. In other words, now that she had rid herself of falsehood, that young woman had only to be herself. Ah, but what is 'herself'? I mean, what is a woman? I assure you, I do not know. I do not believe that you know. I do not believe that anybody can know until she has expressed herself in all the arts and professions open to human skill. That indeed is one of the reasons why I have come here—out of respect for you, who are in process of showing us by your experiments what a woman is, who are in process of providing us, by your failures and successes, with that extremely important piece of information.

But to continue the story of my professional experiences. I made one pound ten and six by my first review; and I bought a Persian cat with the proceeds. Then I grew ambitious. A Persian cat is all very well, I said; but a Persian cat is not enough. I must have a motor-car. And it was thus that I became a novelist—for it is a very strange thing that people will give you a motor-car if you will tell them a story. It is a still stranger thing that there is nothing so delightful in the world as telling stories. It is far pleasanter than writing reviews of famous novels. And yet, if I am to obey your secretary and tell you my professional experiences as a novelist, I must tell you about a very strange experience that befell me as a novelist. And to understand it you must try first to imagine a novelist's state of mind. I hope I am not giving away professional secrets if I say that a novelist's chief desire is to be as unconscious as possible. He has to induce in himself a state of perpetual lethargy. He wants life to proceed with the utmost quiet and regularity. He wants to see the same faces, to read the same books, to do the same things day after day, month after month, while he is writing, so that nothing may break the illusion in which he is living—so that nothing may disturb or disquiet the mysterious nosings about, feelings round, darts, dashes, and sudden discoveries of that very shy and illusive spirit, the imagination. I suspect that this state is the same both for men and women. Be that as it may, I want you to imagine me writing a novel in a state of trance. I want you to figure to yourselves a girl sitting with a pen in her hand, which for minutes, and indeed for hours, she never dips into the inkpot. The image that comes to my mind when I think of this girl is the image of a fisherman lying sunk in dreams on the verge of a deep lake with a rod held out over the water. She was letting her imagination sweep unchecked round every rock and cranny of the world that lies submerged in the depths of our unconscious being. Now came the experience that I believe to be far commoner with women writers than with men. The line raced through the girl's fingers. Her imagination had rushed away. It had sought the pools, the depths, the dark places where the largest fish slumber. And then there was a smash. There was an explosion. There was foam and confusion. The imagination had dashed itself against something hard. The girl was roused from her dream. She was indeed in a state of the most acute and difficult distress. To speak without figure, she had thought of something, something about the body, about the passions which it was unfitting for her as a woman to say. Men, her reason told her, would be shocked. The consciousness of what men will say of a woman who speaks the truth about her passions had roused her from her artist's state of unconsciousness. She could write no more. The trance was over. Her imagination could work no longer. This I believe to be a very common experience with women writers—they are impeded by the extreme conventionality of the other sex. For though men sensibly allow themselves great freedom in these respects, I doubt that they realize or can control the extreme severity with which they condemn such freedom in women.

These then were two very genuine experiences of my own. These were two of the adventures of my professional life. The first—killing the Angel in the House—I think I solved. She died. But the second, telling the truth about my own experiences as a body, I do not think I solved. I doubt that any woman has solved it yet. The obstacles against her are still immensely powerful—and yet they are very difficult to define. Outwardly, what is simpler than to write books? Outwardly, what obstacles are there for a woman rather than for a man? Inwardly, I think, the case is very different; she has still many ghosts to fight, many prejudices to overcome. Indeed it will be a long time still, I think, before a woman can sit down to write a book without finding a phantom to be slain, a rock to be dashed against. And if this is so in literature, the freest of all professions for women, how is it in the new professions which you are now for the first time entering?

Those are the questions that I should like, had I time, to ask you. And indeed, if I have laid stress upon these professional experiences of mine, it is because I believe that they are, though in different forms, yours also. Even when the path is nominally open—when there is nothing to prevent a woman from being a doctor, a lawyer, a civil servant—there are many phantoms and obstacles, as I believe, looming in her way. To discuss and define them is I think of great value and importance; for thus only can the labour be shared, the difficulties be solved. But besides this, it is necessary also to discuss the ends and the aims for which we are fighting, for which we are doing battle with these formidable obstacles. Those aims cannot be taken for granted; they must be perpetually questioned and examined. The whole position, as I see it—here in this hall surrounded by women practising for the first time in history I know not how many different professions—is one of extraordinary interest and importance. You have won rooms of your own in the house hitherto exclusively owned by men. You are able, though not without great labour and effort, to pay the rent. You are earning your five hundred pounds a year. But this freedom is only a beginning; the room is your own, but it is still bare. It has to be furnished; it has to be decorated; it has to be shared. How are you going to furnish it, how are you going to decorate it? With whom are you going to share it, and upon what terms? These, I think are questions of the utmost importance and interest. For the first time in history you are able to ask them; for the first time you are able to decide for yourselves what the answers should be. Willingly would I stay and discuss those questions and answers—but not tonight. My time is up; and I must cease.

1942

JAMES JOYCE
1882–1941

James Joyce was born in Dublin, son of a talented but feckless father, who is accurately described in Joyce's novel *A Portrait of the Artist as a Young Man* (1916) as having been "a medical student, an oarsman, a tenor, an amateur actor, a shouting politician, a small landlord, a small investor, a drinker, a good fellow, a storyteller, somebody's secretary, something in a distillery, a tax-gatherer, a bankrupt, and at present a praiser of his own past." The elder Joyce drifted steadily down the financial and social scale, his family moving from house to house, each one less genteel and more shabby than the previous. James Joyce's primary education was Catholic, from the age of six to the age of nine at Clongowes Wood College and from eleven to sixteen at Belvedere College. Both were Jesuit institutions and were normal roads to the priesthood. He then studied modern languages at University College, Dublin.

From a comparatively young age Joyce regarded himself as a rebel against the shabbiness and philistinism of Dublin. In his last year of school at Belvedere he began to reject his Catholic faith in favor of a literary mission that he saw as involving rebellion and exile. He refused to play any part in the nationalist or other popular activities of his fellow students, and he created some stir by his outspoken articles, one of which, on the Norwegian playwright Henrik Ibsen, appeared in London's *Fortnightly Review* when Joyce was eighteen. He taught himself Dano-Norwegian in order to read Ibsen and to write to him. When an article by Joyce, significantly titled "The Day of the Rabblement," was refused, on instructions of the faculty adviser, by the student magazine that had commissioned it, he had it printed privately. By 1902, when he received his A.B. degree, he was already committed to a career as exile and writer. For Joyce, as for his character Stephen Dedalus, the latter implied the former. To preserve his integrity, to avoid involvement in popular causes, to devote himself to the life of the artist, he felt that he had to go abroad.

Joyce went to Paris after graduation, was recalled to Dublin by his mother's fatal illness, had a short spell there as a schoolteacher, then returned to the Continent in 1904 to teach English at Trieste and then at Zurich. He took with him Nora Barnacle, a woman from Galway with no interest in literature; her vivacity and wit charmed Joyce, and the two lived in devoted companionship until his death, although they were not married until 1931. In 1920 Joyce and Barnacle settled in Paris, where they lived until December 1940, when the war forced them to take refuge in Switzerland; he died in Zurich a few weeks later.

Proud, obstinate, absolutely convinced of his genius, given to fits of sudden gaiety and of sudden silence, Joyce was not always an easy person to get along with, yet he never lacked friends, and throughout his thirty-six years on the Continent he was always the center of a literary circle. Life was hard at first. In Trieste he had very little money, and he did not improve matters by drinking heavily, a habit checked somewhat by his brother Stanislaus, who came out from Dublin to act (as Stanislaus put it much later) as his "brother's keeper." Joyce also suffered from eye diseases and, blind for brief periods, underwent twenty-five operations. In 1917 Edith Rockefeller McCormick and then the lawyer John Quinn, steered in Joyce's direction by Ezra Pound, helped out financially, but a more permanent benefactor was the English feminist and editor Harriet Shaw Weaver, who not only subsidized Joyce generously from 1917 to the end of his life but also occupied herself indefatigably with arrangements for publishing his work.

In spite of doing most of his writing in Trieste, Zurich, and Paris, Joyce paradoxically wrote only and always about Dublin. No writer has ever been more soaked in Dublin, its atmosphere, its history, its topography. He devised ways of expanding his accounts of Dublin, however, so that they became microcosms of human history, geography, and experience.

Joyce began his career by writing a series of stories etching with extraordinary clarity aspects of Dublin life. These stories—published as *Dubliners* in 1914—are sharp realistic sketches of what Joyce called the "paralysis" that beset the lives of people in then-provincial Ireland. The language is crisp, lucid, and detached, and the details are chosen and organized so that carefully interacting symbolic meanings are set up. Some of the stories, such as "Araby," are built around what Joyce called an "epiphany," a dramatic but fleeting moment of revelation about the self or the world. Many end abruptly, without conventional narrative closure, or they lack overt connectives and transitions, leaving multiple possibilities in suspension. The last story in *Dubliners*, "The Dead," was not part of the original draft of the book but was added later, when Joyce was preoccupied with the nature of artistic objectivity. At a festive event, attended by guests whose portraits Joyce draws with precision and economy, a series of jolting events frees the protagonist, Gabriel, from his possessiveness and egotism. The view he attains at the end is the mood of supreme neutrality that Joyce saw as the beginning of artistic awareness. It is the view of art developed by Stephen Dedalus in *A Portrait of the Artist as a Young Man*.

Dubliners represents Joyce's first phase: he had to come to terms with the life he had rejected. Next he had to come to terms with the meaning of his own growth as a man dedicated to imaginative writing, and he did so by writing a novel about the youth and development of an artist, a kind of novel known by the German term *Künstlerroman* (a variation on the *Bildungsroman*). The book's narrative style changes to evoke developments in Stephen's consciousness, from the bare record of a child's tactile experiences to the ironically lush descriptions of artistic illumination to the self-sufficiency of the final diary entries. Joyce wove his autobiography into a novel so finely chiseled and carefully organized, so stripped of everything superfluous, that each word contributes to the presentation of the theme: the parallel movement toward art and toward exile. A part of his first draft was published posthumously under the original title, *Stephen Hero* (1944), and a comparison between it and the final version, *Portrait of the Artist*, shows how carefully Joyce reworked and compressed his material for maximum effect.

In *Portrait* Stephen works out a theory in which art moves from the lyrical form (the simplest, the personal expression of an instant of emotion) through the narrative form (no longer purely personal) to the dramatic (the highest and most nearly perfect form, where "the artist, like the God of creation, remains within or behind or beyond or above his handiwork, invisible, refined out of existence, indifferent, paring his fingernails"). This view of art, which involves the objectivity, even the exile, of the artist—even though the artist uses only the materials provided for him or her by his or her own life—overlaps with the emphasis on masks, impersonality, and ironic detachment in the work of other modernist writers, such as Pound, W. B. Yeats, and T. S. Eliot. Joyce's next novel, *Ulysses* (1922), and his last, *Finnegans Wake* (1939), represent the most consummate craftsmanship, put at the service of a humanely comic vision. His innovations in organization, style, and narrative technique have influenced countless other writers, but these books are unique.

From the beginning Joyce had trouble getting into print. Publication of *Dubliners* was held up for many years while he fought with both English and Irish publishers about words and phrases that they wished to eliminate. *Ulysses* was banned in Britain and America on publication; its earlier serialization in an American magazine, *The Little Review* (March 1918–December 1920), had been stopped abruptly when the U.S. Post Office brought a charge of obscenity against the work. Fortunately Judge John Woolsey's history-making decision in a U.S. district court on December 6, 1933, resulted in the lifting of the ban and the free circulation of *Ulysses* first in America and soon afterward in Britain.

ULYSSES

Ulysses is an account of one day in the lives of Dubliners; it thus describes a limited number of events involving a limited number of people in a limited environment. Yet Joyce's ambition—which took him seven years to realize—is to present the events in such a manner that depth and implication are given to them and they become symbolic. The episodes in *Ulysses* correspond to episodes in Homer's ancient Greek epic *Odyssey*. Joyce regarded Homer's Odysseus, or Ulysses, as the most "complete" man in literature, shown in all his aspects—coward and hero, cautious and reckless, weak and strong, husband and philanderer, father and son, dignified and ridiculous; so he makes his hero, Leopold Bloom, an Irish Jew, into a modern Ulysses. The parallels between the Homeric archetypes and the modern-day characters and events create a host of interpretive complexities. They can seem tight or loose, deflating or ennobling, ironic or heroic, epic or mock-epic, depending on their specific use in different episodes and, to some extent, on the propensities of the reader.

Ulysses opens at eight o'clock on the morning of June 16, 1904. Stephen Dedalus (the same character as in *Portrait,* but two years after the last glimpse of him there) had been summoned back to Dublin by his mother's fatal illness and now lives in an old military tower on the shore with Buck Mulligan, a rollicking medical student, and an Englishman called Haines. In the first three episodes of *Ulysses*, which concentrate on Stephen, he is built up as an aloof, uncompromising artist, rejecting all advances by representatives of the normal world, the incomplete man, to be contrasted later with the complete Leopold Bloom, who is much more "normal" and conciliatory. After tracing Stephen through his early-morning activities and learning the main currents of his mind, we go, in the fourth episode, to the home of Bloom. We follow closely his every activity: attending a funeral, transacting business, eating lunch, walking through the Dublin streets, worrying about his wife's infidelity with Blazes Boylan— and at each point the contents of his mind, including retrospect and anticipation, are presented to us, until his past history is revealed. Finally Bloom and Stephen, who have been just missing each other all day, get together. By this time it is late, and Stephen, who has been drinking with some medical students, is the worse for liquor. Bloom, moved by a paternal feeling toward Stephen (his own son had died in infancy and in a symbolic way Stephen takes his place), follows him during subsequent adventures in the role of protector. The climax of the book comes when Stephen, far gone in drink, and Bloom, worn out with fatigue, succumb to a series of hallucinations, where their unconscious minds surface in dramatic form and their personalities are revealed with a completeness and a frankness unique in literature. Then Bloom takes the unresponsive Stephen home and gives him a meal. After Stephen's departure Bloom retires to bed—it is now two in the morning, June 17—while his wife, Molly, lying in bed, closes the book with a long monologue in which she recalls her romantic and other experiences. Her monologue unfolds in eight flowing, unpunctuated paragraphs, which culminate in the book's final, resonant affirmation, a memory of her response to Bloom's marriage proposal: "and yes I said yes I will Yes."

On the level of realistic description, Ulysses pulses with life and can be enjoyed for its evocation of early-twentieth-century Dublin. On the level of psychological exploration, it gives a profound and moving presentation of the personalities and consciousnesses of Leopold Bloom, Stephen Dedalus, and Molly Bloom. On the level of style, it exhibits the most fascinating linguistic virtuosity, many an episode written in a distinctive way that reflects its subject—e.g., newspaper headlines intruding in a chapter set in a newspaper office (the "Aeolus" episode), the sentimental language of women's magazines dominating a chapter set on a beach where girls are playing ("Nausicaa"), and the pastiche of styles of English literature from its Anglo-Saxon birth to the twentieth century taking over in a chapter set in a maternity hospital ("Oxen of the Sun"). On a deeper symbolic level, the novel explores the paradoxes of human loneliness and sociability (for Bloom is both Jew and Dubliner, both exile and citizen), and it explores the problems posed by the relations between parent and child, between the generations, and between the sexes. At the same time, through its use of themes from Homer, Dante, and Shakespeare and from literature, philosophy, and history, the book weaves a subtle pattern of allusion and suggestion. The more one reads Ulysses the more one finds in it, but at the same time one does not need to probe into the symbolic meaning to relish both its literary artistry and its emotional richness. At the forefront stands Bloom, from one point of view a frustrated and confused outsider in the society in which he moves, from another a champion of kindness and justice whose humane curiosity about his fellows redeems him from mere vulgarity and gives the book its positive human foundation.

Readers who come to Ulysses with expectations about the way the story is to be presented derived from their reading of Victorian novels or even of twentieth-century novelists such as Conrad and Lawrence will find much that is at first puzzling. Joyce presents the consciousness of his characters directly, without any explanatory comment that tells the reader whose consciousness is being rendered (this is the stream of consciousness method, also known as interior monologue). He may move, in the same paragraph and without any sign that he is making such a transition, from a description of a character's action—e.g., Stephen walking along the shore or Bloom entering a restaurant—to an evocation of the character's mental response to this action. That response is always multiple: it derives partly from the character's immediate situation and partly from the whole complex of attitudes created by a personal past history. To suggest this multiplicity, Joyce may vary his style, from the flippant to the serious or from a realistic description to a suggestive set of images that indicate what might be called the general tone of the character's consciousness. Past and present mingle in the texture of the prose because they mingle in the texture of consciousness, and this mingling can be indicated by puns, by sudden breaks into a new kind of style or a new kind of subject matter, or by some other device for keeping the reader constantly in sight of the shifting, kaleidoscopic nature of human awareness. With a little experience the reader learns to follow the implications of Joyce's shifts in manner and content—even to follow that initially bewildering passage in the "Proteus" episode in which Stephen does not go to visit his uncle and aunt but, passing the road that leads to their house, imagines the kind of conversation that would take place in his home if he had gone to visit his uncle and had then returned home and reported that he had done so. Ulysses must not be approached as though it were a traditional novel; we must set aside our preconceptions, follow wherever the author leads us, and let the language tell us what it has to say.

FINNEGANS WAKE

Joyce's final work, *Finnegans Wake* took more than fourteen years to write, and Joyce considered it his masterpiece. In *Ulysses* he had made the symbolic aspect of the novel at least as important as the realistic aspect, but in *Finnegans Wake* he gave up realism altogether. This vast story of a symbolic Irishman's cosmic dream develops by enormous reverberating puns a continuous expansion of meaning, the elements in the puns deriving from every conceivable source in history, literature, mythology, and Joyce's personal experience. The whole book being (on one level at least) a dream, Joyce invents his own dream language, in which words are combined, distorted, created by fitting together bits of other words, used with several different meanings at once, often drawn from several different languages at once, and fused in all sorts of ways to achieve whole clusters of meaning simultaneously. In fact, so many echoing suggestions can be found in every word or phrase that a full annotation of even a few pages would require a large book. Over time, readers and critics of *Finnegans Wake* have sorted out the complex interactions of the multiple puns and pun clusters through which the ideas are projected, and every rereading reveals new meanings. Many readers find the efforts of explication too arduous, but the book has great beauty and fascination even for the casual reader. Newcomers are advised to read aloud— or to listen to the recording of Joyce reading aloud—the extract printed here to appreciate the degree to which the rhythms of the prose assist in conveying the meaning.

To an even greater extent than *Ulysses, Finnegans Wake* aims to embrace all of human history. The title comes from an Irish American ballad about Tom Finnegan, a hod carrier who falls off a ladder when drunk and is apparently killed, but who revives when during the wake (the watch by his dead body) someone spills whiskey on him. The theme of death and resurrection, of cycles of change coming round in the course of history, is central to *Finnegans Wake,* which derives one of its main principles of organization from the cyclical theory of history put forward in 1725 by the Italian philosopher Giambattista Vico. Vico held that history passes through four phases: the divine, or theocratic, when people are governed by their awe of the supernatural; the aristocratic (the "heroic age" reflected in Homer and in *Beowulf*); the democratic and individualistic; and the final stage of chaos, a fall into confusion that startles humanity back into supernatural reverence and starts the process once again. Joyce, like Yeats, saw his own generation as in the final stage awaiting the shock that will bring humans back to the first.

A mere account of the narrative line of *Finnegans Wake* cannot give any idea of the content of the work. If one explains that it opens with Finnegan's fall, then introduces his successor, Humphrey Chimpden Earwicker, who keeps a pub in Chapelizod, a Dublin suburb on the river Liffey, near Phoenix Park; that HCE is feeling guilty about an indecency he committed (or may have committed) in Phoenix Park; that his dream constitutes the novel; that his wife, Anna Livia Plurabelle, or ALP (who is also Eve, Iseult, Ireland, the Liffey), changes her role just as he does; that HCE and ALP have two sons, Shem and Shaun (or Jerry and Kevin), who represent introvert and extrovert, artist and practical man, creator and popularizer, and who symbolize this dichotomy in human nature by all kinds of metamorphoses; and if one adds that, in the four books into which *Finnegans Wake* is divided (after Vico's pattern), actions comic or grotesque or sad or tender or desperate or passionate or terribly ordinary (and very often several of these things at the same time) take place with all the shifting meanings of a dream, so that characters change into others or into inanimate objects and the setting keeps shifting—still one has said very little about what makes *Finnegans Wake* what it is. The dreamer is at once a particular person and a universal figure, his initials also standing for "Here Comes Everybody." His mysterious misdemeanor in Phoenix Park is in a sense Original Sin: Earwicker is Adam as well as a primeval giant, the Hill of Howth, the Great Parent ("Haveth Childers Everywhere" is another expansion of HCE), and Man in History. Other characters who flit and change through the book, such as the Twelve Customers (who are also twelve jurymen and public opinion) and the Four Old Men (who are also judges, the authors of the four Gospels, and the four elements), help weave the texture of multiple significance so characteristic of the work. But always it is the punning language, extending significance downward—rather than the plot, developing it lengthwise—that bears the main load of meaning.

Araby[1]

   North Richmond Street, being blind, was a quiet street except at the hour when the Christian Brothers' School[2] set the boys free. An uninhabited house of two storeys stood at the blind end, detached from its neighbours in a square ground. The other houses of the street, conscious of decent lives within them, gazed at one another with brown imperturbable faces.

   The former tenant of our house, a priest, had died in the back drawing-room. Air, musty from having been long enclosed, hung in all the rooms, and the waste room behind the kitchen was littered with old useless papers. Among these I found a few paper-covered books, the pages of which were curled and damp: *The Abbot*, by Walter Scott, *The Devout Communicant* and *The Memoirs of Vidocq*.[3] I liked the last best because its leaves were yellow. The wild garden behind the house contained a central apple-tree and a few straggling bushes under one of which I found the late tenant's rusty bicycle-pump. He had been a very charitable priest; in his will he had left all his money to institutions and the furniture of his house to his sister.

   When the short days of winter came dusk fell before we had well eaten our dinners. When we met in the street the houses had grown sombre. The space of sky above us was the colour of ever-changing violet and towards it the lamps of the street lifted their feeble lanterns. The cold air stung us and we played till our bodies glowed. Our shouts echoed in the silent street. The career of our play brought us through the dark muddy lanes behind the houses where we ran the gantlet of the rough tribes from the cottages, to the back doors of the dark dripping gardens where odours arose from the ashpits, to the dark odorous stables where a coachman smoothed and combed the horse or shook music from the buckled harness. When we returned to the street light from the kitchen windows had filled the areas. If my uncle was seen turning the corner we hid in the shadow until we had seen him safely housed. Or if Mangan's sister came out on the doorstep to call her brother in to his tea we watched her from our shadow peer up and down the street. We waited to see

1. The third of the fifteen stories in *Dubliners*. This tale of the frustrated quest for beauty in the midst of drabness is both meticulously realistic in its handling of details of Dublin life and the Dublin scene and highly symbolic in that almost every image and incident suggests some particular aspect of the theme (e.g., the suggestion of the Holy Grail in the image of the chalice, mentioned in the fifth paragraph). Joyce was drawing on his own childhood recollections, and the uncle in the story is a reminiscence of Joyce's father. But in all the stories in *Dubliners* dealing with childhood, the child lives not with his parents but with an uncle and aunt—a symbol of that isolation and lack of proper relation between "consubstantial" (in the flesh) parents and children that is a major theme in Joyce's work.
2. The Joyce family moved to 17 North Richmond Street, Dublin, in 1894; and Joyce had earlier briefly attended the Christian Brothers' school a few doors away (the Christian Brothers are a Catholic religious community). The details of the house described here correspond exactly to those of number 17.
3. François Eugéne Vidocq (1775–1857) had an extraordinary career as soldier, thief, chief of the French detective force, and private detective. *The Abbot* is a historical novel dealing with Mary, Queen of Scots. *The Devout Communicant* is a Catholic religious manual.

whether she would remain or go in and, if she remained, we left our shadow and walked up to Mangan's steps resignedly. She was waiting for us, her figure defined by the light from the half-opened door. Her brother always teased her before he obeyed and I stood by the railings looking at her. Her dress swung as she moved her body and the soft rope of her hair tossed from side to side.

Every morning I lay on the floor in the front parlour watching her door. The blind was pulled down to within an inch of the sash so that I could not be seen. When she came out on the doorstep my heart leaped. I ran to the hall, seized my books and followed her. I kept her brown figure always in my eye and, when we came near the point at which our ways diverged, I quickened my pace and passed her. This happened morning after morning. I had never spoken to her, except for a few casual words, and yet her name was like a summons to all my foolish blood.

Her image accompanied me even in places the most hostile to romance. On Saturday evenings when my aunt went marketing I had to go to carry some of the parcels. We walked through the flaring streets, jostled by drunken men and bargaining women, amid the curses of labourers, the shrill litanies of shop-boys who stood on guard by the barrels of pigs' cheeks, the nasal chanting of street-singers, who sang a *come-all-you*[4] about O'Donovan Rossa, or a ballad about the troubles in our native land. These noises converged in a single sensation of life for me: I imagined that I bore my chalice safely through a throng of foes. Her name sprang to my lips at moments in strange prayers and praises which I myself did not understand. My eyes were often full of tears (I could not tell why) and at times a flood from my heart seemed to pour itself out into my bosom. I thought little of the future. I did not know whether I would ever speak to her or not or, if I spoke to her, how I could tell her of my confused adoration. But my body was like a harp and her words and gestures were like fingers running upon the wires.

One evening I went into the back drawing-room in which the priest had died. It was a dark rainy evening and there was no sound in the house. Through one of the broken panes I heard the rain impinge upon the earth, the fine incessant needles of water playing in the sodden beds. Some distant lamp or lighted window gleamed below me. I was thankful that I could see so little. All my senses seemed to desire to veil themselves and, feeling that I was about to slip from them, I pressed the palms of my hands together until they trembled, murmuring: *O love! O love!* many times.

At last she spoke to me. When she addressed the first words to me I was so confused that I did not know what to answer. She asked me was I going to *Araby*.[5] I forgot whether I answered yes or no. It would be a splendid bazaar, she said; she would love to go.

—And why can't you? I asked.

While she spoke she turned a silver bracelet round and round her wrist. She could not go, she said, because there would be a retreat that week in her convent.[6] Her brother and two other boys were fighting for their caps and I was alone at the railings. She held one of the spikes, bowing her head towards me. The light from the lamp opposite our door caught the white curve of her

---

4. Street ballad, so called from its opening words. This one was about the 19th-century Irish nationalist Jeremiah Donovan, popularly known as O'Donovan Rossa.
5. The bazaar, described by its "official catalogue" as a "Grand Oriental Fête," was actually held in Dublin on May 14–19, 1894.
6. I.e., her convent school. "Retreat": period of seclusion from ordinary activities devoted to religious exercises.

neck, lit up her hair that rested there and, falling, lit up the hand upon the railing. It fell over one side of her dress and caught the white border of a petticoat, just visible as she stood at ease.

—It's well for you, she said.

—If I go, I said, I will bring you something.

What innumerable follies laid waste my waking and sleeping thoughts after that evening! I wished to annihilate the tedious intervening days. I chafed against the work of school. At night in my bedroom and by day in the classroom her image came between me and the page I strove to read. The syllables of the word *Araby* were called to me through the silence in which my soul luxuriated and cast an Eastern enchantment over me. I asked for leave to go to the bazaar on Saturday night. My aunt was surprised and hoped it was not some Freemason affair.[7] I answered few questions in class. I watched my master's face pass from amiability to sternness; he hoped I was not beginning to idle. I could not call my wandering thoughts together. I had hardly any patience with the serious work of life which, now that it stood between me and my desire, seemed to me child's play, ugly monotonous child's play.

On Saturday morning I reminded my uncle that I wished to go to the bazaar in the evening. He was fussing at the hallstand, looking for the hat-brush, and answered me curtly:

—Yes, boy, I know.

As he was in the hall I could not go into the front parlour and lie at the window. I left the house in bad humour and walked slowly towards the school. The air was pitilessly raw and already my heart misgave me.

When I came home to dinner my uncle had not yet been home. Still it was early. I sat staring at the clock for some time and, when its ticking began to irritate me, I left the room. I mounted the staircase and gained the upper part of the house. The high cold empty gloomy rooms liberated me and I went from room to room singing. From the front window I saw my companions playing below in the street. Their cries reached me weakened and indistinct and, leaning my forehead against the cool glass, I looked over at the dark house where she lived. I may have stood there for an hour, seeing nothing but the brown-clad figure cast by my imagination, touched discreetly by the lamplight at the curved neck, at the hand upon the railings and at the border below the dress.

When I came downstairs again I found Mrs Mercer sitting at the fire. She was an old garrulous woman, a pawn-broker's widow, who collected used stamps for some pious purpose. I had to endure the gossip of the tea-table. The meal was prolonged beyond an hour and still my uncle did not come. Mrs Mercer stood up to go: she was sorry she couldn't wait any longer, but it was after eight o'clock and she did not like to be out late, as the night air was bad for her. When she had gone I began to walk up and down the room, clenching my fists. My aunt said:

—I'm afraid you may put off your bazaar for this night of Our Lord.

At nine o'clock I heard my uncle's latchkey in the halldoor. I heard him talking to himself and heard the hallstand rocking when it had received the weight of his overcoat. I could interpret these signs. When he was midway through his dinner I asked him to give me the money to go to the bazaar. He had forgotten.

---

7. His aunt shares her Church's distrust of the Freemasons, an old European secret society, reputedly anti-Catholic.

—The people are in bed and after their first sleep now, he said.

I did not smile. My aunt said to him energetically:

—Can't you give him the money and let him go? You've kept him late enough as it is.

My uncle said he was very sorry he had forgotten. He said he believed in the old saying: *All work and no play makes Jack a dull boy.* He asked me where I was going and, when I had told him a second time he asked me did I know *The Arab's Farewell to his Steed.*[8] When I left the kitchen he was about to recite the opening lines of the piece to my aunt.

I held a florin[9] tightly in my hand as I strode down Buckingham Street towards the station. The sight of the streets thronged with buyers and glaring with gas recalled to me the purpose of my journey. I took my seat in a third-class carriage of a deserted train. After an intolerable delay the train moved out of the station slowly. It crept onward among ruinous houses and over the twinkling river. At Westland Row Station a crowd of people pressed to the carriage doors; but the porters moved them back, saying that it was a special train for the bazaar. I remained alone in the bare carriage. In a few minutes the train drew up beside an improvised wooden platform. I passed out on to the road and saw by the lighted dial of a clock that it was ten minutes to ten. In front of me was a large building which displayed the magical name.

I could not find any sixpenny entrance and, fearing that the bazaar would be closed, I passed in quickly through a turnstile, handing a shilling to a weary-looking man. I found myself in a big hall girdled at half its height by a gallery. Nearly all the stalls were closed and the greater part of the hall was in darkness. I recognized a silence like that which pervades a church after a service. I walked into the centre of the bazaar timidly. A few people were gathered about the stalls which were still open. Before a curtain, over which the words *Café Chantant*[1] were written in coloured lamps, two men were counting money on a salver. I listened to the fall of the coins.

Remembering with difficulty why I had come I went over to one of the stalls and examined porcelain vases and flowered tea-sets. At the door of the stall a young lady was talking and laughing with two young gentlemen. I remarked their English accents and listened vaguely to their conversation.

—O, I never said such a thing!

—O, but you did!

—O, but I didn't!

—Didn't she say that?

—Yes. I heard her.

—O, there's a . . . fib!

Observing me the young lady came over and asked me did I wish to buy anything. The tone of her voice was not encouraging; she seemed to have spoken to me out of a sense of duty. I looked humbly at the great jars that stood like eastern guards at either side of the dark entrance to the stall and murmured:

—No, thank you.

The young lady changed the position of one of the vases and went back to the two young men. They began to talk of the same subject. Once or twice the young lady glanced at me over her shoulder.

8. Once-popular sentimental poem by Caroline Norton.
9. A silver coin, now obsolete, worth two shillings.
1. Singing café (French; literal trans.); a café that provided musical entertainment, popular early in the 20th century.

I lingered before her stall, though I knew my stay was useless, to make my interest in her wares seem the more real. Then I turned away slowly and walked down the middle of the bazaar. I allowed the two pennies to fall against the sixpence in my pocket. I heard a voice call from one end of the gallery that the light was out. The upper part of the hall was now completely dark.

Gazing up into the darkness I saw myself as a creature driven and derided by vanity; and my eyes burned with anguish and anger.

1905   1914

The Dead

Lily, the caretaker's daughter, was literally run off her feet. Hardly had she brought one gentleman into the little pantry behind the office on the ground floor and helped him off with his overcoat than the wheezy hall-door bell clanged again and she had to scamper along the bare hallway to let in another guest. It was well for her she had not to attend to the ladies also. But Miss Kate and Miss Julia had thought of that and had converted the bathroom upstairs into a ladies' dressing-room. Miss Kate and Miss Julia were there, gossiping and laughing and fussing, walking after each other to the head of the stairs, peering down over the banisters and calling down to Lily to ask her who had come.

It was always a great affair, the Misses Morkan's annual dance. Everybody who knew them came to it, members of the family, old friends of the family, the members of Julia's choir, any of Kate's pupils that were grown up enough and even some of Mary Jane's pupils too. Never once had it fallen flat. For years and years it had gone off in splendid style as long as anyone could remember; ever since Kate and Julia, after the death of their brother Pat, had left the house in Stoney Batter and taken Mary Jane, their only niece, to live with them in the dark gaunt house on Usher's Island, the upper part of which they had rented from Mr Fulham, the cornfactor[1] on the ground floor. That was a good thirty years ago if it was a day. Mary Jane, who was then a little girl in short clothes, was now the main prop of the household for she had the organ in Haddington Road.[2] She had been through the Academy and gave a pupils' concert every year in the upper room of the Antient Concert Rooms.[3] Many of her pupils belonged to better-class families on the Kingstown and Dalkey line. Old as they were, her aunts also did their share. Julia, though she was quite grey, was still the leading soprano in Adam and Eve's, and Kate, being too feeble to go about much, gave music lessons to beginners on the old square piano in the back room. Lily, the caretaker's daughter, did housemaid's work for them. Though their life was modest they believed in eating well; the best of everything: diamond-bone sirloins, three-shilling tea and the best bottled stout.[4] But Lily seldom made a mistake in the orders so that she got on well with her three mistresses. They were fussy, that was all. But the only thing they would not stand was back answers.

Of course they had good reason to be fussy on such a night. And then it

1. Grain merchant.
2. Haddington Road, like Adam and Eve's below, is a church.

3. Concert hall in Dublin. The academy was the Royal Irish Academy of Music.
4. A dark brown malt liquor, akin to beer.

2508 / James Joyce

was long after ten o'clock and yet there was no sign of Gabriel and his wife. Besides they were dreadfully afraid that Freddy Malins might turn up screwed.[5] They would not wish for worlds that any of Mary Jane's pupils should see him under the influence; and when he was like that it was sometimes very hard to manage him. Freddy Malins always came late but they wondered what could be keeping Gabriel: and that was what brought them every two minutes to the banisters to ask Lily had Gabriel or Freddy come.

—O, Mr Conroy, said Lily to Gabriel when she opened the door for him, Miss Kate and Miss Julia thought you were never coming. Good-night, Mrs Conroy.

—I'll engage[6] they did, said Gabriel, but they forget that my wife here takes three mortal hours to dress herself.

He stood on the mat, scraping the snow from his goloshes, while Lily led his wife to the foot of the stairs and called out:

—Miss Kate, here's Mrs Conroy.

Kate and Julia came toddling down the dark stairs at once. Both of them kissed Gabriel's wife, said she must be perished alive and asked was Gabriel with her.

—Here I am as right as the mail, Aunt Kate! Go on up. I'll follow, called out Gabriel from the dark.

He continued scraping his feet vigorously while the three women went upstairs, laughing, to the ladies' dressing-room. A light fringe of snow lay like a cape on the shoulders of his overcoat and like toecaps on the toes of his goloshes; and, as the buttons of his overcoat slipped with a squeaking noise through the snow-stiffened frieze,[7] a cold fragrant air from out-of-doors escaped from crevices and folds.

—Is it snowing again, Mr Conroy? asked Lily.

She had preceded him into the pantry to help him off with his overcoat. Gabriel smiled at the three syllables she had given his surname and glanced at her. She was a slim, growing girl, pale in complexion and with hay-coloured hair. The gas in the pantry made her look still paler. Gabriel had known her when she was a child and used to sit on the lowest step nursing a rag doll.

—Yes, Lily, he answered, and I think we're in for a night of it.

He looked up at the pantry ceiling, which was shaking with the stamping and shuffling of feet on the floor above, listened for a moment to the piano and then glanced at the girl, who was folding his overcoat carefully at the end of a shelf.

—Tell me, Lily, he said in a friendly tone, do you still go to school?

—O no, sir, she answered. I'm done schooling this year and more.

—O, then, said Gabriel gaily, I suppose we'll be going to your wedding one of these fine days with your young man, eh?

The girl glanced back at him over her shoulder and said with great bitterness:

—The men that is now is only all palaver[8] and what they can get out of you.

Gabriel coloured as if he felt he had made a mistake and, without looking at her, kicked off his goloshes and flicked actively with his muffler at his patent-leather shoes.

He was a stout tallish young man. The high colour of his cheeks pushed

5. Drunk.
6. Bet.

7. A kind of coarse woolen cloth.
8. Empty and deceptive talk.

upwards even to his forehead where it scattered itself in a few formless patches of pale red; and on his hairless face there scintillated restlessly the polished lenses and the bright gilt rims of the glasses which screened his delicate and restless eyes. His glossy black hair was parted in the middle and brushed in a long curve behind his ears where it curled slightly beneath the groove left by his hat.

When he had flicked lustre into his shoes he stood up and pulled his waistcoat down more tightly on his plump body. Then he took a coin rapidly from his pocket.

—O Lily, he said, thrusting it into her hands, it's Christmas-time, isn't it? Just . . . here's a little. . . .

He walked rapidly towards the door.

—O no, sir! cried the girl, following him. Really, sir, I wouldn't take it.

—Christmas-time! Christmas-time! said Gabriel, almost trotting to the stairs and waving his hand to her in deprecation.

The girl, seeing that he had gained the stairs, called out after him:

—Well, thank you, sir.

He waited outside the drawing-room door until the waltz should finish, listening to the skirts that swept against it and to the shuffling of feet. He was still discomposed by the girl's bitter and sudden retort. It had cast a gloom over him which he tried to dispel by arranging his cuffs and the bows of his tie. Then he took from his waistcoat pocket a little paper and glanced at the headings he had made for his speech. He was undecided about the lines from Robert Browning for he feared they would be above the heads of his hearers. Some quotation that they could recognise from Shakespeare or from the Melodies[9] would be better. The indelicate clacking of the men's heels and the shuffling of their soles reminded him that their grade of culture differed from his. He would only make himself ridiculous by quoting poetry to them which they could not understand. They would think that he was airing his superior education. He would fail with them just as he had failed with the girl in the pantry. He had taken up a wrong tone. His whole speech was a mistake from first to last, an utter failure.

Just then his aunts and his wife came out of the ladies' dressing-room. His aunts were two small plainly dressed old women. Aunt Julia was an inch or so the taller. Her hair, drawn low over the tops of her ears, was grey; and grey also, with darker shadows, was her large flaccid face. Though she was stout in build and stood erect her slow eyes and parted lips gave her the appearance of a woman who did not know where she was or where she was going. Aunt Kate was more vivacious. Her face, healthier than her sister's, was all puckers and creases, like a shrivelled red apple, and her hair, braided in the same old-fashioned way, had not lost its ripe nut colour.

They both kissed Gabriel frankly. He was their favourite nephew, the son of their dead elder sister, Ellen, who had married T. J. Conroy of the Port and Docks.[1]

—Gretta tells me you're not going to take a cab back to Monkstown tonight, Gabriel, said Aunt Kate.

—No, said Gabriel, turning to his wife, we had quite enough of that last year, hadn't we? Don't you remember, Aunt Kate, what a cold Gretta got out

9. *Irish Melodies* by Dublin-born Thomas Moore (1779–1852), a collection of songs—including one called "O Ye Dead"—that was extremely popular in late-19th- and early-20th-century Ireland.
1. Board managing the Port of Dublin.

of it? Cab windows rattling all the way, and the east wind blowing in after we passed Merrion. Very jolly it was. Gretta caught a dreadful cold.

Aunt Kate frowned severely and nodded her head at every word.

—Quite right, Gabriel, quite right, she said. You can't be too careful.

—But as for Gretta there, said Gabriel, she'd walk home in the snow if she were let.

Mrs Conroy laughed.

—Don't mind him, Aunt Kate, she said. He's really an awful bother, what with green shades for Tom's eyes at night and making him do the dumb-bells, and forcing Eva to eat the stirabout.[2] The poor child! And she simply hates the sight of it! . . . O, but you'll never guess what he makes me wear now!

She broke out into a peal of laughter and glanced at her husband, whose admiring and happy eyes had been wandering from her dress to her face and hair. The two aunts laughed heartily too, for Gabriel's solicitude was a standing joke with them.

—Goloshes! said Mrs Conroy. That's the latest. Whenever it's wet underfoot I must put on my goloshes. To-night even he wanted me to put them on, but I wouldn't. The next thing he'll buy me will be a diving suit.

Gabriel laughed nervously and patted his tie reassuringly while Aunt Kate nearly doubled herself, so heartily did she enjoy the joke. The smile soon faded from Aunt Julia's face and her mirthless eyes were directed towards her nephew's face. After a pause she asked:

—And what are goloshes, Gabriel?

—Goloshes, Julia! exclaimed her sister. Goodness me, don't you know what goloshes are? You wear them over your . . . over your boots, Gretta, isn't it?

—Yes, said Mrs Conroy. Guttapercha things. We both have a pair now. Gabriel says everyone wears them on the continent.

—O, on the continent, murmured Aunt Julia, nodding her head slowly.

Gabriel knitted his brows and said, as if he were slightly angered:

—It's nothing very wonderful but Gretta thinks it very funny because she says the word reminds her of Christy Minstrels.[3]

—But tell me, Gabriel, said Aunt Kate, with brisk tact. Of course, you've seen about the room. Gretta was saying . . .

—O, the room is all right, replied Gabriel. I've taken one in the Gresham.[4]

—To be sure, said Aunt Kate, by far the best thing to do. And the children, Gretta, you're not anxious about them?

—O, for one night, said Mrs Conroy. Besides, Bessie will look after them.

—To be sure, said Aunt Kate again. What a comfort it is to have a girl like that, one you can depend on! There's that Lily, I'm sure I don't know what has come over her lately. She's not the girl she was at all.

Gabriel was about to ask his aunt some questions on this point but she broke off suddenly to gaze after her sister who had wandered down the stairs and was craning her neck over the banisters.

—Now, I ask you, she said, almost testily, where is Julia going? Julia! Julia! Where are you going?

2. Porridge made by stirring oatmeal in boiling milk or water.
3. Originally the name of a troupe of entertainers imitating African Americans, founded by George Christy of New York. By Joyce's time the meaning had become extended to any group with blackened faces who sang what were known as Negro melodies to banjo accompaniment, interspersed with jokes.
4. The Gresham Hotel, still one of the best hotels in Dublin.

Julia, who had gone halfway down one flight, came back and announced blandly:

—Here's Freddy.

At the same moment a clapping of hands and a final flourish of the pianist told that the waltz had ended. The drawing-room door was opened from within and some couples came out. Aunt Kate drew Gabriel aside hurriedly and whispered into his ear:

—Slip down, Gabriel, like a good fellow and see if he's all right, and don't let him up if he's screwed. I'm sure he's screwed. I'm sure he is.

Gabriel went to the stairs and listened over the banisters. He could hear two persons talking in the pantry. Then he recognised Freddy Malins' laugh. He went down the stairs noisily.

—It's such a relief, said Aunt Kate to Mrs Conroy, that Gabriel is here. I always feel easier in my mind when he's here. . . . Julia, there's Miss Daly and Miss Power will take some refreshment. Thanks for your beautiful waltz, Miss Daly. It made lovely time.

A tall wizen-faced man, with a stiff grizzled moustache and swarthy skin, who was passing out with his partner said:

—And may we have some refreshment, too, Miss Morkan?

—Julia, said Aunt Kate summarily, and here's Mr Browne and Miss Furlong. Take them in, Julia, with Miss Daly and Miss Power.

—I'm the man for the ladies, said Mr Browne, pursing his lips until his moustache bristled and smiling in all his wrinkles. You know, Miss Morkan, the reason they are so fond of me is—

He did not finish his sentence, but, seeing that Aunt Kate was out of earshot, at once led the three young ladies into the back room. The middle of the room was occupied by two square tables placed end to end, and on these Aunt Julia and the caretaker were straightening and smoothing a large cloth. On the sideboard were arrayed dishes and plates, and glasses and bundles of knives and forks and spoons. The top of the closed square piano served also as a sideboard for viands and sweets. At a smaller sideboard in one corner two young men were standing, drinking hop-bitters.

Mr Browne led his charges thither and invited them all, in jest, to some ladies' punch, hot, strong and sweet. As they said they never took anything strong he opened three bottles of lemonade for them. Then he asked one of the young men to move aside, and, taking hold of the decanter, filled out for himself a goodly measure of whisky. The young men eyed him respectfully while he took a trial sip.

—God help me, he said, smiling, it's the doctor's orders.

His wizened face broke into a broader smile, and the three young ladies laughed in musical echo to his pleasantry, swaying their bodies to and fro, with nervous jerks of their shoulders. The boldest said:

—O, now, Mr Browne, I'm sure the doctor never ordered anything of the kind.

Mr Browne took another sip of his whisky and said, with sidling mimicry:

—Well, you see, I'm like the famous Mrs Cassidy, who is reported to have said: *Now, Mary Grimes, if I don't take it, make me take it, for I feel I want it.*

His hot face had leaned forward a little too confidentially and he had assumed a very low Dublin accent so that the young ladies, with one instinct, received his speech in silence. Miss Furlong, who was one of Mary Jane's pupils, asked Miss Daly what was the name of the pretty waltz she had played;

2512 / James Joyce

and Mr Browne, seeing that he was ignored, turned promptly to the two young men who were more appreciative.

A red-faced young woman, dressed in pansy, came into the room, excitedly clapping her hands and crying:

—Quadrilles!⁵ Quadrilles!

Close on her heels came Aunt Kate, crying:

—Two gentlemen and three ladies, Mary Jane!

—O, here's Mr Bergin and Mr Kerrigan, said Mary Jane. Mr Kerrigan, will you take Miss Power? Miss Furlong, may I get you a partner, Mr Bergin. O, that'll just do now.

—Three ladies, Mary Jane, said Aunt Kate.

The two young gentlemen asked the ladies if they might have the pleasure, and Mary Jane turned to Miss Daly.

—O, Miss Daly, you're really awfully good, after playing for the last two dances, but really we're so short of ladies to-night.

—I don't mind in the least, Miss Morkan.

—But I've a nice partner for you, Mr Bartell D'Arcy, the tenor. I'll get him to sing later on. All Dublin is raving about him.

—Lovely voice, lovely voice! said Aunt Kate.

As the piano had twice begun the prelude to the first figure Mary Jane led her recruits quickly from the room. They had hardly gone when Aunt Julia wandered slowly into the room, looking behind her at something.

—What is the matter, Julia? asked Aunt Kate anxiously. Who is it?

Julia, who was carrying in a column of table-napkins, turned to her sister and said, simply, as if the question had surprised her:

—It's only Freddy, Kate, and Gabriel with him.

In fact right behind her Gabriel could be seen piloting Freddy Malins across the landing. The latter, a young man of about forty, was of Gabriel's size and build, with very round shoulders. His face was fleshy and pallid, touched with colour only at the thick hanging lobes of his ears and at the wide wings of his nose. He had coarse features, a blunt nose, a convex and receding brow, tumid and protruded lips. His heavy-lidded eyes and the disorder of his scanty hair made him look sleepy. He was laughing heartily in a high key at a story which he had been telling Gabriel on the stairs and at the same time rubbing the knuckles of his left fist backwards and forwards into his left eye.

—Good-evening, Freddy, said Aunt Julia.

Freddy Malins bade the Misses Morkan good-evening in what seemed an offhand fashion by reason of the habitual catch in his voice and then, seeing that Mr Browne was grinning at him from the sideboard, crossed the room on rather shaky legs and began to repeat in an undertone the story he had just told to Gabriel.

—He's not so bad, is he? said Aunt Kate to Gabriel.

Gabriel's brows were dark but he raised them quickly and answered:

—O no, hardly noticeable.

—Now, isn't he a terrible fellow! she said. And his poor mother made him take the pledge⁶ on New Year's Eve. But come on, Gabriel, into the drawing-room.

---

5. A square dance usually performed by four couples.

6. Sign a solemn promise not to drink alcohol.

Before leaving the room with Gabriel she signalled to Mr Browne by frowning and shaking her forefinger in warning to and fro. Mr Browne nodded in answer and, when she had gone, said to Freddy Malins:

—Now, then, Teddy, I'm going to fill you out a good glass of lemonade just to buck you up.

Freddy Malins, who was nearing the climax of his story, waved the offer aside impatiently but Mr Browne, having first called Freddy Malins' attention to a disarray in his dress, filled out and handed him a full glass of lemonade. Freddy Malins' left hand accepted the glass mechanically, his right hand being engaged in the mechanical readjustment of his dress. Mr Browne, whose face was once more wrinkling with mirth, poured out for himself a glass of whisky while Freddy Malins exploded, before he had well reached the climax of his story, in a kink of high-pitched bronchitic laughter and, setting down his untasted and overflowing glass, began to rub the knuckles of his left fist backwards and forwards into his left eye, repeating words of his last phrase as well as his fit of laughter would allow him.

Gabriel could not listen while Mary Jane was playing her Academy piece, full of runs and difficult passages, to the hushed drawing-room. He liked music but the piece she was playing had no melody for him and he doubted whether it had any melody for the other listeners, though they had begged Mary Jane to play something. Four young men, who had come from the refreshment-room to stand in the door-way at the sound of the piano, had gone away quietly in couples after a few minutes. The only persons who seemed to follow the music were Mary Jane herself, her hands racing along the key-board or lifted from it at the pauses like those of a priestess in momentary imprecation, and Aunt Kate standing at her elbow to turn the page.

Gabriel's eyes, irritated by the floor, which glittered with beeswax under the heavy chandelier, wandered to the wall above the piano. A picture of the balcony scene in *Romeo and Juliet* hung there and beside it was a picture of the two murdered princes in the Tower[7] which Aunt Julia had worked in red, blue and brown wools when she was a girl. Probably in the school they had gone to as girls that kind of work had been taught, for one year his mother had worked for him as a birthday present a waistcoat of purple tabinet,[8] with little foxes' heads upon it, lined with brown satin and having round mulberry buttons. It was strange that his mother had had no musical talent though Aunt Kate used to call her the brains carrier of the Morkan family. Both she and Julia had always seemed a little proud of their serious and matronly sister. Her photograph stood before the pierglass.[9] She held an open book on her knees and was pointing out something in it to Constantine who, dressed in a man-o'-war suit,[1] lay at her feet. It was she who had chosen the names for her sons for she was very sensible of the dignity of family life. Thanks to her, Constantine was now senior curate[2] in Balbriggan and, thanks to her, Gabriel himself had taken his degree in the Royal University. A shadow passed over his face as he remembered her sullen opposition to his marriage. Some slighting phrases she had used still rankled in his memory; she had once spoken of

7. Probably Edward V and his brother Richard, duke of York, reputedly murdered in 1483 by their uncle and successor, Richard III.
8. Silk and wool fabric made chiefly in Ireland.
9. Large tall mirror.
1. Sailor suit, favorite wear for children of both sexes early in the 20th century.
2. Clergyman appointed to assist a parish priest.

Gretta as being country cute and that was not true of Gretta at all. It was
Gretta who had nursed her during all her last long illness in their house at
Monkstown.

He knew that Mary Jane must be near the end of her piece for she was
playing again the opening melody with runs of scales after every bar and while
he waited for the end the resentment died down in his heart. The piece ended
with a trill of octaves in the treble and a final deep octave in the bass. Great
applause greeted Mary Jane as, blushing and rolling up her music nervously,
she escaped from the room. The most vigorous clapping came from the four
young men in the doorway who had gone away to the refreshment-room at the
beginning of the piece but had come back when the piano had stopped.

Lancers[3] were arranged. Gabriel found himself partnered with Miss Ivors.
She was a frank-mannered talkative young lady, with a freckled face and prominent brown eyes. She did not wear a low-cut bodice and the large brooch
which was fixed in the front of her collar bore on it an Irish device.

When they had taken their places she said abruptly:

—I have a crow to pluck with you.

—With me? said Gabriel.

She nodded her head gravely.

—What is it? asked Gabriel, smiling at her solemn manner.

—Who is G. C.? answered Miss Ivors, turning her eyes upon him.

Gabriel coloured and was about to knit his brows, as if he did not understand, when she said bluntly:

—O, innocent Amy! I have found out that you write for The Daily Express.
Now, aren't you ashamed of yourself?

—Why should I be ashamed of myself? asked Gabriel, blinking his eyes and
trying to smile.

—Well, I'm ashamed of you, said Miss Ivors frankly. To say you'd write for
a rag like that. I didn't think you were a West Briton.[4]

A look of perplexity appeared on Gabriel's face. It was true that he wrote a
literary column every Wednesday in The Daily Express, for which he was paid
fifteen shillings. But that did not make him a West Briton surely. The books
he received for review were almost more welcome than the paltry cheque. He
loved to feel the covers and turn over the pages of newly printed books. Nearly
every day when his teaching in the college was ended he used to wander down
the quays to the second-hand booksellers, to Hickey's on Bachelor's Walk, to
Webb's, or Massey's on Aston's Quay, or to O'Clohissey's in the by-street. He
did not know how to meet her charge. He wanted to say that literature was
above politics. But they were friends of many years' standing and their careers
had been parallel, first at the University and then as teachers: he could not
risk a grandiose phrase with her. He continued blinking his eyes and trying to
smile and murmured lamely that he saw nothing political in writing reviews
of books.

When their turn to cross had come he was still perplexed and inattentive.
Miss Ivors promptly took his hand in a warm grasp and said in a soft friendly
tone:

—Of course, I was only joking. Come, we cross now.

3. A square dance for four or more couples.
4. A pejorative term for one who denies a separate

Irish nationality and sees Ireland as simply a western extension of Great Britain.

When they were together again she spoke of the University question[5] and Gabriel felt more at ease. A friend of hers had shown her his review of Browning's poems. That was how she had found out the secret: but she liked the review immensely. Then she said suddenly:

—O, Mr Conroy, will you come for an excursion to the Aran Isles[6] this summer? We're going to stay there a whole month. It will be splendid out in the Atlantic. You ought to come. Mr Clancy is coming, and Mr Kilkelly and Kathleen Kearney. It would be splendid for Gretta too if she'd come. She's from Connacht,[7] isn't she?

—Her people are, said Gabriel shortly.

—But you will come, won't you? said Miss Ivors, laying her warm hand eagerly on his arm.

—The fact is, said Gabriel, I have already arranged to go—

—Go where? asked Miss Ivors.

—Well, you know, every year I go for a cycling tour with some fellows and so—

—But where? asked Miss Ivors.

—Well, we usually go to France or Belgium or perhaps Germany, said Gabriel awkwardly.

—And why do you go to France and Belgium, said Miss Ivors, instead of visiting your own land?

—Well, said Gabriel, it's partly to keep in touch with the languages and partly for a change.

—And haven't you your own language to keep in touch with—Irish? asked Miss Ivors.

—Well, said Gabriel, if it comes to that, you know, Irish is not my language.

Their neighbours had turned to listen to the cross-examination. Gabriel glanced right and left nervously and tried to keep his good humour under the ordeal which was making a blush invade his forehead.

—And haven't you your own land to visit, continued Miss Ivors, that you know nothing of, your own people, and your own country?

—O, to tell you the truth, retorted Gabriel suddenly, I'm sick of my own country, sick of it!

—Why? asked Miss Ivors.

Gabriel did not answer for his retort had heated him.

—Why? repeated Miss Ivors.

They had to go visiting together and, as he had not answered her, Miss Ivors said warmly:

—Of course, you've no answer.

Gabriel tried to cover his agitation by taking part in the dance with great energy. He avoided her eyes for he had seen a sour expression on her face. But when they met in the long chain he was surprised to feel his hand firmly pressed. She looked at him from under her brows for a moment quizzically[8] until he smiled. Then, just as the chain was about to start again, she stood on tiptoe and whispered into his ear:

—West Briton!

When the lancers were over Gabriel went away to a remote corner of the

5. Namely, whether Ireland's elite Protestant universities should be open to Catholics.
6. Three small islands lying across the entrance to Galway Bay, on the west coast of Ireland.

7. Or Connaught, a rural region on the west coast of Ireland.
8. Teasingly.

room where Freddy Malins' mother was sitting. She was a stout feeble old woman with white hair. Her voice had a catch in it like her son's and she stuttered slightly. She had been told that Freddy had come and that he was nearly all right. Gabriel asked her whether she had had a good crossing. She lived with her married daughter in Glasgow and came to Dublin on a visit once a year. She answered placidly that she had had a beautiful crossing and that the captain had been most attentive to her. She spoke also of the beautiful house her daughter kept in Glasgow, and of all the nice friends they had there. While her tongue rambled on Gabriel tried to banish from his mind all memory of the unpleasant incident with Miss Ivors. Of course the girl or woman, or whatever she was, was an enthusiast but there was a time for all things. Perhaps he ought not to have answered her like that. But she had no right to call him a West Briton before people, even in joke. She had tried to make him ridiculous before people, heckling him and staring at him with her rabbit's eyes.

He saw his wife making her way towards him through the waltzing couples. When she reached him she said into his ear:

—Gabriel, Aunt Kate wants to know won't you carve the goose as usual. Miss Daly will carve the ham and I'll do the pudding.

—All right, said Gabriel.

—She's sending in the younger ones first as soon as this waltz is over so that we'll have the table to ourselves.

—Were you dancing? asked Gabriel.

—Of course I was. Didn't you see me? What words had you with Molly Ivors?

—No words. Why? Did she say so?

—Something like that. I'm trying to get that Mr D'Arcy to sing. He's full of conceit, I think.

—There were no words, said Gabriel moodily, only she wanted me to go for a trip to the west of Ireland and I said I wouldn't.

His wife clasped her hands excitedly and gave a little jump.

—O, do go, Gabriel, she cried. I'd love to see Galway again.

—You can go if you like, said Gabriel coldly.

She looked at him for a moment, then turned to Mrs Malins and said:

—There's a nice husband for you, Mrs Malins.

While she was threading her way back across the room Mrs Malins, without adverting to the interruption, went on to tell Gabriel what beautiful places there were in Scotland and beautiful scenery. Her son-in-law brought them every year to the lakes and they used to go fishing. Her son-in-law was a splendid fisher. One day he caught a fish, a beautiful big big fish, and the man in the hotel boiled it for their dinner.

Gabriel hardly heard what she said. Now that supper was coming near he began to think again about his speech and about the quotation. When he saw Freddy Malins coming across the room to visit his mother Gabriel left the chair free for him and retired into the embrasure[9] of the window. The room had already cleared and from the back room came the clatter of plates and knives. Those who still remained in the drawing-room seemed tired of dancing and were conversing quietly in little groups. Gabriel's warm trembling fingers tapped the cold pane of the window. How cool it must be outside! How pleas-

9. Opening for a window in a thick wall.

ant it would be to walk out alone, first along by the river and then through the park! The snow would be lying on the branches of the trees and forming a bright cap on the top of the Wellington Monument.[1] How much more pleasant it would be there than at the supper-table!

He ran over the headings of his speech: Irish hospitality, sad memories, the Three Graces, Paris,[2] the quotation from Browning. He repeated to himself a phrase he had written in his review: *One feels that one is listening to a thought-tormented music*. Miss Ivors had praised the review. Was she sincere? Had she really any life of her own behind all her propagandism? There had never been any ill-feeling between them until that night. It unnerved him to think that she would be at the supper-table, looking up at him while he spoke with her critical quizzing eyes. Perhaps she would not be sorry to see him fail in his speech. An idea came into his mind and gave him courage. He would say, alluding to Aunt Kate and Aunt Julia: *Ladies and Gentlemen, the generation which is now on the wane among us may have had its faults but for my part I think it had certain qualities of hospitality, of humour, of humanity, which the new and very serious and hypereducated generation that is growing up around us seems to me to lack.* Very good: that was one for Miss Ivors. What did he care that his aunts were only two ignorant old women?

A murmur in the room attracted his attention. Mr Browne was advancing from the door, gallantly escorting Aunt Julia, who leaned upon his arm, smiling and hanging her head. An irregular musketry of applause escorted her also as far as the piano and then, as Mary Jane seated herself on the stool, and Aunt Julia, no longer smiling, half turned so as to pitch her voice fairly into the room, gradually ceased. Gabriel recognised the prelude. It was that of an old song of Aunt Julia's—*Arrayed for the Bridal*.[3] Her voice, strong and clear in tone, attacked with great spirit the runs which embellish the air and though she sang very rapidly she did not miss even the smallest of the grace notes. To follow the voice, without looking at the singer's face, was to feel and share the excitement of swift and secure flight. Gabriel applauded loudly with all the others at the close of the song and loud applause was borne in from the invisible supper-table. It sounded so genuine that a little colour struggled into Aunt Julia's face as she bent to replace in the music-stand the old leather-bound song-book that had her initials on the cover. Freddy Malins, who had listened with his head perched sideways to hear her better, was still applauding when everyone else had ceased and talking animatedly to his mother who nodded her head gravely and slowly in acquiescence. At last, when he could clap no more, he stood up suddenly and hurried across the room to Aunt Julia whose hand he seized and held in both his hands, shaking it when words failed him or the catch in his voice proved too much for him.

—I was just telling my mother, he said, I never heard you sing so well, never. No, I never heard your voice so good as it is to-night. Now! Would you believe that now? That's the truth. Upon my word and honour that's the truth. I never

---

1. Tribute to Arthur Wellesley (1769–1852), 1st duke of Wellington, Dublin-born hero of the British army. The obelisk stands in Dublin's Phoenix Park.
2. In Greek mythology Paris was selected by Zeus to choose which of three goddesses was the most beautiful. The Graces were three sister-goddesses—Aglaia, splendor; Euphrosyne, festivity; and Thalia, rejoicing—who together represented loveliness and joy. Gabriel is making a mental note to refer to his two aunts and Mary Jane in a complimentary way.
3. This old song (beginning "Arrayed for the bridal, in beauty behold her") "is replete with long and complicated runs, requiring a sophisticated and gifted singer" (Bowen, *Musical Allusions in the Works of James Joyce*, 1974); the suggestion is that Aunt Julia was a really accomplished singer.

heard your voice sound so fresh and so . . . so clear and fresh, never.

Aunt Julia smiled broadly and murmured something about compliments as she released her hand from his grasp. Mr Browne extended his open hand towards her and said to those who were near him in the manner of a showman introducing a prodigy to an audience:

—Miss Julia Morkan, my latest discovery!

He was laughing very heartily at this himself when Freddy Malins turned to him and said:

—Well, Browne, if you're serious you might make a worse discovery. All I can say is I never heard her sing half so well as long as I am coming here. And that's the honest truth.

—Neither did I, said Mr Browne. I think her voice has greatly improved.

Aunt Julia shrugged her shoulders and said with meek pride:

—Thirty years ago I hadn't a bad voice as voices go.

—I often told Julia, said Aunt Kate emphatically, that she was simply thrown away in that choir. But she never would be said by me.

She turned as if to appeal to the good sense of the others against a refractory child while Aunt Julia gazed in front of her, a vague smile of reminiscence playing on her face.

—No, continued Aunt Kate, she wouldn't be said or led by anyone, slaving there in that choir night and day, night and day. Six o'clock on Christmas morning! And all for what?

—Well, isn't it for the honour of God, Aunt Kate? asked Mary Jane, twisting round on the piano-stool and smiling.

Aunt Kate turned fiercely on her niece and said:

—I know all about the honour of God, Mary Jane, but I think it's not at all honourable for the pope to turn out the women out of the choirs that have slaved there all their lives and put little whipper-snappers of boys over their heads. I suppose it is for the good of the Church if the pope does it. But it's not just, Mary Jane, and it's not right.

She had worked herself into a passion and would have continued in defence of her sister for it was a sore subject with her but Mary Jane, seeing that all the dancers had come back, intervened pacifically:

—Now, Aunt Kate, you're giving scandal to Mr Browne who is of the other persuasion.[4]

Aunt Kate turned to Mr Browne, who was grinning at this allusion to his religion, and said hastily:

—O, I don't question the pope's being right. I'm only a stupid old woman and I wouldn't presume to do such a thing. But there's such a thing as common everyday politeness and gratitude. And if I were in Julia's place I'd tell that Father Healy straight up to his face . . .

—And besides, Aunt Kate, said Mary Jane, we really are all hungry and when we are hungry we are all very quarrelsome.

—And when we are thirsty we are also quarrelsome, added Mr Browne.

—So that we had better go to supper, said Mary Jane, and finish the discussion afterwards.

On the landing outside the drawing-room Gabriel found his wife and Mary Jane trying to persuade Miss Ivors to stay for supper. But Miss Ivors, who had put on her hat and was buttoning her cloak, would not stay. She did not feel

4. I.e., Protestant.

in the least hungry and she had already overstayed her time.

—But only for ten minutes, Molly, said Mrs Conroy. That won't delay you.

—To take a pick itself, said Mary Jane, after all your dancing.

—I really couldn't, said Miss Ivors.

—I am afraid you didn't enjoy yourself at all, said Mary Jane hopelessly.

—Ever so much, I assure you, said Miss Ivors, but you really must let me run off now.

—But how can you get home? asked Mrs Conroy.

—O, it's only two steps up the quay.

Gabriel hesitated a moment and said:

—If you will allow me, Miss Ivors, I'll see you home if you really are obliged to go.

But Miss Ivors broke away from them.

—I won't hear of it, she cried. For goodness sake go in to your suppers and don't mind me. I'm quite well able to take care of myself.

—Well, you're the comical girl, Molly, said Mrs Conroy frankly.

—*Beannacht libh,*[5] cried Miss Ivors, with a laugh, as she ran down the staircase.

Mary Jane gazed after her, a moody puzzled expression on her face, while Mrs Conroy leaned over the banisters to listen for the hall-door. Gabriel asked himself was he the cause of her abrupt departure. But she did not seem to be in ill humour: she had gone away laughing. He stared blankly down the staircase.

At that moment Aunt Kate came toddling out of the supper-room, almost wringing her hands in despair.

—Where is Gabriel? she cried. Where on earth is Gabriel? There's everyone waiting in there, stage to let, and nobody to carve the goose!

—Here I am, Aunt Kate! cried Gabriel, with sudden animation, ready to carve a flock of geese, if necessary.

A fat brown goose lay at one end of the table and at the other end, on a bed of creased paper strewn with sprigs of parsley, lay a great ham, stripped of its outer skin and peppered over with crust crumbs, a neat paper frill round its shin and beside this was a round of spiced beef. Between these rival ends ran parallel lines of side-dishes: two little minsters of jelly, red and yellow; a shallow dish full of blocks of blancmange[6] and red jam, a large green leaf-shaped dish with a stalk-shaped handle, on which lay bunches of purple raisins and peeled almonds, a companion dish on which lay a solid rectangle of Smyrna figs, a dish of custard topped with grated nutmeg, a small bowl full of chocolates and sweets wrapped in gold and silver papers and a glass vase in which stood some tall celery stalks. In the centre of the table there stood, as sentries to a fruit-stand which upheld a pyramid of oranges and American apples, two squat old-fashioned decanters of cut glass, one containing port and the other dark sherry. On the closed square piano a pudding in a huge yellow dish lay in waiting and behind it were three squads of bottles of stout and ale and minerals, drawn up according to the colours of their uniforms, the first two black, with brown and red labels, the third and smallest squad white, with transverse green sashes.

Gabriel took his seat boldly at the head of the table and, having looked to

5. Blessing on you (Gaelic; literal trans.); good-bye.

6. Sweet almond-flavored pudding.

the edge of the carver, plunged his fork firmly into the goose. He felt quite at ease now for he was an expert carver and liked nothing better than to find himself at the head of a well-laden table.

—Miss Furlong, what shall I send you? he asked. A wing or a slice of the breast?

—Just a small slice of the breast.

—Miss Higgins, what for you?

—O, anything at all, Mr Conroy.

While Gabriel and Miss Daly exchanged plates of goose and plates of ham and spiced beef Lily went from guest to guest with a dish of hot floury potatoes wrapped in a white napkin. This was Mary Jane's idea and she had also suggested apple sauce for the goose but Aunt Kate had said that plain roast goose without apple sauce had always been good enough for her and she hoped she might never eat worse. Mary Jane waited on her pupils and saw that they got the best slices and Aunt Kate and Aunt Julia opened and carried across from the piano bottles of stout and ale for the gentlemen and bottles of minerals for the ladies. There was a great deal of confusion and laughter and noise, the noise of orders and counter-orders, of knives and forks, of corks and glass-stoppers. Gabriel began to carve second helpings as soon as he had finished the first round without serving himself. Everyone protested loudly so that he compromised by taking a long draught of stout for he had found the carving hot work. Mary Jane settled down quietly to her supper but Aunt Kate and Aunt Julia were still toddling round the table, walking on each other's heels, getting in each other's way and giving each other unheeded orders. Mr Browne begged of them to sit down and eat their suppers and so did Gabriel but they said there was time enough so that, at last, Freddy Malins stood up and, capturing Aunt Kate, plumped her down on her chair amid general laughter.

When everyone had been well served Gabriel said, smiling:

—Now, if anyone wants a little more of what vulgar people call stuffing let him or her speak.

A chorus of voices invited him to begin his own supper and Lily came forward with three potatoes which she had reserved for him.

—Very well, said Gabriel amiably, as he took another preparatory draught, kindly forget my existence, ladies and gentlemen, for a few minutes.

He set to his supper and took no part in the conversation with which the table covered Lily's removal of the plates. The subject of talk was the opera company which was then at the Theatre Royal. Mr Bartell D'Arcy, the tenor, a dark-complexioned young man with a smart moustache, praised very highly the leading contralto of the company but Miss Furlong thought she had a rather vulgar style of production. Freddy Malins said there was a negro chieftain singing in the second part of the Gaiety pantomime who had one of the finest tenor voices he had every heard.

—Have you heard him? he asked Mr Bartell D'Arcy across the table.

—No, answered Mr Bartell D'Arcy carelessly.

—Because, Freddy Malins explained, now I'd be curious to hear your opinion of him. I think he has a grand voice.

—It takes Teddy to find out the really good things, said Mr Browne familiarly to the table.

—And why couldn't he have a voice too? asked Freddy Malins sharply. Is it because he's only a black?

Nobody answered this question and Mary Jane led the table back to the legitimate opera. One of her pupils had given her a pass for *Mignon*.[7] Of course it was very fine, she said, but it made her think of poor Georgina Burns. Mr Browne could go back farther still, to the old Italian companies that used to come to Dublin—Tietjens, Ilma de Murzka, Campanini, the great Trebelli, Giuglini, Ravelli, Aramburo. Those were the days, he said, when there was something like singing to be heard in Dublin. He told too of how the top gallery of the old Royal used to be packed night after night, of how one night an Italian tenor had sung five encores to *Let Me Like a Soldier Fall*,[8] introducing a high C every time, and of how the gallery boys would sometimes in their enthusiasm unyoke the horses from the carriage of some great *prima donna* and pull her themselves through the streets to her hotel. Why did they never play the grand old operas now, he asked, *Dinorah, Lucrezia Borgia?*[9] Because they could not get the voices to sing them: that was why.

—O, well, said Mr Bartell D'Arcy, I presume there are as good singers to-day as there were then.

—Where are they? asked Mr Browne defiantly.

—In London, Paris, Milan, said Mr Bartell d'Arcy warmly. I suppose Caruso,[1] for example, is quite as good, if not better than any of the men you have mentioned.

—Maybe so, said Mr Browne. But I may tell you I doubt it strongly.

—O, I'd give anything to hear Caruso sing, said Mary Jane.

—For me, said Aunt Kate, who had been picking a bone, there was only one tenor. To please me, I mean. But I suppose none of you ever heard of him.

—Who was he, Miss Morkan? asked Mr Bartell D'Arcy politely.

—His name, said Aunt Kate, was Parkinson. I heard him when he was in his prime and I think he had then the purest tenor voice that was ever put into a man's throat.

—Strange, said Mr Bartell d'Arcy. I never even heard of him.

—Yes, yes, Miss Morkan is right, said Mr Browne. I remember hearing of old Parkinson but he's too far back for me.

—A beautiful pure sweet mellow English tenor, said Aunt Kate with enthusiasm.

Gabriel having finished, the huge pudding was transferred to the table. The clatter of forks and spoons began again. Gabriel's wife served out spoonfuls of the pudding and passed the plates down the table. Midway down they were held up by Mary Jane, who replenished them with raspberry or orange jelly or with blancmange and jam. The pudding was of Aunt Julia's making and she received praises for it from all quarters. She herself said that it was not quite brown enough.

—Well, I hope, Miss Morkan, said Mr Browne, that I'm brown enough for you because, you know, I'm all brown.

All the gentlemen, except Gabriel, ate some of the pudding out of compliment to Aunt Julia. As Gabriel never ate sweets the celery had been left for

7. Opera by Ambroise Thomas first produced in Paris in 1866 and in London in 1870.
8. This song, from the opera *Maritana* by W. Wallace (it actually begins "Yes! let me like a soldier fall"), ends on middle C; it would be a piece of exhibitionism to end on a high C, as Joyce's father, who had a good voice, used to do. Joyce's brother Stanislaus remembered the song as insufferable

rubbish. Mr. Browne is not to be taken seriously as a music critic.
9. An opera by Donizetti, first produced at La Scala, Milan, in 1833. *Dinorah* is an opera by Meyerbeer, first produced in Paris in 1859.
1. Enrico Caruso (1873–1921), the great Italian dramatic tenor.

him. Freddy Malins also took a stalk of celery and ate it with his pudding. He had been told that celery was a capital thing for the blood and he was just then under doctor's care. Mrs Malins, who had been silent all through the supper, said that her son was going down to Mount Melleray in a week or so. The table then spoke of Mount Melleray, how bracing the air was down there, how hospitable the monks were and how they never asked for a penny-piece from their guests.

—And do you mean to say, asked Mr Browne incredulously, that a chap can go down there and put up there as if it were a hotel and live on the fat of the land and then come away without paying a farthing?

—O, most people give some donation to the monastery when they leave, said Mary Jane.

—I wish we had an institution like that in our Church, said Mr Browne candidly.

He was astonished to hear that the monks never spoke, got up at two in the morning and slept in their coffins. He asked what they did it for.

—That's the rule of the order, said Aunt Kate firmly.

—Yes, but why? asked Mr Browne.

Aunt Kate repeated that it was the rule, that was all. Mr Browne still seemed not to understand. Freddy Malins explained to him, as best he could, that the monks were trying to make up for the sins committed by all the sinners in the outside world. The explanation was not very clear for Mr Browne grinned and said:

—I like that idea very much but wouldn't a comfortable spring bed do them as well as a coffin?

—The coffin, said Mary Jane, is to remind them of their last end.

As the subject had grown lugubrious it was buried in a silence of the table during which Mrs Malins could be heard saying to her neighbour in an indistinct undertone:

—They are very good men, the monks, very pious men.

The raisins and almonds and figs and apples and oranges and chocolates and sweets were now passed about the table and Aunt Julia invited all the guests to have either port or sherry. At first Mr Bartell D'Arcy refused to take either but one of his neighbours nudged him and whispered something to him upon which he allowed his glass to be filled. Gradually as the last glasses were being filled the conversation ceased. A pause followed, broken only by the noise of the wine and by unsettlings of chairs. The Misses Morkan, all three, looked down at the tablecloth. Someone coughed once or twice and then a few gentlemen patted the table gently as a signal for silence. The silence came and Gabriel pushed back his chair and stood up.

The patting at once grew louder in encouragement and then ceased altogether. Gabriel leaned his ten trembling fingers on the tablecloth and smiled nervously at the company. Meeting a row of upturned faces he raised his eyes to the chandelier. The piano was playing a waltz tune and he could hear the skirts sweeping against the drawing-room door. People, perhaps, were standing in the snow on the quay outside, gazing up at the lighted windows and listening to the waltz music. The air was pure there. In the distance lay the park where the trees were weighted with snow. The Wellington Monument wore a gleaming cap of snow that flashed westward over the white field of Fifteen Acres.

He began:

—Ladies and Gentlemen.

—It has fallen to my lot this evening, as in years past, to perform a very pleasing task but a task for which I am afraid my poor powers as a speaker are all too inadequate.

—No, no! said Mr Browne.

—But, however that may be, I can only ask you to-night to take the will for the deed and to lend me your attention for a few moments while I endeavour to express to you in words what my feelings are on this occasion.

—Ladies and Gentlemen. It is not the first time that we have gathered together under this hospitable roof, around this hospitable board. It is not the first time that we have been the recipients—or perhaps, I had better say, the victims—of the hospitality of certain good ladies.

He made a circle in the air with his arm and paused. Everyone laughed or smiled at Aunt Kate and Aunt Julia and Mary Jane who all turned crimson with pleasure. Gabriel went on more boldly:

—I feel more strongly with every recurring year that our country has no tradition which does it so much honour and which it should guard so jealously as that of its hospitality. It is a tradition that is unique as far as my experience goes (and I have visited not a few places abroad) among the modern nations. Some would say, perhaps, that with us it is rather a failing than anything to be boasted of. But granted even that, it is, to my mind, a princely failing, and one that I trust will long be cultivated among us. Of one thing, at least, I am sure. As long as this one roof shelters the good ladies aforesaid—and I wish from my heart it may do so for many and many a long year to come—the tradition of genuine warm-hearted courteous Irish hospitality, which our fore-fathers have handed down to us and which we in turn must hand down to our descendants, is still alive among us.

A hearty murmur of assent ran round the table. It shot through Gabriel's mind that Miss Ivors was not there and that she had gone away discourteously: and he said with confidence in himself:

—Ladies and Gentlemen.

—A new generation is growing up in our midst, a generation actuated by new ideas and new principles. It is serious and enthusiastic for these new ideas and its enthusiasm, even when it is misdirected, is, I believe, in the main sincere. But we are living in a sceptical and, if I may use the phrase, a thought-tormented age: and sometimes I fear that this new generation, educated or hypereducated as it is, will lack those qualities of humanity, of hospitality, of kindly humour which belonged to an older day. Listening to-night to the names of all those great singers of the past it seemed to me, I must confess, that we were living in a less spacious age. Those days might, without exaggeration, be called spacious days: and if they are gone beyond recall let us hope, at least, that in gatherings such as this we shall still speak of them with pride and affection, still cherish in our hearts the memory of those dead and gone great ones whose fame the world will not willingly let die.

—Hear, hear! said Mr Browne loudly.

—But yet, continued Gabriel, his voice falling into a softer inflection, there are always in gatherings such as this sadder thoughts that will recur to our minds: thoughts of the past, of youth, of changes, of absent faces that we miss here to-night. Our path through life is strewn with many such sad memories: and were we to brood upon them always we could not find the heart to go on bravely with our work among the living. We have all of us living duties and living affections which claim, and rightly claim, our strenuous endeavours.

2524 / James Joyce

—Therefore, I will not linger on the past. I will not let any gloomy moralising intrude upon us here to-night. Here we are gathered together for a brief moment from the bustle and rush of our everyday routine. We are met here as friends, in the spirit of good-fellowship, as colleagues, also to a certain extent, in the true spirit of *camaraderie*, and as the guests of—what shall I call them?—the Three Graces of the Dublin musical world.

The table burst into applause and laughter at this sally. Aunt Julia vainly asked each of her neighbours in turn to tell her what Gabriel had said.

—He says we are the Three Graces,[2] Aunt Julia, said Mary Jane.

Aunt Julia did not understand but she looked up, smiling, at Gabriel, who continued in the same vein:

—Ladies and Gentlemen.

—I will not attempt to play to-night the part that Paris played on another occasion. I will not attempt to choose between them. The task would be an invidious one and one beyond my poor powers. For when I view them in turn, whether it be our chief hostess herself, whose good heart, whose too good heart, has become a byword with all who know her, or her sister, who seems to be gifted with perennial youth and whose singing must have been a surprise and a revelation to us all to-night, or, last but not least, when I consider our youngest hostess, talented, cheerful, hard-working and the best of nieces, I confess, Ladies and Gentlemen, that I do not know to which of them I should award the prize.

Gabriel glanced down at his aunts and, seeing the large smile on Aunt Julia's face and the tears which had risen to Aunt Kate's eyes, hastened to his close. He raised his glass of port gallantly, while every member of the company fingered a glass expectantly, and said loudly:

—Let us toast them all three together. Let us drink to their health, wealth, long life, happiness and prosperity and may they long continue to hold the proud and self-won position which they hold in their profession and the position of honour and affection which they hold in our hearts.

All the guests stood up, glass in hand, and, turning towards the three seated ladies, sang in unison, with Mr Browne as leader:

> *For they are jolly gay fellows,*
> *For they are jolly gay fellows,*
> *For they are jolly gay fellows,*
> *Which nobody can deny.*

Aunt Kate was making frank use of her handkerchief and even Aunt Julia seemed moved. Freddy Malins beat time with his pudding-fork and the singers turned towards one another, as if in melodious conference, while they sang, with emphasis:

> *Unless he tells a lie,*
> *Unless he tells a lie.*

Then, turning once more towards their hostesses, they sang:

> *For they are jolly gay fellows,*
> *For they are jolly gay fellows,*
> *For they are jolly gay fellows,*
> *Which nobody can deny.*

2. See n. 2, p. 2517.

The acclamation which followed was taken up beyond the door of the supper-room by many of the other guests and renewed time after time, Freddy Malins acting as officer with his fork on high.

The piercing morning air came into the hall where they were standing so that Aunt Kate said:

—Close the door, somebody. Mrs Malins will get her death of cold.

—Browne is out there, Aunt Kate, said Mary Jane.

—Browne is everywhere, said Aunt Kate, lowering her voice.

Mary Jane laughed at her tone.

—Really, she said archly, he is very attentive.

—He has been laid on here like the gas, said Aunt Kate in the same tone, all during the Christmas.

She laughed herself this time good-humouredly and then added quickly:

—But tell him to come in, Mary Jane, and close the door. I hope to goodness he didn't hear me.

At that moment the hall-door was opened and Mr Browne came in from the doorstep, laughing as if his heart would break. He was dressed in a long green overcoat with mock astrakhan cuffs and collar and wore on his head an oval fur cap. He pointed down the snow-covered quay from where the sound of shrill prolonged whistling was borne in.

—Teddy will have all the cabs in Dublin out, he said.

Gabriel advanced from the little pantry behind the office, struggling into his overcoat and, looking round the hall, said:

—Gretta not down yet?

—She's getting on her things, Gabriel, said Aunt Kate.

—Who's playing up there? asked Gabriel.

—Nobody. They're all gone.

—O no, Aunt Kate, said Mary Jane. Bartell D'Arcy and Miss O'Callaghan aren't gone yet.

—Someone is strumming at the piano, anyhow, said Gabriel.

Mary Jane glanced at Gabriel and Mr Browne and said with a shiver:

—It makes me feel cold to look at you two gentlemen muffled up like that. I wouldn't like to face your journey home at this hour.

—I'd like nothing better this minute, said Mr Browne stoutly, than a rattling fine walk in the country or a fast drive with a good spanking goer between the shafts.

—We used to have a very good horse and trap[3] at home, said Aunt Julia sadly.

—The never-to-be-forgotten Johnny, said Mary Jane, laughing.

Aunt Kate and Gabriel laughed too.

—Why, what was wonderful about Johnny? asked Mr Browne.

—The late lamented Patrick Morkan, our grandfather, that is, explained Gabriel, commonly known in his later years as the old gentleman, was a glue-boiler.[4]

—O, now, Gabriel, said Aunt Kate, laughing, he had a starch mill.

—Well, glue or starch, said Gabriel, the old gentleman had a horse by the name of Johnny. And Johnny used to work in the old gentleman's mill, walking

3. A two-wheeled horse-drawn carriage on springs.

4. Glue was made by boiling animal hides and hoofs.

round and round in order to drive the mill. That was all very well; but now comes the tragic part about Johnny. One fine day the old gentleman thought he'd like to drive out with the quality[5] to a military review in the park.

—The Lord have mercy on his soul, said Aunt Kate compassionately.

—Amen, said Gabriel. So the old gentleman, as I said, harnessed Johnny and put on his very best tall hat and his very best stock collar and drove out in grand style from his ancestral mansion somewhere near Back Lane, I think.

Everyone laughed, even Mrs Malins, at Gabriel's manner and Aunt Kate said:

—O now, Gabriel, he didn't live in Back Lane, really. Only the mill was there.

—Out from the mansion of his forefathers, continued Gabriel, he drove with Johnny. And everything went on beautifully until Johnny came in sight of King Billy's statue:[6] and whether he fell in love with the horse King Billy sits on or whether he thought he was back again in the mill, anyhow he began to walk round the statue.

Gabriel paced in a circle round the hall in his goloshes amid the laughter of the others.

—Round and round he went, said Gabriel, and the old gentleman, who was a very pompous old gentleman, was highly indignant. *Go on, sir! What do you mean, sir? Johnny! Johnny! Most extraordinary conduct! Can't understand the horse!*

The peals of laughter which followed Gabriel's imitation of the incident were interrupted by a resounding knock at the hall-door. Mary Jane ran to open it and let in Freddy Malins. Freddy Malins, with his hat well back on his head and his shoulders humped with cold, was puffing and steaming after his exertions.

—I could only get one cab, he said.

—O, we'll find another along the quay, said Gabriel.

—Yes, said Aunt Kate. Better not keep Mrs Malins standing in the draught.

Mrs Malins was helped down the front steps by her son and Mr Browne and, after many manœuvres, hoisted into the cab. Freddy Malins clambered in after her and spent a long time settling her on the seat, Mr Browne helping him with advice. At last she was settled comfortably and Freddy Malins invited Mr Browne into the cab. There was a good deal of confused talk, and then Mr Browne got into the cab. The cabman settled his rug over his knees, and bent down for the address. The confusion grew greater and the cabman was directed differently by Freddy Malins and Mr Browne, each of whom had his head out through a window of the cab. The difficulty was to know where to drop Mr Browne along the route and Aunt Kate, Aunt Julia and Mary Jane helped the discussion from the doorstep with cross-directions and contradictions and abundance of laughter. As for Freddy Malins he was speechless with laughter. He popped his head in and out of the window every moment, to the great danger of his hat, and told his mother how the discussion was progressing till at last Mr Browne shouted to the bewildered cabman above the din of everybody's laughter:

—Do you know Trinity College?

---

5. People of rank or high social position.
6. Statue of King William III of England in front of Trinity College, Dublin. He defeated predomi-nantly Irish Catholic forces in the 1690 Battle of the Boyne.

—Yes, sir, said the cabman.

—Well, drive bang up against Trinity College gates, said Mr Browne, and then we'll tell you where to go. You understand now?

—Yes, sir, said the cabman.

—Make like a bird for Trinity College.

—Right, sir, cried the cabman.

The horse was whipped up and the cab rattled off along the quay amid a chorus of laughter and adieus.

Gabriel had not gone to the door with the others. He was in a dark part of the hall gazing up the staircase. A woman was standing near the top of the first flight, in the shadow also. He could not see her face but he could see the terracotta and salmonpink panels of her skirt which the shadow made appear black and white. It was his wife. She was leaning on the banisters, listening to something. Gabriel was surprised at her stillness and strained his ear to listen also. But he could hear little save the noise of laughter and dispute on the front steps, a few chords struck on the piano and a few notes of a man's voice singing.

He stood still in the gloom of the hall, trying to catch the air that the voice was singing and gazing up at his wife. There was grace and mystery in her attitude as if she were a symbol of something. He asked himself what is a woman standing on the stairs in the shadow, listening to distant music, a symbol of. If he were a painter he would paint her in that attitude. Her blue felt hat would show off the bronze of her hair against the darkness and the dark panels of her skirt would show off the light ones. *Distant Music* he would call the picture if he were a painter.

The hall-door was closed; and Aunt Kate, Aunt Julia and Mary Jane came down the hall, still laughing.

—Well, isn't Freddy terrible? said Mary Jane. He's really terrible.

Gabriel said nothing but pointed up the stairs towards where his wife was standing. Now that the hall-door was closed the voice and the piano could be heard more clearly. Gabriel held up his hand for them to be silent. The song seemed to be in the old Irish tonality and the singer seemed uncertain both of his words and of his voice. The voice, made plaintive by distance and by the singer's hoarseness, faintly illuminated the cadence of the air with words expressing grief:

> O, the rain falls on my heavy locks
> And the dew wets my skin,
> My babe lies cold . . .

—O, exclaimed Mary Jane. It's Bartell D'Arcy singing and he wouldn't sing all the night. O, I'll get him to sing a song before he goes.

—O do, Mary Jane, said Aunt Kate.

Mary Jane brushed past the others and ran to the staircase but before she reached it the singing stopped and the piano was closed abruptly.

—O, what a pity! she cried. Is he coming down, Gretta?

Gabriel heard his wife answer yes and saw her come down towards them. A few steps behind her were Mr Bartell D'Arcy and Miss O'Callaghan.

—O, Mr D'Arcy, cried Mary Jane, it's downright mean of you to break off like that when we were all in raptures listening to you.

—I have been at him all the evening, said Miss O'Callaghan, and Mrs Conroy too and he told us he had a dreadful cold and couldn't sing.

—O, Mr D'Arcy, said Aunt Kate, now that was a great fib to tell.

—Can't you see that I'm as hoarse as a crow? said Mr D'Arcy roughly.

He went into the pantry hastily and put on his overcoat. The others, taken aback by his rude speech, could find nothing to say. Aunt Kate wrinkled her brows and made signs to the others to drop the subject. Mr D'Arcy stood swathing his neck carefully and frowning.

—It's the weather, said Aunt Julia, after a pause.

—Yes, everybody has colds, said Aunt Kate readily, everybody.

—They say, said Mary Jane, we haven't had snow like it for thirty years; and I read this morning in the newspapers that the snow is general all over Ireland.

—I love the look of snow, said Aunt Julia sadly.

—So do I, said Miss O'Callaghan. I think Christmas is never really Christmas unless we have the snow on the ground.

—But poor Mr D'Arcy doesn't like the snow, said Aunt Kate, smiling.

Mr D'Arcy came from the pantry, full swathed and buttoned, and in a repentant tone told them the history of his cold. Everyone gave him advice and said it was a great pity and urged him to be very careful of his throat in the night air. Gabriel watched his wife who did not join in the conversation. She was standing right under the dusty fanlight and the flame of the gas lit up the rich bronze of her hair which he had seen her drying at the fire a few days before. She was in the same attitude and seemed unaware of the talk about her. At last she turned towards them and Gabriel saw that there was colour on her cheeks and that her eyes were shining. A sudden tide of joy went leaping out of his heart.

—Mr D'Arcy, she said, what is the name of that song you were singing?

—It's called *The Lass of Aughrim*,[7] said Mr D'Arcy, but I couldn't remember it properly. Why? Do you know it?

—*The Lass of Aughrim*, she repeated. I couldn't think of the name.

—It's a very nice air, said Mary Jane. I'm sorry you were not in voice tonight.

—Now, Mary Jane, said Aunt Kate, don't annoy Mr D'Arcy. I won't have him annoyed.

Seeing that all were ready to start she shepherded them to the door where good-night was said:

—Well, good-night, Aunt Kate, and thanks for the pleasant evening.

—Good-night, Gabriel. Good-night, Gretta!

—Good-night, Aunt Kate, and thanks ever so much. Good-night, Aunt Julia.

—O, good-night, Gretta, I didn't see you.

—Good-night, Mr D'Arcy. Good-night, Miss O'Callaghan.

—Good-night, Miss Morkan.

—Good-night, again.

—Good-night, all. Safe home.

—Good-night. Good-night.

The morning was still dark. A dull yellow light brooded over the houses and the river; and the sky seemed to be descending. It was slushy underfoot; and only streaks and patches of snow lay on the roofs, on the parapets of the quay and on the area railings. The lamps were still burning redly in the murky air and, across the river, the palace of the Four Courts stood out menacingly against the heavy sky.

7. An Irish version of a ballad about a girl deserted by her lover, whom she later tries to find, bringing the baby she had by him. Other versions are called "Love Gregory" and "Lord Gregory" (the name of the deserting lover), "The Lass of Lochryan," and "The Lass of Ocram."

She was walking on before him with Mr Bartell D'Arcy, her shoes in a brown parcel tucked under one arm and her hands holding her skirt up from the slush. She had no longer any grace of attitude but Gabriel's eyes were still bright with happiness. The blood went bounding along his veins; and the thoughts went rioting through his brain, proud, joyful, tender, valorous.

She was walking on before him so lightly and so erect that he longed to run after her noiselessly, catch her by the shoulders and say something foolish and affectionate into her ear. She seemed to him so frail that he longed to defend her against something and then to be alone with her. Moments of their secret life together burst like stars upon his memory. A heliotrope[8] envelope was lying beside his breakfast-cup and he was caressing it with his hand. Birds were twittering in the ivy and the sunny web of the curtain was shimmering along the floor: he could not eat for happiness. They were standing on the crowded platform and he was placing a ticket inside the warm palm of her glove. He was standing with her in the cold, looking in through a grated window at a man making bottles in a roaring furnace. It was very cold. Her face, fragrant in the cold air, was quite close to his; and suddenly she called out to the man at the furnace:

—Is the fire hot, sir?

But the man could not hear her with the noise of the furnace. It was just as well. He might have answered rudely.

A wave of yet more tender joy escaped from his heart and went coursing in warm flood along his arteries. Like the tender fires of stars moments of their life together, that no one knew of or would ever know of, broke upon and illumined his memory. He longed to recall to her those moments, to make her forget the years of their dull existence together and remember only their moments of ecstasy. For the years, he felt, had not quenched his soul or hers. Their children, his writing, her household cares had not quenched all their souls' tender fire. In one letter that he had written to her then he had said: *Why is it that words like these seem to me so dull and cold? Is it because there is no word tender enough to be your name?*

Like distant music these words that he had written years before were borne towards him from the past. He longed to be alone with her. When the others had gone away, when he and she were in their room in the hotel, then they would be alone together. He would call her softly:

—Gretta!

Perhaps she would not hear at once: she would be undressing. Then something in his voice would strike her. She would turn and look at him. . . .

At the corner of Winetavern Street they met a cab. He was glad of its rattling noise as it saved him from conversation. She was looking out of the window and seemed tired. The others spoke only a few words, pointing out some building or street. The horse galloped along wearily under the murky morning sky, dragging his old rattling box after his heels, and Gabriel was again in a cab with her, galloping to catch the boat, galloping to their honeymoon.

As the cab drove across O'Connell[9] Bridge Miss O'Callaghan said:

—They say you never cross O'Connell Bridge without seeing a white horse.

—I see a white man this time, said Gabriel.

—Where? asked Mr Bartell D'Arcy.

8. Grayish purple.
9. Daniel O'Connell (1775–1847), Irish nation-

alist, statesman, and orator. His statue stands by O'Connell Bridge in Dublin.

Gabriel pointed to the statue, on which lay patches of snow. Then he nodded familiarly to it and waved his hand.

—Good-night, Dan, he said gaily.

When the cab drew up before the hotel Gabriel jumped out and, in spite of Mr Bartell D'Arcy's protest, paid the driver. He gave the man a shilling over his fare. The man saluted and said:

—A prosperous New Year to you, sir.

—The same to you, said Gabriel cordially.

She leaned for a moment on his arm in getting out of the cab and while standing at the curbstone, bidding the others good-night. She leaned lightly on his arm, as lightly as when she had danced with him a few hours before. He had felt proud and happy then, happy that she was his, proud of her grace and wifely carriage. But now, after the kindling again of so many memories, the first touch of her body, musical and strange and perfumed, sent through him a keen pang of lust. Under cover of her silence he pressed her arm closely to his side; and, as they stood at the hotel door, he felt that they had escaped from their lives and duties, escaped from home and friends and run away together with wild and radiant hearts to a new adventure.

An old man was dozing in a great hooded chair in the hall. He lit a candle in the office and went before them to the stairs. They followed him in silence, their feet falling in soft thuds on the thickly carpeted stairs. She mounted the stairs behind the porter, her head bowed in the ascent, her frail shoulders curved as with a burden, her skirt girt tightly about her. He could have flung his arms about her hips and held her still for his arms were trembling with desire to seize her and only the stress of his nails against the palms of his hands held the wild impulse of his body in check. The porter halted on the stairs to settle his guttering candle. They halted too on the steps below him. In the silence Gabriel could hear the falling of the molten wax into the tray and the thumping of his own heart against his ribs.

The porter led them along a corridor and opened a door. Then he set his unstable candle down on a toilet-table and asked at what hour they were to be called in the morning.

—Eight, said Gabriel.

The porter pointed to the tap of the electric-light and began a muttered apology but Gabriel cut him short.

—We don't want any light. We have light enough from the street. And I say, he added, pointing to the candle, you might remove that handsome article, like a good man.

The porter took up his candle again, but slowly for he was surprised by such a novel idea. Then he mumbled good-night and went out. Gabriel shot the lock to.

A ghostly light from the street lamp lay in a long shaft from one window to the door. Gabriel threw his overcoat and hat on a couch and crossed the room towards the window. He looked down into the street in order that his emotion might calm a little. Then he turned and leaned against a chest of drawers with his back to the light. She had taken off her hat and cloak and was standing before a large swinging mirror, unhooking her waist.[1] Gabriel paused for a few moments, watching her, and then said:

—Gretta!

---

1. Shirtwaist; a tailored blouse.

She turned away from the mirror slowly and walked along the shaft of light towards him. Her face looked so serious and weary that the words would not pass Gabriel's lips. No, it was not the moment yet.

—You looked tired, he said.

—I am a little, she answered.

—You don't feel ill or weak?

—No, tired: that's all.

She went on to the window and stood there, looking out. Gabriel waited again and then, fearing that diffidence was about to conquer him, he said abruptly:

—By the way, Gretta!

—What is it?

—You know that poor fellow Malins? he said quickly.

—Yes. What about him?

—Well, poor fellow, he's a decent sort of chap after all, continued Gabriel in a false voice. He gave me back that sovereign I lent him and I didn't expect it really. It's a pity he wouldn't keep away from that Browne, because he's not a bad fellow at heart.

He was trembling now with annoyance. Why did she seem so abstracted? He did not know how he could begin. Was she annoyed, too, about something? If she would only turn to him or come to him of her own accord! To take her as she was would be brutal. No, he must see some ardour in her eyes first. He longed to be master of her strange mood.

—When did you lend him the pound? she asked, after a pause.

Gabriel strove to restrain himself from breaking out into brutal language about the sottish Malins and his pound. He longed to cry to her from his soul, to crush her body against his, to overmaster her. But he said:

—O, at Christmas, when he opened that little Christmas-card shop in Henry Street.

He was in such a fever of rage and desire that he did not hear her come from the window. She stood before him for an instant, looking at him strangely. Then, suddenly raising herself on tiptoe and resting her hands lightly on his shoulders, she kissed him.

—You are a very generous person, Gabriel, she said.

Gabriel, trembling with delight at her sudden kiss and at the quaintness of her phrase, put his hands on her hair and began smoothing it back, scarcely touching it with his fingers. The washing had made it fine and brilliant. His heart was brimming over with happiness. Just when he was wishing for it she had come to him of her own accord. Perhaps her thoughts had been running with his. Perhaps she had felt the impetuous desire that was in him and then the yielding mood had come upon her. Now that she had fallen to him so easily he wondered why he had been so diffident.

He stood, holding her head between his hands. Then, slipping one arm swiftly about her body and drawing her towards him, he said softly:

—Gretta dear, what are you thinking about?

She did not answer nor yield wholly to his arm. He said again, softly:

—Tell me what it is, Gretta. I think I know what is the matter. Do I know?

She did not answer at once. Then she said in an outburst of tears:

—O, I am thinking about that song, *The Lass of Aughrim*.

She broke loose from him and ran to the bed and, throwing her arms across the bed-rail, hid her face. Gabriel stood stock-still for a moment in astonish-

2532 / James Joyce

ment and then followed her. As he passed in the way of the cheval-glass² he caught sight of himself in full length, his broad, well-filled shirt-front, the face whose expression always puzzled him when he saw it in a mirror and his glimmering gilt-rimmed eyeglasses. He halted a few paces from her and said:

—What about the song? Why does that make you cry?

She raised her head from her arms and dried her eyes with the back of her hand like a child. A kinder note than he had intended went into his voice.

—Why, Gretta? he asked.

—I am thinking about a person long ago who used to sing that song.

—And who was the person long ago? asked Gabriel, smiling.

—It was a person I used to know in Galway when I was living with my grandmother, she said.

The smile passed away from Gabriel's face. A dull anger began to gather again at the back of his mind and the dull fires of his lust began to glow angrily in his veins.

—Someone you were in love with? he asked ironically.

—It was a young boy I used to know, she answered, named Michael Furey. He used to sing that song, *The Lass of Aughrim*. He was very delicate.

Gabriel was silent. He did not wish her to think that he was interested in this delicate boy.

—I can see him so plainly, she said after a moment. Such eyes as he had: big dark eyes! And such an expression in them—an expression!

—O then, you were in love with him? said Gabriel.

—I used to go out walking with him, she said, when I was in Galway.

A thought flew across Gabriel's mind.

—Perhaps that was why you wanted to go to Galway with that Ivors girl? he said coldly.

She looked at him and asked in surprise:

—What for?

Her eyes made Gabriel feel awkward. He shrugged his shoulders and said:

—How do I know! To see him perhaps.

She looked away from him along the shaft of light towards the window in silence.

—He is dead, she said at length. He died when he was only seventeen. Isn't it a terrible thing to die so young as that?

—What was he? asked Gabriel, still ironically.

—He was in the gasworks,³ she said.

Gabriel felt humiliated by the failure of his irony and by the evocation of this figure from the dead, a boy in the gasworks. While he had been full of memories of their secret life together, full of tenderness and joy and desire, she had been comparing him in her mind with another. A shameful consciousness of his own person assailed him. He saw himself as a ludicrous figure, acting as a pennyboy for his aunts, a nervous well-meaning sentimentalist, orating to vulgarians and idealising his own clownish lusts, the pitiable fatuous fellow he had caught a glimpse of in the mirror. Instinctively he turned his back more to the light lest she might see the shame that burned upon his forehead.

He tried to keep up his tone of cold interrogation but his voice when he spoke was humble and indifferent.

—I suppose you were in love with this Michael Furey, Gretta, he said.

2. Full-length mirror that can be tilted.
3. Factory where coal gas for heating and lighting is produced.

—I was great with him at that time, she said.

Her voice was veiled and sad. Gabriel, feeling now how vain it would be to try to lead her whither he had purposed, caressed one of her hands and said, also sadly:

—And what did he die of so young, Gretta? Consumption, was it?

—I think he died for me, she answered.

A vague terror seized Gabriel at this answer as if, at that hour when he had hoped to triumph, some impalpable and vindictive being was coming against him, gathering forces against him in its vague world. But he shook himself free of it with an effort of reason and continued to caress her hand. He did not question her again for he felt that she would tell him of herself. Her hand was warm and moist: it did not respond to his touch but he continued to caress it just as he had caressed her first letter to him that spring morning.

—It was in the winter, she said, about the beginning of the winter when I was going to leave my grandmother's and come up here to the convent. And he was ill at the time in his lodgings in Galway and wouldn't be let out and his people in Oughterard were written to. He was in decline, they said, or something like that. I never knew rightly.

She paused for a moment and sighed.

—Poor fellow, she said. He was very fond of me and he was such a gentle boy. We used to go out together, walking, you know, Gabriel, like the way they do in the country. He was going to study singing only for his health. He had a very good voice, poor Michael Furey.

—Well; and then? asked Gabriel.

—And then when it came to the time for me to leave Galway and come up to the convent he was much worse and I wouldn't be let see him so I wrote a letter saying I was going up to Dublin and would be back in the summer and hoping he would be better then.

She paused for a moment to get her voice under control and then went on:

—Then the night before I left I was in my grandmother's house in Nuns' Island, packing up, and I heard gravel thrown up against the window. The window was so wet I couldn't see so I ran downstairs as I was and slipped out the back into the garden and there was the poor fellow at the end of the garden, shivering.

—And did you not tell him to go back? asked Gabriel.

—I implored him to go home at once and told him he would get his death in the rain. But he said he did not want to live. I can see his eyes as well as well! He was standing at the end of the wall where there was a tree.

—And did he go home? asked Gabriel.

—Yes, he went home. And when I was only a week in the convent he died and he was buried in Oughterard where his people came from. O, the day I heard that, that he was dead!

She stopped, choking with sobs, and overcome by emotion, flung herself face downward on the bed, sobbing in the quilt. Gabriel held her hand for a moment longer, irresolutely, and then, shy of intruding on her grief, let it fall gently and walked quietly to the window.

She was fast asleep.

Gabriel, leaning on his elbow, looked for a few moments unresentfully on her tangled hair and half-open mouth, listening to her deep-drawn breath. So she had had that romance in her life: a man had died for her sake. It hardly pained him now to think how poor a part he, her husband, had played in her life. He watched her while she slept as though he and she had never lived together as man and wife. His curious eyes rested long upon her face and on her hair: and, as he thought of what she must have been then, in that time of her first girlish beauty, a strange friendly pity for her entered his soul. He did not like to say even to himself that her face was no longer beautiful but he knew that it was no longer the face for which Michael Furey had braved death.

Perhaps she had not told him all the story. His eyes moved to the chair over which she had thrown some of her clothes. A petticoat string dangled to the floor. One boot stood upright, its limp upper fallen down: the fellow of it lay upon its side. He wondered at his riot of emotions of an hour before. From what had it proceeded? From his aunt's supper, from his own foolish speech, from the wine and dancing, the merry-making when saying good-night in the hall, the pleasure of the walk along the river in the snow. Poor Aunt Julia! She, too, would soon be a shade with the shade of Patrick Morkan and his horse. He had caught that haggard look upon her face for a moment when she was singing *Arrayed for the Bridal*. Soon, perhaps, he would be sitting in that same drawing-room, dressed in black, his silk hat on his knees. The blinds would be drawn down and Aunt Kate would be sitting beside him, crying and blowing her nose and telling him how Julia had died. He would cast about in his mind for some words that might console her, and would find only lame and useless ones. Yes, yes: that would happen very soon.

The air of the room chilled his shoulders. He stretched himself cautiously along under the sheets and lay down beside his wife. One by one they were all becoming shades. Better pass boldly into that other world, in the full glory of some passion, than fade and wither dismally with age. He thought of how she who lay beside him had locked in her heart for so many years that image of her lover's eyes when he had told her that he did not wish to live.

Generous tears filled Gabriel's eyes. He had never felt like that himself towards any woman but he knew that such a feeling must be love. The tears gathered more thickly in his eyes and in the partial darkness he imagined he saw the form of a young man standing under a dripping tree. Other forms were near. His soul had approached that region where dwell the vast hosts of the dead. He was conscious of, but could not apprehend, their wayward and flickering existence. His own identity was fading out into a grey impalpable world: the solid world itself which these dead had one time reared and lived in was dissolving and dwindling.

A few light taps upon the pane made him turn to the window. It had begun to snow again. He watched sleepily the flakes, silver and dark, falling obliquely against the lamplight. The time had come for him to set out on his journey westward. Yes, the newspapers were right: snow was general all over Ireland. It was falling on every part of the dark central plain, on the treeless hills, falling softly upon the Bog of Allen[4] and, farther westward, softly falling into the dark mutinous Shannon waves. It was falling, too, upon every part of the lonely churchyard on the hill where Michael Furey lay buried. It lay thickly drifted on the crooked crosses and headstones, on the spears of the little gate, on the barren thorns. His soul swooned slowly as he heard the snow falling faintly through the universe and faintly falling, like the descent of their last end, upon all the living and the dead.

1914

---

4. The name given to many separate peat bogs between the rivers Liffey (which runs through Dublin) and Shannon (which runs through the central plain of Ireland).

From Ulysses[1]

[PROTEUS][2]

Ineluctable modality of the visible: at least that if no more, thought through my eyes.[3] Signatures of all things[4] I am here to read, seaspawn and seawrack, the nearing tide, that rusty boot. Snotgreen, bluesilver, rust: coloured signs. Limits of the diaphane.[5] But he adds: in bodies. Then he was aware of them bodies before of them coloured. How? By knocking his sconce against them, sure. Go easy. Bald he was and a millionaire, *maestro di color che sanno.*[6] Limit of the diaphane in. Why in? Diaphane, adiaphane.[7] If you can put your five fingers through it, it is a gate, if not a door. Shut your eyes and see.

Stephen closed his eyes to hear his boots crush crackling wrack and shells. You are walking through it howsomever. I am, a stride at a time. A very short space of time through very short times of space. Five, six: the *Nacheinander.*[8] Exactly: and that is the ineluctable modality of the audible. Open your eyes. No. Jesus! If I fell over a cliff that beetles o'er his base,[9] fell through the *Nebeneinander*[1] ineluctably. I am getting on nicely in the dark. My ash sword hangs at my side. Tap with it: they do.[2] My two feet in his boots[3] are at the ends of my legs, *nebeneinander.* Sounds solid: made by the mallet of *Los*

---

1. *Ulysses* was first published in book form on Feb. 2, 1922, Joyce's fortieth birthday. The text given here has been collated with the 1932 Odyssey Press edition.
2. "Proteus," the third of the novel's eigtheen episodes, is so titled because of the deliberate analogies that exist between it and the description of Proteus in Homer's *Odyssey* 4. (Joyce did not title any of the episodes in *Ulysses,* but the names are his; he used them in correspondence and in talk with friends.)
In the *Odyssey* Proteus is the sea god, who continually alters his shape: when Telemachus, Ulysses' son, asks Menelaus for help in finding his father, Menelaus tells him that he encountered Proteus by the seashore on the island of Pharos "in front of Egypt," and that, by holding on to him while he changed from one shape to another, he was able to force him to tell what had happened to Ulysses and the other Greek heroes of the Trojan War. In Joyce's narrative Stephen Dedalus (who, like Homer's Telemachus, is looking for a father, but not in the literal "consubstantial" sense) is walking alone by the Dublin shore, "along Sandymount strand," speculating on the shifting shapes of things and the possibility of knowing truth by appearances.
Stephen meditates first on the "modality of the visible" and on the mystical notion that the Demiurge, God's subordinate, writes his signature on all things; then on the "modality of the audible," closing his eyes and trying to know reality through the sense of hearing. As he continues his walk, the people and objects he sees mingle in his thoughts with memories of his past relations with his family, of his schooldays, of his residence in Paris (from where he was recalled by the death of his mother), of his feeling guilty about his mother's death (he had refused to kneel down and pray at her bedside, because he considered it a betrayal of his integrity as an unbeliever), and also with a variety of speculations about life and reality often derived from mystical works he had read "in the stagnant bay of

Marsh's library" (in Dublin). Stephen's highly theoretical, inquiring, musing mind contrasts sharply with the practical, humane, sensual, concrete imagination of the book's real hero, Leopold Bloom, but significant parallels exist between the streams of consciousness of the two. Some of the more important themes that emerge in Stephen's reverie are pointed out in the footnotes.
3. I.e., the sense of sight provides an unavoidable way ("ineluctable modality") of knowing reality, the knowledge thus provided being a kind of "thought through [the] eyes."
4. From Jakob Böhme (1575–1624), German mystic.
5. Transparency. Stephen is speculating on Aristotle's view of perception as developed in his *De Anima.*
6. One tradition held that Aristotle was bald, with thin legs, small eyes, and a lisp. Aristotle is also traditionally supposed to have inherited considerable wealth and to have been presented with a fortune by his former pupil Alexander the Great. The Italian phrase, Dante's description of Aristotle in the *Inferno,* means "the master of them that know."
7. What is not transparent (opposite of "diaphane").
8. After one another (German). Stephen, with eyes shut, is now sensing reality through the sense of sound only: unlike sight, sound falls on the sense of hearing in chronological sequence, one sound after another.
9. "What if it tempt you toward the flood, my lord, / Or to the dreadful summit of the cliff / That beetles o'er his base into the sea" (*Hamlet* 1.4.50–52). Allusions to *Hamlet* occur often in *Ulysses.*
1. Beside one another (German).
2. Stephen is still walking with his eyes shut, tapping with his "ash sword" (the ash-wood walking stick he carries), as "they" (i.e., blind people) do.
3. I.e., his friend Buck Mulligan's. Stephen, lacking boots of his own, had borrowed a cast-off pair of Mulligan's.

demiurgos.[4] Am I walking into eternity along Sandymount strand? Crush, crack, crik, crick. Wild sea money. Dominie Deasy kens them a'.[5]

> Won't you come to Sandymount,
> Madeline the mare?

Rhythm begins, you see. I hear. A catalectic tetrameter[6] of iambs marching. No, agallop: *deline the mare.*

Open your eyes now. I will. One moment. Has all vanished since? If I open and am for ever in the black adiaphane. *Basta!*[7] I will see if I can see.

See now. There all the time without you: and ever shall be, world without end.

They came down the steps from Leahy's terrace prudently, *Frauenzimmer*:[8] and down the shelving shore flabbily, their splayed feet sinking in the silted sand. Like me, like Algy,[9] coming down to our mighty mother. Number one swung lourdily[1] her midwife's bag, the other's gamp[2] poked in the beach. From the liberties, out for the day. Mrs Florence MacCabe, relict of the late Patk MacCabe,[3] deeply lamented, of Bride Street. One of her sisterhood lugged me squealing into life. Creation from nothing. What has she in the bag? A misbirth with a trailing navelcord, hushed in ruddy wool. The cords of all link back, strandentwining cable of all flesh. That is why mystic monks. Will you be as gods? Gaze in your *omphalos*. Hello. Kinch here. Put me on to Edenville. Aleph, alpha: nought, nought, one.[4]

Spouse and helpmate of Adam Kadmon: Heva,[5] naked Eve. She had no navel. Gaze. Belly without blemish, bulging big, a buckler of taut vellum, no, whiteheaped corn, orient and immortal, standing from everlasting to everlasting. Womb of sin.[6]

---

4. The Demiurge, or demiurgos, supernatural being who, according to Gnostic philosophy, made the world in subordination to God. The mystical notion of the Demiurge, whose mallet fashioned all things and who writes his signature on them, haunts Stephen's mind. The world, sensed by the ear only, "sounds solid," as though made by the Demiurge's hammer. The ending -os gives the word the appearance of a Spanish plural, so Joyce whimsically writes *"Los demiurgos,"* which in Spanish would be "the demiurges."
5. "Dominie": schoolmaster. Mr. Deasy was the headmaster of the school where Stephen taught (the previous episode has shown Stephen teaching). "Kens them a' ": knows them all; Stephen is putting Deasy into a mock-Scottish folk song.
6. The first of the two lines of popular verse that have come into Stephen's head consists metrically of four iambic feet ("tetrameter") with the last foot unlike the first, not defective ("catalectic").
7. Enough! (Italian).
8. Dames, wenches (German). Here, midwives. Stephen sees them coming from Leahy's Terrace, which runs by the beach.
9. Algernon Charles Swinburne, who wrote: "I will go back to the great sweet mother, / Mother and lover of men, the sea. / I will go down to her, I and none other" ("The Triumph of Time," lines 1–3).
1. Heavily (coined by Stephen from the French *lourd*). Stephen, like Joyce, had studied modern languages at University College, Dublin, and his preoccupation with words and languages is part of his character as potential literary artist.

2. Umbrella; and perhaps reference to Mrs. Gamp, the nurse in Dickens's *Martin Chuzzlewit*.
3. Stephen imagines the first midwife is called Mrs. MacCabe. "Relict": widow.
4. Stephen is speculating on the mystical significance of the navel cord, seeing it as linking the generations, the combined navel cords stretching back to Adam and Eve. A mystic gazed in his *omphalos* (navel) to make contact with the first man. Stephen thinks of himself ("Kinch," his nickname) calling up Adam in "Edenville" through his navel, using the line of linked navel cords as a telephone line. Adam's telephone number, "Aleph, alpha: nought, nought, one," begins with the first letters of the Hebrew and of the Greek alphabet to suggest the great primeval number.
5. Hebrew for Eve. Because she was not born in the regular way, but created from Adam's rib, she had no navel. "Adam Kadmon": Adam the Beginner, so called in Hebrew cabalistic literature of the Middle Ages.
6. Stephen is led, through reflection on Eve's navel-less "belly without blemish," to a recollection of the description of the original Eden (Paradise) by Thomas Traherne (ca. 1637–1674), from whose prose *Centuries of Meditation* he quotes: "The corn was orient and immortal wheat, which should never be reaped, nor was ever sown. I thought it had stood from everlasting to everlasting." But immediately afterward Stephen reflects that such language is inappropriate to Eve's body, as hers was the "womb of sin"—i.e., she first ate the fatal apple and brought forth sin.

Wombed in sin darkness I was too, made not begotten. By them, the man with my voice and my eyes and a ghostwoman with ashes on her breath.[7] They clasped and sundered, did the coupler's will. From before the ages He willed me and now may not will me away or ever. A *lex eterna*[8] stays about Him. Is that then the divine substance wherein Father and Son are consubstantial? Where is poor dear Arius[9] to try conclusions? Warring his life long on the contransmagnificandjewbangtantiality.[1] Illstarred heresiarch.[2] In a Greek watercloset he breathed his last: *euthanasia*. With beaded mitre and with crozier, stalled upon his throne, widower of a widowed see, with upstiffed omophorion, with clotted hinderparts.

Airs romped round him, nipping and eager airs. They are coming, waves. The whitemaned seahorses, champing, brightwindbridled, the steeds of Mananaan.[3]

I mustn't forget his letter for the press. And after? The Ship, half twelve. By the way go easy with that money like a good young imbecile. Yes, I must.[4]

His pace slackened. Here. Am I going to aunt Sara's or not? My consubstantial father's voice. Did you see anything of your artist brother Stephen lately? No? Sure he's not down in Strasburg terrace with his aunt Sally? Couldn't he fly a bit higher than that, eh? And and and and tell us Stephen, how is uncle Si? O weeping God, the things I married into. De boys up in de hayloft. The drunken little costdrawer and his brother, the cornet player. Highly respectable gondoliers. And skeweyed Walter sirring his father, no less. Sir. Yes, sir. No, sir. Jesus wept: and no wonder, by Christ.[5]

I pull the wheezy bell of their shuttered cottage: and wait. They take me for a dun, peer out from a coign of vantage.[6]

—It's Stephen, sir.

—Let him in. Let Stephen in.

A bolt drawn back and Walter welcomes me.

—We thought you were someone else.

In his broad bed nuncle Richie, pillowed and blanketed, extends over the

---

7. Stephen is haunted by thoughts of his mother in this guise.

8. Eternal law (Latin). God's eternal law, Stephen reflects, willed his birth from the beginning. He then goes on to speculate on the nature of the divine substance and whether God the Father and God the Son are of the same substance ("consubstantial").

9. Third-century theologian who "tried conclusions" on this matter, maintaining that Christ was less divine than God (Arius's views were condemned as heretical by the Council of Nicaea in 325).

1. Ironic "portmanteau word" made up of terms connected with the Arian controversy—"consubstantial," "transubstantial" (of a substance that changes into another)—and with the facts of Christ's nature (e.g., "Jew"; Jesus was a Jew, as Leopold Bloom in a later episode reminds an anti-Semitic Irishman).

2. Arch-heretic. Arius died suddenly in Constantinople in 336. He was never a bishop, and Stephen's image of him at the moment of death in full episcopal attire seems to combine recollections of other early "heresiarchs." In an earlier reverie Stephen had conjured up in his mind "a horde of heresies fleeing with mitres awry." These heretics are connected in Stephen's mind with argument about the relation between God the Father and God the Son and so with the problem of the true nature of paternity, which haunts him constantly.

3. Mananaan MacLir, Celtic sea god; his steeds are the "whitemaned seahorses." ("White horses" is still the name in Britain for the white foam atop waves.)

4. Mr. Deasy had given Stephen a letter to the press to be taken to the newspaper office. After that he has an appointment with Mulligan at The Ship, a tavern. "That money" is Mr. Deasy's last payment to him.

5. Stephen has been wondering whether to call on his uncle and aunt, Richie and Sara Goulding. He imagines his father interrogating him about the visit as if he had gone; he then pictures his cousins asking after his father, Simon Dedalus (his cousins' "uncle Si"). Simon is contemptuous of his wife's relations (Sara Goulding is his wife's sister). Stephen knows that any mention of them will bring on the familiar abuse of "the things I married into"—at best "highly respectable gondoliers" (from Gilbert and Sullivan's opera *The Gondoliers*). The scene that follows is also Stephen's purely imaginary picture of what the visit would be like.

6. Favorable corner.

2538 / James Joyce

hillock of his knees a sturdy forearm. Cleanchested. He has washed the upper moiety.

—Morrow, nephew.

He lays aside the lapboard whereon he drafts his bills of costs for the eyes of master Goff and master Shapland Tandy, filing consents and common searches and a writ of *Duces Tecum*.[7] A bogoak frame over his bald head: Wilde's *Requiescat*.[8] The drone of his misleading whistle brings Walter back.

—Yes, sir?

—Malt[9] for Richie and Stephen, tell mother. Where is she?

—Bathing Crissie, sir.

Papa's little bedpal. Lump of love.

—No, uncle Richie . . .

—Call me Richie. Damn your lithia water.[1] It lowers. Whusky!

—Uncle Richie, really. . . .

—Sit down or by the law Harry I'll knock you down.

Walter squints vainly for a chair.

—He has nothing to sit down on, sir.

—He has nowhere to put it, you mug. Bring in our chippendale chair. Would you like a bite of something? None of your damned lawdeedaw air here: the rich of a rasher fried with a herring? Sure? So much the better. We have nothing in the house but backache pills.

All'erta![2] He drones bars of Ferrando's *aria di sortita*. The grandest number, Stephen, in the whole opera. Listen.

His tuneful whistle sounds again, finely shaded, with rushes of the air, his fists bigdrumming on his padded knees.

This wind is sweeter.

Houses of decay, mine, his and all. You told the Clongowes gentry you had an uncle a judge and an uncle a general in the army.[3] Come out of them, Stephen. Beauty is not there. Nor in the stagnant bay of Marsh's library where you read the fading prophecies of Joachim Abbas.[4] For whom? The hundred-headed rabble of the cathedral close.[5] A hater of his kind ran from them to the wood of madness, his mane foaming in the moon, his eyeballs stars. Houyhnhnm, horsenostrilled.[6] The oval equine faces, Temple, Buck Mulligan, Foxy Campbell. Lantern jaws. Abbas[7] father, furious dean, what offence laid fire to their brains? Paff! *Descende, calve, ut nimium decalveris.*[8] A garland of grey hair on his comminated head see him me clambering down to the footpace

---

7. You shall take with you (Latin); opening words of a search warrant. Goulding was a law clerk with Messrs. Goff and Tandy.
8. Poem by Oscar Wilde.
9. Whiskey.
1. Mineral water containing lithium salts, often used therapeutically.
2. Look out! (Italian); the first words of the *aria di sortita* (aria sung by a character about to leave the stage) sung by Ferrando, captain of the guard, in Verdi's opera *Il Trovatore*.
3. Stephen, reflecting on the steady social decline of his family, is remembering that, while at school at Clongowes Wood College, he had pretended to have important relations.
4. Abbot Joachim of Floris (the monastery of San Giovanni in Fiore, Italy), 12th-century mystic and theologian, whose prophetic work *Expositio in Apocalypsin* Stephen (like Joyce) had read in Marsh's Library.
5. I.e., the precinct of a cathedral (Marsh's Library

is in the close of St. Patrick's Cathedral).
6. St. Patrick's Close has recalled Jonathan Swift, who was dean of St. Patrick's. Stephen remembers Swift's misanthropy (he was "a hater of his kind") and his creation of the Houyhnhnms (noble horses) in book 4 of *Gulliver's Travels*. Then he thinks of people he knew who have horse faces.
7. Literally: father.
8. Go down, bald-head, lest you become even balder (Latin). This sentence, from Joachim's *Concordia* of the Old and New Testaments, is based on the mocking cry of the children to the prophet Elisha (2 Kings 2.23: "Go up, thou bald head"; Joachim saw Elisha as a forerunner of St. Benedict—both had shaven or baldish heads. Stephen goes on to imagine the "comminated" (threatened) head of Joachim descending, clutching a "monstrance" (receptacle in which the Host [consecrated bread or wafer] is exposed for adoration), in the midst of a nightmare church service.

(*descende*), clutching a monstrance, basiliskeyed. Get down, bald poll! A choir gives back menace and echo, assisting about the altar's horns, the snorted Latin of jackpriests moving burly in their albs, tonsured and oiled and gelded, fat with the fat of kidneys of wheat.

And at the same instant perhaps a priest round the corner is elevating it. Dringdring! And two streets off another locking it into a pyx.[9] Dringadring! And in a ladychapel another taking housel all to his own cheek. Dringdring! Down, up, forward, back. Dan Occam[1] thought of that, invincible doctor. A misty English morning the imp hypostasis tickled his brain. Bringing his host down and kneeling he heard twine with his second bell the first bell in the transept (he is lifting his) and, rising, heard (now I am lifting) their two bells (he is kneeling) twang in diphthong.

Cousin Stephen, you will never be a saint.[2] Isle of saints.[3] You were awfully holy, weren't you? You prayed to the Blessed Virgin that you might not have a red nose. You prayed to the devil in Serpentine avenue that the fubsy widow in front might lift her clothes still more from the wet street. *O si, certo!*[4] Sell your soul for that, do, dyed rags pinned round a squaw. More tell me, more still! On the top of the Howth tram alone crying to the rain: *Naked women!* What about that, eh?

What about what? What else were they invented for?

Reading two pages apiece of seven books every night, eh? I was young. You bowed to yourself in the mirror, stepping forward to applause earnestly, striking face. Hurray for the Goddamned idiot! Hray! No-one saw: tell no-one. Books you were going to write with letters for titles. Have you read his F? O yes, but I prefer Q. Yes, but W is wonderful. O yes, W. Remember your epiphanies[5] on green oval leaves, deeply deep, copies to be sent if you died to all the great libraries of the world, including Alexandria? Someone was to read them there after a few thousand years, a mahamanvantara.[6] Pico della Mirandola[7] like. Ay, very like a whale.[8] When one reads these strange pages of one long gone one feels that one is at one with one who once . . .

The grainy sand had gone from under his feet. His boots trod again a damp crackling mast, razorshells, squeaking pebbles, that on the unnumbered pebbles beats, wood sieved by the shipworm, lost Armada. Unwholesome sandflats waited to suck his treading soles, breathing upward sewage breath. He coasted them, walking warily. A porterbottle stood up, stogged to its waist, in the cakey

9. Vessel in which the Host is kept. Stephen is imagining such a service, with himself officiating (he almost became a priest).
1. William of Occam or Ockham ("Dan" means "master"), 14th-century English theologian, who held that the individual thing is the reality and its name, the universal, an abstraction; he was concerned with hypostasis—the essential part of a thing as distinct from its attributes.
2. A parody of the words of Dryden to his distant relative Swift: "Cousin, you will never make a poet."
3. Ireland was called "*insula sanctorum*" (isle of saints) in the Middle Ages.
4. Oh yes, certainly! (Italian).
5. Joyce's term for the prose poems he wrote as a young man. An epiphany, he said, was the sudden "revelation of the whatness of a thing"—of a gesture, a phrase, or a thought he had experienced; he attempted to express, in the writing, the

moment at which "the soul of the commonest object . . . seems to us radiant." Stephen's recollection of early and exotic literary ambitions is drawn directly from Joyce's ambitions at the same age.
6. Cycle of change and recurrence, in Indian mystical thought. It is connected in Stephen's mind with the constant ebb and flow of the sea by which he is walking.
7. 15th-century mystical philosopher; his *Heptaplus* is a mystical account of the Creation, much influenced by Jewish cabalistic thought.
8. Polonius to Hamlet (*Hamlet* 3.2.351) with reference to the changing shape of a cloud. The Protean theme of constant change, of ebb and flow, and of metempsychosis (i.e., transmigration of souls: a major theme in *Ulysses*), is working in Stephen's mind. The following sentence is a parody of an elegant, condescending modern essay on Pico or some other early mystic.

2540 / James Joyce

sand dough. A sentinel: isle of dreadful thirst.[9] Broken hoops on the shore; at the land a maze of dark cunning nets; farther away chalkscrawled backdoors and on the higher beach a dryingline with two crucified shirts. Ringsend: wigwams of brown steersmen and master mariners. Human shells.

He halted. I have passed the way to aunt Sara's. Am I not going there? Seems not. No-one about. He turned northeast and crossed the firmer sand towards the Pigeonhouse.[1]

—*Qui vous a mis dans cette fichue position?*

—*C'est le pigeon, Joseph.*

Patrice, home on furlough, lapped warm milk with me in the bar Mac-Mahon. Son of the wild goose, Kevin Egan of Paris. My father's a bird, he lapped the sweet *lait chaud* with pink young tongue, plump bunny's face. Lap, *lapin*. He hopes to win in the *gros lots*. About the nature of women he read in Michelet. But he must send me *La Vie de Jésus* by M. Léo Taxil. Lent it to his friend.[2]

—*C'est tordant, vous savez. Moi, je suis socialiste. Je ne crois pas en l'existence de Dieu. Faut pas le dire à mon père.*

—*Il croit?*

—*Mon père, oui.*

Schluss.[3] He laps.

My Latin quarter hat. God, we simply must dress the character. I want puce gloves. You were a student, weren't you? Of what in the other devil's name? Paysayenn. P. C. N., you know: *physiques, chimiques et naturelles.*[4] Aha. Eating your groatsworth of *mou en civet*,[5] fleshpots of Egypt, elbowed by belching cabmen. Just say in the most natural tone: when I was in Paris, *boul'Mich',*[6] I used to. Yes, used to carry punched tickets to prove an alibi if they arrested you for murder somewhere. Justice. On the night of the seventeenth of February 1904 the prisoner was seen by two witnesses. Other fellow did it: other me. Hat, tie, overcoat, nose. *Lui, c'est moi.*[7] You seem to have enjoyed yourself.

Proudly walking. Whom were you trying to walk like? Forget: a dispossessed. With mother's money order, eight shillings, the banging door of the post office slammed in your face by the usher. Hunger toothache. *Encore deux minutes.* Look clock. Must get. *Fermé.* Hired dog! Shoot him to bloody bits with a bang shotgun, bits man spattered walls all brass buttons. Bits all khrrrrklak in place

9. The atmosphere of the sandflats reminds Stephen of a desert island where people die of thirst. (The island of Pharos, where Menelaus found Proteus, was an "island of dreadful hunger.")

1. The Pigeon House in Ringsend, an old structure built on a breakwater in Dublin Bay and which in the course of time has served a great variety of purposes, suggests to Stephen the Dove, which is the symbol of the Holy Spirit, and this in turn suggests an irreverent dialogue (supposedly between Joseph and Mary when Mary is found to be pregnant: "Who has got you into this wretched condition?" "It was the pigeon [i.e., the Holy Dove], Joseph"). This he had picked up in Paris from the blasphemous M. Léo Taxil, whose book *La Vie de Jésus* ("The Life of Jesus") is mentioned in the next paragraph.

2. Stephen had first met Léo Taxil through Patrice, the son of "Kevin Egan of Paris," who in real life was the exiled nationalist Joseph Casey. The phrase "my father's a bird" comes from *The Song of the Cheerful Jesus*, a blasphemous poem by Buck Mulligan (based on Joyce's friend Oliver

Gogarty, who really wrote the poem); Stephen recalls Patrice reciting it as he drank warm milk ("*lait chaud*"), lapping it like a "*lapin*" (rabbit), and expressing the hope that he would win something substantial in the French national lottery (*gros lot:* "first prize"). Jules Michelet (1798–1874), French historian.

3. End (German). Conversation in French between Stephen and Patrice: "It's screamingly funny, you know. I'm a socialist myself. I don't believe in the existence of God. Mustn't tell my father." "He is a believer?" "My father, yes."

4. I.e., the faculty of physics, chemistry, and biology at the École de Médecine in Paris, where Stephen, like Joyce, took a premedical course for a short time. The faculty was popularly known as "P.C.N." (pronounced "Paysayenn").

5. Stew.

6. Popular Parisian abbreviation for the Boulevard Saint Michel.

7. "He is me"—a parody of Louis XIV's remark "*L'état c'est moi*" (I am the state).

clack back. Not hurt? O, that's all right. Shake hands. See what I meant, see? O, that's all right. Shake a shake. O, that's all only all right.[8]

You were going to do wonders, what? Missionary to Europe after fiery Columbanus. Fiacre and Scotus on their creepystools[9] in heaven spilt from their pintpots, loudlatinlaughing: *Euge!*[1] *Euge!* Pretending to speak broken English as you dragged your valise, porter threepence, across the slimy pier at Newhaven. *Comment?* Rich booty you brought back; *Le Tutu,* five tattered numbers of *Pantalon Blanc et Culotte Rouge,*[2] a blue French telegram, curiosity to show:

—Mother dying come home father.[3]

The aunt thinks you killed your mother. That's why she won't.[4]

> *Then here's a health to Mulligan's aunt*
> *And I'll tell you the reason why.*
> *She always kept things decent in*
> *The Hannigan famileye.*

His feet marched in sudden proud rhythm over the sand furrows, along by the boulders of the south wall. He stared at them proudly, piled stone mammoth skulls. Gold light on sea, on sand, on boulders. The sun is there, the slender trees, the lemon houses.

Paris rawly waking, crude sunlight on her lemon streets. Moist pith of farls[5] of bread, the froggreen wormwood, her matin incense, court the air. Belluomo rises from the bed of his wife's lover's wife, the kerchiefed housewife is astir, a saucer of acetic acid in her hand. In Rodot's Yvonne and Madeleine newmake their tumbled beauties, shattering with gold teeth *chaussons* of pastry, their mouths yellowed with the *pus* of *flan breton.*[6] Faces of Paris men go by, their wellpleased pleasers, curled *conquistadores.*[7]

Noon slumbers. Kevin Egan rolls gunpowder cigarettes through fingers smeared with printer's ink,[8] sipping his green fairy as Patrice his white. About us gobblers fork spiced beans down their gullets. *Un demi setier!*[9] A jet of coffee steam from the burnished caldron. She serves me at his beck. *Il est irlandais. Hollandais? Non fromage. Deux irlandais, nous, Irlande, vous savez? Ah, oui!*[1] She thought you wanted a cheese *hollandais.* Your postprandial, do you know that word? Postprandial. There was a fellow I knew once in Barcelona, queer fellow, used to call it his postprandial. Well: *slainte!*[2] Around the slabbed tables

8. A recollection of the occasion when, desperate for money, Stephen had received a money order for eight shillings from his mother. Afflicted with both hunger and toothache, he had gone to cash it at the post office—which was closed, even though, as he expostulated with the man at the door, there were still two minutes (*"encore deux minutes"*) until the official closing time. In his retrospective rage he imagines himself shooting the "hired dog" to bits, and then in a revulsion of feeling has a mental reconciliation with him.
9. Low stools. "Columbanus": 6th-century Irish missionary on the Continent. Fiacre was a 6th-century Irish saint. John Duns Scotus (1266–1308), Scottish scholastic theologian and philosopher.
1. Well done!
2. Like *Le Tutu,* the name of a French popular periodical.
3. This telegram was actually received by Joyce in Paris.

4. Stephen recalls Buck Mulligan's telling him that his (Mulligan's) aunt disapproved of Stephen because, by refusing to pray at his dying mother's bedside, he had hastened her death. Stephen then tries to laugh away his guilty feeling by quoting mentally a (slightly parodied) verse of a popular song.
5. Thin circular cakes.
6. Memories of a restaurant in Paris. "*Chaussons*": pastry turnovers. "*Flan breton*": pastry filled with custard.
7. Conquerors (Spanish).
8. Egan (i.e., Joseph Casey) became a typesetter for the Parisian edition of the *New York Herald.*
9. Abusive Parisian slang for a liquid measure (about one-fourth of a liter)—here, presumably, of wine or beer. "Green Fairy": absinthe, a strong green liqueur.
1. He is Irish. Dutch? Not cheese. We are two Irishmen, Ireland, you understand? Oh, yes!
2. Your health! (Gaelic).

the tangle of wined breaths and grumbling gorges. His breath hangs over our saucestained plates, the green fairy's fang thrusting between his lips. Of Ireland, the Dalcassians, of hopes, conspiracies, of Arthur Griffith now.[3] To yoke me as his yokefellow, our crimes our common cause. You're your father's son. I know the voice. His fustian shirt, sanguineflowered, trembles its Spanish tassels at his secrets. M. Drumont,[4] famous journalist, Drumont, know what he called queen Victoria? Old hag with the yellow teeth. *Vieille ogresse* with the *dents jaunes*. Maud Gonne, beautiful woman, *la Patrie*, M. Millevoye, Félix Faure,[5] know how he died? Licentious men. The *froeken, bonne à tout faire*,[6] who rubs male nakedness in the bath at Upsala. *Moi faire*, she said, *tous les messieurs*.[7] Not this *monsieur*, I said. Most licentious custom. Bath a most private thing. I wouldn't let my brother, not even my own brother, most lascivious thing. Green eyes, I see you. Fang, I feel. Lascivious people.

The blue fuse burns deadly between hands and burns clear. Loose tobacco shreds catch fire: a flame and acrid smoke light our corner. Raw facebones under his peep of day boy's hat. How the head centre got away, authentic version. Got up as a young bride, man, veil, orangeblossoms, drove out the road to Malahide. Did, faith. Of lost leaders, the betrayed, wild escapes. Disguises, clutched at, gone not here.[8]

Spurned lover. I was a strapping young gossoon[9] at that time, I tell you. I'll show you my likeness one day. I was, faith. Lover, for her love he prowled with colonel Richard Burke, tanist of his sept,[1] under the walls of Clerkenwell[2] and, crouching, saw a flame of vengeance hurl them upward in the fog. Shattered glass and toppling masonry. In gay Paree he hides, Egan of Paris, unsought by any save by me. Making his day's stations, the dingy printing-case, his three taverns, the Montmartre lair he sleeps short night in, *rue de la Goutte-d'Or*, damascened with flyblown faces of the gone. Loveless, landless, wifeless. She is quite nicey comfy without her outcast man,[3] madame in *rue Gît-le-Cœur*, canary and two buck lodgers. Peachy cheeks, a zebra skirt, frisky as a young thing's. Spurned and undespairing. Tell Pat[4] you saw me, won't you? I wanted to get poor Pat a job one time. *Mon fils*, soldier of France. I taught him to sing *The boys of Kilkenny are stout roaring blades*. Know that old lay? I taught Patrice that. Old Kilkenny: saint Canice, Strongbow's castle on the Nore.[5] Goes like this. O, O. He takes me, Napper Tandy,[6] by the hand.

> *O, O the boys of*
> *Kilkenny . . .*

3. Two extremes of Irish history. From the Dalcassian line came the early kings of Munster (from 300 C.E. on). Arthur Griffith (1872–1922) was an Irish revolutionary leader, founder of the Sinn Fein ("Ourselves Alone") movement.
4. Edouard Drumont (1844–1917), French politician and bitter anti-Semite.
5. 19th-century French statesman. "Maud Gonne," the beautiful actress and violent Irish nationalist whom W. B. Yeats loved. "*La Patrie*": journal edited by Lucien Millevoye, French nationalist deputy and Maud Gonne's lover.
6. Maid-of-all-work (French). "*Froeken*": *fröken*, unmarried woman or Miss (Swedish).
7. I do all the gentlemen (in broken French).
8. Another Protean theme of change. Egan had told Stephen of his cousin James Stephens's escape from prison disguised as a bride.
9. Boy.

1. Clan. "Tanist": successor-apparent to a Celtic chief.
2. District in east-central London. Stephen is recalling Egan's conversation about the Fenian violence in London that necessitated his fleeing to France.
3. I.e., Egan's wife, who is "quite nicey comfy" in the metaphorical "*rue Gît-le-Cœur*" (i.e., the street where the heart lies dead) back home in Ireland.
4. Patrice, Egan's son.
5. Kilkenny is called after the Irish Saint Canice (its Irish name is Cill Chainnigh), on the river Nore, where Strongbow (the second earl of Pembroke, who invaded Ireland in the 12th century), had his stronghold.
6. James Napper Tandy (1740–1803), Irish revolutionary hero of the song "The Wearing of the Green."

Weak wasting hand on mine. They have forgotten Kevin Egan, not he them. Remembering thee, O Sion.[7]

He had come nearer the edge of the sea and wet sand slapped his boots. The new air greeted him, harping in wild nerves, wind of wild air of seeds of brightness. Here, I am not walking out to the Kish lightship, am I? He stood suddenly, his feet beginning to sink slowly in the quaking soil. Turn back.

Turning, he scanned the shore south, his feet sinking again slowly in new sockets. The cold domed room of the tower[8] waits. Through the barbicans[9] the shafts of light are moving ever, slowly ever as my feet are sinking, creeping duskward over the dial floor. Blue dusk, nightfall, deep blue night. In the darkness of the dome they wait, their pushedback chairs, my obelisk valise, around a board of abandoned platters. Who to clear it? He has the key.[1] I will not sleep there when this night comes. A shut door of a silent tower, entombing their blind bodies, the panthersahib and his pointer.[2] Call: no answer. He lifted his feet up from the suck and turned back by the mole of boulders. Take all, keep all. My soul walks with me, form of forms. So in the moon's midwatches I pace the path above the rocks, in sable silvered, hearing Elsinore's tempting flood.[3]

The flood is following me. I can watch it flow past from here. Get back then by the Poolbeg road to the strand there. He climbed over the sedge and eely oarweeds and sat on a stool of rock, resting his ashplant in a grike.[4]

A bloated carcass of a dog lay lolled on bladderwrack. Before him the gunwale of a boat, sunk in sand. *Un coche ensablé*[5] Louis Veuillot called Gautier's[6] prose. These heavy sands are language tide and wind have silted here. And there, the stoneheaps of dead builders, a warren of weasel rats. Hide gold there. Try it. You have some. Sands and stones. Heavy of the past. Sir Lout's toys. Mind you don't get one bang on the ear. I'm the bloody well gigant rolls all them bloody well boulders, bones for my steppingstones. Feefawfum. I zmellz de bloodz oldz an Iridzman.[7]

A point, live dog, grew into sight running across the sweep of sand. Lord, is he going to attack me? Respect his liberty. You will not be master of others or their slave. I have my stick. Sit tight. From farther away, walking shoreward across from the crested tide, figures, two. The two maries. They have tucked it safe mong the bulrushes. Peekaboo. I see you. No, the dog. He is running back to them. Who?

Galleys of the Lochlanns[8] ran here to beach, in quest of prey, their bloodbeaked prows riding low on a molten pewter surf. Dane vikings, torcs of toma-

7. Cf. Psalm 137.1 (in the King James Bible): "we wept, when we remembered Zion." But "Zion" in the Douay (Roman Catholic) Bible, is spelled "Sion," and the Book of Common Prayer has "When we remembered thee, O Sion."
8. Where Stephen lived with Buck Mulligan.
9. Outworks of a castle.
1. In the preceding episode Mulligan asked for and got the key of the tower from Stephen.
2. I.e., Mulligan and the Englishman Haines, who lived with Stephen in the tower. Stephen thinks of them as calling for him in vain, because he has decided not to return.
3. Cf. *Hamlet* 1.2.241, where the ghost of Hamlet's murdered father is described as having a beard of "sable silver'd."

4. Chink, crevice.
5. A coach embedded in the sand (French).
6. Théophile Gautier, 19th-century French poet, novelist, and critic. Veuillot, 19th-century French journalist.
7. Stephen is thinking of the boulders on the shore as the work of a large but clumsy giant ("Sir Lout"). "They [Sir Lout and his family] were giants right enough. . . . My Sir Lout has rocks in his mouth instead of teeth. He articulates badly" (Joyce to Frank Budgen, reported in Budgen's *James Joyce and the Making of Ulysses*, 1934).
8. Scandinavians (Gaelic). Stephen is meditating on the Vikings who settled Dublin; it was here that they came ashore, he thinks. Malachi (below), king of Meath, had their first leader drowned.

2544 / JAMES JOYCE

hawks aglitter on their breasts when Malachi wore the collar of gold. A school of turlehide whales stranded in hot noon, spouting, hobbling in the shallows. Then from the starving cagework city a horde of jerkined dwarfs, my people, with flayers' knives, running, scaling, hacking in green blubbery whalemeat. Famine, plague and slaughters. Their blood is in me, their lusts my waves. I moved among them on the frozen Liffey, that I, a changeling, among the spluttering resin fires. I spoke to no-one: none to me.

The dog's bark ran towards him, stopped, ran back. Dog of my enemy. I just simply stood pale, silent, bayed about. *Terribilia meditans.*[9] A primrose doublet, fortune's knave, smiled on my fear. For that are you pining, the bark of their applause? Pretenders: live their lives. The Bruce's brother, Thomas Fitzgerald, silken knight, Perkin Warbeck, York's false scion, in breeches of silk of whiterose ivory, wonder of a day, and Lambert Simnel, with a tail of nans and sutlers, a scullion crowned.[1] All kings' sons. Paradise of pretenders then and now. He saved men from drowning[2] and you shake at a cur's yelping. But the courtiers who mocked Guido in Or san Michele were in their own house. House of . . . We don't want any of your medieval abstrusiosities. Would you do what he did? A boat would be near, a lifebuoy. *Natürlich,*[3] put there for you. Would you or would you not? The man that was drowned nine days ago off Maiden's rock. They are waiting for him now. The truth, spit it out. I would want to. I would try. I am not a strong swimmer. Water cold soft. When I put my face into it in the basin at Clongowes. Can't see! Who's behind me? Out quickly, quickly! Do you see the tide flowing quickly in on all sides, sheeting the lows of sands quickly, shellcocoacoloured? If I had land under my feet. I want his life still to be his, mine to be mine. A drowning man. His human eyes scream to me out of horror of his death. I . . . With him together down . . . I could not save her.[4] Waters: bitter death: lost.

A woman and a man. I see her skirties. Pinned up, I bet.

Their dog ambled about a bank of dwindling sand, trotting, sniffing on all sides. Looking for something lost in a past life. Suddenly he made off like a bounding hare, ears flung back, chasing the shadow of a lowskimming gull. The man's shrieked whistle struck his limp ears. He turned, bounded back, came nearer, trotted on twinkling shanks. On a field tenney a buck, trippant, proper, unattired.[5] At the lacefringe of the tide he halted with stiff forehoofs, seawardpointed ears. His snout lifted barked at the wavenoise, herds of seamorse.[6] They serpented towards his feet, curling, unfurling many crests, every ninth, breaking, plashing, from far, from farther out, waves and waves.

Cocklepickers.[7] They waded a little way in the water and, stooping, soused their bags, and, lifting them again, waded out. The dog yelped running to them, reared up and pawed them, dropping on all fours, again reared up at them with mute bearish fawning. Unheeded he kept by them as they came towards the drier sand, a rag of wolf's tongue redpanting from his jaws. His speckled body ambled ahead of them and then loped off at a calf's gallop. The carcass

---

9. Meditating terrible things (Latin).
1. Stephen is meditating on pretenders (i.e., false claimants): the names here are those of pretenders who have figured in English history.
2. Mulligan had saved a man from drowning.
3. Of course (German).
4. A man had been drowned off the coast, and his body had not yet been recovered. As Stephen thinks of the horror of drowning, he recalls once

again his mother's death.
5. The dog is described in the language of heraldry. "On an orange-brown (tawny) background, a buck, tripping, in natural colors, without horns."
6. Seahorses, with a pun on Morse code.
7. Stephen recognizes the man and woman on the beach as gypsy cockle pickers (cockles are edible shellfish, like mussels).

lay on his path. He stopped, sniffed, stalked round it, brother, nosing closer, went round it, sniffing rapidly like a dog all over the dead dog's bedraggled fell. Dogskull, dogsniff, eyes on the ground, moves to one great goal. Ah, poor dogsbody. Here lies poor dogsbody's body.

—Tatters! Outofthat, you mongrel.

The cry brought him skulking back to his master and a blunt bootless kick sent him unscathed across a spit of sand, crouched in flight. He slunk back in a curve. Doesn't see me. Along by the edge of the mole he lolloped, dawdled, smelt a rock and from under a cocked hindleg pissed against it. He trotted forward and, lifting his hindleg, pissed quick short at an unsmelt rock. The simple pleasures of the poor. His hindpaws then scattered sand: then his forepaws dabbled and delved. Something he buried there, his grandmother.[8] He rooted in the sand, dabbling, delving and stopped to listen to the air, scraped up the sand again with a fury of his claws, soon ceasing, a pard,[9] a panther, got in spousebreach,[1] vulturing the dead.

After he woke me last night same dream or was it? Wait. Open hallway. Street of harlots. Remember. Haroun al Raschid.[2] I am almosting it. That man led me, spoke. I was not afraid. The melon he had he held against my face. Smiled: creamfruit smell. That was the rule, said. In. Come. Red carpet spread. You will see who.

Shouldering their bags they trudged, the red Egyptians.[3] His blued feet out of turnedup trousers slapped the clammy sand, a dull brick muffler strangling his unshaven neck. With woman steps she followed: the ruffian and his strolling mort. Spoils[4] slung at her back. Loose sand and shellgrit crusted her bare feet. About her windraw face her hair trailed. Behind her lord his helpmate, bing awast, to Romeville.[5] When night hides her body's flaws calling under her brown shawl from an archway where dogs have mired. Her fancyman is treating two Royal Dublins in O'Loughlin's of Blackpitts. Buss her, wap in rogues' rum lingo, for, O, my dimber wapping dell.[6] A shefiend's whiteness under her rancid rags. Fumbally's lane that night: the tanyard smells.

> White thy fambles, red thy gan
> And thy quarrons dainty is.
> Couch a hogshead with me then.
> In the darkmans clip and kiss.[7]

Morose delectation Aquinas tunbelly calls this, *frate porcospino*.[8] Unfallen Adam rode and not rutted. Call away let him:[9] *thy quarrons dainty is.* Language

---

8. Reference to a joke Stephen had made to his pupils in school that morning about "the fox burying his grandmother under a hollybush."
9. Leopard or panther.
1. I.e., begotten in adultery.
2. Stephen's dream of the famous Caliph of Baghdad, of the "street of harlots," and of his meeting a man with a melon foreshadows his meeting later in the day with Leopold Bloom and his visit to the brothel area of Dublin.
3. I.e., gypsies. As Stephen watches the gypsy cockle pickers with their dog he imagines their vagabond life and recalls fragments of gypsy speech and of thieves' slang.
4. The association of gypsy ("mort": free gypsy woman; harlot) with Egyptian reminds Stephen of the Israelites "spoiling the Egyptians" (Exodus

12.36).
5. Go away to London.
6. 17th-century thieves' slang. "Buss": kiss. "Wap": copulate with. "Rum": good. "Dimber": pretty. "Wapping dell": whore.
7. More thieves' slang. "Fambles": hands. "Gan": mouth. "Quarrons": body. "Couch a hogshead": come to bed. "Darkmans": night. "Clip": kiss. These four lines and some of the phrases in the preceding paragraph are quoted from a song of the period, "The Rogue's Delight in Praise of His Strolling Mort" (cf. n. 3 and n. 4, this page).
8. Brother porcupine (Italian), a reference to the fat ("tunbelly") but prickly 13-century philosopher, St. Thomas Aquinas.
9. The gypsy is calling his dog.

no whit worse than his. Monkwords, marybeads jabber on their girdles: rogue-words, tough nuggets patter in their pockets.

Passing now.

A side-eye at my Hamlet hat. If I were suddenly naked here as I sit? I am not. Across the sands of all the world, followed by the sun's flaming sword, to the west, trekking to evening lands. She trudges, schlepps, trains, drags, tras-cines her load.[1] A tide westering, moondrawn, in her wake. Tides, myriadis-landed, within her, blood not mine, *oinopa ponton*,[2] a winedark sea. Behold the handmaid of the moon. In sleep the wet sign calls her hour, bids her rise. Bridebed, childbed, bed of death, ghostcandled.[3] *Omnis caro ad te veniet.* He comes, pale vampire, through storm his eyes, his bat sails bloodying the sea, mouth to her mouth's kiss.[4]

Here. Put a pin in that chap, will you? My tablets.[5] Mouth to her kiss. No. Must be two of em. Glue em well. Mouth to her mouth's kiss.

His lips lipped and mouthed fleshless lips of air: mouth to her womb. Oomb, allwombing tomb.[6] His mouth moulded issuing breath, unspeeched: ooeeee-hah: roar of cataractic planets, globed, blazing, roaring wayawayawayawaya-awayaway. Paper. The banknotes, blast them. Old Deasy's letter. Here. Thanking you for the hospitality tear the blank end off. Turning his back to the sun he bent over far to a table of rock and scribbled words.[7] That's twice I forgot to take slips from the library counter.

His shadow lay over the rocks as he bent, ending. Why not endless till the farthest star? Darkly they are there behind this light, darkness shining in the brightness, delta of Cassiopeia, worlds. Me sits there with his augur's rod of ash, in borrowed sandals, by day beside a livid sea, unbeheld, in violet night walking beneath a reign of uncouth stars.[8] I throw this ended shadow from me, manshape ineluctable, call it back. Endless, would it be mine, form of my form? Who watches me here? Who ever anywhere will read these written words? Signs on a white field. Somewhere to someone in your flutiest voice. The good bishop of Cloyne[9] took the veil of the temple out of his shovel hat: veil of space with coloured emblems hatched on its field. Hold hard. Coloured on a flat: yes, that's right. Flat I see, then think distance, near, far, flat I see, east, back. Ah, see now. Falls back suddenly, frozen in stereoscope. Click does the trick. You find my words dark. Darkness is in our souls, do you not think? Flutier. Our souls, shamewounded by our sins, cling to us yet more, a woman to her lover clinging, the more the more.

She trusts me, her hand gentle, the longlashed eyes. Now where the blue hell am I bringing her beyond the veil?[1] Into the ineluctable modality of the ineluctable visuality. She, she, she. What she? The virgin at Hodges Figgis'

1. All words suggesting moving or dragging. "'I like that crescendo of verbs,' he [Joyce] said. 'The irresistible tug of the tides'" (Budgen).

2. Winedark sea (Homer).

3. He is thinking of his mother again. The following Latin (from the burial service) means: All flesh will come to thee.

4. Death comes like the Flying Dutchman in a phantom ship to give the fatal kiss.

5. Cf. *Hamlet* 1.5.107: "My tables."

6. Cf. Blake's poem "The Gates of Paradise," esp. the lines "The door of death I open found / And the worm weaving in the ground: / Thou'rt my mother from the womb, / Wife, sister, daughter, to the tomb." Cf. also *Romeo and Juliet* 2.2.9–10: "the earth, that's nature's mother, is her tomb. / What is her burying grave, that is her womb."

7. Stephen tears off the blank end of Mr. Deasy's letter to the press and writes a poem, which is quoted later in the novel.

8. He imagines himself as the constellation Cassiopeia, supposed to represent the wife of Cepheus (an Ethiopian king) seated in a chair and holding up her arms. His ash walking stick he thinks of as an "augur's [Roman soothsayer's] rod of ash."

9. George Berkeley (1685–1753), bishop of Cloyne (in Ireland), who argued that the external world has no objective reality but exists only in the mind of the perceiver. Stephen (as at the opening of this episode) is experimenting again with ways of sensing reality.

1. "She" is Psyche, the soul, whom he is bringing from "beyond the veil." But from metaphysical speculations on reality and the soul Stephen is led

window on Monday looking in for one of the alphabet books you were going to write. Keen glance you gave her. Wrist through the braided jess of her sunshade. She lives in Leeson park with a grief and kickshaws, a lady of letters. Talk that to some else, Stevie: a pickmeup. Bet she wears those curse of God stays suspenders and yellow stockings, darned with lumpy wool. Talk about apple dumplings, *piuttosto*.[2] Where are your wits?

Touch me. Soft eyes. Soft soft soft hand. I am lonely here. O, touch me soon, now. What is that word known to all men? I am quiet here alone. Sad too. Touch, touch me.

He lay back at full stretch over the sharp rocks, cramming the scribbled note and pencil into a pocket, his hat tilted down on his eyes. That is Kevin Egan's movement I made, nodding for his nap, sabbath sleep. *Et vidit Deus. Et erant valde bona.*[3] Alo! *Bonjour.* Welcome as the flowers in May. Under its leaf he watched through peacocktwittering lashes the southing sun. I am caught in this burning scene. Pan's hour, the faunal noon. Among gumheavy serpentplants, milkoozing fruits, where on the tawny waters leaves lie wide. Pain is far.

  And no more turn aside and brood.[4]

His gaze brooded on his broadtoed boots, a buck's castoffs, *nebeneinander*. He counted the creases of rucked leather wherein another's foot had nested warm. The foot that beat the ground in tripudium, foot I dislove. But you were delighted when Esther Osvalt's shoe went on you: girl I knew in Paris. *Tiens, quel petit pied!*[5] Staunch friend, a brother soul: Wilde's love that dare not speak its name.[6] He now will leave me. And the blame? As I am. As I am. All or not at all.

In long lassoes from the Cock lake the water flowed full, covering green-goldenly lagoons of sand, rising, flowing. My ashplant will float away. I shall wait. No, they will pass on, passing chafing against the low rocks, swirling, passing. Better get this job over quick. Listen: a fourworded wavespeech: seesoo, hrss, rsseeiss ooos. Vehement breath of waters amid seasnakes, rearing horses, rocks. In cups of rocks it slops: flop, slop, slap: bounded in barrels. And, spent, its speech ceases. It flows purling, widely flowing, floating foampool, flower unfurling.

Under the upswelling tide he saw the writhing weeds lift languidly and sway reluctant arms, hising up their petticoats,[7] in whispering water swaying and upturning coy silver fronds. Day by day: night by night: lifted, flooded and let fall. Lord, they are weary: and, whispered to, they sigh. Saint Ambrose heard it, sigh of leaves and waves, waiting, awaiting the fullness of their times, *diebus ac noctibus iniurias patiens ingemiscit.*[8] To no end gathered; vainly then released, forthflowing, wending back: loom of the moon. Weary too in sight of lovers, lascivious men, a naked woman shining in her courts, she draws a toil of waters.

(by the Psyche association) to think of "the virgin at Hodges Figgis' [a bookseller's] window."

2. Rather, sooner (Italian).

3. Connecting two phrases from the Vulgate (Latin Bible): "And God saw" (Genesis 1.4) and "And they were very good" (Genesis 1.31).

4. The first line of the second (and last) stanza of Yeats's poem "Who Goes with Fergus?" which is often in Stephen's mind. The line expresses for him the mood, of noontide stillness and of lotos eating in a lush Asian scene, that overcomes him momentarily when he realizes that it is twelve o'clock, the

hour of the Greek nature god Pan, "faunal noon." This Asian lotos-eating theme, which is associated also with Bloom, is important in the *Odyssey*.

5. Look, what a little foot! (French).

6. Asked at his 1895 trial for homosexuality what this line meant, Oscar Wilde defined it as the great spiritual affection of an elder man for a younger man.

7. A phrase from a vulgar song sung by Mulligan earlier that morning.

8. Night and day he patiently groaned forth his wrongs (St. Ambrose).

2548 / James Joyce

Five fathoms out there. Full fathom five thy father lies.[9] At one he said. Found drowned. High water at Dublin bar. Driving before it a loose drift of rubble, fanshoals of fishes, silly shells. A corpse rising salt-white from the undertow, bobbing landward a pace a pace a porpoise. There he is. Hook it quick. Sunk though he be beneath the watery floor. We have him. Easy now.

Bag of corpsegas sopping in foul brine. A quiver of minnows, fat of a spongy titbit, flash through the slits of his buttoned trouserfly. God becomes man becomes fish becomes barnacle goose becomes featherbed mountain. Dead breaths I living breathe, tread dead dust, devour a urinous offal from all dead. Hauled stark over the gunwhale he breathes upward the stench of his green grave, his leprous nosehole snoring to the sun.

A seachange[1] this, brown eyes saltblue. Seadeath, mildest of all deaths known to man. Old Father Ocean. *Prix de Paris:*[2] beware of imitations. Just you give it a fair trial. We enjoyed ourselves immensely.

Come. I thirst. Clouding over. No black clouds anywhere, are there? Thunderstorm. Allbright he falls, proud lightning of the intellect, *Lucifer, dico, qui nescit occasum.*[3] No. My cockle hat and staff and hismy sandal shoon.[4] Where? To evening lands. Evening will find itself.

He took the hilt of his ashplant, lunging with it softly, dallying still. Yes, evening will find itself in me, without me. All days make their end. By the way next when is it? Tuesday will be the longest day. Of all the glad new year, mother,[5] the rum tum tiddledy tum. Lawn Tennyson,[6] gentleman poet. *Già.*[7] For the old hag with the yellow teeth. And Monsieur Drumont, gentleman journalist. *Già.* My teeth are very bad. Why, I wonder? Feel. That one is going too. Shells. Ought I go to a dentist, I wonder, with what money? That one. Toothless Kinch, the superman. Why is that, I wonder, or does it mean something perhaps?

My handkerchief. He threw it. I remember. Did I not take it up?

His hand groped vainly in his pockets. No, I didn't. Better buy one.

He laid the dry snot picked from his nostril on a ledge of rock, carefully. For the rest let look who will.

Behind. Perhaps there is someone.

He turned his face over a shoulder, rere regardant.[8] Moving through the air high spars of a threemaster, her sails brailed up on the crosstrees, homing, upstream, silently moving, a silent ship.

[LESTRYGONIANS][9]

Pineapple rock, lemon platt, butter scotch. A sugarsticky girl shovelling scoopfuls of creams for a christian brother. Some school treat. Bad for their

9. From Ariel's song (*The Tempest* 1.2.400).
1. Another quotation from Ariel's song (1.2.404).
2. Prize of Paris. The reference is probably to the Paris Exposition of 1889, where prizes were awarded in various categories of food and other commodities; the winners bore the seal of the prize on the label (hence, "beware of imitations"). Stephen mentally awards the prize to death by drowning.
3. Lucifer, I say, who knows not his fall (Latin). Thunder and lightning recall the fall of Lucifer.
4. From Ophelia's mad song (*Hamlet* 4.5.23–26): "How should I your true love know / From another one?— / By his cockle hat and staff, / And his sandal shoon." Ophelia, too, was drowned.
5. Cf. Alfred, Lord Tennyson, "The May Queen":

"You must wake and call me early, call me early, mother dear; / Tomorrow 'ill be the happiest time of all the glad New Year."
6. A parody of the poet's name, punning on "lawn tennis," attributed to W. B. Yeats.
7. Let's go (Italian).
8. Looking behind him (heraldic terminology). Stephen, as we leave him sitting by the shore, is described in a highly stylized, heraldic language.
9. The eighth of the novel's eighteen episodes. It is lunchtime in Dublin, and Leopold Bloom, as he walks through the city in no great hurry (for he likes to linger and watch what goes on around him), thinks of food. The Lestrygonians in book 10 of the *Odyssey* are cannibals, and throughout this episode there are suggestions of the slaughter of

tummies. Lozenge and comfit manufacturer to His Majesty the King. God. Save. Our. Sitting on his throne sucking red jujubes white.

A sombre Y. M. C. A. young man, watchful among the warm sweet fumes of Graham Lemon's, placed a throwaway in a hand of Mr Bloom.

Heart to heart talks.

Bloo . . . Me? No.

Blood of the Lamb.[1]

His slow feet walked him riverward, reading. Are you saved? All are washed in the blood of the lamb. God wants blood victim. Birth, hymen, martyr, war, foundation of a building, sacrifice, kidney burntoffering, druids' altars. Elijah is coming. Dr John Alexander Dowie,[2] restorer of the church in Zion, is coming.

Is coming! Is coming!! Is coming!!!
All heartily welcome.

Paying game. Torry and Alexander last year. Polygamy. His wife will put the stopper on that. Where was that ad some Birmingham firm the luminous crucifix. Our Saviour. Wake up in the dead of night and see him on the wall, hanging. Pepper's ghost idea.[3] Iron Nails Ran In.

Phosphorus it must be done with. If you leave a bit of codfish for instance. I could see the bluey silver over it. Night I went down to the pantry in the kitchen. Don't like all the smells in it waiting to rush out. What was it she[4] wanted? The Malaga raisins. Thinking of Spain. Before Rudy[5] was born. The phosphorescence, that bluey greeny. Very good for the brain.

From Butler's monument house corner he glanced along Bachelor's walk. Dedalus' daughter there still outside Dillon's auctionrooms. Must be selling off some old furniture. Knew her eyes at once from the father. Lobbing about waiting for him. Home always breaks up when the mother goes. Fifteen children he had. Birth every year almost. That's in their theology or the priest won't give the poor woman the confession, the absolution. Increase and multiply. Did you ever hear such an idea? Eat you out of house and home. No families themselves to feed. Living on the fat of the land. Their butteries and larders. I'd like to see them do the black fast Yom Kippur.[6] Crossbuns. One meal and a collation for fear he'd collapse on the altar. A housekeeper of one of those fellows if you could pick it out of her. Never pick it out of her. Like

---

living creatures for food or of food as something disgusting, which make somewhat tenuous contact with Homer's description of the cannibals spearing Ulysses' men for food. This episode shows us Bloom's consciousness responding to the sights and sounds of Dublin. His humane curiosity, his desire to learn and to improve the human lot, his sympathetic concern for Mrs. Breen and Mrs. Purefoy, his feeding the gulls, his recollections of a happier time when his daughter was a baby and his relations with his wife were thoroughly satisfactory, his interest in opera, his continuous shying away from thoughts of his wife's rendezvous with the dashing Blazes Boylan—all this helps to build up his character in depth and to differentiate him sharply from Stephen. Unlike Stephen, Bloom's interest in language is confined to simple puns and translations; his interest in poetry is obvious and sentimental; his interest in the nature of reality takes the form of half-forgotten fragments of science remaining in his mind from school days.

Everything about him is concrete, practical, sensual, and middlebrow or lowbrow, as distinct from the abstract, theoretical, esoteric speculations of Stephen in the "Proteus" episode.

1. Bloom has been handed a religious leaflet ("throwaway") containing the phrase "Blood of the Lamb." He at first mistakes "Blood" for "Bloom."

2. Scottish American evangelist (1847–1907), who established the "Christian Catholic Apostolic Church in Zion" in 1896 and founded Zion City, IL, in 1901.

3. A dramatic troupe advertising as "The original Pepper's Ghost! and Spectral Opera Company" was popular in the late-19th century; it seems to have specialized in ghostly special effects, possibly achieved through the use of phosphorescent material on its costumes.

4. I.e., Bloom's wife, Molly, born in Gibraltar.

5. Their son, who had died in infancy eleven years before.

6. Jewish Day of Atonement.

getting L s. d.[7] out of him. Does himself well. No guests. All for number one. Watching his water. Bring your own bread and butter. His reverence. Mum's the word.

Good Lord, that poor child's dress is in flitters. Underfed she looks too. Potatoes and marge, marge and potatoes. It's after they feel it. Proof of the pudding. Undermines the constitution.

As he set foot on O'Connell bridge a puffball of smoke plumed up from the parapet. Brewery barge with export stout. England. Sea air sours it, I heard. Be interesting some day get a pass through Hancock to see the brewery. Regular world in itself. Vats of porter, wonderful. Rats get in too. Drink themselves bloated as big as a collie floating. Dead drunk on the porter. Drink till they puke again like christians. Imagine drinking that! Rats: vats. Well of course if we knew all the things.

Looking down he saw flapping strongly, wheeling between the gaunt quay-walls, gulls. Rough weather outside. If I threw myself down? Reuben J's son must have swallowed a good bellyful of that sewage.[8] One and eightpence too much. Hhhhm. It's the droll way he comes out with the things. Knows how to tell a story too.

They wheeled lower. Looking for grub. Wait.

He threw down among them a crumpled paper ball. Elijah thirtytwo feet per sec is com.[9] Not a bit. The ball bobbed unheeded on the wake of swells, floated under by the bridgepiers. Not such damn fools. Also the day I threw that stale cake out of the Erin's King picked it up in the wake fifty yards astern. Live by their wits. They wheeled, flapping.

> *The hungry famished gull*
> *Flaps o'er the waters dull.*

That is how poets write, the similar sounds. But then Shakespeare has no rhymes: blank verse. The flow of the language it is. The thoughts. Solemn.

> *Hamlet, I am thy father's spirit*
> *Doomed for a certain time to walk the earth.*[1]

—Two apples a penny! Two for a penny!

His gaze passed over the glazed apples serried on her stand. Australians they must be this time of year. Shiny peels: polishes them up with a rag or a handkerchief.

Wait. Those poor birds.

He halted again and bought from the old applewoman two Banbury cakes for a penny and broke the brittle paste and threw its fragments down into the Liffey. See that? The gulls swooped silently two, then all from their heights, pouncing on prey. Gone. Every morsel.

Aware of their greed and cunning he shook the powdery crumb from his hands. They never expected that. Manna.[2] Live on fishy flesh they have to, all

---

7. I.e., cash: L, s., d. are the abbreviations, respectively, for pounds, shillings, and pence.
8. The son of Reuben J. Dodd, Dublin solicitor (lawyer), had been rescued from the river Liffey by a man to whom Reuben J. had given two shillings as a reward—"one and eightpence too much," as Simon Dedalus had remarked to Bloom earlier that morning when they were discussing the incident. In the following sentences Bloom is thinking of

Dedalus's comment.
9. I.e., Elijah is coming, accelerating at the rate of thirty-two feet per second per second, the acceleration rate of falling bodies. ("Elijah is coming" is the legend on the handbill Bloom is tossing away).
1. *Hamlet* 1.5.9–10 (slightly misquoted).
2. The divine food (small, round, and white) that the children of Israel ate in the wilderness (Exodus 16.14–15).

seabirds, gulls, seagoose. Swans from Anna Liffey[3] swim down here sometimes to preen themselves. No accounting for tastes. Wonder what kind is swanmeat. Robinson Crusoe had to live on them.

They wheeled, flapping weakly. I'm not going to throw any more. Penny quite enough. Lot of thanks I get. Not even a caw. They spread foot and mouth disease too. If you cram a turkey, say, on chestnutmeal it tastes like that. Eat pig like pig. But then why is it that saltwater fish are not salty? How is that?

His eyes sought answer from the river and saw a rowboat rock at anchor on the treacly swells lazily its plastered board.

    Kino's
    11/-
    Trousers[4]

Good idea that. Wonder if he pays rent to the corporation. How can you own water really? It's always flowing in a stream, never the same, which in the stream of life we trace. Because life is a stream. All kinds of places are good for ads. That quack doctor for the clap used to be stuck up in all the greenhouses. Never see it now. Strictly confidential. Dr Hy Franks. Didn't cost him a red like Maginni the dancing master self advertisement. Got fellows to stick them up or stick them up himself for that matter on the q.t. running in to loosen a button. Flybynight. Just the place too. POST NO BILLS. POST NO PILLS.[5] Some chap with a dose burning him.

If he . . .

O!

Eh?

No . . . No.

No, no. I don't believe it. He wouldn't surely?

No, no.[6]

Mr Bloom moved forward, raising his troubled eyes. Think no more about that. After one. Timeball on the ballastoffice is down. Dunsink time. Fascinating little book that is of Sir Robert Ball's. Parallax. I never exactly understood.[7] There's a priest. Could ask him. Par it's Greek: parallel, parallax. Met him pike hoses[8] she called it till I told her about the transmigration. O rocks!

Mr Bloom smiled O rocks at two windows of the ballastoffice. She's right after all. Only big words for ordinary things on account of the sound. She's not exactly witty. Can be rude too. Blurt out what I was thinking. Still I don't know. She used to say Ben Dollard had a base barreltone voice. He has legs like barrels and you'd think he was singing into a barrel. Now isn't that wit?

---

3. The Liffey flows from the Wicklow Mountains northeast and east to Dublin Bay.

4. I.e., eleven shillings ("11 / -") for Kino's Trousers. Bloom is a canvasser for advertisements: he receives commissions from newspapers for getting tradesmen to place advertisements with them.

5. The revised text edited by John Kidd (1993) reads, POST NO BILLS. POST 110 PILLS. "Post no bills" can mean either "do not affix any posters" or "mail no accounts." Bloom is punning to himself on the quack doctor's advertising (by posting bills), collecting his money (by mailing accounts), and sending pills to patients by mail.

6. Blazes Boylan, flashy philanderer, is due to call on Molly Bloom that afternoon, to discuss the program of a concert that he is managing for her (Molly is a singer). Bloom knows that Boylan and his wife will commit adultery together. Here it sud-

denly occurs to him that Boylan might give Molly a "dose" of veneral disease, but he puts the thought from him as incredible.

7. The "timeball on the ballastoffice" registers the official time of the observatory at Dunsink (Dublin). Noticing that the timeball is down, which means that it is after one o'clock, Bloom is reminded of the observatory, then of the Irish astronomer Sir Robert Ball's popular book on astronomy, *The Story of the Heavens* (1886), and of the astronomical term *parallax*, which he found in the book but "never exactly understood."

8. Molly's way of pronouncing *metempsychosis*. When Bloom had explained metempsychosis to her that morning, she had exclaimed "O rocks!" at the pretentious term. He now mentally repeats "O rocks!" at the thought of the word *parallax*.

They used to call him big Ben. Not half as witty as calling him base barreltone. Appetite like an albatross. Get outside of a baron of beef. Powerful man he was at stowing away number one Bass.⁹ Barrel of Bass. See? It all works out.

A procession of whitesmocked men marched slowly towards him along the gutter, scarlet sashes across their boards. Bargains. Like that priest they are this morning: we have sinned: we have suffered. He read the scarlet letters on their five tall white hats: H. E. L. Y. S. Wisdom Hely's. Y lagging behind drew a chunk of bread from under his foreboard, crammed it into his mouth and munched as he walked. Our staple food. Three bob a day, walking along the gutters, street after street. Just keep skin and bone together, bread and skilly. They are not Boyl: no: M'Glade's men. Doesn't bring in any business either. I suggested to him about a transparent showcart with two smart girls sitting inside writing letters, copybooks, envelopes, blottingpaper. I bet that would have caught on. Smart girls writing something catch the eye at once. Everyone dying to know what she's writing. Get twenty of them round you if you stare at nothing. Have a finger in the pie. Women too. Curiosity. Pillar of salt.¹ Wouldn't have it of course because he didn't think of it himself first. Or the inkbottle I suggested with a false stain of black celluloid. His ideas for ads like Plumtree's potted under the obituaries, cold meat department. You can't lick 'em. What? Our envelopes. Hello! Jones, where are you going? Can't stop, Robinson, I am hastening to purchase the only reliable inkeraser *Kansell*, sold by Hely's Ltd, 85 Dame street. Well out of that ruck I am. Devil of a job it was collecting accounts of those convents. Tranquilla convent. That was a nice nun there, really sweet face. Wimple suited her small head. Sister? Sister? I am sure she was crossed in love by her eyes. Very hard to bargain with that sort of a woman. I disturbed her at her devotions that morning. But glad to communicate with the outside world. Our great day, she said. Feast of Our Lady of Mount Carmel. Sweet name too: caramel. She knew, I think she knew by the way she. If she had married she would have changed. I suppose they really were short of money. Fried everything in the best butter all the same. No lard for them. My heart's broke eating dripping. They like buttering themselves in and out. Molly tasting it, her veil up. Sister? Pat Claffey, the pawnbroker's daughter. It was a nun they say invented barbed wire.

He crossed Westmoreland street when apostrophe S had plodded by. Rover cycleshop. Those races are on today. How long ago is that? Year Phil Gilligan died. We were in Lombard street west. Wait, was in Thom's. Got the job in Wisdom Hely's year we married. Six years. Ten years ago: ninetyfour he died, yes that's right the big fire at Arnott's. Val Dillon was lord mayor. The Glencree dinner. Alderman Robert O'Reilly emptying the port into his soup before the flag fell, Bobbob lapping it for the inner alderman. Couldn't hear what the band played. For what we have already received may the Lord make us. Milly² was a kiddy then. Molly had that elephantgrey dress with the braided frogs. Mantailored with selfcovered buttons. She didn't like it because I sprained my ankle first day she wore choir picnic at the Sugarloaf. As if that. Old Goodwin's tall hat done up with some sticky stuff. Flies' picnic too. Never put a dress on her back like it. Fitted her like a glove, shoulder and hips. Just beginning to plump it out well. Rabbitpie we had that day. People looking after her.

---

9. A popular British ale.
1. Cf. Genesis 19.1–26, where Lot's wife defies God's order to "look not behind thee" and is turned into "a pillar of salt."
2. Bloom's fifteen-year-old daughter. "For . . . us": cf. the Lord's Prayer, often said before meals.

Happy. Happier then. Snug little room that was with the red wallpaper, Dockrell's, one and ninepence a dozen. Milly's tubbing night. American soap I bought: elderflower. Cosy smell of her bathwater. Funny she looked soaped all over. Shapely too. Now photography.[3] Poor papa's daguerreotype atelier he told me of. Hereditary taste.

He walked along the curbstone.

Stream of life. What was the name of that priestlylooking chap was always squinting in when he passed? Weak eyes, woman. Stopped in Citron's saint Kevin's parade. Pen something. Pendennis? My memory is getting. Pen . . . ? Of course it's years ago. Noise of the trams probably. Well, if he couldn't remember the dayfather's name that he sees every day.

Bartell d'Arcy was the tenor, just coming out then. Seeing her home after practice. Conceited fellow with his waxedup moustache. Gave her that song *Winds that blow from the south.*

Windy night that was I went to fetch her there was that lodge meeting on about those lottery tickets after Goodwin's concert in the supperroom or oakroom of the Mansion house. He and I behind. Sheet of her music blew out of my hand against the High school railings. Lucky it didn't. Thing like that spoils the effect of a night for her. Professor Goodwin linking her in front. Shaky on his pins, poor old sot. His farewell concerts. Positively last appearance on any stage. May be for months and may be for never. Remember her laughing at the wind, her blizzard collar up. Corner of Harcourt road remember that gust. Brrfoo! Blew up all her skirts and her boa nearly smothered old Goodwin. She did get flushed in the wind. Remember when we got home raking up the fire and frying up those pieces of lap of mutton for her supper with the Chutney sauce she liked. And the mulled rum. Could see her in the bedroom from the hearth unclamping the busk of her stays: white.

Swish and soft flop her stays made on the bed. Always warm from her. Always liked to let her self out. Sitting there after till near two taking out her hairpins. Milly tucked up in beddyhouse. Happy. Happy. That was the night . . .

—O, Mr Bloom, how do you do?

—O, how do you do, Mrs Breen?[4]

—No use complaining. How is Molly those times? Haven't seen her for ages.

—In the pink, Mr Bloom said gaily, Milly has a position down in Mullingar, you know.

—Go away! Isn't that grand for her?

—Yes, in a photographer's there. Getting on like a house on fire. How are all your charges?

—All on the baker's list, Mrs Breen said.

How many has she? No other in sight.

—You're in black I see. You have no . . .

—No, Mr. Bloom said. I have just come from a funeral.

Going to crop up all day, I foresee. Who's dead, when and what did he die of ? Turn up like a bad penny.

—O dear me, Mrs Breen said, I hope it wasn't any near relation.

May as well get her sympathy.

---

3. Milly is working at a photographer's.
4. Mrs. Breen had been an old sweetheart of Bloom's.

—Dignam, Mr Bloom said. An old friend of mine. He died quite suddenly, poor fellow. Heart trouble, I believe. Funeral was this morning.

> *Your funeral's tomorrow*
> *While you're coming through the rye.*
> *Diddlediddle dumdum*
> *Diddlediddle . . .*

—Sad to lose the old friends, Mrs Breen's womaneyes said melancholily.

Now that's quite enough about that. Just quietly: husband.

—And your lord and master?

Mrs Breen turned up her two large eyes. Hasn't lost them anyhow.

—O, don't be talking, she said. He's a caution to rattlesnakes. He's in there now with his lawbooks finding out the law of libel. He has me heartscalded. Wait till I show you.

Hot mockturtle vapour and steam of newbaked jampuffs rolypoly poured out from Harrison's. The heavy noonreek tickled the top of Mr Bloom's gullet. Want to make good pastry, butter, best flour, Demerara sugar, or they'd taste it with the hot tea. Or is it from her? A barefoot arab stood over the grating, breathing in the fumes. Deaden the gnaw of hunger that way. Pleasure or pain is it? Penny dinner. Knife and fork chained to the table.

Opening her handbag, chipped leather, hatpin: ought to have a guard on those things. Stick it in a chap's eye in the tram. Rummaging. Open. Money. Please take one. Devils if they lose sixpence. Raise Cain. Husband barging. Where's the ten shillings I gave you on Monday? Are you feeding your little brother's family? Soiled handkerchief: medicinebottle. Pastille that was fell. What is she? . . .

—There must be a new moon out, she said. He's always bad then.[5] Do you know what he did last night?

Her hand ceased to rummage. Her eyes fixed themselves on him, wide in alarm, yet smiling.

—What? Mr. Bloom asked.

Let her speak. Look straight in her eyes. I believe you. Trust me.

—Woke me up in the night, she said. Dream he had, a nightmare. Indiges.[6]

—Said the ace of spades[7] was walking up the stairs.

—The ace of spades! Mr Bloom said.

She took a folded postcard from her handbag.

—Read that, she said. He got it this morning.

—What is it? Mr Bloom asked, taking the card. U. P.?[8]

—U.p.: up, she said. Someone taking a rise out of him. It's a great shame for them whoever he is.

—Indeed it is, Mr Bloom said.

She took back the card, sighing.

—And now he's going round to Mr Menton's office. He's going to take an action for ten thousand pounds, he says.

She folded the card into her untidy bag and snapped the catch.

Same blue serge dress she had two years ago, the nap bleaching. Seen its

---

5. Mr. Breen is mentally disturbed.
6. I.e., indigestion, which Bloom thinks caused Mr. Breen's nightmare.
7. A symbol of death.

8. Expression used in Charles Dickens's *Oliver Twist* (1838) to announce the approaching death of an old woman. It also suggests "you're crazy" or "you've been screwed."

best days. Wispish hair over her ears. And that dowdy toque: three old grapes to take the harm out of it. Shabby genteel. She used to be a tasty dresser. Lines round her mouth. Only a year or so older than Molly.

See the eye that woman gave her, passing. Cruel. The unfair sex.

He looked still at her, holding back behind his look his discontent. Pungent mockturtle oxtail mulligatawny. I'm hungry too. Flakes of pastry on the gusset of her dress: daub of sugary flour stuck to her cheek. Rhubarb tart with liberal fillings, rich fruit interior. Josie Powell that was. In Luke Doyle's long ago, Dolphin's Barn, the charades. U.p.: up.

Change the subject.

—Do you ever see anything of Mrs Beaufoy, Mr Bloom asked.

—Mina Purefoy? she said.

Philip Beaufoy I was thinking. Playgoers' Club[9] Matcham often thinks of the masterstroke. Did I pull the chain? Yes. The last act.

—Yes.

—I just called to ask on the way in is she over it. She's in the lying-in hospital in Holles street. Dr Horne got her in. She's three days bad now.

—O, Mr Bloom said. I'm sorry to hear that.

—Yes, Mrs Breen said. And a houseful of kids at home. It's a very stiff birth, the nurse told me.

—O, Mr Bloom said.

His heavy pitying gaze absorbed her news. His tongue clacked in compassion. Dth! Dth!

—I'm sorry to hear that, he said. Poor thing! Three days! That's terrible for her.

Mrs Breen nodded

—She was taken bad on the Tuesday . . .

Mr Bloom touched her funnybone gently, warning her.

—Mind! Let this man pass.

A bony form strode along the curbstone from the river, staring with a rapt gaze into the sunlight through a heavystringed glass. Tight as a skullpiece a tiny hat gripped his head. From his arm a folded dustcoat, a stick and an umbrella dangled to his stride.

—Watch him, Mr Bloom said. He always walks outside the lampposts. Watch!

—Who is he if it's a fair question? Mrs Breen asked. Is he dotty?

—His name is Cashel Boyle O'Connor Fitzmaurice Tisdall Farrell, Mr Bloom said smiling. Watch!

—He has enough of them, she said. Denis will be like that one of these days.

She broke off suddenly.

—There he is, she said. I must go after him. Goodbye. Remember me to Molly, won't you?

—I will, Mr Bloom said.

He watched her dodge through passers towards the shopfronts. Denis Breen in skimpy frockcoat and blue canvas shoes shuffled out of Harrison's hugging two heavy tomes to his ribs. Blown in from the bay. Like old times. He suffered

9. Bloom is thinking of the story "Matcham's Masterstroke," by "Mr. Philip Beaufoy, Playgoers' Club, London," which he had read on the toilet that morning. He then mentally quotes the opening sentence.

her to overtake him without surprise and thrust his dull grey beard towards her, his loose jaw wagging as he spoke earnestly.

Meshuggah.[1] Off his chump.

Mr Bloom walked on again easily, seeing ahead of him in sunlight the tight skullpiece, the dangling stick, umbrella, dustcoat. Going the two days. Watch him! Out he goes again. One way of getting on in the world. And that other old mosey lunatic in those duds. Hard time she must have with him.

U.p.: up. I'll take my oath that's Alf Bergan or Richie Goulding. Wrote it for a lark in the Scotch house, I bet anything. Round to Menton's office. His oyster eyes staring at the postcard. Be a feast for the gods.

He passed the Irish Times. There might be other answers lying there. Like to answer them all. Good system for criminals. Code. At their lunch now. Clerk with the glasses there doesn't know me. O, leave them there to simmer. Enough bother wading through fortyfour of them. Wanted smart lady typist to aid gentleman in literary work. I called you naughty darling because I do not like that other world. Please tell me what is the meaning. Please tell me what perfume does your wife. Tell me who made the world.[2] The way they spring those questions on you. And the other one Lizzie Twigg.[3] My literary efforts have had the good fortune to meet with the approval of the eminent poet A. E. (Mr Geo. Russell).[4] No time to do her hair drinking sloppy tea with a book of poetry.

Best paper by long chalks for a small ad. Got the provinces now. Cook and general, exc cuisine, housemaid kept. Wanted live man for spirit counter. Resp. girl (R. C.) wishes to hear of post in fruit or pork shop. James Carlisle made that. Six and a half per cent dividend. Made a big deal on Coates's shares. Ca' canny. Cunning old Scotch hunks. All the toady news. Our gracious and popular vicereine.[5] Bought the Irish Field now. Lady Mountcashel has quite recovered after her confinement and rode out with the Ward Union stag-hounds at the enlargement yesterday at Rathoath. Uneatable fox. Pothunters too. Fear injects juices make it tender enough for them. Riding astride. Sit her horse like a man. Weightcarrying huntress. No sidesaddle or pillion for her, not for Joe. First to the meet and in at the death. Strong as a broodmare some of those horsey women. Swagger around livery stables. Toss off a glass of brandy neat while you'd say knife. That one at the Grosvenor this morning. Up with her on the car: wishswish. Stonewall or fivebarred gate put her mount to it. Think that pugnosed driver did it out of spite. Who is this she was like? O yes! Mrs Miriam Dandrade that sold me her old wraps and black under-clothes in the Shelbourne hotel. Divorced Spanish American. Didn't take a feather out of her my handling them. As if I was her clotheshorse. Saw her in the viceregal party when Stubbs the park ranger got me in with Whelan of the

1. Mad (Yiddish).
2. Cf. Marlowe's The Tragical History of Doctor Faustus 5, lines 237–44:

FAUSTUS   . . . Tell me who made the world?
MEPHASTOPHILIS   I will not.
   . . . Think on hell Faustus, for thou art damned.
FAUSTUS   Think, Faustus, upon God, that made the world.

3. Bloom is mentally quoting a letter written to him by the typist Martha Clifford, with whom he is carrying on a purely epistolary love affair (she

had misspelled word as world: "I do not like that other world"). Lizzie Twigg was one of the other typists who had answered his advertisement for a secretary "to aid gentleman in literary work" (Bloom's pretext for beginning such an affair).
4. Æ (George Russell, 1867–1935), the Irish poet mentioned as a reference by Lizzie Twigg when she answered Bloom's advertisement, is later encountered by Bloom with a woman who Bloom speculates might be Lizzie.
5. Wife of the viceroy, who represented the British Crown in Ireland; Bloom is thinking of the society column in the Irish Times.

Express. Scavenging what the quality left. High tea. Mayonnaise I poured on the plums thinking it was custard. Her ears ought to have tingled for a few weeks after. Want to be a bull for her. Born courtesan. No nursery work for her, thanks.

Poor Mrs Purefoy! Methodist husband. Method in his madness. Saffron bun and milk and soda lunch in the educational dairy. Eating with a stopwatch, thirtytwo chews to the minute. Still his muttonchop whiskers grew. Supposed to be well connected. Theodore's cousin in Dublin Castle. One tony relative in every family. Hardy annuals he presents her with. Saw him out at the Three Jolly Topers marching along bareheaded and his eldest boy carrying one in a marketnet. The squallers. Poor thing! Then having to give the breast year after year all hours of the night. Selfish those t.t's[6] are. Dog in the manger. Only one lump of sugar in my tea, if you please.

He stood at Fleet street crossing. Luncheon interval a sixpenny at Rowe's? Must look up that ad in the national library.[7] An eightpenny in the Burton. Better. On my way.

He walked on past Bolton's Westmoreland house. Tea. Tea. Tea. I forgot to tap Tom Kernan.[8]

Sss. Dth, dth, dth! Three days imagine groaning on a bed with a vinegared handkerchief round her forehead, her belly swollen out. Phew! Dreadful simply! Child's head too big: forceps. Doubled up inside her trying to butt its way out blindly, groping for the way out. Kill me that would. Lucky Molly got over hers lightly. They ought to invent something to stop that. Life with hard labour. Twilightsleep idea: queen Victoria was given that. Nine she had. A good layer. Old woman that lived in a shoe she had so many children. Suppose he was consumptive. Time someone thought about it instead of gassing about the what was it the pensive bosom of the silver effulgence.[9] Flapdoddle to feed fools on. They could easily have big establishments. Whole thing quite painless out of all the taxes give every child born five quid at compound interest up to twentyone, five per cent is a hundred shillings and five tiresome pounds, multiply by twenty decimal system, encourage people to put by money save hundred and ten and a bit twentyone years want to work it out on paper come to a tidy sum, more than you think.

Not stillborn of course. They are not even registered. Trouble for nothing.

Funny sight two of them together, their bellies out. Molly and Mrs Moisel. Mothers' meeting. Phthisis retires for the time being, then returns. How flat they look after all of a sudden! Peaceful eyes. Weight off their mind. Old Mrs Thornton was a jolly old soul. All my babies, she said. The spoon of pap in her mouth before she fed them. O, that's nyumyum. Got her hand crushed by old Tom Wall's son. His first bow to the public. Head like a prize pumpkin. Snuffy Dr Murren. People knocking them up at all hours. For God's sake doctor. Wife in her throes. Then keep them waiting months for their fee. To attendance on your wife. No gratitude in people. Humane doctors, most of them.

Before the huge high door of the Irish house of parliament a flock of pigeons flew. Their little frolic after meals. Who will we do it on? I pick the fellow in

---

6. Abbreviation of *teetotalers*, total abstainers from alcohol.
7. Bloom's goal, on his walk through Dublin, is the National Library, where he wants to look up an advertisement in a back number of the *Kilkenny People*.
8. A Dublin tea merchant and friend of Bloom's,

whom Bloom had earlier intended to ask ("tap") for some tea.
9. "Pensive bosom" and "silver effulgence": Bloom recalls two phrases from a public speech that is quoted (via a newspaper account) in "Aeolus," the novel's seventh episode.

2558 / James Joyce

black. Here goes. Here's good luck. Must be thrilling from the air. Apjohn, myself and Owen Goldberg up in the trees near Goose green playing the monkeys. Mackerel they called me.

A squad of constables debouched from College street, marching in Indian file. Goosestep. Foodheated faces, sweating helmets, patting their truncheons. After their feed with a good load of fat soup under their belts. Policeman's lot is oft a happy one.[1] They split up into groups and scattered, saluting towards their beats. Let out to graze. Best moment to attack one in pudding time. A punch in his dinner. A squad of others, marching irregularly, rounded Trinity[2] railings, making for the station. Bound for their troughs. Prepare to receive cavalry. Prepare to receive soup.

He crossed under Tommy Moore's roguish finger. They did right to put him up over a urinal: meeting of the waters.[3] Ought to be places for women. Running into cakeshops. Settle my hat straight. *There is not in this wide world a vallee.* Great song of Julia Morkan's. Kept her voice up to the very last. Pupil of Michael Balfe's wasn't she?

He gazed after the last broad tunic. Nasty customers to tackle. Jack Power could a tale unfold: father a G man. If a fellow gave them trouble being lagged they let him have it hot and heavy in the bridewell.[4] Can't blame them after all with the job they have especially the young hornies. That horsepoliceman the day Joe Chamberlain was given his degree in Trinity he got a run for his money.[5] My word he did! His horse's hoofs clattering after us down Abbey street. Luck I had the presence of mind to dive into Manning's or I was souped. He did come a wallop, by George. Must have cracked his skull on the cobblestones. I oughtn't to have got myself swept along with those medicals. And the Trinity jibs[6] in their mortarboards. Looking for trouble. Still I got to know that young Dixon who dressed that sting for me in the Mater and now he's in Holles street where Mrs Purefoy. Wheels within wheels. Police whistle in my ears still. All skedaddled. Why he fixed on me. Give me in charge. Right here it began.

—Up the Boers!

—Three cheers for De Wet![7]

—We'll hang Joe Chamberlain on a sourapple tree.

Silly billies: mob of young cubs yelling their guts out. Vinegar hill. The Butter exchange band. Few years' time half of them magistrates and civil servants. War comes on: into the army helterskelter: same fellows used to. Whether on the scaffold high.

Never know who you're talking to. Corny Kelleher he has Harvey Duff in his eye. Like that Peter or Denis or James Carey that blew the gaff on the invincibles. Member of the corporation too. Egging raw youths on to get in the know. All the time drawing secret service pay from the castle.[8] Drop him like a hot potato. Why those plainclothes men are always courting slaveys. Easily twig a man used to uniform. Squarepushing up against a backdoor. Maul her a bit. Then the next thing on the menu. And who is the gentleman

1. Cf. W. S. Gilbert, *Pirates of Penzance:* "The policeman's lot is not a happy one."
2. Trinity College, Dublin.
3. "The Meeting of the Waters" was a famous poem by the much-loved Irish poet Thomas Moore (1779–1852), whose statue Bloom now passes.
4. Prison.
5. When Joseph Chamberlain, the British colonial secretary, came to Dublin to receive an honorary

degree from Trinity College, a group of medical students rioted against him and against the Anglo-Boer War (1899–1902), in which the Boers, or Afrikaners, fought and lost to the British Empire.
6. Trinity College students.
7. Boer general. "Up" here as in "up with."
8. I.e., from the British government, whose representative lived at Dublin Castle.

does be visiting there? Was the young master saying anything? Peeping Tom
through the keyhole. Decoy duck. Hotblooded young student fooling round
her fat arms ironing.

—Are those yours, Mary?

—I don't wear such things . . . Stop or I'll tell the missus on you. Out half
the night.

—There are great times coming, Mary. Wait till you see.

—Ah, get along with your great times coming.

Barmaids too. Tobaccoshopgirls.

James Stephens'[9] idea was the best. He knew them. Circles of ten so that a
fellow couldn't round on more than his own ring. Sinn Fein.[1] Back out you
get the knife. Hidden hand. Stay in. The firing squad. Turnkey's daughter got
him out of Richmond, off from Lusk. Putting up in the Buckingham Palace
hotel under their very noses. Garibaldi.[2]

You must have a certain fascination: Parnell. Arthur Griffith[3] is a square-
headed fellow but he has no go in him for the mob. Want to gas about our
lovely land. Gammon[4] and spinach. Dublin Bakery Company's tearoom.
Debating societies. That republicanism is the best form of government. That
the language question should take precedence of the economic question. Have
your daughters inveigling them to your house. Stuff them up with meat and
drink. Michaelmas goose. Here's a good lump of thyme seasoning under the
apron for you. Have another quart of goosegrease before it gets too cold. Half-
fed enthusiasts. Penny roll and a walk with the band. No grace for the carver.
The thought that the other chap pays best sauce in the world. Make themselves
thoroughly at home. Show us over those apricots, meaning peaches. The not
far distant day. Home Rule sun rising up in the northwest.[5]

His smile faded as he walked, a heavy cloud hiding the sun slowly, shadowing Trinity's surly front. Trams passed one another, ingoing, outgoing,
clanging. Useless words. Things go on same; day after day: squads of police
marching out, back: trams in, out. Those two loonies mooching about. Dignam
carted off. Mina Purefoy swollen belly on a bed groaning to have a child tugged
out of her. One born every second somewhere. Other dying every second.
Since I fed the birds five minutes. Three hundred kicked the bucket. Other
three hundred born, washing the blood off, all are washed in the blood of the
lamb, bawling maaaaaa.

Cityful passing away, other cityful coming, passing away too: other coming
on, passing on. Houses, lines of houses, streets, miles of pavements, piledup
bricks, stones. Changing hands. This owner, that. Landlord never dies they
say. Other steps into his shoes when he gets his notice to quit. They buy the
place up with gold and still they have all the gold. Swindle in it somewhere.
Piled up in cities, worn away age after age. Pyramids in sand. Built on bread
and onions. Slaves Chinese wall. Babylon. Big stones left. Round towers. Rest
rubble, sprawling suburbs, jerrybuilt, Kerwan's mushroom houses built of
breeze. Shelter for the night.

No-one is anything.

9. Irish nationalist revolutionary.
1. Ourselves Alone (Gaelic); Irish revolutionary movement.
2. Bloom is thinking of a variety of nationalist conspirators who escaped from danger, among them the 19th-century Italian patriot and general Giuseppe Garibaldi.
3. Founder of Sinn Fein (1872–1922). Charles
Stewart Parnell (1846–1891), Irish nationalist political leader.
4. Ham, bacon.
5. Reference to Griffith's comment on the *Freeman's Journal* masthead, which showed the sun rising in the northwest from behind the Bank of Ireland. Bloom has a *Freeman* in his pocket.

This is the very worst hour of the day. Vitality. Dull, gloomy: hate this hour. Feel as if I had been eaten and spewed.

Provost's house. The reverend Dr Salmon: tinned salmon. Well tinned in there. Wouldn't live in it if they paid me. Hope they have liver and bacon today. Nature abhors a vacuum.

The sun freed itself slowly and lit glints of light among the silverware in Walter Sexton's window opposite by which John Howard Parnell[6] passed, unseeing.

There he is: the brother. Image of him. Haunting face. Now that's a coincidence. Course hundreds of times you think of a person and don't meet him. Like a man walking in his sleep. No-one knows him. Must be a corporation meeting today. They say he never put on the city marshal's uniform since he got the job. Charley Beulger used to come out on his high horse, cocked hat, puffed, powdered and shaved. Look at the woebegone walk of him. Eaten a bad egg. Poached eyes on ghost. I have a pain. Great man's brother: his brother's brother. He'd look nice on the city charger. Drop into the D. B. C. probably for his coffee, play chess there. His brother used men as pawns. Let them all go to pot. Afraid to pass a remark on him. Freeze them up with that eye of his. That's the fascination: the name. All a bit touched. Mad Fanny and his other sister Mrs Dickinson driving about with scarlet harness. Bolt upright like surgeon M'Ardle. Still David Sheehy beat him for south Meath. Apply for the Chiltern Hundreds[7] and retire into public life. The patriot's banquet. Eating orangepeels in the park. Simon Dedalus said when they put him in parliament that Parnell would come back from the grave and lead him out of the House of Commons by the arm.

—Of the twoheaded octopus, one of whose heads is the head upon which the ends of the world have forgotten to come while the other speaks with a Scotch accent. The tentacles . . .

They passed from behind Mr Bloom along the curbstone. Beard and bicycle. Young woman.

And there he is too. Now that's really a coincidence: second time. Coming events cast their shadows before. With the approval of the eminent poet, Mr Geo Russell. That might be Lizzie Twigg with him.[8] A. E.: what does that mean? Initials perhaps. Albert Edward, Arthur Edmund, Alphonsus Eb Ed El Esquire. What was he saying? The ends of the world with a Scotch accent. Tentacles: octopus. Something occult: symbolism. Holding forth. She's taking it all in. Not saying a word. To aid gentleman in literary work.

His eyes followed the high figure in homespun, beard and bicycle, a listening woman at his side. Coming from the vegetarian. Only weggebobbles and fruit. Don't eat a beefsteak. If you do the eyes of that cow will pursue you through all eternity. They say it's healthier. Wind and watery though. Tried it. Keep you on the run all day. Bad as a bloater. Dreams all night. Why do they call that thing they gave me nutsteak? Nutarians. Fruitarians. To give you the idea you are eating rumpsteak. Absurd. Salty too. They cook in soda. Keep you sitting by the tap all night.

6. Charles Parnell's brother.
7. The stewardship of the Chiltern Hundreds (a tract of land in central England owned by the British Crown) is by a legal figment held to be an office of profit under the Crown and is conferred on members of Parliament wishing to resign, which by law they cannot do. Members of Parliament who accept an office of profit under the Crown must vacate their seats.
8. Bloom wonders whether the woman with A. E. might be Lizzie Twigg and then goes on to speculate on the meaning of "A. E." and on Russell's mystical ideas.

Her stockings are loose over her ankles. I detest that: so tasteless. Those literary etherial people they are all. Dreamy, cloudy, symbolistic. Esthetes they are. I wouldn't be surprised if it was that kind of food you see produces the like waves of the brain the poetical. For example one of those policemen sweating Irish stew into their shirts; you couldn't squeeze a line of poetry out of him. Don't know what poetry is even. Must be in a certain mood.

> *The dreamy cloudy gull*
> *Waves o'er the waters dull.*

He crossed at Nassau street corner and stood before the window of Yeates and Son, pricing the fieldglasses. Or will I drop into old Harris's and have a chat with young Sinclair? Wellmannered fellow. Probably at his lunch. Must get those old glasses of mine set right. Gœrz lenses six guineas. Germans making their way everywhere. Sell on easy terms to capture trade. Undercutting. Might chance on a pair in the railway lost property office. Astonishing the things people leave behind them in trains and cloakrooms. What do they be thinking about? Women too. Incredible. Last year travelling to Ennis had to pick up that farmer's daughter's bag and hand it to her at Limerick junction. Unclaimed money too. There's a little watch up there on the roof of the bank to test those glasses by.

His lids came down on the lower rims of his irides. Can't see it. If you imagine it's there you can almost see it. Can't see it.

He faced about and, standing between the awnings, held out his right hand at arm's length towards the sun. Wanted to try that often. Yes: completely. The tip of his little finger blotted out the sun's disk. Must be the focus where the rays cross. If I had black glasses. Interesting. There was a lot of talk about those sunspots when we were in Lombard street west. Terrific explosions they are. There will be a total eclipse this year: autumn some time.

Now that I come to think of it, that ball falls at Greenwich time. It's the clock is worked by an electric wire from Dunsink. Must go out there some first Saturday of the month. If I could get an introduction to professor Joly or learn up something about his family. That would do to: man always feels complimented. Flattery where least expected. Nobleman proud to be descended from some king's mistress. His foremother. Lay it on with a trowel. Cap in hand goes through the land. Not go in and blurt out what you know you're not to: what's parallax? Show this gentleman the door.

Ah.

His hand fell again to his side.

Never know anything about it. Waste of time. Gasballs spinning about, crossing each other, passing. Same old dingdong always. Gas, then solid, then world, then cold, then dead shell drifting around, frozen rock like that pineapple rock. The moon. Must be a new moon out, she said. I believe there is.

He went on by la maison Claire.

Wait. The full moon was the night we were Sunday fortnight exactly there is a new moon. Walking down by the Tolka. Not bad for a Fairview moon. She was humming. The young May moon she's beaming, love. He other side of her. Elbow, arm. He. Glowworm's la-amp is gleaming, love. Touch. Fingers. Asking. Answer. Yes.

Stop. Stop. If it was it was.[9] Must.

---

9. Bloom is thinking again of his wife's infidelity.

Mr Bloom, quickbreathing, slowlier walking passed Adam court.

With deep quiet relief, his eyes took note: this is street here middle of the day Bob Doran's bottle shoulders. On his annual bend, M'Coy said. They drink in order to say or do something or *cherchez la femme*.[1] Up in the Coombe with chummies and streetwalkers and then the rest of the year as sober as a judge.

Yes. Thought so. Sloping into the Empire. Gone. Plain soda would do him good. Where Pat Kinsella had his Harp theatre before Whitbread ran the Queen's.[2] Broth of a boy. Dion Boucicault[3] business with his harvestmoon face in a poky bonnet. Three Purty Maids from School. How time flies eh? Showing long red pantaloons under his skirts. Drinkers, drinking, laughed spluttering, their drink against their breath. More power, Pat. Coarse red: fun for drunkards: guffaw and smoke. Take off that white hat. His parboiled eyes. Where is he now? Beggar somewhere. The harp that once did starve us all.[4]

I was happier then. Or was that I? Or am I now I? Twentyeight I was. She twentythree when we left Lombard street west something changed. Could never like it again after Rudy. Can't bring back time. Like holding water in your hand. Would you go back to then? Just beginning then. Would you? Are you not happy in your home, you poor little naughty boy? Wants to sew on buttons for me. I must answer. Write it in the library.

Grafton street gay with housed awnings lured his senses. Muslin prints silk, dames and dowagers, jingle of harnesses, hoofthuds lowringing in the baking causeway. Thick feet that woman has in the white stockings. Hope the rain mucks them up on her. Countrybred chawbacon. All the beef to the heels were in. Always gives a woman clumsy feet. Molly looks out of plumb.

He passed, dallying, the windows of Brown Thomas, silk mercers. Cascades of ribbons. Flimsy China silks. A tilted urn poured from its mouth a flood of bloodhued poplin: lustrous blood. The huguenots brought that here. *La causa è santa!*[5] Tara tara. Great chorus that. *Tara.* Must be washed in rainwater. Meyerbeer. *Tara: bom bom bom.*

Pincushions. I'm a long time threatening to buy one. Stick them all over the place. Needles in window curtains.

He bared slightly his left forearm. Scrape: nearly gone. Not today anyhow. Must go back for that lotion. For her birthday perhaps. Junejuly augseptember eighth. Nearly three months off. Then she mightn't like it. Women won't pick up pins. Say it cuts lo.

Gleaming silks, petticoats on slim brass rails, rays of flat silk stockings.

Useless to go back. Had to be. Tell me all.

High voices. Sunwarm silk. Jingling harnesses. All for a woman, home and houses, silkwebs, silver, rich fruits, spicy from Jaffa. Agendath Netaim.[6] Wealth of the world.

A warm human plumpness settled down on his brain. His brain yielded. Perfume of embraces all him assailed. With hungered flesh obscurely, he mutely craved to adore.

1. Look for the woman, i.e., in the case (French).
2. The Queen's Theatre.
3. Irish-born American dramatist, manager, and actor.
4. A reference to the lack of financial success of the Harp Theatre through a punning reworking of Moore's famous "Harp That Once Through Tara's Halls."
5. "The cause is sacred," chorus from Meyerbeer's opera *Les Huguenots*, which Bloom is recalling. The Huguenots were 16th- and 17th-century French Protestants, many of whom fled to Britain to escape persecution.
6. Planters' Company (Hebrew). Bloom recalls a leaflet, which he had seen that morning and is still carrying in his pocket, advertising an early Zionist settlement

Duke street. Here we are. Must eat. The Burton. Feel better then.

He turned Combridge's corner, still pursued. Jingling hoofthuds. Perfumed bodies, warm, full. All kissed, yielded: in deep summer fields, tangled pressed grass, in trickling hallways of tenements, along sofas, creaking beds.

—Jack, love!

—Darling!

—Kiss me, Reggy!

—My boy!

—Love![7]

His heart astir he pushed in the door of the Burton restaurant. Stink gripped his trembling breath: pungent meatjuice, slop of greens. See the animals feed. Men, men, men.

Perched on high stools by the bar, hats shoved back, at the tables calling for more bread no charge, swilling, wolfing gobfuls of sloppy food, their eyes bulging, wiping wetted moustaches. A pallid suetfaced young man polished his tumbler knife fork and spoon with his napkin. New set of microbes. A man with an infant's saucestained napkin tucked round him shovelled gurgling soup down his gullet. A man spitting back on his plate: halfmasticated gristle: no teeth to chewchewchew it. Chump chop from the grill. Bolting to get it over. Sad booser's eyes. Bitten off more than he can chew. Am I like that? See ourselves as others see us. Hungry man is an angry man. Working tooth and jaw. Don't! O! A bone! That last pagan king of Ireland Cormac in the school-poem choked himself at Sletty southward of the Boyne.[8] Wonder what he was eating. Something galoptious.[9] Saint Patrick converted him to Christianity. Couldn't swallow it all however.

—Roast beef and cabbage.

—One stew.

Smells of men. His gorge rose. Spaton sawdust, sweetish warmish cigarette-smoke, reek of plug, spilt beer, men's beery piss, the stale of ferment.

Couldn't eat a morsel here. Fellow sharpening knife and fork, to eat all before him, old chap picking his tootles. Slight spasm, full, chewing the cud. Before and after. Grace after meals. Look on this picture then on that. Scoffing up stewgravy with sopping sippets of bread. Lick it off the plate, man! Get out of this.

He gazed round the stooled and tabled eaters, tightening the wings of his nose.

—Two stouts here.

—One corned and cabbage.

That fellow ramming a knifeful of cabbage down as if his life depended on it. Good stroke. Give me the fidgets to look. Safer to eat from his three hands. Tear it limb from limb. Second nature to him. Born with a silver knife in his mouth. That's witty, I think. Or no. Silver means born rich. Born with a knife. But then the allusion is lost.

An illgirt server gathered sticky clattering plates. Rock, the bailiff, standing at the bar blew the foamy crown from his tankard. Well up: it splashed yellow near his boot. A diner, knife and fork upright, elbows on table, ready for a

---

7. Sensual images are leading Bloom to imagine love scenes from a sentimental novel as he enters Burton's restaurant. In the *Odyssey*, the Lestrygonians had used "the handsome daughter of Lestrygonian Antiphates" as a decoy to lure Ulysses' men to her father.

8. Bloom is recalling a "schoolpoem" about a legendary incident in Irish history.

9. I.e., "goluptious," slang for delicious.

second helping stared towards the food-lift across his stained square of news-paper. Other chap telling him something with his mouth full. Sympathetic listener. Table talk. I munched hum un thu Unchster Bunk un Munchday. Ha? Did you, faith?

Mr Bloom raised two fingers doubtfully to his lips. His eyes said:

—Not here. Don't see him.[1]

Out. I hate dirty eaters.

He backed towards the door. Get a light snack in Davy Byrne's. Stopgap. Keep me going. Had a good breakfast.

—Roast and mashed here.

—Pint of stout.

Every fellow for his own, tooth and nail. Gulp. Grub. Gulp. Gobstuff.

He came out into clearer air and turned back towards Grafton street. Eat or be eaten. Kill! Kill!

Suppose that communal kitchen years to come perhaps. All trotting down with porringers and tommycans to be filled. Devour contents in the street. John Howard Parnell example the provost of Trinity every mother's son don't talk of your provosts and provost of Trinity women and children, cabmen, priests, parsons, fieldmarshals, archbishops. From Ailesbury road, Clyde road, artisans' dwellings north Dublin union, lord mayor in his gingerbread coach, old queen in a bathchair. My plate's empty. After you with our incorporated drinking cup. Like sir Philip Crampton's fountain. Rub off the microbes with your handkerchief. Next chap rubs on a new batch with his. Father O'Flynn would make hares of them all. Have rows all the same. All for number one. Children fighting for the scrapings of the pot. Want a souppot as big as the Phoenix park. Harpooning flitches and hindquarters out of it. Hate people all round you. City Arms hotel *table d'hôte* she called it. Soup, joint and sweet. Never know whose thoughts you're chewing. Then who'd wash up all the plates and forks? Might be all feeding on tabloids that time. Teeth getting worse and worse.

After all there's a lot in that vegetarian fine flavour of things from the earth garlic, of course, it stinks Italian organgrinders crisp of onions mushrooms truffles. Pain to animal too. Pluck and draw fowl. Wretched brutes there at the cattlemarket waiting for the poleaxe to split their skulls open. Moo. Poor trembling calves. Meh. Staggering bob. Bubble and squeak. Butchers' buckets wobble lights. Give us that brisket off the hook. Plup. Rawhead and bloody bones. Flayed glasseyed sheep hung from their haunches, sheepsnouts bloody-papered snivelling nosejam on sawdust. Top and lashers going out. Don't maul them pieces, young one.

Hot fresh blood they prescribe for decline. Blood always needed. Insidious. Lick it up smokinghot, thick sugary. Famished ghosts.

Ah, I'm hungry.

He entered Davy Byrne's. Moral pub. He doesn't chat. Stands a drink now and then. But in leapyear once in four. Cashed a cheque for me once.

What will I take now? He drew his watch. Let me see now. Shandygaff?

—Hello, Bloom, Nosey Flynn said from his nook.

—Hello, Flynn.

—How's things?

---

1. He pretends he is looking for someone he cannot see, so that he has an excuse to leave without eating.

—Tiptop . . . Let me see. I'll take a glass of burgundy and . . . let me see.

Sardines on the shelves. Almost taste them by looking. Sandwich? Ham and his descendants mustered and bred there. Potted meats. What is home without Plumtree's potted meat? Incomplete. What a stupid ad! Under the obituary notices they stuck it. All up a plumtree. Dignam's potted mat. Cannibals would with lemon and rice. White missionary too salty. Like pickled pork. Expect the chief consumes the parts of honour. Ought to be tough from exercise. His wives in a row to watch the effect. *There was a right royal old nigger. Who ate or something the somethings of the reverend Mr MacTrigger.* With it an abode of bliss. Lord knows what concoction. Cauls mouldy tripes windpipes faked and minced up. Puzzle find the meat. Kosher. No meat and milk together. Hygiene that was what they call now, Yom Kippur fast spring cleaning of inside. Peace and war depend on some fellow's digestion. Religions. Christmas turkeys and geese. Slaughter of innocents.[2] Eat, drink and be merry. Then casual wards full after. Heads bandaged. Cheese digests all but itself. Mighty cheese.

—Have you a cheese sandwich?

—Yes, sir.

Like a few olives too if they had them. Italian I prefer. Good glass of burgundy; take away that. Lubricate. A nice salad, cool as a cucumber. Tom Kernan can dress. Puts gusto into it. Pure olive oil. Milly served me that cutlet with a sprig of parsley. Take one Spanish onion. God made food, the devil the cooks. Devilled crab.

—Wife well?

—Quite well, thanks . . . A cheese sandwich, then. Gorgonzola, have you?

—Yes, sir.

Nosey Flynn sipped his grog.

—Doing any singing those times?

Look at his mouth. Could whistle in his own ear. Flap ears to match. Music. Knows as much about it as my coachman. Still better tell him. Does no harm. Free ad.

—She's engaged for a big tour end of this month. You may have heard perhaps.

—No. O, that's the style. Who's getting it up?

The curate[3] served.

—How much is that?

—Seven d., sir . . . Thank you, sir.

Mr Bloom cut his sandwich into slender strips. *Mr MacTrigger.* Easier than the dreamy creamy stuff. *His five hundred wives. Had the time of their lives.*

—Mustard, sir?

—Thank you.

He studded under each lifted strip yellow blobs. *Their lives.* I have it. *It grew bigger and bigger and bigger.*

—Getting it up? he said. Well, it's like a company idea, you see. Part shares and part profits.

—Ay, now I remember, Nosey Flynn said, putting his hand in his pocket to scratch his groin. Who is this was telling me? Isn't Blazes Boylan mixed up in it?

2. Cf. Herod's massacre of innocent children after hearing prophecies of Jesus' birth (Matthew 2.16). 3. Bartender.

A warm shock of air heat of mustard hanched on Mr Bloom's heart. He raised his eyes and met the stare of a bilious clock. Two. Pub clock five minutes fast. Time going on. Hands moving. Two. Not yet.[4]

His midriff yearned then upward, sank within him, yearned more longly, longingly.

Wine.

He smellsipped the cordial juice and, bidding his throat strongly to speed it, set his wineglass delicately down.

—Yes, he said. He's the organiser in point of fact.

No fear: no brains.

Nosey Flynn snuffled and scratched. Flea having a good square meal.

—He had a good slice of luck, Jack Mooney was telling me, over that boxing match Myler Keogh won again that soldier in the Portobello barracks. By God, he had the little kipper down in the country Carlow he was telling me. . . .

Hope that dewdrop doesn't come down into his glass. No, snuffled it up.

—For near a month, man, before it came off. Sucking duck eggs by God till further orders. Keep him off the boose, see? O, by God, Blazes is a hairy chap.

Davy Byrne came forward from the hindbar in tuckstitched shirtsleeves, cleaning his lips with two wipes of his napkin. Herring's blush. Whose smile upon each feature plays with such and such replete. Too much fat on the parsnips.

—And here's himself and pepper on him, Nosey Flynn said. Can you give us a good one for the Gold cup?

—I'm off that, Mr Flynn, Davy Byrne answered. I never put anything on a horse.

—You're right there, Nosey Flynn said.

Mr Bloom ate his strips of sandwich, fresh clean bread, with relish of disgust, pungent mustard, the feety savour of green cheese. Sips of his wine soothed his palate. Not logwood that. Tastes fuller this weather with the chill off.

Nice quiet bar. Nice piece of wood in that counter. Nicely planed. Like the way it curves there.

—I wouldn't do anything at all in that line, Davy Byrne said. It ruined many a man, the same horses.

Vintners' sweepstake. Licensed for the sale of beer, wine and spirits for consumption on the premises. Heads I win tails you lose.

—True for you, Nosey Flynn said. Unless you're in the know. There's no straight sport going now. Lenehan gets some good ones. He's giving Sceptre today. Zinfandel's the favourite, lord Howard de Walden's, won at Epsom. Morny Cannon is riding him. I could have got seven to one against Saint Amant a fortnight before.

—That so? Davy Byrne said. . . .

He went towards the window and, taking up the petty cash book, scanned its pages.

—I could, faith, Nosey Flynn said, snuffling. That was a rare bit of horseflesh. Saint Frusquin was her sire. She won in a thunderstorm, Rothschild's filly, with wadding in her ears. Blue jacket and yellow cap. Bad luck to big Ben Dollard and his John O'Gaunt. He put me off it. Ay.

He drank resignedly from his tumbler, running his fingers down the flutes.

4. I.e., not yet time for Boylan to visit Molly.

—Ay, he said, sighing.

Mr Bloom, champing standing, looked upon his sigh. Nosey numbskull. Will I tell him that horse Lenehan?[5] He knows already. Better let him forget. Go and lose more. Fool and his money. Dewdrop coming down again. Cold nose he'd have kissing a woman. Still they might like. Prickly beards they like. Dogs' cold noses. Old Mrs Riordan with the rumbling stomach's Skye terrier in the City Arms hotel. Molly fondling him in her lap. O, the big doggybowwowsywowsy!

Wine soaked and softened rolled pith of bread mustard a moment mawkish cheese. Nice wine it is. Taste it better because I'm not thirsty. Bath of course does that. Just a bite or two. Then about six o'clock I can. Six. Six. Time will be gone then. She . . .

Mild fire of wine kindled his veins. I wanted that badly. Felt so off colour. His eyes unhungrily saw shelves of tins, sardines, gaudy lobsters' claws. All the odd things people pick up for food. Out of shells, periwinkles with a pin, off trees, snails out of the ground the French eat, out of the sea with bait on a hook. Silly fish learn nothing in a thousand years. If you didn't know risky putting anything into your mouth. Poisonous berries. Johnny Magories. Roundness you think good. Gaudy colour warns you off. One fellow told another and so on. Try it on the dog first. Led on by the smell or the look. Tempting fruit. Ice cones. Cream. Instinct. Orangegroves for instance. Need artificial irrigation. Bleibtreustrasse.[6] Yes but what about oysters. Unsightly like a clot of phlegm. Filthy shells. Devil to open them too. Who found them out? Garbage, sewage they feed on. Fizz and Red bank oysters. Effect on the sexual. Aphrodis. He was in the Red bank this morning. Was he oyster old fish at table. Perhaps he young flesh in bed. No. June has no ar no oysters. But there are people like tainted game. Jugged hare. First catch your hare. Chinese eating eggs fifty years old, blue and green again. Dinner of thirty courses. Each dish harmless might mix inside. Idea for a poison mystery. That archduke Leopold was it. No. Yes, or was it Otto one of those Habsburgs? Or who was it used to eat the scruff off his own head? Cheapest lunch in town. Of course, aristocrats, then the others copy to be in the fashion. Milly too rock oil and flour. Raw pastry I like myself. Half the catch of oysters they throw back in the sea to keep up the price. Cheap. No-one would buy. Caviare. Do the grand. Hock in green glasses. Swell blowout. Lady this. Powdered bosom pearls. The *élite. Crème de la crème.*[7] They want special dishes to pretend they're. Hermit with a platter of pulse keep down the stings of the flesh. Know me come eat with me. Royal sturgeon. High sheriff, Coffey, the butcher, right to venisons of the forest from his ex.[8] Send him back the half of a cow. Spread I saw down in the Master of the Rolls' kitchen area. Whitehatted *Chef* like a rabbi. Combustible duck. Curly cabbage *à la duchesse de Parme.* Just as well to write it on the bill of fare so you can know what you've eaten too many drugs spoil the broth. I know it myself. Dosing it with Edwards' desicated soup. Geese stuffed silly for them. Lobsters boiled alive. Do ptake some ptarmigan. Wouldn't mind being a waiter in a swell hotel. Tips, evening dress, halfnaked

5. Bloom is wondering whether to pass on a tip from Lenehan, who wrote for the racing paper *Sport*.
6. The Berlin street that contained the offices of the "Planters' Company" (see n. 6, p. 2562).
7. Cream of the cream (i.e., the very best, socially).

8. All sturgeon caught in or off Britain were the property of the king, according to the ancient traditional rights to certain kinds of fish or game. Bloom goes on to imagine a Dublin butcher having a "right to venisons of the forest from his ex[cellency]"—i.e., the viceroy.

ladies. May I tempt you to a little more filleted lemon sole, miss Dubedat? Yes, do bedad. And she did bedad. Huguenot name I expect that. A miss Dubedat lived in Killiney, I remember. *Du, de la,* French. Still it's the same fish, perhaps old Micky Hanlon of Moore street ripped the guts out of making money, hand over fist, finger in fishes' gills, can't write his name on a cheque, think he was painting the landscape with his mouth twisted. Moooikill A Aitcha Ha. Ignorant as a kish of brogues,[9] worth fifty thousand pounds.

Stuck on the pane two flies buzzed, stuck.

Glowing wine on his palate lingered swallowed. Crushing in the winepress grapes of Burgundy. Sun's heat it is. Seems to a secret touch telling me memory. Touched his sense moistened remembered. Hidden under wild ferns on Howth. Below us bay sleeping sky. No sound. The sky. The bay purple by the Lion's head. Green by Drumleck. Yellowgreen towards Sutton. Fields of undersea, the lines faint brown in grass, buried cities. Pillowed on my coat she had her hair, earwigs in the heather scrub my hand under her nape, you'll toss me all. O wonder! Coolsoft with ointments her hand touched me, caressed: her eyes upon me did not turn away. Ravished over her I lay, full lips full open, kissed her mouth. Yum. Softly she gave me in my mouth the seedcake warm and chewed. Mawkish pulp her mouth had mumbled sweet and sour with spittle. Joy: I ate it: joy. Young life, her lips that gave me pouting. Soft, warm, sticky gumjelly lips. Flowers her eyes were, take me, willing eyes. Pebbles fell. She lay still. A goat. No-one. High on Ben Howth rhododendrons a nannygoat walking surefooted, dropping currants. Screened under ferns she laughed warmfolded. Wildly I lay on her, kissed her, eyes, her lips, her stretched neck, beating, woman's breasts full in her blouse of nun's veiling, fat nipples upright. Hot I tongued her. She kissed me. I was kissed. All yielding she tossed my hair. Kissed, she kissed me.[1]

Me. And me now.

Stuck, the flies buzzed.

His downcast eyes followed the silent veining of the oaken slab. Beauty: it curves: curves are beauty. Shapely goddesses, Venus, Juno: curves the world admires. Can see them library museum standing in the round hall, naked goddesses. Aids to digestion. They don't care what man looks. All to see. Never speaking, I mean to say to fellows like Flynn. Suppose she did Pygmalion and Galatea[2] what would she say first? Mortal! Put you in your proper place. Quaffing nectar at mess with gods, golden dishes, all ambrosial. Not like a tanner lunch we have, boiled mutton, carrots and turnips, bottle of Allsop. Nectar, imagine it drinking electricity: god's food. Lovely forms of women sculped Junonian. Immortal lovely. And we stuffing food in one hole and out behind: food, chyle, blood, dung, earth, food: have to feed it like stoking an engine. They have no. Never looked. I'll look today. Keeper won't see. Bend down let something see if she.

Dribbling a quiet message from his bladder came to go to do not to do there

---

9. A basket of shoes.
1. Bloom is remembering when he first proposed to Molly, on the Hill of Howth, near Dublin. Molly also recalls this in the final episode ("Penelope"), which is her soliloquy: "we were lying among the rhododendrons on Howth head in the gray tweed suit and his straw hat the day I got him to propose to me yes . . . my God after that long kiss I near

lost my breath . . . I saw he understood or felt what a woman is and I knew I could always get round him and I gave him all the pleasure I could leading him on."
2. In Greek mythology Pygmalion, king of Cyprus, sculpted a statue of the goddess Aphrodite that became a mortal woman, Galatea.

to do. A man and ready he drained his glass to the lees and walked, to men too they gave themselves, manly conscious, lay with men lovers, a youth enjoyed her, to the yard.

When the sound of his boots had ceased Davy Byrne said from his book:

—What is this he is? Isn't he in the insurance line?

—He's out of that long ago, Nosey Flynn said. He does canvassing for the *Freeman*.

—I know him well to see, Davy Byrne said. Is he in trouble?

—Trouble? Nosey Flynn said. Not that I heard of. Why?

—I noticed he was in mourning.

—Was he? Nosey Flynn said. So he was, faith. I asked him how was all at home. You're right, by God. So he was.

—I never broach the subject, Davy Byrne said humanely, if I see a gentleman is in trouble that way. It only brings it up fresh in their minds.

—It's not the wife anyhow, Nosey Flynn said. I met him the day before yesterday and he coming out of that Irish farm dairy John Wyse Nolan's wife has in Henry street with a jar of cream in his hand taking it home to his better half. She's well nourished, I tell you. Plovers on toast.

—And is he doing for the *Freeman*? Davy Byrne said.

Nosey Flynn pursed his lips.

—He doesn't buy cream on the ads he picks up. You can make bacon of that.

—How so? Davy Byrne asked, coming from his book.

Nosey Flynn made swift passes in the air with juggling fingers. He winked.

—He's in the craft,[3] he said.

—Do you tell me so? Davy Byrne said.

—Very much so, Nosey Flynn said. Ancient free and accepted order. Light, life and love, by God. They give him a leg up. I was told that by a, well, I won't say who.

—Is that a fact?

—O, it's a fine order, Nosey Flynn said. They stick to you when you're down. I know a fellow was trying to get into it, but they're as close as damn it. By God they did right to keep the women out of it.

Davy Byrne smiledyawnednodded all in one:

—Iiiiiichaaaaaaach!

—There was one woman, Nosey Flynn said, hid herself in a clock to find out what they do be doing. But be damned but they smelt her out and swore her in on the spot a master mason. That was one of the Saint Legers of Doneraile.

Davy Byrne, sated after his yawn, said with tearwashed eyes:

—And is that a fact? Decent quiet man he is. I often saw him in here and I never once saw him, you know, over the line.

—God Almighty couldn't make him drunk, Nosey Flynn said firmly. Slips off when the fun gets too hot. Didn't you see him look at his watch? Ah, you weren't there. If you ask him to have a drink first thing he does he outs with the watch to see what he ought to imbibe. Declare to God he does.

—There are some like that, Davy Byrne said. He's a safe man, I'd say.

---

3. I.e., in the "free and accepted order" of Freemasons, one of the oldest European secret societies; it was not in good repute in predominantly Roman Catholic countries like Ireland.

—He's not too bad, Nosey Flynn said, snuffling it up. He has been known to put his hand down too to help a fellow. Give the devil his due. O, Bloom has his good points. But there's one thing he'll never do.

His hand scrawled a dry pen signature beside his grog.

—I know, Davy Byrne said.

—Nothing in black and white, Nosey Flynn said.

Paddy Leonard and Bantam Lyons came in. Tom Rochford followed frowning, a plaining hand on his claret waistcoat.

—Day, Mr Byrne.

—Day, gentlemen.

They paused at the counter.

—Who's standing? Paddy Leonard asked.

—I'm sitting anyhow, Nosey Flynn answered.

—Well, what'll it be? Paddy Leonard asked.

—I'll take a stone ginger, Bantam Lyons said.

—How much? Paddy Leonard cried. Since when, for God's sake? What's yours, Tom?

—How is the main drainage? Nosey Flynn asked, sipping.

For answer Tom Rochford pressed his hand to his breastbone and hiccupped.

—Would I trouble you for a glass of fresh water, Mr Byrne? he said.

—Certainly, sir.

Paddy Leonard eyed his alemates.

—Lord love a duck, he said, look at what I'm standing drinks to! Cold water and gingerpop! Two fellows that would suck whisky off a sore leg. He has some bloody horse up his sleeve for the Gold cup. A dead snip.

—Zinfandel is it? Nosey Flynn asked.

Tom Rochford spilt powder from a twisted paper into the water set before him.

—That cursed dyspepsia, he said before drinking.

—Breadsoda is very good, Davy Byrne said.

Tom Rochford nodded and drank.

—Is it Zinfandel?

—Say nothing, Bantam Lyons winked. I'm going to plunge five bob on my own.

—Tell us if you're worth your salt and be damned to you, Paddy Leonard said. Who gave it to you?

Mr Bloom on his way out raised three fingers in greeting.

—So long, Nosey Flynn said.

The others turned.

—That's the man now that gave it to me, Bantam Lyons whispered.

—Prrwht! Paddy Leonard said with scorn. Mr Byrne, sir, we'll take two of your small Jamesons[4] after that and a . . . .

—Stone ginger, Davy Byrne added civilly.

—Ay, Paddy Leonard said. A suckingbottle for the baby.

Mr Bloom walked towards Dawson street, his tongue brushing his teeth smooth. Something green it would have to be: spinach say. Then with those Röntgen rays[5] searchlight you could.

At Duke lane a ravenous terrier choked up a sick knuckly cud on the cob-

---

4. Brand of Irish whiskey.   5. X-rays.

blestones and lapped it with new zest. Surfeit. Returned with thanks having fully digested the contents. First sweet then savoury. Mr Bloom coasted warily. Ruminants. His second course. Their upper jaw they move. Wonder if Tom Rochford will do anything with that invention of his. Wasting time explaining it to Flynn's mouth. Lean people long mouths. Ought to be a hall or a place where inventors could go in and invent free. Course then you'd have all the cranks pestering.

He hummed, prolonging in solemn echo, the closes of the bars:

> Don Giovanni, a cenar teco
> M'invitasti.[6]

Feel better. Burgundy. Good pick me up. Who distilled first? Some chap in the blues. Dutch courage. That *Kilkenny People* in the national library now I must.

Bare clean closestools, waiting, in the window of William Miller, plumber, turned back his thoughts. They could: and watch it all the way down, swallow a pin sometimes come out of the ribs years after, tour round the body, changing biliary duct, spleen squirting liver, gastric juice coils of intestines like pipes. But the poor buffer would have to stand all the time with his insides entrails on show. Science.

—A cenar teco.

What does that *teco* mean? Tonight perhaps.

> Don Giovanni, thou hast me invited
> To come to supper tonight,
> The rum the rumdum.

Doesn't go properly.

Keyes: two months if I get Nannetti[7] to. That'll be two pounds ten, about two pounds eight. Three Hynes owes me. Two eleven. Prescott's ad. Two fifteen. Five guineas about. On the pig's back.

Could buy one of those silk petticoats for Molly, colour of her new garters. Today. Today. Not think.[8]

Tour the south then. What about English wateringplaces? Brighton, Margate. Piers by moonlight. Her voice floating out. Those lovely seaside girls. Against John Long's a drowsing loafer lounged in heavy thought, gnawing a crusted knuckle. Handy man wants job. Small wages. Will eat anything.

Mr Bloom turned at Gray's confectioner's window of unbought tarts and passed the reverend Thomas Connellan's bookstore. *Why I left the church of Rome?* Birds' Nest. Women run him. They say they used to give pauper children soup to change to protestants in the time of the potato blight. Society over the way papa went to for the conversion of poor jews. Same bait. *Why we left the church of Rome?*

6. Because Molly is a singer, Bloom is familiar with opera. Here he recalls the song sung by the Commendatore's statue in Mozart's *Don Giovanni* and below he translates accurately the Italian words he quotes, except for *"teco"* (with thee). This opera supplies some of the key themes in *Ulysses*, and the famous duet between Don Giovanni and Zerlina, *"Là ci darèm la mano"* (There we will join hands), haunts Bloom's mind throughout the day. It is on the program of Molly's concert that she is discussing with Boylan that afternoon, and Bloom associates it with her adultery with Boylan.
7. Proofreader and business manager of the *Freeman's Journal* and in charge of the advertising Bloom is trying to get for the paper. If he will add a complimentary reference to Keyes, a grocer, in a gossip column, Keyes promises to renew his advertisement, which means a commission for Bloom.
8. I.e., of Molly and Boylan.

A blind stripling stood tapping the curbstone with his slender cane. No tram in sight. Wants to cross.

—Do you want to cross? Mr Bloom asked.

The blind stripling did not answer. His wallface frowned weakly. He moved his head uncertainly.

—You're in Dawson street, Mr Bloom said. Molesworth street is opposite. Do you want to cross? There's nothing in the way.

The cane moved out trembling to the left. Mr Bloom's eye followed its line and saw again the dyeworks' van drawn up before Drago's. Where I saw his brillantined hair just when I was. Horse drooping. Driver in John Long's. Slaking his drouth.

—There's a van there, Mr Bloom said, but it's not moving. I'll see you across. Do you want to go to Molesworth street?

—Yes, the stripling answered. South Frederick street.

—Come, Mr Bloom said.

He touched the thin elbow gently: then took the limp seeing hand to guide it forward.

Say something to him. Better not do the condescending. They mistrust what you tell them. Pass a common remark.

—The rain kept off.

No answer.

Stains on his coat. Slobbers his food, I suppose. Tastes all different for him. Have to be spoonfed first. Like a child's hand, his hand. Like Milly's was. Sensitive. Sizing me up I daresay from my hand. Wonder if he has a name. Van. Keep his cane clear of the horse's legs tired drudge get his doze. That's right. Clear. Behind a bull: in front of a horse.

—Thanks, sir.

Knows I'm a man. Voice.

—Right now? First turn to the left.

The blind stripling tapped the curbstone and went on his way, drawing his cane back, feeling again.

Mr Bloom walked behind the eyeless feet, a flatcut suit of herringbone tweed. Poor young fellow! How on earth did he know that van was there? Must have felt it. See things in their foreheads perhaps. Kind of sense of volume. Weight would he feel it if something was removed. Feel a gap. Queer idea of Dublin he must have, tapping his way round by the stones. Could he walk in a beeline if he hadn't that cane? Bloodless pious face like a fellow going in to be a priest.

Penrose! That was that chap's name.

Look at all the things they can learn to do. Read with their fingers. Tune pianos. Or we are surprised they have any brains. Why we think a deformed person or a hunchback clever if he says something we might say. Of course the other senses are more. Embroider. Plait baskets. People ought to help. Workbasket I could buy Molly's birthday. Hates sewing. Might take an objection. Dark men they call them.

Sense of smell must be stronger too. Smells on all sides bunched together. Each person too. Then the spring, the summer: smells. Tastes. They say you can't taste wines with your eyes shut or a cold in the head. Also smoke in the dark they say get no pleasure.

And with a woman, for instance. More shameless not seeing. That girl passing the Stewart institution, head in the air. Look at me. I have them all on.

Must be strange not to see her. Kind of a form in his mind's eye. The voice temperature when he touches her with fingers must almost see the lines, the curves. His hands on her hair, for instance. Say it was black for instance. Good. We call it black. Then passing over her white skin. Different feel perhaps. Feeling of white.

Postoffice. Must answer.[9] Fag[1] today. Send her a postal order two shillings half a crown. Accept my little present. Stationer's just here too. Wait. Think over it.

With a gentle finger he felt ever so slowly the hair combed back above his ears. Again. Fibres of fine fine straw. Then gently his finger felt the skin of his right cheek. Downy hair there too. Not smooth enough. The belly is the smoothest. No-one about. There he goes into Frederick street. Perhaps to Levenston's dancing academy piano. Might be settling my braces.

Walking by Doran's public house he slid his hand between waistcoat and trousers and, pulling aside his shirt gently, felt a slack fold of his belly. But I know it's whitey yellow. Want to try in the dark to see.

He withdrew his hand and pulled his dress to.

Poor fellow! Quite a boy. Terrible. Really terrible. What dreams would he have, not seeing. Life a dream for him. Where is the justice being born that way. All those women and children excursion beanfeast burned and drowned in New York.[2] Holocaust. Karma they call that transmigration for sins you did in a past life the reincarnation met him pike hoses.[3] Dear, dear, dear. Pity of course: but somehow you can't cotton on to them someway.

Sir Frederick Falkiner going into the freemasons' hall. Solemn as Troy. After his good lunch in Earlsfort terrace. Old legal cronies cracking a magnum. Tales of the bench and assizes and annals of the bluecoat school.[4] I sentenced him to ten years. I suppose he'd turn up his nose at that stuff I drank. Vintage wine for them, the year marked on a dusty bottle. Has his own ideas of justice in the recorder's court. Wellmeaning old man. Police charge sheets crammed with cases get their percentage manufacturing crime. Sends them to the rightabout. The devil on moneylenders. Gave Reuben J. a great strawcalling. Now he's really what they call a dirty jew. Power those judges have. Crusty old topers in wigs. Bear with a sore paw. And may the Lord have mercy on your soul.

Hello, placard. Mirus bazaar. His excellency the lord lieutenant. Sixteenth today it is. In aid of funds for Mercer's hospital. The *Messiah* was first given for that. Yes. Handel. What about going out there. Ballsbridge. Drop in on Keyes. No use sticking to him like a leech. Wear out my welcome. Sure to know someone on the gate.

Mr Bloom came to Kildare street. First I must. Library.

Straw hat in sunlight. Tan shoes. Turnedup trousers. It is. It is.[5]

His heart quopped[6] softly. To the right. Museum. Goddesses. He swerved to the right.

Is it? Almost certain. Won't look. Wine in my face. Why did I? Too heady. Yes, it is. The walk. Not see. Not see. Get on.

9. Martha Clifford's letter.
1. Nuisance.
2. This terrible disaster on an excursion steamer on a New York City river took place on June 15, 1904, and was reported in the Dublin papers on June 16.
3. I.e., metempsychosis. Bloom is remembering again their morning conversation on this subject, when Molly exclaimed, "O rocks!"
4. Sir Frederick Falkiner wrote the history of the "bluecoat school," in Oxmantown, Dublin, founded by Charles II for poor children.
5. Bloom catches a glimpse of Boylan and tries to avoid an encounter.
6. Throbbed, quivered (dialect, now obsolete).

Making for the museum gate with long windy strides he lifted his eyes. Handsome building. Sir Thomas Deane designed. Not following me?

Didn't see me perhaps. Light in his eyes.

The flutter of his breath came forth in short sighs. Quick. Cold statues: quiet there. Safe in a minute.

No, didn't see me. After two. Just at the gate.

My heart!

His eyes beating looked steadfastly at cream curves of stone. Sir Thomas Deane was the Greek architecture.

Look for something I.

His hasty hand went quick into a pocket, took out, read unfolded Agendath Netaim. Where did I?

Busy looking for.

He thrust back quickly Agendath.

Afternoon she said.

I am looking for that. Yes, that. Try all pockets. Handker. *Freeman.* Where did I? Ah, yes. Trousers. Purse. Potato. Where did I?

Hurry. Walk quietly. Moment more. My heart.

His hand looking for the where did I put found in his hip pocket soap lotion have to call tepid paper stuck. Ah, soap there! Yes. Gate.[7]

Safe!

1914–21   1922

---

7. Anxious to avoid Boylan, Bloom pretends to admire the architecture of the Museum and National Library building and then pretends to be looking for something in his pockets, where he finds the "Agendath Netaim" leaflet. He continues to search desperately in his pockets to avoid looking up and seeing Boylan, discovers the potato he carries as a remedy against rheumatism and a cake of soap he had bought that morning (the soap reminds him that he must call at the chemist's to collect a face lotion he had ordered for Molly). At last he goes through the National Library gate and feels safe.

D. H. LAWRENCE
1885–1930

David Herbert Lawrence was born in the midland mining village of Eastwood, Nottinghamshire. His father was a miner; his mother, better educated than her husband and self-consciously genteel, fought all her married life to lift her children out of the working class. Lawrence was aware from a young age of the struggle between his parents, and allied himself with his mother's delicacy and refinement, resenting his father's coarse and sometimes drunken behavior. In his early novel *Sons and Lovers* (1913), against a background of paternal coarseness conflicting with maternal refinement, Lawrence sets the theme of the demanding mother who has given up the prospect of achieving a true emotional life with her husband and turns to her sons with a stultifying and possessive love. Many years later Lawrence came to feel that he had failed to appreciate his father's vitality and wholeness, even if they were distorted by the culture in which he lived.

Spurred on by his mother, Lawrence escaped from the mining world through education. He won a scholarship to Nottingham high school and later, after working first as a clerk and then as an elementary-school teacher, studied for two years at University College, Nottingham, where he obtained his teacher's certificate. Meanwhile he was reading on his own a great deal of literature and some philosophy and was working on his first novel. Publishing a group of poems in 1909, his first short story and his first novel, *The White Peacock*, in 1910, he was regarded in London literary circles as a promising young writer. He taught school from 1908 to 1912 in Croydon, a southern suburb of London, but he gave this up after falling in love with Frieda von Richthofen Weekley, the German wife of a professor at Nottingham. They went to Germany together and married in 1914, after Frieda's divorce.

Abroad with Frieda, Lawrence finished *Sons and Lovers*, at which he had been working off and on for years. The war brought them back to England, where Frieda's German origins and Lawrence's pacifist objection to the war gave him trouble with the authorities. More and more—especially after the almost immediate banning for indecency of his next novel, *The Rainbow*, in 1915—Lawrence came to feel that the forces of modern civilization were arrayed against him. As soon as he could leave England after the war, he sought refuge in Italy, Australia, Mexico, then again in Italy, and finally in the south of France, often desperately ill, restlessly searching for an ideal, or at least a tolerable, community in which to live. He died of tuberculosis in the south of France at the age of forty-four.

In his poetry and his fiction, Lawrence seeks to express the deep-rooted, the elemental, the instinctual in people and nature. He is at constant war with the mechanical and artificial, with the constraints and hypocrisies that civilization imposes. Because he had new things to say and a new way of saying them, he was not easily or quickly appreciated. Although his early novels are more conventional in style and treatment, from the publication of *The Rainbow* the critics turned away in bewilderment and condemnation. The rest of his life, during which he produced about a dozen more novels and many poems, short stories, sketches, and miscellaneous articles, was, in his own words, "a savage enough pilgrimage," marked by incessant struggle and by periods of frustration and despair. Phrases such as "supreme impulse" and "quickening spontaneous emotion" were characteristic of Lawrence's belief in intuition, in the dark forces of the inner self, that must not be allowed to be swamped by the rational faculties but must be brought into a harmonious relation with them.

The genteel culture of Lawrence's mother came more and more to represent death for Lawrence. In much of his later work, and especially in some of his short stories, he sets the deadening restrictiveness of middle-class conventional living against the forces of liberation that are often represented by an outsider—a peasant, a gypsy, a worker, a primitive of some kind, someone free by circumstance or personal effort. The recurring theme of his short stories—which contain some of his best work—is the distortion of love by possessiveness or gentility or a false romanticism or a false conception of the life of the artist and the achievement of a living relation between a man and a woman against the pressure of class-feeling or tradition or habit or prejudice.

In his two masterpieces, *The Rainbow* and *Women in Love* (both of which developed out of what was originally conceived as a single novel to be called *The Sisters*), Lawrence probes with both subtlety and power into various aspects of relationship— the relationship between humans and their environment, the relationship between the generations, the relationship between man and woman, the relationship between instinct and intellect, and above all the proper basis for the marriage relationship as he conceived it. Lawrence's view of marriage as a struggle, bound up with the deepest rhythms and most profound instincts, derived from his own relationship with his strong-minded wife. He explores this and other kinds of human relationships with a combination of uncanny psychological precision and intense poetic feeling. His novels have an acute surface realism, a sharp sense of time and place, and brilliant topographical detail; at the same time their high symbolism, both of the total pattern of action and of incidents and objects within it, establishes a formal and emotional rhythm.

In poetry as in fiction Lawrence sought out new modes of expression. He began writing in traditional verse forms but, especially after 1912, came to feel that poetry had to be unshackled from habit and fixed form, if it is to make contact with what he called the "insurgent naked throb of the instant moment." Harkening back to the experiments of the American poet Walt Whitman and anticipating the more "open" and "organic" forms of the later twentieth century, Lawrence claimed poetry must be spontaneous, flexible, alive, "direct utterance from the instant, whole man," and should express the "pulsating, carnal self" ("The Poetry of the Present," 1919). To convey the dynamism of animals and people, the emotional intensity of human relationships, his poems repeat and develop symbols or layer clauses in ritualistic cadences or unfold parallels with ancient myths. Vehemently autobiographical, the vital and even ecstatic encounters with nature, sex, and raw feeling in his poems assert the primacy of the unconscious and instinctual self, from which he felt the cerebral-intellectual self had alienated the English middle classes.

In the late 1950s the critic A. Alvarez judged: "The only native English poet of any importance to survive the First World War was D. H. Lawrence." Although there are complex reasons for the posthumous critical triumph of this writer who was so much reviled in his lifetime, there is also a simple and striking reason that must not be forgotten. Lawrence had vision; he responded intensely to life; he had a keen ear and a piercing eye for vitality and color and sound, for landscape—be it of England or Italy or New Mexico—for the individuality and concreteness of things in nature, and for the individuality and concreteness of people. His travel sketches are as impressive in their way as his novels and poems; he seizes both on the symbolic incident and on the concrete reality, and each is interpreted in terms of the other. He looked at the world freshly, with his own eyes, avoiding formulas and clichés; and he forged for himself a kind of utterance that, at his best, was able to convey powerfully and vividly what his original vision showed him. A restless pilgrim, he had uncanny perceptions into the depths of physical things and an uncompromising honesty in his view of human beings and the world.

Odour of Chrysanthemums

I

The small locomotive engine, Number 4, came clanking, stumbling down from Selston with seven full wagons. It appeared round the corner with loud threats of speed, but the colt that it startled from among the gorse,[1] which still flickered indistinctly in the raw afternoon, out-distanced it at a canter. A woman, walking up the railway line to Underwood, drew back into the hedge, held her basket aside, and watched the footplate of the engine advancing. The trucks[2] thumped heavily past, one by one, with slow inevitable movement, as she stood insignificantly trapped between the jolting black wagons and the hedge; then they curved away towards the coppice[3] where the withered oak leaves dropped noiselessly, while the birds, pulling at the scarlet hips beside the track, made off into the dusk that had already crept into the spinney.[4] In the open, the smoke from the engine sank and cleaved to the rough grass. The fields were dreary and forsaken, and in the marshy strip that led to the whimsey,[5] a reedy pit-pond, the fowls had already abandoned their run among the alders, to roost in the tarred fowl-house. The pit-bank loomed up beyond the pond, flames like red sores licking its ashy sides, in the afternoon's stagnant

---

1. Common prickly bush with yellow flowers.
2. Open freight cars.
3. A wood of small trees or shrubs.

4. Thicket.
5. Machine for raising ore or water from a mine.

light. Just beyond rose the tapering chimneys and the clumsy black headstocks of Brinsley Colliery.[6] The two wheels were spinning fast up against the sky, and the winding engine rapped out its little spasms. The miners were being turned up.

The engine whistled as it came into the wide bay of railway lines beside the colliery, where rows of trucks stood in harbour.

Miners, single, trailing and in groups, passed like shadows diverging home. At the edge of the ribbed level of sidings squat a low cottage, three steps down from the cinder track. A large bony vine clutched at the house, as if to claw down the tiled roof. Round the bricked yard grew a few wintry primroses. Beyond, the long garden sloped down to a bush-covered brook course. There were some twiggy apple trees, winter-crack trees, and ragged cabbages. Beside the path hung disheveled pink chrysanthemums, like pink cloths hung on bushes. A woman came stooping out of the felt-covered fowl-house, half-way down the garden. She closed and padlocked the door, then drew herself erect, having brushed some bits from her white apron.

She was a tall woman of imperious mien, handsome, with definite black eyebrows. Her smooth black hair was parted exactly. For a few moments she stood steadily watching the miners as they passed along the railway: then she turned towards the brook course. Her face was calm and set, her mouth was closed with disillusionment. After a moment she called:

"John!" There was no answer. She waited, and then said distinctly:

"Where are you?"

"Here!" replied a child's sulky voice from among the bushes. The woman looked piercingly through the dusk.

"Are you at that brook?" she asked sternly.

For answer the child showed himself before the raspberry-canes that rose like whips. He was a small, sturdy boy of five. He stood quite still, defiantly.

"Oh!" said the mother, conciliated. "I thought you were down at that wet brook—and you remember what I told you——"

The boy did not move or answer.

"Come, come on in," she said more gently, "it's getting dark. There's your grandfather's engine coming down the line!"

The lad advanced slowly, with resentful, taciturn movement. He was dressed in trousers and waistcoat of cloth that was too thick and hard for the size of the garments. They were evidently cut down from a man's clothes.

As they went slowly towards the house he tore at the ragged wisps of chrysanthemums and dropped the petals in handfuls along the path.

"Don't do that—it does look nasty," said his mother. He refrained, and she, suddenly pitiful, broke off a twig with three or four wan flowers and held them against her face. When mother and son reached the yard her hand hesitated, and instead of laying the flower aside, she pushed it in her apron-band. The mother and son stood at the foot of the three steps looking across the bay of lines at the passing home of the miners. The trundle of the small train was imminent. Suddenly the engine loomed past the house and came to a stop opposite the gate.

The engine-driver, a short man with round grey beard, leaned out of the cab high above the woman.

6. Coal mine. "Headstocks" support revolving parts of a machine.

"Have you got a cup of tea?" he said in a cheery, hearty fashion.

It was her father. She went in, saying she would mash.[7] Directly, she returned.

"I didn't come to see you on Sunday," began the little grey-bearded man.

"I didn't expect you," said his daughter.

The engine-driver winced; then, reassuming his cheery, airy manner, he said:

"Oh, have you heard then? Well, and what do you think——?"

"I think it is soon enough," she replied.

At her brief censure the little man made an impatient gesture, and said coaxingly, yet with dangerous coldness:

"Well, what's a man to do? It's no sort of life for a man of my years, to sit at my own hearth like a stranger. And if I'm going to marry again it may as well be soon as late—what does it matter to anybody?"

The woman did not reply, but turned and went into the house. The man in the engine-cab stood assertive, till she returned with a cup of tea and a piece of bread and butter on a plate. She went up the steps and stood near the footplate of the hissing engine.

"You needn't 'a' brought me bread an' butter," said her father. "But a cup of tea"—he sipped appreciatively—"it's very nice." He sipped for a moment or two, then: "I hear as Walter's got another bout[8] on," he said.

"When hasn't he?" said the woman bitterly.

"I heerd tell of him in the 'Lord Nelson' braggin' as he was going to spend that b—— afore he went: half a sovereign[9] that was."

"When?" asked the woman.

"A' Sat'day night—I know that's true."

"Very likely," she laughed bitterly. "He gives me twenty-three shillings."

"Aye, it's a nice thing, when a man can do nothing with his money but make a beast of himself!" said the grey-whiskered man. The woman turned her head away. Her father swallowed the last of his tea and handed her the cup.

"Aye," he sighed, wiping his mouth. "It's a settler,[1] it is——"

He put his hand on the lever. The little engine strained and groaned, and the train rumbled towards the crossing. The woman again looked across the metals. Darkness was settling over the spaces of the railway and trucks: the miners, in grey somber groups, were still passing home. The winding engine pulsed hurriedly, with brief pauses. Elizabeth Bates looked at the dreary flow of men, then she went indoors. Her husband did not come.

The kitchen was small and full of firelight; red coals piled glowing up the chimney mouth. All the life of the room seemed in the white, warm hearth and the steel fender reflecting the red fire. The cloth was laid for tea; cups glinted in the shadows. At the back, where the lowest stairs protruded into the room, the boy sat struggling with a knife and a piece of white wood. He was almost hidden in the shadow. It was half-past four. They had but to await the father's coming to begin tea. As the mother watched her son's sullen little struggle with the wood, she saw herself in his silence and pertinacity; she saw the father in her child's indifference to all but himself. She seemed to be occupied by her husband. He had probably gone past his home, slunk past his

---

7. Steep the tea.
8. Session; i.e., bout of drinking.
9. Gold coin worth twenty shillings. Half a sover-

eign is worth ten. Lord Nelson is the name of a public house (pub).
1. Crushing (or final) blow.

own door, to drink before he came in, while his dinner spoiled and wasted in waiting. She glanced at the clock, then took the potatoes to strain them in the yard. The garden and fields beyond the brook were closed in uncertain darkness. When she rose with the saucepan, leaving the drain steaming into the night behind her, she saw the yellow lamps were lit along the high road that went up the hill away beyond the space of the railway lines and the field.

Then again she watched the men trooping home, fewer now and fewer.

Indoors the fire was sinking and the room was dark red. The woman put her saucepan on the hob,[2] and set a batter-pudding near the mouth of the oven. Then she stood unmoving. Directly, gratefully, came quick young steps to the door. Someone hung on the latch a moment, then a little girl entered and began pulling off her outdoor things, dragging a mass of curls, just ripening from gold to brown, over her eyes with her hat.

Her mother chid her for coming late from school, and said she would have to keep her at home the dark winter days.

"Why, mother, it's hardly a bit dark yet. The lamp's not lighted, and my father's not home."

"No, he isn't. But it's a quarter to five! Did you see anything of him?"

The child became serious. She looked at her mother with large, wistful blue eyes.

"No, mother, I've never seen him. Why? Has he come up an' gone past, to Old Brinsley? He hasn't, mother, 'cos I never saw him."

"He'd watch that," said the mother bitterly, "he'd take care as you didn't see him. But you may depend upon it, he's seated in the 'Prince o' Wales.'[3] He wouldn't be this late."

The girl looked at her mother piteously.

"Let's have our teas, mother, should we?" said she.

The mother called John to table. She opened the door once more and looked out across the darkness of the lines. All was deserted: she could not hear the winding-engines.

"Perhaps," she said to herself, "he's stopped to get some ripping[4] done."

They sat down to tea. John, at the end of the table near the door, was almost lost in the darkness. Their faces were hidden from each other. The girl crouched against the fender[5] slowly moving a thick piece of bread before the fire. The lad, his face a dusky mark on the shadow, sat watching her who was transfigured in the red glow.

"I do think it's beautiful to look in the fire," said the child.

"Do you?" said her mother. "Why?"

"It's so red, and full of little caves—and it feels so nice, and you can fair smell it."

"It'll want mending directly," replied her mother, "and then if your father comes he'll carry on and say there never is a fire when a man comes home sweating from the pit. A public-house is always warm enough."

There was silence till the boy said complainingly: "Make haste, our Annie."

"Well, I am doing! I can't make the fire do it no faster, can I?"

"She keeps wafflin' it about so's to make 'er slow," grumbled the boy.

"Don't have such an evil imagination, child," replied the mother.

---

2. Part of the fireplace.
3. Name of a pub.
4. Taking out or cutting away coal or stone (a min-

ing and quarrying term).
5. Frame that keeps coals in the fireplace.

Soon the room was busy in the darkness with the crisp sound of crunching. The mother ate very little. She drank her tea determinedly, and sat thinking. When she rose her anger was evident in the stern unbending of her head. She looked at the pudding in the fender, and broke out:

"It is a scandalous thing as a man can't even come home to his dinner! If it's crozzled[6] up to a cinder I don't see why I should care. Past his very door he goes to get to a public-house, and here I sit with his dinner waiting for him——"

She went out. As she dropped piece after piece of coal on the red fire, the shadows fell on the walls, till the room was almost in total darkness.

"I canna see," grumbled the invisible John. In spite of herself, the mother laughed.

"You know the way to your mouth," she said. She set the dust pan outside the door. When she came again like a shadow on the hearth, the lad repeated, complaining sulkily:

"I canna see."

"Good gracious!" cried the mother irritably, "you're as bad as your father if it's a bit dusk!"

Nevertheless, she took a paper spill from a sheaf on the mantelpiece and proceeded to light the lamp that hung from the ceiling in the middle of the room. As she reached up, her figure displayed itself just rounding with maternity.

"Oh, mother——!" exclaimed the girl.

"What?" said the woman, suspended in the act of putting the lamp-glass over the flame. The copper reflector shone handsomely on her, as she stood with uplifted arm, turning to face her daughter.

"You've got a flower in your apron!" said the child, in a little rapture at this unusual event.

"Goodness me!" exclaimed the woman, relieved. "One would think the house was afire." She replaced the glass and waited a moment before turning up the wick. A pale shadow was seen floating vaguely on the floor.

"Let me smell!" said the child, still rapturously, coming forward and putting her face to her mother's waist.

"Go along, silly!" said the mother, turning up the lamp. The light revealed their suspense so that the woman felt it almost unbearable. Annie was still bending at her waist. Irritably, the mother took the flowers out from her apron-band.

"Oh, mother—don't take them out!" Annie cried, catching her hand and trying to replace the sprig.

"Such nonsense!" said the mother, turning away. The child put the pale chrysanthemums to her lips, murmuring:

"Don't they smell beautiful!"

Her mother gave a short laugh.

"No," she said, "not to me. It was chrysanthemums when I married him, and chrysanthemums when you were born, and the first time they ever brought him home drunk, he'd got brown chrysanthemums in his buttonhole."

She looked at the children. Their eyes and their parted lips were wondering. The mother sat rocking in silence for some time. Then she looked at the clock.

"Twenty minutes to six!" In a tone of fine bitter carelessness she continued:

6. Curled.

"Eh, he'll not come now till they bring him. There he'll stick! But he needn't come rolling in here in his pit-dirt, for *I* won't wash him. He can lie on the floor——Eh, what a fool I've been, what a fool! And this is what I came here for, to this dirty hole, rats and all, for him to slink past his very door. Twice last week—he's begun now——"

She silenced herself and rose to clear the table.

While for an hour or more the children played, subduedly intent, fertile of imagination, united in fear of the mother's wrath, and in dread of their father's home-coming, Mrs Bates sat in her rocking chair making a "singlet" of thick cream-coloured flannel, which gave a dull wounded sound as she tore off the grey edge. She worked at her sewing with energy, listening to the children, and her anger wearied itself, lay down to rest, opening its eyes from time to time and steadily watching, its ears raised to listen. Sometimes even her anger quailed and shrank, and the mother suspended her sewing, tracing the foot-steps that thudded along the sleepers[7] outside; she would lift her head sharply to bid the children "hush," but she recovered herself in time, and the footsteps went past the gate, and the children were not flung out of their play-world.

But at last Annie sighed, and gave in. She glanced at her wagon of slippers, and loathed the game. She turned plaintively to her mother.

"Mother!"—but she was inarticulate.

John crept out like a frog from under the sofa. His mother glanced up.

"Yes," she said, "just look at those shirt-sleeves!"

The boy held them out to survey them, saying nothing. Then somebody called in a hoarse voice away down the line, and suspense bristled in the room, till two people had gone by outside, talking.

"It is time for bed," said the mother.

"My father hasn't come," wailed Annie plaintively. But her mother was primed with courage.

"Never mind. They'll bring him when he does come—like a log." She meant there would be no scene. "And he may sleep on the floor till he wakes himself. I know he'll not go to work to-morrow after this!"

The children had their hands and faces wiped with a flannel. They were very quiet. When they had put on their night-dresses, they said their prayers, the boy mumbling. The mother looked down at them, at the brown silken bush of intertwining curls in the nape of the girl's neck, at the little black head of the lad, and her heart burst with anger at their father, who caused all three such distress. The children hid their faces in her skirts for comfort.

When Mrs Bates came down, the room was strangely empty, with a tension of expectancy. She took up her sewing and stitched for some time without raising her head. Meantime her anger was tinged with fear.

II

The clock struck eight and she rose suddenly, dropping her sewing on her chair. She went to the stair-foot door, opened it, listening. Then she went out, locking the door behind her.

Something scuffled in the yard, and she started, though she knew it was only the rats with which the place was over-run. The night was very dark. In the great bay of railway lines, bulked with trucks, there was no trace of light,

7. Railroad ties.

2582 / D. H. Lawrence

only away back she could see a few yellow lamps at the pit-top, and the red smear of the burning pit-bank on the night. She hurried along the edge of the track, then, crossing the converging lines, came to the stile by the white gates, whence she emerged on the road. Then the fear which had led her shrank. People were walking up to New Brinsley; she saw the lights in the houses; twenty yards farther on were the broad windows of the "Prince of Wales," very warm and bright, and the loud voices of men could be heard distinctly. What a fool she had been to imagine that anything had happened to him! He was merely drinking over there at the "Prince of Wales." She faltered. She had never yet been to fetch him, and she never would go. So she continued her walk towards the long straggling line of houses, standing back on the highway. She entered a passage between the dwellings.

"Mr Rigley?—Yes! Did you want him? No, he's not in at this minute."

The raw-boned woman leaned forward from her dark scullery[8] and peered at the other, upon whom fell a dim light through the blind of the kitchen window.

"Is it Mrs Bates?" she asked in a tone tinged with respect.

"Yes. I wondered if your Master was at home. Mine hasn't come yet."

" 'Asn't 'e! Oh, Jack's been 'ome an' 'ad 'is dinner an' gone out. 'E's just gone for 'alf an hour afore bed-time. Did you call at the 'Prince of Wales'?"

"No——"

"No, you didn't like——! It's not very nice." The other woman was indulgent. There was an awkward pause. "Jack never said nothink about—about your Master," she said.

"No!—I expect he's stuck in there!"

Elizabeth Bates said this bitterly, and with recklessness. She knew that the woman across the yard was standing at her door listening, but she did not care. As she turned:

"Stop a minute! I'll just go an' ask Jack if 'e knows anythink," said Mrs Rigley.

"Oh no—I wouldn't like to put——!"

"Yes, I will, if you'll just step inside an' see as th' childer doesn't come downstairs and set theirselves afire."

Elizabeth Bates, murmuring a remonstrance, stepped inside. The other woman apologised for the state of the room.

The kitchen needed apology. There were little frocks and trousers and childish undergarments on the squab[9] and on the floor, and a litter of playthings everywhere. On the black American cloth[1] of the table were pieces of bread and cake, crusts, slops, and a teapot with cold tea.

"Eh, ours is just as bad," said Elizabeth Bates, looking at the woman, not at the house. Mrs Rigley put a shawl over her head and hurried out, saying:

"I shanna be a minute."

The other sat, noting with faint disapproval the general untidiness of the room. Then she fell to counting the shoes of various sizes scattered over the floor. There were twelve. She sighed and said to herself: "No wonder!"—glancing at the litter. There came the scratching of two pairs of feet on the yard, and the Rigleys entered. Elizabeth Bates rose. Rigley was a big man, with very large bones. His head looked particularly bony. Across his temple was a blue

8. Back kitchen.
9. Couch.

1. Oilcloth.

scar, caused by a wound got in the pit, a wound in which the coal dust remained blue like tattooing.

" 'Asna 'e come whoam yit?" asked the man, without any form of greeting, but with deference and sympathy. "I couldna say wheer he is—'e's non ower theer!"—he jerked his head to signify the "Prince of Wales."

" 'E's 'appen gone up to th' Yew,"[2] said Mrs Rigley.

There was another pause. Rigley had evidently something to get off his mind: "Ah left 'im finishin' a stint," he began. "Loose-all[3] 'ad bin gone about ten minutes when we com'n away, an' I shouted: 'Are ter comin', Walt?' an' 'e said: 'Go on, Ah shanna be but a'ef a minnit,' so we com'n ter th' bottom, me an' Bowers, thinkin' as 'e wor just behint, an' 'ud come up i' th' next bantle[4]——"

He stood perplexed, as if answering a charge of deserting his mate. Elizabeth Bates, now again certain of disaster, hastened to reassure him:

"I expect 'e's gone up to th' 'Yew Tree,' as you say. It's not the first time. I've fretted myself into a fever before now. He'll come home when they carry him."

"Ay, isn't it too bad!" deplored the other woman.

"I'll just step up to Dick's an' see if 'e is theer," offered the man, afraid of appearing alarmed, afraid of taking liberties.

"Oh, I wouldn't think of bothering you that far," said Elizabeth Bates, with emphasis, but he knew she was glad of his offer.

As they stumbled up the entry, Elizabeth Bates heard Rigley's wife run across the yard and open her neighbour's door. At this, suddenly all the blood in her body seemed to switch away from her heart.

"Mind!" warned Rigley. "Ah've said many a time as Ah'd fill up them ruts in this entry, sumb'dy 'll be breakin' their legs yit."

She recovered herself and walked quickly along with the miner.

"I don't like leaving the children in bed, and nobody in the house," she said.

"No, you dunna!" he replied courteously. They were soon at the gate of the cottage.

"Well, I shanna be many minnits. Dunna you be frettin' now, 'e'll be all right," said the butty.[5]

"Thank you very much, Mr Rigley," she replied.

"You're welcome!" he stammered, moving away. "I shanna be many minnits."

The house was quiet. Elizabeth Bates took off her hat and shawl, and rolled back the rug. When she had finished, she sat down. It was a few minutes past nine. She was startled by the rapid chuff of the winding-engine at the pit, and the sharp whirr of the brakes on the rope as it descended. Again she felt the painful sweep of her blood, and she put her hand to her side, saying aloud: "Good gracious!—it's only the nine o'clock deputy[6] going down," rebuking herself.

She sat still, listening. Half an hour of this, and she was wearied out.

"What am I working myself up like this for?" she said pitiably to herself, "I s'll only be doing myself some damage."

She took out her sewing again.

2. I.e., the Yew Tree (a pub).
3. Signal for end of work.
4. Group.
5. Workmate (cf. "buddy"). Among English coal

miners it means a supervisor intermediary between the employers and the men.
6. Minor coal-mine official.

At a quarter to ten there were footsteps. One person! She watched for the door to open. It was an elderly woman, in a black bonnet and a black woollen shawl—his mother. She was about sixty years old, pale, with blue eyes, and her face all wrinkled and lamentable. She shut the door and turned to her daughter-in-law peevishly.

"Eh, Lizzie, whatever shall we do, whatever shall we do!" she cried.

Elizabeth drew back a little, sharply.

"What is it, mother?" she said.

The elder woman seated herself on the sofa.

"I don't know, child, I can't tell you!"—she shook her head slowly. Elizabeth sat watching her, anxious and vexed.

"I don't know," replied the grandmother, sighing very deeply. "There's no end to my troubles, there isn't. The things I've gone through, I'm sure it's enough——!" She wept without wiping her eyes, the tears running.

"But, mother," interrupted Elizabeth, "what do you mean? What is it?"

The grandmother slowly wiped her eyes. The fountains of her tears were stopped by Elizabeth's directness. She wiped her eyes slowly.

"Poor child! Eh, you poor thing!" she moaned. "I don't know what we're going to do, I don't—and you as you are—it's a thing, it is indeed!"

Elizabeth waited.

"Is he dead?" she asked, and at the words her heart swung violently, though she felt a slight flush of shame at the ultimate extravagance of the question. Her words sufficiently frightened the old lady, almost brought her to herself.

"Don't say so, Elizabeth! We'll hope it's not as bad as that; no, may the Lord spare us that, Elizabeth. Jack Rigley came just as I was sittin' down to a glass afore going to bed, an' 'e said: ' 'Appen you'll go down th' line, Mrs. Bates. Walt's had an accident. 'Appen you'll go an' sit wi' 'er till we can get him home.' I hadn't time to ask him a word afore he was gone. An' I put my bonnet on an' come straight down, Lizzie. I thought to myself: 'Eh, that poor blessed child, if anybody should come an' tell her of a sudden, there's no knowin' what'll 'appen to 'er.' You mustn't let it upset you, Lizzie—or you know what to expect. How long is it, six months—or is it five, Lizzie? Ay!"—the old woman shook her head—"time slips on, it slips on! Ay!"

Elizabeth's thoughts were busy elsewhere. If he was killed—would she be able to manage on the little pension and what she could earn?—she counted up rapidly. If he was hurt—they wouldn't take him to the hospital—how tiresome he would be to nurse!—but perhaps she'd be able to get him away from the drink and his hateful ways. She would—while he was ill. The tears offered to come to her eyes at the picture. But what sentimental luxury was this she was beginning? She turned to consider the children. At any rate she was absolutely necessary for them. They were her business.

"Ay!" repeated the old woman, "it seems but a week or two since he brought me his first wages. Ay—he was a good lad, Elizabeth, he was, in his way. I don't know why he got to be such a trouble, I don't. He was a happy lad at home, only full of spirits. But there's no mistake he's been a handful of trouble, he has! I hope the Lord'll spare him to mend his ways. I hope so, I hope so. You've had a sight o' trouble with him, Elizabeth, you have indeed. But he was a jolly enough lad wi' me, he was, I can assure you. I don't know how it is. . . ."

The old woman continued to muse aloud, a monotonous irritating sound, while Elizabeth thought concentratedly, startled once, when she heard the winding-engine chuff quickly, and the brakes skirr with a shriek. Then she heard the engine more slowly, and the brakes made no sound. The old woman did not notice. Elizabeth waited in suspense. The mother-in-law talked, with lapses into silence.

"But he wasn't your son, Lizzie, an' it makes a difference. Whatever he was, I remember him when he was little, an' I learned to understand him and to make allowances. You've got to make allowances for them——"

It was half-past ten, and the old woman was saying: "But it's trouble from beginning to end; you're never too old for trouble, never too old for that——" when the gate banged back, and there were heavy feet on the steps.

"I'll go, Lizzie, let me go," cried the old woman, rising. But Elizabeth was at the door. It was a man in pit-clothes.

"They're bringin' 'im, Missis," he said. Elizabeth's heart halted a moment. Then it surged on again, almost suffocating her.

"Is he—is it bad?" she asked.

The man turned away, looking at the darkness:

"The doctor says 'e'd been dead hours. 'E saw 'im i' th' lamp-cabin."

The old woman, who stood just behind Elizabeth, dropped into a chair, and folded her hands, crying: "Oh, my boy, my boy!"

"Hush!" said Elizabeth, with a sharp twitch of a frown. "Be still, mother, don't waken th' children: I wouldn't have them down for anything!"

The old woman moaned softly, rocking herself. The man was drawing away. Elizabeth took a step forward.

"How was it?" she asked.

"Well, I couldn't say for sure," the man replied, very ill at ease. " 'E wor finishin' a stint an' th' butties 'ad gone, an' a lot o' stuff come down atop 'n 'im."

"And crushed him?" cried the widow, with a shudder.

"No," said the man, "it fell at th' back of 'im. 'E wor under th' face an' it niver touched 'im. It shut 'im in. It seems 'e wor smothered."

Elizabeth shrank back. She heard the old woman behind her cry:

"What?—what did 'e say it was?"

The man replied, more loudly: " 'E wor smothered!"

Then the old woman wailed aloud, and this relieved Elizabeth.

"Oh, mother," she said, putting her hand on the old woman, "don't waken th' children, don't waken th' children."

She wept a little, unknowing, while the old mother rocked herself and moaned. Elizabeth remembered that they were bringing him home, and she must be ready. "They'll lay him in the parlour," she said to herself, standing a moment pale and perplexed.

Then she lighted a candle and went into the tiny room. The air was cold and damp, but she could not make a fire, there was no fireplace. She set down the candle and looked round. The candlelight glittered on the lustre-glasses, on the two vases that held some of the pink chrysanthemums, and on the dark mahogany. There was a cold, deathly smell of chrysanthemums in the room. Elizabeth stood looking at the flowers. She turned away, and calculated whether there would be room to lay him on the floor, between the couch and the chiffonier. She pushed the chairs aside. There would be room to lay him down and to step round him. Then she fetched the old red tablecloth, and another old cloth, spreading them down to save her bit of carpet. She shivered on leaving the parlour; so, from the dresser drawer she took a clean shirt and put it at the fire to air. All the time her mother-in-law was rocking herself in the chair and moaning.

"You'll have to move from there, mother," said Elizabeth. "They'll be bringing him in. Come in the rocker."

The old mother rose mechanically, and seated herself by the fire, continuing to lament. Elizabeth went into the pantry for another candle, and there, in the little pent-house under the naked tiles, she heard them coming. She stood still in the pantry doorway, listening. She heard them pass the end of the house, and come awkwardly down the three steps, a jumble of shuffling footsteps and muttering voices. The old woman was silent. The men were in the yard.

Then Elizabeth heard Matthews, the manager of the pit, say: "You go in first, Jim. Mind!"

The door came open, and the two women saw a collier backing into the room, holding one end of a stretcher, on which they could see the nailed pit-boots of the dead man. The two carriers halted, the man at the head stooping to the lintel of the door.

"Wheer will you have him?" asked the manager, a short, white-bearded man.

Elizabeth roused herself and came from the pantry carrying the unlighted candle.

"In the parlour," she said.

"In there, Jim!" pointed the manager, and the carriers backed round into the tiny room. The coat with which they had covered the body fell off as they awkwardly turned through the two doorways, and the women saw their man, naked to the waist, lying stripped for work. The old woman began to moan in a low voice of horror.

"Lay th' stretcher at th' side," snapped the manager, "an' put 'im on th' cloths. Mind now, mind! Look you now——!"

One of the men had knocked off a vase of chrysanthemums. He stared awkwardly, then they set down the stretcher. Elizabeth did not look at her husband. As soon as she could get in the room, she went and picked up the broken vase and the flowers.

"Wait a minute!" she said.

The three men waited in silence while she mopped up the water with a duster.

"Eh, what a job, what a job, to be sure!" the manager was saying, rubbing his brow with trouble and perplexity. "Never knew such a thing in my life, never! He'd no business to ha' been left. I never knew such a thing in my life! Fell over him clean as a whistle, an' shut him in. Not four foot of space, there wasn't—yet it scarce bruised him."

He looked down at the dead man, lying prone, half naked, all grimed with coal-dust.

" ' 'Sphyxiated,' the doctor said. It *is* the most terrible job I've ever known. Seems as if it was done o' purpose. Clean over him, an' shut 'im in, like a mouse-trap"—he made a sharp, descending gesture with his hand.

The colliers standing by jerked aside their heads in hopeless comment.

The horror of the thing bristled upon them all.

Then they heard the girl's voice upstairs calling shrilly: "Mother, mother—who is it? Mother, who is it?"

Elizabeth hurried to the foot of the stairs and opened the door:

"Go to sleep!" she commanded sharply. "What are you shouting about? Go to sleep at once—there's nothing——"

Then she began to mount the stairs. They could hear her on the boards, and on the plaster floor of the little bedroom. They could hear her distinctly:

"What's the matter now?—what's the matter with you, silly thing?"—her voice was much agitated, with an unreal gentleness.

"I thought it was some men come," said the plaintive voice of the child. "Has he come?"

"Yes, they've brought him. There's nothing to make a fuss about. Go to sleep now, like a good child."

They could hear her voice in the bedroom, they waited whilst she covered the children under the bedclothes.

"Is he drunk?" asked the girl, timidly, faintly.

"No! No—he's not! He—he's asleep."

"Is he asleep downstairs?"

"Yes—and don't make a noise."

There was silence for a moment, then the men heard the frightened child again:

"What's that noise?"

"It's nothing, I tell you, what are you bothering for?"

The noise was the grandmother moaning. She was oblivious of everything, sitting on her chair rocking and moaning. The manager put his hand on her arm and bade her "Sh—sh! !"

The old woman opened her eyes and looked at him. She was shocked by this interruption, and seemed to wonder.

"What time is it?" the plaintive thin voice of the child, sinking back unhappily into sleep, asked this last question.

"Ten o'clock," answered the mother more softly. Then she must have bent down and kissed the children.

Matthews beckoned to the men to come away. They put on their caps and took up the stretcher. Stepping over the body, they tiptoed out of the house. None of them spoke till they were far from the wakeful children.

When Elizabeth came down she found her mother alone on the parlour floor, leaning over the dead man, the tears dropping on him.

"We must lay him out," the wife said. She put on the kettle, then returning knelt at the feet, and began to unfasten the knotted leather laces. The room was clammy and dim with only one candle, so that she had to bend her face almost to the floor. At last she got off the heavy boots and put them away.

"You must help me now," she whispered to the old woman. Together they stripped the man.

When they arose, saw him lying in the naïve dignity of death, the women stood arrested in fear and respect. For a few moments they remained still, looking down, the old mother whimpering. Elizabeth felt countermanded.[7] She saw him, how utterly inviolable he lay in himself. She had nothing to do with him. She could not accept it. Stooping, she laid her hand on him, in claim. He was still warm, for the mine was hot where he had died. His mother had his face between her hands, and was murmuring incoherently. The old tears fell in succession as drops from wet leaves; the mother was not weeping,

---

7. Contradicted.

merely her tears flowed. Elizabeth embraced the body of her husband, with cheek and lips. She seemed to be listening, inquiring, trying to get some connection. But she could not. She was driven away. He was impregnable.

She rose, went into the kitchen where she poured warm water into a bowl, brought soap and flannel and a soft towel. "I must wash him," she said.

Then the old mother rose stiffly, and watched Elizabeth as she carefully washed his face, carefully brushing his big blond moustache from his mouth with the flannel. She was afraid with a bottomless fear, so she ministered to him. The old woman, jealous, said:

"Let me wipe him!"—and she kneeled on the other side drying slowly as Elizabeth washed, her big black bonnet sometimes brushing the dark head of her daughter-in-law. They worked thus in silence for a long time. They never forgot it was death, and the touch of the man's dead body gave them strange emotions, different in each of the women; a great dread possessed them both, the mother felt the lie was given to her womb, she was denied; the wife felt the utter isolation of the human soul, the child within her was a weight apart from her.

At last it was finished. He was a man of handsome body, and his face showed no traces of drink. He was blond, full-fleshed, with fine limbs. But he was dead.

"Bless him," whispered his mother, looking always at his face, and speaking out of sheer terror. "Dear lad—bless him!" She spoke in a faint, sibilant ecstasy of fear and mother love.

Elizabeth sank down again to the floor, and put her face against his neck, and trembled and shuddered. But she had to draw away again. He was dead, and her living flesh had no place against his. A great dread and weariness held her: she was so unavailing. Her life was gone like this.

"White as milk he is, clear as a twelve-month baby, bless him, the darling!" the old mother murmured to herself. "Not a mark on him, clear and clean and white, beautiful as ever a child was made," she murmured with pride. Elizabeth kept her face hidden.

"He went peaceful, Lizzie—peaceful as sleep. Isn't he beautiful, the lamb? Ay—he must ha' made his peace, Lizzie. 'Appen he made it all right, Lizzie, shut in there. He'd have time. He wouldn't look like this if he hadn't made his peace. The lamb, the dear lamb. Eh, but he had a hearty laugh. I loved to hear it. He had the heartiest laugh, Lizzie, as a lad——"

Elizabeth looked up. The man's mouth was fallen back, slightly open under the cover of the moustache. The eyes, half shut, did not show glazed in the obscurity. Life with its smoky burning gone from him, had left him apart and utterly alien to her. And she knew what a stranger he was to her. In her womb was ice of fear, because of this separate stranger with whom she had been living as one flesh. Was this what it all meant—utter, intact separateness, obscured by heat of living? In dread she turned her face away. The fact was too deadly. There had been nothing between them, and yet they had come together, exchanging their nakedness repeatedly. Each time he had taken her, they had been two isolated beings, far apart as now. He was no more responsible than she. The child was like ice in her womb. For as she looked at the dead man, her mind, cold and detached, said clearly: "Who am I? What have I been doing? I have been fighting a husband who did not exist. *He* existed all the time. What wrong have I done? What was that I have been living with? There lies the reality, this man." And her soul died in her for fear: she knew she had never seen him, he had never seen her, they had met in the dark and had fought in the dark, not knowing whom they met or whom they fought. And now she saw, and turned silent in seeing. For she had been wrong. She had said he was something he was not; she had felt familiar with him. Whereas he was apart all the while, living as she never lived, feeling as she never felt.

In fear and shame she looked at his naked body, that she had known falsely. And he was the father of her children. Her soul was torn from her body and stood apart. She looked at his naked body and was ashamed, as if she had denied it. After all, it was itself. It seemed awful to her. She looked at his face, and she turned her own face to the wall. For his look was other than hers, his way was not her way. She had denied him what he was—she saw it now. She had refused him as himself. And this had been her life, and his life. She was grateful to death, which restored the truth. And she knew she was not dead.

And all the while her heart was bursting with grief and pity for him. What had he suffered? What stretch of horror for this helpless man! She was rigid with agony. She had not been able to help him. He had been cruelly injured, this naked man, this other being, and she could make no reparation. There were the children—but the children belonged to life. This dead man had nothing to do with them. He and she were only channels through which life had flowed to issue in the children. She was a mother—but how awful she knew it now to have been a wife. And he, dead now, how awful he must have felt it to be a husband. She felt that in the next world he would be a stranger to her. If they met there, in the beyond, they would only be ashamed of what had been before. The children had come, for some mysterious reason, out of both of them. But the children did not unite them. Now he was dead, she knew how eternally he was apart from her, how eternally he had nothing more to do with her. She saw this episode of her life closed. They had denied each other in life. Now he had withdrawn. An anguish came over her. It was finished then: it had become hopeless between them long before he died. Yet he had been her husband. But how little!

"Have you got his shirt, 'Lizabeth?"

Elizabeth turned without answering, though she strove to weep and behave as her mother-in-law expected. But she could not, she was silenced. She went into the kitchen and returned with the garment.

"It is aired," she said, grasping the cotton shirt here and there to try. She was almost ashamed to handle him; what right had she or anyone to lay hands on him; but her touch was humble on his body. It was hard work to clothe him. He was so heavy and inert. A terrible dread gripped her all the while: that he could be so heavy and utterly inert, unresponsive, apart. The horror of the distance between them was almost too much for her—it was so infinite a gap she must look across.

At last it was finished. They covered him with a sheet and left him lying, with his face bound. And she fastened the door of the little parlour, lest the children should see what was lying there. Then, with peace sunk heavy on her heart, she went about making tidy the kitchen. She knew she submitted to life, which was her immediate master. But from death, her ultimate master, she winced with fear and shame.

1911, 1914

The Horse Dealer's Daughter

"Well, Mabel, and what are you going to do with yourself?" asked Joe, with foolish flippancy. He felt quite safe himself. Without listening for an answer, he turned aside, worked a grain of tobacco to the tip of his tongue, and spat it out. He did not care about anything, since he felt safe himself.

The three brothers and the sister sat round the desolate breakfast-table, attempting some sort of desultory consultation. The morning's post had given the final tap to the family fortunes, and all was over. The dreary dining-room itself, with its heavy mahogany furniture, looked as if it were waiting to be done away with.

But the consultation amounted to nothing. There was a strange air of ineffectuality about the three men, as they sprawled at table, smoking and reflecting vaguely on their own condition. The girl was alone, a rather short, sullen-looking young woman of twenty-seven. She did not share the same life as her brothers. She would have been good-looking, save for the impressive fixity of her face, "bull-dog," as her brothers called it.

There was a confused tramping of horses' feet outside. The three men all sprawled round in their chairs to watch. Beyond the dark holly bushes that separated the strip of lawn from the high-road, they could see a cavalcade of shire horses swinging out of their own yard, being taken for exercise. This was the last time. These were the last horses that would go through their hands. The young men watched with critical, callous look. They were all frightened at the collapse of their lives, and the sense of disaster in which they were involved left them no inner freedom.

Yet they were three fine, well-set fellows enough. Joe, the eldest, was a man of thirty-three, broad and handsome in a hot, flushed way. His face was red, he twisted his black moustache over a thick finger, his eyes were shallow and restless. He had a sensual way of uncovering his teeth when he laughed, and his bearing was stupid. Now he watched the horses with a glazed look of helplessness in his eyes, a certain stupor of downfall.

The great draught horses swung past. They were tied head to tail, four of them, and they heaved along to where a lane branched off from the high-road, planting their great hoofs floutingly in the fine black mud, swinging their great rounded haunches sumptuously, and trotting a few sudden steps as they were led into the lane, round the corner. Every movement showed a massive, slumbrous strength, and a stupidity which held them in subjection. The groom at the head looked back, jerking the leading rope. And the cavalcade moved out of sight up the lane, the tail of the last horse, bobbed up tight and stiff, held out taut from the swinging great haunches as they rocked behind the hedges in a motion-like sleep.

Joe watched with glazed hopeless eyes. The horses were almost like his own body to him. He felt he was done for now. Luckily he was engaged to a woman as old as himself, and therefore her father, who was steward of a neighbouring estate, would provide him with a job. He would marry and go into harness. His life was over, he would be a subject animal now.

He turned uneasily aside, the retreating steps of the horses echoing in his ears. Then, with foolish restlessness, he reached for the scraps of bacon-rind from the plates, and making a faint whistling sound, flung them to the terrier that lay against the fender. He watched the dog swallow them, and waited till the creature looked into his eyes. Then a faint grin came on his face, and in a high, foolish voice he said:

"You won't get much more bacon, shall you, you little b——?"

The dog faintly and dismally wagged its tail, then lowered its haunches, circled round, and lay down again.

There was another helpless silence at the table. Joe sprawled uneasily in his seat, not willing to go till the family conclave was dissolved. Fred Henry, the second brother, was erect, clean-limbed, alert. He had watched the passing of the horses with more *sang-froid*.[1] If he was an animal, like Joe, he was an animal which controls, not one which is controlled. He was master of any horse, and he carried himself with a well-tempered air of mastery. But he was not master of the situations of life. He pushed his coarse brown moustache upwards, off his lip, and glanced irritably at his sister, who sat impassive and inscrutable.

"You'll go and stop with Lucy for a bit, shan't you?" he asked. The girl did not answer.

"I don't see what else you can do," persisted Fred Henry.

"Go as a skivvy,"[2] Joe interpolated laconically.

The girl did not move a muscle.

"If I was her, I should go in for training for a nurse," said Malcolm, the youngest of them all. He was the baby of the family, a young man of twenty-two, with a fresh, jaunty *museau*.[3]

But Mabel did not take any notice of him. They had talked at her and round her for so many years, that she hardly heard them at all.

The marble clock on the mantelpiece softly chimed the half-hour, the dog rose uneasily from the hearth-rug and looked at the party at the breakfast-table. But still they sat in an ineffectual conclave.

"Oh, all right," said Joe suddenly, apropos of nothing. "I'll get a move on."

He pushed back his chair, straddled his knees with a downward jerk, to get them free, in horsey fashion, and went to the fire. Still he did not go out of the room; he was curious to know what the others would do or say. He began to charge his pipe, looking down at the dog and saying in a high, affected voice:

"Going wi' me? Going wi' me are ter? Tha'rt goin' further than tha counts on just now, dost hear?"

The dog faintly wagged his tail, the man stuck out his jaw and covered his pipe with his hands, and puffed intently, losing himself in the tobacco, looking down all the while at the dog with an absent brown eye. The dog looked up at him in mournful distrust. Joe stood with his knees stuck out, in real horsey fashion.

"Have you had a letter from Lucy?" Fred Henry asked of his sister.

"Last week," came the neutral reply.

"And what does she say?"

There was no answer.

"Does she *ask* you to go and stop there?" persisted Fred Henry.

"She says I can if I like."

"Well, then, you'd better. Tell her you'll come on Monday."

This was received in silence.

1. Cold blood (French, literal trans.); here calm
detachment.
2. Servant girl.
3. Muzzle (French); here face.

"That's what you'll do then, is it?" said Fred Henry, in some exasperation.

But she made no answer. There was a silence of futility and irritation in the room. Malcolm grinned fatuously.

"You'll have to make up your mind between now and next Wednesday," said Joe loudly, "or else find yourself lodgings on the kerbstone."

The face of the young woman darkened, but she sat on immutable.

"Here's Jack Ferguson!" exclaimed Malcolm, who was looking aimlessly out of the window.

"Where?" exclaimed Joe loudly.

"Just gone past."

"Coming in?"

Malcolm craned his neck to see the gate.

"Yes," he said.

There was a silence. Mabel sat on like one condemned, at the head of the table. Then a whistle was heard from the kitchen. The dog got up and barked sharply. Joe opened the door and shouted:

"Come on."

After a moment a young man entered. He was muffled up in overcoat and a purple woollen scarf, and his tweed cap, which he did not remove, was pulled down on his head. He was of medium height, his face was rather long and pale, his eyes looked tired.

"Hello, Jack! Well, Jack!" exclaimed Malcolm and Joe. Fred Henry merely said: "Jack."

"What's doing?" asked the newcomer, evidently addressing Fred Henry.

"Same. We've got to be out by Wednesday. Got a cold?"

"I have—got it bad, too."

"Why don't you stop in?"

"*Me* stop in? When I can't stand on my legs, perhaps I shall have a chance." The young man spoke huskily. He had a slight Scotch accent.

"It's a knock-out, isn't it," said Joe, boisterously, "if a doctor goes round croaking with a cold. Looks bad for the patients, doesn't it?"

The young doctor looked at him slowly.

"Anything the matter with *you*, then?" he asked sarcastically.

"Not as I know of. Damn your eyes, I hope not. Why?"

"I thought you were very concerned about the patients, wondered if you might be one yourself."

"Damn it, no, I've never been patient to no flaming doctor, and hope I never shall be," returned Joe.

At this point Mabel rose from the table, and they all seemed to become aware of her existence. She began putting the dishes together. The young doctor looked at her, but did not address her. He had not greeted her. She went out of the room with the tray, her face impassive and unchanged.

"When are you off then, all of you?" asked the doctor.

"I'm catching the eleven-forty," replied Malcolm. "Are you goin' down wi' th' trap, Joe?"

"Yes, I've told you I'm going down wi' th' trap, haven't I?"

"We'd better be getting her in then. So long Jack, if I don't see you before I go," said Malcolm, shaking hands.

He went out, followed by Joe, who seemed to have his tail between his legs.

"Well, this is the devil's own," exclaimed the doctor, when he was left alone with Fred Henry. "Going before Wednesday, are you?"

"That's the orders," replied the other.

"Where, to Northampton?"

"That's it."

"The devil!" exclaimed Ferguson, with quiet chagrin.

And there was silence between the two.

"All settled up, are you?" asked Ferguson.

"About."

There was another pause.

"Well, I shall miss yer, Freddy, boy," said the young doctor.

"And I shall miss thee, Jack," returned the other.

"Miss you like hell," mused the doctor.

Fred Henry turned aside. There was nothing to say. Mabel came in again, to finish clearing the table.

"What are *you* going to do, then, Miss Pervin?" asked Ferguson. "Going to your sister's, are you?"

Mabel looked at him with her steady, dangerous eyes, that always made him uncomfortable, unsettling his superficial ease.

"No," she said.

"Well, what in the name of fortune *are* you going to do? Say what you mean to do," cried Fred Henry, with futile intensity.

But she only averted her head, and continued her work. She folded the white table-cloth, and put on the chenille cloth.

"The sulkiest bitch that ever trod!" muttered her brother.

But she finished her task with perfectly impassive face, the young doctor watching her interestedly all the while. Then she went out.

Fred Henry stared after her, clenching his lips, his blue eyes fixing in sharp antagonism, as he made a grimace of sour exasperation.

"You could bray[4] her into bits, and that's all you'd get out of her," he said, in a small, narrowed tone.

The doctor smiled faintly.

"What's she *going* to do, then?" he asked.

"Strike me if *I* know!" returned the other.

There was a pause. Then the doctor stirred.

"I'll be seeing you tonight, shall I?" he said to his friend.

"Ay—where's it to be? Are we going over to Jessdale?"

"I don't know. I've got such a cold on me. I'll come round to the 'Moon and Stars,'[5] anyway."

"Let Lizzie and May miss their night for once, eh?"

"That's it—if I feel as I do now."

"All's one——"

The two young men went through the passage and down to the back door together. The house was large, but it was servantless now, and desolate. At the back was a small bricked house-yard and beyond that a big square, gravelled fine and red, and having stables on two sides. Sloping, dank, winter-dark fields stretched away on the open sides.

But the stables were empty. Joseph Pervin, the father of the family, had been a man of no education, who had become a fairly large horse dealer. The stables had been full of horses, there was a great turmoil and come-and-go of horses and of dealers and grooms. Then the kitchen was full of servants. But

4. Grind.   5. Name of a public house (pub).

of late things had declined. The old man had married a second time, to retrieve his fortunes. Now he was dead and everything was gone to the dogs,[6] there was nothing but debt and threatening.

For months, Mabel had been servantless in the big house, keeping the home together in penury for her ineffectual brothers. She had kept house for ten years. But previously it was with unstinted means. Then, however brutal and coarse everything was, the sense of money had kept her proud, confident. The men might be foul-mouthed, the women in the kitchen might have had reputations, her brothers might have illegitimate children. But so long as there was money, the girl felt herself established, and brutally proud, reserved.

No company came to the house, save dealers and coarse men. Mabel had no associates of her own sex, after her sister went away. But she did not mind. She went regularly to church, she attended to her father. And she lived in the memory of her mother, who had died when she was fourteen, and whom she had loved. She had loved her father, too, in a different way, depending upon him, and feeling secure in him, until at the age of fifty-four, he married again. And then she had set hard against him. Now he had died and left them all hopelessly in debt.

She had suffered badly during the period of poverty. Nothing, however, could shake the curious, sullen, animal pride that dominated each member of the family. Now, for Mabel, the end had come. Still she would not cast about her. She would follow her own way just the same. She would always hold the keys of her own situation. Mindless and persistent, she endured from day to day. Why should she think? Why should she answer anybody? It was enough that this was the end, and there was no way out. She need not pass any more darkly along the main street of the small town, avoiding every eye. She need not demean herself any more, going into the shops and buying the cheapest food. This was at an end. She thought of nobody, not even of herself. Mindless and persistent, she seemed in a sort of ecstasy to be coming nearer to her fulfilment, her own glorification, approaching her dead mother, who was glorified.

In the afternoon, she took a little bag, with shears and sponge and a small scrubbing-brush, and went out. It was a grey, wintry day, with saddened, dark green fields and an atmosphere blackened by the smoke of foundries not far off. She went quickly, darkly along the causeway, heeding nobody, through the town to the churchyard.

There she always felt secure, as if no one could see her, although as a matter of fact she was exposed to the stare of everyone who passed along under the churchyard wall. Nevertheless, once under the shadow of the great looming church, among the graves, she felt immune from the world, reserved within the thick churchyard wall as in another country.

Carefully she clipped the grass from the grave, and arranged the pinky-white, small chrysanthemums in the tin cross. When this was done, she took an empty jar from a neighbouring grave, brought water, and carefully, most scrupulously sponged the marble headstone and the coping-stone.

It gave her sincere satisfaction to do this. She felt in immediate contact with the world of her mother. She took minute pains, went through the park in a state bordering on pure happiness, as if in performing this task she came into a subtle, intimate connection with her mother. For the life she followed here

6. Gone wrong (slang).

in the world was far less real than the world of death she inherited from her mother.

The doctor's house was just by the church. Ferguson, being a mere hired assistant, was slave to the country-side. As he hurried now to attend to the out-patients in the surgery, glancing across the graveyard with his quick eye, he saw the girl at her task at the grave. She seemed so intent and remote, it was like looking into another world. Some mystical element was touched in him. He slowed down as he walked, watching her as if spellbound.

She lifted her eyes, feeling him looking. Their eyes met. And each looked away again at once, each feeling, in some way, found out by the other. He lifted his cap and passed on down the road. There remained distinct in his consciousness, like a vision, the memory of her face, lifted from the tombstone in the churchyard, and looking at him with slow, large, portentous eyes. It *was* portentous, her face. It seemed to mesmerise him. There was a heavy power in her eyes which laid hold of his whole being, as if he had drunk some powerful drug. He had been feeling weak and done before. Now the life came back into him, he felt delivered from his own fretted, daily self.

He finished his duties at the surgery as quickly as might be, hastily filling up the bottles of the waiting people with cheap drugs. Then, in perpetual haste, he set off again to visit several cases in another part of his round, before tea-time. At all times he preferred to walk if he could, but particularly when he was not well. He fancied the motion restored him.

The afternoon was falling. It was grey, deadened, and wintry, with a slow, moist, heavy coldness sinking in and deadening all the faculties. But why should he think or notice? He hastily climbed the hill and turned across the dark green fields, following the black cinder-track. In the distance, across a shallow dip in the country, the small town was clustered like smouldering ash, a tower, a spire, a heap of low, raw, extinct houses. And on the nearest fringe of the town, sloping into the dip, was Oldmeadow, the Pervins' house. He could see the stables and the outbuildings distinctly, as they lay towards him on the slope. Well, he would not go there many more times! Another resource would be lost to him, another place gone: the only company he cared for in the alien, ugly little town he was losing. Nothing but work, drudgery, constant hastening from dwelling to dwelling among the colliers and the iron-workers. It wore him out, but at the same time he had a craving for it. It was a stimulant to him to be in the homes of the working people, moving, as it were, through the innermost body of their life. His nerves were excited and gratified. He could come so near, into the very lives of the rough, inarticulate, powerfully emotional men and women. He grumbled, he said he hated the hellish hole. But as a matter of fact it excited him, the contact with the rough, strongly-feeling people was a stimulant applied direct to his nerves.

Below Oldmeadow, in the green, shallow, soddened hollow of fields, lay a square, deep pond. Roving across the landscape, the doctor's quick eye detected a figure in black passing through the gate of the field, down towards the pond. He looked again. It would be Mabel Pervin. His mind suddenly became alive and attentive.

Why was she going down there? He pulled up on the path on the slope above, and stood staring. He could just make sure of the small black figure moving in the hollow of the failing day. He seemed to see her in the midst of such obscurity, that he was like a clairvoyant, seeing rather with the mind's eye than with ordinary sight. Yet he could see her positively enough, whilst he kept his eye attentive. He felt, if he looked away from her, in the thick, ugly falling dusk, he would lose her altogether.

He followed her minutely as she moved, direct and intent, like something transmitted rather than stirring in voluntary activity, straight down the field towards the pond. There she stood on the bank for a moment. She never raised her head. Then she waded slowly into the water.

He stood motionless as the small black figure walked slowly and deliberately towards the centre of the pond, very slowly, gradually moving deeper into the motionless water, and still moving forward as the water got up to her breast. Then he could see her no more in the dusk of the dead afternoon.

"There!" he exclaimed. "Would you believe it?"

And he hastened straight down, running over the wet, soddened fields, pushing through the hedges, down into the depression of callous wintry obscurity. It took him several minutes to come to the pond. He stood on the bank, breathing heavily. He could see nothing. His eyes seemed to penetrate the dead water. Yes, perhaps that was the dark shadow of her black clothing beneath the surface of the water.

He slowly ventured into the pond. The bottom was deep, soft clay, he sank in, and the water clasped dead cold round his legs. As he stirred he could smell the cold, rotten clay that fouled up into the water. It was objectionable in his lungs. Still, repelled and yet not heeding, he moved deeper into the pond. The cold water rose over his thighs, over his loins, upon his abdomen. The lower part of his body was all sunk in the hideous cold element. And the bottom was so deeply soft and uncertain, he was afraid of pitching with his mouth underneath. He could not swim, and was afraid.

He crouched a little, spreading his hands under the water and moving them round, trying to feel for her. The dead cold pond swayed upon his chest. He moved again, a little deeper, and again, with his hands underneath, he felt all around under the water. And he touched her clothing. But it evaded his fingers. He made a desperate effort to grasp it.

And so doing he lost his balance and went under, horribly, suffocating in the foul earthy water, struggling madly for a few moments. At last, after what seemed an eternity, he got his footing, rose again into the air and looked around. He gasped, and knew he was in the world. Then he looked at the water. She had risen near him. He grasped her clothing, and drawing her nearer, turned to take his way to land again.

He went very slowly, carefully, absorbed in the slow progress. He rose higher, climbing out of the pond. The water was now only about his legs; he was thankful, full of relief to be out of the clutches of the pond. He lifted her and staggered on to the bank, out of the horror of wet, grey clay.

He laid her down on the bank. She was quite unconscious and running with water. He made the water come from her mouth, he worked to restore her. He did not have to work very long before he could feel the breathing begin again in her; she was breathing naturally. He worked a little longer. He could feel her live beneath his hands; she was coming back. He wiped her face, wrapped her in his overcoat, looked round into the dim, dark grey world, then lifted her and staggered down the bank and across the fields.

It seemed an unthinkably long way, and his burden so heavy he felt he would never get to the house. But at last he was in the stable-yard, and then in the house-yard. He opened the door and went into the house. In the kitchen he laid her down on the hearth-rug and called. The house was empty. But the fire was burning in the grate.

Then again he kneeled to attend to her. She was breathing regularly, her eyes were wide open and as if conscious, but there seemed something missing in her look. She was conscious in herself, but unconscious of her surroundings.

He ran upstairs, took blankets from a bed, and put them before the fire to warm. Then he removed her saturated, earthy-smelling clothing, rubbed her dry with a towel, and wrapped her naked in the blankets. Then he went into the dining room, to look for spirits. There was a little whisky. He drank a gulp himself, and put some into her mouth.

The effect was instantaneous. She looked full into his face, as if she had been seeing him for some time, and yet had only just become conscious of him.

"Dr. Ferguson?" she said.

"What?" he answered.

He was divesting himself of his coat, intending to find some dry clothing upstairs. He could not bear the smell of the dead, clayey water, and he was mortally afraid for his own health.

"What did I do?" she asked.

"Walked into the pond," he replied. He had begun to shudder like one sick, and could hardly attend to her. Her eyes remained full on him, he seemed to be going dark in his mind, looking back at her helplessly. The shuddering became quieter in him, his life came back to him, dark and unknowing, but strong again.

"Was I out of my mind?" she asked, while her eyes were fixed on him all the time.

"Maybe, for the moment," he replied. He felt quiet, because his strength had come back. The strange fretful strain had left him.

"Am I out of my mind now?" she asked.

"Are you?" he reflected a moment. "No," he answered truthfully. "I don't see that you are." He turned his face aside. He was afraid now, because he felt dazed, and felt dimly that her power was stronger than his, in this issue. And she continued to look at him fixedly all the time. "Can you tell me where I shall find some dry things to put on?" he asked.

"Did you dive into the pond for me?" she asked.

"No," he answered. "I walked in. But I went in overhead as well."

There was silence for a moment. He hesitated. He very much wanted to go upstairs to get into dry clothing. But there was another desire in him. And she seemed to hold him. His will seemed to have gone to sleep, and left him, standing there slack before her. But he felt warm inside himself. He did not shudder at all, though his clothes were sodden on him.

"Why did you?" she asked.

"Because I didn't want you to do such a foolish thing," he said.

"It wasn't foolish," she said, still gazing at him as she lay on the floor, with a sofa cushion under her head. "It was the right thing to do. *I* knew best, then."

"I'll go and shift these wet things," he said. But still he had not the power to move out of her presence, until she sent him. It was as if she had the life of his body in her hands, and he could not extricate himself. Or perhaps he did not want to.

Suddenly she sat up. Then she became aware of her own immediate condition. She felt the blankets about her, she knew her own limbs. For a moment it seemed as if her reason were going. She looked round, with wild eye, as if seeking something. He stood still with fear. She saw her clothing lying scattered.

"Who undressed me?" she asked, her eyes resting full and inevitable on his face.

"I did," he replied, "to bring you round."

For some moments she sat and gazed at him awfully, her lips parted.

"Do you love me, then?" she asked.

He only stood and stared at her, fascinated. His soul seemed to melt.

She shuffled forward on her knees, and put her arms round him, round his legs, as he stood there, pressing her breasts against his knees and thighs, clutching him with strange, convulsive certainty, pressing his thighs against her, drawing him to her face, her throat, as she looked up at him with flaring, humble eyes of transfiguration, triumphant in first possession.

"You love me," she murmured, in strange transport, yearning and triumphant and confident. "You love me. I know you love me, I know."

And she was passionately kissing his knees, through the wet clothing, passionately and indiscriminately kissing his knees, his legs, as if unaware of everything.

He looked down at the tangled wet hair, the wild, bare, animal shoulders. He was amazed, bewildered, and afraid. He had never thought of loving her. He had never wanted to love her. When he rescued her and restored her, he was a doctor, and she was a patient. He had had no single personal thought of her. Nay, this introduction of the personal element was very distasteful to him, a violation of his professional honour. It was horrible to have her there embracing his knees. It was horrible. He revolted from it, violently. And yet— and yet—he had not the power to break away.

She looked at him again, with the same supplication of powerful love, and that same transcendent, frightening light of triumph. In view of the delicate flame which seemed to come from her face like a light, he was powerless. And yet he had never intended to love her. He had never intended. And something stubborn in him could not give way.

"You love me," she repeated, in a murmur of deep, rhapsodic assurance. "You love me."

Her hands were drawing him, drawing him down to her. He was afraid, even a little horrified. For he had, really, no intention of loving her. Yet her hands were drawing him towards her. He put out his hand quickly to steady himself, and grasped her bare shoulder. A flame seemed to burn the hand that grasped her soft shoulder. He had no intention of loving her: his whole will was against his yielding. It was horrible. And yet wonderful was the touch of her shoulders, beautiful the shining of her face. Was she perhaps mad? He had a horror of yielding to her. Yet something in him ached also.

He had been staring away at the door, away from her. But his hand remained on her shoulder. She had gone suddenly very still. He looked down at her. Her eyes were now wide with fear, with doubt, the light was dying from her face, a shadow of terrible greyness was returning. He could not bear the touch of her eyes' question upon him, and the look of death behind the question.

With an inward groan he gave way, and let his heart yield towards her. A sudden gentle smile came on his face. And her eyes, which never left his face, slowly, slowly filled with tears. He watched the strange water rise in her eyes, like some slow fountain coming up. And his heart seemed to burn and melt away in his breast.

He could not bear to look at her any more. He dropped on his knees and caught her head with his arms and pressed her face against his throat. She was very still. His heart, which seemed to have broken, was burning with a kind of agony in his breast. And he felt her slow, hot tears wetting his throat. But he could not move.

He felt the hot tears wet his neck and the hollows of his neck, and he remained motionless, suspended through one of man's eternities. Only now it had become indispensable to him to have her face pressed close to him; he could never let her go again. He could never let her head go away from the close clutch of his arm. He wanted to remain like that for ever, with his heart hurting him in a pain that was also life to him. Without knowing, he was looking down on her damp, soft brown hair.

Then, as it were suddenly, he smelt the horrid stagnant smell of that water. And at the same moment she drew away from him and looked at him. Her eyes were wistful and unfathomable. He was afraid of them, and he fell to kissing her, not knowing what he was doing. He wanted her eyes not to have that terrible, wistful, unfathomable look.

When she turned her face to him again, a faint delicate flush was glowing, and there was again dawning that terrible shining of joy in her eyes, which really terrified him, and yet which he now wanted to see, because he feared the look of doubt still more.

"You love me?" she said, rather faltering.

"Yes." The word cost him a painful effort. Not because it wasn't true. But because it was too newly true, the *saying* seemed to tear open again his newly-torn heart. And he hardly wanted it to be true, even now.

She lifted her face to him, and he bent forward and kissed her on the mouth, gently, with the one kiss that is an eternal pledge. And as he kissed her his heart strained again in his breast. He never intended to love her. But now it was over. He had crossed over the gulf to her, and all that he had left behind had shrivelled and become void.

After the kiss, her eyes again slowly filled with tears. She sat still, away from him, with her face drooped aside, and her hands folded in her lap. The tears fell very slowly. There was complete silence. He too sat there motionless and silent on the hearth-rug. The strange pain of his heart that was broken seemed to consume him. That he should love her? That this was love! That he should be ripped open in this way! Him, a doctor! How they would all jeer if they knew! It was agony to him to think they might know.

In the curious naked pain of the thought he looked again to her. She was sitting there drooped into a muse. He saw a tear fall, and his heart flared hot. He saw for the first time that one of her shoulders was quite uncovered, one arm bare, he could see one of her small breasts; dimly, because it had become almost dark in the room.

"Why are you crying?" he asked, in an altered voice.

She looked up at him, and behind her tears the consciousness of her situation for the first time brought a dark look of shame to her eyes.

"I'm not crying, really," she said, watching him, half frightened.

He reached his hand, and softly closed it on her bare arm.

"I love you! I love you!" he said in a soft, low vibrating voice, unlike himself.

She shrank, and dropped her head. The soft, penetrating grip of his hand on her arm distressed her. She looked up at him.

"I want to go," she said. "I want to go and get you some dry things."

"Why?" he said. "I'm all right."

"But I want to go," she said. "And I want you to change your things."

He released her arm, and she wrapped herself in the blanket, looking at him, rather frightened. And still she did not rise.

"Kiss me," she said wistfully.

He kissed her, but briefly, half in anger.

Then, after a second, she rose nervously, all mixed up in the blanket. He watched her in her confusion as she tried to extricate herself and wrap herself up so that she could walk. He watched her relentlessly, as she knew. And as she went, the blanket trailing, and as he saw a glimpse of her feet and her white leg, he tried to remember her as she was when he had wrapped her in the blanket. But then he didn't want to remember, because she had been nothing to him then, and his nature revolted from remembering her as she was when she was nothing to him.

A tumbling muffled noise from within the dark house startled him. Then he heard her voice: "There are clothes." He rose and went to the foot of the stairs, and gathered up the garments she had thrown down. Then he came back to the fire, to rub himself down and dress. He grinned at his own appearance when he had finished.

The fire was sinking, so he put on coal. The house was now quite dark, save for the light of a street-lamp that shone in faintly from beyond the holly trees. He lit the gas with matches he found on the mantelpiece. Then he emptied the pockets of his own clothes, and threw all his wet things in a heap into the scullery. After which he gathered up her sodden clothes, gently, and put them in a separate heap on the copper-top in the scullery.

It was six o'clock on the clock. His own watch had stopped. He ought to go back to the surgery. He waited, and still she did not come down. So he went to the foot of the stairs and called:

"I shall have to go."

Almost immediately he heard her coming down. She had on her best dress of black voile, and her hair was tidy, but still damp. She looked at him—and in spite of herself, smiled.

"I don't like you in those clothes," she said.

"Do I look a sight?" he answered.

They were shy of one another.

"I'll make you some tea," she said.

"No, I must go."

"Must you?" And she looked at him again with the wide, strained, doubtful eyes. And again, from the pain of his breast, he knew how he loved her. He went and bent to kiss her, gently, passionately, with his heart's painful kiss.

"And my hair smells so horrible," she murmured in distraction. "And I'm so awful, I'm so awful! Oh no, I'm too awful." And she broke into bitter, heart-broken sobbing. "You can't want to love me, I'm horrible."

"Don't be silly, don't be silly," he said, trying to comfort her, kissing her, holding her in his arms. "I want you, I want to marry you, we're going to be married, quickly, quickly—to-morrow if I can."

But she only sobbed terribly, and cried:

"I feel awful. I feel awful. I feel I'm horrible to you."

"No, I want you, I want you," was all he answered, blindly, with that terrible intonation which frightened her almost more than her horror lest he should *not* want her.

1922

Why the Novel Matters

We have curious ideas of ourselves. We think of ourselves as a body with a spirit in it, or a body with a soul in it, or a body with a mind in it. *Mens sana in corpore sano.*[1] The years drink up the wine, and at last throw the bottle away, the body, of course, being the bottle.

It is a funny sort of superstition. Why should I look at my hand, as it so cleverly writes these words, and decide that it is a mere nothing compared to the mind that directs it? Is there really any huge difference between my hand and my brain? Or my mind? My hand is alive, it flickers with a life of its own. It meets all the strange universe in touch, and learns a vast number of things, and knows a vast number of things. My hand, as it writes these words, slips gaily along, jumps like a grasshopper to dot an *i*, feels the table rather cold, gets a little bored if I write too long, has its own rudiments of thought, and is just as much *me* as is my brain, my mind, or my soul. Why should I imagine that there is a *me* which is more *me* than my hand is? Since my hand is absolutely alive, me alive.

Whereas, of course, as far as I am concerned, my pen isn't alive at all. My pen *isn't me* alive. Me alive ends at my finger tips.

Whatever is me alive is me. Every tiny bit of my hands is alive, every little freckle and hair and fold of skin. And whatever is me alive is me. Only my finger-nails, those ten little weapons between me and an inanimate universe, they cross the mysterious Rubicon[2] between me alive and things like my pen, which are not alive, in my own sense.

So, seeing my hand is all alive, and me alive, wherein is it just a bottle, or a jug, or a tin can, or a vessel of clay, or any of the rest of that nonsense? True, if I cut it it will bleed, like a can of cherries. But then the skin that is cut, and the veins that bleed, and the bones that should never be seen, they are all just as alive as the blood that flows. So the tin can business, or vessel of clay, is just bunk.

And that's what you learn, when you're a novelist. And that's what you are very liable *not* to know, if you're a parson, or a philosopher, or a scientist, or a stupid person. If you're a parson, you talk about souls in heaven. If you're a novelist, you know that paradise is in the palm of your hand, and on the end of your nose, because both are alive; and alive, and man alive, which is more than you can say, for certain, of paradise. Paradise is after life, and I for one am not keen on anything that is *after* life. If you are a philosopher, you talk about infinity, and the pure spirit which knows all things. But if you pick up a novel, you realise immediately that infinity is just a handle to this self-same jug of a body of mine; while as for knowing, if I find my finger in the fire, I know that fire burns, with a knowledge so emphatic and vital, it leaves Nirvana[3] merely a conjecture. Oh, yes, my body, me alive, *knows*, and knows intensely. And as for the sum of all knowledge, it can't be anything more than an accumulation of all the things I know in the body, and you, dear reader, know in the body.

---

1. A healthy mind in a healthy body (Latin).
2. When Julius Caesar crossed the river Rubicon (near Rimini, Italy) in 49 B.C.E., in defiance of the Senate, he indicated his intention of advancing against Pompey and thus involving the country in civil war. Hence to "cross the Rubicon" means to take an important and irrevocable decision.
3. In Buddhist theology the extinction of the self and its desires and the attainment of perfect beatitude.

These damned philosophers, they talk as if they suddenly went off in steam, and were then much more important than they are when they're in their shirts. It is nonsense. Every man, philosopher included, ends in his own finger-tips. That's the end of his man alive. As for the words and thoughts and sighs and aspirations that fly from him, they are so many tremulations in the ether, and not alive at all. But if the tremulations reach another man alive, he may receive them into his life, and his life may take on a new colour, like a chameleon creeping from a brown rock on to a green leaf. All very well and good. It still doesn't alter the fact that the so-called spirit, the message or teaching of the philosopher or the saint, isn't alive at all, but just a tremulation upon the ether, like a radio message. All this spirit stuff is just tremulations upon the ether. If you, as man alive, quiver from the tremulation of the ether into new life, that is because you are man alive, and you take sustenance and stimulation into your alive man in a myriad ways. But to say that the message, or the spirit which is communicated to you, is more important than your living body, is nonsense. You might as well say that the potato at dinner was more important.

Nothing is important but life. And for myself, I can absolutely see life nowhere but in the living. Life with a capital L is only man alive. Even a cabbage in the rain is cabbage alive. All things that are alive are amazing. And all things that are dead are subsidiary to the living. Better a live dog than a dead lion. But better a live lion than a live dog. *C'est la vie!*

It seems impossible to get a saint, or a philosopher, or a scientist, to stick to this simple truth. They are all, in a sense, renegades. The saint wishes to offer himself up as spiritual food for the multitude. Even Francis of Assisi[4] turns himself into a sort of angel-cake, of which anyone may take a slice. But an angel-cake is rather less than man alive. And poor St Francis might well apologise to his body, when he is dying: "Oh, pardon me, my body, the wrong I did you through the years!" It was no wafer,[5] for others to eat.

The philosopher, on the other hand, because he can think, decides that nothing but thoughts matter. It is as if a rabbit, because he can make little pills, should decide that nothing but little pills matter. As for the scientist, he has absolutely no use for me so long as I am man alive. To the scientist, I am dead. He puts under the microscope a bit of dead me, and calls it me. He takes me to pieces, and says first one piece, and then another piece, is me. My heart, my liver, my stomach have all been scientifically me, according to the scientist; and nowadays I am either a brain, or nerves, or glands, or something more up-to-date in the tissue line.

Now I absolutely flatly deny that I am a soul, or a body, or a mind, or an intelligence, or a brain, or a nervous system, or a bunch of glands, or any of the rest of these bits of me. The whole is greater than the part. And therefore, I, who am man alive, am greater than my soul, or spirit, or body, or mind, or consciousness, or anything else that is merely a part of me. I am a man, and alive. I am man alive, and as long as I can, I intend to go on being man alive.

For this reason I am a novelist. And being a novelist, I consider myself superior to the saint, the scientist, the philosopher, and the poet, who are all great masters of different bits of man alive, but never get the whole hog.

The novel is the one bright book of life. Books are not life. They are only

---

4. Roman Catholic saint (1181 or 1182–1226).
5. Consumed as Christ's body in Roman Catholic Communion.

tremulations on the ether. But the novel as a tremulation can make the whole man alive tremble. Which is more than poetry, philosophy, science, or any other book-tremulation can do.

The novel is the book of life. In this sense, the Bible is a great confused novel. You may say, it is about God. But it is really about man alive. Adam, Eve, Sarai, Abraham, Isaac, Jacob, Samuel, David, Bath-Sheba, Ruth, Esther, Solomon, Job, Isaiah, Jesus, Mark, Judas, Paul, Peter: what is it but man alive, from start to finish? Man alive, not mere bits. Even the Lord is another man alive, in a burning bush, throwing the tablets of stone at Moses's head.

I do hope you begin to get my idea, why the novel is supremely important, as a tremulation on the ether. Plato makes the perfect ideal being tremble in me. But that's only a bit of me. Perfection is only a bit, in the strange make-up of man alive. The Sermon on the Mount[6] makes the selfless spirit of me quiver. But that, too, is only a bit of me. The Ten Commandments set the old Adam shivering in me, warning me that I am a thief and a murderer, unless I watch it. But even the old Adam is only a bit of me.

I very much like all these bits of me to be set trembling with life and the wisdom of life. But I do ask that the whole of me shall tremble in its wholeness, some time or other.

And this, of course, must happen in me, living.

But as far as it can happen from a communication, it can only happen when a whole novel communicates itself to me. The Bible—but *all* the Bible—and Homer, and Shakespeare: these are the supreme old novels. These are all things to all men. Which means that in their wholeness they affect the whole man alive, which is the man himself, beyond any part of him. They set the whole tree trembling with a new access of life, they do not just stimulate growth in one direction.

I don't want to grow in any one direction any more. And, if I can help it, I don't want to stimulate anybody else into some particular direction. A particular direction ends in a *cul-de-sac*. We're in a *cul-de-sac* at present.

I don't believe in any dazzling revelation, or in any supreme Word. "The grass withereth, the flower fadeth, but the Word of the Lord shall stand for ever."[7] That's the kind of stuff we've drugged ourselves with. As a matter of fact, the grass withereth, but comes up all the greener for that reason, after the rains. The flower fadeth, and therefore the bud opens. But the Word of the Lord, being man-uttered and a mere vibration on the ether, becomes staler and staler, more and more boring, till at last we turn a deaf ear and it ceases to exist, far more finally than any withered grass. It is grass that renews its youth like the eagle, not any Word.

We should ask for no absolutes, or absolute. Once and for all and for ever, let us have done with the ugly imperialism of any absolute. There is no absolute good, there is nothing absolutely right. All things flow and change, and even change is not absolute. The whole is a strange assembly of apparently incongruous parts, slipping past one another.

Me, man alive, I am a very curious assembly of incongruous parts. My yea! of today is oddly different from my yea! of yesterday. My tears of to-morrow will have nothing to do with my tears of a year ago. If the one I love remains unchanged and unchanging, I shall cease to love her. It is only because she changes and startles me into change and defies my inertia, and is herself

6. See Matthew 5.7.   7. Isaiah 40.8.

staggered in her inertia by my changing, that I can continue to love her. If she stayed put, I might as well love the pepper pot.

In all this change, I maintain a certain integrity. But woe betide me if I try to put my finger on it. If I say of myself, I am this, I am that!—then, if I stick to it, I turn into a stupid fixed thing like a lamp-post. I shall never know wherein lies my integrity, my individuality, my me. I *can* never know it. It is useless to talk about my ego. That only means that I have made up an *idea* of myself, and that I am trying to cut myself out to pattern. Which is no good. You can cut your cloth to fit your coat, but you can't clip bits off your living body, to trim it down to your idea. True, you can put yourself into ideal corsets. But even in ideal corsets, fashions change.

Let us learn from the novel. In the novel, the characters can do nothing but *live*. If they keep on being good, according to pattern, or bad, according to pattern, or even volatile, according to pattern, they cease to live, and the novel falls dead. A character in a novel has got to live, or it is nothing.

We, likewise, in life have got to live, or we are nothing.

What we mean by living is, of course, just as indescribable as what we mean by *being*. Men get ideas into their heads, of what they mean by Life, and they proceed to cut life out to pattern. Sometimes they go into the desert to seek God, sometimes they go into the desert to seek cash, sometimes it is wine, woman, and song, and again it is water, political reform, and votes. You never know what it will be next: from killing your neighbour with hideous bombs and gas that tears the lungs, to supporting a Foundlings' Home[8] and preaching infinite Love, and being co-respondent in a divorce.

In all this wild welter, we need some sort of guide. It's no good inventing Thou Shalt Nots!

What then? Turn truly, honourably to the novel, and see wherein you are man alive, and wherein you are dead man in life. You may love a woman as man alive, and you may be making love to a woman as sheer dead man in life. You may eat your dinner as man alive, or as a mere masticating corpse. As man alive you may have shot at your enemy. But as a ghastly simulacrum of life you may be firing bombs into men who are neither your enemies nor your friends, but just things you are dead to. Which is criminal, when the things happen to be alive.

To be alive, to be man alive, to be whole man alive: that is the point. And at its best, the novel, and the novel supremely, can help you. It can help you not to be dead man in life. So much of a man walks about dead and a carcass in the street and house, to-day: so much of women is merely dead. Like a pianoforte with half the notes mute.

But the novel you can see, plainly, when the man goes dead, the woman goes inert. You can develop an instinct for life, if you will, instead of a theory of right and wrong, good and bad.

In life, there is right and wrong, good and bad, all the time. But what is right in one case is wrong in another. And in the novel you see one man becoming a corpse, because of his so-called goodness, another going dead because of his so-called wickedness. Right and wrong is an instinct: but an instinct of the whole consciousness in a man, bodily, mental, spiritual at once. And only in the novel are *all* things given full play, or at least, they may be given full play, when we realize that life itself, and not inert safety, is the reason

8. Orphanage.

for living. For out of the full play of all things emerges the only thing that is anything, the wholeness of a man, the wholeness of a woman, man live, and live woman.

1936

Piano[1]

Softly, in the dusk, a woman is singing to me;
Taking me back down the vista of years, till I see
A child sitting under the piano, in the boom of the tingling strings
And pressing the small, poised feet of a mother who smiles as she sings.

5   In spite of myself, the insidious mastery of song
Betrays me back, till the heart of me weeps to belong
To the old Sunday evenings at home, with winter outside
And hymns in the cozy parlour, the tinkling piano our guide.

So now it is vain for the singer to burst into clamour
10 With the great black piano appassionato.° The glamour   *played with passion*
Of childish days is upon me, my manhood is cast
Down in the flood of remembrance, I weep like a child for the past.

1918

Snake

A snake came to my water-trough
On a hot, hot day, and I in pyjamas for the heat,
To drink there.

In the deep, strange-scented shade of the great dark
    carob-tree°   *Mediterranean evergreen*
5 I came down the steps with my pitcher
And must wait, must stand and wait, for there he was at the trough before
    me.

He reached down from a fissure in the earth-wall in the gloom
And trailed his yellow-brown slackness soft-bellied down, over the edge of
    the stone trough
And rested his throat upon the stone bottom,
10 And where the water had dripped from the tap, in a small clearness,
He sipped with his straight mouth,
Softly drank through his straight gums, into his slack long body,
Silently.

Someone was before me at my water-trough,
15 And I, like a second comer, waiting.

1. For an earlier version of this poem, see "Poems in Process," in the appendices to this volume.

He lifted his head from his drinking, as cattle do,
And looked at me vaguely, as drinking cattle do,
And flickered his two-forked tongue from his lips, and mused a moment,
And stooped and drank a little more,
20 Being earth-brown, earth-golden from the burning bowels of
      the earth
On the day of Sicilian July, with Etna° smoking.   *the volcano*

The voice of my education said to me
He must be killed,
For in Sicily the black, black snakes are innocent, the gold are venomous.

25 And voices in me said, If you were a man
You would take a stick and break him now, and finish him off.

But must I confess how I liked him,
How glad I was he had come like a guest in quiet, to drink at my water-
      trough
And depart peaceful, pacified, and thankless
30 Into the burning bowels of this earth?

Was it cowardice, that I dared not kill him?
Was it perversity, that I longed to talk to him?
Was it humility, to feel so honoured?
I felt so honoured.

35 And yet those voices:
If you were not afraid, you would kill him!

And truly I was afraid, I was most afraid,
But even so, honoured still more
That he should seek my hospitality
40 From out the dark door of the secret earth.

He drank enough
And lifted his head, dreamily, as one who has drunken,
And flickered his tongue like a forked night on the air, so black;
Seeming to lick his lips,
45 And looked around like a god, unseeing, into the air,
And slowly turned his head,
And slowly, very slowly, as if thrice adream
Proceeded to draw his slow length curving round
And climb the broken bank of my wall-face.

50 And as he put his head into that dreadful hole,
And as he slowly drew up, snake-easing his shoulders, and entered farther,
A sort of horror, a sort of protest against his withdrawing into that horrid
      black hole,
Deliberately going into the blackness, and slowly drawing himself after,
Overcame me now his back was turned.

55 I looked round, I put down my pitcher,
I picked up a clumsy log
And threw it at the water-trough with a clatter.

I think it did not hit him;
But suddenly that part of him that was left behind convulsed in undignified
    haste,
60 Writhed like lightning, and was gone
Into the black hole, the earth-lipped fissure in the wall-front
At which, in the intense still noon, I stared with fascination.

And immediately I regretted it.
I thought how paltry, how vulgar, what a mean act!
65 I despised myself and the voices of my accursed human education.

And I thought of the albatross,[1]
And I wished he would come back, my snake.

For he seemed to me again like a king,
Like a king in exile, uncrowned in the underworld,
70 Now due to be crowned again.

And so, I missed my chance with one of the lords
Of life.
And I have something to expiate;
A pettiness.

1923

1. In Coleridge's *Rime of the Ancient Mariner*.

T. S. ELIOT
1888–1965

Thomas Stearns Eliot was born in St. Louis, Missouri, of New England stock. He entered Harvard in 1906 and was influenced there by the anti-Romanticism of Irving Babbitt and the philosophical and critical interests of George Santayana, as well as by the enthusiastic study of Renaissance literature and of South Asian religions. He wrote his Harvard dissertation on the English idealist philosopher F. H. Bradley, whose emphasis on the private nature of individual experience, "a circle enclosed on the outside," influenced Eliot's poetry considerably. He also studied literature and philosophy in France and Germany, before going to England shortly after the outbreak of World War I in 1914. He studied Greek philosophy at Oxford, taught school in London, and then obtained a position with Lloyd's Bank. In 1915 he married an English writer, Vivienne Haigh-Wood, but the marriage was not a success. She suffered from poor emotional and physical health. The strain told on Eliot, too. By November 1921 distress and worry had brought him to the verge of a nervous breakdown, and on medical advice he went to recuperate in a Swiss sanitorium. Two months later he returned, pausing in Paris long enough to give his early supporter and adviser Ezra Pound the manuscript of *The Waste Land*. Eliot left his wife in 1933, and she was eventually committed to a mental home, where she died in 1947. Ten years later he was happily remarried to his secretary, Valerie Fletcher.

Eliot started writing literary and philosophical reviews soon after settling in London and was assistant editor of *The Egoist* magazine from 1917 to 1919. In 1922 he founded the influential quarterly *The Criterion*, which he edited until it ceased publication in 1939. His poetry first appeared in 1915, when, at Pound's urging, "The Love Song of J. Alfred Prufrock" was printed in *Poetry* magazine (Chicago) and a few other short poems were published in the short-lived periodical *Blast*. His first published collection of poems was *Prufrock and Other Observations*, 1917; two other small collections followed in 1919 and 1920; in 1922 *The Waste Land* appeared, first in *The Criterion* in October, then in *The Dial* (in America) in November, and finally in book form. Meanwhile he was also publishing collections of his critical essays. In 1925 he joined the London publishing firm Faber & Gwyer, and he was made a director when the firm was renamed Faber & Faber. He became a British subject and joined the Church of England in 1927.

"Our civilization comprehends great variety and complexity, and this variety and complexity, playing upon a refined sensibility, must produce various and complex results. The poet must become more and more comprehensive, more allusive, more indirect, in order to force, to dislocate if necessary, language into his meaning." This remark, from Eliot's essay "The Metaphysical Poets" (1921), gives one clue to his poetic method from "Prufrock" through *The Waste Land*. When he settled in London he saw poetry in English as exhausted, with no verbal excitement or original craftsmanship. He sought to make poetry more subtle, more suggestive, and at the same time more precise. Like the imagists, he emphasized the necessity of clear and precise images. From the philosopher poet T. E. Hulme and from Pound, he learned to fear what was seen as Romantic self-indulgence and vagueness, and to regard the poetic medium rather than the poet's personality as the important factor. At the same time the "hard, dry" images advocated by Hulme were not enough for him; he wanted wit, allusiveness, irony. He saw in the Metaphysical poets how wit and passion could be combined, and he saw in the French symbolists, such as Charles Baudelaire, Stéphane Mallarmé, Paul Verlaine, and Arthur Rimbaud, how an image could be both absolutely precise in what it referred to physically and endlessly suggestive in its meanings because of its relationship to other images. The combination of precision, symbolic suggestion, and ironic mockery in the poetry of the late-nineteenth-century French poet Jules Laforgue attracted and influenced him, as did Laforgue's verse technique that Eliot described in an interview as "rhyming lines of irregular length, with the rhymes coming in irregular places." He also found in the Jacobean dramatists, such as Thomas Middleton, Cyril Tourneur, and John Webster, a flexible blank verse with overtones of colloquial movement, a way of counterpointing the accent of conversation and the note of terror. Eliot's fluency in French and German, his study of Western and non-Western literary and religious texts in their original languages, his rigorous knowledge of philosophy, his exacting critical intellect, his keen sensitivity to colloquial rhythm and idiom, his ability to fuse anguished emotional states with sharply etched intellectual satire—all of these contributed to his crafting one of the twentieth century's most distinctive and influential bodies of poetry.

Hulme's protests against the Romantic concept of poetry reinforced what Eliot had learned from Babbitt at Harvard; yet for all his severity with poets such as Percy Shelley and Walt Whitman, for all his cultivation of a classical viewpoint and his insistence on order and discipline rather than on mere self-expression in art, one side of Eliot's poetic genius is Romantic. The symbolist influence on his imagery, his elegiac lamentation over loss and fragmentation, his interest in the evocative and the suggestive, lines such as "And fiddled whisper music on those strings / And bats with baby faces in the violet light / Whistled, and beat their wings," and recurring images such as the hyacinth girl and the rose garden show what could be called a Romantic element in his poetry. But it is combined with a dry ironic allusiveness, a play of wit and satire, and a colloquial element, which are not normally found in poets of the Romantic tradition.

Eliot's real novelty—and the cause of much bewilderment when his poems first appeared—was his deliberate elimination of all merely connective and transitional passages, his building up of the total pattern of meaning through the immediate juxtaposition of images without overt explanation of what they are doing, together with his use of oblique references to other works of literature (some of them quite obscure to most readers of his time). "Prufrock" presents a symbolic landscape where the meaning emerges from the mutual interaction of the images, and that meaning is enlarged by echoes, often ironic, of Hesiod and Dante and Shakespeare. *The Waste Land* is a series of scenes and images with no author's voice intervening to tell us where we are but with the implications developed through multiple contrasts and through analogies with older literary works often referred to in a distorted quotation or half-concealed allusion. Furthermore, the works referred to are not necessarily central in the Western literary tradition: besides Dante and Shakespeare there are pre-Socratic philosophers; major and minor seventeenth-century poets and drama-tists; works of anthropology, history, and philosophy; texts of Buddhism and Hinduism; even popular songs and vaudeville. Ancient and modern voices, high and low art, Western and non-Western languages clash, coincide, jostle alongside one another. In a culture where the poet's public might lack a common cultural heritage, a shared knowledge of works of the past, Eliot felt it necessary to accumulate his own body of references. In this his use of earlier literature differs from, say, John Milton's. Both poets are difficult for the modern reader, who needs editorial assistance in recognizing and understanding many of the allusions—but Milton was drawing on a body of knowledge common to educated people in his day. Nevertheless, this aspect of Eliot can be exaggerated; his imagery and the movement of his verse set the tone he requires, establish the area of meaning to be developed, so that even a reader ignorant of most of the literary allusions can often get the feel of the poem and achieve some understanding of what it says.

Eliot's early poetry, until at least the middle 1920s, is mostly concerned in one way or another with the Waste Land, with aspects of cultural decay in the modern Western world. After his formal acceptance of Anglican Christianity, a penitential note appears in much of his verse, a note of quiet searching for spiritual peace, with considerable allusion to biblical, liturgical, and mystical religious literature and to Dante. *Ash Wednesday* (1930), a poem in six parts, much less fiercely concentrated in style than the earlier poetry, explores with gentle insistence a mood both penitential and ques-tioning. The Ariel poems (so called because published in Faber's Ariel pamphlet series) present or explore aspects of religious doubt or discovery or revelation, some-times, as in "Journey of the Magi," drawing on biblical incident. In *Four Quartets* (of which the first, "Burnt Norton," appeared in the *Collected Poems* of 1936, though all four were not completed until 1943, when they were published together), Eliot fur-ther explored essentially religious moods, dealing with the relation between time and eternity and the cultivation of that selfless passivity that can yield the moment of timeless revelation in the midst of time. The mocking irony, the savage humor, the collage of quotations, the deliberately startling juxtaposition of the sordid and the romantic give way in these later poems to a quieter poetic idiom that is less jagged and more abstract, less fragmentary and more formally patterned.

As a critic Eliot worked out in his reading of older literature what he needed as a poet to hold and to admire. He lent the growing weight of his authority to a shift in literary taste that replaced Milton by John Donne as the great seventeenth-century English poet and replaced Alfred, Lord Tennyson in the nineteenth century by Gerard Manley Hopkins. Rewriting English literary history, he saw the late-seventeenth-century "dissociation of sensibility"—the segregation of intellect and emotion—as determining the course of English poetry throughout the eighteenth and nineteenth centuries. This theory also explained what he was aiming at in his own poetry: the reestablishment of that *unified* sensibility he found in Donne and other early-seventeenth-century poets and dramatists, who were able, he suggests in "The Meta-physical Poets," to "feel their thought as immediately as the odour of a rose." His view of tradition, his dislike of the poetic exploitation of the author's personality, his advo-cacy of what he called "orthodoxy," made him suspicious of what he considered eccen-tric geniuses such as William Blake and D. H. Lawrence. On the other side, his dislike of the grandiloquent and his insistence on complexity and on the mingling of the formal with the conversational made him distrust Milton's influence on English poetry. He considered himself a "classicist in literature, royalist in politics, and Anglo-Catholic in religion" (*For Lancelot Andrewes,* 1928), in favor of order against chaos, tradition against eccentricity, authority against rampant individualism; yet his own poetry is in many respects untraditional and certainly highly individual in tone. His conservative and even authoritarian habit of mind, his anti-Semitic remarks and missionary zeal, alienated some who admire—and some whose own poetry has been much influenced by—his poetry.

Eliot's plays address, directly or indirectly, religious themes. *Murder in the Cathedral* (1935) deals in an appropriately ritual manner with the killing of Archbishop Thomas à Becket, using a chorus and presenting its central speech as a sermon by the archbishop. *The Family Reunion* (1939) deals with the problem of guilt and redemption in a modern upper-class English family; combining choric devices from Greek tragedy with a poetic idiom subdued to the accents of drawing-room conversation. In his three later plays, all written in the 1950s, *The Cocktail Party, The Confidential Clerk,* and *The Elder Statesman,* he achieved popular success by casting a serious religious theme in the form of a sophisticated modern social comedy, using a verse that is so conversational in movement that when spoken in the theater it does not sound like verse at all.

Critics differ on the degree to which Eliot succeeded in his last plays in combining box-office success with dramatic effectiveness. But there is no disagreement on his importance as one of the great renovators of poetry in English, whose influence on a whole generation of poets, critics, and intellectuals was enormous. His range as a poet is limited, and his interest in the great middle ground of human experience (as distinct from the extremes of saint and sinner) deficient; but when in 1948 he was awarded the rare honor of the Order of Merit by King George VI and also gained the Nobel Prize in literature, his positive qualities were widely and fully recognized—his poetic cunning, his fine craftsmanship, his original accent, his historical importance as *the* poet of the modern symbolist-Metaphysical tradition.

The Love Song of J. Alfred Prufrock[1]

> *S'io credesse che mia risposta fosse*
> *a persona che mai tornasse al mondo,*
> *questa fiamma staria senza più scosse.*
> *Ma per cio cche giammai di questo fondo*
> *non torno vivo alcun, s'i'odo il vero,*
> *senza tema d'infamia ti rispondo.*[2]

Let us go then, you and I,
When the evening is spread out against the sky
Like a patient etherised upon a table;
Let us go, through certain half-deserted streets,
5   The muttering retreats
Of restless nights in one-night cheap hotels
And sawdust restaurants with oyster shells:
Streets that follow like a tedious argument
Of insidious intent

---

1. The title implies an ironic contrast between the romantic suggestions of "love song" and the dully prosaic name "J. Alfred Prufrock."
2. "If I thought that my reply would be to one who would ever return to the world, this flame would stay without further movement; but since none has ever returned alive from this depth, if what I hear

is true, I answer you without fear of infamy" (Dante, *Inferno* 27.61–66). Guido da Montefeltro, shut up in his flame (the punishment given to false counselors), tells the shame of his evil life to Dante because he believes Dante will never return to earth to report it.

To lead you to an overwhelming question . . .
Oh, do not ask, 'What is it?'
Let us go and make our visit.

In the room the women come and go
Talking of Michelangelo.

The yellow fog that rubs its back upon the window-panes,
The yellow smoke that rubs its muzzle on the window-panes
Licked its tongue into the corners of the evening,
Lingered upon the pools that stand in drains,
Let fall upon its back the soot that falls from chimneys,
Slipped by the terrace, made a sudden leap,
And seeing that it was a soft October night,
Curled once about the house, and fell asleep.

And indeed there will be time[3]
For the yellow smoke that slides along the street,
Rubbing its back upon the window-panes;
There will be time, there will be time
To prepare a face to meet the faces that you meet;
There will be time to murder and create,
And time for all the works and days of hands[4]
That lift and drop a question on your plate;
Time for you and time for me,
And time yet for a hundred indecisions,
And for a hundred visions and revisions,
Before the taking of a toast and tea.

In the room the women come and go
Talking of Michelangelo.

And indeed there will be time
To wonder, 'Do I dare?' and, 'Do I dare?'
Time to turn back and descend the stair,
With a bald spot in the middle of my hair—
(They will say: 'How his hair is growing thin!')
My morning coat, my collar mounting firmly to the chin,
My necktie rich and modest, but asserted by a simple pin—
(They will say: 'But how his arms and legs are thin!')
Do I dare
Disturb the universe?
In a minute there is time
For decisions and revisions which a minute will reverse.

For I have known them all already, known them all—
Have known the evenings, mornings, afternoons,
I have measured out my life with coffee spoons;
I know the voices dying with a dying fall[5]

Line numbers in the margin: 10, 15, 20, 25, 30, 35, 40, 45, 50.

---

3. Cf. Andrew Marvell, "To His Coy Mistress,"
line 1: "Had we but world enough, and time."
4. *Works and Days* is a poem about the farming
year by the Greek poet Hesiod (8th century B.C.E.).
Eliot contrasts useful agricultural labor with the
futile "works and days of hands" engaged in meaningless social gesturing.
5. Cf. Shakespeare's *Twelfth Night* 1.1.4: "That
strain again, it had a dying fall."

Beneath the music from a farther room.
   So how should I presume?

55 And I have known the eyes already, known them all—
The eyes that fix you in a formulated phrase,
And when I am formulated, sprawling on a pin,
When I am pinned and wriggling on the wall,
Then how should I begin
60 To spit out all the butt-ends of my days and ways?
   And how should I presume?

And I have known the arms already, known them all—
Arms that are braceleted and white and bare
(But in the lamplight, downed with light brown hair!)
65 Is it perfume from a dress
That makes me so digress?
Arms that lie along a table, or wrap about a shawl.
   And should I then presume?
   And how should I begin?

         . . . . .

70 Shall I say, I have gone at dusk through narrow streets
And watched the smoke that rises from the pipes
Of lonely men in shirt-sleeves, leaning out of windows? . . .
I should have been a pair of ragged claws
Scuttling across the floors of silent seas.[6]

         . . . . .

75 And the afternoon, the evening, sleeps so peacefully!
Smoothed by long fingers,
Asleep . . . tired . . . or it malingers,
Stretched on the floor, here beside you and me.
Should I, after tea and cakes and ices,
80 Have the strength to force the moment to its crisis?
But though I have wept and fasted, wept and prayed,
Though I have seen my head (grown slightly bald) brought in upon a
     platter,[7]
I am no prophet—and here's no great matter;
I have seen the moment of my greatness flicker,
85 And I have seen the eternal Footman hold my coat, and snicker,
And in short, I was afraid.

And would it have been worth it, after all,
After the cups, the marmalade, the tea,
Among the porcelain, among some talk of you and me,
90 Would it have been worth while,
To have bitten off the matter with a smile,
To have squeezed the universe into a ball[8]

---

6. I.e., he would have been better as a crab on the ocean bed. Perhaps, too, the motion of a crab suggests futility and growing old. Cf. Shakespeare's *Hamlet* 2.2.201–02: "for you yourself, sir, should be old as I am—if, like a crab, you could go backward."

7. Like that of John the Baptist. See Mark 6.17–28 and Matthew 14.3–11.
8. Cf. "To His Coy Mistress," lines 41–44: "Let us roll all our strength and all / Our sweetness up into one ball, / And tear our pleasures with rough strife / Thorough the iron gates of life."

To roll it toward some overwhelming question,
To say: 'I am Lazarus,[9] come from the dead,
Come back to tell you all, I shall tell you all'—
If one, settling a pillow by her head,
    Should say: 'That is not what I meant at all.
    That is not it, at all.'

And would it have been worth it, after all,
Would it have been worth while,
After the sunsets and the dooryards and the sprinkled streets,
After the novels, after the teacups, after the skirts that trail along the floor—
And this, and so much more?—
It is impossible to say just what I mean!
But as if a magic lantern threw the nerves in patterns on a screen:
Would it have been worth while
If one, settling a pillow or throwing off a shawl,
And turning toward the window, should say:
    'That is not it at all,
    That is not what I meant, at all.'

      . . . . .

No! I am not Prince Hamlet, nor was meant to be;
Am an attendant lord, one that will do
To swell a progress,[1] start a scene or two,
Advise the prince; no doubt, an easy tool,
Deferential, glad to be of use,
Politic, cautious, and meticulous;
Full of high sentence,[2] but a bit obtuse;
At times, indeed, almost ridiculous—
Almost, at times, the Fool.

I grow old . . . I grow old . . .
I shall wear the bottoms of my trousers rolled.

Shall I part my hair behind? Do I dare to eat a peach?
I shall wear white flannel trousers, and walk upon the beach.
I have heard the mermaids singing, each to each.

I do not think that they will sing to me.

I have seen them riding seaward on the waves
Combing the white hair of the waves blown back
When the wind blows the water white and black.

We have lingered in the chambers of the sea
By sea-girls wreathed with seaweed red and brown
Till human voices wake us, and we drown.

1910–11   1915, 1917

9. Raised by Jesus from the dead (Luke 16.19–31 and John 11.1–44).
1. In the Elizabethan sense of a state journey made by a royal or noble person. Elizabethan plays sometimes showed such "progresses" crossing the stage. Cf. Chaucer's General Prologue to The Canterbury Tales, line 308.
2. In its older meanings: "opinions," "sententiousness."

The Waste Land   In the essay "*Ulysses*, Order, and Myth" (1923), Eliot hinted at the ambitions of *The Waste Land* when he declared that others would follow James Joyce "in manipulating a continuous parallel between contemporaneity and antiquity. . . . It is simply a way of controlling, of ordering, of giving a shape and a significance to the immense panorama of futility and anarchy which is contemporary history. . . . It is, I seriously believe, a step toward making the modern world possible in art." Eliot labeled this new technique "the mythical method."

He gave another clue to the theme and structure of *The Waste Land* in a general note, in which he stated that "not only the title, but the plan and a good deal of the symbolism of the poem were suggested by Miss Jessie L. Weston's book on the Grail legend: *From Ritual to Romance* [1920]." He further acknowledged a general indebtedness to Sir James Frazer's *Golden Bough* (thirteen volumes, 1890–1915), "especially the . . . volumes *Adonis, Attis, Osiris*," in which Frazer deals with ancient vegetation myths and fertility ceremonies. Drawing on material from Frazer and other anthropologists, Weston traces the relationship of these myths and rituals to Christianity and especially to the legend of the Holy Grail. She finds an archetypal fertility myth in the story of the Fisher King, whose death, infirmity, or impotence (there are many forms of the myth) brought drought and desolation to the land and failure of the power to reproduce themselves among both humans and beasts. This symbolic Waste Land can be revived only if a "questing knight" goes to the Chapel Perilous, situated in the heart of it, and there asks certain ritual questions about the Grail (or Cup) and the Lance—originally fertility symbols, female and male, respectively. The proper asking of these questions revives the king and restores fertility to the land. The relation of this original Grail myth to fertility cults and rituals found in many different civilizations, and represented by stories of a god who dies and is later resurrected (e.g., Tammuz, Adonis, Attis), shows their common origin in a response to the cyclical movement of the seasons, with vegetation dying in winter to be resurrected again in the spring. Christianity, according to Weston, gave its own spiritual meaning to the myth; it "did not hesitate to utilize the already existing medium of instruction, but boldly identified the Deity of Vegetation, regarded as Life Principle, with the God of the Christian Faith." The Fisher King is related to the use of the fish symbol in early Christianity. Weston states "with certainty that the Fish is a Life symbol of immemorial antiquity, and that the title of Fisher has, from the earliest ages, been associated with the Deities who were held to be specially connected with the origin and preservation of Life." Eliot, following Weston, thus uses a great variety of mythological and religious material, both Western and Eastern, to paint a symbolic picture of the modern Waste Land and the need for regeneration. He vividly presents the terror of that desiccated life—its loneliness, emptiness, and irrational apprehensions—as well as its misuse of sexuality, but he paradoxically ends the poem with a benediction. The mass death and social collapse of World War I inform the poem's vision of a Waste Land strewn with corpses, wreckage, and ruin. Another significant general source for the poem is the German composer Richard Wagner's operas *Götterdämmerung (Twilight of the Gods), Parsifal, Das Rheingold,* and *Tristan und Isolde.*

The poem as published owes a great deal to the severe pruning of Ezra Pound; the original manuscript, with Pound's excisions and comments, provides fascinating information about the genesis and development of the poem, and was reproduced in facsimile in 1971, edited by Eliot's widow, Valerie Eliot. Reprinted below is the text as first published in book form in December 1922, including Eliot's notes, which are supplemented by the present editors' notes.

The Waste Land

"NAM Sibyllam quidem Cumis ego ipse oculis meis vidi in ampulla
pendere, et cum illi pueri dicerent: Σίβυλλα τί θέλεις; respondebat
illa: ἀποθανεῖν θέλω."[1]

FOR EZRA POUND
il miglior fabbro[2]

I. *The Burial of the Dead*[3]

April is the cruellest month, breeding
Lilacs out of the dead land, mixing
Memory and desire, stirring
Dull roots with spring rain.
5 Winter kept us warm, covering
Earth in forgetful snow, feeding
A little life with dried tubers.
Summer surprised us, coming over the Starnbergersee[4]
With a shower of rain; we stopped in the colonnade,
10 And went on in sunlight, into the Hofgarten,[5]
And drank coffee, and talked for an hour.
Bin gar keine Russin, stamm' aus Litauen, echt deutsch.[6]
And when we were children, staying at the archduke's,
My cousin's, he took me out on a sled,
15 And I was frightened. He said, Marie,
Marie, hold on tight. And down we went.
In the mountains, there you feel free.
I read, much of the night, and go south in the winter.

What are the roots that clutch, what branches grow
20 Out of this stony rubbish? Son of man,[7]
You cannot say, or guess, for you know only
A heap of broken images, where the sun beats,
And the dead tree gives no shelter, the cricket no relief,[8]
And the dry stone no sound of water. Only

1. From the *Satyricon* of Petronius (1st century
C.E.): "For once I myself saw with my own eyes the
Sibyl at Cumae hanging in a cage, and when the
boys said to her 'Sibyl, what do you want?' she
replied, 'I want to die.'" (The Greek may be trans-
literated, "Síbylla tí théleis?" and "apothanéin
thélo.") The Cumaean Sibyl was the most famous
of the Sibyls, the prophetic old women of Greek
mythology; she guided Aeneas through Hades in
Virgil's *Aeneid*. She had been granted immortality
by Apollo, but because she forgot to ask for perpetual youth, she shrank into withered old age and
her authority declined.
2. The better craftsman (Italian); a tribute originally paid to the Provençal poet Arnaut Daniel in
Dante's *Purgatorio* 26.117. Ezra Pound (1885–
1972), American expatriate poet who was a key figure in the modern movement in poetry, helped
Eliot massively revise the manuscript.
3. The title comes from the Anglican burial service.
4. Lake a few miles south of Munich, where the

"mad" King Ludwig II of Bavaria drowned in 1886
in mysterious circumstances. This romantic, melancholy king passionately admired Richard Wagner and especially Wagner's opera *Tristan und
Isolde*, which plays a significant part in *The Waste
Land*. Ludwig's suffering of "death by water" in the
Starnbergersee thus evokes a cluster of themes
central to the poem. Eliot had met King Ludwig's
second cousin Countess Marie Larisch and talked
with her. Although he had probably not read the
countess's book *My Past*, which discusses King
Ludwig at length, he got information about her life
and times from her in person, and the remarks
made in lines 8–18 are hers.
5. A small public park in Munich.
6. I am not Russian at all; I come from Lithuania,
a true German (German).
7. Cf. Ezekiel II, i [Eliot's note]. God, addressing
Ezekiel, continues: "stand upon thy feet, and I will
speak unto thee."
8. Cf. Ecclesiastes XII, v [Eliot's note]. The verse
Eliot cites is part of the preacher's picture of the

25 There is shadow under this red rock,⁹
 (Come in under the shadow of this red rock),
 And I will show you something different from either
 Your shadow at morning striding behind you
 Or your shadow at evening rising to meet you;
30 I will show you fear in a handful of dust.

    Frisch weht der Wind
    Der Heimat zu,
    Mein Irisch Kind,
    *Wo weilest du?*¹

35 "You gave me hyacinths first a year ago;
 "They called me the hyacinth girl."
 —Yet when we came back, late, from the Hyacinth² garden,
 Yours arms full, and your hair wet, I could not
 Speak, and my eyes failed, I was neither
40 Living nor dead, and I knew nothing,
 Looking into the heart of light, the silence.
 *Oed' und leer das Meer.*³

 Madame Sosostris,⁴ famous clairvoyante,
 Had a bad cold, nevertheless
45 Is known to be the wisest woman in Europe,
 With a wicked pack of cards.⁵ Here, said she,
 Is your card, the drowned Phoenician Sailor,⁶
 (Those are pearls that were his eyes. Look!)
 Here is Belladonna,⁷ the Lady of the Rocks,

---

desolation of old age, "when they shall be afraid of that which is high, and fears shall be in the way and the almond tree shall flourish, and the grasshopper shall be a burden, and desire shall fail."
9. Cf. Isaiah 32.2: the "righteous king" "shall be . . . as rivers of water in a dry place, as the shadow of a great rock in a weary land."
1. V. [see] *Tristan und Isolde*, I, verses 5–8 [Eliot's note]. In Wagner's opera a sailor recalls the girl he has left behind: "Fresh blows the wind to the homeland; my Irish child, where are you waiting?"
2. Name of a young man loved and accidentally killed by Apollo in Greek mythology; from his blood sprang the flower named for him, inscribed with "AI," a cry of grief.
3. Id. [Ibid] III, verse 24 [Eliot's note]. In act 3 of *Tristan und Isolde*, Tristan lies dying. He is waiting for Isolde to come to him from Cornwall, but a shepherd, appointed to watch for her sail, can report only, "Waste and empty is the sea." *Oed'* (or *Öd'*) was originally misspelled *Od'*.
4. A mock Egyptian name (suggested to Eliot by "Sesostris, the Sorceress of Ecbatana," the name assumed by a character in Aldous Huxley's novel *Crome Yellow* [1921] who dresses up as a gypsy to tell fortunes at a fair).
5. I.e., the deck of Tarot cards. The four suits of the Tarot pack, discussed by Jessie Weston in *From Ritual to Romance*, are the cup, lance, sword, and dish—the life symbols found in the Grail story. Weston noted that "today the Tarot has fallen somewhat into disrepute, being principally used for purposes of divination." Some of the cards mentioned in lines 46–56 are discussed by Eliot in

his note to this passage: "I am not familiar with the exact constitution of the Tarot pack of cards, from which I have obviously departed to suit my own convenience. The Hanged Man, a member of the traditional pack, fits my purpose in two ways: because he is associated in my mind with the Hanged God of Frazer, and because I associate him with the hooded figure in the passage of the disciples to Emmaus in part V. The Phoenician Sailor and the Merchant appear later; also the 'crowds of people,' and Death by Water is executed in part IV. The Man with Three Staves (an authentic member of the Tarot pack) I associate, quite arbitrarily, with the Fisher King himself."
6. See part 4. Phlebas the Phoenician and Mr. Eugenides, the Smyrna merchant—both of whom appear later in the poem—are different phases of the same symbolic character, here identified as the "Phoenician Sailor." Mr. Eugenides exports "currants" (line 210); the drowned Phlebas floats in the "current" (line 315). Line 48 draws from Ariel's song in Shakespeare's *The Tempest* (1.2.400–08) to the shipwrecked Ferdinand, who was "sitting on a bank / Weeping again the King my father's wrack," when "this music crept by me on the waters." The song is about the supposed drowning of Ferdinand's father, Alonso. *The Waste Land* contains many references to *The Tempest*. Ferdinand is associated with Phlebas and Mr. Eugenides and, therefore, with the "drowned Phoenician Sailor."
7. Beautiful lady (Italian). The word also suggests Madonna (the Virgin Mary) and, therefore, the Madonna of the Rocks (as in Leonardo da Vinci's

50 The lady of situations.
Here is the man with three staves, and here the Wheel,[8]
And here is the one-eyed merchant,[9] and this card,
Which is blank, is something he carries on his back,
Which I am forbidden to see. I do not find
55 The Hanged Man.[1] Fear death by water.
I see crowds of people, walking round in a ring.
Thank you. If you see dear Mrs. Equitone,
Tell her I bring the horoscope myself:
One must be so careful these days.

60 Unreal City,[2]
Under the brown fog of a winter dawn,
A crowd flowed over London Bridge, so many,[3]
I had not thought death had undone so many.
Sighs, short and infrequent, were exhaled,[4]
65 And each man fixed his eyes before his feet.
Flowed up the hill and down King William Street,
To where Saint Mary Woolnoth kept the hours
With a dead sound on the final stroke of nine.[5]
There I saw one I knew, and stopped him, crying: "Stetson![6]
70 "You who were with me in the ships at Mylae![7]
"That corpse you planted last year in your garden,
"Has it begun to sprout?[8] Will it bloom this year?
"Or has the sudden frost disturbed its bed?
"Oh keep the Dog far hence, that's friend to men,
75 "Or with his nails he'll dig it up again![9]
"You! hypocrite lecteur!—mon semblable—mon frère!"[1]

---

painting); the rocks symbolize the Church. Belladonna is also an eye cosmetic and a poison—the deadly nightshade.
8. I.e., the wheel of fortune, whose turning represents the reversals of human life.
9. I.e., Mr. Eugenides, "one-eyed" because the figure is in profile on the card. Unlike the man with three staves and the wheel, which are Tarot cards, he is Eliot's creation.
1. On his card in the Tarot pack he is shown hanging by one foot from a T-shaped cross. He symbolizes the self-sacrifice of the fertility god who is killed so that his resurrection may restore fertility to land and people.
2. Cf. Baudelaire: "Fourmillante cité, cité pleine de rêves, / Où le spectre en plein jour raccroche le passant" [Eliot's note]. The lines are quoted from "Les Sept Vieillards" ("The Seven Old Men") of Les Fleurs du Mal (The Flowers of Evil), by the French poet Charles Baudelaire (1821–1867): "Swarming city, city full of dreams, / Where the specter in broad daylight accosts the passerby." The word rêve was originally misspelled rève.
3. Cf. Inferno III, 55–57 [Eliot's note]. The note goes on to quote Dante's lines, which may be translated: "So long a train of people, / that I should never have believed / That death had undone so many." Dante, just outside the gate of hell, has seen "the wretched souls of those who lived without disgrace and without praise."
4. Cf. Inferno IV, 25–27 [Eliot's note]. In Limbo, the first circle of hell, Dante has found the virtuous heathens, who lived before Christianity and are, therefore, eternally unable to achieve their desire

of seeing God. Dante's lines, cited by Eliot, mean "Here, so far as I could tell by listening, / there was no lamentation except sighs, / which caused the eternal air to tremble."
5. A phenomenon which I have often noticed [Eliot's note]. St. Mary Woolnoth is a church in the City of London (the financial district); the crowd is flowing across London Bridge to work in the City. According to the Bible, Jesus died at the ninth hour.
6. Presumably representing the "average businessman."
7. The battle of Mylae (260 B.C.E.) in the First Punic War, which, in some measure like World War I, was fought for economic reasons.
8. A distortion of the fertility god's ritual death, which heralded rebirth.
9. Cf. the Dirge in Webster's White Devil [Eliot's note]. In the play by John Webster (d. 1625), the dirge, sung by Cornelia, has the lines "But keep the wolf far thence, that's foe to men, / For with his nails he'll dig them up again." Eliot makes the "wolf" into a "dog," which is not a foe but a friend to humans.
1. V. Baudelaire, Preface to Fleurs du Mal [Eliot's note]. The passage is the last line of the introductory poem "Au Lecteur" ("To the Reader"), in Baudelaire's Fleurs du Mal; it may be translated: "Hypocrite reader!—my likeness—my brother!" "Au Lecteur" describes humans as sunk in stupidity, sin, and evil, but the worst in "each man's foul menagerie of sin" is boredom, the "monstre délicat"—"You know him, reader."

2618 / T. S. ELIOT

II. A Game of Chess[2]

The Chair she sat in, like a burnished throne,[3]
Glowed on the marble, where the glass
Held up by standards wrought with fruited vines
80   From which a golden Cupidon peeped out
      (Another hid his eyes behind his wing)
      Doubled the flames of sevenbranched candelabra
      Reflecting light upon the table as
      The glitter of her jewels rose to meet it,
85   From satin cases poured in rich profusion;
      In vials of ivory and coloured glass
      Unstoppered, lurked her strange synthetic perfumes,
      Unguent, powdered, or liquid—troubled, confused
      And drowned the sense in odours; stirred by the air
90   That freshened from the window, these ascended
      In fattening the prolonged candle-flames,
      Flung their smoke into the laquearia,[4]
      Stirring the pattern on the coffered ceiling.
      Huge sea-wood fed with copper
95   Burned green and orange, framed by the coloured stone,
      In which sad light a carvèd dolphin swam.
      Above the antique mantel was displayed
      As though a window gave upon the sylvan scene[5]
      The change of Philomel,[6] by the barbarous king
100   So rudely forced; yet there the nightingale
      Filled all the desert with inviolable voice
      And still she cried, and still the world pursues,
      "Jug Jug"[7] to dirty ears.
      And other withered stumps of time
105   Were told upon the walls; staring forms
      Leaned out, leaning, hushing the room enclosed.
      Footsteps shuffled on the stair.
      Under the firelight, under the brush, her hair
      Spread out in fiery points
110   Glowed into words, then would be savagely still.

      "My nerves are bad tonight. Yes, bad. Stay with me.
      "Speak to me. Why do you never speak. Speak.

2. The title suggests two plays by Thomas Middleton (1580–1627): A Game at Chess and, more significant, Women Beware Women, which has a scene in which a mother-in-law is distracted by a game of chess while her daughter-in-law is seduced: every move in the chess game represents a move in the seduction.
3. Cf. Antony and Cleopatra, II, ii, l. 190 [Eliot's note]. In Shakespeare's play, Enobarbus's famous description of the first meeting of Antony and Cleopatra begins, "The barge she sat in, like a burnish'd throne, / Burn'd on the water." Eliot's language in the opening lines of part 2 echoes ironically Enobarbus's speech.
4. Laquearia. V. Aeneid, I, 726 [Eliot's note]. Laquearia means "a paneled ceiling," and Eliot's note quotes the passage in the Aeneid that was his

source for the word. The passage may be translated: "Blazing torches hang from the gold-paneled ceiling [laquearibus aureis], and torches conquer the night with flames." Virgil is describing the banquet given by Dido, queen of Carthage, for Aeneas, with whom she fell in love.
5. Sylvan scene. V. Milton, Paradise Lost, IV, 140 [Eliot's note]. The phrase is part of the first description of Eden, seen through Satan's eyes.
6. V. Ovid, Metamorphoses, VI, Philomela [Eliot's note]. Philomela was raped by "the barbarous king" Tereus, husband of her sister, Procne. Philomela was then transformed into a nightingale. Eliot's note for line 100 refers ahead to his elaboration of the nightingale's song.
7. Conventional representation of nightingale's song in Elizabethan poetry.

"What are you thinking of? What thinking? What?"
"I never know what you are thinking. Think."

115 I think we are in rats' alley[8]
Where the dead men lost their bones.

"What is that noise?"
                    The wind under the door.[9]
"What is that noise now? What is the wind doing?"
120   Nothing again nothing.
                                        "Do
"You know nothing? Do you see nothing? Do you remember
"Nothing?"

                    I remember
125 Those are pearls that were his eyes.[1]
"Are you alive, or not? Is there nothing in your head?"
                                                    But
O O O O that Shakespeherian Rag[2]—
It's so elegant
130 So intelligent

"What shall I do now? What shall I do?"
"I shall rush out as I am, and walk the street
"With my hair down, so. What shall we do tomorrow?
"What shall we ever do?"
135   The hot water at ten.
And if it rains, a closed car at four.
And we shall play a game of chess,[3]
Pressing lidless eyes and waiting for a knock upon the door.

When Lil's husband got demobbed,[4] I said—
140 I didn't mince my words, I said to her myself,
HURRY UP PLEASE ITS TIME[5]
Now Albert's coming back, make yourself a bit smart.
He'll want to know what you done with that money he gave you
To get yourself some teeth. He did, I was there.
145 You have them all out, Lil, and get a nice set,
He said, I swear, I can't bear to look at you.
And no more can't I, I said, and think of poor Albert,
He's been in the army four years, he wants a good time,
And if you dont give it him, there's others will, I said.
150 Oh is there, she said. Something o' that, I said.
Then I'll know who to thank, she said, and give me a straight look.
HURRY UP PLEASE ITS TIME

8. Cf. Part III, l. 195 [Eliot's note].
9. Cf. Webster: "Is the wind in that door still?" [Eliot's note]. In John Webster's *The Devil's Law Case* (3.2.162), a physician asks this question on finding that the victim of a murderous attack is still breathing, meaning "Is he still alive?"
1. Cf. Part I, l. 37, 48 [Eliot's note].
2. American ragtime song, which was a hit of Ziegfeld's Follies in 1912. The chorus is "That Shakespherean Rag, most intelligent, very elegant."
3. Cf. the game of chess in Middleton's *Women Beware Women* [Eliot's note]. The significance of this chess game is discussed in the first note to part 2.
4. British slang for "demobilized" (discharged from the army after World War I).
5. The traditional call of the British bartender at closing time.

If you dont like it you can get on with it, I said,
Others can pick and choose if you can't.
155 But if Albert makes off, it wont be for lack of telling.
You ought to be ashamed, I said, to look so antique.
(And her only thirty-one.)
I can't help it, she said, pulling a long face,
It's them pills I took, to bring it off, she said.
160 (She's had five already, and nearly died of young George.)
The chemist[6] said it would be alright, but I've never been the same.
You *are* a proper fool, I said.
Well, if Albert wont leave you alone, there it is, I said,
What you get married for if you dont want children?
165 HURRY UP PLEASE ITS TIME
Well, that Sunday Albert was home, they had a hot gammon,°   *ham, bacon*
And they asked me in to dinner, to get the beauty of it hot—
HURRY UP PLEASE ITS TIME
HURRY UP PLEASE ITS TIME
170 Goonight Bill. Goonight Lou. Goonight May. Goonight.
Ta ta. Goonight. Goonight.
Good night, ladies, good night, sweet ladies, good night, good night.[7]

III. *The Fire Sermon*[8]

The river's tent is broken: the last fingers of leaf
Clutch and sink into the wet bank. The wind
175 Crosses the brown land, unheard. The nymphs are departed.
Sweet Thames, run softly, till I end my song.[9]
The river bears no empty bottles, sandwich papers,
Silk handkerchiefs, cardboard boxes, cigarette ends
Or other testimony of summer nights. The nymphs are departed.
180 And their friends, the loitering heirs of city directors;
Departed, have left no addresses.
By the waters of Leman I sat down and wept[1] . . .
Sweet Thames, run softly till I end my song,
Sweet Thames, run softly, for I speak not loud or long.
185 But at my back in a cold blast I hear[2]
The rattle of the bones, and chuckle spread from ear to ear.

A rat crept softly through the vegetation
Dragging its slimy belly on the bank
While I was fishing in the dull canal
190 On a winter evening round behind the gashouse

6. Pharmacist. "To bring it off": to cause an abortion.
7. Cf. the mad Ophelia's departing words (Shakespeare, *Hamlet* 4.5.69–70). Ophelia, too, met "death by water." Cf. also the popular song lyric "Good night ladies, we're going to leave you now."
8. The Buddha preached the Fire Sermon, against the fires of lust and other passions that destroy people and prevent their regeneration.
9. V. Spenser, *Prothalamion* [Eliot's note]. Eliot's line is the refrain from Edmund Spenser's marriage song, which is also set by the river Thames in London.
1. Cf. Psalms 137.1, in which the exiled Hebrews mourn for their homeland: "By the rivers of Babylon, there we sat down, yea, we wept, when we remembered Zion." Lake Leman is another name for Lake Geneva, in Switzerland; Eliot wrote *The Waste Land* in Lausanne, by that lake. The noun *leman* is an archaic word meaning lover.
2. An ironic distortion of Andrew Marvell's "To His Coy Mistress," lines 21–22: "But at my back I always hear / Time's wingèd chariot hurrying near." Cf. lines 196–97.

Musing upon the king my brother's wreck
And on the king my father's death before him.[3]
White bodies naked on the low damp ground
And bones cast in a little low dry garret,
195 Rattled by the rat's foot only, year to year.
But at my back from time to time I hear
The sound of horns and motors,[4] which shall bring
Sweeney to Mrs. Porter in the spring.[5]
O the moon shone bright on Mrs. Porter
200 And on her daughter
They wash their feet in soda water[6]
Et O ces voix d'enfants, chantant dans la coupole![7]

Twit twit twit
Jug jug jug jug jug jug
205 So rudely forc'd.
Tereu[8]

Unreal City
Under the brown fog of a winter noon
Mr. Eugenides, the Smyrna[9] merchant
210 Unshaven, with a pocket full of currants
C.i.f.[1] London: documents at sight,
Asked me in demotic° French   *colloquial*
To luncheon at the Cannon Street Hotel
Followed by a weekend at the Metropole.[2]

215 At the violet hour, when the eyes and back
Turn upward from the desk, when the human engine waits
Like a taxi throbbing waiting,
I Tiresias,[3] though blind, throbbing between two lives,

3. Cf. *The Tempest*, I, ii [Eliot's note]. See line 48.
4. Cf. Marvell, *To His Coy Mistress* [Eliot's note].
5. Cf. Day, *Parliament of Bees*: "When of the sudden, listening, you shall hear, / A noise of horns and hunting, which shall bring / Actaeon to Diana in the spring, / Where all shall see her naked skin" [Eliot's note]. Actaeon was changed to a stag and hunted to death after he saw Diana, the goddess of chastity, bathing with her nymphs. John Day (1574–ca. 1640), English poet.
6. I do not know the origin of the ballad from which these lines are taken; it was reported to me from Sydney, Australia [Eliot's note]. One of the less bawdy versions of the song, which was popular among Australian troops in World War I, went as follows: "O the moon shines bright on Mrs. Porter / And on the daughter / Of Mrs. Porter. / They wash their feet in soda water / And so they oughter / To keep them clean."
7. V. Verlaine, *Parsifal* [Eliot's note]: "And O those children's voices singing in the dome!" The sonnet by the French poet Paul Verlaine (1844–1896) describes Parsifal, the questing knight, resisting all sensual temptations to keep himself pure for the Grail and heal the Fisher King; Wagner's Parsifal had his feet washed before entering the castle of the Grail.
8. A reference to Tereus, who "rudely forc'd" Phil-

omela; it was also one of the conventional words for a nightingale's song in Elizabethan poetry. Cf. the song from John Lyly's *Alexander and Campaspe* (1564): "Oh, 'tis the ravished nightingale. / *Jug, jug, jug, jug, tereu!* she cries." Cf. also lines 100ff.
9. Now Izmir, a seaport in western Turkey; here associated with Carthage and the ancient Phoenician and Syrian merchants, who spread the old mystery cults.
1. The currants were quoted at a price "carriage and insurance free to London"; and the Bill of Lading etc. were to be handed to the buyer upon payment of the sight draft [Eliot's note]. Another gloss of C.i.f. is "cost, insurance and freight."
2. Luxury hotel in the seaside resort of Brighton. Cannon Street Hotel, near the station that was then chief terminus for travelers to the Continent, was a favorite meeting place for businesspeople going or coming from abroad; it was also a locale for homosexual liaisons.
3. Tiresias, although a mere spectator and not indeed a "character," is yet the most important personage in the poem, uniting all the rest. Just as the one-eyed merchant, seller of currants, melts into the Phoenician Sailor, and the latter is not wholly distinct from Ferdinand Prince of Naples, so all the women are one woman, and the two sexes meet in Tiresias. What Tiresias *sees*, in fact, is the sub-

Old man with wrinkled female breasts, can see
220   At the violet hour, the evening hour that strives
Homeward, and brings the sailor home from sea,[4]
The typist home at teatime, clears her breakfast, lights
Her stove, and lays out food in tins.
Out of the window perilously spread
225   Her drying combinations° touched by the sun's last rays,   *undergarments*
On the divan are piled (at night her bed)
Stockings, slippers, camisoles, and stays.°   *corset*
I Tiresias, old man with wrinkled dugs
Perceived the scene, and foretold the rest—
230   I too awaited the expected guest.
He, the young man carbuncular,° arrives,   *pimply*
A small house agent's clerk, with one bold stare,
One of the low on whom assurance sits
As a silk hat on a Bradford[5] millionaire.
235   The time is now propitious, as he guesses,
The meal is ended, she is bored and tired,
Endeavours to engage her in caresses
Which still are unreproved, if undesired.
Flushed and decided, he assaults at once;
240   Exploring hands encounter no defence;
His vanity requires no response,
And makes a welcome of indifference.
(And I Tiresias have foresuffered all
Enacted on this same divan or bed;
245   I who have sat by Thebes[6] below the wall
And walked among the lowest of the dead.)
Bestows one final patronising kiss,
And gropes his way, finding the stairs unlit . . .

She turns and looks a moment in the glass,
250   Hardly aware of her departed lover;
Her brain allows one half-formed thought to pass:
"Well now that's done: and I'm glad it's over."

---

stance of the poem. The whole passage from Ovid is of great anthropological interest [Eliot's note]. The note then quotes, from the Latin text of Ovid's *Metamorphoses,* the story of Tiresias's change of sex: "[The story goes that once Jove, having drunk a great deal,] jested with Juno. He said, 'Your pleasure in love is really greater than that enjoyed by men.' She denied it; so they decided to seek the opinion of the wise Tiresias, for he knew both aspects of love. For once, with a blow of his staff, he had committed violence on two huge snakes as they copulated in the green forest; and—wonderful to tell—was turned from a man into a woman and thus spent seven years. In the eighth year he saw the same snakes again and said: 'If a blow struck at you is so powerful that it changes the sex of the giver, I will now strike at you again.' With these words she struck the snakes, and again became a man. So he was appointed arbitrator in the playful quarrel, and supported Jove's statement. It is said that Saturnia [i.e., Juno] was quite disproportionately upset, and condemned the arbitrator to perpetual blindness. But the almighty

father (for no god may undo what has been done by another god), in return for the sight that was taken away, gave him the power to know the future and so lightened the penalty paid by the honor."
4. This may not appear as exact as Sappho's lines, but I had in mind the "longshore" or "dory" fisherman, who returns at nightfall [Eliot's note]. Sappho's poem addressed Hesperus, the evening star, as the star that brings everyone home from work to evening rest; her poem is here distorted by Eliot. There is also an echo of the 19th-century Scottish writer Robert Louis Stevenson's "Requiem," line 221: "Home is the sailor, home from sea."
5. Either the Yorkshire woolen manufacturing town, where many fortunes were made in World War I, or the pioneer oil town of Bradford, Pennsylvania, the home of one of Eliot's wealthy Harvard contemporaries, T. E. Hanley.
6. For many generations, Tiresias lived in Thebes, where he witnessed the tragic fates of Oedipus and Creon; he prophesied in the marketplace by the wall of Thebes.

When lovely woman stoops to folly and
Paces about her room again, alone,
255 She smoothes her hair with automatic hand,
And puts a record on the gramophone.[7]

"This music crept by me upon the waters"[8]
And along the Strand, up Queen Victoria Street.
O City, City, I can sometimes hear
260 Beside a public bar in Lower Thames Street,
The pleasant whining of a mandoline
And a clatter and a chatter from within
Where fishmen lounge at noon: where the walls
Of Magnus Martyr hold
265 Inexplicable splendour of Ionian white and gold.[9]

The river sweats[1]
Oil and tar
The barges drift
With the turning tide
270 Red sails
Wide
To leeward, swing on the heavy spar.
The barges wash
Drifting logs
275 Down Greenwich reach
Past the Isle of Dogs.[2]
          Weialala leia
          Wallala leialala

Elizabeth and Leicester[3]
280 Beating oars
The stern was formed
A gilded shell
Red and gold

7. V. Goldsmith, the song in *The Vicar of Wakefield* [Eliot's note]. Olivia, a character in Oliver Goldsmith's 1766 novel, sings the following song when she returns to the place where she was seduced: "When lovely woman stoops to folly / And finds too late that men betray / What charm can soothe her melancholy, / What art can wash her guilt away? / The only art her guilt to cover, / To hide her shame from every eye, / To give repentance to her lover / And wring his bosom—is to die."
8. V. *The Tempest*, as above [Eliot's note]. Cf. line 48. The line is from Ferdinand's speech, continuing after "weeping again the King my father's wrack."
9. The interior of St. Magnus Martyr is to my mind one of the finest among [Sir Christopher] Wren's interiors. See *The Proposed Demolition of Nineteen City Churches*: (P. S. King & Son, Ltd.) [Eliot's note]. In these lines the "pleasant" music, the "fishmen" resting after labor, and the splendor of the church interior suggest a world of true values, where work and relaxation are both real and take place in a context of religious meaning.
1. The Song of the (three) Thames-daughters

begins here. From line 292 to 306 inclusive they speak in turn. V. *Götterdämmerung*, III, i: the Rhinedaughters [Eliot's note]. Eliot parallels the Thames-daughters with the Rhinemaidens in Wagner's opera *Götterdämmerung* (*The Twilight of the Gods*), who lament that, with the gold of the Rhine stolen, the beauty of the river is gone. The refrain in lines 277–78 is borrowed from Wagner.
2. Greenwich is a borough in London on the south side of the Thames; opposite is the Isle of Dogs (a peninsula).
3. The fruitless love of Queen Elizabeth and the earl of Leicester (Robert Dudley) is recalled in Eliot's note: "V. [J. A.] Froude, *Elizabeth*, Vol. I, ch. iv, letter of De Quadra to Philip of Spain: 'In the afternoon we were in a barge, watching the games on the river. (The queen) was alone with Lord Robert and myself on the poop, when they began to talk nonsense, and went so far that Lord Robert at last said, as I was on the spot there was no reason why they should not be married if the queen pleased.'" Queen Elizabeth I was born in the old Greenwich House, by the river, where Greenwich Hospital now stands.

The brisk swell
285　Rippled both shores
Southwest wind
Carried down stream
The peal of bells
White towers
290　　　　　Weialala leia
　　　　　Wallala leialala

"Trams and dusty trees.
Highbury bore me. Richmond and Kew
Undid me.[4] By Richmond I raised my knees
295　Supine on the floor of a narrow canoe."

"My feet are at Moorgate,[5] and my heart
Under my feet. After the event
He wept. He promised 'a new start.'
I made no comment. What should I resent?"

300　"On Margate[6] Sands.
I can connect
Nothing with nothing.
The broken fingernails of dirty hands.
My people humble people who expect
305　Nothing."
　　　　　la la

To Carthage then I came[7]

Burning burning burning burning[8]
O Lord Thou pluckest me out[9]
310　O Lord Thou pluckest

burning

IV. *Death by Water*[1]

Phlebas the Phoenician, a fortnight dead,
Forgot the cry of gulls, and the deep sea swell

4. Cf. *Purgatorio*, V, 133 [Eliot's note]. The *Purgatorio* lines, which Eliot here parodies, may be translated: "Remember me, who am La Pia. / Siena made me, Maremma undid me." "Highbury": a residential London suburb. "Richmond": a pleasant part of London westward up the Thames, with boating and riverside hotels. "Kew": adjoining Richmond, has the famous Kew Gardens.
5. Underground (i.e., subway) station Eliot used daily while working at Lloyds Bank.
6. Popular seaside resort on the Thames estuary.
7. V. St. Augustine's *Confessions*: "to Carthage then I came, where a caldron of unholy loves sang all about mine ears" [Eliot's note]. The passage from the *Confessions* quoted here occurs in St. Augustine's account of his youthful life of lust. Cf. line 92 and its note.
8. The complete text of the Buddha's Fire Sermon (which corresponds in importance to the Sermon on the Mount) from which these words are taken, will be found translated in the late Henry Clarke

Warren's *Buddhism in Translation* (Harvard Oriental Series). Mr. Warren was one of the great pioneers of Buddhist studies in the occident [Eliot's note]. In the sermon, the Buddha instructs his priests that all things "are on fire. . . . The eye . . . is on fire; forms are on fire; eye-consciousness is on fire; impressions received by the eye are on fire; and whatever sensation, pleasant, unpleasant, or indifferent, originates in dependence on impressions received by the eye, that also is on fire. And with what are these on fire? With the fire of passion, say I, with the fire of hatred, with the fire of infatuation." For Jesus' Sermon on the Mount, see Matthew 5–7.
9. From St. Augustine's *Confessions* again. The collocation of these two representatives of eastern and western asceticism, as the culmination of this part of the poem, is not an accident [Eliot's note].
1. This section has been interpreted as signifying death by water without resurrection or as symbolizing the sacrificial death that precedes rebirth.

And the profit and loss.

5   A current under sea
Picked his bones in whispers. As he rose and fell
He passed the stages of his age and youth
Entering the whirlpool.

                 Gentile or Jew
0 O you who turn the wheel and look to windward,
Consider Phlebas, who was once handsome and tall as you.

V. What the Thunder Said[2]

After the torchlight red on sweaty faces
After the frosty silence in the gardens
After the agony in stony places
25 The shouting and the crying
Prison and palace and reverberation
Of thunder of spring over distant mountains
He who was living is now dead[3]
We who were living are now dying
30 With a little patience

Here is no water but only rock
Rock and no water and the sandy road
The road winding above among the mountains
Which are mountains of rock without water
35 If there were water we should stop and drink
Amongst the rock one cannot stop or think
Sweat is dry and feet are in the sand
If there were only water amongst the rock
Dead mountain mouth of carious° teeth that cannot spit   *decayed*
40 Here one can neither stand nor lie nor sit
There is not even silence in the mountains
But dry sterile thunder without rain
There is not even solitude in the mountains
But red sullen faces sneer and snarl
45 From doors of mudcracked houses
                 If there were water
   And no rock
   If there were rock
   And also water
50 And water
   A spring
   A pool among the rock
   If there were the sound of water only
   Not the cicada[4]
55 And dry grass singing

---

2. In the first part of Part V three themes are employed: the journey to Emmaus, the approach to the Chapel Perilous (see Miss Weston's book), and the present decay of eastern Europe [Eliot's note]. On the journey to Emmaus, the resurrected Jesus walks alongside and converses with two disciples, who think he is a stranger until he reveals his identity (Luke 24.13–14).

3. These lines allude to Jesus' agony in the Garden of Gethsemane, his trial, and his crucifixion.

4. Cf. Ecclesiastes' prophecy "the grasshopper shall be a burden, and desire shall fail." Cf. also line 23 and its note.

But sound of water over a rock
Where the hermit-thrush[5] sings in the pine trees
Drip drop drip drop drop drop drop
But there is no water

360 Who is the third who walks always beside you?[6]
When I count, there are only you and I together
But when I look ahead up the white road
There is always another one walking beside you
Gliding wrapt in a brown mantle, hooded
365 I do not know whether a man or a woman
—But who is that on the other side of you?

What is that sound high in the air[7]
Murmur of maternal lamentation
Who are those hooded hordes swarming
370 Over endless plains, stumbling in cracked earth
Ringed by the flat horizon only
What is the city over the mountains
Cracks and reforms and bursts in the violet air
Falling towers
375 Jerusalem Athens Alexandria
Vienna London
Unreal

A woman drew her long black hair out tight
And fiddled whisper music on those strings
380 And bats with baby faces in the violet light
Whistled, and beat their wings
And crawled head downward down a blackened wall
And upside down in air were towers
Tolling reminiscent bells, that kept the hours
385 And voices singing out of empty cisterns and exhausted wells.

In this decayed hole among the mountains
In the faint moonlight, the grass is singing
Over the tumbled graves, about the chapel
There is the empty chapel, only the wind's home.[8]
390 It has no windows, and the door swings,
Dry bones can harm no one.

5. This is *Turdus aonalaschkae pallasii*, the hermit-thrush which I have heard in Quebec County. Chapman says (*Handbook of Birds of Eastern North America*) "it is most at home in secluded woodland and thickety retreats. . . . Its notes are not remarkable for variety or volume, but in purity and sweetness of tone and exquisite modulation they are unequaled." Its "water-dripping song" is justly celebrated [Eliot's note].
6. The following lines were stimulated by the account of one of the Antarctic expeditions (I forget which, but I think one of Shackleton's): it was related that the party of explorers, at the extremity of their strength, had the constant delusion that there was *one more member* than could actually be counted [Eliot's note]. This reminiscence is associated with Jesus' unrecognized presence on the way to Emmaus.
7. Eliot's note for lines 367–77 is: "Cf. Herman Hesse, *Blick ins Chaos* ["A Glimpse into Chaos"]." The note then quotes a passage from the German text, which is translated: "Already half of Europe, already at least half of Eastern Europe, on the way to Chaos, drives drunk in sacred infatuation along the edge of the precipice, sings drunkenly, as though hymn singing, as Dmitri Karamazov [in Dostoyevsky's *Brothers Karamazov*] sang. The offended bourgeois laughs at the songs; the saint and the seer hear them with tears."
8. Suggesting the moment of near despair before the Chapel Perilous, when the questing knight sees nothing there but decay. This illusion of nothingness is the knight's final test.

Only a cock stood on the rooftree
Co co   rico   co co   rico[9]
In a flash of lightning. Then a damp gust
395 Bringing rain

Ganga[1] was sunken, and the limp leaves
Waited for rain, while the black clouds
Gathered far distant, over Himavant.[2]
The jungle crouched, humped in silence.
400 Then spoke the thunder
DA[3]
Datta: what have we given?
My friend, blood shaking my heart
The awful daring of a moment's surrender
405 Which an age of prudence can never retract
By this, and this only, we have existed
Which is not to be found in our obituaries
Or in memories draped by the beneficent spider[4]
Or under seals broken by the lean solicitor°   lawyer
410 In our empty rooms
DA
Dayadhvam: I have heard the key[5]
Turn in the door once and turn once only
We think of the key, each in his prison
415 Thinking of the key, each confirms a prison
Only at nightfall, æthereal rumours
Revive for a moment a broken Coriolanus[6]
DA
Damyata: The boat responded
420 Gaily, to the hand expert with sail and oar
The sea was calm, your heart would have responded
Gaily, when invited, beating obedient
To controlling hands

9. The crowing of the cock signals the departure of ghosts and evil spirits. Cf. *Hamlet* 1.1.157ff. In Matthew 26.34 and 74 the cock crows after Peter betrays Jesus three times.
1. Sanskrit name for the major sacred river in India.
2. I.e., snowy mountain (Sanskrit); usually applied to the Himalayas.
3. Datta, dayadhvam, damyata (Give, sympathize, control). The fable of the meaning of the Thunder is found in the *Brihadaranyaka—Upanishad*, 5, 1. A translation is found in Deussen's *Sechzig Upanishads des Veda*, p. 489 [Eliot's note]. In the Old Indian fable The Three Great Disciplines, the Creator God Prajapati utters the enigmatic syllable DA to three groups. Lesser gods, naturally unruly, interpret it as "Control yourselves" (*Damyata*); humans, naturally greedy, as "Give" (*Datta*); demons, naturally cruel, as "Be compassionate" (*Dayadhvam*); "That very thing is repeated even today by the heavenly voice, in the form of thunder as 'DA' 'DA' 'DA,' which means 'Control yourselves,' 'Give,' and 'Have compassion.' Therefore one should practice these three things: self-control, giving, and mercy." The Upanishads are ancient philosophical dialogues in Sanskrit. They

are primary texts for an early form of Hinduism sometimes called Brahminism.
4. Cf. Webster, *The White Devil*, V, vi: ". . . they'll remarry / Ere the worm pierce your winding-sheet, ere the spider / Make a thin curtain for your epitaphs" [Eliot's note].
5. Cf. *Inferno*, XXXIII, 46 [Eliot's note]. In this passage from the *Inferno* Ugolino recalls his imprisonment in the tower with his children, where they starved to death: "And I heard below the door of the horrible tower being nailed shut." Eliot's note for this line goes on to quote F. H. Bradley, *Appearance and Reality*, p. 346: " 'My external sensations are no less private to myself than are my thoughts or my feelings. In either case my experience falls within my own circle, a circle closed on the outside; and, with all its elements alike, every sphere is opaque to the others which surround it. . . . In brief, regarded as an existence which appears in a soul, the whole world for each is peculiar and private to that soul.' " Eliot wrote his doctoral thesis on Bradley's philosophy.
6. Coriolanus, who acted out of pride rather than duty, exemplifies a man locked in the prison of himself. He led the enemy against his native city out of injured pride (cf. Shakespeare's *Coriolanus*).

2628 / T. S. Eliot

I sat upon the shore
Fishing,[7] with the arid plain behind me
Shall I at least set my lands in order?[8]

London Bridge is falling down falling down falling down[9]
Poi s'ascose nel foco che gli affina[1]
Quando fiam uti chelidon[2]—O swallow swallow[3]
430 *Le Prince d'Aquitaine à la tour abolie*[4]
These fragments I have shored against my ruins
Why then Ile fit you. Hieronymo's mad againe.[5]
Datta. Dayadhvam. Damyata.

Shantih   shantih   shantih[6]

1921   1922

The Hollow Men

Mistah Kurtz—he dead.[1]
A penny for the Old Guy[2]

I

We are the hollow men
We are the stuffed men
Leaning together
Headpiece filled with straw. Alas!
5 Our dried voices, when
We whisper together
Are quiet and meaningless

7. V. Weston: *From Ritual to Romance*; chapter on the Fisher King [Eliot's note].
8. Cf. Isaiah 38.1: "Thus saith the Lord, Set thine house in order, for thou shalt die, and not live."
9. One of the later lines of this nursery rhyme is "Take the key and lock her up, my fair lady."
1. V. *Purgatorio*, XXVI, 148 [Eliot's note]. The note goes on to quote lines 145–148 of the *Purgatorio*, in which the Provençal poet Arnaut Daniel addresses Dante: " 'Now I pray you, by that virtue which guides you to the summit of the stairway, be mindful in due time of my pain.' " Then (in the line Eliot quotes here) "he hid himself in the fire which refines them."
2. V. *Pervigilium Veneris*. Cf. Philomela in parts II and III [Eliot's note]. The Latin phrase in the text, originally misquoting *uti* as *ceu*, means, "When shall I be as the swallow?" It comes from the late Latin poem "*Pervigilium Veneris*" ("Vigil of Venus"), "When will my spring come? When shall I be as the swallow that I may cease to be silent? I have lost the Muse in silence, and Apollo regards me not."
3. Cf. A. C. Swinburne's "Itylus," which begins, "Swallow, my sister, O sister swallow, / How can thine heart be full of spring?" and Tennyson's lyric in *The Princess*: "O Swallow, Swallow, flying, flying south."

4. V. Gerard de Nerval, Sonnet *El Desdichado* [Eliot's note]. The French line may be translated: "The Prince of Aquitaine in the ruined tower." One of the cards in the Tarot pack is "the tower struck by lightning."
5. V. Kyd's *Spanish Tragedy* [Eliot's note]. Subtitled *Hieronymo's Mad Againe*, Kyd's play (1594) is an early example of the Elizabethan tragedy of revenge. Hieronymo, driven mad by the murder of his son, has his revenge when he is asked to write a court entertainment. He replies, "Why then Ile fit you!" (i.e., accommodate you), and assigns the parts in the entertainment so that, in the course of the action, his son's murderers are killed.
6. Shantih. Repeated as here, a formal ending to an Upanishad. "The Peace which passeth understanding" is a feeble translation of the content of this word [Eliot's note]. On the Upanishads see the note to line 401 above.
1. From Joseph Conrad's *Heart of Darkness* (see p. 2380).
2. Every year on Nov. 5, British children build bonfires, on which they burn a scarecrow effigy of the traitor Guido [Guy] Fawkes, who in 1605 attempted to blow up the Parliament buildings. For some days before this, they ask people in the streets for pennies with which to buy fireworks.

As wind in dry glass
Or rats' feet over broken glass
10   In our dry cellar[3]

Shape without form, shade without colour,
Paralysed force, gesture without motion;

Those who have crossed
With direct eyes, to death's other Kingdom
15   Remember us—if at all—not as lost
Violent souls, but only
As the hollow men
The stuffed men.

II

Eyes I dare not meet in dreams
20   In death's dream kingdom[4]
These do not appear:
There, the eyes are
Sunlight on a broken column
There, is a tree swinging
25   And voices are
In the wind's singing
More distant and more solemn
Than a fading star.

Let me be no nearer
30   In death's dream kingdom
Let me also wear
Such deliberate disguises
Rat's coat, crowskin, crossed staves
In a field[5]
35   Behaving as the wind behaves
No nearer—

Not that final meeting
In the twilight kingdom[6]

III

This is the dead land
40   This is cactus land
Here the stone images[7]
Are raised, here they receive

---

3. Cf. *The Waste Land*, lines 115 and 195.
4. At the end of Dante's *Purgatorio* and in *Paradiso* 4, he cannot meet the gaze of Beatrice (see Eliot's 1929 essay "Dante").
5. The traditional British scarecrow is made from two sticks tied in the form of a cross (the vertical one stuck in the ground), dressed in cast-off

clothes, and sometimes draped with dead vermin.
6. Perhaps a reference to Dante's meeting with Beatrice after he has crossed the river Lethe. There reminded of his sins, he is allowed to proceed to Paradise (*Purgatorio* 30).
7. Cf. *The Waste Land*, line 22.

2630   /   T. S. ELIOT

The supplication of a dead man's hand
Under the twinkle of a fading star.

45   Is it like this
In death's other kingdom
Waking alone
At the hour when we are
Trembling with tenderness
50   Lips that would kiss
Form prayers to broken stone.

IV

The eyes are not here
There are no eyes here
In this valley of dying stars
55   In this hollow valley
This broken jaw of our lost kingdoms

In this last of meeting places
We grope together
And avoid speech
60   Gathered on this beach of the tumid river[8]

Sightless, unless
The eyes reappear
As the perpetual star
Multifoliate rose[9]
65   Of death's twilight kingdom
The hope only
Of empty men.

V

Here we go round the prickly pear
Prickly pear prickly pear
70   *Here we go round the prickly pear*
At five o'clock in the morning.[1]

Between the idea
And the reality
Between the motion
75   And the act[2]
Falls the Shadow[3]

For Thine is the Kingdom[4]

8. Dante's Acheron, which encircles hell, and the Congo of Conrad's *Heart of Darkness*.
9. The image of heaven in Dante's *Paradiso* 32.
1. Parodic version of the children's rhyme ending "Here we go round the mulberry bush / On a cold and frosty morning."
2. Cf. Shakespeare's *Julius Caesar* 2.1.63–5: "Between the acting of a dreadful thing / And the

first motion, all the interim is / Like a phantasma or a hideous dream."
3. Cf. Ernest Dowson's "*Non sum qualis eram bonae sub regno Cynarae*," lines 1–2: "Last night, ah, yesternight, betwixt her lips and mine / There fell thy shadow, Cynara!"
4. Cf. The Lord's Prayer.

Between the conception
And the creation
80   Between the emotion
And the response
Falls the Shadow
                    Life is very long

Between the desire
85   And the spasm
Between the potency
And the existence
Between the essence
And the descent
90   Falls the Shadow
                    For Thine is the Kingdom

For Thine is
Life is
For Thine is the

95   *This is the way the world ends*
This is the way the world ends
This is the way the world ends
Not with a bang but a whimper.

1924–25   1925

Journey of the Magi[1]

'A cold coming we had of it,
Just the worst time of the year
For a journey, and such a long journey:
The ways deep and the weather sharp,
5   The very dead of winter.'[2]
And the camels galled, sore-footed, refractory,
Lying down in the melting snow.
There were times we regretted
The summer palaces on slopes, the terraces,
10   And the silken girls bringing sherbet.
Then the camel men cursing and grumbling
And running away, and wanting their liquor and women,
And the night-fires going out, and the lack of shelters,
And the cities hostile and the towns unfriendly
15   And the villages dirty and charging high prices:
A hard time we had of it.

1. One of the wise men who came from the east to Jerusalem to do homage to the infant Jesus (Matthew 2.1–12) is recalling in old age the meaning of the experience.
2. Adapted from a passage in a 1622 Christmas sermon by Bishop Lancelot Andrewes: "A cold coming they had of it at this time of the year, just the worst time of the year to take a journey, and specially a long journey in. The ways deep, the weather sharp, the days short, the sun farthest off, *in solstitio brumali,* 'the very dead of winter.'"

At the end we preferred to travel all night,
Sleeping in snatches,
With the voices singing in our ears, saying
20 That this was all folly.

Then at dawn we came down to a temperate valley,
Wet, below the snow line, smelling of vegetation;
With a running stream and a water mill beating the darkness,
And three trees on the low sky.[3]
25 And an old white horse galloped away in the meadow.
Then we came to a tavern with vine-leaves over the lintel,
Six hands at an open door dicing for pieces of silver,
And feet kicking the empty wine-skins.
But there was no information, and so we continued
30 And arrived at evening, not a moment too soon
Finding the place; it was (you may say) satisfactory.

All this was a long time ago, I remember,
And I would do it again, but set down
This set down
35 This: were we led all that way for
Birth or Death? There was a Birth, certainly,
We had evidence and no doubt. I had seen birth and death,
But had thought they were different; this Birth was
Hard and bitter agony for us, like Death, our death.
40 We returned to our places, these Kingdoms,
But no longer at ease here, in the old dispensation,
With an alien people clutching their gods.
I should be glad of another death.

1927

FROM FOUR QUARTETS

Little Gidding[1]

I

Midwinter spring is its own season
Sempiternal° though sodden towards sundown,   *eternal, everlasting*
Suspended in time, between pole and tropic,
When the short day is brightest, with frost and fire,

3. The "three trees" suggest the three crosses, with Jesus crucified on the center one; the men "dicing for pieces of silver" (line 27) suggest the soldiers dicing for Jesus' garments and Judas's betrayal of him for thirty pieces of silver; the empty wineskins recall one of Jesus' parables of old and new (Mark 2.22).
1. This is the last of Eliot's *Four Quartets,* four related poems each divided into five "movements" in a manner reminiscent of the structure of a quartet or a sonata and each dealing with some aspect of the relation of time and eternity, the meaning of history, the achievement of the moment of timeless insight. Although the *Four Quartets* constitute a unified sequence, they were each written separately and can be read as individual poems. "*Little Gidding* can be understood by itself, without reference to the preceding poems, which it yet so

5 The brief sun flames the ice, on pond and ditches,
In windless cold that is the heart's heat,
Reflecting in a watery mirror
A glare that is blindness in the early afternoon.
And glow more intense than blaze of branch, or brazier,
10 Stirs the dumb spirit: no wind, but pentecostal fire[2]
In the dark time of the year. Between melting and freezing
The soul's sap quivers. There is no earth smell
Or smell of living thing. This is the springtime
But not in time's covenant. Now the hedgerow
15 Is blanched for an hour with transitory blossom
Of snow, a bloom more sudden
Than that of summer, neither budding nor fading,
Not in the scheme of generation.
Where is the summer, the unimaginable
Zero summer?

20   If you came this way,
Taking the route you would be likely to take
From the place you would be likely to come from,
If you came this way in may time, you would find the hedges
White again, in May, with voluptuary sweetness.
25 It would be the same at the end of the journey,
If you came at night like a broken king,[3]
If you came by day not knowing what you came for,
It would be the same, when you leave the rough road
And turn behind the pig-sty to the dull façade
30 And the tombstone. And what you thought you came for
Is only a shell, a husk of meaning
From which the purpose breaks only when it is fulfilled
If at all. Either you had no purpose
Or the purpose is beyond the end you figured
35 And is altered in fulfilment. There are other places
Which also are the world's end, some at the sea jaws,
Or over a dark lake, in a desert or a city[4]—
But this is the nearest, in place and time,
Now and in England.

         If you came this way,
40 Taking any route, starting from anywhere,
At any time or at any season,
It would always be the same: you would have to put off

beautifully completes" (Helen Gardner, *The Composition of Four Quartets*). Each of the four is named after a place. Little Gidding is a village in Huntingdonshire where in 1625 Nicholas Ferrar established an Anglican religious community; the community was broken up in 1647, toward the end of the English Civil War, by the victorious Puritans; the chapel, however, was rebuilt in the 19th century and still exists. Eliot wrote the poem in 1942, when he was taking his turn as a nighttime fire-watcher during the incendiary bombings of London in World War II.
2. On the Pentecost day after the death and resurrection of Jesus, there appeared to his apostles "cloven tongues like as of fire . . . And they were all filled with the Holy Ghost" (Acts 2).
3. King Charles I visited Ferrar's community more than once and is said to have paid his last visit in secret after his final defeat at the battle of Naseby in the civil war.
4. "The 'sea jaws' [Eliot] associated with Iona and St. Columba and with Lindisfarne and St. Cuthbert: the 'dark lake' with the lake of Glendalough and St. Kevin's hermitage in County Wicklow: the desert with the hermits of the Thebaid and St. Antony: the city with Padua and the other St. Antony" (Gardner).

Sense and notion. You are not here to verify,
Instruct yourself, or inform curiosity
45 Or carry report. You are here to kneel
Where prayer has been valid. And prayer is more
Than an order of words, the conscious occupation
Of the praying mind, or the sound of the voice praying.
And what the dead had no speech for, when living,
50 They can tell you, being dead: the communication
Of the dead is tongued with fire beyond the language of the living.
Here, the intersection of the timeless moment
Is England and nowhere. Never and always.

II

Ash on an old man's sleeve
55 Is all the ash the burnt roses leave.
Dust in the air suspended
Marks the place where a story ended.[5]
Dust inbreathed was a house—
The wall, the wainscot, and the mouse.
60 The death of hope and despair,
   This is the death of air.[6]

There are flood and drouth
Over the eyes and in the mouth,
Dead water and dead sand
65 Contending for the upper hand.
The parched eviscerate soil
Gapes at the vanity of toil,
Laughs without mirth.
   This is the death of earth.

70 Water and fire succeed
The town, the pasture, and the weed.
Water and fire deride
The sacrifice that we denied.
Water and fire shall rot
75 The marred foundations we forgot,
Of sanctuary and choir.
   This is the death of water and fire.

In the uncertain hour before the morning[7]
   Near the ending of interminable night
80   At the recurrent end of the unending
After the dark dove with the flickering tongue[8]

---

5. Eliot wrote to a friend: "During the Blitz [bombing] the accumulated debris was suspended in the London air for hours after a bombing. Then it would slowly descend and cover one's sleeves and coat with a fine white ash."
6. "The death of air," like that of "earth" and of "water and fire" in the succeeding stanzas, recalls the theory of the creative strife of the four elements propounded by Heraclitus (Greek philosopher of

4th and 5th centuries B.C.E.): "Fire lives in the death of air; water lives in the death of earth; and earth lives in the death of water."
7. The pattern of indentation in the left margin of lines 78–149, their movement and elevated diction, are meant to suggest the terza rima of Dante's *Divine Comedy*.
8. The German dive bomber.

Had passed below the horizon of his homing
While the dead leaves still rattled on like tin
Over the asphalt where no other sound was
85   Between three districts whence the smoke arose
I met one walking, loitering and hurried
As if blown towards me like the metal leaves
Before the urban dawn wind unresisting.
And as I fixed upon the down-turned face
90   That pointed scrutiny with which we challenge
The first-met stranger in the waning dusk
I caught the sudden look of some dead master
Whom I had known, forgotten, half recalled
Both one and many; in the brown baked features
95   The eyes of a familiar compound ghost⁹
Both intimate and unidentifiable.
So I assumed a double part, and cried
And heard another's voice cry: 'What! are *you* here?'
Although we were not. I was still the same,
100   Knowing myself yet being someone other—
And he a face still forming; yet the words sufficed
To compel the recognition they preceded.
And so, compliant to the common wind,
Too strange to each other for misunderstanding,
105   In concord at this intersection time
Of meeting nowhere, no before and after,
We trod the pavement in a dead patrol.
I said: 'The wonder that I feel is easy,
Yet ease is cause of wonder. Therefore speak:
110   I may not comprehend, may not remember.'
And he: 'I am not eager to rehearse
My thought and theory which you have forgotten.
These things have served their purpose: let them be.
So with your own, and pray they be forgiven
115   By others, as I pray you to forgive
Both bad and good. Last season's fruit is eaten
And the fullfed beast shall kick the empty pail.
For last year's words belong to last year's language
And next year's words await another voice.
120   But, as the passage now presents no hindrance
To the spirit unappeased and peregrine°   *foreign, wandering*
Between two worlds become much like each other,
So I find words I never thought to speak
In streets I never thought I should revisit
125   When I left my body on a distant shore.¹
Since our concern was speech, and speech impelled us
To purify the dialect of the tribe²

9. This encounter with a ghost "compounded" of W. B. Yeats and his fellow Irishman Jonathan Swift is modeled on Dante's meeting with Brunetto Latini (*Inferno* 15), including a direct translation (line 98) of Dante's cry of horrified recognition: "*Siete voi qui, ser Brunetto?*" Cf. also Shakespeare's sonnet 86, line 9: "that affable familiar ghost."

1. Yeats died on Jan. 28, 1939, at Roquebrune in the south of France.
2. A rendering of the line "*Donner un sens plus pur aux mots de la tribu*" in Stéphane Mallarmé's 1877 sonnet "Le Tombeau d'Edgar Poe" ("The Tomb of Edgar Poe").

And urge the mind to aftersight and foresight,
Let me disclose the gifts reserved for age
130   To set a crown upon your lifetime's effort.
First, the cold friction of expiring sense
Without enchantment, offering no promise
But bitter tastelessness of shadow fruit
As body and soul begin to fall asunder.
135   Second, the conscious impotence of rage[3]
At human folly, and the laceration
Of laughter at what ceases to amuse.[4]
And last, the rending pain of re-enactment
Of all that you have done, and been;[5] the shame
140   Of motives late revealed, and the awareness
Of things ill done and done to others' harm
Which once you took for exercise of virtue.
Then fools' approval stings, and honour stains.
From wrong to wrong the exasperated spirit
145   Proceeds, unless restored by that refining fire[6]
Where you must move in measure, like a dancer.'[7]
The day was breaking. In the disfigured street
He left me, with a kind of valediction,
And faded on the blowing of the horn.[8]

III

150   There are three conditions which often look alike
Yet differ completely, flourish in the same hedgerow:
Attachment to self and to things and to persons, detachment
From self and from things and from persons; and, growing between
    them, indifference
Which resembles the others as death resembles life,
155   Being between two lives—unflowering, between
The live and the dead nettle.[9] This is the use of memory:
For liberation—not less of love but expanding
Of love beyond desire, and so liberation
From the future as well as the past. Thus, love of a country
160   Begins as attachment to our own field of action
And comes to find that action of little importance
Though never indifferent. History may be servitude,
History may be freedom. See, now they vanish,

3. Cf. Yeats's "The Spur": "You think it horrible that lust and rage / Should dance attention upon my old age."
4. Cf. Yeats's "Swift's Epitaph" (translated from Swift's own Latin): "Savage indignation there / Cannot lacerate his breast."
5. Cf. Yeats's "Man and the Echo": "All that I have said and done, / Now that I am old and ill, / Turns into a question till / I lie awake night after night / And never get the answer right. / Did that play of mine send out / Certain men the English shot?"
6. Cf. *The Waste Land*, line 428 and its note; also the refining fire in Yeats's "Byzantium," lines 25–32.
7. Cf. Yeats's "Among School Children," line 64: "How can we know the dancer from the dance?"

8. Cf. *Hamlet* 1.2.157: "It faded on the crowing of the cock." The horn is the all-clear signal after an air raid (the dialogue has taken place between the dropping of the last bomb and the sounding of the all clear). Eliot called the section that ends with this line "the nearest equivalent to a canto of the *Inferno* or *Purgatorio*" that he could achieve and spoke of his intention to present "a parallel, by means of contrast, between the *Inferno* and the *Purgatorio* . . . and a hallucinated scene after an air raid."
9. Eliot wrote to a friend: "The dead nettle is the family of flowering plants of which the White Archangel is one of the commonest and closely resembles the stinging nettle and is found in its company."

The faces and places, with the self which, as it could, loved them,
165 To become renewed, transfigured, in another pattern.

Sin is Behovely, but
All shall be well, and
All manner of thing shall be well.[1]
If I think, again, of this place,
170 And of people, not wholly commendable,
Of no immediate kin or kindness,
But some of peculiar genius,
All touched by a common genius,
United in the strife which divided them;
175 If I think of a king at nightfall,[2]
Of three men, and more, on the scaffold
And a few who died forgotten
In other places, here and abroad,
And of one who died blind and quiet[3]
180 Why should we celebrate
These dead men more than the dying?
It is not to ring the bell backward
Nor is it an incantation
To summon the spectre of a Rose.
185 We cannot revive old factions
We cannot restore old policies
Or follow an antique drum.
These men, and those who opposed them
And those whom they opposed
190 Accept the constitution of silence
And are folded in a single party.
Whatever we inherit from the fortunate
We have taken from the defeated
What they had to leave us—a symbol:
195 A symbol perfected in death.
And all shall be well and
All manner of thing shall be well
By the purification of the motive
In the ground of our beseeching.[4]

IV

200 The dove[5] descending breaks the air
With flame of incandescent terror
Of which the tongues declare
The one discharge from sin and error.
The only hope, or else despair

1. A quotation from the 14th-century English mystic Dame Julian of Norwich: "Sin is behovabil [inevitable and fitting], but all shall be well and all shall be well and all manner of thing shall be well."
2. I.e., Charles I. He died "on the scaffold" in 1649, while his principal advisers, Archbishop Laud and Thomas Wentworth, earl of Strafford, were both executed earlier by the victorious parlia- mentary forces.
3. I.e., Milton, who sided with Cromwell against the king.
4. Dame Julian of Norwich was instructed in a vision that "the ground of our beseeching" is love.
5. Both a dive bomber and the Holy Spirit with its Pentecostal tongues of fire.

2638 / T. S. ELIOT

205   Lies in the choice of pyre or pyre—
        To be redeemed from fire by fire.

        Who then devised the torment? Love.
        Love is the unfamiliar Name
        Behind the hands that wove
210   The intolerable shirt of flame[6]
        Which human power cannot remove.
            We only live, only suspire°   breathe, sigh
            Consumed by either fire or fire.

                            V

        What we call the beginning is often the end
215   And to make an end is to make a beginning.
        The end is where we start from. And every phrase
        And sentence that is right (where every word is at home,
        Taking its place to support the others,
        The word neither diffident nor ostentatious,
220   And easy commerce of the old and the new,
        The common word exact without vulgarity,
        The formal word precise but not pedantic,
        The complete consort[7] dancing together)
        Every phrase and every sentence is an end and a beginning,
225   Every poem an epitaph. And any action
        Is a step to the block, to the fire, down the sea's throat
        Or to an illegible stone: and that is where we start.
        We die with the dying:
        See, they depart, and we go with them.
230   We are born with the dead:
        See, they return, and bring us with them.
        The moment of the rose and the moment of the yew-tree[8]
        Are of equal duration. A people without history
        Is not redeemed from time, for history is a pattern
235   Of timeless moments. So, while the light fails
        On a winter's afternoon, in a secluded chapel
        History is now and England.

        With the drawing of this Love and the voice of this Calling[9]

        We shall not cease from exploration
240   And the end of all our exploring
        Will be to arrive where we started
        And know the place for the first time.
        Through the unknown, remembered gate
        When the last of earth left to discover
245   Is that which was the beginning;
        At the source of the longest river

6. Out of love for her husband, Hercules, Deianira gave him the poisoned shirt of Nessus. She had been told that it would increase his love for her, but instead it so corroded his flesh that in his agony he mounted a funeral pyre and burned himself to death.
7. Company; also harmony of sounds.
8. Traditional symbol of death and grief.
9. This line is from the *Cloud of Unknowing*, an anonymous 14th-century mystical work.

The voice of the hidden waterfall
And the children in the apple tree
Not known, because not looked for
250　But heard, half-heard, in the stillness
Between two waves of the sea.[1]
Quick now, here, now, always—
A condition of complete simplicity
(Costing not less than everything)
255　And all shall be well and
All manner of thing shall be well
When the tongues of flame are in-folded
Into the crowned knot of fire
And the fire and the rose are one.

1942   1942, 1943

Tradition and the Individual Talent[1]

I

In English writing we seldom speak of tradition, though we occasionally apply its name in deploring its absence. We cannot refer to 'the tradition' or to 'a tradition'; at most, we employ the adjective in saying that the poetry of So-and-so is 'traditional' or even 'too traditional.' Seldom, perhaps, does the word appear except in a phrase of censure. If otherwise, it is vaguely approbative, with the implication, as to the work approved, of some pleasing archæological reconstruction. You can hardly make the word agreeable to English ears without this comfortable reference to the reassuring science of archæology.

Certainly the word is not likely to appear in our appreciations of living or dead writers. Every nation, every race, has not only its own creative, but its own critical turn of mind; and is even more oblivious of the shortcomings and limitations of its critical habits than of those of its creative genius. We know, or think we know, from the enormous mass of critical writing that has appeared in the French language the critical method or habit of the French; we only conclude (we are such unconscious people) that the French are 'more critical' than we, and sometimes even plume ourselves a little with the fact, as if the French were the less spontaneous. Perhaps they are; but we might remind ourselves that criticism is as inevitable as breathing, and that we should be none the worse for articulating what passes in our minds when we read a book and feel an emotion about it, for criticizing our own minds in their work of criticism. One of the facts that might come to light in this process is our tendency to insist, when we praise a poet, upon those aspects of his work in which he least resembles anyone else. In these aspects or parts of his work we pretend to find what is individual, what is the peculiar essence of the man. We dwell with satisfaction upon the poet's difference from his predecessors,

---

1. The voices of the children in the apple tree sym- bolize the sudden moment of insight. Cf. the con- clusion to "Burnt Norton" (the first of the *Four Quartets*), where the laughter of the children in the garden has a like meaning: "Sudden in a shaft of sunlight / Even while the dust moves / There rises the hidden laughter / Of children in the foliage / Quick now, here, now, always."
1. First published in *The Egoist* magazine (1919) and later collected in *The Sacred Wood* (1920).

especially his immediate predecessors; we endeavour to find something that can be isolated in order to be enjoyed. Whereas if we approach a poet without this prejudice we shall often find that not only the best, but the most individual parts of his work may be those in which the dead poets, his ancestors, assert their immortality most vigorously. And I do not mean the impressionable period of adolescence, but the period of full maturity.

Yet if the only form of tradition, of handing down, consisted in following the ways of the immediate generation before us in a blind or timid adherence to its successes, 'tradition' should positively be discouraged. We have seen many such simple currents soon lost in the sand; and novelty is better than repetition. Tradition is a matter of much wider significance. It cannot be inherited, and if you want it you must obtain it by great labour. It involves, in the first place, the historical sense, which we may call nearly indispensable to any one who would continue to be a poet beyond his twenty-fifth year; and the historical sense involves a perception, not only of the pastness of the past, but of its presence; the historical sense compels a man to write not merely with his own generation in his bones, but with a feeling that the whole of the literature of Europe from Homer and within it the whole of the literature of his own country has a simultaneous existence and composes a simultaneous order. This historical sense, which is a sense of the timeless as well as of the temporal and of the timeless and of the temporal together, is what makes a writer traditional. And it is at the same time what makes a writer most acutely conscious of his place in time, of his own contemporaneity.

No poet, no artist of any art, has his complete meaning alone. His significance, his appreciation is the appreciation of his relation to the dead poets and artists. You cannot value him alone; you must set him, for contrast and comparison, among the dead. I mean this as a principle of æsthetic, not merely historical, criticism. The necessity that he shall conform, that he shall cohere, is not one-sided; what happens when a new work of art is created is something that happens simultaneously to all the works of art which preceded it. The existing monuments form an ideal order among themselves, which is modified by the introduction of the new (the really new) work of art among them. The existing order is complete before the new work arrives; for order to persist after the supervention of novelty, the *whole* existing order must be, if ever so slightly, altered; and so the relations, proportions, values of each work of art toward the whole are readjusted; and this is conformity between the old and the new. Whoever has approved this idea of order, of the form of European, of English literature will not find it preposterous that the past should be altered by the present as much as the present is directed by the past. And the poet who is aware of this will be aware of great difficulties and responsibilities.

In a peculiar sense he will be aware also that he must inevitably be judged by the standards of the past. I say judged, not amputated, by them; not judged to be as good as, or worse or better than, the dead; and certainly not judged by the canons of dead critics. It is a judgment, a comparison, in which two things are measured by each other. To conform merely would be for the new work not really to conform at all; it would not be new, and would therefore not be a work of art. And we do not quite say that the new is more valuable because it fits in; but its fitting in is a test of its value—a test, it is true, which can only be slowly and cautiously applied, for we are none of us infallible judges of conformity. We say: it appears to conform, and is perhaps individual, or it appears individual, and may conform; but we are hardly likely to find that it is one and not the other.

To proceed to a more intelligible exposition of the relation of the poet to the past: he can neither take the past as a lump, an indiscriminate bolus,[2] nor can he form himself wholly on one or two private admirations, nor can he form himself wholly upon one preferred period. The first course is inadmissible, the second is an important experience of youth, and the third is a pleasant and highly desirable supplement. The poet must be very conscious of the main current, which does not at all flow invariably through the most distinguished reputations. He must be quite aware of the obvious fact that art never improves, but that the material of art is never quite the same. He must be aware that the mind of Europe—the mind of his own country—a mind which he learns in time to be much more important than his own private mind—is a mind which changes, and that this change is a development which abandons nothing *en route,* which does not superannuate either Shakespeare, or Homer, or the rock drawing of the Magdalenian[3] draftsmen. That this development, refinement perhaps, complication certainly, is not, from the point of view of the artist, any improvement. Perhaps not even an improvement from the point of view of the psychologist or not to the extent which we imagine; perhaps only in the end based upon a complication in economics and machinery. But the difference between the present and the past is that the conscious present is an awareness of the past in a way and to an extent which the past's awareness of itself cannot show.

Someone said: 'The dead writers are remote from us because we *know* so much more than they did.' Precisely, and they are that which we know.

I am alive to a usual objection to what is clearly part of my programme for the *métier*[4] of poetry. The objection is that the doctrine requires a ridiculous amount of erudition (pedantry), a claim which can be rejected by appeal to the lives of poets in any pantheon. It will even be affirmed that much learning deadens or perverts poetic sensibility. While, however, we persist in believing that a poet ought to know as much as will not encroach upon his necessary receptivity and necessary laziness, it is not desirable to confine knowledge to whatever can be put into a useful shape for examinations, drawing-rooms, or the still more pretentious modes of publicity. Some can absorb knowledge, the more tardy must sweat for it. Shakespeare acquired more essential history from Plutarch[5] than most men could from the whole British Museum. What is to be insisted upon is that the poet must develop or procure the consciousness of the past and that he should continue to develop this consciousness throughout his career.

What happens is a continual surrender of himself as he is at the moment to something which is more valuable. The progress of an artist is a continual self-sacrifice, a continual extinction of personality.

There remains to define this process of depersonalisation and its relation to the sense of tradition. It is in this depersonalization that art may be said to approach the condition of science. I, therefore, invite you to consider, as a suggestive analogy, the action which takes place when a bit of finely filiated[6] platinum is introduced into a chamber containing oxygen and sulphur dioxide.

2. A round mass of anything: a large pill.
3. The most advanced culture of the European Paleolithic period (from discoveries at La Madeleine, France).
4. Vocation (French).

5. Greek biographer (1st century C.E.) of famous Greeks and Romans; from his work Shakespeare drew the plots of his Roman plays.
6. Drawn out like a thread.

II

Honest criticism and sensitive appreciation are directed not upon the poet but upon the poetry. If we attend to the confused cries of the newspaper critics and the susurrus[7] of popular repetition that follows, we shall hear the names of poets in great numbers; if we seek not Blue-book[8] knowledge but the enjoyment of poetry, and ask for a poem, we shall seldom find it. I have tried to point out the importance of the relation of the poem to other poems by other authors, and suggested the conception of poetry as a living whole of all the poetry that has ever been written. The other aspect of this Impersonal theory of poetry is the relation of the poem to its author. And I hinted, by an analogy, that the mind of the mature poet differs from that of the immature one not precisely in any valuation of 'personality,' not being necessarily more interesting, or having 'more to say,' but rather by being a more finely perfected medium in which special, or very varied, feelings are at liberty to enter into new combinations.

The analogy was that of the catalyst.[9] When the two gases previously mentioned are mixed in the presence of a filament of platinum, they form sulphurous acid. This combination takes place only if the platinum is present; nevertheless the newly formed acid contains no trace of platinum, and the platinum itself is apparently unaffected; has remained inert, neutral, and unchanged. The mind of the poet is the shred of platinum. It may partly or exclusively operate upon the experience of the man himself; but, the more perfect the artist, the more completely separate in him will be the man who suffers and the mind which creates; the more perfectly will the mind digest and transmute the passions which are its material.

The experience, you will notice, the elements which enter the presence of the transforming catalyst, are of two kinds: emotions and feelings. The effect of a work of art upon the person who enjoys it is an experience different in kind from any experience not of art. It may be formed out of one emotion, or may be a combination of several; and various feelings, inhering for the writer in particular words or phrases or images, may be added to compose the final result. Or great poetry may be made without the direct use of any emotion whatever: composed out of feelings solely. Canto XV of the *Inferno* (Brunetto Latini)[1] is a working up of the emotion evident in the situation; but the effect, though single as that of any work of art, is obtained by considerable complexity of detail. The last quatrain gives an image, a feeling attaching to an image, which 'came,' which did not develop simply out of what precedes, but which was probably in suspension in the poet's mind until the proper combination arrived for it to add itself to.[2] The poet's mind is in fact a receptacle for seizing and storing up numberless feelings, phrases, images, which remain there until all the particles which can unite to form a new compound are present together.

If you compare several representative passages of the greatest poetry you see how great is the variety of types of combination, and also how completely any semi-ethical criterion of 'sublimity' misses the mark. For it is not the

7. Murmuring, buzzing (Latin).
8. British government publication.
9. Substance that triggers a chemical change without being affected by the reaction.
1. Dante meets in hell his old master, Brunetto Latini, suffering eternal punishment for unnatural lust yet still loved and admired by Dante, who addresses him with affectionate courtesy.

2. Dante's strange interview with Brunetto is over, and Brunetto moves off to continue his punishment: "Then he turned round, and seemed like one of those / Who run for the green cloth [in the footrace] at Verona / In the field; and he seemed among them / Not the loser but the winner."

'greatness,' the intensity, of the emotions, the components, but the intensity of the artistic process, the pressure, so to speak, under which the fusion takes place, that counts. The episode of Paolo and Francesca[3] employs a definite emotion, but the intensity of the poetry is something quite different from whatever intensity in the supposed experience it may give the impression of. It is no more intense, furthermore, than Canto XXVI,[4] the voyage of Ulysses, which has not the direct dependence upon an emotion. Great variety is possible in the process of transmutation of emotion: the murder of Agamemnon, or the agony of Othello,[5] gives an artistic effect apparently closer to a possible original than the scenes from Dante. In the *Agamemnon*, the artistic emotion approximates to the emotion of an actual spectator; in *Othello* to the emotion of the protagonist himself. But the difference between art and the event is always absolute; the combination which is the murder of Agamemnon is probably as complex as that which is the voyage of Ulysses. In either case there has been a fusion of elements. The ode of Keats contains a number of feelings which have nothing particular to do with the nightingale, but which the nightingale, partly, perhaps, because of its attractive name, and partly because of its reputation, served to bring together.

The point of view which I am struggling to attack is perhaps related to the metaphysical theory of the substantial unity of the soul: for my meaning is, that the poet has, not a 'personality' to express, but a particular medium, which is only a medium and not a personality, in which impressions and experiences combine in peculiar and unexpected ways. Impressions and experiences which are important for the man may take no place in the poetry, and those which become important in the poetry may play quite a negligible part in the man, the personality.

I will quote a passage which is unfamiliar enough to be regarded with fresh attention in the light—or darkness—of these observations:

> And now methinks I could e'en chide myself
> For doating on her beauty, though her death
> Shall be revenged after no common action.
> Does the silkworm expend her yellow labours
> For thee? For thee does she undo herself?
> Are lordships sold to maintain ladyships
> For the poor benefit of a bewildering minute?
> Why does yon fellow falsify highways,
> And put his life between the judge's lips,
> To refine such a thing—keeps horse and men
> To beat their valours for her? . . . [6]

In this passage (as is evident if it is taken in its context) there is a combination of positive and negative emotions: an intensely strong attraction toward beauty and an equally intense fascination by the ugliness which is contrasted with it and which destroys it. This balance of contrasted emotion is in the dramatic situation to which the speech is pertinent, but that situation alone is inadequate to it. This is, so to speak, the structural emotion, provided by the drama.

3. Illicit lovers whom Dante meets in the second circle of hell (*Inferno* 5) and at whose punishment and sorrows he swoons with pity.
4. Of the *Inferno*. Ulysses, suffering in hell for "false counseling," tells Dante of his final voyage.
5. Shakespeare's character kills himself after being duped into jealously murdering his wife. In Aeschylus's play *Agamemnon* the title character is murdered by his wife, Clytemnestra.
6. From Cyril Tourneur's *Revenger's Tragedy* 3.4 (1607).

But the whole effect, the dominant tone, is due to the fact that a number of floating feelings, having an affinity to this emotion by no means superficially evident, have combined with it to give us a new art emotion.

It is not in his personal emotions, the emotions provoked by particular events in his life, that the poet is in any way remarkable or interesting. His particular emotions may be simple, or crude, or flat. The emotion in his poetry will be a very complex thing, but not with the complexity of the emotions of people who have very complex or unusual emotions in life. One error, in fact, of eccentricity in poetry is to seek for new human emotions to express; and in this search for novelty in the wrong place it discovers the perverse. The business of the poet is not to find new emotions, but to use the ordinary ones and, in working them up into poetry, to express feelings which are not in actual emotions at all. And emotions which he has never experienced will serve his turn as well as those familiar to him. Consequently, we must believe that 'emotion recollected in tranquillity'[7] is an inexact formula. For it is neither emotion, nor recollection, nor, without distortion of meaning, tranquility. It is a concentration, and a new thing resulting from the concentration, of a very great number of experiences which to the practical and active person would not seem to be experiences at all; it is a concentration which does not happen consciously or of deliberation. These experiences are not 'recollected,' and they finally unite in an atmosphere which is 'tranquil' only in that it is a passive attending upon the event. Of course this is not quite the whole story. There is a great deal, in the writing of poetry, which must be conscious and deliberate. In fact, the bad poet is usually unconscious where he ought to be conscious, and conscious where he ought to be unconscious. Both errors tend to make him 'personal.' Poetry is not a turning loose of emotion, but an escape from emotion; it is not the expression of personality, but an escape from personality. But, of course, only those who have personality and emotions know what it means to want to escape from these things.

III

ὁ δὲ νοῦζ ἴσωζ θειό τερόν τι καὶ ἀπαθέζ ἐστιν.[8]

This essay proposes to halt at the frontier of metaphysics or mysticism, and confine itself to such practical conclusions as can be applied by the responsible person interested in poetry. To divert interest from the poet to the poetry is a laudable aim: for it would conduce to a juster estimation of actual poetry, good and bad. There are many people who appreciate the expression of sincere emotion in verse, and there is a smaller number of people who can appreciate technical excellence. But very few know when there is an expression of *significant* emotion, emotion which has its life in the poem and not in the history of the poet. The emotion of art is impersonal. And the poet cannot reach this impersonality without surrendering himself wholly to the work to be done. And he is not likely to know what is to be done unless he lives in what is not merely the present, but the present moment of the past, unless he is conscious, not of what is dead, but of what is already living.

1919, 1920

---

7. In his preface to *Lyrical Ballads* (2nd ed., 1800), Wordsworth writes that poetry "takes its origin from emotion recollected in tranquility."

8. Aristotle's "De Anima" ("On the Soul") 1.4: "The mind is doubtless something more divine and unimpressionable."

KATHERINE MANSFIELD
1888–1923

Kathleen Mansfield Beauchamp was born in Wellington, New Zealand, daughter of a respected businessman who was later knighted. In 1903 the family moved to London, where Kathleen and her sisters entered Queen's College, the first institution in England founded expressly for the higher education of women. The family returned to New Zealand, leaving the girls in London, but the Beauchamps brought their daughters home in 1906. By this time Kathleen had written a number of poems, sketches, and stories; and after experimenting with different pen names, she adopted that of Katherine Mansfield. She was restless and ambitious and chafed against the narrowness of middle-class life in New Zealand, at that time still very much a new country in the shadow of the British Empire.

In July 1908 Mansfield left again for London; she never returned to New Zealand. In 1909 she suddenly married G. C. Bowden, a teacher of singing and elocution, but left him the same evening. Shortly afterward she became pregnant by another man and went to Germany to await the birth, but she had a miscarriage there. Her experiences in Germany are told in carefully observed sketches full of ironic detail in her first published book, *In a German Pension* (1911).

In 1910 she briefly resumed life with Bowden, who put her in touch with A. R. Orage, editor of the avant-garde periodical *The New Age*. There she published a number of her stories and sketches. At the end of 1911 she met the critic John Middleton Murry, editor of the modernist magazine *Rhythm,* and eventually married him. She developed intense but conflicted friendships with D. H. Lawrence, Virginia Woolf, and other writers of the day. During all this time Mansfield experimented in technique and refined her art, attempting within the short story to illuminate the ambivalences and complexities of friendship and family, gender and class. The death in World War I in October 1915 of her much-loved younger brother sent her imagination back to their childhood days in New Zealand and in doing so gave a fresh charge and significance to her writing. Using her newly developed style with an ever greater subtlety and sensitivity, she now produced her best stories, including "Prelude," "Daughters of the Late Colonel," "At the Bay," and "The Garden Party." With the publication of *The Garden Party and Other Stories* in February 1922, Mansfield's place as a master of the modern short story was ensured. But she was gravely ill with tuberculosis and died suddenly at the age of thirty-four in Fontainebleau, France, where she had gone to try to find a cure by adopting the methods of the controversial mystic George Ivanovich Gurdjieff.

Mansfield produced her best and most characteristic work in her last years, when she combined incident, image, symbol, and structure in a way comparable with, yet interestingly different from, James Joyce's method in *Dubliners,* both writers sharing an influence in the precise and understated art of the Russian writer Anton Chekhov. "Daughters of the Late Colonel," a story of two middle-aged sisters and their devotion to a tyrannical father, shows her working characteristically through suggestion rather than explicit development to illuminate a late-Victorian world, with the subdued elegiac sense of female lives wasted in the service of an outmoded patriarchal order, although the story's ironic surface is restrained comedy. The meaning is achieved most of all through the atmosphere, built up by the accumulation of small strokes, none of which seems more than a shrewdly observed realistic detail. Mansfield also manipulates time masterfully: she makes particularly effective use of the unobtrusive flashback, where we find ourselves in an earlier phase of the action without quite knowing how we got there but fully aware of its relevance to the total action and atmosphere.

The Garden Party[1]

And after all the weather was ideal. They could not have had a more perfect day for a garden party if they had ordered it. Windless, warm, the sky without a cloud. Only the blue was veiled with a haze of light gold, as it is sometimes in early summer. The gardener had been up since dawn, mowing the lawns and sweeping them, until the grass and the dark flat rosettes where the daisy plants had been seemed to shine. As for the roses, you could not help feeling they understood that roses are the only flowers that impress people at garden parties; the only flowers that everybody is certain of knowing. Hundreds, yes, literally hundreds, had come out in a single night; the green bushes bowed down as though they had been visited by archangels.

Breakfast was not yet over before the men came to put up the marquee.

'Where do you want the marquee put, mother?'

'My dear child, it's no use asking me. I'm determined to leave everything to you children this year. Forget I am your mother. Treat me as an honoured guest.'

But Meg could not possibly go and supervise the men. She had washed her hair before breakfast, and she sat drinking her coffee in a green turban, with a dark wet curl stamped on each cheek. Jose, the butterfly, always came down in a silk petticoat and a kimono jacket.

'You'll have to go, Laura; you're the artistic one.'

Away Laura flew, still holding her piece of bread-and-butter. It's so delicious to have an excuse for eating out of doors, and besides, she loved having to arrange things; she always felt she could do it so much better than anybody else.

Four men in their shirt-sleeves stood grouped together on the garden path. They carried staves covered with rolls of canvas, and they had big tool-bags slung on their backs. They looked impressive. Laura wished now that she had not got the bread-and-butter, but there was nowhere to put it, and she couldn't possibly throw it away. She blushed and tried to look severe and even a little bit short-sighted as she came up to them.

'Good morning,' she said, copying her mother's voice. But that sounded so fearfully affected that she was ashamed, and stammered like a little girl, 'Oh—er—have you come—is it about the marquee?'

'That's right, miss,' said the tallest of the men, a lanky, freckled fellow, and he shifted his tool-bag, knocked back his straw hat and smiled down at her. 'That's about it.'

His smile was so easy, so friendly that Laura recovered. What nice eyes he had, small, but such a dark blue! And now she looked at the others, they were smiling too. 'Cheer up, we won't bite,' their smile seemed to say. How very nice workmen were! And what a beautiful morning! She mustn't mention the morning; she must be business-like. The marquee.

'Well, what about the lily-lawn? Would that do?'

And she pointed to the lily-lawn with the hand that didn't hold the bread-and-butter. They turned, they stared in the direction. A little fat chap thrust out his under-lip, and the tall fellow frowned.

---

1. This story draws on an incident from Mansfield's life. In March 1907 her mother gave a garden party in their Wellington house, but a street accident befell a neighbor living in a poor quarter nearby.

'I don't fancy it,' said he. 'Not conspicuous enough. You see, with a thing like a marquee,' and he turned to Laura in his easy way, 'you want to put it somewhere where it'll give you a bang slap in the eye, if you follow me.'

Laura's upbringing made her wonder for a moment whether it was quite respectful of a workman to talk to her of bangs slap in the eye. But she did quite follow him.

'A corner of the tennis-court,' she suggested. 'But the band's going to be in one corner.'

'H'm, going to have a band, are you?' said another of the workmen. He was pale. He had a haggard look as his dark eyes scanned the tennis-court. What was he thinking?

'Only a very small band,' said Laura gently. Perhaps he wouldn't mind so much if the band was quite small. But the tall fellow interrupted.

'Look here, miss, that's the place. Against those trees. Over there. That'll do fine.'

Against the karakas. Then the karaka-trees would be hidden. And they were so lovely, with their broad, gleaming leaves, and their clusters of yellow fruit. They were like trees you imagined growing on a desert island, proud, solitary, lifting their leaves and fruits to the sun in a kind of silent splendour. Must they be hidden by a marquee?

They must. Already the men had shouldered their staves and were making for the place. Only the tall fellow was left. He bent down, pinched a sprig of lavender, put his thumb and forefinger to his nose and snuffed up the smell. When Laura saw that gesture she forgot all about the karakas in her wonder at him caring for things like that—caring for the smell of lavender. How many men that she knew would have done such a thing? Oh, how extraordinarily nice workmen were, she thought. Why couldn't she have workmen for friends rather than the silly boys she danced with and who came to Sunday night supper? She would get on much better with men like these.

It's all the fault, she decided, as the tall fellow drew something on the back of an envelope, something that was to be looped up or left to hang, of these absurd class distinctions. Well, for her part, she didn't feel them. Not a bit, not an atom . . . And now there came the chock-chock of wooden hammers. Some one whistled, some one sang out, 'Are you right there, matey?' 'Matey!' The friendliness of it, the—the—Just to prove how happy she was, just to show the tall fellow how at home she felt, and how she despised stupid conventions, Laura took a big bite of her bread-and-butter as she stared at the little drawing. She felt just like a work-girl.

'Laura, Laura, where are you? Telephone, Laura!' a voice cried from the house.

'Coming!' Away she skimmed, over the lawn, up the path, up the steps, across the veranda, and into the porch. In the hall her father and Laurie were brushing their hats ready to go to the office.

'I say, Laura,' said Laurie very fast, 'you might just give a squiz² at my coat before this afternoon. See if it wants pressing.'

'I will,' said she. Suddenly she couldn't stop herself. She ran at Laurie and gave him a small, quick squeeze. 'Oh, I do love parties, don't you?' gasped Laura.

'Ra-ther,' said Laurie's warm, boyish voice, and he squeezed his sister too,

2. Glance.

and gave her a gentle push. 'Dash off to the telephone, old girl.'

The telephone. 'Yes, yes; oh yes. Kitty? Good morning, dear. Come to lunch? Do, dear. Delighted of course. It will only be a very scratch meal—just the sandwich crusts and broken meringue-shells and what's left over. Yes, isn't it a perfect morning? Your white? Oh, I certainly should. One moment—hold the line. Mother's calling.' And Laura sat back. 'What, mother? Can't hear.'

Mrs Sheridan's voice floated down the stairs. 'Tell her to wear that sweet hat she had on last Sunday.'

'Mother says you're to wear that sweet hat you had on last Sunday. Good. One o'clock. Bye-bye.'

Laura put back the receiver, flung her arms over her head, took a deep breath, stretched and let them fall. 'Huh,' she sighed, and the moment after the sigh she sat up quickly. She was still, listening. All the doors in the house seemed to be open. The house was alive with soft, quick steps and running voices. The green baize[3] door that led to the kitchen regions swung open and shut with a muffled thud. And now there came a long, chuckling absurd sound. It was the heavy piano being moved on its stiff castors. But the air! If you stopped to notice, was the air always like this? Little faint winds were playing chase in at the tops of the windows, out at the doors. And there were two tiny spots of sun, one on the inkpot, one on a silver photograph frame, playing too. Darling little spots. Especially the one on the inkpot lid. It was quite warm. A warm little silver star. She could have kissed it.

The front door bell pealed, and there sounded the rustle of Sadie's print skirt on the stairs. A man's voice murmured; Sadie answered, careless, 'I'm sure I don't know. Wait. I'll ask Mrs Sheridan.'

'What is it, Sadie?' Laura came into the hall.

'It's the florist, Miss Laura.'

It was, indeed. There, just inside the door, stood a wide, shallow tray full of pots of pink lilies. No other kind. Nothing but lilies—canna lilies, big pink flowers, wide open, radiant, almost frighteningly alive on bright crimson stems.

'O-oh, Sadie!' said Laura, and the sound was like a little moan. She crouched down as if to warm herself at that blaze of lilies; she felt they were in her fingers, on her lips, growing in her breast.

'It's some mistake,' she said faintly. 'Nobody ever ordered so many. Sadie, go and find mother.'

But at that moment Mrs Sheridan joined them.

'It's quite right,' she said calmly. 'Yes, I ordered them. Aren't they lovely?' She pressed Laura's arm. 'I was passing the shop yesterday, and I saw them in the window. And I suddenly thought for once in my life I shall have enough canna lilies. The garden party will be a good excuse.'

'But I thought you said you didn't mean to interfere,' said Laura. Sadie had gone. The florist's man was still outside at his van. She put her arm round her mother's neck and gently, very gently, she bit her mother's ear.

'My darling child, you wouldn't like a logical mother, would you? Don't do that. Here's the man.'

He carried more lilies still, another whole tray.

'Bank them up, just inside the door, on both sides of the porch, please,' said Mrs Sheridan. 'Don't you agree, Laura?'

'Oh, I *do* mother.'

3. Coarse woolen.

In the drawing-room Meg, Jose and good little Hans had at last succeeded in moving the piano.

'Now, if we put this chesterfield against the wall and move everything out of the room except the chairs, don't you think?'

'Quite.'

'Hans, move these tables into the smoking-room, and bring a sweeper to take these marks off the carpet and—one moment, Hans—' Jose loved giving orders to the servants, and they loved obeying her. She always made them feel they were taking part in some drama. 'Tell mother and Miss Laura to come here at once.'

'Very good, Miss Jose.'

She turned to Meg. 'I want to hear what the piano sounds like, just in case I'm asked to sing this afternoon. Let's try over "This life is Weary."'

Pom! Ta-ta-ta *Tee*-ta! The piano burst out so passionately that Jose's face changed. She clasped her hands. She looked mournfully and enigmatically at her mother and Laura as they came in.

> This Life is *Wee*-ary,
> A Tear—a Sigh.
> A Love that *Chan*-ges,
>   This Life is *Wee*-ary,
> A Tear—a Sigh.
> A Love that *Chan*-ges,
> And then . . . Good-bye!

But at the word 'Good-bye,' and although the piano sounded more desperate than ever, her face broke into a brilliant, dreadfully unsympathetic smile.

'Aren't I in good voice, mummy?' she beamed.

> This Life is *Wee*-ary,
> Hope comes to Die.
> A Dream—a *Wa*-kening.

But now Sadie interrupted them. 'What is it, Sadie?'

'If you please, m'm, cook says have you got the flags[4] for the sandwiches?'

'The flags for the sandwiches, Sadie?' echoed Mrs Sheridan dreamily. And the children knew by her face that she hadn't got them. 'Let me see.' And she said to Sadie firmly, 'Tell cook I'll let her have them in ten minutes.'

Sadie went.

'Now, Laura,' said her mother quickly. 'Come with me into the smoking-room. I've got the names[5] somewhere on the back of an envelope. You'll have to write them out for me. Meg, go upstairs this minute and take that wet thing off your head. Jose, run and finish dressing this instant. Do you hear me, children, or shall I have to tell your father when he comes home to-night? And—and, Jose, pacify cook if you do go into the kitchen, will you? I'm terrified of her this morning.'

The envelope was found at last behind the dining-room clock, though how it had got there Mrs Sheridan could not imagine.

'One of you children must have stolen it out of my bag, because I remember

4. Little paper flags stuck in a plate of small tri-angular sandwiches indicating what is inside the sandwiches on each plate—an English custom adopted by the New Zealand middle class as a sign of gentility.
5. I.e., the names of the sandwich fillings to be written on each flag.

vividly—cream cheese and lemon-curd. Have you done that?'

'Yes.'

'Egg and—' Mrs Sheridan held the envelope away from her. 'It looks like mice. It can't be mice, can it?'

'Olive, pet,' said Laura, looking over her shoulder.

'Yes, of course, olive. What a horrible combination it sounds. Egg and olive.'

They were finished at last, and Laura took them off to the kitchen. She found Jose there pacifying the cook, who did not look at all terrifying.

'I have never seen such exquisite sandwiches,' said Jose's rapturous voice. 'How many kinds did you say there were, cook? Fifteen?'

'Fifteen, Miss Jose.'

'Well, cook, I congratulate you.'

Cook swept up crusts with the long sandwich knife and smiled broadly.

'Godber's has come,' announced Sadie, issuing out of the pantry. She had seen the man pass the window.

That meant the cream puffs had come. Godber's were famous for their cream puffs. Nobody ever thought of making them at home.

'Bring them in and put them on the table, my girl,' ordered cook.

Sadie brought them in and went back to the door. Of course Laura and Jose were far too grown-up to really care about such things. All the same, they couldn't help agreeing that the puffs looked very attractive. Very. Cook began arranging them, shaking off the extra icing sugar.

'Don't they carry one back to all one's parties?' said Laura.

'I suppose they do,' said practical Jose, who never liked to be carried back. 'They look beautifully light and feathery, I must say.'

'Have one each, my dears,' said cook in her comfortable voice. 'Yer ma won't know.'

Oh, impossible. Fancy cream puffs so soon after breakfast. The very idea made one shudder. All the same, two minutes later Jose and Laura were licking their fingers with that absorbed inward look that only comes from whipped cream.

'Let's go into the garden, out by the back way,' suggested Laura. 'I want to see how the men are getting on with the marquee. They're such awfully nice men.'

But the back door was blocked by cook, Sadie, Godber's man and Hans.

Something had happened.

'Tuk-tuk-tuk,' clucked cook like an agitated hen. Sadie had her hand clapped to her cheek as though she had toothache. Hans's face was screwed up in the effort to understand. Only Godber's man seemed to be enjoying himself; it was his story.

'What's the matter? What's happened?'

'There's been a horrible accident,' said cook. 'A man killed.'

'A man killed! Where? How? When?'

But Godber's man wasn't going to have his story snatched from under his very nose.

'Know those little cottages just below here, miss?' Know them? Of course, she knew them. 'Well, there's a young chap living there, name of Scott, a carter. His horse shied at a traction-engine, corner of Hawke Street this morning, and he was thrown out on the back of his head. Killed.'

'Dead!' Laura stared at Godber's man.

'Dead when they picked him up,' said Godber's man with relish. 'They were taking the body home as I come up here.' And he said to the cook, 'He's left a wife and five little ones.'

'Jose, come here.' Laura caught hold of her sister's sleeve and dragged her through the kitchen to the other side of the green baize door. There she paused and leaned against it. 'Jose!' she said, horrified, 'however are we going to stop everything?'

'Stop everything, Laura!' cried Jose in astonishment. 'What do you mean?'

'Stop the garden party, of course.' Why did Jose pretend?

But Jose was still more amazed. 'Stop the garden party? My dear Laura, don't be so absurd. Of course we can't do anything of the kind. Nobody expects us to. Don't be so extravagant.'

'But we can't possibly have a garden party with a man dead just outside the front gate.'

That really was extravagant, for the little cottages were in a lane to themselves at the very bottom of a steep rise that led up to the house. A broad road ran between. True, they were far too near. They were the greatest possible eyesore, and they had no right to be in that neighbourhood at all. They were little mean dwellings painted a chocolate brown. In the garden patches there was nothing but cabbage stalks, sick hens and tomato cans. The very smoke coming out of their chimneys was poverty-stricken. Little rags and shreds of smoke, so unlike the great silvery plumes that uncurled from the Sheridans' chimneys. Washerwomen lived in the lane and sweeps and a cobbler, and a man whose house-front was studded all over with minute bird-cages. Children swarmed. When the Sheridans were little they were forbidden to set foot there because of the revolting language and of what they might catch. But since they were grown up, Laura and Laurie on their prowls sometimes walked through. It was disgusting and sordid. They came out with a shudder. But still one must go everywhere; one must see everything. So through they went.

'And just think of what the band would sound like to that poor woman,' said Laura.

'Oh, Laura!' Jose began to be seriously annoyed. 'If you're going to stop a band playing every time some one has an accident, you'll lead a very strenuous life. I'm every bit as sorry about it as you. I feel just as sympathetic.' Her eyes hardened. She looked at her sister just as she used to when they were little and fighting together. 'You won't bring a drunken workman back to life by being sentimental,' she said softly.

'Drunk! Who said he was drunk?' Laura turned furiously on Jose. She said, just as they had used to say on those occasions, 'I'm going straight up to tell mother.'

'Do, dear,' cooed Jose.

'Mother, can I come into your room?' Laura turned the big glass door-knob.

'Of course, child. Why, what's the matter? What's given you such a colour?' And Mrs Sheridan turned round from her dressing-table. She was trying on a new hat.

'Mother, a man's been killed,' began Laura.

'Not in the garden?' interrupted her mother.

'No, no!'

'Oh, what a fright you gave me!' Mrs Sheridan sighed with relief, and took off the big hat and held it on her knees.

'But listen, mother,' said Laura. Breathless, half-choking, she told the dreadful story. 'Of course, we can't have our party, can we?' she pleaded. 'The band

and everybody arriving. They'd hear us, mother; they're nearly neighbours!'

To Laura's astonishment her mother behaved just like Jose; it was harder to bear because she seemed amused. She refused to take Laura seriously.

'But, my dear child, use your common sense. It's only by accident we've heard of it. If some one had died there normally—and I can't understand how they keep alive in those poky little holes—we should still be having our party, shouldn't we?'

Laura had to say 'yes' to that, but she felt it was all wrong. She sat down on her mother's sofa and pinched the cushion frill.

'Mother, isn't it really terribly heartless of us?' she asked.

'Darling!' Mrs Sheridan got up and came over to her, carrying the hat. Before Laura could stop her she had popped it on. 'My child!' said her mother, 'the hat is yours. It's made for you. It's much too young for me. I have never seen you look such a picture. Look at yourself!' And she held up her hand-mirror.

'But, mother,' Laura began again. She couldn't look at herself; she turned aside.

This time Mrs Sheridan lost patience just as Jose had done.

'You are being very absurd, Laura,' she said coldly. 'People like that don't expect sacrifices from us. And it's not very sympathetic to spoil everybody's enjoyment as you're doing now.'

'I don't understand,' said Laura, and she walked quickly out of the room into her own bedroom. There, quite by chance, the first thing she saw was this charming girl in the mirror, in her black hat trimmed with gold daisies, and a long black velvet ribbon. Never had she imagined she could look like that. Is mother right? she thought. And now she hoped her mother was right. Am I being extravagant? Perhaps it was extravagant. Just for a moment she had another glimpse of that poor woman and those little children, and the body being carried into the house. But it all seemed blurred, unreal, like a picture in the newspaper. I'll remember it again after the party's over, she decided. And somehow that seemed quite the best plan . . .

Lunch was over by half past one. By half past two they were all ready for the fray. The green-coated band had arrived and was established in a corner of the tennis-court.

'My dear!' trilled Kitty Maitland, 'aren't they too like frogs for words? You ought to have arranged them round the pond with the conductor in the middle on a leaf.'

Laurie arrived and hailed them on his way to dress. At the sight of him Laura remembered the accident again. She wanted to tell him. If Laurie agreed with the others, then it was bound to be all right. And she followed him into the hall.

'Laurie!'

'Hallo!' He was half-way upstairs, but when he turned round and saw Laura he suddenly puffed out his cheeks and goggled his eyes at her. 'My word, Laura! You do look stunning,' said Laurie. 'What an absolutely topping hat!'

Laura said faintly 'Is it?' and smiled up at Laurie, and didn't tell him after all.

Soon after that people began coming in streams. The band struck up; the hired waiters ran from the house to the marquee. Wherever you looked there were couples strolling, bending to the flowers, greeting, moving on over the lawn. They were like bright birds that had alighted in the Sheridans' garden for this one afternoon, on their way to—where? Ah, what happiness it is to be with people who all are happy, to press hands, press cheeks, smile into eyes.

'Darling Laura, how well you look!'

'What a becoming hat, child!'

'Laura, you look quite Spanish. I've never seen you look so striking.'

And Laura, glowing, answered softly, 'Have you had tea? Won't you have an ice? The passion-fruit ices really are rather special.' She ran to her father and begged him. 'Daddy darling, can't the band have something to drink?'

And the perfect afternoon slowly ripened, slowly faded, slowly its petals closed.

'Never a more delightful garden party . . . ' 'The greatest success . . . ' 'Quite the most . . . '

Laura helped her mother with the goodbyes. They stood side by side in the porch till it was all over.

'All over, all over, thank heaven,' said Mrs Sheridan. 'Round up the others, Laura. Let's go and have some fresh coffee. I'm exhausted. Yes, it's been very successful. But oh, these parties, these parties! Why will you children insist on giving parties!' And they all of them sat down in the deserted marquee.

'Have a sandwich, daddy dear. I wrote the flag.'

'Thanks.' Mr Sheridan took a bite and the sandwich was gone. He took another. 'I suppose you didn't hear of a beastly accident that happened to-day?' he said.

'My dear,' said Mrs Sheridan, holding up her hand, 'we did. It nearly ruined the party. Laura insisted we should put it off.'

'Oh, mother!' Laura didn't want to be teased about it.

'It was a horrible affair all the same,' said Mr Sheridan. 'The chap was married too. Lived just below in the lane, and leaves a wife and half a dozen kiddies, so they say.'

An awkward little silence fell. Mrs Sheridan fidgeted with her cup. Really, it was very tactless of father . . .

Suddenly she looked up. There on the table were all those sandwiches, cakes, puffs, all un-eaten, all going to be wasted. She had one of her brilliant ideas.

'I know,' she said. 'Let's make up a basket. Let's send that poor creature some of this perfectly good food. At any rate, it will be the greatest treat for the children. Don't you agree? And she's sure to have neighbours calling in and so on. What a point to have it all ready prepared. Laura!' She jumped up. 'Get me the big basket out of the stairs cupboard.'

'But, mother, do you really think it's a good idea?' said Laura.

Again, how curious, she seemed to be different from them all. To take scraps from their party. Would the poor woman really like that?

'Of course! What's the matter with you today? An hour or two ago you were insisting on us being sympathetic, and now—'

Oh well! Laura ran for the basket. It was filled, it was heaped by her mother.

'Take it yourself, darling,' said she. 'Run down just as you are. No, wait, take the arum lilies too. People of that class are so impressed by arum lilies.'

'The stems will ruin her lace frock,' said practical Jose.

So they would. Just in time. 'Only the basket, then. And, Laura!'—her mother followed her out of the marquee—'don't on any account—'

'What mother?'

No, better not put such ideas into the child's head! 'Nothing! Run along.'

It was just growing dusky as Laura shut their garden gates. A big dog ran by like a shadow. The road gleamed white, and down below in the hollow the little cottages were in deep shade. How quiet it seemed after the afternoon. Here she was going down the hill to somewhere where a man lay dead, and she couldn't realize it. Why couldn't she? She stopped a minute. And it seemed to her that kisses, voices, tinkling spoons, laughter, the smell of crushed grass were somehow inside her. She had no room for anything else. How strange! She looked up at the pale sky, and all she thought was, 'Yes, it was the most successful.'

Now the broad road was crossed. The lane began, smoky and dark. Women in shawls and men's tweed caps hurried by. Men hung over the palings; the children played in the doorways. A low hum came from the mean little cottages. In some of them there was a flicker of light, and a shadow, crab-like, moved across the window. Laura bent her head and hurried on. She wished now she had put on a coat. How her frock shone! And the big hat with the velvet streamer—if only it was another hat! Were the people looking at her? They must be. It was a mistake to have come; she knew all along it was a mistake. Should she go back even now?

No, too late. This was the house. It must be. A dark knot of people stood outside. Beside the gate an old, old woman with a crutch sat in a chair, watching. She had her feet on a newspaper. The voices stopped as Laura drew near. The group parted. It was as though she was expected, as though they had known she was coming here.

Laura was terribly nervous. Tossing the velvet ribbon over her shoulder, she said to a woman standing by, 'Is this Mrs Scott's house?' and the woman, smiling queerly, said, 'It is, my lass.'

Oh, to be away from this! She actually said, 'Help me, God,' as she walked up the tiny path and knocked. To be away from those staring eyes, or to be covered up in anything, one of those women's shawls even. I'll just leave the basket and go, she decided. I shan't even wait for it to be emptied.

Then the door opened. A little woman in black showed in the gloom.

Laura said, 'Are you Mrs Scott?' But to her horror the woman answered, 'Walk in please, miss,' and she was shut in the passage.

'No,' said Laura, 'I don't want to come in. I only want to leave this basket. Mother sent—'

The little woman in the gloomy passage seemed not to have heard her. 'Step this way, please, miss,' she said in an oily voice, and Laura followed her.

She found herself in a wretched little low kitchen, lighted by a smoky lamp. There was a woman sitting before the fire.

'Em,' said the little creature who had let her in. 'Em! It's a young lady.' She turned to Laura. She said meaningly, 'I'm her sister, Miss. You'll excuse 'er, won't you?'

'Oh, but of course!' said Laura. 'Please, please don't disturb her. I—I only want to leave—'

But at that moment the woman at the fire turned round. Her face, puffed up, red, with swollen eyes and swollen lips, looked terrible. She seemed as though she couldn't understand why Laura was there. What did it mean? Why was this stranger standing in the kitchen with a basket? What was it all about? And the poor face puckered up again.

'All right, my dear,' said the other. 'I'll thenk the young lady.'

And again she began, 'You'll excuse her, miss, I'm sure,' and her face, swollen too, tried an oily smile.

Laura only wanted to get out, to get away. She was back in the passage. The door opened. She walked straight through into the bedroom where the dead man was lying.

'You'd like a look at 'im, wouldn't you?' said Em's sister, and she brushed past Laura over to the bed. 'Don't be afraid, my lass,'—and now her voice sounded fond and sly, and fondly she drew down the sheet—' 'e looks a picture. There's nothing to show. Come along, my dear.'

Laura came.

There lay a young man, fast asleep—sleeping so soundly, so deeply, that he was far, far away from them both. Oh, so remote, so peaceful. He was dreaming. Never wake him up again. His head was sunk in the pillow, his eyes were closed; they were blind under the closed eyelids. He was given up to his dream. What did garden parties and baskets and lace frocks matter to him? He was far from all those things. He was wonderful, beautiful. While they were laughing and while the band was playing, this marvel had come to the lane. Happy . . . happy . . . All is well, said that sleeping face. This is just as it should be. I am content.

But all the same you had to cry, and she couldn't go out of the room without saying something to him. Laura gave a loud childish sob.

'Forgive my hat,' she said.

And this time she didn't wait for Em's sister. She found her way out of the door, down the path, past all those dark people. At the corner of the lane she met Laurie.

He stepped out of the shadow. 'Is that you, Laura?'

'Yes.'

'Mother was getting anxious. Was it all right?'

'Yes, quite. Oh, Laurie!' She took his arm, she pressed up against him.

'I say, you're not crying, are you?' asked her brother.

Laura shook her head. She was.

Laurie put his arm round her shoulder. 'Don't cry,' he said in his warm, loving voice. 'Was it awful?'

'No,' sobbed Laura. 'It was simply marvellous. But, Laurie—' She stopped, she looked at her brother. 'Isn't life,' she stammered, 'isn't life—' But what life was she couldn't explain. No matter. He quite understood.

'*Isn't* it, darling?' said Laurie.

1921   1922

JEAN RHYS
1890–1979

Jean Rhys was born Ella Gwendolen Rees Williams on the small island of Dominica in the West Indies. Her father was a Welsh doctor; her mother, a Creole (that is, a white West Indian) descended from wealthy, slave-holding plantation owners. Rhys was educated at a convent school in Roseau, Dominica, before, at the age of seventeen, leaving Dominica to attend the Perse School in Cambridge, England; she returned to her birthplace only once, in 1936. Her feelings toward her Caribbean background and childhood were mixed: she deeply appreciated the rich sensations

2656 / JEAN RHYS

and cross-racial engagements of her tropical experience, yet she was haunted by the knowledge of her violent heritage and carried a heavy burden of historical guilt. As a West Indian she felt estranged from mainstream European culture and identified with the suffering of Afro-Caribbeans, yet as a white Creole she grew up feeling out of place amid the predominantly black population of Dominica.

After studying briefly at the Academy of Dramatic Art in London, Rhys worked as a traveling chorus girl, mannequin, film extra, and—during World War I—volunteer cook. In 1919 she left England to marry the first of three husbands, and for many years she lived abroad, mainly in Paris, where she began to write the stories of her first book, *The Left Bank: Sketches and Studies of Present-Day Bohemian Paris* (1927). It was published with an introduction by the established novelist and poet Ford Madox Ford, who was for a time her lover. Ford grasped the link between her vulnerability as a person and her strength as a writer; he perceived her "terrifying insight . . . and passion for stating the case of the underdog." Rhys declared, "I have only ever written about myself," and indeed much of her writing is semiautobiographical. Her fiction frequently depicts single, economically challenged women, rootless outsiders living in bohemian London or Paris. Her early "sketches" were followed by her first novel, *Postures* (1928, reprinted as *Quartet* in 1969), in part an account of her affair with Ford; *After Leaving Mr. Mackenzie* (1930), about sexual betrayal; *Voyage in the Dark* (1934), an account of a nineteen-year-old chorus girl in London who has come from Dominica; and *Good Morning, Midnight* (1939), another first-person narrative of a lonely drifter, this time in Paris.

She published nothing more for many years, dropping out of sight and often living in poverty, until, following the enthusiastic reception of a radio adaptation of *Good Morning, Midnight* in 1957, she began to work in earnest on her masterpiece, *Wide Sargasso Sea* (1966). In this novel, set in Jamaica and Dominica in the 1830s and 1840s, Rhys returns to her Caribbean childhood and, in a brilliant act of imaginative sympathy, creates a West Indian prehistory for the first Mrs. Rochester, the mad-woman in the attic of Charlotte Brontë's *Jane Eyre*. Altogether Rhys worked on the novel for twenty-one years, amid bouts of depression, loneliness, and alcoholism, but its immediate acclaim gave her the recognition she had so long been denied. She continued to publish works of fiction and autobiography and in the year before her death received the Commander of the Order of the British Empire.

During the long period when she was writing *Wide Sargasso Sea*, Rhys produced only two published stories, both of which draw like the novel on her Caribbean youth. In "The Day They Burned the Books," set in the West Indies, a white girl who only partly understands the painful entanglements of class, race, and cultural prejudice tells how a lower-class Englishman has accumulated a trove of books he values for their cultural prestige, while his mulatto wife, embittered by her husband's racism, comes to despise them as emblems of British imperial oppression. "Let Them Call It Jazz" also has a first-person female narrator, but this time she is a West Indian mulatto, who speaks in West Indian English of her struggle against racial and class barriers after immigrating to London, an outsider in the metropolitan heart of the empire, ultimately jailed—as was Rhys for a few days after assaulting a neighbor—in Royal Holloway Prison. The shattering of a stained-glass window in this story—like the book burning in the first story and the house burning in *Wide Sargasso Sea*—represents an eruption of Afro-Caribbean rage in response to the circumscriptions and deceptions of white racism.

Whether working in Standard or West Indian English, Rhys is one of the great prose stylists of the twentieth century, her language spare yet lyrical, her sentences exactingly written and rewritten to suggest the most in the fewest possible words. Her writing is almost painfully alert to sensory detail, sensitive to the terrible fears and frustrated longings of marginalized people, and fierce in its unmasking of the social and psychic consequences of racial and gender oppression.

The Day They Burned the Books

My friend Eddie was a small, thin boy. You could see the blue veins in his wrists and temples. People said that he had consumption[1] and wasn't long for this world. I loved, but sometimes despised him.

His father, Mr Sawyer, was a strange man. Nobody could make out what he was doing in our part of the world at all. He was not a planter or a doctor or a lawyer or a banker. He didn't keep a store. He wasn't a schoolmaster or a government official. He wasn't—that was the point—a gentleman. We had several resident romantics who had fallen in love with the moon on the Caribees[2]—they were all gentlemen and quite unlike Mr Sawyer who hadn't an 'h' in his composition.[3] Besides, he detested the moon and everything else about the Caribbean and he didn't mind telling you so.

He was agent for a small steamship line which in those days linked up Venezuela and Trinidad[4] with the smaller islands, but he couldn't make much out of that. He must have a private income, people decided, but they never decided why he had chosen to settle in a place he didn't like and to marry a coloured woman. Though a decent, respectable, nicely educated coloured woman, mind you.

Mrs Sawyer must have been very pretty once but, what with one thing and another, that was in days gone by.

When Mr Sawyer was drunk—this often happened—he used to be very rude to her. She never answered him.

'Look at the nigger showing off,' he would say; and she would smile as if she knew she ought to see the joke but couldn't. 'You damned, long-eyed, gloomy half-caste,[5] you don't smell right,' he would say; and she never answered, not even to whisper, 'You don't smell right to me, either.'

The story went that once they had ventured to give a dinner party and that when the servant, Mildred, was bringing in coffee, he had pulled Mrs Sawyer's hair. 'Not a wig, you see,' he bawled. Even then, if you can believe it, Mrs Sawyer had laughed and tried to pretend that it was all part of the joke, this mysterious, obscure, sacred English joke.

But Mildred told the other servants in the town that her eyes had gone wicked, like a soucriant's[6] eyes, and that afterwards she had picked up some of the hair he pulled out and put it in an envelope, and that Mr Sawyer ought to look out (hair is obeah[7] as well as hands).

Of course, Mrs Sawyer had her compensations. They lived in a very pleasant house in Hill Street. The garden was large and they had a fine mango tree, which bore prolifically. The fruit was small, round, very sweet and juicy—a lovely, red-and-yellow colour when it was ripe. Perhaps it was one of the compensations, I used to think.

Mr Sawyer built a room on to the back of this house. It was unpainted inside and the wood smelt very sweet. Bookshelves lined the walls. Every time the

1. Wasting of the body associated with tuberculosis.
2. Or Caribbees: old term for the group of islands in the southeastern West Indies, now called the Lesser Antilles.
3. His pronunciation marks him as lower-class.
4. Formerly British, Caribbean island off northeast Venezuela.
5. Offensive term for a person of mixed racial descent.
6. Female vampire, in Caribbean legend.
7. A charm or fetish used in Afro-Caribbean witchcraft or sorcery.

Royal Mail steamer[8] came in it brought a package for him, and gradually the empty shelves filled.

Once I went there with Eddie to borrow *The Arabian Nights*.[9] That was on a Saturday afternoon, one of those hot, still afternoons when you felt that everything had gone to sleep, even the water in the gutters. But Mrs Sawyer was not asleep. She put her head in at the door and looked at us, and I knew that she hated the room and hated the books.

It was Eddie with the pale blue eyes and straw-coloured hair—the living image of his father, though often as silent as his mother—who first infected me with doubts about 'home', meaning England. He would be so quiet when others who had never seen it—none of us had ever seen it—were talking about its delights, gesticulating freely as we talked—London, the beautiful, rosy-cheeked ladies, the theatres, the shops, the fog, the blazing coal fires in winter, the exotic food (whitebait[1] eaten to the sound of violins), strawberries and cream—the word 'strawberries' always spoken with a guttural and throaty sound which we imagined to be the proper English pronunciation.

'I don't like strawberries,' Eddie said on one occasion.

'You *don't like* strawberries?'

'No, and I don't like daffodils either. Dad's always going on about them. He says they lick the flowers here into a cocked hat[2] and I bet that's a lie.'

We were all too shocked to say, 'You don't know a thing about it.' We were so shocked that nobody spoke to him for the rest of the day. But I for one admired him. I also was tired of learning and reciting poems in praise of daffodils, and my relations with the few 'real' English boys and girls I had met were awkward. I had discovered that if I called myself English they would snub me haughtily: 'You're not English; you're a horrid colonial.' 'Well, I don't much want to be English,' I would say. 'It's much more fun to be French or Spanish or something like that—and, as a matter of fact, I am a bit.' Then I was too killingly funny, quite ridiculous. Not only a horrid colonial, but also ridiculous. Heads I win, tails you lose—that was the English. I had thought about all this, and thought hard, but I had never dared to tell anybody what I thought and I realized that Eddie had been very bold.

But he was bold, and stronger than you would think. For one thing, he never felt the heat; some coldness in his fair skin resisted it. He didn't burn red or brown, he didn't freckle much.

Hot days seemed to make him feel especially energetic. 'Now we'll run twice round the lawn and then you can pretend you're dying of thirst in the desert and that I'm an Arab chieftain bringing you water.'

'You must drink slowly,' he would say, 'for if you're very thirsty and you drink quickly you die.'

So I learnt the voluptuousness of drinking slowly when you are very thirsty— small mouthful by small mouthful, until the glass of pink, iced Coca-Cola was empty.

Just after my twelfth birthday Mr Sawyer died suddenly, and as Eddie's special friend I went to the funeral, wearing a new white dress. My straight

---

8. Ship, owned by the Royal Mail Steam Packet Company, that ferried mail from London to the West Indies beginning in 1841.
9. Also called *The Thousand and One Nights*, a collection of old stories, largely Persian, Arabian, and Indian in origin.

1. Young of a small fish, such as herring, considered a delicacy when cooked whole.
2. From *knocked into a cocked hat*: make them look terrible by comparison. Daffodils are common in English poetry, but do not grow in the West Indies.

hair was damped with sugar and water the night before and plaited into tight little plaits, so that it should be fluffy for the occasion.

When it was all over everybody said how nice Mrs Sawyer had looked, walking like a queen behind the coffin and crying her eyeballs out at the right moment, and wasn't Eddie a funny boy? He hadn't cried at all.

After this Eddie and I took possession of the room with the books. No one else ever entered it, except Mildred to sweep and dust in the mornings, and gradually the ghost of Mr Sawyer pulling Mrs Sawyer's hair faded, though this took a little time. The blinds were always halfway down and going in out of the sun was like stepping into a pool of brown-green water. It was empty except for the bookshelves, a desk with a green baize[3] top and a wicker rocking-chair.

'My room,' Eddie called it. 'My books,' he would say, 'my books.'

I don't know how long this lasted. I don't know whether it was weeks after Mr Sawyer's death or months after, that I see myself and Eddie in the room. But there we are and there, unexpectedly, are Mrs Sawyer and Mildred. Mrs Sawyer's mouth tight, her eyes pleased. She is pulling all the books out of the shelves and piling them into two heaps. The big, fat glossy ones—the good-looking ones, Mildred explains in a whisper—lie in one heap. The *Encyclopaedia Britannica, British Flowers, Birds and Beasts*, various histories, books with maps, Froude's *English in the West Indies*[4] and so on—they are going to be sold. The unimportant books, with paper covers or damaged covers or torn pages, lie in another heap. They are going to be burnt—yes, burnt.

Mildred's expression was extraordinary as she said that—half hugely delighted, half shocked, even frightened. And as for Mrs Sawyer—well, I knew bad temper (I had often seen it), I knew rage, but this was hate. I recognized the difference at once and stared at her curiously. I edged closer to her so that I could see the titles of the books she was handling.

It was the poetry shelf. *Poems*, Lord Byron, *Poetical Works*, Milton, and so on. Vlung, vlung, vlung—all thrown into the heap that were to be sold. But a book by Christina Rossetti, though also bound in leather, went into the heap that was to be burnt, and by a flicker in Mrs Sawyer's eyes I knew that worse than men who wrote books were women who wrote books—infinitely worse. Men could be mercifully shot; women must be tortured.

Mrs Sawyer did not seem to notice that we were there, but she was breathing free and easy and her hands had got the rhythm of tearing and pitching. She looked beautiful, too—beautiful as the sky outside which was a very dark blue, or the mango tree, long sprays of brown and gold.

When Eddie said 'no', she did not even glance at him.

'No,' he said again in a high voice. 'Not that one. I was reading that one.'

She laughed and he rushed at her, his eyes starting out of his head, shrieking, 'Now I've got to hate you too. Now I hate you too.'

He snatched the book out of her hand and gave her a violent push. She fell into the rocking-chair.

Well, I wasn't going to be left out of all this, so I grabbed a book from the condemned pile and dived under Mildred's outstretched arm.

Then we were both in the garden. We ran along the path, bordered with crotons.[5] We pelted down the path though they did not follow us and we could hear Mildred laughing—kyah, kyah, kyah, kyah. As I ran I put the book I had taken into the loose front of my brown holland dress. It felt warm and alive.

---

3. Feltlike fabric.
4. Published in 1888 by the English historian

James Anthony Froude (1818–1894).
5. Tropical plants.

When we got into the street we walked sedately, for we feared the black children's ridicule. I felt very happy, because I had saved this book and it was my book and I would read it from the beginning to the triumphant words 'The End'. But I was uneasy when I thought of Mrs Sawyer.

'What will she do?' I said.

'Nothing,' Eddie said. 'Not to me.'

He was white as a ghost in his sailor suit, a blue-white even in the setting sun, and his father's sneer was clamped on his face.

'But she'll tell your mother all sorts of lies about you,' he said. 'She's an awful liar. She can't make up a story to save her life, but she makes up lies about people all right.'

'My mother won't take any notice of her,' I said. Though I was not at all sure.

'Why not? Because she's . . . because she isn't white?'

Well, I knew the answer to that one. Whenever the subject was brought up—people's relations and whether they had a drop of coloured blood or whether they hadn't—my father would grow impatient and interrupt. 'Who's white?' he would say. 'Damned few.'

So I said, 'Who's white? Damned few.'

'You can go to the devil,' Eddie said. 'She's prettier than your mother. When she's asleep her mouth smiles and she has your curling eyelashes and quantities and quantities and *quantities* of hair.'

'Yes,' I said truthfully. 'She's prettier than my mother.'

It was a red sunset that evening, a huge, sad, frightening sunset.

'Look, let's go back,' I said. 'If you're sure she won't be vexed with you, let's go back. It'll be dark soon.'

At his gate he asked me not to go. 'Don't go yet, don't go yet.'

We sat under the mango tree and I was holding his hand when he began to cry. Drops fell on my hand like the water from the dripstone in the filter[6] in our yard. Then I began to cry too and when I felt my own tears on my hand I thought, 'Now perhaps we're married.'

'Yes, certainly, now we're married,' I thought. But I didn't say anything. I didn't say a thing until I was sure he had stopped. Then I asked, 'What's your book?'

'It's *Kim*,'[7] he said. 'But it got torn. It starts at page twenty now. What's the one you took?'

'I don't know, it's too dark to see,' I said.

When I got home I rushed into my bedroom and locked the door because I knew that this book was the most important thing that had ever happened to me and I did not want anybody to be there when I looked at it.

But I was very disappointed, because it was in French and seemed dull. *Fort Comme La Mort*,[8] it was called. . . .

1960

---

6. Dripstone is a sandstone used as a filter to clean water for household use.

7. Novel (1901) by the English writer Rudyard Kipling (1865–1936), about an Irish orphan boy growing up in India.

8. *Strong as Death*, 1889 novel by the French writer Guy de Maupassant (1850–1893).

SAMUEL BECKETT
1906–1989

Samuel Beckett was born near Dublin. Like W. B. Yeats, Bernard Shaw, and Oscar Wilde, he came from an Anglo-Irish Protestant family. He received a B.A. from Trinity College, Dublin, and after teaching English at the École Normale Supérieure in Paris for two years, returned to Trinity College to take his M.A. in 1931. He gave up teaching in 1932 to write, and having produced an insightful essay on the early stages of James Joyce's *Finnegans Wake* in 1929, he also worked as Joyce's amanuensis (secretary) and translator. In 1937 he settled permanently in Paris, where during World War II he joined an underground group in the anti-Nazi resistance and, after his group was betrayed, barely escaped into unoccupied France. From the mid-1940s he generally wrote in French and subsequently translated some of his work into an eloquent Irish-inflected English. His early novels—*Murphy* (1938; Eng. trans., 1957), *Watt* (1953), and the trilogy, *Molloy* (1951; 1955), *Malone Dies* (1951; 1956), and *The Unnameable* (1953; 1958)—have been hailed as masterpieces and precursors of postmodern fiction; but he is best-known for his plays, especially *Waiting for Godot* (1952; 1954) and *Endgame* (1957; 1958). He received the Nobel Prize in Literature in 1969.

Not much happens in a Beckett play; there is little plot, little incident, and little characterization. Characters engage in dialogue or dialectical monologues that go nowhere. There is no progression, no development, no resolution. Rambling exchanges and repetitive actions enact the lack of a fixed center, of meaning, of purpose, in the lives depicted. Yet the characters persist in their habitual, almost ritualistic, activities; they go on talking, even if only to themselves. In spite of a reiterated theme of nonexistence, the characters go on existing—if minimally: a stream of discourse, of thought and will, a consciousness questioning its own meaning and purpose. In *Waiting for Godot* the main characters wait for an arrival that is constantly deferred. They inhabit a bleak landscape seemingly confined to one road, one tree; they talk of moving on, yet never leave. Subsequent plays restrict the acting space to a room, to urns, to a mound in which the actor is buried; characters are physically confined or disabled, until *Not I* (1973) presents the most minimal embodiment of human consciousness available to theatrical representation: a disembodied mouth.

Beckett focuses his work on fundamental questions of existence and nonexistence, the mind and the body, the self as known from within and as seen from the outside or in retrospect. Joyce's artistic integrity and stream-of-consciousness technique influenced him, but the minimalism of Beckett's plays and fiction contrast with the maximalism of Joyce's *Ulysses* and *Finnegans Wake*. "I realised that Joyce had gone as far as one could in the direction of knowing more, in control of one's material," he told the biographer James Knowlson. "I realised my own way was in impoverishment, in lack of knowledge and in taking away, in subtracting rather than adding."

At the heart of *Endgame* is the vexed relationship between Hamm, the master, and Clov, his servant and nurse. These irritable, resentful, spiteful characters talk of leaving, dying, or otherwise ending, but they continue repetitively in their peevish ways. They live inside a room with two high windows that afford ambiguous views of an exterior world, where everything may or may not be dead. The play's only other characters are Hamm's parents, Nell and Nagg, but they live in two garbage cans and appear from the shoulders up; their relationship is hardly robust. Like other Beckett plays, this one juxtaposes vaudeville, slapstick, and other comic traditions with the intellectual and the grotesque. While denying the audience the comfortable security of a recognizable world, *Endgame* provides laughs, sometimes at the audience's expense. It shares its tragicomic quality with absurdist drama, which disrupts the conventions of realist drama, draws attention to its own fictionality, and refuses to provide hierarchies of significance. Reduced to bare essentials, the maimed, struggling, incomplete characters of *Endgame*—though often behaving as if they were the bumbling protagonists of a farce—raise unsettling questions about meaning and absurdity, power and dependency, time and repetition, language and the void.

Endgame[1]

For Roger Blin[2]

THE CHARACTERS

NAGG
NELL
HAMM
CLOV

Bare interior.
Grey light.
Left and right back, high up, two small windows, curtains drawn.
Front right, a door. Hanging near door, its face to wall, a picture.
Front left, touching each other, covered with an old sheet, two ashbins.
Centre, in an armchair on castors, covered with an old sheet, HAMM.
Motionless by the door, his eyes fixed on HAMM, CLOV. *Very red face.*
Brief tableau.

[CLOV *goes and stands under window left. Stiff, staggering walk. He looks up at window left. He turns and looks at window right. He goes and stands under window right. He looks up at window right. He turns and looks at window left. He goes out, comes back immediately with a small step-ladder, carries it over and sets it down under window left, gets up on it, draws back curtain. He gets down, takes six steps (for example) towards window right, goes back for ladder, carries it over and sets it down under window right, gets up on it, draws back curtain. He gets down, takes three steps towards window left, goes back for ladder, carries it over and sets it down under window left, gets up on it, looks out of window. Brief laugh. He gets down, takes one step towards window right, goes back for ladder, carries it over and sets it down under window right, gets up on it, looks out of window. Brief laugh. He gets down, goes with ladder towards ashbins, halts, turns, carries back ladder and sets it down under window right, goes to ashbins, removes sheet covering them, folds it over his arm. He raises one lid, stoops and looks into bin. Brief laugh. He closes lid. Same with other bin. He goes to* HAMM, *removes sheet covering him, folds it over his arm. In a dressing-gown, a stiff toque*[3] *on his head, a large blood-stained handkerchief over his face, a whistle hanging from his neck, a rug over his knees, thick socks on his feet,* HAMM *seems to be asleep.* CLOV *looks him over. Brief laugh. He goes to door, halts, turns towards auditorium.*]

CLOV [*Fixed gaze, tonelessly.*] Finished, it's finished, nearly finished, it must

---

1. Translated by the author.
2. Frenchman (1907–1984), who directed the premieres of *Waiting for Godot*, *Endgame*, and

other Beckett plays.
3. Small cap with no brim.

be nearly finished. [*Pause.*] Grain upon grain, one by one, and one day, suddenly, there's a heap, a little heap, the impossible heap. [*Pause.*] I can't be punished any more. [*Pause.*] I'll go now to my kitchen, ten feet by ten feet by ten feet, and wait for him to whistle me. [*Pause.*] Nice dimensions, nice proportions, I'll lean on the table, and look at the wall, and wait for him to whistle me. [*He remains a moment motionless, then goes out. He comes back immediately, goes to window right, takes up the ladder and carries it out. Pause.* HAMM *stirs. He yawns under the handkerchief. He removes the handkerchief from his face. Very red face. Black glasses.*]

HAMM Me—[*He yawns.*]—to play.[4] [*He holds the handkerchief spread out before him.*] Old Stancher![5] [*He takes off his glasses, wipes his eyes, his face, the glasses, puts them on again, folds the handkerchief and puts it back neatly in the breast-pocket of his dressing-gown. He clears his throat, joins the tips of his fingers.*] Can there be misery—[*He yawns.*]—loftier than mine? No doubt. Formerly. But now? [*Pause.*] My father? [*Pause.*] My mother? [*Pause.*] My . . . dog? [*Pause.*] Oh I am willing to believe they suffer as much as such creatures can suffer. But does that mean their sufferings equal mine? No doubt. [*Pause.*] No, all is a—[*He yawns.*]—bsolute, [*Proudly.*] the bigger a man is the fuller he is. [*Pause. Gloomily.*] And the emptier. [*He sniffs.*] Clov! [*Pause.*] No, alone. [*Pause.*] What dreams! Those forests! [*Pause.*] Enough, it's time it ended, in the shelter too. [*Pause.*] And yet I hesitate, I hesitate to . . . to end. Yes, there it is, it's time it ended and yet I hesitate to—[*He yawns.*]—to end. [*Yawns.*] God, I'm tired, I'd be better off in bed. [*He whistles. Enter* CLOV *immediately. He halts beside the chair.*] You pollute the air! [*Pause.*] Get me ready, I'm going to bed.

CLOV I've just got you up.

HAMM And what of it?

CLOV I can't be getting you up and putting you to bed every five minutes, I have things to do. [*Pause.*]

HAMM Did you ever see my eyes?

CLOV No.

HAMM Did you never have the curiosity, while I was sleeping, to take off my glasses and look at my eyes?

CLOV Pulling back the lids? [*Pause.*] No.

HAMM One of these days I'll show them to you. [*Pause.*] It seems they've gone all white. [*Pause.*] What time is it?

CLOV The same as usual.

HAMM [*Gesture towards window right.*] Have you looked?

CLOV Yes.

HAMM Well?

CLOV Zero.

HAMM It'd need to rain.

CLOV It won't rain. [*Pause.*]

HAMM Apart from that, how do you feel?

CLOV I don't complain.

HAMM You feel normal?

CLOV [*Irritably.*] I tell you I don't complain.

4. Hamm announces that it is his move, as it were in a game of chess, of which the final stage is called the "endgame."

5. Handkerchief that stanches (checks the flow of) blood.

HAMM   I feel a little queer. [*Pause.*] Clov!

CLOV   Yes.

HAMM   Have you not had enough?

CLOV   Yes! [*Pause.*] Of what?

HAMM   Of this . . . this . . . thing.

CLOV   I always had. [*Pause.*] Not you?

HAMM   [*Gloomily.*] Then there's no reason for it to change.

CLOV   It may end. [*Pause.*] All life long the same questions, the same answers.

HAMM   Get me ready. [CLOV *does not move.*] Go and get the sheet. [CLOV *does not move.*] Clov!

CLOV   Yes.

HAMM   I'll give you nothing more to eat.

CLOV   Then we'll die.

HAMM   I'll give you just enough to keep you from dying. You'll be hungry all the time.

CLOV   Then we won't die. [*Pause.*] I'll go and get the sheet. [*He goes towards the door.*]

HAMM   No! [CLOV *halts.*] I'll give you one biscuit per day. [*Pause.*] One and a half. [*Pause.*] Why do you stay with me?

CLOV   Why do you keep me?

HAMM   There's no one else.

CLOV   There's nowhere else. [*Pause.*]

HAMM   You're leaving me all the same.

CLOV   I'm trying.

HAMM   You don't love me.

CLOV   No.

HAMM   You loved me once.

CLOV   Once!

HAMM   I've made you suffer too much. [*Pause.*] Haven't I?

CLOV   It's not that.

HAMM   [*Shocked.*] I haven't made you suffer too much?

CLOV   Yes!

HAMM   [*Relieved.*] Ah you gave me a fright! [*Pause. Coldly.*] Forgive me. [*Pause. Louder.*] I said, Forgive me.

CLOV   I heard you. [*Pause.*] Have you bled?

HAMM   Less. [*Pause.*] Is it not time for my pain-killer?

CLOV   No. [*Pause.*]

HAMM   How are your eyes?

CLOV   Bad.

HAMM   How are your legs?

CLOV   Bad.

HAMM   But you can move.

CLOV   Yes.

HAMM   [*Violently.*] Then move! [CLOV *goes to back wall, leans against it with his forehead and hands.*] Where are you?

CLOV   Here.

HAMM   Come back! [CLOV *returns to his place beside the chair.*] Where are you?

CLOV   Here.

HAMM   Why don't you kill me?

CLOV   I don't know the combination of the cupboard. [*Pause.*]

HAMM   Go and get two bicycle-wheels.

CLOV   There are no more bicycle-wheels.

HAMM   What have you done with your bicycle?

CLOV   I never had a bicycle.

HAMM   The thing is impossible.

CLOV   When there were still bicycles I wept to have one. I crawled at your feet. You told me to go to hell. Now there are none.

HAMM   And your rounds? When you inspected my paupers. Always on foot?

CLOV   Sometimes on horse. [*The lid of one of the bins lifts and the hands of* NAGG *appear, gripping the rim. Then his head emerges. Nightcap. Very white face.* NAGG *yawns, then listens.*] I'll leave you, I have things to do.

HAMM   In your kitchen?

CLOV   Yes.

HAMM   Outside of here it's death. [*Pause.*] All right, be off. [*Exit* CLOV. *Pause.*] We're getting on.

NAGG   Me Pap![6]

HAMM   Accursed progenitor![7]

NAGG   Me pap!

HAMM   The old folks at home! No decency left! Guzzle, guzzle, that's all they think of. [*He whistles. Enter* CLOV. *He halts beside the chair.*] Well! I thought you were leaving me.

CLOV   Oh not just yet, not just yet.

NAGG   Me pap!

HAMM   Give him his pap.

CLOV   There's no more pap.

HAMM   [*To* NAGG.] Do you hear that? There's no more pap. You'll never get any more pap.

NAGG   I want me pap!

HAMM   Give him a biscuit. [*Exit* CLOV.] Accursed fornicator! How are your stumps?

NAGG   Never mind me stumps. [*Enter* CLOV *with biscuit.*]

CLOV   I'm back again, with the biscuit. [*He gives biscuit to* NAGG *who fingers it, sniffs it.*]

NAGG   [*Plaintively.*] What is it?

CLOV   Spratt's medium.[8]

NAGG   [*As before.*] It's hard! I can't!

HAMM   Bottle him! [CLOV *pushes* NAGG *back into the bin, closes the lid.*]

CLOV   [*Returning to his place beside the chair.*] If age but knew!

HAMM   Sit on him!

CLOV   I can't sit.

HAMM   True. And I can't stand.

CLOV   So it is.

HAMM   Every man his speciality. [*Pause.*] No phone calls? [*Pause.*] Don't we laugh?

CLOV   [*After reflection.*] I don't feel like it.

HAMM   [*After reflection.*] Not I. [*Pause.*] Clov!

CLOV   Yes.

HAMM   Nature has forgotten us.

---

6. Mushy food.
7. Parent.

8. Brand name of a biscuit (cookie).

CLOV There's no more nature.

HAMM No more nature! You exaggerate.

CLOV In the vicinity.

HAMM But we breathe, we change! We lose our hair, our teeth! Our bloom! Our ideals!

CLOV Then she hasn't forgotten us.

HAMM But you say there is none.

CLOV [*Sadly.*] No one that ever lived ever thought so crooked as we.

HAMM We do what we can.

CLOV We shouldn't. [*Pause.*]

HAMM You're a bit of all right,[9] aren't you?

CLOV A smithereen. [*Pause.*]

HAMM This is slow work. [*Pause.*] Is it not time for my pain-killer?

CLOV No. [*Pause.*] I'll leave you, I have things to do.

HAMM In your kitchen?

CLOV Yes.

HAMM What, I'd like to know.

CLOV I look at the wall.

HAMM The wall! And what do you see on your wall? Mene, mene?[1] Naked bodies?

CLOV I see my light dying.

HAMM Your light dying! Listen to that! Well, it can die just as well here, *your* light. Take a look at me and then come back and tell me what you think of *your* light. [*Pause.*]

CLOV You shouldn't speak to me like that. [*Pause.*]

HAMM [*Coldly.*] Forgive me. [*Pause. Louder.*] I said, Forgive me.

CLOV I heard you. [*The lid of* NAGG's *bin lifts. His hands appear, gripping the rim. Then his head emerges. In his mouth the biscuit. He listens.*]

HAMM Did your seeds come up?

CLOV No.

HAMM Did you scratch round them to see if they had sprouted?

CLOV They haven't sprouted.

HAMM Perhaps it's still too early.

CLOV If they were going to sprout they would have sprouted. [*Violently.*] They'll never sprout! [*Pause.* NAGG *takes biscuit in his hand.*]

HAMM This is not much fun. [*Pause.*] But that's always the way at the end of the day, isn't it, Clov?

CLOV Always.

HAMM It's the end of the day like any other day, isn't it, Clov?

CLOV Looks like it. [*Pause.*]

HAMM [*Anguished.*] What's happening, what's happening?

CLOV Something is taking its course. [*Pause.*]

HAMM All right, be off. [*He leans back in his chair, remains motionless.* CLOV *does not move, heaves a great groaning sigh.* HAMM *sits up.*] I thought I told you to be off.

CLOV I'm trying. [*He goes to door, halts.*] Ever since I was whelped.[2] [*Exit* CLOV.]

9. You're pretty good (British slang).
1. "Mene mene, tekel, upharsin": words written by a heavenly hand on the wall during the feast of Balshazzar, king of Babylon. Translated as "Thou art weighed in the balance and found wanting," it foretells his ruin (Daniel 5.25–28).
2. Born (usually applied to puppies: whelps).

HAMM   We're getting on. [*He leans back in his chair, remains motionless.* NAGG *knocks on the lid of the other bin. Pause. He knocks harder. The lid lifts and the hands of* NELL *appear, gripping the rim. Then her head emerges. Lace cap. Very white face.*]

NELL   What is it, my pet? [*Pause.*] Time for love?

NAGG   Were you asleep?

NELL   Oh no!

NAGG   Kiss me.

NELL   We can't.

NAGG   Try. [*Their heads strain towards each other, fail to meet, fall apart again.*]

NELL   Why this farce, day after day? [*Pause.*]

NAGG   I've lost me tooth.

NELL   When?

NAGG   I had it yesterday.

NELL   [*Elegiac.*[3]] Ah yesterday! [*They turn painfully towards each other.*]

NAGG   Can you see me?

NELL   Hardly. And you?

NAGG   What?

NELL   Can you see me?

NAGG   Hardly.

NELL   So much the better, so much the better.

NAGG   Don't say that. [*Pause.*] Our sight has failed.

NELL   Yes. [*Pause. They turn away from each other.*]

NAGG   Can you hear me?

NELL   Yes. And you?

NAGG   Yes. [*Pause.*] Our hearing hasn't failed.

NELL   Our what?

NAGG   Our hearing.

NELL   No. [*Pause.*] Have you anything else to say to me?

NAGG   Do you remember—

NELL   No.

NAGG   When we crashed on our tandem[4] and lost our shanks. [*They laugh heartily.*]

NELL   It was in the Ardennes. [*They laugh less heartily.*]

NAGG   On the road to Sedan.[5] [*They laugh still less heartily.*] Are you cold?

NELL   Yes, perished. And you?

NAGG   [*Pause.*] I'm freezing. [*Pause.*] Do you want to go in?

NELL   Yes.

NAGG   Then go in. [NELL *does not move.*] Why don't you go in?

NELL   I don't know. [*Pause.*]

NAGG   Has he changed your sawdust?

NELL   It isn't sawdust. [*Pause. Wearily.*] Can you not be a little accurate, Nagg?

NAGG   Your sand then. It's not important.

NELL   It is important. [*Pause.*]

NAGG   It was sawdust once.

NELL   Once!

---

3. As though lamenting something lost.
4. A bicycle made for two.
5. Town in northern France where the French Army was defeated in 1870 during the Franco-

Prussian War. Ardennes is a forest in northern France, which was the scene of fierce fighting in both World Wars.

NAGG   And now it's sand. [*Pause.*] From the shore. [*Pause. Impatiently.*] Now
   it's sand he fetches from the shore.

NELL   Now it's sand.

NAGG   Has he changed yours?

NELL   No.

NAGG   Nor mine. [*Pause.*] I won't have it! [*Pause. Holding up the biscuit.*] Do
   you want a bit?

NELL   No. [*Pause.*] Of what?

NAGG   Biscuit. I've kept you half. [*He looks at the biscuit. Proudly.*] Three
   quarters. For you. Here. [*He proffers the biscuit.*] No? [*Pause.*] Do you not
   feel well?

HAMM   [*Wearily.*] Quiet, quiet, you're keeping me awake. [*Pause.*] Talk softer.
   [*Pause.*] If I could sleep I might make love. I'd go into the woods. My eyes
   would see . . . the sky, the earth. I'd run, run, they wouldn't catch me.
   [*Pause.*] Nature! [*Pause.*] There's something dripping in my head. [*Pause.*]
   A heart, a heart in my head. [*Pause.*]

NAGG   [*Soft.*] Do you hear him? A heart in his head! [*He chuckles cautiously.*]

NELL   One mustn't laugh at those things, Nagg. Why must you always laugh
   at them?

NAGG   Not so loud!

NELL   [*Without lowering her voice.*] Nothing is funnier than unhappiness, I
   grant you that. But—

NAGG   [*Shocked.*] Oh!

NELL   Yes, yes, it's the most comical thing in the world. And we laugh, we
   laugh, with a will, in the beginning. But it's always the same thing. Yes, it's
   like the funny story we have heard too often, we still find it funny, but we
   don't laugh any more. [*Pause.*] Have you anything else to say to me?

NAGG   No.

NELL   Are you quite sure? [*Pause.*] Then I'll leave you.

NAGG   Do you not want your biscuit? [*Pause.*] I'll keep it for you. [*Pause.*] I
   thought you were going to leave me.

NELL   I am going to leave you.

NAGG   Could you give me a scratch before you go?

NELL   No. [*Pause.*] Where?

NAGG   In the back.

NELL   No. [*Pause.*] Rub yourself against the rim.

NAGG   It's lower down. In the hollow.

NELL   What hollow?

NAGG   The hollow! [*Pause.*] Could you not? [*Pause.*] Yesterday you scratched
   me there.

NELL   [*Elegiac.*] Ah yesterday!

NAGG   Could you not? [*Pause.*] Would you like me to scratch you? [*Pause.*]
   Are you crying again?

NELL   I was trying. [*Pause.*]

HAMM   Perhaps it's a little vein. [*Pause.*]

NAGG   What was that he said?

NELL   Perhaps it's a little vein.

NAGG   What does that mean? [*Pause.*] That means nothing. [*Pause.*] Will I
   tell you the story of the tailor?

NELL   No. [*Pause.*] What for?

NAGG   To cheer you up.

NELL It's not funny.

NAGG It always made you laugh. [*Pause.*] The first time I thought you'd die.

NELL It was on Lake Como.[6] [*Pause.*] One April afternoon. [*Pause.*] Can you believe it?

NAGG What?

NELL That we once went out rowing on Lake Como. [*Pause.*] One April afternoon.

NAGG We had got engaged the day before.

NELL Engaged!

NAGG You were in such fits that we capsized. By rights we should have been drowned.

NELL It was because I felt happy.

NAGG [*Indignant.*] It was not, it was not, it was my story and nothing else. Happy! Don't you laugh at it still? Every time I tell it. Happy!

NELL It was deep, deep. And you could see down to the bottom. So white. So clean.

NAGG Let me tell it again. [*Raconteur's voice.*] An Englishman, needing a pair of striped trousers in a hurry for the New Year festivities, goes to his tailor who takes his measurements. [*Tailor's voice.*] "That's the lot, come back in four days, I'll have it ready." Good. Four days later. [*Tailor's voice.*] "So sorry, come back in a week, I've made a mess of the seat." Good, that's all right, a neat seat can be very ticklish. A week later. [*Tailor's voice.*] "Frightfully sorry, come back in ten days. I've made a hash of the crotch." Good, can't be helped, a snug crotch is always a teaser. Ten days later. [*Tailor's voice.*] "Dreadfully sorry, come back in a fortnight, I've made a balls of the fly." Good, at a pinch, a smart fly is a stiff proposition. [*Pause. Normal voice.*] I never told it worse. [*Pause. Gloomy.*] I tell this story worse and worse. [*Pause. Raconteur's voice.*] Well, to make it short, the bluebells are blowing and he ballockses[7] the buttonholes. [*Customer's voice.*] "God damn you to hell, Sir, no, it's indecent, there are limits! In six days, do you hear me, six days, God made the world. Yes Sir, no less Sir, the WORLD! And you are not bloody well capable of making me a pair of trousers in three months!" [*Tailor's voice, scandalised.*] "But my dear Sir, my dear Sir, look—[*Disdainful gesture, disgustedly.*]—at the world—[*Pause.*] and look—[*Loving gesture, proudly.*]—at my TROUSERS!" [*Pause. He looks at NELL who has remained impassive, her eyes unseeing, breaks into a high forced laugh, cuts it short, pokes his head towards NELL, launches his laugh again.*]

HAMM Silence!

[*NAGG starts, cuts short his laugh.*]

NELL You could see down to the bottom.

HAMM [*Exasperated.*] Have you not finished? Will you never finish? [*With sudden fury.*] Will this never finish? [*NAGG disappears into his bin, closes the lid behind him. NELL does not move. Frenziedly.*] My kingdom for a nightman![8] [*He whistles. Enter CLOV.*] Clear away this muck! Chuck it in the sea! [*CLOV goes to bins, halts.*]

NELL So white.

---

6. Large lake in northern Italy.
7. Botches.
8. A collector of nightsoil (excrement). Cf. Shake-speare's *Richard III* 5.7.7: "A horse! A horse! My kingdom for a horse!"

HAMM   What? What's she blathering about? [CLOV *stoops, takes* NELL's *hand, feels her pulse.*]

NELL   [*To* CLOV.] Desert! [CLOV *lets go her hand, pushes her back in the bin, closes the lid.*]

CLOV   [*Returning to his place beside the chair.*] She has no pulse.

HAMM   What was she drivelling about?

CLOV   She told me to go away, into the desert.

HAMM   Damn busybody! Is that all?

CLOV   No.

HAMM   What else?

CLOV   I didn't understand.

HAMM   Have you bottled her?

CLOV   Yes.

HAMM   Are they both bottled?

CLOV   Yes.

HAMM   Screw down the lids. [CLOV *goes towards door.*] Time enough. [CLOV *halts.*] My anger subsides, I'd like to pee.

CLOV   [*With alacrity.*] I'll go and get the catheter. [*He goes towards door.*]

HAMM   Time enough. [CLOV *halts.*] Give me my pain-killer.

CLOV   It's too soon. [*Pause.*] It's too soon on top of your tonic, it wouldn't act.

HAMM   In the morning they brace you up and in the evening they calm you down. Unless it's the other way round. [*Pause.*] That old doctor, he's dead naturally?

CLOV   He wasn't old.

HAMM   But he's dead?

CLOV   Naturally. [*Pause.*] You ask *me* that? [*Pause.*]

HAMM   Take me for a little turn. [CLOV *goes behind the chair and pushes it forward.*] Not too fast! [CLOV *pushes chair.*] Right round the world! [CLOV *pushes chair.*] Hug the walls, then back to the centre again. [CLOV *pushes chair.*] I was right in the centre, wasn't I?

CLOV   [*Pushing.*] Yes.

HAMM   We'd need a proper wheel-chair. With big wheels. Bicycle wheels! [*Pause.*] Are you hugging?

CLOV   [*Pushing.*] Yes.

HAMM   [*Groping for wall.*] It's a lie! Why do you lie to me?

CLOV   [*Bearing closer to wall.*] There! There!

HAMM   Stop! [CLOV *stops chair close to back wall.* HAMM *lays his hand against wall.*] Old wall! [*Pause.*] Beyond is the . . . other hell. [*Pause. Violently.*] Closer! Closer! Up against!

CLOV   Take away your hand. [HAMM *withdraws his hand.* CLOV *rams chair against wall.*] There! [HAMM *leans towards wall, applies his ear to it.*]

HAMM   Do you hear? [*He strikes the wall with his knuckles.*] Do you hear? Hollow bricks! [*He strikes again.*] All that's hollow! [*Pause. He straightens up. Violently.*] That's enough. Back!

CLOV   We haven't done the round.

HAMM   Back to my place! [CLOV *pushes chair back to centre.*] Is that my place?

CLOV   Yes, that's your place.

HAMM   Am I right in the centre?

CLOV   I'll measure it.

HAMM   More or less! More or less!

CLOV   [*Moving chair slightly.*] There!

HAMM   I'm more or less in the centre?

CLOV   I'd say so.

HAMM   You'd say so! Put me right in the centre!

CLOV   I'll go and get the tape.

HAMM   Roughly! Roughly! [CLOV *moves chair slightly.*] Bang in the centre!

CLOV   There! [*Pause.*]

HAMM   I feel a little too far to the left. [CLOV *moves chair slightly.*] Now I feel a little too far to the right. [CLOV *moves chair slightly.*] I feel a little too far forward. [CLOV *moves chair slightly.*] Now I feel a little too far back. [CLOV *moves chair slightly.*] Don't stay there, [*I.e., behind the chair.*] you give me the shivers. [CLOV *returns to his place beside the chair.*]

CLOV   If I could kill him I'd die happy. [*Pause.*]

HAMM   What's the weather like?

CLOV   As usual.

HAMM   Look at the earth.

CLOV   I've looked.

HAMM   With the glass?

CLOV   No need of the glass.

HAMM   Look at it with the glass.

CLOV   I'll go and get the glass. [*Exit* CLOV.]

HAMM   No need of the glass! [*Enter* CLOV *with telescope.*]

CLOV   I'm back again, with the glass. [*He goes to window right, looks up at it.*] I need the steps.

HAMM   Why? Have you shrunk? [*Exit* CLOV *with telescope.*] I don't like that, I don't like that. [*Enter* CLOV *with ladder, but without telescope.*]

CLOV   I'm back again, with the steps. [*He sets down ladder under window right, gets up on it, realises he has not the telescope, gets down.*] I need the glass. [*He goes towards door.*]

HAMM   [*Violently.*] But you have the glass!

CLOV   [*Halting, violently.*] No, I haven't the glass! [*Exit* CLOV.]

HAMM   This is deadly. [*Enter* CLOV *with telescope. He goes towards ladder.*]

CLOV   Things are livening up. [*He gets up on ladder, raises the telescope, lets it fall.*] I did it on purpose. [*He gets down, picks up the telescope, turns it on auditorium.*] I see . . . a multitude . . . in transports . . . of joy.[9] [*Pause.*] That's what I call a magnifier. [*He lowers the telescope, turns towards* HAMM.] Well? Don't we laugh?

HAMM   [*After reflection.*] I don't.

CLOV   [*After reflection.*] Nor I. [*He gets up on ladder, turns the telescope on the without.*] Let's see. [*He looks, moving the telescope.*] Zero . . . [*He looks.*] . . . zero . . . [*He looks.*] . . . and zero.

HAMM   Nothing stirs. All is—

CLOV   Zer—

HAMM   [*Violently.*] Wait till you're spoke to! [*Normal voice.*] All is . . . all is . . . all is what? [*Violently.*] All is what?

CLOV   What all is? In a word? Is that what you want to know? Just a moment. [*He turns the telescope on the without, looks, lowers the telescope, turns towards* HAMM.] Corpsed. [*Pause.*] Well? Content?

HAMM   Look at the sea.

---

9. Cf. Revelation 7.9–10: "After this I beheld, and lo, a great multitude, which . . . cried with a loud voice . . . Salvation."

CLOV   It's the same.

HAMM   Look at the ocean! [CLOV *gets down, takes a few steps towards window left, goes back for ladder, carries it over and sets it down under window left, gets up on it, turns the telescope on the without, looks at length. He starts, lowers the telescope, examines it, turns it again on the without.*]

CLOV   Never seen anything like that!

HAMM   [*Anxious.*] What? A sail? A fin? Smoke?

CLOV   [*Looking.*] The light is sunk.

HAMM   [*Relieved.*] Pah! We all knew that.

CLOV   [*Looking.*] There was a bit left.

HAMM   The base.

CLOV   [*Looking.*] Yes.

HAMM   And now?

CLOV   [*Looking.*] All gone.

HAMM   No gulls?

CLOV   [*Looking.*] Gulls!

HAMM   And the horizon? Nothing on the horizon?

CLOV   [*Lowering the telescope, turning towards* HAMM, *exasperated.*] What in God's name could there be on the horizon? [*Pause.*]

HAMM   The waves, how are the waves?

CLOV   The waves? [*He turns the telescope on the waves.*] Lead.

HAMM   And the sun?

CLOV   [*Looking.*] Zero.

HAMM   But it should be sinking. Look again.

CLOV   [*Looking.*] Damn the sun.

HAMM   Is it night already then?

CLOV   [*Looking.*] No.

HAMM   Then what is it?

CLOV   [*Looking.*] Grey. [*Lowering the telescope, turning towards* HAMM, *louder.*] Grey! [*Pause. Still louder.*] GRREY! [*Pause. He gets down, approaches* HAMM *from behind, whispers in his ear.*]

HAMM   [*Starting.*] Grey! Did I hear you say grey?

CLOV   Light black. From pole to pole.

HAMM   You exaggerate. [*Pause.*] Don't stay there, you give me the shivers. [CLOV *returns to his place beside the chair.*]

CLOV   Why this farce, day after day?

HAMM   Routine. One never knows. [*Pause.*] Last night I saw inside my breast. There was a big sore.

CLOV   Pah! You saw your heart.

HAMM   No, it was living. [*Pause. Anguished.*] Clov!

CLOV   Yes.

HAMM   What's happening?

CLOV   Something is taking its course. [*Pause.*]

HAMM   Clov!

CLOV   [*Impatiently.*] What is it?

HAMM   We're not beginning to . . . to . . . mean something?

CLOV   Mean something! You and I, mean something! [*Brief laugh.*] Ah that's a good one!

HAMM   I wonder. [*Pause.*] Imagine if a rational being came back to earth, wouldn't he be liable to get ideas into his head if he observed us long enough. [*Voice of rational being.*] Ah, good, now I see what it is, yes, now I understand what they're at! [CLOV *starts, drops the telescope and begins to scratch his belly with both hands. Normal voice.*] And without going so far as that, we ourselves . . . [*With emotion.*] . . . we ourselves . . . at certain moments . . . [*Vehemently.*] To think perhaps it won't all have been for nothing!

CLOV [*Anguished, scratching himself.*] I have a flea!

HAMM A flea! Are there still fleas?

CLOV On me there's one. [*Scratching.*] Unless it's a crablouse.

HAMM [*Very perturbed.*] But humanity might start from there all over again! Catch him, for the love of God!

CLOV I'll go and get the powder. [*Exit* CLOV.]

HAMM A flea! This is awful! What a day! [*Enter* CLOV *with a sprinkling-tin.*]

CLOV I'm back again, with the insecticide.

HAMM Let him have it! [CLOV *loosens the top of his trousers, pulls it forward and shakes powder into the aperture. He stoops, looks, waits, starts, frenziedly shakes more powder, stoops, looks, waits.*]

CLOV The bastard!

HAMM Did you get him?

CLOV Looks like it. [*He drops the tin and adjusts his trousers.*] Unless he's laying doggo.

HAMM Laying! Lying you mean. Unless he's *lying* doggo.

CLOV Ah? One says lying? One doesn't say laying?

HAMM Use your head, can't you. If he was laying we'd be bitched.

CLOV Ah. [*Pause.*] What about that pee?

HAMM I'm having it.

CLOV Ah that's the spirit, that's the spirit! [*Pause.*]

HAMM [*With ardour.*] Let's go from here, the two of us! South! You can make a raft and the currents will carry us away, far away, to other . . . mammals!

CLOV God forbid!

HAMM Alone, I'll embark alone! Get working on that raft immediately. Tomorrow I'll be gone for ever.

CLOV [*Hastening towards door.*] I'll start straight away.

HAMM Wait! [CLOV *halts.*] Will there be sharks, do you think?

CLOV Sharks? I don't know. If there are there will be. [*He goes towards door.*]

HAMM Wait! [CLOV *halts.*] Is it not yet time for my pain-killer?

CLOV [*Violently.*] No! [*He goes towards door.*]

HAMM Wait! [CLOV *halts.*] How are your eyes?

CLOV Bad.

HAMM But you can see.

CLOV All I want.

HAMM How are your legs?

CLOV Bad.

HAMM But you can walk.

CLOV I come . . . and go.

HAMM In my house. [*Pause. With prophetic relish.*] One day you'll be blind, like me. You'll be sitting there, a speck in the void, in the dark, for ever, like me. [*Pause.*] One day you'll say to yourself, I'm tired, I'll sit down, and you'll go and sit down. Then you'll say, I'm hungry, I'll get up and get something to eat. But you won't get up. You'll say, I shouldn't have sat down, but since I have I'll sit on a little longer, then I'll get up and get something to eat. But you won't go up and you won't get anything to eat. [*Pause.*] You'll look at the wall a while, then you'll say, I'll close my eyes, perhaps have a little sleep, after that I'll feel better, and you'll close them. And when you open them again there'll be no wall any more. [*Pause.*] Infinite emptiness will be all around you, all the resurrected dead of all the ages wouldn't fill it, and there you'll be like a little bit of grit in the middle of the steppe.[1] [*Pause.*] Yes, one day you'll know what it is, you'll be like me, except that you won't have anyone with you, because you won't have had pity on anyone and because there won't be anyone left to have pity on. [*Pause.*]

CLOV   It's not certain. [*Pause.*] And there's one thing you forget.

HAMM   Ah?

CLOV   I can't sit down.

HAMM   [*Impatiently.*] Well you'll lie down then, what the hell! Or you'll come to a standstill, simply stop and stand still, the way you are now. One day you'll say, I'm tired, I'll stop. What does the attitude matter? [*Pause.*]

CLOV   So you all want me to leave you.

HAMM   Naturally.

CLOV   Then I'll leave you.

HAMM   You can't leave us.

CLOV   Then I won't leave you. [*Pause.*]

HAMM   Why don't you finish us? [*Pause.*] I'll tell you the combination of the cupboard if you promise to finish me.

CLOV   I couldn't finish you.

HAMM   Then you won't finish me. [*Pause.*]

CLOV   I'll leave you, I have things to do.

HAMM   Do you remember when you came here?

CLOV   No. Too small, you told me.

HAMM   Do you remember your father?

CLOV   [*Wearily.*] Same answer. [*Pause.*] You've asked me these questions millions of times.

HAMM   I love the old questions. [*With fervour.*] Ah the old questions, the old answers, there's nothing like them! [*Pause.*] It was I was a father to you.

CLOV   Yes. [*He looks at* HAMM *fixedly.*] You were that to me.

HAMM   My house a home for you.

CLOV   Yes. [*He looks about him.*] This was that for me.

HAMM   [*Proudly.*] But for me, [*Gesture towards himself.*] no father. But for Hamm, [*Gesture towards surroundings.*] no home. [*Pause.*]

CLOV   I'll leave you.

HAMM   Did you ever think of one thing?

CLOV   Never.

HAMM   That here we're down in a hole. [*Pause.*] But beyond the hills? Eh? Perhaps it's still green. Eh? [*Pause.*] Flora! Pomona! [*Ecstatically.*] Ceres![2] [*Pause.*] Perhaps you won't need to go very far.

CLOV   I can't go very far. [*Pause.*] I'll leave you.

HAMM   Is my dog ready?

CLOV   He lacks a leg.

HAMM   Is he silky?

CLOV   He's a kind of Pomeranian.

HAMM   Go and get him.

---

1. Level grassy plain devoid of forest, especially in southeast Europe and Siberia.

2. In Roman mythology, respectively, the goddesses of flowers, fruit, and crops.

CLOV He lacks a leg.

HAMM Go and get him! [*Exit* CLOV.] We're getting on. [*Enter* CLOV *holding by one of its three legs a black toy dog.*]

CLOV Your dogs are here. [*He hands the dog to* HAMM *who feels it, fondles it.*]

HAMM He's white, isn't he?

CLOV Nearly.

HAMM What do you mean, nearly? Is he white or isn't he?

CLOV He isn't. [*Pause.*]

HAMM You've forgotten the sex.

CLOV [*Vexed.*] But he isn't finished. The sex goes on at the end. [*Pause.*]

HAMM You haven't put on his ribbon.

CLOV [*Angrily.*] But he isn't finished, I tell you! First you finish your dog and then you put on his ribbon! [*Pause.*]

HAMM Can he stand?

CLOV I don't know.

HAMM Try. [*He hands the dog to* CLOV *who places it on the ground.*] Well?

CLOV Wait! [*He squats down and tries to get the dog to stand on its three legs, fails, lets it go. The dog falls on its side.*]

HAMM [*Impatiently.*] Well?

CLOV He's standing.

HAMM [*Groping for the dog.*] Where? Where is he? [CLOV *holds up the dog in a standing position.*]

CLOV There. [*He takes* HAMM's *hand and guides it towards the dog's head.*]

HAMM [*His hand on the dog's head.*] Is he gazing at me?

CLOV Yes.

HAMM [*Proudly.*] As if he were asking me to take him for a walk?

CLOV If you like.

HAMM [*As before.*] Or as if he were begging me for a bone. [*He withdraws his hand.*] Leave him like that, standing there imploring me. [CLOV *straightens up. The dog falls on its side.*]

CLOV I'll leave you.

HAMM Have you had your visions?

CLOV Less.

HAMM Is Mother Pegg's light on?

CLOV Light! How could anyone's light be on?

HAMM Extinguished!

CLOV Naturally it's extinguished. If it's not on it's extinguished.

HAMM No, I mean Mother Pegg.

CLOV But naturally she's extinguished! [*Pause.*] What's the matter with you today?

HAMM I'm taking my course. [*Pause.*] Is she buried?

CLOV Buried! Who would have buried her?

HAMM You.

CLOV Me! Haven't I enough to do without burying people?

HAMM But you'll bury me.

CLOV No I won't bury you. [*Pause.*]

HAMM She was bonny once, like a flower of the field. [*With reminiscent leer.*] And a great one for the men!

CLOV We too were bonny—once. It's a rare thing not to have been bonny— once. [*Pause.*]

HAMM   Go and get the gaff.[3] [CLOV *goes to door, halts.*]
CLOV   Do this, do that, and I do it. I never refuse. Why?
HAMM   You're not able to.
CLOV   Soon I won't do it any more.
HAMM   You won't be able to any more. [*Exit* CLOV.] Ah the creatures, the creatures, everything has to be explained to them. [*Enter* CLOV *with gaff.*]
CLOV   Here's your gaff. Stick it up. [*He gives the gaff to* HAMM *who, wielding it like a puntpole,[4] tries to move his chair.*]
HAMM   Did I move?
CLOV   No. [HAMM *throws down the gaff.*]
HAMM   Go and get the oilcan.
CLOV   What for?
HAMM   To oil the castors.
CLOV   I oiled them yesterday.
HAMM   Yesterday! What does that mean? Yesterday!
CLOV   [*Violently.*] That means that bloody awful day, long ago, before this bloody awful day. I use the words you taught me. If they don't mean anything any more, teach me others. Or let me be silent. [*Pause.*]
HAMM   I once knew a madman who thought the end of the world had come. He was a painter—and engraver. I had a great fondness for him. I used to go and see him, in the asylum. I'd take him by the hand and drag him to the window. Look! There! All that rising corn! And there! Look! The sails of the herring fleet! All that loveliness! [*Pause.*] He'd snatch away his hand and go back into his corner. Appalled. All he had seen was ashes. [*Pause.*] He alone had been spared. [*Pause.*] Forgotten. [*Pause.*] It appears the case is . . . was not so . . . so unusual.
CLOV   A madman! When was that?
HAMM   Oh way back, way back, you weren't in the land of the living.
CLOV   God be with the days! [*Pause.* HAMM *raises his toque.*]
HAMM   I had a great fondness for him. [*Pause. He puts on his toque again.*] He was a painter—and engraver.
CLOV   There are so many terrible things.
HAMM   No, no, there are not so many now. [*Pause.*] Clov!
CLOV   Yes.
HAMM   Do you not think this has gone on long enough?
CLOV   Yes! [*Pause.*] What?
HAMM   This . . . this . . . thing.
CLOV   I've always thought so. [*Pause.*] You not?
HAMM   [*Gloomily.*] Then it's a day like any other day.
CLOV   As long as it lasts. [*Pause.*] All life long the same inanities.
HAMM   I can't leave you.
CLOV   I know. And you can't follow me. [*Pause.*]
HAMM   If you leave me how shall I know?
CLOV   [*Briskly.*] Well you simply whistle me and if I don't come running it means I've left you. [*Pause.*]
HAMM   You won't come and kiss me goodbye?
CLOV   Oh I shouldn't think so. [*Pause.*]
HAMM   But you might be merely dead in your kitchen.

3. Barbed fishing spear.
4. Long pole, pushed against the bottom of a river to propel a punt (a shallow flat-bottomed boat).

CLOV   The result would be the same.

HAMM   Yes, but how would I know, if you were merely dead in your kitchen?

CLOV   Well . . . sooner or later I'd start to stink.

HAMM   You stink already. The whole place stinks of corpses.

CLOV   The whole universe.

HAMM   [*Angrily.*] To hell with the universe. [*Pause.*] Think of something.

CLOV   What?

HAMM   An idea, have an idea. [*Angrily.*] A bright idea!

CLOV   Ah good. [*He starts pacing to and fro, his eyes fixed on the ground, his hands behind his back. He halts.*] The pains in my legs! It's unbelievable! Soon I won't be able to think any more.

HAMM   You won't be able to leave me. [CLOV *resumes his pacing.*] What are you doing?

CLOV   Having an idea. [*He paces.*] Ah! [*He halts.*]

HAMM   What a brain! [*Pause.*] Well?

CLOV   Wait! [*He meditates. Not very convinced.*] Yes . . . [*Pause. More convinced.*] Yes! [*He raises his head.*] I have it! I set the alarm. [*Pause.*]

HAMM   This is perhaps not one of my bright days, but frankly—

CLOV   You whistle me. I don't come. The alarm rings. I'm gone. It doesn't ring. I'm dead. [*Pause.*]

HAMM   Is it working? [*Pause. Impatiently.*] The alarm, is it working?

CLOV   Why wouldn't it be working?

HAMM   Because it's worked too much.

CLOV   But it's hardly worked at all.

HAMM   [*Angrily.*] Then because it's worked too little!

CLOV   I'll go and see. [*Exit* CLOV. *Brief ring of alarm off. Enter* CLOV *with alarm-clock. He holds it against* HAMM's *ear and releases alarm. They listen to it ringing to the end. Pause.*] Fit to wake the dead! Did you hear it?

HAMM   Vaguely.

CLOV   The end is terrific!

HAMM   I prefer the middle. [*Pause.*] Is it not time for my pain-killer?

CLOV   No! [*He goes to door, turns.*] I'll leave you.

HAMM   It's time for my story. Do you want to listen to my story.

CLOV   No.

HAMM   Ask my father if he wants to listen to my story. [CLOV *goes to bins, raises the lid of* NAGG's, *stoops, looks into it. Pause. He straightens up.*]

CLOV   He's asleep.

HAMM   Wake him. [CLOV *stoops, wakes* NAGG *with the alarm. Unintelligible words.* CLOV *straightens up.*]

CLOV   He doesn't want to listen to your story.

HAMM   I'll give him a bon-bon. [CLOV *stoops. As before.*]

CLOV   He wants a sugar-plum.

HAMM   He'll get a sugar-plum. [CLOV *stoops. As before.*]

CLOV   It's a deal. [*He goes towards door.* NAGG's *hands appear, gripping the rim. Then the head emerges.* CLOV *reaches door, turns.*] Do you believe in the life to come?

HAMM   Mine was always that. [*Exit* CLOV.] Got him that time!

NAGG   I'm listening.

HAMM   Scoundrel! Why did you engender me?

NAGG   I didn't know.

HAMM   What? What didn't you know?

2678 / SAMUEL BECKETT

NAGG   That it'd be you. [*Pause.*] You'll give me a sugar-plum?

HAMM   After the audition.

NAGG   You swear?

HAMM   Yes.

NAGG   On what?

HAMM   My honour. [*Pause. They laugh heartily.*]

NAGG   Two.

HAMM   One.

NAGG   One for me and one for—

HAMM   One! Silence! [*Pause.*] Where was I? [*Pause. Gloomily.*] It's finished, we're finished. [*Pause.*] Nearly finished. [*Pause.*] There'll be no more speech. [*Pause.*] Something dripping in my head, ever since the fontanelles.[5] [*Stifled hilarity of NAGG.*] Splash, splash, always on the same spot. [*Pause.*] Perhaps it's a little vein. [*Pause.*] A little artery. [*Pause. More animated.*] Enough of that, it's story time, where was I? [*Pause. Narrative tone.*] The man came crawling towards me, on his belly. Pale, wonderfully pale and thin, he seemed on the point of—[*Pause. Normal tone.*] No, I've done that bit. [*Pause. Narrative tone.*] I calmly filled my pipe—the meerschaum, lit it with . . . let us say a vesta,[6] drew a few puffs. Aah! [*Pause.*] Well, what is it you want? [*Pause.*] It was an extra-ordinarily bitter day, I remember, zero by the thermometer. But considering it was Christmas Eve there was nothing . . . extra-ordinary about that. Seasonable weather, for once in a way. [*Pause.*] Well, what ill wind blows you my way? He raised his face to me, black with mingled dirt and tears. [*Pause. Normal tone.*] That should do it. [*Narrative tone.*] No, no, don't look at me, don't look at me. He dropped his eyes and mumbled something, apologies I presume. [*Pause.*] I'm a busy man, you know, the final touches, before the festivities, you know what it is. [*Pause. Forcibly.*] Come on now, what is the object of this invasion? [*Pause.*] It was a glorious bright day, I remember, fifty by the heliometer,[7] but already the sun was sinking down into the . . . down among the dead. [*Normal tone.*] Nicely put, that. [*Narrative tone.*] Come on now, come on, present your petition and let me resume my labours. [*Pause. Normal tone.*] There's English for you. Ah well . . . [*Narrative tone.*] It was then he took the plunge. It's my little one, he said. Tsstss, a little one, that's bad. My little boy, he said, as if the sex mattered. Where did he come from? He named the hole. A good half-day, on horse. What are you insinuating? That the place is still inhabited? No no, not a soul, except himself and the child—assuming he existed. Good. I enquired about the situation at Kov,[8] beyond the gulf. Not a sinner. Good. And you expect me to believe you have left your little one back there, all alone, and alive into the bargain? Come now! [*Pause.*] It was a howling wild day, I remember, a hundred by the anemometer.[9] The wind was tearing up the dead pines and sweeping them . . . away. [*Pause. Normal tone.*] A bit feeble, that. [*Narrative tone.*] Come on, man, speak up, what is it you want from me, I have to put up my holly. [*Pause.*] Well to make it short it finally transpired that what he wanted from me was . . . bread for his brat? Bread? But I have no bread, it doesn't agree with me. Good. Then

---

5. Membranous space in infant's skull at the angles of the parietal bones.
6. Vesta is the brand name of a type of match (from Vesta, Roman goddess of the hearth).
7. Literally, a sun meter.

8. Conceivably the town of Kova in southern Siberia (except that it has no gulf); more probably Hamm's invention.
9. A wind meter.

perhaps a little corn? [*Pause. Normal tone.*] That should do it. [*Narrative tone.*] Corn, yes, I have corn, it's true, in my granaries. But use your head. I give you some corn, a pound, a pound and a half, you bring it back to your child and you make him—if he's still alive—a nice pot of porridge, [NAGG *reacts.*] a nice pot and a half of porridge, full of nourishment. Good. The colours come back into his little cheeks—perhaps. And then? [*Pause.*] I lost patience. [*Violently.*] Use your head, can't you, use your head, you're on earth, there's no cure for that! [*Pause.*] It was an exceedingly dry day, I remember, zero by the hygrometer. Ideal weather, for my lumbago.[1] [*Pause. Violently.*] But what in God's name do you imagine? That the earth will awake in spring? That the rivers and seas will run with fish again? That there's manna in heaven still for imbeciles like you? [*Pause.*] Gradually I cooled down, sufficiently at least to ask him how long he had taken on the way. Three whole days. Good. In what condition he had left the child. Deep in sleep. [*Forcibly.*] But deep in what sleep, deep in what sleep already? [*Pause.*] Well to make it short I finally offered to take him into my service. He had touched a chord. And then I imagined already that I wasn't much longer for this world. [*He laughs. Pause.*] Well? [*Pause.*] Well? Here if you were careful you might die a nice natural death, in peace and comfort. [*Pause.*] Well? [*Pause.*] In the end he asked me would I consent to take in the child as well—if he were still alive. [*Pause.*] It was the moment I was waiting for. [*Pause.*] Would I consent to take in the child . . . [*Pause.*] I can see him still, down on his knees, his hands flat on the ground, glaring at me with his mad eyes, in defiance of my wishes. [*Pause. Normal tone.*] I'll soon have finished with this story. [*Pause.*] Unless I bring in other characters. [*Pause.*] But where would I find them? [*Pause.*] Where would I look for them? [*Pause. He whistles. Enter* CLOV.] Let us pray to God.

NAGG   Me sugar-plum!
CLOV   There's a rat in the kitchen!
HAMM   A rat! Are there still rats?
CLOV   In the kitchen there's one.
HAMM   And you haven't exterminated him?
CLOV   Half. You disturbed us.
HAMM   He can't get away?
CLOV   No.
HAMM   You'll finish him later. Let us pray to God.
CLOV   Again!
NAGG   Me sugar-plum!
HAMM   God first! [*Pause.*] Are you right?
CLOV   [*Resigned.*] Off we go.
HAMM   [*To* NAGG.] And you?
NAGG   [*Clasping his hands, closing his eyes, in a gabble.*] Our Father which art—
HAMM   Silence! In silence! Where are your manners? [*Pause.*] Off we go. [*Attitudes of prayer. Silence. Abandoning his attitude, discouraged.*] Well?
CLOV   [*Abandoning his attitude.*] What a hope! And you?
HAMM   Sweet damn all! [*To* NAGG.] And you?
NAGG   Wait! [*Pause. Abandoning his attitude.*] Nothing doing!
HAMM   The bastard! He doesn't exist!

1. Rheumatic pain in the lumbar region of the lower back. "Hygrometer": a moisture meter.

CLOV Not yet.

NAGG Me sugar-plum!

HAMM There are no more sugar-plums! [*Pause.*]

NAGG It's natural. After all I'm your father. It's true if it hadn't been me it would have been someone else. But that's no excuse. [*Pause.*] Turkish Delight,[2] for example, which no longer exists, we all know that, there is nothing in the world I love more. And one day I'll ask you for some, in return for a kindness, and you'll promise it to me. One must live with the times. [*Pause.*] Whom did you call when you were a tiny boy, and were frightened, in the dark? Your mother? No. Me. We let you cry. Then we moved you out of earshot, so that we might sleep in peace. [*Pause.*] I was asleep, as happy as a king, and you woke me up to have me listen to you. It wasn't indispensable, you didn't really need to have me listen to you. [*Pause.*] I hope the day will come when you'll really need to have me listen to you, and need to hear my voice, any voice. [*Pause.*] Yes, I hope I'll live till then, to hear you calling me like when you were a tiny boy, and were frightened, in the dark, and I was your only hope. [*Pause.* NAGG *knocks on lid of* NELL's *bin. Pause.*] Nell! [*Pause. He knocks louder. Pause. Louder.*] Nell! [*Pause.* NAGG *sinks back into his bin, closes the lid behind him. Pause.*]

HAMM Our revels now are ended.[3] [*He gropes for the dog*] The dog's gone.

CLOV He's not a real dog, he can't go.

HAMM [*Groping.*] He's not there.

CLOV He's lain down.

HAMM Give him up to me. [CLOV *picks up the dog and gives it to* HAMM. HAMM *holds it in his arms. Pause.* HAMM *throws away the dog.*] Dirty brute! [CLOV *begins to pick up the objects lying on the ground.*] What are you doing?

CLOV Putting things in order. [*He straightens up. Fervently.*] I'm going to clear everything away! [*He starts picking up again.*]

HAMM Order!

CLOV [*Straightening up.*] I love order. It's my dream. A world where all would be silent and still and each thing in its last place, under the last dust. [*He starts picking up again.*]

HAMM [*Exasperated.*] What in God's name do you think you are doing?

CLOV [*Straightening up.*] I'm doing my best to create a little order.

HAMM Drop it! [CLOV *drops the objects he has picked up.*]

CLOV After all, there or elsewhere. [*He goes towards door.*]

HAMM [*Irritably.*] What's wrong with your feet?

CLOV My feet?

HAMM Tramp! Tramp!

CLOV I must have put on my boots.

HAMM Your slippers were hurting you? [*Pause.*]

CLOV I'll leave you.

HAMM No!

CLOV What is there to keep me here?

HAMM The dialogue. [*Pause.*] I've got on with my story. [*Pause.*] I've got on with it well. [*Pause. Irritably.*] Ask me where I've got to.

CLOV Oh, by the way, your story?

HAMM [*Surprised.*] What story?

2. A sticky sweet candy (originally from Turkey).
3. Words spoken by Prospero in Shakespeare's *The Tempest* 4.1.148.

CLOV The one you've been telling yourself all your days.
HAMM Ah you mean my chronicle?
CLOV That's the one. [*Pause.*]
HAMM [*Angrily.*] Keep going, can't you, keep going!
CLOV You've got on with it, I hope.
HAMM [*Modestly.*] Oh not very far, not very far. [*He sighs.*] There are days like that, one isn't inspired. [*Pause.*] Nothing you can do about it, just wait for it to come. [*Pause.*] No forcing, no forcing, it's fatal. [*Pause.*] I've got on with it a little all the same. [*Pause.*] Technique, you know. [*Pause. Irritably.*] I say I've got on with it a little all the same.
CLOV [*Admiringly.*] Well I never! In spite of everything you were able to get on with it!
HAMM [*Modestly.*] Oh not very far, you know, not very far, but nevertheless, better than nothing.
CLOV Better than nothing! Is it possible?
HAMM I'll tell you how it goes. He comes crawling on his belly—
CLOV Who?
HAMM What?
CLOV Who do you mean, he?
HAMM Who do I mean! Yet another.
CLOV Ah him! I wasn't sure.
HAMM Crawling on his belly, whining for bread for his brat. He's offered a job as gardener. Before— [CLOV *bursts out laughing.*] What is there so funny about that?
CLOV A job as gardener!
HAMM Is that what tickles you?
CLOV It must be that.
HAMM It wouldn't be the bread?
CLOV Or the brat. [*Pause.*]
HAMM The whole thing is comical, I grant you that. What about having a good guffaw the two of us together?
CLOV [*After reflection.*] I couldn't guffaw again today.
HAMM [*After reflection.*] Nor I. [*Pause.*] I continue then. Before accepting with gratitude he asks if he may have his little boy with him.
CLOV What age?
HAMM Oh tiny.
CLOV He would have climbed the trees.
HAMM All the little odd jobs.
CLOV And then he would have grown up.
HAMM Very likely. [*Pause.*]
CLOV Keep going, can't you, keep going!
HAMM That's all. I stopped there. [*Pause.*]
CLOV Do you see how it goes on.
HAMM More or less.
CLOV Will it not soon be the end?
HAMM I'm afraid it will.
CLOV Pah! You'll make up another.
HAMM I don't know. [*Pause.*] I feel rather drained. [*Pause.*] The prolonged creative effort. [*Pause.*] If I could drag myself down to the sea! I'd make a pillow of sand for my head and the tide would come.
CLOV There's no more tide. [*Pause.*]

HAMM   Go and see is she dead. [CLOV *goes to bins, raises the lid of* NELL'S, *stoops, looks into it. Pause.*]

CLOV   Looks like it. [*He closes the lid, straightens up.* HAMM *raises his toque. Pause. He puts it on again.*]

HAMM   [*With his hand to his toque.*] And Nagg? [CLOV *raises lid of* NAGG's *bin, stoops, looks into it. Pause.*]

CLOV   Doesn't look like it. [*He closes the lid, straightens up.*]

HAMM   [*Letting go his toque.*] What's he doing? [CLOV *raises lid of* NAGG's *bin, stoops, looks into it. Pause.*]

CLOV   He's crying. [*He closes lid, straightens up.*]

HAMM   Then he's living. [*Pause.*] Did you ever have an instant of happiness?

CLOV   Not to my knowledge. [*Pause.*]

HAMM   Bring me under the window. [CLOV *goes towards chair.*] I want to feel the light on my face. [CLOV *pushes chair.*] Do you remember, in the beginning, when you took me for a turn? You used to hold the chair too high. At every step you nearly tipped me out. [*With senile quaver.*] Ah great fun, we had, the two of us, great fun. [*Gloomily.*] And then we got into the way of it. [CLOV *stops the chair under window right.*] There already? [*Pause. He tilts back his head.*] Is it light?

CLOV   It isn't dark.

HAMM   [*Angrily*] I'm asking you is it light.

CLOV   Yes. [*Pause.*]

HAMM   The curtain isn't closed?

CLOV   No.

HAMM   What window is it?

CLOV   The earth.

HAMM   I knew it! [*Angrily.*] But there's no light there! The other! [CLOV *stops the chair under window left.* HAMM *tilts back his head.*] That's what I call light! [*Pause.*] Feels like a ray of sunshine. [*Pause.*] No?

CLOV   No.

HAMM   It isn't a ray of sunshine I feel on my face?

CLOV   No. [*Pause.*]

HAMM   Am I very white? [*Pause. Angrily.*] I'm asking you am I very white!

CLOV   Not more so than usual. [*Pause.*]

HAMM   Open the window.

CLOV   What for?

HAMM   I want to hear the sea.

CLOV   You wouldn't hear it.

HAMM   Even if you opened the window?

CLOV   No.

HAMM   Then it's not worth while opening it?

CLOV   No.

HAMM   [*Violently*] Then open it! [CLOV *gets up on the ladder, opens the window. Pause.*] Have you opened it?

CLOV   Yes. [*Pause.*]

HAMM   You swear you've opened it?

CLOV   Yes. [*Pause.*]

HAMM   Well . . . ! [*Pause.*] It must be very calm. [*Pause. Violently.*] I'm asking you is it very calm!

CLOV   Yes.

HAMM   It's because there are no more navigators. [*Pause.*] You haven't much conversation all of a sudden. Do you not feel well?

CLOV   I'm cold.

HAMM   What month are we? [*Pause.*] Close the window, we're going back.
[CLOV *closes the window, gets down, pushes the chair back to its place, remains
standing behind it, head bowed.*] Don't stay there, you give me the shivers!
[CLOV *returns to his place beside the chair.*] Father! [*Pause. Louder.*] Father!
[*Pause.*] Go and see did he hear me. [CLOV *goes to* NAGG's *bin, raises the lid,
stoops. Unintelligible words.* CLOV *straightens up.*]

CLOV   Yes.

HAMM   Both times? [CLOV *stoops. As before.*]

CLOV   Once only.

HAMM   The first time or the second? [CLOV *stoops. As before.*]

CLOV   He doesn't know.

HAMM   It must have been the second.

CLOV   We'll never know. [*He closes lid.*]

HAMM   Is he still crying?

CLOV   No.

HAMM   The dead go fast. [*Pause.*] What's he doing?

CLOV   Sucking his biscuit.

HAMM   Life goes on. [CLOV *returns to his place beside the chair.*] Give me a
rug. I'm freezing.

CLOV   There are no more rugs. [*Pause.*]

HAMM   Kiss me. [*Pause.*] Will you not kiss me?

CLOV   No.

HAMM   On the forehead.

CLOV   I won't kiss you anywhere. [*Pause.*]

HAMM   [*Holding out his hand.*] Give me your hand at least. [*Pause.*] Will you
not give me your hand?

CLOV   I won't touch you. [*Pause.*]

HAMM   Give me the dog. [CLOV *looks round for the dog.*] No!

CLOV   Do you not want your dog?

HAMM   No.

CLOV   Then I'll leave you.

HAMM   [*Head bowed, absently.*] That's right. [CLOV *goes to door, turns.*]

CLOV   If I don't kill that rat he'll die.

HAMM   [*As before.*] That's right. [*Exit* CLOV. *Pause.*] Me to play. [*He takes out
his handkerchief, unfolds it, holds it spread out before him.*] We're getting
on. [*Pause.*] You weep, and weep, for nothing, so as not to laugh, and little
by little . . . you begin to grieve. [*He folds the handkerchief, puts it back in
his pocket, raises his head.*] All those I might have helped. [*Pause.*] Helped!
[*Pause.*] Saved. [*Pause.*] Saved! [*Pause.*] The place was crawling with them!
[*Pause. Violently.*] Use your head, can't you, use your head, you're on earth,
there's no cure for that! [*Pause.*] Get out of here and love one another! Lick
your neighbour as yourself![4] [*Pause. Calmer.*] When it wasn't bread they
wanted it was crumpets. [*Pause. Violently.*] Out of my sight and back to your
petting parties! [*Pause.*] All that, all that! [*Pause.*] Not even a real dog!
[*Calmer.*] The end is in the beginning and yet you go on. [*Pause.*] Perhaps
I could go on with my story, end it and begin another. [*Pause.*] Perhaps I
could throw myself out on the floor. [*He pushes himself painfully off his seat,
falls back again.*] Dig my nails into the cracks and drag myself forward with
my fingers. [*Pause.*] It will be the end and there I'll be, wondering what can

---

4. Parody of Jesus' instruction: "Thou shalt love thy neighbor as thyself" (Matthew 19.19).

have brought it on and wondering what can have . . . [*He hesitates.*] . . . why it was so long coming. [*Pause.*] There I'll be, in the old shelter, alone against the silence and . . . [*He hesitates.*] . . . the stillness. If I can hold my peace, and sit quiet, it will be all over with sound, and motion, all over and done with. [*Pause.*] I'll have called my father and I'll have called my . . . [*He hesitates.*] . . . my son. And even twice, or three times, in case they shouldn't have heard me, the first time, or the second. [*Pause.*] I'll say to myself, He'll come back. [*Pause.*] And then? [*Pause.*] And then? [*Pause.*] He couldn't, he has gone too far. [*Pause.*] And then? [*Pause. Very agitated.*] All kinds of fantasies! That I'm being watched! A rat! Steps! Breath held and then . . . [*He breathes out.*] Then babble, babble, words, like the solitary child who turns himself into children, two, three, so as to be together, and whisper together, in the dark. [*Pause.*] Moment upon moment, pattering down, like the millet grains of . . . [*He hesitates.*] . . . that old Greek,[5] and all life long you wait for that to mount up to a life. [*Pause. He opens his mouth to continue, renounces.*] Ah let's get it over! [*He whistles. Enter* CLOV *with alarm-clock. He halts beside the chair.*] What? Neither gone nor dead?

CLOV In spirit only.
HAMM Which?
CLOV Both.
HAMM Gone from me you'd be dead.
CLOV And vice versa.
HAMM Outside of here it's death! [*Pause.*] And the rat?
CLOV He's got away.
HAMM He can't go far. [*Pause. Anxious.*] Eh?
CLOV He doesn't need to go far. [*Pause.*]
HAMM Is it not time for my pain-killer?
CLOV Yes.
HAMM Ah! At last! Give it to me! Quick! [*Pause.*]
CLOV There's no more pain-killer. [*Pause.*]
HAMM [*Appalled.*] Good . . . ! [*Pause.*] No more pain-killer!
CLOV No more pain-killer. You'll never get any more pain-killer. [*Pause.*]
HAMM But the little round box. It was full!
CLOV Yes. But now it's empty. [*Pause.* CLOV *starts to move about the room. He is looking for a place to put down the alarm-clock.*]
HAMM [*Soft.*] What'll I do? [*Pause. In a scream.*] What'll I do? [CLOV *sees the picture, takes it down, stands it on the floor with its face to the wall, hangs up the alarm-clock in its place.*] What are you doing?
CLOV Winding up.
HAMM Look at the earth.
CLOV Again!
HAMM Since it's calling to you.
CLOV Is your throat sore? [*Pause.*] Would you like a lozenge? [*Pause.*] No. [*Pause.*] Pity. [CLOV *goes, humming, towards window right, halts before it, looks up at it.*]
HAMM Don't sing.
CLOV [*Turning towards* HAMM.] One hasn't the right to sing any more?

---

5. Zeno of Elea (ca. 450 B.C.E.), a Greek philosopher famous for his paradoxes; e.g., "If a grain of millet falling makes no sound, how can a bushel of grains make any sound?" (reported by Aristotle in his *Physics* 5:250 a.19).

HAMM   No.

CLOV   Then how can it end?

HAMM   You want it to end?

CLOV   I want to sing.

HAMM   I can't prevent you. [*Pause.* CLOV *turns towards window right.*]

CLOV   What did I do with that steps? [*He looks around for ladder.*] You didn't
see that steps? [*He sees it.*] Ah, about time. [*He goes towards window left.*]
Sometimes I wonder if I'm in my right mind. Then it passes over and I'm as
lucid as before. [*He gets up on ladder, looks out of window.*] Christ, she's
under water! [*He looks.*] How can that be? [*He pokes forward his head, his
hand above his eyes.*] It hasn't rained. [*He wipes the pane, looks. Pause.*] Ah
what a fool I am! I'm on the wrong side! [*He gets down, takes a few steps
towards window right.*] Under water! [*He goes back for ladder.*] What a fool
I am! [*He carries ladder towards window right.*] Sometimes I wonder if I'm
in my right senses. Then it passes off and I'm as intelligent as ever. [*He sets
down ladder under window right, gets up on it, looks out of window. He turns
towards* HAMM.] Any particular sector you fancy? Or merely the whole thing?

HAMM   Whole thing.

CLOV   The general effect? Just a moment. [*He looks out of window. Pause.*]

HAMM   Clov.

CLOV   [*Absorbed.*] Mmm.

HAMM   Do you know what it is?

CLOV   [*As before.*] Mmm.

HAMM   I was never there. [*Pause.*] Clov!

CLOV   [*Turning towards* HAMM, *exasperated.*] What is it?

HAMM   I was never there.

CLOV   Lucky for you. [*He looks out of window.*]

HAMM   Absent, always. It all happened without me. I don't know what's happened. [*Pause.*] Do you know what's happened? [*Pause.*] Clov!

CLOV   [*Turning towards* HAMM, *exasperated.*] Do you want me to look at this
muckheap, yes or no?

HAMM   Answer me first.

CLOV   What?

HAMM   Do you know what's happened?

CLOV   When? Where?

HAMM   [*Violently.*] When! What's happened? Use your head, can't you! What
has happened?

CLOV   What for Christ's sake does it matter? [*He looks out of window.*]

HAMM   I don't know. [*Pause.* CLOV *turns towards* HAMM.]

CLOV   [*Harshly.*] When old Mother Pegg asked you for oil for her lamp and
you told her to get out to hell, you knew what was happening then, no?
[*Pause.*] You know what she died of, Mother Pegg? Of darkness.

HAMM   [*Feebly.*] I hadn't any.

CLOV   [*As before.*] Yes, you had. [*Pause.*]

HAMM   Have you the glass?

CLOV   No, it's clear enough as it is.

HAMM   Go and get it. [*Pause.* CLOV *casts up his eyes, brandishes his fists. He
loses balance, clutches on to the ladder. He starts to get down, halts.*]

CLOV   There's one thing I'll never understand. [*He gets down.*] Why I always
obey you. Can you explain that to me?

HAMM   No. . . . Perhaps it's compassion. [*Pause.*] A kind of great compassion.

[*Pause.*] Oh you won't find it easy, you won't find it easy. [*Pause.* CLOV *begins to move about the room in search of the telescope.*]

CLOV   I'm tired of our goings on, very tired. [*He searches.*] You're not sitting on it? [*He moves the chair, looks at the place where it stood, resumes his search.*]

HAMM   [*Anguished.*] Don't leave me there! [*Angrily* CLOV *restores the chair to its place.*] Am I right in the centre?

CLOV   You'd need a microscope to find this— [*He sees the telescope.*] Ah, about time. [*He picks up the telescope, gets up on the ladder, turns the telescope on the without.*]

HAMM   Give me the dog.

CLOV   [*Looking.*] Quiet!

HAMM   [*Angrily.*] Give me the dog! [CLOV *drops the telescope, clasps his hands to his head. Pause. He gets down precipitately, looks for the dog, sees it, picks it up, hastens towards* HAMM *and strikes him violently on the head with the dog.*]

CLOV   There's your dog for you! [*The dog falls to the ground. Pause.*]

HAMM   He hit me!

CLOV   You drive me mad, I'm mad!

HAMM   If you must hit me, hit me with the axe. [*Pause.*] Or with the gaff, hit me with the gaff. Not with the dog. With the gaff. Or with the axe. [CLOV *picks up the dog and gives it to* HAMM *who takes it in his arms.*]

CLOV   [*Imploringly.*] Let's stop playing!

HAMM   Never! [*Pause.*] Put me in my coffin.

CLOV   There are no more coffins.

HAMM   Then let it end! [CLOV *goes towards ladder.*] With a bang! [CLOV *gets up on ladder, gets down again, looks for telescope, sees it, picks it up, gets up ladder, raises telescope.*] Of darkness! And me? Did anyone ever have pity on me?

CLOV   [*Lowering the telescope, turning towards* HAMM.] What? [*Pause.*] Is it me you're referring to?

HAMM   [*Angrily.*] An aside, ape! Did you never hear an aside before? [*Pause.*] I'm warming up for my last soliloquy.

CLOV   I warn you. I'm going to look at this filth since it's an order. But it's the last time. [*He turns the telescope on the without.*] Let's see. [*He moves thetelescope.*]Nothing . . . nothing . . . good . . . good . . . nothing . . . goo— [*He starts, lowers the telescope, examines it, turns it again on the without. Pause.*] Bad luck to it!

HAMM   More complications! [CLOV *gets down.*] Not an underplot, I trust. [CLOV *moves ladder nearer window, gets up on it, turns telescope on the without.*]

CLOV   [*Dismayed.*] Looks like a small boy!

HAMM   [*Sarcastic.*] A small . . . boy!

CLOV   I'll go and see. [*He gets down, drops the telescope, goes towards door, turns.*] I'll take the gaff. [*He looks for the gaff, sees it, picks it up, hastens towards door.*]

HAMM   No! [CLOV *halts.*]

CLOV   No? A potential procreator?

HAMM   If he exists he'll die there or he'll come here. And if he doesn't . . . [*Pause.*]

CLOV You don't believe me? You think I'm inventing? [*Pause.*]

HAMM It's the end, Clov, we've come to the end. I don't need you any more.
[*Pause.*]

CLOV Lucky for you. [*He goes towards door.*]

HAMM Leave me the gaff. [CLOV *gives him the gaff, goes towards door, halts,
looks at alarm-clock, takes it down, looks round for a better place to put it,
goes to bins, puts it on lid of* NAGG's *bin. Pause.*]

CLOV I'll leave you. [*He goes towards door.*]

HAMM Before you go . . . [CLOV *halts near door.*] . . . say something.

CLOV There is nothing to say.

HAMM A few words . . . to ponder . . . in my heart.

CLOV Your heart!

HAMM Yes. [*Pause. Forcibly.*] Yes! [*Pause.*] With the rest, in the end, the
shadows, the murmurs, all the trouble, to end up with. [*Pause.*] Clov. . . .
He never spoke to me. Then, in the end, before he went, without my having
asked him, he spoke to me. He said . . .

CLOV [*Despairingly.*] Ah . . . !

HAMM Something . . . from your heart.

CLOV My heart!

HAMM A few words . . . from your heart. [*Pause.*]

CLOV [*Fixed gaze, tonelessly, towards auditorium.*] They said to me, That's
love, yes, yes, not a doubt, now you see how—

HAMM Articulate!

CLOV [*As before.*] How easy it is. They said to me, That's friendship, yes, yes,
no question, you've found it. They said to me, Here's the place, stop, raise
your head and look at all that beauty. That order! They said to me. Come
now, you're not a brute beast, think upon these things and you'll see how
all becomes clear. And simple! They said to me, What skilled attention they
get, all these dying of their wounds.

HAMM Enough!

CLOV [*As before.*] I say to myself—sometimes, Clov, you must learn to suffer
better than that if you want them to weary of punishing you—one day. I say
to myself—sometimes, Clov, you must be there better than that if you want
them to let you go—one day. But I feel too old, and too far, to form new
habits. Good, it'll never end, I'll never go. [*Pause.*] Then one day, suddenly,
it ends, it changes, I don't understand, it dies, or it's me, I don't understand,
that either. I ask the words that remain—sleeping, waking, morning, evening. They have nothing to say. [*Pause.*] I open the door of the cell and go.
I am so bowed I only see my feet, if I open my eyes, and between my legs a
little trail of black dust. I say to myself that the earth is extinguished, though
I never saw it lit. [*Pause.*] It's easy going. [*Pause.*] When I fall I'll weep for
happiness. [*Pause. He goes towards door.*]

HAMM Clov! [CLOV *halts, without turning.*] Nothing. [CLOV *moves on.*] Clov!
[CLOV *halts, without turning.*]

CLOV This is what we call making an exit.

HAMM I'm obliged to you, Clov. For your services.

CLOV [*Turning, sharply.*] Ah pardon, it's I am obliged to you.

HAMM It's we are obliged to each other. [*Pause.* CLOV *goes towards door.*] One
thing more. [CLOV *halts.*] A last favour. [*Exit* CLOV.] Cover me with the sheet.
[*Long pause.*] No? Good. [*Pause.*] Me to play. [*Pause. Wearily.*] Old endgame

2688 / Samuel Beckett

lost of old, play and lose and have done with losing. [*Pause. More animated.*]
Let me see. [*Pause.*] Ah yes! [*He tries to move the chair, using the gaff as
before. Enter* CLOV, *dressed for the road. Panama hat, tweed coat, raincoat
over his arm, umbrella, bag. He halts by the door and stands there, impassive
and motionless, his eyes fixed on* HAMM, *till the end.* HAMM *gives up.*] Good.
[*Pause.*] Discard. [*He throws away the gaff, makes to throw away the dog,
thinks better of it.*] Take it easy. [*Pause.*] And now? [*Pause.*] Raise hat. [*He
raises his toque.*] Peace to our . . . arses. [*Pause.*] And put on again. [*He puts
on his toque.*] Deuce. [*Pause. He takes off his glasses.*] Wipe. [*He takes out
his handkerchief and, without unfolding it, wipes his glasses.*] And put on
again. [*He puts on his glasses, puts back the handkerchief in his pocket.*] We're
coming. A few more squirms like that and I'll call. [*Pause.*] A little poetry.
[*Pause.*] You prayed— [*Pause. He corrects himself.*] You CRIED for night;
it comes— [*Pause. He corrects himself.*] It FALLS: now cry in darkness. [*He
repeats, chanting.*] You cried for night; it falls: now cry in darkness.[6] [*Pause.*]
Nicely put, that. [*Pause.*] And now? [*Pause.*] Moments for nothing, now as
always, time was never and time is over, reckoning closed and story ended.
[*Pause. Narrative tone.*] If he could have his child with him. . . . [*Pause.*] It
was the moment I was waiting for. [*Pause.*] You don't want to abandon him?
You want him to bloom while you are withering? Be there to solace your
last million last moments? [*Pause.*] He doesn't realize, all he knows is hunger, and cold, and death to crown it all. But you! You ought to know what
the earth is like, nowadays. Oh I put him before his responsibilities! [*Pause.
Normal tone.*] Well, there we are, there I am, that's enough. [*He raises the
whistle to his lips, hesitates, drops it. Pause.*] Yes, truly! [*He whistles. Pause.
Louder. Pause.*] Good. [*Pause.*] Father! [*Pause. Louder.*] Father! [*Pause.*]
Good. [*Pause.*] We're coming. [*Pause.*] And to end up with? [*Pause.*] Discard. [*He throws away the dog. He tears the whistle from his neck.*] With my
compliments. [*He throws whistle towards auditorium. Pause. He sniffs. Soft.*]
Clov! [*Long pause.*] No? Good. [*He takes out the handkerchief.*] Since that's
the way we're playing it . . . [*He unfolds handkerchief.*] . . . let's play it that
way . . . [*He unfolds.*] . . . and speak no more about it . . . [*He finishes
unfolding.*] . . . speak no more. [*He holds handkerchief spread out before
him.*] Old stancher! [*Pause.*] You . . . remain. [*Pause. He covers his face with
handkerchief, lowers his arms to armrests, remains motionless.*] [*Brief
tableau.*]

CURTAIN

1958

---

6. Parody of a line from Charles Baudelaire's poem "Meditation" that can be translated as: "You were
calling for evening; it falls; it is here."

W. H. AUDEN
1907–1973

Wystan Hugh Auden was born in York, England, the son of a doctor and of a former nurse. He was educated at private schools and Christ Church, Oxford. After graduation from Oxford he traveled abroad, taught school in England from 1930 to 1935, and later worked for a government film unit. His sympathies in the 1930s were with the left, like those of most intellectuals of his age, and he went to Spain during its Civil War, intending to serve as an ambulance driver on the left-wing Republican side. To his surprise he felt so disturbed by the sight of the many Roman Catholic churches gutted and looted by the Republicans that he returned to England without fulfilling his ambition. He traveled in Iceland and China before moving to the United States in 1939; in 1946 he became an American citizen. He taught at a number of American colleges and was professor of poetry at Oxford from 1956 to 1960. Most of his later life was shared between residences in New York City and in Europe—first in southern Italy, then in Austria.

Auden was the most prominent of the young English poets who, in the late 1920s and early 1930s, saw themselves bringing new techniques and attitudes to English poetry. Stephen Spender, C. Day Lewis, and Louis MacNeice were other liberal and leftist poets in this loosely affiliated group. Auden learned metrical and verbal techniques from Gerard Manley Hopkins and Wilfred Owen, and from T. S. Eliot he took a conversational and ironic tone, an acute inspection of cultural decay. Thomas Hardy's metrical variety, formal irregularity, and fusion of panoramic and intimate perspectives also proved a useful example, and Auden admired W. B. Yeats's "serious reflective" poems of "personal and public interest," though he later came to disavow Yeats's grand aspirations and rhetoric. Auden's English studies at Oxford familiarized him with the rhythms and long alliterative line of Anglo-Saxon poetry. He learned, too, from popular and folk culture, particularly the songs of the English music hall and, later, American blues singers.

The Depression that hit America in 1929 hit England soon afterward, and Auden and his contemporaries looked out at an England of industrial stagnation and mass unemployment, seeing not Eliot's metaphorical Waste Land but a more literal Waste Land of poverty and "depressed areas." Auden's early poetry diagnoses the ills of his country. This diagnosis, conducted in a verse that combines irreverence with craftsmanship, draws on both Freud and Marx to show England now as a nation of neurotic invalids, now as the victim of an antiquated economic system. The intellectual liveliness and nervous force of this work made a great impression, even though the compressed, elliptical, impersonal style created difficulties of interpretation.

Gradually Auden sought to clarify his imagery and syntax, and in the late 1930s he produced "Lullaby," "Musée des Beaux Arts," "In Memory of W. B. Yeats," and other poems of finely disciplined movement, pellucid clarity, and deep yet unsentimental feeling. Some of the poems he wrote at this time, such as "Spain" and "September 1, 1939," aspire to a visionary perspective on political and social change; but as Auden became increasingly skeptical of poetry in the grand manner, of poetry as revelation or as a tool for political change, he removed these poems from his canon. (He came to see as false his claim in "September 1, 1939" that "We must love one another or die.") "Poetry is not magic," he said in the essay "Writing," but a form of truth telling that should "disenchant and disintoxicate." As he continued to remake his style during World War II, he created a voice that, in contrast not only to Romanticism but also to the authoritarianism devastating Europe, was increasingly flat, ironic, and conversational. He never lost his ear for popular speech or his ability to combine elements from popular art with technical formality. He daringly mixed the grave and the flippant, vivid detail and allegorical abstraction. He always experimented, particularly in ways of bringing together high artifice and a colloquial tone.

The poems of Auden's last phase are increasingly personal in tone and combine an air of offhand informality with remarkable technical skill in versification. He turned out, as if effortlessly, poems in numerous verse forms, including sestinas, sonnets, ballads, canzones, syllabics, haiku, the blues, even limericks. As he became ever more mistrustful of a prophetic role for the poet, he embraced the ordinary—the hours of the day, the rooms of a house, a changeable landscape. He took refuge in love and friendship, particularly the love and friendship he shared with the American writer Chester Kallmann. Like Eliot, Auden became a member of the Church of England, and the emotions of his late poetry—sometimes comic, sometimes solemn—were grounded in an ever deepening but rarely obtrusive religious feeling. In the last year of his life he returned to England to live in Oxford, feeling the need to be part of a university community as a protection against loneliness. Auden is now generally recognized as one of the masters of twentieth-century English poetry, a thoughtful, seriously playful poet, combining extraordinary intelligence and immense craftsmanship.

A note on the texts: Auden heavily revised his poems, sometimes omitting stanzas (as in "In Memory of W. B. Yeats") or even entire poems (such as "September 1, 1939"). The texts below are reprinted as they first appeared in book form and again in his *Selected Poems: A New Edition*, ed. Edward Mendelson (1989).

Lullaby[1]

Lay your sleeping head, my love,
Human on my faithless arm;
Time and fevers burn away
Individual beauty from
5   Thoughtful children, and the grave
Proves the child ephemeral:
But in my arms till break of day
Let the living creature lie,
Mortal, guilty, but to me
10   The entirely beautiful.

Soul and body have no bounds:
To lovers as they lie upon
Her tolerant enchanted slope
In their ordinary swoon,
15   Grave the vision Venus° sends   *Roman goddess of love*
Of supernatural sympathy,
Universal love and hope;
While an abstract insight wakes
Among the glaciers and the rocks
20   The hermit's sensual ecstasy.

Certainty, fidelity
On the stroke of midnight pass
Like vibrations of a bell,
And fashionable madmen raise
25   Their pedantic boring cry:
Every farthing[2] of the cost,

1. Title from Auden's later collections.
2. At one time the smallest and least valuable British coin.

All the dreaded cards foretell,
Shall be paid, but from this night
Not a whisper, not a thought,
30   Not a kiss nor look be lost.

Beauty, midnight, vision dies:
Let the winds of dawn that blow
Softly round your dreaming head
Such a day of sweetness show
35   Eye and knocking heart may bless,
Find the mortal world enough;
Noons of dryness see you fed
By the involuntary powers,
Nights of insult let you pass
40   Watched by every human love.

Jan. 1937   1937, 1940

As I Walked Out One Evening[1]

As I walked out one evening,
    Walking down Bristol Street,
The crowds upon the pavement
    Were fields of harvest wheat.

5   And down by the brimming river
    I heard a lover sing
Under an arch of the railway:
    "Love has no ending.

"I'll love you, dear, I'll love you
10   Till China and Africa meet
And the river jumps over the mountain
    And the salmon sing in the street.

"I'll love you till the ocean
    Is folded and hung up to dry
15   And the seven stars[2] go squawking
    Like geese about the sky.

"The years shall run like rabbits
    For in my arms I hold
The Flower of the Ages
20   And the first love of the world."

But all the clocks in the city
    Began to whirr and chime:
"O let not Time deceive you,
    You cannot conquer Time.

1. Title from Auden's later collections.
2. The constellation of the Pleiades, supposed by the ancients to be seven sisters.

25   "In the burrows of the Nightmare
       Where Justice naked is,
   Time watches from the shadow
       And coughs when you would kiss.

   "In headaches and in worry
30   Vaguely life leaks away,
   And Time will have his fancy
       To-morrow or to-day.

   "Into many a green valley
       Drifts the appalling[3] snow;
35   Time breaks the threaded dances
       And the diver's brilliant bow.

   "O plunge your hands in water,
       Plunge them in up to the wrist;
   Stare, stare in the basin
40   And wonder what you've missed.

   "The glacier knocks in the cupboard,
       The desert sighs in the bed,
   And the crack in the tea-cup opens
       A lane to the land of the dead.

45   "Where the beggars raffle the banknotes
       And the Giant is enchanting to Jack,
   And the Lily-white Boy is a Roarer
       And Jill goes down on her back.[4]

   "O look, look in the mirror,
50   O look in your distress;
   Life remains a blessing
       Although you cannot bless.

   "O stand, stand at the window
       As the tears scald and start;
55   You shall love your crooked neighbour
       With your crooked heart."

   It was late, late in the evening,
       The lovers they were gone;
   The clocks had ceased their chiming
60   And the deep river ran on.

Nov. 1937   1938, 1940

---

3. Literally, making white.
4. The giant of "Jack and the Bean Stalk" is trying to seduce Jack; the "lily-white Boy" (presumably pure) becomes a boisterous reveler; Jill, of "Jack and Jill," is seduced.

Musée des Beaux Arts[1]

About suffering they were never wrong,
The Old Masters: how well they understood
Its human position; how it takes place
While someone else is eating or opening a window or just walking dully
    along;
5 How, when the aged are reverently, passionately waiting
For the miraculous birth, there always must be
Children who did not specially want it to happen, skating
On a pond at the edge of the wood:
They never forgot
10 That even the dreadful martyrdom must run its course
Anyhow in a corner, some untidy spot
Where the dogs go on with their doggy life and the torturer's horse
Scratches its innocent behind on a tree.

In Brueghel's *Icarus*,[2] for instance: how everything turns away
15 Quite leisurely from the disaster; the ploughman may
Have heard the splash, the forsaken cry,
But for him it was not an important failure; the sun shone
As it had to on the white legs disappearing into the green
Water; and the expensive delicate ship that must have seen
20 Something amazing, a boy falling out of the sky,
Had somewhere to get to and sailed calmly on.

Dec. 1938   1940

In Memory of W. B. Yeats[1]

(d. January 1939)

I

He disappeared in the dead of winter:
The brooks were frozen, the air-ports almost deserted,
And snow disfigured the public statues;
The mercury sank in the mouth of the dying day.
5 O all the instruments agree
The day of his death was a dark cold day.

Far from his illness
The wolves ran on through the evergreen forests,
The peasant river was untempted by the fashionable quays;

---

1. Museum of Fine Arts (French).
2. *The Fall of Icarus,* by the Flemish painter Pieter Brueghel (ca. 1525–1569), in the Musées Royaux des Beaux Arts in Brussels. In one corner of Brueghel's painting, Icarus's legs are seen disappearing into the sea, his wings having melted when he flew too close to the sun. Auden also alludes to other paintings by Brueghel: the nativity scene in *The Numbering at Bethlehem,* skaters in *Winter Landscape with Skaters and a Bird Trap,* a horse scratching its behind in *The Massacre of the Innocents.*
1. The Irish poet William Butler Yeats, born in 1865, died on January 29, 1939, in Roquebrune (southern France).

10   By mourning tongues
     The death of the poet was kept from his poems.

     But for him it was his last afternoon as himself,
     An afternoon of nurses and rumours;
     The provinces of his body revolted,
15   The squares of his mind were empty,
     Silence invaded the suburbs,
     The current of his feeling failed: he became his admirers.

     Now he is scattered among a hundred cities
     And wholly given over to unfamiliar affections;
20   To find his happiness in another kind of wood[2]
     And be punished under a foreign code of conscience.
     The words of a dead man
     Are modified in the guts of the living.

     But in the importance and noise of to-morrow
25   When the brokers are roaring like beasts on the floor of the Bourse,[3]
     And the poor have the sufferings to which they are fairly accustomed,
     And each in the cell of himself is almost convinced of his freedom;
     A few thousand will think of this day
     As one thinks of a day when one did something slightly unusual.

30   O all the instruments agree
     The day of his death was a dark cold day.

II

     You were silly like us: your gift survived it all;
     The parish of rich women,[4] physical decay,
     Yourself; mad Ireland hurt you into poetry.
35   Now Ireland has her madness and her weather still,
     For poetry makes nothing happen: it survives
     In the valley of its saying where executives
     Would never want to tamper; it flows south
     From ranches of isolation and the busy griefs,
40   Raw towns that we believe and die in; it survives,
     A way of happening, a mouth.

III[5]

     Earth, receive an honoured guest;
     William Yeats is laid to rest:
     Let the Irish vessel lie
45   Emptied of its poetry.

2. Cf. the beginning of Dante's *Inferno:* "In the middle of the journey of our life I came to myself in a dark wood where the straight way was lost" (1.1–3).
3. The French stock exchange.
4. Several wealthy women, including Lady Augusta Gregory (1852–1932), provided financial help to Yeats.
5. The stanza pattern of this section echoes that of Yeats's late poem "Under Ben Bulben." Auden later omitted the section's second, third, and fourth stanzas.

Time that is intolerant
Of the brave and innocent,
And indifferent in a week
To a beautiful physique,

50 Worships language and forgives
Everyone by whom it lives;
Pardons cowardice, conceit,
Lays its honours at their feet.

Time that with this strange excuse
55 Pardoned Kipling[6] and his views,
And will pardon Paul Claudel,[7]
Pardons him for writing well.

In the nightmare of the dark
All the dogs of Europe bark,[8]
60 And the living nations wait,
Each sequestered in its hate;

Intellectual disgrace
Stares from every human face,
And the seas of pity lie
65 Locked and frozen in each eye.

Follow, poet, follow right
To the bottom of the night,
With your unconstraining voice
Still persuade us to rejoice;

70 With the farming of a verse
Make a vineyard of the curse,
Sing of human unsuccess
In a rapture of distress;

In the deserts of the heart
75 Let the healing fountain start,
In the prison of his days
Teach the free man how to praise.

Feb. 1939   1939, 1940

---

6. The British writer Rudyard Kipling (1865–1936) championed imperialism.
7. French author (1868–1955) with extremely conservative politics. Yeats was at times anti-democratic and appeared to favor dictatorship.
8. World War II began in September 1939.

The Unknown Citizen

To JS/07/M/378
This Marble Monument is Erected by the State

He was found by the Bureau of Statistics to be
One against whom there was no official complaint,
And all the reports on his conduct agree
That, in the modern sense of an old-fashioned word, he was a saint,
5   For in everything he did he served the Greater Community.
Except for the War till the day he retired
He worked in a factory and never got fired,
But satisfied his employers, Fudge Motors Inc.
Yet he wasn't a scab or odd in his views,
10   For his Union reports that he paid his dues,
(Our report on his Union shows it was sound)
And our Social Psychology workers found
That he was popular with his mates and liked a drink.
The Press are convinced that he bought a paper every day
15   And that his reactions to advertisements were normal in every way.
Policies taken out in his name prove that he was fully insured,
And his Health-card shows he was once in hospital but left it cured.
Both Producers Research and High-Grade Living declare
He was fully sensible to the advantages of the Installment Plan
20   And had everything necessary to the Modern Man,
A gramophone, a radio, a car and a frigidaire.
Our researchers into Public Opinion are content
That he held the proper opinions for the time of year;
When there was peace, he was for peace; when there was war, he
     went.
25   He was married and added five children to the population,
Which our Eugenist[1] says was the right number for a parent of his
     generation,
And our teachers report that he never interfered with their education.
Was he free? Was he happy? The question is absurd:
Had anything been wrong, we should certainly have heard.

Mar. 1939   1939, 1940

September 1, 1939[1]

I sit in one of the dives
On Fifty-Second Street[2]
Uncertain and afraid
As the clever hopes expire
5   Of a low dishonest decade:
Waves of anger and fear

---

1. An expert in eugenics, a pseudoscience for the
genetic "improvement" of humans.
1. The date of Germany's invasion of Poland and
the outbreak of World War II.
2. In New York City, where Auden was living.

Circulate over the bright
And darkened lands of the earth,
Obsessing our private lives;
10   The unmentionable odour of death
Offends the September night.

Accurate scholarship can
Unearth the whole offence
From Luther[3] until now
15   That has driven a culture mad,
Find what occurred at Linz,[4]
What huge imago[5] made
A psychopathic god:
I and the public know
20   What all schoolchildren learn,
Those to whom evil is done
Do evil in return.

Exiled Thucydides[6] knew
All that a speech can say
25   About Democracy,
And what dictators do,
The elderly rubbish they talk
To an apathetic grave;
Analysed all in his book,
30   The enlightenment driven away,
The habit-forming pain,
Mismanagement and grief:
We must suffer them all again.

Into this neutral air
35   Where blind skyscrapers use
Their full height to proclaim
The strength of Collective Man,
Each language pours its vain
Competitive excuse:
40   But who can live for long
In an euphoric dream;
Out of the mirror they stare,
Imperialism's face
And the international wrong.

45   Faces along the bar
Cling to their average day:
The lights must never go out,
The music must always play,
All the conventions conspire
50   To make this fort assume

---

3. Martin Luther (1483–1546), founder of the
Protestant Reformation.
4. Austrian city where Hitler spent his childhood.
5. Psychoanalytic term for the unconscious representation of a parental figure.

6. Greek general (d. ca. 401 B.C.E.) and historian
of the Peloponnesian War, exiled from Athens
because he failed to prevent the Spartans from
seizing a colony.

The furniture of home;
Lest we should see where we are,
Lost in a haunted wood,
Children afraid of the night
55 Who have never been happy or good.

The windiest militant trash
Important Persons shout
Is not so crude as our wish:
What mad Nijinsky wrote
60 About Diaghilev[7]
Is true of the normal heart;
For the error bred in the bone
Of each woman and each man
Craves what it cannot have,
65 Not universal love
But to be loved alone.

From the conservative dark
Into the ethical life
The dense commuters come,
70 Repeating their morning vow,
"I *will* be true to the wife,
I'll concentrate more on my work,"
And helpless governors wake
To resume their compulsory game:
75 Who can release them now,
Who can reach the deaf,
Who can speak for the dumb?[8]

All I have is a voice
To undo the folded lie,
80 The romantic lie in the brain
Of the sensual man-in-the-street
And the lie of Authority
Whose buildings grope the sky:
There is no such thing as the State
85 And no one exists alone;
Hunger allows no choice
To the citizen or the police;
We must love one another or die.[9]

Defenceless under the night
90 Our world in stupor lies;
Yet, dotted everywhere,
Ironic points of light
Flash out wherever the Just
Exchange their messages:

7. The Russian dancer and choreographer Vaslav Nijinsky (1890–1950) wrote that his former lover the ballet impresario Sergey Diaghilev (1872–1929) "does not want universal love, but to be loved alone."

8. Proverbs 31.8.
9. Auden later revised this line, which struck him as "dishonest." In one version of the poem the line reads "We must love one another and die." Another version leaves out the entire stanza.

95   May I, composed like them
      Of Eros° and of dust,   *Greek god of desire*
      Beleaguered by the same
      Negation and despair,
      Show an affirming flame.

Sept. 1939   1939, 1940

In Praise of Limestone[1]

If it form the one landscape that we the inconstant ones
   Are consistently homesick for, this is chiefly
Because it dissolves in water. Mark these rounded slopes
   With their surface fragrance of thyme and beneath
5 A secret system of caves and conduits; hear these springs
   That spurt out everywhere with a chuckle
Each filling a private pool for its fish and carving
   Its own little ravine whose cliffs entertain
The butterfly and the lizard; examine this region
10   Of short distances and definite places:
What could be more like Mother or a fitter background
   For her son, for the nude young male who lounges
Against a rock displaying his dildo,° never doubting   *penis*
   That for all his faults he is loved, whose works are but
15 Extensions of his power to charm? From weathered outcrop
   To hill-top temple, from appearing waters to
Conspicuous fountains, from a wild to a formal vineyard,
   Are ingenious but short steps that a child's wish
To receive more attention than his brothers, whether
20   By pleasing or teasing, can easily take.

Watch, then, the band of rivals as they climb up and down
   Their steep stone gennels[2] in twos and threes, sometimes
Arm in arm, but never, thank God, in step; or engaged
   On the shady side of a square at midday in
25 Voluble discourse, knowing each other too well to think
   There are any important secrets, unable
To conceive a god whose temper-tantrums are moral
   And not to be pacified by a clever line
Or a good lay: for, accustomed to a stone that responds,
30   They have never had to veil their faces in awe
Of a crater whose blazing fury could not be fixed;
   Adjusted to the local needs of valleys
Where everything can be touched or reached by walking,
   Their eyes have never looked into infinite space
35 Through the lattice-work of a nomad's comb; born lucky,

1. Inspired by the limestone landscape outside Florence, Italy, where Auden and his longtime companion Chester Kallman (1921–1975) were staying; the poem also recalls the poet's native Yorkshire. In a letter to Elizabeth Mayer, Auden wrote: "I hadn't realised till I came how like Italy is to my 'Mutterland', the Pennines [hills in the north of England]. Am in fact starting on a poem, 'In Praise of Limestone', the theme of which is that rock creates the only truly human landscape."
2. Narrow passages between houses (Yorkshire dialect) or, as here, rocks.

Their legs have never encountered the fungi
And insects of the jungle, the monstrous forms and lives
   With which we have nothing, we like to hope, in common.
So, when one of them goes to the bad, the way his mind works
40   Remains comprehensible: to become a pimp
Or deal in fake jewelry or ruin a fine tenor voice
   For effects that bring down the house could happen to all
But the best and the worst of us . . .
                           That is why, I suppose,
   The best and worst never stayed here long but sought
45   Immoderate soils where the beauty was not so external,
   The light less public and the meaning of life
Something more than a mad camp. "Come!" cried the granite wastes,
   "How evasive is your humor, how accidental
Your kindest kiss, how permanent is death." (Saints-to-be
50   Slipped away sighing.) "Come!" purred the clays and gravels
"On our plains there is room for armies to drill; rivers
   Wait to be tamed and slaves to construct you a tomb
In the grand manner: soft as the earth is mankind and both
   Need to be altered." (Intendant Caesars rose and
55 Left, slamming the door.) But the really reckless were fetched
   By an older colder voice, the oceanic whisper:
"I am the solitude that asks and promises nothing;
   That is how I shall set you free. There is no love;
There are only the various envies, all of them sad."

60   They were right, my dear, all those voices were right
And still are; this land is not the sweet home that it looks,
   Nor its peace the historical calm of a site
Where something was settled once and for all: A backward
   And dilapidated province, connected
65   To the big busy world by a tunnel, with a certain
   Seedy appeal, is that all it is now? Not quite:
It has a worldly duty which in spite of itself
   It does not neglect, but calls into question
All the Great Powers assume; it disturbs our rights. The poet,
70   Admired for his earnest habit of calling
The sun the sun, his mind Puzzle, is made uneasy
   By these solid statues which so obviously doubt
His antimythological myth; and these gamins,°   *urchins*
   Pursuing the scientist down the tiled colonnade
75 With such lively offers, rebuke his concern for Nature's
   Remotest aspects: I, too, am reproached, for what
And how much you know. Not to lose time, not to get caught,
   Not to be left behind, not, please! to resemble
The beasts who repeat themselves, or a thing like water
80   Or stone whose conduct can be predicted, these
Are our Common Prayer,[3] whose greatest comfort is music
   Which can be made anywhere, is invisible,
And does not smell. In so far as we have to look forward
   To death as a fact, no doubt we are right: But if

3. The Book of Common Prayer is the liturgical book of the Anglican Church.

85 Sins can be forgiven, if bodies rise from the dead,
These modifications of matter into
Innocent athletes and gesticulating fountains,
Made solely for pleasure, make a further point:
The blessed will not care what angle they are regarded from,
90 Having nothing to hide. Dear, I know nothing of
Either, but when I try to imagine a faultless love
Or the life to come, what I hear is the murmur
Of underground streams, what I see is a limestone landscape.

May 1948   1948, 1951

The Shield of Achilles[1]

She looked over his shoulder
For vines and olive trees,
Marble well-governed cities,
And ships upon untamed seas,
5 But there on the shining metal
His hands had put instead
An artificial wilderness
And a sky like lead.

A plain without a feature, bare and brown,
10 No blade of grass, no sign of neighborhood,
Nothing to eat and nowhere to sit down,
Yet, congregated on its blankness, stood
An unintelligible multitude,
A million eyes, a million boots in line,
15 Without expression, waiting for a sign.

Out of the air a voice without a face
Proved by statistics that some cause was just
In tones as dry and level as the place:
No one was cheered and nothing was discussed;
20 Column by column in a cloud of dust
They marched away enduring a belief
Whose logic brought them, somewhere else, to grief.

She looked over his shoulder
For ritual pieties,
25 White flower-garlanded heifers,
Libation and sacrifice,[2]

1. In Homer's *Iliad* Achilles, the chief Greek hero in the war with Troy, lends his armor to his great friend Patroclus and loses it when Patroclus is killed by Hector. While Achilles is mourning the death of his friend, his mother, the goddess Thetis, goes to Mt. Olympus to beg Hephaestos, the god of fire, to forge new armor for Achilles. The splendid shield of Achilles that Hephaestos then makes is described in book 18 (lines 478–608). On it he depicts the earth, the heavens, the sea, and the planets; a city in peace (with a wedding and a trial) and a city at war; scenes from country life, animal life, and the joyful life of young men and women. The ocean, as the outer border, flows around all these scenes.
2. Cf. John Keats's "Ode on a Grecian Urn" (1820): "Who are these coming to the sacrifice? / To what green altar, O mysterious priest, / Lead'st thou that heifer lowing at the skies, / And all her silken flanks with garlands dressed?" "Libation": sacrifice of wine or other liquid.

But there on the shining metal
    Where the altar should have been,
    She saw by his flickering forge-light
30   Quite another scene.

Barbed wire enclosed an arbitrary spot
    Where bored officials lounged (one cracked a joke)
And sentries sweated, for the day was hot:
    A crowd of ordinary decent folk
35   Watched from without and neither moved nor spoke
As three pale figures were led forth and bound
To three posts driven upright in the ground.

The mass and majesty of this world, all
    That carries weight and always weighs the same,
40 Lay in the hands of others; they were small
    And could not hope for help and no help came:
    What their foes liked to do was done, their shame
Was all the worst could wish; they lost their pride
And died as men before their bodies died.

45   She looked over his shoulder
        For athletes at their games,
    Men and women in a dance
        Moving their sweet limbs
    Quick, quick, to music,
50   But there on the shining shield
    His hands had set no dancing-floor
        But a weed-choked field.

A ragged urchin, aimless and alone,
    Loitered about that vacancy; a bird
55 Flew up to safety from his well-aimed stone:
    That girls are raped, that two boys knife a third,
    Were axioms to him, who'd never heard
Of any world where promises were kept
Or one could weep because another wept.

60   The thin-lipped armorer,
        Hephaestos, hobbled away;
    Thetis of the shining breasts
        Cried out in dismay
    At what the god had wrought
65   To please her son, the strong
    Iron-hearted man-slaying Achilles
        Who would not live long.

1952   1952, 1955

[Poetry as Memorable Speech][1]

Of the many definitions of poetry, the simplest is still the best: 'memorable speech.' That is to say, it must move our emotions, or excite our intellect, for only that which is moving or exciting is memorable, and the stimulus is the audible spoken word and cadence, to which in all its power of suggestion and incantation we must surrender, as we do when talking to an intimate friend. We must, in fact, make exactly the opposite kind of mental effort to that we make in grasping other verbal uses, for in the case of the latter the aura of suggestion round every word through which, like the atom radiating lines of force through the whole of space and time, it becomes ultimately a sign for the sum of all possible meanings, must be rigorously suppressed and its meaning confined to a single dictionary one. For this reason the exposition of a scientific theory is easier to read than to hear. No poetry, on the other hand, which when mastered is not better heard than read is good poetry.

All speech has rhythm, which is the result of the combination of the alternating periods of effort and rest necessary to all living things, and the laying of emphasis on what we consider important; and in all poetry there is a tension between the rhythm due to the poet's personal values, and those due to the experiences of generations crystallised into habits of language such as the English tendency to alternate weak and accented syllables, and conventional verse forms like the hexameter, the heroic pentameter, or the French Alexandrine. Similes, metaphors of image or idea, and auditory metaphors such as rhyme, assonance, and alliteration help further to clarify and strengthen the pattern and internal relations of the experience described.

Poetry, in fact, bears the same kind of relation to Prose, using prose simply in the sense of all those uses of words that are not poetry, that algebra bears to arithmetic. The poet writes of personal or fictitious experiences, but these are not important in themselves until the reader has realised them in his own consciousness.

> Soldier from the war returning,
> Spoiler of the taken town.[2]

It is quite unimportant, though it is the kind of question not infrequently asked, who the soldier is, what regiment he belongs to, what war he had been fighting in, etc. The soldier is you or me, or the man next door. Only when it throws light on our own experience, when these lines occur to us as we see, say, the unhappy face of a stockbroker in the suburban train, does poetry convince us of its significance. The test of a poet is the frequency and diversity of the occasions on which we remember his poetry.

Memorable speech then. About what? Birth, death, the Beatific Vision,[3] the abysses of hatred and fear, the awards and miseries of desire, the unjust walking the earth and the just scratching miserably for food like hens, triumphs, earthquakes, deserts of boredom and featureless anxiety, the Golden Age promised or irrevocably past, the gratifications and terrors of childhood, the impact of nature on the adolescent, the despairs and wisdoms of the mature,

---

1. Excerpted from Auden and John Garrett's introduction to their anthology of verse, *The Poet's Tongue.*
2. Beginning lines of a poem (in which "war" is

plural) by the English poet A. E. Housman (1859–1936).
3. A sight of the glories of heaven.

the sacrificial victim, the descent into Hell, the devouring and the benign mother? Yes, all of these, but not these only. Everything that we remember no matter how trivial: the mark on the wall, the joke at luncheon, word games, these, like the dance of a stoat[4] or the raven's gamble, are equally the subject of poetry.

We shall do poetry a great disservice if we confine it only to the major experiences of life:

> The soldier's pole is fallen,
> Boys and girls are level now with men,
> And there is nothing left remarkable
> Beneath the visiting moon.

> They had a royal wedding.
> All his courtiers wished him well.
> The horses pranced and the dancers danced.
> O Mister it was swell.

> And masculine is found to be
> Hadria the Adriatic Sea,[5]

have all their rightful place, and full appreciation of one depends on full appreciation of the others.

A great many people dislike the idea of poetry as they dislike over-earnest people, because they imagine it is always worrying about the eternal verities.

Those, in Mr Spender's[6] words, who try to put poetry on a pedestal only succeed in putting it on the shelf. Poetry is no better and no worse than human nature; it is profound and shallow, sophisticated and naïve, dull and witty, bawdy and chaste in turn.

In spite of the spread of education and the accessibility of printed matter, there is a gap between what is commonly called 'highbrow' and 'lowbrow' taste, wider perhaps than it has ever been.

The industrial revolution broke up the agricultural communities, with their local conservative cultures, and divided the growing population into two classes: those whether employers or employees who worked and had little leisure, and a small class of shareholders who did no work, had leisure but no responsibilities or roots, and were therefore preoccupied with themselves. Literature has tended therefore to divide into two streams, one providing the first with a compensation and escape, the other the second with a religion and a drug. The Art for Art's sake[7] of the London drawing-rooms of the '90's, and towns like Burnley and Rochdale,[8] are complementary.

Nor has the situation been much improved by the increased leisure and educational opportunities which the population to-day as a whole possess. Were leisure all, the unemployed would have created a second Athens.

Artistic creations may be produced by individuals, and because their work is only appreciated by a few it does not necessarily follow that it is not good; but a universal art can only be the product of a community united in sympathy,

---

4. Weasel.
5. A mnemonic to help remember that Hadria, Latin for the Adriatic Sea, is masculine, despite its typically feminine ending. The first quotation is a remembered version of Cleopatra's speech after Antony dies in Shakespeare's *Antony and Cleopatra*

(4.16.67–70). The source of the middle quotation has not been identified.
6. Stephen Spender (1909–1995), English poet.
7. Phrase associated with aestheticism.
8. Once industrial mill towns in Lancashire, England.

sense of worth, and aspiration; and it is improbable that the artist can do his best except in such a society.

*   *   *

The 'average' man says: 'When I get home I want to spend my time with my wife or in the nursery; I want to get out on to the links[9] go for a spin in the car, not to read poetry. Why should I? I'm quite happy without it.' We must be able to point out to him that whenever, for example, he makes a good joke he is creating poetry, that one of the motives behind poetry is curiosity, the wish to know what we feel and think, and how, as E. M. Forster[1] says, can I know what I think till I see what I say, and that curiosity is the only human passion that can be indulged in for twenty-four hours a day without satiety.

The psychologist maintains that poetry is a neurotic symptom, an attempt to compensate by phantasy for a failure to meet reality. We must tell him that phantasy is only the beginning of writing; that, on the contrary, like psychology, poetry is a struggle to reconcile the unwilling subject and object; in fact, that since psychological truth depends so largely on context, poetry, the parabolic[2] approach, is the only adequate medium for psychology.

The propagandist, whether moral or political, complains that the writer should use his powers over words to persuade people to a particular course of action, instead of fiddling while Rome burns.[3] But Poetry is not concerned with telling people what to do, but with extending our knowledge of good and evil, perhaps making the necessity for action more urgent and its nature more clear, but only leading us to the point where it is possible for us to make a rational and moral choice.

*   *   *

1935

9. Ground on which golf is played.
1. English novelist (1879–1970).
2. I.e., akin to parable.

3. The Roman emperor Nero (37–68) reputedly fiddled while Rome burned.

DYLAN THOMAS
1914–1953

Dylan Thomas was born in Swansea, Wales, and educated at Swansea Grammar School. After working for a time as a newspaper reporter, he was "discovered" as a poet in 1933 through a poetry contest in a popular newspaper. The following year his *Eighteen Poems* caused considerable excitement because of their powerfully suggestive obscurity and the strange violence of their imagery. It looked as though a new kind of visionary Romanticism had been restored to English poetry after the deliberately muted ironic tones of T. S. Eliot and his followers. Over time it became clear that Thomas was also a master of poetic craft, not merely a shouting rhapsodist. His verbal panache played against strict verse forms, such as the villanelle ("Do Not Go Gentle into That Good Night"). "I am a painstaking, conscientious, involved and devious craftsman in words," he wrote in his "Poetic Manifesto." His images were carefully ordered in a patterned sequence, and his major theme was the unity of all life, the continuing *process* of life and death and new life that linked the generations.

Thomas saw the workings of biology as a magical transformation producing unity out of diversity, and again and again in his poetry he sought a poetic ritual to celebrate this unity ("The force that through the green fuse drives the flower / Drives my green age"). He saw men and women locked in cycles of growth, love, procreation, new growth, death, and new life again. Hence each image engenders its opposite in what he called "my dialectical method": "Each image holds within it the seed of its own destruction." Thomas derives his closely woven, sometimes self-contradictory images from the Bible, Welsh folklore and preaching, and Freud. In his poems of reminiscence and autobiographical emotion, such as "Poem in October," he communicates more immediately through compelling use of lyrical feeling and simple natural images. His autobiographical work *Portrait of the Artist as a Young Dog* (1940) and his radio play *Under Milk Wood* (1954) reveal a vividness of observation and a combination of violence and tenderness in expression that show he could handle prose as excitingly as verse.

Thomas was a brilliant talker, an alcoholic, a reckless and impulsive man whose short life was packed with emotional ups and downs. His poetry readings in the United States between 1950 and 1953 were enormous successes, in spite of his sometimes reckless antics. He died suddenly in New York of what was diagnosed as "an insult to the brain," precipitated by alcohol. He played the part of the wild bohemian poet, and while some thought this behavior wonderful, others deplored it. He was a stirring reader of his own and others' poems, and many people who do not normally read poetry were drawn to Thomas's by the magic of his own reading. After his premature death a reaction set in: some critics declared that he had been overrated as a poet because of his sensational life. The "Movement" poets, such as Philip Larkin, repudiated his rhetorical extravagance. Even so, Thomas is still considered an original poet of great power and beauty.

The Force That Through the Green Fuse Drives the Flower

The force that through the green fuse drives the flower
Drives my green age; that blasts the roots of trees
Is my destroyer.
And I am dumb to tell the crooked rose
5   My youth is bent by the same wintry fever.

The force that drives the water through the rocks
Drives my red blood; that dries the mouthing streams
Turns mine to wax.
And I am dumb to mouth unto my veins
10   How at the mountain spring the same mouth sucks.

The hand that whirls the water in the pool[1]
Stirs the quicksand; that ropes the blowing wind
Hauls my shroud sail.
And I am dumb to tell the hanging man
15   How of my clay is made the hangman's lime.[2]

The lips of time leech to the fountain head;
Love drips and gathers, but the fallen blood

---

1. The hand of the angel who troubles the water of the pool Bethesda, thus rendering it curative, in John 5.1–4.

2. Quicklime was sometimes poured into the graves of public hangmen's victims to accelerate decomposition.

Shall calm her sores.
And I am dumb to tell a weather's wind
20   How time has ticked a heaven round the stars.

And I am dumb to tell the lover's tomb
How at my sheet goes the same crooked worm.

1933

Poem in October

It was my thirtieth year to heaven
Woke to my hearing from harbour and neighbour wood
And the mussel pooled and the heron
Priested shore
5   The morning beckon
With water praying and call of seagull and rook°   crow
And the knock of sailing boats on the net webbed wall
Myself to set foot
That second
10   In the still sleeping town and set forth.

My birthday began with the water-
Birds and the birds of the winged trees flying my name
Above the farms and the white horses
And I rose
15   In rainy autumn
And walked abroad in a shower of all my days.
High tide and the heron dived when I took the road
Over the border
And the gates
20   Of the town closed as the town awoke.

A springful of larks in a rolling
Cloud and the roadside bushes brimming with whistling
Blackbirds and the sun of October
Summery
25   On the hill's shoulder,
Here were fond climates and sweet singers suddenly
Come in the morning where I wandered and listened
To the rain wringing
Wind blow cold
30   In the wood faraway under me.

Pale rain over the dwindling harbour
And over the sea wet church the size of a snail
With its horns through mist and the castle
Brown as owls
35   But all the gardens
Of spring and summer were blooming in the tall tales
Beyond the border and under the lark full cloud.
There could I marvel

My birthday
40   Away but the weather turned around.

It turned away from the blithe country
And down the other air and the blue altered sky
Streamed again a wonder of summer
            With apples
45   Pears and red currants
And I saw in the turning so clearly a child's
Forgotten mornings when he walked with his mother
            Through the parables
            Of sun light
50   And the legends of the green chapels

And the twice told fields of infancy
That his tears burned my cheeks and his heart moved in mine.
These were the woods the river and sea
            Where a boy
55   In the listening
Summertime of the dead whispered the truth of his joy
To the trees and the stones and the fish in the tide.
            And the mystery
            Sang alive
60   Still in the water and singingbirds.

And there could I marvel my birthday
Away but the weather turned around. And the true
Joy of the long dead child sang burning
            In the sun.
65   It was my thirtieth
Year to heaven stood there then in the summer noon
Though the town below lay leaved with October blood.
            O may my heart's truth
            Still be sung
70   On this high hill in a year's turning.

1944   1946

Fern Hill[1]

Now as I was young and easy under the apple boughs
About the lilting house and happy as the grass was green,
        The night above the dingle[2] starry,
            Time let me hail and climb
5   Golden in the heydays of his eyes,
And honoured among wagons I was prince of the apple towns
And once below a time I lordly had the trees and leaves
            Trail with daisies and barley
        Down the rivers of the windfall light.

1. Name of the Welsh farmhouse, home of his
aunt Ann Jones, where Thomas spent summer holidays as a boy.
2. Deep dell or hollow, usually wooded.

10 And as I was green and carefree, famous among the barns
About the happy yard and singing as the farm was home,
    In the sun that is young once only,
        Time let me play and be
    Golden in the mercy of his means,
15 And green and golden I was huntsman and herdsman, the calves
Sang to my horn, the foxes on the hills barked clear and cold,
        And the sabbath rang slowly
    In the pebbles of the holy streams.

All the sun long it was running, it was lovely, the hay
20 Fields high as the house, the tunes from the chimneys, it was air
    And playing, lovely and watery
        And fire green as grass.
    And nightly under the simple stars
As I rode to sleep the owls were bearing the farm away,
25 All the moon long I heard, blessed among stables, the night-jars[3]
    Flying with the ricks,° and the horses   *haystacks*
        Flashing into the dark.

And then to awake, and the farm, like a wanderer white
With the dew, come back, the cock on his shoulder: it was all
30   Shining, it was Adam and maiden,[4]
        The sky gathered again
    And the sun grew round that very day.
So it must have been after the birth of the simple light
In the first, spinning place, the spellbound horses walking warm
35   Out of the whinnying green stable
        On to the fields of praise.

And honoured among foxes and pheasants by the gay house
Under the new made clouds and happy as the heart was long,
    In the sun born over and over,
40   I ran my heedless ways,
    My wishes raced through the house high hay
And nothing I cared, at my sky blue trades, that time allows
In all his tuneful turning so few and such morning songs
    Before the children green and golden
45   Follow him out of grace,

Nothing I cared, in the lamb white days, that time would take me
Up to the swallow thronged loft by the shadow of my hand,
    In the moon that is always rising,
        Nor that riding to sleep
50 I should hear him fly with the high fields
And wake to the farm forever fled from the childless land.
Oh as I was young and easy in the mercy of his means,
        Time held me green and dying
    Though I sang in my chains like the sea.

1945   1946

3. Species of bird.   4. Cf. Genesis 1.

Do Not Go Gentle into That Good Night

Do not go gentle into that good night,
Old age should burn and rave at close of day;
Rage, rage against the dying of the light.

Though wise men at their end know dark is right,
5   Because their words had forked no lightning they
Do not go gentle into that good night.

Good men, the last wave by, crying how bright
Their frail deeds might have danced in a green bay,
Rage, rage against the dying of the light.

10   Wild men who caught and sang the sun in flight,
And learn, too late, they grieved it on its way,
Do not go gentle into that good night.

Grave men, near death, who see with blinding sight
Blind eyes could blaze like meteors and be gay,
15   Rage, rage against the dying of the light.

And you, my father, there on the sad height,
Curse, bless, me now with your fierce tears, I pray.
Do not go gentle into that good night.
Rage, rage against the dying of the light.

1951   1952

PHILIP LARKIN
1922–1985

Philip Larkin was born in Coventry; was educated at its King Henry VIII School and at St. John's College, Oxford; and was for many years librarian of the Hull University Library. He wrote the poems of his first book, *The North Ship* (1945), under W. B. Yeats's strong enchantment. Although this influence persisted in the English poet's formal skill and subdued visionary longings, Larkin began to read Thomas Hardy seriously after World War II, and Hardy's rugged language, local settings, and ironic tone helped counter Yeats's influence. "After that," Larkin said, "Yeats came to seem so artificial—all that crap about masks and Crazy Jane and all the rest. It all rang so completely unreal." Also rejecting the international modernism of Eliot and Pound because of its mythical allusions, polyglot discourse, and fragmentary syntax, Larkin reclaimed a more direct, personal, formally regular model of poetry, supposedly rooted in a native English tradition of Wordsworth, Hardy, A. E. Housman, Wilfred Owen, and W. H. Auden. Even so, his poetry is not so thoroughly antimodernist as are his declarations: witness his imagist precision and alienated personae, his blending of revulsion and attraction toward modernity.

Larkin was the dominant figure in what came to be known as "the Movement," a group of university poets that included Kingsley Amis, Donald Davie, and Thom

Gunn, gathered together in Robert Conquest's landmark anthology of 1956, *New Lines*. Their work was seen as counteracting not only the extravagances of modernism but also the influence of Dylan Thomas's high-flown, apocalyptic rhetoric: like Larkin, these poets preferred a civil grammar and rational syntax over prophecy, suburban realities over mythmaking.

No other poet presents the welfare-state world of postimperial Britain so vividly, so unsparingly, and so tenderly. "Poetry is an affair of sanity, of seeing things as they are," Larkin said; "I don't want to transcend the commonplace, I love the commonplace life. Everyday things are lovely to me." Eschewing the grandiose, he writes poetry that, in its everyday diction and melancholy wryness, worldly subjects and regular meters, affirms rather than contravenes the restrictions of ordinary life. Love's failure, the erosion of religious and national abutments, the loneliness of age and death—Larkin does not avert his poetic gaze from these bleak realities. As indicated by the title of his 1955 collection *The Less Deceived*, disillusionment, drabness, and resignation color these poems. Yet Larkin's drearily mundane world often gives way to muted promise, his speakers' alienation to possible communion, his skepticism to encounters even with the sublime. At the end of "High Windows," the characteristically ironic and self-deprecating speaker glimpses both radiant presence and total absence in the sunlit glass: "And beyond it, the deep blue air, that shows / Nothing, and is nowhere, and is endless."

Like Hardy, Larkin wrote novels—*Jill* (1946) and *A Girl in Winter* (1947)—and his poems have a novelist's sense of place and skill in the handling of direct speech. He also edited a controversial anthology, *The Oxford Book of Twentieth-Century English Verse* (1973), which attempted to construct a modern native tradition in England. But his most significant legacy was his poetry, although his output was limited to four volumes. Out of "the commonplace life" he fashioned uncommon poems—some of the most emotionally complex, rhythmically polished, and intricately rhymed poems of the second half of the twentieth century.

Church Going

Once I am sure there's nothing going on
I step inside, letting the door thud shut.
Another church: matting, seats, and stone,
And little books; sprawlings of flowers, cut
5   For Sunday, brownish now; some brass and stuff
Up at the holy end; the small neat organ;
And a tense, musty, unignorable silence,
Brewed God knows how long. Hatless, I take off
My cycle-clips in awkward reverence,

10   Move forward, run my hand around the font.
From where I stand, the roof looks almost new—
Cleaned, or restored? Someone would know: I don't.
Mounting the lectern, I peruse a few
Hectoring large-scale verses,[1] and pronounce
15   "Here endeth" much more loudly than I'd meant.
The echoes snigger briefly. Back at the door
I sign the book, donate an Irish sixpence,[2]
Reflect the place was not worth stopping for.

1. I.e., Bible verses printed in large type for reading aloud.   2. An Irish sixpence has no value in England.

Yet stop I did: in fact I often do,
20   And always end much at a loss like this,
Wondering what to look for; wondering, too,
When churches fall completely out of use
What we shall turn them into, if we shall keep
A few cathedrals chronically on show,
25   Their parchment, plate and pyx³ in locked cases,
And let the rest rent-free to rain and sheep.
Shall we avoid them as unlucky places?

Or, after dark, will dubious women come
To make their children touch a particular stone;
30   Pick simples° for a cancer; or on some   *medicinal herbs*
Advised night see walking a dead one?
Power of some sort or other will go on
In games, in riddles, seemingly at random;
But superstition, like belief, must die,
35   And what remains when disbelief has gone?
Grass, weedy pavement, brambles, buttress, sky,

A shape less recognisable each week,
A purpose more obscure. I wonder who
Will be the last, the very last, to seek
40   This place for what it was; one of the crew
That tap and jot and know what rood-lofts⁴ were?
Some ruin-bibber, randy for antique,
Or Christmas-addict, counting on a whiff
Of gown-and-bands and organ-pipes and myrrh?⁵
45   Or will he be my representative,

Bored, uninformed, knowing the ghostly silt
Dispersed, yet tending to this cross of ground⁶
Through suburb scrub because it held unspilt
So long and equably what since is found
50   Only in separation—marriage, and birth,
And death, and thoughts of these—for which was built
This special shell? For, though I've no idea
What this accoutred frowsty barn is worth,
It pleases me to stand in silence here;

55   A serious house on serious earth it is,
In whose blent air all our compulsions meet,
Are recognised, and robed as destinies.
And that much never can be obsolete,
Since someone will forever be surprising
60   A hunger in himself to be more serious,
And gravitating with it to this ground,

---

3. Box in which communion wafers are kept.
4. Galleries on top of carved screens separating the nave of a church from the choir.
5. Gum resin used in the making of incense; one of three presents given by the Three Wise Men to the infant Jesus. "Gown-and-bands": gown and decorative collar worn by clergypeople.
6. Most churches were built in the shape of a cross.

Which, he once heard, was proper to grow wise in,
If only that so many dead lie round.

1954   1955

MCMXIV[1]

Those long uneven lines
Standing as patiently
As if they were stretched outside
The Oval or Villa Park,[2]
5 The crowns of hats, the sun
On moustached archaic faces
Grinning as if it were all
An August bank Holiday lark;

And the shut shops, the bleached,
10 Established names on the sunblinds,
The farthings and sovereigns,[3]
And dark-clothed children at play
Called after kings and queens,
The tin advertisements
15 For cocoa and twist,° and the pubs   tobacco
Wide open all day;

And the countryside not caring:
The place-names all hazed over
With flowering grasses, and fields
20 Shadowing Domesday lines[4]
Under wheat's restless silence;
The differently-dressed servants
With tiny rooms in huge houses,
The dust behind limousines;

25 Never such innocence,
Never before or since,
As changed itself to past
Without a word—the men
Leaving the gardens tidy,
30 The thousands of marriages
Lasting a little while longer:
Never such innocence again.

1960   1964

---

1. 1914, in Roman numerals, as incised on stone memorials to the dead of World War I.
2. London cricket ground and Birmingham football ground.
3. At that time the least valuable and the most valuable British coins, respectively.
4. The still-visible boundaries of medieval farmers' long and narrow plots, ownership of which is recorded in William the Conqueror's *Domesday Book* (1085–86).

Talking in Bed

Talking in bed ought to be easiest,
Lying together there goes back so far,
An emblem of two people being honest.

Yet more and more time passes silently.
5   Outside, the wind's incomplete unrest
Builds and disperses clouds about the sky,

And dark towns heap up on the horizon.
None of this cares for us. Nothing shows why
At this unique distance from isolation

10   It becomes still more difficult to find
Words at once true and kind,
Or not untrue and not unkind.

1960   1964

Ambulances

Closed like confessionals,[1] they thread
Loud noons of cities, giving back
None of the glances they absorb.
Light glossy grey, arms on a plaque,
5   They come to rest at any kerb:
All streets in time are visited.

Then children strewn on steps or road,
Or women coming from the shops
Past smells of different dinners, see
10   A wild white face that overtops
Red stretcher-blankets momently
As it is carried in and stowed,

And sense the solving emptiness
That lies just under all we do,
15   And for a second get it whole,
So permanent and blank and true.
The fastened doors recede. *Poor soul,*
They whisper at their own distress;

For borne away in deadened air
20   May go the sudden shut of loss
Round something nearly at an end,
And what cohered in it across

---

1. Enclosed stalls in Roman Catholic churches in which priests hear confession.

The years, the unique random blend
Of families and fashions, there

25 At last begin to loosen. Far
From the exchange of love to lie
Unreachable inside a room
The traffic parts to let go by
Brings closer what is left to come,
30 And dulls to distance all we are.

1961   1964

High Windows

When I see a couple of kids
And guess he's fucking her and she's
Taking pills or wearing a diaphragm,
I know this is paradise

5 Everyone old has dreamed of all their lives—
Bonds and gestures pushed to one side
Like an outdated combine harvester,[1]
And everyone young going down the long slide

To happiness, endlessly. I wonder if
10 Anyone looked at me, forty years back,
And thought, *That'll be the life;*
No God any more, or sweating in the dark

About hell and that, or having to hide
What you think of the priest. He
15 *And his lot will all go down the long slide*
Like free bloody birds. And immediately

Rather than words comes the thought of high windows:
The sun-comprehending glass,
And beyond it, the deep blue air, that shows
20 Nothing, and is nowhere, and is endless.

1967   1974

Homage to a Government

Next year we are to bring the soldiers home
For lack of money, and it is all right.
Places they guarded, or kept orderly,
Must guard themselves, and keep themselves orderly.

1. Farm machine for harvesting grain.

5   We want the money for ourselves at home
     Instead of working. And this is all right.

     It's hard to say who wanted it to happen,
     But now it's been decided nobody minds.
     The places are a long way off, not here,
10   Which is all right, and from what we hear
     The soldiers there only made trouble happen.
     Next year we shall be easier in our minds.

     Next year we shall be living in a country
     That brought its soldiers home for lack of money.
15   The statues will be standing in the same
     Tree-muffled squares, and look nearly the same.
     Our children will not know it's a different country.
     All we can hope to leave them now is money.

Jan. 10, 1969   1974

This Be The Verse[1]

     They fuck you up, your mum and dad.
        They may not mean to, but they do.
     They fill you with the faults they had
        And add some extra, just for you.

5   But they were fucked up in their turn
        By fools in old-style hats and coats,
     Who half the time were soppy-stern
        And half at one another's throats.

     Man hands on misery to man.
10   It deepens like a coastal shelf.[2]
     Get out as early as you can,
        And don't have any kids yourself.

Apr. ? 1971   1974

Aubade[1]

     I work all day, and get half-drunk at night.
     Waking at four to soundless dark, I stare.
     In time the curtain-edges will grow light.
     Till then I see what's really always there:
5   Unresting death, a whole day nearer now,

1. Cf. the elegy "Requiem," by Robert Louis Stevenson (1850–1894), of which the final verse reads, "This be the verse you grave for me: / *Here he lies where he longed to be, / Home is the sailor,* *home from sea, / And the hunter home from the hill.*"
2. Underwater land off a coast
1. Music or poem announcing dawn.

Making all thought impossible but how
And where and when I shall myself die.
Arid interrogation: yet the dread
Of dying, and being dead,
10 Flashes afresh to hold and horrify.

The mind blanks at the glare. Not in remorse
—The good not done, the love not given, time
Torn off unused—nor wretchedly because
An only life can take so long to climb
15 Clear of its wrong beginnings, and may never;
But at the total emptiness for ever,
The sure extinction that we travel to
And shall be lost in always. Not to be here,
Not to be anywhere,
20 And soon; nothing more terrible, nothing more true.

This is a special way of being afraid
No trick dispels. Religion used to try,
That vast moth-eaten musical brocade
Created to pretend we never die,
25 And specious stuff that says *No rational being
Can fear a thing it will not feel,* not seeing
That this is what we fear—no sight, no sound,
No touch or taste or smell, nothing to think with,
Nothing to love or link with,
30 The anaesthetic from which none come round.

And so it stays just on the edge of vision,
A small unfocused blur, a standing chill
That slows each impulse down to indecision.
Most things may never happen: this one will,
35 And realisation of it rages out
In furnace-fear when we are caught without
People or drink. Courage is no good:
It means not scaring others. Being brave
Lets no one off the grave.
40 Death is no different whined at than withstood.

Slowly light strengthens, and the room takes shape.
It stands plain as a wardrobe, what we know,
Have always known, know that we can't escape,
Yet can't accept. One side will have to go.
45 Meanwhile telephones crouch, getting ready to ring
In locked-up offices, and all the uncaring
Intricate rented world begins to rouse.
The sky is white as clay, with no sun.
Work has to be done.
50 Postmen like doctors go from house to house.

1977   1977

NADINE GORDIMER
b. 1923

Nadine Gordimer's fiction has given imaginative and moral shape to the recent history of South Africa. Since the publication of her first book, *The Lying Days* (1953), she has charted the changing patterns of response and resistance to apartheid by exploring the place of the European in Africa, selecting representative themes and governing motifs for novels and short stories, and shifting her ideological focus from a liberal to a more radical position. In recognition of this achievement, of having borne untiring and lucid narrative witness, Gordimer was awarded the 1991 Nobel Prize in Literature.

Born to Jewish immigrant parents in the South African mining town of Springs, Gordimer began writing early, from the beginning taking as her subject the pathologies and everyday realities of a racially divided society. Her decision to remain in Johannesburg through the years of political repression reflected her commitment to her subject and to her vision of a postapartheid future. In the years since apartheid was dismantled in 1994, Gordimer has continued to live and write in South Africa, and her recent novels, such as *The House Gun* (1998) and *The Pickup* (2001), retain an uncompromising focus on the inhabitants of a racially fractured culture.

In her nonfiction Gordimer self-consciously places her writing within a tradition of European realism, most notably that defined by the Hungarian philosopher and critic Georg Lukács (1885–1971). Her aim—as shown in her incisive and highly acclaimed novels of the 1970s, *The Conservationist* (1974) and *Burger's Daughter* (1979)—is to evoke by way of the personal and of the precisely observed particular a broader political and historical totality. This method gives her characters, and the stories in which they reside, their representativeness. As Gordimer has famously said, "politics is character in South Africa." Yet throughout the long years of political polarization in that country and the banning of three of her own books, Gordimer has distanced herself from polemics and retained a firm humanist belief in what she variously describes as the objectivity and the inwardness of the writer. Although she has referred to an engagement with political reality as imperative and explores permutations of the question of engagement in novels such as *Burger's Daughter* and *July's People* (1981), she nevertheless asserts the autonomy of the writer's perspective, "the last true judgment." Narrative for Gordimer helps define and clarify historical experience. Her keen sense of history as formation, and as demanding a continual rewriting, has ensured that her novels can be read as at once contemporary in their reference and symbolic of broader social and historical patterns, as in the paranoia surrounding the case of the buried black body on a white farm in *The Conservationist*, or in the psychosocial portrait of Rosa Burger in *Burger's Daughter*.

Gordimer has drawn criticism both for her apparent lack of attention to feminism in favor of race issues and for the wholeness and unfashionable completeness of her novels—their plottedness, meticulous scene paintings, fully realized characters. However, the searching symbolism and complexity of her narratives generally work against such judgments. As the following short story shows, a prominent feature of her writing is to give a number of different perspectives on a situation, in some cases most poignantly those of apartheid's supporters, and in this way to represent the broader anatomy of a diseased politics and, more generally, of the human being in history.

The Moment before the Gun Went Off

Marais Van der Vyver shot one of his farm labourers, dead. An accident, there are accidents with guns every day of the week—children playing a fatal game with a father's revolver in the cities where guns are domestic objects, nowadays, hunting mishaps like this one, in the country—but these won't be reported all over the world. Van der Vyver knows his will be. He knows that the story of the Afrikaner farmer—regional Party leader and Commandant of the local security commando—shooting a black man who worked for him will fit exactly *their* version of South Africa, it's made for them. They'll be able to use it in their boycott and divestment campaigns, it'll be another piece of evidence in their truth about the country. The papers at home will quote the story as it has appeared in the overseas press, and in the back-and-forth he and the black man will become those crudely-drawn figures on anti-apartheid banners, units in statistics of white brutality against the blacks quoted at the United Nations—he, whom they will gleefully be able to call "a leading member" of the ruling Party.

People in the farming community understand how he must feel. Bad enough to have killed a man, without helping the Party's, the government's, the country's enemies, as well. They see the truth of that. They know, reading the Sunday papers, that when Van der Vyver is quoted saying he is "terribly shocked," he will "look after the wife and children," none of those Americans and English, and none of those people at home who want to destroy the white man's power will believe him. And how they will sneer when he even says of the farm boy (according to one paper, if you can trust any of those reporters), "He was my friend, I always took him hunting with me." Those city and overseas people don't know it's true: farmers usually have one particular black boy they like to take along with them in the lands; you could call it a kind of friend, yes, friends are not only your own white people, like yourself, you take into your house, pray with in church and work with on the Party committee. But how can those others know that? They don't want to know it. They think all blacks are like the big-mouth agitators in town. And Van der Vyver's face, in the photographs, strangely opened by distress—everyone in the district remembers Marais Van der Vyver as a little boy who would go away and hide himself if he caught you smiling at him, and everyone knows him now as a man who hides any change of expression round his mouth behind a thick, soft moustache, and in his eyes by always looking at some object in hand, leaf of a crop fingered, pen or stone picked up, while concentrating on what he is saying, or while listening to you. It just goes to show what shock can do; when you look at the newspaper photographs you feel like apologising, as if you had stared in on some room where you should not be.

There will be an inquiry; there had better be, to stop the assumption of yet another case of brutality against farm workers, although there's nothing in doubt—an accident, and all the facts fully admitted by Van der Vyver. He made a statement when he arrived at the police station with the dead man in his bakkie.[1] Captain Beetge knows him well, of course; he gave him brandy. He was shaking, this big, calm, clever son of Willem Van der Vyver, who inherited the old man's best farm. The black was stone dead, nothing to be done for him. Beetge will not tell anyone that after the brandy Van der Vyver wept. He sobbed, snot running onto his hands, like a dirty kid. The Captain was ashamed, for him, and walked out to give him a chance to recover himself.

Marais Van der Vyver left his house at three in the afternoon to cull a buck from the family of kudu[2] he protects in the bush areas of his farm. He is

1. Pickup truck.
2. Large African antelope. The males have long, spirally twisted horns.

interested in wildlife and sees it as the farmers' sacred duty to raise game as well as cattle. As usual, he called at his shed workshop to pick up Lucas, a twenty-year-old farmhand who had shown mechanical aptitude and whom Van der Vyver himself had taught to maintain tractors and other farm machinery. He hooted, and Lucas followed the familiar routine, jumping onto the back of the truck. He liked to travel standing up there, spotting game before his employer did. He would lean forward, braced against the cab below him.

Van der Vyver had a rifle and .300 ammunition beside him in the cab. The rifle was one of his father's, because his own was at the gunsmith's in town. Since his father died (Beetge's sergeant wrote "passed on") no one had used the rifle and so when he took it from a cupboard he was sure it was not loaded. His father had never allowed a loaded gun in the house; he himself had been taught since childhood never to ride with a loaded weapon in a vehicle. But this gun was loaded. On a dirt track, Lucas thumped his fist on the cab roof three times to signal: look left. Having seen the white-ripple-marked flank of a kudu, and its fine horns raking through disguising bush, Van der Vyver drove rather fast over a pot-hole. The jolt fired the rifle. Upright, it was pointing straight through the cab roof at the head of Lucas. The bullet pierced the roof and entered Lucas's brain by way of his throat.

That is the statement of what happened. Although a man of such standing in the district, Van der Vyver had to go through the ritual of swearing that it was the truth. It has gone on record, and will be there in the archive of the local police station as long as Van der Vyver lives, and beyond that, through the lives of his children, Magnus, Helena and Karel—unless things in the country get worse, the example of black mobs in the towns spreads to the rural areas and the place is burned down as many urban police stations have been. Because nothing the government can do will appease the agitators and the whites who encourage them. Nothing satisfies them, in the cities: blacks can sit and drink in white hotels, now, the Immorality Act[3] has gone, blacks can sleep with whites. . . . It's not even a crime any more.

Van der Vyver has a high barbed security fence round his farmhouse and garden which his wife, Alida, thinks spoils completely the effect of her artificial stream with its tree-ferns beneath the jacarandas.[4] There is an aerial soaring like a flag-pole in the back yard. All his vehicles, including the truck in which the black man died, have aerials that swing their whips when the driver hits a pot-hole: they are part of the security system the farmers in the district maintain, each farm in touch with every other by radio, twenty-four hours out of twenty-four. It has already happened that infiltrators from over the border have mined remote farm roads, killing white farmers and their families out on their own property for a Sunday picnic. The pot-hole could have set off a land-mine, and Van der Vyver might have died with his farm boy. When neighbours use the communications system to call up and say they are sorry about "that business" with one of Van der Vyver's boys, there goes unsaid: it could have been worse.

It is obvious from the quality and fittings of the coffin that the farmer has provided money for the funeral. And an elaborate funeral means a great deal to blacks; look how they will deprive themselves of the little they have, in their lifetime, keeping up payments to a burial society so they won't go in boxwood to an unmarked grave. The young wife is pregnant (of course) and another little one, wearing red shoes several sizes too large, leans under her jutting

3. South African government act prohibiting sexual relations between whites and other races.

4. Tropical trees with blue flowers.

belly. He is too young to understand what has happened, what he is witnessing that day, but neither whines nor plays about; he is solemn without knowing why. Blacks expose small children to everything, they don't protect them from the sight of fear and pain the way whites do theirs. It is the young wife who rolls her head and cries like a child, sobbing on the breast of this relative and that.

All present work for Van der Vyver or are the families of those who work; and in the weeding and harvest seasons, the women and children work for him, too, carried—wrapped in their blankets, on a truck, singing—at sunrise to the fields. The dead man's mother is a woman who can't be more than in her late thirties (they start bearing children at puberty) but she is heavily mature in a black dress between her own parents, who were already working for old Van der Vyver when Marais, like their daughter, was a child. The parents hold her as if she were a prisoner or a crazy woman to be restrained. But she says nothing, does nothing. She does not look up; she does not look at Van der Vyver, whose gun went off in the truck, she stares at the grave. Nothing will make her look up; there need be no fear that she will look up; at him. His wife, Alida, is beside him. To show the proper respect, as for any white funeral, she is wearing the navy-blue-and-cream hat she wears to church this summer. She is always supportive, although he doesn't seem to notice it; this coldness and reserve—his mother says he didn't mix well as a child—she accepts for herself but regrets that it has prevented him from being nominated, as he should be, to stand as the Party's parliamentary candidate for the district. He does not let her clothing, or that of anyone else gathered closely, make contact with him. He, too, stares at the grave. The dead man's mother and he stare at the grave in communication like that between the black man outside and the white man inside the cab the moment before the gun went off.

The moment before the gun went off was a moment of high excitement shared through the roof of the cab, as the bullet was to pass, between the young black man outside and the white farmer inside the vehicle. There were such moments, without explanation, between them, although often around the farm the farmer would pass the young man without returning a greeting, as if he did not recognize him. When the bullet went off what Van der Vyver saw was the kudu stumble in fright at the report and gallop away. Then he heard the thud behind him, and past the window saw the young man fall out of the vehicle. He was sure he had leapt up and toppled—in fright, like the buck. The farmer was almost laughing with relief, ready to tease, as he opened his door, it did not seem possible that a bullet passing through the roof could have done harm.

The young man did not laugh with him at his own fright. The farmer carried him in his arms, to the truck. He was sure, sure he could not be dead. But the young black man's blood was all over the farmer's clothes, soaking against his flesh as he drove.

How will they ever know, when they file newspaper clippings, evidence, proof, when they look at the photographs and see his face—guilty! guilty! they are right!—how will they know, when the police stations burn with all the evidence of what has happened now, and what the law made a crime in the past. How could they know that *they do not know*. Anything. The young black callously shot through the negligence of the white man was not the farmer's boy; he was his son.

1991

BRIAN FRIEL
b. 1929

For the renowned playwright Brian Friel, as for his Irish predecessors W. B. Yeats and James Joyce, the vexed issue of language and national identity has been a central preoccupation. His play *Translations* (1980), which reimagines the transitional moment when the language of the colonizer is supplanting the language of the colonized, is one of the richest late-twentieth century meditations on the role of the English language in British colonialism.

Set in 1833 in the rural village of Baile Beag, County Donegal, on the northwest corner of Ireland, the play dramatizes two key processes in the linguistic transformation of a colonized nation: remapping and education. Captain Lancey and Lieutenant Yolland, English officers in the Royal Engineers, have been sent to Ireland to help remap it with anglicized and standardized place-names. An intermediary figure, Owen, originally from Baile Beag but employed by the English as an interpreter, is helping the imperial military, as he puts it, "to translate the quaint, archaic tongue" of the Irish "into the King's good English." To produce Britain's first Ordnance Survey of Ireland, ordered by Parliament in 1824, each Gaelic name is replaced either by a translated English equivalent (Cnoc na Ri becomes Kings Head) or a similar English sound (Druim Dubh becomes Dromduff). Language is crucial in claiming the land for the British crown—ridding it of ambiguity and opacity, making it readable, knowable, taxable, militarily penetrable, evacuating its linguistically embodied history and memory. After Lieutenant Yolland and the Irishwoman Maire fall in love—a cross-linguistic and cross-ethnic romance with tragic consequences—the psychic violence of this colonial renaming becomes a matter of brutal physical force. The play widens the scope of its profound reflection on naming and identity through suggestive parallels with other acts of nomination—the nearly mute Sarah's vocalizing her name, the ritual naming of a baby, Owen's accidental renaming as Roland by the English officers, even an allusion to Adam's naming of the animals.

At the very time when the Ordnance Survey is remaking Irish topography, a new English-language system of National Education is being put into place, and it will supplant the local Irish-speaking schools, or hedge schools, greatly accelerating the anglicization of the still-Gaelic-speaking regions of Ireland. Hugh O'Donnell presides over the hedge school, and while his classroom is a barn where the English language and its literary canon (e.g., William Wordsworth) are unknown, the ancient Greek and Roman gods and goddesses, such as flashing-eyed Athena, are vital and immediate presences in classical languages. The conflicted schoolmaster, who initially dismisses English as useful "for the purposes of commerce" and then seeks employment in the new English schools, foresees the loss of an educational system and, to a significant degree, of a culture; he muses elegiacally but realistically that a community's language cannot remain frozen in the face of massive historical change: "We must learn where we live. We must learn to make [the new English names] our own. We must make them our new home." The English language, the play evocatively suggests, has both dispossessed and rehoused, unified and fragmented, advanced and oppressed the Irish, like the many other peoples remapped and reeducated by the empire.

Friel was born in Omagh, County Tyrone, Northern Ireland, and spent much of his youth in Derry (or Londonderry), Northern Ireland, with vacations across the border in County Donegal, in the Irish Republic, with his maternal relatives. He attended St. Patrick's College, Ireland's national seminary, in Maynooth, but instead of becoming a Roman Catholic priest, taught school in Derry for ten years, before turning full-time to writing in 1960. Having published short stories, essays, and radio plays, he increasingly devoted himself to writing stage dramas, such as *Philadelphia, Here I Come!* (first produced in 1964), *Faith Healer* (1979), and *Dancing at Lughnasa*

(1990), which have been performed and garnered prizes in Derry, Dublin, New York, London, and elsewhere. In 1969 Friel moved across the border from Northern Ireland into Derry's hinterland in County Donegal, and in 1980 he cofounded the Field Day Theatre Company, which has brought professional drama to many parts of Ireland and Northern Ireland, while seeking to break down calcified polarities of Northern Irish politics (Catholic vs. Protestant, Unionist vs. Republican, etc.). *Translations* was Field Day's first production, with the company's cofounder, the actor Stephen Rea, playing the role of Owen, and Liam Neeson playing Doalty.

PRONOUNCING GLOSSARY

As an aid for performance and reading, the following phonetic spellings provide a rough guide to the pronunciation of Irish names and words. Standard Irish diacritical marks are given in the glossary, though omitted by Friel in the playscript.

Anna na mBréag: ANN-na nuh MRAYG

Baile Beag: BOLL-ya bYUG (BOLL rhymes with *doll*)

Baile na gGall: BOLL-ya nuh NOWL (NOWL rhymes with *owl*; *nuh* has the *u* sound as in English *up*)

Beann na Gaoithe: bYOWN na GWEE-ha (YOWN rhymes with *town*)

Buncrana: bunn KRAAH-na (where *AA* is an elongated version of the *a* sound in *apple*)

Bun na hAbhann: BUNN nuh HOW-un

Caitlín Dubh Nic Reactainn: katt-LEEN DUV neek ROK-tin

Carraig na Rí: KORR-ig nuh REE (KORR: the *o* sound as in English *on* and *off*)

Carraig an Phoill: KORR-ig on f-WEEL

Catach: KOTT-ukh

Ceann Balor: kYOWN BA-lor (YOWN as above; "Balor" rhymes with *valor*)

Cnoc na Móna: k-NUKH nuh MOW-na (MOW as in English)

Cnoc na nGabhar: k-NUKH nuh NOW-er (NOW as in English)

Cnoc na Rí: k-NUCK nuh REE

Cúchulainn: KOO-kuhl-lin

Diarmuid: DEER-med

Donegal: dunny-GAWL

Druim Dubh: drimm DUV (the *u* sound of the English *un-*)

Druim Luachra: Drim LOO-krah

Éamon: AIM-en

Grania: GRAW-nya

Inis Meadhon: IN-ish MAAN (where *AA* is an elongated version of the *a* sound in *apple*)

Lag: log (exactly like the English word *log*)

Lis Maol: líss MAY-ull (*liss* rhymes with English *kiss*)

Lis na Muc: LISS nuh MUK

Lis na nGall: Liss nuh nALL

Lis na nGradh: LISS nuh nRAW (a gentle little *n* sound before the *RAW*)

Loch an Iubhair: LUKH un OO-er

Loch na nÉan: LUKH nuh NAY-un

Luachra: LOO-akh-ra

Machaire bán: MOKH-ur-uh BAWN

Machaire Buidhe: MOKH-i-reh bWEE (the middle *i* is short like the English *in*)

Machaire Mór: MOKH-i-reh MOOR

Máire Chatach: MAW-reh KHOTT-ukh

Manus: MAAH-nuss

Mullach Dearg: MULL-ukh JA-rug (hard *J* as in *John*)

Poll na gCaorach: POWL nuh GAY-rukh (POWL rhymes with *cowl*)

Port: purt (rhymes with *hurt*)

Poteen: puh-TCHEEN

Ruadh: ROO-uh

Séamus: SHAY-muss

Seán: shawn

Tobair Bhríain: TUB-er vr-EE-un

Tobair Vree: TUB-er vrEE (the letter V is
    an anglicization)

Tor: tur (as in the first syllable of the
    English word *turret*)

Trá Bhán: trAW VAWN

Tulach Álainn: TULL-ukh AW-linn

Translations

MANUS	BRIDGET
SARAH	HUGH
JIMMY JACK	OWEN
MAIRE	CAPTAIN LANCEY
DOALTY	LIEUTENANT YOLLAND

The action takes place in a hedge-school[1] *in the townland of Baile Beag/Ballybeg,
an Irish-speaking community in County Donegal.*[2]

ACT ONE   *An afternoon in late August 1833.*
ACT TWO   *A few days later.*
ACT THREE   *The evening of the following day.*

Act One

   The hedge-school is held in a disused barn or hay-shed or byre. Along the back
wall are the remains of five or six stalls—wooden posts and chains—where cows
were once milked and bedded. A double door left, large enough to allow a cart
to enter. A window right. A wooden stairway without a banister leads to the
upstairs living-quarters (off) of the schoolmaster and his son. Around the room
are broken and forgotten implements: a cart-wheel, some lobster-pots, farming
tools, a battle[3] of hay, a churn, etc. There are also the stools and bench-seats
which the pupils use and a table and chair for the master. At the door a pail of
water and a soiled towel. The room is comfortless and dusty and functional—
there is no trace of a woman's hand.
   When the play opens, MANUS is teaching SARAH to speak. He kneels beside her.
She is sitting on a low stool, her head down, very tense, clutching a slate on her
knees. He is coaxing her gently and firmly and—as with everything he does—
with a kind of zeal.
   MANUS is in his late twenties/early thirties; the master's older son. He is pale-
faced, lightly built, intense, and works as an unpaid assistant—a monitor—to his
father. His clothes are shabby; and when he moves we see that he is lame.
   SARAH's speech defect is so bad that all her life she has been considered locally
to be dumb and she has accepted this: when she wishes to communicate, she
grunts and makes unintelligible nasal sounds. She has a waiflike[4] appearance
and could be any age from seventeen to thirty-five.
   JIMMY JACK CASSIE—known as the Infant Prodigy—sits by himself, contentedly
reading Homer in Greek and smiling to himself. He is a bachelor in his sixties,
lives alone, and comes to these evening classes partly for the company and partly

---

1. Peasant school in which the Irish language was
the primary medium of instruction; the hedge
school was so called because it was beside a hedge
(or in the open air or in a barn). Such schools were
formed because education of Roman Catholics in
Ireland had been officially proscribed by the Penal
Laws passed in the 17th and 18th centuries.

2. In the northwest corner of Ireland, now in the
Republic of Ireland. Baile Beag/Ballybeg is the
imaginary community in which many of Friel's
plays are set.
3. Compact bundle.
4. Like a homeless child.

for the intellectual stimulation. He is fluent in Latin and Greek but is in no way pedantic—to him it is perfectly normal to speak these tongues.[5] He never washes. His clothes—heavy top coat, hat, mittens, which he wears now—are filthy and he lives in them summer and winter, day and night. He now reads in a quiet voice and smiles in profound satisfaction. For JIMMY *the world of the gods and the ancient myths is as real and as immediate as everyday life in the townland of Baile Beag.*

MANUS *holds* SARAH's *hands in his and he articulates slowly and distinctly into her face.*

MANUS   We're doing very well. And we're going to try it once more—just once more. Now—relax and breathe in . . . deep . . . and out . . . in . . . and out . . .

   [SARAH *shakes her head vigorously and stubbornly.*]
MANUS   Come on, Sarah. This is our secret.
   [*Again vigorous and stubborn shaking of* SARAH's *head.*]
MANUS   Nobody's listening. Nobody hears you.
JIMMY   'Ton d'emeibet epeita thea glaukopis Athene . . .'[6]
MANUS   Get your tongue and your lips working. 'My name—' Come on. One more try. 'My name is—' Good girl.
SARAH   My . . .
MANUS   Great. 'My name—'
SARAH   My . . . my . . .
MANUS   Raise your head. Shout it out. Nobody's listening.
JIMMY   '. . . alla hekelos estai en Atreidao domois . . .'[7]
MANUS   Jimmy, please! Once more—just once more—'My name—' Good girl. Come on now. Head up. Mouth open.
SARAH   My . . .
MANUS   Good.
SARAH   My . . .
MANUS   Great.
SARAH   My name . . .
MANUS   Yes?
   [SARAH *pauses. Then in a rush.*]
SARAH   My name is Sarah.
MANUS   Marvellous! Bloody marvellous!
   [MANUS *hugs* SARAH. *She smiles in shy, embarrassed pleasure.*]
   Did you hear that, Jimmy?—'My name is Sarah'—clear as a bell. [*To* SARAH.]
   The Infant Prodigy doesn't know what we're at.
   [SARAH *laughs at this.* MANUS *hugs her again and stands up.*]
   Now we're really started! Nothing'll stop us now! Nothing in the wide world!
   [JIMMY, *chuckling at his text, comes over to them.*]
JIMMY   Listen to this, Manus.
MANUS   Soon you'll be telling me all the secrets that have been in that head of yours all these years.
   Certainly, James—what is it?

5. Latin and Greek were taught and used in the hedge schools.
6. But the grey-eyed goddess Athene then replied to him (*Odyssey,* XIII, 420) [Friel's note]. Athena, ancient Greek goddess of war, wisdom, and the city, was a tutelary god to the hero Odysseus, also known by the Roman name Ulysses. In this scene of Homer's epic, she plots Odysseus' return home, after his ten-year absence. A disguise, as a dirty and shriveled old man, will enable him to trick and kill the suitors to his wife, Penelope.
7. But he sits at ease in the halls of the Sons of Athens (*Odyssey,* XIII, 423–4) [Friel's note].

[*To* SARAH.] Maybe you'd set out the stools?

[MANUS *runs up the stairs.*]

JIMMY   Wait till you hear this, Manus.

MANUS   Go ahead. I'll be straight down.

JIMMY   'Hos ara min phamene rabdo epemassat Athene—' 'After Athene had said this, she touched Ulysses with her wand. She withered the fair skin of his supple limbs and destroyed the flaxen[8] hair from off his head and about his limbs she put the skin of an old man . . .'! The divil! The divil!

[MANUS *has emerged again with a bowl of milk and a piece of bread.*]

JIMMY   And wait till you hear! She's not finished with him yet!

[*As* MANUS *descends the stairs he toasts* SARAH *with his bowl.*]

JIMMY   'Knuzosen de oi osse—' 'She dimmed his two eyes that were so beautiful and clothed him in a vile ragged cloak begrimed with filthy smoke . . .'! D'you see! Smoke! Smoke! D'you see! Sure look at what the same turf-smoke has done to myself! [*He rapidly removes his hat to display his bald head.*] Would you call that flaxen hair?

MANUS   Of course I would.

JIMMY   'And about him she cast the great skin of a filthy hind,[9] stripped of the hair, and into his hand she thrust a staff and a wallet'! Ha-ha-ha! Athene did that to Ulysses! Made him into a tramp! Isn't she the tight one?

MANUS   You couldn't watch her, Jimmy.

JIMMY   You know what they call her?

MANUS   'Glaukopis Athene.'

JIMMY   That's it! The flashing-eyed Athene! By God, Manus, sir, if you had a woman like that about the house, it's not stripping a turf[1]-bank you'd be thinking about—eh?

MANUS   She was a goddess, Jimmy.

JIMMY   Better still. Sure isn't our own Grania a class of a goddess and—

MANUS   Who?

JIMMY   Grania—Grania—Diarmuid's Grania.[2]

MANUS   Ah.

JIMMY   And sure she can't get her fill of men.

MANUS   Jimmy, you're impossible.

JIMMY   I was just thinking to myself last night: if you had the choosing between Athene and Artemis and Helen of Troy—all three of them Zeus's girls[3]—imagine three powerful-looking daughters like that all in the one parish of Athens!—now, if you had the picking between them, which would you take?

MANUS   [*To* SARAH.]   Which should I take, Sarah?

JIMMY   No harm to Helen; and no harm to Artemis; and indeed no harm to our own Grania, Manus. But I think I've no choice but to go bull-straight for Athene. By God, sir, them flashing eyes would fair keep a man jigged[4] up constant!

---

8. A pale strawlike color. Jimmy is continuing with the same scene of the *Odyssey*.
9. Female red deer.
1. Peat; dried and used for fuel.
2. Young and beautiful Irish princess betrothed to the aged but powerful Fionn mac Cumhaill; many medieval stories recount the flight of Grania and her lover, Dairmud, over the Irish countryside in

their attempt to escape capture by Fionn.
3. I.e., daughters of the most powerful Greek god. As goddess of wild animals, vegetation, and the hunt, Artemis was contrasted with Athena, goddess of the city. Helen's abduction was the legendary cause of the Trojan War.
4. Jerked, caught.

[*Suddenly and momentarily, as if in spasm,* JIMMY *stands to attention and salutes, his face raised in pained ecstasy.*

MANUS *laughs. So does* SARAH. JIMMY *goes back to his seat, and his reading.*]

MANUS   You're a dangerous bloody man, Jimmy Jack.

JIMMY   'Flashing-eyed'! Hah! Sure Homer knows it all, boy. Homer knows it all.

[MANUS *goes to the window and looks out.*]

MANUS   Where the hell has he got to?

[SARAH *goes to* MANUS *and touches his elbow. She mimes rocking a baby.*]

MANUS   Yes, I know he's at the christening; but it doesn't take them all day to put a name on a baby, does it?

[SARAH *mimes pouring drinks and tossing them back quickly.*]

MANUS   You may be sure. Which pub?

[SARAH *indicates.*]

MANUS   Gracie's?

[*No. Further away.*]

MANUS   Con Connie Tim's?

[*No. To the right of there.*]

MANUS   Anna na mBreag's?

[*Yes. That's it.*]

MANUS   Great. She'll fill him up. I suppose I may take the class then.

[MANUS *begins to distribute some books, slates and chalk, texts etc. beside the seats.*

SARAH *goes over to the straw and produces a bunch of flowers she has hidden there.*

During this.]

JIMMY   'Autar o ek limenos prosebe—' 'But Ulysses went forth from the harbour and through the woodland to the place where Athene had shown him he could find the good swineherd who—*o oi biotoio malista kedeto*'—what's that, Manus?

MANUS   'Who cared most for his substance'.

JIMMY   That's it! 'The good swineherd who cared most for his substance above all the slaves that Ulysses possessed . . .'[5]

[SARAH *presents the flowers to* MANUS.]

MANUS   Those are lovely, Sarah.

[*But* SARAH *has fled in embarrassment to her seat and has her head buried in a book.* MANUS *goes to her.*]

MANUS   Flow–ers.

[*Pause.* SARAH *does not look up.*]

MANUS   Say the word: flow–ers. Come on—flow–ers.

SARAH   Flowers.

MANUS   You see?—you're off!

[MANUS *leans down and kisses the top of* SARAH'S *head.*]

MANUS   And they're beautiful flowers. Thank you.

[MAIRE *enters, a strong-minded, strong-bodied woman in her twenties with a head of curly hair. She is carrying a small can of milk.*]

5. At the beginning of book 14 of the *Odyssey*, Odysseus seeks, at Athena's instruction, the field hand who has been most attentive to the hero's estate in his absence.

MAIRE   Is this all's here? Is there no school this evening?

MANUS   If my father's not back, I'll take it.

[MANUS *stands awkwardly, having been caught kissing* SARAH *and with the flowers almost formally at his chest.*]

MAIRE   Well now, isn't that a pretty sight. There's your milk. How's Sarah?

[SARAH *grunts a reply.*]

MANUS   I saw you out at the hay.

[MAIRE *ignores this and goes to* JIMMY.]

MAIRE   And how's Jimmy Jack Cassie?

JIMMY   Sit down beside me, Maire.

MAIRE   Would I be safe?

JIMMY   No safer man in Donegal.

[MAIRE *flops on a stool beside* JIMMY.]

MAIRE   Ooooh. The best harvest in living memory, they say; but I don't want to see another like it. [*Showing* JIMMY *her hands.*] Look at the blisters.

JIMMY   *Esne fatigata?*

MAIRE   *Sum fatigatissima.*

JIMMY   *Bene! Optime!*[6]

MAIRE   That's the height of my Latin. Fit me better if I had even that much English.

JIMMY   English? I thought you had some English?

MAIRE   Three words. Wait—there was a spake[7] I used to have off by heart. What's this it was?

[*Her accent is strange because she is speaking a foreign language and because she does not understand what she is saying.*]

'In Norfolk[8] we besport ourselves around the maypoll.' What about that!

MANUS   Maypole.[9]

[*Again* MAIRE *ignores* MANUS.]

MAIRE   God have mercy on my Aunt Mary—she taught me that when I was about four, whatever it means. Do you know what it means, Jimmy?

JIMMY   Sure you know I have only Irish like yourself.

MAIRE   And Latin. And Greek.

JIMMY   I'm telling you a lie: I know one English word.

MAIRE   What?

JIMMY   Bo–som.

MAIRE   What's a bo–som?

JIMMY   You know—[*He illustrates with his hands.*]—bo–som—bo–som—you know—Diana, the huntress,[1] she has two powerful bosom.

MAIRE   You may be sure that's the one English word you would know. [*Rises.*] Is there a drop of water about?

[MANUS *gives* MAIRE *his bowl of milk.*]

MANUS   I'm sorry I couldn't get up last night.

MAIRE   Doesn't matter.

MANUS   Biddy Hanna sent for me to write a letter to her sister in Nova Scotia. All the gossip of the parish. 'I brought the cow to the bull three times last week but no good. There's nothing for it now but Big Ned Frank.'

MAIRE   [*Drinking.*]   That's better.

---

6. Are you tired? / I am very tired. / Good! Excellent! [Friel's note].
7. Speech.
8. County of eastern England.

9. Tall decorated pole around which traditional English dances were conducted in springtime.
1. Roman goddess, comparable to the Greek Artemis.

MANUS   And she got so engrossed in it that she forgot who she was dictating to: 'The aul drunken schoolmaster and that lame son of his are still footering about in the hedge-school, wasting people's good time and money.'
[MAIRE *has to laugh at this.*]

MAIRE   She did not!

MANUS   And me taking it all down. 'Thank God one of them new national schools[2] is being built above at Poll na gCaorach.' It was after midnight by the time I got back.

MAIRE   Great to be a busy man.
[MAIRE *moves away.* MANUS *follows.*]

MANUS   I could hear music on my way past but I thought it was too late to call.

MAIRE   [*To* SARAH.]   Wasn't your father in great voice last night?
[SARAH *nods and smiles.*]

MAIRE   It must have been near three o'clock by the time you got home?
[SARAH *holds up four fingers.*]

MAIRE   Was it four? No wonder we're in pieces.

MANUS   I can give you a hand at the hay tomorrow.

MAIRE   That's the name of a hornpipe,[3] isn't it?—'The Scholar In The Hay-field'—or is it a reel?[4]

MANUS   If the day's good.

MAIRE   Suit yourself. The English soldiers below in the tents, them sapper[5] fellas, they're coming up to give us a hand. I don't know a word they're saying, nor they me; but sure that doesn't matter, does it?

MANUS   What the hell are you so crabbed[6] about?!
[DOALTY *and* BRIDGET *enter noisily. Both are in their twenties.*
   DOALTY *is brandishing a surveyor's pole. He is an open-minded, open-hearted, generous and slightly thick young man.*
   BRIDGET *is a plump, fresh young girl, ready to laugh, vain, and with a countrywoman's instinctive cunning.*
   DOALTY *enters doing his imitation of the master.*]

DOALTY   Vesperal[7] salutations to you all.

BRIDGET   He's coming down past Carraig na Ri and he's as full as a pig!

DOALTY   *Ignari, stulti, rustici*[8]—pot-boys and peasant whelps[9]—semi-literates and illegitimates.

BRIDGET   He's been on the batter[1] since this morning; he sent the wee ones home at eleven o'clock.

DOALTY   Three questions. Question A—Am I drunk? Question B—Am I sober? [*Into* MAIRE's *face.*] *Responde—responde!*[2]

BRIDGET   Question C, Master—When were you last sober?

MAIRE   What's the weapon, Doalty?

BRIDGET   I warned him. He'll be arrested one of these days.

DOALTY   Up in the bog with Bridget and her aul fella, and the Red Coats were

2. In 1831, two years earlier, a new system of English-speaking schools had been introduced; these would eventually supplant the hedge schools.
3. Vigorous dance performed by a sole person to a wind instrument.
4. Lively dance performed by couples facing each other.
5. Soldier who works in saps, i.e., fortifications, or does field work.
6. Annoyed.
7. Evening.
8. Ignoramuses, fools, peasants [Latin; Friel's note].
9. Young wild animals. "Pot-boys": assistants who serve beer in a pub.
1. On the bottle.
2. Answer—answer! [Latin; Friel's note].

just across at the foot of Cnoc na Mona, dragging them aul chains and peeping through that big machine they lug about everywhere with them—you know the name of it, Manus?

MAIRE Theodolite.[3]

BRIDGET How do you know?

MAIRE They leave it in our byre[4] at night sometimes if it's raining.

JIMMY Theodolite—what's the etymology of that word, Manus?

MANUS No idea.

BRIDGET Get on with the story.

JIMMY *Theo—theos*[5]—something to do with a god. Maybe *thea*—a goddess! What shape's the yoke?

DOALTY 'Shape!' Will you shut up, you aul eejit[6] you! Anyway, every time they'd stick one of these poles into the ground and move across the bog, I'd creep up and shift it twenty or thirty paces to the side.

BRIDGET God!

DOALTY Then they'd come back and stare at it and look at their calculations and stare at it again and scratch their heads. And Cripes[7], d'you know what they ended up doing?

BRIDGET Wait till you hear!

DOALTY They took the bloody machine apart! [*And immediately he speaks in gibberish—an imitation of two very agitated and confused sappers in rapid conversation.*]

BRIDGET That's the image of them!

MAIRE You must be proud of yourself, Doalty.

DOALTY What d'you mean?

MAIRE That was a very clever piece of work.

MANUS It was a gesture.

MAIRE What sort of a gesture?

MANUS Just to indicate . . . a presence.

MAIRE Hah!

BRIDGET I'm telling you—you'll be arrested.

[*When* DOALTY *is embarrassed—or pleased—he reacts physically. He now grabs* BRIDGET *around the waist.*]

DOALTY What d'you make of that for an implement, Bridget? Wouldn't that make a great aul shaft for your churn?

BRIDGET Let go of me, you dirty brute! I've a headline to do before Big Hughie comes.

MANUS I don't think we'll wait for him. Let's get started.

[*Slowly, reluctantly they begin to move to their seats and specific tasks.* DOALTY *goes to the bucket of water at the door and washes his hands.* BRIDGET *sets up a hand-mirror and combs her hair.*]

BRIDGET Nellie Ruadh's baby was to be christened this morning. Did any of yous hear what she called it? Did you, Sarah?

[SARAH *grunts: No.*]

BRIDGET Did you, Maire?

MAIRE No.

BRIDGET Our Seamus says she was threatening she was going to call it after its father.

---

3. A portable instrument for surveying.
4. Barn.
5. God (Greek).

6. Idiot.
7. Christ (mild oath).

DOALTY   Who's the father?

BRIDGET   That's the point, you donkey you!

DOALTY   Ah.

BRIDGET   So there's a lot of uneasy bucks about Baile Beag this day.

DOALTY   She told me last Sunday she was going to call it Jimmy.

BRIDGET   You're a liar, Doalty.

DOALTY   Would I tell you a lie? Hi, Jimmy, Nellie Ruadh's aul fella's looking for you.

JIMMY   For me?

MAIRE   Come on, Doalty.

DOALTY   Someone told him . . .

MAIRE   Doalty!

DOALTY   He heard you know the first book of the Satires of Horace[8] off by heart . . .

JIMMY   That's true.

DOALTY   . . . and he wants you to recite it for him.

JIMMY   I'll do that for him certainly, certainly.

DOALTY   He's busting to hear it.

[JIMMY *fumbles in his pockets.*]

JIMMY   I came across this last night—this'll interest you—in Book Two of Virgil's *Georgics*.[9]

DOALTY   Be God, that's my territory alright.

BRIDGET   You clown you! [*To* SARAH.] Hold this for me, would you? [*Her mirror.*]

JIMMY   Listen to this, Manus. '*Nigra fere et presso pinguis sub vomere terra . . .*'

DOALTY   Steady on now—easy, boys, easy—don't rush me, boys—[*He mimes great concentration.*]

JIMMY   Manus?

MANUS   'Land that is black and rich beneath the pressure of the plough . . .'

DOALTY   Give *me* a chance!

JIMMY   'And with *cui putre*—with crumbly soil—is in the main best for corn.' There you are!

DOALTY   There you are.

JIMMY   'From no other land will you see more wagons wending homeward behind slow bullocks.'[1] Virgil! There!

DOALTY   'Slow bullocks'!

JIMMY   Isn't that what I'm always telling you? Black soil for corn. *That's* what you should have in that upper field of yours—corn, not spuds.

DOALTY   Would you listen to that fella! Too lazy be Jasus to wash himself and he's lecturing me on agriculture! Would you go and take a running race at yourself, Jimmy Jack Cassie! [*Grabs* SARAH.] Come away out of this with me, Sarah, and we'll plant some corn together.

MANUS   Alright—alright. Let's settle down and get some work done. I know Sean Beag isn't coming—he's at the[2] salmon. What about the Donnelly twins? [*To* DOALTY.] Are the Donnelly twins not coming any more?

---

8. Latin lyric poet (65–8 B.C.E.).
9. Four books of poems on farming and rural life by the Roman poet (70–19 B.C.E.).

1. Bulls or, loosely, cattle.
2. Fishing for.

2732 / BRIAN FRIEL

[DOALTY shrugs and turns away.]
Did you ask them?

DOALTY Haven't seen them. Not about these days.

[DOALTY begins whistling through his teeth.
Suddenly the atmosphere is silent and alert.]

MANUS Aren't they at home?

DOALTY No.

MANUS Where are they then?

DOALTY How would I know?

BRIDGET Our Seamus says two of the soldiers' horses were found last night
at the foot of the cliffs at Machaire Buide and . . .

[She stops suddenly and begins writing with chalk on her slate.]
D'you hear the whistles of this aul slate? Sure nobody could write on an aul
slippery thing like that.

MANUS What headline did my father set you?

BRIDGET 'It's easier to stamp out learning than to recall it.'

JIMMY Book Three, the *Agricola* of Tacitus.[3]

BRIDGET God but you're a dose.[4]

MANUS Can you do it?

BRIDGET There. Is it bad? Will he ate me?

MANUS It's very good. Keep your elbow in closer to your side. Doalty?

DOALTY I'm at the seven-times table. I'm perfect, skipper.

[MANUS moves to SARAH.]

MANUS Do you understand those sums?

[SARAH nods: Yes. MANUS leans down to her ear.]

MANUS My name is Sarah.

[MANUS goes to MAIRE. While he is talking to her the others swop books,
talk quietly, etc.]

MANUS Can I help you? What are you at?

MAIRE Map of America. [*Pause.*] The passage money came last Friday.

MANUS You never told me that.

MAIRE Because I haven't seen you since, have I?

MANUS You don't want to go. You said that yourself.

MAIRE There's ten below me to be raised and no man in the house. What do
you suggest?

MANUS Do you want to go?

MAIRE Did you apply for that job in the new national school?

MANUS No.

MAIRE You said you would.

MANUS I said I might.

MAIRE When it opens, this is finished: nobody's going to pay to go to a hedge-
school.

MANUS I know that and I . . . [*He breaks off because he sees* SARAH, *obviously
listening, at his shoulder. She moves away again.*] I was thinking that maybe
I could . . .

MAIRE It's £56 a year you're throwing away.

MANUS I can't apply for it.

---

3. Roman historian (ca. 56–ca. 120 C.E.), author
of *De Vita Julii Agricolae* (*The Life of Julius Agricola*), or the *Agricola*, a biography of his father-in-
law, including an account of his career in Britain.
4. I.e., a dose of medicine, or an unpleasant experience.

MAIRE   You *promised* me you would.

MANUS   My father has applied for it.

MAIRE   He has not!

MANUS   Day before yesterday.

MAIRE   For God's sake, sure you know he'd never—

MANUS   I couldn't—I can't go in against him.

[MAIRE *looks at him for a second. Then.*]

MAIRE   Suit yourself. [*To* BRIDGET.] I saw your Seamus heading off to the Port fair early this morning.

BRIDGET   And wait till you hear this—I forgot to tell you this. He said that as soon as he crossed over the gap at Cnoc na Mona—just beyond where the soldiers are making the maps—the sweet smell was everywhere.

DOALTY   You never told me that.

BRIDGET   It went out of my head.

DOALTY   He saw the crops in Port?

BRIDGET   Some.

MANUS   How did the tops look?

BRIDGET   Fine—I think.

DOALTY   In flower?

BRIDGET   I don't know. I think so. He didn't say.

MANUS   Just the sweet smell—that's all?

BRIDGET   They say that's the way it snakes in, don't they? First the smell; and then one morning the stalks are all black and limp.

DOALTY   Are you stupid? It's the rotting stalks makes the sweet smell for God's sake. That's what the smell is—rotting stalks.

MAIRE   Sweet smell! Sweet smell! Every year at this time somebody comes back with stories of the sweet smell. Sweet God, did the potatoes ever fail in Baile Beag? Well, did they ever—ever? Never! There was never blight here. Never. Never. But we're always sniffing about for it, aren't we?—looking for disaster. The rents are going to go up again—the harvest's going to be lost—the herring have gone away for ever—there's going to be evictions. Honest to God, some of you people aren't happy unless you're miserable and you'll not be right content until you're dead!

DOALTY   Bloody right, Maire. And sure St. Colmcille prophesied there'd never be blight here. He said:

> The spuds will bloom in Baile Beag
> Till rabbits grow an extra lug.[5]

And sure that'll never be. So we're alright.

Seven threes are twenty-one; seven fours are twenty-eight; seven fives are forty-nine— Hi, Jimmy, do you fancy my chances as boss of the new national school?

JIMMY   What's that?—what's that?

DOALTY   Agh, g'way back home to Greece, son.

MAIRE   You ought to apply, Doalty.

DOALTY   D'you think so? Cripes, maybe I will. Hah!

BRIDGET   Did you know that you start at the age of six and you have to stick

---

5. Ear. St. Comcille (521–597), also known as St. Columba, was born in Donegal and established monasteries and churches throughout Ireland and Scotland. Cf. Friel's play about his life, *The Enemy Within* (1962).

at it until you're twelve at least—no matter how smart you are or how much you know.

DOALTY   Who told you that yarn?

BRIDGET   And every child from every house has to go all day, every day, summer or winter. That's the law.

DOALTY   I'll tell you something—nobody's going to go near them—they're not going to take on—law or no law.

BRIDGET   And everything's free in them. You pay for nothing except the books you use; that's what our Seamus says.

DOALTY   'Our Seamus'. Sure your Seamus wouldn't pay anyway. She's making this all up.

BRIDGET   Isn't that right, Manus?

MANUS   I think so.

BRIDGET   And from the very first day you go, you'll not hear one word of Irish spoken. You'll be taught to speak English and every subject will be taught through English and everyone'll end up as cute as the Buncrana[6] people.

[SARAH *suddenly grunts and mimes a warning that the master is coming. The atmosphere changes. Sudden business. Heads down.*]

DOALTY   He's here, boys. Cripes, he'll make yella meal out of me for those bloody tables.

BRIDGET   Have you any extra chalk, Manus?

MAIRE   And the atlas for me.

[DOALTY *goes to* MAIRE *who is sitting on a stool at the back.*]

DOALTY   Swop you seats.

MAIRE   Why?

DOALTY   There's an empty one beside the Infant Prodigy.

MAIRE   I'm fine here.

DOALTY   Please, Maire. I want to jouk[7] in the back here.

[MAIRE *rises.*]

God love you. [*Aloud.*] Anyone got a bloody table-book? Cripes, I'm wrecked.

[SARAH *gives him one.*]

God, I'm dying about you.

[*In his haste to get to the back seat* DOALTY *bumps into* BRIDGET *who is kneeling on the floor and writing laboriously on a slate resting on top of a bench-seat.*]

BRIDGET   Watch where you're going, Doalty!

[DOALTY *gooses*[8] BRIDGET. *She squeals.*

Now the quiet hum of work: JIMMY *reading Homer in a low voice;* BRIDGET *copying her headline;* MAIRE *studying the atlas;* DOALTY, *his eyes shut tight, mouthing his tables;* SARAH *doing sums.*

After a few seconds.]—

BRIDGET   Is this 'g' right, Manus? How do you put a tail on it?

DOALTY   Will you shut up! I can't concentrate!

[*A few more seconds of work. Then* DOALTY *opens his eyes and looks around.*]

False alarm, boys. The bugger's[9] not coming at all. Sure the bugger's hardly fit to walk.

[*And immediately* HUGH *enters. A large man, with residual dignity,*

---

6. Small coastal town northwest of Derry.
7. Perch.

8. Pokes or tickles in an erogenous place.
9. Vulgar term of abuse.

shabbily dressed, carrying a stick. He has, as always, a large quantity of drink taken, but he is by no means drunk. He is in his early sixties.]

HUGH *Adsum,* Doalty, *adsum.*[1] Perhaps not in *sobrietate perfecta*[2] but adequately *sobrius*[3] to overhear your quip. Vesperal salutations to you all.
[*Various responses.*]

JIMMY *Ave,*[4] Hugh.

HUGH James.
[*He removes his hat and coat and hands them and his stick to* MANUS, *as if to a footman.*]
Apologies for my late arrival: we were celebrating the baptism of Nellie Ruadh's baby.

BRIDGET [*Innocently.*] What name did she put on it, Master?

HUGH Was it Eamon? Yes, it was Eamon.

BRIDGET Eamon Donal from Tor! Cripes!

HUGH And after the *caerimonia nominationis*[5]—Maire?

MAIRE The ritual of naming.

HUGH Indeed—we then had a few libations to mark the occasion. Altogether very pleasant. The derivation of the word 'baptise'?—where are my Greek scholars? Doalty?

DOALTY Would it be—ah—ah—

HUGH Too slow. James?

JIMMY 'Baptizein'—to dip or immerse.

HUGH Indeed—our friend Pliny Minor[6] speaks of the 'baptisterium'—the cold bath.

DOALTY Master.

HUGH Doalty?

DOALTY I suppose you could talk then about baptising a sheep at sheep-dipping, could you?
[*Laughter. Comments.*]

HUGH Indeed—the precedent is there—the day you were appropriately named Doalty—seven nines?

DOALTY What's that, Master?

HUGH Seven times nine?

DOALTY Seven nines—seven nines—seven times nine—seven times nine are—Cripes, it's on the tip of my tongue, Master—I knew it for sure this morning—funny that's the only one that foxes[7] me—

BRIDGET [*Prompt.*] Sixty-three.

DOALTY What's wrong with me: sure seven nines are fifty-three, Master.

HUGH Sophocles from Colonus would agree with Doalty Dan Doalty from Tulach Alainn: 'To know nothing is the sweetest life.'[8] Where's Sean Beag?

MANUS He's at the salmon.

HUGH And Nora Dan?

MAIRE She says she's not coming back any more.

HUGH Ah. Nora Dan can now write her name—Nora Dan's education is complete. And the Donnelly twins?

1. I am present [Latin; Friel's note].
2. With complete sobriety [Latin; Friel's note].
3. Sober [Latin; Friel's note].
4. Hail [Latin; Friel's note].
5. Ceremony of naming [Latin; Friel's note].
6. Or Pliny the Younger (61 or 62–ca. 113 C.E.), Roman administrator who wrote an important collection of letters.
7. Befuddles.
8. From *Ajax,* by the ancient Greek playwright Sophocles (ca. 496–406 B.C.E.), born in the village of Colonus, near Athens.

[*Brief pause. Then.*]

BRIDGET They're probably at the turf.[9] [*She goes to* HUGH.] There's the one-and-eight I owe you for last quarter's arithmetic and there's my one-and-six[1] for this quarter's writing.

HUGH *Gratias tibi ago.*[2] [*He sits at his table.*] Before we commence our *studia*[3] I have three items of information to impart to you—[*To* MANUS.] a bowl of tea, strong tea, black—

[MANUS *leaves.*]

Item A: on my perambulations today—Bridget? Too slow. Maire?

MAIRE *Perambulare*—to walk about.

HUGH Indeed—I encountered Captain Lancey of the Royal Engineers who is engaged in the ordnance survey of this area. He tells me that in the past few days two of his horses have strayed and some of his equipment seems to be mislaid. I expressed my regret and suggested he address you himself on these matters. He then explained that he does not speak Irish. Latin? I asked. None. Greek? Not a syllable. He speaks—on his own admission—only English; and to his credit he seemed suitably verecund—James?

JIMMY *Verecundus*—humble.

HUGH Indeed—he voiced some surprise that we did not speak his language. I explained that a few of us did, on occasion—outside the parish of course—and then usually for the purposes of commerce, a use to which his tongue seemed particularly suited—[*Shouts.*] and a slice of soda bread—and I went on to propose that our own culture and the classical tongues made a happier conjugation—Doalty?

DOALTY *Conjugo*—I join together.

[DOALTY *is so pleased with himself that he prods and winks at* BRIDGET.]

HUGH Indeed—English, I suggested, couldn't really express us. And again to his credit he acquiesced to my logic. Acquiesced—Maire?

[MAIRE *turns away impatiently.* HUGH *is unaware of the gesture.*]

Too slow. Bridget?

BRIDGET *Acquiesco.*[4]

HUGH *Procede.*

BRIDGET *Acquiesco, acquiescere, acquievi, acquietum.*

HUGH Indeed—and Item B . . .

MAIRE Master.

HUGH Yes?

[MAIRE *gets to her feet uneasily but determinedly. Pause.*]

Well, girl?

MAIRE We should all be learning to speak English. That's what my mother says. That's what I say. That's what Dan O'Connell[5] said last month in Ennis. He said the sooner we all learn to speak English the better.

[*Suddenly several speak together.*]

JIMMY What's she saying? What? What?

DOALTY It's Irish he uses when he's travelling around scrounging votes.

9. I.e., cutting turf.
1. One and a half shillings—eighteen pennies—in the old British currency. "One-and-eight": one shilling and eight pence, or twenty pennies.
2. I thank you [Latin; Friel's note].
3. Studies [Latin; Friel's note].
4. Acquiescere: to rest, to find comfort in [Latin; Friel's note].

5. Irish lawyer and nationalist leader (1775–1847), born in Kerry and known as the Liberator, who argued for Ireland's adoption of the English language. The first Roman Catholic member of Parliament, he regained civil rights for Irish Catholics and urged the reestablishment of the Irish Parliament in Dublin.

BRIDGET And sleeping with married women. Sure no woman's safe from that fella.

JIMMY Who-who-who? Who's this? Who's this?

HUGH *Silentium!* [*Pause.*] Who is she talking about?

MAIRE I'm talking about Daniel O'Connell.

HUGH Does she mean that little Kerry politician?

MAIRE I'm talking about the Liberator, Master, as you well know. And what he said was this: 'The old language is a barrier to modern progress.' He said that last month. And he's right. I don't want Greek. I don't want Latin. I want English.

[MANUS *reappears on the platform above.*]

I want to be able to speak English because I'm going to America as soon as the harvest's all saved.

[MAIRE *remains standing.* HUGH *puts his hand into his pocket and produces a flask of whisky. He removes the cap, pours a drink into it, tosses it back, replaces the cap, puts the flask back into his pocket. Then.*]

HUGH We have been diverted—*diverto—divertere*—Where were we?

DOALTY Three items of information, Master. You're at Item B.

HUGH Indeed—Item B—Item B—yes—On my way to the christening this morning I chanced to meet Mr George Alexander, Justice of the Peace. We discussed the new national school. Mr Alexander invited me to take charge of it when it opens. I thanked him and explained that I could do that only if I were free to run it as I have run this hedge-school for the past thirty-five years—filling what our friend Euripides[6] calls the '*aplestos pithos*'—James?

JIMMY 'The cask that cannot be filled'.

HUGH Indeed—and Mr Alexander retorted courteously and emphatically that he hopes that is how it will be run.

[MAIRE *now sits.*]

Indeed. I have had a strenuous day and I am weary of you all. [*He rises.*] Manus will take care of you.

[HUGH *goes towards the steps.*

OWEN *enters.* OWEN *is the younger son, a handsome, attractive young man in his twenties. He is dressed smartly—a city man. His manner is easy and charming: everything he does is invested with consideration and enthusiasm. He now stands framed in the doorway, a travelling bag across his shoulder.*]

OWEN Could anybody tell me is this where Hugh Mor O'Donnell holds his hedge-school?

DOALTY It's Owen—Owen Hugh! Look, boys—it's Owen Hugh!

[OWEN *enters. As he crosses the room he touches and has a word for each person.*]

OWEN Doalty! [*Playful punch.*] How are you, boy? *Jacobe, quid agis?*[7] Are you well?

JIMMY Fine. Fine.

OWEN And Bridget! Give us a kiss. Aaaaaah!

BRIDGET You're welcome, Owen.

OWEN It's not—? Yes, it *is* Maire Chatach! God! A young woman!

MAIRE How are you, Owen?

---

6. Greek playwright (ca. 484–406 B.C.E.). 7. James, how are you? [Latin; Friel's note].

[OWEN *is now in front of* HUGH. *He puts his two hands on his father's shoulders.*]

OWEN   And how's the old man himself?

HUGH   Fair—fair.

OWEN   Fair? For God's sake you never looked better! Come here to me. [*He embraces* HUGH *warmly and genuinely.*] Great to see you, Father. Great to be back.

[HUGH's *eyes are moist—partly joy, partly the drink.*]

HUGH   I—I'm—I'm—pay no attention to—

OWEN   Come on—come on—come on—[*He gives* HUGH *his handkerchief.*] Do you know what you and I are going to do tonight? We are going to go up to Anna na mBreag's . . .

DOALTY   Not there, Owen.

OWEN   Why not?

DOALTY   Her poteen's[8] worse than ever.

BRIDGET   They say she puts frogs in it!

OWEN   All the better. [*To* HUGH.] And you and I are going to get footless drunk. That's arranged.

[OWEN *sees* MANUS *coming down the steps with tea and soda bread. They meet at the bottom.*]

And Manus!

MANUS   You're welcome, Owen.

OWEN   I know I am. And it's great to be here. [*He turns round, arms outstretched.*] I can't believe it. I come back after six years and everything's just as it was! Nothing's changed! Not a thing! [*Sniffs.*] Even that smell—that's the same smell this place always had. What is it anyway? Is it the straw?

DOALTY   Jimmy Jack's feet.

[*General laughter. It opens little pockets of conversation round the room.*]

OWEN   And Doalty Dan Doalty hasn't changed either!

DOALTY   Bloody right, Owen.

OWEN   Jimmy, are you well?

JIMMY   Dodging about.

OWEN   Any word of the big day?

[*This is greeted with 'ohs' and 'ahs'.*]

Time enough, Jimmy. Homer's easier to live with, isn't he?

MAIRE   We heard stories that you own ten big shops in Dublin[9]—is it true?

OWEN   Only nine.

BRIDGET   And you've twelve horses and six servants.

OWEN   Yes—that's true. God Almighty, would you listen to them—taking a hand at me!

MANUS   When did you arrive?

OWEN   We left Dublin yesterday morning, spent last night in Omagh and got here half an hour ago.

MANUS   You're hungry then.

HUGH   Indeed—get him food—get him a drink.

OWEN   Not now, thanks; later. Listen—am I interrupting you all?

HUGH   By no means. We're finished for the day.

---

8. Local whiskey illegally distilled to evade British taxation.

9. Ireland's capital was the site of English military and political power.

OWEN Wonderful. I'll tell you why. Two friends of mine are waiting outside the door. They'd like to meet you and I'd like you to meet them. May I bring them in?

HUGH Certainly. You'll all eat and have . . .

OWEN Not just yet, Father. You've seen the sappers working in this area for the past fortnight, haven't you? Well, the older man is Captain Lancey . . .

HUGH I've met Captain Lancey.

OWEN Great. He's the cartographer in charge of this whole area. Cartographer—James?

> [OWEN *begins to play this game—his father's game—partly to involve his classroom audience, partly to show he has not forgotten it, and indeed partly because he enjoys it.*]

JIMMY A maker of maps.

OWEN Indeed—and the younger man that I travelled with from Dublin, his name is Lieutenant Yolland and he is attached to the toponymic department—Father?—*responde*—*responde!*

HUGH He gives names to places.

OWEN Indeed—although he is in fact an orthographer—Doalty?—too slow—Manus?

MANUS The correct spelling of those names.

OWEN Indeed—indeed!

> [OWEN *laughs and claps his hands. Some of the others join in.*]

Beautiful! Beautiful! Honest to God, it's such a delight to be back here with you all again—'civilised' people. Anyhow—may I bring them in?

HUGH Your friends are our friends.

OWEN I'll be straight back.

> [*There is general talk as* OWEN *goes towards the door. He stops beside* SARAH.]

OWEN That's a new face. Who are you?

> [*A very brief hesitation. Then.*]

SARAH My name is Sarah.

OWEN Sarah who?

SARAH Sarah Johnny Sally.

OWEN Of course! From Bun na hAbhann! I'm Owen—Owen Hugh Mor. From Baile Beag. Good to see you.

> [*During this* OWEN–SARAH *exchange.*]

HUGH Come on now. Let's tidy this place up. [*He rubs the top of his table with his sleeve.*] Move, Doalty—lift those books off the floor.

DOALTY Right, Master; certainly, Master; I'm doing my best, Master.

> [OWEN *stops at the door.*]

OWEN One small thing, Father.

HUGH *Silentium!*

OWEN I'm on their pay-roll.

> [SARAH, *very elated at her success, is beside* MANUS.]

SARAH I said it, Manus!

> [MANUS *ignores* SARAH. *He is much more interested in* OWEN *now.*]

MANUS You haven't enlisted, have you?!

> [SARAH *moves away.*]

OWEN Me a soldier? I'm employed as a part-time, underpaid, civilian interpreter. My job is to translate the quaint, archaic tongue you people persist in speaking into the King's good English. [*He goes out.*]

2740 / BRIAN FRIEL

HUGH Move—move—move! Put some order on things! Come on, Sarah—
hide that bucket. Whose are these slates? Somebody take these dishes away.
Festinate! Festinate![1]

> [HUGH *pours another drink.*
> MANUS *goes to* MAIRE *who is busy tidying.*]

MANUS You didn't tell me you were definitely leaving.

MAIRE Not now.

HUGH Good girl, Bridget. That's the style.

MANUS You might at least have told me.

HUGH Are these your books, James?

JIMMY Thank you.

MANUS Fine! Fine! Go ahead! Go ahead!

MAIRE You talk to me about getting married—with neither a roof over your
head nor a sod of ground under your foot. I suggest you go for the new
school; but no—'My father's in for that.' Well now he's got it and now this
is finished and now you've nothing.

MANUS I can always . . .

MAIRE What? Teach classics to the cows? Agh—

> [MAIRE *moves away from* MANUS.
>
> OWEN *enters with* LANCEY *and* YOLLAND. CAPTAIN LANCEY *is middle-
> aged; a small, crisp officer, expert in his field as cartographer but uneasy
> with people—especially civilians, especially these foreign civilians. His
> skill is with deeds, not words.*
>
> LIEUTENANT YOLLAND *is in his late twenties/early thirties. He is tall
> and thin and gangling, blond hair, a shy, awkward manner. A soldier
> by accident.*]

OWEN Here we are. Captain Lancey—my father.

LANCEY Good evening.

> [HUGH *becomes expansive, almost courtly with his visitors.*]

HUGH You and I have already met, sir.

LANCEY Yes.

OWEN And Lieutenant Yolland—both Royal Engineers—my father.

HUGH You're very welcome, gentlemen.

YOLLAND How do you do.

HUGH *Gaudeo vos hic adesse.*[2]

OWEN And I'll make no other introductions except that these are some of the
people of Baile Beag and—what?—well you're among the best people in
Ireland now. [*He pauses to allow* LANCEY *to speak.* LANCEY *does not.*] Would
you like to say a few words, Captain?

HUGH What about a drop, sir?

LANCEY A what?

HUGH Perhaps a modest refreshment? A little sampling of our aqua vitae?[3]

LANCEY No, no.

HUGH Later perhaps when . . .

LANCEY I'll say what I have to say, if I may, and as briefly as possible. Do they
speak *any* English, Roland?

OWEN Don't worry. I'll translate.

LANCEY I see. [*He clears his throat. He speaks as if he were addressing chil-*

---

1. Hurry! [Latin; Friel's note].
2. Welcome! [Latin; Friel's note].

3. "Aqua vitae": spirits; literally, in Latin, water of
life.

dren—a shade too loudly and enunciating excessively.] You may have seen me—seen me—working in this section—section?—working. We are here—here—in this place—you understand?—to make a map—a map—a map and—

JIMMY *Nonne Latine loquitur?*[4]

[HUGH *holds up a restraining hand.*]

HUGH James.

LANCEY [*To* JIMMY.] I do not speak Gaelic, sir. [*He looks at* OWEN.]

OWEN Carry on.

LANCEY A map is a representation on paper—a picture—you understand picture?—a paper picture—showing, representing this country—yes?—showing your country in miniature—a scaled drawing on paper of—of—of—

[*Suddenly* DOALTY *sniggers. Then* BRIDGET. *Then* SARAH. OWEN *leaps in quickly.*]

OWEN It might be better if you *assume* they understand you—

LANCEY Yes?

OWEN And I'll translate as you go along.

LANCEY I see. Yes. Very well. Perhaps you're right. Well. What we are doing is this. [*He looks at* OWEN. OWEN *nods reassuringly.*] His Majesty's government has ordered the first ever comprehensive survey of this entire country—a general triangulation which will embrace detailed hydrographic and topographic information and which will be executed to a scale of six inches to the English mile.

HUGH [*Pouring a drink.*] Excellent—excellent.

[LANCEY *looks at* OWEN.]

OWEN A new map is being made of the whole country.

[LANCEY *looks to* OWEN: *Is that all?* OWEN *smiles reassuringly and indicates to proceed.*]

LANCEY This enormous task has been embarked on so that the military authorities will be equipped with up-to-date and accurate information on every corner of this part of the Empire.

OWEN The job is being done by soldiers because they are skilled in this work.

LANCEY And also so that the entire basis of land valuation can be reassessed for purposes of more equitable taxation.

OWEN This new map will take the place of the estate-agent's map so that from now on you will know exactly what is yours in law.

LANCEY In conclusion I wish to quote two brief extracts from the white paper which is our governing charter: [*Reads.*] 'All former surveys of Ireland originated in forfeiture and violent transfer of property; the present survey has for its object the relief which can be afforded to the proprietors and occupiers of land from unequal taxation.'

OWEN The captain hopes that the public will cooperate with the sappers and that the new map will mean that taxes are reduced.

HUGH A worthy enterprise—*opus honestum!* And Extract B?

LANCEY 'Ireland is privileged. No such survey is being undertaken in England. So this survey cannot but be received as proof of the disposition of this government to advance the interests of Ireland.' My sentiments, too.

OWEN This survey demonstrates the government's interest in Ireland and the captain thanks you for listening so attentively to him.

4. Does he not speak Latin? [Friel's note].

HUGH Our pleasure, Captain.
LANCEY Lieutenant Yolland?
YOLLAND I—I—I've nothing to say—really—
OWEN The captain is the man who actually makes the new map. George's task is to see that the place-names on this map are . . . correct. [*To* YOL-
LAND.] Just a few words—they'd like to hear you. [*To class.*] Don't you want to hear George, too?
MAIRE Has he anything to say?
YOLLAND [*To* MAIRE.] Sorry—sorry?
OWEN She says she's dying to hear you.
YOLLAND [*To* MAIRE.] Very kind of you—thank you . . . [*To class.*] I can only say that I feel—I feel very foolish to—to be working here and not to speak your language. But I intend to rectify that—with Roland's help—indeed I do.
OWEN He wants me to teach him Irish!
HUGH You are doubly welcome, sir.
YOLLAND I think your countryside is—is—is—is very beautiful. I've fallen in love with it already. I hope we're not too—too crude an intrusion on your lives. And I know that I'm going to be happy, very happy, here.
OWEN He is already a committed Hibernophile[5]—
JIMMY He loves—
OWEN Alright, Jimmy—we know—he loves Baile Beag; and he loves you all.
HUGH Please . . . May I . . . ?
        [HUGH *is now drunk. He holds on to the edge of the table.*]
OWEN Go ahead, Father. [*Hands up for quiet.*] Please—please.
HUGH And we, gentlemen, we in turn are happy to offer you our friendship, our hospitality, and every assistance that you may require. Gentlemen—welcome!
        [*A few desultory[6] claps. The formalities are over. General conversation. The soldiers meet the locals.*
        MANUS *and* OWEN *meet down stage.*]
OWEN Lancey's a bloody ramrod but George's alright. How are you anyway?
MANUS What sort of a translation was that, Owen?
OWEN Did I make a mess of it?
MANUS You weren't saying what Lancey was saying!
OWEN 'Uncertainty in meaning is incipient poetry'—who said that?
MANUS There was nothing uncertain about what Lancey said: it's a bloody military operation, Owen! And what's Yolland's function? What's 'incorrect' about the place-names we have here?
OWEN Nothing at all. They're just going to be standardised.
MANUS You mean changed into English?
OWEN Where there's ambiguity, they'll be Anglicised.
MANUS And they call you Roland! They both call you Roland!
OWEN Shhhhh. Isn't it ridiculous? They seemed to get it wrong from the very beginning—or else they can't pronounce Owen. I was afraid some of you bastards would laugh.
MANUS Aren't you going to tell them?
OWEN Yes—yes—soon—soon.
MANUS But they . . .

5. Lover of Ireland (in Latin, Hibernia).   6. Scattered.

OWEN Easy, man, easy. Owen—Roland—what the hell. It's only a name. It's the same me, isn't it? Well, isn't it?

MANUS Indeed it is. It's the same Owen.

OWEN And the same Manus. And in a way we complement each other.

[*He punches* MANUS *lightly, playfully and turns to join the others. As he goes.*]

Alright—who has met whom? Isn't this a job for the go-between?

[MANUS *watches* OWEN *move confidently across the floor, taking* MAIRE *by the hand and introducing her to* YOLLAND.

HUGH *is trying to negotiate the steps.*

JIMMY *is lost in a text.*

DOALTY *and* BRIDGET *are reliving their giggling.*

SARAH *is staring at* MANUS.]

Act Two

SCENE ONE

The sappers have already mapped most of the area. YOLLAND's *official task, which* OWEN *is now doing, is to take each of the Gaelic names—every hill, stream, rock, even every patch of ground which possessed its own distinctive Irish name— and Anglicise it, either by changing it into its approximate English sound or by translating it into English words. For example, a Gaelic name like Cnoc Ban could become Knockban or—directly translated—Fair Hill. These new standardised names were entered into the Name-Book, and when the new maps appeared they contained all these new Anglicised names.* OWEN's *official function as translator is to pronounce each name in Irish and then provide the English translation.*

The hot weather continues. It is late afternoon some days later.

Stage right: an improvised clothes-line strung between the shafts of the cart and a nail in the wall; on it are some shirts and socks.

A large map—one of the new blank maps—is spread out on the floor. OWEN *is on his hands and knees, consulting it. He is totally engrossed in his task, which he pursues with great energy and efficiency.*

YOLLAND's *hesitancy has vanished—he is at home here now. He is sitting on the floor, his long legs stretched out before him, his back resting against a creel,[7] his eyes closed. His mind is elsewhere. One of the reference books—a church registry—lies open on his lap.*

Around them are various reference books, the Name-Book, a bottle of poteen, some cups etc.

OWEN *completes an entry in the Name-Book and returns to the map on the floor.*

OWEN Now. Where have we got to? Yes—the point where that stream enters the sea—that tiny little beach there. George!

YOLLAND Yes. I'm listening. What do you call it? Say the Irish name again?

OWEN Bun na hAbhann.

YOLLAND Again.

OWEN Bun na hAbhann.

YOLLAND Bun na hAbhann.

OWEN That's terrible, George.

---

7. Large wicker basket.

YOLLAND   I know. I'm sorry. Say it again.

OWEN   Bun na hAbhann.

YOLLAND   Bun na hAbhann.

OWEN   That's better. Bun is the Irish word for bottom. And Abha means river. So it's literally the mouth of the river.

YOLLAND   Let's leave it alone. There's no English equivalent for a sound like that.

OWEN   What is it called in the church registry?

[*Only now does* YOLLAND *open his eyes.*]

YOLLAND   Let's see . . . Banowen.

OWEN   That's wrong. [*Consults text.*] The list of freeholders calls it Owen-more—that's completely wrong: Owenmore's the big river at the west end of the parish. [*Another text.*] And in the grand jury lists it's called—God!—Binhone!—wherever they got that. I suppose we could Anglicize it to Bun-owen; but somehow that's neither fish nor flesh.

[YOLLAND *closes his eyes again.*]

YOLLAND   I give up.

OWEN   [*At map.*]   Back to first principles. What are we trying to do?

YOLLAND   Good question.

OWEN   We are trying to denominate and at the same time describe that tiny area of soggy, rocky, sandy ground where that little stream enters the sea, an area known locally as Bun na hAbhann . . . Burnfoot![8] What about Burnfoot?

YOLLAND   [*Indifferently.*]   Good, Roland. Burnfoot's good.

OWEN   George, my name isn't . . .

YOLLAND   B-u-r-n-f-o-o-t?

OWEN   I suppose so. What do you think?

YOLLAND   Yes.

OWEN   Are you happy with that?

YOLLAND   Yes.

OWEN   Burnfoot it is then. [*He makes the entry into the Name-Book.*] Bun na nAbhann—B-u-r-n-

YOLLAND   You're becoming very skilled at this.

OWEN   We're not moving fast enough.

YOLLAND   [*Opens eyes again.*]   Lancey lectured me again last night.

OWEN   When does he finish here?

YOLLAND   The sappers are pulling out at the end of the week. The trouble is, the maps they've completed can't be printed without these names. So London screams at Lancey and Lancey screams at me. But I wasn't intimidated.

[MANUS *emerges from upstairs and descends.*]

'I'm sorry, sir,' I said, 'But certain tasks demand their own tempo. You cannot rename a whole country overnight.' Your Irish air has made me bold. [*To* MANUS.] Do you want us to leave?

MANUS   Time enough. Class won't begin for another half-hour.

YOLLAND   Sorry—sorry?

OWEN   Can't you speak English?

[MANUS *gathers the things off the clothes-line.* OWEN *returns to the map.*]

OWEN   We now come across that beach . . .

YOLLAND   Tra—that's the Irish for beach. [*To* MANUS.] I'm picking up the odd word, Manus.

_____

8. "Burn" is an Ulster-Scots word for river.

MANUS So.

OWEN . . . on past Burnfoot; and there's nothing around here that has any name that I know of until we come down here to the south end, just about here . . . and there should be a ridge of rocks there . . . Have the sappers marked it? They have. Look, George.

YOLLAND Where are we?

OWEN There.

YOLLAND I'm lost.

OWEN Here. And the name of that ridge is Druim Dubh. Put English on that, Lieutenant.

YOLLAND Say it again.

OWEN Druim Dubh.

YOLLAND Dubh means black.

OWEN Yes.

YOLLAND And Druim means . . . what? a fort?

OWEN We met it yesterday in Druim Luachra.

YOLLAND A ridge! The Black Ridge! [To MANUS.] You see, Manus?

OWEN We'll have you fluent at the Irish before the summer's over.

YOLLAND Oh I wish I were. [To MANUS as he crosses to go back upstairs.] We got a crate of orange from Dublin today. I'll send some up to you.

MANUS Thanks. [To OWEN.] Better hide that bottle. Father's just up and he'd be better without it.

OWEN Can't you speak English before your man?

MANUS Why?

OWEN Out of courtesy.

MANUS Doesn't he want to learn Irish? [To YOLLAND.] Don't you want to learn Irish?

YOLLAND Sorry—sorry? I—I—

MANUS I understand the Lanceys perfectly but people like you puzzle me.

OWEN Manus, for God's sake!

MANUS [Still to YOLLAND.] How's the work going?

YOLLAND The work?—the work? Oh, it's—it's staggering along—I think—[To OWEN.]—isn't it? But we'd be lost without Roland.

MANUS [Leaving.] I'm sure. But there are always the Rolands, aren't there? [He goes upstairs and exits.]

YOLLAND What was that he said?—something about Lancey, was it?

OWEN He said we should hide that bottle before Father gets his hands on it.

YOLLAND Ah.

OWEN He's always trying to protect him.

YOLLAND Was he lame from birth?

OWEN An accident when he was a baby: Father fell across his cradle. That's why Manus feels so responsible for him.

YOLLAND Why doesn't he marry?

OWEN Can't afford to, I suppose.

YOLLAND Hasn't he a salary?

OWEN What salary? All he gets is the odd shilling Father throws him—and that's seldom enough. I got out in time, didn't I?

[YOLLAND is pouring a drink.]

Easy with that stuff—it'll hit you suddenly.

YOLLAND I like it.

OWEN Let's get back to the job. Druim Dubh—what's it called in the jury lists? [Consults texts.]

YOLLAND   Some people here resent us.

OWEN   Dramduff—wrong as usual.

YOLLAND   I was passing a little girl yesterday and she spat at me.

OWEN   And it's Drimdoo here. What's it called in the registry?

YOLLAND   Do you know the Donnelly twins?

OWEN   Who?

YOLLAND   The Donnelly twins.

OWEN   Yes. Best fishermen about here. What about them?

YOLLAND   Lancey's looking for them.

OWEN   What for?

YOLLAND   He wants them for questioning.

OWEN   Probably stolen somebody's nets. Dramduffy! Nobody ever called it
Dramduffy. Take your pick of those three.

YOLLAND   My head's addled. Let's take a rest. Do you want a drink?

OWEN   Thanks. Now, every Dubh we've come across we've changed to
Duff. So if we're to be consistent, I suppose Druim Dubh has to become
Dromduff.
       [YOLLAND is now looking out the window.]
You can see the end of the ridge from where you're standing. But D-r-u-m
or D-r-o-m? [Name-Book.] Do you remember—which did we agree on for
Druim Luachra?

YOLLAND   That house immediately above where we're camped—

OWEN   Mm?

YOLLAND   The house where Maire lives.

OWEN   Maire? Oh, Maire Chatach.

YOLLAND   What does that mean?

OWEN   Curly-haired; the whole family are called the Catachs. What about it?

YOLLAND   I hear music coming from that house almost every night.

OWEN   Why don't you drop in?

YOLLAND   Could I?

OWEN   Why not? We used D-r-o-m then. So we've got to call it D-r-o-m-d-u-f-
f—alright?

YOLLAND   Go back up to where the new school is being built and just say the
names again for me, would you?

OWEN   That's a good idea. Poolkerry, Ballybeg—

YOLLAND   No, no; as they still are—in your own language.

OWEN   Poll na gCaorach,
       [YOLLAND repeats the names silently after him.]
Baile Beag, Ceann Balor, Lis Maol, Machaire Buidhe, Baile na gGall, Carraig na Ri, Mullach Dearg—

YOLLAND   Do you think I could live here?

OWEN   What are you talking about?

YOLLAND   Settle down here—live here.

OWEN   Come on, George.

YOLLAND   I mean it.

OWEN   Live on what? Potatoes? Buttermilk?

YOLLAND   It's really heavenly.

OWEN   For God's sake! The first hot summer in fifty years and you think it's
Eden. Don't be such a bloody romantic. You wouldn't survive a mild winter
here.

YOLLAND   Do you think not? Maybe you're right.
       [DOALTY enters in a rush.]

DOALTY   Hi, boys, is Manus about?

OWEN   He's upstairs. Give him a shout.

DOALTY   Manus!

The cattle's going mad in that heat—Cripes, running wild all over the place.

[*To* YOLLAND.] How are you doing, skipper?

[MANUS *appears*.]

YOLLAND   Thank you for—I—I'm very grateful to you for—

DOALTY   Wasting your time. I don't know a word you're saying. Hi, Manus, there's two bucks down the road there asking for you.

MANUS [*Descending*.]   Who are they?

DOALTY   Never clapped eyes on them. They want to talk to you.

MANUS   What about?

DOALTY   They wouldn't say. Come on. The bloody beasts'll end up in Loch an Iubhair if they're not capped.[9] Good luck, boys!

[DOALTY *rushes off.* MANUS *follows him.*]

OWEN   Good luck! What were you thanking Doalty for?

YOLLAND   I was washing outside my tent this morning and he was passing with a scythe across his shoulder and he came up to me and pointed to the long grass and then cut a pathway round my tent and from the tent down to the road—so that my feet won't get wet with the dew. Wasn't that kind of him? And I have no words to thank him . . .

I suppose you're right: I suppose I couldn't live here . . .

Just before Doalty came up to me this morning, I was thinking that at that moment I might have been in Bombay instead of Ballybeg. You see, my father was at his wits end with me and finally he got me a job with the East India Company[1]—some kind of a clerkship. This was ten, eleven months ago. So I set off for London. Unfortunately I—I—I missed the boat. Literally. And since I couldn't face Father and hadn't enough money to hang about until the next sailing, I joined the Army. And they stuck me into the Engineers and posted me to Dublin. And Dublin sent me here. And while I was washing this morning and looking across the Tra Bhan, I was thinking how very, very lucky I am to be here and not in Bombay.

OWEN   Do you believe in fate?

YOLLAND   Lancey's so like my father. I was watching him last night. He met every group of sappers as they reported in. He checked the field kitchens. He examined the horses. He inspected every single report—even examining the texture of the paper and commenting on the neatness of the handwriting. The perfect colonial servant: not only must the job be done—it must be done with excellence. Father has that drive, too; that dedication; that indefatigable energy. He builds roads—hopping from one end of the Empire to the other. Can't sit still for five minutes. He says himself the longest time he ever sat still was the night before Waterloo when they were waiting for Wellington to make up his mind to attack.[2]

OWEN   What age is he?

YOLLAND   Born in 1789—the very day the Bastille fell.[3] I've often thought

---

9. Surpassed.
1. English trade company in India, South Asia, and Southeast Asia, chartered in 1600 and central to 18th- and 19th-century British imperialism in the region.
2. Dublin-born Arthur Wellesley (1769–1852), duke of Wellington, vanquished the French

emperor Napoleon's army on June 18, 1815, in Waterloo, Belgium.
3. The French Revolution began on July 14, 1789, with the storming of the Bastille (a jail in Paris). The French monarchy was later overthrown and replaced by the First Republic.

2748 / Brian Friel

maybe that gave his whole life its character. Do you think it could? He inherited a new world the day he was born—the Year One. Ancient time was at an end. The world had cast off its old skin. There were no longer any frontiers to man's potential. Possibilities were endless and exciting. He still believes that. The Apocalypse is just about to happen . . . I'm afraid I'm a great disappointment to him. I've neither his energy, nor his coherence, nor his belief. Do I believe in fate? The day I arrived in Ballybeg,—no, Baile Beag—the moment you brought me in here, I had a curious sensation. It's difficult to describe. It was a momentary sense of discovery; no—not quite a sense of discovery—a sense of recognition, of confirmation of something I half knew instinctively as if I had stepped . . .

OWEN   Back into ancient time?

YOLLAND   No, no. It wasn't an awareness of *direction* being changed but of experience being of a totally different order. I had moved into a consciousness that wasn't striving nor agitated, but at its ease and with its own conviction and assurance. And when I heard Jimmy Jack and your father swopping stories about Apollo and Cuchulain and Paris and Ferdia[4]—as if they lived down the road—it was then that I thought—I knew—perhaps I could live here . . . [*Now embarrassed.*] Where's the pot-een?

OWEN   Poteen.

YOLLAND   Poteen—poteen—poteen. Even if I did speak Irish I'd always be an outsider here, wouldn't I? I may learn the password but the language of the tribe will always elude me, won't it? The private will always be . . . hermetic,[5] won't it?

OWEN   You can learn to decode us.

[HUGH *emerges from upstairs and descends. He is dressed for the road. Today he is physically and mentally jaunty and alert—almost self-consciously jaunty and alert. Indeed, as the scene progresses, one has the sense that he is deliberately parodying himself.*

The moment HUGH *gets to the bottom of the steps* YOLLAND *leaps respectfully to his feet.*]

HUGH [*As he descends.*]
    Quantumvis cursum longum fessumque moratur
    Sol, sacro tandem carmine vesper adest.
I dabble in verse, Lieutenant, after the style of Ovid.[6]
[*To* OWEN.] A drop of that to fortify me.

YOLLAND   You'll have to translate it for me.

HUGH   Let's see—
    No matter how long the sun may linger on his long and weary journey
    At length evening comes with its sacred song.

YOLLAND   Very nice, sir.

HUGH   English succeeds in making it sound . . . plebeian.[7]

OWEN   Where are you off to, Father?

HUGH   An *expeditio*[8] with three purposes. Purpose A: to acquire a testimonial from our parish priest—[*To* YOLLAND.] a worthy man but barely literate; and

4. Mythical Irish warrior, slain by his foster brother, Cuchulainn, the greatest hero of the medieval Ulster Cycle, an extensive series of stories focused on the warriors of King Conchobar's court in Northern Ireland. "Apollo": Greek god of arts, music, and prophecy, who helped the Trojan

prince Paris kill the greatest Greek hero, Achilles, in the Trojan War.
5. Secret, hidden.
6. Roman poet (43 B.C.E.–17? C.E.).
7. Of the common people.
8. Expedition [Latin; Friel's note].

since he'll ask me to write it myself, how in all modesty can I do myself justice?

[*To* OWEN.] Where did this [*Drink.*] come from?

OWEN   Anna na mBreag's.

HUGH   [*To* YOLLAND.]   In that case address yourself to it with circumspection. [*And* HUGH *instantly tosses the drink back in one gulp and grimaces.*] Aaaaaaagh!

[*Holds out his glass for a refill.*]

Anna na mBreag means Anna of the Lies. And Purpose B: to talk to the builders of the new school about the kind of living accommodation I will require there. I have lived too long like a journeyman[9] tailor.

YOLLAND   Some years ago we lived fairly close to a poet—well, about three miles away.

HUGH   His name?

YOLLAND   Wordsworth—William Wordsworth.[1]

HUGH   Did he speak of me to you?

YOLLAND   Actually I never talked to him. I just saw him out walking—in the distance.

HUGH   Wordsworth? . . . no. I'm afraid we're not familiar with your literature, Lieutenant. We feel closer to the warm Mediterranean.[2] We tend to overlook your island.

YOLLAND   I'm learning to speak Irish, sir.

HUGH   Good.

YOLLAND   Roland's teaching me.

HUGH   Splendid.

YOLLAND   I mean—I feel so cut off from the people here. And I was trying to explain a few minutes ago how remarkable a community this is. To meet people like yourself and Jimmy Jack who actually converse in Greek and Latin. And your place-names—what was the one we came across this morning?—Termon, from Terminus, the god of boundaries.[3] It—it—it's really astonishing.

HUGH   We like to think we endure around truths immemorially posited.

YOLLAND   And your Gaelic literature—you're a poet yourself—

HUGH   Only in Latin, I'm afraid.

YOLLAND   I understand it's enormously rich and ornate.

HUGH   Indeed, Lieutenant. A rich language. A rich literature. You'll find, sir, that certain cultures expend on their vocabularies and syntax acquisitive energies and ostentations entirely lacking in their material lives. I suppose you could call us a spiritual people.

OWEN   [*Not unkindly; more out of embarrassment before* YOLLAND.]   Will you stop that nonsense, Father.

HUGH   Nonsense? What nonsense?

OWEN   Do you know where the priest lives?

HUGH   At Lis na Muc, over near . . .

OWEN   No, he doesn't. Lis na Muc, the Fort of the Pigs, has become Swinefort. [*Now turning the pages of the Name-Book—a page per name.*] And to get to Swinefort you pass through Greencastle and Fair Head and Strandhill

9. Hireling, subservient.
1. Romantic poet (1770–1850), who composed poetry while walking through England's Lake Dis-

trict.
2. I.e., Greek and Latin literature.
3. In Roman mythology.

and Gort and Whiteplains. And the new school isn't at Poll na gCaorach—
it's at Sheepsrock. Will you be able to find your way?

[HUGH *pours himself another drink. Then.*]

HUGH Yes, it is a rich language, Lieutenant, full of the mythologies of fantasy
and hope and self-deception—a syntax opulent with tomorrows. It is our
response to mud cabins and a diet of potatoes; our only method of replying
to . . . inevitabilities.

[*To* OWEN.] Can you give me the loan of half-a-crown? I'll repay you out
of the subscriptions I'm collecting for the publication of my new book. [*To*
YOLLAND.] It is entitled: 'The Pentaglot Preceptor[4] or Elementary Institute
of the English, Greek, Hebrew, Latin and Irish Languages; Particularly Calculated for the Instruction of Such Ladies and Gentlemen as may Wish to
Learn without the Help of a Master'.

YOLLAND [*Laughs.*] That's a wonderful title!

HUGH Between ourselves—the best part of the enterprise. Nor do I, in fact,
speak Hebrew. And that last phrase—'without the Help of a Master'—that
was written before the new national school was thrust upon me—do you
think I ought to drop it now? After all you don't dispose of the cow just
because it has produced a magnificent calf, do you?

YOLLAND You certainly do not.

HUGH The phrase goes. And I'm interrupting work of moment. [*He goes to
the door and stops there.*]

To return briefly to that other matter, Lieutenant. I understand your sense
of exclusion, of being cut off from a life here; and I trust you will find access
to us with my son's help. But remember that words are signals, counters.
They are not immortal. And it can happen—to use an image you'll understand—it can happen that a civilisation can be imprisoned in a linguistic
contour which no longer matches the landscape of . . . fact.

Gentlemen. [*He leaves.*]

OWEN 'An *expeditio* with three purposes': the children laugh at him: he always
promises three points and he never gets beyond A and B.

YOLLAND He's an astute man.

OWEN He's bloody pompous.

YOLLAND But so astute.

OWEN And he drinks too much. Is it astute not to be able to adjust for survival? Enduring around truths immemorially posited—hah!

YOLLAND He knows what's happening.

OWEN What is happening?

YOLLAND I'm not sure. But I'm concerned about my part in it. It's an eviction
of sorts.

OWEN We're making a six-inch map of the country. Is there something sinister in that?

YOLLAND Not in . . .

OWEN And we're taking place-names that are riddled with confusion and . . .

YOLLAND Who's confused? Are the people confused?

OWEN . . . and we're standardising those names as accurately and as sensitively as we can.

YOLLAND Something is being eroded.

OWEN Back to the romance again. Alright! Fine! Fine! Look where we've got

4. I.e., the five-tongued head teacher.

to. [*He drops on his hands and knees and stabs a finger at the map.*] We've come to this crossroads. Come here and look at it, man! Look at it! And we call that crossroads Tobair Vree. And why do we call it Tobair Vree? I'll tell you why. Tobair means a well. But what does Vree mean? It's a corruption of Brian—[*Gaelic pronunciation.*] Brian—an erosion of Tobair Bhriain. Because a hundred-and-fifty years ago there used to be a well there, not at the crossroads, mind you—that would be too simple—but in a field close to the crossroads. And an old man called Brian, whose face was disfigured by an enormous growth, got it into his head that the water in that well was blessed; and every day for seven months he went there and bathed his face in it. But the growth didn't go away; and one morning Brian was found drowned in that well. And ever since that crossroads is known as Tobair Vree—even though that well has long since dried up. I know the story because my grandfather told it to me. But ask Doalty—or Maire—or Bridget—even my father—even Manus—why it's called Tobair Vree; and do you think they'll know? I know they don't know. So the question I put to you, Lieutenant, is this: What do we do with a name like that? Do we scrap Tobair Vree altogether and call it—what?—The Cross? Crossroads? Or do we keep piety with a man long dead, long forgotten, his name 'eroded' beyond recognition, whose trivial little story nobody in the parish remembers?

YOLLAND   Except you.

OWEN   I've left here.

YOLLAND   You remember it.

OWEN   I'm asking you: what do we write in the Name-Book?

YOLLAND   Tobair Vree.

OWEN   Even though the well is a hundred yards from the actual crossroads— and there's no well anyway—and what the hell does Vree mean?

YOLLAND   Tobair Vree.

OWEN   That's what you want?

YOLLAND   Yes.

OWEN   You're certain?

YOLLAND   Yes.

OWEN   Fine. Fine. That's what you'll get.

YOLLAND   That's what you want, too, Roland.
     [*Pause.*]

OWEN [*Explodes.*]   George! For God's sake! *My name is not Roland!*

YOLLAND   What?

OWEN [*Softly.*]   My name is Owen.
     [*Pause.*]

YOLLAND   Not Roland?

OWEN   Owen.

YOLLAND   You mean to say—?

OWEN   Owen.

YOLLAND   But I've been—

OWEN   O-w-e-n.

YOLLAND   Where did Roland come from?

OWEN   I don't know.

YOLLAND   It was never Roland?

OWEN   Never.

YOLLAND   O my God!

[*Pause. They stare at one another. Then the absurdity of the situation strikes them suddenly. They explode with laughter.* OWEN *pours drinks. As they roll about their lines overlap.*]

YOLLAND Why didn't you tell me?
OWEN Do I look like a Roland?
YOLLAND Spell Owen again.
OWEN I was getting fond of Roland.
YOLLAND O my God!
OWEN O-w-e-n.
YOLLAND What'll we write—
OWEN —in the Name-Book?!
YOLLAND R-o-w-e-n!
OWEN Or what about Ol-
YOLLAND Ol- what?
OWEN Oland!
[*And again they explode.*
        MANUS *enters. He is very elated.*]
MANUS What's the celebration?
OWEN A christening!
YOLLAND A baptism!
OWEN A hundred christenings!
YOLLAND A thousand baptisms! Welcome to Eden!
OWEN Eden's right! We name a thing and—bang!—it leaps into existence![5]
YOLLAND Each name a perfect equation with its roots.
OWEN A perfect congruence with its reality.
        [*To* MANUS.] Take a drink.
YOLLAND Poteen—beautiful.
OWEN Lying Anna's poteen.
YOLLAND Anna na mBreag's poteen.
OWEN Excellent, George.
YOLLAND I'll decode you yet.
OWEN [*Offers drink.*] Manus?
MANUS Not if that's what it does to you.
OWEN You're right. Steady—steady—sober up—sober up.
YOLLAND Sober as a judge, Owen.
        [MANUS *moves beside* OWEN.]
MANUS I've got good news! Where's Father?
OWEN He's gone out. What's the good news?
MANUS I've been offered a job.
OWEN Where? [*Now aware of* YOLLAND.] Come on, man—speak in English.
MANUS For the benefit of the colonist?
OWEN He's a decent man.
MANUS Aren't they all at some level?
OWEN Please.
        [MANUS *shrugs.*]
  He's been offered a job.
YOLLAND Where?
OWEN Well—tell us!
MANUS I've just had a meeting with two men from Inis Meadhon.[6] They want

5. Cf. Adam's naming of every creature (Genesis 2.19–20).

6. Middle Island; one of the three Aran Islands, off the west coast of Ireland, south of Donegal.

me to go there and start a hedge-school. They're giving me a free house, free turf, and free milk; a rood[7] of standing corn; twelve drills[8] of potatoes; and— [*He stops.*]

OWEN And what?

MANUS A salary of £42 a year!

OWEN Manus, that's wonderful!

MANUS You're talking to a man of substance.

OWEN I'm delighted.

YOLLAND Where's Inis Meadhon?

OWEN An island south of here. And they came looking for you?

MANUS Well, I mean to say . . .
[OWEN *punches* MANUS.]

OWEN Aaaaagh! This calls for a real celebration.

YOLLAND Congratulations.

MANUS Thank you.

OWEN Where are you, Anna?

YOLLAND When do you start?

MANUS Next Monday.

OWEN We'll stay with you when we're there.
[*To* YOLLAND.] How long will it be before we reach Inis Meadhon?

YOLLAND How far south is it?

MANUS About fifty miles.

YOLLAND Could we make it by December?

OWEN We'll have Christmas together. [*Sings.*] 'Christmas Day on Inis Meadhon . . .'

YOLLAND [*Toast.*] I hope you're very content there, Manus.

MANUS Thank you.
[YOLLAND *holds out his hand.* MANUS *takes it. They shake warmly.*]

OWEN [*Toast.*] Manus.

MANUS [*Toast.*] To Inis Meadhon. [*He drinks quickly and turns to leave.*]

OWEN Hold on—hold on—refills coming up.

MANUS I've got to go.

OWEN Come on, man; this is an occasion. Where are you rushing to?

MANUS I've got to tell Maire.
[MAIRE *enters with her can of milk.*]

MAIRE You've got to tell Maire what?

OWEN He's got a job!

MAIRE Manus?

OWEN He's been invited to start a hedge-school in Inis Meadhon.

MAIRE Where?

MANUS Inis Meadhon—the island! They're giving me £42 a year and . . .

OWEN A house, fuel, milk, potatoes, corn, pupils, what-not!

MANUS I start on Monday.

OWEN You'll take a drink. Isn't it great?

MANUS I want to talk to you for . . .

MAIRE There's your milk. I need the can back.
[MANUS *takes the can and runs up the steps.*]

MANUS [*As he goes.*] How will you like living on an island?

OWEN You know George, don't you?

MAIRE We wave to each other across the fields.

7. A cubic measure.   8. Rows.

YOLLAND Sorry-sorry?

OWEN She says you wave to each other across the fields.

YOLLAND Yes, we do; oh yes, indeed we do.

MAIRE What's he saying?

OWEN He says you wave to each other across the fields.

MAIRE That's right. So we do.

YOLLAND What's she saying?

OWEN Nothing—nothing—nothing.

    [To MAIRE.*]* What's the news?

    *[*MAIRE *moves away, touching the text books with her toe.]*

MAIRE Not a thing. You're busy, the two of you.

OWEN We think we are.

MAIRE I hear the Fiddler O'Shea's about. There's some talk of a dance tomorrow night.

OWEN Where will it be?

MAIRE Maybe over the road. Maybe at Tobair Vree.

YOLLAND Tobair Vree!

MAIRE Yes.

YOLLAND Tobair Vree! Tobair Vree!

MAIRE Does he know what I'm saying?

OWEN Not a word.

MAIRE Tell him then.

OWEN Tell him what?

MAIRE About the dance.

OWEN Maire says there may be a dance tomorrow night.

YOLLAND *[To* OWEN.*]* Yes? May I come?

    [To MAIRE.*]* Would anybody object if I came?

MAIRE *[To* OWEN.*]* What's he saying?

OWEN *[To* YOLLAND.*]* Who would object?

MAIRE *[To* OWEN.*]* Did you tell him?

YOLLAND *[To* MAIRE.*]* Sorry-sorry?

OWEN *[To* MAIRE.*]* He says may he come?

MAIRE *[To* YOLLAND.*]* That's up to you.

YOLLAND *[To* OWEN.*]* What does she say?

OWEN *[To* YOLLAND.*]* She says—

YOLLAND *[To* MAIRE.*]* What-what?

MAIRE *[To* OWEN.*]* Well?

YOLLAND *[To* OWEN.*]* Sorry-sorry?

OWEN *[To* YOLLAND.*]* Will you go?

YOLLAND *[To* MAIRE.*]* Yes, yes, if I may.

MAIRE *[To* OWEN.*]* What does he say?

YOLLAND *[To* OWEN.*]* What is she saying?

OWEN O for God's sake!

    [To MANUS *who is descending with the empty can.]* You take on this job, Manus.

MANUS I'll walk you up to the house. Is your mother at home? I want to talk to her.

MAIRE What's the rush? *[To* OWEN.*]* Didn't you offer me a drink?

OWEN Will you risk Anna na mBreag?

MAIRE Why not.

    *[*YOLLAND *is suddenly intoxicated. He leaps up on a stool, raises his glass and shouts.]*

YOLLAND   Anna na mBreag! Baile Beag! Inis Meadhon! Bombay! Tobair Vree! Eden! And poteen—correct, Owen?

OWEN   Perfect.

YOLLAND   And bloody marvellous stuff it is, too. I love it! Bloody, bloody, bloody marvellous!

[*Simultaneously with his final 'bloody marvellous' bring up very loud the introductory music of the reel. Then immediately go to black. Retain the music throughout the very brief interval.*]

SCENE TWO

The following night.

This scene may be played in the schoolroom, but it would be preferable to lose—by lighting—as much of the schoolroom as possible, and to play the scene down front in a vaguely 'outside' area.

The music rises to a crescendo. Then in the distance we hear MAIRE *and* YOLLAND *approach—laughing and running. They run on, hand-in-hand. They have just left the dance.*

Fade the music to distant background. Then after a time it is lost and replaced by guitar music.

MAIRE *and* YOLLAND *are now down front, still holding hands and excited by their sudden and impetuous escape from the dance.*

MAIRE   O my God, that leap across the ditch nearly killed me.

YOLLAND   I could scarcely keep up with you.

MAIRE   Wait till I get my breath back.

YOLLAND   We must have looked as if we were being chased.

[*They now realise they are alone and holding hands—the beginnings of embarrassment. The hands disengage. They begin to drift apart. Pause.*]

MAIRE   Manus'll wonder where I've got to.

YOLLAND   I wonder did anyone notice us leave.

[*Pause. Slightly further apart.*]

MAIRE   The grass must be wet. My feet are soaking.

YOLLAND   Your feet must be wet. The grass is soaking.

[*Another pause. Another few paces apart. They are now a long distance from one another.*]

YOLLAND [*Indicating himself.*]   George.

[MAIRE *nods: Yes—yes. Then.*]

MAIRE   Lieutenant George.

YOLLAND   Don't call me that. I never think of myself as Lieutenant.

MAIRE   What-what?

YOLLAND   Sorry-sorry? [*He points to himself again.*] George.

[MAIRE *nods: Yes-yes. Then points to herself.*]

MAIRE   Maire.

YOLLAND   Yes, I know you're Maire. Of course I know you're Maire. I mean I've been watching you night and day for the past . . .

MAIRE [*Eagerly.*]   What-what?

YOLLAND [*Points.*]   Maire. [*Points.*] George. [*Points both.*] Maire and George.

[MAIRE *nods: Yes-yes-yes.*]

I—I—I—

MAIRE   Say anything at all. I love the sound of your speech.

YOLLAND [*Eagerly.*]   Sorry-sorry?

[*In acute frustration he looks around, hoping for some inspiration that*

will provide him with communicative means. Now he has a thought: he
tries raising his voice and articulating in a staccato style and with equal
and absurd emphasis on each word.]
Every-morning-I-see-you-feeding-brown-hens-and-giving-meal-to-black-
calf—[The futility of it.]—O my God.
[MAIRE smiles. She moves towards him. She will try to communicate in
Latin.]

MAIRE   Tu es centurio in—in—in exercitu Britannico—[9]

YOLLAND   Yes-yes? Go on—go on—say anything at all—I love the sound of
your speech.

MAIRE   —et es in castris quae—quae—quae sunt in agro[1]—[The futility of
it.]—O my God.
[YOLLAND smiles. He moves towards her.
Now for her English words.] George—water.

YOLLAND   'Water'? Water! Oh yes—water—water—verygood—water—good—
good.

MAIRE   Fire.

YOLLAND   Fire—indeed—wonderful—fire, fire, fire—splendid—splendid!

MAIRE   Ah . . . ah . . .

YOLLAND   Yes? Go on.

MAIRE   Earth.

YOLLAND   'Earth'?

MAIRE   Earth. Earth.
[YOLLAND still does not understand.
MAIRE stoops down and picks up a handful of clay. Holding it out.]
Earth.

YOLLAND   Earth! Of course—earth! Earth. Earth. Good Lord, Maire, your
English is perfect!

MAIRE   [Eagerly.]   What-what?

YOLLAND   Perfect English. English perfect.

MAIRE   George—

YOLLAND   That's beautiful—oh that's really beautiful.

MAIRE   George—

YOLLAND   Say it again—say it again—

MAIRE   Shhh. [She holds her hand up for silence—she is trying to remember
her one line of English. Now she remembers it and she delivers the line as if
English were her language—easily, fluidly, conversationally.] George, in Norfolk we besport ourselves around the maypoll.

YOLLAND   Good God, do you? That's where my mother comes from—Norfolk.
Norwich actually. Not exactly Norwich town but a small village called Little
Walsingham close beside it. But in our own village of Winfarthing we have
a maypole too and every year on the first of May— [He stops abruptly, only
now realising. He stares at her. She in turn misunderstands his excitement.]

MAIRE   [To herself.]   Mother of God, my Aunt Mary wouldn't have taught me
something dirty, would she?
[Pause.

---

9. You are a centurion in the British Army [Latin;
Friel's note]. "Centurion": an officer in command
of a hundred soldiers.

1. And you are in the camp in the field [Latin;
Friel's note].

YOLLAND *extends his hand to* MAIRE. *She turns away from him and moves slowly across the stage.*]

YOLLAND   Maire.

[*She still moves away.*]

YOLLAND   Maire Chatach.

[*She still moves away.*]

YOLLAND   Bun na hAbhann?[2] [*He says the name softly, almost privately, very tentatively, as if he were searching for a sound she might respond to. He tries again.*] Druim Dubh?[3]

[MAIRE *stops. She is listening.* YOLLAND *is encouraged.*]

Poll na gCaorach. Lis Maol.[4]

[MAIRE *turns towards him.*]

Lis na nGall.[5]

MAIRE   Lis na nGradh.[6]

[*They are now facing each other and begin moving—almost imperceptibly—towards one another.*]

MAIRE   Carraig an Phoill.[7]

YOLLAND   Carraig na Ri. Loch na nEan.[8]

MAIRE   Loch an Iubhair. Machaire Buidhe.[9]

YOLLAND   Machaire Mor. Cnoc na Mona.[1]

MAIRE   Cnoc na nGabhar.[2]

YOLLAND   Mullach.[3]

MAIRE   Port.[4]

YOLLAND   Tor.[5]

MAIRE   Lag.[6] [*She holds out her hands to* YOLLAND. *He takes them. Each now speaks almost to himself/herself.*]

YOLLAND   I wish to God you could understand me.

MAIRE   Soft hands; a gentleman's hands.

YOLLAND   Because if you could understand me I could tell you how I spend my days either thinking of you or gazing up at your house in the hope that you'll appear even for a second.

MAIRE   Every evening you walk by yourself along the Tra Bhan and every morning you wash yourself in front of your tent.

YOLLAND   I would tell you how beautiful you are, curly-headed Maire. I would so like to tell you how beautiful you are.

MAIRE   Your arms are long and thin and the skin on your shoulders is very white.

YOLLAND   I would tell you . . .

MAIRE   Don't stop—I know what you're saying.

YOLLAND   I would tell you how I want to be here—to live here—always—with you—always, always.

MAIRE   'Always'? What is that word—'always'?

YOLLAND   Yes-yes; always.

MAIRE   You're trembling.

YOLLAND   Yes, I'm trembling because of you.

2. Mouth of the River?
3. Black Ridge?
4. Pit of the Sheep. Bald Fairy Fort.
5. Fairy Fort of the Foreigner.
6. Fairy Fort of Love.
7. Rock of the Hole.
8. Rock of the King. Lake of the Bird.

9. Lake of the Yew Tree. The Great Plain.
1. The Big Plain. Hill of the Nobles.
2. Hill of the Goat.
3. Summit.
4. Port (i.e., same meaning in Gaelic and English).
5. Bush or heavy.
6. Weak.

MAIRE   I'm trembling, too. [*She holds his face in her hand.*]
YOLLAND   I've made up my mind . . .
MAIRE   Shhhh.
YOLLAND   I'm not going to leave here . . .
MAIRE   Shhh—listen to me. I want you, too, soldier.
YOLLAND   Don't stop—I know what you're saying.
MAIRE   I want to live with you—anywhere—anywhere at all—always—always.
YOLLAND   'Always'? What is that word—'always'?
MAIRE   Take me away with you, George.
      [*Pause.*
      Suddenly they kiss.
      SARAH *enters. She sees them. She stands shocked, staring at them. Her*
      mouth works. Then almost to herself.]
SARAH   Manus . . . Manus!
      [SARAH *runs off.*
      Music to crescendo.]

Act Three

The following evening. It is raining.

SARAH *and* OWEN *alone in the schoolroom.* SARAH, *more waiflike than ever, is*
sitting very still on a stool, an open book across her knee. She is pretending to
read but her eyes keep going up to the room upstairs. OWEN *is working on the*
floor as before, surrounded by his reference books, map, Name-Book etc. But he
has neither concentration nor interest; and like SARAH *he glances up at the*
upstairs room.

After a few seconds MANUS *emerges and descends, carrying a large paper bag*
which already contains his clothes. His movements are determined and urgent.
He moves around the classroom, picking up books, examining each title carefully,
and choosing about six of them which he puts into his bag. As he selects these
books.

OWEN   You know that old limekiln[7] beyond Con Connie Tim's pub, the place
      we call The Murren?—do you know why it's called The Murren?
      [MANUS *does not answer.*]
      I've only just discovered: it's a corruption of Saint Muranus. It seems Saint
      Muranus had a monastery somewhere about there at the beginning of the
      seventh century. And over the years the name became shortened to The
      Murren. Very unattractive name, isn't it? I think we should go back to the
      original—Saint Muranus. What do you think? The original's Saint Muranus.
      Don't you think we should go back to that?
      [*No response.* OWEN *begins writing the name into the Name-Book.*
      MANUS *is now rooting about among the forgotten implements for a piece*
      of rope. He finds a piece. He begins to tie the mouth of the flimsy,
      overloaded bag—and it bursts, the contents spilling out on the floor.]
MANUS   Bloody, bloody, bloody hell!
      [*His voice breaks in exasperation: he is about to cry.*
      OWEN *leaps to his feet.*]

7. Furnace for making lime out of shells or limestone.

OWEN   Hold on. I've a bag upstairs.

[*He runs upstairs.* SARAH *waits until* OWEN *is off. Then.*]

SARAH   Manus . . . Manus, I . . .

[MANUS *hears* SARAH *but makes no acknowledgement. He gathers up his belongings.*

OWEN *reappears with the bag he had on his arrival.*]

OWEN   Take this one—I'm finished with it anyway. And it's supposed to keep out the rain.

[MANUS *transfers his few belongings.* OWEN *drifts back to his task. The packing is now complete.*]

MANUS   You'll be here for a while? For a week or two anyhow?

OWEN   Yes.

MANUS   You're not leaving with the army?

OWEN   I haven't made up my mind. Why?

MANUS   Those Inis Meadhon men will be back to see why I haven't turned up. Tell them—tell them I'll write to them as soon as I can. Tell them I still want the job but that it might be three or four months before I'm free to go.

OWEN   You're being damned stupid, Manus.

MANUS   Will you do that for me?

OWEN   Clear out now and Lancey'll think you're involved somehow.

MANUS   Will you do that for me?

OWEN   Wait a couple of days even. You know George—he's a bloody romantic—maybe he's gone out to one of the islands and he'll suddenly reappear tomorrow morning. Or maybe the search party'll find him this evening lying drunk somewhere in the sandhills. You've seen him drinking that poteen—doesn't know how to handle it. Had he drink on him last night at the dance?

MANUS   I had a stone in my hand when I went out looking for him—I was going to fell him. The lame scholar turned violent.

OWEN   Did anybody see you?

MANUS   [*Again close to tears.*]   But when I saw him standing there at the side of the road—smiling—and her face buried in his shoulder—I couldn't even go close to them. I just shouted something stupid—something like, 'You're a bastard, Yolland.' If I'd even said it in English . . . 'cos he kept saying 'Sorry-sorry?' The wrong gesture in the wrong language.

OWEN   And you didn't see him again?

MANUS   'Sorry?'

OWEN   Before you leave tell Lancey that—just to clear yourself.

MANUS   What have I to say to Lancey? You'll give that message to the island-men?

OWEN   I'm warning you: run away now and you're bound to be . . .

MANUS   [*To* SARAH.]   Will you give that message to the Inis Meadhon men?

SARAH   I will.

[MANUS *picks up an old sack and throws it across his shoulders.*]

OWEN   Have you any idea where you're going?

MANUS   Mayo, maybe. I remember Mother saying she had cousins somewhere away out in the Erris Peninsula.[8] [*He picks up his bag.*] Tell father I took only the Virgil and the Caesar and the Aeschylus[9] because they're mine

8. Northwest corner of County Mayo, south of Donegal.

9. Ancient Greek playwright (525–456 B.C.E.). The surviving works of the Roman general and

anyway—I bought them with the money I get for that pet lamb I reared—
do you remember that pet lamb? And tell him that Nora Dan never returned
the dictionary and that she still owes him two-and-six[1] for last quarter's
reading—he always forgets those things.

OWEN   Yes.

MANUS   And his good shirt's ironed and hanging up in the press and his clean
socks are in the butter-box under the bed.

OWEN   Alright.

MANUS   And tell him I'll write.

OWEN   If Maire asks where you've gone . . . ?

MANUS   He'll need only half the amount of milk now, won't he? Even less
than half—he usually takes his tea black. [Pause.] And when he comes in
at night—you'll hear him; he makes a lot of noise—I usually come down
and give him a hand up. Those stairs are dangerous without a banister.
Maybe before you leave you'd get Big Ned Frank to put up some sort of a
handrail. [Pause.] And if you can bake, he's very fond of soda bread.

OWEN   I can give you money. I'm wealthy. Do you know what they pay me?
Two shillings a day for this—this—this—
[MANUS rejects the offer by holding out his hand.]
Goodbye, Manus.
[MANUS and OWEN shake hands.
Then MANUS picks up his bag briskly and goes towards the door. He
stops a few paces beyond SARAH, turns, comes back to her. He addresses
her as he did in Act One but now without warmth or concern for her.]

MANUS   What is your name? [Pause.] Come on. What is your name?

SARAH   My name is Sarah.

MANUS   Just Sarah? Sarah what? [Pause.] Well?

SARAH   Sarah Johnny Sally.

MANUS   And where do you live? Come on.

SARAH   I live in Bun na hAbhann. [She is now crying quietly.]

MANUS   Very good, Sarah Johnny Sally. There's nothing to stop you now—
nothing in the wide world. [Pause. He looks down at her.] It's alright—it's
alright—you did no harm—you did no harm at all. [He stoops over her and
kisses the top of her head—as if in absolution. Then briskly to the door and
off.]

OWEN   Good luck, Manus!

SARAH [Quietly.] I'm sorry . . . I'm sorry . . . I'm so sorry, Manus . . .
[OWEN tries to work but cannot concentrate. He begins folding up the
map. As he does.]

OWEN   Is there class this evening?
[SARAH nods: yes.]
I suppose Father knows. Where is he anyhow?
[SARAH points.]
Where?
[SARAH mimes rocking a baby.]
I don't understand—where?
[SARAH repeats the mime and wipes away tears. OWEN is still puzzled.]
It doesn't matter. He'll probably turn up.

statesman Julius Caesar (100–44 B.C.E) are his
military commentaries.

1. Two shillings and sixpence—thirty pennies—in
the old British currency.

[BRIDGET *and* DOALTY *enter, sacks over their heads against the rain. They are self-consciously noisier, more ebullient, more garrulous than ever—brimming over with excitement and gossip and brio.*]

DOALTY You're missing the crack,[2] boys! Cripes, you're missing the crack! Fifty more soldiers arrived an hour ago!

BRIDGET And they're spread out in a big line from Sean Neal's over to Lag and they're moving straight across the fields towards Cnoc na nGabhar!

DOALTY Prodding every inch of the ground in front of them with their bayonets and scattering animals and hens in all directions!

BRIDGET And tumbling everything before them—fences, ditches, hay-stacks, turf-stacks!

DOALTY They came to Barney Petey's field of corn—straight through it be God as if it was heather![3]

BRIDGET Not a blade of it left standing!

DOALTY And Barney Petey just out of his bed and running after them in his drawers: 'You hoors[4] you! Get out of my corn, you hoors you!'

BRIDGET First time he ever ran in his life.

DOALTY Too lazy, the wee get,[5] to cut it when the weather was good.

[SARAH *begins putting out the seats.*]

BRIDGET Tell them about Big Hughie.

DOALTY Cripes, if you'd seen your aul fella, Owen.

BRIDGET They were all inside in Anna na mBreag's pub—all the crowd from the wake—

DOALTY And they hear the commotion and they all come out to the street—

BRIDGET Your father in front; the Infant Prodigy footless[6] behind him!

DOALTY And your aul fella, he sees the army stretched across the countryside—

BRIDGET O my God!

DOALTY And Cripes he starts roaring at them!

BRIDGET 'Visigoths! Huns! Vandals!'[7]

DOALTY *'Ignari! Stulti! Rustici!'*[8]

BRIDGET And wee Jimmy Jack jumping up and down and shouting, 'Thermopylae! Thermopylae!'[9]

DOALTY You never saw crack like it in your life, boys. Come away on out with me, Sarah, and you'll see it all.

BRIDGET Big Hughie's fit to take no class. Is Manus about?

OWEN Manus is gone.

BRIDGET Gone where?

OWEN He's left—gone away.

DOALTY Where to?

OWEN He doesn't know. Mayo, maybe.

DOALTY What's on in Mayo?

OWEN [*To* BRIDGET.] Did you see George and Maire Chatach leave the dance last night?

BRIDGET We did. Didn't we, Doalty?

2. Excitement.
3. Plant with small leaves and flowers.
4. Whores.
5. Little bastard or little fool.
6. Barefoot.
7. Nomadic tribes that militarily challenged the (Western) Roman Empire in the 4th and 5th centuries.
8. Ignoramuses! Fools! Peasants! [Latin; Friel's note].
9. A narrow valley on the Aegean Sea, where in 480 B.C.E. a small number of Greek soldiers attempted to stave off a much larger Persian force.

OWEN   Did you see Manus following them out?

BRIDGET   I didn't see him going out but I saw him coming in by himself later.

OWEN   Did George and Maire come back to the dance?

BRIDGET   No.

OWEN   Did you see them again?

BRIDGET   He left her home. We passed them going up the back road—didn't we, Doalty?

OWEN   And Manus stayed till the end of the dance?

DOALTY   We know nothing. What are you asking us for?

OWEN   Because Lancey'll question me when he hears Manus's gone. [*Back to* BRIDGET.] That's the way George went home? By the back road? That's where you saw him?

BRIDGET   Leave me alone, Owen. I know nothing about Yolland. If you want to know about Yolland, ask the Donnelly twins.

   [*Silence.* DOALTY *moves over to the window.*]

   [*To* SARAH.] He's a powerful fiddler, O'Shea, isn't he? He told our Seamus he'll come back for a night at Hallowe'en.

   [OWEN *goes to* DOALTY *who looks resolutely out the window.*]

OWEN   What's this about the Donnellys? [*Pause.*] Were they about last night?

DOALTY   Didn't see them if they were. [*Begins whistling through his teeth.*]

OWEN   George is a friend of mine.

DOALTY   So.

OWEN   I want to know what's happened to him.

DOALTY   Couldn't tell you.

OWEN   What have the Donnelly twins to do with it? [*Pause.*] Doalty!

DOALTY   I know nothing, Owen—nothing at all—I swear to God. All I know is this: on my way to the dance I saw their boat beached at Port. It wasn't there on my way home, after I left Bridget. And that's all I know. As God's my judge.

   The half-dozen times I met him I didn't know a word he said to me; but he seemed a right enough sort . . . [*With sudden excessive interest in the scene outside.*] Cripes, they're crawling all over the place! Cripes, there's millions of them! Cripes, they're levelling the whole land!

   [OWEN *moves away.*

      MAIRE *enters. She is bareheaded and wet from the rain; her hair in disarray. She attempts to appear normal but she is in acute distress, on the verge of being distraught. She is carrying the milk-can.*]

MAIRE   Honest to God, I must be going off my head. I'm half-way here and I think to myself, 'Isn't this can very light?' and I look into it and isn't it empty.

OWEN   It doesn't matter.

MAIRE   How will you manage for tonight?

OWEN   We have enough.

MAIRE   Are you sure?

OWEN   Plenty, thanks.

MAIRE   It'll take me no time at all to go back up for some.

OWEN   Honestly, Maire.

MAIRE   Sure it's better you have it than that black calf that's . . . that . . . [*She looks around.*] Have you heard anything?

OWEN   Nothing.

MAIRE   What does Lancey say?

OWEN   I haven't seen him since this morning.

MAIRE   What does he *think?*

OWEN   We really didn't talk. He was here for only a few seconds.

MAIRE   He left me home, Owen. And the last thing he said to me—he tried to speak in Irish—he said, 'I'll see you yesterday'—he meant to say 'I'll see you tomorrow.' And I laughed that much he pretended to get cross and he said 'Maypoll! Maypoll!' because I said that word wrong. And off he went, laughing—laughing, Owen! Do you think he's alright? What do *you* think?

OWEN   I'm sure he'll turn up, Maire.

MAIRE   He comes from a tiny wee place called Winfarthing. [*She suddenly drops on her hands and knees on the floor—where* OWEN *had his map a few minutes ago—and with her finger traces out an outline map.*]

Come here till you see. Look. There's Winfarthing. And there's two other wee villages right beside it; one of them's called Barton Bendish—it's there; and the other's called Saxingham Nethergate—it's about there. And there's Little Walsingham—that's his mother's townland. Aren't they odd names? Sure they make no sense to me at all. And Winfarthing's near a big town called Norwich. And Norwich is in a county called Norfolk. And Norfolk is in the east of England. He drew a map for me on the wet strand and wrote the names on it. I have it all in my head now: Winfarthing—Barton Bendish—Saxingham Nethergate—Little Walsingham—Norwich—Norfolk. Strange sounds, aren't they? But nice sounds; like Jimmy Jack reciting his Homer.

[*She gets to her feet and looks around; she is almost serene now. To* SARAH.] You were looking lovely last night, Sarah. Is that the dress you got from Boston? Green suits you.

[*To* OWEN.] Something very bad's happened to him, Owen. I know. He wouldn't go away without telling me. Where is he, Owen? You're his friend—where is he? [*Again she looks around the room; then sits on a stool.*]

I didn't get a chance to do my geography last night. The master'll be angry with me. [*She rises again.*]

I think I'll go home now. The wee ones have to be washed and put to bed and that black calf has to be fed . . .

My hands are that rough; they're still blistered from the hay. I'm ashamed of them. I hope to God there's no hay to be saved in Brooklyn.

[*She stops at the door.*] Did you hear? Nellie Ruadh's baby died in the middle of the night. I must go up to the wake. It didn't last long, did it?

[MAIRE *leaves. Silence. Then.*]

OWEN   I don't think there'll be any class. Maybe you should . . .

[OWEN *begins picking up his texts.* DOALTY *goes to him.*]

DOALTY   Is he long gone?—Manus.

OWEN   Half an hour.

DOALTY   Stupid bloody fool.

OWEN   I told him that.

DOALTY   Do they know he's gone?

OWEN   Who?

DOALTY   The army.

OWEN   Not yet.

DOALTY   They'll be after him like bloody beagles. Bloody, bloody fool, limping along the coast. They'll overtake him before night for Christ's sake.

[DOALTY *returns to the window.* LANCEY *enters—now the commanding officer.*]

OWEN   Any news? Any word?

> [LANCEY *moves into the centre of the room, looking around as he does.*]

LANCEY   I understood there was a class. Where are the others?

OWEN   There was to be a class but my father . . .

LANCEY   This will suffice. I will address them and it will be their responsibility to pass on what I have to say to every family in this section.

> [LANCEY *indicates to* OWEN *to translate.* OWEN *hesitates, trying to assess the change in* LANCEY's *manner and attitude.*]

I'm in a hurry, O'Donnell.

OWEN   The captain has an announcement to make.

LANCEY   Lieutenant Yolland is missing. We are searching for him. If we don't find him, or if we receive no information as to where he is to be found, I will pursue the following course of action. [*He indicates to* OWEN *to translate.*]

OWEN   They are searching for George. If they don't find him—

LANCEY   Commencing twenty-four hours from now we will shoot all livestock in Ballybeg.

> [OWEN *stares at* LANCEY.]

At once.

OWEN   Beginning this time tomorrow they'll kill every animal in Baile Beag— unless they're told where George is.

LANCEY   If that doesn't bear results, commencing forty-eight hours from now we will embark on a series of evictions and levelling of every abode in the following selected areas—

OWEN   You're not—!

LANCEY   Do your job. Translate.

OWEN   If they still haven't found him in two days' time they'll begin evicting and levelling every house starting with these townlands.

> [LANCEY *reads from his list.*]

LANCEY   Swinefort.

OWEN   Lis na Muc.

LANCEY   Burnfoot.

OWEN   Bun na hAbhann.

LANCEY   Dromduff.

OWEN   Druim Dubh.

LANCEY   Whiteplains.

OWEN   Machaire Ban.

LANCEY   Kings Head.

OWEN   Cnoc na Ri.

LANCEY   If by then the lieutenant hasn't been found, we will proceed until a complete clearance is made of this entire section.

OWEN   If Yolland hasn't been got by then, they will ravish the whole parish.

LANCEY   I trust they know exactly what they've got to do.

> [*Pointing to* BRIDGET.] I know you. I know where you live.
>
> [*Pointing to* SARAH.] Who are you? Name!
>
> [SARAH's *mouth opens and shuts, opens and shuts. Her face becomes contorted.*]

What's your name?

> [*Again* SARAH *tries frantically.*]

OWEN   Go on, Sarah. You can tell him.

> [*But* SARAH *cannot. And she knows she cannot. She closes her mouth. Her head goes down.*]

OWEN Her name is Sarah Johnny Sally.
LANCEY Where does she live?
OWEN Bun na hAbhann.
LANCEY Where?
OWEN Burnfoot.
LANCEY I want to talk to your brother—is he here?
OWEN Not at the moment.
LANCEY Where is he?
OWEN He's at a wake.
LANCEY What wake?
[DOALTY, *who has been looking out the window all through* LANCEY's *announcements, now speaks—calmly, almost casually.*]
DOALTY Tell him his whole camp's on fire.
LANCEY What's your name? [*To* OWEN.] Who's that lout?
OWEN Doalty Dan Doalty.
LANCEY Where does he live?
OWEN Tulach Alainn.
LANCEY What do we call it?
OWEN Fair Hill. He says your whole camp is on fire.
[LANCEY *rushes to the window and looks out. Then he wheels on* DOALTY.]
LANCEY I'll remember you, Mr Doalty. [*To* OWEN.] You carry a big responsibility in all this. [*He goes off.*]
BRIDGET Mother of God, does he mean it, Owen?
OWEN Yes, he does.
BRIDGET We'll have to hide the beasts somewhere—our Seamus'll know where. Maybe at the back of Lis na nGradh—or in the caves at the far end of the Tra Bhan. Come on, Doalty! Come on! Don't be standing about there!
[DOALTY *does not move.* BRIDGET *runs to the door and stops suddenly. She sniffs the air. Panic.*]
The sweet smell! Smell it! It's the sweet smell! Jesus, it's the potato blight!
DOALTY It's the army tents burning, Bridget.
BRIDGET Is it? Are you sure? Is that what it is? God, I thought we were destroyed altogether. Come on! Come on!
[*She runs off* OWEN *goes to* SARAH *who is preparing to leave.*]
OWEN How are you? Are you alright?
[SARAH *nods: Yes.*]
OWEN Don't worry. It will come back to you again.
[SARAH *shakes her head.*]
OWEN It will. You're upset now. He frightened you. That's all's wrong.
[*Again* SARAH *shakes her head, slowly, emphatically, and smiles at* OWEN. *Then she leaves.*
OWEN *busies himself gathering his belongings.* DOALTY *leaves the window and goes to him.*]
DOALTY He'll do it, too.
OWEN Unless Yolland's found.
DOALTY Hah!
OWEN Then he'll certainly do it.
DOALTY When my grandfather was a boy they did the same thing. [*Simply, altogether without irony.*] And after all the trouble you went to, mapping the place and thinking up new names for it.
[OWEN *busies himself. Pause.*
DOALTY *almost dreamily.*]

2766 / BRIAN FRIEL

I've damned little to defend but he'll not put me out without a fight. And there'll be others who think the same as me.

OWEN That's a matter for you.

DOALTY If we'd all stick together. If we knew how to defend ourselves.

OWEN Against a trained army.

DOALTY The Donnelly twins know how.

HUGH If they could be found.

DOALTY If they could be found. [*He goes to the door.*] Give me a shout after you've finished with Lancey. I might know something then. [*He leaves.*]

> [OWEN *picks up the Name-Book. He looks at it momentarily, then puts it on top of the pile he is carrying. It falls to the floor. He stoops to pick it up—hesitates—leaves it. He goes upstairs.*
>
> As OWEN *ascends,* HUGH *and* JIMMY JACK *enter. Both wet and drunk.* JIMMY *is very unsteady. He is trotting behind* HUGH, *trying to break in on* HUGH's *declamation.*
>
> HUGH *is equally drunk but more experienced in drunkenness: there is a portion of his mind which retains its clarity.*]

HUGH There I was, appropriately dispositioned to proffer my condolences to the bereaved mother . . .

JIMMY Hugh—

HUGH . . . and about to enter the *domus lugubris*[1]—Maire Chatach?

JIMMY The wake house.

HUGH Indeed—when I experience a plucking at my elbow: Mister George Alexander, Justice of the Peace. 'My tidings are infelicitous,' said he—Bridget? Too slow. Doalty?

JIMMY *Infelix*—unhappy.

HUGH Unhappy indeed. 'Master Bartley Timlin has been appointed to the new national school.'

'Timlin? Who is Timlin?'

'A schoolmaster from Cork.[2] And he will be a major asset to the community: he is also a very skilled bacon-curer'!

JIMMY Hugh—

HUGH Ha-ha-ha-ha-ha! The Cork bacon-curer! *Barbarus hic ego sum quia non intelligor ulli*—James?

JIMMY Ovid.

HUGH *Procede.*

JIMMY 'I am a barbarian in this place because I am not understood by anyone.'[3]

HUGH Indeed—[*Shouts.*] Manus! Tea!

I will compose a satire on Master Bartley Timlin, schoolmaster and bacon-curer. But it will be too easy, won't it?

[*Shouts.*] Strong tea! Black!

> [*The only way* JIMMY *can get* HUGH's *attention is by standing in front of him and holding his arms.*]

JIMMY Will you listen to me, Hugh!

HUGH James.

[*Shouts.*] And a slice of soda bread.

---

1. House of mourning [Latin; Friel's note].
2. Influential city on Ireland's south coast.
3. From Ovid's *Tristia*, written after the Roman poet was exiled to live by the Black Sea in what is Romania today.

JIMMY I'm going to get married.

HUGH Well!

JIMMY At Christmas.

HUGH Splendid.

JIMMY To Athene.

HUGH Who?

JIMMY Pallas Athene.

HUGH *Glaukopis Athene?*

JIMMY Flashing-eyed, Hugh, flashing-eyed! [*He attempts the gesture he has made before: standing to attention, the momentary spasm, the salute, the face raised in pained ecstasy—but the body does not respond efficiently this time. The gesture is grotesque.*]

HUGH The lady has assented?

JIMMY She asked *me—I* assented.

HUGH Ah. When was this?

JIMMY Last night.

HUGH What does her mother say?

JIMMY Metis from Hellespont?[4] Decent people—good stock.

HUGH And her father?

JIMMY I'm meeting Zeus tomorrow. Hugh, will you be my best man?

HUGH Honoured, James; profoundly honoured.

JIMMY You know what I'm looking for, Hugh, don't you? I mean to say—you know—I—I—I joke like the rest of them—you know?—[*Again he attempts the pathetic routine but abandons it instantly.*] You know yourself, Hugh—don't you?—You know all that. But what I'm really looking for, Hugh—what I really want—companionship, Hugh—at my time of life, companionship, company, someone to talk to. Away up in Beann na Gaoithe—you've no idea how lonely it is. Companionship—correct, Hugh? Correct?

HUGH Correct.

JIMMY And I always liked her, Hugh. Correct?

HUGH Correct, James.

JIMMY Someone to talk to.

HUGH Indeed.

JIMMY That's all, Hugh. The whole story. You know it all now, Hugh. You know it all.

[*As* JIMMY *says those last lines he is crying, shaking his head, trying to keep his balance, and holding a finger up to his lips in absurd gestures of secrecy and intimacy. Now he staggers away, tries to sit on a stool, misses it, slides to the floor, his feet in front of him, his back against the broken cart. Almost at once he is asleep.*

HUGH *watches all of this. Then he produces his flask and is about to pour a drink when he sees the Name-Book on the floor. He picks it up and leafs through it, pronouncing the strange names as he does. Just as he begins,* OWEN *emerges and descends with two bowls of tea.*]

HUGH Ballybeg. Burnfoot. Kings Head. Whiteplains. Fair Hill. Dunboy. Green Bank.

[OWEN *snatches the book from* HUGH.]

OWEN I'll take that. [*In apology.*] It's only a catalogue of names.

---

4. Renowned for her wisdom, Metis was impregnated by and then swallowed by Zeus, whose head began to ache until Athena sprang from his head.

HUGH   I know what it is.

OWEN   A mistake—my mistake—nothing to do with us. I hope that's strong enough. [*Tea.*]

    [*He throws the book on the table and crosses over to* JIMMY.]

Jimmy. Wake up, Jimmy. Wake up, man.

JIMMY   What—what-what?

OWEN   Here. Drink this. Then go on away home. There may be trouble. Do you hear me, Jimmy? There may be trouble.

HUGH   [*Indicating Name-Book.*]   We must learn those new names.

OWEN   [*Searching around.*]   Did you see a sack lying about?

HUGH   We must learn where we live. We must learn to make them our own. We must make them our new home.

    [OWEN *finds a sack and throws it across his shoulders.*]

OWEN   I know where I live.

HUGH   James thinks he knows, too. I look at James and three thoughts occur to me: A—that it is not the literal past, the 'facts' of history, that shape us, but images of the past embodied in language. James has ceased to make that discrimination.

OWEN   Don't lecture me, Father.

HUGH   B—we must never cease renewing those images; because once we do, we fossilise. Is there no soda bread?

OWEN   And C, Father—one single, unalterable 'fact': if Yolland is not found, we are all going to be evicted. Lancey has issued the order.

HUGH   Ah. *Edictum imperatoris.*[5]

OWEN   You should change out of those wet clothes. I've got to go. I've got to see Doalty Dan Doalty.

HUGH   What about?

OWEN   I'll be back soon.

    [*As* OWEN *exits.*]

HUGH   Take care, Owen. To remember everything is a form of madness. [*He looks around the room, carefully, as if he were about to leave it forever. Then he looks at* JIMMY, *asleep again.*]

The road to Sligo.[6] A spring morning. 1798.[7] Going into battle. Do you remember, James? Two young gallants with pikes across their shoulders and the *Aeneid*[8] in their pockets. Everything seemed to find definition that spring—a congruence, a miraculous matching of hope and past and present and possibility. Striding across the fresh, green land. The rhythms of perception heightened. The whole enterprise of consciousness accelerated. We were gods that morning, James; and I had recently married *my* goddess, Caitlin Dubh Nic Reactainn, may she rest in peace. And to leave her and my infant son in his cradle—that was heroic, too. By God, sir, we were magnificent. We marched as far as—where was it?—Glenties![9] All of twenty-three miles in one day. And it was there, in Phelan's pub, that we got homesick for Athens, just like Ulysses. The *desiderium nostrorum*—the

5. The decree of the commander [Latin; Friel's note].
6. Port town south of County Donegal.
7. That year a force of Catholics and Protestants known as the United Irishmen launched a rebellion throughout Ireland. After the British quashed the uprising, the Irish Parliament was abolished, and two years later the Act of Union incorporated Ireland into the United Kingdom.
8. Virgil's epic, about the Trojan hero Aeneas, who escapes the destruction of Troy and founds Rome.
9. A region of intersecting glens on the coast of central Donegal.

need for our own. Our *pietas*,[1] James, was for older, quieter things. And that was the longest twenty-three miles back I ever made. [*Toasts* JIMMY.] My friend, confusion is not an ignoble condition.

    [MAIRE *enters.*]

MAIRE I'm back again. I set out for somewhere but I couldn't remember where. So I came back here.

HUGH Yes, I will teach you English, Maire Chatach.

MAIRE Will you, Master? I must learn it. I need to learn it.

HUGH Indeed you may well be my only pupil. [*He goes towards the steps and begins to ascend.*]

MAIRE When can we start?

HUGH Not today. Tomorrow, perhaps. After the funeral. We'll begin tomorrow. [*Ascending.*] But don't expect too much. I will provide you with the available words and the available grammar. But will that help you to interpret between privacies? I have no idea. But it's all we have. I have no idea at all. [*He is now at the top.*]

MAIRE Master, what does the English word 'always' mean?

HUGH *Semper—per omnia saecula.*[2] The Greeks called it *'aei'.* It's not a word I'd start with. It's a silly word, girl. [*He sits.*]

    [JIMMY *is awake. He gets to his feet.*

      MAIRE *sees the Name-Book, picks it up, and sits with it on her knee.*]

MAIRE When he comes back, this is where he'll come to. He told me this is where he was happiest.

    [JIMMY *sits beside* MAIRE.]

JIMMY Do you know the Greek word *endogamein*? It means to marry within the tribe. And the word *exogamein* means to marry outside the tribe. And you don't cross those borders casually—both sides get very angry. Now, the problem is this: Is Athene sufficiently mortal or am I sufficiently godlike for the marriage to be acceptable to her people and to my people? You think about that.

HUGH *Urbs antiqua fuit*—there was an ancient city which,'tis said, Juno[3] loved above all the lands. And it was the goddess's aim and cherished hope that here should be the capital of all nations—should the fates perchance allow that. Yet in truth she discovered that a race was springing from Trojan blood to overthrow some day these Tyrian[4] towers—a people *late regem belloque superbum*—kings of broad realms and proud in war who would come forth for Lybia's[5] downfall—such was—such was the course—such was the course ordained—ordained by fate . . . What the hell's wrong with me? Sure I know it backwards. I'll begin again. *Urbs antiqua fuit*—there was an ancient city which,'tis said, Juno loved above all the lands.

    [*Begin to bring down the lights.*]

1. Piety [Friel's note]. The Latin term for the trait associated especially with Virgil's dutiful hero Aeneas. The story of Ulysses', or Odysseus', ten-year wandering on the way home is told in Homer's *Odyssey*.
2. Always—for all time. *Aei*, always [Friel's note].
3. In Roman mythology queen of the gods, who loved ancient Carthage (now in Tunisia) above all. Hugh's recitation is from the beginning of the narrative of Virgil's *Aeneid*. Here Juno angrily foresees the destruction of Carthage by Aeneas's Roman descendants ("a race was springing from Trojan blood") and the extension of Roman rule over this North African colony (Rome and Carthage fought the Punic Wars in the 3rd and 2nd centuries B.C.E.). While vaunting Rome's imperial mission to civilize the world, Virgil's epic also includes a tragic love story: Aeneas and the Carthaginian queen Dido fall in love, but she commits suicide after he abandons her for his imperial duty.
4. I.e., Carthaginian. Carthage had been founded by Phoenicians from the city of Tyre (now in Lebanon).
5. Carthage's.

And it was the goddess's aim and cherished hope that here should be the capital of all nations—should the fates perchance allow that. Yet in truth she discovered that a race was springing from Trojan blood to overthrow some day these Tyrian towers—a people kings of broad realms and proud in war who would come forth for Lybia's downfall . . .
[*Black.*]

DEREK WALCOTT
b. 1930

Derek Walcott was born on the island of Saint Lucia in the British West Indies, where he had a Methodist upbringing in a largely Roman Catholic society. He was educated at St. Mary's College in Saint Lucia and the University of the West Indies in Jamaica. He then moved to Trinidad, where he worked as a book reviewer, art critic, playwright, and artistic director of a theater workshop. Since the early 1980s he has also taught at a number of American colleges and universities, especially Boston University; in 1992 he received the Nobel Prize in Literature.

As a black poet writing from within both the English literary tradition and the history of a colonized people, Walcott has self-mockingly referred to his split allegiances to his Afro-Caribbean and his European inheritances as those of a "schizophrenic," a "mongrel," a "mulatto of style." His background is indeed racially and culturally mixed: his grandmothers were of African descent; his grandfathers were white, a Dutchman and an Englishman. Schooled in the Standard English that is the official language of Saint Lucia, Walcott also grew up speaking the predominantly French Creole (or patois) that is the primary language of everyday life (the island had traded hands fourteen times in colonial wars between the British and the French). In his poetry this cross-cultural inheritance is sometimes the source of pain and ambivalence, as when in "A Far Cry from Africa" he refers to himself as being "poisoned with the blood of both." At other times it fuels a celebratory integration of multiple forms, visions, and energies, as in parts of his long poem *Omeros,* which transposes elements of Homeric epic from the Aegean to the Caribbean.

Even as a schoolboy Walcott knew he was not alone in his effort to sort through his vexed postcolonial affiliations. From a young age he felt a special affinity with Irish writers such as W. B. Yeats, James Joyce, and J. M. Synge, whom he saw as fellow colonials—"They were the niggers of Britain"—with the same paradoxical hatred for the British Empire and worship of the English language. He has repeatedly asked how the postcolonial poet can both grieve the agonizing harm of British colonialism and appreciate the empire's literary gift. Walcott has also acknowledged other English and American writers—T. S. Eliot, Ezra Pound, Hart Crane, W. H. Auden, and Robert Lowell—as enabling influences.

Over the course of his prolific career, Walcott has adapted various European literary archetypes (e.g., the Greek character Philoctetes) and forms (epic, quatrains, terza rima, English meters). He has ascribed his rigorous concern with craft to his youthful Protestantism. At once disciplined and flamboyant as a poet, he insists on the specifically Caribbean opulence of his art: "I come from a place that likes grandeur; it likes large gestures; it is not inhibited by flourish; it is a rhetorical society; it is a society of physical performance; it is a society of style." Although much of his poetry is in a rhetorically elevated Standard English, Walcott adapts the calypso rhythms of a lightly creolized English in "The Schooner *Flight,*" and he braids together West Indian English, Standard English, and French patois in *Omeros.* He has a great passion for metaphor, by which he deftly weaves imaginative connections across cultural and racial boundaries. His plays, written in an accurate and energetic language, are similarly infused with the spirit of syncretism, vividly conjoining Caribbean and European motifs, images, and idioms.

A Far Cry from Africa

A wind is ruffling the tawny pelt
Of Africa. Kikuyu,[1] quick as flies,
Batten upon the bloodstreams of the veldt.[2]
Corpses are scattered through a paradise.
5 Only the worm, colonel of carrion, cries:
"Waste no compassion on these separate dead!"
Statistics justify and scholars seize
The salients of colonial policy.
What is that to the white child hacked in bed?
10 To savages, expendable as Jews?

Threshed out by beaters,[3] the long rushes break
In a white dust of ibises whose cries
Have wheeled since civilization's dawn
From the parched river or beast-teeming plain.
15 The violence of beast on beast is read
As natural law, but upright man
Seeks his divinity by inflicting pain.
Delirious as these worried beasts, his wars
Dance to the tightened carcass of a drum,
20 While he calls courage still that native dread
Of the white peace contracted by the dead.

Again brutish necessity wipes its hands
Upon the napkin of a dirty cause, again
A waste of our compassion, as with Spain,[4]
25 The gorilla wrestles with the superman.
I who am poisoned with the blood of both,
Where shall I turn, divided to the vein?
I who have cursed
The drunken officer of British rule, how choose
30 Between this Africa and the English tongue I love?
Betray them both, or give back what they give?
How can I face such slaughter and be cool?
How can I turn from Africa and live?

1956, 1962

---

1. An east African ethnic group whose members, as Mau Mau fighters, conducted an eight-year campaign of violent resistance against British colonial settlers in Kenya in the 1950s.
2. Open country, neither cultivated nor forest (Afrikaans).
3. In big-game hunting, natives are hired to beat the brush, driving birds—such as ibises—and other animals into the open.
4. The Spanish Civil War (1936–39).

From The Schooner *Flight*

1 Adios, Carenage[1]

In idle August, while the sea soft,
and leaves of brown islands stick to the rim
of this Caribbean, I blow out the light
by the dreamless face of Maria Concepcion
5   to ship as a seaman on the schooner *Flight*.
Out in the yard turning grey in the dawn,
I stood like a stone and nothing else move
but the cold sea rippling like galvanize
and the nail holes of stars in the sky roof,
10   till a wind start to interfere with the trees.
I pass me dry neighbour sweeping she yard
as I went downhill, and I nearly said:
"Sweep soft, you witch, 'cause she don't sleep hard,"
but the bitch look through me like I was dead.
15   A route taxi pull up, park-lights still on.
The driver size up my bags with a grin:
"This time, Shabine, like you really gone!"
I ain't answer the ass, I simply pile in
the back seat and watch the sky burn
20   above Laventille[2] pink as the gown
in which the woman I left was sleeping,
and I look in the rearview and see a man
exactly like me, and the man was weeping
for the houses, the streets, the whole fucking island.

25   Christ have mercy on all sleeping things!
From that dog rotting down Wrightson Road
to when I was a dog on these streets;
if loving these islands must be my load,
out of corruption my soul takes wings,
30   But they had started to poison my soul
with their big house, big car, big-time bohbohl,[3]
coolie, nigger, Syrian, and French Creole,
so I leave it for them and their carnival—
I taking a sea-bath, I gone down the road.
35   I know these islands from Monos to Nassau,[4]
a rusty head sailor with sea-green eyes
that they nickname Shabine, the patois° for   *spoken dialect*
any red nigger, and I, Shabine, saw
when these slums of empire was paradise.
40   I'm just a red nigger who love the sea,
I had a sound colonial education,
I have Dutch, nigger, and English in me,
and either I'm nobody, or I'm a nation.

---

1. Waterfront where schooners are cleaned and repaired. "Adios": goodbye (Spanish).
2. Hillside slum outside Port of Spain, Trinidad.
3. Or *bobol*: corrupt practices or fraud, organized by people in positions of power (Eastern Caribbean English).
4. Capital of the Bahamas. "Monos": island off the northwest coast of Trinidad.

But Maria Concepcion was all my thought
45   watching the sea heaving up and down
as the port side of dories, schooners, and yachts
was painted afresh by the strokes of the sun
signing her name with every reflection;
I knew when dark-haired evening put on
50   her bright silk at sunset, and, folding the sea,
sidled under the sheet with her starry laugh,
that there'd be no rest, there'd be no forgetting.
Is like telling mourners round the graveside
about resurrection, they want the dead back,
55   so I smile to myself as the bow rope untied
and the *Flight* swing seaward: "Is no use repeating
that the sea have more fish. I ain't want her
dressed in the sexless light of a seraph,°   *angel*
I want those round brown eyes like a marmoset,[5] and
60   till the day when I can lean back and laugh,
those claws that tickled my back on sweating
Sunday afternoons, like a crab on wet sand."
As I worked, watching the rotting waves come
past the bow that scissor the sea like silk,
65   I swear to you all, by my mother's milk,
by the stars that shall fly from tonight's furnace,
that I loved them, my children, my wife, my home;
I loved them as poets love the poetry
that kills them, as drowned sailors the sea.

70   You ever look up from some lonely beach
and see a far schooner? Well, when I write
this poem, each phrase go be soaked in salt;
I go draw and knot every line as tight
as ropes in this rigging; in simple speech
75   my common language go be the wind,
my pages the sails of the schooner *Flight*.

                                   1979

The Season of Phantasmal Peace

Then all the nations of birds lifted together
the huge net of the shadows of this earth
in multitudinous dialects, twittering tongues,
stitching and crossing it. They lifted up
5   the shadows of long pines down trackless slopes,
the shadows of glass-faced towers down evening streets,
the shadow of a frail plant on a city sill—
the net rising soundless as night, the birds' cries soundless, until
there was no longer dusk, or season, decline, or weather,
10   only this passage of phantasmal light
that not the narrowest shadow dared to sever.

5. South American monkey.

And men could not see, looking up, what the wild geese drew,
what the ospreys trailed behind them in silvery ropes
that flashed in the icy sunlight; they could not hear
15 battalions of starlings waging peaceful cries,
bearing the net higher, covering this world
like the vines of an orchard, or a mother drawing
the trembling gauze over the trembling eyes
of a child fluttering to sleep;

                         it was the light
20 that you will see at evening on the side of a hill
in yellow October, and no one hearing knew
what change had brought into the raven's cawing,
the killdeer's screech, the ember-circling chough°   *bird in crow family*
such an immense, soundless, and high concern
25 for the fields and cities where the birds belong,
except it was their seasonal passing, Love,
made seasonless, or, from the high privilege of their birth,
something brighter than pity for the wingless ones
below them who shared dark holes in windows and in houses,
30 and higher they lifted the net with soundless voices
above all change, betrayals of falling suns,
and this season lasted one moment, like the pause
between dusk and darkness, between fury and peace,
but, for such as our earth is now, it lasted long.

                                           1981

FROM OMEROS[1]

Book One

Chapter III

III

"Mais qui ça qui rivait-'ous, Philoctete?"[2]

                                  "Moin blessé."[3]
"But what is wrong wif you, Philoctete?"

                                  "I am blest
wif this wound, Ma Kilman,[4] *qui pas ka guérir pièce.*

Which will never heal."

                            "Well, you must take it easy.

1. Modern Greek version of the name Homer. Homer's *Iliad* and *Odyssey* are, along with Dante's *Divine Comedy*, from which Walcott adapts the terza rima stanza, and James Joyce's *Ulysses* (1922), major influences on this Caribbean epic, which moves across centuries and geographies, from Saint Lucia to Africa to Ireland.
2. Pronounced *fee-lock-TET*; a name shared with Philoctetes, who, in the *Iliad* and Sophocles' eponymous play, is abandoned on an island on the way to the Trojan War after receiving a snakebite. The wound never heals and continually torments Philoctetes, who moans uncontrollably. Later the gods decide that the war cannot be won without him, and the Greek soldiers have to go back to the island and beg him to return with them to battle.
3. French patois, punningly mistranslated below, since *blessé* actually means "wounded."
4. The owner of the No Pain Café, Ma Kilman serves in the poem as a sibyl (female prophet) and an obeah woman (one practicing a kind of West Indian sorcery).

5   Go home and lie down, give the foot a lickle°   *little (West Indian English)*
      rest."
    Philoctete, his trouser-legs rolled, stares out to sea

    from the worn rumshop window. The itch in the sore
    tingles like the tendrils of the anemone,
    and the puffed blister of Portuguese man-o'-war.°   *jellyfish*

10 He believed the swelling came from the chained ankles
    of his grandfathers. Or else why was there no cure?
    That the cross he carried was not only the anchor's

    but that of his race, for a village black and poor
    as the pigs that rooted in its burning garbage,
15 then were hooked on the anchors of the abattoir.°   *slaughterhouse*

    Ma Kilman was sewing. She looked up and saw his face
    squinting from the white of the street. He was waiting
    to pass out on the table. This went on for days.

    The ice turned to warm water near the self-hating
20 gesture of clenching his head tight in both hands. She
    heard the boys in blue uniforms, going to school,

    screaming at his elbow: "Pheeloh! Pheelosophee!"
    A mummy embalmed in Vaseline and alcohol.
    In the Egyptian silence she muttered softly:

25 "It have a flower somewhere, a medicine, and ways
    my grandmother would boil it. I used to watch ants
    climbing her white flower-pot. But, God, in which place?"

    Where was this root? What senna,° what tepid   *medicinal herb*
      tisanes,°   *medicinal beverages*
    could clean the branched river of his corrupted blood,
30 whose sap was a wounded cedar's? What did it mean,

    this name that felt like a fever? Well, one good heft
    of his garden-cutlass would slice the damned name clean
    from its rotting yam. He said, *"Merci."*° Then he left.   *Thank you (French)*

Book Six

Chapter XLIX

I

    She bathed him in the brew of the root.[1] The basin
    was one of those cauldrons from the old sugar-mill,
    with its charred pillars, rock pasture, and one grazing

---

1. Ma Kilman is bathing Philoctete to heal his wound.

horse, looking like helmets that have tumbled downhill
5   from an infantry charge. Children rang them with stones.
Wildflowers sprung in them when the dirt found a seam.

She had one in her back yard, close to the crotons,°   *tree or shrub*
agape in its crusted, agonized O: the scream
of centuries. She scraped its rusted scabs, she scoured

10   the mouth of the cauldron, then fed a crackling pyre
with palms and banana-trash. In the scream she poured
tin after kerosene tin, its base black from fire,

of seawater and sulphur. Into this she then fed
the bubbling root and leaves. She led Philoctete
15   to the gurgling lava. Trembling, he entered

his bath like a boy. The lime leaves leeched to his wet
knuckled spine like islands that cling to the basin
of the rusted Caribbean. An icy sweat

glazed his scalp, but he could feel the putrescent shin
20   drain in the seethe like sucked marrow, he felt it drag
the slime from his shame. She rammed him back to his place

as he tried climbing out with: *"Not yet!"* With a rag
sogged in a basin of ice she rubbed his squeezed face
the way boys enjoy their mother's ritual rage,

25   and as he surrendered to her, the foul flower
on his shin whitened and puckered, the corolla
closed its thorns like the sea-egg. What else did it cure?

II

The bow leapt back to the palm of the warrior.
The yoke of the wrong name lifted from his shoulders.
30   His muscles loosened like those of a brown river

that was dammed with silt, and then silkens its boulders
with refreshing strength. His ribs thudded like a horse
cantering on a beach that bursts into full gallop

while a boy yanks at its rein with terrified "Whoas!"
35   The white foam unlocked his coffles, his ribbed shallop
broke from its anchor, and the water, which he swirled

like a child, steered his brow into the right current,
as calm as *In God We Trout*[2] to that other world,
and his flexed palm enclosed an oar with the identi-

---

2. Near the poem's beginning, the character Achille chisels this misspelled phrase into his canoe and then
decides, "Leave it! Is God' spelling and mine" (1.1.2).

40 ical closure of a mouth around its own name,
the way a sea-anemone closes slyly
into a secrecy many mistake for shame.

Centuries weigh down the head of the swamp-lily,
its tribal burden arches the sea-almond's° spine,   *a tree*
45 in barracoon³ back yards the soul-smoke still passes,

but the wound has found her own cure. The soft days spin
the spittle of the spider in webbed glasses,
as she drenches the burning trash to its last flame,

and the embers steam and hiss to the schoolboys' cries
50 when he'd weep in the window for their tribal shame.
A shame for the loss of words, and a language tired

of accepting that loss, and then all accepted.
That was why the sea stank from the frothing urine
of surf, and fish-guts reeked from the government shed,

55 and why God pissed on the village for months of rain.
But now, quite clearly the tears trickled down his face
like rainwater down a cracked carafe from Choiseul,⁴

as he stood like a boy in his bath with the first clay's
innocent prick! So she threw Adam a towel.
60 And the yard was Eden. And its light the first day's.

1990

3. Barracks for housing convicts or slaves.   4. A village in Saint Lucia.

ALICE MUNRO
b. 1931

Alice Munro has become one of the leading short-story writers of her generation. Her fiction combines spareness and realism—an uncompromising look at a panorama of faltering lives—with magisterial vision and expansiveness. Munro's signature approach to the short story, in which she uses a deceptively simple style to produce complex, layered, and emotionally potent effects, has influenced many of her English-language contemporaries, both within and outside Canada. In addition to one novel, *Lives of Girls and Women* (1972), she has published numerous collections of short stories, including *Dance of the Happy Shades* (1968), *Something I've Been Meaning to Tell You* (1974), *The Moons of Jupiter* (1982), *Friend of My Youth* (1990), *The Love of a Good Woman* (1998), *Hateship, Friendship, Courtship, Loveship, Marriage* (2001), and *Runaway* (2004).

    Many of Munro's stories are written in the first person, often from the perspective of women whose voices and experiences suggest the author's history. She was born Alice Anne Laidlaw to a poor family in Wingham, Ontario, and her parents' struggles within a variety of rural occupations continued throughout her childhood. She began

2778 / ALICE MUNRO

writing in her teens and in 1949 enrolled in the University of Western Ontario; she left the university two years later, to marry and raise three daughters. She typically sets her stories in small towns where poverty stamps itself on all facets of life, and where women confront—often in a spirit that combines resignation with stubborn resistance—the triple binds of economic, gender, and cultural confinement. Through a precise and particular emphasis on setting and character, she evokes rural Canadian life in the decades following midcentury, when modernity and the promise of the future are often crowded out by a hardening sense of the past.

In an early writing Munro describes an approach to the outside world that effectively captures her sense of the mystery within the ordinary—the hallmark of her realist style: "It seems as if there are feelings that have to be translated into a next-door language, which might blow them up and burst them altogether; or else they have to be let alone. The truth about them is always suspected, never verified, the light catches but doesn't define them. . . . Yet there is the feeling—I have the feeling—that at some level these things open; fragments, moments, suggestions, open, full of power." This aura of openness and suggestion, conveyed through "next-door language," gives Munro's stories their haunting aspect, their quality of movement, rippling and widening from the small-scale to the magnificent. The story included here, "Walker Brothers Cowboy," exemplifies her ability to imbue "fragments, moments, suggestions" with fullness and power, as we view through a young girl's eyes both the pathos and the degradation of men and women whose lives have fallen into a potentially deadening cycle of promise and decay.

Walker Brothers Cowboy[1]

After supper my father says, "Want to go down and see if the Lake's still there?" We leave my mother sewing under the dining-room light, making clothes for me against[2] the opening of school. She has ripped up for this purpose an old suit and an old plaid wool dress of hers, and she has to cut and match very cleverly and also make me stand and turn for endless fittings, sweaty, itching from the hot wool, ungrateful. We leave my brother in bed in the little screened porch at the end of the front veranda, and sometimes he kneels on his bed and presses his face against the screen and calls mournfully, "Bring me an ice-cream cone!" but I call back, "You will be asleep," and do not even turn my head.

Then my father and I walk gradually down a long, shabby sort of street, with Silverwoods Ice Cream signs standing on the sidewalk, outside tiny, lighted stores. This is in Tuppertown, an old town on Lake Huron,[3] an old grain port. The street is shaded, in some places, by maple trees whose roots have cracked and heaved the sidewalk and spread out like crocodiles into the bare yards. People are sitting out, men in shirtsleeves and undershirts and women in aprons—not people we know but if anybody looks ready to nod and say, "Warm night," my father will nod too and say something the same. Children are still playing. I don't know them either because my mother keeps my brother and me in our own yard, saying he is too young to leave it and I have to mind him. I am not so sad to watch their evening games because the games themselves are ragged, dissolving. Children, of their own will, draw apart, separate into islands of two or one under the heavy trees, occupying themselves in such

---

1. Refers to a traveling salesman for a Canadian company, which is probably modeled on the American direct marketer Watkins Products.
2. In time for.

3. One of the Great Lakes, bordering on Ontario and eastern Michigan. Place-names are both real and invented.

solitary ways as I do all day, planting pebbles in the dirt or writing in it with a stick.

Presently we leave these yards and houses behind; we pass a factory with boarded-up windows, a lumberyard whose high wooden gates are locked for the night. Then the town falls away in a defeated jumble of sheds and small junkyards, the sidewalk gives up and we are walking on a sandy path with burdocks, plantains, humble nameless weeds all around. We enter a vacant lot, a kind of park really, for it is kept clear of junk and there is one bench with a slat missing on the back, a place to sit and look at the water. Which is generally gray in the evening, under a lightly overcast sky, no sunsets, the horizon dim. A very quiet, washing noise on the stones of the beach. Further along, towards the main part of town, there is a stretch of sand, a water slide, floats bobbing around the safe swimming area, a lifeguard's rickety throne. Also a long dark-green building, like a roofed veranda, called the Pavilion, full of farmers and their wives, in stiff good clothes, on Sundays. That is the part of the town we used to know when we lived at Dungannon and came here three or four times a summer, to the Lake. That, and the docks where we would go and look at the grain boats, ancient, rusty, wallowing, making us wonder how they got past the breakwater let alone to Fort William.

Tramps hang around the docks and occasionally on these evenings wander up the dwindling beach and climb the shifting, precarious path boys have made, hanging on to dry bushes, and say something to my father which, being frightened of tramps, I am too alarmed to catch. My father says he is a bit hard up himself. "I'll roll you a cigarette if it's any use to you," he says, and he shakes tobacco out carefully on one of the thin butterfly papers, flicks it with his tongue, seals it and hands it to the tramp, who takes it and walks away. My father also rolls and lights and smokes one cigarette of his own.

He tells me how the Great Lakes came to be. All where Lake Huron is now, he says, used to be flat land, a wide flat plain. Then came the ice, creeping down from the North, pushing deep into the low places. Like *that*—and he shows me his hand with his spread fingers pressing the rock-hard ground where we are sitting. His fingers make hardly any impression at all and he says, "Well, the old ice cap had a lot more power behind it than this hand has." And then the ice went back, shrank back towards the North Pole where it came from, and left its fingers of ice in the deep places it had gouged, and ice turned to lakes and there they were today. They were *new*, as time went. I try to see that plain before me, dinosaurs walking on it, but I am not able even to imagine the shore of the Lake when the Indians were there, before Tuppertown. The tiny share we have of time appalls me, though my father seems to regard it with tranquillity. Even my father, who sometimes seems to me to have been at home in the world as long as it has lasted, has really lived on this earth only a little longer than I have, in terms of all the time there has been to live in. He has not known a time, any more than I, when automobiles and electric lights did not at least exist. He was not alive when this century started. I will be barely alive—old, old—when it ends. I do not like to think of it. I wish the Lake to be always just a lake, with the safe-swimming floats marking it, and the breakwater and the lights of Tuppertown.

My father has a job, selling for Walker Brothers. This is a firm that sells almost entirely in the country, the back country. Sunshine, Boylesbridge, Turnaround—that is all his territory. Not Dungannon where we used to live, Dungannon is too near town and my mother is grateful for that. He sells cough medicine, iron tonic, corn plasters, laxatives, pills for female disorders, mouth-wash, shampoo, liniment, salves, lemon and orange and raspberry concentrate for making refreshing drinks, vanilla, food coloring, black and green tea, gin-ger, cloves, and other spices, rat poison. He has a song about it, with these two lines:

> And have all liniments and oils,
> For everything from corns to boils. . . .

Not a very funny song, in my mother's opinion. A peddler's song, and that is what he is, a peddler knocking at backwoods kitchens. Up until last winter we had our own business, a fox farm. My father raised silver foxes and sold their pelts to the people who make them into capes and coats and muffs. Prices fell, my father hung on hoping they would get better next year, and they fell again, and he hung on one more year and one more and finally it was not possible to hang on anymore, we owed everything to the feed company. I have heard my mother explain this, several times, to Mrs. Oliphant, who is the only neighbor she talks to. (Mrs. Oliphant also has come down in the world, being a schoolteacher who married the janitor.) We poured all we had into it, my mother says, and we came out with nothing. Many people could say the same thing, these days, but my mother has no time for the national calamity, only ours. Fate has flung us onto a street of poor people (it does not matter that we were poor before; that was a different sort of poverty), and the only way to take this, as she sees it, is with dignity, with bitterness, with no reconciliation. No bathroom with a claw-footed tub and a flush toilet is going to comfort her, nor water on tap and sidewalks past the house and milk in bottles, not even the two movie theatres and the Venus Restaurant and Woolworths so mar-vellous it has live birds singing in its fan-cooled corners and fish as tiny as fingernails, as bright as moons, swimming in its green tanks. My mother does not care.

In the afternoons she often walks to Simon's Grocery and takes me with her to help carry things. She wears a good dress, navy blue with little flowers, sheer, worn over a navy-blue slip. Also a summer hat of white straw, pushed down on the side of the head, and white shoes I have just whitened on a newspaper on the back steps. I have my hair freshly done in long damp curls which the dry air will fortunately soon loosen, a stiff large hair ribbon on top of my head. This is entirely different from going out after supper with my father. We have not walked past two houses before I feel we have become objects of universal ridicule. Even the dirty words chalked on the sidewalk are laughing at us. My mother does not seem to notice. She walks serenely like a lady shopping, like a *lady* shopping, past the housewives in loose beltless dresses torn under the arms. With me her creation, wretched curls and flaunt-ing hair bow, scrubbed knees and white socks—all I do not want to be. I loathe even my name when she says it in public, in a voice so high, proud, and ringing, deliberately different from the voice of any other mother on the street.

My mother will sometimes carry home, for a treat, a brick of ice cream—pale Neapolitan; and because we have no refrigerator in our house we wake my brother and eat it at once in the dining room, always darkened by the wall of the house next door. I spoon it up tenderly, leaving the chocolate till last, hoping to have some still to eat when my brother's dish is empty. My mother tries then to imitate the conversations we used to have at Dungannon, going back to our earliest, most leisurely days before my brother was born, when she would give me a little tea and a lot of milk in a cup like hers and we would sit out on the step facing the pump, the lilac tree, the fox pens beyond. She is not able to keep from mentioning those days. "Do you remember when we put you in your sled and Major pulled you?" (Major our dog, that we had to leave with neighbors when we moved.) "Do you remember your sandbox outside the kitchen window?" I pretend to remember far less than I do, wary of being trapped into sympathy or any unwanted emotion.

My mother has headaches. She often has to lie down. She lies on my brother's narrow bed in the little screened porch, shaded by heavy branches. "I look up at that tree and I think I am at home," she says.

"What you need," my father tells her, "is some fresh air and a drive in the country." He means for her to go with him, on his Walker Brothers route.

That is not my mother's idea of a drive in the country.

"Can I come?"

"Your mother might want you for trying on clothes."

"I'm beyond sewing this afternoon," my mother says.

"I'll take her then. Take both of them, give you a rest."

What is there about us that people need to be given a rest from? Never mind. I am glad enough to find my brother and make him go to the toilet and get us both into the car, our knees unscrubbed, my hair unringleted. My father brings from the house his two heavy brown suitcases, full of bottles, and sets them on the back seat. He wears a white shirt, brilliant in the sunlight, a tie, light trousers belonging to his summer suit (his other suit is black, for funerals, and belonged to my uncle before he died), and a creamy straw hat. His salesman's outfit, with pencils clipped in the shirt pocket. He goes back once again, probably to say goodbye to my mother, to ask her if she is sure she doesn't want to come, and hear her say, "No. No thanks, I'm better just to lie here with my eyes closed." Then we are backing out of the driveway with the rising hope of adventure, just the little hope that takes you over the bump into the street, the hot air starting to move, turning into a breeze, the houses growing less and less familiar as we follow the shortcut my father knows, the quick way out of town. Yet what is there waiting for us all afternoon but hot hours in stricken farmyards, perhaps a stop at a country store and three ice-cream cones or bottles of pop, and my father singing? The one he made up about himself has a title—"The Walker Brothers Cowboy"—and it starts out like this:

> Old Ned Fields, he now is dead,
> So I am ridin' the route instead. . . .

Who is Ned Fields? The man he has replaced, surely, and if so he really is dead; yet my father's voice is mournful-jolly, making his death some kind of nonsense, a comic calamity. "Wisht I was back on the Rio Grande,[4] plungin' through the dusky sand." My father sings most of the time while driving the car. Even now, heading out of town, crossing the bridge and taking the sharp turn onto the highway, he is humming something, mumbling a bit of a song to himself, just tuning up, really, getting ready to improvise, for out along the highway we pass the Baptist Camp, the Vacation Bible Camp, and he lets loose:

> Where are the Baptists, where are the Bapists,
> where are all the Baptists today?

4. A large river that begins in Colorado and flows south, becoming the border between Mexico and the United States.

They're down in the water, in Lake Huron water,
    with their sins all a-gittin' washed away.

My brother takes this for straight truth and gets up on his knees trying to
see down to the Lake. "I don't see any Baptists," he says accusingly. "Neither
do I, son," says my father. "I told you, they're down in the Lake."

No roads paved when we left the highway. We have to roll up the windows
because of dust. The land is flat, scorched, empty. Bush lots at the back of
the farms hold shade, black pine-shade like pools nobody can ever get to. We
bump up a long lane and at the end of it what could look more unwelcoming,
more deserted than the tall unpainted farmhouse with grass growing uncut
right up to the front door, green blinds down, and a door upstairs opening on
nothing but air? Many houses have this door, and I have never yet been able
to find out why. I ask my father and he says they are for walking in your sleep.
What? Well, if you happen to be walking in your sleep and you want to step
outside. I am offended, seeing too late that he is joking, as usual, but my
brother says sturdily, "If they did that they would break their necks."

The 1930s. How much this kind of farmhouse, this kind of afternoon seem
to me to belong to that one decade in time, just as my father's hat does, his
bright flared tie, our car with its wide running board (an Essex, and long past
its prime). Cars somewhat like it, many older, none dustier, sit in the farmyards. Some are past running and have their doors pulled off, their seats
removed for use on porches. No living things to be seen, chickens or cattle.
Except dogs. There are dogs lying in any kind of shade they can find, dreaming,
their lean sides rising and sinking rapidly. They get up when my father opens
the car door, he has to speak to them. "Nice boy, there's a boy, nice old boy."
They quiet down, go back to their shade. He should know how to quiet animals, he has held desperate foxes with tongs around their necks. One gentling
voice for the dogs and another, rousing, cheerful, for calling at doors. "Hello
there, missus, it's the Walker Brothers man and what are you out of today?"
A door opens, he disappears. Forbidden to follow, forbidden even to leave the
car, we can just wait and wonder what he says. Sometimes trying to make my
mother laugh, he pretends to be himself in a farm kitchen, spreading out his
sample case. "Now then, missus, are you troubled with parasitic life? Your
children's scalps, I mean. All those crawly little things we're too polite to mention that show up on the heads of the best of families? Soap alone is useless,
kerosene is not too nice a perfume, but I have here—" Or else, "Believe me,
sitting and driving all day the way I do I *know* the value of these fine pills.
Natural relief. A problem common to old folks too, once their days of activity
are over—How about you, Grandma?" He would wave the imaginary box of
pills under my mother's nose and she would laugh finally, unwillingly. "He
doesn't say that really, does he?" I said, and she said no of course not, he was
too much of a gentleman.

One yard after another, then, the old cars, the pumps, dogs, views of gray
barns and falling-down sheds and unturning windmills. The men, if they are
working in the fields, are not in any fields that we can see. The children are
far away, following dry creek beds or looking for blackberries, or else they are
hidden in the house, spying at us through cracks in the blinds. The car seat
has grown slick with our sweat. I dare my brother to sound the horn, wanting
to do it myself but not wanting to get the blame. He knows better. We play I
Spy, but it is hard to find many colors. Gray for the barns and sheds and toilets

and houses, brown for the yard and fields, black or brown for the dogs. The rusting cars show rainbow patches, in which I strain to pick out purple or green; likewise I peer at doors for shreds of old peeling paint, maroon or yellow. We can't play with letters, which would be better, because my brother is too young to spell. The game disintegrates anyway. He claims my colors are not fair, and wants extra turns.

In one house no door opens, though the car is in the yard. My father knocks and whistles, calls, "Hullo there ! Walker Brothers man!" but there is not a stir of reply anywhere. This house has no porch, just a bare, slanting slab of cement on which my father stands. He turns around, searching the barnyard, the barn whose mow must be empty because you can see the sky through it, and finally he bends to pick up his suitcases. Just then a window is opened upstairs, a white pot appears on the sill, is tilted over and its contents splash down the outside wall. The window is not directly above my father's head, so only a stray splash would catch him. He picks up his suitcases with no partic-ular hurry and walks, no longer whistling, to the car. "Do you know what that was?" I say to my brother. "*Pee.*" He laughs and laughs.

My father rolls and lights a cigarette before he starts the car. The window has been slammed down, the blind drawn, we never did see a hand or face. "Pee, pee," sings my brother ecstatically. "Somebody dumped down pee!" "Just don't tell your mother that," my father says. "She isn't liable to see the joke." "Is it in your song?" my brother wants to know. My father says no but he will see what he can do to work it in.

I notice in a little while that we are not turning in any more lanes, though it does not seem to me that we are headed home. "Is this the way to Sunshine?" I ask my father, and he answers, "No, ma'am, it's not." "Are we still in your territory?" He shakes his head. "We're going *fast*," my brother says approvingly, and in fact we are bouncing along through dry puddle-holes so that all the bottles in the suitcases clink together and gurgle promisingly.

Another lane, a house, also unpainted, dried to silver in the sun.

"I thought we were out of your territory."

"We are."

"Then what are we going in here for?"

"You'll see."

In front of the house a short, sturdy woman is picking up washing, which had been spread on the grass to bleach and dry. When the car stops she stares at it hard for a moment, bends to pick up a couple more towels to add to the bundle under her arm, comes across to us and says in a flat voice, neither welcoming nor unfriendly, "Have you lost your way?"

My father takes his time getting out of the car. "I don't think so," he says. "I'm the Walker Brothers man."

"George Golley is our Walker Brothers man," the woman says, "and he was out here no more than a week ago. Oh, my Lord God," she says harshly, "it's you."

"It was, the last time I looked in the mirror," my father says.

The woman gathers all the towels in front of her and holds on to them tightly, pushing them against her stomach as if it hurt. "Of all the people I never thought to see. And telling me you were the Walker Brothers man."

"I'm sorry if you were looking forward to George Golley," my father says humbly.

"And look at me, I was prepared to clean the henhouse. You'll think that's just an excuse but it's true. I don't go round looking like this every day." She is wearing a farmer's straw hat, through which pricks of sunlight penetrate and float on her face, a loose, dirty print smock, and canvas shoes. "Who are those in the car, Ben? They're not yours?"

"Well, I hope and believe they are," my father says, and tells our names and ages. "Come on, you can get out. This is Nora, Miss Cronin. Nora, you better tell me, is it still Miss, or have you got a husband hiding in the woodshed?"

"If I had a husband that's not where I'd keep him, Ben," she says, and they both laugh, her laugh abrupt and somewhat angry. "You'll think I got no manners, as well as being dressed like a tramp," she says. "Come on in out of the sun. It's cool in the house."

We go across the yard ("Excuse me taking you in this way but I don't think the front door has been opened since Papa's funeral, I'm afraid the hinges might drop off"), up the porch steps, into the kitchen, which really is cool, high-ceilinged, the blinds of course down, a simple, clean, threadbare room with waxed worn linoleum, potted geraniums, drinking-pail and dipper, a round table with scrubbed oilcloth. In spite of the cleanness, the wiped and swept surfaces, there is a faint sour smell—maybe of the dishrag or the tin dipper or the oilcloth, or the old lady, because there is one, sitting in an easy chair under the clock shelf. She turns her head slightly in our direction and says, "Nora? Is that company?"

"Blind," says Nora in a quick explaining voice to my father. Then, "You won't guess who it is, Momma. Hear his voice."

My father goes to the front of her chair and bends and says hopefully, "Afternoon, Mrs. Cronin."

"Ben Jordan," says the old lady with no surprise. "You haven't been to see us in the longest time. Have you been out of the country?"

My father and Nora look at each other.

"He's married, Momma," says Nora cheerfully and aggressively. "Married and got two children and here they are." She pulls us forward, makes each of us touch the old lady's dry, cool hand while she says our names in turn. Blind! This is the first blind person I have ever seen close up. Her eyes are closed, the eyelids sunk away down, showing no shape of the eyeball, just hollows. From one hollow comes a drop of silver liquid, a medicine, or a miraculous tear.

"Let me get into a decent dress," Nora says. "Talk to Momma. It's a treat for her. We hardly ever see company, do we, Momma?"

"Not many makes it out this road," says the old lady placidly. "And the ones that used to be around here, our old neighbors, some of them have pulled out."

"True everywhere," my father says.

"Where's your wife then?"

"Home. She's not too fond of the hot weather, makes her feel poorly."

"Well." This is a habit of country people, old people, to say "well," meaning, "Is that so?" with a little extra politeness and concern.

Nora's dress, when she appears again—stepping heavily on Cuban heels down the stairs in the hall—is flowered more lavishly than anything my mother owns, green and yellow on brown, some sort of floating sheer crêpe, leaving her arms bare. Her arms are heavy, and every bit of her skin you can see is covered with little dark freckles like measles. Her hair is short, black, coarse and curly, her teeth very white and strong. "It's the first time I knew there was such a thing as green poppies," my father says, looking at her dress.

"You would be surprised all the things you never knew," says Nora, sending a smell of cologne far and wide when she moves and displaying a change of voice to go with the dress, something more sociable and youthful. "They're not poppies anyway, they're just flowers. You go and pump me some good cold water and I'll make these children a drink." She gets down from the cupboard a bottle of Walker Brothers Orange syrup.

"You telling me you were the Walker Brothers man!"

"It's the truth, Nora. You go and look at my sample cases in the car if you don't believe me. I got the territory directly south of here."

"Walker Brothers? Is that a fact? You selling for Walker Brothers?"

"Yes, ma'am."

"We always heard you were raising foxes over Dungannon way."

"That's what I was doing, but I kind of run out of luck in that business."

"So where're you living? How long've you been out selling?"

"We moved into Tuppertown. I been at it, oh, two, three months. It keeps the wolf from the door. Keeps him as far away as the back fence."

Nora laughs. "Well, I guess you count yourself lucky to have the work. Isabel's husband in Brantford, he was out of work the longest time. I thought if he didn't find something soon I was going to have them all land in here to feed, and I tell you I was hardly looking forward to it. It's all I can manage with me and Momma."

"Isabel married," my father says. "Muriel married too?"

"No, she's teaching school out West. She hasn't been home for five years. I guess she finds something better to do with her holidays. I would if I was her." She gets some snapshots out of the table drawer and starts showing him. "That's Isabel's oldest boy, starting school. That's the baby sitting in her carriage. Isabel and her husband. Muriel. That's her roommate with her. That's a fellow she used to go around with, and his car. He was working in a bank out there. That's her school, it has eight rooms. She teaches Grade Five." My father shakes his head. "I can't think of her any way but when she was going to school, so shy I used to pick her up on the road—I'd be on my way to see you—and she would not say one word, not even to agree it was a nice day."

"She's got over that."

"Who are you talking about?" says the old lady.

"Muriel. I said she's got over being shy."

"She was here last summer."

"No, Momma, that was Isabel. Isabel and her family were here last summer. Muriel's out West."

"I meant Isabel."

Shortly after this the old lady falls asleep, her head on the side, her mouth open. "Excuse her manners," Nora says. "It's old age." She fixes an afghan over her mother and says we can all go into the front room where our talking won't disturb her.

"You two," my father says. "Do you want to go outside and amuse yourselves?"

Amuse ourselves how? Anyway, I want to stay. The front room is more interesting than the kitchen, though barer. There is a gramophone and a pump organ and a picture on the wall of Mary, Jesus' mother—I know that much—in shades of bright blue and pink with a spiked band of light around her head. I know that such pictures are found only in the homes of Roman Catholics and

2786 / Alice Munro

so Nora must be one. We have never known any Roman Catholics at all well, never well enough to visit in their houses. I think of what my grandmother and my Aunt Tena, over in Dungannon, used to always say to indicate that somebody was a Catholic. *So-and-so digs with the wrong foot,* they would say. *She digs with the wrong foot.* That was what they would say about Nora.[5]

Nora takes a bottle, half full, out of the top of the organ and pours some of what is in it into the two glasses that she and my father have emptied of the orange drink.

"Keep it in case of sickness?" my father says.

"Not on your life," says Nora. "I'm never sick. I just keep it because I keep it. One bottle does me a fair time, though, because I don't care for drinking alone. Here's luck!" She and my father drink and I know what it is. Whisky. One of the things my mother has told me in our talks together is that my father never drinks whisky. But I see he does. He drinks whisky and he talks of people whose names I have never heard before. But after a while he turns to a familiar incident. He tells about the chamberpot that was emptied out the window. "Picture me there," he says, "hollering my heartiest. *Oh, lady, it's your Walker Brothers man, anybody home?*" He does himself hollering, grinning absurdly, waiting, looking up in pleased expectation, and then—oh, ducking, covering his head with his arms, looking as if he begged for mercy (when he never did anything like that, I was watching), and Nora laughs, almost as hard as my brother did at the time.

"That isn't true! That's not a word true!"

"Oh, indeed it is, ma'am. We have our heroes in the ranks of Walker Brothers. I'm glad you think it's funny," he says sombrely.

I ask him shyly, "Sing the song."

"What song? Have you turned into a singer on top of everything else?"

Embarrassed, my father says, "Oh, just this song I made up while I was driving around, it gives me something to do, making up rhymes."

But after some urging he does sing it, looking at Nora with a droll, apologetic expression, and she laughs so much that in places he has to stop and wait for her to get over laughing so he can go on, because she makes him laugh too. Then he does various parts of his salesman's spiel. Nora when she laughs squeezes her large bosom under her folded arms. "You're crazy," she says. "That's all you are." She sees my brother peering into the gramophone and she jumps up and goes over to him. "Here's us sitting enjoying ourselves and not giving you a thought, isn't it terrible?" she says. "You want me to put a record on, don't you? You want to hear a nice record? Can you dance? I bet your sister can, can't she?"

I say no. "A big girl like you and so good-looking and can't dance!" says Nora. "It's high time you learned. I bet you'd make a lovely dancer. Here, I'm going to put on a piece I used to dance to and even your daddy did, in his dancing days. You didn't know your daddy was a dancer, did you? Well, he is a talented man, your daddy!"

She puts down the lid and takes hold of me unexpectedly around the waist, picks up my other hand, and starts making me go backwards. "This is the way, now, this is how they dance. Follow me. This foot, see. One and one-two. One and one-two. That's fine, that's lovely, don't look at your feet!

---

5. Relations between Protestants and Catholics within the Irish population in southern Ontario were often strained.

Follow me, that's right, see how easy? You're going to be a lovely dancer!
One and one-two. One and one-two. Ben, see your daughter dancing!"
Whispering while you cuddle near me, Whispering so no one can hear me . . .[6]
    Round and round the linoleum, me proud, intent, Nora laughing and mov-
ing with great buoyancy, wrapping me in her strange gaiety, her smell of
whisky, cologne, and sweat. Under the arms her dress is damp, and little drops
form along her upper lip, hang in the soft black hairs at the corners of her
mouth. She whirls me around in front of my father—causing me to stumble,
for I am by no means so swift a pupil as she pretends—and lets me go,
breathless.
    "Dance with me, Ben."
    "I'm the world's worst dancer, Nora, and you know it."
    "I certainly never thought so."
    "You would now."
    She stands in front of him, arms hanging loose and hopeful, her breasts,
which a moment ago embarrassed me with their warmth and bulk, rising and
falling under her loose flowered dress, her face shining with the exercise, and
delight.
    "Ben."
    My father drops his head and says quietly, "Not me, Nora."
    So she can only go and take the record off. "I can drink alone but I can't
dance alone," she says. "Unless I am a whole lot crazier than I think I am."
    "Nora," says my father, smiling. "You're not crazy."
    "Stay for supper."
    "Oh, no. We couldn't put you to the trouble."
    "It's no trouble. I'd be glad of it."
    "And their mother would worry. She'd think I'd turned us over in a ditch."
    "Oh, well. Yes."
    "We've taken a lot of your time now."
    "Time," says Nora bitterly. "Will you come by ever again?"
    "I will if I can," says my father.
    "Bring the children. Bring your wife."
    "Yes, I will," says my father. "I will if I can."
    When she follows us to the car he says, "You come to see us too, Nora.
We're right on Grove Street, left-hand side going in, that's north, and two
doors this side—east—of Baker Street."
    Nora does not repeat these directions. She stands close to the car in her
soft, brilliant dress. She touches the fender, making an unintelligible mark in
the dust there.

    On the way home my father does not buy any ice cream or pop, but he does
go into a country store and get a package of licorice, which he shares with us.
She digs with the wrong foot, I think, and the words seem sad to me as never
before, dark, perverse. My father does not say anything to me about not mentioning things at home, but I know, just from the thoughtfulness, the pause
when he passes the licorice, that there are things not to be mentioned. The
whisky, maybe the dancing. No worry about my brother, he does not notice
enough. At most he might remember the blind lady, the picture of Mary.

---

6. From the popular song "Whispering," whose original 1920 recording was one of the first records to sell
a million copies.

"Sing," my brother commands my father, but my father says gravely, "I don't know, I seem to be fresh out of songs. You watch the road and let me know if you see any rabbits."

So my father drives and my brother watches the road for rabbits and I feel my father's life flowing back from our car in the last of the afternoon, darkening and turning strange, like a landscape that has an enchantment on it, making it kindly, ordinary and familiar while you are looking at it, but changing it, once your back is turned, into something you will never know, with all kinds of weathers, and distances you cannot imagine.

When we get closer to Tuppertown the sky becomes gently overcast, as always, nearly always, on summer evenings by the Lake.

1968

SEAMUS HEANEY
b. 1939

Seamus Heaney was born into a Roman Catholic family in predominantly Protestant North Ireland (or Ulster), and he grew up on a farm in County Derry bordered on one side by a stream that marked the frontier with the largely Catholic Irish Republic (or Eire) to the south. He won scholarships first to St. Columb's College, a Catholic boarding school, and then to Queen's University in Belfast. There he became one of an extraordinary group of Northern Irish poets from both Protestant and Catholic backgrounds, including Michael Longley and Derek Mahon, who read, discussed, and spurred on one another's work. He taught at Queen's University, before moving in 1972 to the Irish Republic, where he became a citizen and full-time writer. He has been Boylston Professor of Rhetoric and Oratory at Harvard and Professor of Poetry at Oxford, and in 1995 won the Nobel Prize in Literature.

With "Digging," placed appropriately as the first poem of his first book, Heaney defined his territory. He dug into his memory, uncovering first his father and then, going deeper, his grandfather. This idea of poetry as an archaeological process of recovery took on a darker cast after the eruption of internecine violence in Northern Ireland in 1969, culminating in the 1972 Bloody Sunday killing of thirteen Catholic civilians by British paratroopers during a civil rights march in Derry. Across several volumes, especially *North* (1975), Heaney wrote a series of grim "bog poems," about well-preserved Iron Age corpses discovered in the peat of Northern Europe and Ireland. In these poems he sees the bog as a "memory bank," or unconscious, that preserves everything thrown into it, including the victims of ritual killings. He views contemporary violence through the lens of ancient myths, sacrifices, and feuds, an oblique approach that gives his poetry about the Troubles an unusual depth and resonance. He had discovered emblems for the violence in Northern Ireland in *The Bog People*, a book by the Danish archaeologist P. V. Glob, published in translation in 1969, "the year the killing started." Heaney wrote of it:

> It was chiefly concerned with preserved bodies of men and women found in the bogs of Jutland, naked, strangled or with their throats cut, disposed under the peat since early Iron Age times. The author . . . argues convincingly that a number of these, and in particular, the Tollund Man, whose head is now preserved near Aarhus in the museum of Silkeburg, were ritual sacrifices to the Mother Goddess, the goddess of the ground who needed new bridegrooms each winter to bed with her in her sacred place, in the spring. Taken in relation to the tradition

of Irish political martyrdom for the cause whose icon is Kathleen Ni Houlihan [mythic figure emblematic of Mother Ireland], this is more than an archaic barbarous rite: it is an archetypal pattern. And the unforgettable photographs of these victims blended in my mind with photographs of atrocities, past and present, in the long rites of Irish political and religious struggles. ("Feeling into Words")

In the bog poems Heaney reflects on the poet's responsibilities to write about the dead, yet to do so without prettifying or exploiting them. He probes the vexed relations between lyric song and historical suffering, "beauty and atrocity": the need to be true to his calling as artist, but also to represent the irredeemable carnage of modern political violence—"the actual weight / of each hooded victim / slashed and dumped" ("The Grauballe Man"). The result is a tough-minded witnessing, an ethically scrupulous and self-aware mourning of collective loss and sectarian murder. (For more on the Troubles, see "Imagining Ireland" at Norton Literature Online.)

Since the late 1970s Heaney has continued to elegize victims of the Troubles, such as his acquaintance Louis O'Neill, in "Casualty," as well as more personal losses, such as the natural death of his mother, in "Clearances." He has also written poems about domestic love, such as "The Skunk" and "The Sharping Stone." Heaney is thus both a private poet—skillfully kneading grief, love, and wonder into poems about his family and his humble origins—and a public poet, affirming his affinities with the Catholic civil rights movement, which has struggled against British and Protestant domination. Even in his public poetry he refuses slogans, journalistic reportage, and political pieties, scrutinizing instead the wellsprings of collective identity, the ambivalences of individual response to history.

An Irishman writing in the language of the British Empire, he has translated Gaelic poetry and renewed specifically Irish traditions, such as the *aisling,* or vision poem, but he is also steeped in the English literary canon, drawing on British poetry from *Beowulf* (his prize-winning translation appears in volume 1 of this anthology) to the works of William Wordsworth, Gerard Manley Hopkins, and Ted Hughes. Straddling in his verse a multiplicity of divisions, transubstantiating crisscross feelings into unexpected images and intricate sonorities, Heaney has been embraced by popular audiences for his accessible style and yet also admired by poets and academic critics for his lyric subtlety and rigorous technique.

Formally, his poetry ranges from strenuous free verse—the clipped lines and unrhymed quatrains of the bog poems—to more traditional forms, such as the modified terza rima of "Station Island" and the sonnet sequence "Clearances." His poems are earthy and matter-of-fact, saturated with the physical textures, sights, smells, and sounds of farm life, and they are also visionary, lit up by hope and spirit, enacting penitential pilgrimages and unbridled imaginings. That Heaney's poetry is both earthbound and airborne, free and formed, public and private helps explain why he is seen by many as the most gifted English-language poet of his generation.

Digging

Between my finger and my thumb
The squat pen rests; snug as a gun.

Under my window, a clean rasping sound
When the spade sinks into gravelly ground:
5   My father, digging. I look down

Till his straining rump among the flowerbeds
Bends low, comes up twenty years away

Stooping in rhythm through potato drills[1]
Where he was digging.

10   The coarse boot nestled on the lug, the shaft
Against the inside knee was levered firmly.
He rooted out tall tops, buried the bright edge deep
To scatter new potatoes that we picked
Loving their cool hardness in our hands.

15   By God, the old man could handle a spade.
Just like his old man.

My grandfather cut more turf[2] in a day
Than any other man on Toner's bog.
Once I carried him milk in a bottle
20   Corked sloppily with paper. He straightened up
To drink it, then fell to right away
Nicking and slicing neatly, heaving sods
Over his shoulder, going down and down
For the good turf. Digging.

25   The cold smell of potato mould, the squelch and slap
Of soggy peat, the curt cuts of an edge
Through living roots awaken in my head.
But I've no spade to follow men like them.

Between my finger and my thumb
30   The squat pen rests.
I'll dig with it.

1966

The Forge

All I know is a door into the dark.
Outside, old axles and iron hoops rusting;
Inside, the hammered anvil's short-pitched ring,
The unpredictable fantail of sparks
5   Or hiss when a new shoe toughens in water.
The anvil must be somewhere in the centre,
Horned as a unicorn, at one end square,
Set there immoveable: an altar
Where he expends himself in shape and music.
10   Sometimes, leather-aproned, hairs in his nose,
He leans out on the jamb, recalls a clatter
Of hoofs where traffic is flashing in rows;
Then grunts and goes in, with a slam and flick
To beat real iron out, to work the bellows.

1969

1. Small furrows in which seeds are sown.
2. Slabs of peat that, when dried, are a common domestic fuel in Ireland.

The Grauballe Man[1]

As if he had been poured
in tar, he lies
on a pillow of turf
and seems to weep

5   the black river of himself.
The grain of his wrists
is like bog oak,
the ball of his heel

like a basalt egg.
10   His instep has shrunk
cold as a swan's foot
or a wet swamp root.

His hips are the ridge
and purse of a mussel,
15   his spine an eel arrested
under a glisten of mud.

The head lifts,
the chin is a visor
raised above the vent
20   of his slashed throat

that has tanned and toughened.
The cured wound
opens inwards to a dark
elderberry place.

25   Who will say 'corpse'
to his vivid cast?
Who will say 'body'
to his opaque repose?

And his rusted hair,
30   a mat unlikely
as a foetus's.
I first saw his twisted face

in a photograph,
a head and shoulder
35   out of the peat,
bruised like a forceps baby,

but now he lies
perfected in my memory,
down to the red horn
40   of his nails,

---

1. A body exhumed from a Danish bog and photographed in P. V. Glob's book *The Bog People*.

hung in the scales
with beauty and atrocity:
with the Dying Gaul[2]
too strictly compassed

45   on his shield,
with the actual weight
of each hooded victim,
slashed and dumped.

1969

Punishment[1]

I can feel the tug
of the halter at the nape
of her neck, the wind
on her naked front.

5   It blows her nipples
to amber beads,
it shakes the frail rigging
of her ribs.

I can see her drowned
10   body in the bog,
the weighing stone,
the floating rods and boughs.

Under which at first
she was a barked sapling
15   that is dug up
oak-bone, brain-firkin:°   *small cask*

her shaved head
like a stubble of black corn,
her blindfold a soiled bandage,
20   her noose a ring

2. Roman marble reproduction of a Greek bronze sculpture depicting a wounded soldier of Gaul, whose matted hair identifies him as a Celt, in Rome's Capitoline Museum.
1. In 1951 the peat-stained body of a young girl, who lived in the late 1st century C.E., was recovered from a bog in Windeby, Germany. As P. V. Glob describes her in *The Bog People*, she "lay naked in the hole in the peat, a bandage over the eyes and a collar round the neck. The band across the eyes was drawn tight and had cut into the neck and the base of the nose. We may feel sure that it had been used to close her eyes to this world. There was no mark of strangulation on the neck, so that it had not been used for that purpose." Her hair "had been shaved off with a razor on the left side

of the head. . . . When the brain was removed the convolutions and folds of the surface could be clearly seen [Glob reproduces a photograph of her brain]. . . . This girl of only fourteen had had an inadequate winter diet. . . . To keep the young body under, some birch branches and a big stone were laid upon her." According to the Roman historian Tacitus, the Germanic peoples punished adulterous women by shaving off their hair and then scourging them out of the village or killing them. More recently, her "betraying sisters" were sometimes shaved, stripped, tarred, and handcuffed by the Irish Republican Army (IRA) to the railings of Belfast in punishment for keeping company with British soldiers.

to store
the memories of love.
Little adultress,
before they punished you

25   you were flaxen-haired,
undernourished, and your
tar-black face was beautiful.
My poor scapegoat,

I almost love you
30   but would have cast, I know,
the stones of silence.
I am the artful voyeur

of your brain's exposed
and darkened combs,°   *valleys*
35   your muscles' webbing
and all your numbered bones:

I who have stood dumb
when your betraying sisters,
cauled° in tar,   *wrapped, enclosed*
40   wept by the railings,

who would connive
in civilized outrage
yet understand the exact
and tribal, intimate revenge.

1975

Casualty

1

He would drink by himself
And raise a weathered thumb
Towards the high shelf,
Calling another rum
5   And blackcurrant, without
Having to raise his voice,
Or order a quick stout°   *strong dark beer*
By a lifting of the eyes
And a discreet dumb-show
10   Of pulling off the top;
At closing time would go
In waders and peaked cap
Into the showery dark,
A dole-kept¹ breadwinner

1. I.e., receiving unemployment benefits.

2794 / Seamus Heaney

15   But a natural for work.
      I loved his whole manner,
      Sure-footed but too sly,
      His deadpan sidling tact,
      His fisherman's quick eye
20   And turned observant back.
      Incomprehensible
      To him, my other life.
      Sometimes, on his high stool,
      Too busy with his knife
25   At a tobacco plug
      And not meeting my eye
      In the pause after a slug°   gulp of liquor
      He mentioned poetry.
      We would be on our own
30   And, always politic
      And shy of condescension,
      I would manage by some trick
      To switch the talk to eels
      Or lore of the horse and cart
35   Or the Provisionals.[2]

      But my tentative art
      His turned back watches too:
      He was blown to bits
      Out drinking in a curfew
40   Others obeyed, three nights
      After they shot dead
      The thirteen men in Derry.
      PARAS THIRTEEN, the walls said,
      BOGSIDE NIL.[3] That Wednesday
45   Everybody held
      His breath and trembled.

                    2

      It was a day of cold
      Raw silence, wind-blown
      Surplice and soutane:[4]
50   Rained-on, flower-laden
      Coffin after coffin
      Seemed to float from the door
      Of the packed cathedral
      Like blossoms on slow water.
55   The common funeral
      Unrolled its swaddling band,[5]
      Lapping, tightening

2. The Provisional branch of the IRA.
3. This graffito records—in the form of a soccer match score—that the British Army's Parachute Regiment had killed thirteen people; the Roman Catholic inhabitants of Derry's Bogside district, none. The IRA bombing occurred after the killing of Catholic demonstrators on Bloody Sunday, January 30, 1972.
4. Vestments worn by Roman Catholic priests.
5. Long cloth in which babies were once wrapped to restrain and warm them.

Till we were braced and bound
Like brothers in a ring.

60   But he would not be held
At home by his own crowd
Whatever threats were phoned,
Whatever black flags waved.
I see him as he turned
65   In that bombed offending place,
Remorse fused with terror
In his still knowable face,
His cornered outfaced stare
Blinding in the flash.

70   He had gone miles away
For he drank like a fish
Nightly, naturally
Swimming towards the lure
Of warm lit-up places,
75   The blurred mesh and murmur
Drifting among glasses
In the gregarious smoke.
How culpable was he
That last night when he broke
80   Our tribe's complicity?[6]
'Now you're supposed to be
An educated man,'
I hear him say. 'Puzzle me
The right answer to that one.'

3

85   I missed his funeral,
Those quiet walkers
And sideways talkers
Shoaling out of his lane
To the respectable
90   Purring of the hearse . . .
They move in equal pace
With the habitual
Slow consolation
Of a dawdling engine,
95   The line lifted, hand
Over fist, cold sunshine
On the water, the land
Banked under fog: that morning
I was taken in his boat,
100   The screw° purling, turning   *propellor*
Indolent fathoms white,
I tasted freedom with him.
To get out early, haul

---

6. The Roman Catholic community's agreement to obey the curfew (of lines 39–40).

Steadily off the bottom,
105 Dispraise the catch, and smile
As you find a rhythm
Working you, slow mile by mile,
Into your proper haunt
Somewhere, well out, beyond . . .

110 Dawn-sniffing revenant,[7]
Plodder through midnight rain,
Question me again.

1979

The Skunk

Up, black, striped and damasked like the chasuble[1]
At a funeral mass, the skunk's tail
Paraded the skunk. Night after night
I expected her like a visitor.

5   The refrigerator whinnied into silence.
My desk light softened beyond the verandah.
Small oranges loomed in the orange tree.
I began to be tense as a voyeur.

After eleven years I was composing
10   Love-letters again, broaching the word 'wife'
Like a stored cask, as if its slender vowel
Had mutated into the night earth and air

Of California. The beautiful, useless
Tang of eucalyptus spelt your absence.
15   The aftermath of a mouthful of wine
Was like inhaling you off a cold pillow.

And there she was, the intent and glamorous,
Ordinary, mysterious skunk,
Mythologized, demythologized,
20   Snuffing the boards five feet beyond me.

It all came back to me last night, stirred
By the sootfall of your things at bedtime,
Your head-down, tail-up hunt in a bottom drawer
For the black plunge-line nightdress.

1979

7. One returned from the dead.
1. Sleeveless vestment worn by the priest celebrating Mass, its color regulated by the feast of the
day. "Damasked": woven with elaborate designs.

From Station Island[1]

12

Like a convalescent, I took the hand
stretched down from the jetty, sensed again
an alien comfort as I stepped on ground

to find the helping hand still gripping mine,
5   fish-cold and bony, but whether to guide
or to be guided I could not be certain

for the tall man in step at my side
seemed blind, though he walked straight as a rush
upon his ash plant,[2] his eyes fixed straight ahead.

10   Then I knew him in the flesh
out there on the tarmac° among the cars,   *blacktop surface*
wintered hard and sharp as a blackthorn bush.

His voice eddying with the vowels of all rivers[3]
came back to me, though he did not speak yet,
15   a voice like a prosecutor's or a singer's,

cunning,[4] narcotic, mimic, definite
as a steel nib's downstroke, quick and clean,
and suddenly he hit a litter basket

with his stick, saying, "Your obligation
20   is not discharged by any common rite.
What you must do must be done on your own

so get back in harness. The main thing is to write
for the joy of it. Cultivate a work-lust
that imagines its haven like your hands at night

25   dreaming the sun in the sunspot of a breast.
You are fasted now, light-headed, dangerous.
Take off from here. And don't be so earnest,

let others wear the sackcloth and the ashes.[5]
Let go, let fly, forget.
30   You've listened long enough. Now strike your note."

---

1. *Station Island* is a sequence of dream encounters with familiar ghosts, set on Station Island on Lough Derg in Co. Donegal. The island is also known as St. Patrick's Purgatory because of a tradition that Patrick was the first to establish the penitential vigil of fasting and praying which still constitutes the basis of the three-day pilgrimage. Each unit of the contemporary pilgrim's exercises is called a 'station,' and a large part of each station involves walking barefoot and praying round the 'beds,' stone circles which are said to be the remains of early medieval monastic cells [Heaney's note]. In this last section of the poem, the familiar ghost is that of Heaney's countryman James Joyce. Cf. the stanza form and encounter with a ghost in T. S. Eliot's "Little Gidding."
2. Walking stick made of ash, like the one carried by Stephen Dedalus in Joyce's *Ulysses*. (See the opening paragraphs of "Proteus," p. 2535.) Joyce was almost blind.
3. The Anna Livia Plurabelle episode of *Finnegans Wake* resounds with the names of many rivers.
4. "The only arms I allow myself to use—silence, exile, and cunning" (Joyce, *A Portrait of the Artist as a Young Man*).
5. As worn by penitents in biblical times and later.

2798 / Seamus Heaney

It was as if I had stepped free into space
alone with nothing that I had not known
already. Raindrops blew in my face

as I came to. "Old father, mother's son,
35   there is a moment in Stephen's diary
for April the thirteenth, a revelation

set among my stars—that one entry
has been a sort of password in my ears,
the collect of a new epiphany,[6]

40   the Feast of the Holy Tundish."[7] "Who cares,"
he jeered, "any more? The English language
belongs to us. You are raking at dead fires,

a waste of time for somebody your age.
That subject° people stuff is a cod's° game,   *colonized / fool's*
45   infantile, like your peasant pilgrimage.

You lose more of yourself than you redeem
doing the decent thing. Keep at a tangent.
When they make the circle wide, it's time to swim

out on your own and fill the element
50   with signatures on your own frequency,
echo soundings, searches, probes, allurements,

elver-gleams[8] in the dark of the whole sea."
The shower broke in a cloudburst, the tarmac
fumed and sizzled. As he moved off quickly

55   the downpour loosed its screens round his straight walk.

                                                              1984

Clearances

in memoriam M.K.H.,[1] 1911–1984

She taught me what her uncle once taught her:
How easily the biggest coal block split
If you got the grain and hammer angled right.

---

6. Manifestation of a superhuman being, as of the
infant Jesus to the Magi (Matthew 2). In the Christian calendar, the Feast of the Epiphany is January 6. "Epiphany" was also Joyce's term for the
"sudden revelation of the whatness of a thing."
"Collect": short prayer assigned to a particular day.
7. See the end of James Joyce's *Portrait of the Artist as a Young Man* [Heaney's note]: "*13 April:* That

tundish [funnel] has been on my mind for a long
time. I looked it up and find it English and good
old blunt English too. Damn the dean of studies
and his funnel! What did he come here for to teach
us his own language or to learn it from us? Damn
him one way or the other!"
8. Gleams as of young eels.
1. Margaret Kathleen Heaney, the poet's mother.

> The sound of that relaxed alluring blow,
5 > Its co-opted and obliterated echo,
> Taught me to hit, taught me to loosen,
>
> Taught me between the hammer and the block
> To face the music. Teach me now to listen,
> To strike it rich behind the linear black.

1

10 A cobble thrown a hundred years ago
Keeps coming at me, the first stone
Aimed at a great-grandmother's turncoat brow.[2]
The pony jerks and the riot's on.
She's crouched low in the trap
15 Running the gauntlet that first Sunday
Down the brae° to Mass at a panicked gallop.   *steep slope*
He whips on through the town to cries of 'Lundy!'[3]

Call her 'The Convert'. 'The Exogamous[4] Bride'.
Anyhow, it is a genre piece
20 Inherited on my mother's side
And mine to dispose with now she's gone.
Instead of silver and Victorian lace,
The exonerating, exonerated stone.

2

Polished linoleum shone there. Brass taps shone.
25 The china cups were very white and big—
An unchipped set with sugar bowl and jug.
The kettle whistled. Sandwich and teascone
Were present and correct. In case it run,
The butter must be kept out of the sun.
30 And don't be dropping crumbs. Don't tilt your chair.
Don't reach. Don't point. Don't make noise when you stir.

It is Number 5, New Row, Land of the Dead,
Where grandfather is rising from his place
With spectacles pushed back on a clean bald head
35 To welcome a bewildered homing daughter
Before she even knocks. 'What's this? What's this?'
And they sit down in the shining room together.

3

When all the others were away at Mass
I was all hers as we peeled potatoes.
40 They broke the silence, let fall one by one

<hr>

2. Heaney's Protestant great-grandmother married a Catholic.
3. I.e., traitor. In 1688 the Irish colonel Robert Lundy knew that Derry (or Londonderry) would be invaded by the English, but failed to prepare adequate defenses.
4. Married outside the group.

Like solder weeping off the soldering iron:
Cold comforts set between us, things to share
Gleaming in a bucket of clean water.
And again let fall. Little pleasant splashes
45 From each other's work would bring us to our senses.

So while the parish priest at her bedside
Went hammer and tongs at the prayers for the dying
And some were responding and some crying
I remembered her head bent towards my head,
50 Her breath in mine, our fluent dipping knives—
Never closer the whole rest of our lives.

4

Fear of affectation made her affect
Inadequacy whenever it came to
Pronouncing words 'beyond her'. *Bertold Brek.*[5]
55 She'd manage something hampered and askew
Every time, as if she might betray
The hampered and inadequate by too
Well-adjusted a vocabulary.
With more challenge than pride, she'd tell me, 'You
60 Know all them things.' So I governed my tongue
In front of her, a genuinely well-
adjusted adequate betrayal
Of what I knew better. I'd *naw* and *aye*
And decently relapse into the wrong
65 Grammar which kept us allied and at bay.

5

The cool that came off sheets just off the line
Made me think the damp must still be in them
But when I took my corners of the linen
And pulled against her, first straight down the hem
70 And then diagonally, then flapped and shook
The fabric like a sail in a cross-wind,
They made a dried-out undulating thwack.
So we'd stretch and fold and end up hand to hand
For a split second as if nothing had happened
75 For nothing had that had not always happened
Beforehand, day by day, just touch and go,
Coming close again by holding back
In moves where I was x and she was o
Inscribed in sheets she'd sewn from ripped-out flour sacks.

---

5. Bertolt Brecht (1898–1956), German playwright.

6

80 In the first flush of the Easter holidays
The ceremonies during Holy Week
Were highpoints of our *Sons and Lovers*[6] phase.
The midnight fire. The paschal candlestick.[7]
Elbow to elbow, glad to be kneeling next
85 To each other up there near the front
Of the packed church, we would follow the text
And rubrics° for the blessing of the font.[8]   rules
As the hind longs for the streams, so my soul . . .[9]
Dippings. Towellings. The water breathed on.
90 The water mixed with chrism[1] and with oil.
Cruet[2] tinkle. Formal incensation
And the psalmist's outcry taken up with pride:
Day and night my tears have been my bread.[3]

7

In the last minutes he said more to her
95 Almost than in all their life together.
'You'll be in New Row on Monday night
And I'll come up for you and you'll be glad
When I walk in the door . . . Isn't that right?'
His head was bent down to her propped-up head.
100 She could not hear but we were overjoyed.
He called her good and girl. Then she was dead,
The searching for a pulsebeat was abandoned
And we all knew one thing by being there.
The space we stood around had been emptied
105 Into us to keep, it penetrated
Clearances that suddenly stood open.
High cries were felled and a pure change happened.

8

I thought of walking round and round a space
Utterly empty, utterly a source
110 Where the decked chestnut tree had lost its place
In our front hedge above the wallflowers.
The white chips jumped and jumped and skited[4] high.
I heard the hatchet's differentiated
Accurate cut, the crack, the sigh
115 And collapse of what luxuriated
Through the shocked tips and wreckage of it all.
Deep planted and long gone, my coeval[5]
Chestnut from a jam jar in a hole,

6. Novel (1913) by the English writer D. H. Lawrence (1885–1930) that largely centers on the oedipal relationship between a mother and son.
7. Large candle lit during a ceremony on Holy Saturday, which precedes Easter.
8. Receptacle for holy water.

9. Psalms 42.1.
1. Mixture of olive oil and balsam.
2. Small vessel for wine or water.
3. Psalms 42.3.
4. Shot off obliquely.
5. Of the same age.

Its heft and hush become a bright nowhere,
120   A soul ramifying and forever
Silent, beyond silence listened for.

1987

The Sharping Stone[1]

In an apothecary's° chest of drawers,   *pharmacist's*
Sweet cedar that we'd purchased second hand,
In one of its weighty deep-sliding recesses
I found the sharping stone that was to be
5   Our gift to him. Still in its wrapping paper.
Like a baton of black light I'd failed to pass.

•

Airless cinder-depths. But all the same,
The way it lay there, it wakened something too . . .
I thought of us that evening on the logs,
10   Flat on our backs, the pair of us, parallel,
Supported head to heel, arms straight, eyes front,
Listening to the rain drip off the trees
And saying nothing, braced to the damp bark.
What possessed us? The bare, lopped loveliness
15   Of those two winter trunks, the way they seemed
Prepared for launching, at right angles across
A causeway of short fence-posts set like rollers.
Neither of us spoke. The puddles waited.
The workers had gone home, saws fallen silent.
20   And next thing down we lay, babes in the wood,
Gazing up at the flood-face of the sky
Until it seemed a flood was carrying us
Out of the forest park, feet first, eyes front,
Out of November, out of middle age,
25   Together, out, across the Sea of Moyle.[2]

•

Sarcophage des époux.[3] In terra cotta.
Etruscan couple shown side by side,
Recumbent on left elbows, husband pointing
With his right arm and watching where he points,
30   Wife in front, her earrings in, her braids
Down to her waist, taking her sexual ease.
He is all eyes, she is all brow and dream,
Her right forearm and hand held out as if
Some bird she sees in her deep inward gaze
35   Might be about to roost there. Domestic
Love, the artist thought, warm tones and property,

1. Whetstone for sharpening metal blades.
2. Channel between the northwestern coast of
County Antrim in Ireland and the southwestern
coast of Scotland.
3. Coffin for a married couple.

The frangibility of terra cotta . . .
Which is how they figured on the colour postcard
(*Louvre, Département des Antiquités*)[4]
40 That we'd sent him once, then found among his things.

•

He loved inspired mistakes: his Spanish grandson's
English transliteration, thanking him
For a boat trip: 'That was a marvellous
Walk on the water, granddad.' And indeed
45 He walked on air himself, never more so
Than when he had been widowed and the youth
In him, the athlete who had wooed her—
Breasting tapes and clearing the high bars—
Grew lightsome once again. Going at eighty
50 On the bendiest roads, going for broke
At every point-to-point[5] and poker-school,
'He commenced his wild career' a second time
And not a bother on him. Smoked like a train
And took the power mower in his stride.
55 Flirted and vaunted. Set fire to his bed.
Fell from a ladder. Learned to microwave.

•

So set the drawer on freshets° of thaw water   *surges*
And place the unused sharping stone inside it:
To be found next summer on a riverbank
60 Where scythes once hung all night in alder trees
And mowers played dawn scherzos[6] on the blades,
Their arms like harpists' arms, one drawing towards,
One sweeping the bright rim of the extreme.

1996

4. Department of Antiquities, Louvre Museum, Paris, in which this Etruscan funerary statue, known as *The Cerveteri Couple*, is to be found.

5. Horse race over jumps.
6. Vigorous light and playful musical compositions.

J. M. COETZEE
b. 1940

John Michael Coetzee was born in Cape Town, South Africa. His mother was a schoolteacher; his father, a lawyer who became a sheepherder after losing his job. When Coetzee was eight, his family left the provinces, and he chronicles this and other parts of his childhood in third-person memoirs, *Boyhood: Scenes from a Provincial Life* (1997) and *Youth: Scenes from a Provincial Life II* (2002). Coetzee was educated in Cape Town and then lived in London for a few years, working as a computer programmer, before earning his Ph.D. from the University of Texas at Austin, where he wrote a dissertation on the fiction of Samuel Beckett—a major influence along with Kafka and Dostoyevsky, on Coetzee's fiction. He was appointed, first, assistant professor and, subsequently, Butler Professor of English at the State University of New York at Buffalo. In 1984 he returned to South Africa as professor of general literature at the University of Cape Town, and since 2002 he has lived in Australia. Coetzee is the first novelist to win the prestigious Booker Prize twice, and in 2003 he was awarded the Nobel Prize in Literature.

The central concern of Coetzee's fiction—the oppressive nature of colonialism—made its appearance with his first book, *Dusklands* (1974). This consists of two novellas, one set in the U.S. State Department during the Vietnam War, the other in southern Africa two hundred years earlier. The protagonists of these seemingly different stories—Eugene Dawn, an expert in psychological warfare, and Jacobus Coetzee, an explorer and pioneer—are engaged in similar projects, each leading to oppression and murder. Coetzee's subsequent novels include *In the Heart of the Country* (1977), a feminist anticolonial fable in the voice of a mad South African farmwoman; *Life and Times of Michael K* (1983), about a homeless man trying to survive in war-torn Africa; *Foe* (1986), a retelling of Daniel Defoe's *Robinson Crusoe* from the perspective of a female castaway; *The Master of Petersburg* (1994), a fictionalized account of Dostoyevsky's life; *Disgrace* (1999), about sexual harassment, rape, and race relations; and *Elizabeth Costello: Eight Lessons* (2003), which blends essay and fiction. His many essays and works of criticism have concerned censorship, the rights of animals, South African history, and other themes.

Coetzee is at once a passionate political novelist and an intensely literary one, both qualities emerging in his most compelling indictment of colonialism, *Waiting for the Barbarians* (1980). This novel takes its title and theme from a well-known poem by the Greek poet Constantine Cavafy (1863–1933), which ends (in Rae Dalven's translation):

> . . . night is here but the barbarians have not come.
> Some people arrived from the frontiers,
> And they said that there are no longer any barbarians.
>
> And now what shall become of us without any barbarians?
> Those people were a kind of solution.

In Coetzee's novel the rulers of the unnamed empire claim it is threatened by barbarians, but the barbarian threat is, at least in part, a fantasy concocted by the empire to hold itself together. The narrator is a magistrate in charge of a frontier post, poised uneasily between the harmless inhabitants of the region and the empire's ruthless officials, and unable to protect either the natives or himself from his brutal colleague, Colonel Joll. Imprisoned and stripped of his duties, the magistrate becomes increasingly skeptical of the empire's motives. When the imperial army arrives to subdue supposed insurgents, its vicious treatment of prisoners calls into question the relation of "civilization" to "barbarism" and demonstrates, in harrowing scenes of abuse and torture, the ethical dangers of one people's dominance over another. In this medley of realist particularism and allegorical parable, Coetzee leaves the landscape and time of the novel hauntingly unspecified, suggesting that colonialism's degradation and coercion, violence and moral corruption can occur anywhere, at any time.

From Waiting for the Barbarians

First there is the sound of muskets far away, as diminutive as popguns.[1] Then from nearer by, from the ramparts themselves, come volleys of answering shots. There is a stampede of footsteps across the barracks yard. "The barbar-

1. The magistrate, narrator of the novel, listens from the prison in which the empire has incarcerated him.

ians!" someone shouts; but I think he is wrong. Above all the clamour the great bell begins to peal.

Kneeling with an ear to the crack of the door I try to make out what is going on.

The noise from the square mounts from a hubbub to a steady roar in which no single voice can be distinguished. The whole town must be pouring out in welcome, thousands of ecstatic souls. Volleys of musket-shots keep cracking. Then the tenor of the roar changes, rises in pitch and excitement. Faintly above it come the brassy tones of bugles.

The temptation is too great. What have I to lose? I unlock the door. In glare so blinding that I must squint and shade my eyes, I cross the yard, pass through the gate, and join the rear of the crowd. The volleys and the roar of applause continue. The old woman in black beside me takes my arm to steady herself and stands on her toes. "Can you see?" she says. "Yes, I can see men on horseback," I reply; but she is not listening.

I can see a long file of horsemen who, amid flying banners, pass through the gateway and make their way to the centre of the square where they dismount. There is a cloud of dust over the whole square, but I see that they are smiling and laughing: one of them rides with his hands raised high in triumph, another waves a garland of flowers. They progress slowly, for the crowd presses around them, trying to touch them, throwing flowers, clapping their hands above their heads in joy, spinning round and round in private ecstasies. Children dive past me, scrambling through the legs of the grownups to be nearer to their heroes. Fusillade after fusillade comes from the ramparts, which are lined with cheering people.

One part of the cavalcade does not dismount. Headed by a stern-faced young corporal bearing the green and gold banner of the battalion, it passes through the press of bodies to the far end of the square and then begins a circuit of the perimeter, the crowd surging slowly in its wake. The word runs like fire from neighbour to neighbour: *"Barbarians!"*

The standard-bearer's horse is led by a man who brandishes a heavy stick to clear his way. Behind him comes another trooper trailing a rope; and at the end of the rope, tied neck to neck, comes a file of men, barbarians, stark naked, holding their hands up to their faces in an odd way as though one and all are suffering from toothache. For a moment I am puzzled by the posture, by the tiptoeing eagerness with which they follow their leader, till I catch a glint of metal and at once comprehend. A simple loop of wire runs through the flesh of each man's hands and through holes pierced in his cheeks. "It makes them meek as lambs," I remember being told by a soldier who had once seen the trick: "they think of nothing but how to keep very still." My heart grows sick. I know now that I should not have left my cell.

I have to turn my back smartly to avoid being seen by the two who, with their mounted escort, bring up the rear of the procession: the bareheaded young captain whose first triumph this is, and at his shoulder, leaner and darker after his months of campaigning, Colonel of Police Joll.

The circuit is made, everyone has a chance to see the twelve miserable captives, to prove to his children that the barbarians are real. Now the crowd, myself reluctantly in its wake, flows towards the great gate, where a half-moon of soldiers blocks its way until, compressed at front and rear, it cannot budge.

"What is going on?" I ask my neighbour.

"I don't know," he says, "but help me to lift him." I help him to lift the child

he carries on his arm on to his shoulders. "Can you see?" he asks the child.
  "Yes."
  "What are they doing?"
  "They are making those barbarians kneel. What are they going to do to them?"
  "I don't know. Let's wait and see."
  Slowly, titanically, with all my might, I turn and begin to squeeze my body out, "Excuse me . . . excuse me . . ." I say: "the heat—I'm going to be sick." For the first time I see heads turn, fingers point.
  I ought to go back to my cell. As a gesture it will have no effect, it will not even be noticed. Nevertheless, for my own sake, as a gesture to myself alone, I ought to return to the cool dark and lock the door and bend the key and stop my ears to the noise of patriotic bloodlust and close my lips and never speak again. Who knows, perhaps I do my fellow-townsmen an injustice, perhaps at this very minute the shoemaker is at home tapping on his last, humming to himself to drown the shouting, perhaps there are housewives shelling peas in their kitchens, telling stories to occupy their restless children, perhaps there are farmers still going calmly about the repair of the ditches. If comrades like these exist, what a pity I do not know them! For me, at this moment, striding away from the crowd, what has become important above all is that I should neither be contaminated by the atrocity that is about to be committed nor poison myself with impotent hatred of its perpetrators. I cannot save the prisoners, therefore let me save myself. Let it at the very least be said, if it ever comes to be said, if there is ever anyone in some remote future interested to know the way we lived, that in this farthest outpost of the Empire of light there existed one man who in his heart was not a barbarian.
  I pass through the barracks gate into my prison yard. At the trough in the middle of the yard I pick up an empty bucket and fill it. With the bucket held up before me, slopping water over its sides, I approach the rear of the crowd again. "Excuse me," I say, and push. People curse me, give way, the bucket tilts and splashes, I forge forward till in a minute I am suddenly clear in the frontmost rank of the crowd behind the backs of the soldiers who, holding staves between them, keep an arena clear for the exemplary spectacle.
  Four of the prisoners kneel on the ground. The other eight, still roped together, squat in the shade of the wall watching, their hands to their cheeks.
  The kneeling prisoners bend side by side over a long heavy pole. A cord runs from the loop of wire through the first man's mouth, under the pole, up to the second man's loop, back under the pole, up to the third loop, under the pole, through the fourth loop. As I watch a soldier slowly pulls the cord tighter and the prisoners bend further till finally they are kneeling with their faces touching the pole. One of them writhes his shoulders in pain and moans. The others are silent, their thoughts wholly concentrated on moving smoothly with the cord, not giving the wire a chance to tear their flesh.
  Directing the soldier with little gestures of the hand is Colonel Joll. Though I am only one in a crowd of thousands, though his eyes are shaded as ever, I stare at him so hard with a face so luminous with query that I know at once he sees me.
  Behind me I distinctly hear the word *magistrate*. Do I imagine it or are my neighbours inching away from me?
  The Colonel steps forward. Stooping over each prisoner in turn he rubs a handful of dust into his naked back and writes a word with a stick of charcoal.

I read the words upside down: *ENEMY . . . ENEMY . . . ENEMY . . . ENEMY.*
He steps back and folds his hands. At a distance of no more than twenty paces
he and I contemplate each other.

Then the beating begins. The soldiers use the stout green cane staves, bringing them down with the heavy slapping sounds of washing-paddles, raising red
welts on the prisoners' backs and buttocks. With slow care the prisoners extend
their legs until they lie flat on their bellies, all except the one who had been
moaning and who now gasps with each blow.

The black charcoal and ochre dust begin to run with sweat and blood. The
game, I see, is to beat them till their backs are washed clean.

I watch the face of a little girl who stands in the front rank of the crowd
gripping her mother's clothes. Her eyes are round, her thumb is in her mouth:
silent, terrified, curious, she drinks in the sight of these big naked men being
beaten. On every face around me, even those that are smiling, I see the same
expression: not hatred, not bloodlust, but a curiosity so intense that their
bodies are drained by it and only their eyes live, organs of a new and ravening
appetite.

The soldiers doing the beating grow tired. One stands with his hands on his
hips panting, smiling, gesturing to the crowd. There is a word from the Colonel: all four of them cease their labour and come forward offering their canes
to the spectators.

A girl, giggling and hiding her face, is pushed forward by her friends. "Go
on, don't be afraid!" they urge her. A soldier puts a cane in her hand and leads
her to the place. She stands confused, embarrassed, one hand still over her
face. Shouts, jokes, obscene advice are hurled at her. She lifts the cane, brings
it down smartly on the prisoner's buttocks, drops it, and scuttles to safety to
a roar of applause.

There is a scramble for the canes, the soldiers can barely keep order, I lose
sight of the prisoners on the ground as people press forward to take a turn or
simply watch the beating from nearer. I stand forgotten with my bucket
between my feet.

Then the flogging is over, the soldiers reassert themselves, the crowd scram-
bles back, the arena is reconstituted, though narrower than before.

Over his head, exhibiting it to the crowd, Colonel Joll holds a hammer, an
ordinary four-pound hammer used for knocking in tent-pegs. Again his gaze
meets mine. The babble subsides.

"No!" I hear the first word from my throat, rusty, not loud enough. Then
again: "No!" This time the word rings like a bell from my chest. The soldier
who blocks my way stumbles aside. I am in the arena holding up my hands to
still the crowd: "No! No! No!"

When I turn to Colonel Joll he is standing not five paces from me, his arms
folded. I point a finger at him. "You!" I shout. Let it all be said. Let him be the
one on whom the anger breaks. "You are depraving these people!"

He does not flinch, he does not reply.

"You!" My arm points at him like a gun. My voice fills the square. There is
utter silence; or perhaps I am too intoxicated to hear.

Something crashes into me from behind. I sprawl in the dust, gasp, feel the
sear of old pain in my back. A stick thuds down on me. Reaching out to ward
it off, I take a withering blow on my hand.

It becomes important to stand up, however difficult the pain makes it. I
come to my feet and see who it is that is hitting me. It is the stocky man with

the sergeant's stripes who helped with the beatings. Crouched at the knees, his nostrils flaring, he stands with his stick raised for the next blow. "Wait!" I gasp, holding out my limp hand. "I think you have broken it!" He strikes, and I take the blow on the forearm. I hide my arm, lower my head, and try to grope towards him and grapple. Blows fall on my head and shoulders. Never mind: all I want is a few moments to finish what I am saying now that I have begun. I grip his tunic and hug him to me. Though he wrestles, he cannot use his stick; over his shoulder I shout again.

"Not with that!" I shout. The hammer lies cradled in the Colonel's folded arms. "You would not use a hammer on a beast, not on a beast!" In a terrible surge of rage I turn on the sergeant and hurl him from me. Godlike strength is mine. In a minute it will pass: let me use it well while it lasts! "Look!" I shout. I point to the four prisoners who lie docilely on the earth, their lips to the pole, their hands clasped to their faces like monkeys' paws, oblivious of the hammer, ignorant of what is going on behind them, relieved that the offending mark has been beaten from their backs, hoping that the punishment is at an end. I raise my broken hand to the sky. "Look!" I shout. "We are the great miracle of creation! But from some blows this miraculous body cannot repair itself! How—!" Words fail me. "Look at these men!" I recommence. *"Men!"* Those in the crowd who can crane to look at the prisoners, even at the flies that begin to settle on their bleeding welts.

I hear the blow coming and turn to meet it. It catches me full across the face. "I am blind!" I think, staggering back into the blackness that instantly falls. I swallow blood; something blooms across my face, starting as a rosy warmth, turning to fiery agony. I hide my face in my hands and stamp around in a circle trying not to shout, trying not to fall.

What I wanted to say next I cannot remember. A miracle of creation—I pursue the thought but it eludes me like a wisp of smoke. It occurs to me that we crush insects beneath our feet, miracles of creation too, beetles, worms, cockroaches, ants, in their various ways.

I take my fingers from my eyes and a grey world re-emerges swimming in tears. I am so profoundly grateful that I cease to feel pain. As I am hustled, a man at each elbow, back through the murmuring crowd to my cell, I even find myself smiling.

That smile, that flush of joy, leave behind a disturbing residue. I know that they commit an error in treating me so summarily. For I am no orator. What would I have said if they had let me go on? That it is worse to beat a man's feet to pulp than to kill him in combat? That it brings shame on everyone when a girl is permitted to flog a man? That spectacles of cruelty corrupt the hearts of the innocent? The words they stopped me from uttering may have been very paltry indeed, hardly words to rouse the rabble. What, after all, do I stand for besides an archaic code of gentlemanly behaviour towards captured foes, and what do I stand against except the new science of degradation that kills people on their knees, confused and disgraced in their own eyes? Would I have dared to face the crowd to demand justice for these ridiculous barbarian prisoners with their backsides in the air? *Justice:* once that word is uttered, where will it all end? Easier to shout *No!* Easier to be beaten and made a martyr. Easier to lay my head on a block than to defend the cause of justice for the barbarians: for where can that argument lead but to laying down our arms and opening the gates of the town to the people whose land we have raped? The old magistrate, defender of the rule of law, enemy in his own way of the State, assaulted and imprisoned, impregnably virtuous, is not without his own twinges of doubt.

My nose is broken, I know, and perhaps also the cheekbone where the flesh was laid open by the blow of the stick. My left eye is swelling shut.

As the numbness wears off the pain begins to come in spasms a minute or two apart so intense that I can no longer lie still. At the height of the spasm I trot around the room holding my face, whining like a dog; in the blessed valleys between the peaks I breathe deeply, trying to keep control of myself, trying not to make too disgraceful an outcry. I seem to hear surges and lulls in the noise from the mob on the square but cannot be sure that the roar is not simply in my eardrums.

They bring me my evening meal as usual but I cannot eat. I cannot keep still, I have to walk back and forth or rock on my haunches to keep myself from screaming, tearing my clothes, clawing my flesh, doing whatever people do when the limit of their endurance is reached. I weep, and feel the tears stinging the open flesh. I hum the old song about the rider and the juniper bush over and over again, clinging to the remembered words even after they have ceased to make any sense. One, two, three, four . . . I count. It will be a famous victory, I tell myself, if you can last the night.

In the early hours of the morning, when I am so giddy with exhaustion that I reel on my feet, I finally give way and sob from the heart like a child: I sit in a corner against the wall and weep, the tears running from my eyes without stop. I weep and weep while the throbbing comes and goes according to its own cycles. In this position sleep bursts upon me like a thunderbolt. I am amazed to come to myself in the thin grey light of day, slumped in a corner, with not the faintest sense that time has passed. Though the throbbing is still there I find I can endure it if I remain still. Indeed, it has lost its strangeness. Soon, perhaps, it will be as much part of me as breathing.

So I lie quietly against the wall, folding my sore hand under my armpit for comfort, and fall into a second sleep, into a confusion of images among which I search out one in particular, brushing aside the others that fly at me like leaves. It is of the girl. She is kneeling with her back to me before the snow-castle or sandcastle she has built. She wears a dark blue robe. As I approach I see that she is digging away in the bowels of the castle.

She becomes aware of me and turns. I am mistaken, it is not a castle she has built but a clay oven. Smoke curls up from the vent at the back. She holds out her hands to me offering me something, a shapeless lump which I peer at unwillingly through a mist. Though I shake my head my vision will not clear.

She is wearing a round cap embroidered in gold. Her hair is braided in a heavy plait which lies over her shoulder: there is gold thread worked into the braid. "Why are you dressed in your best?" I want to say: "I have never seen you looking so lovely." She smiles at me: what beautiful teeth she has, what clear jet-black eyes! Also now I can see that what she is holding out to me is a loaf of bread, still hot, with a coarse steaming broken crust. A surge of gratitude sweeps through me. "Where did a child like you learn to bake so well in the desert?" I want to say. I open my arms to embrace her, and come to myself with tears stinging the wound on my cheek. Though I scrabble back at once into the burrow of sleep I cannot re-enter the dream or taste the bread that has made my saliva run.

• •

2810 / J. M. COETZEE

Colonel Joll sits behind the desk in my office. There are no books or files;
the room is starkly empty save for a vase of fresh flowers.

The handsome warrant officer whose name I do not know lifts the cedar-
wood chest on to the desk and steps back.

Looking down to refer to his papers, the Colonel speaks. "Among the items
found in your apartment was this wooden chest. I would like you to consider
it. Its contents are unusual. It contains approximately three hundred slips of
white poplar-wood, each about eight inches by two inches, many of them
wound about with lengths of string.[2] The wood is dry and brittle. Some of the
string is new, some so old that it has perished.

"If one loosens the string one finds that the slip splits open revealing two
flat inner surfaces. These surfaces are written on in an unfamiliar script.

"I think you will concur with this description."

I stare into the black lenses. He goes on.

"A reasonable inference is that the wooden slips contain messages passed
between yourself and other parties, we do not know when. It remains for you
to explain what the messages say and who the other parties were."

He takes a slip from the chest and flicks it across the polished surface of
the desk towards me.

I look at the lines of characters written by a stranger long since dead. I do
not even know whether to read from right to left or from left to right. In the
long evenings I spent poring over my collection I isolated over four hundred
different characters in the script, perhaps as many as four hundred and fifty.
I have no idea what they stand for. Does each stand for a single thing, a circle
for the sun, a triangle for a woman, a wave for a lake; or does a circle merely
stand for "circle", a triangle for "triangle", a wave for "wave"? Does each sign
represent a different state of the tongue, the lips, the throat, the lungs, as they
combine in the uttering of some multifarious unimaginable extinct barbarian
language? Or are my four hundred characters nothing but scribal embellish-
ments of an underlying repertory of twenty or thirty whose primitive forms I
am too stupid to see?

"He sends greetings to his daughter," I say. I hear with surprise the thick
nasal voice that is now mine. My finger runs along the line of characters from
right to left. "Whom he says he has not seen for a long time. He hopes she is
happy and thriving. He hopes the lambing season has been good. He has a
gift for her, he says, which he will keep till he sees her again. He sends his
love. It is not easy to read his signature. It could be simply 'Your father' or it
could be something else, a name."

I reach over into the chest and pick out a second slip. The warrant officer,
who sits behind Joll with a little notebook open on his knee, stares hard at me,
his pencil poised above the paper.

"This one reads as follows," I say: " 'I am sorry I must send bad news. The
soldiers came and took your brother away. I have been to the fort every day to
plead for his return. I sit in the dust with my head bare. Yesterday for the first
time they sent a man to speak to me. He says your brother is no longer here.
He says he has been sent away. "Where?" I asked, but he would not say. Do
not tell your mother, but join me in praying for his safety.'

"And now let us see what this next one says." The pencil is still poised, he

---

2. Over the years the magistrate has conducted archaeological digs outside the city, unearthing these poplar
slips and other artifacts.

has not written anything, he has not stirred. " 'We went to fetch your brother yesterday. They showed us into a room where he lay on a table sewn up in a sheet.' " Slowly Joll leans back in his chair. The warrant officer closes his notebook and half-rises; but with a gesture Joll restrains him. " 'They wanted me to take him away like that, but I insisted on looking first. "What if it is the wrong body you are giving me?" I said—"You have so many bodies here, bodies of brave young men." So I opened the sheet and saw that it was indeed he. Through each eyelid, I saw that there was a stitch, "Why have you done that?" I said. "It is our custom," he said. I tore the sheet wide open and saw bruises all over his body, and saw that his feet were swollen and broken. "What happened to him?" I said. "I do not know," said the man, "it is not on the paper; if you have questions you must go to the sergeant, but he is very busy." We have had to bury your brother here, outside their fort, because he was beginning to stink. Please tell your mother and try to console her.'

"Now let us see what the next one says. See, there is only a single character. It is the barbarian character *war*, but it has other senses too. It can stand for *vengeance*, and, if you turn it upside down like this, it can be made to read *justice*. There is no knowing which sense is intended. That is part of barbarian cunning.

"It is the same with the rest of these slips." I plunge my good hand into the chest and stir. "They form an allegory. They can be read in many orders. Further, each single slip can be read in many ways. Together they can be read as a domestic journal, or they can be read as a plan of war, or they can be turned on their sides and read as a history of the last years of the Empire—the old Empire, I mean. There is no agreement among scholars about how to interpret these relics of the ancient barbarians. Allegorical sets like this one can be found buried all over the desert. I found this one not three miles from here in the ruins of a public building. Graveyards are another good place to look in, though it is not always easy to tell where barbarian burial sites lie. It is recommended that you simply dig at random: perhaps at the very spot where you stand you will come upon scraps, shards, reminders of the dead. Also the air: the air is full of sighs and cries. These are never lost: if you listen carefully, with a sympathetic ear, you can hear them echoing forever within the second sphere. The night is best: sometimes when you have difficulty in falling asleep it is because your ears have been reached by the cries of the dead which, like their writings, are open to many interpretations.

"Thank you. I have finished translating."

I have not failed to keep an eye on Joll through all this. He has not stirred again, save to lay a hand on his subordinate's sleeve at the moment when I referred to the Empire and he rose, ready to strike me.

If he comes near me I will hit him with all the strength in my body. I will not disappear into the earth without leaving my mark on them.

The Colonel speaks. "You have no idea how tiresome your behaviour is. You are the one and only official we have had to work with on the frontier who has not given us his fullest co-operation. Candidly, I must tell you I am not interested in these sticks." He waves a hand at the slips scattered on the desk. "They are very likely gambling-sticks. I know that other tribes on the border gamble with sticks.

"I ask you to consider soberly: what kind of future do you have here? You cannot be allowed to remain in your post. You have utterly disgraced yourself. Even if you are not eventually prosecuted—"

"I am waiting for you to prosecute me!" I shout. "When are you going to do it? When are you going to bring me to trial? When am I going to have a chance to defend myself?" I am in a fury. None of the speechlessness I felt in front of the crowd afflicts me. If I were to confront these men now, in public, in a fair trial, I would find the words to shame them. It is a matter of health and strength: I feel my hot words swell in my breast. But they will never bring a man to trial while he is healthy and strong enough to confound them. They will shut me away in the dark till I am a muttering idiot, a ghost of myself; then they will haul me before a closed court and in five minutes dispose of the legalities they find so tiresome.

"For the duration of the emergency, as you know," says the Colonel, "the administration of justice is out of the hands of civilians and in the hands of the Bureau." He sighs. "Magistrate, you seem to believe that we do not dare to bring you to trial because we fear you are too popular a figure in this town. I do not think you are aware of how much you forfeited by neglecting your duties, shunning your friends, keeping company with low people. There is no one I have spoken to who has not at some time felt insulted by your behaviour."

"My private life is none of their business!"

"Nevertheless, I may tell you that our decision to relieve you of your duties has been welcomed in most quarters. Personally I have nothing against you. When I arrived back a few days ago, I had decided that all I wanted from you was a clear answer to a simple question, after which you could have returned to your concubines a free man."

It strikes me suddenly that the insult may not be gratuitous, that perhaps for different reasons these two men might welcome it if I lost my temper. Burning with outrage, tense in every muscle, I guard my silence.

"However, you seem to have a new ambition," he goes on. "You seem to want to make a name for yourself as the One Just Man, the man who is prepared to sacrifice his freedom to his principles.

"But let me ask you: do you believe that that is how your fellow-citizens see you after the ridiculous spectacle you created on the square the other day? Believe me, to people in this town you are not the One Just Man, you are simply a clown, a madman. You are dirty, you stink, they can smell you a mile away. You look like an old beggar-man, a refuse-scavenger. They do not want you back in any capacity. You have no future here.

"You want to go down in history as a martyr, I suspect. But who is going to put you in the history books? These border troubles are of no significance. In a while they will pass and the frontier will go to sleep for another twenty years. People are not interested in the history of the back of beyond."

"There were no border troubles before you came," I say.

"That is nonsense," he says. "You are simply ignorant of the facts. You are living in a world of the past. You think we are dealing with small groups of peaceful nomads. In fact we are dealing with a well organized enemy. If you had travelled with the expeditionary force you would have seen that for yourself."

"Those pitiable prisoners you brought in—are *they* the enemy I must fear? Is that what you say? *You* are the enemy, Colonel!" I can restrain myself no longer. I pound the desk with my fist. "*You* are the enemy, *you* have made the war, and *you* have given them all the martyrs they need—starting not now but a year ago when you committed your first filthy barbarities here! History will bear me out!"

"Nonsense. There will be no history, the affair is too trivial." He seems impassive, but I am sure I have shaken him.

"You are an obscene torturer! You deserve to hang!"

"Thus speaks the judge, the One Just Man," he murmurs.

We stare into each other's eyes.

"Now," he says, squaring the papers before him: "I would like a statement on everything that passed between you and the barbarians on your recent and unauthorized visit to them."

"I refuse."

"Very well. Our interview is over." He turns to his subordinate. "He is your responsibility." He stands up, walks out. I face the warrant officer.

●　　●

The wound on my cheek, never washed or dressed, is swollen and inflamed. A crust like a fat caterpillar has formed on it. My left eye is a mere slit, my nose a shapeless throbbing lump. I must breathe through my mouth.

I lie in the reek of old vomit obsessed with the thought of water. I have had nothing to drink for two days.

In my suffering there is nothing ennobling. Little of what I call suffering is even pain. What I am made to undergo is subjection to the most rudimentary needs of my body: to drink, to relieve itself, to find the posture in which it is least sore. When Warrant Officer Mandel and his man first brought me back here and lit the lamp and closed the door, I wondered how much pain a plump comfortable old man would be able to endure in the name of his eccentric notions of how the Empire should conduct itself. But my torturers were not interested in degrees of pain. They were interested only in demonstrating to me what it meant to live in a body, as a body, a body which can entertain notions of justice only as long as it is whole and well, which very soon forgets them when its head is gripped and a pipe is pushed down its gullet and pints of salt water are poured into it till it coughs and retches and flails and voids itself. They did not come to force the story out of me of what I had said to the barbarians and what the barbarians had said to me. So I had no chance to throw the high-sounding words I had ready in their faces. They came to my cell to show me the meaning of humanity, and in the space of an hour they showed me a great deal.

1980

SALMAN RUSHDIE
b. 1947

The most influential novelist to have come from South Asia in the last fifty years is Ahmed Salman Rushdie, whose dynamic narratives—stories of magic, suffering, and the vitality of human beings in the grip of history—have helped generate the literary renaissance flowering in India today. "I come from Bombay," Rushdie has said, "and from a Muslim family, too. 'My' India has always been based on ideas of multiplicity, pluralism, hybridity: ideas to which the ideologies of the communalists are diametrically opposed. To my mind, the defining image of India is the crowd, and a crowd

2814 / SALMAN RUSHDIE

is by its very nature superabundant, heterogeneous, many things at once." Rushdie was educated at Cathedral School, Bombay (now Mumbai), and from the age of thirteen, at Rugby School, Warwickshire, and King's College, Cambridge. After living briefly in Pakistan, where his prosperous family had moved, Rushdie eventually settled in England, working as an actor and as a freelance advertising copywriter (1970–80).

His first novel, *Grimus* (1979), passed unnoticed, but his second, *Midnight's Children* (1981), announced the arrival of a major writer. Taking its title from those who were born—two months later than its author—around midnight on August 15, 1947, when the independent state of India was born, *Midnight's Children* is a work of prodigious prodigality, a cornucopia as richly fertile in character, incident, and language as the subcontinent that is its setting. The book's triumphant progress across the world culminated in its being judged "the Booker of Bookers," the best novel to have won Britain's premier fiction prize in its first twenty-five years. Rushdie has said that "we're all radio-active with history," and the books that have followed *Midnight's Children* have again shown a form of "magical realism"—learned from Latin American writers such as Jorge Luis Borges and Gabriel García Márquez—deployed in the service of a powerful political-historical imagination.

In 1988 Rushdie found himself at the perilous center of a real, rather than a magical realist, political-historical storm. His novel *The Satanic Verses* provoked riots in India, Pakistan, and South Africa, and was judged by senior religious figures in Iran to have blasphemed the Prophet Muhammad (called by the offensive name "Mahound" in the novel), founder of the Muslim faith, and a fatwa, or legal decree, calling for his death was pronounced. He was obliged to go into hiding, and for almost a decade lived under round-the-clock protection from British Secret Service agents, while governments argued for and against the lifting of the fatwa, and the author himself became symbolic of the vulnerability of the intellectual in the face of fundamentalism. The lifting of the fatwa in 1998 allowed Rushdie to reappear in public, but it is seen as irrevocable by some religious groups, and so his life remains under constant threat. He has defended his book in the essay "In Good Faith" (1990), while defining the irreverently pluralistic vision behind his "mongrel" aesthetic—a vision that has repeatedly resulted in the burning or banning of his books by political nationalists and religious purists in South Asia and other parts of the world:

> If *The Satanic Verses* is anything, it is a migrant's-eye view of the world. It is written from the very experience of uprooting, disjuncture and metamorphosis (slow or rapid, painful or pleasurable) that is the migrant condition, and from which, I believe, can be derived a metaphor for all humanity.
>
> Standing at the centre of the novel is a group of characters most of whom are British Muslims, or not particularly religious persons of Muslim background, struggling with just the sort of great problems of hybridization and ghettoization, of reconciling the old and the new. Those who oppose the novel most vociferously today are of the opinion that intermingling with a different culture will inevitably weaken and ruin their own. I am of the opposite opinion. *The Satanic Verses* celebrates hybridity, impurity, intermingling, the transformation that comes of new and unexpected combinations of human beings, cultures, ideas, politics, movies, songs. It rejoices in mongrelization and fears the absolutism of the Pure. *Mélange*, hotchpotch, a bit of this and a bit of that is *how newness enters the world*. It is the great possibility that mass migration gives the world, and I have tried to embrace it. *The Satanic Verses* is for change-by-fusion, change-by-conjoining. It is a love-song to our mongrel selves.

An earlier story, published the same year as his groundbreaking *Midnight's Children*, had invoked the Prophet uncontroversially. Like *Midnight's Children*, the story "The Prophet's Hair" buoyantly fuses Standard English with an exuberantly Indianized English, peppered with words of Hindi, Persian, Sanskrit, and Arabic origin—

among the many languages that have been used in the extraordinarily polyglot Indian subcontinent. Like *The Satanic Verses*, "The Prophet's Hair" risks playfulness, satire, caricature, and whimsy in its treatment of the religion of his youth (though Rushdie has indicated he was brought up not as a believer but within a relaxed Muslim climate, almost secularized by the variety of other religions surrounding it). The story is at once a moral fable in the tradition of *The Thousand and One Nights* and a magical realist extravaganza, packed with incident, poetic detail ("water to which the cold of the night had given the cloudy consistency of wild honey"), and humor, all brilliantly interwoven at breakneck speed.

The Prophet's[1] Hair

Early in the year 19—, when Srinagar[2] was under the spell of a winter so fierce it could crack men's bones as if they were glass, a young man upon whose cold-pinked skin there lay, like a frost, the unmistakable sheen of wealth was to be seen entering the most wretched and disreputable part of the city, where the houses of wood and corrugated iron seemed perpetually on the verge of losing their balance, and asking in low, grave tones where he might go to engage the services of a dependably professional burglar. The young man's name was Atta, and the rogues in that part of town directed him gleefully into ever darker and less public alleys, until in a yard wet with the blood of a slaughtered chicken he was set upon by two men whose faces he never saw, robbed of the substantial bank-roll which he had insanely brought on his solitary excursion, and beaten within an inch of his life.

Night fell. His body was carried by anonymous hands to the edge of the lake, whence it was transported by shikara[3] across the water and deposited, torn and bleeding, on the deserted embankment of the canal which led to the gardens of Shalimar. At dawn the next morning a flower-vendor was rowing his boat through water to which the cold of the night had given the cloudy consistency of wild honey when he saw the prone form of young Atta, who was just beginning to stir and moan, and on whose now deathly pale skin the sheen of wealth could still be made out dimly beneath an actual layer of frost.

The flower-vendor moored his craft and by stooping over the mouth of the injured man was able to learn the poor fellow's address, which was mumbled through lips that could scarcely move; whereupon, hoping for a large tip, the hawker rowed Atta home to a large house on the shores of the lake, where a beautiful but inexplicably bruised young woman and her distraught, but equally handsome mother, neither of whom, it was clear from their eyes, had slept a wink from worrying, screamed at the sight of their Atta—who was the elder brother of the beautiful young woman—lying motionless amidst the funereally stunted winter blooms of the hopeful florist.

The flower-vendor was indeed paid off handsomely, not least to ensure his silence, and plays no further part in our story. Atta himself, suffering terribly from exposure as well as a broken skull, entered a coma which caused the city's finest doctors to shrug helplessly. It was therefore all the more remark-

---

1. The Prophet Muhammad, founder of the Muslim religion, was born in Mecca about 570 and died in 632.

2. Capital of the state of Kashmir.
3. Long swift Kashmiri boat.

2816 / SALMAN RUSHDIE

able that on the very next evening the most wretched and disreputable part of

able that on the very next evening the most wretched and disreputable part of the city received a second unexpected visitor. This was Huma, the sister of the unfortunate young man, and her question was the same as her brother's, and asked in the same low, grave tones:

'Where may I hire a thief?'

The story of the rich idiot who had come looking for a burglar was already common knowledge in those insalubrious[4] gullies, but this time the young woman added: 'I should say that I am carrying no money, nor am I wearing any jewellery items. My father has disowned me and will pay no ransom if I am kidnapped; and a letter has been lodged with the Deputy Commissioner of Police, my uncle, to be opened in the event of my not being safe at home by morning. In that letter he will find full details of my journey here, and he will move Heaven and Earth to punish my assailants.'

Her exceptional beauty, which was visible even through the enormous welts and bruises disfiguring her arms and forehead, coupled with the oddity of her inquiries, had attracted a sizable group of curious onlookers, and because her little speech seemed to them to cover just about everything, no one attempted to injure her in any way, although there were some raucous comments to the effect that it was pretty peculiar for someone who was trying to hire a crook to invoke the protection of a high-up policeman uncle.

She was directed into ever darker and less public alleys until finally in a gully as dark as ink an old woman with eyes which stared so piercingly that Huma instantly understood she was blind motioned her through a doorway from which darkness seemed to be pouring like smoke. Clenching her fists, angrily ordering her heart to behave normally, Huma followed the old woman into the gloom-wrapped house.

The faintest conceivable rivulet of candlelight trickled through the darkness; following this unreliable yellow thread (because she could no longer see the old lady), Huma received a sudden sharp blow to the shins and cried out involuntarily, after which she at once bit her lip, angry at having revealed her mounting terror to whoever or whatever waited before her, shrouded in blackness.

She had, in fact, collided with a low table on which a single candle burned and beyond which a mountainous figure could be made out, sitting cross-legged on the floor. 'Sit, sit,' said a man's calm, deep voice, and her legs, needing no more flowery invitation, buckled beneath her at the terse command. Clutching her left hand in her right, she forced her voice to respond evenly:

'And you, sir, will be the thief I have been requesting?'

Shifting its weight very slightly, the shadow-mountain informed Huma that all criminal activity originating in this zone was well organised and also centrally controlled, so that all requests for what might be termed freelance work had to be channelled through this room.

He demanded comprehensive details of the crime to be committed, including a precise inventory of items to be acquired, also a clear statement of all

4. Unhealthy.

financial inducements being offered with no gratuities excluded, plus, for filing purposes only, a summary of the motives for the application.

At this, Huma, as though remembering something, stiffened both in body and resolve and replied loudly that her motives were entirely a matter for herself; that she would discuss details with no one but the thief himself; but that the rewards she proposed could only be described as 'lavish'.

'All I am willing to disclose to you, sir, since it appears that I am on the premises of some sort of employment agency, is that in return for such lavish rewards I must have the most desperate criminal at your disposal, a man for whom life holds no terrors, not even the fear of God.

'The worst of fellows, I tell you—nothing less will do!'

At this a paraffin storm-lantern was lighted, and Huma saw facing her a grey-haired giant down whose left cheek ran the most sinister of scars, a cicatrice in the shape of the letter *sín* in the Nastaliq[5] script. She was gripped by the insupportably nostalgic notion that the bogeyman of her childhood nursery had risen up to confront her, because her ayah[6] had always forestalled any incipient acts of disobedience by threatening Huma and Atta: 'You don't watch out and I'll send that one to steal you away—that Sheikh[7] Sín, the Thief of Thieves!'

Here, grey-haired but unquestionably scarred, was the notorious criminal himself—and was she out of her mind, were her ears playing tricks, or had he truly just announced that, given the stated circumstances, he himself was the only man for the job?

Struggling hard against the newborn goblins of nostalgia, Huma warned the fearsome volunteer that only a matter of extreme urgency and peril would have brought her unescorted into these ferocious streets.

'Because we can afford no last-minute backings-out,' she continued, 'I am determined to tell you everything, keeping back no secrets whatsoever. If, after hearing me out, you are still prepared to proceed, then we shall do everything in our power to assist you, and to make you rich.'

The old thief shrugged, nodded, spat. Huma began her story.

Six days ago, everything in the household of her father, the wealthy money-lender Hashim, had been as it always was. At breakfast her mother had spooned khichri[8] lovingly on to the moneylender's plate; the conversation had been filled with those expressions of courtesy and solicitude on which the family prided itself.

Hashim was fond of pointing out that while he was not a godly man he set great store by 'living honourably in the world'. In that spacious lakeside residence, all outsiders were greeted with the same formality and respect, even those unfortunates who came to negotiate for small fragments of Hashim's large fortune, and of whom he naturally asked an interest rate of over seventy per cent, partly, as he told his khichri-spooning wife, 'to teach these people the value of money; let them only learn that, and they will be cured of this

---

5. A Persian cursive script, characterized by rounded forms and elongated horizontal strokes. "Cicatrice": scar of a healed wound.

6. Child's nurse (Anglo-Indian, from Portuguese).
7. Chief (Arabic).
8. Rice and lentils cooked together (Hindi).

fever of borrowing borrowing all the time—so you see that if my plans succeed, I shall put myself out of business!'

In their children, Atta and Huma, the moneylender and his wife had successfully sought to inculcate the virtues of thrift, plain dealing and a healthy independence of spirit. On this, too, Hashim was fond of congratulating himself.

Breakfast ended; the family members wished one another a fulfilling day. Within a few hours, however, the glassy contentment of that household, of that life of porcelain delicacy and alabaster sensibilities, was to be shattered beyond all hope of repair.

The moneylender summoned his personal shikara and was on the point of stepping into it when, attracted by a glint of silver, he noticed a small vial floating between the boat and his private quay. On an impulse, he scooped it out of the glutinous water.

It was a cylinder of tinted glass cased in exquisitely wrought silver, and Hashim saw within its walls a silver pendant bearing a single strand of human hair.

Closing his fist around this unique discovery, he muttered to the boatman that he'd changed his plans, and hurried to his sanctum,[9] where, behind closed doors, he feasted his eyes on his find.

There can be no doubt that Hashim the moneylender knew from the first that he was in possession of the famous relic of the Prophet Muhammad, that revered hair whose theft from its shrine at Hazratbal mosque the previous morning had created an unprecedented hue and cry in the valley.

The thieves—no doubt alarmed by the pandemonium, by the procession through the streets of endless ululating[1] crocodiles of lamentation, by the riots, the political ramifications and by the massive police search which was commanded and carried out by men whose entire careers now hung upon the finding of this lost hair—had evidently panicked and hurled the vial into the gelatine bosom of the lake.

Having found it by a stroke of great good fortune, Hashim's duty as a citizen was clear: the hair must be restored to its shrine, and the state to equanimity and peace.

But the moneylender had a different notion.

All around him in his study was the evidence of his collector's mania. There were enormous glass cases full of impaled butterflies from Gulmarg, three dozen scale models in various metals of the legendary cannon Zamzama, innumerable swords, a Naga spear, ninety-four terracotta camels of the sort sold on railway station platforms, many samovars,[2] and a whole zoology of tiny sandalwood animals, which had originally been carved to serve as children's bathtime toys.

'And after all,' Hashim told himself, 'the Prophet would have disapproved mightily of this relic-worship. He abhorred the idea of being deified! So, by keeping this hair from its distracted devotees, I perform—do I not?—a finer

9. Private room.
1. Howling.

2. Apparatuses for making tea (Russian for self-boilers).

service than I would by returning it! Naturally, I don't want it for its religious value . . . I'm a man of the world, of this world. I see it purely as a secular object of great rarity and blinding beauty. In short, it's the silver vial I desire, more than the hair.

'They say there are American millionaires who purchase stolen art master-pieces and hide them away—they would know how I feel. I must, must have it!'

Every collector must share his treasures with one other human being, and Hashim summoned—and told—his only son Atta, who was deeply perturbed but, having been sworn to secrecy, only spilled the beans when the troubles became too terrible to bear.

The youth excused himself and left his father alone in the crowded solitude of his collections. Hashim was sitting erect in a hard, straight-backed chair, gazing intently at the beautiful vial.

It was well known that the moneylender never ate lunch, so it was not until evening that a servant entered the sanctum to summon his master to the dining-table. He found Hashim as Atta had left him. The same, and not the same—for now the moneylender looked swollen, distended. His eyes bulged even more than they always had, they were red-rimmed, and his knuckles were white.

He seemed to be on the point of bursting! As though, under the influence of the misappropriated relic, he had filled up with some spectral fluid which might at any moment ooze uncontrollably from his every bodily opening.

He had to be helped to the table, and then the explosion did indeed take place.

Seemingly careless of the effect of his words on the carefully constructed and fragile constitution of the family's life, Hashim began to gush, to spume long streams of awful truths. In horrified silence, his children heard their father turn upon his wife, and reveal to her that for many years their marriage had been the worst of his afflictions. 'An end to politeness!' he thundered. 'An end to hypocrisy!'

Next, and in the same spirit, he revealed to his family the existence of a mistress; he informed them also of his regular visits to paid women. He told his wife that, far from being the principal beneficiary of his will, she would receive no more than the eighth portion which was her due under Islamic law. Then he turned upon his children, screaming at Atta for his lack of academic ability—'A dope! I have been cursed with a dope!'—and accusing his daughter of lasciviousness, because she went around the city barefaced, which was unseemly for any good Muslim girl to do. She should, he commanded, enter purdah[3] forthwith.

Hashim left the table without having eaten and fell into the deep sleep of a man who has got many things off his chest, leaving his children stunned, in tears, and the dinner going cold on the sideboard under the gaze of an antic-ipatory bearer.[4]

At five o'clock the next morning the moneylender forced his family to rise,

3. Area of certain traditional Indian houses in which Hindu or Muslim women live secluded from the sight of men outside their family circle.
4. Servant.

wash and say their prayers. From then on, he began to pray five times daily for the first time in his life, and his wife and children were obliged to do likewise.

Before breakfast, Huma saw the servants, under her father's direction, constructing a great heap of books in the garden and setting fire to it. The only volume left untouched was the Qur'an,[5] which Hashim wrapped in a silken cloth and placed on a table in the hall. He ordered each member of his family to read passages from this book for at least two hours per day. Visits to the cinema were forbidden. And if Atta invited male friends to the house, Huma was to retire to her room.

By now, the family had entered a state of shock and dismay; but there was worse to come.

That afternoon, a trembling debtor arrived at the house to confess his inability to pay the latest instalment of interest owed, and made the mistake of reminding Hashim, in somewhat blustering fashion, of the Qur'an's strictures against usury. The moneylender flew into a rage and attacked the fellow with one of his large collection of bullwhips.

By mischance, later the same day a second defaulter came to plead for time, and was seen fleeing Hashim's study with a great gash in his arm, because Huma's father had called him a thief of other men's money and had tried to cut off the wretch's right hand with one of the thirty-eight kukri knives[6] hanging on the study walls.

These breaches of the family's unwritten laws of decorum alarmed Atta and Huma, and when, that evening, their mother attempted to calm Hashim down, he struck her on the face with an open hand. Atta leapt to his mother's defence and he, too, was sent flying.

'From now on,' Hashim bellowed, 'there's going to be some discipline around here!'

The moneylender's wife began a fit of hysterics which continued throughout that night and the following day, and which so provoked her husband that he threatened her with divorce, at which she fled to her room, locked the door and subsided into a raga[7] of sniffling. Huma now lost her composure, challenged her father openly, and announced (with that same independence of spirit which he had encouraged in her) that she would wear no cloth over her face; apart from anything else, it was bad for the eyes.

On hearing this, her father disowned her on the spot and gave her one week in which to pack her bags and go.

By the fourth day, the fear in the air of the house had become so thick that it was difficult to walk around. Atta told his shock-numbed sister: 'We are descending to gutter-level—but I know what must be done.'

That afternoon, Hashim left home accompanied by two hired thugs to extract the unpaid dues from his two insolvent clients. Atta went immediately to his father's study. Being the son and heir, he possessed his own key to the moneylender's safe. This he now used, and removing the little vial from its

---

5. Muslims' sacred book: collection of the Prophet Muhammad's oral revelations.
6. Curved knives broadening toward the point

(Hindi).
7. Musical improvisation (Sanskrit).

hiding-place, he slipped it into his trouser pocket and re-locked the safe door.

Now he told Huma the secret of what his father had fished out of Lake Dal, and exclaimed: 'Maybe I'm crazy—maybe the awful things that are happening have made me cracked—but I am convinced there will be no peace in our house until this hair is out of it.'

His sister at once agreed that the hair must be returned, and Atta set off in a hired shikara to Hazratbal mosque. Only when the boat had delivered him into the throng of the distraught faithful which was swirling around the desecrated shrine did Atta discover that the relic was no longer in his pocket. There was only a hole, which his mother, usually so attentive to household matters, must have overlooked under the stress of recent events.

Atta's initial surge of chagrin was quickly replaced by a feeling of profound relief.

'Suppose', he imagined, 'that I had already announced to the mullahs[8] that the hair was on my person! They would never have believed me now—and this mob would have lynched me! At any rate, it has gone, and that's a load off my mind.' Feeling more contented than he had for days, the young man returned home.

Here he found his sister bruised and weeping in the hall; upstairs, in her bedroom, his mother wailed like a brand-new widow. He begged Huma to tell him what had happened, and when she replied that their father, returning from his brutal business trip, had once again noticed a glint of silver between boat and quay, had once again scooped up the errant relic, and was consequently in a rage to end all rages, having beaten the truth out of her—then Atta buried his face in his hands and sobbed out his opinion, which was that the hair was persecuting them, and had come back to finish the job.

It was Huma's turn to think of a way out of their troubles.

While her arms turned black and blue and great stains spread across her forehead, she hugged her brother and whispered to him that she was determined to get rid of the hair *at all costs*—she repeated this last phrase several times.

'The hair', she then declared, 'was stolen from the mosque; so it can be stolen from this house. But it must be a genuine robbery, carried out by a bona-fide thief, not by one of us who are under the hair's thrall—by a thief so desperate that he fears neither capture nor curses.'

Unfortunately, she added, the theft would be ten times harder to pull off now that their father, knowing that there had already been one attempt on the relic, was certainly on his guard.

'Can you do it?'

Huma, in a room lit by candle and storm-lantern, ended her account with one further question: 'What assurances can you give that the job holds no terrors for you still?'

The criminal, spitting, stated that he was not in the habit of providing references, as a cook might, or a gardener, but he was not alarmed so easily, certainly not by any children's djinni[9] of a curse. Huma had to be content with

---

8. Muslims learned in Islamic theology and sacred law.

9. In Muslim demonology a spirit (genie) with supernatural powers.

2822 / SALMAN RUSHDIE

this boast, and proceeded to describe the details of the proposed burglary.

'Since my brother's failure to return the hair to the mosque, my father has taken to sleeping with his precious treasure under his pillow. However, he sleeps alone, and very energetically; only enter his room without waking him, and he will certainly have tossed and turned quite enough to make the theft a simple matter. When you have the vial, come to my room,' and here she handed Sheikh Sín a plan of her home, 'and I will hand over all the jewellery owned by my mother and myself. You will find . . . it is worth . . . that is, you will be able to get a fortune for it . . .'

It was evident that her self-control was weakening and that she was on the point of physical collapse.

'Tonight,' she burst out finally. 'You must come tonight!'

No sooner had she left the room than the old criminal's body was convulsed by a fit of coughing: he spat blood into an old vanaspati[1] can. The great Sheikh, the 'Thief of Thieves', had become a sick man, and every day the time drew nearer when some young pretender to his power would stick a dagger in his stomach. A lifelong addiction to gambling had left him almost as poor as he had been when, decades ago, he had started out in this line of work as a mere pickpocket's apprentice; so in the extraordinary commission he had accepted from the moneylender's daughter he saw his opportunity of amassing enough wealth at a stroke to leave the valley for ever, and acquire the luxury of a respectable death which would leave his stomach intact.

As for the Prophet's hair, well, neither he nor his blind wife had ever had much to say for prophets—that was one thing they had in common with the moneylender's thunderstruck clan.

It would not do, however, to reveal the nature of this, his last crime, to his four sons. To his consternation, they had all grown up to be hopelessly devout men, who even spoke of making the pilgrimage to Mecca some day. 'Absurd!' their father would laugh at them. 'Just tell me how you will go?' For, with a parent's absolutist love, he had made sure they were all provided with a lifelong source of high income by crippling them at birth, so that, as they dragged themselves around the city, they earned excellent money in the begging business.

The children, then, could look after themselves.

He and his wife would be off soon with the jewel-boxes of the moneylender's women. It was a timely chance indeed that had brought the beautiful bruised girl into his corner of the town.

That night, the large house on the shore of the lake lay blindly waiting, with silence lapping at its walls. A burglar's night: clouds in the sky and mists on the winter water. Hashim the moneylender was asleep, the only member of his family to whom sleep had come that night. In another room, his son Atta lay deep in the coils of his coma with a blood-clot forming on his brain, watched over by a mother who had let down her long greying hair to show her grief, a mother who placed warm compresses on his head with gestures redolent of impotence. In a third bedroom Huma waited, fully dressed, amidst the jewel-heavy caskets of her desperation.

---

1. Vegetable fat used as butter in India.

At last a bulbul[2] sang softly from the garden below her window and, creeping downstairs, she opened a door to the bird, on whose face there was a scar in the shape of the Nastaliq letter *sín*.

Noiselessly, the bird flew up the stairs behind her. At the head of the staircase they parted, moving in opposite directions along the corridor of their conspiracy without a glance at one another.

Entering the moneylender's room with professional ease, the burglar, Sín, discovered that Huma's predictions had been wholly accurate. Hashim lay sprawled diagonally across his bed, the pillow untenanted by his head, the prize easily accessible. Step by padded step, Sín moved towards the goal.

It was at this point that, in the bedroom next door, young Atta sat bolt upright in his bed, giving his mother a great fright, and without any warning—prompted by goodness knows what pressure of the blood-clot upon his brain—began screaming at the top of his voice:

'Thief! Thief! Thief!'

It seems probable that his poor mind had been dwelling, in these last moments, upon his own father; but it is impossible to be certain, because having uttered these three emphatic words the young man fell back upon his pillow and died.

At once his mother set up a screeching and a wailing and a keening and a howling so earsplittingly intense that they completed the work which Atta's cry had begun—that is, her laments penetrated the walls of her husband's bedroom and brought Hashim wide awake.

Sheikh Sín was just deciding whether to dive beneath the bed or brain the moneylender good and proper when Hashim grabbed the tiger-striped swordstick which always stood propped up in a corner beside his bed, and rushed from the room without so much as noticing the burglar who stood on the opposite side of the bed in the darkness. Sín stooped quickly and removed the vial containing the Prophet's hair from its hiding-place.

Meanwhile Hashim had erupted into the corridor, having unsheathed the sword inside his cane. In his right hand he held the weapon and was waving it about dementedly. His left hand was shaking the stick. A shadow came rushing towards him through the midnight darkness of the passageway and, in his somnolent anger, the moneylender thrust his sword fatally through its heart. Turning up the light, he found that he had murdered his daughter, and under the dire influence of this accident he was so overwhelmed by remorse that he turned the sword upon himself, fell upon it and so extinguished his life. His wife, the sole surviving member of the family, was driven mad by the general carnage and had to be committed to an asylum for the insane by her brother, the city's Deputy Commissioner of Police.

Sheikh Sín had quickly understood that the plan had gone awry.

Abandoning the dream of the jewel-boxes when he was but a few yards from its fulfilment, he climbed out of Hashim's window and made his escape during the appalling events described above. Reaching home before dawn, he woke his wife and confessed his failure. It would be necessary, he whispered, for him to vanish for a while. Her blind eyes never opened until he had gone.

2. Asian song thrush.

The noise in the Hashim household had roused their servants and even managed to awaken the night-watchman, who had been fast asleep as usual on his charpoy[3] by the street-gate. They alerted the police, and the Deputy Commissioner himself was informed. When he heard of Huma's death, the mournful officer opened and read the sealed letter which his niece had given him, and instantly led a large detachment of armed men into the light-repellent gullies of the most wretched and disreputable part of the city.

The tongue of a malicious cat-burglar named Huma's fellow-conspirator; the finger of an ambitious bank-robber pointed at the house in which he lay concealed; and although Sín managed to crawl through a hatch in the attic and attempt a roof-top escape, a bullet from the Deputy Commissioner's own rifle penetrated his stomach and brought him crashing messily to the ground at the feet of Huma's enraged uncle.

From the dead thief's pocket rolled a vial of tinted glass, cased in filigree silver.

The recovery of the Prophet's hair was announced at once on All-India Radio. One month later, the valley's holiest men assembled at the Hazratbal mosque and formally authenticated the relic. It sits to this day in a closely guarded vault by the shores of the loveliest of lakes in the heart of the valley which was once closer than any other place on earth to Paradise.

But before our story can properly be concluded, it is necessary to record that when the four sons of the dead Sheikh awoke on the morning of his death, having unwittingly spent a few minutes under the same roof as the famous hair, they found that a miracle had occurred, that they were all sound of limb and strong of wind, as whole as they might have been if their father had not thought to smash their legs in the first hours of their lives. They were, all four of them, very properly furious, because the miracle had reduced their earning powers by 75 per cent, at the most conservative estimate; so they were ruined men.

Only the Sheikh's widow had some reason for feeling grateful, because although her husband was dead she had regained her sight, so that it was possible for her to spend her last days gazing once more upon the beauties of the valley of Kashmir.

1981

3. Light Indian bedstead.

ANNE CARSON
b. 1950

Anne Carson was born in Toronto, Canada, and grew up in Ontario, and she received both her B.A. and her Ph.D. in classics from the University of Toronto. The recipient of a MacArthur Fellowship, she has taught classics at McGill University and the University of Michigan, among other schools. Along with poetry, she has published books of criticism on classical literature; translations from Greek; and a novel-in-verse, *Autobiography of Red* (1998).

In her poetry Carson braids together the ruminative texture of the essay, the narrative propulsion of the novel, the self-analysis of autobiography, and the lapidary compression of lyric. In "The Glass Essay," a long poem that reflects on the dislocations of identity through time, love, and madness, she vividly narrates the end of a love affair, a visit with a difficult mother, and the degeneration of a father with Alzheimer's in a nursing home. Into this semiautobiographical tale she weaves commentary on the writings of Charlotte and Emily Brontë, whose works function—like the classical texts she often incorporates into her poetry—as oblique and remote points of comparison for the poet's experience. Both personal and impersonal, Carson's poetry bridges the gap between private narrative and philosophical speculation, between self-excavation and literary-critical analysis. Tightly wound with crisp diction, studded with striking metaphors, etched with epigrams and ironies, her poems are lucid in feeling and intense in thought. They are as intellectually crystalline as they are emotionally volcanic.

From The Glass Essay

Hero

I can tell by the way my mother chews her toast
whether she had a good night
and is about to say a happy thing
or not.

5   Not.
She puts her toast down on the side of her plate.
You know you can pull the drapes in that room, she begins.

This is a coded reference to one of our oldest arguments,
from what I call The Rules Of Life series.
10 My mother always closes her bedroom drapes tight before going to bed at
     night.

I open mine as wide as possible.
I like to see everything, I say.
What's there to see?

Moon. Air. Sunrise.
15 All that light on your face in the morning. Wakes you up.
I like to wake up.

At this point the drapes argument has reached a delta
and may advance along one of three channels.
There is the What You Need Is A Good Night's Sleep channel,

20 the Stubborn As Your Father channel
and random channel.
More toast? I interpose strongly, pushing back my chair.

Those women! says my mother with an exasperated rasp.
Mother has chosen random channel.
25 Women?

Complaining about rape all the time—
I see she is tapping one furious finger on yesterday's newspaper
lying beside the grape jam.

30   The front page has a small feature
about a rally for International Women's Day—
have you had a look at the Sears Summer Catalogue?

Nope.
Why, it's a disgrace! Those bathing suits—
cut way up to here! (she points) No wonder!

35   You're saying women deserve to get raped
because Sears bathing suit ads
have high-cut legs? Ma, are you serious?

Well someone has to be responsible.
Why should women be responsible for male desire? My voice is high.
40   Oh I see you're one of Them.

One of Whom? My voice is very high. Mother vaults it.
And whatever did you do with that little tank suit you had last year the
        green one?
It looked so smart on you.

The frail fact drops on me from a great height
45   that my mother is afraid.
She will be eighty years old this summer.

Her tiny sharp shoulders hunched in the blue bathrobe
make me think of Emily Brontë's little merlin hawk Hero
that she fed bits of bacon at the kitchen table when Charlotte[1] wasn't
        around.

50   So Ma, we'll go—I pop up the toaster
and toss a hot slice of pumpernickel lightly across onto her plate—
visit Dad today? She eyes the kitchen clock with hostility.

Leave at eleven, home again by four? I continue.
She is buttering her toast with jagged strokes.
55   Silence is assent in our code. I go into the next room to phone the taxi.

My father lives in a hospital for patients who need chronic care
about 50 miles from here.
He suffers from a kind of dementia

characterized by two sorts of pathological change
60   first recorded in 1907 by Alois Alzheimer.[2]
First, the presence in cerebral tissue

---

1. Charlotte Brontë (1816–1855), English novelist, author of *Jane Eyre*, and sister of Emily (1818–
1848), author of *Wuthering Heights*. Throughout
"The Glass Essay," the poet compares her own life
with Emily Brontë's.
2. German neurologist (1864–1915).

of a spherical formation known as neuritic plaque,
consisting mainly of degenerating brain cells.
Second, neurofibrillary snarlings

65 in the cerebral cortex and in the hippocampus.[3]
There is no known cause or cure.
Mother visits him by taxi once a week

for the last five years.
Marriage is for better or for worse, she says,
70 this is the worse.

So about an hour later we are in the taxi
shooting along empty country roads towards town.
The April light is clear as an alarm.

As we pass them it gives a sudden sense of every object
75 existing in space on its own shadow.
I wish I could carry this clarity with me

into the hospital where distinctions tend to flatten and coalesce.
I wish I had been nicer to him before he got crazy.
These are my two wishes.

80 It is hard to find the beginning of dementia.
I remember a night about ten years ago
when I was talking to him on the telephone.

It was a Sunday night in winter.
I heard his sentences filling up with fear.
85 He would start a sentence—about weather, lose his way, start another.
It made me furious to hear him floundering—

my tall proud father, former World War II navigator!
It made me merciless.
I stood on the edge of the conversation,

90 watching him thrash about for cues,
offering none,
and it came to me like a slow avalanche

that he had no idea who he was talking to.
Much colder today I guess. . . .
95 his voice pressed into the silence and broke off,

snow falling on it.
There was a long pause while snow covered us both.
Well I won't keep you,

---

3. Parts of the brain. Neurofibrils are nerve fibers.

he said with sudden desperate cheer as if sighting land.
100   I'll say goodnight now,
I won't run up your bill. Goodbye.

Goodbye.
Goodbye. Who are you?
I said into the dial tone.

105   At the hospital we pass down long pink halls
through a door with a big window
and a combination lock (5–25–3)

to the west wing, for chronic care patients.
Each wing has a name.
110   The chronic wing is Our Golden Mile

although mother prefers to call it The Last Lap.
Father sits strapped in a chair which is tied to the wall
in a room of other tied people tilting at various angles.

My father tilts least, I am proud of him.
115   Hi Dad how y'doing?
His face cracks open it could be a grin or rage

and looking past me he issues a stream of vehemence at the air.
My mother lays her hand on his.
Hello love, she says. He jerks his hand away. We sit.

120   Sunlight flocks through the room.
Mother begins to unpack from her handbag the things she has brought for
    him,
grapes, arrowroot biscuits, humbugs.°   *hard candies*

He is addressing strenuous remarks to someone in the air between us.
He uses a language known only to himself,
125   made of snarls and syllables and sudden wild appeals.

Once in a while some old formula floats up through the wash—
You don't say! or Happy birthday to you!—
but no real sentence

for more than three years now.
130   I notice his front teeth are getting black.
I wonder how you clean the teeth of mad people.

He always took good care of his teeth. My mother looks up.
She and I often think two halves of one thought.
Do you remember that gold-plated toothpick

135   you sent him from Harrod's[4] the summer you were in London? she asks.
Yes I wonder what happened to it.
Must be in the bathroom somewhere.

---

4. Department store.

She is giving him grapes one by one.
They keep rolling out of his huge stiff fingers.
40 He used to be a big man, over six feet tall and strong,

but since he came to hospital his body has shrunk to the merest bone
      house—
except the hands. The hands keep growing.
Each one now as big as a boot in Van Gogh,[5]

they go lumbering after the grapes in his lap.
45 But now he turns to me with a rush of urgent syllables
that break off on a high note—he waits,

staring into my face. That quizzical look.
One eyebrow at an angle.
I have a photograph taped to my fridge at home.

50 It shows his World War II air crew posing in front of the plane.
Hands firmly behind backs, legs wide apart,
chins forward.

Dressed in the puffed flying suits
with a wide leather strap pulled tight through the crotch.
55 They squint into the brilliant winter sun of 1942.

It is dawn.
They are leaving Dover[6] for France.
My father on the far left is the tallest airman,

with his collar up,
60 one eyebrow at an angle.
The shadowless light makes him look immortal,

for all the world like someone who will not weep again.
He is still staring into my face.
Flaps down! I cry.
165 His black grin flares once and goes out like a match.

                                        1995

Epitaph: Zion[1]

Murderous little world once our objects had gazes. Our lives
      Were fragile, the wind
Could dash them away. Here lies the refugee breather
      Who drank a bowl of elsewhere.

                                        2000

---

5. Vincent van Gogh (1853–1890), Dutch postimpressionist, painted *A Pair of Boots* (1887).
6. Port on the English Channel.
1. In the Hebrew Bible the eastern hill of Jerusalem. In Judaism it came to symbolize a promised
homeland; in Christianity, a heavenly or ideal city
of faith.

Poems in Process

Poets have often claimed that their poems were not willed but were inspired, whether by a muse or by divine visitation, or that they emerged full-blown from the poet's unconscious mind. But working manuscripts tell another story, suggesting that, however involuntary the origin of a poem, vision was usually followed by revision, by second thoughts that refined and clarified an original intention or added something new. And revision can be a social as well as a private drama. As noted in section D ("Publishing History, Censorship") of this anthology's "Literary Terminology" glossary, many people participate in the labor that takes texts from the forms in which authors produce them to the forms in which they are presented to readers. In a similar if more limited way, revision, too, as a part of literary history, involves a range of collaborators, both institutional and personal, witting and unwitting: the copyists who recopy drafts so as to prepare fair copies for the printer and who advance suggestions of their own, the advisors who act as sounding boards, and, by the eighteenth century particularly, the critics whose responses the poet anticipates while revising in the hope of preempting them.

Though poets of all periods have revised their work, evidence of this aspect of their labor is sparse until the nineteenth century. It may be that in earlier times, the drafts and proof sheets that recorded revisions were valued only so long as they were useful (to the person preparing the fair copy or the printer setting the text). This emphasis on utility meant that these materials were often discarded once they had served their purpose. (The seventeenth-century term for working drafts, which we still use—"foul papers"—expresses this attitude.) Fascination with anything the author wrote by hand is a distinctly modern phenomenon, a characteristic of an era in which literature has come to be defined by the uniformity of machine-printed books.

Before the introduction of printing into England in 1476, writing was reproduced by hand, in manuscript (literally "written by hand"). Even after printing was introduced, however, certain forms of writing continued to circulate in manuscript. In a manuscript culture, revision was a complicated matter not always instigated or sanctioned by the individuals we would think of as authors. In certain respects, writers and readers were, for many centuries, able, as we are not, to think of all poems as works in process. Thus poets might be at the mercy of scribes who could mistranscribe their work. Chaucer, for example, jokingly promises to curse his scribe Adam unless he should "write truly according to my composition" ("To His Scribe Adam"). Or individuals transcribing poetry into their commonplace books (personalized anthologies) would readily write it down with changes and in so doing blur the lines between authoring and transcribing: sometimes these transcriptions are the only manuscript evidence that has survived.

In the nineteenth century, a relatively new conception of authorship as a career gained widespread acceptance and poets' working drafts began to be preserved with some regularity. The selections from William Blake, Byron, Percy Shelley, John Keats, and Elizabeth Barrett Browning are drafts that were written, emended, crossed out, and rewritten in the heat of first invention; while poems by William Wordsworth, Gerard Manley Hopkins, and Yeats are shown in successive stages of revision over an extended period of time. Shelley's "O World, O Life, O Time" originated in a few key nouns, together with an abstract rhythmic pattern that was only later fleshed out with words. Still other poems—Alfred, Lord Tennyson's "The Lady of Shalott"; Yeats's

"The Sorrow of Love"—were subjected to radical revision long after the initial versions had been committed to print.

Our transcriptions from the poets' drafts attempt to reproduce, as accurately as the change from script to print will allow, the appearance of the manuscript page. A poet's first attempt at a line or phrase is reproduced in larger type, the revisions in smaller type. The line numbers used to identify an excerpt are those of the final form of the complete poem as reprinted in this anthology.

SELECTED BIBLIOGRAPHY

Autograph Poetry in the English Language, 2 vols., 1973, compiled by P. J. Croft, reproduces and transcribes one or more pages of manuscript in the poet's own hand, from the fourteenth century to the present time. Books that discuss the process of poetic composition and revision, with examples from manuscripts and printed versions, are Charles D. Abbott, ed., *Poets at Work*, 1948; Phyllis Bartlett, *Poems in Process*, 1951; A. F. Scott, *The Poet's Craft*, 1957; George Bornstein, *Poetic Remaking: The Art of Browning, Yeats, and Pound*, 1988; and Robert Brinkley and Keith Hanley, eds., *Romantic Revisions*, 1992. In *Word for Word: A Study of Authors' Alterations*, 1965, Wallace Hildick analyzes the composition of prose fiction, as well as poems.

Byron's *"Don Juan,"* ed. T. G. Steffan and W. W. Pratt, 4 vols., 1957, transcribes the manuscript drafts; the Cornell Wordsworth, in process, reproduces, transcribes, and discusses various versions of Wordsworth's poems from the first manuscript drafts to the final publication in his lifetime, and the Cornell Yeats, also in process, does the same for Yeats. The *Bodleian Shelley Manuscripts*, under the general editorship of Donald Reiman, reproduces facsimiles of Percy Shelley's manuscripts. For facsimiles and transcripts of Keats's poems, see *John Keats: Poetry Manuscripts at Harvard*, ed. Jack Stillinger, 1990. Jon Stallworthy, *Between the Lines: Yeats's Poetry in the Making*, 1963, reproduces and analyzes the sequential drafts of a number of Yeats's major poems. Valerie Eliot has edited T. S. Eliot's *The Waste Land: A Facsimile and Transcript of the Original Drafts Including the Annotations of Ezra Pound*, 1971, while Dame Helen Gardner has transcribed and analyzed the manuscript drafts of Eliot's *Four Quartets* in *The Composition of Four Quartets*, 1978.

WILLIAM BLAKE
The Tyger[1]

[First Draft]

The Tyger

1   Tyger Tyger burning bright
In the forests of the night
What immortal hand or eye
~~Dare~~ ~~Could~~ frame thy fearful symmetry

2   Burnt in
~~In what distant~~ deeps or skies
~~The cruel Burnt the~~ fire of thine eyes
On what wings dare he aspire
What the hand dare sieze the fire

3   And what shoulder & what art
Could twist the sinews of thy heart
And when thy heart began to beat
What dread hand & what dread feet

1. These drafts have been taken from a notebook used by William Blake, called the Rossetti MS because it was once owned by Dante Gabriel Rossetti, the Victorian poet and painter; David V. Erdman's edition of *The Notebook of William Blake* (1973) contains a photographic facsimile. The stanza and line numbers were written by Blake in the manuscript.

~~Could fetch it from the furnace deep~~
~~And in thy horrid ribs dare steep~~
~~In the well of sanguine woe~~
~~In what clay & what mould~~
~~Were thy eyes of fury rolld~~

~~Where~~   ~~where~~
4   ~~What~~ the hammer ~~what~~ the chain
In what furnace was thy brain
                                             dread grasp
What the anvil what ~~the arm~~ arm ~~grasp clasp~~
Dare ~~Could~~ its deadly terrors ~~clasp~~ ~~grasp~~ clasp

6   Tyger Tyger burning bright
In the forests of the night
What immortal hand & eye
             frame
Dare ~~form~~ thy fearful symmetry

[*Trial Stanzas*]

Burnt in distant deeps or skies
The cruel fire of thine eye,
Could heart descend or wings aspire
What the hand dare sieze the fire

               dare he smile ~~laugh~~
5 3   And ~~did he laugh~~ his work to see
               ankle
       ~~What the shoulder what the knee~~
       Dare
4   ~~Did~~ he who made the lamb make thee
1   When the stars threw down their spears
2   And waterd heaven with their tears

[*Second Full Draft*]

Tyger Tyger burning bright
In the forests of the night
What Immortal hand & eye
Dare frame thy fearful symmetry

And what shoulder & what art
Could twist the sinews of thy heart
And when thy heart began to beat
What dread hand & what dread feet

When the stars threw down their spears
And waterd heaven with their tears
Did he smile his work to see
Did he who made the lamb make thee

Tyger Tyger burning bright
In the forests of the night
What immortal hand & eye
Dare frame thy fearful symmetry

[*Final Version, 1794*][2]

The Tyger

Tyger Tyger, burning bright,
In the forests of the night;
What immortal hand or eye,
Could frame thy fearful symmetry?

In what distant deeps or skies
Burnt the fire of thine eyes!
On what wings dare he aspire?
What the hand, dare sieze the fire?

And what shoulder, & what art,
Could twist the sinews of thy heart?
And when thy heart began to beat,
What dread hand? & what dread feet?

What the hammer? what the chain,
In what furnace was thy brain?
What the anvil? what dread grasp,
Dare its deadly terrors clasp?

When the stars threw down their spears
And water'd heaven with their tears:
Did he smile his work to see?
Did he who made the Lamb make thee?

Tyger, Tyger burning bright,
In the forests of the night:
What immortal hand or eye,
Dare frame thy fearful symmetry?

WILLIAM WORDSWORTH
She dwelt among the untrodden ways

[*Version in a Letter to Coleridge,
December 1798 or January 1799*][1]

My hope was one, from cities far
    Nursed on a lonesome heath:
Her lips were red as roses are,
    Her hair a woodbine wreath.

---

2. As published in *Songs of Experience.*
1. Printed in Ernest de Selincourt's *Early Letters of William and Dorothy Wordsworth* (1935). By deleting two stanzas, and making a few verbal changes, Wordsworth achieved the terse published form of his great dirge.

She lived among the untrodden ways
  Beside the springs of Dove,
A maid whom there were none to praise,
  And very few to love;

A violet by a mossy stone
  Half-hidden from the eye!
Fair as a star when only one
  Is shining in the sky!

And she was graceful as the broom
  That flowers by Carron's side;²
But slow distemper checked her bloom,
  And on the Heath she died.

Long time before her head lay low
  Dead to the world was she:
But now she's in her grave, and Oh!
  The difference to me!

[*Final Version, 1800*]³

Song

She dwelt among th' untrodden ways
  Beside the springs of Dove,
A Maid whom there were none to praise
  And very few to love.

A Violet by a mossy stone
  Half-hidden from the Eye!
—Fair, as a star when only one
  Is shining in the sky!

She *liv'd* unknown, and few could know
  When Lucy ceas'd to be;
But she is in her Grave, and Oh!
  The difference to me.

LORD BYRON

From Don Juan¹

[*First Draft: Canto 3, Stanza 9*]

~~Life is a play and men.~~
All tragedies are finished by a death,
All Comedies are ended by a marriage,

---

2. The Carron is a river in northwestern Scotland. "Broom" (preceding line) is a shrub with long slender branches and yellow flowers.
3. As published in the second edition of *Lyrical Ballads.*

1. Reproduced from transcripts made of Byron's manuscripts in T. G. Steffan and W. W. Pratt, *Byron's "Don Juan"* (1957). The stanzas were published by Byron in their emended form.

~~For Life can go no further~~
~~These two form the last gasp of Passion's breath.~~
~~All further is a blank— I won't disparage~~
~~That holy state— but certainly beneath~~
~~The Sun— of human things~~
~~These two are levellers, and human breath.~~
~~So~~ ~~These point the epigram of human breath;~~
~~Or any.~~ The future states of both are left to faith,
~~Though Life and love I like not to disparage~~
~~The~~ For authors ~~think~~ description might disparage
       fear
~~Tis strange that poets never try to wreathe~~ [sic?]
~~With eith~~ ~~Tis strange that poets of the Catholic faith~~
~~Neer go beyond— and— but seem to dread miscarriage~~
~~So dramas close with death or settlement for life~~
~~Veiling~~ ~~Leaving the future states of Love and Life~~
~~The paradise beyond like that of life—~~
~~And neer describing either—~~
~~To more conjecture of a devil and or wife.~~
~~And don't say much of paradise or wife.~~
The worlds to come of both—~~&~~ or fall beneath,
And ~~all~~ ~~both the worlds would blame them for miscarriage~~
And then both worlds would punish their miscarriage—
~~So leaving both with priest & prayerbook ready~~
So leaving ~~Clergy both~~ each their Priest and prayerbook ready,
They say no more of death or of the Lady.

[*First Draft: Canto 14, Stanza 95*]

     quote   seldom
Alas! ~~I speak by~~ Experience—~~never~~ yet
~~I had a paramour—and I've had many—~~
         ~~some small—~~
~~To whom I did not cause a deep~~ regret—
~~Whom I had not some reason to~~ regret
~~For Whom— I did not feel myself~~ a Zany—
Alas! by all experience, seldom yet
(I merely quote what I have heard from many)
Had lovers not some reason to regret
The passion which made Solomon a Zany.
~~I also had a wife—~~not to forget—
I've also seen some wives—not to forget—
The marriage state—the best or worst of any—
  were   paragons
Who ~~was~~ the very ~~paragon~~ of wives,
Yet made the misery of ~~both our~~ lives.
        ~~many—~~
        ~~several—~~
        ~~of~~ at least two

PERCY BYSSHE SHELLEY

The three stages of this poem labeled "First Draft" are scattered through one of Shelley's notebooks, now in the Huntington Library, San Marino, California; these drafts have been transcribed and analyzed by Bennett Weaver, "Shelley Works Out the Rhythm of *A Lament*," *PMLA* 47 (1932): 570–76. They show Shelley working with fragmentary words and phrases, and simultaneously with a wordless pattern of pulses that marked out the meter of the single lines and the shape of the lyric stanzas. Shelley left this draft unfinished.

Apparently at some later time, Shelley returned to the poem and wrote what is here called the "Second Draft"; from this he then made, on a second page, a revised fair copy that provided the text that Mary Shelley published in 1824, after the poet's death. These two manuscript pages are now in the Bodleian Library, Oxford; the first page is photographically reproduced and discussed by John Carter and John Sparrow, "Shelley, Swinburne, and Housman," *Times Literary Supplement*, November 21, 1968, pp. 1318–19.

O World, O Life, O Time

[*First Draft, Stage 1*]

Ah time, oh night, oh day
~~Ni nal ni na, na ni~~
~~Ni na ni na, ni na~~
Oh life O death, O time
   Time a di
~~Never Time~~
Ah time, a time O-time
  ~~Time!~~

[*First Draft, Stage 2*]

Oh time, oh night oh day
~~O day oh night, alas~~
  ~~O~~ Death time night ~~oh~~
Oh, Time
Oh time o night oh day

[*First Draft, Stage 3*]

Na na, na na ná na
Nă nă na na na—nă nă
  Nă nă nă nă nā nā
Na na nă nă nâ ă na

Na na na—nă nă—na na
  Na na na na—na na na na na
Na na na na na.
   Na na
Na na na na na

Na na
Na na na na na ˇ na!

Oh time, oh night, o day
      alas
O day ~~serenest~~, o day
O day alas the day
That thou shouldst sleep when we awake to say

O time time—o death—o day
     for
O day, o death life is far from thee
O thou wert never free
For death is now with thee
~~And life is far from~~
O death, o day for life is far from thee

[Second Draft]¹   *I am*
                    despair

Out of the day & night
A joy has taken flight
Fresh spring & summer   & winter hoar
Fill my faint heart with grief, but with
                         delight
        No more—o never more!

~~Wo~~
    O World, o life, o time
~~Will ye~~ On whose last steps I climb
Trembling at those which I have trod² before
When will return the glory of yr prime
    No more   Oh never more

     Out of the day & night
     A joy has taken flight—
             autumn
~~From~~ Green spring, & ~~summer gra~~³ & winter hoar

[FAIR COPY]

O World o Life o Time
On whose last steps I climb
Trembling at that where I had stood before
When will return the glory of yr prime?
    No more, o never more

---

1. Shelley apparently wrote the first stanza of this draft low down on the page, and ran out of space after crowding in the third line of the second stanza; he then, in a lighter ink, wrote a revised form of the whole of the second stanza at the top of the page. In this revision he left a space after "summer" in line 3, indicating that he planned an insertion that would fill out the four-foot meter of this line, and so make it match the five feet in the corresponding line of the first stanza.

In the upper right-hand corner of this manuscript page, Shelley wrote "I am despair"—seemingly to express his bleak mood at the time he wrote the poem.

For this draft and information, and for the transcript of the fair copy that follows, the editors are indebted to Donald H. Reiman.

2. Shelley at first wrote "trod," then overwrote that with "stood." In the following line, Shelley at first wrote "yr," then overwrote "thy."

3. Not clearly legible; it is either "gra" or "gre." A difference in the ink from the rest of the line indicates that Shelley, having left a blank space, later started to fill it in, but thought better of it and crossed out the fragmentary insertion.

2

Out of the day & night
A joy has taken flight
Fresh spring & summer   ⁴ & winter hoar
Move my faint heart with grief but with delight
No more, o, never more

JOHN KEATS
From The Eve of St. Agnes¹

[*Stanza 26*]

But soon his heart revives—her prayers said
She ~~lays aside her veil~~   pearled
       strips her hair of all its   wreath's pearl
~~Unclasps her bosom jewels~~
~~And twist it in one knot upon her head~~

But soon his heart revives—her praying done,   soon
Of all its wreathed pearl she strips her hair
Unclasps her warmed jewels one by one
              her bursting
Loosens ~~the boddice from her~~
              ~~her Boddice lace string~~
              ~~her Boddice and her bosom bar~~
              her

[HERE KEATS BEGINS A NEW SHEET]

Loosens ~~her fragrant boddice and doth bare~~
~~Her~~

26

Anon
~~But soon~~ his heart revives—her praying done,
                                    frees:
Of all its wreathe'd pearl her hair she ~~strips~~
Unclasps her warmed jewels one by one
                              by degrees

4. This fair copy of the second draft retains, and even enlarges, the blank space, indicating that Shelley still hasn't made up his mind what to insert after the word "summer." We may speculate, by reference to the fragmentary version of this stanza in the second draft, that he had in mind as possibilities either an adjective, "gray" or "green," or else the noun "autumn." Mary Shelley closed up this space when she published the poem in 1824, with the result that editors, following her version, have until very recently printed this line as though Shelley had intended it to be one metric foot shorter than the corresponding line of stanza 1.

1. Transcribed from Keats's first draft of all but the first seven stanzas of *The Eve of St. Agnes*; the manuscript is now in the Houghton Library, Harvard University. Keats's published version of the poem contains additional changes in wording. That published version also incorporates revisions introduced by other hands. Because Keats's friend Richard Woodhouse and his publisher, John Taylor, took alarm at the suggestion, made more explicit in one of the stanzas Keats added to his original draft, that the pleasure of which Madeline would dream would include sexual pleasure particularly, they worked over Woodhouse's transcripts of the poem and produced a less risqué text that combined Keats's draft and his revised fair copy along with, as Jack Stillinger has conjectured, their own suggestions.

For a photographic reproduction of the page of the holograph manuscript of *The Eve of St. Agnes* containing the poem's stanza 30, see the color insert.

Loosens her fragrant boddice: ~~and down slips~~ ^to her knees^
Her sweet attire ~~falls light creeps down by~~
        creeps rusteling to her knees
        Mermaid   in sea weed
Half hidden like ~~a Syren of the Sea~~
~~And more melodious~~
        dreaming
She stands awhile in ∧ thought; and sees
                on
In fancy fair Saint Agnes ~~in~~ her bed
But dares not look behind or all the charm is ~~fl~~ dead

[*Stanza 30*]

        But
~~And still she slept~~:
And still she slept an azure-lidded sleep
    In blanched linen, smooth and lavender'd
    While he from frorth the closet brough a heap
        ~~fruits~~
        Of candied ~~sweets sweets, with~~
            apple Quince and plumb and gourd
                        creamed
    With jellies soother than the ~~dairy~~ curd
                tinct
    And lucent syrups ~~smooth~~ with ciannamon
~~And sugar'd dates from that oer Euphrates fard~~
                ~~in Brigantine transferred~~
    Manna and daites in ~~Bragtine transferrd~~
                    ~~and manna wild transferrd~~
~~And Manna wild and Bragantine~~
                    sugar'd dates transferred
~~In Brigantine from Fez~~
    From fez—and spiced danties every one
        ~~glutted~~
    From ~~wealthy~~ Samarchand to cedard lebanon
        silken

argosy

To Autumn[2]

Season of Mists and mellow fruitfulness
    Close bosom friend of the naturring sun;
Conspiring with him how to load and bless
    The Vines with fruit that round the thatch eves run
    To bend with apples the moss'd Cottage trees
        And fill all furuits with sweeness to the core
        To swell the gourd, and plump the hazle shells
    With a white kernel; to set budding more
    And still more later flowers for the bees
    Until they think wam days with never cease
        For Summer has o'erbrimm'd their clammy cells—

2. From an untitled manuscript—apparently Keats's first draft of the poem—in the Houghton Library, Harvard University. The many pen-slips and errors in spelling indicate that Keats wrote rapidly, in a state of creative excitement. Keats made a few further changes before publishing the poem in the form included in the selections above.

oft amid thy stores?
Who hath not seen thee? ~~for thy haunts are many~~
      abroad
  Sometimes whoever seeks ~~for thee~~ may find
Thee sitting careless on a granary floorr
  Thy hair soft lifted by the winnowing wind

                        ~~husky~~
~~While bright the Sun slants through the~~ ^ ~~barn;—~~
     or on a half reap'd furrow sound asleep
~~Or sound asleep in a half reaped field~~
    ~~Dos'd with~~ dead poppies; while thy reaping hook
~~Spares form some slumbrous~~
          ~~minutes while warn slumpers creep~~
  Or on a half reap'd furrow sound asleep
  Dos'd with the fume of poppies, while thy hook
    Spares the next swath and all its twined flowers
~~Spares for some slumbrous minutes the next swath;~~
  And sometimes like a gleans thost dost keep
    Steady thy laden head across the brook;
    Or by a Cyder-press with patent look
  Thou watchest the last oozing hours by hours

Where are the songs of Sping? Aye where are they?
  Think not of them thou hast thy music too—
    barred   bloom
While ~~a gold~~ clouds ~~gilds~~ the soft-dying day
  And   with
~~And~~ Touching ~~the~~ the stibble plains ∧ rosy hue—
  Then in a waiful quire the small gnats mourn
    Among the river sallows, ~~on the~~ borne afots
    Or sinking as the light wind lives and dies;
  And full grown Lambs loud bleat from hilly bourn,
    Hedge crickets sing, and now again full soft
    The Redbreast whistles from a garden croft:
~~And now flock still~~
  And Gather'd Swallows twiter in the Skies—

ALFRED, LORD TENNYSON

From The Lady of Shalott[1]

[*Version of 1832*]

PART THE FIRST.

On either side the river lie
Long fields of barley and of rye,
That clothe the wold, and meet the sky.
And thro' the field the road runs by

1. First published in Tennyson's *Poems* of 1832 (dated 1833 on the title page). The volume was severely criticized by some reviewers; partly in response to this criticism, Tennyson radically revised a number of the poems, including "The Lady of Shalott," before reprinting them in his *Poems* (1842).

Parts 1 and 4 are reproduced here in the version

of 1832. The final form of the poem reprinted in the selections from Tennyson, above, differs from the revised version that Tennyson published in 1842 only in line 157, which in 1842 read "A corse between the houses high"; Tennyson changed the line to "Dead-pale between the houses high" in 1855.

To manytowered Camelot.
The yellowleavèd waterlily,
The greensheathèd daffodilly,
Tremble in the water chilly,
            Round about Shallot.

Willows whiten, aspens shiver,
The sunbeam-showers break and quiver
In the stream that runneth ever
By the island in the river,
            Flowing down to Camelot.
Four gray walls and four gray towers
Overlook a space of flowers,
And the silent isle imbowers
            The Lady of Shallot.

Underneath the bearded barley,
The reaper, reaping late and early,
Hears her ever chanting cheerly,
Like an angel, singing clearly,
            O'er the stream of Camelot.
Piling the sheaves in furrows airy,
Beneath the moon, the reaper weary
Listening whispers, " 'tis the fairy
            Lady of Shalott."

The little isle is all inrailed
With a rose-fence, and overtrailed
With roses: by the marge unhailed
The shallop flitteth silkensailed,
            Skimming down to Camelot.
A pearlgarland winds her head:
She leaneth on a velvet bed,
Full royally apparellèd,
            The Lady of Shalott.

*　*　*

PART THE FOURTH.

In the stormy eastwind straining
The pale-yellow woods were waning,
The broad stream in his banks complaining,
Heavily the low sky raining
            Over towered Camelot:
Outside the isle a shallow boat
Beneath a willow lay afloat,
Below the carven stern she wrote,
            THE LADY OF SHALOTT.

A cloudwhite crown of pearl she dight.
All raimented in snowy white
That loosely flew, (her zone in sight,
Clasped with one blinding diamond bright,)

Her wide eyes fixed on Camelot,
Though the squally eastwind keenly
Blew, with folded arms serenely
By the water stood the queenly
    Lady of Shalott.

With a steady, stony glance—
Like some bold seer in a trance,
Beholding all his own mischance,
Mute, with a glassy countenance—
    She looked down to Camelot.
It was the closing of the day,
She loosed the chain, and down she lay,
The broad stream bore her far away,
    The Lady of Shalott.

As when to sailors while they roam,
By creeks and outfalls far from home,
Rising and dropping with the foam,
From dying swans wild warblings come,
    Blown shoreward; so to Camelot
Still as the boathead wound along
The willowy hills and fields among,
They heard her chanting her deathsong,
    The Lady of Shalott.

A longdrawn carol, mournful, holy,
She chanted loudly, chanted lowly,
Till her eyes were darkened wholly,
And her smooth face sharpened slowly
    Turned to towered Camelot:
For ere she reached upon the tide
The first house by the waterside,
Singing in her song she died,
    The Lady of Shalott.

Under tower and balcony,
By gardenwall and gallery,
A pale, pale corpse she floated by,
Deadcold, between the houses high.
    Dead into towered Camelot.
Knight and burgher, lord and dame,
To the plankèd wharfage came:
Below the stern they read her name,
    "The Lady of Shalott."

They crossed themselves, their stars they blest,
Knight, ministrel, abbot, squire and guest.
There lay a parchment on her breast,
That puzzled more than all the rest,
    The wellfed wits at Camelot.
"The web was woven curiously

The charm is broken utterly,
Draw near and fear not—this is I,
The Lady of Shalott."

From Tithonus[2]

[Lines 1–10]

[TRINITY COLLEGE MANUSCRIPT]

Ay me! Ay me! the woods decay & fall
~~The stars blaze out & never rise again.~~

          the
The vapours weep their substance to ground
Man comes & tills the earth & lies beneath
And after many summers dies the ~~rose~~ swan
Me only fatal immortality
Consumes: I wither slowly in thine arms:
Here at the quiet limit of the world
        e yet
A white-haired shadow roaming like a dream
The ever-silent spaces of the East
Far-folded mists & gleaming halls of morn.

[HEATH MANUSCRIPT]

Tithon

Ay me! ay me! the woods decay and fall,
The vapours weep their substance to the ground,
Man comes and tills the earth and lies beneath,
And after many summers dies the rose.
Me only fatal immortality
Consumes: I wither slowly in thine arms,
Here at the quiet limit of the world,
A white-haired shadow roaming like a dream
The ever-silent spaces of the East,
Far-folded mists, and gleaming halls of morn.

[AS PRINTED IN 1864]

Tithonus

The woods decay, the woods decay and fall,
The vapours weep their burthen to the ground,
Man comes and tills the field and lies beneath,
And after many a summer dies the swan.

2. Three manuscript drafts of "Tithonus" are extant. Two are in Tennyson's Notebooks Nos. 20 and 21, at Trinity College, Cambridge; a third one, written 1833, is in the Commonplace Book compiled by Tennyson's friend J. M. Heath, which is in the Fitzwilliam Museum at Cambridge University. According to Tennyson's editor, Christopher Ricks, the Heath version is later than those in the Trinity Manuscripts. The transcriptions here of

Tennyson's opening lines are from the first draft (Trinity College manuscript, Notebook 20), and from the Heath manuscript, where the poem is titled "Tithon." These are followed by the final version of "Tithonus" Tennyson published in 1864. As late as in the edition of 1860, the opening words had remained "Ay me! ay me!" and "field" (line 3) had remained "earth."

Me only cruel immortality
Consumes: I wither slowly in thine arms,
Here at the quiet limit of the world,
A white-haired shadow roaming like a dream
The ever-silent spaces of the East,
Far-folded mists, and gleaming halls of morn.

ELIZABETH BARRETT BROWNING

From The Runaway Slave at Pilgrim's Point[1]

[*From the British Library manuscript, 1846*]

<u>Why</u>
~~And~~ in that single glance I had
Of my child's face . . I tell you all . .
I saw a look that made me mad—!
The master's look, that used to fall
On my soul like his lash . . or worse:
And so, to save it from my curse
I twisted it round in my shawl.   Does this <u>sound</u> like a slave's article of clothing?[2]

            trembled
And he moaned and ~~struggled~~ from foot to head—
    shivered
He ~~trembled~~ from head to foot—
Till after a time he lay instead
Too suddenly still and mute . .
And I felt, beside, a creeping cold—
I dared to lift up just a fold,
As in lifting a leaf of the mango-fruit.

But <u>my</u> fruit . . . ha, ha—there, had been . .
(I laugh to think on't at this hour . .)
Your fine white angels, (who have seen
God's secrets nearest to His power)
And plucked my fruit to make them wine,
And sucked the soul of that child of mine,
         the soul of
As the hummingbird sucks ∧ the flower.

Ha, ha, for the trick of the angels white!
They freed the white child's spirit so,
I said not a word, but day and night

1. One part of Barrett Browning's manuscript draft of her abolitionist poem is in the British Library in London; another, fittingly, given the poem's initial publication by a Boston abolitionist society, is on the other side of the Atlantic, in the Baylor University's Armstrong Library; a third is in the hands of a private collector. We give six stanzas from the British Library manuscript, along with, first, their counterparts in the initial printed version of the poem in *The Liberty Bell for 1848* (published in December 1847 for the National Anti-Slavery Bazaar), and, then, their counterparts in Barrett Browning's *Poems* of 1850. Barrett Browning added a stanza to the poem after 1847 (the seventh stanza of the 1850 version); stanza 20 in the *Liberty Bell* version corresponds accordingly to stanza 21 in *Poems* and so forth. For discussion of Barrett Browning's revision of the *Liberty Bell* version, see Andrew M. Stauffer, "Elizabeth Barrett Browning's (Re)Vision of Slavery," in *English Language Notes* 34 (1997): 29–48.
2. Written sideways in the right-hand margin of the manuscript, in Robert Browning's handwriting.

I carried the body to and fro—
And it lay on my heart like a stone .. as chill.
The sun may shine out as much as he will.
_{month}
I am cold, though it happened a ~~year~~ ago.

From the white man's house, and the black man's hut
I carried the little body on—
_{'s arms}
The forest ~~trees~~ did around us shut
_{trees}
And silence through the leaves did run—
They asked no questions as I went:
They stood
~~The trees were~~ too high, for astonishment;
They could see God rise on His throne.

My little body, kerchiefed fast,
I bore it on through the forest .. on:
And, when I felt it was tired at last,
I scooped a hole beneath the moon—
Through the forest-tops the angels far
With a white fine finger from every star,
and mock
Did point ⋀ at what was done.

[*First printed version, from* The Liberty Bell *for* 1848]

XX.

Even in that single glance I had
    Of my child's face,—I tell you all,—
I saw a look that made me mad,—
    The master's look, that used to fall
On my soul like this lash, or worse,—
Therefore, to save it from my curse,
    I twisted it round in my shawl.

XXI.

And he moaned and trembled from foot to head,—
    He shivered from head to foot,—
Till, after a time, he lay, instead,
    Too suddenly still and mute;
And I felt, beside, a creeping cold,—
I dared to lift up just a fold,
    As in lifting a leaf of the mango fruit.

XXII.

But MY fruit! ha, ha!—there had been
    (I laugh to think on 't at this hour!)
Your fine white angels,—who have seen
    God's secret nearest to His power,—
And gathered my fruit to make them wine,

And sucked the soul of that child of mine,
   As the humming-bird sucks the soul of the flower.

XXIII.

Ha, ha! for the trick of the angels white!
   They freed the white child's spirit so;
I said not a word, but day and night
   I carried the body to and fro;
And it lay on my heart like a stone—as chill;
The sun may shine out as much as he will,—
   I am cold, though it happened a month ago.

XXIV.

From the white man's house and the black man's hut
   I carried the little body on;
The forest's arms did around us shut,
   And silence through the trees did run!
They asked no questions as I went,—
They stood too high for astonishment,—
   They could see God rise on his throne.

XXV.

My little body, kerchiefed fast,
   I bore it on through the forest—on—
And when I felt it was tired at last,
   I scooped a hole beneath the moon.
Through the forest-tops the angels far,
With a white fine finger in every star
   Did point and mock at what was done.

[*From* Poems, *1850*]

XXI.

Why, in that single glance I had
   Of my child's face, . . . I tell you all,
I saw a look that made me mad!
   The *master's* look, that used to fall
On my soul like his lash . . . or worse!
And so, to save it from my curse,
   I twisted it round in my shawl.

XXII.

And he moaned and trembled from foot to head,
   He shivered from head to foot;
Till after a time, he lay instead
   Too suddenly still and mute.
I felt, beside, a stiffening cold:
I dared to lift up just a fold,
   As in lifting a leaf of the mango-fruit.

XXIII.

But *my* fruit . . . ha, ha!—there, had been
   (I laugh to think on't at this hour!)
Your fine white angels (who have seen
   Nearest the secret of God's power)
And plucked my fruit to make them wine,
And sucked the soul of that child of mine
   As the humming-bird sucks the soul of the flower.

XXIV.

Ha, ha, the trick of the angels white!
   They freed the white child's spirit so.
I said not a word, but day and night
   I carried the body to and fro,
And it lay on my heart like a stone, as chill.
—The sun may shine out as much as he will:
   I am cold, though it happened a month ago.

XXV.

From the white man's house, and the black man's hut,
   I carried the little body on;
The forest's arms did round us shut,
   And silence through the trees did run:
They asked no question as I went,
They stood too high for astonishment,
   They could see God sit on His throne.

XXVI.

My little body, kerchiefed fast,
   I bore it on through the forest, on;
And when I felt it was tired at last,
   I scooped a hole beneath the moon:
Through the forest-tops the angels far,
With a white sharp finger from every star,
   Did point and mock at what was done.

GERARD MANLEY HOPKINS
Thou art indeed just, Lord[1]

*Justus quidem tu es, Domine, si disputem tecum; verumtamen
justa loquar ad te: quare via impiorum prosperatur?* etc.
—Jer. xii 1.

---

1. From a manuscript in the Bodleian Library, Oxford University; it is a clean copy, made after earlier drafts, which Hopkins goes on to revise further. Differences in the ink show that the emendation "lacèd they are" (line 10) was made during the first writing, but that the other verbal changes were made later. The interlinear markings are Hopkins's metrical indicators; he explains their significance in the "Author's Preface," included in *Poems of Gerard Manley Hopkins* (1970), ed. W. H. Gardner and N. H. MacKenzie.
   The epigraph is from the Vulgate translation of Jeremiah 12.1; a literal translation of the Latin is "Thou art indeed just, Lord, [even] if I plead with Thee; nevertheless I will speak what is just to Thee: Why does the way of the wicked prosper? etc."

March 17 1889

Lord, if I
Thou art indeed just, ~~were I to~~ contend
  sir,   plead
With thee; but, ~~Lord~~, so what I ~~speak~~ is just.

Why do sinners' ways prosper? and why must

Disappointment all I endeavour end?
Wert thou my enemy, O thou my friend,
How wouldst thou worse, I wonder, than thou dost
     O the sots and   of
Defeat, thwart me? ~~Ah! sots, revellers~~, thralls to lust
Do in   that
~~In~~ spare hours ~~do~~ more thrive than I ~~who~~ spend,
  great   See,
Sir, ~~my~~ life on thy cause. ~~Look~~, banks and brakes
Now, leavèd   lacèd they are
~~Leavèd~~ how thick! ~~broidered all~~ again
      look
With fretty chervil, ~~now~~, and fresh winds shakes
Them; birds build—but not I build; no, but strain,
Time's eunuch, and not breed one work that wakes.
Mine, O   send my
~~Then send~~, thou lord of life, ~~these~~ roots ~~their~~ rain.

WILLIAM BUTLER YEATS

Yeats usually composed very slowly and with painful effort. He tells us in his autobiography that "five or six lines in two or three laborious hours were a day's work, and
I longed for somebody to interrupt me." His manuscripts show the slow evolution of
his best poems, which sometimes began with a prose sketch, were then versified, and
underwent numerous revisions. In many instances, even after the poems had been
published, Yeats continued to revise them, sometimes drastically, in later printings.

The Sorrow of Love[1]

[*Manuscript, 1891*][2]

The quarrel of the sparrows in the eaves,
The full round moon and the star-laden sky,
The song of the ever-singing leaves,
Had hushed away earth's old and weary cry.

1. Originally composed in Yeats's Pre-Raphaelite
mode of the early 1890s, "The Sorrow of Love" was
one of his most popular poems. Nonetheless, some
thirty years after publication, Yeats rewrote the
lyric in accordance with modernism's emphasis on
precision and colloquial vigor.
2. Manuscript version composed in October
1891, as transcribed by Jon Stallworthy, *Between
the Lines: Yeats's Poetry in the Making* (Oxford University Press, 1963), pp. 47–48.

And then you came with those red mournful lips,
And with you came the whole of the world's tears,
And all the sorrows of her labouring ships,
And all the burden of her million years.

And now the angry sparrows in the eaves,
The withered moon, the white stars in the sky,
The wearisome loud chanting of the leaves,
Are shaken with earth's old and weary cry.

[First Printed Version, 1892][3]

The quarrel of the sparrows in the eaves,
    The full round moon and the star-laden sky,
And the loud song of the ever-singing leaves
    Had hid away earth's old and weary cry.

And then you came with those red mournful lips,
    And with you came the whole of the world's tears,
And all the sorrows of her labouring ships,
    And all burden of her myriad years.

And now the sparrows warring in the eaves,
    The crumbling moon, the white stars in the sky,
And the loud chanting of the unquiet leaves,
    Are shaken with earth's old and weary cry.

[Final Printed Version, 1925][4]

The brawling of a sparrow in the eaves,
The brilliant moon and all the milky sky,
And all that famous harmony of leaves,
Had blotted out man's image and his cry.

A girl arose that had red mournful lips
And seemed the greatness of the world in tears,
Doomed like Odysseus and the labouring ships
And proud as Priam murdered with his peers;

3. From Yeats's *The Countess Kathleen and Various Legends and Lyrics* (1892). In a corrected page proof for this printing, now in the Garvan Collection of the Yale University Library, lines 7–8 originally read "And all the sorrows of his labouring ships, / And all the burden of his married years." Also, in lines 4 and 12, the adjective was "bitter" instead of "weary." In his *Poems* (1895), Yeats inserted the missing "the" in line 8 and changed "sorrows" (line 7) to "trouble"; "burden" (line 8) to "trouble"; and "crumbling moon" (line 10) to "curd-pale moon."
4. From *Early Poems and Stories* (1925). Yeats wrote in his *Autobiographies* (New York, 1999), p. 321, that "in later years" he had "learnt that occasional prosaic words gave the impression of an active man speaking," so that "certain words must be dull and numb. Here and there in correcting my early poems I have introduced such numbness and dullness, turned, for instance, 'the curd-pale moon' into the 'brilliant moon', that all might seem, as it were, remembered with indifference, except some one vivid image." Yeats, however, did not recall his emendations accurately. He had in 1925 altered "the full round moon" (line 2) to "the brilliant moon," and "the curd-pale moon" (line 10, version of 1895) to "a climbing moon."

Arose, and on the instant clamorous eaves,
A climbing moon upon an empty sky,
And all that lamentation of the leaves,
Could but compose man's image and his cry.

Leda and the Swan[5]

[First Version]

Annunciation

Now can the swooping Godhead have his will
Yet hovers, though her helpless thighs are pressed
By the webbed toes; and that all powerful bill
Has suddenly bowed her face upon his breast.
How can those terrified vague fingers push
The feathered glory from her loosening thighs?
All the stretched body's laid on that white rush

        strange
And feels the ~~strong~~ heart beating where it lies
A shudder in the loins engenders there
The broken wall, the burning roof and tower
And Agamemnon dead. . . .
                Being so caught up
Did nothing pass before her in the air?
Did she put on his knowledge with his power
Before the indifferent beak could let her drop
             Sept 18 1923

       swooping
The ~~trembl~~ godhead is half hovering still,
     climbs
Yet ~~climbs~~ upon her trembling body pressed
    webbed
By the toes; & ~~through~~ that all powerful bill
            bowed
Has suddenly ~~bowed~~ her face upon his breast.
How can those terrified vague fingers push
The feathered glory from her loosening thighs
           laid
All the stretched body leans on ~~that~~ white rush
       or
He ~~falling body thrown on the white white rush~~

5. From Yeats's manuscript *Journal*, Sections 248 and 250. This *Journal*, including facsimiles and transcriptions of the drafts of "Leda and the Swan," has been published in W. B. Yeats, *Memoirs*, ed. Denis Donoghue (London, 1972).

The first version, entitled "Annunciation," seems to be a clean copy of earlier drafts; Yeats went on to revise it further, especially the opening octave. Neither of the other two complete drafts, each of which Yeats labeled "Final Version," was in fact final. Yeats crossed out the first draft. The second, although Yeats published it in 1924, was subjected to further revision before he published the poem in *The Tower* (1928), in the final form reprinted in the selections from Yeats, above.

Yeats's handwriting is hasty and very difficult to decipher. The readings of some words in the manuscript are uncertain.

Can feel etc
or Her body can but lean on the white rush

But mounts until her trembling thighs are pressed[6]
B
By the webbed toes; & that all powerful bill
Has suddenly bowed her head on his breast

Final Version

Annunciation

Can hold

The swooping godhead is half hovering still
But mounts, until her trembling thighs are pressed
By the webbed toes, & that all powerful bill
Has hung her helpless body
Has suddenly bowed her head upon his breast.
How can those terrified vague fingers push
The feathered glory from her loosening thighs?
How   now its body leans on
With her body laid on the white rush
all the stretched body laid on the white rush
and Can feel the strange heart beating where it lies?
A shudder in the loins engenders there
The broken wall, the burning roof & tower
And Agamemnon dead . . .
                                    Being mastered so
                          Being so caught up
        So
And mastered by the brute blood of the air
                          Being mastered so
Did nothing pass before her in the air
Did she put on his knowledge with his power
Before the indifferent beak could let her drop.
                          WBY Sept 18 1923
        swoop
A rush upon great wings & hovering still
He sinks until
He has sunk on her down, & her hair
The great bird sinks, till
The bird descends, & her frail thigh thighs are pressed
By the webbed toes, & that all

        that
Now all her body's laid on that white rush[7]
All the stretched body laid on that white rush
Now that whole

6. This passage is written across the blank page opposite the first version; Yeats drew a line indicating that it was to replace the revised lines 2–4, which he had written below the first version.

7. Written on the blank page across from the complete version, with an arrow indicating that it was a revision of the seventh line.

Now t~~⁓⁓⁓⁓⁓⁓⁓⁓⁓~~rush
~~⁓⁓~~an ~~⁓ee~~

Final Version

Leda & the Swan

       A rush, a sudden wheel and
~~A swoop upon great wings~~ & hovering still
      sinks down   ~~bare frail~~
stet The bird ~~descends~~ & her ~~frail~~ thighs are pressed
                  • • •
By the toes webbed toes, & that all powerful bill
     laid
Has ~~driven~~ her helpless face upon his breast.
How can those terrified vague fingers push
The feathered glory from her loosening thighs?
                  s laid
All the stretched body ~~laid~~ on that white rush
And ~~feel~~ feels the strange heart beating where it lies.
A shudder in the loins engenders there
The broken wall, the burning roof & tower
And Agamemnon dead.
                     Being so caught up
So mastered by the ~~br~~ brute blood of the air
Did she put on his knowledge with his power
Before the indifferent beak could let her drop.

D. H. LAWRENCE

The Piano[1]

Somewhere beneath that piano's superb sleek bla~~ck~~
Must hide my mother's piano, little and br~~own~~, with
        the back
      stood close to
That ~~was against~~ the wall, and the front's faded silk, both torn
And the keys with little hollows, that my mother's fingers
        had worn.

Softly, in the shadows, a woman is singing to me
Quietly, through the years I have crept back to see
A child sitting under the piano, in the boom of the
     shaking ~~tingling~~ strings.

---

1. Transcribed from a notebook in which Lawrence at first entered various academic assignments while he was a student at the University College of Nottingham, 1906–8, but then used to write drafts of some of his early poems. These were probably composed in the period from 1906 to 1910. The text reproduced here was revised and published with the title "Piano" in Lawrence's *New Poems*, 1918. A comparison of this draft with "Piano," reprinted above, will show that Lawrence eliminated the first and fourth stanzas (as well as the last two lines of the third stanza); revised the remaining three stanzas, sometimes radically; and most surprisingly, reversed his original conclusion. As Lawrence explained, some of his early poems "had to be altered, where sometimes the hand of commonplace youth had been laid on the mouth of the demon. It is not for technique that these poems are altered: it is to say the real say."

For transcriptions and discussions of this and other poems in Lawrence's early notebook, see Vivian de Sola Pinto, "D. H. Lawrence: Letter-Writer and Craftsman in Verse," in *Renaissance and Modern Studies* 1 (1957): 5–34.

Pressing the little poised feet of the mother who smiles
      as she sings

The full throated woman has chosen a winning, living[2]
      song
And surely the heart that is in me must belong
To the old Sunday evenings, when darkness wandered
      outside
And hymns gleamed on our warm lips, as we watched
      mother's fingers glide

            is
Or is this my sister at home in the old front room
Singing love's first surprised gladness, alone in
      the gloom.
She will start when she sees me, and blushing,
      spread out her hands
To cover my mouth's raillery, till I'm bound in
             heart-spun
    her shame's pleading bands.

A woman is singing me a wild Hungarian
      air
And her arms, and her bosom and the whole
      of her soul is bare
And the great black piano is clamouring as my
      mother's never could clamour
        my mother's [   ]³ tunes are
And the tunes of the past is devoured of this music's
      ravaging glamour.

<hr/>

2. A conjectural reading; the word is not clearly
legible.

3. An undecipherable word is crossed out here.

Selected Bibliographies

The Selected Bibliographies consist of a list of Suggested General Readings on English literature, followed by bibliographies for each of the literary periods in this volume. For ease of reference, the authors within each period are arranged in alphabetical order.

SUGGESTED GENERAL READINGS

Histories of England and of English Literature

New research and new perspectives have made even the most distinguished of the comprehensive general histories written in past generations seem outmoded. Innovative research in social, cultural, and political history has made it difficult to write a single coherent account of England from the Middle Ages to the present, let alone to accommodate in a unified narrative the complex histories of Scotland, Ireland, Wales, and the other nations where writing in English has flourished. Readers who wish to explore the historical matrix out of which the works of literature collected in this anthology emerged are advised to consult the studies of particular periods listed in the appropriate sections of this bibliography. The multivolume *Oxford History of England* and *New Oxford History of England* are useful, as are the three-volume *Peoples of the British Isles: A New History*, ed. Stanford Lehmberg, 1992, the nine-volume *Cambridge Cultural History of Britain*, ed. Boris Ford, 1992, and the multivolume *Penguin History of Britain*, gen. ed. David Cannadine, 1996–. Given the cultural centrality of London, readers may find *The London Encyclopaedia*, ed. Ben Weinreb and Christopher Hibbert, 1986, and Roy Porter's *London: A Social History*, 1994, valuable.

Similar observations may be made about literary history. In the light of such initiatives as women's studies, new historicism, and postcolonialism, the range of authors deemed most significant has expanded in recent years, along with the geographical and conceptual boundaries of literature in English. Attempts to capture in a unified account the great sweep of literature from *Beowulf* to late last night have largely given way to studies of individual genres, carefully delimited time periods, and specific authors. For these more focused accounts, see the listings by period. Among the large-scale literary surveys, *The Cambridge Guide to Literature in English*, 1993, is useful, as is the seven-volume *Penguin History of Literature*, 1993–94. *The Feminist Companion to Literature in English*, ed. Virginia Blain, Isobel Grundy, and Patricia Clements, 1990, is an important resource, and the editorial materials in *The Norton Anthology of Literature by Women*, 2nd ed., 1996, ed. Sandra M. Gilbert and Susan Gubar, constitute a concise history and set of biographies of women authors since the Middle Ages. *Annals of English Literature, 1475–1950*, rev. 1961, lists important publications year by year, together with the significant literary events for each year. Four volumes have been published in the *Oxford English Literary History*, gen. ed. Jonathan Bate, 2002–: James Simpson, *Reform and Cultural Revolution, 1350–1547*; Philip Davis, *The Victorians, 1830–1880*; Randall Stevenson, *The Last of England? 1960–2000*; and Bruce King, *The Internationalization of English Literature, 1948–2000*. See also *The Cambridge History of Medieval English Literature*, ed. David Wallace, 1999, and *The Cambridge History of Early Modern English Literature*, ed. David Loewenstein and Janel Mueller, 2002.

Helpful treatments and surveys of English meter, rhyme, and stanza forms are Paul Fussell Jr., *Poetic Meter and Poetic Form*, rev. 1979; Donald Wesling, *The Chances of Rhyme: Device and Modernity*, 1980; Derek Attridge, *The Rhythms of English Poetry*, 1982; Charles O. Hartman, *Free Verse: An Essay in Prosody*, 1983; John Hollander, *Vision and Resonance: Two Senses of Poetic Form*, rev. 1985; and Robert Pinsky, *The Sounds of Poetry: A Brief Guide*, 1998.

On the development of the novel as a form, see Ian Watt, *The Rise of the Novel*, 1957; *The*

Columbia History of the British Novel, ed. John Richetti, 1994; Margaret Doody, *The True Story of the Novel*, 1996; *Theory of the Novel: A Historical Approach*, ed. Michael McKeon, 2000; and McKeon, *The Origins of the English Novel, 1600–1740*, 15th anniversary ed., 2002. On women novelists and readers, see Nancy Armstrong, *Desire and Domestic Fiction: A Political History of the Novel*, 1987; and Catherine Gallagher, *Nobody's Story: The Vanishing Acts of Women Writers in the Marketplace, 1670–1820*, 1994.

On the history of playhouse design, see Richard Leacroft, *The Development of the English Playhouse: An Illustrated Survey of Theatre Building in England from Medieval to Modern Times*, 1988. For a survey of the plays that have appeared on these and other stages, see Allardyce Nicoll, *British Drama*, rev. 1962, the eight-volume *Revels History of Drama in English*, gen. eds. Clifford Leech and T. W. Craik, 1975–83; and Alfred Harbage, *Annals of English Drama, 975–1700*, 3rd ed., 1989, rev. S. Schoenbaum and Sylvia Wagonheim.

On some of the key intellectual currents that are at once reflected in and shaped by literature, Arthur O. Lovejoy's classic studies *The Great Chain of Being*, 1936, and *Essays in the History of Ideas*, 1948, remain valuable, along with such works as Lovejoy and George Boas, *Primitivism and Related Ideas in Antiquity*, 1935; Ernst Kantorowicz, *The King's Two Bodies: A Study in Medieval Political Theology*, 1957, new ed. 1997; Richard Popkin, *The History of Skepticism from Erasmus to Descartes*, 1960; M. H. Abrams, *Natural Supernaturalism: Tradition and Revolution in Romantic Literature*, 1971; Michel Foucault, *Madness and Civilization: A History of Insanity in the Age of Reason*, Eng. trans. 1965, *The Order of Things: An Archaeology of the Human Sciences*, Eng. trans. 1970; Mikhail Bakhtin, *Rabelais and his World*, Eng. trans. 1968, and *The Dialogic Imagination*, Eng. trans. 1981; Roland Barthes, *The Pleasure of the Text*, Eng. trans. 1975; Jacques Derrida, *Of Grammatology*, Eng. trans. 1976, and *Dissemination*, Eng. trans. 1981; Raymond Williams, *Keywords: A Vocabulary of Culture and Society*, rev. 1983; Pierre Bourdieu, *Distinction: A Social Critique of the Judgment of Taste*, Eng. trans. 1984; Michel de Certeau, *The Practice of Everyday Life*, Eng. trans. 1984; and Sigmund Freud, *Writings on Art and Literature*, ed. Neil Hertz, 1997.

Reference Works

The single most important tool for the study of literature in English is the *Oxford English Dictionary*, 2nd ed., 1989, also available on CD-ROM, and online to subscribers. The OED is written on historical principles: that is, it attempts not only to describe current word use but also to record the history and development of the language from its origins before the Norman conquest to the present. It thus provides, for familiar as well as archaic and obscure words, the widest possible range of meanings and uses, organized chronologically and illustrated with quotations. Beyond the OED there are many other valuable dictionaries, such as *The American Heritage Dictionary*, *The Oxford Dictionary of Etymology*, and an array of reference works from *The Cambridge Encyclopedia of the English Language*, ed. David Crystal, 1995, to guides to specialized vocabularies, slang, regional dialects, and the like.

There is a steady flow of new editions of most major and many minor writers in English, along with a ceaseless outpouring of critical appraisals and scholarship. The *MLA International Bibliography* (also online) is the best way to keep abreast of the most recent work and to conduct bibliographic searches. *The New Cambridge Bibliography of English Literature*, ed. George Watson, 1969–77, updated shorter ed. 1981, is a valuable guide to the huge body of earlier literary criticism and scholarship. *A Guide to English and American Literature*, ed. F. W. Bateson and Harrison Meserole, rev. 1976, is a selected list of editions, as well as scholarly and critical treatments. Further bibliographical aids are described in Arthur G. Kennedy, *A Concise Bibliography for Students of English*, rev. 1972; Richard D. Altick and Andrew Wright, *Selective Bibliography for the Study of English and American Literature*, rev. 1979, and James L. Harner, *Literary Research Guide*, rev. 1998.

For compact biographies of English authors, see the multivolume *Oxford Dictionary of National Biography*, ed. H. C. G. Matthew and Brian Harrison, 2004; condensed biographies will be found in the *Concise Dictionary of National Biography*, 2 parts (1920, 1988). Handy reference books of authors, works, and various literary terms and allusions are *The Oxford Companion to the Theatre*, Phyllis Hartnoll, rev. 1990; *Princeton Encyclopedia of Poetry and Poetics*, ed. Alex Preminger and others, rev. 1993; and *The Oxford Companion to English Literature*, ed. Margaret Drabble, rev. 1998. Handbooks that define and illustrate literary concepts and terms are *The Penguin Dictionary of Literary Terms and Literary Theory*, ed. J. A. Cuddon, 1991; W. F. Thrall and Addison Hibbard, *A Handbook to Literature*, ed. C. Hugh Holman, rev. 1992; *Critical Terms for Literary Study*, ed. Frank Lentricchia and Thomas McLaughlin, rev. 1995; and M. H. Abrams, *A Glossary of Literary Terms*, rev. 1992. Also useful are Richard Lanham, *A Handlist of Rhetorical Terms*, 2nd ed., 1991; Arthur Quinn, *Figures of Speech: 60 Ways to Turn a Phrase*, 1993; and the *Barnhart Concise Dictionary of Etymology*, ed. Robert K. Barnhart, 1995. On the Greek and Roman background, see G. M. Kirkwood, *A Short Guide to Classical Mythology*, 1959; *The*

Oxford Classical Dictionary, rev. 1996; and *The Oxford Companion to Classical Literature*, ed. M. C. Howatson and Ian Chilvers, rev. 1993. Useful online resources include Early English Books Online; University of Pennsylvania's SCETI Furness Shakespeare Library; Michael Best's Internet Shakespeare Editions; and the University of Toronto Early Modern English Dictionaries Database, ed. Ian Lancashire.

Literary Criticism and Theory
Seven volumes of the *Cambridge History of Literary Criticism* have been published, 1989– : *Classical Criticism*, ed. George A. Kennedy; *The Renaissance*, ed. Glyn P. Norton; *The Eighteenth Century*, ed. H. B. Nisbet and Claude Rawson; *Romanticism*, ed. Marshall Brown; *Modernism and the New Criticism*, ed. A. Walton Litz, Louis Menand, and Lawrence Rainey; *From Formalism to Poststructuralism*, ed. Raman Selden; and *Twentieth-Century Historical, Philosophical, and Psychological Perspectives*, ed. Christa Knellwolf and Christopher Norris. See also M. H. Abrams, *The Mirror and the Lamp: Romantic Theory and the Critical Tradition*, 1953; William K. Wimsatt and Cleanth Brooks, *Literary Criticism: A Short History*, 1957; René Wellek, *A History of Modern Criticism: 1750–1950*, 9 vols., 1955–93; Frank Lentricchia, *After the New Criticism*, 1980; *Redrawing the Boundaries: The Transformation of English and American Literary Studies*, ed. Stephen Greenblatt and Giles Gunn, 1992; and J. Hillis Miller, *On Literature*, 2002. Raman Selden, Peter Widdowson, and Peter Brooker have written *A Reader's Guide to Contemporary Literary Theory*, 1997. Other useful resources include *The Johns Hopkins Guide to Literary Theory and Criticism*, ed. Michael Groden and Martin Kreiswirth, 1994 (also online); *Literary Theory, an Anthology*, ed. Julie Rivkin and Michael Ryan, 1998; and *The Norton Anthology of Theory and Criticism*, gen. ed. Vincent Leitch, 2001.

The following is a selection of books in literary criticism that have been notably influential in shaping modern approaches to English literature and literary forms: Lionel Trilling, *The Liberal Imagination*, 1950; T. S. Eliot, *Selected Essays*, 3rd ed. 1951, and *On Poetry and Poets*, 1957; Erich Auerbach, *Mimesis: The Representation of Reality in Western Literature*, 1953; William Empson, *Some Versions of Pastoral*, 1935, rpt. 1986, and *Seven Types of Ambiguity*, 3rd ed. 1953; William K. Wimsatt, *The Verbal Icon*, 1954; Northrop Frye, *Anatomy of Criticism*, 1957; Wayne C. Booth, *The Rhetoric of Fiction*, 1961, rev. ed. 1983; W. J. Bate, *The Burden of the Past and the English Poet*, 1970; Harold Bloom, *The Anxiety of Influence*, 1973; Paul de Man, *Allegories of Reading*, 1979; and Stanley Fish, *Is There a Text in This Class?: The Authority of Interpretive Communities*, 1980.

René Wellek and Austin Warren, *Theory of Literature*, rev. 1970, is a useful introduction to the variety of scholarly and critical approaches to literature up to the time of its publication. Jonathan Culler's *Literary Theory: A Very Short Introduction*, 1997, discusses recurrent issues and debates. See also Terry Eagleton, *After Theory*, 2003. Modern feminist literary criticism was fashioned by such works as Patricia Meyer Spacks, *The Female Imagination*, 1975; Ellen Moers, *Literary Women*, 1976; Elaine Showalter, *A Literature of Their Own*, 1977; and Sandra Gilbert and Susan Gubar, *The Madwoman in the Attic*, 1979. More recent studies include Jane Gallop, *The Daughter's Seduction: Feminism and Psychoanalysis*, 1982; Gayatri Chakravorty Spivak, *In Other Worlds: Essays in Cultural Politics*, 1987; Sandra Gilbert and Susan Gubar, *No Man's Land: The Place of the Woman Writer in the Twentieth Century*, 2 vols., 1988–89; Barbara Johnson, *A World of Difference*, 1989; Judith Butler, *Gender Trouble*, 1990; and the critical views sampled in Elaine Showalter, *The New Feminist Criticism*, 1985; *Feminist Literary Theory: A Reader*, ed. Mary Eagleton, 2nd ed., 1995; and *Feminisms: An Anthology of Literary Theory and Criticism*, ed. Robyn R. Warhol and Diane Price Herndl, 2nd ed. 1997. Gay and lesbian studies and criticism are represented in *The Lesbian and Gay Studies Reader*, ed. Henry Abelove, Michele Barale, and David Halperin, 1993, and by such books as Eve Sedgwick, *Between Men: English Literature and Male Homosocial Desire*, 1985, and *Epistemology of the Closet*, 1990; Diana Fuss, *Essentially Speaking: Feminism, Nature, and Difference*, 1989; Gregory Woods, *A History of Gay Literature: The Male Tradition*, 1998; and David Halperin, *How to Do the History of Homosexuality*, 2002.

Convenient introductions to structuralist literary criticism include Robert Scholes, *Structuralism in Literature: An Introduction*, 1974, and Jonathan Culler, *Structuralist Poetics*, 1975. The poststructuralist challenges to this approach are discussed in Jonathan Culler, *On Deconstruction*, 1982; Fredric Jameson, *Poststructuralism; or the Cultural Logic of Late Capitalism*, 1991; John McGowan, *Postmodernism and Its Critics*, 1991; and *Beyond Structuralism*, ed. Wendell Harris, 1996. For Marxism, see *Selections from the Prison Notebooks of Antonio Gramsci*, ed. and trans. Quintin Hoare and Geoffrey Smith, 1971; Raymond Williams, *Marxism and Literature*, 1977; Fredric Jameson, *The Political Unconscious: Narrative as a Socially Symbolic Act*, 1981; and Terry Eagleton, *Literary Theory: An Introduction*, 1983. New historicism is represented in Stephen Greenblatt, *Learning to Curse*, 1990; in the essays collected in *The New Historicism*, ed. Harold Veeser, 1989, and *New Historical Literary Study: Essays on Reproducing Texts, Representing History*, ed. Jeffrey N. Cox and Larry J.

Reynolds, 1993; and in Catherine Gallagher and Stephen Greenblatt, *Practicing New Historicism*, 2000. The related social and historical dimension of texts is discussed in Jerome McGann, *Critique of Modern Textual Criticism*, 1983; D. F. McKenzie, *Bibliography and Sociology of Texts*, 1986; Roger Chartier, *The Order of Books*, 1994; and *Scholarly Editing: A Guide to Research*, ed. D. C. Greetham, 1995. Characteristic of new historicism is an expansion of the field of literary interpretation extended still further in cultural studies; for a broad sampling of the range of interests, see *The Cultural Studies Reader*, ed. Simon During, 1993, and *A Cultural Studies Reader: History, Theory, Practice*, ed. Jessica Munns and Gita Rajan, 1997. This expansion of the field is similarly reflected in postcolonial studies: see *The Post-Colonial Studies Reader*, ed. Bill Ashcroft, Gareth Griffiths, and Helen Tiffin, 1995, and such influential books as Ranajit Guha and Gayatri Chakravorty Spivak, *Selected Subaltern Studies*, 1988; Edward Said, *Culture and Imperialism*, 1993; Homi Bhabha, *The Location of Culture*, 1994; Anne McClintock, *Imperial Leather: Race, Gender, and Sexuality in the Colonial Contest*, 1995; and Jonathan Goldberg, *Tempest in the Caribbean*, 2004.

Anthologies representing a range of recent approaches include *Modern Criticism and Theory*, ed. David Lodge, 1988, and *Contemporary Literary Criticism*, ed. Robert Con Davis and Ronald Schlieffer, rev. 1998.

THE ROMANTIC PERIOD

Bibliographies and Reference Works
The most convenient starting points are the surveys by Frank Jordan and others in *The English Romantic Poets: A Review of Research and Criticism*, rev. ed. 1985, on Blake, Wordsworth, Coleridge, Byron, Shelley, and Keats; and Carolyn W. Houtchens and Lawrence H. Houtchens, *The English Romantic Poets and Essayists*, rev. ed. 1966, on Blake, the less studied poets, and the essayists. Annual bibliographies of publications about these writers are to be found in *The Romantic Movement: A Selective and Critical Bibliography*, ed. David V. Erdman, 1980–.

See also the topical bibliographies in *The Cambridge Companion to British Romanticism*, ed. Stuart Curran, 1993; *A Companion to Romanticism*, ed. Duncan Wu, 1997; *An Oxford Companion to the Romantic Age*, ed. Iain McCalman, 1999; *The Cambridge Companion to British Literature, 1740–1830*, ed. Thomas Keymer and Jon Mee, 2004; and the Scholarly Resources section of the *Romantic Circles* Web page (www.rc.umd.edu/reference).

Political and Social, and Intellectual Backgrounds
Histories of the political and social events in this period are Asa Briggs, *The Making of Modern England: 1783–1867*, 1959; E. P. Thompson, *The Making of the English Working Class*, 1963, and *Customs in Common*, 1991; James Walvin, *Slavery and British Society, 1776–1834*, 1982; and Linda Colley, *Britons: Forging the Nation, 1707–1837*, 1992. See also Carl Woodring, *Politics in English Romantic Poetry*, 1970; Marilyn Butler, *Romantics, Rebels, and Reactionaries: English Literature and Its Background, 1760–1830*, 1982; Gillian Russell, *The Theatres of War: Performance, Politics, and Society, 1793–1815*, 1995; and James Chandler, *England in 1819: The Politics of Literary Culture and the Case of Romantic Historicism*, 1998.

For English literary relations to the French Revolution, see *The Debate on the French Revolution, 1789–1800*, ed. Alfred Cobban, 2nd ed. 1960; Ronald Paulson, *Representations of Revolution (1789–1820)*, 1983; *Burke, Paine, Godwin, and the Revolution Controversy*, ed. Marilyn Butler, 1984; Olivia Smith, *The Politics of Language, 1791–1819*, 1984; H. T. Dickinson, *British Radicalism and the French Revolution, 1789–1815*, 1985; *The French Revolution and British Popular Politics*, ed. Mark Philp, 1991; Simon Bainbridge, *Napoleon and English Romanticism*, 1995; Kevin Gilmartin, *Print Politics: The Press and Radical Opposition in Early Nineteenth-Century England*, 1996; and John Barrell, *Imagining the King's Death*, 2000.

Illuminating analysis of important intellectual movements will be found in A. O. Lovejoy, *The Great Chain of Being*, 1936, chaps. 9–10. Other useful works on intellectual history are Basil Willey, *Nineteenth Century Studies: Coleridge to Matthew Arnold*, 1949; James Engell, *The Creative Imagination: Enlightenment to Romanticism*, 1981; Marilyn Gaull, *English Romanticism: The Human Context*, 1988; and Robert M. Ryan, *The Romantic Reformation: Religious Politics in English Literature, 1789–1824*, 1997. On Romantic literature in its social matrix, see Raymond Williams, *Culture and Society, 1780–1950*, 1960; Jon Klancher, *The Making of English Reading Audiences, 1790–1832*, 1987; Alan Richardson, *Literature, Education, and Romanticism: Reading as Social Practice, 1780–1832*, 1994; Lee Erickson, *The Economy of Literary Form: English Literature and the Industrialization of Publishing, 1800–1850*, 1996; and Clifford Siskin, *The Work of Writing: Literature and Social Change in Britain, 1700–1830*, 1997.

For literary responses to the expansion in this

era of the Second British Empire, see *Romanticism, Race, and Imperial Culture, 1780–1834*, ed. Alan Richardson and Sonia Hofkosh, 1996, and *Romanticism and Colonialism: Writing and Empire, 1780–1830*, ed. Timothy Fulford and Peter J. Kitson, 1998. Nigel Leask discusses writers' relationship to the Orientalism of the period in *British Romantic Writers and the East*, 1994, as does Saree Makdisi in *Romantic Imperialism: Universal Empire and the Culture of Modernity*, 1997. For discussion of the Romantics and the beginnings of environmentalism, see Jonathan Bate, *Romantic Ecology*, 1991, and James McKusick, *Green Writing: Romanticism and Ecology*, 2000.

Literary History and Criticism
Among the histories of Romantic literature are Ian Jack, *English Literature, 1815–1832*, 1963, and J. R. de J. Jackson, *Poetry of the Romantic Period*, 1980. Douglas Bush, *Mythology and the Romantic Tradition in English Poetry*, 1937, is so broad in its range that it constitutes an excellent survey of Romantic poetry in general. Harold Bloom, *The Visionary Company*, rev. ed. 1971, which relates the poets to the prophetic tradition of Spenser and Milton, includes brief and stimulating commentaries on many important poems; Bloom, *The Ringers in the Tower*, 1971, consists of essays on nineteenth- and twentieth-century "Romantic" writers. David Perkins treats Wordsworth, Shelley, and Keats in *The Quest for Permanence*, 1959. In *Natural Supernaturalism: Tradition and Revolution in Romantic Literature*, 1971, and in *The Correspondent Breeze: Essays on English Romanticism*, 1984, M. H. Abrams deals with persistent themes, concepts, and designs in English and German Romantic literature, and stresses their relation both to the biblical tradition and to the intellectual ambiance of a revolutionary age. Peter L. Thorslev Jr., *The Byronic Hero: Types and Prototypes*, 1962, discusses the alienated hero in other writers as well as Byron; see also Frank Kermode, *Romantic Image*, 1957, on the concept of the poet at odds with society, from the Romantic period to Yeats. Other useful books are Thomas Weiskel, *The Romantic Sublime: Studies in the Structure and Psychology of Transcendence*, 1976; Anne K. Mellor, *English Romantic Irony*, 1980; Thomas McFarland, *Romanticism and the Forms of Ruin: Wordsworth, Coleridge, and Modalities of Fragmentation*, 1981; Jerome J. McGann, *The Romantic Ideology*, 1983; Charles J. Rzepka, *The Self as Mind: Vision and Identity in Wordsworth, Coleridge, and Keats*, 1986; Clifford Siskin, *The Historicity of Romantic Discourse*, 1988; Peter J. Manning, *Reading Romantics: Texts and Contexts*, 1990; William H. Galperin, *The Return of the Visible in British Romanticism*, 1993; McGann, *The Poetics of Sensibility: A Revolution in Literary Style*, 1996; and Lucy Newlyn,

Reading, Writing, and Romanticism: The Anxiety of Reception, 2000. See also the essays in *Romantic Poetry: Recent Revisionary Criticism*, ed. Karl Kroeber and Gene W. Ruoff, 1993. For critical opinions of the poets during their lifetime, see Donald H. Reiman, *The Romantics Reviewed: Contemporary Reviews of British Romantic Writers*, 9 vols., 1972.

Following are studies of various forms of Romantic literature. On literary criticism: M. H. Abrams, *The Mirror and the Lamp: Romantic Theory and the Critical Tradition*, 1953; and *The Cambridge History of Literary Criticism*, vol. 5, *The Romantic Period*, ed. Marshall Brown, 2000. On poetic genres: Stuart Curran, *Poetic Form and British Romanticism*, 1986, and Susan J. Wolfson, *Formal Charges: The Shaping of Poetry in British Romanticism*, 1997. On the fragment: Marjorie Levinson, *The Romantic Fragment Poem*, 1986. On the novel: Robert Kiely, *The Romantic Novel in England*, 1972; Gary Kelly, *English Fiction of the Romantic Period, 1789–1830*, 1989; Ian Duncan, *Modern Romance and Transformations of the Novel*, 1992; Nicola J. Watson, *Revolution and the Form of the British Novel, 1790–1825*, 1994; Katie Trumpener, *Bardic Nationalism: The Romantic Novel and the British Empire*, 1997. On the gothic: Montague Summers, *The Gothic Quest: A History of the Gothic Novel*, 1938; Mario Praz, *The Romantic Agony*, 2nd ed. 1951; E. J. Clery, *The Rise of Supernatural Fiction, 1762–1800*, 1995; and Michael Gamer, *Romanticism and the Gothic: Genre, Reception, and Canon Formation, 1790–1820*, 2000. On drama: Allardyce Nicoll, *History of Early Nineteenth-Century Drama, 1800–50*, 2 vols., rev. ed. 1955; Jeffrey N. Cox, *In the Shadows of Romance: Romantic Tragic Drama in Germany, England, and France*, 1987; Alan Richardson, *A Mental Theatre: Poetic Drama and Consciousness in the Romantic Age*, 1988; and William Jewett, *Fatal Autonomy: Romantic Drama and the Rhetoric of Agency*, 1997. On Romantic prose: Annette Wheeler Cafarelli, *Prose in the Age of Poets: Romanticism and Biographical Narrative from Johnson to De Quincey*, 1990; Mark Parker, *Literary Magazines and British Romanticism*, 2000; and *Romantic Periodicals and Print Culture*, ed. Kim Wheatley, 2003.

On women writers of the period, see Sandra M. Gilbert and Susan Gubar, *The Madwoman in the Attic: The Woman Writer and the Nineteenth-Century Literary Imagination*, 1979; Mary Poovey, *The Proper Lady and the Woman Writer: Ideology as Style in the Works of Mary Wollstonecraft, Mary Shelley, and Jane Austen*, 1984; Margaret Homans, *Bearing the Word: Language and Female Experience in Nineteenth-Century Women's Writing*, 1986; Marlon B. Ross, *The Contours of Masculine Desire: Romanticism and the Rise of Women's Poetry*, 1989;

Gary Kelly, *Women, Writing, and Revolution, 1790–1827*, 1993; Anne K. Mellor, *Romanticism and Gender*, 1993; Judith Pascoe, *Romantic Theatricality: Gender, Poetry, and Spectatorship*, 1997; Mellor, *Mothers of the Nation: Women's Political Writing in England, 1780–1830*, 2002; *Romanticism and Feminism*, ed. Mellor, 1988; *Re-Visioning Romanticism: British Women Writers, 1776–1837*, ed. Carol Shiner Wilson and Joel Haefner, 1994; *Romantic Women Writers: Voices and Countervoices*, ed. Paula R. Feldman and Theresa M. Kelley, 1995; and *Romanticism and Women Poets: Opening the Doors of Perception*, ed. Stephen Behrendt and Harriet Kramer Linkin, 1999. A good starting guide specifically to the poets is J. R. de J. Jackson, *Romantic Poetry by Women: A Bibliography, 1770–1835*, 1993.

Anna Letitia Barbauld

The Poems of Anna Letitia Barbauld, ed. William McCarthy and Elizabeth Kraft, 1994, is now the standard edition. For a biography see Betsy Rodgers, *Georgian Chronicle: Mrs. Barbauld and Her Family*, 1958. Among recent critical essays see Julie Ellison, "The Politics of Fancy in the Age of Sensibility," in *Re-Visioning Romanticism*, ed. Wilson and Haefner, 1994; William Keach, "A Regency Prophecy and the End of Anna Barbauld's Career," *Studies in Romanticism*, 1994; Isobel Armstrong, "The Gush of the Feminine," in *Romantic Women Writers*, ed. Feldman and Kelley, 1995; William McCarthy, "Repression, Desire, and Gender in Anna Letitia Barbauld's Early Poems," also in Feldman and Kelley; and Daniel White, "The 'Joineriana': Anna Barbauld, the Aikin Family Circle, and the Dissenting Public Sphere," *Eighteenth-Century Studies*, 1994.

William Blake

The standard scholarly edition is *The Poetry and Prose of William Blake*, ed. David Erdman and Harold Bloom, rev. ed. 1982, which includes painstaking textual notes and brief commentaries on many of the poems. Erdman also prepared a modernized text of all Blake's verse, with copious explanatory notes by W. H. Stevenson, *The Poems of William Blake* (Longman-Norton Annotated English Poets), 1971. A useful annotated selection of *Blake's Poetry and Designs* has been edited by Mary Lynn Johnson and John E. Grant, 1979. The first full account of Blake's life, Alexander Gilchrist's *The Life of William Blake*, 1863, has been a source for all later biographers and remains widely available. The most recent biographies are James King, *William Blake: His Life*, 1991, and Peter Ackroyd, *Blake*, 1996.

The modern era of the scholarly explication of Blake symbolism was begun by S. Foster Damon, *William Blake: His Philosophy and Symbols*, 1924; Damon also published *Blake Dictionary: The Ideas and Symbols of William Blake*, 1965. Some of the most useful later books are Northrop Frye's classic analysis of Blake's moral allegory, *Fearful Symmetry*, 1947; David V. Erdman's investigation of the relation of Blake's poetry to the historical events of his time, *Blake: Prophet against Empire*, rev. ed. 1969; J. A. Wittreich, *Angel of Apocalypse: Blake's Idea of Milton*, 1975; W. J. T. Mitchell, *Blake's Composite Art: A Study of the Illuminated Poetry*, 1978; Leopold Damrosch Jr., *Symbol and Truth in Blake's Myth*, 1980; Robert N. Essick, *William Blake and the Language of Albion*, 1989; Morris Eaves, *The Counter-Arts Conspiracy: Art and Identity in the Age of Blake*, 1992; Jon Mee, *Dangerous Enthusiasm: William Blake and the Culture of Radicalism in the 1790s*, 1994; Nicholas Williams, *Ideology and Utopia in the Poetry of William Blake*, 1998; and Saree Makdisi, *William Blake and the Impossible History of the 1790s*, 2003.

The Cambridge Companion to William Blake, ed. Morris Eaves, 2003, is a useful general introduction to the man and his work. Studies emphasizing the shorter poems are Robert F. Gleckner, *The Piper and the Bard*, 1959, and E. D. Hirsch Jr., *Innocence and Experience: An Introduction to Blake*, 1964. *Blake's Sublime Allegory*, ed. Stuart Curran and Joseph Anthony Wittreich Jr., 1973, includes essays by various scholars on the major prophecies. On Blake's graphic work see Robert N. Essick, *William Blake, Printmaker*, 1980; Eaves, *William Blake's Theory of Art*, 1982; and Joseph Viscomi, *Blake and the Idea of the Book*, 1993. There is a large and growing list of books that reproduce (some of them in color) Blake's etched poems, drawings, and engravings; especially useful are *The Illuminated Blake*, ed. David V. Erdman, 1974, and Erdman's reproduction, with transcripts and commentary, of *The Notebooks of William Blake*, rev. ed. 1977. See also the excellent website *The Blake Archive* (www.blakearchive.org).

Robert Burns

The standard references for Burns's poems are the Centenary Edition, ed. W. E. Henley and T. F. Henderson, 4 vols., 1896–97, and *The Poems and Songs of Robert Burns*, ed. James Kinsley, 3 vols., 1968. Kinsley also prepared a good one-volume edition, Oxford Standard Authors, 1969. J. De Lancey Ferguson has given us a reliable edition of *The Letters of Robert Burns*, 2 vols., 1931 (2nd ed., ed. G. Ross Roy, 1985), and a brilliant portrait of Burns, *Pride and Passion*, 1939. The most recent among many biographies are James Mackay, *A Biography of Robert Burns*, 1992; Ian McIntyre, *Dirt and Deity: A Life of Robert Burns*, 1995; and Hugh Douglas, *Robert Burns: The Tinder Heart*, 1996. David Daiches, *Robert Burns*, 1950, provides a critical analysis of the major poems, and Thomas Crawford, *Burns: A Study of the Poems and Songs*, 1960, is a detailed and comprehensive commentary. See also Mary Ellen Brown, *Burns and Tradition*, 1984; Raymond Bentman, *Robert Burns*, 1987; *Robert Burns and Cultural Authority*, ed. Robert Crawford, 1997; and Liam McIlvanney, *Burns the Radical*, 2002.

George Gordon, Lord Byron

For the poetry the standard edition is *Lord Byron: The Complete Poetical Works*, ed. Jerome J. McGann, 7 vols., 1980–93; for the letters, *Byron's Letters and Journals*, ed. Leslie A. Marchand, 12 vols., 1973–82 (with a supplementary volume in 1994); Marchand also edited the one-volume *Selected Letters and Journals*, 1982. Ernest J. Lovell Jr., *His Very Self and Voice*, 1954, is a compilation of Byron's conversations. The standard biography is Marchand, *Byron: A Biography*, 3 vols., 1957. Fiona MacCarthy, *Byron: Life and Legend*, 2002, met with much acclaim. See also Louis Crompton, *Byron and Greek Love: Homophobia in 19th-Century England*, 1985.

Among the many useful books on Byron as poet are McGann, *Fiery Dust: Byron's Poetic Development*, 1968; Peter J. Manning, *Byron and His Fictions*, 1978; Jerome Christensen, *Lord Byron's Strength: Romantic Writing and Commercial Society*, 1993; Jane Stabler, *Byron, Politics and History*, 2002. See also *Critical Essays on Lord Byron*, ed. Robert F. Gleckner, 1991, and *Rereading Byron*, ed. Alice Levine and Robert N. Keane, 1993. On Byron's nineteenth-century reception see Andrew Elfenbein, *Byron and the Victorians*, 1995. On Byron and gender see Sonia Hofkosh, "Women and the Romantic Author: The Example of Byron," in *Romanticism and Feminism*, ed. Anne K. Mellor, 1988; Caroline Franklin, *Byron's Heroines*, 1992; and Susan Wolfson, " 'Their She Condition': Cross-Dressing and the Politics of Gender in *Don Juan*," *ELH*, 1987. Other discussions of *Don Juan* include McGann, *"Don Juan" in Context*, 1976; Peter W. Graham, *"Don Juan" and Regency England*, 1990; and Moyra Haslett, *Byron's "Don Juan" and the Don Juan Legend*, 1997.

John Clare

The most recent scholarly presentation of Clare's poems is the series of Oxford English Texts volumes under the general editorship of Eric Robinson: *Later Poems*, 2 vols., 1984; *Early Poems*, 1989; and *Poems of the Middle Period*, 5 vols., 1996–2003. Robinson and his associate David Powell have also produced an Oxford Standard Authors *John Clare*, 1984. An accessible modern-spelling selection has been edited by Jonathan Bate, *"I Am": The Selected Poetry of John Clare*, 2003. J. W. Tibble and Anne Tibble edited Clare's *Prose* and his *Letters*, both 1951. Clare's autobiographical writings have been collected by Eric Robinson in *John Clare by Himself*, 1996. An acclaimed recent biography is Jonathan Bate, *John Clare*, 2003. The essays on

Clare by J. Middleton Murry, collected in his *John Clare and Other Studies*, 1959, indicate the sudden leap forward of Clare's reputation when he was "rediscovered" in the 1920s. For more-recent commentary see John Barrell, *The Idea of Landscape and the Sense of Place, 1730–1840: An Approach to the Poetry of John Clare*, 1972; Mark Storey, *The Poetry of John Clare: A Critical Introduction*, 1974; Elizabeth Helsinger, "Clare and the Place of the Peasant Poet," *Critical Inquiry*, 1987; *John Clare in Context*, ed. Hugh Haughton, Adam Phillips, and Geoffrey Summerfield, 1994; and *John Clare: New Approaches*, ed. John Goodridge and Simon Kövesi, 2000.

Samuel Taylor Coleridge

The Collected Works under the general editorship of Kathleen Coburn is now complete, 16 vols., 1969–2003. E. H. Coleridge, *Complete Poetical Works*, 2 vols., 1912 (with a one-volume edition of *Poetical Works* by the same editor in the Oxford Standard Authors series), has been replaced as the standard by J. C. C. Mays's edition of the poems and plays in volume 16 of the *Collected Works*. The most fully annotated edition of *Biographia Literaria* is that by James Engell and W. Jackson Bate, 2 vols., 1983 (vol. 7 of the *Collected Works*).

Richard Holmes, *Coleridge: Early Visions*, 1989, and *Coleridge: Darker Reflections*, 1998, together constitute the most recent biography, following close upon Rosemary Ashton, *The Life of Samuel Taylor Coleridge: A Critical Biography*, 1987. Walter Jackson Bate, *Coleridge*, 1968, remains valuable. The definitive edition of Coleridge's *Collected Letters* is by E. L. Griggs, 6 vols., 1956–71; see also *Selected Letters*, ed. H. J. Jackson, 1987. Five volumes of Coleridge's *Notebooks* are available, meticulously edited by Kathleen Coburn and associates, 1957–2002. A fascinating one-volume selection from the notebooks has been edited by Seamus Perry, *Coleridge's Notebooks*, 2002.

H. M. Margoliouth has described the most fruitful literary association on record in his *Wordsworth and Coleridge, 1795–1834*, 1953. More sophisticated studies are Paul Magnuson, *Coleridge and Wordsworth: A Lyrical Dialogue*, 1988; Gene W. Ruoff, *Wordsworth and Coleridge: The Making of the Major Lyrics, 1802–1804*, 1989; and Susan Eilenberg, *Strange Power of Speech: Wordsworth, Coleridge, and Literary Possession*, 1992. Studies of Coleridge as a poet include Magnuson, *Coleridge's Nightmare Poetry*, 1974; Reeve Parker, *Coleridge's Meditative Art*, 1975; Kelvin Everest, *Coleridge's Secret Ministry*, 1979; M. H. Abrams, *The Correspondent Breeze*, 1984; and Morton D. Paley, *Coleridge's Later Poetry*, 1996. J. L. Lowes, *The Road to Xanadu*, 1927, rev. ed. 1930, which investigates the sources and composition of *The Ancient Mariner* and "Kubla Khan," is a critical classic. Discussion of Coleridge as critic will be found in M. H. Abrams, *The Mirror and the Lamp*, 1953; for a more recent discussion see Seamus Perry, *Coleridge and the Uses of Division*, 1999. Among the excellent studies of Coleridge's philosophical, theological, and moral interests and achievements are Thomas McFarland's wide-ranging study, *Coleridge and the Pantheist Tradition*, 1969; Owen Barfield, *What Coleridge Thought*, 1971; and Lawrence S. Lockridge, *Coleridge the Moralist*, 1977. Studies of his political views include Nicholas Roe, *Wordsworth and Coleridge: The Radical Years*, 1988; John Morrow, *Coleridge's Political Thought*, 1990; and Patrick J. Keane, *Coleridge's Submerged Politics*, 1994. On his sexual politics, see Karen Swann, "Literary Gentlemen and Lovely Ladies: The Debate on the Character of *Christabel*," *ELH*, 1985, and Julie A. Carlson, *In the Theatre of Romanticism: Coleridge, Nationalism, Women*, 1994. On opium, dreaming, and Coleridge's poetry, see Alethea Hayter, *Opium and the Romantic Imagination*, 1968; M. H. Abrams, *The Milk of Paradise*, rev. ed. 1970; and Jennifer Ford, *Coleridge on Dreaming: Romanticism, Dreams and the Medical Imagination*, 1998. On his developing reputation see *Coleridge: The Critical Heritage*, ed. J. R. de J. Jackson, 2 vols., 1970, 1991. Modern essays in criticism have been collected by, among others, John Beer, *Coleridge's Variety*, 1974; Frederick Burwick, *Coleridge's "Biographia Literaria": Text and Meaning*, 1989; Leonard Orr, *Critical Essays*, 1994; and Lucy Newlyn, ed., *The Cambridge Companion to Coleridge*, 2002.

Felicia Dorothea Hemans

Excellent modern selections are *Felicia Hemans: Selected Poems, Letters, Reception Materials*, ed. Susan J. Wolfson, 2000, and *Felicia Hemans: Selected Poems, Prose, and Letters*, ed. Gary Kelly, 2002. For criticism see Angela Leighton, *Victorian Women Poets: Writing against the Heart*, 1992; Isobel Armstrong, *Victorian Poetry*, 1993; *Felicia Hemans: Reimagining Poetry in the Nineteenth Century*, ed. Nanora Sweet and Julie Melnyk, 2001; Tricia Lootens, "Hemans and Home," *PMLA*, 1994; Sweet, "Hemans and the Post-Napoleonic Moment," in *At the Limits of Romanticism*, ed. Mary A. Favret and Nicola J. Watson, 1994; Susan J. Wolfson, "Felicia Hemans and the Dilemma of Gender," in *Re-Visioning Romanticism*, ed. Carol Shiner Wilson and Joel Haefner, 1994; and Paula R. Feldman, "Felicia Hemans and the Literary Marketplace," *Keats-Shelley Journal*, 1997.

John Keats

The standard edition of the poetry is by Jack Stillinger, *The Poems of John Keats*, 1978. Miriam Allott, *The Poems of John Keats*, 1970, is generously annotated. Hyder E. Rollins, *The Letters of John Keats*, 2 vols., 1958, provides exact texts based on the manuscripts, and a copious *Selected Letters* has been edited by Grant F. Scott, 2002. The most frequently cited biographies are Walter Jackson Bate, *John Keats*, 1963; Robert Gittings, *John Keats*, 1968; and Aileen Ward, *John Keats: The Making of a Poet*, rev. ed. 1986. Andrew Motion, *Keats*, 1997, is the most recent.

Among the many critical studies, the following are especially useful: Earl Wasserman, *The Finer Tone*, 1953 (a close analysis of the major poems); David Perkins, *The Quest for Permanence*, 1959; Jack Stillinger, *The Hoodwinking of Madeline and Other Essays on Keats's Poems*, 1971; Stuart Sperry, *Keats the Poet*, 1973; Christopher Ricks's lively and wide-ranging study, *Keats and Embarrassment*, 1974; Robert M. Ryan's analysis of Keats's personal creed, *Keats: The Religious Sense*, 1976; Helen Vendler, *The Odes of John Keats*, 1983; Leon Waldoff, *Keats and the Silent Work of Imagination*, 1985; Susan J. Wolfson, *The Questioning Presence: Wordsworth, Keats, and the Interrogative Mode in Romantic Poetry*, 1986; John Barnard, *John Keats*, 1987; Marjorie Levinson, *Keats's Life of Allegory*, 1988; Daniel P. Watkins, *Keats's Poetry and the Poetics of Imagination*, 1989; Nicholas Roe, *John Keats and the Culture of Dissent*, 1997; Stillinger, *Reading "The Eve of St. Agnes*," 1999; *The Persistence of Poetry: Bicentennial Essays on Keats*, ed. Robert M. Ryan and Ronald A. Sharp, 1998. On Keats in his social milieu, see Jeffrey N. Cox, *Poetry and Politics in the Cockney School*, 1998. For the poet's nineteenth-century reputation, see *Keats: The Critical Heritage*, ed. G. M. Matthews, 1971. Recent collections of essays include *Critical Essays on John Keats*, ed. Hermione de Almeida, 1990; *Keats and History*, ed. Roe, 1995; and *The Cambridge Companion to Keats*, ed. Susan J. Wolfson, 2001.

Percy Bysshe Shelley

The nearest to a complete collection of Shelley's writings is *The Complete Works*, ed. Roger Ingpen and Walter E. Peck, 10 vols., 1926–30. The most widely used single-volume edition of the poems has been that in the Oxford Standard Authors, ed. Thomas Hutchinson and rev. G. M. Matthews, 1970. *Shelley's Prose* was collected by David Lee Clark in 1954, and *The Letters* was edited by Frederick L. Jones, 2 vols., 1964. Because of the erratic way in which Shelley's poems and essays were published, all the collected editions are faulty; Shelley's writings are now in the process of being revised and reprinted by a number of editors. The best texts are those in *The Lyrics of Shelley*, edited and sensitively interpreted by Judith Chernaik, 1972; and in the large selection, *Shelley's Poetry and Prose*, A Norton Critical Edition, rev. Donald H. Reiman and Neil Fraistat, 2002, which also includes a collection of critical essays. Reiman and Fraistat are currently editing *The Complete Poetry of Percy Bysshe Shelley;* vol. 1 appeared in 2000.

The classic life is Newman Ivey White, *Shelley,* 2 vols., 1940, which is also available in a condensed single volume, *Portrait of Shelley,* 1945. Richard Holmes, *Shelley: The Pursuit,* 1974, is not so detailed as White's biography, but provides a vivid sense of Shelley as a person. Kenneth Neill Cameron, in *The Young Shelley,* 1950, and in the sequel, *Shelley: The Golden Years,* 1974, emphasizes the development of Shelley's radical social and political thinking.

As early as 1900 W. B. Yeats, in "The Philosophy of Shelley's Poetry" (reprinted in *Essays,* 1924), dealt with Shelley as one of the great symbolist poets. Harold Bloom's *Shelley's Mythmaking,* 1959, puts Shelley in the line of visionary poets whose imaginative processes were instinctively mythopoetic. Earl Wasserman, *Shelley: A Critical Reading,* 1971, is a series of close readings of Shelley's most important poems and essays. Other useful critical works are R. G. Woodman, *The Apocalyptic Tradition in the Poetry of Shelley,* 1964; Stuart Curran's study, *Shelley's Annus Mirabilis: The Maturing of an Epic Vision,* 1975; Timothy Webb, *Shelley: A Voice Not Understood,* 1977; Michael Scrivener, *Radical Shelley,* 1982; William Keach, *Shelley's Style,* 1984; Stuart M. Sperry, *Shelley's Major Verse: The Narrative and Dramatic Poetry,* 1988; Stephen C. Behrendt, *Shelley and His Audiences,* 1989; Donald Reiman, *Percy Bysshe Shelley,* rev. ed. 1990; and Susan Wolfson, *Formal Charges,* 1997. Charles Robinson discusses personal and poetic relations in *Byron and Shelley: The Snake and the Eagle Wreathed in Fight,* 1975.

Charlotte Smith

The Poems of Charlotte Smith, ed. Stuart Curran, 1993, is the standard edition. The recent explosion of interest in Smith has led to the republication of a number of her novels in inexpensive scholarly editions. A *Collected Works,* under the general editorship of Curran, is in progress. Judith Phillips Stanton has recently edited *The Collected Letters of Charlotte Smith,* 2002. For a biography see Lorraine Fletcher, *Charlotte Smith: A Critical Biography,* 1998. For commentary see Judith Phillips Stanton, "Charlotte Smith's 'Literary Business,'" *The Age of Johnson,* 1987; Judith Pascoe, "Female Botanists and the Poetry of Charlotte Smith," in *Re-Visioning Romanticism,* ed. Carol Shiner Wilson and Joel Haefner, 1994; Adela Pinch, *Strange Fits of Passion: Epistemologies of Emotion, Hume to Austen,* 1996; Sarah Zimmerman, *Romanticism, Lyricism, and History,* 1999; Anne D. Wallace, "Picturesque Fossils, Sublime Geology? The Crisis of Authority in Charlotte Smith's

Beachy Head," *European Romantic Review,* 2002.

Mary Wollstonecraft

There is a collected edition, *The Works of Mary Wollstonecraft,* ed. Janet Todd and Marilyn Butler, 7 vols., 1989. Todd has also edited *A Wollstonecraft Anthology,* 1989; *Mary Wollstonecraft: Political Writings,* 1993; and a new edition of the *Collected Letters of Mary Wollstonecraft,* 2004. The most important reprints of single works are *A Vindication of the Rights of Men,* facsimile edition by Eleanor Louise Nicholes, 1960; *A Vindication of the Rights of Woman,* Norton Critical Edition by Carol H. Poston, 1988; *Letters Written during a Short Residence in Sweden, Norway, and Denmark,* ed. Poston, 1976; and a reprint in a single volume (ed. Gary Kelly, 1976) of her two novels, the early *Mary, A Fiction,* and *The Wrongs of Woman; or Maria,* which she left unfinished at her death.

Biographers rely for many facts on William Godwin's candid *Memoirs of the Author of "A Vindication of the Rights of Woman,"* 1798, now in a modern edition by Pamela Clemit and Gina Luria Walker, 2001. The first modern critical biography is Ralph Wardle, *Mary Wollstonecraft,* 1951; see also Claire Tomalin, *The Life and Death of Mary Wollstonecraft,* 1974; Emily Sunstein, *A Different Face: The Life of Mary Wollstonecraft,* 1975; and Janet Todd, *Mary Wollstonecraft: A Revolutionary Life,* 2000. An excellent place to begin a review of Wollstonecraft's ideas and writings is *The Cambridge Companion to Mary Wollstonecraft,* ed. Claudia L. Johnson, 2002. Other recent studies include Mary Poovey, *The Proper Lady and the Woman Writer,* 1984; Gary Kelly, *Revolutionary Feminism: The Mind and Career of Mary Wollstonecraft,* 1992; Virginia Sapiro, *A Vindication of Political Virtue: The Political Theory of Mary Wollstonecraft,* 1992; Johnson, *Equivocal Beings: Politics, Gender, and Sentimentality in the 1790s,* 1995; and Barbara Taylor, *Mary Wollstonecraft and the Feminist Imagination,* 2003.

Dorothy Wordsworth

For the journals the best editions are *Journals of Dorothy Wordsworth,* ed. Mary Moorman, 1971, and *The Grasmere Journals,* ed. Pamela Woof, 1991. For the poems consult the appendix of Susan M. Levin's critical study, *Dorothy Wordsworth and Romanticism,* 1987. Dorothy Wordsworth's letters are collected with those of her brother in *The Letters of William and Dorothy Wordsworth,* rev. Chester L. Shaver and others, 7 vols., 1967–92; there is a one-volume selection of her letters, ed. Alan G. Hill, 1985. The standard biography is Robert Gittings and Jo Manton, *Dorothy Wordsworth,* 1985. See also Margaret Homans, *Women Writers and Poetic Identity: Dorothy Wordsworth, Emily Brontë, and Emily Dickinson,* 1980, and the essays by Susan

Wolfson and Kurt Heinzelman in *Romanticism and Feminism*, ed. Anne K. Mellor, 1988.

William Wordsworth
Ernest de Selincourt edited *The Poetical Works* (with Helen Darbishire), 5 vols., 1940–49, and the variorum edition of *The Prelude*, with the texts of 1805 and 1850 on facing pages (rev. Helen Darbishire, 1959). *The Letters of William and Dorothy Wordsworth*, ed. de Selincourt, have been revised by C. L. Shaver, Mary Moorman, and Alan G. Hill, 7 vols., 1967–92. The 1805 and 1850 *Preludes* on facing pages, together with the "Two-Part *Prelude*" of 1799, various manuscript fragments of *The Prelude*, and a selection of recent critical essays on the poem, are available in *The Prelude: 1799, 1805, 1850*, A Norton Critical Edition, ed. Jonathan Wordsworth, M. H. Abrams, and Stephen Gill, 1979. Wordsworth's poems in one volume were edited for the Oxford Authors by Gill, 1984. A comprehensive series, the Cornell Wordsworth, gen. ed. Stephen Parrish, begun in 1975 and now close to completion, prints texts of the poems, together with variant readings from the manuscripts (which are reproduced and transcribed) through the final printings in Wordsworth's lifetime. W. J. B. Owen and Jane Worthington Smyser have edited *The Prose Works*, 3 vols., 1974, and there is a *Selected Prose*, ed. John O. Hayden, 1988. Owen has also printed from his edition a convenient collection of *Wordsworth's Literary Criticism*, 1974. For biography see Gill's reliable *William Wordsworth: A Life*, 1984, and Kenneth R. Johnston's lively and well-researched, if at times speculative, *The Hidden Wordsworth*, 1998, whose emphases are indicated by its subtitle: *Poet, Lover, Rebel, Spy*. Mark L. Reed's dating of Wordsworth's poems, manuscripts, and the events of his daily life has reached two volumes, *Wordsworth: The Chronology of the Early Years*, 1967, and *The Chronology of the Middle Years*, 1975.

For modern discussion of *Lyrical Ballads*, see Stephen M. Parrish, *The Art of the "Lyrical Bal-*

lads," 1973; Mary Jacobus, *Tradition and Experiment in Wordsworth's "Lyrical Ballads,"* 1798, 1976; John E. Jordan, *Why the "Lyrical Ballads"?* 1976; Don H. Bialostosky, *Making Tales*, 1984; and *1798: The Year of "Lyrical Ballads,"* ed. Richard Cronin, 1998. Herbert Lindenberger, *On Wordsworth's "Prelude,"* 1963, explores Wordsworth's major achievement; and Mary Jacobus deals with it from a feminist standpoint in *Romanticism, Writing, and Sexual Difference: Essays on "The Prelude,"* 1989. Aspects of Wordsworth's thought are explored by James A. W. Heffernan, *Wordsworth's Theory of Poetry*, 1969; James K. Chandler, *Wordsworth's Second Nature: A Study of the Poetry and the Politics*, 1984; and Alan Bewell, *Wordsworth and the Enlightenment*, 1989. Prominent critical studies of Wordsworth's poetry are David Perkins, *Wordsworth and the Poetry of Sincerity*, 1964; Geoffrey Hartman's impressive study of *Wordsworth's Poetry, 1787–1814*, 1964, and his *The Unremarkable Wordsworth*, 1987; James H. Averill, *Wordsworth and the Poetry of Human Suffering*, 1980; Kenneth R. Johnston, *Wordsworth and "The Recluse,"* 1984; Marjorie Levinson, *Wordsworth's Great Period Poems*, 1986; Susan J. Wolfson, *The Questioning Presence: Wordsworth, Keats, and the Interrogative Mode in Romantic Poetry*, 1986; David Simpson, *Wordsworth's Historical Imagination*, 1987; Nicholas Roe, *Wordsworth and Coleridge: The Radical Years*, 1988; Theresa M. Kelley, *Wordsworth's Revisionary Aesthetics*, 1988; William H. Galperin, *Revision and Authority in Wordsworth*, 1989; Alan Liu, *Wordsworth, the Sense of History*, 1989; Peter J. Manning, *Reading Romantics*, 1990; and Judith W. Page, *Wordsworth and the Cultivation of Women*, 1994. The range and diversity of critical studies are represented in *The Age of William Wordsworth: Critical Essays on the Romantic Tradition*, ed. Johnston and Gene W. Ruoff, 1987; *Critical Essays on William Wordsworth*, ed. George Gilpin, 1990; and *The Cambridge Companion to Wordsworth*, ed. Gill, 2003.

THE VICTORIAN AGE

General studies and histories of the Victorian age and its frame of mind include Walter E. Houghton, *The Victorian Frame of Mind, 1830–1870*, 1957; Asa Briggs, *The Age of Improvement*, 1962; Richard D. Altick, *Victorian People and Ideas: A Companion for the Modern Reader of Victorian Literature*, 1973; *Victorian Britain: An Encyclopedia*, ed. Sally Mitchell, 1988; Richard L. Stein, *Victoria's Year: English Literature and Culture, 1837–38*, 1988; F. M. L. Thompson, *The Rise of Respectable Society: A Social History of Victorian Britain, 1830–1900*, 1988;

Robin Gilmour, *The Victorian Period: The Intellectual and Cultural Context of Victorian Literature, 1830–1890*, 1993; David Newsome, *The Victorian World Picture: Perceptions and Introspections in a World of Change*, 1997; Philip Davis, *The Victorians*, 2002; and A. N. Wilson, *The Victorians*, 2002. G. M. Young, *Victorian England: Portrait of an Age*, 1936 (republished in 1977 with 215 pages of explanatory notes by George Kitson Clark), is a brilliant synthesis, but it can be incomprehensible to readers who are not yet adequately familiar with the history of the age. Such readers should consult David Thomson, *England in the Nineteenth Century*, 1950, or Derek Beales, *From Castlereagh to Gladstone: 1815–1885*, 1970. The historical spread of Raymond Williams, *Culture and Society, 1780–1950*, 1960, exceeds the Victorian period, but the work continues to be important for those interested in this era.

Some interesting studies of special aspects of the age include Richard Altick, *The English Common Reader*, 1957; E. P. Thompson, *The Making of the English Working Class*, 1963; Steven Marcus, *The Other Victorians: A Study of Sexuality and Pornography in Mid-Nineteenth-Century England*, 1964; *The Victorian City*, ed. H. J. Dyos and Michael Wolff, 2 vols., 1973; Frank M. Turner, *The Greek Heritage in Victorian Britain*, 1981; Jeffrey Weeks, *Sex, Politics and Society: The Regulation of Sexuality since 1800*, 1981; Peter Gay, *The Bourgeois Experience: From Victoria to Freud*, 2 vols., 1984–86; Briggs, *Victorian Things*, 1989; David Cannadine, *The Decline and Fall of the British Aristocracy*, 1990; Christopher Herbert, *Culture and Anomie: Ethnographic Imagination and the Nineteenth Century*, 1991, and *Victorian Relativity: Radical Thought and Scientific Discovery*, 2001; Michael Wheeler, *Death and the Future Life in Victorian Literature and Theology*, 1991; Michael Mason, *The Making of Victorian Sexuality*, 1994; Margaret Homans, *Royal Representations: Queen Victoria and British Culture, 1837–1876*, 1998; and Rick Rylance, *Victorian Psychology and British Culture, 1850–1888*, 2000. Leonore Davidoff and Catherine Hall, *Family Fortunes: Men and Women of the English Middle Class, 1780–1850*, 1987, provides a useful prehistory of this topic for the high Victorian period. For pictures and paintings of the Victorian scene, see Jeremy Maas, *Victorian Painters*, 1969; Christopher Wood, *The Pre-Raphaelites*, 1981; and Julian Treuherz, *Victorian Painting*, 1993. Also revealing are the illustrations for Henry Mayhew, *London Labour and London Poor*, originally published 1851 and reprinted 1967, and Gustav Doré, *London: A Pilgrimage*, originally published 1872 and reprinted 1970. *Nature and the Victorian Imagination*, ed. U. C. Knoepflmacher and G. B. Tennyson, 1977; George Landow, *Victorian Types, Victorian Shadows: Biblical Typology in Victorian Literature, Art, and Thought*, 1980; and *Victorian Literature and the Victorian Visual Imagination*, ed. Carol T. Christ and John O. Jordan, 1995, feature valuable treatments of literature and the visual arts.

Books and collections of writings on Victorian poetry include Robert Langbaum, *The Poetry of Experience*, 1957; Carol T. Christ, *The Finer Optic: The Aesthetic of Particularity in Victorian Poetry*, 1975, and *Victorian and Modern Poetics*, 1984; Angela Leighton, *Victorian Women Poets: Writing against the Heart*, 1992; Isobel Arm-

strong, *Victorian Poetry: Poetry, Poetics, and Politics*, 1993; Antony Harrison, *Victorian Poets and the Politics of Culture*, 1998; *Women's Poetry, Late Romantic to Late Victorian: Gender and Genre 1730–1930*, ed. Armstrong and Virginia Blain, 1999; Yopie Prins, *Victorian Sappho*, 1999; *The Cambridge Companion to Victorian Poetry*, ed. Joseph Bristow, 2000; Matthew Reynolds, *Realms of Verse: English Poetry in a Time of Nation Building*, 2001; and *A Companion to Victorian Poetry*, ed. Richard Cronin, Alison Chapman, and Harrison, 2002.

Studies with a particular interest in the novel include J. Hillis Miller, *The Form of Victorian Fiction*, 1968; Peter Garrett, *The Victorian Multiplot Novel*, 1980; Donald Stone, *The Romantic Impulse in Victorian Fiction*, 1980; George Levine, *The Realistic Imagination*, 1981; Gillian Beer, *Darwin's Plots: Evolutionary Narrative in Darwin, George Eliot and Nineteenth-Century Fiction*, 1983; Peter Brooks, *Reading for the Plot: Design and Intention in Narrative*, 1984; Garrett Stewart, *Death Sentences: Styles of Dying in British Fiction*, 1984; Catherine Gallagher, *The Industrial Reformation of English Fiction: Social Discourse and Narrative Form, 1832–1867*, 1985; D. A. Miller, *The Novel and the Police*, 1988; Joseph W. Childers, *Novel Possibilities: Fiction and the Formation of Early Victorian Culture*, 1995; William A. Cohen, *Sex Scandal: The Private Parts of Victorian Fiction*, 1996; and Nicholas Dames, *Nostalgia, Forgetting and British Fiction, 1810–1870*, 2001. John Sutherland, *The Stanford Companion to Victorian Fiction*, 1989, and *The Cambridge Companion to the Victorian Novel*, ed. Deirdre David, 2000, are useful volumes.

Works that address other prose genres include John Holloway, *The Victorian Sage: Studies in Argument*, 1953; Peter Allan Dale, *The Victorian Critic and the Idea of History*, 1977; Avrom Fleischman, *Figures of Autobiography: The Language of Self in Victorian and Modern England*, 1983; Linda H. Peterson, *Victorian Autobiography: The Tradition of Self-Interpretation*, 1986; Hilary Fraser with David Brown, *English Prose of the Nineteenth Century*, 1997; and *Traditions of Victorian Women's Autobiography: The Poetics and Politics of Life-Writing*, 1999. For drama consult George Rowell, *The Victorian Theatre, 1792–1914: A Survey*, 1956; Michael R. Booth, *Theatre in the Victorian Age*, 1991; Kerry Powell, *Women and the Victorian Theatre*, 1997; and *The Cambridge Companion to Victorian and Edwardian Theatre*, ed. Powell, 2004.

Studies that cut across generic lines include J. Hillis Miller, *The Disappearance of God: Five Nineteenth-Century Writers*, 1963; John R. Reed, *Victorian Conventions*, 1975; John P. McGowan, *Representation and Revelation: Victorian Realism from Carlyle to Yeats*, 1986; and Amanda Anderson, *The Powers of Distance: Cos-*

mopolitanism and the Cultivation of Detachment, 2001. Interesting works focusing on gender and sexuality in Victorian life and literature include *Suffer and Be Still,* 1972, and *A Widening Sphere,* 1977, both ed. Martha Vicinus; Ellen Moers, *Literary Women,* 1976; Elaine Showalter, *A Literature of Their Own,* 1977; Sandra Gilbert and Susan Gubar, *The Madwoman in the Attic,* 1979; Elizabeth Helsinger, Robin Lauterbach Sheets, and William Veeder, *The Woman Question,* 3 vols., 1980; Nina Auerbach, *Woman and the Demon,* 1982, and *Romantic Imprisonment,* 1985; Eve Kosofsky Sedgwick, *Between Men: English Literature and Male Homosexual Desire,* 1985; Margaret Homans, *Bearing the Word: Language and Female Experience in Nineteenth-Century Women's Writing,* 1986; Mary Poovey, *Uneven Developments: The Ideological Work of Gender in Mid-Victorian England,* 1988; Kate Flint, *The Woman Reader: 1837–1914,* 1993; James Eli Adams, *Dandies and Desert Saints: Styles of Victorian Masculinity,* 1995; Elizabeth Langland, *Nobody's Angels: Middle Class Women and Domestic Ideology in Victorian Culture,* 1995; *Victorian Sexual Dissidence,* ed. Richard Dellamora, 1999; and *Women and Literature in Britain, 1800–1900,* ed. Joanne Shattock, 2001. For studies that join a concern with gender or identity with an interest in issues of empire and nation, see Jenny Sharpe, *Allegories of Empire: The Figure of Woman in the Colonial Text,* 1993; Graham Dawson, *Soldier Heroes: British Adventure, Empire and the Imagining of Masculinities,* 1994; Deirdre David, *Rule Britannia: Women, Empire, and Victorian Writing,* 1996; Susan Meyer, *Imperialism at Home: Race and Victorian Women's Fiction,* 1996; and Ian Baucom, *Out of Place: Englishness, Empire, and the Locations of Identity,* 1999. Patrick Brantlinger, *Rule of Darkness: British Literature and Imperialism, 1830–1914,* 1988, provides a good introduction to the topic. *A Companion to Victorian Literature and Culture,* ed. Herbert Tucker, 1999, contains a wide range of interesting and helpful essays. Articles on aspects of Victorian literature and culture appear in many general journals in the field; specialized periodicals include *ELT: English Literature in Transition, 1880–1920; Journal of Victorian Culture; Nineteenth-Century Contexts; Nineteenth-Century Literature; Nineteenth-Century Studies; Novel, Victorian Literature and Culture; Victorian Poetry;* and *Victorian Studies.* Once a year *Victorian Studies* issues a bibliography for the previous year, covering books, articles, and reviews; since 2001 it has been available in a searchable electronic form online. Other useful research tools are the *Victoria Research Web* (www.victorianresearch.org) and specialized bibliographies, which include Richard C. Tobias, *Bibliographies of Studies in Victorian Literature,* 1991; Sharon W. Propas, *Victorian Studies: A Research Guide,* 1992; and Laurence W. Mazzeno, *Victorian Poetry: An Annotated Bibliography,* 1995.

Matthew Arnold

The standard edition of Arnold's poetry is the elaborately annotated *Poems of Arnold,* ed. Miriam Allott, 1979. Cecil Lang has edited *The Letters of Matthew Arnold,* 6 vols., 1996–2001. R. H. Super has produced an authoritative edition of *The Complete Prose Works,* 11 vols., 1960–77. For a study of those prose works, see Joseph Carroll, *The Cultural Theory of Matthew Arnold,* 1982.

The most satisfactory biography is Park Honan's *Matthew Arnold: A Life,* 1981, but see also Nicholas Murray, *A Life of Matthew Arnold,* 1996, and Ian Hamilton, *A Gift Imprisoned: The Poetic Life of Matthew Arnold,* 1998. Lionel Trilling's excellent *Matthew Arnold,* 1949, remains a standard critical and biographical study, but see also G. Robert Stange's *The Poet as Humanist,* 1967, and Dwight Culler's *Imaginative Reason,* 1966. Other assessments include Stefan Collini, *Arnold,* 1988; David G. Riede, *Matthew Arnold and the Betrayal of Language,* 1988; and Alan Grob, *A Longing Like Despair: Arnold's Poetry of Pessimism,* 2002. Two investigations of Arnold's literary and intellectual background are Ruth apRoberts, *Arnold and God,* 1983, and Leon Gottfried, *Matthew Arnold and the Romantics,* 1983. See also the selection of essays edited by Harold Bloom, *Matthew Arnold,* 1987.

Elizabeth Barrett Browning

There is no complete modern standard edition, so readers still rely on the *Complete Works,* ed. Charlotte Porter and Helen Clarke, 6 vols., 1900. Julia Markus edited *Casa Guidi Windows,* 1977, and Margaret Reynolds edited a Norton Critical Edition of *Aurora Leigh,* 1996. Of a projected forty-volume collection, *The Brownings' Correspondence,* ed. Philip Kelley and Ronald Hudson, 1984–, fourteen volumes have been published. The best critical biography is Dorothy Mermin, *Elizabeth Barrett Browning: The Origins of a New Poetry,* 1989. See also Angela Leighton, *Elizabeth Barrett Browning,* 1986, and Rebecca Stott and Simon Avery, *Elizabeth Barrett Browning,* 2003. Interesting discussions of Barrett Browning can be found in Ellen Moers, *Literary Women,* 1976; Sandra Gilbert and Susan Gubar, *The Madwoman in the Attic,* 1979; Deirdre David, *Intellectual Women and Victorian Patriarchy,* 1987; Helen Cooper, *Elizabeth Barrett Browning, Woman and Artist,* 1988; and Marjorie Stone, *Elizabeth Barrett Browning,* 1995. See also the collections of essays edited by Sandra Donaldson, *Critical Essays on Elizabeth Barrett Browning,* 1999, and Harold Bloom, *Elizabeth Barrett Browning,* 2002.

Robert Browning

There are several competing modern editions, some of which are still in progress: *The Complete Works of Robert Browning, with Variant Readings and Annotations*, ed. Roma A. King Jr., 16 vols., 1969–99; *The Poetical Works of Robert Browning*, ed. Ian Jack, 9 vols., 1983–2004; and *The Poems of Browning*, ed. John Woolford and Daniel Karlin, 2 vols., 1991. A convenient two-volume collection is *Robert Browning: The Poems*, ed. John Pettigrew and Thomas J. Collins, 1981. For the Brownings' correspondence see entry under **Elizabeth Barrett Browning**. The standard biography is William Irvine and Park Honan, *The Book, the Ring, and the Poet*, 1974; see also Clyde de L. Ryals, *The Life of Robert Browning: A Critical Biography*, 1993. Gertrude Reese Hudson provides a study of his critical reception in *Robert Browning's Literary Life*, 1993. W. C. DeVane, *A Browning Handbook*, rev. ed. 1955, is a compilation of factual data concerning each of Browning's poems: sources, composition, and reputation. Further information is supplied by Norman B. Crowell, *A Reader's Guide to Robert Browning*, 1972, which also offers simplified summaries of critical discussions for twenty-three monologues.

The critical assessments in G. K. Chesterton, *Robert Browning*, 1903, are colorfully expressed and often shrewd. Robert Langbaum, *The Poetry of Experience*, 1957, begins the modern critical discussion of Browning. See also W. O. Raymond, *The Infinite Moment*, 1965; Donald Hair, *Browning's Experiments with Genre*, 1972; Ian Jack, *Browning's Major Poetry*, 1973; Herbert Tucker, *Browning's Beginnings*, 1980; Loy Martin, *Browning's Dramatic Monologues and the Post-Romantic Subject*, 1985; Joseph Bristow, *Robert Browning*, 1991; Daniel Karlin, *Browning's Hatreds*, 1993; Donald Hair, *Robert Browning's Language*, 1999; and Stefan Hawlin, *The Complete Critical Guide to Robert Browning*, 2002. Useful collections of essays include *The Browning Critics*, ed. Boyd Litzinger and K. L. Knickerbocker, 1965; *Robert Browning: A Collection of Critical Essays*, ed. Philip Drew, 1966; *Browning: The Critical Heritage*, ed. Litzinger and Donald Smalley, 1970; *Robert Browning*, ed. Isobel Armstrong, 1974; *Robert Browning: A Collection of Critical Essays*, ed. Harold Bloom and Adrienne Munich, 1979; *Critical Essays on Robert Browning*, ed. Mary Ellis Gibson, 1992; and *Robert Browning*, ed. Bloom, 2002.

Thomas Carlyle

H. D Traill edited the *Works*, 30 vols., 1898–1901. Twenty-one volumes of the *Collected Letters*, projected to extend to thirty volumes, have been published since 1971 (ed. C. R. Sanders et al.). There is a modern edition of *Sartor Resartus*, ed. Kerry McSweeney and Peter Sabot, 1987. J. A. Froude, *Thomas Carlyle*, 1882–84, for years the standard biography, has been replaced by Fred Kaplan, *Thomas Carlyle*, 1983. Recommended studies are Albert J. LaValley, *Carlyle and the Idea of the Modern*, 1968; Philip Rosenberg, *The Seventh Hero: Thomas Carlyle and the Theory of Radical Activism*, 1974; J. D. Rosenberg, *Carlyle and the Burden of History*, 1985; Ruth apRoberts, *The Ancient Dialect: Thomas Carlyle and Comparative Religion*, 1988; and Chris Vanden Bossche, *Carlyle and the Search for Authority*, 1991. John Holloway, *The Victorian Sage*, 1953, includes a chapter analyzing Carlyle's rhetoric. George B. Tennyson, *Sartor Called Resartus*, 1965, is an important critical study. See also George Levine, *The Boundaries of Fiction*, 1968; the collection of essays edited by K. J. Fielding and Rodger L. Tarr, *Carlyle Past and Present*, 1976; and B. V. Qualls, *The Secular Pilgrims of Victorian Fiction*, 1982. Tarr has also compiled *Thomas Carlyle: A Descriptive Bibliography*, 1990.

Elizabeth Gaskell

The standard edition of Gaskell's fiction is the Knutsford Edition, ed. A. W. Ward, 8 vols., 1906–20; the best modern editions are by Penguin. A modern edition exists of *The Letters of Mrs. Gaskell*, ed. J. A. V. Chapple and Arthur Pollard, rev. ed. 1997, augmented by *Further Letters*, ed. Chapple and A. Shelston, 2000. Biographies include Chapple, *Elizabeth Gaskell: The Early Years*, 1997; Winifred Gerin, *Elizabeth Gaskell*, 1980; and Jenny Uglow, *Elizabeth Gaskell: A Habit of Stories*, 1993. For critical studies see W. A. Craik, *Elizabeth Gaskell and the English Provincial Novel*, 1975; Angus Easson, *Elizabeth Gaskell*, 1979; Patsy Stoneman, *Elizabeth Gaskell*, 1987; *Elizabeth Gaskell: The Critical Heritage*, ed. Angus Easson, 1991; Hilary M. Schor, *Scheherezade in the Marketplace: Elizabeth Gaskell and the Victorian Novel*, 1992; and Deirdre d'Albertis, *Elizabeth Gaskell and the Victorian Social Text*, 1997.

Gerard Manley Hopkins

In 1918 Robert Bridges edited the first (posthumous) edition of Hopkins's poems, which has been the nucleus of all subsequent editions. The most recent is *The Poetical Works of Gerard Manley Hopkins*, ed. Norman H. MacKenzie, 1990. In addition to the poems, Hopkins's letters and parts of his notebooks have been published: *The Letters of Gerard Manley Hopkins to Robert Bridges* and *The Correspondence of G. M. Hopkins and Richard Watson Dixon*, ed. C. C. Abbot, 2 vols., 1935; *Further Letters of Gerard Manley Hopkins*, ed. Abbott, 1938, rev. ed. 1956; *The Journals and Papers of Gerard Manley Hopkins*, ed. Humphry House and Graham Storey, 1969; and *The Sermons and Devotional Writings of Gerard Manley Hopkins*, ed. Christopher Devlin, 1959. A helpful introduction to these works is Norman H. MacKenzie, *A Reader's Guide to Gerard Manley Hopkins*, 1981.

The two best biographies are Robert Bernard Martin, *Gerard Manley Hopkins: A Very Private Life*, 1991, and Norman White, *Hopkins: A Literary Biography*, 1992. Some useful critical studies are W. H. Gardner, *G. M. Hopkins: A Study of Poetic Idiosyncrasy in Relation to Poetic Tradition*, 2 vols., 1944, 1949; Paul L. Mariani, *A Commentary on the Complete Poems of Gerard Manley Hopkins*, 1970; Alison Sulloway, *Gerard Manley Hopkins and the Victorian Temper*, 1972; Daniel Harris, *Inspirations Unbidden: The "Terrible Sonnets" of Gerard Manley Hopkins*, 1982; Walter J. Ong, *Hopkins, the Self, and God*, 1986; Virginia Ridley Ellis, *Gerard Manley Hopkins and the Language of Mystery*, 1991; Julia Saville, *A Queer Chivalry: The Homoerotic Asceticism of Gerard Manley Hopkins*, 2000; and Bernadette Waterman, *Word as World: Philosophical Theology in Gerard Manley Hopkins*, 2002. Two good collections of critical essays are *Hopkins*, ed. Geoffrey Hartmann, 1966, and *Hopkins among the Poets: Studies in Modern Responses to Gerard Manley Hopkins*, ed. Richard F. Giles, 1985.

Rudyard Kipling
The standard complete works is the Sussex Edition, 35 vols., 1937–39. *Rudyard Kipling's Verse: Definitive Edition*, 1940, is supplemented by *Early Verse by Rudyard Kipling, 1879–1889: Unpublished, Uncollated and Rarely Collected Poems*, ed. Andrew Rutherford, 1986. T. S. Eliot edited, with an appreciative and discerning introduction, *A Choice of Kipling's Verse*, 1941. Thomas Pinney edited *The Letters of Rudyard Kipling* (1872–99), 3 vols., 1988–96. Charles E. Carrington, *Rudyard Kipling*, 1955, is the official biography; two recent and worthy ones are Harry Ricketts, *Rudyard Kipling: A Life*, 2001, and David Gilmour, *The Long Recessional*, 2002. Philip Mason, *Kipling: The Glass, the Shadow, and the Fire*, 1975, offers an informative account of Kipling's complex relationship with India. Three important midcentury critics have written interesting essays on Kipling: Edmund Wilson in *The Wound and the Bow*, 1941; George Orwell in *Critical Essays*, 1946; and Lionel Trilling in *The Liberal Imagination*, 1950. Studies of his fiction include Elliot L. Gilbert, *The Good Kipling: Studies in the Short Story*, 1971; Sandra Kemp, *Kipling's Hidden Narratives*, 1987; Mark Paffard, *Kipling's Indian Fiction*, 1989; Zohreh T. Sullivan, *Narratives of Empire: Fictions of Rudyard Kipling*, 1992; and Helen Pike Bauer, *Rudyard Kipling: A Study of the Short Fiction*, 1994. Peter Keating has written a study of his poetry, *Kipling the Poet*, 1994. There are a number of useful collections of critical essays: *Kipling's Mind and Art*, ed. Andrew Rutherford, 1964; *Kipling and the Critics*, ed. E. L. Gilbert, 1965; Roger Lancelyn Green, *Kipling: The Critical Heritage*, 1971; *Rudyard Kip-*

ling, ed. John Gross, 1972; *Critical Essays on Rudyard Kipling*, ed. Harold Orel, 1989; and *Rudyard Kipling*, ed. Harold Bloom, 2004.

Christina Rossetti
The standard variorum edition is *The Complete Poems of Christina Rossetti*, ed. R. W. Crump, 3 vols., 1979–90. Antony Harrison has edited *The Letters of Christina Rossetti*, 3 vols., 1997–2000. See also *Selected Prose of Christina Rossetti*, ed. David A. Kent and P. G. Stanwood, 1998. Two recent biographies are Kathleen Jones, *Learning Not to Be First: The Life of Christina Rossetti*, 1991, and Jan Marsh, *Christina Rossetti: A Writer's Life*, 1995. Virginia Woolf, *Second Common Reader*, 1932, contains an essay on the poet. Dolores Rosenblum, *Christina Rossetti: The Poetry of Endurance*, 1986, and Harrison, *Christina Rossetti in Context*, 1988, are good book-length studies of the poetry. Collections of critical essays are *The Culture of Christina Rossetti: Female Politics and Victorian Contexts*, ed. Mary Arseneau, Harrison, and Lorraine Janzen Kooistra, 1999, and David Kent, *The Achievement of Christina Rossetti*, 1987.

Robert Louis Stevenson
The standard edition of *The Works of Robert Louis Stevenson* was published by Scribner's, 32 vols., 1911–12; Ian Bell edited *The Complete Short Stories*, 1993, and Roger Lewis edited *The Collected Poems*, 2003. There is a Norton Critical Edition of *The Strange Case of Dr. Jekyll and Mr. Hyde*, ed. Katherine Lineham, 2003. Bradford Booth and Ernest Mehew edited *The Letters of Robert Louis Stevenson*, 8 vols., 1994–95. Graham Balfour, *Life of Robert Louis Stevenson*, 1901, has been an important source for subsequent biographers; modern biographies include Jenni Calder, *Robert Louis Stevenson: A Life Study*, 1980, and Bell, *Robert Louis Stevenson: Dreams of Exile*, 1992. For critical studies see David Daiches, *Robert Louis Stevenson*, 1947; Robert Kiely, *Robert Louis Stevenson and the Fiction of Adventure*, 1964; E. Eigner, *Robert Louis Stevenson and the Romantic Tradition*, 1966; Alan Sandison, *Robert Louis Stevenson and the Appearance of Modernism*, 1995; Peter Garrett, *Gothic Reflections*, 2003; and Ann Coley, *Robert Louis Stevenson and the Colonial Imagination*, 2004. For collections of essays see *Dr. Jekyll and Mr. Hyde after One Hundred Years*, ed. William Veeder and Gordon Hirsch, 1988; *Stevenson and Victorian Scotland*, ed. Jenni Calder, 2001; and *Robert Louis Stevenson Reconsidered*, ed. William Jones Jr., 2003.

Alfred, Lord Tennyson
Works was edited by his son Hallam, Lord Tennyson, 9 vols., 1907–08. The poems were edited by Christopher Ricks in one volume, 1969, and

extensively revised in three volumes, 1988. Norton Critical Editions of Tennyson's work are *Tennyson's Poetry*, ed. Robert W. Hill, Jr., 1999, and *In Memoriam*, ed. Erik Gray, 2003. *In Memoriam* has been edited by Susan Shatto and Marion Shaw, 1982. *The Letters of Alfred, Lord Tennyson*, to 1870, are edited by Cecil Y. Lang and Edgar F. Shannon, 4 vols., 1981–91. Hallam Tennyson's *Alfred, Lord Tennyson: A Memoir*, 2 vols., 1897, is a mine of anecdotes and valuable information. *The Tennyson Archive*, ed. Christopher Ricks and Aidan Day, 23 vols., 1987–89, is a monumental production concerning the manuscripts. The standard biography is Robert Martin, *Tennyson*, 1980. Critical studies include Jerome H. Buckley, *Tennyson: The Growth of a Poet*, 1961; Christopher Ricks, *Tennyson*, 1972; F. E. L. Priestley, *Language and Structure in Tennyson's Poetry*, 1973; James R. Kincaid, *Tennyson's Major Poems: The Comic and Ironic Patterns*, 1975; W. David Shaw, *Tennyson's Style*, 1976; and A. Dwight Culler, *The Poetry of Tennyson*, 1977. See also Daniel Albright, *Tennyson: The Muses' Tug-of-War*, 1986; Alan Sinfield, *Alfred Tennyson*, 1986; Herbert F. Tucker, *Tennyson and the Doom of Romanticism*, 1988; Donald S. Hair, *Tennyson's Language*, 1991; and Gerhard Joseph, *Tennyson and the Text: The Weaver's Shuttle*, 1992.

Some of the most interesting discussions are in introductory essays to Tennyson's poems by T. S. Eliot, 1936; W. H. Auden, 1944; and H. Marshall McLuhan, 1956. Also useful are A. C. Bradley, *A Commentary on Tennyson's "In Memoriam,"* 1901; E. D. H. Johnson, *The Alien Vision of Victorian Poetry*, 1952; *Critical Essays on the Poetry of Tennyson*, ed. John Kilham, 1960; *Critical Essays on Alfred Lord Tennyson*, ed. Herbert F. Tucker, 1993; and *Alfred Lord Tennyson*, ed. Harold Bloom, 1999. Book-length studies of the *Idylls* have been published by Clyde de L. Ryals, 1967; John R. Reed, 1969; and John D. Rosenberg, 1973. A collection of critical essays on *In Memoriam* was edited by John Dixon Hunt, 1970, and Timothy Peltason has published a study of the poem, *Reading In Memoriam*, 1985.

Oscar Wilde

There is no standard complete edition, but a convenient one-volume collection is *The Complete Works of Oscar Wilde*, 1989. Merlin Holland and Rupert Hart-Davis edited *Complete Letters*, 2000. The standard biography is Richard Ellmann, *Oscar Wilde*, 1988. See also the psychoanalytic biography by Melissa Knox, *Oscar Wilde: A Long and Lovely Suicide*, 1994, and Barbara Belford, *Oscar Wilde: A Certain Genius*, 2000. Earlier biographies include Hesketh Pearson, *The Life of Oscar Wilde: His Life and Wit*, 1946, and H. Montgomery Hyde, *Oscar Wilde: A Biography*, 1975. *Oscar Wilde, a Pictorial Biography*, by Wilde's son, Vyvyan Holland, 1960, has splendid photographs of Wilde and his contemporaries and also provides a concise factual account of his life. The essays by Ian Fletcher and John Stokes in *Anglo-Irish Literature: A Review of Research*, 1976, and *Recent Research on Anglo-Irish Writers*, 1983, both ed. Richard J. Finneran, provide a full-scale guide to editions of Wilde and studies of his life and work.

Oscar Wilde: A Collection of Critical Essays, ed. Richard Ellmann, 1969, is valuable for its coverage of responses to Wilde by writers such as Yeats and Shaw. *Oscar Wilde: The Critical Heritage*, ed. Karl Beckson, 1970, is especially helpful with regard to the plays; it covers the period 1881–1927. For an account of the contemporary reception of Wilde, see Regenia Gagnier, *Idylls of the Marketplace: Oscar Wilde and the Victorian Public*, 1986. See also Camille Paglia, *Sexual Personae*, 1990; Ed Cohen, *Talk on the Wilde Side: Toward a Genealogy of Discourse on Male Sexualities*, 1993; Gary Schmidgall, *The Stranger Wilde: Interpreting Oscar*, 1994; Lawrence Damson, *Wilde's Intentions: The Artist in His Criticism*, 1997; and Knox, *Oscar Wilde in the 1990s: The Critic as Creator*, 2001. Useful collections of essays are *Critical Essays on Oscar Wilde*, ed. Gagnier, 1991; *The Cambridge Companion to Oscar Wilde*, ed. Peter Raby, 1997; and *Oscar Wilde*, ed. Harold Bloom, 2002. Karl Beckson, *The Oscar Wilde Encyclopedia*, 1998, and Ian Small, *Oscar Wilde: Recent Research*, 2000, are also valuable resources.

THE TWENTIETH CENTURY AND AFTER

The Twentieth Century and After

Martin Gilbert, *A History of the Twentieth Century*, 3 vols., 1997–99, offers a richly informative account of the first half-century, while Peter Conrad, *Modern Times, Modern Places*, 1999, skillfully interweaves the history of the period with its artistic and intellectual movements.

The social and political background is well covered in Robert Graves and Alan Hodge's *The Long Week End: A Social History of Great Brit-* ain, 1918–1939, 1940; *The Baldwin Age*, ed. John Raymond, 1960; Julian Symons's *The Thirties: A Dream Revolved*, 1960, rev. ed. 1975; Hugh Thomas's *The Spanish Civil War*, 1961, 3rd ed. 1986; Malcolm Bradbury's *The Social Context of Modern English Literature*, 1971; *The Twentieth-Century Mind: History, Ideas, and Literature in Britain*, 3 vols., ed. C. B. Cox and A. E. Dyson, 1972; Paul Fussell's *The Great War and Modern Memory*, 1975, and *Wartime:*

Understanding and Behavior in the Second World War, 1989; Samuel Hynes's *The Auden Generation: Literature and Politics in England in the 1930s*, 1976, and *A War Imagined: The First World War and English Culture*, 1991; Valentine Cunningham's *British Writers of the Thirties*, 1988; Alan Sinfield's *Literature, Politics, and Culture in Postwar Britain*, 1989; all of which include useful bibliographies.

The following critical works deal with general aspects of modern English literature: Stephen Spender's *The Struggle of the Modern*, 1963; C. K. Stead's *The New Poetic: Yeats to Eliot*, 1964, rev. ed. 1987, and *Pound, Yeats, Eliot, and the Modernist Movement*, 1986; *The Modern Tradition: Backgrounds of Modern Literature*, ed. Richard Ellmann and Charles Feidelson, 1965; Irving Howe's *The Idea of the Modern in Literature and the Arts*, 1967; Hugh Kenner's *The Pound Era*, 1971; *Modernism 1890–1930*, ed. Malcolm Bradbury and James McFarlane, 1976; David Perkins's *A History of Modern Poetry*, 2 vols., 1976–87; Robert Hughes's *The Shock of the New*, 1981, rev. ed. 1991; Michael Levenson's *A Genealogy of Modernism*, 1984; Carol T. Christ's *Victorian and Modern Poetics*, 1984; Sanford Schwartz's *The Matrix of Modernism: Pound, Eliot and Early Twentieth-Century Thought*, 1985; Maud Ellmann's *The Poetics of Impersonality: T. S. Eliot and Ezra Pound*, 1987; Perry Meisel's *The Myth of the Modern: A Study in British Literature and Criticism after 1850*, 1987; James Longenbach's *Stone Cottage: Pound, Yeats, and Modernism*, 1988; John Bayley's *The Short Story: Henry James to Elizabeth Bowen*, 1988; Sandra M. Gilbert and Susan Gubar's *No Man's Land: The Place of the Woman Writer in the Twentieth Century*, 3 vols., 1988–94; George Watson's *British Literature since 1945*, 1991; Daniel Albright's *Quantum Poetics: Yeats, Pound, Eliot, and the Science of Modernism*, 1997; Lawrence Rainey's *Institutions of Modernism*, 1998; *The Cambridge Companion to Modernism*, ed. Michael Levenson, 1999; Jed Esty's *A Shrinking Island: Modernism and National Culture in England*, 2004; and vols. 11, 12, and 13 of the *Oxford English Literary History*: Chris Baldick's *The Modern Movement*, 2004, which covers 1910–40, Randall Stevenson's *The Last of England?*, 2004, which covers 1960–2000, and Bruce King's *The Internationalization of English Literature*, 2004, which surveys black and Asian British literature from 1948 to 2000.

Useful reference books include John L. Somer and Barbara Eck Cooper's *American and British Literature 1945–1975: An Annotated Bibliography of Contemporary Scholarship*, 1980; Alistair Davies's *An Annotated Critical Bibliography of Modernism*, 1982; *Contemporary Novelists*, ed. D. L. Kirkpatrick and James Vinson, 4th ed. 1986; *Contemporary Dramatists*, ed. K. A. Berney, 5th ed. 1993; *The Oxford Com-*

panion to Twentieth-Century Poetry, ed. Ian Hamilton, 1994; *The Oxford Companion to Irish Literature*, ed. Robert Welch and Bruce Stewart, 1996; *Contemporary Poets*, ed. Thomas Riggs, 7th ed. 2001; Neil Roberts's *A Companion to Twentieth-Century Poetry*, 2001; and entries in the many volumes of the *Dictionary of Literary Biography* (also available online). The British Council/Book Trust Web site (www .contemporarywriters.com) is a useful source of information about contemporary British authors.

W. H. Auden

Auden's *Selected Poems*, ed. Edward Mendelson, 1979, rev. ed. 1989, reprints many of Auden's poems as they first appeared in his volumes of poetry. *The English Auden: Poems, Essays and Dramatic Writings, 1927–1939*, ed. Mendelson, 1977, also reprints Auden's poems in their original versions—all those published in book form in the 1930s—as well as many previously unpublished and uncollected poems and early prose writings. *W. H. Auden: Collected Poems*, ed. Mendelson, 1976, rev. ed. 1991, contains the poems Auden wished to preserve in their final revised form.

The definitive collected editions of Auden's works proceed under Mendelson's editorship: *Plays and Other Dramatic Writings by W. H. Auden, 1928–1938*, 1989; *W. H. Auden and Chester Kallman: Libretti and Other Dramatic Writings by W. H. Auden, 1939–1973*, 1993; *Prose and Travel Books in Prose and Verse, Volume I, 1926–1938*, 1996; and *Prose: Volume II, 1939–1948*, 2002. *Juvenilia 1922–1928*, ed. Katherine Bucknell, 1994, contains Auden's earliest work and appeared in an expanded edition in 2003. "*The Dyer's Hand" and Other Essays*, 1968, is an essential collection of Auden's lectures and essays. Other such collections include *Forewords and Afterwards*, 1973, and two posthumous editions, "*In Solitude, for Company": W. H. Auden after 1940*, ed. Bucknell and Nicholas Jenkins, 1995, and *Lectures on Shakespeare*, ed. Arthur C. Kirsch, 2000. Auden edited a number of anthologies, including *The Poet's Tongue*, with John Garrett, 1935; *The Oxford Book of Light Verse*, 1938; *Poets of the English Language*, with Norman Holmes Pearson, 1950; *An Elizabethan Songbook*, with Noah Greenberg and Chester Kallman, 1955; and *The Elder Edda: A Selection*, 1969. For Auden's life see Humphrey Carpenter's *W. H. Auden: A Biography*, 1981; *The Map of All My Youth: Early Works, Friends, and Influences*, ed. Bucknell and Jenkins, 1990; R. P. T. Davenport-Hines's *Auden*, 1995; Thekla Clark's *Wystan and Chester: A Personal Memoir of W. H. Auden and Chester Kallman*, 1995, rev. ed 1996; and David Garrett Izzo's *W. H. Auden Encyclopedia*, 2002, rev. ed. 2004. The standard bibliography is B. C. Bloomfield and Mendelson's *W. H. Auden: A Bibliography 1924–1969*, 1972, and is updated in *Auden Studies*, ed. Bucknell and Jenkins, 1990–95.

W. H. Auden: The Critical Heritage, ed. John Haffenden, 1983, traces Auden's critical reception and provides contemporary criticism. For helpful glosses on individual poems, see John Fuller's *W. H. Auden: A Commentary*, 1998. Useful studies include Monroe K. Spears's *The Poetry of W. H. Auden*, 1963; Justin Replogle's *Auden's Poetry*, 1969; Samuel Hynes's *The Auden Generation*, 1976, rev. ed. 1992; Edward Mendelson's *Early Auden*, 1981; Edward Callan's *Auden: A Carnival of Intellect*, 1983; Stan Smith's *W. H. Auden*, 1985; Lucy McDiarmid's *Auden's Apologies for Poetry*, 1990; John R. Boly's *Reading Auden: The Returns of Caliban*, 1991; Anthony Hecht's *The Hidden Law*, 1993; Marsha Bryant's *Auden and Documentary in the 1930s*, 1997; Mendelson's *Later Auden*, 1999; Rainer Emig's *W. H. Auden: Towards a Postmodern Poetics*, 2000; Richard R. Bozorth's *Auden's Games of Knowledge: Poetry and the Meanings of Homosexuality*, 2001; Peter Edgerly Firchow's *W. H. Auden: Contexts for Poetry*, 2002; and Susannah Young-ah Gottlieb, *Regions of Sorrow: Anxiety and Messianism in Hannah Arendt and W. H. Auden*, 2003. Useful essays are collected in *Auden: A Collection of Critical Essays*, ed. Monroe K. Spears, 1964, and *Critical Essays on W. H. Auden*, ed. George W. Bahlke, 1991.

Samuel Beckett

Beckett's dramatic works include *Waiting for Godot: Tragicomedy in 2 Acts*, 1954, ed. Dougald McMillan and James Knowlson in the revised edition published in 1994; *Endgame*, 1958, ed. S. E. Gontarski, rev. ed. 1992; *Krapp's Last Tape and Other Dramatic Pieces*, 1960, ed. Knowlson, rev. ed. 1992; *Happy Days: A Play in Two Acts*, 1961; and *The Shorter Plays: With Revised Texts for* Footfalls, Come and Go, *and* What Where, ed. Gontarski, 2000. Beckett's novels include *Murphy*, 1938; *Molloy*, 1951; *Watt*, 1953; *Malone Dies*, 1956; *The Unnamable*, 1958; *Four Novellas*, 1977; and *Nohow On: Three Novels*, 1980. Short prose fiction can be found in *More Pricks than Kicks*, 1930, rev. ed. 1970; *As the Story Was Told: Uncollected and Late Prose*, 1990; *The Complete Short Prose, 1929–1989*, ed. Gontarski, 1995; and *I Can't Go On, I'll Go On: A Selection from Samuel Beckett's Work*, ed. Richard W. Seaver, 1976. Beckett's poetry can be found in *Poems in English*, 1961, and *Collected Poems in English and French*, 1977. Beckett also edited *Our Exagmination Round His Factification for Incamination of Work in Progress*, a symposium on James Joyce's *Finnegans Wake*, 1929, 2nd ed. 1962. The standard biography is Knowlson's *Damned to Fame: The Life of Samuel Beckett*, 1996. Anthony Cronin's *Samuel Beckett: The Last*

Modernist, 1996; *Conversations with and about Beckett*, ed. Mel Gussow, 1996; and Anne Atik's *How It Was: A Memoir of Samuel Beckett*, 2001, are also useful. For biographical background for Beckett's early work, see John Pilling's *Beckett before Godot*, 1997. Bibliographic reference sources include Raymond Federman and John Fletcher's *Samuel Beckett: His Works and His Critics: An Essay in Bibliography*, 1970; P. J. Murphy's *Critique of Beckett Criticism: A Guide to Research in English, French, and German*, 1994; and Ruby Cohn's *A Beckett Canon*, 2001.

Alvarez's *Samuel Beckett*, 1973; Hugh Kenner's *A Reader's Guide to Samuel Beckett*, 1973; and C. J. Ackerly's *The Grove Companion to Samuel Beckett: A Reader's Guide to His Work, Life, and Thought*, 2004, are good introductions to Beckett's work. Criticism of the plays includes Cohn's *Just Play: Beckett's Theatre*, 1980; Beryl Fletcher and John Fletcher's *A Student's Guide to the Plays of Samuel Beckett*, 1985; Gontarksi's *The Intent of Undoing in Samuel Beckett's Dramatic Texts*, 1985; and, specifically on the later drama, Rosemary Pountney's *Theatre of Shadows: Samuel Beckett's Drama 1956–76: From All That Fall to Footfalls with Commentaries on the Late Plays*, 1988.

On *Endgame* see *Twentieth Century Interpretations of* Endgame, ed. B. G. Chevigny, 1969, and Arthur N. Athanason's *Endgame: The Ashbin Play*, 1993. On the later work in general, see Steven Connor's *Samuel Beckett: Repetition Theory and Text*, 1986, and Enoch Brater's *Beyond Minimalism: Beckett's Late Style in the Theatre*, 1987, and *The Drama in the Text: Beckett's Late Fiction*, 1994.

Among many good general studies are Vivian Mercier's *Beckett/Beckett*, 1977; *Samuel Beckett—Humanistic Perspectives*, ed. Morris Beja, 1983; Christopher Ricks's *Beckett's Dying Words*, 1993; and *The Cambridge Companion to Beckett*, ed. John Pilling, 1994. Also very useful is *Samuel Beckett: The Critical Heritage*, ed. Lawrence Graver and Ray Federman, 1979, and David Pattie's *The Complete Critical Guide to Samuel Beckett*, 2000. The Beckett Archive is housed at the University of Reading, and the twice-yearly *Journal of Beckett Studies* began publication in 1976; Gontarski is editor of *The Beckett Studies Reader*, published in 1993.

Anne Carson

Poetry and prose are often combined in Carson's books, which include *Short Talks*, 1992; *Plainwater: Essays and Poetry*, 1995; *Glass, Irony, and God*, 1995; *Autobiography of Red: A Novel in Verse*, 1998; *Men in the Off Hours*, 2000; *The Beauty of the Husband: A Fictional Essay in 29 Tangos*, 2001; and *If Not, Winter: Fragments of Sappho*, 2002. Other works include her classical study *Eros the Bittersweet: An Essay*, 1986, and *Economy of the Unlost: Reading Simonides of Keos with Paul Celan*, 1999. Criticism of her work can be found in *American and Canadian Women Poets, 1930–Present*, ed. Harold Bloom, 2002.

J. M. Coetzee

Dusklands, 1974, consists of two linked novellas. It was followed by the novels *In the Heart of the Country*, 1977; *Waiting for the Barbarians*, 1980; *Life & Times of Michael K.*, 1983; *Foe*, 1986; *Age of Iron*, 1990; *The Master of Petersburg*, 1994; *Disgrace*, 1999; and *Elizabeth Costello*, 2003. Coetzee's nonfiction includes *White Writing: On the Culture of Letters in South Africa*, 1988; *Doubling the Point: Essays and Interviews*, 1992; *Giving Offense: Essays on Censorship*, 1996; the fictionalized lecture *The Lives of Animals*, 1999; and *Stranger Shores: Literary Essays, 1986–1999*, 2001. He coedited, with André Philippus Brink, *A Land Apart: A Contemporary South African Reader*, 1986. He edited and translated *Landscape with Rowers: Poetry from the Netherlands*, 2004, a facing-page collection of six twentieth-century Dutch poets. Kevin Goddard, John Read, and Teresa Dovey's *J. M. Coetzee: A Bibliography*, 1990, is comprehensive of his work to 1990. For Coetzee's life see his fictionalized memoirs *Boyhood: Scenes from Provincial Life*, 1997, and *Youth: Scenes from Provincial Life II*, 2002.

An inclusive overview of Coetzee's fiction is Dominic Head's *J. M. Coetzee*, 1997. Allen Penner's *Countries of the Mind: The Fiction of J. M. Coetzee*, 1989, illuminates work up to and including *Foe*. For a range of criticism see Graham Huggan and Stephen Watson's *Critical Perspectives on J. M. Coetzee*, 1996. Coetzee is examined as a specifically South African postcolonial writer in Susan Gallagher's *A Story of South Africa: J. M. Coetzee's Fiction in Context*, 1991; David Attwell's *J. M. Coetzee: South Africa and the Politics of Writing*, 1993; Sue Kossew's *Critical Essays on J. M. Coetzee*, 1998; and Derek Attridge's *J. M. Coetzee & the Ethics of Reading*, 2004. A special issue of *South Atlantic Quarterly*, 93.1, ed. Michael Valdez Moses, 1994, is devoted to Coetzee's work.

Joseph Conrad

The standard edition of Conrad's works is *The Uniform Edition of the Works of Joseph Conrad*, 22 vols., 1923–38, reprinted 1946–55 as the *Collected Edition of the Works of Joseph Conrad*. Useful essays and notes to the novels are provided by the Norton Critical Editions of *Lord Jim*, ed. Thomas C. Moser, 2nd ed. 1996; *The Nigger of the "Narcissus*," ed. Robert Kimbrough, 1979; and *Heart of Darkness*, ed. Robert Kimbrough, 3rd ed. 1988. The Modern Library edition of *Nostromo*, 1951, also contains an illuminating introductory essay by Robert Penn Warren. Conrad's letters have been published as *The Collected Letters of Joseph Conrad*, 6 vols., ed. Frederick R. Karl and Laurence Davies, 1983–2002, and the selection *Letters from*

Joseph Conrad, 1895–1924, 1 vol., ed. Edward Garnett, 1928; these are supplemented by material in *Joseph Conrad's Letters to R. B. Cunninghame Graham*, ed. C. T. Watts, 1969; the collection *A Portrait in Letters: Correspondence to and about Conrad*, ed. J. H. Stape and Owen Knowles, 1996, is also helpful. Biographies include Zdzislaw Najder's *Joseph Conrad: A Chronicle*, 1983; Cedric Watts's *Joseph Conrad: A Literary Life*, 1989; Jeffrey Meyers's *Joseph Conrad: A Biography*, 1991; and John Batchelor's *The Life of Joseph Conrad: A Critical Biography*, 1994. Memoirs of Conrad include Jessie Conrad's *Joseph Conrad as I Knew Him*, 1926, and *Joseph Conrad and His Circle*, 1935; and Ford Madox Ford's *Joseph Conrad: A Personal Remembrance*, 1965. See also material collected in *Joseph Conrad: Interviews and Recollections*, ed. Martin Ray, 1990. The standard bibliography is *Joseph Conrad: An Annotated Bibliography*, ed. Bruce Teets, 1990.

Ian Watt's *Conrad in the Nineteenth Century*, 1979; Fredric Jameson's *The Political Unconscious: Narrative as a Socially Symbolic Act*, 1981; Jakob Lothe's *Conrad's Narrative Method*, 1989; Vincent P. Pecora's *Self and Form in Modern Narrative*, 1989, and Michael Greaney's *Conrad, Language, and Narrative*, 2002, examine Conrad's narrative strategies. Heliéna Krenn's *Conrad's Lingard Trilogy: Empire, Race and Women in the Malay Novels*, 1990, and Ruth Nadelhaft's *Joseph Conrad*, 1991, offer feminist perspectives, and gender-theoretical criticism includes Andrew Michael Roberts's *Conrad and Gender*, 1993, and *Conrad and Masculinity*, 2000. Christopher GoGwilt's *The Invention of the West: Joseph Conrad and the Double-Mapping of Europe and Empire*, 1995, presents a postcolonial perspective. Peter J. Glassman's *Language and Being: Joseph Conrad and the Literature of Personality*, 1976, offers a psychological analysis. *Conrad on Film*, ed. Gene M. Moore, 1997, is also helpful.

A guide to Conrad's work is *The Cambridge Companion to Joseph Conrad*, ed. J. H. Stape, 1996. In addition to the essays in the Norton Critical Editions, criticism on both *Heart of Darkness* and *The Nigger of the "Narcissus"* can be found in *Conrad: The Critical Heritage*, ed. Norman Sherry, 1973; *Joseph Conrad*, ed. Harold Bloom, 1986; *Joseph Conrad: Critical Assessments*, 4 vols., ed. Keith Carabine, 1992; *A Joseph Conrad Companion*, ed. Leonard Orr and Theodore Billy, 1999; and *Essays on Conrad*, ed. Ian Watt, 2000.

For further reading on *The Nigger of the "Narcissus*," see *Conrad's Manifesto: Preface to a Career: The History of the Preface to* The Nigger of the "Narcissus," *with Facsimiles of the Manuscripts*, ed. David R. Smith and Leonard Baskin, 1966; James W. Parins and Todd K. Bender's *A Concordance to Conrad's* The Nigger of the "Narcissus," 1981; and chapters in

Michael Levenson's *A Genealogy of Modernism*, 1984, and in Michael North's *The Dialect of Modernism*, 1994.

For works concerning *Heart of Darkness*, see Gary Adelman's *Heart of Darkness: Search for the Unconscious*, 1987; *Joseph Conrad's* Heart of Darkness, ed. Harold Bloom, 1987; *Heart of Darkness: A Case Study in Contemporary Criticism*, ed. Ross C. Murfin, 1989; *Marlow*, ed. Harold Bloom, 1992; Nicolas Tredell's *Joseph Conrad: Heart of Darkness*, 1999; Peter Edgerley Firchow's *Envisioning Africa: Racism and Imperialism in Conrad's* Heart of Darkness, 2000; an essay in J. Hillis Miller's *Others*, 2001, and another by Richard J. Ruppel in *Imperial Desire: Dissident Sexualities and Colonial Literature*, ed. Philip Holden and Richard J. Ruppel, 2003.

T. S. Eliot
The *Complete Poems and Plays of T. S. Eliot* was published in 1969. *Inventions of the March Hare: Poems, 1909–1917*, ed. Christopher Ricks, brought early unpublished work to light in 1996. The fascinating manuscripts of *The Waste Land* are available as *The Waste Land: A Facsimile and Transcript of the Original Drafts Including the Annotations of Ezra Pound*, ed. Valerie Eliot, 1971. Also immensely useful is the Norton Critical Edition of *The Waste Land*, ed. Michael North, 2001, which contains contextual documents and criticism in addition to the poem. Eliot's most important critical essays are to be found in *The Sacred Wood: Essays on Poetry and Criticism*, 1920; *The Use of Poetry and the Use of Criticism: Studies in the Relation of Criticism to Poetry in England*, 1933; *The Idea of a Christian Society*, 1939; *Notes towards the Definition of Culture*, 1948; *On Poetry and Poets*, 1957; *To Criticize the Critic and Other Writings*, 1965; and *The Varieties of Metaphysical Poetry*, ed. Ronald Schuchard, 1994. Important biographies include Peter Ackroyd's *T. S. Eliot: A Life*, 1984, and Lyndall Gordon's *T. S. Eliot: An Imperfect Life*, 1999. Also helpful is *The Letters of T. S. Eliot, Vol. I: 1898–1922*, ed. Valerie Eliot, 1988.

Studies of Eliot's work include F. O. Matthiessen's *The Achievement of T. S. Eliot*, 3rd ed. 1958; Northrop Frye's *T. S. Eliot*, 1963; Bernard Bergonzi's *T. S. Eliot*, 1972; Stephen Spender's *T. S. Eliot*, 1976; Ronald Bush's *T. S. Eliot: A Study in Character and Style*, 1983; Robert Crawford's *The Savage and the City in the Work of T. S. Eliot*, 1987; Louis Menand's *Discovering Modernism*, 1987; Richard Shusterman's *T. S. Eliot and the Philosophy of Criticism*, 1988; Christopher Ricks's *T. S. Eliot and Prejudice*, 1988; Eric Sigg's *The American T. S. Eliot: A Study of the Early Writings*, 1989; Michael North's *The Political Aesthetic of Yeats, Eliot, and Pound*, 1991; Jewel Spears Brooker's *Mastery and Escape: T. S. Eliot and the Dialectic*

of Modernism, 1994; Anthony Julius's *T. S. Eliot, Anti-Semitism and Literary Form*, 1995; *T. S. Eliot*, ed. Harriet Davidson, 1999; Ronald Schuchard's *Eliot's Dark Angel: Intersections of Life and Art*, 1999; and Donald J. Childs's *From Philosophy to Poetry: T. S. Eliot's Study of Knowledge and Experience*, 2001.

Valuable collections of essays include *T. S. Eliot: A Collection of Critical Essays*, ed. Hugh Kenner, 1962; *T. S. Eliot: A Collection of Criticism*, ed. Linda Wagner-Martin, 1974; *T. S. Eliot: The Critical Heritage*, ed. Michael Grant, 1982; *T. S. Eliot: Modern Critical Views*, ed. Harold Bloom, 1985; *T. S. Eliot, A Voice Descanting: Centenary Essays*, ed. Shyamal Bagchee, 1990; *T. S. Eliot: The Modernist in History*, ed. Ronald Bush, 1991; *T. S. Eliot*, ed. Harold Bloom, 1999; and *T. S. Eliot and Our Turning World*, ed. Jewel Spears Brooker, 2001. Donald C. Gallup's *T. S. Eliot: A Bibliography*, rev. ed. 1969, is also useful.

Helpful guides to the poetry and plays are Grover Smith's *T. S. Eliot's Poetry and Plays: A Study in Sources and Meanings*, 1956; Carol H. Smith's *T. S. Eliot's Dramatic Theory and Practice, from Sweeney Agonistes to The Elder Statesman*, 1963; *The Cambridge Companion to T. S. Eliot*, ed. A. David Moody, 1994; and *A Concordance to the Complete Poems and Plays of T. S. Eliot*, ed. J. L. Dawson et al., 1995.

For further reading on Eliot's poetry, see Elizabeth Drew's *T. S. Eliot, The Design of His Poetry*, 1949; Helen Gardner's *The Art of T. S. Eliot*, 1950; Hugh Kenner's *The Invisible Poet*, 1959; David Moody's *Thomas Stearns Eliot, Poet*, 1979; Maud Ellmann's *The Poetics of Impersonality: T. S. Eliot and Ezra Pound*, 1987; Lee Oser's *T. S. Eliot and American Poetry*, 1998; and Denis Donoghue's *Words Alone: The Poet, T. S. Eliot*, 2000. On *Four Quartets* see Helen Gardner's *The Composition of* Four Quartets, 1978.

For further reading on *The Waste Land*, see *Eliot in His Time: Essays on the Occasion of the Fiftieth Anniversary of* The Waste Land, ed. A. Walton Litz, 1973; Harriet Davidson's *T. S. Eliot and Hermeneutics: Absence and Interpretation in* The Waste Land, 1985; Calvin Bedient's *He Do the Police in Different Voices: The Waste Land and Its Protagonists*, 1986; *T. S. Eliot's* The Waste Land, ed. Harold Bloom, 1986; Nancy K. Gish's The Waste Land: *A Poem of Memory and Desire*, 1988; and Jewel Spears Brooker and Joseph Bentley's *Reading* The Waste Land: *Modernism and the Limits of Interpretation*, 1990.

Brian Friel
Plays One, 1984, 1996, and *Plays Two*, 1999, draw from Friel's dramatic works, including *The Saucer of Larks*, 1962; *Philadelphia, Here I Come!*, 1965; *The Gold in the Sea*, 1966; *The Loves of Cass McGuire*, 1967; *Lovers*, 1968;

Crystal and Fox, 1970; The Mundy Scheme, 1970; The Gentle Island, 1973; The Freedom of the City, 1974; The Enemy Within, 1975; Living Quarters, 1978; Volunteers, 1979; Aristocrats, 1980; Faith Healer, 1980; Anton Chekhov's Three Sisters: A Translation, 1981; Translations, 1981; The Communication Cord, 1983; Fathers and Sons: After the Novel by Ivan Turgenev, 1987; Making History, 1989; Dancing at Lughnasa, 1990; The London Vertigo, Based on a Play The True Born Irishman, or, The Irish Fine Lady, by Charles Macklin, 1990; A Month in the Country: After Turgenev, 1992; Wonderful Tennessee, 1993; Molly Sweeney, 1994; Give Me Your Answer, Do!, 1997; Uncle Vanya: A Version of the Play by Anton Chekhov, 1998; The Yalta Game: After Chekhov, 2001; Three Plays After, 2002. Friel's fiction can be found in Selected Stories, 1979, and The Diviner: The Best Stories of Brian Friel, 1982. Friel is also editor of Charles McGlinchey's The Last of the Name, 1986, 1999.

For biographical information and criticism see Brian Friel: Essays, Diaries, Interviews, 1964–1999, ed. Christopher Murray, 1999, and Brian Friel in Conversation, ed. Paul Delaney, 2000. Ten Modern Irish Playwrights: A Comprehensive Annotated Bibliography, ed. Kimball King, 1979, is a helpful resource.

Brian Friel: A Reference Guide, 1962–1992, ed. George O'Brien, 1995, provides a useful guide to most of Friel's work. For criticism of Friel's work see D. E. S. Maxwell's Brian Friel, 1973; Seamus Deane's Essays in Modern Irish Literature: 1880–1980, 1985; Ulf Dantanus's Brian Friel: The Growth of an Irish Dramatist, 1985, and Brian Friel: A Study, 1988; Critical Approaches to Anglo-Irish Literature, ed. Michael Allen and Angela Wilcox, 1989; George O'Brien's Brian Friel, 1990; Elmer Kennedy-Andrews's The Art of Brian Friel: Neither Reality nor Dreams, 1995; Brian Friel: A Casebook, ed. William Kerwin, 1997; Nicholas Grene's The Politics of Irish Drama: Plays in Context from Boucicault to Friel, 1999; Richard Pine's The Diviner: The Art of Brian Friel, 2nd ed. 1999; F. C. McGrath's Brian Friel's (Post)Colonial Drama: Language, Illusion, and Politics, 1999; and Tony Corbett's Brian Friel: Decoding the Language of the Tribe, 2002. The Norton Critical Edition Modern Irish Drama, ed. John P. Harrington, 1991, includes backgrounds and criticism for Translations. For criticism of Friel's drama and short stories, see A Companion to Brian Friel, ed. Richard Harp and Robert C. Evans, 2002.

Nadine Gordimer
Gordimer's novels include The Lying Days, 1953; A World of Strangers, 1958; Occasion for Loving, 1963; The Late Bourgeois World, 1966; A Guest of Honour, 1970; The Conservationist, 1974; Burger's Daughter, 1979; July's People,

1981; A Sport of Nature, 1987; My Son's Story, 1990; None to Accompany Me, 1994; The House Gun, 1998; and The Pickup, 2001. Gordimer's short-story collections include Face to Face, 1949; The Soft Voice of the Serpent, 1952; Six Feet of the Country, 1956; Friday's Footprints, 1960; Not for Publication, 1965; Livingstone's Companions, 1971; Some Monday for Sure, 1976; A Soldier's Embrace, 1980; Something Out There, 1984; Jump, 1991; and Loot, and Other Stories, 2003. Collected editions of her stories include Why Haven't You Written?: Selected Stories, 1950–1972, 1992, and Selected Stories, 2000. Gordimer's essays are collected in The Essential Gesture: Writing, Politics and Places, ed. Stephen Clingman, 1988; Writing and Being, 1995; and Living in Hope and History: Notes from Our Century, 1999.

A celebration of Gordimer's work, A Writing Life: Celebrating Nadine Gordimer, ed. Andries Walter Oliphant, was published in 1998. For her life see Conversations with Nadine Gordimer, ed. Nancy Topping Bazin and Marilyn Dallman Seymour, 1990. For a bibliography see Nadine Gordimer: A Bibliography of Primary and Secondary Sources, 1937–1992, ed. Dorothy Driver, 1994.

The following critical accounts include postcolonial, feminist, and political perspectives on Gordimer's work: Abdul R. JanMohamed's Manichean Aesthetics: The Politics of Literature in Colonial Africa, 1983; Stephen Clingman's The Novels of Nadine Gordimer: History from the Inside, 1986; Judie Newman's Nadine Gordimer, 1988; Critical Essays on Nadine Gordimer, ed. Rowland Smith, 1990; The Later Fiction of Nadine Gordimer, ed. Bruce King, 1993; Andrew V. Ettin's Betrayals of the Body Politic: The Literary Commitments of Nadine Gordimer, 1993; Dominic Head's Nadine Gordimer, 1994; Kathrin M. Wagner's Rereading Nadine Gordimer, 1994; Barbara Temple-Thurston's Nadine Gordimer Revisited, 1999; Martine Watson Brownley's Deferrals of Domain: Contemporary Women Novelists and the State, 2000; Joya F. Uraizee's This Is No Place for a Woman: Nadine Gordimer, Buchi Emecheta, and Nayantara Saghal and the Politics of Gender, 2000; and Brighton J. Uledi Kamanga's Cracks in the Wall: Nadine Gordimer's Fiction and the Irony of Apartheid, 2002.

Thomas Hardy
Hardy published over a dozen volumes of poetry in his lifetime. His complete poems can be found in Thomas Hardy: The Complete Poems, ed. James Gibson, 1978, or The Complete Poetical Works of Thomas Hardy, 3 vols., ed. Samuel Lynn Hynes, 1982–95. There are several collected editions of Hardy's complete works, notably the Wessex Edition, 21 vols., 1912–14, and the Mellstock Edition, 37 vols., 1919–20. Useful essays and notes to Hardy's novels are pro-

vided by the Norton Critical Editions of *The Return of the Native*, ed. James Gindin, 1969; *Far from the Madding Crowd*, ed. Robert C. Schweik, 1986; *Tess of the D'Urbervilles*, ed. Scott Elledge, 3rd ed. 1991; *Jude the Obscure*, ed. Norman Page, 2nd ed. 1999; and *The Mayor of Casterbridge*, 2nd ed., ed. Phillip Mallett, 2001. Michael Millgate and Richard Little Purdy have edited *The Collected Letters of Thomas Hardy*, 7 vols., 1978–88. Millgate has also edited *Selected Letters*, 1990, and *Thomas Hardy's Public Voice: The Essays, Speeches, and Miscellaneous Prose*, 2001. Harold Orel has edited *Thomas Hardy's Personal Writings: Prefaces, Literary Opinions, Reminiscences*, 1990. For Hardy's life see Robert Gittings's *Young Thomas Hardy*, 1975, and *Thomas Hardy's Later Years*, 1978; Millgate's *Thomas Hardy: A Biography*, 1982; F. B. Pinion's *Thomas Hardy: His Life and Friends*, 1992; Gibson's *Thomas Hardy: A Literary Life*, 1996; and Paul Turner's *The Life of Thomas Hardy: A Critical Biography*, 1998. *Thomas Hardy: Interviews and Recollections*, ed. Gibson, 1999, is also worth consulting.

The Cambridge Companion to Thomas Hardy, ed. Dale Kramer, 1999, and *The Oxford Reader's Companion to Hardy*, ed. Page, 2000, are good guides to Hardy's work. Pinion's *A Hardy Companion: A Guide to the Works of Thomas Hardy and Their Background*, 1968, continues to be useful. Helpful reference works include Sarah Bird Wright's *Thomas Hardy A to Z: The Essential Reference to His Life and Work*, 2002, and Geoffrey Harvey's *The Complete Critical Guide to Thomas Hardy*, 2003.

For criticism on Hardy's prose and poetry, see *Hardy: A Collection of Critical Essays*, ed. Albert Guérard, 1963; J. Hillis Miller's *Thomas Hardy: Distance and Desire*, 1970; Jean R. Brooks's *Thomas Hardy: The Poetic Structure*, 1971; John Bayley's *An Essay on Hardy*, 1978; *Thomas Hardy: The Writer and His Background*, ed. Page, 1980; *Thomas Hardy*, ed. Harold Bloom, 1982, 2003; and *Thomas Hardy*, ed. Patricia Ingham, 1990, 2003.

For criticism concerning Hardy's poetry, see Hynes's *The Pattern of Hardy's Poetry*, 1956; Donald Davie's *Thomas Hardy and British Poetry*, 1972; Tom Paulin's *Thomas Hardy: The Poetry of Perception*, 1975; *The Poetry of Thomas Hardy*, ed. Patricia Clements and Juliet Grindle, 1980; William Earl Buckler's *The Poetry of Thomas Hardy: A Study in Art and Ideas*, 1983; and James Persoon's *Hardy's Early Poetry: Romanticism through a "Dark Bilberry Eye,"* 2000. For criticism of individual poems J. O. Bailey's *The Poetry of Thomas Hardy: A Handbook and Commentary*, 1970, and Pinion's *A Commentary on the Poems of Thomas Hardy*, 1976, are useful.

For criticism concerning Hardy's fiction see Shirley A. Stave's *The Decline of the Goddess: Nature, Culture, and Women in Thomas Hardy's*

Fiction, 1995; Shanta Dutta's *Ambivalence in Hardy: A Study of His Attitude to Women*, 2000; Rosemary Sumner's *A Route to Modernism: Hardy, Lawrence, Woolf*, 2000; and Joanna Devereux's *Patriarchy and Its Discontents: Sexual Politics in Selected Novels and Stories of Thomas Hardy*, 2003.

The Hardy Centennial Number of *The Southern Review*, 1940, was influential in shaping Hardy's critical reputation; the special Hardy issues of *Agenda*, 1970, and *Victorian Poetry*, 1979, are also notable.

Seamus Heaney

Heaney's volumes of poetry include *Death of a Naturalist*, 1966; *Door into the Dark*, 1969; *Wintering Out*, 1972; *North*, 1975; *Field Work*, 1979; *Sweeney Astray: A Version from the Irish*, 1983; *Station Island*, 1984; *The Haw Lantern*, 1987; *Seeing Things*, 1991; *Sweeney's Flight*, 1992; *The Spirit Level*, 1996; *Opened Ground: Selected Poems, 1966–1996*, 1998; and *Electric Light*, 2001. He is translator of *The Cure at Troy: A Version of Sophocles's Philoctetes*, 1990, and of *The Midnight Verdict*, based on Ovid's *Metamorphoses* and Brian Merriman's *Cúirt an Mheán Oíche*, 1993; he is cotranslator, with Stanislaw Baranczak, of Jan Kochanowski's *Laments*, 1995. His translation of Ozef Kalda's poems set into a song cycle by Leoš Janáček, *Diary of One Who Vanished: A Song Cycle*, was published in 2000; his translation of *Beowulf* was published in 1999 and released in a Norton Critical Edition edited by Daniel Donoghue in 2002. Heaney is also editor of *The Essential Wordsworth*, 1988. Heaney's essays are collected in *Preoccupations: Selected Prose, 1968–1978*, 1980; *The Government of the Tongue: Selected Prose, 1978–1987*, 1988; *The Redress of Poetry: Oxford Lectures*, 1995; and *Finders Keepers: Selected Prose, 1971–2001*, 2002. For his life see Blake Morrison's *Seamus Heaney*, 1982, and Michael Parker's *Seamus Heaney: The Making of the Poet*, 1993. Bibliographical information can be found in Michael J. Durkan and Rand Brandes's *Seamus Heaney: A Reference Guide*, 1996.

For guides to Heaney's poetry see Neil Corcoran's *Seamus Heaney*, 1986, and *Seamus Heaney: Comprehensive Research and Study Guide*, ed. Harold Bloom, 2003. Studies of Heaney's work include Elmer Andrews's *The Poetry of Seamus Heaney: All the Realms of Whisper*, 1988; Thomas C. Foster's *Seamus Heaney*, 1989; Henry Hart's *Seamus Heaney: Poet of Contrary Progressions*, 1992; Bernard O'Donoghue's *Seamus Heaney and the Language of Poetry*, 1994; John Wilson Foster's *The Achievement of Seamus Heaney*, 1995; Helen Vendler's *Seamus Heaney*, 1998; Eugene O'Brien's *Seamus Heaney and the Place of Writing* and *Seamus Heaney: Creating Irelands of the Mind*, 2002; and Floyd Collins's *Seamus Hea-*

ney: The Crisis of Identity, 2003. Collections of essays focusing on Heaney's work include *Seamus Heaney,* ed. Harold Bloom, 1986; *Seamus Heaney: A Collection of Critical Essays,* ed. Andrews, 1992; *The Art of Seamus Heaney,* ed. Tony Curtis, 3rd ed. 1993; and *Critical Essays on Seamus Heaney,* ed. Robert F. Garratt, 1995.

James Joyce
The most reliable edition of *Ulysses,* 1922, is *Ulysses: A Critical and Synoptic Edition,* 3 vols., ed. Hans Walter Gabler with Wolfhard Steppe and Claus Melchoir, 1984, rev. ed. 1986. Annotated editions of *Dubliners,* 1914, and *A Portrait of the Artist as a Young Man,* 1916, are available from Viking, Penguin, and Oxford World's Classics; the Oxford World's Classics edition of *Ulysses,* ed. Jeri Johnson, 1993, uses the 1922 text and has extensive notes and supportive critical material. *Stephen Hero,* ed. John J. Slocum and Herbert Cahoon, 1963, is the novel that provided the basis for *Portrait.* Faber, Minerva, Palladin, and Penguin have all produced good editions of *Finnegans Wake,* which was originally published in 1939. *The Portable James Joyce,* ed. Harry Levin, rev. ed. 1966, conveniently contains selections from *Ulysses* and *Finnegans Wake,* the entire *Portrait,* selections from *Dubliners,* and Joyce's poetry. For Joyce's critical writing see *Critical Writings of James Joyce,* ed. Richard Ellmann and Ellsworth Mason, 1989, and for his poems and shorter pieces see *James Joyce: Poems and Shorter Writings,* ed. Richard Ellmann, A. Walton Litz, and John Whittier-Ferguson, 1991. *The Letters of James Joyce,* 3 vols., was edited by Stuart Gilbert with Ellmann and James F. Spoerri, 1957–66; *Selected Letters of James Joyce,* ed. Ellmann, 1975, is also available. The standard biography of Joyce is Ellmann's *James Joyce,* 3rd ed. 1982. Also useful are Sylvia Beach's *Shakespeare and Company,* 1959; Stanislaus Joyce's *My Brother's Keeper: James Joyce's Early Years,* ed. Ellmann, 1958, and *The Complete Dublin Diary of Stanislaus Joyce,* 1971; Arthur Power's *Conversations with James Joyce,* 1975; *Portraits of the Artist in Exile: Recollections of James Joyce by Europeans,* ed. Willard Potts, 1979; Brenda Maddox's *Nora: A Biography of Nora Joyce,* 1988; and E. H. Mikhail's *James Joyce: Interviews and Recollections,* 1990. The standard bibliography of Joyce's work is *A Bibliography of James Joyce,* ed. Slocum and Cahoon, 2nd ed. 1971. Thomas Jackson Rice's *James Joyce: A Guide to Research,* 1982, and Thomas F. Staley's *An Annotated Critical Bibliography of James Joyce,* 1989, are helpful bibliographies of the secondary literature.
Good general accounts of Joyce's work can be found in Hugh Kenner's *Dublin's Joyce,* 1956, and *Joyce's Voices,* 1978; *James Joyce: The Critical Heritage,* 2 vols., ed. Robert H. Deming, 1970; C. H. Peake's *James Joyce: The Citizen*

and the Artist, 1976; Ellmann's *The Consciousness of Joyce,* 1977; Colin MacCabe's *James Joyce and the Revolution of the Word,* 1979; *James Joyce: New Perspectives,* ed. MacCabe, 1982; *A Companion to Joyce Studies,* ed. Zack Bowen and James F. Carens, 1984; Patrick Parrinder's *James Joyce,* 1984; Vicki Mahaffey's *Reauthorizing Joyce,* 1988; *The Cambridge Companion to James Joyce,* ed. Derek Attridge, 1990, 2nd ed. 2004, and Jean-Michel Rabaté's *James Joyce: Authorized Reader,* 1991.
More-specialized studies include Dominic Manganiello's *Joyce's Politics,* 1980; *Women in Joyce,* ed. Suzette A. Henke and Elaine Unkeless, 1982; Fritz Senn's *Joyce's Dislocations: Essays on Reading as Translation,* 1984; *Post-Structuralist Joyce: Essays from the French,* ed. Attridge and Daniel Ferrer, 1984; Richard Brown's *James Joyce and Sexuality,* 1985; Patrick McGee's *Paperspace: Style as Ideology in Joyce's Ulysses,* 1988; Henke's *James Joyce and the Politics of Desire,* 1990; Margot Norris's *Joyce's Web: The Social Unraveling of Modernism,* 1992; Robert Spoo's *James Joyce and the Language of History: Dedalus's Nightmare,* 1994; Kevin J. H. Dettmar's *The Illicit Joyce of Postmodernism: Reading against the Grain,* 1996; *Semicolonial Joyce,* ed. Attridge and Marjorie Howes, 2000; *Joyce and the City: The Significance of Place,* ed. Michael Begnal, 2002; David Spurr's *Joyce and the Scene of Modernity,* 2002; *Joyce and the Joyceans,* ed. Morton Levitt, 2002; and *James Joyce and the Difference of Language,* ed. Laurent Milesi, 2003.
Don Gifford's *Joyce Annotated: Notes for Dubliners and A Portrait of the Artist as a Young Man,* 2nd ed. 1982, is a useful guide for both works. Studies of *Dubliners* include *Twentieth-Century Interpretations of Dubliners: A Collection of Critical Essays,* ed. Peter K. Garrett, 1968; *James Joyce's Dubliners: Critical Essays,* ed. Clive Hart, 1969. *Concordance to James Joyce's Dubliners: With a Reverse Index, a Frequency List, and a Conversion Tab,* ed. Wilhelm Füger, 1980, provides a unique reference source. Critical studies of *A Portrait of the Artist as a Young Man* include Maud Ellmann's essay in *Untying the Text: A Post-Structuralist Reader,* ed. Robert Young, 1981; *James Joyce's A Portrait of the Artist as a Young Man,* ed. Harold Bloom, 1999; *Readings on A Portrait of the Artist as a Young Man,* ed. Clarice Swisher, 2000; *James Joyce's A Portrait of the Artist as Young Man: A Casebook,* ed. Mark A. Wollaeger, 2003. *A Portrait of the Artist as a Young Man: Complete, Authoritative Text with Biographical and Historical Contexts, Critical History, and Essays from Five Contemporary Critical Perspectives,* ed. R. B. Kershner, 1993, is a helpful compendium.
Critical studies of *Ulysses* include Frank Budgen's *James Joyce and the Making of Ulysses,* 1934, rpt. 1960; Stuart Gilbert's *James Joyce's*

Ulysses: A Study, 2nd. ed. 1952; William Schutte's Joyce and Shakespeare: A Study in the Meaning of Ulysses, 1957; Richard Ellmann's Ulysses on the Liffey, 1972; Weldon Thornton's Allusions in Ulysses: An Annotated List, 1973; Ulysses: Fifty Years, ed. Staley, 1974; James Joyce's Ulysses: Critical Essays, ed. Hart and David Hayman, 1974; Michael Seidel's Epic Geography: James Joyce's Ulysses, 1976; Marilyn French's The Book as World: James Joyce's Ulysses, 1976; Michael Groden's Ulysses in Progress, 1977; James H. Maddox's Joyce's Ulysses and the Assault upon Character, 1978; Karen Lawrence's The Odyssey of Style in Ulysses, 1981; Hayman's Ulysses: The Mechanics of Meaning, rev. ed. 1982; Hugh Kenner's Ulysses, rev. ed. 1987; Gifford and Robert J. Seidman's Ulysses Annotated: Notes for Joyce's Ulysses, 2nd. ed. 1988; Enda Duffy's The Subaltern Ulysses, 1994; A Companion to James Joyce's Ulysses: Biographical and Historical Contexts, Critical History, and Essays from Five Contemporary Critical Perspectives, ed. Norris, 1998; Joycean Cultures, Culturing Joyces, ed. Vincent J. Cheng, Kimberly J. Devlin, and Norris, 1998; Marilyn Reizbaum's James Joyce's Judaic Other, 1999; Paul Schwaber's The Cast of Characters: A Reading of Ulysses, 1999; and Andrew Gibson's Joyce's Revenge: History, Politics, and Aesthetics in Ulysses, 2002. Collections of essays include James Joyce's Ulysses: A Casebook, ed. Attridge, 2004; Leopold Bloom, ed. Harold Bloom, 2004; and James Joyce's Ulysses, ed. Bloom, 2004. David Pierce's James Joyce's Ireland, 1992, provides other useful background material. Phillip F. Herring has edited notes and drafts for the novel and compiled them in Joyce's Ulysses Notesheets in the British Museum, 1972, and Joyce's Notes and Early Drafts for Ulysses: Selections from the Buffalo Collection, 1977.

Studies of Finnegans Wake include Samuel Beckett et al., Our Examination Round His Factification for Incamination of Work in Progress, 2nd ed. 1962; Hart's Structure and Motif in Finnegans Wake, 1962; James S. Atherton's The Books at the Wake: A Study of Literary Allusions in James Joyce's Finnegans Wake, 2nd ed. 1974; Hart's A Concordance to Finnegans Wake, rev. ed. 1974; Adaline Glasheen's A Third Census of Finnegans Wake: An Index of the Characters and Their Roles, 1977; Roland McHugh's Annotations to Finnegans Wake, 1980; John Bishop's Joyce's Book of the Dark: Finnegans Wake, 1986; Kimberly J. Devlin's Wandering and Return in Finnegans Wake: An Integrative Approach to Joyce's Fictions, 1991; Thomas C. Hofheinz's Joyce and the Invention of Irish History: Finnegans Wake in Context, 1995.

Philip Larkin

Larkin's Collected Poems, ed. Anthony Thwaite, 2nd ed. 2004, contains a number of hitherto unpublished poems in addition to the contents of his four collections: The North Ship, 1945; The Less Deceived, 1955; The Whitsun Weddings, 1964; and High Windows, 1974. Philip Larkin: The Whitsun Weddings and Selected Poems, ed. David Punter, was published in 2003. Thwaite edited Selected Letters of Philip Larkin, 1940–1985, 1993, and Further Requirements: Interviews, Broadcasts, Statements, and Book Reviews, 1952–1985, 2001. Larkin's other works include his novels, Jill, 1946, and A Girl in Winter, 1947; a collection of music reviews, All What Jazz: A Record Diary, 1961–1971, 1985; and The Oxford Book of Twentieth-Century English Verse, 1973, which Larkin edited. Previously unpublished material has recently been published in two posthumous collections: Larkin's Jazz: Essays and Reviews, 1940–84, ed. Richard Palmer and John White, 2001, and "Trouble at Willow Gables" and Other Fictions, ed. James Booth, 2002. Required Writing: Miscellaneous Pieces, 1955–1982, 1983, contains much of Larkin's important prose, including recollections, interviews, and essays on literature and jazz. (For further reading on Larkin and jazz, see B. J. Leggett's Larkin's Blues: Jazz, Popular Music, and Poetry, 1999.) The standard biography is Andrew Motion's Philip Larkin: A Writer's Life, 1993. B. C. Bloomfield's Philip Larkin: A Bibliography, 1933–1994, was first published in 1979 and revised and enlarged in 2002.

Studies of Larkin's work include David Timms's Philip Larkin, 1973; Bruce K. Martin's Philip Larkin, 1978; Motion's Philip Larkin, 1982; Terrence Whalen's Philip Larkin and English Poetry, 1986; Salem K. Hassan's Philip Larkin and His Contemporaries: An Air of Authenticity, 1988; Janice Rossen's Philip Larkin: His Life's Work, 1989; Stephen Regan's Philip Larkin, 1992; Booth's Philip Larkin: Writer, 1992; Andrew Swarbrick's Out of Reach: The Poetry of Philip Larkin, 1995; and A. T. Tolley's Larkin at Work: A Study of Larkin's Mode of Composition as Seen in His Workbooks, 1997. Collections of essays include Larkin at Sixty, ed. Thwaite, 1982; Critical Essays on Philip Larkin: The Poems, ed. Linda Cookson and Bryan Loughrey, 1989; Philip Larkin: The Man and His Work, ed. Dale Salwak, 1989; Philip Larkin, ed. Regan, 1997; and New Larkins for Old: Critical Essays, ed. Booth, 2000.

D. H. Lawrence

The Cambridge Edition of Lawrence's works is nearing completion and will prove definitive. Penguin's paperback editions of Lawrence's novels and short fiction are based on the Cambridge Edition; Oxford World's Classics also offers paperbacks of The White Peacock, Sons and Lovers, The Rainbow, and Women in Love, among others. The Portable D. H. Lawrence, ed. Diana Trilling, 1947, offers selections from The Rainbow and Women in Love as well as from

Lawrence's poems, short stories, criticism, and letters. The eight volumes of Lawrence's *Letters*, ed. James T. Boulton et al., were issued by Cambridge between 1979 and 2000. The best edition of Lawrence's poetry remains the third edition of *The Complete Poems*, ed. Vivian de Sola Pinto and Warren Roberts, 1977. For Lawrence's life see the Cambridge triptych: John Worthen's *D. H. Lawrence: The Early Years, 1885–1912*, 1991; Mark Kinkead-Weekes's *D. H. Lawrence: Triumph to Exile, 1912–1922*, 1996; and David Ellis's *D. H. Lawrence: Dying Game, 1922–1930*, 1998.

Recent bibliographies of secondary sources include Paul Poplawski and Worthen's *D. H. Lawrence: A Reference Companion*, 1996, and Warren Roberts and Poplawski's *A Bibliography of D. H. Lawrence*, 3rd ed. 2001.

Pioneering studies include F. R. Leavis's *D. H. Lawrence: Novelist*, 1956; Graham Hough's *The Dark Sun*, 1957; H. M. Daleski's *The Forked Flame*, 1965; George Ford's *Double Measure: A Study of the Novels and Stories of D. H. Lawrence*, 1965; and Colin Clarke's *River of Dissolution: D. H. Lawrence and English Romanticism*, 1969. More recent studies include *D. H. Lawrence: The Critical Heritage*, ed. Ronald P. Draper, 1970; Emile Delavenay's *D. H. Lawrence: The Man and His Work: The Formative Years, 1885–1919*, trans. Katherine M. Delavenay, 1972; Frank Kermode's *D. H. Lawrence*, 1973; *D. H. Lawrence: Novelist, Poet, Prophet*, ed. Stephen Spender, 1973; Paul Delaney's *D. H. Lawrence's Nightmare: The Writer and His Circle in the Years of the Great War*, 1978; *D. H. Lawrence*, ed. Harold Bloom, 1986; Christopher Heywood's *D. H. Lawrence: New Studies*, 1987; *The Challenge of D. H. Lawrence*, ed. Michael Squires and Keith Cushman, 1990; Tony Pinkney's *D. H. Lawrence and Modernism*, 1990; *Rethinking Lawrence*, ed. Keith Brown, 1990; *D. H. Lawrence*, ed. Peter Widdowson, 1992; *The Cambridge Companion to D. H. Lawrence*, ed. Anne Fernihough, 2001; *The Complete Critical Guide to D. H. Lawrence*, ed. Fiona Becket, 2002; *D. H. Lawrence: New Worlds*, ed. Cushman and Earl G. Ingersoll, 2003.

For studies of Lawrence and gender, see *Lawrence and Women*, ed. Anne Smith, 1978; Hilary Simpson's *D. H. Lawrence and Feminism*, 1982; Sheila Macleod's *Lawrence's Men and Women*, 1985; Cornelia Nixon's *Lawrence's Leadership Politics and the Turn Against Women*, 1986; James C. Cowan's *D. H. Lawrence: Self and Sexuality*, 2002; and James J. Miracky's *Regenerating the Novel: Gender and Genre in Woolf, Forster, Sinclair, and Lawrence*, 2003. For studies of Lawrence's poetry, see M. J. Lockwood's *A Study of the Poems of D. H. Lawrence: Thinking in Poetry*, 1987; Holly A. Laird's *Self and Sequence: The Poetry of D. H. Lawrence*, 1988; Sandra Gilbert's *Acts of Atten-*

tion: The Poems of D. H. Lawrence, 2nd ed. 1990; and Amit Chaudhuri, *D. H. Lawrence and 'Difference': Postcoloniality and the Poetry of the Present*, 2003.

For further reading on Lawrence and philosophy, see Aidan Burns's *Nature and Culture in D. H. Lawrence*, 1980; Colin Milton's *Lawrence and Nietzsche: A Study in Influence*, 1987; Michael H. Black's *D. H. Lawrence: The Early Philosophical Works: A Commentary*, 1992; Michael Bell's *D. H. Lawrence: Language and Being*, 1992; and Robert E. Montgomery's *The Visionary D. H. Lawrence: Beyond Philosophy and Art*, 1994. For Lawrence's aesthetics and politics, see Graham Holderness's *D. H. Lawrence: History, Ideology and Fiction*, 1982, and Fernihough's *D. H. Lawrence: Aesthetics and Ideology*, 1993. For Lawrence's theories of the novel, see Scott R. Sanders's *D. H. Lawrence: The World of the Five Major Novels*, 1974; Alastair Niven's *D. H. Lawrence: The Novels*, 1978; Worthen's *D. H. Lawrence and the Idea of the Novel*, 1979; Charles L. Ross's *Women in Love: A Novel of Mythic Realism*, 1991; and *D. H. Lawrence*, ed. Bloom, 2002.

Katherine Mansfield

The Short Stories of Katherine Mansfield, 1937, contains all of Mansfield's stories, and her poetry is contained in *Poems of Katherine Mansfield*, ed. Vincent O'Sullivan, 1988. *The Critical Writings of Katherine Mansfield*, ed. Clare Hanson, was published in 1987. *Journal of Katherine Mansfield*, ed. John Middleton Murry, 1927; *The Collected Letters of Katherine Mansfield*, 4 vols., ed. O'Sullivan and Margaret Scott, 1984–96; and *The Katherine Mansfield Notebooks*, ed. Scott, 1997, 2002, provide autobiographical resources useful in studying Mansfield's work in depth, and Alexandra Johnson's *The Hidden Writer: Diaries and the Creative Life*, 1997, is a supplement to the volumes of Mansfield's life-writing. For biographical accounts of her life, see Antony Alpers's *The Life of Katherine Mansfield*, 1980; Claire Tomalin's *Katherine Mansfield: A Secret Life*, 1988; and Angela Smith's *Katherine Mansfield: A Literary Life*, 2000.

Critical studies of Mansfield's work include Marvin Magalener's *The Fiction of Katherine Mansfield*, 1971; Ian A. Gordon's *Undiscovered Country: The New Zealand Stories of Katherine Mansfield*, 1974; Clare Hanson and Andrew Gurr's *Katherine Mansfield*, 1981; C. A. Hankin's *Katherine Mansfield and Her Confessional Stories*, 1983; Kate Fullbrook's *Katherine Mansfield*, 1986; *Critical Essays on Katherine Mansfield*, ed. Rhoda B. Nathan, 1993; *The Critical Response to Katherine Mansfield*, ed. Jan Pilditch, 1996; Patricia Moran's *Word of Mouth: Body Language in Katherine Mansfield and Virginia Woolf*, 1996; Pamela Dunbar's *Radical Mansfield: Double Discourse in Katherine Mansfield's Short Stories*, 1997; Smith's *Kather-*

ine Mansfield and Virginia Woolf: A Public of Two, 1999; and Deborah Martinson's *In the Presence of Audience: The Self in Diaries and Fiction*, 2003.

Alice Munro

Munro's works include *"Dance of the Happy Shades" and Other Stories*, 1968; *Lives of Girls and Women: A Novel*, 1971; *Something I've Been Meaning to Tell You: Thirteen Stories*, 1974; *Who Do You Think You Are?: Stories*, 1978; *The Beggar Maid: Stories of Flo and Rose*, 1979; *The Moons of Jupiter*, 1983; *The Progress of Love*, 1986; *Friend of My Youth: Stories*, 1990; *Open Secrets: Stories*, 1994; *The Love of a Good Woman: Stories*, 1998; and *Hateship, Friendship, Courtship, Loveship, Marriage: Stories*, 2001. For Munro's life see Catherine Sheldrick Ross's *Alice Munro: A Double Life*, 1992.

Studies of Munro's work include *Probable Fictions: Alice Munro's Narrative Acts*, ed. Louis K. MacKendrick, 1983; W. R. Martin's *Alice Munro: Paradox and Parallel*, 1987; E. D. Blodgett's *Alice Munro*, 1988; Beverly Jean Rasporich's *Dance of the Sexes: Art and Gender in the Fiction of Alice Munro*, 1990; Magdalene Redekop's *Mothers and Other Clowns: The Stories of Alice Munro*, 1992; Karen E. Smythe's *Figuring Grief: Gallant, Munro, and the Poetics of Elegy*, 1992; James Carscallen's *The Other Country: Patterns in the Writing of Alice Munro*, 1993; Ajay Heble's *The Tumble of Reason: Alice Munro's Discourse of Absence*, 1994; Coral Ann Howells's *Alice Munro*, 1998; and *The Rest of the Story: Critical Essays on Alice Munro*, ed. Robert Thacker, 1999. For archival material accompanying criticism see JoAnn McCaig's *Reading In: Alice Munro's Archives*, 2002.

Jean Rhys

Rhys's first collection of short stories is *The Left Bank and Other Stories*, with an introduction by Ford Madox Ford, 1927. Her second collection, *Postures*, 1928, is best-known as the novel *Quartet*, under which title it was republished in 1957. Rhys's other works include *After Leaving Mr. Mackenzie*, 1931; *Voyage in the Dark*, 1934; *Good Morning, Midnight*, 1938; and *Wide Sargasso Sea*, 1966, which appeared with notes, essays, and contextual documents in Judith Raiskin's Norton Critical Edition in 1999. *The Collected Short Stories* was published in 1987 and includes stories from *Tigers Are Better-Looking*, 1968; *My Day: Three Pieces*, 1974; and *Sleep It Off, Lady*, 1976. *Smile Please: An Unfinished Autobiography* was published posthumously in 1979. A selection of her letters, *The Letters of Jean Rhys*, ed. Francis Wyndham and Diana Melly, was published in 1984. For her life see Carole Angier's *Jean Rhys: Life and Work*, 1990, and Elaine Savory's *Jean Rhys*, 1998. Elgin W. Mellown's *Jean Rhys: A Descriptive and*

Annotated Bibliography, 1984, is a useful reference source.

Studies of Rhys's work include Thomas F. Staley's *Jean Rhys: A Critical Study*, 1979; Peter Wolfe's *Jean Rhys*, 1980; Judith Kegan Gardiner's *Rhys, Stead, Lessing and the Politics of Empathy*, 1989; Coral Ann Howells's *Jean Rhys*, 1991; George B. Handley's *Postslavery Literatures in the Americas: Family Portraits in Black and White*, 2000; and Delia Caparoso Konzett's *Ethnic Modernisms: Anzia Yezierska, Zora Neale Hurston, Jean Rhys, and the Aesthetics of Dislocation*, 2002. For readings of Rhys as a specifically Caribbean writer, see Louis James's *Jean Rhys*, 1978; Margaret Paul Joseph's *Caliban in Exile: The Outsider in Caribbean Fiction*, 1992; and Mervyn Morris's *"Is English We Speaking" and Other Essays*, 1999. Helen Nebeker's *Jean Rhys, Woman in Passage: A Critical Study of the Novels of Jean Rhys*, 1981; Nancy R. Harrison's *Jean Rhys and the Novel as Women's Text*, 1988; and Deborah Kelly Kloepfer's *The Unspeakable Mother: Forbidden Discourse in Jean Rhys and H. D*, 1989, offer feminist perspectives on Rhys's work. For analysis of the shorter fiction, see Cheryl Alexander Malcolm and David Malcolm's *Jean Rhys: A Study of the Short Fiction*, 1996. For further reading concerning *Wide Sargasso Sea*, see Selma James's *The Ladies and the Mammies: Jane Austen and Jean Rhys*, 1983, and Veronica Marie Gregg's *Jean Rhys's Historical Imagination: Reading and Writing the Creole*, 1995.

Salman Rushdie

Rushdie's first full-length work of fiction, *Grimus*, 1975, was followed by *Midnight's Children*, 1980; *Shame*, 1983; *The Satanic Verses*, 1988; *The Moor's Last Sigh*, 1995; *The Ground beneath Her Feet*, 1999; and *Fury*, 2001. He also has written the children's novel *Haroun and the Sea of Stories*, 1990, and the volume of short fiction *East, West: Stories*, 1994. Rushdie's nonfiction includes *The Jaguar Smile: A Nicaraguan Journey*, 1987; *In Good Faith*, 1990; *The Wizard of Oz*, 1992; and the collections *Imaginary Homelands: Essays and Criticism, 1981–1991*, 1991, and *Step across This Line: Collected Nonfiction 1992–2002*, 2002. With Elizabeth West, Rushdie is coeditor of *Mirrorwork: Fifty Years of Indian Writing, 1947–1997*, 1997. For biographical material and the author's perspective on his work, see *Conversations with Salman Rushdie*, ed. Michael Reder, 2000, and *Salman Rushdie Interviews: A Sourcebook of His Ideas*, ed. Pradyumna S. Chauhan, 2001. Joel Kuortti's *The Salman Rushdie Bibliography: A Bibliography of Salman Rushdie's Work and Rushdie Criticism*, 1997, is a helpful guide to primary and secondary sources.

Studies of Rushdie's works include Timothy Brennan's *Salman Rushdie and the Third World*, 1989; *The Rushdie File*, ed. Lisa Appignanesi and Sara Maitland, 1989; Malise Ruthven's *A Satanic Affair: Salman Rushdie and the Rage of Islam*, 1990; James Harrison's *Salman Rushdie*, 1992; Catherine Cundy's *Salman Rushdie*, 1996; D. C. R. A. Goonetilleke's *Salman Rushdie*, 1998; *Critical Essays on Salman Rushdie*, ed. M. Keith Booker, 1999; and Sabrina Hassumani's *Salman Rushdie: A Postmodern Reading of His Major Works*, 2002. Criticism of Rushdie's work from a postcolonial perspective includes Fawzia Afzal-Khan's *Cultural Imperialism and the Indo-English Novel: Genre and Ideology in R. K. Narayan, Anita Desai, Kamala Markandaya, and Salman Rushdie*, 1993; Michael Gorra's *After Empire: Scott, Naipaul, Rushdie*, 1997; Anuradha Dingwaney Needham's *Using the Master's Tools: Resistance and the Literature of the African and South-Asian Diasporas*, 2000; Jaina C. Sanga's *Salman Rushdie's Postcolonial Metaphors: Migration, Translation, Hybridity, Blasphemy, and Globalization*, 2001; Deepika Bahri's *Native Intelligence: Aesthetics, Politics, and Postcolonial Literature*, 2003; John Clement Ball's *Satire and the Postcolonial Novel: V. S. Naipaul, Chinua Achebe, Salman Rushdie*, 2003; and Alexandra W. Schultheis's *Regenerative Fictions: Postcolonialism, Psychoanalysis, and the Nation as Family*, 2004.

Dylan Thomas
Collected Poems, ed. Walford Davies and Ralph Maud, 1988, is the standard edition of Thomas's poetry. *Dylan Thomas Selected Poems, 1934–1952* was published in 2003. Thomas also wrote the autobiographical prose work *Portrait of the Artist as a Young Dog*, 1940; a radio play, *Under Milk Wood: A Play for Voices*, 1954; *Quite Early One Morning*, 1954, a collection of stories, essays, and minor pieces broadcast over BBC; and the short-fiction collection *Adventures in the Skin Trade and Other Stories*, 1955. Maud edited *The Notebooks of Dylan Thomas*, 1967; Paul Ferris edited *The Collected Letters of Dylan Thomas*, 1985; and Peter Lynch edited *The Love-Letters of Dylan Thomas*, 2001. For his life see Constantine FitzGibbon's *The Life of Dylan Thomas*, 1965; Ferris's *Dylan Thomas: The Biography*, 1977, 2nd ed. 1999; and Andrew Sinclair's *Dylan the Bard: A Life of Dylan Thomas*, 1999. Bill Read's *The Days of Dylan Thomas*, 1964, supplements a straightforward narrative with many photographs.

For introductions to Thomas see William York Tindall's *A Reader's Guide to Dylan Thomas*, 1962, 3rd ed. 1996; Maud's *Entrances to Dylan Thomas' Poetry*, 1963, and *Where Have All the Old Words Got Me?: Explications of Dylan Thomas's Collected Poems*, 2003; William T. Moynahan's *The Craft and Art of Dylan Thomas*, 1966; and John Ackerman's *A Dylan Thomas Companion*, 1991. For criticism of Thomas's work see C. B. Cox's *Dylan Thomas: A Collec-*

tion of Critical Essays, 1966; R. B. Kershner's *Dylan Thomas*, 1976; *Critical Essays on Dylan Thomas*, ed. Georg Gaston, 1989; Barbara Hardy's *Dylan Thomas: An Original Language*, 2000; and *Dylan Thomas*, ed. John Goodby and Chris Wigginton, 2001.

Derek Walcott
Walcott's *Collected Poems, 1948–1984*, 1986, included selections from *In a Green Night: Poems 1948–60*, 1960; *The Castaway and Other Poems*, 1965; *The Gulf and Other Poems*, 1969; *Another Life*, 1973; *Sea Grapes*, 1976; *The Fortunate Traveler*, 1981; and *Midsummer*, 1984. Subsequent volumes include *The Arkansas Testament*, 1987; *Omeros*, 1990; *The Bounty*, 1997; *Tiepolo's Hound*, 2000; and *The Prodigal*, 2004. His many plays include *Ti-Jean and His Brothers*, 1958; *Dream on Monkey Mountain*, 1967; *The Joker of Seville*, 1978; *O Babylon!*, 1978; *Three Plays: The Last Carnival; Beef, No Chicken; A Branch of the Blue Nile*, 1986; and *The Odyssey*, 1993. *What the Twilight Says: Essays*, 1998, offers a selection of Walcott's essays, and *Conversations with Derek Walcott*, ed. William Baer, 1996, is a collection of interviews. Walcott's autobiography, *Another Life: Fully Annotated*, ed. Edward Baugh and Colbert I. Nepaulsingh, was published in 2004. A fine biography is Bruce King's *Derek Walcott: A Caribbean Life*, 2000. The standard bibliography is Irma E. Goldstraw's *Derek Walcott: An Annotated Bibliography of His Works*, 1984.

Studies of Walcott's work include Edward Baugh's *Derek Walcott: Memory as Vision*, 1978; Ned Thomas's *Derek Walcott: Poet of the Islands*, 1980; *The Art of Derek Walcott*, ed. Stewart Brown, 1991; Rei Terada's *Walcott's Poetry: American Mimicry*, 1992; Robert D. Hamner's *Derek Walcott*, 1981, 2nd ed. 1993; *Postcolonial Literatures: Achebe, Ngugi, Desai, Walcott*, ed. Michael Parker and Roger Starkey, 1995; June D. Bobb's *Beating a Restless Drum: The Poetics of Kamau Brathwaite and Derek Walcott*, 1998; John Thieme's *Derek Walcott*, 1999; Paula Burnett's *Derek Walcott: Politics and Poetics*, 2000; Paul Breslin's *Nobody's Nation: Reading Derek Walcott*, 2001; *Approaches to the Poetics of Derek Walcott*, ed. José Luis Martínez-Dueñas Espejo and José María Pérez Fernández, 2001; Patricia Ismond's *Abandoning Dead Metaphors: The Caribbean Phase of Derek Walcott's Poetry*, 2001; and *Derek Walcott*, ed. Harold Bloom, 2003. An essential collection of primary and secondary materials is *Critical Perspectives on Derek Walcott*, ed. Hamner, 1993. *Verse* 11.2, 1994, *South Atlantic Quarterly* 96.2, 1997, and *Callaloo* 28.1, 2005, are special issues dedicated to Walcott.

For further discussion of *Omeros* see Hamner's *Epic of the Dispossessed: Derek Walcott's Omeros*, 1997; Jahan Ramazani's *The Hybrid Muse*, 2001; and Lance Callahan's *In the Shad-*

ows of Divine Perfection: Derek Walcott's Ome-ros, 2003.

Virginia Woolf

Woolf's ten novels are The Voyage Out, 1915; Night and Day, 1919; Jacob's Room, 1922; Mrs. Dalloway, 1925; To the Lighthouse, 1927; Orlando: A Biography, 1928; The Waves, 1931; Flush: A Biography, 1933; The Years, 1937; and the posthumously published Between the Acts, 1941. Roger Fry: A Biography, 1940, is an actual biography. Mrs. Dalloway's Party: A Short Story Sequence, 1973, and Freshwater: A Comedy, 1976, were both published posthumously; Woolf's short stories have been compiled in The Complete Shorter Fiction, ed. Susan Dick, 1985.

Woolf was a prolific essayist, and A Room of One's Own, 1929, and Three Guineas, 1938, are major works of sociopolitical and literary criticism; The Common Reader, 1925, and The Second Common Reader, 1932, provide selections of her literary criticism; and The Essays of Virginia Woolf, 3 vols., ed. Andrew McNeillie, 1986–88, contains much of her prose. Woolf's complete diaries are available in The Diary of Virginia Woolf, 5 vols., ed. Anne Olivier Bell and Mc-Neillie, 1977–84; the selection A Writer's Diary: Being Extracts from the Diary of Virginia Woolf, ed. Leonard Woolf, 1954, describes the composition of The Years and Three Guineas. Woolf's prolific correspondence is collected in The Letters of Virginia Woolf, 6 vols., ed. Nigel Nicolson and Joanne Trautmann Banks, 1975–80. For Woolf's early development see A Passionate Apprentice: The Early Journals, 1897–1909, ed. Mitchell A. Leaska, 1990. Moments of Being: Unpublished Autobiographical Writings, ed. Jeanne Schulkind, 1976, 2nd ed. 1985, contains her autobiographical writings. Quentin Bell's Virginia Woolf, 1972, is the standard biography, but Lyndall Gordon's Virginia Woolf: A Writer's Life, 1984, and Hermione Lee's Virginia Woolf, 1997, are both useful. Phyllis Rose, Woman of Letters: A Life of Virginia Woolf, 1978, focuses on her feminism, and Louise A. DeSalvo's Virginia Woolf: The Impact of Childhood Sexual Abuse on Her Life and Work, 1989, offers a revised picture of Woolf's childhood and its effect on her writing. For a guide to secondary sources, see B. J. Kirkpatrick and Stuart N. Clarke's A Bibliography of Virginia Woolf, 4th ed. 1997.

Perceptive critical studies of Woolf's work include David Daiches's Virginia Woolf, 1942, rev. ed. 1963; Joan Bennett, Virginia Woolf: Her Art as a Novelist, 2nd ed. 1964; Avrom Fleishman's Virginia Woolf: A Critical Reading, 1975; Lee's The Novels of Virginia Woolf, 1977; New Feminist Essays on Virginia Woolf, ed. Jane Marcus, 1981; Virginia Woolf: New Critical Essays, ed. Patricia Clements and Isobel Grundy, 1983; Alex Zwerdling's Virginia Woolf and the Real World, 1986; Elizabeth Abel's Virginia Woolf and the Fictions of Psychoanalysis, 1989; Virginia

Woolf and War: Fiction, Reality, and Myth, ed. Mark Hussey, 1991; Michael Tratner's Modernism and Mass Politics: Joyce, Woolf, Eliot, Yeats, 1995; Gillian Beer's Virginia Woolf: The Common Ground, 1996; Ambiguous Discourse: Feminist Narratology and British Women Writers, ed. Kathy Mezei, 1996; Juliet Dusinberre's Virginia Woolf's Renaissance: Woman Reader or Common Reader?, 1997; and James J. Miracky's Regenerating the Novel: Gender and Genre in Woolf, Forster, Sinclair, and Lawrence, 2003. Since she was a central member of the "Bloomsbury Group," studies of Woolf may also be aided by Bloomsbury Group: A Collection of Memoirs, Commentary, and Criticism, ed. S. P. Rosenbaum, 1975, and Mary Ann Caws and Sarah Bird Wright's Bloomsbury and France: Art and Friends, 2000.

For further reading on Woolf and feminism, especially regarding A Room of One's Own, see Elaine Showalter's A Literature of Their Own: British Women Novelists from Brontë to Lessing, 1977, 2nd ed. 1999; Ellen Bayuk Rosenman's A Room of One's Own: Women Writers and the Politics of Creativity, 1995; and Rachel Bowlby's Virginia Woolf: Feminist Destinations, 1988, rev. ed. 1997.

William Butler Yeats

In addition to poems and plays, Yeats was author to a number of memoirs, works of short fiction, and essays; with Edwin Ellis he was editor of the first complete works of William Blake, 1893, and in 1936 he selected and introduced the poems for The Oxford Book of Modern Verse. An authoritative edition of Yeats's poetry is available in the revised edition of The Poems, ed. Richard J. Finneran, the first volume of The Collected Works of W. B. Yeats, gen. ed. Finneran and George Mills Harper, 1989. Other published texts in this series include, in order by volume number, The Plays, ed. David R. Clark and Rosalind E. Clark, 2001; Autobiographies, ed. William H. O'Donnell and Douglas N. Archibald, 1999; Later Essays, ed. O'Donnell with Elizabeth Bergmann Loizeaux, 1994; Prefaces and Introductions, ed. O'Donnell, 1989; Letters to the New Island, ed. George Bornstein and Hugh Witemeyer, 1989; The Irish Dramatic Movement, ed. Mary FitzGerald and Finneran, 2003; Early Articles and Reviews, ed. John P. Frayne and Madeleine Marchaterre, 2004; Later Articles and Reviews, ed. Colton Johnson, 2000; and the two short pseudonymous novels, John Sherman and Dhoya, ed. Finneran, 1991. Important scholarly editions include The Variorum Edition of the Poems, ed. Peter Allt and Russell K. Alspach, 1957; and The Variorum Edition of the Plays, ed. Alspach and Catherine C. Alspach, 1966. An excellent paperback selection is the Norton Critical Edition of Yeats's Poetry, Drama, and Prose, ed. James Pethica, 2000, which contains secondary criticism in addition to Yeats's work and reprints the poems in their earlier published versions. Also of note are *Mythologies*, 1959, which contains much of Yeats's prose fiction; *Essays and Introductions*, 1961; and the miscellaneous prose in *Explorations*, 1962; and *Memoirs*, ed. Denis Donoghue, 1973, which contains journals and the first published version of the *Autobiographies*. Yeats's mythological system is available in *A Vision*, first published in 1925, substantially revised and reissued in 1937. John Kelly, Eric Domville, and Ronald Schuchard have to date published three volumes of *The Collected Letters of W. B. Yeats*, 1986, 1994, 1997.

R. F. Foster has published the standard biography, *W. B. Yeats: A Life*, 2 vols., 1997, 2003. Also useful is A. N. Jeffares's *W. B. Yeats: A New Biography*, 1989. Bibliographic information is available in Wade's *A Bibliography of the Writings of W. B. Yeats*, 1958, revised by Alspach 1968.

W. B. Yeats: The Critical Heritage, ed. Jeffares, 1977, provides a reception history and contemporary reviews. Jeffares's *A New Commentary on the Poems of W. B. Yeats*, rev. ed. 1984, and *A Commentary on the Plays of W. B. Yeats*, 1975, are indispensable references. Also valuable are Sam McCready's *A William Butler Yeats Encyclopedia*, 1997, and Lester I. Conner's *A Yeats Dictionary*, 1998.

In the vast body of Yeats criticism, some important studies are Richard Ellmann's *Yeats: The Man and the Masks*, 1948, and *The Identity of Yeats*, 2nd ed. 1964; Thomas Parkinson's *W. B. Yeats, Self-Critic: A Study of his Early Verse*, 1951, rpt. 1971 with *The Later Poetry* and a new foreword; Frank Kermode's *Romantic Image*, 1957; Jon Stallworthy's *Between the Lines: W. B. Yeats's Poetry in the Making*, 1963; Helen Vendler's *Yeats's Vision and Later Plays*, 1963; Thomas R. Whitaker's *Swan and Shadow: Yeats's Dialogue with History*, 1964; Harold Bloom's *Yeats*, 1970; Bornstein's *Yeats and Shelley*, 1970; Donoghue's *William Butler Yeats*, 1971; Mary Helen Thuente's *W. B. Yeats and Irish Folklore*, 1981; Elizabeth Butler Cullingford's *Yeats, Ireland and Fascism*, 1981; Loizeaux's *Yeats and the Visual Arts*, 1986; Paul Scott Stanfield's *Yeats and Politics in the 1930s*, 1988; Finneran's *Editing Yeats's Poems*, 1990; Stan Smith's *W. B. Yeats: A Critical Introduction*, 1990; Jahan Ramazani's *Yeats and the Poetry of Death: Elegy, Self-Elegy, and the Sublime*, 1990; Hazard Adams's *The Book of Yeats's Poems*, 1991; Michael North's *The Political Aesthetic of Yeats, Eliot, and Pound*, 1991; Cullingford's *Gender and History in Yeats's Love Poetry*, 1993; M. L. Rosenthal's *Running to Paradise: Yeats's Poetic Art*, 1994; Marjorie Howes's *Yeats's Nations: Gender, Class, and Irishness*, 1996; Michael J. Sidnell's *Yeats's Poetry and Poetics*, 1996; Vicki Mahaffey's *States of Desire: Wilde, Yeats, Joyce, and the Irish Experiment*, 1998; Bornstein's *Material Modernism: The Politics of the Page*, 2001; Gregory Castle's *Modernism and the Celtic Revival*, 2001; and Richard Greaves's *Transition, Reception, and Modernism in W. B. Yeats*, 2002. Collections of essays include *William Butler Yeats*, ed. Bloom, 1986; *Yeats's Political Identities*, ed. Jonathan Allison, 1996; and *W. B. Yeats: Critical Assessments*, ed. David Pierce, 2000. Many essays have appeared annually in the journals *Yeats* and *Yeats Annual*.

Literary Terminology*

Using simple technical terms can sharpen our understanding and streamline our discussion of literary works. Some terms, such as the ones in Sections A, B, and C of this appendix, help us address the internal style, form, and structure of works. Other terms, such as those in Section D, provide insight into the material forms in which literary works have been produced.

In analyzing what they called "rhetoric," ancient Greek and Roman writers determined the elements of what we call "style" and "structure." Our literary terms are derived, via medieval and Renaissance intermediaries, from the Greek and Latin sources. In the definitions that follow, the etymology, or root, of the word is given when it helps illuminate the word's current usage.

Most of the examples are drawn from texts in this anthology.

Words **boldfaced** within definitions are themselves defined in this appendix. Some terms are defined within definitions; such words are *italicized*.

A. Style

In literary works the manner in which something is expressed contributes substantially to its meaning. The manner of a literary work is its "style," the effect of which is its "tone." We often can intuit the tone of a text; the following terms offer a set of concepts by which we can analyze the stylistic features that produce the tone. The groups within this section move from the micro to the macro level internal to works.

(i) Diction

"Diction," or "lexis" (from, respectively, Latin "dictio" and Greek "lexis," each meaning "word"), designates the actual words used in any utterance—speech, writing, and, for our purposes here, literary works. The choice of words contributes significantly to the style of a given work.

Connotation: To understand connotation, we need to understand **denotation**. While many words can denote the same concept—that is, have the same basic meaning—those words can evoke different associations, or connotations. Contrast, for example, the clinical-sounding term "depression" and the more colorful, musical, even poetic phrase "the blues."

Denotation: A word has a basic, "prosaic" (factual) meaning prior to the associations it connotes (see **connotation**). The word "steed," for example,

---

* This appendix was devised and compiled by James Simpson with the collaboration of all the editors.

might call to mind a horse fitted with battle gear, to be ridden by a warrior, but its denotation is simply "horse."

Lexical set: Words that habitually recur together (e.g., January, February, March, etc.; or red, white, and blue) form a lexical set.

Register: The register of a word is its stylistic level, which can be distinguished by degree of technicality but also by degree of formality. We choose our words from different registers according to context, that is, audience and/or environment. Thus a chemist in a laboratory will say "sodium chloride," a cook in a kitchen "salt." A formal register designates the kind of language used in polite society (e.g., "Mr. President"), while an informal or colloquial register is used in less formal or more relaxed social situations (e.g., "the boss"). In **classical** and medieval rhetoric, these registers of formality were called *high style* and *low style*. A *middle style* was defined as the style fit for narrative, not drawing attention to itself.

(ii) Rhetorical Figures: Figures of Speech

*Literary language often employs patterns perceptible to the eye and/or to the ear. Such patterns are called "figures of speech"; in **classical** rhetoric they were called "**schemes**" (from Greek "schema," meaning "form, figure").*

Alliteration (from Latin "litera," alphabetic letter): the repetition of an initial consonant sound or consonant cluster in consecutive or closely positioned words. This pattern is often an inseparable part of the meter in Germanic languages, where the tonic, or accented **syllable,** is usually the first syllable. Thus all Old English poetry and some varieties of Middle English poetry use alliteration as part of their basic metrical practice. *Sir Gawain and the Green Knight,* line 1: "Sithen the sege and the assaut was sesed at Troye" (see p. 114). Otherwise used for local effects; Stevie Smith, "Pretty," lines 4–5: "And in the pretty pool the pike stalks / He stalks his prey . . ."

Anaphora (Greek "carrying back"): the repetition of words or groups of words at the beginning of consecutive sentences, clauses, or phrases. Blake, "London," lines 5–8: "In every cry of every Man, / In every Infant's cry of fear, / In every voice, in every ban . . ." (see p. 1422); Louise Bennett, "Jamaica Oman," lines 17–20: "Some backa man a push, some side-a / Man a hole him han, / Some a lick sense eena him head, / Some a guide him pon him plan!"

Assonance (Latin "sounding to"): the repetition of identical or near identical stressed vowel sounds in words whose final consonants differ, producing half-rhyme. Tennyson, "The Lady of Shalott," line 100: "His broad clear brow in sunlight glowed" (see p. 1955).

Chiasmus (Greek "crosswise"): the inversion of an already established sequence. This can involve verbal echoes: Pope, "Eloisa to Abelard," line 104, "The crime was common, common be the pain"; or it can be purely a matter of syntactic inversion: Pope, *Epistle to Dr. Arbuthnot,* line 8: "They pierce my thickets, through my grot they glide" (see p. 1164).

Consonance (Latin "sounding with"): the repetition of final consonants in words or stressed syllables whose vowel sounds are different. Herbert, "Easter," line 13: "Consort, both heart and lute . . ."

Homophone (Greek "same sound"): a word that sounds identical to another word but has a different meaning ("bear" / "bare").

Onomatopoeia (Greek "name making"): verbal sounds that imitate and evoke the sounds they denote. Hopkins, "Binsey Poplars," lines 10–12 (about some felled trees): "O if we but knew what we do / When we delve [dig] or hew— / Hack and rack the growing green!" (see p. 2163).

Rhyme: the repetition of identical vowel sounds in stressed syllables whose initial consonants differ ("dead" / "head"). In poetry, rhyme often links the end of one line with another. *Masculine rhyme*: full rhyme on the final syllable of the line ("decays" / "days"). *Feminine rhyme*: full rhyme on syllables that are followed by unaccented syllables ("fountains" / "mountains"). *Internal rhyme*: full rhyme within a single line; Coleridge, *The Rime of the Ancient Mariner*, line 7: "The guests are met, the feast is set" (see p. 1616). *Rhyme riche*: rhyming on **homophones**; Chaucer, *General Prologue*, lines 17/18: "seeke" / "seke." *Off rhyme* (also known as *half rhyme, near rhyme,* or *slant rhyme*): differs from perfect rhyme in changing the vowel sound and/or the concluding consonants expected of perfect rhyme; Byron, "They say that Hope is Happiness," lines 5–7: "most" / "lost" (see p. 1677). *Pararhyme*: stressed vowel sounds differ but are flanked by identical or similar consonants; Owen, "Miners," lines 9–11: "simmer" / "summer."

(iii) Rhetorical Figures: Figures of Thought

Language can also be patterned conceptually, even outside the rules that normally govern it. Literary language in particular exploits this licensed linguistic irregularity. Synonyms for figures of thought are "trope" (Greek "twisting," referring to the irregularity of use) and "conceit" (Latin "concept," referring to the fact that these figures are perceptible only to the mind). Be careful not to confuse "trope" with "topos" (a common error).

Allegory (Greek "saying otherwise"): saying one thing (the "vehicle" of the allegory) and meaning another (the allegory's "tenor"). Allegories may be momentary aspects of a work, as in **metaphor** ("John is a lion"), or, through extended metaphor, may constitute the basis of narrative, as in Bunyan's *Pilgrim's Progress*; this second meaning is the dominant one. See also **symbol** and **type**.

Antithesis (Greek "placing against"): juxtaposition of opposed terms in clauses or sentences that are next to or near each other; Milton, *Paradise Lost* 1.777–80: "They but now who seemed / In bigness to surpass Earth's giant sons / Now less than smallest dwarfs, in narrow room / Throng numberless" (see p. 743).

Bathos (Greek "depth"): a sudden and sometimes ridiculous descent of tone; Pope, *The Rape of the Lock* 3.157–58: "Not louder shrieks to pitying heaven are cast, / When husbands, or when lapdogs breathe their last" (see p. 1147).

Emblem (Greek "an insertion"): a picture allegorically expressing a moral, or a verbal picture open to such interpretation. Donne, "A Hymn to Christ," lines 1–2: "In what torn ship soever I embark, / That ship shall be my emblem of thy ark."

Euphemism (Greek "sweet saying"): the figure by which something distasteful is described in alternative, less repugnant terms (e.g., "he passed away").

Hyperbole (Greek "throwing over"): overstatement, exaggeration; Marvell, "To His Coy Mistress," lines 11–12: "My vegetable love would grow / Vaster than empires, and more slow" (see p. 677); Auden, "As I Walked Out One Evening," lines 9–12: " 'I'll love you, dear, I'll love you / Till China and Africa meet / And the river jumps over the mountain / And the salmon sing in the street" (see p. 2691).

Irony (Greek "dissimulation"): strictly, a subset of allegory: whereas allegory says one thing and means another, irony says one thing and means its opposite; Byron, *Don Juan* 1.1–2: "I want a hero: an uncommon want, / When every year and month sends forth a new one" (see p. 1691). For an extended example of irony, see Swift's "Modest Proposal."

Litotes (from Greek "smooth"): strictly, understatement by denying the contrary; More, *Utopia*: "differences of no slight import." More loosely, understatement; Swift, "A Tale of a Tub": "Last week I saw a woman flayed, and you will hardly believe how much it altered her person for the worse." Stevie Smith, "Sunt Leones," lines 11–12: "And if the Christians felt a little blue— / Well people being eaten often do."

Metaphor (Greek "carrying across," etymologically parallel to Latin "translation"): the identification or implicit identification of one thing with another with which it is not literally identifiable. Blake, "London," lines 11–12: "And the hapless Soldier's sigh / Runs in blood down Palace walls" (see p. 1423).

Metonymy (Greek "change of name"): using a word to **denote** another concept or other concepts, by virtue of habitual association. Thus "The Press," designating printed news media. Fictional names often work by associations of this kind. A figure closely related to **synecdoche.**

Occupatio (Latin "taking possession"): denying that one will discuss a subject while actually discussing it; also known as "praeteritio" (Latin "passing by"). See Chaucer, *Nun's Priest's Tale,* lines 414–32 (see p. 259).

Oxymoron (Greek "sharp blunt"): conjunction of normally incompatible terms; Milton, *Paradise Lost* 1.63: "darkness visible" (see p. 727). Ramanujan, "Foundlings in the Yukon," line 41: "these infants compact with age."

Paradox (Greek "contrary to received opinion"): an apparent contradiction that requires thought to reveal an inner consistency. Chaucer, "Troilus's Song," line 12: "O sweete harm so quainte."

Periphrasis (Greek "declaring around"): circumlocution; the use of many words to express what could be expressed in few or one; Sidney, *Astrophil and Stella* 39.1–4.

Personification, or prosopopoeia (Greek "person making"): the attribution of human qualities to nonhuman forces or objects; Shakespeare, *King Lear* 3.2.1: "Blow winds and crack your cheeks, rage! Blow!"

Pun: a sometimes irresolvable doubleness of meaning in a single word or expression; Shakespeare, Sonnet 135, line 1: "Whoever hath her wish, thou hast thy *Will*" (see p. 507).

Sarcasm (Greek "flesh tearing"): a wounding remark, often expressed ironically; Boswell, *Life of Johnson*: Johnson [asked if any man of the modern age could have written the **epic** poem *Fingal*] replied, "Yes, Sir, many men, many women, and many children."

Simile (Latin "like"): comparison, usually using the word "like" or "as," of one thing with another so as to produce sometimes surprising analogies. Donne, "The Storm," lines 29–30: "Sooner than you read this line did the gale, / Like shot, not feared till felt, our sails assail." Frequently used, in extended

LITERARY TERMINOLOGY / A57

form, in **epic** poetry; Milton, *Paradise Lost* 1.338–46 (see p. 733).

Symbol (Greek "token"): something that stands for something else, and yet seems necessarily to evoke that other thing. Blake, "The Sick Rose," lines 1–8: "O Rose, thou art sick. / The invisible worm / That flies in the night / In the howling storm / Has found out thy bed / Of crimson joy, And his dark secret love / Does thy life destroy" (see p. 1420). In Neoplatonic, and therefore Romantic, theory, to be distinguished from **allegory** thus: whereas allegory involves connections between vehicle and tenor agreed by convention or made explicit, the meanings of a symbol are supposedly inherent to it.

Synecdoche (Greek "to take with something else"): using a part to express the whole, or vice versa; "Donne, "A Hymn to Christ," lines 1–2: "In what torn ship soever I embark / That ship shall be my emblem of thy ark."

Type (Greek "impression, figure"): In Christian allegorical interpretation of the Old Testament, pre-Christian figures were regarded as "types," or fore-shadowings, of Christ or the Christian dispensation. *Typology* has been the source of much visual and literary art in which the parallelisms between old and new are extended to nonbiblical figures; thus the virtuous plowman in *Piers Plowman* becomes a type of Christ.

Zeugma (Greek "a yoking"): a syntactic pun whereby the one word is revealed to have more than one sense in the sentence as a whole; Pope, *Rape of the Lock* 3.7–8, in which the word "take" is used in two senses: "Here thou, great Anna! whom three realms obey, / Dost sometimes counsel take—and sometimes tea" (see p. 1144).

(iv) Meter, Rhythm

Verse (from Latin "versus," turned) is distinguished from prose (from Latin "prorsus," straightforward) as a more compressed form of expression, shaped by metrical norms. **Meter** *(Greek "measure") refers to the regularly recurring sound pattern of verse lines. The means of producing sound patterns across lines differ in different poetic traditions. Verse may be* **quantitative,** *or determined by the quantities of syllables (set patterns of long and short syllables), as in Latin and Greek poetry. It may be* **syllabic,** *determined by fixed numbers of syllables in the line, as in the verse of Romance languages (e.g., French and Italian). It may be* **accentual,** *determined by the number of accents, or stresses in the line, with variable numbers of syllables, as in Old English and some varieties of Middle English alliterative verse. Or it may be* **accentual-syllabic,** *determined by the numbers of accents, but possessing a regular pattern of stressed and unstressed syllables, so as to produce regular numbers of syllables per line. Since Chaucer, English verse has worked primarily within the many possibilities of accentual-syllabic meter. The unit of meter is the* **foot.** *In English verse the number of feet per line corresponds to the number of accents in a line. For the types and examples of different meters, see* **monometer, dimeter, trimeter, tetrameter, pentameter,** *and* **hexameter.** *In the definitions below, "u" designates one unstressed syllable, and "/" one stressed syllable.*

Rhythm *is not absolutely distinguishable from meter. One way of making a clear distinction between these terms is to say that rhythm (from the Greek "to flow") denotes the patterns of sound within the feet of verse lines and the combination of those feet. Very often a particular meter will raise expectations that a given* *rhythm will be used regularly through a whole line or a whole poem. Thus in English verse the pentameter regularly uses an iambic rhythm. Rhythm, however, is much more fluid than meter, and many lines within the same poem using a single meter will frequently exploit different rhythmic possibilities. For examples of different rhythms, see **iamb, trochee, anapest, spondee,** and **dactyl**.*

Accent (synonym "stress"): the special force devoted to the voicing of one syllable in a word over others. In the noun "accent," for example, the stress is on the first syllable.

Alexandrine: in French verse a line of twelve syllables, and, by analogy, in English verse a line of six stresses. See **hexameter.**

Anapest: a three-syllable foot following the rhythmic pattern, in English verse, of two unstressed (uu) syllables followed by one stressed (/). Thus, for example, "Illinois."

Caesura (Latin "cut"): a pause or breathing space within a line of verse, generally occurring between syntactic units; Louise Bennett, "Colonization in Reverse," lines 5–8: "By de hundred, by de tousan, / From country an from town, / By de ship-load, by de plane-load, / Jamaica is Englan boun."

Dactyl (Greek "finger," because of the finger's three joints): a three-syllable foot following the rhythmic pattern, in English verse, of one stressed (/) followed by two unstressed (uu) syllables. Thus, for example, "Oregon."

Dimeter (Greek "two measure"): a two-stress line, rarely used as the meter of whole poems, though used with great frequency in single poems by Skelton, e.g., "The Tunning of Elinour Rumming." Otherwise used for single lines, as in Herbert, "Discipline," line 3: "O my God."

End-stopping: the placement of a complete syntactic unit within a complete metrical pattern; Auden, "In Memory of W. B. Yeats," line 42: "Earth, receive an honoured guest" (see p. 2694). Compare **enjambment.**

Enjambment (French "striding," encroaching): The opposite of **end-stopping,** enjambment occurs when the syntactic unit does not end with the metrical pattern, i.e., when the sense of the line overflows its meter and, therefore, the line break; Auden, "In Memory of W. B. Yeats," lines 44–45: "Let the Irish vessel lie / Emptied of its poetry" (see p. 2694).

Hexameter (Greek "six measure"): The hexameter line (a six-stress line) is the meter of **classical** Latin **epic;** while not imitated in that form for epic verse in English, some instances of the hexameter exist. See, for example, the last line of a Spenserian stanza, *Faerie Queene* 1.1.2: "O help thou my weake wit, and sharpen my dull tong" (p. 370), or Yeats, "The Lake Isle of Innisfree," line 1: "I will arise and go now, and go to Innisfree" (p. 2391).

Hypermetrical (adj.; Greek "over measured"): describes a breaking of the expected metrical pattern by at least one extra syllable.

Iamb: the basic foot of English verse; two syllables following the rhythmic pattern of unstressed (u) followed by stressed (/) and producing a rising effect. Thus, for example, "Vermont."

Monometer (Greek "one measure"): an entire line with just one stress; *Sir Gawain and the Green Knight,* line 15, "wyth (u) wynne (/)" (p. 114).

Pentameter (Greek "five measure"): in English verse, a five-stress line. Between the late fourteenth and the nineteenth centuries, this meter, frequently employing an iambic rhythm, was the basic line of English verse. Chaucer, Shakespeare, Milton, and Wordsworth each, for example, deployed this very flexible line as their primary resource; Milton, *Paradise*

Lost 1.128: "O Prince, O Chief of many thronèd Powers" (see p. 729).

Spondee: a two-syllable foot following the rhythmic pattern, in English verse, of two stressed (//) syllables. Thus, for example, "Utah."

Syllable: the smallest unit of sound in a pronounced word. The syllable that receives the greatest stress is called the *tonic* syllable.

Tetrameter (Greek "four measure"): a line with four stresses. Coleridge, *Christabel*, line 31: "She stole along, she nothing spoke" (see p. 1636).

Trimeter (Greek "three measure"): a line with three stresses. Herbert, "Discipline," line 1: "Throw away thy rod."

Trochee: a two-syllable foot following the pattern, in English verse, of stressed (/) followed by unstressed (u) syllable, producing a falling effect. Thus, for example, "Texas."

(vi) Verse Forms

The terms related to meter and rhythm describe the shape of individual lines. Lines of verse are combined to produce larger groupings, called verse forms. These larger groupings are in the first instance **stanzas** *(***Italian** *"rooms"): groupings of two or more lines, though "stanza" is usually reserved for groupings of at least four lines. Stanzas are often joined by rhyme, often in sequence, where each group shares the same metrical pattern and, when rhymed, rhyme scheme. Stanzas can themselves be arranged into larger groupings. Poets often invent new verse forms, or they may work within established forms, a list of which follows.*

Ballad stanza: usually a **quatrain** in alternating **iambic tetrameter** and **iambic trimeter** lines, rhyming abcb. See "Sir Patrick Spens"; Larkin, "This Be The Verse" (p. 2716).

Ballade: a form consisting usually of three stanzas followed by a four-line envoi (French, "send off"). The last line of the first stanza establishes a **refrain,** which is repeated, or subtly varied, as the last line of each stanza. The form was derived from French medieval poetry; English poets, from the fourteenth to the sixteenth centuries especially, used it with varying stanza forms.

Blank verse: unrhymed **iambic pentameter** lines. Blank verse has no stanzas, but is broken up into uneven units (verse paragraphs) determined by sense rather than form. First devised in English by Henry Howard, Earl of Surrey, in his translation of two books of Virgil's *Aeneid*, this very flexible verse type became the standard form for dramatic poetry in the seventeenth century, as in most of Shakespeare's plays. Milton and Wordsworth, among many others, also used it to create an English equivalent to **classical epic.**

Couplet: in English verse two consecutive, rhyming lines usually containing the same number of stresses. Chaucer first introduced the **iambic pentameter** couplet into English (*Canterbury Tales*); the form was later used in many types of writing, including drama; imitations and translations of **classical epic** (thus *heroic couplet*); essays; and **satire** (see Dryden and Pope). The *distich* (Greek "two lines") is a couplet usually making complete sense; Aemilia Lanyer, *Salve Deus Rex Judaeorum*, lines 5–6: "Read it fair queen, though it defective be, / Your excellence can grace both it and me."

Ottava rima: an eight-line stanza form, rhyming ababbcc, using **iambic pentameter;** Yeats, "Sailing to Byzantium" (see p. 2406). Derived from the Italian poet Boccaccio, an eight-line stanza was used by fifteenth-century

English poets for inset passages (e.g., Christ's speech from the Cross in Lydgate's *Testament*, lines 754–897). The form in this rhyme scheme was used in English poetry for long narrative by, for example, Byron (*Don Juan*; see p. 1690).

Quatrain: a stanza of four lines, usually rhyming abcb, abab, or abba. Of many possible examples, see Crashaw, "On the Wounds of Our Crucified Lord."

Refrain: usually a single line repeated as the last line of consecutive stanzas, sometimes with subtly different wording and ideally with subtly different meaning as the poem progresses. See, for example, Wyatt, "Blame not my lute."

Rhyme royal: a stanza form of seven **iambic pentameter** lines, rhyming ababbcc; first introduced by Chaucer and called "royal" because the form was used by James I of Scotland for his *Kingis Quair* in the early fifteenth century.

Sonnet: a form combining a variable number of units of rhymed lines to produce a fourteen-line poem, usually in rhyming **iambic pentameter** lines. In English there are two principal varieties: the Petrarchan sonnet, formed by an octave (an eight-line stanza, often broken into two **quatrains** having the same rhyme scheme, typically abba abba) and a sestet (a six-line stanza, typically cdecde or cdcdcd); and the Shakespearean sonnet, formed by three quatrains (abab cdcd efef) and a **couplet** (gg). The declaration of a sonnet can take a sharp turn, or "volta," often at the decisive formal shift from octave to sestet in the Petrarchan sonnet, or in the final couplet of a Shakespearean sonnet, introducing a trenchant counterstatement. Derived from Italian poetry, and especially from the poetry of Petrarch, the sonnet was first introduced to English poetry by Wyatt, and initially used principally for the expression of unrequited erotic love, though later poets used the form for many other purposes. See Wyatt, "Whoso list to hunt" (p. 350); Sidney, *Astrophil and Stella* (p. 451); Shakespeare, *Sonnets* (p. 497); Wordsworth, "London, 1802" (p. 1549); Heaney, "Clearances" (p. 2798).

Spenserian stanza: the stanza developed by Spenser for *The Faerie Queene*; nine **iambic** lines, the first eight of which are **pentameters,** followed by one **hexameter,** rhyming ababbcbcc. See also, for example, Shelley, *Adonais* (p. 1772), and Keats, *The Eve of St. Agnes* (p. 1830).

Tercet: a stanza or group of three lines, used in larger forms such as **terza rima,** the **Petrarchan sonnet,** and the **villanelle.**

Terza rima: a sequence of rhymed **tercets** linked by rhyme thus: aba bcb cdc, etc. First used extensively by Dante in *The Divine Comedy,* the form was adapted in English **iambic pentameters** by Wyatt and revived in the nineteenth century. See Wyatt, "Mine own John Poins"; Shelley, "Ode to the West Wind" (p. 1743). For modern adaptations see Eliot, lines 78–149 (though unrhymed) of "Little Gidding" (pp. 2634–36); Heaney, "Station Island" (p. 2797); Walcott, *Omeros* (p. 2774).

Triplet: a **tercet** rhyming on the same sound. Pope inserts triplets among heroic **couplets** to emphasize a particular thought; see *Essay on Criticism,* 315–17 (p. 1131).

Villanelle: a fixed form of usually five **tercets** and a **quatrain** employing only two rhyme sounds altogether, rhyming aba for the tercets and abaa for the quatrain, with a complex pattern of two **refrains.** Derived from a French fixed form. Thomas, "Do Not Go Gentle into That Good Night" (p. 2710).

(v) Syntax

Syntax (Greek "ordering with") designates the rules by which sentences are constructed in a given language. Discussion of meter is impossible without some reference to syntax, since the overall effect of a poem is, in part, always the product of a subtle balance of meter and sentence construction. Syntax is also essential to the understanding of prose style, since prose writers, deprived of the full shaping possibilities of meter, rely all the more heavily on syntactic resources. A working command of syntactical practice requires an understanding of the parts of speech (nouns, verbs, adjectives, adverbs, conjunctions, pronouns, prepositions, and interjections), since writers exploit syntactic possibilities by using particular combinations and concentrations of the parts of speech. The list below offers some useful terms for the description of syntactic features of a work.

Apposition: the repetition of elements serving an identical grammatical function in one sentence. The effect of this repetition is to arrest the flow of the sentence, but in doing so to add extra semantic nuance to repeated elements. This is an especially important feature of Old English poetic style. See, for example, Caedmon's Hymn, where the phrases "heaven kingdom's guardian," "the Measurer's might," "his mind-plans," and "the work of the Glory-Father" each serve an identical syntactic function as the direct objects of "praise."

Hyperbaton (Greek "overstepping"): the rearrangement, or inversion, of the expected word order in a sentence or clause. Gray, "Elegy Written in a Country Churchyard," line 38: "If Memory o'er their tomb no trophies raise" (p. 1333). Poets can suspend the expected syntax over many lines, as in the first sentences of the *Canterbury Tales* (p. 170) and of *Paradise Lost* (p. 726).

Hypotaxis, or subordination (respectively Greek and Latin "ordering under"): the subordination, by the use of subordinate clauses, of different elements of a sentence to a single main verb. Milton, *Paradise Lost* 9.513–15: "As when a ship by skillful steersman wrought / Nigh river's mouth or foreland, where the wind / Veers oft, as oft so steers, and shifts her sail; So varied he" (p. 821). The contrary principle to **parataxis.**

Parataxis, or coordination (respectively Greek and Latin "ordering beside"): the coordination, by the use of coordinating conjunctions, of different main clauses in a single sentence. Malory, "Morte Darthur": "So Sir Lancelot departed and took his sword under his arm, and so he walked in his mantel, that noble knight, and put himself in great jeopardy" (p. 303). The opposite principle to **hypotaxis.**

(vii) Point of View

*All of the many kinds of writing (see "B. Genre and Mode," below) involve a point of view from which a text is, or seems to be, generated. The presence of such a point of view may be powerful and explicit, as in many novels, or deliberately invisible, as in much drama. In some genres, such as the **novel**, the narrator does not necessarily tell the story from a position we can predict; that is, the needs of a particular story, not the **conventions** of the genre, determine the narrator's position. In other genres, the narrator's position is fixed by con-*

vention; in certain kinds of love poetry, for example, the narrating voice is always that of a suffering lover. Not only does the point of view significantly inform the style of a work, but it also informs the structure of that work. Most of the terms below are especially relevant to narrative in either verse or prose, but many also apply to other modes of writing.

Deixis (Greek "pointing"): Every work has, implicitly or explicitly, a "here" and a "now" from which it is narrated. Words that refer to or imply this point from which the voice of the work is projected (such as "here," "there," "this," "that," "now," "then") are examples of deixis, or "deictics." This technique is especially important in drama, where it is used to create a sense of the events happening as the spectator witnesses them.

First-person narration: a narrative in which the voice narrating refers to itself with forms of the first-person pronoun ("I," "me," "my," etc., or possibly "we," "us," "our"), and in which the narrative is determined by the limitations of that voice. Thus Mary Wollstonecraft Shelley, *Frankenstein*.

Frame narrative: Some narratives, particularly collections of narratives, involve a frame narrative that explains the genesis of, and/or gives a perspective on, the main narrative or narratives to follow. Thus Chaucer, *Canterbury Tales*; Mary Wollstonecraft Shelley, *Frankenstein*; or Conrad, *Heart of Darkness*.

Free indirect style: a narratorial voice that manages, without explicit reference, to imply, and often implicitly to comment on, the voice of a **character** in the narrative itself. Virginia Woolf, "A Sketch of the Past," where the voice, although strictly that of the adult narrator, manages to convey the child's manner of perception: "—I begin: the first memory. This was of red and purple flowers on a black background—my mother's dress."

Omniscient narrator (Latin "all-knowing narrator"): a narrator who, in the fiction of the narrative, has complete access to both the deeds and the thoughts of all **characters** in the narrative. Thus Thomas Hardy, "On the Western Circuit."

Order: A story may be told in different orders. A narrator might use the sequence of events as they happened, and thereby follow what **classical** rhetoricians called the *natural order;* alternatively, the narrator might reorder the sequence of events, beginning the narration either in the middle or at the end of the sequence of events, thereby following an *artificial order.* If a narrator begins in the middle of events, he or she is said to begin *in medias res* (Latin "in the middle of the matter"). For a brief discussion of these concepts, see Spenser, *Faerie Queene*, "A Letter of the Authors." Modern narratology makes a related distinction, between *histoire* (French "story") for the natural order that readers mentally reconstruct, and *discours* (French, here "narration") for the narrative as presented.

Plot: the sequence of events in a story as narrated.

Stream of consciousness: usually a **first-person** narrative that seems to give the reader access to the narrator's mind as it perceives or reflects on events, prior to organizing those perceptions into a coherent narrative. Thus (though generated from a **third-person** narrative) Joyce, *Ulysses*, "Lestrygonians" (see p. 2548).

Third-person narration: a narration in which the narrator recounts a narrative of **characters** referred to explicitly or implicitly by third-person pronouns ("he," she," etc.), without the limitation of a **first-person narration.** Thus Johnson, *The History of Rasselas.*

Unities: According to a theory supposedly derived from Aristotle's *Poetics,* the events represented in a play should have unity of time, place, and action: that the play take up no more time than the time of the play, or at most a day; that the space of action should be within a single city; and that there should be no subplot. See Johnson, *The Preface to Shakespeare* (p. 1301).

B. Genre and Mode

The style, structure, and, often, length of a work, when coupled with a certain subject matter, raise expectations that a literary work conforms to a certain **genre** *(French "kind"). Good writers might upset these expectations, but they remain aware of the expectations and thwart them purposefully. Works in different genres may nevertheless participate in the same* **mode,** *a broader category designating the fundamental perspectives governing various genres of writing. For mode, see* **tragic, comic, satiric,** *and* **didactic modes.** *All the other terms in this list refer to more or less specific literary genres. Genres are fluid, sometimes very fluid (e.g., the* **novel***); the word "usually" should be added to almost every statement!*

Animal fable: a short narrative of speaking animals, followed by moralizing comment, written in a low style and gathered into a collection.

Aubade (originally from Spanish "alba," dawn): a lover's dawn song or lyric bewailing the arrival of the day and the necessary separation of the lovers; Donne, "The Sun Rising" (see p. 606). Larkin recasts the genre in "Aubade" (see p. 2716).

Autobiography (Greek "self-life writing"): a narrative of a life written by the subject; Wordsworth, *The Prelude* (see p. 1552). There are subgenres, such as the spiritual autobiography, narrating the author's path to conversion and subsequent spiritual trials, as in Bunyan's *Grace Abounding.*

Beast epic: a continuous, unmoralized narrative, in prose or verse, relating the victories of the wholly unscrupulous but brilliant strategist Reynard the Fox over all adversaries. Chaucer arouses, only to deflate, expectations of the genre in *The Nun's Priest's Tale* (see p. 250).

Biography (Greek "life-writing"): a life as the subject of an extended narrative.

Comedy: a term primarily applied to drama, and derived from ancient drama, in opposition to **tragedy.** Comedy deals with humorously confusing, sometimes ridiculous situations in which the ending is, nevertheless, happy. Shakespeare, *Twelfth Night* (see p. 510).

Comic mode: many genres (e.g., **romance, fabliau, comedy**) involve a happy ending in which justice is done, the ravages of time are arrested, and that which is lost is found. Such genres participate in a comic mode.

Dialogue (Greek "conversation"): Dialogue is a feature of many genres, especially in both the **novel** and drama. As a genre itself, dialogue is used in philosophical traditions especially (most famously in Plato's *Dialogues*), as the representation of a conversation in which a philosophical question is pursued among various speakers.

Didactic mode (Greek "teaching mode"): genres in a didactic mode are designed to instruct or teach, sometimes explicitly (e.g., sermons, philosophical **discourses, georgic**), and sometimes through the medium of fiction (e.g., **animal fable, parable**).

Discourse (Latin "running to and fro"): broadly, any nonfictional speech or writing; as a more specific genre, a philosophical meditation on a set theme. Thus Newman, *The Idea of a University.*

Dramatic monologue (Greek "single speaking"): a poem in which the voice of a historical or fictional **character** speaks, unmediated by any narrator, to an implied though silent audience. See Tennyson, "Ulysses" (p. 1962); Browning, "The Bishop Orders His Tomb" (p. 2059); Eliot, "The Love Song of J. Alfred Prufrock" (p. 2610).

Elegy: In **classical** literature elegy was a form written in elegiac **couplets** (a **hexameter** followed by a **pentameter**) devoted to many possible topics. In Ovidian elegy a lover meditates on the trials of erotic desire (e.g., Ovid's *Amores*). The **sonnet** sequences of both Sidney and Shakespeare exploit this genre, and, while it was still practiced in classical tradition by Donne ("On His Mistress" [see p. 616]), by the later seventeenth century the term came to denote the poetry of loss, especially through the death of a loved person. See Tennyson, *In Memoriam* (p. 1973); Yeats, "In Memory of Major Robert Gregory" (p. 2400); Auden, "In Memory of W. B. Yeats" (p. 2693); Heaney, "Clearances" (p. 2798).

Epic (synonym, *heroic poetry*): an extended narrative poem celebrating martial heroes, invoking divine inspiration, beginning in medias res (see **order**), written in a high style (including the deployment of **epic similes;** on high style, see **register**), and divided into long narrative sequences. Homer's *Iliad* and Virgil's *Aeneid* were the prime models for English writers of epic verse. Thus Milton, *Paradise Lost* (see p. 725); Wordsworth, *The Prelude* (see p. 1552); and Walcott, *Omeros* (see p. 2774). With its precise repertoire of stylistic resources, epic lent itself easily to **parodic** and **burlesque** forms, known as **mock epic;** thus Pope, *The Rape of the Lock* (see p. 1137).

Epigram: a short, pithy poem wittily expressed, often with wounding intent.

Epigraph (Greek "inscription"): any formal statement inscribed on stone; also the brief formulation on a book's title page, or a quotation at the beginning of a poem, introducing the work's themes in the most compressed form possible.

Epistle (Latin "letter"): the letter can be shaped as a literary form, involving an intimate address often between equals. The *Epistles* of Horace provided a model for English writers from the sixteenth century. Thus Wyatt, "Mine own John Poins," or Pope, "Epistle to a Lady." Letters can be shaped to form the matter of an extended fiction, as the eighteenth-century epistolary **novel** (e.g., Samuel Richardson's *Pamela*).

Epitaph: a pithy formulation to be inscribed on a funeral monument.

Epithalamion (Greek "concerning the bridal chamber"): a wedding poem, celebrating the marriage and wishing the couple good fortune. Thus Spenser, *Epithalamion* (see p. 438).

Essay (French "trial, attempt"): an informal philosophical meditation, usually in prose and sometimes in verse. The journalistic periodical essay was developed in the early eighteenth century. Thus Addison and Steele, periodical essays; Pope, *An Essay on Criticism* (see p. 1124).

Fabliau (French "little story," plural *fabliaux*): a short, funny, often bawdy narrative in low style (see **register**) imitated and developed from French models most subtly by Chaucer; see *The Miller's Prologue and Tale* (p. 191).

Farce: a play designed to provoke laughter through the often humiliating antics of stock **characters.**

Georgic (Greek "farming"): Virgil's *Georgics* treat agricultural and occasionally scientific subjects, giving instructions on the proper management of farms. Unlike **pastoral,** which treats the countryside as a place of recreational idleness among shepherds, the georgic treats it as a place of productive labor.

Heroic poetry: see **epic.**

Homily (Greek "discourse"): a sermon, to be preached in church. Writers of literary fiction sometimes exploit the homily, or sermon, as in Chaucer, *The Pardoner's Tale* (see p. 235).

Journal (French "daily"): a diary, or daily record of ephemeral experience, whose perspectives are concentrated on, and limited by, the experiences of single days.

Lai: a short narrative, often characterized by images of great intensity; a French term, and a form practiced by Marie de France (see p. 98).

Legend (Latin "requiring to be read"): a narrative of a celebrated, possibly historical, but mortal **protagonist.** To be distinguished from **myth.** Thus the "Arthurian legend" but the "myth of Proserpine."

Lullaby: a bedtime, sleep-inducing song for children, in simple and regular meter. Adapted by Auden, "Lullaby" (see p. 2690).

Lyric (from Greek "lyre"): Initially meaning a song, "lyric" refers to a short poetic form, without restriction of meter, in which the expression of personal emotion, often by a voice in the first person, is given primacy over narrative sequence. Thus Yeats, "The Wild Swans at Coole" (see p. 2399).

Masque: costly entertainments of the Stuart court, involving dance, song, speech, and elaborate stage effects, in which courtiers themselves participated.

Myth: the narrative of **protagonists** with, or subject to, superhuman powers. A myth expresses some profound foundational truth, often by accounting for the origin of natural phenomena. To be distinguished from **legend.** Thus the "Arthurian legend" but the "myth of Proserpine."

Novel: an extremely flexible genre in both form and subject matter. Usually in prose, giving high priority to narration of events, with a certain expectation of length, novels are preponderantly rooted in a specific, and often complex, social world; sensitive to the realities of material life; and often focused on one **character** or a small circle of central characters. By contrast with chivalric **romance** (the main European narrative genre prior to the novel), novels tend to eschew the marvelous in favor of a recognizable social world and credible action. The novel's openness allows it to participate in all modes, and to be co-opted for a huge variety of subgenres. In English literature the novel dates from the late seventeenth century and has been astonishingly successful in appealing to a huge readership, particularly in the nineteenth and twentieth centuries. The English and Irish tradition of the novel includes, for example, Fielding, Austen, the Brontë sisters, Dickens, George Eliot, Conrad, Woolf, Lawrence, Joyce, to name but a few very great exponents of the genre.

Novella: a short **novel,** often characterized by imagistic intensity. Conrad, *Heart of Darkness* (see p. 2328).

Ode (Greek "song"): a **lyric** poem in elevated, or high style (see **register**), often addressed to a natural force, a person, or an abstract quality. The Pindaric ode in English is made up of **stanzas** of unequal length, while the Horatian ode has stanzas of equal length. For examples of both types, see, respectively, Wordsworth, "Ode: Intimations of Immortality" (p. 1538); and Marvell, "An Horatian Ode" (p. 682), or Keats, "Ode on Melancholy" (p. 1849).

Panegyric: Demonstrative, or epideictic (Greek "showing"), rhetoric was a branch of **classical** rhetoric. Its own two main branches were the rhetoric of praise on the one hand and of vituperation on the other. Panegyric, or eulogy (Greek "sweet speaking"), or encomium (plural *encomia*), is the term used to describe the speeches or writings of praise.

Parable: a simple story designed to provoke, and often accompanied by, **allegorical** interpretation, most famously by Christ as reported in the Gospels.

Pastoral (from Latin "pastor," shepherd): Pastoral is set among shepherds, making often refined **allusion** to other apparently unconnected subjects (sometimes politics) from the potentially idyllic world of highly literary if illiterate shepherds. Pastoral is distinguished from **georgic** by representing recreational rural idleness, whereas the georgic offers instruction on how to manage rural labor. English writers had classical models in the *Idylls* of Theocritus in Greek and Virgil's *Eclogues* in Latin. Pastoral is also called bucolic (from the Greek word for "herdsman").

Romance: From the twelfth to the sixteenth century, the main form of European narrative, in either verse or prose, was that of chivalric romance. Romance, like the later **novel,** is a very fluid genre, but romances are often characterized by (i) a tripartite structure of social integration, followed by disintegration, involving moral tests and often marvelous events, itself the prelude to reintegration in a happy ending, frequently of marriage; (ii) **high-style** diction; (iii) aristocratic social mileux. Thus *Sir Gawain and the Green Knight* (see p. 114); Spenser's (unfinished) *Faerie Queene* (p. 368). The immensely popular, fertile genre was absorbed, in both domesticated and undomesticated form, by the novel. For an adaptation of romance, see Chaucer, *Wife of Bath's Tale* (p. 207).

Satire: In Roman literature (e.g., Juvenal), the communication, in the form of a letter between equals, complaining of the ills of contemporary society. The genre in this form is characterized by a first-person narrator exasperated by social ills; the letter form; a high frequency of contemporary reference; and the use of invective in **low-style** language. Pope practices the genre thus in the *Epistle to Dr. Arbuthnot* (see p. 1163). Wyatt's "Mine own John Poins" draws ultimately on a gentler, Horatian model of the genre.

Satiric mode: Works in a very large variety of genres are devoted to the more or less savage attack on social ills. Thus Swift's travel narrative *Gulliver's Travels* (see p. 974), his **essay** "A Modest Proposal" (p. 1114), Pope's mock-**epic** *The Dunciad*, and Gay's *Beggar's Opera*, to look no further than the eighteenth century, are all within a satiric mode.

Short story: generically similar to, though shorter and more concentrated than, the **novel;** often published as part of a collection. Thus Mansfield, "The Daughters of the Late Colonel."

Topographical poem (Greek "place writing"): a poem devoted to the meditative description of particular places.

Tragedy: a dramatic representation of the fall of kings or nobles, beginning in happiness and ending in catastrophe. Later transferred to other social mileux. The opposite of **comedy.**

Tragic mode: Many genres (**epic** poetry, **legend**ary chronicles, **tragedy,** the **novel**) either do or can participate in a tragic mode, by representing the fall of noble **protagonists** and the irreparable ravages of human society and history.

Tragicomedy: a play in which potentially tragic events turn out to have a happy, or **comic,** ending. Thus Shakespeare, *Measure for Measure.*

C. Miscellaneous

Act: the major subdivision of a play, usually divided into **scenes.**

Aesthetics (from Greek, "to feel, apprehend by the senses"): the philosophy of artistic meaning as a distinct mode of apprehending untranslatable truth, defined as an alternative to rational enquiry, which is purely abstract. Developed in the late eighteenth century by the German philosopher Immanuel Kant especially.

Allusion: Literary allusion is a passing but illuminating reference within a literary text to another, well-known text (often biblical or **classical**). Topical allusions are also, of course, common in certain modes, especially **satire.**

Anagnorisis (Greek "recognition"): the moment of **protagonists'** recognition in a narrative, which is also often the moment of moral understanding.

Apostrophe (from Greek "turning away"): an address, often to an absent person, a force, or a quality. For example, a poet makes an apostrophe to a Muse when invoking her for inspiration.

Blazon: strictly, a heraldic shield; in rhetorical usage, a **topos** whereby the individual elements of a beloved's face and body are singled out for **hyperbolic** admiration. Spenser, *Epithalamion,* lines 167–84 (see p. 441). For an inversion of the **topos,** see Shakespeare, Sonnet 130 (p. 507).

Burlesque (French and Italian "mocking"): a work that adopts the **conventions** of a genre with the aim less of comically mocking the genre than of satirically mocking the society so represented (see **satire**). Thus Pope's *Rape of the Lock* (see p. 1136) does not mock **classical epic** so much as contemporary mores.

Canon (Greek "rule"): the group of texts regarded as worthy of special respect or attention by a given institution. Also, the group of texts regarded as definitely having been written by a certain author.

Catastrophe (Greek "overturning"): the decisive turn in **tragedy** by which the plot is resolved and, usually, the **protagonist** dies.

Catharsis (Greek "cleansing"): According to Aristotle, the effect of **tragedy** on its audience, through their experience of pity and terror, was a kind of spiritual cleansing, or catharsis.

Character (Greek "stamp, impression"): a person, personified animal, or other figure represented in a literary work, especially in narrative and drama. The more a character seems to generate the action of a narrative, and the less he or she seems merely to serve a preordained narrative pattern, the "fuller," or more "rounded," a character is said to be. A "stock" character, common particularly in many comic genres, will perform a predictable function in different works of a given genre.

Classical, Classicism, Classic: Each term can be widely applied, but in English literary discourse, "classical" primarily describes the works of either Greek or Roman antiquity. "Classicism" denotes the practice of art forms inspired by classical antiquity, in particular the observance of rhetorical norms of **decorum** and balance, as opposed to following the dictates of untutored inspiration, as in Romanticism. "Classic" denotes an especially famous work within a given **canon.**

Climax (Greek "ladder"): a moment of great intensity and structural change, especially in drama. Also a figure of speech whereby a sequence of verbally linked clauses is made, in which each successive clause is of greater consequence than its predecessor. Bacon, *Of Studies:* "Studies serve for pastimes, for ornaments, and for abilities. Their chief use for pastimes is in privateness and retiring; for ornament, is in discourse; and for ability, is in judgement."

Convention: a repeatedly recurring feature (in either form or content) of works, occurring in combination with other recurring formal features, constitutes a convention of a particular genre.

Decorum (Latin "that which is fitting"): a rhetorical principle whereby each formal aspect of a work should be in keeping with its subject matter and/or audience.

Denouement (French "unknotting"): the point at which a narrative can be resolved and so ended.

Dramatic irony: a feature of narrative and drama, whereby the audience knows that the outcome of an action will be the opposite of that intended by a **character.**

Ecphrasis (Greek "speaking out"): a **topos** whereby a work of visual art is represented in a literary work. Auden, "Musée des Beaux Arts" (see p. 2693).

Exegesis (Greek "leading out"): interpretation, traditionally of the biblical text, but, by transference, of any text.

Exemplum (Latin "example"): an example inserted into a usually nonfictional writing (e.g., sermon or **essay**) to give extra force to an abstract thesis. Thus Johnson's example of "Sober" in his essay "On Idleness."

Hermeneutics (from the Greek god Hermes, messenger between the gods and humankind): the science of interpretation, first formulated as such by the German philosophical theologian Friedrich Schleiermacher in the early nineteenth century.

Imitation: the practice whereby writers strive ideally to reproduce and yet renew the **conventions** of an older form, often derived from **classical** civilization. Such a practice will be praised in periods of classicism (e.g., the eighteenth century) and repudiated in periods dominated by a model of inspiration (e.g., Romanticism).

Parody: a work that uses the **conventions** of a particular genre with the aim of comically mocking a **topos,** a genre, or a particular exponent of a genre. Shakespeare parodies the topos of **blazon** in Sonnet 130 (see p. 507).

Pathetic fallacy: the attribution of sentiment to natural phenomena, as if they were in sympathy with human feelings. Thus Milton, *Lycidas,* lines 146–47: "With cowslips wan that hang the pensive head, / And every flower that sad embroidery wears" (see p. 710). For critique of the practice, see Ruskin (who coined the term), "Of the Pathetic Fallacy," in *Modern Painters.*

Peripeteia (Greek "turning about"): the sudden reversal of fortune (in both directions) in a dramatic work.

Persona (Latin "sound through"): originally the mask worn in the Roman theater to magnify an actor's voice; in literary discourse persona (plural *personae*) refers to the narrator or speaker of a text, by whose voice the author may mask him- or herself. Eliot, "The Love Song of J. Alfred Prufrock" (see p. 2610).

Protagonist (Greek "first actor"): the hero or heroine of a drama or narrative.

Rhetoric: the art of verbal persuasion. **Classical** rhetoricians distinguished three areas of rhetoric: the forensic, to be used in law courts; the deliberative, to be used in political or philosophical deliberations; and the demonstrative, or epideictic, to be used for the purposes of public praise or blame. Rhetorical manuals covered all the skills required of a speaker, from the management of style and structure to delivery. These manuals powerfully influenced the theory of poetics as a separate branch of verbal practice, particularly in the matter of style.

Scene: a subdivision of an **act,** itself a subdivision of a dramatic performance and/or text. The action of a scene usually occurs in one place.

Sensibility (from Latin, "capable of being perceived by the senses"): as a literary term, an eighteenth-century concept derived from moral philosophy that stressed the social importance of fellow feeling and particularly of sympathy in social relations. The concept generated a literature of "sensibility," such as the sentimental **novel** (the most famous of which was Goethe's *Sorrows of the Young Werther* [1774]), or sentimental poetry, such as Cowper's passage on the stricken deer in *The Task*.

Soliloquy (Latin "single speaking"): a **topos** of drama, in which a **character,** alone or thinking to be alone on stage, speaks so as to give the audience access to his or her private thoughts. Thus Viola's soliloquy in Shakespeare, *Twelfth Night* 2.2.17–41 (p. 528).

Sublime: As a concept generating a literary movement, the sublime refers to the realm of experience beyond the measurable, and so beyond the rational, produced especially by the terrors and grandeur of natural phenomena. Derived especially from the first-century Greek treatise *On the Sublime*, sometimes attributed to Longinus, the notion of the sublime was in the later eighteenth century a spur to Romanticism.

Taste (from Italian "touch"): Although medieval monastic traditions used eating and tasting as a metaphor for reading, the concept of taste as a personal ideal to be cultivated by, and applied to, the appreciation and judgment of works of art in general was developed in the eighteenth century.

Topos (Greek "place," plural *topoi*): a commonplace in the content of a given kind of literature. Originally, in **classical** rhetoric, the topoi were tried-and-tested stimuli to literary invention: lists of standard headings under which a subject might be investigated. In medieval narrative poems, for example, it was commonplace to begin with a description of spring. Writers did, of course, render the commonplace uncommon, as in Chaucer's spring scene at the opening of *The Canterbury Tales* (see p. 170).

Tradition (from Latin "passing on"): A literary tradition is whatever is passed on or revived from the past in a single literary culture, or drawn from others to enrich a writer's culture. "Tradition" is fluid in reference, ranging from small to large referents: thus it may refer to a relatively small aspect of texts (e.g., the tradition of **iambic pentameter**), or it may, at the other extreme, refer to the body of texts that constitute a **canon.**

Translation (Latin "carrying across"): the rendering of a text written in one language into another.

Vernacular (from Latin "verna," servant): the language of the people, as distinguished from learned and arcane languages. From the later Middle Ages especially, the "vernacular" languages and literatures of Europe distinguished themselves from the learned languages and literatures of Latin, Greek, and Hebrew.

Wit: Originally a synonym for "reason" in Old and Middle English, "wit" became a literary ideal in the Renaissance as brilliant play of the full range of mental resources. For eighteenth-century writers, the notion necessarily involved pleasing expression, as in Pope's definition of true wit as "Nature to advantage dressed, / What oft was thought, but ne'er so well expressed" (*Essay on Criticism,* lines 297–98; see p. 1130). Romantic theory of the imagination deprived wit of its full range of apprehension, whence the word came to be restricted to its modern sense, as the clever play of mind that produces laughter.

D. Publishing History, Censorship

By the time we read texts in published books, they have already been treated— that is, changed by authors, editors, and printers—in many ways. Although there are differences across history, in each period literary works are subject to pressures of many kinds, which apply before, while, and after an author writes. The pressures might be financial, as in the relations of author and patron; commercial, as in the marketing of books; and legal, as in, during some periods, the negotiation through official and unofficial censorship. In addition, texts in all periods undergo technological processes, as they move from the material forms in which an author produced them to the forms in which they are presented to readers. Some of the terms below designate important material forms in which books were produced, disseminated, and surveyed across the historical span of this anthology. Others designate the skills developed to understand these processes. The anthology's introductions to individual periods discuss the particular forms these phenomena took in different eras.

Bookseller: In England, and particularly in London, commercial bookmaking and -selling enterprises came into being in the early fourteenth century. These were loose organizations of artisans who usually lived in the same neighborhoods (around St. Paul's Cathedral in London). A bookseller or dealer would coordinate the production of hand-copied books for wealthy patrons (see **patronage**), who would order books to be custom-made. After the introduction of **printing** in the late fifteenth century, authors generally sold the rights to their work to booksellers, without any further **royalties.** Booksellers, who often had their own shops, belonged to the **Stationers' Company.** This system lasted into the eighteenth century. In 1710, however, authors were for the first time granted **copyright,** which tipped the commercial balance in their favor, against booksellers.

Censorship: The term applies to any mechanism for restricting what can be published. Historically, the reasons for imposing censorship are heresy, sedition, blasphemy, libel, or obscenity. External censorship is imposed by institutions having legislative sanctions at their disposal. Thus the pre-Reformation Church imposed the Constitutions of Archbishop Arundel of 1409, aimed at repressing the Lollard "heresy." After the Reformation, some key events in the history of censorship are as follows: 1547, when anti-Lollard legislation and legislation made by Henry VIII concerning treason by writing (1534) were abolished; the Licensing Order of 1643, which legislated that works be licensed, through the Stationers' Company, prior to publication; and 1695, when the last such Act stipulating prepublication licensing lapsed. Postpublication censorship continued in different periods for different reasons. Thus, for example, British publication of D. H. Lawrence's *Lady Chatterley's Lover* (1928) was obstructed (though unsuccessfully) in 1960, under the Obscene Publications Act of 1959. Censorship can also be international: although not published in Iran, Salman Rushdie's *Satanic Verses* (1988) was censored in that country, where the leader, Ayatollah Ruhollah Khomeini, proclaimed a fatwa (religious decree) promising the author's execution. Very often censorship is not imposed externally, however: authors or publishers can censor work in anticipation of what will incur the wrath of readers or the penalties of the law. Victorian and Edwardian publishers of **novels,** for example, urged authors to remove potentially offensive material, especially for serial publication in popular magazines.

Codex (Latin "book"): having the format of a book (usually applied to manuscript books), as distinguished originally from the scroll, which was the standard form of written document in ancient Rome.

Copyright: the legal protection afforded to authors for control of their work's publication, in an attempt to ensure due financial reward. Some key dates in the history of copyright in the United Kingdom are as follows: 1710, when a statute gave authors the exclusive right to publish their work for fourteen years, and fourteen years more if the author were still alive when the first term had expired; 1842, when the period of authorial control was extended to forty-two years; and 1911, when the term was extended yet further, to fifty years after the author's death. In 1995 the period of protection was harmonized with the laws in other European countries to be the life of the author plus seventy years. In the United States no works first published before 1923 are in copyright. Works published since 1978 are, as in the United Kingdom, protected for the life of the author plus seventy years.

Copy text: the particular text of a work used by a textual editor as the basis of an edition of that work.

Folio: Books come in different shapes, depending originally on the number of times a standard sheet of paper is folded. One fold produces a large volume, a *folio* book; two folds produce a *quarto,* four an *octavo,* and six a very small *duodecimo.* Generally speaking, the larger the book, the grander and more expensive. Shakespeare's plays were, for example, first printed in quartos, but were gathered into a folio edition in 1623.

Foul papers: versions of a work before an author has produced, if she or he has, a final copy (a "fair copy") with all corrections removed.

Manuscript (Latin, "written by hand"): Any text written physically by hand is a manuscript. Before the introduction of **printing** with moveable type in 1476, all texts in England were produced and reproduced by hand, in manuscript. This is an extremely labor-intensive task, using expensive materials (e.g., animal skins); the cost of books produced thereby was, accordingly, very high. Even after the introduction of printing, many texts continued to be produced in manuscript. This is obviously true of letters, for example, but until the eighteenth century, poetry written within aristocratic circles was often transmitted in manuscript copies.

Paleography (Greek "ancient writing"): the art of deciphering, describing, and dating forms of handwriting.

Patronage (Latin "protector"): Many technological, legal, and commercial supports were necessary before professional authorship became possible. Although some playwrights (e.g., Shakespeare) made a living by writing for the theater, other authors needed, principally, the large-scale reproductive capacities of **printing** and the security of **copyright** to make a living from writing. Before these conditions obtained, many authors had another main occupation, and most authors had to rely on patronage. In different periods, institutions or individuals offered material support, or patronage, to authors. Thus in Anglo-Saxon England, monasteries afforded the conditions of writing to monastic authors. Between the twelfth and the seventeenth centuries, the main source of patronage was the royal court. Authors offered patrons prestige and ideological support in return for financial support. Even as the conditions of professional authorship came into being at the beginning of the eighteenth century, older forms of direct patronage were not altogether displaced until the middle of the century.

Periodical: Whereas journalism, strictly, applies to daily writing (from French "jour," day), periodical writing appears at larger, but still frequent, intervals, characteristically in the form of the **essay.** Periodicals were developed especially in the eighteenth century.

Printing: Printing, or the mechanical reproduction of books using moveable type, was invented in Germany in the mid-fifteenth century by Johannes Gutenberg; it quickly spread throughout Europe. William Caxton brought printing into England from the Low Countries in 1476. Much greater powers of reproduction at much lower prices transformed every aspect of literary culture.

Publisher: the person or company responsible for the commissioning and publicizing of printed matter. In the early period of **printing,** publisher, printer, and bookseller were often the same person. This trend continued in the ascendancy of the **Stationers' Company,** between the middle of the sixteenth and the end of the seventeenth centuries. Toward the end of the seventeenth century, these three functions began to separate, leading to their modern distinctions.

Royalties: an agreed-upon proportion of the price of each copy of a work sold, paid by the publisher to the author, or an agreed-upon fee paid to the playwright for each performance of a play.

Scribe: in **manuscript** culture, the scribe is the copyist who reproduces a text by hand.

Stationers' Company: The Stationers' Company was an English guild incorporating various tradesmen, including printers, publishers, and booksellers, skilled in the production and selling of books. It was formed in 1403, received its royal charter in 1557, and served as a means both of producing and of regulating books. Authors would sell the manuscripts of their books to individual stationers, who incurred the risks and took the profits of producing and selling the books. The stationers entered their rights over given books in the Stationers' Register. They also regulated the book trade and held their monopoly by licensing books and by being empowered to seize unauthorized books and imprison resisters. This system of licensing broke down in the social unrest of the Civil War and Interregnum (1640–60), and it ended in 1695. Even after the end of licensing, the Stationers' Company continued to be an intrinsic part of the **copyright** process, since the 1710 copyright statute directed that copyright had to be registered at Stationers' Hall.

Subscription: An eighteenth-century system of bookselling somewhere between direct **patronage** and impersonal sales. A subscriber paid half the cost of a book before publication and half on delivery. The author received these payments directly. The subscriber's name appeared in the prefatory pages.

Textual criticism: works in all periods often exist in many subtly or not so subtly different forms. This is especially true with regard to manuscript textual reproduction, but it also applies to printed texts. Textual criticism is the art, developed from the fifteenth century in Italy but raised to new levels of sophistication from the eighteenth century, of deciphering different historical states of texts. This art involves the analysis of textual variants, often with the aim of distinguishing authorial from scribal forms.

Geographic Nomenclature

The British Isles refers to the prominent group of islands off the northwest coast of Europe, especially to the two largest, **Great Britain** and **Ireland**. At present these comprise two sovereign states: **the Republic of Ireland**, or **Éire**, and **the United Kingdom of Great Britain and Northern Ireland**—known for short as the **United Kingdom** or the **U.K.** Most of the smaller islands are part of the **U.K.** but a few, like the **Isle of Man** and the tiny **Channel Islands,** are largely independent. The **U.K.** is often loosely referred to as "Britain" or "Great Britain" and is sometimes called simply, if inaccurately, "England." For obvious reasons, the latter usage is rarely heard among the inhabitants of the other countries of the **U.K.**—**Scotland, Wales,** and **Northern Ireland** (sometimes called **Ulster**). England is by far the most populous part of the kingdom, as well as the seat of its capital, London.

From the first to the fifth century C.E. most of what is now **England** and **Wales** was a province of the Roman Empire called **Britain** (in Latin, **Britannia**). After the fall of Rome, much of the island was invaded and settled by peoples from northern Germany and Denmark speaking what we now call Old English. These peoples are collectively known as the Anglo-Saxons, and the word **England** is related to the first element of their name. By the time of the Norman Conquest (1066) most of the kingdoms founded by the Anglo-Saxons and subsequent Viking invaders had coalesced into the kingdom of **England,** which, in the latter Middle Ages, conquered and largely absorbed the neighboring Celtic kingdom of **Wales.** In 1603 James VI of **Scotland** inherited the island's other throne as James I of **England,** and for the next hundred years—except for the brief period of Puritan rule—**Scotland** (both its English-speaking **Lowlands** and its Gaelic-speaking **Highlands**) and **England** (with **Wales**) were two kingdoms under a single king. In 1707 the Act of Union welded them together as **the United Kingdom of Great Britain. Ireland,** where English rule had begun in the twelfth century and been tightened in the sixteenth, was incorporated by the 1800–1801 Act of Union into **the United Kingdom of Great Britain and Ireland.** With the division of Ireland and the establishment of **the Irish Free State** after World War I, this name was modified to its present form, and in 1949 **the Irish Free State** became **the Republic of Ireland.** In 1999 **Scotland** elected a separate parliament it had relinquished in 1707, and **Wales** elected an assembly it lost in 1409; neither Scotland nor Wales ceased to be part of the **United Kingdom.**

The **British Isles** are further divided into counties, which in **Great Britain** are also known as shires. This word, with its vowel shortened in pronunciation, forms the suffix in the names of many counties, such as **Yorkshire, Wiltshire, Somersetshire.**

The Latin names **Britannia (Britain), Caledonia (Scotland),** and **Hibernia (Ireland)** are sometimes used in poetic diction; so too is **Britain**'s ancient Celtic name, **Albion.** Because of its accidental resemblance to *albus* (Latin for "white"), **Albion** is especially associated with the chalk cliffs that seem to gird much of the English coast like defensive walls.

The British Empire took its name from **the British Isles** because it was created not only by the **English** but also by the **Irish, Scots,** and **Welsh,** as well as by civilians and servicemen from other constituent countries of the empire. Some of the empire's **overseas colonies,** or **crown colonies,** were populated largely by settlers of European origin and their descendants. These predominantly white **settler colonies,** such as **Canada, Australia,** and **New Zealand,** were allowed significant self-government in the nineteenth century and recognized as **dominions** in the early twentieth century.

The **white dominions** became members of **the Commonwealth of Nations**, also called **the Commonwealth, the British Commonwealth,** and **"the Old Commonwealth"** at different times, an association of sovereign states under the symbolic leadership of the British monarch.

Other **overseas colonies** of the empire had mostly indigenous populations (or, in the Caribbean, the descendants of imported slaves, indentured servants, and others). These **colonies** were granted political independence after World War II, later than the **dominions**, and have often been referred to since as **postcolonial** nations. In South and Southeast Asia, **India** and **Pakistan** gained independence in 1947, followed by other countries including **Sri Lanka** (formerly **Ceylon**), **Burma** (now **Myanmar**), **Malaya** (now **Malaysia**), and **Singapore**. In West and East Africa, the **Gold Coast** was decolonized as **Ghana** in 1957, **Nigeria** in 1960, **Sierra Leone** in 1961, **Uganda** in 1962, **Kenya** in 1963, and so forth, while in southern Africa, the white minority government of **South Africa** was already independent in 1931, though majority rule did not come until 1994. In the Caribbean, **Jamaica** and **Trinidad and Tobago** won independence in 1962, followed by **Barbados** in 1966, and other islands of the British West Indies in the 1970s and '80s. Other regions with nations emerging out of British colonial rule included Central America (**British Honduras**, now **Belize**), South America (**British Guiana**, now **Guyana**), the Pacific islands (**Fiji**), and Europe (**Cyprus, Malta**). After decolonization, many of these nations chose to remain within a newly conceived **Commonwealth** and are sometimes referred to as "**New Commonwealth**" countries. Some nations, such as **Ireland, Pakistan,** and **South Africa,** withdrew from the **Commonwealth**, though **South Africa** and **Pakistan** eventually rejoined, and others, such as **Burma** (**Myanmar**), gained independence outside the **Commonwealth**. Britain's last major overseas colony, **Hong Kong,** was returned to Chinese sovereignty in 1997, but while Britain retains only a handful of dependent territories, such as **Bermuda** and **Montserrat**, the scope of the **Commonwealth** remains vast, with 30 percent of the world's population.

British Money

One of the most dramatic changes to the system of British money came in 1971. In the system previously in place, the pound consisted of 20 shillings, each containing 12 pence, making 240 pence to the pound. Since 1971, British money has been calculated on the decimal system, with 100 pence to the pound. Britons' experience of paper money did not change very drastically: as before, 5- and 10-pound notes constitute the majority of bills passing through their hands (in addition, 20- and 50-pound notes have been added). But the shift necessitated a whole new way of thinking about and exchanging coins and marked the demise of the shilling, one of the fundamental units of British monetary history. Many other coins, still frequently encountered in literature, had already passed. These include the groat, worth 4 pence (the word "groat" is often used to signify a trifling sum); the angel (which depicted the archangel Michael triumphing over a dragon), valued at 10 shillings; the mark, worth in its day two-thirds of a pound or 13 shillings 4 pence; and the sovereign, a gold coin initially worth 22 shillings 6 pence, later valued at 1 pound, last circulated in 1932. One prominent older coin, the guinea, was worth a pound and a shilling; though it has not been minted since 1813, a very few quality items or prestige awards (like the purse in a horse race) may still be quoted in guineas. (The table below includes some other well-known, obsolete coins.) Colloquially, a pound was (and is) called a quid; a shilling a bob; sixpence, a tanner; a copper could refer to a penny, a half-penny, or a farthing (¼ penny).

Old Currency	New Currency
1 pound note	1 pound coin (or note in Scotland)
10 shilling (half-pound note)	50 pence
5 shilling (crown)	
2½ shilling (half crown)	20 pence
2 shilling (florin)	10 pence
1 shilling	5 pence
6 pence	
2½ pence	1 penny
2 pence	
1 penny	
½ penny	
¼ penny (farthing)	

In recent years, the British government and people have been contemplating and debating a change even greater than the shift to the decimal system. Britain, a member of the European Union, may adopt the EU's common currency, the Euro, and eventually see the pound itself become obsolete. More than many other EU-member countries, Britain has resisted this change: many people strongly identify their country with its rich commercial history and tend to view their currency patriotically as a national symbol.

Even more challenging than sorting out the values of obsolete coins is calculating for any given period the purchasing power of money, which fluctuates over time by its very nature. At the beginning of the twentieth century, 1 pound was worth about 5 American dollars, though those bought three to four times what they now do. Now, the pound buys anywhere from $1.50 to $1.90. As difficult as it is to generalize, it is clear that money used to be worth much more than it is currently. In Anglo-Saxon times, the most valuable circulating coin was the silver penny: four would buy a sheep. Beyond long-term inflationary trends, prices varied from times of plenty to those marked by poor harvests; from peacetime to wartime; from the country to the metropolis (life in London has always been very expensive); and wages varied according to the availability of labor (wages rose sharply, for instance, during the devastating Black Death in the fourteenth century). The chart below provides a glimpse of some actual prices of given periods and their changes across time, though all the variables mentioned above prevent them from being definitive. Even from one year to the next, an added tax on gin or tea could drastically raise prices, and a lottery ticket could cost much more the night before the drawing than just a month earlier. Still, the prices quoted below do indicate important trends, such as the disparity of incomes in British society and the costs of basic commodities. In the chart below, the symbol £ is used for pound, s. for shilling, d. for a penny (from Latin *denarius*); a sum would normally be written £2.19.3, i.e., 2 pounds, 19 shillings, 3 pence. (This is Leopold Bloom's budget for the day depicted in Joyce's novel *Ulysses* [1922]; in the new currency, it would be about £2.96.)

circa	1390	1590	1650	1750	1815	1875	1950
food and drink	gallon (8 pints) of ale, 1.5d.	tankard of beer, .5d.	coffee, 1d. a dish	"drunk for a penny, dead drunk for twopence" (gin shop sign in Hogarth print)	ounce of laudanum, 3d.	pint of beer, 3d.	pint of Guinness stout, 11d.
	gallon (8 pints) of wine, 3 to 4d.	pound of beef, 2s. 5d.	chicken, 1s. 4d.	dinner at a steakhouse, 1s.	ham and potato dinner for two, 7s.	dinner in a good hotel, 5s.	pound of beef, 2s. 2d.
	pound of cinnamon, 1 to 3s.	pound of cinnamon, 10s. 6d.	pound of tea, £3 10s.	pound of tea, 16s.	Prince Regent's dinner party for 2000, £12.000	pound of tea, 2s.	dinner on railway car, 7s. 6d.
entertainment	no cost to watch a cycle play	admission to public theater, 1 to 3d.	falcon, £11 5s.	theater tickets, 1 to 5s.	admission to Covent Garden theater, 1 to 7s.	theater tickets, 6d. to 7s.	admission to Old Vic theater, 1s. 6d. to 10s. 6d.
	contributory admission to professional troupe theater	cheap seat in private theater, 6d.	billiard table, £25	admission to Vauxhall Gardens, 1s.	annual subscription to Almack's (exclusive club), 10 guineas	admission to Madam Tussaud's waxworks, 1s.	admission to Odeon cinema, Manchester, 1s. 3d.
	maintenance for royal hounds at Windsor, .75d. a day	"to see a dead Indian" (qtd. in *The Tempest*), 1.25d. (ten "doits")	three-quarter-length portrait painting, £31	lottery ticket, £20 (shares were sold)	Jane Austen's piano, 30 guineas	annual fees at a gentleman's club, 7–10 guineas	tropical fish tank, £4 4s.
reading	cheap romance, 1s.	play quarto, 6d.	pamphlet, 1 to 6d.	issue of *The Gentleman's Magazine*, 6d.	issue of *Edinburgh Review*, 6s.	copy of *The Times*, 3d.	copy of *The Times*, 3d.

circa	1390	1590	1650	1750	1815	1875	1950
	a Latin Bible, 2 to £4	Shakespeare's *First Folio* (1623), £1	student Bible, 6s.	cheap edition of Milton, 2s.	membership in circulating library (3rd class), £1 4s. a year	illustrated edition of *Through the Looking-glass*, 6s.	issue of *Eagle* comics, 4.5d.
	payment for illuminating a liturgical book, £22 9s.	Foxe's *Acts and Monuments*, 24s.	Hobbes's *Leviathan*, 8s.	Johnson's *Dictionary*, folio, 2 vols., £4 10s.	1st edition of Austen's *Pride and Prejudice*, 18s.	1st edition of Trollope's *The Way We Live Now*, 2 vols., £1 1s.	Orwell's *Nineteen Eighty Four*, paperback, 3s. 6d.
transportation	night's supply of hay for horse, 2d.	wherry (whole boat) across Thames, 1d.	day's journey, coach, 10s.	boat across Thames, 4d.	coach ride, outside, 2 to 3d. a mile; inside, 4 to 5d. a mile	15-minute journey in a London cab, 1s. 6d.	London tube fare, about 2d. a mile
	coach, £8	hiring a horse for a day, 12d.	coach horse, £30	coach fare, London to Edinburgh, £4 10s.	palanquin transport in Madras, 5s. a day	railway, 3rd class, London to Plymouth, 18s. 8d. (about 1d. a mile)	petrol, 3s. a gallon
	quality horse, £10	hiring a coach for a day, 10s.	fancy carriage, £170	transport to America, £5	passage, Liverpool to New York, £10	passage to India, 1st class, £50	midsize Austin sedan, £449 plus £188 4s. 2d. tax
clothes	clothing allowance for peasant, 3s. a year	shoes with buckles, 8d.	footman's frieze coat, 15s.	working woman's gown, 6s. 6d.	checked muslin, 7s. per yard	flannel for a cheap petticoat, 1s. 3d. a yard	woman's sun frock, £3 13s. 10d.

circa	1390	1590	1650	1750	1815	1875	1950
	shoes for gentry wearer, 4d.	woman's gloves, £1 5s.	falconer's hat, 10s.	gentleman's suit, £8	hiring a dressmaker for a pelisse, 8s.	overcoat for an Eton schoolboy, £1 1s.	tweed sports jacket, £3 16s. 6d.
	hat for gentry wearer, 10d.	fine cloak, £16	black cloth for mourning household of an earl, £100	very fine wig, £30	ladies silk stockings, 12s.	set of false teeth, £2 10s.	"Teddy boy" drape suit, £20
labor/incomes	hiring a skilled building worker, 4d. a day	actor's daily wage during playing season, 1s.	agricultural laborer, 6s. 5d. a week	price of boy slave, £32	lowest-paid sailor on Royal Navy ship, 10s. 9d. a month	seasonal agricultural laborer, 14s. a week	minimum wage, agricultural laborer, £4 14s. per 47-hour week
	wage for professional scribe, £2 3s. 4d. a year + cloak	household servant 2 to £5 a year + food, clothing	tutor to nobleman's children, £30 a year	housemaid's wage, £6 to £8 a year	contributor to Quarterly Review, 10 guineas per sheet	housemaid's wage, £10 to £25 a year	shorthand typist, £367 a year
	minimum income to be called gentleman, £10 a year; for knighthood, 40 to £400	minimum income for eligibility for knighthood, £30 a year	Milton's salary as Secretary of Foreign Tongues, £288 a year	Boswell's allowance, £200 a year	minimum income for a "genteel" family, £100 a year	income of the "comfortable" classes, £800 and up a year	middle manager's salary, £1,480 a year
	income from land of richest magnates, £3,500 a year	income from land of average earl, £4000 a year	Earl of Bedford's income, £8,000 a year	Duke of Newcastle's income, £40,000 a year	Mr. Darcy's income, Pride and Prejudice, £10,000 a year	Trollope's income, £4,000 a year	barrister's salary, £2,032 a year

The British Baronage

The English monarchy is in principle hereditary, though at times during the Middle Ages the rules were subject to dispute. In general, authority passes from father to eldest surviving son, from daughters in order of seniority if there is no son, to a brother if there are no children, and in default of direct descendants to collateral lines (cousins, nephews, nieces) in order of closeness. There have been breaks in the order of succession (1066, 1399, 1688), but so far as possible the usurpers have always sought to paper over the break with a legitimate, i.e., hereditary, claim. When a queen succeeds to the throne and takes a husband, he does not become king unless he is in the line of blood succession; rather, he is named prince consort, as Albert was to Victoria. He may father kings, but is not one himself.

The original Saxon nobles were the king's thanes, ealdormen, or earls, who provided the king with military service and counsel in return for booty, gifts, or landed estates. William the Conqueror, arriving from France, where feudalism was fully developed, considerably expanded this group. In addition, as the king distributed the lands of his new kingdom, he also distributed dignities to men who became known collectively as "the baronage." "Baron" in its root meaning signifies simply "man," and barons were the king's men. As the title was common, a distinction was early made between greater and lesser barons, the former gradually assuming loftier and more impressive titles. The first English "duke" was created in 1337; the title of "marquess," or "marquis" (pronounced "markwis"), followed in 1385, and "viscount" ("vyekount") in 1440. Though "earl" is the oldest title of all, an earl now comes between a marquess and a viscount in order of dignity and precedence, and the old term "baron" now designates a rank just below viscount."Baronets" were created in 1611 as a means of raising revenue for the crown (the title could be purchased for about £1000); they are marginal nobility and have never sat in the House of Lords.

Kings and queens are addressed as "Your Majesty," princes and princesses as "Your Highness," the other hereditary nobility as "My Lord" or "Your Lordship." Peers receive their titles either by inheritance (like Lord Byron, the sixth baron of that line) or from the monarch (like Alfred Lord Tennyson, created first Baron Tennyson by Victoria). The children, even of a duke, are commoners unless they are specifically granted some other title or inherit their father's title from him. A peerage can be forfeited by act of attainder, as for example when a lord is convicted of treason; and, when forfeited, or lapsed for lack of a successor, can be bestowed on another family. Thus in 1605 Robert Cecil was made first earl of Salisbury in the third creation, the first creation dating from 1149, the second from 1337, the title having been in abeyance since 1539. Titles descend by right of succession and do not depend on tenure of land; thus, a title does not always indicate where a lord dwells or holds power. Indeed, noble titles do not always refer to a real place at all. At Prince Edward's marriage in 1999, the queen created him earl of Wessex, although the old kingdom of Wessex has had no political existence since the Anglo-Saxon period, and the name was all but forgotten until it was resurrected by Thomas Hardy as the setting of his novels. (This is perhaps but one of many ways in which the world of the aristocracy increasingly resembles the realm of literature.)

The king and queen	(These are all of the royal line.)
Prince and princess	
Duke and duchess	(These may or may not be of the royal line, but are
Marquess and marchioness	ordinarily remote from the succession.)
Earl and countess	
Viscount and viscountess	
Baron and baroness	
Baronet and lady	

Scottish peers sat in the parliament of Scotland, as English peers did in the parliament of England, till at the Act of Union (1707) Scottish peers were granted sixteen seats in the English House of Lords, to be filled by election. (In 1963, all Scottish lords were allowed to sit.) Similarly, Irish peers, when the Irish parliament was abolished in 1801, were granted the right to elect twenty-eight of their number to the House of Lords in Westminster. (Now that the Republic of Ireland is a separate nation, this no longer applies.) Women members (peeresses) were first allowed to sit in the House as nonhereditary Life Peers in 1958 (when that status was created for members of both genders); women first sat by their own hereditary right in 1963. Today the House of Lords still retains some power to influence or delay legislation, but its future is uncertain. In 1999, the hereditary peers (then amounting to 750) were reduced to 92 temporary members elected by their fellow peers. Holders of Life Peerages remain, as do senior bishops of the Church of England and high-court judges (the "Law Lords").

Below the peerage the chief title of honor is "knight." Knighthood, which is not hereditary, is generally a reward for services rendered. A knight (Sir John Black) is addressed, using his first name, as "Sir John"; his wife, using the last name, is "Lady Black"—unless she is the daughter of an earl or nobleman of higher rank, in which case she will be "Lady Arabella." The female equivalent of a knight bears the title of "Dame." Though the word itself comes from the Anglo-Saxon *cniht*, there is some doubt as to whether knighthood amounted to much before the arrival of the Normans. The feudal system required military service as a condition of land tenure, and a man who came to serve his king at the head of an army of tenants required a title of authority and badges of identity—hence the title of knighthood and the coat of arms. During the Crusades, when men were far removed from their land (or even sold it in order to go on crusade), more elaborate forms of fealty sprang up that soon expanded into orders of knighthood. The Templars, Hospitallers, Knights of the Teutonic Order, Knights of Malta, and Knights of the Golden Fleece were but a few of these companionships; not all of them were available at all times in England.

Gradually, with the rise of centralized government and the decline of feudal tenures, military knighthood became obsolete, and the rank largely honorific; sometimes, as under James I, it degenerated into a scheme of the royal government for making money. For hundreds of years after its establishment in the fourteenth century, the Order of the Garter was the only English order of knighthood, an exclusive courtly companionship. Then, during the late seventeenth, the eighteenth, and the nineteenth centuries, a number of additional orders were created, with names such as the Thistle, Saint Patrick, the Bath, Saint Michael and Saint George, plus a number of special Victorian and Indian orders. They retain the terminology, ceremony, and dignity of knighthood, but the military implications are vestigial.

Although the British Empire now belongs to history, appointments to the Order of the British Empire continue to be conferred for services to that empire at home or abroad. Such honors (commonly referred to as "gongs") are granted by the monarch in her New Year's and Birthday lists, but the decisions are now made by the government in power. In recent years there have been efforts to popularize and democratize the dispensation of honors, with recipients including rock stars and actors. But this does not prevent large sectors of British society from regarding both knighthood and the peerage as largely irrelevant to modern life.

The Royal Lines of England and Great Britain

England

SAXONS AND DANES

Egbert, king of Wessex	802–839
Ethelwulf, son of Egbert	839–858
Ethelbald, second son of Ethelwulf	858–860
Ethelbert, third son of Ethelwulf	860–866
Ethelred I, fourth son of Ethelwulf	866–871
Alfred the Great, fifth son of Ethelwulf	871–899
Edward the Elder, son of Alfred	899–924
Athelstan the Glorious, son of Edward	924–940
Edmund I, third son of Edward	940–946
Edred, fourth son of Edward	946–955
Edwy the Fair, son of Edmund	955–959
Edgar the Peaceful, second son of Edmund	959–975
Edward the Martyr, son of Edgar	975–978 (murdered)
Ethelred II, the Unready, second son of Edgar	978–1016
Edmund II, Ironside, son of Ethelred II	1016–1016
Canute the Dane	1016–1035
Harold I, Harefoot, natural son of Canute	1035–1040
Hardecanute, son of Canute	1040–1042
Edward the Confessor, son of Ethelred II	1042–1066
Harold II, brother-in-law of Edward	1066–1066 (died in battle)

HOUSE OF NORMANDY

William I the Conqueror	1066–1087
William II, Rufus, third son of William I	1087–1100 (shot from ambush)
Henry I, Beauclerc, youngest son of William I	1100–1135

HOUSE OF BLOIS

Stephen, son of Adela, daughter of William I	1135–1154

HOUSE OF PLANTAGENET

Henry II, son of Geoffrey Plantagenet by Matilda, daughter of Henry I	1154–1189
Richard I, Coeur de Lion, son of Henry II	1189–1199
John Lackland, son of Henry II	1199–1216
Henry III, son of John	1216–1272
Edward I, Longshanks, son of Henry III	1272–1307
Edward II, son of Edward I	1307–1327 (deposed)
Edward III of Windsor, son of Edward II	1327–1377
Richard II, grandson of Edward III	1377–1399 (deposed)

HOUSE OF LANCASTER

Henry IV, son of John of Gaunt, son of Edward III	1399–1413
Henry V, Prince Hal, son of Henry IV	1413–1422
Henry VI, son of Henry V	1422–1461 (deposed), 1470–1471 (deposed)

HOUSE OF YORK

Edward IV, great-great-grandson of Edward III	1461–1470 (deposed), 1471–1483
Edward V, son of Edward IV	1483–1483 (murdered)
Richard III, Crookback	1483–1485 (died in battle)

HOUSE OF TUDOR

Henry VII, married daughter of Edward IV	1485–1509
Henry VIII, son of Henry VII	1509–1547
Edward VI, son of Henry VIII	1547–1553
Mary I, "Bloody," daughter of Henry VIII	1553–1558
Elizabeth I, daughter of Henry VIII	1558–1603

HOUSE OF STUART

James I (James VI of Scotland)	1603–1625
Charles I, son of James I	1625–1649 (executed)

COMMONWEALTH & PROTECTORATE

Council of State	1649–1653
Oliver Cromwell, Lord Protector	1653–1658
Richard Cromwell, son of Oliver	1658–1660 (resigned)

HOUSE OF STUART (RESTORED)

Charles II, son of Charles I	1660–1685
James II, second son of Charles I	1685–1688

(INTERREGNUM, 11 DECEMBER 1688 TO 13 FEBRUARY 1689)

William III of Orange, by Mary, daughter of Charles I	1689–1701
and Mary II, daughter of James II	–1694
Anne, second daughter of James II	1702–1714

Great Britain

HOUSE OF HANOVER

George I, son of Elector of Hanover and Sophia, granddaughter of James I	1714–1727
George II, son of George I	1727–1760
George III, grandson of George II	1760–1820
George IV, son of George III	1820–1830
William IV, third son of George III	1830–1837
Victoria, daughter of Edward, fourth son of George III	1837–1901

HOUSE OF SAXE-COBURG AND GOTHA

Edward VII, son of Victoria	1901–1910

HOUSE OF WINDSOR (NAME ADOPTED 17 JULY 1917)

George V, second son of Edward VII	1910–1936
Edward VIII, eldest son of George V	1936–1936 (abdicated)
George VI, second son of George V	1936–1952
Elizabeth II, daughter of George VI	1952–

Religions in England

In the sixth century C.E., missionaries from Ireland and the Continent introduced Christianity to the Anglo-Saxons—actually, reintroduced it, since it had briefly flourished in the southern parts of the British Isles during the Roman occupation, and even after the Roman withdrawal had persisted in the Celtic regions of Scotland and Wales. By the time the earliest poems included in the *Norton Anthology* were composed, therefore, the English people had been Christians for hundreds of years; such Anglo-Saxon poems as "The Dream of the Rood" bear witness to their faith. Our knowledge of the religion of pre-Christian Britain is sketchy, but it is likely that vestiges of paganism assimilated into, or coexisted with, the practice of Christianity: fertility rites were incorporated into the celebration of Easter resurrection, rituals commemorating the dead into All-Hallows Eve and All Saints Day, and elements of winter solstice festivals into the celebration of Christmas. In English literature such "folkloric" elements often elicit romantic nostalgia. Geoffrey Chaucer's Wife of Bath looks back to a magical time before the arrival of Christianity in which the land was "fulfilled of fairye." Hundreds of years later, the seventeenth-century writer Robert Herrick honors the amalgamation of Christian and pagan elements in agrarian British culture in such poems as "Corinna's Gone A-Maying" and "The Hock Cart."

Medieval Christianity was fairly uniform across Western Europe—hence called "catholic," or universally shared—and its rituals and expectations, common to the whole community, permeated everyday life. The Catholic Church was also an international power structure. In its hierarchy of pope, cardinals, archbishops, and bishops, it resembled the feudal state, but the church power structure coexisted alongside a separate hierarchy of lay authorities with a theoretically different sphere of social responsibilities. The sharing out of lay and ecclesiastical authority in medieval England was sometimes a source of conflict. Chaucer's pilgrims are on their way to visit the memorial shrine to one victim of such struggle: Thomas a Becket, Archbishop of Canterbury, who opposed the policies of King Henry III, was assassinated on the king's orders in 1120 and later made a saint. As an international organization, the church conducted its business in the universal language of Latin, and thus although statistically in the period the largest segment of literate persons were monks and priests, the clerical contribution to great writing in English was relatively modest. Yet the lay writers of the period reflect the importance of the church as an institution and the pervasiveness of religion in everyday life.

Beginning in 1517 the German monk Martin Luther, in Wittenberg, Germany, openly challenged many aspects of Catholic practice and by 1520 had completely repudiated the authority of the Pope, setting in train the Protestant Reformation. Luther argued that the Roman Catholic Church had strayed far from the pattern of Christianity laid out in scripture. He rejected Catholic doctrines for which no biblical authority was to be found, such as the belief in Purgatory, and translated the Bible into German, on the grounds that the importance of scripture for all Christians made its translation into the vernacular tongue essential. Luther was not the first to advance such views—followers of the Englishman John Wycliffe had translated the Bible in the fourteenth century. But Luther, protected by powerful German rulers, was able to speak out with impunity and convert others to his views, rather than suffer the persecution usually meted out to heretics. Soon other reformers were following in Luther's footsteps: of these, the Swiss Ulrich Zwingli and the French Jean Calvin would be especially influential for English religious thought.

A86

At first England remained staunchly Catholic. Its king, Henry VIII, was so severe to heretics that the Pope awarded him the title "Defender of the Faith," which British monarchs have retained to this day. In 1534, however, Henry rejected the authority of the Pope to prevent his divorce from his queen, Catherine of Aragon, and his marriage to his mistress, Ann Boleyn. In doing so, Henry appropriated to himself ecclesiastical as well as secular authority. Thomas More, author of *Utopia*, was executed for refusing to endorse Henry's right to govern the English church. Over the following six years, Henry consolidated his grip on the ecclesiastical establishment by dissolving the powerful, populous Catholic monasteries and redistributing their massive landholdings to his own lay followers. Yet Henry's church largely retained Catholic doctrine and liturgy. When Henry died and his young son, Edward, came to the throne in 1547, the English church embarked on a more Protestant path, a direction abruptly reversed when Edward died and his older sister Mary, the daughter of Catherine of Aragon, took the throne in 1553 and attempted to reintroduce Roman Catholicism. Mary's reign was also short, however, and her successor, Elizabeth I, the daughter of Ann Boleyn, was a Protestant. Elizabeth attempted to establish a "middle way" Christianity, compromising between Roman Catholic practices and beliefs and reformed ones.

The Church of England, though it laid claim to a national rather than pan-European authority, aspired like its predecessor to be the universal church of all English subjects. It retained the Catholic structure of parishes and dioceses and the Catholic hierarchy of bishops, though the ecclesiastical authority was now the Archbishop of Canterbury and the Church's "Supreme Governor" was the monarch. Yet disagreement and controversy persisted. Some members of the Church of England wanted to retain many of the ritual and liturgical elements of Catholicism. Others, the Puritans, advocated a more thoroughgoing reformation. Most Puritans remained within the Church of England, but a minority, the "Separatists" or "Congregationalists," split from the established church altogether. These dissenters no longer thought of the ideal church as an organization to which everybody belonged; instead, they conceived it as a more exclusive group of likeminded people, one not necessarily attached to a larger body of believers.

In the seventeenth century, the succession of the Scottish king James to the English throne produced another problem. England and Scotland were separate nations, and in the sixteenth century Scotland had developed its own national Presbyterian church, or "kirk," under the leadership of the reformer John Knox. The kirk retained fewer Catholic liturgical elements than did the Church of England, and its authorities, or "presbyters," were elected by assemblies of their fellow clerics, rather than appointed by the king. James I and his son Charles I, especially the latter, wanted to bring the Scottish kirk into conformity with Church of England practices. The Scots violently resisted these efforts, with the collaboration of many English Puritans, in a conflict that eventually developed into the English Civil War in the mid-seventeenth century. The effect of these disputes is visible in the poetry of such writers as John Milton, Robert Herrick, Henry Vaughan, and Thomas Traherne, and in the prose of Thomas Browne, Lucy Hutchinson, and Dorothy Waugh. Just as in the mid-sixteenth century, when a succession of monarchs with different religious commitments destabilized the church, so the seventeenth century endured spiritual whiplash. King Charles I's highly ritualistic Church of England was violently overturned by the Puritan victors in the Civil War—until 1660, after the death of the Puritan leader, Oliver Cromwell, when the Church of England was restored along with the monarchy.

The religious and political upheavals of the seventeenth century produced Christian sects that de-emphasized the ceremony of the established church and rejected as well its top-down authority structure. Some of these groups were ephemeral, but the Baptists (founded in 1608 in Amsterdam by the English expatriate John Smyth) and Quakers, or Society of Friends (founded by George Fox in the 1640s), flourished outside the established church, sometimes despite cruel persecution. John Bunyan, a Baptist, wrote the Christian allegory *Pilgrim's Progress* while in prison. Some dissenters, like the Baptists, shared the reformed reverence for the absolute authority of scripture but interpreted the scriptural texts differently from their fellow Protestants. Others, like the Quakers, favored, even over the authority of the Bible, the "inner light" or voice of individual conscience, which they took to be the working of the Holy Spirit in the lives of individuals.

The Protestant dissenters were not England's only religious minorities. Despite crushing fines and the threat of imprisonment, a minority of Catholics under Elizabeth and James openly refused to give their allegiance to the new church, and others remained secret adherents to the old ways. John Donne was brought up in an ardently Catholic family, and several other writers converted to Catholicism as adults—Ben Jonson for a considerable part of his career, Elizabeth Carey and Richard Crashaw permanently, and at profound personal cost. In the eighteenth century, Catholics remained objects of suspicion as possible agents of sedition, especially after the "Glorious Revolution" in 1688 deposed the Catholic James II in favor of the Protestant William and Mary. Anti-Catholic prejudice affected John Dryden, a Catholic convert, as well as the lifelong Catholic Alexander Pope. By contrast, the English colony of Ireland remained overwhelmingly Roman Catholic, the fervor of its religious commitment at least partly inspired by resistance to English occupation. Starting in the reign of Elizabeth, England shored up its own authority in Ireland by encouraging Protestant immigrants from Scotland to settle in northern Ireland, producing a virulent religious divide the effects of which are still playing out today.

A small community of Jews had moved from France to London after 1066, when the Norman William the Conqueror came to the English throne. Although despised and persecuted by many Christians, they were allowed to remain as moneylenders to the Crown, until the thirteenth century, when the king developed alternative sources of credit. At this point, in 1290, the Jews were expelled from England. In 1655 Oliver Cromwell permitted a few to return, and in the late seventeenth and early eighteenth centuries the Jewish population slowly increased, mainly by immigration from Germany. In the mid-eighteenth century some prominent Jews had their children brought up as Christians so as to facilitate their full integration into English society: thus the nineteenth-century writer and politician Benjamin Disraeli, although he and his father were members of the Church of England, was widely considered a Jew insofar as his ancestry was Jewish.

In the late seventeenth century, as the Church of England reasserted itself, Catholics, Jews, and dissenting Protestants found themselves subject to significant legal restrictions. The Corporation Act, passed in 1661, and the Test Act, passed in 1673, excluded all who refused to take communion in the Church of England from voting, attending university, or working in government or in the professions. Members of religious minorities, as well as Church of England communicants, paid mandatory taxes in support of Church of England ministers and buildings. In 1689 the dissenters gained the right to worship in public, but Jews and Catholics were not permitted to do so.

During the eighteenth century, political, intellectual, and religious history remained closely intertwined. The Church of England came to accommodate a good deal of variety. "Low church" services resembled those of the dissenting Protestant churches, minimizing ritual and emphasizing the sermon; the "high church" retained more elaborate ritual elements, yet its prestige was under attack on several fronts. Many Enlightenment thinkers subjected the Bible to rational critique and found it wanting: the philosopher David Hume, for instance, argued that the "miracles" described therein were more probably lies or errors than real breaches of the laws of nature. Within the Church of England, the "broad church" Latitudinarians welcomed this rationalism, advocating theological openness and an emphasis on ethics rather than dogma. More radically, the Unitarian movement rejected the divinity of Christ while professing to accept his ethical teachings. Taking a different tack, the preacher

John Wesley, founder of Methodism, responded to the rationalists' challenge with a newly fervent call to evangelism and personal discipline; his movement was particularly successful in Wales. Revolutions in America and France at the end of the century generated considerable millenarian excitement and fostered more new religious ideas, often in conjunction with a radical social agenda. Many important writers of the Romantic period were indebted to traditions of protestant dissent: Unitarian and rationalist protestant ideas influenced William Hazlitt, Anna Barbauld, Mary Wollstonecraft, and the young Samuel Taylor Coleridge. William Blake created a highly idiosyncratic poetic mythology loosely indebted to radical strains of Christian mysticism. Others were even more heterodox: Lord Byron and Robert Burns, brought up as Scots Presbyterians, rebelled fiercely, and Percy Shelley's writing of an atheistic pamphlet resulted in his expulsion from Oxford.

Great Britain never erected an American-style "wall of separation" between church and state, but in practice religion and secular affairs grew more and more distinct during the nineteenth century. In consequence, members of religious minorities no longer seemed to pose a threat to the commonweal. A movement to repeal the Test Act failed in the 1790s, but a renewed effort resulted in the extension of the franchise to dissenting Protestants in 1828 and to Catholics in 1829. The numbers of Roman Catholics in England were swelled by immigration from Ireland, but there were also some prominent English adherents. Among writers, the converts John Newman and Gerard Manley Hopkins are especially important. The political participation and social integration of Jews presented a thornier challenge. Lionel de Rothschild, repeatedly elected to represent London in Parliament during the 1840s and 1850s, was not permitted to take his seat there because he refused to take his oath of office "on the true faith of a Christian"; finally, in 1858, the Jewish Disabilities Act allowed him to omit these words. Only in 1871, however, were Oxford and Cambridge opened to non-Anglicans.

Meanwhile geological discoveries and Charles Darwin's evolutionary theories increasingly cast doubt on the literal truth of the Creation story, and close philological analysis of the biblical text suggested that its origins were human rather than divine. By the end of the nineteenth century, many writers were bearing witness to a world in which Christianity no longer seemed fundamentally plausible. In his poetry and prose, Thomas Hardy depicts a world devoid of benevolent providence. Matthew Arnold's poem "Dover Beach" is in part an elegy to lost spiritual assurance, as the "Sea of Faith" goes out like the tide: "But now I only hear / Its melancholy, long, withdrawing roar / Retreating." For Arnold, literature must replace religion as a source of spiritual truth, and intimacy between individuals substitute for the lost communal solidarity of the universal church.

The work of many twentieth-century writers shows the influence of a religious upbringing or a religious conversion in adulthood. T. S. Eliot and W. S. Auden embrace Anglicanism, William Butler Yeats spiritualism. James Joyce repudiates Irish Catholicism but remains obsessed with it. Yet religion, or lack of it, is a matter of individual choice and conscience, not social or legal mandate. In the past fifty years, church attendance has plummeted in Great Britain. Although 71 percent of the population still identified itself as "Christian" on the 2000 census, only about 7 percent of these regularly attend religious services of any denomination. Meanwhile, immigration from former British colonies has swelled the ranks of religions once alien to the British Isles—Muslim, Sikh, Hindu, Buddhist—though the numbers of adherents remain small relative to the total population.

London in the 19th & 20th centuries

PERMISSIONS ACKNOWLEDGMENTS

W. H. Auden: Introduction to THE POET'S TONGUE [Poetry as a Memorable Speech] by W. H. Auden. Copyright © 1935 by W. H. Auden. Reprinted by permission of Curtis Brown, Ltd. "Lullaby," "Musée des Beaux Arts," "In Memory of W. B. Yeats," "In Praise of Limestone," "The Unknown Citizen," "September 1, 1939," and "The Shield of Achilles" all from W. H. AUDEN: COLLECTED POEMS by W. H. Auden, edited by Edward Mendelson. Copyright © 1937, 1940, 1951, 1952 and renewed 1965, 1968 by W. H. Auden. Reprinted by permission of Random House, Inc., and Faber & Faber Ltd. "As I Walked Out One Evening" copyright © 1940 & renewed 1968 by W. H. Auden, from COLLECTED POEMS by W. H. Auden. Used by permission of Random House, Inc.

Samuel Beckett: *Endgame.* Copyright © 1958 by Samuel Beckett; copyright renewed © 1986 by Samuel Beckett. Used by permission of Grove/Atlantic, Inc., and Faber & Faber Ltd.

William Blake: Poems from THE COMPLETE POETRY AND PROSE OF WILLIAM BLAKE, edited by David V. Erdman, copyright © 1965, 1981, Doubleday & Company. Blake engravings: reproduced from the Lessing J. Rosenwald Collection, Library of Congress.

Robert Burns: Selections from THE POEMS AND SONGS OF ROBERT BURNS, edited by James Kinsley (1968). Reprinted by permission of Oxford University Press.

Lord Byron: Selections as indicated from LORD BYRON: THE COMPLETE POETICAL WORKS, edited by Jerome J. McGann (Vol I., 1980). Reprinted by permission of Oxford University Press.

Anne Carson: "Hero" by Anne Carson, from GLASS IRONY AND GOD, copyright © 1995 by Anne Carson. Reprinted by permission of New Directions Publishing Corp. "Epitaph: Zion" from MEN IN THE OFF HOURS by Anne Carson, copyright © 2000 by Anne Carson. Used by permission of Alfred A. Knopf, a division of Random House, Inc.

John Clare: "Mouse's Nest" and "Pastoral Poesy" from THE POEMS OF JOHN CLARE, edited by J. W. Tibble (J. M. Dent). Reprinted by permission Everyman's Library, London. "The Nightingale's Nest" from SELECTED POEMS AND PROSE OF JOHN CLARE, edited by Eric Robinson and Geoffrey Summerfield. Reproduced with permission of Curtis Brown Ltd., London, on behalf of Eric Robinson. Copyright © Eric Robinson 1984, 1967. All other poems from THE LATER POEMS OF JOHN CLARE 1837–1864, edited by Eric Robinson and David Powell. Reproduced with permission of Curtis Brown Ltd., London, on behalf of Eric Robinson. Copyright © Eric Robinson 1984, 1967.

J. M. Coetzee: Excerpt from WAITING FOR THE BARBARIANS by J. M. Coetzee. Copyright © 1980 by J. M. Coetzee. Used by permission of Viking Penguin, a division of Penguin Putnam, Inc., and Secker and Warburg. Used by permission of The Random House Group Limited.

T. S. Eliot: "The Love Song of J. Alfred Prufrock" and *The Waste Land* from COLLECTED POEMS 1909–1962 by T. S. Eliot. Reprinted by permission of Faber & Faber Ltd. "The Hollow Men" and "Journey of the Magi" from COLLECTED POEMS 1909–1962 by T. S. Eliot, copyright © 1964, 1963 by T. S. Eliot, reprinted by permission of the publishers, Harcourt, Inc., and Faber & Faber Ltd. "Little Gidding" from FOUR QUARTETS, copyright © 1942 by T. S. Eliot and renewed 1970 by Esme Valerie Eliot. Reprinted by permission of Harcourt, Inc., and Faber & Faber Ltd. "Tradition and the Individual Talent" from SELECTED ESSAYS by T. S. Eliot. Reprinted by permission of Faber & Faber Ltd.

Brian Friel: TRANSLATIONS by Brian Friel. Copyright © 1981 by Brian Friel. Reprinted by permission of Faber and Faber, Inc., an affiliate of Farrar, Straus and Giroux, LLC

Nadine Gordimer: "The Moment before the Gun Went Off" from JUMP AND OTHER STORIES by Nadine Gordimer, published by Bloomsbury Publishing PLC in 1991. Copyright © 1991 by Felix Licensing, B.V. Reprinted by permission of Farrar, Straus & Giroux, Inc., Penguin Books Canada Limited, and Bloomsbury Publishing PLC.

Thomas Hardy: "He Never Expected Much" reprinted with the permission of Simon & Schuster from THE COMPLETE POEMS OF THOMAS HARDY, edited by James Gibson. Copyright © 1976 by Macmillan London Ltd.

Seamus Heaney: "Digging," "The Forge," "The Grauballe Man," "Punishment," "Station Island XII," "Clearances," and from SELECTED POEMS 1966–1987 by Seamus Heaney. Copyright © 1998 by Seamus Heaney. "The Sharping Stone" from THE SPIRIT LEVEL by Seamus Heaney. Copyright © 1996 by Seamus Heaney. "Casualty" and "The Skunk" from FIELD WORK All reprinted by permission of Farrar, Straus & Giroux, LLC, and Faber & Faber Ltd.

James Joyce: "Araby" and "The Dead" from DUBLINERS by James Joyce. Copyright © 1916 by B. W. Heubsch. Definitive text copyright © 1967 by the Estate of James Joyce. Used by permission of Viking Penguin, a division of Penguin Putnam, Inc. From ULYSSES by James Joyce. Copyright © 1934 and renewed 1962 by Lucia & George Joyce. Reprinted by permission of Random House, Inc. Reproduced with the permission of the Estate of James Joyce, copyright © Estate of James Joyce.

John Keats: Reprinted by permission of the publisher from JOHN KEATS: COMPLETE POEMS, edited by Jack Stillinger, Cambridge, Mass.: The Belknap Press of Harvard University Press, copyright © 1978, 1982 by the President and Fellows of Harvard College. Reprinted by permission of the publisher from THE LETTERS OF JOHN KEATS 18141821, VOLUMES I and II, edited by Hyder Edward Rollins, Cambridge, Mass.: Harvard University Press, Copyright © 1958 by The President and Fellows of Harvard College.

Rudyard Kipling: "The Man Who Would Be King" from THE MAN WHO WOULD BE KING AND OTHER STORIES (April 1987), Oxford. "The White Man's Burden." Reprinted by permission of A.P. Watt Ltd. on behalf of the National Trust for Places of Historic Interest or Natural Beauty.

Philip Larkin: "Church Going" by Philip Larkin is reprinted from THE LESS DECEIVED by permission of The Marvell Press, England and Australia. "MCMXIV," "Talking in Bed," "Ambulances," "High Windows," "Homage to a Government," "This Be The Verse," and "Aubade" from PHILIP LARKIN: COLLECTED POEMS, edited by Anthony Thwaite.

Copyright © 1988, 2003 by the Estate of Philip Larkin. All reprinted by permission of Farrar, Straus & Giroux, LLC and Faber & Faber Ltd.

D. H. Lawrence: "Odour of Chrysanthemums" copyright © 1933 by the Estate of D. H. Lawrence, renewed © 1961 by Angelo Ravagli and C. M. Weekley, Executors of the Estate of Frieda Lawrence, from COMPLETE SHORT STORIES OF D. H. LAWRENCE. Used by permission of Viking Penguin, a division of Penguin Putnam, Inc., and Laurence Pollinger Ltd. "The Horse Dealer's Daughter," also from THE COMPLETE SHORT STORIES OF D. H. LAWRENCE. Reprinted by permission of the Estate of Frieda Lawrence Ravagli and Laurence Pollinger Ltd. "Why the Novel Matters" from PHOENIX: THE POSTHUMOUS PAPERS OF D. H. LAWRENCE, edited by Edward McDonald. Copyright © 1936 by Frieda Lawrence, renewed © 1964 by the Estate of the late Frieda Lawrence Ravagli. Used by permission of Viking Penguin, a division of Penguin Putnam, Inc., and Laurence Pollinger Ltd. "Piano" and "Snake" from THE COMPLETE POEMS OF D. H. LAWRENCE, edited by V. de Sola Pinto and F. W. Roberts. Copyright © 1964, 1971 by Angelo Ravagli and C. M. Weekley, Executors of the Estate of Frieda Lawrence Ravagli. Used by permission of Viking Penguin, a division of Penguin Putnam, Inc., and Laurence Pollinger Ltd.

Alice Munro: "Walker Brothers Cowboy" from DANCE OF THE HAPPY SHADES by Alice Munro. Copyright © 1968 by Alice Munro. Originally published by McGraw-Hill Ryerson. Reprinted by permission of the William Morris Agency, Inc. on behalf of the Author, and McGraw-Hill Ryerson. All rights reserved.

Jean Rhys: "The Day They Burned the Books" from TIGERS ARE BETTER-LOOKING: WITH A SELECTION FROM THE LEFT BANK by Jean Rhys (First published by Andre Deutsch 1968, Penguin Books 1972.) Copyright © Jean Rhys, 1962.

Christina Rossetti: "Cobwebs," "In an Artist's Studio," "Promises Like Pie-Crust," and "Cardinal Newman" from THE COMPLETE POEMS OF CHRISTINA ROSSETTI, Volume III, edited by R. W. Crump. Copyright © 1979 by Louisiana State University. Reprinted by permission of the Louisiana State University Press.

Salman Rushdie: "The Prophet's Hair" from EAST, WEST: STORIES A DECLARATION by Salman Rushdie. Copyright © 1994 by Salman Rushdie. Reprinted by permission of Pantheon Books, a division of Random House, Inc., and Jonathan Cape.

Percy Bysshe Shelley: Poems from SHELLEY'S POETRY AND PROSE: A NORTON CRITICAL EDITION, edited by Donald Reiman & Sharon Powers. Copyright © 1977 by Donald H. Reiman and Sharon B. Powers. Reprinted by permission of W. W. Norton & Company, Inc.

Dylan Thomas: "The Force That Through the Green Fuse Drives the Flower" by Dylan Thomas. Copyright © 1939, 1943 by New Directions Publishing Corp. "Poem in October" and "Fern Hill" by Dylan Thomas. Copyright © 1945 by The Trustees for the Copyrights of Dylan Thomas, first published in POETRY. "Do Not Go Gentle into That Good Night" by Dylan Thomas. Copyright © 1952 by Dylan Thomas. All from THE POEMS OF DYLAN THOMAS. Reprinted by permission of New Directions Publishing Corp. and David Higham Associates.

Derek Walcott: "A Far Cry from Africa" and "The Season of Phantasmal Peace" from THE COLLECTED POEMS 1948–1984 by Derek Walcott. Copyright © 1986 by Derek Walcott. "III" and "XLIX" from Books One and Six of OMEROS by Derek Walcott. Copyright © 1990 by Derek Walcott. All reprinted by permission of Farrar, Straus & Giroux, Inc. and Faber & Faber Ltd. Excerpt of 77 lines of *The Schooner* Flight from THE COLLECTED POEMS 1948–1984 by Derek Walcott. Copyright © 1986 by Derek Walcott. Reprinted by permission of Farrar, Straus & Giroux, Inc. and Jonathan Cape.

Mary Wollstonecraft: From A VINDICATION OF THE RIGHTS OF WOMAN: A NORTON CRITICAL EDITION, Second Edition, by Mary Wollstonecraft, edited by Carol H. Poston. Copyright © 1988, 1975 by W. W. Norton & Company, Inc. Reprinted by permission of W. W. Norton & Company, Inc.

Virginia Woolf: "The Mark on the Wall" from A HAUNTED HOUSE AND OTHER SHORT STORIES by Virginia Woolf, copyright © 1944 and renewed 1972 by Harcourt, Inc., reprinted by permission of the publisher. "Modern Fiction" from THE COMMON READER by Virginia Woolf, copyright © 1925 by Harcourt, Inc. and renewed 1953 by Leonard Woolf, reprinted by permission of the publisher. "Professions for Women" from THE DEATH OF THE MOTH AND OTHER ESSAYS by Virginia Woolf, copyright © 1942 by Harcourt, Inc. and renewed 1970 by Marjorie T. Parsons, Executrix, reprinted by permission of the publisher. A ROOM OF ONE'S OWN by Virginia Woolf, copyright © 1929 by Harcourt Brace & Company and renewed 1957 by Leonard Woolf, reprinted by permission of the publisher. All reprinted by permission of the publisher and The Society of Authors as the Literary Representative of the Estate of Virginia Woolf.

Dorothy Wordsworth: Selections as indicated from THE GRASMERE JOURNALS, edited by Pamela Woof (1991). Reprinted by permission of Oxford University Press. "Grasmere—A Fragment" and "Thoughts on My Sick Bed" from DOROTHY WORDSWORTH AND ROMANTICISM. Reprinted by permission of The Wordsworth Trust, Dove Cottage, Grasmere.

William Wordsworth: Reprinted from William Wordsworth: THE RUINED COTTAGE AND THE PEDLAR. Edited by James A. Butler. Copyright © 1978 by Cornell University. Copyright © 1978 by Cornell University. Reprinted from William Wordsworth: THE FOURTEEN-BOOK PRELUDE. Edited by W. J. B. Owen. Copyright © 1985 by Cornell University. Both used by permission of the publisher, Cornell University Press.

W. B. Yeats: "The Stolen Child," "The Rose of the World," "The Lake Isle of Innisfree," "The Sorrow of Love," "When You Are Old," "Who Goes with Fergus?," "The Man Who Dreamed of Faeryland," "Adam's Curse," "No Second Troy," "The Fascination of What's Difficult," "A Coat," "September 1913," "The Wild Swans at Coole," and "In Memory of Major Robert Gregory," all from THE POEMS OF W. B. YEATS: A NEW EDITION, edited by Richard J. Finneran. Reprinted by permission of A. P. Watt on the behalf of Michael B. Yeats. "Easter, 1916," "The Second Coming," and "A Prayer for My Daughter" reprinted with the permission of Simon & Schuster and A. P. Watt on the behalf of Michael B. Yeats from THE POEMS OF W. B. YEATS: A NEW EDITION, edited by Richard J. Finneran. Copyright © 1924 by Macmillan Publishing Company, renewed 1952 by Bertha Georgie Yeats. "Leda and the Swan" and "Among School Children" reprinted with the permission of Simon & Schuster and A. P. Watt on the behalf of Michael B. Yeats from THE POEMS

OF W. B. YEATS: A NEW EDITION, edited by Richard J. Finneran. Copyright © 1928 by Macmillan Publishing Company; copyright renewed © 1956 by Georgie Yeats. "A Dialogue of Self and Soul," "Crazy Jane Talks with the Bishop," and "Byzantium" reprinted with the permission of Simon & Schuster and A. P. Watt on the behalf of Michael B. Yeats from THE POEMS OF W. B. YEATS: A NEW EDITION, edited by Richard J. Finneran. Copyright © 1933 by Macmillan Publishing Company; copyright renewed © 1961 by Bertha Georgie Yeats. "Lapis Lazuli," "The Circus Animals' Desertion," and "Under Ben Bulben" reprinted with the permission of Simon & Schuster and A. P. Watt on the behalf of Michael B. Yeats from THE POEMS OF W. B. YEATS: A NEW EDITION, edited by Richard J. Finneran. Copyright © 1940 by Georgie Yeats; copyright renewed © 1968 by Bertha Georgie Yeats, Michael Butler Yeats, and Anne Yeats. "The Sorrow of Love" (transcription of first printed version 12 lines) reprinted by permission of A.P. Watt Ltd on behalf of Michael B. Yeats. Excerpt from "A General Introduction to My Work," reprinted with the permission of Scribner, an imprint of Simon & Schuster Adult Publishing Group, from THE COLLECTED WORKS OF W. B. YEATS. Copyright © 1961 by Mrs. W. B. Yeats.

Every effort has been made to contact the copyright holders of each of the selections. Rights holders of any selections not credited should contact W. W. Norton & Company, Inc., 500 Fifth Avenue, New York, NY 10110 for a correction to be made in the next reprinting of our work.

Index

ARCTIC OCEAN

SIBERIA

ALASKA
(U.S.)

Gree

NORTH AMERICA

Dominion of Canada

NORTH PACIFIC OCEAN

United States
of America

Bermuda (Br.)

NORTH ATL

HAWAIIAN IS. (U.S.)

Mexico

Gulf of Mexico

BAHAMAS (Br.)

Cuba
Haiti Dominican Rep.
Jamaica (Br.) Puerto Rico (U.S.)
VIRGIN IS. (Den.)
Br. Honduras Guadeloupe (Fr.)
Caribbean Sea Dominica (Br.)
Guatemala Honduras
El Salvador Nicaragua Martinique (Fr.) Barbados (Br.)
Grenada (Br.)
Costa Rica Trinidad & Tobago (Br.)
Panama Venezuela Br. Guiana
Dutch Gu
French (

CENTRAL AMERICA

Christmas I. (Br.)
Equator

GILBERT IS. (Br.)

BISMARCK ARCH. (Ger.)

GALAPAGOS IS. (Ecuador)

Colombia
Ecuador

United States
of Brazil

SOLOMON IS. (Br. & Ger.)

FIJI IS. (Br.)

TONGA IS. (Br.)

New Caledonia (Fr.)

Peru

SOUTH AMERICA

Bolivia

Tahiti (Fr.)

Chile Paraguay

Argentina Uruguay

Australia

SOUTH PACIFIC OCEAN

New
Zealand

FALKLAND IS.
(Br.)

SOUTH ATL

S. G

N

W   E

S

MILES

AT EQUATOR   0   1200   2400   3600   4800

0   2400   4800

KILOMETERS

The
Britísh Empire
ca. 1913

Spitzbergen (Nor.)

ARCTIC OCEAN

SIBERIA

Russian Empire · A S I A

Great Britain

Norway
Sweden
Denmark
Netherlands
Germany
Belgium · Lux.
France
Switz.
Austro-Hungary
Italy
Mont.
Serbia
Romania
Bulgaria
Black Sea
Alb.
Greece
Ottoman Empire

MONGOLIA
MANCHURIA

Chinese Republic

Korea (Jap.)
Weihaiwei (Br.)
Japan

Portugal
Spain
Gibraltar (Br.)
Mediterranean Sea
Morocco
Oro.
Algeria
Tunisia
Malta (Br.)
Cyprus (Br.)
Libya

Persia
Afghanistan
TIBET
Nepal
Bhutan

Egypt

Red Sea
Arabia
Bahrein (Br.)
Oman
KURIA MURIA IS. (Br.)
Aden
Fr. Somaliland
Socotra I. (Br.)

BURMA
British India
Siam
Fr. Indo-China
Formosa (Jap.)
Hong Kong (Br.)
Macao (Port.)
Hainan

PACIFIC OCEAN

French W. Africa
Togoland
Gold Coast
Nigeria
Liberia
Sp. Guinea
Cameroons
Fr. Congo
Kabinda

Erltrea
Anglo-Egyptian Sudan
Abyssinia
Br. Somaliland
Italian Somaliland
Equator
Uganda
Br. E. Africa (Kenya)

Arabian Sea
ANDAMAN IS. (Br.)
LACCADIVES (Br.)
MALDIVES (Br.)
NICOBAR IS. (Br.)
Ceylon
Bay of Bengal

PHILIPPINES (U.S.)
Br. N. Borneo
Brunei
Malay States
Sarawak

Dutch East Indies
NEW GUINEA
Papua

Ascension I. (Br.)
Belgian Congo
Angola
Rhodesia
Ger. E. Africa
Zanzibar (Br.)
Nyasaland

SEYCHELLES (Br.)
CHAGOS ARCH. (Br.)
COCOS IS. (Br.)
Christmas I. (Br.)

INDIAN OCEAN

Commonwealth of Australia

St. Helena I. (Br.)
Ger. S.W. Africa
Walvis Bay (Br.)
Bechuanaland
Union of South Africa
Swaziland
Basutoland
Mozambique
Madagascar
Mauritius (Br.)
Rodrigues (Br.)
Réunion (Fr.)

Tasmania

Cunha I. (Br.)

A. Kitzinger